Dear Reader

I was born in 1898. During my hundred years as Bibendum I have accompanied you all over the world, attentive to your safety while travelling and your comfort and enjoyment on and off the road.

The knowledge and experience I acquire each year is summarised for you in the Red Guide.

In this, the 25 th edition, I offer some advice to help you find good food at moderate prices : look for the many restaurants identified by my red face, "Bib Gourmand"!

I look forward to receiving your comments…

I remain at your service for a new century of discoveries.

Bibendum

Contents

Choosing a hotel
or restaurant

*This guide offers a selection of hotels
and restaurants to help the motorist on his travels.
In each category establishments are listed
in order of preference according to the degree
of comfort they offer.*

Categories

🏨	XXXXX	*Luxury in the traditional style*
🏨	XXXX	*Top class comfort*
🏨	XXX	*Very comfortable*
🏨	XX	*Comfortable*
🏨	X	*Quite comfortable*
	🍴	*Traditional pubs serving food*
↑		*Other recommended accommodation*
		(Guesthouses, farmhouses and private homes)
without rest.		*The hotel has no restaurant*
	with rm	*The restaurant also offers accommodation*

Peaceful atmosphere and setting

*Certain establishments are distinguished
in the guide by the red symbols shown below.
Your stay in such hotels will be particularly
pleasant or restful, owing to the character
of the building, its decor, the setting, the welcome
and services offered, or simply the peace
and quiet to be enjoyed there.*

🏨 to ↑	*Pleasant hotels*
XXXXX to X	*Pleasant restaurants*
« Park »	*Particularly attractive feature*
🌢	*Very quiet or quiet, secluded hotel*
🌢	*Quiet hotel*
≤ sea	*Exceptional view*
≤	*Interesting or extensive view*

*The maps located at the beginning of each
regional section in the guide indicate places with
such peaceful, pleasant hotels and restaurants.*

*By consulting them before setting out and sending
us your comments on your return
you can help us with our enquiries.*

Hotel facilities

In general the hotels we recommend have full bathroom and toilet facilities in each room. This may not be the case, however, for certain rooms in categories 🏨, 🏠 and ⤴.

30 rm	*Number of rooms*
|♦|	*Lift (elevator)*
▤	*Air conditioning*
TV	*Television in room*
⊱✳	*Establishment either partly or wholly reserved for non-smokers*
☎	*Telephone in room: direct dialling for outside calls*
♿	*Rooms accessible to disabled people*
🍽	*Meals served in garden or on terrace*
🏊 ⊠	*Outdoor or indoor swimming pool*
🏋 ♨	*Exercise room – Sauna*
🌿	*Garden*
✻ ⛳	*Hotel tennis court – Golf course and number of holes*
⚓	*Landing stage*
⤵	*Fishing available to hotel guests. A charge may be made*
🧑‍🏫 150	*Equipped conference hall: maximum capacity*
🚗	*Hotel garage (additional charge in most cases)*
℗	*Car park for customers only*
🐕	*Dogs are excluded from all or part of the hotel*
Fax	*Telephone document transmission*
May-October	*Dates when open, as indicated by the hotelier*
season	*Probably open for the season – precise dates not available*
	Where no date or season is shown, establishments are open all year round
LL35 OSB	*Postal code*

Animals

It is illegal to bring domestic animals (dogs, cats...) into Great Britain and Ireland.

Cuisine

Stars

*Certain establishments deserve to be brought
to your attention for the particularly fine quality
of their cooking.* **Michelin stars** *are awarded
for the standard of meals served. For such
restaurants we list three culinary specialities
typical of their style of cooking to assist
you in your choice.*

❀❀❀ **Exceptional cuisine, worth a special journey**
*One always eats here extremely well, sometimes
superbly. Fine wines, faultless service, elegant
surroundings. One will pay accordingly !*

❀❀ **Excellent cooking, worth a detour**
*Specialities and wines of first class quality.
This will be reflected in the price.*

❀ **A very good restaurant in its category**
*The star indicates a good place to stop on your journey.
But beware of comparing the star given
to an expensive « de luxe » establishment
to that of a simple restaurant where you can appreciate
fine cooking at a reasonable price.*

The "Bib Gourmand"

Good food at moderate prices
*You may also like to know of other restaurants
with less elaborate, moderately priced menus
that offer good value for money
and serve carefully prepared meals.
We bring them to your attention by marking them
with the* **"Bib Gourmand"** ✍ *and* Meals *in the text of the
Guide, e.g.* Meals 19.00/25.00.

*Please refer to the map of star-rated restaurants
❀❀❀, ❀❀, ❀ and the* **"Bib Gourmand"** ✍,
*located at the beginning of each regional section
in the guide.*

Prices

Prices quoted are valid for autumn 1997. Changes may arise if goods and service costs are revised.

Hotels and restaurants in bold type have supplied details of all their rates and have assumed responsibility for maintaining them for all travellers in possession of this guide.

Prices are given in £ sterling, except for the Republic of Ireland where Irish pounds (punt) are quoted. Where no mention s., t., or st. is shown, prices may be subject to the addition of service charge, V.A.T., or both (V.A.T. does not apply in the Channel Islands).

Your recommendation is self-evident if you always walk into a hotel guide in hand.

Meals

Meals 13.00/28.00	**Set meals**
	Lunch 13.00, *dinner* 28.00 – *including cover charge, where applicable*
Meals 19.00/25.00	*See page 7*
s.	*Service only included*
t.	*V.A.T. only included*
st.	*Service and V.A.T. included*
⌕ 6.00	*Price of 1/2 bottle or carafe of house wine*
Meals a la carte	**A la carte meals**
20.00/35.00	*The prices represent the range of charges from a simple to an elaborate 3 course meal and include a cover charge where applicable*
⌕ 8.50	*Charge for full cooked breakfast (i.e. not included in the room rate)*
	Continental breakfast may be available at a lower rate

↑ : *Dinner in this category of establishment will generally be offered from a fixed price menu of limited choice, served at a set time to residents only. Lunch is rarely offered. Many will not be licensed to sell alcohol.*

8

Rooms

rm 50.00/80.00

*Lowest price 50.00 per room for a comfortable
single and highest price 80.00 per room
for the best double or twin*

suites

Check with the hotelier for prices

rm ☺ 55.00/85.00

*Full cooked breakfast (whether taken or not)
is included in the price of the room*

Short breaks (SB.)

*Many hotels offer a special rate for a stay
of two or more nights which comprises dinner,
room and breakfast usually for a minimum
of two people. Please enquire at hotel for rates.*

Alcoholic beverages-conditions of sale

*The sale of alcoholic drinks is governed
in Great Britain and Ireland by licensing laws
which vary greatly from country to country.*

*Allowing for local variations, restaurants may stay
open and serve alcohol with a bona fide meal
during the afternoon. Hotel bars and public houses
are generally open between 11am and 11pm
at the discretion of the licensee. Hotel residents,
however, may buy drinks outside the permitted
hours at the discretion of the hotelier.*

*Children under the age of 14 are not allowed
in bars.*

Deposits

*Some hotels will require a deposit, which confirms
the commitment of customer and hotelier alike.
Make sure the terms of the agreement are clear.*

Credit cards

*Credit cards accepted by the establishment:
MasterCard (Eurocard) – American Express – Diners
Club – Visa – Japan Credit Bureau*

Towns

✉ York	*Postal address*
401 M 27, ⑩	*Michelin map and co-ordinates or fold*
West Country G.	*See the Michelin Green Guide* *England : The West Country*
pop. 1057	*Population. (Crown copyright 1991. Published* *by permission of the Controller of Her Majesty's* *Stationery Office.)*
BX **A**	*Letters giving the location of a place* *on the town plan*
ⓘ₁₈	*Golf course and number of holes (handicap usually* *required, telephone reservation strongly advised)*
☀, ≤	*Panoramic view, viewpoint*
✈	*Airport*
⛴	*Shipping line*
⛵	*Passenger transport only*
🛈	*Tourist Information Centre*

Standard Time

In winter standard time throughout the British Isles
is Greenwich Mean Time (G.M.T.). In summer
British clocks are advanced by one hour to give
British Summer Time (B.S.T.). The actual dates
are announced annually but always occur over
weekends in March and October.

Sights

Star-rating

★★★	*Worth a journey*
★★	*Worth a detour*
★	*Interesting*
AC	*Admission charge*

Location

See	*Sights in town*
Envir.	*On the outskirts*
Exc.	*In the surrounding area*
N, S, E, W	*The sight lies north, south, east or west of the town*
A 22	*Take road A 22, indicated by the same symbol on the Guide map*
2 m.	*Mileage*

Car, tyres

The wearing of seat belts in Great Britain
is obligatory for drivers, front seat passengers
and rear seat passengers where seat belts are fitted.
It is illegal for front seat passengers
to carry children on their lap.

In the Republic of Ireland seat belts are
compulsory, if fitted, for drivers and front seat
passengers. Children under 12 are not allowed in
front seats unless in a suitable safety restraint.

Michelin tyre suppliers
ATS Tyre dealers

The location of the nearest ATS tyre dealer can
be obtained by contacting the address below
between 9am and 5pm.

> ATS HOUSE
> 180-188 Northolt Rd.
> Harrow,
> Middlesex HA2 0ED
> (0181) 423 2000

Motoring organisations

The major motoring organisations in Great Britain
and Ireland are the Automobile Association and the
Royal Automobile Club. Each provides services
in varying degrees for non-resident members
of affiliated clubs.

AUTOMOBILE ASSOCIATION
Fanum House
BASINGSTOKE, Hants.,
RG21 2EA
☎ (01256) 320123

ROYAL AUTOMOBILE CLUB
RAC House, Lansdowne Rd.
CROYDON, Surrey CR9 2JA
☎ (0181) 686 2525

AUTOMOBILE ASSOCIATION
23 Rock Hill
BLACKROCK
Co-Dublin
☎ (01) 283 3555

ROYAL AUTOMOBILE CLUB
RAC IRELAND
New Mount House
22-24 Lower Mount St.
DUBLIN 2
☎ (01) 676 0113

Town plans

@ ●a   *Hotels – Restaurants*

Sights

  Place of interest and its main entrance
🏛 ⚱   *Interesting place of worship*

Roads

M 1   *Motorway*
④ ④   *Junctions : complete, limited*
        Dual carriageway with motorway characteristics
        Main traffic artery
        Primary route
A 2   *- (network currently being reclassified)*
◄ ⋮⋮⋮⋮⋮ *One-way street – Unsuitable for traffic, street subject to restrictions*
        Pedestrian street
Piccadilly 🅿 *Shopping street – Car park*
⊹ ⊣⊢ ⊣⊢ *Gateway – Street passing under arch – Tunnel*
15.6   *Low headroom (16'6" max.) on major through routes*
🚉   *Station and railway*
□⁺⁺⁺⁺⁺□ □-■-■-□ *Funicular – Cable-car*
△ Ⓑ   *Lever bridge – Car ferry*

Various signs

🛈   *Tourist Information Centre*
☪ 🕎   *Mosque – Synagogue*
Υ ∴   *Communications tower or mast – Ruins*
        Garden, park, wood – Cemetery
◯ 🏇 🏌 *Stadium – Racecourse – Golf course*
⏵   *Golf course (with restrictions for visitors)*
⋖ 🎇   *View – Panorama*
■ ◉ ✚   *Monument – Fountain – Hospital*
⚓ ⛋   *Pleasure boat harbour – Lighthouse*
✈ ⊖ ●   *Airport – Underground station*
        Ferry services :
⛴   *- passengers and cars*
✉   *Main post office with poste restante, telephone*
        Public buildings located by letter :
C H   *- County Council Offices – Town Hall*
M T U *- Museum – Theatre – University, College*
POL.   *- Police (in large towns police headquarters)*

London

BRENT WEMBLEY *Borough – Area*
        Borough boundary – Area boundary

13

Ami lecteur

C'est en 1898 que je suis né. Voici donc cent ans que, sous le nom de Bibendum, je vous accompagne sur toutes les routes du monde, soucieux du confort de votre conduite, de la sécurité de votre déplacement, de l'agrément de vos étapes.

L'expérience et le savoir-faire que j'ai acquis, c'est au Guide Rouge que je les confie chaque année.

Et dans cette 25e édition, pour trouver de bonnes adresses à petits prix, un conseil : suivez donc les nombreux restaurants que vous signale mon visage de "Bib Gourmand" !

N'hésitez pas à m'écrire...

Je reste à votre service pour un nouveau siècle de découvertes.

En toute confiance,

Bibendum ———

Sommaire

Le choix d'un hôtel, d'un restaurant

Ce guide vous propose une sélection d'hôtels et restaurants établie à l'usage de l'automobiliste de passage. Les établissements, classés selon leur confort, sont cités par ordre de préférence dans chaque catégorie.

Catégories

🏨	XXXXX	*Grand luxe et tradition*
🏨	XXXX	*Grand confort*
🏚	XXX	*Très confortable*
🏚	XX	*De bon confort*
🏠	X	*Assez confortable*
	🍺	*Traditionnel "pub" anglais servant des repas*
⌂		*Autre ressource hôtelière conseillée (Logis à la ferme, maison d'hôtes et cottages)*
without rest.		*L'hôtel n'a pas de restaurant*
	with rm	*Le restaurant possède des chambres*

Agrément et tranquillité

Certains établissements se distinguent dans le guide par les symboles rouges indiqués ci-après. Le séjour dans ces hôtels se révèle particulièrement agréable ou reposant. Cela peut tenir d'une part au caractère de l'édifice, au décor original, au site, à l'accueil et aux services qui sont proposés, d'autre part à la tranquillité des lieux.

🏨 à ⌂		*Hôtels agréables*
XXXXX à X		*Restaurants agréables*
« Park »		*Élément particulièrement agréable*
	🍃	*Hôtel très tranquille ou isolé et tranquille*
	🍃	*Hôtel tranquille*
	⩽ sea	*Vue exceptionnelle*
	⩽	*Vue intéressante ou étendue.*

Les localités possédant des établissements agréables ou tranquilles sont repérées sur les cartes placées au début de chacune des régions traitées dans ce guide.

Consultez-les pour la préparation de vos voyages et donnez-nous vos appréciations à votre retour, vous faciliterez ainsi nos enquêtes.

L'installation

Les chambres des hôtels que nous recommandons possèdent, en général, des installations sanitaires complètes. Il est toutefois possible que dans les catégories 🏠, 🏠 et 🏠, certaines chambres en soient dépourvues.

30 rm	Nombre de chambres
🛗	Ascenseur
▤	Air conditionné
TV	Télévision dans la chambre
⚡	Établissement entièrement ou en partie réservé aux non-fumeurs
☎	Téléphone dans la chambre, direct avec l'extérieur
🦽	Chambres accessibles aux handicapés physiques
🍽	Repas servis au jardin ou en terrasse
⌁ ⌁	Piscine : de plein air ou couverte
🏋 ⌁s	Salle de remise en forme – Sauna
🌿	Jardin de repos
⚡ ⌁8	Tennis à l'hôtel – Golf et nombre de trous
⚓	Ponton d'amarrage
⌁	Pêche ouverte aux clients de l'hôtel (éventuellement payant)
🏛 150	Salles de conférences : capacité maximum
🚗	Garage dans l'hôtel (généralement payant)
🅿	Parking réservé à la clientèle
🐕	Accès interdit aux chiens (dans tout ou partie de l'établissement)
Fax	Transmission de documents par télécopie
May-October	Période d'ouverture, communiquée par l'hôtelier
season	Ouverture probable en saison mais dates non précisées. En l'absence de mention, l'établissement est ouvert toute l'année.
LL35 OSB	Code postal de l'établissement

Animaux

L'introduction d'animaux domestiques (chiens, chats...) est interdite en Grande-Bretagne et en Irlande.

La table

Les étoiles

*Certains établissements méritent d'être signalés
à votre attention pour la qualité de leur cuisine.
Nous les distinguons par les étoiles de bonne table.
Nous indiquons, pour ces établissements,
trois spécialités culinaires qui pourront orienter
votre choix.*

🏵🏵🏵 Une des meilleures tables, vaut le voyage
*On y mange toujours très bien, parfois
merveilleusement. Grands vins, service impeccable,
cadre élégant... Prix en conséquence.*

🏵🏵 Table excellente, mérite un détour
*Spécialités et vins de choix...
Attendez-vous à une dépense en rapport.*

🏵 Une très bonne table dans sa catégorie
*L'étoile marque une bonne étape
sur votre itinéraire.
Mais ne comparez pas l'étoile d'un établissement
de luxe à prix élevés avec celle d'une petite maison
où à prix raisonnables, on sert également
une cuisine de qualité.*

😋 Le "Bib Gourmand"

Repas soignés à prix modérés

*Vous souhaitez parfois trouver des tables plus
simples, à prix modérés ; c'est pourquoi nous avons
sélectionné des restaurants proposant, pour un
rapport qualité-prix particulièrement favorable,
un repas soigné.
Ces restaurants sont signalés par le* "Bib Gourmand" 😋
et Meals
Ex Meals *19.00/25.00.*

*Consultez les cartes des étoiles de bonne table
🏵🏵🏵, 🏵🏵, 🏵 et des* "Bib Gourmand" 😋*,
placées au début de chacune des régions traitées
dans ce guide.*

Les prix

Les prix que nous indiquons dans ce guide
ont été établis en automne 1997. Ils sont susceptibles
de modifications, notamment en cas de variations
des prix des biens et services.

Les prix sont indiqués en livres sterling
(1 £ = 100 pence), sauf en République d'Irlande
où ils sont donnés en « Punts ».
Lorsque les mentions s., t., ou st. ne figurent pas,
les prix indiqués peuvent être majorés
d'un pourcentage pour le service, la T.V.A.,
ou les deux (la T.V.A. n'est pas appliquée
dans les Channel Islands).
Les hôtels et restaurants figurent en gros caractères
lorsque les hôteliers nous ont donné tous leurs prix
et se sont engagés, sous leur propre responsabilité,
à les appliquer aux touristes de passage porteurs
de notre guide.

Entrez à l'hôtel le guide à la main, vous montrerez
ainsi qu'il vous conduit là en confiance.

Repas

Meals 13.00/28.00	**Repas à prix fixe**
	Déjeuner 13.00, dîner 28.00. Ces prix s'entendent couvert compris
Meals 19.00/25.00	*Voir page 19*
s.	*Service compris*
t.	*T.V.A. comprise*
st.	*Service et T.V.A. compris (prix nets)*
⌐ 6.00	*Prix de la 1/2 bouteille ou carafe de vin ordinaire*
Meals à la carte 20.00/35.00	**Repas à la carte**
	Le 1er prix correspond à un repas simple mais soigné, comprenant : petite entrée, plat du jour garni, dessert. Le 2e prix concerne un repas plus complet, comprenant : entrée, plat principal, fromage ou dessert. Ces prix s'entendent couvert compris
⌣ 8.50	*Prix du petit déjeuner à l'anglaise, s'il n'est pas compris dans celui de la chambre. Un petit déjeuner continental peut être obtenu à moindre prix.*

↑ : *Dans les établissements de cette catégorie,
le dîner est servi à heure fixe exclusivement
aux personnes ayant une chambre. Le menu,
à prix unique, offre un choix limité de plats.
Le déjeuner est rarement proposé.
Beaucoup de ces établissements ne sont pas autorisés
à vendre des boissons alcoolisées.*

Chambres

rm 50.00/80.00

*Prix minimum 50.00 d'une chambre pour une
personne et prix maximum 80.00 de la plus belle
chambre occupée par deux personnes*

suites
Se renseigner auprès de l'hôtelier

rm ⊆ 55.00/85.00
*Le prix du petit déjeuner à l'anglaise est inclus
dans le prix de la chambre,
même s'il n'est pas consommé*

« Short breaks » (SB.)

*Certains hôtels proposent des conditions
avantageuses ou « Short Break » pour un séjour
minimum de 2 nuits. Ce forfait calculé
par personne, pour 2 personnes au minimum,
comprend la chambre, le dîner et le petit déjeuner.
Se renseigner auprès de l'hôtelier.*

La vente de boissons alcoolisées

*En Grande-Bretagne et en Irlande, la vente
de boissons alcoolisées est soumise à des lois
pouvant varier d'une région à l'autre.
D'une façon générale, les restaurants peuvent
demeurer ouverts l'après-midi et servir des boissons
alcoolisées dans la mesure où elles accompagnent
un repas suffisamment consistant. Les bars d'hôtel
et les pubs sont habituellement ouverts de 11 heures
à 23 heures. Néanmoins, l'hôtelier a toujours
la possibilité de servir, à sa clientèle,
des boissons alcoolisées en dehors des heures légales.
Les enfants au-dessous de 14 ans n'ont pas accès
aux bars.*

Les arrhes

*Certains hôteliers demandent le versement d'arrhes.
Il s'agit d'un dépôt-garantie qui engage l'hôtelier
comme le client. Bien faire préciser les dispositions
de cette garantie.*

Cartes de crédit

*Cartes de crédit acceptées par l'établissement :
MasterCard (Eurocard) – American Express –
Diners Club – Visa – Japan Credit Bureau*

Les villes

✉ York	*Bureau de poste desservant la localité*
401 M 27, ⑩	*Numéro des cartes Michelin et carroyage ou numéro du pli*
West Country G.	*Voir le guide vert Michelin England : The West Country*
pop. 1057	*Population*
BX A	*Lettres repérant un emplacement sur le plan*
18	*Golf et nombre de trous (Handicap généralement demandé, réservation par téléphone vivement recommandée)*
✻, ⋞	*Panorama, point de vue*
✈	*Aéroport*
⛴	*Transports maritimes*
⛴	*Transports maritimes (pour passagers seulement)*
ℹ	*Information touristique*

Heure légale

Les visiteurs devront tenir compte de l'heure officielle
en Grande-Bretagne : une heure de retard sur l'heure française.

Les curiosités

Intérêt

★★★	*Vaut le voyage*
★★	*Mérite un détour*
★	*Intéressant*
AC	*Entrée payante*

Situation

See	*Dans la ville*
Envir.	*Aux environs de la ville*
Exc.	*Excursions dans la région*
N, S, E, W	*La curiosité est située :* *au Nord, au Sud, à l'Est, à l'Ouest*
A 22	*On s'y rend par la route A 22, repérée* *par le même signe sur le plan du Guide*
2 m.	*Distance en miles*

La voiture, les pneus

En Grande-Bretagne, le port de la ceinture
de sécurité est obligatoire pour le conducteur
et le passager avant ainsi qu'à l'arrière, si le
véhicule en est équipé. La loi interdit au passager
avant de prendre un enfant sur ses genoux.

En République d'Irlande, le port de la ceinture
de sécurité est obligatoire pour le conducteur
et le passager avant, si le véhicule en est équipé.
Les enfants de moins de 12 ans ne sont pas
autorisés à s'asseoir à l'avant, sauf si le véhicule
est muni d'un système d'attache approprié.

Fournisseurs de pneus michelin
ATS Spécialistes du pneu

Des renseignements sur le plus proche point
de vente de pneus ATS pourront être obtenus
en s'informant entre 9 h et 17 h à l'adresse
indiquée ci-dessous.

> ATS HOUSE
> 180-188 Northolt Rd.
> Harrow,
> Middlesex HA2 OED
> (0181) 423 2000

Automobile clubs

Les principales organisations de secours automobile
dans le pays sont l'Automobile Association et le
Royal Automobile Club, toutes deux offrant certains
de leurs services aux membres de clubs affiliés.

AUTOMOBILE ASSOCIATION
Fanum House
BASINGSTOKE, Hants.,
RG21 2EA
☏ (01256) 320123

ROYAL AUTOMOBILE CLUB
RAC House, Lansdowne Rd,
CROYDON, Surrey CR9 2JA
☏ (0181) 686 2525

AUTOMOBILE ASSOCIATION
23 Rock Hill
BLACKROCK
Co-Dublin
☏ (01) 283 3555

ROYAL AUTOMOBILE CLUB
RAC IRELAND New Mount
House
22-24 Lower Mount St.
DUBLIN 2
☏ (01) 676 0113

Les plans

ⓐ ●a   *Hôtels – Restaurants*

Curiosités

Bâtiment intéressant et entrée principale
Édifice religieux intéressant

Voirie

M 1   *Autoroute*
④   ④   *- échangeurs : complet, partiel*
Route à chaussées séparées de type autoroutier
Grand axe de circulation
A 2   *Itinéraire principal (Primary route)*
- réseau en cours de révision
Sens unique – Rue impraticable, réglementée
Rue piétonne
Piccadilly P   *Rue commerçante – Parc de stationnement*
Porte – Passage sous voûte – Tunnel
15.5   *Passage bas (inférieur à 16′6″) sur les grandes voies de circulation*
Gare et voie ferrée
Funiculaire – Téléphérique, télécabine
△ B   *Pont mobile – Bac pour autos*

Signes divers

🛈   *Information touristique*
ŏ ✡   *Mosquée – Synagogue*
Tour ou pylône de télécommunication – Ruines
Jardin, parc, bois – Cimetière
Stade – Hippodrome – Golf
Golf (réservé)
Vue – Panorama
Monument – Fontaine – Hôpital
Port de plaisance – Phare
Aéroport – Station de métro
Transport par bateau :
- passagers et voitures
✉   *Bureau principal de poste restante, téléphone*
Bâtiment public repéré par une lettre :
C   H   *- Bureau de l'Administration du Comté – Hôtel de ville*
M   T   U   *- Musée – Théâtre – Université, grande école*
POL.   *- Police (commissariat central)*

Londres

BRENT WEMBLEY   *Nom d'arrondissement (borough) – de quartier (area)*
Limite de « borough » – d'« area »

Amico lettore

E' nel 1898 che sono nato e da cento anni quindi, con il nome di Bibendum, vi accompagno per le strade del mondo, attendo al comfort della vostra guida, alla sicurezza dei vostri spostamenti, alla piacevolezza delle vostre soste.

L'esperienza ed il savoir-faire acquisiti li affido ogni anno alla Guida Rossa.

E, in questa 25^{esima} edizione, un consiglio per trovare dei buoni indirizzi a prezzi interessanti : cercate i tanti ristoranti contrassegnati dal mio faccino di "Bib Gourmand" !

Non esitate a scrivermi...

Resto al vostro servizio per un nuovo secolo di scoperte.

Cordialmente.

Bibendum _____

Sommario

La scelta di un albergo, di un ristorante

Questa guida propone una selezione di alberghi e ristoranti per orientare la scelta dell'automobilista. Gli esercizi, classificati in base al confort che offrono, vengono citati in ordine di preferenza per ogni categoria.

Categorie

🏨	XXXXX	*Gran lusso e tradizione*
🏨	XXXX	*Gran confort*
🏨	XXX	*Molto confortevole*
🏨	XX	*Di buon confort*
🏨	X	*Abbastanza confortevole*
	🍴	*Pub tradizionali con cucina*
⌂		*Altra forme di alloggio consigliate (Pensioni, Fattorie e Casa private)*
without rest.		*L'albergo non ha ristorante*
	with rm	*Il ristorante dispone di camere*

Amenità e tranquillità

Alcuni esercizi sono evidenziati nella guida dai simboli rossi indicati qui di seguito. Il soggiorno in questi alberghi si rivela particolarmente ameno o riposante.
Ciò può dipendere sia dalle caratteristiche dell'edificio, dalle decorazioni non comuni, dalla sua posizione e dal servizio offerto, sia dalla tranquillità dei luoghi.

🏨 a ⌂	*Alberghi ameni*
XXXXX a X	*Ristoranti ameni*
« Park »	*Un particolare piacevole*
🦅	*Albergo molto tranquillo o isolato e tranquillo*
🦅	*Albergo tranquillo*
≤ sea	*Vista eccezionale*
≤	*Vista interessante o estesa*

Le località che possiedono degli esercizi ameni o tranquilli sono riportate sulle carte che precedono ciascuna delle regioni trattate nella guida.
Consultatele per la preparazione dei vostri viaggi e, al ritorno, inviateci i vostri pareri ; in tal modo agevolerete le nostre inchieste.

Installazioni

Le camere degli alberghi che raccomandiamo possiedono, generalmente, delle installazioni sanitarie complete. È possibile tuttavia che nelle categorie 🏨, 🏠 *e* ⌂ *alcune camere ne siano sprovviste.*

30 rm	*Numero di camere*
🛗	*Ascensore*
▤	*Aria condizionata*
TV	*Televisione in camera*
⇸	*Esercizio riservato completamente o in parte ai non fumatori*
☎	*Telefono in camera comunicante direttamente con l'esterno*
ⴕ	*Camere di agevole accesso per portatori di handicap*
🀆	*Pasti serviti in giardino o in terrazza*
⌇ ⊠	*Piscina : all'aperto, coperta*
⌘ ⇋	*Palestra – Sauna*
🎐	*Giardino*
⚹ ⛳	*Tennis appartenente all'albergo – Golf e numero di buche*
⚓	*Pontile d'ormeggio*
⤳	*Pesca aperta ai clienti dell'albergo (eventualmente a pagamento)*
🏛 150	*Sale per conferenze : capienza massima*
🚗	*Garage nell'albergo (generalmente a pagamento)*
🅿	*Parcheggio riservato alla clientela*
🐕	*Accesso vietato ai cani (in tutto o in parte dell'esercizio)*
Fax	*Trasmissione telefonica di documenti*
May-October	*Periodo di apertura, comunicato dall'albergatore*
season	*Probabile apertura in stagione, ma periodo non precisato. Gli esercizi senza tali menzioni sono aperti tutto l'anno.*
LL35 OSB	*Codice postale dell'esercizio*

Animali

L'introduzione di animali domestici (cani, gatti...), in Gran Bretagna e in Irlanda, è vietata.

La tavola

Le stelle

*Alcuni esercizi meritano di essere segnalati alla
vostra attenzione per la qualità particolare della
loro cucina ; li abbiamo evidenziati
con le « stelle di ottima tavola ».
Per ognuno di questi ristoranti indichiamo
tre specialità culinarie e alcuni vini locali
che potranno aiutarvi nella scelta.*

❀❀❀ **Una delle migliori tavole, vale il viaggio**
*Vi si mangia sempre molto bene, a volte
meravigliosamente. Grandi vini, servizio impeccabile,
ambientazione accurata... Prezzi conformi.*

❀❀ **Tavola eccellente, merita una deviazione**
*Specialità e vini scelti...
Aspettatevi una spesa in proporzione.*

❀ **Un'ottima tavola nella sua categoria**
*La stella indica una tappa gastronomica
sul vostro itinerario.
Non mettete però a confronto la stella di un esercizio
di lusso, dai prezzi elevati, con quella di un piccolo
esercizio dove, a prezzi ragionevoli, viene offerta
una cucina di qualità.*

Il "Bib Gourmand"

Pasti accurati a prezzi contenuti

*Per quando desiderate trovare delle tavole più
semplici a prezzi contenuti abbiamo selezionato
dei ristoranti che, per un rapporto qualità-prezzo
particolarmente favorevole, offrono un pasto
accurato.
Questi ristoranti sono evidenziali nel testo con
il "Bib Gourmand"* 🅰 *e* Meals, *evidenziata in rosso,
davanti ai prezzi.
Ex.* Meals *19.00/25.00*

Consultate le carte delle stelle ❀❀❀, ❀❀, ❀
e con il "Bib Gourmand" 🅰, *che precedono
ciascuna delle regioni trattate nella guida.*

I prezzi

*I prezzi che indichiamo in questa guida sono stati
stabiliti nell'autunno 1997 e potranno pertanto
subire delle variazioni in relazione ai
cambiamenti dei prezzi di beni e servizi.*

*Gli alberghi e i ristoranti vengono menzionati in
carattere grassetto quando gli albergatori ci hanno
comunicato tutti i loro prezzi e si sono impegnati,
sotto la propria responsabilità, ad applicarli ai
turisti di passaggio, in possesso della nostra guida.
I prezzi sono indicati in lire sterline
(1 £ = 100 pence) ad eccezione per la Repubblica
d'Irlanda dove sono indicati in « punts ».
Quando non figurano le lettere s., t., o st. i prezzi
indicati possono essere maggiorati per il servizio
o per l'I.V.A. o per entrambi. (L'I.V.A. non viene
applicata nelle Channel Islands).*

*Entrate nell'albergo o nel ristorante con la guida
in mano, dimostrando in tal modo la fiducia
in chi vi ha indirizzato.*

Pasti

Meals 13.00/28.00   **Prezzo fisso**
Pranzo 13.00, *cena* 28.00. *Questi prezzi comprendono
il coperto*

Meals 19.00/25.00   *Vedere p. 31*

s.   *Servizio compreso*

t.   *I.V.A. compresa*

st.   *Servizio èd I.V.A. compresi (prezzi netti)*

🍷 6.00   *Prezzo della mezza bottiglia o di una caraffa di vino*

Meals a la carte   **Alla carta**
20.00/35.00   *Il 1° prezzo corrisponde ad un pasto semplice
comprendente : primo piatto, piatto del giorno
con contorno, dessert. Il 2° prezzo corrisponde
ad un pasto più completo comprendente : antipasto,
piatto principale, formaggio o dessert
Questi prezzi comprendono il coperto*

🍵 8.50   *Prezzo della prima colazione inglese se non
è compreso nel prezzo della camera. Una prima
colazione continentale può essere ottenuta a minor prezzo*

↑ : *Negli alberghi di questa categoria, la cena
viene servita, ad un'ora stabilita, esclusivamente
a chi vi alloggia. Il menu, a prezzo fisso, offre
una scelta limitata di piatti. Raramente viene
servito anche il pranzo. Molti di questi esercizi
non hanno l'autorizzazione a vendere alcolici.*

Camere

rm 50.00/80.00

suites

rm ⌖ 55.00/85.00

Prezzo minimo 50.00 per una camera singola e prezzo massimo 80.00 per la camera più bella per due persone
Informarsi presso l'albergatore
Il prezzo della prima colazione inglese è compreso nel prezzo della camera anche se non viene consumata

« Short breaks » (SB.)

Alcuni alberghi propongono delle condizioni particolarmente vantaggiose o short break per un soggiorno minimo di due notti.
Questo prezzo, calcolato per persona e per un minimo di due persone, comprende : camera, cena e prima colazione. Informarsi presso l'albergatore.

La vendita di bevande alcoliche

La vendita di bevande alcoliche in Gran Bretagna è regolata da leggi che variano considerevolmente da regione a regione.

Eccezion fatta per varianti locali, i ristoranti possomo rimanere aperti o servire bevande alcoliche con i pasti il pomeriggio. I bar degli hotel e i pub sono generalmente aperti dalle 11 alle 23, a discrezione del gestore. I clienti dell'hotel, comunque, possono acquistare bevande al di fuori delle ore stabilite se il direttore lo permette.

I bambini al di sotto del 14 anni non possono entrare nei bar.

La caparra

Alcuni albergatori chiedono il versamento di una caparra. Si tratta di un deposito-garanzia che impegna tanto l'albergatore che il cliente.
Vi consigliamo di farvi precisare le norme riguardanti la reciproca garanzia di tale caparra.

Carte di credito

⊕ AE ⊕ VISA JCB

Carte di credito accettate dall'esercizio
MasterCard (Eurocard) – American Express – Diners Club – Visa – Japan Credit Bureau

Le città

⊠ York	*Sede dell'ufficio postale*
401 M 27, ⑩	*Numero della carta Michelin e del riquadro o numero della piega*
West Country G.	*Vedere la Guida Verde Michelin England : The West Country*
pop. 1057	*Popolazione*
BX A	*Lettere indicanti l'ubicazione sulla pianta*
⌐18	*Golf e numero di buche (handicap generalmente richiesto, prenotazione telefonica vivamente consigliata)*
☀, ≼	*Panorama, vista*
✈	*Aeroporto*
⛴	*Trasporti marittimi*
⛴	*Trasporti marittimi (solo passeggeri)*
🛈	*Ufficio informazioni turistiche*

Ora legale

I visitatori dovranno tenere in considerazione l'ora ufficiale in Gran Bretagna : un'ora di ritardo sull'ora italiana.

Le curiosità

Grado di interesse

★★★	*Vale il viaggio*
★★	*Merita una deviazione*
★	*Interessante*
AC	*Entrata a pagamento*

Ubicazione

See	*Nella città*
Envir.	*Nei dintorni della città*
Exc.	*Nella regione*
N, S, E, W	*La curiosità è situata : a Nord, a Sud, a Est, a Ovest*
A 22	*Ci si va per la strada A 22 indicata con lo stesso segno sulla pianta*
2 m.	*Distanza in miglia*

L'automobile, I pneumatici

In Gran Bretagna, l'uso delle cinture di sicurezza
è obbligatorio per il conducente ed il passeggero del
sedile anteriore, nonchè per i sedili posteriori, se ne sono
equipaggiati. La legge non consente al passaggero
davanti di tenere un bambino sulle ginocchia.
Nella Repubblica d'Irlanda, l'uso delle cinture di
sicurezza è obbligatorio per il conducente e il
passeggero davanti, se il veicolo ne è equipaggiato.
I bambini di meno di 12 anni non sono
autorizzati a viaggiare sul sedile anteriore, a meno
che questo non sia dotato di un sistema
di sicurezza espressamente concepito.

Rivenditori di pneumatici Michelin
ATS Specialista in pneumatici

Potrete avere delle informazioni sul più vicino
punto vendita di pneumatici ATS, rivolgendovi, tra
le 9 e le 17, all'indirizzo indicato qui di seguito :

ATS HOUSE
180-188 Northolt Rd.
Harrow,
Middlesex HA2 OED
(0181) 423 2000

Automobile clubs

Le principali organizzazioni di soccorso
automobilistico sono l'Automobile Association ed il
Royal Automobile Club : entrambe offrono alcuni
servizi ai membri affiliati.

AUTOMOBILE ASSOCIATION
Fanum House
BASINGSTOKE. Hants.,
RG21 2EA
☏ (01256) 320123

ROYAL AUTOMOBILE CLUB
RAC House, Lansdowne Rd,
CROYDON, Surrey CR9 2JA
☏ (0181) 686 2525

AUTOMOBILE ASSOCIATION
23 Rock Hill
BLACKROCK
Co-Dublin
☏ (01) 283 3555

ROYAL AUTOMOBILE CLUB
RAC IRELAND
New Mount House
22-24 Lower Mount St.
DUBLIN 2
☏ (01) 676 0113

Le piante

@ ● a   *Alberghi – Ristoranti*

Curiosità

    Edificio interessante ed entrata principale
🏛 ⚲   *Costruzione religiosa interessante*

Viabilità

    Autostrada
❹ ❹   *- svincoli : completo, parziale,*
   Strada a carreggiate separate di tipo autostradale
   Asse principale di circolazione
A 2   *Itinerario principale*
   - (« Primary route », rete stradale in corso di revisione)
◄ ⟹⟹   *Senso unico – Via impraticabile, a circolazione regolamentata*
   Via pedonale
Piccadilly 🅿   *Via commerciale – Parcheggio*
╪ ╡╞ ╡╞   *Porta – Sottopassaggio – Galleria*
16'3   *Sottopassaggio (altezza inferiore a 16'6") sulle grandi vie di circolazione*
   Stazione e ferrovia
⬦⊶⊶⊶ ⬦⬛⬛⬛   *Funicolare – Funivia, Cabinovia*
⚠ 🅱   *Ponte mobile – Traghetto per auto*

Simboli vari

🛈   *Ufficio informazioni turistiche*
☪ ✡   *Moschea – Sinagoga*
ⵟ ∴   *Torre o pilone per telecomunicazioni – Ruderi*
🌳 ⸬   *Giardino, parco, bosco – Cimitero*
◯ 🏇 ⓡ   *Stadio – Ippodromo – Golf*
ⲣ   *Golf riservato*
⊰ ✵   *Vista – Panorama*
■ ◉ ✚   *Monumento – Fontana – Ospedale*
⚓ ⚑   *Porto per imbarcazioni da diporto – Faro*
✈ ⊖ ●   *Aeroporto – Stazione della Metropolitana*
⛴   *Trasporto con traghetto :*
   - passeggeri ed autovetture
✉   *Ufficio centrale di fermo posta, telefono*
▦   *Edificio pubblico indicato con lettera :*
C H   *- Sede dell'Amministrazione di Contea – Municipio*
M T U   *- Museo – Teatro – Università, grande scuola*
POL.   *- Polizia (Questura, nelle grandi città)*

Londra

BRENT WEMBLEY   *Nome del distretto amministrativo (borough) – del quartiere (area)*
   Limite del « borough » – di « area »

Lieber Leser

Im Jahre 1898 habe ich das Licht der Welt erblickt. So bin ich schon seit hundert Jahren als Bibendum Ihr treuer Wegbegleiter auf all Ihren Reisen und sorge für Ihre Sicherheit während der Fahrt und für Ihre Bequemlichkeit bei Ihren Aufenthalten in Hotels und Restaurants.

Es sind meine Erfahrungen und mein Know how, die alljährlich in den Roten Hotelführer einfliessen.

Um in dieser 25. Ausgabe gute Restaurants mit kleinen Preisen zu finden, hier mein Typ : folgenSie meinem fröhlichen **"Bib Gourmand"** *Gesicht, es wird Ihnen den Weg zu zahlreichen Restaurants mir besonders günstigem Preis-/Leistungsverhältnis weisen ! Ihre Kommentare sind uns jederzeit herzlich willkommen.*

Stets zu Diensten im Hinblick auf ein neues Jahrhundert voller Entdeckungen.

Mit freundlichen Grüssen.

Bibendum _____

Inhaltsverzeichnis

Wahl eines Hotels, eines Restaurants

Die Auswahl der in diesem Führer aufgeführten Hotels und Restaurants ist für Durchreisende gedacht. In jeder Kategorie drückt die Reihenfolge der Betriebe (sie sind nach ihrem Komfort klassifiziert) eine weitere Rangordnung aus.

Kategorien

🏨	🎋🎋🎋🎋🎋	*Großer Luxus und Tradition*
🏨	🎋🎋🎋🎋	*Großer Komfort*
🏨	🎋🎋🎋	*Sehr komfortabel*
🏨	🎋🎋	*Mit gutem Komfort*
🏨	🎋	*Mit Standard Komfort*
	🍴	*Traditionelle Pubs die Speisen anbieten*
↑		*Andere empfohlene Übernachtungsmöglichkeiten (Gästehäuser, Bauernhäuser und Private Übernachtungsmöglichkeiten) und Pensionen*
without rest.		*Hotel ohne Restaurant*
with rm		*Restaurant vermietet auch Zimmer*

Annehmlichkeiten

Manche Häuser sind im Führer durch rote Symbole gekennzeichnet (s. unten). Der Aufenthalt in diesen ist wegen der schönen, ruhigen Lage, der nicht alltäglichen Einrichtung und Atmosphäre sowie dem gebotenen Service besonders angenehm und erholsam.

🏨 bis ↑		*Angenehme Hotels*
🎋🎋🎋🎋🎋 bis 🎋		*Angenehme Restaurants*
« Park »		*Besondere Annehmlichkeit*
⊗		*Sehr ruhiges, oder abgelegenes und ruhiges Hotel*
⊗		*Ruhiges Hotel*
⩽ sea		*Reizvolle Aussicht*
⩽		*Interessante oder weite Sicht*

Die den einzelnen Regionen vorangestellten Übersichtskarten, auf denen die Orte mit besonders angenehmen oder ruhigen Häusern eingezeichnet sind, helfen Ihnen bei der Reisevorbereitung. Teilen Sie uns bitte nach der Reise Ihre Erfahrungen und Meinungen mit. Sie helfen uns damit, den Führer weiter zu verbessern.

41

Einrichtung

Die meisten der empfohlenen Hotels verfügen über Zimmer, die alle oder doch zum größten Teil mit einer Naßzelle ausgestattet sind. In den Häusern der Kategorien 🏨, 🏠 und ⌂ kann diese jedoch in einigen Zimmern fehlen.

30 rm	Anzahl der Zimmer
🛗	Fahrstuhl
▤	Klimaanlage
📺	Fernsehen im Zimmer
⚞⚟	Hotel ganz oder teilweise reserviert für Nichtraucher
☎	Zimmertelefon mit direkter Außenverbindung
♿	Für Körperbehinderte leicht zugängliche Zimmer
⌂	Garten-, Terrassenrestaurant
⋛ ⊠	Freibad, Hallenbad
🏋 ⊆s	Fitneßraum – Sauna
⚘	Liegewiese, Garten
✗ ⌐18	Hoteleigener Tennisplatz – Golfplatz und Lochzahl
⚓	Bootssteg
◁	Angelmöglichkeit für Hotelgäste, evtl. gegen Gebühr
🏛 150	Konferenzräume : Höchstkapazität
⌥	Hotelgarage (wird gewöhnlich berechnet)
℗	Parkplatz reserviert für Gäste
🐕̸	Hunde sind unerwünscht (im ganzen Haus bzw. in den Zimmern oder im Restaurant)
Fax	Telefonische Dokumentenübermittlung
May-October	Öffnungszeit, vom Hotelier mitgeteilt
season	Unbestimmte Öffnungszeit eines Saisonhotels. Die Häuser, für die wir keine Schließungszeiten angeben, sind im allgemeinen ganzjährig geöffnet
LL35 OSB	Angabe des Postbezirks (hinter der Hoteladresse)

Tiere

Das Mitführen von Haustieren (Hunde, Katzen u. dgl.) bei der Einreise in Großbritannien und Irland ist untersagt.

Küche

Die Sterne

*Einige Häuser verdienen wegen ihrer
überdurchschnittlich guten Küche Ihre besondere
Beachtung. Auf diese Häuser weisen die Sterne hin.
Bei den mit « Stern » ausgezeichneten Betrieben
nennen wir drei kulinarische Spezialitäten,
die Sie probieren sollten.*

❀❀❀ ### Eine der besten Küchen : eine Reise wert
*Man ißt hier immer sehr gut, öfters auch
exzellent, edle Weine, tadelloser Service, gepflegte
Atmosphäre ... entsprechende Preise.*

❀❀ ### Eine hervorragende Küche : verdient einen Umweg
Ausgesuchte Menus und Weine ... angemessene Preise.

❀ ### Eine sehr gute Küche : verdient Ihre besondere Beachtung
*Der Stern bedeutet eine angenehme Unterbrechung
Ihrer Reise.*
*Vergleichen Sie aber bitte nicht den Stern eines sehr
teuren Luxusrestaurants mit dem Stern eines kleineren
oder mittleren Hauses, wo man Ihnen zu einem
annehmbaren Preis eine ebenfalls vorzügliche Mahlzeit
reicht.*

Der "Bib Gourmand"

Sorgfältig zubereitete, preiswerte Mahlzeiten

*Für Sie wird es interessant sein, auch solche Häuser
kennenzulernen, die eine etwas einfachere, Küche
zu einem besonders günstigen Preis/Leistungs-
Verhältnis bieten.*
*Im Text sind die betreffenden Restaurants durch die
Angabe "Bib Gourmand"* ☺ *und* Meals *kenntlich gemacht,
z. B* Meals *19.00/25.00.*

Siehe Karten mit « Stern » ❀❀❀, ❀❀, ❀ *und
"Bib Gourmand"* ☺, *die den einzelnen im Führer
behandelten Regionen vorangestellt sind.*

Preise

Die in diesem Führer genannten Preise wurden uns im Herbst 1997 angegeben. Sie können sich mit den Preisen von Waren und Dienstleistungen ändern.

Die Preise sind in Pfund Sterling angegeben (1 £ = 100 pence) mit Ausnahme der Republik Irland wo sie in Punts angegeben sind.

Wenn die Buchstaben **s.**, **t.**, oder **st.** nicht hinter den angegebenen Preisen aufgeführt sind, können sich diese um den Zuschlag für Bedienung und/oder MWSt erhöhen (keine MWSt auf den Channel Islands).

Die Namen der Hotels und Restaurants, die ihre Preise genannt haben, sind fett gedruckt.

Gleichzeitig haben sich diese Häuser verpflichtet, die von den Hoteliers selbst angegebenen Preise den Benutzern des Michelin-Führers zu berechnen.

Halten Sie beim Betreten des Hotels den Führer in der Hand. Sie zeigen damit, daß Sie aufgrund dieser Empfehlung gekommen sind.

Mahlzeiten

Meals 13.00/28.00	**Feste Menupreise**
	Mittagessen 13.00, *Abendessen* 28.00 *(inkl. Couvert)*
Meals 19.00/25.00	*Siehe Seite 43*
s.	*Bedienung inkl.*
t.	*MWSt inkl.*
st.	*Bedienung und MWSt inkl.*
▯ 6.00	*Preis für 1/2 Flasche oder eine Karaffe Tafelwein*
Meals a la carte 20.00/35.00	**Mahlzeiten « à la carte »**
	Der erste Preis entspricht einer einfachen aber sorgfältig zubereiteten Mahlzeit, bestehend aus kleiner Vorspeise, Tagesgericht mit Beilage und Nachtisch. Der zweite Preis entspricht einer reichlicheren Mahlzeit mit Vorspeise, Hauptgericht, Käse oder Nachtisch (inkl. Couvert)
⌑ 8.50	*Preis des englischen Frühstücks, wenn dieser nicht im Übernachtungspreis enthalten ist. Einfaches, billigeres Frühstück (Continental breakfast) erhältlich*

↑ : In dieser Hotelkategorie wird ein Abendessen normalerweise nur zu bestimmten Zeiten für Hotelgäste angeboten. Es besteht aus einem Menu mit begrenzter Auswahl zu festgesetztem Preis. Mittagessen wird selten angeboten. Viele dieser Hotels sind nicht berechtigt, alkoholische Getränke auszuschenken.

Zimmer

rm 50.00/80.00

Mindestpreis 50.00 für ein Einzelzimmer und
Höchstpreis 80.00 für das schönste Doppelzimmer

suites

Preise auf Anfrage

rm ⌑ 55.00/85.00

Übernachtung mit englischem Frühstück, selbst wenn
dieses nicht eingenommen wird

« Short breaks » (SB.)

Einige Hotels bieten Vorzugskonditionen für einen
Mindestaufenthalt von zwei Nächten oder mehr
(Short Break). Der Preis ist pro Person kalkuliert,
bei einer Mindestbeteiligung von zwei Personen
und schließt das Zimmer, das Abendessen
und das Frühstück ein.

Ausschank alkoholischer Getränke

In Großbritanien und Irland unterliegt der Ausschank
alkoholischer Getränke gesetzlichen Bestimmungen
die von Land zu Land sehr verschieden sind.

Restaurants können nachmittags geöffnet sein und
alkoholische Getränke ausschenken, wenn diese zu einer
entsprechenden Mahlzeit genossen werden. Hotelbars und
Pubs sind generell von 11 Uhr vormittags bis 23 Uhr
abends geöffnet: Hotelgäste können alkoholische Getränke
jedoch auch außerhalb der Öffnungszeiten serviert
werden.

Kindern unter 14 Jahren ist der Aufenthalt in Bars
untersagt.

Anzahlung

Einige Hoteliers verlangen eine Anzahlung.
Diese ist als Garantie sowohl für den Hotelier
als auch für den Gast anzusehen.

Kreditkarten

⊙ⓔ AE ① VISA JCB

Vom Haus akzeptierte Kreditkarten :
MasterCard (Eurocard) – American Express –
Diners Club – Visa – Japan Credit Bureau

Städte

✉ York	*Zuständiges Postamt*
401 M 27, ⑩	*Nummer der Michelin-Karte und Koordinaten* *des Planfeldes oder Faltseite*
West Country G.	*Siehe auch den grünen Michelinführer* *« England : The West Country »*
pop. 1057	*Einwohnerzahl*
BX A	*Markierung auf dem Stadtplan*
⌐₁₈	*Öffentlicher Golfplatz und Lochzahl* *(Handicap erforderlich, telefonische Reservierung* *empfehlenswert)*
❋, ≼	*Rundblick, Aussichtspunkt*
✈	*Flughafen*
⛴	*Autofähre*
⛴	*Personenfähre*
🛈	*Informationsstelle*

Uhrzeit

In Großbritannien ist eine Zeitverschiebung
zu beachten und die Uhr gegenüber der deutschen
Zeit um 1 Stunde zurückzustellen.

Sehenswürdigkeiten

Bewertung

★★★	*Eine Reise wert*
★★	*Verdient einen Umweg*
★	*Sehenswert*
AC	*Eintritt (gegen Gebühr)*

Lage

See	*In der Stadt*
Envir.	*In der Umgebung der Stadt*
Exc.	*Ausflugsziele*
N, S, E, W	*Im Norden (N), Süden (S), Osten (E), Westen (W) der Stadt*
A 22	*Zu erreichen über die Straße A 22*
2 m.	*Entfernung in Meilen*

Das Auto, die Reifen

*In Großbritannien herrscht Anschnallpflicht für
Fahrer, Beifahrer und auf dem Rücksitz, wenn
Gurte vorhanden sind. Es ist verboten, Kinder auf
den Vordersitzen auf dem Schoß zu befördern.
In Irland besteht für den Fahrer und den Beifahrer
Anschnallpflicht, wenn Gurte vorhanden sind.
Kinder unter 12 Jahren dürfen allerdings nicht
auf den Vordersitzen befördert werden, es sei
denn es existiert ein entsprechender Kindersitz.*

Lieferanten von Michelin-Reifen
ATS Reifenhändler

*Die Anschrift der nächstgelegenen ATS-Verkaufsstelle
erhalten Sie auf Anfrage (9-17 Uhr) bei*

> ATS HOUSE
> 180-188 Northolt Rd.
> Harrow, Middlesex HA2 OED
> (0181) 423 2000

Automobilclubs

*Die wichtigsten Automobilclubs des Landes sind die
Automobile Association und der Royal Automobile
Club, die den Mitgliedern der der FIA
angeschlossenen Automobilclubs Pannenhilfe leisten
und einige ihrer Dienstleistungen anbieten.*

*AUTOMOBILE ASSOCIATION
Fanum House
BASINGSTOKE, Hants.,
RG21 2EA
℘ (01256) 320123*

*ROYAL AUTOMOBILE CLUB
RAC House, Lansdowne Rd.
CROYDON, Surrey CR9 2JA
℘ (0181) 686 2525*

*AUTOMOBILE ASSOCIATION
23 Rock Hill
BLACKROCK
Co-Dublin
℘ (01) 283 3555*

*ROYAL AUTOMOBILE CLUB
RAC IRELAND
New Mount House
22-24 Lower Mount St.
DUBLIN 2
℘ (01) 676 0113*

Stadtpläne

@ ●a   *Hotels – Restaurants*

Sehenswürdigkeiten

Sehenswertes Gebäude mit Haupteingang
Sehenswerter Sakralbau

Straßen

M 1   *Autobahn*
❹ ❹   *- Anschlußstellen : Autobahneinfahrt und/oder-ausfahrt,*
Schnellstraße mit getrennten Fahrbahnen
Hauptverkehrsstraße
A 2   *Fernverkehrsstraße (Primary route)*
- Netz wird z.z. neu eingestuft
◄ ⊏≡≡≡⊐   *Einbahnstraße – Gesperrte Straße, mit*
Verkehrsbeschränkungen
⊏⊐ ≡≡   *Fußgängerzone*
Piccadilly 🅿   *Einkaufsstraße – Parkplatz, Parkhaus*
⊹ ⊐⊏ ⊐⊏⊏   *Tor – Passage – Tunnel*
15.3   *Unterführung (Höhe angegeben bis 16'6")*
auf Hauptverkehrsstraßen
🚂   *Bahnhof und Bahnlinie*
⊶⊹⊹⊹⊹⊶ ⊐■■■⊏   *Standseilbahn – Seilschwebebahn*
⚠ 🅱   *Bewegliche Brücke – Autofähre*

Sonstige Zeichen

🛈   *Informationsstelle*
ᚼ ⊠   *Moschee – Synagoge*
Ṫ ⸬   *Funk-, Fernsehturm – Ruine*
▦ ⊞   *Garten, Park, Wäldchen – Friedhof*
◯ 🐎 ⛳   *Stadion – Pferderennbahn – Golfplatz*
ᛈ   *Golfplatz (Zutritt bedingt erlaubt)*
⩤ ⊀   *Aussicht – Rundblick*
■ ◉ ✚   *Denkmal – Brunnen – Krankenhaus*
⚓ 🗼   *Jachthafen – Leuchtturm*
✈ ⊖ ●   *Flughafen – U-Bahnstation*
⛴   *Schiffsverbindungen : Autofähre*
✉   *Hauptpostamt (postlagernde Sendungen), Telefon*
▢▢   *Öffentliches Gebäude, durch einen Buchstaben gekennzeichnet :*
C H   *- Sitz der Grafschaftsverwaltung – Rathaus*
M T U   *- Museum – Theater – Universität, Hochschule*
POL.   *- Polizei (in größeren Städten Polizeipräsidium)*

London

BRENT WEMBLEY   *Name des Verwaltungsbezirks (borough) –*
des Stadtteils (area)
Grenze des « borough » – des « area »

49

Beer

Beer is one of the oldest and most popular alcoholic drinks in the world. Traditional draught beer is made by grinding malted barley, heating it with water and adding hops which add the familiar aroma and bitterness.

Beers in Britain can be divided into 2 principal types: Ales and Lagers which differ principally in their respective warm and cool fermentations. In terms of sales the split between the two is approximately equal. Beer can also be divided into keg or cask.

Keg beer - is filtered, pasteurised and chilled and then packed into pressurised containers from which it gets its name.

Cask beer – or 'Real Ale' as it is often referred to, is not filtered, pasteurised or chilled and is served from casks using simple pumps. It is considered by some to be a more characterful, flavoursome and natural beer.

There are several different beer styles in Britain and Ireland:

Bitter – whilst it is the most popular traditional beer in England and Wales it is now outsold by lager. Although no precise definition exists it is usually paler and dryer than Mild with a high hop content and slightly bitter taste.

Mild – is largely found in Wales, the West Midlands and the North West of England. The name refers to the hop character as it is a gentle, sweetish and full flavoured beer. It is generally lower in alcohol and sometimes darker in colour, caused by the addition of caramel or by using dark malt.

Stout - the great dry stouts are brewed in Ireland and are instantly recognisable by their black colour and creamy head. They have a pronounced roast flavour with plenty of hop bitterness.

In Scotland the beers produced are full bodied and malty and are often known simply as Light, Heavy, or Export which refers to the body and strength of the beer.

Although Ireland is most famous for its stouts, it also makes a range of beers which have variously been described as malty, buttery, rounded and fruity with a reddish tinge.

Whisky

The term whisky is derived from the Scottish Gaelic *uisage beatha and the Irish Gaelic* uisce beathadh, *both meaning "water of life". When spelt without an e it usually refers to Scotch Whisky which can only be produced in Scotland by the distillation of malted and unmalted barley, maize, rye, and mixtures of two or more of these. Often simply referred to as Scotch it can be divided into 2 basic types: malt whisky and grain whisky.*

Malt whisky – *is made only from malted barley which is traditionally dried over peat fires. The malt is then milled and mixed with hot water before mashing turns the starches into sugars and the resulting liquid, called wort, is filtered out. Yeast is added and fermentation takes place followed by two distilling processes using a pot still. The whisky is matured in oak, ideally sherry casks, for at least three years which affects both its colour and flavour. All malts have a more distinctive smell and intense flavour than grain whiskies and each distillery will produce a completely individual whisky of great complexity. A single malt is the product of an individual distillery. There are approximately 100 malt whisky distilleries in Scotland.*

Grain whisky – *is made from a mixture of any malted or unmalted cereal such as maize or wheat and is distilled in the Coffey, or patent still, by a continuous process. Very little grain whisky is ever drunk unblended.*

Blended whisky - *is a mix of more than one malt whisky or a mix of malt and grain whiskies to produce a soft, smooth and consistent drink. There are over 2000 such blends which form the vast majority of Scottish whisky production.*

Irish Whiskey - *differs from Scotch whisky both in its spelling and method of production. It is traditionally made from cereals, distilled three times and matured for at least 7 years. The different brands are as individual as straight malt and considered by some to be gentler in character.*

La bière

La bière est l'une des plus anciennes et populaires boissons alcoolisées dans le monde. Pour produire la bière pression traditionnelle, on écrase l'orge malté que l'on chauffe ensuite avec de l'eau à laquelle on ajoute le houblon. C'est ce qui lui donne son arôme et son goût amer bien connus.

Deux types de bières sont principalement vendues en Grande Bretagne : les Ales *fermentées à chaud* et les Lagers *fermentées à froid*. Elles se divisent en « keg beer » et en « cask beer ».

Bière en keg : elle est filtrée, pasteurisée et refroidie, puis versée dans des tonnelets pressurisés appelés kegs.

Bière en cask ou « Real Ale » : elle n'est ni filtrée, ni pasteurisée, ni refroidie mais tirée directement du tonneau à l'aide d'une simple pompe. Selon certains, cette bière, de qualité bien distincte, a plus de saveur et est plus naturelle.

Types de bières vendues au Royaume-Uni et en Irlande :

Bitter – C'est la bière traditionnelle la plus populaire en Angleterre et au pays de Galles mais ses ventes diminuent au profit des lagers. La Bitter est généralement plus pâle et son goût plus sec que la Mild. Son contenu en houblon est élevé et elle a un goût légèrement amer.

La Mild se consomme surtout au pays de Galles, dans le Midlands de l'Ouest et dans le Nord Ouest de l'Angleterre. On l'appelle ainsi en raison de son goût moelleux légèrement douceâtre conféré par le houblon. Cette bière, généralement moins alcoolisée est plus foncée par le caramel qui lui est ajouté ou par l'utilisation de malt plus brun.

Stout – les grandes marques de bières brunes sont brassées en Irlande et sont reconnaissables par leur couleur noire rehaussée de mousse crémeuse. Elles ont un goût prononcé de houblon grillé et une saveur amère.

Celles produites en Écosse sont maltées ; elles ont du corps et se dénomment le plus souvent Light, Heavy ou Export en référence au corps et à leur teneur en alcool.

Whisky

Le mot whisky est un dérivé du gaélique écossais *uisage beatha* et du gaélique irlandais *uisce beathadh* signifiant tous deux "eau de vie". Quand il est écrit sans e, il se réfère au whisky écossais qui ne peut être produit qu'en Ecosse par la distillation de céréales maltées ou non comme l'orge, le maïs, le seigle ou d'un mélange de deux ou plus de ces céréales. Souvent appelé tout simplement Scotch il se réfère à deux types de whisky : whisky pur malt ou whisky de grain.

Le whisky pur malt est fait seulement à partir d'orge maltée qui est traditionnellement séchée au-dessus de feux de tourbe. Le malt est moulu et mélangé avec de l'eau chaude, puis le brassage transforme l'amidon en sucre ; le moût est ensuite filtré. On y ajoute de la levure et après la fermentation on fait distiller deux fois dans un alambic. Le whisky est alors vieilli pendant au moins trois ans dans des fûts de chêne, ayant contenu de préférence du sherry, ce qui transforme son goût et sa couleur. Tous les whisky pur malt ont un arôme particulier et une saveur plus intense que les whisky de grain et chaque distillerie produit son propre whisky avec des qualités bien distinctes. Il y a environ une centaine de distilleries de whisky pur malt en Ecosse.

Le whisky de grain est fait d'un mélange de céréales, maltées ou non, comme le maïs ou le froment et est distillé dans un alambic de type Coffey suivant un procédé continu. Très peu de whisky de grain est consommé à l'état pur. On procède à des mélanges pour la consommation.

Blended whisky est le mélange d'un ou de plusieurs whisky pur malt et de whisky de grain afin de produire un alcool léger, moëlleux et de qualité. Il existe plus de 200 marques de blended whisky qui forment la majeure partie de la production écossaise.

Le whiskey irlandais, différent du whisky écossais par sa fabrication, est traditionnellement produit à partir de céréales ; il est ensuite distillé trois fois et vieilli pendant au moins sept ans. Certains le trouvent plus moëlleux.

Birra

La birra è una delle bevande alcoliche più antiche e popolari. La tradizionale birra alla spina si ottiene macinando l'orzo, riscaldandolo con l'acqua e aggiungendo il luppolo, che le conferiscono l'aroma e il tipico sapore amaro.

Le birre britanniche si dividono in due tipi principali : Ales e Lagers, che differiscono essenzialmente per la fermentazione, rispettivamente calda e fredda. In termini di vendita, i due tipi approssimativamente si equivalgono. La birra può anche dividersi in keg (lett. barilotto), e cask (lett. botte).

La keg beer è filtrata, pastorizzata e raffreddata, e poi messa in contenitori pressurizzati, da cui deriva il nome.

La cask beer, o Real Ale, come viene comunemente indicata, non è filtrata, pastorizzata o raffreddata, ed è servita dalle botti, usando semplici pompe. Alcuni la considerano una birra più ricca di carattere e di gusto e più naturale.

In Gran Bretagna e Irlanda, le birre si caratterizzano anche in base a « stili » diversi.

Le bitter costituisce la birra tradizionalmente più popolare in Inghilterra e nel Galles, ma è ora « superata » dalla lager. Non esiste definizione specifica per la birra bitter, ma si può dire che si tratta in genere di una birra più pallida e secca della mild, dall'alto contenuto di luppolo e dal gusto leggermente amaro.

La mild è diffusa in Galles, West Midlands e Inghilterra nord-occidentale. Il nome richiama il carattere del luppolo, essendo delicata, dolce e dal gusto pieno. Contiene solitamente una limitata quantità di alcol ed è talvolta scura per l'aggiunta di caramello e per l'impiego di malto scuro.

La secche stouts vengono prodotte in Irlanda e sono immediatamente riconoscibili dal colore nero e dalla schiuma cremosa. Hanno una decisa fragranza di tostatura e un gusto amaro di luppolo.

Whisky

Il termine whisky deriva dal gaelico scozzese uisage beatha *e dal gaelico irlandese* uisce beathadh, *che significano « acqua di vita ». Se scritto senza la* e, *indica di solito lo* Scotch Whisky, *che può essere unicamente prodotto in Scozia dalla distillazione di malto e orzo, granturco e segale, e dall'unione di due o più di questi ingredienti. Spesso chiamato semplicemente Scoveri, si divide in due tipi :* malt whisky e grain whisky.

Il malt whisky *viene prodotto unicamente con malto, tradizionalmente seccato su fuochi alimentati con torba. Il malto viene poi macinato e gli viene aggiunta acqua bollente prima che l'impasto muti gli amidi in zuccheri e il liquido che ne deriva, chiamato* wort *(mosto di malto), venga filtrato. Si amalgama poi il lievito e avviene la fermentazione, seguita da due processi di distillazione nell'alambicco. Il whisky è lasciato invecchiare in legno di quercia, idealmente in botti di sherry, per almeno tre anni, perchè acquisti colore e sapore. Ogni tipo di* malt whisky *ha un profumo più distintivo e un gusto più intenso del* grain whisky. *Ogni distilleria produce un whisky dal carattere individuale, che richiede un processo di grande complessità. Un solo* malt whisky *è il prodotto di una specifica distilleria. In Scozia, esistono circa 100 distillerie di* malt whisky.

Il grain whisky *è il risultato della fusione di qualsiasi cereale con o senza malto, come il granturco o il frumento, e viene distillato nel Coffey, o alambicco brevettato, grazie ad un processo continuo. È molto scarsa la quantità di* grain whisky *che si beve puro.*

Il blended whisky *nasce dalla fusione di più di un* malt whisky, *o da quella di* malt e grain whiskies. *Il risultato è una bevanda dal gusto delicato, dolce e pieno. Esistono più di 2000 whisky di questo tipo, che costituiscono la parte più consistente della produzione scozzese.*

Bier

Bier ist eines der ältesten und beliebtesten alkoholischen Getränke der Welt. Das traditionelle Faßbier wird aus gemahlener und gemalzter Gerste hergestellt, die in Wasser erhitzt wird. Durch Beigabe von Hopfen werden das bekannte Aroma und der typische bittere Geschmack erzeugt.

Die Biersorten in Großbritannien unterteilen sich in zwei Hauptgruppen : Ales und Lagers, wobei die Art der Gärung – im einen Fall warm, im anderen kalt – ausschlaggebend für das Endresultat ist. Beide Sorten haben hierzulande einen ungefähr gleichen Marktanteil. Da sich die meisten Brauvorgänge anfangs gleichen, entscheiden erst die Endphasen des Brauens, welche der verschiedenen Biersorten entsteht.

Darüber hinaus kann das englische Bier auch nach der Art seiner Abfüllung in Keg- *bzw.* Cask-*Bier unterschieden werden :*

Keg beer *wird gefiltert, pasteurisiert, abgekühlt und anschließend in luftdichte, unter Druck gesetzte Metallbehälter gefüllt, von denen das Bier auch seinen Namen erhält.*

Cask beer, *gewöhnlich* Real Ale *genannt, wird weder gefiltert, noch pasteurisiert oder gekühlt, sondern mit einfachen (zumeist Hand-) Pumpen vom Faß gezapft.*

Es gibt folgende Biersorten in Großbritannien und Irland :
Bitter *ist das meistbekannte traditionelle Bier in England und Wales. Eine genaue Definition, was ein Bitter ausmacht, sucht man vergeblich ; es ist gewöhnlich heller und trockener als das* Mild, *hat einen hohen Hopfenanteil und einen leicht bitteren Geschmack. In den letzten Jahren hat das – meist importierte oder in Lizenz gebraute –* Lager *ihm jedoch den Rang abgelaufen.*

Mild *ist übergiegend in Wales, in den westlichen Midlands und Nordwestengland zu finden. Der Name bezieht sich auf den Hopfenanteil, der es zu einem milden, etwas süßlichen und vollmundigen Bier macht. Es hat einen geringeren Alkoholgehalt und besitzt wegen der Zugabe von Karamel oder dunklem Malz bisweilen eine dunklere Farbe.*

Stouts *von hervorragendem trockenem Geschmack werden in Irland gebraut und sind unmittelbar an ihrer schwarzen Farbe und der cremigen Blume erkennbar. Sie haben einen ausgesprochen starken Geschmack nach bitterem Hopfen.*

In Schottland hergestellte Biere sind alkoholstark und malzig ; sie sind oft einfach bekannt als: Light, Heavy *oder* Export *– Bezeichnungen, die auf Körper und Stärke des Bieres hinweisen.*

Whisky

Die Bezeichnung Whisky entstammt dem Gälischen, wo im Schottischen der Ausdruck uisage beatha, im Irischen des Ausdruck uisce beathadh jeweils « Wasser des Lebens » bedeuten. Wird Whisky ohne ein e am Ende geschrieben, ist Scotch Whisky gemeint, der nur in Schottland aus gemalzter und ungemalzter Gerste. Mais, Roggen oder aus Mischungen zweier oder mehrerer dieser Zutaten gebrannt werden darf. Oft auch nur als Scotch bezeichnet, kann dieser in zwei Grundarten unterschieden werden : malt whisky und grain whisky.

Malt (Malz) whisky wird nur aus gemalzter Gerste hergestellt, die traditionell über Torffeuern getrocknet wird. Danach wird das Malz gemahlen und mit heißem Wasser vermischt, wonach in der Maische die Stärke in Zucker umgewandelt wird. Die dadurch entstandene Flüssigkeit, "wort" genannt, wird gefiltert und mit Hefe versetzt, was den Gärungsprozess einleitet. Anschließend folgen zwei Destillierungen im herkömmlichen Topf über offenem Feuer. Der Whisky reift danach mindestens drei Jahre lang in Eichenholz, idealerweise in Sherry-Fässern, was sich sowohl auf Farbe wie auf Geschmack des Whiskys auswirkt. Alle malts haben einen ausgeprägteren Geruch und intensiveren Geschmack als die grain-Whiskies ; und jede Destillerie erzeugt einen völlig eigenen Whisky mit individueller Geschmacksnote und großer Komplexität. Ein sogenannter single malt enstammt aus einer einzigen Destillerie. Es gibt ungefähr 100 Malt Whisky-Destillerien in Schottland.

Grain (Korn) whisky wird aus Mischungen von gemalzten und ungemalzten Getreidesorten, wie Mais oder Weizen, hergestellt und wird in einem kontinuierlichen Prozeß in dem sogenannten "Coffey" destilliert. Nur sehr wenige Kornwhisky-Sorten sind nicht das Ergebnis von blending, dem Abstimmen des Geschmacks durch Mischung.

Blended whisky wird aus mehr als einer Sorte Malt Whisky oder aus Malt und Grain Whiskies gemischt, um ein weiches, geschamcklich harmonisches Getränk von beständiger Güte zu garantieren. Die über 2000 im Handel zu findenden blends stellen den Großteil der schottischen Whiskyerzeugung dar.

Irish Whiskey unterscheidet sich vom Scotch Whisky sowohl in der Schreibweise wie auch dem Herstellungsverfahren. Er wird traditionell aus Getreide hergestellt, wird dreifach destilliert und reift mindestens sieben Jahre lang. Die verschiedenen Sorten sind so individuell ausgeprägt wie reine Malt Whiskies und werden oft als weicher und gefälliger empfunden.

Starred establishments
Les établissements à étoiles
Gli esercizi con stelle
Die Stern-Restaurants

England

Bray-on-Thames	*Waterside Inn*
London	*Chez Nico at Ninety Park Lane*
	(at Grosvenor House H.)

London	*The Oak Room Marco Pierre White*
	(at Le Meridien Piccadilly H.)
–	*La Tante Claire*

England

Bath	*Lettonie*
London	*Aubergine*
–	*Le Gavroche*
	Pied à Terre
–	*The Square*
Oxford	*Le Manoir aux Quat' Saisons*
Reading	*L'Ortolan*

Scotland

Ullapool	*Altnaharrie Inn*

Ireland

Republic of Ireland

Dublin	*Patrick Guilbaud*

England

Altrincham	*Juniper*
Baslow	*Fischer's at Baslow Hall*
Bath	*Homewood Park*
Blackburn	*Northcote Manor*
Bourton-on-the-Water	*Lords of the Manor*
–	*Lower Slaughter Manor*
Bradford	*Restaurant Nineteen*
Bristol	*Harveys*
–	*Hunstrete House*
Broadway	*Buckland Manor*
Brockenhurst	*Le Poussin*
Chagford	*Gidleigh Park*
Channel Islands	
Gorey (Jersey)	*Village Bistro*
St Saviour (Jersey)	*Longueville Manor*
Cheltenham	*Le Champignon Sauvage*
Chester	*Arkle (at Chester Grosvenor H.)*
East Grinstead	*Gravetye Manor*
Emsworth	*36 on the Quay*
Falmouth	*Pennypots*
Faversham	*Read's*
Folkestone	*La Terrasse*
	(at Sandgate H.)
Grantham	*Harry's Place*
Grasmere	*Michaels Nook Country House*

Great Malvern	*Croque-en-Bouche*
Haslemere	*Fleur de Sel*
Ilkley	*Box Tree*
Leeds	*Pool Court at 42*
–	*Rascasse*
London	*The Café Royal Grill Room*
–	*The Canteen*
–	*Capital*
–	*Chavot*
–	*City Rhodes*
–	*Connaught*
–	*L'Escargot*
–	*The Halkin*
–	*Leith's*
–	*Nobu (at The Metropolitan H.)*
–	*L'Oranger*
–	*Oriental (at Dorchester H.)*
–	*Quo Vadis*
–	*River Café*
–	*Les Saveurs de Jean-Christophe Novelli W1*
Longridge	*Paul Heathcote's*
Ludlow	*Merchant House*
Lymington	*Gordleton Mill*
Minster Lovell	*Lovells at Windrush Farm*

Newcastle upon Tyne	*21 Queen Street*
New Milton	*Chewton Glen*
Norwich	*Adlard's*
Oakham	*Hambleton Hall*
Plymouth	*Chez Nous*
Shepton Mallet	*Charlton House*
Storrington	*Manley's*
Taplow	*Waldo's (at Cliveden H.)*
Tavistock	*Horn of Plenty*
Ullswater	*Sharrow Bay Country House*
Waterhouses	*Old Beams*
Winteringham	*Winteringham Fields*

Scotland

Aberfoyle	*Braeval*
Achiltibuie	*Summer Isles*
Balloch	*Georgian Room*
	(at Cameron House H.)
Fort William	*Inverlochy Castle*

Glasgow	*One Devonshire Gardens*
Gullane	*La Potinière*
Port Appin	*Airds*
Portpatrick	*Knockinaam Lodge*

Wales

Llyswen	*Llangoed Hall*

Ireland

Northern Ireland

Bangor	*Shanks*
Belfast	*Deanes*
–	*Roscoff*

Republic of Ireland

Ahakista	*Shiro*
Dublin	*Peacock Alley*
–	*Thornton's*
Kenmare	*Park*
–	*Sheen Falls Lodge*

60

"Bib Gourmand"

Good food at moderate prices

Repas soignés à prix modérés

Pasti accurati a prezzi contenuti

Sorgfältig zubereitete, preiswerte Mahzeiten

😊 Meals

England

Baslow	*Café-Max*	London	*Malabar*
Bath	*Moody Goose*	–	*Monsieur Max*
Blackpool	*September Brasserie*	–	*MPW*
Blakeney	*Morston Hall*	–	*Nico Central*
Bridgnorth	*Old Vicarage*	–	*Novelli W8*
Brighton and Hove	*Black Chapati*	–	*Simply Nico*
Bristol	*Markwicks*	–	*Sugar Club*
Cambridge	*22 Chesterton Road*	–	*Woz*
Channel Islands		Ludlow	*Oaks*
Gorey (Jersey)	*Jersey Pottery*	Maiden Newton	*Le Petit Canard*
	(Garden Rest.)	Maldon	*Chigborough Lodge*
–	*Village Bistro*	Manchester	*Mash*
Devizes	*George and Dragon*	–	*Simply Heathcotes*
Drewsteignton	*Hunts Tor*	Milford-on-Sea	*Rocher's*
Durham	*Bistro 21*	Nayland	*White Hart*
Eastbourne	*Hungry Monk*	Newcastle upon Tyne	*Café 21*
Fordingbridge	*Three Lions*	–	*Forsters*
Fowey	*Food for Thought*	Old Burghclere	*Dew Pond*
Halifax	*Design House*	Oldham	*Brasserie (at White Hart Inn)*
Harrogate	*The Bistro*	Oxford	*Le Petit Blanc*
Haworth	*Weaver's*	Painswick	*Country Elephant*
Helmsley	*Star Inn*	Pateley Bridge	*Dusty Miller*
Kendal	*Punch Bowl Inn*	Preston	*Heathcotes Brasserie*
Kenilworth	*Simpson's*	Rushlake Green	*Stone House*
Keswick	*Swinside Lodge*	St Albans	*Sukiyaki*
King's Lynn	*Rococo*	St Ives	*Pig "n" Fish*
Leeds	*Leodis*	Salisbury	*Howard's House*
–	*Rascasse*	Sheffield	*Rafters*
London	*L'Accento*	–	*Smith's of Sheffield*
–	*Alastair Little Lancaster Road*	Shepton Mallet	*Bowlish House*
–	*Atelier*	Skipton	*Bar Brasserie (at Angel Inn)*
–	*Blue Print Café*	Southend-on-Sea	*Paris*
–	*Cafe Spice Namaste*	Stanton	*Leaping Hare*
–	*Chapter One*	Storrington	*Old Forge*
–	*Chez Bruce*	Tadworth	*Gemini*
–	*Chutney Mary*	Towcester	*Vine House*
–	*L'Escargot (Ground Floor)*	Virginstow	*Percy's at Coombshead*
–	*Kensington Place*	Winkleigh	*Pophams*

Winsford	Savery's at Karslake House
Wiveliscombe	Langley House
Wokingham	Rose Street Wine Bar

Scotland

Dalry	Braidwoods
Edinburgh	Atrium
–	(fitz) Henry
Lochinver	The Albannach
Muir of Ord	Dower House
Skye (Isle of)	Harlosh House

Wales

Llanrwst	Chandler's Brasserie
Llansanffraid Glan Conwy	Old Rectory
Llanwrtyd Wells	Carlton House

Ireland

Northern Ireland

| Portrush | Ramore |

Republic of Ireland

Ballyconneely	Erriseask House
Castlebaldwin	Cromleach Lodge
Dingle	Doyle's Seafood Bar
Dublin	Chapter One
–	L'Ecrivain
–	Ernie's
–	Roly's Bistro
Dungarvan	The Tannery
Dun Laoghaire	Morels Bistro
Kenmare	An Leath Phingin
–	d'Arcy's
–	Lime Tree

Particularly pleasant Hotels
Hôtels agréables
Alberghi ameni
Angenehme Hotels

England

London	Claridge's	New Milton	Chewton Glen
-	Dorchester	Taplow	Cliveden
-	The Savoy		

Ireland Republic of Ireland

Straffan	Kildare H. & Country Club

England

Aylesbury	Hartwell House
Bath	Lucknam Park
-	The Royal Crescent
Ipswich	Hintlesham Hall
London	Connaught
Melton Mowbray	Stapleford Park
Oxford	Le Manoir aux Quat' Saisons

Scotland

Dunkeld	Kinnaird
Fort William	Inverlochy Castle
Glasgow	One Devonshire Gardens

Wales

Llyswen	Llangoed Hall

Ireland Republic of Ireland

Dublin	The Merrion
Kenmare	Park
-	Sheen Falls Lodge

England

Abberley	The Elms
Amberley	Amberley Castle
Bath	Homewood Park
Birmingham	Mill House
Bolton Abbey	Devonshire Arms Country House
Bourton-on-the-Water	Lords of the Manor
-	Lower Slaughter Manor
Bristol	Hunstrete House
Broadway	Buckland Manor
Castle Combe	Manor House
Chagford	Gidleigh Park
Channel Islands	
La Pulente (Jersey)	Atlantic
St Saviour (Jersey)	Longueville Manor
Chipping Campden	Charingworth Manor
East Grinstead	Gravetye Manor
Evershot	Summer Lodge
Gillingham	Stock Hill Country House
Grasmere	Michaels Nook Country House
Kidderminster	Brockencote Hall
Leeds	42 The Calls
London	Blakes
-	Capital
-	Covent Garden
-	Durley House
-	Goring
-	The Halkin
-	Pelham
-	22 Jermyn Street
Newbury	Hollington House
Oakham	Hambleton Hall

Sandiway	Nunsmere Hall
Scilly *(Isles of)*	
St Martin's	St Martin's on the Isle
Tresco	The Island
Shepton Mallet	Charlton House
Sutton Coldfield	New Hall
Tetbury	The Close
Ullswater	Sharrow Bay Country House
York	Middlethorpe Hall

Scotland

Arisaig	Arisaig House
Dunblane	Cromlix House

Edinburgh	The Howard
Eriska *(Isle of)*	Isle of Eriska
Inverness	Culloden House
Port Appin	Airds

Wales

Llandudno	Bodysgallen Hall

Ireland *Republic of Ireland*

Dublin	The Clarence
Gorey	Marlfield House
Mallow	Longueville House
Wicklow	Tinakilly House

England

Bradford-on-Avon	Woolley Grange
Brampton	Farlam Hall
Cheltenham	On the Park
Cuckfield	Ockenden Manor
King's Lynn	Congham Hall
Lewdown	Lewtrenchard Manor
Liskeard	Well House
Littlehampton	Bailiffscourt
London	Sloane
–	Sydney House
Oxford	Old Parsonage
Prestbury	White House Manor
Purton	Pear Tree at Purton
South Molton	Whitechapel Manor
Tetbury	Calcot Manor
Ullswater	Old Church
Wareham	Priory
Wight *(Isle of)*	
Yarmouth	George
Windermere	Gilpin Lodge
–	Holbeck Ghyll
Woodstock	Feathers

Scotland

Achiltibuie	Summer Isles
Arran (Isle of)	Kilmichael Country House

Gullane	Greywalls
Lewis & Harris *(Isle of)*	Ardvourlie
Ardvourlie (Harris)	Castle
Mull *(Isle of)*	Killiechronan House
Portpatrick	Knockinaam Lodge
Strontian	Kilcamb Lodge
Ullapool	Altnaharrie Inn
Whitebridge	Knockie Lodge

Wales

Llandrillo	Tyddyn Llan Country House
Machynlleth	Ynyshir Hall
Swansea	Fairyhill
Talsarnau	Maes-y-Neuadd

Ireland *Republic of Ireland*

Ballingarry	Mustard Seed at Echo Lodge
Cashel Bay	Cashel House
Castlebaldwin	Cromleach Lodge
Donegal	St Ernan's House
Glin	Glin Castle
Kanturk	Assolas Country House
Shanagarry	Ballymaloe House
Skibbereen	Liss Ard Lake Lodge

England

Ashwater	Blagdon Manor Country H.
Blakeney	Morston Hall
Bury St Edmunds	Twelve Angel Hill (without rest)
Buttermere	Pickett Howe
Calstock	Danescombe Valley
Chipping Campden	Malt House
Dulverton	Ashwick House
Horley	Langshott Manor
Keswick	Swinside Lodge
Leominster	The Marsh
Porlock	Oaks
Rushlake Green	Stone House
Salisbury	Howard's House
Staverton	Kingston House

Teignmouth	*Thomas Luny House*
	(without rest)
Tintagel	*Trebrea Lodge*
Winchester	*Wykeham Arms*
Wiveliscombe	*Langley House*

Scotland

Kentallen	*Ardsheal House*
Lochinver	*The Albannach*
Maybole	*Ladyburn*
Muir of Ord	*Dower House*
Mull *(Isle of)*	*Ardfenaig House*
Perth	*Dupplin Castle*

Wales

Betws-y-Coed *Tan-y-Foel Country House*
Llansanffraid Glan Conwy *Old Rectory*

Ireland

Northern Ireland
Holywood	*Rayanne House*

Republic of Ireland
Bagenalstown	*Kilgraney*
	Country House
Leenane	*Delphi Lodge*
Riverstown	*Coopershill*
Wicklow	*Old Rectory*

England

Alnmouth	*High Buston Hall*
Askrigg	*Helm Country House*
Bethersden	*Little Hodgeham*
	(without rest)
Billingshurst	*Old Wharf (without rest)*
Boroughbridge	*Brafferton Hall*
Broadway	*Old Rectory (without rest)*
Calne	*Chilvester Hill House*
Canterbury	*Thruxted Oast (without rest)*
Carlisle	*Number Thirty One*
Caxton	*Church Farm*
Cockermouth	*Low Hall (without rest)*
–	*New House Farm*
Coniston	*Appletree Holme*
Crackington Haven	*Manor Farm*
Cranbrook	*Old Cloth Hall*
East Hoathly	*Old Whyly*
East Retford	*Old Plough*
Faversham	*Frith Farm House*
Grindon	*Porch Farmhouse*
Hayling Island	*Cockle Warren Cottage*
Honiton	*Cokesputt House*
Iron Bridge	*Severn Lodge (without rest)*
Lewes	*Millers (without rest)*
Lizard	*Landewednack House*
Melksham	*Sandridge Park*
North Bovey	*Gate House*
Norwich	*Old Rectory (without rest)*
Otley	*Bowerfield House*
Plymouth	*The Barn*
St Blazey	*Nanscawen House*
	(without rest)
Seaford	*Old Parsonage*
	(without rest)
Stow-on-the-Wold	*College House*
Tavistock	*Quither Mill*
Tetbury	*Tavern House (without rest)*
Thame	*Upper Green Farm*
	(without rest)

Thoralby	*Littleburn*
Veryan	*Crugsillick Manor*
Wiveliscombe	*Jews Farm House*
Worcester	*Upton House*
York	*4 South Parade (without rest)*

Scotland

Arran *(Isle of)*	*Apple Lodge*
Banff	*Eden House*
Earlston	*Birkhill*
Edinburgh	*Drummond House*
	(without rest)
–	*17 Abercromby Place*
	(without rest)
–	*Sibbet House (without rest)*
–	*27 Heriot Row (without rest)*
Fort William	*The Grange (without rest)*
Glenborrodale	*Feorag House*
Islay *(Isle of)*	*Kilmeny Farmhouse*
Marnoch	*Old Manse of Marnoch*

Wales

Bala	*Fron Feuno Hall*
Betws-y-Coed	*Penmachno Hall*

Ireland

Northern Ireland
Belfast	*Cottage (without rest)*
Coleraine	*Greenhill House*
Dungannon	*Grange Lodge*

Republic of Ireland
Castlelyons	*Ballyvolane House*
Castlerea	*Clonalis House*
Inistioge	*Berryhill*
Kanturk	*Glenlohane*
Kenmare	*Sallyport House (without rest)*
Kilkenny	*Blanchville House*

Particularly pleasant Restaurants
Restaurants agréables
Ristoranti ameni
Angenehme Restaurants

XXXXX

England

London — The Oak Room Marco Pierre White (at Le Meridien Piccadilly H.)

XXXX

England

Bray-on-Thames	Waterside Inn (with rm)	Taplow	Waldo's (at Cliveden H.)
London	Oriental (at Dorchester H.)	Winteringham	Winteringham Fields (with rm)

XXX

England

Baslow	Fischer's at Baslow Hall (with rm)	Moulsford	Beetle & Wedge (with rm)
Emsworth	36 on the Quay	Reading	L'Ortolan
Leeds	Pool Court at 42	Romsey	Old Manor House
London	Goode's at Thomas Goode	Sheffield	Old Vicarage
–	Grill Room (at Dorchester H.)	Wight (Isle of)	
–	Oxo Tower	Yarmouth	George Restaurant
–	Le Pont de la Tour		
–	Quaglino's		
Lymington	Gordleton Mill (with rm)		

Scotland

Kingussie	The Cross (with rm)

XX

England

Eastbourne	Hungry Monk
Fowey	Food for Thought
Goring	Leatherne Bottel
Grantham	Harry's Place
Great Yeldham	White Hart
Moreton-in-Marsh	Marsh Goose
Newcastle upon Tyne	Horton Grange (with rm)
Padstow	Seafood (with rm)
Painswick	Country Elephant
Waterhouses	Old Beams (with rm)

Scotland

Aberfoyle	Braeval

Wales

Llanrwst	Cae'r Berllan (with rm)

Ireland

Republic of Ireland

Ahakista	Shiro

X

England

Channel Islands

Gorey (Jersey)	Jersey Pottery (Garden Rest.)
Fordingbridge	Three Lions (with rm)
Thirsk	Crab & Lobster

Scotland

Gullane	La Potinière

Ireland

Republic of Ireland

Kenmare	Lime Tree

England

Channel Islands,

Isle of Man

Local government in England, Scotland and Wales is being reorganised with effect from April 1996. The names and boundaries of local authorities, as listed in this guide, may be subject to change.

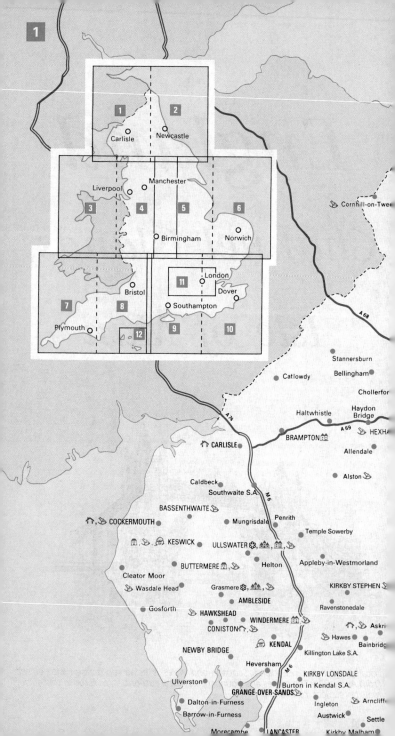

1

| 1 | 2 |

Carlisle   Newcastle

| 3 | 4 | 5 | 6 |

Liverpool   Manchester

Birmingham   Norwich

Cornhill-on-Twee

| 11 | London |

Bristol   Dover

| 7 | 8 | | 9 | 10 |

Southampton

Plymouth | 12 |

A 68

Stannersburn

Catlowdy   Bellingham

Chollerfor

Haltwhistle   Haydon Bridge

BRAMPTON   A 69   HEXHA

CARLISLE

Allendale

Alston

Caldbeck

Southwaite S.A.

BASSENTHWAITE

COCKERMOUTH   Mungrisdale   Penrith

KESWICK   Temple Sowerby

ULLSWATER

BUTTERMERE   Helton   Appleby-in-Westmorland

Cleator Moor

Wasdale Head   Grasmere   KIRKBY STEPHEN

AMBLESIDE

Gosforth   HAWKSHEAD   Ravenstonedale

WINDERMERE

CONISTON   Askri

KENDAL   Hawes   Bainbridg

NEWBY BRIDGE   Killington Lake S.A.

Heversham

Ulverston   KIRKBY LONSDALE

Burton in Kendal S.A.

GRANGE-OVER-SANDS

Dalton-in-Furness   Ingleton   Arncliff

Barrow-in-Furness   Austwick   Settle

Morecambe   LANCASTER   Kirkby Malham

Place with at least _____

a hotel or restaurant   ● Ripon
a pleasant hotel or restaurant   🏨, ⌂, ✗
a quiet, secluded hotel   🦢
a restaurant with   ✿, ✿✿, ✿✿✿, 🍽 Meals
*See this town for establishments
located in its vicinity*   LEICESTER

Localité offrant au moins _____

une ressource hôtelière   ● Ripon
un hôtel ou restaurant agréable   🏨, ⌂, ✗
un hôtel très tranquille, isolé   🦢
une bonne table à   ✿, ✿✿, ✿✿✿, 🍽 Meals
*Localité groupant dans le texte
les ressources de ses environs*   LEICESTER

La località possiede come minimo _____

una risorsa alberghiera   ● Ripon
Albergo o ristorante ameno   🏨, ⌂, ✗
un albergo molto tranquillo, isolato   🦢
un'ottima tavola con   ✿, ✿✿, ✿✿✿, 🍽 Meals
*La località raggruppa nel suo testo
le risorse dei dintorni*   LEICESTER

Ort mit mindestens _____

einem Hotel oder Restaurant   ● Ripon
ein angenehmes Hotel oder Restaurant   🏨, ⌂, ✗
einem sehr ruhigen und abgelegenen Hotel   🦢
einem Restaurant mit   ✿, ✿✿, ✿✿✿, 🍽 Meals
*Ort mit Angaben über Hotels und Restaurants
in der Umgebung*   LEICESTER

Berwick-upon-Tweed

Belford · BAMBURGH
Seahouses

ALNWICK
⌂ Alnmouth

Rothbury

Kirkwhelpington
Ashington
Morpeth
A 696
Whitley Bay
Tynemouth
orbridge · NEWCASTLE UPON TYNE ✿, 🍽, ✗✗ with rm.
GATESHEAD
Ebchester
Sunderland
Washington
Carterway Heads
Washington S.A.
Blanchland
Chester-le-Street

🍽 DURHAM
Crook
Bowburn
Hamsterley 🦢
Sedgefield
HARTLEPOOL
Bishop Auckland
Rushyford

STOCKTON-ON-TEES
ARNARD CASTLE
Thornaby-on-Tees
Staithes
Greta Bridge
Middlesbrough
Loftus 🦢
DARLINGTON 🦢
Yarm
WHITBY
Stokesley
Ingleby Greenhow 🦢
Scotch Corner
Great Broughton
eeth
Moulton
Goathland
🦢 RICHMOND
Rosedale Abbey
Patrick Brompton
NORTHALLERTON 🦢
Hutton-le-Hole
oralby
W. Witton
Leeming Bar
Lastingham 🦢
SCARBOROUGH 🦢
Bedale
Pickhill
Kirkbymoorside
MIDDLEHAM
E. Witton
Appleton
PICKERING 🦢
le Moors
THIRSK ✗
Filey
Masham
HELMSLEY
🍽
ettlewell
Hovingham
Ripon
EASINGWOLD
MALTON
🍽 PATELEY BRIDGE
Bridlington

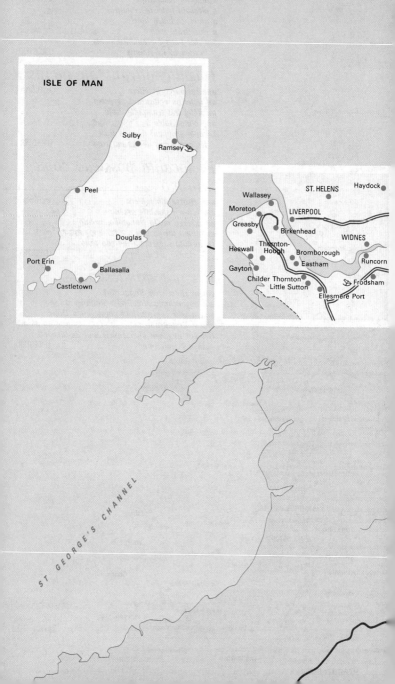

ISLE OF MAN

Sulby
Ramsey
Peel
Douglas
Port Erin
Ballasalla
Castletown

Wallasey
ST. HELENS
Haydock
Moreton
LIVERPOOL
Greasby
Birkenhead
WIDNES
Thornton-Hough
Heswall
Bromborough
Gayton
Eastham
Runcorn
Childer Thornton
Little Sutton
Frodsham
Ellesmere Port

ST GEORGE'S CHANNEL

NORTH SEA

Sutton-on-Sea

Burgh-le-Marsh

Wells-next-the-Sea

West Runton

Burnham Market

BLAKENEY 🏛, 👤

CROMER

Hunstanton

Little Walsingham

Binham

Holt

Great Snoring

Barney

Erpingham

Thorpe Market

Fakenham

Foulsham

North Walsham

Sandringham 🐾

Reepham

Cawston

Long Sutton

Elsing

Coltishall

Wroxham

KING'S LYNN
🏛, 🐾, 👤

EAST DEREHAM

A 47

South Walsham

Horning

Acle

Wisbech

SWAFFHAM

Wymondham

NORWICH
❄ 🏠

GREAT YARMOUTH

March

Attleborough

LOWESTOFT

Great Hockham

A 11

Thetford

Pulham Market

SOUTHWOLD

ELY

Mildenhall

🐾 Stanton

DISS

Walberswick

Barton Mills

Eye

Gislingham

Middleton

Westleton

BURY ST. EDMUNDS 🏛

Theberton 🐾

NEWMARKET

A 14

FRAMLINGHAM

Kelsale

STOWMARKET

Otley 🏠, 🐾

Aldeburgh

CAMBRIDGE 🐾

Needham Market

WOODBRIDGE 🐾

A 11

Lavenham

Long Melford

IPSWICH 🏛 🐾

Clare

Sudbury

Hadleigh

Capel St. Mary

SAFFRON WALDEN 🐾

Stoke-by-Nayland

Dedham

XX Great Yeldham

Nayland

Higham

Felixstowe

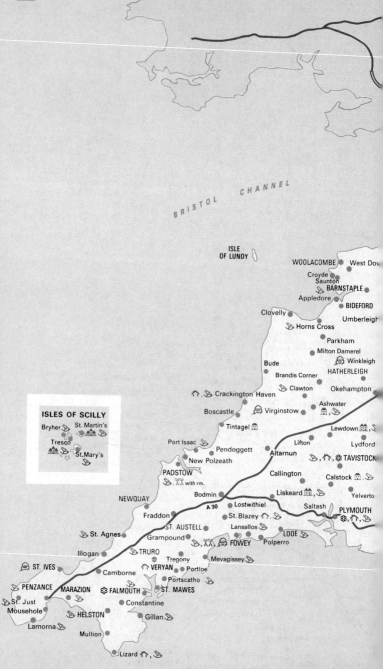

BRISTOL CHANNEL

ISLE OF LUNDY

WOOLACOMBE • West Dov
Croyde
Saunton
BARNSTAPLE
Appledore
BIDEFORD
Clovelly
Umberleigh
Horns Cross
Parkham
Milton Damerel
Winkleigh
Bude
HATHERLEIGH
Brandis Corner
Clawton
Okehampton
Crackington Haven
Ashwater
Boscastle
Virginstow
Tintagel
Lewdown
Port Isaac
Lifton
Lydford
Pendoggett
Altarnun
TAVISTOCK
New Polzeath
PADSTOW
Callington
Calstock
with rm.
Bodmin
Liskeard
Yelverto
NEWQUAY
A 30
Lostwithiel
Saltash
PLYMOUTH
Fraddon
St. Blazey
ST. AUSTELL
Lansallos
LOOE
St. Agnes
Grampound
FOWEY
Polperro
Illogan
TRURO
Tregony
Mevagissey
ST. IVES
Camborne
VERYAN
Portloe
PENZANCE
MARAZION
Portscatho
St. Just
FALMOUTH
ST. MAWES
Mousehole
Constantine
Lamorna
HELSTON
Gillan
Mullion
Lizard

ISLES OF SCILLY
Bryher
St. Martin's
Tresco
St. Mary's

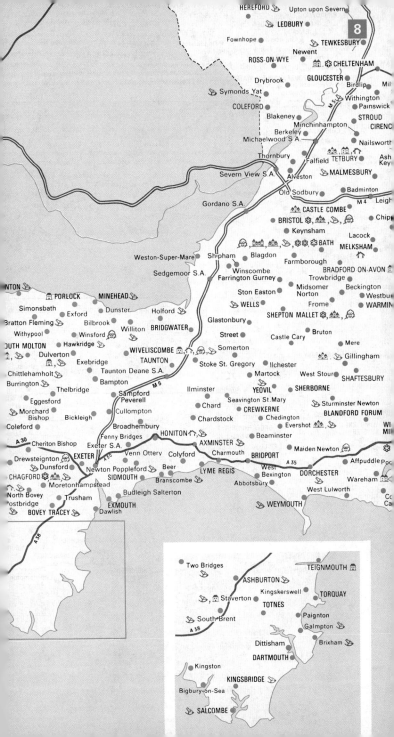

Melbourn
Baldock
Clavering
SHOP'S STORTFORD
Ware
Hertford
STANSTED AIRPORT
SAFFRON WALDEN
Great Yeldham
Thaxted
Wethersfield
Great
Dunmow
Felsted
Braintree
Earls Colne
Coggeshall
Clare
Sudbury
Hadleigh
IPSWICH
Stoke-by-Nayland
Nayland
Higham
Dedham
Capel St. Mary
Felixstowe
Harwich and
Dovercourt
Wix
Manningtree
COLCHESTER

CHELMSFORD
MALDON
Burnham-on-Crouch
Clacton-on-Sea

LONDON
BASILDON
Rochford
Southend-on-Sea
Horndon-on-the-Hill
North Stifford
Gravesend
Rochester
Medway S.A.
Cobham
Newington
Sittingbourne
FAVERSHAM
WHITSTABLE
Herne Bay
Birchington
Broadstairs
RAMSGATE
Sandwich
CANTERBURY
Deal

M 25
M 20
MAIDSTONE
LENHAM
Pluckley
ASHFORD
Wye
Bethersden
DOVER
FOLKESTONE
Channel Tunnel

Edenbridge
Horley
Turners Hill
Penshurst
ROYAL TUNBRIDGE WELLS
EAST GRINSTEAD
AWLEY
FOREST ROW
rdingly
Hartfield
Crowborough
Mayfield
Cuckfield
Uckfield
Wadhurst
Hawkhurst
Ticehurst
CRANBROOK
Tenterden
Hythe
New Romney

wards
eath
ickstead
Lewes
Newick
East Hoathly
Rushlake Green
Battle
Herstmonceux
Sedlescombe
Brede
Wittersham
RYE
Winchelsea
New Romney

GHTON AND HOVE
Alfriston
Newhaven
SEAFORD
HAILSHAM
Bexhill
Pevensey
EASTBOURNE
Hastings and St. Leonards

ENGLISH CHANNEL

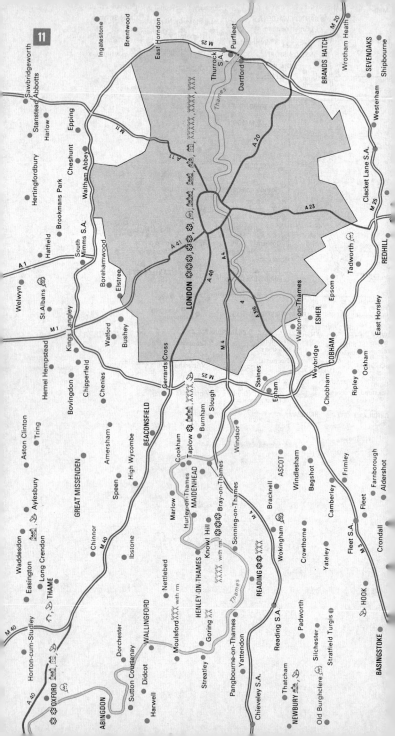

Channel Islands

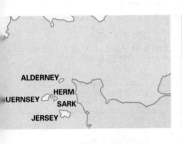

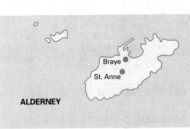

ALDERNEY

ALDERNEY
HERM
GUERNSEY
SARK
JERSEY

Braye
St. Anne

GUERNSEY

Pembroke Bay ● l'Ancresse

HERM

● Vazon Bay

St. Peter Port

St. Saviour

St. Peter in the Wood ● ● St. Martin

Forest ● Fermain Bay

SARK

JERSEY

Grève de Lecq ●

Bouley Bay ● ● Rozel Bay

St. Martin

St. Lawrence

St. Peter ●

St. Saviour ✿, 🏛 Gorey✿, ✕, 🍺

La Haule ●

🏛 La Pulente ● ● La Haule St. Aubin

St. Helier ● Grouville

Corbière St. Brelade's Bay

St. Clement

ABBERLEY Worcestershire 403 404 M 27 – pop. 654 – ⊠ Worcester.
London 137 – Birmingham 27 – Worcester 13.

🏨 **The Elms** ≫, WR6 6AT, W : 2 m. on A 443 ℘ (01299) 896666, Fax (01299) 896804, ≤, 🎭,
« Queen Anne mansion », park – 💥 rest, 📺 ☎ 🅿 – 🔬 30. 🟠 🗚 ⓞ ☑☑
Meals 12.50/25.00-29.50 st. ♦ 7.50 – **16 rm** ☑ 75.00/135.00 st. – SB.

🏠 **Manor Arms** ≫, Abberley Village, WR6 6BN, ℘ (01299) 896507, Fax (01299) 896723, 🎭
– 📺 ☎ 🅿. 🟠 ☑☑
Meals a la carte 9.45/17.25 st. ♦ 4.50 – **8 rm** ☑ 35.00/60.00 st. – SB.

ABBOTSBURY Dorset 403 404 M 32 The West Country G. – pop. 422.
See : Town★★ - Chesil Beach★★ - Swannery★ AC – Sub-Tropical Gardens★ AC.
Env. : St. Catherine's Chapel★, ½ m. uphill (30 mn rtn on foot).
Exc. : Maiden Castle★★ (≤★) NE : 7 ½ m.
London 146 – Exeter 50 – Bournemouth 44 – Weymouth 10.

🏠 **Ilchester Arms**, 9 Market St., DT3 4JR, ℘ (01305) 871243, Fax (01305) 871225 – 💥 rest,
📺 ☎ 🅿. 🟠 🗚 ⓞ ☑☑. 🦮
Meals a la carte 9.30/17.35 t. ♦ 4.95 – **9 rm** 42.25/52.25 t. – SB.

🏠 **Abbey House** ≫ without rest., Church St., DT3 4JJ, ℘ (01305) 871330,
Fax (01305) 871088, « Part 15C abbey infirmary », 🎭 – 💥 📺 🅿. 🦮
4 rm ☑ 54.00/60.00 st., 1 suite.

ABBOT'S SALFORD Warks. 403 404 O 27 – see Evesham (Worcestershire).

ABINGDON Oxon. 403 404 Q 28 Great Britain G. – pop. 35 234.
See : Town★ – County Hall★.
🏌, 🏌 Drayton Park, Steventon Rd, Drayton ℘ (01235) 550607/528989.
🚩 25 Bridge St., OX14 3HN ℘ (01235) 522711.
London 64 – Oxford 6 – Reading 25.

🏨 **Upper Reaches**, Thames St., OX14 3JA, ℘ (01235) 522311, Fax (01235) 555182 – 💥 📺
☎ 🅿. 🟠 🗚 ⓞ ☑☑ 🇯🇨🇧. 🦮
Meals (light lunch)/dinner 18.95 st. – ☑ 9.95 – **31 rm** 95.00/130.00 st. – SB.

🏨 **Abingdon Four Pillars**, Marcham Rd, OX14 1TZ, W : 1 m. on A 415 ℘ (01235) 553456,
Fax (01235) 554117 – 💥 rm, 📺 ☎ 🅿 – 🔬 140. 🟠 🗚 ⓞ ☑☑. 🦮
Meals (carving lunch) 12.95/14.95 st. and a la carte – ☑ 6.95 – **63 rm** 75.00/86.00 st. – SB.

at Frilford W : 3 ¾ m. on A 415 – ⊠ Abingdon.

🏠 **Dog House**, Frilford Heath, OX13 6QJ, NE : 1 ¼ m. by A 338 on Cothill rd
℘ (01865) 390830, Fax (01865) 390860, 🎭 – 💥 rm, 📺 ☎ & 🅿. 🟠 🗚 ⓞ ☑☑
Meals a la carte 5.20/10.40 t. ♦ 5.60 – **19 rm** ☑ 69.00/79.00 t.

at Kingston Bagpuize W : 7 m. by A 415 – ⊠ Abingdon.

🏠 **Fallowfields** ≫, Faringdon Rd, OX13 5BH, ℘ (01865) 820416, Fax (01865) 821275, 🏊,
🎭 – 💥 📺 ☎ 🅿. 🟠 🗚 ☑☑ 🇯🇨🇧
Meals (dinner only) a la carte approx. 26.50 t. ♦ 12.50 – **3 rm** ☑ 95.00/120.00 st.

at Cothill NW : 3 ¼ m. by A 415 – ⊠ Abingdon.

🍴 **Merry Miller**, OX13 6JW, ℘ (01865) 390390, Fax (01865) 390040 – 💥 🍽 🅿. 🟠 ☑☑ 🇯🇨🇧
Meals a la carte 9.65/17.85 t. ♦ 5.65.

ACLE Norfolk 404 Y 26 Great Britain G. – pop. 2 208.
Env. : The Broads★.
London 118 – Great Yarmouth 8 – Norwich 11.

🏠 **Travelodge**, Acle bypass, NR13 3BE, on A 47 at junction with B 1140 ℘ (01493) 751970,
Reservations (Freephone) 0800 850950 – 💥 rm, 📺 & 🅿. 🟠 🗚 ⓞ ☑☑ 🇯🇨🇧. 🦮
Meals (grill rest.) – **40 rm** 39.95 t.

ACTON GREEN Herefordshire 403 404 M 27 – see Bromyard.

ADDERBURY Oxon. 403 404 Q 27 – see Banbury.

ADLINGTON Ches. – see Macclesfield.

ADLINGTON Lancs. 402 404 M 23 – pop. 8 556.
London 217 – Liverpool 35 – Manchester 21 – Preston 16.

🏠 **Gladmar Country,** Railway Rd, PR6 9RG, ℰ (01257) 480398, Fax (01257) 482681, 🛲 –
📺 ☎ 🅿. 🚗 AE ① VISA. ✱
Meals (closed Friday to Sunday) (residents only) (dinner only) 12.50 **st.** 🍷 6.95 – **20 rm**
⇄ 37.00/58.00 **st.**

AFFPUDDLE Dorset 403 404 N 31 The West Country G. – pop. 447 – ✉ Dorchester.
Env. : Moreton Church★★, S : 2 ½ m. by B 3390 – Bere Regis★ (St. John the Baptist
Church★), NE : 3 ½ m. by B 3390 and A 35.
London 121 – Bournemouth 19 – Exeter 60 – Southampton 47 – Weymouth 14.

🏠 **Old Vicarage** ✈ without rest., DT2 7HH, ℰ (01305) 848315, Fax (01305) 848315,
« Georgian house », 🛲 – 📺 🅿. ✱
closed 25 December-1 January – **3 rm** ⇄ 28.00/45.00.

ALBRIGHTON Shrops. 402 403 L 25 – see Shrewsbury.

ALBURY Surrey – see Guildford.

ALCESTER Warks. 403 404 O 27 – pop. 6 282.
London 104 – Birmingham 20 – Cheltenham 27 – Stratford-upon-Avon 8.

🏨 **Kings Court,** Kings Coughton, B49 5QQ, N : 1 ½ m. on A 435 ℰ (01789) 763111,
Fax (01789) 400242, 🛲 – 📺 ☎ & 🅿 – 🔬 130. 🚗 AE VISA
closed 24 to 30 December – Meals (buffet lunch)/dinner a la carte 13.80/17.35 **st.** – **42 rm**
⇄ 52.00/78.00 **st.**

🏠 **Throckmorton Arms,** Coughton, B49 5HX, N : 2 ¼ m. on A 435 ℰ (01789) 762879,
Fax (01789) 762654 – 📺 ☎ 🅿. 🚗 AE ① VISA JCB. ✱
closed 25 December – Meals (closed Sunday dinner and Monday) 9.95 **t.**
(lunch) and a la carte 10.25/17.25 **t.** – **10 rm** ⇄ 48.00/65.00 **t.**

ALDBOURNE Wilts. 403 404 P 29 – pop. 1 682.
London 77 – Oxford 36 – Southampton 53 – Swindon 9.

✕✕ **Raffles,** 1 The Green, SN8 2BW, ℰ (01672) 540700, Fax (01672) 540038 – 🚗 AE ① VISA
closed Saturday lunch, Sunday dinner, Monday, 2 weeks August-September, 25 to 31
December and Bank Holidays – Meals a la carte 14.60/24.20 **t.** 🍷 4.00.

ALDEBURGH Suffolk 404 Y 27 – pop. 2 654.
🏌 Thorpeness Golf Hotel, Thorpeness ℰ (01728) 452176.
🛈 The Cinema, High St., IP15 5AU ℰ (01728) 453637 (summer only).
London 97 – Ipswich 24 – Norwich 41.

🏨🏨 **Wentworth,** Wentworth Rd, IP15 5BD, ℰ (01728) 452312, Fax (01728) 454343, ≤ –
❦ rm, 📺 ☎ 🅿. 🚗 AE ① VISA
closed 27 December-11 January – Meals 13.50/16.25 **t.** – **38 rm** ⇄ (dinner included) 73.00/
144.00 **t.** – SB.

🏨 **Brudenell,** The Parade, IP15 5BU, ℰ (01728) 452071, Fax (01728) 454082, ≤ – 📱 ❦ 📺 ☎
🅿. 🚗 AE ① VISA JCB. ✱
Meals (light lunch Monday to Friday in summer, carving lunch Saturday and bar lunch in
winter)/dinner 17.95 **t.** 🍷 5.75 – ⇄ 8.95 – **47 rm** 65.00/85.00 **st.** – SB.

🏨 **White Lion,** Market Cross Pl., IP15 5BJ, ℰ (01728) 452720, Fax (01728) 452986, ≤ – 📺 ☎
🅿 – 🔬 100. 🚗 AE ① VISA JCB
Meals (bar lunch Monday to Saturday)/dinner 17.95 **st.** and a la carte 🍷 6.35 – **38 rm**
⇄ 59.50/98.00 **st.** – SB.

✕ **Lighthouse,** 77 High St., IP15 5AU, ℰ (01728) 453377, Fax (01728) 453377 – ❦. 🚗 VISA
JCB
closed 1 week late January and 1 week October – Meals 15.75 **t.** (dinner)
and lunch a la carte 11.45/16.95 **t.** 🍷 6.75.

✕ **Regatta,** 171-173 High St., IP15 5AN, ℰ (01728) 452011, Fax (01728) 452011 – 🚗 AE VISA
restricted opening October-Easter – Meals a la carte 12.85/21.95 **t.** 🍷 4.75.

The Guide is updated annually so renew your Guide every year.

ALDERLEY EDGE *Ches.* 402 403 404 N 24 – *pop. 5 280.*

🏌 *Wilmslow, Great Warford, Mobberley* ℘ *(01565) 872148 –* 🏌 *Brook Lane* ℘ *(01625) 585583.*

London 187 – Chester 34 – Manchester 14 – Stoke-on-Trent 25.

🏰 **Alderley Edge,** Macclesfield Rd, SK9 7BJ, ℘ *(01625) 583033, Fax (01625) 586343,* 🌳 – 📺 ☎ 🅿 – 🔏 120. 🌐 AE ⓞ VISA. 🕸
Meals – (see **The Alderley** below) – 🍽 8.50 – **32 rm** 89.50/125.00 t. – SB.

🍴🍴🍴 **The Alderley** (at Alderley Edge H.), Macclesfield Rd, SK9 7BJ, ℘ *(01625) 583033,* Fax (01625) 586343, 🌳 – ▤ 🅿 🌐 AE ⓞ VISA
Meals 16.50/23.95 t. and a la carte 🍷 7.50.

ALDERNEY 403 Q 33 and 230 ⑨ – *see Channel Islands.*

ALDERSHOT *Hants.* 404 R 30.
London 45 – Portsmouth 38 – Reading 22 – Winchester 32.

🏠 **Travel Inn,** Wellington Av., GU11 1SQ, E : on A 323 ℘ *(01252) 344063, Fax (01252) 344073* – 🕸 rm, 📺 ♿ 🅿. 🌐 AE ⓞ VISA. 🕸
Meals (grill rest.) – **40 rm** 36.50 t.

ALDRIDGE *W. Mids.* 402 403 404 O 26 – *pop. 16 862 –* ✉ *Walsall.*
London 130 – Birmingham 12 – Derby 32 – Leicester 40 – Stoke-on-Trent 38.

Plan : see Birmingham p.3

🏰 **Fairlawns,** 178 Little Aston Rd, WS9 0NU, E : 1 m. on A 454 ℘ *(01922) 55122, Fax (01922) 743210,* 🌳 – ▤ rest, 📺 ☎ 🅿 – 🔏 80. 🌐 AE ⓞ VISA CT n
Meals *(closed Saturday lunch, Sunday dinner and Bank Holidays)* 16.95/22.95 **st.** and a la carte 🍷 5.95 – **31 rm** 🛏 49.50/89.50 **st.**, 4 suites – SB.

🅰 ATS 106 Leighswood Rd ℘ *(01922) 51968/53970*

ALDWINCLE *Northants.* 402 404 S 26 – *pop. 310 –* ✉ *Oundle.*
London 84 – Cambridge 40 – Leicester 40 – Northampton 26 – Peterborough 18.

⌂ **The Maltings** 🌿 without rest., Main St., NN14 3EP, ℘ *(01832) 720233, Fax (01832) 720326,* 🌳 – 🕸 🅿. 🌐 VISA. 🕸
closed 1 week Christmas – **3 rm** 🛏 35.00/49.00.

ALFRETON *Derbs.* 402 403 404 P 24 – *pop. 22 822.*
🏌 *Shirland, Lower Delves* ℘ *(01773) 834935 –* 🏌 *Ormonde Fields, Nottingham Rd, Codnor, Ripley* ℘ *(01773) 742987.*
London 134 – Derby 13 – Nottingham 19 – Sheffield 27.

🏠 **Travelodge,** Old Swanwick Colliery Rd, DE55 1HJ, S : ¾ m. by A 61 at junction with A 38 ℘ *(01773) 520040, Fax (01773) 520040,* Reservations (Freephone) 0800 850950 – 🕸 rm, ▤ rest, 📺 ♿ 🅿 – 🔏 50. 🌐 AE ⓞ VISA JCB. 🕸
Meals (grill rest.) – **60 rm** 44.95 t.

ALFRISTON *E. Sussex* 404 U 31 – *pop. 1 721 –* ✉ *Polegate.*
London 66 – Eastbourne 9 – Lewes 10 – Newhaven 8.

🏰 **Star Inn,** High St., BN26 5TA, ℘ *(01323) 870495, Fax (01323) 870922 –* 🕸 📺 ☎ 🅿 – 🔏 30. 🌐 AE ⓞ VISA. 🕸
Meals (bar lunch Monday to Saturday)/dinner 18.95 **st.** 🍷 8.50 – 🛏 9.95 – **34 rm** 72.50/102.50 **st.** – SB.

🍴🍴 **Moonrakers,** High St., BN26 5TD, ℘ *(01323) 870472 –* 🌐 AE VISA JCB
closed 25 December and first 2 weeks January – **Meals** (dinner only) 12.95 t. and a la carte 🍷 4.95.

ALLENDALE *Northd.* 401 402 N 19 – *pop. 2 123 –* ✉ *Hexham.*
🏌 *High Studdon, Allenheads Rd* ℘ *(01434) 345005.*
London 314 – Carlisle 39 – Newcastle upon Tyne 33.

⌂ **Thornley House,** NE47 9NH, W : ¾ m. on Whitfield rd ℘ *(01434) 683255,* 🌳 – 🕸 🅿. 🕸
Meals (by arrangement) (communal dining) 11.00 **st.** – **3 rm** 🛏 26.50/37.00.

ALLESLEY *W. Mids.* 403 404 P 26 – *see Coventry.*

ALNMOUTH Northd. 🅰🅰🅰 🅰🅰🅰 P 17 *Great Britain G. – pop. 586.*
　　Env. : *Warkworth Castle★ AC, S : 4 m. by B 1338 and A 1068.*
　　🏌 *Alnmouth Village, Marine Rd. ℘ (01665) 830370.*
　　London 314 – Edinburgh 90 – Newcastle upon Tyne 37.

🏠　**Marine House,** 1 Marine Rd, NE66 2RW, ℘ (01665) 830349, ≤, 🚗 – ⅙※ 📺 🄿. 🐵 🆚🅸🆂🅰
　　Meals (by arrangement) 13.00 t. ▒ 6.50 – **10 rm** �🍽 (dinner included) 76.00 t. – SB.

⌂　**High Buston Hall** ⤫, High Buston, NE66 3QH, SW: 2 ¼ m. by B 1338 off A 1068
　　℘ (01665) 830341, Fax (01665) 830341, ≤, « Georgian house », 🚗 – ⅙※ 📺 🄿. 🛇
　　closed December and January – **Meals** (by arrangement) (communal dining) 25.00 st. –
　　3 rm ⍾ 40.00/60.00 st.

⌂　**The Grange** without rest., 20 Northumberland St., NE66 2RJ, ℘ (01665) 830401,
　　Fax (01665) 830401, ≤, 🚗 – ⅙※ 📺 🄿. 🛇
　　closed December and January – **5 rm** ⍾ 22.00/54.00 st.

ALNWICK Northd. 🅰🅰🅰 🅰🅰🅰 O 17 *Great Britain G. – pop. 7 419.*
　　See : *Town ★ – Castle★★ AC.*
　　Exc. : *Dunstanburgh Castle★ AC, NE : 8 m. by B 1340 and Dunstan rd (last 2½ m. on foot).*
　　🏌 *Swansfield Park ℘ (01665) 602632.*
　　🅱 *The Shambles, NE66 1TN ℘ (01665) 510665.*
　　London 320 – Edinburgh 86 – Newcastle upon Tyne 34.

🏨　**White Swan,** Bondgate Within, NE66 1TD, ℘ (01665) 602109, Fax (01665) 510400,
　　« Furnishings from SS Olympic » – ⅙※ 📺 ☎ 🄿 – 🔬 150. 🐵 🄰🄴 🆚🅸🆂🅰
　　Meals (bar lunch Monday to Saturday)/dinner 17.95 t. ▒ 6.70 – **55 rm** ⍾ 69.00/79.00 t. –
　　SB.

🏠　**Oaks,** South Rd, NE66 2PN, SE : ½ m. ℘ (01665) 510014, Fax (01665) 603219 – 📺 ☎ 🄿.
　　🐵 🆚🅸🆂🅰
　　Meals a la carte 10.85/13.15 t. ▒ 3.50 – **12 rm** ⍾ 39.50/50.00 t.

⌂　**Charlton House,** 2 Aydon Gdns., South Rd, NE66 2NT, SE : ½ m. ℘ (01665) 605185 – ⅙※
　　📺 🄿. 🛇
　　Meals (by arrangement) 11.00 st. – **4 rm** ⍾ 18.00/40.00 st.

⌂　**Bondgate House,** 20 Bondgate Without, NE66 1PN, ℘ (01665) 602025,
　　Fax (01665) 602025 – ⅙※ rest, 📺 🄿. 🆚🅸🆂🅰 🄹🄲🄱. 🛇
　　Meals (by arrangement) 12.00 t. ▒ 5.50 – **8 rm** ⍾ 25.00/44.00 st. – SB.

at Newton on the Moor *S : 5½ m. on A 1 –* ⊠ *Alnwick.*

🍴🍴　**Cook and Barker Inn** with rm, NE65 9JY, ℘ (01665) 575234 – 📺 🄿. 🐵 🄰🄴 🆚🅸🆂🅰 🄹🄲🄱
　　Meals a la carte 18.25/27.10 st. ▒ 5.00 – **4 rm** ⍾ 37.50/70.00 st.

ALPORT Derbs. – see Bakewell.

ALSAGER Ches. 🅰🅰🅰 🅰🅰🅰 🅰🅰🅰 N 24 *Great Britain G. – pop. 13 435 –* ⊠ *Stoke-on-Trent (Staffs.).*
　　Env. : *Little Moreton Hall★★ AC, NE : 4 m. by A 50 and A 34.*
　　London 180 – Chester 36 – Liverpool 49 – Manchester 32 – Stoke-on-Trent 11.

🏨　**Manor House,** Audley Rd, ST7 2QQ, SE : ¾ m. ℘ (01270) 884000, Fax (01270) 882483, 🔲
　　– ⅙※ rm, 📺 ☎ 🄿 – 🔬 200. 🐵 🄰🄴 🅾 🆚🅸🆂🅰. 🛇
　　Meals *(closed Saturday lunch)* 14.00/21.00 t. and a la carte ▒ 6.45 – **56 rm** ⍾ 74.00/
　　104.00 t. – SB.

⌂　**Sappho Cottage,** 118 Crewe Rd, ST7 2JA, ℘ (01270) 882033, Fax (01270) 883556, 🚗 –
　　⅙※ 📺 🄿. 🛇
　　Meals (by arrangement) (communal dining) 14.00 st. – **3 rm** ⍾ 30.00/45.00 st.

ALSTON Cumbria 🅰🅰🅰 🅰🅰🅰 M 19 – *pop. 2 065.*
　　🏌 *Alston Moor, The Hermitage ℘ (01434) 381675.*
　　🅱 *The Railway Station, CA9 3JB ℘ (01434) 381696 (summer only).*
　　London 309 – Carlisle 28 – Newcastle upon Tyne 45.

🏨　**Lovelady Shield Country House** ⤫, Nenthead Rd, CA9 3LF, E : 2 ½ m. on A 689
　　℘ (01434) 381203, Fax (01434) 381515, ≤, 🚗 – ⅙※ rest, 📺 ☎ 🄿. 🐵 🄰🄴 🅾 🆚🅸🆂🅰. 🛇
　　closed 3 to 31 January – **Meals** (bar lunch)/dinner 26.95 t. ▒ 7.90 – **12 rm** ⍾ (dinner
　　included) 52.00/170.00 t. – SB.

🏠　**Nent Hall Country House,** CA9 3LQ, E : 2 ½ m. on A 689 ℘ (01434) 381584,
　　Fax (01434) 382668, 🚗 – ⅙※ rest, 📺 ☎ ら 🄿. 🐵 🆚🅸🆂🅰
　　restricted opening in winter – **Meals** (dinner only) 12.50 st. and a la carte ▒ 7.75 – **18 rm**
　　⍾ 60.00/75.00 st. – SB.

⌂ **High Windy Hall** ॐ, Middleton in Teesdale Rd, CA9 3EZ, ☞ (01434) 381547, Fax (01434) 382477, ← – ❄ ⊡ ℗. ⓌⓈ 𝘝𝘐𝘚𝘈 J̄C̄B̄. ℀
mid March-November – **Meals** (by arrangement) 18.95 **t.** ≬ 6.00 – **5 rm** ⌖ 35.00/65.00 **t.** – SB.

ALTARNUN Cornwall 403 G 32 The West Country G. – pop. 2 405 – ✉ Launceston.
See : Church★.
Env. : Bodmin Moor★★, Laneast (St. Sidwell's★), N : 2½ m. by minor roads.
London 279 – Exeter 56 – Plymouth 36 – Truro 39.

🏛 **Penhallow Manor Country House** ॐ, PL15 7SJ, ☞ (01566) 86206, Fax (01566) 86179, ↘, ☞ – ❄ rest, ⊡ ☎ ℗. ⓌⓈ 𝘈𝘌 𝘝𝘐𝘚𝘈. ℀
closed 3 January-14 February – **Meals** (bar lunch)/dinner 20.50 **st.** ≬ 6.00 – **6 rm** ⌖ 52.50/85.00 **st.** – SB.

ALTON Hants. 404 R 30 – pop. 16 005.
🛇 Old Odiham Rd ☞ (01420) 82042.
🛈 7 Cross and Pillory Lane, GU34 1HL ☞ (01420) 88448.
London 53 – Reading 24 – Southampton 29 – Winchester 18.

🏛🏛 **Swan,** High St., GU34 1AT, ☞ (01420) 83777, Fax (01420) 87975 – ❄ ⊡ ☎ ℗ – 🔬 50. ⓌⓈ 𝘈𝘌 ⓪ 𝘝𝘐𝘚𝘈 J̄C̄B̄
Meals (bar lunch)/dinner 17.95 **t.** – ⌖ 9.25 – **36 rm** 65.00/78.00 **st.** – SB.

🏛🏛 **Alton Grange,** London Rd, GU34 4EG, NE : 1 m. on A 339 ☞ (01420) 86565, Fax (01420) 541346, ☞ – ❄ ⊡ ☎ ℗ – 🔬 80. ⓌⓈ 𝘈𝘌 ⓪ 𝘝𝘐𝘚𝘈 J̄C̄B̄. ℀
closed 26 to 30 December – **Meals** a la carte 18.15/26.85 **t.** ≬ 4.95 – **29 rm** ⌖ 57.50/85.00 **t.**

🏛🏛 **Alton House,** Normandy St., GU34 1DW, ☞ (01420) 80033, Fax (01420) 89222, ☍, ☞, ℀ – ⊡ ☎ ℗ – 🔬 120. ⓌⓈ 𝘈𝘌 ⓪ 𝘝𝘐𝘚𝘈. ℀
closed 26 December – **Meals** 12.95 **t.** and a la carte ≬ 4.50 – ⌖ 6.50 – **39 rm** 55.00/85.00 **t.** – SB.

ALTON TOWERS Staffs. 402 403 404 O 25.
London 158 – Birmingham 48 – Derby 23 – Stafford 24 – Stoke-on-Trent 13.

🏛🏛🏛 **Alton Towers,** ST10 4DB, ☞ (01538) 704600, Fax (01538) 704657, ←, « Fantasy themed », ☎, ⃞, ☞, park – ﹫ ❄, ▤ rest, ⊡ ☎ ♿ ℗ – 🔬 200. ⓌⓈ 𝘈𝘌 𝘝𝘐𝘚𝘈 J̄C̄B̄. ℀
closed 1 week Christmas – **Secret Garden :** Meals a la carte 14.15/23.15 **st.** ≬ 9.95 – ⌖ 4.95 – **175 rm** 98.00/118.00 **st.** – SB.

ALTRINCHAM Gtr. Manchester 402 403 404 N 23 – pop. 40 042.
🛇 Altrincham Municipal, Stockport Rd, Timperley ☞ (0161) 928 0761 – Dunham Forest, Oldfield Lane ☞ (0161) 928 2605 – 🛇 Ringway, Hale Mount, Hale Barns ☞ (0161) 904 9609.
🛈 20 Stamford New Rd, WA14 1EJ ☞ (0161) 912 5931.
London 191 – Chester 30 – Liverpool 30 – Manchester 8.

🏛🏛 **Cresta Court,** Church St., WA14 4DP, on A 56 ☞ (0161) 927 7272, Fax (0161) 926 9194, ﹫ – ﹫, ❄ rest, ▤ rest, ⊡ ☎ ℗ – 🔬 250. ⓌⓈ 𝘈𝘌 ⓪ 𝘝𝘐𝘚𝘈
Meals a la carte 12.00/16.00 **st.** ≬ 5.95 – **138 rm** ⌖ 72.50/92.50 **st.** – SB.

🏛🏛 **Woodland Park,** Wellington Rd, WA15 7RG, off A 560 ☞ (0161) 928 8631, Fax (0161) 941 2821 – ▤ rest, ⊡ ☎ ℗ – 🔬 200. ⓌⓈ 𝘈𝘌 ⓪ 𝘝𝘐𝘚𝘈 J̄C̄B̄. ℀
The Terrace : Meals (closed Sunday) 14.95 **t.** and dinner a la carte ≬ 8.50 – **45 rm** ⌖ 75.00/110.00 **t.**

🏛🏛 **Bowdon,** Langham Rd, WA14 2HT, SW : 1 m. ☞ (0161) 928 7121, Fax (0161) 927 7560 – ❄ ⊡ ☎ ℗ – 🔬 150. ⓌⓈ 𝘈𝘌 ⓪ 𝘝𝘐𝘚𝘈
Meals (buffet lunch Monday to Friday and bar lunch Saturday)/dinner 17.95 **t.** and a la carte ≬ 6.95 – ⌖ 9.50 – **89 rm** 70.00/100.00 **st.** – SB.

🏛🏛 **George and Dragon - Premier Lodge,** Manchester Rd, WA14 4PH, on A 56 ☞ (0161) 928 9933, Fax (0161) 929 8060 – ﹫, ❄ rm, ⊡ ☎ ℗ – 🔬 40. ⓌⓈ 𝘈𝘌 ⓪ 𝘝𝘐𝘚𝘈 J̄C̄B̄. ℀
Meals (closed Saturday lunch) (grill rest.) 6.55 **t.** and a la carte ≬ 3.85 – ⌖ 4.95 – **46 rm** 44.25 **t.** – SB.

🏛 **Pelican Inn - Premier Lodge,** Manchester Rd, West Timperley, WA14 5NH, N : 2 m. on A 56 ☞ (0161) 962 7414, Fax (0161) 962 3456 – ❄ rm, ⊡ ☎ ℗ – 🔬 50. ⓌⓈ 𝘈𝘌 ⓪ 𝘝𝘐𝘚𝘈. ℀
Meals (grill rest.) a la carte 15.35/16.35 **st.** ≬ 4.50 – ⌖ 4.95 – **48 rm** 44.25 **t.** – SB.

XX **Juniper**, 21 The Downs, WA14 2QD, ℘ (0161) 929 4008, Fax (0161) 929 4009 – ▤. **WS** **AE**
✓ **VISA** **JCB**
closed Monday and Saturday lunch, Sunday and Bank Holidays – **Meals** 15.00/25.00 **t.**
and a la carte 17.00/27.50 **t.** ₰ 10.00
Spec. Cornish brill with scallop ravioli and artichoke. Panfried pork fillet with black pudding,
brandy and sultanas. Hot rice pudding soufflé.

⌂ **Old Packet House** with rm, Navigation Rd, Broadheath, WA14 1LW, N : 1 m. by A 56
℘ (0161) 929 1331, Fax (0161) 929 1331 – **TV** **P**. **WS** **VISA**
Meals (in bar) a la carte 12.40/16.85 **t.** – **4 rm** ⊇ 47.50/65.00 **t.**

at Hale SE : 1 m. on B 5163 – ⊠ Altrincham.

X **Est, Est, Est**, 183 Ashley Rd, WA15 9SD, ℘ (0161) 928 1811 – ▤. **WS** **AE** **VISA**
closed 25 and 26 December – **Meals** - Italian - 9.95 **t.** and a la carte.

at Halebarns SE : 3 m. on A 538 – ⊠ Altrincham.

🏨 **Four Seasons**, Manchester Airport, Hale Rd, WA15 8XW, ℘ (0161) 904 0301,
Fax (0161) 980 1787, ☞ – ▐, ✓ rm, ▤ rest, **TV** ☎ **P** – ▲ 120. **WS** **AE** **①** **VISA**. ⁒
The Four Seasons : **Meals** (closed Saturday lunch) 15.95/18.95 **st.** and a la carte ₰ 6.95 –
⊇ 10.50 – **90 rm** 98.50/118.50 **st.**, 4 suites.

Ⓐ ATS 74 Oakfield Rd ℘ (0161) 928 7024

ALVELEY Shrops. – see Bridgnorth.

ALVERSTONE I.O.W. **403** **404** Q 32 – see Wight (Isle of).

ALVESTON South Gloucestershire **403** **404** M 29 – pop. 2 525 – ⊠ Bristol.
London 127 – Bristol 11 – Gloucester 23 – Swindon 42.

🏨 **Alveston House**, BS12 2LJ, on A 38 ℘ (01454) 415050, Fax (01454) 415425, ☞ – **TV** ☎
P – ▲ 85. **WS** **AE** **①** **VISA** **JCB**
Meals 18.75 **st.** and a la carte ₰ 6.50 – **30 rm** ⊇ 75.00/95.00 **st.** – SB.

🏨 **Forte Posthouse Alveston**, Thornbury Rd, BS12 2LL, on A 38 ℘ (01454) 412521,
Fax (01454) 413920, ⛲, ☞ – ✓ rm, **TV** ☎ **P** – ▲ 100. **WS** **AE** **①** **VISA**. ⁒
Meals a la carte 11.80/25.65 **st.** ₰ 7.95 – ⊇ 8.95 – **74 rm** 69.00/158.00 **st.** – SB.

ALWALTON Cambs. **402** **404** T 26 – see Peterborough.

AMBERLEY Glos. **403** **404** N 28 – see Stroud.

AMBERLEY W. Sussex **404** S 31 Great Britain G. – pop. 525 – ⊠ Arundel.
Env. : Bignor Roman Villa (mosaics★) AC, NW : 3½ m. by B 2139 via Bury.
London 56 – Brighton 24 – Portsmouth 31.

🏨 **Amberley Castle** ⚲, BN18 9ND, SW : ½ m. on B 2139 ℘ (01798) 831992,
Fax (01798) 831998, « 14C castle, 12C origins », ☞, park – ✓ rest, **TV** ☎ **P** – ▲ 40. **WS** **AE**
① **VISA**. ⁒
Queen's Room : **Meals** (booking essential) 18.10/29.50 **t.** and dinner a la carte 35.40/
52.20 **t.** ₰ 8.95 – **15 rm** ⊇ 130.00/300.00 **t.** – SB.

AMBLESIDE Cumbria **402** L 20 Great Britain G. – pop. 2 905.
Env. : Lake Windermere★★ – Dove Cottage, Grasmere★ AC AY **A** – Brockhole National Park
Centre★ AC, SE : 3 m. by A 591 AZ.
Exc. : Wrynose Pass★★, W : 7½ m. by A 593 AY – Hard Knott Pass★★, W : 10 m. by A 593 AY
🛈 Old Courthouse, Church St., LA22 0BT ℘ (015394) 32582 (closed Sunday and Monday in
winter) AZ – Main Car Park, Waterhead, LA22 0EN ℘ (015394) 32729 (summer only) BY.
London 278 – Carlisle 47 – Kendal 14.

Plan on next page

🏨 **Rothay Manor**, Rothay Bridge, LA22 0EH, S : ½ m. on A 593 ℘ (015394) 33605,
Fax (015394) 33607, ≤, ☞ – ✓ rest, **TV** ☎ **P**. **WS** **AE** **①** **VISA**. ⁒   BY **r**
closed 3 January-6 February – **Meals** (buffet lunch Monday to Saturday)/dinner 28.00 **t.**
₰ 6.50 – **15 rm** ⊇ 79.00/137.00 **t.**, 3 suites – SB.

🏨 **Ambleside Salutation**, Lake Rd, LA22 9BX, ℘ (015394) 32244, Fax (015394) 34157 –
✓ rest, **TV** ☎ **P** – ▲ 30. **WS** **AE** **①** **VISA**   AZ **r**
Meals (bar lunch)/dinner 19.50 **t.** and a la carte ₰ 5.25 – **36 rm** ⊇ 47.00/94.00 **t.** – SB.

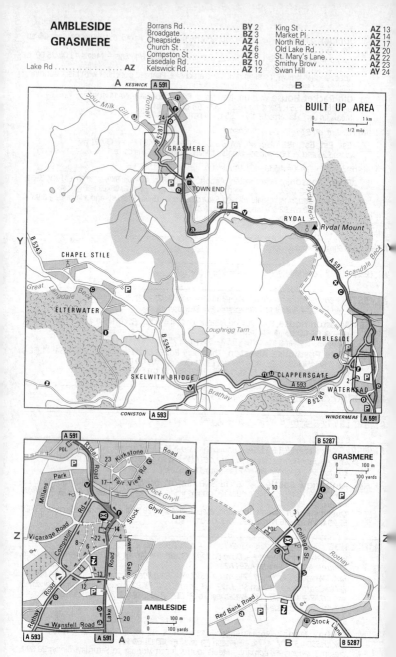

AMBLESIDE
GRASMERE

BUILT UP AREA

KESWICK A 591

A 591

Town plans: roads most used by traffic and those on which guide listed hotels and restaurants stand are fully drawn; the beginning only of lesser roads is indicated.

86

🏨 **Kirkstone Foot Country House,** Kirkstone Pass Rd, LA22 9EH, NE : ¼ m.
𝒫 (015394) 32232, Fax (015394) 32805, 🖼 – ⁑⁑ rest, 📺 ☎ 🅿. 🆗 🄰🄴 ⓪ 𝐕𝐈𝐒𝐀 𝐉𝐂𝐁.
AZ c
🦌
closed 3 to 31 January – **Meals** (dinner only) 21.95 **t.** ₰ 5.00 – **13 rm** ⌑ (dinner included)
67.00/134.00 **t.** – SB.

🏠 **Borrans Park,** Borrans Rd, LA22 0EN, *𝒫 (015394) 33454, Fax (015394) 33003,* 🖼 – ⁑⁑
📺 ☎ 🅿. 🆗 𝐕𝐈𝐒𝐀 𝐉𝐂𝐁.
BY a
closed 1 week Christmas – **Meals** (dinner only) 17.50 **st.** ₰ 4.95 – **12 rm** ⌑ 50.00/80.00 **st.** –
SB.

🏠 **Elder Grove,** Lake Rd, LA22 0DB, *𝒫 (015394) 32504, Fax (015394) 32504* – ⁑⁑ rest, 📺 ☎
🅿. 🆗 🄰🄴 ⓪ 𝐕𝐈𝐒𝐀. 🦌
AZ a
mid February-mid November – **Meals** (dinner only) 17.00 **t.** and a la carte ₰ 5.00 – **12 rm**
⌑ (dinner included) 45.00/90.00 **t.** – SB.

🏠 **Rothay Garth,** Rothay Rd, LA22 0EE, *𝒫 (015394) 32217, Fax (015394) 34400,* 🖼 – ⁑⁑ 📺
☎ 🅿. 🆗 🄰🄴 ⓪ 𝐕𝐈𝐒𝐀 𝐉𝐂𝐁. 🦌
AZ e
Meals 9.50/15.50 **st.** and lunch a la carte ₰ 5.90 – **15 rm** ⌑ (dinner included) 53.00/
118.00 **st.**, 1 suite – SB.

🏠 **Laurel Villa,** Lake Rd, LA22 0DB, *𝒫 (015394) 33240* – ⁑⁑ 📺 🅿. 🆗 🄰🄴 𝐕𝐈𝐒𝐀. 🦌 AZ s
Meals (booking essential) (residents only) (dinner only) 20.00 **t.** – **8 rm** ⌑ 50.00/80.00 **t.**

🏠 **Riverside** 🦢 without rest., Under Loughrigg, LA22 9LJ, *𝒫 (015394) 32395,*
Fax (015394) 32395, 🖼 – 📺 🅿. 🆗 𝐕𝐈𝐒𝐀. 🦌
BY s
March-November – **4 rm** ⌑ 40.00/60.00 **st.**

🏠 **Crow How** 🦢, Rydal Rd, LA22 9PN, NW : ½ m. on A 591 *𝒫 (015394) 32193,*
Fax (015394) 32193, ≤, 🖼 – ⁑⁑ rest, 📺 🅿. 🆗 🄰🄴 𝐕𝐈𝐒𝐀
BY x
closed December-January and restricted opening February and November – **Meals** (dinner
only) 14.00 **st.** ₰ 4.75 – **9 rm** ⌑ 25.00/64.00 **st.** – SB.

🏠 **Rowanfield Country House** 🦢, Kirkstone Rd, LA22 9ET, NE : ¾ m.
𝒫 (015394) 33686, Fax (015394) 31569, ≤ Lake Windermere and Coniston Old Man, 🖼 –
⁑⁑ 📺 🅿. 🆗 𝐕𝐈𝐒𝐀 𝐉𝐂𝐁. 🦌
AZ u
April-mid November and Christmas-New Year – **Meals** (by arrangement) 17.00 **t.** – **8 rm**
⌑ 60.00 **st.** – SB.

🏠 **Scandale Brow** without rest., Rydal Rd, LA22 9PL, NW : ½ m. on A 591
𝒫 (015394) 34528, Fax (015394) 34528, 🖼 – ⁑⁑ 📺 🅿
BY c
3 rm ⌑ 37.00/50.00 **s.**

✗ **Glass House,** Rydal Rd, LA22 9AN, *𝒫 (015394) 32137, Fax (015394) 31139,* « Converted
mill » – 🦌. 🆗 𝐕𝐈𝐒𝐀
AZ v
Meals a la carte 11.70/20.25 **t.** ₰ 4.95.

🍴 **Drunken Duck Inn** with rm, Barngates, LA22 0NG, SW : 3 m. by A 593 and B 5286 on
Tarn Hows rd *𝒫 (015394) 36347, Fax (015394) 36781,* ≤, « Part 16C » – ⁑⁑ rest, 📺 ☎ 🅿.
🆗 🄰🄴 𝐕𝐈𝐒𝐀 𝐉𝐂𝐁
closed 25 December – **Meals** (bar lunch Monday to Saturday)/dinner a la carte 16.40/
22.75 **t.** – **9 rm** ⌑ 55.00/75.00 **t.**

at Waterhead *S : 1 m. on A 591* – BY – ✉ Ambleside.

🏨 **Wateredge,** Borrans Rd, LA22 0EP, *𝒫 (015394) 32332, Fax (015394) 31878,* ≤, « Part 17C
fishermen's cottages, lakeside setting », 🖼 – ⁑⁑ rest, 📺 ☎ 🅿. 🆗 🄰🄴 𝐕𝐈𝐒𝐀 𝐉𝐂𝐁. 🦌
BY o
closed mid December-mid January – **Meals** (light lunch)/dinner 27.90 **t.** ₰ 8.80 – **22 rm**
⌑ (dinner included) 80.00/188.00 **t.** – SB.

🏨 **Regent,** LA22 0ES, *𝒫 (015394) 32254, Fax (015394) 31474,* 🔲 – ⁑⁑ rest, 📺 ☎ 🅿. 🆗 𝐕𝐈𝐒𝐀
𝐉𝐂𝐁
BY e
Meals 20.00 **st.** and a la carte ₰ 7.95 – **25 rm** ⌑ 59.00/140.00 **t.** – SB.

at Clappersgate *W : 1 m. on A 593* – BY – ✉ Ambleside.

🏨 **Nanny Brow Country House** 🦢, LA22 9NF, *𝒫 (015394) 32036, Fax (015394) 32450,*
≤, « Landscaped gardens », 🦢 – ⁑⁑ 📺 ☎ 🅿. 🆗 🄰🄴 ⓪ 𝐕𝐈𝐒𝐀 𝐉𝐂𝐁
BY u
Meals (dinner only) 19.50 **t.** and a la carte ₰ 8.00 – **15 rm** ⌑ (dinner included) 65.00/
161.00 **t.**, 3 suites – SB.

🏠 **Grey Friar Lodge,** LA22 9NE, *𝒫 (015394) 33158, Fax (015394) 33158,* ≤, 🖼 – ⁑⁑ 📺 🅿.
🦌
BY n
April-October and weekends only in March – **Meals** (residents only) (dinner only) 16.50 **st.** –
8 rm ⌑ (dinner included) 49.50/99.00 **st.** – SB.

at Skelwith Bridge W : 2½ m. on A 593 – AY – ✉ Ambleside.

🏛 **Skelwith Bridge,** LA22 9NJ, ℘ (015394) 32115, Fax (015394) 34254 – ✦ rest, 📺 ☎ 🅿.
⬛⬛ 💳
AY v
closed 12 to 26 December – Meals (bar lunch Monday to Saturday)/dinner 18.75 st. ⓘ 6.95 –
29 rm ⬱ 47.00/84.00 st. – SB.

⌂ **Greenbank** without rest., LA22 9NW, on A 593 ℘ (015394) 33236, ≤, ⌦ – ✦ 📺 🅿
closed Christmas and restricted opening in winter – 3 rm ⬱ 25.00/42.00 st.

at Elterwater W : 4½ m. by A 593 off B 5343 – AY – ✉ Ambleside.

🏛 **Langdale H. & Country Club,** Great Langdale, LA22 9JD, NW : 1 ¼ m. on B 5343
℘ (015394) 37302, Fax (015394) 37694, Ⅰ₆, ☎, ☎, 🔲, 🦰, park, 🍴, squash – ✦ rest, ▤ rest,
📺 ☎ 🅿 – 🔬 90. ⬛⬛ 🅰🅴 ⓞ 💳 💳. 🦰
AY c
Meals (light lunch)/dinner 18.50 st. and a la carte ⓘ 8.95 – 65 rm ⬱ 115.00/190.00 st. – SB.

🏛 **Eltermere Country House** 🦡, LA22 9HY, ℘ (015394) 37207, ≤, ⌦ – ✦ rest, 📺 🅿.
🦰
AY i
closed 3 weeks Christmas – Meals (dinner only) 17.50 t. ⓘ 5.50 – 18 rm ⬱ (dinner included)
49.00/105.00 st. – SB.

at Little Langdale W : 4½ m. by A 593 – ✉ Langdale.

🏠 **Three Shires Inn** 🦡 with rm, LA22 9NZ, ℘ (015394) 37215, ≤, ⌦ – ✦ rest, 🅿. ⬛⬛ 💳.
🦰
restricted opening January and December – Meals (bar lunch)/dinner 18.00 st.
and a la carte ⓘ 4.95 – 10 rm ⬱ 35.00/70.00 st. – SB.

at Great Langdale W : 6 m. by A 593 on B 5343 – AY – ✉ Ambleside.

⌂ **Long House** 🦡 without rest., LA22 9JS, ℘ (015394) 37222, ≤ Langdale valley, ⌦ – ✦
🅿. ⬛⬛ 💳. 🦰
restricted opening in winter – 3 rm ⬱ 27.00/48.00 s.

AMERSHAM (Old Town) Bucks. 404 S 28 – pop. 21 711.
London 29 – Aylesbury 16 – Oxford 33.

🏛 **Crown,** 16 High St., HP7 0DH, ℘ (01494) 721541, Fax (01494) 431283, « Part 16C former
coaching inn », ⌦ – ✦ 📺 ☎ 🅿 – 🔬 30. ⬛⬛ 🅰🅴 ⓞ 💳 💳. 🦰
Meals 13.95/19.95 t. ⓘ 7.75 – ⬱ 8.95 – 23 rm 110.00/140.00 t. – SB.

✕✕ **King's Arms,** High St., HP7 0DJ, ℘ (01494) 726333, Fax (01494) 433480, « Part 15C inn »
– 🅿. ⬛⬛ 🅰🅴 ⓞ 💳 💳
closed Sunday dinner, Monday and 26-30 December – Meals 12.50/25.00 t. and a la carte
ⓘ 4.40.

AMESBURY Wilts. 403 404 O 30 The West Country G. – pop. 6 333.
Env. : Stonehenge★★★ AC, W : 2 m. by A 303.
Exc. : Wilton Village★ (Wilton House★★ AC, Wilton Carpet Factory★ AC), SW : 13 m. by
A 303, B 3083 and A 36.
🛈 Redworth House, Flower Lane, SP4 7HG ℘ (01980) 622833.
London 87 – Bristol 52 – Taunton 66.

🏛 **Travelodge,** SP4 7AS, N : ¼ m. at junction of A 303 with A 345 ℘ (01980) 624966,
Reservations (Freephone) 0800 850950 – ✦ rm, 📺 ⬥ 🅿. ⬛⬛ 🅰🅴 ⓞ 💳 💳. 🦰
Meals (grill rest.) – 32 rm 44.95 t.

⌂ **Mandalay** without rest., 15 Stonehenge Rd, SP4 7BA, ℘ (01980) 623733,
Fax (01980) 626642, ⌦ – ✦ 📺 ☎ 🅿. ⬛⬛ 🅰🅴 ⓞ 💳 💳. 🦰
5 rm ⬱ 28.00/38.00 s.

AMPFIELD Hants. 403 404 P 30 – pop. 1 523 – ✉ Romsey.
🛏 Ampfield (Par Three), Winchester Rd ℘ (01794) 368480.
London 79 – Bournemouth 31 – Salisbury 19 – Southampton 11 – Winchester 7.

🏛 **Potters Heron,** Winchester Rd, SO51 9ZF, on A 31 ℘ (01703) 266611,
Fax (01703) 251359, ☎ – ▯ ✦ 📺 ☎ ⬥ 🅿 – 🔬 150. ⬛⬛ 🅰🅴 ⓞ 💳
Meals 12.95/17.95 st. and a la carte ⓘ 5.25 – ⬱ 8.95 – 54 rm 75.00/85.00 st. – SB.

✕✕ **Keats,** Winchester Rd, SO51 9BQ, on A 31 ℘ (01794) 368252 – 🅿. ⬛⬛ 🅰🅴 ⓞ 💳 💳
closed Sunday, Monday and 25-26 December – Meals - Italian - 11.15 t. (lunch)
and a la carte 17.70/26.70 t. ⓘ 5.70.

AMPNEY CRUCIS Glos. 403 404 O 28 – see Cirencester.

L'ANCRESSE *Guernsey (Channel Islands)* [403] P 33 and [230] ⑩ – *see Channel Islands.*

ANDOVER *Hants.* [403] [404] P 30 – *pop. 34 647.*
⛳9 *51 Winchester Rd* ✆ *(01264) 323980.*
[i] *Town Mill House, Bridge St., SP10 1BL* ✆ *(01264) 324320.*
London 74 – Bath 53 – Salisbury 17 – Winchester 11.

🏨 **White Hart,** Bridge St., SP10 1BH, ✆ (01264) 352266, *Fax (01264) 323767* – 🚭 rm, [TV] ☎ [P] – 🧑‍🏫 65. [MC] [AE] [D] [VISA]
Meals 15.95 **st.** and a la carte 🍷 5.95 – ☕ 7.95 – **27 rm** 65.00/75.00 **st.** – SB.

🏨 **Ashley Court,** Micheldever Rd, SP11 6LA, by London St. and Wolversdene Rd ✆ (01264) 357344, *Fax (01264) 356755*, 🌳 – [TV] ☎ [P] – 🧑‍🏫 120. [MC] [AE] [VISA]. 🐕
Meals *(closed Sunday dinner)* (bar lunch)/dinner 15.90 **t.** and a la carte 🍷 5.90 – **35 rm** ☕ 54.50/64.50 **t.**

ATS 51a New St. ✆ (01264) 323606/7

ANSTY *Warks. – see Coventry (W. Mids.).*

APPLEBY-IN-WESTMORLAND *Cumbria* [402] M 20 – *pop. 2 570 (inc. Bongate).*
⛳18 *Appleby, Brackenber Moor* ✆ *(017683) 51432.*
[i] *Moot Hall, Boroughgate, CA16 6XD* ✆ *(017683) 51177.*
London 285 – Carlisle 33 – Kendal 24 – Middlesbrough 58.

🏨 **Appleby Manor Country House** 🐦, Roman Rd, CA16 6JB, E : 1 m. by B 6542 and Station Rd ✆ (017683) 51571, *Fax (017683) 52888*, ≤, 🏊, 🌳 – 🚭 rest, [TV] ☎ [P] – 🧑‍🏫 40. [MC] [AE] [D] [VISA] [JCB]. 🐕
closed 24 to 26 December – **Meals** a la carte 16.35/26.35 **st.** 🍷 5.95 – **30 rm** ☕ 76.00/112.00 **st.** – SB.

🏨 **Tufton Arms,** Market Sq., CA16 6XA, ✆ (017683) 51593, *Fax (017683) 52761*, 🎣 – [TV] ☎ [P] – 🧑‍🏫 100. [MC] [AE] [D] [VISA] [JCB]
Meals 20.50 **t.** (dinner) and a la carte 11.35/24.40 **t.** 🍷 4.50 – **19 rm** ☕ 47.50/90.00 **t.**, 2 suites – SB.

🏨 **Royal Oak Inn,** Bongate, CA16 6UN, SE : ½ m. on B 6542 ✆ (017683) 51463, *Fax (017683) 52300*, « Part 16C and 17C » – 🚭 rest, [TV] ☎ [P]. [MC] [AE] [D] [VISA] [JCB]
closed 24 and 25 December – **Meals** a la carte 13.00/20.00 **t.** 🍷 5.00 – **9 rm** ☕ 33.00/84.00 **t.** – SB.

APPLEDORE *Devon* [403] H 30 *The West Country G.* – *pop. 2 187.*
See : *Town*★.
London 228 – Barnstaple 12 – Exeter 46 – Plymouth 61 – Taunton 63.

🏠 **West Farm,** Irsha St., EX39 1RY, W : ¼ m. ✆ (01237) 425269, *Fax (01237) 425207*, « 17C house », 🌳 – 🚭 rm, [TV]. 🐕
Meals (by arrangement) (communal dining) 22.50 – **3 rm** ☕ 45.00/60.00.

APPLETON LE MOORS *N. Yorks* [402] R 21 – *pop. 178.*
London 242 – Middlesbrough 37 – Scarborough 26 – York 37.

🏨 **Appleton Hall Country House** 🐦, YO6 6TF, ✆ (01751) 417227, *Fax (01751) 417540*, 🌳 – |♦|, 🚭 rest, [TV] ☎ [P]. [MC] [AE] [VISA] [JCB]. 🐕
Meals (dinner only) 19.50 **t.** 🍷 5.00 – **7 rm** ☕ (dinner included) 75.00/130.00 **t.**, 2 suites.

ARDINGLY *W. Sussex* [404] T 30 – *pop. 1 594.*
London 37 – Brighton 20 – Crawley 11.

🍺 Ardingly Inn with rm, Street Lane, RH17 6UA, ✆ (01444) 892214, *Fax (01444) 892942*, 🌳 – [TV] [P]
6 rm.

ARKESDEN *Essex – see Saffron Walden.*

When looking for a quiet hotel
use the maps found in the introduction
or look for establishments with the sign 🐦 *or* 🐦.

ENGLAND

ARNCLIFFE N. Yorks. **402** N 21 – pop. 79 – ✉ Skipton.
London 232 – Kendal 41 – Leeds 41 – Preston 50 – York 52.

🏠 **Amerdale House** ⓢ, BD23 5QE, ℘ (01756) 770250, Fax (01756) 770250, ≤, 龺 –
✥ rest, 📺 🅿. 🐵 🆅🆂🅰. ✼
mid March-mid November – Meals (dinner only) 27.00 **st.** ⌕ 5.50 – **11 rm** ⌷ (dinner
included) 69.50/125.00 **st.**

ARUNDEL W. Sussex **404** S 31 Great Britain G. – pop. 3 033.
See : Castle★★ AC.
🏴 61 High St., BN18 9AJ ℘ (01903) 882268.
London 58 – Brighton 21 – Southampton 41 – Worthing 9.

🏠 **Norfolk Arms**, 22 High St., BN18 9AD, ℘ (01903) 882101, Fax (01903) 884275 – ✥ rest,
📺 ☎ 🅿 – 🔬 100. 🐵 🆎 ⓪ 🆅🆂🅰
Meals 9.95/18.00 **st.** and dinner a la carte ⌕ 5.65 – **34 rm** ⌷ 70.00/100.00 **st.** – SB.

🏠 **Swan**, 27-29 High St., BN18 9AG, ℘ (01903) 882314, Fax (01903) 883759 – ✥ rest,
🍴 rest, 📺 ☎ 🅿. 🐵 🆎 ⓪ 🆅🆂🅰
Meals 13.95 **st.** and a la carte ⌕ 5.25 – **15 rm** ⌷ 50.00/75.00 **st.** – SB.

🏠 **Comfort Inn**, Crossbush, BN17 7QQ, SE : 1 ¼ m. by A 27 on A 284 ℘ (01903) 840840,
Fax (01903) 849849 – ✥ rm, 🍴 rest, 📺 ☎ 🅿 – 🔬 30. 🐵 🆎 ⓪ 🆅🆂🅰
Meals 9.75 **st.** and dinner a la carte ⌕ 5.75 – **53 rm** 40.50/49.50 **st.** – SB.

🏠 **Travel Inn**, Crossbush, BN18 9PQ, E : 1 m. on A 27 ℘ (01903) 882655, Fax (01903) 884381
– ✥ 📺 ⌖ 🅿. 🐵 🆎 ⓪ 🆅🆂🅰. ✼
Meals (grill rest.) – **30 rm** 36.50 **t.**

↑ **Portreeves Acre** without rest., The Causeway, BN18 9JL, ℘ (01903) 883277, 龺 – 📺 🅿
closed 1 week Christmas – **3 rm** ⌷ 30.00/42.00 **s.**

at Burpham NE : 3 m. by A 27 – ✉ Arundel.

🏠 **Burpham Country** ⓢ, BN18 9RJ, ℘ (01903) 882160, Fax (01903) 884627, ≤, 龺 –
✥ rest, 📺 ☎ 🅿. 🐵 🆎 🆅🆂🅰. ✼
closed 1 week January and 1 week October – Meals (closed Monday) (dinner only) 22.00 **t.**
⌕ 6.50 – **10 rm** ⌷ 37.00/92.00 **t.** – SB.

XX **George and Dragon**, BN18 9RR, ℘ (01903) 883131, Fax (01903) 883341 – 🐵 🆎 🆅🆂🅰
🅹🅲🅱
closed Sunday dinner and 25 December – Meals (bar lunch Monday to Saturday)/
dinner 19.50 **t.** ⌕ 5.75.

at Walberton W : 3 m. by A 27 off B 2132 – ✉ Arundel.

🏠 **Stakis Avisford Park**, Yapton Lane, BN18 0LS, on B 2132 ℘ (01243) 551215,
Fax (01243) 552481, ≤, 🏋, 🏊, 🏊, 🏊, 🛏, 龺, park, ✼, squash – ✥ 📺 ☎ 🅿 – 🔬 300. 🐵
🆎 ⓪ 🆅🆂🅰
Meals (closed Saturday lunch) (buffet lunch) 16.50/23.75 **st.** and dinner a la carte –
⌷ 10.50 – **134 rm** 98.00/115.00 **st.**, 5 suites – SB.

🍴 **Royal Oak**, Yapton Lane, BN18 0LS, on B 2132 ℘ (01243) 552865 – 🅿. 🐵 🆅🆂🅰 🅹🅲🅱
closed Monday except Bank Holidays – Meals a la carte 12.75/23.00 **t.** ⌕ 5.95.

ASCOT Windsor & Maidenhead **404** R 29 – pop. 15 761 (inc. Sunningdale).
🛏 Mill Ride, North Ascot ℘ (01344) 886777.
London 36 – Reading 15.

🏛 **Royal Berkshire** ⓢ, London Rd, Sunninghill, SL5 0PP, E : 2 m. on A 329
℘ (01344) 23322, Fax (01344) 27100, « Queen Anne mansion », 🏋, 🏊, 🏊, 龺, park, ✼,
squash – 📺 ☎ 🅿 – 🔬 70. 🐵 🆎 ⓪ 🆅🆂🅰 🅹🅲🅱
Meals – (see *Stateroom* below) – ⌷ 15.50 – **60 rm** 149.00/174.00 **t.**, 3 suites – SB.

🏛 Berystede, Bagshot Rd, Sunninghill, SL5 9JH, S : 1 ½ m. on A 330 ℘ (01344) 23311,
Fax (01344) 872301, 🏊, 龺 – 🛗, ✥ rm, 📺 ☎ 🅿 – 🔬 120
90 rm, 1 suite.

XXX **Stateroom** (at Royal Berkshire H.), London Rd, Sunninghill, SL5 0PP, E : 2 m. on A 329
℘ (01344) 23322, Fax (01344) 27100, 龺 – ✥ 🅿. 🐵 🆎 ⓪ 🆅🆂🅰 🅹🅲🅱
Meals (closed Saturday lunch) (booking essential) 24.75/34.50 **st.** and a la carte ⌕ 14.95.

XX **Ciao Ninety**, 6 Hermitage Par., High St., SL5 7TE, ℘ (01344) 22285 – 🍴. 🐵 🆎 ⓪ 🆅🆂🅰
Meals - Italian - 14.00/23.00 **t.** and a la carte ⌕ 8.50.

at Sunninghill S : 1½ m. by A 329 on B 3020 – ✉ Ascot.

XX **Jade Fountain**, 38 High St., SL5 9NE, ℘ (01344) 27070 – 🍴. 🐵 🆎 ⓪ 🆅🆂🅰 🅹🅲🅱
closed 24 to 27 December – Meals - Chinese (Canton, Peking) - a la carte 22.00/35.00 **t.**

ASENBY N. Yorks. – see Thirsk.

ASHBOURNE Derbs. 402 403 404 O 24 Great Britain G. – pop. 6 300.

Env. : Dovedale★★ (Ilam Rock★) NW : 6 m. by A 515.

🏗 13 Market Pl., DE6 1EU 🖉 (01335) 343666.

London 146 – Derby 14 – Manchester 48 – Nottingham 33 – Sheffield 44.

🏛 **Callow Hall** ⑤, Mappleton Rd, DE6 2AA, W : ¾ m. by Union St. (off Market Pl.) 🖉 (01335) 343403, Fax (01335) 343624, ≼, « Victorian country house », ⤳, ☞, park – ↳ rest, 📺 ☎ ♿ ⓟ. 🐵 🅰🅴 ① 𝘝𝘐𝘚𝘈, ✀
closed 25-26 December and 1 week February – **Meals** (closed Sunday dinner to non-residents) (dinner only and Sunday lunch)/dinner 33.00 **t.** and a la carte ⓘ 5.75 – **15 rm** ⚏ 73.00/136.50 **t.**, 1 suite – SB.

🏛 **Hanover International**, Derby Rd, DE6 1XH, SE : 1 m. following signs for the A 52 (Derby) 🖉 (01335) 346666, Fax (01335) 346549, Ⓕ₅, ≋, 🔲 – 📳, ↳ rm, 📺 ☎ ♿ ⓟ – 🔏 200. 🐵 🅰🅴 ① 𝘝𝘐𝘚𝘈 𝘑𝘊𝘉. ✀
Meals a la carte approx. 18.30 **st.** ⓘ 6.15 – ⚏ 8.50 – **48 rm** 70.00/96.00 **st.**, 2 suites – SB.

🞭 ATS Airfield Ind. Est., Blenheim Rd 🖉 (01335) 344644

ASHBURTON Devon 403 I 32 The West Country G. – pop. 3 660.

Env. : Dartmoor National Park★★.

London 220 – Exeter 20 – Plymouth 23.

🏛 **Holne Chase** ⑤, TQ13 7NS, W : 3 m. on Two Bridges rd 🖉 (01364) 631471, Fax (01364) 631453, ≼, ⤳, ☞, park – 📺 ☎ ⓟ. 🐵 🅰🅴 ① 𝘝𝘐𝘚𝘈
Meals – (see below) – ⚏ 4.25 – **12 rm** 60.00/130.00 **st.**, 6 suites – SB.

🏠 **Dartmoor Lodge**, Peartree Cross, TQ13 7JW, 🖉 (01364) 652232, Fax (01364) 653990 – 📳, ↳ rm, 📺 ☎ ♿ ⓟ – 🔏 100. 🐵 🅰🅴 𝘝𝘐𝘚𝘈
Meals 10.45 **st.** and a la carte ⓘ 5.65 – ⚏ 4.95 – **30 rm** 35.00/60.00 **st.** – SB.

🛖 **Gages Mill**, Buckfastleigh Rd, TQ13 7JW, SW : 1 m. 🖉 (01364) 652391, Fax (01364) 652391, ☞ – ↳ rest, ⓟ. ✀
March-mid November – **Meals** (by arrangement) 12.00 ⓘ 4.00 – **8 rm** ⚏ 23.00/46.00 **t.** – SB.

🗙🗙 **Holne Chase** (at Holne Chase H.), TQ13 7NS, W : 3 m. on Two Bridges rd 🖉 (01364) 631471, Fax (01364) 631453, ☞ – ↳ ⓟ. 🐵 🅰🅴 ① 𝘝𝘐𝘚𝘈
Meals (booking essential) 20.00/29.50 **st.** ⓘ 7.90.

at Holne W : 4½ m. by Two Bridges rd – ✉ Ashburton.

🛖 **Wellpritton Farm** ⑤, TQ13 7RX, E : 1 m. 🖉 (01364) 631273, park – ↳ rest, ⓟ. ✀
Meals 8.00 **st.** – **4 rm** ⚏ 18.00/36.00 **st.**

at Poundsgate W : 5 m. on Princetown rd – ✉ Newton Abbot.

🏠 **Leusdon Lodge** ⑤, Lower Town, TQ13 7PE, NE : 1 m. by Princetown rd, off Leusdon rd 🖉 (01364) 631304, Fax (01364) 631599, ≼, ☞ – ↳ 📺 ☎ ⓟ. 🐵 🅰🅴 𝘝𝘐𝘚𝘈
March-November – **Meals** (dinner only) 25.00 **st.** – **6 rm** ⚏ 45.00/95.00 **t.**

ASHBY DE LA ZOUCH Leics. 402 403 404 P 25 – pop. 10 595.

🏊 Willesley Park, Measham Rd 🖉 (01530) 411532.

🏗 North St., LE65 1HU 🖉 (01530) 411767.

London 119 – Birmingham 29 – Leicester 18 – Nottingham 22.

🏛 **Fallen Knight**, Kilwardby St., LE65 2FQ, 🖉 (01530) 412230, Fax (01530) 417596 – 📳 📺 ☎ ⓟ – 🔏 70. 🐵 🅰🅴 ① 𝘝𝘐𝘚𝘈 𝘑𝘊𝘉. ✀
Meals 14.95/18.50 **t.** and a la carte ⓘ 6.95 – **24 rm** ⚏ 62.00/112.00 **st.** – SB.

🗙🗙 **Rajni**, 48 Tamworth Rd, LE65 2PR, S : ½ m. on B 5006 🖉 (01530) 560349 – 🞶 ⓟ. 🐵 🅰🅴 ①
𝘝𝘐𝘚𝘈
closed Friday lunch and 25 December – **Meals** - Indian - a la carte 7.15/15.00 **t.**

🞭 ATS Kilwardby St. 🖉 (01530) 412791

Benutzen Sie für weite Fahrten in Europa die **Michelin-Länderkarten** :

970 Europa, 976 Tschechische Republik-Slowakische Republik,
980 Griechenland, 984 Deutschland, 985 Skandinavien-Finnland,
986 Großbritannien-Irland, 987 Deutschland-Österreich-Benelux, 988 Italien,
989 Frankreich, 990 Spanien-Portugal, 991 Jugoslawien.

ASHFORD *Kent* [404] W 30 – *pop. 52 002.*
ℹ *18 The Churchyard, TN23 1QG ☎ (01233) 629165.*
London 56 – Canterbury 14 – Dover 24 – Hastings 30 – Maidstone 19.

Eastwell Manor 🌿, Eastwell Park, Boughton Lees, TN25 4HR, N : 3 m. by A 28 on A 25 ☎ (01233) 219955, *Fax (01233) 635530*, ≤, « Reconstructed period mansion in form gardens », park, 🎾 – |‡|, ⊁ rest, [TV] ☎ [P] – 🧑‍🏫 80. [MC] [AE] [D] [VISA] [JCB]. ⊁
Meals 16.60/28.50 **t.** and a la carte – **20 rm** ☕ 160.00/210.00 **t.**, 3 suites – SB.

Ashford International, Simone Weil Av., TN24 8UX, N : 1 ½ m. by A 2 ☎ (01233) 219988, *Fax (01233) 627708*, 🏋, ≘s, 🏊 – |‡|, ⊁ rm, [TV] ☎ ♿ [P] – 🧑‍🏫 400. [MC] [AE] [D] [VISA]
Meals (carving lunch) 15.95/17.95 **st.** 🍷 7.50 – ☕ 10.50 – **198 rm** 110.00/120.00 **st.**, 2 suite – SB.

Forte Posthouse Ashford, Canterbury Rd, TN24 8QQ, ☎ (01233) 62579 *Fax (01233) 643176*, 🌳 – ⊁ rm, [TV] ☎ ♿ [P] – 🧑‍🏫 100. [MC] [AE] [D] [VISA] [JCB]. ⊁
Meals a la carte 14.55/25.65 **st.** 🍷 7.25 – ☕ 8.95 – **103 rm** 69.00 **st.** – SB.

Master Spearpoint, Canterbury Rd, Kennington, TN24 9QR, NE : 2 m. on A 2 ☎ (01233) 636863, *Fax (01233) 610119*, 🌳 – [TV] ☎ [P] – 🧑‍🏫 60. [MC] [AE] [D] [VISA]
Meals *(closed Saturday lunch)* (carving lunch)/dinner 15.00 **t.** and a la carte 🍷 5.50 – ☕ 7.2 – **34 rm** 65.00/75.00 **st.** – SB.

at Hothfield *NW : 3½ m. by A 20 – ✉ Ashford.*

Holiday Inn Garden Court, Maidstone Rd, TN26 1AR, N : 1 m. on A 2 ☎ (01233) 713333, *Fax (01233) 712082*, 🏋, 🌳 – |‡|, ⊁ rm, ▤ rest, [TV] ☎ ♿ [P] – 🧑‍🏫 25. [MC] [AE] [D] [VISA] [JCB]
Meals (dinner only and Sunday lunch)/dinner 10.95 **st.** and a la carte 🍷 4.50 – ☕ 4.50 **104 rm** 69.50 **st.**

Travel Inn, Maidstone Rd, Hothfield Common, TN26 1AP, on A 20 ☎ (01233) 71257 *Fax (01233) 713945* – ⊁ rm, [TV] ♿ [P]. [MC] [AE] [D] [VISA]. ⊁
Meals (grill rest.) – **40 rm** 36.50 **t.**

Ⓜ ATS Henwood Ind. Est., Hythe Rd, Henwood ☎ (01233) 622450/624891

ASHFORD-IN-THE-WATER *Derbs.* [402] [403] [404] O 24 – *see Bakewell.*

ASHINGTON *Northd.* [401] [402] P 18.
London 303 – Edinburgh 102 – Newcastle upon Tyne 17.

Woodhorn Grange, Queen Elizabeth 11 Country Park, Woodhorn, NE63 9AT, N : ½ m by A 197 on A 189 ☎ (01670) 862332, *Fax (01670) 860986* – [TV] [P]. [MC] [VISA]. ⊁
Meals (grill rest.) a la carte approx. 11.00 **st.** – ☕ 5.45 – **13 rm** 36.50 **t.**

ASHINGTON *W. Sussex* [404] S 31 – *pop. 2 852 – ✉ Pulborough.*
London 50 – Brighton 20 – Worthing 9.

Mill House 🌿, Mill Lane, RH20 3BZ, ☎ (01903) 892426, *Fax (01903) 892855*, 🌳 – [TV] ☎ [P] – 🧑‍🏫 40. [MC] [AE] [VISA]
Meals (bar lunch)/dinner a la carte 17.50/24.50 **t.** 🍷 4.50 – **10 rm** ☕ 47.00/87.00 **st.** – SB.

ASHPRINGTON *Devon* [403] I 32 – *see Totnes.*

ASHTON-IN-MAKERFIELD *Gtr. Manchester* [402] M 23 – *pop. 28 105 – ✉ Wigan.*
London 199 – Liverpool 21 – Manchester 20.

Bay Horse - Premier Lodge, 53 Warrington Rd, WN4 9PJ, S : ½ m. on A 49 ☎ (01942) 725032, *Fax (01942) 719302* – ⊁ rm, [TV] ☎ ♿ [P]. [MC] [AE] [D] [VISA]. ⊁
Meals (grill rest.) a la carte approx. 13.60 **st.** 🍷 4.25 – ☕ 4.95 – **28 rm** 44.25 **st.** – SB.

ASHTON KEYNES *Wilts.* [403] [404] O 29 – *pop. 1 682.*
London 98 – Bristol 40 – Gloucester 27 – Oxford 42 – Swindon 14.

Two Cove House, SN6 6NS, off Park Place ☎ (01285) 861221, 🌳 – ⊁ rest, [P]. ⊁
closed 25 December – **Meals** (by arrangement) (communal dining) 17.50 **st.** – **3 rm** ☕ 34.00/54.00 **st.**

ASHTON-UNDER-LYNE *Gtr. Manchester* **402 403 404** N 23 – *pop. 43 906.*
London 209 – Leeds 40 – Manchester 7 – Sheffield 34.

🏨 **York House**, York Pl., off Richmond St., OL6 7TT, ℰ (0161) 330 9000, *Fax (0161) 343 1613,*
🚗 – ▥ ☎ ❷ – 🔬 40. **◑◐ AE ◍ VISA JCB**
closed 26 December – **Meals** *(closed Saturday lunch, Sunday and Bank Holidays)* 8.75 **st.**
(lunch) and a la carte 12.55/20.05 **st.** ₰ 4.95 – **34 rm** � 49.00/72.00 **st.** – SB.

⚲ **Woodlands** without rest., 33 Shepley Rd, Audenshaw, M34 5DL, SW : 2 m. by A 635 and
A 6017 on B 6169 ℰ (0161) 336 4241 – ▥ ☎ ❷. **◑◐ VISA**. ⚘
closed 1 week Christmas and 1 week spring – **3 rm** 40.00/60.00 **s.**

ASHWATER *Devon* **403** H 31 – *pop. 623.*
London 238 – Bideford 26 – Exeter 43 – Launceston 7 – Plymouth 34.

🏛 **Blagdon Manor Country H.** ⚘, EX21 5DF, NW : 2 m. by Holsworthy rd on Blagdon rd
ℰ (01409) 211224, *Fax (01409) 211634*, ≤, « Part 17C », 🚗 – ⊁ ▥ ☎ ❷. **◑◐ AE VISA JCB**.
⚘
closed 25 and 26 December – **Meals** (residents only) (communal dining) (dinner only)
18.50 **t.** ₰ 7.50 – **7 rm** ⊘ 60.00/110.00 **t.**

ASKRIGG *N. Yorks.* **402** N 21 – *pop. 1 002* – ✉ *Leyburn.*
London 251 – Kendal 32 – Leeds 70 – York 63.

🏨 **King's Arms**, Market Pl., DL8 3HQ, ℰ (01969) 650258, « Part 18C,
part 19C coaching inn » – ⊁ rest, ▥ ☎ ❷. **◑◐ AE VISA JCB**. ⚘
Clubroom : **Meals** (dinner only and Sunday lunch)/dinner 25.00 **st.** ₰ 7.50 – *Silks Grill :*
Meals a la carte 11.70/21.70 **st.** ₰ 4.50 – **11 rm** ⊘ 50.00/125.00 **st.** – SB.

🏛 **Winville**, Main St., DL8 3HG, ℰ (01969) 650515, *Fax (01969) 650594*, 🚗 – ▥ ☎ ❷. **◑◐ ◍**
VISA
Meals *(closed Monday)* 19.50 **st.** (dinner) and a la carte 11.50/17.50 **st.** ₰ 3.75 – **10 rm**
⊘ 36.00/52.00 **st.** – SB.

⚲ **Helm Country House** ⚘, Helm, DL8 3JF, W : 1 ¼ m., turning right at No Through Rd
sign ℰ (01969) 650443, *Fax (01969) 650443*, ≤, « Part 17C stone cottage » – ⊁ ▥ ❷. **◑◐**
VISA. ⚘
closed November and December – **Meals** 16.00 ₰ 6.75 – **3 rm** ⊘ 46.00/68.00 – SB.

ASPLEY GUISE *Beds.* **404** S 27 – *pop. 2 236.*
🏌 Woburn Sands, West Hill ℰ (01908) 582264 – 🏌 Millbrook, Ampthill ℰ (01525) 840252.
London 52 – Bedford 13 – Luton 16 – Northampton 22.

🏰 **Moore Place**, The Square, MK17 8DW, ℰ (01908) 282000, *Fax (01908) 281888,*
« Georgian mansion », 🚗 – ▥ ☎ ❷ – 🔬 50. **◑◐ AE ◍ VISA**. ⚘
Meals (bar lunch Saturday) 19.95 **st.** and a la carte ₰ 7.95 – **53 rm** ⊘ 75.00/95.00 **st.**,
1 suite.

ASTON CLINTON *Bucks.* **404** R 28 – *pop. 3 467* – ✉ *Aylesbury.*
London 42 – Aylesbury 4 – Oxford 26.

🏰 **Bell Inn**, London Rd, HP22 5HP, ℰ (01296) 630252, *Fax (01296) 631250,* « Part 17C former
coaching inn » – ⊁ rest, ▥ ☎ ❷ – 🔬 30. **◑◐ AE VISA**. ⚘
Meals 15.00/39.00 **t.** and a la carte ₰ 12.00 – ⊘ 9.50 – **15 rm** 60.00/80.00 **st.**, 5 suites – SB.

🏛 **West Lodge**, London Rd, HP22 5HL, ℰ (01296) 630362, *Fax (01296) 630151,* ☎s, ▤ –
⊁ rest, ▥ ☎ ❷. **◑◐ AE ◍ VISA JCB**. ⚘
Montgolfier : **Meals** (residents only Sunday to Thursday) (dinner only) 30.00 **t.** ₰ 9.00 –
7 rm ⊘ 32.00/60.00 **t.**

ATHERSTONE *Warks.* **403 404** P 26 – *pop. 10 677.*
London 120 – Birmingham 22 – Coventry 15 – Leicester 30.

XX **Chapel House** with rm, Friar's Gate, CV9 1EY, ℰ (01827) 718949, *Fax (01827) 717702,*
« Part Georgian former dower house », 🚗 – ▥ ☎. **◑◐ AE ◍ VISA JCB**. ⚘
closed 25 and 26 December – **Meals** *(closed lunch Monday, Tuesday and Saturday and
Sunday dinner)* 12.00 **st.** (lunch) and a la carte 18.00/30.40 **st.** ₰ 8.00 – **13 rm** ⊘ 47.50/
75.00 **st.**

Pour les grands voyages d'affaires ou de tourisme,
Guide Rouge **MICHELIN : EUROPE.**

93

ATTLEBOROUGH *Norfolk* 404 X 26 – *pop. 6 530.*
London 94 – Cambridge 47 – Norwich 15.

Sherbourne Country House, Norwich Rd, NR17 2JX, NE : ½ m. ✆ (01953) 454363, *Fax (01953) 453509*, – rest, TV ☎ P. MC VISA
Meals 16.95 **st.** and a la carte 6.25 – **8 rm** 35.00/68.00 **st.** – SB.

ATS London Rd ✆ (01953) 453883

AUSTWICK *N. Yorks.* 402 M 21 – *pop. 467* – ✉ *Lancaster (Lancs.).*
London 259 – Kendal 28 – Lancaster 20 – Leeds 46.

The Traddock, LA2 8BY, ✆ (015242) 51224, *Fax (015242) 51224*, – TV ☎ P – 70. MC VISA.
Meals (dinner only) 20.00 **st.** 4.00 – **11 rm** 42.00/72.00 **st.** – SB.

Wood View, The Green, LA2 8BB, ✆ (015242) 51268, – TV P.
Meals (by arrangement) 15.00 **st.** – **6 rm** 35.00/50.00 **st.** – SB.

AVON *Hants. – see Ringwood.*

AVON DASSETT *Warks. – pop. 191* – ✉ *Leamington Spa*
London 82 – Birmingham 37 – Coventry 22 – Oxford 34.

Crandon House without rest., CV33 0AA, NE : 1 ¼ m. by Fenny Compton rd on Farnborough rd ✆ (01295) 770652, *Fax (01295) 770652*, ←, park – TV P. MC VISA JCB
closed Christmas – **5 rm** 25.00/46.00.

AXMINSTER *Devon* 403 L 31 *The West Country G.* – *pop. 3 472.*
Env. : *Lyme Regis★ - The Cobb★, SE : 5½ m. by A 35 and A 3070.*
The Old Courthouse, Church St., EX13 5AQ ✆ (01297) 34386 (summer only).
London 156 – Exeter 27 – Lyme Regis 5.5 – Taunton 22 – Yeovil 24.

Fairwater Head Country House, Hawkchurch, EX13 5TX, NE : 5 ¼ m. by B 3261 and A 35 off B 3165 ✆ (01297) 678349, *Fax (01297) 678459*, ← Axe Vale, – rest, TV ☎ P. MC AE O VISA.
closed January and February – **Meals** 11.50/20.00 **st.** and dinner a la carte 6.50 – **21 rm** 60.00/120.00 **st.** – SB.

at Membury *N : 4½ m. by A 35 and Stockland rd* – ✉ *Axminster.*

Lea Hill, EX13 7AQ, S : ½ m. ✆ (01404) 881881, ←, « Part 14C Devon longhouse », – rm, TV ☎ P. MC AE O VISA
Meals (bar lunch)/dinner 18.00 **t.** and a la carte 6.50 – **11 rm** (dinner included) 76.00/148.00 **t.** – SB.

AYLESBURY *Bucks.* 404 R 28 *Great Britain G.* – *pop. 58 058.*
Env. : *Waddesdon Manor (Collection★★) NW : 5½ m. by A 41.*
18 *Weston Turville, New Rd ✆ (01296) 24084* – 9 *Hulcott Lane, Bierton ✆ (01296) 393644.*
8 Bourbon St., HP20 2RR ✆ (01296) 330559.
London 46 – Birmingham 72 – Northampton 37 – Oxford 22.

Hartwell House, Oxford Rd, HP17 8NL, SW : 2 m. on A 418 ✆ (01296) 747444, *Fax (01296) 747450*, ←, « Part Jacobean, part Georgian house, former residence of Louis XVIII », park, – TV ☎ P – 80. MC AE VISA.
Meals 26.50/42.00 **st.** 11.50 – 14.00 – **32 rm** 110.00/180.00 **st.**, 13 suites 280.00/500.00 **st.** – SB.

Forte Posthouse Aylesbury, Aston Clinton Rd, HP22 5AA, SE : 2 m. on A 41 ✆ (01296) 393388, *Fax (01296) 392211*, – rm, TV ☎ P – 100. MC AE O VISA
Meals a la carte 16.70/24.85 **t.** 7.25 – 9.95 – **92 rm** 79.00 **t.**, 2 suites – SB.

Holiday Inn Garden Court, Buckingham Rd, HP19 3FY, N : 1 m. on A 413 ✆ (01296) 398839, *Fax (01296) 394108*, – rm, TV ☎ P – 30. MC AE O VISA JCB.
Meals (dinner only) (residents only) a la carte approx. 13.45 **st.** – 8.50 – **40 rm** 69.00 **st.**

Bottle & Glass, Gibraltar, HP17 8TY, SW : 5 m. on A 418 ✆ (01296) 748488, *Fax (01296) 747673*, « 17C thatched inn » – P. MC AE O VISA JCB
closed Sunday dinner and 25-26 December – **Meals** – Seafood specialities – a la carte 15.00/30.00 **st.**

ATS Gatehouse Way ✆ (01296) 433177

BABBACOMBE *Torbay* 🔢 J 32 – *see Torquay.*

BADBY *Northants. – see Daventry.*

BADINGHAM *Suffolk* 🔢 Y 27 – *see Framlingham.*

BADMINTON *South Gloucestershire* 🔢🔢 N 29 – *pop. 2 167.*
London 114 – Bristol 19 – Gloucester 26 – Swindon 33.

🏠 **Petty France,** Dunkirk, GL9 1AF, NW : 3 m. on A 46 *ℰ* (01454) 238361, Fax (01454) 238768, *☞ – ↳⇌* rest, 📺 ☎ 🅿 – 🔏 25. 🐵 🄰🄴 🄾 *VISA*
Meals 17.95 **st.** and a la carte 👤 6.95 – *☲* 3.50 – **20 rm** 69.00/120.00 **st.** – SB.

🏠 **Bodkin House,** Dunkirk, GL9 1AF, NW : 3 m. on A 46 *ℰ* (01454) 238310, Fax (01454) 238422 – ↳⇌ rest, 📺 ☎ 🅿. 🐵 🄰🄴 🄾 *VISA* 🄹🄲🄱. 🛇
Meals 14.95 **t.** and a la carte 👤 6.00 – **8 rm** *☲* 49.95/70.00 **t.** – SB.

BAGINTON *Warks.* 🔢🔢 P 26 – *see Coventry.*

BAGSHOT *Surrey* 🔢 R 29 – *pop. 5 190.*
London 37 – Reading 17 – Southampton 49.

🏰 **Pennyhill Park** 🛇, London Rd, GU19 5ET, SW : 1 m. on A 30 *ℰ* (01276) 471774, Fax (01276) 473217, *≼, ⤓, 🅵₉, ⤸, ☞,* park, *🛇 – ↳⇌* 📺 ☎ 🅿 – 🔏 60. 🐵 🄰🄴 🄾 *VISA* 🛇
Meals 26.00/38.00 **st.** and a la carte 👤 13.00 – **79 rm** 135.00/175.00 **st.**, 10 suites – SB.

🏠 **Travel Inn,** London Rd, GU19 5HR, N : ½ m. on A 30 *ℰ* (01276) 473196, Fax (01276) 451357, *☞ – ↳⇌* rm, 📺 ☎ 🅿. 🐵 🄰🄴 🄾 *VISA*. 🛇
Meals (grill rest.) – **39 rm** 36.50 **t.**

BAINBRIDGE *N. Yorks.* 🔢 N 21 – *pop. 474 –* ✉ *Wensleydale.*
London 249 – Kendal 31 – Leeds 68 – York 61.

🍴 **Rose and Crown** with rm, DL8 3EE, *ℰ* (01969) 650225, Fax (01969) 650735 – 📺 🅿. 🐵 *VISA*
closed 25 December and 1 January – **Meals** (bar lunch Monday to Saturday)/dinner a la carte 11.85/23.35 **t.** 👤 5.45 – **11 rm** *☲* 30.00/60.00 **t.** – SB.

BAKEWELL *Derbs.* 🔢🔢🔢 O 24 *Great Britain G. – pop. 3 818.*
Env. : *Chatsworth*★★★ *(Park and Garden*★★★*) AC, NE : 2½ m. by A 619 – Haddon Hall*★★ *AC, SE : 2 m. by A 6.*
🅱 *Old Market Hall, Bridge St., DE45 1DS ℰ* (01629) 813227.
London 160 – Derby 26 – Manchester 37 – Nottingham 33 – Sheffield 17.

🏠 **Rutland Arms,** The Square, DE45 1BT, *ℰ* (01629) 812812, Fax (01629) 812309 – ↳⇌ rest, 📺 ☎ 🅿 – 🔏 100. 🐵 🄰🄴 🄾 *VISA*. 🛇
Meals 16.95 **t.** (dinner) and lunch a la carte 10.15/13.65 **t.** 👤 6.95 – **36 rm** *☲* 55.00/75.00 **t.** – SB.

🏠 **Milford House,** Mill St., DE45 1DA, *ℰ* (01629) 812130, *☞ –* 📺 🅿. 🐵 *VISA*. 🛇
April-October – **Meals** *(closed November-March except December)* (bar lunch)/dinner 12.00 and a la carte 👤 4.70 – **12 rm** *☲* 40.00/75.00 **st.** – SB.

XX **Renaissance,** Bath St., DE45 1BX, *ℰ* (01629) 812687 – ↳⇌. 🐵 *VISA*
closed Sunday dinner, Monday, first 2 weeks August and 2 weeks Christmas – **Meals** - French - 17.95 **t.** 👤 4.90.

at Hassop N : 3½ m. by A 619 on B 6001 – ✉ *Bakewell.*

🏰 **Hassop Hall** 🛇, DE45 1NS, *ℰ* (01629) 640488, Fax (01629) 640577, *≼, « Part 16C »,* ☞, park, *🛇 –* ▮🛗▮ 📺 ☎ 🅿. 🐵 🄰🄴 🄾 *VISA* 🄹🄲🄱. 🛇
accommodation closed 3 days at Christmas – **Meals** *(closed Monday lunch and Sunday dinner)* 14.90/25.75 **t.** 👤 6.75 – *☲* 8.95 – **13 rm** 70.00/125.00 **t.**

at Great Longstone N : 4 m. by A 619 off B 6001 – ✉ *Bakewell.*

🏠 **Croft** 🛇, DE45 1TF, *ℰ* (01629) 640278, *☞ –* ▮🛗▮, ↳⇌ rest, 📺 🅿. 🐵 *VISA* 🄹🄲🄱. 🛇
closed 2 January-12 February – **Meals** (dinner only) 22.50 **t.** 👤 4.50 – **9 rm** *☲* 60.00/97.50 **t.**

at Alport S : 4 m. by A 6 off B 5056 – ✉ *Bakewell.*

🏠 **Rock House** without rest., DE45 1LG, *ℰ* (01629) 636736, *☞ – ↳⇌* 🅿. 🛇
3 rm *☲* 20.00/40.00.

at Ashford-in-the-Water NW : 1 ¾ m. by A 6 and A 6020 on B 6465 – ✉ Bakewell.

🏠 **Riverside Country House,** Fennel St., DE45 1QF, ✆ (01629) 814275, Fax (01629) 812873, 🌲 – ❄️ 📺 🚰 📵, 🅰🅴 ⑩ 𝚅𝙸𝚂𝙰
Meals 18.95/27.00 t. ⬥ 6.40 – ☲ 10.00 – **15 rm** 75.00/150.00 st. – SB.

BALDERSTONE Lancs. – see Blackburn.

BALDOCK Herts. 🟦🟦🟦 T 28 – pop. 9 232.
London 42 – Bedford 20 – Cambridge 21 – Luton 15.

🏠 **Travelodge,** A 1 Great North Road, Hinxworth (southbound carriageway), SG7 5EX, NW : 3 m. by A 507 on A 1 ✆ (01462) 835329, Fax (01462) 835329, Reservations (Freephone) 0800 850950 – ❄️ rm, 📺 🚰 📵, 🅰🅴 ⑩ 𝚅𝙸𝚂𝙰 𝙹𝙲𝙱, ✀
Meals (grill rest.) – **40 rm** 44.95 t.

BALLASALLA Isle of Man 🟦🟦🟦 G 21 – see Man (Isle of).

BALSALL COMMON W. Mids. – see Coventry.

BAMBER BRIDGE Lancs. 🟦🟦🟦 M 22 – see Preston.

BAMBURGH Northd. 🟦🟦🟦 🟦🟦🟦 O 17 Great Britain G. – pop. 582.
See : Castle★ AC.
London 337 – Edinburgh 77 – Newcastle upon Tyne 51.

🏠 **Lord Crewe Arms,** Front St., NE69 7BL, ✆ (01668) 214243, Fax (01668) 214273 – ❄️ rest, 📺 📵, 🅰🅴 𝚅𝙸𝚂𝙰 𝙹𝙲𝙱
Easter-October – Meals (bar lunch)/dinner 15.75 st. ⬥ 4.25 – **22 rm** ☲ 37.00/74.00 st. – SB.

at Waren Mill W : 2 ¾ m. on B 1342 – ✉ Belford.

🏠 **Waren House** ⚘, NE70 7EE, ✆ (01668) 214581, Fax (01668) 214484, ≤, 🌲 – ❄️ 📺 ☎ 📵 – 🔼 30. 🅰🅴 ⑩ 𝚅𝙸𝚂𝙰 𝙹𝙲𝙱
Meals (dinner only) 22.45 st. ⬥ 6.50 – **8 rm** ☲ 80.00/130.00 st., 2 suites – SB.

BAMPTON Devon 🟦🟦🟦 J 31 – pop. 1 617 London 189.
Exeter 18 – Minehead 21 – Taunton 15.

🏠 **Bark House,** Oakfordbridge, EX16 9HZ, W : 3 m. by B 3227 on A 396 ✆ (01398) 351236, 🌲 – ❄️ rest, 📺 ☎ 📵
restricted opening in winter – Meals (light lunch and Sunday lunch in winter)/dinner 17.50 st. ⬥ 4.75 – **5 rm** ☲ 29.50/39.00 st. – SB.

BANBURY Oxon. 🟦🟦🟦 🟦🟦🟦 P 27 Great Britain G. – pop. 39 906.
Exc. : Upton House★ AC, NW : 7 m. by A 422.
🟥 Cherwell Edge, Chacombe ✆ (01295) 711591.
🟦 Banbury Museum, 8 Horsefair, OX16 0AA ✆ (01295) 259855.
London 76 – Birmingham 40 – Coventry 25 – Oxford 23.

🏠 **Whately Hall,** Horsefair, by Banbury Cross, OX16 0AN, ✆ (01295) 263451, Fax (01295) 271736, « Part 17C », 🌲 – ❄️ 📺 ☎ 📵 – 🔼 80. 🅰🅴 ⑩ 𝚅𝙸𝚂𝙰 𝙹𝙲𝙱, ✀
Meals (closed lunch Saturday and Bank Holidays) 13.95/21.50 st. and a la carte ⬥ 8.75 – ☲ 9.95 – **68 rm** 75.00/80.00 st., 4 suites – SB.

🏠 **Banbury House,** 27-29 Oxford Rd, OX16 9AH, ✆ (01295) 259361, Fax (01295) 270954 – ❄️ rm, 📺 ☎ 📵 – 🔼 70. 🅰🅴 ⑩ 𝚅𝙸𝚂𝙰, ✀
closed 24 to 30 December – Meals (bar lunch)/dinner 17.00 st. and a la carte ⬥ 7.50 – ☲ 8.50 – **48 rm** 71.00/110.00 st. – SB.

at Adderbury S : 3 m. on A 4260 – ✉ Banbury.

🏠 **Red Lion,** The Green, OX17 3LU, ✆ (01295) 810269, Fax (01295) 811906, « Part 16C inn » – 📺 ☎ 📵, 🅰🅴 ⑩ 𝚅𝙸𝚂𝙰 𝙹𝙲𝙱
Meals a la carte 18.75/22.70 t. – **14 rm** ☲ 52.50/70.00 t.

at North Newington W : 2 ¼ m. by B 4035 – ✉ Banbury.

🏠 **La Madonette Country Guest House** ⚘ without rest., OX15 6AA, ✆ (01295) 730212, Fax (01295) 730363, 🌲 – 📺 ☎ 📵, 🅰🅴 ⑩ 𝚅𝙸𝚂𝙰 𝙹𝙲𝙱, ✀
5 rm ☲ 37.50/55.00 st.

at Wroxton NW : 3 m. by B 4100 on A 422 – ⊠ Banbury.

🏛 **Wroxton House,** Silver St., OX15 6QB, 𝒫 (01295) 730777, Fax (01295) 730800 – ⇆ 🖵
☎ 🅿 – 🔏 50. 🕮 🕮 ① 𝑉𝐼𝑆𝐴 JCB. ℅
Meals 15.50/22.50 **st.** and dinner a la carte 🍴 7.95 – ☲ 7.50 – **32 rm** 85.00/120.00 **st.** – SB.

at Shenington NW : 6 m. by B 4100 off A 422 – ⊠ Banbury.

⌂ **Sugarswell Farm** 🕸, OX15 6HW, NW : 2 ¼ m. on Edge Hill rd 𝒫 (01295) 680512,
Fax (01295) 688149, ≤, 🛲, park – ⇆ 🅿. ℅
Meals (by arrangement) (communal dining) 19.00 **st.** – **3 rm** ☲ 38.00/55.00 **st.**

🔘 ATS Beaumont Ind. Est., Beaumont Close 𝒫 (01295) 253525

BANTHAM Devon – see Kingsbridge.

BARDWELL Suffolk 𝟜𝟘𝟜 W 27 – see Bury St. Edmunds.

BARFORD Warks. 𝟜𝟘𝟛 𝟜𝟘𝟜 P 27 – see Warwick.

BAR HILL Cambs. 𝟜𝟘𝟜 U 27 – see Cambridge.

---

*Great Britain and Ireland is now covered
by an Atlas at a scale of 1 inch to 4.75 miles.*

Three easy to use versions: Paperback, Spiralbound and Hardback.

BARNARD CASTLE Durham 𝟜𝟘𝟚 O 20 Great Britain G. – pop. 6 084.

See : Bowes Museum★ AC.
Exc. : Raby Castle★ AC, NE : 6 ½ m. by A 688.
🎋 Harmire Rd 𝒫 (01833) 638355.
🚩 Woodleigh, Flatts Rd, DL12 8AA 𝒫 (01833) 690909.
London 258 – Carlisle 63 – Leeds 68 – Middlesbrough 31 – Newcastle upon Tyne 39.

🏠 **Jersey Farm** 🕸, Darlington Rd, DL12 8TA, E : 1 ½ m. on A 67 𝒫 (01833) 638223,
Fax (01833) 631988, park – 🖵 ☎ 🅿 – 🔏 150. 🕮 𝑉𝐼𝑆𝐴
Meals (closed Saturday lunch) (carving rest.) 14.00 **t.** 🍴 5.00 – **16 rm** ☲ 52.00/70.00 **t.**,
4 suites – SB.

⌂ **Homelands,** 85 Galgate, DL12 8ES, 𝒫 (01833) 638757, 🛲 – 🖵 ☎. ℅
closed 24 December-2 January – **Meals** (by arrangement) 11.95 **st.** 🍴 4.50 – **4 rm** ☲ 24.00/
42.00 **st.**

at Romaldkirk NW : 6 m. by A 67 on B 6277 – ⊠ Barnard Castle.

🏛 **Rose and Crown,** DL12 9EB, 𝒫 (01833) 650213, Fax (01833) 650828, « Part 18C
coaching inn » – ⇆ rest, 🖵 ☎ 🅿. 🕮 𝑉𝐼𝑆𝐴
closed 25 and 26 December – **Meals** (closed Sunday dinner) (bar lunch Monday to
Saturday)/dinner 23.00 **t.** 🍴 5.50 – **10 rm** ☲ 60.00/70.00 **t.**, 2 suites – SB.

BARNARD GATE Oxon. 𝟜𝟘𝟛 𝟜𝟘𝟜 P 28 – see Witney.

BARNEY Norfolk 𝟜𝟘𝟜 W 25 – ⊠ Fakenham.
London 187 – Cambridge 71 – King's Lynn 21 – Norwich 29.

⌂ **Old Brick Kilns,** Little Barney Lane, NR21 0NL, E : ¾ m. 𝒫 (01328) 878305,
Fax (01328) 878948, 🛲 – ⇆ 🖵 ☎ 🅿. 🕮 𝑉𝐼𝑆𝐴 JCB. ℅
closed Christmas and New Year – **Meals** (by arrangement) (communal dining) 15.00 **st.**
🍴 3.60 – **3 rm** ☲ 24.00/48.00 **st.** – SB.

BARNSDALE BAR W. Yorks. 𝟜𝟘𝟚 𝟜𝟘𝟜 Q 23 – ⊠ Pontefract.
London 181 – Leeds 22 – Nottingham 53 – Sheffield 26.

🏠 **Travelodge,** WF8 3JB, on A 1 (southbound carriageway) 𝒫 (01977) 620711, Reservations
(Freephone) 0800 850950 – ⇆ rm, 🖵 🕭 🅿. 🕮 🕮 ① 𝑉𝐼𝑆𝐴 JCB. ℅
Meals (grill rest.) – **56 rm** 44.95 **t.**

BARNSLEY Glos. 𝟜𝟘𝟛 𝟜𝟘𝟜 O 28 – see Cirencester.

BARNSLEY S. Yorks. 402 404 P 23 – pop. 75 120.

[18] Wakefield Rd, Staincross ℰ (01226) 382856 – [18] Silkstone, Field Head, Elmhirst Lane ℰ (01226) 790328 – [18] Wombwell Hillies, Wentworth View, Wombwell ℰ (01226) 754433.

🖪 56 Eldon St., S70 2JL ℰ (01226) 206757.

London 177 – Leeds 21 – Manchester 36 – Sheffield 15.

🏛 **Ardsley House,** Doncaster Rd, Ardsley, S71 5EH, E: 2 ¾ m. on A 635 ℰ (01226) 309955, Fax (01226) 205374, ☞ – ⇔ rm, ▤ rest, ▥ ☎ 🅿 – 🔬 350. 🕮 ㉕ ⓪ 𝓥𝓘𝓢𝓐
Meals (closed lunch Saturday and Bank Holidays) 11.50/21.50 t. and a la carte ₪ 4.70 – ☑ 8.75 – **73 rm** 67.00/83.00 st. – SB.

🏛 **Travel Inn,** Maple Rd, Tankersley, S74 3DL, SW : 6 ½ m. by A 61 at A 61/A 616 roundabout ℰ (01226) 350035, Fax (01226) 741524 – ⇔ rm, ▥ 🕭 🅿. **Meals** (grill rest.) – **42 rm** 36.50 t.

🏛 **Travelodge,** Doncaster Rd, S70 3PE, E: 2 ½ m. on A 635 ℰ (01226) 298799, Reservations (Freephone) 0800 850950 – ▥ 🕭 🅿. 🕮 ㉕ ⓪ 𝓥𝓘𝓢𝓐 𝓙𝓬𝓫. ☒
Meals (grill rest.) – **32 rm** 35.95 t.

🔘 ATS Huddersfield Rd ℰ (01226) 281888/287406   ATS Wombwell Lane, Aldham Bridge, Wombwell ℰ (01226) 753511

BARNSTAPLE Devon 403 H 30 The West Country G. – pop. 27 691.

See : Town★ - Long Bridge★.

Env. : Arlington Court★★ (Carriage Collection★) AC, NE : 6 m. by A 39.

[18], [19] Chulmleigh, Leigh Rd ℰ (01769) 580519.

🖪 North Devon Library, Tuly St., EX31 1EL ℰ (01271) 388583.

London 222 – Exeter 40 – Taunton 51.

🏛 **Barnstaple,** Braunton Rd, EX31 1LE, W: 1 ½ m. on A 361 ℰ (01271) 76221, Fax (01271) 24101, ╠♂, ╩♠, ♒, ☐ – ▤ rest, ▥ ☎ 🅿 – 🔬 350. 🕮 ㉕ ⓪ 𝓥𝓘𝓢𝓐
Meals 9.00/16.00 st. and a la carte ₪ 4.95 – ☑ 5.00 – **60 rm** 52.00/87.00 st. – SB.

XX **Lynwood House** with rm, Bishops Tawton Rd, EX32 9EF, S : 1 ½ m. by A 361 and Newport rd ℰ (01271) 43695, Fax (01271) 79340 – ⇔ rest, ▥ ☎ 🅿. 🕮 ㉕ ⓪ 𝓥𝓘𝓢𝓐
Meals (closed Sunday to non-residents) a la carte 16.85/50.50 t. ₪ 9.00 – **5 rm** ☑ 47.50/67.50 st. – SB.

at Bishop's Tawton S : 2 ¾ m. by A 39 on A 377 – ⊠ Barnstaple.

🏛 **Downrew House** ⏏, EX32 0DY, SE : 1 ½ m. on Chittlehampton rd ℰ (01271) 42497, Fax (01271) 23947, ≤, ╩, ☞, park – ▥ ☎ 🅿 – 🔬 40. 🕮 𝓥𝓘𝓢𝓐
closed 28 December-5 February – **Meals** (bar lunch Saturday) 7.95/17.50 t. and dinner a la carte ₪ 4.75 – **12 rm** ☑ (dinner included) 66.00/125.00 t. – SB.

🏛 **Halmpstone Manor** ⏏, EX32 0EA, SE : 3 m. by Chittlehampton rd ℰ (01271) 830321, Fax (01271) 830826, ≤, ☞, park – ⇔ rest, ▥ ☎ 🅿. 🕮 ㉕ ⓪ 𝓥𝓘𝓢𝓐
closed November and January – **Meals** (lunch by arrangement)/dinner 35.00 st. ₪ 8.50 – **5 rm** ☑ 70.00/130.00 st. – SB.

🔘 ATS Pottington Ind. Est., Braunton Rd ℰ (01271) 42294/5

BARROW-IN-FURNESS Cumbria 402 K 21 – pop. 48 947.

[18] Rakesmoore Lane, Hawcoat ℰ (01229) 825444 – [18] Furness, Walney Island ℰ (01229) 471232.

🖪 Forum 28, Duke St., LA14 1HU ℰ (01229) 870156.

London 295 – Kendal 34 – Lancaster 47.

🏛 **Arlington House,** 200/202 Abbey Rd, LA14 5LD, N : 1 m. ℰ (01229) 831976, Fax (01229) 870990, ╩ – ▥ ☎ 🅿. 🕮 𝓥𝓘𝓢𝓐. ☒
closed 25 December – **Meals** (closed Sunday) (dinner only) a la carte 15.75/22.75 t. ₪ 5.25 – **8 rm** ☑ 55.00/75.00 t.

🔘 ATS 149-151 Ainslie St. ℰ (01229) 828513

BARTON MILLS Suffolk. 404 V 26 – pop. 832.

London 72 – Cambridge 21 – Ipswich 37 – Norwich 40.

🏛 **Travelodge,** Fiveways Roundabout, IP28 6AE, on A 11 ℰ (01638) 717675, Reservations (Freephone) 0800 850950 – ▥ 🕭 🅿. 🕮 ㉕ ⓪ 𝓥𝓘𝓢𝓐 𝓙𝓬𝓫. ☒
32 rm 44.95 t.

BARTON STACEY *Hants.* **403 404** P 30 – *pop. 741.*
London 76 – Andover 10 – Bath 60 – Salisbury 22 – Winchester 8.

🏠 **Travelodge,** SO21 3NP, N : 1 ¼ m. on A 303 (westbound carriageway) ℰ (01264) 720260, Reservations (Freephone) 0800 850950 – 📺 Ꮬ **P**. **MO AE O VISA JCB**. ⚘
20 rm 44.95 t.

BARTON UNDER NEEDWOOD *Staffs.* – *see Burton-upon-Trent.*

BARWICK *Somerset* **403 404** M 31 – *see Yeovil.*

BASFORD *Staffs.* – *see Stoke-on-Trent.*

BASILDON *Essex* **404** V 29 – *pop. 100 924.*
🔝 Clayhill Lane, Sparrow's Hearne ℰ (01268) 533297 – 🔝, 🔝 Langdon Hills, Lower Dunton Rd, Bulphan ℰ (01268) 548444/544300.
London 30 – Chelmsford 17 – Southend-on-Sea 13.

🏠 **Campanile,** A 127 Southend Arterial Rd, Pipp's Hill, SS14 3AE, NW : 1 m. by A 176 at junction with A 127 ℰ (01268) 530810, *Fax (01268) 286710* – ⚘ rm, 📺 Ꮬ **P** – 🔼 30. **MO AE O VISA**
Meals 10.55 **st.** and a la carte 🍷 5.40 – ⚌ 4.50 – **97 rm** 38.00 **st.**

🏠 **Travel Inn,** High Rd, Fobbing, SS17 9NR, SW : 2 ¼ m. by A 176 at junction with A 13 ℰ (01268) 554500, *Fax (01268) 581752* – ⚘ rm, 📺 Ꮬ **P**. **MO AE O VISA**
Meals (grill rest.) – **60 rm** 36.50 t.

🏠 **Travel Inn,** Felmores, East Mayne, SS13 1BW, N : 1 ½ m. on A 132 ℰ (01268) 522227, *Fax (01268) 530092* – ⚘ rm, 📺 Ꮬ **P**. **MO AE O VISA**. ⚘
Meals (grill rest.) – **32 rm** 36.50 t.

at Wickford N : 5 ¼ m. by A 132 – ✉ *Basildon.*

🏠🏠 **Chichester,** Old London Rd, Rawreth, SS11 8UE, E : 2 ¾ m. by A 129 ℰ (01268) 560555, *Fax (01268) 560580,* ⚘ – ⚘ rest, 🍽 rest, 📺 Ꮬ **P** – 🔼 100. **MO AE O VISA**. ⚘
Meals (bar lunch Saturday) 11.50/14.25 – ⚌ 7.95 – **35 rm** 59.50/62.50 t.

🅐 ATS Archers Field ℰ (01268) 525177

BASINGSTOKE *Hants.* **403 404** Q 30 – *pop. 77 837.*
🔝 Test Valley, Micheldever Rd, Overton ℰ (01256) 771737 – 🔝 Weybrook Park, Aldermaston Rd, Sherborne St John ℰ (01256) 20347.
🅱 Willis Museum, Old Town Hall, Market Pl., RG21 7QD ℰ (01256) 817618.
London 55 – Reading 17 – Southampton 31 – Winchester 18.

Plan on next page

🏠🏠🏠 **Audleys Wood** ⚘, Alton Rd, RG25 2JT, S : 1 ½ m. on A 339 ℰ (01256) 817555, *Fax (01256) 817500,* « Gothic Renaissance mansion », park – ⚘ rm, 📺 Ꮬ Ꮬ **P** – 🔼 50. **MO AE VISA JCB**. ⚘ Z v
Meals *(closed Saturday lunch)* 17.95/27.00 **st.** and a la carte 🍷 8.50 – ⚌ 10.50 – **69 rm** 110.00/145.00 **st.**, 2 suites – SB.

🏠🏠 **Hilton National,** Old Common Rd, Black Dam, RG21 3PR, ℰ (01256) 460460, *Fax (01256) 840441,* 🦽, ᏔᏔ – ⚘ rm, 🍽 rest, 📺 Ꮬ Ꮬ **P** – 🔼 150. **MO AE O VISA JCB**
Meals *(closed lunch Saturday and Bank Holidays)* (carving rest.) 14.50/18.50 **st.** and a la carte 🍷 6.50 – ⚌ 10.95 – **141 rm** 104.00 **st.** Z i

🏠🏠 **Forte Posthouse Basingstoke,** Grove Rd, RG21 3EE, S : 1 m. on A 339 ℰ (01256) 468181, *Fax (01256) 840081* – ⚘ rm, 📺 Ꮬ **P** – 🔼 150. **MO AE O VISA JCB**
Meals a la carte 17.40/23.85 **st.** 🍷 7.95 – ⚌ 9.95 – **84 rm** 79.00 **st.** – SB. Z e

🏠 **Travel Inn,** Worting Rd, RG22 6PG, ℰ (01256) 811477, *Fax (01256) 819329* – ⚘ rm, 📺 Ꮬ **P**. **MO AE O VISA**. ⚘ Z c
Meals (grill rest.) – **49 rm** 36.50 t.

🏠 **Travelodge,** Winchester Rd, RG22 5HN, SW : 2 ¼ m. by A 30 ℰ (01256) 843566, Reservations (Freephone) 0800 850950 – ⚘ rm, 📺 Ꮬ **P**. **MO AE O VISA JCB**. ⚘ Z u
32 rm 44.95 t.

🏠 **Fernbank** without rest., 4 Fairfields Rd, RG21 3DR, ℰ (01256) 321191, *Fax (01256) 321191* – ⚘ 📺 Ꮬ **P**. **MO VISA**. ⚘ Y a
closed 2 weeks Christmas – **16 rm** ⚌ 47.00/60.00.

BASINGSTOKE

London Street . . . . **Y** 19
Upper Church Street . . . . **Y** 24
Walks (The) Shopping Centre . **Y**
Winchester Street . . . . **Y** 27

Aldermaston Road . . . . **Z** 2
Beaconsfield Road . . . . **Y** 3
Buckland Avenue . . . . **Z** 5
Chequers Road . . . . **Y** 6
Church Street . . . . **Y** 7
Churchill Way . . . . **Z** 9
Churchill Way East . . . . **Z** 10
Council Road . . . . **Y** 12
Cross Street . . . . **Y** 13
Fairfields Road . . . . **Y** 14
Houndmills Road . . . . **Z** 17
New Road . . . . **Y** 20
Reading Road . . . . **Z** 22
Southern Ringway . . . . **Z** 23
Victoria Street . . . . **Y** 25
Wote Street . . . . **Y** 28

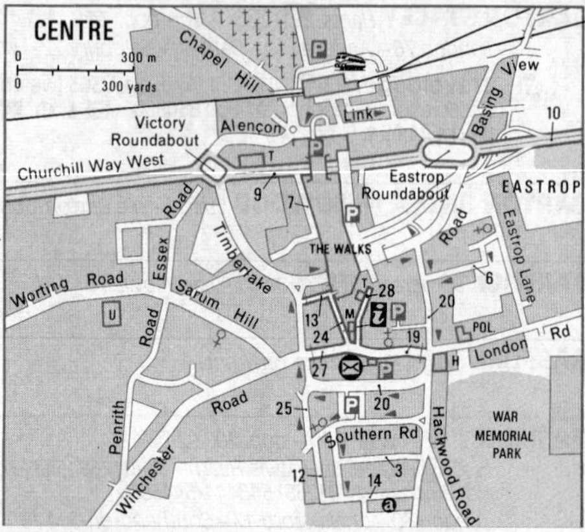

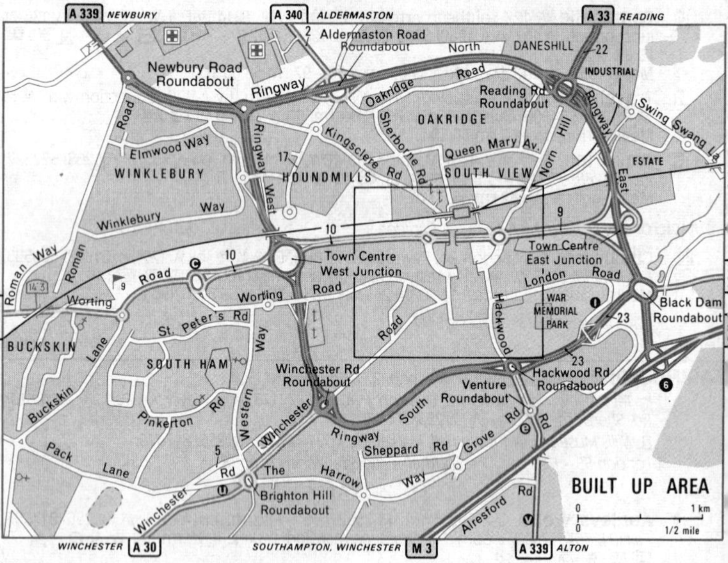

at Oakley *W : 4¾ m. on B 3400 – Z.*

Beach Arms, RG23 7EP, on B 3400 ☎ (01256) 780210, *Fax (01256) 780557,* – TV ☎ & – 25. MC AE VISA
Meals 12.50 **st.** and a la carte – 6.00 – **32 rm** 54.00 **st.**

ATS Moniton Trading Est., West Ham Lane ☎ (01256) 51431

ATS Armstrong Rd, Daneshill East ☎ (01256) 462448

When visiting Scotland,
use the ***Michelin Green Guide*** **"Scotland".**

- *Detailed descriptions of places of interest*
- *Touring programmes*
- *Maps and street plans*
- *The history of the country*
- *Photographs and drawings of monuments, beauty spots, houses...*

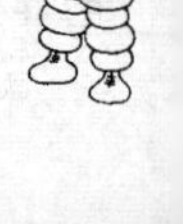

BASLOW Derbs. 402 403 404 P 24 *Great Britain G.* – pop. 1 184 – ⊠ Bakewell.
See : *Chatsworth*★★★ *(Park and Garden*★★★*) AC.*
London 161 – Derby 27 – Manchester 35 – Sheffield 13.

🏨 **Cavendish,** DE45 1SP, on A 619 ℘ (01246) 582311, *Fax (01246) 582312,* ≼ Chatsworth
Park, « Collection of paintings and fine art », ⚲, 寿 – ⅙⅞ rest, 🆃🆅 ☎ 🅿 – 🔬 25. 🆀🅾 🆃🅴 🅾
VISA. 🏵
Meals 32.25 **t.** and a la carte ⅃ 11.95 – 🖙 9.20 – **22 rm** 84.00/124.00 **t.**, 1 suite – SB.

🏵🏵🏵 **Fischer's at Baslow Hall** (Fischer) with rm, Calver Rd, DE45 1RR, on A 623
℘ (01246) 583259, *Fax (01246) 583818,* « Edwardian manor house », 寿 – ⅙⅞ rest, 🆃🆅 ☎
🅿. 🆀🅾 🆃🅴 🅾 *VISA*. 🏵
closed 25 and 26 December – **Meals** *(closed Saturday lunch and Sunday dinner)* 22.00/
42.00 **t.** – 🖙 7.25 – **5 rm** 80.00/120.00 **st.**, 1 suite – SB
Spec. Tomato risotto with roasted scallops, herb salad and brown butter vinaigrette. Squab
pigeon and foie gras wrapped in savoy cabbage. Apricot and vanilla soufflé with an apricot
compote.

🏵 🏵🏵 **Café-Max :** Meals *(closed Saturday dinner and Sunday)* a la carte 18.50/27.75 **t.**

When visiting Great Britain,
use the **Michelin Green Guide** **"Great Britain".**
- *Detailed descriptions of places of interest*
- *Touring programmes*
- *Maps and street plans*
- *The history of the country*
- *Photographs and drawings of monuments,*
  beauty spots, houses...

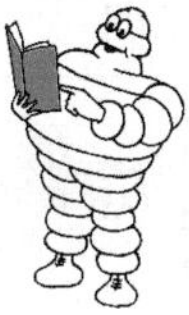

BASSENTHWAITE Cumbria 401 402 K 19 – pop. 433.
London 300 – Carlisle 24 – Keswick 7.

🏨 **Armathwaite Hall** 🏊, CA12 4RE, W : 1 ½ m. on B 5291, ⊠ Keswick ℘ (017687) 76551,
Fax (017687) 76220, ≼ Bassenthwaite Lake, « Part 18C mansion in extensive grounds », ℔,
≘, ☒, ⚲, 寿, park, ℁ – ⅃ ⅙⅞ rest, 🆃🆅 ☎ 🅿 – 🔬 100. 🆀🅾 🆃🅴 🅾 *VISA* 🆃🅲🅱
Meals 14.95/32.95 **t.** and dinner a la carte ⅃ 9.00 – **42 rm** 🖙 55.00/205.00 **t.** – SB.

🏨 **Castle Inn,** CA12 4RG, W : 1 m. on A 591 at junction with B 5291, ⊠ Keswick
℘ (017687) 76401, *Fax (017687) 76604,* ℔, ≘, ☒, 寿, ℁ – ⅙⅞ rest, 🆃🆅 ☎ 🅿 – 🔬 200.
🆀🅾 🆃🅴 🅾 *VISA*
Meals *(bar lunch)/dinner* 18.95 **st.** ⅃ 8.00 – **45 rm** 🖙 64.00/140.00 **st.**, 3 suites – SB.

🏨 **Overwater Hall** 🏊, CA5 1HH, NE : 2 ¾ m. by A 591 off Uldale rd, ⊠ Carlisle
℘ (017687) 76566, *Fax (017687) 76566,* ≼, « 19C mansion », 寿, park – ⅙⅞ rest, 🆃🆅 ☎ 🅿.
🆀🅾 *VISA*
Meals *(dinner only and Sunday lunch)/dinner* 18.50 **st.** ⅃ 4.95 – **13 rm** 🖙 *(dinner included)*
55.00/110.00 **st.** – SB.

🏠 **Pheasant Inn,** CA13 9YE, SW : 3 ¼ m. by B 5291 and A 66 on Wythop Mill rd, ⊠
Cockermouth ℘ (017687) 76234, *Fax (017687) 76002,* « 16C », 寿, park – ⅙⅞ rest, 🅿. 🆀🅾
VISA
closed 24 and 25 December – **Meals** 13.00/22.00 **st.** ⅃ 5.75 – **20 rm** 🖙 67.00/108.00 **st.** –
SB.

🏠 **Ravenstone Lodge,** CA12 4QG, S : 1 ½ m. on A 591 ℘ (017687) 76629,
Fax (017687) 76629, ≼, 寿 – 🆃🆅 🅿. 🆀🅾 *VISA* 🆃🅲🅱
Meals *(residents only) (dinner only)* 15.00 **st.** ⅃ 4.50 – **10 rm** 🖙 30.50/61.00 **st.**

at Ireby N : 5 m. by A 591 on Ireby rd – ⊠ Carlisle.

🏠 **Woodlands** 🏊, CA5 1EX, NW : ¼ m. on Mealsgate rd ℘ (016973) 71791,
Fax (016973) 71482, 寿 – ⅙⅞ 🆃🆅 🅿. 🆀🅾 *VISA* 🆃🅲🅱. 🏵
closed January, February and December except Christmas and New Year – **Meals**
(by arrangement) 12.50 **s.** – **7 rm** 🖙 27.50/60.00 **s.** – SB.

at Boltongate N : 6 ½ m. by A 591 and Ireby rd on Mealsgate rd – ⊠ Carlisle.

🏠 **Boltongate Old Rectory** 🏊, CA5 1DA, ℘ (016973) 71647, *Fax (016973) 71798,* ≼,
« Part 15C », 寿 – ⅙⅞ 🅿. 🆀🅾 *VISA*. 🏵
closed 20 December-6 January – **Meals** *(by arrangement) (communal dining)* 21.00 ⅃ 8.00 –
3 rm 🖙 42.00/74.00.

BATH Bath & North East Somerset **403 404** M 29 *The West Country G.* – pop. 85 202.

See : City★★★ – Royal Crescent★★★ AV (No 1 Royal Crescent★★ AC AV D) – The Circus★★★ AV – Museum of Costume★★★ AC AV M2 – Royal Photographic Society National Centre of Photography★★ AC BV M4 – Roman Baths★★ AC BX B – Holburne Museum and Crafts Study Centre★★ AC Y M1 – Pump Room★ BX A - Assembly Rooms★ AV – Bath Abbey★ BX – Pulteney Bridge★ BV – Bath Industrial Heritage Centre★ AC AV M3 – Landsdown Crescent★★ (Somerset Place★) Y – Camden Crescent★ Y – Beckford Tower and Museum AC (prospect★) Y M6 – Museum of East Asian Art★ AV – Orange Grove★ BX.

Env. : – Claverton (American Museum★★ AC, Claverton Pumping Station★ AC) E : 3 m. by A 36 Y.

Exc. : Corsham Court★★ AC, NE : 8 ½ m. by A 4 – Dyrham Park★ AC, N : 6 ½ m. by A 4 and A 46.

🐦, 🐦, 🐦, Tracy Park, Bath Rd, Wick ℘ (0117) 937 2251 – 🐦 Lansdown ℘ (01225) 425007 – 🐦 Entry Hill ℘ (01225) 834248.

🏛 Abbey Chambers, Abbey Churchyard, BA1 1LY ℘ (01225) 477101.

London 119 – Bristol 13 – Southampton 63 – Taunton 49.

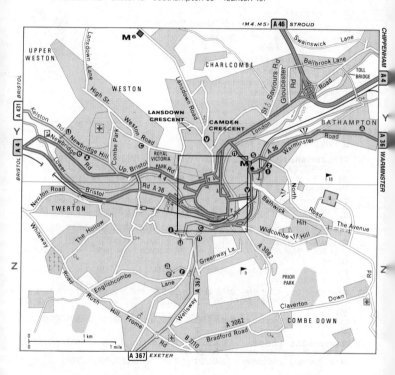

🏨🏨🏨 **Bath Spa** ⤣, Sydney Rd, BA2 6JF, ℘ (01225) 444424, *Fax (01225) 444006*, « Part 19C mansion in landscaped gardens », ₤₅, ⇌₅, 🏊, ⚒ – 🛗 ⇄ 📺 ☎ & 🅿 – 🔬 120. 🆎 🆎 📺
VISA JCB
Y Z
Alfresco in the Colonnade : Meals a la carte 21.90/34.95 **t.** – (see also **Vellore** below) – ⚁ 14.25 – **90 rm** 139.00/199.00 **t.**, 8 suites – SB.

🏨🏨 **The Royal Crescent**, 16 Royal Cres., BA1 2LS, ℘ (01225) 823333, *Fax (01225) 339401*, ≤, « Restored 18C town houses in magnificent Georgian crescent », ⚘ – 🛗, ⇄ rest, 🗏 📺
☎ ⟷ – 🔬 60. 🆎 🆎 📺 **VISA**
AV a
Pimpernel's : Meals *(closed Sunday and Monday)* (dinner only) 42.00 **t.** ₰ 13.00 –
The Brasserie : Meals 19.50/29.00 **t.** and a la carte 23.50/39.00 **t.** ₰ 13.00 – ⚁ 13.50 –
28 rm 165.00/235.00 **t.**, 14 suites 330.00/675.00 **t.** – SB.

BATH

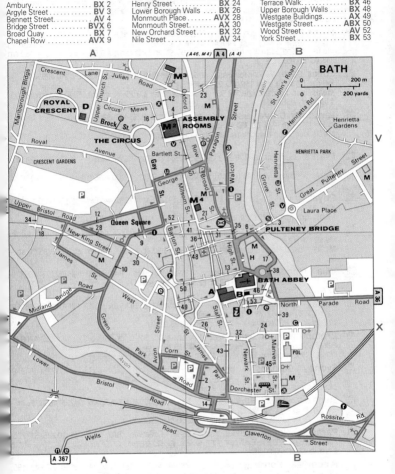

Homewood Park, BA3 6BB, SE : 6 ½ m. on A 36 ℰ (01225) 723731, *Fax (01225) 723820*, ≤, « Part Georgian country house », ⌇, ☞, park, ℀ – ⇔ rest, ⊡ ☎ 🅿. 🕦 AE ① *VISA* JCB. ✻
Meals 21.50 **st.** (lunch) and dinner a la carte 38.00/50.00 **st.** – **17 rm** ⇌ 98.00/198.00 **st.**, 2 suites – SB
Spec. Confit of foie gras with bay jelly and brioche toast. Breast of Trelough duck with celeriac and Calvados sauce. Tiramisu with espresso sauce and chocolate spaghetti.

The Priory, Weston Rd, BA1 2XT, ℰ (01225) 331922, *Fax (01225) 448276*, ≤, *Fб*, ☜, ⌇, 🔄, ☞ – ⇔ rest, ⊡ ☎ ৬ 🅿. 🕦 ① *VISA*. ✻
Meals 16.50/32.50 **t.** and a la carte ▯ 8.00 – **28 rm** ⇌ 130.00/250.00 **st.** – SB.

Queensberry, Russel St., BA1 2QF, ℰ (01225) 447928, *Fax (01225) 446065*, « Georgian town houses » – |✿| ⊡ ☎. 🕦 *VISA*. ✻
closed 1 week Christmas – Meals – (see *Olive Tree* below) – ⇌ 7.50 – **22 rm** 95.00/185.00 **st.** – SB.

AV **X**

Y **C**

Francis, Queen Sq., BA1 2HH, ☎ (01225) 424257, *Fax (01225) 319715* – |≴| ⇌ 📺 ☎ ❶ – 🔏 80. 🆘 🆎 ⓪ 𝘝𝘐𝘚𝘈
AV i
Meals 21.95 (dinner) and a la carte 13.00/18.00 ᾦ 7.50 – ⊇ 9.75 – **93 rm** 89.00/109.00 t., 1 suite – SB.

Fountain House without rest., 9-11 Fountain Buildings, Lansdown Rd, BA1 5DV, ☎ (01225) 338622, *Fax (01225) 445855* – |≴| 📺 ☎. 🆘 🆎 ⓪ 𝘝𝘐𝘚𝘈
BV e
13 suites 100.00/200.00 st.

Hilton National, Walcot St., BA1 5BJ, ☎ (01225) 463411, *Fax (01225) 464393*, ℔, 🕿, 🔲 – |≴| ⇌ 📺 ☎ ⟵ ❶ – 🔏 240. 🆘 🆎 ⓪ 𝘝𝘐𝘚𝘈 𝘑𝘊𝘉
BV i
Meals *(closed Saturday lunch)* 15.00/18.00 st. and a la carte ᾦ 6.50 – ⊇ 10.75 – **150 rm** 113.00/200.00 st. – SB.

Stakis Bath, Widcombe Basin, BA2 4JP, ☎ (01225) 338855, *Fax (01225) 428941* – |≴|, ⇌ rm, 📺 ☎ ❶ – 🔏 130. 🆘 🆎 ⓪ 𝘝𝘐𝘚𝘈
BX r
Meals (bar lunch)/dinner 17.95 st. and a la carte ᾦ 8.25 – ⊇ 10.95 – **106 rm** 98.00/118.00 st. – SB.

Lansdown Grove, Lansdown Rd, BA1 5EH, ☎ (01225) 483888, *Fax (01225) 483838*, � – |≴| ⇌ 📺 ☎ ❶ – 🔏 80. 🆘 🆎 𝘝𝘐𝘚𝘈
Y v
Meals (bar lunch Monday to Saturday)/dinner a la carte 15.25/24.50 st. – **48 rm** ⊇ 72.50/160.00 st. – SB.

Pratt's, South Par., BA2 4AB, ☎ (01225) 460441, *Fax (01225) 448807* – |≴|, ⇌ rm, 📺 ☎ – 🔏 50. 🆘 🆎 ⓪ 𝘝𝘐𝘚𝘈
BX c
Meals (bar lunch Monday to Saturday)/dinner 16.25 st. ᾦ 6.00 – **46 rm** ⊇ 62.50/120.00 st. – SB.

Royal, Manvers St., BA1 1JP, ☎ (01225) 463134, *Fax (01225) 442931* – |≴| 📺 ☎. 🆘 🆎 ⓪ 𝘝𝘐𝘚𝘈. 🞨
BX a
Meals (grill rest.) 8.75 st. and a la carte ᾦ 3.95 – **30 rm** ⊇ 45.00/70.00 st. – SB.

Abbey, 1 North Par., BA1 1LG, ☎ (01225) 461603, *Fax (01225) 447758* – |≴|, ⇌ rest, 📺 ☎. 🆘 🆎 ⓪ 𝘝𝘐𝘚𝘈. 🞨
BX e
Meals *(closed lunch Monday to Friday)* 8.85/16.50 st. ᾦ 4.50 – **56 rm** ⊇ 59.00/95.00 st. – SB.

Villa Magdala without rest., Henrietta Rd, BA2 6LX, ☎ (01225) 466329, *Fax (01225) 483207*, � – ⇌ 📺 ☎ ❶. 🆘 🆎 𝘝𝘐𝘚𝘈 𝘑𝘊𝘉. 🞨
BV r
17 rm ⊇ 55.00/90.00 st.

Apsley House without rest., 141 Newbridge Hill, BA1 3PT, ☎ (01225) 336966, *Fax (01225) 425462*, � – 📺 ☎ ❶. 🆘 𝘝𝘐𝘚𝘈 𝘑𝘊𝘉. 🞨
Y x
closed 24 to 28 December – **7 rm** ⊇ 50.00/95.00 st.

Brompton House without rest., St. John's Rd, Bathwick, BA2 6PT, ☎ (01225) 420972, *Fax (01225) 420505*, � – ⇌ 📺 ☎ ❶. 🆘 🆎 𝘝𝘐𝘚𝘈 𝘑𝘊𝘉. 🞨
Y n
closed Christmas and New Year – **18 rm** ⊇ 38.00/80.00 st.

Sydney Gardens without rest., Sydney Rd, BA2 6NT, ☎ (01225) 464818, *Fax (01225) 484347*, ≼, � – ⇌ 📺 ☎ ❶. 🆘 🆎 𝘝𝘐𝘚𝘈 𝘑𝘊𝘉
Y i
closed January – **6 rm** ⊇ 59.00/69.00 st.

Siena without rest., 25 Pulteney Rd, BA2 4EZ, ☎ (01225) 425495, *Fax (01225) 469029*, � – ⇌ 📺 ☎ ❶ – 🔏 25. 🆘 🆎 ⓪ 𝘝𝘐𝘚𝘈 𝘑𝘊𝘉
Z v
closed 25 December – **14 rm** ⊇ 45.00/82.50 st., 1 suite.

Paradise House without rest., 86-88 Holloway, BA2 4PX, ☎ (01225) 317723, *Fax (01225) 482005*, ≼ Bath, � – 📺 ☎ ⟵ ❶. 🆘 🆎 𝘝𝘐𝘚𝘈. 🞨
Z c
8 rm ⊇ 45.00/80.00 st.

Bloomfield House without rest., 146 Bloomfield Rd, BA2 2AS, ☎ (01225) 420105, *Fax (01225) 481958*, ≼, « Georgian house », 🌫 – ⇌ 📺 ☎ ❶. 🆘 𝘝𝘐𝘚𝘈 𝘑𝘊𝘉. 🞨
Z r
8 rm ⊇ 40.00/75.00 st.

Holly Lodge without rest., 8 Upper Oldfield Park, BA2 3JZ, ☎ (01225) 424042, *Fax (01225) 481138*, ≼, 🌫 – ⇌ 📺 ☎ ❶. 🆘 🆎 ⓪ 𝘝𝘐𝘚𝘈. 🞨
Z i
7 rm ⊇ 48.00/89.00 st.

Meadowland without rest., 36 Bloomfield Park, BA2 2BX, ☎ (01225) 311079, *Fax (01225) 304507*, 🌫 – ⇌ 📺 ❶. 🆘 𝘝𝘐𝘚𝘈. 🞨
Z e
3 rm ⊇ 50.00/70.00.

Cranleigh without rest., 159 Newbridge Hill, BA1 3PX, ☎ (01225) 310197, *Fax (01225) 423143* – ⇌ 📺 ❶. 🆘 𝘝𝘐𝘚𝘈. 🞨
Y e
booking essential in January – **5 rm** ⊇ 45.00/75.00 st.

Leighton House without rest., 139 Wells Rd, BA2 3AL, ☎ (01225) 314769, *Fax (01225) 443079*, 🌫 – 📺 ☎ ❶. 🆘 𝘝𝘐𝘚𝘈. 🞨
AX e
8 rm ⊇ 47.00/72.00 st.

🏠 **Haydon House** without rest., 9 Bloomfield Park, off Bloomfield Rd, BA2 2BY, *℘* (01225) 444919, *Fax* (01225) 427351, *☞* – ✭↫ 📺 ☎. ⚫🔟 Æ *VISA* 🇯🇨🇧. ✳ Z a
5 rm ⊃ 55.00/80.00 **st.**

🏠 **Dorian House** without rest., 1 Upper Oldfield Park, BA2 3JX, *℘* (01225) 426336, *Fax* (01225) 444699, ≼, *☞* – 📺 ☎ 🅿. ⚫🔟 Æ ⓞ *VISA*. ✳ Z u
8 rm ⊃ 47.00/75.00 **st.**

🏠 **Laura Place** without rest., 3 Laura Pl., Great Pulteney St., BA2 4BH, *℘* (01225) 463815, *Fax* (01225) 310222 – ✭↫ 📺 ☎ 🅿. ⚫🔟 Æ *VISA*. ✳ BV v
closed 20 December-1 March – **8 rm** ⊃ 55.00/88.00 **st.**

🏠 **Orchard Lodge** without rest., Warminster Rd, Bathampton, BA2 6XG, E : 1 ½ m. on A 36 *℘* (01225) 466115, *Fax* (01225) 446050, ☎s – 📺 ☎ 🅿. ⚫🔟 *VISA* Y a
14 rm ⊃ 45.00/62.00 **st.**

↥ **Cheriton House** without rest., 9 Upper Oldfield Park, BA2 3JX, *℘* (01225) 429862, *Fax* (01225) 428403, *☞* – ✭↫ 📺 🅿. ⚫🔟 Æ ⓞ *VISA*. ✳ Z u
9 rm ⊃ 42.00/72.00 **st.**

↥ **Kennard** without rest., 11 Henrietta St., BA2 6LL, *℘* (01225) 310472, *Fax* (01225) 460054 – ✭↫ 📺 ☎. ⚫🔟 Æ ⓞ *VISA* 🇯🇨🇧. ✳ BV u
13 rm ⊃ 45.00/85.00 **st.**

↥ **Greenways** without rest., 1 Forester Rd, Bathwick, BA2 6QF, *℘* (01225) 310132, *Fax* (01225) 310132 – 📺 🅿 Y s
closed 24 and 25 December – **3 rm** ⊃ 40.00/55.00.

↥ **Blairgowrie House** without rest., 55 Wellsway, BA2 4RT, *℘* (01225) 332266 – 📺. ✳ Z n
3 rm ⊃ 35.00/52.00.

↥ **Oakleigh** without rest., 19 Upper Oldfield Park, BA2 3JX, *℘* (01225) 315698, *Fax* (01225) 448223 – 📺 🅿. ⚫🔟 Æ *VISA*. ✳ Z i
4 rm ⊃ 35.00/65.00 **st.**

↥ **Brocks** without rest., 32 Brock St., BA1 2LN, *℘* (01225) 338374, *Fax* (01225) 334245 – 📺. ⚫🔟 *VISA*. ✳ AV e
closed 2 weeks January – **6 rm** ⊃ 50.00/68.00 **t.**

↥ **Oldfields** without rest., 102 Wells Rd, BA2 3AL, *℘* (01225) 317984, *Fax* (01225) 444471, *☞* – 📺 🅿. ⚫🔟 *VISA* 🇯🇨🇧. ✳ AX n
closed January – **14 rm** ⊃ 48.00/70.00.

XXXX **Vellore** (at Bath Spa H.), Sydney Rd, BA2 6JF, *℘* (01225) 444424, *Fax* (01225) 444006, *☞* – ✭↫ rest, ▤ 🅿. ⚫🔟 Æ ⓞ *VISA* 🇯🇨🇧 Y z
Meals (dinner only and Sunday lunch)/dinner a la carte 24.45/36.50 **t.** ⓘ 9.50.

XX **Lettonie** (Blunos) with rm, 35 Kelston Rd, BA1 3QH, *℘* (01225) 446676, ✿✿✿ *Fax* (01225) 447541, ≼, *☞* – ✭↫ rest, 📺 ☎ 🅿. ⚫🔟 Æ ⓞ *VISA* Y u
closed Sunday, Monday, 2 weeks August and 2 weeks Christmas – **Meals** 21.95/38.50 **t.** ⓘ 15.00 – **5 rm** 75.00/135.00 **t.**
Spec. Borsch terrine with shredded beef, piragi and soured cream. Calves sweetbreads with ham and chicken mousse, lemon cream sauce. Apple and vanilla parfait with an apple sorbet.

XX **Hole in the Wall,** 16 George St., BA1 2EH, *℘* (01225) 425242, *Fax* (01225) 425242 – ✭↫. ⚫🔟 Æ *VISA* AV u
closed Sunday dinner and 25-26 December – **Meals** 11.50 **t.** (lunch) and a la carte 22.00/24.50 **t.** ⓘ 11.00.

XX **Moody Goose,** 7A Kingsmead Sq., BA1 2AB, *℘* (01225) 466688 – ⚫🔟 ⓞ *VISA*
closed Sunday, Bank Holidays except 25 December and 2 weeks spring – **Meals** 10.00/19.50 **t.** and a la carte 18.50/28.50 **t.** ⓘ 9.00. AX e

XX **Clos du Roy,** 1 Seven Dials, Saw Close, BA1 1EN, *℘* (01225) 444450, *Fax* (01225) 404044 – ⚫🔟 Æ ⓞ *VISA* 🇯🇨🇧 AX r
closed 26 December and 1 January – **Meals** 12.95/19.50 **t.** and a la carte ⓘ 7.50.

XX **Olive Tree** (at Queensberry H.), Russel St., BA1 2QF, *℘* (01225) 447928, *Fax* (01225) 446065 – ✭↫ ▤. ⚫🔟 *VISA* AV x
closed lunch Sunday and Bank Holidays and 1 week Christmas – **Meals** 13.50/19.00 **t.** and a la carte ⓘ 10.00.

XX **Rajpoot,** Rajpoot House, Argyle St., BA2 4BA, *℘* (01225) 466833, *Fax* (01225) 442462 – ▤. ⚫🔟 Æ ⓞ *VISA* BV s
closed 25 and 26 December – **Meals** - Indian - 15.50/18.95 **t.** and a la carte.

XX **Sukhothai,** 90a Walcot St., BA1 5BG, *℘* (01225) 462463, *Fax* (01225) 462463 – ▤. ⚫🔟 Æ ⓞ *VISA* 🇯🇨🇧 BV a
closed Sunday and Bank Holidays – **Meals** - Thai - 6.90/16.00 **t.** and a la carte.

X **Tilleys Bistro,** 3 North Parade Passage, BA1 1NX, ✆ (01225) 484200 – ✦✦, ⓦⓞ VISA JCB
closed Sunday lunch and 1 week at Christmas – **Meals** 6.90 t. (lunch) and dinner
a la carte 12.50/20.00 t. ₰ 8.90.   BX i

X **Woods,** 9-13 Alfred St., BA1 2QX, ✆ (01225) 314812, Fax (01225) 443146 – ⓦⓞ VISA
closed Sunday dinner – **Meals** a la carte 16.75/25.25 t. ₰ 5.00.   AV v

X **N°. 5 Bistro,** 5 Argyle St., BA2 4BA, ✆ (01225) 444499, Fax (01225) 318668 – ⓦⓞ AE ⓞ VISA
JCB
closed Monday lunch, Sunday and 25-29 December – **Meals** a la carte 15.15/25.95 t. ₰ 5.95.
                                                                                     BV s

at Box (Wilts.) NE : 5½ m. on A 4 – Y – ⊠ Corsham.

⌂ **Hermitage** without rest., Bath Rd, SN13 8DT, ✆ (01225) 744187, Fax (01225) 743447, ⤢,
⚘ – ✦✦ ⓣⓥ ⓟ. ⅏
closed 22 December-6 January – **5 rm** ⊊ 37.00/48.00 st.

⌂ **Manor Farm** without rest., Wadswick, SN13 8JB, SE : 2 m. by A 365 off B 3109
✆ (01225) 810700, Fax (01225) 810307, « Working farm », ⚘, park – ✦✦ ⓣⓥ ⓟ. ⓦⓞ VISA
JCB. ⅏
April-September – **3 rm** ⊊ 30.00/45.00.

at Colerne (Wilts.) NE : 6½ m. by A 4 – Y – , Batheaston rd and Bannerdown Rd – ⊠ Chippenham.

🏨 **Lucknam Park** ⤢, SN14 8AZ, N : ½ m. on Marshfield rd ✆ (01225) 742777,
Fax (01225) 743536, ≼, « Early 18C country house in park », ₤₅, ⓢ, ⤢, ⚘, ⅍ – ✦✦ rest,
ⓣⓥ ☎ ⓟ – ₰ 25. ⓦⓞ AE ⓞ VISA JCB. ⅏
Meals 24.50/40.00 st. and a la carte 40.00/59.00 st. ₰ 12.00 – ⊊ 18.00 – **38 rm** 130.00/
250.00 st., 4 suites – SB.

at Bathford E : 3½ m. by A 4 – Y – off A 363 – ⊠ Bath.

🏠 **Lodge** without rest., Bathford Hill, BA1 7SL, ✆ (01225) 858467, Fax (01225) 858172, ⤢, ⚘
– ⓣⓥ ☎ ⓟ. ⓦⓞ VISA
4 rm ⊊ 55.00/110.00 st., 1 suite.

at Monkton Combe SE : 4½ m. by A 36 – Y – ⊠ Bath.

🏠 **Monkshill** ⤢ without rest., Shaft Rd, BA2 7HL, ✆ (01225) 833028, Fax (01225) 833028
≼ Limpley Stoke Valley, « Antiques », ⚘ – ✦✦ ⓣⓥ ⓟ. ⓦⓞ VISA. ⅏
closed 2 weeks Christmas and New Year – **3 rm** ⊊ 45.00/70.00 st.

at Limpley Stoke (Lower) SE : 5½ m. by A 36 – Y – off B 3108 – ⊠ Bath.

🏨 **Cliffe,** Cliffe Drive, Crowe Hill, BA3 6HY, ✆ (01225) 723226, Fax (01225) 723871, ≼, ⤢, ⚘ –
✦✦ rest, ⓣⓥ ☎ ⓟ. ⓦⓞ AE VISA JCB
Meals 15.00 t. (lunch) and dinner a la carte 19.00/27.25 t. ₰ 5.75 – **11 rm** ⊊ 68.00/105.00 t
– SB.

at Hinton Charterhouse S : 5¾ m. by A 367 – Z – on B 3110 – ⊠ Bath.

⌂ **Green Lane House** without rest., Green Lane, BA3 6BL, ✆ (01225) 723631
Fax (01225) 723773 – ⓦⓞ AE VISA. ⅏
4 rm ⊊ 42.00/54.00.

at Norton St. Philip (Somerset) S : 7¼ m. by A 367 – Z – on B 3110 – ⊠ Bath.

⌂ **The Plaine** without rest., BA3 6LE, ✆ (01373) 834723, Fax (01373) 834101, « 16C
cottages » – ✦✦ ⓣⓥ ⓟ. ⓦⓞ VISA JCB. ⅏
closed 25 and 26 December – **3 rm** ⊊ 40.00/58.00 st.

⌂ **Monmouth Lodge** without rest., BA3 6LH, on B 3110 ✆ (01373) 834367, ⚘ – ✦✦ ⓣⓥ
ⓟ. ⓦⓞ VISA. ⅏
March-November – **3 rm** ⊊ 45.00/60.00.

🔘 ATS London Rd ✆ (01225) 338899

BATHFORD Bath & North East Somerset 403 404 M 29 – see Bath.

BATLEY W. Yorks. 402 O 22 – pop. 48 030.
London 205 – Leeds 9 – Manchester 40 – Middlesbrough 76 – Sheffield 31.

🏨 **Alder House,** Towngate Rd, Healey Lane, WF17 7HR, ✆ (01924) 444777
Fax (01924) 442644, ⚘ – ⓣⓥ ☎ ⓟ – ₰ 80. ⓦⓞ AE ⓞ VISA. ⅏
Meals (bar lunch Monday to Saturday and Sunday dinner)/dinner 16.50 t. ₰ 5.50 – **20 rm**
⊊ 49.00/75.00 t. – SB.

The Guide is updated annually so renew your Guide every year.

BATTLE E. Sussex 404 V 31 *Great Britain G.* – pop. 5 235.
 See : *Town*★ – *Abbey and Site of the Battle of Hastings*★ *AC*.
 🖪 88 High St., TN33 0AQ ℘ (01424) 773721.
 London 55 – Brighton 34 – Folkestone 43 – Maidstone 30.

🏨 **Netherfield Place** ⌂, TN33 9PP, NW : 2 m. by A 2100 on Netherfield rd
 ℘ (01424) 744455, *Fax (01424) 774024*, ≤, « Georgian style country house, gardens »,
 park, ※ – 📺 ☎ ₱ – 🛦 50. 🐠 🕮 ⓪ 𝘝𝘐𝘚𝘈
 closed last week December and first week January – **Meals** 15.00/27.00 **t.** and a la carte
 🛢 8.00 – **13 rm** ⊡ 70.00/160.00 **t.** – SB.

🏨 **Powdermills** ⌂, Powdermill Lane, TN33 0SP, S : 1 ½ m. by A 2100 on B 2095
 ℘ (01424) 775511, *Fax (01424) 774540*, ≤, « Part Georgian gunpowdermill, antiques », ⌁,
 ☞, park – 📺 ☎ ₱ – 🛦 250. 🐠 🕮 ⓪ 𝘝𝘐𝘚𝘈
 Meals – (see *Orangery below*) – **35 rm** ⊡ 65.00/150.00 **t.** – SB.

🏠 **Burnt Wood House** ⌂, Powdermill Lane, TN33 0SU, S : 2 m. on A 2100 on B 2095
 ℘ (01424) 775151, *Fax (01424) 775151*, ≤, ⬰, ☞, park, ※ – ⥆ rest, 📺 ☎ ₱. 🐠 🕮 ⓪
 𝘝𝘐𝘚𝘈
 Meals 10.66/19.50 **t.** 🛢 5.50 – **10 rm** ⊡ 45.00/85.00 **t.** – SB.

🏠 **George**, 23 High St., TN33 0EA, ℘ (01424) 774466, *Fax (01424) 774853* – 📺 ☎ ₱ – 🛦 50.
 🐠 🕮 ⓪ 𝘝𝘐𝘚𝘈
 Meals a la carte 9.45/16.40 **st.** 🛢 4.25 – **18 rm** ⊡ 50.00/75.00 **st.** – SB.

🍴🍴 **Orangery** (at Powdermills H.), Powdermill Lane, TN33 0SP, S : 1 ½ m. by A 2100 on B 2095
 ℘ (01424) 775511, *Fax (01424) 774540*, ☞ – ₱. 🐠 🕮 ⓪ 𝘝𝘐𝘚𝘈
 Meals *(closed Sunday dinner January-February)* 14.95/19.50 and dinner a la carte 🛢 6.50.

*Your recommendation is self-evident if you always walk into a
hotel Guide in hand.*

BEACONSFIELD Bucks. 404 S 29 – pop. 12 292.
 London 26 – Aylesbury 19 – Oxford 32.

🏨 **De Vere Bellhouse**, Oxford Rd, HP9 2XE, E : 1 ¾ m. on A 40 ℘ (01753) 887211,
 Fax (01753) 888231, 🖩, ⛉, 🏊, ☞, squash – 🖩 ⥆ 📺 ☎ ₱ – 🛦 450. 🐠 🕮 ⓪ 𝘝𝘐𝘚𝘈. ※
 Archways : **Meals** *(closed Saturday lunch)* 17.00/21.50 **st.** and dinner a la carte 🛢 7.00 –
 Brasserie : **Meals** a la carte 16.00/25.25 **st.** 🛢 7.00 – **133 rm** ⊡ 140.00/180.00 **st.**, 3 suites
 – SB.

🍴🍴 **Leigh House**, 53 Wycombe End, HP9 1LX, ℘ (01494) 676348, *Fax (01494) 676348* – ▥.
 🐠 🕮 ⓪ 𝘝𝘐𝘚𝘈 𝗝𝗖𝗕
 closed 25 and 26 December – **Meals** - Chinese (Peking) - 12.00/19.00 **t.** and a la carte.

at Wooburn Common SW : 3½ m. by A 40 – ✉ Beaconsfield.

🏠 **Chequers Inn** ⌂, Kiln Lane, HP10 0JQ, SW : 1 m. on Bourne End rd ℘ (01628) 529575,
 Fax (01628) 850124 – 📺 ☎ ₱ – 🛦 45. 🐠 🕮 ⓪ 𝘝𝘐𝘚𝘈. ※
 Meals 16.95/19.00 **t.** and a la carte 🛢 8.75 – **17 rm** ⊡ 82.50/87.50 **t.** – SB.

 🅐 ATS Warwick Rd ℘ (01494) 671338

BEAMINSTER Dorset 403 L 31 – pop. 2 769.
 London 154 – Exeter 45 – Taunton 30 – Weymouth 29.

🏨 **Bridge House**, DT8 3AY, ℘ (01308) 862200, *Fax (01308) 863700*, ☞ – ⥆ rest, 📺 ☎ ₱.
 🐠 🕮 ⓪ 𝘝𝘐𝘚𝘈 𝗝𝗖𝗕
 Meals 14.50/20.50 **t.** 🛢 5.00 – **14 rm** ⊡ 58.00/107.00 **t.** – SB.

🏠 **The Lodge**, 9 Tunnel Rd, DT8 3BL, on A 3066 ℘ (01308) 863468, « Georgian country
 house », ☞, ※ – 📺 ₱. 🐠 ⓪ 𝘝𝘐𝘚𝘈 𝗝𝗖𝗕
 closed Christmas – **Meals** *(closed Sunday)* (residents only) (dinner only) 20.00 **st.** 🛢 8.00 –
 3 rm ⊡ 50.00/80.00 **st.**

BEARSTED Kent 404 V 30 – see Maidstone.

BEAULIEU Hants. 403 404 P 31 *Great Britain G.* – pop. 726 – ✉ Brockenhurst.
 See : *Town*★★ - *National Motor Museum*★★ *AC*.
 Env. : *Buckler's Hard*★ *(Maritime Museum*★ *AC) SE : 2 m.*
 London 102 – Bournemouth 24 – Southampton 13 – Winchester 23.

🏨 **Montagu Arms**, Palace Lane, SO42 7ZL, ℘ (01590) 612324, *Fax (01590) 612188*,
 « Part 18C inn, gardens » – 📺 ☎ ₱ – 🛦 40. 🐠 🕮 ⓪ 𝘝𝘐𝘚𝘈. ※
 Meals 24.90 **t.** (dinner) and a la carte 14.95/35.40 **t.** – **22 rm** ⊡ 69.00/129.00, 2 suites – SB.

at Bucklers Hard S : 2½ m. – ⊠ Brockenhurst.

🏠 **Master Builder's House,** SO42 7XB, ℰ (01590) 616253, Fax (01590) 616297, ≼, 斎, 屛 – ✦⊞ ⊞ ☎ ℗ – 🔬 40. 🐾 🕮 ① 𝘝𝘐𝘚𝘈. 🌿
Meals 16.95 t. and a la carte 🍴 8.15 – **23 rm** ⊆ 61.95/121.25 t. – SB.

BECKINGHAM Lincs. 🗺️🗺️🗺️ R 24 – pop. 263 – ⊠ Fenton Claypole.
London 124 – Leicester 43 – Lincoln 20 – Nottingham 28 – Sheffield 46.

XX **Black Swan,** Hillside, LN5 0RF, ℰ (01636) 626474, 屛 – ✦⊞ ℗. 🐾 𝘝𝘐𝘚𝘈
closed Sunday dinner, Monday, 1 week February and 2 weeks August – **Meals** (booking essential) (lunch by arrangement Monday to Saturday)/dinner a la carte 17.50/28.00 t.
🍴 7.85.

BECKINGTON Somerset 🗺️🗺️🗺️ N 30 – pop. 903 – ⊠ Bath (Bath & North East Somerset).
London 110 – Bristol 27 – Southampton 54 – Swindon 37.

🏠 **Travelodge,** BA3 6SF, on A 36 ℰ (01373) 830251, Reservations (Freephone) 0800 850950 – ✦⊞ rm, ⊞ ఉ ℗. 🐾 🕮 ① 𝘝𝘐𝘚𝘈 𝐽𝐶𝐵. 🌿
40 rm 44.95 t.

XX **Woolpack Inn** with rm, Warminster Rd, BA3 6SP, ℰ (01373) 831244, Fax (01373) 831223, « Part 16C », 屛 – ✦⊞ rest, ⊞ ☎ ℗. 🐾 🕮 𝘝𝘐𝘚𝘈. 🌿
Meals a la carte 20.65/26.90 t. 🍴 5.50 – **12 rm** ⊆ 54.50/64.50 t. – SB.

When looking for a quiet hotel
use the maps found in the introduction
or look for establishments with the sign ⅋ or ⅋.

BEDALE N. Yorks. 🗺️🗺️ P 21 – pop. 2 828 – ⊠ Darlington.
🏌 Leyburn Rd ℰ (01677) 422568.
🅱 Bedale Hall, DL8 1AA ℰ (01677) 424604 (summer only).
London 225 – Leeds 45 – Newcastle Upon Tyne 30 – York 38.

🏠 **Hyperion House** without rest., 88 South End, DL8 2DS, ℰ (01677) 422334, 屛 – ✦⊞ ⊞ ℗. 🌿
closed Christmas, New Year and February – **3 rm** ⊆ 25.00/42.00 st.

BEDFORD Beds. 🗺️🗺️ S 27 – pop. 73 917.
🏌 Bedfordshire, Bromham Rd, Biddenham ℰ (01234) 353241 Y – 🏌 Mowsbury, Kimboltor Rd ℰ (01234) 216374/771041.
🅱 10 St. Paul's Sq., MK40 1SL ℰ (01234) 215226.
London 59 – Cambridge 31 – Colchester 70 – Leicester 51 – Lincoln 95 – Luton 20 – Oxford 52 – Southend-on-Sea 85.

Plan opposite

🏰 **Barns,** Cardington Rd, MK44 3SA, E : 2 m. on A 603 ℰ (01234) 270044, Fax (01234) 273102 ≼⅋, 屛 – ✦⊞ ⊞ ☎ ఉ ℗ – 🔬 120. 🐾 🕮 ① 𝘝𝘐𝘚𝘈   Y n
Meals (bar lunch Saturday) 19.50 t. 🍴 6.95 – ⊆ 8.95 – **48 rm** 78.00/140.00 t. – SB.

🏠 **Bedford Swan,** The Embankment, MK40 1RW, ℰ (01234) 346565, Fax (01234) 212009 🖵 – 📱, 🍴 rest, ⊞ ☎ ℗ – 🔬 300. 🐾 🕮 ① 𝘝𝘐𝘚𝘈. 🌿   X a
Meals 15.50 st. and a la carte 🍴 8.00 – ⊆ 6.50 – **114 rm** 72.00/79.50 st., 1 suite – SB.

🏠 **Wayfarer,** 403 Goldington Rd, Goldington, MK41 0DS, E : 2 m. on A 428 ℰ (01234) 272707, Fax (01234) 272707 – ⊞ ☎ ఉ ℗. 🐾 🕮 ① 𝘝𝘐𝘚𝘈. 🌿   Y v
closed 24 to 27 and 31 December and 1 January – **Meals** (grill rest.) a la carte 9.20/20.70 t. – **29 rm** ⊆ 55.00/65.00 t. – SB.

at Elstow S : 2 m. by A 6 off A 5134 – ⊠ Bedford.

XX **St. Helena,** High St., MK42 9XP, ℰ (01234) 344848, « Part 16C house », 屛 – ℗. 🐾 🕮 ① 𝘝𝘐𝘚𝘈 𝐽𝐶𝐵   Y
closed Saturday lunch, Sunday, Monday and 1 week Christmas – **Meals** 17.75/28.00 t 🍴 8.50.

at Houghton Conquest S : 6½ m. by A 6 – Y – ⊠ Bedford.

XX **Knife and Cleaver** with rm, The Grove, MK45 3LA, ℰ (01234) 740387 Fax (01234) 740900, 斎, 屛 – ✦⊞ ℗. 🐾 🕮 𝘝𝘐𝘚𝘈 𝐽𝐶𝐵. 🌿
closed 27 to 30 December – **Meals** (closed dinner Sunday and Bank Holidays) (bar lunch Saturday) 13.95/18.50 t. and a la carte 🍴 6.35 – **9 rm** ⊆ 45.00/69.00 t. – SB.

BEDFORD

Great Britain and Ireland is now covered by an Atlas at a scale of 1 inch to 4.75 miles.

Three easy to use versions: Paperback, Spiralbound and Hardback.

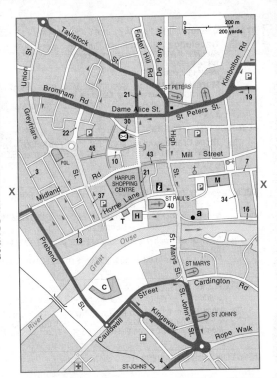

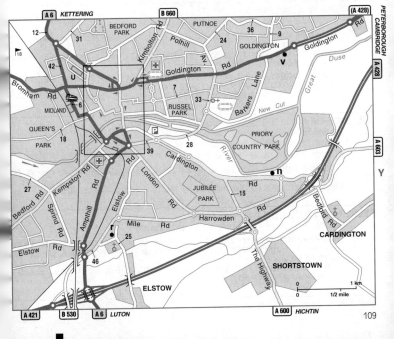

109

at Marston Moretaine SW : 6¼ m. by A 6 – Y – off A 421 – ⊠ Bedford.

🏠 **Travelodge**, Beancroft Rd junction, MK43 0PZ, on A 421 ℘ (01234) 766755, Fax (01234) 766755, Reservations (Freephone) 0800 850950 – ⚡ rm, 📺 ⅃ 🅿. ⓴⓽ 🅰🅴 ⓪ VISA JCB. ⅜
Meals (grill rest.) – **32 rm** 44.95 **t.**

✗✗ **Moreteyne Manor**, Woburn Rd, MK43 0NG, ℘ (01234) 767003, ㈜, « 16C moated manor house », ☞ – ⚡ 🅿. ⓴⓽ 🅰🅴 ⓪ VISA
closed 26 to 30 December – **Meals** (by arrangement Monday) 16.95/26.50 **t.** and a la carte ⅃ 5.00.

at Turvey W : 8 m. on A 428 – Y – ⊠ Bedford.

🏠 **Three Cranes** with rm, MK43 8EP, ℘ (01234) 881305 – ⚡ rm, 📺 🅿. 📺 ⓴⓽ 🅰🅴 VISA. ⅜
Meals (in bar) a la carte 11.20/16.95 **t.** ⅃ 5.50 – **4 rm** � 35.00/48.00 **t.**

🅰 ATS 3 London Rd ℘ (01234) 358838

BEER Devon **403** K 31 The West Country G. – pop. 1 415 – ⊠ Seaton.
Env. : Seaton (≤★★) N : ¾ m.
🅸🆂 Axe Cliff, Squires Lane, Axmouth, Seaton ℘ (01297) 24371.
London 170 – Exeter 22 – Taunton 28.

🏠 **Anchor Inn** with rm, Fore St., EX12 3ET, ℘ (01297) 20386, Fax (01297) 24474, ≤ – 📺. ⓴⓽ VISA JCB. ⅜
Meals a la carte 11.00/24.50 **t.** ⅃ 5.50 – **8 rm** ⊏ 50.00/65.00 **t.**

BEESTON Ches. **402 403 404** L 24 – pop. 196 – ⊠ Tarporley.
London 186 – Chester 15 – Liverpool 40 – Shrewsbury 32.

🏛 **Wild Boar**, Whitchurch Rd, CW6 9NW, on A 49 ℘ (01829) 260309, Fax (01829) 261081, « Part 17C timbered house » – ⚡ rm, 🍴 rest, 📺 ☎ ⅃ 🅿 – ⨜ 50. ⓴⓽ 🅰🅴 VISA
Meals 14.50/24.00 **st.** and a la carte ⅃ 5.50 – **37 rm** ⊏ 59.00/125.00 **st.** – SB.

BEESTON Notts. **402 403 404** Q 25 – see Nottingham.

BELFORD Northd. **401 402** O 17 – pop. 1 177.
London 335 – Edinburgh 71 – Newcastle upon Tyne 49.

🏛 **Blue Bell**, Market Pl., NE70 7NE, ℘ (01668) 213543, Fax (01668) 213787, ☞ – ⚡ rest, 📺 ☎ ⅃ 🅿. ⓴⓽ 🅰🅴 VISA
Meals (bar lunch Monday to Saturday)/dinner 21.00 **t.** and a la carte ⅃ 4.95 – **17 rm** ⊏ 44.00/96.00 **t.**

🏠 **Purdy Lodge**, Adderstone Services, NE70 7JU, on A 1 at junction with B 1341 ℘ (01668) 213000, Fax (01668) 213111 – 📺 ⅃ 🅿. ⓴⓽ 🅰🅴 ⓪ VISA
Meals (bar lunch)/dinner a la carte 9.55/23.55 ⅃ 4.95 – ⊏ 5.25 – **20 rm** 39.50 **st.**

BELLINGHAM Northd. **401 402** N 18 – pop. 1 164 – ⊠ Hexham.
🅸🆂 Boggle Hole ℘ (01434) 220530.
🄱 Main St., NE48 2BQ ℘ (01434) 220616.
London 315 – Carlisle 48 – Newcastle upon Tyne 33.

⌂ **Westfield House**, NE48 2DP, ℘ (01434) 220340, Fax (01434) 220340, ☞ – ⚡ 🅿. ⓴⓽ VISA. ⅜
Meals (by arrangement) (communal dining) 14.50 **s.** – **5 rm** ⊏ 40.00/52.00 **s.**

BELPER Derbs. **402 403 404** P 24 – pop. 18 213.
London 141 – Derby 8 – Manchester 55 – Nottingham 17.

🏛 **Makeney Hall Country House** ⌂, Makeney, Milford, DE56 0RS, S : 2 m. by A 6 on Makeney rd ℘ (01332) 842999, Fax (01332) 842777, ☞ – ⅃|, ⚡ rm, 📺 ☎ ⅃ 🅿 – ⨜ 180. ⓴⓽ 🅰🅴 ⓪ VISA JCB
Meals (closed Saturday lunch and Sunday dinner) 13.00/22.50 **st.** and a la carte – ⊏ 8.50 – **45 rm** 88.00/147.00 **st.** – SB.

BEPTON W. Sussex – see Midhurst.

BERKELEY *Glos.* **403 404** M 28 *Great Britain G. – pop. 1 550.*

See : *Berkeley Castle★★ AC.*

Exc. : *Wildfowl and Wetlands Trust, Slimbridge★ AC, NE : 6 ½ m. by B 4066 and A 38.*

London 129 – Bristol 20 – Cardiff 50 – Gloucester 18.

🏨 **Prince of Wales,** Berkeley Rd, GL13 9HD, NE : 2 ½ m. by B 4066 on A 38
℘ (01453) 810474, *Fax* (01453) 511370, ☞ – ⇔ rm, 📺 ☎ 🅿 – 🔬 200. 🆎 🆑 ① *VISA*
Meals (dinner only) 13.00 **st.** and a la carte ⅙ 6.20 – ⇌ 6.00 – **41 rm** 45.00/55.00 **st.** – SB.

🏠 **Old School House,** 34 Canonbury St., GL11 9BG, *℘* (01453) 811711, *Fax* (01453) 511761
– ⇔ rest, 📺 ☎ 🅿 🆎 *VISA* **JCB**
Meals 15.95 **t.** (dinner) and a la carte 13.70/15.95 **t.** ⅙ 4.40 – **7 rm** ⇌ 40.00/48.50 **st.**

BERKSWELL *W. Mids.* **403 404** P 26 – *see Coventry.*

BERWICK-UPON-TWEED *Northd.* **401 402** O 16 *Great Britain and Scotland G. – pop. 13 544.*

See : *Town★ - Walls★.*

Env. : *Foulden★, NW : 5 m. – Paxton House (Chippendale furniture★) AC, W : 5 m. by A 6105, A 1 and B 6461.*

Exc. : *St. Abb's Head★★ (≤★), NW : 12 m. by A 1, A 1107 and B 6438 – SW : Tweed Valley★★ – Eyemouth Museum★ AC, N : 7 ½ m. by A 1 and A 1107 – Holy Island★ (Priory ruins★ AC, Lindisfarne Castle★ AC), SE : 9 m. by A 1167 and A 1 – Manderston★ (stables★), W : 13 m. by A 6105 – Ladykirk (Kirk o'Steil★), SW : 8 ½ m. by A 698 and B 6470.*

🏌 *Goswick Beal ℘* (01289) 387256 – 🏌 *Magdalene Fields ℘* (01289) 306384.

🛈 *Castlegate Car Park, TD15 1JS ℘* (01289) 330733.

London 349 – Edinburgh 57 – Newcastle upon Tyne 63.

🏨 **Marshall Meadows Country House** 🌤, TD15 1UT, N : 2 ¾ m. by A 1
℘ (01289) 331133, *Fax* (01289) 331438, ☞, park, ※ – ⇔ rest, 📺 ☎ 🅿 – 🔬 180. 🆎 *VISA*
JCB
Meals 20.00 **t.** (dinner) and a la carte 13.00/25.70 **t.** ⅙ 6.00 – **18 rm** ⇌ 65.00/90.00 **t.**,
1 suite – SB.

⌂ **Harberton,** 181 Main St., Spittal, TD15 1RP, SE : 2 ¼ m. by A 1167 *℘* (01289) 308813, ≤,
☞ – ⇔ 📺 🅿
closed Christmas and New Year – **Meals** 10.00 – **5 rm** ⇌ 18.50/46.00.

🅰 ATS 78-80 Church St. *℘* (01289) 308222

BETHERSDEN *Kent* **404** W 30 – *pop. 1 341 – ⊠ Ashford.*
London 63 – Folkestone 20 – Maidstone 27.

⌂ **Little Hodgeham** 🌤 *without rest.,* Smarden Rd, TN26 3HE, W : 2 m. *℘* (01233) 850323,
« *15C cottage, antique furniture* », ☞ – 🅿. ※
mid March-August – **3 rm** ⇌ 45.50/71.00 **s.**

BEVERLEY *East Riding* **402** S 22 *Great Britain G. – pop. 23 632 – ⊠ Kingston-upon-Hull.*

See : *Town★ - Minster★★ – St. Mary's Church★.*

🏌 *The Westwood ℘* (01482) 867190.

🛈 *The Guildhall, Register Sq., HU17 9AU ℘* (01482) 867430.

London 188 – Kingston-upon-Hull 8 – Leeds 52 – York 29.

🏨 **Beverley Arms,** North Bar Within, HU17 8DD, *℘* (01482) 869241, *Fax* (01482) 870907 – 🛗
⇔ 📺 ☎ 🅿 – 🔬 70. 🆎 🆑 ① *VISA*
Meals 9.25/17.95 **st.** and a la carte ⅙ 6.00 – **57 rm** ⇌ 65.00/85.00 **st.** – SB.

🏠 **Lairgate,** 30 Lairgate, HU17 8EP, *℘* (01482) 882141, *Fax* (01482) 861067 – 📺 ☎ 🅿. 🆎
VISA
Meals 13.95 **t.** and a la carte ⅙ 5.00 – **22 rm** ⇌ 50.00/80.00 **st.** – SB.

XX **Cerutti 2,** Beverley Station, Station Sq., HU17 0AS, *℘* (01482) 866700 – 🅿. 🆎 *VISA*
closed Sunday, 1 week Christmas and Bank Holidays – **Meals** a la carte 16.45/21.75 **t.** ⅙ 5.00.

at Tickton NE : 3½ m. by A 1035 – ⊠ Kingston-upon-Hull.

🏨 **Tickton Grange,** HU17 9SH, on A 1035 *℘* (01964) 543666, *Fax* (01964) 542556, ☞ – 📺
☎ 🅿 – 🔬 80. 🆎 🆑 ① *VISA*
closed 26 to 30 December – **Meals** 14.50/19.50 **t.** – ⇌ 7.50 – **17 rm** 52.50/79.50 **t.** – SB.

at Walkington *SW : 3½ m. by A 164 – ✉ Beverley.*

🍴🍴🍴 **Manor House** ⚘ with rm, Northlands, Newbald Rd, HU17 8RT, NE : 1 m. by Northgate ☏ (01482) 881645, *Fax (01482) 866501,* « Late 19C house, conservatory », 🌳 – TV ☎ Ⓟ. MC VISA JCB. 🚫🐕
closed 25 December and Bank Holidays – **Meals** *(closed Sunday)* (dinner only) 17.50 **t.** and a la carte 🍷 8.50 – ☕ 8.50 – **7 rm** 70.00/100.00 **t.** – SB.

⚙ ATS 379 Grovehill Rd ☏ (01482) 868655

BEXHILL *E. Sussex* **404** V 31 – *pop. 38 905.*

⛳18 *Cooden Beach ☏ (01424) 842040* – ⛳18 *Highwoods, Ellerslie Lane ☏ (01424) 212625.*
ℹ *51 Marina, TN40 1BQ ☏ (01424) 732208.*
London 66 – Brighton 32 – Folkestone 42.

🏨 **Jarvis Cooden Beach,** Cooden Sea Rd, Cooden Beach, TN39 4TT, W : 2 m. on B 2182 ☏ (01424) 842281, *Fax (01424) 846142,* ≤, ≘s, 🏊, 🏊, 🌳 – 🚭 rm, TV ☎ Ⓟ – 👥 140. MC AE ⓓ VISA
Meals 12.75/15.95 **st.** and a la carte 🍷 4.50 – **41 rm** ☕ 75.00/99.00 – SB.

🍴 **Leet Lychgates,** 5a Church St., Old Town, TN40 2HE, ☏ (01424) 212193 – 🚭. MC VISA
closed Tuesday lunch, Sunday dinner, Monday and 25 December – **Meals** a la carte approx. 18.95 🍷 6.25.

BIBURY *Glos.* **403** **404** O 28 *Great Britain G. – pop. 570 – ✉ Cirencester.*

See : *Village*★.
London 86 – Gloucester 26 – Oxford 30.

🏨 **Swan,** GL7 5NW, ☏ (01285) 740695, *Fax (01285) 740473,* « Attractively furnished inn with gardens and trout stream », 🎣 – 🛗 🚭 TV ☎. MC AE VISA JCB. 🚫🐕
Meals (dinner only and Sunday lunch)/dinner 24.50 **st.** 🍷 10.00 – ***Jankowski's Brasserie :*** **Meals** a la carte 11.90/17.85 **st.** 🍷 10.00 – **18 rm** ☕ 109.00/220.00 **st.** – SB.

⌂ **Cotteswold House** without rest., Arlington, GL7 5ND, on B 4425 ☏ (01285) 740609, *Fax (01285) 740609* – 🚭 TV Ⓟ. 🚫🐕
3 rm ☕ 25.00/40.00.

BICKLEIGH *Devon* **403** J 31 *The West Country G. – pop. 3 595 – ✉ Tiverton.*

See : *Village*★★ *- Devonshire's Centre, Bickleigh Mill*★★ *AC – Bickleigh Castle*★ *AC.*
Env. : *– Knightshayes Court*★ *AC, N : 4 m. by A 396.*
Exc. : *Uffculme (Coldharbour Mill*★★ *AC) NE : 7 ½ m.*
⛳18 *Post Hill, Tiverton ☏ (01884) 252114.*
London 195 – Exeter 9 – Taunton 31.

🏠 **Fisherman's Cot,** EX16 8RW, on A 396 ☏ (01884) 855289, *Fax (01884) 855241,* « Riverside setting », 🎣, 🌳 – 🚭 rm, TV ☎ Ⓟ. MC AE VISA
Meals (carving lunch)/dinner a la carte 12.20/17.40 **t.** – **21 rm** ☕ 46.00/66.00 **t.** – SB.

🏠 **Bickleigh Cottage,** Bickleigh Bridge, EX16 8RJ, on A 396 ☏ (01884) 855230, « Part 17C thatched cottage, riverside setting », 🌳 – 🚭 rest, Ⓟ. MC VISA. 🚫🐕
April-October – **Meals** (residents only) (dinner only) 11.50 🍷 3.75 – **8 rm** ☕ 22.50/47.50.

BICKLEY MOSS *Ches.* **402** **404** L 24 – *✉ Malpas.*

London 180 – Birmingham 63 – Chester 16 – Shrewsbury 27 – Stoke-on-Trent 25.

🍴 **Cholmondeley Arms** with rm, Cholmondeley, SY14 8BT, N : 1 ½ m. on A 49 ☏ (01829) 720300, *Fax (01829) 720123,* « Converted schoolhouse », 🌳 – TV ☎ Ⓟ. MC VISA
Meals *(closed 25 December)* a la carte 10.45/19.20 **t.** – ☕ 7.50 – **6 rm** 35.00/41.00 **t.** – SB.

BIDEFORD *Devon* **403** H 30 *The West Country G. – pop. 14 326.*

See : *Bridge*★★ *– Burton Art Gallery*★ *AC.*
Env. : *Appledore*★, *N : 2 m.*
Exc. : *Clovelly*★★, *W : 11 m. by A 39 and B 3237 – Lundy Island*★★, *NW : by ferry – Rosemoor*★ *– Great Torrington (Dartington Crystal*★ *AC) SE : 7½ m. by A 386.*
⛳18 *Royal North Devon, Golf Links Rd, Westward Ho ☏ (01237) 473824* – ⛳9 *Torrington, Weare Trees ☏ (01805) 622229.*
⛴ *to Lundy Island (Lundy Co. Ltd) (2 h 15 mn).*
ℹ *Victoria Park, The Quay, EX39 2QQ ☏ (01237) 477676.*
London 231 – Exeter 43 – Plymouth 58 – Taunton 60.

🏛 **Yeoldon House** ⬧, Durrant Lane, EX39 2RL, N : 1 ½ m. by B 3235 off A 386
🖉 (01237) 474400, Fax (01237) 476618, ≤, 🍽, park – 🍽 rest, 📺 ☎ 🅿. 🐠 🖭 ⓞ 𝘝𝘐𝘚𝘈
closed 24 December-2 January – **Meals** (dinner only and Sunday lunch)/dinner
a la carte 14.50/23.70 **t.** ⓘ 6.50 – **10 rm** ⭤ 42.00/95.00 **t.**

🏛 **Newbridge,** Heywood Rd, Northam, EX39 3QA, N : 1 ¼ m. by B 3235 on A 386
🖉 (01237) 474989, Fax (01237) 474989 – 🍽 rest, 📺 ☎ 🅿. 🐠 𝘝𝘐𝘚𝘈. �️
Meals (closed Sunday dinner to non-residents) (dinner only and Sunday lunch)/dinner
14.95 **st.** and a la carte ⓘ 4.50 – **10 rm** ⭤ 35.00/70.00 **t.** – SB.

at Instow N : 3 m. by A 386 on B 3233 – ⊠ Bideford.

🏢 **Commodore,** Marine Par., EX39 4JN, 🖉 (01271) 860347, Fax (01271) 861233, ≤ Taw and
Torridge estuaries, 🍽 – 📺 ☎ 🅿 – 🔏 200. 🐠 🖭 ⓞ 𝘝𝘐𝘚𝘈. �️
closed 24 to 27 December – **Meals** 11.00/18.00 **t.** and a la carte ⓘ 4.00 – **20 rm** ⭤ 50.00/
100.00 – SB.

at Eastleigh NE : 2½ m. by A 386 (via Old Barnstaple Rd) – ⊠ Bideford.

🏠 **Pines,** EX39 4PA, 🖉 (01271) 860561, Fax (01271) 861248, ≤, 🍽 – 🍽 📺 ☎ 🅿. 🐠 𝘝𝘐𝘚𝘈
closed November – **Meals** (by arrangement) 14.00 **st.** ⓘ 3.50 – **7 rm** ⭤ 40.00/75.00 **st.** – SB.

🅰 ATS New Rd 🖉 (01237) 472451

BIGBURY-ON-SEA Devon 403 I 33 – pop. 600 – ⊠ Kingsbridge.
London 196 – Exeter 42 – Plymouth 17.

🏛 **Henley** ⬧, Folly Hill, TQ7 4AR, 🖉 (01548) 810240, Fax (01548) 810020, ≤ Bigbury Bay and
Bolt Tail, 🍽 – 🍽 📺 ☎ 🅿. 🐠 🖭 𝘝𝘐𝘚𝘈
April-October – **Meals** (residents only) (dinner only) 16.50 ⓘ 4.75 – **7 rm** ⭤ 34.00/64.00 **st.** –
SB.

BIGGLESWADE Beds. 404 T 27 – pop. 12 350.
London 44 – Bedford 11 – Cambridge 23 – Peterborough 37.

🏛 **Stratton House,** London Rd, SG18 8ED, 🖉 (01767) 312442, Fax (01767) 600416 – ▤ rest,
📺 ☎ 🅿 – 🔏 40. 🐠 🖭 𝘝𝘐𝘚𝘈
Meals a la carte 8.50/22.00 **st.** ⓘ 4.50 – **31 rm** ⭤ 44.00/65.00 **st.**

BILBROOK Somerset 403 J 30 The West Country G. – ⊠ Minehead.
Env. : Washford – Cleeve Abbey★★ AC, E : 1 m. by A 39 – Dunster★★ – Castle★★ AC (upper
rooms ≤★) Water Mill★ AC, St. George's Church★, Dovecote★, NW : 3 m. by A 39.
London 179 – Bristol 56 – Minehead 7 – Taunton 17.

🍴 **Dragon House** with rm, TA24 6HQ, on A 39 🖉 (01984) 640215, Fax (01984) 641340,
« Part 18C », 🍽 – 📺 ☎ 🅿. 🐠 🖭 𝘝𝘐𝘚𝘈
Meals (lunch by arrangement) a la carte 13.25/22.90 **t.** – **9 rm** ⭤ 30.00/46.00 **t.**

BILBROUGH N. Yorks. 402 Q 22 – see York.

BILLESLEY Warks. – see Stratford-upon-Avon.

BILLINGSHURST W. Sussex 404 S 30 – pop. 4 980.
London 44 – Brighton 24 – Guildford 25 – Portsmouth 40.

🏛 **Travelodge,** Five Oaks, Staines St., RH14 9AE, N : 1 m. on A 29 🖉 (01403) 782711,
Reservations (Freephone) 0800 850950 – 🍽 rm, 📺 🔥 🅿. 🐠 🖭 ⓞ 𝘝𝘐𝘚𝘈 𝗝𝗖𝗕. �️
26 rm 44.95 **t.**

🏠 **Old Wharf** ⬧ without rest., Wharf Farm, Newbridge, RH14 0JG, W : 1 ¾ m. on A 272
🖉 (01403) 784096, Fax (01403) 784096, ≤, « Restored canalside warehouse », ⬧, 🍽, park,
🌳 – 🍽 📺 🅿. 🐠 🖭 𝘝𝘐𝘚𝘈. �️
closed 10 days Christmas-New Year – **4 rm** ⭤ 40.00/70.00 **st.**

🍴🍴 **Gables,** Pulborough Rd, Parbrook, RH14 9EU, S : ½ m. on A 29 🖉 (01403) 782571,
Fax (01403) 784094, « 15C timbered house » – 🅿. 🐠 🖭 𝘝𝘐𝘚𝘈
closed Sunday dinner, Monday and 25 December – **Meals** (dinner only and Sunday lunch)/
dinner 23.00 **t.** ⓘ 7.50.

BILSBURROW Lancs. – see Garstang.

BINBROOK Lincs. 402 404 T 23 – pop. 1 605.
London 162 – Great Grimsby 10 – Lincoln 26 – Scunthorpe 32.

⌂ **Hoe Hill,** Swinhope, LN8 6HX, NE : 1 m. on B 1203 ℰ (01472) 398206, ⇙ – ⁕ **₽**. ⅋
closed January – **Meals** (by arrangement) (communal dining) 14.00 – **4 rm** ⊇ 18.00/
50.00 **s**.

BINGHAM Notts. 402 404 R 25 – pop. 7 057.
London 125 – Lincoln 28 – Nottingham 11 – Sheffield 35.

🏠 **Yeung Sing,** Market St., NG13 8AB, ℰ (01949) 831831, Fax (01949) 838833 – ⬚ 📺 ☎ **₽**.
🆔 AE VISA. ⅋
closed 25 and 26 December – **Meals** – (see below) – **15 rm** ⊇ 39.00/50.00 **t**.

✗✗ **Yeung Sing** (at Yeung Sing H.), Market St., NG13 8AB, ℰ (01949) 831222,
Fax (01949) 838833 – ▤ **₽**. 🆔 AE VISA
closed 25 and 26 December – **Meals** - Chinese (Canton) - (dinner only and Sunday lunch)/
dinner 18.00 **t**. and a la carte.

🔟 ATS 1 Moorbridge Rd ℰ (01949) 837717

BINGLEY W. Yorks. 402 O 22 – pop. 19 585 – ✉ Bradford.
🏌 St. Ives Est. ℰ (01274) 562436.
London 204 – Bradford 6 – Skipton 13.

🏨 **Jarvis Bankfield,** Bradford Rd, BD16 1TU, SE : 1 ½ m. on A 650 ℰ (01274) 567123,
Fax (01274) 551331, ⇙ – ⬚, ⁕ rm, ▤ rest, 📺 ☎ & **₽** – ⛟ 200. 🆔 AE ⓞ VISA JCB.
Meals (carving rest.) (bar lunch Saturday) 9.95/16.95 **st**. and a la carte – ⊇ 8.50 – **103 rm**
82.00/92.00 **t**. – SB.

🏠 **Five Rise Locks,** Beck Lane, BD16 4DD, ℰ (01274) 565296, Fax (01274) 568828, ⇙ – ⁕
📺 ☎ **₽**. 🆔 VISA JCB. ⅋
closed Christmas and New Year – **Meals** (residents only) (dinner only) 12.50 **st**. ⚬ 3.00 – **9 rm**
⊇ 46.00/55.00 **t**. – SB.

⌂ **Holroyd House** ⅏ without rest., Beck Rd, Micklethwaite, BD16 3JN, N : 1 ¾ m. by A 650
and Micklethwaite Lane ℰ (01274) 562464, ⸜, ⇙ – ⁕ 📺 **₽**. ⅋
3 rm ⊇ 18.00/36.00 **s**.

✗ **Christophers',** 7-9 Chapel Lane, BD16 2NG, ℰ (01274) 510742 – 🆔 ⓞ VISA JCB
closed Sunday, Monday, 1 week August and 1 week January – **Meals** 10.95/11.95 **st**.
and a la carte ⚬ 6.45.

BINHAM Norfolk 404 W 25 – pop. 281 – ✉ Fakenham.
London 123 – Cambridge 75 – King's Lynn 31 – Norwich 29.

⌂ **Field House** ⅏, Walsingham Rd, NR21 0BU, SW : 1 ½ m. on B 1388 ℰ (01328) 830639,
« Georgian farmhouse », ⇙ – ⁕ 📺 **₽**. ⅋
closed 24 to 26 December – **Meals** (by arrangement) 15.00 **s**. – **3 rm** ⊇ 34.00/52.00 **s**. – SB

BINLEY W. Mids. – see Coventry.

BINTON Warks. – see Stratford-upon-Avon.

BIRCHINGTON Kent 404 X 29 – pop. 9 859.
London 71 – Dover 20 – Maidstone 40 – Margate 5.

🏠 **Crown Inn (Cherry Brandy House),** Ramsgate Rd, Sarre, CT7 0LF, SW : 4 m. on A 28
ℰ (01843) 847808, Fax (01843) 847914, ⇙ – 📺 ☎ & **₽**. 🆔 AE ⓞ
Meals (bar lunch Monday to Saturday)/dinner 15.00 **t**. and a la carte ⚬ 5.50 – **12 rm**
⊇ 43.50/66.75 **t**. – SB.

BIRCH SERVICE AREA Gtr. Manchester 402 ㉒ 403 ③ 404 ⑩ – ✉ Heywood (Lancs.).

🏠 **Travelodge** without rest., OL10 2HQ, on M 62 between junctions 18 and 19
ℰ (0161) 655 3403, Fax (0161) 655 3358, Reservations (Freephone) 0800 850950 – ⁕ 📺 ☎
& **₽**. 🆔 AE ⓞ VISA JCB. ⅋
55 rm 46.95 **t**.

🏠 **Travelodge** without rest., OL10 2HQ, M 62 (westbound) between junctions 18 and 19
ℰ (0161) 643 9419, Reservations (Freephone) 0800 850950 – ⁕ 📺 ☎ & **₽**. 🆔 AE ⓞ VISA
JCB. ⅋
35 rm 46.95 **t**.

BIRDLIP _Glos._ 🗺️ N 28 _Great Britain G._ – ✉️ _Gloucester._
Env. : _Crickley Hill Country Park_ (≤★) _N : 1½ m. by B 4070 and A 417._
London 107 – Bristol 51 – Gloucester 9 – Oxford 44 – Swindon 24.

🏨 **Royal George**, GL4 8JH, ℘ (01452) 862506, Fax (01452) 862277, 🌳 – ⇔ rm, 📺 ☎ 🅿 –
🔚 100. 🆗 ⁂ ① _VISA_. ⁒
Meals (dinner only) 16.95 **st.** and a la carte ⅛ 4.50 – **34 rm** ⊆ 59.50/78.00 **st.** – SB.

✗ **Kingshead House**, GL4 8JH, ℘ (01452) 862299 – 🅿. 🆗 ⁂ ① _VISA_
closed Saturday lunch, Sunday dinner, Monday, 25-27 December and 1 January – **Meals**
a la carte 17.50/29.00 **t.** ⅛ 6.50.

BIRKENHEAD _Mersey._ 🗺️ K 23 – _pop. 93 087._
🏌️ _Arrowe Park, Woodchurch_ ℘ (0151) 677 1527 – 🏌️ _Prenton, Golf Links Rd, Prenton_
℘ (0151) 608 1461.
Mersey Tunnels (toll).
⛴️ to _Liverpool and Wallasey (Mersey Ferries)._
🛈 _Woodside Visitors Centre, Woodside Ferry Terminal, L41 6DU_ ℘ (0151) 647 6780.
London 222 – Liverpool 2.

Plan : see Liverpool p. 3

🏨 **Bowler Hat**, 2 Talbot Rd, Oxton, L43 2HH, ℘ (0151) 652 4931, Fax (0151) 653 8127, 🌳 –
📺 ☎ 🅿 – 🔚 200. 🆗 ⁂ ① _VISA_
Meals (bar lunch Saturday and Bank Holidays) 13.50 **st.** and a la carte ⅛ 5.50 – ⊆ 8.50 –
32 rm 65.00/90.00 **st.** – SB.

✗ **Beadles**, 15 Rosemount, Oxton, L43 5SG, ℘ (0151) 653 9010 – ⇔. 🆗 _VISA_ _JCB_
closed Sunday to Tuesday, 2 weeks February and 2 weeks August-September – **Meals**
(dinner only) a la carte approx. 22.00 **t.** ⅛ 5.50.

🔧 ATS 40 Mill Lane, Wallasey, Wirral ℘ (0151) 638 1949/8606

BIRMINGHAM

W. Mids. **403 404** O 26 *Great Britain G. – pop. 965 928.*

London 122 – Bristol 91 – Liverpool 103 – Manchester 86 – Nottingham 50.

TOURIST INFORMATION

🖬 *Convention & Visitor Bureau, 2 City Arcade, B2 4TX* ℰ *(0121) 643 2514, Fax (0121) 616 1038*
🖬 *Convention & Visitor Bureau, National Exhibition Centre, B40 1NT* ℰ *(0121) 780 4321*
🖬 *Birmingham Airport, Information Desk, B26 3QJ* ℰ *(0121) 767 7145/7146.*

PRACTICAL INFORMATION

🖥 *Edgbaston, Church Road* ℰ *(0121) 454 1736,* FX.
🖥 *Hilltop, Park Lane, Handsworth* ℰ *(0121) 554 4463,* CU.
🖥 *Hatchford Brook, Coventry Road, Sheldon* ℰ *(0121) 743 9821.*
🖥 *Brand Hall, Heron Road, Oldbury, Warley* ℰ *(0121) 552 2195,* BU.
🖥 *Harborne Church Farm, Vicarage Road, Harborne* ℰ *(0121) 427 1204,* EX.
✈ *Birmingham International Airport :* ℰ *(0121) 767 5511, E : 6½ m. by A 45* DU.

SIGHTS

See : *City★ – Museum and Art Gallery★★* JZ **M2** *– Barber Institute of Fine Arts★★ (at Birmingham University)* EX *– Cathedral of St. Philip (stained glass portrayals★)* KYZ.
Env. : *Aston Hall★★* FV **M.**
Exc. : *Black Country Museum★ , Dudley, NW : 10 m. by A 456 and A 4123* AU.

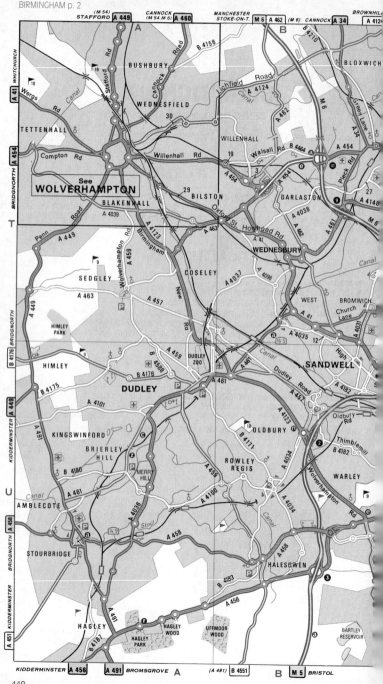

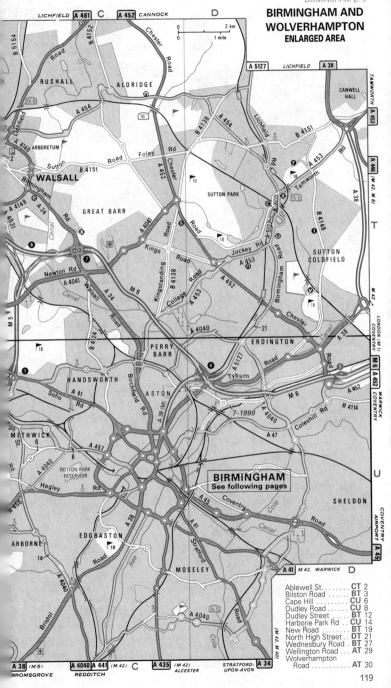

BIRMINGHAM AND WOLVERHAMPTON
ENLARGED AREA

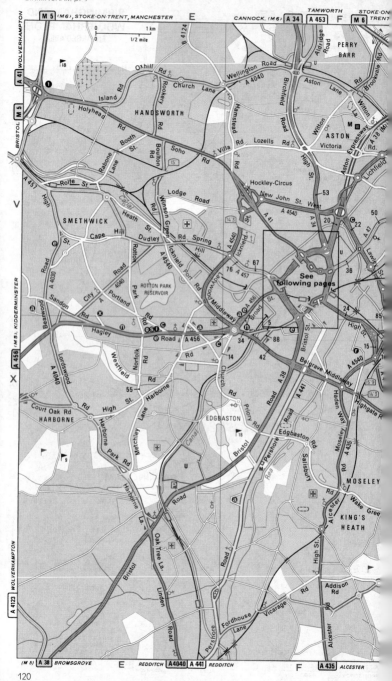

See following pages

BUILT UP AREA

For Street Index
see Birmingham p. 7

121

CENTRE

«**Short Breaks**»
Many hotels now offer a special rate for a stay of 2 nights
which includes dinner, bed and breakfast.

STREET INDEX TO BIRMINGHAM TOWN PLANS

«Short Breaks» (SB)
De nombreux hôtels proposent des conditions avantageuses
pour un séjour de deux nuits comprenant la chambre, le dîner et le petit déjeuner.

Town plans : Birmingham pp. 2-7
Except where otherwise stated see pp. 6 and 7

Hyatt Regency, 2 Bridge St., B1 2JZ, ℰ (0121) 643 1234, Fax (0121) 616 2323, ≤, 16, ≦s, ☒ – |\$|, ⫯⫯ rm, ☰ ⊡ ☎ ⇔ – 🛦 250. ⬤❸ 🖭 ⓪ 𝘝𝘐𝘚𝘈, ⫯⫯
Meals – (see **Number 282** below) – ☲ 12.00 – **308 rm** 155.00/180.00 st., 11 suites.
JZ a

Swallow, 12 Hagley Rd, B16 8SJ, ℰ (0121) 452 1144, Fax (0121) 456 3442, ☒ – |\$|, ⫯⫯ rm, ☰ ⊡ ☎ & 🅿 – 🛦 25. ⬤❸ 🖭 ⓪ 𝘝𝘐𝘚𝘈
p. 4 FX c
Langtrys : Meals (closed Sunday) a la carte 24.15/30.00 t. ⫯ 8.50 – (see also **Sir Edward Elgar's** below) – **94 rm** ☲ 150.00/190.00 st., 4 suites – SB.

Holiday Inn Crowne Plaza, Central Sq., Holliday St., B1 1HH, ℰ (0121) 631 2000, Fax (0121) 643 9018, 16, ≦s, ☒ – |\$|, ⫯⫯ rm, ☰ ⊡ ☎ & 🅿 – 🛦 150. ⬤❸ 🖭 ⓪ 𝘝𝘐𝘚𝘈 𝗝𝗖𝗕. ⫯⫯
JZ z
Meals (closed Saturday lunch) (carving lunch) 15.95/19.50 st. and dinner a la carte ⫯ 9.00 – ☲ 11.95 – **281 rm** 135.00/145.00 st., 3 suites – SB.

Copthorne, Paradise Circus, B3 3HJ, ℰ (0121) 200 2727, Fax (0121) 200 1197, 16, ≦s, ☒ – |\$|, ⫯⫯ rm, ☰ rest, ⊡ ☎ 🅿 – 🛦 180. ⬤❸ 🖭 ⓪ 𝘝𝘐𝘚𝘈. ⫯⫯
JZ e
Meals 21.95 st. (dinner) and a la carte 13.85/25.70 st. – ☲ 11.75 – **209 rm** 120.00/150.00 st., 3 suites – SB.

Jonathan's, 16-24 Wolverhampton Rd, Oldbury, B68 0LH, W : 4 m. by A 456 ℰ (0121) 429 3757, Fax (0121) 434 3107, « Authentic Victorian furnishings and memorabilia » – ⫯⫯ rest, ⊡ ☎ 🅿. ⬤❸ 🖭 ⓪ 𝘝𝘐𝘚𝘈
p. 2 BU e
Meals - English - (closed Sunday dinner) 15.90 t. and a la carte ⫯ 6.75 – **21 rm** ☲ 75.00/85.00 st., 11 suites 125.00 st. – SB.

The Burlington, 6 Burlington Arcade, 126 New St., B2 4JQ, ℰ (0121) 643 9191, Fax (0121) 643 5075, 16, ≦s – |\$|, ⫯⫯ rm, ☰ rest, ⊡ ☎ – 🛦 450. ⬤❸ 🖭 ⓪ 𝘝𝘐𝘚𝘈
KY a
closed 25 December – **Berlioz : Meals** (closed lunch Saturday and Sunday) 17.95 st. and a la carte ⫯ 6.50 – ☲ 10.95 – **107 rm** 105.00/115.00 st., 5 suites – SB.

Grand, Colmore Row, B3 2DA, ℰ (0121) 607 9988, Fax (0121) 233 1465 – |\$|, ⫯⫯ rm, ☰ rest, ⊡ ☎ – 🛦 500. ⬤❸ 🖭 ⓪ 𝘝𝘐𝘚𝘈 𝗝𝗖𝗕
JKY c
Meals 12.00/14.50 st. and a la carte. ⫯ 8.00 – ☲ 10.50 – **170 rm** 110.00/135.00 st., 2 suites – SB.

Plough and Harrow, 135 Hagley Rd, Edgbaston, B16 8LS, ℰ (0121) 454 4111, Fax (0121) 454 1868, ☞ – |\$| ⫯⫯ ⊡ ☎ 🅿 – 🛦 70. ⬤❸ 🖭 ⓪ 𝘝𝘐𝘚𝘈 𝗝𝗖𝗕. ⫯⫯
p. 4 EX a
Meals (closed Saturday lunch) a la carte 18.40/26.70 st. ⫯ 6.45 – ☲ 9.25 – **42 rm** 85.00/100.00 st., 2 suites – SB.

Forte Posthouse Birmingham City, Smallbrook, Queensway, B5 4EW, ℰ (0121) 643 8171, Fax (0121) 631 2528, 16, ≦s, ☒, squash – |\$|, ⫯⫯ rm, ☰ ⊡ ☎ 🅿 – 🛦 630. ⬤❸ 🖭 ⓪ 𝘝𝘐𝘚𝘈 𝗝𝗖𝗕
KZ o
Meals 12.95/16.25 t. and a la carte ⫯ 8.85 – ☲ 9.95 – **252 rm** 94.00 st., 1 suite – SB.

Strathallan Thistle, 225 Hagley Rd, Edgbaston, B16 9RY, ℰ (0121) 455 9777, Fax (0121) 454 9432 – |\$|, ⫯⫯ rm, ☰ rest, ⊡ ☎ 🅿 – 🛦 170. ⬤❸ 🖭 ⓪ 𝘝𝘐𝘚𝘈 𝗝𝗖𝗕. ⫯⫯
p. 4 EX i
Meals (closed Saturday lunch) 17.25 st. (dinner) and a la carte 15.50/27.45 st. ⫯ 5.85 – ☲ 10.50 – **148 rm** 97.00/131.00 st., 3 suites – SB.

Apollo, 243 Hagley Rd, Edgbaston, B16 9RA, ℰ (0121) 455 0271, Fax (0121) 456 2394 – |\$|, ⫯⫯ rm, ☰ rest, ⊡ ☎ 🅿 – 🛦 150. ⬤❸ 🖭 ⓪ 𝘝𝘐𝘚𝘈 𝗝𝗖𝗕
p. 4 EX o
Meals (closed Saturday lunch) (carving lunch) 12.95/14.95 st. and a la carte ⫯ 5.50 – ☲ 9.50 – **124 rm** 75.00/105.00 st., 2 suites – SB.

Quality Norfolk, 267 Hagley Rd, B16 9NA, ℰ (0121) 454 8071, Fax (0121) 455 6149 – |\$|, ⫯⫯ rm, ☰ rest, ⊡ ☎ & 🅿 – 🛦 100. ⬤❸ 🖭 ⓪ 𝘝𝘐𝘚𝘈
p. 4 EX n
Meals (closed Sunday lunch) (carving rest.) 8.50/15.00 st. and dinner a la carte ⫯ 6.00 – **166 rm** ☲ 59.50/69.50 st. – SB.

Novotel, 70 Broad St., B1 2HT, ℰ (0121) 643 2000, Fax (0121) 643 9796, 16, ≦s – |\$|, ⫯⫯ rm, ☰ rest, ⊡ ☎ & 🅿 – 🛦 250. ⬤❸ 🖭 ⓪ 𝘝𝘐𝘚𝘈. ⫯⫯
p. 4 FV e
Meals 15.00 st. and a la carte ⫯ 5.75 – ☲ 8.95 – **148 rm** 79.00/85.00 st.

Chamberlain, Alcester St., B12 0PJ, ℰ (0121) 606 9000, Fax (0121) 606 9001 – |\$| ⫯⫯, ☰ rest, ⊡ ☎ ⇔ – 🛦 400. ⬤❸ 🖭 ⓪ 𝘝𝘐𝘚𝘈 𝗝𝗖𝗕. ⫯⫯
p. 4 FX r
Meals (closed Saturday lunch) (carving rest.) 6.00/10.00 st. – **250 rm** ☲ 35.00/80.00 st.

Asquith House, 19 Portland Rd, off Hagley Rd, Edgbaston, B16 9HN, ℰ (0121) 454 5282, Fax (0121) 456 4668, « Attractive furnishings », ☞ – ⫯⫯ ⊡ ☎. ⬤❸ 🖭 𝘝𝘐𝘚𝘈
closed 25-26 December and 1 January – **Meals** (by arrangement Saturday and Sunday) 15.95/25.95 st. and a la carte ⫯ 4.50 – **10 rm** ☲ 70.00/83.00 t.
p. 4 EX c

Westbourne Lodge, 27-29 Fountain Rd, Edgbaston, B17 8NJ, ℰ (0121) 429 1003, Fax (0121) 429 7436, ☞ – ⫯⫯ rm, ⊡ ☎ 🅿. ⬤❸ 🖭 𝘝𝘐𝘚𝘈 𝗝𝗖𝗕
p. 4 EV x
Meals (bar lunch)/dinner 14.95 t. ⫯ 5.50 – **18 rm** ☲ 48.00/58.00 t.

Copperfield House, 60 Upland Rd, Selly Park, B29 7JS, ℰ (0121) 472 8344, Fax (0121) 415 5655, ⌕ – ⇔ rest, ⊡ ☎ ℗. ⓪ ⒶⒺ ⓋⒾⓈⒶ   p. 4 FX a
Meals (closed Sunday dinner) (bar lunch)/dinner 16.95 t. ⓵ 5.00 – **17 rm** ⌷ 52.50/72.50 t. – SB.

Bearwood Court, 360-366 Bearwood Rd, Bearwood, B66 4ET, ℰ (0121) 429 9731, Fax (0121) 429 6175 – ⊡ ☎ ℗. ⓪ ⓋⒾⓈⒶ ⒿⒸⒷ. ⅍   p. 4 EV e
closed 25 December – **Meals** (closed Saturday and Sunday dinner) 6.50/12.50 st. and a la carte ⓵ 5.00 – **24 rm** ⌷ 35.00/50.00 st.

Travel Inn, Richard St., Waterlinks, B7 4AA, ℰ (0121) 333 6484, Fax (0121) 333 6490 – ⁅§⁆ ⇔, ▤ rest, ⊡ ⅚ ℗. ⓪ ⒶⒺ ⓪ ⓋⒾⓈⒶ. ⅍   p. 4 FV c
Meals (grill rest.) – **60 rm** 36.50 t.

Travel Inn, 20-22 Bridge St., B1 2JH, ℰ (0121) 633 4820, Fax (0121) 633 4779 – ⁅§⁆ ⇔ rm, ⊡ ⅚ ℗ – ⚏ 40. ⓪ ⒶⒺ ⓪ ⓋⒾⓈⒶ. ⅍   JZ c
Meals (grill rest.) – **54 rm** 36.50 t.

Quality Cobden, 166-174 Hagley Rd, Edgbaston, B16 9NZ, ℰ (0121) 454 6621, Fax (0121) 456 2935, ℔, ⇌, ▨, ⌕ – ⁅§⁆, ⇔ rm, ⊡ ☎ ℗ – ⚏ 100. ⓪ ⒶⒺ ⓪ ⓋⒾⓈⒶ   p. 4 EX e
Meals 10.00/15.00 st. and dinner a la carte ⓵ 6.00 – ⌷ 8.75 – **230 rm** 59.50/69.50 st. – SB.

Hagley Court, 229 Hagley Rd, Edgbaston, B16 9RP, ℰ (0121) 454 6514, Fax (0121) 456 2722 – ⊡ ☎ ℗. ⓪ ⒶⒺ ⓪ ⓋⒾⓈⒶ ⒿⒸⒷ. ⅍   p. 4 EX s
closed 24 December-2 January – **Meals** (closed Friday to Sunday) (dinner only) 15.00 st. and a la carte ⓵ 6.50 – **27 rm** ⌷ 45.00/68.00 st.

Campanile, 55 Irving St., B1 1DH, ℰ (0121) 622 4925, Fax (0121) 622 4195 – ⇔ rm, ⊡ ☎ ⅚ ℗ – ⚏ 35. ⓪ ⒶⒺ ⓪ ⓋⒾⓈⒶ ⒿⒸⒷ   p. 4 FX e
Meals (grill rest.) 10.55 st. and a la carte ⓵ 6.60 – ⌷ 4.50 – **46 rm** 38.00 st.

Travelodge without rest., 230 Broad St., B15 1AY, ℰ (0121) 644 5266, Fax (0121) 644 5251, Reservations (Freephone) 0800 850950 – ⁅§⁆ ⇔ ⊡ ☎ ⅚ ℗. ⓪ ⒶⒺ ⓪ ⓋⒾⓈⒶ ⒿⒸⒷ. ⅍   p. 4 FV n
136 rm 49.95 t.

XXXX **Sir Edward Elgar's** (at Swallow H.), 12 Hagley Rd, B16 8SJ, ℰ (0121) 452 1144, Fax (0121) 456 3442 – ▤ ℗. ⓪ ⒶⒺ ⓪ ⓋⒾⓈⒶ   p. 4 FX c
closed Saturday lunch – **Meals** 21.50/27.00 t. and a la carte ⓵ 8.50.

XX **Leftbank,** 79 Broad St., B15 1QA, ℰ (0121) 643 4464, Fax (0121) 643 4464 – ⓪ ⒶⒺ ⓪ ⓋⒾⓈⒶ ⒿⒸⒷ   p. 4 FV a
closed Saturday lunch, Sunday, 25 December-10 January and Bank Holidays – **Meals** 14.50 t. (lunch) and dinner a la carte 20.30/30.50 t. ⓵ 6.50.

XX **Number 282** (at Hyatt Regency H.), 2 Bridge St., B1 2JZ, ℰ (0121) 643 1234, Fax (0121) 616 2323 – ▤ ⇎. ⓪ ⒶⒺ ⓪ ⓋⒾⓈⒶ   JZ a
closed Saturday – **Meals** 16.00/17.00 st.

XX **Shimla Pinks,** 214 Broad St., B15 1AY, ℰ (0121) 633 0366, Fax (0121) 633 0366 – ▤. ⓪ ⒶⒺ ⓪ ⓋⒾⓈⒶ   p. 4 FX n
closed lunch Saturday and Sunday, 25 December and 1 January – **Meals** - Indian - 6.95/19.95 t. and a la carte ⓵ 6.95.

XX **Henry's,** 27 St. Paul's Sq., B3 1RB, ℰ (0121) 200 1136, Fax (0121) 200 1190 – ▤. ⓪ ⒶⒺ ⓪ ⓋⒾⓈⒶ   JY a
Meals - Chinese (Canton) - 15.00 t. and a la carte ⓵ 7.00.

XX **Dynasty,** 93-103 Hurst St., B5 4TE, ℰ (0121) 622 1410, Fax (0121) 622 1410 – ⓪ ⒶⒺ ⓪ ⓋⒾⓈⒶ ⒿⒸⒷ   KZ e
closed Christmas and Bank Holidays – **Meals** - Chinese - (lunch by arrangement)/dinner a la carte 14.00/24.00 t.

XX **Maharaja,** 23-25 Hurst St., B5 4AS, ℰ (0121) 622 2641, Fax (0121) 662 4021 – ▤. ⓪ ⒶⒺ ⓪ ⓋⒾⓈⒶ   KZ i
closed Sunday and Bank Holidays – **Meals** - North Indian - a la carte 9.00/11.85 t. ⓵ 6.25.

XX **Franzl's,** 151 Milcote Rd, Bearwood, Smethwick, B67 5BN, ℰ (0121) 429 7920, Fax (0121) 429 1615 – ⓪ ⒶⒺ ⓪ ⓋⒾⓈⒶ ⒿⒸⒷ   p. 4 EV a
closed Sunday, Monday and August – **Meals** - Austrian - (dinner only) 13.45/19.45 t. ⓵ 5.15.

at Hall Green SE : 5¾ m. by A 41 on A 34 – ⊠ Birmingham.

🏠🏠 **Robin Hood,** Stratford Rd, B28 9ES, ℰ (0121) 745 9900, Fax (0121) 733 1075 – ⇔ ⊡ ☎ ℗. ⓪ ⒶⒺ ⓋⒾⓈⒶ   GX a
closed 1 week Christmas – **Meals** (grill rest.) a la carte approx. 12.20 st. ⓵ 4.95 – **30 rm** ⌷ 70.00/85.00 st. – SB.

at Birmingham Airport SE : 9 m. by A 45 – DU – ⊠ Birmingham.

🏨 **Novotel,** Passenger Terminal, B26 3QL, ℰ (0121) 782 7000, Fax (0121) 782 0445 – 🛗, ✳rm, 🍴 rest, 📺 ☎ ৬ – 🕰 35. 🐵 🆎 ① 𝘝𝘐𝘚𝘈
closed 25 December – Meals 8.00/16.00 st. and a la carte ₪ 5.55 – ⚏ 8.75 – **195 rm** 88.00 st. – SB.

🏨 **Forte Posthouse Birmingham Airport,** Coventry Rd, B26 3QW, on A 45 ℰ (0121) 782 8141, Fax (0121) 782 2476 – ✳rm, 📺 ☎ 🅿 – 🕰 130. 🐵 🆎 ① 𝘝𝘐𝘚𝘈 ᴶᶜᴮ
Meals a la carte 18.10/25.40 st. – ⚏ 9.95 – **136 rm** 79.00 st. – SB.

at National Exhibition Centre SE : 9½ m. on A 45 – DU – ⊠ Birmingham.

🏨 **Birmingham Metropole,** Bickenhill, B40 1PP, ℰ (0121) 780 4242, Fax (0121) 780 3923, Ⅰᵇ, ⛱, ☒ – 🛗, ✳rm, 🍴 📺 ☎ ৬ 🅿 – 🕰 2000. 🐵 🆎 ① 𝘝𝘐𝘚𝘈
closed 25 and 26 December – Meals (carving rest.) 24.75 t. and a la carte ₪ 12.00 –
Primavera : Meals - Italian - (closed Saturday lunch and Sunday) a la carte 18.60/40.55 t. ₪ 8.50 – **787 rm** ⚏ 187.00/235.00 t., 15 suites – SB.

🏨 **Arden,** Coventry Rd, B92 0EH, ℰ (01675) 443221, Fax (01675) 443221, Ⅰᵇ, ⛱, ☒ – 🛗, ✳rm, 📺 ☎ ৬ 🅿 – 🕰 170. 🐵 🆎 ① 𝘝𝘐𝘚𝘈, ✻
Meals (bar lunch Saturday) 15.00 st. and a la carte ₪ 6.35 – ⚏ 9.00 – **146 rm** 79.00/ 129.00 st.

at Northfield SW : 6 m. by A 38 – CU – ⊠ Birmingham.

🏨 **Norwood,** 87-89 Bunbury Rd, B31 2ET, via Church rd ℰ (0121) 411 2202, Fax (0121) 411 2202, ☞ – 📺 ☎ 🅿. 🐵 🆎 ① 𝘝𝘐𝘚𝘈 ᴶᶜᴮ
closed 24 to 26 December – Meals (closed Friday to Sunday) (dinner only) 16.50 st. ₪ 4.50 – **18 rm** ⚏ 69.00/74.00 st.

at Kings Norton SW : 7 m. on A 441 – EX – ⊠ Birmingham.

🏨 **Mill House,** 180 Lifford Lane, B30 3NT, ℰ (0121) 459 5800, Fax (0121) 459 8553, ☞ – ✳ 📺 ☎ 🅿. 🐵 🆎 ① 𝘝𝘐𝘚𝘈 ᴶᶜᴮ. ✻
closed 1 to 16 January – Meals – (see **Lombard Room** below) – **8 rm** ⚏ 95.00/105.00 t., 1 suite – SB.

🏨 **Lombard Room,** 180 Lifford Lane, B30 3NT, ℰ (0121) 459 5800, Fax (0121) 459 8553, ✸ – ✳⊓ 🅿. 🐵 🆎 𝘝𝘐𝘚𝘈 ᴶᶜᴮ
closed lunch Monday and Saturday, Sunday dinner, 1-16 January and Bank Holidays –
Meals 16.85/23.50 t.

at Oldbury W : 7¾ m. by A 456 on A 4123 – ⊠ Birmingham.

🏨 **Travelodge,** Wolverhampton Rd, B69 2BH, on A 4123 ℰ (0121) 552 2967, Reservations (Freephone) 0800 850950 – 📺 ৬ 🅿. 🐵 🆎 ① 𝘝𝘐𝘚𝘈 ᴶᶜᴮ. ✻   BU n
33 rm 44.95 t.

at Great Barr NW : 6 m. on A 34 – ⊠ Birmingham.

🏨 **Forte Posthouse Birmingham,** Chapel Lane, B43 7BG, ℰ (0121) 357 7444, Fax (0121) 357 7503, Ⅰᵇ, ⛱, ☒ – ✳rm, 📺 ☎ 🅿 – 🕰 120. 🐵 🆎 ① 𝘝𝘐𝘚𝘈   CT x
Meals a la carte 19.00/26.00 ₪ 7.00 – ⚏ 9.95 – **192 rm** 89.00 st. – SB.

at West Bromwich NW : 6 m. on A 41 – ⊠ Birmingham.

🏨 **Moat House Birmingham,** Birmingham Rd, B70 6RS, ℰ (0121) 609 9988, Fax (0121) 525 7403, Ⅰᵇ – 🛗, ✳rm, 🍴 rest, 📺 ☎ 🅿 – 🕰 180. 🐵 🆎 ① 𝘝𝘐𝘚𝘈
Meals 13.95 st. and a la carte – ⚏ 8.50 – **168 rm** 99.00/114.00 st. – SB.   BU c

🔵 ATS 1558 Pershore Rd., Stirchley
ℰ (0121) 458 2951
ATS 158 Slade Rd, Erdington ℰ (0121) 327 2783
ATS 1189 Chester Rd, Erdington
ℰ (0121) 373 6104/382 7533
ATS 94 Aldrige Rd, Perry Barr ℰ (0121) 356 5925/ 6632
ATS 314 Bearwood Rd, Bearwood
ℰ (0121) 420 2000
ATS 427 Bordesley Green, Bordesley Green
ℰ (0121) 772 6514

ATS 43 Whitmore Rd, Small Heath
ℰ (0121) 772 2571
ATS 341 Dudley Rd, Winson Green
ℰ (0121) 454 2588/2536
ATS Dudley Rd, Halesowen ℰ (0121) 550 2464
ATS 947 Bristol Rd South, Northfield
ℰ (0121) 475 1244
ATS 87 Old Meeting St., West Bromwich
ℰ (0121) 553 3495

BIRMINGHAM AIRPORT W. Mids. 🔢403🔢 🔢404🔢 O 26 – see Birmingham.

Pas de publicité payée dans ce guide.

BIRMINGHAM NORTH SERVICE AREA W. Mids. – ⊠ Wolverhampton.

🏨 **Travelodge** without rest., WV11 2AT, M 6 between junctions 10A and 11
ℰ (01922) 414100, Fax (01922) 418762, Reservations (Freephone) 0800 850950 – ⇌ 📺 ♿
📿 🕮 🝙 ① *VISA* JCB. ⅏
64 rm 46.95 t.

BIRTLE Gtr. Manchester – see Bury.

BISHOP AUCKLAND Durham 401 402 P 20 – pop. 23 154.

🛇 High Plains, Durham Rd *ℰ* (01388) 602198 – 🛇 Oakleaf, School Aycliffe Lane, Newton
Aycliffe *ℰ* (01325) 310820 – 🛇 Woodham G. & C.C., Burnhill Way, Newton Aycliffe *ℰ* (01325)
320574.
London 253 – Carlisle 73 – Middlesbrough 24 – Newcastle upon Tyne 28 – Sunderland 25.

🏨 **Park Head,** Park View Terr., New Coundon, DL14 8QB, NE : 1 ¾ m. by A 689 on A 688
ℰ (01388) 661727, Fax (01388) 661727 – ⇌ rm, 📺 🕿 📿 🕮 🝙 *VISA*. ⅏
closed 25 December – **Meals** (bar lunch Monday to Saturday)/dinner 8.95 **st.** and a la carte
§ 5.25 – **31 rm** ⊇ 43.00/68.00 **st.** – SB.

🔘 ATS Cockton Hill *ℰ* (01388) 603681

BISHOP'S HULL Somerset – see Taunton.

BISHOP'S STORTFORD Herts. 404 U 28 – pop. 28 403.

✈ Stansted Airport : *ℰ* (01279) 680500, NE : 3 ½ m.
🛃 The Old Monastery, Windhill, CM23 2ND *ℰ* (01279) 655831.
London 34 – Cambridge 27 – Chelmsford 19 – Colchester 33.

🏨 **The Cottage** ⌂ without rest., 71 Birchanger Lane, CM23 5QA, NE : 2 ¼ m. by B 1383 on
Birchanger rd *ℰ* (01279) 812349, Fax (01279) 812349, « Part 17C and 18C cottages », 🌳 –
⇌ 📺 📿 🕮 *VISA*. ⅏
closed 24 to 27 December – **15 rm** ⊇ 26.00/50.00 **st.**

✗ **The Lemon Tree,** 14-16 Water Lane, CM23 2LB, *ℰ* (01279) 757788, Fax (01279) 757766 –
🕮 🝙 JCB
closed Sunday dinner, Monday, Christmas and 1 to 8 January – **Meals** a la carte 14.75/
21.50 **t.** § 5.50.

at Hatfield Heath (Essex) SE : 6 m. on A 1060 – ⊠ Bishop's Stortford.

🏰 **Down Hall Country House** ⌂, CM22 7AS, S : 1 ½ m. by Matching Lane
ℰ (01279) 731441, Fax (01279) 730416, ≼, « 19C Italianate mansion », 🖪, ≋, 🖾, 🌳,
park, ⅏ – 🖹 📺 🕿 📿 – 🔬 250. 🕮 🝙 ① *VISA* JCB. ⅏
Meals (carving lunch) 17.50/22.00 **t.** – **Downham** : **Meals** (closed lunch Monday to Friday)
17.50/22.00 and a la carte – ⊇ 10.25 – **103 rm** 115.00/192.00 **t.**

🔘 ATS Unit 7, Twyford Business Park, London Rd *ℰ* (01279) 507915

BISHOP'S TAWTON Devon 403 H 30 – see Barnstaple.

BLABY Leics. 402 403 404 Q 26 – pop. 6 538.

London 100 – Coventry 10 – Leicester 4 – Northampton 38.

🏨 **Time Out,** 15 Enderby Rd, LE8 4GD, *ℰ* (01162) 787898, Fax (01162) 781974, 🖪, ≋, 🖾 –
🖹 rest, 📺 🕿 ♿ 📿 – 🔬 40. 🕮 🝙 ① *VISA* JCB
Meals 13.95/16.95 **t.** and a la carte § 6.50 – ⊇ 9.25 – **25 rm** 68.00/80.00 – SB.

BLACKBURN 402 M 22 – pop. 105 994.

🛇 Pleasington *ℰ* (01254) 202177 – 🛇 Wilpshire, 72 Whalley Rd *ℰ* (01254) 248260 – 🛇 Great
Harwood, Harwood Bar *ℰ* (01254) 884391.
🛃 King George's Hall, Northgate, BB2 1AA *ℰ* (01254) 53277.
London 228 – Leeds 47 – Liverpool 39 – Manchester 24 – Preston 11.

✗ **Beetlestones,** 16 Town Hall St., BB2 1AG, *ℰ* (01254) 682670, Fax (01254) 682670 – 🕮 🝙
① *VISA*
closed Monday dinner, Sunday, 25-26 December, 1 January and Bank Holidays – **Meals**
9.50 **t.** (dinner) and a la carte 14.45/30.00 **t.** § 7.95.

at Langho N : 4½ m. on A 666 – ⊠ Whalley.

🏛 **Mytton Fold Farm H. and Golf Club,** Whalley Rd, BB6 8AB, NE : 1 m. by A 66 on Whalley rd ☏ (01254) 240662, Fax (01254) 248119, ⓑ, ⌖ – ⑂ rest, ⓉⓋ ☎ ⓟ – ⚙ 250. ⓒⓞ ⒜⒠ ⓥⒾⓢⒶ, ⅋

closed 24 December-2 January – **Meals** (bar lunch Monday to Saturday)/dinner 15.00 **t.** ⅋ 5.25 – **27 rm** ⊇ 48.00/74.00 **t.** – SB.

🏛 **Petre Lodge,** Northcote Rd, BB6 8BG, NE : ½ m. ☏ (01254) 245506, Fax (01254) 245506 – ⑂ ⓉⓋ ☎ ⓟ. ⓒⓞ ⒜⒠ ⓥⒾⓢⒶ.

Meals (residents only) (dinner only) a la carte 9.95/15.40 **st.** ⅋ 4.50 – **9 rm** ⊇ 49.00/59.00 **st.**

XXX **Northcote Manor** (Haworth) with rm, Northcote Rd, BB6 8BE, N : ½ m. on A 59 at ⅋ junction with A 666 ☏ (01254) 240555, Fax (01254) 246568, ⌖ – ⑂ rest, ⓉⓋ ☎ ⓟ. ⓒⓞ ⒜⒠ ⓞ ⓥⒾⓢⒶ.

closed 25 December and 1 January – **Meals** 17.00 **t.** (lunch) and a la carte 28.50/43.90 **t.** – **14 rm** ⊇ 80.00/140.00 **t.** – SB

Spec. Bury black pudding and pink trout with mustard and nettle dressing. Assiette of new season's lamb, minted pesto. Apple crumble soufflé with Lancashire cheese ice cream.

at Clayton-le-Dale N : 4¾ m. by A 666 on B 6245 – ⊠ Blackburn.

XX **Shajan,** Longsight Rd, BB1 9EX, SW : ½ m. on A 59 ☏ (01254) 813234 – ▤ ⓟ. ⓒⓞ ⒜⒠ ⓞ ⓥⒾⓢⒶ

Meals - Indian - a la carte 13.60/18.10 **t.** ⅋ 4.25.

at Mellor NW : 4 m. by A 677 – ⊠ Blackburn.

🏛 **Millstone,** Church Lane, BB2 7JR, ☏ (01254) 813333, Fax (01254) 812628 – ⑂ ⓉⓋ ☎ ⓟ – ⚙ 25. ⓒⓞ ⒜⒠ ⓞ ⓥⒾⓢⒶ

Millers : **Meals** (bar lunch Saturday) 21.00 **st.** (dinner) and a la carte 19.50/27.50 **st.** ⅋ 6.00 – **22 rm** ⊇ 75.00/90.00 **st.**, 2 suites – SB.

at Balderstone NW : 6½ m. by A 677 off A 59 – ⊠ Blackburn.

🏛 **Boddington Arms,** Myerscough Rd, BB2 7LE, on A 59 ☏ (01254) 813900, Fax (01254) 814079 – ⑂ rm, ▤ rest, ⓉⓋ ☎ ⓕ ⓟ. ⓒⓞ ⒜⒠ ⓞ ⓥⒾⓢⒶ. ⅋

Meals (grill rest.) (in bar) a la carte 7.30/14.75 **s.** ⅋ 4.25 – ⊇ 4.95 – **20 rm** 42.25 **st.** – SB.

ⓐ ATS Pendle St., Copy Nook ☏ (01254) 55963/59272/665115

BLACKPOOL 🄬🄾🄼 K 22 Great Britain G. – pop. 146 262.

See : Tower★ AC AY A.

ⓑ Blackpool Park, North Park Drive, no telephone booking BY – ⓑ Poulton-le-Fylde, Myrtle Farm, Breck Rd ☏ (01253) 892444.

✈ Blackpool Airport : ☏ (01253) 343434, S : 3 m. by A 584.

🄱 1 Clifton St., FY1 1LY ☏ (01253) 21623 – Pleasure Beach, Unit 25, Ocean Boulevard, FY4 1PL ☏ (01253) 403223 (summer only).

London 246 – Leeds 88 – Liverpool 56 – Manchester 51 – Middlesbrough 123.

Plan opposite

🏨 **Stakis Blackpool,** North Promenade, FY1 2JQ, ☏ (01253) 23434, Fax (01253) 27864, ≤, 🖂 – ⑂ rm, ▤ rest, ⓉⓋ ☎ ⓕ ⓟ – ⚙ 750. ⓒⓞ ⒜⒠ ⓞ ⓥⒾⓢⒶ   AY **x**
The Promenade : **Meals** (closed Saturday lunch) (carving rest.) 18.50 – **The Crystal Room :** **Meals** (dinner only) 17.50 **st.** and a la carte – ⊇ 9.50 – **268 rm** 140.00/160.00 **st.**, 6 suites – SB.

🏨 **Imperial,** North Promenade, FY1 2HB, ☏ (01253) 23971, Fax (01253) 751784, ≤, Ⓕ⅋, ⇌, 🖂 – ⅋–⅋, ⑂ rm, ⓉⓋ ☎ ⓟ – ⚙ 400. ⓒⓞ ⒜⒠ ⓞ ⓥⒾⓢⒶ. ⅋   AY **c**
Palm Court : **Meals** 17.50 **t.** (dinner) and a la carte 21.95/45.95 **t.** ⅋ 7.50 – ⊇ 12.75 – **173 rm** 129.00/144.00 **t.**, 10 suites – SB.

🏨 **De Vere,** East Park Drive, FY3 8LL, ☏ (01253) 838866, Fax (01253) 798800, Ⓕ⅋, ⇌, 🖂, ⓑ, ⅋⅋, squash – ⅋– ⑂ rm, ▤ rest, ⓉⓋ ☎ ⓕ ⓟ – ⚙ 500. ⓒⓞ ⒜⒠ ⓞ ⓥⒾⓢⒶ. ⅋   BZ **a**
Meals (bar lunch)/dinner 18.95 **st.** and a la carte – **162 rm** ⊇ 120.00/140.00 **st.**, 2 suites – SB.

🏨 **Savoy,** Queens Promenade, FY2 9SJ, ☏ (01253) 352561, Fax (01253) 500735 – ⅋ ⓉⓋ ☎ ⓟ – ⚙ 300. ⓒⓞ ⒜⒠ ⓞ ⓥⒾⓢⒶ   AY **a**
Meals (bar lunch Monday to Saturday)/dinner 12.50 **st.** and a la carte – **128 rm** ⊇ 80.00/120.00 **st.**, 3 suites – SB.

🏨 **Libertys on the Square** without rest., Cocker Sq., North Promenade, FY1 1RX, ☏ (01253) 291155, Fax (01253) 752271, ≤ – ⅋ ⓉⓋ ☎ ⓟ. ⓒⓞ ⒜⒠ ⓥⒾⓢⒶ. ⅋   AY **n**
38 rm ⊇ 39.50/59.50 **t.**

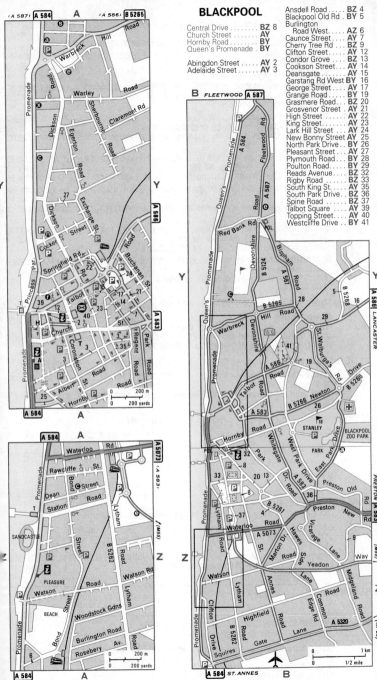

BLACKPOOL

🏨 **Berwyn**, 1-2 Finchley Rd, Gynn Sq., FY1 2LP, ℰ (01253) 352896, Fax (01253) 594391 – 📺
☎. 🐽 VISA. ⌖
AY e
Meals (residents only) (dinner only) 15.00 **t.** – **20 rm** ⌸ 28.00/56.00 **t.** – SB.

🏨 **Travel Inn**, Devonshire Rd, Bispham, FY2 0AR, ℰ (01253) 354942, Fax (01253) 590498 –
⌖ rm, ▤ rest, 📺 ⌖ ℗ – ⌖ 40. 🐽 AE ① VISA
BY e
Meals (grill rest.) – **40 rm** 36.50 **t.**

🏨 **Travel Inn**, Yeadon Way, South Shore, FY1 6BF, ℰ (01253) 341415, Fax (01253) 343805 –
⌖ rm, ▤ rest, 📺 ⌖ ℗ – ⌖ 40. 🐽 AE ① VISA. ⌖
AZ e
Meals (grill rest.) – **40 rm** 36.50 **t.**

⌂ **Sunray**, 42 Knowle Av., off Queens Promenade, FY2 9TQ, ℰ (01253) 351937,
Fax (01253) 593307 – ⌖ rest, 📺 ☎ 🐽 AE ① VISA
BY c
closed 15 December-5 January – **Meals** (by arrangement) 12.00 **s.** – **9 rm** ⌸ 28.00/
56.00 **st.** – SB.

⌂ **Burlees**, 40 Knowle Av., off Queen's Promenade, FY2 9TQ, ℰ (01253) 354535,
Fax (01253) 354535 – ⌖ 📺 ℗. 🐽 VISA. ⌖
BY c
February-October – **Meals** (by arrangement) 8.00 **st.** ⅄ 4.00 – **9 rm** ⌸ 24.00/48.00 **st.** – SB.

⌂ **Grosvenor View**, 7-9 King Edward Av., FY2 9TD, ℰ (01253) 352851 – ⌖ ℗. 🐽 AE VISA.
⌖
AY s
closed January and February – **Meals** (by arrangement) 6.00 **st.** – **17 rm** ⌸ 20.00/44.00 **st.**
– SB.

⌂ **Bambi** without rest., 27 Bright St., South Shore, FY4 1BS, ℰ (01253) 343756,
Fax (01253) 343756 – 📺. 🐽 AE ① VISA. ⌖
AZ c
restricted opening in winter – **5 rm** ⌸ 18.00/35.00 **s.**

✗ **September Brasserie**, 15-17 Queen St., FY1 1PU, ℰ (01253) 23282, Fax (01253) 299455
– 🐽 AE ① VISA JCB
AY r
closed 1 week in spring and 1 week in autumn – **Meals** 16.95 **t.** (dinner) and a la carte
18.00/24.25 **t.** ⅄ 6.75.

at Little Thornton NE : 5 m. by A 586 – BY – off A 588 – ⌧ Blackpool.

✗✗ **River House** ⤳ with rm, Skippool Creek, Wyre Rd, FY5 5LF, ℰ (01253) 883497,
Fax (01253) 892083, ≤, ⌗ – 📺 ☎ ℗. 🐽 VISA
closed 25-26 December and 1 January – **Meals** (closed Sunday) (booking essential)
20.00 **t.** and a la carte ⅄ 7.50 – **5 rm** ⌸ 65.00/80.00 **t.** – SB.

at Little Singleton NE : 6 m. by A 586 – BY – on A 585 – ⌧ Blackpool.

🏨 **Mains Hall**, 86 Mains Lane, FY6 7LE, ℰ (01253) 885130, Fax (01253) 894132, ⌗ – ⌖ rm,
📺 ☎ ℗. 🐽 AE ① VISA
Meals (light lunch Monday to Friday)/dinner 16.00 **st.** ⅄ 4.00 – **10 rm** ⌸ 40.00/100.00 **st.** –
SB.

at Singleton NE : 7 m. by A 586 – BY – on B 5260 – ⌧ Blackpool.

🏨 **Singleton Lodge** ⤳, Lodge Lane, FY6 8LT, N : ¼ m. on B 5260 ℰ (01253) 883854,
Fax (01253) 894432, ⌗ – 📺 ☎ ℗. 🐽 AE VISA
closed 25 to 26 December and 1 January – **Meals** (dinner only and Sunday lunch)/dinner
a la carte 14.50/22.55 **t.** ⅄ 5.00 – **12 rm** ⌸ 52.00/70.00 **t.** – SB.

🔘 ATS Clifton Rd ℰ (01253) 695033

BLACKROD Lancs. 402 404 M 23 – pop. 5 681.
London 220 – Burnley 25 – Liverpool 31 – Manchester 16 – Preston 18.

🏩 **Georgian House**, Manchester Rd, BL6 5RU, SE : 1 ½ m. by B 5408 on A 6
ℰ (01942) 814598, Fax (01942) 813427, ⅄, ≋, 🔲 – 🛗, ⌖ rm, 📺 ☎ ℗ – ⌖ 250. 🐽 AE
① VISA
Regency : Meals (bar lunch Saturday and Bank Holidays) 12.00/17.95 **st.** and a la carte
⅄ 6.10 – ⌸ 8.95 – **98 rm** 89.00/125.00 **st.** – SB.

BLACKWATER Cornwall 403 E 33 – see Truro.

BLAGDON North Somerset 403 L 30 – pop. 1 900 – ⌧ Bristol.
London 140 – Bristol 18 – Taunton 24.

⌂ **Butcombe Farm** ⤳ without rest., Aldwick Lane, BS18 6UW, N : 1 ½ m. by Station Rd
ℰ (01761) 462380, Fax (01761) 462300, ≤, « Farmhouse of 15C origin », ⌶, ⌗, park – 📺
☎ ℗. 🐽 VISA JCB
5 rm ⌸ 39.00/49.00 **st.**

BLAKENEY *Glos.* 403 404 M 28.
> *London 134 – Bristol 31 – Gloucester 16 – Newport 31.*

🏠 **Viney Hill Country Guesthouse,** Viney Hill, GL15 4LT, W : ¾ m. by A 48
$\mathscr{C}$ (01594) 516000, *Fax* (01594) 516018, *≤* – ⃰ ⃰ 🔟 ❷. 🚳 *VISA*. ⃰
Meals (by arrangement) 16.50 **st.** ₰ 8.00 – **6 rm** ⌸ 32.00/46.00 **st.** – SB.

BLAKENEY *Norfolk* 404 X 25 – *pop. 1 628* – ⊠ *Holt.*
> *London 127 – King's Lynn 37 – Norwich 28.*

🏨 **Blakeney,** The Quay, NR25 7NE, $\mathscr{C}$ (01263) 740797, *Fax* (01263) 740795, *≤*, *Ӻ₅*, *≏s*, *🔲*,
≋ – 🛗, ⃰ ⃰ rest, 🔟 ☎ ❷ – ⚖ 200. 🚳 ஈ ⓪ *VISA*
Meals (light lunch Monday to Saturday)/dinner 17.00 **t.** and a la carte ₰ 4.50 – **60 rm**
⌸ 75.00/210.00 **st.** – SB.

🏠 **Manor,** The Quay, NR25 7ND, $\mathscr{C}$ (01263) 740376, *Fax* (01263) 741116, *≋* – ⃰ ⃰ rest, 🔟 ☎
❷
closed 3 to 26 January – **Meals** (bar lunch Monday to Saturday)/dinner 15.50 **t.**
and a la carte ₰ 4.00 – **37 rm** ⌸ 32.00/84.00 **t.** – SB.

🍴 **White Horse** with rm, 4 High St., NR25 7AL, $\mathscr{C}$ (01263) 740574, *Fax* (01263) 741303 – 🔟
❷. 🚳 ஈ *VISA*. ⃰
Meals (*closed Sunday, Monday and 25-26 December*) (bar lunch)/dinner a la carte 14.75/
20.45 **t.** ₰ 4.95 – **9 rm** ⌸ 30.00/70.00 **t.**

at Cley next the Sea *E : 1½ m. on A 149* – ⊠ *Holt.*

⌂ **Cley Mill** *⅍*, NR25 7NN, $\mathscr{C}$ (01263) 740209, *Fax* (01263) 740209, *≤*, « 18C redbrick
windmill on saltmarshes », *≋* – ❷. 🚳 *VISA* *JCB*. ⃰
closed Christmas – **Meals** (by arrangement) (communal dining) 15.00 **st.** – **6 rm** ⌸ 30.00/
69.00 **st.** – SB.

🍴 **George & Dragon** with rm, High St., NR25 7RN, $\mathscr{C}$ (01263) 740652, *Fax* (01263) 741275,
≋ – 🔟 ❷
closed 25 December – **Meals** a la carte 9.75/18.50 **t.** – **8 rm** ⌸ 35.00/67.50 **t.**

at Morston *W : 1½ m. on A 149* – ⊠ *Holt.*

🏠 **Morston Hall** *⅍*, NR25 7AA, $\mathscr{C}$ (01263) 741041, *Fax* (01263) 740419, *≋* – 🔟 ☎ ❷. 🚳
☕ ஈ *VISA*
closed 1 January-6 February – Meals (dinner only and Sunday lunch)/dinner 27.50 **st.** ₰ 5.50
– **6 rm** ⌸ (dinner included) 100.00/160.00 **st.** – SB.

BLANCHLAND *Northd.* 401 402 N 19 – *pop. 135* – ⊠ *Consett (Durham).*
> *London 298 – Carlisle 47 – Newcastle upon Tyne 24.*

🏨 **Lord Crewe Arms** *⅍*, DH8 9SP, $\mathscr{C}$ (01434) 675251, *Fax* (01434) 675337, « Part 13C
abbey », *≋* – 🔟 ☎. 🚳 ஈ ⓪ *VISA*
Meals (bar lunch Monday to Saturday)/dinner a la carte 27.00/29.00 **t.** ₰ 7.00 – **20 rm**
⌸ 75.00/110.00 **t.** – SB.

BLANDFORD FORUM *Dorset* 403 404 N 31 *The West Country G.* – *pop. 8 880.*
> See : *Town★.*
> Env. : *Kingston Lacy★★ AC, SE : 5 ½ m. by B 3082 – Royal Signals Museum★, NE : 2 m. by*
> *B 3082.*
> Exc. : *Milton Abbas★, SW : 8 m. by A 354 – Sturminster Newton★, NW : 8 m. by A 357.*
> 🏌 *Ashley Wood, Tarrant Rawston* $\mathscr{C}$ (01258) 452253.
> 🚩 *Marsh & Ham Car Park, West St., DT11 7AW* $\mathscr{C}$ (01258) 454770.
> *London 124 – Bournemouth 17 – Dorchester 17 – Salisbury 24.*

🏨 **Crown,** West St., DT11 7AJ, $\mathscr{C}$ (01258) 456626, *Fax* (01258) 451084, *◝*, *≋* – ⃰ ⃰ rm, 🔟 ☎
❷ – ⚖ 200. 🚳 ஈ *VISA*
closed 1 week Christmas – **Meals** (*closed Saturday lunch*) 13.95 **t.** and a la carte ₰ 4.80 –
32 rm ⌸ 62.00/90.00 **t.** – SB.

at Pimperne *NE : 2½ m. on A 354* – ⊠ *Blandford Forum.*

🏠 **Anvil,** Salisbury Rd, DT11 8UQ, $\mathscr{C}$ (01258) 453431, *Fax* (01258) 480182 – 🔟 ☎ ❷. 🚳 ஈ ⓪
VISA
Meals a la carte 9.45/22.40 **t.** ₰ 5.50 – **10 rm** ⌸ 47.50/75.00 **t.**

at Tarrant Monkton *NE : 5½ m. by A 354* – ⊠ *Blandford Forum.*

🍴 **Langton Arms** with rm, DT11 8RX, $\mathscr{C}$ (01258) 830225, *Fax* (01258) 830053, *≋* – 🔟 ☎
❷. 🚳 *VISA*
Meals (bar lunch Monday to Saturday) (in bar Monday and Tuesday dinner) a la carte 11.95/
16.95 **t.** ₰ 4.00 – **6 rm** ⌸ 39.00/54.00 **t.**

at Farnham NE : 7½ m. by A 354 – ⊠ Blandford Forum.

🛏️ **Museum** with rm, DT11 8DE, ℰ (01725) 516261, ☞ – 📺 ☎ 🅿️. ⓦⓢ VISA
closed 25 December – **Meals** a la carte 12.15/22.20 **t.** – **4 rm** ⊑ 45.00/65.00 **t.**

at Chettle NW : 7¼ m. by A 354 – ⊠ Blandford Forum.

XX **Castleman** ⤢ with rm, DT11 8DB, ℰ (01258) 830096, Fax (01258) 830051, ≼, « Part 16C dower house with Victorian additions », ☞ – ⥤ rest, 📺 ☎ 🅿️. ⓦⓢ VISA
closed 26 December, 1 January and February – **Meals** (dinner only and Sunday lunch)/
dinner a la carte 13.50/20.50 **t.** ⧍ 4.00 – **8 rm** ⊑ 35.00/65.00 **t.**

BLAWITH Cumbria 402 K 21 – see Coniston.

BLEDINGTON Glos. 403 404 P 28 – see Stow-on-the-Wold.

BLOCKLEY Glos. 403 404 O 27 – pop. 1 668 – ⊠ Moreton-in-Marsh.
London 89 – Birmingham 40 – Gloucester 29 – Oxford 33.

🏠 **Crown Inn**, High St., GL56 9EX, ℰ (01386) 700245, Fax (01386) 700247, « Converted 15C coach house and cottages », ☞ – 📺 ☎ 🅿️. ⓦⓢ AE ① VISA
Meals a la carte 13.85/31.85 **t.** – **21 rm** ⊑ 64.00/128.00 **t.**

THE CHANNEL TUNNEL Map Guide

260 *French edition*
  with tourist sights in England

261 *English edition*
  with tourist sights on the Continent

BLUNSDON Wilts. 403 404 O 29 – see Swindon.

BLYTH Notts. 402 403 404 Q 23 – pop. 1 867 – ⊠ Worksop.
London 166 – Doncaster 13 – Lincoln 30 – Nottingham 32 – Sheffield 20.

🏠 **Charnwood**, Sheffield Rd, S81 8HF, W : ¾ m. on A 634 ℰ (01909) 591610,
Fax (01909) 591429, ☞ – ⥤ rm, 📺 ☎ 🅿️ – ⧌ 120. ⓦⓢ AE ① VISA JCB. ⌗
Meals 11.50/17.50 **t.** and a la carte ⧍ 6.95 – **34 rm** ⊑ 60.00/80.00 **st.**

🏠 **Travelodge** without rest., Hilltop roundabout, S81 8HG, N : ¾ m. by B 6045 at junction of
A 1 (M) with A 614 ℰ (01909) 591841, Fax (01909) 591831, Reservations (Freephone) 0800
850950 – ⥤ 📺 ☎ & 🅿️. ⓦⓢ AE ① VISA JCB. ⌗
39 rm 42.95 **t.**

🏠 **Travelodge**, A1 southbound, S81 8EL, SE : 1 m. by A 634 on A 1 ℰ (01909) 591775,
Reservations (Freephone) 0800 850950 – 📺 & 🅿️. ⓦⓢ AE ① VISA JCB. ⌗
32 rm 42.95 **t.**

BODINNICK-BY-FOWEY Cornwall – see Fowey.

BODMIN Cornwall 403 F 32 The West Country G. – pop. 12 553.
See : St. Petroc Church★.
Env. : Bodmin Moor★★ – Lanhydrock★★, S : 3 m. by B 3269 – Blisland★ (Church★), N :
5 ½ m. by A 30 and minor roads – Pencarrow★, NW : 4 m. by A 389 and minor roads –
Cardinham (Church★), NE : 4 m. by A 30 and minor rd – St. Mabyn (Church★), N : 5 ½ m. by
A 389, B 3266 and minor rd.
Exc. : St. Tudy★, N : 7 m. by A 389, B 3266 and minor rd.
🛈 Shire House, Mount Folly Sq., PL31 2DQ ℰ (01208) 76616.
London 270 – Newquay 18 – Plymouth 32 – Truro 23.

⌂ **Mount Pleasant Moorland** ⤢, Mount, PL30 4EX, E : 7¼ m. by A 30 on Warleggan rd
ℰ (01208) 821342, Fax (01208) 821417, ≼, ⤢, ☞ – ⥤ 🅿️. ⓦⓢ VISA JCB. ⌗
April-September – **Meals** 12.00 **s.** – **7 rm** ⊑ 23.00/52.00.

◉ ATS Church Sq. ℰ (01208) 74353/73757

BODYMOOR HEATH Staffs. 402 403 404 O 26 – see Tamworth.

BOGNOR REGIS W. Sussex 404 R 31 – pop. 19 836.
🛈 Belmont St., PO21 1BJ ℘ (01243) 823140.
London 65 – Brighton 29 – Portsmouth 24 – Southampton 36.

🏨 **Robin Hood,** Shripney Rd, PO22 9PA, N : 3 m. on A 29 ℘ (01243) 822323,
Fax (01243) 841430 – 📺 ☎ 🄿. 🐠 AE ⓞ VISA JCB
Meals a la carte 13.50/19.15 t. ⓘ 5.75 – **24 rm** ⊏ 45.00/70.00 st. – SB.

🏠 **Inglenook,** 255 Pagham Rd, Nyetimber, PO21 3QB, W : 2 ½ m. ℘ (01243) 262495,
Fax (01243) 262668, « Part 16C », �ுர் – 📺 ☎ 🄿 – 🔬 100. 🐠 AE ⓞ VISA
Meals 12.95/14.95 t. and a la carte ⓘ 4.50 – **18 rm** ⊏ 40.00/100.00 t. – SB.

BOLDON Tyne and Wear 401 402 O 19 – see Newcastle upon Tyne.

BOLLINGTON Ches. 402 403 404 N 24 – see Macclesfield.

BOLTON Gtr. Manchester 402 404 M 23 – pop. 139 020.
🏌 Regent Park, Links Rd, Chorley New Road ℘ (01204) 844170 – 🏌 Lostock Park ℘ (01204)
843278 – 🏌 Bolton Old Links, Chorley Old Rd, Montserrat ℘ (01204) 840050.
🛈 Town Hall, Victoria Sq, BL1 1RU ℘ (01204) 364333.
London 214 – Burnley 19 – Liverpool 32 – Manchester 11 – Preston 23.

🏨 **Bolton Moat House,** 1 Higher Bridge St., BL1 2EW, ℘ (01204) 879988,
Fax (01204) 380777, « Cloisters restaurant in 19C church », 🏋, ☎, 🔲 – 🛗, 🌿 rm, 🍽 rest,
📺 ☎ & 🄿 – 🔬 300. 🐠 AE ⓞ VISA JCB
Meals (closed Saturday lunch) 15.50 t. (dinner) and a la carte 14.70/29.45 t. ⓘ 6.00 – ⊏ 9.95
– **126 rm** 99.00/117.00 t., 2 suites – SB.

🏨 **Pack Horse,** Nelson Sq., Bradshawgate, BL1 1DP, ℘ (01204) 527261, Fax (01204) 364352
– 🛗, 🌿 rm, 📺 ☎ – 🔬 250. 🐠 AE ⓞ VISA JCB. 🌿
Meals (closed Sunday dinner) 19.95 st. (dinner) and a la carte 12.00/21.00 st. ⓘ 6.50 –
⊏ 8.75 – **72 rm** 72.00/82.00 st. – SB.

🏨 **Beaumont,** Beaumont Rd, BL3 4TA, SW : 2 ½ m. by A 676 on A 58 ℘ (01204) 651511,
Fax (01204) 61064 – 🌿 rm, 📺 ☎ 🄿 – 🔬 120. 🐠 AE ⓞ VISA
Meals (closed Sunday lunch) a la carte 13.15/28.50 st. ⓘ 7.25 – ⊏ 8.95 – **96 rm** 69.00 st. –
SB.

🏮 **Cheetham Arms** with rm, 987 Blackburn Rd, Sharples, BL1 7LG, N : 2 ¾ m. on A 666
℘ (01204) 301372, Fax (01204) 598209 – 📺 🄿. 🐠 AE VISA
Meals (closed Sunday dinner to non-residents) (in bar) 7.90/13.40 t. ⓘ 3.75 – **4 rm** ⊏ 32.00/
44.00 t.

at Egerton N : 3½ m. on A 666 – ⊠ Bolton.

🏨 **Egerton House,** Blackburn Rd, BL7 9PL, ℘ (01204) 307171, Fax (01204) 593030, 🌿 –
🌿 📺 ☎ 🄿 – 🔬 150. 🐠 AE ⓞ VISA. 🌿
Meals (closed Saturday lunch) 14.00/22.95 st. and a la carte ⓘ 6.50 – ⊏ 8.95 – **32 rm** 87.50/
110.00 t. – SB.

at Bromley Cross N : 3¼ m. by A 676 on B 6472 – ⊠ Bolton.

🏨 **Last Drop Village,** Hospital Rd, BL7 9PZ, NW: 1 m. by B 6472 on Hospital Rd
℘ (01204) 591131, Fax (01204) 304122, « Village created from restored farm buildings »,
🏋, ☎, 🔲, 🌿, squash – 🌿 rm, 📺 ☎ 🄿 – 🔬 200. 🐠 AE ⓞ VISA JCB
Meals 10.75/19.50 st. and a la carte – **83 rm** ⊏ 85.00/95.00 t., 3 suites – SB.

🏠 **Quarlton Manor Farm** �, Plantation Rd, Edgworth, BL7 0DD, NE : 4 ¾ m. by B 6472
and B 6391 following signs for Edgeworth and Blackburn ℘ (01204) 852277,
Fax (01204) 852286, ≤, « Part 17C farmhouse », 🌿, park – 🌿 📺 🄿
Meals 17.00/19.00 st. ⓘ 4.00 – **5 rm** ⊏ 39.00/79.00 st. – SB.

@ ATS Foundry St. ℘ (01204) 522144/527841/
388681
ATS Moss Bank Way, Astley Bridge, Bolton (ASDA car
park) ℘ (01204) 300057

ATS Chorley Rd, Fourgates, Westhoughton
℘ (01204) 813024

BOLTON ABBEY N. Yorks. 402 O 22 Great Britain G. – pop. 117 – ⊠ Skipton.
See : Bolton Priory★ AC.
London 216 – Harrogate 18 – Leeds 23 – Skipton 6.

🏨 **Devonshire Arms Country House** �, BD23 6AJ, ℘ (01756) 710441,
Fax (01756) 710564, ≤, « Part 17C restored coaching inn », 🏋, ☎, 🔲, 🌿, park, 🌿 – 🌿
📺 ☎ & 🄿 – 🔬 150. 🐠 AE ⓞ VISA
Burlington : Meals 18.95/37.50 t. ⓘ 10.00 – **38 rm** ⊏ 125.00/175.00 st., 3 suites – SB.

BOLTONGATE Cumbria – see Bassenthwaite.

BOREHAMWOOD Herts. 404 T 29 – pop. 29 837.
London 10 – Luton 20.

Plan : see Greater London (North West)

🏨 **Elstree Moat House,** Barnet bypass, WD6 5PU, at junction of A 5135 with A 1
℘ (0181) 214 9988, Fax (0181) 207 3194, ℔, ☎, 🖳 – 🛗, ⇄ rm, ▤ rest, 🆃🆅 ☎ ᕕ 🅿 –
🔬 400. 🆀🆂 🅰🅴 🅾 🆅🅸🆂🅰. ⋙
CT s
Meals 13.50/15.95 **t.** and a la carte ᐁ 5.25 – **131 rm** ⇆ 121.00/175.00 **st.** – SB.

🏨 **Oaklands Toby,** Studio Way, WD6 5JY, off Elstree Way (A 5135) ℘ (0181) 905 1455,
Fax (0181) 905 1370 – ⇄ rm, ▤ rest, 🆃🆅 ☎ ᕕ 🅿 – 🔬 35. 🆀🆂 🅰🅴 🆅🅸🆂🅰. ⋙
CT i
Meals (closed dinner 25 December) (grill rest.) a la carte 12.00/18.50 **t.** ᐁ 5.95 – **38 rm**
⇆ 85.00/95.00 **t.** – SB.

BOROUGHBRIDGE N.Yorks 402 P 21 – pop. 1 903.
London 215 – Leeds 19 – Middlesbrough 36 – York 16.

🏨 **Rose Manor,** Horsefair, YO5 9LL, ℘ (01423) 322245, Fax (01423) 324920, 🌰 – ⇄ rm, 🆃🆅
☎ 🅿 – 🔬 200. 🆀🆂 🅰🅴 🆅🅸🆂🅰. ⋙
closed 26 to 30 December – **Meals** 17.50 **st.** (dinner) and a la carte 16.45/21.00 **st.** ᐁ 4.25 –
17 rm ⇆ 71.75/99.50 **st.** – SB.

🏨 **Crown,** Horsefair, YO5 9LB, ℘ (01423) 322328, Fax (01423) 324512 – 🛗 🆃🆅 ☎ ᕕ 🅿 –
🔬 180. 🆀🆂 🅰🅴 🅾 🆅🅸🆂🅰
Meals (carving lunch)/dinner 18.95 **st.** and a la carte – **40 rm** ⇆ 50.00/90.00 **t.** – SB.

at Brafferton Helperby NE : 5 m. by B 6265 and Easingwold rd on Helperby rd – ✉ York.

⌂ **Brafferton Hall** ⌂, YO6 2NZ, by Hall Lane ℘ (01423) 360352, Fax (01423) 360352, 🌰 –
⇄ 🆃🆅 🅿 🆀🆂 🅰🅴 🆅🅸🆂🅰
Meals (by arrangement) (communal dining) 18.50 **s.** – **4 rm** ⇆ 30.00/60.00 **s.**

⌂ **Laurel Manor Farm** ⌂, YO6 2NZ, by Hall Lane ℘ (01423) 360436, Fax (01423) 360436,
🐎, 🌰, park, ⋘ – 🆃🆅 🅿
Meals (by arrangement) (communal dining) 20.00 **st.** ᐁ 2.00 – **3 rm** ⇆ 25.00/50.00 **st.**

BORROWDALE Cumbria 402 K 20 – see Keswick.

BOSCASTLE Cornwall 403 F 31 The West Country G..
See : Village★.
Env. : Church★ – Old Post Office★.
London 260 – Bude 14 – Exeter 59 – Plymouth 43.

🏠 **Bottreaux House,** PL35 0BG, S : ¾ m. by B 3263 on B 3266 ℘ (01840) 250231,
Fax (01840) 250170 – ⇄ 🆃🆅 🅿 ☎. 🆀🆂 🆅🅸🆂🅰 🆓
restricted opening in winter – **Meals** (closed Sunday) (dinner only) a la carte 12.75/16.00 **t.**
ᐁ 4.00 – **7 rm** ⇆ 25.00/51.00 **t.** – SB.

⌂ **Trerosewill Farm** ⌂, Paradise, PL35 0DL, S : 1 m. off B 263 ℘ (01840) 250545,
Fax (01840) 250545, ⋖, « Working farm », 🌰, park – ⇄ 🆃🆅 🅿 🆀🆂 🆅🅸🆂🅰 🆓
closed Christmas and New Year – **Meals** 17.00 **st.** – **7 rm** ⇆ 21.00/59.00 **st.** – SB.

⌂ **St. Christopher's,** High St., PL35 0BD, S : ¾ m. by B 3263 off B 3266 ℘ (01840) 250412 –
⇄ 🆃🆅 🅿 🆀🆂 🆅🅸🆂🅰 🆓
closed mid December-mid February – **Meals** 11.50 **st.** ᐁ 3.00 – **9 rm** ⇆ 21.00/42.00 – SB.

BOSHAM W. Sussex 404 R 31 – see Chichester.

BOSTON Lincs. 402 404 T 25 Great Britain G. – pop. 34 606.
See : St. Botolph's Church★.
Exc. : Tattershal Castle★, NW : 15 m. by A 1121, B 1192 and A 153.
🛅 Cowbridge, Horncastle Rd ℘ (01205) 362306.
🅱 Market Pl., PE21 6NN ℘ (01205) 356656.
London 122 – Lincoln 35 – Nottingham 55.

🏨 **Comfort Friendly Inn**, Donnington Rd, Bicker Bar Roundabout, PE20 3AN, SW : 8 m. at junction of A 17 with A 52 *β* (01205) 820118, *Fax (01205) 820228* – ⤢ rm, 📺 rest, 📺 ☎ &
🅿 – 🔥 90. 🏧 🆎 ⓪ 𝘝𝘐𝘚𝘈
Meals *(bar lunch)/dinner* 9.75 **st.** and a la carte ▯ 4.25 – ☲ 5.75 – **55 rm** 39.75 **st.** – SB.

ⓐ ATS London Rd *β* (01205) 362854

BOTLEY *Hants.* 🔢 🔢 Q 31 – *pop. 2 297* – ⊠ *Southampton.*
🛆 *Botley Park H. & C.C., Winchester Rd, Boorley Green β (01489) 780888 ext : 444.*
London 83 – Portsmouth 17 – Southampton 6 – Winchester 11.

🏨 **Botley Park**, Winchester Rd, Boorley Green, SO32 2UA, NW : 1 ½ m. on B 3354
β (01489) 780888, *Fax (01489) 789242*, *Ƒ₆*, ☎ₛ, 🔲, 🛆, park, ⚒, squash – ⤢, 📺 rest, 📺
☎ & 🅿 – 🔥 250. 🏧 🆎 ⓪ 𝘝𝘐𝘚𝘈. ⚒
Meals *(closed lunch Saturday and Bank Holiday Mondays)* *(dancing Saturday evenings in winter)* 22.50 **st.** *(dinner)* and a la carte 16.85/31.15 **st.** ▯ 6.95 – ☲ 9.95 – **100 rm** 103.00/150.00 **st.** – SB.

BOUGHTON *Kent* – *see Faversham.*

BOUGHTON MONCHELSEA *Kent* – *see Maidstone.*

BOULEY BAY *Jersey (Channel Islands)* 🔢 P 33 and 🔢 ⑪ – *see Channel Islands.*

BOURNE *Lincs.* 🔢 🔢 S 25 – *pop. 8 777.*
London 101 – Leicester 42 – Lincoln 35 – Nottingham 42.

🏠 **Bourne Eau House**, 30 South St., PE10 9LY, on A 15 *β* (01778) 423621, « Part Elizabethan and Georgian house », ☞ – ⤢ 📺 🅿. ⚒
closed Easter weekend and 15 December-15 January – **Meals** *(closed Sunday)* *(residents only)* *(communal dining)* *(dinner only)* 22.50 **st.** – **3 rm** ☲ 35.00/70.00 **s.**

at Toft *SW : 3 m. by A 151 on A 6121* – ⊠ *Bourne.*

🏨 **Toft House**, Main Rd, Toft, PE10 0JT, *β* (01778) 590614, *Fax (01778) 590264*, 🛆, ☞ – 📺
☎ 🅿 – 🔥 70. 🏧 𝘝𝘐𝘚𝘈. ⚒
closed 25 and 26 December – **Meals** *(closed Sunday dinner)* 9.00/14.50 **t.** ▯ 3.80 – **22 rm** ☲ 43.00/65.00 **t.**

ⓐ ATS 18 Abbey Rd *β* (01778) 422811

BOURNEMOUTH 🔢 🔢 O 31 *The West Country G.* – *pop. 155 488.*
See : *Compton Acres*★★ *(English Garden* ≤★★★*) AC* AX – *Russell-Cotes Art Gallery and Museum*★★ *AC* DZ - *Shelley Rooms AC* EX.
🛆 *Queens Park, Queens Park West Drive β (01202) 396198/302611, DV –* 🛆 *Meyrick Park, Central Drive β (01202) 290307,* CY.
✈ *Bournemouth (Hurn) Airport : β (01202) 593939, N : 5 m. by Hurn -* DV.
🔢 *Westover Rd, BH1 2BU β (01202) 451700.*
London 114 – Bristol 76 – Southampton 34.

Plans on following pages

🏨 **Carlton**, Meyrick Rd, East Overcliff, BH1 3DN, *β* (01202) 552011, *Fax (01202) 299573*, ≤,
⌂, *Ƒ₆*, ☎ₛ, 🔲, 🔲, ☞ – 📺 rest, 📺 rest, 📺 ☎ 🅿 – 🔥 160. 🏧 🆎 ⓪ 𝘝𝘐𝘚𝘈   EZ a
Meals 16.50/21.50 **st.** and a la carte ▯ 7.50 – ☲ 9.50 – **65 rm** 85.00/150.00 **st.**, 5 suites – SB.

🏨 **Royal Bath**, Bath Rd, BH1 2EW, *β* (01202) 555555, *Fax (01202) 554158*, ≤, *Ƒ₆*, ☎ₛ, 🔲,
☞ – ▯ 📺 ☎ ⇔ – 🔥 400. 🏧 🆎 ⓪ 𝘝𝘐𝘚𝘈. ⚒   DZ a
Meals 23.00 **st.** *(dinner)* and a la carte 23.00/33.00 ▯ 8.00 – *(see also Oscars below)* –
124 rm ☲ *(dinner included)* 148.00/296.00 **st.**, 7 suites – SB.

🏨 **Swallow Highcliff**, St. Michael's Rd, West Cliff, BH2 5DU, *β* (01202) 557702,
Fax (01202) 292734, ≤, *Ƒ₆*, ☎ₛ, 🔲, 🔲, ☞, ⚒ – ▯, ⤢ rm, 📺 ☎ 🅿 – 🔥 450. 🏧 🆎 ⓪
𝘝𝘐𝘚𝘈. ⚒   CZ z
Meals 11.75/20.00 **st.** – **154 rm** ☲ 85.00/145.00 **st.**, 3 suites – SB.

🏨 **Norfolk Royale**, Richmond Hill, BH2 6EN, *β* (01202) 551521, *Fax (01202) 299729*, ☎ₛ,
🔲 – ▯, ⤢ rm, 📺 rest, 📺 ☎ ⇔ – 🔥 90. 🏧 🆎 ⓪ 𝘝𝘐𝘚𝘈. ⚒   CY u
Meals 12.95/24.50 **st.** and a la carte ▯ 9.50 – **90 rm** ☲ 95.00/145.00 **st.**, 5 suites – SB.

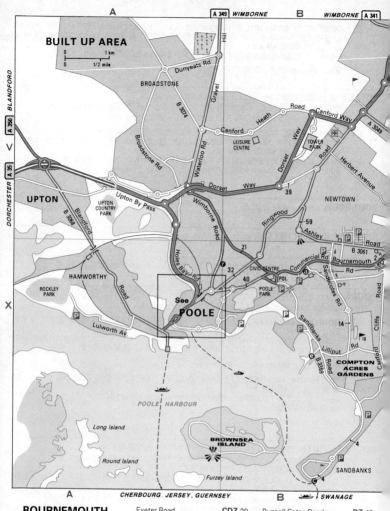

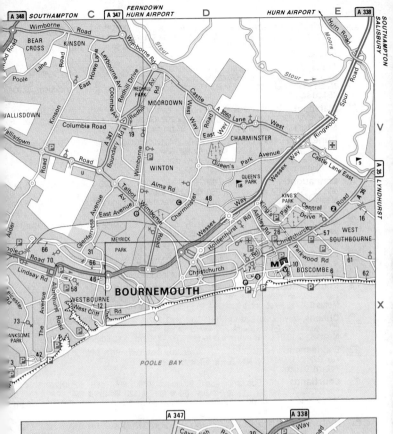

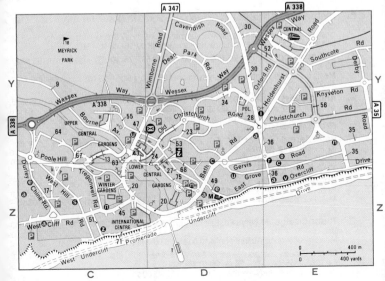

Stakis Bournemouth, Westover Rd, BH1 2BZ, ℰ (01202) 557681, *Fax (01202) 554918*,
≼, ℐ₅, ☎s, ▨, –‖ ▥ ☎ ⇦ – ⚒ 100. ⬤⬤ Æ ⓪ ₥₤₳ ᴊᴄᴮ
DZ z
Meals 12.50/18.50 **t.** and dinner a la carte ⦙ 7.75 – ☲ 9.50 – **104 rm** 95.00/109.00 **t.**,
6 suites – SB.

Chine, Boscombe Spa Rd, BH5 1AX, ℰ (01202) 396234, *Fax (01202) 391737*, ≼, ☎s, ℐ, ▨,
▱ –‖ ▥ ☎ ℗ – ⚒ 120. ⬤⬤ Æ ⓪ ₥₤₳. ⚞
DX e
Meals (bar lunch Saturday) 14.50/17.50 **st.** ⦙ 5.00 – **86 rm** ☲ (dinner included) 70.00/
154.00 **st.** – SB.

Marsham Court, Russell-Cotes Rd, East Cliff, BH1 3AB, ℰ (01202) 552111,
Fax (01202) 294744, ≼, ℐ, –‖ ▥ ☎ ℗ – ⚒ 200. ⬤⬤ Æ ⓪ ₥₤₳. ⚞
DZ e
Meals (bar lunch)/dinner 17.00 **t.** ⦙ 7.00 – **85 rm** ☲ 53.00/86.00 **st.**, 1 suite – SB.

Durley Hall, Durley Chine Rd, BH2 5JS, ℰ (01202) 751000, *Fax (01202) 757585*, ℐ₅, ☎s,
ℐ, ▨, –‖ ▥ ☎ ℗ – ⚒ 200. ⬤⬤ Æ ⓪ ₥₤₳ ᴊᴄᴮ
CZ e
Meals (buffet lunch Monday to Saturday)/dinner a la carte 16.50/25.00 **t.** ⦙ 4.70 – **81 rm**
☲ (dinner included) 55.00/130.00 **st.** – SB.

Connaught, West Hill Rd, West Cliff, BH2 5PH, ℰ (01202) 298020, *Fax (01202) 298028*, ℐ₅,
☎s, ℐ, ▨, –‖ ▥ ☎ ⅋ ℗ – ⚒ 250. ⬤⬤ Æ ⓪ ₥₤₳
CZ s
Meals (bar lunch Monday to Saturday)/dinner 19.50 **st.** and a la carte ⦙ 4.95 – **55 rm**
☲ 52.00/110.00 **st.**, 1 suite – SB.

Miramar, 19 Grove Rd, East Overcliff, BH1 3AL, ℰ (01202) 556581, *Fax (01202) 291242*, ≼,
▱ –‖, ⚞ rest, ▥ ☎ ℗ – ⚒ 80. ⬤⬤ Æ ₥₤₳ ᴊᴄᴮ
DZ u
Meals 8.25/17.25 **t.** – **38 rm** ☲ 65.00/120.00 **t.** – SB.

East Cliff Court, East Overcliff Drive, BH1 3AN, ℰ (01202) 554545, *Fax (01202) 557456*,
≼, ℐ, –‖, ⚞ rest, ▥ ☎ ℗ – ⚒ 100. ⬤⬤ Æ ⓪ ₥₤₳
EZ v
Meals 6.95/14.95 **st.** ⦙ 4.50 – **70 rm** ☲ (dinner included) 65.00/130.00 **st.** – SB.

Round House, Meyrick Rd, The Lansdowne, BH1 2PR, ℰ (01202) 553262,
Fax (01202) 557698 –‖, ⚞ rm, ▥ ☎ ℗ – ⚒ 100. ⬤⬤ Æ ⓪ ₥₤₳
DY a
Meals 8.95/15.95 **st.** and a la carte ⦙ 8.95 – **98 rm** 45.00/60.00 **st.** – SB.

Queens, Meyrick Rd, East Cliff, BH1 3DL, ℰ (01202) 554415, *Fax (01202) 294810*, ℐ₅, ☎s,
▨ –‖, ▤ rest, ▥ ☎ ℗ – ⚒ 200. ⬤⬤ Æ ⓪ ₥₤₳
EYZ r
Meals 8.95/18.95 **t.** and dinner a la carte ⦙ 5.00 – **110 rm** ☲ 52.50/140.00 **t.** – SB.

Bournemouth Heathlands, 12 Grove Rd, East Cliff, BH1 3AY, ℰ (01202) 553336,
Fax (01202) 555937, ℐ₅, ☎s, ℐ, –‖ ▥ ☎ ℗ – ⚒ 250
EZ c
112 rm, 2 suites.

Courtlands, 16 Boscombe Spa Rd, East Cliff, BH5 1BB, ℰ (01202) 302442,
Fax (01202) 309880, ☎s, ℐ, –‖, ⚞ rest, ▥ ☎ ℗ – ⚒ 120. ⬤⬤ Æ ⓪ ₥₤₳
DX o
Meals (bar lunch Monday to Saturday)/dinner 13.50 **t.** and a la carte ⦙ 4.50 – **58 rm**
☲ 45.00/94.00 **t.** – SB.

Hinton Firs, 9 Manor Rd, East Cliff, BH1 3HB, ℰ (01202) 555409, *Fax (01202) 299607*, ☎s,
ℐ, ▨ ☎ ℗. ⬤⬤ ₥₤₳. ⚞
EY n
closed 4 to 30 January – Meals (bar lunch except Sunday October-May)/dinner 13.75 **st.**
and a la carte ⦙ 4.20 – **52 rm** ☲ (dinner included) 48.00/102.00 **st.** – SB.

Collingwood, 11 Priory Rd, BH2 5DF, ℰ (01202) 557575, ☎s, ▨ –‖, ⚞ rest, ▥ ☎ ℗.
⬤⬤ ₥₤₳. ⚞
CZ n
Meals (bar lunch Monday to Saturday)/dinner 16.95 **t.** ⦙ 5.15 – **53 rm** ☲ (dinner included)
48.00/100.00 **t.** – SB.

Anglo-Swiss, 16 Gervis Rd, East Cliff, BH1 3EQ, ℰ (01202) 554794, *Fax (01202) 299615*,
☎s, ▨ –‖ ▥ ☎ ℗ – ⚒ 80. ⬤⬤ Æ ⓪ ₥₤₳ ᴊᴄᴮ
EY e
Meals (bar lunch Monday to Saturday)/dinner 19.00 **t.** and a la carte ⦙ 5.25 – ☲ 8.75 –
63 rm 57.50/69.50 **t.** – SB.

Belvedere, 14 Bath Rd, BH1 2EU, ℰ (01202) 297556, *Fax (01202) 294699* – ‖ ▥ ☎ ℗ –
⚒ 80. ⬤⬤ Æ ⓪ ₥₤₳ ᴊᴄᴮ. ⚞
DYZ c
Meals (bar lunch Monday to Saturday)/dinner 15.50 **t.** and a la carte ⦙ 4.95 – **61 rm**
☲ 45.00/94.00 **t.** – SB.

Boltons, 9 Durley Chine Road South, West Cliff, BH2 5JT, ℰ (01202) 751517,
Fax (01202) 751629, ℐ, ▱ – ▥ ☎ ℗. ⬤⬤ ₥₤₳
CZ a
March-October – Meals (residents only) (dinner only) 12.00 **st.** – **11 rm** ☲ 26.00/52.00 **st.** –
SB.

Tudor Grange, 31 Gervis Rd, East Cliff, BH1 3EE, ℰ (01202) 291472, ▱ – ▥ ☎ ℗. ⬤⬤
₥₤₳
EY o
Meals (residents only) (dinner only) 10.00 **st.** ⦙ 5.00 – **11 rm** ☲ 28.00/58.00 **st.** – SB.

Silver Trees without rest., 57 Wimborne Rd, BH3 7AL, ℰ (01202) 556040,
Fax (01202) 556040, ▱ – ▥ ℗. ⬤⬤ Æ ₥₤₳. ⚞
CV e
closed Christmas and New Year – **5 rm** ☲ 25.00/43.00 **s.**

🏠 **Valberg,** 1A Wollstonecraft Rd, Boscombe, BH5 1JQ, ☎ (01202) 394644, 🌳 – ⊬ rest, [TV] [P]. ⊬ EX V
Meals (by arrangement) 7.00 – **10 rm** ☕ 39.00/50.00 – SB.

🍴🍴🍴 **Oscars** (at Royal Bath H.), Bath Rd, BH1 2EW, ☎ (01202) 555555, *Fax (01202) 554158* – 🚗. [MC] [AE] [D] [VISA] DZ a
closed Sunday dinner – **Meals** 16.50/28.50 **st.** and a la carte 🍷 8.00.

🍴🍴 **Salathai,** 1066 Christchurch Rd, Boscombe East, BH7 6DS, ☎ (01202) 420772 – ❄. [MC] [AE] [VISA] [JCB] EV z
closed Sunday, 25-26 December and 1 January – **Meals** - Thai - 7.95 **st.** (lunch) and a la carte 12.95/22.95 **st.** 🍷 7.00.

🍴🍴 **Noble House,** 3-5 Lansdowne Rd, BH1 1RZ, ☎ (01202) 291277 – ❄. [MC] [AE] [D] [VISA] [JCB] DEY i
closed Sunday lunch and 25-26 December – **Meals** - Chinese - 5.80/19.00 **st.** and a la carte.

🍴 **Helvetia,** 61 Charminster Rd, BH8 8UE, ☎ (01202) 555447, *Fax (01202) 319722* – ❄. [MC] [AE] [D] [VISA] DV c
Meals - Swiss - 8.95/13.95 **st.** and a la carte 🍷 5.90.

[M] ATS 892 Christchurch Rd, Boscombe ☎ (01202) 424457

ATS 1 Fernside Rd, Poole ☎ (01202) 733301/733326

BOURTON *Shrops.* [402] [403] M 26 – *see Much Wenlock.*

Halten Sie beim Betreten des Hotels oder des Restaurants den Führer in der Hand.
Sie zeigen damit, daß Sie aufgrund dieser Empfehlung gekommen sind.

BOURTON-ON-THE-WATER *Glos.* [403] [404] O 28 *Great Britain G.* – *pop. 2 239.*

See : *Town*★.
Env. : *Northleach (Church of SS. Peter and Paul*★*, Wool Merchants' Brasses*★ *), SW : 5 m. by A 429.*
London 91 – Birmingham 47 – Gloucester 24 – Oxford 36.

🏨 **Dial House,** The Chestnuts, High St., GL54 2AN, ☎ (01451) 822244, *Fax (01451) 810126,* 🌳 – ⊬ [TV] ☎ [P]. [MC] [AE] [VISA] [JCB]. ⊬
Meals a la carte 12.45/23.40 **t.** 🍷 7.00 – **10 rm** ☕ 45.00/110.00 **t.** – SB.

🏠 **Coombe House** without rest., Rissington Rd, GL54 2DT, ☎ (01451) 821966, *Fax (01451) 810477,* 🌳 – ⊬ [TV] [P]. [MC] [AE] [VISA]. ⊬
closed 24, 25 and 31 December – **7 rm** ☕ 46.00/71.00 **st.**

🏠 **Lansdowne Villa,** Lansdowne, GL54 2AT, ☎ (01451) 820673, *Fax (01451) 822099* – ⊬ [TV] [P]. [MC] [VISA] [JCB]. ⊬
closed December and January – **Meals** 12.50 **st.** 🍷 3.75 – **12 rm** ☕ 26.00/42.00 **st.**

🏠 **Broadlands,** Clapton Row, GL54 2DN, ☎ (01451) 822002, *Fax (01451) 821776* – ⊬ rest, [TV] [P]. [MC] [VISA] [JCB]. ⊬
closed 25 December and 1 week January – **Meals** (by arrangement) 12.50 **st.** – **11 rm** ☕ 40.00/58.00 **st.**

🏠 **The Lawns** without rest., Station Rd, GL54 2ER, ☎ (01451) 821195 – ⊬ [TV] [P]
closed 25 and 26 December – **5 rm** ☕ 40.00/50.00.

at Great Rissington *SE : 3¼ m.* – ✉ *Cheltenham.*

🍺 **Lamb Inn** with rm, GL54 2LP, ☎ (01451) 820388, *Fax (01451) 820724,* « Part 17C Cotswold stone inn », 🌳 – [P]. [MC] [AE] [VISA]
closed 25 and 26 December – **Meals** a la carte 12.50/17.50 **t.** 🍷 6.50 – **14 rm** ☕ 38.00/75.00.

at Lower Slaughter *NW : 1¾ m. by A 429* – ✉ *Cheltenham.*

🏨 ✿ **Lower Slaughter Manor** 🐦, GL54 2HP, ☎ (01451) 820456, *Fax (01451) 822150,* ←, « 17C manor house, gardens », 🏊, 🎾 – ⊬ rest, [TV] ☎ [P] – 👥 25. [MC] [AE] [D] [VISA]. ⊬
Meals 19.95/39.50 **t.** and a la carte 28.50/41.50 **t.** 🍷 15.00 – **12 rm** ☕ 130.00/300.00 **t.**, 3 suites – SB
Spec. Pressed crab and scallops with crispy vegetables and spinach sauce. Ginger roasted pigeon with foie gras, crispy potato and juniper scented sauce. Hot blackberry soufflé with a compote of fresh figs.

🏨 **Washbourne Court,** GL54 2HS, ☎ (01451) 822143, *Fax (01451) 821045,* 🍽, « Part 17C house », 🌳, 🎾 – ⊬ rest, [TV] ☎ [P]. [MC] [AE] [D] [VISA]. ⊬
Meals 21.50/36.50 **t.** – **19 rm** ☕ 120.00/190.00 **t.**, 9 suites – SB.

at Upper Slaughter NW : 2¾ m. by A 429 – ⊠ Cheltenham.

 Lords of the Manor ⤢, GL54 2JD, ℰ (01451) 820243, Fax (01451) 820696, ≼, « Part 17C manor house », ⤢, ⌨, park – ⤢ rest, 📺 ☎ 🅿 – 🕮 30. 🆗 🅰🅴 ⓞ 🆅🅸🆂🅰 🅹🅲🅱. ⋇
Meals 19.95/29.50 **t.** and a la carte 35.70/47.45 **t.** ⫷ 8.00 – **27 rm** ⊃ 90.00/245.00 **st.** – SB
Spec. Consommé of duck confit, beetroot and truffle oil. Pot roasted rabbit with home dried tomatoes, rösti potatoes and lentil sauce. Vacherin of red berries, roasted almonds and wild strawberry jus.

BOVEY TRACEY Devon 403 I 32 *The West Country G.* – pop. 3 492 – ⊠ Newton Abbot.
See : *St. Peter, St. Paul and St. Thomas of Canterbury Church*★.
Env. : *Dartmoor National Park*★★.
🖪 Newton Abbot ℰ (01626) 52460.
London 214 – Exeter 14 – Plymouth 32.

🏨 **Edgemoor,** Haytor Rd, TQ13 9LE, W : 1 m. on B 3387 ℰ (01626) 832466, Fax (01626) 834760, ⌨ – ⤢ rest, 📺 ☎ 🅿 – 🕮 90. 🆗 🅰🅴 ⓞ 🆅🅸🆂🅰 🅹🅲🅱
closed 1 week after Christmas – **Meals** (booking essential) 15.95/22.50 **t.** ⫷ 4.25 – **17 rm** ⊃ 52.50/99.95 **t.** – SB.

🏠 **Coombe Cross,** Coombe Cross, TQ13 9EY, E : ½ m. on B 3344 ℰ (01626) 832476, Fax (01626) 835298, ≼, 🛌, 🏊, 🎾, ⌨ – ⤢ rest, 📺 ☎ 🅿. 🆗 🅰🅴 ⓞ 🆅🅸🆂🅰 🅹🅲🅱
closed 20 November-26 December – **Meals** (bar lunch)/dinner 19.95 ⫷ 6.45 – **20 rm** ⊃ 40.00/66.00 **t.** – SB.

⤒ **Front House Lodge,** East St., TQ13 9EL, ℰ (01626) 832202, Fax (01626) 832202, ⌨ – ⤢ 📺 🅿. 🆗 🅰🅴 ⓞ 🆅🅸🆂🅰 🅹🅲🅱. ⋇
Meals (by arrangement) 15.00 **s.** – **6 rm** ⊃ 25.00/48.00 **s.**

at Haytor W : 2½ m. on B 3387 – ⊠ Bovey Tracey.

🏨 **Bel Alp House** ⤢, TQ13 9XX, on B 3387 ℰ (01364) 661217, Fax (01364) 661292, ≼ countryside, « Country house atmosphere », ⌨ – ⤢ rest, 📺 ☎ ⅋ 🅿. 🆗 🅰🅴 ⓞ 🆅🅸🆂🅰 🅹🅲🅱
restricted opening December to March – **Meals** (booking essential to non-residents) (light lunch)/dinner 30.00 **st.** ⫷ 8.00 – **8 rm** ⊃ 60.00/140.00 **st.**

at Haytor Vale W : 3½ m. by B 3387 – ⊠ Newton Abbot.

🏠 **Rock Inn,** TQ13 9XP, ℰ (01364) 661305, Fax (01364) 661242, « 18C », ⌨ – ⤢ 📺 ☎ 🅿. 🆗 🅰🅴 ⓞ 🆅🅸🆂🅰
Four Seasons : Meals 14.95/21.95 **t.** and a la carte ⫷ 6.25 – **9 rm** ⊃ 45.95/91.00 **t.** – SB.

BOVINGDON Herts. 404 S 28 – pop. 4 491 London 35.
Aylesbury 29 – Maidenhead 21 – Oxford 31.

🏨 **Bobsleigh Inn,** Hempstead Rd, HP3 0DS, on B 4505 ℰ (01442) 833276, Fax (01442) 832471, 🏊, ⌨ – 📺 ☎ ⅋ 🅿 – 🕮 60. 🆗 🅰🅴 ⓞ 🆅🅸🆂🅰 🅹🅲🅱
closed Monday lunch and Sunday to non-residents – **Meals** 15.95/19.95 **st.** and a la carte ⫷ 6.25 – **44 rm** ⊃ 60.00/85.00 **st.**

BOWBURN Durham 401 402 P 19 – pop. 3 296.
London 265 – Durham 3 – Middlesbrough 20.

🏠 **RoadChef Lodge** without rest., Tursdale Rd, DH6 5NP, at junction 61 of A 1(M) ℰ (0191) 377 3666, Fax (0191) 377 1448, Reservations (Freephone) 0800 834719 – ⤢ 📺 ☎ ⅋ 🅿. 🆗 🅰🅴 ⓞ 🆅🅸🆂🅰. ⋇
closed 25 December and 1 January – ⊃ 4.00 – **38 rm** 43.50 **st.**

BOWNESS-ON-WINDERMERE Cumbria 402 L 20 – see Windermere.

BOX Wilts. 403 404 M 29 – see Bath (Bath & North East Somerset).

BRACKENTHWAITE Cumbria – see Buttermere.

Dans ce guide
un même symbole, un même mot,
imprimé en **noir** ou en **rouge**, en maigre ou en **gras**,
n'ont pas tout à fait la même signification.
Lisez attentivement les pages explicatives.

BRACKLEY Northants. 403 404 Q 27 – pop. 9 113.

🔹 2 Bridge St., NN13 7AP ℘ (01280) 700111.
London 67 – Birmingham 53 – Northampton 21 – Oxford 21.

🏠 **Crown,** 20 Market Pl., NN13 7DP, ℘ (01280) 702210, Fax (01280) 701840 – 📺 ☎ – 🏛 60.
🐵 🝗 ⓪ 💳
Meals (closed dinner 24 December) 10.25/11.50 **st.** and dinner a la carte ↥ 4.95 – ⚏ 6.00 –
19 rm 50.00/65.00 **st.**

🔹 ATS Station Building, Northampton Rd ℘ (01280) 702000/703188

BRACKNELL Bracknell Forest 404 R 29 – pop. 60 895.

🔹 Downshire, Easthampstead Park, Wokingham ℘ (01344) 302030.
🔹 The Look Out, Nine Mile Ride, RG12 7QW ℘ (01344) 868196.
London 35 – Reading 11.

🏯 **Coppid Beech,** John Nike Way, RG12 8TF, NW : 3 m. by A 329 on B 3408
℘ (01344) 303333, Fax (01344) 301200, ↥⌀, 🝘, 🖳 – 🛗, 🌡 rm, 🍽 rest, 📺 ☎ 🕭 🕭 –
🏛 350. 🐵 🝗 ⓪ 💳 🇯 🍸
Rowans : **Meals** (closed Saturday lunch) 18.50/22.50 **t.** and a la carte ↥ 7.50 – **205 rm**
⚏ 135.00/345.00 **st.** – SB.

🏨 **Hilton National Bracknell,** Bagshot Rd, RG12 0QJ, S : 2 m. on A 322
℘ (01344) 424801, Fax (01344) 487454, 🝘 – 🛗, 🌡 rm, 🍽 rest, 📺 ☎ 🕭 – 🏛 450. 🐵 🝗
⓪ 💳 🇯 🍸
Meals (closed Saturday lunch) 14.50/16.95 **st.** and dinner a la carte – ⚏ 12.95 – **167 rm**
137.00/167.00 **st.** – SB.

🏠 **Travel Inn,** Arlington Sq., Wokingham Rd, RG12 1WA, W : ½ m. on A 329 at "3.M."
roundabout ℘ (01344) 486320, Fax (01344) 486172 – 🌡 rm, 📺 🕭 🕭. 🐵 🝗 ⓪ 💳
Meals (grill rest.) – **40 rm** 36.50 **t.**

Le Guide change, changez de **guide Michelin** *tous les ans.*

BRADFIELD COMBUST Suffolk – see Bury St. Edmunds.

BRADFORD W. Yorks. 402 O 22 Great Britain G. – pop. 289 376.

See : City★.
🔹 West Bowling, Newall Hall, Rooley Lane ℘ (01274) 724449 BY – 🔹 Woodhall Hills,
Woodhall Rd, Calverley, Pudsley ℘ (0113) 256 4771 – 🔹 Bradford Moor, Scarr Hall, Pollard
Lane ℘ (01274) 638313 BX – 🔹 East Bierley, South View Rd ℘ (01274) 681023 BX –
🔹 Queensbury, Brighouse Rd ℘ (01274) 882155, AY.
✈ Leeds and Bradford Airport : ℘ (0113) 250 9696, NE : 6 m. by A 658 BX.
🔹 National Museum of Photography, Film & TV, Pictureville, BD1 1NQ ℘ (01274) 753678.
London 212 – Leeds 9 – Manchester 39 – Middlesbrough 75 – Sheffield 45.

Plan of Enlarged Area : see Leeds

🏯 **Cedar Court,** Mayo Av., off Rooley Lane, BD5 8HZ, ℘ (01274) 406606, Fax (01274) 406600,
↥⌀, 🝘, 🖳 – 🛗, 🌡 rm, 🍽 rest, 📺 ☎ 🕭 🕭 – 🏛 640. 🐵 🝗 ⓪ 💳 🇯   BY a
Meals (closed Saturday lunch) 14.50/19.95 **st.** and a la carte ↥ 9.95 – ⚏ 9.50 – **122 rm**
95.00 **st.**, 5 suites – SB.

🏯 **Victoria,** Bridge St., BD1 1JX, ℘ (01274) 728706, Fax (01274) 736358, ↥⌀, 🝘 – 🛗, 🌡 rm,
📺 ☎ 🕭 🕭 – 🏛 150. 🐵 🝗 ⓪ 💳   BZ a
Vic and Bert's : **Meals** (closed lunch Saturday and Sunday) 13.90 **st.** and a la carte ↥ 6.50 –
⚏ 10.00 – **57 rm** 60.50/73.00 **st.**, 3 suites – SB.

🏯 **Stakis Bradford,** Hall Ings, BD1 5SH, ℘ (01274) 734734, Fax (01274) 306146 – 🛗, 🌡 rm,
🍽 rest, 📺 ☎ – 🏛 700. 🐵 🝗 ⓪ 💳 🇯 🍸   BZ e
Meals (closed Sunday lunch) a la carte 16.00/23.00 **st.** ↥ 5.50 – ⚏ 8.95 – **116 rm** 85.00/
95.00 **st.**, 4 suites – SB.

🏨 **Courtyard by Marriott Leeds/Bradford,** The Pastures, Tong Lane, BD4 0RP,
SE : 4 ¾ m. by A 650 and B 6135 on Tong Lane ℘ (0113) 2854646, Fax (0113) 2853661, 🝘,
🌫 – 🛗, 🌡 rm, 📺 🕭 🕭 – 🏛 250. 🐵 🝗 ⓪ 💳   on Leeds town plan BX e
Meals (bar lunch Saturday) a la carte 15.50/24.45 **st.** ↥ 6.75 – ⚏ 8.95 – **49 rm** 74.00 **st.**,
1 suite – SB.

🏨 **Guide Post,** Common Rd, Low Moor, BD12 0ST, S : 3 m. by A 641 off A 638
℘ (01274) 607866, Fax (01274) 671085 – 📺 ☎ 🕭 – 🏛 100. 🐵 🝗 ⓪ 💳
Meals (closed Saturday lunch and Sunday dinner) 8.95/14.95 **t.** and dinner a la carte ↥ 3.95
– **43 rm** ⚏ 55.00/85.00 **t.**   on Leeds town plan AX c

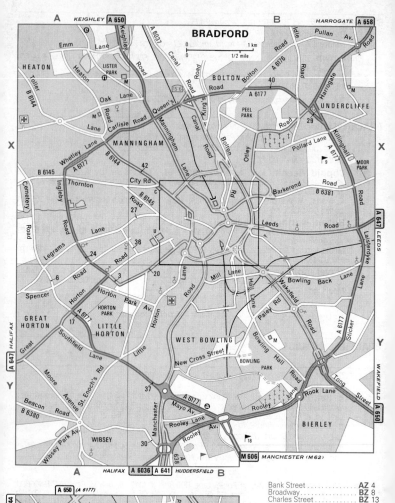

BRADFORD

1 km
1/2 mile

Novotel Bradford, Euroway Trading Estate, Merrydale Rd, BD4 6SA, S : 3 ½ m. by A 641 and A 6117 off M 606 _℘ (01274) 683683, Fax (01274) 651342,_ ⏋ – 劇, ↝ rm, ⊡ 🅟 & 🅟 – 🔏 300. ⓄⒸ 🅰🅴 ⓄⒾ 𝘝𝘐𝘚𝘈
on Leeds town plan AX   **a**
Meals 14.50 **st.** (dinner) and a la carte 13.15/21.15 ∬ 5.15 – ⌷ 7.95 – **125 rm** 55.00/ 67.50 **st.** – SB.

Travel Inn, Whitehall Rd, Cleckheaton, BD19 6HG, _℘ (01274) 862828, Fax (01274) 852973_ – ↝ rm, ⊡ & 🅟. ⓄⒸ 🅰🅴 ⓄⒾ 𝘝𝘐𝘚𝘈. �
on Leeds town plan BX   **c**
Meals (grill rest.) – **40 rm** 36.50 **t.**

Park Drive, 12 Park Drive, Heaton, BD9 4DR, _℘ (01274) 480194, Fax (01274) 484869,_ 🞪 – ↝ rest, ⊡ ☎ 🅟. ⓄⒸ 🅰🅴 𝘝𝘐𝘚𝘈. �
AX   **e**
Meals (residents only) (dinner only) 12.50 **st.** and a la carte – **11 rm** ⌷ 47.00/57.00 **st.** – SB.

Brow Top Farm without rest., Baldwin Lane, Clayton, BD14 6PS, SW : 4 ½ m. by A 647 off Baldwin Lane _℘ (01274) 882178,_ « Working farm », 🞪 – ⊡ 🅟. �
closed Christmas – **3 rm** ⌷ 20.00/35.00.

Restaurant Nineteen (Smith) with rm, 19 North Park Rd, Heaton, BD9 4NT, _℘ (01274) 492559, Fax (01274) 483827_ – ⊡ 🅟. ⓄⒸ 🅰🅴 𝘝𝘐𝘚𝘈. �
AX   **n**
❀
closed Sunday, Monday, 1 week spring, 1 week August and 2 weeks December-January –
Meals (dinner only) 28.00 **t.** ∬ 10.50 – ⌷ 7.50 – **4 rm** 75.00/90.00 **t.**
Spec. Red pepper, goat's cheese and olive tart. Sea bass with leeks, sweet potato chips and red Thai sauce. Sicilian cassata.

at Gomersal SE : 7 m. by A 650 on A 651 – BY – ✉ Bradford.

Gomersal Park, Moor Lane, BD19 4LJ, NW : 1 ½ m. by A 651 off A 652 _℘ (01274) 869386, Fax (01274) 861042,_ 𝑓𝑎, ☎, ⏋ – ⊡ ☎ 🅟 – 🔏 200. ⓄⒸ 🅰🅴 ⓄⒾ 𝘝𝘐𝘚𝘈
accommodation closed 26 to 30 December – **Meals** _(closed Saturday lunch)_ 9.95/15.95 **t.** and a la carte – ⌷ 8.25 – **49 rm** 75.00/85.00 **t.**, 1 suite.

🛠 ATS 8 Cranmer Rd _℘ (01274) 632233/632106_   ATS Tong Street (ASDA) _℘ (01274) 680155_
ATS 177 Thornton Rd _℘ (01274) 731141/723015_

BRADFORD-ON-AVON Wilts. �403 �404 N 29 The West Country G. – pop. 8 815.

See : Town★★ - Saxon Church of St. Lawrence★★ - Tithe Barn★ – Bridge★.

Env. : Great Chalfield Manor★ (All Saints★) AC, NE : 3 m. by B 3109 – Westwood Manor★ AC, S : 1 ½ m. by B 3109 – Top Rank Tory (≤★).

Exc. : Bath★★★, NW : 7 ½ m. by A 363 and A 4 – Corsham Court★★ AC, NE : 6 ½ m. by B 3109 and A 4.

🅱 34 Silver St., BA15 1JX _℘ (01225) 865797._
London 118 – Bristol 24 – Salisbury 35 – Swindon 33.

Woolley Grange, Woolley Green, BA15 1TX, NE : ¾ m. by B 3107 on Woolley St. _℘ (01225) 864705, Fax (01225) 864059,_ ≤, 🞪 « 17C manor house, special facilities for young children », ⏋, 🞪, ✿ – ↝ rest, ⊡ ☎ 🅟 – 🔏 40. ⓄⒸ 𝘝𝘐𝘚𝘈 𝗝𝗖𝗕
Meals 15.50/29.00 **st.** ∬ 6.00 – **20 rm** ⌷ 90.00/195.00 **st.**, 3 suites – SB.

Widbrook Grange, Trowbridge Rd, Widbrook, BA15 1UH, SE : 1 m. on A 363 _℘ (01225) 864750, Fax (01225) 862890,_ « Georgian farmhouse and converted out-buildings », 𝑓𝑎, ⏋, 🞪, park – ↝ rest, ⊡ ☎ & 🅟 – 🔏 25. ⓄⒸ 🅰🅴 ⓄⒾ 𝘝𝘐𝘚𝘈 𝗝𝗖𝗕. ✿
Meals _(closed Friday to Sunday)_ (residents only) (dinner only) a la carte approx. 22.50 **t.** ∬ 7.00 – **19 rm** ⌷ 35.00/99.00 **t.**

Georgian Lodge, 25 Bridge St., BA15 1BY, _℘ (01225) 862268, Fax (01225) 862218_ – ⊡ ☎. ⓄⒸ 🅰🅴 ⓄⒾ 𝘝𝘐𝘚𝘈. ✿
closed 24 and 25 December – **Meals** _(closed Monday lunch)_ a la carte 11.50/24.00 **st.** ∬ 4.50 – **10 rm** ⌷ 35.00/75.00 **st.**

Bradford Old Windmill, 4 Masons Lane, BA15 1QN, on A 363 _℘ (01225) 866842, Fax (01225) 866648,_ ≤, 🞪 – ↝ ⊡ 🅟. ⓄⒸ 🅰🅴 𝘝𝘐𝘚𝘈. ✿
restricted opening in winter – **Meals** - Ethnic Vegetarian - (by arrangement) (communal dining) 18.00 **s.** – **4 rm** ⌷ 65.00/89.00.

Priory Steps, Newtown, off Market St., BA15 1NQ, _℘ (01225) 862230, Fax (01225) 866248,_ ≤, « 17C weavers cottages », 🞪 – ⊡ 🅟. ⓄⒸ 𝘝𝘐𝘚𝘈. ✿
Meals (by arrangement) (communal dining) 18.00 **st.** ∬ 4.00 – **5 rm** ⌷ 50.00/66.00 **s.**

Midway Cottage without rest., Farleigh Wick, BA15 2PU, NW : 2 ¾ m. on A 363 _℘ (01225) 863932,_ 🞪 – ⊡ ☎ 🅟
3 rm ⌷ 25.00/38.00 **st.**

at Winsley W : 2½ m. by A 363 on B 3108 – ✉ Bradford-on-Avon.

Burghope Manor ⌂ without rest., BA15 2LA, off B 3108 _℘ (01225) 723557, Fax (01225) 723113,_ « 13C manor house », 🞪 – ↝ ⊡ 🅟. ⓄⒸ 🅰🅴 𝘝𝘐𝘚𝘈 𝗝𝗖𝗕. ✿
closed Christmas and New Year – **5 rm** ⌷ 60.00/75.00 **st.**

at Monkton Farleigh NW : 4 m. by A 363 – ⊠ Bradford-on-Avon.

⌂ **Fern Cottage** without rest., BA15 2QJ, ℰ (01225) 859412, Fax (01225) 859018, ☞ – ⇖
🔲 **ℙ**. ⁒
3 rm ⊑ 30.00/50.00 st.

BRADWELL Derbs. 402 403 404 O 24 – pop. 1 728 – ⊠ Sheffield.
London 181 – Derby 51 – Manchester 32 – Sheffield 16 – Stoke-on-Trent 41.

⌂ **Stoney Ridge** ⤸ without rest., Granby Rd, S33 9HU, W : ¾ m. by Gore Lane
ℰ (01433) 620538, 🔟, ☞ – 🔲 **ℙ**. ⓪⓪ 𝚅𝙸𝚂𝙰
3 rm ⊑ 28.00/50.00 st.

BRAFFERTON HELPERBY N. Yorks 402 P 21 – see Boroughbridge.

BRAINTREE Essex 404 V 28 – pop. 33 229.
🏌 Kings Lane, Stisted ℰ (01376) 346079 – 🏌 Towerlands, Panfield Rd ℰ (01376) 326802.
🛈 Town Hall Centre, Market Sq., CM7 6YG ℰ (01376) 550066.
London 45 – Cambridge 38 – Chelmsford 12 – Colchester 15.

🏨 **White Hart**, Bocking End, CM7 9AB, ℰ (01376) 321401, Fax (01376) 552628, ⇋ – ⇖ rm,
🔲 ☎ **ℙ** – 🕭 40. ⓪⓪ 𝙰𝙴 ⓪ 𝚅𝙸𝚂𝙰. ⁒
Meals (grill rest.) a la carte 9.50/18.90 t. – ⊑ 5.95 – **31 rm** 59.50/71.00 t.

🏨 **Travel Inn**, Galley's Corner, CM7 8GG, SE : 2 m. by B 1018 on A 120 ℰ (01376) 340914,
Fax (01376) 370437 – ⇖ rm, 🔲 ⴕ **ℙ**. ⓪⓪ 𝙰𝙴 ⓪ 𝚅𝙸𝚂𝙰
Meals (grill rest.) – **40 rm** 36.50 t.

Ⓜ ATS 271-275 Rayne Rd ℰ (01376) 323306

BRAITHWAITE Cumbria 401 402 K 20 – see Keswick.

BRAMHALL Gtr. Manchester 402 403 404 N 23 – pop. 39 730 (inc. Hazel Grove) – ⊠ Stockport.
London 190 – Chesterfield 35 – Manchester 11.

🏨 **County H. Bramhall**, Bramhall Lane South, SK7 2EB, on A 5102 ℰ (0161) 455 9988,
Fax (0161) 440 8071 – 🔲 ☎ ⴕ **ℙ** – 🕭 250. ⓪⓪ 𝙰𝙴 ⓪ 𝚅𝙸𝚂𝙰. ⁒
Meals (bar lunch Saturday) a la carte 12.30/20.90 st. ⅋ 4.00 – ⊑ 9.50 – **65 rm** 95.00/
110.00 st.

BRAMHOPE W. Yorks. 402 P 22 – see Leeds.

BRAMLEY S. Yorks. 402 403 404 Q 23 – see Rotherham.

BRAMPTON Cumbria 401 402 L 19 Great Britain G. – pop. 3 957.
Env. : Hadrian's Wall★★, NW : by A 6077.
🏌 Talkin Tarn ℰ (016977) 2255.
🛈 Moot Hall, Market Pl., CA8 IRW ℰ (016977) 3433 (summer only).
London 317 – Carlisle 9 – Newcastle upon Tyne 49.

🏨 **Farlam Hall** ⤸, CA8 2NG, SE : 2 ¾ m. on A 689 ℰ (016977) 46234, Fax (016977) 46683,
≤, « Gardens » – 🔲 ☎ **ℙ**. ⓪⓪ 𝙰𝙴 𝚅𝙸𝚂𝙰
closed 26 to 30 December – **Meals** (dinner only) 29.50/30.50 t. ⅋ 6.75 – **12 rm** ⊑ (dinner
included) 120.00/240.00 t. – SB.

🏨 **Kirby Moor Country House**, Longtown Rd, CA8 2AB, N : ½ m. on A 6071
ℰ (016977) 3893, Fax (016977) 41847, ☞ – ⇖ rest, 🔲 ☎ **ℙ**. ⓪⓪ 𝙰𝙴 𝚅𝙸𝚂𝙰. ⁒
closed one week January and one week February – **Meals** (light lunch)/dinner 15.45 t.
and a la carte ⅋ 6.25 – **6 rm** ⊑ 37.00/60.00 t. – SB.

at Kirkcambeck N : 7 ¾ m. by A 6071 and Walton rd – ⊠ Brampton.

⌂ **Cracrop Farm** ⤸ without rest., CA8 2BW, W : 1 m. by B 6318 on Stapleton rd
ℰ (016977) 48245, Fax (016977) 48333, ≤, « Working farm », ⇋, ☞, park – ⇖ 🔲 **ℙ**. ⓪⓪
𝙰𝙴 𝚅𝙸𝚂𝙰. ⁒
closed 25 December – **4 rm** ⊑ 25.00/55.00 st.

BRANDESBURTON *East Riding* 402 T 22 – pop. 1 835 – ⊠ *Great Driffield*.
London 197 – Kingston-upon-Hull 16 – York 37.

🏛 **Burton Lodge**, YO25 8RU, S : ½ m. on Brandesburton Hospital rd (old A 165)
ℰ (01964) 542847, Fax (01964) 542847, 🐎, 🐎, ℀ – ᔐ rest, 📺 ☎ 📵. 🚳 ㏂ 𝚅𝙸𝚂𝙰 𝙹𝙲𝙱
closed 25 December – **Meals** *(residents only) (dinner only)* 13.50 **st.** – **9 rm** ⊑ 35.00/48.00.

BRANDIS CORNER *Devon* – ⊠ *Holsworthy*
London 232 – Barnstaple 33 – Exeter 42 – Plymouth 37 – Truro 71.

🏚 **Bickford Arms**, EX22 7XY, ℰ (01409) 221318, Fax (01409) 221781, « Part 17C thatched
inn » – 📺 ☎ 📵. 🚳 𝚅𝙸𝚂𝙰 𝙹𝙲𝙱. ℀
Meals 8.95 and a la carte ‖ 8.95 – **5 rm** ⊑ 35.00/60.00 **st.** – SB.

BRANDON *Warks.* 403 404 P 26 – *see Coventry (W. Mids.)*.

BRANDS HATCH *Kent* – ⊠ *Dartford*.
📍 *Corinthian, Gay Dawn Farm, Fawkham, Dartford* ℰ (01474) 707559.
London 22 – Maidstone 18.

🏬 **Brands Hatch Thistle**, DA3 8PE, on A 20 ℰ (01474) 854900, Fax (01474) 853220 –
ᔐ rm, ▤ rest, 📺 ☎ 📵 – 🔬 270. 🚳 ㏂ ⓞ 𝚅𝙸𝚂𝙰 𝙹𝙲𝙱
Genevieves : **Meals** *(closed Saturday lunch and Bank Holidays)* 16.50/22.50 **t.** and a la carte
‖ 8.00 – **Bugatti Brasserie :** **Meals** a la carte 13.00/19.00 **t.** ‖ 8.00 – ⊑ 10.50 – **129 rm**
89.00/120.00 **t.** – SB.

at Fawkham Green *E* : 1½ m. by A 20 – ⊠ *Ash Green*.

🏠 **Brands Hatch Place**, DA3 8NQ, ℰ (01474) 872239, Fax (01474) 879652, 🖴, 🛎, 🗔, 🐎,
park, ℀, squash – ᔐ rm, 📺 ☎ 📵 – 🔬 120. 🚳 ㏂ ⓞ 𝚅𝙸𝚂𝙰
Meals *(closed Saturday lunch)* 14.75/19.95 **st.** and a la carte ‖ 6.00 – **41 rm** ⊑ 89.00/
99.00 **st.** – SB.

BRANSCOMBE *Devon* 403 K 31 *The West Country G.* – pop. 501 – ⊠ *Seaton*.
See : *Village★*.
Env. : *Seaton (⩽★★), NW : 3 m – Colyton★*.
London 167 – Exeter 20 – Lyme Regis 11.

🏛 **The Look Out** 🗲, EX12 3DN, S : ¾ m. by Beach rd ℰ (01297) 680262,
Fax (01297) 680272, ⩽ cliffs and Beer Head, « Converted coastguards cottages », 🐎 – 📺
☎ 📵
closed 1 week Christmas – **Meals** *(closed Monday) (dinner only)* 25.00 **t.** ‖ 6.25 – **5 rm**
⊑ 60.00/92.00 **t.**

🏛 **Masons Arms**, EX12 3DJ, ℰ (01297) 680300, Fax (01297) 680500, « 14C inn » – 📺 ☎ 📵
– 🔬 100. 🚳 𝚅𝙸𝚂𝙰
Meals *(bar lunch Monday to Saturday)/dinner* 18.00 **t.** and a la carte ‖ 9.50 – **21 rm**
⊑ 22.00/96.00 – SB.

BRANSTON *Lincs.* 402 404 S 24 – *see Lincoln.*

BRANSTON *Staffs.* – *see Burton-upon-Trent.*

BRATTON FLEMING *Devon* 403 I 30 *The West Country G.* – pop. 1 813 – ⊠ *Barnstaple*.
Env. : *Exmoor National Park★★*.
London 228 – Barnstaple 6 – Exeter 46 – Taunton 36.

🏛 **Bracken House** 🗲, EX31 4TG, ℰ (01598) 710320, ⩽, 🐎 – ᔐ rest, 📺 & 📵. 🚳 𝚅𝙸𝚂𝙰
late March-early November – **Meals** *(residents only) (dinner only)* 16.00 **t.** ‖ 3.00 – **8 rm**
⊑ *(dinner included)* 66.00/102.00 **t.** – SB.

BRAYE *Alderney (Channel Islands)* 403 Q 33 and 230 ⑨ – *see Channel Islands.*

Les prix   Pour toutes précisions sur les prix indiqués dans ce guide,
reportez-vous aux pages de l'introduction.

BRAY-ON-THAMES Windsor & Maidenhead **404** R 29 – pop. 8 121 – ⊠ Maidenhead.
London 34 – Reading 13.

Plan : see Maidenhead

🏥 **Monkey Island**, SL6 2EE, SE : ¾ m. by Upper Bray Rd and Old Mill Lane ℰ (01628) 23400, Fax (01628) 784732, ≤, 斎, « Island on River Thames », ℩ら, ℩, 屛 – ⊡ ☎ ℗ – 🔏 150. ◑◐ 🖭 ⓪ 𝘝𝘐𝘚𝘈. ✵
closed 26 December-15 January – **Meals** (closed Saturday lunch) 20.00/28.00 **t.**
and a la carte ℩ 10.00 – ⊑ 11.50 – **23 rm** 95.00/135.00 **t.**, 2 suites – SB.

🏥 **Chauntry House**, 1 High St., SL6 2AB, ℰ (01628) 673991, Fax (01628) 773089, 屛 –
✵ rest, ⊡ ☎ ℗. ◑◐ 🖭 ⓪ 𝘝𝘐𝘚𝘈. ✵   X a
closed 24 December-2 January – **Meals** (closed Sunday dinner and Bank Holidays)
a la carte 27.50/39.00 **st.** ℩ 6.00 – **13 rm** ⊑ 90.00/135.00 **st.**

XXXX **Waterside Inn** (Roux) with rm, Ferry Rd, SL6 2AT, ℰ (01628) 620691, Fax (01628) 784710,
❀❀❀ « ≤ Thames-side setting » – 🔽, 🍽 rest, ⊡ ☎ ℗. ◑◐ 🖭 ⓪ 𝘝𝘐𝘚𝘈 𝘑𝘊𝘉. ✵   X s
closed 26 December-30 January – **Meals** - French - (closed Tuesday lunch, Sunday dinner
from mid October-mid April, Monday and Bank Holidays) 30.50-45.50/
69.50 **st.** and a la carte 59.80/88.50 **st.** ℩ 9.50 – **8 rm** 140.00/170.00 **st.**, 1 suite
Spec. Tronçonnettes de homard poêlées minute au Porto blanc. Filets de lapereau grillés
aux marrons glacés. Soufflé chaud aux framboises.

XX **Fat Duck**, High St., SL6 2AQ, ℰ (01628) 580333, Fax (01628) 776188, 屛 – ◑◐ 🖭 𝘝𝘐𝘚𝘈
closed Sunday dinner, Monday and 2 weeks Christmas – **Meals** 19.50 **t.** (lunch)
and a la carte 30.75/45.00 **t.** ℩ 7.50.   X e

BREADSALL Derby – see Derby.

BREDE E. Sussex **404** V 31 – pop. 1 764
London 62 – Brighton 43 – Canterbury 41 – Hastings 7 – Maidstone 25.

↑ **Arndale Cottage** without rest., Broad Oak, TN31 6EP, N : 1 ¼ m. on A 28
ℰ (01424) 882813, 屛 – ✵ ⊡ ℗. ✵
closed 24 to 26 December – **4 rm** ⊑ 25.00/48.00 **s.**

BREDWARDINE Herefordshire **403** L 27 – ⊠ Hereford.
London 150 – Hereford 12 – Newport 51.

🏠 **Brobury House** ⊗ without rest., Brobury, HR3 6BS, ℰ (01981) 500595,
Fax (01981) 500229, ℩, 屛 – ℗. ◑◐ 𝘝𝘐𝘚𝘈. ✵
closed 25 December and 1 January – **4 rm** ⊑ 20.00/80.00.

↑ **Bredwardine Hall** ⊗, HR3 6DB, ℰ (01981) 500596, 屛 – ✵ ⊡ ℗
closed : 10 December-10 January – **Meals** (by arrangement) 14.00 **st.** ℩ 5.95 – **5 rm**
⊑ 30.00/52.00 **st.** – SB.

BRENTWOOD Essex **404** V 29 – pop. 49 463
🏌 Bentley G. & C.C., Ongar Road ℰ (01277) 373179 – 🏌, 🏌, Warley Park, Magpie Lane, Little
Warley ℰ (01277) 224891.
🚩 44 High St., CM14 4AG ℰ (01277) 200300.
London 22 – Chelmsford 11 – Southend-on-Sea 21.

🏨 **Marygreen Manor**, London Rd, CM14 4NR, SW : 1 ¼ m. on A 1023 ℰ (01277) 225252,
Fax (01277) 262809, 屛 – ✵ rm, ⊡ ☎ & ℗ – 🔏 50. ◑◐ 🖭 ⓪ 𝘝𝘐𝘚𝘈. ✵
Meals 17.00/27.00 **st.** and a la carte ℩ 6.50 – ⊑ 9.50 – **32 rm** 99.00/119.00 **st.**, 1 suite.

🏨 **Forte Posthouse Brentwood**, Brook St., CM14 5NF, SW : 1 ½ m. on A 1023
ℰ (01277) 260260, Fax (01277) 264264, ℩ら, ☎, 🏊 – 🔽, ✵ rm, ⊡ ☎ ℗ – 🔏 100. ◑◐ 🖭
⓪ 𝘝𝘐𝘚𝘈 𝘑𝘊𝘉. ✵
Meals a la carte 10.00/17.50 **st.** ℩ 6.00 – ⊑ 9.95 – **145 rm** 99.00/119.00 **st.** – SB.

⊕ ATS Fairfield Rd ℰ (01277) 211079   ATS Unit 30, Wash Rd, Hutton Ind. Est., Hutton
                                               ℰ (01277) 262877

BRETFORTON Worcestershire **403 404** O 27 – see Evesham.

BRIDGNORTH Shrops. **402 403 404** M 26 Great Britain G. – pop. 11 229.
Exc. : Ironbridge Gorge Museum★★ AC (The Iron Bridge★★ - Coalport China Museum★★ -
Blists Hill Open Air Museum★★ - Museum of the River and Visitor Centre★) NW : 8 m. by
B 4373.
🏌 Stanley Lane ℰ (01746) 763315.
🚩 The Library, Listley St., WV16 4AW ℰ (01746) 763358.
London 146 – Birmingham 26 – Shrewsbury 20 – Worcester 29.

🏠 **Cross Lane House**, Astley Abbotts, WV16 4SJ, N : 1 ¾ m. on B 4373 🐾 (01746) 764887, Fax (01746) 768667, ≤, 🐾 – ⁕ 📺 📞 🅿. 🐵 🖭 *VISA* 𝖩𝖢𝖡
Meals (residents only) (lunch by arrangement)/dinner 17.50 st. ≬ 6.50 – **9 rm** ⇌ 42.50/58.00 st. – SB.

at Worfield NE : 4 m. by A 454 – ✉ Bridgnorth.

🏨 **Old Vicarage** ≫, WV15 5JZ, 🐾 (01746) 716497, Fax (01746) 716552, 🐾 – ⁕ 📺 📞 ♿
🅿. 🐵 🖭 ① *VISA*
Meals (residents only Sunday dinner) (dinner only and Wednesday and Sunday lunch)/dinner 25.00/32.50 st. ≬ 13.50 – **13 rm** ⇌ 70.00/152.50 st., 1 suite – SB.

at Alveley SE : 7 m. by A 442 – ✉ Bridgnorth.

🏰 **Mill**, Birdsgreen, WV15 6HL, NE : ¾ m. 🐾 (01746) 780437, Fax (01746) 780850, 🐾 – 📲,
⁕ rest, 📺 📞 🅿 – 🔬 200. 🐵 🖭 ① *VISA*. ✻
Meals 11.50/21.00 t. and a la carte ≬ 7.85 – ⇌ 6.50 – **21 rm** 58.00/100.00 t. – SB.

BRIDGWATER Somerset 408 L 30 The West Country G. – pop. 34 610.
See : Town★ – Castle Street★ – St. Mary's★ – Admiral Blake Museum★ AC.
Env. : Westonzoyland (St. Mary's Church★★) SE : 4 m. by A 372 – North Petherton (Church Tower★★) S : 3 ½ m. by A 38.
Exc. : Stogursey Priory Church★★, NW : 14 m. by A 39.
🏌 Enmore Park,Enmore 🐾 (01278) 671244.
🚺 50 High St., TA6 3BL 🐾 (01278) 427652 (summer only).
London 160 – Bristol 39 – Taunton 11.

🏠 **Friarn Court**, 37 St. Mary St., TA6 3LX, 🐾 (01278) 452859, Fax (01278) 452988 – 📺 📞 🅿.
🐵 🖭 ① *VISA* 𝖩𝖢𝖡
Meals (closed Sunday) (dinner only) a la carte 13.30/21.05 st. ≬ 4.50 – **16 rm** ⇌ 39.90/59.90 st. – SB.

at North Petherton S : 3 m. on A 38 – ✉ Bridgwater.

🏨 **Walnut Tree**, TA6 6QA, 🐾 (01278) 662255, Fax (01278) 663946 – ⁕ rm, 🔲 rest, 📺 📞 🅿
– 🔬 90. 🐵 🖭 ① *VISA* 𝖩𝖢𝖡. ✻
Meals 10.50/14.00 t. and a la carte ≬ 4.70 – ⇌ 7.00 – **31 rm** 63.00/88.00 t., 1 suite – SB.

🅐 ATS Friarn St. 🐾 (01278) 455891/455795

BRIDLINGTON East Riding 402 T 21 Great Britain G. – pop. 31 334.
Env. : Flamborough Head★, NE : 5 ½ m. by B 1255 and B 1259 – Burton Agnes Hall★ AC, SW : 6 m. by A 166.
🏌 Belvedere Rd 🐾 (01262) 672092/606367 – 🏌 Flamborough Head, Lighthouse Rd, Flamborough 🐾 (01262) 850333/850417.
🚺 25 Prince St., YO15 2NP 🐾 (01262) 673474.
London 236 – Kingston-upon-Hull 29 – York 41.

🏨 **Expanse**, North Marine Drive, YO15 2LS, 🐾 (01262) 675347, Fax (01262) 604928, ≤ – 📲 📺
📞 🅿. 🐵 🖭 ① *VISA*. ✻
Meals 8.75/14.50 st. and dinner a la carte ≬ 4.05 – **48 rm** ⇌ 29.50/80.00 st. – SB.

⌂ **Tennyson**, 19 Tennyson Av., YO15 2EU, 🐾 (01262) 604382, Fax (01262) 604382 – ⁕ 📺
🅿. 🐵 🖭 ① *VISA* 𝖩𝖢𝖡
Meals (by arrangement) approx. 9.00 s. ≬ 3.90 – **6 rm** ⇌ 24.95/44.00 s.

🅐 ATS Springfield Av. 🐾 (01262) 675571

BRIDPORT Dorset 408 L 31 The West Country G. – pop. 11 667.
Env. : Parnham House★★ AC, N : 6 m. by A 3066 – Mapperton Gardens★, N : 4 m. by A 3066 and minor rd.
Exc. : Lyme Regis★ – The Cobb★, W : 11 m. by A 35 and A 3052.
🏌 Bridport and West Dorset, East Cliff, West Bay 🐾 (01308) 422597.
🚺 32 South St., DT6 3NQ 🐾 (01308) 424901.
London 150 – Exeter 38 – Taunton 33 – Weymouth 19.

🏠 **Roundham House**, Roundham Gdns, West Bay Rd, DT6 4BD, S : 1 m. by B 3157
🐾 (01308) 422753, Fax (01308) 421145, ≤, 🐾 – ⁕ rest, 📺 📞 🅿. 🐵 *VISA* 𝖩𝖢𝖡
closed January and February – Meals (dinner only and Sunday lunch)/dinner 17.50 t. and a la carte ≬ 6.50 – **8 rm** ⇌ 35.00/65.00 t. – SB.

⌂ **Britmead House,** West Bay Rd, DT6 4EG, S : 1 m. on B 3157 ℘ (01308) 422941, *Fax (01308) 422516*, 🌺 – ✝⅞ rest, 📺 🅿. 🆎 ⓄⓌ *VISA*. 🌼
Meals 13.50 **st.** ◊ 4.30 – **7 rm** ⌥ 36.00/58.00 **st.** – SB.

✗ **Riverside,** West Bay, DT6 4EZ, S : 1 ¾ m. by B 3157 ℘ (01308) 422011, *Fax (01308) 458808* – ⓄⓌ *VISA* 🇯CB
closed Sunday dinner, Monday except Bank Holidays and 1 December-28 February –
Meals - Seafood - (booking essential) a la carte 19.00/27.50 **t.** ◊ 6.75.

at Shipton Gorge *SE : 3 m. by A 35 –* ✉ *Bridport.*

⌂ **Innsacre Farmhouse** 🍃, Shipton Lane, DT6 4LJ, N : 1 m. ℘ (01308) 456137, *Fax (01308) 456137*, 🌺 – ✝⅞ 📺 🅿. ⓄⓌ *VISA*
closed Christmas – **Meals** (by arrangement) 11.50 **s.** ◊ 6.50 – **4 rm** ⌥ 45.00/65.00 **s.**

🅰 ATS Victoria Grove ℘ (01308) 423661

BRIGHOUSE *W. Yorks.* 402 O 22 – *pop. 32 198.*
London 213 – Bradford 12 – Burnley 28 – Manchester 35 – Sheffield 39.

🏨 **Forte Posthouse Brighouse,** Clifton Village, HD6 4HW, SE : 1 m. on A 644 ℘ (01484) 400400, *Fax (01484) 400068*, ƒ₅, ⌂, 🏊 – ✝⅞ rm, 📺 ☎ ⅙ 🅿 – 🔬 200. ⓄⓌ 🆎 Ⓞ *VISA*
Meals 10.00 **st.** (lunch) and a la carte 8.00/20.00 **st.** ◊ 6.95 – ⌥ 10.95 – **92 rm** 89.00 **st.**, 2 suites – SB.

✗ **Brook's,** 6 Bradford Rd, HD6 1RW, ℘ (01484) 715284, *Fax (01484) 712641* – ✝⅞. ⓄⓌ *VISA*
closed Sunday, 1 week August and 2 weeks January – **Meals** (dinner only and lunch in December) 21.00 **t.** ◊ 5.95.

BRIGHTON AND HOVE 404 T 31 *Great Britain G. – pop. 192 453.*

See : *Town★★* - *Royal Pavilion★★★ AC* CZ – *Seafront★★* – *The Lanes★* BCZ – *St. Bartholomew's★ AC* CX **B** – *Art Gallery and Museum (20C decorative arts★)* CY **M.**
Env. : *Devil's Dyke (⩽★) NW : 5 m. by Dyke Rd (B 2121)* BY.

🔟 *East Brighton, Roedean Rd* ℘ (01273) 604838 CV – 🔟 *The Dyke, Devil's Dyke, Dyke Rd* ℘ (01273) 857296, BV – 🔟 *Hollingbury Park, Ditchling Rd* ℘ (01273) 552010, CV – 🔟 *Waterhall, Devils Dyke Rd* ℘ (01273) 508658, AV.

✈ *Shoreham Airport :* ℘ (01273) 452304, W : 8 m. by A 27 AV.

🛈 *10 Bartholomew Sq., BN1 1JS* ℘ (01273) 323755.
London 53 – Portsmouth 48 – Southampton 61.

Plans on following pages

🏨 **Grand,** Kings Rd, BN1 2FW, ℘ (01273) 321188, *Fax (01273) 202694*, ⩽, ƒ₅, ⌂, 🏊 – ⅙ 📺 ☎ ⅙ ⥂ – 🔬 800. ⓄⓌ 🆎 *VISA*
Meals 18.00/25.50 **t.** and a la carte – **195 rm** ⌥ 145.00/270.00 **st.**, 5 suites – SB.   BZ **V**

🏨 **Brighton Thistle,** Kings Rd, BN1 2GS, ℘ (01273) 206700, *Fax (01273) 820692*, ⩽, ƒ₅, ⌂, 🏊 – ⅙ ✝⅞ rm, ☰ 📺 ⅙ ⥂ ⥂⥂ – 🔬 300. ⓄⓌ 🆎 Ⓞ *VISA*   CZ **n**
Promenade :* Meals** 16.50 **st.** and a la carte 16.20/24.40 ◊ 7.00 – (see also ***La Noblesse below) – ⌥ 10.50 – **200 rm** 142.00/192.00 **st.**, 4 suites – SB.

🏨 **Stakis Brighton Metropole,** Kings Rd, BN1 2FU, ℘ (01273) 775432, *Fax (01273) 207764*, ⩽, ƒ₅, ⌂, 🏊 – ⅙ ✝⅞ rm, ☰ 📺 ⥂⥂ – 🔬 1200. ⓄⓌ 🆎 Ⓞ *VISA* BZ **s**
Meals 19.00/19.50 **t.** and a la carte ◊ 9.50 – **314 rm** ⌥ 170.00/190.00 **st.**, 10 suites – SB.

🏨 **Stakis Bedford,** Kings Rd, BN1 2JF, ℘ (01273) 329744, *Fax (01273) 775877*, ⩽, ƒ₅, ⌂, 🏊 – ⅙ ☰ rest, 📺 ☎ ⥂⥂ – 🔬 450. ⓄⓌ 🆎 Ⓞ *VISA*   BZ **c**
Meals (carving rest.) 14.95/17.95 **st.** ◊ 8.00 – ⌥ 7.50 – **125 rm** 108.00/135.00 **st.**, 4 suites – SB.

🏨 **Old Ship,** Kings Rd, BN1 1NR, ℘ (01273) 329001, *Fax (01273) 820718* – ⅙, ✝⅞ rm, 📺 ☎ ⥂⥂ – 🔬 300. ⓄⓌ 🆎 Ⓞ *VISA*. 🌼   CZ **c**
Meals (dancing Saturday evening) 14.50/19.90 **st.** and a la carte – **152 rm** ⌥ 80.00/150.00 **st.** – SB.

🏨 **Brighton Oak,** West St., BN1 2RQ, ℘ (01273) 220033, *Fax (01273) 778000* – ⅙, ✝⅞ rm, ☰ rest, 📺 ☎ ⅙ – 🔬 200. ⓄⓌ 🆎 Ⓞ *VISA*   BZ
Meals (bar lunch)/dinner 14.75 **st.** and a la carte ◊ 6.50 – ⌥ 7.95 – **136 rm** 52.00/105.00 **st.**, 2 suites – SB.

🏨 **Jarvis Norfolk,** 149 Kings Rd, BN1 2PP, ℘ (01273) 738201, *Fax (01273) 821752*, ⌂, 🏊 – ⅙, ✝⅞ rm, 📺 ☎ 🅿 – 🔬 180. ⓄⓌ 🆎 Ⓞ *VISA*   BZ
Meals (bar lunch Monday to Saturday)/dinner 16.95 **t.** and a la carte ◊ 5.95 – ⌥ 8.50 – **120 rm** 89.00/125.00 **t.** – SB.

Jarvis Preston Park, 216 Preston Rd, BN1 6UU, N : 1 ½ m. on A 23 ✆ (01273) 507853, *Fax (01273) 540039*, ≘, ☒ – ⇷ ▭ ☎ Ⓟ – 🕮 60. ⓂⒸ AE ⓓ VISA BV a
Meals (bar lunch Monday to Saturday)/dinner 15.95 **st.** 🍷 7.00 – ☕ 8.95 – **33 rm** 79.00/ 95.00 **st.** – SB.

Topps without rest., 17 Regency Sq., BN1 2FG, ✆ (01273) 729334, *Fax (01273) 203679* – ⇅ ▭ ☎. ⓂⒸ AE ⓓ VISA. ⚹ BZ a
15 rm ☕ 45.00/99.00 **st.**

Adelaide without rest., 51 Regency Sq., BN1 2FF, ✆ (01273) 205286, *Fax (01273) 220904* – ▭ ☎. ⓂⒸ VISA. ⚹ BZ z
closed 25 December and first 2 weeks January – **12 rm** ☕ 39.00/78.00 **st.**

Allendale, 3 New Steine, BN2 1PB, ✆ (01273) 675436, *Fax (01273) 602603* – ⇷ rest, ▭ ☎. ⓂⒸ AE VISA CZ u
closed 25 and 26 December – **Meals** (by arrangement) (dinner only) 15.00 **st.** 🍷 2.50 – **12 rm** ☕ 25.00/70.00 **t.**

Prince Regent without rest., 29 Regency Sq., BN1 2FH, ✆ (01273) 329962, *Fax (01273) 748162* – ▭ ☎. ⓂⒸ AE VISA JCB. ⚹ BZ u
closed 24 to 26 December – **20 rm** ☕ 35.00/90.00 **t.**

Amblecliff without rest., 35 Upper Rock Gdns., BN2 1QF, ✆ (01273) 681161, *Fax (01273) 676945* – ⇷ ▭ ☎. ⓂⒸ AE VISA. ⚹ CZ s
restricted opening January and December – **8 rm** ☕ 40.00/60.00 **t.**

Ainsley House, 28 New Steine, BN2 1PD, ✆ (01273) 605310, *Fax (01273) 688604* – ⇷ rest, ▭ ☎. ⓂⒸ AE ⓓ VISA JCB. ⚹ CZ r
closed 1 week Christmas – **Meals** (by arrangement) (dinner only) 15.00 **st.** – **11 rm** ☕ 24.00/68.00 **st.**

Kempton House, 33-34 Marine Par., BN2 1TR, ✆ (01273) 570248, *Fax (01273) 570248*, ≤ – ▭ ☎. ⓂⒸ VISA CZ a
Meals *(closed Sunday)* (dinner only) 15.50 **st.** – **12 rm** ☕ 32.00/56.00 **st.**

New Steine without rest., 12a New Steine, BN2 1PB, ✆ (01273) 681546 – ▭. ⚹
closed January and February – **11 rm** ☕ 19.00/45.00 **st.** CZ v

La Noblesse (at Brighton Thistle H.), Kings Rd, BN1 2GS, ✆ (01273) 206700, *Fax (01273) 820692* – ▤ 🚗. ⓂⒸ AE ⓓ VISA CZ n
Meals *(closed Saturday lunch, Sunday and Monday)* 18.50/27.50 **st.** 🍷 7.00.

One Paston Place, 1 Paston Pl., Kemp Town, BN2 1HA, ✆ (01273) 606933, *Fax (01273) 675685* – ▤. ⓂⒸ AE ⓓ VISA JCB CV a
closed Sunday, Monday, first 2 weeks January and first 2 weeks August – **Meals** 16.50 **t.** (lunch) and a la carte 24.50/31.50 **t.** 🍷 8.85.

La Marinade, 77 St. Georges Rd, Kemp Town, BN2 1EF, ✆ (01273) 600992, *Fax (01273) 600992* – ▤. ⓂⒸ AE ⓓ VISA CV c
closed Sunday dinner, Monday and 2 weeks in winter – **Meals** - French - 12.80/18.50 **t.** 🍷 5.00.

Whytes, 33 Western St., BN1 2PG, ✆ (01273) 776618 – ⓂⒸ AE VISA BZ o
closed Sunday and 2 weeks February-March – **Meals** (booking essential Monday) (dinner only) 19.50 **t.** 🍷 6.75.

Black Chapati, 12 Circus Par., off New England Rd, BN1 4GW, ✆ (01273) 699011 – ⓂⒸ AE VISA CX a
closed Sunday, Monday, 2 weeks July and 2 weeks Christmas – **Meals** - Asian specialities - (dinner only) a la carte 16.95/20.15 **t.**

Terre à Terre, 71 East St., BN1 1HQ, ✆ (01273) 729051, *Fax (01273) 327561* – ⓂⒸ VISA CZ e
closed Monday lunch and 25-26 December – **Meals** - Vegetarian - (light lunch)/dinner a la carte 14.50/17.25 **t.** 🍷 6.00.

at Hove.

Imperial, First Av., BN3 2GU, ✆ (01273) 777320, *Fax (01273) 777310* – ⇅ ▭ ☎ – 🕮 100. ⓂⒸ AE ⓓ VISA AZ e
Meals 13.95 **st.** and a la carte 🍷 7.50 – **75 rm** ☕ 70.00/90.00 **st.** – SB.

Claremont House, Second Av., BN3 2LL, ✆ (01273) 735161, *Fax (01273) 735161*, 🌳 – ▭ ☎. ⓂⒸ AE ⓓ VISA JCB AY c
Meals (bar lunch)/dinner 9.50 **st.** and a la carte 🍷 3.50 – **12 rm** ☕ 45.00/78.00 **st.** – SB.

Le Classique, 37 Waterloo St., BN3 1AY, ✆ (01273) 734140 – ⇷. ⓂⒸ AE ⓓ VISA BY i
closed Sunday – **Meals** - French - (dinner only) 15.25 **t.** and a la carte.

Quentin's, 42 Western Rd, BN3 1JD, ✆ (01273) 822734 – ⓂⒸ AE ⓓ VISA AZ a
closed Saturday lunch, Sunday, Monday, last week August and 1st week September – **Meals** 17.95 **t.** 🍷 4.50.

ATS 40 Bristol Gdns ✆ (01273) 680150/686344
ATS Franklin Rd, Portslade ✆ (01273) 415327/414488

BRIGHTON AND HOVE

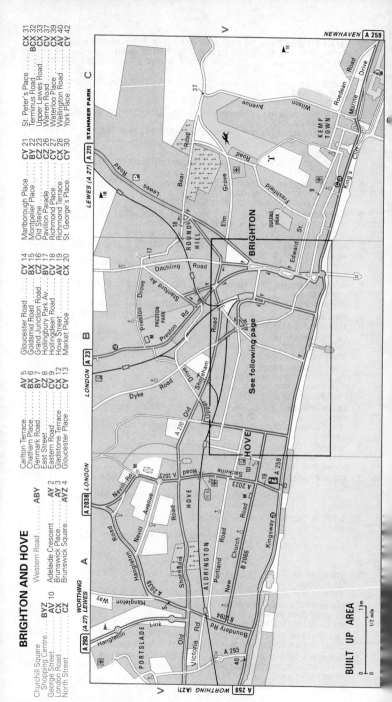

See following page

BRIMFIELD *Herefordshire* 403 404 L 27 *Great Britain G.* – *pop. 626* – ⊠ *Ludlow (Shrops.)*.
Env. : *Berrington Hall* ★ *AC, S : 3 m. by A 49*.
London 149 – Birmingham 41 – Hereford 21 – Shrewsbury 32 – Worcester 33.

🏨 **Travelodge,** Woofferton, SY8 4AL, N : ½ m. on A 49 *&* (01584) 711695, Reservations (Freephone) 0800 850950 – ⅙ rm, 🔟 ⅗ & ⇔ – ⚊ 300. 🐵 🖭 ⓪ 𝘝𝘐𝘚𝘈 ᴊᴄʙ. ⅍
32 rm 39.95 **t.**

🍽 **Roebuck Inn** with rm, SY8 4NE, *&* (01584) 711230, *Fax (01584) 711654,* ☆ – 🔟 ☎ 🄿. 🐵 𝘝𝘐𝘚𝘈 ᴊᴄʙ. ⅍
closed 25 December – **Meals** 12.50 **t.** (lunch) and a la carte 12.95/25.75 **t.** ⅃ 5.40 – **3 rm** ⌑ 40.00/60.00 **t.** – SB.

BRIMSCOMBE *Glos.* 403 404 N 28 – *see Stroud.*

BRISTOL *Bristol* 403 404 M 29 *The West Country G.* – *pop. 407 992.*
See : *City* ★★ – *St. Mary Redcliffe* ★★ DZ – *Brandon Hill* ★★ AX – *Georgian House* ★★ AX A – *Harbourside Industrial Museum* ★★ CZ **M2** – *SS Great Britain* ★★ *AC* AX B – *The Old City* ★ CYZ : *Theatre Royal* ★★ CZ T – *Merchant Seamen's Almshouses* ★ K – *St. Stephen's City* ★ CY D – *St. John the Baptist* ★ CY – *College Green* ★ CYZ (*Bristol Cathedral* ★, *Lord Mayor's Chapel* ★) – *The Exploratory Hands-on Science Centre* ★ DZ – *City Museum and Art Gallery* ★ AX **M**.
Env. : *Clifton* ★★ AX (*Suspension Bridge* ★★ (toll), R.C. *Cathedral of St. Peter and St. Paul* ★★ F, *Bristol Zoological Gardens* ★ *AC, Village* ★) – *Blaise Hamlet* ★★ – *Blaise Castle House Museum* ★, NW : 5 m. by A 4018 and B 4057 AV.
Exc. : *Bath* ★★★, SE : 13 m. by A 4 BX – *Chew Magna* ★ (*Stanton Drew Stone Circles* ★ AC, S : 8 m. by A 37 – BX – and B 3130 – *Clevedon* ★ (*Clevedon Court* ★ AC, ⩽★) W : 11 ½ m. by A 370, B 3128 – AX – and B 3130.
⛳ Mangotsfield, Carsons Rd *&* (0117) 956 5501, BV – ⛳ Beggar Bush Lane, Failand, Clifton *&* (01275) 393117/393474, AX – ⛳ Knowle, Fairway, West Town Lane, Brislington *&* (0117) 977 6341, BX – ⛳ Long Ashton, Clarken Coombe *&* (01275) 392229, AX – ⛳ Stockwood Vale, Stockwood Lane, Keynsham *&* (0117) 986 6505, BX.
Severn Bridge (toll).
✈ Bristol Airport : *&* (01275) 474444, SW : 7 m. by A 38 AX.
🛈 St. Nicholas Church, St. Nicholas St., BS1 1UE *&* (0117) 926 0767 – Bristol Airport, BS19 3DY *&* (01275) 474444.
London 121 – Birmingham 91.

Plans on following pages

🏨 **Swallow Royal,** College Green, BS1 5TA, *&* (0117) 925 5200, *Fax (0117) 925 1515,* ⅃₆ ⅗s, 🔲 – ⧍, ⅙ rm, 🔟 ☎ & ⇔ – ⚊ 300. 🐵 🖭 ⓪ 𝘝𝘐𝘚𝘈 ᴊᴄʙ
CZ a
Terrace : **Meals** 20.00 **t.** (lunch) and a la carte 25.20/30.20 **t.** ⅃ 10.25 – **Palm Court :** **Meals** *(closed Sunday and Bank Holidays)* (dinner only) 24.00 **st.** and a la carte ⅃ 10.25 – **230 rm** ⌑ 132.50/142.50 **st.**, 12 suites – SB.

🏨 **Bristol Marriott,** 2 Lower Castle St., Old Market, BS1 3AD, *&* (0117) 929 4281 *Fax (0117) 922 5838,* ⩽, ⅃₆, ⅗s, 🔲 – ⧍, ⅙ rm, 🔟 ☎ & 🄿 – ⚊ 600. 🐵 🖭 ⓪ 𝘝𝘐𝘚𝘈 ᴊᴄʙ
⅍
DY s
Le Chateau : **Meals** *(closed Sunday and Bank Holidays)* (dinner only) 19.50 **t.** and a la carte 20.50/34.00 **t.** ⅃ 7.25 – **The Brasserie :** **Meals** *(closed Saturday lunch)* 15.95 **t.** and a la carte ⅃ 7.25 – ⌑ 10.95 – **281 rm** 97.00 **st.**, 8 suites – SB.

🏨 **Grand Thistle,** Broad St., BS1 2EL, *&* (0117) 929 1645, *Fax (0117) 922 7619* – ⧍, ⅙ rm 🔟 ☎ 🄿 – ⚊ 600. 🐵 🖭 ⓪ 𝘝𝘐𝘚𝘈
CY a
Meals *(closed Saturday lunch)* 15.50/18.50 **st.** and a la carte ⅃ 5.60 – ⌑ 10.00 – **178 rm** 100.00/120.00 **st.**, 4 suites – SB.

🏨 **Holiday Inn Crowne Plaza Bristol,** Victoria St., BS1 6HY, *&* (0117) 976 9988 *Fax (0117) 925 5040,* ⅃₆ – ⧍, ⅙ rm, 🗐 rest, 🔟 ☎ & 🄿 – ⚊ 180. 🐵 🖭 ⓪ 𝘝𝘐𝘚𝘈 ᴊᴄʙ
DZ a
Meals (bar lunch)/dinner 16.95 **st.** ⅃ 6.00 – ⌑ 10.00 – **128 rm** 110.00/210.00 **st.** – SB.

🏨 **Jurys Bristol,** Prince St., BS1 4QF, *&* (0117) 923 0333, *Fax (0117) 923 0300* – ⧍, ⅙ rm 🗐 rest, 🔟 ☎ 🄿 – ⚊ 300. 🐵 🖭 ⓪ 𝘝𝘐𝘚𝘈
CZ e
Meals 10.50/17.95 **st.** and a la carte ⅃ 6.95 – ⌑ 10.50 – **187 rm** 105.00 **st.** – SB.

🏨 **Hilton National Bristol,** Redcliffe Way, BS1 6NJ, *&* (0117) 926 0041 *Fax (0117) 923 0089,* ⅃₆, ⅗s, 🔲 – ⧍, ⅙ rm, 🗐 rest, 🔟 ☎ 🄿 – ⚊ 300. 🐵 🖭 ⓪ 𝘝𝘐𝘚𝘈 ᴊᴄʙ
DZ r
Meals *(closed Saturday lunch)* 18.00/23.75 **t.** and a la carte ⅃ 6.15 – ⌑ 12.50 – **201 rm** 110.00/150.00 **t.** – SB.

🏨 **Westbury Park** without rest., 37 Westbury Rd, BS9 3AU, *&* (0117) 962 0465 *Fax (0117) 962 8607* – 🔟 ☎. 🐵 🖭 ⓪ 𝘝𝘐𝘚𝘈
AV u
8 rm ⌑ 32.50/49.00 **st.**

🏠 **Travelodge** without rest., Cribbs Causeway, BS10 7TL, N : 6 ¾ m. on A 4018, ℰ (0117) 501530, Reservations (Freephone) 0800 850950 – ⇄ rm, 📺 &, 🅿. 🐾 🅰🅴 ① 𝑉𝐼𝑆𝐴 𝐽𝐶𝐵. ✦
AV e
40 rm 49.95 t.

✗✗✗ **Harveys,** 12 Denmark St., BS1 5DQ, ℰ (0117) 927 5034, Fax (0117) 927 5003, « Medieval cellars and wine museum » – 🗐. 🐾 🅰🅴 ① 𝑉𝐼𝑆𝐴
CY c
🏵 closed Saturday lunch, Sunday, 24 to 29 December and Bank Holidays – **Meals** 16.95 st. (lunch) and a la carte 30.30/49.75 st.
Spec. Grilled scallops with caviar and a light mussel and lobster jus. Roast farm pigeon with sauté potatoes, sherry vinegar jus. Warm apple, raisin and almond gateau with vanilla sauce.

✗✗ **Markwicks,** 43 Corn St., BS1 1HT, ℰ (0117) 926 2658, Fax (0117) 926 2658 – 🐾 🅰🅴 𝑉𝐼𝑆𝐴
CY i
🕭 𝐽𝐶𝐵
closed Saturday lunch, Sunday, Monday, 1 week Easter, 1 week Christmas-New Year and 2 weeks August – **Meals** 16.00/23.50 st. and a la carte 23.50/29.95 t. ﺎ 5.50.

✗✗ **Hunt's,** 26 Broad St., BS1 2HG, ℰ (0117) 926 5580, Fax (0117) 926 5580 – 🐾 🅰🅴 𝑉𝐼𝑆𝐴
closed Saturday lunch, Sunday, Monday, 1 week Easter, 1 week late August and 24 December-2 January – **Meals** a la carte 22.15/28.20 t. ﺎ 9.25.   CY r

✗✗ **Glass Boat,** Welsh Back, nr. Bristol Bridge, BS1 4SB, ℰ (0117) 929 0704, Fax (0117) 929 7338, ≼ – 🗐. 🐾 🅰🅴 ① 𝑉𝐼𝑆𝐴
DY a
closed Saturday lunch, Sunday and 24 December-5 January – **Meals** 10.95/17.50 t. and a la carte ﺎ 9.25.

✗✗ **Redcliffs,** Redcliff Quay, 125 Redcliff St., BS1 6HQ, ℰ (0117) 987 2270, Fax (0117) 930 4255, ≼, � – 🐾 🅰🅴 ① 𝑉𝐼𝑆𝐴
DZ e
closed Saturday lunch, Sunday dinner and 1 week Christmas – **Meals** 12.95/16.95 t. and a la carte ﺎ 5.95.

✗✗ **China Palace,** 18a Baldwin St., BS1 1SE, ℰ (0117) 926 2719, Fax (0117) 925 6168 – 🗐. 🐾 🅰🅴 𝑉𝐼𝑆𝐴 𝐽𝐶𝐵
CY x
Meals - Chinese - 22.50 t. (dinner) and a la carte 15.30/34.50 t.

✗✗ **Jameson's,** 30-32 Upper Maudlin St., BS2 8DJ, ℰ (0117) 927 6565, Fax (0117) 929 1790 – 🐾 🅰🅴 ① 𝑉𝐼𝑆𝐴
CY e
closed Saturday lunch, Sunday dinner and Bank Holidays – **Meals** 21.90 t. (dinner) and a la carte 21.80/28.80 t. ﺎ 4.95.

✗✗ **Michaels,** 129 Hotwell Rd, BS8 4RU, ℰ (0117) 927 6190, Fax (0117) 925 3629 – ⇄. 🐾 🅰🅴 ① 𝑉𝐼𝑆𝐴
AX z
closed Sunday dinner and 1 weekend late August – **Meals** (dinner only and Sunday lunch)/ dinner 14.95 st. ﺎ 4.95.

✗✗ **Du Gourmet,** 43 Whiteladies Rd, BS8 2LS, ℰ (0117) 973 6230, Fax (0117) 923 7394 – 🐾 🅰🅴 ① 𝑉𝐼𝑆𝐴
AX v
closed Saturday lunch, Sunday, 24 December-2 January and Bank Holidays – **Meals** - French - a la carte 14.95/21.70 t. ﺎ 7.00.

✗ **Red Snapper,** 1 Chandos Rd, Redland, BS6 6PG, ℰ (0117) 973 7999 – 🐾 🅰🅴 𝑉𝐼𝑆𝐴 AX c
closed Sunday dinner, Monday, 10 days August-September, 25 December-1 January and 10 days January – **Meals** 12.00 t. (lunch) and a la carte 19.00/23.50 t.

✗ **Oliveto,** 21 Cotham Road South, Kingsdown, BS6 5TZ, ℰ (0117) 942 1744, Fax (0117) 944 1613 – 🐾 🅰🅴 ① 𝑉𝐼𝑆𝐴
AX s
closed Saturday and Sunday lunch and Monday – **Meals** - Italian - a la carte 16.45/23.10 st. ﺎ 5.95.

at Patchway (South Gloucestershire) N : 6½ m. on A 38 – BV – ⊠ Bristol.

🏩 **Aztec,** Aztec West Business Park, BS12 4TS, N : 1 m. by A 38 ℰ (01454) 201090, Fax (01454) 201593, 𝐼₆, ≘ₛ, 🔲, 🖉, squash – 🛗, ⇄ rm, 📺 ☎ &, 🅿 – 🔬 200. 🐾 🅰🅴 ① 𝑉𝐼𝑆𝐴
closed 26 to 29 December – **Meals** (closed lunch Saturday and Bank Holidays) 16.95/ 23.00 st. and dinner a la carte ﺎ 9.95 – **102 rm** ⊑ 119.00/140.00 st., 7 suites – SB.

🏨 **Stakis Bristol,** Woodlands Lane, Bradley Stoke, BS12 4JF, N : 1 m. by A 38 ℰ (01454) 201144, Fax (01454) 612022, 𝐼₆, ≘ₛ, 🔲 – ⇄ rm, 🗐 rest, 📺 ☎ &, 🅿 – 🔬 200. 🐾 🅰🅴 ① 𝑉𝐼𝑆𝐴. ✦
Meals (closed Saturday lunch) (carving rest.) 12.50/17.25 st. and dinner a la carte ﺎ 7.50 – ⊑ 9.95 – **142 rm** 99.00/113.00 st. – SB.

at Hambrook (South Gloucestershire) NE : 5½ m. by M 32 on A 4174 – ⊠ Bristol.

🏩 **Forte Posthouse Bristol,** Filton Rd, BS16 1QX, ℰ (0117) 956 4242, Fax (0117) 956 9735, 𝐼₆, ≘ₛ, 🔲, 🖉, park – 🛗, ⇄ rm, 🗐 rest, 📺 ☎ 🅿 – 🔬 120. 🐾 🅰🅴 ① 𝑉𝐼𝑆𝐴
BV o
Meals (closed Saturday lunch) 15.50/17.95 st. and a la carte ﺎ 7.50 – ⊑ 9.95 – **190 rm** 89.00 st., 4 suites – SB.

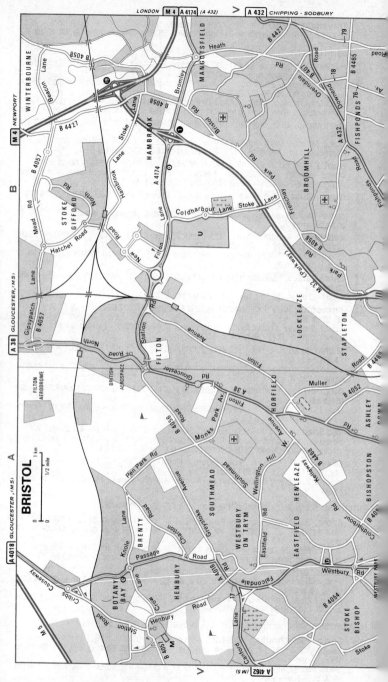

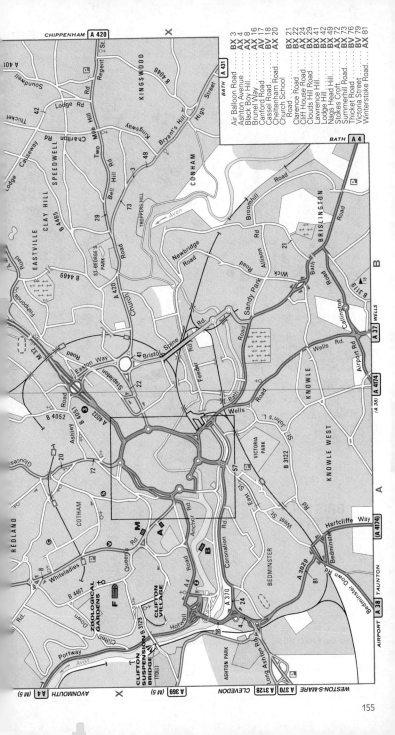

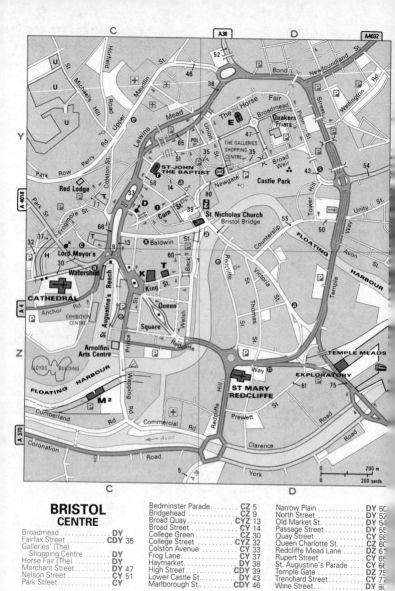

When travelling for business or pleasure
in England, Wales, Scotland and Ireland :

– use the series of five maps
  (nos **401**, **402**, **403**, **404** and **923**) at a scale of 1:400 000

– they are the perfect complement to this Guide

at Mangotsfield NE : 5 ¾ m. by M 32 on A 4174 – BV – ✉ Bristol.

🏨 **Travel Inn,** 200-202 Westerleigh Rd, BS16 7AN, E : ¾ m. off A 4174 ℰ (0117) 956 4755, Fax (0117) 956 4644 – ⇔ rm, �📺 ₺ 🅿. ⚫ 🅰🅴 ① 🆅🅸🆂🅰
Meals (grill rest.) – **40 rm** 36.50 **t.**

at Winterbourne (South Gloucestershire) NE : 7 ½ m. by M 32 and A 4174 on B 4058 – BV – ✉ Bristol.

🏨🏨 **Jarvis Grange H. & Country Club,** Northwoods, BS17 1RP, NW : 2 m. by B 4057 on B 4427 ℰ (01454) 777333, Fax (01454) 777447, ☎, 🔲, park – ⇔ 📺 ☎ 🅿 – 🔬 150. ⚫ 🅰🅴 ① 🆅🅸🆂🅰
Meals (closed Saturday lunch) 16.95/20.50 **st.** and a la carte ⌀ 7.00 – 立 9.50 – **62 rm** 110.00/125.00 **st.** – SB.

at Saltford (Bath & North East Somerset) SE : 7½ m. on A 4 – BX – ✉ Bristol.

🏨 **Brunel's Tunnel House,** High St., BS18 3BQ, off Beech Rd ℰ (01225) 873873, Fax (01225) 874875, 🌲 – 📺 ☎ 🅿. ⚫ 🆅🅸🆂🅰 🅹🅲🅱. ⛛
closed 25 December – **Meals** (closed Friday to Sunday) (booking essential) (dinner only) 16.00 **st.** – **8 rm** 立 50.00/60.00 **st.** – SB.

at Chelwood (Bath & North East Somerset) SE : 8½ m. by A 37 – BX – on A 368 – ✉ Bristol.

🏨🏨 **Chelwood House,** BS18 4NH, SW : ¾ m. on A 37 ℰ (01761) 490730, Fax (01761) 490730, ≼, 🌲 – ⇔ rest, 📺 ☎ 🅿. ⚫ 🅰🅴 ① 🆅🅸🆂🅰 ⛛
Meals (closed Sunday) (dinner only) a la carte 14.20/24.50 **st.** ⌀ 5.50 – **10 rm** 立 47.50/88.00 **st.** – SB.

at Hunstrete (Bath & North East Somerset) SE : 10 m. by A 4 and A 37 – BX – off A 368 – ✉ Bristol.

🏨🏨 **Hunstrete House** ⋟, BS18 4NS, ℰ (01761) 490490, Fax (01761) 490732, ≼, « Late 17C country house, gardens and deer park », 🔲, 🌲 – ⇔ rest, 📺 ☎ 🅿 – 🔬 40. ⚫ 🅰🅴 ① 🆅🅸🆂🅰 🅹🅲🅱, ⛛
✿
Meals 19.95/55.00 **st.** and a la carte 40.00/49.50 **st.** ⌀ 7.00 – **22 rm** 立 115.00/180.00 **st.**, 1 suite – SB
Spec. Salted cod and spiced sweetbreads with coriander and sauternes sauce. Blade of beef with buttered cabbage, crisp potato and foie gras sauce. Apple tart with caramel sauce, Calvados and sultana ice cream.

at Stanton Wick (Bath & North East Somerset) S : 9 m. by A 37 and A 368 on Stanton Wick rd – BX – ✉ Bristol.

🏨 **Carpenters Arms,** BS18 4BX, ℰ (01761) 490202, Fax (01761) 490763 – ⇔ rm, 📺 ☎ 🅿. ⚫ 🅰🅴 ① 🆅🅸🆂🅰, ⛛
Meals a la carte 13.50/21.00 **t.** ⌀ 7.10 – **12 rm** 立 52.50/69.50 **t.** – SB.

ⓂⒶ ATS 68-72 Avon St. ℰ (0117) 971 8140
ATS 551 Gloucester Rd, Horfield ℰ (0117) 951 4525
ATS 58-60 Broad St., Staple Hill ℰ (0117) 956 4741/ 956 5396/956 4594 957 1483
ATS 34-38 St. Johns Lane, Bedminster ℰ (0117) 977 6418/977 0674

BRIXHAM Devon 403 J 32 The West Country G. – pop. 15 865.
Env. : Berry Head★ (≼★★★) NE : 1 ½ m.
🅱 The Old Market House, The Quay, TQ5 8TB ℰ (01803) 852861.
London 230 – Exeter 30 – Plymouth 32 – Torquay 8.

🏨🏨 **Berry Head** ⋟, Berry Head Rd, TQ5 9AJ, ℰ (01803) 853225, Fax (01803) 882084, ≼ Torbay, 🌲 – 📺 ☎ 🅿 – 🔬 300. ⚫ 🅰🅴 ①
Meals 9.50/18.00 **st.** and a la carte ⌀ 4.60 – **16 rm** 立 (dinner included) 48.00/120.00 **t.** – SB.

🏨 **Quayside,** 41 King St., TQ5 9TJ, ℰ (01803) 855751, Fax (01803) 882733, ≼ – ⇔ rest, 📺 ☎ 🅿. ⚫ 🅰🅴 ① 🆅🅸🆂🅰 🅹🅲🅱
Meals (bar lunch)/dinner a la carte 20.80/23.30 **t.** ⌀ 4.75 – **29 rm** 立 47.00/78.00 **t.** – SB.

BROAD CAMPDEN Glos. – see Chipping Campden.

BROADHEMBURY Devon 403 K 31 – pop. 617 – ✉ Honiton.
London 191 – Exeter 17 – Honiton 5 – Taunton 23.

🍴 **Drewe Arms,** EX14 0NF, ℰ (01404) 841267, Fax (01404) 841267, « Part 13C thatched inn », 🌲 – 🅿
closed 25 December – **Meals** - Seafood - 21.00 **st.** and a la carte ⌀ 5.50.

BROADSTAIRS Kent **404** Y 29 – pop. 22 116.

 North Foreland, Convent Rd, Broadstairs ℘ (01843) 862140.

🛈 6b High St., CT10 1LH ℘ (01843) 862242.

London 78 – Dover 21 – Maidstone 47.

🏨 Castlemere, 15 Western Esplanade, CT10 1TD, S : 1 m. by Queens Rd (A 255) and West Cliffe Rd ℘ (01843) 861566, Fax (01843) 866379, ≤, 🐴 – 📺 ☎ 🅿 **🕸 VISA**
Meals (bar lunch)/dinner 12.50 s. ⅜ 4.50 – **26 rm** ⇌ 39.00/74.00 st. – SB.

XX Marchesi, 18 Albion St., CT10 1LU, ℘ (01843) 862481, Fax (01843) 861509, ≤ – ⅜⇐ 🅿. **🕸**
AE ① VISA
closed Sunday dinner except mid June-mid September and 27 to 30 December –
Meals 10.50/15.50 st. and a la carte ⅜ 5.50.

BROADWAY Worcestershire **403 404** O 27 Great Britain G. – pop. 2 328.

See : Town★.

Env. : Country Park (Broadway Tower ⁂★★), SE : 2 m. by A 44 – Snowshill Manor★ (Terrace Garden★) AC, S : 2 ½ m.

🛈 1 Cotswold Court, WR12 7AA ℘ (01386) 852937 (summer only).

London 93 – Birmingham 36 – Cheltenham 15 – Worcester 22.

🏨 Lygon Arms, High St., WR12 7DU, ℘ (01386) 852255, Fax (01386) 858611, « Part 16C inn », ₭₰, ⇌s, 🔲, 🐴, ℀ – 📺 ☎ 🅿 – 🔬 80. **🕸 🕸 AE ① VISA JCB**
Meals 25.00/39.00 t. and a la carte ⅜ 9.00 – ⇌ 9.20 – **60 rm** 105.00/163.00, 5 suites – SB.

🏨 Broadway, The Green, WR12 7AA, ℘ (01386) 852401, Fax (01386) 853879, 🐴 – ⅜⇐ 📺 ☎
🅿 **🕸 AE ① VISA**. ℀
Meals 10.95/19.95 t. and a la carte – **19 rm** ⇌ 47.50/95.00 t. – SB.

🏠 Collin House ⑤, Collin Lane, WR12 7PB, NW : 1 ¼ m. by A 44 ℘ (01386) 858354,
« 17C », 🐴 – 🅿. **🕸 VISA**. ℀
closed 24 to 28 December – Meals 16.00 st. (lunch) and a la carte 16.00/24.00 st. ⅜ 5.00 –
7 rm ⇌ 46.00/98.00 st. – SB.

↑ Barn House without rest., 152 High St., WR12 7AJ, ℘ (01386) 858633,
Fax (01386) 858633, « 17C », 🔲, 🐴, park – ⅜⇐ 📺 🅿
3 rm ⇌ 35.00/75.00 st., 1 suite.

↑ Windrush House without rest., Station Rd, WR12 7DE, ℘ (01386) 853577, 🐴 – ⅜⇐ 📺
🅿
closed Christmas and restricted opening in winter – **5 rm** ⇌ 35.00/44.00 s.

↑ Olive Branch without rest., 78 High St., WR12 7AJ, ℘ (01386) 853440,
Fax (01386) 853440, 🐴 – 📺 🅿. **AE**. ℀
7 rm ⇌ 19.50/48.00 st.

↑ Small Talk Lodge, Keil Close, 32 High St., WR12 7DP, ℘ (01386) 858953 – ⅜⇐ rest, 📺 🅿.
🕸 VISA JCB
Meals (by arrangement) 15.00 st. ⅜ 4.00 – **8 rm** ⇌ 38.00/56.00 st. – SB.

↑ Whiteacres without rest., Station Rd, WR12 7DE, ℘ (01386) 852320, 🐴 – ⅜⇐ 📺 🅿. ℀
March-October – **6 rm** ⇌ 42.00 t.

at Willersey (Glos.) N : 2 m. on B 4632 – ⊠ Broadway.

↑ Old Rectory ⑤ without rest., Church St., WR12 7PN, ℘ (01386) 853729,
Fax (01386) 858061, « Part 17C », 🐴 – ⅜⇐ 📺 🅿. **🕸 VISA**. ℀
closed 22 to 27 December – **8 rm** ⇌ 50.00/95.00 st.

at Willersey Hill (Glos.) E : 2 m. by A 44 – ⊠ Broadway.

🏨 Dormy House, WR12 7LF, ℘ (01386) 852711, Fax (01386) 858636, ₭₰, ⇌s, 🐴 – 📺 ☎ 🅿
– 🔬 200. **🕸 AE ① VISA**
closed 25 and 26 December – Meals (bar lunch Saturday) 28.50 t. and dinner a la carte
⅜ 9.65 – **46 rm** ⇌ 65.00/157.00 t., 3 suites – SB.

at Buckland (Glos.) SW : 2¼ m. by B 4632 – ⊠ Broadway.

🏨 Buckland Manor ⑤, WR12 7LY, ℘ (01386) 852626, Fax (01386) 853557, ≤, « Part 13C
manor house in extensive gardens », 🔲, ℀ – ⅜⇐ rest, 📺 ☎ 🅿. **🕸 AE ① VISA**. ℀
Meals 27.50 t. (lunch) and a la carte 32.50/51.25 t. ⅜ 7.50 – **13 rm** ⇌ 170.00/325.00 t. – SB
Spec. Pastry case of scallops, mussels and langoustines with a light cream sauce. Roasted
rack of English lamb, garlic and herb crust with a rosemary jus. Peach tarte Tatin with
caramel sauce and lime sorbet.

at Wormington (Glos.) SW : 4¼ m. by B 4632 on Wormington rd – ⊠ Broadway.

↑ Leasow House ⑤ without rest., Laverton Meadow, WR12 7NA, E : 1 ¼ m.
℘ (01386) 584526, Fax (01386) 584596, ≤, 🐴 – 📺 ☎ ᴚ 🅿. **🕸 AE VISA**
7 rm ⇌ 35.00/62.00 s.

BROADWELL *Glos.* 🅰🅾🅱 🅰🅾🅴 O 28 – *see Stow-on-the-Wold.*

BROCKDISH *Norfolk* 🅰🅾🅴 X 26 – *see Diss.*

BROCKENHURST *Hants.* 🅰🅾🅱 🅰🅾🅴 P 31 *Great Britain G.* – pop. 3 048.

Env. : *New Forest*★★ (*Rhinefield Ornamental Drive*★★ , *Bolderwood Ornamental Drive*★★).

London 99 – Bournemouth 17 – Southampton 14 – Winchester 27.

🏨 **Rhinefield House** ⬦, Rhinefield Rd, SO42 7QB, NW : 3 m. ℰ (01590) 622922, *Fax (01590) 622800*, « Victorian country mansion, formal gardens », ℄, ⇆, ⌧, park, ℀ – ⇆ 📺 ☎ 🅿 – 🕍 120. 🐵 🆎 ① 𝘝𝘐𝘚𝘈. ℅

Armada : Meals 16.95/24.50 **st.** and a la carte ⓘ 7.25 – **34 rm** ⌐ 100.00/195.00 **st.** – SB.

🏨 **New Park Manor** ⬦, Lyndhurst Rd, SO42 7QH, N : 1½ m. on A 337 ℰ (01590) 623467, *Fax (01590) 622268*, ⌧, ⇌, ℀ – ⇆ 📺 ☎ 🅿 – 🕍 75. 🐵 🆎 ① 𝘝𝘐𝘚𝘈 𝘑𝘊𝘉. ℅

Stag Head : Meals 17.50/29.50 **st.** and dinner a la carte ⓘ 9.00 – **21 rm** ⌐ 85.00/160.00 **st.** – SB.

🏨 **Careys Manor,** Lyndhurst Rd, SO42 7RH, on A 337 ℰ (01590) 623551, *Fax (01590) 622799*, ℄, ⇆, ⌧, ⇌ – ⇆ 📺 ☎ 🅿 – 🕍 100. 🐵 🆎 ① 𝘝𝘐𝘚𝘈 𝘑𝘊𝘉.

Meals 15.75/21.95 **t.** and a la carte ⓘ 10.95 – *Le Blaireau :* Meals - French - a la carte 13.65/19.20 **t.** ⓘ 6.50 – **79 rm** ⌐ 73.00/169.00 **t.** – SB.

🏨 **Whitley Ridge** ⬦, Beaulieu Rd, SO42 7QL, E : 1 m. on B 3055 ℰ (01590) 622354, *Fax (01590) 622856*, ≤, ⇌, ℀ – 📺 ☎ 🅿. 🐵 🆎 ① 𝘝𝘐𝘚𝘈 𝘑𝘊𝘉

Meals (bar lunch Monday to Saturday)/dinner 19.50 **st.** and a la carte ⓘ 6.40 – **13 rm** ⌐ 60.00/130.00 **st.** – SB.

🏠 **Cloud,** Meerut Rd, SO42 7TD, ℰ (01590) 622165, *Fax (01590) 622818* – ⇆ rest, 📺 ☎ 🅿. 🐵 𝘝𝘐𝘚𝘈

closed first 3 weeks January – Meals 9.95/17.00 **t.** ⓘ 4.75 – **16 rm** ⌐ 50.00/80.00 **st.** – SB.

🏠 **Thatched Cottage,** 16 Brookley Rd, SO42 7RR, ℰ (01590) 623090, *Fax (01590) 623479*, « 17C farmhouse » – ⇆ rest, 📺 ☎ 🅿. 🐵 𝘝𝘐𝘚𝘈 𝘑𝘊𝘉

closed January – Meals *(closed Sunday dinner and Monday)* 26.50 **t.** (dinner) and lunch a la carte 26.50/29.50 ⓘ 7.50 – **5 rm** ⌐ 90.00/135.00 **st.**

🏠 **Cottage** without rest., Sway Rd, SO42 7SH, ℰ (01590) 622296, *Fax (01590) 623014*, ⇌ – ⇆ 📺 🅿. 🐵 𝘝𝘐𝘚𝘈

closed January and December – **7 rm** ⌐ 49.00/82.00 **st.**

🍴 **Le Poussin** (Aitken), The Courtyard, rear of 49-51 Brookley Rd, SO42 7RB, ℰ (01590) 623063, *Fax (01590) 623144*, ⇛ – ⇆. 🐵 𝘝𝘐𝘚𝘈

🏵 closed Monday and Tuesday – Meals (booking essential) 20.50/28.00 **t.** ⓘ 8.25

Spec. Wild mushroom and rabbit boudin. Saddle of New Forest venison on a cabbage and onion confit, red wine sauce. Hot passion fruit soufflé.

at Sway SW : 3 m. by B 3055 – ✉ Lymington.

🏠 **Nurse's Cottage,** Station Rd, SO41 6BA, ℰ (01590) 683402, *Fax (01590) 683402*, ⇌ – ⇆ 📺 🅿. 🐵 🆎 𝘝𝘐𝘚𝘈 𝘑𝘊𝘉

closed 15 November-15 December – Meals (by arrangement) 17.25 ⓘ 3.95 – **3 rm** ⌐ 50.00/90.00 – SB.

BROMBOROUGH *Mersey.* 🅰🅾🅲 🅰🅾🅱 L 24 – pop. 14 518 – ✉ Wirral.

🏌 *Raby Hall Rd* ℰ (0151) 334 2155.

London 210 – Chester 14 – Liverpool 6.5 – Manchester 46.

🏨 **The Village H. & Leisure Club,** Pool Lane, L62 4UE, on A 41 ℰ (0151) 643 1616, *Fax (0151) 643 1420*, ℄, ⇆, ⌧, ℀, squash – 📟 ⇆, ▤ rest, 📺 ☎ ♿ 🅿 – 🕍 200. 🐵 🆎 ① 𝘝𝘐𝘚𝘈. ℅

Meals a la carte 11.35/23.55 **st.** ⓘ 3.90 – **91 rm** ⌐ 84.00/98.00 **st.** – SB.

🏠 **Travel Inn,** High St., L62 7HZ, ℰ (0151) 334 2917, *Fax (0151) 334 0443* – ⇆ rm, 📺 🅿 – 🕍 80. 🐵 🆎 ① 𝘝𝘐𝘚𝘈. ℅

Meals (grill rest.) – **32 rm** 36.50 **t.**

BROME *Suffolk* 🅰🅾🅴 X 26 – *see Diss (Norfolk).*

BROMLEY CROSS *Gtr. Manchester* 🅰🅾🅲 🅰🅾🅴 M 23 – *see Bolton.*

Benutzen Sie den Hotelführer des laufenden Jahres.

BROMSGROVE Worcestershire 403 404 N 26 – pop. 26 366.

🛈 Bromsgrove Museum, 26 Birmingham Rd, B61 0DD 🖉 (01527) 831809.
London 117 – Birmingham 14 – Bristol 71 – Worcester 13.

🏬 **Stakis Bromsgrove,** Birmingham Rd, B61 0JB, N : 2 ½ m. on A 38 🖉 (0121) 447 7888,
Fax (0121) 447 7273, ₤5, 🏖, 🏊, 🛲 – ₩ rm, 🍴 rest, 📺 ☎ 🅿 – 🛦 200. 🍱 🖭 ⓐ 🚾.
🛠
Meals (closed Saturday lunch) 13.95/18.95 **st.** and dinner a la carte ₰ 7.50 – ☲ 9.75 –
137 rm 108.00/123.00 **st.**, 2 suites – SB.

🏬 **Pine Lodge,** 85 Kidderminster Rd, B61 9AB, W : 1 m. on A 448 🖉 (01527) 576600,
Fax (01527) 878981, ₤5, 🏖, 🏊, – 🛏 ₩ , 🍴 rest, 📺 ☎ & 🅿 – 🛦 200. 🍱 🖭 ⓐ 🚾
Meals (closed Saturday lunch) 15.50/17.75 **st.** and a la carte ₰ 8.75 – **112 rm** ☲ 92.50/
102.50 **st.**, 2 suites.

🏛 **Grafton Manor,** Grafton Lane, B61 7HA, SW : 1 ¾ m. by Worcester Rd 🖉 (01527) 579007,
Fax (01527) 575221, « 16C and 18C manor », 🛲 , park – ₩ rest, 📺 ☎ 🅿. 🍱 🖭 ⓐ 🚾.
🛠
Meals (closed Saturday lunch) 20.50/25.95 **t.** ₰ 12.90 – **7 rm** ☲ 85.00/125.00 **t.**, 2 suites –
SB.

🏛 **Perry Hall,** 13 Kidderminster Rd, B61 7JN, 🖉 (01527) 579976, Fax (01527) 575998, 🛲 –
₩ rm, 📺 ☎ 🅿 – 🛦 70. 🍱 🖭 ⓐ 🚾
Meals 11.95/16.95 **st.** and a la carte – ☲ 8.50 – **58 rm** 82.00/102.00 **st.** – SB.

🏠 **Bromsgrove Country,** 249 Worcester Rd, Stoke Heath, B61 7JA, SW : 2 m
🖉 (01527) 835522, Fax (01527) 871257, 🛲 – ₩ rm, 📺 🅿. 🍱 🚾. 🛠
closed Christmas-New Year – **Meals** (residents only) (dinner only) a la carte approx. 10.00
₰ 4.50 – ☲ 5.00 – **9 rm** 45.00/49.00 **st.**

| Prices | For notes on the prices quoted in this Guide, see the introduction. |

BROMYARD Herefordshire 403 404 M 27 – pop. 3 117.
🛈 T.I.C. & Heritage Centre, 1 Rowberry St., HR7 4DX 🖉 (01885) 488528.
London 138 – Hereford 15 – Leominster 13 – Worcester 14.

🏛 **Falcon,** Broad St., HR7 4BT, 🖉 (01885) 483034, Fax (01885) 488818 – ₩ 📺 ☎ 🅿. 🍱 ⓐ
🚾
Meals (closed Sunday dinner) (carving rest.) 4.50/10.50 **st.** and dinner a la carte ₰ 5.50 –
8 rm ☲ 39.50/49.50 **st.** – SB.

🏠 **Granary** ⬥, Church House Farm, Collington, HR7 4NA, N : 4 ¼ m. by B 4214, Edvin Loach
rd and Ripplewood rd 🖉 (01885) 410345, « Working farm » – 📺 🅿. 🛠
Meals (by arrangement) 9.00 **st.** – **5 rm** ☲ 20.00/40.00 **t.**

at Acton Green SE : 4 ¾ m. by A 44 on B 4220 – ⊠ Bromyard.

🏠 **Hidelow House** ⬥, Acton Beauchamp, WR6 5AH, S : ¼ m. 🖉 (01886) 884547,
Fax (01886) 884060, 🛲 – ₩ rm, 📺 🅿
closed 25 December – **Meals** (by arrangement) (communal dining) 11.50 **st.** – **3 rm**
☲ 20.00/80.00 **st.**

BROOK Hants. 403 404 P 31 – ⊠ Lyndhurst.
London 92 – Bournemouth 24 – Southampton 14.

🏛 **Bell Inn,** SO43 7HE, 🖉 (01703) 812214, Fax (01703) 813958, ₤8 – ₩ 📺 ☎ 🅿 – 🛦 40. 🍱
🖭 ⓐ 🚾 🗷
Meals (bar lunch Monday to Saturday)/dinner 24.50 **st.** and a la carte – **25 rm** ☲ 49.00/
75.00 **st.** – SB.

BROOKMANS PARK Herts. 404 T 28 – pop. 3 315.
London 21 – Luton 21.

🍽🍽 **Villa Rosa,** 3 Great North Rd, AL9 6LB, SE : 1 ¾ m. on A 1000 🖉 (01707) 651444,
Fax (01707) 654970 – 🅿. 🍱 🖭 ⓐ 🚾 🗷
closed Saturday lunch, Sunday and Bank Holidays – **Meals** - Italian - a la carte 17.50/22.50 **t**

BROUGHTON Lancs. 402 L 22 – see Preston.

BROUGHTON North Lincolnshire 402 S 23 – see Scunthorpe.

BROUGHTON ASTLEY *Leics.* 403 Q 26 – *pop. 6 487*
London 100 – Coventry 22 – Leicester 11 – Northampton 30.

🏛 **Mill on the Soar,** Coventry Rd, Sutton in the Elms, LE9 6JU, NW : 1 ½ m. by B 581 on B 4114 ℰ (01455) 282419, *Fax* (01455) 285937, ⌇, ⌂ rm, ⊡ ☎ ℗ – 🔥 40. ⬤❸ ⬛ ⬤ *VISA*
Meals (in bar) (buffet lunch) a la carte approx. 10.60 **t.** – ⌸ 4.95 – **20 rm** 39.50 **st.**

BROXTED *Essex* 404 U 28 – *see Stansted Airport.*

BROXTON *Ches.* 402 403 L 24 – *pop. 417.*
London 197 – Birmingham 68 – Chester 12 – Manchester 44 – Stoke-on-Trent 29.

🏛 **Carden Park** ⌂, CH3 9DQ, W : 1 ½ m. on A 534 ℰ (01829) 731000, *Fax* (01829) 731032, ⌂, 【ۃ, ☎, ⬚, ▥, ⌇, ⌲, park, ※ – ⧠ ⌂, ▤ rest, ⊡ ☎ ⅙ ℗ – 🔥 400. ⬤❸ ⬛ ⬤ *VISA* *JCB.* ⌘
Meals *(closed Sunday)* a la carte approx. 14.00 **t.** ⅙ 6.00 – **Garden Restaurant :** Meals (dinner only and Sunday lunch)/dinner 21.95 **t.** ⅙ 6.00 – ⌸ 10.95 – **120 rm** 110.00/250.00 **t.,** 5 suites.

🏛 **Broxton Hall Country House,** Whitchurch Rd, CH3 9JS, on A 41 at junction with A 534 ℰ (01829) 782321, *Fax* (01829) 782330, « Part 17C timbered house », ⌲ – ⊡ ☎ ℗. ⬤❸ ⬛ ⬤ *VISA*
closed 25 December and 1 January – **Meals** 15.90/23.90 **t.** and lunch a la carte ⅙ 10.75 – **10 rm** ⌸ 60.00/105.00 **t.** – SB.

Prices	For notes on the prices quoted in this Guide, see the introduction.

BRUTON *Somerset* 403 404 M 30 *The West Country G.* – *pop. 2 111.*
Exc. : *Stourhead*★★★ *AC, W : 8 m. by B 3081.*
London 118 – Bristol 27 – Bournemouth 44 – Salisbury 35 – Taunton 36.

✕✕ **Truffles,** 95 High St., BA10 0AR, ℰ (01749) 812255 – ⬤❸ *VISA*
closed Sunday dinner, Monday, 2 weeks February and 2 weeks October – **Meals** 13.50/ 22.95 **st.** ⅙ 5.95.

BRYHER *Cornwall* 403 ㉚ – *see Scilly (Isles of).*

BUCKDEN *Cambs.* 404 T 27 – *pop. 2 534* – ✉ *Huntingdon.*
London 65 – Bedford 15 – Cambridge 20 – Northampton 31.

🏛 **George Coaching Inn,** Olde Great North Rd, PE18 9XA, ℰ (01480) 810307, *Fax* (01480) 811274 – ⊡ ☎ ℗. ⬤❸ ⬛ ⬤ *VISA*
Meals 12.00 **st.** and a la carte ⅙ 6.50 – **16 rm** ⌸ 58.00/84.00 **st.**

🏛 **Lion,** High St., PE18 9XA, ℰ (01480) 810313, *Fax* (01480) 811070, « Part 15C inn » – ⊡ ☎ ℗. ⬤❸ ⬛ ⬤ *VISA* *JCB*
Meals 8.75/16.00 **t.** and a la carte ⅙ 4.00 – **15 rm** ⌸ 59.50/85.00 **t.** – SB.

BUCKINGHAM *Bucks.* 403 404 Q 27 *Great Britain G.* – *pop. 10 168.*
Exc. : *Claydon House*★ *AC, S : 8 m. by A 413.*
⛳ Silverstone, Silverstone Rd, Stowe ℰ (01280) 850005 – ⛳ Tingewick Rd ℰ (01280) 813282.
London 64 – Birmingham 61 – Northampton 20 – Oxford 25.

🏛 **Villiers,** 3 Castle St., MK18 1BS, ℰ (01280) 822444, *Fax* (01280) 822113 – ⧠, ▤ rest, ⊡ ☎ ℗ – 🔥 250. ⬤❸ ⬛ ⬤ *VISA.* ⌘
Henry's : Meals (dinner only and Sunday lunch)/dinner 23.25 **st.** and a la carte ⅙ 8.70 – **Café Porcini :** Meals - Italian - (a la carte) 10.00/20.00 **st.** ⅙ 4.50 – **34 rm** ⌸ 80.00/94.00 **st.,** 4 suites – SB.

🏛 **Buckingham Four Pillars,** Buckingham Ring Rd, MK18 1RY, S : 1 ¼ m. by Bridge St. on A 421 ℰ (01280) 822622, *Fax* (01280) 823074, 【ۃ, ☎, ⬚ – ⅙ rm, ▤ rest, ⊡ ☎ ⅙ ℗ – 🔥 160. ⬤❸ ⬛ ⬤ *VISA*
Meals (carving lunch Sunday and carving dinner Tuesday and Saturday) 10.95/14.95 **st.** and a la carte – ⌸ 6.95 – **70 rm** 75.00/86.00 **st.** – SB.

BUCKLAND *Glos.* 403 404 O 27 – *see Broadway (Worcestershire).*

BUCKLAND Oxon. 408 404 P 28 – ⊠ Faringdon.
London 78 – Oxford 16 – Swindon 15.

🏚 **Lamb Inn** with rm, Lamb Lane, SN7 8QN, ℰ (01367) 870484, Fax (01367) 810475 – 🖵 ☎
🅿 ⬤❸ 🖭 VISA JCB ⋙
closed 24 to 26 December – **Meals** (restricted menu Monday) (bar lunch Monday to
Saturday)/dinner a la carte 13.25/27.15 **t**. ⬧ 5.95 – **4 rm** � 45.00/50.00 **t**.

BUCKLERS HARD Hants. 408 404 P 31 – see Beaulieu.

BUDE Cornwall 408 G 31 The West Country G. – pop. 3 681.
See : The Breakwater★★ – Compass Point (⩽★).
Env. : Poughill★ (church★★), N : 2 ½ m. – E : Tamar River★★ – Kilkhampton (Church★),
NE : 5 ½ m. by A 39 – Stratton (Church★), E : 1 ½ m. – Launcells (Church★), E : 3 m. by
A 3072 – Marhamchurch (St. Morwenne's Church★), SE : 2 ½ m. by A 39 – Poundstock★
(⩽★★, church★, guildhouse★), S : 4 ½ m. by A 39.
Exc. : Morwenstow (cliffs★★, church★), N : 8 ½ m. by A 39 and minor roads – Jacobstow
(Church★), S : 7 m. by A 39.
🔟 Burn View ℰ (01288) 352006.
🖪 Bude Visitor Centre, The Crescent, EX23 8LE ℰ (01288) 354240.
London 252 – Exeter 51 – Plymouth 44 – Truro 53.

🏨🏨 **Falcon**, Breakwater Rd, EX23 8SD, ℰ (01288) 352005, Fax (01288) 356359, ⩽, 🐎 – 🖵 ☎
🅿 ⬤❸ 🖭 ⬤ VISA
closed 25 December – **Meals** (bar lunch Monday to Saturday)/dinner 16.00 **st**. and a la carte
⬧ 4.00 – **22 rm** ⊇ (dinner included) 47.50/99.00 **st**. – SB.

🏨🏨 **Hartland**, Hartland Terr., EX23 8JY, ℰ (01288) 355661, Fax (01288) 355664, ⩽, 🔟 – 🛗
⋙ rm, 🖵 ☎ 🅿
Easter-October and Christmas – **Meals** (bar lunch)/dinner 19.00 **t**. ⬧ 4.75 – **29 rm** ⊇ 45.00/
70.00 **t**. – SB.

🏨 **Cliff**, Crooklets Beach, EX23 8NG, ℰ (01288) 353110, Fax (01288) 353110, 🔲, 🐎, ⋇ –
⋙ rest, 🖵 ☎ 🅿 ⬤❸ VISA JCB
May-September – **Meals** (bar lunch)/dinner 10.00 **t**. ⬧ 4.00 – **15 rm** ⊇ 32.00/65.00 **st**. –
SB.

🏨 **Camelot**, Downs View, EX23 8RE, ℰ (01288) 352361, Fax (01288) 355470, 🐎 – ⋙ rest.
🖵 ☎ 🅿 ⬤❸ VISA ⋙
March-October – **Meals** (bar lunch)/dinner 15.00 **st**. and a la carte ⬧ 4.95 – **21 rm** ⊇ 28.00/
56.00 **st**. – SB.

🏨 **Bude Haven**, Flexbury Av., EX23 8NS, ℰ (01288) 352305 – ⋙ 🖵 🅿 ⬤❸ 🖭 VISA ⋙
closed 29 December-5 January – **Meals** (bar lunch)/dinner 10.00 **st**. ⬧ 3.75 – **12 rm**
⊇ 28.00/50.00 **st**. – SB.

BUDLEIGH SALTERTON Devon 408 K 32 The West Country G. – pop. 3 759.
Env. : East Budleigh (Church★), N : 2 ½ m. by A 376 – Bicton★ (Gardens★) AC, N : 3 m. by
A 376.
🔟 East Devon, North View Rd ℰ (01395) 443370.
🖪 Fore St., EX9 6NG ℰ (01395) 445275.
London 182 – Exeter 16 – Plymouth 55.

🏠 **Long Range**, 5 Vales Rd, EX9 6HS, by Raleigh Rd ℰ (01395) 443321, Fax (01395) 445220
🐎 – ⋙ 🖵 🅿 ⋙
Meals 15.00 **st**. – **6 rm** ⊇ 50.00/55.00 **st**. – SB.

BUDOCK WATER Cornwall – see Falmouth.

BURFORD Oxon. 408 404 P 28 – pop. 1 171.
🔟 ℰ (01993) 822149.
🖪 The Brewery, Sheep St., OX18 4LP ℰ (01993) 823558.
London 76 – Birmingham 55 – Gloucester 32 – Oxford 20.

🏨🏨 **Bay Tree**, 12-14 Sheep St., OX18 4LW, ℰ (01993) 822791, Fax (01993) 823008,
« 16C house, antique furnishings », 🐎 – ⋙ rest, 🖵 ☎ 🅿 – 🔏 40. ⬤❸ 🖭 ⬤ VISA JCB ⋙
Meals 13.95/21.95 **st**. and dinner a la carte – **20 rm** ⊇ 60.00/120.00 **st**., 2 suites – SB.

🏨 **Lamb Inn**, Sheep St., OX18 4LR, ℰ (01993) 823155, Fax (01993) 822228, « Part 14C
antique furnishings », 🐎 – ⋙ rest, 🖵 ☎ ⬤❸ VISA
closed 25 and 26 December – **Meals** (bar lunch Monday to Friday)/dinner 24.00 **t**. ⬧ 7.50 –
15 rm ⊇ 62.50/110.00 – SB.

Golden Pheasant, 91 High St., OX18 4QA, ☎ (01993) 823223, *Fax (01993) 822621* – rest, TV ☎ P. MC AE VISA.
Meals (bar lunch Monday to Saturday)/dinner a la carte 14.50/24.85 **t.** – **12 rm** 50.00/110.00 **t.** – SB.

Burford House without rest., 99 High St., OX18 4QA, ☎ (01993) 823151, *Fax (01993) 823240,* – TV. MC AE VISA.
7 rm 65.00/105.00 **t.**

Inn For All Seasons, The Barringtons, OX18 4TN, W : 3 ¼ m. on A 40 ☎ (01451) 844324, *Fax (01451) 844375,* – TV ☎ P – 35. MC AE VISA.
closed 25 and 26 December – **Meals** 16.50 **t.** (dinner) and a la carte 14.00/20.75 **t.** 4.95 – **10 rm** 42.50/79.00 **st.** – SB.

Travelodge, Bury Barn, OX7 5TB, on A 40 (Burford roundabout) ☎ (01993) 822699, Reservations (Freephone) 0800 850950 – TV P. MC AE VISA JCB.
Meals (grill rest.) – **40 rm** 44.95 **t.**

at Fulbrook *NE : ¾ m. on A 361 – ✉ Burford.*

Elm House, Meadow Lane, OX18 4BW, ☎ (01993) 823611, *Fax (01993) 823937,* – TV ☎ P. MC VISA JCB
Meals (residents only) (dinner only) 18.50 5.25 – **7 rm** 41.00/70.50 **t.** – SB.

BURGH-LE-MARSH *Lincs.* 402 404 U 24 – *pop. 2 718*
London 110 – Boston 29 – Great Grimsby 38 – Lincoln 25.

Windmill, 46 High St., PE24 5JT, ☎ (01754) 810281, *Fax (01754) 810281* – P. MC AE VISA
closed Sunday dinner, Monday and 1 week February – **Meals** (dinner only and Sunday lunch)/dinner 19.50 **t.** 5.75.

BURLAND *Ches. – see Nantwich.*

BURLEY *Hants.* 403 404 O 31 *Great Britain G.* – *pop. 1 438 – ✉ Ringwood.*
Env. : *New Forest★★ (Rhinefield Ornamental Drive★★, Bolderwood Ornamental Drive★★).*
London 102 – Bournemouth 17 – Southampton 17 – Winchester 30.

Toad Hall, The Cross, BH24 4AB, ☎ (01425) 403448, *Fax (01425) 402505* – TV ☎ P. MC AE VISA.
Meals *(closed Sunday dinner)* 12.95/16.95 **st.** and a la carte 4.95 – **8 rm** 45.00/65.00 **st.** – SB.

BURLEY IN WHARFEDALE *W. Yorks.* 402 O 22 – *pop. 5 528.*
London 218 – Bradford 14 – Harrogate 15 – Leeds 14 – Preston 52.

David Woolley's, 78 Main St., LS29 7BT, ☎ (01943) 864602 – P. MC VISA
closed Sunday, Monday, 25-26 December and 1 January – **Meals** (dinner only) 14.95 **t.** and a la carte 4.75.

BURNHAM *Bucks.* 404 S 29 – *pop. 11 169.*
London 33 – Oxford 37 – Reading 17.

County H. Burnham Beeches, Grove Rd, SL1 8DP, NW : 1 m. by Britwell Rd ☎ (01628) 429955, *Fax (01628) 603994,* park, – rm, TV ☎ P – 180. MC AE VISA.
***Grays* :** **Meals** (bar lunch Saturday and Sunday) 22.50 **st.** and a la carte 6.20 – 10.00 – **73 rm** 130.00/150.00 **t.**, 2 suites – SB.

BURNHAM MARKET *Norfolk* 404 W 25 *Great Britain G.* – *pop. 898.*
Env. : *Holkham Hall★★ AC, E : 3 m. by B 1155.*
London 128 – Cambridge 71 – Norwich 36.

Hoste Arms, The Green, PE31 8HD, ☎ (01328) 738777, *Fax (01328) 730103,* « 17C inn », – TV ☎ P. MC VISA
Meals – (see below) – **19 rm** 60.00/98.00 **t.**

Railway Inn without rest., Creake Rd, PE31 8EN, ☎ (01328) 730505, *Fax (01328) 730103* – TV P. MC VISA
Meals – (see ***Hoste Arms*** below) – **6 rm** 42.00/58.00 **t.**

Hoste Arms (at Hoste Arms H.), The Green, PE31 8HD, ☎ (01328) 738777, *Fax (01328) 730103* – P. MC VISA
Meals (booking essential) a la carte 13.45/22.20 **t.** 8.50.

BURNHAM-ON-CROUCH Essex 404 W 29 – pop. 7 067.
London 52 – Chelmsford 19 – Colchester 32 – Southend-on-Sea 25.

XXX **Contented Sole**, 80 High St., CM0 8AA, ☎ (01621) 782139 – **M⊙** VISA
closed Sunday dinner, Monday, 1 week late summer and 2 weeks January – Meals 12.95 t
and a la carte ₡ 6.00.

BURNLEY Lancs. 402 N 22 – pop. 74 661.
🏌18, 🏌9 Towneley, Towneley Park, Todmorden Rd ☎ (01282) 451636 – 🏌18 Glen View ☎ (01282)
421045.
🔒 Burnley Mechanics, Manchester Rd, BB11 1JA ☎ (01282) 455485.
London 236 – Bradford 32 – Leeds 37 – Liverpool 55 – Manchester 25 – Middlesbrough 104
– Preston 22 – Sheffield 68.

🏨 **Oaks,** Colne Rd, Reedley, BB10 2LF, NE : 2 ½ m. on A 56 ☎ (01282) 414141
Fax (01282) 433401, 🛵, 全§, 🔲, 🐎 – 🛬 rm, 📺 🕿 🅿 – 🔬 120. **M⊙** AE
Meals – **Quills :** Meals (dinner only) 22.00 st. and a la carte ₡ 10.95 – 53 rm ⬚ 90.00,
110.00 st. – SB.

🏨 **Rosehill House,** Rosehill Av., Manchester Rd, BB11 2PW, S : 1 ¼ m. by A 56
☎ (01282) 453931, Fax (01282) 455628, 🐎 – 🛬 📺 🕿 🅿. **M⊙** AE VISA
closed 1 January – Meals a la carte 13.25/23.40 st. ₡ 5.45 – 22 rm ⬚ 35.00/65.00 st. – SB.

🏨 **The Alexander,** 2 Tarleton Av., off Todmorden Rd, BB11 3ET, S : ¾ m. by A 671
☎ (01282) 422684, Fax (01282) 424094, 🐎 – 📺 🕿 🅿. **M⊙** AE ⓪ VISA. ⁑
Meals (closed Saturday lunch) 7.95 st. (lunch) and a la carte 10.45/19.75 st. ₡ 4.95 – 16 rm
⬚ 39.50/58.00 st. – SB.

🏨 **Travel Inn,** Queen Victoria, Queen Victoria Rd, BB10 3EF, E : ¾ m. by A 671 on A 6114
☎ (01282) 450250, Fax (01282) 452811 – 🛬 rm, 🍴 rest, 📺 🛠 🅿 – 🔬 40. **M⊙** AE ⓪ VISA
⁑
Meals (grill rest.) – 40 rm 36.50 t.

🏨 **Travelodge,** Cavalry Barracks, Barracks Rd, BB11 4AS, W : ½ m. at junction of A 671 with
A 679 ☎ (01282) 416039, Fax (01282) 416039, Reservations (Freephone) 0800 850950 –
🛬 rm, 📺 🛠 🅿. **M⊙** AE ⓪ VISA JCB. ⁑
Meals (grill rest.) – 32 rm 39.95 t.

🔧 ATS Healey Wood Rd ☎ (01282) 422409/38423/451624

BURNSALL N. Yorks. 402 O 21 – pop. 108 – ⊠ Skipton.
London 223 – Bradford 26 – Leeds 29.

🏨 **Red Lion,** BD23 6BU, ☎ (01756) 720204, Fax (01756) 720292, ≼ – 🛬 📺 🕿 🅿. **M⊙** AE VISA
⁑
Meals – (see below) – 11 rm ⬚ 48.00/85.00 t. – SB.

XX **Red Lion** (at Red Lion H.), BD23 6BU, ☎ (01756) 720204, Fax (01756) 720292 – 🛬 🅿. **M⊙**
AE VISA
Meals (dinner only and Sunday lunch)/dinner 22.50 t. ₡ 6.95.

BURNT YATES N. Yorks. – see Ripley.

BURPHAM W. Sussex 404 S 30 – see Arundel.

BURRINGTON Devon 403 I 31 – pop. 533.
London 260 – Barnstaple 14 – Exeter 28 – Taunton 50.

🏨 **Northcote Manor** ⤡, EX37 9LZ, NW : 1 ½ m. by Barnstaple rd ☎ (01769) 560501
Fax (01769) 560770, ≼, « 17C manor house », 🐎, park, ⁑ – 🛬 rest, 📺 🕿 🅿. **M⊙** AE ⓪
VISA JCB
closed 5 January-5 February – Meals (booking essential) 18.00/30.00 st. and a la carte –
11 rm ⬚ 69.50/109.50 st., 1 suite – SB.

BURSLEM Staffs. 402 403 404 N 24 – see Stoke-on-Trent.

BURSTALL Suffolk – see Ipswich.

BURTON-IN-KENDAL SERVICE AREA *Cumbria* 402 L 21 – ⊠ *Carnforth.*

🏨 **Travelodge** without rest., LA6 1JF, on M 6 northbound carriageway between junctions 35 and 36 ℘ (01524) 784012, *Fax (01524) 784014,* Reservations (Freephone) 0800 850950 – ⅍ ⊠ ☎ ₺ ₽. ⓦⓢ ℀ ⓞ ⓥⓢⓐ ℘. ℀
47 rm 46.95 **t.**

BURTON-UPON-TRENT *Staffs.* 402 403 404 O 25 – *pop. 60 525.*

　🏌 Branston G. & C.C., Burton Rd ℘ (01283) 512211 – 🏌 Craythorne, Craythorne Rd, Stretton ℘ (01283) 564329.

　🛈 Unit 40, Octagon Centre, New St., DE14 3TN ℘ (01283) 516609/508589.

　London 128 – Birmingham 29 – Leicester 27 – Nottingham 27 – Stafford 27.

🏨 Stanhope Arms, Ashby Road East, DE15 0PU, SE : 2 ½ m. on A 50 ℘ (01283) 217954, *Fax (01283) 226199* – ⊠ ☎ ₽ – 🔬 150
23 rm.

at Stretton *N : 3½ m. by A 50 off A 5121* – ⊠ *Burton-upon-Trent.*

XXX **Dovecliff Hall** ⚶ with rm, Dovecliff Rd, DE13 0DJ, NE : 1 m. ℘ (01283) 531818, *Fax (01283) 516546,* ≤, 斎, « Restored Georgian house, gardens », ⬦, park – ⊠ ☎ ₽. ⓦⓢ ℀ ⓞ ⓥⓢⓐ. ℀
closed 1 week Easter, 1 week May, 2 weeks in summer and 1 week Christmas – **Meals** *(closed lunch Monday and Saturday and Sunday dinner)* 13.50/21.50 **t.** and dinner a la carte ₫ 9.00 – **7 rm** ⊷ 55.00/105.00 **t.** – SB.

at Rolleston-on-Dove *N : 3¾ m. by A 50 on Rolleston Rd* – ⊠ *Burton-upon-Trent.*

🏨 **Brookhouse Inn,** Brookside, DE13 9AA, ℘ (01283) 814188, *Fax (01283) 813644,* « Part 17C house, antiques », 綿 – ⊠ ☎ ₽. ⓦⓢ ℀ ⓞ ⓥⓢⓐ
Meals *(closed Saturday lunch and Sunday dinner)* 9.95 **t.** (lunch) and a la carte 19.25/32.95 **t.** ₫ 4.95 – **19 rm** ⊷ 69.00/95.00 **t.** – SB.

at Newton Solney *NE : 3 m. by A 50 on B 5008* – ⊠ *Burton-upon-Trent.*

🏨 **Newton Park,** Newton Rd, DE15 0SS, ℘ (01283) 703568, *Fax (01283) 703214,* 綿 – 🛗, ⅍ rm, ⊠ ☎ ₺ ₽ – 🔬 100. ⓦⓢ ℀ ⓞ ⓥⓢⓐ. ℀
Meals *(bar lunch Monday to Saturday)/dinner* 16.95 **st.** ₫ 5.75 – ⊷ 8.95 – **51 rm** 95.00/105.00 **st.** – SB.

at Branston *SW : 1½ m. on A 5121* – ⊠ *Burton-upon-Trent.*

🏨 **Riverside,** Riverside Drive, off Warren Lane, DE14 3EP, ℘ (01283) 511234, *Fax (01283) 511441,* ⬦, 綿 – ⊠ ☎ ₽ – 🔬 150. ⓦⓢ ℀ ⓥⓢⓐ
Meals *(closed Saturday lunch)* 17.50 **t.** (dinner) and a la carte 11.20/26.90 **t.** ₫ 5.50 – **22 rm** ⊷ 59.50/69.50 **t.**

at Barton-under-Needwood *SW : 5 m. by A 5121 on A 38* – ⊠ *Burton-upon-Trent.*

🏨 **Travelodge,** Lichfield Rd, DE13 8EG, on A 38 (northbound carriageway) ℘ (01283) 716343, *Fax (01283) 716343,* Reservations (Freephone) 0800 850950 – ⅍ rm, ⊠ ₺ ₽. ⓦⓢ ℀ ⓞ ⓥⓢⓐ ℘. ℀
Meals (grill rest.) – **20 rm** 39.95 **t.**

🏨 **Travelodge,** DE13 8EH, on A 38 (southbound carriageway) ℘ (01283) 716784, Reservations (Freephone) 0800 850950 – ⅍ rm, ⊠ ₺ ₽. ⓦⓢ ℀ ⓞ ⓥⓢⓐ ℘. ℀
Meals (grill rest.) – **40 rm** 39.95 **t.**

　⓪ ATS All Saints Rd ℘ (01283) 565994/563170

BURTONWOOD SERVICE AREA *Ches.* 402 M 23 – ⊠ *Warrington.*

🏨 **Welcome Lodge,** WA5 3AX, M 62 (westbound carriageway) ℘ (01925) 710376, *Fax (01925) 710378,* Reservations (Freephone) 0800 7314466 – ⅍ rm, ⊠ ₺ ₽. ⓦⓢ ℀ ⓞ ⓥⓢⓐ. ℀
Meals (grill rest.) – **40 rm** 45.00 **t.**

BURY *Gtr. Manchester* 402 N 23 403 ② 404 N 23 – *pop. 62 633.*

　🏌 Greenmount ℘ (01204) 883712.

　🛈 The Mets Art Centre, Market St., BL9 0BW ℘ (0161) 253 5111.

　London 211 – Leeds 45 – Liverpool 35 – Manchester 9.

X **Est, Est, Est,** 703 Manchester Rd, BL9 0ED, S : 2 m. on A 56 ℘ (0161) 766 4869, *Fax (0161) 766 4869* – ▤ ₽. ⓦⓢ ℀ ⓥⓢⓐ
closed 25 and 26 December – **Meals** - Italian - a la carte 11.65/19.95 **t.** ₫ 5.65.

at Walmersley N : 1 ¾ m. on A 56 – ⊠ Bury.

🏛 **Red Hall**, Manchester Rd, BL9 5NA, N : 1 ¼ m. on A 56 – ℰ (01706) 822476
Fax (01706) 828086 – 🍴 rest, 🖵 ☎ 🅿 – 🔬 45. 🝙 🆎 ⓪ 🝮 🝭. ⍟
closed 24 December-3 January – **Meals** (closed lunch Monday and Saturday) 13.50 t
and a la carte 🍴 6.00 – **20 rm** 🖃 50.00/62.00 t.

at Birtle NE : 3 m. by B 6222 – ⊠ Bury.

🏛 **Normandie** ⍤, Elbut Lane, BL9 6UT, ℰ (0161) 764 1170, Fax (0161) 764 4866, ≼ – 📶 🖵
☎ 🅿. 🝙 🆎 ⓪ 🝮 🝭. ⍟
closed 9 to 14 April and 26 December-4 January – **Meals** – (see below) – 🖃 6.95 – **23 rm**
49.00/79.00.

🍴🍴🍴 **Normandie** (at Normandie H.), Elbut Lane, BL9 6UT, ℰ (0161) 764 117C
Fax (0161) 764 4866, ≼ – 🅿. 🝙 🆎 ⓪ 🝮 🝭
closed Saturday lunch, Sunday and Bank Holidays except 25 December – **Meals** (booking
essential) 12.50/15.00 t. and a la carte 🍴 5.00.

🔧 ATS John St. ℰ (0161) 764 2830/6860

BURY ST. EDMUNDS Suffolk 404 W 27 Great Britain G. – pop. 31 237.
See : Town★ – Abbey and Cathedral★.
Env. : Ickworth House★ AC, SW : 3 m. by A 143.
📍 Suffolk G. & C.C., St. John's Hill Plantation, The Street ℰ (01284) 706777.
🎫 6 Angel Hill, IP33 1UZ ℰ (01284) 764667.
London 79 – Cambridge 27 – Ipswich 26 – Norwich 41.

🏛 **Angel**, 3 Angel Hill, IP33 1LT, ℰ (01284) 753926, Fax (01284) 750092 – 🍴 rm, 🖵 ☎ 🅿
🔬 140. 🝙 🆎 ⓪ 🝮
Meals (closed Sunday dinner) 16.00/21.00 **st.** and dinner a la carte – 🖃 10.50 – **41 rm**
62.00/110.00 t., 1 suite.

🏛 **Priory**, Tollgate, IP32 6EH, N : 1 ¾ m. by A 1101 on B 1106 ℰ (01284) 76618
Fax (01284) 767604, ⍤ – 🍴 🖵 ☎ 🅿 – 🔬 60. 🝙 🆎 ⓪ 🝮. ⍟
closed 26 December – **Meals** (closed lunch Saturday and Sunday) 19.50 **t.** and a la carte
🍴 4.95 – **25 rm** 🖃 65.00/97.00 **st.** – SB.

🏛 **Butterfly**, Symonds Rd, IP32 7BW, SE : 1 ½ m. by A 1302 and A 134 at junction with A 14
ℰ (01284) 760884, Fax (01284) 755476 – 🍴 rm, 🖵 ☎ 🅿 – 🔬 60. 🝙 🆎 ⓪ 🝮 🝭. ⍟
Meals 12.50 **st.** and a la carte – 🖃 6.95 – **66 rm** 59.50/80.00 **st.**

🏛 **Twelve Angel Hill** without rest., 12 Angel Hill, IP33 1UZ, ℰ (01284) 70408
Fax (01284) 725549, ⍤ – 🍴 🖵 ☎ 🅿. 🝙 🆎 ⓪ 🝮. ⍟
closed January – **6 rm** 🖃 45.00/80.00 **st.**

🏛 **Ounce House** without rest., 13 Northgate St., IP33 1HP, ℰ (01284) 76177
Fax (01284) 768315, ⍤ – 🍴 🖵 ☎ 🅿. 🝙 🝮. ⍟
4 rm 🖃 45.00/75.00 s.

🏛 **Abbey** without rest., 35 Southgate St., IP33 2AZ, ℰ (01284) 762020, Fax (01284) 724770
🍴 🖵 ☎ 🅿. 🝙 🆎 ⓪ 🝮 🝭. ⍟
10 rm 🖃 48.00/65.00 **st.**, 2 suites.

at Ixworth NE : 7 m. by A 143 – ⊠ Bury St. Edmunds.

🍴🍴 **Theobalds**, 68 High St., IP31 2HJ, ℰ (01359) 231707, Fax (01359) 231707, ⍤ – 🝙 🝮
closed Saturday lunch, Sunday dinner, Monday and 2 weeks August – **Meals** 16.50 t
(lunch) and dinner a la carte 23.50/29.25 **t.** 🍴 7.50.

at Bardwell NE : 9 ¾ m. by A 143 and A 1088 on Bardwell rd – ⊠ Bury St. Edmunds.

🏠 **Six Bells Country Inn** with rm, The Green, IP31 1AW, ℰ (01359) 25082C
Fax (01359) 250820, ⍤ – 🖵 ☎ 🅿. 🝙 🝮 🝭. ⍟
closed 25 and 26 December – **Meals** (bar lunch Monday) 12.50 **st.** (dinner
and a la carte 13.05/18.40 **st.** 🍴 4.50 – **8 rm** 🖃 45.00/60.00 **st.** – SB.

at Rougham Green SE : 4 m. by A 1302 and A 134 off A 14 – ⊠ Bury St. Edmunds.

🏛 **Ravenwood Hall**, IP30 9JA, ℰ (01359) 270345, Fax (01359) 270788, 🍲, ⍤, park, ⍥
🍴 🖵 ☎ 🅿 – 🔬 150. 🝙 🆎 ⓪ 🝮
Meals 18.95 **t.** and a la carte 🍴 4.75 – **14 rm** 🖃 59.00/109.00 **t.** – SB.

at Bradfield Combust SE : 4 ½ m. on A 134 – ⊠ Bury St. Edmunds.

🏛 **Bradfield House**, Sudbury Rd, IP30 0LR, ℰ (01284) 386301, ⍤ – 🍴 rest, 🖵 ☎ 🅿. ⍥
⓪ 🝮 🝭
Meals (closed Saturday lunch, Sunday dinner and Monday) 21.50 **t.** and a la carte – **4 rm**
🖃 55.00/85.00 **t.** – SB.

at Horringer SW : 3 m. on A 143 – ⊠ Bury St. Edmunds.

🏠 **Beehive,** IP29 5SN, ℘ (01284) 735260, Fax (01284) 830321, 斧 – **₽**. **◍③** **𝘝𝘐𝘚𝘈**
Meals a la carte 13.20/20.15 **t.**

at Fornham All Saints NW : 3¼ m. by A 1101 on B 1106 – ⊠ Bury St. Edmunds.

🏠 **Fornham Hall** without rest., IP28 6JJ, ℘ (01284) 725266, « Part Georgian house, Tudor origins », 斧 – 锋 **₽**. **◍③** **𝘝𝘐𝘚𝘈**. ※
3 rm ⊇ 35.00/70.00 **st.,** 1 suite.

🔩 ATS Units 1 and 3, Ailwin Rd, Moreton Hall Ind. Est. ℘ (01284) 705610

BUSHEY Herts. **404** S 29 London 18.
Luton 21 – Watford 3.

Plan : see Greater London (North-West)

✗✗ **st James,** 30 High St., WD2 3DN, ℘ (0181) 950 2480, Fax (0181) 950 4107 – ▤. **◍③** **AE** **𝘝𝘐𝘚𝘈**
closed Sunday – Meals 14.95 **t.** (lunch) and a la carte 20.45/22.75 **t.** ₰ 7.00.

BUTTERMERE Cumbria **402** K 20 – pop. 139 – ⊠ Cockermouth.
London 306 – Carlisle 35 – Kendal 43.

🏠 **Bridge,** CA13 9UZ, ℘ (017687) 70252, Fax (017687) 70252, ≼ – 锋 rest, ☎ **₽**. **◍③** **𝘝𝘐𝘚𝘈**. ※
Meals (booking essential) (bar lunch)/dinner 21.00 **t.** ₰ 5.90 – **22 rm** ⊇ (dinner included) 62.50/125.00 **t.** – SB.

at Brackenthwaite NW : 4 m. on B 5289 – ⊠ Cockermouth.

🏠 **Pickett Howe** ⊗, CA13 9UY, ℘ (01900) 85444, Fax (01900) 85209, ≼, « Part 17C longhouse », 斧 – 锋 **₽**. **◍③** **𝘝𝘐𝘚𝘈**. ※
April-October – Meals (residents only) (communal dining) (dinner only) 22.50 **st.** ₰ 4.40 – **4 rm** ⊇ 70.00/75.00 **st.**

BUTTERTON Staffs. – see Leek.

BUXTON Derbs. **402** **403** **404** O 24 – pop. 19 854.
🏌 Buxton and High Peak, Townend ℘ (01298) 23453.
🅱 The Cresent, SK17 6BQ ℘ (01298) 25106.
London 172 – Derby 38 – Manchester 25 – Stoke-on-Trent 24.

🏨🏨 **Palace,** Palace Rd, SK17 6AG, ℘ (01298) 22001, Fax (01298) 72131, ₤₃, 숎, ⬜, 斧 – 🛗 📺
☎ 👍 **₽** – 🔬 400. **◍③** **𝘝𝘐𝘚𝘈**
Meals (bar lunch)/dinner 17.95 **st.** ₰ 6.95 – **118 rm** ⊇ 85.00/98.00, 4 suites – SB.

🏛 **Lee Wood,** The Park, SK17 6TQ, on A 5004 ℘ (01298) 23002, Fax (01298) 23228, 斧 – 🛗,
锋 rm, 📺 ☎ **₽** – 🔬 100. **◍③** **AE** **◍** **𝘝𝘐𝘚𝘈** **JCB** – ⊇ 8.00 – **37 rm** 60.00/82.00 **st.** – SB.
Meals 13.50/23.50 **st.** and a la carte ₰ 6.75 –

🏠 **Coningsby,** 6 Macclesfield Rd, SK17 9AH, ℘ (01298) 26735, Fax (01298) 26735, 斧 –
锋 rest, 📺 **₽**. ※
March-October – Meals (by arrangement) 15.50 **st.** – **3 rm** ⊇ 42.50/55.00 **s.**

🏠 **Lakenham** without rest., 11 Burlington Rd, SK17 9AL, ℘ (01298) 79209 – 📺 **₽**
6 rm ⊇ 35.00/52.00.

🔩 ATS Staden Lane Ind. Park, off Ashbourne Rd ℘ (01298) 25608/25655

BYFORD Herefordshire **403** L 27 – see Hereford.

CADNAM Hants. **403** **404** P 31 – pop. 1 866.
London 91 – Salisbury 16 – Southampton 8 – Winchester 19.

🏠 **Walnut Cottage** without rest., Old Romsey Rd, SO40 2NP, off A 31 ℘ (01703) 812275,
Fax (01703) 812275, 斧 – 📺 **₽**. ※
closed 24 to 26 December – **3 rm** ⊇ 28.00/43.00.

CAISTOR ST. EDMUND Norfolk **404** X 26 – see Norwich.

CALCOT Glos. – see Tetbury.

CALDBECK Cumbria **401** **402** K 19 – pop. 688 – ⊠ Wigton.
London 308 – Carlisle 13 – Keswick 16 – Workington 23.

⌂ **Parkend** ⌖, Park End, CA7 8HH, SW : 1 ½ m. on B 5299 ℘ (016974) 78494, « Converted 17C farmhouse », ⌖ – ⌖ rest, **TV** **℗**, **◍◍** **AE** **①** **VISA**
closed 5 January-1 February – **Meals** (by arrangement) approx. 14.00 **st.** ⌂ 4.75 – **3 rm** ⌖ 32.00/48.00 **st.**

CALLINGTON Cornwall **403** H 32 – pop. 4 265 London 239.
Exeter 48 – Plymouth 14 – Truro 45.

⌂ **East Cornwall Farmhouse** ⌖, Fullaford Rd, PL17 8AN, E : 1 ¾ m. by A 390 or Harrowbarrow rd ℘ (01579) 350018, ⌖, ⌖ – ⌖ **TV** **℗**
March-November – **Meals** (by arrangement) (communal dining) 10.00 ⌂ 4.50 – **5 rm** ⌖ 18.00/42.00 **s.** – SB.

CALNE Wilts. **403** **404** O 29 The West Country G. – pop. 11 516.
Env. : Bowood House★ AC, (Library ⩽★) SW : 2 m. by A 4 – Avebury★★ (The Stones★ Church★) E : 6 m. by A 4.
London 91 – Bristol 33 – Swindon 17.

⌂ **Chilvester Hill House,** SN11 0LP, W : ¾ m. by A 4 on Bremhill rd ℘ (01249) 813981 Fax (01249) 814217, ⌖ – ⌖ rest, **TV** **℗**, **◍◍** **AE** **①** **VISA**, ⌖
Meals (by arrangement) (communal dining) 18.00 **st.** ⌂ 5.50 – **3 rm** ⌖ 45.00/85.00 **st.**

⊚ ATS Unit 4, Maundrell Rd., Portemarsh Ind. Est. ℘ (01249) 821622

Great Britain and Ireland is now covered by an Atlas at a scale of 1 inch to 4.75 miles.

Three easy to use versions: Paperback, Spiralbound and Hardback.

CALSTOCK Cornwall **403** H 32 The West Country G. – pop. 5 964 – ⊠ Tavistock.
Env. : Tamar River★★ – Cotehele★ AC, SW : 1 m. - Morwellham★ AC, NE : 1 ½ m.
London 246 – Exeter 48 – Plymouth 22.

⌂ **Danescombe Valley** ⌖, Lower Kelly, PL18 9RY, W : ½ m. ℘ (01822) 832414 Fax (01822) 832446, ⩽ Viaduct and Tamar Valley, « Country house atmosphere » – ⌖ rest **℗**, **◍◍** **AE** **①** **VISA**, ⌖
March-October – **Meals** (booking essential to non-residents) (dinner only) 33.00 **st.** ⌂ 5.00 – **5 rm** ⌖ 72.50/125.00 **st.**

CAMBERLEY Surrey **404** R 29 – pop. 46 120 (inc. Frimley).
London 40 – Reading 13 – Southampton 48.

⌂ **Frimley Hall** ⌖, Lime Av. via Conifer Drive, GU15 2BG, E : ¾ m. off Portsmouth Rd (A 325 ℘ (01276) 28321, Fax (01276) 691253, ⌖ – ⌖ **TV** **☎** **℗** – ⌖ 60. **◍◍** **AE** **①** **VISA** **JCB**
Meals a la carte 15.00/20.00 **t.** and a la carte ⌂ 6.00 – ⌖ 12.50 – **66 rm** 105.00/115.00 **st.** – SB.

⌂ **Travel Inn,** 221 Yorktown Rd, GU15 4RT, W : 2 m. by A 30 and A 321 on A 3095 ℘ (01276) 878181, Fax (01276) 890648 – ⌖ rm, **TV** ⌖ **℗**, **◍◍** **AE** **①** **VISA**, ⌖
Meals (grill rest.) – **40 rm** 36.50 **t.**

CAMBORNE Cornwall **403** E 33 The West Country G. – pop. 35 915 (inc. Redruth).
Env. : Carn Brea (⩽★★), NE : 3 m. by A 3047 and minor rd.
London 299 – Falmouth 14 – Penzance 16 – Truro 14.

⌂ **Tyack's,** 27 Commercial St., TR14 8LD, ℘ (01209) 612424, Fax (01209) 612435 – ⌖ rm, **TV** ⌖ **℗**, **◍◍** **AE** **①** **VISA** **JCB**, ⌖
Meals 15.00 **t.** and a la carte ⌂ 4.50 – **13 rm** ⌖ 42.00/72.00 **t.**, 2 suites.

CAMBRIDGE Cambs. **404** U 27 Great Britain G. – pop. 95 682.
See : Town★★★ – St. John's College★★★ AC Y – King's College★★ (King's College Chapel★★★) Z The Backs★★ YZ – Fitzwilliam Museum★★ Z M1 – Trinity College★★ Y – Clare College★ Z B – Kettle's Yard★ Y M2 – Queen's College★ AC Z.
⌖ Cambridgeshire Moat House Hotel, Bar Hill ℘ (01954) 780555 X.
⌖ Cambridge Airport : ℘ (01223) 373737, E : 2 m. on A 1303 X.
⌖ Wheeler St., CB2 3QB ℘ (01223) 322640.
London 55 – Coventry 88 – Kingston-upon-Hull 137 – Ipswich 54 – Leicester 74 – Norwich 6 – Nottingham 88 – Oxford 100.

CAMBRIDGE

COLLEGES

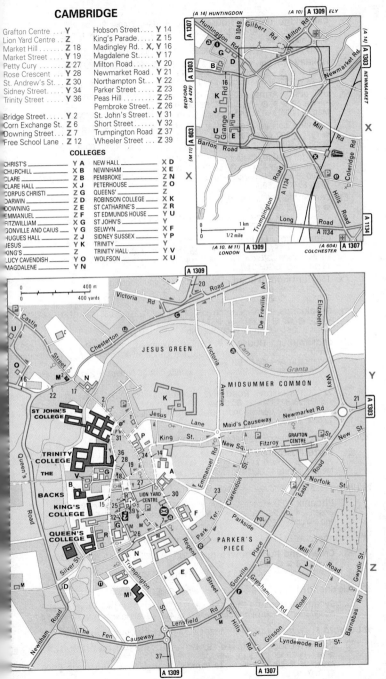

Cambridge Garden House Moat House, Granta Pl., off Mill Lane, CB2 1RT, ℰ (01223) 259988, *Fax (01223) 316605*, ≤, *Ib*, ≦s, ◻, 屏 – 劇, ⇔ rm, ⊡ ☎ ❷ – ⚑ 250. ⬣◗ ⚑ *VISA* ⬤
Meals 14.55/18.00 t. ⒤ 6.50 – ⚏ 12.95 – **117 rm** 115.00/185.00 t. – SB.
Z n

Holiday Inn, Downing St., CB2 3DT, ℰ (01223) 464466, *Fax (01223) 464440* – 劇, ⇔ rm ▦ ⊡ ☎ & ❷ – ⚑ 150. ⬣◗ ⚑ ❶ *VISA* ᴊᴄʙ
Meals 15.95 and a la carte – ⚏ 10.95 – **194 rm** 118.00/160.00 st., 2 suites – SB.
Z a

University Arms, Regent St., CB2 1AD, ℰ (01223) 351241, *Fax (01223) 315256* – 劇, ⇔ rm, ⊡ ☎ & ❷ – ⚑ 300. ⬣◗ ⚑ ❶ *VISA*
Meals 11.00/19.00 st. and a la carte ⒤ 4.75 – **114 rm** ⚏ 100.00/125.00 st., 1 suite – SB.
Z e

Gonville, Gonville Pl., CB1 1LY, ℰ (01223) 366611, *Fax (01223) 315470* – 劇 ⇔, ▦ rest, ⊡ ☎ ❷ – ⚑ 200. ⬣◗ ⚑ ❶ *VISA* ⬤
Meals 13.50/16.95 st. and a la carte ⒤ 7.00 – **64 rm** ⚏ 82.00/101.00 st. – SB.
Z r

Arundel House, Chesterton Rd, CB4 3AN, ℰ (01223) 367701, *Fax (01223) 367721* – ⇔ ▦ rest, ⊡ ☎ ❷ – ⚑ 50. ⬣◗ ⚑ ❶ *VISA* ⬤
closed 25 and 26 December – Meals 10.95/15.95 t. and a la carte ⒤ 4.65 – ⚏ 3.25 – **105 rm** 39.50/89.00 t. – SB.
Y u

Centennial, 63-71 Hills Rd, CB2 1PG, ℰ (01223) 314652, *Fax (01223) 315443* – ⇔ rm, ⊡ ☎ ❷ – ⚑ 25. ⬣◗ ⚑ ❶ *VISA* ⬤
closed 1 week Christmas – Meals (dinner only) 15.50 st. and a la carte ⒤ 3.25 – **39 rm** ⚏ 69.00/90.00 t. – SB.
X x

Cambridge Lodge, 139 Huntingdon Rd, CB3 0DQ, ℰ (01223) 352833 *Fax (01223) 355166*, 屏 – ⊡ ☎ ❷ – ⚑ 25. ⬣◗ ⚑ ❶ *VISA*. ⬤
Meals *(closed Saturday lunch and Sunday dinner)* 15.95/20.50 t. and a la carte ⒤ 5.00 – **13 rm** ⚏ 60.00/90.00 t.
X

↑ **136 Huntingdon Road** without rest., 136 Huntingdon Rd, CB3 0HL, ℰ (01223) 365285 *Fax (01223) 461142*, 屏 – ⇔ ⊡ ❷. ⬣◗ *VISA*. ⬤
3 rm ⚏ 36.00/56.00 s.
X a

↑ **Brooklands**, 95 Cherry Hinton Rd, CB1 4BS, ℰ (01223) 242035, *Fax (01223) 242035*, ≦s – ⇔ ⊡ ❷. ⬣◗ ⚑ ❶ *VISA* ᴊᴄʙ. ⬤
Meals 9.00 st. – **5 rm** ⚏ 30.00/48.00 st.
X e

XXX **Midsummer House**, Midsummer Common, CB4 1HA, ℰ (01223) 369299 *Fax (01223) 302672*, « Attractively situated beside River Cam, overlooking Midsummer Common », 屏 – ⬣◗ ⚑ ❶ *VISA* ᴊᴄʙ
closed Saturday lunch, Sunday dinner, Monday and 26 December-2 January – Meals 23.00/ 33.00 t. ⒤ 9.95.
Y a

XX **22 Chesterton Road**, 22 Chesterton Rd, CB4 3AX, ℰ (01223) 351880 *Fax (01223) 323814* – ▦. ⬣◗ ⚑ *VISA*
closed Sunday, Monday and 1 week Christmas – Meals (booking essential) (dinner only) 22.50 t. ⒤ 6.95.
Y c

at Impington N : 2 m. on B 1049 at junction with A 14 – X – ⊠ Cambridge.

Forte Posthouse Cambridge, Lakeview, Bridge Rd, CB4 4PH, ℰ (01223) 237000 *Fax (01223) 233426*, *Ib*, ≦s, ◻, 屏 – ⇔ rm, ⊡ ☎ & ❷ – ⚑ 70. ⬣◗ ⚑ ❶ *VISA* ᴊᴄʙ
Meals a la carte 17.00/25.00 st. ⒤ 7.00 – ⚏ 9.95 – **118 rm** 89.00 st. – SB.

at Histon N : 3 m. on B 1049 – X – ⊠ Cambridge.

XX **Phoenix**, 20 The Green, CB4 4JA, ℰ (01223) 233766 – ▦ ❷. ⬣◗ ⚑ *VISA*
closed 24 to 26 December – Meals - Chinese (Peking, Szechuan) - 14.50/25.50 t. and a la carte ⒤ 9.00.

at Horningsea NE : 4 m. by A 1303 – X – and B 1047 on Horningsea rd – ⊠ Cambridge.

Crown and Punchbowl Inn, CB5 9JG, ℰ (01223) 860643, *Fax (01223) 441814*, 屏 – ⇔ rm, ⊡ ☎ ❷. ⬣◗ *VISA* ᴊᴄʙ. ⬤
Meals a la carte 12.50/25.15 t. ⒤ 3.95 – **5 rm** ⚏ 43.50/70.00 t.

at Little Shelford S : 5½ m. by A 1309 – X – off A 10 – ⊠ Cambridge.

XX **Sycamore House**, 1 Church St., CB2 5HG, ℰ (01223) 843396 – ⇔ ❷. ⬣◗ *VISA*
closed Sunday, Monday and Christmas-New Year – Meals (dinner only) 22.50 t. ⒤ 4.75.

at Duxford S : 9½ m. by A 1309 – X – A 1301 and A 505 on B 1379 – ⊠ Cambridge.

Duxford Lodge, Ickleton Rd, CB2 4RU, ℰ (01223) 836444, *Fax (01223) 832271*, 屏 – ⊡ ☎ ❷ – ⚑ 30. ⬣◗ ⚑ *VISA* ᴊᴄʙ
closed 25 to 30 December – **Le Paradis :** Meals 18.50 st. and a la carte ⒤ 5.00 – **15 rm** ⚏ 70.00/95.00 st. – SB.

at Madingley *W : 4½ m. by A 1303* – **X.**

XX **Three Horseshoes,** High St., CB3 8AB, ℘ *(01954) 210221, Fax (01954) 212043,* 🏡 – **℗.**
 ⑩ ᴬᴱ ⓪ VISA
 Meals *(closed Sunday dinner)* a la carte 16.50/25.25 **t.** ⓵ 5.00.

at Bar Hill *NW : 5½ m. by A 1307* – **X** – *off A 14.*

🏨 **Cambridgeshire Moat House,** CB3 8EU, ℘ *(01954) 249988, Fax (01954) 780010,* ⅃₅,
 🗵, ᴴₛ, ≋, ⁏ – ᛏᛉ rm, 🔟 ☎ ℗ – 🔏 200. **⑩ ᴬᴱ ⓪ VISA JCB**
 Meals 16.50 **st.** (dinner) and a la carte 12.00/29.50 **st.** ⓵ 6.00 – ⊊ 9.50 – **99 rm** 95.00/
 110.00 **st.** – SB.

at Lolworth Service Area *NW : 6 m. by A 1307* – **X** – *on A 14* – ✉ *Cambridge.*

🏨 **Travelodge,** CB3 8DR, (northbound carriageway) ℘ *(01954) 781335, Reservations (Freephone)* 0800 850950 – ᛏᛉ rm, 🔟 ᵴ ℗. **⑩ ᴬᴱ ⓪ VISA JCB.** ⁒
 20 rm 44.95 **t.**

at Swavesey Service Area *NW : 8 m. by A 1307 on A 14* – **X** – ✉ *Cambridge.*

🏨 **Travelodge,** CB4 5QA, (southbound carriageway) ℘ *(01954) 789113, Reservations (Freephone)* 0800 850950 – ᛏᛉ rm, 🔟 ᵴ ℗. **⑩ ᴬᴱ ⓪ VISA JCB.** ⁒
 36 rm 44.95 **t.**

 🅰 ATS 143 Histon Rd ℘ *(01223) 351431/361695*

CANNOCK *Staffs.* **④⓪② ④⓪③ ④⓪④** N 25 *Great Britain G.* – *pop. 60 106.*
 Exc. : *Weston Park★★ AC, W : 11 m. by A 5.*
 ᴴₛ *Cannock Park, Stafford Rd* ℘ *(01543) 578850.*
 *London 135 – Birmingham 20 – Derby 36 – Leicester 51 – Shrewsbury 32 – Stoke-on-Trent
 28.*

🏨 **Roman Way,** Watling St., Hatherton, WS11 1SH, SW: 1 ¼ m. by A 4601 on A 5
 ℘ *(01543) 572121, Fax (01543) 502742* – ᛏᛉ rm, 🔟 ☎ ᵴ ℗ – 🔏 120. **⑩ ᴬᴱ ⓪ VISA JCB**
 Meals *(closed Saturday lunch)* (carving lunch)/dinner 15.00 **st.** and a la carte ⓵ 6.85 –
 ⊊ 9.25 – **56 rm** 80.00/120.00 **st.** – SB.

🏨 **Travel Inn,** Watling St., WS11 1SJ, SW : 1 m. at junction of A 4601 with A 5
 ℘ *(01543) 572721, Fax (01543) 466130* – ᛏᛉ rm, 🔟 ᵴ ℗ – 🔏 100. **⑩ ᴬᴱ ⓪ VISA.** ⁒
 Meals (grill rest.) – **38 rm** 36.50 **t.**

 🅰 ATS Cannock Rd, Chadsmoor ℘ *(01543) 574580/   ATS Cannock Rd, Heath Hayes ℘ (01543) 274200*
 504985

CANON PYON *Herefordshire* **④⓪③** L 27 – *see Hereford.*

CANTERBURY *Kent* **④⓪④** X 30 *Great Britain G.* – *pop. 36 464.*
 See : *City★★★ - Cathedral★★★ Y - St. Augustine's Abbey★★ AC YZ K – King's School★ Y B –
 Mercery Lane★ Y 12 - Christ Church Gate★ Y A – Weavers★ Y D – Hospital of St. Thomas the
 Martyr, Eastbridge★ Y E – Poor Priests Hospital★ AC Y M1 – St. Martin's Church★ Y N –
 West Gate★ AC Y R.*
 🅱 *34 St. Margaret's St., CT1 2TG* ℘ *(01227) 766567.*
 London 59 – Brighton 76 – Dover 15 – Maidstone 28 – Margate 17.

Plan on next page

🏨 **County,** High St., CT1 2RX, ℘ *(01227) 766266, Fax (01227) 451512* – 📶 🔟 ☎ ⇔ ℗ –
 🔏 140. **⑩ ᴬᴱ ⓪ VISA.** ⁒   Y n
 Sullys : **Meals** 17.00/21.00 **st.** and a la carte ⓵ 10.00 – ⊊ 8.95 – **72 rm** 80.00/115.00 **st.,**
 1 suite – SB.

🏨 **Falstaff,** 8-12 St. Dunstan's St., CT2 8AF, ℘ *(01227) 462138, Fax (01227) 463525* – ᛏᛉ 🔟
 ☎ ℗ – 🔏 50. **⑩ ᴬᴱ ⓪ VISA.** ⁒   Y a
 Meals 14.00 **st.** and a la carte ⓵ 5.95 – ⊊ 8.95 – **24 rm** 75.00 **st.** – SB.

🏨 **Chaucer,** Ivy Lane, CT1 1TU, ℘ *(01227) 464427, Fax (01227) 450397* – ᛏᛉ 🔟 ☎ ℗ –
 🔏 100. **⑩ ᴬᴱ ⓪ VISA**   Z c
 Meals a la carte 18.75/21.40 **st.** ⓵ 7.25 – ⊊ 8.75 – **42 rm** 70.00/85.00 **st.** – SB.

🏨 **Thanington** without rest., 140 Wincheap, CT1 3RY, ℘ *(01227) 453227,*
 Fax (01227) 453225, 🗵, ⁏ – ᛏᛉ 🔟 ☎ ℗. **⑩ ᴬᴱ ⓪ VISA JCB**   Z s
 16 rm ⊊ 46.00/70.00 **st.**

🏨 **Ebury,** 65-67 New Dover Rd, CT1 3DX, ℘ *(01227) 768433, Fax (01227) 459187,* 🗵, ⁏ – 🔟
 ☎ ℗. **⑩ ᴬᴱ VISA**   Z r
 closed 21 December-14 January – **Meals** (dinner only) (light dinner Sunday) a la carte 12.45/
 15.55 **t.** ⓵ 5.10 – **15 rm** ⊊ 45.00/68.00 **t.** – SB.

CANTERBURY

Burgate . . . . Y
Butchery Lane . . . . Y 5
Guildhall Street . . . . Y 6
High Street . . . . Y 8
Mercery Lane . . . . Y 12

Palace Street . . . . Y
St. George's Street . . . . Z 17
St. Margaret's Street . . . . . . YZ 18
St. Peter's Street . . . . Y 20

Beercart Lane . . . . YZ 2
Borough (The) . . . . Y 4
Lower Bridge Street . . . . Z 9

Lower Chantry Lane . . . . Z 10
Rhodaus Town . . . . Z 13
Rosemary Lane . . . . Z 14
St. George's Place . . . . Z 16
St. Mary's Street . . . . Z 19
St. Radigund's Street . . . . . . Y 21
Upper Bridge Street . . . . Z 23
Watling Street . . . . Z 25

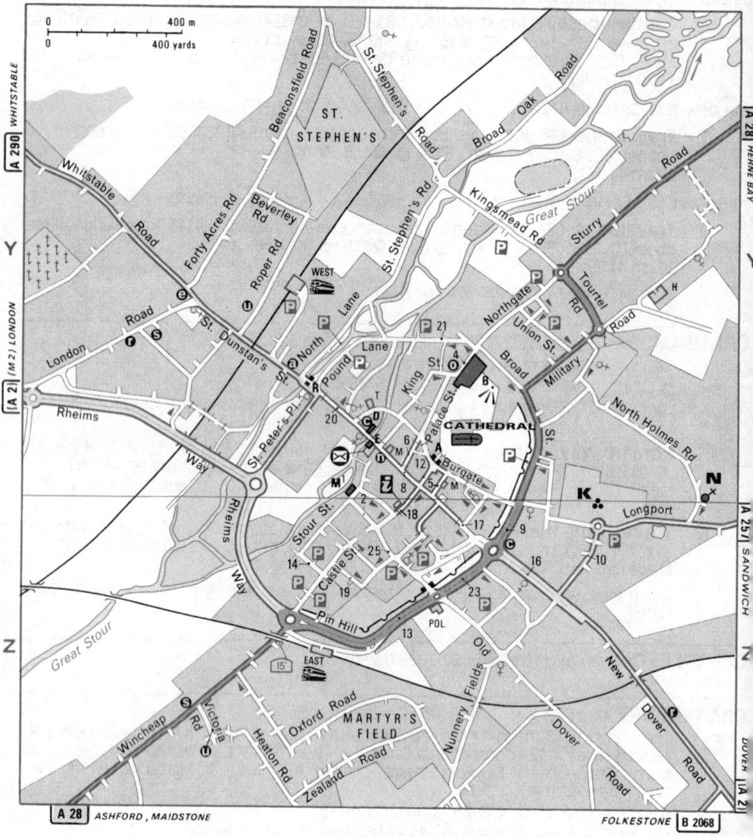

Pointers, 1 London Rd, CT2 8LR, ☎ (01227) 456846, *Fax (01227) 831131* – TV ☎ P. MC AE
Diners VISA JCB — Y e
closed 23 December-mid January – **Meals** (dinner only) 13.95 **t.** 4.50 – **12 rm** 45.00/
60.00 **t.** – SB.

Pilgrims, 18 The Friars, CT1 2AS, ☎ (01227) 464531, *Fax (01227) 762514* – TV ☎. MC VISA.
— Y c
Meals (dinner only) a la carte 11.50/18.50 **t.** 6.95 – **14 rm** 45.00/80.00 **t.**

Magnolia House, 36 St. Dunstan's Terr., CT2 8AX, ☎ (01227) 765121,
Fax (01227) 765121, – TV P. MC AE VISA. — Y s
Meals (by arrangement) 18.00 **t.** – **7 rm** 36.00/70.00 **t.**

Clare Ellen without rest., 9 Victoria Rd, CT1 3SG, ☎ (01227) 760205, *Fax (01227) 784482*,
– TV P. MC VISA JCB. — Z u
6 rm 22.00/48.00 **s.**

Zan Stel Lodge without rest., 140 Old Dover Rd, CT1 3NX, ☎ (01227) 453654, –
TV P. — Z e
closed 25-26 and 31 December and 1 January – **4 rm** 30.00/50.00.

↑ **Alexandra House** without rest., 1 Roper Rd, CT2 7EH, ℰ (01227) 767011, Fax (01227) 786617, ⌨ – 🖵 🅿. ⌦   **Y u**
7 rm ⌂ 24.00/48.00.

↑ **Ann's House** without rest., 63 London Rd, CT2 8JZ, ℰ (01227) 768767, Fax (01227) 768172 – ✠ 🖵. ⓌⓈ 𝗩𝗜𝗦𝗔. ⌦   **Y r**
18 rm ⌂ 22.00/48.00 st.

XX **Tuo e Mio**, 16 The Borough, CT1 2DR, ℰ (01227) 761471 – ⓌⓈ 𝔸𝔼 ⓪ 𝗩𝗜𝗦𝗔 𝗝𝗖𝗕   **Y o**
closed Tuesday lunch, Monday, last 2 weeks February and last 2 weeks August – **Meals** - Italian - a la carte 12.00/23.50 **t.** ◊ 4.25.

at Littlebourne *E : 3 ¾ m. on A 257* – **Z** – ✉ *Canterbury*.

▥ **Bow Window,** 50 High St., CT3 1ST, ℰ (01227) 721264, Fax (01227) 721250 – ✠ rest, 🖵 ☎ 🅿. ⓌⓈ 𝔸𝔼 𝗩𝗜𝗦𝗔. ⌦
Meals a la carte 13.00/20.50 **t.** ◊ 5.00 – **8 rm** ⌂ 44.00/60.00 **t.** – SB.

at Chartham *SW : 3 ¼ m. by A 28* – **Z** – ✉ *Canterbury*.

↑ **Thruxted Oast** ⌂ without rest., Mystole, CT4 7BX, SW : 1 ½ m. by Rattington St., turning right at T-junction after ½ m. on Mystole Lane ℰ (01227) 730080, ≤, ⌨ – ✠ 🖵 ☎ 🅿. ⓌⓈ 𝔸𝔼 𝗩𝗜𝗦𝗔. ⌦
closed 25 December – **3 rm** ⌂ 68.00/78.00 st.

↑ **Old Rectory,** Ashford Rd, CT4 7HS, on A 28 ℰ (01227) 730075, Fax (01227) 731929, ⌨ – ✠ 🅿. ⓌⓈ 𝗩𝗜𝗦𝗔. ⌦
restricted opening in winter – **Meals** (by arrangement) (communal dining) 18.00 st. – **3 rm** ⌂ 30.00/60.00 st.

at Chartham Hatch *W : 3 ¼ m. by A 28* – **Z** – ✉ *Canterbury*.

▦ **Howfield Manor,** Howfield Lane, CT4 7HQ, SE : 1 m. ℰ (01227) 738294, Fax (01227) 731535, ⌨ – 🖵 ☎ 🅿 – ⌴ 100. ⓌⓈ 𝔸𝔼 𝗩𝗜𝗦𝗔 𝗝𝗖𝗕. ⌦
Old Well : Meals 13.95/18.95 st. and a la carte ◊ 6.50 – **15 rm** ⌂ 70.00/90.00 st. – SB.

at Gate Service Area *W : 4 ½ m. on A 2* – **Y** – ✉ *Faversham*.

▥ **Travelodge,** Dunkirk, ME13 9LN, (westbound carriageway) ℰ (01227) 752781, Reservations (Freephone) 0800 850950 – ✠ 🖵 ໕ 🅿. ⓌⓈ 𝔸𝔼 ⓪ 𝗩𝗜𝗦𝗔 𝗝𝗖𝗕. ⌦
40 rm 44.95 **t.**

  ◉ ATS 29 Sturry Rd ℰ (01227) 464867/765021

CAPEL ST. MARY *Suffolk* 𝟜𝟘𝟜 X 27 – *pop. 3 176* – ✉ *Ipswich*.
    London 78 – Cambridge 52 – Colchester 18 – Ipswich 3.

▥ **Travelodge,** Bentley Services, IP9 2JP, W ½ m. on A 12 ℰ (01473) 312157, Fax (01473) 312157, Reservations (Freephone) 0800 850950 – ✠ rm, 🖵 ໕ 🅿. ⓌⓈ 𝔸𝔼 ⓪ 𝗩𝗜𝗦𝗔 𝗝𝗖𝗕. ⌦
closed 24 and 25 December – **Meals** (grill rest.) – **32 rm** 39.95 **t.**

CARBIS BAY *Cornwall* 𝟜𝟘𝟛 D 33 – *see St. Ives*.

CARCROFT *S. Yorks.* 𝟜𝟘𝟚 𝟜𝟘𝟛 𝟜𝟘𝟜 Q 23 – *see Doncaster*.

CARLISLE *Cumbria* 𝟜𝟘𝟙 𝟜𝟘𝟚 L 19 *Great Britain G.* – *pop. 72 439*.
    See : *Town*★ - *Cathedral*★ *(Painted Ceiling*★ *)* AY E – *Tithe Barn*★ BY A.
    Env. : *Hadrian's Wall*★★ , *N : by A 7* AY.
    ▮₁₈ Aglionby ℰ (01228) 513303 BY – ▮₁₆ Stony Holme, St. Aidan's Rd ℰ (01228) 34856, BY – ▮₉ Dalston Hall, Dalston ℰ (01228) 710165, AZ.
    ✈ Carlisle Airport ℰ (01228) 573641, NW : 5 ½ m. by A 7 – BY – and B 6264 – **Terminal :** *Bus Station, Lowther Street.*
    🄳 Carlisle Visitor Centre, Old Town Hall, Green Market, CA3 8JH ℰ (01228) 512444.
    London 317 – Blackpool 95 – Edinburgh 101 – Glasgow 100 – Leeds 124 – Liverpool 127 – Manchester 122 – Newcastle upon Tyne 59.

Plan on next page

▦▦ **Cumbrian,** Court Sq., CA1 1QY, ℰ (01228) 531951, Fax (01228) 547799 – 🛗, ✠ rm, 🖵 ☎ ໕ – ⌴ 300. ⓌⓈ 𝔸𝔼 ⓪ 𝗩𝗜𝗦𝗔   **BZ a**
Meals (bar lunch)/dinner a la carte approx. 15.95 **st.** ◊ 6.95 – **70 rm** ⌂ 68.00/88.00 st. – SB.

▦▦ **Cumbria Park,** 32 Scotland Rd, CA3 9DG, N : 1 m. on A 7 ℰ (01228) 522887, Fax (01228) 514796 – 🛗, ✠ rm, 🖵 ☎ 🅿 – ⌴ 150. ⓌⓈ 𝔸𝔼 ⓪ 𝗩𝗜𝗦𝗔 𝗝𝗖𝗕. ⌦
closed 25 and 26 December – **Meals** *(closed Sunday lunch)* 12.50/16.95 **t.** and a la carte – **48 rm** ⌂ 69.00/120.00 **t.**

CARLISLE

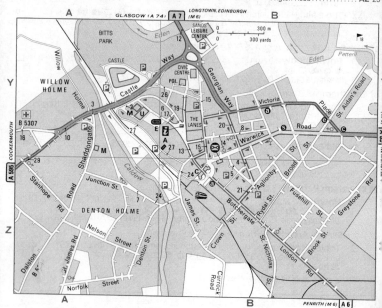

🏠 **Gosling Bridge - Premier Lodge,** Kingstown Rd, CA3 0AT, N : 1 ¾ m. on A 7
ℰ (01228) 515294, Fax (01228) 515220 – ❖ rm, 📺 ☎ ♿ ₱. ⬥ 🆎 ① 𝗩𝗜𝗦𝗔 ❄
Meals (grill rest.) a la carte approx. 19.15 ₰ 4.25 – ⊑ 4.95 – **30 rm** 44.25 st.

🏠 **Number Thirty One,** 31 Howard Pl., CA1 1HR, *ℰ (01228) 597080, Fax (01228) 597080,*
« Victorian town house » – ❖ 📺 ⬥ 🆎 ① 𝗩𝗜𝗦𝗔   BY a
April-November – Meals (by arrangement) 20.00 st. – **3 rm** ⊑ 40.00/80.00 st. – SB.

🏠 **Beeches** without rest., Wood St., CA1 2SF, E : 1 ½ m. by A 69 off Victoria Rd
ℰ (01228) 511962, 🌳 – 📺 ₱
3 rm ⊑ 30.00/40.00 st.

🏠 **Courtfield House** without rest., 169 Warwick Rd, CA1 1LP, *ℰ (01228) 522767* – 📺
4 rm ⊑ 25.00/38.00 s.   BY c

🏠 **Fern Lee,** 9 St. Aidan's Rd, CA1 1LT, *ℰ (01228) 511930* – ❖ rm, 📺 ₱. ❄   BY e
closed 24 and 25 December – Meals (by arrangement) 8.00 st. – **8 rm** ⊑ 25.00/40.00 st. –
SB.

🏠 **Langleigh House** without rest., 6 Howard Pl., CA1 1HR, *ℰ (01228) 530440,*
Fax (01228) 530440 – 📺 ₱. ❄   BY s
closed 23 to 28 December – **3 rm** ⊑ 25.00/39.00 st.

✗✗ **No. 10,** 10 Eden Mount, Stanwix, CA3 9LY, N : ¾ m. on A 7. *ℰ (01228) 524183* – ⬥ 🆎 𝗩𝗜𝗦𝗔
closed Sunday, one week late October and February – Meals (dinner only) a la carte 14.70/
21.00 t. ₰ 4.80.

at Kingstown *N : 3 m. by A 7 – BY – at junction 44 of M 6 –* ✉ *Carlisle.*

🏨 **Forte Posthouse Carlisle,** Park House Rd, Kingstown, CA3 0HR, on A 7
ℰ (01228) 531201, Fax (01228) 543178, Ⅰ₅, ≘ₛ, ▦ – ❖ rm, 📺 ☎ ♿ ₱ – 🔏 60. ⬥ 🆎 ①
𝗩𝗜𝗦𝗔 𝗝𝗖𝗕.
Meals (closed Saturday lunch) a la carte 14.55/25.65 t. ₰ 7.95 – ⊑ 9.95 – **127 rm** 79.00 st. –
SB.

174

at High Crosby NE : 5 m. by A 7 and B 6264 – **BY** – off A 689 – ✉ Carlisle.

🏠 **Crosby Lodge Country House** 🐾, CA6 4QZ, ℰ (01228) 573618, Fax (01228) 573428, ≼, « 18C country mansion », 🦌 – ↦ rest, 📺 ☎ 🅿, ⓦⓢ ⒶⒺ 𝘝𝘐𝘚𝘈 ⒿⒸⒷ, ⚘
closed 24 December-20 January – **Meals** (Sunday dinner residents only) 16.50/28.00 **t.** and a la carte ⓘ 9.00 – **11 rm** ⊇ 75.00/125.00 **t.** – SB.

at Wetheral E : 6¼ m. by A 69 – **BZ** – on B 6263 – ✉ Carlisle.

🏠 **Crown**, CA4 8ES, ℰ (01228) 561888, Fax (01228) 561637, Ⅰ₅, ⓢ, ⬚, 🦌, squash – ↦ rm, 📺 ☎ & 🅿 – 🔏 175. ⓦⓢ ⒶⒺ ⓞ 𝘝𝘐𝘚𝘈
Meals (bar lunch Saturday) 10.95/18.00 **t.** and a la carte ⓘ 7.95 – **49 rm** ⊇ 97.00/116.00 **st.**, 2 suites – SB.

🔧 ATS Rosehill Ind. Est., Montgomery Way ℰ (01228) 25277

CARLTON N. Yorks. 402 O 21 – see Middleham.

CARLYON BAY Cornwall 403 F 33 – see St. Austell.

CARNFORTH Lancs. 402 L 21 – see Lancaster.

CARTERWAY HEADS Northd 401 402 O 19 – ✉ Shotley Bridge.
London 272 – Carlisle 59 – Newcastle upon Tyne 21.

🍴 **Manor House Inn**, DH8 9LX, on A 68 ℰ (01207) 255268 – ↦ 🅿, ⓦⓢ ⒶⒺ 𝘝𝘐𝘚𝘈. ⚘
closed 25 December – **Meals** a la carte 12.40/17.60 **st.** ⓘ 3.75.

CARTMEL Cumbria 402 L 21 – see Grange-over-Sands.

CARTMELL FELL Cumbria 402 L 21 – see Newby Bridge.

CASTLE ASHBY Northants. 404 R 27 – pop. 138 – ✉ Northampton.
London 76 – Bedford 15 – Northampton 11.

🏠 **Falcon** 🐾, NN7 1LF, ℰ (01604) 696200, Fax (01604) 696673, 🌳, « Part 16C inn », 🦌 – 📺 ☎ & 🅿, ⓦⓢ ⒶⒺ 𝘝𝘐𝘚𝘈 ⒿⒸⒷ
Meals 19.50 **t.** and a la carte ⓘ 4.50 – **16 rm** ⊇ 70.00/77.50 **t.** – SB.

CASTLE CARY Somerset 403 404 M 30 – pop. 2 904.
London 125 – Bristol 28 – Taunton 31 – Yeovil 13.

🏠 **George**, Market Pl., BA7 7AH, ℰ (01963) 350761, Fax (01963) 350035 – 📺 ☎ 🅿, ⓦⓢ ⒶⒺ 𝘝𝘐𝘚𝘈
Meals (bar meals Monday to Saturday lunch and Sunday dinner) 9.95 **t.** (lunch) and dinner a la carte 11.70/22.95 **t.** – **15 rm** ⊇ 45.00/85.00 **t.** – SB.

✕✕ **Bond's** with rm, Ansford Hill, Ansford, BA7 7JP, N : ¾ m. by Ansford Rd on A 371 ℰ (01963) 350464, Fax (01963) 350464, 🦌 – 📺 ☎ 🅿, ⓦⓢ 𝘝𝘐𝘚𝘈. ⚘
closed 1 week Christmas – **Meals** (light lunch)/dinner 13.50 **st.** and a la carte ⓘ 5.00 – **7 rm** ⊇ 38.00/80.00 **st.** – SB.

CASTLE COMBE Wilts. 403 404 N 29 The West Country G. – pop. 347 – ✉ Chippenham.
See : Village★★.
London 110 – Bristol 23 – Chippenham 6.

🏠 **Manor House** 🐾, SN14 7HR, ℰ (01249) 782206, Fax (01249) 782159, « Part 14C manor house in park », ⬚, Ⅰ₈, ⬚, 🦌, ✕ – 📺 ☎ 🅿 – 🔏 50. ⓦⓢ ⒶⒺ ⓞ 𝘝𝘐𝘚𝘈. ⚘
Meals 18.95/35.00 **t.** and dinner a la carte 40.50/56.95 **t.** ⓘ 13.50 – ⊇ 12.00 – **43 rm** 140.00/350.00 **t.** – SB.

🏠 **Castle Inn**, SN14 7HN, ℰ (01249) 783030, Fax (01249) 782315, « Part 12C » – ↦ 📺 ☎. ⓦⓢ ⒶⒺ ⓞ 𝘝𝘐𝘚𝘈. ⚘
Meals a la carte 11.45/17.00 **t.** ⓘ 6.50 – **11 rm** ⊇ 60.00/100.00 **t.** – SB.

at Ford S : 1¾ m. on A 420 – ✉ Chippenham.

🏠 **White Hart Inn**, SN14 8RP, ℰ (01249) 782213, Fax (01249) 783075 – 📺 ☎ 🅿, ⓦⓢ ⒶⒺ ⓞ 𝘝𝘐𝘚𝘈
Meals a la carte 19.40/22.70 **t.** ⓘ 6.25 – **11 rm** ⊇ 45.00/70.00 **t.** – SB.

at Nettleton Shrub W : 2 m. by B 4039 on Nettleton rd (Fosse Way) – ⊠ Chippenham.

⋔ **Fosse Farmhouse,** SN14 7NJ, ℰ (01249) 782286, Fax (01249) 783066, 🌼 – ⅙⊷ rest, 📺
🅿. ⬛️ 🅰🅴 𝑉𝐼𝑆𝐴 𝐽𝐶𝐵. ⅏
Meals 25.00 t. 🛈 7.00 – **5 rm** ⊆ 55.00/125.00 t. – SB.

CASTLE DONINGTON Leics. 𝟜𝟘𝟚 𝟜𝟘𝟛 𝟜𝟘𝟜 P 25 – pop. 6 007 – ⊠ Derby.
🛫 East Midlands Airport : ℰ (01332) 852852, S : by B 6540 and A 453.
London 123 – Birmingham 38 – Leicester 23 – Nottingham 13.

🏨 **Hilton National,** East Midlands Airport, Derby Rd, Lockington, DE74 2YW, E : 6 ½ m. by
High St. and A 453 on A 6 at junction 24 of M 1 ℰ (01509) 674000, Fax (01509) 672412, 𝐼𝟨,
≦s, ⬛️ – 🛗, ⅙⊷ rm, ▤ 📺 ☎ �&Ꮣ 🅿 – 🔬 350. ⬛️ 🅰🅴 𝐽𝐶𝐵
Meals (closed Saturday lunch) 15.75/18.75 **st.** and a la carte 🛈 6.50 – ⊆ 10.75 – **151 rm**
109.00 **st.**, 1 suite – SB.

🏛 **Donington Thistle,** East Midlands Airport, DE74 2SH, SE : 3 ¼ m. by High St. on A 453
ℰ (01332) 850700, Fax (01332) 850823, 𝐼𝟨, ≦s, ⬛️ – ⅙⊷, ▤ rest, 📺 ☎ �&Ꮣ 🅿 – 🔬 220. ⬛️
🅰🅴 ⓪ 𝑉𝐼𝑆𝐴 𝐽𝐶𝐵
Meals (bar lunch Saturday and Bank Holidays) 14.00/21.00 **st.** and a la carte 🛈 6.25 –
⊆ 10.00 – **110 rm** 106.00/138.00 **st.** – SB.

🏦 **Priest House on the River,** Kings Mills, DE74 2RR, W : 1 ¾ m. by Park Lane
ℰ (01332) 810649, Fax (01332) 811141, ≺, « Riverside setting », ⅏, park – ⅙⊷ rest, 📺 ☎
🅿 – 🔬 130. ⬛️ 🅰🅴 ⓪ 𝑉𝐼𝑆𝐴
Meals (bar lunch Saturday) 13.95/20.50 **t.** and a la carte – ⊆ 9.50 – **43 rm** 90.00/105.00 **st.**,
2 suites – SB.

🏦 **Donington Manor,** High St., DE74 2PP, ℰ (01332) 810253, Fax (01332) 850330 – 📺 ☎
🅿 – 🔬 80. ⬛️ 🅰🅴 ⓪ 𝑉𝐼𝑆𝐴. ⅏
closed 24 to 30 December – Meals 8.00/12.00 **st.** and a la carte – **27 rm** ⊆ 60.00/80.00 **st.**

CASTLETON Derbs. 𝟜𝟘𝟚 𝟜𝟘𝟛 𝟜𝟘𝟜 O 23 Great Britain G. – pop. 689 – ⊠ Sheffield (S. Yorks.).
Env. : Blue John Caverns★ AC, W : 1 m.
London 181 – Derby 49 – Manchester 30 – Sheffield 16 – Stoke-on-Trent 39.

🏛 **Ye Olde Nags Head,** Cross St., S33 8WH, ℰ (01433) 620248, Fax (01433) 620614 – 📺 ☎
🅿. ⬛️ 🅰🅴 ⓪ 𝑉𝐼𝑆𝐴. ⅏
Meals 15.95 **t.** (dinner) and a la carte approx. 18.00 **t.** – **8 rm** ⊆ 59.50/109.50 **t.** – SB.

CASTLETOWN Isle of Man 𝟜𝟘𝟚 G 21 – see Man (Isle of).

CATLOWDY Cumbria 𝟜𝟘𝟙 𝟜𝟘𝟚 L 18 – ⊠ Carlisle.
London 333 – Carlisle 16 – Dumfries 36 – Hawick 31 – Newcastle upon Tyne 65.

⋔ **Bessiestown Farm** ⅏, CA6 5QP, ℰ (01228) 577219, Fax (01228) 577219, « Working
farm », ⬛️, 🌼, park – ⅙⊷ 📺 🅿. ⬛️ 𝑉𝐼𝑆𝐴. ⅏
closed 25 and 26 December – Meals (by arrangement) 18.00 **st.** 🛈 5.95 – **8 rm** ⊆ 21.00/
60.00 **st.** – SB.

CAWSTON Norfolk 𝟜𝟘𝟜 X 25 Great Britain G. – pop. 2 265 – ⊠ Norwich.
Env. : Blicking Hall★★ AC, NE : 5 m. by B 1145 and B 1354.
London 122 – Cromer 15 – King's Lynn 42 – Norwich 13.

🏛 **Grey Gables** ⅏, Norwich Rd, NR10 4EY, S : 1 m. ℰ (01603) 871259, Fax (01603) 871259,
🌼, ⅍ – ⅙⊷ rm, 📺 ☎ 🅿. ⬛️ 𝑉𝐼𝑆𝐴
closed 25 and 26 December – Meals (lunch by arrangement)/dinner 12.50/18.00 **st.** 🛈 5.95
– **8 rm** ⊆ 21.00/60.00 **st.** – SB.

⋔ **The Walnuts** without rest., 8-12 New St., NR10 4AL, ℰ (01603) 871357,
Fax (01603) 871357, ⬛️, 🌼 – ⅙⊷ 🅿
closed 25 and 26 December – **3 rm** ⊆ 32.00/44.00 **s.**

CAXTON Cambs.
London 67 – Bedford 18 – Cambridge 12 – Huntingdon 7.

⋔ **Church Farm** ⅏, Gransden Rd, CB3 8PL, ℰ (01954) 719543, Fax (01954) 718999, « Part
17C farmhouse », 🌼, ⅍ – ⅙⊷ 🅿. ⬛️ 𝑉𝐼𝑆𝐴. ⅏
closed 2 weeks in spring and 2 weeks in autumn – Meals (communal dining) 18.50 – **4 rm**
⊆ 32.50/65.00.

CHADDESLEY CORBETT *Worcestershire* [403] [404] N 26 – *see Kidderminster.*

CHAGFORD *Devon* [403] I 31 *The West Country G.* – *pop. 1 417.*
Env. : *Dartmoor National Park★★.*
London 218 – Exeter 17 – Plymouth 28.

Gidleigh Park ⛰, TQ13 8HH, NW : 2 m. by Gidleigh Rd ☎ (01647) 432367, *Fax (01647) 432574,* ≤ Teign Valley, woodland and Meldon Hill, « Timbered country house, water garden », 🐟, park, 🎾 – ⊁ rest, [TV] ☎ [P]. [MC] [AE] [O] [VISA]
Meals (booking essential) 33.00-57.50/57.50-62.50 **st.** 🍷 9.00 – **13 rm** ☕ (dinner included) 225.00/425.00 **st.**, 2 suites
Spec. Roast quail with raviolo of spinach and parmesan. John Dory with a galette of aubergine tomato and courgette, lemon thyme sauce. Apple mousse with apple ice cream and a cider coulis.

Glendarah House without rest., Lower St., TQ13 8BZ, ☎ (01647) 433270, *Fax (01647) 433483,* ≤, 🌳 – ⊁ [TV] [P]. [MC] [VISA]. ⊁
closed Christmas and 2 weeks in winter – **6 rm** ☕ 30.00/60.00 **st.**

Thornworthy House ⛰, Thornworthy, TQ13 8EY, SW : 3 m. by Fernworthy rd on Thornworthy rd ☎ (01647) 433297, *Fax (01647) 433297,* ≤, « Country house atmosphere », 🌳, park, 🎾 – ⊁ [TV] [P]. ⊁
closed 4 to 31 January – **Meals** (by arrangement) 17.00 **st.** 🍷 4.50 – ☕ 5.50 – **3 rm** 27.00/55.00 **st.**

🍴 **22 Mill Street** with rm, 22 Mill St., TQ13 8AW, ☎ (01647) 432244 – ⊁ [TV]. [MC] [VISA]
closed Sunday dinner and Monday except Bank Holidays when closed Monday dinner and Tuesday, 5 to 20 January and 25 December – **Meals** (light lunch)/dinner 24.50 **st.** – **2 rm** ☕ 30.00/40.00 **st.**

at Sandypark *NE : 2¼ m. on A 382 – ✉ Chagford.*

Mill End, TQ13 8JN, on A 382 ☎ (01647) 432282, *Fax (01647) 433106,* « Country house with water mill », 🐟, 🌳 – ⊁ rest, [TV] ☎ 🚗 [P]. [MC] [AE] [VISA] [JCB]
Meals 14.50/23.50 **t.** 🍷 6.95 – **17 rm** ☕ 47.00/95.00 **t.** – SB.

Great Tree ⛰, TQ13 8JS, on A 382 ☎ (01647) 432491, *Fax (01647) 432562,* ≤, 🐟, 🌳, park – ⊁ rest, [TV] ☎ [P]. [MC] [AE] [O] [VISA]
Meals (bar lunch)/dinner 21.00 **t.** 🍷 5.85 – **10 rm** ☕ 50.00/98.00 **t.** – SB.

at Easton *NE : 1½ m. on A 382 – ✉ Chagford.*

Easton Court, TQ13 8JL, ☎ (01647) 433469, *Fax (01647) 433654,* « Part 15C thatched house », 🌳 – ⊁ rest, [TV] ☎. [MC] [AE] [VISA]
closed January – **Meals** (dinner only) 22.00 🍷 6.00 – **8 rm** ☕ (dinner included) 70.00/138.00 **t.** – SB.

CHALE *I.O.W.* – *see Wight (Isle of).*

CHANNEL ISLANDS [403] OPQ 33 and [230] ⑨ ⑩ ⑪ *The West Country G.* – *pop. 145 920.*

ALDERNEY

[403] Q 33 and [230] ⑨ *The West Country G.* – *pop. 2 297.*

See : *Braye Bay★ – Mannez Garenne (≤★ from Quesnard Lighthouse) – Telegraph Bay★ – Vallee des Trois Vaux★ – Clonque Bay★.*
✈ ☎ *(01481) 822551 - Booking Office : Aurigny Air Services ☎ (01481) 822888.*
⛴ *to Weymouth, (Guernsey) St. Peter Port and France (St. Malo) (Condor Ferries Ltd) daily.*
⛴ *to France (St. Malo) (Condor Ferries Ltd) weekly.*
[i] *States Office, Queen Elizabeth II St. GY9 3AA ☎ (01481) 822994/822811.*

Braye.

🍴 **First and Last,** GY9 3TH, ☎ (01481) 823162, ≤ harbour – [MC] [AE] [O] [VISA]
23 March-27 October – **Meals** *(closed Monday except Bank Holidays)* 11.95 and a la carte 🍷 3.50.

St. Anne.

Chez André, Victoria St., GY9 3TA, ☎ (01481) 822777, *Fax (01481) 822962* – ⊁ rm, [TV] ☎. [MC] [AE] [O] [VISA]
Meals a la carte 13.00/32.00 🍷 4.95 – ☕ 6.80 – **11 rm** 46.00/92.00 – SB.

🏠 **Inchalla** ॐ, Le Val, GY9 3UL, ℰ (01481) 823220, *Fax (01481) 824045*, ⛅, ☞ – ⅙ rest, 📺 ☎ 🅿. 🐵 AE *VISA* JCB. ✹
closed 2 weeks Christmas and New Year – **Meals** *(closed Sunday)* (dinner only) 16.00
a la carte ⅄ 4.75 – **9 rm** ⊇ 78.00/86.00.

🏠 **Belle Vue**, The Butes, GY9 3UN, ℰ (01481) 822844, *Fax (01481) 823601* – ⅙ 📺 ☎. 🐵
VISA JCB. ✹
closed 24 to 26 December – **Meals** 7.50/12.50 and a la carte ⅄ 3.20 – **27 rm** ⊇ 42.50/85.00
– SB.

↑ **Chez Nous** without rest., Les Venelles, GY9 3TW, ℰ (01481) 823633, *Fax (01481) 823732* –
⅙ 📺 ☎. AE. ✹
March-November – **3 rm** ⊇ 32.00/56.00 s.

✗ **Georgian House**, Victoria St., GY9 3UF, ℰ (01481) 822471, *Fax (01481) 822471* – 🐵 AE
① *VISA* JCB
Meals *(closed Tuesday dinner)* 10.75 (lunch) and a la carte 11.25/20.00 ⅄ 4.25.

🏠 **Rose and Crown** with rm, Le Huret, GY9 3TR, ℰ (01481) 823414, *Fax (01481) 823615*,
☞ – 📺 ☎. 🐵 AE ① *VISA* JCB. ✹
booking essential in winter – **Meals** a la carte 7.65/16.75 s. ⅄ 2.75 – **6 rm** ⊇ 38.00/80.00 s.

GUERNSEY

📕📕📕 OP 33 and 📕📕 ⑨ ⑩ *The West Country G.* – pop. 58 867.

See : *Island★ – Pezeries Point★★ – Icart Point★★ – Côbo Bay★★ – St. Martin's Point★★ –
St. Apolline's Chapel★ – Vale Castle★ – Fort Doyle★ – La Gran'mere du Chimquiere★ –
Rocquaine Bay★ – Jerbourg Point★.*

✈ *Service Air* ℰ (01481) 37682, Aurigny Air ℰ (01481) 37426.

⛴ *from St. Peter Port to France (St. Malo) via Jersey (St. Helier) (Emeraude Lines)
(summer only) (3 h 50 mn) – from St. Peter Port to Jersey (St. Helier) (Condor Ferries Ltd)
2 daily (1 h 15 mn) – from St. Peter Port to Jersey (St. Helier) and Poole (Condor Ferries Ltd).*

⛴ *from St. Peter Port to France (St. Malo, Granville and Carteret) (Emeraude Lines) (sum-
mer only) – from St. Peter Port to France (St. Malo) via Sark and Jersey (St. Helier) (Condor
Ferries Ltd) 2 weekly – from St. Peter Port to Herm (Herm Seaway) (25 mn) – from St. Peter
Port to Sark (Isle of Sark Shipping Co. Ltd) (summer only) (45 mn) – from St. Peter Port to
Jersey (St. Helier) (Condor Ferries Ltd) (50 mn) – from St. Peter Port to Jersey (St. Helier) via
Sark (Condor Ltd) weekly.*

🚹 *P.O. Box 23, North Esplanade, GY1 3AN ℰ (01481) 723552 – The Airport, La Villiaze, Forest
ℰ (01481) 37267.*

L'Ancresse.
St. Peter Port 4.

🏛 **Symphony House** ॐ, Hacse Lane, GY3 5DS, ℰ (01481) 45418, *Fax (01481) 43581*, ☆,
☞ – 📺 ☎ 🅿. 🐵 *VISA* JCB. ✹
Symphony's : **Meals** (dinner only and Sunday lunch) 10.50/14.50 and a la carte ⅄ 7.95 –
15 rm ⊇ 40.00/80.00 – SB.

Fermain Bay – ✉ St. Peter Port.

🏰 **La Favorita** ॐ, Fermain Lane, GY4 6SD, ℰ (01481) 35666, *Fax (01481) 35413*, ⩽, ☆,
⛅, 🏊, ☞ – 🛗 ⅙ 📺 ☎ 🅿. 🐵 AE ① *VISA*. ✹
closed January-mid February – **Meals** 14.50 s. (dinner) and a la carte 13.50/17.65 s. ⅄ 4.50 –
37 rm ⊇ 50.50/91.00 s. – SB.

🏨 **Le Chalet** ॐ, GY4 6SD, ℰ (01481) 35716, *Fax (01481) 35718*, ⛅ – 📺 ☎ 🅿. 🐵 AE ① *VISA*
8 April-18 October – **Meals** (bar meals Monday to Saturday lunch and Sunday dinner)/
dinner 17.00 and a la carte ⅄ 6.00 – **40 rm** ⊇ 50.50/101.00, 1 suite – SB.

Forest – pop. 1 386.

↑ **Tudor Lodge Deer Farm** without rest., Forest Rd, GY8 0AG, ℰ (01481) 37849,
Fax (01481) 35662, ☞, park – 📺 ☎ 🅿. *VISA*. ✹
closed December-mid January – **5 rm** ⊇ 35.00/60.00.

↑ **Mon Plaisir** without rest., Rue des Landes, GY8 0DY, ℰ (01481) 64498, *Fax (01481) 63493*,
☞ – 📺 🅿. ✹
restricted opening in winter – **5 rm** ⊇ 27.00/48.00.

Pembroke Bay – ✉ *Vale.*

St. Peter Port 5.

🏛 **Pembroke Bay** ⤢, GY3 5BY, ℰ (01481) 47573, Fax (01481) 48838, ≤, ⊒, ☞, ℀ – ⇆ 📺 ☎ 🅿. ⓪ VISA
April-mid October – Meals – (see *Melting Pot* below) – **12 rm** ⇌ 60.00/98.00 **s.**

✕ **Melting Pot** (at Pembroke Bay H.), GY3 5BY, ℰ (01481) 41175, Fax (01481) 48838, ☞ – 🅿. ⓪ VISA JCB
closed Monday to Thursday November-April – Meals 13.50 **s.** (dinner) and a la carte 13.50/22.50 **s.** ⅋ 5.50.

St. Martin – *pop. 6 082.*

St. Peter Port 2.

🏛 **Green Acres** ⤢, Les Hubits, GY4 6LS, ℰ (01481) 35711, Fax (01481) 35978, ⊒, ☞ – ⇆ rest, ▤ rest, 📺 ☎ 🅿 – 🔬 40. ⓪ VISA ℀
mid February-October – Meals (bar lunch)/dinner 14.50 ⅋ 4.50 – **48 rm** ⇌ 33.00/94.00 – SB.

🏛 **Idlerocks** ⤢, Jerbour Point, GY4 6BJ, ℰ (01481) 37711, Fax (01481) 35592, ≤ sea and neighbouring Channel Islands, ⊒, ☞ – ⇆ rm, 📺 ☎ 🅿. ⓪ ℀ VISA
Meals (bar lunch Monday to Saturday)/dinner 14.50 and a la carte ⅋ 5.25 – **28 rm** ⇌ (dinner included) 51.00/184.00 – SB.

🏛 **St. Margarets Lodge**, Forest Rd, GY4 6UE, ℰ (01481) 35757, Fax (01481) 37594, ☎ₛ, ⊒, ☞ – 🛗, ⇆ rest, 📺 ☎ 🅿 – 🔬 80. ⓪ ℀ ① VISA JCB ℀
Meals (bar lunch Monday to Saturday)/dinner 15.95 and a la carte ⅋ 3.95 – **47 rm** ⇌ 38.00/76.00 **s.** – SB.

🏛 **Bon Port** ⤢, Moulin Huet Bay, GY4 6EW, ℰ (01481) 39249, Fax (01481) 39596, ≤ Moulin Huet Bay and Jerbour Point, ☎ₛ, ☞ – ⇆ rest, 📺 ☎ 🅿. ⓪ ℀ VISA ℀
Renoir View : Meals 15.00 (dinner) and a la carte 14.25/23.45 ⅋ 5.50 – **14 rm** ⇌ 70.20/108.00, 4 suites.

🏛 **Saints Bay** ⤢, Icart, GY4 6JG, ℰ (01481) 38888, Fax (01481) 35558, ⊒, ☞ – 📺 ☎ 🅿. ⓪ VISA ℀
Meals (bar lunch)/dinner 14.50 **s.** and a la carte ⅋ 4.50 – **36 rm** ⇌ (dinner included) 75.00/104.00 **s.**

🏛 **Bella Luce**, La Fosse, Moulin Huet, GY4 6EB, ℰ (01481) 38764, Fax (01481) 39561, ☎ₛ, ⊒, ☞ – ▤ rest, 📺 ☎ 🅿. ⓪ ℀ VISA
Meals (bar lunch Monday to Saturday)/dinner 13.00 and a la carte ⅋ 5.50 – **31 rm** ⇌ 50.00/97.00 – SB.

🏛 **La Cloche** ⤢ without rest., Les Traudes, GY4 6LR, ℰ (01481) 35421, Fax (01481) 38258, ⊒, ☞ – ⇆ 📺 ☎ 🅿. ⓪ VISA. ℀
May-October – **10 rm** ⇌ (dinner included) 71.25/95.00 **s.**

🏛 **La Michele** ⤢, Les Hubits, GY4 6NB, ℰ (01481) 38065, Fax (01481) 39492, ⊒, ☞ – ⇆ rest, 📺 ☎ 🅿. ⓪ ℀ VISA. ℀
9 April-October – Meals (residents only) (dinner only) 8.95 **s.** ⅋ 3.80 – **13 rm** ⇌ (dinner included) 45.00/80.00 **s.** – SB.

🏛 **La Barbarie** ⤢, Saints Bay, GY4 6ES, ℰ (01481) 35217, Fax (01481) 35208, ⊒, ☞ – 📺 ☎ 🅿. ⓪ VISA. ℀
Meals (bar lunch Monday to Saturday)/dinner 14.50 and a la carte ⅋ 4.95 – **22 rm** ⇌ 47.00/74.00, 1 suite – SB.

🏛 **Farnborough** without rest., Les Damouettes Lane, GY1 1ZN, off Les Hubits ℰ (01481) 37756, Fax (01481) 34082, ☞ – 📺 ☎ 🅿. ⓪ VISA. ℀
April-September – **11 rm** ⇌ 35.00/60.00 **s.**

St. Peter in the Wood – *pop. 2 242* – ✉ *St. Peters.*

St. Peter Port 6.

✕✕ **Café Du Moulin**, Rue du Quanteraine, GY7 9DP, ℰ (01481) 65944, Fax (01481) 65708, ⌖ – ⓪ VISA
closed Sunday dinner and Monday except July-August – Meals a la carte 15.65/25.65 ⅋ 4.95.

St. Peter Port *The West Country G.* – *pop. 16 648.*

See : Town★★ – St. Peter's Church★ Z – Hauteville House★ AC Z – Castle Cornet★ (≤★) AC Z.
Env. : Saumarez Park★ (Guernsey Folk Museum★), W : 2 m. by road to Catel Z – Little Chapel★, SW : 2 ¼ m. by Mount Durand road Z.
🛆 Rohais, St. Pierre Park ℰ (01481) 727039, Z.

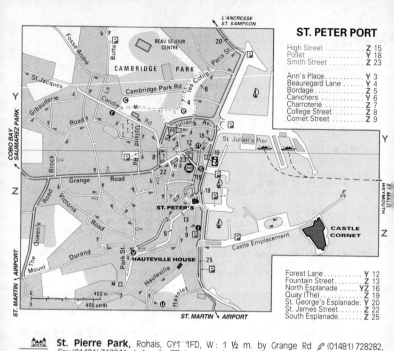

ST. PETER PORT

St. Pierre Park, Rohais, GY1 1FD, W : 1 ½ m. by Grange Rd ℰ (01481) 728282, Fax (01481) 712041, ≤, 🏋️, 🖙, 🔲, 📶, 🐎, park, ℅ – 🛗, 🔄 rm, ▤ rest, 📺 ☎ 🅿 – 🔬 200. 🕸️ 🅰🅴 ⓪ 𝖵𝖨𝖲𝖠. 🕸️
Café Renoir : Meals 15.00 **s.** (dinner) and a la carte 13.00/29.00 **s.** 🍴 4.50 – (see also **Victor Hugo** below) – **132 rm** ⊇ 115.00/165.00 **s.**, 3 suites.

Duke of Richmond, Cambridge Park, GY1 1UY, ℰ (01481) 726221, Fax (01481) 728945, ≤, 🔲 – 🛗, ▤ rest, 📺 ☎ – 🔬 100. 🕸️ 🅰🅴 ⓪ 𝖵𝖨𝖲𝖠
Meals 9.50/15.00 **s.** and a la carte 🍴 5.00 – **74 rm** ⊇ 55.00/85.00 **s.**, 1 suite – SB.　　　**Y c**

De Havelet, Havelet, GY1 1BA, ℰ (01481) 722199, Fax (01481) 714057, 🖙, 🔲, 🐎 – 📺 ☎ 🅿 🕸️ 🅰🅴 ⓪ 𝖵𝖨𝖲𝖠　　　**Z u**
Wellington Boot : Meals (dinner only and Sunday lunch)/dinner 16.50 and a la carte 🍴 6.50 – *Havelet Grill :* Meals (closed Sunday lunch and Monday dinner) a la carte 13.00/26.00 🍴 6.50 – **34 rm** ⊇ 58.00/114.00 – SB.

Moore's Central, Le Pollet, GY1 1WH, ℰ (01481) 724452, Fax (01481) 714037, 🏋️, 🖙 – 🖨 📺 🅿 . 🕸️ 🅰🅴 ⓪ 𝖵𝖨𝖲𝖠. 🕸️　　　**Y n**
Library : Meals (carving rest.) a la carte 10.70/28.00 🍴 5.00 – *Conservatory :* Meals 9.75/15.50 and a la carte 🍴 6.00 – **49 rm** ⊇ 49.00/155.00 – SB.

La Frégate 🗭, Les Cotils, GY1 1UT, ℰ (01481) 724624, Fax (01481) 720443, ≤ town and harbour, 🐎 – 📺 ☎ 🅿 . 🕸️ 🅰🅴 ⓪ 𝖵𝖨𝖲𝖠 𝖩𝖢𝖡. 🕸️　　　**Y e**
Meals 12.50/20.00 and a la carte 🍴 5.00 – **13 rm** ⊇ 55.00/95.00.

Midhurst House, Candie Rd, GY1 1UP, ℰ (01481) 724391, Fax (01481) 729451, 🐎 – 📺 ☎ . 🕸️ 𝖵𝖨𝖲𝖠. 🕸️　　　**Y r**
Easter-mid October – Meals (closed Wednesday and Saturday) (residents only) (dinner only) 12.50 🍴 4.00 – **7 rm** ⊇ 68.00 **s.** – SB.

Victor Hugo (at St. Pierre Park H.), Rohais, GY1 1FD, W : 1 ½ m. by Grange Rd ℰ (01481) 728282, Fax (01481) 712041 – ▤ 🅿 . 🕸️ 🅰🅴 ⓪ 𝖵𝖨𝖲𝖠 𝖩𝖢𝖡
closed Saturday lunch and Sunday dinner – Meals - Seafood - 14.50/19.95 **s.** and a la carte 🍴 4.50.

Le Nautique, Quay Steps, GY1 2LE, ℰ (01481) 721714, Fax (01481) 721786, ≤ – 🕸️ 🅰🅴 ⓪ 𝖵𝖨𝖲𝖠 𝖩𝖢𝖡　　　**Z s**
closed Sunday and 25 December-10 January – Meals a la carte 17.00/23.50 **s.** 🍴 5.35.

Four Seasons, Albert House, South Esplanade, GY1 1AJ, ℰ (01481) 727444 – 🕸️ 𝖵𝖨𝖲𝖠　　　**Z i**
closed Tuesday dinner, Sunday, February and Bank Holidays – Meals 10.00/15.00 and a la carte 🍴 4.75.

XX **The Absolute End,** Longstore, GY1 2BG, N : ¾ m. by St. George's Esplanade
 ℰ (01481) 723822, *Fax (01481) 729129* – **CB** **AE** **VISA**
 closed Sunday and January – **Meals** - Seafood - a la carte 15.25/26.00 **s.** ⌖ 5.00.

XX **La Piazza,** Trinity Sq., GY1 1LX, ℰ (01481) 725085, 😊 – **CB** **AE** **VISA**   Z   v
 closed Sunday and 24 December-24 January – **Meals** - Italian - a la carte 15.30/25.20 ⌖ 3.60.

St. Saviour – *pop. 2 419.*
 St. Peter Port 4.

🏛 **L'Atlantique,** Perelle Bay, GY7 9NA, ℰ (01481) 64056, *Fax (01481) 63800*, ≤, ⊒, ☞ – **TV**
 ☎ **P**. **CB** **AE** **VISA**. �
 March-October – **Meals** *(closed 2 January-28 February)* (bar lunch Monday to Saturday)/
 dinner 15.50 and a la carte ⌖ 4.85 – **23 rm** ☞ 40.00/85.00 – SB.

🏠 **Les Piques Country** ⌖, Rue des Piques, GY7 9FW, ℰ (01481) 64515,
 Fax (01481) 65857, « Part 15C farmhouse », ☞s, ⊒, ☞ – **TV** ☎ **P**. **CB** **VISA**. �
 March-October – **Meals** (dinner only and lunch Saturday and Sunday)/dinner 13.95
 and a la carte ⌖ 3.95 – **20 rm** ☞ 50.00/150.00.

🏠 **Auberge du Val** ⌖, Sous L'Eglise, GY7 9FX, ℰ (01481) 63862, *Fax (01481) 64835*, 😊,
 « Converted 19C farmhouse, herb garden », ☞s – **TV** ☎ **P**. **CB** **AE** **VISA**. �
 Meals *(closed Sunday dinner and Monday except lunch Bank Holidays)* a la carte 15.20/
 18.95 – **7 rm** ☞ 30.00/60.00 **s.**

Vazon Bay – ✉ Catel.

🏛 **La Grande Mare,** Vazon Coast Rd, GY5 7BD, ℰ (01481) 56576, *Fax (01481) 56532*, ≤, ⊒,
 🏌, ⊐, ☞ – ▯ **TV** ☎ **P**. **CB** **AE** **①** **VISA**. �
 Meals 12.50/15.95 and dinner a la carte ⌖ 6.50 – **11 rm** ☞ 48.00/120.00, **13 suites** 124.00/
 176.00.

HERM

403 P 33 and **230** ⑩ *The West Country G.* – *pop. 113.*

See : *Le Grand Monceau*★.

⛴ to Guernsey (St. Peter Port) (Herm Seaway) (25 mn).

🛈 *Administrative Office, GY1 3HR* ℰ (01481) 700334.

🏛 **White House** ⌖, GY1 3HR, ℰ (01481) 722159, *Fax (01481) 710066*, « Private island
 setting ≤ Belle Greve Bay and Guernsey », ⊒, ☞, park, ✖ – ✖ rest. **CB** **AE** **VISA**. �
 Easter-5 October – **Meals** (booking essential to non-residents) 13.00/17.25 ⌖ 7.95 – **38 rm**
 ☞ (dinner included) 68.00/136.00.

JERSEY

403 0P 33 and **230** ⑪ *The West Country G.* – *pop. 84 082.*

See : *Island*★★ – *Jersey Zoo*★★ *AC* – *Jersey Museum*★ – *Eric Young Orchid Foundation*★ –
St. Catherine's Bay★ *(≤*★★*)* – *Grosnez Point*★ – *Devil's Hole*★ – *St. Matthews Church,
Millbrook (glasswork*★*)* – *La Hougue Bie*★ *(Neolithic tomb*★ *AC)* – *Waterworks Valley* -
Hamptonne Country Life Museum★ – *St. Catherine's Bay*★ *(≤*★★*)* – *Noirmont Point*★.

✈ *States of Jersey Airport :* ℰ (01534) 492000.

🚢 *from St. Helier to France (St. Malo) (Emeraude Lines) (summer only) (2 h 30 mn) –
from St. Helier to France (St. Malo) and Poole (Condor Ferries Ltd) daily – from St. Helier to
Sark (Condor Ferries Ltd) 3 weekly (45 mn) – from St. Helier to Guernsey (St. Peter Port) and
Poole (Condor Ferries Ltd).*

⛴ *from St. Helier to France (Granville and St. Malo) (Emeraude Lines and Condor Ferries
Ltd) (summer only) – from St. Helier to France (St. Malo) (Condor Ferries Ltd) 3 weekly –
from Gorey to France (Portbail and Carteret) (Emeraude Lines) (summer only) (30-40 mn) –
from St. Helier to Guernsey (St. Peter Port) (50 mn), to Sark (45 mn) (Condor Ferries Ltd) –
from St. Helier to Guernsey (St. Peter Port) via Sark (Condor Ltd) weekly.*

🛈 *Liberation Square, St. Helier, JE1 1BB* ℰ (01534) 500777.

Bouley Bay – ✉ Trinity.
 St. Helier 5.

🏛 **Water's Edge,** JE3 5AS, ℰ (01534) 862777, *Fax (01534) 863645*, ≤ Bouley Bay, ☞s, ⊒,
 ☞ – ▯, ✖ rest. **TV** ☎ **P**. **CB** **AE** **①** **VISA** **JCB**
 mid April-October – **Meals** 10.50/15.50 **s.** and a la carte ⌖ 3.75 – **47 rm** ☞ 58.50/113.00 **s.**,
 4 suites – SB.

Corbiere – ⊠ St. Brelade.
St. Helier 8.

🏯🏯🏯 **Sea Crest** 🌊 with rm, Petit Port, JE3 8HH, ✆ (01534) 46353, Fax (01534) 47316, ≤, 斎, 🌳 – ■ rest, 🔟 ☎ 🅿. 🐠 🆎 𝑉𝐼𝑆𝐴. ❋
closed mid January-mid February – **Meals** (closed Sunday dinner November-March and Monday) 12.00/20.00 and a la carte ₰ 8.00 – **7 rm** 🖙 52.00/110.00 s.

L'Etacq.

🏠 **Lobster Pot** 🌊, JE3 2DL, ✆ (01534) 482888, Fax (01534) 481574, ≤, 斎 – ■ rest, 🔟 ☎ 🅿. 🐠 🆎 ⓪ 𝑉𝐼𝑆𝐴 𝐽𝐶𝐵. ❋
Brasserie : Meals 15.50 and a la carte 19.95/39.45 ₰ 9.00 – (see also **Restaurant** below) – **12 rm** 🖙 77.00/132.00 s. – SB.

🏯🏯 **Restaurant** (at Lobster Pot H.), JE3 2DL, ✆ (01534) 482888, Fax (01534) 481574 – ■ 🅿. 🐠 🆎 ⓪ 𝑉𝐼𝑆𝐴 𝐽𝐶𝐵.
closed Sunday to Tuesday – **Meals** (dinner only) 35.00 ₰ 12.50.

Gorey The West Country G. – ⊠ St. Martin.
See : Mont Orgueil Castle★ (≤★★) AC.
St. Helier 4.

🏠 **Old Court House**, Gorey Village, JE3 9FS, ✆ (01534) 854444, Fax (01534) 853587, ≘s, 🟰, 🌳 – 🛗 🔟 ☎ ₺ 🅿. 🐠 🆎 ⓪ 𝑉𝐼𝑆𝐴 𝐽𝐶𝐵. ❋
mid April-mid October – **Meals** (bar lunch)/dinner 13.50 s. and a la carte ₰ 4.00 – **58 rm** 🖙 (dinner included) 54.50/117.00.

🏠 **Moorings**, Gorey Pier, JE3 6EW, ✆ (01534) 853633, Fax (01534) 857618 – ■ rest, 🔟 ☎. 🐠 🆎 𝑉𝐼𝑆𝐴 𝐽𝐶𝐵. ❋
Meals 11.00/15.00 s. and a la carte ₰ 3.75 – **16 rm** 🖙 34.00/95.00 s. – SB.

🏠 **Trafalgar Bay**, Gorey Village, JE3 9ES, ✆ (01534) 856643, Fax (01534) 856922, 🟰, 🌳 – ❋ rest, 🔟 🅿. 🐠 🆎 𝑉𝐼𝑆𝐴. ❋
May-October – **Meals** (bar lunch)/dinner 10.00 ₰ 4.50 – **27 rm** 🖙 (dinner included) 48.00/102.00 s.

🏠 **Maison Gorey**, Gorey Village, JE3 9EP, ✆ (01534) 857775, Fax (01534) 857779 – ❋ rest, 🔟 ☎. 🐠 🆎 ⓪ 𝑉𝐼𝑆𝐴. ❋
closed October – **Meals** (bar lunch)/dinner 8.00 ₰ 4.90 – **30 rm** 🖙 45.00/90.00 s. – SB.

🏯 **Suma's**, Gorey Hill, JE3 6ET, ✆ (01534) 853291, Fax (01534) 851913, ≤, 斎 – ■. 🐠 🆎 ⓪ 𝑉𝐼𝑆𝐴
closed Sunday dinner, Monday and 24 December-31 January – **Meals** 13.75 s. (lunch) and a la carte 17.00/23.50 s.

🏯 **Jersey Pottery (Garden Restaurant)**, Gorey Village, JE3 9EP, ✆ (01534) 851119, Fax (01534) 856403, « Working pottery », 🌳 – ❋ 🅿. 🐠 🆎 ⓪ 𝑉𝐼𝑆𝐴 𝐽𝐶𝐵.
closed Sunday and 10 days Christmas – **Meals** - Seafood - (lunch only) 19.00 s. and a la carte 19.40/33.95 s. ₰ 7.15.

🏯 **Village Bistro** (Cameron), Gorey Village, JE3 9EP, ✆ (01534) 853429, Fax (01534) 853429, 斎 – 🐠 𝑉𝐼𝑆𝐴
closed Monday except Bank Holidays, last 2 weeks February and last 2 weeks October – Meals (dinner booking essential) 12.50 (lunch) and a la carte 21.90/28.20 ₰ 5.50
Spec. Scallops with carrot and basil. Braised lamb with parmesan risotto. Chocolate pavé.

Grève De Lecq – ⊠ St. Ouen.

🏠 **Des Pierres**, JE3 2DT, on B 65 ✆ (01534) 481858, Fax (01534) 485273 – 🔟 🅿. 🐠 𝑉𝐼𝑆𝐴. ❋
closed 15 December-15 January – **Meals** (residents only) (dinner only) 8.00 s. ₰ 5.50 – **16 rm** 🖙 (dinner included) 35.00/70.00 s. – SB.

Grouville – pop. 4 297.

🏠 **Lavender Villa**, Rue a Don, JE3 9DX, on A 3 ✆ (01534) 854937, Fax (01534) 856147, 🌳 – ❋ rest, 🔟 🅿. 🐠 🆎 𝑉𝐼𝑆𝐴. ❋
mid March-October – **Meals** (residents only) (dinner only) 8.00 ₰ 3.50 – **21 rm** 🖙 (dinner included) 35.00/70.00 s.

La Haule – ⊠ St. Brelade.

🏯🏯 **La Place** 🌊, Route du Coin, JE3 8BT, by B 25 on B 43 ✆ (01534) 44261, Fax (01534) 45164, ≘s, 🟰, 🌳 – ❋ rm, 🔟 ☎ 🅿 – 🔬 100. 🐠 🆎 ⓪ 𝑉𝐼𝑆𝐴 𝐽𝐶𝐵. ❋
Knights : Meals (dinner only and Sunday lunch)/dinner 23.10 s. and a la carte ₰ 7.50 – **43 rm** 🖙 102.00/152.00 s.

🏰 **La Haule Manor,** St. Aubin's Bay, JE3 8BS, ℘ (01534) 41426, Fax (01534) 45501, ≤, 🌳 –
📺 ☎ 📞. 🐱 ⅢⅢ VISA. ⊗
Meals 11.95/16.50 and a la carte 👖 4.90 – **14 rm** ⊑ 65.00/129.00.

⌂ **Au Caprice,** Route de la Haule, JE3 8BA, on A 1 ℘ (01534) 22083, Fax (01534) 26199 –
↳ rest, 📺. 🐱 ⅢⅢ VISA. ⊗
Easter-October – **Meals** (by arrangement) 6.00 **s.** – **12 rm** ⊑ 54.00 **s.** – SB.

La Pulente – ⊠ St. Brelade.

🔝 Les Mielles G. & C.C., St. Ouens Bay ℘ (01534) 482787.
St. Helier 7.

🏰 **Atlantic** ⊗, JE3 8HE, ℘ (01534) 44101, Fax (01534) 44102, ≤, 🌤, 🏋, ☎s, 🏊, 🏊, 🌳, ⊗
– 📳 📺 ☎ 📞 – 🔔 60. 🐱 ⅢⅢ ⑪ VISA. ⊗
closed January and February – **Meals** 15.00/23.50 and dinner a la carte 25.65/37.50 👖 9.00 –
49 rm ⊑ 125.00/220.00, 1 suite – SB.

Rozel Bay – ⊠ St. Martin.
St. Helier 6.

🏰 **Chateau La Chaire** ⊗, Rozel Valley, JE3 6AJ, ℘ (01534) 863354, Fax (01534) 865137,
« Victorian country house », 🌳 – 📺 ☎ 📞. 🐱 ⅢⅢ ⑪ VISA JCB. ⊗
Meals – (see below) – **13 rm** ⊑ 95.00/150.00, 1 suite – SB.

🏰 **Beau Couperon,** JE3 6AN, ℘ (01534) 865522, Fax (01534) 865332, ≤, 🏊 – 📺 ☎ 📞. 🐱
ⅢⅢ ⑪ VISA JCB. ⊗
9 April-mid October – **Meals** 18.95 **s.** (dinner) and a la carte 13.00/20.00 **s.** 👖 5.50 – **35 rm**
⊑ 77.50/110.00 **s.**

XXX **Chateau La Chaire** (at Chateau La Chaire H.), Rozel Valley, JE3 6AJ, ℘ (01534) 863354,
Fax (01534) 865137 – ↳ 📞. 🐱 ⅢⅢ ⑪ VISA JCB
Meals 21.50/28.20 and a la carte 👖 6.80.

St. Aubin.
St. Helier 4.

🏰 **La Tour,** High St., JE3 8BZ, ℘ (01534) 43770, Fax (01534) 47143, ≤ St. Aubin's Fort and
Bay, 🌳 – 📺 ☎ 📞. 🐱 VISA. ⊗
closed 2 January-15 March – **Rooks : Meals** (closed Sunday and Monday) (dinner only)
10.50 and a la carte 👖 5.00 – **24 rm** ⊑ 40.50/88.00, 1 suite.

🏰 **Somerville,** Mont du Boulevard, JE3 8AD, S : ¾ m. via harbour ℘ (01534) 41226,
Fax (01534) 46621, ≤ St. Aubin's Bay, 🏊 – 📳 📺 ☎ 📞. 🐱 ⅢⅢ ⑪ VISA. ⊗
closed 3 January to March – **Meals** (bar lunch)/dinner 13.75 **s.** and a la carte 👖 5.00 – **59 rm**
⊑ 47.00/94.00 **s.**

🏰 **Mont de La Roque,** Mont de La Roque, JE3 8BQ, ℘ (01534) 42942, Fax (01534) 47841,
≤ St. Aubin's Fort and Bay, 🌤 – 🔳 rest, 📺 ☎ 📞. 🐱 ⅢⅢ VISA. ⊗
closed January and February – **Le Mirage : Meals** (dinner only and Sunday lunch)
15.50 and a la carte 👖 3.50 – **24 rm** ⊑ 32.50/150.00 **s.**

🏠 **Panorama** without rest., High St., JE3 8BZ, ℘ (01534) 42429, Fax (01534) 45940,
≤ St. Aubin's Fort and Bay, 🌳 – 📺. 🐱 ⅢⅢ ⑪ VISA. ⊗
Easter-mid December – **17 rm** ⊑ 44.00/88.00.

🏠 **St. Magloire,** High St., JE3 8BZ, ℘ (01534) 41302, Fax (01534) 44148 – ↳ rest, 📺. 🐱
VISA. ⊗
mid March-mid October – **Meals** (residents only) (dinner only) 7.00 **s.** 👖 2.50 – **12 rm**
⊑ 30.00/51.00 **s.**

🏠 **Bon Viveur,** The Bulwarks, JE3 8AB, ℘ (01534) 41049, Fax (01534) 47540, ≤ – 📺. 🐱 ⅢⅢ
VISA. ⊗
March-October – **Meals** 10.00 and a la carte 👖 3.25 – **19 rm** ⊑ 26.50/53.00.

⌂ **Sabots d'or,** High St., JE3 8BR, ℘ (01534) 43732, Fax (01534) 490142 – 📺. 🐱 ⅢⅢ ⑪ VISA.
⊗
restricted opening in winter – **Meals** 7.00 **s.** – **12 rm** ⊑ 22.00/48.00 **s.**

🏠 **Old Court House Inn** with rm, St. Aubin's Harbour, JE3 8AB, ℘ (01534) 46433,
Fax (01534) 45103, ≤, 🌤 – 📺 ☎ 📞. 🐱 ⅢⅢ VISA. ⊗
Meals 9.95/16.50 and a la carte 👖 5.00 – **8 rm** ⊑ 40.00/80.00 **s.**, 1 suite.

St. Brelade's Bay The West Country G. – pop. 9 331 – ⊠ St. Brelade.
See : Fishermen's Chapel (frescoes★).
St. Helier 6.

🏰 **L'Horizon,** JE3 8EF, ℘ (01534) 43101, Fax (01534) 46269, ≤ St. Brelade's Bay, 🌤, 🏋, ☎s,
🏊 – 📳 📺 ☎ 👤 📞 – 🔔 150. 🐱 ⅢⅢ ⑪ VISA. ⊗
Crystal Room : Meals (dinner only) 24.00 **s.** and a la carte 👖 6.50 – (see also **The Grill**
below) – **104 rm** ⊑ 125.00/215.00 **s.**, 3 suites – SB.

ENGLAND

St. Brelade's Bay, Rue de la Baie, JE3 8EF, ℘ (01534) 46141, *Fax (01534) 47278*, ≤ St. Brelade's Bay, ☎, ⅃, ✦, ✕ – │☼│ ⊡ ☎ ℗. ⓪ VISA. ✦
May-September – Meals 12.00/20.00 and a la carte ╻ 6.00 – **80 rm** ☑ (dinner included) 111.30/247.20, 1 suite.

Golden Sands, La Route de la Baie, JE3 8EF, ℘ (01534) 41241, *Fax (01534) 499366*, ≤ – │☼│ ⊡ ☎. ⓪ ⌿Ǝ VISA. ✦
Easter-31 October – Meals (residents only) (dinner only) 15.00 s. ╻ 6.00 – **62 rm** ☑ 34.00/120.00 s.

Chateau Valeuse, Rue de la Valeuse, JE3 8EE, ℘ (01534) 46281, *Fax (01534) 47110*, ⅃, ✦ – ⊡ ☎ ℗. ⓪ VISA JCB. ✦
7 April-15 October – Meals *(closed Sunday dinner)* 11.00/18.70 and dinner a la carte ╻ 5.50 – **34 rm** ☑ (dinner included) 54.00/132.00 – SB.

XXX **The Grill** (at L'Horizon H.), JE3 8EF, ℘ (01534) 490082, *Fax (01534) 46269* – ▤ ℗. ⓪ ⌿Ǝ ⓪ VISA
Meals a la carte 21.00/35.00 s. ╻ 6.50.

St. Clement – pop. 7 393.

⌐₉ St. Clements ℘ (01534) 821938.
St. Helier 2.

Playa D'Or without rest., Greve d'Azette, JE2 6SA, W : 2 m. on A 4 ℘ (01534) 22861, *Fax (01534) 69668* – ✦✕ ⊡ ℗. ⓪ ⌿Ǝ ⓪ VISA. ✦
closed December and January – **15 rm** ☑ 27.50/55.00 s.

Rocque-Berg View, Rue de Samares, JE2 6LS, ℘ (01534) 852642, *Fax (01534) 851694* – ✦✕ rest, ⊡ ℗. ✦
restricted opening in winter – Meals (by arrangement) 8.00 s. – **9 rm** ☑ 45.00/48.00 s.

St. Helier *The West Country G.* – pop. 28 123.

See : Jersey Museum★ *AC* Z – Elizabeth Castle (≤★) *AC* Z – Fort Regent (≤★ *AC*) Z.
Env. : St. Peter's Valley - German Underground Hospital★ *AC*, NW : 4 m. by A 1, A 11 St. Peter's Valley rd and C 112.

Plan opposite

De Vere Grand, Esplanade, JE4 8WD, ℘ (01534) 22301, *Fax (01534) 37815*, ≤, ╞ձ, ☎, ☒ – │☼│, ▤ rest, ⊡ ☎ ♿ – ⌿ը 180. ⓪ ⌿Ǝ ⓪ VISA. ✦
Y u
Meals 15.50/22.75 and a la carte ╻ 7.00 – (see also *Victoria's* below) – **110 rm** ☑ 100.00/170.00 s., 5 suites – SB.

Pomme d'Or, Liberation Sq., JE2 3NR, ℘ (01534) 880110, *Fax (01534) 37781* – │☼│, ✦✕ rm, ▤ rest, ⊡ ☎ ♿ – ⌿ը 180. ⓪ ⌿Ǝ ⓪ VISA. ✦
Z u
Harbour Room : Meals (carving rest.) 12.50/16.00 s. ╻ 4.00 – (see also *La Petite Pomme* below) – **145 rm** ☑ 75.00/120.00 s., 2 suites – SB.

De la Plage, Havre des Pas, JE2 4UQ, ℘ (01534) 23474, *Fax (01534) 68642*, ≤, ╞ձ – │☼│ ⊡ ☎ ℗. ⓪ ⌿Ǝ ⓪ VISA JCB. ✦
Z s
26 April-12 October – Meals (bar lunch)/dinner 16.50 and a la carte ╻ 4.50 – **78 rm** ☑ 42.50/113.00 – SB.

Apollo, 9 St. Saviour's Rd, JE2 4LA, ℘ (01534) 25441, *Fax (01534) 22120*, ╞ձ, ☎, ☒ – │☼│ ⊡ ☎ ℗. ⓪ ⌿Ǝ ⓪ VISA. ✦
Z e
Meals (dinner only) 12.50 and a la carte ╻ 7.50 – **85 rm** ☑ 65.50/99.00 – SB.

Laurels, La route du Fort, JE2 4PA, ℘ (01534) 36444, *Fax (01534) 59904* – ✦✕ rest, ⊡ ☎ ℗. ⓪ ⌿Ǝ ⓪ VISA
Z v
mid March-October – Meals (residents only) (dinner only) 9.50 ╻ 4.90 – **37 rm** ☑ 57.50/105.00 s.

Queens, Queens Rd, JE2 3GR, ℘ (01534) 22239, *Fax (01534) 21930* – │☼│, ✦✕ rest, ⊡ ☎ ℗. ⓪ ⌿Ǝ ⓪ VISA JCB. ✦
Y x
Meals (residents only) (dinner only) 8.00 s. ╻ 4.00 – **37 rm** ☑ (dinner included) 45.00/90.00 s.

Washington, Clarendon Rd, JE2 3YS, ℘ (01534) 37981, *Fax (01534) 89899*, ⅃ – ✦✕ rest, ⊡ ☎ ℗. ⓪ ⌿Ǝ ⓪ VISA
Y e
April-October – Meals (residents only) (dinner only) 9.50 s. ╻ 4.90 – **36 rm** ☑ 57.50/95.00 – SB.

Mornington, 60-68 Don Rd, JE2 4QD, ℘ (01534) 24452, *Fax (01534) 34131* – │☼│, ✦✕ rest, ⊡ ☎ ℗. ⓪ ⌿Ǝ ⓪ VISA JCB. ✦
Z c
April-October – Meals (dinner only) 9.50 s. ╻ 4.00 – **31 rm** ☑ (dinner included) 76.00 s.

Chateau de la Mer, Havre des Pas, JE2 4UQ, ℘ (01534) 33366, *Fax (01534) 36544*, ≤ – ⊡ ☎ ℗. ⓪ ⌿Ǝ ⓪ VISA JCB. ✦
Z o
closed 23 December-1 February – Meals *(closed Sunday November-June and Monday November-March)* (dinner only and Sunday lunch)/dinner 15.50 and a la carte ╻ 4.95 – **5 rm** ☑ 54.00/88.00 s. – SB.

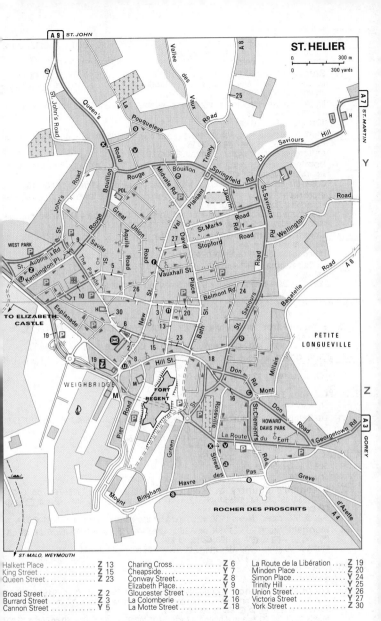

ST. HELIER

A 9 ST. JOHN
A 7 ST. MARTIN
A 6
A 3 GOREY

TO ELIZABETH CASTLE

WEST PARK

PETITE LONGUEVILLE

WEIGHBRIDGE

FORT REGENT

HOWARD DAVIS PARK

ROCHER DES PROSCRITS

ST. MALO, WEYMOUTH

Uplands, St. John's Rd, JE2 3LE, ℘ (01534) 873006, Fax (01534) 68804, ⤲ – ⚭ rest, 📺 Y a
🕾 🅿. ⬤⑧ Æ ① VISA. ⚅
closed 2 January-20 February – **Meals** (residents only) (bar lunch)/dinner 9.50 **s.** ⬩ 3.95 – **43 rm** ⊇ (dinner included) 41.50/83.00 **s.**

Greenwood Lodge, Roseville St., JE2 4PL, ℘ (01534) 67073, Fax (01534) 67876, ⤲ – ⚭ Z x
📺 🕾. ⬤⑧ Æ VISA JCB
March-mid November – **Meals** (bar lunch)/dinner 7.50 ⬩ 3.30 – **35 rm** ⊇ (dinner included) ⊇ 41.00/70.00.

185

ENGLAND

🏠 **Almorah**, 1 Almorah Cres., Lower Kings Cliff, JE2 3GU, ℰ (01534) 21648,
Fax (01534) 509724, ☞ – 🆃🆅 ☎ 🅿, 🕽🕽 VISA. ⋙
Meals (residents only) (dinner only) 8.75 ᐁ 4.00 – **14 rm** ⊑ 37.00/54.00 – SB.
Y o

🏠 **Brookfield**, 24 Raleigh Av., JE2 3ZG, ℰ (01534) 23168, Fax (01534) 21543 – 🆃🆅, 🕽🕽 VISA. ⋙
March-November – **Meals** (residents only) (dinner only) 7.00 s. ᐁ 2.80 – **20 rm** ⊑ (dinner included) 29.50/59.00 s.
Y v

⌂ **La Bonne Vie** without rest., Roseville St., JE2 4PL, ℰ (01534) 35955, Fax (01534) 33357 –
⋙ 🆃🆅, 🕽🕽 VISA. ⋙
10 rm ⊑ 25.00/50.00 s.
Z a

⌂ **Glen** ⤳ without rest., Vallee des Vaux, JE2 3GB, N : 1 ¼ m. by A 8 ℰ (01534) 32062,
Fax (01534) 880738, ☞ – 🆃🆅 🅿, VISA. ⋙
restricted opening in winter – **7 rm** ⊑ 28.00/53.00 s.

⌂ **Domino** without rest., Vauxhall St. (Rue du Val), JE2 4TJ, ℰ (01534) 30360,
Fax (01534) 31546 – 🆃🆅 🅿, VISA. ⋙
closed Christmas, New Year and restricted opening in winter – **13 rm** ⊑ 35.00/60.00 s.
Y r

XXX **Victoria's** (at De Vere Grand H.), Peirson Rd, JE4 8WD, ℰ (01534) 872255,
Fax (01534) 37815 – ▤, 🕽🕽 AE ① VISA
closed Saturday lunch, Sunday dinner and dinner 25-26 December – **Meals** (live music and dancing Friday and Saturday) 15.50/22.75 and a la carte ᐁ 7.00.
Y z

XXX **La Petite Pomme** (at Pomme d'Or H.), Liberation Sq., JE2 3NR, ℰ (01534) 66608 – ▤.
🕽🕽 AE ① VISA
closed Sunday and 25 December – **Meals** 14.50/16.50 s. and a la carte ᐁ 4.00.
Z u

XX **La Capannina**, 65-67 Halkett Pl., JE2 4WG, ℰ (01534) 34602, Fax (01534) 877628 – 🕽🕽 AE
① VISA
closed Sunday – **Meals** - Italian - 17.00 (dinner) and a la carte 11.70/28.50 ᐁ 5.50.
Z n

St. Lawrence – pop. 4 561.
St. Helier 3.

🏠 **Elmdale Farm**, Ville Emphrie, JE3 1EA, ℰ (01534) 34779, Fax (01534) 601115, ⟍, ☞ –
🆃🆅 ☎ 🅿, 🕽🕽 VISA. ⋙
Meals 8.25/13.50 and a la carte ᐁ 4.00 – **19 rm** ⊑ 35.00/70.00.

⌂ **Villa d'Oro** without rest., La Grande Route de St. Laurent, JE3 1NJ, on A 10
ℰ (01534) 862262, Fax (01534) 863012, ☞ – 🆃🆅, 🕽🕽 AE VISA JCB. ⋙
May-September – **12 rm** ⊑ 25.00/46.00 s.

St. Martin – pop. 3 258.
St. Helier 4.

⌂ **Le Relais de St. Martin**, Grande Route de Faldouet, JE3 6UG, ℰ (01534) 853271,
Fax (01534) 855241, ☞ – ⋙ rest, 🆃🆅 🅿, 🕽🕽 VISA. ⋙
April-October – **Meals** 9.25 s. ᐁ 3.75 – **11 rm** ⊑ 27.00/54.00.

St. Peter The West Country G. – pop. 4 231.
See : Living Legend★.
St. Helier 5.

🏨 **Greenhill's Country** ⤳, Coin Varin, Mont de l'Ecole, JE3 7EL, on C 112
ℰ (01534) 481042, Fax (01534) 485322, « Part 17C farmhouse », ⟍, ☞ – ▤ rest, 🆃🆅 ☎ 🅿.
🕽🕽 AE ① VISA. ⋙
5 April-17 October – **Meals** 13.50/19.50 and a la carte ᐁ 5.20 – **25 rm** ⊑ 45.00/110.00 s.

🏨 **Mermaid**, Airport Rd, JE3 7BN, on B 36 ℰ (01534) 41255, Fax (01534) 45826, 🎣, ⟲s, ⟍,
⟍, ☞, ⁒ – 🆃🆅 ☎ 🅿 – 🔬 120. 🕽🕽 AE ① VISA. ⋙
Meals 12.50 (dinner) and a la carte 13.00/19.50 – **68 rm** ⊑ 48.00/97.00 – SB.

St. Saviour – pop. 12 747.
St. Helier 1.

🏰 **Longueville Manor**, Longueville Rd, JE2 7WF, on A 3 ℰ (01534) 25501,
Fax (01534) 31613, « Former manor house with Jacobean panelling », ⟍, ☞, park, ⁒ – ⫽,
⋙ rest, ▤ rest, 🆃🆅 ☎ 🅿, 🕽🕽 AE ① VISA
Meals 20.00/35.00 s. and dinner a la carte 32.75/40.25 s. ᐁ 12.50 – **30 rm** ⊑ 175.00/
245.00 s., 2 suites – SB
Spec. Gateau of crab and garden vegetables with a marinated tomato terrine. Grilled panaché of seafood and vegetables, tomato compote and aioli. Pot roasted chicken with griddled asparagus and pancetta.

⌂ **Champ Colin** ⤳ without rest., Rue du Champ Colin, Houge Bie, JE2 7UN,
ℰ (01534) 851877, Fax (01534) 854902, « Part 19C farmhouse, antiques », ☞ – ⋙ 🆃🆅 🅿.
🕽🕽 AE VISA JCB. ⋙
3 rm ⊑ 34.50/46.00.

SARK

[403] P 33 and [230] [10] *The West Country G.* – *pop. 560.*

See : *Island★★ – La Coupée★★★ – Port du Moulin★★ – Creux Harbour★ – La Seigneurie★ AC – Pilcher Monument★ – Hog's Back★.*

⛴ *to St. Helier (Condor Ferries Ltd) 3 weekly (45 mn).*

⛴ *to France (St. Malo) via Jersey (St. Helier) (Condor Ferries Ltd) 3 weekly – to Guernsey (St. Peter Port) (Isle of Sark Shipping Co. Ltd and Condor Ferries Ltd) (summer only) (45 mn).*

[i] *Harbour Hill, GY9 0SB ☎ (01481) 832345.*

🏨 **Dixcart** 🌿, GY9 0SD, ☎ (01481) 832015, *Fax (01481) 832164*, 🌳, « Part 16C farmhouse », 🌲, park – [MC] [AE] [VISA] [JCB]
Meals (booking essential in winter) 14.00 (dinner) and a la carte 14.00/25.00 🍷 4.00 – **15 rm** 🛏 42.00/84.00.

🏨 **Stocks Island** 🌿, GY9 0SD, ☎ (01481) 832001, *Fax (01481) 832130*, 🏊, 🌲 – [MC] [AE] [D] [VISA] [JCB]
9 April-3 October – **Meals** 9.00/15.00 **s.** and a la carte 🍷 5.00 – **24 rm** 🛏 (dinner included) 59.00/118.00 **s.** – SB.

🏨 **Petit Champ** 🌿, GY9 0SF, ☎ (01481) 832046, *Fax (01481) 832469*, ≤ coast, Herm, Jetou and Guernsey, 🏊, 🌲 – 🚭 rest. [MC] [AE] [D] [VISA]. 🐕
9 April-3 October – **Meals** 17.25 **s.** (dinner) and a la carte 9.50/25.05 **s.** 🍷 4.25 – **16 rm** 🛏 (dinner included) 51.00/108.00.

🏠 **Les Quatre Vents,** GY9 0SE, off Harbour Hill ☎ (01481) 832247, *Fax (01481) 832332*, ≤, 🌲 – 🚭 [TV]. 🐕
Meals (by arrangement) 15.00 **s.** – **4 rm** 🛏 20.00/40.00 **s.**

🍴 **La Sablonnerie** 🌿 with rm, Little Sark, GY9 0SD, ☎ (01481) 832061, *Fax (01481) 832408*, 🌳, « Part 16C farmhouse », 🌲 – [MC] [AE] [VISA]. 🐕
Easter-mid October – **Meals** 20.80/23.80 and a la carte 🍷 5.50 – **21 rm** 🛏 (dinner included) 55.50/131.00, 1 suite.

🍴 **Founiais,** Harbour Hill, GY9 0SB, ☎ (01481) 832626, *Fax (01481) 832642*, 🌳 – [MC] [VISA]
March-October – **Meals** a la carte 14.95/21.90 **s.** 🍷 4.00.

CHANNEL TUNNEL *Kent* [404] X 30 – *see Folkestone.*

CHAPELTOWN *N. Yorks.* [402] [403] [404] P 23 – *see Sheffield.*

CHARD *Somerset* [403] L 31 – *pop. 13 086.*

[i] *The Guildhall, Fore St., TA20 1PP ☎ (01460) 67463.*

London 157 – Exeter 32 – Lyme Regis 12 – Taunton 18 – Yeovil 17.

🏨 **Lordleaze,** Lordleaze Lane, TA20 2HW, SE : 1 ½ m. by A 358 off Forton rd ☎ (01460) 61066, *Fax (01460) 66468* – [TV] ☎ [P] – 🎤 120. [MC] [AE] [VISA]
Meals (bar lunch)/dinner 16.95 **st.** and a la carte 🍷 4.50 – **16 rm** 🛏 45.00/68.00 **st.** – SB.

CHARDSTOCK *Devon* [403] L 31 *The West Country G.* – *pop. 725* – ✉ *Axminster.*

Env. : *Chard (Museum★) AC, N : 3 m. by A 358.*

London 160 – Exeter 31 – Lyme Regis 9.5 – Taunton 20 – Yeovil 21.

🏨 **Tytherleigh Cot,** EX13 7BN, ☎ (01460) 221170, *Fax (01460) 221291*, 🏋, 🏊, 🌲 – 🚭 rest, [TV] ☎ [P] – 🎤 30. [MC] [VISA]
Meals (dinner only) 15.95 **st.** 🍷 7.50 – **19 rm** 🛏 55.00/123.00 **st.** – SB.

CHARINGWORTH *Glos.* – *see Chipping Campden.*

Gli alberghi o ristoranti ameni sono indicati nella guida con un **simbolo rosso.**
Contribuite a mantenere la guida aggiornata segnalandoci gli alberghi ed i ristoranti dove avete soggiornato piacevolmente.

🏨 ... 🏠

🍴🍴🍴🍴🍴 ... 🍴

CHARLBURY Oxon. 403 404 P 28 – pop. 2 694.
London 72 – Birmingham 50 – Oxford 15.

🏛 **Bell**, Church St., OX7 3PP, ✆ (01608) 810278, Fax (01608) 811447 – 📺 ☎ 🅿 – 🕍 50. 🆗 🆎 ① 🆅🆂🅰 🅹🅲🅱. ✖
Meals a la carte 18.50/23.50 – **17 rm** ⌑ 65.00/95.00 st. – SB.

🍴 **Bull Inn** with rm, Sheep St., OX7 3RR, ✆ (01608) 810689 – 📺 🅿. 🆗 🆅🆂🅰. ✖
closed Sunday dinner, Monday, 25 December and 1 January – **Meals** a la carte 12.65/25.00 **t.** – **3 rm** ⌑ 50.00/60.00 **t.**

CHARLECOTE Warks. 403 404 P 27 – see Stratford-upon-Avon.

CHARLESTOWN Cornwall 403 F 32 – see St. Austell.

CHARLTON W. Sussex 404 R 31 – see Chichester.

CHARLWOOD Surrey 404 T 30 – pop. 1 969 – ✉ Horley.
London 30 – Brighton 29 – Royal Tunbridge Wells 28.

🏨 **Stanhill Court** ⌖, Stan Hill, RH6 0EP, NW : 1 m. ✆ (01293) 862166, Fax (01293) 862773, ⌖, ⌖, ⌖, park – ✖ 📺 ☎ 🅿 – 🕍 100. 🆗 🆎 ① 🆅🆂🅰 🅹🅲🅱. ✖
Meals (bar lunch Saturday) a la carte 20.00/35.00 **st.** ‖ 5.95 – ⌑ 10.75 – **13 rm** 89.00/125.00 **st.**

Großbritannien und Irland
ein Atlas in drei Ausgaben : Paperback, gebunden, spiralgebunden

---

CHARMOUTH Dorset 403 L 31 – pop. 1 497 – ✉ Bridport.
London 157 – Dorchester 22 – Exeter 31 – Taunton 27.

🏛 **Thatch Lodge**, The Street, DT6 6PQ, ✆ (01297) 560407, Fax (01297) 560407, « Part 14C thatched cottage » , ⌖ – ✖ 📺 🅿. 🆗 🆅🆂🅰. ✖
closed February – **Meals** (by arrangement) (dinner only) 19.50 **t.** ‖ 6.45 – **7 rm** ⌑ 47.50/90.00 **st.** – SB.

🏛 **White House**, 2 Hillside, The Street, DT6 6PJ, ✆ (01297) 560411, Fax (01297) 560702 – 📺 ☎ 🅿. 🆗 🆎 ① 🆅🆂🅰 🅹🅲🅱. ✖
Meals (dinner only) 14.00 **st.** ‖ 6.00 – **10 rm** ⌑ (dinner included) 48.50/110.00 **st.** – SB.

⌂ **Hensleigh**, Lower Sea Lane, DT6 6LW, ✆ (01297) 560830 – ✖ rest, 📺 🅿. 🆗 🆎 🆅🆂🅰
mid March-October – **Meals** (by arrangement) 14.00 **st.** ‖ 4.95 – **11 rm** ⌑ 27.00/54.00 – SB.

CHARTHAM Kent 404 X 30 – see Canterbury.

CHARTHAM HATCH Kent 404 X 30 – see Canterbury.

CHATTERIS Cambs. 402 404 U 26 – pop. 7 261.
London 85 – Cambridge 26 – Norwich 71.

🍴 **Cross Keys** with rm, 12-16 Market Hill, PE16 6BA, ✆ (01354) 693036, Fax (01354) 693036, « Part 17C inn » – 📺 ☎ 🅿. 🆗 🆎 ① 🆅🆂🅰 🅹🅲🅱
Meals 8.95 **t.** (lunch) and a la carte 15.00/19.00 **t.** ‖ 4.50 – **7 rm** ⌑ 32.50/55.00 **st.** – SB.

CHEADLE Ches. 402 403 N 23.
London 200 – Manchester 7 – Stoke-on-Trent 33.

🏨 **Village H. & Leisure Club**, Cheadle Rd, SK8 1HW, S : ¾ m. by A 5149 ✆ (0161) 428 0404, Fax (0161) 428 1191, 🄵🅳, ☎, 🗔, squash – ▐, ✖ rm, ▤ rest, 📺 ☎ ⅙ 🅿 – 🕍 200. 🆗 🆎 ① 🆅🆂🅰. ✖
Meals (grill rest.) a la carte 12.35/23.95 **t.** ‖ 6.00 – **73 rm** ⌑ 86.00/99.00 **st.**

🏛 **Travel Inn**, Royal Crescent, Cheadle Royal Retail Park, SK8 3FE, SW : 2 m. by A 560 off A 34 ✆ (0161) 491 5884, Fax (0161) 491 5896 – ▐, ✖ rm, ▤ rest, 📺 ⅙ 🅿. 🆗 🆎 ① 🆅🆂🅰. ✖
Meals (grill rest.) – **40 rm** 36.50 **t.**

⌂ **Spring Cottage** without rest., 60 Hulme Hall Rd, Cheadle Hulme, SK8 6JZ, S : 2 ¼ m. by A 5149 on B 5095 ✆ (0161) 485 1037 – 📺 🅿. 🆗 🆅🆂🅰
6 rm ⌑ 20.00/39.00 **s.**

CHEDDLETON Staffs. 402 403 404 N 24 – pop. 3 534 – ⊠ Leek.
London 125 – Birmingham 48 – Derby 33 – Manchester 42 – Stoke-on-Trent 11.

⌂ **Choir Cottage** without rest., Ostlers Lane, via Hollows Lane (opposite Red Lion on A 520), ST13 7HS, ℘ (01538) 360561 – 📺 🅿. ⚘
closed Christmas and New Year – **3 rm** ⊊ 30.00/55.00 st.

CHEDINGTON Dorset 403 L 31 – pop. 100 – ⊠ Beaminster.
🏌 Halstock, Common Lane ℘ (01935) 891689 – 🏌 Chedington Court, South Perrott, Beaminster ℘ (01935) 891413.
London 148 – Dorchester 17 – Taunton 25.

🏦 **Hazel Barton** ⑤, DT8 3HY, ℘ (01935) 891613, Fax (01935) 891370, ≤, ⛭ – 📺 📺 ☎ 🅿. ⚘
restricted opening in winter – **Meals** (by arrangement) 25.00 st. ⫙ 6.00 – **4 rm** ⊊ 110.00/120.00 st.

CHELMSFORD Essex 404 V 28 – pop. 97 451.
🅱 E Block, County Hall, Market Rd, CM1 1GG ℘ (01245) 283400.
London 33 – Cambridge 46 – Ipswich 40 – Southend-on-Sea 19.

🏛 **County**, 29 Rainsford Rd, CM1 2QA, ℘ (01245) 491911, Fax (01245) 492762 – 📺 ☎ 🅿 –
🔺 200. ◍◍ 🆎 ① 𝘝𝘐𝘚𝘈. ⚘
closed Christmas-New Year – **Meals** a la carte 20.50/30.90 ⫙ 7.00 – **34 rm** ⊊ 68.00/80.00 st., 1 suite.

🏛 **Travel Inn**, Chelmsford Service Area, Colchester Rd, Springfield, CM2 5PY, NE : at junction of A 12 with A 138 and A 130 ℘ (01245) 464008, Fax (01245) 464010 – 📶, ⥮ rm, 📺 ᴅ 🅿 –
🔺 35. ◍◍ 🆎 ① 𝘝𝘐𝘚𝘈. ⚘
Meals (grill rest.) – **61 rm** 36.50 t.

at Great Baddow SE : 3 m. by A 414 – ⊠ Chelmsford.

🏛 **Pontlands Park** ⑤, West Hanningfield Rd, CM2 8HR, ℘ (01245) 476444, Fax (01245) 478393, ≤, ⥮, ⌇, 🔲, ⛭ – 📺 ☎ 🅿 – 🔺 40. ◍◍ 🆎 ① 𝘝𝘐𝘚𝘈 𝘑𝘊𝘉. ⚘
closed 27 to 30 December – **The Conservatory : Meals** (closed Monday and Saturday lunch and Sunday dinner to non-residents) (dancing Friday evening) 17.00 t. and a la carte ⫙ 5.50 – ⊊ 9.00 – **16 rm** 90.00/125.00 st., 1 suite.

⑩ ATS 375 Springfield Rd ℘ (01245) 257795
ATS Chelmer Village Centre, Springfield (ASDA car park) ℘ (01245) 465676

ATS Town Centre, Inchbonnie Rd, South Woodham Ferrers (ASDA car park) ℘ (01245) 324999

CHELTENHAM Glos. 403 404 N 28 Great Britain G. – pop. 91 301.
See : Town★ – Pitville Pump Room★ AC A A.
Exc. : Sudeley Castle★ (Paintings★) AC, NE : 7 m. by B 4632 A.
🏌 Cleeve Hill ℘ (0124 267) 2025 A – 🏌 Cotswold Hills, Ullenwood ℘ (01242) 522421, A.
🅱 77 Promenade, GL50 1PP ℘ (01242) 522878.
London 99 – Birmingham 48 – Bristol 40 – Gloucester 9 – Oxford 43.

Plan on next page

🏛 **Queen's**, Promenade, GL50 1NN, ℘ (01242) 514724, Fax (01242) 224145, ⛭ – 📶 ⥮ 📺 ☎ 🅿 – 🔺 200. ◍◍ 🆎 ① 𝘝𝘐𝘚𝘈 𝘑𝘊𝘉   B n
Regency : Meals a la carte 17.45/22.75 t. ⫙ 9.50 – ⊊ 10.75 – **74 rm** 90.00/145.00 t. – SB.

🏛 **Golden Valley Thistle**, Gloucester Rd, GL51 0TS, W : 2 m. on A 40 ℘ (01242) 232691, Fax (01242) 221846, ⌕₆, ⥮, 🔲, ⛭, ❊ – 📶, ⥮ rm, ▤ rest, 📺 ☎ 🅿 – 🔺 220. ◍◍ 🆎 ① 𝘝𝘐𝘚𝘈 𝘑𝘊𝘉. ⚘
Burford Room : Meals 15.50/22.50 t. and a la carte ⫙ 5.50 – ⊊ 10.00 – **118 rm** 99.00/133.00 st., 4 suites.

🏛 **Cheltenham Park**, Cirencester Rd, Charlton Kings, GL53 8EA, ℘ (01242) 222021, Fax (01242) 226935, ⌕₆, ⥮, 🔲, ⛭ – ⥮, ▤ rest, 📺 ☎ ᴅ 🅿 – 🔺 350. ◍◍ 🆎 ① 𝘝𝘐𝘚𝘈. ⚘
Meals (closed Saturday lunch) 12.50/21.50 **st.** and a la carte ⫙ 6.50 – **143 rm** ⊊ 90.00/120.00 st., 1 suite. – SB.   A e

🏦 **On the Park**, 38 Evesham Rd, GL52 2AH, ℘ (01242) 518898, Fax (01242) 511526, « Regency town house », ⛭ – 📺 ☎. ◍◍ 🆎 ① 𝘝𝘐𝘚𝘈. ⚘   C r
Meals (booking essential) 26.50 **t.** (dinner) and lunch a la carte 21.50/28.50 t. ⫙ 10.00 – ⊊ 8.25 – **12 rm** 77.50/112.50 t. – SB.

🏦 **Prestbury House**, The Burgage, GL52 3DN, NE : 1 ½ m. by Prestbury Rd (B 4632) off Tatchley Lane ℘ (01242) 529533, Fax (01242) 227076, ⛭ – ⥮ rm, 📺 ☎ 🅿 – 🔺 30. ◍◍ 🆎 ① 𝘝𝘐𝘚𝘈. ⚘   A r
Meals 24.50 **st.** and a la carte ⫙ 5.00 – **16 rm** ⊊ 67.00/83.00 **st.** – SB.

CHELTENHAM

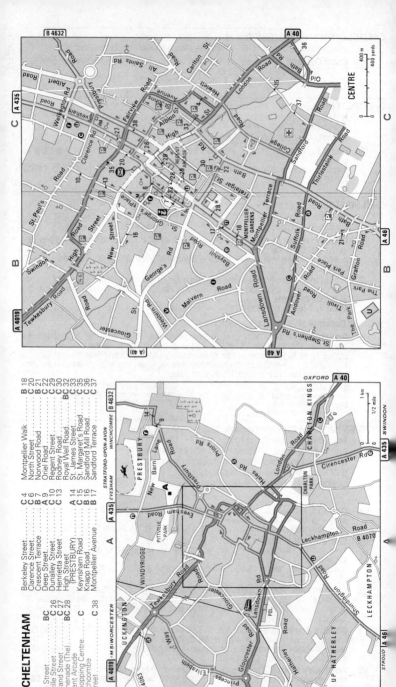

190

🏠 **Charlton Kings,** London Rd, Charlton Kings, GL52 6UU, ☎ (01242) 231061, *Fax (01242) 241900*, 🚗 – 🌾 📺 ☎ 🅿. 🆎 ⭕ VISA. ⅏
A c
Meals (dinner only) 16.95 **t.** ₰ 7.40 – **14 rm** ⌕ 55.50/94.00 **st.** – SB.

🏠 **Lypiatt House,** Lypiatt Rd, GL50 2QW, ☎ (01242) 224994, *Fax (01242) 224996* – 📺 ☎ 🅿. 🆎 🅰🅴 VISA. ⅏
B c
Meals (by arrangement) (dinner only) 19.75 **st.** ₰ 6.00 – **10 rm** ⌕ 49.00/70.00 **st.**

🏠 **Milton House,** 12 Royal Parade, Bayshill Rd, GL50 3AY, ☎ (01242) 582601, *Fax (01242) 222326* – 🌾 📺 ☎ 🅿. 🆎 ⭕ VISA
B e
closed 25 December-2 January – **Meals** (by arrangement) (dinner only) 25.00 **st.** ₰ 4.00 – **8 rm** ⌕ 38.50/68.00 **st.**

🏠 **Regency House,** 50 Clarence Sq., GL50 4JR, ☎ (01242) 582718, *Fax (01242) 262697*, 🚗 – 🌾 📺 ☎. 🆎 🅰🅴 VISA. ⅏
C c
closed 24 December-2 January – **Meals** *(closed Sunday dinner)* 12.95 **t.** and a la carte ₰ 6.00 – **8 rm** ⌕ 36.00/58.00 **st.** – SB.

🏠 **Wyastone,** Parabola Rd, GL50 3BG, ☎ (01242) 245549, *Fax (01242) 522659* – 🌾 rest, 📺 ☎ 🚗 🅿. 🆎 🅰🅴 VISA. ⅏
B i
closed 23 December-4 January – **Meals** (dinner only) 18.00 **st.** ₰ 6.00 – **13 rm** ⌕ 49.00/69.00 **st.**

🏠 **Stretton Lodge,** Western Rd, GL50 3RN, ☎ (01242) 570771, *Fax (01242) 528724*, 🚗 – 🌾 📺 ☎ 🅿. 🆎 🅰🅴 VISA JCB. ⅏
B v
Meals a la carte 12.50/16.50 **st.** ₰ 6.00 – **5 rm** ⌕ 45.00/75.00 **st.** – SB.

🏠 **Beaumont House,** Shurdington Rd, GL53 0JE, ☎ (01242) 245986, *Fax (01242) 520044*, 🚗 – 🌾 rest, 📺 ☎ 🅿. 🆎 🅰🅴 VISA JCB. ⅏
A u
Meals (dinner only) 19.95 **st.** ₰ 4.70 – **15 rm** ⌕ 39.00/60.00 **st.** – SB.

🏠 **Travel Inn,** Tewkesbury Rd, Uckington, GL51 9SL, NW : 1 ¾ m. on A 4019 at junction with B 4634 ☎ (01242) 233847, *Fax (01242) 244887* – 🌾 📺 ₰ 🅿. 🆎 🅰🅴 ⭕ VISA. ⅏ A a
Meals (grill rest.) – **40 rm** 36.50 **t.**

↑ **Hannaford's,** 20 Evesham Rd, GL52 2AB, ☎ (01242) 515181, *Fax (01242) 257571* – 🌾 rest, 📺 ☎ 🅿. 🆎 🅰🅴 VISA. ⅏
C u
closed 24 December-2 January – **Meals** (by arrangement) 15.00 – **8 rm** ⌕ 38.00/60.00 **t.**

↑ **Hunting Butts Farm,** Swindon Lane, GL50 4NZ, N : 1½ m. by A 435 ☎ (01242) 524982, *Fax (01242) 251507*, ⩽, « Working farm », 🚗 – 🌾 rest, 📺 🅿
A n
Meals (by arrangement) 10.00 **st.** – **7 rm** ⌕ 22.50/40.00 **st.**

↑ **Hollington House,** 115 Hales Rd, GL52 6ST, ☎ (01242) 256652, *Fax (01242) 570280*, 🚗 – 🌾 rest, 📺 🅿. 🆎 🅰🅴 VISA. ⅏
A s
Meals (by arrangement) approx. 17.00 **t.** ₰ 5.00 – **9 rm** ⌕ 35.00/60.00 **t.** – SB.

XXX **81 Restaurant,** 81 The Promenade (1st Floor), GL51 1PJ, ☎ (01242) 222466, *Fax (01242) 222474* – 🌾 🆎 🅰🅴 VISA JCB
B u
closed Sunday dinner, Monday and 26 December-2 January – **Meals** 18.00 **t.** (lunch) and a la carte 26.20/31.45 **t.** ₰ 8.95 – (see also **81 Bistro** below).

XX ✾ **Le Champignon Sauvage** (Everitt-Matthias), 24-26 Suffolk Rd, GL50 2AQ, ☎ (01242) 573449, *Fax (01242) 573449* – 🆎 🅰🅴 ⭕ VISA JCB
B a
closed Saturday lunch, Sunday, 2 weeks in summer, 1 week Christmas and Bank Holidays – **Meals** 18.50/32.00 **t.** ₰ 5.25
Spec. Ballottine of duck confit with pickled apple Tatin and foie gras sauce. Salmon poached in goose fat, fresh pea velouté. Feuillantine of mango, Thai spiced cream and red wine syrup.

XX **Mayflower,** 32-34 Clarence St., GL50 3NX, ☎ (01242) 522426, *Fax (01242) 251667* – ▣. 🆎 🅰🅴 ⭕ VISA JCB
B r
closed Sunday lunch and 24 to 26 December – **Meals** - Chinese - 6.50/17.00 **t.** and a la carte ₰ 6.95.

XX **81 Bistro,** 81 The Promenade (Ground floor), GL51 1PJ, ☎ (01242) 222466, *Fax (01242) 222474* – 🆎 🅰🅴 VISA JCB
B u
closed Sunday dinner, Monday and 26 December-2 January – **Meals** a la carte 15.20/23.35 **t.**

at Woolstone N : 6 ¼ m. by A 435 – A – ✉ Cheltenham.

↑ **Old Rectory** 🦢 without rest., GL52 4RG, ☎ (01242) 673766, ⩽, 🚗 – 🌾 📺 🅿. ⅏
March-November – **3 rm** ⌕ 28.00/40.00 **st.**

at Cleeve Hill NE : 4 m. on B 4632 – A – ✉ Cheltenham.

🏠 **Rising Sun,** GL52 3PX, ☎ (01242) 676281, *Fax (01242) 673069*, ⩽, 🍴, 🚗 – 🌾 📺 ☎ 🅿. 🆎 🅰🅴 VISA. ⅏
accommodation closed 25 and 26 December – **Meals** (dinner only and Sunday lunch)/ dinner 13.50 **t.** and a la carte – **24 rm** ⌕ 59.50/79.50 **t.** – SB.

🏠 **Cleeve Hill** without rest., GL52 3PR, ☎ (01242) 672052, ⩽, 🚗 – 🌾 📺 ☎ 🅿. 🆎 🅰🅴 VISA. ⅏
9 rm ⌕ 48.00/75.00 **st.**

at Shurdington SW : 3 ¾ m. on A 46 – A – ⊠ Cheltenham.

🏛 **Greenway** ⤝, GL51 5UG, ℰ (01242) 862352, Fax (01242) 862780, ≼, « Part 16C Cotswold country house, gardens » – ⭒ rm, 📺 ☎ 🅿 – 🔬 30. 🐠 🖭 ⑩ 𝘝𝘐𝘚𝘈. ⚹
Meals (closed lunch Saturday and Bank Holiday Monday) 19.45/32.00 t. ▯ 12.75 – 19 rm ⤆ 90.00/225.00 t. – SB.

🏛 **Cheltenham and Gloucester Moat House,** Shurdington Rd, GL3 4PB, SW : 1 ¼ m. on A 46 ℰ (01452) 519988, Fax (01452) 519977, 🏤, 𝕱𝕤, 🕿, 🔲 – 🕸, ⭒ rm, 🍽 rest, 📺 ☎ 🕭 🅿 – 🔬 340. 🐠 🖭 ⑩ 𝘝𝘐𝘚𝘈
Meals (closed Saturday lunch) 17.00/20.00 st. and a la carte ▯ 8.00 – ⤆ 10.00 – 94 rm 90.00/105.00 st., 2 suites – SB.

at Staverton W : 4 ¼ m. by A 40 – ⊠ Cheltenham.

🏛 **White House,** Gloucester Rd, GL51 0ST, on B 4063 ℰ (01452) 713226, Fax (01452) 857590 – 📺 ☎ 🅿 – 🔬 200. 🐠 🖭 ⑩ 𝘝𝘐𝘚𝘈 𝗃𝖼𝖻
closed 24-25, 28 to 30 December and 1 January – Meals 12.50/16.50 st. and a la carte ▯ 5.50 – 47 rm ⤆ 70.00/90.00 st., 2 suites – SB.

🔞 ATS Chosen View Rd ℰ (01242) 521288   ATS 99-101 London Rd ℰ (01242) 519814

CHELWOOD Bath & North East Somerset – see Bristol.

CHENIES Bucks. 𝟜𝟘𝟜 S 28 – pop. 258 – ⊠ Rickmansworth (Herts.).
London 30 – Aylesbury 18 – Watford 7.

🏠 **Bedford Arms,** WD3 6EQ, ℰ (01923) 283301, Fax (01923) 284825, 🏤, 🌳 – ⭒ rm, 📺 ☎ 🅿. 🐠 🖭 ⑩ 𝘝𝘐𝘚𝘈 𝗃𝖼𝖻. ⚹
Meals (bar lunch Saturday) 18.00/23.00 t. and a la carte ▯ 12.50 – ⤆ 10.50 – 10 rm 120.00/ 139.00 t.

Per spostarvi più rapidamente utilizzate le **carte Michelin "Grandi Strade"** :

n° 𝟗𝟳𝟬 Europa, n° 𝟗𝟳𝟲 Rep. Ceca/Slovacchia, n° 𝟗𝟴𝟬 Grecia,

n° 𝟗𝟴𝟰 Germania, n° 𝟗𝟴𝟱 Scandinavia-Finlandia,

n° 𝟗𝟴𝟲 Gran Bretagna-Irlanda, n° 𝟗𝟴𝟳 Germania-Austria-Benelux,

n° 𝟗𝟴𝟴 Italia, n° 𝟗𝟴𝟵 Francia, n° 𝟗𝟵𝟬 Spagna-Portogallo, n° 𝟗𝟵𝟭 Jugoslavia.

CHERITON BISHOP Devon 𝟜𝟘𝟛 I 31 The West Country G. – pop. 754 – ⊠ Exeter.
Env. : Dartmoor National Park★★.
Exc. : Crediton (Holy Cross Church★) NE : 6 ½ m. by A 30.
London 211 – Exeter 10 – Plymouth 51.

🍴 **Old Thatch Inn** with rm, EX6 6HJ, ℰ (01647) 24204, Fax (01647) 24584, « Part 16C » – 📺 🅿. 🐠 𝘝𝘐𝘚𝘈. ⚹
Meals (in bar) a la carte 9.85/16.50 st. ▯ 4.50 – 2 rm ⤆ 34.50/46.00 st.

CHERWELL VALLEY SERVICE AREA Oxon. – ⊠ Bicester.

🏠 **Travelodge** without rest., Northampton Rd, Ardley, OX6 9RD, M 40, junction 10 ℰ (01869) 346060, Fax (01869) 345030, Reservations (Freephone) 0800 850950 – ⭒ 📺 ☎ 🕭 🅿. 🐠 🖭 ⑩ 𝘝𝘐𝘚𝘈 𝗃𝖼𝖻. ⚹
98 rms 46.95 t.

CHESHUNT Herts. 𝟜𝟘𝟜 T 28 – pop. 51 998 – ⊠ Broxbourne.
🅸𝟾 Cheshunt, Park Lane ℰ (01992) 29777.
London 22 – Cambridge 40 – Ipswich 70 – Luton 34 – Southend-on-Sea 39.

🏛 **Cheshunt Marriott,** Halfhide Lane, Turnford, EN10 6NG, NW : 1 ¼ m. off B 176 ℰ (01992) 451245, Fax (01992) 440120, 𝕱𝕤, 🔲, 🌳 – 🕸 ⭒ 🍽 📺 ☎ 🕭 🅿 – 🔬 120. 🐠 🖭 ⑩ 𝘝𝘐𝘚𝘈 𝗃𝖼𝖻
Meals (dinner only) 19.50 t. and a la carte ▯ 6.25 – ⤆ 9.50 – 130 rm 110.00 st., 12 suites – SB.

CHESTER Ches. 𝟜𝟘𝟸 𝟜𝟘𝟛 L 24 Great Britain G. – pop. 80 110.
See : City★★ - The Rows★★ – Cathedral★ – City Walls★.
Env. : Chester Zoo★ AC, N : 3 m. by A 5116.
🅸𝟾 Upton-by-Chester, Upton Lane ℰ (01244) 381183 – 🅸𝟾 Curzon Park ℰ (01244) 675130.
🄳 Town Hall, Northgate St., CH1 2HJ ℰ (01244) 317962 – Chester Visitor Centre, Vicars Lane, CH1 1QX ℰ (01244) 351609/318916.
London 207 – Birkenhead 7 – Birmingham 91 – Liverpool 19 – Manchester 40 – Preston 52 – Sheffield 76 – Stoke-on-Trent 38.

CHESTER

Chester Grosvenor, Eastgate, CH1 1LT, ℘ (01244) 324024, *Fax (01244) 313246*, ⌶♠, ⇌ – ⧄ ▤ 🆃🆅 ☎ & 🅿 – ♨ 250. 🅜🅢 🅐🅔 🅞 𝘝𝘐𝘚𝘈 🅹🅲🅱. ⌀
closed 25 and 26 December – Meals – (see **Arkle** and **La Brasserie** below) – ⌹ 12.50 – **82 rm** 120.00/210.00, 3 suites – SB.

Crabwall Manor ⌂, Parkgate Rd, Mollington, CH1 6NE, NW : 2 ¼ m. on A 540
℘ (01244) 851666, *Fax (01244) 851400*, « Part 16C manor », ⌖, park – ▤ rest, 🆃🆅 ☎ 🅿 – ♨ 100. 🅜🅢 🅐🅔 🅞 𝘝𝘐𝘚𝘈 🅹🅲🅱. ⌀
Meals – (see **Crabwall Manor** below) – ⌹ 10.00 – **42 rm** 110.00/150.00 t., 6 suites.

Moat House Chester, Trinity St., CH1 2BD, ℘ (01244) 899988, *Fax (01244) 316118*, ⌶♠, ⇌ – ⧄ – ⧄ rm, ▤ rest, 🆃🆅 ☎ & 🅿 – ♨ 500. 🅜🅢 🅐🅔 🅞 𝘝𝘐𝘚𝘈. ⌀
The Paddocks : Meals (dinner only and Sunday lunch)/dinner a la carte 20.00/35.00 t.
⌷ 7.00 – ⌹ 9.50 – **149 rm** 110.00/150.00 t., 3 suites – SB.

Mollington Banastre, Parkgate Rd, Mollington, CH1 6NN, NW : 2 ¼ m. on A 540
℘ (01244) 851471, *Fax (01244) 851165*, ⌶♠, ⇌, ⌧, ⌖, squash – ⧄ ⌀ ⊨, ▤ rest, 🆃🆅 ☎ 🅿 – ♨ 250. 🅜🅢 🅐🅔 🅞 𝘝𝘐𝘚𝘈
Meals 17.00/21.00 st. and a la carte ⌷ 5.95 – ⌹ 9.25 – **63 rm** 84.00/105.00 st. – SB.

Hoole Hall, Warrington Rd, Hoole, CH2 3PD, NE : 2 m. on A 56 ℘ (01244) 350011,
Fax (01244) 320251, ⌖ – ⧄ ⌀ ⊨ 🆃🆅 ☎ & 🅿 – ♨ 150. 🅜🅢 🅐🅔 🅞 𝘝𝘐𝘚𝘈
Dudleys : Meals *(closed Saturday lunch)* (buffet lunch Monday to Friday) 7.50/
17.95 st. and dinner a la carte ⌷ 5.95 – ⌹ 9.25 – **97 rm** 75.00/90.00 st. – SB.

🏨 **The Queen**, City Rd, CH1 3AH, ℰ (01244) 350100, *Fax (01244) 318483*, 🚗 – 🛗 🕸 📺 ☎
 ⓦ 🅿 – 🛗 220. 🐵 🖭 ⑩ 𝘝𝘐𝘚𝘈
 i
 The Garden : Meals 13.95/16.95 st. and a la carte ⓵ 5.50 – **127 rm** ⯑ 90.00/110.00 st.,
 1 suite – SB.

🏨 **Blossoms**, St. John St., CH1 1HL, ℰ (01244) 323186, *Fax (01244) 346433* – 🛗 🕸 📺 ☎ –
 🛗 100. 🐵 🖭 ⑩ 𝘝𝘐𝘚𝘈 𝙅𝘾𝘽
 e
 Meals a la carte 15.00/23.00 st. ⓵ 7.50 – ⯑ 9.25 – **63 rm** 75.00/90.00 t., 1 suite – SB.

🏨 **Redland** without rest., 64 Hough Green, CH4 8JY, SW : 1 m. by A 483 on A 5104
 ℰ (01244) 671024, *Fax (01244) 681309*, « Victorian town house », 🚗 – 🕸 📺 ☎ 🅿. 🐵
 𝘝𝘐𝘚𝘈. 🛇
 12 rm ⯑ 45.00/75.00 t.

🏨 **Cavendish**, 42-44 Hough Green, CH4 8JQ, SW : 1 m. by A 483 on A 5104
 ℰ (01244) 675100, *Fax (01244) 678844*, 🚗 – 🕸 rest, 📺 ☎ 🅿. 🐵 𝘝𝘐𝘚𝘈. 🛇
 Meals (lunch by arrangement) (residents only) 20.00 t. ⓵ 5.50 – **16 rm** ⯑ 50.00/70.00 t. –
 SB.

🏨 **Green Bough**, 60 Hoole Rd, CH2 3NL, on A 56 ℰ (01244) 326241, *Fax (01244) 326265* –
 🕸 📺 ☎ 🅿. 🐵 𝘝𝘐𝘚𝘈. 🛇
 Meals (bar lunch)/dinner 12.75 st. and a la carte ⓵ 6.50 – **20 rm** ⯑ 40.00/60.00 st. – SB.

🏨 **Alton Lodge**, 78 Hoole Rd, CH2 3NT, on A 56 ℰ (01244) 310213, *Fax (01244) 319206* – 🕸
 📺 ☎ 🅿. 🐵 𝘝𝘐𝘚𝘈 𝙅𝘾𝘽. 🛇
 closed Christmas and New Year – Meals *(closed Friday to Sunday)* (residents only) (dinner
 only) a la carte 10.45/18.70 t. ⓵ 3.95 – **16 rm** ⯑ 39.50/49.50 t.

🏨 **Ye Olde King's Head**, 48-50 Lower Bridge St., CH1 1RS, ℰ (01244) 324855,
 Fax (01244) 315693, « 16C inn » – 📺 ☎ 🚗. 🐵 🖭 ⑩ 𝘝𝘐𝘚𝘈. 🛇
 s
 April-December – Meals (grill rest.) 6.55 t. and a la carte – ⯑ 4.95 – **8 rm** 44.25 t. – SB.

🏨 **Chester Court**, 48 Hoole Rd, CH2 3NL, on A 56 ℰ (01244) 320779, *Fax (01244) 344795* –
 📺 ☎ 🅿. 🐵 🖭 𝘝𝘐𝘚𝘈
 Meals (dinner only) 15.00 t. ⓵ 6.95 – **20 rm** ⯑ 40.00/60.00 t. – SB.

🏠 **Mitchell's of Chester** without rest., Green Gables, 28 Hough Green, CH4 8JU, SW : 1 m.
 by A 483 on A 5104 ℰ (01244) 679004, *Fax (01244) 679004*, 🚗 – 🕸 📺 🅿. 🐵. 🛇
 closed 24 to 26 December – **4 rm** ⯑ 25.00/40.00 st.

🏠 **Chester Town House** without rest., 23 King St., CH1 2AH, ℰ (01244) 350021,
 Fax (01244) 342095 – 🕸 📺 𝘝𝘐𝘚𝘈. 🛇
 z
 closed Christmas and New Year – **5 rm** ⯑ 35.00/50.00 st.

🏠 **Castle House** without rest., 23 Castle St., CH1 2DS, ℰ (01244) 350354,
 Fax (01244) 350354, « Part Elizabethan town house » – 🕸 📺. 🐵 𝘝𝘐𝘚𝘈
 x
 5 rm ⯑ 22.00/44.00 s.

🏠 **Edwards House**, 61-63 Hoole Rd, CH2 3NJ, on A 56 ℰ (01244) 318055,
 Fax (01244) 319888 – 🕸 📺 ☎ 🅿. 🐵 𝘝𝘐𝘚𝘈. 🛇
 Meals (by arrangement) 9.45 st. ⓵ 3.95 – **11 rm** ⯑ 25.00/50.00 st. – SB.

🏠 **Stone Villa** without rest., 3 Stone Pl., CH2 3NR, by Hoole Way off Hoole Rd
 ℰ (01244) 345014 – 🕸 📺 🅿. 🐵 𝘝𝘐𝘚𝘈. 🛇
 closed 1 week at Christmas – **10 rm** ⯑ 32.00/52.00 st.

🕱🕱🕱🕱 **Arkle** (at Chester Grosvenor H.), Eastgate, CH1 1LT, ℰ (01244) 324024, *Fax (01244) 313246*
 ⣏ – 🕸 🍽 📠. 🐵 🖭 ⑩ 𝘝𝘐𝘚𝘈 𝙅𝘾𝘽
 a
 closed Monday lunch, Sunday dinner and 25-26 December – Meals 25.00/45.00 t.
 and a la carte 45.00/57.50 t. ⓵ 10.75
 Spec. Duo of Landes duck liver. Fillets of sea bass, scallops and oyster beignets with a
 coriander brandade. Hot coffee soufflé with Tia Maria ice cream.

🕱🕱🕱 **Crabwall Manor** (at Crabwall Manor H.), Parkgate Rd, Mollington, CH1 6NE, NW : 2 ¼ m.
 on A 540 ℰ (01244) 851666, *Fax (01244) 851400*, 🚗 – 🍽 🅿. 🐵 🖭 ⑩ 𝘝𝘐𝘚𝘈 𝙅𝘾𝘽
 Meals a la carte 29.50/37.50 t. ⓵ 7.00.

🕱🕱 **La Brasserie** (at Chester Grosvenor H.), Eastgate, CH1 1LT, ℰ (01244) 324024,
 Fax (01244) 313246 – 🍽 📠. 🐵 🖭 ⑩ 𝘝𝘐𝘚𝘈
 a
 closed 25 and 26 December – Meals 9.50 t. (lunch) and a la carte 20.00/28.50 t. ⓵ 5.75.

🕱 **Est, Est, Est**, Newgate House, Newgate St., CH1 1DE, ℰ (01244) 400507,
 Fax (01244) 400507 – 🍽. 🐵 🖭
 c
 closed 25 and 26 December – Meals - Italian - a la carte 15.50/20.25 t. ⓵ 4.95.

🕱 **Blue Bell**, 65 Northgate St., CH1 2HQ, ℰ (01244) 317758, *Fax (01244) 317759*, 🍴,
 « Converted 15C inn » – 🕸 📺. 🐵 𝙅𝘾𝘽
 n
 closed 25-26 December and 1 January – Meals 15.00 st. (dinner) and a la carte 19.70/
 28.95 st. ⓵ 7.50.

at Mickle Trafford NE : 2 ½ m. by A 56 – ✉ Chester.

🏨 **Royal Oak**, Warrington Rd, CH2 4EX, on A 56 ℰ (01244) 301391, *Fax (01244) 301948*, 🚗 –
 🕸 📺 ☎ 🅿. 🐵 𝘝𝘐𝘚𝘈.
 Meals (grill rest.) a la carte 10.30/15.10 st. ⓵ 4.45 – **36 rm** ⯑ 62.00/72.00 st. – SB.

at Rowton SE : 3 m. by A 41 – ⊠ Chester.

🏨 **Rowton Hall**, Whitchurch Rd, CH3 6AD, 𝒫 (01244) 335262, Fax (01244) 335464, ℩₅, ⇌,
🔲, 🐎, 🛁 – 🔟 ☎ 🕭 🅿 – 🔬 200. 🆎 🕮 ⊙ 𝒱𝒮𝒜
Meals 13.00/20.00 **t.** and a la carte ⓘ 6.50 – **42 rm** ⌸ 75.00/95.00 **t.** – SB.

at Sealand (Clwyd) NW : 4 m. on A 548 – ⊠ Deeside.

🏨 **Gateway to Wales**, Welsh Rd, CH5 2HX, NW : 1 ½ m. at junction of A 550 with A 548
𝒫 (01244) 830332, Fax (01244) 836190, ℩₅, ⇌, 🔲 – 🛗 🛬 🔟 ☎ 🕭 🅿 – 🔬 120. 🆎 🕮 ⊙
𝒱𝒮𝒜
The Regency : Meals 17.50 **t.** and a la carte ⓘ 5.50 – **38 rm** ⌸ 65.00/90.00 **st.**, 1 suite – SB.

at Two Mills NW : 5 ¾ m. on A 540 at junction with A 550 – ⊠ Ledsham.

🏨 **Tudor Rose Lodge**, Parkgate Rd, L66 9PD, 𝒫 (0151) 339 2399, Fax (0151) 347 1725 – 🛗,
🛬 rm, 🔟 ☎ 🕭 🅿. 🆎 🕮 ⊙ 𝒱𝒮𝒜. 🐎
Meals (grill rest.) 10.95/12.95 **t.** and a la carte – ⌸ 4.95 – **31 rm** 44.25 **st.**

at Puddington NW : 7¼ m. by A 540 – ⊠ South Wirral.

🗙🗙🗙 **Craxton Wood** ⊱ with rm, Parkgate Rd, L66 9PB, on A 540 𝒫 (0151) 339 4717,
Fax (0151) 339 1740, ≤, 🐎, park – 🔟 ☎ 🅿. 🆎 🕮 ⊙ 𝒱𝒮𝒜. 🐎
closed Sunday, first week January, last two weeks August and Bank Holidays –
Meals 19.85 **st.** and a la carte ⓘ 6.45 – **13 rm** ⌸ 63.85/106.85 **st.**, 1 suite – SB.

🕭 ATS 7 Bumpers Lane, Sealand Trading Est. 𝒫 (01244) 375154

CHESTERFIELD Derbs. 🏷🏷🏷 P 24 Great Britain G. – pop. 71 945.

Env. : Bolsover Castle★ AC, E : 5 m. by A 632.

℩₈, ℩₉ Chesterfield Municipal, Murray House, Crow Lane 𝒫 (01246) 273887 – ℩₈ Grassmoor,
North Wingfield Rd 𝒫 (01246) 856044.
🅱 Peacock Information Centre, Low Pavement, S40 1PB 𝒫 (01246) 345777/345770.
London 152 – Derby 24 – Nottingham 25 – Sheffield 12.

🏨 **Travelodge**, Brimington Road North, Wittington Moor, S41 9BE, N : 2 m. on A 61
𝒫 (01246) 455411, Reservations (Freephone) 0800 850950 – 🔟 🕭 🅿. 🆎 🕮 ⊙ 𝒱𝒮𝒜 𝒥𝒞ℬ.
🐎
20 rm 44.95 **t.**

🕭 ATS 512 Sheffield Rd 𝒫 (01246) 452281

CHESTER-LE-STREET Durham 🏷🏷 P 19 – pop. 35 123.

℩₈ Lumley Park 𝒫 (0191) 388 3218 – ℩₈ Roseberry Grange, Grange Villa 𝒫 (0191) 370 0670.
London 275 – Durham 7 – Newcastle upon Tyne 8.

🏰 **Lumley Castle**, DH3 4NX, E : 1 m. on B 1284 𝒫 (0191) 389 1111, Fax (0191) 387 1437,
« 13C », 🐎 – 🛬 rm, 🔟 ☎ 🅿 – 🔬 150. 🆎 🕮 ⊙ 𝒱𝒮𝒜 𝒥𝒞ℬ. 🐎
closed 25-26 December and 1 January – **Meals** (closed Saturday lunch) 13.50/22.50 **st.**
and a la carte ⓘ 8.50 – **61 rm** ⌸ 82.50/160.00 **st.**, 1 suite – SB.

CHESTERTON Oxon. 🏷🏷 Q 28 – pop. 806 – ⊠ Bicester.

℩₈ Chesterton , Bicester 𝒫 (01869) 241204.
London 69 – Birmingham 65 – Northampton 36 – Oxford 15.

🏨 **Bignell Park**, OX6 8UE, on A 4095 𝒫 (01869) 241444, Fax (01869) 241444, 🐎 – 🔟 ☎ 🅿.
🆎 🕮 ⊙ 𝒱𝒮𝒜
Meals (closed Saturday lunch) 17.50 **t.** and a la carte ⓘ 6.25 – **15 rm** ⌸ 62.50/90.00 **t.** – SB.

CHETTLE Dorset – see Blandford Forum.

CHICHESTER W. Sussex 🏷🏷 R 31 Great Britain G. – pop. 26 572.

See : City★ – Cathedral★ BZ **A** – St. Mary's Hospital★ BY **D** – Pallant House★ AC BZ **M**.
Env. : Fishbourne Roman Palace (mosaics★) AC AZ **R**.
Exc. : Weald and Downland Open Air Museum★ AC, N : 6 m. by A 286 AY.

℩₈ Goodwood 𝒫 (01243) 785012, AY – ℩₈, ℩₈, ℩₉ Chichester Golf Centre, Hunston Village
𝒫 (01243) 533833, AZ.
🅱 29a South St., PO19 1AH 𝒫 (01243) 775888.
London 69 – Brighton 31 – Portsmouth 18 – Southampton 30.

CHICHESTER

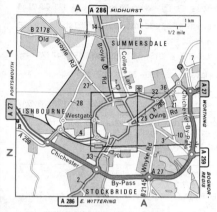

🏨 **Jarvis Chichester,** Westhampnett, PO19 4UL, ✆ (01243) 786351, *Fax (01243) 782371,*
⩬, 🔲 – ⅙✕ 📺 ☎ ₲ 🅿 – 🛐 300. 🅞🅞 🅰🅴 🅾 *VISA*   AY e
Meals (bar lunch Saturday) 15.95 **st.** and a la carte ⅊ 5.95 – ⌐ 8.95 – **76 rm** 95.00/
120.00 **st.**, 1 suite – SB.

🏨 **Suffolk House,** 3 East Row, PO19 1PD, ✆ (01243) 778899, *Fax (01243) 787282,* 🍽 –
⅙✕ rest, 📺 ☎. 🅞🅞 🅰🅴 🅾 *VISA*. ✛   BY a
Meals (dinner only) 14.75 **st.** and a la carte ⅊ 5.25 – **10 rm** ⌐ 55.00/110.00 **st.** – SB.

🏨 **Crouchers Bottom,** Birdham Rd, Apuldram, PO20 7EH, SW: 2 ½ m. on A 286
✆ (01243) 784995, *Fax (01243) 539797,* ⩤, 🍽 – ⅙✕ 📺 ☎ ₲ 🅿. 🅞🅞 🅰🅴 🅾 *VISA*
Meals (dinner only) 20.50 **st.** ⅊ 6.50 – **9 rm** ⌐ 52.00/85.00 **st.** – SB.

XX **Comme ça,** 67 Broyle Rd, PO19 4BD, on A 286 ✆ (01243) 788724, *Fax (01243) 530052,* 🍽
– 🅿. 🅞🅞 🅰🅴 *VISA*   AY c
closed Sunday dinner and Monday – **Meals** - French - 17.75 **st.** (lunch) and a la carte 19.15/
25.65 **st.** ⅊ 6.25.

at Charlton N: 6¼ m. by A 286 – **AY** – ⊠ Chichester.

🏨 **Woodstock House,** PO18 0HU, ✆ (01243) 811666, *Fax (01243) 811666,* 🍽 – ⅙✕ rm, 📺
☎ 🅿. 🅞🅞 🅰🅴 *VISA*. ✛
closed 25 and 26 December – **Meals** (dinner only) 19.95 **st.** ⅊ 6.25 – **10 rm** ⌐ 38.50/
92.00 **st.** – SB.

at Chilgrove N: 6½ m. by A 286 – **AY** – on B 2141 – ⊠ Chichester.

⌂ **Forge Cottage,** at White Horse Inn, PO18 9HX, ✆ (01243) 535333, *Fax (01243) 535363*
« Converted 17C forge », 🍽 – ⅙✕ 📺 ☎ 🅿. 🅞🅞 🅰🅴 🅾 *VISA* JCB. ✛
closed 2 weeks February and last week October – **Meals** – (see *White Horse Inn* below) –
5 rm ⌐ 35.00/79.00 **st.**

XX **White Horse Inn,** 1 High St., PO18 9HX, ✆ (01243) 535219, *Fax (01243) 535301* – 🅿. 🅞🅞
🅾 *VISA*
closed Sunday dinner, Monday, February and last week October – **Meals** 19.50/23.50 **t**
⅊ 5.75.

at Halnaker NE: 3¼ m. on A 285 – **BY** – ⊠ Chichester.

⌂ **Old Store** without rest., Stane St., PO18 0QL, on A 285 ✆ (01243) 531977
Fax (01243) 531977, 🍽 – 📺 🅿. 🅞🅞 *VISA*. ✛
closed 2 weeks February-March and 1 week at Christmas – **7 rm** ⌐ 28.00/55.00 **st.**

at Goodwood NE : 3½ m. by A 27 – AY – on East Dean Rd – ✉ Chichester.

🏨 **Marriott Goodwood Park H. & Country Club,** PO18 0QB, ℰ (01243) 775537, Fax (01243) 520120, ✻, ≘s, ⌧, ⅓, ☞, park, ✵, squash – ⇌ 📺 ☎ ℗ – ⚿ 120. ⓪ 匯 ⓪ *VISA* ᴊᴄʙ. ✵
Meals 21.95 **st.** and a la carte – **93 rm** ☑ 108.00 **st.,** 1 suite – SB.

at Bosham W : 4 m. by A 259 – AZ – ✉ Chichester.

🏨 **Millstream,** Bosham Lane, PO18 8HL, ℰ (01243) 573234, Fax (01243) 573459, ☞ – ⇌ 📺 ☎ ℗ – ⚿ 45. ⓪ 匯 ⓪ *VISA*
Meals 13.50/19.95 **t.** ⅙ 5.50 – **33 rm** ☑ 69.00/139.00 **t.** – SB.

⌂ **Hatpins** without rest., Bosham Lane, PO18 8HG, ℰ (01243) 572644, ≘s, ☞ – 📺 ℗. ✵
3 rm ☑ 25.00/70.00 **s.**

at Chidham W : 6 m. by A 259 – AZ – ✉ Chichester.

⌂ **Old Rectory** ⧖ without rest., Cot Lane, West Chidham, PO18 8TA, ℰ (01243) 572088, Fax (01243) 572088, ☞ – ⇌ 📺 ℗
closed 3 weeks February-March – **4 rm** ☑ 22.00/50.00.

    ⦿ ATS Terminus Rd Ind Est. ℰ (01243) 773100

CHIDHAM W. Sussex – see Chichester.

CHIEVELEY SERVICE AREA Newbury – ✉ Thatcham.

🏠 **Travelodge** without rest., Oxford Rd, Hermitage, RG18 9XX, at junction 13 of M 4 ℰ (01635) 248024, Fax (01635) 247886, Reservations (Freephone) 0800 850950 – ⇌ 📺 ⅓ ℗. ⓪ 匯 ⓪ *VISA* ᴊᴄʙ. ✵
44 rm 49.95 **t.**

CHILDER THORNTON Ches. – ✉ Wirral.
London 200 – Birkenhead 7 – Chester 12.

🏠 **Travel Inn,** New Chester Rd, L66 1QW, on A 41 ℰ (0151) 339 8101, Fax (0151) 347 1401 – ⇌ rm, 📺 ⅓ ℗. ⓪ 匯 ⓪ *VISA*. ✵
Meals (grill rest.) – **31 rm** 36.50 **t.**

CHILGROVE W. Sussex 404 R 31 – see Chichester.

CHILLINGTON Devon 403 I 33 – see Kingsbridge.

CHINLEY Derbs. 402 403 404 O 23 – ✉ Stockport (Ches.).
London 187 – Manchester 24 – Sheffield 25.

⌂ **Ashen Clough** ⧖, SK23 6AH, N : 1 ½ m. by Maynestone Rd ℰ (01663) 750311, ≤, ☞, park – ⇌ rm, ℗. ✵
Meals (by arrangement) (communal dining) 19.50 **s.** – **3 rm** ☑ 42.00/64.00.

CHINNOR Oxon. 404 R 28 The West Country G. – pop. 5 599.
Exc. : Ridgeway Path★★.
London 45 – Oxford 19.

⌂ **Cross Lanes Cottage** without rest., West Lane, Bledlow, HP27 9PF, NE : 1 ½ m. on B 4009 ℰ (01844) 345339, « Part 16C », ☞ – ⇌ 📺 ℗. ✵
3 rm ☑ 40.00/50.00 **st.**

✗ **Sir Charles Napier Inn,** Sprig's Alley, by Bledlow Ridge rd, OX9 4BX, SE : 2 ½ m. ℰ (01494) 483011, Fax (01494) 485434, ஜ, « Characterful inn », ☞ – ℗. ⓪ 匯 *VISA*
closed Sunday dinner and Monday – Meals a la carte 21.50/27.50 **t.** ⅙ 6.00.

CHIPPENHAM Wilts. 403 404 N 29 The West Country G. – pop. 25 961.
See : Yelde Hall★.
Env. : Corsham Court★★ AC, SW : 4 m. by A 4 – Sheldon Manor★ AC, W : 1 ½ m. by A 420 – Biddestone★, W : 3 ½ m. – Bowood House★ AC (Library ≤★) SE : 5 m. by A 4 and A 342.
Exc. : Castle Combe★★, NW : 6 m. by A 420 and B 4039.
⅓ Monkton Park (Par Three) ℰ (01249) 653928.
🛈 The Citadel, Bath Rd, SN15 2AA ℰ (01249) 657733.
London 106 – Bristol 27 – Southampton 64 – Swindon 21.

🏛 **Stanton Manor**, Stanton St. Quintin, SN14 6DQ, N : 5 m. by A 429 𝄡 (01666) 837552, Fax (01666) 837022, 🐴 – 📺 ☎ 🅿. 🕪 ⏣ ⑩ VISA. ⅍
closed 2 weeks August and 26 December-5 January – **Meals** (closed Sunday) 22.00 **st.**
🍴 7.50 – **10 rm** ⇄ 75.00/95.00 **st.** – SB.

Ⓐ ATS Cocklebury Rd 𝄡 (01249) 653541

CHIPPERFIELD Herts. 404 ⑫ – pop. 1 680 – ✉ Kings Langley.
London 27 – Hemel Hempstead 5 – Watford 6.

🏛 **Two Brewers Inn**, The Common, WD4 9BS, 𝄡 (01923) 265266, Fax (01923) 261884 – ⅍✳ 📺 ☎ 🅿 – 🔬 25. 🕪 ⏣ ⑩ VISA
Meals a la carte 12.30/16.90 **st.** 🍴 8.00 – ⇄ 9.45 – **20 rm** 85.00/100.00 **st.** – SB.

CHIPPING Lancs. 402 M 22 – pop. 1 392 – ✉ Preston.
London 233 – Lancaster 30 – Leeds 54 – Manchester 40 – Preston 12.

🏛 **Gibbon Bridge** ⏍, PR3 2TQ, E : 1 m. on Clitheroe rd 𝄡 (01995) 61456, Fax (01995) 61277, ⟨, 🛵, ⅀, 🐴, park, ⅍ – 🛏 📺 ☎ 🕭 🅿 – 🔬 30. 🕪 ⏣ ⑩ VISA. ⅍
Meals 14.00/20.00 **st.** and dinner a la carte – **12 rm** ⇄ 70.00/100.00 **st.**, **18 suites** 130.00/200.00 **st.** – SB.

CHIPPING CAMPDEN Glos. 403 404 O 27 Great Britain G. – pop. 1 741.
See : Town★.
Env. : Hidcote Manor Garden★★ AC, NE : 2 ½ m.
🗎 The Guildhall, OX7 5NJ 𝄡 (01608) 644379.
London 93 – Cheltenham 21 – Oxford 37 – Stratford-upon-Avon 12.

🏛 **Cotswold House**, The Square, GL55 6AN, 𝄡 (01386) 840330, Fax (01386) 840310, « Attractively converted Regency town house », 🐴 – ⅍✳ rest, 📺 ☎ 🅿 – 🔬 30. 🕪 ⏣ ⑩ VISA. ⅍
closed 23 to 26 December – **Garden Room :** Meals (dinner only and Sunday lunch)/dinner 20.00 **t.** and a la carte 🍴 8.50 – **Forbes Brasserie :** Meals a la carte 12.25/16.15 **t.** – **15 rm** ⇄ 55.00/144.00 **st.** – SB.

🏛 **Seymour House**, High St., GL55 6AH, 𝄡 (01386) 840429, Fax (01386) 840369, « Mature grapevine in restaurant », 🐴 – ⅍✳ rest, 📺 ☎ 🅿. 🕪 ⏣ VISA. ⅍
Meals 15.50/22.95 **st.** and lunch a la carte 🍴 7.00 – **13 rm** ⇄ 65.00/110.00 **st.**, 3 suites – SB.

🏛 **Noel Arms**, High St., GL55 6AT, 𝄡 (01386) 840317, Fax (01386) 841136 – ⅍✳ rest, 📺 ☎ 🅿 – 🔬 40. 🕪 ⏣ ⑩ VISA JCB
Meals (bar lunch Monday to Saturday)/dinner 21.95 **st.** 🍴 6.95 – **26 rm** ⇄ 70.00/109.00 **st.** – SB.

at Mickleton N : 3 ¼ m. by B 4035 and B 4081 on B 4632 – ✉ Chipping Campden.

🏛 **Three Ways House**, GL55 6SB, 𝄡 (01386) 438429, Fax (01386) 438118, 🐴 – ⅍✳ rest, 📺 ☎ 🅿 – 🔬 80. 🕪 ⏣ ⑩ VISA JCB. ⅍
Meals (bar lunch Monday to Saturday)/dinner 20.00 **t.** 🍴 7.00 – **41 rm** ⇄ 60.00/105.00 **t.** – SB.

at Charingworth E : 3 m. by B 4035 – ✉ Chipping Campden.

🏛 **Charingworth Manor** ⏍, GL55 6NS, on B 4035 𝄡 (01386) 593555, Fax (01386) 593353, ⟨, « Part early 14C manor house with Jacobean additions », ⅀, ⬛ 🐴, park, ⅍ – ⅍✳ rest, 📺 ☎ 🅿 – 🔬 30. 🕪 ⏣ ⑩ VISA
Meals 17.50/37.50 **st.** 🍴 8.00 – **26 rm** ⇄ 105.00/260.00 **st.** – SB.

at Broad Campden S : 1 ¼ m. by B 4081 – ✉ Chipping Campden.

🏛 **Malt House** ⏍, GL55 6UU, 𝄡 (01386) 840295, Fax (01386) 841334, « 17C », 🐴 – 📺 🅿 🕪 VISA JCB
Meals (closed Tuesday) (dinner only) 25.50 **st.** 🍴 8.50 – **7 rm** ⇄ 49.50/97.50 **st.**, 1 suite – SB

⌂ **Orchard Hill House** ⏍ without rest., GL55 6UU, 𝄡 (01386) 841473, Fax (01386) 841030, « 17C farmhouse » – ⅍✳ 📺 🅿. ⅍
closed 24 to 26 December – **4 rm** ⇄ 43.00/57.00 **s.**

⌂ **Marnic House** without rest., GL55 6UR, 𝄡 (01386) 840014, Fax (01386) 840441, 🐴 – ⅍✳ 📺 🅿
closed 23 December-2 January – **3 rm** ⇄ 35.00/46.00 **t.**

When looking for a quiet hotel
use the maps found in the introduction
or look for establishments with the sign ⏍ *or* ⏍

CHIPPING NORTON *Oxon* [403] [404] P 28 *Great Britain G. – pop. 5 386.*

Env. : *Chastleton House★★, NW : 4 m. by A 44.*

⛳18 *Lyneham* ☎ *(01993) 831841 –* ⛳18 *Southcombe* ☎ *(01608) 642383.*

London 77 – Birmingham 44 – Gloucester 36 – Oxford 21.

🍴🍴 **Morel's,** 2 Horsefair, OX7 5AQ, ☎ (01608) 641075 – ⊬. [MC] [VISA] [JCB]
closed Sunday dinner, Monday, 2 to 23 January and 1 week September – **Meals** - French - (dinner only and Sunday lunch)/dinner 22.00 **t.** 🍷 7.50.

CHISELDON *Wilts.* [403] [404] O 29 – *see Swindon.*

CHITTLEHAMHOLT *Devon* [403] I 31 – *pop. 194 – ✉ Umberleigh.*

London 216 – Barnstaple 14 – Exeter 28 – Taunton 45.

🏨 **Highbullen** 🌿, EX37 9HD, ☎ (01769) 540561, *Fax (01769) 540492*, ⩽, ≘s, ⛱, ⛱, ⛳18, ⛳, 🌳, park, 🎾indoor/outdoor, squash – ⊬ rest, [TV] ☎ [P] – 🪑 25. [MC] [VISA]. ⊁
Meals (bar lunch)/dinner 18.50 **st.** 🍷 4.75 – ☕ 3.00 – **35 rm** (dinner included) 60.00/160.00 **st.**

CHOBHAM *Surrey* [404] S 29 – *pop. 3 411 – ✉ Woking.*

London 35 – Reading 21 – Southampton 53.

⌂ **Knaphill Manor** 🌿 without rest., Carthouse Lane, GU21 4XT, SW : 1 m. by Castle Grove Rd and Guildford Rd ☎ (01276) 857962, *Fax (01276) 855503*, ⩽, 🌳, 🎾 – [TV] [P]. [MC] [VISA]. ⊁
closed Easter, Christmas and New Year – **3 rm** ☕ 45.00/70.00.

🍴🍴 **Quails,** 1 Bagshot Rd, GU24 8BP, ☎ (01276) 858491, *Fax (01276) 858491* – ▤. [MC] [AE] [D] [VISA]
closed Saturday lunch, Sunday dinner, Monday, 26 December and 1 January – **Meals** 14.95/19.95 **t.** and a la carte 🍷 4.95.

CHOLLERFORD *Northd.* [401] [402] N 18 *Great Britain G. – ✉ Hexham.*

Env. : *Hadrian's Wall★★ – Chesters★ (Bath House★)* **AC**, *W : ½ m. by B 6318.*

London 303 – Carlisle 36 – Newcastle upon Tyne 21.

🏨 **George,** NE46 4EW, ☎ (01434) 681611, *Fax (01434) 681727*, ⩽, « Riverside gardens », 🏋, ≘s, ⛱, ⛳ – ⊬ rm, [TV] ☎ ♿ [P] – 🪑 65. [MC] [AE] [D] [VISA]. ⊁
Meals 15.00/24.95 **st.** and a la carte 🍷 7.00 – **46 rm** ☕ 90.00/145.00 **st.** – SB.

CHORLEY *Lancs.* [402] [404] M 23 – *pop. 33 536.*

⛳18 *Duxbury Park, Duxbury Hall Rd* ☎ *(01257) 265380 –* ⛳18 *Shaw Hill Hotel G. & C.C., Preston Rd, Whittle-le-Woods* ☎ *(01257) 269221.*

London 222 – Blackpool 30 – Liverpool 32 – Manchester 26.

🏨 **Yarrow Bridge - Premier Lodge,** Bolton Rd, PR7 4AB, S : 1 m. on A 6 ☎ (01257) 265989, *Fax (01257) 230821* – ⊬ [TV] ☎ ♿ [P]. [MC] [AE] [D] [VISA] [JCB]. ⊁
Meals (grill rest.) a la carte 7.60/20.80 **t.** 🍷 4.25 – ☕ 4.95 – **29 rm** 42.25 **st.** – SB.

at Whittle-le-Woods *N : 2 m. on A 6 – ✉ Chorley.*

🏨 **Shaw Hill H. Golf & Country Club** 🌿, Preston Rd, PR6 7PP, ☎ (01257) 269221, *Fax (01257) 261223*, ⛳18 – [TV] ☎ [P] – 🪑 200. [MC] [AE] [VISA]
Vardon : **Meals** (bar lunch Saturday) 13.50/19.50 **t.** and a la carte 🍷 6.95 – **30 rm** ☕ 70.00/128.00 **t.** – SB.

🏨 **Parkville Country House,** 174 Preston Rd, PR6 7HE, ☎ (01257) 261881, *Fax (01257) 273171*, 🌳 – [TV] ☎ [P]. [MC] [AE] [D] [VISA] [JCB]. ⊁
closed 25 December – **Meals** *(closed Sunday)* (dinner only) 15.95 **t.** and a la carte 🍷 4.95 – **13 rm** ☕ 55.00/75.00 **st.**

🔧 ATS 18 Westminster Rd ☎ (01257) 262000/265472

CHORLTON CUM HARDY *Gtr. Manchester* [402] [403] [404] N 23 – *see Manchester.*

CHRISTCHURCH *Dorset* [403] [404] O 31 *The West Country G. – pop. 36 379.*

See : *Town★ – Priory★* – Env. : *Hengistbury Head★ (⩽★★) SW : 4 ½ m. by A 35 and B 3059.*

⛳18 *Highcliffe Castle, 107 Lymington Rd, Highcliffe-on-Sea* ☎ *(01425) 272953 –* ⛳9 *Barrack Rd, Iford* ☎ *(01202) 473817.*

[i] *23 High St., BH23 1AB* ☎ *(01202) 471780.*

London 111 – Bournemouth 6 – Salisbury 26 – Southampton 24 – Winchester 39.

Travel Inn, Somerford Rd, BH23 3QG, E : 2 m. by A 35 on B 3059 ✆ (01202) 485376, *Fax (01202) 474939* – ⇔ rm, TV ♿ P. MC AE ① VISA. ✻
Meals (grill rest.) – **38 rm** 36.50 **t.**

Splinters, 12 Church St., BH23 1BW, ✆ (01202) 483454, *Fax (01202) 483454* – MC AE ① VISA JCB
closed Sunday dinner, Monday and 26 to 31 December – **Meals** 15.95/27.95 **t.** 6.50.

at Mudeford *SE : 2 m. – ✉ Christchurch.*

Avonmouth, 95 Mudeford, BH23 3NT, ✆ (01202) 483434, *Fax (01202) 479004*, ≤, ⛱, – ⇔ TV ☎ P – 60. MC AE ① VISA JCB
Meals (bar lunch Monday to Saturday)/dinner 19.95 **st.** 7.50 – **40 rm** (dinner included) 84.00/168.00 **st.** – SB.

Waterford Lodge, 87 Bure Lane, Friars Cliff, BH23 4DN, ✆ (01425) 272940, *Fax (01425) 279130*, – TV ☎ P – 80. MC AE ① VISA. ✻
closed 28 December-2 January – **Meals** 13.95/23.00 **t.** – 9.00 – **17 rm** 74.00/90.00 **t.** – SB.

CHURCHILL *Oxon.* 403 404 P 28 – *pop. 502* – ✉ *Chipping Norton.*
London 79 – Birmingham 46 – Cheltenham 29 – Oxford 23 – Swindon 31.

The Forge without rest., OX7 6NJ, ✆ (01608) 658173, *Fax (01608) 659262* – TV P. MC VISA. ✻
5 rm 40.00/60.00 **st.**

CHURCH STRETTON *Shrops.* 402 403 L 26 *Great Britain G.* – *pop. 3 435.*
Env. : *Wenlock Edge*★, *E : by B 4371.*
18 *Trevor Hill* ✆ *(01694) 722281.*
London 166 – Birmingham 46 – Hereford 39 – Shrewsbury 14.

Mynd House, Ludlow Rd, Little Stretton, SY6 6RB, SW : 1 ¼ m. on B 4370 ✆ (01694) 722212, *Fax (01694) 724180*, – ⇔ TV ☎ P. MC AE VISA
closed 22 December-1 February and 3 weeks in summer – **Meals** (booking essential) (bar lunch)/dinner a la carte approx. 28.00 **st.** 6.00 – **5 rm** 40.00/80.00 **st.**, 2 suites – SB.

Inwood Farm ⛰, All Stretton, SY6 6LA, N : 1 ½ m. by B 4370 ✆ (01694) 724046, ≤, , park – ⇔ TV P. ✻
Meals (communal dining) (dinner only) 18.00 **st.** 5.00 – **3 rm** 35.00/55.00 **st.**

Belvedere, Burway Rd, SY6 6DP, ✆ (01694) 722232, *Fax (01694) 722232*, – P. MC VISA
closed 17 to 29 December – **Meals** (dinner only) 10.00 **st.** – **12 rm** 23.00/50.00 **st.**

at Woolstaston *NW : 5 ½ m. by A 49.*

Rectory Farm ⛰ without rest., SY6 6NN, ✆ (01694) 751306, ≤, « 17C timbered house », – TV P. ✻
March-November – **3 rm** 26.00/44.00.

ATS Crossways ✆ (01694) 722526/722112

CHURT *Surrey* 404 R 30 – *see Farnham.*

CIRENCESTER *Glos.* 403 404 O 28 *Great Britain G.* – *pop. 15 221.*
See : *Town*★ – *Church of St. John the Baptist*★ – *Corinium Museum*★ *(Mosaic pavements*★*) AC.*
Env. : *Fairford : Church of St. Mary*★ *(stained glass windows*★★*) E : 7 m. by A 417.*
18 *Cheltenham Rd* ✆ *(01285) 653939.*
Corn Hall, Market Pl., GL7 2NW ✆ *(01285) 654180.*
London 97 – Bristol 37 – Gloucester 19 – Oxford 37.

Jarvis Fleece, Market Pl., GL7 2NZ, ✆ (01285) 658507, *Fax (01285) 651017* – ⇔ rest, TV ☎ P – 25. MC AE ① VISA
Meals (bar lunch Monday to Saturday)/dinner 13.95 **t.** and a la carte 8.50 – 8.50 – **30 rm** 75.00/89.00 **t.** – SB.

Wimborne House, 91 Victoria Rd, GL7 1ES, ✆ (01285) 653890, *Fax (01285) 653890*, – ⇔ TV P. ✻
closed 2 weeks Christmas – **Meals** (by arrangement) 7.50 – **5 rm** 30.00/45.00 **st.** – SB.

The Ivy House without rest., 2 Victoria Rd, GL7 1EN, ✆ (01285) 656626 – ⇔ TV. ✻
closed 25 December – **4 rm** 28.00/42.00 **st.**

Harry Hare's, 3 Gosditch St., GL7 2AG, ✆ (01285) 652375, *Fax (01285) 641691*, – MC AE VISA
closed 1 to 7 January – **Meals** a la carte 14.85/24.95 **t.**

at Barnsley NE : 4 m. by A 429 on B 4425 – ⊠ Cirencester.

🍽 **Village Pub** with rm, GL7 5EF, ℰ (01285) 740421 – 📺 ☎ 🅿. �👀 🖭 𝘝𝘐𝘚𝘈
closed 25 December – Meals a la carte 10.50/15.50 st. ₰ 4.50 – **5 rm** � 30.00/45.00 st.

at Ampney Crucis E : 2¾ m. by A 417 – ⊠ Cirencester.

🏨 **Crown of Crucis,** GL7 5RS, on A 417 ℰ (01285) 851806, Fax (01285) 851735, 🌳 –
☆ rm, 📺 ☎ 🅿 – 🔬 80. 👀 🖭 ① 𝘝𝘐𝘚𝘈
closed 24 to 30 December – Meals (bar lunch)/dinner 16.45 t. and a la carte – **25 rm**
⊠ 56.00/80.00 t. – SB.

⌂ **Waterton Garden Cottage** ⤳, GL7 5RX, S : ½ m. by Driffield rd turning right into
unmarked driveway ℰ (01285) 851303, « Converted Victorian stables, walled garden » –
🅿.
Meals (by arrangement) (communal dining) 20.00 s. – **3 rm** ⊠ 22.50/45.00 s.

at Ewen SW : 3¼ m. by A 429 – ⊠ Cirencester.

🍽 **Wild Duck Inn** with rm, Drake's Island, GL7 6BY, ℰ (01285) 770310, Fax (01285) 770924,
« Part 16C former farm buildings », 🌳 – 📺 ☎ 🅿. 👀 🖭 𝘝𝘐𝘚𝘈. ⌘
closed 25 December – Meals a la carte 11.90/20.90 t. – ⊠ 5.00 – **10 rm** 49.50/90.00 t.

at Kemble SW : 4 m. by A 433 on A 429 – ⊠ Cirencester.

⌂ **Smerrill Barns** without rest., GL7 6BW, N : 1¼ m. on A 429 ℰ (01285) 770907,
Fax (01285) 770706, « Converted 18C barn » – ☆ 📺 🅿. 👀 𝘝𝘐𝘚𝘈 𝙅𝘊𝘉. ⌘
7 rm ⊠ 35.00/55.00 st.

at Stratton NW : 1¼ m. on A 417 – ⊠ Cirencester.

🏨 **Stratton House,** Gloucester Rd, GL7 2LE, ℰ (01285) 651761, Fax (01285) 640024, 🌳 –
☆ 📺 ☎ 🅿 – 🔬 150. 👀 🖭 ① 𝘝𝘐𝘚𝘈
Meals (bar lunch Monday to Saturday)/dinner 18.50 st. and a la carte ₰ 6.75 – **41 rm**
⊠ 85.00/110.00 t. – SB.

🔧 ATS 1 Mercian Close, Watermoor End ℰ (01285) 657761

CLACKET LANE SERVICE AREA Surrey 404 U 30 – ⊠ Westerham.

🏨 **RoadChef Lodge** without rest., TN16 2ER, M 25 between junctions 5 and 6
ℰ (01959) 565789, Fax (01959) 561311, Reservations (Freephone) 0800 834719 – ☆ 📺 ☎
🔬 🅿. 👀 🖭 ① 𝘝𝘐𝘚𝘈. ⌘
closed 24 to 26 December – ⊠ 5.00 – **58 rm** 47.50 st.

CLACTON-ON-SEA Essex 404 X 28 – pop. 45 065.
🏌 West Rd ℰ (01255) 424331.
🛈 23 Pier Av., CO15 1QD ℰ (01255) 423400.
London 76 – Chelmsford 37 – Colchester 14 – Ipswich 28.

🏠 **Chudleigh,** 13 Agate Rd, Marine Parade West, CO15 1RA, ℰ (01255) 425407,
Fax (01255) 425407 – 📺 🅿. 👀 🖭 ① 𝘝𝘐𝘚𝘈 𝙅𝘊𝘉
Meals (closed Friday to Sunday October-Easter) (dinner only) 12.00 st. ₰ 3.75 – **10 rm**
⊠ 32.50/50.00 st.

🔧 ATS 46 High St. ℰ (01255) 420659

CLANFIELD Oxon. 403 404 P 28 – pop. 1 709 (inc. Shilton).
London 75 – Oxford 24 – Swindon 16.

XXX **Plough at Clanfield** with rm, Bourton Rd, OX18 2RB, on A 4095 ℰ (01367) 810222,
Fax (01367) 810596, « Elizabethan manor house », 🌳 – ☆ 📺 ☎ 🅿. 👀 🖭 ① 𝘝𝘐𝘚𝘈 𝙅𝘊𝘉.
⌘
closed 27 to 29 December – Meals (closed Monday lunch) 18.50/28.50 t. ₰ 7.50 – **6 rm**
⊠ 70.00/150.00 t. – SB.

CLAPPERSGATE Cumbria – see Ambleside.

CLARE Suffolk 404 V 27 – pop. 1 976 – ⊠ Sudbury.
London 67 – Cambridge 27 – Colchester 24 – Ipswich 32 – Bury St.Edmunds 16.

⌂ **Ship Stores,** 22 Callis St., CO10 8PX, ℰ (01787) 277834 – ☆ rm, 📺. 👀 𝘝𝘐𝘚𝘈 𝙅𝘊𝘉. ⌘
Meals (by arrangement) 8.50 s. – **5 rm** ⊠ 32.00/44.00 s.

CLAVERING *Essex* 404 U 28 – *pop. 1 663* – ⊠ *Saffron Walden.*
London 44 – Cambridge 25 – Colchester 44 – Luton 29.

🏠 **Cricketers** with rm, CB11 4QT, ℘ (01799) 550442, *Fax (01799) 550882,* 🐾 – 📺 ☎ 🕭 🄿.
🔵 🖭 *VISA*. ⅋
closed 25 and 26 December – **Meals** (lunch in bar)/dinner 23.00 **t.** and a la carte ₰ 7.05 –
6 rm � 60.00/80.00 **t.**

CLAWTON *Devon* 403 H 31 *The West Country G.* – *pop. 292* – ⊠ *Holsworthy.*
Env. : *W : Tamar River*★★.
London 240 – Exeter 39 – Plymouth 36.

🏠 **Court Barn Country House** ⍯, EX22 6PS, W : ½ m. ℘ (01409) 271219,
Fax (01409) 271309, 🐾, ⅋ – ⅋ rm, 📺 ☎ 🄿. 🔵 🖭 ⑩ *VISA* 🄹🄲🄱
closed 2 to 7 January – **Meals** (booking essential) 12.50/18.00 **s.** ₰ 4.95 – **8 rm** ⊊ 39.00/
84.00 – SB.

CLAYDON *Suffolk* 404 X 27 – *see Ipswich.*

CLAYGATE *Surrey* 404 ⓐ – *see Esher.*

CLAYTON-LE-DALE *Lancs.* – *see Blackburn.*

CLAYTON-LE-MOORS *Lancs.* 402 M 22 – *pop. 6 961* – ⊠ *Accrington.*
London 232 – Blackburn 3.5 – Lancaster 37 – Leeds 44 – Preston 14.

🏨 **Dunkenhalgh,** Blackburn Rd, BB5 5JP, SW : 1 ½ m. on A 678 ℘ (01254) 398021,
Fax (01254) 872230, ₭, ⅙, 📞, 🔲, 🐾, park – ⅋ 📺 ☎ 🄿 – 🔬 400. 🔵 🖭 ⑩ *VISA* 🄹🄲🄱
Cameo : **Meals** 11.95/21.95 **t.** and a la carte ₰ 6.50 – ⊊ 8.95 – **120 rm** 105.00/115.00 **st.**,
1 suite – SB.

🏠 **Sparth House,** Whalley Rd, BB5 5RP, ℘ (01254) 872263, *Fax (01254) 872263,* 🐾 –
⅋ rest, 📺 ☎ 🄿 – 🔬 100. 🔵 *VISA*. ⅋
Meals 5.95/16.95 **t.** and a la carte ₰ 5.00 – **16 rm** ⊊ 48.25/78.50 **t.** – SB.

CLAYTON-LE-WOODS *Lancs.* – *pop. 14 173* – ⊠ *Chorley.*
London 220 – Liverpool 31 – Manchester 26 – Preston 5.5.

🏨 **The Pines,** Preston Rd, PR6 7ED, on A 6 at junction with B 5256 ℘ (01772) 338551,
Fax (01772) 629002, 🐾 – ⅋ rm, 📺 ☎ 🄿 – 🔬 200. 🔵 🖭 ⑩ *VISA*. ⅋
closed 25 and 26 December – **Meals** 12.00/16.50 **t.** and a la carte ₰ 6.95 – **36 rm** ⊊ 50.00/
75.00 **t.**, 2 suites – SB.

🏠 **Travelodge,** Preston Rd, PR6 7JB, on A 6 ℘ (01772) 311963, *Fax (01772) 311963*
Reservations (Freephone) 0800 850950 – ⅋ rm, 📺 🕭 🄿. 🔵 🖭 ⑩ *VISA* 🄹🄲🄱. ⅋
Meals (grill rest.) – **40 rm** 44.95 **t.**

CLAYTON WEST *W. Yorks* 402 404 P 23 – *pop. 7 988* (inc. Skelmanthorpe) – ⊠ *Huddersfield.*
London 190 – Leeds 19 – Manchester 35 – Sheffield 24.

🏨 **Bagden Hall,** Wakefield Rd, Scissett, HD8 9LE, SW : 1 m. on A 636 ℘ (01484) 865330
Fax (01484) 861001, ≤, ₨, 🐾, park – 🔲 rest, 📺 ☎ 🄿 – 🔬 90. 🔵 🖭 ⑩ *VISA*. ⅋
Meals (closed Sunday dinner) 11.95/16.95 **t.** and dinner a la carte ₰ 5.50 – **17 rm** ⊊ 60.00/
100.00 **t.**

CLEARWELL *Glos.* – *see Coleford.*

CLEATOR MOOR *Cumbria* 402 J 20 – *pop. 6 410.*
London 317 – Carlisle 31 – Keswick 25 – Whitehaven 7.

🏨 **Ennerdale Country House,** Cleator, CA23 3DT, S : 1 ½ m. by B 5295 on A 5086
℘ (01946) 813907, *Fax (01946) 815260,* 🐾 – ⅋ rest, 📺 ☎ 🄿 – 🔬 150. 🔵 🖭 ⑩ *VISA* 🄹🄲🄱
Meals 10.95/18.50 **st.** and a la carte ₰ 8.75 – **28 rm** ⊊ 80.00/90.00 **st.**, 2 suites – SB.

CLEETHORPES *North East Lincolnshire* 402 404 U 23 – *pop. 32 719.*
✈ Humberside Airport : ℘ (01652) 688456, W : 16 m. by A 46 and A 18 Y.
🔡 42-43 Alexandra Rd, DN35 8LE ℘ (01472) 323111/323112.
London 171 – Boston 49 – Lincoln 38 – Sheffield 77.

🏠 **Kingsway,** Kingsway, DN35 0AE, ℰ (01472) 601122, Fax (01472) 601381, ≼ – 📺 ☎ ⇔
P. ⓂⒺ ⒶⒺ ⓄⒹ **VISA** ⚙
closed 25 and 26 December – **Meals** 14.75/17.95 **t.** and a la carte ⓖ 5.25 – **50 rm** ⊑ 66.00/
90.00 **t.** – SB.

CLEEVE HILL *Glos.* 🔢🔢 N 28 – *see Cheltenham.*

CLEY NEXT THE SEA *Norfolk* 🔢 X 25 – *see Blakeney.*

CLIMPING *W. Sussex* 🔢 S 31 – *see Littlehampton.*

CLITHEROE *Lancs* 🔢 M 22 – *pop. 13 548.*
　　　🏌 *Whalley Rd* ℰ (01200) 422618.
　　　🛈 *12-14 Market Pl., BB7 2DA* ℰ (01200) 425566.
　　　London 64 – Blackpool 35 – Manchester 31.

↑ **Brooklyn,** 32 Pimlico Rd, BB7 2AH, ℰ (01200) 428268 – ⇝ rm, 📺. ⓂⒺ **VISA** **JCB**. ⚙
Meals *(by arrangement)* 10.00 **st.** – **4 rm** ⊑ 25.00/40.00 **st.**

✗ **Auctioneer,** New Market St., BB7 2JW, ℰ (01200) 427153, Fax (01200) 427153 – ⓂⒺ ⒶⒺ
VISA
closed Monday – **Meals** 9.95/21.75 **t.** and lunch a la carte ⓖ 5.50.

at Waddington *N : 1¾ m. on B 6478* – ⊠ *Clitheroe.*

↑ **Peter Barn** ⊗ *without rest.,* Rabbit Lane, via Cross Lane, BB7 3JH, NW : 1½ m. by B 6478
　ℰ (01200) 428585, ⇜ – ⇝ **P.** ⚙
　closed Christmas-New Year – **3 rm** ⊑ 25.00/44.00.

　ⓘ ATS Salthill Rd ℰ (01200) 23011

CLOVELLY *Devon* 🔢 G 31 *The West Country G.* – *pop. 439* – ⊠ *Bideford.*
　　See : *Village★★.*
　　Env. : *SW : Tamar River★★.*
　　Exc. : *Hartland : Hartland Church★ – Hartland Quay★ (viewpoint★★) – Hartland Point ≼★★★,
　　W : 6½ m. by B 3237 and B 3248 – Morwenstow (Church★, cliffs★★), SW : 11½ m. by A 39.*
　　⇌ *to Isle of Lundy (Lundy Co. Ltd) (summer only) (1 h 30 mn).*
　　London 241 – Barnstaple 18 – Exeter 52 – Penzance 92.

🏠 **Red Lion** ⊗, The Quay, EX39 5TF, ℰ (01237) 431237, Fax (01237) 431044, ≼ – 📺 ☎ **P.**
ⓂⒺ ⒶⒺ **VISA**. ⚙
Meals *(bar lunch November-April)* 17.50 **t.** *(dinner) and lunch a la carte approx.* 12.00 **t.** –
11 rm ⊑ 56.50/83.00 **t.** – SB.

🏠 **New Inn,** High St., EX39 5TQ, ℰ (01237) 431303, Fax (01237) 431636, « 17C » – 📺 ☎. ⓂⒺ
ⒶⒺ **VISA**
Meals *(bar lunch)/dinner* 17.50 **t.** ⓖ 6.30 – **8 rm** ⊑ 38.50/72.50 **t.** – SB.

COATHAM MUNDEVILLE *Durham* 🔢 P 20 – *see Darlington.*

COBHAM *Kent* 🔢 V 29 – *pop. 1 586 (inc. Luddesdown)* – ⊠ *Gravesend.*
　　London 27 – Maidstone 13 – Rochester 6.

🏠 **Leather Bottle,** The Street, DA12 3BZ, ℰ (01474) 814327, Fax (01474) 812086, « 17C
inn », ⇜ – 📺 ☎ **P.** ⓂⒺ ⒶⒺ ⓄⒹ **VISA**. ⚙
closed 24 December – **Meals** a la carte 10.75/16.30 **st.** – ⊑ 5.50 – **6 rm** 45.00/60.00 **st.**

COBHAM *Surrey* 🔢 S 30 – *pop. 15 254 (inc. Oxshott).*
　　London 24 – Guildford 10.

🏠 **Hilton National,** Seven Hills Road South, KT11 1EW, W : 1½ m. by A 245
　ℰ (01932) 864471, Fax (01932) 868017, ⓕ, ⊜, ☐, ⇜, park, ⚘, squash – |⧢|, ⇝ rm, 📺 ☎
　P. – 🅰 300. ⓂⒺ ⒶⒺ ⓄⒹ **VISA** **JCB**
Meals *(bar lunch Saturday) (dancing Saturday evening)* 17.50/21.95 **st.** and a la carte ⓖ 6.50
– ⊑ 11.50 – **148 rm** 159.00/191.00 **st.**, 1 suite.

🏠 **Cedar House,** Mill Rd, KT11 3AN, ℰ (01932) 863424, Fax (01932) 862023, ⇜ – 📺 ☎ **P.**
ⓂⒺ ⒶⒺ ⓄⒹ **VISA**. ⚙
Meals *(closed Saturday lunch and Sunday dinner)* 15.00/20.00 **t.** and a la carte – **6 rm**
⊑ 80.00/105.00 **t.**

at Stoke D'Abernon SE : 1½ m. on A 245 – ⊠ Cobham.

🏛 **Woodlands Park,** Woodlands Lane, KT11 3QB, on A 245 ℰ (01372) 843933, Fax (01372) 842704, ☞, park, ※ – 📳 📺 ☎ 🅿 – 🔬 280. 🐠 🖭 ⓪ 𝘝𝘐𝘚𝘈. ※
Meals (closed Saturday lunch and Sunday dinner) 14.95/20.50 **t.** and a la carte ⬧ 6.95 – ☲ 10.00 – **57 rm** 125.00/155.00 **t.**, 1 suite – SB.

COCKERMOUTH Cumbria **401 402** J 20 – pop. 7 702.

🔞 Embleton ℰ (017687) 76223/76941.
🛈 Town Hall, Market St., CA13 9NP ℰ (01900) 822634.
London 306 – Carlisle 25 – Keswick 13.

🏠 **Trout,** Crown St., CA13 0EJ, ℰ (01900) 823591, Fax (01900) 827514, ☜, ☞ – ☀ 📺 ☎ 🅿 – 🔬 50. 🐠 🖭 𝘝𝘐𝘚𝘈
Meals 11.95/18.95 **t.** and a la carte – **34 rm** ☲ 59.95/140.00 **t.** – SB.

⌂ **Low Hall** ⬡ without rest., Brandlingill, CA13 0RE, S : 3 ¼ m. by A 5086 on Embleton rd ℰ (01900) 826654, ≤, « Part 17C farmhouse », ☞ – ☀ 🅿. 🐠 𝘝𝘐𝘚𝘈 𝘑𝘊𝘉. ※
closed Christmas – **3 rm** ☲ 25.00/60.00 **st.**

at Lorton SE : 4¼ m. by B 5292 – ⊠ Cockermouth.

⌂ **New House Farm** ⬡, CA13 9UU, S : 1 ¼ m. on B 5289 ℰ (01900) 85404, Fax (01900) 85404, ≤, « Part 17C and 19C farmhouse », ☞, park – ☀ 🅿. ※
Meals 20.00 **st.** ⬧ 5.50 – **3 rm** ☲ 40.00/70.00 **st.** – SB.

⌂ **Winder Hall** ⬡ without rest., Low Lorton, CA13 9UP, on B 5289 ℰ (01900) 85107, « Part 17C manor house », ☞ – ☀ 📺 🅿
closed December and January – **5 rm** ☲ 30.00/60.00 **s.**

COGGESHALL Essex **404** W 28 – pop. 3 927 – ⊠ Colchester.
London 49 – Braintree 6 – Chelmsford 16 – Colchester 9.

🏛 **White Hart,** Market End, C06 1NH, ℰ (01376) 561654, Fax (01376) 561789, « Part 15C guildhall », ☞ – 📺 🅿 🐠 🖭 𝘝𝘐𝘚𝘈 𝘑𝘊𝘉. ※
Meals - Italian - (in bar Sunday dinner) 14.95 **t.** (dinner) and a la carte 19.00/28.15 **t.** ⬧ 6.95 – **18 rm** ☲ 61.50/97.00 **t.**

✗✗ **Baumann's Brasserie,** 4-6 Stoneham St., CO6 1TT, ℰ (01376) 561453, Fax (01376) 563762 – 🐠 🖭 𝘝𝘐𝘚𝘈
closed Saturday lunch, Sunday dinner, Monday and first 2 weeks January – **Meals** 9.95 **st.** (lunch) and a la carte 17.85/24.40 **st.**

COLCHESTER Essex **404** W 28 Great Britain G. – pop. 96 063.

See : Castle and Museum⋆ AC.
🔞 Birch Grove, Layer Rd ℰ (01206) 734276.
🛈 1 Queen St., CO1 2PJ ℰ (01206) 282920.
London 52 – Cambridge 48 – Ipswich 18 – Luton 76 – Southend-on-Sea 41.

🏠 **George,** 116 High St., CO1 1TD, ℰ (01206) 578494, Fax (01206) 761732 – ☀ rm, ▤ rest, 📺 ☎ 🅿 – 🔬 80. 🐠 🖭 ⓪ 𝘝𝘐𝘚𝘈
Meals 16.95 **t.** (dinner) and a la carte 14.50/30.95 **t.** ⬧ 5.95 – ☲ 8.25 – **45 rm** 70.00/75.00 **st.** – SB.

🏠 **Rose and Crown,** East St., Eastgates, CO1 2TZ, ℰ (01206) 866677, Fax (01206) 866616, « Part 15C inn » – ☀ rm, 📺 ☎ ꜛ 🅿 – 🔬 100. 🐠 🖭 ⓪ 𝘝𝘐𝘚𝘈. ※
closed 26 to 28 December – **Meals** (bar meals Saturday lunch, Sunday dinner and Monday) a la carte 22.50/34.75 **t.** – **28 rm** ☲ 62.50 **t.** – SB.

🏠 **Red Lion,** 43 High St., CO1 1DJ, ℰ (01206) 577986, Fax (01206) 578207, « Part 15C inn » – 📺 ☎ – 🔬 40. 🐠 🖭 ⓪ 𝘝𝘐𝘚𝘈 𝘑𝘊𝘉. ※
The Parliament : Meals a la carte 15.15/21.95 **t.** ⬧ 6.95 – **22 rm** ☲ 67.50/75.00 **st.** – SB.

🏠 **Butterfly,** Old Ipswich Rd, CO7 7QY, NE : 4 ¼ m. by A 1232 at junction of A 12 with A 120 (via sliproad to A 120) ℰ (01206) 230900, Fax (01206) 231095 – ☀ rm, 📺 ☎ ꜛ 🅿 – 🔬 80. 🐠 🖭 ⓪ 𝘝𝘐𝘚𝘈 𝘑𝘊𝘉. ※
Meals 12.50 and a la carte – ☲ 6.95 – **50 rm** 59.50/80.00 **st.**

🏠 **Travel Inn,** Severalls Business Park, Ipswich Rd, CO4 4NP, N : 2 ¾ m. on A 1232 ℰ (01206) 855001, Fax (01206) 211388 – ☀ rm, 📺 ꜛ 🅿. 🐠 🖭 ⓪ 𝘝𝘐𝘚𝘈
Meals (grill rest.) – **40 rm** 36.50 **t.**

🏠 **D'Arcy House,** 3-5 Culver Street East, CO1 1LD, ℰ (01206) 768111, Fax (01206) 763938 – 📺. 🐠 𝘝𝘐𝘚𝘈
Meals (closed Sunday dinner, 25-26 December and Bank Holidays) 12.50/15.00 **t** and a la carte – **3 rm** ☲ 30.00/52.00 **t.** – SB.

⌂ **Four Sevens,** 28 Inglis Rd, CO3 3HU, off Maldon Rd (B 1022) *℘ (01206) 546093,*
Fax (01206) 546093, ☞ – ⅍ rest, ⊡. ⅏
closed 25 December-2 January – **Meals** (by arrangement) 15.00 **s.** – **6 rm** �*z* 30.00/45.00 **s.**

XX **North Hill Exchange Brasserie,** 19-20 North Hill, CO1 1DZ, *℘ (01206) 769988,*
Fax (01206) 766898 – ⊕❾ Æ ⊕ VISA
closed Sunday – **Meals** 9.95 **st.** and a la carte.

X **Warehouse Brasserie,** 12a Chapel St. North, CO2 7AT, *℘ (01206) 765656,*
Fax(01206) 765656 – ▤. ⊕❾ Æ ⊕ VISA
closed Sunday dinner and 25-26 December – **Meals** 10.95 **t.** (lunch) and a la carte 15.00/
19.95 **t.** ⍧ 4.50.

at Eight Ash Green *W : 4 m. by A 604 –* ⊠ *Colchester.*

🏨 **Forte Posthouse Colchester,** Abbotts Lane, CO6 3QL, at junction of A 604 with A 12
℘ (01206) 767740, Fax (01206) 766577, Ⅰ₆, ⇌, ⬚ – ⅍ rm, ⊡ ☎ & ❷ – 🕍 150. ⊕❾ Æ
⊕ VISA
Meals a la carte 16.50/24.45 **t.** ⍧ 7.25 – ⊡ 8.95 – **110 rm** 59.00 **st.** – SB.

at Marks Tey *W : 5 m. by A 12 at junction with A 120 –* ⊠ *Colchester.*

🏨 **Marks Tey,** London Rd, CO6 1DU, on B 1408 *℘ (01206) 210001, Fax (01206) 212167, Ⅰ₆,*
⇌, ⬚, ⅏ – ⅍ rm, ▤ rest, ⊡ ☎ ❷ – 🕍 200. ⊕❾ Æ ⊕ VISA JCB. ⅏
closed 28 to 30 December – **Meals** 15.50 **st.** and a la carte ⍧ 8.00 – ⊡ 7.50 – **109 rm**
67.50/75.00 **st.,** 1 suite – SB.

ⓐ ATS East Hill *℘ (01206) 866484/867471*　　　ATS Telford Way, Severalls Park Ind. Est.
ATS 451 Ipswich Rd *℘ (01206) 841404*　　　　*℘ (01206) 845641*

COLDRED *Kent – see Dover.*

COLEFORD *Devon* 🄳🄰🄳 I 31 – ⊠ *Crediton.*
London 214 – Barnstaple 29 – Exeter 14 – Taunton 42.

🏠 **New Inn** with rm, EX17 5BZ, *℘ (01363) 84242, Fax (01363) 85044, « Part 13C thatched*
inn » – ⅍ rm, ⊡ ❷. ⊕❾ Æ ⊕ VISA JCB. ⅏
closed 25 and 26 December – **Meals** (in bar) a la carte 14.40/20.85 **t.** ⍧ 4.50 – **5 rm**
⊡ 42.00/62.00 **st.**

COLEFORD *Glos.* 🄳🄰🄳 🄳🄰🄳 M 28 *Great Britain G. –* pop. 9 567.
Env. : *W : Wye Valley*★.
🄸₈ *Forest of Dean, Lords Hills ℘ (01594) 832583 –* ⌥₈ *Forest Hills, Mile End Rd ℘ (01594)*
810620.
🄳 *High St., GL16 8HG ℘ (01594) 812388.*
London 143 – Bristol 28 – Gloucester 19 – Newport 29.

🏨 **Speech House,** Forest of Dean, GL16 7EL, NE : 3 m. by B 4028 on B 4226
℘ (01594) 822607, Fax (01594) 823658, ☞ – ⅍ ⊡ ☎ ❷ – 🕍 40. ⊕❾ Æ ⊕ VISA
Meals (bar lunch Monday to Saturday)/dinner a la carte 14.15/23.05 **t.** ⍧ 4.25 – ⊡ 8.50 –
13 rm 65.00/95.00 **t.,** 1 suite – SB.

at Clearwell *S : 2 m. by B 4228 –* ⊠ *Coleford.*

🏨 **Wyndham Arms,** GL16 8JT, *℘ (01594) 833666, Fax (01594) 836450 – ⅍ rest, ⊡ ☎ ❷ –*
🕍 55. ⊕❾ Æ ⊕ VISA JCB
Meals 13.75/18.25 **t.** and a la carte ⍧ 5.50 – **17 rm** ⊡ 52.50/65.00 **t.** – SB.

🏠 **Tudor Farmhouse,** High St., GL16 8JS, *℘ (01594) 833046, Fax (01594) 837093, « Part*
13C and 16C », ☞ – ⅍ ⊡ ☎ ❷. ⊕❾ Æ ⊕ VISA ⅏
closed 24 to 30 December – **Meals** (closed Sunday) (dinner only) 18.25 **st.** and a la carte
⍧ 4.95 – **10 rm** ⊡ 47.50/67.00 **st.,** 3 suites – SB.

COLERNE *Wilts.* 🄳🄰🄳 🄳🄰🄳 M 29 – *see Bath (Bath & North East Somerset).*

COLESHILL *Warks.* 🄳🄰🄳 🄳🄰🄳 O 26 – pop. 6 324 – ⊠ *Birmingham (W. Mids.).*
London 109 – Birmingham 8 – Coventry 11.

🏨 **Swan,** High St., B46 3BL, *℘ (01675) 464107, Fax (01675) 467493 – ⊡ ☎ ❷ – 🕍 60. ⊕❾ Æ*
⊕ VISA JCB. ⅏
Meals (closed Saturday dinner) 13.95 **st.** and a la carte – ⊡ 6.00 – **32 rm** 54.00 **st.**

🏨 **Coleshill,** 152 High St., B46 3BG, *℘ (01675) 465527, Fax (01675) 464013 – ⊡ ☎ ❷ –*
🕍 150. ⊕❾ Æ ⊕ VISA JCB. ⅏
Meals (grill rest.) 13.50 **st.** and a la carte ⍧ 4.95 – **23 rm** ⊡ 75.00/85.00 **st.** – SB.

COLNE *Lancs.* 402 N 22 – *pop. 18 776.*

🏌 *Law Farm, Skipton Old Rd ℘ (01282) 863391 –* 🏌 *Ghyll Brow, Barnoldswick ℘ (01282) 842466.*

London 234 – Manchester 29 – Preston 26.

🏠 **Higher Slipper Hill Farm** ⌂, Foulridge, BB8 7LY, NW : 3 ¾ m. by A 56 and B 6251 on Barrowford rd ℘ (01282) 863602, ≤, 🗚 – 🖕 rm, 🆅 ☎ ℗, 🅾 🆎 🆅🆂🅰. ⌘
closed 1 week Christmas-New Year – **Meals** *(closed Friday to Sunday)* (residents only) (dinner only) a la carte 11.95/18.50 **s.** ⌀ 5.95 – **9 rm** ⌯ 36.00/50.00 **s.**

@ ATS North Valley Road ℘ (01282) 870645

COLN ST. ALDWYNS *Glos.* – *pop. 260* – ✉ *Cirencester.*
London 101 – Bristol 53 – Gloucester 20 – Swindon 15.

🏠 **New Inn**, GL7 5AN, ℘ (01285) 750651, *Fax* (01285) 750657, « *16C coaching inn* » – 🖕 rest, 🆅 ☎ ℗, 🅾 🆎 🆅🆂🅰 🅹🅲🅱. ⌘
Meals (lunch in bar Monday to Saturday) 22.50 **t.** and a la carte 14.15/22.50 **t.** ⌀ 10.25 – **14 rm** ⌯ 59.00/104.00 **t.** – SB.

COLSTERWORTH *Lincs.* 402 404 S 25 – *pop. 1 452.*
London 105 – Grantham 8 – Leicester 29 – Nottingham 32 – Peterborough 14.

🏠 **Travelodge** without rest., Granada Service Area, NG33 5JR, at A 151/A 1 (southbound carriageway) ℘ (01476) 861077, *Fax* (01476) 861078, Reservations (Freephone) 0800 850950 – 🖕 rm 🆅 ☎ ℗ – ⌀ 30. 🅾 🆎 🅾 🆅🆂🅰 🅹🅲🅱. ⌘
31 rm 39.95 **t.**

🏠 **Travelodge**, NG33 5JJ, E : ½ m. by B 6403 on A 1 (southbound carriageway) ℘ (01476) 861181, *Fax* (01476) 861181, Reservations (Freephone) 0800 850950 – 🖕 rm, 🆅 ⌀ ℗, 🅾 🆎 🅾 🆅🆂🅰 🅹🅲🅱. ⌘
Meals (grill rest.) – **32 rm** 42.95 **t.**

🏠 **Travelodge**, New Fox, South Witham, NG33 5LN, S : 3 m. by B 6403 on A 1 (northbound carriageway) ℘ (01572) 767586, *Fax* (01572) 767586, Reservations (Freephone) 0800 850950 – 🖕 rm, 🆅 ⌀ ℗, 🅾 🆎 🅾 🆅🆂🅰 🅹🅲🅱. ⌘
Meals (grill rest.) – **32 rm** 39.95 **t.**

COLSTON BASSETT *Notts.* 402 404 R 25 – *pop. 239* – ✉ *Nottingham*
London 129 – Lincoln 40 – Nottingham 15 – Sheffield 51.

🍴 **Martins Arms** with rm, School Lane, NG12 3FD, ℘ (01949) 81361, *Fax* (01949) 81361, 🗚, 🗚 – ℗, 🅾 🆅🆂🅰. ⌘
closed 25 December – **Meals** *(closed Sunday dinner)* 16.95 **t.** (lunch) and a la carte 20.85/35.85 **t.** ⌀ 7.50 – **2 rm** ⌯ 35.00/65.00 **t.**

COLTISHALL *Norfolk* 404 Y 25 *Great Britain G.* – *pop. 1 992* – ✉ *Norwich.*
Env. : The Broads★.
London 133 – Norwich 8.

🏨 **Norfolk Mead** ⌂, Church Loke, NR12 7DN, ℘ (01603) 737531, *Fax* (01603) 737521, ⌇, ⌇, 🗚 – 🖕 🆅 ☎ ℗, 🅾 🆎 🆅🆂🅰
Meals (light lunch) 12.95/17.95 **t.** and a la carte ⌀ 6.95 – **9 rm** ⌯ 65.00/99.00 **t.** – SB.

COLWALL *Herefordshire* – see *Great Malvern.*

COLYFORD *Devon Great Britain G.* – ✉ *Colyton.*
Env. : Colyton★ (Church★), N : 1 m. on B 3161 – Axmouth (≤★), S : 1 m. by A 3052 and B 3172.
London 168 – Exeter 21 – Taunton 30 – Torquay 46 – Yeovil 32.

🏠 **Swallows Eaves**, EX13 6QJ, ℘ (01297) 553184, *Fax* (01297) 553574, 🗚 – 🖕 🆅 ℗, 🅾 🆅🆂🅰. ⌘
Meals (dinner only) 19.00 **st.** ⌀ 7.45 – **8 rm** ⌯ 38.00/76.00 **st.** – SB.

COMBE *Devon* – see *Salcombe.*

COMPTON ABBAS *Dorset* – see *Shaftesbury.*

CONGLETON *Ches.* [402] [403] [404] N 24 *Great Britain G.* – *pop. 24 897.*

Env. : *Little Moreton Hall★★* **AC**, *SW : 3 m. by A 34.*

⛳ *Biddulph Rd* ☎ *(01260) 273540.*

ℹ *Town Hall, High St., CW12 1BN* ☎ *(01260) 271095.*

London 183 – Liverpool 50 – Manchester 25 – Sheffield 46 – Stoke-on-Trent 13.

🏠 **Sandhole Farm** 🐦 without rest., Hulme Walfield, CW12 2JH, N : 2 ¼ m. on A 34 ☎ (01260) 224419, *Fax (01260) 224766*, 🌳, park – 🚭 [TV] ☎ [P]. [MC] [AE] [D] [VISA]. 🐕
18 rm ☕ 37.00/47.00 **st.**

ATS Brookside ☎ (01260) 273720

CONISTON *Cumbria* [402] K 20 *Great Britain G.* – *pop. 1 304.*

Env. : *Coniston Water★* – *Brantwood★* **AC**, *SE : 2 m. on east side of Coniston Water.*

Exc. : *Hard Knott Pass★★, Wrynose Pass★★, NW : 10 m. by A 593 and minor road.*

ℹ *Ruskin Av., LA21 8EH* ☎ *(015394) 41533 (summer only).*

London 285 – Carlisle 55 – Kendal 22 – Lancaster 42.

🏨 **Coniston Lodge,** Station Rd, LA21 8HH, ☎ (015394) 41201, *Fax (015394) 41201* – 🚭 [TV] ☎ [P]. [MC] [AE] [VISA]. 🐕
closed 23 to 28 December – **Meals** *(closed Sunday and Monday)* (dinner only) 18.50 **st.** 🍷 7.25 – **6 rm** ☕ 44.00/74.00 **t.**

at Water Yeat *S : 6½ m. by A 593 on A 5084* – ✉ *Ulverston.*

🏠 **Water Yeat,** LA12 8DJ, ☎ (01229) 885306, *Fax (01229) 885306*, 🌳 – 🚭 [P]. 🐕
closed mid December-mid February and 1 week July – **Meals** (by arrangement) 17.00 **st.** 🍷 8.50 – **5 rm** ☕ 36.00/56.00 **st.** – SB.

at Blawith *S : 7¼ m. by A 593 on A 5084* – ✉ *Ulverston.*

🏠 **Appletree Holme** 🐦, LA12 8EL, W : 1 m. taking unmarked road opposite church and then right hand fork ☎ (01229) 885618, ⩽, 🌳 – 🚭 [TV] [P]. [MC] [VISA]. 🐕
Meals 22.50 – **4 rm** ☕ (dinner included) 65.50/131.00 **st.** – SB.

at Torver *SW : 2¼ m. on A 593* – ✉ *Coniston.*

🏨 **Wheelgate Country House** without rest., Little Arrow, LA21 8AU, NE : ¾ m. on A 593 ☎ (015394) 41418, *Fax (015394) 41114*, « Part 17C farmhouse », 🌳 – 🚭 [TV] [P]. [MC] [VISA]. 🐕
March-November – **5 rm** ☕ 30.00/60.00 **st.**

🏨 **Old Rectory** 🐦, LA21 8AX, NE : ¼ m. by A 593 ☎ (015394) 41353, *Fax (015394) 41156*, ⩽, 🌳 – 🚭 [TV] [P]. [MC] [VISA] [JCB]
Meals (residents only) (dinner only) 16.50 **t.** 🍷 4.95 – **7 rm** ☕ 30.00/60.00 **t.**, 1 suite – SB.

🏠 **Arrowfield Country** without rest., Little Arrow, LA21 8AU, NE : ¾ m. on A 593 ☎ (015394) 41741, ⩽, 🌳 – 🚭 [TV] [P]. 🐕
closed December and January – **5 rm** ☕ 23.00/46.00 **st.**

CONSTANTINE *Cornwall* [403] E 33 – ✉ *Falmouth.*

Env. : *Mawgan-in-Meneage (Church★), S : 3 m. by minor roads.*

London 303 – Falmouth 15 – Penzance 25 – Truro 24.

🍴 **Trengilly Wartha** with rm, Nancenoy, TR11 5RP, S : 1 ½ m. by Fore St. off Port Navas rd ☎ (01326) 340332, *Fax (01326) 340332*, 🌳 – [TV] ☎ [P]. [MC] [AE] [D] [VISA] [JCB]
Meals *(closed 25 December)* (bar lunch)/dinner 21.50 **st.** 🍷 6.10 – **6 rm** ☕ 42.00/62.00 **st.** – SB.

CONSTANTINE BAY *Cornwall* [403] E 32 – *see Padstow.*

COOKHAM *Windsor & Maidenhead* [404] R 29 *Great Britain G.* – *pop. 6 096* – ✉ *Maidenhead.*

See : *Stanley Spencer Gallery★* **AC**.

London 32 – High Wycombe 7 – Reading 16.

🍴🍴 **Alfonso's,** 19 Station Hill Par., SL6 9BR, ☎ (01628) 525775 – [MC] [AE] [D] [VISA]
closed Saturday lunch, Sunday, 2 weeks August and Bank Holidays – **Meals** 12.50 **t.** (lunch) and a la carte 19.50/35.00 **t.** 🍷 8.00.

COPDOCK *Suffolk* [404] X 27 – *see Ipswich.*

COPTHORNE *W. Sussex* [404] T 30 – *see Crawley.*

CORBIERE Jersey (Channel Islands) 403 P 33 and 230 ⑩ ⑪ – see Channel Islands.

CORBRIDGE Northd. 401 402 N 19 Great Britain G. – pop. 2 719.

Env. : Hadrian's Wall★★, N : 3 m. by A 68 – Corstopitum★ AC, NW : ½ m.

🗗 Hill St., NE45 5AA 𝒫 (01434) 632815 (summer only).

London 300 – Hexham 3 – Newcastle upon Tyne 18.

🏠 **Angel Inn**, Main St., NE45 5LA, 𝒫 (01434) 632119, Fax (01434) 632119, « 18C former posting inn » – ✦ rest, ⊡ ☎ 🅿, ⑩ 쪼 ① 𝘝𝘐𝘚𝘈, ⅏
closed 25 December and 1 January – Meals 15.95 t. and a la carte ⅄ 4.20 – 5 rm ⊇ 42.00/64.00 t.

🏠 **Riverside** without rest., Main St., NE45 5LE, 𝒫 (01434) 632942, Fax (01434) 633883 – ⊡
☎ 🅿, ⑩ 쪼 𝘝𝘐𝘚𝘈 𝘑𝘊𝘉
closed 2 weeks November and Christmas-New Year – 10 rm ⊇ 25.00/50.00 st.

🏠 **Lion of Corbridge**, Bridge End, NE45 5AX, 𝒫 (01434) 632504, Fax (01434) 632571 –
✦ rest, ⊡ ☎ 🕭 🅿, ⑩ 쪼 ① 𝘝𝘐𝘚𝘈 𝘑𝘊𝘉, ⅏
closed 25 December and 1 January – Meals a la carte 9.40/19.45 t. ⅄ 4.95 – 14 rm ⊇ 45.00/68.00 t. – SB.

XXX **Ramblers Country House**, Farnley, NE45 5RN, S : 1 m. on Riding Mill Rd
𝒫 (01434) 632424, Fax (01434) 633656 – 🅿, ⑩ 쪼 ① 𝘝𝘐𝘚𝘈
closed Sunday dinner, Monday, 25 December and 1 January – Meals (dinner only and Sunday lunch)/dinner 14.95 t. and a la carte ⅄ 4.15.

XX **Valley**, The Old Station House, Station Rd, NE45 5AY, S : ½ m. by Riding Mill Rd
𝒫 (01434) 633434, Fax (01434) 633923 – ⑩ 쪼 ① 𝘝𝘐𝘚𝘈
closed Sunday – Meals - Indian - (dinner only) a la carte 13.65/23.45 t.

CORBY Northants. 404 R 26 Great Britain G. – pop. 49 053.

Env. : Boughton House★★ AC, S : 5 ½ m. by A 6116 and A 43.

🏌 Stamford Rd, Weldon 𝒫 (01536) 260756.

🗗 Civic Centre, George St., NN17 1QB 𝒫 (01536) 407507.

London 100 – Leicester 26 – Northampton 22 – Peterborough 24.

🏨 **Stakis Corby**, Geddington Rd, NN18 8ET, E : 2 ½ m. on A 6116 𝒫 (01536) 401020, Fax (01536) 400767, ℉₆, ≘s, ⊠ – 🛗, ✦ rm, 🍽 rest, ⊡ ☎ 🕭 🅿 – 🔬 190. ⑩ 쪼 ① 𝘝𝘐𝘚𝘈 𝘑𝘊𝘉
Meals (carving lunch Monday to Friday) (bar lunch Saturday) (live music and dancing Saturday evening) 16.50 and a la carte ⅄ 7.00 – ⊇ 9.50 – 101 rm 85.00/95.00 t., 2 suites – SB.

🏨 **Rockingham Forest**, Rockingham Rd, NN17 1AE, N : 2 ½ m. on A 6116
𝒫 (01536) 401348, Fax (01536) 266383 – ✦ rm, ⊡ ☎ 🅿 – 🔬 400. ⑩ 쪼 ① 𝘝𝘐𝘚𝘈 𝘑𝘊𝘉
Meals (bar lunch Monday to Saturday)/dinner a la carte 15.45/22.95 t. ⅄ 5.75 – ⊇ 8.50 –
70 rm 60.00/85.00 st. – SB.

🅖 ATS St. James Rd 𝒫 (01536) 269519

CORFE CASTLE Dorset 403 404 N 32 The West Country G. – pop. 1 335 – ✉ Wareham.

See : Castle★ (≤★★) AC.

London 129 – Bournemouth 18 – Weymouth 23.

🏨 **Mortons House**, 45 East St., BH20 5EE, 𝒫 (01929) 480988, Fax (01929) 480820, ≤, « Elizabethan manor », � – ✦ rest, ⊡ ☎ 🅿, ⑩ 쪼 ① 𝘝𝘐𝘚𝘈
Meals 15.50/20.00 t. and dinner a la carte ⅄ 5.50 – 16 rm ⊇ 65.00/80.00 t., 1 suite – SB.

CORNHILL-ON-TWEED Northd. 401 402 N 17 Scotland G. – pop. 317.

Env. : Ladykirk (Kirk o'Steil★), NE : 6 m. by A 698 and B 6470.

London 345 – Edinburgh 49 – Newcastle upon Tyne 59.

🏨 **Tillmouth Park** ♨, TD12 4UU, NE : 2 ½ m. on A 698 𝒫 (01890) 882255, Fax (01890) 882540, ≤, « 19C country house », 🐟, 🌳, park – ⊡ ☎ 🅿, ⑩ 쪼 ① 𝘝𝘐𝘚𝘈
closed 26 December – Meals 8.50/25.00 t. and a la carte ⅄ 6.25 – 14 rm ⊇ 80.00/150.00 t. – SB.

🏠 **Coach House**, Crookham, TD12 4TD, E : 4 m. on A 697 𝒫 (01890) 820293, Fax (01890) 820284, 🌳 – ✦ rest, ⊡ 🕭 🅿, ⑩ 𝘝𝘐𝘚𝘈, ⅏
Easter-October – Meals (by arrangement) 16.50 t. ⅄ 3.95 – 9 rm ⊇ 23.00/72.00 t.

CORSE LAWN Worcestershire – see Tewkesbury (Glos.).

COSGROVE Northants. 404 R 27 – see Stony Stratford.

COSHAM Portsmouth 403 404 Q 31 – see Portsmouth and Southsea.

COTHILL Oxon. – see Abingdon.

COVENEY Cambs. – see Ely.

COVENTRY W. Mids. 403 404 P 26 Great Britain G. – pop. 299 316.
See : City★ - Cathedral★★★ AC AV – Old Cathedral★ AV A – Museum of British Road Transport★ AC AV M1.
Windmill Village, Birmingham Rd, Allesley ℘ (01203) 404041 – Sphinx, Sphinx Drive ℘ (01203) 451361.
🛈 Bayley Lane, CV1 5RN ℘ (01203) 832303/832304.
London 100 – Birmingham 18 – Bristol 96 – Nottingham 52.

Plans on following pages

De Vere, Cathedral Sq., CV1 5RP, ℘ (01203) 633733, Fax (01203) 225299 – ▮, rm, rest, 📺 ☎ 🅿 – 400. 🟦 AE ⓪ VISA — AV n
Meals (closed Saturday lunch) 16.50 st. (dinner) and a la carte 20.25/27.25 st. ▯ 5.25 – 170 rm ⊇ 105.00/115.00 st., 10 suites – SB.

Brooklands Grange, Holyhead Rd, CV5 8HX, NW : 2 ½ m. on A 4114 ℘ (01203) 601601, Fax (01203) 601277, ☞ – 📺 ☎ 🅿. 🟦 AE VISA. ⸙ — AY e
Meals (closed Saturday lunch) 17.95 st. and a la carte ▯ 6.25 – 30 rm ⊇ 85.00/105.00 st.

Leofric, Broadgate, CV1 1LZ, ℘ (01203) 221371, Fax (01203) 551352 – ▮, rm, rest, 📺 ☎ 🅿 – 600. 🟦 AE ⓪ VISA — AV r
Meals (bar lunch Sunday) 9.95/14.50 st. and a la carte ▯ 5.95 – ⊇ 7.95 – 89 rm 86.00/110.00 st., 5 suites – SB.

Travel Inn, Rugby Rd, Binley Woods, CV3 2TA, at junction of A 46 with A 428 ℘ (01203) 636585, Fax (01203) 431178 – rm, 📺 �& 🅿. 🟦 AE ⓪ VISA. ⸙ — BZ n
Meals (grill rest.) – 50 rm 36.50 t.

Ashbourne without rest., 33 St Patricks Rd, CV1 2LP, ℘ (01203) 229518 – 📺. ⸙ — AV a
closed 1 week Christmas – 5 rm ⊇ 20.00/38.00 t.

Crest without rest., 39 Friars Rd, CV1 2LJ, ℘ (01203) 227822, Fax (01203) 227244 – 📺. ⸙ — AV e
closed 25 and 26 December – 4 rm ⊇ 23.00/45.00 s.

at Longford N : 4 m. on B 4113 – ✉ Coventry.

Novotel, Wilsons Lane, CV6 6HL, ℘ (01203) 365000, Fax (01203) 362422, ⚊, ☞ – ▮, rm, rest, 📺 ☎ �& 🅿 – 200. 🟦 AE ⓪ VISA — BV v
Meals 12.50/14.50 st. and a la carte ▯ 6.00 – ⊇ 8.00 – 98 rm 55.00 st.

at Walsgrave NE : 3 m. on A 4600 – ✉ Coventry.

Hilton National, Paradise Way, The Triangle, CV2 2ST, NE : 1 m. by A 4600 at junction 2 of M 6 ℘ (01203) 603000, Fax (01203) 603011, 🇮6, ☎s, ⚊ – ▮, rm, rest, 📺 ☎ �& 🅿 – 600. 🟦 AE ⓪ VISA JCB — BX c
Meals 12.50/17.50 st. and a la carte – ⊇ 10.95 – 169 rm 115.00 st., 3 suites – SB.

at Ansty (Warks.) NE : 5 ¾ m. by A 4600 – BY – on B 4065 – ✉ Coventry.

Ansty Hall, CV7 9HZ, ℘ (01203) 612222, Fax (01203) 602155, « Part 17C mansion », ☞ – rm 📺 ☎ 🅿 – 80. 🟦 AE ⓪ VISA. ⸙
Meals (buffet lunch) 13.95/20.95 st. and dinner a la carte ▯ 6.50 – ⊇ 8.50 – 29 rm 83.00/115.00 st. – SB.

at Binley E : 3½ m. on A 428 – BY – ✉ Coventry.

Coombe Abbey ⸙, Brinklow Rd, CV3 2AB, E : 2 m. on B 4027 ℘ (01203) 450450, Fax (01203) 635401, ≤, « Former Cistercian abbey of 12C origins with formal gardens by Capability Brown », ⸙, park – ▮, rm, 📺 ☎ �& 🅿 – 120. 🟦 AE ⓪ VISA JCB. ⸙
Meals (bar lunch Monday to Saturday)/dinner 24.50 st. and a la carte ▯ 7.50 – ⊇ 10.50 – 61 rm 120.00/130.00 st., 1 suite – SB.

at Brandon (Warks.) E : 6 m. on A 428 – BZ – ✉ Coventry.

Brandon Hall ⸙, Main St., CV8 3FW, ℘ (01203) 542571, Fax (01203) 544909, ☞, park, squash – rm 📺 ☎ 🅿 – 100. 🟦 AE ⓪ VISA JCB. ⸙
Meals (bar lunch Saturday) 10.95/18.95 st. and dinner a la carte ▯ 8.00 – ⊇ 9.75 – 60 rm 85.00/110.00 t. – SB.

209

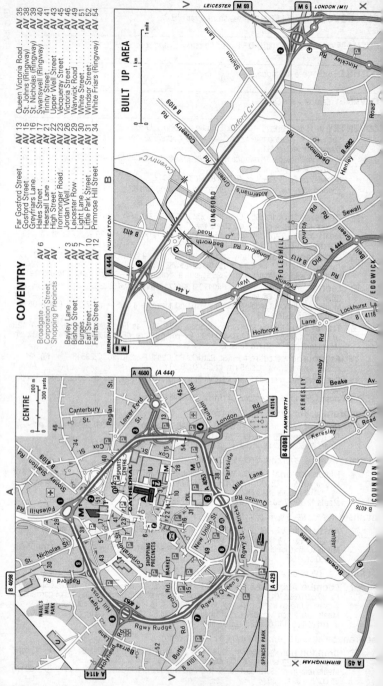

COVENTRY

Broadgate .... AV 6
Corporation Street ...... AV
Shopping Precincts ...... AV

Bayley Lane .... AV 3
Bishop Street .... AV 5
Burges .... AV 7
Earl Street .... AV 10
Fairfax Street .... AV 12

Far Gosford Street ...... AV 13
Gosford Street .... AV 15
Greyfriars Lane .... AV 16
Hales Street .... AV 17
Hearsall Lane .... AV 21
High Street .... AV 22
Ironmonger Road .... AV 23
Jordan Well .... AV 26
Leicester Row .... AV 29
Light Lane .... AV 30
Little Park Street .... AV 31
Primrose Hill Street ..... AV 34

Queen Victoria Road .... AV 35
St. Johns (Ringway) ..... AV 38
St. Nicholas (Ringway) ... AV 39
Swanswell (Ringway) .... AV 40
Trinity Street .... AV 41
Upper Well Street .... AV 43
Vecqueray Street .... AV 45
Victoria Street .... AV 46
Warwick Road .... AV 49
White Street .... AV 51
Windsor Street .... AV 52
White Friars (Ringway) ... AV 54

BUILT UP AREA

CENTRE

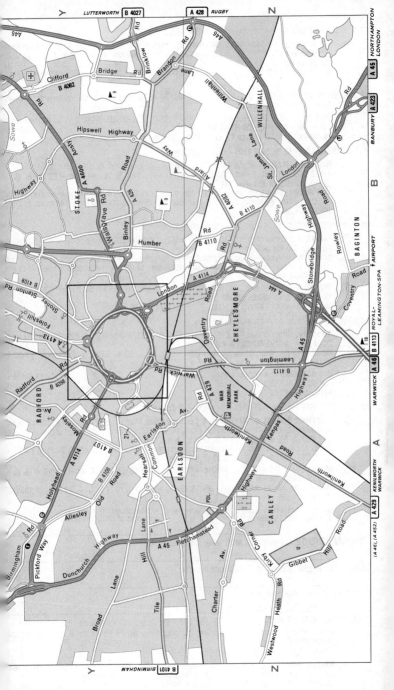

at Ryton on Dunsmore *SE : 4 ¾ m. by A 45 – ✉ Coventry.*

Courtyard by Marriott Coventry, London Rd, CV8 3DY, on A 45 (northbound carriageway) ℘ (01203) 301585, *Fax (01203) 301610* – ⇔ rm, ▤ rest, TV ☎ & P – 🏛 250. MC AE D VISA. ✻ BZ u
Meals (bar lunch Saturday) a la carte 15.05/19.70 **t.** 🍷 6.95 – ☕ 8.95 – **47 rm** 75.00 **t.**, 2 suites – SB.

at Baginton *(Warks.) S : 3 m. by A 4114 and A 444 off A 45 (off westbound carriageway and Howes Lane turning) – ✉ Coventry.*

Old Mill, Mill Hill, CV8 3AH, ℘ (01203) 302241, *Fax (01203) 307070,* « Converted corn mill », ⛱ – TV ☎ P. MC AE D VISA. ✻ BZ e
Meals (grill rest.) a la carte 12.50/17.70 **t.** – **20 rm** ☕ 70.00/80.00 **t.** – SB.

at Berkswell *W : 6 ½ m. by B 4101 – AY – ✉ Coventry.*

Nailcote Hall, Nailcote Lane, CV7 7DE, S : 1 ½ m. on B 4101 ℘ (01203) 466174, *Fax (01203) 470720,* « Part 17C timbered house », Fø, 🏊, ⛳9, ⛱, 🎾 – TV ☎ & P – 🏛 100. MC AE D VISA JCB. ✻
Oak Room : **Meals** *(closed Saturday lunch and Sunday dinner)* (booking essential) 19.50/28.50 **t.** – ***Rick's :*** **Meals** (booking essential) a la carte 25.00/40.00 **t.** – **38 rm** ☕ 125.00/195.00 **t.** – SB.

at Balsall Common *W : 6 ¾ m. by B 4101 – AY – ✉ Coventry.*

Haigs, 273 Kenilworth Rd, CV7 7EL, on A 452 ℘ (01676) 533004, *Fax (01676) 535132,* ⛱ – TV ☎ P. MC VISA JCB. ✻
closed 26 December-4 January and 2 weeks in summer – ***Poppy's :*** **Meals** *(closed Sunday dinner)* (dinner only and Sunday lunch)/dinner 17.95 **t.** and a la carte 🍷 5.95 – **15 rm** ☕ 52.50/72.50 **t.**

Travel Inn, Kenilworth Rd, CV7 7EX, on A 452 ℘ (01676) 533118, *Fax (01676) 535926* – ⇔ rm, TV & P. MC AE D VISA
Meals (grill rest.) – **42 rm** 36.50 **t.**

at Allesley *NW : 3 m. on A 4114 – ✉ Coventry.*

Allesley, Birmingham Rd, CV5 9GP, ℘ (01203) 403272, *Fax (01203) 405190* – ⬍, ▤ rest, TV ☎ P – 🏛 450. MC AE D VISA. ✻ AY r
Meals *(closed Saturday lunch and Bank Holidays)* 14.50/17.50 **st.** and a la carte 🍷 7.00 – **90 rm** ☕ 102.00/130.00 **st.** – SB.

Brookfields without rest., 134 Butt Lane, CV5 9FF, ℘ (01203) 404866, *Fax (01203) 402022,* ⛱ – P. ✻ AX s
4 rm ☕ 25.00/60.00 **st.**

at Meriden *NW : 6 m. by A 45 on B 4104 – AX – ✉ Coventry.*

Marriott Forest of Arden H. & Country Club, Maxstoke Lane, CV7 7HR, NW : 2 ¾ m. by Maxstoke rd ℘ (01676) 522335, *Fax (01676) 523711,* Fø, ≘s, 🏊, ⛳18, 🎣, park, 🎾 – ⬍ ⇔, ▤ rest, TV ☎ & P – 🏛 400. MC AE D VISA JCB
Meals *(closed Saturday lunch)* 16.50 **t.** (lunch) and dinner a la carte 13.80/21.75 **t.** 🍷 7.25 – ☕ 10.95 – **152 rm** 135.00/145.00 **st.**, 2 suites – SB.

Manor, Main Rd, CV7 7NH, ℘ (01676) 522735, *Fax (01676) 522186,* ⛱ – ⇔ TV ☎ & P – 🏛 275. MC AE D VISA
Meals (bar lunch Saturday) 17.95/18.75 **st.** and a la carte 🍷 6.00 – **74 rm** ☕ 105.00/150.00 **st.** – SB.

ATS Ashmore Lake Way, Willenhall ℘ (01902) 602555/605098
ATS Kingswood Close, off Holbrook Lane, Holbrooks ℘ (01203) 638554

COWAN BRIDGE *Cumbria* 402 M 21 – *see Kirkby Lonsdale.*

COWES *I.O.W.* 403 404 PQ 31 – *see Wight (Isle of).*

COWLEY *Oxon. – see Oxford.*

CRACKINGTON HAVEN *Cornwall* 403 G 31 *The West Country G.* – ✉ *Bude.*

Env. : *Poundstock★ (≤★★, church★, guildhouse★), NE : 5 ½ m. by A 39 – Jacobstow (Church★), E : 3 ½ m.*

London 262 – Bude 11 – Truro 42.

Manor Farm 🐎, EX23 0JW, SE : 1 ¼ m. taking first left onto Church Park Rd then take first right ℘ (01840) 230304, ≤, « Part 11C manor », ⛱, park – ⇔ P. ✻
closed 25 December – **Meals** (communal dining) 15.00 **s.** – **5 rm** ☕ 35.00/70.00 **s.** – SB.

↑ **Trevigue** ♨, EX23 0LQ, SE : 1 ¼ m. on High Cliff rd ℰ (01840) 230418,
Fax (01840) 230418, « 16C farmhouse, working farm » – ⅍ ❄ **P**.
March-October – **Meals** (by arrangement) (communal dining) 18.00 **t**. 🛭 4.25 – **4 rm**
⌂ 52.50/80.00 **t**.

↑ **Treworgie Barton** ♨, St. Gennys, EX23 0NL, E : 2 ¼ m. turning left onto Dizzard rd
approx. ¼ m. after white church and then onto Treworgie rd ℰ (01840) 230233,
Fax (01840) 230233, ≤, « 16C farmhouse », ♨, park – ❄ ⅍ **TV** **P**. ⅍
closed October, December and January and booking essential February, March and November – **Meals** (by arrangement) 15.00 **st**. – **3 rm** ⌂ 40.00/46.00 **st**., 1 suite – SB.

CRANBORNE Dorset **403** **404** O 31 – pop. 667.
🛇, 🛇 Crane Valley, Verwood ℰ (01202) 814088.
London 107 – Bournemouth 21 – Salisbury 18 – Southampton 30.

🏠 **Fleur De Lys** with rm, Wimborne St., BH21 5PP, on B 3078 ℰ (01725) 517282,
Fax (01725) 517631 – **TV** ☎ **P**. **◖◗** **AE** **VISA**. ⅍
Meals (bar lunch)/dinner 12.95 **t**. and a la carte 🛭 4.95 – **8 rm** ⌂ 27.00/65.00 **t**. – SB.

CRANBROOK Kent **404** V 30 Great Britain G. – pop. 3 522.
Env. : Sissinghurst Castle★ AC, NE : 2 ½ m. by A 229 and A 262.
🛈 Vestry Hall, Stone St., TN17 3HA ℰ (01580) 712538 (summer only).
London 53 – Hastings 19 – Maidstone 15.

🏠 **Kennel Holt** ♨, Goudhurst Rd, TN17 2PT, NW : 2 ¼ m. by A 229 on A 262
ℰ (01580) 712032, Fax (01580) 715495, « Gardens » – ⅍ ❄ **P**. **◖◗** **AE** **VISA** **JCB**. ⅍
closed 3 weeks January – **Meals** (closed Sunday dinner to non-residents and Monday)
(lunch by arrangement)/dinner 22.50 **t**. 🛭 6.50 – **9 rm** ⌂ 85.00/150.00 **t**.

🏠 **Hartley Mount**, TN17 3QX, S : ½ m. on A 229 ℰ (01580) 712230, Fax (01580) 715733, ♨,
⅍ – ❄ **TV** ☎ ⇔ **P**. **◖◗** **AE** **VISA** **JCB**. ⅍
Meals (lunch by arrangement) 15.50/17.50 **st**. and a la carte 🛭 6.00 – **6 rm** ⌂ 60.00/
100.00 **st**. – SB.

↑ **Old Cloth Hall** ♨, TN17 3NR, E : 1 m. by Tenterden Rd ℰ (01580) 712220,
Fax (01580) 712220, ≤, « Tudor manor house, gardens », park – ❄ rm, **TV** **P**. ⅍
closed Christmas – **Meals** (by arrangement) 22.00 **st**. – **3 rm** ⌂ 45.00/95.00 **st**.

↑ **Hancocks Farmhouse** ♨, Tilsden Lane, TN17 3PH, E : ¾ m. by Tenterden Rd off
Benenden rd taking first left turn ℰ (01580) 714645, Fax (01580) 714645, ≤, « 16C half
timbered farmhouse », ♨ – ❄ **TV** **P**
closed 24-26 December, 1 week in spring and 1 week in summer – **Meals** (by arrangement)
22.00 **s**. – **3 rm** ⌂ 35.00/70.00 **st**.

✗ **Soho South**, 23 Stone St., TN17 3HF, ℰ (01580) 714666, Fax (01580) 715653 – **◖◗** **VISA**
closed Sunday to Tuesday, 25 December and 1 week in autumn – **Meals** a la carte 17.70/
25.95 **t**. 🛭 8.65.

at Sissinghurst NE : 1 ¾ m. by B 2189 on A 262 – ✉ Cranbrook.

✗ **Rankins**, The Street, TN17 2JH, ℰ (01580) 713964 – **◖◗** **VISA**
closed Sunday dinner, Monday, Tuesday, 1 week May, 1 week September and Bank Holidays –
Meals (dinner only and Sunday lunch)/dinner 26.00 **t**. 🛭 4.80.

CRANTOCK Cornwall **403** E 32 – see Newquay.

CRAVEN ARMS Shrops. **402** **403** L 26 Great Britain G. – pop. 1 892.
Env. : Wenlock Edge★, NE : by B 4368.
London 170 – Birmingham 47 – Hereford 32 – Shrewsbury 21.

↑ **Old Rectory** ♨, Hopesay, SY7 8HD, W : 4 m. by B 4368 ℰ (01588) 660245,
Fax (01588) 660502, ≤, « Part 17C », ♨ – ❄ **TV** **P**. ⅍
closed Christmas and New Year – **Meals** (by arrangement) (communal dining) 18.00 **s**.
🛭 6.00 – **3 rm** ⌂ 32.00/64.00 **s**.

CRAWLEY W. Sussex **404** T 30 – pop. 88 203.
🛇, 🛇 Cottesmore, Buchan Hill, Pease Pottage ℰ (01293) 528256 – 🛇, 🛇 Tilgate Forest,
Titmus Drive, Tilgate ℰ (01293) 530103 – 🛇 Gatwick Manor, London Rd, Lowfield Heath
ℰ (01293) 538587 – 🛇 Pease Pottage, Horsham Rd ℰ (01293) 521706.
London 33 – Brighton 21 – Lewes 23 – Royal Tunbridge Wells 23.

Plan of enlarged Area : see Gatwick

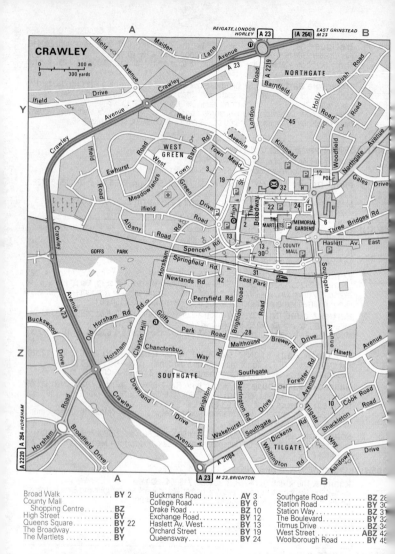

CRAWLEY

REIGATE, LONDON HORLEY **A 23** **(A 264)** EAST GRINSTEAD M 23

NORTHGATE

WEST GREEN

THE MARTLETS

MEMORIAL GARDENS

COUNTY MALL

GOFFS PARK

SOUTHGATE

TILGATE

A 2220 A 264 HORSHAM

A 23 M 23, BRIGHTON

Holiday Inn Gatwick West, Langley Drive, Tushmore Roundabout, RH11 7SX
℘ (01293) 529991, *Fax (01293) 515913*, ⅃᳅, ⇄, 🔲 – 🛗, ⅙ rm, 🔳 📺 ☎ ♿ 🅿 – 🔼 250. **⽊**🅖
ⒶⒺ ⓪ 𝚅𝙸𝚂𝙰 𝙹𝙲𝙱. ❀
BY r
Colonnade : Meals (dinner only and Sunday lunch)/dinner 18.50 **st.** and a la carte ⅃ 7.50 –
La Brasserie : Meals a la carte 11.75/21.20 **st.** ⅃ 7.50 – ☷ 12.50 – **215 rm** 120.00 **st.** –
2 suites – SB.

Europa Gatwick, Balcombe Rd, Maidenbower, RH10 7ZR, E : 2 ½ m. by Haslett Av. and
Worth Rd on B 2036 ℘ (01293) 886666, *Fax (01293) 886781*, ⅃᳅, ⇄, 🔲, ⌇ – 🛗, ⅙ rm, 📺
☎ ♿ 🅿 – 🔼 150. **⽊**🅖 ⒶⒺ ⓪ 𝚅𝙸𝚂𝙰. ❀
on Gatwick town plan Z a
Mediterranee : Meals (dinner only and Sunday lunch)/dinner 13.50 **st.** – ☷ 9.95 – **207 rm**
75.00/79.00 **st.**, 4 suites – SB.

George, High St., RH10 1BS, ℘ (01293) 524215, *Fax (01293) 548565* – ⅙ 📺 ☎ 🅿 –
🔼 50. **⽊**🅖 ⒶⒺ ⓪ 𝚅𝙸𝚂𝙰
BY c
Meals (bar lunch Monday to Saturday)/dinner a la carte 14.25/21.75 **t.** ⅃ 8.95 – ☷ 8.95 –
80 rm 65.00 **st.**

214

🏛 **Goffs Park - Premier Lodge**, Goffs Park Rd, Southgate, RH11 8AX, ℘ (01293) 535447, *Fax* (01293) 542050, 🌼 – ✺ rm, ≣ rest, 🔟 ☎ ❷ – 益 150. ◍◐ AE ◐ VISA. ⋘   **AZ a**
Meals (grill rest.) 6.55/12.95 **t.** and a la carte – 🍷 4.95 – **57 rm** 44.25/65.00 **st.**

at Copthorne NE : 4½ m. on A 264 – BY.

🏛 **Copthorne London Gatwick**, Copthorne Way, RH10 3PG, ℘ (01342) 714971, *Fax* (01342) 717375, ƒ₅, ⩵s, ⊠, 🌼, park, ⋘, squash – ✺ rm, 🔟 ☎ ❷ – 益 110. ◍◐ AE
◐ VISA JCB.
Lion D'Or : *Meals* (closed Saturday lunch, Sunday and Bank Holidays) 18.95/22.95 **t.** and a la carte 🍷 9.50 – **Brasserie :** *Meals* (carving lunch) 16.95 **t.** and dinner a la carte 🍷 9.50 – 🍷 12.50 – **227 rm** 105.00/195.00 **st.**

🏛 **Copthorne Effingham Park**, West Park Rd, RH10 3EU, on B 2028 ℘ (01342) 714994, *Fax* (01342) 716039, ⩽, ƒ₅, ⩵s, ⊠, 🏌, 🌼, park – 🔋, ✺ rm, 🔟 ☎ & ❷ – 益 600. ◍◐ AE ◐
VISA.
Terrace : *Meals* (bar lunch)/dinner a la carte 12.40/26.25 **st.** 🍷 6.50 – 🍷 11.95 – **120 rm** 115.00/145.00 **st.**, 2 suites.

at Three Bridges E : 1 m. on Haslett Avenue East – BY – ✉ Crawley.

🏛 Jarvis International H. Gatwick, Tinsley Lane South, RH11 1NP, N : ½ m. by Hazelwick Av.
℘ (01293) 561186, *Fax* (01293) 561169, ƒ₅, ⩵s, ⊠ – 🔋, ✺ rm, ≣ 🔟 ☎ & ❷ – 益 210
151 rm.   on Gatwick town plan **Y n**

◎ ATS Reynolds Rd, West Green ℘ (01293) 533151/2

Benutzen Sie die Grünen Michelin-Reiseführer.
wenn Sie eine Stadt oder Region kennenlernen wollen.

CREWE Ches. 402 403 404 M 24 – pop. 63 351.
🏌 Queen's Park, Queen's Park Drive ℘ (01270) 666724 – 🏌 Fields Rd, Haslington ℘ (01270) 584227.
London 174 – Chester 24 – Liverpool 49 – Manchester 36 – Stoke-on-Trent 15.

🏠 **Travel Inn**, Coppenhall Lane, Woolstanwood, CW2 8SD, W : 2 m. on A 532 at junction with A 530 ℘ (01270) 251126, *Fax* (01270) 256316 – ✺ 🔟 & ❷. ◍◐ AE ◐ VISA. ⋘
Meals (grill rest.) – **41 rm** 36.50 **t.**

🏠 **Travelodge**, Alsager Rd, Barthomley, CW2 5PT, SE : 5½ m. by A 5020 on A 500 at junction with M 6 ℘ (01270) 883157, *Fax* (01270) 883157, Reservations (Freephone) 0800 850950 – ✺ rm, 🔟 & ❷. ◍◐ AE ◐ VISA JCB. ⋘
Meals (grill rest.) – **42 rm** 44.95 **t.**

◎ ATS Gresty Rd ℘ (01270) 256285

CREWKERNE Somerset 403 L 31 *The West Country G.* – pop. 7 142.
See : Church★.
Env. : Forde Abbey★ *AC, SW :* 8 m. by B 3165 and B 3162 – Clapton Court Gardens★ *AC, S :* 3 ½ m. by B 3165.
Exc. : Montacute House★★ *AC, NE :* 7 m. by A 30 – Parnham House★★ *AC, SE :* 7 ½ m. by A 356 and A 3066.
🏌 Windwhistle G. & C.C., Cricket St. Thomas, Chard ℘ (01460) 30231.
London 145 – Exeter 38 – Southampton 81 – Taunton 20.

🏠 **Broadview Gardens**, 43 East St., TA18 7AG, ℘ (01460) 73424, *Fax* (01460) 73424, 🌼 –
✺ 🔟 ❷. ◍◐ VISA. ⋘
Meals (by arrangement) (communal dining) 14.00 – **3 rm** 🍷 25.00/56.00 **st.** – SB.

at Middle Chinnock NE : 3 ¾ m. by A 30 off West Chinnock rd – ✉ Crewkerne.

🏠 **Chinnock House** ⌂, TA18 7PN, ℘ (01935) 881229, « Georgian house », 🍏, 🌼 – ❷. ⋘
closed 25 December and 2 weeks spring – Meals (by arrangement) (communal dining) 22.00 **s.** – **3 rm** 🍷 35.00/55.00 **s.**

at North Perrot E : 3½ m. by A 30 on A 3066 – ✉ Crewkerne.

🏠 **Manor Arms** with rm, TA18 7SG, ℘ (01460) 72901, *Fax* (01460) 72901, « 16C inn » – ✺
🔟 ❷ – 益 25. ◍◐ AE ◐ VISA JCB. ⋘
Meals (in bar Sunday dinner and Monday) a la carte 9.00/16.00 **st.** – **5 rm** 🍷 38.00/48.00 **st.** – SB.

CRICK Northants. 403 404 Q 26 – see Rugby.

CRICKLADE *Wilts* 403 404 O 29 – *pop. 3 808.*

      🛆 *Cricklade Hotel, Common Hill ℰ (01793) 750751.*
      London 90 – Bristol 45 – Gloucester 27 – Oxford 34 – Swindon 6.

🏰 **Cricklade H. & Country Club,** Common Hill, SN6 6HA, SW : 1 m. on B 4040
    ℰ *(01793) 750751, Fax (01793) 751767,* ≼, *Ⅰ₆,* 🔲*,* 🛆*, park,* ❦ *–* 📺 ☎ 🅿 *–* 🔬 120. 🆗 🆎
    VISA. 🛠
    Meals 15.50/20.00 **t.** and a la carte ⓙ 6.50 **– 46 rm** ⊇ 78.00/115.00 **t.** – SB.

CROCKERTON *Wilts. – see Warminster.*

CROFT-ON-TEES *Durham* 402 P 20 – *see Darlington.*

CROMER *Norfolk* 404 X 25 – *pop. 7 267.*

      🛆 *Royal Cromer, Overstrand Rd ℰ (01263) 512884.*
      🖪 *Bus Station, Prince of Wales Rd, NR27 9HS ℰ (01263) 512497.*
      London 132 – Norwich 23.

⌂ **Morden House,** 20 Cliff Av., NR27 0AN, ℰ *(01263) 513396,* 🚗 *–* ⚡ 📺 🅿. ⓞ
    Meals 12.00 ⓙ 5.00 **– 6 rm** ⊇ 22.50/45.00 – SB.

⌂ **Birch House,** 34 Cabbell Rd, NR27 9HX, ℰ *(01263) 512521 –* ⚡ 📺. 🆗 *VISA.* 🛠
    closed 23 to 30 December – **Meals** (by arrangement) 8.00 **s.** ⓙ 4.50 **– 8 rm** ⊇ 17.00/40.00 **s.**

at Northrepps *SE : 2 ¾ m. by B 1159 and Northrepps rd –* ⊠ *Cromer.*

⌂ **Shrublands Farm,** NR27 0AA, ℰ *(01263) 579297, Fax (01263) 579297,* « Working
    farm », 🚗*, park –* ⚡ 🅿. 🛠
    closed last 2 weeks December – **Meals** (by arrangement) (communal dining) 14.00 **s. – 3 rm**
    ⊇ 24.00/44.00 **s.**

      For the quickest route use the **Michelin Main Road Maps:**

      970 Europe, 974 Poland, 976 Czech Republic-Slovak Republic, 980 Greece,
      984 Germany, 985 Scandinavia-Finland, 986 Great Britain and Ireland,
      987 Germany-Austria-Benelux, 988 Italy, 989 France,
      990 Spain-Portugal.

CRONDALL *Hants.* 404 R 30 – *pop. 6 113.*
      London 56 – Reading 21 – Winchester 30.

❦❦ **Chesa,** Bowling Alley, GU10 5RJ, N : 1 m. ℰ *(01252) 850328, Fax (01252) 850328 –* 🅿. 🆗
    🆎 *VISA* 🇯🇨🇧
    closed Saturday lunch, Sunday dinner, Monday, Tuesday and first 3 weeks January – **Meals**
    (booking essential) (lunch by arrangement)/dinner a la carte 24.50/29.00 ⓙ 6.10.

CRONTON *Mersey.* 402 403 404 L 23 – *see Widnes.*

CROOK *Durham* 401 402 O 19 – *pop. 8 246 –* ⊠ *Bishop Auckland.*
      🛆 *Low Job's Hill ℰ (01388) 762429.*
      London 261 – Carlisle 65 – Middlesbrough 34 – Newcastle upon Tyne 27.

🏠 **Duke of York Inn,** Fir Tree, DL15 8DG, SW : 3 ½ m. by A 689 off A 68 ℰ *(01388) 762848 –*
    📺 ☎ 🅿. 🆗 ⓞ *VISA.* 🛠
    Meals a la carte 14.45/20.70 **t.** ⓙ 4.95 **– 4 rm** ⊇ 50.00/65.00 **t.** – SB.

⌂ **Greenhead Country House** without rest., Fir Tree, DL15 8BL, SW : 3 ½ m. by A 689 of
    A 68 ℰ *(01388) 763143, Fax (01388) 763143,* 🚗 *–* 📺 🅿. 🆗 *VISA.* 🛠
    7 rm ⊇ 40.00/60.00 **s.**

CROSBY *Mersey.* 402 403 K 23 – *see Liverpool.*

CROSBY GARRETT *Cumbria – see Kirkby Stephen.*

CROSTHWAITE *Cumbria* 402 L 21 – *see Kendal.*

CROWBOROUGH E. Sussex 404 U 30 – pop. 19 563.
  London 45 – Brighton 25 – Maidstone 26.

🏨 **Winston Manor**, Beacon Rd, TN6 1AD, on a A 26 ℰ (01892) 652772, Fax (01892) 665537, ≤s, ≋s, 🏊, 🎾 – ⧈ 🗹 ☎ 🄿 – 🔬 300. 🐵 🆎 ① 𝘝𝘐𝘚𝘈. ⫝̸
  closed 25 to 30 December – **Meals** (bar lunch Monday to Saturday)/dinner 19.50 t. ⋔ 5.45 – 50 rm � 80.00/100.00 t. – SB.

⌂ **Lye Green House** ⮥ without rest., Lye Green, TN6 1UU, N : 2 ¼ m. on Groombridge rd ℰ (01892) 652018, Fax (01892) 652018, « Lutyens house, gardens », ⤏, ☞ – ⥺ 🗹 🄿. ⫝̸
  closed December and January – **3 rm** ⊶ 45.00/55.00.

  ⓜ ATS Church Rd ℰ (01892) 662100

CROWTHORNE Bracknell Forest 404 R 29 – pop. 21 500.
  London 42 – Reading 15.

✗✗ **Beijing**, 103 Old Wokingham Rd, RG45 6LH, NE : ¾ m. by A 3095 ℰ (01344) 778802 – ▤ 🄿. 🐵 🆎 𝘝𝘐𝘚𝘈 𝗝𝗖𝗕
  closed Sunday lunch, 25-26 December, 1 January and Bank Holidays – **Meals** - Chinese - 15.50/18.50 t. and a la carte.

CROXDALE Durham – see Durham.

CROYDE Devon 403 H 30 – ⊠ Braunton.
  London 232 – Barnstaple 10 – Exeter 50 – Taunton 61.

🏨 **Croyde Bay House** ⮥, Moor Lane, Croyde Bay, EX33 1PA, NW : 1 m. by Baggy Point rd ℰ (01271) 890270, ≤ Croyde Bay, ☞ – ⥺ rest, 🗹 🄿. 🐵 🆎 𝘝𝘐𝘚𝘈 𝗝𝗖𝗕
  March-mid November – **Meals** (dinner only) 18.50 t. ⋔ 4.25 – **7 rm** ⊶ (dinner included) 54.00/108.00 t. – SB.

🏨 **Kittiwell House**, St. Mary's Rd, EX33 1PG, ℰ (01271) 890247, Fax (01271) 890469, « 16C thatched Devon longhouse » – ⥺ rm, 🗹 ☎ 🄿. 🐵 🆎 𝘝𝘐𝘚𝘈 𝗝𝗖𝗕
  closed mid January-mid February – **Meals** (dinner only and Sunday lunch)/dinner 18.50 t. and a la carte – **12 rm** ⊶ (dinner included) 64.00/114.00 t. – SB.

⌂ **Whiteleaf** without rest., Hobbs Hill, EX33 1PN, ℰ (01271) 890266, ☞ – 🗹 🄿. 🐵 𝘝𝘐𝘚𝘈 𝗝𝗖𝗕
  4 rm ⊶ 35.00/56.00 s.

CRUDWELL Wilts. 403 404 N 29 – see Malmesbury.

CUCKFIELD W. Sussex 404 T 30 – pop. 2 879.
  London 40 – Brighton 15.

🏨 **Ockenden Manor** ⮥, Ockenden Lane, RH17 5LD, ℰ (01444) 416111, Fax (01444) 415549, « Part 16C manor house », ☞ – ⥺ rest, 🗹 ☎ 🄿 – 🔬 50. 🐵 🆎 ① 𝘝𝘐𝘚𝘈. ⫝̸
  Meals 18.50/29.50 t. and a la carte 30.50/49.00 t. ⋔ 6.50 – ⊶ 5.00 – **20 rm** 90.00/235.00 t., 2 suites – SB.

CULLOMPTON Devon 403 J 31 The West Country G. – pop. 5 676.
  See : Town★ – St. Andrew's Church★.
  Env. : Uffculme (Coldharbour Mill★★ AC) NE : 5 ½ m. by B 3181 and B 3391.
  Exc. : Killerton★★, SW : 6 ½ m. by B 3181 and B 3185.
  ⓫ Padbrook Park ℰ (01884) 38286.
  London 197 – Exeter 15 – Taunton 29.

🏨 **Manor**, 2-4 Fore St., EX15 1JL, ℰ (01884) 32281, Fax (01884) 38344 – 🗹 ☎ 🄿. 🐵 𝘝𝘐𝘚𝘈
  Meals (closed Sunday dinner to non-residents) (bar lunch)/dinner a la carte 15.70/21.15 t. ⋔ 6.50 – **10 rm** ⊶ 43.50/58.50 t. – SB.

CUMNOR Oxon. 403 404 P 28 – see Oxford.

CURDWORTH W. Mids. – see Sutton Coldfield.

DALTON-IN-FURNESS Cumbria 402 K 21 – pop. 7 550.

📍 The Dunnerholme, Duddon Rd, Askham-in-Furness ℰ (01229) 262675.
London 283 – Barrow-in-Furness 3.5 – Kendal 30 – Lancaster 41.

🏠 Clarence House Country, Skelgate, LA15 8BQ, NW : ½ m. on Askam rd
ℰ (01229) 462508, Fax (01229) 467177, ☞ – 📺 ☎ 🅿 – 🔬 40. 🌐 🅰🅴 🆅🅸🆂🅰 🅹🅲🅱. �
closed 25 and 26 December – **Meals** a la carte 13.70/26.65 **t.** – **17 rm** ⊊ 60.00/110.00 **t.** –
SB.

DARESBURY Warrington 402 403 404 M 23 – pop. 1 579 – ⊠ Warrington.
London 197 – Chester 16 – Liverpool 22 – Manchester 25.

🏨 Daresbury Park, Chester Rd, WA4 4BB, on A 56 ℰ (01925) 267331, Fax (01925) 265615,
🛏, ⇌, 🏊, squash – 😤, ⇚ rm, 📺 ☎ 🅿 – 🔬 300. 🌐 🅰🅴 ① 🆅🅸🆂🅰. ✘
The Looking Glass : **Meals** (closed Saturday lunch) (carving rest.) 15.00/18.00 **st.** –
The Terrace : **Meals** (closed Sunday and Monday) (dinner only) 28.00 **st.** and a la carte –
⊊ 8.25 – **140 rm** 110.00/160.00 **st.** – SB.

DARGATE Kent – see Faversham.

DARLINGTON Darlington 402 P 20 – pop. 86 767.

📍 Blackwell Grange, Briar Close ℰ (01325) 464464 – 📍 Stressholme, Snipe Lane ℰ (01325)
461002.
✈ Teesside Airport : ℰ (01325) 332811, E : 6 m. by A 67.
🛈 13 Horsemarket, DL1 5PW ℰ (01325) 388666.
London 251 – Leeds 61 – Middlesbrough 14 – Newcastle upon Tyne 35.

🏨 Blackwell Grange, Blackwell Grange, DL3 8QH, SW : 1 m. on A 167 ℰ (01325) 509955,
Fax (01325) 380899, 🛏, ⇌, 🏊, 📍, ☞ – 😤, ⇚ rm, 📺 ☎ 🅿 – 🔬 300. 🌐 🅰🅴 ① 🆅🅸🆂🅰. ✘
Meals (closed Saturday lunch) 15.95 **st.** (dinner) and a la carte 13.50/22.95 **st.** 🍴 4.00 –
⊊ 9.75 – **99 rm** 85.00/105.00 **st.** – SB.

🏠 Balmoral without rest., 63 Woodland Rd, DL3 7BQ, ℰ (01325) 461908,
Fax (01325) 461908 – ⇚ 📺. ✘
8 rm ⊊ 21.00/42.00.

at Coatham Mundeville N : 4 m. on A 167 – ⊠ Darlington.

🏨 Hall Garth Golf & Country Club, DL1 3LU, E : ¼ m. on Brafferton rd ℰ (01325) 300400,
Fax (01325) 310083, 🛏, ⇌, 🏊, 📍, ☞, ✘ – ⇚ rm, 📺 ☎ 🅿 – 🔬 300. 🌐 🅰🅴 ① 🆅🅸🆂🅰. ✘
Meals 10.95/21.95 **t.** and dinner a la carte 🍴 7.50 – **40 rm** ⊊ 91.00/120.00 **t.**, 1 suite – SB.

at Croft-on-Tees S : 3½ m. on A 167 – ⊠ Darlington.

🏠 Clow Beck House ⅋ without rest., Monk End Farm, DL2 2SW, W : ½ m. by South
Parade ℰ (01325) 721075, Fax (01325) 720419, ≤, « Working farm », 🔫, ☞, park – 📺 ☎
🔬 🅿. 🌐 🅰🅴 🆅🅸🆂🅰. ✘
10 rm ⊊ 35.00/50.00 **t.**

at Headlam NW : 6 m. by A 67 – ⊠ Gainford.

🏨 Headlam Hall ⅋, DL2 3HA, ℰ (01325) 730238, Fax (01325) 730790, ≤, « Part Jacobean
and part Georgian manor house », ⇌, 🏊, ☞, park, ✘ – ⇚ rest, 📺 ☎ 🅿 – 🔬 150. 🌐
🅰🅴 ① 🆅🅸🆂🅰. ✘
closed 24 to 26 December – **Meals** 12.00/17.50 **st.** and dinner a la carte 🍴 3.60 – **24 rm**
⊊ 60.00/90.00 **st.**, 2 suites – SB.

at Heighington NW : 6 m. by A 68 off A 6072 – ⊠ Darlington.

🏠 Eldon House without rest., East Green, DL5 6PP, ℰ (01325) 312270, ☞, ✘ – 🅿
3 rm ⊊ 30.00/50.00 **s.**

at Redworth NW : 7 m. by A 68 on A 6072 – ⊠ Bishop Auckland.

🏨 Redworth Hall H. & Country Club ⅋, DL5 6NL, on A 6072 ℰ (01388) 772442,
Fax (01388) 775112, « Part 18C and 19C manor house of Elizabethan origins », 🛏, ⇌, 🏊,
☞, park, ✘, squash – 😤, ⇚ rm, 🍽 rest, 📺 ☎ 🔬 🅿 – 🔬 300. 🌐 🅰🅴 ① 🆅🅸🆂🅰
Conservatory : **Meals** 13.75/21.75 **t.** and a la carte 🍴 7.95 – (see also **Blue Room** below) –
⊊ 9.95 – **96 rm** 105.00/155.00 **st.**, 4 suites – SB.

🍴 Blue Room (at Redworth Hall H. & Country Club), DL5 6NL, on A 6072 ℰ (01388) 772442,
Fax (01388) 775112, « Part 18C and 19C manor house of Elizabethan origins », ☞, park –
⇚ 🅿. 🌐 🅰🅴 ① 🆅🅸🆂🅰
closed Sunday and Bank Holiday Mondays – **Meals** (dinner only) 32.95 **t.** and a la carte
🍴 8.95.

🅰 ATS Albert St., off Neasham Rd ℰ (01325) 469271/469693

DARTFORD Kent **404** U 29 – pop. 59 411.

Dartford Tunnel and Bridge (toll).

🚪 *The Clocktower, Suffolk Rd, DA1 1EJ* ☎ *(01322) 343243.*

London 20 – Hastings 51 – Maidstone 22.

🏨 **Stakis Dartford Bridge,** Masthead Close, Crossways Business Park, DA2 6QF, NE : 2½ m. by A 226, Cotton Lane and Crossways Boulevard ☎ (01322) 284444, Fax (01322) 288225, 14, ⇌s, 🔲, ℀ – ⬚, ⤙ rm, ▤ 🔟 ☎ & 🅿 – 🕿 240. 🐠 ⅍ ⓪ 𝘝𝘐𝘚𝘈. ℀
Meals *(closed Saturday lunch)* 18.45/21.00 **t.** and a la carte ▯ 11.00 – � 10.50 – **171 rm** 99.00/109.00 **st.**, 4 suites – SB.

🏨 **Campanile,** Dartford Bridge, Clipper Boulevard West, Edison's Park, Crossways, DA2 6QN, NE : 3 m. by A 226, Cotton Lane and Galleon Boulevard ☎ (01322) 278925, Fax (01322) 278948 – ⤙ rm, 🔟 ☎ & 🅿 – 🕿 30. 🐠 ⅍ ⓪ 𝘝𝘐𝘚𝘈
Meals 11.00 **st.** and a la carte ▯ 4.50 – � 4.50 – **80 rm** 38.00 **t.**

DARTINGTON Devon **403** I 32 – see Totnes.

DARTMOUTH Devon **403** J 32 The West Country G. – pop. 5 676.

See : *Town★★ (⩽★) – Old Town - Butterwalk★ - Dartmouth Castle (⩽★★★) AC.*

Exc. : *Start Point (⩽★) S : 13 m. (including 1 m. on foot).*

🚪 *The Engine House, Mayor's Av., TQ6 9YY* ☎ *(01803) 834224.*

London 236 – Exeter 36 – Plymouth 35.

🏨 **Royal Castle,** 11 The Quay, TQ6 9PS, ☎ (01803) 833033, Fax (01803) 835445, ⩽ – ⤙ rest, 🔟 ☎. 🐠 ⅍ ⓪ 𝘝𝘐𝘚𝘈
Meals *(bar lunch Monday to Saturday)/dinner* 18.45 **t.** and a la carte ▯ 6.00 – **25 rm** � 58.45/131.90 **t.** – SB.

🏨 **Dart Marina,** Sandquay, TQ6 9PH, ☎ (01803) 832580, Fax (01803) 835040, ⩽ Dart Marina – ℀, ▤ rest, 🔟 ☎ 🅿. 🐠 ⅍ ⓪ 𝘝𝘐𝘚𝘈. ℀
Meals a la carte 23.75/28.60 **t.** – � 9.95 – **50 rm** 65.00/143.00 **t.** – SB.

🏠 **Ford House,** 44 Victoria Rd, TQ6 9DX, ☎ (01803) 834047, Fax (01803) 834047, ℀ – 🔟 ☎ 🅿. 🐠 ⅍ ⅍
March-November – **Meals** *(residents only) (communal dining) (dinner only) (unlicensed)* 25.00 **st.** – **3 rm** ⊆ 50.00/70.00 **st.** – SB.

🏠 **Boringdon House** without rest., 1 Church Rd, TQ6 9HQ, ☎ (01803) 832235, « Georgian house », ℀ – ⤙ 🔟 🅿
closed February and March – **3 rm** ⊆ 39.00/50.00 **st.**

🏠 **Wadstray House** ⧖ without rest., Blackawton, TQ9 7DE, W : 4 ½ m. on A 3122 ☎ (01803) 712539, ℀ – ⤙ 🔟 🅿. ℀
3 rm ⊆ 50.00 **st.**

🏠 **Hedley House** without rest., Newcomen Rd, TQ6 9BN, ☎ (01803) 835849, ⩽ Dart Estuary and Kingswear – ⤙. ℀
3 rm ⊆ 50.00/80.00.

🏠 **Woodside Cottage** ⧖ without rest., Blackawton, TQ9 7BL, W : 5 ½ m. by A 3122 on Blackawton rd ☎ (01803) 712375, Fax (01803) 712605, ⩽, ℀ – ⤙ 🔟 🅿. ℀
March-October – **3 rm** ⊆ 24.00/44.00 **s.**

✗✗ **Carved Angel,** 2 South Embankment, TQ6 9BH, ☎ (01803) 832465, Fax (01803) 835141, ⩽ Dart Estuary – 🐠 𝘝𝘐𝘚𝘈
closed Sunday dinner, Monday, 1 January-13 February and 5 days Christmas – **Meals** 30.00/ 48.00 **st.** ▯ 8.50.

✗✗ **Aragua,** St. Saviours Sq., TQ6 9DH, ☎ (01803) 832224, Fax (01803) 832224 – 🅿. 🐠 𝘝𝘐𝘚𝘈
closed dinner Sunday and Monday-Tuesday in winter, last 2 weeks March, last week June, first 3 weeks December, 25 December and 1 January – **Meals** *(dinner only and lunch Friday to Sunday)/dinner* a la carte 22.00/33.75 **st.**

✗ **Billy Budd's,** 7 Foss St., TQ6 9DW, ☎ (01803) 834842, Fax (01803) 834842 – 🐠 𝘝𝘐𝘚𝘈
closed Sunday, Monday except Bank Holidays, 6 weeks January-February, 1 week November and Christmas – **Meals** *(booking essential) (light lunch)/dinner* a la carte approx. 19.45 **t.**

at Stoke Fleming SW : 3 m. on A 379 – ✉ Dartmouth.

🏨 **Stoke Lodge,** Cinders Lane, TQ6 0RA, ☎ (01803) 770523, Fax (01803) 770851, ⩽, ⇌s, 🔟, 🔲, ℀, ℀ – 🔟 ☎ 🅿. 🐠 ⅍ 𝘝𝘐𝘚𝘈. ℀
Meals 10.50/16.95 **t.** and a la carte ▯ 5.50 – **25 rm** ⊆ 45.00/88.00 **t.** – SB.

Pour les grands voyages d'affaires ou de tourisme,
Guide Rouge MICHELIN : EUROPE.

DAVENTRY Northants **404** Q 27 – pop. 18 099.

  ⌐ Norton Rd ℘ (01327) 702829 – ⌐ɓ, ⌐ɓ Hellidon Lakes Hotel & C.C., Hellidon ℘ (01327) 62550 – ⌐ɓ Staverton Park, Staverton ℘ (01327) 302000/302118.

  🛈 Moot Hall, Market Sq., NN11 4BH ℘ (01327) 300277.

  London 79 – Coventry 23 – Northampton 13 – Oxford 46.

🏨 **Hanover International H. and Club Daventry,** Sedgemoor Way, off Ashby Rd, NN11 5SG, N : 2 m. on A 361 ℘ (01327) 301777, Fax (01327) 706313, ₤ɕ, ⇌ₛ, ☒ – ◙ ✳, ▤ rest, ⊡ ☎ ₺ ☻ – 🛦 600. ⬛⬤ 🆎 ⓘ 𝘝𝘐𝘚𝘈 𝘑𝘊𝘉
  Meals (closed 24 to 29 December) 21.00 t. (dinner) and a la carte 20.40/29.40 t. ₤ 7.50 – ⛌ 10.50 – **136 rm** 95.00/110.00 t., 2 suites – SB.

🏨 Chasley, London Rd, NN11 4EN, SE : ¾ m. on A 45 ℘ (01327) 77333, Fax (01327) 300420 – ◙ ✳ ⊡ ☎ ☻ – 🛦 350
  144 rm, 4 suites.

at Flore E : 6 m. on A 45 – ✉ Northampton.

🏨 Courtyard by Marriott Daventry, High St., NN7 4LP, E : ½ m. on A 45 ℘ (01327) 349022, Fax (01327) 349017, ₤ɕ – ✳ rm, ▤ rest, ⊡ ☎ ₺ ☻ – 🛦 80
  53 rm.

at Everdon SE : 7 m. by A 45, A 361 and B 4037 on Everdon rd – ✉ Daventry.

⌂ **Threeways House,** NN11 6BL, ℘ (01327) 361631, Fax (01327) 361359, ☞ – ✳ rest, ⊡ ☻
  Meals (by arrangement) (communal dining) 15.00 st. – **3 rm** ⛌ 25.00/45.00 st.

at Badby S : 3½ m. by A 45 on A 361 – ✉ Daventry.

🏮 **Windmill Inn,** Main St., NN11 3AN, ℘ (01327) 702363, Fax (01327) 311521 – ⊡ ☎ ☻ – 🛦 50. ⬛⬤ 🆎 𝘝𝘐𝘚𝘈 𝘑𝘊𝘉
  Meals a la carte 11.65/18.95 t. ₤ 5.50 – **8 rm** ⛌ 45.00/65.00 t. – SB.

at Hellidon SW : 6½ m. by A 45 and A 361 on Hellidon rd – ✉ Daventry.

🏨 **Hellidon Lakes H. & Country Club** ⤢, NN11 6LN, SW : ¾ m. ℘ (01327) 262550, Fax (01327) 262559, ≤, ₤ɕ, ☒, ⌐ɓ, ⌐ɓ, ⟋, park, ✼ – ⊡ ☎ ₺ ☻ – 🛦 200. ⬛⬤ 🆎 ⓘ 𝘝𝘐𝘚𝘈. ✼
  Meals 18.95 t. (dinner) and a la carte approx. 24.20 t. ₤ 5.85 – **43 rm** ⛌ 89.50/140.00 t., 2 suites – SB.

DAWLISH Devon **403** J 32 – pop. 9 648.

  ⌐ɓ Warren ℘ (01626) 862255.

  🛈 The Lawn, EX7 9PW ℘ (01626) 863589.

  London 215 – Exeter 13 – Plymouth 40 – Torquay 11.

🏨 **Langstone Cliff,** Dawlish Warren, EX7 0NA, N : 2 m. by A 379 ℘ (01626) 865155, Fax (01626) 867166, ⤢, ☒, ☞, park, ✼ – ◙ ⊡ ☎ ☻ – 🛦 400. ⬛⬤ 🆎 ⓘ 𝘝𝘐𝘚𝘈
  Meals (lunch by arrangement Monday to Saturday) 11.00/14.50 st. ₤ 4.00 – **67 rm** ⛌ 49.00/98.00 st. – SB.

DEAL Kent **404** Y 30 – pop. 28 504.

  ⌐ɓ Walmer & Kingsdown, The Leas, Kingsdown ℘ (01304) 373256.

  🛈 Town Hall, High St., CT14 6BB ℘ (01304) 369576.

  London 78 – Canterbury 19 – Dover 8.5 – Margate 16.

🏨 **Royal,** Beach St., CT14 6JD, ℘ (01304) 375555, Fax (01304) 372270, ≤, ⌂ – ✳ rm, ⊡ ☎.
  ⬛⬤ 🆎 𝘝𝘐𝘚𝘈. ✼
  The Boathouse : **Meals** (closed Sunday dinner and Monday) (residents only) 10.75/ 12.50 st. and a la carte ₤ 4.50 – **12 rm** ⛌ 45.00/75.00 st. – SB.

⌂ **Sutherland House,** 186 London Rd, CT14 9PT, ℘ (01304) 362853, Fax (01304) 381146 – ✳ rm, ⊡ ☻. ⬛⬤ 🆎 𝘝𝘐𝘚𝘈 𝘑𝘊𝘉
  Meals (by arrangement) 18.50 st. ₤ 4.50 – **3 rm** ⛌ 35.00/50.00 st. – SB.

✕✕ **Dunkerley's** with rm, 19 Beach St., CT14 7AH, ℘ (01304) 375016, Fax (01304) 380187, ≤ – ✳ rest, ⊡ ☎. ⬛⬤ 🆎 ⓘ 𝘝𝘐𝘚𝘈. ✼
  closed Monday lunch – **Meals** 9.50 t. (lunch) and a la carte 20.85/32.40 t. ₤ 4.50 – **6 rm** ⛌ 40.00/60.00 t. – SB.

  ⓐ ATS 40 Gilford Rd ℘ (01304) 361543

Pas de publicité payée dans ce guide.

DEDDINGTON *Oxon.* **403 404** Q 28 – *pop. 2 319.*
London 72 – Birmingham 46 – Coventry 33 – Oxford 18.

🏠 **Holcombe,** High St., OX15 0SL, ℰ *(01869) 338274, Fax (01869) 337167,* 🐴 – 📺 ☎ 🅿. 🟠🟢
AE VISA JCB
closed 2 to 11 January and 26 to 30 December – **Meals** 11.95/22.95 **st.** and a la carte ⓘ 6.50
– **17 rm** ⊊ 62.50/110.00 **st.** – SB.

✗ **Dexter's,** 37 Market Pl., OX15 0SE, ℰ *(01869) 338813* – 🟠🟢 AE VISA JCB
closed 25 December-4 January – **Meals** 14.00/19.95 **t.** and a la carte ⓘ 9.50.

DEDHAM *Essex* **404** W 28 *Great Britain G.* – *pop. 1 847* – ✉ *Colchester.*
Env. : *Stour Valley★ – Flatford Mill★, E : 6 m. by B 1029, A 12 and B 1070.*
London 63 – Chelmsford 30 – Colchester 8 – Ipswich 12.

🏠🏠 **Maison Talbooth** ⤴, Stratford Rd, CO7 6HN, W : ½ m. ℰ *(01206) 322367,*
Fax (01206) 322752, ≤, 🐴 – 📺 ☎ 🅿. 🟠🟢 AE VISA ✳
Meals – (see *Le Talbooth* below) – ⊊ 7.50 – **9 rm** 90.00/170.00 **t.**, 1 suite – SB.

✗✗✗ **Le Talbooth,** Gun Hill, CO7 6HP, W : 1 m. ℰ *(01206) 323150, Fax (01206) 322309,* « Part
Tudor house in attractive riverside setting », 🐴 – 🅿. 🟠🟢 VISA
closed Sunday dinner September-May – **Meals** 18.50/23.50 **t.** and a la carte ⓘ 6.95.

✗✗ **Fountain House & Dedham Hall** ⤴ with rm, Brook St., CO7 6AD, ℰ *(01206) 323027,*
Fax (01206) 323293, 🐴 – ✳ rest, 📺 🅿. 🟠🟢 VISA ✳
closed 25 and 26 December – **Meals** *(closed Sunday dinner and Monday)* (dinner only and
Sunday lunch)/dinner 19.50 **t.** ⓘ 9.00 – **5 rm** ⊊ 40.00/60.00 **t.**

DENMEAD *Hants.* **403** Q 31 – *pop. 5 626.*
London 70 – Portsmouth 11 – Southampton 27.

✗✗ **Barnard's,** Hambledon Rd, PO7 6NU, ℰ *(01705) 257788, Fax (01705) 257788,* 🐴 – ✳.
🟠🟢 AE VISA JCB
closed Saturday lunch, Sunday, Monday, 1 week August and 1 week Christmas –
Meals 10.00/17.50 **t.** and a la carte ⓘ 5.00.

DENTON *Gtr. Manchester* **402 404** N 23 – *pop. 37 785.*
🔵 *Denton, Manchester Rd* ℰ *(0161) 336 3218.*
London 196 – Chesterfield 41 – Manchester 6.

🏠 **Old Rectory,** Meadow Lane, Haughton Green, M34 1GD, S : 2 m. by A 6017, Two Trees
Lane and Haughton Green Rd ℰ *(0161) 336 7516, Fax (0161) 320 3212,* 🐴 – ✳, ▤ rest, 📺
☎ 🅿 – 🔏 100. 🟠🟢 AE ⓞ
Meals *(closed Saturday lunch)* 11.95/16.50 **st.** and a la carte ⓘ 7.50 – **36 rm** ⊊ 67.00/
82.00 **st.** – SB.

🏠 **Travel Inn,** Manchester Rd, M34 3SJ, W : 1 m. by A 57 at junction of M 66 and M 67
ℰ *(0161) 320 1116, Fax (0161) 320 1098* – ✳ rm, ▤ rest, 📺 ⓑ 🅿. 🟠🟢 AE ⓞ VISA
Meals (grill rest.) – **40 rm** 36.50 **t.**

DERBY **402 403 404** P 25 *Great Britain G.* – *pop. 223 836.*
See : *City★ – Museum and Art Gallery★ (Collection of Derby Porcelain★)* YZ **M1** – *Royal
Crown Derby Museum★ AC* Z **M2.**
Env. : *Kedleston Hall★★ AC, NW : 4 ½ m. by Kedleston Rd* X.
🔵 *Wilmore Rd, Sinfin* ℰ *(01332) 766323* – 🔵 *Mickleover, Uttoxeter Rd* ℰ *(01332) 513339* –
🔵 *Kedleston Park* ℰ *(01332) 840035* – 🔵, 🔵 *Breadsall Priory Hotel G. & C.C., Moor Rd,
Morley* ℰ *(01332) 832235* – 🔵 *Allestree Park, Allestree Hall, Allestree* ℰ *(01332) 550616.*
✈ *East Midlands Airport, Castle Donington :* ℰ *(01332) 852852, SE : 12 m. by A 6* X.
🛈 *Assembly Rooms, Market Pl., DE1 3AH* ℰ *(01332) 255802.*
*London 132 – Birmingham 40 – Coventry 49 – Leicester 29 – Manchester 62 – Nottingham
16 – Sheffield 47 – Stoke-on-Trent 35.*

Plan on next page

🏠🏠 **Midland,** Midland Rd, DE1 2SQ, ℰ *(01332) 345894, Fax (01332) 293522,* 🐴 – 📱, ✳ rm,
📺 ☎ ⓑ 🅿 – 🔏 150. 🟠🟢 AE ⓞ VISA ✳   Z i
closed 24 to 26 December – **Meals** *(closed lunch Saturday)* 12.95/17.35 **st.**
and lunch a la carte ⓘ 8.25 – ⊊ 10.00 – **97 rm** 72.00/94.00 **st.**, 1 suite – SB.

🏠 **La Gondola,** 220 Osmaston Rd, DE23 8JX, ℰ *(01332) 332895, Fax (01332) 384512* – 📺 ☎
🅿 – 🔏 70. 🟠🟢 AE ⓞ VISA ✳   X c
Meals - Italian - *(closed Sunday)* (dancing Saturday) 7.50/12.50 **t.** and a la carte ⓘ 5.75 –
19 rm ⊊ 46.00/56.00 **st.**, 1 suite – SB.

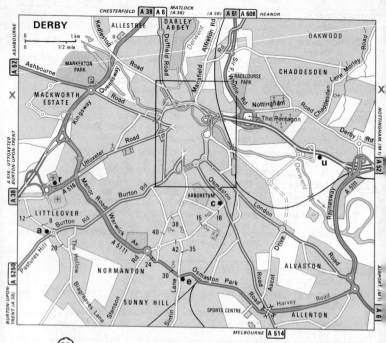

DERBY

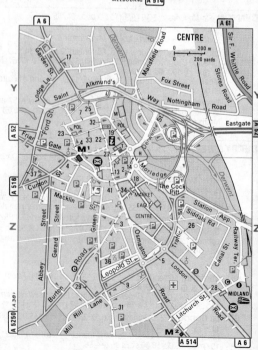

CENTRE

222

Oast House - Premier Lodge, Foresters Leisure Park, 220 Osmaston Park Rd, DE23 8AG, ✆ (01332) 270027, *Fax (01332) 270528* – ⇐ rm, 📺 ☎ ᖴ 🅿 – 🔬 40. 🆗 🅰🅴 🅰🅳🅸 *VISA* 🅹🅲🅱. ✻
X e
Meals (grill rest.) 6.55/10.95 **st.** and a la carte – ⇄ 4.95 – **26 rm** 42.25 **st.** – SB.

Royal Stuart, 119 London Rd, DE1 2QR, ✆ (01332) 340633, *Fax (01332) 293502* – ⇐ 📺 ☎ 🅿 – 🔬 150. 🆗 🅰🅴 *VISA*. ✻
Z o
closed Christmas and New Year – **Meals** *(closed lunch Saturday and Bank Holidays)* 8.95/ 15.95 **st.** and a la carte 🛈 6.45 – ⇄ 7.50 – **101 rm** 51.00/58.00 **st.** – SB.

European Inn without rest., Midland Rd, DE1 2SL, ✆ (01332) 292000, *Fax (01332) 293940* – 🔃 ⇐ 📺 ☎ ᖴ 🅿 – 🔬 120. 🆗 🅰🅴 🅾 *VISA*. ✻
Z c
⇄ 6.00 – **86 rm** 42.50 **t.**

Travel Inn, Wyvern Business Park, DE21 6BF, ✆ (01332) 667826, *Fax (01332) 667827* – 🔃, ⇐ rm, ▤ rest, 📺 ᖴ 🅿. 🆗 🅰🅴 🅾 *VISA*. ✻
X u
Meals (grill rest.) – **82 rm** 36.50 **t.**

Travel Inn, Manor Park Way, Uttoxeter New Rd, DE22 3NA, ✆ (01332) 203003, *Fax (01332) 207506* – ⇐ rm, ▤ rest, 📺 ᖴ 🅿. 🆗 🅰🅴 🅾 *VISA*. ✻
X r
Meals (grill rest.) – **43 rm** 36.50 **t.**

XX **New Water Margin,** 72-74 Burton Rd, DE1 1TG, ✆ (01332) 364754, *Fax (01332) 290482* – ▤ 🅿. 🆗 🅰🅴 🅾 *VISA*
Z e
Meals - Chinese (Canton) - 11.00/14.80 **t.** and a la carte.

at Breadsall *NE : 4 m. by A 52 off A 61* – X – ✉ *Derby.*

Marriott Breadsall Priory H. & Country Club ⬎, Moor Rd, Morley, DE7 6DL, NE : 1 ¼ m. by Rectory Lane ✆ (01332) 832235, *Fax (01332) 833509*, ≼, 📶, 🛋, ☎, 🔲, 🛋, 🐎, ✻ – 🔃 ⇐, ▤ rest, 📺 ☎ ᖴ 🅿 – 🔬 120. 🆗 🅰🅴 🅾 *VISA*. ✻
Priory : **Meals** *(closed Saturday lunch)* a la carte 20.00/30.00 **st.** – *Long Weekend :* Meals a la carte 15.00/20.00 **st.** – ⇄ 9.00 – **107 rm** 94.00/103.00 **st.**, 5 suites – SB.

at Littleover *SW : 2½ m. on A 5250* – X – ✉ *Derby.*

La Villa, 222 Rykneld Rd, DE3 7AP, SW : 1 ¾ m. on A 5250 ✆ (01332) 510161, *Fax (01332) 514010* – ▤ rm, 📺 ☎ 🅿. 🆗 🅰🅴 *VISA* 🅹🅲🅱. ✻
Meals - Italian - *(closed lunch Monday and Sunday)* 12.75/19.95 **st.** and dinner a la carte – **14 rm** ⇄ 55.00/85.00 **st.**

at Mickleover *SW : 3 m. by A 38 and A 516* – X – ✉ *Derby.*

Mickleover Court, Etwall Rd, DE3 5XX, ✆ (01332) 521234, *Fax (01332) 521238*, 📶, ☎, 🔲 – 🔃, ⇐ rm, ▤ 📺 ☎ ᖴ 🅿 – 🔬 200. 🆗 🅰🅴 🅾 *VISA*
Avesbury : **Meals** a la carte 15.95/28.95 **st.** 🛈 7.00 – *Stelline Trattoria :* **Meals** - Italian - a la carte 12.25/21.95 **st.** 🛈 6.50 – **72 rm** ⇄ 115.00/135.00 **st.**, 8 suites – SB.

at Mackworth *NW : 2¾ m. by A 52* – X – ✉ *Derby.*

Mackworth, Ashbourne Rd, DE22 4LY, on A 52 ✆ (01332) 824324, *Fax (01332) 824692*, 🐎 – 📺 ☎ 🅿 – 🔬 60. 🆗 🅰🅴 *VISA*
closed 24 to 26 December and 1 January – **Meals** (carving rest.) 8.95/12.50 **t.** and a la carte 🛈 5.25 – **14 rm** ⇄ 44.50/72.00 **t.**

at Kedleston *NW : 4 m. by Kedleston Rd* – X – ✉ *Derby.*

Kedleston Country House, Kedleston Rd, DE22 5JD, E : 2 m. ✆ (01332) 559202, *Fax (01332) 558822*, ≼ – 📺 ☎ ᖴ 🅿. 🆗 🅰🅴 🅾 *VISA* 🅹🅲🅱. ✻
Meals *(closed Sunday dinner)* 9.95 **t.** and a la carte 🛈 6.00 – **14 rm** ⇄ 45.00/60.00 **t.** – SB.

🛈 ATS   Gosforth   Rd,   off   Ascot   Drive   ATS 67 Bridge St. ✆ (01332) 347327
✆ (01332) 340854   ATS 59 Kedleston Rd ✆ (01332) 297878

DESBOROUGH *Northants.* 🔢 R 26 – pop. 7 351.
London 83 – Birmingham 52 – Leicester 20 – Northampton 20.

Travelodge, Harborough Rd, NN14 2UG, N : 1 ½ m. on A 6 ✆ (01536) 762034, *Fax (01536) 762034*, Reservations (Freephone) 0800 850950 – ⇐ rm, 📺 ᖴ 🅿. 🆗 🅰🅴 🅾 *VISA* 🅹🅲🅱. ✻
Meals (grill rest.) – **32 rm** 39.95 **t.**

DETHICK *Derbs.* – see Matlock.

Entrez à l'hôtel le Guide à la main, vous montrerez ainsi,
qu'il vous conduit là en confiance.

DEVIZES Wilts. 403 404 O 29 The West Country G. – pop. 13 205.

See : St. John's Church★★ – Market Place★ – Devizes Museum★ AC.

Env. : Potterne (Porch House★★) S : 2 ½ m. by A 360 – E : Vale of Pewsey★.

Exc. : Stonehenge★★★ AC, SE : 16 m. by A 360 and A 344 – Avebury★★ (The Stones★, Church★) NE : 7 m. by A 361.

🏌 Erlestoke Sands, Erlestoke ℰ (01380) 831069.

🖪 39 St. John's St., SN10 1BL ℰ (01380) 729408.

London 98 – Bristol 38 – Salisbury 25 – Swindon 19.

at Market Lavington S : 6 m. by A 360 on B 3098 – ✉ Devizes.

⌂ **Old Coach House** without rest., 21 Church St., SN10 4DU, ℰ (01380) 812879, Fax (01380) 812879, 🚗 – ❧ 📺 🅿. ❀
closed 12 December-6 January and booking essential February and October – **3 rm** ⊇ 26.00/43.50 **s.**

at Erlestoke SW : 8 m. by A 360 on B 3098 – ✉ Devizes.

⌂ **Longwater** ❧, Lower Rd, SN10 5UE, ℰ (01380) 830095, Fax (01380) 830095, ⬗, 🚗, park – 📺 🅿
closed Christmas-New Year – **Meals** (by arrangement) (communal dining) 12.00 **s.** ⊹ 3.00 – **5 rm** ⊇ 28.00/44.00 **s.** – SB.

at Rowde NW : 2 m. by A 361 on A 342 – ✉ Devizes.

🍴 **George & Dragon**, High St., SN10 2PN, on A 342 ℰ (01380) 723053, Fax (01380) 724738, 🚗 – ❧ 🅿. 🝙 𝘝𝘐𝘚𝘈.
closed Sunday, Monday, 25-26 December and 1 January – **Meals** (booking essential) 10.00 **t.** (lunch) and a la carte 15.00/28.50 **t.** ⊹ 9.25.

Les prix	Pour toutes précisions sur les prix indiqués dans ce guide, reportez-vous aux pages de l'introduction.

DEWSBURY W. Yorks. 402 P 22 – pop. 50 168.

London 205 – Leeds 9 – Manchester 40 – Middlesbrough 76 – Sheffield 31.

🏠 **Heath Cottage**, Wakefield Rd, WF12 8ET, E : ¾ m. on A 638 ℰ (01924) 465399, Fax (01924) 459405 – ❧ 📺 𝘝𝘐𝘚𝘈 𝘑𝘊𝘉. ❀
Meals (closed Sunday dinner to non-residents) (booking essential Bank Holiday Mondays) 9.95/12.95 **st.** and a la carte ⊹ 4.50 – **28 rm** ⊇ 48.00/65.00 **st.** – SB.

DIDCOT Oxon. 403 404 Q 29 – ✉ Abingdon.

🖪 The Car Park, Station Rd, OX11 7NR ℰ (01235) 813243.

London 58 – Oxford 15 – Reading 20 – Swindon 31.

🏠 **Travel Inn**, Milton Heights, Milton, OX14 4DP, NW : 3 ¼ m. by B 4493 on A 4130 ℰ (01235) 835168, Fax (01235) 835187 – ❧ rm, ▤ rest, 📺 🕭 🅿. 🝙 🝘 𝘈𝘌 🝜 𝘝𝘐𝘚𝘈. ❀
Meals (grill rest.) – **40 rm** 36.50 **t.**

DIDDLEBURY Shrops. 402 403 L 26 Great Britain G. – pop. 911 – ✉ Craven Arms.

Env. : NW : Wenlock Edge★.

London 169 – Birmingham 46.

🏠 **Delbury Hall** ❧, SY7 9DH, entrance on B 4368 beside lodge, opposite 40 mph sign ℰ (01584) 841267, Fax (01584) 841441, ≼, « Georgian mansion, country house atmosphere », ⬗, 🚗, park, ❀ – ❧ 📺 🕭 🅿. 🝙 𝘝𝘐𝘚𝘈 𝘑𝘊𝘉. ❀
closed Christmas – **Meals** (by arrangement) (communal dining) (dinner only) 27.00 **s.** ⊹ 7.50 – **3 rm** ⊇ 55.00/90.00 **s.**

DIDSBURY Gtr. Manchester 402 403 404 N 23 – see Manchester.

DISLEY Ches. 402 403 404 N 23 – pop. 3 743 – ✉ Stockport.

London 187 – Chesterfield 35 – Manchester 12.

🏨 **Stakis Moorside** ❧, Mudhurst Lane, Higher Disley, SK12 2AP, SE : 2 m. by Buxton Old Rd ℰ (01663) 764151, Fax (01663) 762794, ≼, ℐ₅, ⌘, 🝏, ❀, squash – ⧮, ❧ rm, 📺 🕭 🅿 – 🝙 300. 🝙 𝘈𝘌 🝜 𝘝𝘐𝘚𝘈. ❀
Meals (bar lunch Saturday) 13.00/19.95 **st.** and a la carte ⊹ 7.95 – ⊇ 8.95 – **93 rm** 85.00/100.00 **st.**, 1 suite – SB.

ENGLAND

DISS _Norfolk_ 404 X 26 – _pop. 6 538._
  🛈 _Meres Mouth, Mere St., IP22 3AG_ 𝒫 _(01379) 650523._
  London 98 – Ipswich 25 – Norwich 21 – Thetford 17.

  ⌂ **Malt House,** Palgrave, IP22 1AE, SW: 1 m. by Denmark St. 𝒫 (01379) 642107,
  Fax (01379) 640315, « Gardens » – 🛏 📺 🅿. 🆑 ⓞ 𝘝𝘐𝘚𝘈 JCB. ✄
  closed 15 December-5 January – **Meals** (by arrangement) (communal dining) 20.00 **s.** –
  3 rm ⯁ 35.00/60.00 **s.**

  ✕ **Weavers,** Market Hill, IP22 3JZ, 𝒫 (01379) 642411 – 🆑 AE ⓞ 𝘝𝘐𝘚𝘈 JCB
  closed Saturday and Monday lunch, Sunday, last 2 weeks August and 1 week Christmas –
  Meals 10.75/12.00 **t.** and dinner a la carte 🛢 9.75.

at Scole _E : 2½ m. by A 1066 –_ ✉ _Diss._

  🏨 **Scole Inn,** Norwich Rd, IP21 4DR, 𝒫 (01379) 740481, Fax (01379) 740762, « 17C » –
  ▤ rest, 📺 ☎ 🅿 – ⛟ 40. 🆑 AE 𝘝𝘐𝘚𝘈
  Meals (bar lunch Saturday) 14.95 **t.** and a la carte 🛢 4.85 – **23 rm** ⯁ 52.00/76.00 **t.** – SB.

at Brockdish _E : 7 m. by A 1066, A 140 and A 143 –_ ✉ _Diss._

  ⌂ **Grove Thorpe,** Grove Rd, IP21 4JE, N : ¾ m. 𝒫 (01379) 668305, Fax (01379) 668305,
  « 17C bailiffs house », ⚲, 🐎 – 🅿. ✄
  closed 25 December – **Meals** (by arrangement) (communal dining) 15.00 **s.** – **3 rm**
  ⯁ 32.00/58.00 **s.** – SB.

at Brome _(Suffolk) SE : 2¾ m. by A 1066 on B 1077 –_ ✉ _Eye._

  🏨 **Cornwallis Arms** ⚲, IP23 8AJ, 𝒫 (01379) 870326, Fax (01379) 870051, « Part 16C
  house, topiary gardens », park – 📺 ☎ 🅿 – ⛟ 30. 🆑 AE ⓞ 𝘝𝘐𝘚𝘈 JCB
  Oaksmere : Meals a la carte 15.70/28.85 **st.** 🛢 8.95 – **11 rm** ⯁ 59.50/105.00 **st.** – SB.

at Wingfield _SE : 7 m. by A 1066 and B 1118._

  🏠 **De La Pole Arms,** Church Rd, IP21 5RA, 𝒫 (01379) 384545, Fax (01379) 384377, « Part
  17C inn » – 🅿. 🆑 𝘝𝘐𝘚𝘈
  Meals a la carte 12.95/22.15 **t.** 🛢 11.75.

at Fersfield _NW : 7 m. by A 1066 –_ ✉ _Diss._

  ⌂ **Strenneth** ⚲ without rest., Airfield Rd, IP22 2BP, 𝒫 (01379) 688182,
  Fax (01379) 688260, ⚘ – 🛏 📺 🅿. 🆑 𝘝𝘐𝘚𝘈
  7 rm 25.00/60.00.

  🅐 ATS Shelfanger Rd 𝒫 (01379) 642861

DITTISHAM _Devon_ 403 J 32 – _pop. 463 –_ ✉ _Dartmouth_
  London 214 – Exeter 33 – Plymouth 34.

  🏠 **Red Lion Inn** with rm, TQ6 0ES, 𝒫 (01803) 722235, ≼ – 📺 ☎ 🅿. 🆑 𝘝𝘐𝘚𝘈
  accommodation closed 24 to 26 December – **Meals** (in bar Monday dinner) a la carte 8.90/
  17.40 **t.** 🛢 4.50 – **6 rm** ⯁ 29.50/64.00 **t.**

DITTON PRIORS _Shrops._ 403 404 M 26 – _pop. 680 –_ ✉ _Bridgnorth._
  London 154 – Birmingham 34 – Ludlow 13 – Shrewsbury 21.

  ⌂ **Middleton Lodge** ⚲ without rest., Middleton Priors, WV16 6UR, NE : 1 ¼ m.
  𝒫 (01746) 712228, Fax (01746) 712675, « Part 17C hunting lodge », ⚘ – 🛏 📺 🅿. ✄
  closed Christmas – **3 rm** ⯁ 30.00/50.00.

  ✕✕ **Howard Arms,** WV16 6SQ, 𝒫 (01746) 712200, ⚘ – 🛏 🅿. 🆑 𝘝𝘐𝘚𝘈
  closed Sunday dinner, Monday and 2 weeks September – **Meals** (dinner only and Sunday
  lunch)/dinner 25.00 **t.** 🛢 5.00.

DODDISCOMBSLEIGH _Devon – see Exeter._

DONCASTER _S. Yorks._ 402 403 404 Q 23 – _pop. 71 595._
  🏌 _Doncaster Town Moor, Bawtry Rd, Belle Vue_ 𝒫 _(01302) 533778 –_ 🏌 _Crookhill Park,
  Conisborough_ 𝒫 _(01709) 862979 –_ 🏌 _Wheatley, Amthorpe Rd_ 𝒫 _(01302) 831655 –_
  🏌 _Owston Park, Owston Hall, Owston_ 𝒫 _(01302) 330821._
  🛈 _Central Library, Waterdale, DN1 3JE_ 𝒫 _(01302) 734309._
  London 173 – Kingston-upon-Hull 46 – Leeds 30 – Nottingham 46 – Sheffield 19.

  🏨 **Doncaster Moat House,** Warmsworth, DN4 9UX, SW: 2 ¾ m. on A 630
  𝒫 (01302) 799988, Fax (01302) 310197, 🛢, ⚐, 🔲 – �ⷮ, 🛏 rm, 📺 ☎ & 🅿 – ⛟ 400. 🆑 AE
  ⓞ 𝘝𝘐𝘚𝘈
  Meals _(closed Saturday lunch)_ (buffet lunch) 12.50/16.95 **t.** and a la carte 🛢 6.25 – ⯁ 8.50 –
  98 rm 95.00/110.00 **t.**, 2 suites – SB.

225

🏨 **Mount Pleasant,** Great North Rd, DN11 0HP, SE : 6 m. on A 638 ✆ (01302) 868219, *Fax (01302) 865130,* 🏋, 🌳 – 🚭 rest, [TV] ☎ ♿ [P] – 👥 60. [MC] [AE] [DC] VISA JCB. 🚫
closed 25 December – **Meals** 12.00/18.50 🍾 4.50 – **28 rm** ☕ 53.00/79.00 **t.**, 1 suite – SB.

🏨 **Danum Swallow,** High St., DN1 1DN, ✆ (01302) 342261, *Fax (01302) 329034* – ⇕, 🚭 rm, [TV] ☎ [P] – 👥 350. [MC] [AE] [DC] VISA
Meals *(closed Saturday lunch)* 9.50/16.95 **st.** 🍾 6.50 – **64 rm** ☕ 55.00/75.00 **st.**, 2 suites – SB.

🏨 **Grand St. Leger,** Racecourse Roundabout, Bennetthorpe, DN2 6AX, SE : 1 ½ m. on A 638 ✆ (01302) 364111, *Fax (01302) 329865* – [TV] ☎ [P]. [MC] [AE] [DC] VISA
Meals 11.95/17.95 **st.** and a la carte 🍾 4.50 – **20 rm** ☕ 66.00/80.00 **st.** – SB.

🏨 **Punch's,** Bawtry Rd, Bessacarr, DN4 7BS, SE : 3 m. on A 638 ✆ (01302) 370037, *Fax (01302) 532281* – 🚭 [TV] ☎ ♿ [P] – 👥 40. [MC] [AE] VISA
Meals (grill rest.) 9.95 **st.** and a la carte 🍾 4.45 – **24 rm** ☕ 55.00/74.00 **st.** – SB.

🏨 **Campanile,** Doncaster Leisure Park, Bawtry Rd, DN4 7PD, SE : 2 m. on A 638 ✆ (01302) 370770, *Fax (01302) 370813* – 🚭 rm, [TV] ☎ ♿ [P] – 👥 30. [MC] [AE] [DC] VISA
Meals 10.55 **st.** and a la carte 🍾 4.95 – ☕ 4.50 – **50 rm** 36.50 **st.**

🏨 **Travel Inn,** South Entry Drive, White Rose Way, DN4 5JH, S : 1 ½ m. by A 6182 ✆ (01302) 361134, *Fax (01302) 364811* – 🚭 rm, [TV] ♿ [P]. [MC] [AE] [DC] VISA
Meals (grill rest.) – **42 rm** 36.50 **t.**

🍴🍴 **Aagrah,** Great North Rd, Woodlands, DN6 7RA, NW : 4 m. on A 638 ✆ (01302) 728888 – [P]. [MC] [AE] VISA
closed 25 December – **Meals** - Indian - (dinner only) a la carte 10.80/16.30 **t.**

at Carcroft *NW : 6½ m. on A 1 –* ✉ *Doncaster.*

🏨 **Travelodge,** Great North Rd, (northbound carriageway) ✆ (01302) 330841, Reservations (Freephone) 0800 850950 – [TV] ♿ [P]. [MC] [AE] [DC] VISA JCB. 🚫
40 rm 39.95 **t.**

⊛ ATS Heavens Walk ✆ (01302) 367337/367338/360249/340797

DORCHESTER *Dorset* [403] [404] M 31 *The West Country G.* – *pop. 15 037.*

See : *Town★ - Dorset County Museum★ AC.*

Env. : *Maiden Castle★★ (≤★) SW : 2 ½ m. – Puddletown Church★, NE : 5 ½ m. by A 35.*

Exc. : *Moreton Church★★, E : 7 ½ m. – Bere Regis★ (St. John the Baptist Church★ - Roof★★) NE : 11 m. by A 35 – Athelhampton House★ AC, NE : 6 ½ m. by A 35 - Cerne Abbas★, N : 7 m. by A 352.*

⛳18 *Came Down ✆ (01305) 812531.*

ℹ *Unit 11, Antelope Walk, Dorchester, DT1 1BE ✆ (01305) 267992.*

London 135 – Bournemouth 27 – Exeter 53 – Southampton 53.

🏨 **King's Arms,** 30 High East St., DT1 1HF, ✆ (01305) 265353, *Fax (01305) 260269* – ⇕, 🚭 rm, [TV] ☎ [P] – 👥 80. [MC] [AE] VISA. 🚫
Meals 10.95 **t.** and a la carte – ☕ 4.95 – **33 rm** 44.25 **t.**

🏨 **Wessex Royale,** 32 High West St., DT1 1UP, ✆ (01305) 262660, *Fax (01305) 251941* – [TV] ☎ – 👥 100. [MC] [AE] [DC] VISA JCB
Meals (bar lunch)/dinner a la carte 17.00/20.00 **st.** 🍾 5.00 – **25 rm** ☕ 39.95/59.00 **st.**, 1 suite.

🏨 **Casterbridge** without rest., 49 High East St., DT1 1HU, ✆ (01305) 264043, *Fax (01305) 260884,* « Georgian town house » – 🚭 [TV] ☎. [MC] [AE] [DC] VISA JCB. 🚫
closed 25 and 26 December – **14 rm** ☕ 38.00/75.00.

🏨 **Yalbury Cottage** 🛋, Lower Bockhampton, DT2 8PZ, E : 2 ¼ m. by B 3150 and Bockhampton rd ✆ (01305) 262382, *Fax (01305) 266412,* 🌳 – 🚭 [TV] ☎ [P]. [MC] VISA JCB
closed 27 December-22 January – **Meals** (dinner only) 19.00 **t.** 🍾 7.00 – **8 rm** ☕ 46.00/72.00 **st.** – SB.

🏨 **Westwood House** without rest., 29 High West St., DT1 1UP, ✆ (01305) 268018, *Fax (01305) 250282* – [TV] ☎. [MC] [AE] VISA
7 rm ☕ 37.50/62.50 **st.**

🍴🍴 **Mock Turtle,** 34 High West St., DT1 1UP, ✆ (01305) 264011 – [MC] VISA
closed 1 January and 25-26 December – **Meals** *(closed lunch Saturday and Monday and Sunday)* 14.45/22.20 **t.** 🍾 6.00.

at Winterbourne Steepleton *W : 4 ¾ m. by B 3150 and A 35 on B 3159 –* ✉ *Dorchester.*

⌂ **Old Rectory** without rest., DT2 9LG, ✆ (01305) 889468, *Fax (01305) 889737,* 🌳 – 🚭 [P]. 🚫
closed 23 to 30 December – **3 rm** ☕ 30.00/80.00 **st.**

at Frampton *NW : 6 m. by B 3147 and A 37 on A 356 –* ✉ *Dorchester.*

🏠 **Hyde Farm House** ⏾, DT2 9NG, NW : ½ m. on A 356 ℘ (01300) 320272, ≼, « Part 18C and 19C », ⌖ – ✝⇇ rm, ❷. ✍
Meals (residents only) (dinner only) (unlicensed) 15.00 ⏴ 8.50 – **3 rm** ⌑ 27.50/55.00 **s.**

ⓐ ATS Unit 4, Great Western Ind. Centre ATS Units 1/2, Jonson Trading Est.
℘ (01305) 264756   ℘ (01305) 264308

DORCHESTER *Oxon.* 🄰🄾🄳 🄰🄾🄴 Q 29 *Great Britain G. –* pop. 1 5037.
See : *Town*★.
Exc. : *Ridgeway Path*★★.
London 51 – Abingdon 6 – Oxford 8 – Reading 17.

🏨 **George,** 23 High St., OX10 7HH, ℘ (01865) 340404, *Fax (01865) 341620,* « Part 14C coaching inn », ⌖ – 🆃🆅 ☎ ❷ – 🍴 40. 🆆🆂 🆁🅴 *VISA* 🅹🅲🅱
Meals 11.95/21.50 **st.** ⏴ 5.20 – **17 rm** ⌑ 52.50/75.00 **st.** – SB.

🏨 **White Hart,** 26 High St., OX10 7HN, ℘ (01865) 340074, *Fax (01865) 341082,* « 17C coaching inn » – 🆃🆅 ☎ ❷ – 🍴 35. 🆆🆂 🆁🅴 🅾 *VISA*
Meals 15.00 **t.** and a la carte ⏴ 7.00 – **15 rm** ⌑ 65.00/85.00 **t.,** 4 suites – SB.

DORKING *Surrey* 🄰🄾🄴 T 30 – pop. 15 658.
London 26 – Brighton 39 – Guildford 12 – Worthing 33.

🏰 **Burford Bridge,** Box Hill, RH5 6BX, N : 1 ½ m. on A 24 ℘ (01306) 884561, *Fax (01306) 880386,* ⌔, ⌖ – ✝⇇ 🆃🆅 ☎ ❷ – 🍴 150. 🆆🆂 🆁🅴 🅾 *VISA* 🅹🅲🅱
Meals a la carte 21.15/36.45 **t.** ⏴ 7.50 – ⌑ 10.50 – **48 rm** 110.00/125.00 **st.** – SB.

🏨 **White Horse,** High St., RH4 1BE, ℘ (01306) 881138, *Fax (01306) 887241 –* ✝⇇ 🆃🆅 ☎ ❷ – 🍴 50. 🆆🆂 🆁🅴 🅾 *VISA* 🅹🅲🅱
Meals a la carte 14.50/21.50 **st.** ⏴ 6.00 – ⌑ 8.50 – **68 rm** 90.00/110.00 **t.** – SB.

🏠 **Travelodge,** Reigate Rd, RH4 1QB, E : ½ m. on A 25 ℘ (01306) 740361, Reservations (Freephone) 0800 850950 – ✝⇇ 🆃🆅 ⓺ ❷. 🆆🆂 🆁🅴 🅾 *VISA* 🅹🅲🅱. ✍
29 rm 49.95 **t.**

✕✕ **Partner's and Sons,** 2-4 West St., RH4 1BL, ℘ (01306) 882826, *Fax (01306) 885741 –* ✝⇇ ▤. 🆆🆂 🆁🅴 🅾 *VISA*
closed Sunday dinner, Tuesday and January – **Meals** 16.00 **t.** (lunch) and a la carte 17.85/30.40 **t.** ⏴ 5.50.

DORRINGTON *Shrops.* 🄰🄾🄶 🄰🄾🄴 L 26 – *see Shrewsbury.*

DOULTING *Somerset* 🄰🄾🄶 🄰🄾🄴 M 30 – *see Shepton Mallet.*

DOVER *Kent* 🄰🄾🄴 Y 30 *Great Britain G. –* pop. 34 179.
See : *Castle*★★ AC Y.
⛴ to France (Calais) (P & O/Stena Line) (1 h 30 mn) – to France (Calais) (SeaFrance Ltd) frequent services (1 h 30 mn) – to France (Calais) (Hoverspeed Ltd) frequent services daily (35 mn).
🅱 *Townwall St., CT16 1JR* ℘ (01304) 205108.
London 76 – Brighton 84.

Plan on next page

🏨 **Churchill,** Dover Waterfront, CT17 9BP, ℘ (01304) 203633, *Fax (01304) 216320,* ≼ – ▮ ✝⇇ 🆃🆅 ☎ ❷ – 🍴 120. 🆆🆂 🆁🅴 🅾 *VISA*. ✍ .   Z a
Meals 12.95/15.50 **t.** and dinner a la carte ⏴ 6.25 – ⌑ 8.00 – **68 rm** 55.00/90.00 **st.**

🏨 **Forte Posthouse Dover,** Singledge Lane, Whitfield, CT16 3LF, NW : 3 ½ m. by A 256 on A 2 ℘ (01304) 821222, *Fax (01304) 825576 –* ✝⇇ rm, 🆃🆅 ⓺ ❷ – 🍴 40. 🆆🆂 🆁🅴 🅾 *VISA* 🅹🅲🅱
Meals a la carte 13.15/25.65 **st.** ⏴ 7.50 – ⌑ 8.95 – **67 rm** 69.00 **st.** – SB.   Z o

🏠 **Travel Inn,** Folkestone Rd, CT15 7AB, SW : 2 ½ m. on B 2011 ℘ (01304) 213339, *Fax (01304) 214504 –* ✝⇇ rm, 🆃🆅 ⓺ ❷. 🆆🆂 🆁🅴 🅾 *VISA*. ✍
closed 24 and 25 December – **Meals** (grill rest.) – **62 rm** 36.50 **t.**

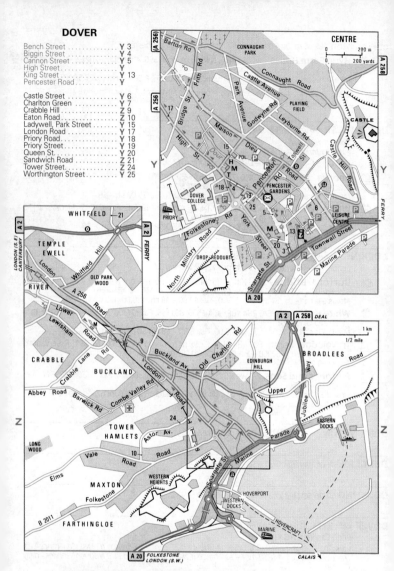

DOVER

命 **East Lee** without rest., 108 Maison Dieu Rd, CT16 1RT, ℰ (01304) 210176,
Fax (01304) 210176 – ⚡ 📺 ☎. ⬢⬢ 𝘝𝘐𝘚𝘈. ✻   Y o
4 rm ⊡ 35.00/45.00.

命 **Number One** without rest., 1 Castle St., CT16 1QH, ℰ (01304) 202007, 🌳 – 📺 ⇌. ✻
closed 24 to 26 December – **5 rm** ⊡ 30.00/44.00.   Y u

at St. Margaret's at Cliffe NE : 4 m. by A 258 – Z – on B 2058 – ⊠ Dover.

🏨 **Wallett's Court**, West Cliffe, CT15 6EW, NW : ¾ m. on B 2058 ℰ (01304) 852424,
Fax (01304) 853430, « Part 17C manor house », 🌳, ⚒ – ⚡ 📵 ⬢⬢ 🅐🅔 ⓪ 𝘝𝘐𝘚𝘈. ✻
closed 4 days Christmas – **Meals** – (see below) – **10 rm** ⊡ 55.00/90.00.

XX **Wallett's Court** (at Wallett's Court H.), West Cliffe, CT15 6EW, NW : ¾ m. on B 2058
ℰ (01304) 852424, Fax (01304) 853430, 🌳 – ⚡ ⓟ. ⬢⬢ 🅐🅔 ⓪ 𝘝𝘐𝘚𝘈
closed 4 days Christmas – **Meals** (dinner only) 24.00 t. and a la carte ⬧ 8.50.

228

at Coldred NW : 6 m. by A 256 off A 2 – Z – ⊠ Dover.

⌂ **Coldred Court** ⌂, Church Rd, CT15 5AQ, ℘ (01304) 830816, Fax (01304) 830816, « 17C farmhouse », ☞ – 📺 🅿. ✻
closed Christmas – **Meals** (by arrangement) 15.00 – **3 rm** � 50.00/70.00.

DOVERIDGE Derbs. 402 403 404 O 25 – see Uttoxeter.

DOWN HATHERLEY Glos. – see Gloucester.

DOWNTON Wilts. 403 404 O 31 – see Salisbury.

DREWSTEIGNTON Devon 403 I 31 The West Country G. – pop. 668.
Env. : Dartmoor National Park★★.
London 216 – Exeter 15 – Plymouth 46.

⌂ **Hunts Tor**, EX6 6QW, ℘ (01647) 281228 – ✺ rest, 📺
March-October – **Meals** (booking essential-minimum 24 hours notice required) 20.00 **st.** –
3 rm 42.50/75.00 **st.**

DRIFFIELD East Riding 402 S 21 – see Great Driffield.

DRIFT Cornwall – see Penzance.

DROITWICH Worcestershire 403 404 N 27 – pop. 20 966.
📍 Ombersley, Bishopswood Rd ℘ (01905) 620747 – 📍 Ford Lane ℘ (01905) 770129.
🅱 St. Richard's House, Victoria Sq., WR9 8DS ℘ (01905) 774312.
London 129 – Birmingham 20 – Bristol 66 – Worcester 6.

🏨 **Travelodge**, Rashwood Hill, WR9 8DA, NE : 1 ½ m. on A 38 ℘ (01527) 861545, Reservations (Freephone) 0800 850950 – ✺ rm, 📺 ⅙ 🅿. 🆎 🅰🅴 ⓞ 𝒱𝐼𝒮𝒜 𝐽𝐶𝐵. ✻
32 rm 44.95 **t.**

✕✕ **Rossini's**, 6 Worcester Rd, WR9 8AB, ℘ (01905) 794799 – 🅿. 🆎 🅰🅴 𝒱𝐼𝒮𝒜
closed Sunday and 25-26 December – **Meals** - Italian - 11.50/16.90 **t.** and a la carte ⓐ 4.90.

at Feckenham E : 7¼ m. on B 4090 – ⊠ Redditch.

⌂ **Steps**, 6 High St., B96 6HS, ℘ (01527) 892678 – ✺ rm,
Meals (by arrangement) 9.95 **s.** – **3 rm** ⊠ 20.00/40.00 **s.** – SB.

at Smite S : 3¾ m. by B 4090 and A 38 off A 4538 – ⊠ Worcester.

🏨 **Pear Tree**, WR3 8SY, ℘ (01905) 756565, Fax (01905) 756777 – ✺ rm, 📺 ☎ ⅙ 🅿 –
⅙ 250. 🆎 🅰🅴 ⓞ 𝒱𝐼𝒮𝒜. ✻
Meals a la carte 14.00/22.95 **st.** – **21 rm** ⊠ 75.00/95.00 **st.**, 3 suites.

at Hadley Heath SW : 4 m. by Ombersley Way, A 4133 and Ladywood rd – ⊠ Droitwich.

🏨 Hadley Bowling Green Inn, WR9 0AR, ℘ (01905) 620294, Fax (01905) 620771 – ✺ rest,
📺 ☎ 🅿
14 rm.

DRONFIELD Derbs. 402 403 404 P 24 – pop. 22 985 – ⊠ Sheffield (S. Yorks.).
London 158 – Derby 30 – Nottingham 31 – Sheffield 6.

🏨 **Manor House**, 10-15 High St., S18 6PY, ℘ (01246) 413971, Fax (01246) 412104 – ✺ 📺
☎ 🅿 – ⅙ 25. 🆎 🅰🅴 𝒱𝐼𝒮𝒜
closed 25 and 26 December – **Meals** (lunch by arrangement) 17.50 **t.** and a la carte ⓐ 7.95 –
8 rm ⊠ 49.50/69.50 **t.**, 2 suites – SB.

🏨 **Chantry**, Church St., S18 1QB, ℘ (01246) 413014, Fax (01246) 413014, ☞ – 📺 🅿. 🆎 🅰🅴
𝒱𝐼𝒮𝒜.
Meals (closed Monday lunch and Sunday dinner) (residents only) (bar lunch)/dinner
14.95 **st.** and a la carte ⓐ 5.50 – **8 rm** ⊠ 44.00/60.00 **st.**

⌂ **Horsleygate Hall** ⌂ without rest., Horsleygate Lane, Holmesfield, S18 7WD, W : 3 ½ m.
by B 5056 off B 6054 ℘ (0114) 2890333, « Part Victorian, part Georgian house », ☞, park –
✺ 🅿. ✻
closed 1 week Christmas and New Year – **3 rm** ⊠ 25.00/44.00 **st.**

DRYBROOK *Glos.* 403 404 M 28 – *pop. 2 742.*
London 149 – Bristol 34 – Gloucester 12 – Newport 35.

✕✕ **Cider Press,** The Cross, GL17 9EB, ✆ (01594) 544472 – 🚭. MC VISA
closed Tuesday and first 3 weeks January – **Meals** (by arrangement Sunday and Monday) a la carte 18.30/24.50 **t.** 🍷 5.95.

DUDDENHOE END *Essex* 404 U 27 – *see Saffron Walden.*

DUDDINGTON *Northants.* 402 404 S 26 – *see Stamford (Lincs.).*

DUDLEY *W. Mids.* 402 403 404 N 26 *Great Britain G.* – *pop. 304 615.*
See : *Black Country Museum★.*
ℹ *39 Churchill Shopping Centre, DY2 7BL,* ✆ *(01384) 812830.*
London 132 – Birmingham 10 – Wolverhampton 6.

Plan : see Birmingham p. 2

⌂⌂⌂ **Copthorne Merry Hill,** The Waterfront, Level St., Brierley Hill, DY5 1UR, SW : 2 ¼ m. by A 461 ✆ (01384) 482882, *Fax (01384) 482773,* 🏋, ≘s, 🏊 – 🛗, 🚭 rm, ▤ rest, TV ☎ ♿ Ⓟ – 👥 250. MC AE ⓓ VISA JCB. 🚫🐕 AU z
Meals a la carte 15.40/29.15 **st.** 🍷 7.95 – ☕ 12.50 – **129 rm** 120.00/130.00 **st.**, 9 suites.

⌂⌂ Ward Arms, Birmingham Rd, DY1 4RN, NE : ¾ m. on A 461 ✆ (01384) 458070, *Fax (01384) 457502* – 🚭 rm, TV ☎ ♿ Ⓟ – 👥 100 BT a
72 rm.

⌂ **Travelodge** without rest., Dudley Rd, Brierley Hill, DY5 1LQ, SW : 2 m. on A 461 ✆ (01384) 481579, Reservations (Freephone) 0800 850950 – 🚭 TV ♿ Ⓟ. MC AE ⓓ VISA JCB. 🚫🐕 AU c
32 rm 44.95 **t.**

⚙ ATS Oakeywell St. ✆ (01384) 238047

DULVERTON *Somerset* 403 J 30 *The West Country G.* – *pop. 1 870 (inc. Brushford).*
See : *Village★.*
Env. : *Exmoor National Park★★ – Tarr Steps★★, NW : 6 m. by B 3223.*
London 198 – Barnstaple 27 – Exeter 26 – Minehead 18 – Taunton 27.

⌂⌂ **Carnarvon Arms,** TA22 9AE, SE : 1 ½ m. on B 3222 ✆ (01398) 323302, *Fax (01398) 324022,* 🏊, 🎣, 🌳, park, 🎾 – TV ☎ Ⓟ – 👥 100. MC AE VISA
Meals (lunch by arrangement)/dinner 24.25 **t.** – **24 rm** ☕ 45.00/80.00 **t.**, 1 suite.

⌂ **Ashwick House** 🐦, TA22 9QD, NW : 4 ¼ m. by B 3223 ✆ (01398) 323868, *Fax (01398) 323868,* ⩽, ⛱, « Country house atmosphere », 🌳 – 🚭 rest, TV ☎ Ⓟ. 🚫🐕
Meals (dinner only and Sunday lunch)/dinner 19.75 **t.** 🍷 6.50 – **6 rm** ☕ (dinner included) 68.00/124.00 **t.** – SB.

DUNCHURCH *Warks.* 403 404 Q 26 – *pop. 2 251* – ✉ *Rugby.*
London 90 – Coventry 12 – Leicester 24 – Northampton 26.

⌂ **Travelodge,** London Rd, Thurlaston, CV23 9LG, NW : 2 ½ m. on A 45 ✆ (01788) 521538, Reservations (Freephone) 0800 850950 – 🚭 rm, TV ♿ Ⓟ. MC AE ⓓ VISA JCB. 🚫🐕
Meals (grill rest.) – **40 rm** 44.95 **t.**

DUNSFORD *Devon* 403 I 31 *The West Country G.* – *pop. 1212.*
Env. : *Dartmoor National Park★★.*
London 206 – Exeter 6 – Plymouth 35.

⌃ **Rock House** 🐦, EX6 7EP, SE : 1 ½ m. by B 3212 off Christow rd ✆ (01647) 252514, ⩽, 🌳, park – Ⓟ
Meals 25.00 **st.** 🍷 4.00 – **3 rm** ☕ 37.50/60.00 **st.**

DUNSLEY *N. Yorks.* – *see Whitby.*

DUNSTABLE *Beds.* 404 S 28 – *pop. 49 666.*
⛳18 *Tilsworth, Dunstable Rd* ✆ *(01525) 210721/210722.*
ℹ *The Library, Vernon Pl., LU5 4HA* ✆ *(01582) 471012.*
London 40 – Bedford 24 – Luton 4.5 – Northampton 35.

🏛 **Old Palace Lodge,** Church St., LU5 4RT, 𝒫 (01582) 662201, *Fax (01582) 696422* – 📶,
⇔ rm, 🍴 rest, 📺 ☎ 🅿 – 🔬 35. 🆎 AE ⓪ VISA JCB
Meals *(closed Saturday lunch)* 19.50 **t.** and a la carte ⅙ 11.00 – ☲ 8.75 – **68 rm** 82.50/
102.50 **t.**

🏛 **Highwayman,** London Rd, LU6 3DX, SE : 1 m. on A 5 𝒫 (01582) 601122,
Fax (01582) 603812 – 📺 ☎ ♿ 🅿 – 🔬 50. 🆎 AE ⓪ VISA. ✜
Meals (lunch by arrangement Monday to Saturday)/dinner 10.95 **t.** and a la carte ⅙ 4.50 –
51 rm ☲ 49.00/65.00 **t.**

🏛 **Travel Inn,** 350 Luton Rd, LU5 4LL, NE : 1 ¾ m. on A 505 𝒫 (01582) 609938,
Fax (01582) 664114 – ⇔ rm, 🍴 rest, 📺 ♿ 🅿. 🆎 AE ⓪ VISA
Meals (grill rest.) – **42 rm** 36.50 **t.**

🏛 **Travel Inn,** Watling St., Kensworth, LU6 3QP, SE : 2 ½ m. on A 5 𝒫 (01582) 840509,
Fax (01582) 842811 – ⇔ rm, 📺 ♿ 🅿. 🆎 AE ⓪ VISA. ✜
Meals (grill rest.) – **40 rm** 36.50 **t.**

at Hockliffe NW : 3 ¼ m. on A 5 – ✉ Dunstable.

🏛 **Travelodge,** LU7 9LZ, SE : ¾ m. on A 5 𝒫 (01525) 211177, *Fax (01525) 211177*, Reservations (Freephone) 0800 850950 – ⇔ rm, 📺 ♿ 🅿. 🆎 AE ⓪ VISA JCB. ✜
Meals (grill rest.) – **28 rm** 49.95 **t.**

DUNSTER Somerset **403** J 30 *The West Country G.* – *pop. 848* – ✉ Minehead.

See : Town★★ – Castle★★ AC (Upper rooms ≤★) – Dunster Water Mill★ AC – St. George's
Church★ – Dovecote★.
Env. : Exmoor National Park★★ (Dunkery Beacon★★★ (≤★★★), Watersmeet★, Valley of the
Rocks★, Vantage Point★) – Cleeve Abbey★★ AC, SE : 5 m. by A 39 – Timberscombe
(Church★) SW : 3 ½ m. by A 396.
London 184 – Bristol 61 – Exeter 40 – Taunton 22.

🏛 **Luttrell Arms,** 36 High St., TA24 6SG, 𝒫 (01643) 821555, *Fax (01643) 821567*, « Part 15C
inn », 🌳 – ⇔ 📺 ☎ ⇦, 🆎 AE ⓪ VISA JCB. ✜
Meals 19.95 **st.** (dinner) and a la carte 9.85/16.65 **st.** ⅙ 6.95 – ☲ 9.50 – **27 rm** 75.00/
120.00 **t.** – SB.

🏛 **The Exmoor House,** West St., TA24 6SN, 𝒫 (01643) 821268, *Fax (01643) 821267*, 🌳 –
⇔ 📺 ☎. 🆎 AE VISA JCB
Meals (lunch only) a la carte 11.15/15.15 **t.** – ***The Garden Room :*** **Meals** (dinner only)
23.95 **t.** – **6 rm** ☲ 45.00/90.00 **st.** – SB.

DURHAM Durham **401 402** P 19 *Great Britain G.* – *pop. 36 937.*

See : City★★★ - Cathedral★★★ (Nave★★★, Chapel of the Nine Altars★★★, Sanctuary
Knocker★) B – Oriental Museum★★ AC (at Durham University by A 167) B – City and
Riverside (Prebends' Bridge ≤★★ A , Framwellgate Bridge ≤★★ B) – Monastic Buildings
(Cathedral Treasury★, Central Tower ≤★) B – Castle★ (Norman chapel★) AC B.
🏌 Mount Oswald, South Rd 𝒫 (0191) 386 7527.
🅱 Market Pl., DH1 3NJ 𝒫 (0191) 384 3720.
London 267 – Leeds 77 – Middlesbrough 23 – Sunderland 12.

Plan on next page

🏨 **Ramside Hall,** Carrville, DH1 1TD, NE : 3 m. on A 690 𝒫 (0191) 386 5282,
Fax (0191) 386 0399, 🏌, 🌳, park – 📶, ⇔ rm, 📺 ☎ ♿ 🅿 – 🔬 300. 🆎 AE ⓪ VISA. ✜
Meals 16.00 **st.** and a la carte – **78 rm** ☲ 90.00/110.00 **st.**, 2 suites – SB.

🏨 **Royal County,** Old Elvet, DH1 3JN, 𝒫 (0191) 386 6821, *Fax (0191) 386 0704*, 🛌, 🏊, 🔲 –
📶, ⇔ rm, 🍴 rest, 📺 ☎ ♿ 🅿 – 🔬 120. 🆎 AE ⓪ VISA   **B a**
County : **Meals** 14.50/23.50 **st.** and a la carte ⅙ 6.50 – ***Bowes :*** **Meals** 18.50 **st.** (dinner)
and a la carte 12.25/24.75 **st.** ⅙ 6.50 – **149 rm** ☲ 95.00/145.00 **st.**, 1 suite – SB.

🏨 **Three Tuns Swallow,** New Elvet, DH1 3AQ, 𝒫 (0191) 386 4326, *Fax (0191) 386 1406* –
⇔ rm, 📺 ☎ 🅿 – 🔬 350. 🆎 AE ⓪ VISA   **B e**
Meals 13.50/18.75 **st.** ⅙ 7.00 – **46 rm** ☲ 95.00/115.00 **st.**, 1 suite – SB.

🏛 **Travel Inn,** Arnison Retail Centre, DH1 5GB, N : 3 m. by A 167 𝒫 (0191) 383 9140,
Fax (0191) 383 9107 – 🅿. 🆎 AE ⓪ VISA
40 rm 36.50 **t.**

✗ **Bistro 21,** Aykley Heads House, Aykley Heads, DH1 5TS, NW : 1 ½ m. by A 691 and B 6532
🏵 𝒫 (0191) 384 4354, *Fax (0191) 384 1149*, 🌱 – 🅿. 🆎 AE ⓪ VISA
closed Sunday, Monday, 25-26 December and Bank Holidays – **Meals** 13.50 **t.**
(lunch) and a la carte 17.50/24.50 **t.**

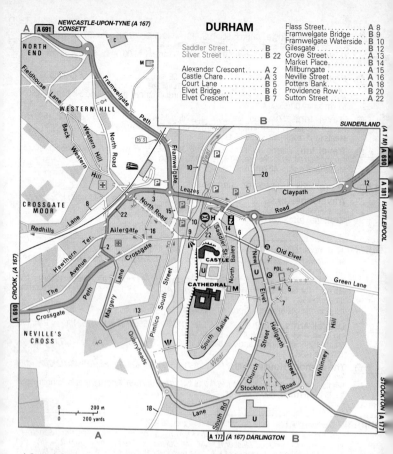

Flass Street.............. **A** 8
Framwelgate Bridge .... **B** 9
Framwelgate Waterside . **B** 10
Gilesgate .... **B** 12
Grove Street............. **A** 13
Market Place.............. **B** 14
Millburngate .... **A** 15
Neville Street .... **A** 16
Potters Bank............. **A** 18
Providence Row.......... **A** 20
Sutton Street .... **A** 22

Saddler Street........... **B**
Silver Street .... **B** 22

Alexander Crescent..... **A** 2
Castle Chare............ **A** 3
Court Lane .... **B** 5
Elvet Bridge .... **B** 6
Elvet Crescent .... **B** 7

DURHAM

at Croxdale *S : 3 m. on A 167 –* **B** *–* ⌧ *Durham.*

🏨 **Bridge Toby,** DH1 3SP, ✆ (0191) 378 0524, Fax (0191) 378 9981 – 📺 ☎ 🅿 – 🔏 50. 🆎 🆎
🆅🆂🅰, ✀
   accommodation closed 1 January and 24 to 26 December – **Meals** (grill rest.) 5.00 **t.**
   and a la carte 👖 5.00 – **46 rm** ⌑ 52.00/62.00 **t.** – SB.

   🔧 ATS Finchale Rd, Newton Hall ✆ (0191) 384 1810   ATS Mill Rd, Langley Moor ✆ (0191) 378 0262

DUXFORD *Cambs.* 🔢 U 27 *– see Cambridge.*

EAGLESCLIFFE *Stockton-on-Tees* 🔢 P 20 *– see Stockton-on-Tees.*

EARL'S COLNE *Essex* 🔢 W 28 *– pop. 3 420 –* ⌧ *Colchester.*
London 55 – Cambridge 33 – Chelmsford 22 – Colchester 10.

🏠 **Elm House,** 14 Upper Holt St., CO6 2PG, on A 604 ✆ (01787) 222197, 🌳 – ↩ rm. ✀
   closed Easter and 25-26 December – **Meals** (by arrangement) (communal dining) 18.00 **s.** –
   3 rm ⌑ 19.00/50.00 **s.** – SB.

Die Namen der wichtigsten Einkaufsstraßen sind
am Anfang des Straßenverzeichnisses in Rot aufgeführt.

EASINGTON Bucks.

London 54 – Aylesbury 13 – Oxford 18.

🍴 **Mole & Chicken,** The Terrace, HP18 9EY, ℰ (01844) 208387, Fax (01844) 208387, « Characterful inn » – **ℙ**. **⬤ 0̸** AE VISA
closed 25 December – **Meals** a la carte 12.95/23.40 t. ⓕ 7.75.

EASINGWOLD N. Yorks. 402 Q 21 – pop. 2 816 – ✉ York.

🏌 Stillington Rd ℰ (01347) 821486.

🛈 Chapel Lane, YO6 3AE ℰ (01347) 821530 (summer only).

London 217 – Middlesbrough 37 – York 14.

🏠 **Garth,** York Rd, YO6 3PG, S : 1¼ m. ℰ (01347) 822988 – 🖙 rm, 📺 ☎ **ℙ**. **⬤** VISA. ⁂
Meals - Italian - (closed Sunday) (dinner only) a la carte 11.00/17.00 t. – **9 rm** ⊇ 35.00/
49.50 t. – SB.

🏠 **Old Vicarage** without rest., Market Pl., YO6 3AL, ℰ (01347) 821015, ☞ – 🖙 🖙 📺 **ℙ**. ⁂
closed December and January – **6 rm** ⊇ 27.50/60.00 st.

at Raskelf W : 2¾ m. – ✉ York.

🏠 **Old Farmhouse,** YO6 3LF, ℰ (01347) 821971 – 🖙 rest, 📺 ☎ **ℙ**
closed 23 December-31 January – **Meals** (closed Sunday to non-residents) (dinner only)
16.50 st. ⓕ 6.50 – **10 rm** ⊇ (dinner included) 45.00/82.00 st. – SB.

EASTBOURNE E. Sussex 404 U 31 Great Britain G. – pop. 94 793.

See : Seafront★.

Env. : Beachy Head★★★, SW : 3 m. by B 2103 Z.

🏌 Royal Eastbourne, Paradise Drive ℰ (01323) 729738 Z – 🏌 Eastbourne Downs, East
Dean Rd ℰ (01323) 720827 – 🏌 Eastbourne Golfing Park, Lottbridge Drove ℰ (01323)
520400.

🛈 3 Cornfield Rd, BN21 4QL ℰ (01323) 411400.

London 68 – Brighton 25 – Dover 61 – Maidstone 49.

Plan on next page

🏨 **De Vere Grand,** King Edward's Par., BN21 4EQ, ℰ (01323) 412345, Fax (01323) 412233,
≤, ⓕ₅, ≘s, ⌁, ⊠, ☞ – ⏸ 📺 ☎ **ℙ** – 🕍 400. **⬤** AE **0̸** VISA   Z x
Garden Restaurant : Meals (dinner only and lunch Sunday and Monday) 19.50/
25.00 st. and a la carte ⓕ 8.00 – (see also **Mirabelle** below) – **149 rm** ⊇ 115.00/160.00 st.,
15 suites – SB.

🏨 **Cavendish,** 37-40 Grand Par., BN21 4DH, ℰ (01323) 410222, Fax (01323) 410941
≤, ⓕ₅, – ⏸, 🖙 rm, 📺 ☎ **ℙ** – 🕍 170. **⬤** AE **0̸** VISA. ⁂   X r
Meals 10.50/21.50 st. and dinner a la carte – **108 rm** ⊇ 90.00/110.00 st., 4 suites – SB.

🏨 **Lansdowne,** King Edward's Par., BN21 4EE, ℰ (01323) 725174, Fax (01323) 739721, ≤ –
⏸ 📺 ☎ ⟵ – 🕍 130. **⬤** AE **0̸** VISA JCB   Z z
closed 1 to 15 January – **Meals** (bar lunch Monday to Saturday)/dinner 15.50 st. ⓕ 4.75 –
122 rm ⊇ 52.00/98.00 st. – SB.

🏨 **Langham,** Royal Par., BN22 7AH, ℰ (01323) 731451, Fax (01323) 646623, ≤ – ⏸ 📺 ☎. **⬤**
AE VISA JCB   Z e
closed 13 December-12 February – **Meals** 7.50/11.50 st. and a la carte ⓕ 5.55 – **88 rm**
⊇ 36.00/72.00 st. – SB.

🏨 **Chatsworth,** Grand Par., BN21 3YR, ℰ (01323) 411016, Fax (01323) 643270, ≤ – ⏸,
🖙 rm, 📺 ☎ – 🕍 100. **⬤** AE **0̸** VISA   X e
Meals 11.50/15.50 st. ⓕ 4.75 – **46 rm** ⊇ 46.00/86.00 st., 1 suite – SB.

🏨 **Brownings,** 28 Upperton Rd, BN21 1JS, ℰ (01323) 724558, Fax (01323) 731288, ⌁ – 📺
☎ **ℙ** – 🕍 40. **⬤** VISA JCB. ⁂   Z a
Meals a la carte 12.00/21.00 st. ⓕ 5.00 – **10 rm** ⊇ 45.00/70.00 st.

🏨 **Oban,** King Edward's Par., BN21 4DS, ℰ (01323) 731581, Fax (01323) 721994 – ⏸, 🖙 rest,
📺 ☎ AE VISA JCB. ⁂   X a
closed January and February – **Meals** (bar lunch)/dinner 13.95 t. ⓕ 4.25 – **30 rm** ⊇ 28.00/
56.00 t. – SB.

🏠 **Cherry Tree,** 15 Silverdale Rd, BN20 7AJ, ℰ (01323) 722406, Fax (01323) 648838 –
🖙 rest, 📺 ☎. **⬤** AE VISA. ⁂   Z u
closed January – **Meals** (by arrangement) 12.00 t. ⓕ 4.00 – **10 rm** ⊇ 24.00/58.00 t. – SB.

🏠 **Brayscroft** without rest., 13 South Cliff Av., BN20 7AH, ℰ (01323) 647005 – 🖙   Z n
5 rm ⊇ 21.00/42.00 s.

🏠 **Southcroft,** 15 South Cliff Av., BN20 7AH, ℰ (01323) 729071 – 🖙. ⁂   Z n
closed Christmas – **Meals** (by arrangement) 9.00 st. ⓕ 3.00 – **4 rm** ⊇ 21.00/42.00 st. – SB.

233

EASTBOURNE

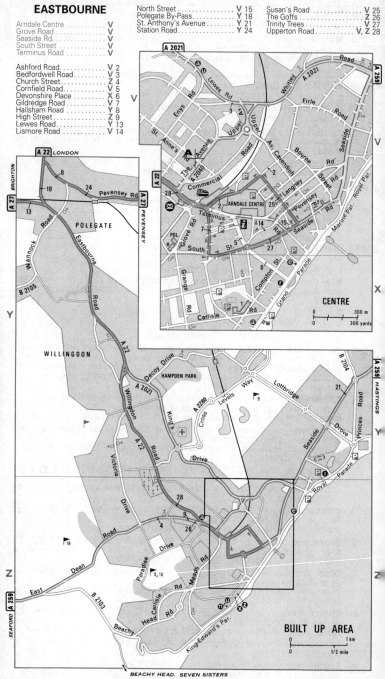

CENTRE

0   300 m
0   300 yards

BUILT UP AREA

0   1 km
0   1/2 mile

BEACHY HEAD, SEVEN SISTERS

234

⌂ **Camelot Lodge,** 35 Lewes Rd, BN21 2BU, ℘ (01323) 725207 – ⤬ rest, 📺 🅿. ⓦⓢ 𝗩𝗜𝗦𝗔
🇯🇨🇧. ⌘   V u
April-October – **Meals** *(by arrangement)* 8.00 **st.** – **7 rm** � 35.00/45.00 **st.**

⌂ **Far End,** 139 Royal Par., BN22 7LH, ℘ (01323) 725666 – ⤬ rest, 📺 🅿   Y   i
restricted opening in winter – **Meals** *(by arrangement)* 7.00 – **10 rm** ⊏ 17.00/42.00 – SB.

ⅩⅩⅩⅩ **Mirabelle** (at De Vere Grand H.), King Edward's Par., BN21 4EQ, ℘ (01323) 410771,
Fax (01323) 412233 – ▤ 🅿. ⓦⓢ 𝗔𝗘 ⓞ 𝗩𝗜𝗦𝗔   Z   x
closed Sunday, Monday, first 2 weeks January and first 2 weeks August – **Meals** 18.50/
29.50 **st.** and dinner a la carte ¦ 9.50.

ⅩⅩ **Downland** with rm, 37 Lewes Rd, BN21 2BU, ℘ (01323) 732689, *Fax (01323) 720321* – 📺
☎ 🅿. ⓦⓢ 𝗔𝗘 ⓞ 𝗩𝗜𝗦𝗔 🇯🇨🇧. ⌘   V   a
closed 23 to 30 December – **Meals** *(closed Sunday and Monday to non-residents)*
(dinner only) 17.50 **t.** and a la carte ¦ 8.00 – **14 rm** ⊏ 40.00/70.00 **t.** – SB.

at Jevington *NW : 6 m. by A 259* – Z – *on B 2105* – ⊠ *Polegate.*

ⅩⅩ **Hungry Monk,** The Street, BN26 5QF, ℘ (01323) 482178, *Fax (01323) 483989,* « *Part*
⌂ *Elizabethan cottages* », 🚗 – ⤬ ▤ 🅿. 𝗔𝗘
closed 24 to 26 December and Bank Holiday Mondays – **Meals** *(booking essential)*
(dinner only and Sunday lunch)/dinner 24.00 **t.** ¦ 7.00.

at Wilmington *NW : 6½ m. by A 22 on A 27* – Y – ⊠ *Eastbourne.*

ⅩⅩ **Crossways** with rm, Lewes Rd, BN26 5SG, ℘ (01323) 482455, *Fax (01323) 487811,* 🚗 –
⤬ rest, 📺 ☎ 🅿. ⓦⓢ 𝗔𝗘 𝗩𝗜𝗦𝗔 🇯🇨🇧. ⌘
closed 23 December-23 January – **Meals** *(closed Sunday and Monday) (dinner only)* 26.95 **t.**
¦ 7.25 – **7 rm** ⊏ 46.00/75.00 **st.** – SB.

🅐 ATS Langney Rise ℘ (01323) 761971

EAST BUCKLAND *Devon* 𝟰𝟬𝟯 I 30 – *see South Molton.*

EAST DEREHAM *Norfolk* 𝟰𝟬𝟰 W 25 – *pop. 12 974.*
London 109 – Cambridge 57 – King's Lynn 27 – Norwich 16.

🏠 **George,** Swaffham Rd, NR19 2AZ, ℘ (01362) 696801, *Fax (01362) 695711* – 📺 ☎ 🅿. ⓦⓢ
𝗔𝗘 ⓞ 𝗩𝗜𝗦𝗔 🇯🇨🇧
Meals a la carte 12.00/23.00 **st.** ¦ 5.50 – **7 rm** ⊏ 42.50/52.50 **st.,** 1 suite.

⌂ **Peacock House** without rest., Peacock Lane, Old Beetley, NR20 4DG, N : 3 ½ m. by
B 1110 ℘ (01362) 860371, « *Part 17C farmhouse* », 🚗 – ⤬ 🅿
closed 2 weeks January-February and 2 weeks November – **3 rm** ⊏ 18.00/38.00 **s.**

at Wendling *W : 5½ m. by A 47.*

⌂ **Greenbanks Country,** Swaffham Rd, NR19 2AR, ℘ (01362) 687742, ⌇, 🚗 – ⤬ rest,
📺 🅿. ⓦⓢ 𝗩𝗜𝗦𝗔
Meals 17.50 **st.** ¦ 5.50 – **5 rm** ⊏ 38.00/58.00 **st.** – SB.

EAST GRINSTEAD *W. Sussex* 𝟰𝟬𝟰 T 30 – *pop. 24 383.*
🅱 *Copthorne, Borers Arm Rd* ℘ (01342) 712508.
London 48 – Brighton 30 – Eastbourne 32 – Lewes 21 – Maidstone 37.

🏨 Jarvis Felbridge, London Rd, RH19 2BH, NW: 1 ½ m. on A 22 ℘ (01342) 326992,
Fax (01342) 410778, 𝟣𝟦, ⌇, ⌇, ▦, 🚗, ⅔ – ⤬ rm, 📺 ☎ ⅙ 🅿 – 🔬 350
90 **rm.**

🏨 **Woodbury House,** Lewes Rd, RH19 3UD, SE : ½ m. on A 22 ℘ (01342) 313657,
Fax (01342) 314801, 🚗 – 📺 ☎ 🅿. ⓦⓢ 𝗔𝗘 ⓞ 𝗩𝗜𝗦𝗔. ⌘
Chauffers : **Meals** 9.95 **t.** and a la carte ¦ 5.00 – *Bistro :* **Meals** 9.95 **t.** and a la carte ¦ 5.00
– **14 rm** ⊏ 70.00/85.00 **st.** – SB.

at Gravetye *SW : 4 ½ m. by B 2110 taking second turn left towards West Hoathly* – ⊠ *East*
Grinstead.

🏨 **Gravetye Manor** ⌇, Vowels Lane, RH19 4LJ, ℘ (01342) 810567, *Fax (01342) 810080,* ≤,
❀ « *16C manor house with gardens and grounds by William Robinson* », ⌇, park – ⤬ rest,
📺 ☎ 🅿. 𝗔𝗘 𝗩𝗜𝗦𝗔. ⌘
Meals *(booking essential)* 24.00/30.00 **s.** and a la carte 34.50/59.50 **s.** ¦ 10.50 – ⊏ 11.50 –
18 rm 110.00/248.00 **s.**
Spec. Terrine of chicken "Shakazia". Assiette of lamb. Tian of white chocolate with ragout of
cherries and sugared pistachios.

🅐 ATS London Rd, North End ℘ (01342) 410740

EAST HADDON Northants. 403 404 Q 27 – pop. 607 – ⊠ Northampton
London 78 – Birmingham 47 – Leicester 32 – Northampton 6.

🏠 **Red Lion** with rm, High St., NN6 8BU, ℰ (01604) 770223, Fax (01604) 770767, « Part 17C », 🐜 – 🔟 ☎ 🅿. 🍷 ⬥ 🅰 💳 🃏 💳
closed 25 and 26 December – **Meals** (closed Sunday dinner) 17.85 **t.** (lunch) and a la carte 20.45/30.15 **t.** ₫ 7.00 – **5 rm** ⊇ 50.00/65.00 **t.**

EASTHAM Mersey. 402 403 L 24 – pop. 15 011 – ⊠ Wirral.
London 209 – Birmingham 45 – Chester 13 – Liverpool 7.5 – Manchester 45.

🏨 **Travelodge,** New Chester Rd, L62 9AQ, at junction of A 41 with M 53 ℰ (0151) 327 2489, Fax (0151) 327 2489, Reservations (Freephone) 0800 850950 – ⬥ rm, 🔟 ♿ 🅿. 🍷 🅰 💳 💳 🃏. 🞨
Meals (grill rest.) – **31 rm** 39.95 **t.**

EAST HOATHLY E. Sussex 404 U 31 – pop. 1 206
London 60 – Brighton 16 – Eastbourne 13 – Hastings 25 – Maidstone 32.

🏠 **Old Whyly** 🐦, BN8 6EL, W : ½ m., turning right after post box on right, taking centre gravel drive after approx. 400 metres ℰ (01825) 840216, Fax (01825) 840738, ⬅, « Georgian manor house, antiques », 🅹, 🐜, 🞦 – ⬥ rm, 🅿. 🞨
Meals (by arrangement) (communal dining) 20.00 – **3 rm** ⊇ 67.50/90.00.

Si vous cherchez un hôtel tranquille,
consultez d'abord les cartes de l'introduction
ou repérez dans le texte les établissements indiqués avec le signe 🐦 ou 🐦

EAST HORNDON Essex.
London 21 – Chelmsford 13 – Southend-on-Sea 17.

🏨 **Travelodge,** CM13 3LL, on A 127 (eastbound carriageway) ℰ (01277) 810819, Reservations (Freephone) 0800 850950 – 🔟 ♿ 🅿. 🍷 🅰 💳 💳 🃏. 🞨
22 rm 49.95 **t.**

EAST HORSLEY Surrey 404 S 30 – ⊠ Leatherhead.
London 31 – Guildford 8 – Reigate 21.

🏨 **Jarvis Thatchers,** Epsom Rd, KT24 6TB, on A 246 ℰ (01483) 284291, Fax (01483) 284222, 🅹, 🐜 – ⬥ rm, 🔟 ☎ 🅿 – 🔏 60. 🍷 🅰 💳 💳
Meals (closed Saturday lunch) 14.50/19.50 **t.** and a la carte ₫ 7.50 – **54 rm** ⊇ 95.00/190.00 **st.** – SB.

EASTLEIGH Devon 403 H 30 – see Bideford.

EASTLEIGH Hants. 403 P 31 – pop. 49 934.
🏌 Fleming Park, Magpie Lane ℰ (01703) 612797.
✈ Southampton (Eastleigh) Airport : ℰ (01703) 620021.
🛈 Town Hall Centre, Leigh Rd, SO50 9DE ℰ (01703) 641261.
London 74 – Winchester 8 – Southampton 4.

🏨 **Forte Posthouse Southampton/Eastleigh,** Leigh Rd, SO50 9PG, ℰ (01703) 619700, Fax (01703) 643945, 🗐, 🛎, 🞖 – 🗐, ⬥ rm, 🍽 rest, 🔟 ☎ ♿ 🅿 – 🔏 200. 🍷 🅰 💳 💳 🃏
Meals a la carte 15.80/25.65 **st.** ₫ 7.95 – ⊇ 9.95 – **113 rm** 69.00 **st.**, 3 suites – SB.

🏨 **Travel Inn,** Leigh Rd, SO50 9YX, W : ½ m. on A 335 ℰ (01703) 650541, Fax (01703) 650531 – 🗐, ⬥ rm, 🔟 ♿ 🅿. 🍷 🅰 💳 💳
Meals (grill rest.) – **60 rm** 36.50 **t.**

🏨 **Travelodge,** Twyford Rd, SO50 4LF, N : 1 m. on A 335 ℰ (01703) 616813, Reservations (Freephone) 0800 850950 – 🔟 ♿ 🅿. 🍷 🅰 💳 💳 🃏. 🞨
32 rm 49.95 **t.**

🔧 ATS Dutton Lane, Bishopstoke Rd ℰ (01703) 613027/613393

EASTLING Kent 404 W 30 – see Faversham.

EASTON Devon 403 I 31 – see Chagford.

EAST RETFORD *Notts.* **402 404** R 24 – *pop. 20 679.*
   London 148 – Lincoln 23 – Nottingham 31 – Sheffield 27.

⌂ **Old Plough** ♨, Top St., North Wheatley, DN22 9DB, NE : 5 m. by A 620
   ℘ (01427) 880916, ≼, 🐾 – ⅌ 🖃 📺 ❶. ⋘
   Meals (by arrangement) (communal dining) 14.50 **s.** ⬩ 4.00 – **3 rm** ⊑ 35.00/70.00 **s.**

   🚗 ATS Babworth Rd ℘ (01777) 706501

EAST WITTERING *W. Sussex* **404** R 31 – *pop. 4 630* – ✉ *Chichester.*
   London 74 – Brighton 37 – Portsmouth 25.

✗ **Clifford's Cottage,** Bracklesham Lane, Bracklesham Bay, PO20 8JA, E : 1 m. by B 2179 on
   B 2198 ℘ (01243) 670250 – 🖃 ❶. 🆇 🆎 ⓞ 🆅🆂🅰
   closed Sunday dinner, Monday, Tuesday, first week May and 2 weeks November – **Meals**
   (dinner only and Sunday lunch)/dinner 17.95 **t.** and a la carte ⬩ 4.25.

EAST WITTON *N. Yorks.* **402** O 21 – *pop. 153* – ✉ *Leyburn.*
   London 238 – Leeds 45 – Middlesbrough 30 – York 39.

⌂ **Holly Tree,** DL8 4LS, ℘ (01969) 622383, « *16C cottage* », 🐾 – ⅌ ❶
   March-October – **Meals** (by arrangement) (communal dining) 15.00 **st.** ⬩ 6.50 – **4 rm**
   ⊑ 40.00/54.00 **s.**

✗✗ **Blue Lion** with rm, DL8 4SN, ℘ (01969) 624273, *Fax (01969) 624189,* « *19C inn* », 🐾 – 📺
   ☎ ❶. 🆇 🆅🆂🅰
   Meals (in bar Tuesday to Saturday lunch, Sunday dinner and Monday) dinner
   a la carte 17.85/26.15 **t.** ⬩ 6.95 – **12 rm** ⊑ 50.00/80.00 **t.** – SB.

EBCHESTER *Durham* **401 402** O 19 – ✉ *Consett.*
   ⬡ Consett and District, Elmfield Rd, Consett ℘ (01207) 502186.
   London 275 – Carlisle 64 – Newcastle upon Tyne 16.

🏛 **Raven Country,** Broomhill, DH8 6RY, SE : ¾ m. on B 6309 ℘ (01207) 562562,
   Fax (01207) 560262, ≼ – 📺 ☎ ⅖ ❶. 🆇 🆎 ⓞ 🆅🆂🅰. ⋘
   Meals (bar lunch Monday to Saturday)/dinner 19.95 **st.** and a la carte ⬩ 4.95 – **28 rm**
   ⊑ 52.00/69.00 **st.** – SB.

ECCLES *Gtr. Manchester* **402 403 404** M 23 – *see Manchester.*

ECCLESHALL *Staffs.* **402 403 404** N 25 – *pop. 2 748.*
   London 149 – Birmingham 33 – Derby 40 – Shrewsbury 26 – Stoke-on-Trent 12.

🍴 **Badger Inn** with rm, Green Lane, ST21 6BA, S : ¼ m. by A 519 ℘ (01785) 850564 –
   ⅌ rest. 📺 ❶. 🆇 🆅🆂🅰 🆓🆒🅱
   Meals a la carte 8.45/15.35 **t.** – **4 rm** ⊑ 25.00/50.00 **t.**

ECCLESTON *Mersey.* **402** ㉝ **403** ⑬ – *see St. Helens.*

EDENBRIDGE *Kent* **404** U 30 *Great Britain G.* – *pop. 7 196.*
   Env. : Hever Castle★ AC, E : 2 ½ m. – Chartwell★ AC, N : 3 m. by B 2026.
   ⬡, ⬡, ⬡ Crouch House Rd ℘ (01732) 867381.
   London 35 – Brighton 36 – Maidstone 29.

✗✗✗ **Honours Mill,** 87 High St., TN8 5AU, ℘ (01732) 866757, « *Carefully renovated 18C mill* »
   – 🆇 🆅🆂🅰
   closed Saturday lunch, Sunday dinner, Monday and 2 weeks Christmas – **Meals** 15.50/
   32.75 **t.** ⬩ 5.95.

EGERTON *Gtr. Manchester* **402** ㉑ **403** ② **404** ⑨ – *see Bolton.*

EGGESFORD *Devon* **403** I 31.
   London 215 – Barnstaple 18 – Exeter 22 – Taunton 48.

🏠 **Fox and Hounds,** EX18 7JZ, ℘ (01769) 580345, *Fax (01769) 580262,* ⬡, ⬡, 🐾, park –
   📺 ❶ – ⚱ 80. 🆇 🆅🆂🅰 🆓🆒🅱. ⋘
   Meals 13.50 **t.** and a la carte ⬩ 3.75 – **19 rm** ⊑ 36.50/68.00 **t.** – SB.

EGHAM *Surrey* 404 S 29 – *pop. 23 816.*
London 29 – Reading 21.

🏛 **Runnymede,** Windsor Rd, TW20 0AG, on A 308 ℘ *(01784) 436171, Fax (01784) 436340,*
£5, ⬭, ◨, *≋,* ✗ – ᰙ, ✚ rm, ▤ ☎ ❷ – ▵ 350. ◍◉ ﷼ ◉ ᴠɪsᴀ. ✖
Meals *(bar lunch Saturday) (dancing Saturday evening)* a la carte 26.00/33.75 **t.** ₰ 8.50 –
� 12.95 – **171 rm** 129.00/175.00 **st.** – SB.

🏛 **Great Fosters,** Stroude Rd, TW20 9UR, S : 1 ¼ m. by B 388 ℘ *(01784) 433822,*
Fax (01784) 472455, « Elizabethan mansion, gardens », *£5,* ◨, park, *✗* – ᴛᴠ ☎ ❷ –
▵ 100. ◍◉ ﷼ ◉ ᴠɪsᴀ. ✖
Meals 15.50/25.00 **t.** and a la carte ₰ 5.50 – **42 rm** ⊒ 93.00/165.00 **t.**, 2 suites.

EIGHT ASH GREEN *Essex* 404 W 28 – *see Colchester.*

ELLESMERE PORT *Mersey.* 402 403 L 24 – *pop. 64 504.*
London 211 – Birkenhead 9 – Chester 9 – Liverpool 11 – Manchester 44.

🏨 **Holiday Inn Ellesmere Port Chester,** Centre Island, Waterways, Lower Mersey St.,
L65 2AL, NE : 1 ½ m. by A 5032 (M 53 junction 9) ℘ *(0151) 356 8111, Fax (0151) 356 8444,*
« Marina setting overlooking Boat Museum », *£5,* ⬭, ◨ – ᰙ, ✚ rm, ▤ rest, ᴛᴠ ☎ ₺ ❷ –
▵ 120. ◍◉ ﷼ ◉ ᴠɪsᴀ ᴊᴄʙ. ✖
Waterways : **Meals** *(closed lunch Saturday and Sunday)* 11.95 **t.** (lunch)
and a la carte 16.45/25.15 **t.** ₰ 9.50 – ⊒ 8.50 – **83 rm** 85.00/105.00 **t.**

⊚ ATS 1 Rossfield Rd, Rossmore Trading Est. ℘ *(0151) 855 8144*

ELMDON *Essex* 404 U 27 – *see Saffron Walden.*

ELSING *Norfolk* 404 X 25 – *pop. 261 –* ✉ *East Dereham.*
London 118 – Cambridge 66 – King's Lynn 33 – Norwich 15.

🏠 **Bartles Lodge** ⌖ without rest., Church St., NR20 3EA, ℘ *(01362) 637177,* ✎, *≋* – ᴛᴠ
❷. ◍◉ ᴠɪsᴀ
7 rm ⊒ 27.00/56.00 **st.**

ELSLACK *N. Yorks.* 402 N 22 – *see Skipton.*

ELSTOW *Beds.* 404 S 27 – *see Bedford.*

ELSTREE *Herts.* 404 T 29 – *pop. 2 196.*
⛳ *Watling St.* ℘ *(0181) 953 6115.*
London 10 – Luton 22.

Plan : see Greater London (North West)

🏛 **Edgwarebury,** Barnet Lane, WD6 3RE, ℘ *(0181) 953 8227, Fax (0181) 207 3668, ≋,*
park, *✗* – ✚ rm, ᴛᴠ ☎ ❷ – ▵ 80. ◍◉ ﷼ ◉ ᴠɪsᴀ. ✖   CT e
Meals – (see *The Cavendish* below) – ⊒ 8.95 – **47 rm** 92.00/170.00 **t.** – SB.

✗✗✗ **The Cavendish** (at Edgwarebury H.), Barnet Lane, WD6 3RE, ℘ *(0181) 953 8227,*
Fax (0181) 207 3668, ≋, park ✚ ❷. ◍◉ ﷼ ◉ ᴠɪsᴀ
Meals *(closed Saturday lunch to non-residents)* (booking essential) 26.95 **st.**
and a la carte 18.85/30.75 **st.** ₰ 6.95.

ELTERWATER *Cumbria – see Ambleside.*

ELY *Cambs.* 404 U 26 *Great Britain G. – pop. 10 329.*
See : *Cathedral★★ AC.*
Exc. : *Wicken Fen★, SE : 9 m. by A 10 and A 1123.*
⛳ *Cambridge Rd* ℘ *(01353) 662751.*
🛈 *Oliver Cromwells House, 29 St. Mary's St., CB7 4HF* ℘ *(01353) 662062.*
London 74 – Cambridge 16 – Norwich 60.

🏛 **Travelodge,** Witchford Rd, CB6 3NN, W : 1 m. on A 10/A 142 roundabout, Ely bypass
℘ *(01353) 668499, Reservations (Freephone) 0800 850950 –* ✚ rm, ᴛᴠ ₺ ❷. ◍◉ ﷼ ◉ ᴠɪsᴀ
ᴊᴄʙ. ✖
39 rm 39.95 **t.**

✗ **Old Fire Engine House,** 25 St. Mary's St., CB7 4ER, ☏ (01353) 662582, *Fax (01353) 664869,* 🌾 – ⭐ 🅿. 🔟 *VISA*
closed Sunday dinner, 2 weeks Christmas-New Year and Bank Holidays – **Meals** *-* English *-* (booking essential) a la carte 19.50/22.50 ⓖ 5.00.

at Littleport *N : 5 ¾ m. on A 10 –* ✉ *Ely.*

✗✗ **Fen House,** 2 Lynn Rd, CB6 1QG, ☏ (01353) 860645 – ⭐ 🔟 🔟 *VISA*
closed Sunday to Tuesday and 25-26 December – **Meals** (booking essential) (dinner only) 26.00 t. ⓖ 5.75.

at Coveney *NW : 4 m. by West Fen rd –* ✉ *Ely.*

⌂ **Hill House Farm** without rest., 9 Main St., CB6 2DJ, ☏ (01353) 778369, 🌾 – ⭐ 🔟 🅿. ✑
closed 25 and 26 December – **3 rm** ⊇ 30.00/42.00 **s.**

🔘 ATS 11 Broad St. ☏ (01353) 662758/662801

EMPINGHAM *Leics.* 402 404 *S 26 – see Stamford (Lincs.).*

EMSWORTH *Hants.* 404 *R 31 – pop. 18 310 (inc. Southbourne).*
London 75 – Brighton 37 – Portsmouth 10.

🏨 **Brookfield,** 93-95 Havant Rd, PO10 7LF, ☏ (01243) 373363, *Fax (01243) 376342,* 🌾 – ▤ rest, 🔟 ☎ 🅿 – ⚞ 50. 🔟 🔟 🔟 *VISA* 🔟 ✑
closed 24 December-1 January – **Hermitage :** **Meals** 15.95 t. and a la carte ⓖ 4.95 – **40 rm** ⊇ 54.00/79.00 t. – SB.

🏠 **Travelodge,** PO10 7RB, E : ½ m. on A 27 (eastbound carriageway) ☏ (01243) 370877, Reservations (Freephone) 0800 850950 – ⭐ rm, 🔟 ➏ 🅿. 🔟 🔟 🔟 *VISA* 🔟 ✑
36 rm 44.95 **t.**

✗✗✗ **36 on the Quay** (Farthing), 47 South St., The Quay, PO10 7EG, ☏ (01243) 375592, ✿ *Fax (01243) 374429 –* 🔟 🔟 🔟 *VISA*
closed lunch Monday and Saturday, Sunday, 5 to 18 January, 5 to 11 October and Bank Holidays – **Meals** 19.00/29.95 t. ⓖ 7.50
Spec. Scallops wrapped in skate with a basil and coral cream. Breasts of wood pigeon with goose liver, plums and a game reduction. Banana ice cream with caramelised galette and a toffee sauce.

✗✗ **Spencer's,** 36 North St., PO10 7DG, ☏ (01243) 372744, *Fax (01243) 372744 –* ▤. 🔟 🔟 🔟 *VISA*
closed Sunday, Monday and 25-26 December – **Meals** (dinner only) 22.00 t. ⓖ 5.00.

✗ **Downstairs at Spencer's** (☏ *(01243) 379017)* **: Meals** *-* Brasserie *- (closed Sunday, 25-26 December and Bank Holidays)* a la carte 11.70/18.00 t. ⓖ 3.95.

ENSTONE *Oxon.* 403 404 *P 28 – pop. 1 523 –* ✉ *Chipping Norton.*
London 73 – Birmingham 48 – Gloucester 32 – Oxford 18.

⌂ **Swan Lodge** without rest., OX7 4NE, on A 44 ☏ (01608) 678736, *Fax (01608) 677963,* 🌾 – ⭐ rest, 🔟 🅿. ✑
3 rm ⊇ 30.00/40.00.

EPPING *Essex* 404 *U 28 – pop. 9 922.*
London 18 – Cambridge 40 – Chelmsford 21 – Southend-on-Sea 37.

✗ **Neil's,** 142 High St., CM16 4AG, ☏ (01992) 576767 – 🔟 *VISA*
closed Sunday and Monday – **Meals** (booking essential) a la carte 19.00/28.00 t. ⓖ 5.00.

EPSOM *Surrey* 404 ③⓪ *– pop. 64 405 (inc. Ewell).*
🏌 *Longdown Lane South, Epsom Downs* ☏ *(01372) 721666 –* 🏌 *Horton Park C.C., Hook Rd* ☏ *(0181) 393 8400.*
London 17 – Guildford 16.

🏠 **Travel Inn,** Dorking Rd, KT18 7LB, SW : ½ m. on A 24 ☏ (01372) 739786 – ⭐ rm, 🔟 ➏ 🅿. 🔟 🔟 🔟 *VISA*
Meals (grill rest.) – **40 rm** 36.50 **t.**

✗✗ **Le Raj,** 211 Fir Tree Rd, Epsom Downs, KT19 3LB, SE : 2 ¼ m. by B 289 and B 284 on B 291 ☏ (01737) 371371, *Fax (01737) 211903 –* ▤. 🔟 🔟 🔟 *VISA*
closed 25 and 26 December – **Meals** *-* Indian *-* a la carte 22.00/33.90 **t.**

EPWORTH North Lincolnshire 402 404 R 23 – pop. 3 359 – ✉ Doncaster.
London 170 – Leeds 48 – Lincoln 31 – Sheffield 39.

X **Epworth Tap,** 9-11 Market Pl., DN9 1EU, ℰ (01427) 873333, Fax (01427) 875020 – 🔟
🔟
closed Sunday to Wednesday and 2 weeks Christmas-New Year – **Meals** (booking essential)
(dinner only) a la carte 16.00/22.95 **t.** ♦ 6.95.

ERLESTOKE Wilts. 403 404 N 30 – see Devizes.

ERPINGHAM Norfolk 404 X 25 – pop. 1 871.
London 123 – Cromer 8 – King's Lynn 46 – Norwich 16.

X **The Ark** ⌂ with rm, The Street, NR11 7QB, ℰ (01263) 761535, ⟐ – ⟐ 🔟 🅿. ⟐
closed 25 to 30 December – **Meals** (closed Sunday dinner and Monday) (dinner only and
Sunday lunch)/dinner 23.50 **t.** and a la carte ♦ 6.00 – **3 rm** ☲ (dinner included) 70.00/
125.00 **t.**

🍴 **Saracens Head,** with rm, Wolterton, NR11 7LX, W : 1 ½ m. ℰ (01263) 768909, ⟐ –
⟐ rm, 🅿. 🄰🄴 🔟. ⟐
Meals (residents only 25 December) a la carte approx. 14.85 **t.** ♦ 4.50 – **4 rm** ☲ 40.00/
60.00 **st.**

ESCRICK N. Yorks. 402 Q 22 – see York.

ESHER Surrey 404 S 29 – pop. 46 599 (inc. Molesey).
⛳ Thames Ditton & Esher, Portsmouth Rd ℰ (0181) 398 1551 BZ – ⛳ Moore Place,
Portsmouth Rd ℰ (01372) 463533 BZ – ⛳, ⛳ Sandown Park, More Lane ℰ (01372) 461234
BZ.
London 20 – Portsmouth 58.

Plan : see Greater London (South-West)

XX **Good Earth,** 14-18 High St., KT10 9RT, ℰ (01372) 462489, Fax (01372) 465588 – ▤. 🔟 🄰🄴
🔟 🔟   BZ **e**
closed 24 to 27 December – **Meals** - Chinese - 18.00/26.50 **t.** and a la carte ♦ 10.00.

X **La Orient,** 63 High St., KT10 9RQ, ℰ (01372) 466628 – ▤. 🔟 🄰🄴 🔟 🔟   BZ **a**
closed 25 to 28 December – **Meals** - South East Asian - 15.50 **t.** and a la carte ♦ 4.95.

at Claygate SE : 1 m. by A 244 – ✉ Esher.

XX **Mi Piache,** 7 High St., KT10 0JW, ℰ (01372) 462200, Fax (01372) 464882 – ▤. 🔟 🄰🄴
🔟   BZ **n**
closed Saturday lunch and Sunday dinner – **Meals** 9.95/14.95 **t.** and a la carte ♦ 4.25.

XX **Le Petit Pierrot,** 4 The Parade, KT10 0NU, ℰ (01372) 465105, Fax (01372) 467642 – 🔟
🄰🄴 🔟 🔟   BZ **r**
closed Saturday lunch, Sunday, 1 week Christmas-New Year and Bank Holidays – **Meals** -
French - 18.75/21.75 **t.** ♦ 5.15.

L'ETACQ Jersey (Channel Islands) 403 P 33 – see Channel Islands.

EVERCREECH Somerset 403 404 M 30 – see Shepton Mallet.

EVERDON Northants. – see Daventry.

EVERSHOT Dorset 403 404 M 31 – pop. 225 – ✉ Dorchester.
London 149 – Bournemouth 39 – Dorchester 12 – Salisbury 53 – Taunton 30 – Yeovil 10.

🏛 **Summer Lodge** ⌂, Summer Lane, DT2 0JR, ℰ (01935) 83424, Fax (01935) 83005,
« Part Georgian dower house », ⌂, ⟐, ⟐ – ⟐ rest, 🔟 ☎ 🅿. 🔟 🄰🄴 🔟 🔟
🅹🄲🄱
Meals 12.50/32.50 **t.** and a la carte 34.50/48.00 **t.** – **17 rm** ☲ 117.50/225.00 **t.** – SB.

⌂ **Rectory House,** Fore St., DT2 0JW, ℰ (01935) 83273, Fax (01935) 83273, ⟐ – ⟐ 🔟 🅿
🔟 🔟. ⟐
closed January and December – **Meals** (by arrangement) 18.00 – **5 rm** ☲ 45.00/90.00 **s.**

⌂ **Church Farm** ⌂ without rest., Stockwood, DT2 0NG, NE : 3 ½ m. by The Common and
A 37 off Stockwood rd ℰ (01935) 83221, Fax (01935) 83771, « Working farm », ⟐ – ⟐ 🔟
🅿
3 rm ☲ 28.00/40.00 **st.**

EVESHAM Worcestershire 403 404 O 27 – pop. 17 823.

🗓 The Almonry, Abbey Gate, WR11 4BG ℰ (01386) 446944.
London 99 – Birmingham 30 – Cheltenham 16 – Coventry 32.

🏨 **Evesham,** Coopers Lane, off Waterside, WR11 6DA, off Waterside ℰ (01386) 765566, Fax (01386) 765443, Reservations (Freephone) 0800 716969, 🔆, 🐎 – 🔲 🕿 🅿. 🐵 ᴀᴇ ⓘ 𝗩𝗜𝗦𝗔. 🛠
closed 25 and 26 December – **Meals** a la carte 14.50/23.25 **st.** 🍷 4.80 – **40 rm** ⊑ 60.00/90.00 **st.** – SB.

🏨 **Waterside,** 56-59 Waterside, WR11 6JZ, ℰ (01386) 442420, Fax (01386) 446272, 🐋, 🐎 – 🔲 🕿 🅿. 🐵 ᴀᴇ 𝗩𝗜𝗦𝗔
closed 24 December-2 January – **Meals** a la carte 9.10/15.20 **t.** – **15 rm** ⊑ 40.60/75.00 **t.** – SB.

⌂ **Church House** without rest., Greenhill Park Rd, WR11 4NL, ℰ (01386) 40498, 🐎 – 🔲 🅿
3 rm ⊑ 30.00/46.00 **st.**

⌂ **The Croft** without rest., 54 Greenhill Park Rd, WR11 4NF, ℰ (01386) 446035, 🐎 – 🔲 🅿
3 rm ⊑ 35.00/46.00 **s.**

🍴 **Riverside** with rm, The Parks, Offenham Rd, WR11 5JP, NW : 2 m. by Waterside and B 4035 off B 4510 ℰ (01386) 446200, Fax (01386) 40021, <, 🐋, 🐎 – 🖐 rest, 🔲 🕿 🅿. 🐵 𝗩𝗜𝗦𝗔
closed Sunday dinner, Monday and 25 December – **Meals** 16.95/24.95 **st.** 🍷 7.30 – **7 rm** ⊑ 60.00/80.00 **st.** – SB.

at Harvington NE : 4½ m. by A 4184 and B 4088 off Bidford rd – ✉ Evesham.

🏨 **Mill at Harvington** 🐾, Anchor Lane, WR11 5NR, SE : 1 ½ m. ℰ (01386) 870688, Fax (01386) 870688, <, « 18C mill with riverside garden », 🏊, 🐋, 🍴 – 🖐 rest, 🔲 🕿 🅿. 🐵 ᴀᴇ ⓘ 𝗩𝗜𝗦𝗔 JCB. 🛠
closed 24 to 28 December – **Meals** 13.95/22.95 **st.** 🍷 5.25 – **21 rm** ⊑ 58.00/107.00 **st.** – SB.

at Abbot's Salford (Warks.) NE : 5 m. by A 4184 and B 4088 on Bidford rd – ✉ Evesham.

🏨 **Salford Hall,** WR11 5UT, ℰ (01386) 871300, Fax (01386) 871301, « Tudor mansion with early 17C extension and gatehouse », 🈸, 🐎, 🍴 – 🖐 rest, 🔲 🕿 🅿 – 🛡 50. 🐵 ᴀᴇ ⓘ 𝗩𝗜𝗦𝗔 JCB. 🛠
closed 24 to 30 December – **Meals** 15.25/27.50 **st.** 🍷 8.75 – ⊑ 8.50 – **34 rm** 80.00/150.00 **st.** – SB.

at Bretforton E : 3½ m. by B 4035 – ✉ Evesham.

⌂ **The Pond House** 🐾 without rest., Lower Fields, Weston Rd, WR11 5QA, SE : 2 m. by B 4035 ℰ (01386) 831687, <, 🐎 – 🖐 🔲 🅿. 🛠
4 rm ⊑ 38.00/48.00 **s.**

🔧 ATS Worcester Rd ℰ (01386) 765313

EWEN Glos. 403 404 O 28 – see Cirencester.

EXEBRIDGE Somerset 403 J 30 The West Country G. – ✉ Dulverton.
Env. : Exmoor National Park★★.
London 194 – Exeter 23 – Minehead 19 – Taunton 23.

🍴 **Anchor Inn** with rm, TA22 9AZ, NW : ¼ m. on B 3222 ℰ (01398) 323433, Fax (01398) 323808, « Riverside setting », 🐋, 🐎 – 🔲 🕿 🅿. 🐵 𝗩𝗜𝗦𝗔
Meals (bar lunch)/dinner 21.95 **t.** and a la carte – **6 rm** ⊑ 35.00/70.00 **t.** – SB.

EXETER Devon 403 J 31 The West Country G. – pop. 94 717.
See : City★★ – Cathedral★★ Z – Royal Albert Memorial Museum★ Y.
Exc. : Killerton★★ AC, NE : 7 m. by B 3181 V – Ottery St. Mary★ (St. Mary's★) E : 12 m. by B 3183 – Y – A 30 and B 3174 – Crediton (Holy Cross Church★), NW : 9 m. by A 377.
🏌 Downes Crediton, Hookway ℰ (01363) 773991.
✈ Exeter Airport : ℰ (01392) 367433, E : 5 m. by A 30 V – **Terminal :** St. David's and Central Stations.
🗓 Civic Centre, Paris St., EX1 IRP ℰ (01392) 265700 – Exeter Services, Sidmouth Rd, EX2 7HF ℰ (01392) 437581/279088.
London 201 – Bournemouth 83 – Bristol 83 – Plymouth 46 – Southampton 110.

Plan on next page

EXETER
BUILT UP AREA

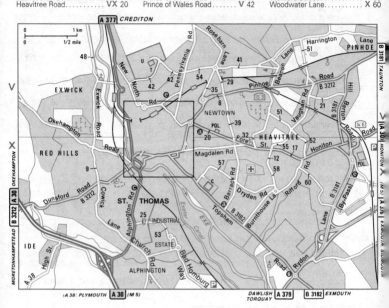

Southgate, Southernhay East, EX1 1QF, ℰ (01392) 412812, Fax (01392) 413549, ⅃₅, ⌖s, ⬚ – |₿|, ✳ rm, ▤ rest, ⊡ ☎ ℗ – ⌂ 150. ⬤⬤ ⒜⒠ ⓪ *VISA* ⰘⰘ   Z a
Meals *(closed Saturday lunch)* 12.95/19.50 **st.** and a la carte – ⌂ 10.95 – **109 rm** 95.00 **st.**, 1 suite – SB.

Rougemont Thistle, Queen St., EX4 3SP, ℰ (01392) 254982, Fax (01392) 420928 – |₿|, ✳ rm, ▤ rest, ⊡ ☎ ℗ – ⌂ 300. ⬤⬤ ⒜⒠ ⓪ *VISA*   Y x
Meals 9.95/18.95 and a la carte ⅃ 4.90 – **88 rm** ⌂ 89.00/113.00 **st.**, 2 suites.

County H. Exeter Royal Clarence, Cathedral Yard, EX1 1HD, ℰ (01392) 319955, Fax (01392) 439423 – |₿| ✳ ⊡ ☎ – ⌂ 120. ⬤⬤ ⒜⒠ ⓪ *VISA*. ✳   Y z
Meals a la carte 10.85/24.40 **st.** ⅃ 6.50 – ⌂ 9.50 – **55 rm** 88.00/110.00 **st.**, 1 suite – SB.

Gipsy Hill ⌦, Gipsy Hill Lane, via Pinn Lane, EX1 3RN, E : 2 m. by Honiton Rd (A 30) off Pinhoe rd ℰ (01392) 465252, Fax (01392) 464302, ≤, ☞ – ✳ rm, ⊡ ☎ ℗ – ⌂ 120. ⬤⬤ ⒜⒠ *VISA*. ✳
closed 24 to 30 December – **Meals** 9.50/16.50 **st.** and a la carte ⅃ 4.50 – **37 rm** ⌂ 70.00/ 90.00 **st.** – SB.

Buckerell Lodge, Topsham Rd, EX2 4SQ, ℰ (01392) 221111, Fax (01392) 441111, ☞ – ✳ rm, ⊡ ☎ ♿ ℗ – ⌂ 60. ⬤⬤ ⒜⒠ ⓪ *VISA* ⰘⰘ   X a
Meals *(closed Saturday lunch)* 12.50/18.50 **st.** and dinner a la carte ⅃ 5.95 – ⌂ 9.95 – **53 rm** 42.00/79.00 **st.** – SB.

St. Olaves Court, Mary Arches St., EX4 3AZ, ℰ (01392) 217736, Fax (01392) 413054, ☞ – ⊡ ☎ ℗. ⬤⬤ ⒜⒠ ⓪ *VISA*. ✳   Z e
Meals – (see *Golsworthy's* below) – ⌂ 6.00 – **15 rm** 70.00/95.00 **t.** – SB.

Exeter Arms Toby, Rydon Lane, Middlemoor, EX2 7HL, E : 3 m. on B 318 ℰ (01392) 435353, Fax (01392) 420826 – ✳ rest, ⊡ ☎ ♿ ℗ – ⌂ 80. ⬤⬤ ⒜⒠ *VISA*. ✳
Meals (grill rest.) a la carte 10.75/16.10 **t.** ⅃ 4.45 – **37 rm** ⌂ 52.50/62.50 **t.**   X e

Devon, Matford, EX2 8XU, S : 3 m. by A 377 on A 379 ℰ (01392) 259268 Fax (01392) 413142 – ✳ rest, ⊡ ☎ ℗ – ⌂ 160. ⬤⬤ ⒜⒠ ⓪ *VISA*
Meals (carving lunch) a la carte 12.65/16.20 **t.** – **41 rm** ⌂ 62.00/85.00 **t.**

🏨 **St. Andrews,** 28 Alphington Rd, EX2 8HN, ☎ (01392) 276784, Fax (01392) 250249 – ⚡
📺 ☎ 🐕 🅿. 🆓 AE ⓪ VISA. ⚹
X c
closed Christmas-New Year – **Meals** (bar lunch)/dinner a la carte 14.00/21.45 **t.** ⬥ 3.95 –
16 rm ⊑ 42.00/61.50 **t.** – SB.

🏨 **The Edwardian** without rest., 30-32 Heavitree Rd, EX1 2LQ, ☎ (01392) 276102,
Fax (01392) 54699 – 📺 ☎. 🆓 AE VISA. ⚹
V a
closed 24 to 26 December – **13 rm** ⊑ 24.00/52.00 **st.**

🏨 **Travel Inn,** 398 Topsham Rd, EX2 6HE, ☎ (01392) 875441, Fax (01392) 876174 – ⚡ rm,
📺 🐕 🅿. 🆓 AE ⓪ VISA. ⚹
X o
Meals (grill rest.) – **45 rm** 36.50 **t.**

🏠 **The Grange** ⧖ without rest., Stoke Hill, EX4 7JH, N : 1 ¾ m. by Old Tiverton Rd.
☎ (01392) 259723, ⤋, 🌾 – ⚡ 📺 🅿. ⚹
3 rm ⊑ 20.00/37.00 **t.**

EXETER
CENTRE

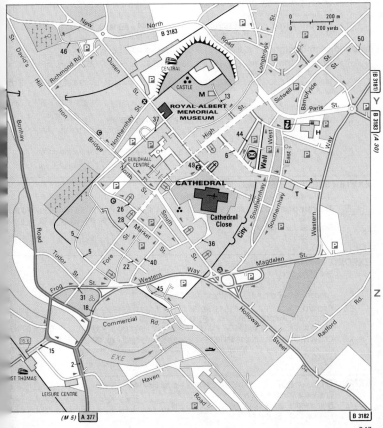

☆ **Raffles,** 11 Blackall Rd, EX4 4HD, ℰ (01392) 270200, Fax (01392) 270200 – 📺 🚗. **⬤◎** **AE**
① **VISA**
Meals (by arrangement) 14.00 **st.** ⌕ 3.75 – **7 rm** ⊆ 32.00/46.00 **st.** – SB.
V e

✗✗ **Golsworthy's** (at St. Olaves Court H.), Mary Arches St., EX4 3AZ, ℰ (01392) 217736,
Fax (01392) 413054, 🍴 – **📵**. **⬤◎** **AE** **VISA** **JCB**
closed lunch Saturday and Sunday – Meals 15.00 **t.** and a la carte ⌕ 5.25.
Z e

✗ **Lamb's,** 15 Lower North St., EX4 3ET, ℰ (01392) 54269, Fax (01392) 431145 – ✲✲. **⬤◎** **AE**
VISA **JCB**
closed Saturday lunch, Sunday, Monday, 2 weeks August, 1 week autumn and Christmas –
Meals 19.00 **t.** and a la carte ⌕ 5.00.
Y c

at Stoke Canon N : 5 m. by A 377 off A 396 – V – ⊠ Exeter.

🏠 **Barton Cross** ⬔, Huxham, EX5 4EJ, ℰ (01392) 841245, Fax (01392) 841942, « Part 17C
thatched cottages », 🍴 – ✲✲ rest, 📺 ☎ **📵**. **⬤◎** **AE** **VISA** **JCB**
Meals (closed Sunday dinner) (dinner only and Sunday lunch)/dinner 22.50 **t.** and a la carte
⌕ 6.00 – **7 rm** ⊆ 63.50/85.00 **t.** – SB.

at Whimple NE : 9 m. by A 30 – V – ⊠ Exeter.

🏠 **Woodhayes** ⬔, EX5 2TD, ℰ (01404) 822237, Fax (01404) 822337, « Georgian country
house », 🍴 – ✲✲ rest, 📺 ☎ **📵**. **⬤◎** **AE** **①** **VISA**. 🛇
closed 1 week Christmas – Meals (booking essential) (lunch residents only) 27.50 **st.** ⌕ 6.20
– **5 rm** ⊆ (dinner included) 90.00/140.00 **st.**

at Kennford S : 5 m. on A 38 – X – ⊠ Exeter.

🏠 **Fairwinds,** EX6 7UD, ℰ (01392) 832911, Fax (01392) 832911 – ✲✲ 📺 ☎ **📵**. **⬤◎** **VISA**. 🛇
closed 5 December-6 January – Meals (residents only) (bar lunch)/dinner 11.95 ⌕ 3.95 –
7 rm ⊆ 24.00/49.00 – SB.

🛏 **Gissons Arms** with rm, EX6 7UD, ℰ (01392) 832444 – 📺 ☎ **📵**. **⬤◎** **VISA**. 🛇
Meals a la carte 10.95/16.90 **st.** – **6 rm** ⊆ 30.00/45.00 **t.**

at Doddiscombsleigh SW : 10 m. by B 3212 off B 3193 – X – ⊠ Exeter.

🛏 **Nobody Inn** with rm, EX6 7PS, ℰ (01647) 252394, Fax (01647) 252978, ≼, « Part 16C »,
🍴 – ☎ **📵**. **⬤◎** **VISA**. 🛇
Meals (in bar Sunday and Monday) (bar lunch) a la carte 11.10/18.45 **t.** ⌕ 3.60 – **7 rm**
⊆ 30.00/59.00 **t.**

at Ide SW : 3 m. by A 377 – X – ⊠ Exeter.

✗✗ **Old Mill,** 20 High St., EX2 9RN, ℰ (01392) 259480 – **📵**. **⬤◎** **VISA**
closed Sunday, Monday, 26 to 29 December and 1 January – Meals (dinner only)
a la carte 16.85/24.15 **t.** ⌕ 4.55.

◎ ATS 276/280 Pinhoe Road, Polsloe Bridge   ATS Unit 3, Bittern Way, Sowton Ind. Est.
ℰ (01392) 255465   ℰ (01392) 216026

EXETER SERVICE AREA Devon **403** J 31 – ⊠ Exeter.
🔢 Sandygate, EX2 7NJ ℰ (01392) 437581.

🏠 **Travelodge,** Moor Lane, Sandygate, EX2 4AR, M 5 junction 30 ℰ (01392) 74044
Fax (01392) 410406, Reservations (Freephone) 0800 850950 – ✲✲ rm, 📺 ☎ ♿ **📵** – ⚒ 70
⬤◎ **AE** **①** **VISA** **JCB**. 🛇
76 rm 55.95 **t.**

EXFORD Somerset **403** J 30 The West Country G.
See : Church★.
Env. : Exmoor National Park★★.
London 193 – Exeter 41 – Minehead 14 – Taunton 33.

🏠🏠 **Crown,** TA24 7PP, ℰ (01643) 831554, Fax (01643) 831665, « Attractively furnished
country inn, water garden », 🔄 – 📺 ☎ **📵**. **⬤◎** **AE** **VISA** **JCB**
Meals (in bar) 13.00/17.00 **t.** ⌕ 5.90 – (see also below) – **17 rm** ⊆ 35.00/76.00 **t.**

✗✗ **Crown,** TA24 7PP, ℰ (01643) 831554, Fax (01643) 831665 – **📵**. **⬤◎** **AE** **VISA** **JCB**
closed Sunday dinner – Meals (dinner only and Sunday lunch)/dinner a la carte 18.50/35.75
⌕ 5.90.

EXMOUTH Devon **403** J 32 The West Country G. – pop. 28 414.
Env. : A la Ronde★ AC, N : 2 m. by B 3180.
🔢 Alexandra Terr., EX8 1NZ ℰ (01395) 222299.
London 210 – Exeter 11.

🏛 **Imperial**, The Esplanade, EX8 2SW, ✆ (01395) 274761, Fax (01395) 265161, ≤, ⊒, 🐾, ✖ – 📱 ⅙ 📺 ☎ ℗, 🐠 AE ⓪ *VISA*
Meals (bar lunch Monday to Saturday)/dinner a la carte 18.95/25.00 **st.** ⒤ 8.00 – ⌸ 9.00 –
57 rm 57.50/80.50 **st.** – SB.

🏠 **Barn** ♨, Foxholes Hill, EX8 2DF, E : 1 m. via Esplanade and Queens Dr. ✆ (01395) 224411,
Fax (01395) 225445, ≤, 🐾 – 🐾 📺 ☎ ℗ – 🛦 50. 🐠 *VISA*. ✀
closed 20 December-10 January – **Meals** (bar lunch Monday to Saturday)/dinner 14.00 **t.**
⒤ 5.95 – **11 rm** ⌸ 33.00/66.00 – SB.

✖✖ **The Seafood**, 9 Tower St., EX8 1NT, ✆ (01395) 269459 – 🐠 AE *VISA* JCB
closed 15 February-6 March – **Meals** - Seafood - (dinner only and lunch Wednesday to
Friday) a la carte 15.95/27.75 ⒤ 7.50.

at Lympstone N : 3 m. by A 376 – ✉ Exmouth.

✖✖ **River House** with rm, The Strand, EX8 5EY, ✆ (01395) 265147, ≤ Exe Estuary – ⅙ rest,
📺, 🐠 AE *VISA*, ✀
closed 1-2 January, 25-27 December and Bank Holiday Mondays – **Meals** (closed Sunday and
Monday to non-residents) 33.00 **t.** and lunch a la carte ⒤ 6.95 – ⌸ 7.00 – **3 rm** 59.00/
96.00 **t.** – SB.

EYAM Derbs. 402 403 404 O 24 – pop. 1 018 – ✉ Sheffield.
London 163 – Derby 29 – Manchester 32 – Sheffield 12.

🏠 **Miners Arms** with rm, Water Lane, S32 5RG, ✆ (01433) 630853 – 📺 ℗, 🐠 *VISA*. ✀
closed first 2 weeks January – **Meals** (closed Sunday dinner and Monday) (bar lunch Tuesday
to Saturday) a la carte 14.75/17.95 ⒤ 3.95 – **7 rm** ⌸ 25.00/50.00 **st.**

EYE Cambs. 402 404 T 26 – see Peterborough.

EYE Suffolk 404 X 27 – pop. 1 741.
London 94 – Ipswich 19 – Thetford 23.

🏠 **Four Horseshoes** with rm, Thornham Magna, IP23 8HD, SW : 5 m. by B 1117 off A 140
✆ (01379) 678777, Fax (01379) 678134, 🐾 – ⅙ rest, 📺 ☎ ℗. 🐠 AE *VISA*
closed 25 December – **Meals** (bar lunch Monday to Saturday)/dinner a la carte 12.00/
18.00 **t.** ⒤ 7.00 – **8 rm** ⌸ 35.00/65.00 **st.**

EYTON Herefordshire – see Leominster.

FAKENHAM Norfolk 404 W 25 – pop. 6 471.
London 111 – Cambridge 64 – Norwich 27.

🏠 **Sculthorpe Mill** ♨, Lynn Rd, Sculthorpe, NR21 9QG, W : 2 ½ m. by A 148
✆ (01328) 856161, Fax (01328) 856651, « Converted late 18C watermill », 🐾 – ⅙ rm, 📺
☎ ℗. 🐠 AE ⓪ *VISA*
Meals (bar lunch)/dinner a la carte 11.60/16.45 **st.** – **6 rm** ⌸ 40.00/60.00 **st.**

FALFIELD South Gloucestershire 403 404 M 29.
London 132 – Bristol 16 – Gloucester 22.

🏛 **Gables Inn**, Bristol Rd, GL12 8DL, on A 38 ✆ (01454) 260502, Fax (01454) 261821, 🛦, ☎ –
⅙ rest, 📺 ☎ ₰ ℗ – 🛦 150. 🐠 AE *VISA* JCB. ✀
Meals 9.95/16.50 **st.** and dinner a la carte ⒤ 5.50 – ⌸ 4.50 – **32 rm** 53.50 **st.** – SB.

FALMOUTH Cornwall 403 E 33 The West Country G. – pop. 20 297.
See : Town★ – Pendennis Castle★ (≤★★) AC B.
Env. : Glendurgan Garden★★ AC – Trebah Garden★, SW : 4 ½ m. by Swanpool Rd A –
Mawnan Parish Church★ (≤★★) S : 4 m. by Swanpool Rd A – Cruise along Helford River★.
Exc. : Trelissick★★ (≤★★) NW : 13 m. by A 39 and B 3289 A – Carn Brea (≤★★) NW : 10 m. by
A 393 A – Gweek (Setting★, Seal Sanctuary★) SW : 8 m. by A 39 and Treverva rd – Wendron
(Poldark Mine★) AC, SW : 12 ½ m. by A 39 – A – and A 394.
🏌 Swanpool Rd ✆ (01326) 311262/314296 A – 🏌 Budock Vean Hotel ✆ (01326) 250288.
🛈 28 Killigrew St., TR11 3PN ✆ (01326) 312300.
London 308 – Penzance 26 – Plymouth 65 – Truro 11.

Plan on next page

FALMOUTH

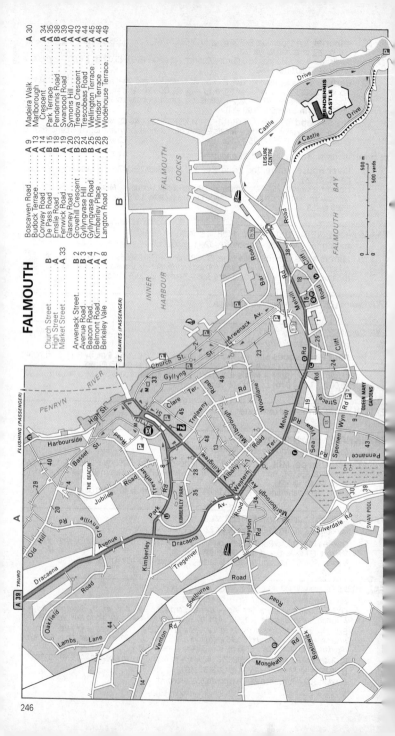

246

Royal Duchy, Cliff Rd, TR11 4NX, ℰ (01326) 313042, *Fax (01326) 319420*, ≤, ☎, 🔲, ✿
– 📶 📺 ☎ 🅿. 🅿🅘 🅰🅴 ⓞ *VISA*. ✿
B a
Meals 9.75/20.00 **t.** and a la carte ₐ 5.75 – **41 rm** ⌿ (dinner included) 80.50/178.50 **t.**,
2 suites – SB.

Greenbank, Harbourside, TR11 2SR, ℰ (01326) 312440, *Fax (01326) 211362*, ≤ harbour,
🛵, ☎ – 📶, ✿ rm, 📺 ☎ ⇐ 🅿 – 🔬 40. 🅿🅘 🅰🅴 ⓞ *VISA*
A a
closed 24 December-13 January – **Nightingales :** **Meals** 9.50/17.50 **t.** and a la carte ₐ 6.50 –
61 rm ⌿ 64.00/160.00 **t.** – SB.

Penmere Manor ◈, Mongleath Rd, TR11 4PN, ℰ (01326) 211411, *Fax (01326) 317588*,
☎, 🔲, 🔲, ✿ – ✿ rm, 📺 ☎ 🅿 – 🔬 60. 🅿🅘 🅰🅴 ⓞ *VISA* *JCB*
A e
closed 24 to 27 December – **Bolitho's :** **Meals** *(dinner only)* 22.00 **t.** and a la carte ₐ 5.50 –
38 rm ⌿ 59.00/114.00 **t.** – SB.

Carthion, Cliff Rd, TR11 4AP, ℰ (01326) 313669, *Fax (01326) 212828*, ≤, ✿ – 📺 ☎ 🅿. 🅿🅘
🅰🅴 ⓞ *VISA*. ✿
B v
closed 23 December-1 February – **Meals** (bar lunch Monday to Saturday)/dinner 12.00 **t.**
and a la carte ₐ 4.95 – **18 rm** ⌿ (dinner included) 51.00/102.00 **t.**

Broadmead, 66-68 Kimberley Park Rd, TR11 2DD, ℰ (01326) 315704, *Fax (01326) 311048*
– ✿ rest, 📺 ☎ 🅿. 🅿🅘 🅰🅴 *VISA* *JCB*
A u
closed Christmas-New Year – **Meals** (bar lunch)/dinner 12.75 **t.** ₐ 4.95 – **12 rm** ⌿ 26.50/
53.00 **t.** – SB.

Prospect House without rest., 1 Church Rd, Penryn, TR10 8DA, NW : 2 m. by A 39 on
B 3292 ℰ (01326) 373198, *Fax (01326) 373198*, ✿ – 🅿. 🅿🅘 *VISA*
3 rm ⌿ 30.00/55.00.

Rosemullion without rest., Gyllyngvase Hill, TR11 4DF, ℰ (01326) 314690 – ✿ 📺 🅿
June-early October – **13 rm** ⌿ 22.50/45.00 **s.**
B c

Melvill House, 52 Melvill Rd, TR11 4DQ, ℰ (01326) 316645, *Fax (01326) 211608* – ✿ 📺
🅿. ✿
B o
closed 22 to 29 December – **Meals** (by arrangement) 8.50 – **7 rm** ⌿ 25.00/44.00 – SB.

Chelsea House, 2 Emslie Rd, TR11 4BG, ℰ (01326) 212230, ≤, ✿ – ✿ rest, 📺 🅿. 🅿🅘
VISA *JCB*. ✿
B s
May-September – **Meals** 8.95 **s.** – **7 rm** ⌿ 27.00/42.00 **s.**

Esmond House without rest., 5 Emslie Rd, TR11 4BG, ℰ (01326) 313214 – ✿ 📺. ✿
closed 25 December – **7 rm** ⌿ 18.00/36.00.
B e

Trevaylor, 8 Pennance Rd, TR11 4EA, ℰ (01326) 313041, ≤ – ✿ rest, 📺 🅿
A r
7 rm.

at Mylor Bridge N : 4½ m. by A 39 and B 3292 on Mylor rd – A – ✉ *Falmouth.*

Pandora Inn, Restronguet Creek, PR11 5ST, NE : 1 m. by Passage Hill off Restronguet Hill
ℰ (01326) 372678, *Fax (01326) 372678*, ≤, « Thatched inn of 13C origins » – 🚤 🅿. 🅿🅘 🅰🅴
VISA
closed 25 December – **Meals** (bar lunch)/dinner a la carte 16.70/24.95 **st.** ₐ 4.00.

at Mawnan Smith SW : 5 m. by Trescobeas Rd – A – ✉ *Falmouth.*

Meudon ◈, TR11 5HT, E : ½ m. by Carwinion Rd ℰ (01326) 250541, *Fax (01326) 250543*,
« ≤ Terraced gardens landscaped by Capability Brown », park – 📶 📺 ☎ 🅿. 🅿🅘 🅰🅴 ⓞ
VISA
March-4 November – **Meals** 15.00/25.00 **t.** and lunch a la carte ₐ 10.00 – **27 rm** ⌿ (dinner
included) 100.00/180.00 **t.**, 2 suites – SB.

Nansidwell Country House ◈, TR11 5HU, SE : ¼ m. by Carwinion Rd
ℰ (01326) 250340, *Fax (01326) 250440*, ≤, « Country house atmosphere, gardens », park,
✿ – 📺 ☎ 🅿. 🅿🅘 *VISA*
closed 2 to 31 January – **Meals** 15.75/27.50 **t.** and dinner a la carte ₐ 7.75 – ⌿ 4.00 – **12 rm**
90.00/168.00 **t.** – SB.

Trelawne ◈, Maenporth Rd, TR11 5HS, E : ¾ m. by Carwinion Rd ℰ (01326) 250226,
Fax (01326) 250909, ≤, 🔲, ✿ – ✿ rest, 📺 ☎ 🅿. 🅿🅘 🅰🅴 ⓞ *VISA*. ✿
closed 22 December-12 February – **The Hutches :** **Meals** *(bar lunch)/dinner* 18.50 **t.** ₐ 4.90
– **14 rm** ⌿ 45.00/102.00 **t.** – SB.

Pennypots (Viner), Maenporth Beach, TR11 5HN, E : 1 m. by Carwinion Rd
ℰ (01326) 250251, *Fax (01326) 250251*, ≤ – 🅿. 🅿🅘 🅰🅴 ⓞ *VISA* *JCB*
closed Sunday, Monday and 4 weeks in winter – **Meals** (dinner only) 26.50 **t.** ₐ 5.50
Spec. Sautéed foie gras with pasta, on a white wine jus. Steamed fillet of sea bass with a
lobster sauce. Bread and butter pudding with clotted cream.

at Budock Water W : 2¼ m. by Trescobeas Rd – A – ✉ Falmouth.

🏨 **Crill Manor** �, TR11 5BL, S : ¾ m. ℘ (01326) 211880, Fax (01326) 211229, ☂, 🍽 – 🔆
📺 ☎ 🅿. 🆗 🄰🄴 VISA JCB. ✀
Meals (bar lunch)/dinner 18.50 st. ↕ 5.25 – **14 rm** ⌷ 39.00/78.00 st. – SB.

🏨 **Penmorvah Manor** ⍀, TR11 5ED, S : ¾ m. ℘ (01326) 250277, Fax (01326) 250509, 🍽
– 🔆 rm, 📺 ☎ 🅿. 🆗 🄰🄴 VISA JCB
Meals (bar lunch)/dinner 17.50 st. – **27 rm** ⌷ 45.00/90.00 st. – SB.

🔧 ATS Dracaena Av. ℘ (01326) 319233

FAREHAM Hants. 403 404 Q 31 Great Britain G. – pop. 54 866 (inc. Portchester).
Env. : Portchester castle★ AC, SE : 2 ½ m. by A 27.
🛈 Westbury Manor, West St., PO16 0JJ ℘ (01329) 221342.
London 77 – Portsmouth 9 – Southampton 13 – Winchester 19.

🏨 **Solent**, Rookery Av., Whiteley, PO15 7AJ, NW : 5 m. by A 27 ℘ (01489) 880000,
Fax (01489) 880007, 🐚, ≘s, 🔲, park, ✼, squash – 🛗, 🔆 rm, 📺 ☎ ₢ 🅿 – 🔬 250. 🆗 🄰🄴
VISA. ✀
Meals 12.95/20.00 st. and dinner a la carte ↕ 10.95 – **84 rm** ⌷ 98.00/119.00 st., 4 suites –
SB.

🏨 **Forte Posthouse Fareham**, Cartwright Drive, Titchfield, PO15 5RJ, W : 2 ¾ m. on A 27
℘ (01329) 844644, Fax (01329) 844666, 🐚, ≘s, 🔲 – 🔆 rm, 📺 ☎ ₢ 🅿 – 🔬 140. 🆗 🄰🄴
⑩ VISA
Meals a la carte 12.05/25.65 st. ↕ 8.45 – ⌷ 10.95 – **125 rm** 69.00 st. – SB.

🏨 **Red Lion**, East St., PO16 0BP, ℘ (01329) 822640, Fax (01329) 823579, ≘s – 📺 ☎ ₢ 🅿 –
🔬 80. 🆗 🄰🄴 ⑩ VISA. ✀
Meals a la carte 13.40/25.65 t. – **42 rm** ⌷ 62.50/75.00 t. – SB.

🏨 **Lysses House**, 51 High St., PO16 7BQ, ℘ (01329) 822622, Fax (01329) 822762, 🍽 – 🛗,
🔆 rest, 📺 ☎ 🅿 – 🔬 100. 🆗 🄰🄴 ⑩ VISA. ✀
closed 24 December-2 January and Bank Holidays – Meals (closed Saturday lunch and
Sunday) 13.95/18.50 st. and a la carte ↕ 5.10 – **21 rm** ⌷ 60.00/75.00 st. – SB.

🏨 **Travel Inn**, Southampton Rd, Park Gate, SO3 6AF, W : 4 m. by A 27 ℘ (01489) 579857,
Fax (01489) 577238 – 🔆 rm, 📺 ₢ 🅿. 🆗 🄰🄴 ⑩ VISA. ✀
Meals (grill rest.) – **40 rm** 36.50 t.

🏨 **Springfield** without rest., 67 The Avenue, PO14 1PE, W : 1 m. on A 27 ℘ (01329) 828325,
🍽 – 🔆 📺 ☎ 🅿. 🆗 VISA
closed 2 weeks Christmas – **6 rm** ⌷ 39.00/48.00 st.

🏨 **Avenue House** without rest., 22 The Avenue, PO14 1NS, W : ½ m. on A 27
℘ (01329) 232175, Fax (01329) 232196, 🍽 – 🔆 📺 ☎ ₢ 🅿. 🆗 🄰🄴 ⑩ VISA. ✀
17 rm ⌷ 41.50/48.00.

🔧 ATS Queens Rd ℘ (01329) 234941/280032

FARMBOROUGH Bath & North East Somerset 403 M 29 The West Country G. – pop. 1 084 –
✉ Bath.
Exc. : Bath★★★, NE : 7 ½ m. by A 39 and A 4.
London 137 – Bath 7.5 – Bristol 12 – Wells 13.

🏨 **Streets**, The Street, BA3 1AR, ℘ (01761) 471452, Fax (01761) 471452, ☂, 🍽 – 📺 ☎ 🅿.
🆗 🄰🄴 VISA. ✀
closed 20 December-1 January – Meals (dinner only) 14.80 st. ↕ 4.60 – **8 rm** ⌷ 46.00/
58.00 st.

FARNBOROUGH Hants. 404 R 30 – pop. 52 535.
🛈 Southwood, Ively Rd ℘ (01252) 548700.
London 41 – Reading 17 – Southampton 44 – Winchester 33.

🏨 **Forte Posthouse Farnborough**, Lynchford Rd, GU14 6AZ, S : 1 ½ m. on
Farnborough Rd (A 325) ℘ (01252) 545051, Fax (01252) 377210, 🐚, ≘s, 🔲 – 🔆 rm, 📺
☎ 🅿 – 🔬 120. 🆗 🄰🄴 ⑩ VISA. ✀
Meals (closed Saturday lunch) a la carte 14.25/25.65 t. ↕ 11.45 – ⌷ 10.95 – **143 rm**
109.00 t. – SB.

🏨 **Falcon**, 68 Farnborough Rd, GU14 6TH, S : ¾ m. on A 325 ℘ (01252) 545378,
Fax (01252) 522539 – 📺 ☎ 🅿. 🆗 🄰🄴 ⑩ VISA. ✀
restricted opening Christmas-New Year – Meals (closed lunch Saturday and Sunday)
17.95 st. and a la carte ↕ 5.75 – **30 rm** ⌷ 73.75/86.75 st.

XX **Wings Cottage,** 32 Alexandra Rd, GU14 6DA, S : 1 ¼ m. by A 325 off Boundary Rd
ℰ *(01252) 544141, Fax (01252) 549361* – 🗐. **MO** **AE** **①** **VISA** **JCB**
closed Sunday lunch – **Meals** - Chinese - 19.00/24.50 and a la carte.

FARNHAM *Dorset* **403** **404** N 31 – *see Blandford Forum.*

FARNHAM *Surrey* **404** R 30 – *pop. 36 178.*

🕤 *Farnham Park (Par Three)* ℰ *(01252) 715216.*
🎯 *Vernon House, 28 West St., GU9 7DR* ℰ *(01252) 715109.*
London 45 – Reading 22 – Southampton 39 – Winchester 28.

🏨 **Bush,** The Borough, GU9 7NN, ℰ *(01252) 715237, Fax (01252) 733530, 🛲 – ⅍ rm,* 🗎 ☎
🄿 – 🔬 60. **MO** **AE** **①** **VISA** **JCB**
Thackeray's : **Meals** (dinner only and Sunday lunch)/a la carte 21.00/25.00 **st.** 🖗 7.00 –
Café bar Tabac : **Meals** *(closed Sunday)* a la carte 10.25/15.45 **t.** – ☲ 9.50 – **65 rm**
85.00/115.00 **st.** – SB.

🏨 **Bishop's Table,** 27 West St., GU9 7DR, ℰ *(01252) 710222, Fax (01252) 733494, 🛲 –* 🗎
☎. **MO** **AE** **①** **VISA**. ⋘
closed 26 to 30 December – **Meals** *(closed Saturday lunch)* 18.00 🖗 8.95 – **17 rm** ☲ 83.00/
132.00 **st.** – SB.

XX **Banaras,** 40 Downing St., GU9 7PH, ℰ *(01252) 734081* – **MO** **AE** **VISA**
closed 25 and 26 December – **Meals** - Indian - (buffet lunch Sunday) a la carte 16.35/27.05
🖗 3.75.

at Churt *S : 5 ¾ m. on A 287.*

🏨 **Pride of the Valley,** Tilford Rd, GU10 2LE, E : 1 ½ m. by Hale House Lane
ℰ *(01428) 605799, Fax (01428) 605875, 🛲 –* 🗎 ☎ 🄿. **MO** **VISA**
Meals 15.95 **st.** and a la carte 🖗 4.65 – **11 rm** ☲ 50.00/85.00 **st.**

FARRINGTON GURNEY *Bath & North East Somerset* **403** **404** M 30 *The West Country G. –*
pop. 780 – ✉ *Bristol.*
Env. : Downside Abbey★ (Abbey Church★) SE : 5 m. by A 37 and B 3139.
Exc. : Wells★★ - Cathedral★★★, Vicars' Close★, Bishop's Palace★ AC (≤★★) SW : 8 m. by A 39
– Chew Magna★ (Stanton Drew Stone Circles★ AC) NW : 9 ½ m. by A 37 and B 3130.
London 132 – Bath 13 – Bristol 12 – Wells 8.

🏠 **Country Ways,** Marsh Lane, BS18 5TT, ℰ *(01761) 452449, Fax (01761) 452706, 🛲 –*
⅍ rest, 🗎 ☎ 🄿. **MO** **VISA**. ⋘
closed 1 week Christmas – **Meals** *(closed Sunday)* (dinner only) a la carte 18.80/22.25 **st.**
🖗 7.00 – **6 rm** ☲ 60.00/85.00 **st.** – SB.

FAR SAWREY *Cumbria* **402** L 20 – *see Hawkshead.*

FAVERSHAM *Kent* **404** W 30 – *pop. 17 070.*
🎯 *Fleur de Lis Heritage Centre, 13 Preston St., ME13 8NS* ℰ *(01795) 533261.*
London 52 – Dover 26 – Maidstone 21 – Margate 25.

↑ **Preston Lea** without rest., Canterbury Rd, ME13 8XA, E : 1 m. on A 2 ℰ *(01795) 535266,*
Fax (01795) 533388, 🛲 – ⅍ 🗎 🄿. **MO** **VISA** **JCB**. ⋘
3 rm ☲ 35.00/48.00 **st.**

at Dargate *NE : 3 m. by A 299 –* ✉ *Faversham.*

🍴 **Dove Inn,** Plum Pudding Lane, ME13 9HB, ℰ *(01227) 751360, Fax (01227) 751360, 🛲 –*
🄿. **MO** **VISA** **JCB**
closed dinner Sunday and Monday – **Meals** a la carte 13.95/21.00 **st.**

at Boughton *SE : 3 m. by A 2 –* ✉ *Faversham.*

🏠 **Garden,** 167-169 The Street, ME13 9BH, ℰ *(01227) 751411, Fax (01227) 751801, 🛲 –*
🗐 rest, 🗎 ☎ 🄿. **MO** **AE** **VISA** **JCB**
Meals (residents only Sunday dinner) 12.50/18.95 **t.** and a la carte 🖗 6.00 – **10 rm** ☲ 60.00/
80.00 **t.** – SB.

🍴 **White Horse Inn** with rm, The Street, ME13 9AX, ℰ *(01227) 751343, Fax (01227) 751090,*
🛲 – 🗎 ☎ 🄿
12 rm.

at Plumford *S : 2 ½ m. by A 2 and Brogdale Rd on Plumford Lane –* ✉ *Faversham.*

↑ **The Granary** ⬙ without rest., Plumford Lane, ME13 0DS, ℰ *(01795) 538416,*
Fax (01795) 538416, ≤, 🛲 – ⅍ 🗎 🄿. **MO** **VISA** **JCB**
closed 25 and 26 December – **3 rm** ☲ 30.00/44.00.

at Painter's Forstal *SW : 2¼ m. by A 2 and Brogdale Rd – ✉ Faversham.*

🍴🍴🍴 ✿ **Read's** (Pitchford), ME13 0EE, ☎ (01795) 535344, *Fax (01795) 591200*, ⛱, 🌳 – [MC] [AE] [D] [VISA] [JCB]
closed Sunday, Monday and first week January – **Meals** 17.50/21.00 **t.** and a la carte 32.50/36.00 **t.** 🍷 7.50
Spec. Lobster bouillabaisse with crème fraîche and spring onion broth. Choice cuts of lamb, roasted pink, with buttered fondant and rosemary sauce. Hot Drambuie soufflé with local raspberries.

at Eastling *SW : 5 m. by A 2 – ✉ Faversham.*

🏠 **Frith Farm House** 🐦, Otterden, ME13 0DD, SW : 2 m. by Otterden rd on Newnham rd ☎ (01795) 890701, *Fax (01795) 890009*, 🌳 – 🚭 [TV] [P]. [MC] [VISA]. 🐕
Meals (by arrangement) (communal dining) 19.50 **s.** – **3 rm** ☕ 35.00/58.00 **s.** – SB.

ATS 20 North Lane ☎ (01795) 534039

FAWKHAM GREEN *Kent – see Brands Hatch.*

FECKENHAM *Worcestershire* [403] [404] O 27 – *see Droitwich.*

FELIXSTOWE *Suffolk* [404] Y 28 – *pop. 28 606.*

⛳18, ⛳9 *Felixstowe Ferry, Ferry Rd ☎ (01394) 283060.*
[i] *Leisure Centre, Undercliff Road West, IP11 8AB ☎ (01394) 276770.*
London 84 – Ipswich 11.

🏨 **Orwell,** Hamilton Rd, IP11 7DX, ☎ (01394) 285511, *Fax (01394) 670687*, 🌳 – [lift], 🚭 rest, [TV] ☎ [P] – 🎤 250. [MC] [AE] [D] [VISA]
Meals 13.50/16.50 **st.** and a la carte 🍷 7.25 – ☕ 8.95 – **57 rm** 55.00/65.00 **st.**, 1 suite – SB.

🏨 **Waverley,** Wolsey Gdns., IP11 7DF, ☎ (01394) 282811, *Fax (01394) 670185*, ≤ – [TV] ☎ [P] – 🎤 70. [MC] [AE] [D] [VISA]
Meals 15.95 **t.** (dinner) and a la carte 7.75/23.75 **t.** 🍷 7.95 – ☕ 8.50 – **19 rm** 54.95/72.95 **t.** – SB.

ATS 4-8 Sunderland Rd, Carr Rd Ind. Est. ☎ (01394) 675604
ATS Crescent Rd ☎ (01394) 277596/277888

FELSTED *Essex* [404] V 28 – *pop. 2 512 – ✉ Great Dunmow.*
London 39 – Cambridge 31 – Chelmsford 9 – Colchester 24.

🍴 **Rumbles Cottage,** Braintree Rd, CM6 3DJ, ☎ (01371) 820996 – [MC] [VISA]
closed Saturday lunch, Sunday dinner, Monday and 2 weeks February – **Meals** (lunch by arrangement)/dinner 14.00 **t.** and a la carte 🍷 4.50.

FELTON *Herefordshire – pop. 93.*
London 130 – Birmingham 54 – Hereford 14 – Shrewsbury 50 – Worcester 27.

🏠 **Felton House** 🐦 without rest., HR1 3PH, ☎ (01432) 820366, 🌳 – 🚭 [P]
closed January – **4 rm** ☕ 21.00/42.00.

FENNY BRIDGES *Devon* [403] K 31 – ✉ *Honiton.*
London 166 – Exeter 12.

🍺 **Greyhound Inn** with rm, EX14 0BJ, on A 30 ☎ (01404) 850380, *Fax (01404) 850812* « 17C thatched inn », 🌳 – [TV] ☎ [P]. [MC] [AE] [VISA]. 🐕
Meals (bar lunch Monday to Saturday)/dinner a la carte 10.95/22.65 **t.** 🍷 5.95 – **10 rm** ☕ 45.00/65.00 **t.**

FERMAIN BAY *Guernsey (Channel Islands)* [403] P 33 and [230] ⑩ – *see Channel Islands.*

FERNDOWN *Dorset* [403] [404] O 31 – *pop. 25 177.*
London 108 – Bournemouth 6 – Dorchester 27 – Salisbury 23.

🏨 **Dormy,** New Rd, BH22 8ES, on A 347 ☎ (01202) 872121, *Fax (01202) 895388*, 🏋, 🧖, 🏊, ⛳18, 🌳, 🎾, squash – [lift], 🚭 rm, [TV] ☎ [P] – 🎤 250. [MC] [AE] [D] [VISA]
Meals *(closed Saturday lunch)* 14.50/19.50 **st.** and a la carte – **123 rm** ☕ 110.00/135.00 **st** 5 suites – SB.

🏨 **Travel Inn**, Ringwood Rd, Tricketts Cross, BH22 9BB, NE : 1 m. on A 347 🖉 (01202) 874210 – 🛬 rm, 📺 ⅃ 🅿. 🆎 AE ⓪ VISA. 🛬
Meals (grill rest.) – **32 rm** 36.50 **t.**

FERRENSBY *N. Yorks. – see Knaresborough.*

FERRYBRIDGE SERVICE AREA *W. Yorks. – ✉ Leeds.*
London 178 – Leeds 14 – Doncaster 14 – Rotherham 28 – York 28.

🏨 **Travelodge**, WF11 0AF, at junction 33 of M 62 with A 1 🖉 (01977) 670488, Reservations (Freephone) 0800 850950 – 🛬 📺 ☎ ⅃ 🅿. 🆎 AE ⓪ VISA JCB. 🛬
35 rm 46.95 **t.**

FERSFIELD *Norfolk – see Diss.*

FILEY *N. Yorks.* 402 *T 21 – pop. 6 619 London 238.*
Kingston-upon-Hull 42 – Leeds 68 – Middlesbrough 58.

🏨 **Downcliffe House**, The Beach, YO14 9LA, 🖉 (01723) 513310, Fax (01723) 516141, ≤ – 🛬 rest, 📺 ☎ 🅿 VISA. 🛬
closed 2 to 23 January – **Meals** (bar lunch Monday to Saturday)/dinner a la carte 13.85/22.85 **t.** ⅃ 5.25 – **10 rm** ⌂ 38.00/76.00 **t.** – SB.

FINDON *W. Sussex* 404 *S 31 – pop. 1 776 – ✉ Worthing.*
London 49 – Brighton 13 – Southampton 50 – Worthing 4.

🏨🏨 **Findon Manor**, High St., BN14 0TA, off A 24 🖉 (01903) 872733, Fax (01903) 877473, « Part 16C stone and flint house », 🌳 – 📺 ☎ 🅿 – ⅃ 40. 🆎 AE VISA. 🛬
Meals 14.95/17.95 **t.** ⅃ 7.00 – **11 rm** ⌂ 47.50/70.00 **t.** – SB.

FINEDON *Northants.* 404 *S 26 – see Wellingborough.*

FLAMSTEAD *Herts.* 404 *S 28 – pop. 1 399 – ✉ St. Albans.*
London 32 – Luton 5.

🏨🏨 **Hertfordshire Moat House**, London Rd, AL3 8HH, on A 5 🖉 (01582) 449988, Fax (01582) 842282, ⅃ᵦ – 🛬, ▤ rest, 📺 ☎ 🅿 – ⅃ 300. 🆎 AE ⓪ VISA JCB
Meals *(closed Saturday lunch)* a la carte 16.70/27.40 **st.** ⅃ 8.00 – ⌂ 9.50 – **89 rm** 115.00/135.00 **st.** – SB.

FLEET *Hants.* 404 *R 30 – pop. 30 391.*
London 40 – Basingstoke 11 – Reading 17.

🏨🏨 **Lismoyne**, Church Rd, GU13 8NA, 🖉 (01252) 628555, Fax (01252) 811761, 🌳 – 🛬 rest, 📺 ☎ 🅿 – ⅃ 100. 🆎 AE ⓪ VISA JCB
Meals 14.00/19.95 **st.** and a la carte ⅃ 7.50 – ⌂ 9.95 – **45 rm** 67.00/80.00 **st.** – SB.

⊚ ATS 113-115 Kings Rd 🖉 (01252) 616412/620028

FLEET SERVICE AREA *Hants. – ✉ Basingstoke.*

🏨 **Welcome Lodge**, Hartley Witney, RG27 8BN, M 3 between junctions 4a and 5 (southbound carriageway) 🖉 (01252) 815587, Fax (01252) 815587, Reservations (Freephone) 0800 7314466 – 📺 ⅃ 🅿. 🆎 AE ⓪ VISA. 🛬
60 rm 50.00 **t.**

FLEETWOOD *Lancs.* 402 *K 22 – pop. 27 227.*
🏌 *Fleetwood, Golf House, Princes Way* 🖉 (01253) 873114.
🚢 *to the Isle of Man (Douglas) (Isle of Man Steam Packet Co. Ltd) (summer only) (3 h 20 mn).*
🚪 *Old Ferry Office, The Esplanade, FY7 6DL* 🖉 (01253) 773953.
London 245 – Blackpool 10 – Lancaster 28 – Manchester 53.

🏨🏨 **North Euston**, The Esplanade, FY7 6BN, 🖉 (01253) 876525, Fax (01253) 777842, ≤ – 🛗 📺 ☎ 🅿 – ⅃ 150. 🆎 AE ⓪ VISA JCB. 🛬
Meals (bar lunch Saturday) 11.50/17.50 and a la carte ⅃ 6.00 – **54 rm** ⌂ 49.00/70.00 **t.** – SB.

⊚ ATS 238 Dock St. 🖉 (01253) 771211

FLITWICK *Beds.* 404 S 27 – *pop. 11 063.*
London 45 – Bedford 13 – Luton 12 – Northampton 28.

Flitwick Manor, Church Rd, MK45 1AE, off Dunstable Rd (01525) 712242, *Fax (01525) 718753*, « 18C manor house », park.
Meals 20.95/37.50 **t.** 7.50 – 12.50 – **15 rm** 95.00/225.00 **t.** – SB.

FLORE *Northants.* 403 404 Q 27 – *see Daventry.*

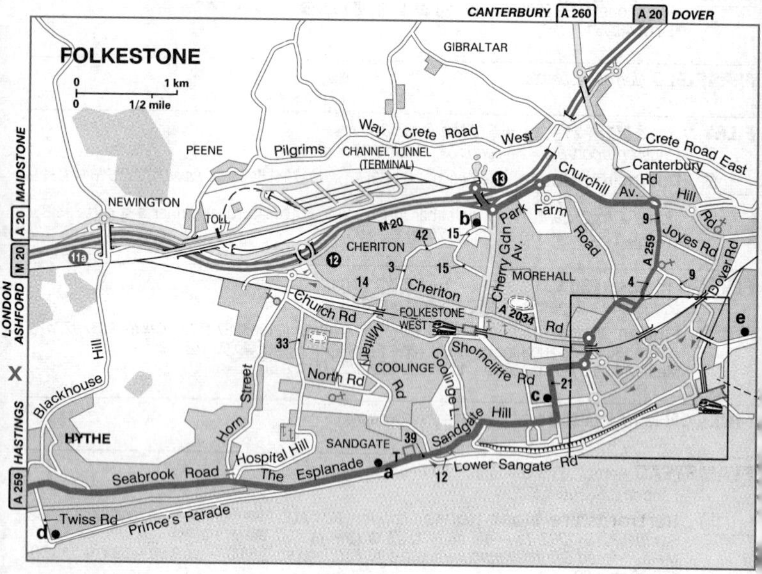

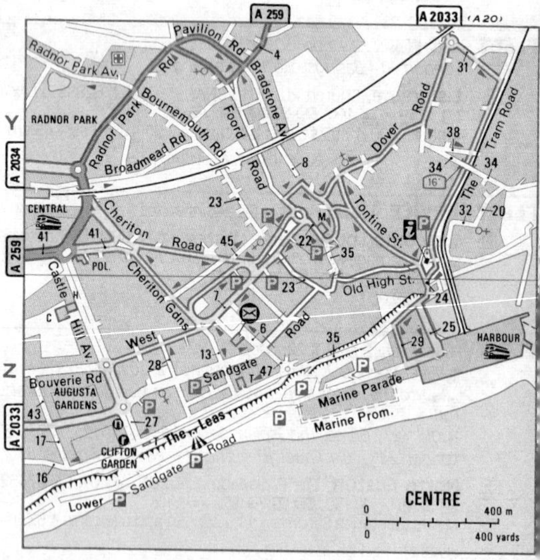

Guildhall Street . . . . . YZ 23
Rendezvous Street . . YZ 37
Sandgate Road . . . . Z
Tontine Street . . . . Y

Ashley Avenue . . . . X 3
Black Bull Road . . . . X, Y 4
Bouverie Place . . . . Z 6
Bouverie Road East . . . Z 7
Bradstone Road . . . . . . Y 8
Canterbury Road . . . . . X 9
Castle Road . . . . X 12
Cheriton Place . . . . Z 13
Cheriton High Street . . X 14
Cherry Garden Lane . . X 15
Clifton Crescent . . . . . . Z 16
Clifton Road . . . . Z 17
Durlocks (The) . . . . Y 20
Earl's Av . . . . X 21
Grace Hill. . . . . Y 22
Harbour Street . . . . Z 24
Harbour App. Road . . . Z 25
Langhorne Gardens . . . Z 27
Manor Road . . . . Z 28
Marine Terrace . . . . Z 29
Morrison Road . . . . Y 31
North Street . . . . Y 32
Pond Hill Rd . . . . X 33
Radnor Bridge Road . . Y 34
Remembrance (Rd of) . Z 35
Ryland Place . . . . Y 38
Sandgate High Street . X 39
Shorncliffe Road . . . . . Y 41
Tilekiln Lane . . . . X 42
Trinity Gardens . . . . Z 43
Victoria Grove . . . . Y 45
West Terrace . . . . Z 47

FOLKESTONE Kent 404 X 30 *Great Britain G.* – pop. 45 587.

See : *The Leas★ (≤★)Z.*

Channel Tunnel : Le Shuttle information and reservations 𝒫 (0990) 353535.

🚢 to France (Boulogne) (Hoverspeed Ltd) 4-6 daily (55 mn).

🚩 Harbour St., CT20 1QN 𝒫 (01303) 258594.

London 76 – Brighton 76 – Dover 8 – Maidstone 33.

Plan opposite

🏤 **Clifton,** The Leas, CT20 2EB, 𝒫 (01303) 851231, Fax (01303) 851231, ≤, � – ▐☆▌ 🖵 ☎ – 🔏 80. 🐼 🖭 ⓘ 𝑽𝑰𝑺𝑨 JCB. ❤️
Z r
Meals 10.50/17.00 **t.** and a la carte 🍷 4.75 – ☲ 8.50 – **80 rm** 49.50/72.00 **t.** – SB.

🏠 **Wards,** 39 Earls Av., CT20 2HB, 𝒫 (01303) 245166, Fax (01303) 254480 – 🖵 ☎ 🅿 – 🔏 50. 🐼 🖭 ⓘ 𝑽𝑰𝑺𝑨. ❤️
X c
closed 1 January – Meals *(closed Sunday dinner and Bank Holidays)* a la carte 10.95/17.70 **t.** 🍷 4.25 – **10 rm** ☲ 52.00/85.00 **t.**

🏠 **Travel Inn,** Cherry Garden Lane, CT19 4AP, NW : 1 ¼ m. by A 259 at junction 13 of M 20 𝒫 (01303) 273620, Fax (01303) 273641 – 🌴 🖵 ♿ 🅿. 🐼 🖭 ⓘ 𝑽𝑰𝑺𝑨. ❤️
X b
Meals (grill rest.) – **40 rm** 36.50 **t.**

⌂ **Harbourside** without rest., 13-14 Wear Bay Rd, CT19 6AT, 𝒫 (01303) 256528, Fax (01303) 241299, ≤, ⇌, 🌫 – 🌴 🖵 🐼 🖭 𝑽𝑰𝑺𝑨. ❤️
X e
6 rm ☲ 30.00/60.00.

✗✗ **La Tavernetta,** Leaside Court, Clifton Gdns., CT20 2ED, 𝒫 (01303) 254955, Fax (01303) 244732 – 🐼 🖭 ⓘ
Z n
closed Sunday, 25-26 December and Bank Holidays – Meals - Italian - 9.50 **t.** (lunch) and a la carte 17.40/24.75 **t.** 🍷 5.55.

at Sandgate W : 1 ¾ m. on A 259 – ✉ Folkestone.

🏠 **Sandgate,** The Esplanade, CT20 3DY, W : ½ m. 𝒫 (01303) 220444, Fax (01303) 220496, ≤ – ▐☆▌ 🖵 ☎. 🐼 🖭 ⓘ 𝑽𝑰𝑺𝑨. ❤️
X a
closed mid January-mid February and first week October – Meals – (see **La Terrasse** below) – **15 rm** ☲ 39.00/69.00 **t.** – SB.

✗✗✗ **La Terrasse** (Gicqueau) (at Sandgate H.), The Esplanade, CT20 3DY, W : ½ m. 𝒫 (01303) 220444, Fax (01303) 220496, ≤, � – 🌴. 🐼 🖭 ⓘ 𝑽𝑰𝑺𝑨. ❤️
X a
❃ closed Sunday dinner and Monday except Bank Holidays, mid January-mid February and first week October – Meals - French - (booking essential) 19.50/28.50 **t.** and a la carte 28.50/35.50 **t.** 🍷 7.50
Spec. Pan fried scallops with a purée of potatoes, black truffle jus. Roasted turbot with girolle mushrooms and a light poultry jus. Valhrona chocolate dessert with almond cream and verbena ice cream.

🔧 ATS 318/324 Cheriton Rd 𝒫 (01303) 275198/275121

FONTWELL W. Sussex – ✉ Arundel.

🚩 Little Chef Complex, BN18 0SD 𝒫 (01243) 543269.

London 60 – Chichester 6 – Worthing 15.

🏠 **Travelodge,** BN18 0SB, at A 27/A 29 roundabout 𝒫 (01243) 543973, Reservations (Free-phone) 0800 850950 – 🌴 rm, 🖵 ♿ 🅿. 🐼 🖭 ⓘ 𝑽𝑰𝑺𝑨 JCB. ❤️
32 rm 44.95 **t.**

FORD Wilts. – see Castle Combe.

FORDINGBRIDGE Hants. 403 404 O 31 – pop. 4 301.

🚩 Salisbury St., SP6 1AB 𝒫 (01425) 654560 (summer only).

London 101 – Bournemouth 17 – Salisbury 11 – Winchester 30.

✗✗ **Hour Glass,** Salisbury Rd, Burgate, SP6 1LX, N : 1 m. on A 338 𝒫 (01425) 652348, « 14C thatched cottage », 🌫 – 🌴 🅿. 🐼 ⓘ 𝑽𝑰𝑺𝑨
closed Sunday dinner, Monday, 1 week February and 2 weeks November – Meals 19.95 **t.** (dinner) and lunch a la carte 🍷 5.00.

🍴 **The Augustus John,** 116 Station Rd, SP6 1DG, 𝒫 (01425) 652098 – 🅿. 🐼 𝑽𝑰𝑺𝑨 JCB
closed Sunday dinner – Meals a la carte 12.85/14.85 **t.** 🍷 4.00.

at Stuckton SE : 1 m. by B 3078 – ✉ Fordingbridge.

✗ **Three Lions** with rm, Stuckton Rd, SP6 2HF, 𝒫 (01425) 652489, Fax (01425) 656144, 🌫 – 🌴 rm, 🖵 🅿. 🐼 𝑽𝑰𝑺𝑨 JCB
closed 19 January-11 February – Meals *(closed Sunday dinner and Monday)* a la carte 18.75/29.25 **st.** 🍷 9.00 – ☲ 4.75 – **3 rm** 67.50/75.00 **st.** – SB.

FOREST Guernsey (Channel Islands) 403 P 33 and 230 ⑨ ⑩ – see Channel Islands.

FOREST ROW E. Sussex 404 U 30 – pop. 3 508.

ᴵ₈, ᴵ₈ Royal Ashdown Forest, Chapel Lane, Forest Row ℘ (01342) 822018.
London 35 – Brighton 26 – Eastbourne 30 – Maidstone 32.

🏨 **Brambletye,** The Square, RH18 5EZ, ℘ (01342) 824144, Fax (01342) 824833 – 📺 ☎ 🅿.
🕳 AE VISA JCB
closed 25 to 30 December – Meals 15.00 t. and a la carte ⅃ 5.00 – **22 rm** ⊇ 56.00/69.50 st.
– SB.

🏨 **Chequers Inn,** The Square, RH18 5ES, ℘ (01342) 823333, Fax (01342) 825454 – 📺 ☎
⟵, 🕳 AE ⓪ VISA, ⅜
Meals 11.50/13.95 t. and dinner a la carte ⅃ 8.95 – **20 rm** ⊇ 55.00/75.00 st.

at Wych Cross S : 2½ m. on A 22 – ⊠ Forest Row.

🏰🏰 **Ashdown Park** ॐ, RH18 5JR, E : ¾ m. on Hartfield rd ℘ (01342) 824988,
Fax (01342) 826206, ≤, « Part 19C manor house in extensive gardens », Iₐ, ⓢ, 🔲, Iₐ,
park, ✵, squash – 📺 ☎ 🕭 🅿 – 🕳 150. 🕳 AE ⓪ VISA JCB. ⅜
Anderida : Meals 21.00/31.00 st. and a la carte ⅃ 9.25 – **89 rm** ⊇ 110.00/285.00, 6 suites –
SB.

FORNHAM ALL SAINTS Suffolk 404 W 27 – see Bury St. Edmunds.

FOTHERINGHAY Northants. 404 S 26 – see Oundle.

FOULSHAM Norfolk – pop. 1 379 – ⊠ East Dereham.
London 121 – Cambridge 69 – King's Lynn 31 – Norwich 18.

✕✕ **The Gamp,** Claypit Lane, NR20 5RW, ℘ (01362) 684114, 🌫 – ⅙ 🅿. 🕳 VISA
closed Tuesday lunch, Sunday dinner, Monday and first 2 weeks January – Meals 10.95/
11.50 st. and a la carte ⅃ 5.65.

FOUR MARKS Hants. 403 404 Q 30 – pop. 3 843 (inc. Medstead) – ⊠ Alton.
London 58 – Guildford 24 – Reading 29 – Southampton 24.

🏨 **Travelodge,** 156 Winchester Rd, GU34 5HZ, on A 31 ℘ (01420) 562659, Reservations
(Freephone) 0800 850950 – 📺 🕭 🅿. 🕳 AE ⓪ VISA JCB. ⅜
31 rm 44.95 t.

FOWEY Cornwall 403 G 32 The West Country G. – pop. 1 939.
See : Town★★.
Env. : Gribbin Head★★ (≤★★) 6 m. rtn on foot – Bodinnick (≤★★) - Lanteglos Church★
E : 5 m. by ferry – Polruan (≤★★) SE : 6 m. by ferry – Polkerris★, W : 2 m. by A 3082.
🗓 The Post Office, 4 Custom House Hill, PL23 1AA ℘ (01726) 833616.
London 277 – Newquay 24 – Plymouth 34 – Truro 22.

🏨 **Marina,** 17 The Esplanade, PL23 1HY, ℘ (01726) 833315, Fax (01726) 832779, ≤ Fowey
river and harbour, 🌫 – ⅙ rest, 📺 ☎. 🕳 VISA
closed 20 December-24 February – Meals (dinner only) 17.00 t. and a la carte ⅃ 6.95 -
11 rm ⊇ 40.00/92.00.

🏨 **Carnethic House** ॐ, Lambs Barn, PL23 1HQ, NW : ¾ m. on A 3082 ℘ (01726) 833336
Fax (01726) 833336, 🔲, 🌫, ✵ – ⅙ rest, 📺 🅿. 🕳 AE ⓪ VISA. ⅜
closed December and January – Meals (bar lunch)/dinner 15.00 st. ⅃ 4.00 – **8 rm** ⊇ 40.00/
62.00 st. – SB.

⌂ **Ocean View** without rest., 24 Tower Park, PL23 1JB, ℘ (01726) 832283, ≤, 🌫 – ⅙. ⅜
Easter-September – **4 rm** ⊇ 25.00/40.00 s.

✕✕ **Food for Thought,** 4 Town Quay, PL23 1AT, ℘ (01726) 832221, Fax (01726) 832077
« Converted coastguard's cottage on quayside » – 🕳 VISA
closed Sunday, Christmas, January and February – Meals (dinner only) 19.95 t
and a la carte 22.85/37.85 t.

at Golant N : 3 m. by B 3269 – ⊠ Fowey.

🏨 **Cormorant** ॐ, PL23 1LL, ℘ (01726) 833426, Fax (01726) 833426, ≤ River Fowey, 🌫
– 📺 ☎ 🅿. 🕳 AE VISA JCB
Meals (light lunch)/dinner 18.00 t. ⅃ 8.05 – **11 rm** ⊇ 52.00/84.00 t.

at Bodinnick-by-Fowey *E : ¼ m. via car ferry* – ⊠ *Fowey*.

🏠 **Old Ferry Inn** with rm, PL23 1LX, ℰ *(01726) 870237, Fax (01726) 870116*, ≤ Fowey Estuary and town, « Part 16C » – 📺 ❷. 🌐 *VISA* **JCB**
Meals (bar lunch)/dinner a la carte 14.95/19.70 **t.** – **12 rm** ⚏ 30.00/70.00 **t.**

FOWNHOPE *Herefordshire* 🗺️🗺️ M 27 – *pop. 900* – ⊠ *Hereford*.
London 132 – Cardiff 46 – Hereford 6 – Gloucester 27.

🏠 **Green Man Inn,** Market Hill, HR1 4PE, ℰ *(01432) 860243, Fax (01432) 860207*, 🔌, 🌳 – ❄️ rest, 📺 ☎ ❷. 🌐 AE ① *VISA*. 🕸️
Meals (bar lunch)/dinner a la carte 14.05/18.85 **t.** ┆ 4.85 – **19 rm** ⚏ 33.50/54.50 **t.** – SB.

FRADDON *Cornwall* 🗺️ F 32 – ⊠ *St. Columbus Major*.
London 264 – Exeter 77 – Penzance 35 – Newquay 7 – Plymouth 44 – Truro 12.

🏠 **Travel Inn,** Penhale, TR9 6NA, on A 30 (eastbound carriageway) ℰ *(01726) 861148, Fax (01726) 861336* – ❄️ rm, 📺 ᵬ ❷. 🌐 AE ① *VISA*. 🕸️
Meals (grill rest.) – **40 rm** 36.50 **t.**

FRAMLINGHAM *Suffolk* 🗺️ Y 27 – *pop. 2 697* – ⊠ *Woodbridge*.
London 92 – Ipswich 19 – Norwich 42.

🏨 **Crown,** Market Hill, IP13 9AN, ℰ *(01728) 723521, Fax (01728) 724274*, « 16C inn » – ❄️ 📺 ☎ ❷. 🌐 AE ① *VISA*
Meals *(bar lunch Monday to Saturday)* a la carte 13.90/24.95 **t.** ┆ 5.25 – **13 rm** ⚏ 40.00/95.00 **t.**

at Badingham *NE : 3¼ m. by B 1120 on A 1120* – ⊠ *Woodbridge*.

🏠 **Colston Hall** 🌿 without rest., IP13 8LB, E : ¾ m. by A 1120 on Bruisyard rd ℰ *(01728) 638375*, 🔌, 🌳, park – ❄️ ❷. 🕸️
6 rm ⚏ 30.00/50.00 **t.**

FRAMPTON *Dorset* 🗺️🗺️ M 31 – *see Dorchester*.

FRANKLEY SERVICE AREA *W. Mids.* 🗺️🗺️ ⑲ – ⊠ *Birmingham*.

Plan : see Birmingham p. 2

🏠 **Travelodge** without rest., B32 4AR, M 5 between junctions 3 and 4 (southbound carriageway) ℰ *(0121) 550 3261, Fax (0121) 501 2880*, Reservations (Freephone) 0800 850950 – ❄️ 📺 ☎ ᵬ ❷. 🌐 AE ① *VISA* **JCB**. 🕸️   BU a
62 rm 46.95 **t.**

FRANT *E. Sussex* 🗺️ U 30 – *see Royal Tunbridge Wells*.

FRESHWATER BAY *I.O.W.* 🗺️🗺️ P 31 – *see Wight (Isle of)*.

FRILFORD *Oxon.* 🗺️🗺️ P 28-29 – *see Abingdon*.

FRIMLEY *Surrey* 🗺️ R 30 – *pop. 5 661* – ⊠ *Camberley*.
London 39 – Reading 17 – Southampton 47.

🏨 **One Oak Toby,** 114 Portsmouth Rd, GU15 1HS, NE : 1 m. on A 325 ℰ *(01276) 691939, Fax (01276) 676088* – ❄️ 📺 ☎ ❷ – ┴ 30. 🌐 AE *VISA*. 🕸️
closed 24 December-2 January – **Meals** (grill rest.) a la carte 10.30/16.10 **t.** – **40 rm** ⚏ 73.00/83.00 **t.** – SB.

FRODSHAM *Ches.* 🗺️🗺️🗺️ L 24 – *pop. 8 903* – ⊠ *Warrington*.
London 203 – Chester 11 – Liverpool 21 – Manchester 29 – Stoke-on-Trent 42.

🏨 **Forest Hills,** Overton Hill, WA6 6HH, S : 1 ¾ m. by B 5152 on Simons Lane ℰ *(01928) 735255, Fax (01928) 735517*, ≤, 🔌, 🔌, 🏊, squash – ❄️ rm, 📺 ☎ ❷ – ┴ 200. 🌐 AE ① *VISA* **JCB**
Meals *(closed Saturday lunch)* 13.45/22.15 **st.** ┆ 4.95 – ⚏ 8.50 – **57 rm** 83.00 **st.** – SB.

🏨 **Old Hall,** Main St., WA6 7AB, ℘ (01928) 732052, Fax (01928) 739046, ☞ – ⇆ rm, 📺 ☎ 🅿
– ⚒ 30. 🆖 🄰🄴 ⓪ 𝗩𝗜𝗦𝗔
Meals *(closed Bank Holidays)* 11.50/16.95 **t.** and a la carte ⌀ 5.95 – **20 rm** ⏛ 57.50/73.00 **t.**,
1 suite.

🏠 **Heathercliffe Country House** ⌂, Manley Rd, WA6 6HB, S : 1 ½ m. by B 5152
℘ (01928) 733722, Fax (01928) 735667, ≤, ☞, park – 📺 ☎ 🅿, 🆖 🄰🄴 ⓪ 𝗩𝗜𝗦𝗔
closed 2 days Christmas – **Meals** *(closed Saturday lunch and Bank Holidays)* a la carte 11.85/
22.85 **t.** – **9 rm** ⏛ 64.00/95.00 **t.** – SB.

🔘 ATS Brooklyn Garage, Chester Rd ℘ (01928) 733555

FROME Somerset 🄘🄓🄔 🄘🄓🄙 N 30 *The West Country G.* – *pop. 23 159.*
Exc. : Farleigh Hungerford★ - St. Leonard's Chapel★, N : 9 m. by A 361, A 36 and A 366.
🛈 The Round Tower, Justice Lane, BA11 2JW ℘ (01373) 467271.
London 119 – Bath 16 – Bristol 24 – Southampton 51 – Swindon 43 – Taunton 41.

✕ **Crofts,** 21 Fromefield, BA11 2HE, NE : ½ m. on B 3090 ℘ (01373) 472149 – ⇆, 🆖 𝗩𝗜𝗦𝗔
closed Monday and Tuesday dinner and 26 December-2 January – **Meals** 15.95 **t.** ⌀ 4.50.

FULBROOK Oxon. 🄘🄓🄔 🄘🄓🄙 P 28 – see Burford.

GALMPTON Devon 🄘🄓🄔 J 32 – ✉ Brixham.
London 229 – Plymouth 32 – Torquay 6.

🏠 **Maypool Park** ⌂, Maypool, TQ5 0ET, SW : 1 m. by Greenway Rd ℘ (01803) 842442,
Fax (01803) 845782, ≤, ☞ – ⇆ 📺 ☎ 🅿, 🆖 🄰🄴 𝗩𝗜𝗦𝗔, ⋇
closed 22 December-2 January – **Meals** *(residents only) (dinner only)* 17.50 **st.** ⌀ 5.00 –
10 rm ⏛ 39.50/85.00 **st.** – SB.

GARFORTH W. Yorks. 🄘🄔🄙 P 22 – see Leeds.

GARSTANG Lancs. 🄘🄔🄙 L 22 – *pop. 5 697.*
🛈 Discovery Centre, Council Offices, High St., PR3 1FU ℘ (01995) 602125.
London 233 – Blackpool 13 – Manchester 41.

🏨 **Garstang Country H. and Golf Club,** Bowgreave, PR3 1YE, S : 1 ¼ m. on B 6430
℘ (01995) 600100, Fax (01995) 600950, 🛏 – 🛗 ⇆ 📺 ☎ 🅿 – ⚒ 200. 🆖 🄰🄴 ⓪ 𝗩𝗜𝗦𝗔, ⋇
Meals 9.95/14.50 **st.** ⌀ 4.95 – **32 rm** ⏛ 45.00/70.00 **st.**

🏨 **Crofters,** Cabus, PR3 1PH, W : ¾ m. on A 6 ℘ (01995) 604128, Fax (01995) 601646 –
⇆ rest, 📺 ☎ 🅿 – ⚒ 200. 🆖 🄰🄴 ⓪ 𝗩𝗜𝗦𝗔 🄹🄲🄱
Meals *(dancing Saturday evening) (bar lunch Monday to Saturday)*/dinner a la carte 13.05/
18.85 **t.** ⌀ 5.00 – ⏛ 5.00 – **19 rm** 35.00/65.00 **t.**

🏠 **Pickering Park,** Garstang Rd, Catterall, PR3 0HD, S : 1 ½ m. on B 6430
℘ (01995) 600999, Fax (01995) 602100, ☞ – ⇆ rest, 📺 ☎ 🅿 – ⚒ 25. 🆖 🄰🄴 ⓪ 𝗩𝗜𝗦𝗔
Meals 12.50 **t.** and a la carte ⌀ 6.50 – **16 rm** ⏛ 55.00/80.00 **st.** – SB.

at Bilsborrow S : 3¾ m. by B 6430 on A 6 – ✉ Preston.

🏨 **Guy's Thatched Hamlet,** Canalside, St. Michaels Rd, PR3 0RS, off A 6
℘ (01995) 640010, Fax (01995) 640141 – 📺 ☎ 🅿, 🆖 🄰🄴 𝗩𝗜𝗦𝗔 🄹🄲🄱
closed 25 December – **Meals** 6.00/10.00 **st.** and a la carte ⌀ 4.40 – ⏛ 5.50 – **53 rm** 36.00 **st.**
– SB.

🏠 **Olde Duncombe House** without rest., Garstang Rd, PR3 0RE, ℘ (01995) 640336,
Fax (01995) 640336 – 📺 ☎ 🅿, 🆖 🄰🄴 𝗩𝗜𝗦𝗔
9 rm ⏛ 32.50/49.50 **st.**

GATE SERVICE AREA Kent – see Canterbury.

Remember the speed limits that apply in the United Kingdom, unless otherwise
signposted.

- 60 mph on single carriageway roads
- 70 mph on dual carriageway roads and motorways

GATESHEAD Tyne and Wear **401 402** P 19 *Great Britain G.* – pop. 83 159.

EXC. : *Beamish : North of England Open Air Museum*★★ *AC, SW : 6 m. by A 692 and A 6076* BX.

🏌 *Ravensworth, Moss Heaps, Wrekenton* ℰ *(0191) 487 6014/487 2843* – 🏌 *Heworth, Gingling Gate* ℰ *(0191) 469 2137* BX.

Tyne Tunnel (toll).

🛈 *Central Library, Prince Consort Rd, NE8 4LN* ℰ *(0191) 477 3478* BX – *Metrocentre, Portcullis, 7 The Arcade, NE11 9YL* ℰ *(0191) 460 6345* AX.

London 282 – Durham 16 – Middlesbrough 38 – Newcastle upon Tyne 1 – Sunderland 11.

Plan : see Newcastle upon Tyne

🏨 **Newcastle/Gateshead Marriott,** Cameron Park, Metro Centre, NE11 9XF, ℰ (0191) 493 2233, Fax (0191) 493 2030, 𝄃𝄃, 🚭, 🔲 – 📱, 🌤 rm, 🗐 📺 ☎ 🕭 🅟 – 🔏 450.
🆄🅎 🅰🅴 ⓞ 𝚅𝚂𝙰 𝙹𝙲𝙱
AX e
Meals (bar lunch)/dinner 16.50 **st.** and a la carte – ⊑ 10.95 – **146 rm** 94.00 **st.,** 2 suites.

🏨 **Gibside Arms,** Front St., Whickham, NE16 4JG, ℰ (0191) 488 9292, Fax (0191) 488 8000 –
🗐 rest, 📺 ☎ 🕭 🚐 – 🔏 100. 🆄🅎 🅰🅴 ⓞ 𝚅𝚂𝙰
AX s
closed 23 to 28 December – **Meals** (bar lunch)/dinner 14.95 **st.** and a la carte 🕽 4.75 –
⊑ 8.50 – **45 rm** 53.50/64.00 **st.** – SB.

🏨 **Travel Inn,** Derwenthaugh Rd, NE16 3BL, ℰ (0191) 414 6308, Fax (0191) 414 5032 – 📱 🌤
📺 🕭. 🆄🅎 🅰🅴 ⓞ 𝚅𝚂𝙰
AX c
40 rm 36.50 **t.**

at Low Fell S : 2 m. by A 167 and Belle Vue Bank – BX – ✉ Gateshead.

🏨 **Eslington Villa,** 8 Station Rd, NE9 6DR, ℰ (0191) 487 6017, Fax (0191) 420 0667, 🌳 –
🌤 rest, 📺 ☎ 🅟. 🆄🅎 🅰🅴 ⓞ 𝚅𝚂𝙰 𝙹𝙲𝙱
closed 25 and 26 December – **Meals** (closed Sunday dinner and Bank Holidays) 16.70/
21.95 **t.** and a la carte 🕽 5.50 – **12 rm** ⊑ 59.50/69.50 **t.** – SB.

🅐 ATS Earlsway, First Av., Team Valley Trading Est. ℰ (0191) 4910081

Pour voyager rapidement, utilisez les **cartes Michelin "Grandes Routes"** :

970 Europe, **976** République Tchèque-République Slovaque, **980** Grèce,
984 Allemagne, **985** Scandinavie-Finlande, **986** Grande-Bretagne-Irlande,
987 Allemagne-Autriche-Benelux,
988 Italie, **989** France, **990** Espagne-Portugal, **991** Yougoslavie.

GATWICK AIRPORT W. Sussex **404** T 30 – ✉ Crawley.

✈ Gatwick Airport : ℰ (01293) 535353.

🛈 International Arrivals, South Terminal, RH6 0NP ℰ (01293) 560108.

London 29 – Brighton 28.

Plan on next page

🏨 **London Gatwick Airport Hilton,** South Terminal, RH6 0LL, ℰ (01293) 518080,
Fax (01293) 528980, 𝄃𝄃, 🚭, 🔲 – 📱, 🌤 rm, 🗐 📺 ☎ 🕭 🅟 – 🔏 500. 🆄🅎 🅰🅴 ⓞ 𝚅𝚂𝙰 Y u
Meals 22.95/25.95 **st.** and a la carte – ⊑ 12.95 – **547 rm** 187.00/217.00 **st.,** 3 suites.

🏨 **Ramada H. Gatwick,** Povey Cross Rd, RH6 0BE, ℰ (01293) 820169, Fax (01293) 820259,
𝄃𝄃, 🚭, 🔲, squash – 📱, 🌤 rm, 🗐 📺 ☎ 🅟 – 🔏 180. 🆄🅎 🅰🅴 ⓞ 𝚅𝚂𝙰 𝙹𝙲𝙱 Y a
Meals (closed lunch Saturday and Sunday) 16.50/17.50 **st.** and a la carte – ⊑ 11.00 –
250 rm 85.00 **st.,** 5 suites.

🏨 **Le Meridien London Gatwick,** Gatwick Airport (North Terminal), RH6 0PH,
ℰ (01293) 567070, Fax (01293) 567739, 𝄃𝄃, 🚭, 🔲 – 📱, 🌤 rm, 🗐 📺 ☎ 🕭 🅟 – 🔏 350. 🆄🅎
🅰🅴 ⓞ 𝚅𝚂𝙰 𝙹𝙲𝙱
Y e
New Fortune : Meals - Chinese - 25.00 **t.** and a la carte – **Brasserie :** Meals (closed Sunday
lunch) 14.95/18.95 **t.** and dinner a la carte 🕽 6.95 – ⊑ 10.95 – **468 rm** 159.00 **st.,** 6 suites –
SB.

🏨 **Forte Posthouse Gatwick,** Povey Cross Rd, RH6 0BA, ℰ (01293) 771621,
Fax (01293) 771054 – 📱, 🌤 rm, 🗐 rest, 📺 ☎ 🅟 – 🔏 120. 🆄🅎 🅰🅴 ⓞ 𝚅𝚂𝙰 𝙹𝙲𝙱 Y c
Meals 16.95/14.95 **st.** and a la carte 🕽 7.50 – ⊑ 9.95 – **210 rm** 90.00 **st.** – SB.

🏨 **Travel Inn,** Longbridge Way, Gatwick Airport (North Terminal), RH6 0NX,
ℰ (01293) 568158, Fax (01293) 568278 – 📱, 🌤 rm, 🗐 rest, 📺 🕭 🅟 – 🔏 35. 🆄🅎 🅰🅴 ⓞ 𝚅𝚂𝙰
Y s
🌤
Meals (grill rest.) – **121 rm** 36.50 **t.**

🏨 **Travelodge** without rest., Church Rd, Lowfield Heath, RH11 0PQ, ℰ (01293) 533441,
Fax (01293) 535369, Reservations (Freephone) 0800 850950 – 🗐 rm, 📺 ☎ 🕭 🅟. 🆄🅎 🅰🅴 ⓞ
𝚅𝚂𝙰 𝙹𝙲𝙱 🌤
Y r
126 rm 49.95 **t.**

🅐 ATS Building 238B, Perimeter Rd South ℰ (01293) 568333/568555

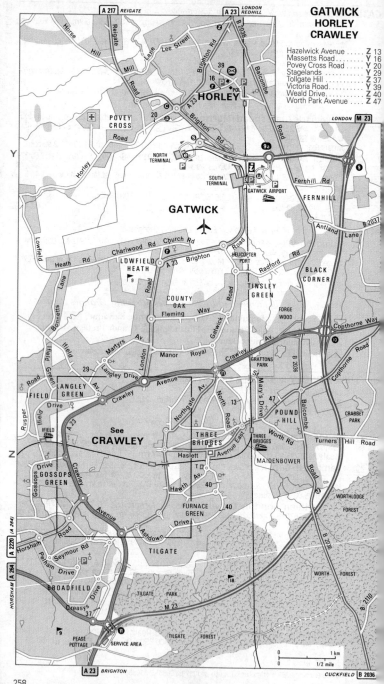

GATWICK
HORLEY
CRAWLEY

258

GAYTON *Mersey.* – ✉ *Wirral.*
London 206 – Birkenhead 12 – Chester 13 – Liverpool 10.

Travel Inn, Chester Rd, L60 3FD, on A 540 at junction with A 551 ☎ (0151) 342 1982, *Fax (0151) 342 8983* – rm, TV ♿ P. MC AE D VISA.
Meals (grill rest.) – **37 rm** 36.50 **t.**

GEDNEY DYKE *Lincs.*
London 109 – Lincoln 45 – Leicester 62 – Norwich 62.

The Chequers, Main St., PE12 0AJ, ☎ (01406) 362666, *Fax (01406) 362666,* – P. MC AE D VISA JCB
closed 25 and 26 December – **Meals** a la carte 13.90/23.45 **t.** 6.50.

GERRARDS CROSS *Bucks.* 404 S 29 – *pop. 19 523 (inc. Chalfont St. Peter).*
London 22 – Aylesbury 22 – Oxford 36.

Bull, Oxford Rd, SL9 7PA, on A 40 ☎ (01753) 885995, *Fax (01753) 885504,* – rm, TV ☎ P – 200. MC AE D VISA.
Meals *(closed Saturday lunch)* 16.50/19.95 **st.** and a la carte 7.85 – **93 rm** 135.00/175.00 **st.**, 2 suites – SB.

GILLAN *Cornwall* 403 E 33 – ✉ *Helston.*
London 301 – Falmouth 23 – Penzance 25 – Truro 26.

Tregildry , TR12 6HG, ☎ (01326) 231378, *Fax (01326) 231561,* ←, – TV ☎ P. MC VISA JCB
March-October – ***Herra :*** **Meals** (dinner only) 21.50 **st.** 6.75 – **10 rm** (dinner included) 75.00/120.00 **st.** – SB.

GILLINGHAM *Dorset* 403 404 N 30 *The West Country G.* – *pop. 6 404.*
Exc. : *Stourhead★★★ AC, N : 9 m. by B 3092, B 3095 and B 3092.*
London 116 – Bournemouth 34 – Bristol 46 – Southampton 52.

Stock Hill Country House , Stock Hill, SP8 5NR, W : 1 ½ m. on B 3081 ☎ (01747) 823626, *Fax (01747) 825628,* « Victorian country house, antiques », , , , park, – rest, TV ☎ P. MC AE D VISA.
Meals *(closed Monday lunch)* (booking essential) 20.00/32.00 **t.** 9.10 – **9 rm** (dinner included) 115.00/280.00 **t.** – SB.

GISLINGHAM *Suffolk* 404 X 27 – *pop. 822* – ✉ *Eye.*
London 93 – Cambridge 45 – Ipswich 20 – Norwich 30.

Old Guildhall, Mill St., IP23 8JT, ☎ (01379) 783361, « 15C former guildhall », – TV P.
closed January – **Meals** (by arrangement) 12.50 – **3 rm** 37.50/55.00 – SB.

GLASTONBURY *Somerset* 403 L 30 *The West Country G.* – *pop. 7 747.*
See : *Town★★ - Abbey★★ (Abbot's Kitchen★) AC – St. John the Baptist Church★★ – Somerset Rural Life Museum★ AC – Glastonbury Tor★ (←★★★).*
Env. : *Wells★★ - Cathedral★★★, Vicars' Close★, Bishop's Palace★ AC (←★★) NE : 5 ½ m. by A 39.*
Exc. : *Wookey Hole★ (Caves★ AC, Papermill★) NE : 8 m. by A 39.*
The Tribunal, 9 High St., BA6 9DP ☎ (01458) 832954.
London 136 – Bristol 26 – Taunton 22.

Lion at Pennard with rm, West Pennard, BA6 8NH, E : 3 ½ m. on A 361 ☎ (01458) 832941, *Fax (01458) 832941,* « Part 15C inn » – TV ☎ P. MC AE VISA.
Meals (in bar) a la carte 11.50/16.00 **t.** – **7 rm** 25.00/45.00 **t.** – SB.

GLENFIELD *Leicester* 402 403 404 Q 26 – *see Leicester.*

Dieser Führer ist kein vollständiges Hotel- und Restaurantverzeichnis.
Um den Ansprüchen aller Touristen gerecht zu werden,
haben wir uns auf eine Auswahl in jeder Kategorie beschränkt.

GLEWSTONE Herefordshire – see Ross-on-Wye.

GLOOSTON Leics. – see Market Harborough.

GLOSSOP Derbs. ⓐⓑⓒ O 23 – pop. 30 771 (inc. Hollingworth).
  ⛳ Sheffield Rd ℰ (01457) 865247.
  🅱 The Gatehouse, Victoria St., SK13 8HT ℰ (01457) 855920.
  London 194 – Manchester 18 – Sheffield 25.

🏨 **Wind in the Willows** ⌂, Hurst Rd, Derbyshire Level, SK13 9PT, E : 1 m. by A 57 ℰ (01457) 868001, Fax (01457) 853354, ✍ – 📺 ☎ 🅿. 🕮 🖭 ① VISA
closed 1 week Christmas-New Year – **Meals** (residents only) (dinner only) 21.00 **st.** ▯ 7.95 –
12 rm ⚏ 65.00/105.00 **st.**

GLOUCESTER Glos. ⓑⓒ N 28 Great Britain G. – pop. 114 003.
  See : City★ - Cathedral★★ Y – The Docks★ Y – Bishop Hooper's Lodging★ AC Y M.
  ⛳, ⛳ Gloucester Hotel, Matson Lane ℰ (01452) 525653.
  🅱 St Michael's Tower, The Cross, GL1 1PD ℰ (01452) 421188.
  London 106 – Birmingham 52 – Bristol 38 – Cardiff 66 – Coventry 57 – Northampton 83 –
  Oxford 48 – Southampton 98 – Swansea – Swindon 35.

Plan opposite

🏨 **Jarvis Gloucester H. & Country Club**, Robinswood Hill, GL4 6EA, SE : 3 m. by B 4073 ℰ (01452) 525653, Fax (01452) 307212, ₤₅, ⛨, 🔲, ⛳, ⛳, ※, squash – ﬀ rm, 📺 ☎ 🅿 – ▵ 180. 🕮 🖭 ① VISA   Z c
Meals (closed Saturday lunch) 9.75/17.50 **t.** and a la carte ▯ 5.75 – ⚏ 8.50 – **102 rm** 95.00/109.00 **t.**, 5 suites – SB.

🏨 **The Twigworth**, Tewksbury Rd, Twigworth, GL2 9PG, NE : 2 ½ m. on A 38 ℰ (01452) 730266, Fax (01452) 730099 – ﬀ rm, 📺 ☎ ৬ 🅿 – ▵ 40. 🕮 🖭 ① VISA. ※
Meals (grill rest.) a la carte 7.90/14.45 **st.** ▯ 4.55 – ⚏ 4.95 – **52 rm** 42.25 **t.**

🏨 **Travel Inn**, Tewksbury Rd, Longford, GL2 9BE, N : 1 ¾ m. on A 38 ℰ (01452) 523519, Fax (01452) 300924 – ﬀ rm, 📺 ৬ 🅿. 🕮 🖭 ① VISA. ※
Meals (grill rest.) – **60 rm** 36.50 **t.**

※※ **Yeungs**, St. Oswald's Rd, Cattle Market, GL1 2SR, ℰ (01452) 309957 – ▤. 🕮 🖭 VISA
closed Monday lunch, Sunday, 25-26 December and 1 January – **Meals** - Chinese - 14.50/18.00 **t.** and a la carte ▯ 5.50.   Z e

at Down Hatherley NE : 3 ¼ m. by A 38 – Z – ✉ Gloucester.

🏨 **Hatherley Manor**, Down Hatherley Lane, GL2 9QA, ℰ (01452) 730217, Fax (01452) 731032, ₤₅, ✍ – ﬀ rest, 📺 ৬ 🅿 – ▵ 330. 🕮 🖭 ① VISA
Meals (closed Saturday lunch) 12.75/17.00 **st.** ▯ 6.00 – **56 rm** ⚏ 80.00/95.00 **st.** – SB.

at Upton St. Leonards SE : 3 ½ m. by B 4073 – Z – ✉ Gloucester.

🏨 **Hatton Court**, Upton Hill, GL4 8DE, S : ¾ m. on B 4073 ℰ (01452) 617412, Fax (01452) 612945, ≤, 🔲, ✍ – ﬀ rest, ▤ rest, 📺 ☎ 🅿 – ▵ 60. 🕮 🖭 ① VISA JCB. ※
Carringtons : Meals 14.50/22.50 **t.** and a la carte ▯ 9.50 – **45 rm** ⚏ 90.00/145.00 **t.** – SB.

🏨 **Jarvis Bowden Hall**, Bondend Lane, GL4 8ED, E : 1 m. by Bondend rd ℰ (01452) 614121, Fax (01452) 611885, ≤, ⛨, 🔲, ✍, park – ﬀ 📺 ☎ 🅿 – ▵ 85. 🕮 🖭 ① VISA
Meals (dinner only and Sunday lunch)/dinner 17.95 **t.** ▯ 7.00 – ⚏ 8.50 – **72 rm** 99.00/115.00 **st.**

🏠 **Bullens Manor Farm** without rest., High St., GL4 8DL, SE : ½ m. ℰ (01452) 616463, ≤, « Working farm », park – ﬀ 📺 🅿. ※
closed 1 week Christmas – **3 rm** ⚏ 22.00/40.00 **t.**

at Witcombe SE : 7 m. by A 40 on A 417 – Z – off A 46 – ✉ Gloucester.

🏨 **Travel Inn**, GL3 4SS, ℰ (01452) 862521, Fax (01452) 864926 – ﬀ rm, 📺 ৬ 🅿. 🕮 🖭 ①
VISA. ※
closed 24 to 27 December – **Meals** (grill rest.) – **39 rm** 36.50 **t.**

  Ⓜ ATS St. Oswalds Rd ℰ (01452) 527329

Bitte beachten Sie die Geschwindigkeitsbeschränkungen in Großbritannien
- 60 mph (= 96 km/h) außerhalb geschlossener Ortschaften
- 70 mph (= 112 km/h) auf Straßen mit getrennten Fahrbahnen und Autobahnen.

GLOUCESTER

Benutzen Sie auf Ihren Reisen in Europa
die **Michelin-Länderkarten** 1 : 1 000 000.

GOATHLAND *N. Yorks.* 402 R 20 – *pop. 444* – *Whitby.*
London 248 – Middlesbrough 36 – York 38.

Mallyan Spout, The Common, YO22 5AN, (01947) 896486, *Fax (01947) 896327*, – .
closed 25 December – **Meals** (bar lunch Monday to Saturday)/dinner 19.50 **t.** 4.75 – **24 rm** 50.00/130.00 **t.** – SB.

Whitfield House, Darnholm, YO22 5LA, NW : 3/4 m. (01947) 896215, – .
closed 4 days Christmas – **Meals** (dinner only) 11.50 **t.** and a la carte 3.85 – **8 rm** 28.00/56.00 **t.**

Heatherdene, The Common, YO22 5AN, (01947) 896334, – rest,
Meals (light lunch)/dinner a la carte approx. 11.10 6.50 – **8 rm** 40.00/70.00.

GODALMING *Surrey* 404 S 30 – *pop. 20 630.*
18 *West Surrey, Enton Green (01483) 421275* – 9 *Shillinglee Park, Chiddingfold (01428) 653237.*
London 38 – Guildford 5 – Southampton 51.

Inn on the Lake, Ockford Rd, GU7 1RH, (01483) 415575, *Fax (01483) 860445*, – – 120.
accommodation closed 25 December – **Meals** *(closed Sunday dinner)* a la carte approx. 25.95 **t.** 7.95 – **19 rm** 80.00/90.00 **t.** – SB.

Kings Arms and Royal, High St., GU7 1EB, (01483) 421545, *Fax (01483) 415403*, – – 40. .
Meals (grill rest.) a la carte 9.25/21.90 **t.** – **15 rm** 60.00/66.00 **t.**

at Hascombe *SE : 3 1/2 m. on B 2130* – *Godalming.*

White Horse, The Street, GU8 4JA, (01483) 208258, *Fax (01483) 208200*, –
closed Sunday dinner and 25 December – **Meals** 22.00 **t.** and a la carte 5.00.

ATS Meadrow (01483) 421845/422219

Die Preise — Einzelheiten über die in diesem Reiseführer angegebenen Preise finden Sie in der Einleitung.

GODSTONE *Surrey* 404 T 30 – *pop. 2 399.*
London 22 – Brighton 36 – Maidstone 28.

Tutu L'Auberge, Tilburstow Hill, South Godstone, RH9 8JY, S : 2 1/4 m. (01342) 892318, *Fax (01342) 893435*, – .
closed Sunday dinner, Monday and 26 to 29 December – **Meals** - French - 15.00 and a la carte 6.00.

GOLANT *Cornwall* 403 G 32 – *see Fowey.*

GOLCAR *W. Yorks.* – *see Huddersfield.*

GOMERSAL *W. Yorks.* 402 O 22 – *see Bradford.*

GOODWOOD *W. Sussex* 404 R 31 – *see Chichester.*

GOOSNARGH *Lancs.* 402 L 22 – *pop. 1 087* – *Preston.*
London 238 – Blackpool 18 – Preston 6.

Solo, Goosnargh Lane, PR3 2BP, (01772) 865206, *Fax (01772) 865206* – .
closed 26 December and 1 January – **Meals** (dinner only and Sunday lunch)/dinner 23.00 **st.** 5.40.

Ye Horns Inn with rm, Horns Lane, PR3 2FJ, NE : 2 1/2 m. by B 5269 and Beacon Fell rd following obvious signposting (01772) 865230, *Fax (01772) 864299*, – .
closed Monday lunch except Bank Holidays – **Meals** 10.50/15.95 **t.** and a la carte 6.25 – **6 rm** 45.00/70.00 **t.** – SB.

ENGLAND

GORDANO SERVICE AREA *North Somerset* – ✉ *Bristol.*
Severn Bridge (toll).

🏠 **Welcome Lodge,** BS20 9XG, M 5 junction 19 ☎ (01275) 373709, *Fax (01275) 374104,* Reservations (Freephone) 0800 7314466 – 🚭 rm, [TV] ♿ [P]. [MC] [AE] [D] [VISA]. 🐕
62 rm 50.00 **t.**

GOREY *Jersey (Channel Islands)* [403] P 33 and [230] [11] – *see Channel Islands.*

GORING *Oxon.* [403] [404] Q 29 *The West Country G.* – *pop. 4 193 (inc. Streatley).*
Exc. : *Ridgeway Path*★★.
London 56 – Oxford 16 – Reading 12.

🍴🍴 **Leatherne Bottel,** RG8 0HS, N : 1 ½ m. by B 4009 ☎ (01491) 872667, *Fax (01491) 875308,* ≤, 🌳, « Thames-side setting » – [P]. [MC] [AE] [VISA]
closed Sunday dinner and 25 December – **Meals** (booking essential) a la carte 20.95/36.75 **t.**

GORLESTON-ON-SEA *Norfolk* [404] Z 26 – *see Great Yarmouth.*

GOSFORTH *Cumbria* [402] J 20 – *pop. 1 568* – ✉ *Seascale.*
London 317 – Kendal 55 – Workington 21.

🏠 **Westlakes,** Gosforth Rd, CA20 1HP, SW : ¼ m. on B 5344 ☎ (019467) 25221, *Fax (019467) 25099,* 🌳 – [TV] ☎ [P]. [MC] [AE] [VISA] [JCB]. 🐕
closed 22 December-4 January – **Meals** *(closed Sunday lunch)* a la carte 12.50/24.00 **st.**
🍷 4.50 – **9 rm** ☕ 47.50/55.00 **st.**

Wenn Sie ein ruhiges Hotel suchen,
benutzen Sie zuerst die Karte in der Einleitung
oder wählen Sie im Text ein Hotel mit dem Zeichen 🐴 *oder* 🐴.

GOSFORTH *Tyne and Wear* [401] [402] P 18 – *see Newcastle upon Tyne.*

GOVETON *Devon* [403] I 33 – *see Kingsbridge.*

GRAMPOUND *Cornwall* [403] F 33 *The West Country G.* – ✉ *Truro.*
Env. : *Trewithen*★★★ *AC, W : 2 m. by A 390 – Probus*★ *(tower*★, *Country Demonstration Garden*★ *AC) W : 2 ½ m. by A 390.*
London 287 – Newquay 16 – Plymouth 44 – Truro 8.

🍴🍴 **Eastern Promise,** 1 Moor View, TR2 4RT, ☎ (01726) 883033 – 🚭 [P]. [MC] [AE] [D] [VISA] [JCB]
closed Wednesday – **Meals** - Chinese - (booking essential) (dinner only) 18.50 **st.** and a la carte 🍷 3.95.

GRANGE-IN-BORROWDALE *Cumbria* [402] K 20 – *see Keswick.*

GRANGE-OVER-SANDS *Cumbria* [402] L 21 *Great Britain G.* – *pop. 4 473.*
Env. : *Cartmel Priory*★, *NW : 3 m.*
⛳18 *Meathop Rd* ☎ *(015395) 33180* – ⛳9 *Grange Fell, Fell Rd* ☎ *(015395) 32536.*
[i] *Victoria Hall, Main St., LA11 6DP* ☎ *(015395) 34026 (restricted opening in winter).*
London 268 – Kendal 13 – Lancaster 24.

🏠 **Netherwood,** Lindale Rd, LA11 6ET, ☎ (015395) 32552, *Fax (015395) 34121,* ≤ Morecambe Bay, 🏊, 🌳, park – 🛗 🚭, ▤ rest, [TV] ☎ [P] – 🎤 150. [MC] [VISA]
Meals 13.50/22.25 **t.** 🍷 4.75 – **29 rm** ☕ 43.00/120.00 **t.** – SB.

at Lindale *NE : 2 m. on B 5277* – ✉ *Grange-over-Sands.*

🏠 **Greenacres** without rest., LA11 6LP, ☎ (015395) 34578, *Fax (015395) 34578* – 🚭 [TV] [P].
[MC] [VISA]. 🐕
5 rm ☕ 34.00/58.00 **s.**

at Witherslack *NE : 5 m. by B 5277 off A 590.*

🏠 **Old Vicarage** 🐴, Church Rd, LA11 6RS, NW : ¾ m. ☎ (015395) 52381, *Fax (015395) 52373,* « Part Georgian country house », 🌳, 🎾 – 🚭 rest, [TV] ☎ [P]. [MC] [AE] [VISA] [JCB]
Meals (booking essential) (dinner only and Sunday lunch) 27.50 **t.** 🍷 6.50 – **14 rm** ☕ 59.00/158.00 **t.** – SB.

ENGLAND

at Cartmel *NW : 3 m.*

🏦 **Aynsome Manor** ⬙, LA11 6HH, N : ¾ m. by Newby Bridge rd and Wood Broughton rd
ℱ (015395) 36653, Fax (015395) 36016, ☞ – ⵟ rest, 🔟 ☎ 🅿. 🕪 🕮 𝘝𝘐𝘚𝘈
closed 2 to 28 January – **Meals** *(closed Sunday dinner to non-residents)* (dinner only and
Sunday lunch)/dinner 16.00 t. ⌀ 5.50 – **12 rm** ⌑ (dinner included) 62.00/108.00 – SB.

🏠 **Uplands** ⬙, Haggs Lane, LA11 6HD, E : 1 m. ℱ (015395) 36248, Fax (015395) 36848, ≼,
☞ – ⵟ rest, 🔟 ☎ 🅿. 🕪 🕮 𝘝𝘐𝘚𝘈
closed January and February – **Meals** *(closed Monday and lunch Tuesday to Wednesday)*
(booking essential) 16.00/27.50 t. ⌀ 5.50 – **5 rm** ⌑ (dinner included) 82.00/140.00 t.

GRANTHAM *Lincs.* **402 404** S 25 *Great Britain G.* – *pop. 33 243.*

See : *St. Wulfram's Church*★.

Env. : *Belton House*★ *AC, N : 2 ½ m. by A 607.*

Exc. : *Belvoir Castle*★★ *AC, W : 6 m. by A 607.*

🖥, 🖥, 🖥 Belton Park, Belton Lane, Londonthorpe Rd ℱ (01476) 567399 – 🖥, 🖥, 🖥 Belton
Woods Hotel ℱ (01476) 593200.

🖪 *The Guildhall Centre, St. Peter's Hill, NG31 6PZ* ℱ (01476) 566444.

London 113 – Leicester 31 – Lincoln 29 – Nottingham 24.

🏨 **De Vere Belton Woods,** Belton, NG32 2LN, N : 2 m. on A 607 ℱ (01476) 593200,
Fax (01476) 574547, 😋, 🕍, ⌬, 🔲, 🖥, 🖥, ☞, park, ⚒, squash – ⫟ ⵟ 🔟 ☎ 🕹 🅿 –
🏛 275. 🕪 🕮 𝘝𝘐𝘚𝘈 𝘑𝘊𝘉.
Manor : **Meals** *(closed Sunday)* (dinner only) 21.00 and a la carte ⌀ 8.90 – **Plus Fours :**
Meals 16.50 st. and a la carte ⌀ 8.95 – **132 rm** ⌑ 115.00/125.00 t., 4 suites – SB.

🏛 **Swallow,** Swingbridge Rd, NG31 7XT, S : 1 ¼ m. at junction of A 607 with A 1 southbound
sliproad ℱ (01476) 593000, Fax (01476) 592592, 😋, 🕍, ⌬, 🔲 – ⵟ rm, 🍴 rest, 🔟 ☎ 🕹
🅿 – 🏛 200. 🕪 🕮 ⓞ 𝘝𝘐𝘚𝘈
Tapestry : **Meals** 10.50/19.00 st. and a la carte – **90 rm** ⌑ 90.00/130.00 st. – SB.

🏦 **Angel and Royal,** High St., NG31 6PN, ℱ (01476) 565816, Fax (01476) 567149, « Part
13C » – ⵟ 🔟 ☎ 🅿 – 🏛 30. 🕪 🕮 ⓞ 𝘝𝘐𝘚𝘈
Meals *(bar lunch Monday to Saturday)*/dinner a la carte 13.00/19.25 st. ⌀ 5.95 – ⌑ 9.45 –
29 rm 60.00/85.00 st. – SB.

at Hough-on-the-Hill *N : 6 ¾ m. by A 607 on Hough Rd –* ✉ *Grantham.*

🍴 **Brownlow Arms** with rm, NG32 2AZ, ℱ (01400) 250234, Fax (01400) 250772, « Part 17C
inn », ☞ – 🔟 ☎ 🅿. 🕪 🕮 ⓞ 𝘝𝘐𝘚𝘈 𝘑𝘊𝘉. ⌀⌀
Meals *(closed lunch Monday to Friday and Sunday dinner)* a la carte 11.40/19.85 t. ⌀ 4.00 –
7 rm ⌑ 40.00/52.00 t.

at Great Gonerby *NW : 2 m. on B 1174 –* ✉ *Grantham.*

🍴🍴 **Harry's Place** (Hallam), 17 High St., NG31 8JS, ℱ (01476) 561780 – ⵟ 🅿. 🕪 𝘝𝘐𝘚𝘈
✿ closed Sunday, Monday and 25-26 December – **Meals** (booking essential) a la carte 33.50/
50.00 t. ⌀ 10.00
Spec. Salad of Filey lobster with truffle oil dressing. Loin of West Country lamb with
madeira, rosemary and tarragon sauce. Hot apricot and cognac soufflé.

at Grantham Service Area *NW : 3 m on B 1174 at junction with A 1 –* ✉ *Grantham.*

🏠 **Travelodge,** NG32 2AB, ℱ (01476) 77500, Fax (01476) 77500, Reservations (Freephone)
0800 850950 – ⵟ rm, 🔟 🕹 🅿. 🕪 🕮 ⓞ 𝘝𝘐𝘚𝘈 𝘑𝘊𝘉. ⌀⌀
Meals (grill rest.) – **40 rm** 42.95 t.

⬣ ATS East St. ℱ (01476) 590222   ATS Elmer St. South ℱ (01476) 590444

GRASMERE *Cumbria* **402** K 20 *Great Britain G.* – ✉ *Ambleside.*

See : *Dove Cottage*★ *AC* AY **A.**

Env. : *Lake Windermere*★★, *SE : by A 591* AZ.

🖪 *Redbank Rd, LA22 9SW* ℱ (015394) 35245 *(summer only)* BZ.

London 282 – Carlisle 43 – Kendal 18.

Plans : see Ambleside

🏛 **Michaels Nook Country House** ⬙, LA22 9RP, NE : ½ m. off A 591, turning by
✿ Swan H. ℱ (015394) 35496, Fax (015394) 35645, ≼ mountains and countryside,
« Antiques and gardens », park – ⵟ rest, 🔟 ☎ 🅿. 🕪 🕮 ⓞ 𝘝𝘐𝘚𝘈 𝘑𝘊𝘉. ⌀⌀   AY **e**
Meals (booking essential) 31.50/41.50 t. ⌀ 8.00 – **12 rm** ⌑ (dinner included) 140.00/
280.00 st., 2 suites – SB
Spec. Langoustine ravioli, tarragon froth. Confit of duck, claret and truffle glaze. Hot
chocolate soufflé, chocolate sorbet.

Wordsworth, Stock Lane, LA22 9SW, ℰ (015394) 35592, *Fax (015394) 35765*, ☎, 🔲, 🎐
– ﹩, ❧ rest, 🗏 rest, 📺 ☎ 🅿 – 🔬 130. 🐵 🇦 ⓪ 𝘝𝘐𝘚𝘈. ✿
BZ s
Prelude : Meals 13.50 t. (lunch) and a la carte ⓵ 8.75 – **35 rm** � 65.00/160.00 t., 2 suites –
SB.

Swan, LA22 9RF, on A 591 ℰ (015394) 35551, *Fax (015394) 35741*, ≼, 🎐 – ❧ 📺 ☎ 🅿
AY r
37 rm.

Prince of Wales, Keswick Rd, LA22 9PR, on A 591 ℰ (015394) 35666,
Fax (015394) 35565, ≼, « Lakeside setting », 🎐, 🎐 – ❧ 📺 ☎ 🅿 – 🔬 100. 🐵 🇦 ⓪
𝘝𝘐𝘚𝘈
AY e
Meals (bar lunch)/dinner 21.00 t. and a la carte ⓵ 5.50 – **72 rm** � 85.00/120.00 t. – SB.

Gold Rill, Red Bank Rd, LA22 9PU, ℰ (015394) 35486, *Fax (015394) 35486*, ≼, 🔲, 🎐 –
❧ rest, 📺 ☎ 🅿. ✿
BZ a
closed 6 to 21 January and 2 weeks December – **Meals** (bar lunch)/dinner 18.50 st.
and a la carte ⓵ 6.50 – **24 rm** ⊒ (dinner included) 59.00/118.00 **st.**, 1 suite – SB.

White Moss House, Rydal Water, LA22 9SE, S : 1 ½ m. on A 591 ℰ (015394) 35295,
Fax (015394) 35516, 🎐, 🎐 – ❧ rest, 📺 ☎ 🅿. 🐵 𝘝𝘐𝘚𝘈 𝘑𝘊𝘉. ✿
BY v
6 March-9 December – **Meals** (closed Sunday) (booking essential) (dinner only) 27.50 t.
⓵ 7.95 – **7 rm** ⊒ (dinner included) 89.00/178.00 **st.**, 1 suite – SB.

Red Lion, Red Lion Sq., LA22 9SS, ℰ (015394) 35456, *Fax (015394) 35579*, 𝘑₅, ☎ – ﹩,
❧ rest, 📺 ☎ 🅿 – 🔬 60. 🐵 🇦 ⓪ 𝘝𝘐𝘚𝘈. ✿
BZ c
Meals (bar lunch)/dinner 19.50 t. and a la carte ⓵ 5.25 – **36 rm** ⊒ 44.00/94.00 t. – SB.

Oak Bank, Broadgate, LA22 9TA, ℰ (015394) 35217, *Fax (015394) 35685*, 🎐 – ❧ rest, 📺
☎ 🅿. 🐵 𝘝𝘐𝘚𝘈 𝘑𝘊𝘉
BZ e
closed January and Christmas – **Meals** (bar lunch)/dinner 18.50 ⓵ 5.75 – **15 rm** ⊒ (dinner
included) 60.00/140.00 **st.** – SB.

Grasmere, Broadgate, LA22 9TA, ℰ (015394) 35277, *Fax (015394) 35277*, 🎐 – ❧ rest,
📺 ☎ 🅿. 🐵 🇦 𝘝𝘐𝘚𝘈 𝘑𝘊𝘉
BZ r
closed January – **Meals** (dinner only) 15.00 t. ⓵ 5.00 – **12 rm** ⊒ (dinner included) 47.00/
100.00 t. – SB.

Lancrigg Vegetarian Country House 🎐, Easedale Rd, LA22 9QN, W : ½ m. on
Easedale Rd ℰ (015394) 35317, *Fax (015394) 35058*, ≼ Easedale Valley, 🎐, park – ❧ rest,
📺 ☎ 🅿. 🐵 𝘝𝘐𝘚𝘈 𝘑𝘊𝘉
AY u
Meals (dinner only) 20.00 **st.** ⓵ 9.25 – **13 rm** ⊒ (dinner included) 60.00/180.00 **st.** – SB.

Bridge House, Stock Lane, LA22 9SN, ℰ (015394) 35425, *Fax (015394) 35523*, 🎐 –
❧ rest, 📺 ☎ 🅿. 🐵 𝘝𝘐𝘚𝘈 𝘑𝘊𝘉. ✿
BZ n
closed January – **Meals** (dinner only) 15.00 **st.** ⓵ 5.50 – **18 rm** ⊒ (dinner included) 44.00/
88.00 **st.** – SB.

Rothay Lodge 🎐 without rest., White Bridge, LA22 9RH, ℰ (015394) 35341, 🎐 – ❧
📺 🅿. ✿
AY o
March-October – **5 rm** ⊒ 40.00/52.00.

Banerigg without rest., Lake Rd, LA22 9PW, S : ¾ m. on A 591 ℰ (015394) 35204, ≼, 🎐 –
❧ 🅿. ✿
AY a
March-November – **7 rm** ⊒ 24.50/48.00 **st.**

GRASSENDALE *Mersey* 🄬🄬🄬 L 23 – *see Liverpool.*

GRASSINGTON *N. Yorks.* 🄬🄬 O 21 – *pop. 1 102 – ⊠ Skipton.*
🄰 *National Park Centre, Colvend, Hebden Rd, BD23 5LB ℰ (01756) 752774 (summer only).*
London 240 – Bradford 30 – Burnley 28 – Leeds 37.

Ashfield House, BD23 5AE, ℰ (01756) 752584, *Fax (01756) 752584*, 🎐 – ❧ 📺 🅿. 🐵
𝘝𝘐𝘚𝘈. ✿
restricted opening in winter – **Meals** (by arrangement) 15.00 **st.** ⓵ 5.00 – **7 rm** ⊒ 24.50/
52.00 – SB.

GRAVESEND *Kent* 🄬🄬🄬 V 29 – *pop. 51 435.*
≈ to Tilbury (White Horse Ferries Ltd) frequent services daily (6 mn).
🄰 *10 Parrock St., DA12 1ET ℰ (01474) 337600.*
London 25 – Dover 54 – Maidstone 16 – Margate 53.

🏨🏨 **Manor,** Hever Court Rd, Singlewell, DA12 5UQ, SE : 2 ½ m. by A 227 off A 2 *𝄞* (01474) 353100, *Fax* (01474) 354978, ℩₆, 😤, 🔲 – ⅙ rm, 🍴 rest, 🖵 ☎ 🅿 – 🔏 200. 🅾🕄 🇦🇪 𝘝𝘐𝘚𝘈. ⋘
Meals *(closed Saturday, Sunday, Christmas and Bank Holidays)* (bar lunch)/dinner 17.95 **t.** and a la carte ₰ 5.50 – **53 rm** ☲ 68.50/85.50 **st.** – SB.

🏠 **Overcliffe,** 15-16 Overcliffe, DA11 0EF, *𝄞* (01474) 322131, *Fax* (01474) 536737 – 🖵 ☎ 🅿. 🅾🕄 🇦🇪 ⓸ 𝘝𝘐𝘚𝘈. ⋘
Meals (dinner only) a la carte 17.90/23.05 **t.** – **28 rm** ☲ 62.50/75.00 **t.**

GRAVETYE *W. Sussex – see East Grinstead.*

GRAZELEY GREEN *Wokingham – see Reading.*

GREASBY *Mersey.* 𝟺𝟶𝟸 ㉒ 𝟺𝟶𝟹 ⑫ *– pop. 56 077 (inc. Moreton) –* ✉ *Wirral.*
London 220 – Liverpool 9.

🏨🏨 **Twelfth Man Lodge,** Greasby Rd, L49 2PP, on B 5139 *𝄞* (0151) 677 5445, *Fax* (0151) 678 5085 – ⅙ rm, 🖵 ☎ & 🅿. 🅾🕄 🇦🇪 ⓸ 𝘝𝘐𝘚𝘈. ⋘
closed 25 December – **Meals** (grill rest.) a la carte approx. 19.15 **st.** – ☲ 4.95 – **30 rm** 42.25 **st.**

GREAT BADDOW *Essex* 𝟺𝟶𝟺 V 28 *– see Chelmsford.*

GREAT BARR *W. Mids.* 𝟺𝟶𝟹 𝟺𝟶𝟺 O 26 *– see Birmingham.*

GREAT BROUGHTON *N. Yorks.* 𝟺𝟶𝟸 Q 20 *– pop. 937 (inc. Little Broughton) –* ✉ *Middlesbrough.*
London 241 – Leeds 61 – Middlesbrough 10 – York 54.

🏠 **Wainstones,** 31 High St., TS9 7EW, *𝄞* (01642) 712268, *Fax* (01642) 711560 – 🖵 ☎ & 🅿 – 🔏 100. 🅾🕄 🇦🇪 ⓸ 𝘝𝘐𝘚𝘈. ⋘
Meals 14.95 **st.** (dinner) and a la carte 14.70/22.20 ₰ 5.25 – **24 rm** ☲ 55.95/69.95 – SB.

GREAT CHESTERFORD *Essex* 𝟺𝟶𝟺 U 27 *– see Saffron Walden.*

GREAT DRIFFIELD *East Riding* 𝟺𝟶𝟸 S 21 *Great Britain G. – pop. 9 463 –* ✉ *York.*
Exc. : *Burton Agnes Hall*★ *AC, NE : 6 m. by A 166 – Sledmere House*★ *AC, NW : 8 m. by A 166 and B 1252.*
🇮🇦 *Driffield, Sunderlandwick* *𝄞* (01377) 253116 – 🇮🇦 *Hainsworth Park, Brandesburton 𝄞* (01964) 542362.
London 201 – Kingston-upon-Hull 21 – Scarborough 22 – York 29.

🏠 **Star Inn,** Warter Rd, North Dalton, YO25 9UX, SW : 7 m. by A 164 and A 163 on B 1246 *𝄞* (01377) 217688 – 🖵 ☎ 🅿. 🅾🕄 𝘝𝘐𝘚𝘈 ᴶᶜᴮ
Meals (bar lunch Monday) 10.95/12.95 **t.** and dinner a la carte ₰ 4.95 – **7 rm** ☲ 35.00/ 44.50 **t.** – SB.

at Lockington *S : 9 ¾ m. by A 164 –* ✉ *Great Driffield.*

✗✗ **Rockingham Arms,** 52 Front St., YO25 9SH, *𝄞* (01430) 810607, *Fax* (01430) 810734 – 🅿. 🅾🕄 𝘝𝘐𝘚𝘈
closed Sunday, Monday, 1 week Christmas and Bank Holidays – **Meals** (dinner only) 25.95 **t.** ₰ 6.95.

🅾 ATS 14 Westgate *𝄞* (01377) 252386/253628

GREAT DUNMOW *Essex* 𝟺𝟶𝟺 V 28 *– pop. 4 907.*
London 42 – Cambridge 27 – Chelmsford 13 – Colchester 24.

🏨🏨 **Saracen's Head,** High St., CM6 1AG, *𝄞* (01371) 873901, *Fax* (01371) 875743 – ⅙ 🖵 ☎ 🅿 – 🔏 60. 🅾🕄 🇦🇪 ⓸ 𝘝𝘐𝘚𝘈
Meals 16.95 **st.** and a la carte ₰ 5.75 – ☲ 8.95 – **22 rm** 65.00/95.00 **st.** – SB.

✗✗✗ **The Starr** with rm, Market Pl., CM6 1AX, *𝄞* (01371) 874321, *Fax* (01371) 876337 – 🖵 ☎ 🅿 – 🔏 35. 🅾🕄 🇦🇪 ⓸ 𝘝𝘐𝘚𝘈
closed 2 to 9 January – **Meals** *(closed Saturday lunch and Sunday dinner)* 19.80/32.50 **t.** and lunch a la carte ₰ 7.95 – **8 rm** ☲ 60.00/105.00 **t.**

GREAT GONERBY *Lincs.* 𝟺𝟶𝟸 𝟺𝟶𝟺 S 25 *– see Grantham.*

GREAT HOCKHAM Norfolk 404 W 26 – ✉ Attleborough.
London 86 – Cambridge 41 – Norwich 23.

⌂ **Church Cottage** without rest., Breckles, NR17 1EW, N : 1 ½ m. by A 1075 on B 111
𝒫 (01953) 498286, Fax (01953) 498320, 🏊, ⌦, 🐾 – 🅿. ⍟
closed 20 December-5 January – **3 rm** 🖙 18.00/36.00 **s.**

GREAT LANGDALE Cumbria – see Ambleside.

GREAT LONGSTONE Derbs. 402 403 404 O 24 – see Bakewell.

GREAT MALVERN Worcestershire 403 404 N 27 – pop. 31 537.
🖪 21 Church St., WR14 2AA 𝒫 (01684) 892289 B.
London 127 – Birmingham 34 – Cardiff 66 – Gloucester 24.

Plan on next page

🏨 **Red Gate** without rest., 32 Avenue Rd, WR14 3BJ, 𝒫 (01684) 565013, Fax (01684) 565013,
⌦ – ✺ 📺 🅿. ⓜⓢ 𝒱𝐼𝒮𝐴 ᴊᴄʙ. ⍟   B r
closed Christmas and restricted opening in winter – **6 rm** 🖙 30.00/52.00 **st.**

🏨 **Pembridge,** 114 Graham Rd, WR14 2HX, 𝒫 (01684) 574813, Fax (01684) 574813, ⌦ –
✺ rest, 📺 🅿. ⓜⓢ 𝔸𝔼 𝒱𝐼𝒮𝐴. ⍟   B a
Meals (closed Sunday dinner) (by arrangement) 11.95/17.00 **t.** ⓖ 6.95 – **8 rm** 🖙 42.00/
65.00 **t.** – SB.

⌂ **Sidney House** without rest., 40 Worcester Rd, WR14 4AA, 𝒫 (01684) 574994, ≼, ⌦ – 📺
🅿. ⓜⓢ 𝔸𝔼 𝒱𝐼𝒮𝐴. ⍟   B s
closed last week December and first 2 weeks January – **8 rm** 🖙 20.00/59.00 **st.**

✕✕ **Anupam,** 85 Church St., WR14 2AE, 𝒫 (01684) 573814, Fax (01684) 893988 – 🍽. ⓜⓢ 𝔸𝔼 ⓓ
𝒱𝐼𝒮𝐴.   B e
closed 25 and 26 December – **Meals** - Indian - a la carte 13.50/19.90 **t.**

at Welland SE : 4½ m. by A 449 on A 4104 – A – ✉ Great Malvern.

🏨 **Holdfast Cottage** ⌂⌂, Marlbank Rd, WR13 6NA, W : ¾ m. on A 4104 𝒫 (01684) 310288,
Fax (01684) 311117, « 17C country cottage », ⌦ – ✺ 📺 ☎ 🅿. ⓜⓢ 𝒱𝐼𝒮𝐴   A e
closed Christmas and first 2 weeks January – **Meals** (closed Sunday dinner) (dinner only)
18.00 **st.** ⓖ 5.75 – **8 rm** 🖙 44.00/85.00 **st.** – SB.

🏨 **Welland Court** ⌂⌂, WR8 0ST, E: 1 ½ m. by A 4104 𝒫 (01684) 594426,
Fax (01684) 594426, ≼ The Malvern Hills, « Part 15C and 18C manor house », 🐾, ⌦, park –
📺 🅿. ⍟
closed 25 December – **Meals** (by arrangement) (residents only) (communal dining) (dinner
only) (unlicensed) 30.00 **st.** – **3 rm** 🖙 42.50/65.00.

at Malvern Wells S : 2 m. on A 449 – ✉ Malvern.

🏨🏨 **Cottage in the Wood** ⌂⌂, Holywell Rd, WR14 4LG, 𝒫 (01684) 575859,
Fax (01684) 560662, ≼ Severn and Evesham Vales, ⌦ – ✺ rest, 🍽 rest, 📺 ☎ 🅿. ⓜⓢ 𝔸𝔼
𝒱𝐼𝒮𝐴 ᴊᴄʙ   A z
Meals 11.95 **st.** (lunch) and a la carte 23.25/26.60 **st.** ⓖ 7.50 – **20 rm** 🖙 69.00/139.00 **st.** –
SB.

⌂ **Old Vicarage,** Hanley Rd, WR14 4PH, 𝒫 (01684) 572585, Fax (01684) 572585, ≼, ⌦ –
✺ rest, 📺 🅿   A c
restricted opening November-March – **Meals** (by arrangement) 14.50 **st.** ⓖ 4.50 – **5 rm**
🖙 32.00/48.00 **st.**

✕✕ **Croque-en-Bouche** (Marion Jones), 221 Wells Rd, WR14 4HF, 𝒫 (01684) 565612,
❀ Fax (01684) 565612 – ✺. ⓜⓢ 𝒱𝐼𝒮𝐴   A u
closed Sunday to Wednesday, 1 week May, 1 week September and Christmas-New Year –
Meals (booking essential) (dinner only) 23.00/36.00 ⓖ 6.50
Spec. Crab and lobster croustade with bouillabaisse sauce. Roast leg of Welsh lamb with
aubergine and braised garlic. Salads and herbs from the garden.

✕ **Planters,** 191-193 Wells Rd, WR14 4HE, 𝒫 (01684) 575065 – ⓜⓢ 𝒱𝐼𝒮𝐴   A a
closed Sunday, Monday, 25-26 December and restricted opening in winter – **Meals** -
South East Asian - (booking essential) (dinner only) a la carte 17.75/22.50 **t.** ⓖ 7.95.

at Wynds Point S : 4 m. on A 449 – ✉ Malvern.

🏨 **Malvern Hills,** British Camp, WR13 6DW, 𝒫 (01684) 540237, Fax (01684) 540327, ⌦ – 📺
☎ 🅿. ⓜⓢ 𝒱𝐼𝒮𝐴   A s
Meals (dinner only and Sunday lunch)/dinner 18.50 **st.** and a la carte – **16 rm** 🖙 40.00/
75.00 **st.** – SB.

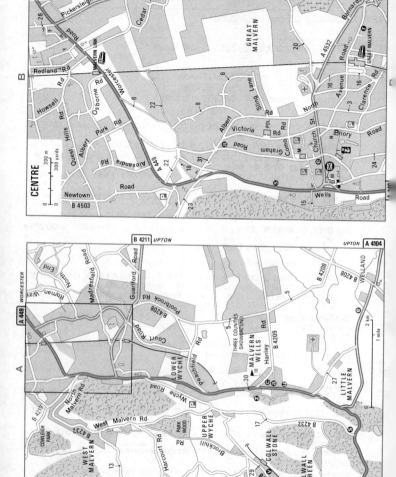

GREAT MALVERN

Town plans
roads most used
by traffic and those
on which guide listed
hotels and restaurants
stand are fully drawn;
the beginning only
of lesser roads
is indicated.

268

at Colwall SW : 3 m. on B 4218 – ⊠ Great Malvern.

🏨 **Colwall Park,** WR13 6QG, ℰ (01684) 540206, Fax (01684) 540847, ☞ – TV ☎ 🅿 – 🔬 120. 📠 AE ⓞ VISA JCB
A V
Meals 15.00/25.00 **t.** and a la carte ⓘ 9.50 – **20 rm** ⊃ 59.50/115.00 **st.** – SB.

GREAT MILTON Oxon. 403 404 Q 28 – see Oxford.

GREAT MISSENDEN Bucks. 404 R 28 – pop. 7 980 (inc. Prestwood).
London 34 – Aylesbury 10 – Maidenhead 19 – Oxford 35.

XX **La Petite Auberge,** 107 High St., HP16 0BB, ℰ (01494) 865370 – 📠 ⓞ VISA
closed Sunday, 2 weeks Christmas and Bank Holidays – **Meals** - French - (dinner only)
a la carte 23.60/29.60 **t.**

at Little Hampden NW : 2½ m. by Princes Risborough Rd – ⊠ Great Missenden.

🍴 **Rising Sun,** HP16 9PS, ℰ (01494) 488393, ☞ – 📠 VISA JCB
closed Sunday dinner and Monday – **Meals** a la carte 14.65/18.15 **st.**

GREAT RISSINGTON Glos. – see Bourton-on-the-Water.

GREAT SNORING Norfolk 404 W 25 – pop. 191 – ⊠ Fakenham.
London 115 – Cambridge 68 – Norwich 28.

🏠 **Old Rectory** ≫, Barsham Rd, NR21 0HP, ℰ (01328) 820597, Fax (01328) 820048, « Part
15C manor house », ☞ – ⊱ rest, TV ☎ 🅿. 📠 AE VISA JCB. ⋇
closed 24 to 27 December – **Meals** (booking essential) (dinner only) 23.00 **st.** ⓘ 5.25 – **6 rm**
⊃ 69.50/92.00 **t.** – SB.

GREAT TEW Oxon. 403 404 P 28 – pop. 145.
London 75 – Birmingham 50 – Gloucester 42 – Oxford 21.

🍴 **Falkland Arms** with rm, OX7 4DB, ℰ (01608) 683653, Fax (01608) 683656, « 17C inn in
picturesque village », ☞ – ⊱ rm, TV. 📠 VISA. ⋇
closed 25 December and 1 January – **Meals** (closed Sunday dinner) (in bar) a la carte 10.70/
15.95 **t.** – **4 rm** ⊃ 40.00/55.00 **t.**

GREAT WITLEY Worcestershire 403 404 M 27 – pop. 484.
London 137 – Birmingham 32 – Hereford 30 – Worcester 11.

⌂ **Ribston House** ≫, Bank Rd, Little Witley, WR6 6LS, SW : 3 m. by A 443
ℰ (01886) 888750, Fax (01886) 888925, ☞ – 🅿. ⋇
booking essential – **Meals** (communal dining) 18.00 **st.** ⓘ 4.00 – **3 rm** ⊃ 25.00/50.00 **st.**

GREAT YARMOUTH Norfolk 404 Z 26 Great Britain G. – pop. 56 190.
Env. : The Broads★.
🏌 Gorleston, Warren Rd ℰ (01493) 661911 – 🏌 Beach House, Caister-on-Sea ℰ (01493)
720421.
🛈 Marine Parade, NR30 2EJ ℰ (01493) 842195 (summer only).
London 126 – Cambridge 81 – Ipswich 53 – Norwich 20.

🏨 **Regency Dolphin,** 14-15 Albert Sq., NR30 3JH, ℰ (01493) 855070, Fax (01493) 853798,
♨, ☞ – TV ☎ 🅿 – 🔬 120. 📠 AE VISA. ⋇
Boulevard : Meals 14.95 **t.** and dinner a la carte ⓘ 5.50 – **48 rm** ⊃ 65.00/95.00 **t.** – SB.

🏨 **Imperial,** North Drive, NR30 1EQ, ℰ (01493) 851113, Fax (01493) 852229 – 🛗, ⊱ rm,
⊟ rest, TV AE ⓞ VISA
Rambouillet : Meals (closed lunch Saturday and Bank Holidays) 12.50/
19.50 **st.** and a la carte ⓘ 6.00 – **39 rm** ⊃ 62.00/77.00 **st.** – SB.

🏠 Two Bears, Southtown Rd, NR31 0HU, ℰ (01493) 603198, Fax (01493) 440486, ☞ – TV ☎
🅿 – 🔬 25
11 rm.

at Gorleston-on-Sea S : 3 m. on A 12 – ⊠ Great Yarmouth.

🏨 **Cliff,** Cliff Hill, NR31 6DH, ℰ (01493) 662179, Fax (01493) 653617, ☞ – ⊱ rm, TV ☎ 🅿 –
🔬 170. 📠 AE ⓞ VISA. ⋇
Meals 16.00 **t.** and a la carte ⓘ 5.95 – **38 rm** ⊃ 62.00/96.00 **t.**, 1 suite – SB.

🅐 ATS Suffling Rd ℰ (01493) 858211

GREAT YELDHAM Essex 404 V 27 – pop. 1 513 – ⊠ Colchester.
London 58 – Cambridge 29 – Chelmsford 24 – Colchester 21 – Ipswich 37.

XX **White Hart,** Poole St., CO9 4HJ, ℰ (01787) 237250, Fax (01787) 238044, « 16C inn », 龠 –
✦ ℗. ⚫❿ 䍐 ⓪ ⱱⱭ JCB
closed dinner Sunday, Monday, 25-26 December, 1, 4 and 5 January – **Meals**
a la carte 13.00/27.50 t. ﹩ 11.00.

GRENOSIDE S. Yorks. 402 403 404 P 23 – see Sheffield.

GRETA BRIDGE Durham 402 O 20.
London 253 – Carlisle 63 – Leeds 63 – Middlesbrough 32.

🏨 **Morritt Arms,** DL12 9SE, ℰ (01833) 627232, Fax (01833) 627392, ⬧, 龠 – ✦ 📺 ☎ 🚗
℗ – 🔏 150. ⚫❿ 䍐 ⓪ ⱱⱭ
Meals 15.95 t. and a la carte ﹩ 4.95 – **18 rm** ⊡ 49.50/79.50 t. – SB.

GRÈVE DE LECQ Jersey (Channel Islands) 403 P 33 and 230 ⑪ – see Channel Islands.

GRIMSTON Norfolk – see King's Lynn.

GRINDLEFORD Derbs. 402 403 404 P 24 – ⊠ Sheffield (S. Yorks.).
London 165 – Derby 31 – Manchester 34 – Sheffield 10.

🏨 **Maynard Arms,** Main Rd, S32 2HE, on A 625 ℰ (01433) 630321, Fax (01433) 630445, ≤,
龠 – ✦ rest, 📺 ☎ ℗ – 🔏 150. ⚫❿ 䍐 ⱱⱭ
Meals 16.50 t. ﹩ 6.75 – **9 rm** ⊡ 59.00/79.00 t., 1 suite – SB.

GRINDON Staffs. – pop. 242 – ⊠ Leek.
London 118 – Birmingham 70 – Derby 26 – Manchester 42 – Stoke-on-Trent 20.

↑ **Porch Farmhouse** ⬧, ST13 7TP, ℰ (01538) 304545, Fax (01538) 304545, « Part 17C »,
龠 – ✦ ℗. ⚫❿ ⱱⱭ
closed Christmas-New Year – **Meals** (by arrangement) (communal dining) (unlicensed)
18.00 s. – **3 rm** ⊡ 30.00/50.00 s. – SB.

GRINGLEY Notts. 402 S 23 – ⊠ Doncaster.
London 163 – Leeds 43 – Lincoln 24 – Nottingham 42 – Sheffield 26.

↑ **Old Vicarage,** DN10 4RF, on High St. ℰ (01777) 817248, Fax (01777) 817248, ≤, 龠, ⋇ –
✦ rm, ℗. ⚫❿ ⱱⱭ
closed 1 January, 25-26 and 31 December – **Meals** (by arrangement) (communal dining)
18.00 s. ﹩ 5.60 – **3 rm** ⊡ 31.00/52.00 s.

GRIZEDALE Cumbria 402 K 20 – see Hawkshead.

GROUVILLE Jersey (Channel Islands) 403 P 33 and 230 ⑪ – see Channel Islands.

GUERNSEY 403 OP 33 and 230 ⑨ ⑩ – see Channel Islands.

GUILDFORD Surrey 404 S 30 – pop. 65 998.
🛈 14 Tunsgate, GU1 3QT ℰ (01483) 444333 Y.
London 33 – Brighton 43 – Reading 27 – Southampton 49.

Plan opposite

🏨 **Angel Posting House and Livery,** High St., GU1 3DP, ℰ (01483) 564555,
Fax (01483) 533770, « 16C coaching inn with 13C vaulted cellar restaurant » – 📺 ☎ & –
🔏 70. ⚫❿ 䍐 ⓪ ⱱⱭ   Y e
Meals 15.00/18.50 t. and a la carte ﹩ 7.50 – ⊡ 9.50 – **14 rm** 135.00 st., 7 suites – SB.

🏨 **Forte Posthouse Guildford,** Egerton Rd, GU2 5XZ, ℰ (01483) 574444,
Fax (01483) 302960, 🖪, ⇌, ⬧, – ✦ rm, 📺 ☎ & ℗ – 🔏 180. ⚫❿ 䍐 ⓪ ⱱⱭ
Meals (closed Saturday and Bank Holiday lunch) 9.95 **st.** (lunch) and a la carte 16.45/
22.90 st. – ⊡ 10.95 – **109 rm** 109.00/129.00 st., 2 suites – SB.   Z v

🏨 **Travel Inn,** Stoke Rd, GU1 1UP, N : 1 ½ m. by A 320 on A 25 ℰ (01483) 304932,
Fax (01483) 304935 – ✦ rm, 📺 & ℗. ⚫❿ 䍐 ⓪ ⱱⱭ, ⋇
Meals (grill rest.) – **60 rm** 36.50 t.   Z a

GUILDFORD

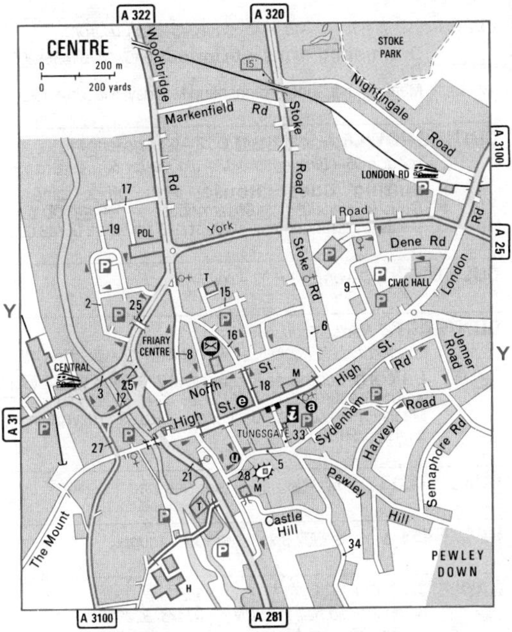

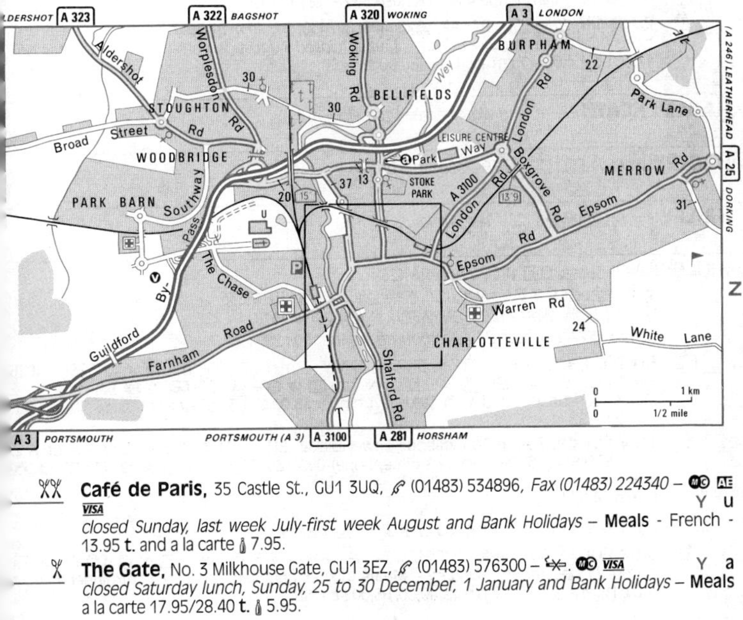

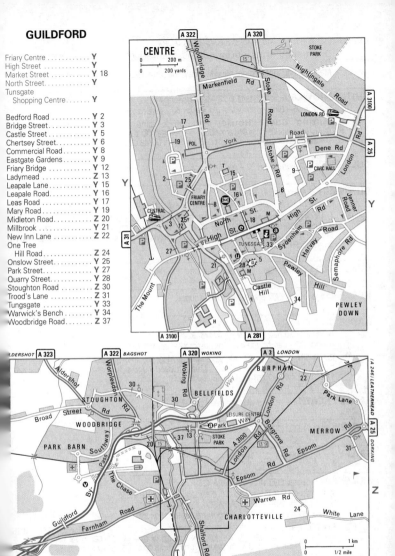

🍴🍴 **Café de Paris,** 35 Castle St., GU1 3UQ, ☎ (01483) 534896, *Fax (01483) 224340* – [MC] [AE] [VISA] Y u
closed Sunday, last week July-first week August and Bank Holidays – **Meals** - French - 13.95 **t.** and a la carte 🍷 7.95.

🍴 **The Gate,** No. 3 Milkhouse Gate, GU1 3EZ, ☎ (01483) 576300 – 🚭. [MC] [VISA] Y a
closed Saturday lunch, Sunday, 25 to 30 December, 1 January and Bank Holidays – **Meals** a la carte 17.95/28.40 **t.** 🍷 5.95.

at Shere *E : 6 ¾ m. by A 246 off A 25 – Z – ✉ Guildford.*

🍴🍴 **Kinghams,** Gomshall Lane, GU5 9HB, ☎ (01483) 202168, « 17C cottage » – [P]. [MC] [AE] [VISA]
closed Sunday dinner, Monday and 25 December-3 January – **Meals** a la carte 15.40/21.40 **t.** 🍷 5.00.

at Albury *E : 6 ¾ m. by A 25 – Z – on A 248 – ✉ Guildford.*

Drummond Arms with rm, GU5 9AG, ☎ (01483) 202039, *Fax (01483) 202039* – . VISA.
Meals (in bar Sunday dinner and Monday) a la carte 13.50/21.00 **st.** – **7 rm** 38.00/50.00.

GUITING POWER *Glos.* 403 404 O 28 – ✉ *Cheltenham.*
London 95 – Birmingham 47 – Gloucester 30 – Oxford 39.

Guiting Guest House, Post Office Lane, GL54 5TZ, ☎ (01451) 850470, *Fax (01451) 850034,* « 16C farmhouse » – . VISA JCB
Meals (by arrangement) 16.00 **st.** – **3 rm** 28.00/48.00 **st.**

GULWORTHY *Devon* 403 H 32 – *see Tavistock.*

GUNTHORPE *Notts. – pop. 646.*
London 132 – Lincoln 32 – Nottingham 12 – Sheffield 40.

Unicorn, Gunthorpe Bridge, NG14 7FB, SE : 1 ½ m. by A 6097 and Gunthorpe (riverside) rd ☎ (0115) 966 3612, *Fax (0115) 966 4801,* – rest, . AE VISA.
Meals (grill rest.) (bar lunch Monday to Saturday)/dinner a la carte 14.15/19.70 **t.** – **16 rm** 49.50/59.50 **t.**

GUNWALLOE *Cornwall* 403 E 33 – *see Helston.*

HACKNESS *N. Yorks.* 402 S 21 – *see Scarborough.*

HADLEIGH *Suffolk* 404 W 27 – *pop. 6 595.*
Toppesfield Hall, IP7 5DN ☎ (01473) 822922.
London 72 – Cambridge 49 – Colchester 17 – Ipswich 10.

Edgehill, 2 High St., IP7 5AP, ☎ (01473) 822458, – .
closed Christmas and New Year – **Meals** *(closed August)* (by arrangement) (dinner only) 17.50 **st.** 4.00 – **7 rm** 40.00/80.00 **st.** – SB.

HADLEY HEATH *Heref. and Worcs. – see Droitwich.*

HAGLEY *W. Mids.* 403 404 N 26 – *see Stourbridge.*

HAILEY *Oxon.* 403 404 P 28 – *see Witney.*

HAILSHAM *E. Sussex* 404 U 31 – *pop. 18 426.*
18 *Wellshurst G. & C.C., North St., Hellingly ☎ (01435) 813636.*
The Library, Western Rd, BN27 3DN ☎ (01323) 844426.
London 57 – Brighton 23 – Eastbourne 7 – Hastings 20.

Boship Farm, Lower Dicker, BN27 4AT, NW : 3 m. by A 295 on A 22 ☎ (01323) 844826 *Fax (01323) 843945,* – rm, – 120. AE VISA
Meals (bar lunch Monday to Saturday)/dinner 18.00 **t.** 5.95 – **44 rm** 55.00/90.00 **t.** 2 suites – SB.

Travelodge, Boship Roundabout, Lower Dicker, BN27 4DT, NW : 3 m. by A 295 on A 22 ☎ (01323) 844556, Reservations (Freephone) 0800 850950 – . AE VISA JCB.
40 rm 44.95 **t.**

at Magham Down *NE : 2 m. by A 295 on A 271 – ✉ Hailsham.*

Olde Forge, BN27 1PN, ☎ (01323) 842893, *Fax (01323) 842893* – . AE VISA
closed 25 December-2 January – **Meals** (dinner only and Sunday lunch)/dinner 14.50 **t** and a la carte 3.95 – **7 rm** 40.00/65.00 **st.** – SB.

HALE *Gtr. Manchester* 402 403 404 M 23 – *see Altrincham.*

HALEBARNS *Gtr. Manchester – see Altrincham.*

HALIFAX W. Yorks. 402 O 22 – pop. 91 069.

⊓ Halifax Bradley Hall, Holywell Green ℘ (01422) 374108 – ⊓ Halifax West End, Paddock Lane, Highroad Well ℘ (01422) 353608, ⊓ Union Lane, Ogden ℘ (01422) 244171 – ⊓ Ryburn, Norland, Sowerby Bridge ℘ (01422) 831355 – ⊓ Elland, Hammerstones Leach Lane, Hullen Edge ℘ (01422) 372505 – ⊓ Lightcliffe, Knowle Top Rd ℘ (01422) 202459.

🖪 Piece Hall, HX1 1RE ℘ (01422) 368725.

London 205 – Bradford 8 – Burnley 21 – Leeds 15 – Manchester 28.

🏥 **Holdsworth House,** Holmfield, HX2 9TG, N : 3 m. by A 629 and Shay Lane ℘ (01422) 240024, Fax (01422) 245174, « Part 17C », ⌂ – ⁕ 📺 ☎ ₤ 🅿 – 🔬 150. 🐵 🖭 🔘 💳 . ⁒
closed 26 to 30 December – **Meals** (closed Saturday and Sunday lunch) a la carte 19.20/27.40 **st.** ₤ 8.95 – ⚏ 6.50 – **36 rm** 77.50/97.50 **st.**, 4 suites – SB.

🏨 **Imperial Crown,** 42-46 Horton St., HX1 1BR, ℘ (01422) 342342, Fax (01422) 349866 – 📺 ☎ – 🔬 150. 🐵 🖭 🔘 💳 🗀
Meals (dinner only) 16.00 **st.** and a la carte – **39 rm** ⚏ 69.00/85.00 **st.**, 2 suites – SB.

🏛 **Imperial Crown Lodge,** 31 Square Rd, HX1 1QG, ℘ (01422) 342342, Fax (01422) 349866, « American diner, rock music memorabilia » – 📺 🅿 . 🐵 🖭 🔘 💳 🗀
Meals 6.95 **st.** (lunch) and a la carte 12.15/15.20 **st.** – **15 rm** ⚏ 49.50/64.50 **st.** – SB.

✗ **Design House** (Restaurant), Dean Clough (Gate 5), HX3 5AX, ℘ (01422) 383242, Fax (01422) 322732 – 🍴 🅿 . 🐵 🖭 💳
closed Saturday lunch, Sunday, 25-26 December and 1-2 January – **Meals** 12.95 **st.** (lunch) and a la carte 16.40/24.95 **t.** ₤ 6.50.

⊛ ATS Hope St. ℘ (01422) 365892/360819

I nomi delle principali vie commerciali sono scritti in rosso all'inizio dell'indice toponomastico delle piante di città.

HALL GREEN W. Mids. 402 403 404 O 26 – see Birmingham.

HALNAKER W. Sussex – see Chichester.

HALTWHISTLE Northd. 401 402 M 19 Great Britain G. – pop. 3 773.

Env. : Hadrian's Wall★★, N : 4 ½ m. by A 6079 – Housesteads★★ AC, NE : 6 m. by B 6318 – Roman Army Museum★ AC, NW : 5 m. by A 69 and B 6318 – Vindolanda (Museum★) AC, NE : 5 m. by A 69 – Steel Rig (≤★) NE : 5 ½ m. by B 6318.

⊓ Banktop, Greenhead ℘ (016977) 47367.

🖪 Church Hall, Main St., NE49 0BE ℘ (01434) 322002 (April-October) – Haltwhistle Swimming and Leisure Club, Greencroft, NE49 9DP ℘ (01434) 322002 (November-March).

London 335 – Carlisle 22 – Newcastle upon Tyne 37.

⌂ **Ashcroft** without rest., Lantys Lonnen, NE49 0DA, ℘ (01434) 320213, « Gardens » – ⁕ 🅿 . 🐵 💳 . ⁒
8 rm ⚏ 18.00/45.00 **s.**

HAMBLETON Rutland – see Oakham.

HAMBROOK South Gloucestershire 403 404 M 29 – see Bristol.

HAMSTEAD MARSHALL Newbury 403 404 P 29 – see Newbury.

HAMSTERLEY Durham 401 402 O 19 – pop. 397 – ⊠ Bishop Auckland.

London 260 – Carlisle 75 – Middlesbrough 30 – Newcastle upon Tyne 22.

⌂ **Grove House** ⌂, Hamsterley Forest, DL13 3NL, W : 3 ¾ m. via Bedburn on Hamsterley Forest Toll rd ℘ (01388) 488203, ⌂ – ⁕ 🅿 . ⁒
closed Christmas and New Year – **Meals** (by arrangement) 16.00 **s.** – **3 rm** ⚏ 28.00/46.00 **s.**

HANDFORTH Ches. 402 403 404 N 23 – see Wilmslow.

HANWOOD Shrops. 402 403 L 25 – see Shrewsbury.

HAREWOOD *W. Yorks.* [402] P 22 – *pop. 3 222* – ✉ *Leeds.*
London 214 – Harrogate 9 – Leeds 10 – York 20.

🏨 **Harewood Arms,** Harrogate Rd, LS17 9LH, on A 61 📞 (0113) 288 6566, *Fax (0113) 288 6064,* 🌳 – [TV] ☎ [P]. [MC] [AE] [D] [VISA]
Meals 9.50/16.95 **t.** and a la carte 🍷 5.95 – **24 rm** ☕ 65.00/78.00 **t.**

HARLOW *Essex* [404] U 28 – *pop. 74 629.*
⛳18 *Nazeing, Middle St.* 📞 *(01992) 893798/893915.*
London 22 – Cambridge 37 – Ipswich 60.

🏨 **Churchgate Manor,** Churchgate St., Old Harlow, CM17 0JT, E : 3 ¼ m. by A 414 and B 183 📞 (01279) 420246, *Fax (01279) 437720,* 🏋, ♨, 🏊, 🌳 – 🚭 [TV] ☎ [P] – 👥 170. [MC] [AE] [D] [VISA] [JCB]
Meals (bar lunch Saturday) 18.95/19.95 **t.** and a la carte 🍷 5.95 – ☕ 9.75 – **82 rm** 79.00/115.00 **t.**, 3 suites – SB.

🏨 **Harlow Moat House,** Southern Way, CM18 7BA, SE : 2 ¼ m. by A 1025 on A 414 📞 (01279) 829988, *Fax (01279) 635094* – 🚭 rm, [TV] ☎ [P] – 👥 150. [MC] [AE] [D] [VISA] [JCB]. 🚫🐕
Meals (carving rest.) (bar lunch Saturday) a la carte 17.45/22.50 **t.** – ☕ 9.50 – **118 rm** 75.00/90.00 **t.** – SB.

🏨 **Travel Inn,** Cambridge Rd, Old Harlow, CM20 2EP, NE : 3 ¼ m. by A 414 on A 1184 📞 (01279) 442545, *Fax (01279) 452169* – 🚭 rm, [TV] ♿ [P]. [MC] [AE] [D] [VISA]. 🚫🐕
Meals (grill rest.) – **38 rm** 36.50 **t.**

ATS 14 Burnt Mill 📞 (01279) 421965

HARNHAM *Wilts.* [403] [404] O 30 – *see Salisbury.*

HAROME *N. Yorks.* – *see Helmsley.*

HARPENDEN *Herts.* [404] S 28 – *pop. 28 097.*
London 32 – Luton 6.

🏨 **Glen Eagle,** 1 Luton Rd, AL5 2PX, 📞 (01582) 760271, *Fax (01582) 460819,* 🌳 – ⇅, 🚭 rm, ❄ rest, [TV] ☎ [P] – 👥 80. [MC] [AE] [D] [VISA] [JCB]. 🚫🐕
Meals (bar meals Saturday lunch, Sunday dinner and Bank Holidays) 21.95 **st.** and a la carte 🍷 7.00 – ☕ 8.75 – **58 rm** 82.50/102.50, 2 suites.

🏨 **County H. Harpenden House,** 18 Southdown Rd, AL5 1PE, 📞 (01582) 449955, *Fax (01582) 769858,* 🌳 – 🚭 rm, [TV] ☎ [P] – 👥 150. [MC] [AE] [D] [VISA]. 🚫🐕
Meals (lunch booking essential) (bar meals Saturday lunch) 12.95 **t.** and a la carte 🍷 7.50 – ☕ 10.00 – **52 rm** 99.00/125.00 **st.**, 1 suite – SB.

🍴🍴 **Chef Peking,** 5-6 Church Green, AL5 2TP, 📞 (01582) 769358, *Fax (01582) 462094* – ❄. [MC] [AE] [D] [VISA]
Meals - Chinese (Peking, Szechuan) - 15.00 **st.** and a la carte 🍷 4.00.

🍴 **Le Zou,** 1a Clayton House, Vaughan Rd, AL5 4HU, 📞 (01582) 763318 – [MC] [AE] [VISA]
closed Sunday, Monday and last 3 weeks August – **Meals** (booking essential) (dinner only) 18.50 **t.** and a la carte 🍷 5.75.

HARROGATE *N. Yorks.* [402] P 22 *Great Britain G.* – *pop. 66 178.*
See : *Town*★.
Exc. : *Fountains Abbey*★★★ *AC :- Studley Royal*★★ *AC (≤★ from Anne Boleyn's Seat) - Fountains Hall (Façade*★*), N : 13 m. by A 61 and B 6265* AY – *Harewood House*★★ *(The Gallery*★*) AC, S : 7½m. by A 61* BZ.
⛳18 *Forest Lane Head* 📞 *(01423) 863158* – ⛳18 *Follifoot Rd, Pannal* 📞 *(01423) 871641* – ⛳18 *Oakdale* 📞 *(01423) 567162* – ⛳9 *Crimple Valley, Hookstone Wood Rd* 📞 *(01423) 883485.*
[i] *Royal Baths Assembly Rooms, Crescent Rd, HG1 2RR* 📞 *(01423) 537300.*
London 211 – Bradford 18 – Leeds 15 – Newcastle Upon Tyne 76 – York 22.

Plan opposite

🏨 **Rudding Park** 🌙, Rudding Park, Follifoot, HG3 1JH, SE : 6 ½ m. by A 61 off A 658 📞 (01423) 871350, *Fax (01423) 872286,* ⛱, ⛳18, 🌳, park – ⇅, 🚭 rm, [TV] ☎ ♿ [P] – 👥 300. [MC] [AE] [VISA]. 🚫🐕
Meals a la carte 16.95/24.85 **st.** 🍷 8.00 – **48 rm** ☕ 99.00/129.00 **st.**, 2 suites – SB.

🏨 **Old Swan,** Swan Rd, HG1 2SR, 📞 (01423) 500055, *Fax (01423) 501154,* 🌳 – ⇅ [TV] ☎ [P] – 👥 450. [MC] [AE] [D] [VISA] AY e
Wedgewood Room : **Meals** (dinner only and Sunday lunch)/dinner 19.95 **t.** and a la carte 🍷 5.95 – ***Library :*** **Meals** (lunch only) 19.50 **t.** 🍷 5.95 – ☕ 10.50 – **127 rm** 97.50/126.00 **st.**, 9 suites – SB.

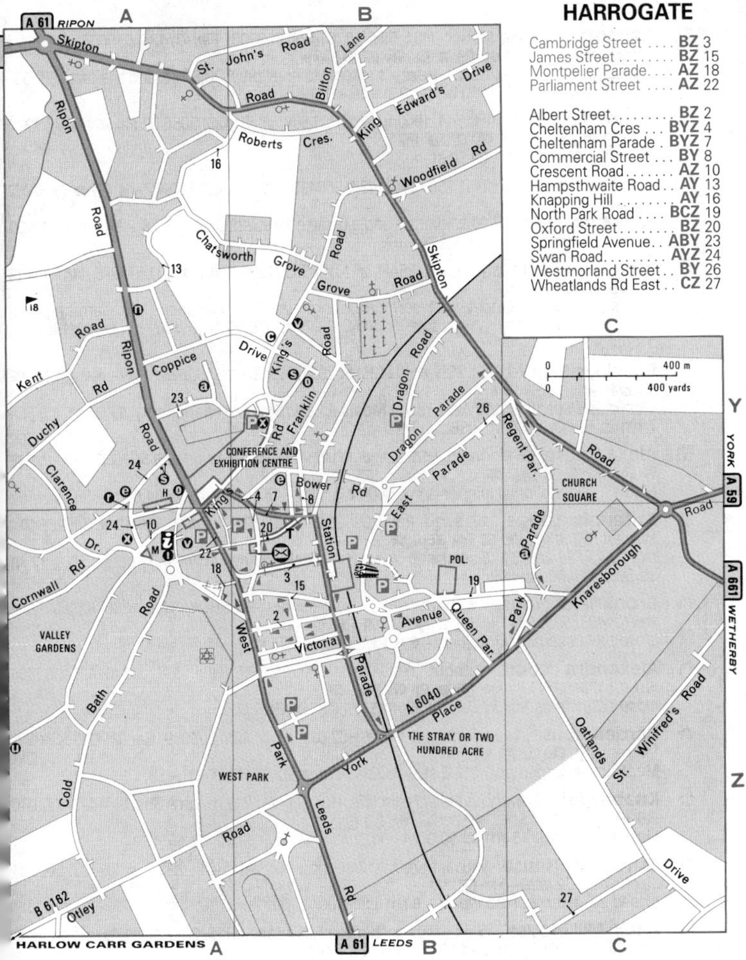

HARROGATE

Cambridge Street .... BZ 3
James Street .... BZ 15
Montpelier Parade.... AZ 18
Parliament Street .... AZ 22

Albert Street......... BZ 2
Cheltenham Cres ... BYZ 4
Cheltenham Parade . BYZ 7
Commercial Street ... BY 8
Crescent Road........ AZ 10
Hampsthwaite Road .. AY 13
Knapping Hill .... AY 16
North Park Road .... BCZ 19
Oxford Street......... BZ 20
Springfield Avenue.. ABY 23
Swan Road......... AYZ 24
Westmorland Street .. BY 26
Wheatlands Rd East .. CZ 27

Harrogate Moat House, Kings Rd, HG1 1XX, ☎ (01423) 849988, *Fax (01423) 524435*, ≤ – |♦|, ⊁ rm, ≡ rest, TV ☎ ♿ P – 400. MC AE D VISA. ✂ BY x
Abbey : **Meals** (carving rest.) (dinner only) 15.00 **t.** 6.00 – ***Boulevard :*** **Meals** *(closed Monday lunch)* 15.00/17.00 **t.** and dinner a la carte 6.00 – ☐ 9.50 – **205 rm** 99.00/134.00 **st.**, 9 suites – SB.

St. George, 1 Ripon Rd, HG1 2SY, ☎ (01423) 561431, *Fax (01423) 530037*, ♦, ≘s, ☐ – |♦|, ⊁ rm, TV ☎ P – 200. MC AE D VISA AY o
Meals (bar lunch)/dinner 17.50 **st.** and a la carte 6.00 – **89 rm** ☐ 90.00/110.00 **st.**, 1 suite – SB.

Crown, Crown Pl., HG1 2RZ, ☎ (01423) 567755, *Fax (01423) 502284* – |♦|, ⊁ rm, TV ☎ P – 300. MC AE D VISA JCB AZ i
Meals (bar lunch Monday to Saturday)/dinner 19.00 **st.** and a la carte 5.75 – ☐ 9.50 – **116 rm** 85.00/105.00 **st.**, 5 suites – SB.

Grants, Swan Rd, HG1 2SS, ☎ (01423) 560666, *Fax (01423) 502550* – |♦|, ⊁ rm, ≡ rest, TV ☎ P – 70. MC AE D VISA JCB AY s
Chimney Pots : **Meals** 11.50/17.50 **t.** 5.75 – **41 rm** ☐ 96.50/147.00 **t.**, 1 suite – SB.

🏨 **Balmoral,** Franklin Mount, HG1 5EJ, ℰ (01423) 508208, Fax (01423) 530652, « Antique furnishings » – ⇔ rest, ⊡ ☎ 📵. 🍽 AE VISA JCB
BY v
closed Christmas-New Year – **Henry's :** Meals (dinner only) 20.00 st. and a la carte ≬ 5.65 – ⌸ 8.50 – **18 rm** 85.00/110.00 st.,, 2 suites – SB.

🏨 **Kimberley** without rest., 11-19 Kings Rd, HG1 5JY, ℰ (01423) 505613, Fax (01423) 530276 – ≬ ⊡ ☎ 📵 – 🕮 25. 🍽 AE ⓞ VISA
BY c
⌸ 7.95 – **48 rm** 59.50/89.50 st.

🏨 **Studley,** 28 Swan Rd, HG1 2SE, ℰ (01423) 560425, Fax (01423) 530967 – ≬ ⊡ ☎ 📵. 🍽 AE ⓞ VISA. ⇔
AZ x
Le Breton : Meals 17.00 t. (dinner) and a la carte 19.95/22.95 t. ≬ 5.75 – **34 rm** ⌸ 68.00/98.00 t., 2 suites – SB.

🏨 **White House,** 10 Park Par., HG1 5AH, ℰ (01423) 501388, Fax (01423) 527973, ⇔ – ⇔ ⊡ ☎. 🍽 AE JCB. ⇔
CZ a
Meals (closed Sunday dinner) (booking essential) (lunch by arrangement) 15.50 t. (lunch) and a la carte approx. 24.75 t. ≬ 5.75 – **9 rm** ⌸ 88.50/128.50 t., 1 suite – SB.

🏦 **Ruskin,** 1 Swan Rd, HG1 2SS, ℰ (01423) 502045, Fax (01423) 506131, ⇔ – ⇔ ⊡ 📵. 🍽 AE VISA. ⇔
AY s
closed 25 December and New Year – **Meals** (closed Sunday) (dinner only) 17.95 st. ≬ 6.50 – **7 rm** ⌸ 59.00/95.00 st.

🏦 **Alexa House,** 26 Ripon Rd, HG1 2JJ, ℰ (01423) 501988, Fax (01423) 504086 – ⇔ rm, ⊡ ☎ 📵. 🍽 AE ⓞ VISA. ⇔
AY n
Meals (residents only) (dinner only) 14.00 t. ≬ 5.00 – **13 rm** ⌸ 48.00/64.00 t. – SB.

🏦 **Britannia Lodge,** 16 Swan Rd, HG1 2SA, ℰ (01423) 508482, Fax (01423) 526840 – ⇔ rest, ⊡ ☎ 📵. 🍽 AE VISA JCB. ⇔
AYZ r
closed 25, 26 and 31 December-1 January – **Meals** (dinner only) 14.50 st. ≬ 4.50 – **12 rm** ⌸ 50.00/70.00 st. – SB.

⌂ **Brookfield House** without rest., 5 Alexandra Rd, HG1 5JS, ℰ (01423) 506646, Fax (01423) 523151 – ⇔ ⊡ ☎ 📵. 🍽 VISA. ⇔
BY s
closed 24 December-2 January – **6 rm** ⌸ 38.00/55.00 st.

⌂ **Alexandra Court** without rest., 8 Alexandra Rd, HG1 5JS, ℰ (01423) 502764, Fax (01423) 523151 – ⇔ ⊡ ☎ 📵. 🍽 VISA. ⇔
BY o
closed Christmas and 31 December – **13 rm** ⌸ 38.00/60.00 t.

⌂ **Garden House,** 14 Harlow Moor Drive, HG2 0JX, ℰ (01423) 503059, Fax (01423) 503059 – ⇔ rest, ⊡. 🍽 AE ⓞ VISA. ⇔
AZ u
Meals (by arrangement) 11.00 st. ≬ 4.00 – **7 rm** ⌸ 22.00/47.00 st. – SB.

⌂ **Knabbs Ash** ⬂ without rest., Felliscliffe, HG3 2LT, W : 5 ½ m. on A 59 ℰ (01423) 771040, Fax (01423) 771515, ≤, ⇔, park – ⇔ ⊡ 📵. ⇔
closed Christmas – **3 rm** ⌸ 30.00/42.00.

⌂ **Ashwood House** without rest., 7 Spring Grove, HG1 2HS, ℰ (01423) 560081, Fax (01423) 527928 – ⇔ ⊡. ⇔
AY a
closed 24 December-2 January – **8 rm** ⌸ 30.00/45.00.

⌂ **Knox Mill House** ⬂ without rest., Knox Mill Lane, HG3 2AE, N : 1 ½ m. by A 61 ℰ (01423) 560650, Fax (01423) 560560, ≤ – ⇔ 📵. ⇔
closed Christmas and New Year – **3 rm** ⌸ 30.00/40.00 s.

XX **La Bergerie,** 11-13 Mount Par., HG1 1BX, ℰ (01423) 500089, Fax (01423) 560837 – 🍽 VISA
BY e
closed Sunday and 25 December – **Meals** - French - (dinner only) 15.75/17.75 t.

X **The Bistro,** 1 Montpellier Mews, HG1 2TG, ℰ (01423) 530708, Fax (01423) 567000, 😼 – 🍽 VISA
AZ v
closed Sunday, Monday and 1 week Christmas – **Meals** a la carte 19.00/23.50 t. ≬ 6.95.

X **Drum and Monkey,** 5 Montpellier Gdns, HG1 2TF, ℰ (01423) 502650, Fax (01423) 522469 – 🍽 VISA
AZ v
closed Sunday and 24 December-2 January – **Meals** - Seafood - (booking essential) a la carte 12.95/29.05 t. ≬ 6.45.

at Markington NW : 8 ¾ m. by A 61 – AY – ⊠ Harrogate.

🏨 **Hob Green** ⬂, HG3 3PJ, SW : ½ m. ℰ (01423) 770031, Fax (01423) 771589, ≤, « Country house in extensive parkland », ⇔ – ⊡ ☎ 📵. 🍽 AE VISA JCB
Meals 14.95/21.50 st. and dinner a la carte ≬ 7.50 – **11 rm** ⌸ 80.00/99.00 st., 1 suite – SB.

🔧 ATS Leeds Rd, Pannal ℰ (01423) 879194

HARTFIELD *E. Sussex* **404** U 30 – pop. 2 026.
London 47 – Brighton 28 – Maidstone 25.

⌂ **Bolebroke Mill** ⌂ without rest., Edenbridge Rd, TN7 4JP, N : 1 ¼ m. by B 2026 on unmarked rd ℘ (01892) 770425, Fax (01892) 770425, « Part early 17C cornmill, original features », ⌖ – ⌖ 📺 ℗. ⫯ 🆎 *VISA*. ⫰
February-mid December – **5 rm** ⌖ 52.00/74.00 **s.**

HARTFORD *Ches.* **402 403 404** M 24 – pop. 4 605.
London 188 – Chester 15 – Liverpool 31 – Manchester 25.

🏨 **Hartford Hall**, 81 School Lane, CW8 1PW, ℘ (01606) 75711, Fax (01606) 782285, ⌖ – 📺 ☎ ℗ – ⚒ 35. ⫯ 🆎 ⓞ *VISA*. ⫰
Meals 9.95 **t.** (lunch) and a la carte 13.40/20.95 **t.** – ⌖ 6.95 – **19 rm** 59.95, 1 suite – SB.

HARTINGTON *Derbs.* **402 403 404** O 24 – pop. 1 604 (inc. Dovedale) – ✉ *Buxton.*
London 168 – Derby 36 – Manchester 40 – Sheffield 34 – Stoke-on-Trent 22.

🏛 **Biggin Hall** ⌂, Biggin, SK17 0DH, SE : 2 m. by B 5054 ℘ (01298) 84451, Fax (01298) 84681, ⌖, « 17C », ⌖ – ⌖ rest, 📺 ℗ ⫯ *VISA*. ⫰
Meals *(booking essential to non-residents)* (dinner only) 14.50 ⌖ 4.50 – ⌖ 3.50 – **17 rm** 35.00/80.00 **st.** – SB.

HARTLEBURY *Worcestershire* **403** N 26 – pop. 2 253.
London 135 – Birmingham 20 – Worcester 11.

🏨 **Travelodge**, Crossway Green, DY13 9SH, S : 2 ½ m. by B 4193 on A 449 (southbound carriageway) ℘ (01299) 250553, Reservations (Freephone) 0800 850950 – ⌖ rm, 📺 ⚹ ℗. ⫯ 🆎 ⓞ *VISA* *JCB*. ⫰
32 rm 44.95 **t.**

Jährlich eine neue Ausgabe
Aktuellste Informationen, jährlich für Sie!

HARTLEPOOL *Hartlepool* **402** Q 19 – pop. 87 310.
🏌, 🏌 *Seaton Carew, Tees Rd ℘ (01429) 266249/261040 – 🏌 Castle Eden & Peterlee*
℘ (01429) 836220 – 🏌 Hart Warren ℘ (01429) 274398.
✈ *Teesside Airport : ℘ (01325) 332811, SW : 20 m. by A 689, A 1027, A 135 and A 67.*
🛈 *Hartlepool Art Gallery & Infor, Church Sq., TS24 7EQ ℘ (01429) 869706.*
London 263 – Durham 19 – Middlesbrough 9 – Sunderland 21.

🏨 **Grand**, Swainson St., TS24 8AA, ℘ (01429) 266345, Fax (01429) 265217 – 📶 📺 ☎ ℗ – ⚒ 200. ⫯ 🆎 ⓞ *VISA*. ⫰
Meals *(closed Sunday dinner)* (bar lunch Monday to Saturday)/dinner 14.50 **t.** ⌖ 4.75 – **47 rm** ⌖ 49.95/85.00 **t.** – SB.

🏛 **Travel Inn**, Old West Quay, Hartlepool Marina, TS24 0XZ, ℘ (01429) 890115, Fax (01429) 868674, ⌖ – ⌖ rm, 📺 ⚹ ℗. ⫯ 🆎 ⓞ *VISA*. ⫰
Meals (grill rest.) – **40 rm** 36.50 **t.**

at Seaton Carew *SE : 2 m. on A 178.*

🏨 **Marine**, 5-7 The Front, TS25 1BS, ℘ (01429) 266244, Fax (01429) 864144, ⌖ – 📺 ☎ ℗ – ⚒ 50. ⫯ 🆎 ⓞ *VISA*. ⫰
closed 25 December – **Meals** (bar lunch Saturday) (carving rest.) 8.75 **st.** and a la carte ⌖ 5.25 – **25 rm** ⌖ 48.00/68.00 **st.** – SB.

✗ **Krimo's**, 8 The Front, TS25 1BS, ℘ (01429) 266120 – ⫯ *VISA*
closed Saturday lunch, Sunday, Monday, 1 January, last 2 weeks August and 25-26 December – **Meals** 13.95 **st.** (dinner) and a la carte 12.55/23.90 **st.** ⌖ 4.35.

 ⓐ ATS York Rd ℘ (01429) 275552

HARTSHEAD MOOR SERVICE AREA *W. Yorks.* **402** O 22 – ✉ *Brighouse.*
London 213 – Bradford 8 – Burnley 31 – Manchester 35 – Sheffield 39.

🏛 **Welcome Lodge**, Clifton, HD6 4JX, M 62 between junctions 25 and 26 (eastbound carriageway) ℘ (01274) 851706, Fax (01274) 855169, Reservations (Freephone) 0800 7314466 – 📺 ⚹ ℗. ⫯ 🆎 ⓞ *VISA*. ⫰
40 rm 45.00 **t.**

HARVINGTON *Worcestershire* **403 404** O 27 – see Evesham.

HARWELL *Oxon.* [403] [404] Q 29 – *pop. 2 236.*
London 64 – Oxford 16 – Reading 18 – Swindon 22.

🏨 **Kingswell,** Reading Rd, OX11 0LZ, S : ¾ m. on A 417 ☎ (01235) 833043, *Fax (01235) 833193* – 📺 ☎ [P] – 🎤 30. [MC] [AE] [D] VISA. 🚫
Meals 15.95/17.95 **st.** and a la carte 🍷 4.00 – **19 rm** ☕ 81.00/102.00 **st.** – SB.

HARWICH and DOVERCOURT *Essex* [404] X 28 – *pop. 18 436 (Harwich).*
⛳9 *Station Rd, Parkeston ☎ (01255) 503616.*
⛴ *to Germany (Hamburg) (Scandinavian Seaways) daily (20 h) – to Denmark (Esbjerg) (Scandinavian Seaways) (20 h) – to The Netherlands (Hook of Holland) (Stena Line) 2 daily (6 h 30 mn) day, (8 h 30 mn) night – to Sweden (Gothenburg) (Scandinavian Seaways) (24 h).*
[i] *Iconfield Park, Parkeston, CO12 4EN ☎ (01255) 506139.*
London 78 – Chelmsford 41 – Colchester 20 – Ipswich 23.

🍴🍴 **Pier at Harwich** with rm, The Quay, CO12 3HH, ☎ (01255) 241212, *Fax (01255) 551922,* ← – 📺 ☎ [P]. [MC] [AE] [D] VISA. 🚫
accommodation closed 24 to 26 December – **Meals** - Seafood - 14.00/18.00 **t.** and a la carte 🍷 6.95 – ☕ 4.00 – **6 rm** 52.50/85.00 **st.** – SB.

Ⓜ ATS 723 Main Rd, Dovercourt ☎ (01255) 508314

HASCOMBE *Surrey – see Godalming.*

HASLEMERE *Surrey* [404] R 30 – *pop. 12 218.*
London 47 – Brighton 46 – Southampton 44.

🏨 **Lythe Hill,** Petworth Rd, GU27 3BQ, E : 1 ½ m. on B 2131 ☎ (01428) 651251, *Fax (01428) 644131,* ←, 🎣, 🌳, park, 🎾 – 🚭 rest, 📺 ☎ [P] – 🎤 60. [MC] [AE] [D] VISA JCB
Meals *(closed Sunday lunch and Saturday dinner)* 19.50 **st.** and a la carte 🍷 8.00 – ***Auberge de France :*** **Meals** - French - *(closed Monday)* (dinner only and Sunday lunch)/dinner 24.50 **st.** and a la carte 🍷 8.00 – ☕ 9.00 – **28 rm** 94.00/105.00 **st.**, 12 suites – SB.

🏨 **Georgian,** High St., GU27 2JY, ☎ (01428) 651555, *Fax (01428) 661304,* 🌳 – 📺 ☎ [P]. [MC] [AE] [D] VISA
Meals 12.50/15.95 **st.** and a la carte 🍷 6.95 – ☕ 9.50 – **25 rm** 69.00/83.00 **st.** – SB.

🍴🍴🍴 ✿ **Fleur de Sel** (Perraud), 23-27 Lower St., GU27 2NY, ☎ (01428) 651462, *Fax (01428) 661568* – [MC] [AE] VISA
closed Saturday lunch, Sunday dinner, Monday and last 2 weeks August – **Meals** - French - 12.50/26.00 **t.** 🍷 7.50
Spec. Carpaccio of salmon and smoked haddock marinated in lemon and dill. Roast crispy duck with a honey and ginger sauce. Assiette of desserts.

HASLINGDEN *Lancs.* [402] N 22
London 228 – Blackpool 40 – Burnley 9 – Leeds 39 – Manchester 28 – Liverpool 52.

🏨 **Sykeside Country House,** Rawtenstall Road End, BB4 6QE, S : 1 m. by A 680 on A 681 ☎ (01706) 831163, *Fax (01706) 830090,* 🌳 – 🚭 📺 ☎ ♿ [P]. [MC] [AE] [D] VISA. 🚫
closed 26 December, 1 January and Bank Holidays – **Meals** *(closed Saturday lunch and Sunday dinner)* 9.95 **st.** (lunch) and dinner a la carte 17.45/23.20 **st.** 🍷 5.95 – **10 rm** ☕ 57.00/85.00 **st.**

HASSOP *Derbs. – see Bakewell.*

HASTINGS and ST. LEONARDS *E. Sussex* [404] V 31 – *pop. 81 139 (Hastings).*
⛳18 *Beauport Park, Battle Rd, St. Leonards-on-Sea ☎ (01424) 852977.*
[i] *4 Robertson Terr., TN34 1JE ☎ (01424) 781111 – Fishmarket, The Stade, TN34 1JE ☎ (01424) 781111 (summer only).*
London 65 – Brighton 37 – Folkestone 37 – Maidstone 34.

Plan opposite

🏨 **Beauport Park** 🐴, Battle Rd, TN38 8EA, NW : 3 ½ m. at junction of A 2100 with B 2159 ☎ (01424) 851222, *Fax (01424) 852465,* ←, « Formal garden », 🏊, ⛳18, park, 🎾 – 🚭 rest, 📺 ☎ [P] – 🎤 60. [MC] [AE] [D] VISA JCB
Meals 16.00/21.50 **st.** and a la carte 🍷 5.00 – **23 rm** ☕ 75.00/100.00 **t.**, 1 suite – SB.

🏨 Cinque Ports, Summerfields, Bohemia Rd, TN34 1ET, ☎ (01424) 439222 *Fax (01424) 437277* – 📺 ☎ [P] – 🎤 250 AZ a
40 rm.

HASTINGS
AND ST. LEONARDS

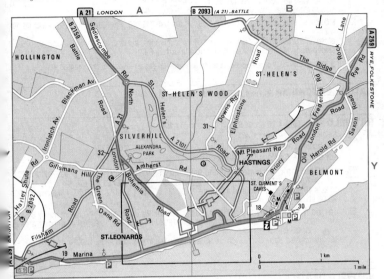

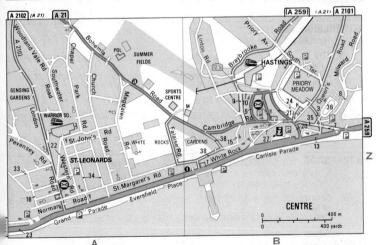

CENTRE

Dieser Führer ist kein vollständiges Hotel- und Restaurantverzeichnis.
Um den Ansprüchen aller Touristen gerecht zu werden,
haben wir uns auf eine Auswahl in jeder Kategorie beschränkt.

🏠 **Tower House**, 26-28 Tower Road West, TN38 0RG, ☎ (01424) 427217,
Fax (01424) 427217, 🌧 – ⇔ 📺 ☎. ◉◉ 🖭 ◉ 𝘝𝘐𝘚𝘈. ⚘
Meals (residents only) (dinner only) 12.50 ≬ 4.00 – **11 rm** ⊑ 34.00/69.00 st. – SB.
AY **c**

🏠 **Parkside House** without rest., 59 Lower Park Rd, TN34 2LD, ☎ (01424) 433096,
Fax (01424) 421431, 🌧 – ⇔ 📺 📺. ◉◉ 𝘝𝘐𝘚𝘈. ⚘
5 rm ⊑ 26.00/52.00 st.
BY **e**

🏠 **Filsham Farmhouse** without rest., 111 Harley Shute Rd, TN38 8BY, ☎ (01424) 433109,
Fax (01424) 461061, « Part 17C », 🌧 – ⇔ 📺 ℗
closed Christmas and New Year – **3 rm** ⊑ 25.00/60.00.
AY **u**

XX **Röser's**, 64 Eversfield Pl., TN37 6DB, ☎ (01424) 712218, Fax (01424) 712218 – ◉◉ 🖭 ◉
𝘝𝘐𝘚𝘈
closed Saturday lunch, Sunday, Monday, first 2 weeks January, last 2 weeks June and 25-26
December – Meals 18.95/21.95 st. and a la carte ≬ 6.50.
BZ **i**

ⓐ ATS Menzies Rd, Pondswood Ind. Est., St. Leonards-on-Sea ☎ (01424) 427780/424567

HATCH BEAUCHAMP Somerset **403** K 30 – see Taunton.

HATFIELD Herts. **404** T 28 Great Britain G. – pop. 31 104.
See : Hatfield House★★ AC.
ⓑ Hatfield London C.C., Bedwell Park, Essendon ☎ (01707) 642624.
London 27 – Bedford 38 – Cambridge 39.

🏨 **Hatfield Oak**, Roehyde Way, AL10 9AF, S : 2 m. by B 6426 on A 1001 ☎ (01707) 275701,
Fax (01707) 266033 – ⇔ rm, 📧 rest, 📺 ☎ ♿ ℗ – 🔬 120. ◉◉ 🖭 ◉ 𝘝𝘐𝘚𝘈. ⚘
Meals 18.50 st. (dinner) and a la carte 15.50/21.00 st. ≬ 5.50 – ⊑ 8.75 – **76 rm** 75.00/
90.00 st.

🏨 **Jarvis International Hatfield**, 301 St. Albans Rd West, AL10 9RH, W : 1 m. by B 6426
on A 1057 at junction with A 1001 ☎ (01707) 265411, Fax (01707) 264019 – ⇔ rm, 📺 ☎ ℗
– 🔬 150. ◉◉ 🖭 ◉ 𝘝𝘐𝘚𝘈. ⚘
Meals (closed Saturday lunch) 16.95 st. and a la carte ≬ 7.00 – ⊑ 8.00 – **101 rm** 89.00/
99.00 st. – SB.

HATFIELD HEATH Essex **404** U 28 – see Bishop's Stortford (Herts.).

HATHERLEIGH Devon **403** H 31 – pop. 1 542 – ⊠ Okehampton.
London 230 – Exeter 29 – Plymouth 38.

🍴 **The Tally Ho** with rm, 14 Market St., EX20 3JN, ☎ (01837) 810306, Fax (01837) 811079,
« Part 16C inn » – ⇔ 📺 ℗. ◉◉ 𝘝𝘐𝘚𝘈. ⚘
closed 22 December-5 January – Meals (closed Wednesday and Thursday) (bar lunch)/
dinner a la carte 17.25/29.95 t. ≬ 6.95 – **3 rm** ⊑ 30.00/60.00 t. – SB.

at Sheepwash NW : 5½ m. by A 3072 – ⊠ Beaworthy.

🏠 **Half Moon Inn**, The Square, EX21 5NE, ☎ (01409) 231376, Fax (01409) 231673, « 17C »,
🎣 – 📺 ☎ ℗. ◉◉ 𝘝𝘐𝘚𝘈
Meals (bar lunch)/dinner 19.25 t. ≬ 5.00 – **14 rm** ⊑ 37.50/75.00 t.

HATHERSAGE Derbs. **402 403 404** P 24 – pop. 2 858 – ⊠ Sheffield (S. Yorks.).
ⓑ Sickleholme, Bamford ☎ (01433) 651306 London 177.
Derby 39 – Manchester 34 – Sheffield 11 – Stoke-on-Trent 44.

🏨 **George**, S32 1BB, ☎ (01433) 650436, Fax (01433) 650099, 🎣 – ⇔ rest, 📺 ☎ ℗. ◉◉ 🖭
◉ 𝘝𝘐𝘚𝘈. ⚘
Meals 14.95/18.95 t. and dinner a la carte ≬ 7.05 – ⊑ 9.50 – **19 rm** 59.50/79.50 t. – SB.

HATTON Warks. – see Warwick.

La HAULE Jersey (Channel Islands) **230** ⑪ – see Channel Islands.

Keine bezahlte Reklame im Michelin-Führer.

HAWES N. Yorks.  N 21 – pop. 1 117.

🛈 Dales Countryside Museum, Station Yard, DL8 3NT 🖉 (01969) 667450 (summer only).
London 253 – Kendal 27 – Leeds 72 – York 65.

🏛 **Simonstone Hall** ⚘, Simonstone, DL8 3LY, N : 1 ½ m. on Muker rd 🖉 (01969) 667255,
Fax (01969) 667741, <, « Part 18C country house », 🐎 – ⇔ 📺 ☎ 🅿. 🕮 🚾 🗷
Meals (bar lunch Monday to Saturday) 14.50/17.00 t. 🔋 8.10 – **18 rm** ☲ 45.00/120.00 t.,
1 suite – SB.

🏠 **Stone House** ⚘, Sedbusk, DL8 3PT, N : 1 m. by Muker rd on Askrigg rd
🖉 (01969) 667571, Fax (01969) 667720, <, 🐎 – ⇔ rest, 📺 ☎ 🅿. 🕮 🚾 🗷
closed January – **Meals** (dinner only) 16.95 t. 🔋 4.95 – **22 rm** ☲ 33.50/67.00 st. – SB.

🏠 **Rookhurst Georgian Country House** ⚘, Gayle, DL8 3RT, S : ½ m. by Gayle rd
🖉 (01969) 667454, Fax (01969) 667454, 🐎 – ⇔ 📺 🅿. 🕮 🚾. 🗷
closed 21 to 29 December and 4 January-5 February – **Meals** (booking essential) (residents
only) (dinner only) 🔋 7.50 – **5 rm** ☲ (dinner included) 70.00/120.00 s. – SB.

🏠 **Cockett's**, Market Pl., DL8 3RD, 🖉 (01969) 667312, Fax (01969) 667162, 🐎 – ⇔ 📺 ☎.
🕮 🕮 🕮 🕮 🚾 🗷. 🗷
closed Christmas and first 2 weeks January – **Meals** (closed lunch Friday and Saturday)
a la carte 12.50/22.50 st. 🔋 6.00 – **8 rm** ☲ 45.00/69.00 st. – SB.

🏠 **Herriot's**, Main St., DL8 3QU, 🖉 (01969) 667536 – ⇔ rest, 📺. 🕮 🚾. 🗷
closed Christmas and January – **Meals** (closed Wednesday and Thursday lunch and Monday
except Bank Holidays) 12.95 t. (dinner) and a la carte 9.70/19.70 t. 🔋 4.45 – **7 rm** ☲ 25.00/
50.00 st. – SB.

🏠 **Brandymires**, Muker Rd, DL8 3PR, N : ¼ m. 🖉 (01969) 667482 – ⇔ 🅿
February-October – **Meals** (by arrangement) 12.00 st. 🔋 4.75 – **4 rm** ☲ 27.00/38.00 st.

| I prezzi | Per ogni chiarimento sui prezzi riportati in guida, consultate le pagine dell'introduzione. |

HAWKHURST Kent ██ V 30 Great Britain G. – pop. 3 463.
Env. : Bodiam Castle★★ AC, SE : 3 ½ m. by B 2244.
London 47 – Folkestone 34 – Hastings 14 – Maidstone 19.

🏛 **Tudor Court**, Rye Rd, TN18 5DA, E : ¾ m. on A 268 🖉 (01580) 752312,
Fax (01580) 753966, <, 🐎, 🗷 – ⇔ 📺 ☎ 🅿 – 🔬 60. 🕮 🕮 🕮 🚾 🗷. 🗷
Meals 17.50 t. 🔋 5.50 – **16 rm** ☲ 50.00/90.00 t. – SB.

HAWKRIDGE Somerset ██ J 30 The West Country G. – ✉ Dulverton.
Env. : Tarr Steps★★, NE : 2 ½ m.
Exc. : Exmoor National Park★★.
London 203 – Exeter 32 – Minehead 17 – Taunton 32.

🏠 **Tarr Steps** ⚘, TA22 9PY, NE : 1 ½ m. 🖉 (01643) 851293, Fax (01643) 851218, <, 🦆, 🐎,
park – ☎ 🅿. 🕮 🚾 🗷
closed 2 weeks February – **Meals** (booking essential) (dinner only and Sunday lunch)/
dinner 23.25 t. 🔋 6.90 – **11 rm** ☲ (dinner included) 62.00/124.00 t. – SB.

HAWKSHEAD Cumbria ██ L 20 Great Britain G. – pop. 570 – ✉ Ambleside.
See : Village★.
Env. : Lake Windermere★★ – Coniston Water★ (Brantwood★, on east side), SW : by B 5285.
🛈 Main Car Park, LA22 0NT 🖉 (015394) 36525 (summer only).
London 283 – Carlisle 52 – Kendal 19.

🏠 **Highfield House** ⚘, Hawkshead Hill, LA22 0PN, W : ¾ m. on B 5285 (Coniston rd)
🖉 (015394) 36344, Fax (015394) 36793, < Kirkstone Pass and Fells, 🐎 – ⇔ rest, 📺 ☎ 🅿.
🕮 🚾 🗷
closed 2 to 30 January and 24 to 26 December – **Meals** (bar lunch)/dinner 17.50 st. – **11 rm**
☲ 40.50/87.00 st. – SB.

🏠 **Rough Close Country House** ⚘, LA22 0QF, S : 1 ½ m. on Newby Bridge rd
🖉 (015394) 36370, 🐎 – ⇔ 📺 🅿. 🕮 🚾. 🗷
April-October and restricted opening March – **Meals** (by arrangement) 14.00 t. 🔋 4.50 –
5 rm ☲ (dinner included) 51.50/83.00 t.

🏠 **Ivy House**, Main St., LA22 0NS, 🖉 (015394) 36204, 🦆 – ⇔ rest, 📺 🅿. 🕮 🚾
mid March-early November – **Meals** 12.00 t. 🔋 3.90 – **11 rm** ☲ 31.00/62.00 t. – SB.

🏠 **Bracken Fell** ⚘ without rest., Barngates Rd, Outgate, LA22 0NH, N : 1 m. by B 5286 on
Barngates rd 🖉 (015394) 36289, 🐎 – ⇔ 🅿. 🗷
7 rm ☲ 45.00 st.

at Near Sawrey SE : 2 m. on B 5285 – ⊠ Ambleside.

🏠 **Sawrey Country House** ॐ, LA22 0LF, ℰ (015394) 36387, Fax (015394) 36010, ⩻ Esthwaite Water and Grizedale Forest, ⬎, ⩘ – ⫟ 🔟 ☎ 🅿. 🐵 VISA JCB. ⅍
restricted opening in winter – Meals (booking essential) (dinner only) 20.00 st. ⅄ 6.00 –
10 rm ⊡ (dinner included) 60.00/130.00 st. – SB.

🏠 **Ees Wyke Country House** ॐ, LA22 0JZ, ℰ (015394) 36393, Fax (015394) 36393, ⩻ Esthwaite Water and Grizedale Forest, ⩘ – ⫟ rest, 🔟 🅿. 🅰🅴
closed January and February – Meals (booking essential) (dinner only) 20.00 t. ⅄ 6.00 – **8 rm**
⊡ (dinner included) 56.00/112.00 t.

at Far Sawrey SE : 2½ m. on B 5285 – ⊠ Ambleside.

🏠 **West Vale**, LA22 0LQ, ℰ (015394) 42817, ⩻ – ⫟ rest, 🅿. ⅍
March-October – Meals (by arrangement) 11.00 st. ⅄ 4.50 – **8 rm** ⊡ 23.00/46.00 st.

at Grizedale SW : 2¾ m. – ⊠ Ambleside.

🏠 **Grizedale Lodge** ॐ, LA22 0QL, ℰ (015394) 36532, Fax (015394) 36572 – ⫟ 🔟 🅿. 🐵
🅰🅴 VISA JCB
closed 3 January-mid February – Meals (bar lunch)/dinner 15.50 st. ⅄ 5.50 – **9 rm**
⊡ (dinner included) 57.50/127.00 st. – SB.

HAWNBY N. Yorks 402 Q 21 – see Helmsley.

Per i grandi viaggi d'affari o di turismo,
Guida MICHELIN rossa : EUROPE.

HAWORTH W. Yorks. 402 O 22 Great Britain G. – pop. 4 956 – ⊠ Keighley.
See : Haworth Parsonage and the Brontës★ AC.
🛈 2-4 West Lane, BD22 8EF ℰ (01535) 642329.
London 213 – Burnley 22 – Leeds 22 – Manchester 34.

🏠 **Old White Lion**, 6 West Lane, BD22 8DU, ℰ (01535) 642313, Fax (01535) 646222 – 🔟 ☎
🅿 – 🔬 70. 🐵 🅰🅴 ⓞ VISA. ⅍
Meals (bar lunch Monday to Saturday)/dinner 16.50 t. and a la carte ⅄ 4.30 – **14 rm**
⊡ 60.00/85.00 t. – SB.

🏠 **Ferncliffe**, Hebden Rd, BD22 8RS, on A 6033 ℰ (01535) 643405, ⩻ – 🔟 🅿. 🐵 VISA
closed 23 December-2 January – Meals (by arrangement) 9.75 t. ⅄ 4.95 – **6 rm** ⊡ 19.50/
39.00 t.

✕✕ **Weaver's** with rm, 15 West Lane, BD22 8DU, ℰ (01535) 643822, Fax (01535) 644832,
« Converted weavers cottages » – ⫟ rest, 🔟 ☎. 🐵 🅰🅴 ⓞ VISA JCB. ⅍
closed last week June and 25 December-2 January – Meals (closed Sunday and Monday)
(dinner only) a la carte 13.85/23.85 t. ⅄ 5.55 – **3 rm** ⊡ 49.50/69.50 st. – SB.

HAYDOCK Mersey. 402 403 404 M 23 – pop. 16 705 – ⊠ St Helens.
London 198 – Liverpool 17 – Manchester 18.

🏨 **Haydock Thistle**, Penny Lane, WA11 9SG, NE : ½ m. on A 599 ℰ (01942) 272000
Fax (01942) 711092, ⅙, ⩶, ⬜, ⩘ – ⫟ rm, 🍽 rest, 🔟 ☎ 🅖 🅿 – 🔬 300. 🐵 🅰🅴 ⓞ VISA
⅍
The Restaurant : Meals (bar lunch Saturday) 19.50 st. (dinner) and a la carte 23.00/
32.00 st. ⅄ 6.50 – ⊡ 9.75 – **135 rm** 95.00/114.00 st., 4 suites – SB.

🏨 **Forte Posthouse Haydock**, Lodge Lane, Newton-le-Willows, WA12 0JG, NE : 1 m. on
A 49 ℰ (01942) 717878, Fax (01942) 718419, ⅙, ⩶, ⬜, ⩘ – 🛗, ⫟ rm, 🍽 rest, 🔟 ☎ 🅖
🅿 – 🔬 180. 🐵 🅰🅴 ⓞ VISA
Meals (closed lunch Saturday and Sunday) a la carte 15.50/20.85 st. ⅄ 6.00 – ⊡ 9.95 –
138 rm 79.00 st.

🏠 **Travelodge**, Piele Rd, WA11 9TL, on A 580 ℰ (01942) 272055, Fax (01942) 272067
Reservations (Freephone) 0800 850950 – ⫟ rm, 🔟 🅖 🅿. 🐵 🅰🅴 ⓞ VISA JCB. ⅍
Meals (grill rest.) – **62 rm** 39.95 t.

HAYDON BRIDGE Northd. 401 402 N 19 – pop. 1 784 – ⊠ Hexham.
London 344 – Carlisle 31 – Newcastle upon Tyne 27.

🏠 **Geeswood House**, Whittis Rd, NE47 6AQ, ℰ (01434) 684220, ⩘ – ⫟. ⅍
closed 25 December – Meals (communal dining) 10.50 st. – **3 rm** ⊡ 22.00/36.00 st. – SB.

HAYFIELD Derbs. 402 403 404 O 23 – pop. 2 293 – ⊠ Stockport (Ches.).
London 191 – Manchester 22 – Sheffield 29.

🏨 **Waltzing Weasel,** New Mills Rd, Birch Vale, SK22 1BT, W : ½ m. on A 6015
☎ (01663) 743402, Fax (01663) 743402, ≼, ⌖ – 📺 ☎ 🅿. ◐◑ 🝆 *VISA*
Meals (dinner only) 24.50 **st.** ⋕ 4.50 – **8 rm** ⊇ 35.00/95.00 **st.**

✗ Bridge End, 7 Church St., SK12 5JE, ☎ (01663) 747321, Fax (01663) 742121 – 🅿.

HAYLING ISLAND Hants. 404 R 31 – pop. 14 054.
🏌 Links Lane ☎ (01705) 463712/463777.
🄱 Beachlands, Seafront, PO11 OAG ☎ (01705) 467111 (summer only).
London 77 – Brighton 45 – Southampton 28.

⌂ **Cockle Warren Cottage,** 36 Seafront, PO11 9HL, ☎ (01705) 464961,
Fax (01705) 464838, ⌗, ⌖ – ⌁ 📺 ☎ 🅿. ◐◑ 🝆 🄓 *VISA*. ⌖
closed 1 week April and 1 week October – **Meals** (by arrangement) 27.50 **st.** ⋕ 5.50 – ⊇ 4.50
– **5 rm** 58.00/98.00 **st.**

HAYTOR Devon – see Bovey Tracey.

HAYTOR VALE Devon – see Bovey Tracey.

HAYWARDS HEATH W. Sussex 404 T 31 – pop. 28 923.
🏌 Paxhill Park, East Mascalls Lane, Lindfield ☎ (01444) 484467.
London 41 – Brighton 16.

🏨 **Birch,** Lewes Rd, RH17 7SF, E : ¾ m. on A 272 ☎ (01444) 451565, Fax (01444) 440109 –
⌁ rest, 📺 ☎ ⌖ 🅿 – ⌁ 60. ◐◑ 🝆 🄓 *VISA*
Meals (bar lunch Saturday) 16.95/25.00 **t.** ⋕ 5.00 – **51 rm** ⊇ 65.00/99.00 **t.**

◉ ATS Gower Rd ☎ (01444) 412640/454189

HEADLAM Durham – see Darlington.

HEATHROW AIRPORT Middx. – see Hillingdon (Greater London).

HEBDEN BRIDGE W. Yorks. 402 N 22 – pop. 3 681 – ⊠ Halifax
🏌 Wadsworth ☎ (01422) 842896.
🄱 1 Bridge Gate, HX7 8EX ☎ (01422) 843831.
London 223 – Burnley 13 – Leeds 24 – Manchester 25.

🏨 **Carlton,** Albert St., HX7 8ES, ☎ (01422) 844400, Fax (01422) 843117 – ⧉, ⌁ rest, 📺 ☎ –
⌁ 100. ◐◑ 🝆 *VISA* *JCB*
Meals 8.50/9.95 **st.** and a la carte ⋕ 6.25 – **16 rm** ⊇ 49.00/75.00 **st.** – SB.

⌂ **Redacre Mill,** Mytholmroyd, HX7 5DQ, SE : 1 ½ m. by A646 off Westfield Terr.
☎ (01422) 885563, Fax (01422) 885563, ≼, « Converted canalside warehouse », ⌖ – ⌁
📺 🅿. ◐◑ *VISA*. ⌖
closed Christmas-New Year and Saturday and Sunday in December – **Meals** (residents only)
(dinner only) 14.50 **s.** ⋕ 4.50 – **5 rm** ⊇ 37.50/55.00 **st.** – SB.

✗ **Kitties,** 52 Market St., HX7 6AA, ☎ (01422) 842956 – ◐◑ 🝆 *VISA*
closed 25 December and 3 to 30 January – **Meals** (dinner only) a la carte 16.30/21.95 **t.**
⋕ 5.50.

HEDON East Riding 402 T 22 – see Kingston-upon-Hull.

HEIGHINGTON Durham 402 P20 – see Darlington.

HELLIDON Northants. 404 Q 27 – see Daventry.

HELMSLEY N. Yorks. 402 Q 21 Great Britain G. – pop. 1 833.
Env. : Rievaulx Abbey★★ AC, NW : 2 ½ m. by B 1257.
🏌 Ampleforth College, 56 High St. ☎ (01439) 770678.
🄱 Town Hall, Market Pl., YO6 5BL ☎ (01439) 770173 (summer only).
London 239 – Middlesbrough 28 – York 24.

🏰 **Black Swan**, Market Pl., YO6 5BJ, ℰ (01439) 770466, *Fax (01439) 770174*, « Part 16C inn », 🚗 – ⚑ 📺 ☎ 🅿. 🕥 🖭 ⓪ 🆚
   Meals 15.00/21.00 **st.** and dinner a la carte 🍷 7.50 – 🍽 10.00 – **44 rm** 105.00/135.00 **st.** – SB.

🏠 **Carlton Lodge**, Bondgate, YO6 5EY, ℰ (01439) 770557, *Fax (01439) 770623*, 🚗 – ⚑ rest, 📺 ☎ 🅿. 🕥
   Meals 15.95 **t.** 🍷 5.25 – **12 rm** 🍽 (dinner included) 47.50/96.00 **t.** – SB.

🏠 **Feathers**, Market Pl., YO6 5BH, ℰ (01439) 770275, *Fax (01439) 771101*, 🚗 – 📺 🅿. 🕥 🆚
   Meals a la carte 9.95/15.95 **st.** 🍷 5.00 – **14 rm** 🍽 40.00/80.00 **st.** – SB.

at Nawton *E : 3 ¼ m. on A 170 –* ✉ *York.*

⛺ **Plumpton Court**, High St., YO6 5TT, ℰ (01439) 771223, 🚗 – ⚑ 🅿. 🕸
   Meals (by arrangement) 12.00 **st.** – **7 rm** 🍽 33.50/50.00 **st.** – SB.

at Harome *SE : 2 ¾ m. by A 170 –* ✉ *York.*

🏰 **Pheasant**, YO6 5JG, ℰ (01439) 771241, *Fax (01439) 771744*, 🔲, 🚗 – ⚑ rest, 📺 ☎ 🅿. 🕥 🖭 🆚 JCB. 🕸
   March-November – **Meals** (bar lunch)/dinner 20.00 **t.** 🍷 4.80 – **12 rm** 🍽 (dinner included) 60.00/120.00 **t.**, 2 suites – SB.

🍴 **Star Inn**, YO6 5JE, ℰ (01439) 770397, « Part 14C thatched inn », 🚗 – ⚑ 🅿. 🕥 🆚
   closed Monday except lunch April-September and 2 weeks January – **Meals** (booking essential) a la carte 18.95/25.95 **t.** 🍷 7.50.

at Old Byland *NW : 5 m. by B 1257.*

⛺ **Valley View Farm** 🐾, YO6 5LG, ℰ (01439) 798221, *Fax (01439) 798221*, ≤, « Working farm », 🚗, park – 📺 🅿. 🕥 🆚. 🕸
   Meals 12.50 **s.** – **4 rm** 🍽 27.00/54.00 – SB.

at Hawnby *NW : 6 ¼ m. by B 1257 –* ✉ *Helmsley.*

🏠 **Hawnby** 🐾, YO6 5QS, ℰ (01439) 798202, *Fax (01439) 798344*, ≤, 🎣, 🚗 – 📺 ☎ 🅿. 🕥 🆚. 🕸
   closed February and restricted opening in winter – **Meals** (bar lunch Monday to Saturday)/dinner 12.50 **st.** 🍷 3.50 – **6 rm** 🍽 (dinner included) 42.50/80.00 **st.**

at Laskill *NW : 6 ¼ m. by B 1257 –* ✉ *Hawnby.*

⛺ **Laskill Farm**, YO6 5BN, ℰ (01439) 798268, « Working farm », 🚗 – ⚑ rest, 📺 🅿
   Meals (by arrangement) (communal dining) 11.00 **st.** – **7 rm** 🍽 22.00/50.00 **st.** – SB.

HELSTON *Cornwall* 403 *E 33 The West Country G. – pop. 8 505.*
   See : *The Flora Day Furry Dance★★.*
   Env. : *Lizard Peninsula★ – Gunwalloe Fishing Cove★, S : 4 m. by A 3083 and minor rd – Culdrose (Flambards Village Theme Park★), SE : 1 m. – Wendron (Poldark Mine★), NE : 2 ½ m. by B 3297 – Gweek (Seal Sanctuary★ – setting★), E : 4 m. by A 394 and minor rd.*
   London 306 – Falmouth 13 – Penzance 14 – Truro 17.

🏠 **Nansloe Manor** 🐾, Meneage Rd, TR13 0SB, ℰ (01326) 574691, *Fax (01326) 564680*, 🚗 – ⚑ rest, 📺 ☎ 🅿. 🕥 🆚 JCB. 🕸
   Meals (bar lunch Monday to Saturday)/dinner a la carte approx. 25.00 **t.** 🍷 5.95 – **7 rm** 🍽 50.00/100.00 **t.** – SB.

✗✗ **Crahan**, Trevenen, TR13 0ND, NE : 2 ¾ m. on A 394 ℰ (01326) 573090, 🚗 – 🅿. 🕥 🆚
   closed Tuesday to Thursday lunch, Sunday, Monday, 25-26 December and 5 to 19 January – **Meals** 15.00/21.00 **st.** 🍷 5.45.

at Gunwalloe *S : 5 m. by A 394 off A 3083 –* ✉ *Helston.*

🍴 **The Halzephron Inn** with rm, TR12 7QB, ℰ (01326) 240406 – ⚑ rest, 📺 🅿. 🕥 🆚
   closed 25 December – **Meals** a la carte 12.40/20.75 **t.** 🍷 3.50 – **2 rm** 🍽 35.00/59.00 **t.**

   🅰 ATS Clodgey Lane ℰ (01326) 562656

HELTON *Cumbria* 401 402 *L 20 –* ✉ *Penrith.*
   London 287 – Carlisle 26 – Kendal 24 – Workington 43.

🏰 **Beckfoot Country House** 🐾, CA10 2QB, S : 1 ¼ m. ℰ (01931) 713241, *Fax (01931) 713391*, ≤, 🚗 – ⚑ 📺 🅿. 🕥 🖭 🆚. 🕸
   March-November – **Meals** (dinner only) 16.00 **s.** – **6 rm** 🍽 32.00/64.00 **s.** – SB.

The Guide is updated annually so renew your Guide every year.

HEMEL HEMPSTEAD Herts. **404** S 28 – pop. 79 235.

 ⓡ Little Hay Golf Complex, Box Lane, Bovingdon ℰ (01442) 833798 – ⓡ Boxmoor, 18 Box Lane ℰ (01442) 242434.

 🗊 Dacorum Information Centre, HP1 1DT ℰ (01442) 234222.

 London 30 – Aylesbury 16 – Luton 10 – Northampton 46.

🏤 **Forte Posthouse Hemel Hempstead,** Breakspear Way, HP2 4UA, E : 2 ½ m. on A 414 ℰ (01442) 251122, Fax (01442) 211812, ⓕₔ, ⓢ, 🔲 – 🕸, ⅍ rm, 🔟 ☎ ⅙ ⓟ – ⚑ 60. **◗◗** 🅰🅴 **①** **VISA** **JCB**
Meals a la carte 14.25/24.65 t. ⓙ 7.95 – ☑ 10.95 – **146 rm** 99.00 t. – SB.

🏠 **Boxmoor Lodge,** London Rd, HP1 2RA, W : 1 m. on A 4251 ℰ (01442) 230770, Fax (01442) 252230, 🌫 – ⅍ rm, 🔟 ☎ ⅙ ⓟ – ⚑ 35. **◗◗** 🅰🅴 **①** **VISA**
Meals (closed lunch Monday and Sunday) 17.00/19.00 t. and a la carte ⓙ 6.00 – **24 rm** ☑ 55.00/95.00 st.

🏠 **Travel Inn,** Stoney Lane, Bourne End, HP1 2SB, W : 3 ½ m. by A 4251 off A 41 ℰ (01442) 879149, Fax (01442) 879147 – 🕸, ⅍ rm, 🔟 ⅙ ⓟ – ⚑ 35. **◗◗** 🅰🅴 **①** **VISA**. ⅗
Meals (grill rest.) – **60 rm** 36.50 t.

HENFIELD W. Sussex **404** T 31 – pop. 4 111.

 London 47 – Brighton 10 – Worthing 11.

🏠 **Tottington Manor,** Edburton, BN5 9LJ, SE : 3 ½ m. by A 2037 on Fulking rd ℰ (01903) 815757, Fax (01903) 879331, ⟨, 🌫 – 🔟 ☎ ⓟ. **◗◗** 🅰🅴 **①** **VISA** **JCB**. ⅗
closed last week December – Meals (closed Sunday dinner) 25.00 t. (dinner) and a la carte 20.10/28.40 t. – **6 rm** ☑ 50.00/85.00 t. – SB.

at Wineham NE : 3½ m. by A 281, B 2116 and Wineham Lane – ⊠ Henfield.

⌂ **Frylands** ☞ without rest., BN5 9BP, W : ¼ m. taking left turn at telephone box ℰ (01403) 710214, Fax (01403) 711449, ⟨, « Part Elizabethan farmhouse », ⌇, ⟍, 🌫, park – 🔟 ⓟ. ⅗
closed 20 December-2 January – **3 rm** ☑ 20.00/38.00 s.

Prices   For notes on the prices quoted in this Guide, see the introduction.

HENLADE Somerset – see Taunton.

HENLEY-IN-ARDEN Warks. **403** **404** O 27 – pop. 2 803.

 London 104 – Birmingham 15 – Stratford-upon-Avon 8 – Warwick 8.5.

🏤 **Ardencote Manor H. & Country Club** ☞, Lye Green Rd, Claverdon, CV35 8LS, E : 3 ¾ m. by A 4189 on Shrewley rd ℰ (01926) 843111, Fax (01926) 842646, ⓕₔ, ⓢ, 🔲, ⟍, 🌫, park, ⅗, squash – ⅍ rest, 🔟 ☎ ⓟ – ⚑ 45. **◗◗** 🅰🅴 **①** **VISA** **JCB**. ⅗
Oak Room : Meals (closed Saturday lunch) (booking essential) 14.95/21.95 t. ⓙ 5.50 –
Palms : Meals 14.95/21.95 t. ⓙ 5.50 – **18 rm** ☑ 87.50/135.00 t. – SB.

HENLEY-ON-THAMES Oxon. **404** R 29 – pop. 10 558.

 ⓡ Huntercombe, Nuffield ℰ (01491) 641207.

 🗊 Town Hall, Market Pl., RG9 2AQ ℰ (01491) 578034.

 London 40 – Oxford 23 – Reading 9.

🏨 **Red Lion,** RG9 2AR, ℰ (01491) 572161, Fax (01491) 410039 – 🔟 ☎ ⓟ – ⚑ 30. **◗◗** 🅰🅴 **VISA**
Meals 17.50 t. and a la carte ⓙ 5.75 – ☑ 9.75 – **26 rm** 82.50/115.00 st.

XX **Villa Marina,** 18 Thameside, RG9 1BH, ℰ (01491) 575262, Fax (01491) 411394 – **◗◗** 🅰🅴 **①** **VISA**
closed 26 December-1 January – Meals - Italian - 12.00 t. (lunch) and a la carte 17.00/21.70 t. ⓙ 5.00.

at Stonor N : 4 m. by A 4130 on B 480 – ⊠ Henley-on-Thames.

🏨 **Stonor Arms,** RG9 6HE, ℰ (01491) 638866, Fax (01491) 638863, 🌫 – 🔟 ☎ ⓟ. **◗◗** 🅰🅴 **VISA**
Stonor : Meals a la carte 18.50/27.50 t. ⓙ 6.50 – **10 rm** ☑ 90.00/105.00 t. – SB.

at Skirmett (Bucks.) NE : 7 m. by A 4155 – ⊠ Henley-on-Thames.

X **Old Crown,** RG9 6TD, ℰ (01491) 638435, Fax (01491) 638435, « 18C cottage », 🌫 – ⅍. **◗◗** **VISA**
closed Sunday dinner, Monday except Bank Holidays and 25 December – Meals a la carte 15.25/26.75 t. ⓙ 6.00.

HEREFORD *Herefordshire* **403** L 27 *Great Britain G. – pop. 54 326.*

See : *City★ - Cathedral★★ (Mappa Mundi★) A* **A** *– Old House★ A* **B**.

Exc. : *Kilpeck (Church of SS. Mary and David★★) SW : 8 m. by A 465* **B**.

[18] *Raven's Causeway, Wormsley & (01432) 830219 –* [18] *Belmont Lodge, Belmont & (01432) 352666 –* [18] *Burghill Valley, Tillington Rd, Burghill & (01432) 760456 –* [9] *Hereford Municipal, Holmer Rd & (01432) 278178* **B**.

🅱 *1 King St., HR4 9BW & (01432) 268430.*

London 133 – Birmingham 51 – Cardiff 56.

HEREFORD

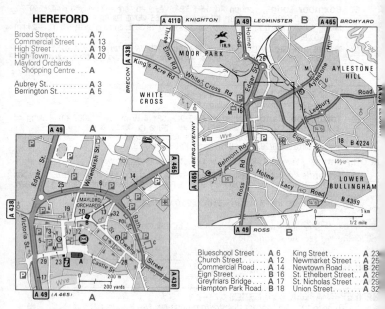

🏰🏰 **Green Dragon,** Broad St., HR4 9BG, & (01432) 272506, *Fax (01432) 352139* – |‡| ✝= 📺 ☎
〈⊃ – ⚱ 200. 🅼🅂 🄰🄴 ① 𝘝𝘐𝘚𝘈.
A 6
Meals a la carte 16.75/23.45 **st.** ◊ 7.00 – ⊆ 8.95 – **80 rm** 50.00/60.00 **st.**, 3 suites – SB.

🏨 **Three Counties,** Belmont Rd, HR2 7BP, SW : 1 ½ m. on A 465 & (01432) 299955,
Fax (01432) 275114 – ✝= rm, 📺 ☎ & 🄿 – ⚱ 350. 🅼🅂 🄰🄴 ① 𝘝𝘐𝘚𝘈. ⋇
B 0
Meals (bar lunch Monday to Saturday)/dinner 15.50 **st.** and a la carte ◊ 5.25 – **60 rm**
⊆ 57.50/75.50 **st.** – SB.

🏠 **Aylestone Court,** Aylestone Hill, HR1 1HS, & (01432) 341891, *Fax (01432) 267691,* 🐎 -
📺 ☎ 🄿. 🅼🅂 🄰🄴 ① 𝘝𝘐𝘚𝘈
B
Meals *(closed Sunday)* 14.00 **s.** and a la carte ◊ 6.45 – **10 rm** ⊆ 38.80/58.00 **t.**

🏠 **Travel Inn,** Holmer Rd, Holmer, HR4 9RS, N : 1 ¾ m. on A 49 & (01432) 274853,
Fax (01432) 343002 – ✝= rm, 📺 & 🄿. 🅼🅂 🄰🄴 ① 𝘝𝘐𝘚𝘈. ⋇
Meals (grill rest.) – **39 rm** 36.50 **t.**

⌂ **Collins House** without rest., 19 Owen St., HR1 2JB, & (01432) 272416,
Fax (01432) 357717 – ✝= 📺 ☎ 🄿. 🅼🅂 𝘝𝘐𝘚𝘈 🄹🄲🄱. ⋇
A 0
⊆ 3.00 – **3 rm** 30.00/40.00 **s.**

at Marden *N : 5 ¾ m. by A 49 –* **B** *– ⊠ Hereford.*

⌂ **The Vauld Farm** ⌔, HR1 3HA, NE : 1 ½ m. by Litmarsh rd & (01568) 797898,
« *16C timbered farmhouse* », 🐎 – ✝= rest, 🄿. ⋇
Meals (by arrangement) (communal dining) 16.50 **s.** – **3 rm** ⊆ 25.00/50.00 **s.**, 1 suite.

at Canon Pyon *N : 7 m. on A 4110 –* **B** *– ⊠ Hereford.*

⌂ **Hermitage Manor** ⌔ without rest., HR4 8NR, S : 1 m. on A 4110 & (01432) 760317,
< Vale of Hereford, 🐎 – ✝= 📺 🄿. ⋇
mid March-October – **3 rm** ⊆ 25.00/50.00.

at Orcop S : 8¼ m. by A 49 – B – off A 466 – ⊠ Hereford.

⌂ **The Burnett** ⬧, Orcop Hill, HR2 8SF, NW : ½ m. ℘ (01981) 540526, ≤, « Part 16C farmhouse », ⌔ – ⤫ ❷
Meals (residents only) (dinner only) 22.50 **st.** ₰ 5.00 – **3 rm** ⌑ 25.00/60.00 **st.**

at Ruckhall W : 5 m. by A 49 off A 465 – B – ⊠ Eaton Bishop.

🍴 **Ancient Camp Inn** ⬧ with rm, HR2 9QX, ℘ (01981) 250449, Fax (01981) 251581, ≤ River Wye and countryside, ⬧ – 🆃🆅 ☎ ❷. 🕮 🆅🆂🅰.
Meals (closed Sunday dinner and Monday to non-residents) a la carte 15.00/24.00 **t.** ₰ 4.75 – **5 rm** ⌑ 40.00/60.00 **t.**

at Byford W : 7½ m. by A 438 B – ⊠ Hereford.

⌂ **Old Rectory**, HR4 7LD, ℘ (01981) 590218, Fax (01981) 590499, ⌔ – ⤫ 🆃🆅 ❷. ⬧
March-November – **Meals** (by arrangement) 15.00 **s.** – **3 rm** ⌑ 25.00/40.00 **s.**

  🔘 ATS 6 Kyrle St. ℘ (01432) 265491

HERM 🔢 P 33 and 🔢 ⑩ – see Channel Islands.

HERMITAGE Dorset – see Sherborne.

HERNE BAY Kent 🔢 X 29 – pop. 31 861.
  🏌 Herne Bay, Eddington ℘ (01227) 374097.
  🅱 12 William St., CT6 5EJ ℘ (01227) 361911.
  London 63 – Dover 24 – Maidstone 32 – Margate 13.

⌂ **Northdown** without rest., 14 Cecil Park, CT6 6DL, off Canterbury Rd ℘ (01227) 372051, Fax (01227) 372051, ⌔ – 🆃🆅 ☎ ❷. 🕮 🆎 🆅🆂🅰. ⬧
5 rm ⌑ 20.00/44.00 **st.**

HERSTMONCEUX E. Sussex 🔢 U 31 – pop. 3 898.
  London 63 – Eastbourne 12 – Hastings 14 – Lewes 16.

🍴🍴 **Sundial**, Gardner St., BN27 4LA, ℘ (01323) 832217, « Converted 16C cottage », ⌔ – ⤫
❷. 🕮 🆎 🆅🆂🅰 🆓
closed Sunday dinner, Monday, 10 August-early September and 24 December-20 January –
Meals - French - 19.50/27.50 **t.** and a la carte ₰ 6.25.

HERTFORD Herts. 🔢 T 28 – pop. 21 665.
  🅱 The Castle, SG14 1HR ℘ (01992) 584322.
  London 24 – Cambridge 35 – Luton 26.

⌂ **Hall House** ⬧, Broad Oak End, SG14 2JA, NW : 1 ¾ m. by A 119 and Bramfield Rd
℘ (01992) 582807, Fax (01992) 582807, ⌔ – ⤫ 🆃🆅 ❷. 🕮 🆅🆂🅰. ⬧
closed Christmas-New Year – **Meals** (by arrangement) 20.00 **s.** – **3 rm** ⌑ 48.00/65.00 **s.**

HERTINGFORDBURY Herts. 🔢 T 28 – pop. 633 – ⊠ Hertford.
  London 26 – Luton 18.

🏨 **White Horse**, Hertingfordbury Rd, SG14 2LB, ℘ (01992) 586791, Fax (01992) 550809, ⌔
– ⤫, 🍽 rest, 🆃🆅 ☎ ❷ – 🔬 50. 🕮 🆎 🆓 🆅🆂🅰
Meals (closed Saturday lunch) 10.50/12.50 **st.** ₰ 8.00 – ⌑ 8.75 – **42 rm** 80.00/95.00 **st.** – SB.

HESWALL Mersey 🔢 🔢 K 24 – pop. 16 569 London 212.
  Birkenhead 12 – Chester 14 – Liverpool 14.

🍴 **Est, Est, Est,** 146-148 Telegraph Rd, L60 0AH, ℘ (0151) 342 9550, Fax (0151) 342 9551 –
🍽. 🕮 🆎 🆓 🆅🆂🅰
closed 25 and 26 December – **Meals** - Italian - 9.95 **t.** (dinner) and a la carte 16.00/21.00 **t.**
₰ 5.75.

HETHERSETT Norfolk 🔢 X 26 – see Norwich.

HETTON N. Yorks. 🔢 N 21 – see Skipton.

HEVERSHAM Cumbria 402 L 21 – pop. 639 – ✉ Milnthorpe.
London 270 – Kendal 7 – Lancaster 18 – Leeds 72.

🏨 **Blue Bell,** Princes Way, LA7 7EE, on A 6 ℰ (015395) 62018, Fax (015395) 62455, ☞ –
✦✦ rest, 📺 ☎ 🅿 – 🔬 80. 🐼 🅰🅴 ⓪ 𝗩𝗜𝗦𝗔
Meals 11.50/19.95 t. and a la carte ≬ 6.95 – **21 rm** ⚏ 39.50/64.00 t. – SB.

HEXHAM Northd. 401 402 N 19 Great Britain G. – pop. 11 008.
See : Abbey★ (Saxon Crypt★★, Leschman chantry★).
Env. : Hadrian's Wall★★, N : 4 ½ m. by A 6079.
Exc. : Housesteads★★, NW : 12 ½ m. by A 6079 and B 6318.
🏌 Spital Park ℰ (01434) 602057 – 🏌 Slaley Hall G. & C.C., Slaley ℰ (01434) 673350 –
🏌 Tynedale, Tyne Green ℰ (01434) 608154.
🅱 The Manor Office, Hallgate, NE46 1XD ℰ (01434) 605225.
London 304 – Carlisle 37 – Newcastle upon Tyne 21.

🏨 **Beaumont,** Beaumont St., NE46 3LT, ℰ (01434) 602331, Fax (01434) 606184 – 📠 ✦✦ 📺
– 🔬 80. 🐼 🅰🅴 ⓪ 𝗩𝗜𝗦𝗔 🦺
closed 25 December – **Meals** 17.50 t. (dinner) and a la carte 11.45/25.75 t. ≬ 5.00 – ⚏ 6.50
– **23 rm** 53.00/76.00 t. – SB.

↑ **East Peterel Field Farm** ⌕, NE46 2JT, S : by B 6306 off Whiteley Chapel Rd
ℰ (01434) 607209, Fax (01434) 601753, ≼, ☞, park – 📺 🅿. 🦺
Meals (by arrangement) (communal dining) 17.50 st. – **4 rm** ⚏ 30.00/56.00.

↑ **Middlemarch** without rest., Hencotes, NE46 2EB, ℰ (01434) 605003, Fax (01434) 605003
– ✦✦ 📺 🅿. 🦺
3 rm ⚏ 26.00/50.00 st.

↑ **Wallbank House,** 7 Woodlands, NE46 1HT, ℰ (01434) 602548 – ✦✦ 📺
Meals (by arrangement) (communal dining) 12.00 s. – **3 rm** ⚏ 17.00/38.00 s.

↑ **West Close House** without rest., Hextol Terr., NE46 2AD, by Allendale Rd
ℰ (01434) 603307, ☞ – ✦✦ 🅿. 🦺
4 rm ⚏ 18.00/48.00.

at Slaley SE : 5 ½ m. by B 6306 – ✉ Hexham.

🏨 **Slaley Hall** ⌕, NE47 0BY, SE : 2 ¼ m. ℰ (01434) 673350, Fax (01434) 673962, ≼, ℔, ≘ₛ,
🔲, 🏌, ☞, park – 📠 ✦✦ 🖽 📺 ☎ & 🅿 – 🔬 450. 🐼 🅰🅴 ⓪ 𝗩𝗜𝗦𝗔
Meals 15.95/19.75 t. and a la carte ≬ 8.50 – **129 rm** ⚏ 130.00/185.00 t. – SB.

🅐 ATS Haugh Lane ℰ (01434) 602394

HEYTESBURY Wilts. 403 404 N 30 – see Warminster.

HICKSTEAD W. Sussex.
London 40 – Brighton 8.

🏨 **Travelodge,** Jobs Lane, RH17 5NX, off A 23 ℰ (01444) 881377, Reservations (Freephone)▶
0800 850950 – 📺 & 🅿. 🐼 🅰🅴 ⓪ 𝗩𝗜𝗦𝗔 𝗝𝗖𝗕. 🦺
40 rm 44.95 t.

HIGHAM Suffolk 404 W 28 – pop. 119 – ✉ Colchester.
London 55 – Colchester 10 – Ipswich 11.

↑ **Old Vicarage** ⌕ without rest., CO7 6JY, ℰ (01206) 337248, ≼, « 16C former vicarage »
🔾, ⌔, ☞, park, 🦺 – 📺 🅿
3 rm ⚏ 26.00/56.00 t.

HIGH CROSBY Cumbria 401 402 L 19 – see Carlisle.

HIGH WYCOMBE Bucks. 404 R 29 – pop. 71 718.
🏌 Hazlemere G & C.C., Penn Rd, Hazlemere ℰ (01494) 714722 – 🏌, 🏌 Wycombe Heights▶
Rayners Av., Loudwater ℰ (01494) 816686.
🅱 Paul's Row, HP11 2HQ ℰ (01494) 421892.
London 34 – Aylesbury 17 – Oxford 26 – Reading 18.

🏠 **Forte Posthouse High Wycombe,** Handy Cross, HP11 1TL, SW : 1 ½ m. by A 404
℘ (01494) 442100, Fax (01494) 439071 – ⁕ rm, ☰ rest, 📺 ☎ & ℗ – 🛎 100. ◖◗ 🖭 ①
𝘝𝘐𝘚𝘈 𝙅𝘊𝘽. ✂
Meals a la carte 19.50/28.35 st. ∦ 7.25 – ☑ 10.95 – **106 rm** 99.00/139.00 st. – SB.

🏠 **Alexandra,** Queen Alexandra Rd, HP11 2JX, ℘ (01494) 463494, Fax (01494) 463560 –
⁕ rm, 📺 ☎ & ℗. ◖◗ 🖭 𝘝𝘐𝘚𝘈. ✂
Meals (closed Friday to Sunday) (dinner only) a la carte 14.00/19.70 st. – ☑ 8.90 – **29 rm**
75.00 st., 1 suite.

⑩ ATS Copyground Lane ℘ (01494) 525101/   ATS Station Approach, Crendon St.
438019   ℘ (01494) 532718

HILLSFORD BRIDGE Devon – see Lynton.

HINCKLEY Leics. 402 403 404 P 26 – pop. 40 608.
🛈 Hinckley Library, Lancaster Rd, LE10 0AT ℘ (01455) 635106.
London 103 – Birmingham 31 – Coventry 12 – Leicester 14.

🏠 **Sketchley Grange,** Sketchley Lane, LE10 3HU, S : 1 ½ m. by B 4109 (Rugby Rd)
℘ (01455) 251133, Fax (01455) 631384, ☞ – ⁕ 📺 ☎ ℗ – 🛎 280. ◖◗ 🖭 ① 𝘝𝘐𝘚𝘈
Meals (bar dinner Sunday) 11.95/18.95 st. and a la carte ∦ 7.95 – ☑ 8.95 – **38 rm** 79.00/
115.00 st. – SB.

⑩ ATS 5 Leicester Rd ℘ (01455) 632022/635835

HINTLESHAM Suffolk 404 X 27 – see Ipswich.

HINTON CHARTERHOUSE Bath & North East Somerset – see Bath.

HISTON Cambs. 404 U 27 – see Cambridge.

HITCHIN Herts. 404 T 28 – pop. 32 221.
London 40 – Bedford 14 – Cambridge 26 – Luton 9.

🏠 **Lord Lister,** 1 Park St., SG4 9AH, ℘ (01462) 432712, Fax (01462) 438506 – ⁕ 📺 ☎ ℗. ◖◗
🖭 ① 𝘝𝘐𝘚𝘈. ✂
Meals (dinner only) 10.75 t. and a la carte ∦ 3.95 – **19 rm** ☑ 49.00/65.00 st. – SB.

✗ **Just 32,** 32 Sun St., SG5 1AH, ℘ (01462) 455666 – ◖◗ 🖭 ① 𝘝𝘐𝘚𝘈 𝙅𝘊𝘽
closed Saturday lunch, Sunday, 25-26 December and Bank Holiday Mondays – **Meals**
a la carte 16.50/22.50 t. ∦ 6.00.

at Little Wymondley SE : 2½ m. by A 602 – ✉ Hitchin.

🏠 **Blakemore Thistle,** Blakemore End Rd, SG4 7JJ, ℘ (01438) 355821, Fax (01438) 742114,
⬟, ☞ – |𝄐|, ⁕ rm, 📺 ☎ ℗ – 🛎 200. ◖◗ 🖭 ① 𝘝𝘐𝘚𝘈
Meals 15.95/18.95 t. ∦ 8.50 – ☑ 9.75 – **80 rm** 85.00/101.00, 2 suites – SB.

✗✗ **Redcoats Farmhouse** with rm, Redcoats Green, SG4 7JR, S : ½ m. ℘ (01438) 729500,
Fax (01438) 723322, « Part 15C », ☞ – ⁕ rm, 📺 ☎ ℗. ◖◗ 🖭 ① 𝘝𝘐𝘚𝘈. ✂
closed 1 week Christmas and Bank Holiday Mondays – **Meals** (closed Saturday lunch and
Sunday dinner) 15.00 t. (lunch) and a la carte 25.75/32.50 t. ∦ 5.50 – **14 rm** ☑ 65.00/
95.00 st. – SB.

HOCKLEY HEATH W. Mids. 403 404 O 26 – pop. 14 538 – ✉ Solihull.
London 117 – Birmingham 11 – Coventry 17.

🏠 **Nuthurst Grange Country House,** Nuthurst Grange Lane, B94 5NL, S : ¾ m. by
A 3400 ℘ (01564) 783972, Fax (01564) 783919, ☞ – 📺 ☎ ℗ – 🛎 70. ◖◗ 🖭 ① 𝘝𝘐𝘚𝘈. ✂
closed 25 December – **Meals** – (see below) – **15 rm** ☑ 120.00/165.00 t. – SB.

🏠 **Travel Inn,** Stratford Rd, B94 6NX, on A 3400 ℘ (01564) 782144, Fax (01564) 783197 –
⁕ rm, 📺 & ℗ – 🛎 40. ◖◗ 🖭 ① 𝘝𝘐𝘚𝘈. ✂
Meals (grill rest.) – **40 rm** 36.50 t.

✗✗✗ **Nuthurst Grange** (at Nuthurst Grange Country House), Nuthurst Grange Lane, B94 5NL,
S : ¾ m. by A 3400 ℘ (01564) 783972, Fax (01564) 783919, ☞ – ⁕ ℗. ◖◗ 🖭 ① 𝘝𝘐𝘚𝘈
Meals (closed Saturday lunch) 29.50 t. (dinner) and lunch a la carte 18.50/27.50 t. ∦ 8.50.

HOCKLIFFE Beds. 404 S 28 – see Dunstable.

HOLBROOK *Suffolk* 404 X 28 – *see Ipswich.*

HOLFORD *Somerset* 403 K 30 *Great Britain G. – pop. 307 –* ✉ *Bridgwater.*
Env. : *Stogursey Priory Church★★, W : 4 ½ m.*
London 171 – Bristol 48 – Minehead 15 – Taunton 22.

🏠 **Combe House** ⤜, Holford Combe, TA5 1RZ, SW : 1 m., turning off A 39 at Elf petrol station ℘ (01278) 741382, Fax (01278) 741382, ⇌, 🔲, ☞, ✗ – ✗ rest, 📺 ☎ 🅿. 🝉 🄰🄴 𝗩𝗜𝗦𝗔, ✗
closed January – **Meals** *(bar lunch)/dinner* 18.25 **st.** ₰ 5.95 – **16 rm** � 38.00/76.00 **st.**, 1 suite – SB.

HOLMES CHAPEL *Ches.* 402 403 404 M 24 – *pop. 5 465.*
London 181 – Chester 25 – Liverpool 41 – Manchester 24 – Stoke-on-Trent 20.

🏨 **Old Vicarage**, Knutsford Rd, Cranage, CW4 8EF, NW : ½ m. on a 50 ℘ (01477) 532041, Fax (01477) 535728 – ✗ rest, 📺 ☎ ᪲ 🅿. – ⚿ 30. 🝉 🄰🄴 𝗩𝗜𝗦𝗔, ✗
Church's Brasserie : Meals 14.50 **st.** and a la carte ₰ 6.00 – **25 rm** ⊑ 68.50/80.00 **st.** – SB.

🏨 **Holly Lodge**, 70 London Rd, CW4 7AS, on A 50 ℘ (01477) 537033, Fax (01477) 535823 – ✗ 📺 ☎ 🅿. – ⚿ 120. 🝉 🄰🄴 𝗩𝗜𝗦𝗔, ✗
Meals *(closed Saturday lunch)* (bar meals Sunday dinner) (dancing Friday evening) a la carte 11.85/21.90 **st.** ₰ 7.50 – **38 rm** ⊑ 69.50/80.00 **st.**

🏨 **Cottage Rest. and Lodge**, London Rd, Allostock, WA16 9LU, N : 3 m. on A 50 ℘ (01565) 722470, Fax (01565) 722749 – ✗ rm, 📺 ☎ 🅿. 🝉 🄰🄴 𝗩𝗜𝗦𝗔, ✗
closed 26 and 27 December – **Meals** *(closed Sunday dinner to non-residents)* a la carte approx. 18.95 **t.** ₰ 6.95 – **12 rm** ⊑ 65.00/75.00 **t.**

HOLMFIRTH *W. Yorks.* 402 404 O 23 – *pop. 21 979 (inc. Honley) –* ✉ *Huddersfield.*
🛈 49-51 Huddersfield Rd, HD7 1JP ℘ (01484) 687603.
London 195 – Leeds 23 – Manchester 25 – Sheffield 22.

🏠 **Holme Castle**, Holme, HD7 1QG, SW : 2 ½ m. on A 6024 ℘ (01484) 680680, Fax (01484) 686764, ⩽, ☞ – ✗ 📺 🅿. 🝉 🄰🄴 𝗩𝗜𝗦𝗔, ✗
Meals *(by arrangement)* 19.00 ₰ 6.40 – **8 rm** ⊑ 30.00/70.00 – SB.

HOLNE *Devon* 403 I 32 – *see Ashburton.*

HOLT *Norfolk* 404 X 25 – *pop. 2 972.*
London 124 – King's Lynn 34 – Norwich 22.

✗✗ **Yetman's**, 37 Norwich Rd, NR25 6SA, ℘ (01263) 713320 – ✗. 🝉 🄰🄴 𝗩𝗜𝗦𝗔
closed Monday except dinner in summer, Tuesday, 25 December and 3 weeks October November – **Meals** *(dinner only and Sunday lunch)* 25.50 **t.**
🝟 ATS Hempstead Rd Ind. Est. ℘ (01263) 712015

HOLYWELL *Cambs.* 404 T 27 – *see St. Ives.*

HONILEY *Warks.* – *see Warwick*

HONITON *Devon* 403 K 31 *The West Country G. – pop. 7 859.*
See : *All Hallows Museum★ AC.*
Env. : *Ottery St. Mary★ (St. Mary's★) SW : 5 m. by A 30 and B 3177.*
Exc. : *Faraway Countryside Park (⩽★) AC, SE : 6 ½ m. by A 375 and B 3174.*
🛈 Lace Walk Car Park, EX14 8LT ℘ (01404) 43716.
London 186 – Exeter 17 – Southampton 93 – Taunton 18.

🏨 **Deer Park** ⤜, Buckerell Village, Weston, EX14 0PG, W : 2 ½ m. by A 30 ℘ (01404) 41266, Fax (01404) 46598, ⩽, ⇌, 🛆, ⚲, ☞, park, ✗, squash – 📺 ☎ 🅿. – ⚿ 70. 🝉 🄰🄴 🄾 𝗩𝗜𝗦.✗
Meals 16.00/26.00 **st.** and a la carte ₰ 6.00 – **22 rm** ⊑ 45.00/240.00 **s.** – SB.

at Yarcombe NE : 8 m. on A 30 – ✉ *Honiton.*

🏠 **Belfry Country H.**, EX14 9BD, on A 30 ℘ (01404) 861234, Fax (01404) 861579, ⩽ – ✗ 📺 ☎ 🅿. 🝉 🄰🄴 𝗩𝗜𝗦𝗔 𝗝𝗖𝗕
Meals *(dinner only)* 18.95 **st.** and a la carte ₰ 5.50 – **6 rm** ⊑ 44.00/68.00 **st.** – SB.

at Wilmington E : 3 m. on A 35 – ⊠ Honiton.

🏠 **Home Farm**, EX14 9JR, on A 35 ℰ (01404) 831278, Fax (01404) 831411, « Part 16C thatched farm », 🌾 – ⅙ rest, 📺 ☎ 🅿. 🇲🇶 🇦🇪 ⑩ 𝑉𝐼𝑆𝐴 𝐽𝐶𝐵
closed 23 and 28 December – Meals 14.50 t. and a la carte ᵭ 4.85 – **13 rm** ⊃ 32.00/60.00 t.

at Payhembury NW : 7½ m. by A 30 – ⊠ Honiton.

🏠 **Cokesputt House** ⅌, EX14 0HD, ℰ (01404) 841289, ≼, « Part 17C and 18C, gardens » – ⅙ 𝑉𝐼𝑆𝐴 𝐽𝐶𝐵. ⅍
closed Christmas – Meals (booking essential) (communal dining) 19.50 s. – **3 rm** ⊃ 30.50/60.00 s.

HONLEY W. Yorks. 402 404 O 23 – see Huddersfield.

HOO GREEN Ches. – see Knutsford.

HOOK Hants. 404 R 30 – pop. 6 471 – ⊠ Basingstoke.
London 47 – Reading 13 – Southampton 35.

🏨 **Basingstoke Country**, Scures Hill, Nately Scures, RG27 9JS, W : 1 m. on A 30 ℰ (01256) 764161, Fax (01256) 768341, ₤₅, ☎, 🔲, 🌾 – ⸗, ⅙ rm, 🔲 rest, 📺 ☎ ⅙ 🅿 – 🔬 170. 🇲🇶 🇦🇪 ⑩ 𝑉𝐼𝑆𝐴 ⅍
Meals (closed Saturday lunch and Sunday dinner) 15.25/24.50 st. and a la carte ᵭ 7.25 – ⊃ 9.95 – **100 rm** 88.50/149.50 st. – SB.

🏨 **Raven**, Station Rd, RG27 9HS, ℰ (01256) 762541, Fax (01256) 768677 – ⅙ rm, 📺 ☎ 🅿 – 🔬 100. 🇲🇶 🇦🇪 ⑩ 𝑉𝐼𝑆𝐴. ⅍
Meals (closed Saturday lunch and Sunday dinner) a la carte 11.15/25.40 t. ᵭ 4.25 – **38 rm** ⊃ 65.00/75.00 t. – SB.

🏠 **White Hart**, London Rd, RG27 9DZ, on A 30 ℰ (01256) 762462, Fax (01256) 768351, 🌾 – 📺 ☎ 🅿. 🇲🇶 🇦🇪 ⑩ 𝑉𝐼𝑆𝐴
Meals a la carte 9.40/17.75 st. – ⊃ 6.00 – **21 rm** 54.00 st.

🏠 **Hook House**, London Rd, RG27 9EQ, E : ½ m. on A 30 ℰ (01256) 762630, Fax (01256) 760232, « Part Georgian house », 🌾 – ⅙ 📺 ☎ 🅿. 🇲🇶 🇦🇪 ⑩ 𝑉𝐼𝑆𝐴 𝐽𝐶𝐵. ⅍
closed Christmas – Meals (residents only) (dinner only) a la carte approx. 15.00 t. ᵭ 4.00 – **13 rm** ⊃ 55.50/74.50 st.

at Rotherwick N : 2 m. by A 30 and B 3349 on Rotherwick rd – ⊠ Basingstoke.

🏨 **Tylney Hall** ⅌, RG27 9AZ, S : 1½ m. by Newnham rd on Ridge Lane ℰ (01256) 764881, Fax (01256) 768141, « 19C mansion in extensive gardens by Gertrude Jekyll », ₤₅, ☎, 🔲, 🔲, park, ⅍ – 📺 ☎ 🅿 – 🔬 100. 🇲🇶 🇦🇪 ⑩ 𝑉𝐼𝑆𝐴 𝐽𝐶𝐵. ⅍
Meals 21.00/31.00 st. and a la carte ᵭ 8.50 – **101 rm** ⊃ 110.00/185.00 st., 9 suites – SB.

HOOK Wilts. – see Swindon.

HOPE Derbs. 402 403 404 O 23 – ⊠ Sheffield.
London 180 – Derby 50 – Manchester 31 – Sheffield 15 – Stoke-on-Trent 40.

🏠 **Underleigh** ⅌, S33 6RF, N : 1 m. by Edale rd ℰ (01433) 621372, Fax (01433) 621324, ≼, 🌾 – ⅙ rest, 📺 ☎ 🅿. 🇲🇶 𝑉𝐼𝑆𝐴. ⅍
Meals (by arrangement) (communal dining) 16.50 s. ᵭ 4.50 – **6 rm** ⊃ 40.00/62.00 s. – SB.

HOPE COVE Devon 403 I 33 – see Salcombe.

HOPTON WAFERS Shrops. 403 404 M 26 – pop. 609 – ⊠ Kidderminster.
London 150 – Birmingham 32 – Shrewsbury 38.

🏠 **Crown Inn**, DY14 0NB, on A 4117 ℰ (01299) 270372, Fax (01299) 271127 – ⅙ rm, 📺 ☎ 🅿. 🇲🇶 𝑉𝐼𝑆𝐴. ⅍
Meals 17.50/24.50 st. ᵭ 4.75 – **8 rm** ⊃ 47.50/75.00 st. – SB.

HOPWOOD W. Mids. – ⊠ Birmingham.
London 131 – Birmingham 8.

🏨 **Westmead**, Redditch Rd, B48 7AL, on A 441 ℰ (0121) 445 1202, Fax (0121) 445 6163, ☎ – ⅙ rm, 🔲 rest, 📺 ☎ 🅿 – 🔬 250. 🇲🇶 🇦🇪 ⑩ 𝑉𝐼𝑆𝐴 𝐽𝐶𝐵. ⅍
Meals a la carte 11.25/21.35 st. ᵭ 6.95 – ⊃ 8.95 – **56 rm** 75.00 st., 2 suites – SB.

HORLEY Surrey 404 T 30 – pop. 19 267.

London 27 – Brighton 26 – Royal Tunbridge Wells 22.

Plan : see Gatwick

🏛 **Chequers Thistle,** Brighton Rd, RH6 8PH, on A 23 ℰ (01293) 786992, Fax (01293) 820625 – ⇔, ▤ rest, 📺 ☎ 🅿 – ⚖ 60. ◑ AE ⓪ VISA JCB. ⋘   Y z
Meals (closed Saturday lunch) 12.50/17.95 t. and a la carte ⬩ 5.50 – ⬡ 9.75 – **78 rm** 97.00/120.00 t. – SB.

🏛 **Langshott Manor,** Langshott, RH6 9LN, N : by A 23 turning right at Chequers Thistle onto Ladbroke Rd ℰ (01293) 786680, Fax (01293) 783905, « Part Elizabethan manor house », ᾗ – ⇔ 📺 ☎ 🅿. ◑ AE ⓪ VISA. ⋘
closed 25 to 30 December – Meals (booking essential) (lunch by arrangement) 24.00/32.50 t. ⬩ 7.30 – **10 rm** ⬡ 105.00/145.00 t. – SB.

↑ **Lawn** without rest., 30 Massetts Rd, RH6 7DE, ℰ (01293) 775751, Fax (01293) 821803, ᾗ – ⇔ 📺 🅿. ◑ AE VISA   Y r
7 rm ⬡ 35.00/45.00 t.

HORNCASTLE Lincs. 402 404 T 24 – pop. 4 994.

London 140 – Boston 19 – Great Grimsby 31 – Lincoln 21.

🏛 **Admiral Rodney,** North St., LN9 5DX, ℰ (01507) 523131, Fax (01507) 523104 – ⧄, ⇔ rm, 📺 ☎ 🅿 – ⚖ 140. ◑ ⓪ VISA JCB. ⋘
Meals (carving lunch)/dinner 12.95 t. ⬩ 4.95 – **31 rm** ⬡ 45.00/80.00 t. – SB.

XX **Magpies,** 71-75 East St., LN9 6AA, ℰ (01507) 527004, Fax (01507) 524064 – ⇔. ◑ VISA
closed Saturday and Tuesday lunch, Sunday, Monday, 2 weeks October and restricted opening January – Meals 12.00/25.00 t. ⬩ 9.75.

HORNDON-ON-THE-HILL Essex 404 V 29

London 25 – Chelmsford 22 – Maidstone 34 – Southend-on-Sea 16.

🏚 **Bell Inn** with rm, High Rd, SS17 8LD, ℰ (01375) 642463, Fax (01375) 361611, « 16C coaching inn » – ⇔ rm, 🅿. ◑ AE VISA JCB
Meals (closed 25 and 26 December) a la carte 13.80/23.95 t. ⬩ 6.95 – ⬡ 6.25 – **4 rm** 45.00/65.00 t.

HORNING Norfolk 404 Y 25 Great Britain G. – pop. 1 070 – ✉ Norwich.

Env. : The Broads★.

London 122 – Great Yarmouth 17 – Norwich 11.

🏛 **Petersfield House** ⬏, Lower St., NR12 8PF, ℰ (01692) 630741, Fax (01692) 630745, ᾗ – 📺 ☎ 🅿. ◑ AE ⓪ VISA
Meals (dancing Saturday evening) 13.50/15.50 t. and a la carte ⬩ 5.00 – **18 rm** ⬡ 58.00/85.00 t. – SB.

HORNINGSEA Cambs. 404 U 27 – see Cambridge.

HORNINGSHAM Wilts. 403 404 N 30 – see Warminster.

HORNS CROSS Devon 403 H 31 The West Country G. – ✉ Bideford.

Exc. : Clovelly★★, NW : 7 m. by A 39 and B 3237.

London 237 – Barnstaple 15 – Exeter 48.

🏛 **Foxdown Manor** ⬏, Foxdown, EX39 5PJ, S : 1 m. ℰ (01237) 451325, Fax (01237) 451525, ≤, ⬠s, ⬝, ᾗ, park, ⋇ – 📺 ☎ 🅿. ◑ ⓪ VISA
closed February – Meals (bar lunch)/dinner a la carte 21.50/32.75 st. ⬩ 8.00 – **7 rm** ⬡ 50.00/120.00 st., 1 suite.

↑ **Lower Waytown** without rest., EX39 5DN, NE : 1 ¼ m. on A 39 ℰ (01237) 451787, Fax (01237) 451787, « Part 17C thatched cottage », ᾗ – ⇔ 📺 🅿. ⋘
closed Christmas, New Year and restricted opening in winter – **3 rm** ⬡ 35.00/50.00 s. – SB.

HORRINGER Suffolk 404 W 27 – see Bury St. Edmunds.

HORSFORTH W. Yorks. 402 P 22 – see Leeds.

HORSHAM W. Sussex 404 T 30 – pop. 42 552.

ⓑ, ⓑ Mannings Heath, Fullers, Hammerpond Rd ℘ (01403) 210228.

🛈 9 Causeway, RH12 1HE ℘ (01403) 211661.

London 39 – Brighton 23 – Guildford 20 – Lewes 25 – Worthing 20.

South Lodge ⚘, Brighton Rd, Lower Beeding, RH13 6PS, SE : 5 m. on A 281 ℘ (01403) 891711, Fax (01403) 891766, ≤, « Victorian mansion, gardens », ⓑ, ⚘, park, ✵ – ✵ rest, 📺 ☎ 🅿 – 🕍 80. ⓪ 🄰🄴 ⓞ 𝘝𝘐𝘚𝘈 𝐉𝐂𝐁. ✸
Meals 15.00/25.00 **st.** and dinner a la carte ⓘ 7.50 – ⚌ 10.95 – **37 rm** 130.00/195.00 **t.**, 2 suites – SB.

Cisswood House, Sandygate Lane, Lower Beeding, RH13 6NF, SE : 3 ¾ m. on A 281 ℘ (01403) 891216, Fax (01403) 891621, 🔧, 🌺 – 📺 ☎ 🅿 – 🕍 150. ⓪ 🄰🄴 ⓞ 𝘝𝘐𝘚𝘈. ✸
closed Easter, Christmas-New Year and August Bank Holiday – **Meals** (closed Sunday) 23.50/25.50 **t.** ⓘ 5.50 – ⚌ 5.00 – **30 rm** 75.00/95.00 **st.**, 2 suites – SB.

Travel Inn, The Station, 57 North St., RH12 1RB, ℘ (01403) 250141, Fax (01403) 270797 – ✵ rm, 📺 ⓖ 🅿. ⓪ 🄰🄴 ⓞ 𝘝𝘐𝘚𝘈. ✸
Meals (grill rest.) – **40 rm** 36.50 **t.**

Jeremy's (at the Crabtree), Brighton Rd, Lower Beeding, RH13 6PT, SE : 5 ¼ m. on A 281 ℘ (01403) 891257, Fax (01403) 891606, �, 🌺 – ✵ 🅿. ⓪ 🄰🄴 𝘝𝘐𝘚𝘈
closed dinner Sunday and Bank Holidays and 25 December – **Meals** 25.00 **t.** (dinner) and lunch a la carte approx. 17.50 **st.**

at Southwater S : 3 m. by B 2237 – ✉ Horsham.

Cole's, Worthing Rd, RH13 7BS, ℘ (01403) 730456 – ✵ 🅿. ⓪ 🄰🄴 ⓞ 𝘝𝘐𝘚𝘈 𝐉𝐂𝐁
closed Saturday lunch, Sunday dinner, Monday, 1 week spring and 2 weeks late summer – Meals 15.00 **t.** (lunch) and a la carte 19.00/28.15 **t.** ⓘ 6.50.

at Slinfold W : 4 m. by A 281 off A 264 – ✉ Horsham.

Random Hall, Stane St., RH13 7QX, W : ½ m. on A 29 ℘ (01403) 790558, Fax (01403) 791046, « Part 16C farmhouse » – ✵ rest, 📺 ☎ 🅿. ⓪ 🄰🄴 𝘝𝘐𝘚𝘈. ✸
closed 27 December-4 January – Meals 14.60/20.65 **st.** ⓘ 6.50 – ⚌ 8.50 – **15 rm** 62.50 **st.** – SB.

🔧 ATS Nightingale Road ℘ (01403) 267491/251736

HORTON Northants. 404 R 27 – pop. 574 – ✉ Northampton.

London 66 – Bedford 18 – Northampton 6.

French Partridge, Newport Pagnell Rd, NN7 2AP, ℘ (01604) 870033, Fax (01604) 870032 – 🅿
closed Sunday, Monday, 2 weeks Easter, 3 weeks July-August and 2 weeks Christmas – Meals (booking essential) (dinner only) 26.00 **st.** ⓘ 5.50.

HORTON-CUM-STUDLEY Oxon. 403 404 Q 28 – pop. 453 – ✉ Oxford.

London 57 – Aylesbury 23 – Oxford 7.

Studley Priory ⚘, OX33 1AZ, ℘ (01865) 351203, Fax (01865) 351613, ≤, « Elizabethan manor house in park », ⓑ, 🌺, ✵ – ✵ 📺 ☎ 🅿 – 🕍 30. ⓪ 🄰🄴 ⓞ 𝘝𝘐𝘚𝘈 𝐉𝐂𝐁. ✸
Meals a la carte 25.00/34.00 **st.** ⓘ 8.50 – ⚌ 7.50 – **17 rm** 105.00/185.00 **st.**, 1 suite – SB.

HOTHFIELD Kent 404 W 30 – see Ashford.

HOUGH-ON-THE-HILL Lincs. – see Grantham.

HOUGHTON CONQUEST Beds. 404 S 27 – see Bedford.

HOVE E. Sussex 404 T 31 – see Brighton and Hove.

HOVINGHAM N. Yorks. 402 R 21 – pop. 322 – ✉ York.

London 235 – Middlesbrough 36 – York 25.

Worsley Arms, YO6 4LA, ℘ (01653) 628234, Fax (01653) 628130, « Part 19C coaching inn », 🌺 – ✵ 📺 ☎ ⚏ 🅿 – 🕍 25. ⓪ 🄰🄴 𝘝𝘐𝘚𝘈
Wyvern : Meals (dinner only and Sunday lunch)/dinner 23.50 **t.** and a la carte – **Cricketer's Bistro :** Meals a la carte 14.30/22.00 **t.** – **18 rm** ⚌ 60.00/80.00 – SB.

HOWTOWN Cumbria – see Ullswater.

HUDDERSFIELD W. Yorks. 402 404 O 23 – pop. 143 726.

$\overline{18}$, $\overline{9}$ Bradley Park, Bradley Rd & (01484) 223772 – $\overline{18}$ Woodsome Hall, Fenay Bridge & (01484) 602971 – $\overline{18}$ Outlane, Slack Lane & (01422) 374762 A – $\overline{18}$ Meltham, Thick Hollins Hall & (01484) 850227 – $\overline{18}$ Fixby Hall, Lightridge Rd & (01484) 420110 B – $\overline{18}$ Crosland Heath, Felks Stile Rd & (01484) 653216 A.

🛈 High Street Building, 3-5 Albion St., HD1 2NW & (01484) 223200.

London 191 – Bradford 11 – Leeds 15 – Manchester 25 – Sheffield 26.

HUDDERSFIELD

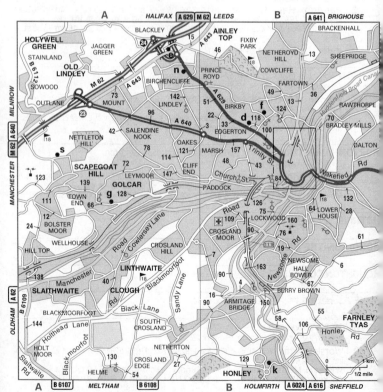

Pour un bon usage des plans de ville, voir les signes conventionnels.

HUDDERSFIELD

*Great Britain and
Ireland is now covered
by an Atlas at a scale
of 1 inch to 4.75 miles.*

*Three easy
to use versions:
Paperback, Spiralbound
and Hardback.*

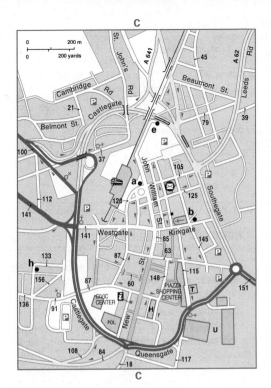

Hilton National Huddersfield/Halifax, Ainley Top, HD3 3RH, NW : 3 m. at junction of A 629 with A 643 ℰ (01484) 375431, *Fax* (01484) 310067, ⅙, ☎, ⬚ – ⧉ ⅏, ▤ rest, �📺 ☎ ❻ – ⚿ 400. 🆆🅂 🅰🅴 ⓪ 𝑽𝑰𝑺𝑨 𝐉𝐂𝐁
                      A e
Meals *(closed Saturday lunch)* 12.95/17.50 **st.** and a la carte ⓰ 6.50 – ⬚ 10.25 – **113 rm** 93.00 **st.**, 1 suite.

George, St. George's Sq., HD1 1JA, ℰ (01484) 515444, *Fax* (01484) 435056 – ⧉, ⚿ rm, 📺 ☎ ⅙ ❻ – ⚿ 120. 🆆🅂 🅰🅴 ⓪ 𝑽𝑰𝑺𝑨
                      C a
closed 2 to 4 January – **Meals** *(closed Saturday lunch)* 7.95/14.95 **st.** and a la carte ⓰ 5.25 – **59 rm** ⬚ 79.00/99.00 **st.**, 1 suite – SB.

Lodge, 48 Birkby Lodge Rd, Birkby, HD2 2BG, N : 1 ½ m. by A 629 and Blacker Rd ℰ (01484) 431001, *Fax* (01484) 421590, ≈ – ⚿ 📺 ☎ ❻ – ⚿ 30. 🆆🅂 🅰🅴 ⓪ 𝑽𝑰𝑺𝑨 𝐉𝐂𝐁 ⚘
                      B f
closed 25 to 29 December – **Meals** *(closed Sunday dinner)* 14.95/24.95 **t.** ⓰ 6.00 – **13 rm** ⬚ 60.00/70.00 **t.**

Huddersfield, 37-47 Kirkgate, HD1 1QT, ℰ (01484) 512111, *Fax* (01484) 435262, ☎ – ⧉, ▤ rest, 📺 ☎ ❻. 🆆🅂 𝑽𝑰𝑺𝑨 𝐉𝐂𝐁
                      C b
Meals 6.50/14.50 **st.** and a la carte ⓰ 5.00 – **46 rm** ⬚ 47.50/67.50 **st.** – SB.

Briar Court, Halifax Rd, Birchencliffe, HD3 3NT, NW : 2 m. on A 629 ℰ (01484) 519902, *Fax* (01484) 431812 – ⚿ rm, 📺 ☎ ❻ – ⚿ 150
                      A n
43 rm, 4 suites.

Elm Crest, 2 Queens Rd, HD2 2AG, off Edgerton Rd (A 629) ℰ (01484) 530990, *Fax* (01484) 516227 – ⚿ 📺 ☎ ❻. 🆆🅂 🅰🅴 ⓪ 𝑽𝑰𝑺𝑨. ⚘
                      B d
Meals *(closed Sunday lunch)* 12.00/14.00 **st.** and a la carte ⓰ 5.00 – **8 rm** ⬚ 35.00/60.00 **st.** – SB.

The Mallows without rest., 55 Spring St., Springwood, HD1 4AZ, ℰ (01484) 544684 – ⚿ 📺 ❻. ⚘
                      C h
closed 22 December-4 January – **6 rm** ⬚ 17.50/40.00 **st.**

Cafe Pacific, 3 Viaduct St., HD1 5DL, ℰ (01484) 559055, *Fax* (01484) 559155 – 🆆🅂 𝑽𝑰𝑺𝑨
                      C e
closed Sunday, Monday, 25 December and 1 January – **Meals** 10.95 **t.** and a la carte ⓰ 4.25.

at Honley S : 4 m. by A 616 – ⊠ Huddersfield.

⋇ **Mustard and Punch,** 6 Westgate, HD7 2AA, 𝒫 (01484) 662066 – ⓤⓢ 𝗩𝗜𝗦𝗔   B k
closed Saturday lunch, Sunday and Monday – **Meals** 16.50/26.00 t. ⅋ 4.75.

at Golcar W : 3½ m. by A 62 on B 6111 – ⊠ Huddersfield.

⋇⋇ **Weaver's Shed,** Knowl Rd, via Scar Lane, HD7 4AN, 𝒫 (01484) 654284,
Fax (01484) 654284, « Converted 18C woollen mill » – ⓟ. ⓤⓢ ⒶⒺ 𝗩𝗜𝗦𝗔   A g
closed Saturday lunch, Sunday, Monday, 2 weeks January, 2 weeks July-August and Bank
Holidays – **Meals** 13.95 t. (lunch) and a la carte 20.85/31.85 t. ⅋ 10.75.

at Outlane NW : 4 m. on A 640 – ⊠ Huddersfield.

🏨 **Old Golf House,** New Hey Rd, HD3 3YP, 𝒫 (01422) 379311, Fax (01422) 372694, ⇝ –
⋇⋇, ▤ rest, ⓣⓥ ☎ ⓟ – 🔏 100. ⓤⓢ ⒶⒺ ⓞ 𝗩𝗜𝗦𝗔 𝗝𝗖𝗕   A s
Meals 16.95 **st.** (dinner) and a la carte 11.65/19.95 **st.** ⅋ 6.50 – ⊐ 8.95 – **49 rm** 75.00 **st.** –
SB.

ⓐ ATS Leeds Rd 𝒫 (01484) 534441

HULL Kingston-upon-Hull**402** S 22 – see Kingston-upon-Hull.

HUNGERFORD Newbury**403 404** P 29 The West Country G. – pop. 5 046.
Exc. : Savernake Forest★★ (Grand Avenue★★★), W : 7 m. by A 4 – Crofton Beam Engines★,
SW : 8 m. by A 338 and minor roads.
London 74 – Bristol 57 – Oxford 28 – Reading 26 – Southampton 46.

🏨 **Bear at Hungerford,** 17 Charnham St., RG17 0EL, on A 4 𝒫 (01488) 682512,
Fax (01488) 684357, 🌳 – ⋇⋇ ⓣⓥ ☎ ⓟ – 🔏 75. ⓤⓢ ⒶⒺ ⓞ 𝗩𝗜𝗦𝗔
Meals 14.95/18.95 **st.** and a la carte ⅋ 6.50 – ⊐ 8.25 – **41 rm** 79.00/130.00 **st.** – SB.

🏨 **Three Swans,** 117 High St., RG17 0LZ, 𝒫 (01488) 682721, Fax (01488) 681708 – ⋇⋇ rm,
ⓣⓥ ☎ ⓟ – 🔏 70. ⓤⓢ ⒶⒺ ⓞ 𝗩𝗜𝗦𝗔 𝗝𝗖𝗕
Meals a la carte 11.40/25.15 **st.** ⅋ 4.50 – ⊐ 6.50 – **15 rm** 55.00/70.00 **st.** – SB.

⌂ **Marshgate Cottage** without rest., Marsh Lane, RG17 0QX, W : ¾ m. by Church St.
𝒫 (01488) 682307, Fax (01488) 685475, ≼, 🌳 – ⋇⋇ ⓣⓥ ☎ ⓟ. ⓤⓢ 𝗩𝗜𝗦𝗔 𝗝𝗖𝗕. ⅍
6 rm ⊐ 35.50/55.00 **t.**

⋇ **Just William's,** 50 Church St., RG17 0JH, 𝒫 (01488) 681199 – ⓤⓢ ⒶⒺ 𝗩𝗜𝗦𝗔 𝗝𝗖𝗕
closed Sunday, Good Friday, Bank Holiday Mondays and 25 December-2 January – **Meals**
a la carte 17.40/25.20 **t.** ⅋ 5.95.

HUNSTANTON Norfolk**402 404** V 25 – pop. 4 634.
🏌 Golf Course Road 𝒫 (01485) 532811.
🚩 Town Hall, The Green, PE36 5BQ 𝒫 (01485) 532610.
London 120 – Cambridge 60 – Norwich 45.

🏨 **Le Strange Arms,** Golf Course Rd, PE36 6JJ, N : 1 m. by A 149 𝒫 (01485) 534411
Fax (01485) 534724, ≼, 🌳 – ⓣⓥ ☎ ⓟ – 🔏 150. ⓤⓢ ⒶⒺ ⓞ 𝗩𝗜𝗦𝗔
Meals (bar lunch Monday to Saturday)/dinner 16.50 **t.** and a la carte ⅋ 6.10 – **33 rm**
⊐ 53.00/80.00 **t.**, 3 suites – SB.

⌂ **Claremont** without rest., 35 Greevegate, PE36 6AF, 𝒫 (01485) 533171
Fax (01485) 533171 – ⋇⋇ ⓣⓥ. ⅍
7 rm ⊐ 23.50/48.00.

HUNSTRETE Bath & North East Somerset**403 404** M 29 – see Bristol.

HUNTINGDON Cambs.**404** T 26 – pop. 15 575.
🏌 Brampton Park, Buckden Rd 𝒫 (01480) 434700 – 🏌 Hemingford Abbots, New Farm
Lodge, Cambridge Rd 𝒫 (01480) 495000.
🚩 The Library, Princes St., PE18 6PH 𝒫 (01480) 388588.
London 69 – Bedford 21 – Cambridge 16.

🏨 **Old Bridge,** 1 High St., PE18 6TQ, 𝒫 (01480) 452681, Fax (01480) 411017, 🏠, 🌳 –
⋇⋇ rest, ⓣⓥ ☎ ⓟ – 🔏 50. ⓤⓢ ⒶⒺ ⓞ 𝗩𝗜𝗦𝗔
Meals a la carte 17.45/25.00 **st.** ⅋ 4.95 – **25 rm** ⊐ 79.50/120.00 **st.**

🏨 **George,** George St., PE18 6AB, 𝒫 (01480) 432444, Fax (01480) 453130 – ⋇⋇ ⓣⓥ ☎ ⓟ
🔏 150. ⓤⓢ ⒶⒺ ⓞ 𝗩𝗜𝗦𝗔 𝗝𝗖𝗕.
Meals (bar lunch Monday to Saturday)/dinner a la carte 16.95/24.70 **st.** ⅋ 6.25 – ⊐ 9.25
24 rm 70.00/85.00 **st.** – SB.

🏨 **Travelodge**, PE18 9JF, SE : 5 ½ m. on A 14 (eastbound carriageway) ℰ (01954) 230919, *Fax (01954) 230919*, Reservations (Freephone) 0800 850950 – ⊱ rm, 📺 ⅋ ℗. ⒶⓈ ⒶⒺ ⓪ *VISA* *JCB*. ⚘
Meals (grill rest.) – **40 rm** 44.95 **t.**

🔧 ATS Nursery Rd ℰ (01480) 451031/451515

HURLEY-ON-THAMES *Windsor & Maidenhead* **404** R 29 – *pop. 1 712 –* ⊠ *Maidenhead.*
London 38 – Oxford 26 – Reading 12.

🏛 **Ye Olde Bell**, High St., SL6 5LX, ℰ (01628) 825881, *Fax (01628) 825939*, « Part 12C inn »,
⛲ – 📺 ☎ ℗ – 🔬 130. ⒶⓈ ⒶⒺ ⓪ *VISA*
Meals 17.95/23.50 **st.** and a la carte ⅄ 7.50 – �️ 9.50 – **41 rm** 115.00/135.00 **st.**, 1 suite –
SB.

HURSTBOURNE TARRANT *Hants.* **403** **404** P 30 – *pop. 700 –* ⊠ *Andover.*
London 77 – Bristol 77 – Oxford 38 – Southampton 33.

🏨 **Esseborne Manor** ⚘, SP11 0ER, NE : 1 ½ m. on A 343 ℰ (01264) 736444,
Fax (01264) 736725, ⛲, ⚘ – 📺 ☎ ℗. ⒶⓈ ⒶⒺ ⓪ *VISA*. ⚘
Meals 17.00 **st.** and a la carte 20.00/34.00 **st.** ⅄ 8.25 – **10 rm** ⊝ 88.00/135.00 **st.** – SB.

HURST GREEN *Lancs.* **402** M 22 – ⊠ *Clitheroe.*
London 236 – Blackburn 12 – Burnley 13 – Preston 12.

🏛 **Shireburn Arms**, Whalley Rd, BB7 9QJ, on B 6243 ℰ (01254) 826518,
Fax (01254) 826208, ⛲ – 📺 ☎ ℗. ⒶⓈ ⒶⒺ *VISA*
Meals (bar lunch Saturday) 5.95/14.95 **t.** and dinner a la carte ⅄ 6.50 – **18 rm** ⊝ 40.00/
55.00 **t.** – SB.

🍴 **Bayley Arms** with rm, Avenue Rd, BB7 9QB, ℰ (01254) 826478, *Fax (01254) 826797* – 📺
℗. ⒶⓈ ⒶⒺ *VISA*. ⚘
closed 25 December – **Meals** (in bar) a la carte 10.20/21.45 **t.** ⅄ 4.50 – **7 rm** ⊝ 35.00/
45.00 **st.**

Les prix	Pour toutes précisions sur les prix indiqués dans ce guide, reportez-vous aux pages de l'introduction.

HUTTON-LE-HOLE *N. Yorks.* **402** R 21 – *pop. 162.*
London 244 – Scarborough 27 – York 33.

⌂ **Hammer and Hand**, YO6 6UA, ℰ (01751) 417300, *Fax (01751) 417711* – ⊱ 📺 ℗
Meals (by arrangement) 12.50 ⅄ 4.50 – **3 rm** ⊝ 24.00/46.00 **s.** – SB.

HUYTON *Mersey.* **402** **403** L 23 – *see Liverpool.*

HYDE *Gtr. Manchester* **402** **403** **404** N 23 – *pop. 30 666.*
London 202 – Manchester 10.

🏨 **Village Leisure**, Captain Clarke Rd, Dukinfield, SK14 4QG, NW : 1 ¼ m. by A 627
ℰ (0161) 368 1456, *Fax (0161) 367 8343*, ⅃₆, ⇔, squash – ≣, ⊱ rest, 📺 ☎ ℗ – 🔬 150.
ⒶⓈ ⒶⒺ ⓪ *VISA*
Meals (grill rest.) a la carte 10.55/24.30 **st.** ⅄ 3.90 – **89 rm** ⊝ 69.00/81.00 **st.**

HYTHE *Hants.* **403** **404** P 31 – *pop. 19 293 (inc. Dibden) –* ⊠ *Southampton.*
⛴ *to Southampton (White Horse Ferries Ltd) frequent services daily (12 mn).*
London 100 – Bournemouth 22 – Portsmouth 41 – Salisbury 27 – Southampton 17.

🍴 **The Boathouse**, 29 Shamrock Way, Hythe Marina Village, SO45 6DY, ℰ (01703) 845594,
Fax (01703) 846017, ≼, ⛲ – ≣ ℗. ⒶⓈ *VISA*
closed Sunday dinner, Monday and first 2 weeks February – **Meals** - Brasserie - 10.50 **st.**
(lunch) and a la carte 16.00/20.50 **st.**

HYTHE *Kent* **404** X 30 – *pop. 14 569.*
🅑 *Sene Valley, Sene, Folkestone* ℰ (01303) 268513.
🅑 *En Route Travel, Red Lion Sq., CT21 5AU* ℰ (01303) 267799 (summer only).
London 68 – Folkestone 6 – Hastings 33 – Maidstone 31.

Plan : see Folkestone

🏛️ **Hythe Imperial,** Prince's Par., CT21 6AE, ℰ (01303) 267441, Fax (01303) 264610, ≤, ₤₆, ≘ₛ, 🏊, 🏌, 🎯, ✕, squash – 📱, ⊱ rest, 📺 ☎ ⅙ ℗ – 🕍 250. 🆎 ℹ️ 🆅🆂🅰. 🕸
The Restaurant : Meals 16.00/22.00 **t.** and a la carte – *Churchills :* Meals a la carte approx. 12.80 **t.** – 🖙 8.50 – **98 rm** 85.00/100.00 **t.,** 2 suites – SB.   X d

🏛️ **Stade Court,** West Par., CT21 6DT, ℰ (01303) 268263, Fax (01303) 261803, ≤ – 📱, ⊱ rm, 📺 ☎ ℗ – 🕍 35. 🆎 ℹ️ 🆅🆂🅰. 🕸
Meals 12.95/17.50 **t.** and a la carte ᵢ 6.60 – 🖙 9.50 – **42 rm** 59.00/79.00 **t.** – SB.

IBSTONE Bucks 🆄🅾🅰 R 29 – pop. 254 – ⊠ High Wycombe.
London 39 – Oxford 20 – Reading 19.

🏠 **Fox of Ibstone Country,** HP14 3GG, ℰ (01491) 638722, Fax (01491) 638873, 🎯 – 📺 ℗ ℗. 🆎 ℹ️ 🆅🆂🅰. 🕸
closed 25-26 December and 1 January – Meals (in bar Sunday dinner) a la carte 16.00/21.00 **t.** ᵢ 5.00 – **9 rm** 🖙 45.00/76.00 **t.**

IDE Devon 🆄🅾🅳 J 31 – see Exeter.

IFFLEY Oxon – see Oxford.

ILCHESTER Somerset 🆄🅾🅳 L 30 – pop. 1 733.
London 138 – Bridgwater 21 – Exeter 48 – Taunton 24 – Yeovil 5.

🏠 **Ilchester Arms,** The Square, BA22 8LN, ℰ (01935) 840220, Fax (01935) 841353 – 📺 ☎ ℗. 🆎 🆅🆂🅰. 🕸
closed 25 December – Meals a la carte 12.15/23.40 **t.** ᵢ 4.50 – **8 rm** 🖙 49.50/67.50 – SB.

ILKLEY W. Yorks. 🆄🅾🅽 O 22 – pop. 13 530.
🏌 Myddleton ℰ (01943) 607277.
🅑 Station Rd, LS29 8HA ℰ (01943) 602319.
London 210 – Bradford 13 – Harrogate 17 – Leeds 16 – Preston 46.

🏛️ **Rombalds,** 11 West View, Wells Rd, LS29 9JG, ℰ (01943) 603201, Fax (01943) 816586 – ⊱ 📺 ☎ ℗ – 🕍 50. 🆎 ℹ️ 🆅🆂🅰 🅹🅲🅱
closed 27 to 29 December – Meals a la carte 12.70/20.00 **st.** ᵢ 6.25 – **11 rm** 🖙 67.50/97.50 **st.,** 4 suites – SB.

🏠 **Grove,** 66 The Grove, LS29 9PA, ℰ (01943) 600298, Fax (01943) 600298 – ⊱ rest, 📺 ☎ ℗. 🆎 ℹ️ 🆅🆂🅰 🅹🅲🅱
closed 1 week Christmas – Meals (bar lunch)/dinner 13.50 **st.** ᵢ 5.00 – **6 rm** 🖙 39.00/54.00 **st.** – SB.

✕✕✕ **Box Tree,** 37 Church St., LS29 9DR, ℰ (01943) 608484, Fax (01943) 607186, « 18C stone
❀ farmhouse, collection of paintings, sculpture and objets d'art » – 🆎 ℹ️ 🆅🆂🅰
closed Sunday dinner, Monday, last 2 weeks January and 26 to 30 December – Meals 22.50/29.50 **st.** and lunch a la carte 22.50/72.00 **st.** ᵢ 6.60
Spec. Sautéed scallops served with a fruit chutney and lemon sauce. Roasted calves sweetbreads with broad beans and hazelnut oil. Fillet of lamb with a herb crust and a tomato and rosemary sauce.

ILLOGAN Cornwall 🆄🅾🅳 E 33 The West Country G. – pop. 13 095 – ⊠ Redruth.
Env. : Portreath★, NW : 2 m. by B 3300 – Hell's Mouth★, SW : 5 m. by B 3301.
London 305 – Falmouth 14 – Penzance 17 – Truro 11.

🏠 **Aviary Court** ⅛, Mary's Well, TR16 4QZ, NW : ¾ m. by Alexandra Rd ℰ (01209) 842256 Fax (01209) 843744, 🎯 – ⊱ rest, 📺 ☎ ℗. 🆎 🆅🆂🅰. 🕸
Meals (dinner only and Sunday lunch)/dinner 13.00 **t.** and a la carte ᵢ 5.25 – **6 rm** 🖙 42.00/60.00 **t.**

ILMINSTER Somerset 🆄🅾🅳 L 31 The West Country G. – pop. 4 162.
See : Town★ – Minster★★.
Env. : Barrington Court Gardens★ AC, NE : 3 ½ m. by B 3168 – Chard (Museum★), S : 6 m by B 3168 and A 358.
London 145 – Taunton 12 – Yeovil 17.

🏠 **Travelodge,** Southfield Roundabout, Horton Cross, TA19 9PT, NW : 1 ½ m. at junction c A 303 with A 358 ℰ (01460) 53748, Reservations (Freephone) 0800 850950 – 📺 ⅙ ℗. 🆎 🅰 ℹ️ 🆅🆂🅰 🅹🅲🅱. 🕸
32 rm 44.95 **t.**

IMPINGTON *Cambs. – see Cambridge.*

INGATESTONE *Essex* [404] V 28 – *pop. 6 002* – ✉ *Chelmsford.*
London 27 – Chelmsford 6.

🏨 **Ivy Hill,** Writtle Rd, Margaretting, CM4 0EH, NE : 2 ¼ m. by A 12 ✆ (01277) 353040, *Fax (01277) 355038,* 🏊, 🌳, 🎾 – [TV] ☎ [P] – 🎤 80. [MC] [AE] [D] [VISA]. 🚫
Meals *(closed Saturday lunch and Sunday dinner)* 21.95 **t.** and a la carte 🍷 7.75 – **34 rm** ☕ 85.00/120.00 **t.**

INGLEBY GREENHOW *N. Yorks.* [402] Q 20 – *pop. 391.*
London 262 – Darlington 28 – Leeds 62 – Middlesbrough 12 – Scarborough 50 – York 49.

🏠 **Manor House Farm** 🌿, TS9 6RB, S : 1 m. via lane to manor, next to church ✆ (01642) 722384, ≤, « Working farm », 🌳 – 🚭 [P]. [MC] [VISA] [JCB]. 🚫
closed 20 to 29 December – **Meals** (by arrangement) 🍷 5.95 – **3 rm** ☕ (dinner included) 53.00/86.00 **st.** – SB.

INGLETON *N. Yorks.* [402] M 21 – *pop. 1 979* – ✉ *Carnforth (Lancs.).*
ℹ *Community Centre Car Park, LA6 3HG ✆ (015242) 41049 (summer only).*
London 266 – Kendal 21 – Lancaster 18 – Leeds 53.

🏨 **Pines Country House,** Kendal Rd, LA6 3HN, NW : ¼ m. on A 65 ✆ (015242) 41252, *Fax (015242) 41252,* 🏊, 🌳 – 🚭 [TV] [P]. [MC] [VISA]
closed December and January – **Meals** (booking essential) (residents only) (dinner only) 13.50 **st.** 🍷 4.00 – **8 rm** ☕ 34.00/52.00 **s.** – SB.

🏠 **Ferncliffe House,** 55 Main St., LA6 3HJ, ✆ (015242) 42405 – 🚭 rest, [TV] [P]. [MC] [VISA]
restricted opening in winter – **Meals** 12.50 **st.** – **5 rm** ☕ 28.00/44.00 **st.** – SB.

🏠 **Riverside Lodge** without rest., 24 Main St., LA6 3HJ, ✆ (015242) 41359, ≤, 🏊, 🎣, 🌳 – 🚭 [TV] [P]. [MC] [VISA]
closed 25 December – **8 rm** ☕ 32.00/44.00.

INSTOW *Devon* [403] H 30 – *see Bideford.*

IPSWICH *Suffolk* [404] X 27 *Great Britain G.* – *pop. 130 157.*
See : *Christchurch Mansion (collection of paintings★)* X B.
⛳18 *Rushmere, Rushmere Heath ✆ (01473) 727109* – ⛳18, ⛳9 *Purdis Heath, Bucklesham Rd ✆ (01473) 727474* – ⛳18 *Fynn Valley, Witnesham ✆ (01473) 785267.*
ℹ *St. Stephens Church, St. Stephens Lane, IP1 1DP ✆ (01473) 258070.*
London 76 – Norwich 43.

Plan on next page

🏨 **Belstead Brook Manor,** Belstead Rd, IP2 9HB, SW : 2 ½ m. ✆ (01473) 684241, *Fax (01473) 681249,* 🏋, 🏊, 🏊, 🌳 – 🛗 🚭 [TV] ☎ ♿ [P] – 🎤 200. [MC] [AE] [D] [VISA] Z u
Meals *(closed Saturday lunch)* 20.00 **st.** and a la carte 🍷 8.95 – ☕ 9.75 – **74 rm** 79.00/85.00 **st.**, 2 suites – SB.

🏨 **Courtyard by Marriott Ipswich,** The Havens, Ransomes Europark, IP3 9SJ, SE : 3 ½ m. by A 1156 and Nacton Rd at junction with A 14 ✆ (01473) 272244, *Fax (01473) 272484,* 🏋 – 🛗, 🚭 rm, ❄ rest, [TV] ☎ ♿ [P] – 🎤 180. [MC] [AE] [D] [VISA] [JCB]. 🚫
Meals 14.00/18.00 **st.** and a la carte 🍷 6.95 – ☕ 8.95 – **60 rm** 59.00/75.00 **st.** – SB.

🏨 **Marlborough,** Henley Rd, IP1 3SP, ✆ (01473) 257677, *Fax (01473) 226927,* 🌳 – 🚭 rest, [TV] ☎ [P] – 🎤 50. [MC] [AE] [D] [VISA] Y e
Meals 14.50/19.85 **t.** and a la carte 🍷 8.65 – ☕ 10.15 – **21 rm** 65.00/68.00 **t.**, 1 suite – SB.

🏨 **Novotel,** Greyfriars Rd, IP1 1UP, ✆ (01473) 232400, *Fax (01473) 232414* – 🛗, 🚭 rm, [TV] ☎ ♿ [P] – 🎤 180. [MC] [AE] [D] [VISA] [JCB] X c
Meals 14.00 **st.** and a la carte 🍷 5.95 – ☕ 8.75 – **100 rm** 72.50 **st.** – SB.

🏨 **Highview House,** 56 Belstead Rd, IP2 8BE, ✆ (01473) 601620, *Fax (01473) 688659,* 🌳 – [TV] ☎ [P]. [MC] [VISA] [JCB]. 🚫 Z c
Meals *(closed Friday to Sunday)* (dinner only) a la carte 7.95/13.40 **st.** – **11 rm** ☕ 33.00/45.00 **st.**

🏨 **Travel Inn,** Bourne Hill, Wherstead, IP2 8ND, S : 1 ¾ m. by A 137 (Wherstead Rd) ✆ (01473) 692372, *Fax (01473) 692283* – 🚭 rm, [TV] ♿ [P]. [MC] [AE] [D] [VISA]
Meals (grill rest.) – **40 rm** 36.50 **t.**

🏠 **Mount Pleasant** without rest., 103 Anglesea Rd, IP1 3PJ, ✆ (01473) 251601, *Fax (01473) 252198,* 🌳 – [TV] [P] Y a
closed 24 December-2 January – **3 rm** ☕ 30.00/50.00 **s.**

IPSWICH

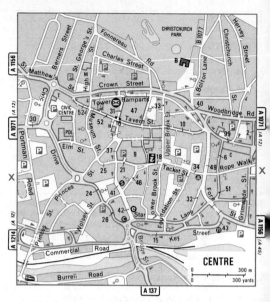

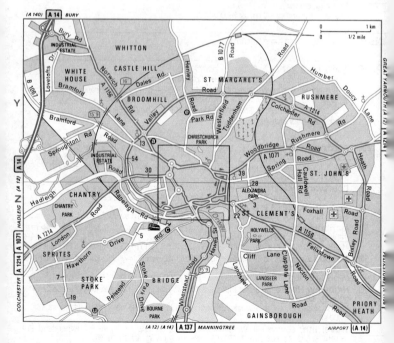

Europe

If the name of the hotel
is not in bold type,
on arrival ask the hotelier his prices.

300

XX **Dhaka,** 6 Orwell Pl., IP4 1BB, 𝒫 (01473) 251397 – **◑◉** 🄰🄴 _VISA_   X a
closed 25 and 26 December – **Meals** - Indian - 6.95/16.50 and a la carte.

X **Mortimer's on the Quay,** Wherry Quay, IP4 1AS, 𝒫 (01473) 230225,
Fax (01473) 761611 – **◑◉** 🄰🄴 ⓪ _VISA_ 🄹🄲🄱   X n
*closed Saturday lunch, Sunday, 2 weeks late August, 24 December-6 January and 2 days at
Bank Holidays* – **Meals** - Seafood - a la carte 15.15/25.85 t. ⓵ 4.50.

X **Galley,** 25 St. Nicholas St., IP1 1TW, 𝒫 (01473) 281131, *Fax* (01473) 281131, 🌂 – ⇔, **◑◉**
🄰🄴 _VISA_ _VISA_   X s
closed Sunday and Bank Holidays – **Meals** a la carte 15.95/22.95 t. ⓵ 6.95.

at Claydon NW : 4½ m. by A 1156 off A 14 – Y – ✉ Ipswich.

🏨 **Claydon Country House,** 16-18 Ipswich Rd, IP6 0AR, 𝒫 (01473) 830382,
Fax (01473) 832476, 🌿 – 📺 ☎ 🄿. **◑◉** 🄰🄴 _VISA_. ⅍
closed 26 December-2 January – **Meals** a la carte 12.85/22.85 t. ⓵ 7.50 – **14 rm** ⌸ 54.00/
59.00 t. – SB.

🏠 **Travel Inn,** Mockbeggars Hall Farm, Paper Mill Lane, IP6 0AP, SW : ½ m. off A 14 round-
about 𝒫 (01473) 833125, *Fax* (01473) 833127 – |⟊|, ⇔ rm, 📺 ⅋ 🄿. **◑◉** 🄰🄴 ⓪ _VISA_
Meals (dinner only) – **59 rm** 36.50 t.

at Holbrook S : 5¾ m. by A 137 – Z – and B 1456 on B 1080 – ✉ Ipswich.

⋔ **Highfield** ◕ without rest., Harkstead Rd, IP9 2RA, E : ½ m. by Fishponds Lane
𝒫 (01473) 328250, ≼, 🌿 – ⇔ 📺 🄿
closed Christmas-New Year – **3 rm** ⌸ 27.00/42.00.

at Copdock SW : 4 m. by A 1214 off A 1071 – Z – ✉ Ipswich.

🏨 **County H. Ipswich,** London Rd, IP8 3JD, 𝒫 (01473) 209988, *Fax* (01473) 730801, 🕩, 🛱
– |⟊| rm, 📺 ☎ ⅋ 🄿 – ⚖ 500. **◑◉** 🄰🄴 ⓪ _VISA_. ⅍
Meals 14.50 st. and a la carte ⓵ 5.50 – ⌸ 8.95 – **73 rm** 70.00/85.00 st. – SB.

at Burstall W : 4½ m. by A 1214 off A 1071 – Y – ✉ Ipswich.

⋔ **Mulberry Hall** ◕, IP8 3DP, 𝒫 (01473) 652348, *Fax* (01473) 652110, « 16C farmhouse »,
🌿, ⅍ – ⇔ 🄿. ⅍
closed 1 week Christmas – **Meals** (by arrangement) (communal dining) 15.00 s. – **3 rm**
⌸ 18.00/36.00 st.

at Hintlesham W : 5 m. by A 1214 on A 1071 – Y – ✉ Ipswich.

🏨 **Hintlesham Hall** ◕, IP8 3NS, 𝒫 (01473) 652334, *Fax* (01473) 652463, ≼, « Georgian
country house of 16C origins », 🕩, 🛱, ⚒, 🛁, ⅊, 🌿, park, ⅍ – ⇔ rest, 📺 ☎ 🄿 –
⚖ 80. **◑◉** 🄰🄴 ⓪ _VISA_. ⅍
Meals (residents only Saturday lunch) 19.50/25.00 st. and a la carte 29.25/43.25 st. ⓵ 6.50 –
⌸ 7.50 – **29 rm** 89.00/210.00 st., 4 suites – SB.

     🅐 ATS White Elm St. 𝒫 (01473) 217157

IREBY Cumbria 🄼🄾🄸 🄼🄾🄸 K 19 – *see Bassenthwaite.*

IRON BRIDGE Wrekin 🄼🄾🄸 🄼🄾🄸 M 26 *Great Britain G.* – *pop. 2 184.*
See : *Ironbridge Gorge Museum** AC (The Iron Bridge**, Coalport China Museum**,
Blists Hill Open Air Museum**, Museum of the River and visitors centre*).
🄴 4 The Wharfage, TF8 7AW 𝒫 (01952) 432166.
London 135 – Birmingham 36 – Shrewsbury 18.

🏨 **Valley,** Buildwas Rd, TF7 8DW, on B 4380 𝒫 (01952) 432727, *Fax* (01952) 432308, 🌿 –
⇔ rest, 📺 ☎ ⅋ 🄿 – ⚖ 250. **◑◉** 🄰🄴 ⓪ _VISA_. ⅍
closed 26 December-1 January – **Meals** 18.50 st. and a la carte ⓵ 4.50 – **35 rm** ⌸ 67.00/
80.00 st. – SB.

⋔ **Severn Lodge** ◕ without rest., New Rd, TF8 7AS, 𝒫 (01952) 432148,
Fax (01952) 432148, 🌿 – ⇔ 📺 🄿. ⅍
closed 24 to 27 December – **3 rm** ⌸ 39.00/52.00 st.

⋔ **Bridge House** without rest., Buildwas, TF8 7BN, W : 2 m. on B 4380 𝒫 (01952) 432105,
« 17C cottage », 🌿 – 🄿. ⅍
closed Christmas-New Year – **4 rm** ⌸ 32.00/52.00.

ISLE OF MAN 🄼🄾🄸 FG 21 – *see Man (Isle of).*

IVY HATCH Kent – *see Sevenoaks.*

IXWORTH Suffolk 404 W 27 – see Bury St. Edmunds.

JERSEY 403 OP 33 and 230 ⑩ ⑪ – see Channel Islands.

JEVINGTON E. Sussex 404 U 31 – see Eastbourne.

KEDLESTON Derbs. 402 403 404 P 25 – see Derby.

KEIGHLEY W. Yorks. 402 O 22 – pop. 49 567.

⯈ Branshaw, Branshaw Moor, Oakworth ℰ (01535) 643235 – ⯈ Riddlesden, Howden Rough ℰ (01535) 602148.

London 200 – Bradford 10 – Burnley 20.

🏨 **Beeches,** Bradford Rd, BD21 4BB, ℰ (01535) 610611, Fax (01535) 610037 – ⇥ 📺 ☎ ℷ. **℗** – ⚇ 30. ⬢ 🆎 𝘝𝘐𝘚𝘈. ℀
closed 25 and 26 December – **Meals** (grill rest.) a la carte approx. 12.00 **st.** – **43 rm** ⚏ 60.00/70.00 **st.** – SB.

🏨 **Dalesgate,** 406 Skipton Rd, Utley, BD20 6HP, ℰ (01535) 664930, Fax (01535) 611253 – 📺 ☎ ℗. ⬢ 🆎 ① 𝘝𝘐𝘚𝘈
closed 10 days Christmas – **Meals** (closed Sunday) (dinner only) 11.50 and a la carte – **19 rm** ⚏ 42.00/60.00 **st.** – SB.

⑪ ATS 69-73 Bradford Rd, Riddlesden ℰ (01535) 607533/607933

Le Guide change, changez de **guide Michelin** *tous les ans.*

KELSALE Suffolk – pop. 1 309 – ⬚ Saxmundham
London 103 – Cambridge 68 – Ipswich 23 – Norwich 37.

⯅ **Mile Hill Barn,** North Green, IP17 2RG, N : 1 ½ m. on (main) A 12 ℰ (01728) 668519, 🚗 – ⇥ 📺 ℗
Meals (by arrangement) 13.00 **s.** – **3 rm** ⚏ 45.00/55.00 **s.**

✕ **Hedgehogs,** IP17 2RF, N : 1 m. on (main) A 12 ℰ (01728) 604444, Fax (01728) 604499, « 16C house » – ⇥ ℗. ⬢ 🆎 𝘝𝘐𝘚𝘈
closed Monday lunch, Sunday dinner and 2 to 15 January – **Meals** 9.95 **t.** and dinner a la carte 14.60/19.75 **t.**

KEMBLE Glos. 403 404 N 28 – see Cirencester.

KEMERTON Glos. – see Tewkesbury.

KENDAL Cumbria 402 L 21 Great Britain G. – pop. 25 461.
Env. : Levens Hall and Garden★ AC, S : 4 ½ m. by A 591, A 590 and A 6.
Exc. : Lake Windermere★★, NW : 8 m. by A 5284 and A 591.
⯈ The Heights ℰ (01539) 724079.
🄷 Town Hall, Highgate, LA9 4DL ℰ (01539) 725758.
London 270 – Bradford 64 – Burnley 63 – Carlisle 49 – Lancaster 22 – Leeds 72 – Middlesbrough 77 – Newcastle upon Tyne 104 – Preston 44 – Sunderland 88.

🏨 **Stonecross Manor,** Milnthorpe Rd, LA9 5HP, S : 1 ½ m. on A 6 ℰ (01539) 733559, Fax (01539) 736386, ⬒, 🔲 – 🛗 📺 ☎ ℗ – ⚇ 140. ⬢ 🆎 ① 𝘝𝘐𝘚𝘈. ℀
Meals (bar lunch Monday to Saturday)/dinner 17.50 **t.** �ℷ 6.75 – **30 rm** ⚏ 57.00/98.00 **st.** – SB.

🏨 **Lane Head House,** Helsington, LA9 5RJ, S : 2 m. off A 6 ℰ (01539) 731283, Fax (01539) 721023, ≤, 🚗 – ⇥ 📺 ☎ ℗. ⬢ 🆎 𝘝𝘐𝘚𝘈 𝘑𝘊𝘉
Meals (dinner only) 17.00 ℷ 5.20 – **6 rm** ⚏ 35.00/70.00 – SB.

⯅ **Burrow Hall** without rest., Plantation Bridge, LA8 9JR, NW : 3 ¼ m. by A 5284 on A 591 ℰ (01539) 821711, 🚗 – ⇥ 📺 ℗. ⬢ 🆎 𝘝𝘐𝘚𝘈 𝘑𝘊𝘉
March-November – **3 rm** ⚏ 30.00/44.00 **st.**, 1 suite.

at Selside N : 6 m. on A 6 – ⬚ Kendal.

⯅ **Low Jock Scar** ⬙, LA8 9LE, off A 6 ℰ (01539) 823259, Fax (01539) 823259, 🚗 – ⇥ ℗
March-October – **Meals** (by arrangement) 15.50 **st.** ℷ 4.00 – **5 rm** ⚏ 30.00/54.00 **st.**

at Underbarrow W : 3½ m. via All Hallows Lane on Crosthwaite rd – ✉ Kendal.

⬠ **Tullythwaite House** ⬱, LA8 8BB, S : ¾ m. by Brigster rd ℘ (015395) 68397, ≤,
« Georgian house », ☞ – ⇚ rest, 📺 **❶**
closed December and January and booking essential February – **Meals** (by arrangement)
13.00 – **3 rm** �□ 27.00/48.00.

at Crosthwaite W : 5¼ m. via All Hallows Lane on Crosthwaite rd – ✉ Kendal.

⬠ **Crosthwaite House,** LA8 8BP, ℘ (015395) 68264, ≤ – ⇚ rest, 📺. 🄰🄴
February-mid November – **Meals** (by arrangement) 12.00 **st.** ⓘ 5.00 – **6 rm** �□ 22.00/
44.00 **st.**

🏠 **Punch Bowl Inn** with rm, LA8 8HR, ℘ (015395) 68237, *Fax (015395) 68875* – ⇚ 📺 **❶**.
🄌 🆅🆂🅰. ⬱
closed 25-26 December and 1 January – **Meals** (booking essential) a la carte 13.40/18.50 **st.**
ⓘ 6.00 – **3 rm** �□ 35.00/50.00 **st.**

🄌 ATS Mintsfeet Est. ℘ (01539) 721559

KENILWORTH Warks. 🄸🄾🄸 🄸🄾🄸 P 26 *Great Britain G.* – *pop. 21 623.*
See : *Castle★ AC.*
🄱 *The Library, 11 Smalley Pl., CV8 1QG ℘ (01926) 852595.*
London 102 – Birmingham 19 – Coventry 5 – Warwick 5.

🏨 **De Montfort,** The Square, CV8 1ED, ℘ (01926) 855944, *Fax (01926) 857830* – 🛗 ⇚ 📺 ☎
❶ – 🔬 300. 🄌 🄰🄴 🆅🆂🅰
Meals 12.50/19.95 **st.** and a la carte ⓘ 5.95 – �□ 9.25 – **105 rm** 99.00/115.00 **st.** – SB.

🏨 **Chesford Grange,** Chesford Bridge, CV8 2LD, SE : 1 ¾ m. on A 452 ℘ (01926) 859331,
Fax (01926) 859075, 🕰, 🔲, ☞, park – 🛗, ⇚ rm, 📺 ☎ **❶** – 🔬 860. 🄌 🄰🄴 🄾 🆅🆂🅰
Meals *(closed Saturday lunch)* 16.50 **st.** and a la carte ⓘ 5.25 – **154 rm** �□ 95.00/135.00 **st.** –
SB.

🏠 **Victoria Lodge,** 180 Warwick Rd, CV8 1HU, ℘ (01926) 512020, *Fax (01926) 858703,* ☞ –
⇚ 📺 ☎ **❶**. 🄌 🄰🄴 🆅🆂🅰 🅹🅲🅱. ⬱
Meals (dinner only) 14.95 **st.** ⓘ 2.75 – **7 rm** �□ 37.50/52.50 **st.**

🏠 **Castle Laurels,** 22 Castle Rd, CV8 1NG, ℘ (01926) 856179, *Fax (01926) 854954* – ⇚ 📺
☎ **❶**. 🄌 🆅🆂🅰. ⬱
closed 21 December-1 January – **Meals** (residents only) (dinner only) 12.25 **t.** ⓘ 5.30 – **12 rm**
�□ 33.60/53.50 **st.** – SB.

⬠ **Abbey** without rest., 41 Station Rd, CV8 1JD, ℘ (01926) 512707, *Fax (01926) 859148* – ⇚
📺. ⬱
7 rm �□ 21.00/42.00.

🆇🆇 **Simpson's,** 101-103 Warwick Rd, CV8 1HL, ℘ (01926) 864567, *Fax (01926) 864510* – ▤ **❶**.
🄌 🄰🄴 🄾 🆅🆂🅰 🅹🅲🅱
closed Saturday lunch, Sunday, 24 to 27 December, 1 January and Bank Holidays – **Meals** 15.00/23.50 **t.** ⓘ 6.95.

🆇🆇 **Bosquet,** 97a Warwick Rd, CV8 1HP, ℘ (01926) 852463 – 🄌 🄰🄴 🆅🆂🅰 🅹🅲🅱
closed Sunday, Monday, 3 weeks August and 1 week Christmas – **Meals** - French - (lunch by
arrangement) 22.00 **t.** and a la carte ⓘ 5.75.

KENNFORD Devon 🄸🄾🄸 J 32 – *see Exeter.*

KERNE BRIDGE Herefordshire – *see Ross-on-Wye.*

KESWICK Cumbria 🄸🄾🄸 K 20 *Great Britain G.* – *pop. 4 836.*
Env. : *Derwentwater★ X – Thirlmere (Castlerigg Stone Circle★), E : 1 ½ m. X A.*
🄱 *Threlkeld Hall ℘ (017687) 79324/79010.*
🄱 *Moot Hall, Market Sq., CA12 5JR ℘ (017687) 72645 – at Seatoller, Seatoller Barn, Borrow-
dale, Keswick, CA12 5XN ℘ (017687) 77294 (summer only).*
London 294 – Carlisle 31 – Kendal 30.

Plan on next page

🏨 **Underscar Manor** ⬱, Applethwaite, CA12 4PH, N : 1 ¾ m. by A 591 on Underscar rd
℘ (017687) 75000, *Fax (017687) 74904,* ≤ Derwent Water and Fells, « Victorian Italianate
country house », ☞, park – 📺 ☎ **❶**. 🄌 🄰🄴 🆅🆂🅰. ⬱
Meals – (see below) – **11 rm** �□ (dinner included) 95.00/250.00 **t.** – SB.

KESWICK

North is at the top on all town plans.

Les plans de villes sont disposés le Nord en haut.

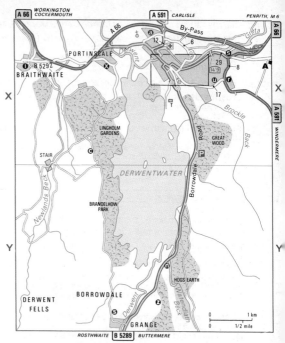

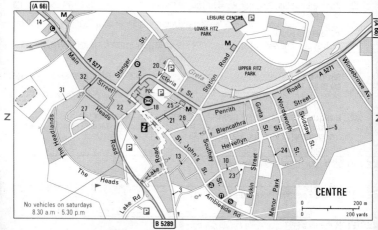

🏨 **Lyzzick Hall** ⚘, Underskiddaw, CA12 4PY, NW : 2 ½ m. on A 591 ℰ (017687) 72277 *Fax (017687) 72278*, ≤, ⇌s, ⬚, ⚘ – ⅍ rest, 📺 ☎ 🅿. 🅼🅲 🅰🅴 *VISA* 🅹🅲🅱. ⅍ *closed 24 to 26 December and 4 weeks late January-early February* – **Meals** 10.75. 14.00 **t.** and a la carte ⦙ 4.60 – **29 rm** ⇌ 40.00/84.00 **t.**

🏛 **Dale Head Hall Lakeside** ⚘, Thirlmere, CA12 4TN, SE : 5 ¾ m. on A 59 ℰ (017687) 72478, *Fax (017687) 71070*, ≤ Lake Thirlmere, « Lakeside setting », ⚘, ⚘ ⅍ ☎ 🅿. 🅼🅲 🅰🅴 *VISA* 🅹🅲🅱. ⅍ *closed January* – **Meals** (dinner only) 25.00 **st.** ⦙ 7.00 – **9 rm** ⇌ (dinner included) 87.50 125.00 **st.** – SB.

Grange Country House 🔇, Manor Brow, Ambleside Rd, CA12 4BA, ☎ (017687) 72500, ≤, 🌳 – 🚭 [TV] ☎ [P]. [MC] [VISA] X u
5 March-4 November – **Meals** (light lunch)/dinner 19.00 **st.** 🍷 6.25 – **10 rm** ☕ (dinner included) 62.50/105.00 **st.** – SB.

Applethwaite Country House 🔇, Underskiddaw, CA12 4PL, NW : 1 ¾ m. by A 591 on Ormathwaite rd ☎ (017687) 72413, *Fax (017687) 75706*, ≤, 🌳 – 🚭 [TV] [P]. [MC] [VISA]. 🐕
16 February-November – **Meals** (dinner only) 16.50 **t.** 🍷 4.95 – **12 rm** ☕ 33.00/66.00 **t.** – SB.

Lairbeck 🔇, Vicarage Hill, CA12 5QB, ☎ (017687) 73373, 🌳 – 🚭 [TV] ☎ [P]. [MC] [VISA]. 🐕 X a
closed January and February – **Meals** (dinner only) 14.00 **st.** 🍷 6.00 – **14 rm** ☕ 34.00/68.00 **st.** – SB.

Chaucer House, Derwentwater Pl., CA12 4DR, ☎ (017687) 72318, *Fax (017687) 75551* – |‡|, 🚭 rest, [TV] [P]. [MC] [AE] [VISA] [JCB] Z a
closed December and January – **Meals** (lunch by arrangement)/dinner 17.00 **t.** and a la carte 🍷 5.75 – **34 rm** ☕ 38.00/70.00 **t.** – SB.

Brackenrigg Country House, Thirlmere, CA12 4TF, SE : 3 m. on A 591 ☎ (017687) 72258, 🌳 – 🚭 rest, [TV] [P]. 🐕
Easter-October – **Meals** (by arrangement) 16.00 – **6 rm** ☕ 26.00/54.00 – SB.

Craglands, Penrith Rd, CA12 4LJ, ☎ (017687) 74406, ≤ – 🚭 [TV] [P]. 🐕 X s
closed Christmas and restricted bookings in winter – **Meals** (by arrangement) 19.50 **st.** – **5 rm** ☕ 30.00/50.00.

Acorn House without rest., Ambleside Rd, CA12 4DL, ☎ (017687) 72553, *Fax (017687) 75332* – 🚭 [TV] [P]. [MC] [VISA]. 🐕 Z s
closed January and November – **10 rm** ☕ 35.00/60.00 **st.**

Abacourt House without rest., 26 Stanger St., CA12 5JU, ☎ (017687) 72967 – 🚭 [TV] [P]
5 rm ☕ 42.00 **st.** Z e

Claremont House, Chestnut Hill, CA12 4LT, ☎ (017687) 72089, ≤, 🌳 – 🚭 rest, [P]. 🐕
closed 24 to 26 December – **Meals** (by arrangement) 11.70/19.00 **s.** 🍷 5.95 – **5 rm** ☕ 39.00/52.00 **s.** – SB. X r

Greystones without rest., Ambleside Rd, CA12 4DP, ☎ (017687) 73108 – 🚭 [TV] [P]. [MC] [VISA]. 🐕 Z n
closed December – **8 rm** ☕ 23.50/47.00 **st.**

🍴🍴🍴 **Underscar Manor** (at Underscar Manor H.), Applethwaite, CA12 4PH, N : 1 ¾ m. by A 591 on Underscar rd ☎ (017687) 75000, *Fax (017687) 74904*, ≤ Derwent Water and Fells, « Victorian Italianate country house », 🌳, park – 🚭 [P]. [MC] [AE] [VISA]
Meals 21.00 **t.** (lunch) and a la carte 30.00/36.00 **t.** 🍷 7.00.

at Threlkeld *E : 4 m. by A 66 – X – ✉ Keswick.*

Scales Farm without rest., CA12 4SY, NE : 1 ¾ m. off A 66 ☎ (017687) 79660, *Fax (017687) 79660*, « Part 17C », 🌳 – 🚭 [TV] [P]
closed Christmas – **5 rm** ☕ 26.00/46.00 – SB.

at Borrowdale *S : on B 5289 – ✉ Keswick.*

Stakis Keswick Lodore, CA12 5UX, ☎ (017687) 77285, *Fax (017687) 77343*, ≤, 🏋, ≘s, 🏊, 🏊, 🌳, park, 🎾, squash – |‡|, 🚭 rest, [TV] ☎ 🚗 [P] – 🏛 70. [MC] [AE] [DC] [VISA]. 🐕 Y n
Meals (bar lunch Monday to Saturday)/dinner a la carte 8.00/22.50 **st.** 🍷 9.00 – **74 rm** ☕ (dinner included) 77.00/152.00 **st.**, 1 suite – SB.

Greenbank Country House 🔇, CA12 5UY, ☎ (017687) 77215, *Fax (017687) 77215*, ≤, 🌳 – 🚭 rm, [P]. [MC] [VISA]. 🐕 Y z
closed January and December – **Meals** (residents only) (dinner only) 12.00 **t.** 🍷 4.30 – **10 rm** ☕ (dinner included) 42.00/84.00 **st.** – SB.

at Grange-in-Borrowdale *S : 4 ¾ m. by B 5289 – ✉ Keswick.*

Borrowdale Gates Country House 🔇, CA12 5UQ, ☎ (017687) 77204, *Fax (017687) 77254*, ≤ Borrowdale Valley, 🌳 – 🚭 rest, [TV] ☎ [P]. [MC] [AE] [VISA]. 🐕 Y s
closed January and 7 to 17 December – **Meals** 14.00/25.50 **t.** and lunch a la carte 🍷 6.75 – **28 rm** ☕ (dinner included) 75.00/145.00 **t.**

at Rosthwaite *S : 6 m. on B 5289 – Y – ✉ Keswick.*

Hazel Bank 🔇, CA12 5XB, ☎ (017687) 77248, *Fax (017687) 77373*, ≤, 🌳 – 🚭 [TV] [P]. [MC] [VISA] [JCB]
April-October – **Meals** (residents only) (dinner only) 🍷 3.90 – **6 rm** ☕ (dinner included) 46.00/92.00 **st.**

at Seatoller *S : 8 m. on B 5289* – Y – ✉ *Keswick.*

🏠 **Seatoller House,** CA12 5XN, ✆ (017687) 77218, ⇐ Borrowdale, 🌳 – 🚭 [P]
April-October – **Meals** (by arrangement) (communal dining) 10.00 **t.** 🍾 7.00 – **9 rm** 🛏 28.50/55.00 **t.**

at Portinscale *W : 1½ m. by A 66* – ✉ *Keswick.*

🏠 **Swinside Lodge** 🪑, Newlands, CA12 5UE, S : 1 ½ m. on Grange Rd ✆ (017687) 72948, *Fax (017687) 72948,* ⇐ Catbells and Causey Pike, 🌳 – 🚭 [TV] [P]. 🚫🐕 X c
closed December except 4 days Christmas-mid February – **Meals** (booking essential) (dinner only) (unlicensed) 25.00 **t.** – **7 rm** 🛏 (dinner included) 72.00/160.00 **t.** – SB.

🏠 **Derwent Cottage** 🪑, CA12 5RF, ✆ (017687) 74838, 🌳 – 🚭 [TV] [P]. [MC] [VISA] [JCB]. 🚫🐕 X x
March-October – **Meals** (by arrangement) 14.00 **st.** 🍾 3.50 – **6 rm** 🛏 41.00/72.00 **st.** – SB.

at Braithwaite *W : 2 m. by A 66 on B 5292* – ✉ *Keswick.*

🏠 **Ivy House,** CA12 5SY, ✆ (017687) 78338, *Fax (017687) 78113* – 🚭 rest, [TV] ☎ [P]. [MC] [AE] [D] [VISA] [JCB] X i
closed January – **Meals** (dinner only) 21.95 **t.** 🍾 5.25 – **12 rm** 🛏 37.00/84.00 **t.**

🏠 **Cottage in The Wood** 🪑, Whinlatter Pass, CA12 5TW, NW : 1 ¾ m. on B 5292 ✆ (017687) 78409, ⇐, 🌳 – 🚭 [P]. [MC] [VISA] [JCB]
mid March-mid November – **Meals** (dinner only) 16.50 **st.** 🍾 5.00 – **7 rm** 🛏 (dinner included) 58.00/92.00 **st.**

at Thornthwaite *W : 3½ m. by A 66* – X – ✉ *Keswick.*

🏠 **Thwaite Howe** 🪑, CA12 5SA, ✆ (017687) 78281, *Fax (017687) 78529,* ⇐ Skiddaw and Derwent Valley, 🌳 – 🚭 [TV] ☎ [P]. [MC] [VISA]
March-October – **Meals** (residents only) (dinner only) 17.50 **t.** 🍾 7.20 – **8 rm** 🛏 (dinner included) 68.50/97.00 **st.** – SB.

KETTERING *Northants.* [404] R 26 – *pop. 47 186.*

[i] *The Coach House, Sheep St., NN16 0AN* ✆ *(01536) 410266.*
London 88 – Birmingham 54 – Leicester 16 – Northampton 24.

🏨 **Kettering Park,** Kettering Parkway, NN15 6XT, S : 2 ¼ m. by A 509 (Wellingborough rd) at junction with A 14 ✆ (01536) 416666, *Fax (01536) 416171,* 🏋, ♨, 🏊, 🌳, squash – 🛗 🚭 ▤ [TV] ☎ ♿ [P] – 🧑‍🏫 200. [MC] [AE] [D] [VISA]
Langberrys : **Meals** (bar lunch Saturday and Bank Holiday Monday) 13.95 **t.** (lunch) and a la carte 22.25/31.00 **t.** – **119 rm** 🛏 107.00/128.00 **st.** – SB.

🏨 **Royal,** Market Pl., NN16 0AJ, ✆ (01536) 520732, *Fax (01536) 411036* – 🚭 rm, [TV] ☎ [P] – 🧑‍🏫 170. [MC] [VISA] [JCB]
Meals (dinner only) 12.50 **t.** and a la carte 🍾 4.95 – 🛏 6.50 – **40 rm** 52.00/62.00 **t.**, 1 suite – SB.

🏠 **Travel Inn,** Rothwell Rd, NN16 8XF, NW : 1 ¼ m. at junction of A 14 with A 43 ✆ (01536) 310082, *Fax (01536) 310104* – 🚭 rm, [TV] ♿ [P]. [MC] [AE] [D] [VISA]. 🚫🐕
Meals (grill rest.) – **39 rm** 36.50 **t.**

ATS Northfield Av. ✆ (01536) 512832

KETTLEWELL *N. Yorks.* [402] N 21 – *pop. 297 (inc. Starbotton)* – ✉ *Skipton.*

London 237 – Bradford 33 – Leeds 40.

🏠 **Cam Lodge** 🪑, BD23 5QU, ✆ (01756) 760276, 🌳 – 🚭 [P]. 🚫🐕
April-September – **Meals** 12.00 **s.** – **4 rm** 🛏 22.50/45.00 **s.**

🏠 **Langcliffe Country House** 🪑, BD23 5RJ, by Church rd on access only rd ✆ (01756) 760243, ⇐, 🌳 – 🚭 rest, [TV] ☎ [P]. [MC] [VISA]. 🚫🐕
Meals (by arrangement) 16.00 **s.** 🍾 4.25 – **5 rm** 🛏 40.00/58.00 **st.** – SB.

KETTON *Lincs.* [402] [404] S 26 – *see Stamford.*

KEXBY *N. Yorks.* – *see York.*

KEYNSHAM *Bristol* [403] [404] M 29 – *pop. 15 813* – ✉ *Bristol.*

London 123 – Bath 9 – Bristol 6 – Gloucester 44.

🏠 **Grange,** 42 Bath Rd, BS18 1SN, ✆ (0117) 986 9181, *Fax (0117) 986 6373,* 🌳 – 🚭 rm, [TV] ☎ [P]. [MC] [VISA]
Meals 10.75 **st.** (dinner) and a la carte 11.05/16.05 🍾 5.75 – **29 rm** 🛏 46.00/80.00 **st.**

KEYSTON *Cambs.* **404** S 26 – *pop. 257 (inc. Bythorn)* – ⊠ *Huntingdon.*
London 75 – Cambridge 29 – Northampton 24.

XX **Pheasant Inn,** Village Loop Rd, PE18 0RE, ℰ (01832) 710241, Fax (01832) 710340 – ⇔
ℙ. ℂ ℀ ℗ ⓥ VISA JCB
closed dinner 25 December – **Meals** 11.75 **st.** (lunch) and a la carte 12.25/25.20 **st.**

KIDDERMINSTER *Worcestershire* **403 404** N 26 – *pop. 54 644.*
🖪 *Severn Valley Railway Station, Comberton Hill, DY10 1QX* ℰ *(01562) 829400 (summer only).*
London 139 – Birmingham 17 – Shrewsbury 34 – Worcester 15.

🏨 **Stone Manor,** Stone, DY10 4PJ, SE : 2 ½ m. on A 448 ℰ (01562) 777555, Fax (01562) 777834, ≤, ☞, park, ⅋ – ⇔ rest, 📺 ☎ ℗ – 🔬 150. ℂ ℀ ℗ ⓥ VISA. ℅
Meals 14.50/17.50 **t.** and a la carte ⅃ 6.45 – ⊊ 7.95 – **51 rm** 49.50/110.00 **t.**, 1 suite – SB.

🏨 **Gainsborough House,** Bewdley Hill, DY11 6BS, ℰ (01562) 820041, Fax (01562) 66179 – ⇔ rm, 📺 ☎ ℗ – 🔬 240. ℂ ℀ ℗ ⓥ VISA
Meals (bar lunch Monday to Saturday)/dinner 16.50 **t.** and a la carte ⅃ 7.50 – ⊊ 9.50 – **42 rm** 68.00/85.00 **st.** – SB.

at Chaddesley Corbett *SE : 4½ m. by A 448* – ⊠ *Kidderminster.*

🏨 **Brockencote Hall** ⧈, DY10 4PY, on A 448 ℰ (01562) 777876, Fax (01562) 777872, ≤, « Part 19C mansion in park », ☞ – ⇔ rest, 📺 ☎ ⅋ ℗ – 🔬 25. ℂ ℀ ℗ ⓥ VISA. ℅
Meals (closed Saturday lunch) 20.50/43.50 **st.** ⅃ 6.50 – **17 rm** ⊊ 90.00/145.00 **st.** – SB.

🔘 ATS Park St. ℰ (01926) 744668/744843

KILLINGTON LAKE SERVICE AREA *Cumbria* **402** M 21 – ⊠ *Kendal.*

🏠 **RoadChef Lodge** without rest., LA8 0NW, M 6 between junctions 36 and 37 (southbound carriageway) ℰ (01539) 621666, Fax (01539) 621660, Reservations (Freephone) 0800 834719 – ⇔ 📺 ☎ ⅋ ℗. ℂ ℀ ℗ ⓥ VISA. ℅
closed Christmas and New Year – **36 rm** 43.50 **st.**

KIMBOLTON *Herefordshire* **403** L 27 – *see Leominster.*

KINGHAM *Oxon.* **403 404** P 28 – *pop. 1 434.*
London 81 – Gloucester 32 – Oxford 25.

🏨 **Mill House** ⧈, OX7 6UH, ℰ (01608) 658188, Fax (01608) 658492, ⧖, ☞ – ⇔ rest, 📺 ☎ ℗ – 🔬 70. ℂ ℀ ℗ ⓥ VISA JCB
Meals 13.95/22.75 **st.** and a la carte ⅃ 9.50 – **23 rm** ⊊ (dinner included) 84.95/159.90 **st.**

KINGSBRIDGE *Devon* **403** I 33 *The West Country G.* – *pop. 5 258.*
See : *Town★ – Boat Trip to Salcombe★★ AC.*
Exc. : *Prawle Point (≤★★★) SE : 10 m. around coast by A 379.*
🖪 *Thurlestone* ℰ (01548) 560405.
🖪 *The Quay, TQ7 1HS* ℰ (01548) 853195.
London 236 – Exeter 36 – Plymouth 20 – Torquay 21.

🏠 **Kings Arms,** Fore St., TQ7 1AB, ℰ (01548) 852071, Fax (01548) 852977, ◫ – ⇔ rm, 📺 ☎ ℗ – 🔬 250. ℂ ℀ ⓥ VISA JCB
Meals a la carte 10.00/16.00 **st.** ⅃ 4.25 – **12 rm** ⊊ 35.00/65.00 **st.** – SB.

at Goveton *NE : 2½ m. by A 381* – ⊠ *Kingsbridge.*

🏨 **Buckland-Tout-Saints** ⧈, TQ7 2DS, ℰ (01548) 853055, Fax (01548) 856261, ≤, « Queen Anne mansion », ☞, park – ⇔ rest, 📺 ☎ ℗. ℂ ℀ ⓥ VISA
Meals (booking essential) 16.50/30.00 **st.** ⅃ 7.00 – **13 rm** ⊊ 60.00/160.00 **t.**

at Chillington *E : 5 m. on A 379* – ⊠ *Kingsbridge.*

🏠 **White House,** TQ7 2JX, ℰ (01548) 580580, Fax (01548) 581124, ☞ – ⇔ rest, 📺 ☎ ℗. ℂ ℀ ℗
April-28 December – **Meals** (bar lunch residents only)/dinner 13.95 **st.** ⅃ 5.80 – **8 rm** ⊊ 47.00/94.00 **st.** – SB.

at Thurlestone *W : 4 m. by A 381* – ⊠ *Kingsbridge.*

🏨 **Thurlestone** ⧈, TQ7 3NN, ℰ (01548) 560382, Fax (01548) 561069, ≤, 🏋, 🏊, 🏊, ◫, 🎣, ☞, ⅋, squash – 🛗, ⇔ rest, 🍴 rest, 📺 ☎ ⊷ ℗ – 🔬 100. ℂ ℀ ℗ ⓥ VISA JCB. ℅
closed 4 to 16 January – **Meals** 12.50/24.00 **st.** and a la carte ⅃ 7.50 – **65 rm** ⊊ (dinner included) 94.00/188.00 **t.** – SB.

at Bantham W : 5 m. by A 379 – ⊠ Kingsbridge.

Sloop Inn with rm, TQ7 3AJ, ℰ (01548) 560489, Fax (01548) 561940 – ⊺⊻ ℗
closed 25 and 26 December – **Meals** a la carte 11.30/15.30 **t.** – **5 rm** ⊇ 35.00/62.00 **t.**

ATS Union Rd ℰ (01548) 853247/852699

KING'S CLIFFE Northants. 404 S 26 – ⊠ Peterborough.
London 93 – Leicester 21 – Northampton 19 – Peterborough 7.

King's Cliffe House, 31 West St., PE8 6XB, ℰ (01780) 470172, ⌖ – ⊱⊱ ℗ ℗
closed Sunday to Tuesday, 1 January, 25-26 December, 2 weeks in spring and 2 weeks in autumn – **Meals** (booking essential) (dinner only) a la carte 15.75/26.45 **st.** � 4.95.

KINGSKERSWELL Devon 403 J 32 – pop. 3 672 – ⊠ Torquay.
London 219 – Exeter 21 – Plymouth 33 – Torquay 4.

Pitt House, 2 Church End Rd, TQ12 5DS, ℰ (01803) 873374, « 15C thatched dower house », ⌖ – ⊱⊱ ℗. 🆂🆂 🆅🅸🆂🅰
closed Sunday dinner, Monday, 2 weeks in winter and 1 week in summer – **Meals** (light lunch) a la carte 16.75/24.45 **t.**

KINGS LANGLEY Herts. 404 S 28 – pop. 8 144.
London 26 – Luton 14.

Langleys - Lodge Inn, Hempstead Rd, WD4 8BR, ℰ (01923) 263150, Fax (01923) 264061 – ⊱⊱ rm, ⊺⊻ ℅ ℗. 🆂🆂 🆅🅸🆂🅰 🆂🆂
Meals (grill rest.) a la carte 10.00/14.65 **st.** ⓵ 7.95 – ⊇ 5.50 – **60 rm** 37.50 **st.**

KING'S LYNN Norfolk 402 404 V 25 Great Britain G. – pop. 41 281.
Exc. : Houghton Hall★★ AC, NE : 14 ½ m. by A 148 – Four Fenland Churches★ (Terrington St. Clement, Walpole St. Peter, West Walton, Walsoken) SW : by A 47.
🟆 Eagles, School Rd, Tilney All Saints ℰ (01553) 827147.
🅱 The Old Gaol House, Saturday Market Pl., PE30 5DQ ℰ (01553) 763044.
London 103 – Cambridge 45 – Leicester 75 – Norwich 44.

Knights Hill, Knights Hill Village, South Wootton, PE30 3HQ, NE : 4 ½ m. on A 148 at junction with A 149 ℰ (01553) 675566, Fax (01553) 675568, ℉, ≘s, 🅂, ⌖, ℀ – ⊱⊱ ⊺⊻ ☎ ℗ – 🕰 300. 🆂🆂 🅰🅴 🅾 🆅🅸🆂🅰. ℀
Garden : Meals (dinner only and Sunday lunch)/dinner 16.95 **st.** and a la carte ⓵ 4.95 – **Farmers Inn :** Meals (carving lunch) a la carte 9.60/20.20 **st.** ⓵ 3.95 – ⊇ 7.50 – **55 rm** 80.00/120.00 **st.** – SB.

Duke's Head, Tuesday Market Pl., PE30 1JS, ℰ (01553) 774996, Fax (01553) 763556 – 📳 ⊱⊱ ⊺⊻ ☎ ℗ – 🕰 200. 🆂🆂 🅰🅴 🅾 🆅🅸🆂🅰 🆓🅲🅱. ℀
Meals (closed Saturday lunch) 10.95/18.95 **st.** and a la carte ⓵ 6.00 – **Griffins :** Meals a la carte 9.60/17.90 **st.** ⓵ 5.00 – ⊇ 9.25 – **71 rm** 70.00/85.00 **st.** – SB.

Butterfly, Beveridge Way, PE30 4NB, SE : 2 ¼ m. by Hardwick Rd at junction of A 10 with A 47 ℰ (01553) 771707, Fax (01553) 768027 – ⊺⊻ ☎ ℗ – 🕰 40. 🆂🆂 🅰🅴 🅾 🆅🅸🆂🅰
Meals 12.25 **st.** and a la carte ⓵ 9.75 – ⊇ 6.95 – **50 rm** 59.50 **st.** – SB.

Old Rectory without rest., 33 Goodwins Rd, PE30 5QX, ℰ (01553) 768544, ⌖ – ⊱⊱ ⊺⊻ ℗
4 rm ⊇ 28.00/38.00.

Fairlight Lodge without rest., 79 Goodwins Rd, PE30 5PE, ℰ (01553) 762234 Fax (01553) 770280, ⌖ – ⊱⊱ ⊺⊻ ℗
closed 24 to 26 December – **7 rm** ⊇ 18.00/40.00.

Rococo, 11 Saturday Market Pl., Old Town, PE30 5DQ, ℰ (01553) 771483 Fax (01553) 771483 – 🆂🆂 🅾 🆅🅸🆂🅰 🆓🅲🅱
closed Monday lunch, Sunday, 25-26 December and 1 week May – **Meals** (booking essential) 13.50 /25.00-27.50 **t.** ⓵ 9.00.

at Grimston E : 6 ¼ m. by A 148 – ⊠ King's Lynn.

Congham Hall ⊱, Lynn Rd, PE32 1AH, ℰ (01485) 600250, Fax (01485) 601191, ≼, « Part Georgian manor house, herb garden », 🅂, ⌖, park, ℀ – ⊱⊱ rest, ⊺⊻ ☎ ℗ – 🕰 25. 🆂🆂 🅰 🅾 🆅🅸🆂🅰 🆓🅲🅱. ℀
Orangery : Meals (closed Saturday lunch) 13.50/32.00 **t.** and lunch a la carte 14.25/31.50 **t.** ⓵ 7.50 – **12 rm** ⊇ 74.00/145.00 **t.**, 2 suites – SB.

ATS 4 Oldmedow Rd, Hardwick Rd Trading Est. ℰ (01553) 774035

KINGS NORTON W. Mids. 402 ⑩ 403 ㉛ 404 ⑳ – see Birmingham.

KINGSTON Devon 403 I 33 – pop. 364 – ✉ Kingsbridge.
London 237 – Exeter 41 – Plymouth 11.

⌂ **Trebles Cottage** ⟨⟩, TQ7 4PT, ℘ (01548) 810268, Fax (01548) 810268, ☞ – ⥂ rest, 📺
🅿. ◍ 🅰🅴 𝗩𝗜𝗦𝗔
Meals (by arrangement) 16.00 **st.** ⅃ 6.50 – **5 rm** ⊇ 35.00/74.00 **st.** – SB.

KINGSTON BAGPUIZE Oxon. 403 404 P 28 – see Abingdon.

KINGSTON-UPON-HULL Kingston-upon-Hull 402 S 22 Great Britain G. – pop. 310 636.
Exc. : Burton Constable★ AC, NE : 9 m. by A 165 and B 1238 Z.
📗 Springhead Park, Willerby Rd ℘ (01482) 656309 – 📗 Sutton Park, Salthouse Rd ℘ (01482)
374242.
Humber Bridge (toll).
✈ Humberside Airport : ℘ (01652) 688456, S : 19 m. by A 63 – **Terminal** : Coach Service.
🚢 to The Netherlands (Rotterdam) (North Sea Ferries) (13 h 30 mn) – to The Netherlands
(Zeebrugge) (North Sea Ferries) (13 h 45 mn).
🛈 1 Paragon St., HU1 3NA ℘ (01482) 223344 – King George Dock, Hedon Rd, HU9 5PR
℘ (01482) 702118 – 1 Paragon St., HU1 3NA ℘ (01482) 223559.
London 183 – Leeds 61 – Nottingham 94 – Sheffield 68.

Plan on next page

🏨 **Forte Posthouse Hull Marina,** The Marina, Castle St., HU1 2BX, ℘ (01482) 225221,
Fax (01482) 213299, ≼, 🛵, 🚌, 🏊, – 🛏 ⥂ 📺 ☎ 🅿 – 🔬 120. ◍ 🅰🅴 🅾 𝗩𝗜𝗦𝗔 🅹🅲🅱 Y n
Meals (closed Saturday lunch) a la carte 9.95/15.50 **st.** ⅃ 8.95 – ⊇ 9.95 – **99 rm** 89.00/
99.00 **st.** – SB.

🏨 **Quality Royal,** Ferensway, HU1 3UF, ℘ (01482) 325087, Fax (01482) 323172, 🛵, 🚌, 🏊
– 🛏 ⥂ 📺 ☎ & 🅿 – 🔬 450. ◍ 🅰🅴 🅾 𝗩𝗜𝗦𝗔 Y a
Meals 9.50/16.00 **st.** and a la carte ⅃ 5.75 – ⊇ 9.50 – **155 rm** 63.50/102.50 **st.** – SB.

🏨 **Travel Inn,** Kingswood Park, Ennerdale Link Rd, HU7 0HS, N : 5 m. on A 1033 by A 1079
℘ (01482) 820225, Fax (01482) 820300, ☞ – ⥂ rm, 📺 & 🅿. ◍ 🅰🅴 🅾 𝗩𝗜𝗦𝗔
Meals (grill rest.) – **42 rm** 36.50 **t.**

🏨 **Travel Inn,** Ferriby Rd, Hessle, HU13 0JA, W : 7 m. by A 63 off A 164 ℘ (01482) 645285,
Fax (01482) 645299 – ⥂ rm, 📺 & 🅿. ◍ 🅰🅴 🅾 𝗩𝗜𝗦𝗔. ⚘
Meals (grill rest.) – **40 rm** 36.50 **t.**

🏨 **Campanile,** Beverley Rd, Freetown Way, HU2 9AN, ℘ (01482) 325530,
Fax (01482) 587538 – 📺 & 🅿 – 🔬 30. ◍ 🅰🅴 🅾 𝗩𝗜𝗦𝗔 X a
Meals 10.55 **st.** and a la carte ⅃ 5.95 – ⊇ 4.50 – **48 rm** 36.50 **st.**

✗✗ **Cerutti's,** 10 Nelson St., HU1 1XE, ℘ (01482) 328501, Fax (01482) 587597 – 🅿. ◍ 𝗩𝗜𝗦𝗔
closed Saturday lunch, Sunday, 1 week Christmas and Bank Holidays – **Meals** - Seafood -
a la carte 16.00/22.00 **t.** ⅃ 6.00. Y o

at Hedon E : 6½ m. by A 63 on A 1033 – Z – ✉ Kingston-upon-Hull.

🏨 **Kingstown,** Hull Rd, HU12 8DJ, W : 1 m. on A 1033 ℘ (01482) 890461, Fax (01482) 890713
– 📺 ☎ & 🅿. ◍ 🅰🅴 🅾 𝗩𝗜𝗦𝗔 🅹🅲🅱. ⚘
Meals (in bar Monday to Saturday lunch and Sunday)/dinner a la carte 8.30/16.85 **st.** –
34 rm ⊇ 62.00/85.00 **st.**

at Willerby W : 5 m. by A 1079, Spring Bank – Z – and Willerby Rd – ✉ Kingston-upon-Hull.

🏨 **Willerby Manor,** Well Lane, HU10 6ER, ℘ (01482) 652616, Fax (01482) 653901, 🛵, 🚌,
🏊, ☞ – 📺 ☎ 🅿 – 🔬 500. ◍ 🅰🅴 𝗩𝗜𝗦𝗔. ⚘
closed 25 December – **Meals** (closed Saturday lunch and Sunday dinner) 12.50/14.50 **st.**
and a la carte ⅃ 8.95 – ⊇ 8.50 – **51 rm** 65.00/82.00 **st.**

at North Ferriby W : 7 m. on A 63 – Z – ✉ Kingston-upon-Hull.

🏨 **Forte Posthouse Hull,** Ferriby High Rd, HU14 3LG, ℘ (01482) 645212,
Fax (01482) 643332 – ⥂ rm, 🍽 rest, 📺 ☎ 🅿 – 🔬 100. ◍ 🅰🅴 🅾 𝗩𝗜𝗦𝗔
Meals a la carte 16.70/25.65 **t.** ⅃ 7.95 – ⊇ 8.95 – **95 rm** 69.00 **st.** – SB.

at Little Weighton NW : 9 m. by A 1079 – Z – and B 1233 via Skidby – ✉ Cottingham.

🏨 **Rowley Manor** ⟨⟩, HU20 3XR, SW : ½ m. by Rowley Rd ℘ (01482) 848248,
Fax (01482) 849900, ≼, « Georgian manor house », ☞ – 📺 ☎ 🅿 – 🔬 80. ◍ 🅰🅴 🅾 𝗩𝗜𝗦𝗔
Meals 19.95 **st.** ⅃ 5.45 – **16 rm** ⊇ 65.00/95.00 **st.** – SB.

ⓐ ATS Great Union St. ℘ (01482) 329044 ATS Waverley St. ℘ (01482) 329370/225502

KINGSTON-UPON-HULL

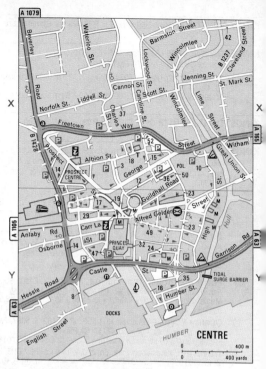

CENTRE

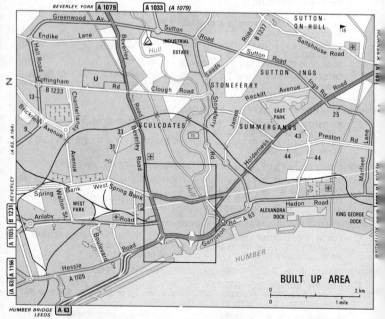

BUILT UP AREA

KINGSTOWN *Cumbria – see Carlisle.*

KINGTON *Herefordshire* 403 K 27 – *pop. 2 197.*
London 152 – Birmingham 61 – Hereford 19 – Shrewsbury 54.

🏠 **Penrhos Court,** HR5 3LH, E : 1 ½ m. on A 44 ℰ (01544) 230720, Fax (01544) 230754,
« Part 15C and 16C house with medieval cruck hall », 🐾 – ⇌ 📺 ☎ 🅿 – 🔏 25. 🅬🅢 🄰🄴 𝘝𝘐𝘚𝘈
🛇
closed February – **Meals** *(booking essential) (lunch by arrangement)* 25.00 **t.** � 6.00 – **19 rm**
⊇ 55.00/95.00 **t.** – SB.

🄰 ATS 20-22 Bridge St. ℰ (01544) 230350

KINVER *Staffs.* 403 404 N 26 – *see Stourbridge (W. Mids).*

KIRBY HILL *N. Yorks. – see Richmond.*

KIRKBURTON *W. Yorks.* 402 404 O 23 ⑳ – *pop. 4 121 –* ✉ *Huddersfield.*
London 195 – Leeds 20 – Manchester 32 – Sheffield 22.

🏠 **Hanover International H. Huddersfield,** Penistone Rd, HD8 0PE, on A 629
ℰ (01484) 607788, Fax (01484) 607961 – ⇌ rm, 📺 ☎ 🅿 – 🔏 140. 🅬🅢 🄰🄴 🄾 𝘝𝘐𝘚𝘈 𝗝𝗖𝗕
Meals *(bar lunch Monday to Saturday)/dinner* 17.95 **st.** and a la carte � 6.95 – **46 rm**
⊇ 69.00/95.00 **st.** – SB.

KIRKBY LONSDALE *Cumbria* 402 M 21 – *pop. 2 076 –* ✉ *Carnforth (Lancs.).*
🟦 Scaleber Lane, Barbon ℰ (015242) 76365 – 🟦 Casterton, Sedbergh Rd ℰ (015242) 71592.
🅱 24 Main St., LA6 2AE ℰ (015242) 71437 *(restricted opening in winter).*
London 259 – Carlisle 62 – Kendal 13 – Lancaster 17 – Leeds 58.

🏠 **Whoop Hall Inn,** Burrow with Burrow, LA6 2HP, SE : 1 m. on A 65 ℰ (015242) 71284,
Fax (015242) 72154, 🐾 – 📺 ☎ 🅿 – 🔏 140. 🅬🅢 🄰🄴 🄾 𝘝𝘐𝘚𝘈 𝗝𝗖𝗕. 🛇
Meals 8.95/15.95 **t.** and a la carte � 4.50 – **23 rm** ⊇ 50.00/70.00 **t.** – SB.

🏠 **Pheasant Inn,** Casterton, LA6 2RX, NE : 1 ¼ m. on A 683 ℰ (015242) 71230,
Fax (015242) 71230, 🐾 – ⇌ rest, 📺 ☎ 🅕 🅿. 🅬🅢 🄾 𝘝𝘐𝘚𝘈 𝗝𝗖𝗕
closed 25 December – **Meals** *(closed Sunday November-March and Monday) (bar lunch)/*
dinner a la carte 12.70/23.00 **st.** � 6.00 – **10 rm** ⊇ 37.50/64.00 **t.**

🍴 **Snooty Fox Tavern** with rm, 33 Main St., LA6 2AH, ℰ (015242) 71308,
Fax (015242) 72642, « Jacobean inn » – 📺 🅿. 🅬🅢 🄰🄴 𝘝𝘐𝘚𝘈. 🛇
Meals a la carte 10.75/20.65 **st.** � 5.50 – **9 rm** ⊇ 30.00/55.00 **st.**

at Cowan Bridge *(Lancs.)* SE : 2 m. on A 65 – ✉ *Carnforth (Lancs.).*

🏠 **Hipping Hall,** LA6 2JJ, SE : ½ m. on A 65 ℰ (015242) 71187, Fax (015242) 72452,
« Former 15C hamlet », 🐾 – ⇌ rest, 📺 ☎ 🅿. 🅬🅢 🄰🄴 𝘝𝘐𝘚𝘈
March-October – **Meals** *(residents only) (communal dining) (dinner only)* 24.00 **st.** � 8.00 –
5 rm ⊇ 69.00/84.00 **st.**, 2 suites – SB.

KIRKBY MALHAM *N. Yorks.* 402 N 21 – *pop. 70 –* ✉ *Skipton.*
London 235 – Bradford 25 – Burnley 30 – Carlisle 97 – Harrogate 25 – York 47.

🏠 **Holgate Head** 🕭, BD23 4JT, ℰ (01729) 830376, Fax (01729) 830576, ≤, 🐾 – ⇌ 📺 🅿.
🛇
March-mid October – **Meals** *(communal dining)* 21.00 **st.** ⓐ 4.50 – **3 rm** ⊇ 50.00/70.00 **st.**

KIRKBYMOORSIDE *N. Yorks.* 402 R 21 – *pop. 2 650.*
🟦 Manor Vale ℰ (01751) 431525.
London 244 – Scarborough 26 – York 33.

🏠 **George and Dragon,** 17 Market Pl., YO6 6AA, ℰ (01751) 433334, Fax (01751) 433334,
« Part 17C coaching inn », 🐾 – ⇌ rest, 📺 ☎ 🅿. 🅬🅢 𝘝𝘐𝘚𝘈
Meals a la carte 13.60/21.65 **t.** ⓐ 5.00 – **17 rm** ⊇ 49.00/90.00 **t.** – SB.

KIRKBY STEPHEN *Cumbria* 402 M 20 – *pop. 1 619.*
🅱 Market St., CA17 4QN ℰ (017683) 71199 *(summer only).*
London 285 – Carlisle 48 – Kendal 24.

🏠 **Ing Hill Lodge** 🕭, Mallerstang Dale, CA17 4JT, S : 4 ½ m. on B 6259 ℰ (017683) 71153,
Fax (017683) 71153, ≤ Mallerstang Dale, 🐾 – ⇌ 📺 🅿
Meals *(by arrangement)* 12.50 **st.** ⓐ 3.50 – **3 rm** ⊇ 50.00 **st.** – SB.

at Crosby Garrett *NW : 4½ m. by Silver St. – ✉ Kirkby Stephen.*

🏠 **Old Rectory** 🌄, CA17 4PW, ✆ (017683) 72074, « Part 17C », 🌳 – 🚭 [P]
closed Christmas and New Year – **Meals** (by arrangement) (communal dining) 11.00 **st.** – **3 rm** ☕ 31.00/42.00 **st.**

KIRKCAMBECK *Cumbria* [401] [402] L 18 – *see Brampton.*

KIRKHAM *Lancs.* [402] L 22 – *pop. 9 038* – ✉ *Preston.*
London 240 – Blackpool 9 – Preston 7.

🍴🍴 **Cromwellian,** 16 Poulton St., PR4 2AB, ✆ (01772) 685680, *Fax (01772) 685680* – [MC] [AE] [D] [VISA] [JCB]
closed Sunday, Monday, 1 week June and 2 weeks September – **Meals** (dinner only) 15.00 **st.** 🍷 5.25.

KIRKWHELPINGTON *Northd.* [401] [402] N/O 18 *Great Britain G.* – *pop. 353* – ✉ *Morpeth.*
Env. : *Wallington House★ AC, E : 3 ½ m. by A 696 and B 6342.*
London 305 – Carlisle 46 – Newcastle upon Tyne 20.

🏠 **Shieldhall** 🌄, Wallington, NE61 4AQ, SE : 2 ½ m. by A 696 on B 6342 ✆ (01830) 540387, *Fax (01830) 540387*, 🌳 – 🚭 [P]. [MC] [VISA]. 🐕
restricted opening in winter – **Meals** (by arrangement) 14.75 **s.** – **4 rm** ☕ 30.00/43.00.

KNARESBOROUGH *N. Yorks.* [402] P 21 – *pop. 13 380.*
⛳18 *Boroughbridge Rd* ✆ *(01423) 863219.*
[i] *35 Market Place, HG5 8AL* ✆ *(01423) 866886 (summer only).*
London 217 – Bradford 21 – Harrogate 3 – Leeds 18 – York 18.

🏨 **Dower House,** Bond End, HG5 9AL, ✆ (01423) 863302, *Fax (01423) 867665*, 🏋, ♨, 🏊, 🌳 – 🚭 [TV] ☎ [P] – 🎤 65. [MC] [AE] [D] [VISA]. 🐕
Meals (bar lunch Monday to Saturday)/dinner 19.50 **st.** and a la carte 🍷 5.25 – ☕ 8.00 – **31 rm** 52.00/75.00 **st.**, 1 suite – SB.

at Ferrensby *NE : 3 m. on A 6055.*

🍴🍴 **General Tarleton Inn** with rm, Boroughbridge Rd, HG5 0QB, ✆ (01423) 340284 *Fax (01423) 340288* – 🚭 rest, [TV] ☎ [P] – 🎤 40. [MC] [AE] [VISA]
closed 25 December – ***The Dining Room :*** **Meals** (dinner only and Sunday lunch)/dinner 24.85 **t.** 🍷 9.10 – ☕ 9.50 – **14 rm** 52.50 **t.** – SB.
🍴 **Bar/Brasserie : Meals** *(closed 25 December)* a la carte 17.65/26.85 **t.** 🍷 9.10.

KNIGHTWICK *Worcestershire* [403] [404] M 27 – *pop. 87* – ✉ *Worcester.*
London 132 – Hereford 20 – Leominster 18 – Worcester 8.

🍺 **Talbot** with rm, WR6 5PH, on B 4197 ✆ (01886) 821235, *Fax (01886) 821060*, ♨, 🎣, squash – [TV] ☎ [P]. [MC] [VISA]. 🐕
closed 25 December – **Meals** 12.95 **st.** (lunch) and dinner a la carte 14.45/23.70 **st.** 🍷 4.80 – **10 rm** ☕ 35.00/65.00 **st.** – SB.

KNOWLE *W. Mids.* [403] [404] O 26 – *pop. 17 588* – ✉ *Solihull.*
London 108 – Birmingham 9 – Coventry 10 – Warwick 11.

🏨 **Greswolde Arms,** 1657 High St., B93 0LL, ✆ (01564) 772711, *Fax (01564) 770354* – 🚭 rm, [TV] ☎ ♿ [P] – 🎤 150. [MC] [AE] [D] [VISA] [JCB]. 🐕
Meals 14.95 **st.** and a la carte 🍷 6.50 – ☕ 6.00 – **36 rm** 54.00 **t.** – SB.

KNOWL HILL *Windsor & Maidenhead* [404] R 29 – ✉ *Twyford.*
⛳18, ⛳9, *Hennerton, Crazies Hill Rd, Wargrave* ✆ *(01734) 401000/404778.*
London 38 – Maidenhead 5 – Reading 8.

🏨 **Bird in Hand,** Bath Rd, RG10 9UP, ✆ (01628) 826622, *Fax (01628) 826748*, 🌳 – [TV] ☎ [P]. [MC] [AE] [D] [VISA] [JCB]
closed 24 to 30 December – **Meals** 15.00 **st.** and a la carte 🍷 5.50 – **15 rm** ☕ 75.00/100.00 **st.** – SB.

KNUTSFORD *Ches.* 402 403 404 M 24 – *pop. 13 352.*

🛈 *Council Offices, Toft Rd, WA16 6TA &ℰ (01565) 632611.*
London 187 – Chester 25 – Liverpool 33 – Manchester 18 – Stoke-on-Trent 30.

🏨 **Cottons,** Manchester Rd, WA16 0SU, NW : 1 ½ m. on A 50 &ℰ (01565) 650333,
Fax (01565) 755351, ₤₆, ☎, 🔲, ⚲, squash – |≢|, ⇔ rm, 🔲 ☎ & ❿ – 🔬 200. 🐠 🅰🅴 ⓞ
𝘝𝘐𝘚𝘈. ⅏
Magnolia : Meals *(closed lunch Saturday and Bank Holidays)* a la carte 18.95/31.25 **t.** ₤ 7.95
– **90 rm** ⛁ 104.00/124.00 **t.,** 9 suites – SB.

🏨 **Royal George,** King St., WA16 6EE, &ℰ (01565) 634151, *Fax (01565) 634955* – |≢|, ⇔ rm,
🔲 ☎ ❿ – 🔬 120. 🐠 🅰🅴 ⓞ 𝘝𝘐𝘚𝘈
Meals (bar lunch Monday to Saturday)/dinner 11.45 **st.** and a la carte – ⛁ 6.95 – **31 rm**
49.00/59.00 **st.** – SB.

🏨 **Longview,** 55 Manchester Rd, WA16 0LX, &ℰ (01565) 632119, *Fax (01565) 652402* –
⇔ rest, 🔲 ☎ ❿. 🐠 🅰🅴 ⓞ 𝘝𝘐𝘚𝘈
closed Christmas and New Year – **Meals** *(closed Sunday and Bank Holidays)* (bar lunch)/
dinner a la carte 16.85/23.15 **st.** ₤ 5.25 – **23 rm** ⛁ 57.00/85.00 **t.** – SB.

🏨 **Travelodge,** Chester Rd, Tabley, WA16 0PP, NW : 2 ¾ m. by A 5033 on A 556
&ℰ (01565) 652187, *Fax (01565) 652187,* Reservations (Freephone) 0800 850950 – ⇔ rm,
🔲 & ❿. 🐠 🅰🅴 ⓞ 𝘝𝘐𝘚𝘈 𝘑𝘊𝘉. ⅏
Meals (grill rest.) – **32 rm** 49.95 **t.**

🍴🍴 **Belle Epoque Brasserie** with rm, 60 King St., WA16 6DT, &ℰ (01565) 633060,
Fax (01565) 634150, « Art Nouveau », ☞ – 🔲 ☎ – 🔬 60. 🐠 🅰🅴 ⓞ 𝘝𝘐𝘚𝘈. ⅏
closed 25-26 December and 1 January – **Meals** *(closed Saturday lunch, Sunday and Bank
Holidays)* a la carte 12.20/22.50 **st.** – ⛁ 5.00 – **7 rm** 40.00/50.00 **st.**

🍴🍴 **Treasure Village,** 84 King St., WA16 6EG, &ℰ (01565) 651537, *Fax (01565) 632820* – ▤. 🐠
🅰🅴 𝘝𝘐𝘚𝘈 𝘑𝘊𝘉
closed 25 and 26 December – **Meals** - Chinese - 5.20 **t.** (lunch) and a la carte 10.50/17.30 **t.**
₤ 6.50.

🍴 **Est, Est, Est,** 81 King St., WA16 6DX, &ℰ (01565) 755487, *Fax (01565) 651151* – ▤. 🐠 🅰🅴
𝘝𝘐𝘚𝘈
closed 25 and 26 December – **Meals** - Italian - 9.95 **t.** and a la carte ₤ 5.65.

at Mobberley *NE : 2½ m. by A 537 on B 5085 –* ✉ *Knutsford.*

🏠 **Hinton,** Town Lane, WA16 7HH, on B 5085 &ℰ (01565) 873484, *Fax (01565) 873484,* ☞ –
⇔ 🔲 ☎ ❿. 🐠 🅰🅴 ⓞ 𝘝𝘐𝘚𝘈. ⅏
Meals (by arrangement) 11.00 – **5 rm** ⛁ 35.00/48.00.

🏠 **Laburnum Cottage** without rest., Knutsford Rd, WA16 7PU, W : ¾ m. on B 5085
&ℰ (01565) 872464, *Fax (01565) 872464,* ☞ – ⇔ 🔲 ❿. ⅏
5 rm ⛁ 39.00/50.00 **st.**

at Over Peover *SE : 5 m. by A 50 and Stocks Lane –* ✉ *Knutsford.*

🍴 **The Dog** with rm, Wellbank Lane, Peover Heath, WA16 8UP, SE : ½ m. &ℰ (01625) 861431,
Fax (01625) 861421 – ⇔ rest, 🔲 ❿. 🐠 𝘝𝘐𝘚𝘈
Meals (in bar) a la carte 12.65/14.95 – **3 rm** ⛁ 50.00/70.00 **t.**

at Hoo Green *NW : 3½ m. on A 50 –* ✉ *Knutsford.*

🏨 **The Kilton Inn - Premier Lodge,** Warrington Rd, WA16 0PZ, &ℰ (01565) 830420,
Fax (01565) 830411 – ⇔ rm, 🔲 ☎ & ❿. 🐠 🅰🅴 ⓞ 𝘝𝘐𝘚𝘈. ⅏
Meals (grill rest.) a la carte 9.50/15.00 **t.** – ⛁ 4.95 – **28 rm** 44.25 **t.** – SB.

🔧 ATS Malt St. &ℰ (01565) 652224

LACOCK *Wilts.* 403 404 N 29 *The West Country G. – pop. 1 068 –* ✉ *Chippenham.*
See : *Village★★* - *Lacock Abbey★ AC* - *High St.★, St. Cyriac★, Fox Talbot Museum of
Photography★ AC.*
London 109 – Bath 16 – Bristol 30 – Chippenham 3.

🏨 **Sign of the Angel,** 6 Church St., SN15 2LB, &ℰ (01249) 730230, *Fax (01249) 730527,*
« Part 14C and 15C former wool merchant's house in National Trust village », ☞ – 🔲 ☎
❿. 🐠 🅰🅴 𝘝𝘐𝘚𝘈
closed 1 week Christmas – **Meals** - English - *(closed Monday lunch)* a la carte 14.50/26.00 **t.**
₤ 5.00 – **10 rm** ⛁ 60.00/80.00 **t.** – SB.

LAMORNA *Cornwall* 403 D 33 *London 303.*
Falmouth 30 – Penzance 5 – Plymouth 83 – Truro 32.

🏨 **The Lamorna Cove** 🌊, TR19 9XH, &ℰ (01736) 731411, ≤, 🔟, ☞ – |≢| ⇔ 🔲 ☎ ❿. 🐠
🅰🅴 𝘝𝘐𝘚𝘈
restricted opening in winter – **Meals** (booking essential to non-residents) (bar lunch)/
dinner 17.50 **t.** ₤ 4.75 – **12 rm** ⛁ (dinner included) 49.50/120.00 **t.**

LANCASTER *Lancs.* 402 L 21 *Great Britain G. – pop. 44 497.*

See : *Castle*★ *AC.*

🏌 *Ashton Hall, Ashton-with-Stodday ℰ (01524) 752090 –* 🏌₉ *Lansil, Caton Rd ℰ (01524) 39269.*

🖪 *29 Castle Hill, LA1 1YN ℰ (01524) 32878.*

London 252 – Blackpool 26 – Bradford 62 – Burnley 44 – Leeds 71 – Middlesbrough 97 – Preston 26.

🏨 **Lancaster House,** Green Lane, Ellel, LA1 4GJ, S : 3 ¼ m. by A 6 ℰ (01524) 844822, Fax (01524) 844766, ₤₰, ⓢ, 🔲, ⭲↝, 🍴 rest, 🔟 ☎ ₤ ₽ – ₤ 120. 🕦 🆎 ⓞ 𝒱𝒮𝒜. ✦
Gressingham : Meals 12.95 st. (lunch) and a la carte 16.60/26.50 st. ₤ 7.25 – ⌚ 8.45 – 80 rm 84.00 st. – SB.

🏨 **Forte Posthouse Lancaster,** Waterside Park, Caton Rd, LA1 3RA, NE : 1 ½ m. on A 683 at junction 34 of M 6 ℰ (01524) 65999, Fax (01524) 841265, ₤₰, ⓢ, 🔲, ⚞ – ⫻, ⭲↝ rm, 🔟 ☎ ₤ ₽ – ₤ 120. 🕦 🆎 ⓞ 𝒱𝒮𝒜. ✦
Meals a la carte 15.00/24.50 st. ₤ 7.95 – ⌚ 8.95 – **155 rm** 69.00/99.00 st. – SB.

↑ **Edenbreck House** without rest., Sunnyside Lane, off Ashfield Av., LA1 5ED, by Westbourne Rd, near the station ℰ (01524) 32464, ⚞ – 🔟 ₽. ✦
April-October – **3 rm** ⌚ 30.00/50.00.

at Carnforth N : 6 ¼ m. on A 6.

↑ **New Capernwray Farm** ⤸, Capernwray, LA6 1AD, NE : 3 m. by B 6254 ℰ (01524) 734284, Fax (01524) 734284, ≤, « 17C former farmhouse », ⚞ – ⭲↝ 🔟 ₽. 🕦 𝒱𝒮𝒜 ᴊᴄʙ
Meals (communal dining) 21.00 – **3 rm** ⌚ 43.00/66.00.

LANCASTER SERVICE AREA *Lancs. –* ✉ *Forton.*

🖪 *(M 6) Forton, Bay Horse, LA2 9DU ℰ (01524) 792181.*

🏩 **Travelodge,** LA2 9DU, on M 6 between junctions 32 and 33 ℰ (01524) 792227 Fax (01524) 791703, Reservations (Freephone) 0800 850950 – ⭲↝ 🔟 ₤ ₽. 🕦 🆎 ⓞ 𝒱𝒮𝒜 ᴊᴄʙ. ✦
Meals (grill rest.) – **53 rm** 46.95 t.

LANCING *W. Sussex* 404 S 31 *– pop. 29 575 (inc. Sompting).*
London 59 – Brighton 9 – Southampton 53.

🏨 **Sussex Pad,** Old Shoreham Rd, BN15 0RH, E : 1 m. off A 27 ℰ (01273) 454647 Fax (01273) 453010, ⚞ – 🔟 ☎ ₤ ₽. 🕦 🆎 ⓞ 𝒱𝒮𝒜
Meals 20.50 t. ₤ 6.50 – **19 rm** ⌚ 50.00/90.00 t.

LANGHO *Lancs.* 402 M 22 *– see Blackburn.*

LANSALLOS *Cornwall* 403 G 32 *– pop. 1 625 –* ✉ *Fowey.*
London 273 – Plymouth 30.

↑ **Carneggan House** ⤸, Lanteglos-by-Fowey, PL23 1NW, NW : 2 m. on Polruan rd ℰ (01726) 870327, Fax (01726) 870327, ≤, ⚞ – ⭲↝ rest, 🔟 ₽. 🕦 🆎 𝒱𝒮𝒜
closed 20 to 28 December – Meals (by arrangement) (communal dining) 17.00 st. ₤ 3.00 – **3 rm** ⌚ 30.00/55.00 st.

LARKFIELD *Kent* 404 V 30 *– see Maidstone.*

LASKILL *N. Yorks. – see Helmsley.*

LASTINGHAM *N. Yorks.* 402 R 21 *– pop. 87 –* ✉ *York.*
London 244 – Scarborough 26 – York 32.

🏨 **Lastingham Grange** ⤸, YO6 6TH, ℰ (01751) 417345, Fax (01751) 417358, ≤ « Country house atmosphere », ⚞, park – ⭲↝ rest, 🔟 ☎ ₤. ✦
March-November – Meals (light lunch Monday to Saturday)/dinner 27.75 t. ₤ 3.75 – **12 rm** ⌚ 76.00/143.00 t. – SB.

LAVENHAM *Suffolk* 404 W 27 *Great Britain G. – pop. 1 231 –* ✉ *Sudbury.*
See : *Town*★★ *– Church of St. Peter and St. Paul*★.
🖪 *Lady St., CO10 9RA ℰ (01787) 248207 (summer only).*
London 66 – Cambridge 39 – Colchester 22 – Ipswich 19.

Swan, High St., CO10 9QA, ℰ (01787) 247477, Fax (01787) 248286, « Part 14C timbered inn », ⇄ – ✦ 🗺 ☎ ℗ – 🕭 45. 🐵 🖭 ⑩ 𝘝𝘐𝘚𝘈
Meals 17.95/24.95 **st.** and a la carte 🖟 8.00 – 🖙 9.95 – **44 rm** 75.00/120.00 **st.**, 2 suites – SB.

Angel, Market Pl., CO10 9QZ, ℰ (01787) 247388, Fax (01787) 248344, « 15C inn », ⇄ – 🗺
☎ ℗. 🐵 🖭 𝘝𝘐𝘚𝘈
closed 25 and 26 December – **Meals** a la carte 13.45/18.00 **t.** 🖟 4.95 – **8 rm** 🖙 37.50/65.00 **t.** – SB.

Great House with rm, Market Pl., CO10 9QZ, ℰ (01787) 247431, Fax (01787) 248007, « Part 14C timbered house » – 🗺 ☎. 🐵 🖭 𝘝𝘐𝘚𝘈 🗾🖙
closed 3 weeks January – **Meals** - French - (closed Sunday dinner and Monday to non-residents) 13.95/17.95 **t.** and a la carte 🖟 6.90 – **1 rm** 🖙 55.00/98.00 **t.**, **3 suites** 68.00/98.00 **t.** – SB.

LEA Lancs. – see Preston.

LEAMINGTON SPA Warks. 403 404 P 27 – see Royal Leamington Spa.

LEDBURY Herefordshire 403 404 M 27 – pop. 6 216.
🖪 3 The Homend, HR8 1BN – ℰ (01531) 636147.
London 119 – Hereford 14 – Newport 46 – Worcester 16.

Feathers, High St., HR8 1DS, ℰ (01531) 635266, Fax (01531) 632001, « Timbered 16C inn », squash – 🗺 ☎ ℗ – 🕭 120. 🐵 🖭 𝘝𝘐𝘚𝘈
Meals a la carte 14.15/25.15 **st.** 🖟 7.00 – **11 rm** 🖙 65.00/85.00 **st.** – SB.

Barn House without rest., New St., HR8 2DX, ℰ (01531) 632825, « Part 17C », ⇄ – ✦
🗺 ℗ – 🕭 30. 🐵 𝘝𝘐𝘚𝘈. 🛠
closed 25 and 26 December – **3 rm** 🖙 42.00/54.00.

Wall Hills 🛏, Hereford Rd, HR8 2PR, NW : 1 ¼ m. by Hereford Rd on A 438
ℰ (01531) 632833, ≤, ⇄ – ✦ ℗. 🐵 𝘝𝘐𝘚𝘈. 🛠
closed Christmas and New Year – **Meals** 15.75 **st.** 🖟 4.90 – **3 rm** 🖙 35.00/52.00 **st.** – SB.

at Wellington Heath N : 2 m. by B 4214 – ⊠ Ledbury.

Hope End 🛏, Hope End, HR8 1JQ, N : ¾ m. ℰ (01531) 633613, Fax (01531) 636366, « 18C house, restored Georgian gardens », park – ✦ rest, ☎ ℗. 🐵 𝘝𝘐𝘚𝘈 🗾. 🛠
closed mid December-first week February – **Meals** (booking essential) (dinner only) 30.00 **st.** 🖟 8.00 – **8 rm** 🖙 87.00/144.00 **st.** – SB.

at Preston SW : 3¼ m. by A 449 on B 4215 – ⊠ Ledbury.

Preston Priory 🛏 without rest., HR8 2LL, ℰ (01531) 660247, Fax (01531) 660247, ≤,
⇄ – ✦ 🗺 ℗. 🛠
3 rm 🖙 30.00/44.00 s.

LEEDS W. Yorks. 402 P 22 Great Britain G. – pop. 424 194.
See : City★ – City Art Gallery★ AC DZ M.
Env. : Kirkstall Abbey★ AC, NW : 3 m. by A 65 BV – Templenewsam★ (decorative arts★) AC, E : 5 m. by A 64 and A 63 CX D.
Exc. : Harewood House★★ (The Gallery★) AC, N : 8 m. by A 61 CV.
🖾, 🖾 Temple Newsam, Temple Newsam Rd, Halton ℰ (0113) 264 5624 CV – 🖾 Gotts Park, Armley Ridge Rd, Armley ℰ (0113) 234 2019 BV – 🖾 Middleton Park, Ring Rd, Beeston Park, Middleton ℰ (0113) 270 9506 CX – 🖾, 🖾 Moor Allerton, Coal Rd, Wike ℰ (0113) 266 1154 – 🖾 Howley Hall, Scotchman Lane, Morley ℰ (01924) 472432 – 🖾 Roundhay, Park Lane ℰ (0113) 266 2695, CV.
✈ Leeds - Bradford Airport : ℰ (0113) 250 9696, NW : 8 m. by A 65 and A 658 BV.
🖪 The Arcade, City Station, LS1 1PL ℰ (0113) 242 5242.
London 204 – Liverpool 75 – Manchester 43 – Newcastle upon Tyne 95 – Nottingham 74.

Plans on following pages

Oulton Hall, Rothwell Lane, Oulton, LS26 8HN, SE : 5 ½ m. by A 61 and A 639
ℰ (0113) 282 1000, Fax (0113) 282 8066, ≤, 🖆, 🚿, 🏊, 🖾, 🖾, ⇄, squash – 🛗✦, ≡ rest,
🗺 ☎ ℗ – 🕭 330. 🐵 🖭 𝘝𝘐𝘚𝘈
CX a
Bronte : Meals (closed Saturday lunch) 14.00/22.50 **st.** and dinner a la carte – **150 rm**
🖙 130.00/150.00 **st.**, 2 suites – SB.

Leeds Marriott, 4 Trevelyan Sq., Boar Lane, LS1 6ET, ℰ (0113) 236 6366,
Fax (0113) 236 6367, 🖆, 🚿, 🖾 – 🛗, ✦ rm, ≡ 🗺 ☎ ⚓ ℗ – 🕭 300. 🐵 🖭 ⑩ 𝘝𝘐𝘚𝘈
🗾
DZ x
Dyson's (ℰ (0113) 236 6444) : Meals (closed Sunday dinner) 15.95 **st.** (dinner) and a la carte 16.90/21.90 **t.** 🖟 7.50 – 🖙 10.95 – **240 rm** 89.00/99.00 **st.**, 4 suites – SB.

315

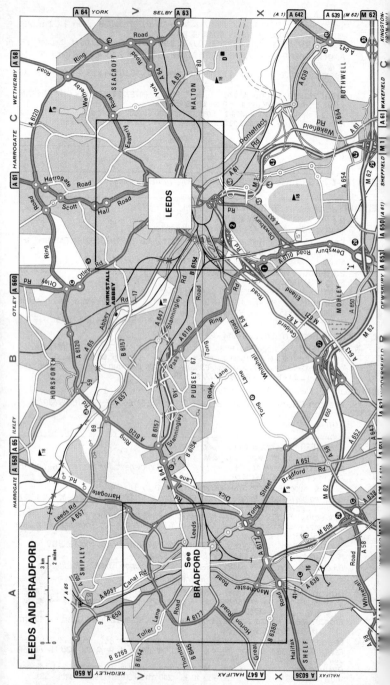

LEEDS AND BRADFORD

LEEDS

See BRADFORD

KIRKSTALL ABBEY

PUDSEY

HORSFORTH

MORLEY

ROTHWELL

HALTON

SHELF

3 km
2 miles

316

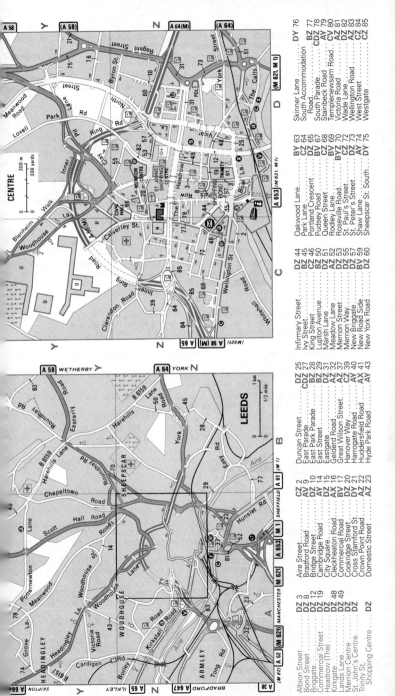

317

42 The Calls, 42 The Calls, LS2 7EW, ℰ (0113) 244 0099, Fax (0113) 234 4100, ≤, « Converted riverside grain mill » – |≢|, ⇔ rm, ⊡ ☎ ⇔ – ⚿ 55. ◉ᴼ ㎒ ⑪ 𝓥𝓢𝓐. ⅍ closed 5 days Christmas – Meals – (see **Pool Court at 42** below) – (see also **Brasserie Forty Four** below) – ⊈ 11.50 – **38 rm** 95.00/145.00 st., 3 suites – SB.
DZ z

Holiday Inn Crown Plaza, Wellington St., LS1 4DL, ℰ (0113) 244 2200, Fax (0113) 244 0460, ₣₰, ⇔s, ⊠ – |≢|, ⇔ rm, ▤ ☎ & ⓟ – ⚿ 200. ◉ᴼ ㎒ ⑪ 𝓥𝓢𝓐. ⅍
CZ c
Meals 14.95/17.95 t. and a la carte ⅃ 5.95 – ⊈ 11.95 – **120 rm** 120.00 st., 5 suites – SB.

Hilton National Leeds, Neville St., LS1 4BX, ℰ (0113) 244 2000, Fax (0113) 243 3577, ₣₰, ⇔s, ⊠ – |≢|, ⇔ rm, ▤ ⊡ ☎ & ⓟ – ⚿ 400. ◉ᴼ ㎒ ⑪ 𝓥𝓢𝓐 ᴶᶜᴮ
AZ r
Meals 11.95/16.95 t. and a la carte ⅃ 6.50 – ⊈ 11.95 – **186 rm** 115.00 st., 20 suites.

Queen's, City Sq., LS1 1PL, ℰ (0113) 243 1323, Fax (0113) 242 5154 – |≢|, ⇔ rm, ▣ ⊡ & ⓟ – ⚿ 600. ◉ᴼ ㎒ ⑪ 𝓥𝓢𝓐 ᴶᶜᴮ. ⅍
DZ a
Meals (carving rest.) 12.50/15.70 st. ⅃ 6.25 – **Harewood :** Meals (closed Saturday lunch) 10.50/17.50 and a la carte ⅃ 6.25 – ⊈ 11.50 – **184 rm** 85.00/95.00 st., 6 suites – SB.

Village H. and Leisure Club, Otley Rd, Headingley, LS16 5PR, NW : 3 ½ m. on A 660 ℰ (0113) 278 1000, Fax (0113) 278 1111, ₣₰, ⇔s, ⊿, ⊠, squash – |≢| ⇔ ▤ ▣ ☎ & ⓟ – ⚿ 250. ◉ᴼ ㎒ ⑪ 𝓥𝓢𝓐. ⅍
Meals (grill rest.) a la carte 9.90/23.40 t. ⅃ 3.90 – **94 rm** 86.00/119.00 t.

Weetwood Hall, Otley Rd, LS16 5PS, NW : 4 m. on A 660 ℰ (0113) 230 6000, Fax (0113) 230 6095, ⅏ – |≢| ⇔, ▤ rest, ▣ ☎ & ⓟ – ⚿ 150. ◉ᴼ ㎒ ⑪ 𝓥𝓢𝓐. ⅍
BV c
Meals 12.95/15.25 st. and dinner a la carte ⅃ 6.95 – ⊈ 8.25 – **108 rm** 72.50/120.00 st.

Haley's, Shire Oak Rd, Headingley, LS6 2DE, NW : 2 m. off Otley Rd (A 660) ℰ (0113) 278 4446, Fax (0113) 275 3342 – ⇔ rm, ▣ ☎ ⓟ – ⚿ 25. ◉ᴼ ㎒ ⑪ 𝓥𝓢𝓐 ᴶᶜᴮ. ⅍ CV s closed 26 to 30 December – Meals (closed Sunday dinner to non-residents) (dinner only and Sunday lunch June-September)/dinner a la carte 22.25/26.75 st. ⅃ 6.75 – **22 rm** ⊈ 110.00/150.00 st. – SB.

Merrion Thistle, Merrion Centre, 17 Wade Lane, LS2 8NH, ℰ (0113) 243 9191, Fax (0113) 242 3527 – |≢| ⇔, ▤ rest, ▣ ☎ ⓟ – ⚿ 80. ◉ᴼ ㎒ ⑪ 𝓥𝓢𝓐 ᴶᶜᴮ
DZ e
Meals 14.75 t. (dinner) and a la carte 20.45/27.40 t. ⅃ 5.40 – ⊈ 9.75 – **108 rm** 99.00/120.00 st., 1 suite.

Metropole, King St., LS1 2HQ, ℰ (0113) 245 0841, Fax (0113) 242 5156 – |≢|, ⇔ rm, ▣ ☎ & ⓟ – ⚿ 200. ◉ᴼ ㎒ 𝓥𝓢𝓐
CZ e
Meals (closed Sunday lunch and Bank Holidays) 15.95 t. (dinner) and a la carte 16.00/25.00 st. ⅃ 5.25 – ⊈ 9.95 – **104 rm** 89.00/150.00 st., 1 suite – SB.

Golden Lion, 2 Lower Briggate, LS1 4AE, ℰ (0113) 243 6454, Fax (0113) 242 9327 – |≢|, ⇔ rm, ▣ ☎ ⓟ – ⚿ 120. ◉ᴼ ㎒ ⑪ 𝓥𝓢𝓐 ᴶᶜᴮ
DZ v
Meals (bar lunch)/dinner 16.25 t. and a la carte ⅃ 4.65 – **89 rm** ⊈ 91.00/111.00 – SB.

Holiday Inn Express, Aberford Rd, Oulton, LS26 8EJ, SE : 5 ½ m. by A 61 on A 639 ℰ (0113) 282 6201, Fax (0113) 282 9243 – ⇔ rm, ▣ & ⓟ – ⚿ 60
CX e
49 rm.

Travel Inn, Citygate, Wellington St., LS3 1LH, ℰ (0113) 242 8104, Fax (0113) 242 8105 – |≢| ⇔ rm, ▣ & ⓟ. ◉ᴼ ㎒ ⑪ 𝓥𝓢𝓐. ⅍
AZ v
Meals (grill rest.) – **84 rm** 36.50 t.

Pinewood, 78 Potternewton Lane, LS7 3LW, ℰ (0113) 262 2561, Fax (0113) 262 2561, ⅏ – ▤ rest, ▣ ◉ᴼ ㎒ 𝓥𝓢𝓐. ⅍
AY a
Meals (by arrangement) 9.95 t. – **10 rm** ⊈ 35.00/42.00 t.

Pool Court at 42 (at 42 The Calls H.), 44 The Calls, LS2 7EW, ℰ (0113) 244 4242, Fax (0113) 234 3332, 斎, « Riverside setting » – ▤. ◉ᴼ ㎒ 𝓥𝓢𝓐
DZ z
closed Saturday lunch, Sunday, 1 week Christmas and Bank Holidays – Meals 17.00/29.50 t. ⅃ 8.95
Spec. Chicken and crab boudin with steamed seaweed and lobster velouté. Duckling breast with duck confit and foie gras pie, port wine sauce. Bitter-sweet chocolate "St. Emilion" with crème anglaise.

Rascasse (Gueller), Canal Wharf, Water Lane, LS11 5BB, ℰ (0113) 244 6611 Fax (0113) 244 0736, ≤, « Converted grain warehouse, canalside setting » – ▤. ◉ᴼ ㎒ ⑪ 𝓥𝓢𝓐
AZ c
closed Saturday lunch, Sunday, 1 week after Christmas and Bank Holiday Mondays – Meals 17.00/18.00 t. and a la carte 21.75/31.25 t. ⅃ 7.00
Spec. Marinière of monkfish and calamari, fresh coriander. Papillotes of squab pigeon "Rascasse", essence of ceps. Caramelised lemon tart, raspberry sorbet.

Leodis, Victoria Mill, Sovereign St., LS1 4BJ, ℰ (0113) 242 1010, Fax (0113) 243 0432, 斎 « Converted riverside warehouse » – ▤. ◉ᴼ ㎒ ⑪ 𝓥𝓢𝓐 ᴶᶜᴮ
AZ e
closed Saturday lunch, Sunday, 25-26 December and 1 January – Meals 13.95 t. and a la carte 15.90/25.30 t. ⅃ 6.45.

XX **Brasserie Forty Four** (at 42 The Calls H.), 44 The Calls, LS2 7EW, ℰ (0113) 234 3232,
Fax (0113) 234 3332 – ■. **M③** **AE** **①** **VISA**   DZ z
closed Saturday lunch, Sunday, 1 week Christmas and Bank Holidays – **Meals** 11.95 t.
(lunch) and dinner a la carte 17.35/21.90 t. ⓘ 7.70.

XX **Fourth Floor** (at Harvey Nichols), 107-111 Briggate, LS1 6AZ, ℰ (0113) 204 8000,
Fax (0113) 204 8080 – ■. **M③** **AE** **①** **VISA** **JCB**   DZ s
closed dinner Monday to Wednesday, Sunday, 25-26 December and 1 January – **Meals**
a la carte 16.25/26.50 t. ⓘ 7.50.

XX **Maxi's,** 6 Bingley St., LS3 1LX, off Kirkstall Rd ℰ (0113) 244 0552, Fax (0113) 234 3902,
« Pagoda, ornate decor » – ■ **Ⓟ**. **M③** **AE** **①** **VISA**   AZ a
Meals - Chinese (Canton, Peking) - 17.50 t. and a la carte.

XX **Lucky Dragon,** Templar Lane, LS2 7LP, ℰ (0113) 245 0520, Fax (0113) 245 0520 – ■. **M③**
AE **VISA**   DZ u
closed 25 December – **Meals** - Chinese (Cantonese) - 15.50 t. ⓘ 4.75.

X **The Calls Grill,** Calls Landing, 38 The Calls, LS2 7EW, ℰ (0113) 245 3870,
Fax (0113) 243 9035, « Converted riverside warehouse » – ■ **Ⓟ**. **M③** **AE** **①** **VISA**   DZ c
closed Sunday lunch – **Meals** (grill rest.) 11.00 t. (dinner) and a la carte 13.10/25.95 t.
ⓘ 6.95.

X **Sous le nez en ville,** Quebec House, Quebec St., LS1 2HA, ℰ (0113) 244 0108,
Fax (0113) 245 0240 – **M③** **AE** **VISA**   CZ a
closed Sunday, 25-26 December and Bank Holidays – **Meals** 14.95 st. (dinner)
and a la carte 17.40/24.15 ⓘ 5.75.

X **Est, Est, Est,** 151 Otley Old Rd, LS16 6HN, NW : 4 ½ m. by A 660 off Cookridge rd
ℰ (0113) 267 2100 – ■ **Ⓟ**. **M③** **AE** **VISA**
Meals - Italian - a la carte 7.30/21.35 t. ⓘ 5.05.

X **Shears Yard,** The Calls, LS2 7EY, ℰ (0113) 244 4144 – ■. **M③** **AE** **VISA** **JCB**   DZ a
closed Sunday and 25 to 30 December – **Meals** 10.95 t. (dinner) and a la carte 17.10/
22.85 t. ⓘ 5.75.

at Seacroft *NE : 5½ m. at junction of A 64 with A 6120* – ✉ *Leeds.*

🏨 Stakis Leeds, Ring Rd, LS14 5QF, ℰ (0113) 273 2323, Fax (0113) 232 3018 – ▐, ⁵⁺ rm, 📺
☎ **Ⓟ** – 🔬 250   CV a
100 rm.

at Garforth *E : 6 m. by A 63* – CV – *at junction with A 642* – ✉ *Leeds.*

🏨 Hilton National, Wakefield Rd, LS25 1LH, ℰ (0113) 286 6556, Fax (0113) 286 8326, **Fↄ**, **⊆s**,
▣ – ⁵⁺ rm, ■ rest, 📺 ☎ & **Ⓟ** – 🔬 350
144 rm.

XX **Aagrah,** Aberford Rd, LS25 1BA, on A 642 ℰ (0113) 287 6606 – **Ⓟ**. **M③** **AE** **VISA**
closed 25 December – **Meals** - Indian - (dinner only) a la carte 10.80/16.30 t.

at Pudsey *W : 5 ¾ m. by A 647* – AZ – ✉ *Leeds.*

XX **Aagrah,** 483 Bradford Rd, LS28 8ED, on A 647 ℰ (01274) 668818, Fax (01274) 669803 – **Ⓟ**.
M③ **AE** **VISA**   BV e
closed 25 December – **Meals** - Indian - (dinner only) a la carte 10.80/16.30 t.

at Horsforth *NW : 5 m. by A 65 off A 6120* – ✉ *Leeds.*

X **Paris,** Calverley Bridge, Calverley Lane, Rodley, LS13 1NP, SW : 1 m. by A 6120
ℰ (0113) 258 1885, Fax (0113) 239 0651 – ■ **Ⓟ** – 🔬 40. **M③** **AE** **①** **VISA**   BV a
closed Saturday lunch and 26 December – **Meals** 11.95 t. and a la carte ⓘ 6.00.

at Bramhope *NW : 8 m. on A 660* – BV – ✉ *Leeds.*

🏨 **Forte Posthouse Leeds/Bradford,** Leeds Rd, LS16 9JJ, ℰ (0113) 284 2911,
Fax (0113) 284 3451, ≤, **Fↄ**, **⊆s**, ▣, 🌫, park – ▐, ⁵⁺ rm, 📺 ☎ **Ⓟ** – 🔬 160. **M③** **AE** **①** **VISA**
Meals a la carte 9.95/24.55 st. ⓘ 6.95 – ☲ 10.95 – **123 rm** 89.00 st., 1 suite – SB.

🏨 **Jarvis Parkway H. and Country Club,** Otley Rd, LS16 8AG, S : 2 m. on A 660
ℰ (0113) 267 2551, Fax (0113) 267 4410, **Fↄ**, **⊆s**, ▣, 🌫, ✗ – ▐, ⁵⁺ rm, 📺 ☎ & **Ⓟ** –
🔬 300. **M③** **AE** **①** **VISA**
Meals 13.50/16.80 t. and dinner a la carte ⓘ 6.00 – ☲ 10.50 – **105 rm** 99.00/109.00 st. – SB.

at Yeadon *NW : 8 m. by A 65 on A 658* – BV – ✉ *Leeds.*

🏨 **Travel Inn,** Victoria Av., LS19 7AW, on A 658 ℰ (0113) 250 4284, Fax (0113) 250 5838 –
⁵⁺ rm, 📺 & **Ⓟ**. **M③** **AE** **①** **VISA**. 🌫
Meals (grill rest.) – **40 rm** 36.50 t.

🔧 ATS Cross Green Lane ℰ (0113) 245 9423   ATS 2 Regent St. ℰ (0113) 243 0652

La guida cambia, cambiate la guida ogni anno.

LEEK Staffs. **402** **403** **404** N 24 – pop. 18 167.

᠊᠍᠍᠍ Westwood, Newcastle Rd, Wallbridge ℘ (01538) 398385.

🖪 Market Pl., ST13 5HH ℘ (01538) 381000.

London 122 – Derby 30 – Manchester 39 – Stoke-on-Trent 12.

↑ **Country Cottage** ⟩, Back Lane Farm, Winkhill, ST13 7PJ, SE : 5 ½ m. by A 523 (turning left opposite Little Chef) ℘ (01538) 308273, Fax (01538) 308098, ≤, ⌁, park – ⥲ 📺 🅿. ⅍

Meals 12.50 st. – **4 rm** � 19.00/39.00 st.

at Butterton E : 8 m. by A 523 off B 5053 – ✉ Leek.

᠊ **Black Lion Inn** with rm, ST13 7ST, ℘ (01538) 304232, « 18C », ⌁ – 📺 🅿. �🔟 VISA. ⅍
Meals (closed Wednesday lunch) (in bar except Friday and Saturday dinner and Sunday lunch) a la carte 10.25/14.25 t. – **3 rm** ⊇ 35.00/50.00 t.

LEEMING BAR N. Yorks. **402** P 21 – pop. 1 824 – ✉ Northallerton.

London 235 – Leeds 44 – Middlesbrough 30 – Newcastle upon Tyne 52 – York 37.

᠊ **White Rose**, DL7 9AY, ℘ (01677) 422707, Fax (01677) 425123 – 📺 ☎ 🅿. �🔟 🅰🅴 ⓪ VISA
Meals (bar lunch) a la carte 9.75/14.25 st. – **18 rm** ⊇ 34.00/46.00 st.

LEICESTER
BUILT UP AREA

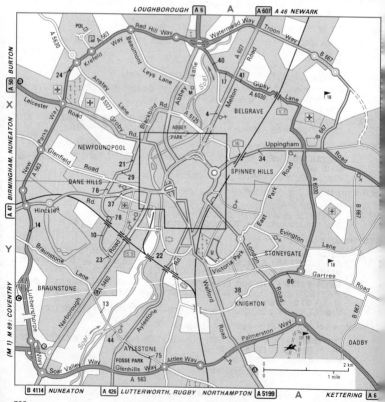

LEICESTER 402 403 404 Q 26 *Great Britain G. – pop. 318 518.*

See : *Guildhall*★ BY **B** – *Museum and Art Gallery*★ CY **M2** – *St. Mary de Castro Church*★ BY **A**.

☐ Leicestershire, Evington Lane ℘ (0116) 273 6035, AY – ☐ Western Park, Scudamore Rd ℘ (0116) 287 6158/287 2339 – ☐ Humberstone Heights, Gipsy Lane ℘ (0116) 276 1905/3680, AX – ☐ Oadby, Leicester Road Racecourse ℘ (0116) 270 0215/270 9052, AY.

✈ East Midlands Airport, Castle Donington : ℘ (01332) 852852 NW : 22 m. by A 50 – AX – and M1.

🏢 7-9 Every St., Town Hall Sq., LE1 6AG ℘ (0116) 265 0555.

London 107 – Birmingham 43 – Coventry 24 – Nottingham 26.

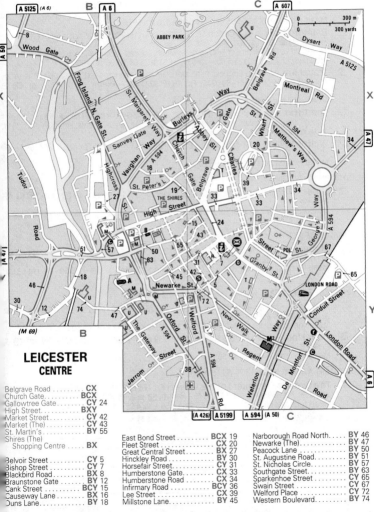

LEICESTER
CENTRE

Belgrave Road .... **CX**
Church Gate .... **BCX**
Gallowtree Gate .... **CY** 24
High Street .... **BXY**
Market Street .... **CY** 42
Market (The) .... **CY** 43
St. Martin's .... **BY** 55
Shires (The)
  Shopping Centre ..... **BX**

Belvoir Street .... **CY** 5
Bishop Street .... **CY** 7
Blackbird Road .... **BX** 8
Braunstone Gate .... **BY** 12
Cank Street .... **BCY** 15
Causeway Lane .... **BX** 16
Duns Lane .... **BY** 18

East Bond Street .... **BCX** 19	Narborough Road North..... **BY** 46
Fleet Street .... **CX** 20	Newarke (The)............. **BY** 47
Great Central Street........ **BX** 27	Peacock Lane .... **BY** 50
Hinckley Road .... **CY** 31	St. Augustine Road........ **BY** 51
Horsefair Street........... **CY** 33	St. Nicholas Circle........ **BY** 57
Humberstone Gate........ **CX** 33	Southgate Street.......... **BY** 63
Humberstone Road .... **CX** 34	Sparkenhoe Street........ **CY** 65
Infirmary Road .... **BCY** 36	Swain Street .... **CY** 67
Lee Street .... **CX** 39	Welford Place .... **BY** 72
Millstone Lane............ **BY** 45	Western Boulevard........ **BY** 74

🏨 **Stakis Leicester**, Junction 21 Approach, Braunstone, LE3 2WQ, SW : 3 ½ m. by A 5460 at junction with A 563 ℘ (0116) 263 0066, *Fax* (0116) 263 0627, ☏, 🍸, 🔲, 🐾 – 🛬 rm, ▤ rest, 🆃🆅 🕿 🕭 🖃 – 🕍 200. 🏧 AE ⓪ 🆅🆂🅰 🆓🅲🅱 AY **e**
Meals (bar lunch Saturday) 13.50/19.50 **st.** and a la carte ᵃ 8.00 – � 9.95 – **168 rm** 101.00/111.00 **st.**, 2 suites – SB.

Holiday Inn Leicester, 129 St. Nicholas Circle, LE1 5LX, ☎ (0116) 253 1161, *Fax (0116) 251 3169*, ⅙, ⌂, ▣ – ▤, ⅍ rm, ▤ ⅏ ☎ ⅙ ⅌ – ⅍ 280. ◍◐ ᴀᴇ ① ᴠⁱˢᴀ ᴊᶜᴮ. ⅍
BY c
The Hayloft : Meals 12.95/18.25 t. and a la carte ⅙ 6.50 – ⌂ 9.95 – **187 rm** 110.00/120.00 st., 1 suite.

Grand, 73 Granby St., LE1 6ES, ☎ (0116) 255 5599, *Fax (0116) 254 4736* – ▤, ⅍ rm, ▤ ☎ ⅌ – ⅍ 450. ◍◐ ᴀᴇ ① ᴠⁱˢᴀ
CY o
Meals *(closed 1 January)* (bar lunch Monday to Saturday)/dinner 17.95 st. and a la carte ⅙ 10.75 – ⌂ 9.95 – **91 rm** 95.00/120.00 st., 1 suite – SB.

Forte Posthouse Leicester, Braunstone Lane East, LE3 2FW, SW : 2 m. on A 5460 ☎ (0116) 263 0500, *Fax (0116) 282 3623* – ▤, ⅍ rm, ▤ rest, ▤ ☎ ⅌ – ⅍ 80. ◍◐ ᴀᴇ ① ᴠⁱˢᴀ
AY u
Meals a la carte 17.45/23.95 st. – ⌂ 8.95 – **170 rm** 69.00 st. – SB.

Belmont House, De Montfort St., LE1 7GR, ☎ (0116) 254 4773, *Fax (0116) 247 0804* – ▤, ⅍ rm, ▤ ☎ ⅌ – ⅍ 100. ◍◐ ᴀᴇ ① ᴠⁱˢᴀ ᴊᶜᴮ. ⅍
CY c
closed 25 to 29 December – **Cherry's :** Meals *(closed Saturday lunch and Bank Holiday Mondays)* 12.75/19.50 t. ⅙ 5.80 – ⌂ 8.50 – **65 rm** 75.00/93.00 st. – SB.

Travel Inn, Meridian Business Park, Meridian Way, Braunstone, LE3 2LW, SW : 3 ¾ m. by A 47 off A 563 ☎ (0116) 289 0945, *Fax (0116) 282 7486* – ⅍ rm, ▤ rm, ▤ ⅙ ⅌. ◍◐ ᴀᴇ ① ᴠⁱˢᴀ
AY c
Meals (grill rest.) – **51 rm** 36.50 t.

The Tiffin, 1 De Montfort St., LE1 7GA, ☎ (0116) 247 0420 – ▤. ◍◐ ᴀᴇ ① ᴠⁱˢᴀ
CY r
closed lunch Saturday and Bank Holidays and Sunday – Meals - Indian - 17.25 t. and a la carte.

Welford Place, 9 Welford Place, LE1 6ZH, ☎ (0116) 247 0758, *Fax (0116) 247 1843* – ◍◐ ᴀᴇ ① ᴠⁱˢᴀ
CY s
Meals 11.50 st. and a la carte ⅙ 7.20.

at Rothley N : 5 m. by A 6 – AX – on B 5328 – ⊠ Leicester.

Limes, 35 Mountsorrel Lane, LE7 7PS, ☎ (0116) 230 2531 – ⅍ rest, ▤ ▤ ☎ ⅌. ◍◐ ᴀᴇ ᴠⁱˢᴀ ᴊᶜᴮ. ⅍
closed 22 December-5 January – Meals (residents only) (dinner only) a la carte approx. 11.50/18.40 st. – **11 rm** ⌂ 42.50/60.00 st.

at Wigston SE : 3 ¼ m. on A 50 – ⊠ Leicester.

Stage, Leicester Rd, LE18 1JW, ☎ (0116) 288 6161, *Fax (0116) 281 1874*, ⅙, ⌂, ▣ – ⅍ rm, ▤ rest, ▤ ☎ ⅙ ⅌ – ⅍ 250. ◍◐ ᴀᴇ ① ᴠⁱˢᴀ. ⅍
AY a
Meals (carving lunch Sunday) 9.95/16.95 st. and a la carte ⅙ 7.95 – ⌂ 8.50 – **75 rm** 69.00/89.00 st. – SB.

at Leicester Forest East W : 3 m. on A 47 – AY – ⊠ Leicester.

Red Cow, Hinckley Rd, LE3 3PG, ☎ (0116) 238 7878, *Fax (0116) 238 6539* – ⅍ rm, ▤ ☎ ⅙ ⅌. ◍◐ ᴀᴇ ① ᴠⁱˢᴀ. ⅍
Meals (grill rest.) a la carte 10.85/19.15 t. ⅙ 4.10 – ⌂ 4.95 – **31 rm** 39.50 t.

Travel Inn, Hinckley Rd, LE3 3GD, ☎ (0116) 239 4677, *Fax (0116) 239 3429* – ⅍ rm, ▤ ⅙ ⅌. ◍◐ ᴀᴇ ① ᴠⁱˢᴀ. ⅍
Meals (grill rest.) – **40 rm** 36.50 t.

at Glenfield NW : 4 ¾ m. by A 50 – ⊠ Leicester.

The Gynsills - Premier Lodge, Leicester Rd, LE3 8HB, NE : ¾ m. by Station Rd off A 50 ☎ (0116) 231 3693, *Fax (0116) 321148* – ⅍ rm, ▤ ☎ ⅙ ⅌. ◍◐ ᴀᴇ ① ᴠⁱˢᴀ. ⅍
AX a
Meals (grill rest.) a la carte 8.40/15.15 st. ⅙ 4.55 – ⌂ 4.95 – **43 rm** 42.25 st. – SB.

◎ ATS 16 Wanlip St. ☎ (0116) 262 4281   ATS 31 Woodgate ☎ (0116) 262 5611

LEICESTER FOREST EAST Leics. 402 403 404 Q26 – see Leicester.

LEIGH Dorset 403 404 M 31 – see Sherborne.

Particularly pleasant hotels and restaurants
are shown in the Guide by a red symbol.

Please send us the names
of anywhere you have enjoyed your stay.

Your **Michelin Guide** will be even better.

🏠🏠🏠 ... 🏠

XXXXX ... X

LEIGH DELAMERE SERVICE AREA Wilts. – ✉ Chippenham.

🏨 **Travelodge** without rest., SN14 6LB, M 4 between junctions 18 and 17 (eastbound carriageway) ℰ (01666) 837691, Fax (01666) 837112, Reservations (Freephone) 0800 850950 – ✚ ⊤⊽ ☎ ♿ 🅿. ⓪ ℀ ⓪ 𝑉𝐼𝑆𝐴 J̄C̄B̄. ℀
51rm 46.95 **t.**

LEIGHTON BUZZARD Beds. 404 S 28 – pop. 32 610.
  ⯆ Plantation Rd ℰ (01525) 373811/373812 – ⯆ Aylesbury Vale, Wing ℰ (01525) 240196.
  London 47 – Bedford 20 – Luton 12 – Northampton 30.

🏠 **Grove Farm** ℀, Grove, LU7 0QU, S : 3 ½ m. by A 4146, A 505 and B 488 on Grove Church rd ℰ (01525) 372225, Fax (01525) 854565, ≼, 🐎, 🔲, 🌿, park – ⊤⊽ 🅿. ⓪ ℀ 𝑉𝐼𝑆𝐴. ℀
Meals (by arrangement) (communal dining) 17.50 **st.** – **3 rm** ⊇ 35.00/70.00 **st.**

  ⓪ ATS Grovebury Road ℰ (01525) 376158

LEINTWARDINE Shrops. 403 L 26 – ✉ Craven Arms.
  London 156 – Birmingham 55 – Hereford 24 – Worcester 40.

🏠 **Upper Buckton Farm** ℀, Buckton, SY7 0JU, W : 2 m. by A 4113 and Buckton rd ℰ (01547) 540634, ≼, « Working farm », 🌿 – 🅿. ℀
Meals (by arrangement) 18.00 **s.** – **3 rm** ⊇ 35.00/50.00.

🏠 **Lower House** ℀, Adforton, SY7 0NF, S : 2 ¼ m. by A 4113 off B 4530 ℰ (01568) 770223, Fax (01568) 770592, 🌿 – ✚ 🅿. ℀
Meals (communal dining) 16.00 **st.** – **4 rm** ⊇ 26.00/52.00.

Pour les grands voyages d'affaires ou de tourisme,
Guide Rouge MICHELIN : EUROPE.

LENHAM Kent 404 W 30 – pop. 2 167 – ✉ Maidstone.
  London 45 – Folkestone 28 – Maidstone 9.

XX **Lime Tree** with rm, 8-10 The Limes, The Square, ME17 2PQ, ℰ (01622) 859509, Fax (01622) 850096 – ⊤⊽ ☎ ⓪ ℀ ⓪ 𝑉𝐼𝑆𝐴 J̄C̄B̄. ℀
closed Monday lunch and Sunday dinner – **Meals** 17.95/19.95 **t.** and a la carte ♦ 9.50 – **10 rm** ⊇ 42.50/56.50 **st.**

at Warren Street NE : 2 m. on Warren Street rd – ✉ Maidstone.

🏨 **Harrow Inn**, ME17 2ED, ℰ (01622) 858727, Fax (01622) 850026, 🌿 – ⊤⊽ ☎ 🅿. ⓪ ℀ 𝑉𝐼𝑆𝐴. ℀
closed 25 and 26 December – **Meals** (in bar Sunday dinner) a la carte 16.00/19.00 **t.** – **13 rm** ⊇ 39.50/49.50 **t.** – SB.

LEOMINSTER Herefordshire 403 L 27 Great Britain G. – pop. 9 543.
  Env. : Berrington Hall★ AC, N : 3 m. by A 49.
  ⯆ Ford Bridge ℰ (01568) 612863.
  🎫 1 Corn Sq., HR6 8LR ℰ (01568) 616460 (summer only).
  London 141 – Birmingham 47 – Hereford 13 – Worcester 26.

🏠 **Heath House** ℀, Stoke Prior, HR6 0NF, SE : 3 ¾ m. by A 44 on Risbury rd ℰ (01568) 760385, Fax (01568) 760385 – ✚ 🅿. ℀
March-November – **Meals** (by arrangement) (communal dining) 15.00 **st.** ♦ 3.00 – **3 rm** ⊇ 24.00/48.00 **st.**

at Kimbolton NE : 3 m. by A 49 on A 4112.

🏠 **Lower Bache House** ℀, HR6 0ER, E : 1 ¾ m. by A 4112 ℰ (01568) 750304, « Part 17C farmhouse », 🌿, park – ✚ ⊤⊽ 🅿. ℀
Meals (communal dining) 15.50 **st.** ♦ 5.00 – **3 rm** ⊇ 31.50/53.00 **st.** – SB.

at Eyton NW : 2 m. by B 4361 – ✉ Leominster.

🏨 **The Marsh** ℀, HR6 0AG, ℰ (01568) 613952, « Part 14C timbered house », 🌿 – ✚ ⊤⊽ ☎ 🅿. ⓪ ℀ ⓪ 𝑉𝐼𝑆𝐴. ℀
closed January – **Meals** (booking essential) (dinner only and Sunday lunch) 25.50 **st.** ♦ 7.50 – **4 rm** ⊇ 90.00/125.00 **st.** – SB.

  ⓪ ATS Market Mill, Dishley St. ℰ (01568) 612679/ 614114

LETCHWORTH Herts. 🔢 T 28 – pop. 31 418.
London 40 – Bedford 22 – Cambridge 22 – Luton 14.

🏠 **Broadway Toby,** The Broadway, SG6 3NZ, ℘ (01462) 480111, Fax (01462) 481563 – 📳,
🍴 rm, 📺 ☎ 🅿 – 🔬 200. 🔟 🕰 ⑩ 💳 ⛷
Meals (grill rest.) a la carte 8.00/14.50 **st.** – **34 rm** ⊇ 62.50/75.50 **st.** – SB.

⑩ ATS Unit 21, Jubilee Trade Centre, Works Rd ℘ (01462) 670517

LEWDOWN Devon 🔢 H 32 The West Country G.
Env. : Lydford★★, E : 4 m.
Exc. : Launceston★ - Castle★ (≤★) St. Mary Magdalene★, W : 8 m. by A 30 and A 388.
London 238 – Exeter 37 – Plymouth 22.

🏠 **Lewtrenchard Manor** ⬎, EX20 4PN, S : ¾ m. by Lewtrenchard rd ℘ (01566) 783256,
Fax (01566) 783332, « 17C manor house and gardens », ⬎, park – 🍴 rest, 📺 ☎ 🅿 –
🔬 50. 🔟 🕰 ⑩ 💳 ⛷
Meals (lunch by arrangement Monday to Saturday)/dinner 28.00 **t.** ₰ 5.00 – **9 rm** ⊇ 80.00/
140.00 **t.**

LEWES E. Sussex 🔢 U 31 Great Britain G. – pop. 15 376.
See : Town★ (High Street★, Keere Street★) – Castle (≤★) AC.
Exc. : Sheffield Park Garden★ AC, N : 9 ½ m. by A 275.
🔢 Chapel Hill ℘ (01273) 473245.
🎫 187 High St., BN7 2DE ℘ (01273) 483448.
London 53 – Brighton 8 – Hastings 29 – Maidstone 43.

🏨 **Shelleys,** High St., BN7 1XS, ℘ (01273) 472361, Fax (01273) 483152, 🍴, 🌳 – 📺 ☎ 🅿 –
🔬 50. 🔟 🕰 ⑩ 💳 💳 ⛷
Meals 17.50/25.00 **st.** and a la carte ₰ 8.50 – ⊇ 11.50 – **18 rm** 115.00/204.00 **st.**, 1 suite –
SB.

🏠 **Millers** without rest., 134 High St., BN7 1XS, ℘ (01273) 475631, Fax (01273) 486226, 🌳 –
🍴 📺 ⛷
closed 4-5 November and 20 December-5 January – **3 rm** ⊇ 45.00/50.00 **s.**

✗ **Pailin,** 20 Station St., BN7 2DB, ℘ (01273) 473906, Fax (01273) 622665 – 🔟 🕰 ⑩ 💳 💳
closed Sunday and 25-26 December – **Meals** - Thai - a la carte 12.45/17.45 **t.**

⑩ ATS 18 North St. ℘ (01273) 477972

LEYLAND Lancs. 🔢 L 22 – pop. 3 729 London 224.
Blackburn 12 – Lancaster 30 – Leeds 68 – Preston 7.

🏠 **Jarvis Leyland,** Leyland Way, PR5 2JX, E : ¾ m. on B 5256 ℘ (01772) 422922,
Fax (01772) 622282, ☎, 🔳 – 🍴 📺 ☎ 🅿 – 🔬 230. 🔟 🕰 ⑩ 💳
Meals (bar lunch Saturday) 9.95/13.95 **st.** and a la carte ₰ 5.75 – ⊇ 5.75 – **93 rm** 69.00/
79.00 **st.** – SB.

LICHFIELD Staffs. 🔢 🔢 🔢 O 25 Great Britain G. – pop. 28 666.
See : City★ - Cathedral★★ AC.
🔢, 🔢 Seedy Mill, Elmhurst ℘ (01543) 417333.
🎫 Donegal House, Bore St., WS13 6NE ℘ (01543) 252109.
London 128 – Birmingham 16 – Derby 23 – Stoke-on-Trent 30.

🏠 **Little Barrow,** Beacon St., WS13 7AR, ℘ (01543) 414500, Fax (01543) 415734 – 📺 ☎ 🅿 –
🔬 100. 🔟 🕰 ⑩ 💳 ⛷
closed 25 December – **Meals** 11.00/15.50 **t.** and a la carte ₰ 5.50 – **24 rm** ⊇ 55.00/65.00 **t.**
– SB.

✗✗ **Thrales,** 40-44 Tamworth St., WS13 6JJ, (corner of Backcester Lane) ℘ (01543) 255091
Fax (01543) 415352 – 🔟 💳
closed Sunday dinner, Bank Holiday Mondays and 31 December – **Meals** 9.50/11.50 **t.**
and a la carte ₰ 6.00.

✗ **Chandlers Grande Brasserie,** Corn Exchange, Conduit St., WS13 6JU,
℘ (01543) 416688, Fax (01543) 417887 – 🔟 🕰 💳
Meals 9.90/12.50 **st.** and a la carte ₰ 4.25.

⑩ ATS Eastern Av. ℘ (01543) 414200

---

*To visit a town or region: use the **Michelin** Green Guides.*

LIFTON Devon **403** H 32 *The West Country G.* – *pop. 964.*

Env. : *Launceston★ – Castle★ (≼★) St. Mary Magdalene★, W : 4 ½ m. by A 30 and A 388.*

London 238 – Bude 24 – Exeter 37 – Launceston 4 – Plymouth 32.

🏨 **Lifton Hall,** PL16 0DR, ℘ (01566) 784863, *Fax (01566) 784770* – ⅍ rest, 📺 ☎ 🅿. 🆖 🅐🅔 ① 🆅🆂🅰. ⅍
Herbs : Meals (bar meals except Friday and Saturday dinner) 23.50 **st.** ▯ 7.95 – **11 rm** ⍁ 50.00/90.00 **st.** – SB.

🏨 **Arundell Arms,** Fore St., PL16 0AA, ℘ (01566) 784666, *Fax (01566) 784494*, ⤚, ☞ – ⅍ rest, 📺 ☎ 🅿 – 🔏 100. 🆖 🅐🅔 ① 🆅🆂🅰
closed Christmas – Meals – (see below) – **28 rm** ⍁ 68.00/108.00 **st.** – SB.

🏠 **Thatched Cottage** ⌂, Sprytown, PL16 0AY, E : 1 ¼ m. by old A 30 ℘ (01566) 784224, *Fax (01566) 784334*, ☞ – ⅍ rest, 📺 ☎ 🅿. 🆖 🅐🅔 ① 🆅🆂🅰 🅹🅲🅱
Meals a la carte 11.95/23.85 **t.** ▯ 7.95 – **5 rm** ⍁ 38.50/99.00 **st.** – SB.

XX **Arundell Arms** (at Arundell Arms H.), Fore St., PL16 0AA, ℘ (01566) 784666, *Fax (01566) 784494* – ⅍
closed dinner 25 and 26 December – Meals 19.00/27.50 **t.** ▯ 6.00.

When travelling through **Europe**
use the **Michelin** *red-cover* **map series,** *nos* **980** *to* **991**.

LIMPLEY STOKE Bath & North East Somerset – *see Bath.*

LINCOLN Lincs. **402 404** S 24 *Great Britain G.* – *pop. 80 281.*

See : *City★★ – Cathedral and Precincts★★★ AC Y – High Bridge★★ Z 9 – Usher Gallery★★ AC YZ M1 – Jew's House★ Y – Castle★ AC Y.*

Env. : *Doddington Hall★ AC, W : 6 m. by B 1003 – Z – and B 1190.*

Exc. : *Gainsborough Old Hall★ AC, NW : 19 m. by A 57 – Z – and A 156.*

🏌 *Carholme, Carholme Rd* ℘ (01522) 523725.

✈ *Humberside Airport :* ℘ (01652) 688456, *N : 32 m. by A 15 – Y – M 180 and A 18.*

🛈 *9 Castle Hill, LN1 3AA* ℘ (01522) 529828.

London 140 – Bradford 81 – Cambridge 94 – Kingston-upon-Hull 44 – Leeds 73 – Leicester 53 – Norwich 104 – Nottingham 38 – Sheffield 48 – York 82.

Plan on next page

🏨🏨 **White Hart,** Bailgate, LN1 3AR, ℘ (01522) 526222, *Fax (01522) 531798*, « Antique furniture » – ▯ ⅍ 📺 🅿 ⟷ – 🔏 70. 🆖 🅐🅔 ① 🆅🆂🅰 🅹🅲🅱   Y c
Meals 12.95 **t.** (lunch) and a la carte 20.20/31.45 **t.** ▯ 6.25 – ⍁ 9.50 – **44 rm** 70.00/90.00 **t.**, 3 suites – SB.

🏨🏨 **Courtyard by Marriott,** Brayford Wharf North, LN1 1YW, ℘ (01522) 544244, *Fax (01522) 560805*, 🏋 – ▯ ⅍ rm, 🍽 📺 ☎ 🕭 🅿 – 🔏 30. 🆖 🅐🅔 ① 🆅🆂🅰 🅹🅲🅱   Z a
Meals a la carte 11.85/23.75 **t.** ▯ 6.95 – ⍁ 8.00 – **95 rm** 66.00 **t.** – SB.

🏨 **Forte Posthouse Lincoln,** Eastgate, LN2 1PN, ℘ (01522) 520341, *Fax (01522) 510780* – ▯, ⅍ rm, 📺 ☎ 🅿 – 🔏 90. 🆖 🅐🅔 ① 🆅🆂🅰 🅹🅲🅱   Y z
Meals a la carte 15.80/25.70 **t.** ▯ 8.45 – ⍁ 8.95 – **70 rm** 69.00 **st.** – SB.

🏠 **D'Isney Place** without rest., Eastgate, LN2 4AA, ℘ (01522) 538881, *Fax (01522) 511321*, ☞ – ⅍ 📺 ☎. 🆖 🅐🅔 ① 🆅🆂🅰 🅹🅲🅱   Y e
17 rm ⍁ 49.00/92.00 **t.**

🏠 **Damons Motel,** 997 Doddington Rd, LN6 3SE, SW : 4 ¼ m. by A 15 on B 1190 at junction with A 46 ℘ (01522) 500422, *Fax (01522) 689719*, 🏋 – ⅍ rm, 📺 ☎ 🕭 🅿. 🆖 🅐🅔 ① 🆅🆂🅰. ⅍
Meals (grill rest.) (booking essential) a la carte 15.50/23.50 **st.** – **47 rm** ⍁ 43.00/49.50 **st.**

🏠 **Hillcrest,** 15 Lindum Terr., LN2 5RT, ℘ (01522) 510182, *Fax (01522) 510182*, ≼, ☞ – ⅍ 📺 ☎ 🅿. 🆖 🅐🅔 🅹🅲🅱   Y o
closed 21 December-4 January – Meals *(closed Sunday)* (bar lunch)/dinner 14.00 **t.** and a la carte ▯ 4.50 – **16 rm** ⍁ 48.00/69.00 **t.** – SB.

🏠 **Minster Lodge** without rest., 3 Church Lane, LN2 1QJ, ℘ (01522) 513220, *Fax (01522) 513220* – 📺 ☎ 🅿. 🆖 🆅🆂🅰 🅹🅲🅱.   Y a
6 rm ⍁ 45.00/55.00 **t.**

🏠 **Carline** without rest., 1-3 Carline Rd, LN1 1HL, ℘ (01522) 530422 – ⅍ 📺 🅿. ⅍   Y i
closed Christmas and New Year – **9 rm** ⍁ 20.00/40.00 **t.**

🏠 **Tennyson** without rest., 7 South Park Av., LN5 8EN, ℘ (01522) 521624, *Fax (01522) 521624* – 📺 ☎ 🅿. 🆖 🅐🅔 ① 🆅🆂🅰. ⅍
closed 1 week Christmas and New Year – **8 rm** ⍁ 26.00/41.00 **st.**

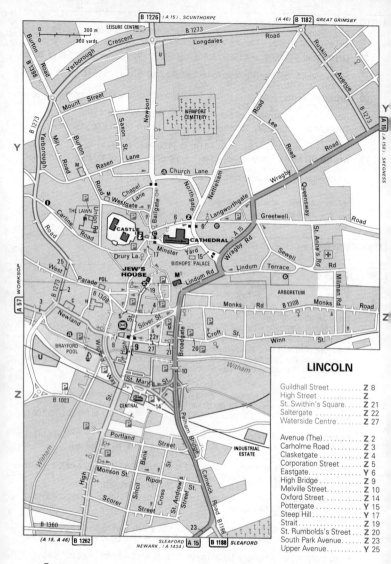

LINCOLN

Travel Inn, Lincoln Rd, Canwick Hill, LN4 2RF, SE : 1 ¾ m. on B 1188 ℰ (01522) 525216, Fax (01522) 542521 – ⅍ rm, 📺 ⅌ ℗ ⓂⓈ ⒜Ⓔ ⓪ 𝘝𝘐𝘚𝘈, ⅏
Meals (grill rest.) – 40 rm 36.50 **t.**

Jew's House, Jew's House, 15 The Strait, LN2 1JD, ℰ (01522) 524851, « 12C town house » – ⅍ ⓂⓈ ⒜Ⓔ ⓪ 𝘝𝘐𝘚𝘈. ⅏
YZ x
closed Sunday, Monday and 1 week Christmas – **Meals** 12.95/19.95 **t.** and a la carte ⅃ 5.00.

at Washingborough E : 3 m. by B 1188 – Z – on B 1190 – ⊠ Lincoln.

Washingborough Hall ⅊, Church Hill, LN4 1BE, ℰ (01522) 790340, Fax (01522) 792936, ⅃, ⅏ – ⅍ 📺 ☎ ℗ – ⅍ 50. ⓂⓈ ⒜Ⓔ ⓪ 𝘝𝘐𝘚𝘈
closed Christmas – **Meals** (booking essential) (bar lunch Monday to Saturday)/dinner 15.00 **t.** and a la carte – **12 rm** ⊇ 56.50/91.50 **st.** – SB.

at Branston *SE : 3 m. on B 1188 –* **Z.**

🏠 Moor Lodge, Sleaford Rd, LN4 1HU, ℰ (01522) 791366, Fax (01522) 794389 – 📺 ☎ 🅿 –
🔥 150
24 rm.

🅰 ATS Crofton Rd, Allenby Trading Est. ℰ (01522) 527225

LINDALE *Cumbria* **402** *L 21 – see Grange-over-Sands.*

LIPHOOK *Hants.* **404** *R 30.*
London 51 – Brighton 48 – Guildford 16 – Portsmouth 30 – Southampton 41 – Winchester 30.

🏠 **Travelodge,** GU30 7TT, SW : 2 m. by B 2131 on A 3 (northbound carriageway)
ℰ (01428) 727619, Reservations (Freephone) 0800 850950 – ⏱ rm, 📺 ♿ 🅿. 🆎 🔤 ⓪ 𝗩𝗜𝗦𝗔
🔤 ✻
Meals (grill rest.) – **40 rm** 39.95 **t.**

LISKEARD *Cornwall* **403** *G 32 The West Country G. – pop. 7 044.*
See : Church★.
Exc. : Lanhydrock★★, W : 11 ½ m. by A 38 and A 390 – NW : Bodmin Moor★★ - St. Endellion
Church★★ - Altarnun Church★ - St. Breward Church★ - Blisland★ (church★) - Camelford★ -
Cardinham Church★ - Michaelstow Church★ - St. Kew★ (church★) - St. Mabyn Church★ -
St. Neot★ (Parish Church★★) - St. Sidwell's, Laneast★ - St. Teath Church★ - St. Tudy★ -
Launceston★ – Castle★ (≤★) St. Mary Magdalene★, NE : 19 m. by A 390 and A 388.
London 261 – Exeter 59 – Plymouth 18 – Truro 37.

🏠 **Well House** ⬦, St. Keyne, PL14 4RN, S : 3 ½ m. by B 3254 on St. Keyne Well rd
ℰ (01579) 342001, Fax (01579) 343891, ≤, « Victorian country house », 🏊, 🎾, ✻ – 📺 ☎
🅿. 🆎 🔤 ⓪ 𝗩𝗜𝗦𝗔 🔤
Meals (booking essential) 26.95 **t.** 🍷 4.45 – **9 rm** 70.00/145.00 **t.**

🏠 **Old Rectory** ⬦, Duloe Rd, St. Keyne, PL14 4RL, S : 3 ¼ m. on B 3254 ℰ (01579) 342617,
Fax (01579) 342293, 🎾 – ⏱ 📺 🅿. 🆎 𝗩𝗜𝗦𝗔
closed Christmas – **Meals** (booking essential) (dinner only) 18.50 **st.** – **8 rm** 🖵 30.00/
75.00 **st.** – SB.

🅰 ATS 10 Dean St. ℰ (01579) 345489/345247

LITTLEBOURNE *Kent* **404** *X 30 – see Canterbury.*

LITTLEBURY GREEN *Essex* **404** *O 27 – see Saffron Walden.*

LITTLE HAMPDEN *Bucks. – see Great Missenden.*

LITTLEHAMPTON *W. Sussex* **404** *S 31 – pop. 50 408.*
London 64 – Brighton 18 – Portsmouth 31.

🏠 **Bailiffscourt** ⬦, Climping St., Climping, BN17 5RW, W : 2 ¾ m. by A 259
ℰ (01903) 723511, Fax (01903) 723107, « Reconstructed "medieval" house », 🎾, park, ✻
– ⏱ rest, 📺 ☎ 🅿 – 🔥 35. 🆎 🔤 𝗩𝗜𝗦𝗔
Meals 17.50/32.50 **st.** 🍷 12.75 – **27 rm** 🖵 130.00/255.00 **st.** – SB.

🏠 **Travelodge,** Worthing Rd, Rustington, BN17 6JN, E : 1 ¼ m. on B 2187
ℰ (01903) 733150, Reservations (Freephone) 0800 850950 – ⏱ rm, 📺 ♿ 🅿. 🆎 🔤 ⓪ 𝗩𝗜𝗦𝗔
🔤 ✻
Meals (grill rest.) – **36 rm** 35.95 **st.**

🏠 **Amberley Court** without rest., Crookthorn Lane, Climping, BN17 5QU, W : 1 ¾ m. by
B 2187 off A 259 ℰ (01903) 725131, Fax (01903) 734555, 🎾 – ⏱ 📺 🅿. ✻
closed 25 and 26 December – **3 rm** 🖵 35.00/54.00 **st.**

🅰 ATS Church St. ℰ (01903) 713085/716919

LITTLE LANGDALE *Cumbria* **402** *K 20 – see Ambleside.*

LITTLE LANGFORD *Wilts. – see Salisbury.*

LITTLEOVER Derbs. 402 403 404 P 25 – *see Derby.*

LITTLE PETHERICK Cornwall 403 F 32 – *see Padstow.*

LITTLEPORT Cambs 404 U 26 – *see Ely.*

LITTLE SHELFORD Cambs. 404 U 27 – *see Cambridge.*

LITTLE SINGLETON Lancs. – *see Blackpool.*

LITTLE SUTTON Ches. – ⊠ South Wirral.
London 208 – Chester 12 – Liverpool 9 – Manchester 48.

🏨 **Woodhey,** Berwick Rd, L66 4PS, on A 550 ℰ (0151) 339 5121, *Fax (0151) 339 3214*, ⌕,
⬛ – ⇖, 🍽 rest, 📺 ☎ ᒼ 🄿 – 🕍 200. 🄫🄮 🄰🄴 ① 𝘝𝘐𝘚𝘈
Meals *(closed Saturday lunch)* 17.25 **t.** and a la carte – ⚏ 9.85 – **53 rm** 72.80/88.50 **t.** – SB.

LITTLE THORNTON Lancs. 402 L 22 – *see Blackpool.*

LITTLE WALSINGHAM Norfolk 404 W 25 – ⊠ Walsingham.
London 117 – Cambridge 67 – Cromer 21 – Norwich 32.

✗ **Old Bakehouse** with rm, 33-35 High St., NR22 6BZ, ℰ (01328) 820454,
Fax (01328) 820454 – ⇖ rest, 📺. 🄫🄮 𝘝𝘐𝘚𝘈. ⅍
closed 2 weeks March, 25-26 December and restricted opening in winter – **Meals** *(closed
Monday and Tuesday)* (dinner only) 14.00 **t.** and a la carte ⚏ 5.50 – **3 rm** ⚏ 25.00/45.00 **t.**

🅟 **White Horse Inn** with rm, Fakenham Rd, East Barsham, NR21 0LH, S : 2 ¼ m. by High St.
on Fakenham rd ℰ (01328) 820645, *Fax (01328) 820645* – ⇖ rest, 📺 🄿. 🄫🄮 𝘝𝘐𝘚𝘈
Meals a la carte 13.75/18.95 **t.** ⚏ 3.95 – **3 rm** ⚏ 30.00/48.00 **t.**

LITTLE WEIGHTON East Riding 402 S 22 – *see Kingston-upon-Hull.*

LITTLEWICK GREEN Windsor & Maidenhead 404 R 29 – *see Maidenhead.*

LITTLE WYMONDLEY Herts. 404 T 28 – *see Hitchin.*

GREEN TOURIST GUIDES
Picturesque scenery, buildings
Attractive routes
Touring programmes
Plans of towns and buildings.

LIVERPOOL *Mersey.* 402 403 L 23 *Great Britain G. – pop. 481 786.*

See : *City★ – Walker Art Gallery★★ DY M2 – Liverpool Cathedral★★ (Lady Chapel★) EZ – Metropolitan Cathedral of Christ the King★★ EY – Albert Dock★ CZ (Merseyside Maritime Museum★ AC M1 - Tate Gallery Liverpool★).*

Exc. : *Speke Hall★ AC, SE : 8 m. by A 561 BX.*

�15, ☐5 *Allerton Municipal, Allerton Rd* ♟ *(0151) 428 1046 –* ☐5 *Liverpool Municipal, Ingoe Lane, Kirkby* ♟ *(0151) 546 5435,* BV – ☐5 *Bowring, Bowring Park, Roby Rd, Huyton* ♟ *(0151) 489 1901.*

Mersey Tunnels (toll) AX.

✈ *Liverpool Airport :* ♟ *(0151) 486 8877, SE : 6 m. by A 561 BX* – **Terminal** : *Pier Head.*

⛴ *to Isle of Man (Douglas) (Isle of Man Steam Packet Co. Ltd) (4 h) – to Northern Ireland (Belfast) (Norse Irish Ferries Ltd) (11 h).*

⛴ *to Birkenhead (Mersey Ferries) – to Wallasey (Mersey Ferries).*

🛈 *Merseyside Welcome Centre, Clayton Square Shopping Centre, L1 1QR* ♟ *(0151) 709 3631 – Atlantic Pavilion, Albert Dock, L3 4AE* ♟ *(0151) 708 8854.*

London 219 – Birmingham 103 – Leeds 75 – Manchester 35.

Town plans : Liverpool pp. 2-5

🏨🏨 **Liverpool Moat House,** Paradise St., L1 8JD, ♟ (0151) 471 9988, *Fax (0151) 709 2706,* ₺₆, ⌂ₛ, ⬚, – |⫯|, ※ rm, ⬛ 🗍 ☎ 🅿 – 🕍 400. 🐾 🖽 ⓞ 𝗩𝗜𝗦𝗔 𝗝𝗖𝗕
        DZ n
Meals a la carte 15.95/23.40 st. ₰ 5.95 – ⊆ 9.50 – **244 rm** 105.00/125.00 st., 7 suites – SB.

🏨🏨 **Atlantic Tower Thistle,** 30 Chapel St., L3 9RE, ♟ (0151) 227 4444, *Fax (0151) 236 3973,* ⇐ – |⫯|, ※ rm, ⬛ 🗍 ☎ 🅿 – 🕍 100. 🐾 🖽 ⓞ 𝗩𝗜𝗦𝗔. ⅏
        CY r
Meals 17.50 t. and a la carte – ⊆ 10.25 – **223 rm** 99.00/119.00 st., 3 suites – SB.

🏨 **The Park - Premier Lodge,** Dunningsbridge Rd, L30 6YN, N : 6 ¾ m. by A 59 on A 5036
♟ (0151) 525 7555, *Fax (0151) 525 2481* – |⫯|, ※ rm, ⬛ 🗍 ☎ 🅿 – 🕍 200. 🐾 🖽 ⓞ 𝗩𝗜𝗦𝗔. ⅏
Meals (grill rest.) 6.55 st. and a la carte ₰ 3.95 – ⊆ 6.95 – **60 rm** 42.25 st. – SB.

🏨 **Devonshire House,** 293-297 Edge Lane, L7 9LD, E : 2 ¼ m. on A 5047
♟ (0151) 260 2414, *Fax (0151) 263 2109,* ⇌ – |⫯| ⬛ 🗍 ☎ & 🅿 – 🕍 300. 🐾 🖽 ⓞ 𝗩𝗜𝗦𝗔. ⅏
        BX a
Meals 8.95/16.00 t. and a la carte – **54 rm** ⊆ 80.00/100.00 t.

🏠 **Travel Inn,** Northern Perimeter Rd, L30 7PT, N : 6 m. by A 59 on A 5036
♟ (0151) 531 1497, *Fax (0151) 520 1842* – ※ rm, ⬛ rest, ⬛ & 🅿. 🐾 🖽 ⓞ 𝗩𝗜𝗦𝗔. ⅏
Meals (grill rest.) – **43 rm** 36.50 t.

🏠 **Travel Inn,** Queens Dr., West Derby, L13 0DL, E : 4 m. on A 5058 (Ringroad)
♟ (0151) 228 4724, *Fax (0151) 220 7610* – ※ rm, ⬛ rest, ⬛ & 🅿. 🐾 🖽 ⓞ 𝗩𝗜𝗦𝗔. ⅏
        BV a
Meals (grill rest.) – **40 rm** 36.50 t.

🏠 **Campanile,** Wapping and Chaloner St., L3 4AJ, ♟ (0151) 709 8104, *Fax (0151) 709 8725* –
※ rm, ⬛ ☎ & 🅿 – 🕍 30. 🐾 🖽 ⓞ 𝗩𝗜𝗦𝗔
        CZ a
Meals (grill rest.) 10.55 st. and a la carte ₰ 5.25 – ⊆ 4.50 – **78 rm** 38.00 st.

✗✗ **Becher's Brook,** 29a Hope St., L1 9BQ, ♟ (0151) 707 0005, *Fax (0151) 708 7011* – ※. 🐾
🖽 𝗩𝗜𝗦𝗔
        EZ a
closed Saturday lunch, Sunday, 2 to 9 August, 25-26 December, 1 January and Bank Holidays
– **Meals** 16.50 t. (lunch) and a la carte 23.50/28.00 t. ₰ 9.00.

at Crosby N : 5½ m. on A 565 – AV.

🏨 **Blundellsands,** The Serpentine, Blundellsands, L23 6YB, W : 1 ¼ m. via College Rd,
Mersey Rd and Agnes Rd ♟ (0151) 924 6515, *Fax (0151) 931 5364* – |⫯|, ※ rm, ⬛ ☎ 🅿 –
🕍 250. 🐾 🖽 ⓞ 𝗩𝗜𝗦𝗔
Meals (bar lunch Saturday) 10.25/14.50 t. and a la carte ₰ 5.25 – ⊆ 7.95 – **37 rm** 45.00/
100.00 st. – SB.

at Huyton E : 8¼ m. by A 5047 and A 5080 – BX – on B 5199 – ✉ *Liverpool.*

🏨🏨 **Village H. and Leisure Club,** Fallows Way, L35 1RZ, SE : 3 ¼ m. by A 5080 off Windy
Arbor Rd ♟ (0151) 449 2341, *Fax (0151) 449 3832,* ₺₆, ⌂ₛ, ⬚, squash – |⫯|, ※ rm, ⬛ ☎ &
🅿 – 🕍 250. 🐾 🖽 ⓞ 𝗩𝗜𝗦𝗔. ⅏
Meals *(closed lunch Saturday and Bank Holidays)* 15.95/18.50 st. and a la carte ₰ 6.25 –
62 rm ⊆ 84.00/110.00 st.

🏠 **Derby Lodge - Premier Lodge,** Roby Rd, L36 4HD, SW : 1 m. on A 5080
♟ (0151) 480 4440, *Fax (0151) 443 0932,* ⇌ – ⬛ rest, ⬛ ☎ 🅿 – 🕍 35. 🐾 🖽 ⓞ 𝗩𝗜𝗦𝗔. ⅏
Meals (grill rest.) 12.95 t. and a la carte – ⊆ 4.95 – **8 rm** ⊆ 44.25 t.

🏠 **Travel Inn,** Wilson Rd, Tarbock, L36 6AD, SE : 2 ¼ m. on A 5080 ♟ (0151) 480 9614,
Fax (0151) 480 9361 – ※ rm, ⬛ rest, ⬛ & 🅿. 🐾 🖽 ⓞ 𝗩𝗜𝗦𝗔. ⅏
Meals (grill rest.) – **40 rm** 36.50 t.

at Grassendale SE : 4½ m. on A 561 – BX – ✉ *Liverpool.*

✗✗✗ **Gulshan,** 544-548 Aigburth Rd, L19 3QG, on A 561 ♟ (0151) 427 2273 – ⬛. 🐾 🖽 ⓞ 𝗩𝗜𝗦𝗔
closed 25 December – **Meals** - Indian - (dinner only) 16.00 t. and a la carte.

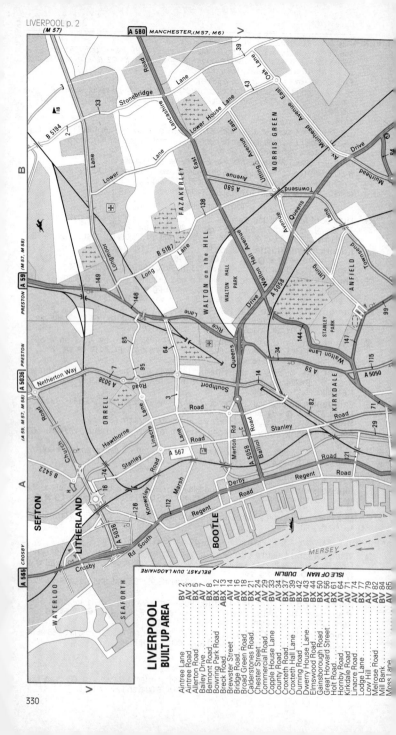

A 580 MANCHESTER, (M 57, M 6)

A 565 CROSBY | (A 59, M 57, M 58) PRESTON | A 5036 PRESTON | A 59 (M 57, M 58) PRESTON

BELFAST, DUN LAOGHAIRE
DUBLIN
ISLE OF MAN

LIVERPOOL
BUILT UP AREA

WATERLOO
SEAFORTH
SEFTON
LITHERLAND
Crosby
BOOTLE
MERSEY
ORRELL
WALTON on the HILL
WALTON HALL PARK
FAZAKERLEY
NORRIS GREEN
ANFIELD
STANLEY PARK
KIRKDALE

330

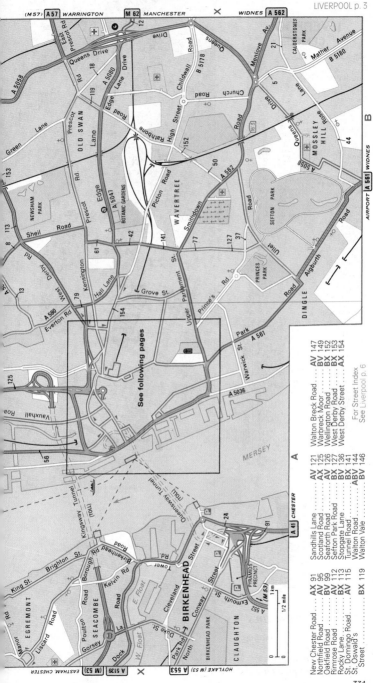

331

LIVERPOOL
CENTRE

GREEN TOURIST GUIDES

Picturesque scenery, buildings
Attractive routes
Touring programmes
Plans of towns and buildings.

332

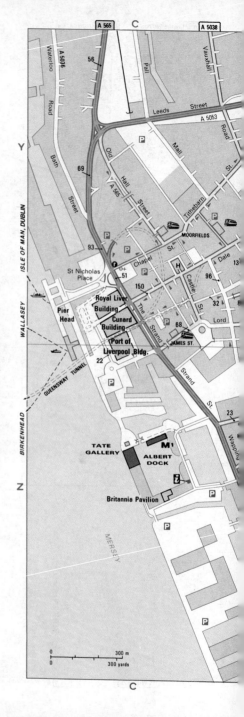

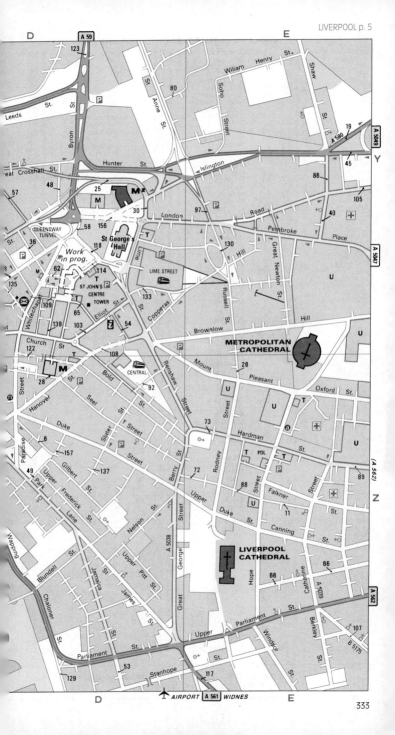

STREET INDEX TO LIVERPOOL TOWN PLANS

The names of main shopping streets are indicated in red
at the beginning of the list of streets.

at Woolton *SE : 6 m. by A 562* – **BX** – *, A 5058 and Woolton Rd* – ✉ *Liverpool.*

Woolton Redbourne, Acrefield Rd, L25 5JN, ☎ (0151) 421 1500, *Fax (0151) 421 1501,* « Victorian house, antiques », – rest, TV ☎ P. MC AE ① VISA JCB
Meals (residents only) (dinner only) 22.95 **t.** 6.95 – **25 rm** 63.00/92.00 **t.**, 1 suite – SB.

ATS 15/37 Caryl St. ☎ (0151) 709 8032
ATS Wilson Road, Huyton ☎ (0151) 489 8386
ATS 190-194 St. Mary's Rd, Garston ☎ (0151) 427 3665
ATS 73-77 Durning Rd, Wavertree ☎ (0151) 263 7604
ATS Musker St., Crosby ☎ (0151) 931 3166
ATS Unit E, Liver Ind. Est., Long Lane, Aintree ☎ (0151) 524 1000

LIZARD *Cornwall* 403 E 34 *The West Country G.*

Env. : *Lizard Peninsula★ - Mullion Cove★★ (Church★) - Kynance Cove★★ - Cadgwith★ - Coverack★ – Cury★ (Church★) - Gunwalloe Fishing Cove★ - St. Keverne (Church★) - Landewednack★ (Church★) – Mawgan-in-Meneage (Church★) - Ruan Minor (Church★) - St. Anthony-in-Meneage★.*

London 326 – Penzance 24 – Truro 29.

Landewednack House, Church Cove, TR12 7PQ, ☎ (01326) 290909, *Fax (01326) 290192,* « Part 17C, antique furnished, former rectory overlooking Church Cove », – TV ☎ P. MC VISA.
closed 1 week in autumn, 1 week in spring and Christmas – **Meals** (by arrangement) 18.95 **st.** 6.00 – **3 rm** 40.00/42.00 **t.**

Housel Bay, Housel Bay, TR12 7PG, ☎ (01326) 290417, *Fax (01326) 290359,* Housel Cove – |, rest, TV ☎ P. MC AE VISA.
Meals (bar lunch Monday to Saturday)/dinner 19.50 **t.** 5.50 – **21 rm** 30.00/49.00 **t.** – SB.

Penmenner House, Penmenner Rd, TR12 7NR, ☎ (01326) 290370, , – TV P. MC VISA.
closed January – **Meals** (by arrangement) 12.50 **st.** – **6 rm** 25.00/47.00 **st.**

South Parc without rest., TR12 7NL, ☎ (01326) 290441, , – TV P.
3 rm 26.00/44.00 **st.**

LOCKINGTON *East Riding – see Great Driffield.*

LOFTUS *Redcar & Cleveland* 402 R 20 – *pop. 5 931* – ✉ *Saltburn-by-the-Sea.*

London 264 – Leeds 73 – Middlesbrough 17 – Scarborough 36.

Grinkle Park, Easington, TS13 4UB, SE : 3 ½ m. by A 174 on Grinkle rd ☎ (01287) 640515, *Fax (01287) 641278,* , , park, – TV ☎ P. MC AE ① VISA.
Meals 10.95/18.00 **st.** and dinner a la carte 7.55 – **20 rm** 68.50/90.00 **st.** – SB.

LOLWORTH SERVICE AREA *Cambs. – see Cambridge.*

When travelling for business or pleasure
in **England, Wales, Scotland** *and* **Ireland** *:*

- use the series of five maps
  (nos 401, 402, 403, 404 and 923) at a scale of 1:400 000
- they are the perfect complement to this Guide

LONDON

folds ㊷ to ㊹ – *London G. – pop. 6 679 699*

PRACTICAL INFORMATION

🛈 *British Travel Centre, 12 Regent St., Piccadilly Circus, SW1Y 4PQ ℘ (0171) 971 0026.*

✈ *Heathrow, ℘ (0181) 759 4321, p. 8* AX *–* **Terminal** : *Airbus (A1) from Victoria, Airbus (A2) from Paddington – Underground (Piccadilly line) frequent service daily.*

✈ *Gatwick, ℘ (01293) 535353, p. 9 : by A 23* EZ *and M 23 –* **Terminal** : *Coach service from Victoria Coach Station (Flightline 777, hourly service) – Railink (Gatwick Express) from Victoria (24 h service).*

✈ *London City Airport ℘ (0171) 646 0000, p. 7 :* HV.

✈ *Stansted, at Bishop's Stortford, ℘ (01279) 680500, Fax 662066, NE : 34 m. p. 7 : by M 11* JT *and A 120.*

British Airways, Victoria Air Terminal : *115 Buckingham Palace Rd, SW1, ℘ (0171) 834 9411, Fax 828 7142, p. 32* BX

SIGHTS

HISTORIC BUILDINGS AND MONUMENTS

*Palace of Westminster*** : House of Lords★★, Westminster Hall★★ (hammerbeam roof***), Robing Room★, Central Lobby★, House of Commons★, Big Ben★, Victoria Tower★ p. 26* LY *– Tower of London*** (Crown Jewels***, White Tower or Keep***, St. John's Chapel★★, Beauchamp Tower★* Tower Hill Pageant★ *) p. 27* PVX.

Banqueting House★★ p. 26 LX *– Buckingham Palace★★ (Changing of the Guard★★, Royal Mews★★) p. 32* BVX *– Kensington Palace★★ p. 24* FX *– Lincoln's Inn★★ p. 33* EV *– London Bridge★ p. 27* PVX *– Royal Hospital Chelsea★★ p. 31* FU *– St. James's Palace★ p. 29* EP *– Somerset House★★ p. 33* EXY *– South Bank Arts Centre★★ (Royal Festival Hall★, National Theatre★, County Hall★) p. 26* MX *– The Temple★★ (Middle Temple Hall★) p. 22* MV *– Tower Bridge★★ p. 27* PX.

Albert Memorial★ p. 30 CQ *– Apsley House★ p. 28* BP *– Burlington House★ p. 29* EM *– Charterhouse★ p. 23* NOU *– George Inn★, Southwark p. 27* PX *– Gray's Inn★ p. 22* MU *– Guildhall★ (Lord Mayor's Show★★) p. 23* OU *– International Shakespeare Globe Centre★ p. 27* OX T *– Dr Johnson's House★ p. 23* NUV A *– Lancaster House★ p. 29* EP *– Leighton House★ p. 24* EY *– Linley Sambourne House★ p. 24* EY *– Lloyds Building★★ p. 23* PV *– Mansion House★ (plate and insignia★★) p. 23* PV P *– The Monument★ (✳★) p. 23* PV G *– Old Admiralty★ p. 26* KLX *– Royal Albert Hall★ p. 30* CQ *– Royal Exchange★ p. 23* PV V *– Royal Opera Arcade★ (New Zealand House) p. 29* FGN *– Royal Opera House★ (Covent Garden) p. 33* DX *– Spencer House★★ p. 29* DP *– Staple Inn★ p. 22* MU Y *– Theatre Royal★ (Haymarket) p. 29* GM *– Westminster Bridge★ p. 26* LY.

CHURCHES

The City Churches

*St. Paul's Cathedral*** (Dome ⩽★★★) p. 23* NOV.

St. Bartholomew the Great★★ (choir★) p. 23 OU K *– St. Dunstan-in-the-East★★ p. 23* PV F *– St. Mary-at-Hill★★ (woodwork★★, plan★) p. 23* PV B *– Temple Church★★ p. 22* MV.

All Hallows-by-the-Tower (font cover★★ brasses★) p. 23 PV Y *– Christ Church★. p. 23* OU E *– St. Andrew Undershaft (monuments★) p. 23* PV A *– St. Bride★ (steeple★★) p. 23* NV J *– St. Clement Eastcheap (panelled interior★★) p. 23* PV E *– St. Edmund the King and Martyr (tower and spire★) p. 23* PV D *– St-Giles Cripplegate★ p. 23* OU N *– St. Helen Bishopsgate★ (monuments★★) p. 23* PUV R *– St. James Garlickhythe (tower and spire★, sword rests★) p. 23* OV R *– St. Magnus the Martyr (tower★, sword rest★) p. 23* PV K *– St. Margaret Lothbury★ (tower and spire★, woodwork★, screen★, font★) p. 23* PU S *– St. Margaret Pattens (spire★, woodwork★) p. 23* PV N *– St. Martin-within-Ludgate (tower and spire★, door cases★) p. 23* NOV B *– St. Mary Abchurch★ (reredos★★, tower and spire★, dome★) p. 23* PV X *– St. Mary-le-Bow (tower and steeple★★) p. 23* OV G *– St. Michael Paternoster Royal (tower and spire★) p. 23* OV D *– St. Nicholas Cole Abbey (tower and spire★) p. 23* OV F *– St. Olave★ p. 23* PV S *– St. Peter upon Cornhill (screen★) p. 23* PV L *– St. Stephen Walbrook★ (tower and steeple★, dome★), p. 23* PV Z *– St. Vedast (tower and spire★, ceiling★), p. 23* OU E.

Other Churches

*Westminster Abbey*** (Henry VII Chapel***, Chapel of Edward the Confessor★★, Chapter House★★, Poets' Corner★) p. 26* LY.

Southwark Cathedral★★ p. 27 PX.

Queen's Chapel★ p. 29 EP *– St. Clement Danes★ p. 33* EX *– St. James's★ p. 29* EM *– St. Margaret's★ p. 26* LY A *– St. Martin-in-the-Fields★ p. 33* DY *– St. Paul's★ (Covent Garden) p. 33* DX *– Westminster Roman Catholic Cathedral★ p. 26* KY B.

PARKS

*Regent's Park*** p. 21* HI (terraces★★), Zoo★★.

Hyde Park – Kensington Gardens★★ (Orangery★) pp. 24 and 25 – St. James's Park★★ p. 26 KXY.

STREETS AND SQUARES

The City★★★ *p. 23* NV.

Bedford Square★★ *p. 22* KLU – *Belgrave Square*★★ *p. 32* AVX – *Burlington Arcade*★★ *p. 29* DM – *Covent Garden*★★ *(The Piazza*★★ *) p. 33* DX – *The Mall*★★ *p. 29* FP – *Piccadilly*★ *p. 29* EM – *The Thames*★★ *pp. 25-27* – *Trafalgar Square*★★ *p. 33* DY – *Whitehall*★★ *(Horse Guards*★ *) p. 26* LX

Barbican★ *p. 23* OU – *Bond Street*★ *pp. 28-29* CK-DM – *Canonbury Square*★ *p. 23* NS – *Carlton House Terrace*★ *p. 29* GN – *Cheyne Walk*★ *p. 25* GHZ – *Fitzroy Square*★ *p. 22* KU – *Jermyn Street*★ *p. 29* EN – Leicester Square★ *p. 29* GM – *Merrick Square*★ *p. 27* OY – *Montpelier Square*★ *p. 31* EQ – *Neal's Yard*★ *p. 33* DV – *Piccadilly Arcade*★ *p. 29* DEN – *Portman Square*★ *p. 28* AJ – *Queen Anne's Gate*★ *p. 26* KY – Regent Street★ *p. 29* EM – *Piccadilly Circus*★ *p. 29* FM – *St. James's Square*★ *p. 29* FN – *St. James's Street*★ *p. 29* EN – *Shepherd Market*★ *p. 28* CN – *Soho*★ *p. 29* – *Trinity Church Square*★ *p. 27* OY – *Victoria Embankment gardens*★ *p. 33* DEXY – *Waterloo Place*★ *p. 29* FN.

MUSEUMS

British Museum★★★ *p. 22* LU – *National Gallery*★★★ *p. 29* GM – *Science Museum*★★★ *p. 30* CR – *Tate Gallery*★★★ *p. 26* LZ – *Victoria and Albert Museum*★★★ *p. 31* DR – *Wallace Collection*★★★ *p. 28* AH.

Courtauld Institute Galleries★★ *(Somerset House) p. 33* EXY – *Museum of London*★★ *p. 23* OU M – *National Portrait Gallery*★★ *p. 29* GM – *Natural History Museum*★★ *p. 30* CS – *Sir John Soane's Museum*★★ *p. 22* MU M.

Clock Museum★ *(Guildhall) p. 22* OU – *Imperial War Museum*★ *p. 27* NY – *London Transport Museum*★ *p. 33* DX – *Madame Tussaud's*★ *p. 21* IU M – *Museum of Mankind*★ *p. 29* DM – *National Army Museum*★ *p. 31* FU – *Percival David Foundation of Chinese Art*★ *p. 22* KLT M – *Planetarium*★ *p. 21* IU M – *Wellington Museum*★ *(Apsley House) p. 28* BP.

OUTER LONDON

Blackheath *p. 11* HX *terraces and houses*★ , *Eltham Palace*★ **A**
Brentford *p. 8* BX *Syon Park*★★ , *gardens*★
Bromley *p. 10* GY *The Crystal Palace Park*★
Chiswick *p. 9* CV *Chiswick Mall*★★ , *Chiswick House*★ **D**, *Hogarth's House*★ **E**
Dulwich *p. 10* *Picture Gallery*★ FX **X**
Greenwich *pp. 10 and 11 : Cutty Sark*★★ GV **F**, *Footway Tunnel*(≤ ★★ *) – Fan Museum*★ *p. 6* GV **A**, – *National Maritime Museum*★★ *(Queen's House*★★ *)* GV **M**, *Royal Naval College*★★ *(Painted Hall*★ , *the Chapel*★ *)* GV **G**, *The Park and Old Royal Observatory*★ *(Meridian Building : collection*★★ *)* HV **K**, *Ranger's House*★ GX **N**
Hampstead *Kenwood House*★★ *(Adam Library*★★ , *paintings*★★ *) p. 5* EU **P**, *Fenton House*★★ , *p. 20* ES
Hampton Court *p. 8* BY *(The Palace*★★★ , *gardens*★★★ , *Fountain Court*★ , *The Great Vine*★ *)*
Kew *p. 9* CX *Royal Botanic Gardens*★★★ *: Palm House*★★ , *Temperate House*★ , *Kew Palace or Dutch House*★★ , *Orangery*★ , *Pagoda*★ , *Japanese Gateway*★
Hendon★ *p. 5*, *Royal Air Force Museum*★★ CT **M**
Hounslow *p. 8* BV *Osterley Park*★★
Lewisham *p. 10* GX *Horniman Museum*★ **M**
Richmond *pp. 8 and 9 : Richmond Park*★★ , ❄★★★ CX, *Richmond Hill*❄★★ CX, *Richmond Bridge*★★ BX **R**, *Richmond Green*★★ BX **S** *(Maids of Honour Row*★★ , *Trumpeter's House*★ *)*, *Asgill House*★ BX **B**, *Ham House*★★ BX **V**
Shoreditch *p. 6* FU *Geffrye Museum*★ **M**
Tower Hamlets *p. 6* GV *Canary Wharf*★★ B, *Isle of Dogs*★ *St. Katharine Dock*★ **Y**
Twickenham *p. 8* BX *Marble Hill House*★ **Z**, *Strawberry Hill*★ **A** .

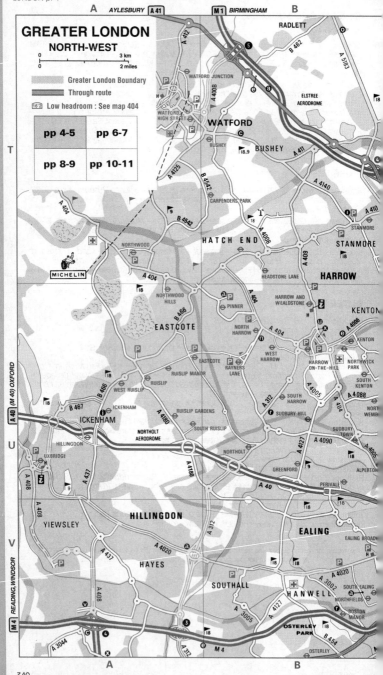

GREATER LONDON
NORTH-WEST

0 ——— 3 km	
0 ——— 2 miles	

Greater London Boundary

Through route

16·2 Low headroom : See map 404

pp 4-5	pp 6-7
pp 8-9	pp 10-11

MICHELIN

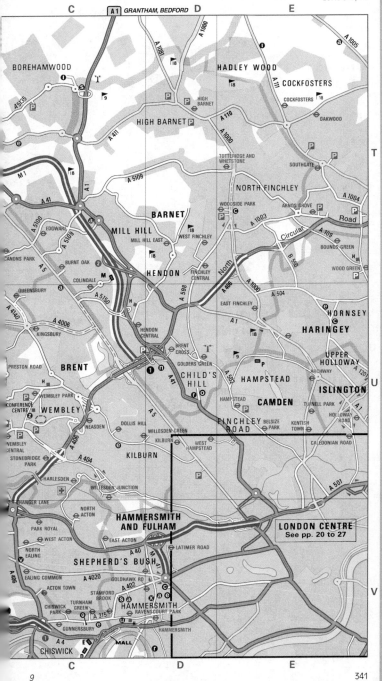

LONDON CENTRE
See pp. 20 to 27

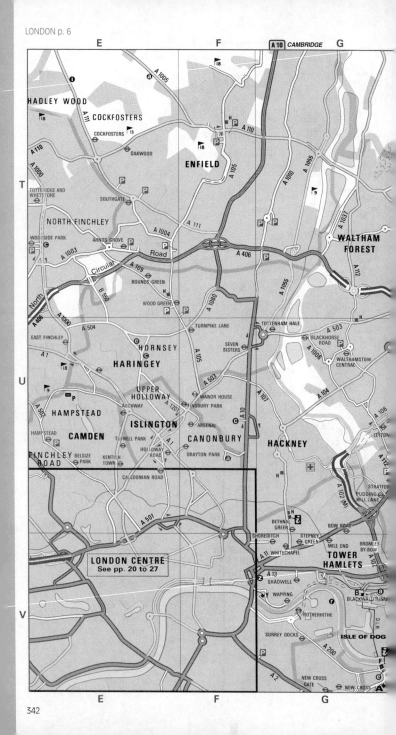

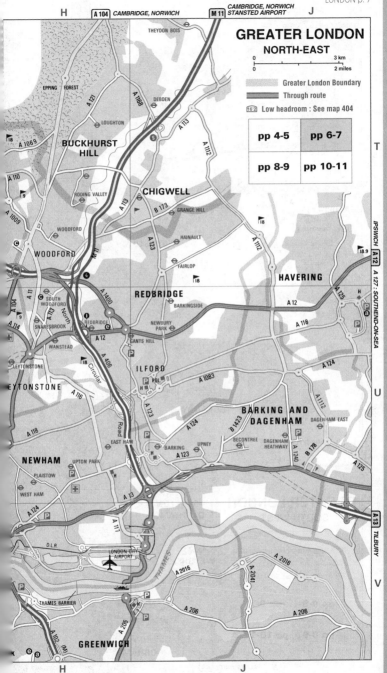

GREATER LONDON
NORTH-EAST

0   3 km
0   2 miles

Greater London Boundary

Through route

16.2 Low headroom : See map 404

| pp 4-5 | pp 6-7 |
| pp 8-9 | pp 10-11 |

H   A 104   CAMBRIDGE, NORWICH
M 11   CAMBRIDGE, NORWICH STANSTED AIRPORT
J

THEYDON BOIS

EPPING FOREST

DEBDEN

LOUGHTON

BUCKHURST HILL

RODING VALLEY

CHIGWELL

GRANGE HILL

WOODFORD

HAINAULT

FAIRLOP

WOODFORD

SOUTH WOODFORD

SNARESBROOK

WANSTEAD

LEYTONSTONE

REDBRIDGE

BARKINGSIDE

NEWBURY PARK

GANTS HILL

ILFORD

HAVERING

EYTONSTONE

Circular

Road

EAST HAM

NEWHAM

UPTON PARK

PLAISTOW

WEST HAM

BARKING AND DAGENHAM

BECONTREE

DAGENHAM EAST

DAGENHAM HEATHWAY

UPNEY

BARKING

D.L.R.

LONDON CITY AIRPORT

THAMES

THAMES BARRIER

GREENWICH

IPSWICH   A 12   A 127 : SOUTHEND-ON-SEA

A 13   TILBURY

T

U

V

H   J

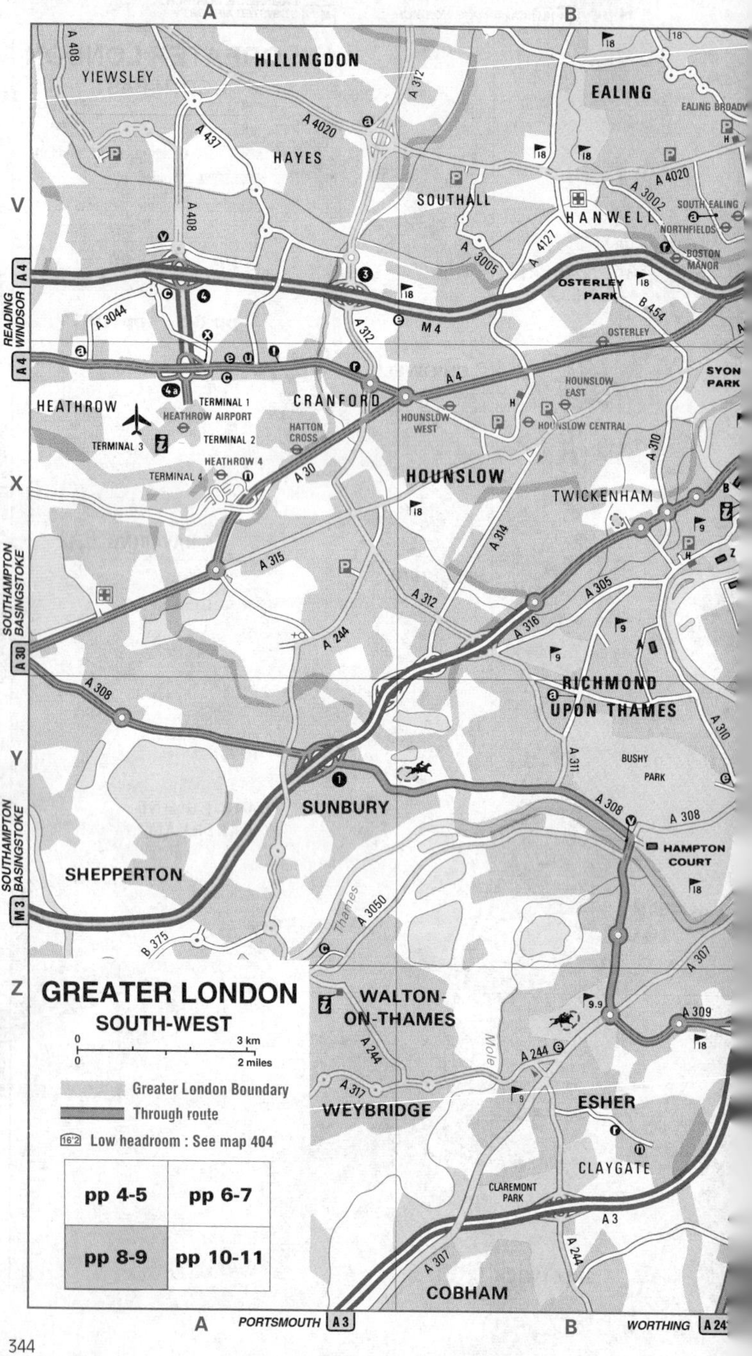

A
B
V
X
Y
Z
HILLINGDON
YIEWSLEY
EALING
EALING BROADW
HAYES
SOUTHALL
HANWELL
SOUTH EALING
NORTHFIELDS
BOSTON MANOR
OSTERLEY PARK
OSTERLEY
SYON PARK
HEATHROW
TERMINAL 1
HEATHROW AIRPORT
TERMINAL 2
TERMINAL 3
HEATHROW 4
TERMINAL 4
HATTON CROSS
CRANFORD
HOUNSLOW WEST
HOUNSLOW EAST
HOUNSLOW CENTRAL
HOUNSLOW
TWICKENHAM
RICHMOND UPON THAMES
BUSHY PARK
SUNBURY
SHEPPERTON
HAMPTON COURT
Thames
Mole
WALTON-ON-THAMES
WEYBRIDGE
ESHER
CLAYGATE
CLAREMONT PARK
COBHAM
READING WINDSOR
SOUTHAMPTON BASINGSTOKE
SOUTHAMPTON BASINGSTOKE
PORTSMOUTH A 3
WORTHING A 24
A 4
A 4
A 30
M 3
M 4
A 408
A 437
A 4020
A 312
A 3002
A 3005
A 4127
B 454
A 3044
A 30
A 315
A 314
A 310
A 305
A 316
A 244
A 308
A 311
A 3050
B 375
A 307
A 309
A 317
A 3
GREATER LONDON
SOUTH-WEST
0 3 km
0 2 miles
Greater London Boundary
Through route
16'2 Low headroom : See map 404
pp 4-5
pp 6-7
pp 8-9
pp 10-11

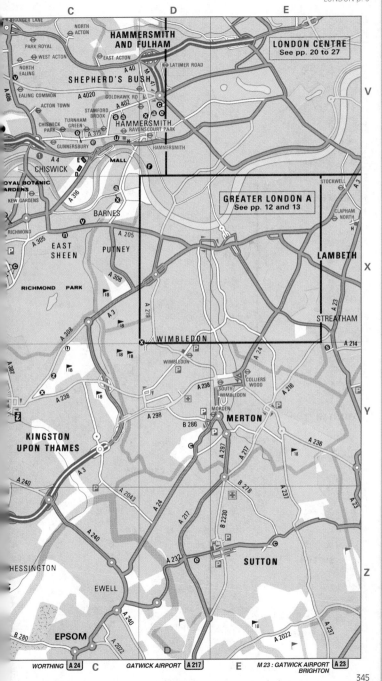

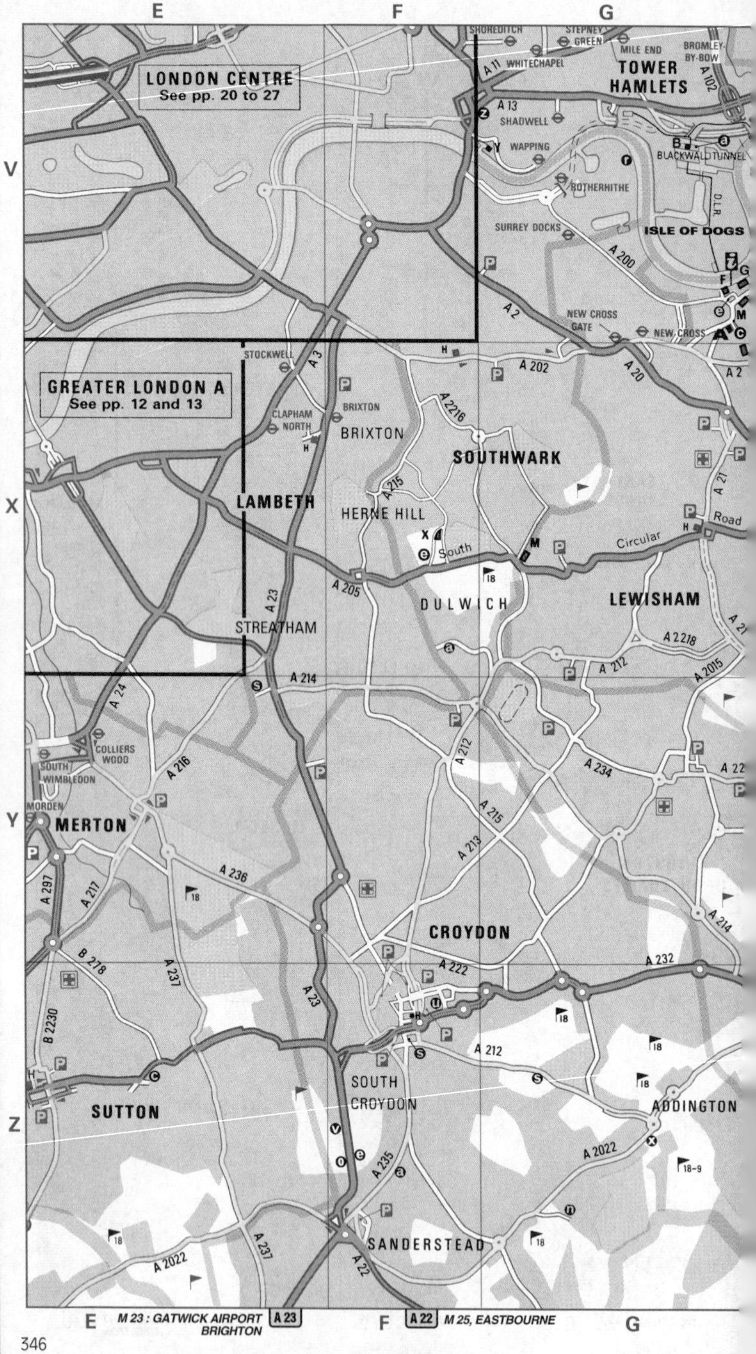

E F G

LONDON CENTRE
See pp. 20 to 27

V

SHOREDITCH STEPNEY GREEN MILE END BROMLEY-BY-BOW
A 11 WHITECHAPEL TOWER A 102
A 13 SHADWELL HAMLETS
WAPPING BLACKWALL TUNNEL
ROTHERHITHE D.L.R.
SURREY DOCKS ISLE OF DOGS
A 200
NEW CROSS
A 2 GATE NEW CROSS A 2

GREATER LONDON A
See pp. 12 and 13

STOCKWELL A 202 A 20
A 3 A 2216
CLAPHAM BRIXTON
NORTH SOUTHWARK A 21
BRIXTON

X

LAMBETH A 215 A 2
HERNE HILL Circular Road
A 205 South M LEWISHAM
18 A 2218 A 21
STREATHAM DULWICH
A 212 A 2015
A 214 A 22

COLLIERS
WOOD A 216 A 212 A 234
SOUTH A 215
WIMBLEDON A 213
MORDEN A 214

Y

MERTON
A 297 A 217 A 236
CROYDON
B 278 A 237 A 23 A 222 A 232
B 2230
A 212
SOUTH A 2022 ADDINGTON
CROYDON
SUTTON 18-9

Z

A 235
SANDERSTEAD
A 2022 A 22
A 237

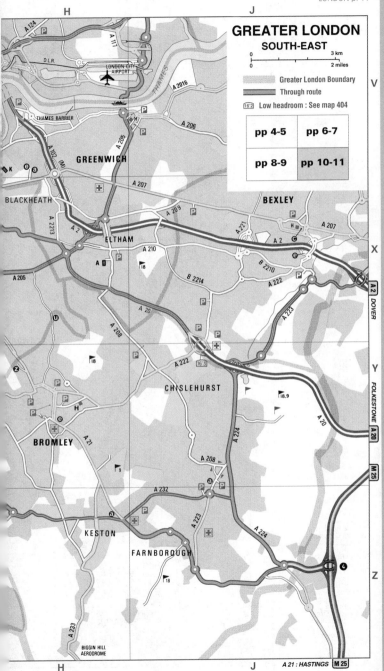

GREATER LONDON
SOUTH-EAST

0 ___ 3 km
0 ___ 2 miles

Greater London Boundary
Through route
16:2 Low headroom : See map 404

| pp 4-5 | pp 6-7 |
| pp 8-9 | pp 10-11 |

THAMES BARRIER

GREENWICH

BLACKHEATH

ELTHAM

BEXLEY

CHISLEHURST

BROMLEY

KESTON

FARNBOROUGH

BIGGIN HILL AERODROME

LONDON CITY AIRPORT

D.L.R.

THAMES

A 124
A 111
A 2016
A 206
A 705
A 207
A 2
A 209
A 221
A 207
A 2
A 210
B 2210
A 222
B 2214
A 205
A 20
A 208
A 222
A 223
A 224
A 208
A 232
A 223
A 224
A 21
A 233
A 2213
A 102 (M)

DOVER A 2
FOLKESTONE A 20
M 25

A 21 : HASTINGS M 25

347

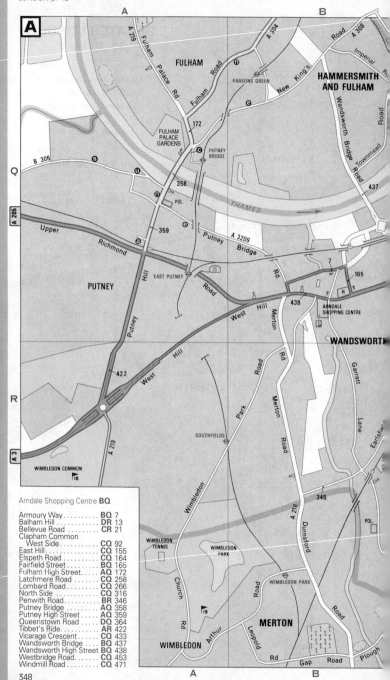

A

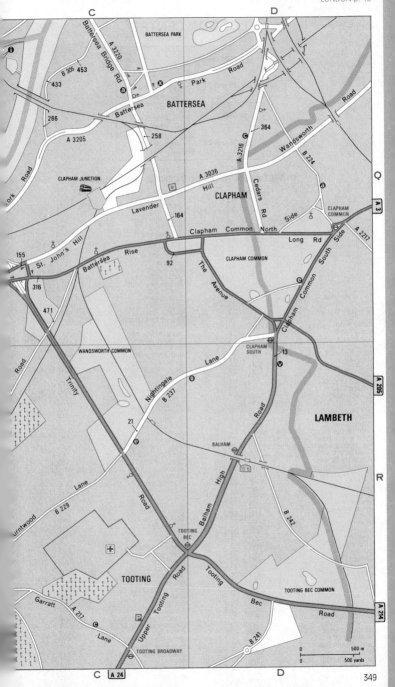

LONDON CENTRE

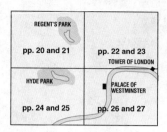

STREET INDEX TO LONDON CENTRE TOWN PLANS

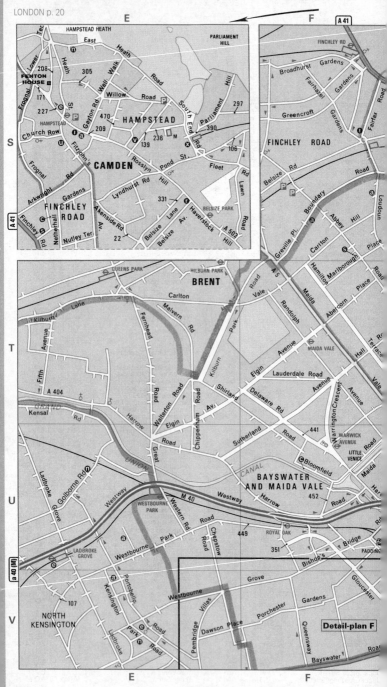

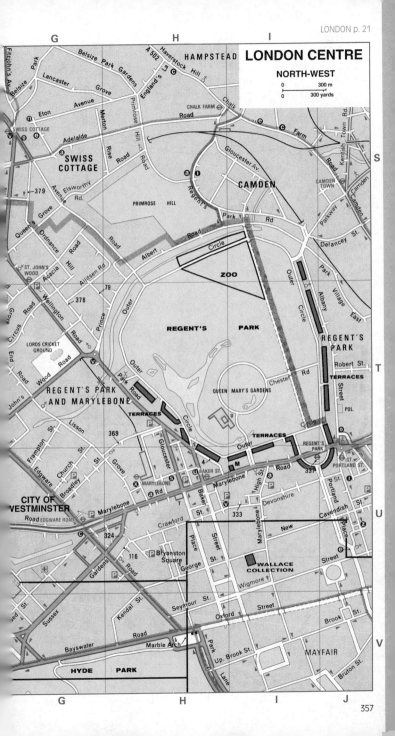

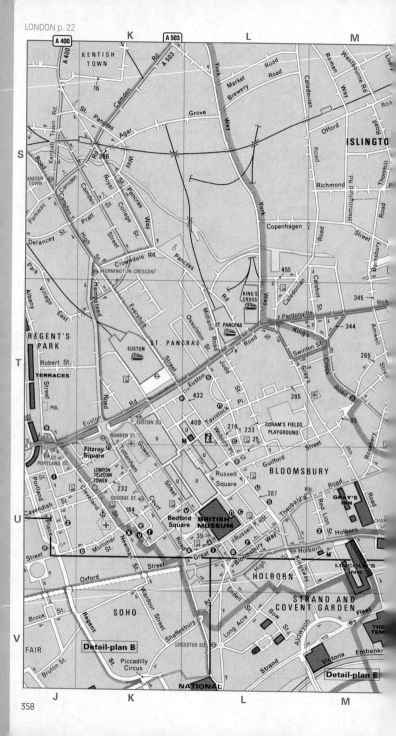

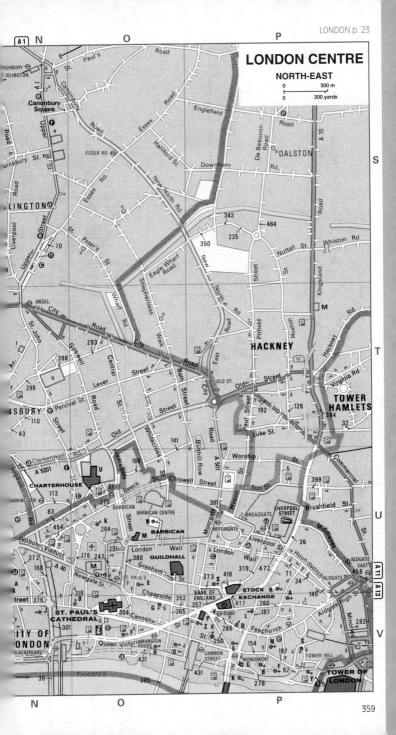

LONDON CENTRE

NORTH-EAST

| 0 | 300 m |
| 0 | 300 yards |

E F

Grove Gloucester

Westbourne Porchester Gardens

V 107 Kensington Pembridge Villas Dawson Place Queensway

NORTH KENSINGTON Park Road Detail-plan F

Portobello Bayswater Road

Clarendon Rd Lansdowne Notting Hill Gate Kensington

Walk Park Avenue

X Holland Camden Church Kensington A ROUND POND

37 Holland HOLLAND PARK Sheffield Ter. Gardens KENSINGTO

A 40 224 Holland Park Hill KENSINGTON PALACE KENSINGTO

Abbotsbury HOLLAND PARK Holland Street High Street

M 41 Addison Road KENSINGTON Holland St 229

Holland Villas 3 LINLEY SAMBOURNE High HIGHT STREET KENSINGTON

Y Kensington Road Melbury Rd HOUSE 225 Kensington ROYAL BOROUGH OF Elvaston Pl

A 3220 LEIGHTON St. KENSINGTON AND

326 HOUSE High POL CHELSEA Gloucester

OLYMPIA Kensington Warwick 158 Scarsdale Villas Marloes

A 315 North Pembroke 342 SOUTH

207 End Rd 719 Road Cromwell Collingham Rd KENSINGTON

Edith Road West Cromwell 298 410 245 Brompton Drayton Ga

182 203 Warwick EARL'S COURT 299 426 Gliston

A 4 Talgarth Rd North 348 347 Redcliffe

BARONS COURT Baron's Court End WEST KENSINGTON 151 Old Finborough Gardens Edith Grove

Star Road EARLS COURT EXHIBITION BLDG Gardens 202

Z Greyhound Road WEST BROMPTON BROMPTON CEMETERY Fulham

HAMMERSMITH Musard Rd Seagrave Road

AND FULHAM Ryston Lillie Halford Rd

Lillie Road Estcourt Rd Road Vanston

Munster Road Dawes Rd Filmer Rd Bishops Rd FULHAM Dawes Rd Fulham Rd A 304 FULHAM BROADWAY Harwood King's A 217 Lots Rd Lots

A 4 E F

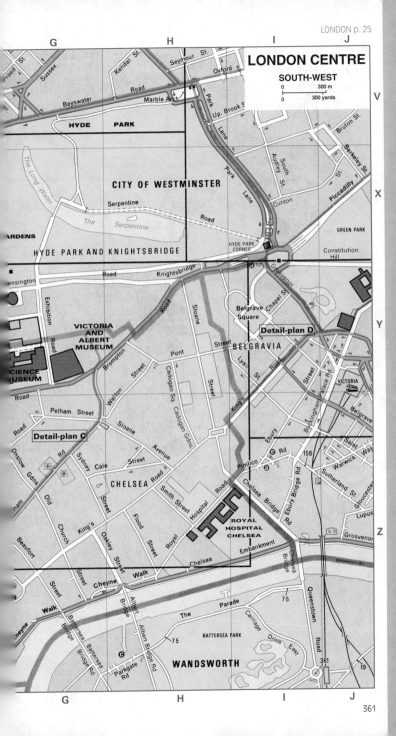

LONDON CENTRE

SOUTH-WEST

0 _____ 300 m
0 _____ 300 yards

HYDE PARK

CITY OF WESTMINSTER

The Long Water

Serpentine

The Serpentine Road

GARDENS

HYDE PARK AND KNIGHTSBRIDGE

HYDE PARK CORNER

GREEN PARK

Constitution Hill

Kensington

Road

Knightsbridge

Road

Exhibition Road

VICTORIA AND ALBERT MUSEUM

Sloane

Belgrave Square

Chapel St.

Detail-plan D

Grosvenor Pl.

BELGRAVIA

SCIENCE MUSEUM

Road

Pelham Street

Brompton

Walton Street

Pont Street

Cadogan Sq.

Cadogan Gdns.

Street

Lyall St.

King's Road

Eaton Square

VICTORIA

Buckingham Palace Rd

Belgrave

Detail-plan C

Sloane Avenue

Street

Onslow Gdns

Old

Sydney Street

Cale Street

CHELSEA

Smith Street

Hospital Road

Ebury

Pimlico Rd

Chelsea Bridge Rd

156

Warwick Way

Sutherland St.

Gloucester

Pelham

Church Street

King's Road

Flood Street

Oxley Street

Royal

ROYAL HOSPITAL CHELSEA

Chelsea Embankment

Chelsea Bridge

Lupus

Grosvenor

14 9

Beaufort

Street

Cheyne Walk

Chelsea Walk

Albert Bridge

The Parade

Queenstown Road

Z

Cheyne Walk

Battersea Bridge

Battersea Bridge Rd

Albert Bridge Rd

Parkgate Rd

75

BATTERSEA PARK

Carriage Drive East

75

WANDSWORTH

361

Sussex

Praed St.

Kendal St.

Seymour St.

Oxford St.

Bayswater Road

Marble Arch

Up. Brook S

Park Lane

South Audley St.

Bruton St.

Berkeley St.

Curzon

Piccadilly

J K L M

V

SOHO

STRAND AND COVENT GARDEN

Fleet

Brook St.

Wardour Street

Shaftesbury

Long Acre

Bow St.

Aldwych

Victoria Embankme

THE TEMP

FAIR

Detail-plan B

LEICESTER SQ.

Strand

Detail-plan E

Bruton St.

St.

Piccadilly Circus

Regent St.

NATIONAL GALLERY

CHARING CROSS

Berkeley St.

St.

Trafalgar Square

X

Piccadilly

ST. JAMES'S St.

ST. JAMES'S

The Mall

Pall Mall

OLD ADMIRALTY

HORSE GUARDS

Whitehall

317

462 460

228

SOUTH BANK ARTS CENTRE

Start

108

GREEN PARK

The Mall

ST. JAMES'S PARK

BANQUETING HOUSE

23

WATERLOO

WATER

Constitution Hill

BUCKINGHAM PALACE

Queen Anne's Gate

340

193

WESTMINSTER

COUNTY HALL

York Road

277

WESTMINSTER BRIDGE

Westminster B

LAMBETH NORTH

Birdcage Walk

Buckingham Gate

Petty France

Tothill St.

402

52

A

Y

ST. JAMES'S PARK

WESTMINSTER ABBEY

196

PALACE OF WESTMINSTER

Lambeth Palace Road

219

LAMBETH

NEW SCOTLAND YARD

Great

Peter Street

Marsham

Millbank

LAMBETH PALACE

Lambeth Rd

200

Horseferry

St.

Victoria

Francis

Rochester St.

Row

Page St.

Lambeth Bridge

Fitzalan S

VICTORIA

H

Vincent Sq.

Rd.

Lambeth Walk

Belgrave

Wilton Rd.

Vincent Sq.

Regency St.

Islip St.

Embankment

Vauxhall Walk

Black Prince Roa

LAMBET

alace Rd

Warwick Way

Saint

Way

Tachbrook Street

Vauxhall Bridge

436

John

Millbank

TATE GALLERY

Tyers

Newburn St.

Sutherland St.

George's

Drive

Denbigh St.

Street

Claverton St.

30

PIMLICO

G

Lupus St.

a

St.George's Square

Rd

Vauxhall Bridge

49

Albert

Kennington Lane

Z

Grosvenor

14 9

VAUXHALL

341

150

Harleyford Road

Clayton

Kennington Oval

THE OVAL

Elms

Lane

Road

290

Lambeth

SOUTH LAMBETH

Fentiman

Road

211 OVAL

Nine

P

NEW COVENT GARDEN MARKET

Wandsworth

Road

South

Dorset

Rd

Clapham

61

19

J K L A3 M

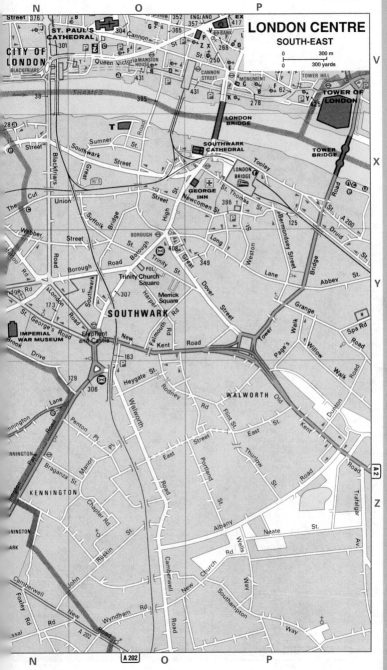

LONDON CENTRE
SOUTH-EAST

| 0 | 300 m |
| 0 | 300 yards |

ST. PAUL'S CATHEDRAL

CITY OF LONDON

BLACKFRIARS

ENGLAND

BANK

MONUMENT

TOWER HILL

TOWER OF LONDON

THAMES

LONDON BRIDGE

SOUTHWARK CATHEDRAL

TOWER BRIDGE

Sumner St.

Southwark Street

LONDON BRIDGE

Tooley St.

A 200

The Cut

Union

Suffolk

Blackfriars Bridge

High Street

BOROUGH

St. Thomas St.

Newcomen St.

GEORGE INN

Druid St.

Webber Street

Borough Road

BOROUGH

Trinity St.

Great Dover Street

Long Lane

Weston St.

Bermondsey Street

Grange Road

Bridge

Abbey St.

Trinity Church Square

POL.

Harper Rd.

Merrick Square

SOUTHWARK

St. George's Road

Borough Road

London Road

IMPERIAL WAR MUSEUM

Elephant and Castle

New Kent Road

Falmouth Rd.

Grange

Tower Bridge

Page's Walk

Willow Walk

Spa Rd.

Brook Drive

Heygate St.

Rodney Rd.

WALWORTH

Old Kent Road

Dunton Road

Trafalgar

KENNINGTON

Lane

Penton Pl.

Walworth Road

Braganza St.

Manor Pl.

East Street

Portland St.

Thurlow St.

Flint St.

East St.

KENNINGTON PARK

Chapter Rd.

Ruskin

Albany Rd.

Neate St.

Wells

Av.

Camberwell

Foxley Rd.

New

John

Wyndham Rd.

A 202

Church

Camberwell Road

New Church

Southampton Way

Way

A 202

B

A   B   C

Dorset St.

Gloucester Place

Baker Street

Manchester Street

Aybrook St.

New Cavendish St.

Cavendish St.

Harley Street

Portland Place

H

Montagu Square

Blandford Street

George Street

WALLACE COLLECTION

287

413

281

Welbeck Street

Wimpole Street

Queen Anne Street

Chandos

REGENT'S PARK AND MARYLEBONE

Cavendish Sq.

J

Portman Square

Wigmore

287

Street

Street

Henrietta Pl.

Holles St.

Vere St.

K

Seymour St.

POL.

Bryanston St.

188

Orchard Street

Portman Street

Oxford Street

Duke Street

James Street

BOND ST.

35

175

South Molton Street

New Bond St.

210

MARBLE ARCH

North Row

Park Street

Row

314

Green Street

Lees Pl.

Weighhouse St.

Davies Street

175

35

Brook Street

Brook's Mews

12

Street

CITY OF WESTMINSTER

L

149

Woods Mews

Upper Brook St.

Culross Street

Grosvenor Square

Grosvenor Street

Carlos St.

Mount Row

Street

Bruton

M

Upper Grosvenor Street

Reeves Mews

Mount

South Street

Adam's Row

St.

Pl.

St.

MAYFAIR

Berkeley Square

St.

Aldford St.

South Street

Chapley St.

Farm Street

Mews

Charles Street

Curzon

Bolton St.

HYDE PARK

132

421

Hill

Waveton St.

Hay's

Street

Street

Half Moon St.

N

Curzon

Street

Shepherd Market

HYDE PARK AND KNIGHTSBRIDGE

Shepherd Street

P

Serpentine Road

205

220

Brick Street

Old Park Lane

Piccadilly

Street

GREEN PARK

0   200 m
0   200 yards

APSLEY HOUSE WELLINGTON MUSEUM

A   B   C

Oxford Street is closed to private traffic, Mondays to Saturdays : from 7 am to 7 pm between Portman Street and St. Giles Circus

365

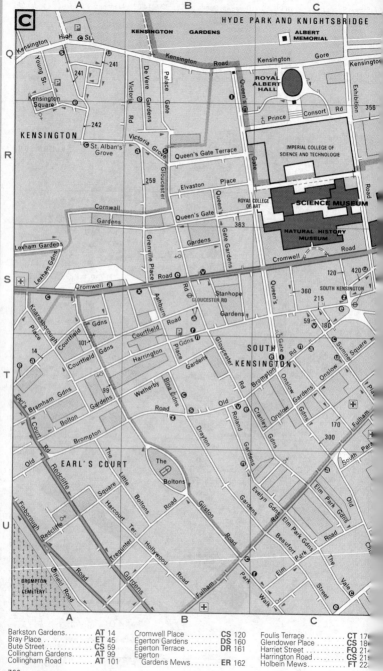

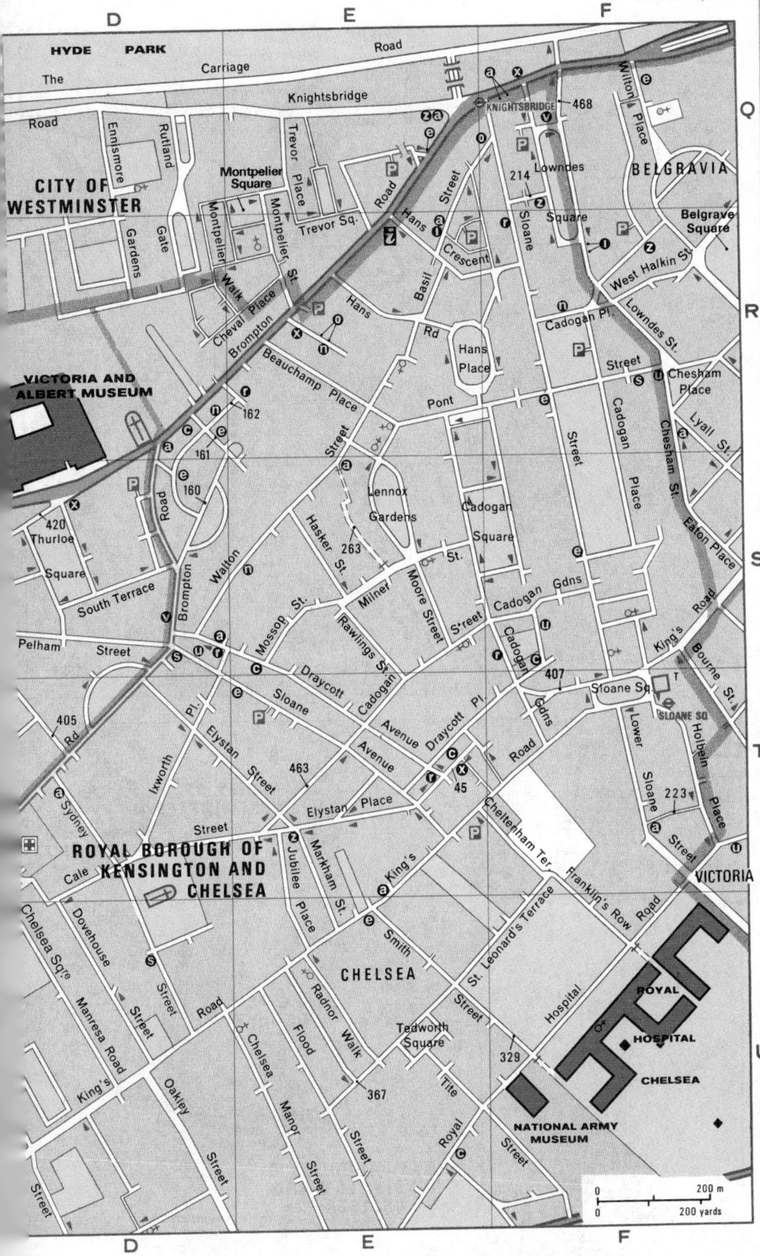

D
E
F
HYDE PARK
The
Carriage
Road
Knightsbridge
KNIGHTSBRIDGE
468
Q
Wilton Place
BELGRAVIA
Belgrave Square
CITY OF WESTMINSTER
Ennismore
Rutland
Gate
Gardens
Montpelier Square
Montpelier Walk
Montpelier St.
Trevor Place
Trevor Sq.
Road
Hans
Crescent
Basil
Street
Sloane
214
Lowndes
Square
West Halkin St.
Cheval Place
Brompton
Hans
Rd
Hans Place
Cadogan Pl.
Lowndes St.
R
VICTORIA AND ALBERT MUSEUM
Beauchamp Place
162
Pont
Street
Chesham Place
Lyall St.
161
160
Cadogan Place
Chesham St.
Lennox Gardens
Cadogan Square
Eaton Place
420
Thurloe
Square
Road
263
Hasker St.
Walton
St.
S
South Terrace
Milner
Moore Street
Mossop St.
Cadogan Gdns
Brompton
Rawlings St.
Street
Cadogan
King's Road
Pelham
Street
Draycott
Cadogan
407
Sloane Sq.
Bourne St.
Sloane
Avenue
Draycott Pl.
Gdns
SLOANE SQ
405
Rd
Pl.
Elystan
Street
Road
Lower
Holbein
T
Ixworth
463
Avenue
45
Sloane
223
Place
Sydney
Elystan Place
Cheltenham Ter.
Street
Street
ROYAL BOROUGH OF KENSINGTON AND CHELSEA
Cale
Jubilee
Markham St.
King's
Franklin's Row
Road
VICTORIA
Chelsea Sq're
Dovehouse
Place
Smith
St. Leonard's Terrace
CHELSEA
Street
Radnor
Street
Road
Hospital
ROYAL
Manresa Road
Street
Walk
Tedworth Square
HOSPITAL
U
Chelsea
Flood
329
CHELSEA
King's
Oakley
367
Tite
Manor
Street
Royal
NATIONAL ARMY MUSEUM
Street
Street
Street
Street
0
200 m
0
200 yards

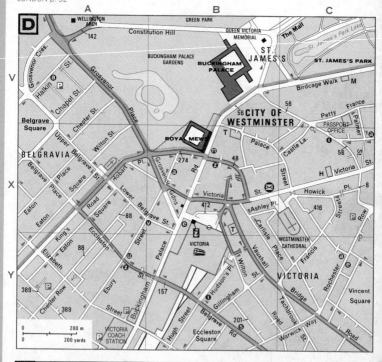

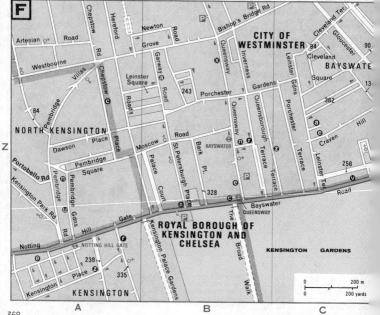

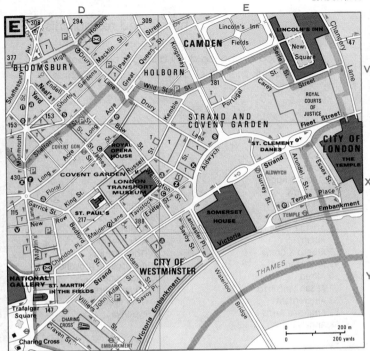

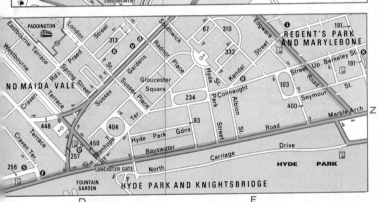

Alphabetical list of hotels and restaurants
Liste alphabétique des hôtels et restaurants
Elenco alfabetico degli alberghi e ristoranti
Alphabetisches Hotel- und Restaurantverzeichnis

T

U - V - W

X - Y - Z

Alphabetical list of areas included
Liste alphabétique des quartiers cités
Elenco alfabetico dei quartieri citati
Liste der erwähnten Bezirke

Starred establishments in London
Les établissements à étoiles de Londres
Gli esercizi con stelle a Londra
Die Stern-Restaurants in London

❀ ❀ ❀

75 *Mayfair*	XXXXX	The Oak Room Marco Pierre White (at Le Meridien Piccadilly H.)	75 *Mayfair*	XXXXX Chez Nico at Ninety Park Lane (at Grosvenor House H.)
			60 *Chelsea*	XXXX La Tante Claire

❀ ❀

75 *Mayfair*	XXXX	Le Gavroche	60 *Chelsea*	XXX Aubergine
75 *Mayfair*	XXX	The Square	50 *Bloomsbury*	XX Pied à Terre

❀

74 *Mayfair*	🏛	Connaught	52 *City of London*	XXX City Rhodes
59 *Chelsea*	🏛	Capital	80 *Soho*	XXX L'Escargot
73 *Belgravia*	🏛	The Halkin	80 *Soho*	XXX Quo Vadis
80 *Soho*	XXXX	The Café Royal Grill Room	64 *North Kensington*	XXX Leith's
75 *Mayfair*	XXXX	Oriental (at Dorchester H.)	80 *St James's*	XX L'Oranger
75 *Mayfair*	XXXX	Les Saveurs de Jean-Christophe Novelli W1	61 *Chelsea*	XX Chavot
			55 *Hammersmith*	XX River Café
			76 *Mayfair*	XX Nobu (at The Metropolitan H.)
60 *Chelsea*	XXX	The Canteen		

"Bib Gourmand"
Good food at moderate prices
Repas soignés à prix modérés
Pasti accurati a prezzi contenuti
Sorgfältig zubereitete, preiswerte Mahlzeiten

😊 Meals

49 *Farnborough*	XXX Chapter One	64 *Kensington*	X Kensington Place
51 *Chelsea*	XXX Chutney Mary		
80 *Soho*	XXX L'Escargot (Ground Floor)	64 *Kensington*	X Novelli W8
		64 *Kensington*	X Malabar
81 *Soho*	XX Atelier	64 *North Kensington*	X Woz
78 *Regent's Park & Marylebone*		64 *North Kensington*	X Sugar Club
70 *Canary Wharf*	XX Nico Central	65 *North Kensington*	X Alastair Little Lancaster Road
70 *Whitechapel*	XX MPW		
	XX Cafe Spice Namaste	72 *Bayswater & Maida Vale*	X L'Accento
83 *Victoria*	XX Simply Nico	68 *Richmond*	X Monsieur Max
71 *Wandsworth*	XX Chez Bruce	69 *Bermondsey*	X Blue Print Café

377

Particularly pleasant hotels and restaurants
Hôtels et restaurants agréables
Alberghi e ristoranti ameni
Angenehme Hotels und Restaurants

🏰🏰🏰

| 73 *Mayfair* | Claridge's | 81 *Strand* | The Savoy |
| 73 *Mayfair* | Dorchester | *& Covent Garden* | |

🏰🏰🏰

| 74 *Mayfair* | Connaught |

🏰🏰🏰

50 *Bloomsbury*	Covent Garden	65 *South*	
59 *Chelsea*	Capital	*Kensington*	Pelham
59 *Chelsea*	Durley House	73 *Belgravia*	The Halkin
65 *South*		79 *St. James's*	22 Jermyn Street
Kensington	Blakes	82 *Victoria*	Goring

🏰🏰

| 59 *Chelsea* | Sloane | 59 *Chelsea* | Sydney House |

XXXXX

| 72 *Mayfair* | The Oak Room Marco Pierre White (at Le Meridien Piccadilly H.) |

XXXX

| 75 *Mayfair* | Oriental (at Dorchester H.) |

XXX

69 *Bermondsey*	Le Pont de la Tour	79 *St. James's*	Quaglino's
75 *Mayfair*	Goode's at Thomas Goode	70 *Southwark*	Oxo Tower
75 *Mayfair*	Grill Room (at Dorchester H.)		

Restaurants classified according to type
Restaurants classés suivant leur genre
Ristoranti classificati secondo il loro genere
Restaurants nach Art und Einrichtung geordnet

Bistros

66 *South Kensington*	ⅹ Bangkok	58 *Finsbury*	ⅹ Stephen Bull's Bistro

Seafood

76 *Mayfair*	ⅹⅹⅹ Scotts	61 *Chelsea*	ⅹⅹ Poissonnerie de l'Avenue
76 *Mayfair*	ⅹⅹ Bentley's	82 *Strand & Covent Garden*	ⅹⅹ Sheekey's
66 *South Kensington*	ⅹⅹ Downstairs at One Ninety	58 *Islington*	ⅹ Fisk (Scandinavian)
67 *Kingston*	ⅹⅹ Gravier's	67 *Kennington*	ⅹ Lobster Pot
72 *Bayswater & Maida Vale*	ⅹⅹ Jason's	70 *Southwark*	ⅹ Livebait

Chinese

75 *Mayfair*	ⅹⅹⅹⅹ ✿ Oriental (at Dorchester H.)	53 *Ealing*	ⅹⅹ Maxim
73 *Hyde Park & Knightsbridge*	ⅹⅹⅹ Mr Chow	56 *Stanmore*	ⅹⅹ Mr Tang's Mandarin
73 *Hyde Park & Knightsbridge*	ⅹⅹⅹ Pearl of Knightsbridge	49 *Bromley*	ⅹⅹ Peking Diner
76 *Mayfair*	ⅹⅹⅹ Princess Garden	72 *Bayswater & Maida Vale*	ⅹⅹ Poons
60 *Chelsea*	ⅹⅹⅹ L'Oriental (at La Belle Epoque)	61 *Chelsea*	ⅹⅹ Red of Knightsbridge
81 *Strand & Covent Garden*	ⅹⅹⅹ West ZENders	71 *Putney*	ⅹⅹ Royal China
59 *Richmond*	ⅹⅹ Four Regions	72 *Bayswater & Maida Vale*	ⅹⅹ Royal China
48 *Mill Hill*	ⅹⅹ Good Earth	56 *Central Harrow*	ⅹⅹ Taste of China
61 *Chelsea*	ⅹⅹ Good Earth	54 *Greenwich*	ⅹⅹ Treasure of China
68 *South Woodford*	ⅹⅹ Ho-Ho	51 *Hampstead*	ⅹⅹ Vegetarian Cottage
83 *Victoria*	ⅹⅹ Hunan	53 *Addington*	ⅹⅹ Willow
52 *City of London*	ⅹⅹ Imperial City	49 *Orpington*	ⅹⅹ Xian
83 *Victoria*	ⅹⅹ Ken Lo's Memories of China	51 *Hampstead*	ⅹⅹ ZeNW3
83 *Kensington*	ⅹⅹ Ken Lo's Memories of China	81 *Soho*	ⅹ Fung Shing
		64 *Kensington*	ⅹ Mandarin
65 *Fulham*	ⅹⅹ Mao Tai	81 *Soho*	ⅹ Poons
		53 *Croydon*	ⅹ Tai Tung

English

75 *Mayfair*	ⅹⅹⅹ Grill Room (at Dorchester H.)	81 *Strand & Covent Garden*	ⅹⅹ Rules
83 *Victoria*	ⅹⅹⅹ Shepherd's	50 *Bloomsbury*	ⅹ Alfred
61 *Chelsea*	ⅹⅹ English Garden		

French

75 *Mayfair*	XXXXX	✿✿✿ Chez Nico at Ninety Park Lane	67 *Kingston*	XX Gravier's
75 *Mayfair*	XXXX	✿✿ (Le) Gavroche	61 *Chelsea*	XX Grill St. Quentin
75 *Mayfair*	XXXX	✿ (Les) Saveurs de Jean-Christophe Novelli W1	50 *Bloomsbury*	XX Mon Plaisir
			61 *Chelsea*	XX Poissonnerie de l'Avenue
60 *Chelsea*	XXXX	✿✿✿ (La) Tante Claire	63 *Kensington*	XX (La) Pomme d'Amour
83 *Victoria*	XXX	Auberge de Provence	52 *City of London*	XX (Le) Quai
55 *Crouch End*	XX	(Les) Associés	73 *Belgravia*	XX Vong (French Thai)
61 *Chelsea*	XX	Brasserie St. Quentin	79 *Regent's Park & Marylebone*	X (L') Aventure
61 *Chelsea*	XX	✿ Chavot	51 *Hampstead*	X (La) Grignote
64 *North Kensington*	XX	Chez Moi	67 *Kennington*	X Lobster Pot
61 *Chelsea*	XX	(La) Ciboulette	82 *Strand & Covent Garden*	X Magno's Brasserie
57 *Chiswick*	XX	(La) Dordogne	68 *Hampston Hill*	X Monsieur Max
63 *Kensington*	XX	(L') Escargot Doré	79 *Regent's Park & Marylebone*	X (Le) Muscadet
82 *Strand & Covent Garden*	XX	(L') Estaminet	83 *Victoria*	X (La) Poule au Pot
			54 *Dalston*	X Soulard

Greek

72 *Bayswater & Maida Vale*	X Kalamaras	62 *Chelsea*	X Cafe O

Hungarian

81 *Soho*	XX Gay Hussar

Indian & Pakistani

69 *Bermondsey*	XXX Bengal Clipper	66 *South Kensington*	XX Memories of India
66 *South Kensington*	XXX Bombay Brasserie	78 *Regent's Park & Marylebone*	XX (La) Porte des Indes
61 *Chelsea*	XXX Chutney Mary (Anglo-Indian)	80 *Soho*	XX Red Fort
66 *South Kensington*	XX Café Lazeez	71 *Wandsworth*	XX Tabaq
70 *Whitechapel*	XX Cafe Spice Namaste	76 *Mayfair*	XX Tamarind
		55 *Hammersmith*	XX Tandoori Nights
76 *Mayfair*	XX Chor Bizarre	61 *Chelsea*	XX Vama
66 *South Kensington*	XX Delhi Brasserie	71 *Wandsworth*	X Bombay Bicycle Club
78 *Regent's Park & Marylebone*	XX Gaylord	56 *South Harrow*	X Jaflong
54 *Ealing*	XX Gitanjli - Mayfair	64 *Kensington*	X Malabar
81 *Soho*	XX Gopal's	49 *Willesden Green*	X Sabras (Indian Vegetarian)
66 *South Kensington*	XX Khan's of Kensington	81 *Soho*	X Soho Spice
50 *Bloomsbury*	XX Malabar Junction	66 *South Kensington*	X Star of India
		77 *Mayfair*	X Veeraswamy

Irish

76 *Mayfair*	XX	Mulligans

Italian

73 *Belgravia*	🏛 ❀	(The) Halkin		61 *Chelsea*	XX	Toto's
60 *Chelsea*	XXX	Grissini		56 *Central Harrow*	XX	Trattoria Sorrentina
83 *Victoria*	XXX	(L') Incontro		70 *Carshalton*	XX	(La) Veranda
83 *Victoria*	XXX	Santini		73 *Belgravia*	XX	Zafferano
72 *Bayswater & Maida Vale*	XX	Al San Vincenzo		73 *Bayswater & Maida Vale*	X	(L') Accento
78 *Regent's Park & Marylebone*	XX	Bertorelli's		72 *Bayswater & Maida Vale*	X	Assaggi
82 *Strand & Covent Garden*	XX	Bertorelli's		69 *Bermondsey*	X	Cantina Del Ponte
78 *Regent's Park & Marylebone*	XX	Caldesi		64 *Kensington*	X	Cibo
61 *Chelsea*	XX	Caraffini		71 *Putney*	X	Del Buongustaio
61 *Chelsea*	XX	Daphne's		71 *Putney*	X	Enoteca
69 *Dulwich*	XX	Luigi's		55 *Crouch End*	X	Florians
64 *North Kensington*	XX	Orsino		53 *Croydon*	X	Mario
63 *Kensington*	XX	Osteria del Parco		83 *Victoria*	X	Olivo
61 *Chelsea*	XX	Osteria Le Fate		68 *Barnes*	X	Riva
55 *Hammersmith*	XX ❀	River Café		57 *Ickenham*	X	Roberto's

Japanese

79 *St. James's*	XXX	Suntory		80 *St. James's*	XX	Matsuri
52 *City of London*	XXX	Tatsuso		52 *City of London*	XX	Miyama
78 *Regent's Park & Marylebone*	XX	Asuka		76 *Mayfair*	XX	Shogun
51 *Hampstead*	XX	Benihana		48 *Colindale*	X	Abeno
51 *Chelsea*	XX	Benihana		51 *Holborn*	X	Holborn Imari
76 *Mayfair*	XX	Benihana		52 *City of London*	X	Imari
76 *Mayfair*	XX ❀	Nobu		62 *Chelsea*	X	T'Su

Lebanese

73 *Belgravia*	XX	Al Bustan		63 *Kensington*	XX	Phoenicia
61 *Chelsea*	XX	Beit Eddine				

Moroccan

76 *Mayfair*	X	Momo

Polish

64 *Kensington*	X	Wódka

Pubs

55 *Hammersmith*	Anglesea Arms		55 *Hammersmith*	Havelock Tavern
62 *Chelsea*	Chelsea Ram		52 *Regent's Park*	(The) Queens
60 *Battersea*	Duke of Cambridge			

Spanish

60 *Chelsea*	XXX Albero & Grana	66 *South Kensington*	X Cambio De Tercio

Swedish

58 *Canonbury* X Anna's Place

Thai

55 *Fulham*	XX Blue Elephant	73 *Belgravia*	XX Vong (French Thai)
61 *Chelsea*	XX Busabong Too	67 *Kingston*	X Ayudhya
70 *Battersea*	XX Chada	66 *South Kensington*	X Bangkok
72 *Bayswater & Maida Vale*	XX Nipa	71 *Tooting*	X Oh Boy
52 *City of London*	XX Sri Siam City	81 *Soho*	X Sri Siam
66 *South Kensington*	XX Tui	62 *Swiss Cottage*	X Thai Pepper

Vegetarian

51 *Hampstead*	XX Vegetarian Cottage	49 *Willesden Green*	X Sabras (Indian)

Vietnamese

81 *Soho* X Saigon

Boroughs and areas

Greater London *is divided, for administrative purposes, into 32 boroughs plus the City : these sub-divide naturally into minor areas, usually grouped around former villages or quarters, which often maintain a distinctive character.*

BARNET pp. 4 and 5.

Brent Cross – ✉ NW2.

🏨 **Holiday Inn Garden Court,** Tilling Rd, NW2 1LP, ℰ (0181) 201 8686, *Fax (0181) 455 4660* – |‡|, ✻ rm, ☰ ☑ ☎ ዿ ℗ – 🕍 50. ⓶⓿ ⒶⒺ ⓪ 𝘝𝘐𝘚𝘈 ᴊᴄʙ DU n
Meals (bar lunch)/dinner 12.95 **st.** and a la carte ⌀ 5.25 – ⊑ 10.95 – **153 rm** 119.00 **st.** – SB.

Child's Hill – ✉ NW2.

✗ **Quincy's,** 675 Finchley Rd, NW2 2JP, ℰ (0171) 794 8499 – ☰. ⓶⓿ ⒶⒺ 𝘝𝘐𝘚𝘈 DU r
closed Sunday, Monday and Christmas – **Meals** (booking essential) (dinner only) 25.00 **t.**
⌀ 4.50.

✗ **Laurent,** 428 Finchley Rd, NW2 2HY, ℰ (0171) 794 3603 – ⓶⓿ ⒶⒺ 𝘝𝘐𝘚𝘈 DU o
closed Sunday, first 3 weeks August and Bank Holidays – **Meals** - Couscous - a la carte approx. 13.95 **t.**

Mill Hill – ✉ NW7.

🏴 100 Barnet Way, Mill Hill ℰ (0181) 959 2282 CT.

✗✗ **Good Earth,** 143 The Broadway, NW7 4RN, ℰ (0181) 959 7011, *Fax (0181) 959 1464* – ☰.
⓶⓿ ⒶⒺ ⓪ 𝘝𝘐𝘚𝘈 CT a
closed 24 to 28 December – **Meals** - Chinese - 19.80 **t.** and a la carte ⌀ 8.00.

BEXLEY pp. 10 and 11.

Bexley – ✉ Kent.

🏨 **Forte Posthouse Bexley,** Black Prince Interchange, Southwold Rd, DA5 1ND, on A 2
ℰ (01322) 526900, *Fax (01322) 526113* – |‡|, ✻ rm, ☑ ☎ ዿ ℗ – 🕍 70. ⓶⓿ ⒶⒺ ⓪ 𝘝𝘐𝘚𝘈 ᴊᴄʙ
Meals 8.95 **st.** (lunch) and a la carte 16.95/24.85 **st.** ⌀ 7.50 – ⊑ 9.95 – **104 rm** 89.00 **st.** –
SB. JX e

Bexleyheath – ✉ Kent.

🏨🏨 **Swallow,** 1 Broadway, DA6 7JZ, ℰ (0181) 298 1000, *Fax (0181) 298 1234,* ℔, ☒ – |‡|,
✻ rm, ☰ ☑ ☎ ዿ ℗ – 🕍 200. ⓶⓿ ⒶⒺ ⓪ 𝘝𝘐𝘚𝘈 JX c
Galleria : **Meals** *(closed Saturday lunch, Sunday and Bank Holidays)* a la carte 24.05/
33.20 **st.** ⌀ 6.50 – **Copper :** **Meals** *(closed 1 January)* a la carte 18.75/30.00 **st.** ⌀ 6.50 –
142 rm ⊑ 100.00/180.00 **st.** – SB.

BRENT pp. 4 and 5.

Colindale – ✉ Middx.

✗ **Abeno,** Yaohan Plaza, 399 Edgware Rd, NW9 0JJ, ℰ (0181) 205 1131, *Fax (0181) 446 537*
– ✻ ☰ ℗. ⓶⓿ 𝘝𝘐𝘚𝘈 ᴊᴄʙ CU
closed lunch Monday and Tuesday, Easter Sunday and 25 December – **Meals** - Japanese
(Okonomi-Yaki) - 7.80/18.80 **t.** and a la carte.

Wembley – ✉ *Middx.*

Hilton National Wembley, Empire Way, HA9 8DS, ☎ (0181) 902 8839, *Fax (0181) 900 2201,* ⅃₆, ≘, ▢ – |‡|, ⅏ rm, ▤ rest, TV ☎ P – 🏛 300. MO AE D VISA JCB
Celebrities : **Meals** *(closed Saturday lunch)* (carving rest.) 15.95/19.95 **st.** and a la carte – ***Terracotta :*** **Meals** - Italian - (dinner only) a la carte 18.25/24.95 **st.** – ☕ 12.00 – **301 rm** 140.00/160.00 **st.** – SB. CU z

Willesden Green – ✉ *Middx.*

Sabras, 263 High Rd, NW10 2RX, ☎ (0181) 459 0340 CU e
closed Monday and 25 December – **Meals** - Indian Vegetarian - (dinner only) 10.00/15.00 **t.** and a la carte.

BROMLEY *pp. 10 and 11.*

⛳18, ⛳9 *Cray Valley, Sandy Lane, St. Paul's Cray, Orpington ☎ (01689) 831927,* **JY.**

Bromley – ✉ *Kent.*

⛳9 *Magpie Hall Lane ☎ (0181) 462 7014* **HY.**

Bromley Court, Bromley Hill, BR1 4JD, ☎ (0181) 464 5011, *Fax (0181) 460 0899,* ⅃₆, ≘, ⛲ – |‡|, ⅏ rm, TV ☎ P – 🏛 150. MO AE D VISA. ✗ HY z
Meals *(closed Saturday lunch)* 14.95/17.95 **t.** and a la carte 🍷 4.65 – **115 rm** ☕ 86.00/98.00 **t.**, 1 suite.

Peking Diner, 71 Burnt Ash Lane, BR1 5AA, ☎ (0181) 464 7911 – ▤. MO AE D VISA
Meals - Chinese (Peking) - a la carte 13.00/19.50 🍷 3.75. HX u

Farnborough – ✉ *Kent.*

Chapter One, Farnborough Common, Locksbottom, BR6 8NF, ☎ (01689) 854848, *Fax (01689) 858439* – ▤ P. MO AE D VISA JCB HZ a
Meals 19.50 **t.** (lunch) and dinner a la carte approx. 22.95 **t.** 🍷 7.50.

Orpington – ✉ *Kent.*

⛳18 *High Elms, High Elms Rd, Downe, Orpington ☎ (01689) 858175.*

Xian, 324 High St., BR6 0NG, ☎ (01689) 871881 – ▤. MO AE D VISA JCB JY a
closed Sunday lunch, 25-26 December and 1 week summer – **Meals** - Chinese (Peking, Szechuan) - 7.50/13.00 **t.** and a la carte.

CAMDEN *Except where otherwise stated see pp. 20-23.*

Bloomsbury – ✉ *NW1/W1/WC1.*

ℹ *34-37 Woburn Pl., WC1H 0JR ☎ (0171) 580 4599.*

Holiday Inn Kings Cross, 1 Kings Cross Rd, WC1X 9HX, ☎ (0171) 833 3900, *Fax (0171) 917 6163,* ⩽, ⅃₆, ≘, ▢, squash – |‡|, ⅏ rm, ▤ TV ☎ ♿ – 🏛 220. MO AE D VISA JCB. ✗ MT a
Meals *(closed Sunday lunch)* 17.95 **st.** (dinner) and a la carte 18.00/30.00 **st.** 🍷 7.00 – ☕ 9.75 – **403 rm** 170.00 **st.**, 2 suites – SB.

Marlborough, 9-14 Bloomsbury St., WC1B 3QD, ☎ (0171) 636 5601, *Fax (0171) 636 0532* – |‡|, ⅏ rm, ▤ rest, TV ☎ ♿ – 🏛 200. MO AE D VISA. ✗ LU i
Meals 17.00 **st.** and a la carte 🍷 7.50 – ☕ 14.00 – **166 rm** 158.00/196.00 **s.**, 7 suites.

Russell, Russell Sq., WC1B 5BE, ☎ (0171) 837 6470, *Fax (0171) 837 2857* – |‡|, ⅏ rm, ▤ rest, TV ☎ – 🏛 400. MO AE D VISA JCB. ✗ LU o
Fitzroy Doll's : **Meals** a la carte approx. 21.00 **st.** 🍷 7.50 – ***Virginia Woolf's :*** **Meals** *(closed Sunday dinner)* a la carte 12.85/19.85 **st.** 🍷 6.95 – ☕ 10.95 – **327 rm** 130.00/155.00 **st.**, 2 suites – SB.

Grafton, 130 Tottenham Court Rd, W1P 9HP, ☎ (0171) 388 4131, *Fax (0171) 387 7394* – |‡|, ⅏ rm, ▤ rest, TV ☎ – 🏛 100. MO AE D VISA. ✗ KU n
Meals 17.50 **st.** and a la carte 🍷 7.50 – ☕ 11.00 – **320 rm** 119.00/162.00 **s.**, 4 suites.

Mountbatten, 20 Monmouth St., WC2H 9HD, ☎ (0171) 836 4300, *Fax (0171) 240 3540* – |‡|, ⅏ rm, ▤ rest, TV ☎ – 🏛 75. MO AE D VISA. ✗ p. 33 DV o
Meals 19.00 **st.** and a la carte 🍷 7.50 – ☕ 14.00 – **120 rm** 187.00/226.00 **s.**, 7 suites.

Montague, 15 Montague St., WC1B 5BJ, ☎ (0171) 637 1001, *Fax (0171) 637 2516,* ⛲ – |‡|, ⅏ rm, ▤ rest, TV ☎ ♿ – 🏛 120. MO AE D VISA JCB. ✗ LU c
Meals *(closed lunch Saturday and Sunday)* a la carte 16.00/25.95 **t.** 🍷 11.00 – ☕ 11.50 – **102 rm** 120.00/160.00 **s.**, 2 suites.

🏠🏠🏠 **Covent Garden,** 10 Monmouth St., WC2H 9HB, ℰ (0171) 806 1000, *Fax (0171) 806 1100,* ⨍₆ – 🛗 🗏 📺 ☎, 🐾 🆎 *VISA*, ⛾   p. 33 DV n
Meals a la carte 16.50/29.15 **t.** – 🖵 14.50 – **48 rm** 165.00/245.00 **s.**, 2 suites.

🏠🏠🏠 **Kingsley,** Bloomsbury Way, WC1A 2SD, ℰ (0171) 242 5881, *Fax (0171) 831 0225* – 🛗, ⇆ rm, 🗏 rest, 📺 ☎ – 🔏 90. 🐾 🆎 ⓞ *VISA* ᴶᶜᴮ   LU r
Meals *(closed lunch Saturday, Sunday and Bank Holidays)* 16.00 **t.** and a la carte ⅙ 5.30 – 🖵 11.25 – **137 rm** 125.00/240.00 **st.**

🏠🏠🏠 **Forte Posthouse Bloomsbury,** Coram St., WC1N 1HT, ℰ (0171) 837 1200, *Fax (0171) 837 5374* – 🛗, ⇆ rm, 🗏 rest, 📺 ☎ ⅙ ⓟ – 🔏 750. 🐾 🆎 ⓞ *VISA* ᴶᶜᴮ ⛾   LT c
Meals a la carte 18.00/26.00 **st.** ⅙ 7.95 – 🖵 11.95 – **282 rm** 119.00/129.00 **st.**, 2 suites – SB.

🏠🏠 **Kenilworth,** 97 Great Russell St., WC1B 3LB, ℰ (0171) 637 3477, *Fax (0171) 631 3133* – 🛗, ⇆ rm, 🗏 rest, 📺 ☎ – 🔏 65. 🐾 🆎 ⓞ *VISA*. ⛾   LU a
Meals 16.95 **st.** and a la carte ⅙ 7.50 – 🖵 11.00 – **187 rm** 123.00/166.00 **s.**

🏠🏠 **Blooms** without rest., 7 Montague St., WC1B 5BP, ℰ (0171) 323 1717, *Fax (0171) 636 6498* – 🛗 📺 🐾 🆎 ⓞ *VISA* ᴶᶜᴮ. ⛾   LU n
27 rm 🖵 110.00/165.00 **st.**

🏠🏠 **Bonnington in Bloomsbury,** 92 Southampton Row, WC1B 4BH, ℰ (0171) 242 2828, *Fax (0171) 831 9170* – 🛗, ⇆ rm, 🗏 rest, 📺 ☎ ⅙ – 🔏 250. 🐾 🆎 ⓞ *VISA* ᴶᶜᴮ   LU s
Meals *(closed lunch Saturday and Sunday)* 11.50/19.75 **st.** and a la carte ⅙ 8.20 – **215 rm** 🖵 105.00/133.00 **t.**

🏠🏠 **Bloomsbury Park,** 126 Southampton Row, WC1B 5AD, ℰ (0171) 430 0434, *Fax (0171) 242 0665* – 🛗, ⇆ rm, 📺 ☎ – 🔏 25. 🐾 🆎 ⓞ *VISA* ᴶᶜᴮ. ⛾   LU u
Meals 14.95 **t.** (dinner) and a la carte 13.85/17.95 **t.** ⅙ 4.90 – 🖵 10.95 – **95 rm** 101.00/145.00 **st.**

🏠 **Academy,** 17-21 Gower St., WC1E 6HG, ℰ (0171) 631 4115, *Fax (0171) 636 3442,* 🌿 – 🗏 rest, 📺 ☎. 🐾 🆎 ⓞ *VISA* ᴶᶜᴮ. ⛾   KLU v
GHQ : Meals *(closed Saturday and Sunday)* a la carte 15.75/21.00 **t.** ⅙ 6.90 – 🖵 9.95 – **48 rm** 95.00/170.00 **st.**

🏠 **Harlingford** without rest., 61-63 Cartwright Gdns., WC1H 9EL, ℰ (0171) 387 1551, *Fax (0171) 387 4616,* 🌿, ⛾ – 📺 ☎. 🐾 🆎 *VISA* ᴶᶜᴮ. ⛾   LT n
42 rm 🖵 65.00/80.00 **st.**

🏠 **Mabledon Court** without rest., 10-11 Mabledon Pl., WC1H 9AZ, ℰ (0171) 388 3866, *Fax (0171) 387 5686* – 🛗 📺 ☎. 🐾 🆎 *VISA* ᴶᶜᴮ. ⛾   LT s
31 rm 🖵 60.00/70.00 **st.**

XX **Pied à Terre,** 34 Charlotte St., W1P 1HJ, ℰ (0171) 636 1178, *Fax (0171) 916 1171* – 🗏. 🐾
🆎 ⓞ *VISA* ᴶᶜᴮ   KU e
£3£3 closed Saturday lunch, Sunday, last 2 weeks August, 2 weeks Christmas and Bank Holidays –
Meals 23.00/29.50 **t.** and a la carte 39.50/49.50 **t.** ⅙ 10.50
Spec. Ballottine of duck confit with foie gras and sauté potato salad. Seared scallops with gazpacho, confit tomatoes and ratatouille. Steamed pigeon breast, fondant potato and choucroute.

XX **Neal Street,** 26 Neal St., WC2H 9PS, ℰ (0171) 836 8368, *Fax (0171) 497 1361* – 🐾 🆎 ⓞ *VISA* ᴶᶜᴮ   p. 33 DV s
closed Sunday, 1 week Christmas and Bank Holidays – Meals a la carte 26.00/39.00 **t.** ⅙ 9.00.

XX **Malabar Junction,** 107 Great Russell St., WC1B 3NA, ℰ (0171) 580 5230 – 🗏. 🐾 🆎 *VISA*   LU x
closed 25 and 26 December – Meals - South Indian - 8.50/9.50 **st.** and a la carte.

XX **Mon Plaisir,** 21 Monmouth St., WC2H 9DD, ℰ (0171) 836 7243, *Fax (0171) 379 0121* – 🐾 🆎 ⓞ *VISA* ᴶᶜᴮ   p. 33 DV a
closed Saturday lunch, Sunday, 1 week Christmas-New Year, Easter and Bank Holidays –
Meals - French - 14.95/19.95 **st.** and a la carte ⅙ 5.95.

XX **Bleeding Heart,** Bleeding Heart Yard, EC1N 8SJ, off Greville St., Hatton Garden, ℰ (0171) 242 2056, *Fax (0171) 831 1402,* 🏠 – 🐾 🆎 ⓞ *VISA*   NU e
closed Saturday, Sunday, 10 days Christmas-New Year and Bank Holidays – Meals a la carte 17.85/26.40 **t.** ⅙ 4.25.

X **Alfred,** 245 Shaftesbury Av., WC2H 8EH, ℰ (0171) 240 2566, *Fax (0171) 497 0672,* 🏠 – 🗏. 🐾 🆎 ⓞ *VISA*   p. 33 DV k
closed Saturday lunch, Sunday, Christmas and Bank Holidays – Meals - English - 12.95/15.95 **t.** and a la carte ⅙ 6.95.

X **Museum Street Cafe,** 47 Museum St., WC1A 1LY, ℰ (0171) 405 3211, *Fax (0171) 405 3211* – ⇆. 🐾 🆎 *VISA*   LU ×
closed Monday dinner, Saturday, Sunday, 1 week Spring, 2 weeks summer and 1 week Christmas – Meals 17.50/23.50 **t.** and a la carte.

Euston – ✉ WC1.

Euston Plaza, 17/18 Upper Woburn Pl., WC1H 0HT, ☎ (0171) 383 4105, *Fax (0171) 383 4106*, ⅟, – |₿|, ⇔ rm, ▤ TV ☎ ♿ – 🏛 150. MC AE ⓓ VISA JCB. ✗
Three Crowns: **Meals** 18.95 **t.** and dinner a la carte 6.50 – ***Terrace:*** **Meals** *(closed Saturday and Sunday)* 13.00 **t.** (dinner) and a la carte 11.00/17.95 **t.** 6.50 – ☕ 12.00 – **150 rm** 141.00/190.00 **st.** – SB. KLT e

Hampstead – ✉ NW3.

Winnington Rd, Hampstead ☎ (0181) 455 0203.

Swiss Cottage without rest., 4 Adamson Rd, NW3 3HP, ☎ (0171) 722 2281, *Fax (0171) 483 4588*, « Antique furniture » – |₿| TV ☎ – 🏛 50. MC AE ⓓ VISA. ✗ GS n
58 rm ☕ 75.00/140.00 **st.**, 5 suites.

Forte Posthouse Hampstead, 215 Haverstock Hill, NW3 4RB, ☎ (0171) 794 8121, *Fax (0171) 435 5586* – |₿|, ⇔ rm, ▤ rest, TV ☎ P – 🏛 30. MC AE ⓓ VISA JCB ES r
Meals (bar lunch Monday to Saturday)/dinner a la carte 14.55/25.65 **t.** 7.25 – ☕ 10.95 – **140 rm** 99.00 **st.** – SB.

Sandringham, 3 Holford Rd, Hampstead Village, NW3 1AD, ☎ (0171) 435 1569, *Fax (0171) 431 5932*, – ⇔ TV ☎. MC AE VISA JCB. ✗ ES n
Meals (room service only) – ☕ 5.00 – **17 rm** 70.00/140.00 **s.**

Langorf without rest., 20 Frognal, NW3 6AG, ☎ (0171) 794 4483, *Fax (0171) 435 9055* – |₿| TV ☎. MC AE ⓓ VISA. ✗ ES c
31 rm 68.00/95.00 **st.**

Charles Bernard, 5-7 Frognal, NW3 6AL, ☎ (0171) 794 0101, *Fax (0171) 794 0100* – |₿| TV ☎ P. MC AE ⓓ VISA JCB. ✗ ES s
Meals *(closed Sunday)* (dinner only) a la carte 12.50/24.00 **st.** – **57 rm** ☕ 69.00/79.00 **st.**

XX **Byron's,** 3a Downshire Hill, NW3 1NR, ☎ (0171) 435 3544, *Fax (0171) 431 3544* – MC AE VISA ES v
closed 25 and 26 December – **Meals** a la carte 19.75/36.95 **t.** 7.50.

XX **Benihana,** 100 Avenue Rd, NW3 3HF, ☎ (0171) 586 9508, *Fax (0171) 586 6740* – ▤. MC AE ⓓ VISA JCB GS o
closed 25 December – **Meals** - Japanese (Teppan-Yaki) - 10.00/14.00 **st.** and a la carte.

XX **ZeNW3,** 83-84 Hampstead High St., NW3 1RE, ☎ (0171) 794 7863, *Fax (0171) 794 6956* – ▤. MC AE ⓓ VISA JCB ES a
closed Christmas – **Meals** - Chinese - 12.50/27.00 **t.** and a la carte.

XX Vegetarian Cottage, 91 Haverstock Hill, NW3 4RL, ☎ (0171) 586 1257 – ▤ HS c
Meals - Chinese Vegetarian rest.

X **Café des Arts,** 82 Hampstead High St., NW3 1RE, ☎ (0171) 435 3608 – ⇔. MC AE ⓓ VISA ES i
closed 25 and 26 December – **Meals** 7.95 **t.** (lunch) and a la carte 14.10/19.20 **t.** 6.50.

X **Cucina,** 45a South End Rd, NW3 2QB, ☎ (0171) 435 7814, *Fax (0171) 435 7815* – ▤. MC AE VISA ES x
closed 25 December – **Meals** 13.95/15.95 **t.** and a la carte 5.95.

X **Gresslin's,** 13 Heath St., NW3 6TP, ☎ (0171) 794 8386, *Fax (0171) 433 3282* – ▤. MC VISA JCB ES u
closed Monday lunch, Sunday dinner and Bank Holidays – **Meals** 10.95 **t.** (lunch) and a la carte 20.00/26.00 **t.**

X **La Grignote,** 77 Heath St., NW3 6UG, ☎ (0171) 433 3455 – MC VISA ES e
closed lunch Monday to Friday, Sunday dinner, 24 to 30 December and 12 to 26 August – **Meals** - French - 17.75/19.50 6.00.

Holborn – ✉ WC2.

Drury Lane Moat House, 10 Drury Lane, High Holborn, WC2B 5RE, ☎ (0171) 208 9988, *Fax (0171) 831 1548*, ⅟ – |₿|, ⇔ rm, ▤ TV ☎ ♿ P – 🏛 60. MC AE ⓓ VISA JCB p. 33 DV c
Meals 15.50/16.75 **t.** and a la carte 6.95 – ☕ 10.75 – **163 rm** 145.00/175.00 **st.** – SB.

X Holborn Imari, 71 Red Lion St., WC1R 4NA, ☎ (0171) 405 0486, *Fax (0171) 431 8071* – ▤ MU z
Meals - Japanese rest.

Regent's Park – ✉ NW1.

White House, Albany St., NW1 3UP, ☎ (0171) 387 1200, *Fax (0171) 388 0091*, ⅟, – |₿|, ⇔ rm, ▤ rest, TV ☎ – 🏛 110. MC AE ⓓ VISA JCB. ✗ JT o
The Restaurant: **Meals** a la carte 25.75/68.95 **t.** 7.25 – ***Garden Cafe:*** **Meals** *(closed Sunday)* a la carte 16.10/28.20 **t.** 7.25 – ☕ 12.95 – **582 rm** 145.00/152.00 **st.**, 2 suites.

XX **Odette's,** 130 Regent's Park Rd, NW1 8XL, ☎ (0171) 586 5486, *Fax (0171) 586 2575* – 🆖
🆎 ⓪ 𝚟𝚒𝚜𝚊
HS   i
closed Saturday lunch, Sunday, 10 days Christmas and Bank Holidays – **Meals** 10.00 t.
(lunch) and a la carte 23.75/28.25 t. ◊ 5.50.

X **Belgo Noord,** 72 Chalk Farm Rd, NW1 8AN, ☎ (0171) 267 0718, *Fax (0171) 267 7508* – 🆖
🆎 ⓪ 𝚟𝚒𝚜𝚊 𝙹𝙲𝙱
IS   e
closed dinner 24 December and 25 December – **Meals** a la carte 16.85/30.40 t.

X **Luna,** 48 Chalk Farm Rd, NW1 8AJ, ☎ (0171) 482 4667, *Fax (0171) 284 0818*, ☞ – 🆖 𝚟𝚒𝚜𝚊
IS   c
closed 25 to 27 December – **Meals** a la carte 15.95/18.85 t.

▥ **The Queens,** 49 Regent's Park Rd, NW1 8XE, ☎ (0171) 586 0408, *Fax (0171) 586 5677*, ☞
– 🆖 𝚟𝚒𝚜𝚊
HS   a
Meals a la carte 6.45/24.85 t.

Swiss Cottage – ✉ NW3.

🏨 **Regents Park Marriott,** 128 King Henry's Rd, NW3 3ST, ☎ (0171) 722 7711,
Fax (0171) 586 5822, ↕, ☎, ▦ – ▯, ↔ rm, ▤ 📺 ☎ ♿ ☻ – 🔔 400. 🆖 🆎 ⓪ 𝚟𝚒𝚜𝚊 𝙹𝙲𝙱,
⚹
GS   a
Meals 18.95 t. and a la carte – ☞ 12.95 – **298 rm** 180.00/190.00 s., 5 suites – SB.

XX **Peter's Chateaubriand,** 65 Fairfax Rd, NW6 4EE, ☎ (0171) 624 5804 – ▤. 🆖 🆎 ⓪
𝚟𝚒𝚜𝚊 𝙹𝙲𝙱
FS   i
closed Saturday lunch, 26 December and 1 January – **Meals** 14.95 t. and a la carte.

XX **Bradley's,** 25 Winchester Rd, NW3 3NR, ☎ (0171) 722 3457 – ▤. 🆖 🆎 𝚟𝚒𝚜𝚊   GS   e
closed Saturday lunch, 1 week Christmas and Bank Holidays – **Meals** 15.00 t.
(lunch) and a la carte 21.90/26.90 t. ◊ 10.00.

X **Thai Pepper,** 115 Finchley Rd, NW3 6HY, ☎ (0171) 722 0026 – ▤. 🆖 🆎 ⓪ 𝚟𝚒𝚜𝚊   GS   v
closed lunch Saturday and Sunday and Bank Holidays – **Meals** - Thai - 17.00 t. and a la carte
◊ 3.90.

CITY OF LONDON p. 23.

XXX **Tatsuso,** 32 Broadgate Circle, EC2M 2QS, ☎ (0171) 638 5863, *Fax (0171) 638 5864* – ▤. 🆖
🆎 ⓪ 𝚟𝚒𝚜𝚊 𝙹𝙲𝙱
PU   u
closed Saturday, Sunday, late December and Bank Holidays – **Meals** - Japanese - (booking
essential) 50.00 t. and a la carte.

XXX **Gladwins,** Minister Court, Mark Lane, EC3R 7AA, ☎ (0171) 444 0004, *Fax (0171) 444 0001*
– ▤. 🆖 🆎 𝚟𝚒𝚜𝚊
PV   e
closed Saturday, Sunday and Bank Holidays – **Meals** (lunch only) 32.50 t.

XXX **City Rhodes,** 1 New Street Sq., EC4A 3BF, ☎ (0171) 583 1313, *Fax (0171) 353 1662* – ▤.
🆖 🆎 ⓪ 𝚟𝚒𝚜𝚊
NU   u
⚘
closed Saturday, Sunday and Bank Holidays – **Meals** a la carte 22.55/34.30 t. ◊ 13.95.
Spec. Escalope of salmon, black treacle, juniper and sherry dressing. Steak and "kidney pie".
"Jaffa Cake" pudding.

XX **Brasserie Rocque,** 37 Broadgate Circle, EC2M 2QS, ☎ (0171) 638 7919.
Fax (0171) 628 5899, ☞ – ▤. 🆖 🆎 ⓪ 𝚟𝚒𝚜𝚊
PU   ↓
closed Saturday, Sunday and Bank Holidays – **Meals** (lunch only) 27.50 t. and a la carte
◊ 5.00.

XX **Le Quai,** Riverside Walkway, 1 Broken Wharf, High Timber St., EC4V 3QQ
☎ (0171) 236 6480, *Fax (0171) 236 6479* – ▤. 🆖 🆎 ⓪ 𝚟𝚒𝚜𝚊 𝙹𝙲𝙱
OV   a
closed Saturday, Sunday, 2 weeks Christmas and Bank Holidays – **Meals** - French - (dinner
booking essential) 32.50 t.

XX **Miyama,** 17 Godliman St., EC4V 5BD, ☎ (0171) 489 1937, *Fax (0171) 236 0325* – ▤. 🆖 🆎
⓪ 𝚟𝚒𝚜𝚊 𝙹𝙲𝙱
OV   e
closed Saturday dinner, Sunday and Christmas-New Year – **Meals** - Japanese - 40.00 t.
and a la carte ◊ 7.50.

XX **Imperial City,** Royal Exchange, Cornhill, EC3V 3LL, ☎ (0171) 626 3437.
Fax (0171) 338 0125 – ▤. 🆖 🆎 ⓪ 𝚟𝚒𝚜𝚊
PV   ↓
closed Saturday, Sunday, 25 December and Bank Holidays – **Meals** - Chinese - 19.95/24.95 t.
and a la carte.

XX **Sri Siam City,** 85 London Wall, EC2M 7AD, ☎ (0171) 628 5772, *Fax (0171) 628 3395* – ▤
🆖 🆎 ⓪ 𝚟𝚒𝚜𝚊
PU
closed Saturday, Sunday and Bank Holidays – **Meals** - Thai - 15.50/24.95 t. and a la carte
◊ 8.00.

X **Imari,** 20 Copthall Av., EC2R 7DN, ☎ (0171) 628 3611, *Fax (0171) 431 8071* – ▤
Meals - Japanese rest.
PU

388

CROYDON *pp. 10 and 11.*

Addington – ⊠ *Surrey.*

╓₁₈, ╓₁₈, ╓₉ *Addington Court, Featherbed Lane* ℘ *(0181) 657 0281/2/3,* GZ –
╓₁₈ *The Addington, Shirley Church Rd* ℘ *(0181) 777 1055* GZ.

XX **Willow,** 88 Selsdon Park Rd, CR2 8JT, ℘ (0181) 657 4656 – ▤ 🅿. ◍ 🆎 ⑩ 𝐕𝐈𝐒𝐀   GZ **x**
closed 25 to 27 December – **Meals** - Chinese (Peking, Szechuan) - 16.50 **t.** and a la carte
⏧ 5.00.

Coulsdon – ⊠ *Surrey.*

🏨 **Coulsdon Manor** ⌖, Coulsdon Court Rd, via Stoats Nest Rd, CR5 2LL,
℘ (0181) 668 0414, *Fax (0181) 668 3118,* ╟₆, ⓢ, ╓₁₈, ℀, squash – |𝄞| 📺 ☎ 🅿 – 🔬 180. ◍
🆎 ⑩ 𝐕𝐈𝐒𝐀 𝐉𝐂𝐁. ℀   EZ **e**
Manor House : **Meals** 16.00/38.00 **t.** and a la carte ⏧ 8.00 – **35 rm** ⯐ 89.00/105.00 **t.** – SB.

Croydon – ⊠ *Surrey.*

🛈 *Croydon Clocktower, Katherine St., CR9 1ET* ℘ *(0181) 253 1009.*

🏨 **Hilton National,** Waddon Way, Purley Way, CR9 4HH, ℘ (0181) 680 3000,
Fax (0181) 681 6171, ╟₆, ⓢ, 🄻 – |𝄞|, ⇆ rm, ▤ 📺 ☎ ⅊ 🅿 – 🔬 400. ◍ 🆎 ⑩ 𝐕𝐈𝐒𝐀 𝐉𝐂𝐁. ℀
Meals *(closed Saturday lunch)* 14.00/17.50 **st.** and a la carte ⏧ 6.95 – ⯐ 12.00 – **168 rm**
120.00/160.00 **st.**   FZ **e**

🏨 **Croydon Park,** 7 Altyre Rd, CR9 5AA, ℘ (0181) 680 9200, *Fax (0181) 760 0426,* ⓢ,
🄻, squash – |𝄞|, ⇆ rm, ▤ 📺 ☎ 🅿 – 🔬 300. ◍ 🆎 ⑩ 𝐕𝐈𝐒𝐀 𝐉𝐂𝐁. ℀   FZ **u**
Oscars : **Meals** 15.95/16.95 **st.** and a la carte ⏧ 8.00 – **210 rm** ⯐ 99.00 **st.**, 1 suite – SB.

🏨 **Forte Posthouse Croydon,** Purley Way, CR9 4LT, ℘ (0181) 688 5185,
Fax (0181) 681 6438, ⟿ – ⇆ rm, ▤ rest, 📺 ☎ 🅿 – 🔬 140. ◍ 🆎 ⑩ 𝐕𝐈𝐒𝐀   FZ **o**
Meals a la carte 18.00/20.50 **st.** – ⯐ 9.95 – **83 rm** 89.00/129.00 **st.** – SB.

🏨 **Windsor Castle Toby,** 415 Brighton Rd, South Croydon, CR2 6ES, ℘ (0181) 680 4559,
Fax (0181) 680 5121, ⟿ – ⇆ rm, 📺 ☎ 🅿. ◍ 🆎 𝐕𝐈𝐒𝐀. ℀   FZ **a**
Meals (carving rest.) a la carte 10.15/15.10 **t.** ⏧ 4.45 – **29 rm** ⯐ 69.00/79.00 **t.** – SB.

🏨 **Travel Inn,** 104 Coombe Rd, CR0 5RB, on A 212 ℘ (0181) 686 2030, *Fax (0181) 686 6435,*
⟿ – ⇆ rm, 📺 ⅊ 🅿. ◍ 🆎 ⑩ 𝐕𝐈𝐒𝐀. ℀   GZ **s**
Meals (grill rest.) – **39 rm** 36.50 **t.**

X **Mario,** 299 High St., CR0 1QL, ℘ (0181) 686 5624 – ◍ 🆎 𝐕𝐈𝐒𝐀   FZ **s**
*closed Saturday lunch, Monday dinner, Sunday, last 2 weeks August, 25 December and Bank
Holidays* – **Meals** - Italian - a la carte 16.95/29.75 **t.** ⏧ 6.70.

X **Tai Tung,** Unit 1A, Wing Yip Centre, 550 Purley Way, CR0 4RF, ℘ (0181) 688 3668,
Fax (0181) 688 0116 – ▤ 🅿. ◍ 🆎 𝐕𝐈𝐒𝐀   FZ **v**
closed 24 to 26 December – **Meals** - Chinese (Canton) - a la carte 9.50/23.00 **t.** ⏧ 5.50.

Sanderstead – ⊠ *Surrey.*

╓₁₈ *Selsdon Park Hotel, Addington Rd, Sanderstead* ℘ *(0181) 657 8811* GZ.

🏨 **Selsdon Park,** Addington Rd, CR2 8YA, ℘ (0181) 657 8811, *Fax (0181) 651 6171,* ≤, ╟₆,
ⓢ, ⿴, 🄻, ╓₁₈, ⟿, park, ℀, squash – |𝄞|, ⇆ rm, 📺 ☎ 🅿 – 🔬 150. ◍ 🆎 ⑩ 𝐕𝐈𝐒𝐀 𝐉𝐂𝐁.
℀   GZ **n**
Meals (dancing Friday and Saturday) 19.50/22.50 **st.** and a la carte ⏧ 8.00 – ⯐ 12.95 –
192 rm 94.00/138.00 **t.**, 7 suites – SB.

EALING *pp. 4 and 5.*

Ealing – ⊠ *W5.*

╓₁₈ *West Middlesex, Greenford Rd* ℘ *(0181) 574 3450* BV – ╓₉ *Horsenden Hill, Woodland Rise*
℘ *(0181) 902 4555* BU.

🏨 **Jarvis Carnarvon,** Ealing Common, W5 3HN, ℘ (0181) 992 5399, *Fax (0181) 992 7082* –
|𝄞|, ⇆ rm, 📺 ☎ 🅿 – 🔬 200. ◍ 🆎 ⑩ 𝐕𝐈𝐒𝐀 𝐉𝐂𝐁. ℀   CV **v**
Meals *(closed Saturday lunch)* a la carte 19.50/30.50 **t.** ⏧ 7.50 – ⯐ 11.50 – **145 rm** 108.00/
120.00 **t.** – SB.

XX **Maxim,** 153-155 Northfield Av., W13 9QT, ℘ (0181) 567 1719, *Fax (0181) 932 7067* – ▤.
◍ 🆎 ⑩ 𝐕𝐈𝐒𝐀 𝐉𝐂𝐁   BV **a**
closed Sunday lunch and 25 to 28 December – **Meals** - Chinese (Peking) - 12.00/15.00 **t.**
and a la carte.

XX **Gitanjli - Mayfair,** 18-19 The Mall, Ealing Broadway, W5 2PJ, 𝒫 (0181) 810 0006, Fax (0181) 810 0005 – ▤, ◍◉ Ⓐ Ⓞ 𝘝𝘐𝘚𝘈   CV s
closed 26 December – **Meals** - North Indian - a la carte 13.10/25.20 **t.**

X **Noughts 'n' Crosses,** 77 The Grove, W5 5LL, 𝒫 (0181) 840 7568, Fax (0181) 840 1905 –
◍◉ Ⓐ 𝘝𝘐𝘚𝘈 𝗝𝗖𝗕   BV u
closed Sunday dinner, Monday, August and 26 December-5 January – **Meals** (dinner only and Sunday lunch)/dinner 16.90/21.50 **t.** ▯ 5.30.

Hanwell – ⊠ W7.

▯ᵦ Brent Valley, Church Rd, 𝒫 (0181) 567 1287 BV.

🏠 **Wellmeadow Lodge,** 24 Wellmeadow Rd, W7 2AL, 𝒫 (0181) 567 7294, Fax (0181) 566 3468, ≈ – ▤ ◍◉ Ⓐ 𝘝𝘐𝘚𝘈. ⍥   BV r
Meals (booking essential) (residents only) (communal dining) (dinner only) 20.00 **st.** – 10 rm ⌁ 70.00/120.00 **st.**

ENFIELD pp. 6 and 7.

▯ᵦ Lee Valley, Picketts Lock Lane, Edmonton 𝒫 (0181) 803 3611 GT.

Enfield – ⊠ Middx.

▯ᵦ Whitewebbs, Beggars Hollow, Clay Hill 𝒫 (0181) 363 4454/2951, N : 1 m. FT.

🏠🏠 **Royal Chace,** The Ridgeway, EN2 8AR, 𝒫 (0181) 366 6500, Fax (0181) 367 7191, ⌁, ≈ –
📺 ☎ 🅟 – 🔏 270. ◍◉ Ⓐ Ⓞ 𝘝𝘐𝘚𝘈. ⍥   ET a
Meals (closed Saturday lunch, Sunday dinner and Bank Holidays) 15.95/18.95 **st.** and dinner a la carte ▯ 6.15 – **92 rm** ⌁ 85.00/120.00 **st.**

Hadley Wood – ⊠ Herts.

🏠🏠🏠 **West Lodge Park** ⍦, off Cockfosters Rd, EN4 0PY, 𝒫 (0181) 440 8311, Fax (0181) 449 3698, ≤, ≈, park – ▤ ⍢ 📺 ☎ ⅙ 🅟 – 🔏 80. ◍◉ Ⓐ 𝘝𝘐𝘚𝘈. ⍥   ET i
The Cedar : Meals 19.95/24.95 **st.** ▯ 7.25 – ⌁ 10.50 – **46 rm** 84.50/240.00 **st.** – SB.

The Guide is updated annually so renew your Guide every year.

GREENWICH pp. 10 and 11.

Blackheath – ⊠ SE3.

🏠🏠 **Bardon Lodge,** 15 Stratheden Rd, SE3 7TH, 𝒫 (0181) 853 4051, Fax (0181) 858 7387, ≈
– ⍢ rest, 📺 ☎ 🅟 – 🔏 30. ◍◉ Ⓐ 𝘝𝘐𝘚𝘈   HV a
Lamplight : Meals (dinner only) 16.50 **t.** and a la carte ▯ 5.95 – **30 rm** ⌁ 60.00/90.00 **st.**

Greenwich – ⊠ SE10.

🛈 46 Greenwich Church St., SE10 9BL 𝒫 (0181) 858 6376.

XX **Treasure of China,** 10-11 Nelson Rd, SE10 9JB, 𝒫 (0181) 858 9884, Fax (0181) 293 5327
– ▤, ◍◉ Ⓐ Ⓞ 𝘝𝘐𝘚𝘈 𝗝𝗖𝗕   GV e
closed 25 and 26 December – **Meals** - Chinese (Peking, Szechuan) - 12.00/25.00 **t.** and a la carte.

XX **Spread Eagle,** 1-2 Stockwell St., SE10 9JN, 𝒫 (0181) 853 2333, Fax (0181) 305 1666 – ▤
◍◉ Ⓐ Ⓞ 𝘝𝘐𝘚𝘈 𝗝𝗖𝗕   GV c
closed Sunday dinner and 1 week Christmas – **Meals** 17.00 **st.** and a la carte ▯ 5.00.

HACKNEY p.23.

Dalston – ⊠ N 1.

X **Soulard,** 113 Mortimer Rd, N1 4JY, 𝒫 (0171) 254 1314 – ◍◉ 𝘝𝘐𝘚𝘈   PS e
closed Sunday, Monday and 15 August-second week September – **Meals** - French - (dinner only and lunch in December) 16.95 **t.** ▯ 4.75.

Stoke Newington – ⊠ N16.

X **Mesclun,** 24 Stoke Newington Church St., N16 0LU, 𝒫 (0171) 249 5029 – ◍◉ 𝘝𝘐𝘚𝘈.
𝗝𝗖𝗕   FU e
closed Sunday dinner and 25 to 31 December – **Meals** (dinner only) a la carte 16.15/19.40 **t**
▯ 4.50.

HAMMERSMITH and FULHAM *Except where otherwise stated see pp. 24-25.*

Fulham – ✉ *SW6.*

La Reserve, 422-428 Fulham Rd, SW6 1DU, ✆ (0171) 385 8561, *Fax (0171) 385 7662* – |$|, ⇸ rm, TV ☎. MC AE ⓓ VISA JCB. ✈ FZ a
closed 25 and 26 December – **Meals** a la carte 14.00/21.20 **t.** 5.95 – ☕ 3.50 – **41 rm** 79.00/110.00 **st.** – SB.

Travel Inn Capital, 3 Putney Bridge Approach, SW6 3JD, ✆ (0171) 471 8300, *Fax (0171) 471 8315* – |$|, ⇸ rm, TV ♿. MC AE ⓓ VISA AQ c
Meals (grill rest.) – **154 rm** 49.50 **t.**

Blue Elephant, 4-6 Fulham Broadway, SW6 1AA, ✆ (0171) 385 6595, *Fax (0171) 386 7665* – ▤. MC AE ⓓ VISA EZ z
closed Saturday lunch and 24 to 27 December – **Meals** - Thai - (booking essential) 28.00/ 34.00 **st.** and a la carte.

755, 755 Fulham Rd, SW6 5UU, ✆ (0171) 371 0755, *Fax (0171) 371 0695* – ▤. MC AE VISA
closed Monday lunch, Sunday dinner, 2 weeks summer, 1 week Christmas and Bank Holidays – **Meals** 14.00/22.00 **t.** and a la carte 6.95. p. 12 BQ n

Mao Tai, 58 New Kings Rd., Parsons Green, SW6 4UG, ✆ (0171) 731 2520 – ▤. MC AE ⓓ VISA p. 12 BQ e
closed 24 to 26 December – **Meals** - Chinese (Szechuan) - 19.50 **t.** and a la carte.

Hammersmith – ✉ *W6/W12/W14.*

River Café (Ruth Rogers/Rose Gray), Thames Wharf, Rainville Rd, W6 9HA, ✆ (0171) 381 8824, *Fax (0171) 381 6217*, ☂ – MC AE VISA p. 9 DV r
✿ *closed Sunday dinner, 1 week Christmas and Bank Holidays* – **Meals** - Italian - (booking essential) a la carte 33.50/40.00
Spec. Crab risotto with tomato, lemon and basil. Roast loin of organic pork with salsa verde. Almond tart.

Tandoori Nights, 319-321 King St., W6 9NH, ✆ (0181) 741 4328, *Fax (0181) 741 4328* – ▤. MC AE ⓓ VISA JCB p. 9 CV u
closed 25 and 26 December – **Meals** - Indian - a la carte 10.30/20.00 **t.** 6.50.

Snows on the Green, 166 Shepherd's Bush Rd, Brook Green, W6 7PB, ✆ (0171) 603 2142, *Fax (0171) 602 7553* – MC AE ⓓ VISA p. 9 DV x
closed Saturday lunch, Sunday dinner, 1 week Christmas and Bank Holiday Mondays – **Meals** 15.50 **st.** (lunch) and a la carte 19.00/23.00 **st.**

The Brackenbury, 129-131 Brackenbury Rd, W6 0BQ, ✆ (0181) 748 0107, *Fax (0181) 741 0905*, ☂ – MC AE VISA JCB p. 9 CV a
closed Saturday lunch, Sunday dinner and Christmas – **Meals** a la carte 18.00/20.00 **t.** 9.50.

Havelock Tavern, 57 Masbro Rd, W14 0LS, ✆ (0171) 603 5374, *Fax (0171) 602 1163*, ☂
closed 25 and 26 December – **Meals** a la carte approx. 15.00 **st.** p. 9 DV e

Anglesea Arms, 35 Wingate Rd, W6 0UR, ✆ (0181) 749 1291, *Fax (0181) 749 1291* – MC VISA p. 9 CV s
closed 1 week Christmas and Bank Holidays – **Meals** (bookings not accepted) a la carte 12.75/18.45 **t.** 8.50.

Shepherd's Bush – ✉ *W12/W14.*

Chinon, 23 Richmond Way, W14 0AS, ✆ (0171) 602 5968, *Fax (0171) 602 4082* – ▤. MC AE VISA p. 9 DV c
closed Sunday and 24 to 29 December – **Meals** (dinner only) 17.50 **t.** and a la carte 7.50.

Wilsons, 236 Blythe Rd, W14 0HJ, ✆ (0171) 603 7267 – MC VISA p. 9 DV a
closed Saturday lunch and Sunday dinner – **Meals** a la carte 18.25/23.70 **t.** 4.25.

HARINGEY *pp. 6 and 7.*

Crouch End – ✉ *N 8.*

Les Associés, 172 Park Rd, N8 8JY, ✆ (0181) 348 8944 – MC VISA EU e
closed Saturday lunch, Monday, 10 days January and 10 days September – **Meals** - French - 12.50 **t.** (lunch) and dinner a la carte 17.00/21.80 **t.** 7.10.

Florians, 4 Topsfield Par., Middle Lane, N8 8RP, ✆ (0181) 348 8348 – MC VISA EU c
closed 25-26 December and 1 January – **Meals** - Italian - 9.95 **t.** and a la carte 6.00.

HARROW pp. 4 and 5.

Central Harrow – ✉ Middx.

🖼 Civic Centre, Station Rd, HA4 7XW ℘ (0181) 424 1100/2/3 BU

🏨 **Cumberland**, 1 St. John's Rd, HA1 2EF, ℘ (0181) 863 4111, Fax (0181) 861 5668, ☎ – ✸ rm, 📺 ☎ 🅿 – 🔬 130. ● AE ① VISA JCB. ✗
Meals 10.50/14.50 t. and a la carte ≬ 7.75 – ☲ 8.50 – **84 rm** 87.50/92.50 t. BU x

XX **Taste of China**, 174 Station Rd, HA1 2RH, ℘ (0181) 863 2080 – ■. ● AE ① VISA JCB
closed lunch Sunday and Bank Holidays – **Meals** - Chinese - 14.00 t. and a la carte. BU u

XX **Trattoria Sorrentina**, 6 Manor Par., Sheepcote Rd, HA1 2JN, ℘ (0181) 427 9411, Fax (0181) 427 9411 – ■. ● AE ① VISA BU x
closed Saturday lunch and Sunday – **Meals** - Italian - 15.95 t. and a la carte ≬ 4.50.

Kenton – ✉ Middx.

🏠 **Travel Inn**, Kenton Rd, HA3 8AT, ℘ (0181) 907 4069, Fax (0181) 909 1604 – ✸ rm, 📺 & 🅿. ● AE ① VISA. ✗ BU e
Meals (grill rest.) – **44 rm** 36.50 t.

North Harrow – ✉ Middx.

XX **Percy's**, 66-68 Station Rd, HA2 7SJ, ℘ (0181) 427 2021, Fax (0181) 427 8134 – ✸. ● AE ① VISA BU n
closed Sunday, Monday, 27 to 30 December and Bank Holidays – **Meals** (booking essential) 19.50 t.

Pinner – ✉ Middx.

XX **Friends**, 11 High St., HA5 5PJ, ℘ (0181) 866 0286, Fax (0181) 866 0286 – ✸. ● AE ① VISA
closed Sunday dinner, 25 December and Bank Holidays – **Meals** 14.95/18.95 t. and a la carte ≬ 8.95. BU a

South Harrow – ✉ Middx.

X **Jaflong**, 299 Northolt Rd, HA2 8JA, ℘ (0181) 864 7345 – ■. ● AE ① VISA BU r
Meals - Indian - 5.50/13.00 t. and a la carte.

Stanmore – ✉ Middx.

XX **Mr Tang's Mandarin**, 28 The Broadway, HA7 4DW, ℘ (0181) 954 0339 – ■. ● AE ① VISA BT i
Meals - Chinese (Peking) - a la carte 14.50/18.00 t.

HAVERING pp. 6 and 7.

Hornchurch by A 12 – JT – on A 127 – ✉ Essex.

🏨 **Palms**, Southend Arterial Rd (A 127), RM11 3UJ, ℘ (01708) 346789, Fax (01708) 341719, ☞ – ✸ rm, 📺 & 🅿 – 🔬 270. ● AE ① VISA. ✗
Meals (bar lunch Saturday) (dancing Friday evening) 9.95/18.00 st. and a la carte ≬ 6.50 – ☲ 9.95 – **137 rm** 92.00/150.00 st.

Romford – ✉ Essex.

🛆, 🛆 Havering, Risebridge, Risebridge Chase, Lower Bedfords Rd ℘ (01708) 741429, JT.

🏠 **Travel Inn**, Mercury Gdns., RM1 3EN, ℘ (01708) 760548, Fax (01708) 760456 – 📳, ✸ rm, 📺 & 🅿. ● AE ① VISA JU a
Meals (grill rest.) – **40 rm** 36.50 t.

HILLINGDON pp. 4 and 8.

🛆 Haste Hill, The Drive, Northwood ℘ (01923) 825224 AU.

Hayes – ✉ Middx.

🏠 **Travel Inn**, 362 Uxbridge Rd, UB4 0HF, ℘ (0181) 573 7479, Fax (0181) 569 1204 – ✸ rm, 📺 & 🅿. ● AE ① VISA. ✗ AV a
Meals (grill rest.) – **62 rm** 36.50 t.

Heathrow Airport – ⊠ Middx.

Radisson Edwardian, 140 Bath Rd, Hayes, UB3 5AW, ℘ (0181) 759 6311, Fax (0181) 759 4559, ₣₆, ⓪, ◻ – ▮, ⅙ rm, ▤ ⓣⓥ ☎ ℗ – ▨ 550. ⓪ⓐ ⅍ ⓞ ⓥⓘⓢⓐ. ⅏
Henleys : Meals a la carte 34.50/39.00 st. ◮ 8.00 – **Brasserie :** Meals a la carte approx. 20.50 st. ◮ 8.00 – ⌣ 14.00 – **442 rm** 157.00/200.00 s., 17 suites.
AX e

Holiday Inn Crowne Plaza Heathrow London, Stockley Rd, West Drayton, UB7 9NA, ℘ (01895) 445555, Fax (01895) 445122, ₣₆, ⓪, ◻, ▯ – ▮, ⅙ rm, ▤ ⓣⓥ ☎ ⅌ ℗ – ▨ 200. ⓪ⓐ ⅍ ⓞ ⓥⓘⓢⓐ ⱼ⶜⶛
AV v
Marlowe : Meals a la carte 24.75/36.20 st. ◮ 7.50 – **Cafe Galleria :** Meals a la carte 18.15/ 27.95 st. ◮ 7.50 – ⌣ 12.95 – **372 rm** 175.00/185.00 st., 2 suites.

Sheraton Skyline, Bath Rd, Hayes, UB3 5BP, ℘ (0181) 759 2535, Fax (0181) 750 9150, ₣₆, ◻ – ▮, ⅙ rm, ▤ ⓣⓥ ☎ ⅌ ℗ – ▨ 500. ⓪ⓐ ⅍ ⓞ ⓥⓘⓢⓐ. ⅏
Colony Room : Meals (closed Sunday) (dinner only) a la carte 26.25/35.75 st. ◮ 11.50 – **Le Jardin :** Meals 18.75 st. and a la carte ◮ 11.50 – ⌣ 15.50 – **346 rm** 185.00/224.50 st., 5 suites.

London Heathrow Hilton, Terminal 4, TW6 3AF, ℘ (0181) 759 7755, Fax (0181) 759 7579, ₣₆, ⓪, ◻ – ▮, ⅙ rm, ▤ ⓣⓥ ☎ ⅍ ℗ – ▨ 240. ⓪ⓐ ⅍ ⓞ ⓥⓘⓢⓐ ⱼ⶜⶛. ⅏
AX n
Brasserie : Meals 20.95/22.75 st. and a la carte ◮ 12.00 – **Zen Oriental :** Meals - Chinese - 25.80/27.50 t. and a la carte ◮ 14.80 – ⌣ 14.95 – **390 rm** 185.00 st., 5 suites – SB.

Forte Crest, Sipson Rd, West Drayton, UB7 0JU, ℘ (0181) 759 2323, Fax (0181) 897 8659 – ▮, ⅙ rm, ▤ ⓣⓥ ☎ ⅍ ℗ – ▨ 100. ⓪ⓐ ⅍ ⓞ ⓥⓘⓢⓐ ⱼ⶜⶛. ⅏
AV c
Meals (closed Saturday lunch) (carving rest.) 17.50 st. ◮ 7.25 – **Sampans :** Meals - Chinese - (dinner only) 17.95 t. and a la carte ◮ 7.95 – **Tutto :** Meals (closed lunch Saturday, Sunday and Bank Holidays) 9.99 t. and a la carte ◮ 8.95 – ⌣ 11.50 – **521 rm** 125.00/135.00 st., 6 suites – SB.

Excelsior Heathrow, Bath Rd, West Drayton, UB7 0DU, ℘ (0181) 759 6611, Fax (0181) 759 3421, ₣₆, ⓪, ◻ – ▮, ⅙ rm, ▤ ⓣⓥ ☎ ⅍ ℗ – ▨ 700. ⓪ⓐ ⅍ ⓞ ⓥⓘⓢⓐ. ⅏
Meals (carving rest.) 17.95 st. and dinner a la carte ◮ 5.75 – **Wheeler's :** Meals - Seafood - (closed lunch Saturday and Sunday and Bank Holidays) a la carte 21.00/37.00 st. ◮ 6.75 – ⌣ 12.50 – **817 rm** 125.00/130.00 st., 10 suites – SB.
AX x

Ramada H. Heathrow, Bath Rd, TW6 2AQ, ℘ (0181) 897 6363, Fax (0181) 897 1113, ₣₆, ⓪ – ▮, ⅙ rm, ▤ ⓣⓥ ☎ ⅍ ℗ – ▨ 550. ⓪ⓐ ⅍ ⓞ ⓥⓘⓢⓐ ⱼ⶜⶛. ⅏
AX c
Meals 17.50/20.50 st. and a la carte ◮ 6.00 – ⌣ 11.25 – **634 rm** 150.00 st., 6 suites.

Sheraton Heathrow, Colnbrook bypass, West Drayton, UB7 0HJ, ℘ (0181) 759 2424, Fax (0181) 759 2091 – ▮, ⅙ rm, ▤ ⓣⓥ ☎ ⅍ ℗ – ▨ 60. ⓪ⓐ ⅍ ⓞ ⓥⓘⓢⓐ. ⅏
AVX a
Meals a la carte 15.45/28.70 st. ◮ 9.50 – ⌣ 13.50 – **427 rm** 170.00/180.00 st., 4 suites.

Forte Posthouse Heathrow, Bath Rd, Hayes, UB3 5AJ, ℘ (0181) 759 2552, Fax (0181) 564 9265 – ▮, ⅙ rm, ▤ ⓣⓥ ☎ ℗ – ▨ 45. ⓪ⓐ ⅍ ⓞ ⓥⓘⓢⓐ ⱼ⶜⶛. ⅏
AX i
Meals a la carte 14.25/25.65 st. ◮ 7.25 – ⌣ 10.95 – **186 rm** 109.00 st. – SB.

ckenham – ⊠ Middx.

X **Roberto's,** 15 Long Lane, UB10 8AX, ℘ (01895) 632519 – ▤. ⓪ⓐ ⅍ ⓥⓘⓢⓐ ⱼ⶜⶛
AU i
closed Sunday – Meals - Italian - a la carte 14.50/26.00 t. ◮ 7.50.

IOUNSLOW pp. 8 and 9.

▮₈ Wyke Green, Syon Lane, Isleworth ℘ (0181) 560 8777 BV – ▮₈ Airlinks, Southall Lane ℘ (0181) 561 1418 ABV – ▮₈ Hounslow Heath, Staines Rd ℘ (0181) 570 5271 BX.
🛈 24 The Treaty Centre, Hounslow High St., TW3 1ES ℘ (0181) 572 8279.

hiswick – ⊠ W4.

XX **La Dordogne,** 5 Devonshire Rd, W4 2EU, ℘ (0181) 747 1836, Fax (0181) 994 9144 – ⓪ⓐ ⅍ ⓞ ⓥⓘⓢⓐ
CV o
closed lunch Saturday and Sunday and Bank Holidays – Meals - French - a la carte 18.90/ 30.30 t. ◮ 5.10.

X **The Chiswick,** 131 Chiswick High Rd, W4 2ED, ℘ (0181) 994 6887, Fax (0181) 747 8708 – ⓪ⓐ ⅍ ⓥⓘⓢⓐ
CV e
closed Saturday lunch, Sunday dinner and 4 days Christmas – Meals 9.50 t. and a la carte ◮ 4.75.

ranford – ⊠ Middx.

🏠 **Jarvis International Heathrow,** Bath Rd, TW5 9QE, ℘ (0181) 897 2121, Fax (0181) 897 7014, ☞ – ▮, ⅙ rm, ⓣⓥ ☎ ℗ – ▨ 100. ⓪ⓐ ⅍ ⓞ ⓥⓘⓢⓐ. ⅏
AX r
Meals (closed lunch Saturday and Sunday) 12.50/15.95 t. and a la carte ◮ 6.50 – ⌣ 10.95 – **72 rm** 109.00/125.00 st., 1 suite – SB.

Heston Service Area – ⊠ Middx.

🏠 **Travelodge** without rest., TW5 9NB, on M 4 (between junctions 2 and 3 westbound carriageway) ℘ (0181) 580 2000, Fax (0181) 580 2006, Reservations (Freephone) 0800 850950 – ❄ 📺 ☎ ዿ ℗. ⓂⓈ ◯ VISA JCB. ⅍ ABV e
95 rm 55.95 **t**.

ISLINGTON Except where otherwise stated see pp. 20-23.

Canonbury – ⊠ N1.

 ✗ **Anna's Place**, 90 Mildmay Park, N1 4PR, ℘ (0171) 249 9379 p. 6 FU a
closed Sunday dinner, lunch 2 weeks August, Monday, 1 week Easter and 2 weeks Christmas
– **Meals** - Swedish - (booking essential) a la carte 18.75/27.50 **t**.

Clerkenwell – ⊠ EC1.

 ✗✗ **Maison Novelli**, 29 Clerkenwell Green, EC1R 0DU, ℘ (0171) 251 6606, Fax (0171) 490 1083 – ⓂⓈ Ⓐ ◯ VISA JCB NU a
closed Saturday lunch, Sunday, New Year and Bank Holidays – **Meals** a la carte 25.00/40.00 **t**.
♦ 12.60.

 ✗ **Novelli EC1**, 30 Clerkenwell Green, EC1R 0DU, ℘ (0171) 251 6606 – ⓂⓈ Ⓐ ◯ VISA
JCB NU a
Meals (closed Saturday lunch, Sunday and Bank Holidays) a la carte 14.30/22.30 **t**. ♦ 10.50.

Finsbury – ⊠ WC1/EC1/EC2.

 ✗ **Stephen Bull's Bistro**, 71 St. John St., EC1M 4AN, ℘ (0171) 490 1750 Fax (0171) 490 3128 – ▤. ⓂⓈ Ⓐ VISA NU r
closed Saturday lunch, Sunday, 24 December-2 January and Bank Holidays – **Meals**
a la carte 19.50/25.00 **t**. ♦ 11.50.

 ✗ **Quality Chop House**, 94 Farringdon Rd, EC1R 3EA, ℘ (0171) 837 5093 MT n
closed Saturday lunch and 10 days Christmas – **Meals** a la carte 18.00/26.25 **t**. ♦ 8.00.

 ✗ **Moro**, 34-36 Exmouth Market, EC1R 4QE, ℘ (0171) 833 8336, Fax (0171) 833 9338 – ▤. ⓂⓈ
VISA NT a
closed Sunday and 24 December-3 January – **Meals** a la carte 16.50/20.50 **t**.

 ✗ **St. John**, 26 St. John St., EC1M 4AY, ℘ (0171) 251 0848, Fax (0171) 251 4090 – ⓂⓈ Ⓐ ◯
VISA OU c
closed Saturday lunch, Sunday, Easter and Christmas – **Meals** a la carte 19.00/26.00 **t**.
♦ 10.00.

 ▯ **Peasant**, 240 St. John St., EC1V 4PH, ℘ (0171) 336 7726, Fax (0171) 251 4476 – ⓂⓈ Ⓐ
VISA
closed Saturday lunch, Sunday, 24 December-2 January and Bank Holidays – **Meal**
a la carte 16.80/21.90 **t**. NT

Islington – ⊠ N1.

 🏨 **Stakis London Islington**, Upper St., N1 0UY, ℘ (0171) 354 7700, Fax (0171) 354 7711
❄ rm, ▤ 📺 ☎ ዿ – 🔒 35. ⓂⓈ Ⓐ ◯ VISA. ⅍ NS
Meals a la carte 19.95/30.45 **t**. ♦ 7.00 – ⌍ 11.50 – **183 rm** 135.00/210.00 **st**. – SB.

 ✗✗ **Frederick's**, Camden Passage, N1 8EG, ℘ (0171) 359 2888, Fax (0171) 359 5173, 綠 , 綠
– ▤. ⓂⓈ Ⓐ ◯ VISA NS
closed Sunday, 1 week Christmas-New Year and Bank Holidays – **Meals** a la carte 24.00
30.00 **st**. ♦ 7.50.

 ✗✗ **Lola's**, 359 Upper St., N1 0PD, ℘ (0171) 359 1932, Fax (0171) 359 2209 – ⓂⓈ Ⓐ ◯ VIS
JCB NS
closed Sunday dinner – **Meals** 16.50 **t**. (lunch) and a la carte 19.25/26.50 **t**. ♦ 7.75.

 ✗ **Granita**, 127 Upper St., N1 1PQ, ℘ (0171) 226 3222, Fax (0171) 226 4833 – ▤. ⓂⓈ VISA
closed Tuesday lunch, Monday, 1 week Easter, 2 weeks August and 10 days Christmas
Meals 13.95 **t**. (lunch) and dinner a la carte 21.50/24.50 **t**. NS

 ✗ **Fisk**, 265 Upper St., N1 2UQ, ℘ (0171) 359 1022 – ⓂⓈ Ⓐ VISA JCB NS
closed Sunday, Monday, 24-26 and 31 December and 1 January – **Meals** - Scandinavian
Seafood - (light lunch)/dinner a la carte 21.50/44.90 **t**. ♦ 4.75.

 ✗ **Euphorium**, 203 Upper St., N1 1RQ, ℘ (0171) 704 6909, Fax (0171) 226 0241 – ⓂⓈ Ⓐ VI
JCB NS
closed Sunday dinner – **Meals** 17.00 **t**. (lunch) and dinner a la carte 23.50/30.00 **t**.

KENSINGTON and CHELSEA *(Royal Borough of).*

Chelsea – ⊠ *SW1/SW3/SW10 – Except where otherwise stated see pp. 30 and 31.*

Hyatt Carlton Tower, 2 Cadogan Pl., SW1X 9PY, ℰ *(0171) 235 1234,*
Fax (0171) 235 9129, ≤, *I₅,* ⊆s, ⊠, ☞, ℀ – ▐╢, ⁕ rm, ▤ ☎ ⇦ – ⚄ 250. ⓌⓈ ⅍ ⓪
VISA JCB. ⅗
FR n
Rib Room *(ℰ (0171) 824 7053) :* Meals 26.50/32.50 **t.** and a la carte ▒ 15.00 – (see also
Grissini below) – ⊊ 16.50 – **191 rm** 265.00/320.00, 29 suites.

Conrad International London, Chelsea Harbour, SW10 0XG, ℰ *(0171) 823 3000,*
Fax (0171) 351 6525, ≤, *I₅,* ⊆s, ⊠ – ▐╢, ⁕ rm, ▤ ▤ ☎ ⅙ ⇦ – ⚄ 180. ⓌⓈ ⅍ ⓪ _VISA_
JCB
p. 13 CQ i
The Brasserie : Meals 22.50 (dinner) and a la carte 19.50/34.00 ▒ 16.00 – ⊊ 17.00 –,
159 suites 250.00/280.00.

Sheraton Park Tower, 101 Knightsbridge, SW1X 7RN, ℰ *(0171) 235 8050,*
Fax (0171) 235 8231, ≤ – ▐╢, ⁕ rm, ▤ ▤ ☎ ⅙ ⇦ – ⚄ 60. ⓌⓈ ⅍ ⓪ _VISA JCB_. ⅗
101 Knightsbridge *(ℰ (0171) 235 6067) :* Meals 23.50/34.00 **t.** and a la carte ▒ 15.50 – ⊊
17.00 – **267 rm** 262.00/378.00 **s.,** 22 suites – SB.
FQ v

Capital, 22-24 Basil St., SW3 1AT, ℰ *(0171) 589 5171, Fax (0171) 225 0011* – ▐╢ ▤ ▤ ☎
⇦ – ⚄ 25. ⓌⓈ ⅍ ⓪ _VISA_. ⅗
ER a
✿ Meals (booking essential) 28.00/55.00 **t.** and a la carte 50.50/55.50 **t.** ▒ 9.00 – ⊊ 17.50 –
48 rm 167.00/310.00 **s.**
Spec. Asparagus tuile with a sauternes, truffle and lime sabayon. Braised duckling in
orange, fennel, cinnamon and honey with flat beans. Assiette of vanilla.

Durley House, 115 Sloane St., SW1X 9PJ, ℰ *(0171) 235 5537, Fax (0171) 259 6977,*
« Georgian town house », ☞, ℀ – ▐╢ ▤ ☎. ⓌⓈ ⅍ _VISA_. ⅗
FS e
Meals (room service only) a la carte 18.00/25.50 **t.** ▒ 9.95 – ⊊ 14.50, **11 suites** 220.00/
395.00 **s.**

Cadogan, 75 Sloane St., SW1X 9SG, ℰ *(0171) 235 7141, Fax (0171) 245 0994,* ☞, ℀ – ▐╢,
⁕ rm, ▤ rest, ▤ ☎ – ⚄ 40. ⓌⓈ ⅍ _VISA_. ⅗
FR e
Meals *(closed Saturday lunch)* 17.90/25.50 **t.** and a la carte ▒ 6.75 – ⊊ 14.50 – **61 rm**
140.00/215.00 **st.,** 4 suites – SB.

Cliveden Town House, 24-26 Cadogan Gdns., SW3 2RP, ℰ *(0171) 730 6466,*
Fax (0171) 730 0236, ☞ – ▐╢ ▤ rm, ▤ ☎. ⓌⓈ ⅍ ⓪ _VISA_
FS c
Meals (room service only) – ⊊ 17.50 – **31 rm** 120.00/250.00 **s.,** 4 suites.

Franklin, 28 Egerton Gdns., SW3 2DB, ℰ *(0171) 584 5533, Fax (0171) 584 5449,*
« Tastefully furnished Victorian town house », ☞ – ▐╢ ▤ ▤ ☎. ⓌⓈ ⅍ ⓪ _VISA_. ⅗
DS e
Meals (room service only) a la carte 20.00/28.00 **st.** ▒ 8.00 – ⊊ 14.00 – **46 rm** 140.00/
275.00 **s.,** 1 suite.

Basil Street, 8 Basil St., SW3 1AH, ℰ *(0171) 581 3311, Fax (0171) 581 3693* – ▐╢ ▤ ☎ –
⚄ 55. ⓌⓈ ⅍ ⓪ _VISA JCB_. ⅗
FQ o
Meals (carving lunch Saturday) 11.00/19.50 **t.** and a la carte ▒ 7.50 – ⊊ 13.50 – **93 rm**
115.00/170.00 **s.**

Chelsea, 17-25 Sloane St., SW1X 9NU, ℰ *(0171) 235 4377, Fax (0171) 235 3705* – ▐╢,
⁕ rm, ▤ ▤ ☎ – ⚄ 100. ⓌⓈ ⅍ ⓪ _VISA JCB_. ⅗
FR r
The Restaurant : Meals *(closed Sunday dinner)* 19.50 **t.** (lunch) and a la carte 19.50/
32.00 **t.** – ⊊ 13.75 – **219 rm** 180.00/230.00 **s.,** 5 suites.

Sydney House, 9-11 Sydney St., SW3 6PU, ℰ *(0171) 376 7711, Fax (0171) 376 4233,*
« Tastefully furnished Victorian town house » – ▐╢ ▤ ☎. ⓌⓈ ⅍ ⓪ _VISA_
DT a
Meals (room service only) – ⊊ 14.10 – **21 rm** 150.00/200.00 **s.**

Egerton House, 17-19 Egerton Terr., SW3 2BX, ℰ *(0171) 589 2412, Fax (0171) 584 6540,*
« Tastefully furnished Victorian town house » – ▐╢ ▤ ▤ ☎. ⓌⓈ ⅍ ⓪ _VISA_. ⅗
DR e
Meals (room service only) a la carte 17.50/29.00 **t.** ▒ 10.00 – ⊊ 14.00 – **29 rm** 140.00/
210.00.

Sloane, 29 Draycott Pl., SW3 2SH, ℰ *(0171) 581 5757, Fax (0171) 584 1348,* « Victorian
town house, antiques » – ▐╢ ▤ ▤ ☎. ⓌⓈ ⅍ ⓪ _VISA JCB_. ⅗
ET c
Meals (room service only) – ⊊ 12.00 – **12 rm** 130.00/225.00 **s.**

Eleven Cadogan Gardens, 11 Cadogan Gdns., SW3 2RJ, ℰ *(0171) 730 7000,*
Fax (0171) 730 5217, I₅ – ▐╢ ▤ ☎. ⓌⓈ ⅍ ⓪ _VISA JCB_. ⅗
FS u
Meals (room service only) a la carte 15.00/20.00 ▒ 7.05 – ⊊ 11.75 – **55 rm** 138.65/220.90 **t.,**
5 suites.

The London Outpost of the Carnegie Club without rest., 69 Cadogan Gdns.,
SW3 2RB, ℰ *(0171) 589 7333, Fax (0171) 581 4958,* ☞ – ▐╢ ⁕ ▤ ▤ ☎. ⓌⓈ ⅍ ⓪
VISA. ⅗
FS r
⊊ 14.75 – **11 rm** 150.00/235.00.

Beaufort without rest., 33 Beaufort Gdns., SW3 1PP, ℘ (0171) 584 5252, Fax (0171) 589 2834, « English floral watercolour collection » – 🛗 ▤ 📺 ☎. ⬢⬢ 𝔸𝔼 ⓞ 𝘝𝘐𝘚𝘈 JCB. ⬢
ER n
28 rm 130.00/240.00 **s.**

Parkes without rest., 41 Beaufort Gdns., SW3 1PW, ℘ (0171) 581 9944, Fax (0171) 581 1999 – 🛗 📺 ☎. ⬢⬢ 𝔸𝔼 ⓞ 𝘝𝘐𝘚𝘈 JCB. ⬢
ER x
18 rm ⊇ 115.00/180.00 **s.**, 15 suites 210.00/265.00 **s.**

Claverley without rest., 13-14 Beaufort Gdns., SW3 1PS, ℘ (0171) 589 8541, Fax (0171) 584 3410 – 🛗 ⬢ 📺 ☎. ⬢⬢ 𝔸𝔼 ⓞ 𝘝𝘐𝘚𝘈 JCB. ⬢
ER o
29 rm ⊇ 60.00/215.00 **t.**

Knightsbridge, 12 Beaufort Gdns., SW3 1PT, ℘ (0171) 589 9271, Fax (0171) 823 9692, 𝑓⬧, ☎ – 🛗 📺 ☎. ⬢⬢ 𝔸𝔼 ⓞ 𝘝𝘐𝘚𝘈 JCB. ⬢
ER o
Meals (room service only) – **44 rm** ⊇ 90.00/135.00 **st.**, 6 suites.

L'Hotel, 28 Basil St., SW3 1AT, ℘ (0171) 589 6286, Fax (0171) 225 0011 – 🛗 📺 ☎. ⬢⬢ 𝔸𝔼 ⓞ 𝘝𝘐𝘚𝘈 JCB. ⬢
ER i
Le Metro : Meals 15.00 **t.** and a la carte – **12 rm** 144.50/169.00 **s.**

La Tante Claire (Koffmann), 68-69 Royal Hospital Rd, SW3 4HP, ℘ (0171) 352 6045, Fax (0171) 352 3257 – ▤. ⬢⬢ 𝔸𝔼 𝘝𝘐𝘚𝘈
EU c
closed Saturday, Sunday, 10 days Easter, 3 weeks August, 10 days Christmas and Bank Holidays – **Meals** - French - (booking essential) 28.00 **st.** (lunch) and a la carte 54.00/64.00 **st.** ⬧ 14.00
Spec. Coquilles St. Jacques à la planche, sauce encre. Pied de cochon aux morilles, pomme purée. Croustade de pommes à la fleur d'oranger.

Aubergine (Ramsay), 11 Park Walk, SW10 0AJ, ℘ (0171) 352 3449, Fax (0171) 351 1770 – ▤. ⬢⬢ 𝔸𝔼 ⓞ 𝘝𝘐𝘚𝘈
CU r
closed Saturday lunch, Sunday, 2 weeks August, 2 weeks Christmas and Bank Holidays – **Meals** (booking essential) 24.00/45.00-55.00 **t.** ⬧ 15.00
Spec. Tartare of scallops with crème fraîche and caviar in a basil consommé. Braised turbot with a herb and lettuce tortellini and a sea urchin sauce. Tart Tatin of pineapple caramelised with vanilla.

The Canteen, Harbour Yard, Chelsea Harbour, SW10 0XD, ℘ (0171) 351 7330, Fax (0171) 351 6189 – ▤. ⬢⬢ 𝔸𝔼 ⓞ 𝘝𝘐𝘚𝘈
p. 13 CQ i
closed Saturday lunch, Sunday dinner and Bank Holidays – **Meals** 19.50 **t.** (lunch) and a la carte 24.95/27.40 **t.** ⬧ 7.50
Spec. Warm salad of sea scallops, apple and cashew nuts. Seared Cajun tuna with a salad of couscous, peppers and olives. Crêpe Suzette soufflé.

Bibendum, Michelin House, 81 Fulham Rd, SW3 6RD, ℘ (0171) 581 5817, Fax (0171) 823 7925 – ▤. ⬢⬢ 𝔸𝔼 ⓞ 𝘝𝘐𝘚𝘈
DS s
closed 25-26 December and 1 January – **Meals** 28.00 **t.** (lunch) and dinner a la carte 39.00/50.00 **t.**

Fifth Floor (at Harvey Nichols), Knightsbridge, SW1X 7RJ, ℘ (0171) 235 5250, Fax (0171) 823 2207 – ▤. ⬢⬢ 𝔸𝔼 ⓞ 𝘝𝘐𝘚𝘈 JCB
FQ a
closed dinner Sunday and Bank Holidays and 25 December – **Meals** 22.50 **t.** (lunch) and dinner a la carte 24.75/41.50 **t.** ⬧ 7.50.

La Belle Epoque, 151 Draycott Av., SW3 3AL, ℘ (0171) 460 5000, Fax (0171) 460 5001 – ▤. ⬢⬢ 𝔸𝔼 𝘝𝘐𝘚𝘈
ES e
closed 25 and 26 December – *La Salle :* Meals a la carte 21.25/34.00 **st.** ⬧ 9.00 – (see also *L'Oriental* below).
✗ *La Brasserie* (℘ (0171) 460 5105) : Meals (closed 25 and 26 December) a la carte 17.00/24.50 **st.**

L'Oriental (at La Belle Epoque), 151 Draycott Av., SW3 3AL, ℘ (0171) 460 5010, Fax (0171) 460 5001 – ▤. ⬢⬢ 𝔸𝔼 𝘝𝘐𝘚𝘈
ES e
closed Sunday and 25-26 December – **Meals** - Eastern specialities - (dinner only) a la carte 32.00/45.50 **st.**

Grissini (at Hyatt Carlton Tower H.), Cadogan Pl., SW1X 9PY, ℘ (0171) 858 7171, Fax (0171) 235 9129 – ▤. ⬢⬢ 𝔸𝔼 ⓞ 𝘝𝘐𝘚𝘈 JCB
FR a
closed Saturday lunch – **Meals** - Italian - 19.00 **t.** (lunch) and a la carte 22.00/39.00 **t.** ⬧ 9.00.

Albero & Grana, Chelsea Cloisters, 89 Sloane Av., SW3 3DX, ℘ (0171) 225 1048, Fax (0171) 581 3259 – ▤. ⬢⬢ 𝔸𝔼 ⓞ 𝘝𝘐𝘚𝘈
ET e
Meals - Spanish - (dinner only and Saturday lunch) a la carte approx. 40.00 **t.**

Turner's, 87-89 Walton St., SW3 2HP, ℘ (0171) 584 6711, Fax (0171) 584 4441 – ▤. ⬢⬢ 𝔸 ⓞ 𝘝𝘐𝘚𝘈
ES e
closed Saturday lunch and Bank Holidays – **Meals** 15.00/29.50 **t.** and a la carte ⬧ 9.50.

XXX
@
Chutney Mary, 535 King's Rd, SW10 0SZ, ℰ (0171) 351 3113, Fax (0171) 351 7694 – ▤.
p. 24 FZ v
🐵 AE ⓪ VISA JCB
closed 25 December dinner and 26 December – Meals - Anglo-Indian - 14.50 t.
(lunch) and dinner a la carte 23.90/28.05 t. ⌂ 8.75.

XX
❀
Chavot (Chavot), 257-259 Fulham Rd, SW3 6HY, ℰ (0171) 351 7823, Fax (0171) 376 4971 –
CU a
🐵 AE VISA
closed Saturday lunch and Sunday – Meals - French - 22.50 t. (lunch) and a la carte 32.00/
40.50 t.
Spec. Roasted scallops with mustard oil and horseradish potatoes. Venison cutlet wtih
braised cabbage. Citrus terrine with chocolate samosa.

XX
Bluebird, 350 King's Rd, SW3 5UU, ℰ (0171) 559 1000, Fax (0171) 559 1111 – |♣| ▤. 🐵 AE
⓪ VISA
CU e
closed 25-26 December and lunch 1 January – Meals 15.75 t. (lunch) and a la carte 17.00/
44.50 t.

XX
English Garden, 10 Lincoln St., SW3 2TS, ℰ (0171) 584 7272, Fax (0171) 581 2848 – ▤.
ET x
🐵 AE ⓪ VISA JCB
Meals - English - 16.50 t. (lunch) and a la carte 27.00/30.75 t. ⌂ 5.50.

XX
Benihana, 77 King's Rd, SW3 4NX, ℰ (0171) 376 7799, Fax (0171) 376 7377 – ▤. 🐵 AE ⓪
VISA JCB
EU e
Meals - Japanese (Teppan-Yaki) - 10.00/14.00 and a la carte.

XX
La Ciboulette, 138a King's Rd, SW3 4XB, ℰ (0171) 823 7444, Fax (0171) 823 7457 – ▤.
ET a
🐵 AE VISA JCB
closed Sunday dinner and Bank Holidays – Meals - French - 13.50/18.50 t. and a la carte
⌂ 8.75.

XX
Brasserie St. Quentin, 243 Brompton Rd, SW3 2EP, ℰ (0171) 589 8005,
Fax (0171) 584 6064 – ▤. 🐵 AE ⓪ VISA JCB
DR a
Meals - French - a la carte 22.80/38.40 t. ⌂ 6.90.

XX
Poissonnerie de l'Avenue, 82 Sloane Av., SW3 3DZ, ℰ (0171) 589 2457,
Fax (0171) 581 3360 – ▤. 🐵 AE ⓪ VISA JCB
DS u
closed Sunday, 25-26 December and Bank Holidays – Meals - French Seafood - 18.50 t.
(lunch) and a la carte 26.00/34.50 t. ⌂ 6.50.

XX
Daphne's, 112 Draycott Av., SW3 3AE, ℰ (0171) 589 4257, Fax (0171) 581 2232 – ▤. 🐵 AE
⓪ VISA
DS a
closed 1 week Christmas – Meals - Italian - a la carte 24.50/30.00 ⌂ 8.50.

XX
Vama, 438 King's Rd, SW10 0LJ, ℰ (0171) 351 4118, Fax (0171) 565 8501 – ▤. 🐵 AE ⓪ VISA
Meals - Indian - 9.95 t. (lunch) and a la carte 20.50/24.75 t. ⌂ 4.75.
GZ e

XX
The Collection, 264 Brompton Rd, SW3 2AS, ℰ (0171) 225 1212, Fax (0171) 225 1050 –
▤. 🐵 AE ⓪ VISA
DS v
closed Sunday, 25 December and 1 January – Meals a la carte 18.00/31.50 t.

XX
Caraffini, 61-63 Lower Sloane St., SW1W 8DH, ℰ (0171) 259 0235 – ▤. 🐵 AE VISA
closed Sunday and Bank Holidays – Meals - Italian - a la carte 19.40/27.40 t. ⌂ 7.75.
FT a

XX
Osteria Le Fate, 5 Draycott Av., SW3, ℰ (0171) 591 0071 – 🐵 VISA
ET r
closed Sunday – Meals - Italian - 18.00/28.00 st. and a la carte.

XX
Grill St. Quentin, 3 Yeoman's Row, SW3 2AL, ℰ (0171) 581 8377, Fax (0171) 584 6064 –
▤. 🐵 AE ⓪ VISA JCB
ER r
Meals - French - a la carte 19.00/25.90 t. ⌂ 6.90.

XX
Busabong Too, 1a Langton St., SW10 0JL, ℰ (0171) 352 7414, Fax (0171) 352 7414 – ▤.
p. 24 FZ x
🐵 AE ⓪ VISA JCB
closed 24 and 25 December – Meals - Thai - (dinner only) 22.25 t. and a la carte.

XX
Toto's, Walton House, Walton St., SW3 2JH, ℰ (0171) 589 0075, Fax (0171) 581 9668 – ▤.
🐵 AE ⓪ VISA JCB
ES a
closed 25 to 27 December – Meals - Italian - 19.50/30.00 st. and a la carte ⌂ 7.00.

XX
Red of Knightsbridge, 8 Egerton Garden Mews, SW3 2EH, ℰ (0171) 584 7007 –
Meals - Chinese - 10.00/15.00 t. and a la carte.
DR n

XX
Good Earth, 233 Brompton Rd, SW3 2EP, ℰ (0171) 584 3658, Fax (0171) 823 8769 – ▤.
🐵 AE ⓪ VISA JCB
DR c
closed 24 to 27 December – Meals - Chinese - 10.95/18.50 t. and a la carte ⌂ 8.00.

XX
Dan's, 119 Sydney St., SW3 6NR, ℰ (0171) 352 2718, Fax (0171) 352 3265 – 🐵 AE VISA
JCB
DU s
closed Sunday dinner and 24 December-2 January – Meals a la carte 23.25/29.25 t.

XX
Beit Eddine, 8 Harriet St., SW1X 9JW, ℰ (0171) 235 3969, Fax (0171) 245 6335 – 🐵 AE ⓪
VISA
FQ z
Meals - Lebanese - a la carte approx. 20.00 t. ⌂ 7.50.

✗ **Drones of Pont Street,** 1 Pont St., SW1X 9EJ, ℰ (0171) 259 6166, *Fax (0171) 259 6177* – 🗐. **🐵 AE ⓪ VISA**
FR s
closed 24 to 27 December – **Meals** 12.95 t. (lunch) and a la carte 23.40/43.20 t.

✗ **Thierry's,** 342 King's Rd, SW3 5UR, ℰ (0171) 352 3365, *Fax (0171) 352 3365* – 🗐. **🐵 AE ⓪ VISA JCB**
CU c
closed 1 week Christmas – **Meals** a la carte 15.50/27.25 t. ⓵ 6.50.

✗ **Kartouche,** 329-331 Fulham Rd, SW10 9QL, ℰ (0171) 823 3515, *Fax (0171) 823 3991* – 🗐. **🐵 AE VISA JCB**
BU c
closed 24 December-2 January – **Meals** 14.50 t. (lunch) and a la carte 13.95/20.50 t. ⓵ 11.75.

✗ **Foundation** (at Harvey Nichols), Knightsbridge, SW1 7RJ, ℰ (0171) 201 8000, *Fax (0171) 201 8080* – 🗐. **🐵 AE ⓪ VISA JCB**
FQ a
closed Sunday dinner and 25-26 December – **Meals** 16.50 t. (lunch) and a la carte 18.00/26.50 t.

✗ **Monkey's,** 1 Cale St., Chelsea Green, SW3 3QT, ℰ (0171) 352 4711 – 🗐. **🐵 VISA**
ET z
closed Sunday dinner, Easter, 3 weeks August and Christmas – **Meals** 20.00/35.00 t. ⓵ 8.00.

✗ **Cafe O,** 163 Draycott Av., SW3 3AJ, ℰ (0171) 584 5950, *Fax (0171) 581 8753* – **🐵 AE VISA JCB**
DS r
closed Sunday lunch, 25 December, 1 January and Bank Holidays – **Meals** - Greek - a la carte 15.35/17.75 t.

✗ **T'Su,** 118 Draycott Av., SW3 3AE, ℰ (0171) 581 1699, *Fax (0171) 581 8716* – 🗐. **🐵 AE VISA**
DS a
closed August Bank Holiday, 25 December and 1 January – **Meals** - Japanese - a la carte 10.00/30.00 t.

🍴 **Chelsea Ram,** 32 Burnaby St., SW10 0PL, ℰ (0171) 351 4008, *Fax (0171) 349 0884* – **🐵 VISA**
FZ r
Meals a la carte approx. 17.35 st.

Earl's Court – ✉ SW5/SW10 – *Except where otherwise stated see pp. 30 and 31.*

🏨 **Barkston Gardens,** 34-44 Barkston Gdns., SW5 0EW, ℰ (0171) 373 7851, *Fax (0171) 370 6570* – 🛗, ⬚s, 🖐↔ rm, 📺 ☎ – 🔏 100. **🐵 AE ⓪ VISA JCB.** ❀
AT e
Meals 7.95 st. (dinner) and a la carte 12.50/19.40 st. ⓵ 5.00 – ☲ 8.75 – **82 rm** 80.00/90.00 st.

🏨 **Albany,** 4-12 Barkston Gdns., SW5 0EN, ℰ (0171) 370 6116, *Fax (0171) 244 8024* – 🛗, 🗐 rest, 📺 ☎ – 🔏 30. **🐵 AE ⓪ VISA JCB**
AT a
Meals a la carte 10.50/17.00 t. ⓵ 4.50 – ☲ 6.00 – **78 rm** 90.00/110.00 st. – SB.

🏠 **Henley House** without rest., 30 Barkston Gdns., SW5 0EN, ℰ (0171) 370 4111, *Fax (0171) 370 0026,* ⌘ – 📺 ☎. **🐵 AE ⓪ VISA JCB.** ❀
AT e
☲ 3.40 – **20 rm** 69.00/95.00 st.

🏠 **Rushmore** without rest., 11 Trebovir Rd, SW5 9LS, ℰ (0171) 370 3839, *Fax (0171) 370 0274* – 📺 ☎. **🐵 AE VISA JCB.** ❀
p. 24 EZ c
☲ 5.00 – **22 rm** 65.00/79.00 st.

🏠 **Amsterdam** without rest., 7 and 9 Trebovir Rd, SW5 9LS, ℰ (0171) 370 2814, *Fax (0171) 244 7608,* ⌘ – 🛗 📺 ☎. **🐵 AE VISA JCB.** ❀
p. 24 EZ c
☲ 2.75 – **14 rm** 70.00/90.00 st., 6 suites.

✗ **Chezmax,** 168 Ifield Rd, SW10 9AF, ℰ (0171) 835 0874 – **🐵 AE VISA**
AU c
closed lunch Saturday and Monday, Sunday, Easter, 25-26 December and 2 weeks August – **Meals** 23.50 t. (dinner) and lunch a la carte 13.50/32.45 t.

Kensington – ✉ SW7/W8/W11/W14 – *Except where otherwise stated see pp. 24-27.*

🏨🏨 **Royal Garden,** 2-24 Kensington High St., W8 4PT, ℰ (0171) 937 8000, *Fax (0171) 938 4532,* ≤, **Ⅰ₆**, ⬚s, – 🛗, 🖐↔ rm, 🗐 📺 ☎ 🕭 🅟 – 🔏 600. **🐵 AE ⓪ VISA JCB.** ❀
The Tenth (ℰ (0171) 361 1910) : **Meals** *(closed Saturday lunch and Sunday.* 19.50 t. (lunch) and a la carte 20.70/38.75 t. ⓵ 10.50 – **Park Terrace** : **Meals** 18.25 (lunch) and a la carte 17.00/31.00 t. ⓵ 10.50 – ☲ 16.50 – **385 rm** 175.00/215.00, 15 suites.
p. 30 AQ x

🏨🏨 **Copthorne Tara,** Scarsdale Pl., W8 5SR, ℰ (0171) 937 7211, *Fax (0171) 937 7100* – 🛗, 🖐↔ rm, 🗐 📺 ☎ 🕭 🅟 – 🔏 500. **🐵 AE ⓪ VISA JCB.** ❀
FY u
Brasserie : **Meals** 18.00 st. and a la carte ⓵ 6.50 – **Jerome K. Jerome** : **Meals** *(closed Sunday)* (dinner only) a la carte 22.20/32.30 st. ⓵ 6.50 – ☲ 13.00 – **815 rm** 170.00/210.00 st., 10 suites.

🏨🏨 **Halcyon,** 81 Holland Park, W11 3RZ, ℰ (0171) 727 7288, *Fax (0171) 229 8516* – 🛗 🗐 📺 ☎ **🐵 AE ⓪ VISA.** ❀
EX u
Meals – (see **The Room** below) – ☲ 14.00 – **40 rm** 170.00/260.00 st., 3 suites.

The Milestone, 1-2 Kensington Court, W8 5DL, ℰ (0171) 917 1000, Fax (0171) 917 1010, ⅃⅌, ⇆ – 🛗 🖥 📺 ☎. 🕮 🆎 ⑩ 𝘝𝘐𝘚𝘈. ⚞   p. 30 AQ u
Meals (closed Saturday, Sunday and Bank Holidays) 18.00/26.00 t. and a la carte ⅄ 12.00 – ⚏ 15.00 – **48 rm** 220.00/270.00 st., 5 suites.

London Kensington Hilton, 179-199 Holland Park Av., W11 4UL, ℰ (0171) 603 3355, Fax (0171) 602 9397 – 🛗, ⇆ rm, 🖥 📺 ☎ ♿ 🅿 – 🔬 300. 🕮 🆎 ⑩ 𝘝𝘐𝘚𝘈 𝖩𝖢𝖡. ⚞
Meals 20.00 st. (dinner) and a la carte 15.00/30.00 st. ⅄ 9.50 – **Hiroko : Meals** - Japanese - 15.00/32.00 st. and a la carte ⅄ 7.00 – ⚏ 14.50 – **603 rm** 170.00/250.00 st. – SB.   EX s

Kensington Park Thistle, 16-32 De Vere Gdns., W8 5AG, ℰ (0171) 937 8080, Fax (0171) 937 7616 – 🛗, ⇆ rm, 🖥 rest, 📺 ☎ ♿ – 🔬 120. 🕮 🆎 ⑩ 𝘝𝘐𝘚𝘈. ⚞
Moniques Brasserie : Meals 15.75 t. and a la carte ⅄ 6.00 – **Cairngorm Grill : Meals** (closed Sunday, Monday, August and Bank Holidays) (dinner only) 21.00 t. and a la carte ⅄ 8.50 – ⚏ 13.50 – **346 rm** 139.00/200.00 st., 6 suites – SB.   p. 30 BQ e

Hilton National London Olympia, 380 Kensington High St., W14 8NL, ℰ (0171) 603 3333, Fax (0171) 603 4846, ⅃⅌, ⇆ – 🛗, ⇆ rm, 🖥 rest, 📺 ☎ 🅿 – 🔬 450   EY a
395 rm, 10 suites.

Forte Posthouse Kensington, Wrights Lane, W8 5SP, ℰ (0171) 937 8170, Fax (0171) 937 8289, ⅃⅌, ⇆, 🔲, ⚲, squash – 🛗, ⇆ rm, 🖥 rest, 📺 ☎ 🅿 – 🔬 180. 🕮 🆎 ⑩ 𝘝𝘐𝘚𝘈 𝖩𝖢𝖡. ⚞   FY c
~~Meals~~ 16.95 t. and a la carte ⅄ 7.50 – ⚏ 11.00 – **547 rm** 129.00 t.

Comfort Inn Kensington, 22-32 West Cromwell Rd, SW5 9QJ, ℰ (0171) 373 3300, Fax (0171) 835 2040 – 🛗, ⇆ rm, 🖥 📺 ☎ – 🔬 80. 🕮 🆎 ⑩ 𝘝𝘐𝘚𝘈 𝖩𝖢𝖡. ⚞   EZ n
Meals (bar lunch)/dinner a la carte 9.00/18.00 st. ⅄ 6.00 – ⚏ 8.95 – **125 rm** 85.00/99.00 st.

Holland Court without rest., 31-33 Holland Rd, W14 8HJ, ℰ (0171) 371 1133, Fax (0171) 602 9114, ⚲ – 🛗 📺 ☎. 🕮 🆎 ⑩ 𝘝𝘐𝘚𝘈 𝖩𝖢𝖡. ⚞   EY e
22 rm ⚏ 75.00/105.00.

The Room (at Halcyon H.), 129 Holland Park Av., W11 3UT, ℰ (0171) 221 5411, Fax (0171) 229 8516, ⚘ – 🖥. 🕮 🆎 ⑩ 𝘝𝘐𝘚𝘈   EX u
closed Saturday lunch, 25 to lunch 31 December and Bank Holidays – **Meals** 26.00/ 37.00 t. and a la carte 26.00/45.00 ⅄ 7.00.

Clarke's, 124 Kensington Church St., W8 4BH, ℰ (0171) 221 9225, Fax (0171) 229 4564 – 🖥. 🕮 𝘝𝘐𝘚𝘈   EX c
closed Saturday, Sunday, 2 weeks August and Christmas – **Meals** 29.00/40.00 st. ⅄ 8.50.

Launceston Place, 1a Launceston Pl., W8 5RL, ℰ (0171) 937 6912, Fax (0171) 938 2412 – 🖥. 🕮 🆎 𝘝𝘐𝘚𝘈 𝖩𝖢𝖡   p. 30 BR a
closed Saturday lunch, Sunday dinner, Easter, 25 December, 1 January and Bank Holidays – **Meals** 17.50 t. and a la carte ⅄ 6.00.

Belvedere in Holland Park, Holland House, off Abbotsbury Rd, W8 6LU, ℰ (0171) 602 1238, Fax (0171) 610 4382, ⚘, « 19C orangery in park » – 🖥. 🕮 🆎 ⑩ 𝘝𝘐𝘚𝘈 𝖩𝖢𝖡   EY u
closed Sunday dinner, 25 December and 1 January – **Meals** a la carte 17.00/26.00 t. ⅄ 8.00.

Arcadia, Kensington Court, 35 Kensington High St., W8 5EB, ℰ (0171) 937 4294, Fax (0171) 937 4393 – 🖥. 🕮 ⑩ 𝘝𝘐𝘚𝘈   p. 30 AQ s
closed Saturday lunch, 24-26 December and 1 January – **Meals** 15.95 t. (lunch) and dinner a la carte 17.70/23.00 t. ⅄ 6.75.

La Pomme d'Amour, 128 Holland Park Av., W11 4UE, ℰ (0171) 229 8532, Fax (0171) 221 4096 – 🖥. 🕮 🆎 ⑩ 𝘝𝘐𝘚𝘈   EX e
closed Saturday lunch, Sunday and Bank Holidays – **Meals** - French - 14.20/18.30 t. and a la carte ⅄ 5.00.

L'Escargot Doré, 2-4 Thackeray St., W8 5ET, ℰ (0171) 937 8508, Fax (0171) 937 8508 – 🖥 🕮 🆎 ⑩ 𝘝𝘐𝘚𝘈 𝖩𝖢𝖡   p. 30 AQR e
closed Saturday lunch, Sunday last 2 weeks August, 1 week Christmas and Bank Holidays – **Meals** 16.00 t. and a la carte ⅄ 5.80.

Osteria del Parco, 148 Holland Park Av., W11 4UE, ℰ (0171) 221 6090, Fax (0171) 221 4096 – 🖥. 🕮 ⑩ 𝘝𝘐𝘚𝘈   EX v
closed 25 December – **Meals** - Italian - a la carte 13.50/19.70 t. ⅄ 4.50.

Ken Lo's Memories of China, 353 Kensington High St., W8 6NW, ℰ (0171) 603 6951, Fax (0171) 603 0848 – 🖥. 🕮 🆎 ⑩ 𝘝𝘐𝘚𝘈 𝖩𝖢𝖡   EY v
closed Sunday lunch, 24 December-2 January and Bank Holidays – **Meals** - Chinese - (booking essential) 17.50/25.50 t. and a la carte ⅄ 11.00.

Phoenicia, 11-13 Abingdon Rd, W8 6AH, ℰ (0171) 937 0120, Fax (0171) 937 7668 – 🖥. 🕮 🆎 ⑩ 𝘝𝘐𝘚𝘈 𝖩𝖢𝖡   EY n
closed 25 and 26 December – **Meals** - Lebanese - (buffet lunch) a la carte 15.00/22.85 t. ⅄ 5.80.

X
ⓐ **Kensington Place**, 201 Kensington Church St., W8 7LX, ℰ (0171) 727 3184, Fax (0171) 229 2025 – ▤. ⓂⓈ ⒶⒺ Ⓥ𝘐𝘚𝘈 JCB
p. 32 AZ z
closed 25-26 December and 1 January – **Meals** (booking essential) 14.50 **t**. (lunch) and a la carte 21.00/36.00 **t**. ⅄ 5.75.

X
ⓐ **Novelli W8**, 122 Palace Gardens Terr., W8 4RT, ℰ (0171) 229 4024, Fax (0171) 243 1826, 🍴 – ⓂⓈ ⒶⒺ Ⓞ Ⓥ𝘐𝘚𝘈 JCB
p. 32 AZ r
closed Sunday, Christmas and New Year – **Meals** (booking essential) 14.50 **t**. (lunch) and a la carte 20.20/29.70 **t**. ⅄ 11.00.

X **Cibo**, 3 Russell Gdns., W14 8EZ, ℰ (0171) 371 6271, Fax (0171) 602 1371 – ⓂⓈ ⒶⒺ Ⓞ Ⓥ𝘐𝘚𝘈 JCB
EY o
closed Saturday lunch, Sunday dinner and 23 to 29 December – **Meals** - Italian - 16.75 **t**. (lunch) and a la carte 19.95/33.75 **t**.

X **The Abingdon**, 54 Abingdon Rd, W8 6AP, ℰ (0171) 937 3339, Fax (0171) 795 6388 – ▤. ⓂⓈ ⒶⒺ Ⓥ𝘐𝘚𝘈
EY z
closed 25-26 December and 1 January – **Meals** a la carte 19.15/24.25 **t**.

X
ⓐ **Malabar**, 27 Uxbridge St., W8 7TQ, ℰ (0171) 727 8800 – ⓂⓈ Ⓥ𝘐𝘚𝘈
p. 32 AZ e
closed last week August and 4 days Christmas – **Meals** - Indian - (booking essential) (buffet lunch Sunday) 15.75 **st**. and a la carte 14.95/28.30 **st**. ⅄ 4.75.

X **Wódka**, 12 St. Albans Grove, W8 5PN, ℰ (0171) 937 6513, Fax (0171) 937 8621 – ⓂⓈ ⒶⒺ Ⓞ Ⓥ𝘐𝘚𝘈
p. 30 AR c
closed lunch Saturday, Sunday and Bank Holidays – **Meals** - Polish - 12.50 **t**. (lunch) and a la carte 16.70/23.90 **t**. ⅄ 7.90.

X **Mandarin**, 197c Kensington High St., W8 6BA, ℰ (0171) 937 1551 – ▤. ⓂⓈ ⒶⒺ Ⓞ Ⓥ𝘐𝘚𝘈 JCB
closed 24 to 26 December – **Meals** - Chinese - 9.00/16.50 **t**. and a la carte ⅄ 6.00. EY s

North Kensington – ⊠ W2/W10/W11 – Except where otherwise stated see pp. 20-23.

🏢 **Pembridge Court**, 34 Pembridge Gdns., W2 4DX, ℰ (0171) 229 9977, Fax (0171) 727 4982, « Collection of antique clothing » – 🛗, ▤ rest, 📺 ☎. ⓂⓈ ⒶⒺ Ⓞ Ⓥ𝘐𝘚𝘈
Meals (residents only) (restricted menu) (dinner only) a la carte approx. 19.00 **st**. ⅄ 4.95 –
20 rm ⊇ 110.00/175.00 **st**.
p. 32 AZ n

🏢 **Abbey Court** without rest., 20 Pembridge Gdns., W2 4DU, ℰ (0171) 221 7518, Fax (0171) 792 0858, « Tastefully furnished Victorian town house » – ✦≡ 📺 ☎. ⓂⓈ ⒶⒺ Ⓞ Ⓥ𝘐𝘚𝘈 JCB. ✄
22 rm ⊇ 88.00/145.00 **t**.
p. 32 AZ u

🏠 Portobello, 22 Stanley Gdns., W11 2NG, ℰ (0171) 727 2777, Fax (0171) 792 9641, « Attractive town house in Victorian terrace » – 🛗 📺 ☎
EV n
22 rm.

XXX
❀ **Leith's**, 92 Kensington Park Rd, W11 2PN, ℰ (0171) 229 4481, Fax (0171) 221 1246 – ▤. ⓂⓈ ⒶⒺ Ⓞ Ⓥ𝘐𝘚𝘈 JCB
EV e
closed lunch Saturday and Monday, Sunday, 2 weeks August, 2 weeks Christmas-New Year and Bank Holidays except Good Friday – **Meals** 19.50/35.00 **t**. and dinner a la carte 33.00/43.75 **t**. ⅄ 8.25
Spec. Roast scallops with spiced lemon couscous, artichokes and a light curry butter. Wild salmon with oxtail consommé, lentil and mushroom dumplings. Braised squab pigeon with pancetta and greens, celeriac fondant.

XX **Chez Moi**, 1 Addison Av., Holland Park, W11 4QS, ℰ (0171) 603 8267, Fax (0171) 603 3898 – ▤. ⓂⓈ ⒶⒺ Ⓞ Ⓥ𝘐𝘚𝘈
p. 24 EX n
closed Saturday lunch, Sunday and Bank Holidays – **Meals** - French - 15.00 **t**. (lunch) and a la carte 22.25/31.75 **t**. ⅄ 5.50.

XX **Orsino**, 119 Portland Rd, W11 4LN, ℰ (0171) 221 3299, Fax (0171) 229 9414 – ▤. ⓂⓈ ⒶⒺ Ⓥ𝘐𝘚𝘈
p. 24 EX x
closed 24 and 25 December – **Meals** - Italian - (booking essential) 15.50 **t**. (lunch) and a la carte 17.00/28.00 **t**. ⅄ 5.50.

X
ⓐ **Woz**, 46 Golborne Rd, W10 5PR, ℰ (0181) 968 2200, Fax (0181) 968 0550 – ⓂⓈ ⒶⒺ Ⓥ𝘐𝘚𝘈 JCB
closed Monday lunch, Sunday dinner, 1 week April, 2 weeks August and 1 week Christmas – **Meals** 12.95/22.95 **t**. and lunch a la carte 14.45/20.20 **t**. EU n

X
ⓐ **Sugar Club**, 33a All Saints Rd, W11 1HE, ℰ (0171) 221 3844, Fax (0171) 229 2759, 🍴 – ✦≡. ⓂⓈ ⒶⒺ Ⓞ Ⓥ𝘐𝘚𝘈
EU a
closed 1 week Christmas and August Bank Holiday – **Meals** 15.50 **t**. (lunch) and a la carte 19.60/29.40 **t**.

✗ **Alastair Little Lancaster Road,** 136a Lancaster Rd, W11 1QU, ℘ (0171) 243 2220 – ⬤⬤
⬛⬛ **VISA**   EU e
closed Sunday and Bank Holidays – **Meals** 19.00/25.00 **t.**

✗ **192,** 192 Kensington Park Rd, W11 2ES, ℘ (0171) 229 0482 – ⬤⬤ ⬛⬛ ⬤ **VISA**   EV a
closed 25-26 December and August Bank Holiday – **Meals** 12.50 **t.** (lunch)
and a la carte 21.50/26.00 **t.**

South Kensington – ✉ SW5/SW7/W8 – *Except where otherwise stated see pp. 30 and 31.*

🏨 **Gloucester,** 4-18 Harrington Gdns., SW7 4LH, ℘ (0171) 373 6030, *Fax (0171) 373 0409,* ╠ᵴ
– |桑|, ⇔ rm, ▤ �📺 ☎ 🅿 – 🔬 650. ⬤⬤ ⬛⬛ ⬤ **VISA** **JCB**. ⬤   BS r
Meals 9.95 **t.** (lunch) and a la carte 16.00/22.50 **t.** ▯ 12.00 – ☲ 14.50 – **542 rm** 185.00/
205.00 **st.**, 6 suites.

🏨 **Pelham,** 15 Cromwell Pl., SW7 2LA, ℘ (0171) 589 8288, *Fax (0171) 584 8444,* « Tastefully
furnished Victorian town house » – |桑| ▤ �📺 ☎. ⬤⬤ ⬛⬛ **VISA**. ⬤   CS z
Kemps : **Meals** *(closed Saturday)* 12.95/15.95 **t.** and a la carte 16.95/22.20 **t.** – ☲ 13.25 –
38 rm 140.00/215.00 **s.**, 3 suites.

🏨 **Blakes,** 33 Roland Gdns., SW7 3PF, ℘ (0171) 370 6701, *Fax (0171) 373 0442,* « Antique
oriental furnishings » – |桑|, ▤ rest, �📺 ☎ 🅿. ⬤⬤ ⬛⬛ ⬤ **VISA**. ⬤   BU n
Meals a la carte 30.25/61.25 **st.** ▯ 11.00 – ☲ 17.00 – **46 rm** 150.00/340.00 **st.**, 5 suites.

🏨 **Harrington Hall,** 5-25 Harrington Gdns., SW7 4JW, ℘ (0171) 396 9696,
Fax (0171) 396 9090, ▭, ⇌ᵴ – |桑|, ⇔ rm, ▤ 📺 ☎ – 🔬 250. ⬤⬤ ⬛⬛ ⬤ **VISA** **JCB**. ⬤ BT n
Wetherby's : **Meals** 19.75 **st.** and a la carte ▯ 7.50 – ☲ 13.50 – **200 rm** 160.00/175.00 **st.**

🏨 **Bailey's,** 140 Gloucester Rd, SW7 4QH, ℘ (0171) 373 6000, *Fax (0171) 370 3760* – |桑|,
⇔ rm, ▤ 📺 ☎ – 🔬 440. ⬤⬤ ⬛⬛ ⬤ **VISA** **JCB**. ⬤   BS a
Olives : **Meals** (dinner only) a la carte 15.75/18.75 **t.** ▯ 8.50 – ☲ 12.50 – **212 rm** 99.90/
293.75 **t.**

🏨 **Rembrandt,** 11 Thurloe Pl., SW7 2RS, ℘ (0171) 589 8100, *Fax (0171) 225 3363,* ╠ᵴ, ⇌ᵴ,
▣ – |桑|, ⇔ rm, ▤ rest, 📺 ☎ – 🔬 250. ⬤⬤ ⬛⬛ ⬤ **VISA** **JCB**. ⬤   DS x
Meals 16.95 **st.** and a la carte – ☲ 10.75 – **195 rm** 150.00/200.00 **st.**

🏨 **Regency,** 100 Queen's Gate, SW7 5AG, ℘ (0171) 370 4595, *Fax (0171) 370 5555,* ╠ᵴ, ⇌ᵴ –
|桑|, ⇔ rm, ▤ rest, 📺 ☎ – 🔬 100. ⬤⬤ ⬛⬛ ⬤ **VISA** **JCB**. ⬤   CT e
Meals *(closed lunch Saturday and Sunday)* (carving lunch) 21.00 **st.** and a la carte ▯ 6.00 –
☲ 12.00 – **192 rm** 139.00 **s.**, 6 suites – SB.

🏨 **Swallow International,** Cromwell Rd, SW5 0TH, ℘ (0171) 973 1000,
Fax (0171) 244 8194, ╠ᵴ, ⇌ᵴ, ▣ – |桑|, ⇔ rm, ▤ 📺 ☎ – 🔬 200. ⬤⬤ ⬛⬛ ⬤ **VISA**. ⬤
Blayneys : **Meals** (dinner only) a la carte 30.25/39.50 **st.** – ☲ 12.75 – **417 rm** 120.00/ AS c
155.00 **st.**, 2 suites – SB.

🏨 **Holiday Inn Kensington,** 100 Cromwell Rd, SW7 4ER, ℘ (0171) 373 2222,
Fax (0171) 373 0559, ╠ᵴ – |桑|, ⇔ rm, ▤ 📺 ☎ ♿ – 🔬 130. ⬤⬤ ⬛⬛ ⬤ **VISA** **JCB**. ⬤
Meals *(closed lunch Saturday and Sunday)* a la carte 20.50/28.65 **t.** ▯ 7.50 – ☲ 11.95 –
143 rm 164.00/184.00 **st.**, 19 suites.   BS e

🏨 **Jury's Kensington,** 109-113 Queen's Gate, SW7 5LR, ℘ (0171) 589 6300,
Fax (0171) 581 1492 – |桑|, ⇔ rm, 📺 ☎ – 🔬 80. ⬤⬤ ⬛⬛ ⬤ **VISA**. ⬤   CT i
closed 25 to 28 December – **Meals** 15.00/20.00 **st.** and a la carte – ☲ 11.95 – **172 rm**
145.00/250.00 **st.**

🏨 **Vanderbilt,** 68-86 Cromwell Rd, SW7 5BT, ℘ (0171) 589 2424, *Fax (0171) 225 2293* – |桑|,
⇔ rm, ▤ rest, 📺 ☎ – 🔬 120. ⬤⬤ ⬛⬛ ⬤ **VISA**. ⬤   BS v
Meals 17.50 **st.** and a la carte ▯ 7.50 – ☲ 11.00 – **223 rm** 115.00/140.00 **s.**

🏨 **Forum,** 97 Cromwell Rd, SW7 4DN, ℘ (0171) 370 5757, *Fax (0171) 373 1448,* ≤, ╠ᵴ – |桑|,
⇔ rm, ▤ rest, 📺 ☎ ♿ 🅿 – 🔬 400. ⬤⬤ ⬛⬛ ⬤ **VISA** **JCB**. ⬤   BS x
Meals 18.00 **st.** (dinner) and a la carte 13.45/23.50 **st.** ▯ 7.00 – ☲ 12.25 – **906 rm** 160.00/
180.00 **st.**, 4 suites.

🏨 **Gore,** 189 Queen's Gate, SW7 5EX, ℘ (0171) 584 6601, *Fax (0171) 589 8127,* « Attractive
decor » – |桑|, ⇔ rm, 📺 ☎. ⬤⬤ ⬛⬛ ⬤ **VISA** **JCB**   BR n
closed 25 and 26 December – **Bistrot 190 :** **Meals** (only members and residents may book)
a la carte 16.90/28.20 **t.** – (see also **Downstairs at One Ninety** below) – ☲ 9.00 – **54 rm**
125.00/280.00 **st.**

🏨 **John Howard,** 4 Queen's Gate, SW7 5EH, ℘ (0171) 581 3011, *Fax (0171) 589 8403* – |桑| ▤
📺 ☎. ⬤⬤ ⬛⬛ ⬤ **VISA** **JCB**. ⬤   BQ i
Meals *(closed Sunday)* (dinner only) 20.00 **t.** and a la carte ▯ 6.50 – ☲ 11.50 – **43 rm** 89.00/
119.00 **st.**, 9 suites.

🏗🏗 **Cranley,** 10-12 Bina Gdns., SW5 0LA, ✆ (0171) 373 0123, *Fax (0171) 373 9497,*
« Antiques » – 🛗 🗄 📺 ☎. 🆎 ⓪ 𝘝𝘐𝘚𝘈 JCB. ✵ BT c
Meals (room service only) 🍴 7.50 – ⌚ 12.95 – **33 rm** 140.00/160.00 **st.**, 4 suites.

🏗🏗 **Number Sixteen** without rest., 16 Sumner Pl., SW7 3EG, ✆ (0171) 589 5232,
Fax (0171) 584 8615, « Attractively furnished Victorian town houses », 🌳 – 🛗 📺 ☎. 🆎 🆎
⓪ 𝘝𝘐𝘚𝘈. ✵ CT c
⌚ 8.00 – **36 rm** 80.00/190.00 **st.**

🏗🏗 **Cranley Gardens** without rest., 8 Cranley Gdns., SW7 3DB, ✆ (0171) 373 3232,
Fax (0171) 373 7944 – 🛗 📺 ☎. 🆎 🆎 ⓪ 𝘝𝘐𝘚𝘈 JCB BT e
⌚ 5.50 – **85 rm** 75.00/105.00 **st.**

🏗 **Five Sumner Place** without rest., 5 Sumner Pl., SW7 3EE, ✆ (0171) 584 7586,
Fax (0171) 823 9962 – 🛗 📺 ☎. 🆎 🆎 𝘝𝘐𝘚𝘈 JCB. ✵ CT u
13 rm ⌚ 88.00/139.00 **st.**

🏗 **Aster House** without rest., 3 Sumner Pl., SW7 3EE, ✆ (0171) 581 5888,
Fax (0171) 584 4925, 🌳 – ✵ 📺 ☎. 🆎 𝘝𝘐𝘚𝘈 JCB. ✵ CT u
12 rm ⌚ 80.00/145.00 **st.**

XXX **Bombay Brasserie,** Courtfield Rd, SW7 4UH, ✆ (0171) 370 4040, *Fax (0171) 835 1669,*
« Raj-style decor, conservatory » – 🗄. 🆎 ⓪ 𝘝𝘐𝘚𝘈 BS a
closed 25 and 26 December – **Meals** - Indian - (buffet lunch) 15.95 **t.** (lunch) and
dinner a la carte 23.25/29.10 **t.** 🍴 7.25.

XX **Hilaire,** 68 Old Brompton Rd, SW7 3LQ, ✆ (0171) 584 8993, *Fax (0171) 581 2949* – 🗄. 🆎
🆎 𝘝𝘐𝘚𝘈 JCB CT n
closed Saturday lunch, Sunday and Bank Holidays – **Meals** (booking essential) 23.00/34.50 **t.**
🍴 10.50.

XX **Shaw's,** 119 Old Brompton Rd, SW7 3RN, ✆ (0171) 373 7774, *Fax (0171) 370 5102* – 🗄
🆎 🆎 ⓪ 𝘝𝘐𝘚𝘈 JCB BT v
closed Saturday lunch, Sunday, Easter, 1 week August and 1 week Christmas-New Year –
Meals 18.50/32.95 **t.** 🍴 9.00.

XX **Downstairs at One Ninety** (at Gore H.), 190 Queen's Gate, SW7 5EU,
✆ (0171) 581 5666, *Fax (0171) 581 8172* – 🗄. 🆎 🆎 ⓪ 𝘝𝘐𝘚𝘈 JCB BR n
closed Saturday lunch, Sunday and Christmas – **Meals** - Seafood - (booking essential)
22.50 **t.** (lunch) and a la carte 28.25/50.25 **t.**

XX **Café Lazeez,** 93-95 Old Brompton Rd, SW7 3LD, ✆ (0171) 581 9993, *Fax (0171) 581 8200*
– 🗄. 🆎 ⓪ 𝘝𝘐𝘚𝘈 JCB CT a
Restaurant : Meals - North Indian - a la carte 17.95/25.55 **t.**
X **Cafe :** Meals a la carte 17.95/25.55 **t.**

XX **Tui,** 19 Exhibition Rd, SW7 2HE, ✆ (0171) 584 8359 – 🆎 🆎 ⓪ 𝘝𝘐𝘚𝘈 JCB CS u
closed 5 days at Christmas and Bank Holiday Mondays – **Meals** - Thai - 10.00 **st.**
(lunch) and a la carte 16.60/26.65 **t.** 🍴 4.75.

XX **Delhi Brasserie,** 134 Cromwell Rd, SW7 4HA, ✆ (0171) 370 7617, *Fax (0171) 244 8639* –
🗄. 🆎 🆎 ⓪ 𝘝𝘐𝘚𝘈 AS a
closed 25 and 26 December – **Meals** - Indian - 6.95/14.95 **t.** and a la carte.

XX **Khan's of Kensington,** 3 Harrington Rd, SW7 3ES, ✆ (0171) 581 2900
Fax (0171) 581 2900 – 🗄. 🆎 🆎 𝘝𝘐𝘚𝘈 CS e
closed 25 and 26 December – **Meals** - Indian - 7.95/16.50 **t.** and a la carte.

XX **Memories of India,** 18 Gloucester Rd, SW7 4RB, ✆ (0171) 589 6450
Fax (0171) 584 4438 – 🗄. 🆎 🆎 ⓪ 𝘝𝘐𝘚𝘈 JCB BR :
closed 25 December – **Meals** - Indian - 7.95/15.50 **t.** and a la carte.

X **Star of India,** 154 Old Brompton Rd, SW5 0BE, ✆ (0171) 373 2901, *Fax (0171) 373 5664* –
🗄. 🆎 🆎 ⓪ 𝘝𝘐𝘚𝘈 JCB BT :
closed Bank Holidays – **Meals** - Indian - a la carte 24.85/36.10 **t.**

X **Cambio de Tercio,** 163 Old Brompton Rd, SW5 0LJ, ✆ (0171) 244 8970
Fax (0171) 244 8970 – 🆎 🆎 𝘝𝘐𝘚𝘈 BT :
Meals - Spanish - a la carte 15.75/23.50 **t.** 🍴 7.50.

X **Bangkok,** 9 Bute St., SW7 3EY, ✆ (0171) 584 8529, *Fax (0171) 823 7883* – 🗄. 🆎 𝘝𝘐𝘚𝘈
closed Sunday, Christmas and Bank Holidays – **Meals** - Thai Bistro - a la carte 17.00/21.75 **t.**
🍴 6.75. CS :

KINGSTON UPON THAMES pp. 8 and 9.
🏌 *Home Park, Hampton Wick* ✆ (0181) 977 6645, BY.

Chessington – ✉ *Surrey.*

🏗 **Travel Inn,** Leatherhead Rd, KT9 2NE, on A 243 ✆ (01372) 744060, *Fax (01372) 720889*
✵ rm, 📺 ᎬᏂ. 🅿. 🆎 🆎 ⓪ 𝘝𝘐𝘚𝘈. ✵ BZ
Meals (grill rest.) – **42 rm** 36.50 **t.**

Kingston – ✉ Surrey.

🏨 **Kingston Lodge,** Kingston Hill, KT2 7NP, ✆ (0181) 541 4481, Fax (0181) 547 1013 – ⇖ rm, ▤ rest, 📺 ☎ ♿ ♿ – ⚿ 60. ◉ AE ◉ VISA JCB
CY u
Meals (bar lunch Monday to Saturday)/dinner a la carte 14.70/22.25 t. ⚬ 6.50 – ☲ 9.75 – 62 rm 115.00 t.

✗✗ Gravier's, 9 Station Rd, Norbiton, KT2 7AA, ✆ (0181) 549 5557   CY x
Meals - French Seafood rest.

✗ **Ayudhya,** 14 Kingston Hill, KT2 7NH, ✆ (0181) 549 5984, Fax (0181) 549 5984 – ◉ AE ◉
VISA   CY z
closed Monday, Easter Sunday, 25-26 December, 1 January and Bank Holidays – Meals - Thai - a la carte 14.55/27.10 t. ⚬ 6.00.

LAMBETH Except where otherwise stated see pp.10-11 and pp.26-27.

Clapham Common – ✉ SW4.

🏨 **Windmill on the Common,** Clapham Common South Side, SW4 9DE, ✆ (0181) 673 4578, Fax (0181) 675 1486, ﹡ – ⇖ rm, ▤ rest, 📺 ☎ ♿ ♿. ◉ AE ◉ VISA
Meals (bar lunch Monday to Saturday)/dinner 15.95 t. and a la carte – 29 rm ☲ 88.00/
115.00 t.   p. 13 DQ e

✗ The Grafton, 45 Old Town, SW4 0JL, ✆ (0171) 627 1048, Fax (0171) 652 0268 – ◉ AE VISA
JCB   p. 13 DQ a
closed Monday and 3 weeks Christmas – Meals 12.50/18.95 t. and a la carte ⚬ 5.00.

Kennington – ✉ SE11.

✗ **Lobster Pot,** 3 Kennington Lane, SE11 4RG, ✆ (0171) 582 5556 – ◉ AE ◉ VISA JCB
closed Sunday, Monday and 24 December-5 January – Meals - French Seafood - 15.50/
22.50 st. and a la carte ⚬ 8.50.   NZ e

Lambeth – ✉ SE1.

🏨 **Novotel London Waterloo,** 113 Lambeth Rd, SE1 7LS, ✆ (0171) 793 1010, Fax (0171) 793 0202, ⚿, ⚿ – ⚑, ⇖ rm, 📺 ☎ ♿ ♿ – ⚿ 40. ◉ AE ◉ VISA. ✺ LYZ a
Meals 14.50 st. and a la carte ⚬ 5.55 – ☲ 11.00 – 185 rm 112.00/132.00 st., 2 suites.

Streatham – ✉ SW16.

⌂ **Barrow House** without rest., 45 Barrow Rd, SW16 5PF, ✆ (0181) 677 1925, Fax (0181) 677 1925, « Victoriana », ﹡ – ⇖. ✺   EY s
closed 24 to 26 December – 4 rm ☲ 30.00/45.00 st.

Waterloo – ✉ SE1.

✗✗ **People's Palace,** Level 3, The Royal Festival Hall, SE1 8XX, ✆ (0171) 928 9999, Fax (0171) 928 2355, ≼ Victoria Embankment and River Thames – ▤. ◉ AE ◉ VISA
Meals 14.50/16.50 t. and a la carte.   MX e

✗✗ RSJ, 13a Coin St., SE1 8YQ, ✆ (0171) 928 4554 – ▤. ◉ AE ◉ VISA   NX e
closed Saturday lunch, Sunday and Bank Holidays – Meals 15.95 st. and a la carte ⚬ 5.95.

LONDON HEATHROW AIRPORT – see Hillingdon, London p. 56.

MERTON pp. 8 and 9.

Morden – ✉ Morden.

🏨 **Travelodge,** Epsom Rd, SM4 5PH, SW : on A 24 ✆ (0181) 640 8227, Reservations (Free-phone) 0800 850950 – ⇖ rm, 📺 ♿ ♿. ◉ AE ◉ VISA JCB. ✺   DY c
Meals (grill rest.) – 32 rm 49.95 t.

Wimbledon – ✉ SW19.

🏨🏨 **Cannizaro House** ⚐, West Side, Wimbledon Common, SW19 4UE, ✆ (0181) 879 1464, Fax (0181) 879 7338, ≼, « 18C country house in Cannizaro Park », ﹡ – ⚑, ⇖ rm, 📺 ☎ ♿
– ⚿ 60. ◉ AE ◉ VISA JCB. ✺   DXY x
Meals 25.75 t. and a la carte ⚬ 10.50 – ☲ 13.50 – 44 rm 150.00/249.00 t., 2 suites – SB.

REDBRIDGE pp. 6 and 7.
🖬 Town Hall, High Rd, IG1 1DD ✆ (0181) 478 3020 ext 2126.

Ilford – ⊠ Essex.

🖪 Wanstead Park Rd ✆ (0181) 554 2930, HU – 🖪, 🖪 Fairlop Waters, Forest Rd, Barkingside ✆ (0181) 500 9911 JT.

🏛 **Travel Inn**, Redbridge Lane East, IG4 5BG, ✆ (0181) 550 6451, Fax (0181) 550 6214 – ﹩₩ rm, 🔟 ₺ 🅿. ⓿⑨ 🆎 ⓪ 🆅🆂🅰. ⅖
Meals (grill rest.) – **44 rm** 36.50 t.　　　　　　　　　　　　　　HU i

🏛 **Travelodge**, Beehive Lane, IG4 5DR, ✆ (0181) 550 4248, Reservations (Freephone) 0800 850950 – ﹩₩ rm, 🔟 ₺ 🅿. ⓿⑨ 🆎 ⓪ 🆅🆂🅰 🅹🅲🅱. ⅖
Meals (grill rest.) – **32 rm** 49.95 t.　　　　　　　　　　　　　　HU e

South Woodford – ⊠ Essex.

🍴🍴 **Ho-Ho**, 20 High Rd, E18 2QL, ✆ (0181) 989 1041 – 🍽. ⓿⑨ 🆎 ⓪ 🆅🆂🅰 🅹🅲🅱　　HU c
closed 25 and 26 December – **Meals** - Chinese (Peking, Szechuan) - a la carte 30.20/46.90 **st.**

Woodford – ⊠ Essex.

🖪 2 Sunset Av., Woodford Green ✆ (0181) 504 0553/4254.
London 13 – Brentwood 16 – Harlow 16.

🏛 **County H. Epping Forest**, 30 Oak Hill, Woodford Green, IG8 9NY, ✆ (0181) 787 9988, Fax (0181) 506 0941 – 🗐, ﹩₩ rm, 🍽 rest, 🔟 ☎ 🅿 – 🔬 200. ⓿⑨ 🆎 ⓪ 🆅🆂🅰 🅹🅲🅱. ⅖
Meals (closed Saturday lunch) 15.95 **t.** (dinner) and a la carte 14.75/24.15 **t.** ₪ 9.95 – ⊊ 9.50 – **99 rm** 85.00/100.00 **st.** – SB.　　　　　　　　　　　　　　HT c

---

RICHMOND-UPON-THAMES pp. 8 and 9.

Barnes – ⊠ SW13.

🍴🍴 **Sonny's**, 94 Church Rd, SW13 0DQ, ✆ (0181) 748 0393, Fax (0181) 748 2698 – 🍽. ⓿⑨ 🆎 🆅🆂🅰
closed Sunday dinner and Bank Holidays – **Meals** a la carte 20.70/29.90 **t.**　　CX x

🍴 **Riva**, 169 Church Rd, SW13 9HR, ✆ (0181) 748 0434, Fax (0181) 748 0434 – ⓿⑨ 🆎 🆅🆂🅰 🅹🅲🅱
closed Saturday lunch, Easter, last 2 weeks August, Christmas and Bank Holidays – **Meals** - Italian - a la carte 17.15/29.75 **t.** ₪ 6.95.　　　　　　　　　　　　CX a

East Sheen – ⊠ SW14.

🍴🍴 **Redmond's**, 170 Upper Richmond Road West, SW14 8AW, ✆ (0181) 878 1922, Fax (0181) 878 1133 – ⓿⑨ 🆅🆂🅰 🅹🅲🅱　　　　　　　　　　　　　　　　　　CX v
closed Saturday lunch, Sunday dinner, 25-26 December, first week January and Bank Holidays – **Meals** 23.00 **t.** ₪ 5.00.

🍴🍴 **Crowther's**, 481 Upper Richmond Rd West, SW14 7PU, ✆ (0181) 876 6372 – 🍽. ⓿⑨ 🆅🆂🅰
closed Saturday lunch, Sunday, Monday, 2 weeks August and 1 week Christmas – **Meals** (booking essential) 18.50/23.00 ₪ 5.25.　　　　　　　　　　　　CX n

Hampton Court – ⊠ Surrey.

🏨 **Mitre**, Hampton Court Rd, KT8 9BN, ✆ (0181) 979 9988, Fax (0181) 979 9777, ≼, « Riverside setting » – 🗐, ﹩₩ rm, 🔟 ☎ 🅿 – 🔬 25. ⓿⑨ 🆎 ⓪ 🆅🆂🅰　　　　　BY v
Meals (bar lunch Saturday) 16.75/23.50 **st.** ₪ 4.90 – **36 rm** ⊊ 115.00/195.00 **st.** – SB.

Hampton Hill – ⊠ Middx.

🍴 **Monsieur Max**, 133 High St., TW12 1NJ, ✆ (0181) 979 5546, Fax (0181) 979 5546
closed Saturday lunch and 3 days Christmas – Meals - French - 14.00/23.00 **t.**　　BY a

Hampton Wick – ⊠ Surrey.

🏛 **Chase Lodge**, 10 Park Rd, KT1 4AS, ✆ (0181) 943 1862, Fax (0181) 943 9363 – 🔟 ☎. ⓿⑨ 🆎 ⓪ 🆅🆂🅰 🅹🅲🅱
Meals a la carte 12.30/18.45 **t.** ₪ 5.95 – **11 rm** ⊊ 62.00/85.00 **t.** – SB.　　BY e

Richmond – ⊠ Surrey.

🖪, 🖪 Richmond Park, Roehampton Gate ✆ (0181) 876 3205/1795 CX – 🖪 Sudbrook Par ✆ (0181) 940 1463 CX.
🖬 Old Town Hall, Whittaker Av., TW9 1TP ✆ (0181) 940 9125.

🏨 **Petersham** 🌿, Nightingale Lane, TW10 6UZ, ☎ (0181) 940 7471, *Fax (0181) 939 1098*, <, 🌳 – 🛗 📺 ☎ [P] – 🎤 50. [MO] [AE] [D] [VISA] [JCB]. 🚭 CX c
Meals – (see ***Nightingales*** below) – **57 rm** ☕ 115.00/145.00 **t.** – SB.

🏨 **Richmond Gate,** 158 Richmond Hill, TW10 6RP, ☎ (0181) 940 0061, *Fax (0181) 332 0354*, 🏋, ♨, 🏊, 🌳 – 🚭 📺 ☎ [P] – 🎤 45. [MO] [AE] [D] [VISA]. 🚭 CX c
Gates On The Park **:** Meals *(closed Saturday lunch)* 18.50/25.50 **t.** and a la carte 🍷 9.30 –
Gates Bistro **:** Meals *(closed Saturday and Sunday)* (dinner only) a la carte 15.20/28.85 **t.** 🍷 9.50 – **65 rm** ☕ 122.00/144.00 **t.**, 1 suite – SB.

🏨 **Richmond Hill,** Richmond Hill, TW10 6RW, ☎ (0181) 940 2247, *Fax (0181) 940 5424*, 🏋, ♨, 🏊 – 🛗, ❄ rest, 📺 ☎ [P] – 🎤 200. [MO] [AE] [D] [VISA] [JCB] CX r
Pembrokes **:** Meals 14.00/19.50 **t.** and a la carte 🍷 12.50 – **118 rm** ☕ 110.00/155.00 **t.**, 5 suites – SB.

🏨 **Rose of York,** Petersham Rd, TW10 6UY, ☎ (0181) 948 5867, *Fax (0181) 332 6986* – 📺 ☎ [P]. [MO] [AE] [VISA] [JCB]. 🚭 CX z
Meals (in bar) a la carte 11.40/17.40 **t.** – **12 rm** ☕ 58.00/80.00 **st.**

🍴🍴🍴 **Nightingales** (at Petersham H.), Nightingale Lane, TW10 6UZ, ☎ (0181) 940 7471, *Fax (0181) 939 1098*, <, 🌳 – [P]. [MO] [AE] [D] [VISA] [JCB] CX c
Meals (residents only Sunday dinner) 18.50/25.00 **t.** 🍷 7.50.

🍴🍴 **Four Regions,** 102-104 Kew Rd, TW9 2PQ, ☎ (0181) 940 9044, *Fax (0181) 332 6130*, ⛱ – ❄. [MO] [AE] [VISA] CX e
closed 25 and 26 December – **Meals** - Chinese - 15.50/25.00 **t.** and a la carte.

SOUTHWARK *Except where otherwise stated see pp.10-11 and pp.26-27.*

Bermondsey – ✉ *SE1.*

🍴🍴🍴 **Le Pont de la Tour,** 36d Shad Thames, Butlers Wharf, SE1 2YE, ☎ (0171) 403 8403, *Fax (0171) 403 0267*, <, ⛱, « Riverside setting » – ❄. [MO] [AE] [D] [VISA] PX c
closed Saturday lunch – **Meals** 27.50 **t.** (lunch) and dinner a la carte 31.50/38.50 **t.**

🍴🍴🍴 **Bengal Clipper,** Cardamom Building, Shad Thames, Butlers Wharf, SE1 2YR, ☎ (0171) 357 9001, *Fax (0171) 357 9002* – ❄. [MO] [AE] [D] [VISA] [JCB] PX e
closed 25 and 26 December – **Meals** - Indian - a la carte 13.85/28.35 **t.**

🍴 **Blue Print Café,** Design Museum, Shad Thames, Butlers Wharf, SE1 2YD, ☎ (0171) 378 7031, *Fax (0171) 378 6540*, ⛱, « Riverside setting, < Tower Bridge » – [MO] [AE] [D] [VISA] PX u
closed Sunday dinner – Meals a la carte approx. 23.55 **t.**

🍴 **Butlers Wharf Chop House,** 36e Shad Thames, Butlers Wharf, SE1 2YE, ☎ (0171) 403 3403, *Fax (0171) 403 3414*, « Riverside setting, < Tower Bridge » – [MO] [AE] [D] [VISA] PX n
closed Saturday lunch and Sunday dinner – **Meals** 22.75 **t.** (lunch) and dinner a la carte 24.50/31.75 **t.**

🍴 **Cantina Del Ponte,** 36c Shad Thames, Butlers Wharf, SE1 2YE, ☎ (0171) 403 5403, *Fax (0171) 403 0267*, <, ⛱, « Riverside setting » – [MO] [AE] [D] [VISA] PX c
Meals - Italian-Mediterranean - a la carte 10.50/25.25 **t.**

🍴 **Café dell'Ugo,** 56-58 Tooley St., SE1 2SZ, ☎ (0171) 407 6001, *Fax (0171) 357 8806* – ❄. [MO] [AE] [D] [VISA] PX r
closed Saturday lunch, Sunday and Bank Holidays – **Meals** 15.00 **t.** (dinner) and a la carte 17.45/26.75 **t.**

Dulwich – ✉ *SE19.*

🍴🍴 **Belair House,** Gallery Rd, Dulwich Village, SE21 7AB, ☎ (0181) 299 9788, *Fax (0181) 299 6793*, ⛱, « Georgian summer house », 🌳 – [P]. [MO] [AE] [D] [VISA] [JCB]
closed Monday – **Meals** 19.95 **t.** (lunch) and a la carte 23.40/50.45 **t.** 🍷 10.00. FX e

🍴🍴 **Luigi's,** 129 Gipsy Hill, SE19 1QS, ☎ (0181) 670 1843 – ❄. [MO] [AE] [D] [VISA] [JCB] FX a
closed Sunday – **Meals** - Italian - a la carte 16.20/24.15 **t.** 🍷 4.90.

Rotherhithe – ✉ *SE16.*

🏨 **Holiday Inn at Nelson Dock,** 265 Rotherhithe St., Nelson Dock, SE16 1EJ, ☎ (0171) 231 1001, *Fax (0171) 231 0599*, <, ⛱, « Riverside setting », 🏋, ♨, 🏊, 🎾 – 🛗, 🚭 rm, ❄ rest, 📺 ☎ ♿ [P] – 🎤 350. [MO] [AE] [D] [VISA] [JCB]. 🚭 GV r
closed 22 to 28 December – **Meals** 21.50 **st.** and dinner a la carte 🍷 7.50 – ☕ 10.50 – **362 rm** 115.00/135.00 **st.**, 4 suites.

Southwark – ✉ SE1.

Oxo Tower (8th floor), Oxo Tower Wharf, Barge House St., SE1 9PH, ℘ (0171) 803 3888, Fax (0171) 803 3838, ≼ London skyline and River Thames, ☆ – 🛗 ▤. 🐵 🖭 ⓪ 𝖵𝖨𝖲𝖠 𝖩𝖢𝖡.
closed Saturday lunch, 25-26 December and 1 January – **Meals** 24.50 st. (lunch) and dinner a la carte 26.50/36.50 t. 🍷 10.00.
NX a

X **Brasserie :** **Meals** (closed 23 to 26 December and 1 January) a la carte 19.50/26.00 t.

X **Livebait**, 43 The Cut, SE1 8LF, ℘ (0171) 928 7211, Fax (0171) 928 2279 – 🐵 𝖵𝖨𝖲𝖠
closed Sunday – **Meals** - Seafood - a la carte approx. 31.00 t.
NX c

SUTTON pp. 8 and 9.

Carshalton – ✉ Surrey.

XX **La Veranda**, 18-19 Beynon Rd, SM5 3RL, ℘ (0181) 647 4370 – ▤. 🐵 🖭 ⓪ 𝖵𝖨𝖲𝖠
closed Sunday and Bank Holidays – **Meals** - Italian - a la carte 21.70/24.00 t. 🍷 6.80.
EZ c

Sutton – ✉ Surrey.

🏌, 🏌 Oak Sports Centre, Woodmansterne Rd, Carshalton ℘ (0181) 643 8363.

🏨 **Holiday Inn**, Gibson Rd, SM1 2RF, ℘ (0181) 770 1311, Fax (0181) 770 1539, 🛌, 🚲, 🔲 - 🛗 ⇆, ▤ rest, 🔲 ☎ ᵫ 🅿 – 🔬 220. 🐵 🖭 ⓪ 𝖵𝖨𝖲𝖠 𝖩𝖢𝖡. ⋇
Meals (closed lunch Saturday) 14.95 st. and a la carte 🍷 6.95 – ⎓ 11.95 – **115 rm** 139.00/155.00 st., 1 suite.
EZ a

🏠 **Thatched House**, 135-141 Cheam Rd, SM1 2BN, ℘ (0181) 642 3131, Fax (0181) 770 0684, 🌸 – 🔲 ☎ 🅿 – 🔬 50. 🐵 ⓪ 𝖵𝖨𝖲𝖠 𝖩𝖢𝖡. ⋇
Meals (closed dinner Saturday and Sunday and Bank Holidays) 10.95/13.50 t. and lunch a la carte 🍷 4.95 – **32 rm** ⎓ 45.50/85.00 t.
DZ e

TOWER HAMLETS – p. 6.

Canary Wharf – ✉ E14.

XX **MPW**, Second Floor, Cabot Place East, E14 4QT, ℘ (0171) 513 0513, Fax (0171) 513 0551, ▤. 🐵 🖭 ⓪ 𝖵𝖨𝖲𝖠
closed Saturday, Sunday, 25-26 December and 1 January – **Meals** a la carte 18.50/31.45 t. 🍷 9.00.
GV

Whitechapel – ✉ E1.

XX **Cafe Spice Namaste**, 16 Prescot St., E1 8AZ, ℘ (0171) 488 9242, Fax (0171) 488 9339, ▤. 🐵 🖭 ⓪ 𝖵𝖨𝖲𝖠 𝖩𝖢𝖡
closed Saturday lunch, Sunday, 1 week Christmas and Bank Holiday Mondays – **Meals** Indian - a la carte 18.70/32.55 t. 🍷 6.50.
GV

WANDSWORTH Except where otherwise stated see pp. 12 and 13.

Battersea – ✉ SW8/SW11.

🏠 **Travelodge**, without rest., 200 York Rd, SW11 3SA, ℘ (0171) 228 5508, Fax (0171) 228 5508, Reservations (Freephone) 0800 850950 – 🛗, ⇆ 🔲 ☎ ᵫ 🅿. 🐵 🖭 🄫 𝖵𝖨𝖲𝖠 𝖩𝖢𝖡. ⋇
80 rm 49.95 t.
CQ

XX **Ransome's Dock**, 35-37 Parkgate Rd, SW11 4NP, ℘ (0171) 223 1611, Fax (0171) 924 2614, ☆ – 🐵 ⓪ 𝖵𝖨𝖲𝖠
closed Sunday dinner and 1 week Christmas – **Meals** a la carte 19.50/27.75 (lunch) and a la carte 17.75/27.00 t. 🍷 6.25.
p. 25 HZ

XX **Chada**, 208-210 Battersea Park Rd, SW11 4ND, ℘ (0171) 622 2209, Fax (0171) 924 2178, ▤. 🐵 🖭 ⓪ 𝖵𝖨𝖲𝖠 𝖩𝖢𝖡
closed Saturday lunch and Bank Holidays – **Meals** - Thai - a la carte 12.40/25.15 st.
CQ

X **The Stepping Stone**, 123 Queenstown Rd, SW8 3RH, ℘ (0171) 622 0555, Fax (0171) 622 4230 – ▤. 🐵 🖭 ⓪ 𝖵𝖨𝖲𝖠
closed Saturday lunch, Sunday dinner, 1 week Christmas and Bank Holiday Mondays
Meals 13.75 t. (lunch) and a la carte 18.75/22.10 t. 🍷 5.00.
DQ

🍴 **Duke of Cambridge**, 228 Battersea Bridge Rd, SW11 3AA, ℘ (0171) 223 5662, Fax (0171) 801 9684, ☆ – 🐵 𝖵𝖨𝖲𝖠
Meals a la carte approx. 17.35 st.
CQ

Putney – ⊠ SW15.

XX **Putney Bridge,** Lower Richmond Rd, SW15 1LB, ℰ (0181) 780 1811, *Fax (0181) 780 1211*, ≼, « Riverside setting » – **⚙⊙** **VISA**
AQ u
Meals 17.50 **t.** (lunch) and a la carte 18.00/31.50 **t.** ⅞ 9.00.

XX Royal China, 3 Chelverton Rd, SW15 1RN, ℰ (0181) 788 0907 – ▤
AQ a
Meals - Chinese rest.

XX **The Phoenix,** Pentlow St., SW15 1LY, ℰ (0181) 780 3131, *Fax (0181) 780 1114* – ▤. **⚙⊙** **AE** **VISA**
AQ s
closed 25-26 December and Bank Holidays – **Meals** 12.50 **t.** (lunch) and a la carte 15.20/22.75 **t.** ⅞ 4.75.

X **Del Buongustaio,** 283 Putney Bridge Rd, SW15 2PT, ℰ (0181) 780 9361, *Fax (0181) 789 9659* – ▤. **⚙⊙** **AE** **VISA**
AQ e
closed lunch Saturday and Sunday July-August and 10 days Christmas-New Year – **Meals** - Italian - a la carte 18.35/22.90 **t.** ⅞ 5.95.

X **Enoteca,** 28 Putney High St., SW15 1SQ, ℰ (0181) 785 4449, *Fax (0181) 785 4449* – **⚙⊙** **AE** **⊙** **VISA**
AQ n
closed lunch Saturday and Bank Holidays, Sunday and 25 to 30 December – **Meals** - Italian - a la carte 20.65/24.25 **t.** ⅞ 5.00.

Tooting – ⊠ SW17.

X **Oh Boy,** 843 Garratt Lane, SW17 0PG, ℰ (0181) 947 9760, *Fax (0181) 879 7867* – ▤. **⚙⊙** **AE** **⊙** **VISA** **JCB**
CR c
closed 25 December and 1 January – **Meals** - Thai - (dinner only) 20.00 **t.** and a la carte ⅞ 4.25.

Wandsworth – ⊠ SW12/SW17/SW18.

XXX **Chez Bruce,** 2 Bellevue Rd, SW17 7EG, ℰ (0181) 672 0114, *Fax (0181) 767 6648* – ▤. **⚙⊙** **AE** **⊙** **VISA**
CR e
closed Sunday dinner, 1 week Christmas and Bank Holidays – **Meals** 18.00/25.00 **t.**

XX **Tabaq,** 47 Balham Hill, SW12 9DR, ℰ (0181) 673 7820, *Fax (0181) 673 2701* – ▤. **⚙⊙** **AE** **⊙** **VISA** **JCB**
DR v
closed Sunday and 25 December – **Meals** - Indian - a la carte 14.45/24.50 **t.** ⅞ 4.75.

X **Bombay Bicycle Club,** 95 Nightingale Lane, SW12 8NX, ℰ (0181) 673 6217, *Fax (0181) 673 9100* – **⚙⊙** **AE** **⊙** **VISA**
DR o
closed Sunday, Easter and 25 December – **Meals** - Indian - (dinner only) a la carte 16.00/21.50 **t.** ⅞ 8.00.

WESTMINSTER (City of).

Bayswater and Maida Vale – ⊠ W2/W9 – Except where otherwise stated see pp. 32 and 33.

🏨 **Royal Lancaster,** Lancaster Terr., W2 2TY, ℰ (0171) 262 6737, *Fax (0171) 724 3191*, ≼ – ⧫, ⇇ rm, ▤ **⚙ ☎ ☏** – 🔬 1400. **⚙⊙** **AE** **⊙** **VISA** **JCB**. ⚘
DZ e
Park : **Meals** (closed Saturday lunch and Sunday dinner) 23.50 **st.** and a la carte ⅞ 11.00 – *Pavement Cafe :* **Meals** a la carte 13.70/17.20 **st.** ⅞ 10.00 – (see also **Nipa** below) – ⊟ 14.50 – **398 rm** 210.00/230.00 **st.**, 20 suites.

🏨 **Stakis London Metropole,** Edgware Rd, W2 1JU, ℰ (0171) 402 4141, *Fax (0171) 724 8866*, ≼, **₭**, ⊜, ▨ – ⧫, ⇇ rm, ▤ **⚙ ☎** – 🔬 1200. **⚙⊙** **AE** **⊙** **VISA** **JCB**. ⚘
p. 21 GU c
Meals (buffet rest.) 20.50/30.50 **t.** and a la carte – (see also **Aspects** below) ⅞ 8.00 – ⊟ 17.95 – **721 rm** 150.00/200.00 **st.**, 26 suites – SB.

🏨 **The Hempel** ⚘, Hempel Garden Sq., 31-35 Craven Hill Gdns., W2 3EA, ℰ (0171) 298 9000, *Fax (0171) 402 4666*, « Minimalist », ☞ – ⧫ ▤ **⚙ ☎ ♿ ☏** – 🔬 40. **⚙⊙** **AE** **⊙** **VISA**. ⚘
CZ a
I-Thai : **Meals** - Thai-Italian - a la carte 27.00/40.00 **t.** – ⊟ 17.00 – **41 rm** 220.00/255.00 **s.**, 6 suites.

🏨 **Whites,** Bayswater Rd, 90-92 Lancaster Gate, W2 3NR, ℰ (0171) 262 2711, *Fax (0171) 262 2147* – ⧫, ⇇ rm, ▤ **⚙ ☎ ☏** – 🔬 30. **⚙⊙** **AE** **⊙** **VISA** **JCB**. ⚘
CZ v
Meals (closed Saturday lunch) 17.50/20.50 **t.** and a la carte ⅞ 7.90 – ⊟ 12.50 – **52 rm** 167.00/247.00 **st.**, 2 suites – SB.

🏨 **Jarvis London Embassy,** 150 Bayswater Rd, W2 4RT, ℰ (0171) 229 1212, *Fax (0171) 229 2623* – ⧫, ⇇ rm, ▤ rest, **⚙ ☎ ☏** – 🔬 100. **⚙⊙** **AE** **⊙** **VISA**
BZ o
Meals (carving rest.) 14.95 **st.** and a la carte ⅞ 6.50 – ⊟ 9.50 – **193 rm** 115.00/135.00 **st.**, 1 suite – SB.

🏨🏨 **Plaza on Hyde Park**, 1-7 Lancaster Gate, W2 3LG, ✆ (0171) 262 5022,
Fax (0171) 724 8666 – 🛗, ↩ rm, 📺 ☎ – 🔏 30. ⚙ 🆎 ⓪ 𝗩𝗜𝗦𝗔 𝗝𝗖𝗕, ⋙ DZ r
Meals a la carte 14.40/25.65 st. ⓰ 6.70 – ☲ 10.95 – **402 rm** 125.00/140.00 st.

🏨🏨 **Stakis London Coburg**, 129 Bayswater Rd, W2 4RJ, ✆ (0171) 221 2217,
Fax (0171) 229 0557 – 🛗, ↩ rm, 📺 ■ rest, 📺 ☎ – 🔏 100. ⚙ 🆎 ⓪ 𝗩𝗜𝗦𝗔, ⋙ BZ c
Meals 15.95 st. and a la carte – ☲ 9.95 – **128 rm** 125.00/150.00 st., 1 suite – SB.

🏨🏨 **Hyde Park Towers**, 41-51 Inverness Terr., W2 3JN, ✆ (0171) 221 8484,
Fax (0171) 792 3201 – 🛗, ■ rest, 📺 ☎ – 🔏 45. ⚙ 🆎 ⓪ 𝗩𝗜𝗦𝗔, ⋙ BZ r
Meals 10.95/13.95 t. ⓰ 5.50 – ☲ 7.50 – **114 rm** 110.00/150.00 t. – SB.

🏨 **Mornington** without rest., 12 Lancaster Gate, W2 3LG, ✆ (0171) 262 7361,
Fax (0171) 706 1028 – 🛗 ↩ 📺 ☎. ⚙ 🆎 ⓪ 𝗩𝗜𝗦𝗔 𝗝𝗖𝗕 DZ s
66 rm ☲ 99.00/140.00.

🏨 **Byron** without rest., 36-38 Queensborough Terr., W2 3SH, ✆ (0171) 243 0987,
Fax (0171) 792 1957 – 🛗 ■ 📺 ☎. ⚙ 🆎 ⓪ 𝗩𝗜𝗦𝗔 𝗝𝗖𝗕. CZ z
44 rm ☲ 75.50/96.00 st., 1 suite.

🏨 **Delmere**, 130 Sussex Gdns., W2 1UB, ✆ (0171) 706 3344, *Fax (0171) 262 1863* – 🛗 📺 ☎
⚙ 🆎 ⓪ 𝗩𝗜𝗦𝗔 𝗝𝗖𝗕. ⋙ DZ v
Meals *(closed Sunday)* (dinner only) 12.95 t. and a la carte ⓰ 6.00 – ☲ 6.00 – **38 rm** 78.00/98.00 st.

🏨 **Gresham** without rest., 116 Sussex Gdns., W2 1UA, ✆ (0171) 402 2920,
Fax (0171) 402 3137 – 🛗 📺 ☎. ⚙ 🆎 ⓪ 𝗩𝗜𝗦𝗔 𝗝𝗖𝗕. ⋙ DZ a
☲ 5.00 – **38 rm** 60.00/75.00 st.

🏨 **Norfolk Plaza** without rest., 29-33 Norfolk Sq., W2 1RX, ✆ (0171) 723 0792,
Fax (0171) 224 8770 – 🛗 📺 ☎. ⚙ 🆎 ⓪ 𝗩𝗜𝗦𝗔 𝗝𝗖𝗕. ⋙ DZ z
☲ 6.00 – **81 rm** 98.00/118.00 st., 6 suites.

🏨 **Comfort Inn** without rest., 18-19 Craven Hill Gdns., W2 3EE, ✆ (0171) 262 6644,
Fax (0171) 262 0673 – 🛗 ↩ 📺 ☎. ⚙ 🆎 ⓪ 𝗩𝗜𝗦𝗔. ⋙ CZ e
☲ 4.50 – **64 rm** 73.00/93.00 st.

XXX **Aspects** (at Stakis London Metropole H.), Edgware Rd, W2 1JU, ✆ (0171) 402 4141,
Fax (0171) 724 8866, ≼ London – ■. ⚙ 🆎 ⓪ 𝗩𝗜𝗦𝗔 𝗝𝗖𝗕 p. 21 GU
closed Sunday – **Meals** 20.50/30.50 t. and a la carte ⓰ 8.00.

XX **Nipa** (at Royal Lancaster H.), Lancaster Terr., W2 2TY, ✆ (0171) 262 6737,
Fax (0171) 724 3191 – ■ 🅿. ⚙ 🆎 ⓪ 𝗩𝗜𝗦𝗔 𝗝𝗖𝗕 DZ c
closed Saturday lunch and Sunday – **Meals** - Thai - 23.00 st. and a la carte ⓰ 10.00.

XX **Poons**, Unit 205, Whiteleys, Queensway, W2 4YN, ✆ (0171) 792 2884 – ■. ⚙ 🆎 ⓪ 𝗩𝗜𝗦𝗔
closed 25 and 26 December – **Meals** - Chinese - 15.00/25.00 t. and a la carte. BZ

XX **Al San Vincenzo**, 30 Connaught Sq., W2 2AE, ✆ (0171) 262 9623 – ⚙ 𝗩𝗜𝗦𝗔 EZ
closed Saturday lunch and Sunday – **Meals** - Italian - (booking essential) a la carte 22.00/34.50 t. ⓰ 7.50.

XX **Jason's**, Blomfield Rd, Little Venice, W9 2PD, ✆ (0171) 286 6752, *Fax (0171) 266 4332*, 🌂
« Canalside setting » – ⚙ 🆎 𝗩𝗜𝗦𝗔 𝗝𝗖𝗕 p. 20 FU
closed Sunday dinner – **Meals** - Seafood - 14.95/18.95 t. and a la carte.

XX **Royal China**, 13 Queensway, W2 4QJ, ✆ (0171) 221 2535 – ■. ⚙ 🆎 ⓪ 𝗩𝗜𝗦𝗔
closed 25 December – **Meals** - Chinese - 22.00 t. (dinner) and a la carte. BZ

X **Assaggi**, 39 Chepstow Pl., W2 4TS, ✆ (0171) 792 5501 – ⚙ 🆎 𝗩𝗜𝗦𝗔 𝗝𝗖𝗕 AZ
closed Sunday dinner, Monday, Christmas, New Year and Bank Holidays – **Meals** - Italian -
a la carte 21.75/31.75 t.

X **L'Accento**, 16 Garway Rd, W2 4NH, ✆ (0171) 243 2201, *Fax (0171) 243 2201* – ⚙ 𝗩𝗜𝗦𝗔
🍷 𝗝𝗖𝗕
Meals - Italian - 15.25 t. and a la carte 18.75/23.25 t. BZ

X **Kalamaras**, 76-78 Inverness Mews, W2 3JQ, ✆ (0171) 727 9122, *Fax (0171) 221 9411* – ⚙
🆎 ⓪ 𝗩𝗜𝗦𝗔 BZ
closed Sunday lunch – **Meals** - Greek - a la carte 15.00/25.00 t.

Belgravia – ✉ SW1 – *Except where otherwise stated see pp. 30 and 31.*

🏨🏨🏨🏨 **The Lanesborough**, 1 Lanesborough Pl., SW1X 7TA, ✆ (0171) 259 5599,
Fax (0171) 259 5606, 🛏 – 🛗, ↩ rm, ■ 📺 ☎ & 🅿 – 🔏 90. ⚙ 🆎 ⓪ 𝗩𝗜𝗦𝗔 𝗝𝗖𝗕
The Conservatory: Meals 24.50/31.50 st. and a la carte ⓰ 13.50 – ☲ 17.00 – **86 rm**
205.00/395.00 s., 9 suites. p. 25 IY

🏨🏨🏨🏨 **The Berkeley**, Wilton Pl., SW1X 7RL, ✆ (0171) 235 6000, *Fax (0171) 235 4330*, 🛏, ≋, 🔥
– 🛗, ↩ rm, ■ 📺 ☎ ⟷ – 🔏 220. ⚙ 🆎 ⓪ 𝗩𝗜𝗦𝗔 𝗝𝗖𝗕. ⋙ FQ
Restaurant: Meals 26.50/33.00 st. and a la carte ⓰ 10.00 – (see also **Vong** below) –
☲ 18.50 – **130 rm** 265.00/320.00 s., 26 suites.

The Halkin, 5 Halkin St., SW1X 7DJ, ℰ (0171) 333 1000, *Fax (0171) 333 1100,* « Contemporary interior design » – |≜|, ✑ rm, ▤ ▥ ☎ ℗ – ⚌ 25. ⫽⊙ ⅍ ⑩ 𝗩𝗜𝗦𝗔 ᴊᴄʙ. ✑
Stefano Cavallini Restaurant at The Halkin : Meals - Italian - *(closed lunch Saturday and Sunday, Easter and 25 December)* (booking essential) 25.00 **st.** (lunch) and a la carte 40.00/
53.00 **st.** ⓘ 9.50 – ⌫ 14.25 – **36 rm** 250.00/330.00 **s.**, 5 suites – SB   p. 32 AV   a
Spec. Duck ravioli with savoy cabbage and foie gras. Lobster and pigeon with pea ravioli. Risotto of fried herbs and onions.

Sheraton Belgravia, 20 Chesham Pl., SW1X 8HQ, ℰ (0171) 235 6040,
Fax (0171) 259 6243 – |≜|, ✑ rm, ▤ ▥ ☎ ℗ – ⚌ 50. ⫽⊙ ⅍ ⑩ 𝗩𝗜𝗦𝗔 ᴊᴄʙ. ✑   FR   u
Chesham's : Meals a la carte 26.00/32.00 **st.** ⓘ 6.00 – ⌫ 15.00 – **82 rm** 210.00/310.00 **s.**,
7 suites.

Lowndes, 21 Lowndes St., SW1X 9ES, ℰ (0171) 823 1234, *Fax (0171) 235 1154,* ✑ – |≜|,
✑ rm, ▤ ▥ ☎ ℗ – ⚌ 25. ⫽⊙ ⅍ ⑩ 𝗩𝗜𝗦𝗔 ᴊᴄʙ. ✑   FR   i
Brasserie 21 : Meals 17.00 **t.** and a la carte ⓘ 9.50 – ⌫ 13.50 – **77 rm** 235.00/255.00 **s.**,
1 suite.

Diplomat without rest., 2 Chesham St., SW1X 8DT, ℰ (0171) 235 1544,
Fax (0171) 259 6153 – |≜| ▥ ☎ ℗. ⫽⊙ ⅍ ⑩ 𝗩𝗜𝗦𝗔 ᴊᴄʙ. ✑   FR   a
26 rm ⌫ 85.00/150.00 **t.**

Zafferano, 15 Lowndes St., SW1X 9EY, ℰ (0171) 235 5800, *Fax (0171) 235 1971* – ▤. ⫽⊙
⅍ 𝗩𝗜𝗦𝗔   FR   i
closed Sunday, 2 weeks August and Bank Holidays – Meals - Italian - 21.50/25.50 **t.**
and a la carte ⓘ 9.50.

Vong (at The Berkeley H.), Wilton Pl., SW1X 7RL, ℰ (0171) 235 1010, *Fax (0171) 235 1011* –
▤. ⫽⊙ ⅍ ⑩ 𝗩𝗜𝗦𝗔 ᴊᴄʙ   FQ   e
closed Sunday lunch and 25 December – Meals - French-Thai - 22.00 **t.**
(lunch) and a la carte 23.75/39.00 **t.**

Al Bustan, 27 Motcomb St., SW1X 8JU, ℰ (0171) 235 8277, *Fax (0171) 235 1668* – ▤. ⫽⊙
⅍ ⑩ 𝗩𝗜𝗦𝗔   FR   z
closed 23 December-4 January – Meals - Lebanese - 13.00 **t.** (lunch) and a la carte 19.50/
22.25 **t.** ⓘ 10.00.

Hyde Park and Knightsbridge – ✉ SW1/SW7 – pp. 30 and 31.

Mandarin Oriental Hyde Park, 66 Knightsbridge, SW1X 7LA, ℰ (0171) 235 2000,
Fax (0171) 235 4552, ≤, ₣₆ – |≜|, ✑ rm, ▤ ▥ ☎ ♿ – ⚌ 250. ⫽⊙ ⅍ ⑩ 𝗩𝗜𝗦𝗔. ✑   FQ   x
Restaurant On The Park : Meals a la carte 21.95/43.95 **t.** ⓘ 14.00 – ⌫ 16.50 – **166 rm**
240.00/260.00 **s.**, 19 suites.

Knightsbridge Green without rest., 159 Knightsbridge, SW1X 7PD, ℰ (0171) 584 6274,
Fax (0171) 225 1635 – |≜| ▤ ▥ ☎. ⫽⊙ ⅍ ⑩ 𝗩𝗜𝗦𝗔. ✑   EQ   z
closed 24 to 26 December – ⌫ 9.50 – **15 rm** 90.00/130.00 **st.**, 12 suites 150.00 **st.**

Pearl of Knightsbridge, 22 Brompton Rd, SW1X 7QN, ℰ (0171) 225 3888,
Fax (0171) 225 0252 – ▤. ⫽⊙ ⅍ ⑩ 𝗩𝗜𝗦𝗔   EQ   e
closed 25 and 26 December – Meals - Chinese - 10.80/22.80 **t.** and a la carte.

Mr. Chow, 151 Knightsbridge, SW1X 7PA, ℰ (0171) 589 7347, *Fax (0171) 584 5780* – ▤.
⫽⊙ ⅍ ⑩ 𝗩𝗜𝗦𝗔 ᴊᴄʙ   EQ   a
closed 24 to 26 December – Meals - Chinese - a la carte 30.00/35.00 **t.**

Mayfair – ✉ W1 – pp. 28 and 29.
    DN   e

Dorchester, Park Lane, W1A 2HJ, ℰ (0171) 629 8888, *Fax (0171) 409 0114,* ₣₆, ⇆ – |≜|,
✑ rm, ▤ ▥ ☎ ♿ ⟺ – ⚌ 550. ⫽⊙ ⅍ ⑩ 𝗩𝗜𝗦𝗔 ᴊᴄʙ. ✑   BN   a
Meals – (see *Oriental* and *Grill Room* below) – ⌫ 18.50 – **197 rm** 240.00/300.00 **s.**,
47 suites.

Claridge's, Brook St., W1A 2JQ, ℰ (0171) 629 8860, *Fax (0171) 499 2210,* ₣₆ – |≜|, ✑ rm,
▤ ▥ ☎ ♿ – ⚌ 200. ⫽⊙ ⅍ ⑩   BL   c
Restaurant : Meals 29.00/38.00 **st.** and a la carte 29.00/45.00 **st.** ⓘ 10.50 – *Causerie :*
Meals *(closed Saturday and Sunday)* a la carte 30.00/36.00 **st.** ⓘ 10.50 – ⌫ 18.00 – **138 rm**
255.00/365.00 **s.**, 60 suites – SB.

Four Seasons, Hamilton Pl., Park Lane, W1A 1AZ, ℰ (0171) 499 0888,
Fax (0171) 493 1895, ₣₆ – |≜|, ✑ rm, ▤ ▥ ☎ ⟺ – ⚌ 500. ⫽⊙ ⅍ ⑩ 𝗩𝗜𝗦𝗔 ᴊᴄʙ. ✑
Lanes : Meals 32.00 **st.** (lunch) and a la carte 26.00/45.00 **st.** ⓘ 8.00 – (see also *Four
Seasons* below) – ⌫ 17.75 – **201 rm** 250.00/305.00 **s.**, 26 suites.   BP   a

Le Meridien Piccadilly, 21 Piccadilly, W1V 0BH, ℰ (0171) 734 8000,
Fax (0171) 437 3574, ⇆, ☒, squash – |≜|, ✑ rm, ▤ ▥ ☎ ♿ – ⚌ 250. ⫽⊙ ⅍ ⑩ 𝗩𝗜𝗦𝗔
ᴊᴄʙ. ✑   EM   a
Terrace Garden : Meals 19.95 **t.** and a la carte ⓘ 12.00 – (see also *The Oak Room Marco
Pierre White* below) – ⌫ 16.50 – **248 rm** 275.00/335.00, 18 suites.

Grosvenor House, Park Lane, W1A 3AA, ℰ (0171) 499 6363, Fax (0171) 493 3341, ℔, ⇌, ◱ – ⧏, ⇖ rm, ▤ ▥ ☎ & ⇐ – ⛤ 1500. ⓌⓄ ㏂ ⓪ 𝓥𝓘𝓢𝓐 𝓙𝓒𝓑. ⌘
AM a
Café Nico : Meals 29.50 st. – *Pasta Vino :* Meals - Italian - *(closed Saturday and Sunday)* a la carte 32.50/40.75 t. – (see also *Chez Nico at Ninety Park Lane* below) – ⇌ 19.50 – **382 rm** 210.00/345.00, 72 suites.

London Hilton on Park Lane, 22 Park Lane, W1Y 4BE, ℰ (0171) 493 8000, Fax (0171) 493 4957, « Panoramic ≤ of London », ℔ – ⧏, ⇖ rm, ▤ ▥ ☎ & – ⛤ 1000. ⓌⓄ ㏂ ⓪ 𝓥𝓘𝓢𝓐 𝓙𝓒𝓑.
BP e
*Trader Vics (*ℰ (0171) 208 4113) :* Meals (dinner only) a la carte 19.00/54.50 t. ▤ 9.00 – *Park Brasserie :* Meals 25.50 t. and a la carte ▤ 9.75 – (see also *Windows* below) – ⇌ 17.00 – **394 rm** 340.00, 52 suites.

Connaught, Carlos Pl., W1Y 6AL, ℰ (0171) 499 7070, Fax (0171) 495 3262 – ⧏ ▤ ▥ ☎. ⓌⓄ ㏂ ⓪ 𝓥𝓘𝓢𝓐. ⌘
BM e
❀
The Restaurant : Meals *(booking essential)* 25.00/55.00 t. and a la carte 28.10/56.60 t. ▤ 12.00 – *Grill Room :* Meals *(closed Saturday lunch)* (booking essential) 25.00/35.00 t. and a la carte 25.10/56.60 t. ▤ 12.00 – **66 rm** 225.00/340.00 s., 24 suites
Spec. Sole "Jubilée". Prélude gourmande Connaught. Sherry trifle "Wally Ladd".

47 Park Street, 47 Park St., W1Y 4EB, ℰ (0171) 491 7282, Fax (0171) 491 7281 – ⧏ ▤ ▥ ☎. ⓌⓄ ㏂ ⓪ 𝓥𝓘𝓢𝓐 𝓙𝓒𝓑. ⌘
AM c
Meals *(room service)* – (see also *Le Gavroche* below) – ⇌ 19.00 – **52 suites** 255.00/500.00 s.

Brown's, Albemarle St., W1X 4BP, ℰ (0171) 493 6020, Fax (0171) 493 9381 – ⧏ ▥ ☎ – ⛤ 70. ⓌⓄ ㏂ ⓪ 𝓥𝓘𝓢𝓐 𝓙𝓒𝓑. ⌘
DM e
Meals *(closed lunch Saturday, Sunday and Bank Holidays)* 24.00/29.00 st. and a la carte ▤ 11.00 – ⇌ 17.50 – **112 rm** 240.00/268.00, 6 suites – SB.

Park Lane, Piccadilly, W1Y 8BX, ℰ (0171) 499 6321, Fax (0171) 499 1965 – ⧏, ⇖ rm, ▥ ☎ ℗ – ⛤ 300. ⓌⓄ ㏂ ⓪ 𝓥𝓘𝓢𝓐 𝓙𝓒𝓑
CP x
*Brasserie on the Park (*ℰ (0171) 290 7364) :* Meals 15.95 st. and a la carte ▤ 8.25 – (see also *Bracewells* below) – ⇌ 17.00 – **286 rm** 220.50/263.00 s., 20 suites.

Britannia, Grosvenor Sq., W1A 3AN, ℰ (0171) 629 9400, Fax (0171) 629 7736, ℔ – ⧏, ⇖ rm, ▤ ▥ ☎ – ⛤ 100. ⓌⓄ ㏂ ⓪ 𝓥𝓘𝓢𝓐 𝓙𝓒𝓑. ⌘
BM x
Adams : Meals *(closed Saturday and Sunday)* 26.00 t. and a la carte ▤ 13.50 – (see also *Shogun* below) – ⇌ 13.95 – **306 rm** 205.00/295.00 s., 12 suites.

May Fair Inter-Continental, Stratton St., W1A 2AN, ℰ (0171) 629 7777, Fax (0171) 629 1459, ℔, ⇌, ◱ – ⧏, ⇖ rm, ▤ ▥ ☎ & – ⛤ 290. ⓌⓄ ㏂ ⓪ 𝓥𝓘𝓢𝓐 𝓙𝓒𝓑. ⌘
DN z
*May Fair Café (*ℰ (0171) 915 2842) :* Meals a la carte 18.00/34.00 t. – (see also *Opus 70* below) – ⇌ 16.00 – **262 rm** 269.00/299.00 st., 12 suites.

Inter-Continental, 1 Hamilton Pl., Hyde Park Corner, W1V 0QY, ℰ (0171) 409 3131, Fax (0171) 493 3476, ℔, ⇌ – ⧏, ⇖ rm, ▤ ▥ ☎ & ⇐ – ⛤ 1000. ⓌⓄ ㏂ ⓪ 𝓥𝓘𝓢𝓐 𝓙𝓒𝓑. ⌘
BP c
Meals 22.00/26.00 t. and a la carte ▤ 9.75 – (see also *Le Soufflé* below) – ⇌ 18.30 – **410 rm** 265.00 s., 48 suites.

Athenaeum, 116 Piccadilly, W1V 0BJ, ℰ (0171) 499 3464, Fax (0171) 493 1860, ℔, ⇌ – ⧏, ⇖ rm, ▤ ▥ ☎ – ⛤ 55. ⓌⓄ ㏂ ⓪ 𝓥𝓘𝓢𝓐 𝓙𝓒𝓑. ⌘
CP x
Bulloch's at 116 : Meals *(closed lunch Saturday and Sunday)* a la carte 30.40/34.40 t. ▤ 9.50 – ⇌ 16.50 – **121 rm** 225.00/295.00 s., 35 suites.

The Metropolitan, Old Park Lane, W1Y 4LB, ℰ (0171) 447 1000, Fax (0171) 447 1100, ≤ « Contemporary interior design », ℔ – ⧏, ⇖ rm, ▤ ▥ ☎ ⇐. ⓌⓄ ㏂ ⓪ 𝓥𝓘𝓢𝓐 𝓙𝓒𝓑. ⌘
BP c
Meals *(residents and members only)* (light lunch)/dinner a la carte 19.50/28.00 t. – (see also *Nobu* below) – ⇌ 15.00 – **152 rm** 195.00/275.00 s., 3 suites.

Westbury, Bond St., W1A 4UH, ℰ (0171) 629 7755, Fax (0171) 495 1163 – ⧏, ⇖ rm, ▤ ▥ ☎ – ⛤ 110. ⓌⓄ ㏂ ⓪ 𝓥𝓘𝓢𝓐
DM a
La Mediterranée (closed Saturday and Sunday lunch) a la carte approx. 28.50 t. ▤ 15.50 – ⇌ 14.75 – **231 rm** 180.00/230.00 s., 13 suites.

London Marriott Grosvenor Square, Duke St., Grosvenor Sq., W1A 4AW, ℰ (0171) 493 1232, Fax (0171) 491 3201, ℔ – ⧏, ⇖ rm, ▤ ▥ ☎ – ⛤ 600. ⓌⓄ ㏂ ⓪ 𝓥𝓘𝓢, 𝓙𝓒𝓑. ⌘
BL z
Diplomat : Meals *(closed Saturday lunch)* 19.50 t. (lunch) and a la carte 17.75/27.75 t. ▤ 12.75 – ⇌ 12.95 – **210 rm** 235.00 s., 11 suites – SB.

Chesterfield, 35 Charles St., W1X 8LX, ℰ (0171) 491 2622, Fax (0171) 491 4793 – ⧏ ⇖ rm, ▤ rest, ▥ ☎ – ⛤ 110. ⓌⓄ ㏂ ⓪ 𝓥𝓘𝓢𝓐. ⌘
CN x
Butlers : Meals *(closed Saturday lunch)* 8.95/15.95 st. and a la carte ▤ 11.00 – ⇌ 16.00 – **106 rm** 145.00/210.00 s., 4 suites.

Washington, 5-7 Curzon St., W1Y 8DT, ℰ (0171) 499 7000, Fax (0171) 495 6172 – ⧏ ⇖ rm, ▤ ▥ ☎ – ⛤ 80. ⓌⓄ ㏂ ⓪ 𝓥𝓘𝓢𝓐 𝓙𝓒𝓑
CN x
Meals a la carte 14.00/20.00 st. – ⇌ 13.95 – **169 rm** 160.00/205.00 s., 4 suites – SB.

Holiday Inn Mayfair, 3 Berkeley St., W1X 6NE, ℰ (0171) 493 8282, Fax (0171) 629 2827
– |‡|, ⇔ rm, ▤ ▥ ☎ – 🔬 60. ◉◎ ஊ ① VISA JCB. ℅ DN r
Meals (closed Saturday lunch) 22.00 **t.** and a la carte 🍴 8.00 – ⇄ 12.95 – **181 rm** 160.00/210.00.

Flemings, 7-12 Half Moon St., W1Y 7RA, ℰ (0171) 499 2964, Fax (0171) 629 4063 – |‡|,
▤ rest, ▥ ☎ – 🔬 50. ◉◎ ஊ ① VISA JCB. ℅ CN z
Meals 9.95/23.50 **st.** and a la carte 🍴 9.00 – ⇄ 11.50 – **120 rm** 130.00/175.00, 10 suites.

Green Park, Half Moon St., W1Y 8BP, ℰ (0171) 629 7522, Fax (0171) 491 8971 – |‡|,
⇔ rm, ▤ rest, ▥ ☎ – 🔬 70. ◉◎ ஊ ① VISA JCB. ℅ CN a
Meals (closed lunch Saturday, Sunday and Bank Holidays) a la carte 17.95/31.20 **st.** 🍴 6.75 –
⇄ 10.95 – **160 rm** 135.00/182.00 **st.**, 1 suite.

London Mews Hilton, 2 Stanhope Row, W1Y 7HE, ℰ (0171) 493 7222,
Fax (0171) 629 9423 – |‡|, ⇔ rm, ▤ ▥ ☎ ⇌ – 🔬 50. ◉◎ ஊ ① VISA JCB. ℅ BP u
Meals (dinner only) 19.00 **st.** and a la carte 🍴 9.45 – ⇄ 15.00 – **71 rm** 180.00/216.00 **st.**,
1 suite – SB.

The Oak Room Marco Pierre White (at Le Meridien Piccadilly H.), 21 Piccadilly,
W1V 0BH, ℰ (0171) 437 0202 – ▤. ◉◎ ஊ ① VISA JCB EM a
closed Saturday lunch, Sunday, last 2 weeks August and 2 weeks Christmas-New Year –
Meals (booking essential) 29.50/75.00 **t.** 🍴 15.00
Spec. Foie gras en surprise. Contre-filet "Molly Parkin". Caramelised pineapple with vanilla.

Chez Nico at Ninety Park Lane (Ladenis) (at Grosvenor House H.), Park Lane,
W1A 3AA, ℰ (0171) 409 1290, Fax (0171) 355 4877 – ▤. ◉◎ ஊ ① VISA AM e
closed Saturday lunch, Sunday, 4 days at Easter, 10 days at Christmas and Bank Holiday
Mondays – **Meals** - French - (booking essential) 32.00/62.00 **t.**
Spec. Langoustine ravioli with lobster sauce. Escalope of sea bass with a basil coulis. Glazed
lemon tart with raspberry coulis.

Le Gavroche (Roux), 43 Upper Brook St., W1Y 1PF, ℰ (0171) 408 0881,
Fax (0171) 409 0939 – ▤. ◉◎ ஊ ① VISA JCB AM c
closed Saturday, Sunday, Christmas-New Year and Bank Holidays – **Meals** - French -
(booking essential) 40.00 **st.** (lunch) and a la carte 60.00/94.20 **st.** 🍴 15.00
Spec. Terrine de foie gras et confit de canard aux fruits secs et épices. Gibiers suivant
la chasse. Bar en papillote farci au fenouil.

Oriental (at Dorchester H.), Park Lane, W1A 2HJ, ℰ (0171) 317 6328, Fax (0171) 409 0114 –
▤. ◉◎ ஊ ① VISA JCB BN a
closed Saturday lunch, Sunday and August – **Meals** - Chinese (Canton) - 25.50/37.00
st. and a la carte 30.00/63.50 **st.** 🍴 14.00
Spec. Fried prawns with cashew nuts in a lemon sauce. Stir fried beef with lemon grass and
black pepper. Deep fried mixed seafood wrapped in rice paper with mango.

Four Seasons (at Four Seasons H.), Hamilton Pl., Park Lane, W1A 1AZ, ℰ (0171) 499 0888,
Fax (0171) 493 1895 – |‡| ▤ ⇌. ◉◎ ஊ ① VISA JCB BP a
Meals a la carte 26.00/48.00 **st.** 🍴 19.00.

Windows (at London Hilton on Park Lane), 22 Park Lane, W1Y 4BE, ℰ (0171) 208 4020,
« Panoramic ≤ of London » – ▤. ◉◎ ஊ ① VISA JCB BP e
closed Saturday lunch and Sunday dinner – **Meals** 33.95/33.50 **t.** and dinner a la carte
🍴 13.00.

Les Saveurs de Jean-Christophe Novelli W1, 37a Curzon St., W1Y 7AF,
ℰ (0171) 491 8919, Fax (0171) 491 3658 – ▤. ◉◎ ஊ VISA JCB BN o
closed Saturday lunch and Sunday – **Meals** - French - 28.00/35.00 **t.** and a la carte 22.00/46.50 **t.** 🍴 14.00.
Spec. Cured trout tartare with croque of cucumber, soft quail egg and caviar. Roast sea
bass with sun dried tomatoes, pickled aubergine and picholine olives. Hot and cold, dark
and white chocolate plate "Liz Mc Grath".

The Square, 6-10 Bruton St., W1X 7AG, ℰ (0171) 495 7100, Fax (0171) 495 7150 – ▤. ◉◎
ஊ ① VISA CM v
closed lunch Saturday and Sunday and 1 week Christmas – **Meals** 45.00 **t.** (dinner)
and lunch a la carte 29.50/35.50 **t.** 🍴 11.50
Spec. Steamed cod with leeks, oysters and caviar. Cappuccino of shellfish with cannelloni
of lobster. Saddle of lamb with a herb crust, purée of shallots and rosemary.

Grill Room (at Dorchester H.), Park Lane, W1A 2HJ, ℰ (0171) 317 6336,
Fax (0171) 409 0114 – ▤. ◉◎ ஊ ① VISA JCB BN a
Meals - English - 28.00/37.00 **st.** and a la carte 34.00/56.00 **st.** 🍴 14.00.

Goode's at Thomas Goode, 19 South Audley St., W1Y 6BN, ℰ (0171) 409 7242,
Fax (0171) 629 4230 – ▤. ◉◎ ஊ ① VISA BM c
closed Saturday, Sunday, first 3 weeks August, 1 week Christmas and Bank Holidays – **Meals**
(lunch only) 37.50 **t.** 🍴 15.20.

Le Soufflé (at Inter-Continental H.), 1 Hamilton Pl., Hyde Park Corner, W1V 0QY,
ℰ (0171) 409 3131, Fax (0171) 409 7460 – ▤ ⇌. ◉◎ ஊ ① VISA JCB BP o
closed Saturday lunch, Sunday dinner, Monday, 3 weeks January and Bank Holidays –
Meals 29.50/45.00 **t.** and a la carte 🍴 10.00.

411

XXXX **Bracewells** (at Park Lane H.), Piccadilly, W1Y 8BX, ℘ (0171) 753 6725, *Fax (0171) 499 1965*
– **ℙ**. **M◎ AE ◎ VISA JCB**
CP x
closed Saturday lunch, Sunday, August and Bank Holidays – **Meals** 26.50 **t.**
(lunch) and a la carte 33.95/43.95 **t.** ₰ 9.00.

XXXX **Princess Garden,** 8-10 North Audley St., W1Y 1WF, ℘ (0171) 493 3223,
Fax (0171) 629 3130 – ▤. **M◎ AE ◎ VISA JCB**
AL z
closed 4 days Christmas – **Meals** - Chinese (Peking, Szechuan) - 30.00 **t.** (dinner)
and a la carte 29.00/45.00 **t.** ₰ 9.50.

XXXX **Opus 70** (at May Fair Inter-Continental H.), Stratton St., W1A 2AN, ℘ (0171) 915 2842,
Fax (0171) 629 1459 – ▤. **M◎ AE ◎ VISA JCB**
DN z
closed Saturday lunch – **Meals** a la carte 20.00/40.50 **t.**

XXXX **Scotts,** 20 Mount St., W1Y 6HE, ℘ (0171) 629 5248, *Fax (0171) 499 8246* – ▤. **M◎ AE ◎**
VISA JCB
BM a
Meals - Seafood - a la carte 21.70/41.00 **t.** ₰ 7.00.

XX **Nobu** (at The Metropolitan H.), 19 Old Park Lane, W1Y 4LB, ℘ (0171) 447 4747,
✤ *Fax (0171) 447 4749,* ≤ – ▤. **M◎ AE ◎ VISA JCB**
BP c
closed lunch Saturday and Sunday – **Meals** - New style Japanese with South American
influences - 40.00/50.00 **t.** and a la carte 60.00/100.00 **t.** ₰ 8.50
Spec. Lobster ceviche. Black cod with miso. Snow crab with spicy cream sauce.

XX **L'Odéon,** 65 Regent St., W1R 7HH, ℘ (0171) 287 1400, *Fax (0171) 287 1300* – ▤. **M◎ AE ◎**
VISA JCB
EM r
closed Saturday lunch, 25-26 December, 1 January and Bank Holidays – **Meals** 17.50 **t.**
and a la carte ₰ 8.90.

XX **Tamarind,** 20 Queen St., W1X 7PJ, ℘ (0171) 629 3561, *Fax (0171) 499 5034* – **M◎ AE ◎**
VISA
CN e
closed Saturday lunch, 25 December and 1 January – **Meals** - Indian - 16.50 **t.**
(lunch) and a la carte 27.00/38.50 **t.** ₰ 6.75.

XX **Greenhouse,** 27a Hay's Mews, W1X 7RJ, ℘ (0171) 499 3331, *Fax (0171) 499 5368* – ▤. **M◎**
AE ◎ VISA
BN e
closed Saturday lunch and 25 December – **Meals** a la carte 30.40/35.00 **t.** ₰ 6.00.

XX **Bentley's,** 11-15 Swallow St., W1R 7HD, ℘ (0171) 734 4756, *Fax (0171) 287 2972* – ▤. **M◎**
AE ◎ VISA JCB
EM
closed Sunday, 25-26 December and 1 January – **Meals** - Seafood - a la carte 25.50/40.25 **t.**
₰ 11.00.

XX **Nicole's,** 158 New Bond St., W1V 9PA, ℘ (0171) 499 8408, *Fax (0171) 409 0381* – ▤. **M◎ AE**
◎ VISA JCB
DM n
closed Saturday dinner, Sunday and Bank Holidays – **Meals** a la carte 25.50/28.50 **t.**

XX Langan's Brasserie, Stratton St., W1X 5FD, ℘ (0171) 491 8822 – ▤

XX **Marquis,** 121A Mount St., W1Y 5HB, ℘ (0171) 499 1256, *Fax (0171) 493 4460* – **M◎ AE ◎**
VISA JCB
BM u
*closed Saturday lunch, Sunday, 21 August-1 September, 23 December-4 January and Bank
Holidays* – **Meals** 19.50 **t.** and a la carte ₰ 6.10.

XX **Chor Bizarre,** 16 Albemarle St., W1X 3HA, ℘ (0171) 629 9802, *Fax (0171) 493 7756*
« Authentic Indian decor and furnishings » – **M◎ AE ◎ VISA JCB**
DM s
closed Sunday, 24 to 26 December and 1 January – **Meals** - Indian - 12.95/31.00 **t**
and a la carte.

XX **Benihana,** 37 Sackville St., Piccadilly, W1X 2DQ, ℘ (0171) 494 2525, *Fax (0171) 494 1456* –
▤. **M◎ AE ◎ VISA JCB**
EM s
Meals - Japanese (Teppan-Yaki) - 10.00/14.00 **st.** and a la carte.

XX **Mulligans,** 13-14 Cork St., W1X 1PF, ℘ (0171) 409 1370, *Fax (0171) 409 2732* – **M◎ AE ◎**
VISA
DM c
closed Sunday, 1 week Christmas-New Year and Bank Holidays – **Meals** - Irish -
a la carte 19.95/28.85 **t.**

XX **Shogun** (at Britannia H.), Adams Row, W1Y 5DE, ℘ (0171) 493 1255 – ▤. **M◎ AE ◎ VISA**
JCB
BM x
closed Monday – **Meals** - Japanese - (dinner only) a la carte 22.00/36.00 **st.**

X **The Cafe** (at Sotheby's), 34-35 New Bond St., W1A 2AA, ℘ (0171) 408 5077 ✤. **M◎ AE ◎**
VISA
DL
closed Saturday, Sunday, Good Friday, 2 weeks August and Christmas-New Year – **Meal**
(booking essential) (lunch only) a la carte 18.00/24.50 **st.**

X **Momo,** 25 Heddon St., W1R 7LG, ℘ (0171) 434 4040, *Fax (0171) 287 0404* – ▤. **M◎ AE ◎**
VISA
EM
Meals - Moroccan - 13.50 **t.** (lunch) and a la carte approx. 22.00 **t.** ₰ 6.00.

X **Veeraswamy**, Victory House, 101 Regent St., W1R 8RS, ☎ (0171) 734 1401, Fax (0171) 439 8434 – 🖿. 🐼 🖭 ① *VISA* JCB.
EM c
closed 25 and 26 December – **Meals** - Indian - 13.00 **t.** (lunch) and a la carte 16.50/20.00 **t.** ⓐ 5.00.

X **Zinc Bar and Grill**, 20 Heddon St., W1R 7LF, ☎ (0171) 255 8899, Fax (0171) 255 8888 – 🖿 🐼 🖭 ① *VISA*
EM x
closed 25 and 26 December – **Meals** (Sunday dinner by arrangement) 12.50 **t.** (lunch) and dinner a la carte 13.95/29.25 **t.**

Regent's Park and Marylebone – ⊠ NW1/NW6/NW8/W1 – Except where otherwise stated see pp. 28 and 29.
🖪 Basement Services Arcade, Selfridges Store, Oxford St., W1 ☎ (0171) 824 8844.

🏨🏨🏨 **Landmark London**, 222 Marylebone Rd, NW1 6JQ, ☎ (0171) 631 8000, Fax (0171) 631 8080, « Victorian Gothic architecture, atrium and winter garden », ↻, ⇆, 🔄 – 🖩, ⇆ rm, 🖿 🔟 ☎ 🕹 ⇔ – 🔬 350. 🐼 🖭 ① *VISA* JCB. ⋊ p. 21 HU a
The Dining Room : Meals (closed Saturday lunch and Sunday dinner) 24.00/ 34.00 **st.** and a la carte ⓐ 8.50 – ⊑ 18.00 – **288 rm** 245.00/310.00 **s.**, 9 suites.

🏨🏨🏨 **Churchill Inter-Continental**, 30 Portman Sq., W1A 4ZX, ☎ (0171) 486 5800, Fax (0171) 486 1255, ⇆ – 🖩, ⇆ rm, 🖿 🔟 ☎ 🕹 – 🔬 200. 🐼 🖭 ① *VISA* JCB. ⋊ AJ x
Clementine's : Meals (closed Saturday lunch) 23.00 **t.** and a la carte 8.00 – ⊑ 16.50 – **415 rm** 280.00, 33 suites.

🏨🏨🏨 **Langham Hilton**, 1 Portland Pl., Regent St., W1N 4JA, ☎ (0171) 636 1000, Fax (0171) 323 2340, ↻, ⇆ – 🖩, ⇆ rm, 🖿 🔟 🕹 – 🔬 250. 🐼 🖭 ① *VISA* JCB. ⋊ p. 21 JU e
Memories : Meals 24.50/31.00 **st.** and dinner a la carte ⓐ 16.00 – **Tsar's** : Meals (closed Sunday) a la carte 20.80/34.80 **st.** ⓐ 16.00 – ⊑ 17.50 – **359 rm** 250.00 **s.**, 20 suites.

🏨🏨🏨 **Selfridge**, Orchard St., W1H 0JS, ☎ (0171) 408 2080, Fax (0171) 629 8849 – 🖩, ⇆ rm, 🖿 🔟 ☎ – 🔬 220. 🐼 🖭 ① *VISA* JCB. ⋊ AK e
Fletchers : Meals (closed Saturday lunch, Sunday, 3 weeks August and Bank Holidays) 20.00 **t.** and a la carte ⓐ 14.00 – **Orchard** : Meals 10.95 **t.** and a la carte ⓐ 11.50 – ⊑ 12.50 – **290 rm** 175.00/225.00 **st.**, 4 suites – SB.

🏨🏨 **The Leonard**, 15 Seymour St., W1H 5AA, ☎ (0171) 935 2010, Fax (0171) 935 6700, « Attractively furnished Georgian town houses » – 🖩 🖿 🔟 ☎ – 🔬 30. 🐼 🖭 ① *VISA*. ⋊ AK n
Meals (room service only) – ⊑ 13.50 – **6 rm** 160.00/180.00 **s.**, **20 suites** 225.00/375.00 **s.**

🏨🏨 **Radisson SAS Portman**, 22 Portman Sq., W1H 9FL, ☎ (0171) 208 6000, Fax (0171) 208 6001, ↻, ⇆, ⋊ – 🖩, ⇆ rm, 🖿 rest, 🔟 ☎ – 🔬 350. 🐼 🖭 ① *VISA* JCB. ⋊ AJ o
Meals 16.50 **st.** (lunch) and a la carte 22.95/36.00 **st.** ⓐ 10.00 – ⊑ 15.50 – **272 rm** 195.00/ 288.00 **st.**, 7 suites.

🏨🏨 **London Regent's Park Hilton**, 18 Lodge Rd, NW8 7JT, ☎ (0171) 722 7722, Fax (0171) 483 2408 – 🖩, ⇆ rm, 🖿 🔟 ☎ 🕹 – 🔬 150. 🐼 🖭 ① *VISA* JCB. ⋊
Minsky's : Meals 19.50/20.95 **st.** and a la carte ⓐ 10.50 – **Kashinoki** : Meals - Japanese - (closed Monday) 18.50/32.50 **t.** and a la carte ⓐ 16.00 – ⊑ 15.50 – **376 rm** 155.00/ 175.00 **st.**, 1 suite. p. 21 GT v

🏨🏨 **Montcalm**, Great Cumberland Pl., W1A 2LF, ☎ (0171) 402 4288, Fax (0171) 724 9180 – 🖩, ⇆ rm, 🖿 🔟 ☎ – 🔬 80. 🐼 🖭 ① *VISA* JCB. p. 33 EZ x
Meals - (see **The Crescent** below) – ⊑ 15.95 – **110 rm** 175.00/230.00 **s.**, 10 suites.

🏨🏨 **Clifton Ford**, 47 Welbeck St., W1M 8DN, ☎ (0171) 486 6600, Fax (0171) 486 7492 – 🖩 🖿 🔟 ☎ 🕹 ⇔ – 🔬 150. 🐼 🖭 ① *VISA*
BH a
Meals (closed lunch Saturday and Sunday) a la carte approx. 22.00 **t.** ⓐ 6.50 – ⊑ 14.50 – **183 rm** 210.00/225.00 **s.**, 2 suites.

🏨🏨 **Berners**, 10 Berners St., W1A 3BE, ☎ (0171) 666 2000, Fax (0171) 666 2001 – 🖩, ⇆ rm, 🖿 rest, 🔟 ☎ 🕹 – 🔬 150. 🐼 🖭 ① *VISA* JCB. ⋊ EJ r
Meals 16.95 **t.** (lunch) and a la carte 20.65/33.70 **st.** ⓐ 7.50 – ⊑ 14.95 – **214 rm** 150.00/ 185.00 **st.**, 3 suites.

🏨🏨 **Marble Arch Marriott**, 134 George St., W1H 6DN, ☎ (0171) 723 1277, Fax (0171) 402 0666, ↻, ⇆, 🔄 – 🖩, ⇆ rm, 🖿 🔟 ☎ 🕹 🕹 – 🔬 150. 🐼 🖭 ① *VISA* JCB. ⋊ p. 33 EZ i
Meals 16.00/20.00 **st.** and a la carte ⓐ 6.50 – ⊑ 12.95 – **240 rm** 190.00/210.00 **s.** – SB.

🏨🏨 **Berkshire**, 350 Oxford St., W1N 0BY, ☎ (0171) 629 7474, Fax (0171) 629 8156 – 🖩, ⇆ rm, 🖿 🔟 ☎ – 🔬 40. 🐼 🖭 ① *VISA* JCB. ⋊ BK n
Meals 19.00 **st.** and a la carte ⓐ 7.50 – ⊑ 14.00 – **145 rm** 187.00/226.00 **s.**, 2 suites.

🏨🏨 **Forte Posthouse Regent's Park**, Carburton St., W1P 8EE, ☎ (0171) 388 2300, Fax (0171) 387 2806 – 🖩, ⇆ rm, 🖿 rest, 🔟 ☎ 🕹 – 🔬 320. 🐼 🖭 ① *VISA* JCB. ⋊
Meals (closed lunch Saturday and Sunday) 16.95 **st.** (dinner) and a la carte 18.80/28.75 **st.** ⓐ 6.95 – ⊑ 10.95 – **322 rm** 129.00/149.00 **st.**, 3 suites – SB. p. 21 JU i

Saint Georges, Langham Pl., W1N 8QS, ℘ (0171) 580 0111, *Fax (0171) 436 7997*, ≤ – |聲|, ⛛ rm, 🔟 ☎ – 🔏 25. 🐠 🖭 ⑩ 💳 🗂. ✻
p. 21 JU a
Meals a la carte 19.00/26.50 st. 🍴 7.00 – ☲ 12.95 – **83 rm** 145.00/155.00 st., 3 suites – SB.

Dorset Square, 39-40 Dorset Sq., NW1 6QN, ℘ (0171) 723 7874, *Fax (0171) 724 3328*, « Attractively furnished Regency town houses », ☞ – |聲| 🔟 ☎. 🐠 🖭 💳. ✻
The Potting Shed : Meals *(closed Sunday lunch and Saturday)* 14.95 t. and a la carte – ☲ 12.50 – **37 rm** 98.00/180.00 s.
p. 21 HU s

Durrants, 26-32 George St., W1H 6BJ, ℘ (0171) 935 8131, *Fax (0171) 487 3510*, « Converted Georgian houses with Regency façade » – |聲|, ≡ rest, 🔟 ☎ – 🔏 100. 🐠 🖭 💳. ✻
AH e
Meals 19.50 t. and a la carte 🍴 8.00 – ☲ 10.75 – **89 rm** 95.00/140.00 st., 3 suites.

Rathbone without rest., Rathbone St., W1P 2LB, ℘ (0171) 636 2001, *Fax (0171) 636 3882* – |聲| ⛛ ≡ 🔟 ☎
p. 22 KU x
72 rm.

Savoy Court, Granville Pl., W1H 0EH, ℘ (0171) 408 0130, *Fax (0171) 493 2070* – |聲|, ≡ rest, 🔟 ☎. 🐠 🖭 ⑩ 💳 🗂. ✻
AK i
Meals 12.00 st. (dinner) and a la carte 14.50/20.50 st. 🍴 6.50 – ☲ 11.00 – **95 rm** 111.00/145.00 s.

Langham Court, 31-35 Langham St., W1N 5RE, ℘ (0171) 436 6622, *Fax (0171) 436 2303* – |聲| 🔟 ☎ – 🔏 80. 🐠 🖭 ⑩ 💳 🗂. ✻
p. 21 JU z
Meals 19.75 st. and a la carte – ☲ 11.50 – **56 rm** 129.00/145.00 st. – SB.

Stakis London Harewood, Harewood Row, NW1 6SE, ℘ (0171) 262 2707, *Fax (0171) 262 2975* – |聲|, ⛛ rm, ≡ rest, 🔟 ☎. 🐠 🖭 ⑩ 💳. ✻
p. 21 HU x
Meals (dinner only) 15.00 st. and a la carte 🍴 7.50 – ☲ 10.50 – **92 rm** 98.00/135.00 st. – SB

Hart House without rest., 51 Gloucester Pl., W1H 3PE, ℘ (0171) 935 2288, *Fax (0171) 935 8516* – 🔟 ☎. 🐠 🖭 💳. ✻
AH a
16 rm ☲ 60.00/85.00 st.

Orrery, 55 Marylebone High St., W1M 3AE, ℘ (0171) 616 8000, *Fax (0171) 616 8080*, « Converted 19C stables, contemporary interior » – |聲| ≡. 🐠 🖭 ⑩ 💳
IU a
closed 25 December and 1 January – Meals (booking essential) 23.50 t. (lunch) and dinner a la carte 26.00/41.50 t. 🍴 13.00.

Interlude, 5 Charlotte St., W1P 1HD, ℘ (0171) 637 0222, *Fax (0171) 637 0224* – ≡. 🐠 🖭 ⑩ 💳 🗂.
p. 22 KU r
closed Saturday lunch, Sunday, 2 weeks August, 1 week Christmas-New Year and Bank Holidays – Meals 22.50 t. (lunch) and a la carte 25.00/47.00 t.

The Crescent (at Montcalm H.), Great Cumberland Pl., W1A 2LF, ℘ (0171) 402 4288, *Fax (0171) 724 9180* – ≡. 🐠 🖭 ⑩ 💳 🗂.
EZ x
closed Saturday lunch and Sunday – Meals 18.00 t.

Nico Central, 35 Great Portland St., W1N 5DD, ℘ (0171) 436 8846, *Fax (0171) 436 3455* – ≡. 🐠 🖭 ⑩ 💳.
DJ r
closed Saturday lunch, Sunday and 23 December-1 January – Meals 25.00/27.00 st. 🍴 8.00.

Oceana, Jason Court, 76 Wigmore St., W1H 9DQ, ℘ (0171) 224 2992, *Fax (0171) 486 1211* – ≡. 🐠 🖭 ⑩ 💳 🗂.
BJ r
closed Saturday, Sunday and Bank Holidays – Meals a la carte 15.50/26.50 t. 🍴 8.00.

La Porte des Indes, 32 Bryanston St., W1H 7AE, ℘ (0171) 224 0055, *Fax (0171) 224 1144* – ≡. 🐠 🖭 ⑩ 💳
AK r
closed Saturday lunch and 25-26 December – Meals - Indian - 20.00/31.00 t. and a la carte 🍴 4.75.

Caldesi, 15-17 Marylebone Lane, W1M 5FE, ℘ (0171) 935 9226, *Fax (0171) 929 0924* – ≡ 🐠 🖭 ⑩ 💳 🗂.
BJ r
closed Saturday lunch, Sunday and Bank Holidays – Meals - Italian - 15.00 t. and a la carte 🍴 7.00.

Bertorelli's, 19-23 Charlotte St., W1P 1HP, ℘ (0171) 636 4174, *Fax (0171) 467 8902* ≡
p. 22 KU r
Meals Italian rest.

Stephen Bull, 5-7 Blandford St., W1H 3AA, ℘ (0171) 486 9696, *Fax (0171) 490 3128* – ≡ 🐠 🖭 💳
BH r
closed Saturday lunch, Sunday, 24 December-2 January and Bank Holidays – Meals a la carte 22.75/32.00 t. 🍴 10.50.

Asuka, Berkeley Arcade, 209a Baker St., NW1 6AB, ℘ (0171) 486 5026, *Fax (0171) 224 1741* – ≡. 🐠 🖭 💳 🗂.
p. 21 HU r
closed Saturday lunch, Sunday and Bank Holidays – Meals - Japanese - 13.50/23.90 t. and a la carte 🍴 9.70.

Gaylord, 79-81 Mortimer St., W1N 7TB, ℘ (0171) 580 3615, *Fax (0171) 636 0860* – ≡. 🐠 🖭 ⑩ 💳
p. 22 KU r
Meals - Indian - 16.95 t. and a la carte.

✗ **Justin de Blank,** 120-122 Marylebone Lane, W1M 5FZ, ℰ (0171) 486 5250, *Fax (0171) 935 4046* – ⚏ ⚍ 𝗩𝗜𝗦𝗔
BH u
closed Saturday, Sunday, Christmas, New Year and Bank Holidays – **Meals** a la carte 14.45/19.95 **t.**

✗ **The Blenheim,** 21 Loudoun Rd, NW8 0NB, ℰ (0171) 625 1222, *Fax (0171) 328 1593*, 🌣 –
⚏ ⚍ ⓞ 𝗩𝗜𝗦𝗔
p. 20 FS a
closed 24-25 December and 1 January – **Meals** a la carte 18.15/21.15 **t.**

✗ **L'Aventure,** 3 Blenheim Terr., NW8 0EH, ℰ (0171) 624 6232, *Fax (0171) 625 5548* – ⚏ ⚍
𝗩𝗜𝗦𝗔
p. 20 FS s
closed Saturday lunch, 4 days Easter and first 2 weeks January – **Meals** - French - 18.50/26.50 **t.** ⓘ 7.50.

✗ **Union Café,** 96 Marylebone Lane, W1M 5FP, ℰ (0171) 486 4860 – ⚏ 𝗩𝗜𝗦𝗔 𝗝𝗖𝗕
BH c
closed Sunday, Christmas-New Year and Bank Holidays – **Meals** a la carte 17.00/24.00 **t.**

✗ **Zoe,** 3-5 Barrett St., St. Christopher's Pl., W1M 5HH, ℰ (0171) 224 1122, *Fax (0171) 935 5444* – ▤. ⚏ ⚍ ⓞ 𝗩𝗜𝗦𝗔
BJ a
closed Sunday and Bank Holidays – **Meals** 12.50 **t.** and a la carte.

✗ **Le Muscadet,** 25 Paddington St., W1M 3RF, ℰ (0171) 935 2883, *Fax (0171) 935 2883* – ▤.
⚏ 𝗩𝗜𝗦𝗔 𝗝𝗖𝗕
p. 21 HU v
closed Saturday lunch, Sunday, Easter, last 3 weeks August and 25-31 December – **Meals** - French - 19.50 **t.** and a la carte ⓘ 10.00.

St. James's – ✉ W1/SW1/WC2 – pp. 28 and 29.

🏨🏨🏨 **Ritz,** 150 Piccadilly, W1V 9DG, ℰ (0171) 493 8181, *Fax (0171) 493 2687*, 🌣 – |❚|, ⧖ rm, ▤
▦ ☎ – 🔏 50. ⚏ ⚍ ⓞ 𝗩𝗜𝗦𝗔 𝗝𝗖𝗕. ⬥
DN a
Italian Garden : **Meals** (summer only) 29.00/38.50 **st.** and a la carte – (see also *The Restaurant* below) – ⧖ 19.50 – **116 rm** 225.00/325.00 **s.,** 14 suites – SB.

🏨🏨 **Dukes** ⧖, 35 St. James's Pl., SW1A 1NY, ℰ (0171) 491 4840, *Fax (0171) 493 1264* – |❚| ▤
▦ ☎ – 🔏 50. ⚏ ⚍ ⓞ 𝗩𝗜𝗦𝗔 𝗝𝗖𝗕. ⬥
EP x
Meals *(closed Saturday lunch)* (residents only) a la carte 24.45/33.95 ⓘ 7.00 – ⧖ 14.00 – **73 rm** 165.00/215.00 **s.,** 8 suites.

🏨🏨 **Stafford** ⧖, 16-18 St. James's Pl., SW1A 1NJ, ℰ (0171) 493 0111, *Fax (0171) 493 7121* –
|❚| ▤ ▦ ☎ – 🔏 35. ⚏ ⚍ ⓞ 𝗩𝗜𝗦𝗔 𝗝𝗖𝗕. ⬥
DN u
Meals *(closed Saturday lunch)* 23.50/26.25 **st.** and a la carte ⓘ 8.50 – ⧖ 15.50 – **75 rm** 190.00/245.00, 5 suites.

🏨🏨 **22 Jermyn Street,** 22 Jermyn St., SW1Y 6HL, ℰ (0171) 734 2353, *Fax (0171) 734 0750* –
|❚| ▦ ☎. ⚏ ⚍ ⓞ 𝗩𝗜𝗦𝗔 𝗝𝗖𝗕. ⬥
FM e
Meals (room service only) – ⧖ 16.50 – **5 rm** 195.00 **s.,** **13 suites** 250.00/285.00 **s.**

🏨🏨 **Cavendish,** 81 Jermyn St., SW1Y 6JF, ℰ (0171) 930 2111, *Fax (0171) 839 2125* – |❚|,
⧖ rm, ▤ rest, ▦ ☎ ⇔ – 🔏 80. ⚏ ⚍ ⓞ 𝗩𝗜𝗦𝗔 𝗝𝗖𝗕. ⬥
EN i
Meals *(closed Saturday lunch)* 19.50 **st.** (lunch) and dinner a la carte approx. 24.50 **st.** ⓘ 8.95 – ⧖ 13.50 – **253 rm** 150.00/170.00 **s.,** 2 suites – SB.

🏨 **Pastoria,** 3-6 St. Martin's St., off Leicester Sq., WC2H 7HL, ℰ (0171) 930 8641, *Fax (0171) 925 0551* – |❚|, ⧖ rm, ▤ rest, ▦ ☎ – 🔏 60. ⚏ ⚍ ⓞ 𝗩𝗜𝗦𝗔. ⬥
GM v
Meals a la carte 16.00/23.00 **st.** ⓘ 7.50 – ⧖ 11.00 – **58 rm** 140.00/191.00 **s.**

🏨 **Royal Trafalgar Thistle,** Whitcomb St., WC2H 7HG, ℰ (0171) 930 4477, *Fax (0171) 925 2149* – |❚|, ⧖ rm, ▤ rest, ▦ ☎. ⚏ ⚍ ⓞ 𝗩𝗜𝗦𝗔 𝗝𝗖𝗕. ⬥
GM r
Meals 13.50/17.50 **st.** and a la carte ⓘ 5.75 – ⧖ 13.50 – **108 rm** 127.00/165.00 **st.** – SB.

🏨 **Hospitality Inn Piccadilly** without rest., 39 Coventry St., W1V 8EL, ℰ (0171) 930 4033, *Fax (0171) 925 2586* – |❚| ⧖ ▦ ☎. ⚏ ⚍ ⓞ 𝗩𝗜𝗦𝗔 𝗝𝗖𝗕. ⬥
FGM a
⧖ 12.50 – **91 rm** 137.00/170.00 **st.**

✗✗✗✗✗ **The Restaurant** (at Ritz H.), 150 Piccadilly, W1V 9DG, ℰ (0171) 493 8181, *Fax (0171) 493 2687*, 🌣, « Elegant restaurant in Louis XVI style » – ▤. ⚏ ⚍ ⓞ 𝗩𝗜𝗦𝗔
𝗝𝗖𝗕
DN a
Meals (dancing Friday and Saturday evenings) 29.00/38.50 **st.** and a la carte 42.50/93.50 **st.**

✗✗✗ **Quaglino's,** 16 Bury St., SW1Y 6AL, ℰ (0171) 930 6767, *Fax (0171) 839 2866* – ▤. ⚏ ⚍
ⓞ 𝗩𝗜𝗦𝗔
EN r
Meals (booking essential) 14.50 (lunch) and a la carte 19.50/50.50 ⓘ 10.50.

✗✗✗ **Suntory,** 72-73 St. James's St., SW1A 1PH, ℰ (0171) 409 0201, *Fax (0171) 499 0208* – ▤.
⚏ ⚍ ⓞ 𝗩𝗜𝗦𝗔 𝗝𝗖𝗕
EP z
closed Sunday, Easter, 25-26 December, 1 January and Bank Holidays – **Meals** - Japanese - 15.00/49.80 **st.** and a la carte ⓘ 12.00.

✗✗✗ **33,** 33 St. James's St., SW1A 1HD, ℰ (0171) 930 4272, *Fax (0171) 930 7618* – ▤. ⚏ ⚍ ⓞ
𝗩𝗜𝗦𝗔
EN n
closed Saturday lunch, Sunday, Christmas and Bank Holidays – **Meals** a la carte 22.90/43.95 **st.** ⓘ 16.00.

XX **L'Oranger,** 5 St. James's St., SW1A 1EF, ☏ (0171) 839 3774, Fax (0171) 839 4330, 斎 – ▤.
🔅 **⓪ AE ⓪ VISA JCB**
EP a
closed Sunday lunch and 1 week Christmas – **Meals** 22.00/29.50 t. 🍷 8.00
Spec. Marinated tuna in crushed black pepper with white radish and green salad. Roasted sea bass with confit of peppers and aubergine crisps. Loin of pork and Toulouse sausage with piquant mustard grain sauce.

XX **Criterion Brasserie Marco Pierre White,** 224 Piccadilly, W1V 9LB, ☏ (0171) 930 0488, Fax (0171) 930 8190, « 19C Neo-Byzantine decor » – ⓪ AE VISA
closed 24-25 December and 1 January – **Meals** 17.95 t. (lunch) and a la carte 24.75/32.95 t.
🍷 14.00.
FM c

XX **Le Caprice,** Arlington House, Arlington St., SW1A 1RT, ☏ (0171) 629 2239, Fax (0171) 493 9040 – ▤. ⓪ AE ⓪ VISA
DN c
closed dinner 24 to 26 December, 1 January and August Bank Holiday – **Meals** a la carte 25.00/44.75 t. 🍷 8.50

XX **Cave** (at Caviar House), 161 Piccadilly, W1V 9DF, ☏ (0171) 409 0445, Fax (0171) 493 1667 –
▤. ⓪ AE ⓪ VISA
DN s
closed Sunday, 25-26 December and 1 January – **Meals** 25.25 t. (lunch) and dinner a la carte 31.75/36.75 t. 🍷 10.75.

XX **The Avenue,** 7-9 St. James's St., SW1A 1EE, ☏ (0171) 321 2111, Fax (0171) 321 2500 – ▤.
⓪ AE ⓪ VISA
EP e
Meals 19.50 t. (lunch) and dinner a la carte 18.85/31.20 t.

XX **Matsuri,** 15 Bury St., SW1Y 6AL, ☏ (0171) 839 1101, Fax (0171) 930 7010 – ▤. ⓪ AE ⓪
VISA JCB
EN r
closed Sunday, 25 December and Bank Holidays – **Meals** - Japanese (Teppan-Yaki, Sushi) - 20.00/35.00 t. and a la carte 🍷 9.50.

Soho – ✉ W1/WC2 – pp. 28 and 29.

🏨 **Hampshire,** Leicester Sq., WC2H 7LH, ☏ (0171) 839 9399, Fax (0171) 930 8122 – 🛗
✦ rm, ▤ 📺 ☏ – 🔄 80. ⓪ AE ⓪ VISA. ✦
GM s
Meals 18.00 st. and a la carte 🍷 8.00 – ☐ 14.00 – **119 rm** 243.00/298.00 s., 5 suites.

🏛 **Hazlitt's** without rest., 6 Frith St., W1V 5TZ, ☏ (0171) 434 1771, Fax (0171) 439 1524
« Early 18C town houses » – 📺 ☏. ⓪ AE ⓪ VISA JCB. ✦
FK u
closed 24 to 26 December – **22 rm** 115.00/148.00 s., 1 suite.

XXXX **The Café Royal Grill Room,** 68 Regent St., W1R 6EL, ☏ (0171) 437 1177, « Rococo
🔅 decoration » – ▤. ⓪ AE ⓪ VISA
EM e
closed Saturday lunch and Sunday – **Meals** 22.50 t. (lunch) and a la carte 35.00/45.00 t.
🍷 10.15
Spec. Aspic of oyster Moscovite. Noisettes of lamb Edouard VII. Marjolaine.

XXX **Richard Corrigan at Lindsay House,** 21 Romilly St., W1V 5TG, ☏ (0171) 439 0450
Fax (0171) 439 7849 – ▤. ⓪ ⓪ VISA
GL
closed Saturday lunch, Sunday and 25-26 December – **Meals** a la carte 24.00/40.00 t. 🍷 7.00

XXX **L'Escargot,** 48 Greek St., W1V 5LQ, ☏ (0171) 437 2679, Fax (0171) 437 0790 – ▤. ⓪ AE
🔅 ⓪ VISA JCB
🏵 GK s
Ground Floor : Meals (closed Saturday lunch, Sunday, 25-26 December and 1 January)
17.50/23.45 t. and a la carte 23.45/29.45 t. 🍷 9.50 – **First Floor :** Meals (closed Saturday lunch, Sunday, Monday and August) 23.50/38.00 t. 🍷 9.50
Spec. Carpaccio of beef, parmesan crackling and herb dressing. Breast of duck with Anna potatoes and carrot, red wine jus. Ginger brûlée with a warm rhubarb compote.

XXX **Quo Vadis,** 26-29 Dean St., W1A 6LL, ☏ (0171) 437 9585, Fax (0171) 434 9972 – ▤. ⓪ AE
🔅 VISA
FK s
closed lunch Saturday and Sunday – **Meals** 17.95 t. (lunch) and a la carte 24.50/43.00 t.
🍷 9.00.
Spec. Grilled scallops gros sel, citrus fruits and beurre orange. Escalope of calf's liver with bacon and sage, pomme purée and sauce diable. Marquise of bitter chocolate with caramel sauce.

XX **Red Fort,** 77 Dean St., W1V 5HA, ☏ (0171) 437 2115, Fax (0171) 434 0721 – ▤. ⓪ AE ⓪
VISA
FJK
Meals - Indian - (buffet lunch) 12.50/25.00 t. and a la carte 🍷 7.50.

XX **Mezzo,** Lower ground floor, 100 Wardour St., W1V 3LE, ☏ (0171) 314 4000
Fax (0171) 314 4040 – ▤. ⓪ AE ⓪ VISA
FK
closed lunch Saturday and 1 January and 25-26 December – **Meals** 15.50 (lunch) and a la carte 21.00/35.50 t.

XX **Soho Soho,** (first floor), 11-13 Frith St., W1V 5TS, ☏ (0171) 494 3491
Fax (0171) 437 3091, 斎 – ▤. ⓪ AE ⓪ VISA JCB
FK
closed Saturday lunch, Sunday, 25 December and Bank Holidays – **Meals** 15.50 (dinner) and a la carte 20.25/30.40 t. 🍷 9.00.

XX **Lexington,** 45 Lexington St., W1R 3LG, ℰ (0171) 434 3401, Fax (0171) 287 2997 – ▤. 🆕
🆎 Ⓞ 𝚅𝙸𝚂𝙰 𝙹𝙲𝙱
EK e
closed Saturday lunch, Sunday and Bank Holidays – **Meals** a la carte 18.50/23.70 t. ⅄ 7.50.

XX **Gopal's,** 12 Bateman St., W1V 5TD, ℰ (0171) 434 0840 – ▤. 🆕 🆎 𝚅𝙸𝚂𝙰
FK e
closed 25 and 26 December – **Meals** - Indian - a la carte 15.95/23.40 t.

XX **Gay Hussar,** 2 Greek St., W1V 6NB, ℰ (0171) 437 0973, Fax (0171) 437 4631 – ▤. 🆕 🆎
Ⓞ 𝚅𝙸𝚂𝙰
GJ c
closed Sunday and Bank Holidays – **Meals** - Hungarian - 16.00 t. (lunch) and a la carte 19.25/
24.95 t. ⅄ 6.50.

XX **Atelier,** 41 Beak St., W1R 3LE, ℰ (0171) 287 2057, Fax (0171) 287 1767 – 🆕 🆎 Ⓞ 𝚅𝙸𝚂𝙰
🍽️
closed Saturday lunch, Sunday, 1 week Christmas and Bank Holidays – Meals 19.50 t.
and a la carte 25.75/28.00 t. ⅄ 8.25.
EL a

X **dell 'Ugo,** 56 Frith St., W1V 5TA, ℰ (0171) 734 8300, Fax (0171) 734 8784 – 🆕 🆎 Ⓞ 𝚅𝙸𝚂𝙰
closed Saturday lunch, Sunday and Bank Holidays – **Meals** 12.50 t. (lunch)
and a la carte 16.95/25.90 t.
FK z

X **Soho Spice,** 124-126 Wardour St., W1V 3LA, ℰ (0171) 434 0808, Fax (0171) 434 0799 – 🆕
🆎 Ⓞ 𝚅𝙸𝚂𝙰
FJ e
closed Sunday – **Meals** - Indian - 14.95 t. and a la carte.

X **Sri Siam,** 16 Old Compton St., W1V 5PE, ℰ (0171) 434 3544, Fax (0171) 287 1311 – ▤. 🆕
🆎 Ⓞ 𝚅𝙸𝚂𝙰
GK r
closed Sunday lunch, 25-26 December and 1 January – **Meals** - Thai - 11.50/16.80 t.
and a la carte ⅄ 8.00.

X **Alastair Little,** 49 Frith St., W1V 5TE, ℰ (0171) 734 5183 – 🆕 🆎 𝚅𝙸𝚂𝙰 𝙹𝙲𝙱
FK o
closed Saturday lunch, Sunday and Bank Holidays – **Meals** (booking essential) 25.00/30.00 t.
⅄ 14.50.

X **Bistrot Soho,** 64 Frith St., W1V 5TA, ℰ (0171) 734 4545, Fax (0171) 287 1027 – ▤. 🆕 🆎
Ⓞ 𝚅𝙸𝚂𝙰
FK z
closed Sunday, 25-26 December and 1 January – **Meals** 16.50 (lunch) and a la carte 18.00/
31.25 ⅄ 8.75.

X **Poons,** 4 Leicester St., Leicester Sq., WC2H 7BL, ℰ (0171) 437 1528 – ▤. 🆕 🆎 𝚅𝙸𝚂𝙰 𝙹𝙲𝙱
closed 24 to 26 December – **Meals** - Chinese - a la carte 9.50/13.60 t.
GM e

X **Fung Shing,** 15 Lisle St., WC2H 7BE, ℰ (0171) 734 0284, Fax (0171) 734 0284 – ▤. 🆕 🆎
Ⓞ 𝚅𝙸𝚂𝙰
GL a
closed 24 to 26 December – **Meals** - Chinese (Canton) - 15.00 t. and a la carte ⅄ 5.00.

X **Saigon,** 45 Frith St., W1V 5TE, ℰ (0171) 437 7109, Fax (0171) 734 1668 – ▤. 🆕 🆎 Ⓞ
𝚅𝙸𝚂𝙰
FGK x
closed Sunday, Easter, Christmas and Bank Holidays – **Meals** - Vietnamese - a la carte 13.10/
16.50.

Strand and Covent Garden – ✉ WC2 – *Except where otherwise stated see p. 33.*

🏨🏨 **The Savoy,** Strand, WC2R 0EU, ℰ (0171) 836 4343, Fax (0171) 240 6040, 🛁, 🛎, 🔲 – 📶,
🔄 rm, ▤ 📺 ☎ 🅿️ – 🔬 500. 🆕 🆎 Ⓞ 𝚅𝙸𝚂𝙰 𝙹𝙲𝙱. 🍽️
DEY a
Grill : Meals *(closed Saturday lunch, Sunday and August)* 29.75 t. (dinner)
and a la carte 35.00/50.50 st. ⅄ 9.95 – **River :** Meals 28.50/37.50 st.
and a la carte 43.50/55.00 st. ⅄ 9.95 – ☕ 17.50 – **154 rm** 240.00/365.00 s., 48 suites –
SB.

🏨🏨 **Le Meridien Waldorf,** Aldwych, WC2B 4DD, ℰ (0171) 836 2400, Fax (0171) 836 7244 –
📶, 🔄 rm, ▤ rm, 📺 ☎ – 🔬 450. 🆕 🆎 Ⓞ 𝚅𝙸𝚂𝙰 𝙹𝙲𝙱. 🍽️
EX x
Meals a la carte 20.40/31.45 t. ⅄ 12.00 – ☕ 15.00 – **286 rm** 210.00/280.00 s., 6 suites – SB.

🏨🏨 **The Howard,** Temple Pl., WC2R 2PR, ℰ (0171) 836 3555, Fax (0171) 379 4547, ≤ – 📶,
🔄 rm, ▤ 📺 ☎ 🅿️ – 🔬 100. 🆕 🆎 Ⓞ 𝚅𝙸𝚂𝙰 𝙹𝙲𝙱. 🍽️
EX e
Meals 28.50 st. and a la carte – ☕ 18.00 – **133 rm** 200.00/260.00 st., 2 suites.

XXX **Ivy,** 1 West St., WC2H 9NE, ℰ (0171) 836 4751, Fax (0171) 497 3644 – ▤. 🆕 🆎 Ⓞ 𝚅𝙸𝚂𝙰
closed dinner 24 to 26 December, 1 January and August Bank Holiday – **Meals**
a la carte 25.00/44.25 t. ⅄ 9.50.
p. 29 GK z

XXX **WestZENders,** 4a Upper St. Martin's Lane, WC2H 9EA, ℰ (0171) 497 0376,
Fax (0171) 497 0378 – ▤. 🆕 🆎 Ⓞ 𝚅𝙸𝚂𝙰 𝙹𝙲𝙱
DX x
closed 25 and 26 December – **Meals** - Chinese - 19.80 t. (dinner) and a la carte 17.30/
32.50 t.

XX **Rules,** 35 Maiden Lane, WC2E 7LB, ℰ (0171) 836 5314, Fax (0171) 497 1081, « London's
oldest restaurant with collection of antique cartoons, drawings and paintings » – 🆕 🆎 Ⓞ
𝚅𝙸𝚂𝙰
DX n
closed 4 days Christmas – **Meals** - English - a la carte 25.45/29.15 t. ⅄ 5.95.

417

XX **Bank**, 1 Kingsway, Aldwych, ℰ (0171) 379 9797, Fax (0171) 379 9014 – ⓜⓢ ⒶⒺ ⓞ 𝗩𝗜𝗦𝗔
closed 25-26 December and Bank Holidays – **Meals** 16.50 t. (lunch) and a la carte 16.00/
29.00 t.
EX s

XX **Christopher's**, 18 Wellington St., WC2 7DD, ℰ (0171) 240 4222, Fax (0171) 240 3357 –
▤. ⓜⓢ ⒶⒺ ⓞ 𝗩𝗜𝗦𝗔 𝗝𝗖𝗕
EX z
closed Sunday, 25-26 December and Bank Holidays – **Meals** a la carte 22.00/33.50 t. ≬ 9.00.

XX **L'Estaminet**, 14 Garrick St., off Floral St., WC2 9BJ, ℰ (0171) 379 1432 – ⓜⓢ ⒶⒺ 𝗩𝗜𝗦𝗔 𝗝𝗖𝗕
closed Sunday, Easter, 25 December and Bank Holidays – **Meals** - French - a la carte 18.95/
28.20 t. ≬ 7.00.
DX a

XX **Sheekey's**, 28-32 St. Martin's Court, WC2N 4AL, ℰ (0171) 240 2565, Fax (0171) 240 8114 –
▤. ⓜⓢ ⒶⒺ ⓞ 𝗩𝗜𝗦𝗔
DX v
closed Sunday, Easter, 25 December and Bank Holidays – **Meals** - Seafood - 14.75/
17.95 t. and a la carte.

XX **Bertorelli's**, 44a Floral St., WC2E 9DA, ℰ (0171) 836 3969, Fax (0171) 836 1868 – ▤. ⓜⓢ
ⒶⒺ ⓞ 𝗩𝗜𝗦𝗔 𝗝𝗖𝗕
DX c
closed Sunday and 25 December – **Meals** - Italian - a la carte approx. 23.50 t. ≬ 7.50.

X **Stephen Bull St. Martin's Lane**, 12 Upper St. Martin's Lane, WC2 H9DL,
ℰ (0171) 379 7811 – ▤. ⓜⓢ ⒶⒺ 𝗩𝗜𝗦𝗔
DX r
closed Saturday lunch, Sunday, 1 week Christmas-New Year and Bank Holidays – **Meals**
a la carte 22.95/27.95 t. ≬ 8.25.

X **Le Café du Jardin**, 28 Wellington St., WC2E 7BD, ℰ (0171) 836 8769,
Fax (0171) 836 4123 – ▤. ⓜⓢ ⒶⒺ ⓞ 𝗩𝗜𝗦𝗔
EX a
Meals 13.50 t. and a la carte ≬ 7.00.

X **Magno's Brasserie**, 65a Long Acre, WC2E 9JH, ℰ (0171) 836 6077, Fax (0171) 379 6184
– ▤. ⓜⓢ ⒶⒺ ⓞ 𝗩𝗜𝗦𝗔 𝗝𝗖𝗕
DV e
Meals - French - 16.95 t. and a la carte ≬ 7.95.

X **Joe Allen**, 13 Exeter St., WC2E 7DT, ℰ (0171) 836 0651, Fax (0171) 497 2148 – ▤. ⓜⓢ ⒶⒺ
𝗩𝗜𝗦𝗔
EX c
closed 24 and 25 December – **Meals** 13.00 t. (lunch) and a la carte 19.00/28.00 t. ≬ 5.50.

Victoria – ✉ SW1 – Except where otherwise stated see p. 32.
🛈 Victoria Station Forecourt, SW1V 1JU ℰ (0171) 824 8844.

🏨🏨🏨 **St. James Court**, 45 Buckingham Gate, SW1E 6AF, ℰ (0171) 834 6655,
Fax (0171) 630 7587, 🐟, ☎ – 🛗, ✲ rm, ▤ 📺 ☎ – 🔬 180. ⓜⓢ ⒶⒺ ⓞ 𝗩𝗜𝗦𝗔 𝗝𝗖𝗕.
❀
CX i
Café Mediterranée : Meals 15.00 t. (lunch) and a la carte 21.95/28.50 t. ≬ 8.50 – **Inn of
Happiness** : Meals - Chinese - (closed Saturday lunch) 15.50/18.50 t. and a la carte ≬ 8.50 –
(see also **Auberge de Provence** below) – ☲ 15.00 – **372 rm** 120.00/185.00 s., 18 suites.

🏨🏨🏨 **Royal Horseguards Thistle**, 2 Whitehall Court, SW1A 2EJ, ℰ (0171) 839 3400,
Fax (0171) 925 2263 – 🛗, ✲ rm, ▤ 📺 ☎ – 🔬 180. ⓜⓢ ⒶⒺ ⓞ 𝗩𝗜𝗦𝗔 𝗝𝗖𝗕. ❀ p. 26 LX a
Meals 22.50 t. and a la carte ≬ 6.95 – ☲ 13.50 – **278 rm** 179.00/275.00 st., 3 suites.

🏨🏨🏨 **Stakis London St. Ermin's**, Caxton St., SW1H 0QW, ℰ (0171) 222 7888,
Fax (0171) 222 6914 – 🛗, ✲ rm, ▤ rest, 📺 ☎ – 🔬 250. ⓜⓢ ⒶⒺ ⓞ 𝗩𝗜𝗦𝗔 𝗝𝗖𝗕. ❀ CX x
Cloisters : Meals (closed lunch Saturday and Sunday) 17.95/19.95 st. and a la carte –
Caxton Grill : Meals (closed Saturday lunch, Sunday and Bank Holidays) a la carte
25.50/38.40 st. – ☲ 11.95 – **288 rm** 140.00/185.00 st., 2 suites – SB.

🏨🏨 **Goring**, 15 Beeston Pl., Grosvenor Gdns., SW1W 0JW, ℰ (0171) 396 9000,
Fax (0171) 834 4393 – 🛗, ▤ rm, 📺 ☎ – 🔬 50. ⓜⓢ ⒶⒺ ⓞ 𝗩𝗜𝗦𝗔. ❀
BX a
Meals 27.50/36.00 st. ≬ 9.00 – ☲ 14.50 – **72 rm** 155.00/180.00 s., 4 suites.

🏨🏨 **Grosvenor Thistle**, 101 Buckingham Palace Rd, SW1W 0SJ, ℰ (0171) 834 9494,
Fax (0171) 630 1978 – 🛗, ✲ rm, 📺 ☎ – 🔬 200. ⓜⓢ ⒶⒺ ⓞ 𝗩𝗜𝗦𝗔 𝗝𝗖𝗕. ❀
BX e
Meals (carving rest.) 17.85 st. and a la carte ≬ 6.75 – ☲ 13.50 – **363 rm** 127.00/185.00 st.,
3 suites.

🏨🏨 **Royal Westminster Thistle**, 49 Buckingham Palace Rd, SW1W 0QT,
ℰ (0171) 834 1821, Fax (0171) 931 7542 – 🛗, ✲ rm, ▤ 📺 ☎ – 🔬 180. ⓜⓢ ⒶⒺ ⓞ 𝗩𝗜𝗦𝗔 𝗝𝗖𝗕.
❀
BX z
Meals 12.95/21.95 st. and a la carte ≬ 8.00 – ☲ 12.50 – **134 rm** 145.00/200.00 st. – SB.

🏨🏨 **Dolphin Square**, Dolphin Sq., SW1V 3LX, ℰ (0171) 834 3800, Fax (0171) 798 8735, 🐟,
☎, 🏊, 🎾, ✎, squash – 🛗, ▤ rest, 📺 ☎ 🖘 🅿 – 🔬 50. ⓜⓢ ⒶⒺ ⓞ 𝗩𝗜𝗦𝗔. ❀
Meals 15.70 st. and a la carte 12.20/23.75 st. ≬ 7.75 – ☲ 12.50 – **15 rm** 100.00/180.00 st.
137 suites 115.00/180.00 st.
p. 26 KZ a

🏨🏨 **Rubens**, 39-41 Buckingham Palace Rd, SW1W 0PS, ℰ (0171) 834 6600,
Fax (0171) 828 5401 – 🛗, ✲ rm, ▤ rest, 📺 ☎ – 🔬 75. ⓜⓢ ⒶⒺ ⓞ 𝗩𝗜𝗦𝗔. ❀
BX c
Meals (closed lunch Saturday and Sunday) (carving lunch) 15.95 st. and dinner a la carte –
☲ 10.95 – **178 rm** 99.00/155.00 s., 1 suite.

Rochester, 69 Vincent Sq., SW1P 2PA, ℘ (0171) 828 6611, *Fax (0171) 233 6724* – 🛗,
▤ rest, 📺 ☎ – 🔥 60
CY e
80 rm.

Holiday Inn London Victoria, 2 Bridge Pl., SW1V 1QA, ℘ (0171) 834 8123,
Fax (0171) 828 1099, ℔, ⊜s, ⬚ – 🛗, ⚞⚟ rm, ▤ 📺 ☎ – 🔥 180. 🆎 🆎 ⓪ 𝙑𝙄𝙎𝘼 𝙅𝘾𝘽.
❀
BY i
Meals 17.95/25.00 **st.** and dinner a la carte – � 11.50 – **212 rm** 150.00/160.00 **st.**

Winchester without rest., 17 Belgrave Rd, SW1V 1RB, ℘ (0171) 828 2972,
Fax (0171) 828 5191 – 📺. ❀
BY s
closed 25 December – **18 rm** � 65.00/85.00 **st.**

Auberge de Provence (at St. James Court H.), 45 Buckingham Gate, SW1E 6AF,
℘ (0171) 821 1899, *Fax (0171) 630 7587* – ▤. 🆎 🆎 ⓪ 𝙑𝙄𝙎𝘼 𝙅𝘾𝘽.
CX i
Meals - French - a la carte 24.65/30.75 **t.** ⓖ 8.00.

L'Incontro, 87 Pimlico Rd, SW1W 8PH, ℘ (0171) 730 6327, *Fax (0171) 730 5062* – ▤. 🆎
🆎 𝙅𝘾𝘽
p. 31 FT u
closed lunch Saturday and Sunday and 25-26 December – **Meals** - Italian - 20.50 **t.**
(lunch) and a la carte 27.50/51.50 **t.** ⓖ 11.50.

Santini, 29 Ebury St., SW1W 0NZ, ℘ (0171) 730 4094, *Fax (0171) 730 0544* – ▤. 🆎 🆎 ⓪
𝙑𝙄𝙎𝘼 𝙅𝘾𝘽
ABX v
closed lunch Saturday and Sunday and 25-26 December – **Meals** - Italian - 19.75 **t.**
(lunch) and a la carte 25.00/51.75 **t.** ⓖ 11.00.

Shepherd's, Marsham Court, Marsham St., SW1P 4LA, ℘ (0171) 834 9552,
Fax (0171) 233 6047 – ▤. 🆎 🆎 ⓪ 𝙑𝙄𝙎𝘼
p. 26 LZ z
closed Saturday, Sunday and Bank Holidays – **Meals** - English - (booking essential) 23.95 **t.**
ⓖ 5.50.

Simply Nico, 48a Rochester Row, SW1P 1JU, ℘ (0171) 630 8061 – ▤. 🆎 🆎 ⓪ 𝙑𝙄𝙎𝘼
𝙅𝘾𝘽
CY a
closed Saturday lunch, Sunday, 10 days Christmas, Easter and Bank Holidays –
Meals (booking essential) 25.00/27.00 **st.** ⓖ 10.00.

The Atrium, 4 Millbank, SW1P 3JA, ℘ (0171) 233 0032, *Fax (0171) 233 0010* – ▤. 🆎 🆎
⓪ 𝙑𝙄𝙎𝘼
p. 26 LY s
closed Saturday, Sunday, 25 December and 1 January – **Meals** a la carte 20.50/25.95 **t.**

Ken Lo's Memories of China, 67-69 Ebury St., SW1W 0NZ, ℘ (0171) 730 7734,
Fax (0171) 730 2992 – ▤. 🆎 🆎 ⓪ 𝙑𝙄𝙎𝘼 𝙅𝘾𝘽
AY u
closed Sunday lunch, 24 December-1 January and Bank Holidays – **Meals** - Chinese - 20.50/
24.50 **t.** and a la carte.

Hunan, 51 Pimlico Rd, SW1W 8NE, ℘ (0171) 730 5712, *Fax (0171) 730 8265* – 🆎 🆎 𝙑𝙄𝙎𝘼
closed Sunday lunch, 25-26 December and Bank Holidays – **Meals** - Chinese (Hunan) -
a la carte 11.40/48.80.
p. 25 IZ a

Tate Gallery, Tate Gallery, Millbank, SW1P 4RG, ℘ (0171) 887 8877, *Fax (0171) 887 8007*,
« Rex Whistler murals » – ▤. 🆎 🆎 𝙑𝙄𝙎𝘼 𝙅𝘾𝘽
p. 26 LZ c
closed Sunday and 24 to 26 December – **Meals** (booking essential) (lunch only) 25.00 **t.**

Olivo, 21 Eccleston St., SW1W 9LX, ℘ (0171) 730 2505, *Fax (0171) 824 8190* – ▤. 🆎 🆎 𝙑𝙄𝙎𝘼
closed lunch Saturday and Sunday and Bank Holidays – **Meals** - Italian - 16.00 **t.**
(lunch) and dinner a la carte 22.50/29.00 **t.** ⓖ 8.00.
AY z

La Poule au Pot, 231 Ebury St., SW1W 8UT, ℘ (0171) 730 7763, *Fax (0171) 259 9651*, ⛲
– ▤. 🆎 🆎 ⓪ 𝙑𝙄𝙎𝘼 𝙅𝘾𝘽
p. 25 IZ e
Meals - French - 13.95 **t.** (lunch) and a la carte 24.85/36.60 **t.** ⓖ 5.50.

LONGBRIDGE *Warks. – see Warwick.*

LONG CRENDON *Bucks.* 🗺️403 404 R 28 – *pop. 2 505 –* ✉ *Aylesbury.*
London 50 – Aylesbury 11 – Oxford 15.

🍴 **Angel Inn** with rm, Bicester Rd, HP18 9EE, ✆ (01844) 208268, Fax (01844) 202497, 🌫️, « Part 16C » – ⇄ rm, 📺 ☎ 🅿. 🐧 🟦 *VISA*. ℅
Meals *(closed Sunday dinner)* a la carte 16.25/23.50 **t.** ⓛ 7.20 – ⌂ 5.00 – **3 rm** 45.00/55.00 **t.**

LONG EATON *Derbs.* 🗺️402 403 404 Q 25 – *see Nottingham (Notts.).*

LONGFORD *W. Mids.* 🗺️403 404 P 26 – *see Coventry.*

LONG MARSTON *N. Yorks.* 🗺️402 Q 22 – *see York.*

LONG MELFORD *Suffolk* 🗺️404 W 27 *Great Britain G. – pop. 2 808.*
See : *Melford Hall★ AC.*
London 62 – Cambridge 34 – Colchester 18 – Ipswich 24.

🏛️ **Bull,** Hall St., CO10 9JG, ✆ (01787) 378494, Fax (01787) 880307, « Part 15C coaching inn » – ⇄ rm, 📺 ☎ 🅿 – 🔏 60. 🐧 🟦 *VISA*
Meals 15.95/19.95 **st.** and a la carte ⓛ 7.40 – ⌂ 9.95 – **25 rm** 65.00/110.00 **st.** – SB.

🏛️ **Countrymen,** The Green, CO10 9DN, ✆ (01787) 312356, Fax (01787) 374557 – ⇄ rest, 📺 ☎ 🅿. 🐧 🟦 *VISA* 🇯🇨🇧
closed January – **Countrymen :** Meals *(closed Sunday dinner and Monday)* 9.95 **t.** and a la carte ⓛ 5.00 – **8 rm** ⌂ 55.00/95.00 **t.**, 1 suite – SB.

🏠 **George and Dragon,** Hall St., CO10 9JB, ✆ (01787) 371285, Fax (01787) 312428, 🌫️ – 📺 ☎ 🅿 – 🔏 30. 🐧 🟦 *VISA*
Meals a la carte 10.15/18.15 **st.** ⓛ 5.95 – **7 rm** ⌂ 30.00/50.00 **st.**

🍴🍴🍴 **Chimneys,** Hall St., CO10 9JR, ✆ (01787) 379806, Fax (01787) 312294, « Part 16C cottage », 🌫️ – 🐧 🟦 *VISA*
closed Sunday dinner – **Meals** 16.50/27.50 **st.**

🍴 **Scutchers Bistro,** Westgate St., CO10 9DP, on A 1092 ✆ (01787) 310200 Fax (01787) 310620, 🌫️ – 🐧 🟦 *VISA*
closed Sunday, Monday and first 10 days January – **Meals** a la carte 17.90/23.30 **t.**

LONG PRESTON *N. Yorks.* 🗺️402 N 21 – ✉ *Skipton.*
London 232 – Bradford 28 – Kendal 36 – Leeds 47.

🏠 **Country House,** BD23 4NJ, ✆ (01729) 840246, Fax (01729) 840246, ⇄s, 🌫️ – ⇄ 📺 🅿 ℅
closed mid December-first weekend of February – **Meals** *(residents only) (dinner only) (unlicensed)* 14.00 **st.** – **7 rm** ⌂ 32.50/54.00 **t.**

LONGRIDGE *Lancs.* 🗺️402 M 22 – *pop. 7 351.*
London 241 – Blackburn 12 – Burnley 18.

🍴🍴🍴 **Paul Heathcote's** (Heathcote), 104-106 Higher Rd, PR3 5SY, NE : ½ m. by B 526 ✿ following signs for Jeffrey Hill ✆ (01772) 784969, Fax (01772) 785713 – ⇄, 🐧 🟦 ⓞ *VISA*
closed Monday – **Meals** *(dinner only and lunch Friday and Sunday)* 25.00/38.00 **t.** and dinner a la carte 32.00/40.00 **t.** ⓛ 14.00
Spec. Roast scallops with cauliflower purée and sherry caramel. Suckling pig with cider and sage. Marmalade rice pudding with damson and lychee compote.

LONG SUTTON *Lincs.* 🗺️404 U 25 – *pop. 4 185.*
London 100 – Lincoln 51 – Leicester 67 – Norwich 54.

🏠 **Travelodge,** Wisbech Rd, PE12 9AG, SE : 1 m. at junction of A 17 with A 110 ✆ (01406) 362230, Reservations (Freephone) 0800 850950 – ⇄ rm, 📺 🔥 🅿. 🐧 🟦 ⓞ *VISA* 🇯🇨🇧. ℅
Meals *(grill rest.)* – **40 rm** 44.95 **t.**

The Guide is updated annually so renew your Guide every year.

LOOE Cornwall **403** G 32 *The West Country G.* – pop. 5 022.

See : *Town*★ – *Monkey Sanctuary*★ *AC.*

🏌 *Bin Down ℘ (01503) 240239* – 🏌 *Whitsand Bay Hotel, Portwrinkle, Torpoint ℘ (01503) 230276.*

🛈 *The Guildhall, Fore St., PL13 1AA ℘ (01503) 262072 (summer only).*

London 264 – Plymouth 21 – Truro 39.

🏨 **Klymiarven** ⌂, Barbican Hill, East Looe, PL13 1BH, E : 2 m. by A 387 off B 3253 or access from town on foot ℘ (01503) 262333, *Fax (01503) 262333*, < Looe and harbour, 🌧 – ✤ rest, 🔟 ☎ 🅿. 🝙 *VISA*
Meals (bar lunch Monday to Friday)/dinner 15.50 **st.** and a la carte ⌂ 4.00 – **14 rm** � 41.00/82.00 **st.** – SB.

🏨 **Commonwood Manor** ⌂, St. Martins Rd, East Looe, PL13 1LP, NE : ½ m. by A 387 on B 3253 ℘ (01503) 262929, *Fax (01503) 262632*, < Looe Valley, 🏊, 🌧 – 🔟 ☎ 🅿. 🝙 *AE VISA* *JCB*
closed 22 to 30 December – **Meals** (bar lunch)/dinner 17.00 **st.** ⌂ 5.25 – **9 rm** ⊂ 38.00/76.00 **st.**, 2 suites – SB.

🏠 **Bucklawren Farm** ⌂, St. Martin-by-Looe, PL13 1NZ, NE : 3 ½ m. by A 387 and B 3253 truning right onto single track road signposted to monkey sanctuary ℘ (01503) 240738, *Fax (01503) 240481*, <, « Working farm », 🌧, park – ✤ rest, 🅿. 🝙 *VISA*
28 March-30 October – **Meals** (by arrangement) 10.00 **s.** – **6 rm** ⊂ 26.00/42.00 **s.** – SB.

🏠 **Harescombe Lodge** ⌂ without rest., Watergate, PL13 2NE, NW : 2 ¾ m. by A 387 turning right opposite Waylands Farm onto single track road ℘ (01503) 263158, 🌧 – 🅿. ✿
3 rm ⊂ 40.00 **st.**

🍴 **Trawlers**, Buller Quay, East Looe, PL13 1AH, ℘ (01503) 263593 – 🝙 *VISA*
closed Sunday, Monday and restricted opening November-February – **Meals** - Seafood - (dinner only) a la carte 16.75/22.75 **t.** ⌂ 4.50.

at Sandplace N : 2 ¼ m. on A 387 – ✉ Polperro.

🏨 **Polraen Country House**, PL13 1PJ, ℘ (01503) 263956, *Fax (01503) 264389*, 🌧 – ✤ rest, 🔟 🅿. 🝙 *VISA JCB*
Meals (dinner only and Sunday lunch)/dinner 17.50 **st.** and a la carte ⌂ 4.75 – **5 rm** ⊂ 35.00/60.00 **t.** – SB.

at Widegates NE : 3½ m. on B 3253 – ✉ Looe.

🏠 **Coombe Farm** ⌂, PL13 1QN, on B 3253 ℘ (01503) 240223, *Fax (01503) 240895*, < countryside, 🏊, 🌧, park – ✤ 🔟 ☎ 🅿. 🝙 *AE* ⓞ *VISA*. ✿
March-October – **Meals** (by arrangement) 15.00 **st.** ⌂ 3.75 – **10 rm** ⊂ 36.00/72.00 **st.** – SB.

at Talland Bay SW : 4 m. by A 387 – ✉ Looe.

🏨 **Talland Bay** ⌂, PL13 2JB, ℘ (01503) 272667, *Fax (01503) 272940*, <, « Country house atmosphere », 🏊, 🏊, 🌧 – ✤ rest, 🔟 ☎ 🅿. 🝙 *AE* ⓞ *VISA*. ✿
closed January – **Meals** (bar lunch)/dinner 21.00 **t.** and a la carte ⌂ 6.65 – **17 rm** ⊂ (dinner included) 65.00/188.00 **t.**, 2 suites – SB.

🏨 **Allhays Country House** ⌂, PL13 2JB, ℘ (01503) 272434, *Fax (01503) 272929*, <, 🌧 – ✤ 🔟 ☎ 🅿. 🝙 *AE* ⓞ *VISA JCB*
closed 12 days Christmas – **Meals** (bar lunch)/dinner 16.00 **st.** ⌂ 5.45 – **6 rm** ⊂ 28.00/77.00 **st.** – SB.

at Pelynt NW : 4 m. by A 387 on B 3359 – ✉ Looe.

🏨 **Jubilee Inn**, Pelynt, PL13 2JZ, ℘ (01503) 220312, *Fax (01503) 220920*, « Part 16C » – 🔟 ☎ 🅿. 🝙 *VISA JCB*
Meals a la carte 14.10/24.40 **t.** ⌂ 5.50 – **9 rm** ⊂ 36.00/59.00 **t.** – SB.

LORTON Cumbria **402** K 20 – *see Cockermouth.*

LOSTWITHIEL Cornwall **403** G 32 *The West Country G.* – pop. 2 452.

Env. : *Lanhydrock*★★, N : 4 m. by B 3268 – *Restormel Castle*★ *AC* (※★) N : 1 m. – *Bodmin* (*St. Petroc Church*★) NW : 6 m. by B 3268.

🏌 *Lostwithiel G & C.C., Lower Polscoe ℘ (01208) 873550* – 🏌 *Lanhydrock, Lostwithiel Road, Bodmin ℘ (01208) 73600.*

🛈 *Community Centre, Liddicoat Rd, PL22 0HE ℘ (01208) 872207.*

London 273 – Plymouth 30 – Truro 23.

🏨 **Restormel Lodge**, 17 Castle Hill, PL22 0DD, on A 390 ℘ (01208) 872223, *Fax (01208) 873568*, 🏊, 🌧 – 🔟 ☎ 🅿. 🝙 *AE* ⓞ *VISA*
Meals (bar lunch)/dinner 15.00 **t.** and a la carte ⌂ 4.50 – ⊂ 6.00 – **32 rm** 40.00/52.00 **st.**

LOUGHBOROUGH Leics. 402 403 404 Q 25 – pop. 46 867.

18 Lingdale, Joe Moore's Lane, Woodhouse Eaves ℰ (01509) 890703.
🖪 John Storer House, Wards End, LE11 3HA ℰ (01509) 218113.
London 117 – Birmingham 41 – Leicester 11 – Nottingham 15.

🏛 **Quality Friendly,** New Ashby Rd, LE11 0EX, W : 2 m. on A 512 ℰ (01509) 211800, Fax (01509) 211868, 16, ⌂, 🏊, 🐎 – ⅙ rm, 📺 ☎ ⅙ 🅿 – 🔏 225. 🐠 AE ① VISA
Meals 9.00/14.50 t. and dinner a la carte 🕯 8.75 – ⌂ 8.75 – **94 rm** 67.50/97.50 **st.** – SB.

🏛 **Cedars,** Cedar Rd, LE11 2AB, SE : 1 m. by A 6 ℰ (01509) 214459, Fax (01509) 233573, ⌂, 🏊, 🐎 – 📺 ☎ 🅿. 🐠 AE ① VISA
Meals (closed Sunday dinner, 26 to 29 December and Bank Holidays) 14.95 t. and a la carte 🕯 7.75 – **36 rm** ⌂ 50.00/65.00 t.

↑ **Garendon Lodge,** 136 Leicester Rd, LE11 2AQ, SE : ¾ m. on A 6 ℰ (01509) 211120 – ⅙ 📺 🅿. 🐠 VISA
Meals 9.50 s. – **5 rm** ⌂ 22.00/36.00 s.

↑ **Garendon Park,** 92 Leicester Rd, LE11 2AQ, SE : ½ m. on A 6 ℰ (01509) 236557, Fax (01509) 265559 – 📺 🅿. 🐠 AE VISA JCB. ⅜
Meals approx. 9.50 **st.** – **9 rm** ⌂ 28.00/45.00 **st.**

at Quorndon SE : 3 m. by A 6 – ✉ Loughborough.

🏛 **Quorn Country,** 66 Leicester Rd, LE12 8BB, ℰ (01509) 415050, Fax (01509) 415557, 🐎 – ⅙ rm, 🍴 rm, 📺 ☎ ⅙ 🅿 – 🔏 120. 🐠 AE ① VISA
Shires : Meals (closed Saturday lunch) 20.00 t. (dinner) and a la carte 23.50/36.15 t. 🕯 5.85 – **Orangery :** Meals (closed Saturday lunch and dinner Sunday and Monday) 12.50 t. (lunch) and a la carte 16.25/19.45 t. 🕯 5.85 – ⌂ 8.95 – **18 rm** 94.00/104.00 t., 2 suites – SB.

🏛 **Quorn Grange,** 88 Wood Lane, LE12 8DB, SE : ¾ m. ℰ (01509) 412167, Fax (01509) 415621, 🐎 – 📺 ☎ ⅙ 🅿 – 🔏 100. 🐠 AE ① VISA JCB
closed 26 December and 1 January – Meals (closed Saturday lunch) 12.35/18.95 **st.** and a la carte 🕯 8.95 – ⌂ 7.85 – **14 rm** 78.00/92.00 **st.**, 1 suite.

ⓐ ATS Bridge St. ℰ (01509) 218447/218472

LOUTH Lincs. 402 404 U 23 – pop. 14 248.
London 156 – Boston 34 – Great Grimsby 17 – Lincoln 26.

🏛 **Kenwick Park** ⌂, LN11 8NR, SE : 2 ¼ m. by B 1520 on A 157 ℰ (01507) 608806, Fax (01507) 608027, ≤, 16, ⌂, 🏊, 18, 🐎, park, ⅜, squash – 📺 ☎ 🅿 – 🔏 30. 🐠 AE ① VISA
Meals 18.50 **st.** and a la carte 🕯 5.95 – **24 rm** ⌂ 79.50/120.00 **st.** – SB.

🏛 **Beaumont,** 66 Victoria Rd, LN11 0BX, ℰ (01507) 605005, Fax (01507) 607768 – 📲 📺 ☎ 🅿 – 🔏 90. 🐠 AE VISA
Meals 10.95 **st.** (dinner) and a la carte 11.95/24.50 **st.** 🕯 5.50 – **17 rm** ⌂ 40.00/75.00 **st.** – SB.

🏛 **Brackenborough Arms,** Cordeaux Corner, Brackenborough, LN11 0SZ, N : 2 m. by A 16 ℰ (01507) 609169, Fax (01507) 609413 – 📺 ☎ 🅿 – 🔏 30. 🐠 AE ① VISA. ⅜
closed 25 and 26 December – Meals a la carte 9.65/22.75 t. 🕯 8.95 – **24 rm** ⌂ 60.00/72.50 t. – SB.

ⓐ ATS 179 Newmarket ℰ (01507) 601975

LOWER ODDINGTON Glos. 403 404 P 28 – see Stow-on-the-Wold.

LOWER SLAUGHTER Glos. 403 404 O 28 – see Bourton-on-the-Water.

LOWESTOFT Suffolk 404 Z 26 Great Britain G. – pop. 62 907.
Env. : The Broads★.
18, 18 Rookery Park, Carlton Colville ℰ (01502) 560380.
🖪 East Point Pavillion, Royal Plain, NR33 0AP ℰ (01502) 523000.
London 116 – Ipswich 43 – Norwich 30.

🏛 **Hatfield,** Esplanade, NR33 0QP, ℰ (01502) 565337, Fax (01502) 511885 – 📲 📺 ☎ 🅿 – 🔏 100. 🐠 AE ① VISA. ⅜
Meals (closed dinner 25 December) 13.50 t. and a la carte 🕯 4.95 – **33 rm** ⌂ 49.00/99.00 t. – SB.

🏛 **Travel Inn,** 249 Yarmouth Rd, NR32 4AA, N : 2 ½ m. on A 12 ℰ (01502) 572441 – ⅙ rm 📺 ⅙ 🅿. 🐠 AE VISA. ⅜
Meals (grill rest.) – **41 rm** 35.50 t.

at Oulton NW : 2 m. by B 1074 – ⊠ Lowestoft.

🏨 **Parkhill**, Parkhill, NR32 5DQ, N : ½ m. on A 1117 ℰ (01502) 730322, Fax (01502) 731695,
🚗 – ⇄ rm, 📺 ☎ ❷ 🅿 – ⚖ 150. 🆀🆂 🅰🅴 ⓪ 𝓥𝐼𝑆𝐴 𝐽𝐶𝐵
Meals 13.90 **t.** and a la carte ᵇ 5.00 – **16 rm** ⇆ 48.00/60.00 **t.**, 2 suites – SB.

⊚ ATS 263 Whapload Rd ℰ (01502) 561581

LOW FELL Tyne and Wear – see Gateshead.

LOW LAITHE N. Yorks. – see Pateley Bridge.

LUDLOW Shrops. 𝟒𝟎𝟑 L 26 Great Britain G. – pop. 9 040.
See : Town★ – Castle★ AC – Feathers Hotel★ – St. Laurence's Parish Church★
(Misericords★).
Exc. : Stokesay Castle★ AC, NW : 6 ½ m. by A 49.
🛈 Castle St., SY8 1AS ℰ (01584) 875053.
London 162 – Birmingham 39 – Hereford 24 – Shrewsbury 29.

🏨🏨 **Feathers**, Bull Ring, SY8 1AA, ℰ (01584) 875261, Fax (01584) 876030, 🍴, « Part
Elizabethan house » – 🛗 ⇄, ▤ rest, 📺 ☎ ❷ 🅿 – ⚖ 100. 🆀🆂 🅰🅴 ⓪ 𝓥𝐼𝑆𝐴 𝐽𝐶𝐵
Meals 13.50/19.95 **t.** and dinner a la carte ᵇ 5.95 – **38 rm** ⇆ 55.00/120.00 **t.**, 1 suite – SB.

🏨 **Dinham Hall**, Dinham, SY8 1EJ, ℰ (01584) 876464, Fax (01584) 876019, 🍴, 🚗 –
⇄ rest, 📺 ☎ ❷ 🅿, 🆀🆂 🅰🅴 ⓪ 𝓥𝐼𝑆𝐴 𝐽𝐶𝐵
Meals 11.50/21.50 **st.** ᵇ 6.85 – **12 rm** ⇆ 65.00/125.00 **st.** – SB.

🏨 **Overton Grange**, Hereford Rd, SY8 4AD, S : 1 ¾ m. on B 4361 ℰ (01584) 873500,
Fax (01584) 873524, ≤, – 📺 ☎ ❷ 🅿 – ⚖ 160. 🆀🆂 𝓥𝐼𝑆𝐴. 🛇
Meals 20.00 **t.** (dinner) and lunch a la carte approx. 16.75 **t.** ᵇ 5.50 – **16 rm** ⇆ (dinner
included) 64.00/128.00 **t.** – SB.

🏨 **Cliffe** ⌂, Dinham, SY8 2JE, W : ½ m. via Dinham Bridge ℰ (01584) 872063,
Fax (01584) 873991, 🚗 – ⇄ rest, 📺 ☎ 🅿, 🆀🆂 🅰🅴 𝓥𝐼𝑆𝐴
Meals (closed Sunday dinner) (bar lunch Monday to Saturday)/dinner 13.95 **t.** ᵇ 5.00 – **9 rm**
⇆ 30.00/58.00 **t.**

⌂ **Number Twenty Eight** without rest., 28 Lower Broad St., SY8 1PQ, ℰ (01584) 876996,
Fax (01584) 876860, 🚗 – ⇄ 📺 ☎, 🆀🆂 🅰🅴 𝓥𝐼𝑆𝐴. 🛇
4 rm ⇆ 45.00/65.00 **st.**

⌂ **Cecil**, Sheet Rd, SY8 1LR, ℰ (01584) 872442, Fax (01584) 872442, 🚗 – ⇄ 📺 🅿. 🆀🆂 𝓥𝐼𝑆𝐴
closed Christmas – Meals (by arrangement) 12.00 **st.** – **9 rm** ⇆ 19.00/52.00 **st.** – SB.

⌂ **Dinham Weir**, Dinham Bridge, SY8 1EH, ℰ (01584) 874431, ≤, 🚗 – ⇄ rm, 📺 ☎ 🅿. 🆀🆂
🅰🅴 𝓥𝐼𝑆𝐴. 🛇
Meals 12.50 **st.** – **8 rm** ⇆ 50.00/65.00 **st.** – SB.

XX **Merchant House** (Hill), Lower Corve St., SY8 1DU, ℰ (01584) 875438,
🏵 Fax (01584) 875438, « Jacobean house » – ⇄. 🆀🆂 🅰🅴 𝓥𝐼𝑆𝐴 𝐽𝐶𝐵
closed Sunday, Monday and 2 weeks in spring – Meals (dinner only and lunch Friday and
Saturday) 27.50 **st.** ᵇ 9.00
Spec. Sautéed monkfish with mustard and cucumber. Bourride of chicken. Nectarine and
brioche summer pudding.

XX **Oaks**, 17 Corve St., SY8 1DA, ℰ (01584) 872325 – ⇄. 🆀🆂 𝓥𝐼𝑆𝐴
⌘ closed Sunday, Monday, 1 week in spring and 1 week in autumn – Meals (dinner only) 22.50 **t.** ᵇ 5.95.

X **Courtyard**, 2 Quality Sq., SY8 1AR, ℰ (01584) 878080 – ⇄
closed Sunday, 25-26 December, New Year, 2 weeks January, May Bank Holiday and 1 week
October – Meals (light lunch) (dinner Thursday to Saturday and Sunday lunch October-
May)/dinner a la carte 17.40/20.40 **t.** ᵇ 5.35.

⊚ ATS Weeping Cross Lane ℰ (01584) 872401

Particularly pleasant hotels and restaurants
are shown in the Guide by a red symbol.

Please send us the names
of anywhere you have enjoyed your stay.

Your **Michelin Guide** will be even better.

🏨🏨🏨 ... ⌂

XXXXX ... X

LUTON 404 S 28 *Great Britain G. – pop. 171 671.*

See : *Luton Hoo★ (Wernher Collection★★) AC* X.

🔋 *Stockwood Park, London Rd* ℰ *(01582) 413704, X –* 🔋, 🔋 *South Beds, Warden Hill Rd* ℰ *(01582) 575201.*

✈ *Luton International Airport :* ℰ *(01582) 405100, E : 1 ½ m.* X – **Terminal :** *Luton Bus Station.*

🗗 *The Bus Station, 65-67 Bute St., LU1 2EY* ℰ *(01582) 401579.*

London 35 – Cambridge 36 – Ipswich 93 – Oxford 45 – Southend-on-Sea 63.

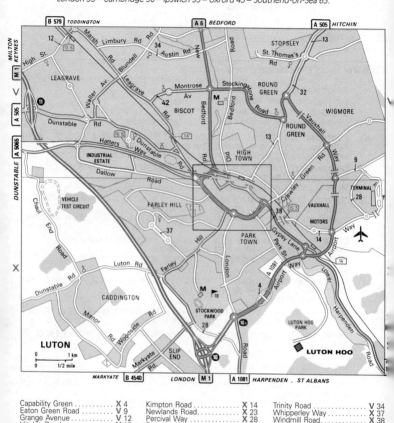

Capability Green . . . . **X** 4	Kimpton Road . . . . **X** 14	Trinity Road . . . . **V** 34
Eaton Green Road . . . . **V** 9	Newlands Road. . . . . **X** 23	Whipperley Way . . . . **X** 37
Grange Avenue . . . . **V** 12	Percival Way . . . . **X** 28	Windmill Road. . . . . **X** 38
Hitchin Road . . . . **V** 13	Stopsley Way . . . . **X** 32	Woodland Avenue . . . . **V** 42

🏨 **Strathmore Thistle,** Arndale Centre, LU1 2TR, ℰ (01582) 734199, Fax (01582) 402528 –
📱, 🔄 rm, 🍽 rest, 📺 ☎ & 🅿 – 🔬 300. ᴹⓈ ᴬᴱ ① 𝘝𝘐𝘚𝘈   Y n
Meals 18.50 **st.** and a la carte ⌀ 5.50 – ☲ 9.75 – **147 rm** 90.00/119.00 **st.,** 3 suites – SB.

🏨 **Shannon,** 40a Guildford St., LU1 2PA, ℰ (01582) 482119, Fax (01582) 482818 – 📺 ☎ ᴹⓈ
ᴬᴱ ① 𝘝𝘐𝘚𝘈 ᴶᴄʙ, 🛇   Y e
closed 25 and 26 December – **Meals** (closed Sunday) (bar lunch)/dinner a la carte 7.35/
11.80 **t.** – **28 rm** ☲ 49.50/59.50 **t.**

ⓐ ATS 67 Kingsway ℰ (01582) 597519   ATS High St., Oakley Rd, Leagrave
                                                ℰ (01582) 507020/592381

Prices	For notes on the prices quoted in this Guide, see the introduction.

LUTON

.UTTERWORTH Leics. 403 404 Q 26 – pop. 7 380.

🏌 Ullesthorpe Court Hotel, Frolesworth Rd ✆ (01455) 209023.

London 93 – Birmingham 34 – Coventry 14 – Leicester 16.

🏨 **Denbigh Arms**, 24 High St., LE17 4AD, ✆ (01455) 553537, Fax (01455) 556627 – 📺 ☎ 🅿
– 🔬 50. ⬤⬤ 🄰🄴 ⓞ 𝓥𝓘𝓢𝓐 𝓙𝓒𝓑. ⬤%
Meals (bar lunch Saturday) 8.95/13.95 **st.** and a la carte ⅙ 5.50 – ☷ 7.50 – **32 rm** 70.00/
80.00 **st.** – SB.

.YDFORD Devon 403 H 32 The West Country G. – pop. 1 734 – ✉ Okehampton.

See : Village★★.

Env. : Dartmoor National Park★★.

London 234 – Exeter 33 – Plymouth 24.

🏨 **Moor View House**, Vale Down, EX20 4BB, NE : 1½ m. on A 386 ✆ (01822) 820220, 🐎 –
✣📺 🅿
Meals (booking essential to non-residents) (dinner only) 25.00 **st.** ⅙ 5.50 – **4 rm** ☷ 50.00/
95.00 **st.** – SB.

🍴 **Castle Inn** with rm, EX20 4BH, ✆ (01822) 820242, Fax (01822) 820454, « 16C », 🐎 – 📺
🅿. ⬤⬤ 🄰🄴 ⓞ 𝓥𝓘𝓢𝓐 𝓙𝓒𝓑
closed 25 December – **Meals** (bar lunch)/dinner 15.95 **t.** and a la carte ⅙ 4.65 – **10 rm**
☷ 32.50/72.50 **t.** – SB.

YME REGIS Dorset 403 L 31 The West Country G. – pop. 3 851.

See : Town★ – The Cobb★.

🏌 Timber Hill ✆ (01297) 442963/442043.

🅱 Guildhall Cottage, Church St., DT7 3BS ✆ (01297) 442138.

London 160 – Dorchester 25 – Exeter 31 – Taunton 27.

🏛 **Alexandra,** Pound St., DT7 3HZ, ℘ (01297) 442010, Fax (01297) 443229, ≤, 辇 – 🺧 ☎ 🅿.
⬛ AE ⑩ VISA. ॐ
closed Christmas and New Year – **Meals** 12.50/22.50 **t.** and a la carte ⓘ 6.15 – **27 rm**
⌑ (dinner included) 48.00/145.00 **t.**

🏛 **Kersbrook,** Pound Rd, DT7 3HX, ℘ (01297) 442596, Fax (01297) 442596, 辇 – ⅙ rest,
🺧 🅿. ⬛ VISA
closed 8 January-8 February – **Meals** (bar lunch Monday, Friday and Saturday) (restricted
menu Sunday dinner residents only) 8.95/16.50 **t.** and dinner a la carte ⓘ 6.50 – **10 rm**
⌑ 55.00/82.00 **t.** – SB.

⬆ **Red House** without rest., Sidmouth Rd, DT7 3ES, W : ¾ m. on A 3052 ℘ (01297) 442055,
Fax (01297) 442055, 辇 – ⅙ 🺧 🅿. 辇. ॐ
mid March-mid October – **3 rm** ⌑ 30.00/50.00 **s.**

⬆ **White House** without rest., 47 Silver St., DT7 3HR, ℘ (01297) 443420, ≤ – 🺧 🅿
Easter-September – **7 rm** ⌑ 24.00/42.00.

at Uplyme (Devon) NW : 1¼ m. on B 3165 (A 3070) – ⊠ Lyme Regis.

⬆ **Amherst Lodge Farm** ॐ, DT7 3XH, NW : 1¼ m. by B 3165 (A 3070), taking left turn in
Yawl to Cathole ℘ (01297) 442773, Fax (01297) 442625, « Working farm », ⬤, 辇, park –
⅙ rm, 🺧 🅿. ॐ
closed Christmas – **Meals** (by arrangement) 23.00 **st.** ⓘ 6.00 – **3 rm** ⌑ 35.00/68.00 **st.**

LYMINGTON Hants. 👧👦👦 P 31 – pop. 13 508.

⟿ to the Isle of Wight (Yarmouth) (Wightlink Ltd) frequent services daily (30 mn).

🅱 St. Barb Museum & Visitor Information Centre, New St., SO41 9TW ℘ (01590) 672422
(summer only).

London 103 – Bournemouth 18 – Southampton 19 – Winchester 32.

🏛 **Stanwell House,** 15 High St., SO41 9AA, ℘ (01590) 677123, Fax (01590) 677756, 辇 –
⅙ rm, 🺧 ☎ – 🔏 40. ⬛ AE ⑩ VISA. ॐ
Meals (closed Sunday dinner) 16.50/20.00 **t.** and a la carte – **27 rm** ⌑ 50.00/140.00 **t.**,
1 suite.

🏛 **Passford House** ॐ, Mount Pleasant Lane, Mount Pleasant, SO41 8LS, NW : 2 m. by
A 337 and Sway rd ℘ (01590) 682398, Fax (01590) 683494, ≤, 👪, ☎, ⬛, ⬛, 辇, park, ॐ –
⅙ rest, 🺧 ☎ 🅿 – 🔏 100. ⬛ AE ⑩ VISA JCB
Meals 22.50 **t.** (dinner) and a la carte 19.00/27.50 **t.** ⓘ 6.50 – **54 rm** ⌑ 75.00/140.00 **t.**,
1 suite – SB.

⬆ **Albany House,** 3 Highfield, SO41 9GB, ℘ (01590) 671900, 辇 – ⅙ rest, 🺧 🅿. ॐ
closed 5 days Christmas – **Meals** (by arrangement) 14.50 – **3 rm** ⌑ 38.00/59.00.

⬆ **Efford Cottage,** Everton, SO41 0JD, W : 2 m. on A 337 ℘ (01590) 642315
Fax (01590) 642315, 辇 – ⅙ rest, 🺧 🅿
Meals (by arrangement) 15.00 **s.** – **3 rm** ⌑ 42.00/44.00 **s.**

XXX **Gordleton Mill** with rm, Silver St., Hordle, SO41 6DJ, NW : 3½ m. by A 337 and Sway Rc
🕸 ℘ (01590) 682219, Fax (01590) 683073, 綸, « Part 17C water mill, gardens » – ⅙, ▤ rest
🺧 ☎ 🅿. ⬛ AE ⑩ VISA
closed first 2 weeks November – **Provence :** **Meals** (closed Sunday dinner and Monday
(booking essential) 19.50-28.00 **t.** (lunch) and a la carte 43.50/50.50 **t.** ⓘ 9.50 – **6 rm**
⌑ 97.00/129.00 **t.**, 1 suite – SB
Spec. Salad of roast scallops with tomato sorbet and lemon vinaigrette. Smoked fillet ot
beef with a watercress purée, lentils and sauce bordelaise. Iced apple parfait with a vanilla
coulis.

✗ **Limpets,** 9 Gosport St., SO41 9BG, ℘ (01590) 675595, Fax (01590) 675595 – ⬛ VISA
closed Sunday and Monday – **Meals** 12.00/20.00 **t.** and a la carte ⓘ 7.25.

🔘 ATS Marsh Lane ℘ (01590) 675938/9

LYMM Ches. 👦👦👦 M 23 – pop. 2 583.
London 197 – Chester 26 – Liverpool 29 – Manchester 15.

🏛 **Lymm,** Whitbarrow Rd, WA13 9AQ, via Brookfield Rd ℘ (01925) 752233
Fax (01925) 756035, 辇 – ⅙ 🺧 ☎ 🅿 – 🔏 120. ⬛ AE ⑩ VISA
Meals (bar lunch Monday to Saturday)/dinner 18.50 **t.** ⓘ 5.50 – **62 rm** ⌑ 85.00/110.00 – SE

Demandez chez votre libraire le catalogue des **publications Michelin**

LYMPSTONE Devon 🔢 J 32 – *see Exmouth.*

LYNDHURST Hants. 🔢 🔢 P 31 *Great Britain G.* – *pop. 2 381.*
Env. : *New Forest*★★ *(Bolderwood Ornamental Drive*★★*, Rhinefield Ornamental Drive*★★ *).*
🏌, 🏌 *Dibden, Main Rd* ℘ *(01703) 845596* – 🏌 *New Forest, Southampton Rd* ℘ *(01703) 282752.*
🛈 *New Forest Museum & Visitor Centre, Main Car Park, SO43 7NY* ℘ *(01703) 282269.*
London 95 – Bournemouth 20 – Southampton 10 – Winchester 23.

🏨 **Parkhill** ⌂, Beaulieu Rd, SO43 7FZ, SE : 1 ¼ m. on B 3056 ℘ (01703) 282944, Fax (01703) 283268, ≼, �, « Tastefully furnished country house », 🌊, 🌊, 🌲, park – ℀ rest, 📺 ☎ 🅿 – 🔒 50. 🐵 🝍 ⑩ 🆅🆂🅰 🅹🅲🅱. 🛇
Meals 16.00/27.00 t. and a la carte ⌁ 7.95 – **18 rm** ⌑ 75.00/126.00 t., 2 suites – SB.

🏨 **Crown**, 9 High St., SO43 7NF, ℘ (01703) 282922, Fax (01703) 282751, 🌲 – ▐ 📺 ☎ 🅿 – 🔒 70. 🐵 🝍 ⑩ 🆅🆂🅰 🅹🅲🅱
Meals (bar lunch Monday to Saturday)/dinner 17.00 t. and a la carte ⌁ 8.00 – **38 rm** ⌑ 70.00/153.00 t., 1 suite – SB.

🏠 **Beaulieu**, Beaulieu Rd, SO42 7YQ, SE : 3 ½ m. on B 3056 ℘ (01703) 293344, Fax (01703) 292729, 🌊, 🌲 – 📺 ☎ 🅿 – 🔒 40. 🐵 🝍 ⑩ 🆅🆂🅰
Meals (dinner only) 18.50 t. and a la carte ⌁ 5.95 – **17 rm** ⌑ 65.00/125.00 st., 1 suite – SB.

🏠 **Ormonde House**, Southampton Rd, SO43 7BT, ℘ (01703) 282806, Fax (01703) 282004, 🌲 – ℀ 📺 ☎ 🅿. 🐵 🆅🆂🅰 🅹🅲🅱
closed 4 days Christmas – **Meals** (by arrangement) (residents only) (dinner only) 14.00 st. ⌁ 4.50 – **17 rm** ⌑ 31.00/62.00 st. – SB.

🏠 **Whitemoor House**, Southampton Rd, SO43 7BU, ℘ (01703) 282186, Fax (01703) 282186 – ℀ 📺 🅿. 🐵 🆅🆂🅰
closed Christmas-early February – **Meals** (by arrangement) 12.50 st. ⌁ 5.00 – **8 rm** ⌑ 30.00/55.00 st. – SB.

LYNMOUTH Devon 🔢 I 30 – *see Lynton.*

LYNTON Devon 🔢 I 30 *The West Country G.* – *pop. 1 870 (inc. Lynmouth).*
See : *Town*★ *(≼*★*).*
Env. : *Valley of the Rocks*★*, W : 1 m. – Watersmeet*★*, E : 1 ½ m. by A 39.*
Exc. : *Exmoor National Park*★★ *– Doone Valley*★*, SE : 7 ½ m. by A 39 (access from Oare on foot).*
🛈 *Town Hall, Lee Rd, EX35 6BT* ℘ *(01598) 752225.*
London 206 – Exeter 59 – Taunton 44.

🏨 **Lynton Cottage** ⌂, North Walk Hill, EX35 6ED, ℘ (01598) 752342, Fax (01598) 752597, ≼ bay and Countisbury Hill, 🌲 – 📺 ☎ 🅿. 🐵 🆅🆂🅰.
closed January – **Meals** (light lunch)/dinner 21.50 st. and a la carte ⌁ 4.90 – **16 rm** ⌑ (dinner included) 63.00/150.00 t. – SB.

🏨 **Hewitt's** ⌂, North Walk, EX35 6HJ, ℘ (01598) 752293, Fax (01598) 752489, ≼ bay and Countisbury Hill, « Victorian house in wooded cliffside setting », park – ℀ 📺 ☎ 🅿. 🐵 🆅🆂🅰 🅹🅲🅱
closed January and December – **Meals** (residents only) (dinner only) 16.50 st. – **10 rm** ⌑ 35.00/90.00 st. – SB.

🏠 **Highcliffe House**, Sinai Hill, EX35 6AR, ℘ (01598) 752235, Fax (01598) 752235, ≼ bay and Countisbury Hill, « Victorian residence, antiques », 🌲 – ℀ 📺 🅿. 🐵 🆅🆂🅰. 🛇
February-October – **Meals** (closed Sunday) (booking essential to non-residents) (dinner only) 25.00 st. ⌁ 8.75 – **6 rm** ⌑ 53.00/84.00 st.

🏠 **Castle Hill House**, Castle Hill, EX35 6JA, ℘ (01598) 752291, Fax (01598) 752291 – ℀ rest, 📺. 🐵 🆅🆂🅰 🛇
booking essential in winter – **Meals** (dinner only) a la carte 13.40/17.85 st. ⌁ 4.95 – **9 rm** ⌑ 27.50/60.00 st. – SB.

🏠 **Seawood** ⌂, North Walk, EX35 6HJ, ℘ (01598) 752272, ≼ bay and headland – ℀ rest, 📺 🅿
April-October – **Meals** (dinner only) 12.00 st. ⌁ 4.25 – **12 rm** ⌑ 28.00/58.00 st. – SB.

🏠 **Chough's Nest** ⌂, North Walk, EX35 6HJ, ℘ (01598) 753315, Fax (01598) 763529, ≼ bay and Countisbury Hill – ℀ 📺 🅿. 🐵 🆅🆂🅰 🅹🅲🅱. 🛇
March-November – **Meals** (dinner only) 18.00 st. – **12 rm** ⌑ 30.00/60.00 st.

🏠 **Victoria Lodge**, 30-31 Lee Rd, EX35 6BS, ℘ (01598) 753203, Fax (01598) 753203, 🌲 – ℀ 📺 🅿. 🐵 🆅🆂🅰. 🛇
closed November-January and restricted opening February-March – **Meals** (by arrangement) 16.00 st. – **9 rm** ⌑ 30.00/64.00 st. – SB.

⌂ **Longmead House,** 9 Longmead, EX35 6DQ, ✆ (01598) 752523, *Fax (01598) 752523*, 🌳 – ⊁ 🅿. [MC] VISA
16 March-31 October – **Meals** 13.00 **st.** 🍷 4.50 – **7 rm** ☕ 20.00/44.00 **st.** – SB.

⌂ **Rockvale** 🐌, Lee Rd, EX35 6HW, off Lee Rd ✆ (01598) 752279, ⩽ – ⊁ [TV] ☎ 🅿. [MC] VISA. 🐕
March-October – **Meals** (by arrangement) 14.00 **st.** 🍷 5.50 – **8 rm** ☕ (dinner included) 35.00/80.00 **st.** – SB.

at Lynmouth.

🏨 **Tors** 🐌, EX35 6NA, ✆ (01598) 753236, *Fax (01598) 752544*, ⩽ Lynmouth and bay, 🏊, 🌳 – |\$| [TV] ☎ 🅿 – 🎓 80. [MC] [AE] [D] VISA JCB
closed 3 January-3 March – **Meals** (bar lunch Monday to Saturday)/dinner 20.00 **st.** and a la carte 🍷 8.00 – **35 rm** ☕ 62.00/100.00 **st.** – SB.

🏨 **Rising Sun,** Harbourside, EX35 6EQ, ✆ (01598) 753223, *Fax (01598) 753480*, ⩽, « Part 14C thatched inn », 🌳 – ⊁ [TV] ☎. [MC] [AE] [D] VISA JCB. 🐕
Meals – (see below) – **15 rm** ☕ 55.00/120.00 **t.**, 1 suite – SB.

⌂ **Countisbury Lodge** 🐌 without rest., Tors Park, EX35 6NB, off Countisbury Hill ✆ (01598) 752388, ⩽ – ⊁ 🅿. [MC] VISA
April-October – **6 rm** ☕ 46.00/57.00 **st.**

⌂ **Heatherville** 🐌, Tors Park, EX35 6NB, by Tors Rd ✆ (01598) 752327, ⩽ – [TV] 🅿
March-October – **Meals** 15.00 **t.** – **8 rm** ☕ 24.00/37.00.

⌂ **Seaview Villa,** 6 Summerhouse Path, EX35 6ES, off Watersmeet Rd ✆ (01598) 753460 – ⊁ [TV]
closed December – **Meals** (communal dining) 13.00 **s.** 🍷 3.50 – **6 rm** ☕ 19.00/44.00 **s.** – SB.

🍴🍴 **Rising Sun** (at Rising Sun H.), Harbourside, EX35 6EQ, ✆ (01598) 753223, *Fax (01598) 753480*, « Part 14C thatched inn », 🌳 – ⊁. [MC] [AE] [D] VISA JCB
Meals (booking essential) (bar lunch)/dinner 25.00 **t.** and a la carte 🍷 6.80.

at Hillsford Bridges *SE : 4½ m. by A 39 – ✉ Lynton.*

🏨 **Combe Park** 🐌, EX35 6LE, ✆ (01598) 752356, *Fax (01598) 753484*, 🌳 – ⊁ rest, 🅿
April-October – (dinner only) 19.50 **t.** 🍷 9.25 – **9 rm** ☕ (dinner included) 60.00/110.00 **t.** – SB.

at Martinhoe *W : 4¼ m. via Coast rd (toll) – ✉ Barnstaple.*

🏨 **Old Rectory** 🐌, EX31 4QT, ✆ (01598) 763368, *Fax (01598) 763567*, 🌳 – ⊁ [TV] 🅿. 🐕
Easter-October – **Meals** (dinner only) 26.50 🍷 6.50 – **8 rm** ☕ (dinner included) 65.00/130.00 **t.** – SB.

LYTHAM *Lancs.* [402] L 22 – *see Lytham St. Anne's.*

LYTHAM ST. ANNE'S *Lancs.* [402] L 22 – *pop. 40 866.*
⛳ Fairhaven, Lytham Hall Park, Ansdell ✆ (01253) 736741 – ⛳ St. Annes Old Links, Highbury Rd ✆ (01253) 723597.
ℹ 290 Clifton Drive South, FY8 1LH ✆ (01253) 725610.
London 237 – Blackpool 7 – Liverpool 44 – Preston 13.

🏨 **Dalmeny,** 19-33 South Promenade, FY8 1LX, ✆ (01253) 712236, *Fax (01253) 724447*, ⩽ 🏋, ♨, 🏊, squash – |\$| [TV] ☎ 🅿 – 🎓 200. [MC] [AE] VISA. 🐕
closed 24 to 26 December – ***C'est la vie :*** **Meals** *(closed Sunday dinner to Wednesday)* (dinner only and Sunday lunch)/dinner 14.95 **st.** and a la carte 🍷 6.95 – ***Carvery :*** **Meals** (dinner only) 12.00 **st.** – **109 rm** ☕ 47.50/83.00 **t.**

🏨 **The Grand,** South Promenade, FY8 1NB, ✆ (01253) 721288, *Fax (01253) 714459*, ⩽ – |\$| ⊁ rm, [TV] ☎ 🅿 – 🎓 140. [MC] [AE] VISA
closed 24 to 26 December – ***The Bistro :*** **Meals** (bar lunch Monday to Saturday)/dinner a la carte 18.45/26.10 **t.** 🍷 7.00 – **40 rm** ☕ 55.00/90.00 **t.**

🏨 **Glendower,** North Promenade, FY8 2NQ, ✆ (01253) 723241, *Fax (01253) 723241*, ⩽, 🏋 ♨, 🏊 – |\$|, ⊁ rest, [TV] ☎ 🅿 – 🎓 150. [MC] [AE] [D] VISA
closed Christmas – **Meals** (bar lunch)/dinner 14.95 🍷 6.95 – **58 rm** ☕ 40.00/84.00 – SB.

🏨 **Bedford,** 307-311 Clifton Drive South, FY8 1HN, ✆ (01253) 724636, *Fax (01253) 729244* 🏋, ♨ – |\$|, ⊁ rest, [TV] ☎ 🅿 – 🎓 120. [MC] [AE] [D] VISA JCB
Meals (bar lunch)/dinner 15.00 **t.** and a la carte 🍷 4.25 – **36 rm** ☕ 45.00/70.00 **t.** – SB.

at Lytham *SE : 3 m. by A 584.*

🏨 **Clifton Arms,** West Beach, FY8 5QJ, ✆ (01253) 739898, *Fax (01253) 730657*, ⩽ – |\$| [TV] ☎ 🅿 – 🎓 150. [MC] [AE] [D] VISA. 🐕
Meals 14.50/21.50 **t.** and a la carte 🍷 7.50 – **40 rm** ☕ 75.00/115.00 **t.**, 4 suites – SB.

🏠 **The County-Premier Lodge,** Church Rd, FY8 5LH, ☎ (01253) 795128, *Fax (01253) 795149* – [TV] ☎. [MC] [AE] [D] VISA
Meals (grill rest.) 6.55 **t.** and a la carte – ☕ 4.95 – **21 rm** 44.25 **t.** – SB.

ATS Hove Rd, Off St. David's Road South ☎ (01253) 721300/711249

MACCLESFIELD *Ches.* [402] [403] [404] N 24 – *pop. 50 270.*

The Tytherington Club ☎ (01625) 434562 – Shrigley Hall, Shrigley Park, Pott Shrigley ☎ (01625) 575757.

Town Hall, SK10 1DX ☎ (01625) 504114.

London 186 – Chester 38 – Manchester 18 – Stoke-on-Trent 21.

🏠 **Sutton Hall** ⛶, Bullocks Lane, Sutton, SK11 0HE, SE : 2 m. by A 523 ☎ (01260) 253211, *Fax (01260) 252538,* – [TV] ☎ [P]. [MC] [AE] VISA.
Meals 10.95/19.95 **t.** and a la carte 🍷 5.75 – **9 rm** ☕ 75.00/90.00 **st.**

🏠 **Rising Sun - Premier Lodge,** Congleton Rd, Gawsworth, SK11 7XD, SW : 2 m. by A 537 on A 536 ☎ (01625) 422906, *Fax (01625) 434215* – rm, [TV] ☎ ♿ [P]. [MC] [AE] [D] VISA JCB.
Meals (grill rest.) a la carte 10.75/14.55 **t.** 🍷 3.95 – ☕ 4.95 – **28 rm** 42.25 **t.**

🏠 **Chadwick House,** 55 Beech Lane, SK10 2DS, N : ¼ m. on A 538 ☎ (01625) 615558, *Fax (01625) 610265,* – [TV] [P]. [MC] [AE] [D] VISA.
Meals (residents only) (dinner only) 8.95 **st.** 🍷 4.00 – **13 rm** ☕ 35.00/55.00 **st.**

🏠 **Travel Inn,** Titherington Business Park, Springwood Way, SK10 2XA, NE : 2 ½ m. by A 523 ☎ (01625) 427809, *Fax (01625) 422874* – rm, rest, [TV] ♿ [P]. [MC] [AE] [D] VISA
Meals (grill rest.) – **40 rm** 36.50 **t.**

at Adlington *N : 5 m. on A 523 – ✉ Macclesfield.*

🏠 **Travelodge,** London Road South, SK12 4NA, on A 523 ☎ (01625) 875292, Reservations (Freephone) 0800 850950 – rm, [TV] ♿ [P]. [MC] [AE] [D] VISA JCB.
Meals (grill rest.) – **32 rm** 44.95 **t.**

at Bollington *NE : 3½ m. by A 523 on B 5090 – ✉ Macclesfield.*

🍴🍴 **Mauro's,** 88 Palmerston St., SK10 5PW, ☎ (01625) 573898 – [MC] [AE] VISA JCB
closed Saturday lunch, Sunday, 25-26 December and 2 weeks August – **Meals** - Italian - a la carte 14.60/24.25 **t.** 🍷 6.75.

🍴 **Beasdales,** 22 Old Market Pl., High St., SK10 5PH, ☎ (01625) 575058 – [MC] VISA JCB
closed Sunday, Monday and 2 weeks August – **Meals** - Bistro - (dinner only) a la carte 15.20/23.20 **t.** 🍷 4.40.

at Pott Shrigley *NE : 4 ¾ m. by A 523 on B 5090 – ✉ Macclesfield.*

🏠 **Shrigley Hall** ⛶, Shrigley Park, SK10 5SB, N : ¼ m. ☎ (01625) 575757, *Fax (01625) 573323,* « Part 19C country house in park », – rm, [TV] ☎ [P] – 220. [MC] [AE] [D] VISA
Oakridge : **Meals** (dinner only) 23.00 **st.** and a la carte 🍷 6.50 – **150 rm** ☕ 99.00/150.00 **st.** – SB.

ATS 115 Hurdsfield Rd ☎ (01625) 425481/425233/424237

MACKWORTH *Derbs.* [402] [403] [404] P 25 – *see Derby.*

MADINGLEY *Cambs.* [404] U 27 – *see Cambridge.*

MAGHAM DOWN *E. Sussex – see Hailsham.*

MAIDENCOMBE *Devon* [403] J 32 – *see Torquay.*

When travelling for business or pleasure in **England, Wales, Scotland** *and* **Ireland**:

- use the series of five maps (nos [401], [402], [403], [404] and [923]) at a scale of 1:400 000
- they are the perfect complement to this Guide

MAIDENHEAD

*For business
or tourist interest:*
**MICHELIN Red Guide
EUROPE.**

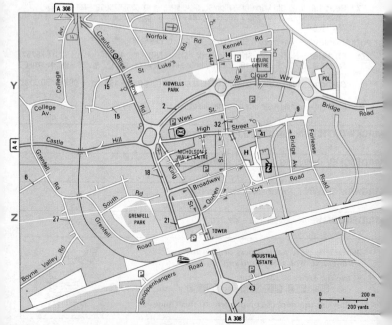

430

MAIDENHEAD Windsor & Maidenhead 404 R 29 – pop. 59 605.

🇷 Bird Hills, Drift Rd, Hawthorn Hill ℘ (01628) 771030/75588/26035 – 🇷 Shoppenhangers Rd ℘ (01628) 24693 X.

🇧 The Library, St. Ives Rd, SL6 1QU ℘ (01628) 781110.

London 33 – Oxford 32 – Reading 13.

Plans opposite

🏛 **Holiday Inn Maidenhead,** Manor Lane, SL6 2RA, ℘ (01628) 23444, Fax (01628) 770035, ⅃₆, ⅀ₛ, 🌀, ≪, squash – 📲 ↹, 🍽 rest, 📺 ☎ ᵴ ❹ – 🔬 400. 🆗🆎 ⑩ 𝘷𝘪𝘴𝘢. ⅍   X n
Promenade: Meals (closed Saturday lunch) 17.50/19.50 st. and a la carte – ⌸ 12.95 – 187 rm 145.00 st., 2 suites – SB.

🏛 **Fredrick's,** Shoppenhangers Rd, SL6 2PZ, ℘ (01628) 635934, Fax (01628) 771054, ⌲ –
📺 ☎ ❹ – 🔬 150. 🆗🆎 ⑩ 𝘷𝘪𝘴𝘢. ⅍   X c
closed 24 December-3 January – Meals – (see below) – 36 rm ⌸ 168.00/198.00 t., 1 suite.

🏚 **Thames Riviera,** at the bridge, SL6 8DW, ℘ (01628) 74057, Fax (01628) 776586, ≤, 🏖,
⌲ – 📺 ☎ ❹ – 🔬 50. 🆗🆎 ⑩ 𝘷𝘪𝘴𝘢. ⅍   V e
closed 26 to 30 December – **Jerome's:** Meals (light lunch Saturday) 10.50/ 18.50 t. and a la carte ⅃ 5.50 – ⌸ 8.95 – 52 rm 88.00/98.00 t. – SB.

🏚 **Walton Cottage,** Marlow Rd, SL6 7LT, ℘ (01628) 24394, Fax (01628) 773851 – 📲,
↹ rest, 📺 ☎ ❹ – 🔬 30. 🆗🆎 ⑩ 𝘷𝘪𝘴𝘢 𝘫𝘤𝘣. ⅍   Y e
closed 24 December-5 January – Meals (closed Friday to Sunday) (dinner only) 16.75 st. ⅃ 7.50 – 64 rm ⌸ 84.00/140.00 st.

↑ **Beehive Manor** without rest., Cox Green Lane, SL6 3ET, SW : 1 ½ m. by Shoppenhangers Rd, off Cox Green Rd ℘ (01628) 620980, Fax (01628) 621840, « Part 16C manor house », ⌲ – ↹.
closed 1 week Christmas – 3 rm ⌸ 38.00/58.00 s.

XXX **Fredrick's** (at Fredrick's H.), Shoppenhangers Rd, SL6 2PZ, ℘ (01628) 635934, Fax (01628) 771054, ⌲ – 🍽 ❹. 🆗🆎 ⑩ 𝘷𝘪𝘴𝘢   X c
closed Saturday lunch and 24 December-3 January – Meals 23.50/33.50 t. and a la carte ⅃ 8.00.

at Littlewick Green W : 3 ¼ m. by A 4 – V – ✉ Maidenhead.

🏚 **Riders Country House,** Bath Rd, SL6 3RQ, on A 4 ℘ (01628) 822085, Fax (01628) 829211 – 📺 ☎ ❹ – 🔬 30. 🆗🆎 𝘷𝘪𝘴𝘢. ⅍
Meals a la carte 13.00/19.50 t. ⅃ 4.50 – 19 rm ⌸ 75.00/90.00 st.

🅐 ATS Denmark St., Cordwallis Est. ℘ (01628) 20161

MAIDEN NEWTON Dorset 403 404 M 31 The West Country G. – pop. 937 – ✉ Dorchester.

Env. : Cerne Abbas★, NE : 5 ½ m.

London 143 – Bournemouth 35 – Bristol 55 – Taunton 34 – Weymouth 16.

XX **Le Petit Canard,** Dorchester Rd, DT2 0BE, ℘ (01300) 320536 – 🆗🆎 𝘷𝘪𝘴𝘢
closed Sunday, Monday, first week January and 1 week June – Meals (booking essential) (dinner only) 23.50 t. ⅃ 6.50.

MAIDSTONE Kent 404 V 30 Great Britain G. – pop. 90 878.

Env. : Leeds Castle★ AC, SE : 4 ½ m. by A 20 and B 2163.

🇷 Tudor Park Hotel, Ashford Rd, Bearsted ℘ (01622) 734334 – 🇷 Cobtree Manor Park, Chatham Rd, Boxley ℘ (01622) 753276.

🇧 The Gatehouse, The Old Palace Gardens, Mill St., ME15 6YE ℘ (01622) 673581.

London 36 – Brighton 64 – Cambridge 84 – Colchester 72 – Croydon 36 – Dover 45 – Southend-on-Sea 49.

🏛 **Stakis Maidstone,** Bearsted Rd, ME14 5AA, NE : 1 ½ m. by A 249 ℘ (01622) 734322, Fax (01622) 734600, ⅃₆, ⅀ₛ, 🌀 – ↹ rm, 🍽 rest, 📺 ☎ ᵴ ❹ – 🔬 90. 🆗🆎 ⑩ 𝘷𝘪𝘴𝘢. ⅍
Meals (closed lunch Saturday and Bank Holidays) 13.25/18.25 st. and dinner a la carte ⅃ 7.50 – ⌸ 10.25 – 136 rm 98.00/108.00 st., 3 suites – SB.

🏚 **Grangemoor,** 4-8 St. Michael's Rd, ME16 8BS, off Tonbridge Rd ℘ (01622) 677623, Fax (01622) 678246, ⌲ – 📺 ☎ ❹ – 🔬 100. 🆗🆎 𝘷𝘪𝘴𝘢
closed 25 to 30 December – Meals 12.50 t. and a la carte ⅃ 4.95 – 47 rm ⌸ 45.00/54.00 t. – SB.

🏚 **Travel Inn,** London Rd, ME16 0HG, NW : 2 m. on A 20 ℘ (01622) 752515, Fax (01622) 672469 – ↹ rm, 📺 ᵴ ❹. 🆗🆎 ⑩ 𝘷𝘪𝘴𝘢. ⅍
Meals (grill rest.) – 40 rm 36.50 t.

at Bearsted E : 3 m. by A 249 off A 20 – ⊠ Maidstone.

🏨🏨🏨 **Marriott Tudor Park H. & Country Club,** Ashford Rd, ME14 4NQ, on A 20
℘ (01622) 734334, Fax (01622) 735360, ≼, ₤₅, ☎s, ◪, ₨, ☞, park, ℀ – 🛊 ⤫ 🄿 🖻 ᵭ 🄿
– 🖾 300. **🐠** 🖭 ◑ **VISA** **JCB**. ✿
Meals (closed Saturday lunch) 20.00 **t.** (dinner) and a la carte 13.80/21.95 **t.** ⓝ 7.25 –
⌷ 10.75 – **117 rm** 95.00 **st.,** 1 suite – SB.

✕✕ **Soufflé,** The Green, ME14 4DN, off Yeoman Lane ℘ (01622) 737065, Fax (01622) 737065 –
🄿. **🐠** 🖭 **VISA**
closed Saturday lunch, Sunday dinner, 1 January and Bank Holidays – **Meals** 14.50/
18.90 **t.** and a la carte.

at Boughton Monchelsea S : 4½ m. by A 229 on B 2163 – ⊠ Maidstone.

🏛 **Tanyard** ॐ, Wierton Hill, ME17 4JT, S : 1 ½ m. by Park Lane on Wierton Rd
℘ (01622) 744705, Fax (01622) 741998, ≼, « 14C tannery », ☞ – ⤫ rest, 🖭 ☎ 🄿. **🐠** 🖭
◑ **VISA**. ✿
closed 25 December-late January – **Meals** (closed Monday, Tuesday and Saturday
lunch) 22.50/27.50 **t.** ⓝ 5.40 – **6 rm** ⌷ 65.00/140.00 **t.**

at Wateringbury SW : 4½ m. on A 26 – ⊠ Maidstone.

🏨🏨 **Wateringbury,** Tonbridge Rd, ME18 5NS, ℘ (01622) 812632, Fax (01622) 812720, ☎s,
☞ – ⤫ rm, 🖭 ☎ 🄿 – 🖾 75. **🐠** 🖭 ◑ **VISA** **JCB**. ✿
Meals a la carte 8.45/14.45 **t.** ⓝ 4.95 – **40 rm** 42.25 **t.**

at Larkfield W : 3¼ m. on A 20 – ⊠ Maidstone.

🏨🏨 **Larkfield Priory,** 812 London Rd, ME20 6HJ, ℘ (01732) 846858, Fax (01732) 846786 –
⤫ 🖭 ☎ 🄿 – 🖾 80. **🐠** 🖭 ◑ **VISA**
Meals (bar lunch Monday to Saturday)/dinner 17.50 **st.** and a la carte ⓝ 6.50 – ⌷ 9.00 –
51 rm 72.00 **st.** – SB.

🅐 ATS 165 Upper Stone St. ℘ (01622) 758738/758664

To visit a town or region: use the **Michelin** *Green Guides.*

MALDON Essex **404** W 28 – pop. 15 841.

🔏 Forrester Park, Beckingham Rd, Great Totham ℘ (01621) 891406 – 🔏, 🔏 Bunsay Downs,
Little Baddow Rd, Woodham Walter ℘ (01245) 412648/412369.
🄱 Coach Lane, CM9 7UH ℘ (01621) 856503.
London 42 – Chelmsford 9 – Colchester 17.

🏨🏨 **Blue Boar,** Silver St., CM9 4QE, ℘ (01621) 852681, Fax (01621) 856202 – ⤫ 🖭 ☎ 🄿 –
🖾 30. **🐠** 🖭 ◑ **VISA** **JCB**
Meals 11.75/17.50 **t.** and a la carte ⓝ 5.75 – ⌷ 8.95 – **28 rm** 65.00/80.00 **t.** – SB.

✕ **Chigborough Lodge,** Chigborough Rd, Heybridge, CM9 4RE, NE : 2 ½ m. by A 414 off
B 1026 ℘ (01621) 853590 – 🄿. **🐠** **VISA**
closed Saturday lunch, Sunday dinner, Monday, Tuesday, 2 weeks in summer and 2 weeks
in winter – Meals (booking essential) a la carte 16.00/22.00 **t.** ⓝ 6.20.

at Tolleshunt Knights NE : 7 m. by B 1026 – ⊠ Maldon.

🏨🏨🏨 **Five Lakes H. Golf & Country Club,** Colchester Rd, Tolleshunt Knights, CM9 8HX,
N : 1 ¼ m. by B 1026 ℘ (01621) 868888, Fax (01621) 869696, ₤₅, ☎s, ◪, ₨, park,
℀ indoor/outdoor, squash – 🛊, 🗏 rest, 🖭 ☎ ᵭ 🄿 – 🖾 450. **🐠** 🖭 ◑ **VISA**
Camelot : Meals (closed Sunday dinner) (dinner only and Sunday lunch)/dinner
23.50 **t.** and a la carte ⓝ 7.95 – **Bejerano's Brasserie :** Meals 17.50 **t.** and a la carte ⓝ 7.95 –
⌷ 8.95 – **110 rm** 85.00/115.00 **t.,** 4 suites – SB.

🅐 ATS 143-147 High St. ℘ (01621) 856541

MALMESBURY Wilts. **403 404** N 29 The West Country G. – pop. 4 439.

See : Town★ – Market Cross★★ – Abbey★.
🄱 Town Hall, Market Lane, SN16 9BZ ℘ (01666) 823748.
London 108 – Bristol 28 – Gloucester 24 – Swindon 19.

🏨🏨🏨 **Whatley Manor** ॐ, Easton Grey, SN16 0RB, W : 2 ½ m. on B 4040 ℘ (01666) 822888
Fax (01666) 826120, ≼, « Part 18C manor house », ☎s, ⌁, ☝, ☞, park, ℀ – 🖭 ☎ 🄿 –
🖾 40. **🐠** 🖭 ◑ **VISA**
Meals 16.00/29.00 **t.** ⓝ 7.00 – **29 rm** ⌷ 74.00/120.00 **t.** – SB.

🏠 **Old Bell,** Abbey Row, SN16 0AG, ☎ (01666) 822344, Fax (01666) 825145, « Part 13C former abbots hostel », 🌤 – 🍴 rest, 📺 ☎ 🅿 – 🔬 35. 🆎 🆎 ⓘ 🆚 🇯🇨🇧
Meals 15.00/26.00 st. ⅄ 11.00 – **30 rm** ⊃ 70.00/145.00 st., 1 suite – SB.

🏠 **Knoll House,** Swindon Rd, SN16 9LU, on B 4042 ☎ (01666) 823114, Fax (01666) 823897, ⬛, 🌤 – 🍴 rest, 📺 ☎ 🅿 – 🔬 35. 🆎 🆎 ⓘ 🆚
Meals 24.00 st. (dinner) and a la carte 15.00/21.50 st. ⅄ 5.00 – **22 rm** ⊃ 60.00/82.50 st. – SB.

at Crudwell N : 4 m. on A 429 – ✉ Malmesbury.

🏠 **Mayfield House,** SN16 9EW, on A 429 ☎ (01666) 577409, Fax (01666) 577977, 🌤 – 🍴 rest, 📺 ☎ 🅿 – 🔬 30. 🆎 🆎 ⓘ 🆚
closed first 2 weeks January – **Meals** (bar lunch Monday to Saturday)/dinner 15.95 t. ⅄ 4.95 – **20 rm** ⊃ 44.00/65.00 t. – SB.

MALPAS Ches. 🗺️🗺️ L 24 – pop. 3 684.
London 177 – Birmingham 60 – Chester 15 – Shrewsbury 26 – Stoke-on-Trent 30.

⌂ **Tilston Lodge** 🦢 without rest., Tilston, SY14 7DR, NW : 3 m. on Tilston Rd ☎ (01829) 250223, Fax (01829) 250223, « Rare breed farm animals », 🌤 – 🍴 📺 🅿. 🎇
3 rm ⊃ 35.00/64.00 s.

MALTON N. Yorks. 🗺️ R 21 Great Britain G. – pop. 4 294.
Env. : Castle Howard★★ (Park★★★) AC, W : 6 m.
🏌️, 🏌️, 🏌️ Malton & Norton, Welham Park, Welham Rd, Norton ☎ (01653) 692959.
🏢 58 Market Place, YO17 0LW ☎ (01653) 600048.
London 229 – Kingston-upon-Hull 36 – Scarborough 24 – York 17.

🏠 **Green Man,** 15 Market St., YO17 0LY, ☎ (01653) 600370, Fax (01653) 696006 – 📺 ☎ 🅿.
🆎 🆎 ⓘ 🆚. 🎇
Meals (grill rest.) 15.50 st. and a la carte ⅄ 5.95 – **23 rm** ⊃ 45.00/90.00 st., 1 suite.

🏠 **Talbot,** Yorkersgate, YO17 0AA, ☎ (01653) 694031, Fax (01653) 693355, 🌤 – 📺 ☎ 🅿 –
🔬 40. 🆎 🆎 ⓘ 🆚
Meals (bar lunch)/dinner 16.50 t. and a la carte ⅄ 6.95 – **30 rm** ⊃ 42.50/85.00 t., 1 suite – SB.

🏠 **Greenacres Country,** Amotherby, YO17 0TG, W : 2 ½ m. on B 1257 ☎ (01653) 693623, Fax (01653) 693623, 🔲, 🌤 – 🍴 📺 🅿. 🆎 🆚. 🎇
March-26 October – **Meals** (closed Sunday) (residents only) (dinner only) 12.25 st. ⅄ 3.50 – **9 rm** ⊃ 27.50/55.00 st. – SB.

at Wharram-Le-Street SE : 6 m. on B 1248 – ✉ Malton.

⌂ **Red House,** YO17 9TL, ☎ (01944) 768455, 🌤, 🎇 – 🍴 📺 🅿
closed 1 week Christmas – **Meals** (by arrangement) 15.00 st. ⅄ 3.00 – **3 rm** ⊃ 25.00/50.00 – SB.

🅰️ ATS 27 Commercial St., Norton ☎ (01653) 692567/693525

MALVERN Worcestershire 🗺️🗺️ N 27 – see Great Malvern.

MALVERN WELLS Worcestershire 🗺️🗺️ N 27 – see Great Malvern.

MAN (Isle of) 🗺️ FG 21 Great Britain G. – pop. 69 788.
See : Laxey Wheel★★ – Snaefell★ (☀️ ★★★) – Cregneash Folk Museum★.
⛴️ from Douglas to Belfast (Isle of Man Steam Packet Co. Ltd) (summer only) (4 h 30 mn) – from Douglas to Republic of Ireland (Dublin) (Isle of Man Steam Packet Co. Ltd) (4 h 30 mn) – from Douglas to Fleetwood (Isle of Man Steam Packet Co. Ltd) (summer only) (3 h 20 mn) – from Douglas to Heysham (Isle of Man Steam Packet Co. Ltd) (3 h 45 mn) – from Douglas to Liverpool (Isle of Man Steam Packet Co. Ltd) (4 h) – from Douglas to Ardrossan (Caledonian MacBrayne Ltd) (summer only) weekly (8 h).

Ballasalla.

🍴🍴 **Haworths,** Main Rd, IM9 2DA, ☎ (01624) 822940 – 🆎 🆚
closed Saturday lunch, Sunday and 3 weeks January – **Meals** 14.95/25.00 st. ⅄ 9.00.

Castletown – pop. 3 152.

🖪 Town Hall ℘ (01624) 825005.
Douglas 10.

Ⓧ **Chablis Cellar,** 21 Bank St., IM9 1AT, ℘ (01624) 823527 – ◍ 𝑉𝐼𝑆𝐴
closed Sunday dinner – **Meals** a la carte 10.15/25.15 **t.** ♦ 8.00.

Douglas – pop. 22 214.

🖪 Douglas Municipal, Pulrose Park ℘ (01624) 661558 – 🖪 King Edward Bay, Groudle Rd, Onchan ℘ (01624) 620430/673821.

✈ Ronaldsway Airport : ℘ (01624) 821600, SW : 7 m. – **Terminal** : Coach service from Lord St.

🖪 Sea Terminal Building ℘ (01624) 686766.

🏛 **Mount Murray H. & Country Club,** Santon, IM4 2HT, SW : 4 ¾ m. by A 5 ℘ (01624) 661111, Fax (01624) 611116, ⅙, ⌾, 🔲, 🖪, park, ℘, squash – |♦|, ↝ rm, ◫ ☎ ♦ 𝐏 – 🕮 300. ◍ 𝔸𝔼 ◍ 𝑉𝐼𝑆𝐴. ⌘
Meals 13.75/21.00 **st.** and a la carte ♦ 7.00 – **Murray's :** **Meals** (closed Sunday dinner) (dinner only and Sunday lunch)/dinner 21.00 **st.** and a la carte ♦ 7.00 – **90 rm** ⌐ 80.00/120.00 **st.** – SB.

🏛 **Regency,** Queens Promenade, IM2 4NN, ℘ (01624) 680680, Fax (01624) 680690, ⩽ – |♦|, ↝ rm, ◫ ☎ – 🕮 70. ◍ 𝔸𝔼 ◍ 𝑉𝐼𝑆𝐴. ⌘
Five Continents : **Meals** 12.50 **st.** (lunch) and a la carte 18.50/25.50 **st.** ♦ 8.50 – ⌐ 7.50 – **28 rm** 65.00/90.00 **st.**, 4 suites.

🏛 **Sefton,** Harris Promenade, IM1 2RW, ℘ (01624) 626011, Fax (01624) 676004, ⩽, ⅙, ⌾, 🔲 – |♦|, ↝ rm, ◫ ☎ ♦ 𝐏 – 🕮 80. ◍ 𝔸𝔼 ◍ 𝑉𝐼𝑆𝐴. ⌘
Meals (bar lunch Monday to Friday)/dinner 14.00 **st.** and a la carte ♦ 6.00 – **77 rm** ⌐ 55.00/79.00 **st.**, 1 suite – SB.

🏛 **Empress,** Central Promenade, IM2 4RA, ℘ (01624) 661155, Fax (01624) 673554, ⅙, ⌾, 🔲 – |♦|, ▤ rest, ◫ ☎ – 🕮 150. ◍ 𝔸𝔼 ◍ 𝑉𝐼𝑆𝐴. ⌘
Meals 12.50 **t.** (dinner) and a la carte 17.00/25.00 **st.** ♦ 6.00 – ⌐ 7.50 – **99 rm** 65.00/75.00 **t.**, 3 suites – SB.

🏛 Admirals House, 12 Loch Promenade, IM1 2LX, ℘ (01624) 629551, Fax (01624) 675021 – |♦| ◫ ☎
Meals - Spanish rest. – **12 rm.**

🔧 ATS Mount Vernon, Peel Rd ℘ (01624) 622661   ATS 5-7 South Quay ℘ (01624) 676532

Peel – pop. 3 829.

🖪 Town Hall, Derby Rd ℘ (01624) 842341.
Douglas 11.

↑ **Haven,** 10 Peveril Av., IM5 1QB, ℘ (01624) 842585, Fax (01624) 842585 – ↝ ◫. ◍ 𝑉𝐼𝑆𝐴 ⌘
Meals (by arrangement) (communal dining) 10.50 **st.** – **3 rm** ⌐ 30.00/40.00 **st.** – SB.

Port Erin.

↑ **Rowany Cottier** without rest., Spaldrick, IM9 6PE, ℘ (01624) 832287, ⩽ Port Erin Bay, ⋐ – ↝ ◫ 𝐏. ⌘
5 rm ⌐ 35.00/51.00 **st.**

Ramsey.

↑ **The River House** ⌾, IM8 3DA, N : ¼ m. turning left after bridge before Bridge Inn o Bowring Rd ℘ (01624) 816412, ⩽, « Part Georgian house, riverside setting », ⋐ – ◫ 𝐏
Meals (by arrangement) (communal dining) 23.00 – **3 rm** ⌐ 45.00/70.00 **st.**

↑ **Rose Cottage** ⌾, St. Judes, IM7 3BX, NW : 4 ½ m. off A 13 ℘ (01624) 880610, ⋐ – ↝ ◫ 𝐏
closed 25 December – **Meals** (by arrangement) (communal dining) 13.20 **st.** – **3 rm** ⌐ 24.00/48.00 **st.**

Sulby – ⊠ Lezayre.
Douglas 16.

↑ **Kerrowmoar House** ⌾, IM7 2AX, E : ½ m. on Ramsey rd ℘ (01624) 89754? Fax (01624) 897927, « Part Georgian house, antiques », 🔲, ⋐, park, ℘ – ◫ ☎ 𝐏. 𝔸𝔼.
closed 24 December-2 January – **Meals** (by arrangement) (communal dining) 15.00 **s.** **4 rm** ⌐ 48.00/90.00 **s.**

MANCHESTER

Gtr. Manchester **402** **403** **404** N 23 *Great Britain G. – pop. 402 889*

London 202 – Birmingham 86 – Glasgow 221 – Leeds 43 – Liverpool 35 – Nottingham 72.

TOURIST INFORMATION

🛈 *Manchester Visitor Centre, Town Hall Extension, M60 2LA ℘ (061) 234 3157/8.*
🛈 *Manchester Airport, International Arrivals Hall, Terminal 1, M90 3NY ℘ (0161) 436 3344 –*
Manchester Airport, International Arrivals Hall, Terminal 2, M90 4TU ℘ (061) 489 6412.

PRACTICAL INFORMATION

🛏 *Heaton Park, Prestwick ℘ (0161) 798 0295,* **ABV**
🛏 *Houldsworth Park, Houldsworth St., Reddish, Stockport ℘ (0161) 442 9611.*
🛏 *Chorlton-cum-Hardy, Barlow Hall, Barlow Hall Rd ℘ (0161) 881 3139.*
🛏 *William Wroe, Pennybridge Lane, Flixton ℘ (0161) 748 8680.*
✈ *Manchester International Airport : ℘ (0161) 489 3000, S : 10 m. by A 5103 –* **AX** *–*
and M 56 – Terminal : *Coach service from Victoria Station.*

SIGHTS

See : *City★ - Castlefield Heritage Park★* **CZ** *– Town Hall★* **CZ** *– City Art Gallery★* **CZ M2** *–*
Cathedral★ (Stalls and Canopies★) **CY**

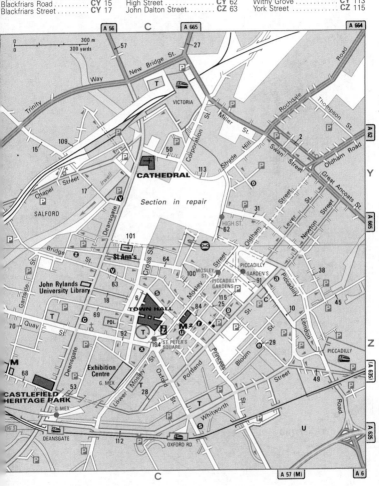

GREEN TOURIST GUIDES

Picturesque scenery, buildings

Attractive routes

Touring programmes

Plans of towns and buildings.

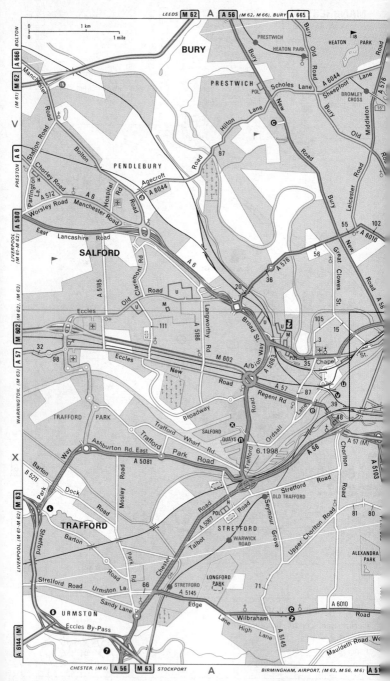

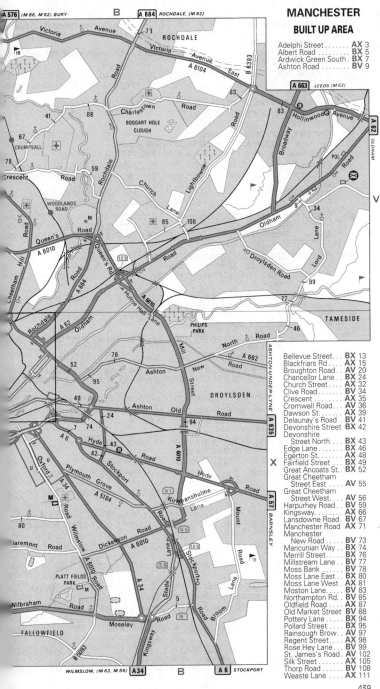

MANCHESTER
BUILT UP AREA

439

Victoria and Albert, Water St., M3 4JQ, ℰ (0161) 832 1188, *Fax (0161) 834 2484*, « Converted 19C warehouse, television themed interior », ₤₅, ☎, – ฿, ✻ rm, ▤ ☎ ₺,
🅿 – 🔬 300. 🐵 🝏 ⓞ 𝘝𝘐𝘚𝘈, ✺
AX u
Café Maigret : Meals a la carte 17.50/31.50 **t.** ₰ 10.50 – (see also *Sherlock Holmes* below)
– ☲ 10.50 – **152 rm** 149.00 **st.**, 4 suites – SB.

Holiday Inn Crowne Plaza Midland, Peter St., M60 2DS, ℰ (0161) 236 3333,
Fax (0161) 932 4100, ₤₅, ☎, 🔲, squash – ฿, ✻ rm, ▤ 🆅 ₺ ₺ 🅿 – 🔬 600. 🐵 🝏 ⓞ 𝘝𝘐𝘚𝘈
JᴄB, ✺
CZ x
French rest. : Meals (dinner only) 32.50 **t.** and a la carte – *Trafford Room :* Meals *(closed Saturday lunch)* (carving rest.) 18.95 **t.** and a la carte – ☲ 11.95 – **296 rm** 150.00/170.00 **t.**,
7 suites – SB.

Ramada, Blackfriars St., Deansgate, M3 2EQ, ℰ (0161) 835 2555, *Fax (0161) 835 3077* – ฿,
✻ rm, ▤ rest, 🆅 ☎ ₺ 🅿 – 🔬 400. 🐵 🝏 ⓞ 𝘝𝘐𝘚𝘈 JᴄB, ✺
CY v
Meals 12.50/19.50 **st.** and a la carte – ☲ 10.50 – **195 rm** 128.00 **st.**, 5 suites.

Palace, Oxford St., M60 7HA, ℰ (0161) 288 1111, *Fax (0161) 288 2222*, « Victorian Gothic architecture, former Refuge Assurance building » – ฿, ✻ rm, 🆅 ☎ – 🔬 850. 🐵 🝏 ⓞ
𝘝𝘐𝘚𝘈
Waterhouses : Meals *(closed lunch Saturday and Sunday)* 14.95/16.95 **t.** and dinner a la carte ₰ 5.95 – ☲ 10.50 – **169 rm** 109.00/149.00 **st.** CZ s

Copthorne Manchester, Clippers Quay, Salford Quays, M5 2XP, ℰ (0161) 873 7321,
Fax (0161) 873 7318, ₤₅, ☎, 🔲 – ฿, ✻ rm, ▤ rest, 🆅 ☎ ₺ 🅿 – 🔬 150. 🐵 🝏 ⓞ
𝘝𝘐𝘚𝘈, ✺ – *Chandlers :* Meals 17.50/19.50 **st.** and a la carte ₰ 9.50 – ☲ 11.95 – **166 rm**
140.00/175.00 **st.** AX n

Portland Thistle, 3-5 Portland St., Piccadilly Gdns., M1 6DP, ℰ (0161) 228 3400
Fax (0161) 228 6347, ☎ – ฿, ✻ rm, 🆅 ☎ 🅿 – 🔬 300. 🐵 🝏 ⓞ 𝘝𝘐𝘚𝘈 CZ a
Winston's : Meals 16.45/20.45 **st.** and a la carte ₰ 6.95 – ☲ 11.25 – **204 rm** 108.00/
143.00 **st.**, 1 suite – SB.

Castlefield, Liverpool Rd, M3 4JR, ℰ (0161) 832 7073, *Fax (0161) 839 0326,* ₤₅, ☎, 🔲 –
฿, ▤ rest, 🆅 ☎ ₺ 🅿 – 🔬 60. 🐵 🝏 ⓞ 𝘝𝘐𝘚𝘈, ✺
AX v
closed 25 and 26 December – Meals (bar lunch)/dinner 14.95 **t.** and a la carte ₰ 4.45 –
48 rm ☲ 74.00/80.00 **t.** – SB.

Campanile, 55 Ordsall Lane, M5 4RS, ℰ (0161) 833 1845, *Fax (0161) 833 1847* – ✻ 🆅 ☎
₺ 🅿 – 🔬 60. 🐵 🝏 ⓞ 𝘝𝘐𝘚𝘈 JᴄB AX e
Meals 10.55 **st.** and a la carte ₰ 4.95 – ☲ 4.50 – **105 rm** 38.00.

Comfort Friendly Inn, Birch St., Hyde Rd, West Gorton, M12 5NT, SE : 2 ½ m
by A 57 ℰ (0161) 220 8700, *Fax (0161) 220 8848* – ✻ 🆅 ☎ ₺ 🅿 – 🔬 100. 🐵 🝏 ⓞ
𝘝𝘐𝘚𝘈
BX z
Meals (bar lunch)/dinner 9.75 **st.** and a la carte ₰ 4.50 – ☲ 5.75 – **90 rm** 38.50 **st.** – SB.

Travel Inn, Basin 8, The Quays, Salford Quays, M5 4SQ, ℰ (0161) 872 4026
Fax (0161) 876 0094 – ✻ rm, 🆅 ₺ 🅿. 🐵 🝏 ⓞ 𝘝𝘐𝘚𝘈, ✺
AX z
Meals (grill rest.) – **52 rm** 36.50 **t.**

Sherlock Holmes (at Victoria and Albert H.), Water St., M3 4JQ, ℰ (0161) 832 1188
Fax (0161) 832 2484 – ▤ 🅿. 🐵 🝏 ⓞ 𝘝𝘐𝘚𝘈 AX r
Meals *(closed Sunday)* 18.00/34.00 **t.** and dinner a la carte ₰ 10.95.

Simply Heathcotes, Jackson Row, M2 5WB, ℰ (0161) 835 3536, *Fax (0161) 835 3534*
▤, 🐵 🝏 𝘝𝘐𝘚𝘈 JᴄB CZ c
closed 25-26 December, 1 January and Bank Holidays – Meals 11.50/17.50 ₰
and a la carte 21.50/26.50 **t.** ₰ 6.50.

Air, 40 Chorlton St., M1 3HW, ℰ (0161) 661 1111, *Fax (0161) 661 1112* – ▤. 🐵 🝏 𝘝𝘐𝘚𝘈
closed lunch July and August, Sunday, 25-26 December, 1 January and Easter Sunday
Meals a la carte 21.90/27.40 **t.** CZ c

Brasserie St Pierre, 57-63 Princess St., M2 4EQ, ℰ (0161) 228 0231, *Fax (0161) 228 023*
– 🝏 🝏 𝘝𝘐𝘚𝘈 CZ e
closed Saturday lunch, Monday dinner, Sunday and 24 December-2 January – Mea
13.95 **t.** and a la carte.

Est, Est, Est, 5 Ridgefield, M2 6EG, ℰ (0161) 833 9400 – ▤ rest. 🐵 🝏 ⓞ 𝘝𝘐𝘚𝘈 JᴄB
closed 25 and 26 December – Meals - Italian - a la carte 10.50/17.50 ₰ 4.80. CZ c

Giulio's Terrazza, 14 Nicholas St., M1 4EJ, ℰ (0161) 236 4033, *Fax (0161) 228 6501* – ▤
🐵 🝏 ⓞ 𝘝𝘐𝘚𝘈 JᴄB CZ c
closed Sunday, 25 December and Bank Holidays – Meals - Italian - 9.50/12.50
and a la carte ₰ 5.80.

Koreana, Kings House, 40a King St. West, M3 2WY, ℰ (0161) 832 433
Fax (0161) 832 2293 – 🐵 🝏 ⓞ 𝘝𝘐𝘚𝘈 CZ c
closed lunch Saturday and Bank Holidays, Sunday and 1 week Christmas – Meals - Korea
- 5.50/13.50 **t.** and a la carte.

XX **Royal Orchid,** 36 Charlotte St., M1 4FD, ℰ (0161) 236 5183, *Fax (0161) 236 8830* – 🆖 🆎
🇴 *VISA*　　　　　　　　　　　　　　　　　　　　　　　　　　　　　CZ　o
closed lunch Monday and Saturday, Sunday and 25-26 December – **Meals** - Thai - 8.50 **t.**
(lunch) and a la carte 12.25/19.70 **t.** ⓐ 4.50.

X **Market,** 104 High St., M4 1HQ, ℰ (0161) 834 3743, *Fax (0161) 834 3743* – 🆖 🆎 🇴 *VISA*
JCB　　　　　　　　　　　　　　　　　　　　　　　　　　　　　　CY　o
closed Sunday to Tuesday, 1 week Easter, August and 1 week Christmas – **Meals** - Bistro -
(dinner only) a la carte 16.85/24.35 **t.** ⓐ 4.95.

X **Mash,** 40 Chorlton St., M1 3HW, ℰ (0161) 661 6161, *Fax (0161) 661 6060* – 🖃. 🆖 🆎
🈂️　　*VISA*　　　　　　　　　　　　　　　　　　　　　　　　　　CZ　e
closed Easter Sunday, 25-26 December and 1 January – Meals a la carte 13.50/20.50 **t.**

X **The Colony,** 16 Princess St., M1 4NB, ℰ (0161) 236 4516 – 🆖 🆎 🇴 *VISA*　　　CZ　u
closed Saturday lunch, Sunday and Bank Holidays – **Meals** - South-east Asian -
a la carte 12.25/16.25 **t.** ⓐ 8.00.

X **Chiang Rai,** 16 Princess St., M1 4NB, ℰ (0161) 237 9511 – 🆖 🆎 🇴 *VISA*　　　CZ　u
closed Sunday lunch and Bank Holidays – **Meals** - Thai - a la carte 13.40/18.95 ⓐ 8.00.

at Northenden *S : 5¼ m. by A 5103* – AX – ✉ *Manchester*.

🏨 **Forte Posthouse Manchester,** Palatine Rd, M22 4FH, ℰ (0161) 998 7090,
Fax (0161) 946 0139 – 🛗, ✱ rm, 📺 ☎ 🅿 – 🔬 150. 🆖 🆎 🇴 *VISA* *JCB*
closed 24 December-3 January – **Meals** (bar lunch Saturday and Sunday) a la carte 17.75/
26.20 **st.** ⓐ 7.25 – ☲ 8.95 – **190 rm** 69.00 **st.** – SB.

at Didsbury *S : 5½ m. by A 5103* – AX – *on A 5145* – ✉ *Manchester*.

X **Est, Est, Est,** 756 Wilmslow Rd, M20 0RN, ℰ (0161) 445 8209 – 🖃. 🆖 🆎 *VISA*
closed 25 and 26 December – **Meals** - Italian - 9.95 **t.** and a la carte ⓐ 5.65.

X **Chiang Rai,** (first floor) 762-766 Wilmslow Rd, M20 2DR, ℰ (0161) 448 2277 – 🆖 🆎 🇴
VISA
closed Monday and Tuesday – **Meals** - Thai - (dinner only) a la carte 13.40/18.95 ⓐ 8.00.

at Manchester Airport *S : 9 m. by A 5103* – AX – *off M 56* – ✉ *Manchester*.

🏨 **Manchester Airport Hilton,** Outwood Lane (Terminal One), M90 4WP,
ℰ (0161) 435 3000, *Fax (0161) 435 3040*, 🇮🇴, ✿, 🔲 – 🛗, ✱ rm, 🖃 📺 ☎ 🕭 🅿 – 🔬 300.
🆖 🆎 🇴 *VISA* *JCB*. ✛
Meals 18.50 **t.** (lunch) and a la carte 23.20/28.45 **t.** ⓐ 10.50 – **Portico :** Meals *(closed
Sunday and Bank Holidays)* (dinner only) 29.00 **t.** ⓐ 11.50 – ☲ 13.95 – **222 rm** 150.00/
210.00 **st.**, 1 suite – SB.

🏨 **Forte Posthouse Manchester Airport,** Outwood Lane (Terminal One), M90 3NS,
ℰ (0161) 437 5811, *Fax (0161) 436 2340*, 🇮🇴, ✿, 🔲 – 🛗, ✱ rm, 🖃 📺 ☎ 🅿 – 🔬 75. 🆖
🆎 🇴 *VISA* *JCB*. ✛
Meals (bar lunch Monday to Saturday)/dinner 12.95 **t.** and a la carte – ☲ 10.95 – **284 rm**
89.00/129.00 **st.**, 1 suite – SB.

🏨 **Etrop Grange,** Thorley Lane, M90 4EG, ℰ (0161) 499 0500, *Fax (0161) 499 0790* – ✱ rm,
📺 ☎ 🕭 🅿 – 🔬 40. 🆖 🆎 🇴 *VISA* *JCB*
Meals *(closed Saturday lunch)* 17.50/30.00 **st.** ⓐ 7.50 – ☲ 10.75 – **37 rm** 110.00/160.00 **st.**,
2 suites – SB.

🏨 **Holiday Inn Garden Court,** Outwood Lane (Terminal One), M90 4HL,
ℰ (0161) 498 0333, *Fax (0161) 498 0222* – 🛗, ✱ rm, 📺 ☎ 🕭 🅿. 🆖 🆎 🇴 *VISA* *JCB*.
✛
Meals *(closed lunch Saturday and Sunday)* (bar lunch)/dinner 14.00 **st.** and a la carte
– ☲ 5.95 – **163 rm** 57.00 **st.**

🏨 **Travel Inn,** Finney Lane, Heald Green, SK8 2QH, E : 2 m. by B 5166 ℰ (0161) 499 1944,
Fax (0161) 437 4910 – ✱ rm, 📺 🕭 🅿 – 🔬 70. 🆖 🆎 🇴 *VISA*. ✛
Meals (grill rest.) – **60 rm** 36.50 **t.**

XXX **Moss Nook,** Ringway Rd, Moss Nook, M22 5WD, ℰ (0161) 437 4778, *Fax (0161) 498 8089*
– 🅿. 🆖 🆎 🇴 *VISA*
closed Saturday lunch, Sunday, Monday and 2 weeks Christmas – **Meals** 16.95/29.95 **t.**
and a la carte ⓐ 7.00.

t Chorlton-Cum-Hardy *SW : 5 m. by A 5103 on A 6010* – ✉ *Manchester*.

⌂ **Sabre D'or** without rest., 392 Wilbraham Rd, M21 0UH, ℰ (0161) 881 5055,
Fax (0161) 881 1546 – 📺 ☎ 🅿　　　　　　　　　　　　　　　　　　AX　c
16 rm ☲ 35.00/50.00.

⌂ **Abbey Lodge** without rest., 501 Wilbraham Rd, M21 0UJ, ℰ (0161) 862 9266,
Fax (0161) 862 9266, 🌳 – 📺 🅿. ✛　　　　　　　　　　　　　　　AX　z
4 rm ☲ 35.00/45.00 **s.**

at Eccles W : 4 m. by M 602 – **AX** – ⊠ Manchester.

🏛 **Highbury,** 113 Monton Rd, M30 9HQ, NW : 1 ¼ m. by A 576 on B 5229 ℘ (0161) 787 8545, Fax (0161) 787 9023 – ✲ rest, 📺 ☎ 🅿. ⚫ ⚫ ⚫ 🆚. ✲
closed 24 December-1 January – **Meals** (by arrangement) (residents only) (dinner only)
a la carte 10.50/12.50 **st.** – **15 rm** ⊇ 38.00/52.00 **st.**

at Worsley W : 7 ¼ m. by M 602 – **AV** – and M 62 (eastbound) on A 572 – ⊠ Manchester.

🏨 **Novotel Manchester West,** Worsley Brow, M28 2YA, at junction 13 of M 62 ℘ (0161) 799 3535, Fax (0161) 703 8207, ⏋ – |₤|, ✲ rm, 🔳 rest, 📺 ☎ 🕭 🅿 – 🔬 220. ⚫ ⚫ 🆚
Meals 16.00 **st.** and a la carte ⅙ 5.35 – ⊇ 8.95 – **119 rm** 69.00 **st.**

✕✕ **Tung Fong,** 2 Worsley Rd, M28 4NL, on A 572 ℘ (0161) 794 5331, Fax (0161) 727 9598 – ▤. ⚫ ⚫ 🆚
closed lunch Saturday and Sunday – **Meals** - Chinese (Peking) - 5.90/15.50 **st.** and a la carte.

at Pendlebury NW : 4 m. by A 6 on A 666 – ⊠ Manchester.

🏨 **Henry Boddington,** 219 Bolton Rd, M27 8TG, ℘ (0161) 736 5143, Fax (0161) 737 2786 – 📺 ☎ 🕭 🅿. ⚫ ⚫ ⚫ 🆚. ✲
Meals (grill rest.) 6.55 **t.** and a la carte – ⊇ 4.95 – **30 rm** 44.25 **t.**
AV a

at Swinton NW : 4 m. by A 580 – **AV** – and A 572 on B 5231 – ⊠ Manchester.

🏨 **New Ellesmere - Premier Lodge,** East Lancs Rd, M27 8AA, SW : ½ m. on A 580 ℘ (0161) 728 2791, Fax (0161) 794 8222 – ✲ rm, 📺 ☎ 🕭 🅿. ⚫ ⚫ ⚫ 🆚. ✲
Meals (grill rest.) a la carte 8.55/14.30 **st.** ⅙ 4.25 – ⊇ 4.95 – **27 rm** 44.25 **st.**

ⓐ ATS Chester St. ℘ (0161) 236 5505
ATS 98 Wilmslow Rd, Rusholme ℘ (0161) 224 6296
ATS Warren Rd, Trafford Park ℘ (0161) 872 7631

ATS 122 Higher Rd, Urmston ℘ (0161) 748 6990/5923
ATS 20/28 Waterloo Rd ℘ (0161) 832 7752

MANCHESTER AIRPORT Gtr. Manchester 402 403 404 N 23 – see Manchester.

MANGOTSFIELD Bristol 403 404 M 29 – see Bristol.

MANNINGTREE Essex 404 X 28 – pop. 5 043 – ⊠ Colchester.
London 67 – Colchester 10 – Ipswich 12.

🏠 **Aldhams** without rest., Bromley Rd, Lawford, CO11 2NE, SW : 2 ½ m. by B 1352 and A 137 on Bromley Rd ℘ (01206) 393210, Fax (01206) 393210, « Lutyens style house, walled garden », ✿ – ✲ 📺 🅿. ✲
closed 24 to 26 December – **3 rm** ⊇ 25.00/45.00 **s.**

✕ **Stour Bay Café,** 39-43 High St., CO11 1AH, ℘ (01206) 396687, Fax (01206) 395462 – ⚫ ⚫ 🆚
closed lunch Tuesday to Thursday, Sunday, Monday, 2 weeks in winter and 2 weeks in summer – **Meals** a la carte 14.15/22.45 **t.** ⅙ 6.95.

MARAZION Cornwall 403 D 33 The West Country G. – pop. 1 381 – ⊠ Penzance.
Env. : St. Michael's Mount★★ (≤★★) – Ludgvan★ (Church★) N : 2 m. by A 30 – Chysauster Village★, N : 2 m. by A 30 – Gulval★ (Church★) W : 2 ½ m – Prussia Cove★, SE : 5 ½ m by A 30 and minor rd.
ⓕ Praa Sands ℘ (01736) 763445.
London 318 – Penzance 3 – Truro 26.

🏛 **Mount Haven,** Turnpike Rd, TR17 0DQ, ℘ (01736) 710249, Fax (01736) 71165 ≤ St. Michael's Mount and Mount's Bay – ✲ rest, 📺 ☎ 🅿. ⚫ ⚫ 🆚
closed 1 week Christmas – **Meals** (dinner only and Sunday lunch)/dinner 19.00 **s** and a la carte ⅙ 4.75 – **17 rm** ⊇ 39.00/77.00 **st.**

at St. Hilary E : 2 ½ m. by Turnpike Rd, on B 3280 – ⊠ Penzance.

🏠 **Enny's** ❦, Trewhella Lane, TR20 9BZ, ℘ (01736) 740262, Fax (01736) 740262, « 17 manor house, working farm », ⏋, ✿, park, ✕ – ✲ rm, 📺 🅿. ⚫ ⚫ 🆚. ✲
closed Christmas – **Meals** (by arrangement) 18.00 – **5 rm** ⊇ 40.00/60.00 **t.**

at Perranuthnoe SE : 1 ¾ m. by A 394 – ⊠ Penzance.

🏠 **Ednovean Farm** ❦ without rest., TR20 9LZ, ℘ (01736) 711883, « Converte 17C barn », ✿, park – ✲ 📺 🅿. ✲
closed 25 and 26 December – **3 rm** ⊇ 35.00/50.00.

MARCH Cambs. 402 404 U 26 – *pop. 16 221*.
　ᵣ₅ *Frogs Abbey, Grange Rd ℰ (01354) 652364.*
　London 93 – Cambridge 34 – Norwich 63.

　🏠 **Olde Griffin,** High St., PE15 9JS, ℰ (01354) 652517, Fax (01354) 650086 – 📺 ☎ 🅿 –
　🔏 100. 🔞 🆎 ⓪ 𝘝𝘐𝘚𝘈. 🦶
　Meals (bar lunch)/dinner 12.95 **st.** and a la carte – **20 rm** ⊆ 38.50/55.00 **st.** – SB.

MARDEN Herefordshire – see Hereford.

MARKET BOSWORTH Leics. 402 403 404 P 26 – *pop. 2 019* – ✉ Nuneaton.
　London 109 – Birmingham 30 – Coventry 23 – Leicester 22.

　🏠 **Softleys,** Market Pl., CV13 0JS, ℰ (01455) 290464, Fax (01455) 290464 – ⇔ 📺 ☎ 🔞 🆎
　⓪ 𝘝𝘐𝘚𝘈. 🦶
　closed 25 December – **Meals** (in bar) a la carte 13.25/19.75 **t.** ₆ 6.25 – **3 rm** ⊆ 45.00/
　55.00 **s.**

MARKET HARBOROUGH Leics. 404 R 26 – *pop. 16 563*.
　ᵣ₅ *Great Oxendon Rd ℰ (01858) 463684.*
　🅱 *Pen Lloyd Library, Adam and Eve St., LE16 7LT ℰ (01858) 468106.*
　London 88 – Birmingham 47 – Leicester 15 – Northampton 17.

　🏛 **Angel,** High St., LE16 7NL, ℰ (01858) 462702, Fax (01858) 410464 – 📺 ☎ 🔥 🅿 – 🔏 100.
　🔞 🆎 ⓪ 𝘝𝘐𝘚𝘈. 🦶
　Meals 14.50 **st.** and a la carte ₆ 5.25 – ⊆ 7.95 – **30 rm** 64.50/79.50 **st.** – SB.

at Glooston NE : 7½ m. by B 6047 off Hallaton rd – ✉ Market Harborough.

　🍴 **Old Barn Inn** with rm, LE16 7ST, ℰ (01858) 545215 – ⇔ rm, 📺 🅿. 🔞 🆎 𝘝𝘐𝘚𝘈
　Meals *(closed lunch Monday to Friday and Sunday dinner)* a la carte 12.15/21.70 **st.** ₆ 5.00 –
　3 rm ⊆ 37.50/49.50 **st.**

at Marston Trussell (Northants.) W : 3½ m. by A 4304 – ✉ Market Harborough.

　🏠 **Sun Inn,** Main St., LE16 9TY, ℰ (01858) 465531, Fax (01858) 433155 – 📺 ☎ 🅿 – 🔏 80. 🔞
　🆎 𝘝𝘐𝘚𝘈
　Meals a la carte 17.75/26.00 **t.** ₆ 4.95 – **19 rm** ⊆ 45.00/60.00 **t.**

　🔘 ATS 47-49 Kettering Rd ℰ (01858) 464535

MARKET LAVINGTON Wilts. 403 404 O 29 – see Devizes.

MARKET RASEN Lincs. 402 404 T 23 – *pop. 2 948*.
　London 156 – Boston 41 – Great Grimsby 19 – Lincoln 16.

　🏠 **Bleasby House,** Legsby, LN8 3QN, SE : 4 ¼ m. by B 1202 ℰ (01673) 842383,
　Fax (01673) 844808, « Working farm », �🐾, 🐎, park, ✼ – ⇔ 📺 🅿. 🦶
　closed 1 week Christmas – **Meals** (by arrangement) 12.00 **st.** – **3 rm** ⊆ 20.00/40.00 **st.**

MARKET WEIGHTON East Riding 402 R/S 22 – *pop. 4 371* – ✉ York.
　London 206 – Kingston-upon-Hull 19 – York 20.

　🏛 **Londesborough Arms,** 44 High St., YO4 3AH, ℰ (01430) 872214, Fax (01430) 872214 –
　📺 ☎ 🅿 – 🔏 150. 🔞 🆎 ⓪ 𝘝𝘐𝘚𝘈. 🦶
　Meals 13.95 **t.** and a la carte ₆ 4.75 – **18 rm** ⊆ 37.50/55.00 **t.** – SB.

MARKFIELD Leics. 402 403 404 Q 25 – *pop. 3 897*.
　London 113 – Birmingham 45 – Leicester 6 – Nottingham 24.

　🏛 **Field Head,** Markfield Lane, LE67 9PS, on B 5327 ℰ (01530) 245454, Fax (01530) 243740 –
　⇔ 📺 ☎ 🔥 🅿 – 🔏 50. 🔞 🆎 ⓪ 𝘝𝘐𝘚𝘈 𝘑𝘊𝘉. 🦶
　Meals *(closed Saturday lunch and Sunday dinner)* a la carte 10.00/24.00 **st.** – **28 rm**
　⊆ 79.00/95.00 **st.** – SB.

　🏠 **Travelodge,** Littleshaw Lane, LE67 0PP, NW : 1 m. on A 50 at junction 22 of M 1
　ℰ (01530) 244777, Fax (01530) 244580, Reservations (Freephone) 0800 850950 – ⇔ 📺 ☎
　🔥 🅿. 🔞 🆎 ⓪ 𝘝𝘐𝘚𝘈 𝘑𝘊𝘉. 🦶
　Meals (grill rest.) – **40 rm** 46.95 **t.**

MARKHAM MOOR *Notts. – ⊠ Retford.*

London 143 – Lincoln 18 – Nottingham 28 – Sheffield 27.

🏛 **Travelodge**, DN22 0QU, on A 1 (northbound carriageway) *℘ (01777) 838091*, Reservations (Freephone) 0800 850950 – ✦✦ rm, 📺 🕭 🅿. 🕮 🕮 ◯ *VISA* 🚕. ✦
Meals (grill rest.) – **40 rm** 39.95 **t.**

MARKINGTON *N. Yorks.* 402 P 21 – *see Harrogate.*

MARKS TEY *Essex* 404 W 28 – *see Colchester.*

MARLBOROUGH *Wilts.* 403 404 O 29 *The West Country G. – pop. 6 429.*

See : *Town★*.

Env. : *Savernake Forest★★ (Grand Avenue★★★), SE : 2 m. by A 4 – Whitehorse (≼★), NW : 5 m – West Kennett Long Barrow★, Silbury Hill★, W : 6 m. by A 4.*

Exc. : *Ridgeway Path★★ – Avebury★★ (The Stones★, Church★), W : 7 m. by A 4 – Crofton Beam Engines★ AC, SE : 9 m. by A 346 – Wilton Windmill★ AC, SE : 9 m. by A 346, A 338 and minor rd.*

🔒 *The Common ℘ (01672) 512147.*

🖸 *George Lane Car Park, SN8 1EE ℘ (01672) 513989.*

London 84 – Bristol 47 – Southampton 40 – Swindon 12.

🏰 **Ivy House,** High St., SN8 1HJ, *℘ (01672) 515333, Fax (01672) 515338* – 📺 ☎ 🅿 – 🔬 50. 🕮 🕮 *VISA*. ✦
Garden : **Meals** 10.95/18.00 **t.** and a la carte 🍴 4.75 – **Options :** **Meals** a la carte 8.00/ 13.25 **t.** 🍴 4.75 – **30 rm** ⊆ 62.00/99.00 **t.** – SB.

🏰 **Castle and Ball,** High St., SN8 1LZ, *℘ (01672) 515201, Fax (01672) 515895* – ✦✦ 📺 ☎ 🅿 – 🔬 45. 🕮 🕮 ◯ *VISA*
Meals 11.50/19.75 **t.** and dinner a la carte 🍴 7.05 – ⊆ 7.25 – **34 rm** 85.00/115.00 **t.** – SB.

at Ogbourne St. George *NE : 3¾ m. by A 346 – ⊠ Marlborough.*

🏠 **Laurel Cottage** without rest., Southend, SN8 1SG, S : ½ m. on A 346 *℘ (01672) 841288*, « 16C thatched cottage », *🌿* – ✦✦ 📺 🅿. ✦
Easter-September – **3 rm** ⊆ 35.00/50.00.

🚗 ATS 120/121 London Rd *℘ (01672) 512274*

MARLOW *Bucks.* 404 R 29 – *pop. 17 771.*

🖸 *31 High St., SL6 1AU ℘ (01628) 483597 (summer only).*

London 35 – Aylesbury 22 – Oxford 29 – Reading 14.

🏛 **Danesfield House** 🌊, Henley Rd, SL7 2EY, SW : 2 ½ m. on A 4155 *℘ (01628) 891010, Fax (01628) 890408,* « Italian Renaissance style mansion, ≼ terraced gardens and River Thames », 🏊, park, ✗ – 🛗 🕭, ✦✦ rest, 🖳 rest, 📺 ☎ 🅿 – 🔬 80. 🕮 🕮 ◯ *VISA* 🚕. ✦
Oak Room : **Meals** 24.50/35.50 **t.** and a la carte 🍴 10.00 – *Orangery :* **Meals** a la carte 17.45/22.40 **t.** 🍴 10.00 – **86 rm** ⊆ 145.00/175.00 **t.**, 1 suite – SB.

🏛 **Compleat Angler,** Marlow Bridge, Bisham Rd, SL7 1RG, *℘ (01628) 484444, Fax (01628) 486388,* ≼ River Thames, « Riverside setting », ⤵, ✗ – 🛗, ✦✦ rm, 📺 ☎ 🅿 – 🔬 120. 🕮 🕮 🚕
Riverside Valaisan : **Meals** 24.95/34.50 **t.** and a la carte 🍴 7.50 – ⊆ 14.00 – **60 rm** 135.00/ 205.00 **t.**, 2 suites – SB.

🏛 Country House without rest., Bisham Rd, SL7 1RP, *℘ (01628) 890606, Fax (01628) 890983,* 🌿 – 📺 ☎ 🅿
10 rm.

🏠 **Holly Tree House** without rest., Burford Close, Marlow Bottom, SL7 3NF, N : 2 m. by A 4155 and Wycombe Rd, off Marlow Bottom *℘ (01628) 891110, Fax (01628) 481278,* 🏊 🌿 – 📺 ☎ 🅿. 🕮 🕮 *VISA*
5 rm ⊆ 64.50/79.50 **st.**

MARPLE *Gtr. Manchester* 402 403 404 N 23 – *pop. 19 829.*

London 190 – Chesterfield 35 – Manchester 11.

🏛 **Springfield,** 99 Station Rd, SK6 6PA, *℘ (0161) 449 0721, Fax (0161) 449 0766,* 🌿 – ✦✦ rm, 📺 ☎ 🅿. 🕮 🕮 *VISA*. ✦
Meals *(closed Friday to Sunday)* (dinner only) 15.00 🍴 6.00 – **7 rm** ⊆ 35.00/50.00 **st.**

MARSDEN *W. Yorks.* [402] [404] O 23 – *pop. 3 873* – ✉ *Huddersfield.*
London 195 – Leeds 22 – Manchester 18 – Sheffield 30.

Hey Green Country House ⛰, Waters Rd, HD7 6NG, NW : 1 ¼ m. by Station Rd and Reddisher Rd ☎ (01484) 844235, *Fax (01484) 847605*, 🌳 – [TV] ☎ [P]. [MC] [AE] [D] [VISA] [JCB]. 🐕
Meals a la carte 15.35/21.45 **t.** 🍷 6.50 – ☕ 8.50 – **10 rm** 49.00/70.00 **t.**

MARSTON MORETAINE *Beds.* [404] S 27 – *see Bedford.*

MARSTON TRUSSELL *Northants.* [404] R 26 – *see Market Harborough.*

MARTINHOE *Devon* – *see Lynton.*

MARTOCK *Somerset* [403] L 31 *The West Country G.* – *pop. 4 051.*
See : *Village★ – All Saints★★.*
Env. : *Montacute House★★ AC, SE : 4 m. – Muchelney★★ (Parish Church★★), NW : 4 ½ m. by B 3165 – Ham Hill (≤★★), S : 2 m. by minor roads.*
Exc. : *Martock – Barrington Court Garden★ AC, SW : 7 ½ m. by B 3165 and A 303.*
London 148 – Taunton 19 – Yeovil 6.

Hollies, Bower Hinton, TA12 6LG, S : 1 m. on B 3165 ☎ (01935) 822232, *Fax (01935) 822249*, 🌳 – [TV] ☎ ♿ [P] – 🎤 175. [MC] [AE] [D] [VISA]. 🐕
Meals (bar lunch Monday to Saturday and Sunday dinner)/dinner 16.50 **t.** and a la carte 🍷 5.00 – **28 rm** ☕ 60.00/78.00 **t.**, 2 suites – SB.

MASHAM *N. Yorks.* [402] P 21 – *pop. 1 171* – ✉ *Ripon.*
London 231 – Leeds 38 – Middlesbrough 37 – York 32.

King's Head, Market Pl., HG4 4EF, ☎ (01765) 689295, *Fax (01765) 689070* – [TV] ☎ – 🎤 30. [MC] [AE] [D] [VISA]. 🐕
Meals a la carte 8.20/15.85 **t.** – **9 rm** ☕ 39.00/58.00 **t.** – SB.

🍴 **Floodlite,** 7 Silver St., HG4 4DX, ☎ (01765) 689000 – [MC] [AE] [VISA]
closed Tuesday to Thursday lunch, Monday and 2 weeks January – **Meals** 10.50 **t.** (lunch) and a la carte 14.25/26.70 **t.** 🍷 5.25.

MATLOCK *Derbs.* [402] [403] [404] P 24 *Great Britain G.* – *pop. 14 680.*
Exc. : *Hardwick Hall★★ AC, E : 12 ½ m. by A 615 and B 6014.*
[i] *The Pavilion, DE4 3NR ☎ (01629) 55082.*
London 153 – Derby 17 – Manchester 46 – Nottingham 24 – Sheffield 24.

Riber Hall ⛰, DE4 5JU, SE : 3 m. by A 615 ☎ (01629) 582795, *Fax (01629) 580475*, « Part Elizabethan manor house », 🌳, 🎾 – 🚭 rest, [TV] ☎ [P]. [MC] [AE] [D] [VISA] [JCB]
Meals 16.00/32.00 **t.** 🍷 7.75 – ☕ 8.00 – **14 rm** 89.00/158.00 **t.** – SB.

New Bath, New Bath Rd, Matlock Bath, DE4 3PX, S : 1 ½ m. on A 6 ☎ (01629) 583275, *Fax (01629) 580268*, ♨, 🏊, 🏊, 🌳, 🎾 – 🚭 [TV] ☎ [P] – 🎤 130. [MC] [AE] [D] [VISA]. 🐕
Meals *(closed Saturday lunch)* 10.95/18.95 **st.** and dinner a la carte 🍷 8.70 – ☕ 9.25 – **55 rm** 75.00/130.00 **st.** – SB.

Temple, Matlock Bath, DE4 3PG, S : 1 ¾ m. by A 6 ☎ (01629) 583911, *Fax (01629) 580851*, ≤, 🌳 – 🚭 rest, [TV] ☎ [P]. [MC] [AE] [D] [VISA]. 🐕
Meals 14.50 **st.** (dinner) and a la carte 17.50/26.80 **st.** 🍷 5.00 – **14 rm** ☕ 39.00/69.00 **st.** – SB.

Hodgkinson's, 150 South Par., Matlock Bath, DE4 3NR, S : 1 ¼ m. on A 6 ☎ (01629) 582170, *Fax (01629) 584891*, « Victoriana » – [TV] ☎ [P]. [MC] [AE] [VISA] [JCB]
closed 25 and 26 December – **Meals** *(closed Sunday)* (dinner only) 19.50/24.50 **t.** 🍷 4.95 – **7 rm** ☕ 35.00/90.00 **st.** – SB.

at Tansley *E : 1 ¾ m. on A 615* – ✉ *Matlock.*

Lane End House, Green Lane, DE4 5FJ, off Church St. ☎ (01629) 583981, *Fax (01629) 583981*, 🌳 – 🚭 [TV] [P]. [MC] [VISA]
closed Christmas and New Year – **Meals** (by arrangement) (communal dining) 15.95 **s.** – **4 rm** ☕ 30.00/57.00 **s.** – SB.

at Dethick *SE : 4 m. by A 615* – ✉ *Matlock.*

Manor Farmhouse ⛰, DE4 5GG, ☎ (01629) 534246, ≤, 🌳, park – 🚭 [TV] [P]. 🐕
restricted opening in winter – **Meals** (by arrangement) 10.50 **st.** – **3 rm** ☕ 30.00/50.00 **st.**

MATTERDALE END *Cumbria* – *see Ullswater.*

MAWDESLEY *Lancs.* 402 L 23 – *pop. 1 750* – ✉ *Ormskirk.*
London 217 – Liverpool 28 – Manchester 28 – Preston 15.

🏨 **Mawdesley's Eating House and H.,** Hall Lane, L40 2QZ, N : ½ m. ℰ (01704) 822552,
Fax (01704) 822096, ℰ♣, ⇌, ☒ – ☜ ☎ ⅋ ⅙ ℗ – 🛆 50. ⅏ 🆎 ⅏ 𝗩𝗜𝗦𝗔. ⅏
accommodation closed 25 and 26 December – **Meals** (grill rest.) 10.00 **t.** *and a la carte*
⅄ 4.75 – **44 rm** ☲ 43.50/53.50 **t.** – SB.

MAWNAN SMITH *Cornwall* 403 E 33 – *see Falmouth.*

MAYFIELD *E. Sussex* 404 U 30 – *pop. 1 954.*
London 46 – Brighton 25 – Eastbourne 22 – Lewes 17 – Royal Tunbridge Wells 9.

🏠 **Coles Hall,** Five Ashes, TN20 6JH, SW : 3 ½ m. on A 267 ℰ (01825) 830274, ℛ, park – ☜
℗
Meals (by arrangement) (communal dining) 15.00 **st.** – **3 rm** ☲ 20.00/36.00 **st.**

MEADOW HEAD *S. Yorks.* – *see Sheffield.*

MEDWAY SERVICE AREA *Medway* – ✉ *Gillingham.*
London 39 – Canterbury 22 – Maidstone 11.

🏨 **Travelodge,** ME8 8PQ, on M 2 between junctions 4 and 5 ℰ (01634) 233343,
Fax (01634) 263187, Reservations (Freephone) 0800 850950 – ☜ rm, ☒ ☎ ⅙ ℗. ⅏ 🆎 ⅏
𝗩𝗜𝗦𝗔 𝖩𝖢𝖡. ⅏
Meals (grill rest.) – **58 rm** 46.95 **t.**

MELBOURN *Cambs.* 404 U 27 – *pop. 4 006* – ✉ *Royston (Herts.).*
London 44 – Cambridge 10.

🏨 **Melbourn Bury** ⅏, Royston Rd, SG8 6DE, SW : ¾ m. ℰ (01763) 261151,
Fax (01763) 262375, ⪕, « *Country house of Tudor origin* », ℛ, park – ☜ rm, ☒ ℗. ⅏ 🆎
𝗩𝗜𝗦𝗔. ⅏
closed Easter, 2 weeks in autumn and Christmas-New Year – **Meals** *(closed Sunday dinner)*
(booking essential) (residents only) (communal dining) (dinner only) 17.00 **st.** ⅄ 6.50 – **3 rm**
☲ 52.00/84.00 **st.**

🏠 **Chiswick House** *without rest.,* 3 Chiswick End, SG8 6LZ, NW : 1 m. by Meldreth rd, off
Whitecroft Rd ℰ (01763) 260242, ℛ – ☜ ℗
6 rm ☲ 35.00/42.00.

𝗫𝗫𝗫 **Sheen Mill** *with rm,* Station Rd, SG8 6DX, ℰ (01763) 261393, *Fax* (01763) 261376, ⪕,
« *Restored 17C water mill* », ℛ – ☒ ☎ ℗. ⅏ 🆎 ⅏ 𝗩𝗜𝗦𝗔. ⅏
Meals *(closed Sunday dinner and Bank Holidays)* 16.95/23.50 **t.** *and a la carte* ⅄ 5.25 – **8 rm**
☲ 60.00/85.00 **t.**

𝗫𝗫 **Pink Geranium,** 25 Station Rd, SG8 6DX, ℰ (01763) 260215, *Fax* (01763) 262110, ℛ –
☜ ℗. ⅏ 🆎 ⅏ 𝗩𝗜𝗦𝗔
closed Sunday dinner and 1 January – **Meals** 16.00/25.00 **t.** *and a la carte.*

MELKSHAM *Wilts.* 403 404 N 29 *The West Country G.* – *pop. 13 074.*
Env. : *Corsham Court★★ AC, NW : 4 ½ m. by A 365 and B 3353 – Lacock★★ (Lacock Abbey★*
AC, High Street★, St. Cyriac★, Fox Talbot Museum of Photography★ AC) N : 3 ½ m.
by A 350.
🅱 *Church St., SN12 6LS* ℰ (01225) 707424.
London 113 – Bristol 25 – Salisbury 35 – Swindon 28.

🏨 **Shurnhold House** *without rest.,* Shurnhold, SN12 8DG, NW : 1 m. on A 36.
ℰ (01225) 790555, *Fax* (01225) 793147, « *Jacobean manor house, gardens* » – ☜ ☒ ☎
℗. ⅏ 🆎 𝗩𝗜𝗦𝗔. ⅏
☲ 5.25 – **4 rm** ☲ 48.00/98.00 **s.**

🏠 **Sandridge Park** ⅏, Sandridge Hill, SN12 7QU, E : 2 m. on A 3102 ℰ (01225) 706897,
Fax (01225) 702838, ⪕, « *Early Victorian mansion* », ℛ, park – ☜ rm, ☒ ℗. ⅏ 𝗩𝗜𝗦𝗔. ⅏
closed Christmas – **Meals** (booking essential) (communal dining) 20.00 ⅄ 3.50 – **3 rm**
☲ 40.00/80.00.

𝗫 **Toxique** *with rm,* 187 Woodrow Rd, SN12 7AY, NE : 1 ¼ m. by A 3102 and Forest rd
ℰ (01225) 702129, « *Contemporary interior design* », ℛ – ℗. ⅏ 🆎 ⅏ 𝗩𝗜𝗦𝗔 𝖩𝖢𝖡. ⅏
Meals *(closed Sunday dinner, Monday and Tuesday)* (booking essential) (dinner only and
Sunday lunch)/dinner 28.00 **st.** ⅄ 7.50 – **4 rm** ☲ (dinner included) 95.00/150.00 **st.**

at Shaw NW : 1½ m. on A 365 – ⊠ Melksham.

🏠 **Shaw Country,** Bath Rd, SN12 8EF, on A 365 ℘ (01225) 702836, Fax (01225) 790275, 🌤 – 🐾 rest, 📺 ☎ 🅿. 🕮 ⬜ ⬜ ⬜ ⬜
closed 26 to 28 December – **Meals** 12.50/17.95 **t.** and a la carte ₰ 6.00 – **13 rm** ⊡ 42.00/92.00 **t.** – SB.

MELLOR Lancs. – see Blackburn.

MELTON MOWBRAY Leics. 402 404 R 25 – pop. 24 348.

🏌 Waltham Rd, Thorpe Arnold ℘ (01664) 62118.

🖪 Melton Carnegie Museum, Thorpe End, LE13 1RB ℘ (01664) 480992.

London 113 – Leicester 15 – Northampton 45 – Nottingham 18.

🏰 **Stapleford Park** ♨, LE14 2EF, E : 5 m. by B 676 on Stapleford rd ℘ (01572) 787522, Fax (01572) 787651, ≼, « Part 16C and 19C mansion in park », ₰, ⬛, ⬜, ⬜, ⬛, 🌤, ⬜ – 🛗 🐾 📺 ☎ 🅿 – 🔬 200. ⬜ ⬜ ⬜ ⬜
Meals (residents only) (light lunch Monday to Saturday)/dinner 37.50 **st.** ₰ 16.00 – **50 rm** ⊡ 165.00/240.00 **s.**, 1 suite.

🏠 **Quorn Lodge,** 46 Asfordby Rd, LE13 0HR, ℘ (01664) 66660, Fax (01664) 480660 – 🐾 📺 ☎ 🅿 – 🔬 80. ⬜ ⬜ ⬜ ⬜
closed 26 December-1 January – **Meals** (closed Sunday dinner) 9.50/15.75 **t.** and dinner a la carte ₰ 3.95 – **18 rm** ⊡ 45.00/65.00 **t.** – SB.

at Old Dalby NW : 8½ m. by A 6006 – ⊠ Melton Mowbray.

🏠 **Home Farm** ♨ without rest., 9 Church Lane, LE14 3LB, ℘ (01664) 822622, Fax (01664) 823155, 🌤 – 🐾 📺 🅿. ⬜ ⬜
5 rm ⊡ 28.50/45.00.

🔧 ATS Leicester Rd ℘ (01664) 62072

The Guide is updated annually so renew your Guide every year.

MEMBURY Devon – see Axminster.

MEMBURY SERVICE AREA Newbury 403 404 P 29 – ⊠ Newbury.

🏠 **Welcome Lodge,** Membury, Lambourn Woodlands, RG16 7TU, M 4 between junctions 14 and 15 (westbound carriageway) ℘ (01488) 71881, Fax (01488) 72336, Reservations (Freephone) 0800 7314466 – 🐾 rm, 📺 ♿ 🅿. ⬜ ⬜ ⬜ ⬜
Meals (grill rest.) – **40 rm** 45.00 **t.**

MENDLESHAM GREEN Suffolk 404 W 27 – see Stowmarket.

MERE Wilts. 403 404 N 30 The West Country G. – pop. 2 257.

Env. : Stourhead★★★ AC, NW : 4 m. by B 3095 and B 3092.

Exc. : Longleat House★★★ AC, N : 9½ m. by A 303 and B 3092.

🖪 The Square, BA12 6JJ ℘ (01747) 861211.

London 113 – Exeter 65 – Salisbury 26 – Taunton 40.

🏠 **Chetcombe House,** Chetcombe Rd, BA12 6AZ, NE : ½ m. by B 3095 ℘ (01747) 860219, Fax (01747) 860111, 🌤 – 🐾 📺 🅿. ⬜ ⬜ ⬜ ⬜
closed 25-26 December and 1 January – **Meals** (lunch by arrangement)/dinner a la carte 14.50 **s.** ₰ 3.75 – **5 rm** ⊡ 29.00/50.00 **s.** – SB.

MERIDEN W. Mids. 403 404 P 26 – see Coventry.

MEVAGISSEY Cornwall 403 F 33 The West Country G. – pop. 2 272.

See : Town★★.

London 287 – Newquay 21 – Plymouth 44 – Truro 20.

🏠 **Mevagissey House** ♨ without rest., Vicarage Hill, PL26 6SZ, ℘ (01726) 842402, Fax (01726) 844327, ≼, 🌤 – 🐾 📺 🅿. ⬜ ⬜ ⬜ ⬜
April-October – **4 rm** ⊡ 32.00/54.00 **st.**

MEYSEY HAMPTON *Glos.* – ✉ *Cirencester.*
London 101 – Bristol 44 – Gloucester 26 – Oxford 29.

🏠 **Masons Arms** with rm, High St., GL7 5JT, ☎ (01285) 850164, *Fax* (01285) 850164 – ✤ rest, 📺 🅿. 🅾️③ *VISA*
Meals *(closed Sunday dinner)* a la carte 10.10/14.20 **t.** – **8 rm** ⊒ 34.00/56.00 **t.**

MICHAELWOOD SERVICE AREA *Glos.* 🔢 M 29 – ✉ *Dursley.*

🏠 **Welcome Lodge** without rest., Lower Wick, GL11 6DD, M 5 (northbound carriageway)
☎ (01454) 261513, *Fax* (01454) 260331, Reservations (Freephone) 0800 7314466 – ✤ 📺 ♿
🅿. 🅾️③ 🄰🄴 ① *VISA*. ✤
40 rm 45.00 **t.**

MICKLEOVER *Derbs.* 🔢🔢🔢 P 25 – see Derby.

MICKLETON *Glos.* 🔢🔢 O 27 – see Chipping Campden.

MICKLE TRAFFORD *Ches.* – see Chester.

MIDDLE CHINNOCK *Somerset* 🔢 L 31 – see Crewkerne.

Le Guide change, changez de **guide Michelin** *tous les ans.*

MIDDLEHAM *N. Yorks.* 🔢 O 21 – pop. 754.
London 233 – Kendal 45 – Leeds 47 – York 45.

🏨 **Miller's House,** Market Pl., DL8 4NR, ☎ (01969) 622630, *Fax* (01969) 623570, ✿ –
✤ rest, 📺 ☎ 🅿. 🅾️③ *VISA*. ✤
closed 2 to 31 January – **Meals** *(dinner only)* 19.50 **t.** ₰ 5.10 – **7 rm** ⊒ *(dinner included)*
54.50/109.00 **t.** – SB.

🏠 **Waterford House,** 19 Kirkgate, DL8 4PG, ☎ (01969) 622090, *Fax* (01969) 624020, « Part
17C house, antiques », ✿ – ✤ rest, 📺 🅿. 🅾️③ *VISA* JCB
Meals *(lunch by arrangement)/dinner* 19.50 **st.** and a la carte ₰ 5.00 – **5 rm** ⊒ 55.00/
85.00 **st.**

at Carlton *SW : 4½ m. on Coverdale Rd* – ✉ *Leyburn.*

🗙🗙 **Foresters Arms** with rm, DL8 4BB, ☎ (01969) 640272, *Fax* (01969) 640272 – 📺 🅿. 🅾️③
VISA. ✤
closed 2 weeks January – **Meals** *(closed Sunday dinner and Monday)* a la carte 16.85/
26.40 **t.** – **3 rm** ⊒ 35.00/60.00 **t.**

MIDDLESBROUGH 🔢 Q 20 – pop. 147 430.
🏌 *Middlesbrough Municipal, Ladgate Lane* ☎ (01642) 315533 – 🏌 *Brass Castle Lane, Marton*
☎ (01642) 316430.
Cleveland Transporter Bridge (toll) **BY**.
✈ *Teesside Airport :* ☎ (01325) 332811, SW : 13 m. by A 66 – **AZ** – and A 19 on A 67.
🛈 *51 Corporation Rd, TS1 1LT* ☎ (01642) 243425.
London 246 – Kingston-upon-Hull 89 – Leeds 66 – Newcastle upon Tyne 41.

Plan opposite

🏨 **Baltimore,** 250 Marton Rd, TS4 2EZ, ☎ (01642) 224111, *Fax* (01642) 226156 – 📺 ☎ 🅿
🛗 25. 🅾️③ 🄰🄴 ① *VISA*. ✤
BZ
Meals *(closed lunch Saturday and Sunday)* 13.75 **st.** and a la carte ₰ 5.50 – ⊒ 9.50 – **30 rm**
66.50/85.00 **st.**, 1 suite – SB.

🏠 **Grey House,** 79 Cambridge Rd, TS5 5NL, ☎ (01642) 817485, *Fax* (01642) 817485, ✿ –
☎ 🅿. 🅾️③ 🄰🄴 *VISA*
AZ
Meals *(by arrangement)* 12.00 **st.** – **9 rm** ⊒ 35.00/50.00 **s.**

🗙 **Purple Onion,** 80 Corporation Rd, TS1 2RF, ☎ (01642) 222250, *Fax* (01642) 248088 –
🅾️③ *VISA*
BY
closed Sunday dinner, 25-26 December and 1 January – **Meals** - Brasserie - a la carte 11.70/
29.15 **t.** ₰ 5.95.

🅾 ATS Murdock Rd (off Sotherby Rd), Cargo St. ☎ (01642) 249245/6

MIDDLESBROUGH

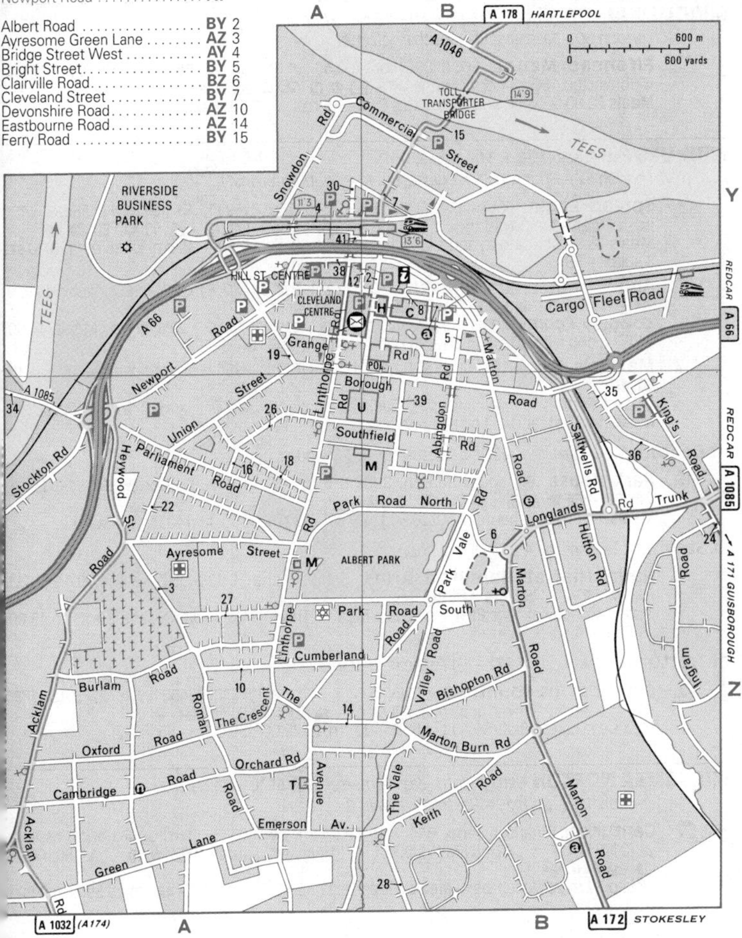

La guida cambia, cambiate la guida ogni anno.

MIDDLETON *N.Yorks. – see Pickering.*

MIDDLETON *Suffolk – pop. 380 –* ✉ *Saxmundham.*
London 108 – Cambridge 73 – Ipswich 27 – Norwich 37.

⌂ **Rose Farm** 🐦 without rest., Mill St., IP17 3NG, ☎ (01728) 648456, 🌳 – ⊁ [TV] Ⓟ. 🐕
21 February-October – **3 rm** ☕ 45.00/50.00 **s.**

⌂ **Little Orchard** 🐦, IP17 3NT, ☎ (01728) 648385, 🌳 – ⊁ [TV] Ⓟ. 🐕
closed 24 December-1 January – **Meals** (by arrangement) 12.00 **s.** – **3 rm** ☕ 20.00/40.00 **s.**

MIDDLETON STONEY *Oxon.* 403 404 Q 28 – *pop. 304.*
  London 66 – Northampton 30 – Oxford 12.

🏛 **Jersey Arms,** OX6 8SE, ℰ (01869) 343234, Fax (01869) 343565, ✿ – ⤪ rest, 📺 ☎ 🅿. ⓪ 🆎 *VISA* JCB. ⚡
  Meals a la carte 20.00/27.50 **t.** ⬩ 6.95 – **13 rm** ⊇ 69.00/85.00 **t.**, 3 suites – SB.

MIDDLE WALLOP *Hants.* 403 404 P 30 – ✉ *Stockbridge.*
  London 80 – Salisbury 11 – Southampton 21.

🏛🏛 **Fifehead Manor,** SO20 8EG, on A 343 ℰ (01264) 781565, Fax (01264) 781400,
  « Converted 16C manor house », ✿ – 📺 ☎ 🅿. ⓪ 🆎 *VISA*. ⚡
  Meals 20.00/25.00 **t.** and a la carte ⬩ 8.00 – **15 rm** ⊇ 70.00/130.00 **t.**

MIDHURST *W. Sussex* 404 R 31 – *pop. 6 451.*
  London 57 – Brighton 38 – Chichester 12 – Southampton 41.

🏛🏛🏛 **Spread Eagle,** South St., GU29 9NH, ℰ (01730) 816911, Fax (01730) 815668, « 15C
  hostelry, antique furnishings », 🇫🇷, ⬥, ⬛ – ⤪ rest, 📺 ☎ 🅿 – 🔏 50. ⓪ 🆎 ⓞ *VISA*
  Meals 28.50 **st.** (dinner) and a la carte 28.50/36.50 **st.** ⬩ 9.50 – **36 rm** ⊇ 85.00/120.00 **st.**,
  3 suites – SB.

🏛🏛 **Angel,** North St., GU29 9DN, ℰ (01730) 812421, Fax (01730) 815928, « 16C coaching inn »,
  ✿ – ⤪ rm, 📺 ☎ ⬥ 🅿 – 🔏 60. ⓪ 🆎 ⓞ *VISA*. ⚡
  Cowdray Room : **Meals** 14.50/21.00 **t.** and a la carte ⬩ 13.50 – *Brasserie :* **Meals** 14.50/
  21.00 **t.** and a la carte ⬩ 13.50 – **28 rm** ⊇ 80.00/155.00 **t.** – SB.

✗ **Maxine's,** Red Lion St., GU29 9PB, ℰ (01730) 816271, « 15C timbered cottage » – ⤪. ⓪
  🆎 *VISA*
  closed Sunday dinner, Monday, Tuesday, 2 weeks January and 2 weeks October –
  Meals 14.95 **st.** and a la carte ⬩ 5.95.

at Bepton *SW : 2½ m. by A 286 on Bepton rd* – ✉ *Midhurst.*

🏛 **Park House** ⏳, South Bepton, GU29 0JB, ℰ (01730) 812880, Fax (01730) 815643, ⬛,
  ✿, ✗ – 📺 ☎ ⬥ 🅿 – 🔏 70. ⓪ 🆎 *VISA*
  Meals (by arrangement) 12.50/20.50 **t.** ⬩ 6.50 – **13 rm** ⊇ 65.00/140.00 **t.**, 1 suite.

at Stedham *W : 2 m. by A 272* – ✉ *Midhurst.*

✗ **Nava Thai at Hamilton Arms,** School Lane, GU29 0NZ, ℰ (01730) 812555
  Fax (01730) 817459 – 🅿. ⓪ *VISA* JCB
  closed Monday except Bank Holidays – **Meals** - Thai - 17.00 **t.** (dinner) and a la carte 13.00/
  19.00 **t.** ⬩ 4.50.

at Trotton *W : 3¼ m. on A 272* – ✉ *Petersfield (Hants.).*

🏛🏛 **Southdowns Country** ⏳, GU31 5JN, S : 1 m. ℰ (01730) 821521, Fax (01730) 821790
  ⬛⬛, ⬛, ✿, ✗ – ⤪ rm, ▦ rest, 📺 ☎ 🅿 – 🔏 100. ⓪ 🆎 ⓞ *VISA*. ⚡
  Meals a la carte 18.00/33.40 **t.** ⬩ 5.95 – **20 rm** ⊇ 79.00/139.00 **t.** – SB.

MIDSOMER NORTON *Bath & North East Somerset* 403 M 30 – ✉ *Bath.*
  London 129 – Bath 10 – Bristol 15 – Wells 8.

🏛🏛 **Centurion,** Charlton Lane, BA3 4BD, SE : 1 m. by B 3355, Charlton Rd and Fosseway
  ℰ (01761) 417711, Fax (01761) 418357, ⬥, ⬛, ⬥, ✿, squash – 📺 ☎ 🅿 – 🔏 180. ⓪ 🆎
  ⓞ *VISA* JCB. ⚡
  closed 24 to 26 December – **Meals** a la carte 11.45/19.50 **t.** ⬩ 5.50 – **44 rm** ⊇ 59.50/69.50 **t.**
  – SB.

MILBORNE PORT *Dorset* 403 404 M 31 – *see Sherborne.*

MILDENHALL *Suffolk* 404 V 26 – *pop. 12 827.*
  London 72 – Cambridge 24 – Ipswich 37 – Norwich 45.

🏛🏛 **Riverside,** Mill St., IP28 7DP, ℰ (01638) 717274, Fax (01638) 715997, ✿ – ⬛ 📺 ☎ 🅿 –
  🔏 60. ⓪ 🆎 ⓞ *VISA* JCB
  Meals 18.00 and a la carte ⬩ 7.00 – **21 rm** ⊇ 54.00/82.00 **t.** – SB.

Si vous cherchez un hôtel tranquille,
consultez d'abord les cartes de l'introduction
ou repérez dans le texte les établissements indiqués avec le signe ⏳ *ou* ⏳

MILFORD-ON-SEA Hants. 403 404 P 31 – pop. 4 434 – ⌖ Lymington.
London 109 – Bournemouth 15 – Southampton 24 – Winchester 37.

🏨 **Westover Hall** ⌖, Park Lane, SO41 0PT, ℘ (01590) 643044, Fax (01590) 644490, ≤ Christchurch Bay, Isle of Wight and The Needles, « Victorian mansion built by Arnold Mitchell », ☞ – ⌖ rest, 📺 ☎ 🄿, 🕮 ⒶⒺ ⓪ 𝚅𝙸𝚂𝙰 𝙹𝙲𝙱
Meals - Italian 19.50 **st.** – **13 rm** ⌕ 50.00/110.00 **st.**

🏨 **South Lawn,** Lymington Rd, SO41 0RF, ℘ (01590) 643911, Fax (01590) 644820, ☞ – ⌖ rest, 📺 ☎ 🄿, 🕮 𝚅𝙸𝚂𝙰, ⌖
closed 21 December-19 January – **Meals** (closed Monday lunch) 18.50 **t.** (dinner) and lunch a la carte 12.00/19.00 **t.** ≬ 8.50 – **24 rm** ⌕ 49.00/98.00 **t.** – SB.

✕✕ **Rocher's,** 69-71 High St., SO41 0QG, ℘ (01590) 642340 – 🕮 ⒶⒺ ⓪ 𝚅𝙸𝚂𝙰
closed Sunday dinner, Monday, Tuesday, 2 weeks June and 25-26 December – Meals - French - (dinner only and Sunday lunch)/dinner 17.50/23.50 **st.** ≬ 7.00.

MILNROW Gtr. Manchester 402 404 N 23 – see Rochdale.

MILTON DAMEREL Devon 403 H 31 – pop. 451.
London 249 – Barnstaple 21.

🏨 **Woodford Bridge,** EX22 7LL, N : 1 m. on A 388 ℘ (01409) 261481, Fax (01409) 261585, ↳, ⌕, ⌧, ☞, squash – 📺 ☎ 🄿, 🕮 ⒶⒺ 𝚅𝙸𝚂𝙰, ⌖
Meals (bar lunch Monday to Saturday)/dinner 13.00 **t.** and a la carte ≬ 5.50 – ⌕ 5.00 – **8 rm** 45.00/105.00 **t.**

MILTON KEYNES 404 R 27 – pop. 156 148.
↳ Abbey Hill, Monks Way, Two Mile Ash ℘ (01908) 563845 AV – ↳ Windmill Hill, Tattenhoe Lane, Bletchley ℘ (01908) 648149 BX – ↳, ↳ Wavendon Golf Centre, Lower End Rd, Wavendon ℘ (01908) 281811 CV.
🛈 411 Secklow Gate East, The Food Hall, MK9 3NE ℘ (01908) 232525 FY.
London 56 – Birmingham 72 – Bedford 16 – Northampton 18 – Oxford 37.

Plans on following pages

🏨 **Forte Posthouse Milton Keynes,** 500 Saxon Gate West, Central Milton Keynes, MK9 2HQ, ℘ (01908) 667722, Fax (01908) 674714, ↳, ⌕, ⌧ – ᵇ, ⌖ rm, ▤ 📺 ☎ ⅙ 🄿 – ⌂ 150. 🕮 ⒶⒺ ⓪ 𝚅𝙸𝚂𝙰 𝙹𝙲𝙱   EYZ a
Brasserie Mondiale : Meals a la carte 14.55/25.85 **st.** ≬ 7.25 – ⌕ 10.95 – **151 rm** 99.00 **st.**, 2 suites – SB.

🏨 **Hilton National Milton Keynes,** Timbold Drive, Kents Hill Park, MK7 6HL, SE : 4 m. by B 4034 and A 421 off Brickhill St. (V10) ℘ (01908) 694433, Fax (01908) 695533, ↳, ⌕, ⌧ – ᵇ, ⌖ rm, ▤ rest, 📺 ☎ ⅙ 🄿 – ⌂ 300. 🕮 ⒶⒺ ⓪ 𝚅𝙸𝚂𝙰 𝙹𝙲𝙱   CVX d
New Horizons : Meals 12.50/18.95 **st.** ≬ 6.50 – ⌕ 10.95 – **138 rm** 120.00/220.00 **t.** – SB.

🏨 **Courtyard by Marriott Milton Keynes,** London Rd, Newport Pagnell, NE : 4 ¼ m. on A 509 ℘ (01908) 613688, Fax (01908) 617335, ↳, ☞ – ⌖ 📺 ☎ ⅙ 🄿 – ⌂ 200. 🕮 ⒶⒺ ⓪ 𝚅𝙸𝚂𝙰, ⌖   CV r
Meals (bar lunch Saturday) a la carte 13.00/23.00 **t.** ≬ 8.00 – ⌕ 8.95 – **49 rm** 85.00 **st.** – SB.

🏨 **Quality Friendly,** Monks Way, Two Mile Ash, MK8 8LY, NW : 2 m. by A 509 and A 5 at junction with A 422 ℘ (01908) 561666, Fax (01908) 568303, ↳ ⌖ rm, – ⌖ rm, 📺 ☎ ⅙ 🄿 – ⌂ 120. 🕮 ⒶⒺ ⓪ 𝚅𝙸𝚂𝙰 𝙹𝙲𝙱   AV e
Meals (closed Saturday lunch) (carving rest.) 12.00/14.50 **t.** and a la carte ≬ 4.50 – ⌕ 8.75 – **88 rm** 67.50/107.50 **st.** – SB.

🏨 **Caldecotte Arms - Premier Lodge,** Bletcham Way (H10), MK7 8HP, SE : 5 ½ m. by A 509 and A 5, taking 2nd junction left signposted Milton Keynes (South and East) ℘ (01908) 366188, Fax (01908) 366603, « Windmill feature, lakeside setting » – ⌖ rm, 📺 ☎ ⅙ 🄿, 🕮 ⒶⒺ ⓪ 𝚅𝙸𝚂𝙰 𝙹𝙲𝙱, ⌖   CX h
Meals (grill rest.) a la carte 10.15/15.15 **t.** ≬ 4.55 – ⌕ 4.95 – **40 rm** 44.25 **t.** – SB.

🏨 **Shenley Church Inn,** Burchard Cres., Shenley Church End, MK5 6HQ, SW : 2 m. by A 509 and Portway (H5) off Watling St. (V4) ℘ (01908) 505467, Fax (01908) 502308 – ᵇ, ⌖ rm, 📺 ☎ ⅙ 🄿 – ⌂ 100. 🕮 𝚅𝙸𝚂𝙰, ⌖   BVX f
Meals (carving rest.) a la carte 10.75/15.10 **t.** ≬ 4.45 – **50 rm** ⌕ 69.50/79.50 **t.** – SB.

🏨 **Peartree Bridge Inn,** Milton Keynes Marina, Waterside, Peartree Bridge, MK6 3PE, SE : 2 m. by B 4034 ℘ (01908) 691515, Fax (01908) 690274, « Marina setting beside the Grand Union Canal » – ⌖ 📺 ☎ ⅙ 🄿, 🕮 ⒶⒺ 𝚅𝙸𝚂𝙰, ⌖   BCV k
Meals (grill rest.) a la carte 11.80/16.10 **st.** ≬ 4.95 – **39 rm** ⌕ 65.00/75.00 **st.** – SB.

🏨 **Broughton,** Broughton Village, MK10 9AA, E : 4 m. by A 509 off A 5130 ℘ (01908) 667726, Fax (01908) 604844, ☞ – 📺 ☎ 🄿, 🕮 ⒶⒺ ⓪ 𝚅𝙸𝚂𝙰 𝙹𝙲𝙱, ⌖   CV m
Meals (closed Sunday dinner) (bar lunch Monday to Saturday)/dinner 13.95 **t.** and a la carte ≬ 4.75 – **31 rm** ⌕ 80.00/100.00 **t.**

MILTON KEYNES

For the quickest route use the
Michelin Main Road Maps:

970	Europe,
976	Czech Republic-Slovak Republic,
980	Greece,
984	Germany,
985	Scandinavia-Finland,
986	Great Britain and Ireland,
987	Germany-Austria-Benelux,
988	Italy,
989	France,
990	Spain-Portugal and
991	Yugoslavia.

452

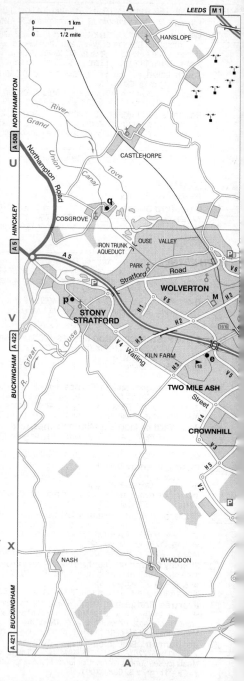

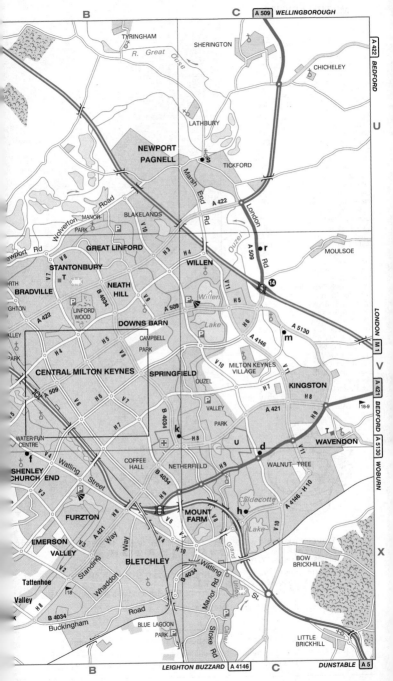

MILTON KEYNES

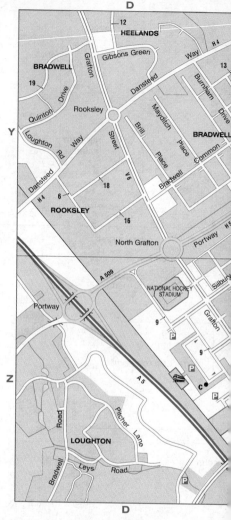

🏠 **Travel Inn,** Secklow Gate West, Central Milton Keynes, MK9 3BZ, ✆ (01908) 66338
Fax (01908) 607481 – ✡ rm, 📺 ☎ ⅙ 🅿 – 🔬 30. 🆎 🅰🅴 ⑩ 𝘝𝘐𝘚𝘈. ✨
Meals (grill rest.) – **38 rm** 36.50 t.   FY

XX **Jaipur,** Elder House, 502 Eldergate, Station Sq., MK9 1LR, ✆ (01908) 669796
Fax (01908) 694464 – ▤, 🆎 🅰🅴 ⑩ 𝘝𝘐𝘚𝘈
closed 25 December – **Meals** - Indian - (buffet lunch Sunday) a la carte 15.75/25.20 t.   DZ

🔘 ATS 38 Victoria Rd, Bletchley ✆ (01908) 640420

Bitte beachten Sie die Geschwindigkeitsbeschränkungen in Großbritannien
- 60 mph (= 96 km/h) außerhalb geschlossener Ortschaften
- 70 mph (= 112 km/h) auf Straßen mit getrennten Fahrbahnen und Autobahnen.

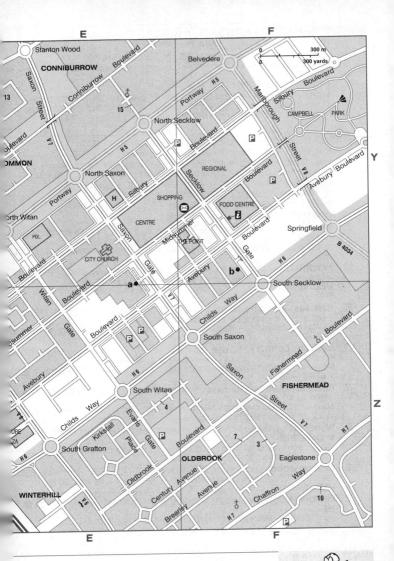

MILTON-UNDER-WYCHWOOD Oxon. – pop. 2 030.
London 83 – Birmingham 52 – Gloucester 35 – Oxford 27.

🏢 **Hillborough,** The Green, OX7 6JH, ℘ (01993) 830501, Fax (01993) 832005, 🌦 – ⚡ rest,
📺 ☎ 🅿. 🆎 𝘝𝘐𝘚𝘈
closed January – Meals *(closed Sunday and Monday)* 13.75/16.00 **t.** and a la carte ┃ 6.00 –
10 rm ⊆ 35.00/54.00 **t.**

455

MINCHINHAMPTON *Glos.* 403 404 N 28 – *pop. 3 201.*
London 115 – Bristol 26 – Gloucester 11 – Oxford 51.

⌂ **Hunters Lodge** without rest., Dr Brown's Rd, GL6 9BT, ✆ (01453) 883588, *Fax (01453) 731449,* ≼, « Cotswold stone house on Minchinhampton common », ⚘ – 🚭 📺 Ⓟ. ⊗
closed Christmas – **3 rm** 🛏 26.00/44.00.

✗ **Markey's,** The Old Ram, Market Sq., GL6 9BW, ✆ (01453) 882287 – 🚭. MC AE VISA
Closed Tuesday lunch, Sunday, Monday, 2 weeks in summer and 2 weeks in autumn – **Meals** 9.95 **t.** (lunch) and dinner a la carte 16.40/22.40 **t.** 🍷 6.95.

MINEHEAD *Somerset* 403 J 30 *The West Country G.* – *pop. 9 158.*
See : *Town*★ - *Higher Town (Church Steps*★, *St. Michael's*★*).*
Env. : *Dunster*★★ - *Castle*★★ **AC** *(upper rooms* ≼★*) Water Mill*★ **AC**, *St. George's Church*★, *Dovecote*★, *SE : 2 ½ m. by A 39* – *Selworthy*★ *(Church*★, ≼★★*) W : 4 ½ m. by A 39.*
Exc. : *Exmoor National Park*★★ – *Cleeve Abbey*★★ **AC**, *SE : 6 ½ m. by A 39.*
⛳18 *The Warren, Warren Rd* ✆ *(01643) 702057.*
ℹ *17 Friday St., TA24 5UB* ✆ *(01643) 702624.*
London 187 – Bristol 64 – Exeter 43 – Taunton 25.

🏨 **Periton Park** ☾, Middlecombe, TA24 8SW, W : 1 ½ m. by A 39 ✆ (01643) 706885, *Fax (01643) 706885,* ≼, ⚘ – 🚭 📺 ☎ Ⓟ. MC AE VISA JCB. ⊗
closed January – **Meals** (dinner only) 21.50 **st.** – **8 rm** 🛏 (dinner included) 52.00/96.00 **st.** – SB.

🏨 **Northfield** ☾, Northfield Rd, TA24 5PU, ✆ (01643) 705155, *Fax (01643) 707715,* ≼ bay « Gardens », 🏋, 🏊 – ⇅, 🚭 rest, 📺 ☎ Ⓟ – 👥 70. MC AE ① VISA JCB. ⊗
Meals (bar lunch Monday to Saturday)/dinner 18.00 **t.** 🍷 5.25 – **29 rm** 🛏 50.00/110.00 **t.** – SB.

🏨 **Benares** ☾, Northfield Rd, TA24 5PT, ✆ (01643) 704911, *Fax (01643) 706373,* ≼ « Gardens » – 🚭 rest, 📺 ☎ Ⓟ. MC AE ① VISA
21 March-6 November – **Meals** (bar lunch)/dinner 19.00 **st.** 🍷 4.70 – **19 rm** 🛏 48.00/89.00 **st.** – SB.

🏠 **Beacon Country House** ☾, Beacon Rd, TA24 5SD, ✆ (01643) 703476 *Fax (01643) 707007,* ≼, ⚘, park – 🚭 rest, 📺 ☎ Ⓟ. MC VISA JCB
Meals (lunch by arrangement)/dinner 19.50 **st.** and a la carte 🍷 3.90 – **9 rm** 🛏 68.00/136.00 **st.** – SB.

🏠 **Channel House** ☾, Church Path, TA24 5QG, off Northfield Rd ✆ (01643) 703229, ≼, ⚘ – 📺 ☎ Ⓟ. MC ① VISA JCB. ⊗
March-October and Christmas – **Meals** (dinner only) 20.00 **st.** and a la carte 🍷 4.90 – **8 rm** 🛏 (dinner included) 80.00/120.00 **st.** – SB.

🏠 **Wyndcott** ☾, Martlet Rd, TA24 5QE, ✆ (01643) 704522, *Fax (01643) 703210,* ≼, ⚘ – 📺 ☎ Ⓟ. MC AE VISA
Meals (booking essential to non-residents) (lunch by arrangement) 9.95/18.95 **st.** 🍷 4.95 – **11 rm** 🛏 (dinner included) 45.95/107.90 **st.** – SB.

🏠 **Beaconwood** ☾, Church Rd, North Hill, TA24 5SB, ✆ (01643) 702032 *Fax (01643) 702032,* ≼ sea and Minehead, ⛱, ⚘, 🎾 – 🚭 rest, 📺 ☎ Ⓟ. MC VISA
Meals (bar lunch)/dinner 14.00 **st.** 🍷 4.00 – **12 rm** 🛏 36.00/80.00 **st.** – SB.

🏠 **Rectory House,** Northfield Rd, TA24 5QH, ✆ (01643) 702611, ⚘ – 🚭 rest, 📺 Ⓟ. MC VISA
March-October – **Meals** (dinner only May-September) 18.50 – **7 rm** 🛏 25.00/50.00.

◉ ATS Bampton St. ✆ (01643) 704808/9

MINSTER *Kent* 404 Y 29 – *see Ramsgate.*

MINSTERLEY *Shrops.* 402 403 L 26 – *pop. 1 397.*
London 174 – Birmingham 57 – Hereford 55 – Shrewsbury 10.

⌂ **Cricklewood Cottage** without rest., Plox Green, SY5 0HT, SW : 1 m. on A 488 ✆ (01743) 791229, ⚘ – 🚭 Ⓟ. ⊗
closed 24 and 25 December – **3 rm** 🛏 29.00/44.00 **s.**

Bitte beachten Sie die Geschwindigkeitsbeschränkungen in Großbritannien
- 60 mph (= 96 km/h) außerhalb geschlossener Ortschaften
- 70 mph (= 112 km/h) auf Straßen mit getrennten Fahrbahnen und Autobahnen.

MINSTER LOVELL Oxon. 408 404 P 28 – pop. 1 613 – ⊠ Witney.
London 72 – Gloucester 36 – Oxford 16.

XXX **Lovells at Windrush Farm** with rm, Windrush Farm, Old Minster Lovell, OX8 5RN
ॐ (expected move in February 1988 to 7 Horsefair, Chipping Norton, OX7 5AL,
ℰ (01608) 644490), E : ¾ m. by B 4047 on Old Minster rd ℰ (01993) 779802,
Fax (01993) 776212, ☞ – ⅍ rest, 🅿. ⃝⃝ ⅋⃝ ⃝ ⅦⅦⅅ on
closed January – **Meals** (closed Monday) (booking essential) (dinner only and lunch by
arrangement Friday and Sunday) 21.00/35.00 **t.** ⅓ 11.00 – 3 rm ⊃ (dinner included) 95.00/
175.00 **t.**
Spec. Lobster hollandaise. Breast of duck on braised cabbage with fondant potatoes and
a grenadine jus. Assiette of summer fruit desserts.

MOBBERLEY Ches. 402 408 404 N 24 – see Knutsford.

MONK FRYSTON N. Yorks. 402 Q 22 – pop. 722 – ⊠ Lumby.
London 190 – Kingston-upon-Hull 42 – Leeds 13 – York 20.

🏨 **Monk Fryston Hall**, LS25 5DU, ℰ (01977) 682369, Fax (01977) 683544, « Italian
garden », park – ⅍ rest, 📺 ☎ 🅿 – 🔬 50. ⃝⃝ ⅋⃝ ⃝ ⅦⅦⅅ ⅉⅭⅮ
Meals 13.75/23.00 **t.** and a la carte ⅓ 5.75 – 28 rm ⊃ 73.50/108.00 **t.** – SB.

MONKTON COMBE Bath & North East Somerset – see Bath.

MONKTON FARLEIGH Wilts. 408 404 N 29 – see Bradford-on-Avon.

MONTACUTE Somerset 408 L 31 – see Yeovil.

MOONFLEET Dorset – see Weymouth.

MORCHARD BISHOP Devon 408 I 31 – pop. 978 – ⊠ Crediton.
London 217 – Barnstaple 28 – Exeter 17 – Taunton 40.

⌂ **Wigham** ⌖, EX17 6RJ, NE : 1 m. on Eastington rd ℰ (01363) 877350, Fax (01363) 877350,
≼, « 16C longhouse, working farm », ⅏ – ⅍ 📺 ☎ 🅿. ⃝⃝ ⅋⃝ ⃝ ⅦⅦⅅ ⅉⅭⅮ. ⅍
booking essential and restricted opening December-March – **Meals** (communal
dining) 20.00 **st.** – 5 rm ⊃ (dinner included) 92.00/138.00 **st.** – SB.

MORCOTT SERVICE AREA Rutland – see Uppingham.

MORECAMBE Lancs. 402 L 21 – pop. 46 657.
🏌 Bare ℰ (01524) 418050 – 🏌 Heysham, Trumacar Park, Middleton Rd ℰ (01524) 851011.
🛈 Station Buildings, Central Promenade, LA4 4DB ℰ (01524) 582808/9.
London 248 – Blackpool 29 – Carlisle 66 – Lancaster 4.

🏨 **Strathmore**, Marine Rd, East Promenade, LA4 5AP, ℰ (01524) 421234,
Fax (01524) 414242, ≼ – ᶘ, ▤ rest, 📺 ☎ 🅿 – 🔬 200. ⃝⃝ ⅋⃝ ⃝ ⅦⅦⅅ. ⅍
Meals 9.95/16.95 **st.** – 51 rm ⊃ 61.00/87.00 **st.** – SB.

Ⓓ ATS Northgate, White Lund Ind. Est.
ℰ (01524) 68075/62011

MORETON Mersey. 402 408 K 23 – pop. 12 053.
London 225 – Birkenhead 4 – Liverpool 5.

XX **Lee Ho**, 308 Hoylake Rd, L46 6DE, W : ¼ m. on A 553 ℰ (0151) 677 6440 – ▤. ⃝⃝ ⅋⃝ ⅦⅦⅅ
closed Sunday, Monday, 25-26 December, 1 January and Bank Holidays – **Meals** - Chinese -
(dinner only) 17.50 **st.** and a la carte ⅓ 4.45.

Ⓓ ATS 83 Hoylake Rd ℰ (0151) 678 2393

MORETONHAMPSTEAD Devon 408 I 32 The West Country G. – pop. 1 380 – ⊠ Newton
Abbot.
Env. : Dartmoor National Park★★.
🏌 Manor House Hotel ℰ (01647) 440998.
London 213 – Exeter 13 – Plymouth 28.

Manor House ⊗, TQ13 8RE, SW : 2 m. on B 3212 ℰ (01647) 440355, Fax (01647) 440961, ≤, « Part 19C », 🕞, ℞, ℛ, park, ℀ – ⊫, ✦ rest, ⊤⊽ ☎ 🄿 – 🛱 120. ⓪ AE ① VISA
Meals (bar lunch Monday to Saturday)/dinner 18.95 t. and a la carte ⓘ 5.95 – **90 rm** ⊆ 80.00/110.00 t. – SB.

Wray Barton Manor without rest., TQ13 8SE, SE : 1 ½ m. on A 382 ℰ (01647) 440467, Fax (01647) 440628, ≤, ℛ – ✦ ⊤⊽ 🄿
April-October – **6 rm** ⊆ 18.00/48.00 st.

Moorcote without rest., TQ13 8LS, NW : ¼ m. on A 382 ℰ (01647) 440966, ℛ – ✦ ⊤⊽ 🄿. ℀
April-30 October – **6 rm** ⊆ 28.00/38.00 st.

MORETON-IN-MARSH Glos. 403 404 O 28 Great Britain G. – pop. 1 895.
Env. : Chastleton House★★, SE : 5 m. by A 44.
London 86 – Birmingham 40 – Gloucester 31 – Oxford 29.

Manor House, High St., GL56 0LJ, ℰ (01608) 650501, Fax (01608) 651481, « 16C manor house, gardens », ☎, 🔲 – ⊫, ✦ rest, ⊤⊽ ☎ 🄿 – 🛱 75. ⓪ AE ① VISA JCB. ℀
Meals 12.50/21.90 t. and dinner a la carte ⓘ 9.95 – **38 rm** ⊆ 65.00/125.00 st., 1 suite – SB.

Redesdale Arms, High St., GL56 0AW, ℰ (01608) 650308, Fax (01608) 651843 – ⊤⊽ ☎ 🄿 – 🛱 80. ⓪ AE ① VISA. ℀
Meals a la carte 13.45/19.50 st. – ⊆ 5.95 – **16 rm** 42.25 st., 1 suite – SB.

Treetops without rest., London Rd, GL56 0HE, ℰ (01608) 651036, Fax (01608) 651036, ℛ – ✦ ⊤⊽ 🄿. ⓪ VISA. ℀
6 rm ⊆ 30.00/42.00.

Marsh Goose, High St., GL56 0AX, ℰ (01608) 652111, Fax (01608) 652403 – ✦. ⓪ AE ① VISA JCB
closed Sunday dinner, Monday, 26 December and 1 January – **Meals** 13.50/25.00 t and a la carte 19.00/35.00 t. ⓘ 4.90.

Annies, 3 Oxford St., GL56 0LA, ℰ (01608) 651981, Fax (01608) 651981 – ⓪ AE ① VISA
closed Sunday and late January-early February – **Meals** (dinner only) a la carte 23.30/31.75 st. ⓘ 6.25.

MORPETH Northd. 401 402 O 18 – pop. 14 393.
🕞 The Common ℰ (01670) 504942.
🄑 The Chantry, Bridge St., NE61 1PJ ℰ (01670) 511323.
London 301 – Edinburgh 93 – Newcastle upon Tyne 15.

Linden Hall ⊗, Longhorsley, NE65 8XF, NW : 7 ½ m. by A 192 on A 697 ℰ (01670) 516611, Fax (01670) 788544, ≤, « Country house in extensive grounds », 🕭, 🔲 🕞, ℛ, park – ⊫, ✦ rest, ⊤⊽ ☎ & 🄿 – 🛱 300. ⓪ AE ① VISA JCB. ℀
Meals 16.95/25.00 st. and a la carte – **49 rm** ⊆ 97.50/130.00 st., 1 suite – SB.

ⓐ ATS Coopies Lane Ind. Est. ℰ (01670) 514627

MORSTON Norfolk – see Blakeney.

MORTEHOE Devon 403 H 30 – see Woolacombe.

MOTCOMBE Dorset 403 404 N 30 – see Shaftesbury.

MOULSFORD Oxon. 403 404 Q 29 The West Country G. – pop. 491.
Exc. : Ridgeway Path★★.
London 58 – Oxford 17 – Reading 13 – Swindon 37.

Beetle and Wedge with rm, Ferry Lane, OX10 9JF, ℰ (01491) 65138? Fax (01491) 651376, ≤, « Thames-side setting », 🕭, ℛ – ⬇ ✦ ⊤⊽ ☎ 🄿. ⓪ AE ① VIS JCB
closed 25 December – **The Dining Room :** Meals (closed Sunday dinner and Monda (booking essential) 27.50/35.00 t. – **10 rm** ⊆ 90.00/135.00 t. – SB.

℀ **Boathouse :** Meals (closed 25 December) (booking essential) a la carte 21.20/31.20 t

MOULSOE *Bucks. – pop. 251.*
London 57 – Bedford 13 – Luton 21 – Northampton 15.

🍴 **Carrington Arms** with rm, Cranfield Rd, MK16 0HB, ☎ (01908) 218050, *Fax (01908) 217850* – [TV] [P]. [MC] [AE] [DC] [VISA] [JCB]
Meals (dinner bookings not accepted) a la carte approx. 18.00 **t.** – **8 rm** 38.50/48.50 **t.**

MOULTON *Northants.* [404] R 27 – *see Northampton.*

MOULTON *N. Yorks.* [402] P 20 – *pop. 197* – ✉ *Richmond.*
London 243 – Leeds 53 – Middlesbrough 25 – Newcastle upon Tyne 43.

🍴🍴 **Black Bull Inn,** DL10 6QJ, ☎ (01325) 377289, *Fax (01325) 377422,* « Brighton Belle Pullman coach » – [P]. [MC] [AE] [DC] [VISA] [JCB]
closed Sunday and 24 to 27 December – **Meals** 14.95 **t.** (lunch) and a la carte 21.70/30.70 **st.** 🍷 6.50.

MOUSEHOLE *Cornwall* [403] D 33 *The West Country G.* – ✉ *Penzance.*
See : *Village★.*
Env. : *Penwith★★ – Lamorna (The Merry Maidens and The Pipers Standing Stone★) SW : 3 m. by B 3315.*
Exc. : *Land's End★ (cliff scenery★★★) W : 9 m. by B 3315.*
London 321 – Penzance 3 – Truro 29.

🏨 **The Old Coastguard,** TR18 6PR, ☎ (01736) 731222, *Fax (01736) 731720,* ≤, 🌳 – 🚭 [TV] ☎ [P]. [MC] [VISA]
Meals *(closed weekday lunches November-February)* 18.95 **t.** (dinner) and a la carte 14.00/20.00 **t.** 🍷 4.50 – **21 rm** ☕ 32.00/64.00 **st.** – SB.

MUCH WENLOCK *Shrops.* [402] [403] M26 *Great Britain G.* – *pop. 1 921.*
See : *Priory★ AC.*
Env. : *Ironbridge Gorge Museum★★ AC (The Iron Bridge★★ - Coalport China Museum★★ - Blists Hill Open Air Museum★★ – Museum of the River and Visitor Centre★) NE : 4 ½ m. by A 4169 and B 4380.*
[i] *The Museum, High St., TF13 6HR ☎ (01952) 727679 (summer only).*
London 154 – Birmingham 34 – Shrewsbury 12 – Worcester 37.

🏨 **Raven,** Barrow St., TF13 6EN, ☎ (01952) 727251, *Fax (01952) 728416,* 🌳 – 🚭 rest, [TV] ☎ [P]. [MC] [AE] [DC] [VISA] [JCB]. 🐕
closed 25 December – **Meals** (light lunch Monday to Saturday)/dinner a la carte 20.50/26.75 **t.** 🍷 7.00 – **15 rm** ☕ 48.00/85.00 **t.** – SB.

at Bourton *SW : 2 ¾ m. on B 4378* – ✉ *Much Wenlock.*

🏨 **Bourton Manor** 🌙, TF13 6QE, ☎ (01746) 785531, *Fax (01746) 785683,* ≤, 🌳 – 🚭 rest, [TV] ☎ [P] – 🎪 40. [MC] [AE] [DC] [VISA]
Meals (bar lunch Monday to Saturday)/dinner a la carte 17.25/21.45 **t.** 🍷 5.50 – **8 rm** ☕ 48.00/110.00 **t.** – SB.

MUDEFORD *Dorset* [403] [404] O 31 – *see Christchurch.*

MULLION *Cornwall* [403] E 33 *The West Country G.* – *pop. 2 040* – ✉ *Helston.*
See : *Mullion Cove★★ (Church★) – Lizard Peninsula★.*
Env. : *Kynance Cove★★, S : 5 m. – Cury★ (Church★), N : 2 m. by minor roads.*
Exc. : *Helston (The Flora Day Furry Dance★★) (May), N : 7 ½ m. by A 3083 – Culdrose (Flambards Village Theme Park★) AC, N : 6 m. by A 3083 – Wendron (Poldark Mine★), N : 9 ½ m. by A 3083 and B 3297.*
London 323 – Falmouth 21 – Penzance 21 – Truro 26.

🏨 **Polurrian,** TR12 7EN, SW : ½ m. ☎ (01326) 240421, *Fax (01326) 240083,* ≤ Mounts Bay, 🏋, 🧖, 🏊, 🏊, 🌳, 🎾, squash – 🚭 rest, [TV] ☎ [P] – 🎪 120. [MC] [AE] [DC] [VISA]
closed January – **Meals** (bar lunch Monday to Saturday)/dinner 21.00 **st.** and a la carte 🍷 5.50 – **38 rm** ☕ (dinner included) 76.00/180.00, 1 suite – SB.

Your recommendation is self-evident if you always walk into a hotel Guide in hand.

MUNGRISDALE Cumbria **401 402** L 19 20 – pop. 330 – ⊠ Penrith.

London 301 – Carlisle 33 – Keswick 8.5 – Penrith 13.

🏠 **Mill** ⍛, CA11 0XR, ℰ (017687) 79659, Fax (017687) 79155, ⌘, ⌹ – 灬 rest, �📺 **℗**
27 February-October – **Meals** (dinner only) 25.00 t. ⓘ 4.95 – **7 rm** ⊇ 60.00/70.00 t.

🏠 **Mosedale House** ⍛, Mosedale, CA11 0XQ, N : 1 m. by Mosedale rd ℰ (017687) 79371 –
灬 📺 ₺ **℗**
closed 25 and 26 December – **Meals** 13.00 st. ⓘ 4.65 – **5 rm** ⊇ (dinner included) 37.00/
90.00 st.

MYLOR BRIDGE Cornwall **403** E 33 – see Falmouth.

NAILSWORTH Glos. **403 404** N 28 – pop. 5 242.

London 120 – Bristol 30 – Swindon 41.

🏛 **Egypt Mill**, GL6 0AE, ℰ (01453) 833449, Fax (01453) 836098, « Part 16C converted mill »,
⌹ – 📺 ☎ **℗** – ⚿ 100. **⊘0** ⚞ **VISA**. �００
Restaurant : Meals 10.50/16.50 st. ⓘ 6.25 – **Cellar Bistro :** Meals a la carte 12.25/18.65 t.
ⓘ 5.90 – **16 rm** ⊇ 42.50/95.00 st. – SB.

🏠 **Aaron Farm**, Nympsfield Rd, GL6 0ET, W : ¾ m. by Spring Hill ℰ (01453) 833598,
Fax (01453) 833598 – 灬 📺 **℗**
Meals 12.00 st. – **3 rm** ⊇ 28.00/40.00 st.

XX **Waterman's**, Old Market, GL6 0BX, ℰ (01270) 832808 – **⊘0** ⚞ **①** **VISA** **JCB**
closed Sunday and Monday – **Meals** (dinner only) a la carte 15.25/25.45 t. ⓘ 4.50.

X **William's Bistro**, 3 Fountain St., GL6 0BL, ℰ (01453) 835507, Fax (01453) 835950 – **⊘0**
VISA
closed Sunday, Monday, 2 weeks Christmas and New Year – **Meals** - Seafood - (dinner only)
a la carte 18.00/28.00 t.

Si vous cherchez un hôtel tranquille,
consultez d'abord les cartes de l'introduction
ou repérez dans le texte les établissements indiqués avec le signe ⍛ *ou* ⍛

NANTWICH Ches. **402 403 404** M 24 – pop. 11 695.

🛈 Church House, Church Walk, CW5 5RG ℰ (01270) 610983/610880.

London 176 – Chester 20 – Liverpool 45 – Stoke-on-Trent 17.

🏛 **Rookery Hall** ⍛, Worleston, CW5 6DQ, N : 2 ½ m. by A 51 on B 5074 ℰ (01270) 610016
Fax (01270) 626027, ≼, « Part 19C country house », ⌘, ⌹, park, � – ⯊ 灬 📺 ☎ ₺ **℗** ·
⚿ 70. **⊘0** ⚞ **①** **VISA**
Meals (booking essential) 17.50/37.50 st. ⓘ 9.50 – **42 rm** ⊇ 120.00/160.00 st., 3 suites -
SB.

🏛 **The Peacock - Premier Lodge**, 221 Crewe Rd, CW5 6NE, NE : 1 ¼ m. on A 53◄
ℰ (01270) 624069, Fax (01270) 610113 – 灬 rm, 📺 ☎ ₺ **℗**. **⊘0** ⚞ **①** **VISA**. ⍠
Meals (grill rest.) a la carte 8.00/15.00 st. – ⊇ 4.95 – **37 rm** 42.25 st. – SB.

🏠 **Oakland House** without rest., 252 Newcastle Rd, Blakelow, Shavington, CW5 7ET, E
2 ½ m. by A 51 on A 500 ℰ (01270) 567134, Fax (01270) 651752, ⌹ – 灬 📺 **℗**. **⊘0** **VISA**. ⍠
5 rm ⊇ 26.00/38.00 st.

🏠 **The Limes** without rest., 5 Park Rd, CW5 7AQ, ℰ (01270) 624081, Fax (01270) 624081, ⌹
– 灬 📺 **℗**
restricted opening December and January – **3 rm** ⊇ 30.00/45.00 st.

XX **Churche's Mansion**, Hospital St., CW5 5RY, E : ¼ m. ℰ (01270) 625933
Fax (01270) 627831, ⍉, « Timbered Elizabethan house », ⌹ – 灬 **℗**. **⊘0** ⚞ **①** **VISA**
closed Sunday dinner, Monday and 2 weeks January – **Meals** 18.95/28.50 t. ⓘ 9.00.

at Burland W : 2 ½ m. on A 534 – ⊠ Nantwich.

🏠 **Burland Farm** without rest., Wrexham Rd, CW5 8ND, W : ¾ m. on A 53◄
ℰ (01270) 524210, Fax (01270) 524419, « Working farm », ⌹ – 📺 **℗**
closed mid December-mid January – **3 rm** ⊇ 30.00/50.00.

NATIONAL EXHIBITION CENTRE W. Mids. **403 404** O 26 – see Birmingham.

NAWTON N. Yorks. – see Helmsley.

NAYLAND Suffolk 404 W 28.
London 64 – Bury St. Edmunds 24 – Cambridge 54 – Colchester 6 – Ipswich 19.

↑ **Gladwins Farm** ᯓ, Harpers Hill, CO6 4NU, NW : ½ m. on A 134 ℘ (01206) 262261, *Fax (01206) 263001*, ←, 🖘, 🖵, ᯓ, 🛋, park, 🎾 – ↳ rm, 📺 🄿, 🟥 *VISA*
closed 10 days Christmas and New Year – **Meals** (by arrangement) 12.50 – **4 rm** � 20.00/72.00 **st.**

✗ **Martha's Vineyard,** 18 High St., CO6 4JF, ℘ (01206) 262888 – 🟥 *VISA*
closed Sunday dinner, Monday to Wednesday, 2 weeks summer, 2 weeks winter and 25 December – **Meals** (dinner only and Sunday lunch)/dinner 22.00 **t.** ℹ 10.00.

✗ **White Hart,** High St., CO6 4JF, ℘ (01206) 263382, *Fax (01206) 263638* – 🄿, 🟥 🆎 ⓞ *VISA*
🍺 *closed 26 December and 1-2 January* – **Meals** 16.00 **t.** (lunch) and a la carte 18.50/21.50 **t.** ℹ 8.50.

NEAR SAWREY Cumbria 402 L 20 – see Hawkshead.

NEEDHAM MARKET Suffolk 404 X 27 – pop. 4 312.
London 77 – Cambridge 47 – Ipswich 8.5 – Norwich 38.

🏨 **Travelodge,** Norwich Rd, IP6 8LP, Beacon Hill Service Area, at junction of A 14 with A 140 ℘ (01449) 721640, *Fax (01449) 721640*, Reservations (Freephone) 0800 850950 – ↳ rm, 📺 🕭 🄿, 🟥 🆎 ⓞ *VISA* JCB, 🞰
Meals (grill rest.) – **40 rm** 35.95 **t.**

↑ **Pipps Ford,** Norwich Rd roundabout, IP6 8LJ, SE : 1 ¾ m. by B 1078 at junction of A 14 with A 140 ℘ (01449) 760208, *Fax (01449) 760561*, « Elizabethan farmhouse », 🛋, 🛋, 🎾 – ↳ 🄿. 🞰
closed mid December-mid January – **Meals** (by arrangement) (communal dining) 17.50 ℹ 6.50 – **7 rm** ☞ 37.50/65.00.

The Guide is updated annually so renew your Guide every year.

NETTLETON SHRUB Wilts. 403 404 N 29 – see Castle Combe.

NEW ALRESFORD Hants. 403 404 Q 30 – pop. 5 041 – ✉ Alresford.
London 63 – Portsmouth 40 – Reading 33 – Southampton 20.

✗ **Hunters** with rm, 32 Broad St., SO24 9AQ, ℘ (01962) 732468, *Fax (01962) 732468*, « Former coaching inn », 🛋 – ↳ rm, 📺 – ᵴ 60. 🟥 🆎 ⓞ *VISA*. 🞰
closed 1 week Christmas – **Meals** (closed Sunday lunch June-August and Sunday dinner) 14.95 **t.** (dinner) and a la carte 21.40/26.40 **t.** ℹ 4.50 – **3 rm** ☞ 37.50/47.50 **st.** – SB.

NEWARK-ON-TRENT Notts. 402 404 R 24 Great Britain G. – pop. 35 129.
See : St. Mary Magdalene★.
🏌 Kelwick, Coddington ℘ (01636) 626241.
🖪 The Gilstrap Centre, Castlegate, NG24 1BG ℘ (01636) 78962.
London 127 – Lincoln 16 – Nottingham 20 – Sheffield 42.

🏨 **Grange,** 73 London Rd, NG24 1RZ, S : ½ m. on Grantham rd (A 1) ℘ (01636) 703399, *Fax (01636) 702328*, 🛋 – ↳ 📺 🕭 🄿, 🟥 🆎 ⓞ *VISA* JCB, 🞰
closed 24 December-2 January – **Meals** (lunch by arrangement)/dinner 13.50 **st.** and a la carte ℹ 4.95 – **15 rm** ☞ 44.95/72.95 **st.** – SB.

at North Muskham N : 4½ m. by A 46 and A 1 – ✉ Newark-on-Trent.

🏨 **Travelodge,** NG23 6HT, N : ½ m. on A 1 (southbound carriageway) ℘ (01636) 703635, *Fax (01636) 703635*, Reservations (Freephone) 0800 850950 – ↳ rm, 📺 🄿. 🟥 🆎 ⓞ *VISA* JCB, 🞰
Meals (grill rest.) – **30 rm** 39.95 **t.**

🔘 ATS 70 William St. ℘ (01636) 77531

NEWBURGH Lancs. 402 L 23.
London 217 – Liverpool 26 – Manchester 39 – Preston 20 – Southport 13.

🏨 **Red Lion,** Ash Brow, WN8 7NG, on A 5209 ℘ (01257) 462336, *Fax (01257) 462827* – 📺 🕭 🄿 – ᵴ 45. 🟥 🆎 *VISA* JCB
Meals (grill rest.) (in bar) 7.25 **st.** and a la carte ℹ 4.95 – ☞ 4.95 – **13 rm** 28.00/35.00 **st.**

NEWBURY 403 404 Q 29 – pop. 33 273.

🏌 *Newbury and Crookham, Bury's Bank Rd, Greenham Common ℘ (01635) 40035 AX –*
🏌 *Donnington Valley, Old Oxford Rd ℘ (01635) 32488 AV.*

🛈 *The Wharf, RG14 5AS ℘ (01635) 30267.*

London 67 – Bristol 66 – Oxford 28 – Reading 17 – Southampton 38.

NEWBURY

Kennett Schopping Centre **BZ**

*There is no paid
advertising in this Guide.*

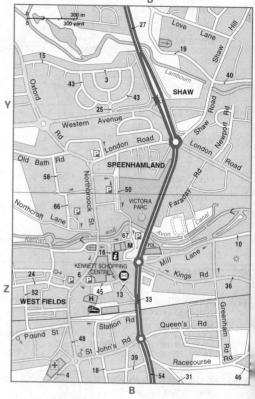

🏨 **Donnington Valley H. & Golf Course,** Old Oxford Rd, Donnington, RG14 3AG,
N : 1 ¾ m. by A 4 on B 4494 ℘ (01635) 551199, *Fax (01635) 551123,* 🏌, park – 🛏 ❄ 📺 ☎
⅙ 🅿 – 🔬 140. 🅿🄾 🄰🄴 ⓪ 𝗩𝗜𝗦𝗔   AV a
Gallery : Meals 17.50/19.50 st. and a la carte ↓ 5.95 – � 9.50 – **58 rm** 95.00/130.00 st. –
SB.

🏨 **Jarvis Elcot Park H. and Country Club,** RG20 8NJ, W : 5 m. by A 4
℘ (01488) 658100, *Fax (01488) 658288,* ≤, ↓⅙, ≘s, 🔲, 🌳, park, 🎾 – ❄ rm, 🍽 rest, 📺 ☎
⅙ 🅿 – 🔬 110. 🅿🄾 🄰🄴 ⓪ 𝗩𝗜𝗦𝗔 ⅍
Meals *(closed lunch Saturday and Bank Holidays)* 19.95 st. and a la carte ↓ 8.00 – ⊏ 9.50 –
75 rm 104.00/150.00 st. – SB.

🏨 **Stakis Newbury,** Oxford Rd, RG20 8XY, N : 3 ¼ m. on A 34 ℘ (01635) 247010,
Fax (01635) 247077, ↓⅙, ≘s, 🔲 – ❄ rm, 🍽 rest, 📺 ☎ ⅙ 🅿 – 🔬 200. 🅿🄾 🄰🄴 ⓪ 𝗩𝗜𝗦𝗔 ⅉꞔ
Meals *(closed Saturday lunch)* (carving lunch) 12.00/16.95 **t.** and dinner a la carte -
⊏ 10.75 – **108 rm** 105.00/115.00 st., 2 suites – SB.

🏨 **Hilton National,** Pinchington Lane, RG14 7HL, S : 2 m. by A 34 ℘ (01635) 529000,
Fax (01635) 529337, ↓⅙, ≘s, 🔲 – ❄ rm, 🍽 rest, 📺 ☎ ⅙ 🅿 – 🔬 200. 🅿🄾 🄰🄴 ⓪ 𝗩𝗜𝗦𝗔 ⅉꞔ
Meals *(bar lunch Saturday)* 13.95/17.50 st. and dinner a la carte ↓ 6.50 – ⊏ 10.75 – **109 rm**
115.00/155.00 st. – SB.   AX

🏨 Foley Lodge, Stockcross, RG20 8JU, NW : 2 m. by A 4 on B 4000 ℘ (01635) 528770,
Fax (01635) 528398, 🔲, 🌳 – 🛏, ❄ rm, 📺 ☎ 🅿 – 🔬 220   AV b
67 rm, 1 suite.

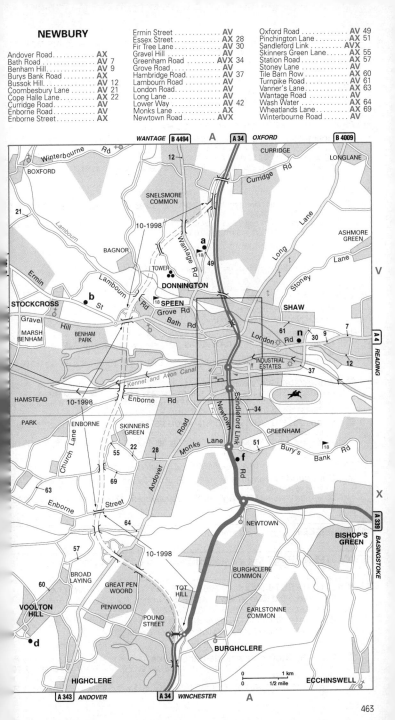

NEWBURY

Andover Road............ **AX**
Bath Road .... **AV** 7
Benham Hill............ **AV** 9
Burys Bank Road....... **AX**
Bussok Hill............. **AV** 12
Coombesbury Lane ..... **AV** 21
Cope Halle Lane........ **AX** 22
Curridge Road.......... **AV**
Enborne Road.......... **AV**
Enborne Street......... **AX**

Ermin Street .... **AV**
Essex Street............ **AX** 28
Fir Tree Lane .... **AV** 30
Gravel Hill .... **AV**
Greenham Road ..... **AVX** 34
Grove Road .... **AX**
Hambridge Road........ **AV** 37
Lambourn Road......... **AV**
London Road........... **AV**
Long Lane .... **AV**
Lower Way .... **AV** 42
Monks Lane .... **AX**
Newtown Road .... **AVX**

Oxford Road .... **AV** 49
Pinchington Lane ...... **AX** 51
Sandleford Link .... **AVX**
Skinners Green Lane..... **AX** 55
Station Road .... **AX** 57
Stoney Lane .... **AV**
Tile Barn Row .... **AV** 60
Turnpike Road.......... **AV** 61
Vanner's Lane.......... **AX** 63
Wantage Road .... **AV**
Wash Water .... **AV** 64
Wheatlands Lane....... **AX** 69
Winterbourne Road .... **AV**

🏠 **Blue Boar Inn,** North Heath, RG20 8UE, N : 4 ¾ m. by A 4 on B 4494 ℘ (01635) 248236, Fax (01635) 248506 – 🎛 ☎ 🅿. 🕮 🆎 ⓪ 𝘝𝘐𝘚𝘈 ᴶᶜᴮ. ⌘
Meals (closed 25 and 26 December) (in bar Sunday dinner) a la carte 18.00/26.15 **t.** ⓝ 5.95 – 15 rm ⌐ 53.00/63.00. – SB.

🏠 **Limes,** 368 London Rd, RG14 2QH, E : ½ m. on A 4 ℘ (01635) 33082, Fax (01635) 580023, 🚗 – 🎛 ☎ 🅿. 🕮 🆎 𝘝𝘐𝘚𝘈 ᴶᶜᴮ. ⌘   AV n
closed 25 December – Meals (by arrangement) (dinner only) a la carte 13.60/17.25 **st.** – 15 rm ⌐ 38.00/58.00.

at Woolton Hill SW : 4½ m. by A 34 off A 343 – ✉ Newbury.

🏛 **Hollington House** ⍐, RG20 9XA, SW : ½ m. on East End rd ℘ (01635) 255100, Fax (01635) 255075, ≤, « Edwardian country house, gardens », ⌑, park, ⌘ – ▮, ⭰ rm, 🎛 ☎ 🅿 – 🔬 45. 🕮 🆎 ⓪ 𝘝𝘐𝘚𝘈 ᴶᶜᴮ. ⌘   AX d
Meals 14.50/26.50 **t.** and a la carte 30.00/41.50 **t.** – ⌐5.00 – 19 rm 99.00/185.00 **t.**, 1 suite – SB.

at Hamstead Marshall SW : 5½ m. by A 4 – AV – ✉ Newbury.

🏠 **White Hart Inn,** Kintbury Rd, RG20 0HW, ℘ (01488) 658201, Fax (01488) 657192, 🚗 – 🎛 ☎ 🅿. 🕮 𝘝𝘐𝘚𝘈. ⌘
closed 2 weeks summer, 25-26 December and 1 January – Meals - Italian - (closed Sunday) a la carte 14.50/25.00 **t.** – 6 rm ⌐ 50.00/75.00 **t.**

🔧 ATS 30 Queens Rd ℘ (01635) 42250

Le Guide change, changez de **guide Michelin** *tous les ans.*

NEWBY BRIDGE Cumbria 🔢 L 21 Great Britain G. – ✉ Ulverston.
Env. : Lake Windermere★★.
London 270 – Kendal 16 – Lancaster 27.

🏛 **Lakeside,** Lakeside, LA12 8AT, NE : 1 m. on Hawkshead rd ℘ (015395) 31207, Fax (015395) 31699, ≤, « Lakeside setting », ⌒, 🚗 – ▮ ⭰ 🎛 ☎ 🅿 – 🔬 100. 🕮 🆎 ⓪ 𝘝𝘐𝘚𝘈
Meals (bar lunch Monday to Saturday)/dinner 28.00 **st.** ⓝ 9.95 – 70 rm ⌐ 95.00/160.00 **st.** – SB.

🏛 **Whitewater,** The Lakeland Village, LA12 8PX, SW : 1 ½ m. by A 590 ℘ (015395) 31133, Fax (015395) 31881, ⅃ぶ, ≘ʂ, ⬛, ⌘, squash – ▮ 🎛 ☎ 🅿 – 🔬 70. 🕮 🆎 ⓪ 𝘝𝘐𝘚𝘈. ⌘
closed 4 to 9 January – Meals (bar lunch Monday to Saturday)/dinner 19.00 **t.** and a la carte ⓝ 5.75 – 35 rm ⌐ 70.00/100.00 **st.** – SB.

🏛 **Swan,** LA12 8NB, ℘ (015395) 31681, Fax (015395) 31917, ≤, ⌒, 🚗 – ⭰ rest, 🎛 ☎ 🅿 – 🔬 65. 🕮 🆎 𝘝𝘐𝘚𝘈. ⌘
Meals (bar lunch Monday to Saturday)/dinner 18.75 **t.** and a la carte ⓝ 6.95 – 35 rm ⌐ 62.00/100.00 **t.**, 1 suite – SB.

at Cartmell Fell NE : 3¼ m. by A 590 off A 592 – ✉ Grange-over-Sands.

🏠 **Lightwood Farmhouse** ⍐, LA11 6NP, ℘ (015395) 31454, Fax (015395) 31454, ≤, 🚗 – ⭰ 🎛 🅿. 🕮 𝘝𝘐𝘚𝘈. ⌘
closed Christmas-mid February – Meals (by arrangement) 12.00 **s.** ⓝ 4.00 – 5 rm ⌐ 32.00/ 52.00 **s.** – SB.

NEWBY WISKE N. Yorks. – see Northallerton.

NEWCASTLE AIRPORT Tyne and Wear 🔢 🔢 O 19 – see Newcastle upon Tyne.

NEWCASTLE-UNDER-LYME Staffs. 🔢 🔢 🔢 N 24 Great Britain G. – pop. 73 731.
Exc. : Wedgwood Visitor's Centre★ AC, SE : 6 ½ m. by A 34 Z.
▸ Newcastle Municipal, Keele Rd ℘ (01782) 627596.
🚪 Ironmarket, ST5 1AT ℘ (01782) 297313/717137.
London 161 – Birmingham 46 – Liverpool 56 – Manchester 43.

Plan of Built up Area : see Stoke-on-Trent

🏛 **Forte Posthouse Newcastle-under-Lyme,** Clayton Rd, Clayton, ST5 4DL, S : 2 m on A 519 ℘ (01782) 717171, Fax (01782) 717138, ⅃ぶ, ≘ʂ, ⬛, 🚗 – ⭰ rm, 🎛 ☎ 🅿 – 🔬 70 🕮 🆎 ⓪ 𝘝𝘐𝘚𝘈 ᴶᶜᴮ. ⌘   on Stoke-on-Trent town plan   V   ▮
Meals (closed lunch Saturday) a la carte 14.00/23.50 **st.** ⓝ 5.95 – ⌐ 10.95 – 119 rm 69.00 st – SB.

NEWCASTLE-UNDER-LYME
CENTRE

High Street .... YZ
Roebuck Centre .... YZ 61

Albert Street .... Y
Barracks Road .... YZ
Blackfriars Road .... Z 9
Brook Lane .... Z
Brunswick Street .... Y
Church Street .... Y 20
Friarswood Road .... Z
George Street .... Y
Hassell Street .... Y
Higherland .... Z 37
Iron Market .... Y 38
King Street .... Y
Lancaster Road .... Z
Liverpool Road .... Y 41
Lower Street .... YZ
Merrial Street .... Y 47
Parkstone Avenue .... Z
Pool Dam .... Z
Queen Street .... Y
Ryecroft .... Y
Vessey Terrace .... Z 73
Victoria Road .... Z

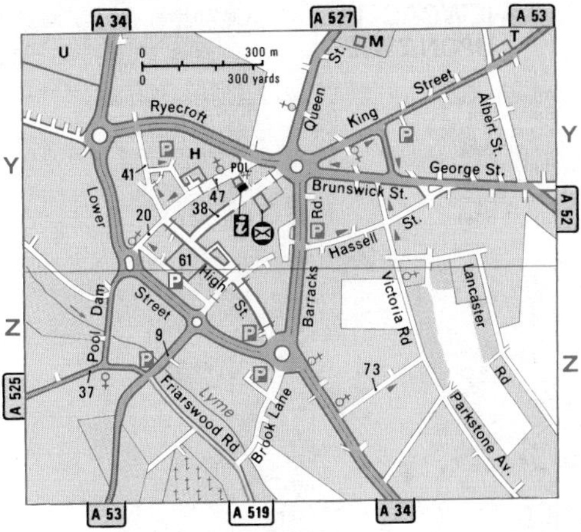

A 34
A 527
A 53
U
M
T
0 300 m
0 300 yards
Ryecroft
Queen St.
King
Street
Albert St.
Y
George St.
Brunswick St.
Hassell
St.
H
POL
41
20
38
47
61
Lower
High St.
Street
Pool Dam
Barracks Rd.
Victoria Rd
Lancaster Rd
Z
9
73
37
Friarswood Rd
Lyme
Brook Lane
Parkstone Av.
A 525
A 52
A 53
A 519
A 34

🏨 **Clayton Lodge,** Clayton Rd, Clayton, ST5 4AF, S : 1 ¼ m. on A 519 ☎ (01782) 613093, *Fax (01782) 711896* – ⊁ rm, [TV] ☎ [P] – 🏨 280. [M] [AE] [D] VISA
Meals (bar lunch Saturday and Bank Holidays) 15.95 **st.** 🍷 6.50 – ☕ 8.95 – **50 rm** 79.00/119.00 **t.** – SB. on Stoke-on-Trent town plan V e

🍴 **Bauhinia,** Parklands, ST4 6NW, ☎ (01782) 719709 – ▤ [P]. [M] [AE] VISA JCB
closed Sunday lunch and 25-26 December – **Meals** - Chinese - 5.95/13.45 **t.** and a la carte 🍷 5.15. on Stoke-on-Trent town plan V u

ATS Lower St. ☎ (01782) 622431

NEWCASTLE UPON TYNE *Tyne and Wear* [401] [402] O 19 *Great Britain G.* – *pop. 189 150.*

See : *City*★★ – *Grey Street*★ CZ – *Quayside*★ CZ : *Composition*★, *All Saints Church*★ *(interior*★*)* – *Castle Keep*★ *AC* CZ – *Laing Art Gallery and Museum*★ *AC* CY **M1** – *Museum of Antiquities*★ CY **M2.**

Env. : *Hadrian's Wall*★★, *W : by A 69* AV.

Exc. : *Beamish : North of England Open-Air Museum*★★ *AC, SW : 7 m. by A 692 and A 6076* AX – *Seaton Delaval Hall*★ *AC, NE : 11 m. by A 189* – BV – *and A 190*

Broadway East, Gosforth ☎ (0191) 285 6710, BV – *City of Newcastle, Three Mile Bridge, Gosforth ☎ (0191) 285 1775,* – *Wallsend, Rheydt Av., Bigges Main ☎ (0191) 262 1973, NE : by A 1058* BV – *Whickham, Hollinside Park ☎ (0191) 488 7309.*

Tyne Tunnel (toll).

✈ *Newcastle Airport : ☎ (0191) 286 0966, NW : 5 m. by A 696* AV – **Terminal :** *Bus Assembly : Central Station Forecourt.*

⛴ *to Norway (Bergen, Haugesund and Stavanger) (Color Line) – to Sweden (Gothenburg) (Scandinavian Seaways) weekly (22 h) – to Germany (Hamburg) (Scandinavian Seaways) daily (23 h) – to The Netherlands (Amsterdam) (Scandinavian Seaways) daily (14 h).*

ℹ *Central Library, Princess Sq., NE99 1DX ☎ (0191) 261 0610 – Main Concourse, Central Station, NE1 5DL ☎ (0191) 230 0030.*

London 276 – Edinburgh 105 – Leeds 95.

Plans on following pages

🏨 **Copthorne Newcastle,** The Close, Quayside, NE1 3RT, ☎ (0191) 222 0333, *Fax (0191) 230 1111,* ≤, Fø, ≘s, 🏊 – ⬍, ⊁ rm, ▤ rest, [TV] ☎ ♿ [P] – 🏨 200. [M] [AE] [D] VISA JCB CZ z
Le Rivage : **Meals** *(closed Sunday)* (dinner only) a la carte 28.85/30.40 **st.** 🍷 7.65 – ***Harry's :*** **Meals** *(closed Saturday lunch)* a la carte 18.90/30.95 **st.** 🍷 7.65 – ☕ 11.95 – **156 rm** 135.00/160.00 **st.**

🏨 **Vermont,** Castle Garth (off St. Nicholas St.), NE1 1RQ, ☎ (0191) 233 1010, *Fax (0191) 233 1234,* ≤, Fø – ⬍, ⊁ rm, [TV] ☎ ♿ [P] – 🏨 200. [M] [AE] [D] VISA CZ s
Brasserie : **Meals** 13.50/15.50 **st.** and a la carte 🍷 6.50 – (see also ***Blue Room*** below) – ☕ 10.50 – **95 rm** 125.00/135.00 **st.**, 6 suites – SB.

🏨 **Imperial Swallow,** Jesmond Rd, NE2 1PR, ☎ (0191) 281 5511, *Fax (0191) 281 8472,* Fø, ≘s, 🏊 – ⬍, ⊁ rm, ▤ rest, [TV] ☎ [P] – 🏨 150. [M] [AE] [D] VISA CY e
Meals *(closed Saturday lunch)* 9.50/18.00 **st.** 🍷 8.00 – **122 rm** ☕ 85.00/105.00 **st.** – SB.

NEWCASTLE
UPON TYNE

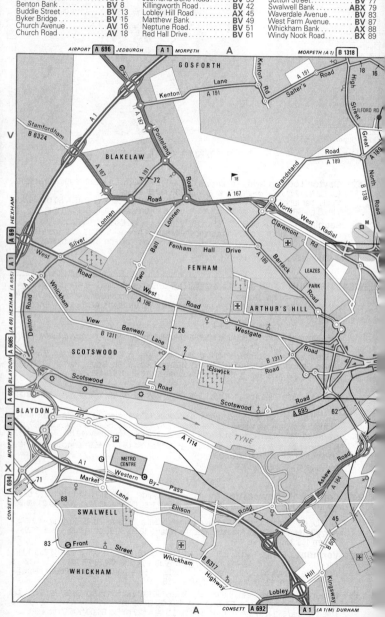

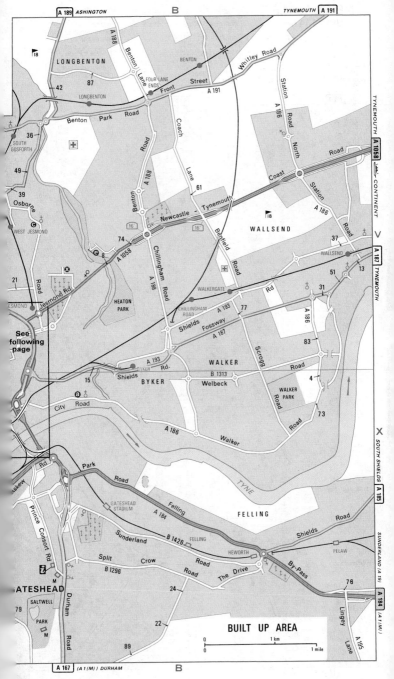

NEWCASTLE
UPON TYNE

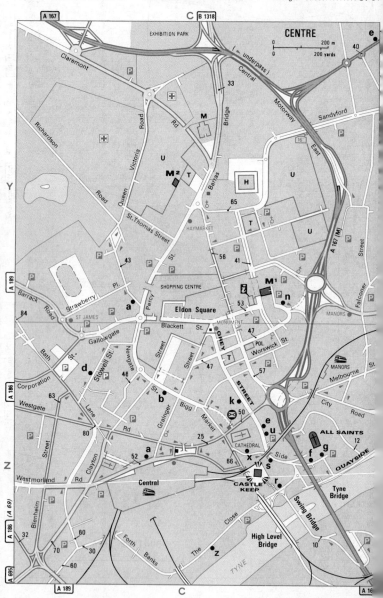

Forte Posthouse Newcastle upon Tyne, 1 New Bridge Street West, NE1 8BS, *℘ (0191) 232 6191, Fax (0191) 261 8529* – 🛗, ✤ rm, 🍴 rest, 🖭 ☎ 🔥 🅿 – 🔬 400. 🍽 🎫 ⑩ 𝑉𝐼𝑆𝐴 JCB
CY n
closed 25 December – **Meals** 8.95 **st.** and a la carte 🍷 11.45 – ⬡ 9.95 – **166 rm** 79.00/109.00. – SB.

Novotel, Ponteland Rd, Kenton, NE3 3HZ, at junction of A 1 (M) with A 696 *℘ (0191) 214 0303, Fax (0191) 214 0633,* ☎, ⬛ – 🛗, ✤ rm, 🍴 rest, 🖭 ☎ 🔥 🅿 – 🔬 220. 🍽 🎫 ⑩ 𝑉𝐼𝑆𝐴
AV a
Meals 14.00 **st.** and a la carte – ⬡ 9.00 – **126 rm** 69.00 **st.**

County Thistle, Neville St., NE99 1AH, *℘ (0191) 232 2471, Fax (0191) 232 1285* – 🛗, ✤ rm, 🖭 ☎ 🅿 – 🔬 130. 🍽 🎫 ⑩ 𝑉𝐼𝑆𝐴 JCB
CZ a
Meals (bar lunch Saturday) 10.95/18.50 **st.** and dinner a la carte 🍷 5.95 – ⬡ 10.00 – **115 rm** 92.00/114.00. – SB.

Swallow, 1 Newgate Arcade, Newgate St., NE1 5SX, *℘ (0191) 232 5025, Fax (0191) 232 8428* – 🛗, ✤ rm, 🖭 ☎ 🅿 – 🔬 100. 🍽 🎫 ⑩ 𝑉𝐼𝑆𝐴
CZ b
Meals 10.25/17.25 **st.** and a la carte 🍷 6.50 – **93 rm** ⬡ 90.00/100.00 **st.** – SB.

Bank Top Toby, Ponteland Rd., Kenton, NE3 3TY, at junction of A 1 (M) with A 696 *℘ (0191) 214 0877, Fax (0191) 214 0095* – ✤, 🍴 rest, 🖭 ☎ 🔥 🅿 – 🔬 50. 🍽 🎫 𝑉𝐼𝑆𝐴 ✤
AV a
closed Christmas – **Meals** a la carte 10.65/16.10 **st.** 🍷 4.95 – **30 rm** ⬡ 62.00/72.00 **st.** – SB.

Surtees, 12-16 Dean St., NE1 1PG, *℘ (0191) 261 7771, Fax (0191) 230 1322* – 🛗 🖭 ☎. 🍽 🎫 ⑩ 𝑉𝐼𝑆𝐴 JCB
CZ u
Meals - Café-restaurant - (dinner only and Sunday lunch)/dinner a la carte 12.80/16.85 **st.** 🍷 3.95 – **27 rm** ⬡ 67.50/77.50 **st.**

Waterside, 48-52 Sandhill, Quayside, NE1 3JF, *℘ (0191) 230 0111, Fax (0191) 230 1615* – 🛗 🖭 ☎. 🍽 🎫 ⑩ 𝑉𝐼𝑆𝐴 JCB
CZ r
Meals - Café-restaurant - *(closed Sunday and Bank Holidays)* 6.95 **st.** 🍷 3.95 – ⬡ 9.95 – **26 rm** 57.00/83.00 **st.**

New Kent, 127 Osborne Rd, Jesmond, NE2 2TB, *℘ (0191) 281 1083, Fax (0191) 281 3369* – 🖭 ☎ 🅿. 🍽 🎫 ⑩ 𝑉𝐼𝑆𝐴 JCB. ✤
BV c
Meals (bar lunch)/dinner 12.95 **t.** and a la carte 🍷 5.00 – **32 rm** ⬡ 59.50/85.00 **t.** – SB.

Travelodge, Whitemare Pool, NE10 8YB, SE : 4 m. at junction of A 194 with A 184 *℘ (0191) 438 3333, Reservations (Freephone) 0800 850950* – ✤ rm, 🖭 🔥 🅿. 🍽 🎫 ⑩ 𝑉𝐼𝑆𝐴 JCB. ✤
Meals (grill rest.) – **71 rm** 44.95 **t.**

Travel Inn, City Rd, Quayside, NE2 2AQ, *℘ (0191) 232 6533, Fax (0191) 232 6557* – ✤ rm, 🔥 🅿. 🍽 🎫 ⑩ 𝑉𝐼𝑆𝐴
BX a
Meals (grill rest.) – **82 rm** 36.50 **t.**

Avenue without rest., 2 Manor House Rd, NE2 2LU, at junction with Osborne Av. *℘ (0191) 281 1396, Fax (0191) 281 6588* – 🖭 ☎ 🅿. 🍽 🎫 𝑉𝐼𝑆𝐴 JCB
BV x
closed 1 week Christmas – **11 rm** ⬡ 29.50/39.50 **st.**

Blue Room (at Vermont H.), Castle Garth (off St. Nicholas St.), NE1 1RQ, *℘ (0191) 233 1010, Fax (0191) 233 1234* – 🍴 🅿. 🍽 🎫 ⑩ 𝑉𝐼𝑆𝐴
CZ s
closed Sunday, one week January and two weeks July-August – **Meals** 16.50 **st.** (lunch) and dinner a la carte 29.95/36.45 **st.** 🍷 6.50.

Fisherman's Lodge, Jesmond Dene, Jesmond, NE7 7BQ, *℘ (0191) 281 3281, Fax (0191) 281 6410* – ✤ 🅿. 🍽 🎫 ⑩ 𝑉𝐼𝑆𝐴 JCB
BV e
closed Saturday lunch, Sunday and Bank Holidays – **Meals** 18.00/28.50 **t.** and a la carte 🍷 6.00.

21 Queen Street (Laybourne), 21 Queen St., Quayside, NE1 3UG, *℘ (0191) 222 0755, Fax (0191) 221 0761* – 🍴 🎫 ⑩ 𝑉𝐼𝑆𝐴
CZ f
❀
closed Saturday lunch, Sunday and Bank Holidays – **Meals** 17.50 **t.** (lunch) and a la carte 29.50/37.50 **t.** 🍷 6.50
Spec. Thin tomato tart with pistou and a friture of garden herbs. Roast fillet of beef stuffed with braised oxtail, Newcastle Brown Ale sauce. Hot caramel soufflé, orange sorbet and a salad of oranges.

Vujon, 29 Queen St., Quayside, NE1 3UG, *℘ (0191) 221 0601, Fax (0191) 221 0602* – 🍴. 🍽 🎫 ⑩ 𝑉𝐼𝑆𝐴
CZ g
closed Sunday lunch and 25-26 December – **Meals** - Indian - 20.00 **st.** (dinner) and a la carte 18.00/24.00 **st.** 🍷 4.50.

The Blackgate, The Side, NE1 3JE, *℘ (0191) 261 7356* – 🍽 🎫 ⑩ 𝑉𝐼𝑆𝐴 JCB
CZ x
closed Saturday lunch, Monday dinner, Sunday and Bank Holidays – **Meals** 11.50 **t.** (lunch) and a la carte 15.25/27.15 **t.** 🍷 5.95.

Leela's, 20 Dean St., NE1 1PG, *℘ (0191) 230 1261* – ✤. 🍽 🎫 ⑩ 𝑉𝐼𝑆𝐴
CZ e
closed Sunday, 2 weeks early January and Bank Holidays – **Meals** - South Indian - 9.95/16.95 **t.** and a la carte 🍷 7.00.

XX **King Neptune,** 34-36 Stowell St., NE1 4XB, ℘ (0191) 261 6657 – 🍴 AE ⊙ VISA   CZ d
closed 25 December and 1 January – **Meals** - Chinese (Peking) and Seafood - 6.50/
14.80 t. and a la carte.

X **The Metropolitan,** 35 Grey St., NE1 6EE, ℘ (0191) 230 2306, Fax (0191) 230 2307 – 🍴
AE VISA   CZ k
closed Sunday and Bank Holidays – **Meals** 10.95 t. (lunch) and a la carte 15.15/20.65 t.

X **Barn Again Bistro,** 21a Leazes Park Rd, NE1 4PF, ℘ (0191) 230 3338 – 🍴 VISA   CY a
closed Saturday lunch, Sunday, 1 week Christmas and Bank Holiday Mondays –
Meals 10.95 t. (lunch) and a la carte 13.20/22.85 t. ⓘ 3.85.

at Gosforth N : 4¾ m. by B 1318 – AV – ✉ Tyneside.

🏨 **Swallow Gosforth Park,** High Gosforth Park, NE3 5HN, on B 1318 ℘ (0191) 236 4111,
Fax (0191) 236 8192, ≤, ₤₅, ≘s, ☒, ☞, park, ℀, squash – 🛏 ⇥, 🍴 rest, TV ☎ & ⊙ –
🛎 600. 🍴 AE ⊙ VISA JCB
Brandling : Meals 18.50/24.50 st. and a la carte ⓘ 8.00 – **Conservatory :** Meals a la carte
15.00/20.00 st. ⓘ 8.00 – **173 rm** ⊇ 115.00/130.00 st., 5 suites – SB.

at Seaton Burn N : 8 m. by B 1318 – AV – ✉ Newcastle upon Tyne.

🏨 **Holiday Inn,** Great North Rd, NE13 6BP, N : ¾ m. at junction with A 1 ℘ (0191) 201 9988,
Fax (0191) 236 8091, ₤₅, ≘s, ☒ – ⇥ rm, 🍴 TV ☎ & ⊙ – 🛎 400. 🍴 AE ⊙ VISA JCB. ℀
Meals 15.50/17.50 st. and a la carte ⓘ 7.50 – ⊇ 9.95 – **149 rm** 110.00/120.00 st., 1 suite –
SB.

at Boldon E : 7¾ m. by A 184 – BX.

🏨 **Quality Friendly,** Witney Way, Boldon Business Park, NE35 9PE, ℘ (0191) 519 1999,
Fax (0191) 519 0655, ₤₅, ≘s – ⇥ rm, 🍴 rest, TV ☎ & ⊙ – 🛎 230. 🍴 AE ⊙ VISA JCB
Meals (closed Saturday lunch) 8.25/14.50 st. and a la carte – ⊇ 8.75 – **82 rm** 67.50/
87.50 st. – SB.

XX **Forsters,** 2 St. Bedes, Station Rd, East Boldon, NE36 OLE, ℘ (0191) 519 0929 – 🍴 AE ⊙
🏵 VISA
closed Sunday, Monday, 2 weeks June, 1 week August, Christmas, New Year and Bank
Holidays – **Meals** (dinner only) 17.00 t. and a la carte 18.50/24.85 st. ⓘ 4.25.

at Newcastle Airport NW : 6¾ m. by A 167 off A 696 – AV – ✉ Newcastle upon Tyne.

🏨 **Airport Moat House,** Woolsington, NE13 8DJ, ℘ (0191) 401 9988, Fax (01661) 860157 –
🛏, ⇥ rm, 🍴 rest, TV ☎ ⊙ – 🛎 400. 🍴 AE ⊙ VISA JCB
Meals a la carte 14.45/26.20 st. ⓘ 6.20 – ⊇ 9.50 – **98 rm** 90.00/120.00 st., 2 suites – SB.

at Ponteland NW : 8¼ m. by A 167 on A 696 – AV – ✉ Newcastle upon Tyne.

XX **Horton Grange** with rm, Seaton Burn, NE13 6BU, NE : 3 ½ m. by Morpeth rd
℘ (01661) 860686, Fax (01661) 860308, ☞ – ⇥ rest, TV ☎ ⊙. 🍴 AE VISA JCB. ℀
closed 1 week Christmas and 1 January – **Meals** (closed Sunday) (booking essential) (dinner
only) 34.00 t. ⓘ 6.50 – **9 rm** ⊇ 59.00/90.00 t.

X **Café 21,** 35 The Broadway, Darras Hall Estate, NE20 9PW, SW : 1 ½ m. by B 6323 and
🏵 Callerton Lane ℘ (01661) 820357, Fax (01661) 820357 – 🍴 AE ⊙ VISA
closed Sunday, Monday and Bank Holidays – **Meals** - Bistro - 14.50 t. (lunch) and dinner
a la carte 13.50/22.50 t. ⓘ 6.50.

⊕ ATS 80/90 Blenheim St. ℘ (0191) 232 3921/   ATS Newton Park Garage, Newton Rd, Heaton
232 5031   ℘ (0191) 281 2243

NEWENT Glos. 403 404 M 28 – pop. 4 111.
London 109 – Gloucester 10 – Hereford 22 – Newport 44.

↑ **Orchard House** ⌂, Aston Ingham Rd, Kilcot, GL18 1NP, SW : 2 ¼ m. by B 4221 on B 4222
℘ (01989) 720417, Fax (01989) 720770, ☞ – ⊙. 🍴 VISA JCB. ℀
Meals (communal dining) 17.50 s. ⓘ 5.00 – **4 rm** ⊇ 32.00/69.00 s.

NEWHAVEN E. Sussex 404 U 31 – pop. 11 208.
⛴ to France (Dieppe) (P &O Stena Line) 4 daily (4 h).
London 63 – Brighton 9 – Eastbourne 14 – Lewes 7.

🏨 **Travel Inn,** Avis Rd, BN9 0AG, E : ½ m. on A 259 ℘ (01273) 612356, Fax (01273) 612359
⇥ rm, TV & ⊙. 🍴 AE ⊙ VISA
Meals (grill rest.) – **40 rm** 36.50 t.

La guida cambia, cambiate la guida ogni anno.

NEWICK E. Sussex 404 U 31 – pop. 2 445.
London 57 – Brighton 14 – Eastbourne 20 – Hastings 34 – Maidstone 30.

🏨 **Newick Park** ⟋, BN8 4SB, SE : 1 ½ m. following signs for Newick Park
𝒫 (01825) 723633, Fax (01825) 723969, ≤, « Georgian house, extensive grounds », 🏊, 🐎,
park, 🎾 – ↩ rest, 📺 ☎ 🅿. 🅾 🆎 ⑪ 𝘝𝘐𝘚𝘈. 🕸
Meals (booking essential to non-residents) 18.50/27.50 **t.** and a la carte ₰ 10.25 – **13 rm**
⌷ 95.00/245.00 **t.** – SB.

NEWINGTON Kent 404 V/W 29 – pop. 2 454.
London 40 – Canterbury 20 – Maidstone 13.

🏠 **Newington Manor,** Callaways Lane, ME9 7LU, 𝒫 (01795) 842053, Fax (01795) 844273,
« Part 14C and 16C manor house », 🐎 – 📺 ☎ 🅿. 🅾 🆎 ⑪ 𝘝𝘐𝘚𝘈. 🕸
closed 24 December-3 January – **Meals** *(closed Saturday lunch, Sunday dinner and Bank
Holiday Mondays)* 15.50 **st.** and a la carte ₰ 6.50 – ⌷ 10.00 – **12 rm** 55.00/95.00 **st.**

NEWLYN Cornwall 403 D 33 – see Penzance.

NEWMARKET Suffolk 404 V 27 – pop. 16 498.
🏌 Links, Cambridge Rd 𝒫 (01638) 662708.
🛈 63 The Rookery, CB8 8HT 𝒫 (01638) 667200.
London 64 – Cambridge 13 – Ipswich 40 – Norwich 48.

🏨 **Bedford Lodge,** Bury Rd, CB8 7BX, NE : ½ m. on A 1304 𝒫 (01638) 663175,
Fax (01638) 667391, 🖪, 🈺, 🏊, 🐎 – ☳ 📺 ☎ 🅿 – 🔬 200. 🅾 🆎 ⑪ 𝘝𝘐𝘚𝘈
Meals 16.95 **st.** and a la carte ₰ 7.00 – **49 rm** ⌷ 75.00/100.00 **st.**, 7 suites – SB.

🏠 **Heath Court,** Moulton Rd, CB8 8DY, 𝒫 (01638) 667171, Fax (01638) 666533 – ☳, ↩ rm,
📺 ☎ 🅿 – 🔬 130. 🅾 🆎 ⑪ 𝘝𝘐𝘚𝘈
Meals (bar lunch Saturday) a la carte 16.70/27.05 **t.** ₰ 6.25 – **41 rm** ⌷ 72.00/140.00 **st.** – SB.

at Six Mile Bottom *(Cambs.) SW : 6 m. on A 1304 –* ✉ *Newmarket.*

🏨 **Swynford Paddocks,** CB8 0UE, 𝒫 (01638) 570234, Fax (01638) 570283, ≤, 🐎, park,
🎾 – ↩ rest, 📺 ☎ 🅿 – 🔬 25. 🅾 🆎 ⑪ 𝘝𝘐𝘚𝘈 𝗝𝗖𝗕. 🕸
Meals 24.95 **t.** (dinner) and a la carte 15.40/30.40 **t.** ₰ 6.95 – **15 rm** ⌷ 85.00/143.00 **t.** – SB.

🅐 ATS 2 Exeter Rd 𝒫 (01638) 662521

NEWMILLERDAM W. Yorks. – see Wakefield.

NEW MILTON Hants. 403 404 P 31 – pop. 24 324 (inc. Barton-on-Sea).
🏌 Barton-on-Sea, Milford Rd 𝒫 (01425) 615308.
London 106 – Bournemouth 12 – Southampton 21 – Winchester 34.

🏨 **Chewton Glen** ⟋, Christchurch Rd, BH25 6QS, W : 2 m. by A 337 and Ringwood Rd on
Chewton Farm Rd 𝒫 (01425) 275341, Fax (01425) 272310, ≤, 🍴, « Gardens », 🖪, 🈺, 🏊,
🏊, 🏌, park, 🎾indoor/outdoor – ↩ rest, 🍽 rest, 📺 ☎ 🅿 – 🔬 120. 🅾 𝘝𝘐𝘚𝘈. 🕸
Marryat Room and Conservatory : **Meals** 23.50/45.00 **t.** ₰ 9.00 – **40 rm** ⌷ (dinner
included) 280.00/460.00 **t.**, 13 suites
Spec. Double baked Emmenthal soufflé with a fondue sauce. Braised pork cheeks and
lobster with vegetables, lemon grass and coriander. Hot chocolate fondant with chocolate
mint ice cream.

NEW POLZEATH Cornwall 403 F 32 – ✉ Wadebridge.
London 283 – Newquay 27 – Plymouth 49 – Truro 36.

🏠 **Cornish Cottage,** PL27 6UF, 𝒫 (01208) 862213, Fax (01208) 862259, 🏊 – 📺 ☎ 🅿. 🅾
🆎 ⑪ 𝘝𝘐𝘚𝘈 𝗝𝗖𝗕. 🕸
closed January – **The Gourmet :** **Meals** (dinner only and Sunday lunch)/dinner
28.50 **t.** and a la carte – **12 rm** ⌷ (dinner included) 70.00/140.00 **t.** – SB.

NEWPORT Wrekin 402 403 404 M 25 Great Britain G. – pop. 10 964.
Exc. : Weston Park★★, SE : 6 ½ m. by A 41 and A 5.
London 150 – Birmingham 33 – Shrewsbury 18 – Stoke-on-Trent 21.

🏠 **Royal Victoria,** St. Mary's St., TF10 7AB, 𝒫 (01952) 820331, Fax (01952) 820209 – 📺 ☎
🅿 – 🔬 140. 🅾 🆎 ⑪ 𝘝𝘐𝘚𝘈
Meals *(closed Sunday dinner)* (bar lunch)/dinner 14.50 **t.** ₰ 3.95 – **24 rm** ⌷ 39.50/52.50 **t.** –
SB.

NEWPORT PAGNELL *Bucks.* 404 R 27 – *pop. 12 285.*

London 57 – Bedford 13 – Luton 21 – Northampton 15.

Plan : see Milton Keynes

🏨 **Swan Revived,** High St., MK16 8AR, ✆ (01908) 610565, *Fax (01908) 210995* – |‡| 📺 ☎ ℗ – 🛏 70. **M⊙ AE ① VISA** on Milton Keynes town plan CU S *closed 26 December* – **Meals** a la carte 13.00/23.30 **st.** – **40 rm** ⌂ 64.00/68.00 **st.**, 2 suites – SB.

NEWQUAY *Cornwall* 403 E 32 *The West Country G.* – *pop. 17 390.*

Env. : *Penhale Point and Kelsey Head★ (≤★★), SW : by A 3075 Y – Trerice★ AC, SE : 3 ½ m. by A 392 – Y – and A 3058.*

Exc. : *St. Agnes – St. Agnes Beacon★★ (※★★), SW : 12 ½ m. by A 3075 – Y – and B 3285.*

🏌 Tower Rd ✆ (01637) 872091, Z – 🏌 Treloy ✆ (01637) 878554 – 🏌 Merlin, Mawgan Porth ✆ (01841) 540222.

✈ Newquay Airport : ✆ (01637) 860551 Y.

🛈 Municipal Offices, Marcus Hill, TR7 1BD ✆ (01637) 871345.

London 291 – Exeter 83 – Penzance 34 – Plymouth 48 – Truro 14.

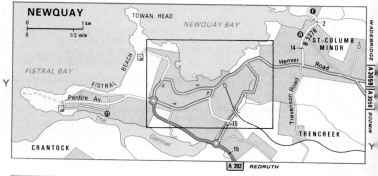

🏨 **The Bristol,** Narrowcliff, TR7 2PQ, ℘ (01637) 875181, *Fax (01637) 879347*, ≼, ⇌, 🔄 – ☷
📺 📞 – 🔥 200. 🌐 AE ① *VISA* JCB
Z r
Meals 11.50/18.50 **t.** and a la carte ⓙ 6.00 – **73 rm** ⊑ 52.00/104.00 **t.**, 1 suite – SB.

🏨 **Trebarwith,** Trebarwith Cres., TR7 1BZ, ℘ (01637) 872288, *Fax (01637) 875431*,
≼ bay and coast, ⇌, 🔄, ☞ – ↩ rest, 📺 ☎ 📞. 🌐 AE *VISA*. ⋘
Z a
Easter-October – **Meals** (bar lunch)/dinner 13.50 **st.** and a la carte ⓙ 7.50 – **41 rm** ⊑ (dinner included) 48.00/100.00 **st.** – SB.

🏨 **Kilbirnie,** Narrowcliff, TR7 2RS, ℘ (01637) 875155, *Fax (01637) 850769*, ⇌, 🔄, 🔄 – ☷ 📺
☎ 📞 – 🔥 150. 🌐 AE ① *VISA* JCB
Z e
Meals (bar lunch)/dinner 12.50 **t.** – **66 rm** ⊑ (dinner included) 36.00/80.00 **t.**

🏠 **Trenance Lodge,** 83 Trenance Rd, TR7 2HW, ℘ (01637) 876702, *Fax (01637) 872034*, 🔄,
☞ – ↩ rest, 📺 📞. 🌐 *VISA*. ⋘
Z u
Meals (lunch by arrangement) 10.00/15.00 **t.** and dinner a la carte ⓙ 5.95 – **5 rm** ⊑ 35.00/56.00 – SB.

🏠 **Whipsiderry,** Trevelgue Rd, Porth, TR7 3LY, NE : 2 m. by A 392 off B 3276
℘ (01637) 874777, *Fax (01637) 874777*, ≼, ⇌, 🔄, ☞ – ↩ rest, 📺 📞. 🌐 AE *VISA*
closed January, February and November – **Meals** (bar lunch)/dinner 13.95 **t.** ⓙ 6.95 – **24 rm** ⊑ (dinner included) 44.00/88.00 **t.**

🏠 **Windward,** Alexandra Rd, Porth Bay, TR7 3NB, ℘ (01637) 873185, *Fax (01637) 852436* –
↩ rest, 📺 📞. 🌐 AE *VISA*. ⋘
Y r
Easter-October – **Meals** (residents only) (bar lunch)/dinner 10.00 **st.** – **14 rm** ⊑ (dinner included) 43.00/74.00 **st.**

🏠 **Corisande Manor** ⋙, Riverside Av., Pentire, TR7 1PL, ℘ (01637) 872042,
Fax (01637) 874557, ≼ Gannel Estuary, ☞ – ↩ rest, 📺 ☎ 📞. 🌐 *VISA*. ⋘
Y n
Meals (dinner only) 17.50 **st.** ⓙ 4.95 – **12 rm** ⊑ 39.00/79.00 **st.** – SB.

🏠 **Porth Veor Manor,** Porth Way, TR7 3LW, ℘ (01637) 873274, *Fax (01637) 851690*, ☞ –
↩ rest, 📺 📞. 🌐 *VISA* JCB
Y a
Meals (closed lunch October-April) 6.95/10.95 **st.** and dinner a la carte ⓙ 4.50 – **17 rm** ⊑ (dinner included) 35.00/90.00 **st.** – SB.

⌂ **Wheal Treasure,** 72 Edgcumbe Av., TR7 2NN, ℘ (01637) 874136 – ↩ rest, 📺 📞.
⋘
Z z
June-September – **Meals** (by arrangement) – **12 rm** ⊑ (dinner included) 56.00 **st.**

⌂ **Copper Beech,** 70 Edgcumbe Av., TR7 2NN, ℘ (01637) 873376 – ↩ rest, 📺 📞. ⋘
Easter-late October – **Meals** (residents only) ⓙ 4.75 – **15 rm** ⊑ (dinner included) 24.00/57.00 **st.**
Z s

⌂ **Chynoweth Lodge,** 1 Eliot Gdns., TR7 2QE, ℘ (01637) 876684, ☞ – ↩ 📺 📞
Z u
mid March-mid October – **Meals** 7.00 – **9 rm** ⊑ 24.00/48.00 **st.**

⌂ **Towan Beach,** 7 Trebarwith Cres., TR7 1DX, ℘ (01637) 872093, *Fax (01637) 872093* –
↩ rest, 📺. 🌐 *VISA* JCB. ⋘
Z v
Meals (by arrangement) 9.50 **st.** ⓙ 3.50 – **6 rm** ⊑ 23.00/50.00 **st.**

at St. Newlyn East *S : 5½ m. by A 392 –* Y *– off A 3058 – ✉ Newquay.*

⌂ **Trewerry Mill** ⋙ without rest., TR8 5HS, NE : 1½ m. ℘ (01872) 510345, ☞ – ↩ 📞. ⋘
March-October – **6 rm** ⊑ 19.00/48.00 **st.**

at Crantock *SW : 4 m. by A 3075 –* Y *– ✉ Newquay.*

🏠 **Crantock Bay** ⋙, West Pentire, TR8 5SE, W : ¾ m. ℘ (01637) 830229,
Fax (01637) 831111, ≼ Crantock Bay, 🄵, ⇌, 🔄, ☞, ⋇ – ↩ rest, 📺 ☎ 📞. 🌐 AE ① *VISA*
JCB
restricted opening November-mid March – **Meals** (buffet lunch)/dinner 17.95 **t.** ⓙ 4.90 –
34 rm ⊑ (dinner included) 46.50/128.00 **t.** – SB.

⌂ **Crantock Plains Farmhouse,** Cubert, TR8 5PH, SE : 1½ m. bearing right at the fork in
the road ℘ (01637) 830253, ☞ – ↩ 📞. ⋘
closed January and February – **Meals** (by arrangement) 9.00 **s.** ⓙ 6.00 – **6 rm** ⊑ 19.00/44.00 **s.**

NEW ROMNEY *Kent* 🔢 W 31.
London 71 – Brighton 60 – Folkestone 17 – Maidstone 36.

🏠 **Romney Bay House** ⋙, Coast Rd, Littlestone, TN28 8QY, E : 2¼ m. off B 2071
℘ (01797) 364747, *Fax (01797) 367156*, ≼, ☞, ⋇ – ↩ 📺 📞. 🌐 ① *VISA*. ⋘
closed Christmas – **Meals** (light lunch by arrangement)/dinner 28.00 **t.** ⓙ 8.50 – **7 rm** ⊑ 45.00/105.00 **t.**

NEWTON ON THE MOOR *Northd.* 🔢 🔢 O 17 – *see Alnwick.*

NEWTON POPPLEFORD Devon **403** K 31 – pop. 1 765 (inc. Harpford) – ⊠ Ottery St. Mary.
London 208 – Exeter 10 – Sidmouth 4.

🏠 **Coach House** ⮞, Southerton, EX11 1SE, N : 1 m. by Venn Ottery Rd ℘ (01395) 568577,
☞ – 📺 ☎ ℗, ⓦ 🍴, ✂
Meals (dinner only) 13.00 **t.** ⑂ 5.50 – **6 rm** ☑ 36.00/74.00 **t.**

NEWTON SOLNEY Derbs. **402 403 404** P 25 – see Burton-upon-Trent (Staffs.).

NITON I.O.W. **403 404** Q 32 – see Wight (Isle of).

NOMANSLAND Wilts. **403 404** P 31 – ⊠ Salisbury.
London 96 – Bournemouth 26 – Salisbury 13 – Southampton 14 – Winchester 25.

🍴 **Les Mirabelles,** Forest Edge Rd, SP5 2BN, ℘ (01794) 390205, Fax (01794) 390205 – ⓦ
VISA
closed Sunday dinner, Monday and 1 to 20 January – **Meals** - French - a la carte 13.80/
22.70 **t.** ⑂ 8.00.

NORMAN CROSS Peterborough **404** T 26 – see Peterborough.

NORMANTON PARK Rutland – see Stamford.

NORTHALLERTON N. Yorks. **402** P 20 – pop. 13 774.
🚹 The Applegarth Car Park, DL7 8LZ ℘ (01609) 776864.
London 238 – Leeds 48 – Middlesbrough 24 – York 33.

🏨 **Golden Lion,** 114 High St., DL7 8PP, ℘ (01609) 777411, Fax (01609) 773250 – ✣ 📺 ☎ ℗
– 🛗 150. ⓦ ⒶⒺ **VISA** **JCB**. ✂
Meals (bar lunch Monday to Saturday)/dinner 14.95 **t.** and a la carte ⑂ 6.50 – ☑ 9.50 –
24 rm 55.00/86.00 **t.** – SB.

⤒ **Windsor,** 56 South Par., DL7 8SL, ℘ (01609) 774100 – 📺. ⓦ **VISA**. ✂
closed 1 week Christmas – **Meals** (by arrangement) 9.50 – **6 rm** ☑ 20.00/42.00 **st.**

🍴🍴 **Romanby Court,** High St., DL7 8PG, ℘ (01609) 774918 – ⓦ ⒶⒺ ① **VISA** **JCB**
closed Sunday, Monday, 2 weeks January, 2 weeks summer and 25-26 December – **Meals** -
Italian - 9.95 **t.** (dinner) and a la carte 14.85/23.40 **t.** ⑂ 5.95.

at Staddlebridge NE : 7½ m. by A 684 on A 19 at junction with A 172 – ⊠ Northallerton.

🍴🍴 **McCoys at the Tontine** with rm, DL6 3JB, on southbound carriageway (A 19
℘ (01609) 882671, Fax (01609) 882660, « 1930's decor » – 🗎 📺 ☎ ℗, ⓦ ⒶⒺ ① **VISA**
closed 25-26 December and 1 January – **Meals** (closed Sunday to Wednesday) (dinner only)
a la carte 21.15/33.15 **t.** – **6 rm** ☑ 79.00/99.00 **t.**
🍴 **Bistro :** Meals (closed 25-26 December and 1 January) a la carte 18.85/32.15 **t.** ⑂ 7.00.

at Newby Wiske S : 2½ m. by A 167 – ⊠ Northallerton.

🏨 **Solberge Hall** ⮞, DL7 9ER, NW : 1 ¼ m. on Warlaby rd ℘ (01609) 779191,
Fax (01609) 780472, <, ☞, park – ✣ rest, 📺 ☎ ℗ – 🛗 100. ⓦ ⒶⒺ ① **VISA**
Meals 7.25/21.00 **t.** and dinner a la carte ⑂ 6.50 – **24 rm** ☑ 57.00/89.00 **t.**, 1 suite – SB.

NORTHAMPTON Northants. **404** R 27 Great Britain G. – pop. 179 596.
Exc. : All Saints, Brixworth★, N : 7 m. on A 508 Y.
🏌, 🏌 Delapre, Eagle Drive, Nene Valley Way ℘ (01604) 764036/763957, Z – 🏌 Collingtree
Park, Windingbrook Lane ℘ (01604) 700000.
🚹 Mr Grant's House, 10 St. Giles Sq., NN1 1DA ℘ (01604) 22677.
London 69 – Cambridge 53 – Coventry 34 – Leicester 42 – Luton 35 – Oxford 41.

Plan opposite

🏨 **Swallow,** Eagle Drive, NN4 7HW, SE : 2 m. by A 428 off A 45 ℘ (01604) 768700,
Fax (01604) 769011, 🖽, 🖾, 🔲 – ✣ rm, 🗎 rest, 📺 ☎ ⓺ ℗ – 🛗 220. ⓦ ⒶⒺ ① **VISA** **JCB**
Spires : Meals (closed Saturday lunch) 14.00/21.00 **st.** and a la carte ⑂ 7.25 – **La Fontana**
Meals - Italian - (closed Saturday lunch) 14.00/21.00 **st.** and a la carte ⑂ 7.25 – **118 rm**
☑ 103.00/115.00 **st.**, 2 suites – SB.
Z a

🏨 **Stakis Northampton,** 100 Watering Lane, Collingtree, NN4 0XW, S : 3 m. on A 508
℘ (01604) 700666, Fax (01604) 702850, 🖽, 🖾, 🔲, ☞ – ✣ rm, 🗎 rest, 📺 ☎ ⓺ ℗ –
🛗 300. ⓦ ⒶⒺ ① **VISA**
Meals (closed Saturday lunch) (carving lunch) 14.75/19.95 **t.** and dinner a la carte ⑂ 7.00 –
☑ 10.25 – **136 rm** 99.00/120.00 **t.**, 3 suites – SB.

NORTHAMPTON

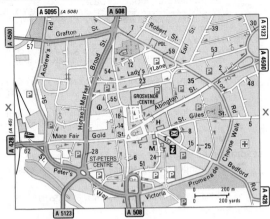

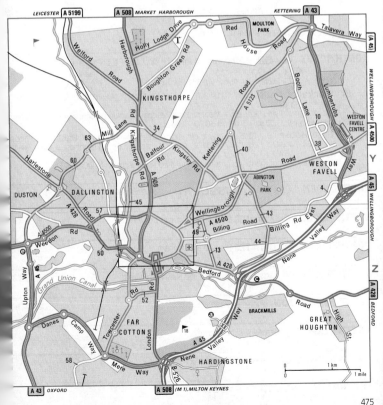

475

Courtyard by Marriott, Bedford Rd, NN4 7YF, SE : 1 ½ m. on A 428 *&* (01604) 22777, Fax (01604) 35454, ⅃₅ – ⬚, ⅙⩹ rm, ▤ ▥ ☎ ఉ ⊕ – ⚤ 40. ⬤⊙ ⒶⒺ ⓪ 𝘝𝘐𝘚𝘈   Z c
Meals a la carte approx. 16.00 **t**. ⅃ 6.95 – ⊇ 8.95 – **104 rm** 85.00/105.00 **t**. – SB.

Northampton Moat House, Silver St., NN1 2TA, *&* (01604) 739988, Fax (01604) 230614, ⅃₅, ⊜ₛ – ⬚, ⅙⩹ rm, ▥ ☎ ⊕ – ⚤ 600. ⬤⊙ ⒶⒺ ⓪ 𝘝𝘐𝘚𝘈   X n
Meals (closed lunch Saturday and Bank Holidays) a la carte 15.20/21.50 **st**. ⅃ 6.00 – ⊇ 9.50 – **136 rm** 90.00/105.00 **st**., 4 suites – SB.

Midway Toby, London Rd, Wootton, NN4 0TG, S : 2 ½ m. on A 508 *&* (01604) 769676, Fax (01604) 769523 – ⅙⩹ rm, ▤ rest, ▥ ☎ ఉ ⊕ – ⚤ 100. ⬤⊙ ⒶⒺ 𝘝𝘐𝘚𝘈. ⅗
closed 25-26 December and 1 January – Meals (grill rest.) a la carte 9.30/16.10 **t**. – **31 rm** ⊇ 65.00/75.00 **t**. – SB.

Travel Inn, Harpole Turn, Weedon Rd, NN7 4DD, W : 3 ¾ m. on A 45 *&* (01604) 832340, Fax (01604) 831807 – ⅙⩹ rm, ▥ ఉ ⊕ – ⚤ 60. ⬤⊙ ⒶⒺ ⓪ 𝘝𝘐𝘚𝘈. ⅗
Meals (grill rest.) – **51 rm** 36.50 **t**.

Travelodge, Upton Way (Ring Rd), NN5 6EG, SW : 1 ¾ m. by A 45 *&* (01604) 758395, Fax (01604) 758395, Reservations (Freephone) 0800 850950 – ⅙⩹ rm, ▥ ఉ ⊕. ⬤⊙ ⒶⒺ ⓪ 𝘝𝘐𝘚𝘈 𝙅𝘊𝘉. ⅗   Z e
Meals (grill rest.) – **60 rm** 44.95 **t**.

at Spratton N : 7 m. by A 508 off A 50 – Y – ⊠ Northampton.

Broomhill Country House ⋙, Holdenby Rd, NN6 8LD, SW : 1 m. on Holdenby rd *&* (01604) 845959, Fax (01604) 845834, ≤, ⅃, ☞, park, ⅗ – ▥ ☎ ⊕. ⬤⊙ ⒶⒺ ⓪ 𝘝𝘐𝘚𝘈. ⅗
closed 25 and 26 December – Meals (closed Sunday dinner to non-residents) 14.95/18.95 **t**. and a la carte ⅃ 6.00 – **13 rm** ⊇ 65.00/85.00 **t**. – SB.

at Moulton NE : 4½ m. by A 43 – Y – ⊠ Northampton.

Poplars, 33 Cross St., NN3 7RZ, *&* (01604) 643983, Fax (01604) 790233, ☞ – ▥ ☎ ⊕. ⬤⊙ ⒶⒺ 𝘝𝘐𝘚𝘈
closed 1 week Christmas – Meals (by arrangement) 13.50 **t**. ⅃ 3.50 – **18 rm** ⊇ 45.00/50.00 **t**. – SB.

ⓜ ATS Kingsthorpe Rd *&* (01604) 713303

NORTH BOVEY Devon ⁴⁰³ I 32 The West Country G. – pop. 254 – ⊠ Newton Abbot.
Env. : Dartmoor National Park★★.
London 214 – Exeter 13 – Plymouth 31 – Torquay 21.

Blackaller House ⋙, TQ13 8QY, *&* (01647) 440322, Fax (01647) 440322, ≤, ☞ – ⅙⩹ rest, ▥ ⊕
closed January and February – Meals (closed Monday) (booking essential to non-residents) (dinner only) 21.00 **st**. – **5 rm** ⊇ 30.00/72.00 **st**.

Gate House ⋙, TQ13 8RB, just off village green, past "Ring of Bells" public house *&* (01647) 440479, Fax (01647) 440479, ≤, « 15C thatched Devon hallhouse », ☞ – ⅙⩹ ▥ ⊕. ⅗
Meals (by arrangement) (communal dining) 14.00 **st**. – **3 rm** ⊇ 32.00/50.00 **st**.

NORTHENDEN Gtr. Manchester ⁴⁰² ⁴⁰³ ⁴⁰⁴ N 23 – see Manchester.

NORTH FERRIBY East Riding ⁴⁰² S 22 – see Kingston-upon-Hull.

NORTHFIELD W. Mids. ⁴⁰³ ㉒ ⁴⁰⁴ ⑳ – see Birmingham.

NORTH MUSKHAM Notts. ⁴⁰² ⁴⁰⁴ R 24 – see Newark-on-Trent.

NORTH NEWINGTON Oxon – see Banbury.

NORTH PERROT Somerset – see Crewkerne.

NORTH PETHERTON Somerset ⁴⁰³ K 30 – see Bridgwater.

NORTHREPPS Norfolk ⁴⁰⁴ Y 25 – see Cromer.

NORTH STIFFORD Essex **404** ④ – ✉ Grays.

London 22 – Chelmsford 24 – Southend-on-Sea 20.

🏨🏨 **Stifford Moat House**, High Rd, RM16 5UE, at junction of A 13 with A 1012
ℰ (01708) 719988, Fax (01375) 390426, 余, ℁ – 🛊, ⅙‑ rm, 📺 ☎ ਓ **ℙ** – 🔬 150. **◑⑨ Œ ⓪**
VISA
Meals (closed Saturday lunch and Sunday dinner) 17.50 **st.** (dinner) and a la carte 23.00/
35.75 **st.** ᵻ 6.00 – ⌷ 9.50 – **96 rm** 94.00/130.00 **st.** – SB.

NORTH STOKE Oxon. – see Wallingford.

NORTH WALSHAM Norfolk **403 404** Y 25 Great Britain G. – pop. 9 534.

Exc. : Blicking Hall★★ **AC**, W : 8 ½ m. by B 1145, A 140 and B 1354.

London 125 – Norwich 16.

🏛 **Beechwood**, 20 Cromer Rd, NR28 0HD, *ℰ* (01692) 403231, Fax (01692) 407284, 余 – ⅙‑
📺 ☎ **ℙ**. **◑⑨ VISA**
Meals (closed Saturday lunch) 8.00/16.50 **st.** ᵻ 6.00 – **9 rm** ⌷ 42.00/76.00 **s.** – SB.

NORTHWICH Ches. **402 403 404** M 24 – pop. 4 243.

London 188 – Chester 19 – Liverpool 29 – Manchester 25.

🏛 **Quincey's - Premier Lodge**, London Rd, Leftwich, CW9 8EG, S : 1 ½ m. on A 533
ℰ (01606) 45524, Fax (01606) 330350, 余 – ⅙‑ rm, 📺 ☎ ਓ **ℙ** – 🔬 35. **◑⑨ Œ ⓪ VISA**. ℁
Meals (grill rest.) a la carte 12.85/19.60 **t.** – ⌷ 4.95 – **32 rm** 44.25 **t.** – SB.

NORTON Shrops. – see Telford.

NORTON ST PHILIP Somerset **403 404** N 30 – see Bath (Bath & North East Somerset).

When looking for a quiet hotel
use the maps found in the introduction
or look for establishments with the sign ⧼⧽ or ⧼⧽

NORWICH Norfolk **404** Y 26 Great Britain G. – pop. 171 304.

See : City★★ - Cathedral★★ Y – Castle (Museum and Art Gallery★ **AC**) Z – Market Place★ Z.

Env. : Sainsbury Centre for Visual Arts★ **AC**, W : 3 m. by B 1108 X.

Exc. : Blicking Hall★★ **AC**, N : 11 m. by A 140 – V – and B 1354 – NE : The Broads★ .

🏌 Royal Norwich, Drayton High Rd, *ℰ* (01603) 425712, V – 🏌 Sprowston Park,
Wroxham Rd *ℰ* (01603) 410657 – 🏌 Costessey Park, Costessey *ℰ* (01603) 746333 –
🏌 Bawburgh, Glen Lodge, Marlingford Rd *ℰ* (01603) 740404.

✈ Norwich Airport : *ℰ* (01603) 411923, N : 3 ½ m. by A 140 V.

🚺 The Guildhall, Gaol Hill, NR2 1NF *ℰ* (01603) 666071.

London 109 – Kingston-upon-Hull 148 – Leicester 117 – Nottingham 120.

Plans on following pages

🏰🏰 **Sprowston Manor**, Wroxham Rd, NR7 8RP, NE : 3 ¼ m. on A 1151 *ℰ* (01603) 410871,
Fax (01603) 423911, ᴸ₆, ⓯, 🏊, 🏌, 余, park – 🛊 ⅙‑, ▤ rest, 📺 ☎ **ℙ** – 🔬 120. **◑⑨ Œ ⓪**
VISA
Meals 19.95 **st.** and a la carte ᵻ 11.00 – ⌷ 9.95 – **93 rm** 91.00/129.00 **st.**, 1 suite – SB.

🏨🏨 **Dunston Hall H. Golf & Country Club**, Ipswich Rd, NR14 8PQ, S : 4 m. on A 140
ℰ (01508) 470444, Fax (01508) 471499, ᴸ₆, ⓯, 🏊, 🏌, park, ℁ – 🛊, ⅙‑ rest, 📺 ☎ **ℙ** –
🔬 300. **◑⑨ Œ ⓪ VISA**
Meals (carving rest.) a la carte 9.95/23.15 **st.** ᵻ 5.00 – **La Fontaine :** Meals (closed Sunday)
(dinner only) 18.95 **st.** and a la carte ᵻ 5.00 – **72 rm** ⌷ 79.00/125.00 **st.** – SB.

🏨🏨 **Nelson**, Prince of Wales Rd, NR1 1DX, *ℰ* (01603) 760260, Fax (01603) 620008, ≤, ᴸ₆, ⓯,
🏊, 🛊 – 🛊, ⅙‑ rm, ▤ rest, 📺 ☎ ਓ **ℙ** – 🔬 90. **◑⑨ Œ ⓪ VISA**. ℁   Z a
Trafalgar : Meals (closed Saturday lunch) 15.50 **st.** (dinner) and a la carte 15.65/27.15 **st.**
ᵻ 4.85 – **Quarter-deck :** Meals a la carte 10.25/17.40 **st.** ᵻ 4.85 – **132 rm** ⌷ 77.50/99.00 **st.**
– SB.

🏛 **County H. Norwich Maids Head**, Tombland, NR3 1LB, *ℰ* (01603) 209955,
Fax (01603) 613688 – 🛊, ⅙‑ rm, 📺 ☎ **ℙ** – 🔬 210. **◑⑨ Œ ⓪ VISA**. ℁   Y u
Meals 15.95 **st.** (dinner) and a la carte 9.85/32.85 **st.** ᵻ 6.95 – ⌷ 8.75 – **81 rm** 75.00/
95.00 **st.**, 1 suite – SB.

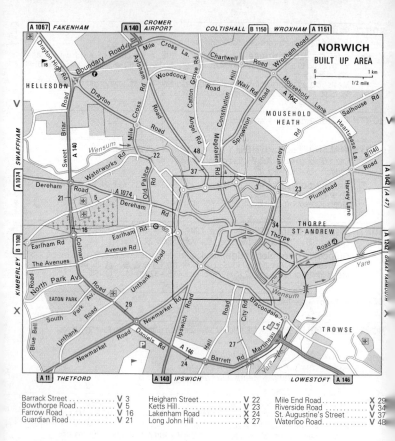

Stakis Norwich, Cromer Rd, NR6 6JA, N : 3 m. by A 140 ℰ (01603) 410544,
Fax (01603) 789935, Fᵃ, ⇆s, ◲, – ⌷ ⅍ rm, ▤ rest, ◱ ☎ ⅁ ⅁ – ⚗ 450. ⱽ⅁ ᴬᴱ ⅁ *VISA* ᴶᶜᴮ, ⅍
Meals 11.00/14.00 **st.** and a la carte ⌗ 4.75 – *The Wallbro* : **Meals** *(closed Saturday and
Sunday)* (dinner only) a la carte 18.95 **st.** ⌗ 4.75 – ⌷ 8.95 – **108 rm** 77.00/140.00 **st.** – SB.

Quality Friendly, 2 Barnard Rd, Bowthorpe, NR5 9JB, W : 3 ½ m. on A 1074,
ℰ (01603) 741161, *Fax (01603) 741500*, Fᵃ, ⇆s, ◲, – ⅍ rm, ▤ rest, ◱ ☎ ⅁ ⅁ – ⚗ 180.
ⱽ⅁ ᴬᴱ ⅁ *VISA* ᴶᶜᴮ
Meals (carving rest.) 9.95/14.50 **st.** and a la carte ⌗ 4.50 – ⌷ 8.75 – **78 rm** 67.50/87.50 **st.** –
SB.

Forte Posthouse Norwich, Ipswich Rd, NR4 6EP, S : 2 ¼ m. on A 140,
ℰ (01603) 456431, *Fax (01603) 506400*, Fᵃ, ⇆s, ◲, – ⅍ rm, ◱ ☎ ⅁ – ⚗ 65. ⱽ⅁ ᴬᴱ ⅁ *VISA*
Meals a la carte 13.25/23.85 **st.** ⌗ 7.50 – ⌷ 8.95 – **116 rm** 69.00 **st.** – SB.

Norwich, 121 Boundary Rd, NR3 2BA, on A 140 ℰ (01603) 787260, *Fax (01603) 400466*,
Fᵃ, ⇆s, ◲, – ⅍ rm, ▤ rest, ◱ ☎ ⅁ ⅁ – ⚗ 300. ⱽ⅁ ᴬᴱ ⅁ *VISA* ᴶᶜᴮ, ⅍   V
Meals (carving lunch)/dinner 15.50 **st.** and a la carte ⌗ 5.80 – ⌷ 8.50 – **107 rm** 67.00/
100.00 **st.** – SB.

Catton Old Hall, Lodge Lane, Old Catton, NR6 7HG, N : 3 ¼ m. by Catton Grove Rd and St
Faiths Rd ℰ (01603) 419379, *Fax (01603) 400339*, « 17C farmhouse », ⌔ – ◱ ☎ ⅁. ⱽ⅁ ᴬ
⅁ *VISA* ᴶᶜᴮ, ⅍
closed 13 December-2 January – **Meals** (booking essential) (residents only) (dinner only)
21.50 t. ⌗ 6.00 – **5 rm** ⌷ 42.50/90.00 **st.** – SB.

Beeches, 4-6 Earlham Rd, NR2 3DB, ℰ (01603) 621167, *Fax (01603) 620151*, ⌔ – ⅍ ◱
☎ ⅁ ⅁. ⱽ⅁ ᴬᴱ ⅁ *VISA*. ⅍   VX
closed 1 week Christmas – **Meals** (dinner only) 12.00 **st.** and a la carte ⌗ 6.00 – **25 rm**
⌷ 54.00/70.00 **t.** – SB.

🏨 **Annesley House,** 6 Newmarket Rd, NR2 2LA, ℰ (01603) 624553, *Fax (01603) 621577,* 🍴
– 🌿 rest, 📺 ☎ 🅿. 🆀🆂 🅰🅴 ⓪ *VISA* 🄹🄲🄱, 🛇
Z c
closed 24 to 27 December – **Meals** (dinner only) 17.50 **t.** and a la carte ⓵ 4.25 – **26 rm**
🍴 62.50/75.00 **t.** – SB.

🏨 **Cumberland,** 212-216 Thorpe Rd, NR1 1TJ, ℰ (01603) 434550, *Fax (01603) 433355* – 📺
X a
☎ 🅿. 🆀🆂 🅰🅴 ⓪ *VISA* 🄹🄲🄱, 🛇
closed 26 December-4 January – **Meals** *(closed Saturday and Sunday lunch)*
(booking essential) 9.95/19.95 **t.** and dinner a la carte ⓵ 5.95 – **25 rm** 🍴 42.50/99.00 **st.** –
SB.

🏨 **Travel Inn,** Longwater Interchange, New Costessey, NR5 0TL, NW : 5 ¼ m. on A 1047
(junction with A 47) ℰ (01603) 749140, *Fax (01603) 749 1219* – 🌿 rm, 📺 🅱 🅿. 🆀🆂 🅰🅴 ⓪
VISA
Meals (grill rest.) – **40 rm** 36.50 **t.**

NORWICH

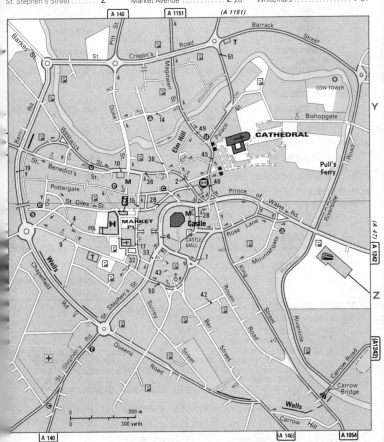

⌂ **Old Rectory** without rest., Watton Rd, Little Melton, NR9 3PB, W : 5 ½ m. on B 1108
    ℰ (01603) 812121, Fax (01603) 812521, 💐 – ⇥ 📺 🅿. ⓪. ✵
    closed 24 December to 2 January – **3 rm** � 38.00/68.00 **st.**

⌂ **Kingsley Lodge** without rest., 3 Kingsley Rd, NR1 3RB, ℰ (01603) 615819,
    Fax (01603) 615819 – ⇥ 📺. ✵   Z r
    closed Christmas-January – **4 rm** ⊆ 24.00/40.00 **s.**

XX **Adlard's** (Adlard), 79 Upper St. Giles St., NR2 1AB, ℰ (01603) 633522 – 🅾🅾 🅰🅴 ⓪ 𝘝𝘐𝘚𝘈 𝗝𝗖𝗕
❀   closed Monday lunch, Sunday, 2 weeks August and 1 week Christmas – **Meals** 19.00/
    32.00 **t.** ⓷ 8.00   Z e
    Spec. Pâté of foie gras with wild mushroom salad. Steamed sea bass with caviar, herb salad
    and a basil coulis. Pistachio ice cream with chocolate wafers.

XX **Marco's**, 17 Pottergate, NR2 1DS, ℰ (01603) 624044 – ⇥✖. 🅾🅾 🅰🅴 𝘝𝘐𝘚𝘈   Y e
    closed Sunday, Monday and Bank Holidays – **Meals** - Italian - 14.00 **t.** (lunch)
    and a la carte 23.60/30.00 **t.** ⓷ 5.80.

XX **By Appointment** with rm, 25-29 St. Georges St., NR3 1AB, ℰ (01603) 630730 – ⇥✖ 📺
    ☎. 𝘝𝘐𝘚𝘈   Y a
    accommodation closed 25 and 26 December – **Meals** (closed Sunday and Monday) (dinner
    only) a la carte 20.80/29.70 **t.** ⓷ 6.75 – **4 rm** ⊆ 65.00/85.00 **t.**

XX **Brasted's**, 8-10 St. Andrew's Hill, NR2 1AD, ℰ (01603) 625949, Fax (01603) 766445 – 🅾🅾
    🅰🅴 ⓪ 𝘝𝘐𝘚𝘈   Y c
    closed Saturday lunch, Sunday and 24 December-2 January – **Meals** a la carte 20.25/
    31.50 **t.**

XX **Green's Seafood Rest.**, 82 Upper St. Giles St., NR2 1LT, ℰ (01603) 623733,
    Fax (01603) 615268 – 🍽. 🅾🅾 𝘝𝘐𝘚𝘈   Z s
    closed Saturday lunch, Sunday, Monday, 1 week Christmas and Bank Holidays – **Meals** -
    Seafood - 16.00 **t.** (lunch) and dinner a la carte 20.00/25.30 **t.**

X **St. Benedicts**, 9 St. Benedicts St., NR2 4PE, ℰ (01603) 765377, Fax (01603) 765377 – 🅾🅾
    🅰🅴 ⓪ 𝘝𝘐𝘚𝘈   Y v
    closed Sunday, Monday and 25 to lunch 31 December – **Meals** a la carte 14.90/21.45 **st.**
    ⓷ 5.75.

at Caistor St. Edmund S : 4¼ m. by A 140 – X – ✉ Norwich.

⌂ **Old Rectory** ☜, NR14 8QS, ℰ (01508) 492490, Fax (01508) 495172, « Georgian
    rectory », 💐, park – 📺 🅿. 🅾🅾 𝘝𝘐𝘚𝘈 𝗝𝗖𝗕. ✵
    closed Christmas – **Meals** (communal dining) 18.00 **s.** – **3 rm** ⊆ 35.00/60.00 **s.**

at Stoke Holy Cross S : 5¾ m. by A 140 – X – ✉ Norwich.

ⓘ▷ **Wildebeest Arms**, 82-86 Norwich Rd, NR14 8QJ, ℰ (01508) 492497, 💐 – 🅿. 🅾🅾 🅰🅴 ⓪
    𝘝𝘐𝘚𝘈
    closed 25 and 26 December – **Meals** 12.00 **t.** (lunch) and a la carte 16.50/22.25 **t.** ⓷ 6.95.

at Hethersett SW : 6 m. by A 11 – X – ✉ Norwich.

🏨 **Park Farm**, NR9 3DL, on B 1172 ℰ (01603) 810264, Fax (01603) 812104, 【ゟ, ☎, 🔳, 💐,
    park, ✵ – ⇥✖ rest, 🍽 rest, 📺 ☎ 🅿. – ⚖ 150. 🅾🅾 🅰🅴 ⓪ 𝘝𝘐𝘚𝘈. ✵
    Meals 12.25/17.50 **t.** and a la carte ⓷ 6.50 – **38 rm** ⊆ 68.00/135.00 **t.** – SB.

🏛 **Travelodge**, Thickthorn Service Area, NR9 3AU, at junction of A 11 with A 47
    ℰ (01603) 457549, Reservations (Freephone) 0800 850950 – ⇥✖ rm, 📺 🅖 🅿. 🅾🅾 🅰🅴 ⓪ 𝘝𝘐𝘚𝘈
    𝗝𝗖𝗕. ✵
    Meals (grill rest.) – **40 rm** 44.95 **t.**

    ◉ ATS Mason Rd, Mile Cross Lane ℰ (01603) 423471   ATS Aylsham Way, Aylsham Rd ℰ (01603) 426316

NOTTINGHAM 402 403 404 Q 25 Great Britain G. – pop. 270 222.

    See : Castle Museum★ (alabasters★) AC, CZ M.
    Env. : Wollaton Hall★ AC, W : 3 m. by A 609 AZ M.
    Exc. : Newstead Abbey★ AC, N : 9 m. by A 611 – AY – and B 683.
    ▣ Bulwell Forest, Hucknall Rd ℰ (0115) 977 0576, AY – ▣ Wollaton Park ℰ (0115) 978 7574
    AZ – ▣ Mapperley, Central Av., Plains Rd ℰ (0115) 955 6672, BY – ▣ Nottingham City,
    Lawton Drive, Bulwell ℰ (0115) 927 8021 – ▣ Beeston Fields, Beeston ℰ (0115) 925 7062 –
    ▣ Ruddington Grange, Wilford Rd, Ruddington ℰ (0115) 984 6141, BZ – 🔒,🔒 Edwalton,
    ℰ (0115) 923 4775, BZ - 🔒, 🔒, 🔒 Cotgrave Place G & C.C., Stragglethorpe ℰ (0115) 933
    3344/5500.
    ✈ East Midlands Airport, Castle Donington : ℰ (01332) 852852 SW : 15 m. by A 453 AZ.
    🚩 1-4 Smithy Row, NG1 2BY ℰ (0115) 947 0661 – at West Bridgford : County Hall,
    Loughborough Rd, NG2 7QP ℰ (0115) 977 3558.
    London 135 – Birmingham 50 – Leeds 74 – Manchester 72.

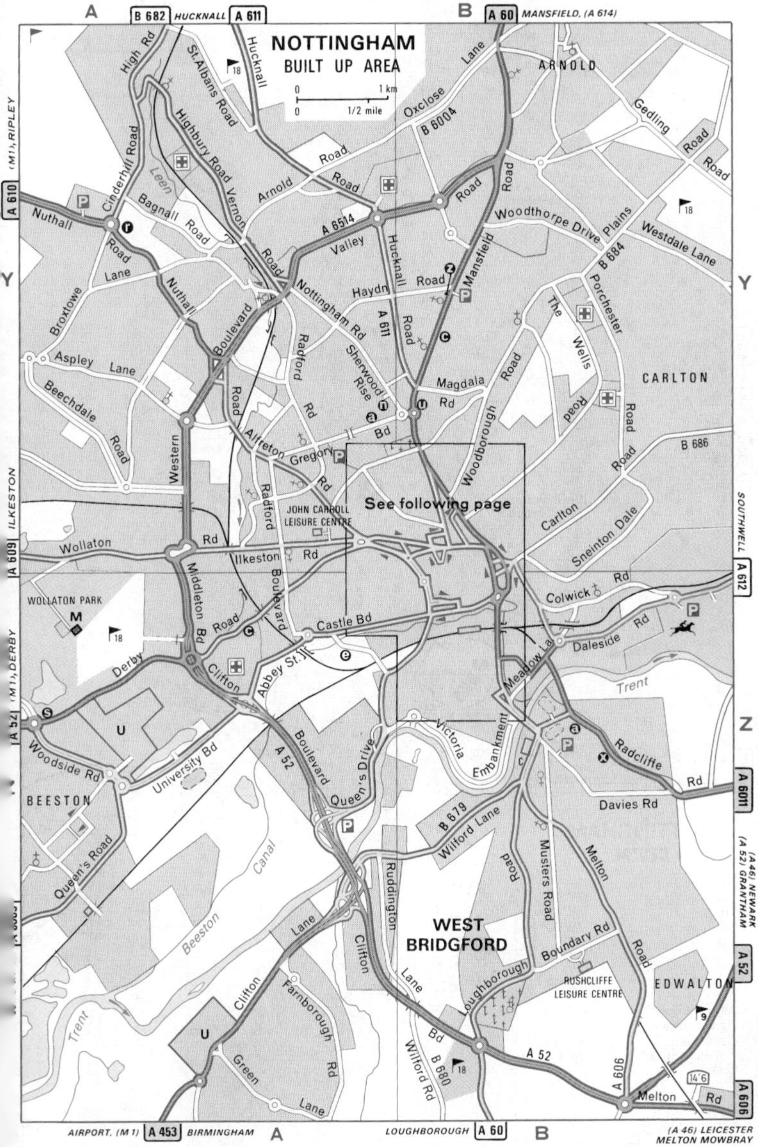

Forte Posthouse Nottingham City, St. James's St., NG1 6BN, ☏ (0115) 947 0131, *Fax (0115) 948 4366* – |‡|, ⋟ rm, ▤ TV ☎ P – 🎭 600. ⓂⒸ AE Ⓓ VISA JCB CY a
closed 25 and 26 December – **Meals** *(closed Saturday lunch)* 12.50/15.95 **st.** and a la carte 🍾 7.50 – ☕ 10.95 – **129 rm** 79.00/89.00 **st.**, 1 suite – SB.

Nottingham Gateway, Nuthall Rd, NG8 6AZ, ☏ (0115) 979 4949, *Fax (0115) 979 4744* – |‡|, ⋟ rm, ▤ rest, TV ☎ ♿ P – 🎭 250. ⓂⒸ AE Ⓓ VISA. ✂ AY r
Meals (carving rest.) 7.95/11.95 **st.** and a la carte 🍾 5.50 – ☕ 8.50 – **108 rm** 65.00/85.00 **st.** – SB.

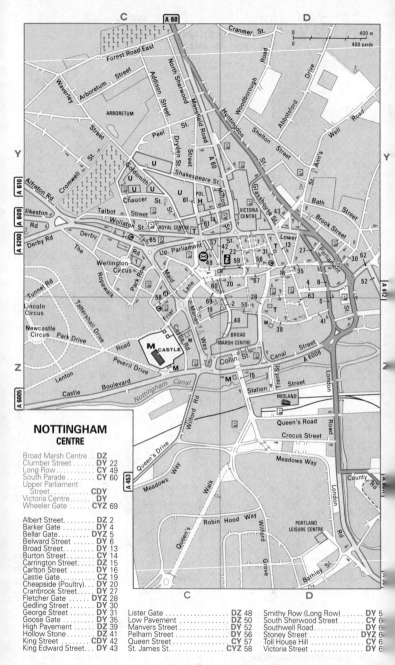

NOTTINGHAM
CENTRE

If you find you cannot take up a hotel booking you have made,
please let the hotel know immediately.

🏛️ **Nottingham Moat House**, 296 Mansfield Rd, NG5 2BT, ℰ (0115) 935 9988, *Fax (0115) 969 1506* – 📶, ⁕ rm, 🍴 rest, 📺 ☎ 🅿 – 🔬 180. 🆗 🄰🄴 🄾 *VISA* 　　BY u
Meals (grill rest.) 6.95/9.95 and a la carte – *Churchills* : Meals 9.75/13.95 t. and a la carte
🍷 5.75 – 🖙 9.50 – **169 rm** 90.00/110.00 st., 3 suites – SB.

🏛️ **Rutland Square**, St. James's St., NG1 6FJ, ℰ (0115) 941 1114, *Fax (0115) 941 0014* – 📶, ⁕ rm, 🍴 rest, 📺 ☎ 🅿 – 🔬 150. 🆗 🄰🄴 *VISA* 　　CZ c
Meals (bar lunch Monday to Saturday)/dinner 14.95 st. 🍷 7.95 – **104 rm** 75.00/90.00 st.,
1 suite – SB.

🏛️ **Strathdon Thistle**, 44 Derby Rd, NG1 5FT, ℰ (0115) 941 8501, *Fax (0115) 948 3725* – 📶, ⁕ rm, 🍴 rest, 📺 ☎ ♿ 🅿 – 🔬 120. 🆗 🄰🄴 🄾 *VISA* 🄹🄲🄱. ⁒　　CY c
Meals (bar lunch Saturday) 15.30/17.10 st. and a la carte 🍷 5.50 – 🖙 10.00 – **68 rm** 88.00/
118.00 st. – SB.

🏛️ **Holiday Inn Garden Court**, Castle Marina Park, off Castle Boulevard, NG7 1GX, ℰ (0115) 993 5000, *Fax (0115) 993 4000* – 📶, ⁕ rm, 🍴 rest, 📺 ☎ ♿ 🅿 – 🔬 45. 🆗 🄰🄴 🄾 *VISA* 🄹🄲🄱　　AZ e
Meals *(closed lunch Saturday and Sunday)* (bar lunch Monday to Friday)/dinner 14.50 st. and a la carte 🍷 7.50 – 🖙 8.50 – **100 rm** 79.50 st. – SB.

🏛️ **Woodville**, 340 Mansfield Rd, NG5 2EF, ℰ (0115) 960 6436, *Fax (0115) 985 6846* – 🍴 rest, 📺 ☎ 🅿 – 🔬 90. 🆗 🄰🄴 🄾 *VISA* 🄹🄲🄱　　BY c
Meals *(closed Saturday lunch and Sunday)* 9.95/12.95 st. and a la carte 🍷 5.00 – **45 rm** 🖙 50.00/60.00 st. – SB.

🏛️ **Stage**, Gregory Boulevard, NG7 6LB, ℰ (0115) 960 3261, *Fax (0115) 969 1040* – ⁕ rm, 📺 ☎ 🅿 – 🔬 40. 🆗 🄰🄴 🄾 *VISA*　　AY a
Meals *(closed Sunday)* (bar lunch)/dinner 11.95 t. 🍷 4.95 – **52 rm** 🖙 44.50/54.50 t.

🏛️ **Priory Toby**, Derby Rd, Wollaton Vale, NG8 2NR, W : 3 m. on A 52 ℰ (0115) 922 1691, *Fax (0115) 925 6224* – ⁕ rm 📺 ☎ 🅿. 🆗 🄰🄴 *VISA*. ⁒　　AZ s
Meals (grill rest.) a la carte 11.90/16.10 st. 🍷 4.45 – **31 rm** 🖙 64.00/74.00 st. – SB.

🏠 **Greenwood Lodge City**, Third Av., Sherwood Rise, NG7 6JH, ℰ (0115) 962 1206, *Fax (0115) 962 1206*, 🌳 – ⁕ rm 📺 🅿. 🆗 *VISA*. ⁒　　AY n
Meals (residents only) (communal dining) (dinner only) a la carte 15.95/22.00 s. 🍷 5.50 – 6 rm 🖙 30.00/50.00 s.

🏠 **Lucieville St. James**, 349 Derby Rd, NG7 2DZ, ℰ (0115) 978 7389, *Fax (0115) 979 0346*, 🌳 – ⁕ rm 📺 ☎ 🅿. 🆗 🄰🄴 🄾 *VISA*. ⁒　　AZ c
Meals (residents only) (dinner only)/22.50 s. and a la carte 🍷 8.00 – 🖙 9.50 – 6 rm 55.00/
135.00 s. – SB.

🏠 **Travel Inn**, Phoenix Centre, Millenium Way West, NG8 6AS, NW : 4 m. on A 610 ℰ (0115) 951 9971, *Fax (0115) 977 0113* – 📶, ⁕ rm, 🍴 rest, 📺 ♿ 🅿. 🆗 🄰🄴 🄾 *VISA*. ⁒　　AY r
Meals (grill rest.) – **60 rm** 36.50 t.

🍴🍴 **Sonny's**, 3 Carlton St., NG1 1NL, ℰ (0115) 947 3041, *Fax (0115) 950 7776* – 🍴. 🆗 🄰🄴 *VISA*
closed 1 January, 25 December and Bank Holidays – Meals 13.95 t. (lunch) and a la carte
18.65/24.45 t.　　DY c

🍴🍴 **Saagar**, 473 Mansfield Rd, Sherwood, NG5 2DR, ℰ (0115) 962 2014 – 🍴. 🆗 🄰🄴 *VISA* 🄹🄲🄱　　BY z
closed Sunday lunch and 25 December – Meals - Indian - a la carte 13.65/17.50 t. 🍷 5.50.

at West Bridgford SE : 2 m. on A 52 – ✉ Nottingham.

🏛️ **Windsor Lodge**, 116 Radcliffe Rd, NG2 5HG, ℰ (0115) 952 8528, *Fax (0115) 952 0020* – 📺 ☎ 🅿 – 🔬 40. 🆗 🄰🄴 🄾 *VISA*. ⁒　　BZ x
closed 25 and 26 December – Meals *(closed Sunday and Bank Holidays)* (residents only) (dinner only) 11.75 st. 🍷 4.50 – **47 rm** 🖙 39.50/58.00 st.

🏠 **Swans**, 84-90 Radcliffe Rd, NG2 5HH, ℰ (0115) 981 4042, *Fax (0115) 945 5745* – 📶 📺 ☎ 🅿 – 🔬 50. 🆗 🄰🄴 🄾 *VISA*. ⁒　　BZ a
closed 25 to 29 December – Meals *(closed lunch Monday and Saturday and Sunday dinner)* 13.95 t. and a la carte 🍷 5.00 – **30 rm** 🖙 50.00/60.00 t., 1 suite.

at Plumtree SE : 5¾ m. by A 60 – BZ – off A 606 – ✉ Nottingham.

🍴 **Perkins**, Old Railway Station, Station Rd, NG12 5NA, ℰ (0115) 937 3695, *Fax (0115) 937 6405* – 🅿. 🆗 🄰🄴 🄾 *VISA* 🄹🄲🄱
closed Sunday, Monday, 1 week Christmas and 2 weeks August – Meals - Bistro - a la carte 16.30/20.30 t.

at Beeston SW : 4¼ m. on A 6005 – AZ – ✉ Nottingham.

🏛️ **Village H. & Leisure Club**, Brailsford Way, Chilwell Meadows, NG9 6DL, SW : 2¾ m. by A 6005 ℰ (0115) 946 4422, *Fax (0115) 946 4428*, 🏋, ☎, 🏊, squash – 📶 ⁕, 🍴 rest, 📺 ☎ ♿ 🅿 – 🔬 220. 🆗 🄰🄴 🄾 *VISA*. ⁒
Meals (grill rest.) a la carte 10.35/17.85 st. 🍷 4.50 – **92 rm** 🖙 86.00/115.00 st.

at Risley SW : 7½ m. by A 52 – AZ – on B 5010 – ✉ Derby.

🏨 **Risley Hall,** Derby Rd, DE72 3SS, ℘ (0115) 939 9000, Fax (0115) 939 9766, ⅃₀, ≋s, ⬛, ☞ – |₿|, ⅍ rest, 🆃🆅 ☎ 🅿 – 🕍 150. 🚇 🆎 Ⓞ 🆅🅸🆂🅰
Meals (residents only Sunday dinner) 11.95/16.95 **st.** and a la carte ₰ 8.95 – ☑ 7.50 – **16 rm** 65.00/150.00 **st.** – SB.

at Sandiacre (Derbs.) SW : 7½ m. by A 52 – AZ – on B 5010 – ✉ Nottingham.

🏨 **Forte Posthouse Nottingham/Derby,** Bostocks Lane, NG10 5NJ, SW : ¾ m. at junction 25 of M 1 ℘ (0115) 939 7800, Fax (0115) 949 0469 – ⅍ rm, ▤ rest, 🆃🆅 ☎ 🅿 – 🕍 50. 🚇 🆎 Ⓞ 🆅🅸🆂🅰 🅹🅲🅱
Meals 15.95 **st.** (dinner) and a la carte 14.25/25.65 **st.** – ☑ 9.95 – **91 rm** 69.00/109.00 **st.** – SB.

at Long Eaton (Derbs.) SW : 8 m. on A 6005 – AZ.

🏨 **Novotel,** Bostock Lane, NG10 4EP, NW : 1 ¾ m. by A 6005 on B 6002 ℘ (0115) 946 5111, Fax (0115) 946 5900, ⬛, ☞ – |₿|, ⅍ rm, 🆃🆅 ☎ ♿ 🅿 – 🕍 200. 🚇 🆎 Ⓞ 🆅🅸🆂🅰 ⅍
Meals 16.00 **st.** (dinner) and a la carte 12.15/24.75 **st.** ₰ 5.35 – ☑ 7.75 – **105 rm** 59.50 **st.**

🏨 **Jarvis Nottingham,** Bostock Lane, NG10 5NL, NW : 1 ¾ m. by A 6005 on B 6002 ℘ (0115) 946 0000, Fax (0115) 946 0726 – ⅍ rm, 🆃🆅 ☎ ♿ 🅿 – 🕍 60. 🚇 🆎 Ⓞ 🆅🅸🆂🅰 ⅍ closed 24 to 26 December – Meals (grill rest.) a la carte 12.95/29.40 **t.** ₰ 4.95 – ☑ 6.50 – **101 rm** 60.95 **t.** – SB.

🅖 ATS 116 Highbury Rd, Bulwell ℘ (0115) 927 8824   ATS Oxford St., Long Eaton, Derbs.
ATS 66 Castle Boulevard ℘ (0115) 947 6678   ℘ (0115) 973 2156
ATS 126-132 Derby Rd, Stapleford
℘ (0115) 939 2986

NUNEATON Warks. 🔢🔢 P 26 – pop. 66 715.
🛇 Purley Chase, Pipers Lane, Ridge Lane ℘ (01203) 393118.
🅱 Nuneaton Library, Church St., CV11 4DR ℘ (01203) 384027.
London 107 – Birmingham 25 – Coventry 10 – Leicester 18.

🏨 **Travel Inn,** Coventry Rd, CV10 7PJ, S : 2 ½ m. by A 444 on B 4113 ℘ (01203) 343583, Fax (01203) 327156, ☞ – 🆃🆅 ♿ 🅿. 🚇 🆎 Ⓞ 🆅🅸🆂🅰 ⅍
Meals (grill rest.) – **48 rm** 36.50 **t.**

🏨 **Travelodge** without rest., CV10 7TF, S : 1 ½ m. on A 444 (southbound carriageway) ℘ (01203) 382541, Fax (01203) 382541, Reservations (Freephone) 0800 850950 – ⅍ 🆃🆅 ♿ 🅿. 🚇 🆎 Ⓞ 🆅🅸🆂🅰 🅹🅲🅱. ⅍
40 rm 35.95 **t.**

🏨 **Travelodge** without rest., St. Nicholas Park Drive, CV11 6EN, NE : 1 ½ m. by A 47 (Hinkley Rd) ℘ (01203) 353885, Fax (01203) 353885, Reservations (Freephone) 0800 850950 – ⅍ 🆃🆅 ♿ 🅿. 🚇 🆎 Ⓞ 🆅🅸🆂🅰 🅹🅲🅱. ⅍
28 rm 35.95 **t.**

at Sibson (Leics.) N : 7 m. on A 444 – ✉ Nuneaton.

🏨 **Millers',** Twycross Rd, CV13 6LB, ℘ (01827) 880223, Fax (01827) 880223 – 🆃🆅 ☎ 🅿. 🚇 🆎 Ⓞ 🆅🅸🆂🅰 🅹🅲🅱
Meals (closed Sunday dinner) 9.95 **st.** and a la carte ₰ 4.95 – **40 rm** ☑ 47.50/54.50 **st.** – SB.
🅖 ATS Weddington Rd ℘ (01203) 341130/341139

OAKHAM Rutland 🔢🔢 R 25 – pop. 8 691.
🅱 Flore's House, 34 High St., LE15 6AL ℘ (01572) 724329.
London 103 – Leicester 26 – Northampton 35 – Nottingham 28.

🏨 **Barnsdale Lodge,** The Avenue, Rutland Water, LE15 8AH, E : 2 ½ m. on A 60... ℘ (01572) 724678, Fax (01572) 724961, « Converted part 17C farmhouse » – ⅍ 🆃🆅 ☎ 🅿 – 🕍 300. 🚇 🆎 🆅🅸🆂🅰 🅹🅲🅱. ⅍
residents only 25 and 26 December – Meals a la carte 16.35/23.35 **t.** ₰ 9.95 – **29 rm** ☑ 58.00/90.00 **t.** – SB.

🏨 **Whipper-In,** Market Pl., LE15 6DT, ℘ (01572) 756971, Fax (01572) 757759 – ⅍ rest, 🆃🆅 ☎ – 🕍 50. 🚇 🆎 Ⓞ 🆅🅸🆂🅰 ⅍
Meals 11.95/16.50 **t.** and dinner a la carte – **24 rm** ☑ 59.00/84.00 **st.** – SB.

🏨 **Boultons,** 4 Catmose St., LE15 6HW, ℘ (01572) 722844, Fax (01572) 724473 – 🆃🆅 ☎ ♿ 🅿 – 🕍 60. 🚇 🆎 Ⓞ 🆅🅸🆂🅰 🅹🅲🅱. ⅍
Meals 15.00/18.50 **st.** and a la carte ₰ 7.00 – **25 rm** ☑ 60.00/80.00 **st.** – SB.

🏨 **Lord Nelson's House,** Market Pl., LE15 6DT, ℘ (01572) 723199, Fax (01572) 72319... « 17C town house » – ⅍ rm, 🆃🆅 ☎. 🚇 🆅🅸🆂🅰. ⅍
closed 25 and 26 December – Meals (closed Sunday and dinner Monday to Thursday t... non-residents) (light lunch)/dinner 18.50 **st.** – **5 rm** ☑ 49.00/79.00 **st.**

at Hambleton *E : 3 m. by A 606 – ✉ Oakham.*

🏨 [✿] **Hambleton Hall** 🐦, LE15 8TH, ☎ (01572) 756991, *Fax (01572) 724721,* « Victorian country house, ≤ Rutland Water », 🏊, 🌳, park, 🎾 – |♿| [TV] ☎ [P]. [MC] [AE] [D] [VISA]
Meals 19.50/35.00 **st.** and a la carte 47.50/58.00 **st.** 🍷 12.50 – ☕ 12.00 – **15 rm** 145.00/ 295.00 **st.** – SB
Spec. Langoustine tails with chilled tomato juice and basil. Lamb sweetbreads with chicken and morel tortellini, asparagus, madeira sauce. Caramelised apple tart with blackberry compote and vanilla ice cream.

OAKLEY *Hants.* [403] [404] Q 30 – *see Basingstoke.*

OBORNE *Dorset* [403] [404] M 31 – *see Sherborne.*

OCKHAM *Surrey* [404] S 30 – *pop. 407* – ✉ *Ripley.*
London 27 – Guildford 9.

🏨 **Hautboy** 🐦, Ockham Lane, GU23 6NP, ☎ (01483) 225355, *Fax (01483) 211176,* 🌳 – ▤ rest, [TV] ☎ [P]. [MC] [AE] [VISA]. 🚫
closed 25 December – **Meals** 18.00/26.00 **t.** and a la carte 🍷 5.50 – ☕ 7.50 – **5 rm** 98.00/ 125.00 **st.**

Per spostarvi più rapidamente utilizzate le ***carte Michelin "Grandi Strade"*** *:*

n° **[970] Europa,** *n°* **[976] Rep. Ceca/Slovacchia,** *n°* **[980] Grecia,**
n° **[984] Germania,** *n°* **[985] Scandinavia-Finlandia,**
n° **[986] Gran Bretagna-Irlanda,** *n°* **[987] Germania-Austria-Benelux,**
n° **[988] Italia,** *n°* **[989] Francia,** *n°* **[990] Spagna-Portogallo,** *n°* **[991] Jugoslavia.**

ODIHAM *Hants.* [404] R 30 – *pop. 3 531* – ✉ *Hook.*
London 51 – Reading 16 – Winchester 25.

🏨 **George,** 100 High St., RG29 1LP, ☎ (01256) 702081, *Fax (01256) 704213,* « 15C inn » – 🚭 rm, [TV] ☎ [P]. [MC] [AE] [D] [VISA]
Meals *(closed Saturday lunch and Sunday dinner)* 14.25 **t.** (lunch) and a la carte 19.50/ 27.00 **t.** 🍷 6.50 – **18 rm** ☕ 70.00/95.00 **t.**

🍴 **Grapevine,** 121 High St., RG29 1LA, ☎ (01256) 701122 – ▤. [MC] [VISA]
closed Saturday lunch, Sunday, 1 January, 25-26 December, 1 week Easter, first 2 weeks October and Bank Holiday Monday – **Meals** 7.50/12.95 **t.** and a la carte 🍷 4.50.

OGBOURNE ST. GEORGE *Wilts.* [403] [404] O 29 – *see Marlborough.*

OKEHAMPTON *Devon* [403] H 31 *The West Country G.* – *pop. 4 841.*
Exc. : *S : Dartmoor National Park★★ – Lydford★★, S : 8 m. by B 3260 and A 386.*
⛳18 *Okehampton ☎ (01837) 52113* – ⛳18, ⛳18, ⛳18 *Ashbury, Fowley Cross ☎ (01837) 55453.*
[i] *3 West St., EX20 1HQ ☎ (01837) 53020 (summer only).*
London 226 – Exeter 25 – Plymouth 30.

🏨 **Travelodge,** Sourton Cross, EX20 4LY, SW : 4 ½ m. by B 3260 and A 30 on A 386 ☎ (01837) 52124, Reservations (Freephone) 0800 850950 – 🚭 rm, [TV] ♿ [P]. [MC] [AE] [D] [VISA] [JCB]. 🚫
Meals (grill rest.) – **42 rm** 44.95 **t.**

🏨 **Travelodge,** Whiddon Down, EX20 2QT, E : 7 ¾ m. by A 30 on A 382 ☎ (01837) 231626, Reservations (Freephone) 0800 850950 – 🚭 rm, [TV] ♿ [P]. [MC] [AE] [D] [VISA] [JCB]. 🚫
Meals (grill rest.) – **40 rm** 39.95 **t.**

🛞 ATS 46 North Rd ☎ (01837) 53277

OLD *Northants.* – *pop. 290.*
London 77 – Birmingham 58 – Leicester 26 – Northampton 6.

🏠 **Wold Farm** 🐦, Harrington Rd, NN6 9RJ, ☎ (01604) 781258, « Working farm », 🌳, park – 🚭 [P]. 🚫
Meals (by arrangement) (communal dining) 15.00 **st.** – **6 rm** ☕ 25.00/50.00 **st.**

OLD BROWNSOVER *Warks.* – *see Rugby.*

OLD BURGHCLERE *Hants.* [404] Q 29 – ✉ *Newbury.*
London 77 – Bristol 76 – Newbury 10 – Reading 27 – Southampton 28.

🍴🍴 **Dew Pond,** RG20 9LH, ☎ (01635) 278408, *Fax (01635) 278408,* ≤ – ⊁ [P]. [MC] [VISA]
closed Sunday, Monday, 24 to 27 December, first 2 weeks January and 2 weeks August – **Meals** (dinner only) 25.00 **st.** 🍷 6.50.

OLDBURY *W. Mids. – see Birmingham.*

OLD BYLAND *N.Yorks. – see Helmsley.*

OLD DALBY *Leics.* [402] [404] R 25 – *see Melton Mowbray.*

Per visitare una città o una regione : utilizzate le guide verdi ***Michelin.***

OLDHAM *Gtr. Manchester* [402] [404] N 23 – *pop. 103 931.*
Crompton and Royton, High Barn, Royton ☎ (0161) 624 2154 – Werneth, Green Lane, Garden Suburb ☎ (0161) 624 1190 – Lees New Rd ☎ (0161) 624 4986.
[i] 11 Albion St., OL1 3BD ☎ (0161) 627 1024.
London 212 – Leeds 36 – Manchester 7 – Sheffield 38.

Plan : see Manchester

Smokies Park, Ashton Rd, Bardsley, OL8 3HX, S : 2 ¾ m. on A 627 ☎ (0161) 624 3405, *Fax (0161) 627 5262,* Ⅰ₅, ≘ – [TV] ☎ [P] – 🏛 150. [MC] [AE] [D] [VISA]. ✗
Meals (dancing Friday and Saturday evenings) (buffet lunch) 4.25 **t.** and a la carte 9.10/20.85 **t.** 🍷 5.60 – **47 rm** ☕ 60.00/80.00 **t.** – SB.

Bower, Hollinwood Av., Chadderton, OL9 8DE, SW : 3 ¼ m. by A 62 on A 6104 ☎ (0161) 682 7254, *Fax (0161) 683 4605,* 🌳 – ⊁ [TV] ☎ [P] – 🏛 200. [MC] [AE] [D] [VISA]
Meals (bar lunch Saturday) 9.50/18.50 **st.** and a la carte 🍷 6.50 – ☕ 7.95 – **63 rm** 73.00/150.00 **st.** – SB. BV e

Avant, Windsor Rd, off Manchester St., OL8 4AS, ☎ (0161) 627 5500, *Fax (0161) 627 5896* – |≑|, ⊁ rm, ▤ rest, [TV] ☎ ♿ [P] – 🏛 250. [MC] [AE] [D] [VISA] [JCB]
closed 25 and 26 December – **Meals** *(closed Sunday lunch)* 9.50/16.75 **st.** and a la carte 🍷 6.75 – ☕ 8.50 – **101 rm** 75.00/85.00 **st.**, 2 suites.

Pennine Way, Manchester St., OL8 1UZ, ☎ (0161) 624 0555, *Fax (0161) 627 2031,* Ⅰ₅ – |≑|, ⊁ rm, [TV] ☎ [P] – 🏛 320. [MC] [AE] [D] [VISA]
Meals (bar lunch Monday to Saturday)/dinner 16.95 **st.** and a la carte 🍷 6.45 – **130 rm** ☕ 75.00/95.00 **st.** – SB.

Travel Inn, The Broadway, Chadderton, OL9 8DW, SW : 3 ½ m. by A 62 on A 6104 at junction with A 663 ☎ (0161) 681 1373, *Fax (0161) 682 7974* – ⊁ rm, ▤ rest, [TV] ♿ [P]. [MC] [AE] [D] [VISA]. ✗ BV e
Meals (grill rest.) – **40 rm** 36.50 **t.**

🍴🍴 **White Hart Inn** with rm, 51 Stockport Rd (1st floor), Lydgate, OL4 4JJ, E : 3 m. by A 669 on A 6050 ☎ (01457) 872566, *Fax (01457) 875190* – ⊁ [TV] ☎ [P]. [MC] [AE] [VISA]. ✗
closed Sunday dinner and Monday – **Meals** (dinner only and Sunday lunch)/dinner 25.00 **st.** 🍷 7.75 – (see also ***Brasserie*** below) – **5 rm** ☕ 60.00/80.00 **t.**

🍴 **Brasserie** (at White Hart Inn), 51 Stockport Rd, Lydgate, OL4 4JJ, E : 3 m. by A 669 on A 6050 ☎ (01457) 872566, *Fax (01457) 875190* – [P]. [MC] [AE] [VISA]
Meals 11.00 **t.** (lunch) and a la carte 13.00/24.00 **t.** 🍷 7.75.

ATS 169-171 Huddersfield Rd ☎ (0161) 633 1551
ATS 179-185 Hollins Rd ☎ (0161) 627 0180/665 1958

OLD SODBURY *South Gloucestershire* [403] [404] M 29 – ✉ *Bristol.*
Chipping Sodbury ☎ (01454) 312024.
London 110 – Bristol 14 – Gloucester 30 – Swindon 29.

Sodbury House without rest., Badminton Rd, BS17 6LU, on A 432 ☎ (01454) 312847 *Fax (01454) 273105,* 🌳 – ⊁ [TV] ☎ [P] – 🏛 25. [MC] [AE] [VISA]. ✗
closed 24 December-3 January – **13 rm** ☕ 43.00/90.00 **st.**

Dornden ≫, 15 Church Lane, BS17 6NB, ☎ (01454) 313325, *Fax (01454) 312263,* ≤, 🌳 ✗ – [TV] [P]
closed 3 weeks September-October and 2 weeks Christmas-New Year – **Meal** (by arrangement) 10.00 **t.** – **9 rm** ☕ 26.00/52.00 **t.**

OMBERSLEY *Worcestershire* 403 404 N 27 – *pop. 2 089.*
London 148 – Birmingham 42 – Leominster 33.

↑ **Greenlands** ⬳ without rest., Uphampton, WR9 0JP, NW : 1 ½ m. by A 449 turning left at the Reindeer pub ℘ *(01905) 620873,* ⬱, « 16C cottage », ☞ – ⬲ 📺 🅿. ⬳
3 rm ⌧ 18.00/43.00 **st.**

ORCOP *Herefordshire* 403 L 27 – *see Hereford.*

ORMSKIRK *Lancs.* 402 L 23 – *pop. 23 425.*
London 219 – Liverpool 12 – Preston 18.

🏨 **Beaufort,** High Lane, Burscough, L40 7SN, NE : 1 ¾ m. by B 5319 on A 59 ℘ *(01704) 892655, Fax (01704) 895135* – ⬲ rm, 📺 🅿 🔥 🅿 – ⬕ 40. 🆎 🆎 ⓞ 𝗩𝗜𝗦𝗔. ⬳
Meals 11.95/15.95 **st.** and dinner a la carte ⬩ 5.50 – **21 rm** ⌧ 57.50/75.00 **t.** – SB.

OSWESTRY *Shrops.* 402 403 K 25 – *pop. 15 612.*
🏌 *Aston Park* ℘ *(01691) 610221* – 🏌 *Llanymynech, Pant* ℘ *(01691) 830542.*
🅱 *Mile End Services, SY11 4JA* ℘ *(01691) 662488* – *The Heritage Centre, 2 Church Terr., SY11 2TE* ℘ *(01691) 662753.*
London 182 – Chester 28 – Shrewsbury 18.

🏨 **Wynnstay,** Church St., SY11 2SZ, ℘ *(01691) 655261, Fax (01691) 670606,* 🔥, 🛎, 🔲, ☞
– 📺 ☎ 🅿 – ⬕ 180. 🆎 🆎 ⓞ 𝗩𝗜𝗦𝗔. ⬳
Meals a la carte 16.65/25.60 **st.** ⬩ 5.25 – ⌧ 8.95 – **26 rm** 65.00/80.00 **st.**, 1 suite – SB.

🏨 **Travelodge,** Mile End Service Area, SY11 4JA, SE : 1 ¼ m. at junction of A 5 with A 483 ℘ *(01691) 658178,* Reservations (Freephone) 0800 850950 – ⬲ rm, 📺 🔥 🅿. 🆎 🆎 ⓞ 𝗩𝗜𝗦𝗔 𝗝𝗖𝗕. ⬳
Meals (grill rest.) – **40 rm** 39.95 **t.**

✕✕ **Sebastian's** with rm, 45 Willow St., SY11 1AQ, ℘ *(01691) 655444, Fax (01691) 653452* –
⬲ 📺 ☎. 🆎 🆎 𝗩𝗜𝗦𝗔. ⬳
closed 1 January and 25-26 December – **Meals** *(closed Sunday and Monday)* (dinner only) 18.95 **t.** and a la carte ⬩ 4.95 – ⌧ 7.95 – **3 rm** 33.00/42.00 **t.**

at Rhydycroesau *W : 3¼ m. on B 4580* – ⊠ *Oswestry.*

🏨 **Pen-Y-Dyffryn Country** ⬳, SY10 7DT, SE : ¼ m. by B 4580 ℘ *(01691) 653700,* Fax *(01691) 653700,* ⬱, 🐾, ☞ – ⬲ rest, 📺 🅿. 🆎 🆎 𝗩𝗜𝗦𝗔 𝗝𝗖𝗕. ⬳
closed January – **Meals** (dinner only) 18.00 **t.** and a la carte ⬩ 5.00 – **8 rm** ⌧ 47.00/74.00 **t.** – SB.

🔧 ATS Oswald Rd ℘ *(01691) 653540/653256*

OTLEY *Suffolk* 404 X 27 – *pop. 1 381* – ⊠ *Ipswich.*
London 83 – Ipswich 7.5 – Norwich 43.

↑ **Bowerfield House** ⬳, Helmingham Rd, IP6 9NR, ℘ *(01473) 890742,* Fax *(01473) 890059,* « Converted 17C stable and barn », ☞ – ⬲ 📺 🅿. ⬳
Easter-October – **Meals** (by arrangement) (communal dining) 18.50 **st.** – **3 rm** ⌧ 36.00/46.00 **st.**

OTLEY *W. Yorks.* 402 O 22 – *pop. 13 596.*
🏌 *West Busk Lane* ℘ *(01943) 461015.*
🅱 *Council Offices, 8 Boroughgate, LS21 3AH* ℘ *(0113) 247 7707.*
London 216 – Harrogate 14 – Leeds 12 – York 28.

🏨 **Chevin Lodge** ⬳, Yorkgate, LS21 3NU, S : 2 m. by East Chevin Rd ℘ *(01943) 467818,* Fax *(01943) 850335,* « Pine log cabin village », 🔥, 🛎, 🔲, 🐾, ☞, park, ⬳ – 📺 ☎ 🔥 🅿 –
⬕ 120. 🆎 🆎 𝗩𝗜𝗦𝗔
Meals 11.75/18.50 **t.** and a la carte ⬩ 5.00 – **46 rm** ⌧ 89.00/99.00 **t.**, 4 suites – SB.

OULTON Suffolk – see Lowestoft.

OUNDLE Northants. 404 S 26 – pop. 3 996 – ⊠ Peterborough.

🏌 Benefield Rd ℘ (01832) 273267.

🛈 14 West St., PE8 4EF ℘ (01832) 274333.

London 89 – Leicester 37 – Northampton 30.

🏠 **Talbot,** New St., PE8 4EA, ℘ (01832) 273621, Fax (01832) 274545, ℛ – ఈ▥ 🎜 ☎ 🅿 –
🔏 100. ◖◗ 🆎 ⑩ 𝘝𝘐𝘚𝘈 J͞C͞B
Meals (bar lunch Monday to Saturday)/dinner a la carte 12.40/19.90 **t.** ⅞ 8.00 – ⇌ 9.50 –
38 rm 70.00/85.00 **t.,** 1 suite – SB.

at Fotheringhay N : 3¾ m. by A 427 off A 605 – ⊠ Peterborough (Cambs.).

⤒ **Castle Farm,** PE8 5HZ, ℘ (01832) 226200, « Riverside garden » – ఈ rm, 🎜 🅿. ℀
Meals (by arrangement) 12.50 **t.** – **6 rm** ⇌ 31.00/50.00 **st.**

at Upper Benefield W : 4 m. on A 427 – ⊠ Peterborough (Cambs.).

🏛 **Wheatsheaf,** PE8 5AN, ℘ (01832) 205254, Fax (01832) 205245, ℛ – 🎜 ☎ 🅿. ◖◗ 🆎 ⑩
𝘝𝘐𝘚𝘈 J͞C͞B ℀
Meals a la carte 11.70/23.20 **t.** – **9 rm** ⇌ 50.00/60.00 **t.**

When visiting Great Britain,
use the Michelin Green Guide **"Great Britain".**
- *Detailed descriptions of places of interest*
- *Touring programmes*
- *Maps and street plans*
- *The history of the country*
- *Photographs and drawings of monuments,*
  beauty spots, houses...

OUTLANE W. Yorks. – see Huddersfield.

OVER PEOVER Ches. 402 403 404 M 24 – see Knutsford.

OXFORD Oxon. 403 404 Q 28 Great Britain G. – pop. 118 795.

See : City★★★ - Christ Church★★ (Hall★★ AC, Tom Quad★, Tom Tower★, Cathedral★ AC -
Choir Roof★) BZ – Merton College★★ AC BZ - Magdalen College★★ BZ – Ashmolean
Museum★★ BY M2 – Bodleian Library★★ (Ceiling★★, Lierne Vaulting★) AC BZ F – St. John's
College★ BY - The Queen's College★ BZ – Lincoln College★ BZ - Trinity College (Chapel★)
BY – New College (Chapel★) AC, BZ – Radcliffe Camera★ BZ A – Sheldonian Theatre★ AC,
BZ G – University Museum★ BY M3 – Pitt Rivers Museum★ BY M4.

Env. : Iffley Church★ AZ A.

Exc. : Woodstock : Blenheim Palace★★★ (The Grounds★★★) AC, NW : 8 m. by A 4144 and
A 34 AY.

Swinford Bridge (toll).

🛈 The Old School, Gloucester Green, OX1 2DA ℘ (01865) 726871.

London 59 – Birmingham 63 – Brighton 105 – Bristol 73 – Cardiff 107 – Coventry 54 –
Southampton 64.

Plans on following pages

🏨 **Randolph,** Beaumont St., OX1 2LN, ℘ (01865) 247481, Fax (01865) 791678 – 🛗, ఈ rm
🎜 ☎ – 🔏 250. ◖◗ 🆎 ⑩ 𝘝𝘐𝘚𝘈 J͞C͞B
BY r
Spires : Meals 20.00/27.00 **st.** and a la carte – ⇌ 12.75 – **116 rm** 125.00/155.00 **st.**
5 suites – SB.

🏨 **Oxford Moat House,** Wolvercote Roundabout, OX2 8AL, ℘ (01865) 489988,
Fax (01865) 310259, 𝑓ₐ, ⸙, 🏊, squash – ఈ rm, ▤ rest, 🎜 ☎ 🅿 – 🔏 150. ◖◗ 🆎 ⑩ 𝘝𝘐𝘚𝘈
J͞C͞B ℀
AY e
Meals 14.50 **st.** ⅞ 7.00 – ⇌ 10.00 – **155 rm** 99.00/129.00 **st.** – SB.

🏠 **Old Parsonage,** 1 Banbury Rd, OX2 6NN, ℘ (01865) 310210, Fax (01865) 311262, ㎡,
« Part 17C house », ℛ – 🎜 ☎ 🅿. ◖◗ 🆎 ⑩ 𝘝𝘐𝘚𝘈 J͞C͞B ℀
BY e
closed 24 to 27 December – **Meals** (room service and meals in bar only) a la carte 16.05/
27.40 **st.** ⅞ 6.10 – **30 rm** ⇌ 125.00/225.00 **st.**

🏨 **Eastgate,** Merton St., OX1 4BE, ✆ (01865) 248244, *Fax (01865) 791681* – 📶 ✸✱, ≣ rest,
📺 ☎ 🅿. 🕼 ஊ ① VISA JCB. ⅙
BZ **c**
Meals (bar lunch Monday to Saturday)/dinner 15.95 **st.** ₆ 7.95 – ☲ 9.95 – **45 rm** 95.00/
130.00 **st.** – SB.

🏨 **Linton Lodge,** Linton Rd, OX2 6UJ, ✆ (01865) 553461, *Fax (01865) 310365*, ≈ – 📶,
✸✱ rm, 📺 ☎ 🅿 – 🔬 120. 🕼 ஊ ① VISA. ⅙
AY **n**
Meals (bar lunch)/dinner 17.25 **st.** and a la carte ₆ 5.95 – ☲ 10.25 – **70 rm** 99.00/139.00 **st.**
– SB.

🏠 **Bath Place,** 4-5 Bath Pl., OX1 3SU, ✆ (01865) 791812, *Fax (01865) 791834*, « 17C Flemish
weavers cottages » – ✸✱ rest, ≣ rest, 📺 ☎ 🅿. 🕼 ஊ VISA JCB. ⅙
BY **a**
closed last week December and first week January – Meals (closed Tuesday lunch, Sunday
dinner and Monday) 17.50/29.50 **t.** and a la carte ₆ 6.95 – ☲ 8.50 – **10 rm** 80.00/140.00 **t.**,
2 suites.

🏠 **Marlborough House** without rest., 321 Woodstock Rd, OX2 7NY, ✆ (01865) 311321,
Fax (01865) 515329 – ✸✱ 📺 ☎ 🅿. 🕼 VISA JCB. ⅙
AY **v**
closed 23 December-2 January – **16 rm** 59.50/69.50 **st.**

🏠 **Cotswold House** without rest., 363 Banbury Rd, OX2 7PL, ✆ (01865) 310558,
Fax (01865) 310558, ≈ – ✸✱ 📺 🅿. ⅙
AY **c**
closed 10 days Christmas – **7 rm** ☲ 42.00/62.00 **st.**

🏠 **Chestnuts** without rest., 45 Davenant Rd, OX2 8BU, ✆ (01865) 553375,
Fax (01865) 553375 – ✸✱ 📺 🅿. ⅙
AY **s**
closed 22 December-7 January – **5 rm** ☲ 37.00/63.00 **s.**

🏠 **Mount Pleasant,** 76 London Rd., Headington, OX3 9AJ, ✆ (01865) 762749,
Fax (01865) 762749 – ✸✱ 📺 ☎ 🅿. 🕼 ஊ ① VISA JCB. ⅙
AY **a**
Meals 8.50 **t.** – **8 rm** ☲ 45.00/65.00 **t.**

🏠 **Dial House** without rest., 25 London Rd, Headington, OX3 7RE, ✆ (01865) 769944,
Fax (01865) 769944, ≈ – ✸✱ 📺 🅿
AY **o**
8 rm ☲ 45.00/60.00.

🏠 **Tilbury Lodge** without rest., 5 Tilbury Lane, Botley, OX2 9NB, W : 2 m. by A 420 off B 4044
✆ (01865) 862138, *Fax (01865) 863700*, ≈ – ✸✱ 📺 ☎ 🅿. 🕼 VISA. ⅙
AZ **e**
closed 23 December-1 January – **9 rm** ☲ 45.00/82.00 **st.**

🏠 **Pine Castle,** 290-292 Iffley Rd, OX4 4AE, ✆ (01865) 241497, *Fax (01865) 727230* – ✸✱ 📺
☎ 🅿. 🕼 VISA JCB. ⅙
Z **r**
closed 1 week Christmas – Meals 10.50 **st.** – **8 rm** ☲ 55.00/65.00 **st.**

✕✕ **Gee's,** 61 Banbury Rd, OX2 6PE, ✆ (01865) 553540, *Fax (01865) 310308*, « Conservatory »
– ≣. 🕼 ஊ ① VISA
AY **r**
closed 25 and 26 December – Meals 9.75 **t.** (lunch) and a la carte 18.60/24.10 **t.** ₆ 8.50.

✕ **Le Petit Blanc,** 71-72 Walton St., OX2 6AG, ✆ (01865) 510999, *Fax (01865) 510700* – ≣.
🕼 ஊ ① VISA JCB
AY **z**
closed 25 December – Meals - Brasserie - 14.00 **t.** (lunch) and a la carte 14.80/25.20 **t.**

at **Stanton St. John** *NE : 7 m. by A 40* – AY – ✉ Oxford.

🍴 **Talkhouse** with rm, OX33 1EX, on B 4027 ✆ (01865) 351648, *Fax (01865) 351085*, ❦ , ≈
– 📺 ☎ 🅿. 🕼 ஊ ① VISA. ⅙
closed 25 December – **Meals** (buffet lunch) 7.95 **t.** and a la carte 13.40/20.40 **t.** ₆ 7.75 –
4 rm ☲ 45.50/59.50 **t.**

at **Wheatley** *E : 7 m. by A 40* – AY – ✉ Oxford.

🏠 **Travelodge** without rest., London Rd, OX33 1JH, ✆ (01865) 875705, Reservations (Freephone) 0800 850950 – ✸✱ 📺 ♿ 🅿. 🕼 ஊ ① VISA JCB. ⅙
36 rm 49.95 **t.**

at **Iffley** *SE : 2 m. by A 4158* – ✉ Oxford.

🏨 Hawkwell House, Church Way, OX4 4DZ, ✆ (01865) 749988, *Fax (01865) 748525*, ≈ –
✸✱ rest, 📺 ☎ 🅿 – 🔬 200
AZ **c**
27 rm.

🏠 **The Tree,** Church Way, OX4 4EY, ✆ (01865) 775974, *Fax (01865) 747554*, ≈ – ✸✱ rm, 📺
☎ 🅿. 🕼 VISA. ⅙
AZ **a**
closed 25 and 26 December – Meals (bar lunch)/dinner 12.50 **st.** and a la carte – **8 rm**
☲ 55.00/75.00 **st.**

Cowley *SE : 2½ m. by B 480* – ✉ Oxford.

🏠 **Travel Inn,** Garsington Rd, OX4 2JZ, ✆ (01865) 779230, *Fax (01865) 775887* – 📶, ✸✱ rm,
📺 ♿ 🅿. 🕼 ஊ ① VISA. ⅙
AZ **s**
Meals (grill rest.) – **120 rm** 36.50 **t.**

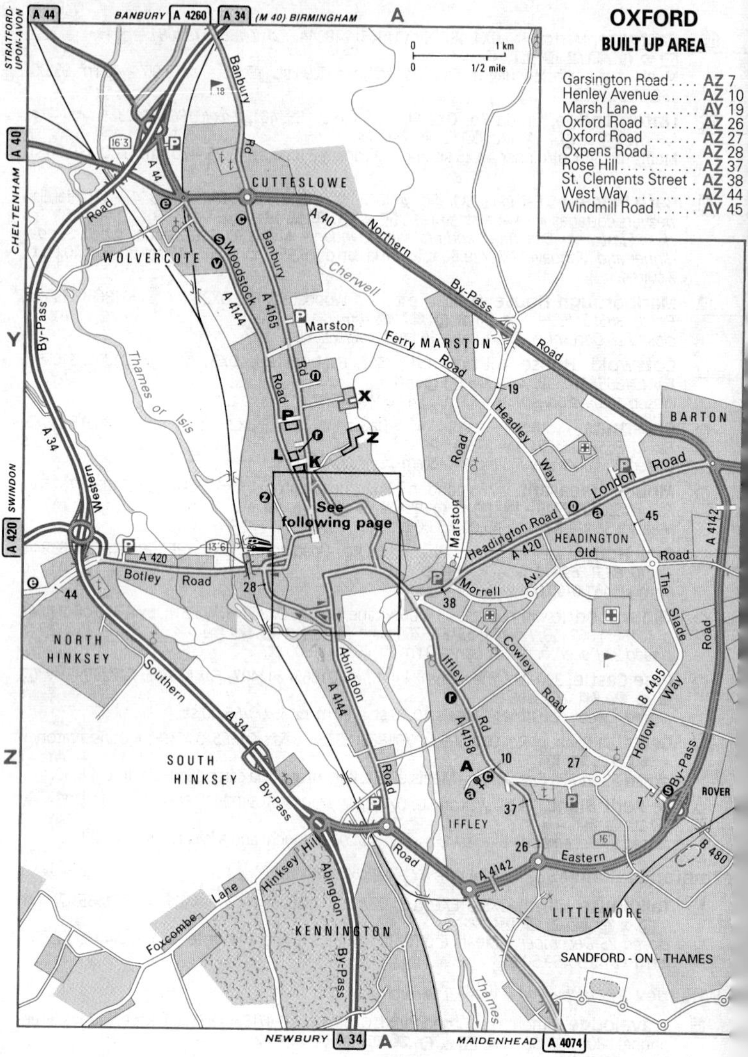

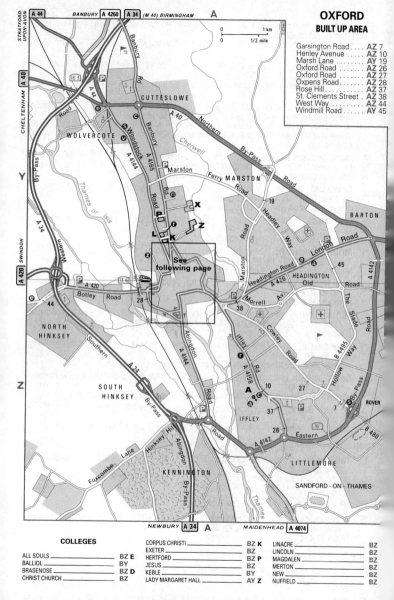

COLLEGES

ALL SOULS	BZ	E
BALLIOL	BY	
BRASENOSE	BZ	D
CHRIST CHURCH	BZ	
CORPUS CHRISTI	BZ	K
EXETER	BZ	
HERTFORD	BZ	P
JESUS	BZ	
KEBLE	BY	
LADY MARGARET HALL	AY	Z
LINACRE	BZ	
LINCOLN	BZ	
MAGDALEN	BZ	
MERTON	BZ	
NEW	BZ	
NUFFIELD	BZ	

at Great Milton *SE : 12 m. by A 40 off A 329 – AY –* ✉ *Oxford.*

Le Manoir aux Quat' Saisons (Blanc) ⚘, Church Rd, OX44 7PD, ☎ (01844) 27888
Fax (01844) 278847, ←, « Part 15C and 16C manor house, gardens », park, 🎾 – ⇔ re
▤ rest, [TV] ☎ [P] – 🏛 35. [MC] [AE] [O] [VISA] [JCB]. ✱
closed 5 to 19 January – **Meals** - French - 32.00 **t.** (lunch Monday to Saturday) and a la ca
63.00/78.00 **t.** – ☕ 13.50 – **16 rm** 195.00/295.00 **t.**, 3 suites – SB
Spec. Aiguillette de saumon sauvage en gelée, sauce aigre doux au caviar. Assiet
d'agneau de lait et jus de cuisson. Soufflé à la pistache et sorbet cacao amer.

OXFORD

CENTRE

0 ___ 200 m
0 ___ 200 yards

t Cumnor W : 4 ¼ m. by A 420 – AY – on B 4017 – ⊠ Oxford.

✕ **Bear and Ragged Staff,** Appleton Rd, OX2 9QH, ✆ (01865) 862329, Fax (01865) 865366
– **P. ⬛⬛ AE VISA**
Meals *(closed 3-4 days Christmas-New Year)* a la carte 18.00/28.85 **t**.

Ⓜ ATS Pony Rd, Horspath Trading Est., Cowley ATS 2 Stephen Rd, Headington ✆ (01865) 61732
✆ (01865) 777188

491

OXHILL *Warks.* [403] [404] P 27 – *pop. 303* – ✉ *Stratford-upon-Avon.*
London 85 – Birmingham 32 – Oxford 25.

Nolands Farm 🐎, CV35 0RJ, on A 422 ☎ (01926) 640309, *Fax (01926) 641662,* 🐟, 🌳 – 🚭 rest, [TV] [P]. [MC] [VISA]. 🐕
closed Christmas and New Year – **Meals** (by arrangement) 16.95 **st.** 🍷 3.00 – **8 rm** 🛏 30.00/44.00 **st.**

PADSTOW *Cornwall* [403] F 32 *The West Country G.* – *pop. 2 460.*
See : *Town*★.
Env. : *Trevone (Cornwall Coast Path*★★*) W : 3 m. by B 3276 – Trevose Head*★ *(<*★★*) W : 6 m. by B 3276.*
Exc. : *Bedruthan Steps*★, *SW : 7 m. by B 3276 – Pencarrow*★, *SE : 11 m. by A 389.*
⛳18, ⛳9, ⛳9 *Trevose, Constantine Bay* ☎ *(01841) 520208.*
[i] *Red Brick Building, North Quay, PL28 8AF* ☎ *(01841) 533449 (summer only).*
London 288 – Exeter 78 – Plymouth 45 – Truro 23.

Metropole, Station Rd, PL28 8DB, ☎ (01841) 532486, *Fax (01841) 532867,* < Came Estuary, 🏊, 🌳 – [lift] 🚭 [TV] ☎ ♿ [P] – 🎤 50. [MC] [AE] [DC] [VISA]
Meals (bar lunch Monday to Saturday)/dinner a la carte 14.45/21.25 **t.** 🍷 6.95 – 🛏 8.75 – **50 rm** 75.00/150.00 **t.** – SB.

St. Petroc's House, 4 New St., PL28 8EA, ☎ (01841) 532700, *Fax (01841) 532942* – [TV] ☎ [P]. [MC] [VISA]
closed 1 week Christmas – ***St. Petrocs Bistro :*** **Meals** *(closed Monday)* (booking essential 18.95 **t.** 🍷 7.50 – **13 rm** 🛏 33.00/105.00 **t.** – SB.

Dower House without rest., Fentonluna Lane, PL28 8BA, ☎ (01841) 532317 *Fax (01841) 532667* – 🚭 [TV] ☎ [P]. [MC] [VISA]. 🐕 – *March-November* – **6 rm** 🛏 42.00 80.00 **st.**

Old Custom House Inn, South Quay, PL28 8ED, ☎ (01841) 532359, *Fax (01841) 533372* < Camel Estuary and harbour – 🚭 rest, ▤ rest, [TV] ☎. [MC] [AE] [DC] [VISA]
Meals (bar lunch Monday to Saturday) (carving lunch Sunday) a la carte 15.35/23.95 **t** 🍷 5.70 – **26 rm** 🛏 71.00/100.00 **t.**

Middle Street Cafe, Middle St., PL28 8AP, ☎ (01841) 532777, *Fax (01841) 533566,* 🍽 – 🚭 rest, [TV]. [MC] [VISA]
closed 3 weeks January – **Meals** *(closed Sunday)* (light lunch)/dinner 14.95 **t.** – **3 rm** 🛏 37.00/70.00 **t.**

Woodlands, Treator, PL28 8RU, W : 1 ¼ m. by A 389 on B 3276 ☎ (01841) 532426 *Fax (01841) 532426,* <, 🌳 – 🚭 [TV] [P]. 🐕
April-30 October – **Meals** (by arrangement) 12.00 🍷 6.75 – **9 rm** 🛏 30.00/54.00 **s.** – SB.

Treverbyn House without rest., Station Rd, PL28 8AD, ☎ (01841) 532855, <, 🌳 – [TV] [P]. 🐕 – *closed January* – **3 rm** 🛏 40.00/70.00 **t.**

🍴🍴 **Seafood** with rm, Riverside, PL28 8BY, ☎ (01841) 532485, *Fax (01841) 533344,* < « Attractively converted granary on quayside » – [TV] ☎ [P]. [MC] [VISA]
closed 1 week Christmas and 30 December-7 February – **Meals** - Seafood - *(closed Sunday)* (booking essential) 26.50/32.50 **t.** and a la carte 37.55/54.75 **t.** 🍷 7.50 – **10 rm** 🛏 48.75 125.00 **t.** – SB.

🍴 **Bistro Margot Thomas,** 11 Duke St., PL28 8AB, ☎ (01841) 533441 – 🚭. [MC] [VISA]
closed January – **Meals** (booking essential) (dinner only) 22.95 **t.**

at Little Petherick *S : 3 m. on A 389* – ✉ *Wadebridge.*

Molesworth Manor without rest., PL27 7QT, ☎ (01841) 540292, <, « Part 17C and 19 rectory », 🌳 – [P]. 🐕 – *closed November and December* – **10 rm** 🛏 20.00/56.00 **st.**

Old Mill Country House without rest., PL27 7QT, ☎ (01841) 540388, « Part 16C cor mill », 🌳 – [P]. [MC] [AE] [VISA]. 🐕 – *March-October* – **6 rm** 🛏 57.00/61.00.

at St. Issey *S : 3½ m. on A 389* – ✉ *Wadebridge.*

Olde Treodore House 🐎 without rest., PL27 7QS, N : ¼ m. off A 38 ☎ (01841) 540291, <, 🌳 – 🚭 [TV] [P]
closed Christmas and restricted opening during winter – **3 rm** 🛏 38.00/52.00.

at Constantine Bay *SW : 4 m. by B 3276* – ✉ *Padstow.*

Treglos 🐎, PL28 8JH, ☎ (01841) 520727, *Fax (01841) 521163,* <, 🏊, 🌳 – [lift] 🚭, ▤ res [TV] ☎ 🚗 [P]. [MC] [VISA]
12 March-7 November – **Meals** 12.00/22.50 **t.** and dinner a la carte – **41 rm** 🛏 (dinn included) 74.00/148.00 **st.**, 3 suites – SB.

PADWORTH *Berks.* [403] [404] Q 29 – *pop. 545* – ✉ *Reading.*
London 58 – Basingstoke 12 – Reading 10.

Courtyard by Marriott Reading, Bath Rd, RG7 5HT, on A 4 ☎ (01189) 71441 *Fax (01189) 714442,* 🏋 – 🚭 ▤ [TV] ☎ ♿ [P] – 🎤 180. [MC] [AE] [DC] [VISA]. 🐕
Meals a la carte 12.85/21.25 **t.** 🍷 6.95 – **50 rm** 🛏 80.00/110.00 **t.** – SB.

PAIGNTON *Torbay* 403 J 32 *The West Country G.* – pop. 42 989.

See : Torbay★ - Kirkham House★ *AC* Y **B.**

Env. : *Paignton Zoo★★ AC, SW :* ½ m. by A 3022 AY *(see Plan of·Torbay)* – Cockington★, N : 3 m. by A 3022 and minor roads.

🛈 The Esplanade, TQ4 6BN 🖉 (01803) 558383.

London 226 – Exeter 26 – Plymouth 29.

Plan of Built up Area : see Torbay

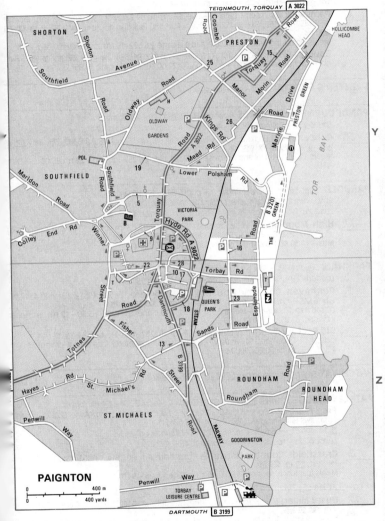

Hyde Road	Y	Church Street	Y 9	Great Western Way	Z 18
Torbay Road	Z	Commercial Road	Z 10	Higher Polsham Road	Y 19
Torquay Road	Y	Elmsleigh Road	Z 13	Palace Avenue	Z 22
Victoria Road	Z 28	Eugene Road	Y 15	Queen's Road	Z 23
		Garfield Road	Y 16	Upper Manor Road	Y 25
Cecil Road	Y 5	Gerston Road	Z 17	Upper Morin Road	Y 26

493

Redcliffe, 4 Marine Drive, TQ3 2NL, ℰ (01803) 526397, Fax (01803) 528030, ≤ Torbay, ♣, ⇌, ⃗, ▣, ⌀ – ▤, ⎗ rest, 🅣 ☎ 🅟 – ♨ 200. ⅏ 🆄 𝚅𝙸𝚂𝙰. ⅏
Meals (bar lunch Monday to Saturday/dinner 15.75 **st.** and a la carte ▯ 5.50 – **58 rm** ⌂ 42.00/110.00 **st.** – SB.

Ⓐ ATS Orient Rd ℰ (01803) 556888

PAINSWICK Glos. 🄰🄾🄱 🄰🄾🄲 N 28 Great Britain G. – pop. 1 628.
See : Town★.
London 107 – Bristol 35 – Cheltenham 10 – Gloucester 7.

Painswick ⌂, Kemps Lane, GL6 6YB, SE : ½ m. by Bisley St., St. Marys St. and Tibbiwell ℰ (01452) 812160, Fax (01452) 814059, « Part 18C Palladian house », 🌳 – 🅣 ☎ 🅟. ⅏ 🆄 𝚅𝙸𝚂𝙰. ⅏
Meals (light lunch)/dinner 24.50 **t.** and a la carte ▯ 6.50 – **19 rm** ⌂ 75.00/150.00 **t.** – SB.

Country Elephant, New St., GL6 6XH, ℰ (01452) 813564, 🌳 – ⎗. ⅏ 🆄 ⓞ 𝚅𝙸𝚂𝙰 𝙹𝙲𝙱
closed Sunday and Monday – Meals 13.00/22.00 **st.** and a la carte 26.85/33.45 **st.** ▯ 8.75.

PAINTER'S FORSTAL Kent – see Faversham.

PANGBOURNE-ON-THAMES Newbury 🄰🄾🄱 🄰🄾🄲 Q 29 – ✉ Reading.
London 53 – Basingstoke 18 – Newbury 16 – Oxford 22 – Reading 6.

Copper Inn, Church Rd, RG8 7AR, ℰ (01189) 842244, Fax (01189) 845542, 🍴, 🌳 – 🅣 ☎ ♨ – ♨ 60. ⅏ 🆄 ⓞ 𝚅𝙸𝚂𝙰. ⅏
Meals 14.50 **t.** (lunch) and a la carte 19.15/24.15 **t.** ▯ 6.25 – ⌂ 9.50 – **22 rm** 85.00/115.00 **t.** – SB.

PARBOLD Lancs. 🄰🄾🄴 L 23 Great Britain G. – pop. 2 872 – ✉ Wigan.
Env. : Rufford Old Hall★ (Great Hall★) AC, NW : 4 m. by B 5246.
London 212 – Liverpool 25 – Manchester 24 – Preston 19.

High Moor Inn, High Moor Lane, WN6 9QA, NE : 3 m. by B 5246 and Chorley Rd ℰ (01257) 252364, Fax (01257) 255120 – ⎗ 🅟. ⅏ 🆄 ⓞ 𝚅𝙸𝚂𝙰
Meals 11.50 **st.** (lunch) and dinner a la carte 17.00/23.00 **t.**

PARKHAM Devon 🄰🄾🄱 H 31 – ✉ Bideford.
London 229 – Barnstaple 14 – Exeter 87 – Plymouth 58.

Penhaven Country House ⌂, Rectory Lane, EX39 5PL, ℰ (01237) 451711, Fax (01237) 451878, 🌳, park – ⎗ rest, 🅣 ☎ 🅟. ⅏ 🆄 ⓞ 𝚅𝙸𝚂𝙰
closed 4 to 30 January – Meals 9.95/13.95 **t.** and dinner a la carte ▯ 5.50 – **12 rm** ⌂ (dinner included) 62.95/135.90 **st.** – SB.

Old Rectory ⌂, Rectory Lane, EX39 5PL, ℰ (01237) 451443, 🌳 – ⎗ 🅟. 🆄. ⅏
closed 11 December-14 January – Meals (by arrangement) (communal dining) 23.00 **s.** ▯ 5.00 – **3 rm** ⌂ 50.00/78.00 **s.**

PATCHWAY South Gloucestershire 🄰🄾🄱 🄰🄾🄲 M 29 – see Bristol.

PATELEY BRIDGE N. Yorks. 🄰🄾🄴 O 21 Great Britain G. – pop. 2 504 – ✉ Harrogate.
Exc. : Fountains Abbey★★★ AC - Studley Royal★★ AC (≤★ from Anne Boleyn's Seat) -
Fountains Hall (Façade★), NE : 8½ m. by B 6265.
🄱 14 High St., HG3 5AW ℰ (01423) 711147 (summer only).
London 225 – Leeds 28 – Middlesbrough 46 – York 32.

Grassfields Country House ⌂, Low Wath Rd, HG3 5HL, ℰ (01423) 711412, 🌳 –
⎗ rest, 🅟. ⅏ 𝚅𝙸𝚂𝙰
Meals (bar lunch)/dinner 13.00 **t.** and a la carte ▯ 4.25 – **9 rm** ⌂ 29.50/59.00 **st.**

at Low Laithe SE : 2¾ m. on B 6165 – ✉ Harrogate.

Dusty Miller, Main Rd, Summerbridge, HG3 4BU, ℰ (01423) 780837, Fax (01423) 780065
– 🅟. ⅏ 🆄 𝚅𝙸𝚂𝙰
closed Sunday, Monday, 25-26 December and 1 January – Meals (dinner only) 24.00 **t.** and a la carte 25.30/35.40 **t.** ▯ 4.45.

Carters Knox Manor with rm, Summer Bridge, HG3 4DQ, ℰ (01423) 780607 – ⎗ rm
🅣 🅟. ⅏ 𝚅𝙸𝚂𝙰
closed 25 and 26 December – Meals 12.50 **st.** and a la carte ▯ 4.50 – **4 rm** ⌂ 42.50/70.00 **st.** – SB.

at Wath-in-Nidderdale NW : 2 ¼ m. by Low Wath Rd – ⊠ Harrogate.

XX **Sportsman's Arms** ⤳ with rm, HG3 5PP, ℰ (01423) 711306, Fax (01423) 712524, �́ – ᐧᐧ 🆑 ⊡ 🅿. 🕦 𝘝𝘐𝘚𝘈. ✻
closed 25 December – **Meals** (in bar Monday to Saturday lunch and Sunday dinner)/
dinner 21.00 **st.** and a la carte 👌 5.80 – **7 rm** � 40.00/65.00 **st.** – SB.

at Ramsgill-in-Nidderdale NW : 5 m. by Low Wath Rd – ⊠ Harrogate.

🏛 **Yorke Arms** ⤳, HG3 5RL, ℰ (01423) 755243, Fax (01423) 755330 – ᐧᐧ rest, ⊡ ☎ 🅿. 🕦
🅰🅴 𝘝𝘐𝘚𝘈. ✻
Meals (bar lunch Monday to Saturday)/dinner 21.95 **t.** and a la carte 👌 4.95 – **13 rm**
� 40.00/60.00 **t.** – SB.

PATRICK BROMPTON N. Yorks. 402 P 21 – pop. 145 – ⊠ Bedale.
London 228 – Leeds 48 – Newcastle upon Tyne 33 – York 41.

🏛 **Elmfield House** ⤳, Arrathorne, DL8 1NE, NW : 2 ¼ m. by A 684 on Richmond rd
ℰ (01677) 450558, Fax (01677) 450557, 🌿, park – ᐧᐧ rest, ⊡ ☎ & 🅿. 🕦 𝘝𝘐𝘚𝘈. ✻
Meals (dinner only) 11.50 **st.** 👌 4.00 – **9 rm** � 31.00/60.00 **st.** – SB.

PAULERSPURY Northants. 403 404 R 27 – see Towcester.

PAYHEMBURY Devon – see Honiton.

PEASMARSH E. Sussex 404 W 31 – see Rye.

PEEL Isle of Man 402 F 21 – see Man (Isle of).

PELYNT Cornwall 403 G 32 – see Looe.

PEMBROKE BAY Guernsey (Channel Islands) 403 P 33 and 230 ⑩ – see Channel Islands.

PEMBURY Kent 404 U 30 – see Royal Tunbridge Wells.

PENDLEBURY Gtr. Manchester 402 403 404 N 23 – see Manchester.

PENDOGGETT Cornwall 403 F 32 – ⊠ Port Isaac.
London 264 – Newquay 22 – Truro 30.

🏠 **Cornish Arms** with rm, PL30 3HH, on B 3314 ℰ (01208) 880263, Fax (01208) 880335,
« Retaining 16C features » – ⊡ ☎ 🅿. 🕦 🅰🅴 ⓪ 𝘝𝘐𝘚𝘈 𝙅𝘊𝘽
Meals (bar lunch Monday to Saturday)/dinner 16.50 **t.** and a la carte 👌 6.50 – **7 rm** � 40.00/
70.00 **t.** – SB.

PENKRIDGE Staffs. 402 403 404 N 25 – pop. 7 212 – ⊠ Stafford.
London 140 – Birmingham 25 – Derby 41 – Leicester 56 – Shrewsbury 27 –
Stoke-on-Trent 23.

🏛 **Bridge House,** Stone Cross, ST19 5AS, on A 449 ℰ (01785) 714426, 🌿 – ⊡ 🅿
Meals a la carte 11.55/18.50 **st.** 👌 3.50 – **8 rm** � 25.00/40.00 **st.**

PENRITH Cumbria 401 402 L 19 – pop. 12 049.
🏌 Salkeld Rd ℰ (01768) 891919/65429.
🅱 Robinsons School, Middlegate, CA11 7PT ℰ (01768) 867466.
London 290 – Carlisle 24 – Kendal 31 – Lancaster 48.

🏛🏛 **North Lakes,** Ullswater Rd, CA11 8QT, S : 1 m. by A 592 at junction 40 of M 6
ℰ (01768) 868111, Fax (01768) 868291, 🏊, ☎, 🏊, squash – 📶, ᐧᐧ rm, ⊡ ☎ & 🅿 –
🔏 200. 🕦 🅰🅴 ⓪ 𝘝𝘐𝘚𝘈 𝙅𝘊𝘽
Meals (closed Saturday lunch) 12.95/19.50 **st.** and a la carte 👌 7.95 – **84 rm** � 92.00/
146.00 **st.** – SB.

🏨 **Travelodge,** Redhills, CA11 0DT, SW : 1 ½ m. by A 592 on A 66 *&* (01768) 866958, Reservations (Freephone) 0800 850950 – ⇔ rm, 📺 ও 🄿. 🕮 🖭 ① 𝘝𝘐𝘚𝘈 𝗷𝗰𝗯. ⫝̸
Meals (grill rest.) – **40 rm** 44.95 **t.**

🔘 ATS Gilwilly Ind. Est. *&* (01768) 865656/7

PENSHURST Kent ⁪⁪⁪ U 30 *Great Britain G.* – pop. 1 509.
Env. : *Hever Castle*⋆ *AC*, W : 6 m. by B 2176 and B 2027.
London 38 – Maidstone 19 – Royal Tunbridge Wells 6.

⌂ **Swale Cottage** ॐ without rest., Poundsbridge Lane, TN11 8AH, SE : 1 m. by B 2176 off Poundsbridge Lane *&* (01892) 870738, ≤, 🞥 – ⇔ 📺 🄿. ⫝̸
3 rm ⊇ 45.00/65.00.

Dieser Führer ist kein vollständiges Hotel- und Restaurantverzeichnis.
Um den Ansprüchen aller Touristen gerecht zu werden,
haben wir uns auf eine Auswahl in jeder Kategorie beschränkt.

PENZANCE Cornwall ⁪⁪⁪ D 33 *The West Country G.* – pop. 19 709.
See : *Town*⋆ - *Outlook*⋆⋆⋆ – *Western Promenade* (≤⋆⋆⋆) YZ – *National Lighthouse Centre*⋆ *AC*Y – *Chapel St.*⋆ Y – *Maritime Museum*⋆ *AC*Y M1.
Env. : *St. Buryan*⋆⋆ (church tower⋆⋆), SW : 5 m. by A 30 and B 3283 – *Penwith*⋆⋆ – Sancreed - *Church*⋆⋆ (Celtic Crosses⋆⋆) - Carn Euny⋆, W : 3½ m. by A 30 Z – *St. Michael's Mount*⋆⋆ (≤⋆⋆), E : 4 m. by B 3311 – Y – and A 30 – *Gulval*⋆ (Church⋆), NE : 1 m. – *Ludgvan*⋆ (Church⋆), NE : 3½ m. by A 30 – *Chysauster Village*⋆, N : 3½ m. by A 30, B 3311 and minor rd – *Newlyn*⋆ - *Pilchard Works*⋆, SW : 1½ m. by B 3315 Z – *Lanyon Quoit*⋆, NW : 3½ m. by St. Clare Street – *Men-an-Tol*⋆, NW : 5 m. by B 3312 – *Madron Church*⋆, NW : 1½ m. by St. Clare Street Y.
Exc. : *Morvah* (≤⋆⋆), NW : 6½ m. by St. Clare Street Y – *Zennor* (Church⋆), NW : 6 m. by B 3311 Y – *Prussia Cove*⋆, E : 8 m. by B 3311 – Y – and A 394 – *Land's End*⋆ (cliff scenery⋆⋆⋆), SW : 10 m. by A 30 Z – *Porthcurno*⋆, SW : 8½ m. by A 30, B 3283 and minor rd.
Access to the Isles of Scilly by helicopter *&* (01736) 63871, Fax (01736) 64293.
⚓ to the Isles of Scilly (Hugh Town) (Isles of Scilly Steamship Co. Ltd) (summer only) (2 h 40 mn).
🛈 Station Rd, TR18 2NF *&* (01736) 362207.
London 319 – Exeter 113 – Plymouth 77 – Taunton 155.

Plan opposite

🏨 **Abbey,** Abbey St., TR18 4AR, *&* (01736) 366906, Fax (01736) 351163, « Attractively furnished 17C house », 🞥 – 📺 🄿. 🕮 🖭 𝘝𝘐𝘚𝘈   Y u
Meals (booking essential) (dinner only) 24.50 **st.** ♦ 6.50 – **6 rm** ⊇ 70.00/135.00 **t.**, 1 suite – SB.

🏨 **Beachfield,** The Promenade, TR18 4NW, *&* (01736) 362067, Fax (01736) 331100, ≤ – 📺 ☎. 🕮 🖭 𝘝𝘐𝘚𝘈   Z a
closed Christmas-New Year – Meals (bar lunch)/dinner 13.95 **t.** and a la carte – **18 rm** ⊇ 39.50/79.00 **t.** – SB.

🏨 **Tarbert,** 11 Clarence St., TR18 2NU, *&* (01736) 363758, Fax (01736) 331336 – ⇔ rest, 📺 ☎. 🕮 𝘝𝘐𝘚𝘈. ⫝̸   Y i
closed 25 December-2 January – Meals (dinner only) 15.50 **t.** and a la carte ♦ 5.50 – **12 rm** ⊇ 34.00/68.00 **t.** – SB.

⌂ **Estoril,** 46 Morrab Rd, TR18 4EX, *&* (01736) 362468, Fax (01736) 367471 – ⇔ 📺 ☎ 🄿. 🕮 𝘝𝘐𝘚𝘈. ⫝̸   Y o
closed December and January – Meals 14.00 **t.** ♦ 4.00 – **10 rm** ⊇ 27.00/54.00 **t.** – SB.

⌂ **Chy-An-Mor** without rest., 15 Regent Terr., TR18 4DW, *&* (01736) 363441, Fax (01736) 363441, ≤, 🞥 – ⇔ 📺 🄿. 🕮 𝘝𝘐𝘚𝘈 𝗷𝗰𝗯   Y e
March-October – **10 rm** ⊇ 27.00/49.00 **st.**

✗✗ **Harris's,** 46 New St., TR18 2LZ, *&* (01736) 364408, Fax (01736) 333273 – 🕮 🖭 𝘝𝘐𝘚𝘈 𝗷𝗰𝗯   Y a
closed Monday lunch, Monday dinner November-June, Sunday, 1 January, 25-26 December and 3 weeks winter – Meals a la carte 23.95/34.90 **st.** ♦ 9.50.

at Newlyn SW : 1½ m. on B 3315 – Z – ✉ Penzance.

🏨 **Higher Faugan** ॐ, TR18 5NS, SW : ¾ m. on B 3315 *&* (01736) 362076, Fax (01736) 351648, 🏊, 🞥, park, ✗ – ⇔ rest, 📺 ☎ 🄿. 🕮 🖭 ① 𝘝𝘐𝘚𝘈 𝗷𝗰𝗯
restricted opening in winter – Meals (by arrangement November-February) (bar lunch)/dinner 17.25 **st.** ♦ 4.25 – **11 rm** ⊇ 50.00/99.00 **st.** – SB.

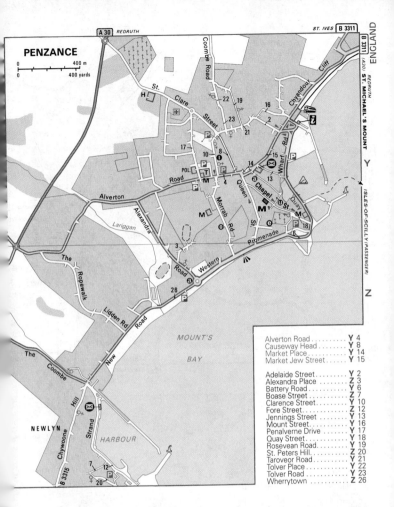

PENZANCE

0 — 400 m
0 — 400 yards

Alverton Road	Y	4
Causeway Head	Y	8
Market Place	Y	14
Market Jew Street	Y	15

Adelaide Street	Y	2
Alexandra Place	Z	3
Battery Road	Y	6
Boase Street	Z	7
Clarence Street	Y	10
Fore Street	Z	12
Jennings Street	Y	13
Mount Street	Y	16
Penalverne Drive	Y	17
Quay Street	Y	18
Rosevean Road	Y	19
St. Peters Hill	Z	20
Taroveor Road	Y	21
Tolver Place	Y	22
Tolver Road	Y	23
Wherrytown	Z	26

t **Drift** *SW : 2½ m. on A 30* – **Z** – ⊠ *Penzance*.

↑ **Rose Farm** ⤳ without rest., Chyanhal, Buryas Bridge, TR19 6AN, SW : ¾ m. on
Chyanhal rd ℘ (01736) 731808, *Fax (01736) 731808*, « Working farm », ☞ – 📺 ❷. ⛝
closed 25 and 26 December – **3 rm** ⌷ 25.00/42.00 **st.**

  🔘 ATS Jelbert Way, Eastern Green
  ℘ (01736) 362768

  ATS Units 25-26, Stable Hobba Ind. Est., Newlyn
  ℘ (01736) 369100

ERRANUTHNOE *Cornwall* 403 D 33 – *see Marazion.*

ETERBOROUGH 402 404 T 26 *Great Britain G.* – *pop.* 134 788.

See : *Cathedral*★★ *ACY.*

🛋 Thorpe Wood, Nene Parkway ℘ (01733) 267701, BX – 🛋 Peterborough Milton, Milton
Ferry ℘ (01733) 380204, BX – 🛋 Orton Meadows, Ham Lane ℘ (01733) 237478, BX.

🚩 45 Bridge St., PE1 1HA ℘ (01733) 452336.

London 85 – Cambridge 35 – Leicester 41 – Lincoln 51.

497

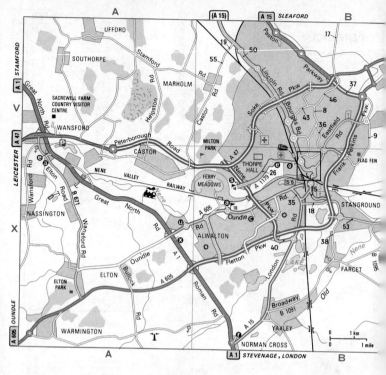

PETERBOROUGH

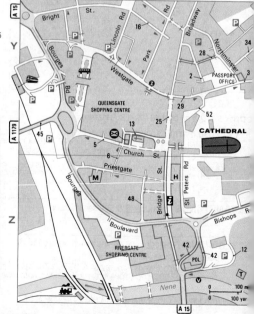

🏨 **Orton Hall,** The Village, Orton Longueville, PE2 7DN, SW : 2 ½ m. by Oundle Rd (A 605) ℘ (01733) 391111, *Fax (01733) 231912*, 🌳, park – ⇔ 📺 ☎ 🅿 – 🔬 120. 🆗 🄰🄴 ⓪ 𝗩𝗜𝗦𝗔
BX c
The Huntly Restaurant : Meals *(closed Saturday lunch and Sunday dinner)* 16.95 **st.** and dinner a la carte ⓘ 5.35 – ☲ 7.95 – **49 rm** 80.00/120.00 **st.** – SB.

🏨 **Peterborough Moat House,** Thorpe Wood, PE3 6SG, SW : 2 ¼ m. at roundabout 33 ℘ (01733) 289988, *Fax (01733) 262737*, Ⅰ₅, ≘s – |𝖍|, ⇔ rm, 🍽 rest, 📺 ☎ & 🅿 – 🔬 400.
BX s
🆗 🄰🄴 ⓪ 𝗩𝗜𝗦𝗔 𝗝𝗖𝗕
Meals *(bar lunch Saturday)* 14.95 **st.** and a la carte ⓘ 7.50 – ☲ 9.50 – **121 rm** 85.00/ 100.00 **st.**, 4 suites – SB.

🏨 **Bull,** Westgate, PE1 1RB, ℘ (01733) 61364, *Fax (01733) 557304* – ⇔ rm, 🍽 rest, 📺 ☎ 🅿
Y z
– 🔬 200. 🆗 🄰🄴 ⓪ 𝗩𝗜𝗦𝗔 𝗝𝗖𝗕. ❀
closed Christmas and New Year – **Meals** *(dancing Saturday evening)* 13.50 and a la carte ⓘ 6.25 – **102 rm** ☲ 68.50/79.00 **t.**, 1 suite – SB.

🏨 **Butterfly,** Thorpe Meadows, off Longthorpe Parkway, PE3 6GA, W : 1 m. by Thorpe Rd ℘ (01733) 64240, *Fax (01733) 65538* – ⇔ rm, 📺 ☎ & 🅿 – 🔬 80. 🆗 🄰🄴 ⓪ 𝗩𝗜𝗦𝗔 𝗝𝗖𝗕
Meals 13.75 **st.** *(dinner)* and a la carte 15.20/24.45 **st.** ⓘ 5.75 – ☲ 6.95 – **70 rm** 62.50 **st.** – SB.
BX e

🏨 **Thorpe Lodge,** 83 Thorpe Rd, PE3 6JQ, ℘ (01733) 348759, *Fax (01733) 891598* – 📺 ☎
🅿. 🆗 🄰🄴 ⓪ 𝗩𝗜𝗦𝗔. ❀
BX o
closed 1 week Christmas-New Year – **Meals** *(closed Saturday and Sunday)* a la carte 9.45/ 15.25 **st.** ⓘ 4.25 – **18 rm** ☲ 39.00/47.50 **st.**

🏨 **Travel Inn,** Ham Lane, Orton Meadows, PE2 0UU, SW : 3 ½ m. by Oundle Rd (A 605) ℘ (01733) 235794, *Fax (01733) 391055* – ⇔ rm, 🍽 rest, 📺 & 🅿. 🆗 🄰🄴 ⓪ 𝗩𝗜𝗦𝗔. ❀
Meals *(grill rest.)* – **40 rm** 36.50 **t.**
BX a

✕✕ **Grain Barge,** The Quayside, Embankment Rd, PE1 1EG, ℘ (01733) 311967 – 🍽. 🆗 🄰🄴 ⓪
𝗩𝗜𝗦𝗔
Z v
closed 25 and 26 December – **Meals** - Chinese (Peking) - *(buffet lunch Sunday)* 14.00 **st.** *(dinner)* and a la carte 13.90/23.20 **st.**

t Eye NE : 4 m. by A 47 – BV – ✉ Peterborough.

✕ **I Toscanini,** 2 Peterborough Rd, PE6 7YB, ℘ (01733) 223221, *Fax (01733) 755355*, 🍴 –
🅿. 🆗 🄰🄴 ⓪ 𝗩𝗜𝗦𝗔
closed Sunday dinner, Monday and 26 December – **Meals** - Italian - *(live music Thursday to Saturday evenings)* 13.50/20.00 **t.** and a la carte.

t Norman Cross S : 5 ¾ m. on A 15 at junction with A 1 – ✉ Peterborough.

🏨 **Forte Posthouse Peterborough,** Great North Rd, PE7 3TB, ℘ (01733) 240209, *Fax (01733) 244455*, Ⅰ₅, ≘s, ▨ – ⇔ rm, 🍽 rest, 📺 ☎ & 🅿 – 🔬 50. 🆗 🄰🄴 ⓪ 𝗩𝗜𝗦𝗔
BX r
𝗝𝗖𝗕
Meals a la carte 15.80/25.65 **st.** ⓘ 8.45 – ☲ 9.95 – **93 rm** 69.00/89.00 **st.** – SB.

t Alwalton SW : 5 ¾ m. on Oundle Rd (A 605) – ✉ Peterborough.

🏨 **Swallow,** Peterborough Business Park, Lynch Wood, PE2 6GB, (opposite East of England Showground) ℘ (01733) 371111, *Fax (01733) 236725*, Ⅰ₅, ≘s, ▨, 🌳 – ⇔, 🍽 rest, 📺 ☎
& 🅿 – 🔬 350. 🆗 🄰🄴 ⓪ 𝗩𝗜𝗦𝗔
AX u
Emperor : Meals 19.75 **st.** and a la carte ⓘ 5.50 – ***Laurels :*** Meals 15.50/18.00 **st.** and a la carte ⓘ 5.50 – **161 rm** ☲ 99.00/115.00 **st.**, 2 suites – SB.

🏨 **Travelodge,** Great North Rd, PE7 3UR, A 1 (southbound carriageway) ℘ (01733) 231109, *Fax (01733) 231109*, Reservations (Freephone) 0800 850950 – ⇔ rm, 📺 & 🅿. 🆗 🄰🄴 ⓪
𝗩𝗜𝗦𝗔 𝗝𝗖𝗕. ❀
AX x
Meals *(grill rest.)* – **32 rm** 44.95 **t.**

t Wansford W : 8½ m. by A 47 – ✉ Peterborough.

🏨 **Haycock,** PE8 6JA, ℘ (01780) 782223, *Fax (01780) 783031*, 🍴, « Part 17C coaching inn », 🌳 – ⇔ rm, 📺 ☎ & 🅿 – 🔬 150. 🆗 🄰🄴 ⓪ 𝗩𝗜𝗦𝗔
AX e
Meals a la carte 16.05/29.30 **st.** ⓘ 5.35 – **50 rm** ☲ 85.00/160.00 **st.** – SB.

⌂ **Stoneacre** ⟩ without rest., Elton Rd, PE8 6JT, S : ½ m. on unmarked drive ℘ (01780) 783283, 🌳 – ⇔ 📺 🅿
AX a
5 rm ☲ 30.00/50.00 **s.**

🔘 ATS Wareley Rd (off George St.) ℘ (01733) 67112/3

ETERSFIELD Hants. 𝟦𝟢𝟦 R 30 – *pop.* 12 177.

Ⅰ₈, Ⅰ₅ Heath Rd ℘ (01730) 263725.

🅱 County Library, 27 The Square, GU32 3HH ℘ (01730) 268829.
London 59 – Brighton 45 – Guildford 25 – Portsmouth 19 – Southampton 32 – Winchester 19.

🏨 **Langrish House** ⤴, Langrish, GU32 1RN, W : 3 ½ m. by A 272, ℰ (01730) 266941,
Fax (01730) 260543, ≤, ☞, park – 📺 ☎ 🅿 – 🔬 60. 🝿 🌃 🗛 ① 🗺. ⚡
closed 24 December-2 January – **Meals** (closed Bank Holidays) (bar lunch)/dinner 13.95 **t**
and a la carte ⒥ 3.95 – **18 rm** ⊆ 48.00/95.00 **t.** – SB.

🝿 ATS 15 Dragon St. ℰ (01730) 265151

PETERSTOW Herefordshire 🝿🝿 🝿🝿 M 28 – see Ross-on-Wye.

PETWORTH W. Sussex 🝿🝿 S 31 Great Britain G. – pop. 2 156.
See : Petworth House★★ AC.
🝿 Osiers Farm ℰ (01798) 344097.
London 54 – Brighton 31 – Portsmouth 33.

✗ **Horse Guards Inn** with rm, Upperton Rd, Tillington, GU28 9AF, W : 1 ½ m. by A 272,
ℰ (01798) 342332, ☞ – ⤧ rm, 📺. 🝿 🗛 🗺. ⚡
closed 25 December – **Meals** (booking essential) a la carte 15.75/25.00 **t.** ⒥ 7.50 – **3 rm**
⊆ 62.00 **t.**

at Sutton S : 5 m. by A 283 – ⊠ Pulborough.

🍴 **White Horse Inn** with rm, The Street, RH20 1PS, ℰ (01798) 869221, Fax (01798) 869291,
☞ – 📺 ☎ 🅿. 🝿 🗛 ① 🗺. ⚡
Meals a la carte 13.00/21.80 **t.** ⒥ 6.50 – **6 rm** ⊆ 48.00/68.00 **st.** – SB.

PEVENSEY E. Sussex 🝿🝿 V 31 – pop. 2 833.
London 74 – Brighton 25 – Folkestone 49.

🏠 **Priory Court**, BN24 5LG, ℰ (01323) 763150, Fax (01323) 769030, ☞ – 📺 🅿. 🝿 🗺. ⚡
Meals 9.95/11.95 **st.** and a la carte – **10 rm** ⊆ 35.00/70.00 **st.** – SB.

PEWSEY Wilts. 🝿🝿 🝿🝿 O 29 – pop. 2 831.
London 88 – Bristol 53 – Salisbury 21 – Swindon 19.

✗✗✗ **London House**, Market Pl., SN9 5AB, ℰ (01672) 564775, Fax (01672) 564785 – ⤧. 🝿 🗛
① 🗺
closed Monday lunch, Sunday, Bank Holidays and 18-19 September – **Meals** 24.00
(lunch) and a la carte 28.00/38.00 **t.** ⒥ 8.00.

🍴 **Seven Stars**, Bottlesford, SN9 6LU, W : 3 ½ m. by Wilcot Rd off Woodborough rd
ℰ (01672) 851325, Fax (01672) 851583, « 18C thatched inn », ☞ – 🅿. 🝿 🗺 🗛
closed Sunday dinner, Monday and 2 weeks February – **Meals** a la carte 13.65/20.75
⒥ 6.25.

PICKERING N. Yorks. 🝿🝿 R 21 – pop. 5 914.
🝿 Eastgate Car Park, YO18 7DU ℰ (01751) 473791.
London 237 – Middlesbrough 43 – Scarborough 19 – York 25.

🏨 **Forest and Vale**, Malton Rd, YO18 7DL, ℰ (01751) 472722, Fax (01751) 472972, ☞
⤧ rest, 📺 ☎ 🅿 – 🔬 40. 🝿 🗛 ① 🗺
Meals 8.55/16.25 **t.** and a la carte ⒥ 6.95 – **17 rm** ⊆ 53.00/73.00 **t.** – SB.

🏠 **White Swan**, Market Pl., YO18 7AA, ℰ (01751) 472288, Fax (01751) 475554 – ⤧ 📺
🅿. 🝿 🗛 🗺
Meals (lunch by arrangement Monday to Saturday)/dinner a la carte 14.45/22.50 **t.** ⒥ 5.50
11 rm ⊆ 50.00/80.00 **t.**, 1 suite – SB.

🏠 **Burgate House**, 17 Burgate, YO18 7AU, ℰ (01751) 473463, Fax (01751) 473463, ☞ – 🝿
☎ 🅿. 🝿 🗺
closed 24 to 27 December – **Meals** 10.00/13.00 **st.** ⒥ 3.50 – **6 rm** ⊆ 40.00/60.00 **st.** – SB.

✗ **The Lodge** with rm, Middleton Rd, YO18 8NQ, W : ½ m. ℰ (01751) 472971,
Fax (01751) 476852, ☞ – 📺 ☎ 🅿. 🝿 🗺 🗛
Meals (closed Monday) a la carte 14.95/25.25 **t.** ⒥ 5.50 – **8 rm** ⊆ 42.00/56.00 **t.** – SB.

at Middleton NW : 1½ m. on A 170 – ⊠ Pickering.

🏠 **Cottage Leas** ⤴, Nova Lane, YO18 8PN, N : 1 m. ℰ (01751) 472129, Fax (01751) 474938,
☞, ✗, – 📺 ☎ 🅿. 🝿 🗺 🗛
closed 25 and 26 December – **Meals** (dinner only) a la carte 13.85/22.75 **t.** ⒥ 5.95 – **12 rm**
⊆ 40.00/70.00 **t.** – SB.

⚲ **Sunnyside**, Carr Lane, YO18 8PD, ℰ (01751) 476104, Fax (01751) 476104, ☞ – ⤧ rest,
📺 🝿 🗺
closed December and January – **Meals** (by arrangement) 12.00 – **3 rm** ⊆ 26.00/40.00 **st.** –
SB.

at Sinnington NW : 4 m. by A 170 – ⊠ York.

🏛 **Fox and Hounds,** Main St., YO6 6SQ, ☎ (01751) 431577, Fax (01751) 432791, 🐴 – ⤢
📺 ☎ 🅿. 🐾 VISA
Meals a la carte 15.40/22.40 **t.** ⅟ 7.55 – **10 rm** ⊑ 42.00/64.00 **t.**

PICKHILL N. Yorks. 402 P 21 – pop. 412 – ⊠ Thirsk.
London 229 – Leeds 41 – Middlesbrough 30 – York 34.

🏛 **Nags Head Country Inn,** YO7 4JG, ☎ (01845) 567391, Fax (01845) 567212, « Part
18C », 🐴 – ⤢ 📺 ☎ 🅿. 🐾 VISA JCB. ⅙
Meals (lunch by arrangement Monday to Saturday) (in bar Sunday dinner)/dinner 17.00 **t.**
and a la carte ⅟ 4.95 – **15 rm** ⊑ 36.00/50.00 **t.**

PILLING Lancs. 402 L 22 – pop. 2 204 – ⊠ Preston.
London 243 – Blackpool 11 – Burnley 43 – Manchester 49.

🏛 **Springfield House** ⅌, Wheel Lane, PR3 6HL, ☎ (01253) 790301, Fax (01253) 790907,
🐴 – ⤢ rest, 📺 ☎ 🅿. 🐾 VISA JCB
Meals 9.95/15.95 **t.** ⅟ 5.50 – **8 rm** ⊑ 35.00/59.50 **t.** – SB.

PIMPERNE Dorset 403 404 N 31 – see Blandford Forum.

Benutzen Sie für weite Fahrten in Europa die **Michelin-Länderkarten** :

970 Europa, 976 Tschechische Republik-Slowakische Republik,
980 Griechenland, 984 Deutschland, 985 Skandinavien-Finnland,
986 Großbritannien-Irland, 987 Deutschland-Österreich-Benelux, 988 Italien,
989 Frankreich, 990 Spanien-Portugal, 991 Jugoslawien.

PLUCKLEY Kent 404 W 30 – pop. 883.
London 53 – Folkestone 25 – Maidstone 18.

↑ **Elvey Farm** ⅌, TN27 0SU, W : 2 m. by Smarden rd and Marley Farm rd, off Mundy Bois rd
☎ (01233) 840442, Fax (01233) 840726, ≼, « Converted oast house and barn », 🐴 – 📺 🅿.
🐾 VISA JCB
Meals (by arrangement) 16.75 **st.** ⅟ 6.50 – **9 rm** ⊑ 45.50/65.50 **st.** – SB.

🍴 **Dering Arms,** TN27 0RR, S : 1 ½ m. on Bethersden rd ☎ (01233) 840371,
Fax (01233) 840498, 🐴 – 🅿. 🐾 AE VISA
closed Sunday dinner, Monday and 26 to 28 December – **Meals** a la carte 15.65/26.40 **t.**
⅟ 5.45.

PLUMFORD Kent – see Faversham.

PLUMTREE Notts. – see Nottingham.

PLYMOUTH Devon 403 H 32 The West Country G. – pop. 245 295.
See : Town★★ – Smeaton's Tower (≼★★) AC BZ A – Plymouth Dome★ AC BZ – Royal
Citadel (Ramparts≼★★) AC BZ – City Museum and Art Gallery★ BZ M.
Env. : – Saltram House★★ AC, E : 3½ m. BY A – Tamar River★★ – Anthony House★ AC, W :
5 m. by A 374 – Mount Edgcumbe (≼★) AC, SW : 2 m. by passenger ferry from Stonehouse
AZ
Exc. : NE : Dartmoor National Park★★ – Buckland Abbey★ AC, N : 7½ m. by A 386 ABY
🏌 Staddon Heights, Plymstock ☎ (01752) 402475 – 🏌 Elfordleigh Hotel G & C.C., Colebrook,
Plympton ☎ (01752) 336428.
Tamar Bridge (toll) AY
✈ Plymouth City (Roborough) Airport : ☎ (01752) 772752, N : 3½ m. by A 386 ABY
⛴ to France (Roscoff) (Brittany Ferries) 1-3 daily (6 h) – to Spain (Santander) (Brittany
Ferries) 2 weekly (24 h).
🛈 Island House, 9 The Barbican, PL1 2LS ☎ (01752) 264849.
London 242 – Bristol 124 – Southampton 161.

Plans on following pages

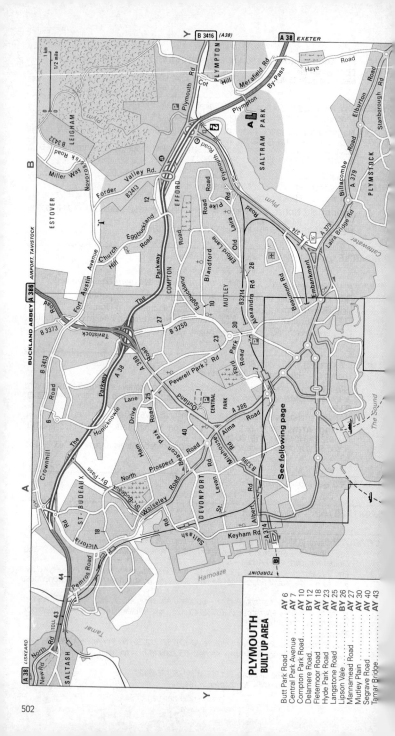

502

PLYMOUTH
BUILT UP AREA

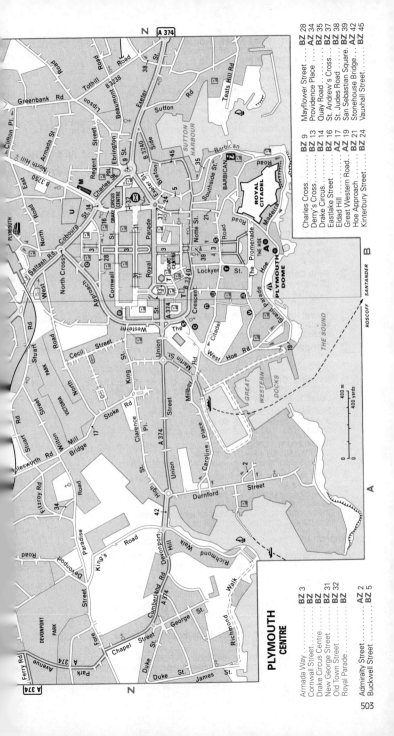

PLYMOUTH CENTRE

503

🏨 **Plymouth Hoe Moat House,** Armada Way, PL1 2HJ, ℰ (01752) 639988
Fax (01752) 673816, ≤ city and Plymouth Sound, ₤s, ⇌s, ⬛ – ▯ ⟨×⟩, ▤ rest, ⧆ ⬛ & ⇆
– ₰ 400. 🐵 ᴀᴇ ⓪ 𝘝𝘐𝘚𝘈. ⌘
BZ
Blue Riband : Meals (closed Saturday lunch) 14.00/19.50 st. and dinner a la carte ₰ 7.50 –
⌑ 10.50 – **209 rm** 105.00/145.00 st. – SB.

🏨 **Copthorne Plymouth,** Armada Centre, Armada Way, PL1 1AR, (via Western Approach
southbound) ℰ (01752) 224161, Fax (01752) 670688, ₤s, ⬛ – ▯, ⟨×⟩ rm, ▤ rest, ⧆ ⬛ &
🅿 – ₰ 150. 🐵 ᴀᴇ ⓪ 𝘝𝘐𝘚𝘈 𝐉𝐂𝐁. ⌘
BZ
Meals (dinner only) 18.95 st. and a la carte ₰ 6.85 – **Burlington :** Meals (dinner only and
Sunday lunch)/dinner 18.95 st. and a la carte ₰ 6.85 – ⌑ 10.95 – **135 rm** 95.00/160.00 st. –
SB.

🏨 **The Duke of Cornwall,** Millbay Rd, PL1 3LG, ℰ (01752) 266256, Fax (01752) 600062
▯, ⟨×⟩ rm, ⧆ ⬛ 🅿 – ₰ 300. 🐵 ᴀᴇ ⓪ 𝘝𝘐𝘚𝘈 𝐉𝐂𝐁
AZ
closed 23 to 30 December – **Meals** (bar lunch Saturday) 21.25 st. ₰ 6.65 – **67 rm** ⌑ 69.50
89.50 st., 3 suites – SB.

🏨 **Grand,** Elliot St., The Hoe, PL1 2PT, ℰ (01752) 661195, Fax (01752) 600653, ≤ – ▯ ⟨×⟩ ⧆
☎ 🅿 – ₰ 70. 🐵 ᴀᴇ 𝘝𝘐𝘚𝘈
BZ
Meals (residents only Saturday lunch) (dancing Saturday evening) 10.50/17.50 st.
and a la carte ₰ 6.25 – **77 rm** ⌑ 75.00/135.00 st. – SB.

🏨 **Forte Posthouse Plymouth,** Cliff Rd, The Hoe, PL1 3DL, ℰ (01752) 662828
Fax (01752) 660974, ≤ Plymouth Sound, ⬛ – ▯, ⟨×⟩ rm, ⧆ ☎ 🅿 – ₰ 100. 🐵 ᴀᴇ ⓪ 𝘝𝘐𝘚𝘈
Meals 8.95 st. (lunch) and dinner a la carte approx. 20.00 st. ₰ 7.25 – ⌑ 8.95 – **106 rm**
69.00 st. – SB.

🏨 **New Continental,** Millbay Rd, PL1 3LD, ℰ (01752) 220782, Fax (01752) 227013, ₤s, ⇌s
⬛ – ▯, ⟨×⟩ rm, ⧆ ☎ 🅿 – ₰ 400. 🐵 ᴀᴇ ⓪ 𝘝𝘐𝘚𝘈
AZ
closed 24 December-2 January – **Meals** (bar lunch Saturday and Bank Holidays) 9.95
16.25 t. and a la carte – **99 rm** ⌑ 69.00/130.00 t. – SB.

🏨 **Travel Inn,** 300 Plymouth Rd, Crabtree, PL3 6RW, ℰ (01752) 600660 – ⟨×⟩ rm, ⧆ &
🐵 ᴀᴇ ⓪ 𝘝𝘐𝘚𝘈. ⌘
BY
Meals (grill rest.) – **40 rm** 36.50 t.

🏨 **Campanile,** Longbridge Rd, Marsh Mills, PL6 8LD, ℰ (01752) 601087, Fax (01752) 2232
– ⟨×⟩ rm, ⧆ ☎ & 🅿 – ₰ 30. 🐵 ᴀᴇ ⓪ 𝘝𝘐𝘚𝘈
BY
Meals 10.55 st. and a la carte ₰ 5.50 – ⌑ 4.50 – **50 rm** 36.50 st.

🏠 **Bowling Green** without rest., 9-10 Osborne Pl., Lockyer St., The Hoe, PL1 2PB
ℰ (01752) 209090, Fax (01752) 209092 – ⧆ ☎. 🐵 ᴀᴇ ⓪ 𝘝𝘐𝘚𝘈
BZ
closed 24 to 26 December – **12 rm** ⌑ 36.00/48.00 st.

🏠 **Berkeley's of St. James** without rest., 4 St. James Place East, The Hoe, PL1 3AS
ℰ (01752) 221654 – ⟨×⟩ ⧆. 🐵 𝘝𝘐𝘚𝘈. ⌘
AZ
closed 3 days Christmas – **5 rm** ⌑ 25.00/40.00 s.

🏠 **Athenaeum Lodge** without rest., 4 Athenaeum St., The Hoe, PL1 2RQ
ℰ (01752) 665005 – ⟨×⟩ ⧆ 🅿. 🐵 𝘝𝘐𝘚𝘈. ⌘
BZ
closed 26 December and 1 January – **10 rm** ⌑ 17.00/38.00.

✕ **Chez Nous** (Marchal), 13 Frankfort Gate, PL1 1QA, ℰ (01752) 266793, Fax (01752) 2667
💠 – 🐵 ᴀᴇ ⓪ 𝘝𝘐𝘚𝘈
AZ
closed Sunday, Monday, first 3 weeks February, first 3 weeks September and Bank Holidays
Meals - French - 29.50 t. ₰ 10.50
Spec. Médaillons de lotteau coulis de tomate. Suprême de caneton aux lentilles. Meringu
et sa glace au citron vert avec coulis de pruneaux.

at Plympton NE : 5 m. by A 374 on B 3416 – BY – ✉ Plymouth.

🏨 **Boringdon Hall** ⏞, Boringdon Hill, PL7 4DP, N : 1 ½ m. by Glen Rd ℰ (01752) 344455
Fax (01752) 346578, « Part 16C manor », ⇌s, ⬛, park, ✕ – ⟨×⟩ ⧆ ☎ 🅿 – ₰ 150. 🐵
𝘝𝘐𝘚𝘈 𝐉𝐂𝐁. ⌘
The Gallery : Meals (bar lunch Saturday) (carving lunch Sunday) 15.00/18.95
and a la carte ₰ 5.75 – **40 rm** ⌑ 70.00/90.00 t. – SB.

🏠 **The Barn** ⏞, Hemerdon, PL7 5BU, NE : 2 ½ m. by Glen Rd and B 3417, turning left beside
telephone box after Miners Arms in Hemerdon ℰ (01752) 347016, Fax (01752) 33567
« Converted 19C barn », ⟨↗⟩ – ⟨×⟩ 🅿
closed Christmas and New Year – **Meals** (by arrangement) (communal dining) 19.00 s
₰ 4.70 – **3 rm** ⌑ 28.00/64.00 st.

🏠 **Windwhistle Farm** ⏞, Hemerdon, PL7 5BU, NE : 2 ½ m. by Glen Rd and B 3417
turning left beside telephone box after Miners Arms in Hemerdon ℰ (01752) 340600, ⟨↗⟩
⟨×⟩ ⧆ 🅿. ⌘
closed 22 to 29 December – **Meals** (by arrangement) (communal dining) 14.00 st. – **3 rm**
⌑ 22.00/44.00 st.

at Yealmpton *E : 8 m. by A 374 on A 379 –* BY *–* ⊠ *Plymouth*.

🏯 **Kitley** ⟡, The Kitley Estate, PL8 2NW, W : ½ m. on A 379 ℰ (01752) 881555, *Fax (01752) 881667*, ⟨, « *17C mansion* », 🐎, park – 📺 ☎ 🅿 – 🔬 150. 🆎 ⚏ *VISA* **Meals** (bar lunch Monday to Saturday)/dinner 23.50 **t.** and a la carte ⧍ 7.50 – **10 rm** ⊐ 68.00/78.00 **t.**, 1 suite – SB.

🅰 ATS Teats Hill Rd, Coxside ℰ (01752) 266217/ 227964 ATS Miller Way, Novorossisk Rd, Estover ℰ (01752) 769123

ATS Strode Rd, Newnham Ind. Est., Plympton ℰ (01752) 331001

PLYMPTON *Devon* 🔢 H 32 *– see Plymouth*.

PODIMORE *Somerset – see Yeovil*.

POLPERRO *Cornwall* 🔢 G 33 *The West Country G. –* ⊠ *Looe*.

See : *Village*★.

London 271 – Plymouth 28.

🏠 **Trenderway Farm** ⟡ *without rest.*, Pelynt, PL13 2LY, NE : 2 m. by A 387 ℰ (01503) 272214, *Fax (01503) 272991*, ⟨, « *16C farmhouse, working farm* », 🐎, park – 🕊 📺 🅿. ⟡ *closed Christmas-New Year –* **4 rm** ⊐ 45.00/65.00 **st.**

✗ **Kitchen**, The Coombes, PL13 2RQ, ℰ (01503) 272780 – 🕊. 🆎 *VISA* *Easter-October –* **Meals** *(closed Sunday)* (dinner only) a la carte 17.50/22.50 **t.** ⧍ 6.50.

I nomi delle principali vie commerciali sono scritti in rosso all'inizio dell'indice toponomastico delle piante di città.

PONTEFRACT *N. Yorks*. 🔢 Q 22.

London 194 – Leeds 16 – Manchester 53 – Nottingham 64 – Sheffield 29 – York 25.

🏨 **Travel Inn**, Knottingley Rd, Knottingley, WF11 0BU, NE : 2 ½ m. by A 645 ℰ (01977) 607946, *Fax (01977) 607954 –* 🕊 rm, 📺 ⅙ 🅿. 🆎 ⚏ ⓪ *VISA* **Meals** (grill rest.) – **40 rm** 36.50 **t.**

PONTELAND *Tyne and Wear* 🔢 🔢 O 19 *– see Newcastle upon Tyne*.

POOLE 🔢 🔢 O 31 *The West Country G. –* pop. 138 479.

See : *Town*★ *(Waterfront* **M1** *, Scaplen's Court* **M2** *)*.

Env. : *Compton Acres*★★★, *(English Garden* ⟨★★★*) AC*, SE : 3 m. by B 3369 BX *(on Bournemouth town plan) – Brownsea Island*★ *(Baden-Powell Stone* ⋇★★*) AC, by boat from Poole Quay or Sandbanks* BX *(on Bournemouth town plan)*.

🏌 *Parkstone, Links Rd* ℰ (01202) 707138 – 🏌 *Bulbury Woods, Lytchett Matravers* ℰ (01929) 459574.

🚢 *to France (Cherbourg) (Brittany Ferries Truckline) 1-2 daily (4 h 15 mn) day (5 h 45 mn) night – to France (St. Malo) (Brittany Ferries) (winter only) 4 weekly (8 h) – to France (St. Malo) via Jersey (St. Helier) (Condor Ferries Ltd) daily – to Guernsey (St. Peter Port) and Jersey (St. Helier) (Condor Ferries Ltd)*.

🛈 *The Quay, BH15 1HE* ℰ (01202) 253253 – *Dolphin Shopping Centre, BH15 1SZ*.

London 116 – Bournemouth 4 – Dorchester 23 – Weymouth 28.

Plan of Built up Area : see Bournemouth

🏯 **Haven**, Banks Rd, Sandbanks, BH13 7QL, SE : 4 ¼ m. on B 3369 ℰ (01202) 707333, *Fax (01202) 708796*, ⟨ Ferry, Old Harry Rocks and Poole Bay, 🛁, ⟰, ⧌, 🔲, ⟡, squash – 🛗 📺 ☎ 🅿 – 🔬 160. 🆎 ⚏ ⓪ *VISA*. ⟡ on Bournemouth town plan BX **c** **Meals** 15.00/22.50 **st.** and dinner a la carte ⧍ 6.00 – *Conservatory :* **Meals** (lunch only) a la carte 18.50/29.00 **st.** ⧍ 7.00 – (see also *La Roche* below) – **90 rm** ⊐ 75.00/232.00 **st.**, 2 suites – SB.

🏨 **Salterns**, 38 Salterns Way, Lilliput, BH14 8JR, ℰ (01202) 707321, *Fax (01202) 707488*, ⟨, « *Harbourside setting* », 🐎 – 🕊 rm, ▤ rest, 📺 ☎ 🅿 – 🔬 80. 🆎 ⚏ ⓪ *VISA* **Meals** 15.50/19.50 **t.** and dinner a la carte ⧍ 5.50 – ⊐ 9.50 – **20 rm** 76.00/120.00 **t.** – SB. on Bournemouth town plan BX **e**

POOLE

Dolphin Shopping Centre
High Street

Church Street 3

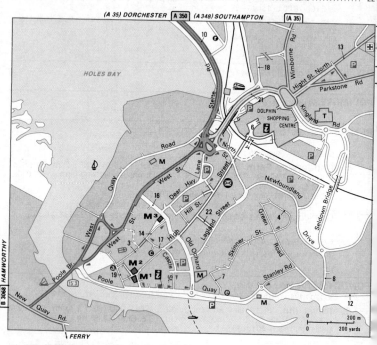

Mansion House, 7-11 Thames St., BH15 1JN, off Poole Quay *ℰ* (01202) 685666, Fax (01202) 665709, « 18C town house » – ▤ rest, 📺 ☎ 🅿 – 🔬 40. 🌑 🅰🅴 ⓞ 𝘝𝘐𝘚𝘈 🄹🄲🄱. ✁

Benjamin's : Meals *(closed Saturday lunch and Sunday dinner)* 13.50/22.50 **t.** ⌂ 6.25 –
JJ's Bistro : Meals *(closed Sunday dinner and Bank Holiday Mondays)* (residents only)
11.85 **t.** (dinner) and lunch a la carte 11.50/17.50 **t.** ⌂ 4.50 – **28 rm** ⌸ 82.50/125.00 **st.** – SB.

Quay Thistle, The Quay, BH15 1HD, *ℰ* (01202) 666800, Fax (01202) 684470, ≤ – |🛗|
✁ rm, 📺 ☎ 🅿 – 🔬 60. 🌑 🅰🅴 ⓞ 𝘝𝘐𝘚𝘈 🄹🄲🄱. ✁
Octagon : Meals 17.50/21.00 **t.** and a la carte ⌂ 6.00 – ⌸ 11.00 – **68 rm** 98.00/114.00 **st.** –
SB.

Arndale Court, 62-66 Wimborne Rd, BH15 2BY, *ℰ* (01202) 683746, Fax (01202) 668838 –
📺 ☎ 🅿 – 🔬 30. 🌑 🅰🅴 ⓞ 𝘝𝘐𝘚𝘈   on Bournemouth town plan ABX
Meals (bar lunch Monday to Saturday and Sunday dinner)/dinner a la carte 13.45/19.65 **st.**
⌂ 4.25 – **32 rm** ⌸ 51.00/70.00 **st.**

Travel Inn, Holesbay Rd, BH15 2BD, *ℰ* (01202) 669944, Fax (01202) 669954 – ✁ rm, 📺
& 🅿. 🌑 🅰🅴 ⓞ 𝘝𝘐𝘚𝘈. ✁
Meals (grill rest.) – **40 rm** 36.50 **t.**

La Roche (at Haven H.), Banks Rd, Sandbanks, BH13 7QL, *ℰ* (01202) 707333,
Fax (01202) 708796 – ✁ 🅿. 🌑 🅰🅴 ⓞ 𝘝𝘐𝘚𝘈   on Bournemouth town plan BX
closed Sunday and Monday – **Meals** (dinner only) a la carte 32.00/37.50 **st.** ⌂ 7.00.

John B's, 20 High St., Old Town, BH15 1BP, *ℰ* (01202) 672440, Fax (01202) 672440 – 🌑 🅰🅴
ⓞ 𝘝𝘐𝘚𝘈
closed Sunday except at Bank Holidays – **Meals** (dinner only) a la carte 19.50/27.50 **t.** ⌂ 6.50.

Isabel's, 32 Station Rd, Lower Parkstone, BH14 8UD, *ℰ* (01202) 747885 – 🌑 🅰🅴 ⓞ 𝘝𝘐𝘚𝘈
closed Sunday, Monday, 25-26 December and 1-2 January – **Meals** (dinner only) 18.00 **t.**
and a la carte ⌂ 4.95.   on Bournemouth town plan BX

🔘 ATS 1 Fernside Rd *ℰ* (01202) 733301/733326

506

ENGLAND

POOLEY BRIDGE Cumbria 401 402 L 20 – see Ullswater.

PORLOCK Somerset 403 J 30 The West Country G. – pop. 1 395 (inc. Oare) – ✉ Minehead.
See : Village★ – Porlock Hill (≤★★) – St. Dubricius Church★ – Env. : Dunkery Beacon★★★ (≤★★★), S : 5½ m. – Exmoor National Park★★ – Selworthy★ (≤★★, Church★), E : 2 m. by A 39 and minor rd – Luccombe★ (Church★), E : 3 m. by A 39 – Culbone★ (St. Beuno), W : 3½ m. by B 3225, 1½ m. on foot – Doone Valley★, W : 6 m. by A 39, access from Oare on foot.
London 190 – Bristol 67 – Exeter 46 – Taunton 28.

🏠 **Oaks**, TA24 8ES, ℘ (01643) 862265, Fax (01643) 862265, ≤ Porlock Bay, 🐎 – ⅍ 📺 ☎ 🅿.
⁽⁾ 🆅🆂🅰
April-October – **Meals** (booking essential to non-residents) (dinner only) 24.00 **st.** ⅍ 5.00 –
9 rm ⊇ 55.00/90.00 **st.** – SB.

⌂ **Bales Mead** ⌂ without rest., West Porlock, TA24 8NX, NW : 1 m. on B 3225
℘ (01643) 862565, ≤, 🐎 – ⅍ 📺 🅿. ⅍
closed Christmas and New Year – **3 rm** ⊇ 36.00/52.00.

at Porlock Weir NW : 1½ m. – ✉ Minehead.

🏠🏠 **Anchor and Ship Inn**, TA24 8PB, ℘ (01643) 862753, Fax (01643) 862843, ≤, 🐎 – 📺 ☎
🅿. ⁽⁾ 🅰🅴 🆅🆂🅰 – closed January – **Meals** (bar lunch)/dinner 19.75 **t.** and a la carte ⅍ 7.50 –
20 rm ⊇ (dinner included) 87.75/155.50 **st.** – SB.

PORLOCK WEIR Somerset 403 J 30 – see Porlock.

PORT ERIN Isle of Man 402 F 21 – see Man (Isle of).

PORTINSCALE Cumbria – see Keswick.

PORT ISAAC Cornwall 403 F 32 The West Country G. – Env. : St. Endellion (church★★), S : 2½ m. by B 3267 on B 3314 – St. Kew★ (church★), SE : 3 m. by B 3267, B 3314 and minor roads.
Exc. : – Pencarrow★, SE : 12 m. by B 3267, B 3314 and A 389.
London 266 – Newquay 24 – Tintagel 14 – Truro 32.

🏠 **Port Gaverne**, Port Gaverne, PL29 3SQ, S : ½ m. ℘ (01208) 880244, Fax (01208) 880151,
« Retaining 17C features » – ⅍ rest, 📺 ☎ 🅿. ⁽⁾ 🅰🅴 🆅🆂🅰 🅹🅲🅱
closed 3 January-14 February – **Meals** (bar lunch)/dinner a la carte 18.95/25.25 **t.** ⅍ 5.10 –
17 rm ⊇ (dinner included) 60.00/132.00 **t.** – SB.

🏠 **Castle Rock**, PL29 3SB, ℘ (01208) 880300, Fax (01208) 880219, ≤ Port Isaac Bay and
Tintagel Head – ⅍ rest, 📺 ☎ 🅿. ⁽⁾ 🅰🅴 🆅🆂🅰 – closed January – **Meals** (bar lunch)/
dinner 15.00 **t.** and a la carte ⅍ 4.95 – **17 rm** ⊇ 32.00/74.00 **t.** – SB.

⌂ **Archer Farm** ⌂ without rest., Trewetha, PL29 3RU, SE : ½ m. by B 3267
℘ (01208) 880522, ≤, 🐎 – 📺 ☎ 🅿 – May-September – **5 rm** ⊇ 25.00/60.00 **s.**

🍴 **Slipway** with rm, Harbour Front, PL29 3RH, ℘ (01208) 880264, Fax (01208) 880264, 🌦,
« Part 16C inn » – 🅿. ⁽⁾ 🅰🅴 🆅🆂🅰. ⅍
closed 3 weeks January and February – **Meals** (restricted opening during winter) (bar
lunch)/dinner a la carte 16.00/23.75 **t.** ⅍ 4.95 – **9 rm** ⊇ 24.00/100.00 **t.** – SB.

PORTLOE Cornwall 403 F 33 – ✉ Truro – London 296 – St. Austell 15 – Truro 15.

🏠 **Lugger**, TR2 5RD, ℘ (01872) 501322, Fax (01872) 501691, ≤, 🏖 – ⅍ rest, 📺 ☎ 🅿. ⁽⁾
🅰🅴 ① 🆅🆂🅰 🅹🅲🅱. ⅍
early March-early October – **Meals** (bar lunch Monday to Saturday)/dinner 25.00 **t.**
and a la carte ⅍ 4.50 – **19 rm** ⊇ (dinner included) 70.00/150.00 **t.** – SB.

PORTSCATHO Cornwall 403 F 33 The West Country G. – ✉ Truro – Env. : St. Just-in-Roseland
Church★★, W : 4 m. by A 3078 – St. Anthony-in-Roseland (≤★★) S : 3½ m.
London 298 – Plymouth 55 – Truro 16.

🏠🏠 **Roseland House** ⌂, Rosevine, TR2 5EW, N : 2 m. by A 3078 ℘ (01872) 580644,
Fax (01872) 580801, ≤ Gerrans Bay, 🐎 – ⅍ rest, 📺 🅿. ⁽⁾ 🅰🅴 🆅🆂🅰. ⅍
closed Christmas and New Year – **Meals** (booking essential January and November) (bar
lunch)/dinner 15.00 **t.** ⅍ 5.00 – **14 rm** ⊇ (dinner included) 54.00/108.00 **t.** – SB.

🏠 **Gerrans Bay**, 12 Tregassick Rd, TR2 5ED, ℘ (01872) 580338, Fax (01872) 580250, ≤, 🐎 –
⅍ rest, 📺 🅿. ⁽⁾ 🅰🅴 🆅🆂🅰 🅹🅲🅱. ⅍ – April-October – **Meals** (bar lunch Monday to Saturday)/
dinner 19.50 **st.** ⅍ 5.00 – **14 rm** ⊇ (dinner included) 49.00/108.00 **st.**

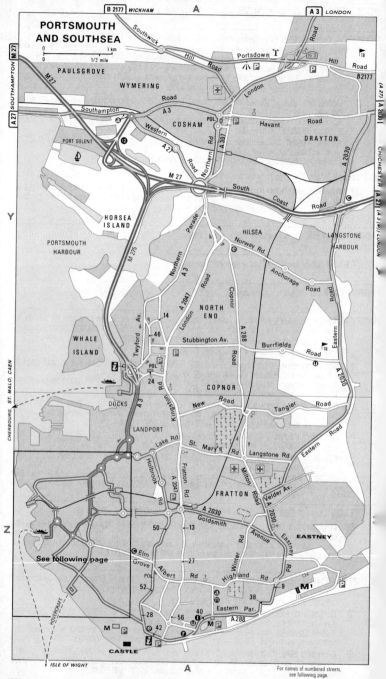

PORTSMOUTH AND SOUTHSEA

0   1 km
0   1/2 mile

See following page

For names of numbered streets,
see following page.

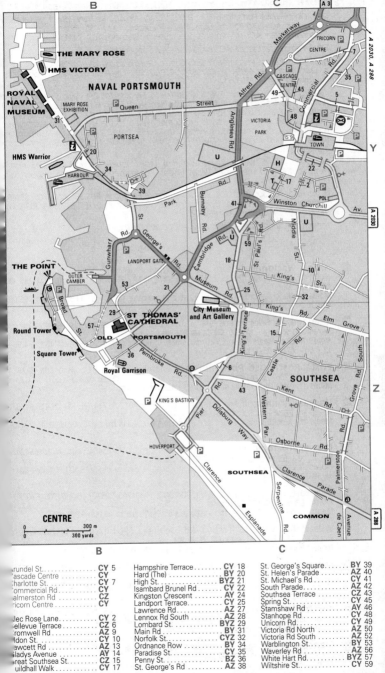

CENTRE

See : *City★ – Naval Portsmouth* BY : *H.M.S. Victory★★★ AC, The Mary Rose★★, Royal Naval Museum★★ AC – Old Portsmouth★* BYZ : *The Point (≤★★) - St. Thomas Cathedral★ – Southsea (Castle★ AC)* AZ – *Royal Marines Museum, Eastney★ AC*, AZ **M**1.

Env. : *Portchester Castle★ AC, NW :* 5½ *m. by A 3 and A 27* AY.

🔟 *Great Salterns, Portsmouth Golf Centre, Burrfields Rd 🕿 (01705) 664549* AY – 🔟 *Crookhorn Lane, Widley 🕿 (01705) 372210/372299* – 🔟 *Southwick Park, Pinsley Drive, Southwick 🕿 (01705) 380131.*

🚢 *to France (Cherbourg) (P & O European Ferries Ltd) 2-4 daily (5 h) day, (7 h) night – to France (Le Havre) (P & O European Ferries Ltd) 3 daily (5 h 30 mn) day, (7 h 30 mn) night – to France (Caen) (Brittany Ferries) 2-3 daily (6 h) day (6 h 15 mn) night, (St. Malo) daily (8 h 45 mn) day (10 h 30 mn) night – to the Isle of Wight (Fishbourne) (Wightlink Ltd) frequent services daily (35 mn) – to Spain (Santander) (Brittany Ferries) winter only (30 h) – to Spain (Bilbao) (P & O European Ferries Ltd) 1-2 weekly (30 h).*

🚢 *to the Isle of Wight (Ryde) (Wightlink Ltd) frequent services daily (15 mn) – from Southsea to the Isle of Wight (Ryde) (Hovertravel Ltd) frequent services daily (10 mn).*

🖪 *The Hard, PO1 3QJ 🕿 (01705) 826722 – Clarence Esplanade, PO5 3ST 🕿 (01705) 832464 (summer only) – Terminal Building, Portsmouth Ferryport 🕿 (01705) 838635 – 102 Commercial Rd, PO1 1EJ 🕿 (01705) 838382.*

London 78 – Brighton 48 – Salisbury 44 – Southampton 21.

Plans on preceding pages

🏨 **Hilton National,** Eastern Rd, Farlington, PO6 1UN, NE : 5 m. on A 2030 🕿 *(01705) 219111, Fax (01705) 210762,* 🛵, 🚗, 🔲, 🎾 – 쓪 rm, 🔟 🕿 ♿ 🅿 – 🔏 230. 🐵 AE ⓪ VISA. 🕸
AY c
Meals *(bar lunch Saturday)* 14.50/18.50 **st.** *and a la carte* ▯ 7.00 – ⚌ 11.50 – **118 rm** 95.00/ 115.00 **st.** – SB.

🏨 **Innlodge,** Burrfields Rd, PO3 5HH, 🕿 *(01705) 650510, Fax (01705) 693458,* 🐎 – 쓪 rm ▤ rest, 🔟 🕿 ♿ 🅿 – 🔏 150. 🐵 AE ⓪ VISA. 🕸
AY u
Beiderbecks : Meals *(closed Saturday lunch)* (grill rest.) *a la carte* 6.85/11.15 **t.** ▯ 4.95 – ⚌ 6.50 – **73 rm** 45.00 **t.**

🏨 **Forte Posthouse Portsmouth,** Pembroke Rd, PO1 2TA, 🕿 *(01705) 827651 Fax (01705) 756715,* 🛵, 🚗, 🔲 – ▮ 쓪 🔟 🕿 🅿 – 🔏 250. 🐵 AE ⓪ VISA
CZ e
Meals *a la carte* 14.35/25.45 **st.** – ⚌ 9.95 – **163 rm** 69.00 **st.** – SB.

🏨 **Hospitality Inn,** South Par., Southsea, PO4 0RN, 🕿 *(01705) 731281, Fax (01705) 817572* ≤ – ▮▮ 쓪 🔟 🕿 – 🔏 300. 🐵 AE ⓪ VISA JCB
AZ
Meals *(bar lunch)/dinner* 15.50 **t.** *and a la carte* ▯ 8.60 – **113 rm** ⚌ 78.00/93.00 **st.**, 2 suite – SB.

🏨 **Green Farm Toby,** Copnor Rd, Hilsea, PO3 5HS, 🕿 *(01705) 654645, Fax (01705) 654287* 쓪, ▤ rest, 🔟 🕿 ♿ 🅿 – 🔏 35. 🐵 AE ⓪ VISA. 🕸
AY
closed 24 December-2 January – Meals (grill rest.) *a la carte* 11.55/15.10 **t.** ▯ 4.45 – **30 rm** ⚌ 59.00/69.00 **st.** – SB.

🏠 **Beaufort,** 71 Festing Rd, Southsea, PO4 0NQ, 🕿 *(01705) 823707, Fax (01705) 870270* 쓪 rm, 🔟 🕿 🅿 🐵 AE ⓪ VISA. 🕸
AZ
Meals *(dinner only)* 14.50 **st.** *and a la carte* ▯ 5.25 – **20 rm** ⚌ 48.00/69.00 – SB.

🏠 **Westfield Hall,** 65 Festing Rd, Southsea, PO4 0NQ, 🕿 *(01705) 826971* Fax (01705) 870200 – 🔟 🕿 🅿 🐵 AE ⓪ VISA. 🕸
AZ
Meals *(dinner only)* 14.95 **t.** *and a la carte* ▯ 4.95 – **23 rm** ⚌ 46.00/70.00 **t.**

🏠 **Seacrest,** 11-12 South Par., Southsea, PO5 2JB, 🕿 *(01705) 733192, Fax (01705) 832523,* – ▮▮, 쓪 rest, 🔟 🕿 🅿 🐵 AE ⓪ VISA. 🕸
AZ
Meals *(residents only) (dinner only)* 12.95 **t.** *and a la carte* ▯ 3.95 – **28 rm** ⚌ 48.00/68.00 – SB.

↥ **Fortitude Cottage** without rest., 51 Broad St., Old Portsmouth, PO1 2JD 🕿 *(01705) 823748, Fax (01705) 823748* – 쓪 🔟. 🐵 AE VISA JCB. 🕸
BY
closed 25 and 26 December – **3 rm** ⚌ 27.00/46.00.

↥ **Glencoe** without rest., 64 Whitwell Rd, Southsea, PO4 0QS, 🕿 *(01705) 737413* Fax (01705) 737413 – 쓪 🔟. 🐵 VISA
AZ
7 rm ⚌ 18.50/38.00.

XX **Tang's,** 127 Elm Grove, Southsea, PO5 1LJ, ℘ (01705) 826000, Fax (01705) 838323 – ▤. ✆❸
AE ⓪ VISA
AZ c
closed Monday and 25-26 December – **Meals** - Chinese - (dinner only) 15.00 **t.** and a la carte.

XX **Bistro Montparnasse,** 103 Palmerston Rd, Southsea, PO5 3PS, ℘ (01705) 816754,
Fax (01705) 816754 – ✆❸ AE VISA
CZ a
closed Sunday, Monday and 25-26 December – **Meals** (dinner only) 14.90 **st.** and a la carte
▯ 6.95.

at Cosham N : 4½ m. by A 3 and M 275 on A 27 – ⊠ Portsmouth.

🏨 **Portsmouth Marriott,** North Harbour, PO6 4SH, ℘ (01705) 383151, Fax (01705)
388701, ₤₅, ≋s, ◲, squash – ▯, ⇌ rm, ▤ ▥ ☎ ₺ ❶ – 🔬 280. ✆❸ AE ⓪ VISA ⌧₸ A₹% a
Meals 18.95 **st.** ▯ 7.25 – ⌑ 10.95 – **169 rm** 69.00/96.00 **st.,** 1 suite – SB.

🏨 **Travel Inn,** 1 Southampton Rd, North Harbour, PO6 4SA, ℘ (01705) 321122,
Fax (01705) 215780 – ⇌ rm, ▥ ₺ ❶. ✆❸ AE ⓪ VISA. ⅍
AY a
Meals (grill rest.) – **40 rm** 36.50 **t.**

🔧 ATS Sharps Close, off Williams Rd ℘ (01705) 665959

POSTBRIDGE Devon ⁴⁰³ I 32 The West Country G. – ⊠ Yelverton.
Env. : Dartmoor National Park★★.
London 205 – Exeter 21 – Plymouth 19.

🏨 **Lydgate House** ♨, PL20 6TJ, ℘ (01822) 880209, Fax (01822) 880202, ≤, ⌇, ☞, park –
⇌ rest, ▥ ❶. ✆❸ VISA
closed 4 January-1 March – **Meals** (dinner only) 16.50 **t.** ▯ 5.25 – **8 rm** ⌑ 31.50/63.00 **t.**

The Guide is updated annually so renew your Guide every year.

POTT SHRIGLEY Ches. – see Macclesfield.

POUNDSGATE Devon – see Ashburton.

POYNTON Ches. ⁴⁰² ⁴⁰³ N 23 – pop. 14 768.
London 193 – Chester 44 – Manchester 12 – Stoke-on-Trent 28.

🏨 **The Spinney** without rest., 59-61 Chester Rd, SK12 1HB, W : ¼ m. on A 5149
℘ (01625) 871397, Fax (01625) 872143, ☞ – ⇌ ▥ ❶. ✆❸ AE VISA ⌧₸
closed 2 weeks Christmas – **13 rm** ⌑ 49.50/66.50 **st.**

PRESTBURY Ches. ⁴⁰² ⁴⁰³ ⁴⁰⁴ N 24 – pop. 3 346.
▯₈ Mottram Hall Hotel, Wilmslow Rd, Mottram St. Andrews ℘ (01625) 828135.
London 184 – Liverpool 43 – Manchester 17 – Stoke-on-Trent 25.

🏨 **De Vere Mottram Hall,** Wilmslow Rd, Mottram St. Andrew, SK10 4QT, NW : 2 ¼ m. on
A 538 ℘ (01625) 828135, Fax (01625) 829284, ≤, « Part 18C mansion », ₤₅, ≋s, ◲, ▯₈, ☞,
park, ⅍, squash – ▯, ⇌ rm, ▥ ☎ ₺ ❶ – 🔬 275. ✆❸ AE ⓪ VISA
Meals (dancing Friday and Saturday evenings) (bar lunch Saturday) 19.00/24.00 **st.**
and a la carte ▯ 9.00 – **Oak :** **Meals** (closed Saturday lunch) 19.00/24.00 **st.** and a la carte
▯ 9.00 – **129 rm** ⌑ 125.00/160.00 **st.,** 3 suites – SB.

🏨 **White House Manor,** The Village, SK10 4HP, ℘ (01625) 829376, Fax (01625) 828627, ☞
– ▥ ☎ ❶. ✆❸ AE ⓪ VISA. ⅍
closed 25 December – **Meals** – (room service or see **White House** below) – ⌑ 8.50 – **11 rm**
70.00/95.00 **t.** – SB.

🏨 **The Bridge,** The Village, SK10 4DQ, ℘ (01625) 829326, Fax (01625) 827557, ☞ – ▥ ☎ ₺
❶ – 🔬 100. ✆❸ AE ⓪ VISA ⌧₸. ⅍
Meals 10.75/13.25 **t.** and a la carte ▯ 6.50 – ⌑ 8.50 – **23 rm** 40.00/100.00 **t.** – SB.

XX **White House,** The Village, SK10 4DG, ℘ (01625) 829376, Fax (01625) 828627 – ❶. ✆❸ AE
⓪ VISA
closed Monday lunch, Sunday dinner and 25 December – **Meals** 12.95/
16.95 **t.** and a la carte ▯ 5.95.

RESTON Herefordshire ⁴⁰³ ⁴⁰⁴ M 27 – see Ledbury.

PRESTON *Lancs.* 402 L 22 – *pop. 177 660.*

🏌 *Fulwood Hall Lane, Fulwood* ℰ *(01772) 700436* – 🏌 *Ingol, Tanterton Hall Rd, Ingol*
ℰ *(01772) 734556* – 🏌 *Aston & Lea, Tudor Av., Blackpool Rd* ℰ *(01772) 726480* –
🏌 *Penwortham, Blundell Lane* ℰ *(01772) 743207.*

🛈 *The Guildhall, Lancaster Rd, PR1 1HT* ℰ *(01772) 253731.*

London 226 – Blackpool 18 – Burnley 22 – Liverpool 30 – Manchester 34 – Stoke-on-Trent 65.

🏨 **Forte Posthouse Preston,** The Ringway, PR1 3AU, ℰ (01772) 259411,
Fax (01772) 201923 – 📶, ❊ rm, 📺 ☎ 🅿 – 🔬 120. 🚗 🅰🅴 ⓪ 𝒱𝒾𝒮𝒜 🆓ᴄ🅱. ❊
Meals a la carte 16.00/26.00 – 🖃 8.95 – **119 rm** 69.00/109.00 **st.** – SB.

🏨 **Claremont,** 516 Blackpool Rd, Ashton, PR2 1HY, NW : 2 m. by A 6 on A 5085
ℰ (01772) 729738, Fax (01772) 726274, 🐎 – ❊ rest, 📺 ☎ 🅿. 🚗 🅰🅴 ⓪ 𝒱𝒾𝒮𝒜. ❊
Meals 9.95/11.95 **st.** and dinner a la carte ₰ 5.00 – **14 rm** 🖃 37.50/51.00 **st.**

🍴🍴 **Heathcotes Brasserie,** 23 Winckley Sq., PR1 3JJ, ℰ (01772) 252732,
Fax (01772) 203433 – ▤. 🚗 🅰🅴 𝒱𝒾𝒮𝒜
Meals 12.50 **t.** (lunch) and a la carte 20.00/27.50 **t.** ₰ 5.50.

at Broughton *N : 3 m. on A 6 – ⊠ Preston.*

🏰 **Preston Marriott,** 418 Garstang Rd, PR3 5JB, ℰ (01772) 864087, Fax (01772) 861728,
🛌, 🚿, 🔲, 🐎 – 📶 ❊ rm, 📺 ☎ 🅿 – 🔬 150. 🚗 🅰🅴 ⓪ 𝒱𝒾𝒮𝒜 🆓ᴄ🅱. ❊
Broughton Park : Meals (closed Saturday lunch) 13.95/18.95 **t.** and dinner a la carte
₰ 7.25 – 🖃 10.95 – **97 rm** 75.00/87.00 **t.,** 1 suite – SB.

at Samlesbury *E : 2½ m. by A 59 – ⊠ Preston.*

🏨 **Tickled Trout,** Preston New Rd, PR5 0UJ, W : 1 m. on A 59 ℰ (01772) 877671,
Fax (01772) 877463, ≼, 🚿, 🔥 – ❊ rm 📺 ☎ 🅿 – 🔬 150. 🚗 🅰🅴 ⓪ 𝒱𝒾𝒮𝒜 🆓ᴄ🅱
Meals (closed Saturday lunch) 18.95 **st.** and a la carte ₰ 7.00 – 🖃 9.95 – **72 rm** 90.00/
110.00 **st.** – SB.

🏨 **Swallow,** Preston New Rd, PR5 0UL, E : 1 m. at junction of A 59 with A 677
ℰ (01772) 877351, Fax (01772) 877424, 🚿, 🔲, squash – 📶 ❊, ▤ rest, 📺 ☎ 🅿 – 🔬 250.
🚗 🅰🅴 ⓪ 𝒱𝒾𝒮𝒜 🆓ᴄ🅱
Meals (bar lunch Saturday) 9.50/18.50 **st.** ₰ 9.00 – **78 rm** 🖃 80.00/130.00 **st.** – SB.

at Walton le Dale *SE : 2 m. by A 6, A 675, B 6230 (Bamber Bridge rd) on B 6258 – ⊠ Preston.*

🏨 **The Vineyard,** Cinnamon Hill, PR5 4JN, ℰ (01772) 254646, Fax (01772) 258967 – 📺 ☎ 🅿
– 🔬 100. 🚗 🅰🅴 ⓪ 𝒱𝒾𝒮𝒜. ❊
Meals (grill rest.) a la carte 12.00/18.00 **t.** – 🖃 6.95 – **16 rm** 45.00 **t.** – SB.

at Bamber Bridge *S : 5 m. by A 6 on B 6258 – ⊠ Preston.*

🏨 **Novotel,** Reedfield Place, Walton Summit, PR5 8AA, SE : ¾ m. by A 6 at junction 29 of M 61
ℰ (01772) 313331, Fax (01772) 627868, 🔲, 🐎 – 📶, ❊ rm, ▤ rest, 📺 ☎ 🅿 – 🔬 180. 🚗
🅰🅴 ⓪ 𝒱𝒾𝒮𝒜
Meals 13.50 **st.** and a la carte – 🖃 9.50 – **98 rm** 55.00 **st.**

🏨 **The Poachers Tavern - Lodge Inn,** Lobstock Lane, PR5 6BA, S : ½ m. on A 6
ℰ (01772) 324100, Fax (01772) 629525 – ❊ rm, ▤ rest, 📺 & 🅿. 🚗 🅰🅴 ⓪ 𝒱𝒾𝒮𝒜. ❊
Meals (grill rest.) a la carte 8.50/12.50 **t.** ₰ 3.95 – 🖃 5.50 – **40 rm** 37.50 **t.** – SB.

at Lea *W : 3½ m. on A 583 – ⊠ Preston.*

🏨 **Travel Inn,** Blackpool Rd, PR4 0XL, on A 583 ℰ (01772) 720476, Fax (01772) 729971 –
❊ rm, ▤ rest, 📺 & 🅿. 🚗 🅰🅴 ⓪ 𝒱𝒾𝒮𝒜. ❊
Meals (grill rest.) – **38 rm** 36.50 **t.**

🅰 ATS 296-298 Aqueduct St, Ashton ℰ (01772) 257688

PRESTWICH *Gtr. Manchester* 402 403 404 N 23 – *pop. 31 801 – ⊠ Manchester.*
London 205 – Leeds 40 – Liverpool 30 – Manchester 5.

Plan : see Manchester

🏨 **Village H & Leisure Club,** George St., M25 9WS, S : 1 ¾ m. by A 56 ℰ (0161) 798 8905,
Fax (0161) 773 5562, 🛌, 🚿, squash – ❊, ▤ rest, 📺 ☎ 🅿 – 🔬 120. 🚗 🅰🅴 ⓪ 𝒱𝒾𝒮𝒜
Meals (grill rest.) a la carte 13.85/26.40 **t.** – **39 rm** 🖃 67.00/74.00 **t.,** 1 suite – SB.   AV

🏨 **Travel Inn,** Bury New Rd, M25 3AJ, NW : ½ m. on A 56 ℰ (0161) 798 0827,
Fax (0161) 773 8099 – ❊ rm, 📺 & 🅿. 🚗 🅰🅴 ⓪ 𝒱𝒾𝒮𝒜. ❊
Meals (grill rest.) – **60 rm** 36.50 **t.**

PRIDDY *Somerset* 403 L 30 – *see Wells.*

PUCKRUP *Glos. – see Tewkesbury.*

PUDDINGTON *Ches.* 402 403 K 24 *– see Chester.*

PUDSEY *W. Yorks.* 402 P 22 *– see Leeds.*

PULBOROUGH *W. Sussex* 404 S 31 *– pop. 3 497.*
 18, 9 *West Chiltington, Broadford Bridge Rd* ℰ *(01798) 813574.*
 London 49 – Brighton 25 – Guildford 25 – Portsmouth 35.

🏛 **Chequers,** Church Pl., RH20 1AD, NE : ¼ m. on A 29 ℰ (01798) 872486, Fax (01798) 872715, ⇌ – 😾 📺 ☎ 🄿. 🌐 🄰🄴 ① 𝘝𝘐𝘚𝘈
 Meals (dinner only) 18.95 **t.** and a la carte ⫘ 5.95 – **11 rm** ⛭ 59.50/89.00 **t.** – SB.

✗✗ **Stane Street Hollow,** Codmore Hill, RH20 1BG, NE : 1 m. on A 29 ℰ (01798) 872819 – 😾 🄿. 🌐 𝘝𝘐𝘚𝘈 🄹🄲🄱
 closed Saturday lunch, Sunday dinner, Monday, Tuesday, 2 weeks late May, 2 weeks late October and 24 December-5 January – **Meals** - Swiss - (booking essential) 15.50 **t.** (lunch) and a la carte 20.50/25.00 **t.** ⫘ 8.50.

at West Chiltington E : 2 ¾ m. by A 283 on West Chiltington rd – ⊠ *Pulborough.*

⌂ **New House Farm** without rest., Broadford Bridge Rd, RH20 2LA, ℰ (01798) 812215, ⇌ – 😾 📺 🄿. 🌣
 closed Christmas – **3 rm** ⛭ 35.00/50.00 **st.**

La PULENTE *Jersey (Channel Islands)* 403 P 33 and 230 ⑪ *– see Channel Islands.*

PULHAM MARKET *Norfolk* 404 X 26 *– pop. 919 –* ⊠ *Diss.*
 London 106 – Cambridge 58 – Ipswich 29 – Norwich 16.

⌂ **Old Bakery,** Church Walk, IP21 4SJ, ℰ (01379) 676492, Fax (01379) 676492, ⇌ – 😾 📺. 🌣
 closed Christmas and New Year – **Meals** (by arrangement) 14.00 ⫘ 4.00 – **3 rm** ⛭ 35.00/ 48.00 **s.**

PURFLEET *Essex* 404 ⑭.
 Dartford Tunnel and Bridge (toll).
 London 16 – Hastings 56 – Maidstone 26 – Southend-on-Sea 24.

🏨 **Travel Inn,** High St., RM16 1QA, ℰ (01708) 865432, Fax (01708) 860852 – 😾 rm, 📺 ᬓ 🄿. 🌐 🄰🄴 ① 𝘝𝘐𝘚𝘈 🌣
 Meals (grill rest.) – **30 rm** 36.50 **t.**

PURTON *Wilts.* 403 404 O 29 *– pop. 3 879 –* ⊠ *Swindon.*
 London 94 – Bristol 41 – Gloucester 31 – Oxford 38 – Swindon 5.

🏛 **Pear Tree at Purton,** Church End, SN5 9ED, S : ½ m. by Church St. on Lydiard Millicent rd ℰ (01793) 772100, Fax (01793) 772369, ≼, « Conservatory restaurant », ⇌ – 📺 ☎ 🄿 – ⫘ 60. 🌐 🄰🄴 ① 𝘝𝘐𝘚𝘈 🄹🄲🄱
 closed 26 to 30 December – **Meals** *(closed Saturday lunch)* 17.50/27.50 **t.** ⫘ 6.00 – **16 rm** ⛭ 85.00/105.00 **t.**, 2 suites.

QUORNDON *Leics. – see Loughborough.*

RAINHILL *Mersey.* 402 ㉝ 403 ⑬ *– see St. Helens.*

RAMSBOTTOM *Gtr. Manchester* 402 N 23 *– pop. 17 318.*
 London 223 – Blackpool 39 – Burnley 12 – Leeds 46 – Manchester 13 – Liverpool 39.

✗ **Village,** 18 Market Pl., BL0 9HT, ℰ (01706) 825070, Fax (01706) 822005 – 😾. 🌐 🄰🄴 ① 𝘝𝘐𝘚𝘈 🄹🄲🄱
 closed Sunday dinner, Monday, Tuesday, 26 December and 1 January – **Meals** 7.50/21.00 **st.** and lunch a la carte ⫘ 4.75.

RAMSEY *Isle of Man* 402 G 21 *– see Man (Isle of).*

RAMSGATE Kent **404** Y 30 – pop. 37 895.

    ⟶ – to Belgium (Ostend) (Holyman Sally Ferries) 2 daily (4 h) – to France (Dunkerque) (Holyman Sally Ferries) 3-4 daily (1 h 15 mn).

    ⟶ to Belgium (Ostend) (Holyman Sally Ferries) 5-7 daily (1 h 40 mn).

    🛈 19-21 Harbour St., CT11 8HA ℘ (01843) 583333.

    London 77 – Dover 19 – Maidstone 45 – Margate 4.5.

🏨 **Jarvis Marina**, Harbour Par., CT11 8LJ, ℘ (01843) 588276, Fax (01843) 586866, ≤, ⚓, 🖼 – ❘﹩❘, 🍽 rest, 📺 ☎ 🅿 – 🔬 120. 🆎 🅰🅴 ⑩ 𝘝𝘐𝘚𝘈. ﹪
    Meals (bar lunch Monday to Saturday)/dinner 13.00 **st.** and a la carte ⓙ 5.75 – **58 rm** ⊇ 76.50/94.00 **st.** – SB.

🏨 **San Clu**, Victoria Par., East Cliff, CT11 8DT, ℘ (01843) 592345, Fax (01843) 580157, ≤ – ❘﹩❘ 📺 ☎ 🅿, 🆎 🅰🅴 ⑩ 𝘝𝘐𝘚𝘈. ﹪
    Meals (bar lunch Monday to Saturday)/dinner 12.50 **st.** and a la carte – **44 rm** ⊇ 45.00/140.00 **st.** – SB.

at Minster W : 5½ m. by A 253 on B 2048 – ✉ Ramsgate.

🍴 **Morton's Fork** with rm, 42 Station Rd, CT12 4BZ, ℘ (01843) 823000, Fax (01843) 821224 – ❘﹩❘ 📺 ☎ 🅿. 🆎 🅰🅴 ⑩ 𝘝𝘐𝘚𝘈 𝐉𝐂𝐁. ﹪
    closed 24 December-2 January – **Meals** (closed Sunday dinner and Monday) 12.95 **t.** and a la carte – **6 rm** ⊇ 39.00/63.00 **t.** – SB.

    🅰 ATS 82-84 Bellevue Rd ℘ (01843) 595829

RAMSGILL-IN-NIDDERDALE N. Yorks. **402** O 21 – see Pateley Bridge.

RASKELF N. Yorks. – see Easingwold.

RAVENSTONEDALE Cumbria **402** M 20 – pop. 886 – ✉ Kirkby Stephen.
    London 280 – Carlisle 43 – Kendal 19 – Kirkby Stephen 5.

🏨 **Black Swan**, CA17 4NG, ℘ (015396) 23204, Fax (015396) 23604, ⚲, 🐎 – ᐸ﹩ rest, 📺 ☎ 🕭 🅿. 🆎 🅰🅴 ⑩ 𝘝𝘐𝘚𝘈 𝐉𝐂𝐁
    Meals 9.75/23.00 **t.** and a la carte ⓙ 5.00 – **15 rm** ⊇ 50.00/80.00 **t.** – SB.

🍴 **Fat Lamb** with rm, Crossbank, CA17 4LL, SE : 2 m. by Sedburgh rd on A 683 ℘ (015396) 23242, Fax (015396) 23285, ≤, 🐎, park – ᐸ﹩ 🅿. 🆎 𝘝𝘐𝘚𝘈
    Meals 11.50/17.00 **t.** and a la carte ⓙ 3.75 – **12 rm** ⊇ 35.00/60.00 **t.** – SB.

READING **403** **404** Q 29 – pop. 213 474.
    🏌 Calcot Park, Bath Rd, Calcot ℘ (01734) 427124.
    Whitchurch Bridge (toll).
    🛈 Town Hall, Blagrave St., RG1 1QH ℘ (0118) 956 6226.
    London 43 – Brighton 79 – Bristol 78 – Croydon 47 – Luton 62 – Oxford 28 – Portsmouth 67 – Southampton 46.

Plan opposite

🏨 **Holiday Inn Reading**, Caversham Bridge, Richfield Av., RG1 8BD, ℘ (01189) 259988, Fax (01189) 391665, ≤, « Thames-side setting », 𝐼𝐬, ⚓, 🖼 – ❘﹩❘, ᐸ﹩ rm, 📺 ☎ 🕭 🅿 – 🔬 250. 🆎 🅰🅴 ⑩ 𝘝𝘐𝘚𝘈 𝐉𝐂𝐁   X e
    Meals 17.95 **st.** and a la carte ⓙ 6.50 – ⊇ 9.25 – **109 rm** 106.00/126.00 **st.**, 2 suites – SB.

🏨 **Ramada**, Oxford Rd, RG1 7RH, ℘ (01189) 586222, Fax (01189) 597842, 𝐼𝐬, ⚓, 🖼 – ❘﹩❘, ᐸ﹩ rm, 📺 ☎ 🅿 – 🔬 220. 🆎 🅰🅴 ⑩ 𝘝𝘐𝘚𝘈 𝐉𝐂𝐁. ﹪   Z j
    Meals (buffet lunch Monday to Saturday)/dinner a la carte 13.50/28.30 **t.** ⓙ 5.95 – ⊇ 8.95 – **193 rm** 110.00 **st.**, 1 suite.

🏨 **Forte Posthouse Reading**, 500 Basingstoke Rd, RG2 0SL, S : 2 ½ m. on A 33 ℘ (01189) 875485, Fax (01189) 311958, 𝐼𝐬, ⚓, 🖼 – ᐸ﹩ rm, 📺 ☎ 🅿 – 🔬 100. 🆎 🅰🅴 ⑩ 𝘝𝘐𝘚𝘈 𝐉𝐂𝐁   X a
    Meals a la carte 14.55/25.65 **st.** ⓙ 7.50 – ⊇ 9.95 – **202 rm** 99.00 **st.**

🏨 **Upcross**, 68 Berkeley Av., RG1 6HY, ℘ (01189) 590796, Fax (01189) 576517, 🐎 – ᐸ﹩ rest, 📺 ☎ 🅿 – 🔬 45. 🆎 🅰🅴 ⑩ 𝘝𝘐𝘚𝘈   Z c
    Meals (closed Saturday lunch) 12.50/15.00 **st.** and a la carte – **22 rm** ⊇ 59.00/69.00 **st.**

🏨 **Hillingdon Prince**, 39 Christchurch Rd, RG2 7AN, ℘ (01189) 311391, Fax (01189) 756357 – ❘﹩❘ 📺 ☎ 🅿 – 🔬 100. 🆎 🅰🅴 𝘝𝘐𝘚𝘈   X v
    Meals a la carte 11.45/21.45 **st.** ⓙ 6.50 – **36 rm** ⊇ 65.00/95.00 **st.**

🏨 **Rainbow Corner**, 132-138 Caversham Rd, RG1 8AY, ℘ (01189) 588140, Fax (01189) 586500 – 📺 ☎ 🅿. 🆎 🅰🅴 ⑩ 𝘝𝘐𝘚𝘈. ﹪   X u
    Meals (closed Sunday dinner and Bank Holidays) 12.95 **st.** and a la carte ⓙ 3.95 – ⊇ 5.95 – **32 rm** 60.00/76.00 **st.** – SB.

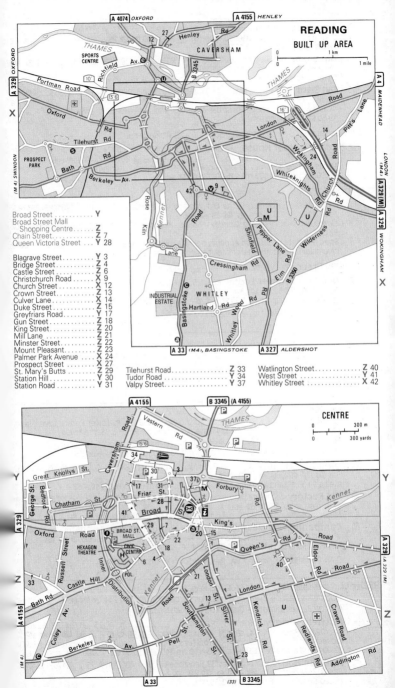

READING

BUILT UP AREA

0 ——— 1 km
0 ——— 1 mile

Broad Street .... Y
Broad Street Mall
  Shopping Centre...... Z
Chain Street.............. Z 7
Queen Victoria Street ... Y 28

Blagrave Street.......... Y 3
Bridge Street............. Z 4
Castle Street............. Z 6
Christchurch Road ..... X 9
Church Street............ X 12
Crown Street............. Z 13
Culver Lane.............. X 14
Duke Street.............. Z 15
Greyfriars Road.......... Y 17
Gun Street............... Z 18
King Street............... Z 20
Mill Lane .... Z 21
Minster Street........... Z 22
Mount Pleasant......... Z 23
Palmer Park Avenue .... X 24
Prospect Street .... X 27
St. Mary's Butts .... Z 29
Station Hill .... Y 30
Station Road .... Y 31

Tilehurst Road................ Z 33
Tudor Road .... Y 34
Valpy Street................. Y 37

Watlington Street............. Z 40
West Street .... Y 41
Whitley Street............... X 42

CENTRE

0 ——— 300 m
0 ——— 300 yards

🏛 **Travelodge**, 387 Basingstoke Rd, RG2 0JE, S : 2 m. on A 33 *€* (01189) 750618, Reservations (Freephone) 0800 850950 – ⅏ rm, 📺 ♿ 🄿 🕮 🆎 ① 𝖵𝖨𝖲𝖠 𝖩𝖢𝖡 ⌘
X c
Meals (grill rest.) – **36 rm** 49.95 **t.**

⌂ **Dittisham** without rest., 63 Tilehurst Rd, RG30 2JL, *€* (01189) 569483, ☞ – 📺 🄿 🕮 𝖵𝖨𝖲𝖠 ⌘
X s
5 rm ⊆ 22.50/40.00 **s.**

XX **Old Siam**, King's Walk, King St., RG1 2HG, *€* (01189) 512600, *Fax (01189) 596300* – 🕮 🆎 ① 𝖵𝖨𝖲𝖠 𝖩𝖢𝖡
Z a
closed Sunday, 2 weeks Christmas-New Year and Bank Holidays – **Meals** - Thai - 14.50/ 19.50 **st.** and a la carte.

at Sindlesham SE : 5 m. by A 329 on B 3030 – X – ⊠ Wokingham.

🏰 **Reading Moat House**, Mill Lane, RG41 5DF, NW : ½ m. by Mole Rd *€* (01189) 499988, *Fax (01189) 666530*, 🖪, 🖘 – 🛗, ⅏ rm, 📺 ☎ ♿ 🄿 – 🔬 80. 🕮 🆎 ① 𝖵𝖨𝖲𝖠 𝖩𝖢𝖡 ⌘
Meals *(closed Saturday lunch)* (booking essential Bank Holidays) 18.00 **st.** and a la carte
🍷 8.00 – ⊆ 10.00 – **100 rm** 115.00/135.00 **st.** – SB.

at Shinfield S : 4¼ m. on A 327 – X – ⊠ Reading.

XXX **L'Ortolan** (Burton-Race), The Old Vicarage, Church Lane, RG2 9BY, *€* (01189) 883783, ❀ ❀ *Fax (01189) 885391*, ☞ – 🄿 🕮 🆎 ① 𝖵𝖨𝖲𝖠
closed Sunday dinner and Monday – **Meals** - French - 19.90/39.50 **t.** and a la carte 64.50/ 82.00 **t.** 🍷 11.00
Spec. Papillote de saumon et petits pois à la française. Pigeon sauvage rôti et sa garniture hivernale. Tarte soufflée au chocolat amer et sa glace au chocolat blanc.

at Grazeley Green SW : 5½ m. by A 33 – X – ⊠ Reading.

🏛 **Old Bell - Premier Lodge**, RG7 1LS, *€* (01189) 883115, *Fax (01189) 886225* – ⅏ rm, 📺 ☎ ♿ 🄿 🕮 ① 𝖵𝖨𝖲𝖠 ⌘
Meals a la carte approx. 11.50 **st.** 🍷 4.75 – ⊆ 4.95 – **32 rm** 44.25 **st.**

🅐 ATS Basingstoke Rd *€* (01189) 759500

READING SERVICE AREA Newbury – ⊠ Reading.

🏛 **Travelodge** without rest., RG30 3UQ, M 4 eastbound between junctions 11 and 12 *€* (01189) 566966, *Fax (01189) 508427*, Reservations (Freephone) 0800 850950 – ⅏ 📺 ☎ ♿ 🄿 🕮 🆎 ① 𝖵𝖨𝖲𝖠 𝖩𝖢𝖡 ⌘
45 rm 49.95 **t.**

REDDITCH Worcestershire 🅴🅾🅱 🅴🅾🅸 O 27 – pop. 73 372.
🖪 Abbey Park G & C.C., Dagnell End Rd *€* (01527) 63918 – 🖪 Lower Grinsty, Green Lane, Callow Hill *€* (01527) 543309 – 🖪 Pitcheroak, Plymouth Rd *€* (01527) 541054.
🖪 Civic Square, Alcester St., B98 8AH *€* (01527) 60806.
London 111 – Birmingham 15 – Cheltenham 33 – Stratford-upon-Avon 15.

🏨 **Quality Friendly** ♨, Pool Bank, Southcrest, B97 4JS, *€* (01527) 541511, *Fax (01527) 402600*, ☞ – 📺 ☎ 🄿 – 🔬 70. 🕮 🆎 ① 𝖵𝖨𝖲𝖠
Meals 14.50 **st.** and a la carte 🍷 5.75 – ⊆ 9.75 – **58 rm** 66.50/90.25 **st.** – SB.

🏛 **Old Rectory** ♨, Ipsley Lane, Ipsley, B98 0AP, *€* (01527) 523000, *Fax (01527) 517003*, ☞ – ⅏ rest. 🄿 🄿 🕮 🆎 ① 𝖵𝖨𝖲𝖠 ⌘
Meals (in bar Sunday) (dinner only) 16.95 **st.** – **10 rm** ⊆ 45.00/85.00 **st.** – SB.

🏛 **Campanile**, Far Moor Lane, Winyates Green, B98 0SD, E : 2 ½ m. by A 4023 *€* (01527) 510710, *Fax (01527) 517269* – ⅏ rm, 📺 ☎ ♿ 🄿 – 🔬 25. 🕮 🆎 ① 𝖵𝖨𝖲𝖠 ⌘
Meals 10.55 **t.** and a la carte 🍷 4.95 – ⊆ 4.50 – **47 rm** 36.50 **t.** – SB.

🅐 ATS Pipers Rd, Park Farm Ind. Est., Park Farm South *€* (01527) 502002

REDHILL Surrey 🅴🅾🅸 T 30 – pop. 47 602 (inc. Reigate).
🖪 Redhill & Reigate, Clarence Lodge, Pendleton Rd *€* (01737) 244626/244433.
London 22 – Brighton 31 – Guildford 20 – Maidstone 34.

🏰 **Nutfield Priory**, Nutfield, RH1 4EN, E : 2 m. on A 25 *€* (01737) 822066 *Fax (01737) 823321*, ≤, 🖪, 🖘, 🏊, ☞, park, squash – 🛗 📺 ☎ 🄿 – 🔬 80. 🕮 🆎 ① 𝖵𝖨𝖲𝖠
closed 26 to 30 December – **Cloisters : Meals** *(closed Saturday lunch)* 16.00/ 22.00 **t.** and a la carte 🍷 6.95 – ⊆ 9.95 – **59 rm** 110.00/130.00 **st.**, 1 suite – SB.

⌂ **Ashleigh House** without rest., 39 Redstone Hill, RH1 4BG, on A 25 *€* (01737) 764763 *Fax (01737) 780308*, 🏊, ☞ – 📺 🄿 🕮 𝖵𝖨𝖲𝖠 ⌘
closed Christmas – **8 rm** ⊆ 30.00/55.00 **t.**

516

at Salfords *S : 2½ m. on A 23 – ⊠ Redhill.*

🏠 **Travel Inn,** Brighton Rd, RH1 5BT, ℘ (01737) 767277, Fax (01737) 778099 – 📺 ☎ ੬ 🅿.
🐼 AE ⑩ VISA. ✻
Meals (grill rest.) – **42 rm** 36.50 **t.**

REDWORTH *Durham – see Darlington.*

REEPHAM *Norfolk* 404 X 25 – *pop. 2 405 – ⊠ Norwich.*
London 125 – Cromer 26 – King's Lynn 34 – Norwich 14.

🏠 **Westwood Barn** ⟫, Crabgate Lane South, Wood Dalling, NR11 6SW, N : 3 m. by Station
Rd and Wood Dalling Rd ℘ (01263) 584108, ≼, ⊯ – ✻ rm, 📺 🅿. ✻
Meals (by arrangement) 16.00 **st.** – **3 rm** ⊡ 32.00/48.00 **st.**

REETH *N. Yorks.* 402 O 20 – *pop. 939 – ⊠ Richmond.*
London 253 – Leeds 53 – Middlesbrough 36.

🏨 **Burgoyne,** On The Green, DL11 6SN, ℘ (01748) 884292, Fax (01748) 884292, ≼, ⊯ – ✻
📺 ☎ ੬ 🅿. 🐼 VISA
closed 2 January-mid February – Meals (dinner only) 23.50 **t.** ₰ 5.25 – **9 rm** ⊡ 57.50/
100.00 **t.** – SB.

🏠 **Arkleside,** DL11 6SG, ℘ (01748) 884200, Fax (01748) 884200, ≼, ⊯ – 📺 🅿. 🐼 VISA
closed 25 December and January – Meals (dinner only) 17.00 **t.** ₰ 6.50 – **8 rm** ⊡ 40.00/
60.00 **t.,** 1 suite – SB.

REIGATE *Surrey* 404 T 30 – *pop. 47 602 (inc. Redhill).*
London 26 – Brighton 33 – Guildford 20 – Maidstone 38.

🏨 **Bridge House,** Reigate Hill, RH2 9RP, N : 1 ¼ m. on A 217 ℘ (01737) 246801,
Fax (01737) 223756, ≼ – 📺 ☎ 🅿 – ⚱ 50. 🐼 AE ⑩ VISA. ✻
Meals *(closed 27 to 29 December, 2 January and Bank Holidays)* (dancing Wednesday to
Saturday evenings) 16.50/23.00 **t.** and a la carte – ⊡ 10.50 – **37 rm** 60.00/95.00 **t.** – SB.

🏠 **Cranleigh,** 41 West St., RH2 9BL, ℘ (01737) 223417, Fax (01737) 223734, ☀, ⊯, ✻ – 📺
☎ 🅿. 🐼 AE ⑩ VISA JCB. ✻
closed 1 week Christmas – Meals *(closed Friday to Sunday)* (dinner only) a la carte
approx. 16.00 **st.** ₰ 5.00 – **9 rm** ⊡ 62.00/82.00 **st.** – SB.

✕✕ **The Dining Room,** 59a High St., RH2 9AE, ℘ (01737) 226650 – ✻ ▤. 🐼 AE VISA
*closed Saturday lunch, Sunday, 1 week Easter, 2 weeks August, 1 week Christmas and Bank
Holidays* – Meals 10.00/19.90 **t.** and a la carte ₰ 7.95.

✕ **La Barbe,** 71 Bell St., RH2 7AN, ℘ (01737) 241966, Fax (01737) 226387 – 🐼 AE VISA JCB
closed Saturday lunch, Sunday, 26 to 28 December and Bank Holidays – Meals - French
- 18.95/24.95 **st.** ₰ 6.95.

RETFORD *Notts. – see East Retford.*

REYDON *Suffolk – see Southwold.*

RHYDYCROESAU *Shrops.* 402 403 K 25 – *see Oswestry.*

RICHMOND *N. Yorks.* 402 O 20 *Great Britain G. – pop. 7 862.*
See : Castle★ AC – Georgian Theatre Royal and Museum★.
🏌 Bend Hagg ℘ (01748) 825319 – 🏌 Catterick, Leyburn Rd ℘ (01748) 833401.
🅱 Friary Gardens, Victoria Rd ℘ (01748) 850252.
London 243 – Leeds 53 – Middlesbrough 26 – Newcastle upon Tyne 44.

🏨 **King's Head,** Market Pl., DL10 4HS, ℘ (01748) 850220, Fax (01748) 850635 – ✻ 📺 ☎ 🅿
– ⚱ 150. 🐼 AE ⑩ VISA JCB
Meals (bar lunch Monday to Saturday)/dinner 18.95 **t.** and a la carte ₰ 5.50 – **28 rm**
⊡ 50.00/100.00 **t.** – SB.

🏠 **West End,** 45 Reeth Rd., DL10 4EX, W : ½ m. on A 6108 ℘ (01748) 824783, ⊯ – ✻ 📺 🅿
closed 2 weeks Christmas-New Year – Meals 12.00 **st.** ₰ 4.30 – **5 rm** ⊡ 21.00/42.00 **st.**

🏠 **Whashton Springs Farm** ⟫ without rest., DL11 7JS, NW : 3 ½ m. on Ravensworth rd
℘ (01748) 822884, Fax (01748) 826285, « Working farm », ⊯, park – ✻ ☎ 🅿. ✻
closed Christmas-1 February – **8 rm** ⊡ 26.00/42.00 **s.**

517

at Kirby Hill NW : 4½ m. by Ravensworth rd – ⊠ Richmond.

🍴 **Shoulder of Mutton Inn** with rm, DL11 7JH, ℰ (01748) 822772 – 📺 🅿. ✵
closed 25 December – **Meals** (bar lunch)/dinner a la carte 8.55/15.45 **st.** – **5 rm** 🖙 25.00/
39.00 **st.**

@ ATS Reeth Rd ℰ (01748) 824182/3

RIDGEWAY Derbs. – see Sheffield (S. Yorks.).

RINGWOOD Hants. 403 404 O 31 – pop. 11 959.
🅱 The Furlong, BH24 1AZ ℰ (01425) 470896 (summer only).
London 102 – Bournemouth 11 – Salisbury 17 – Southampton 20.

🏠 **Moortown Lodge,** 244 Christchurch Rd, BH24 3AS, ℰ (01425) 471404,
Fax (01425) 476052 – ✵ 📺 ☎ 🅿. 🆎 🗚 𝓥𝓘𝓢𝓐. ✵
closed 24 December-mid January – **Meals** (closed Sunday) (dinner only) 18.95 **t.** ⫶ 5.95 –
6 rm 🖙 32.00/80.00 **t.** – SB.

at Avon S : 4 m. on B 3347 – ⊠ Christchurch.

🏠🏠 **Tyrrells Ford** ﹩, BH23 7BH, ℰ (01425) 672646, Fax (01425) 672262, ☞, park – ✵ rest,
📺 ☎ 🅿 – 🔬 25. 🆎 🗚 ⓞ 𝓥𝓘𝓢𝓐. ✵
Meals 15.95/19.95 **t.** and dinner a la carte ⫶ 5.95 – **16 rm** 🖙 65.00/100.00 **t.** – SB.

RIPLEY N. Yorks. 402 P 21 – pop. 193 – ⊠ Harrogate.
London 213 – Bradford 21 – Leeds 18 – Newcastle upon Tyne 79.

🏠🏠 **Boar's Head**, HG3 3AY, ℰ (01423) 771888, Fax (01423) 771509, « 18C coaching inn within
estate village of Ripley Castle », ﹩, ✵ – ✵ rm, 📺 ☎ 🅗 🅿. 🆎 🗚 ⓞ 𝓥𝓘𝓢𝓐
Meals 17.50/36.00 **t.** ⫶ 6.50 – **25 rm** 🖙 105.00/120.00 **t.** – SB.

at Burnt Yates W : 2¾ m. on B 6165 – ⊠ Harrogate.

🏠 **Bay Horse Inn**, HG3 3EJ, on B 6165 ℰ (01423) 770230, ☞ – ✵ 📺 ☎ 🅿. 🆎 𝓥𝓘𝓢𝓐. ✵
Meals 10.50/15.95 **t.** and a la carte ⫶ 5.95 – **16 rm** 🖙 40.00/55.00 **t.** – SB.

⌂ **High Winsley Cottage** ﹩, HG3 3EP, NW : 1 m. by Brimham Rocks rd
ℰ (01423) 770662, ≼, ☞ – ✵ 🅿. ✵
closed January and February – **Meals** (communal dining) 12.50 **st.** – **5 rm** 🖙 34.50/
47.00 **st.** – SB.

RIPLEY Surrey 404 S 30 – pop. 1 697.
London 28 – Guildford 6.

XXX **Michels'**, 13 High St., GU23 6AQ, ℰ (01483) 224777, Fax (01483) 222940, ☞ – 🆎 🗚 𝓥𝓘𝓢𝓐
closed Saturday lunch, Sunday dinner, Monday, early January and 2 weeks August –
Meals 21.00/23.00 **t.** and a la carte ⫶ 4.50.

RIPON N. Yorks. 402 P 21 Great Britain G. – pop. 13 806.
See : Town★ - Cathedral★ (Saxon Crypt★★) AC.
Env. : Fountains Abbey★★★ AC :- Studley Royal★★ AC (≼★ from Anne Boleyn's Seat) -
Fountains Hall (Façade★), SW : 2½ m. by B 6265 – Newby Hall (Tapestries★) AC, SE : 3½ m.
by B 6265.
🅢 Ripon City, Palace Rd ℰ (01765) 603640.
🅱 Minster Rd, HG4 1LT ℰ (01765) 604625 (summer only).
London 222 – Leeds 26 – Middlesbrough 35 – York 23.

🏠🏠 **Ripon Spa**, Park St., HG4 2BU, E : ¼ m. on B 6265 ℰ (01765) 602172, Fax (01765) 690770,
☞ – ⫶ 📺 ☎ 🅿 – 🔬 150. 🆎 🗚 ⓞ 𝓥𝓘𝓢𝓐 𝓙𝓒𝓑
Meals 12.45/16.75 **st.** and a la carte ⫶ 5.50 – 🖙 8.75 – **40 rm** 65.00/95.00 **st.** – SB.

XX **Old Deanery** with rm, Minster Rd, HG4 1QS, ℰ (01765) 603518, Fax (01765) 603518,
« 17C former deanery », ☞ – ✵ rest, 📺 🅿. 🆎 🗚 ⓞ 𝓥𝓘𝓢𝓐 𝓙𝓒𝓑. ✵
Meals (closed Sunday dinner and Monday) 19.95/30.00 **t.** and a la carte ⫶ 6.25 – **3 rm**
🖙 (dinner included) 75.00/130.00 **st.**

@ ATS Dallamires Lane ℰ (01765) 601579

RISLEY Notts. – see Nottingham.

ROADE *Northants. – pop. 2 239.*
London 66 – Coventry 36 – Northampton 5.5.

XX **Roade House** with rm, 16 High St., NN7 2NW, ℰ (01604) 863372 – ⇔ **℗**. **◍③ 俹 VISA**
Meals 16.00 **st.** (lunch) and dinner a la carte 19.25/24.25 **st.** ⅋ 7.00 – **6 rm** ⊂ 65.00/
75.00 **st.**

ROCHDALE *Gtr. Manchester 402 N 23 – pop. 94 313.*
⯈ Edenfield Rd, Bagslate ℰ (01706) 46024 – ⯈ Marland, Springfield Park, Bolton Rd
ℰ (01706) 49801 – ⯈, ⯈ Castle Hawk, Chadwick Lane, Castleton ℰ (01706) 40841.
🛈 The Clock Tower, Town Hall, OL16 1AB ℰ (01706) 356592.
London 224 – Blackpool 40 – Burnley 11 – Leeds 45 – Manchester 12 – Liverpool 40.

🏛 **Norton Grange,** Manchester Rd, Castleton, OL11 2XZ, SW : 3 m. by A 58 on A 664
ℰ (01706) 30788, *Fax (01706) 49313,* ⌘ – ▮, ⇔ rm, ▤ rest, ▥ ☎ ₺ ℗ – ⫞ 150. **◍③ 俹**
① VISA
Meals 10.95/19.95 **st.** and a la carte ⅋ 5.75 – ⊂ 8.75 – **50 rm** 90.00/107.00 **st.,** 1 suite – SB.

🏛 **Royal Toby Lodge,** Manchester Rd, Castleton, OL11 3HF, SW : 2 m. by A 58 on A 664
ℰ (01706) 861861, *Fax (01706) 868428,* ⌘ – ▮, ▤ rest, ▥ ☎ ₺ ℗, **◍③ 俹 ① VISA.** ⅏
closed 25 December – **Meals** 10.25/17.55 **t.** and a la carte – ***Fallen Angel :*** **Meals** - Italian -
(dinner only) a la carte 15.00/20.00 **t.** ⅋ 4.95 – ⊂ 4.95 – **41 rm** 55.00/70.00.

🏛 **Castleton,** Manchester Rd, Castleton, OL11 2XX, SW : 3 m. by A 58 on A 664
ℰ (01706) 357888, *Fax (01706) 525757,* ⌘ – ▥ ☎ ℗. **◍③ 俹 ① VISA.** ⅏
Meals *(closed lunch Monday and Saturday)* 9.50/14.50 **t.** and a la carte ⅋ 5.00 – **13 rm**
⊂ 50.00/70.00 **t.**

XX **Nutters,** Edenfield Rd, Cheesden, Norden, OL12 7TY, W : 5 m. on A 680 ℰ (01706) 650167,
Fax (01706) 650167, ← – ⇔ ℗. **◍③ 俹 VISA**
closed Tuesday and first 2 weeks August – **Meals** a la carte 21.35/26.05 **t.**

XXX **After Eight,** 2 Edenfield Rd, OL11 5AA, W : 1 m. on A 680 ℰ (01706) 46432 – ⇔. **◍③ 俹**
VISA
closed Sunday, Monday, 2 weeks May, 25 December and 1 January – **Meals** (dinner only)
a la carte 18.90/23.30 **st.** ⅋ 5.90.

at Milnrow *SE : 3 m. by A 640 –* ⊠ *Rochdale.*

🏛 **Travel Inn,** Newhey Rd, OL16 4JF, ℰ (01706) 299999, *Fax (01706) 299074 –* ⇔ rm,
▤ rest, ▥ ₺ ℗. **◍③ 俹 ① VISA.** ⅏
Meals (grill rest.) – **40 rm** 36.50 **t.**

🛢 ATS Royds St. ℰ (01706) 32411/49935   ATS Castleton Moor, Nixon St. (ASDA)
                                                ℰ (01706) 57068

ROCHESTER *Medway 404 V 29 Great Britain G. – pop. 23 971 –* ⊠ *Chatham.*
See : *Castle★ AC – Cathedral★ AC.*
🛈 95 High St., ME1 1LX ℰ (01634) 843666.
London 30 – Dover 45 – Maidstone 8 – Margate 46.

🏛 **Bridgewood Manor,** Maidstone Rd, ME5 9AX, SE : 3 m. by A 2 and A 229 on A 2045
ℰ (01634) 201333, *Fax (01634) 201300,* ₺, ⇌, ▥, ⅏ – ▮ ⇔, ▤ rest, ▥ ☎ ₺ ℗ –
⫞ 200. **◍③ 俹 ① VISA.** ⅏
Meals *(closed Saturday lunch)* 18.50/25.00 **t.** and a la carte ⅋ 7.75 – ⊂ 9.50 – **96 rm** 89.00/
105.00 **t.,** 4 suites – SB.

🏛 **Forte Posthouse Rochester,** Maidstone Rd, ME5 9SF, SE : 2 ½ m. by A 2 on A 229
ℰ (01634) 687111, *Fax (01634) 864876,* ₺, ⇌, ▥, ⌘ – ▮, ⇔ rm, ▤ rest, ▥ ☎ ₺ ℗ –
⫞ 110. **◍③ 俹 ① VISA JCB.** ⅏
Meals a la carte 16.70/24.85 **t.** ⅋ 7.95 – ⊂ 9.95 – **105 rm** 89.00 **st.** – SB.

ROCHFORD *Essex 404 W 29 – pop. 15 081.*
London 46 – Chelmsford 19 – Colchester 39 – Southend-on-Sea 3.

🏛 **Renouf,** Bradley Way, SS4 1BU, ℰ (01702) 541334, *Fax (01702) 549563,* ⌘ – ▤ rest, ▥ ☎
℗ – ⫞ 30. **◍③ 俹 VISA**
closed 26 to 30 December – **Meals** (residents only Sunday dinner and Bank Holidays)
17.50 **st.** and a la carte ⅋ 5.50 – **23 rm** ⊂ 59.50/79.50 **st.**

Si vous cherchez un hôtel tranquille,
consultez d'abord les cartes de l'introduction
ou repérez dans le texte les établissements indiqués avec le signe ⊱ *ou* ⊱

ROGATE *W. Sussex* 404 R 30 – *pop. 1 785 –* ⊠ *Petersfield (Hants.).*
London 63 – Brighton 42 – Guildford 29 – Portsmouth 23 – Southampton 36.

⌂ **Mizzards Farm** ⊗ *without rest.,* GU31 5HS, SW : 1 m. by Harting rd ℘ (01730) 821656, Fax (01730) 821655, ≤, « 17C farmhouse », ⊒, ☞, park – ⇄ ⊡ **P**. ℀
closed Christmas – **3 rm** ⊑ 35.00/60.00 st.

ROLLESTON-ON-DOVE *Staffs.* 402 403 404 P 25 – *see Burton-upon-Trent.*

ROMALDKIRK *Durham* 402 N 20 – *see Barnard Castle.*

ROMSEY *Hants.* 403 404 P 31 *Great Britain G. – pop. 17 032.*
See : *Abbey★ (interior★★).*
Env. : *Broadlands★ AC, S : 1 m.*
☗ Dunwood Manor, Shootash Hill ℘ (01794) 340549 – ☗ Nursling ℘ (01703) 732218 – ☗, ☗ Wellow, Ryedown Lane, East Wellow ℘ (01794) 322872.
☗ 1 Latimer St., SO51 8DF ℘ (01794) 512987.
London 82 – Bournemouth 28 – Salisbury 16 – Southampton 8 – Winchester 10.

🏨 **White Horse,** Market Pl., SO51 8ZJ, ℘ (01794) 512431, Fax (01794) 517485 – ⇄ rm, ⊡ ☎ **P** – 🛋 30. ◑◐ 歴 ⓪ 𝚅𝙸𝚂𝙰
Meals (dinner only and Sunday lunch)/dinner a la carte 8.95/20.40 t. ⋬ 7.50 – ⊑ 8.95 –
33 rm 70.00/90.00 t. – SB.

⌂ **Spursholt House** ⊗, Salisbury Rd, SO51 6DJ, W : 1 ¼ m. by A 3090 (old A 31) on A 27 ℘ (01794) 512229, Fax (01794) 523142, « Part 17C mansion, gardens » – ⇄ **P**
closed 24 December-2 January – **Meals** (by arrangement) (communal dining) 15.00 st. –
3 rm ⊑ 30.00/48.00 st.

⌂ **Highfield House** ⊗, Newtown Rd, Awbridge, SO51 0GG, NW : 3 ½ m. by A 3090 (old A 31) and A 27 ℘ (01794) 340727, Fax (01794) 341450, ☞ – ⇄ rm, ⊡ ☎ **P**.
Meals (by arrangement) (communal dining) 15.00 s. – **3 rm** ⊑ 45.00/50.00 s.

✗✗✗ **Old Manor House,** 21 Palmerston St., SO51 8GF, ℘ (01794) 517353, « Timbered 16C house » – **P**. ◑◐ 歴 𝚅𝙸𝚂𝙰 𝙹𝙲𝙱
closed Sunday dinner, Monday and 1 week Christmas-New Year – **Meals** 17.50/
19.50 st. and a la carte 21.50/29.50 st. ⋬ 6.00.

ROSEDALE ABBEY *N. Yorks.* 402 R 20 *Great Britain G. – pop. 332 (Rosedale) –* ⊠ *Pickering.*
Env. : ≤★ *on road to Hutton-le-Hole.*
London 247 – Middlesbrough 27 – Scarborough 25 – York 36.

🏨 **Blacksmith's Arms,** Hartoft End, YO18 8EN, SE : 2 ½ m. on Pickering rd ℘ (01751) 417331, Fax (01751) 417167, ≤, ☞ – ⇄ rest, ⊡ ☎ **P**. ◑◐ 歴 ⓪ 𝚅𝙸𝚂𝙰
Meals (bar lunch)/dinner 15.50 t. ⋬ 5.95 – **14 rm** ⊑ (dinner included) 60.00/100.00 st. –
SB.

🏨 **Milburn Arms,** YO18 8RA, ℘ (01751) 417312, Fax (01751) 417312, ☞ – ⇄ rest, ⊡ ☎ **P**. ◑◐ ⓪ 𝚅𝙸𝚂𝙰
closed last 2 weeks January and 25 December – **Priory : Meals** (bar lunch Monday to Saturday)/dinner a la carte 20.25/26.15 t. ⋬ 6.30 – **11 rm** ⊑ 47.50/80.00 t.

🏨 **White Horse Farm,** YO18 8SE, NW : ¼ m. by Thorgill rd ℘ (01751) 417239, Fax (01751) 417781, ≤, ☞ – ⊡ ☎ **P**. ◑◐ 歴 ⓪ 𝚅𝙸𝚂𝙰
closed 24 and 25 December – **Meals** (bar lunch Monday to Saturday)/dinner 16.00 t.
and a la carte ⋬ 6.00 – **15 rm** ⊑ 45.00/70.00 st. – SB.

ROSS-ON-WYE *Herefordshire* 403 404 M 28 *Great Britain G. – pop. 9 606.*
See : *Market House★ – Yat Rock (≤★).*
Env. : *SW : Wye Valley★ – Goodrich Castle★ AC, SW : 3½ m. by A 40.*
☗ Swan House, Eddie Cross St., HR9 7BZ ℘ (01989) 562768.
London 118 – Gloucester 15 – Hereford 15 – Newport 35.

🏨 **Chase,** Gloucester Rd, HR9 5LH, ℘ (01989) 763161, Fax (01989) 768330, ☞ – ⊡ ☎ **P** – 🛋 250. ◑◐ 歴 ⓪ 𝚅𝙸𝚂𝙰. ℀
closed 26 and 27 December – **Meals** 11.20/23.50 t. ⋬ 4.95 – **39 rm** ⊑ 70.00/120.00 st. – SB.

🏨 **Royal,** Palace Pound, HR9 5HZ, ℘ (01989) 565105, Fax (01989) 768058, ≤, ☞ – ⇄ ⊡ ☎ **P** – 🛋 80. ◑◐ 歴 ⓪ 𝚅𝙸𝚂𝙰
Meals (bar lunch Monday to Saturday)/dinner a la carte 15.40/22.70 st. ⋬ 7.55 – ⊑ 8.75 –
39 rm 75.00/85.00 st. – SB.

🏨 **Travel Inn**, Ledbury Rd, HR9 7QJ, NE : 1 ½ m. by A 40 at junction with A 449 and M 50 *℘* (01989) 563861, *Fax (01989) 566124* – ⇆ rm, 📺 ₺ 🅿. 🆎 🅰🅴 💳 📼 �. �
Meals (grill rest.) – **43 rm** 36.50 t.

⌂ **Arches**, Walford Rd, HR9 5PT, on B 4234 *℘* (01989) 563348, 🍽 – ⇆ 📺 🅿. �
Meals (by arrangement) 12.00 **st.** – **7 rm** �♎ 19.00/46.00 **st.**

⌂ **Sunnymount**, Ryefield Rd, HR9 5LU, off Gloucester Rd *℘* (01989) 563880 – ⇆ rest, 🅿.
🆎 🅰🅴 💳
closed 21 to 31 December – **Meals** (by arrangement) 15.00 **st.** ₰ 4.00 – **6 rm** ⏛ 27.00/
50.00 **st.** – SB.

💥💥 **Pheasants**, 52 Edde Cross St., HR9 7BZ, *℘* (01989) 565751 – ⇆. 🆎 🅰🅴 🅾 💳
closed Sunday, Monday, 25 December-2 January and 7 to 14 June – **Meals** (lunch
by arrangement) 26.00 t. ₰ 6.50.

at Kerne Bridge *S : 3 ¾ m. on B 4234* – ✉ *Ross-on-Wye.*

⌂ **Lumleys** without rest., HR9 5QT, *℘* (01600) 890040, 🍽 – ⇆ 📺 ☎ 🅿
closed January – **3 rm** ⏛ 30.00/50.00.

at Glewstone *SW : 3 ¼ m. by A 40* – ✉ *Ross-on-Wye.*

🏨 **Glewstone Court**, HR9 6AW, *℘* (01989) 770367, *Fax (01989) 770282*, ≤, « Part Georgian
and Victorian country house », 🍽 – 📺 ☎ 🅿. 🆎 🅰🅴 💳 📼
closed 25 and 26 December – **Meals** (bar lunch Monday to Saturday)/dinner 24.00 **st.** ₰ 5.00
– **7 rm** ⏛ 45.00/95.00 **st.** – SB.

at Peterstow *W : 2 ½ m. on A 49* – ✉ *Ross-on-Wye.*

🏨🏨 **Pengethley Manor** ⚘, HR9 6LL, NW : 1 ½ m. on A 49 *℘* (01989) 730211,
Fax (01989) 730238, ≤, ⚒, 🍽, park – 📺 ☎ ₺ 🅿 – 🔬 50. 🆎 🅰🅴 🅾 💳
Meals 16.00/25.00 **st.** and a la carte ₰ 9.95 – **21 rm** ⏛ 75.00/120.00 **t.**, 3 suites – SB.

🅰 ATS Ind. Est., Alton Rd *℘* (01989) 564638

ROSTHWAITE *Cumbria* 🔢🔢 K 20 – *see Keswick.*

ROTHBURY *Northd* 🔢🔢🔢 O 18 *Great Britain G. – pop. 1 805 –* ✉ *Morpeth.*
See : *Cragside House★ (interior★) AC.*
🅱 *National Park Information Centre, Church House, Church St., NE65 7UP ℘ (01669)*
620887 (summer only).
London 311 – Edinburgh 84 – Newcastle upon Tyne 29.

⌂ **Orchard** without rest., High St., NE65 7TL, *℘* (01669) 620684, 🍽 – 📺. �
March-November – **6 rm** ⏛ 21.00/46.00.

ROTHERHAM *S. Yorks.* 🔢🔢🔢 P 23 – *pop. 121 380.*
🏌 *Thrybergh Park ℘ (01709) 850466 –* 🏌 *Grange Park, Upper Wortley Rd, Kimberworth*
℘ (01709) 558884 – 🏌 *Phoenix, Pavilion Lane, Brinsworth ℘ (01709) 363788.*
🅱 *Central Library, Walker Pl., S65 1JH ℘ (01709) 823611.*
London 166 – Kingston-upon-Hull 61 – Leeds 36 – Sheffield 6.

🏨🏨 **Hellaby Hall**, Old Hellaby Lane, Hellaby, S66 8SN, E : 5 ¼ m. on A 631 *℘* (01709) 702701,
Fax (01709) 700979, 🍽 – 📳, ⇆ rm, 📺 ₺ 🅿 – 🔬 140. 🆎 🅰🅴 🅾 💳 📼
Attic : **Meals** (dancing Friday and Saturday evenings) (bar lunch Saturday) 12.50/
19.50 **t.** and a la carte ₰ 6.50 – **51 rm** ⏛ 85.00/98.00 **t.**, 1 suite – SB.

🏨🏨 **County H. Rotherham Carlton Park**, 102-104 Moorgate Rd, S60 2BG,
℘ (01709) 849955, *Fax (01709) 368960*, 🔧, ☎ – 📳, ⇆ rm, ▤ rest, 📺 ☎ 🅿 – 🔬 120. 🆎
🅰🅴 🅾 💳. �
Meals 10.95/15.95 **t.** and a la carte ₰ 6.00 – ⏛ 9.50 – **75 rm** 70.00/85.00 **st.**

🏨🏨 **Swallow**, West Bawtry Rd, S60 4NA, SE : 2 ¼ m. on A 630 *℘* (01709) 830630,
Fax (01709) 830549, 🔧, ▨ – 📳, ⇆ rm, 📺 ☎ ₺ 🅿 – 🔬 300. 🆎 🅰🅴 🅾 💳
Meals (bar lunch Saturday) 12.95/17.75 **st.** ₰ 7.00 – **98 rm** ⏛ 95.00/110.00 **st.**, 2 suites –
SB.

🏨 **Travel Inn**, Bawtry Rd, S65 3JB, E : 2 m. by A 6021 on A 631 *℘* (01709) 543216,
Fax (01709) 531546 – ⇆ rm, 📺 ₺ 🅿. 🆎 🅰🅴 🅾 💳. �
Meals (grill rest.) – **37 rm** 36.50 t.

🏨 **Campanile**, Lowton Way, Hellaby Ind. Est., S66 8RY, E : 5 m. by A 6021 and A 631 off
Denby Way *℘* (01709) 700255, *Fax (01709) 545169* – ⇆ rm, 📺 ☎ ₺ 🅿 – 🔬 30. 🆎 🅰🅴 🅾
💳
Meals 10.55 **t.** and a la carte ₰ 4.95 – ⏛ 4.50 – **50 rm** 36.50 **t.**

at Bramley E : 4 m. by A 6021 off A 631 – ⌧ Rotherham.

🏨 **Elton,** Main St., S66 0SF, ℰ (01709) 545681, Fax (01709) 549100 – ⇆ rm, 📺 ☎ 🅿. 🕸 AE ① VISA JCB
   Meals 11.50/20.50 **st.** and a la carte ₰ 5.45 – ⌸ 8.50 – **29 rm** 50.00/75.00 **st.** – SB.

   🅐 ATS Eastwood Works, Fitzwilliam Rd
   ℰ (01709) 371556/372391

ROTHERWICK Hants – see Hook.

ROTHLEY Leics. 402 403 404 Q 25 – see Leicester.

ROUGHAM GREEN Suffolk – see Bury St. Edmunds.

ROWDE Wilts. 403 404 N 29 – see Devizes

ROWNHAMS SERVICE AREA Hants. 403 404 P 31 – ⌧ Southampton.
   🚩 M 27 Services (westbound), S01 8AW ℰ (01703) 730345.

🏨 **RoadChef Lodge** without rest., S016 8AP, M 27 between junctions 3 and 4 (southbound carriageway) ℰ (01703) 741144, Fax (01703) 740204, Reservations (Freephone) 0800 834719 – ⇆ 📺 ☎ ♿ 🅿. 🕸 AE ① VISA. ⋇
   closed 25 December – ⌸ 5.00 – **39 rm** 43.50 **st.**

ROWSLEY Derbs. 402 403 404 P 24 Great Britain G. – pop. 451 – ⌧ Matlock.
   Env. : Chatsworth★★★ (Park and Garden★★★) AC, N : by B 6012.
   London 157 – Derby 23 – Manchester 40 – Nottingham 30.

🏨 **Peacock,** Bakewell Rd, DE4 2EB, ℰ (01629) 733518, Fax (01629) 732671, « 17C stone house, antiques », ⚲, ⌖ – 📺 ☎ 🅿. 🕸 AE ① VISA. ⋇
   Meals 16.00/19.50 **t.** ₰ 8.50 – **14 rm** ⌸ 85.00/105.00 **t.** – SB.

🏨 **East Lodge** ⚥, DE4 2EF, on A 6 ℰ (01629) 734474, Fax (01629) 733949, ⌖, park – 📺 ☎ ♿ 🅿. 🕸 AE VISA. ⋇
   Meals 12.90/19.95 **t.** ₰ 6.95 – **15 rm** ⌸ 63.00/110.00 **t.** – SB.

ROWTON Ches. 402 403 L 24 – see Chester.

ROYAL LEAMINGTON SPA Warks. 403 404 P 27 – pop. 55 396.
   🏌 Leamington and County, Golf Lane, Whitnash ℰ (01926) 425961 (on plan of Warwick).
   🚩 Jephson Lodge, Jephson Gardens, The Parade, CV32 4AB ℰ (01926) 311470.
   London 99 – Birmingham 23 – Coventry 9 – Warwick 3.

Plan opposite

🏨 **Mallory Court** ⚥, Harbury Lane, Bishop's Tachbrook, CV33 9QB, S : 2 ¼ m. by B 408 (Tachbrook Rd) ℰ (01926) 330214, Fax (01926) 451714, ≼, 🍴, « Country house in extensive gardens », ⚲, squash – ⇆ rest, 📺 ☎ ⟵ 🅿. 🕸 AE ① VISA. ⋇
   Meals (booking essential) 25.00/32.50 **st.** and a la carte ₰ 9.75 – ⌸ 12.00 – **10 rm** 140.00 225.00 **st.** – SB.

🏨 **Regent,** 77 Parade, CV32 4AX, ℰ (01926) 427231, Fax (01926) 450728 – ▐, ⇆, ▤ rest, 📺 ☎ 🅿 – 🔬 100. 🕸 AE ① VISA JCB
   Meals 11.75/16.50 **st.** and a la carte ₰ 5.50 – **80 rm** ⌸ 75.00/125.00 **st.** – SB.

🏨 **Courtyard by Marriott,** Olympus Av., Tachbrook Park, CV34 6RJ, SW : 1 ½ m. by A 45 ℰ (01926) 425522, Fax (01926) 881322, 🐥 – ▐, ⇆ rm, ▤ rest, 📺 ☎ ♿ 🅿 – 🔬 50. 🕸 AE
   VISA JCB. ⋇   on Warwick town plan   Z
   Meals (closed Saturday and Sunday lunch) a la carte 12.95/21.25 **st.** ₰ 6.95 – ⌸ 8.25 **94 rm** 75.00/90.00 **st.** – SB.

🏨 **Angel,** 143 Regent St., CV32 4NZ, ℰ (01926) 881296, Fax (01926) 881296 – ▐ 📺 ☎ 🅿 🔬 40. 🕸 AE ① VISA
   Meals (closed Sunday dinner) 9.50/14.50 **t.** and a la carte ₰ 3.50 – **48 rm** ⌸ 55.00/65.00 **t.**

🏨 **Leamington H. & Bistro,** 64 Upper Holly Walk, CV32 4JL, ℰ (01926) 88377 Fax (01926) 330467, ⌖ – 📺 ☎ 🅿 – 🔬 40. 🕸 AE VISA. ⋇   U
   Meals 11.95/15.95 **t.** and a la carte ₰ 10.00 – ⌸ 5.50 – **21 rm** 60.00/90.00 **t.**

ROYAL LEAMINGTON SPA

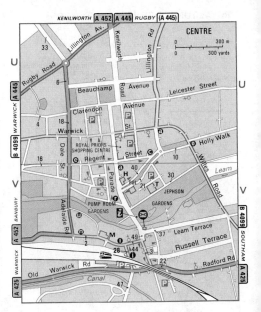

🏨 **Eaton Court,** 1-7 St. Marks Rd, CV32 6DL, ℘ (01926) 885848, *Fax (01926) 885848*, 🐎 –
⇌✦ 📺 ☎ 🅿 – 🔬 100. 🕮 🖭 ⓪ 𝚅𝙸𝚂𝙰 𝙹𝙲𝙱, ⅍   on Warwick town plan   Z e
closed 24 December-3 January – **Meals** (dinner only) 14.50 **t.** and a la carte 🍷 5.25 – **36 rm**
⊆ 45.00/75.00 **st.** – SB.

🏨 **Lansdowne,** 87 Clarendon St., CV32 4PF, ℘ (01926) 450505, *Fax (01926) 421313* –
⇌✦ rest, 📺 ☎ 🅿, 𝚅𝙸𝚂𝙰, ⅍   U a
closed 24-25 and 31 December-1 January – **Meals** (dinner only) 17.95 **st.** 🍷 4.95 – **14 rm**
⊆ 49.95/63.90 **st.** – SB.

🏨 **Adams,** 22 Avenue Rd, CV31 3PQ, ℘ (01926) 450742, *Fax (01926) 313110*, 🐎 – 📺 ☎ 🅿.
🕮 🖭 𝚅𝙸𝚂𝙰, ⅍   V n
Meals (bar lunch)/dinner 18.50 **t.** and a la carte 🍷 6.50 – **12 rm** ⊆ 46.00/68.00 **t.** – SB.

↑ **York House,** 9 York Rd, CV31 3PR, ℘ (01926) 424671, *Fax (01926) 832272* – ⇌✦ 📺 ☎, 🕮
🖭 𝚅𝙸𝚂𝙰, ⅍   V u
closed 23 December-1 January – **Meals** (by arrangement) 12.50 **t.** – **8 rm** ⊆ 25.00/52.00 **t.**
– SB.

↑ **Coverdale** without rest., 8 Portland St., CV32 5HE, ℘ (01926) 330400,
Fax (01926) 833388 – 📺 ☎, 🕮 ⓪ 𝚅𝙸𝚂𝙰   U e
7 rm ⊆ 38.00/48.00 **st.**

XX **Les Plantagenets,** 15 Dormer Pl., CV32 5AA, ℘ (01926) 451792, *Fax (01926) 453171* –
🕮 🖭 𝚅𝙸𝚂𝙰   V r
closed Saturday lunch, Sunday and Bank Holidays – **Meals** - French - 9.95/18.50 **t.** and
dinner a la carte 🍷 6.95.

XX **The Emperors,** Bath Pl., CV31 3BP, ℘ (01926) 313030, *Fax (01926) 435966* – 🍽 rest. 🕮
🖭 ⓪ 𝚅𝙸𝚂𝙰   V i
closed Sunday and Bank Holidays – **Meals** - Chinese (Peking and Cantonese) - a la carte
15.50/23.60 **t.** 🍷 4.40.

🔘 ATS 52-54 Morton St. ℘ (01926) 339643/4

ROYAL TUNBRIDGE WELLS Kent 🟦🟦 U 30 *Great Britain G.* – *pop. 60 272.*

See : *The Pantiles*★ B **26** – *Calverley Park*★ B.

🟩 *Langton Rd ℘ (01892) 523034* A.

🅱 *The Old Fish Market, The Pantiles, TN2 5TN ℘ (01892) 515675.*

London 36 – Brighton 33 – Folkestone 46 – Hastings 27 – Maidstone 18.

ROYAL TUNBRIDGE WELLS

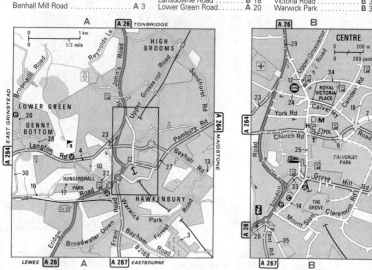

Spa, Mount Ephraim, TN4 8XJ, ☏ (01892) 520331, *Fax* (01892) 510575, 🛌, ⇔, 🔲, ⬎, 🐎 park, ※ – 🛗, ⇔ rm, 📺 ☎ ⴟ ⴗ – 🔬 250. ⬤🕲 ⵏ ⴕ 𝑉𝐼𝑆𝐴
A   v
Meals *(closed Saturday lunch)* 14.50/19.00 **t.** and a la carte ⫶ 10.50 – ⛫ 9.00 – **70 rm** 79.00/
140.00 **st.**, 4 suites – SB.

Swan, The Pantiles, TN2 5TD, ☏ (01892) 541450, *Fax* (01892) 541465 – 📺 ☎ ⴗ – 🔬 55
⬤🕲 ⵏ ⴕ 𝑉𝐼𝑆𝐴. ⌖
A   a
Meals 10.95/14.95 **t.** and a la carte ⫶ 4.25 – **19 rm** ⛫ 55.00/100.00 **t.** – SB.

Danehurst, 41 Lower Green Rd, Rusthall, TN4 8TW, W : 1 ¾ m. by A 264
☏ (01892) 527739, *Fax* (01892) 514804, 🐎 – ⇔ 📺 ⴗ. ⬤🕲 ⵏ 𝑉𝐼𝑆𝐴. ⌖
A   e
closed last week August – **Meals** (by arrangement) 19.95 **s.** – **4 rm** ⛫ 35.00/65.00 **st.**

Signor Franco, 5a High St., TN1 1UL, ☏ (01892) 549199, *Fax* (01892) 541378 – ▤. ⬤🕲 ⴕ
𝑉𝐼𝑆𝐴
B
closed Sunday and Bank Holidays – **Meals** - Italian - a la carte 20.90/31.70 **t.** ⫶ 8.10.

Chi, 26 London Rd, TN1 1DA, ☏ (01892) 513888, *Fax* (01892) 662489 – ⬤🕲 ⵏ 𝑉𝐼𝑆𝐴
B
closed Sunday and 24 to 26 December – **Meals** - Chinese - 17.50 **t.** and a la carte.

Xian, 54 High St., TN1 1XF, ☏ (01892) 522930, *Fax* (01892) 540322 – ⬤🕲 ⵏ 𝑉𝐼𝑆𝐴
B
closed Sunday and 25-26 December – **Meals** - Chinese - 10.50/17.00 **t.** ⫶ 4.60.

at Pembury *NE : 4 m. by A 264 off B 2015* – A – ⊠ *Royal Tunbridge Wells.*

Jarvis Pembury, 8 Tonbridge Rd, TN2 4QL, ☏ (01892) 823567, *Fax* (01892) 823931, ⇔
🔲 – ⇔ rm, 📺 ☎ ⴙ ⴗ – 🔬 200. ⬤🕲 ⵏ ⴕ 𝑉𝐼𝑆𝐴
A
Meals 12.50/17.95 **t.** and dinner a la carte ⫶ 7.00 – ⛫ 9.50 – **74 rm** 99.00/109.00 **st.**
5 suites – SB.

at Frant *S : 2½ m. on A 267* – A – ⊠ *Royal Tunbridge Wells.*

Old Parsonage ⌂ without rest., Church Lane, TN3 9DX, ☏ (01892) 750773
Fax (01892) 750773, ≼, « Georgian rectory », 🐎 – ⇔ 📺 ⴗ. ⬤🕲 𝑉𝐼𝑆𝐴
3 rm ⛫ 52.00/67.00 **st.**

Bassetts, 37 High St., TN3 9DT, ☏ (01892) 750635, *Fax* (01892) 750913, « 15C » – ⇔. ⬤
𝑉𝐼𝑆𝐴
closed Sunday, Monday and 1 week in spring – **Meals** 17.50/28.50 **t.** ⫶ 5.00.

ROZEL BAY Jersey (Channel Islands) 403 P 33 and 230 ⑪ – see Channel Islands.

RUAN-HIGH-LANES Cornwall 403 F 33 – see Veryan.

RUCKHALL Herefordshire – see Hereford.

RUGBY Warks. 403 404 Q 26 – pop. 61 106.
  Whitefields Hotel, Coventry Rd, Thurlaston ℰ (01788) 521800.
  The Library, St. Matthews St., CV21 3BZ ℰ (01788) 535348.
  London 88 – Birmingham 33 – Leicester 21 – Northampton 20 – Warwick 17.

Rugby Grosvenor, 81-87 Clifton Rd, CV21 3QQ, on B 5414 ℰ (01788) 535686, Fax (01788) 541297, ⅙, ≘s, ⬛ – �📺 ☎ 🅿. 🕦 ঊ ⓪ 🆅🆂🅰 🌀
  closed 25 December – Meals (closed lunch Saturday and Sunday) a la carte 16.85/22.95 t. – 20 rm 🖙 69.50/79.50 t., 1 suite.

Mr Chan's, 3-5 Castle St., CV21 2TP, ℰ (01788) 542326, Fax (01788) 542326 – ▤. 🕦 ঊ 🆅🆂🅰 🌀
  Meals - Chinese - (buffet lunch Sunday) 5.50/15.00 t. and a la carte ⌘ 5.00.

at Old Brownsover N : 2 m. by A 426 and Brownsover Rd – ⊠ Rugby.

Brownsover Hall, Brownsover Lane, CV21 1HU, ℰ (01788) 546100, Fax (01788) 579241, « 19C Gothic style hall », ☞, park – ⥼ rm, 📺 ☎ 🅿 – ♨ 80. 🕦 ঊ ⓪ 🆅🆂🅰
  Meals (closed lunch Sunday and Bank Holidays) 11.95/16.95 t. and dinner a la carte ⌘ 6.50 – 🖙 9.25 – 31 rm 80.00/90.00 t. – SB.

at Crick SE : 6 m. on A 428.

Forte Posthouse Rugby/Northampton, NN6 7XR, W : ½ m. on A 428 ℰ (01788) 822101, Fax (01788) 823955, ⅙, ≘s, ⬛ – ⥼ rm, ▤ rest, 📺 ☎ 🅿 – ♨ 200. 🕦 ঊ ⓪ 🆅🆂🅰 🌀
  Meals a la carte 17.40/25.20 st. ⌘ 7.50 – 🖙 8.95 – 88 rm 89.00 st. – SB.

at West Haddon (Northants.) SE : 10 m. on A 428.

Pytchley Inn, 23 High St., NN6 7AP, ℰ (01788) 510426, Fax (01788) 510209, ☞ – 📺 ☎ 🅿. 🕦 ঊ 🆅🆂🅰. 🌀
  Meals (grill rest.) a la carte 7.40/15.65 t. ⌘ 4.50 – 17 rm 🖙 39.00/80.00.

  🔘 ATS 73 Bath St. ℰ (01788) 574705

RUGELEY Staffs. 402 403 404 O 25 – pop. 22 975.
  London 134 – Birmingham 31 – Derby 29 – Stoke-on-Trent 22.

Travelodge, Western Springs Rd, WS15 2AS, at junction of A 51 with A 460 ℰ (01889) 570096, Reservations (Freephone) 0800 850950 – ⥼ rm, 📺 🅿 🅿. 🕦 ঊ ⓪ 🆅🆂🅰 🌀
  Meals (grill rest.) – 32 rm 44.95 t.

  🔘 ATS Mill Lane ℰ (01889) 582500/578600

RUMWELL Somerset – see Taunton.

RUNCORN Ches. 402 403 L 23 – pop. 64 154.
  Clifton Rd ℰ (01928) 572093.
  London 202 – Liverpool 14 – Manchester 29.

Forte Posthouse Warrington/Runcorn, Wood Lane, Beechwood, WA7 3HA, SE : ½ m. off junction 12 of M 56 ℰ (01928) 714000, Fax (01928) 714611, ⅙, ≘s, ⬛, ☞ – ▤, ⥼ rm, 📺 ☎ 🅿 – ♨ 500. 🕦 ঊ ⓪ 🆅🆂🅰 🌀
  Meals a la carte 15.15/26.20 st. – 🖙 9.95 – 136 rm 79.00 st. – SB.

Campanile, Lowlands Rd, WA7 5TP, beside the railway station ℰ (01928) 581771, Fax (01928) 581730 – ⥼ rm, 📺 ☎ 🅖 🅿 – ♨ 30. 🕦 ঊ 🆅🆂🅰. 🌀
  Meals 10.55 t. and a la carte ⌘ 4.95 – 🖙 4.50 – 53 rm 36.50 t.

Travel Inn, Chester Rd, Preston Brook, WA7 3BB, SE : 6 m. by A 533 on A 56 ℰ (01928) 716829, Fax (01928) 719852 – ⥼ rm, ▤ rest, 📺 🅖 🅿 – ♨ 40. 🕦 ঊ ⓪ 🆅🆂🅰. 🌀
  Meals (grill rest.) – 40 rm 36.50 t.

  🔘 ATS Sandy Lane, Weston Point ℰ (01928) 567715

RUSHDEN Northants. 404 S 27 – pop. 23 854.

London 74 – Cambridge 42 – Northampton 14 – Peterborough 25.

🏠 **Travelodge**, NN10 9EP, on A 45 (eastbound carriageway) ℰ (01933) 357008, Fax (01933) 411325, Reservations (Freephone) 0800 850950 – ⇔ rm, 📺 ⅙ ℗, ⑩ 🇦🇪 ⓪ VISA JCB. ✍
Meals (grill rest.) – **40 rm** 35.95 **t.**

RUSHLAKE GREEN E. Sussex 404 U 31 – ✉ Heathfield.

London 54 – Brighton 26 – Eastbourne 13.

🏠 **Stone House** ⬎, TN21 9QJ, north-east corner of the green ℰ (01435) 830553, Fax (01435) 830726, « Part 15C, part Georgian country house, antiques », ⬎, ☞, park – 📺 ☎ ℗
closed 2 to 26 February and 21 December-7 January – Meals (residents only) (dinner only) 24.95 **st.** ⅄ 5.10 – **6 rm** ⬷ 75.00/179.50 **st.**, 1 suite – SB.

RUSHYFORD Durham 401 402 P 20.

London 269 – Carlisle 82 – Middlesbrough 14 – Newcastle upon Tyne 26 – Sunderland 22.

🏨 **Eden Arms**, DL17 0LL, ℰ (01388) 720541, Fax (01388) 721871, 🖅, ⇌s, 🔲 – ⇔ rm, 📺 ☎ ℗ – 🔬 100. ⑩ 🇦🇪 ⓪ VISA
Meals (closed Saturday lunch) 12.50/19.50 **st.** and a la carte ⅄ 8.00 – **46 rm** ⬷ 85.00/125.00 **st.** – SB.

RYDE I.O.W. 403 404 Q 31 – see Wight (Isle of).

RYE E. Sussex 404 W 31 Great Britain G. – pop. 3 708.

See : Old Town★★ : Mermaid Street★, St. Mary's Church (≤★).
🔢 The Heritage Centre, Strand Quay, TN31 7AY ℰ (01797) 226696.
London 61 – Brighton 49 – Folkestone 27 – Maidstone 33.

🏨 **George**, High St., TN31 7JP, ℰ (01797) 222114, Fax (01797) 224065 – ⇔ 📺 ☎ – 🔬 60. ⑩ 🇦🇪 ⓪ VISA. ✍
Meals (residents only 25 and 26 December) (bar lunch Monday to Saturday)/dinner 16.00 **st.** and a la carte ⅄ 6.20 – ⬷ 8.95 – **22 rm** 70.00/100.00 **st.** – SB.

🏨 **Mermaid Inn**, Mermaid St., TN31 7EY, ℰ (01797) 223065, Fax (01797) 225069, « 15C » – 📺 ☎ ℗. ⑩ 🇦🇪 ⓪ VISA JCB. ✍
Meals 14.95/21.00 **t.** and a la carte ⅄ 8.00 – **28 rm** ⬷ 62.00/128.00 **t.** – SB.

🏠 **Rye Lodge**, Hilders Cliff, TN31 7LD, ℰ (01797) 223838, Fax (01797) 223585 – ⇔ rest, 📺 ☎ ℗. ⑩ 🇦🇪 ⓪ VISA JCB
Meals (bar lunch)/dinner 19.50 **s.** and a la carte ⅄ 6.75 – **15 rm** ⬷ 47.50/105.00 **st.** – SB.

🏠 **Jeake's House** without rest., Mermaid St., TN31 7ET, ℰ (01797) 222828, Fax (01797) 222623 – 📺 ☎. ⑩ VISA
12 rm ⬷ 24.50/87.00 **st.**

🏠 **Little Orchard House** without rest., West St., TN31 7ES, ℰ (01797) 223831, Fax (01797) 223831, ☞ – ⇔ 📺 📺. ⑩ VISA. ✍
3 rm ⬷ 45.00/84.00 **st.**

🏠 **Old Vicarage** without rest., 66 Church Sq., TN31 7HF, ℰ (01797) 222119, Fax (01797) 227466, ☞ – ⇔ 📺 ℗. ✍
closed Christmas – **6 rm** ⬷ 40.00/60.00 **st.**

XX **Flushing Inn**, 4 Market St., TN31 7LA, ℰ (01797) 223292, « 15C inn with 16C mural » – ⇔. ⑩ 🇦🇪 ⓪ VISA
closed Monday dinner, Tuesday and first 2 weeks January – Meals - Seafood - 15.00/26.00 **t.** and lunch a la carte ⅄ 5.50.

X **Landgate Bistro**, 5-6 Landgate, TN31 7LH, ℰ (01797) 222829 – ⑩ 🇦🇪 ⓪ VISA JCB
closed Sunday, Monday, 2 weeks in summer and 1 week Christmas – Meals (dinner only) 14.90 **st.** and a la carte ⅄ 4.20.

at Rye Foreign NW : 2 m. on A 268 – ✉ Rye.

🏠 **Broomhill Lodge**, TN31 7UN, on A 268 ℰ (01797) 280421, Fax (01797) 280402, ⇌s, ☞ – 📺 ☎ ℗ – 🔬 40. ⑩ ⓪ VISA. ✍
Meals (bar lunch)/dinner 21.50 **st.** ⅄ 4.80 – **11 rm** ⬷ 47.00/84.00 **st.** – SB.

at Peasmarsh NW : 4 m. on A 268 – ✉ Rye.

🏨 **Flackley Ash**, London Rd, TN31 6YH, ℰ (01797) 230651, Fax (01797) 230510, 🖅, ⇌s, 🔲 ☞ – ⇔ rest, 📺 ☎ ℗ – 🔬 100. ⑩ 🇦🇪 ⓪ VISA JCB
Meals 12.95/22.00 **st.** – **30 rm** ⬷ 69.00/108.00 **st.**, 2 suites – SB.

RYE FOREIGN *E. Sussex – see Rye.*

RYLSTONE *N. Yorks.* 402 N 21 – *see Skipton.*

RYTON ON DUNSMORE *W. Mids.* 403 404 P 28 – *see Coventry.*

SAFFRON WALDEN *Essex* 404 U 27 *Great Britain G. – pop. 13 201.*
> See : *Audley End★★ AC.*
> ⊟ *1 Market Pl., Market Sq., CB10 1HR* ℘ *(01799) 510444.*
> *London 46 – Cambridge 15 – Chelmsford 25.*

↑ **Bridge End Orchard** *without rest., 35 Bridge St., CB10 1BT,* ℘ *(01799) 522001,* ☞ –
⊱ 🖵 🅿. 🌑 VISA. ⌘
3 rm ⌑ 55.00/60.00 **st.**

at Great Chesterford NE : 3 ¾ m. by B 184 – ⊠ Saffron Walden.

↑ **The Delles** ⤸ *without rest., Carmen St., CB10 1NR,* ℘ *(01799) 530256,*
Fax (01799) 530256, « *Part 16C farmhouse* », ☞ – ⊱ 🖵 🅿. ⌘
3 rm ⌑ 30.00/44.00 **st.**

at Arkesden SW : 5½ m. by B 1052 and B 1383 off B 1039 – ⊠ Saffron Walden.

🍴 **Axe and Compasses,** *CB11 4EX,* ℘ *(01799) 550272,* « *Part 17C inn* » – 🅿. 🌑 VISA. ⌘
Meals *a la carte* 11.00/21.45 **t.** ⌀ 6.00.

at Littlebury Green W : 4½ m. by B 1383 – ⊠ Saffron Walden.

↑ **Elmdon Lee,** *CB11 4XB,* ℘ *(01763) 838237, Fax (01763) 838237,* ☞ – 🖵 🅿. 🌑 ⓪ VISA.
⌘
closed 25 December – **Meals** *(by arrangement) (communal dining)* 16.50 **s.** ⌀ 4.00 – **4 rm**
⌑ 30.00/60.00 **s.**

at Duddenhoe End W : 7½ m. by B 1052 and B 1383 off B 1039 – ⊠ Saffron Walden.

↑ **Duddenhoe End Farm** *without rest., CB11 4UU,* ℘ *(01763) 838258,* ☞, *park –* ⊱ 🖵
🅿. ⌘
closed Christmas-New Year – **3 rm** ⌑ 25.00/42.00 **s.**

at Elmdon W : 7½ m. by B 1052 and B 1383 off B 1039 – ⊠ Saffron Walden.

↑ **Elmdon Bury** ⤸, *CB11 4NF,* ℘ *(01763) 838220, Fax (01763) 838504,* 🔲, ☞, *park,* ⌘ –
⊱ *rm,* 🅿. ⌘
closed 23 December-3 January – **Meals** *(by arrangement) (communal dining) (dinner only)*
(unlicensed) 17.00 **st.** – **3 rm** ⌑ 30.00/50.00 **st.**

🔘 ATS Station Rd ℘ *(01799) 521426*

ST. AGNES *Cornwall* 403 E 33 *The West Country G. – pop. 2 899.*
> See : *St. Agnes Beacon★★ (*⁂★★*).*
> Env. : *Portreath★, SW : 5 ½ m.*
> 🇹🇭 *Perranporth, Budnic Hill* ℘ *(01872) 572454.*
> *London 302 – Newquay 12 – Penzance 26 – Truro 9.*

🏨 **Rose-in-Vale** ⤸, *Mithian, TR5 0QD, E : 2 m. by B 3285* ℘ *(01872) 552202,*
Fax (01872) 552700, 🔲, ☞ – ⊱ *rest,* 🖵 ☎ 🅿. 🌑 🄰🄴 ⓪ VISA
closed January and February – **Meals** *(bar lunch)/dinner* 19.95 **st.** *and a la carte* ⌀ 4.25 –
19 rm ⌑ 45.00/116.00 **st.** – SB.

ST. ALBANS *Herts.* 404 T 28 *Great Britain G. – pop. 80 376.*
> See : *City★ - Cathedral★ – Verulamium★ (Museum★ AC).*
> Env. : *Hatfield House★★ AC, E : 6 m. by A 1057.*
> 🇹🇭 *Batchwood Hall, Batchwood Drive* ℘ *(01727) 833349 –* 🇹🇭, 🇹🇭 *Kinsbourne Green Lane,*
> *Redbourn* ℘ *(01582) 793493.*
> ⊟ *Town Hall, Market Pl., AL3 5DJ* ℘ *(01727) 864511.*
> *London 27 – Cambridge 41 – Luton 10.*

🏨🏨 **Sopwell House** ⤸, *Cottonmill Lane, AL1 2HQ, SE : 1 ½ m. by A 1081 and Mile House*
Lane ℘ *(01727) 864477, Fax (01727) 844741,* 🏛, *Ⅰ₆,* 🈂, 🔲, ☞, *park –* 📶 🖵 ☎ 🅿 –
🔬 400. 🌑 🄰🄴 ⓪ VISA
Bejerano's Brasserie : *Meals a la carte* 11.15/20.40 **t.** *– (see also **Magnolia***
***Conservatory** below) –* ⌑ 9.95 – **90 rm** 104.75/145.00 **st.,** *2 suites –* SB.

Noke Thistle, Watford Rd, AL2 3DS, SW : 2 ½ m. at junction of A 405 with B 4630 ℘ (01727) 854252, *Fax (01727) 841906,* 🏋 – 🚭 rm, ▤ rest, [TV] ☎ [P] – 🎤 50. [MC] [AE] [DC] [VISA]
Meals *(closed Saturday lunch)* 19.50/23.00 **t.** and a la carte 🍷 5.95 – ☕ 10.00 – **109 rm** 102.00/122.00 **t.**, 2 suites – SB.

The Manor 'St. Michael's Village', Fishpool St., AL3 4RY, ℘ (01727) 864444, *Fax (01727) 848909,* <, « Part 16C, part William and Mary manor house, lake and gardens » – 🚭 rm, [TV] ☎ [P]. [MC] [AE] [VISA]. 🐾
Meals 19.50/27.50 **t.** 🍷 7.00 – **22 rm** ☕ 98.00/175.00 **t.**, 1 suite – SB.

Pré, Redbourn Rd, AL3 6JZ, NW : 1 ¼ m. on A 5183 ℘ (01727) 855259, *Fax (01727) 852239,* 🌳 – 🚭 rest, [TV] ☎ [P]. [MC] [AE] [DC] [VISA]. 🐾
closed 24 and 25 December – **Meals** (grill rest.) a la carte 12.00/16.50 **t.** 🍷 4.50 – **11 rm** ☕ 49.50/59.50 **t.**

Nonna Rosa, 3 Manor Rd, AL1 3ST, ℘ (01727) 853613, *Fax (01727) 853613,* 🌳 – [TV] ☎ [P]. [MC] [AE] [DC] [VISA]. 🐾
Meals 12.00 **st.** and a la carte 🍷 4.00 – **10 rm** ☕ 42.00/51.00 **st.**

Ardmore House, 54 Lemsford Rd, AL1 3PR, ℘ (01727) 859313, *Fax (01727) 859313,* 🌳 – [TV] ☎ [P]. [MC] [AE] [VISA]. 🐾
Meals (dinner only) a la carte 14.75/19.95 **t.** – **26 rm** ☕ 49.50/75.00 **st.**

Black Lion Inn, 198 Fishpool St., AL3 4SB, ℘ (01727) 851786, *Fax (01727) 859243* – [TV] ☎ ♿ [P]. [MC] [AE] [VISA]
Meals - Italian - *(closed Monday lunch and Sunday dinner)* a la carte 20.75/25.25 **t.** 🍷 6.00 – **16 rm** ☕ 52.00/65.00 **t.**

Orchard House 🐦 without rest., Orchard House Lane, Holywell Hill, AL1 1BX, ℘ (01727) 856520, *Fax (01727) 840957,* 🌳 – 🚭 [TV] [P]. 🐾
closed 25 and 26 December – **3 rm** ☕ 40.00/55.00 **st.**

XXX **Magnolia Conservatory** (at Sopwell House H.), Cottonmill Lane, AL1 2HQ, SE : 1 ½ m. by A 1081 and Mile House Lane ℘ (01727) 864477, *Fax (01727) 844741* – 🚭 [P]. [MC] [AE] [DC] [VISA]
closed Saturday lunch and Sunday dinner – **Meals** 14.95/23.50 **t.** and a la carte.

X **Sukiyaki,** 6 Spencer St., AL3 5EG, ℘ (01727) 865009 – [MC] [AE] [DC] [VISA] [JCB]
closed Sunday, Monday, 25 December, 1 January, 2 weeks in summer and Bank Holidays – Meals - Japanese - (dinner only) a la carte 16.00/26.00 **t.** 🍷 5.50.

⊙ ATS 163 Victoria St. ℘ (01727) 835174 ATS Lyon Way, Hatfield Rd ℘ (01727) 852314

ST. ANNE *Alderney (Channel Islands)* [403] Q 33 and [230] ⑨ – *see Channel Islands.*

ST. AUBIN *Jersey (Channel Islands)* [403] P 33 and [230] ⑪ – *see Channel Islands.*

ST. AUSTELL *Cornwall* [403] F 32 *The West Country G.* – *pop. 21 622.*

See : *Holy Trinity Church*★.

Env. : *St. Austell Bay*★★ *(Gribbin Head*★★*) E : by A 390 and A 3082 – Carthew : Wheal Martyn China Clay Heritage Centre*★★ *AC, N : 2 m. by A 391 – Mevagissey*★★ *- Lost Gardens of Heligan*★*, S : 5 m. by B 3273 – Charlestown*★*, SE : 2 m. by A 390.*

Exc. : *Trewithen*★★★ *AC, NE : 7 m. by A 390 – Lanhydrock*★★*, NE : 11 m. by A 390 and B 3269 – Polkerris*★*, E : 7 m. by A 390 and A 3082.*

⛳18 *Carlyon Bay* ℘ *(01726) 814250.*

London 281 – Newquay 16 – Plymouth 38 – Truro 14.

White Hart, Church St., PL25 4AT, ℘ (01726) 72100, *Fax (01726) 74705* – [TV] ☎ – 🎤 45. [MC] [AE] [DC] [VISA] [JCB]. 🐾
closed 25 and 26 December – **Meals** 7.75/11.00 **t.** – **18 rm** ☕ 40.00/63.00 **t.** – SB.

Poltarrow Farm without rest., St. Mewan, PL26 7DR, SW : 1 ¾ m. by A 390 ℘ (01726) 67111, *Fax (01726) 67111,* « Working farm », 🌳, park – 🚭 [TV] [P]. [MC] [VISA]. 🐾
closed Christmas – **5 rm** ☕ 22.00/44.00.

at Tregrehan *E : 2½ m. by A 390 –* ✉ *St. Austell.*

Boscundle Manor, PL25 3RL, ℘ (01726) 813557, *Fax (01726) 814997,* « Converted 18C manor, gardens », 🏊, 🏊, park – 🚭 rest, [TV] ☎ [P]. [MC] [AE] [VISA] [JCB]
mid March-October – **Meals** *(closed Sunday to non-residents)* (dinner only) 25.00 **st.** 🍷 5.00 – **7 rm** ☕ 75.00/130.00 **st.**, 3 suites – SB.

Anchorage House, Nettles Corner, Boscundle, PL25 3RH, ℘ (01726) 814071, 🌳 – 🚭 [TV] [P]. 🐾
closed November, 25 December and 1 January – **Meals** (by arrangement) (communal dining) 22.50 **s.** – **3 rm** ☕ 36.00/60.00 **s.**

at Carlyon Bay *E : 2½ m. by A 3601 – ✉ St. Austell.*

Carlyon Bay, PL25 3RD, ✆ (01726) 812304, *Fax (01726) 814938,* < Carlyon Bay, « Extensive gardens », ♨, 🏊, [🏊], ⛳18, 🎾 – ⇅ [TV] ☎ [P] – 👥 65. [MC] [AE] [DC] [VISA]. 🚫
Meals 16.50/24.50 **t.** and a la carte 🍷 5.75 – **72 rm** ☕ (dinner included) 93.00/186.00 **t.** – SB.

Cliff Head, Sea Rd, PL25 3RB, ✆ (01726) 812345, *Fax (01726) 815511,* ♨, [🏊], 🌳 – [TV] ☎ [P] – 👥 230. [MC] [AE] [DC] [VISA]. 🚫
Meals 5.95/15.95 **st.** and a la carte 🍷 3.75 – **61 rm** ☕ 40.00/70.00 **t.**

Wheal Lodge without rest., 91 Sea Rd, PL25 3SH, ✆ (01726) 815543, *Fax (01726) 815543,* 🌳 – [TV] [P]. [MC] [VISA]. 🚫
closed 1 week Christmas – **6 rm** ☕ 45.00/70.00 **st.**

at Charlestown *SE : 2 m. by A 390 – ✉ St. Austell.*

Pier House, PL25 3NJ, ✆ (01726) 67955, *Fax (01726) 69246,* < – [TV] ☎ [P]. [MC] [VISA]. 🚫
Meals *(closed 25 December)* a la carte 12.80/14.45 🍷 3.75 – **25 rm** ☕ 33.00/65.00 **t.**

T' Gallants without rest., 6 Charlestown Rd, PL25 3NJ, ✆ (01726) 70203, 🌳 – [TV] [P]. [MC] [VISA]. 🚫
8 rm ☕ 25.00/38.00.

Rashleigh Arms with rm, PL25 3NJ, ✆ (01726) 73635, *Fax (01726) 69246,* 🌳 – [TV] [P]. [MC] [AE] [VISA]. 🚫
Meals 4.95 **t.** (lunch) and a la carte 8.70/17.15 – **5 rm** ☕ 24.00/48.00 **st.**

⊚ ATS Gover Rd ✆ (01726) 65685/6

ST. BLAZEY *Cornwall* [403] F 32 – *pop. 8 837 (inc. Par).*
London 276 – Newquay 21 – Plymouth 33 – Truro 19.

Nanscawen House 🔇 without rest., Prideaux Rd, PL24 2SR, W : ¾ m. following signs for Luxulyan ✆ (01726) 814488, *Fax (01726) 814488,* <, 🏊, 🌳 – 🚭 [TV] ☎ [P]. [MC] [VISA] [JCB]. 🚫
closed 25 and 26 December – **3 rm** ☕ 40.00/78.00 **s.**

ST. BRELADE'S BAY *Jersey (Channel Islands)* [403] P 33 and [230] ⑪ – *see Channel Islands.*

ST. CLEMENT *Jersey (Channel Islands)* [403] P 33 and [230] ⑪ – *see Channel Islands.*

ST. HELENS *Mersey.* [402] [403] L 23 – *pop. 106 293.*
⛳18 *Sherdley Park Municipal, Sherdley Park ✆ (01744) 813149.*
London 207 – Liverpool 12 – Manchester 27.

Stakis St. Helens, Linkway West, WA10 1NG, ✆ (01744) 453444, *Fax (01744) 454655,* 🏋, ♨, [🏊] – ⇅, 🚭 rm, ❄ [TV] ☎ [P] – 👥 200. [MC] [AE] [DC] [VISA]
The Chalon : **Meals** (dancing Friday and Saturday evenings) 10.00/16.00 **t.** and dinner a la carte 🍷 7.00 – ☕ 9.95 – **81 rm** 101.00/104.00 **st.**, 3 suites – SB.

Waterside, East Lancashire Rd, WA11 7LX, N : 1 ¾ m. at junction of A 580 with A 571 ✆ (01744) 23333, *Fax (01744) 454231,* Reservations (Freephone) 0800 118833 – 🚭 rm, [TV] ☎ ♿ [P] – 👥 80. [MC] [AE] [DC] [VISA]. 🚫
closed 25 December – **Meals** (grill rest.) 6.55/12.95 **st.** and a la carte – ☕ 6.95 – **43 rm** 44.25 **st.** – SB.

at Rainhill *SW : 3½ m. by A 58 and B 5413 – ✉ St. Helens.*

The Ship, 804 Warrington Rd, L35 6PE, SE : 1 m. on A 57 ✆ (0151) 426 4165, *Fax (0151) 426 2831,* Reservations (Freephone) 0800 118833, 🌳 – 🚭 rm, [TV] ☎ ♿ [P]. [MC] [AE] [DC] [VISA]. 🚫
Meals (grill rest.) 12.95 **st.** (dinner) and a la carte 9.75/18.70 🍷 7.75 – ☕ 4.95 – **34 rm** 42.25 **st.** – SB.

at Eccleston *W : 3 m. by A 570 on B 5201 – ✉ St. Helens.*

Griffin Inn, Church Lane, WA10 5AD, on B 5201 ✆ (01744) 27907, *Fax (01744) 453475,* Reservations (Freephone) 0800 118833, 🌳 – 🚭 rm, [TV] ☎ [P]. [MC] [AE] [DC] [VISA]. 🚫
Meals (grill rest.) 6.55/12.95 **st.** and a la carte – ☕ 4.95 – **11 rm** 42.25 **st.**

⊚ ATS Sutton Rd ✆ (01744) 613434

ATS Blackbrook Rd, Blackbrook ✆ (01744) 754175

ST. HELIER *Jersey (Channel Islands)* [403] P 33 and [230] ⑪ – *see Channel Islands.*

ST. HILARY Cornwall – see Marazion.

ST. ISSEY Cornwall 408 F 32 – see Padstow.

ST. IVES Cambs. 404 T 27 – pop. 16 510 – ⊠ Huntingdon.
London 75 – Cambridge 14 – Huntingdon 6.

📖 **Slepe Hall,** Ramsey Rd, PE17 4RB, ℰ (01480) 463122, Fax (01480) 300706 – ⥾ rest, 📺 ☎
℗ – 🔥 40. 👁 Æ ① VISA. ⋘
closed 25 to 29 December and New Year – **Meals** 13.95/14.95 **st.** and a la carte ⬩ 5.00 –
16 rm ⋥ 62.00/85.00 **st.**

📖 **Dolphin,** Bridge Foot, London Rd, PE17 4EP, ℰ (01480) 466966, Fax (01480) 495597 – 📺
☎ ℗ – 🔥 150. 👁 Æ ① VISA. ⋘
closed 24 December-4 January – **Meals** 17.50 **t.** (dinner) and a la carte 9.45/24.95 **t.** ⬩ 4.50 –
47 rm ⋥ 65.00/85.00 **t.** – SB.

📖 **Oliver's Lodge,** Needingworth Rd, PE17 4JP, ℰ (01480) 463252, Fax (01480) 461150 –
≣ rest, 📺 ☎ ℗ – 🔥 40. 👁 Æ ① VISA JCB
closed 1 to 3 January – **Meals** a la carte 11.20/19.05 **t.** ⬩ 4.50 – **15 rm** ⋥ 62.00/92.50 **t.** –
SB.

at Holywell E : 3 m. by A 1123 – ⊠ Huntingdon.

📖 **Old Ferryboat Inn** with rm, PE17 3TG, ℰ (01480) 463227, Fax (01480) 494885, ⋞ –
⥾ rest, 📺 ℗. 👁 VISA. ⋘
Meals a la carte 10.70/16.25 **st.** – **7 rm** ⋥ 44.50/73.00 **st.**

⑩ ATS East St. ℰ (01480) 465572

ST. IVES Cornwall 408 D 33 The West Country G. – pop. 10 092.
See : Town★★ - Barbara Hepworth Museum★★ AC Y M1 – Tate Gallery ★★ - St. Nicholas
Chapel (⋞★★) Y – Parish Church★ Y A.
Env. : S : Penwith★★ Y.
Exc. : St. Michael's Mount★★ (⋞★★) S : 10 m. by B 3306 – Y – B 3311, B 3309 and A 30.
🏌 Tregenna Castle Hotel ℰ (01736) 795254 ext: 121 Y – 🏌 West Cornwall, Lelant ℰ (01736)
753401.
🛈 The Guildhall, Street-an-Pol, TR26 2DS ℰ (01736) 796297.
London 319 – Penzance 10 – Truro 25.

Plan opposite

📖 **Porthminster,** The Terrace, TR26 2BN, ℰ (01736) 795221, Fax (01736) 797043, ⋞, Fa
≡s, ⌁, ⌁, ⋞ – ∣∥ 📺 ☎ ℗. 👁 Æ ① VISA JCB
Y
closed 2 to 8 January – **Meals** (bar lunch Monday to Saturday)/dinner 20.00 **st.**
and a la carte ⬩ 4.95 – **47 rm** ⋥ 64.00/142.00 **st.**

📖 **Countryman at Trink,** Old Coach Rd, TR26 3JQ, S : 2 ½ m. by B 3306 and B 3311 o
Hayle rd ℰ (01736) 797571, Fax (01736) 797571, ⋞ – ⥾ 📺 ℗. 👁 Æ ① VISA JCB. ⋘
Meals (dinner only) a la carte 13.45/15.75 – **6 rm** ⋥ 38.00/60.00 – SB.

↑ **Old Vicarage** without rest., Parc-an-Creet, TR26 2ET, ℰ (01736) 796124,
Fax (01736) 796124, ⋞ – ⥾ 📺 ℗. 👁 Æ VISA JCB
Easter-October – **8 rm** ⋥ 23.00/48.00 **t.**

↑ **Blue Hayes,** Trelyon Av., TR26 2AD, ℰ (01736) 797129, ⋞, ⋞ – ⥾ rest, 📺 ℗. 👁 VI
JCB. ⋘
Y
mid March-mid October – **Meals** 16.00 **st.** ⬩ 4.00 – **9 rm** ⋥ 36.00/88.00 **t.** – SB.

↑ **Trewinnard,** 4 Parc Av., TR26 2DN, ℰ (01736) 794168, Fax (01736) 794168, ⋞ – ⥾ 📺 ℗
👁 VISA JCB. ⋘
Y
April-October – **Meals** (by arrangement) 12.00 **st.** ⬩ 2.75 – **7 rm** ⋥ 27.50/55.00 **st.**

↑ **Pondarosa,** 10 Porthminster Terr., TR26 2DQ, ℰ (01736) 795875 – ⥾ 📺 ℗. ⋘
Y
Meals 8.50 **s.** ⬩ 4.50 – **9 rm** ⋥ 21.00/42.00 **s.** – SB.

✕ **Pig'n'Fish,** Norway Lane, TR26 1LZ, ℰ (01736) 794204 – 👁 VISA
Y
closed Sunday to Thursday November-mid December and mid December-February
Meals - Seafood - (dinner only) 19.50 **t.** and a la carte 21.00/37.75 **t.** ⬩ 9.00.

at Carbis Bay S : 1 ¾ m. on A 3074 – ⊠ St. Ives.

📖 **Boskerris,** Boskerris Rd, TR26 2NQ, ℰ (01736) 795295, Fax (01736) 798632, ⋞, ⌁, ⋞
⥾ rest, 📺 ☎ ℗. 👁 Æ ① VISA JCB
Z
Easter-1 November – **Meals** (bar lunch)/dinner 18.00 **st.** ⬩ 5.90 – **19 rm** ⋥ (dinner
included) 38.00/82.50 – SB.

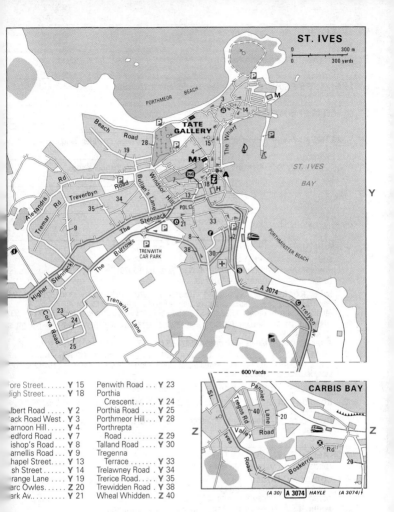

ST. IVES

ST. IVES BAY

CARBIS BAY

Pour un bon usage des plans de ville, voir les signes conventionnels.

T. JUST Cornwall **403** C 33 The West Country G. – pop. 2 092.

See : Church★.

Env. : Penwith★★ – Sancreed – Church★★ (Celtic Crosses★★), SE : 3 m. by A 3071 – St. Buryan★★ (Church Tower★★), SE : 5 ½ m. by B 3306 and A 30 – Land's End★ (cliff scenery★★★), S : 5 ½ m. by B 3306 and A 30 – Cape Cornwall★ (≤★★), W : 1 ½ m. – Morvah (≤★★), NE : 4 ½ m. by B 3306 – Geevor Tin Mine★ **AC**, N : 3 m. by B 3306 – Carn Euny★, SE : 3 m. by A 3071 – Wayside Cross★ – Sennen Cove★ (≤★), S : 5 ½ m. by B 3306 and A 30.

Exc. : – Porthcurno★, S : 9 ½ m. by B 3306, A 30 and B 3315.

☒₁₈ Cape Cornwall G & C.C., ℰ (01736) 788611.

London 325 – Penzance 7.5 – Truro 35.

🏠 **Boscean Country** ≫, TR19 7QP, NW : ½ m. by Boswedden Rd ℰ (01736) 788748, Fax (01736) 788748, ≤, 🐎 – ⊁※ rest, **🅿** **M③** **VISA**. ✵

Meals (dinner only) (residents only) ₺ 3.50 – **12 rm** ⌑ (dinner included) 37.00/66.00 **t.**

T. JUST IN ROSELAND Cornwall – see St. Mawes.

ST. LAWRENCE *I.O.W. – see Wight (Isle of).*

ST. LAWRENCE *Jersey (Channel Islands)* 403 P 33 *and* 230 ⑪ *– see Channel Islands.*

ST. LEONARDS *E. Sussex* 404 V 31 *– see Hastings and St. Leonards.*

ST. MARGARET'S AT CLIFFE *Kent* 404 Y 30 *– see Dover.*

ST. MARTIN *Guernsey (Channel Islands)* 403 P 33 *and* 230 ⑩ *– see Channel Islands.*

ST. MARTIN *Jersey (Channel Islands)* 403 P 33 *and* 230 ⑪ *– see Channel Islands.*

ST. MARTIN'S *Cornwall* 403 ㉚ *– see Scilly (Isles of).*

ST. MARY'S *Cornwall* 403 ㉚ *– see Scilly (Isles of).*

ST. MAWES *Cornwall* 403 E 33 *The West Country G.* – ✉ *Truro.*
  See : *Town★ - Castle★ AC (≤★).*
  Env. : *St. Just-in-Roseland Church★★, N : 2 ½ m. by A 3078.*
  London 299 – Plymouth 56 – Truro 18.

🏨 **Idle Rocks,** Harbourside, 1 Tredenham Rd, TR2 5AN, ℰ (01326) 270771
  Fax (01326) 270062, ≤ harbour and estuary – ⇔ rest, ⊡ ☎ ⑳ ☒ ☒
  Meals (bar lunch)/dinner 25.95 **t.** ▯ 5.05 – **24 rm** ⌑ (dinner included) 69.00/138.00 **t.** – SB.

🏨 **Rising Sun,** The Square, TR2 5DJ, ℰ (01326) 270233, *Fax (01326) 270198* – ⇔ rm, ⊡ ☎
  ☻. ⑳ ☒. ✀
  Riser Brasserie : **Meals** a la carte 14.35/20.55 **t.** – **7 rm** ⌑ 55.00/110.00 **t.,** 1 suite – SB.

🏠 **St. Mawes,** The Seafront, TR2 5DW, ℰ (01326) 270266, ≤ – ⊡ ☎. ⑳ ☒ ᴊᴄʙ
  closed December and January – **Meals** (bar lunch)/dinner 18.00 **st.** ▯ 6.00 – **7 rm** ⌑ (dinner included) 60.00/120.00 **st.** – SB.

at St. Just in Roseland *N : 2½ m. on A 3078 –* ✉ *Truro.*

🏠 **Rose da Mar** ⌕, TR2 5JB, N : ¼ m. on B 3289 ℰ (01326) 270450, *Fax (01326) 270450,* ≤
  ⇆ – ⇔ ☻
  Easter-October – **Meals** (booking essential) (dinner only) 14.00 **st.** ▯ 5.95 – **7 rm** ⌑ 25.00
  60.00 **st.**

ST.MICHAELS-ON-WYRE *Lancs.* 402 L 22.
  London 235 – Blackpool 24 – Burnley 35 – Manchester 43.

🏠 **Compton House** without rest., Garstang Rd, PR3 0TE, ℰ (01995) 679378
  Fax (01995) 679378, ⇆ – ⊡ ☻
  closed 2 weeks Christmas – **3 rm** ⌑ 20.00/40.00.

%% **Mallards,** Garstang Rd, PR3 0TE, ℰ (01995) 679661 – ☻. ⑳ ☒ ᴊᴄʙ
  closed Sunday dinner and 1 week January, July and October – **Meals** (dinner only an
  Sunday lunch)/dinner 19.00 **t.** ▯ 5.50.

ST. NEOTS *Cambs.* 404 T 27 *Great Britain G.* – *pop. 13 471.*
  See : *Town★.*
  Env. : *Parish Church★★.*
  ᴛ₁₈, ᴛ₁₈ Abbotsley, Eynesbury Hardwicke ℰ (01480) 474000.
  London 60 – Bedford 11 – Cambridge 17 – Huntingdon 9.

🏠 **Eaton Oak,** Crosshall Rd, PE19 4AG, NW : 1 m. on B 1048 at junction with A
  ℰ (01480) 219555, *Fax (01480) 407520 –* ⇔ rest, ⊡ ☎ ☻. ⑳ ☒ ☒. ✀
  closed 25 December – **Meals** (grill rest.) a la carte 8.90/18.95 **t.** – **9 rm** ⌑ 40.00/50.00 **t.**
  ⓐ ATS Brook St. ℰ (01480) 472920

ST. NEWLYN EAST *Cornwall* 403 E 32 *– see Newquay.*

ST. PETER *Jersey (Channel Islands)* 403 P 33 *and* 230 ⑪ *– see Channel Islands.*

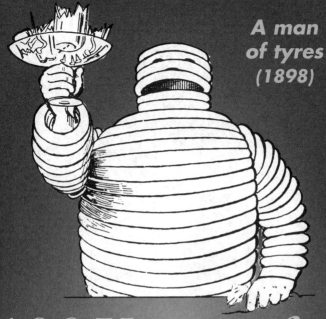

A man
of tyres
(1898)

100 Years of
BIBENDUM *!*

He moves with the times...

And he's
ver looked
o young!

Without **BIBENDUM**
there would be no wheels

From bicycle tyres...

...to the space shuttle!

Making tyres to suit every need

An international figure...

BIBENDUM
makes the world go round !

BIBENDUM,
your travel companion...

...taking you into the 21st century

Happy Birthday Bibendum

1998
BIBENDUM

100 Years of Innovation

Everybody knows the Michelin Man, or Bibendum as he is officially called, and this year, he will celebrate his 100th

birthday at events all over the world. But not everyone knows how he came about, or where he got his name.

In fact, the origins of the Michelin Man go back to 1894 when the two original Michelin brothers, Edouard and André, were visiting an exhibition in France. Finding themselves in front of a stack of tyres, Edouard commented that if you added arms and legs, the pile of tyres would look like a man.

Four years later, fantasy was turned into reality with an advertising poster of a figure made completely of tyres tucking into a feast of nails, bolts and broken glass. The message read that Michelin tyres swallow all obstacles.

The advertisement also carried the words 'Nunc est

bibendum' - which in Latin means 'now is the time to drink.' So successful was the campaign that people soon linked the tyre man with the word Bibendum, until eventually the association stuck. So, if you aren't already acquainted, meet Bibendum, or even better, Bib.

Michelin kick off the World Cup

If there's one thing that's clear about Bibendum it's that he's a winner. And when he's not busy lifting awards for the quality of his tyres, he's taking the top prizes in the world's most prestigious motor races.

In fact, Bibendum is an expert at everything he tries, and regularly drives faster, further, and with heavier loads than anyone else. Not bad for a man entering his second century.

How appropriate that with all this energy and vitality, Michelin has been chosen as the official tyre of the 1998 Football World Cup, kicking off this summer in France.

FRANCE 98 WORLD CUP

OFFICIAL TYRE OF THE 1998 WORLD CUP

III

The best trips start with Michelin

There's far more to Michelin travel information than the famous Guides to hotels and restaurants. Michelin has over 250 different publications designed to make sure your next holiday or business trip runs smooth from start to finish.

Before you leave, you can plan your route with **Michelin maps and atlases** which are clear and easy to use, and annually revised to include all the latest route information.

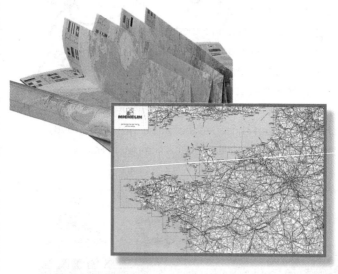

Once you arrive, if you're on a weekend or short break, you'll find all you need to know in **Michelin In Your Pocket Guides.** Entertaining and colourful they put all the facts at your fingertips with detailed maps to help you find your way around.

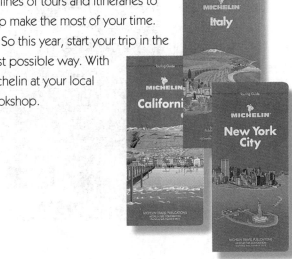

For a more detailed look at a destination, **Michelin Green Tourist Guides** explain history, economy, geography and the arts and include outlines of tours and itineraries to help make the most of your time.

So this year, start your trip in the best possible way. With Michelin at your local bookshop.

The leading edge

In 1997, as in previous years, Michelin products excelled in the highest levels of motorsport. If it had wheels and it was winning, it was probably on Michelin.

But the rewards of this success are not the broken records or the additions to the trophy cabinet. Michelin's domination of the sporting world is of real benefit to the everyday motorist, and helps the company provide higher standards of service, develop cutting edge technology and show without doubt that Michelin tyres really are world beaters.

In the RAC Auto Trader British Touring Car Championship, Michelin continues to lead the way and in 1997, seven out of the 8 teams elected to drive on Michelin Pilot tyres. Leading the charge was Alain Menu in his Renault, adding to Michelin's unequalled record of wins in five years of competition.

Michelin has also dominated the international rally scene for well over 20 years and throughout 1997, Michelin tyres carried the sport's top teams through the mud, dust, grit and snow of the world's toughest terrain.

It was the same story on two wheels, and Mick Doohan's fourth successive World Grand Prix title with Honda and Michelin earned him a place amongst motorcycling's legends.

Michelin is revving up for 1998, and looking forward to an equally impressive crop of victories.

NEW MICHELIN ENERGY

While most people only think about their tyres when they need changing, they are one of the most important parts of your car, and help you steer, brake and accelerate as well as affecting comfort, noise and fuel consumption. In other words, choose a better tyre and you directly influence safety, performance and economy.

Michelin products have a reputation for exemplary road-holding and durability, and the latest range is no exception.

New Michelin Energy car tyres have been developed in direct response to drivers' demands for increased safety and handling all year round. By fitting Michelin Energy tyres, you will benefit from enhanced dry road performance as well as improved grip and braking on wet, greasy and even snowy roads.

Furthermore, thanks to the silica based tread compounds, Energy tyres create less rolling resistance and up to 5% fuel savings. For these reasons, Michelin Energy is a popular choice among manufacturers looking for tyres to complement the performance of their most up to date cars.

For further information on the Michelin Energy range, contact your nearest tyre dealer.

ST. PETER IN THE WOOD *Guernsey (Channel Islands)* **403** P 33 and **230** ⑨ – *see Channel Islands.*

ST. PETER PORT *Guernsey (Channel Islands)* **403** P 33 and **230** ⑩ – *see Channel Islands.*

ST. SAVIOUR *Guernsey (Channel Islands)* **403** P 33 and **230** ⑨ – *see Channel Islands.*

ST. SAVIOUR *Jersey (Channel Islands)* **403** P 33 and **230** ⑪ – *see Channel Islands.*

SALCOMBE *Devon* **403** I 33 *The West Country G.* – *pop. 1 921.*

Env. : *Sharpitor (Overbecks Museum and Garden★) (⩽★★) AC, S : 2 m. by South Sands Z.*
Exc. : *Prawle Point (⩽★★★) E : 16 m. around coast by A 381 – Y – and A 379.*
🛈 *Council Hall, Market St., TQ8 8DE ℰ (01548) 842736/843927 (summer only).*
London 243 – Exeter 43 – Plymouth 27 – Torquay 28.

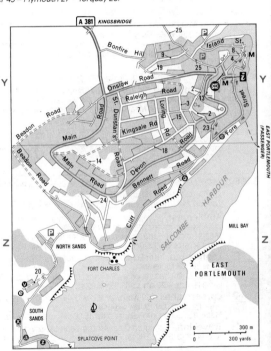

SALCOMBE

Fore Street . . . . **Y**

Allenhayes Road.	**Y** 2
Bonaventure Road.	**Y** 3
Buckley Street	**Y** 4
Camperdown Road	**Y** 7
Church Street	**Y** 8
Coronation Road.	**Y** 9
Devon Road	**Y** 13
Fortescue Road.	**Z** 14
Grenville Road	**Y** 15
Herbert Road.	**Z** 18
Knowle Road.	**Y** 19
Moult Road	**Z** 20
Newton Road	**Y** 23
Sandhills Road.	**Z** 24
Shadycombe Road.	**Y** 25

Town plans
roads most used
by traffic and those
on which guide listed
hotels and restaurants
stand are fully drawn;
the beginning only
of lesser roads
is indicated.

🏨 **Tides Reach,** South Sands, TQ8 8LJ, ℰ (01548) 843466, *Fax (01548) 843954*, ⩽ estuary, ‡, ⇌, 🔲, ⇗, squash – ‡ 🔟, ⇖ rest, 📺 ☎ 📵, ⓐ⓮ 🅰🅴 ⓞ *VISA JCB*
closed December and January – **Meals** (bar lunch)/dinner 24.75 **st.** and a la carte ‡ 7.45 –
38 rm ⇆ (dinner included) 94.00/188.00 **st.** – SB.
Z X

🏨 **Marine,** Cliff Rd, TQ8 8JH, ℰ (01548) 844444, *Fax (01548) 843109*, ⩽ estuary, ‡, ⇌, 🔲 –
‡, ⇖ rest, 📺 ☎ 📵, ⓐ⓮ 🅰🅴 ⓞ *VISA*
Meals 11.50/24.00 **t.** and a la carte ‡ 7.95 – ⇆ 8.50 – **51 rm** 70.00/125.00 **t.** – SB.
Y e

🏨 **South Sands,** South Sands, TQ8 8LL, ℰ (01548) 843741, *Fax (01548) 842112*, ⩽, 🔲 – ⬇,
⇖ rest, 📺 ☎ 📵, ⓐ⓮ *VISA JCB*
April-October – **Meals** (bar lunch)/dinner 21.00 **st.** and a la carte ‡ 5.15 – **30 rm** ⇆ (dinner
included) 80.00/170.00 **st.** – SB.
Z a

Bolt Head ⚓, South Sands, TQ8 8LL, ℘ (01548) 843751, Fax (01548) 843060, ≤ estuary, ⤴ – 📺 ☎ 📧 🏧 ⑩ 💳 🎴 ⚘
21 March-9 November – **Meals** (buffet lunch)/dinner 24.00 **st.** ⅜ 8.95 – **28 rm** ⌷ (dinner included) 92.00/195.00 **st.** – SB.
Z z

Grafton Towers, Moult Rd, TQ8 8LG, ℘ (01548) 842882, ≤ estuary, ⩟ – ⇜ rest, 📺 🅿.
📧 💳
April-October – **Meals** (dinner only) 16.95 **st.** ⅜ 5.50 – **12 rm** ⌷ (dinner included) 48.00/54.00 **st.** – SB.
Z v

The Wood ⚓, De Courcy Rd, Moult Hill, TQ8 8LQ, by Moult Rd ℘ (01548) 842778, Fax (01548) 844277, ≤ estuary, ⩟ – ⇜ 📺 ☎ 🅿. 🏧
April-November – **Meals** (by arrangement) 16.00 **st.** – **6 rm** ⌷ 30.00/80.00 **st.** – SB.
Z e

Bay View without rest., Bennett Rd, TQ8 8JJ, ℘ (01548) 842238, ≤ estuary – 🅿. ⚘
May-September (minimum 2 nights stay) – **3 rm** ⌷ 35.00/54.00 **s.**
Z o

at Combe SW : 3¾ m. by A 381 – Y – turning at Shell petrol station in Marlborough village, following signs for Sharpitor – ✉ Salcombe.

Old Walls ⚓, TQ7 3DN, ℘ (01548) 844440, « 17C cob and thatched cottages », ⩟ – ⇜ 📺 🅿. ⚘
Meals (by arrangement) (communal dining) 17.50 **st.** – **3 rm** ⌷ 70.00/80.00 **st.** – SB.

at Soar Mill Cove SW : 4¼ m. by A 381 via Malborough village – Y – ✉ Salcombe.

Soar Mill Cove ⚓, TQ7 3DS, ℘ (01548) 561566, Fax (01548) 561223, ≤, ⤴, 🔲, ⩟, ⚙ – ⇜ rest, 📺 ☎ 🅿. 📧 💳 ⚘
closed 3 January-5 February and 1 November-20 December – **Meals** (booking essential to non-residents) (light lunch)/dinner 35.00 **t.** and a la carte ⅜ 7.00 – **21 rm** ⌷ 112.00/260.00 **t.** – SB.

at Hope Cove W : 4 m. by A 381 via Malborough village – Y – ✉ Kingsbridge.

Lantern Lodge ⚓, TQ7 3HE, by Grand View Rd ℘ (01548) 561280, Fax (01548) 561736, ≤, 🛁, 🔲, ⩟ – ⇜ rest, 📺 ☎ 🅿. 📧 💳 🎴 ⚘
March-November – **Meals** (bar lunch)/dinner 14.50 **t.** ⅜ 5.95 – **14 rm** ⌷ (dinner included) 53.90/120.00 **t.** – SB.

Port Light ⚓ with rm, Bolberry Down, TQ7 3DY, SE : 2 ¼ m. via Inner Hope ℘ (01548) 561384, ≤, ⩟ – 📺 🅿. 📧 💳
closed January – **Meals** a la carte 13.70/20.35 **t.** ⅜ 4.95 – **5 rm** ⌷ (dinner included) 37.00/76.00 **t.** – SB.

SALE Gtr. Manchester **402 403 404** N 23 – pop. 56 052 – ✉ Manchester.
🏌 Sale Lodge, Golf Rd ℘ (0161) 973 3404.
London 212 – Liverpool 36 – Manchester 6 – Sheffield 43.

Amblehurst, 44 Washway Rd, M33 7QZ, on A 56 ℘ (0161) 973 8800, Fax (0161) 905 1697, ⩟ – ⇜ rm, 🍴 rest, 📺 ☎ 🅿. 📧 🏧 ⑩ 💳 ⚘
Meals (closed Saturday lunch, Sunday dinner and Bank Holidays) 13.95 **t.** (dinner) and a la carte 14.75/20.95 **t.** ⅜ 5.45 – **42 rm** ⌷ 70.00/105.00 **t.**

Lennox Lea, Irlam Rd, M33 2BH, ℘ (0161) 973 1764, Fax (0161) 969 6059, ⩟ – ⇜ rest, 📺 ☎ 🅿. 📧 🏧 ⑩ 💳
closed 25-26 December and 1 January – **Meals** (closed Sunday) (dinner only) 12.95 **t.** and a la carte ⌷ 45.95/55.95 **st.**

Cornerstones, 230 Washway Rd, M33 4RA, ℘ (0161) 283 6909, Fax (0161) 283 6909, ⩟ – ⇜ 📺 ☎ 🅿. 📧 ⑩ 💳 🎴 ⚘
Meals (residents only) (dinner only) 15.00 **s.** – ⌷ 3.00 – **9 rm** 23.00/46.00 **s.** – SB.

Travel Inn, Carrington Lane, Ashton-upon-Mersey, M33 5BL, NW : 1 ½ m. by B 5166 or A 6144 ℘ (0161) 962 8113, Fax (0161) 905 1742 – ⇜ rm, 📺 ६ 🅿 – 🔏 40. 📧 🏧 ⑩ 💳 ⚘
Meals (grill rest.) – **40 rm** 36.50 **t.**

Summer Palace, 11-15 Tatton Rd, M33 1EB, ℘ (0161) 973 9980, Fax (0161) 976 2243 – 🍴
Meals - Chinese (Peking) rest.

SALFORDS Surrey **404** T 30 – see Redhill.

THE CHANNEL TUNNEL Map Guide

260 French edition
with tourist sights in England

261 English edition
with tourist sights on the Continent

SALISBURY Wilts. 403 404 O 30 *The West Country G. – pop. 39 268.*

See : *City★★ – Cathedral★★★ AC Z – Salisbury and South Wiltshire Museum★ AC Z M2 – Close★ Z : Mompesson House★ AC Z A – Sarum St. Thomas Church★ Y B – Royal Gloucestershire, Berkshire and Wiltshire Regiment Museum★.*

Env. : *Wilton Village★ (Wilton House★★ AC, Wilton Carpet Factory★ AC), W : 3 m. by A 30 Y – Old Sarum★, N : 2 m. by A 345 Y – Woodford (Heale House Garden★) AC, NW : 4 ½ m. by Stratford Rd Y.*

Exc. : *Stonehenge★★★ AC, NW : 10 m. by A 345 – Y – and A 303 – Wardour Castle★ AC, W : 15 m. by A 30 Y.*

ₙₛ, ₙₛ *Salisbury & South Wilts., Netherhampton ℘ (01722) 742645 –* ₙₛ *High Post, Great Durnford ℘ (01722) 782231.*

🖪 *Fish Row, SP1 1EJ ℘ (01722) 334956.*

London 91 – Bournemouth 28 – Bristol 53 – Southampton 23.

Plan on next page

🏛 **Milford Hall,** 206 Castle St., SP1 3TE, ℘ (01722) 417411, Fax (01722) 419444 – 📺 ☎ 🅿 – 🏛 25. 🆗 🆎 𝘝𝘐𝘚𝘈 𝙅𝘾𝘽   Y a
Meals 9.95/15.50 **st.** and dinner a la carte 🖢 5.00 – **35 rm** ⚌ 55.00/69.00 **st.** – SB.

🏛 **White Hart,** 1 St. John's St., SP1 2SD, ℘ (01722) 327476, Fax (01722) 412761 – ⅓⅓ 📺 ☎ 🅿 – 🏛 80. 🆗 🆎 ⓞ 𝘝𝘐𝘚𝘈 𝙅𝘾𝘽. ⅍   Z s
Meals *(closed Saturday lunch)* a la carte 19.25/30.75 **t.** 🖢 6.95 – ⚌ 10.25 – **68 rm** 90.00/120.00 **t.** – SB.

🏛 **Red Lion,** 4 Milford St., SP1 2AN, ℘ (01722) 323334, Fax (01722) 325756 – 📱, ⅓⅓ rest, 📺 ☎ – 🏛 100. 🆗 🆎 ⓞ 𝘝𝘐𝘚𝘈 𝙅𝘾𝘽. ⅍   Z c
Meals (dinner only and Sunday lunch)/dinner 17.50 **t.** and a la carte 🖢 7.95 – ⚌ 9.00 – **54 rm** 85.00/125.00 **t.** – SB.

🏠 **Byways House** without rest., 31 Fowlers Rd, off Milford Hill, SP1 2QP, ℘ (01722) 328364, Fax (01722) 322146, 🌱 – 📺 🅿. 🆗 𝘝𝘐𝘚𝘈. ⅍   Z e
closed Christmas-New Year – **23 rm** ⚌ 24.00/53.50 **st.**

🏠 **Cricket Field Cottage,** Wilton Rd, SP2 7NS, W : 1 ¼ m. on A 36 ℘ (01722) 322595, Fax (01722) 322595 – ⅓⅓ rest, 📺 🛆 🅿. ⅍
Meals *(closed Sunday)* (booking essential) (residents only) (dinner only) (unlicensed) 18.00 **st.** – **13 rm** ⚌ 29.50/45.00 **st.**

⌂ **Stratford Lodge,** 4 Park Lane, SP1 3NP, off Castle Rd ℘ (01722) 325177, Fax (01722) 325177, 🌱 – 📺 ☎ 🅿. 🆗 🆎 ⓞ 𝘝𝘐𝘚𝘈 𝙅𝘾𝘽. ⅍
closed 1 week Christmas – **Meals** (by arrangement) 18.00 **st.** 🖢 5.50 – **8 rm** ⚌ 36.50/56.00 **st.**

⌂ **Old House,** 161 Wilton Rd, SP2 7JQ, W : 1 m. on A 36 ℘ (01722) 333433, Fax (01722) 416144, 🌱 – ⅓⅓ 📺 🅿. ⅍
Meals (by arrangement) 18.00 **st.** 🖢 2.50 – **7 rm** ⚌ 35.00/60.00 **st.** – SB.

⌂ **Malvern** without rest., 31 Hulse Rd, SP1 3LU, ℘ (01722) 327995, 🌱 – ⅓⅓ 📺. ⅍   Y x
3 rm ⚌ 30.00/42.00 **st.**

⌂ **Glen Lyn** without rest., 6 Bellamy Lane, Milford Hill, SP1 2SP, ℘ (01722) 327880, Fax (01722) 327880 – ⅓⅓ 📺 🅿. ⅍   YZ x
closed 2 weeks Christmas-New Year – **6 rm** ⚌ 31.00/43.00 **st.**

at Whiteparish SE : 7½ m. by A 36 – Z – on A 27 – ✉ Salisbury.

⌂ **Brickworth Farmhouse** without rest., Brickworth Lane, SP5 2QE, NW : 1 ½ m. off A 36 ℘ (01794) 884663, Fax (01794) 884581, 🌱 – 📺 🅿. ⅍
closed 23 December-2 January – **4 rm** ⚌ 25.00/40.00.

⌂ **Newton Farmhouse,** Southampton Rd, SP5 2QL, SW : 1 ½ m. on A 36 ℘ (01794) 884416, 🌱 – ⅓⅓ 📺 🅿. ⅍
Meals (by arrangement) 16.00 **s.** – **7 rm** ⚌ 25.00/50.00 **s.**

at Downton S : 6 m. by A 338 – Z – on B 3080.

⌂ **Warren** without rest., 15 High St., SP5 3PG, ℘ (01725) 510263, 🌱 – 🅿
closed 20 December-6 January – **6 rm** ⚌ 28.00/45.00 **t.**

at Woodfalls S : 7¾ m. by A 338 – Z – on B 3080 – ✉ Salisbury.

🏠 **Woodfalls Inn,** The Ridge, SP5 2LN, ℘ (01725) 513222, Fax (01725) 513220 – ⅓⅓ rest, 📺 ☎ 🅿 – 🏛 150. 🆗 🆎 𝘝𝘐𝘚𝘈
Meals 14.95/17.50 **t.** and dinner a la carte 🖢 7.95 – **8 rm** ⚌ 52.95/72.50 **t.**, 2 suites.

at Harnham SW : 1½ m. by A 3094 – ✉ Salisbury.

🏛 **County H. Salisbury Rose & Crown,** Harnham Rd, SP2 8JQ, ℘ (01722) 399955, Fax (01722) 339816, ≤, 🌿, « Part 13C inn, riverside setting », 🌱 – 📺 ☎ 🅿 – 🏛 80. 🆗 🆎 ⓞ 𝘝𝘐𝘚𝘈 𝙅𝘾𝘽. ⅍   Z u
Meals 8.50 **st.** (lunch) and a la carte 17.70/21.75 **st.** 🖢 5.00 – ⚌ 9.50 – **28 rm** 105.00/130.00 **st.** – SB.

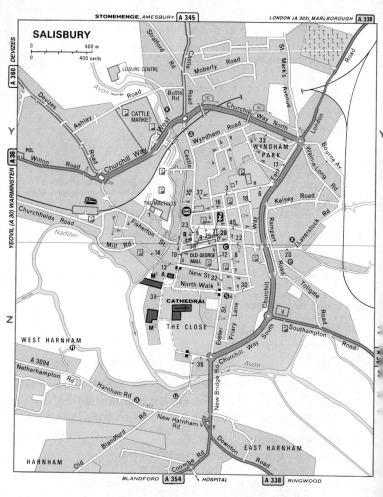

SALISBURY

A 360 DEVIZES

YEOVIL (A 30) WARMINSTER **A 36**

BLANDFORD **A 354** ✝ HOSPITAL **A 338** RINGWOOD

GREEN TOURIST GUIDES

Picturesque scenery, buildings

Attractive routes

Touring programmes

Plans of towns and buildings.

536

Grasmere, 70 Harnham Rd, SP2 8JN, ☎ (01722) 338388, *Fax (01722) 333710*, ≤, – 80. VISA JCB. Z a
Meals 12.50/17.50 **st.** and a la carte 6.50 – **20 rm** 60.50/125.00 **st.**

Old Mill, Town Path, SP2 8EU, ☎ (01722) 327517, *Fax (01722) 333367*, ≤, « Part 12C water mill », – . VISA. Z n
Meals a la carte 11.10/18.60 **t.** 6.50 – **10 rm** 45.00/70.00 **t.** – SB.

at Teffont *W : 10¼ m. by A 36 – Y – and A 30 on B 3089 – ✉ Salisbury.*

Howard's House , Teffont Evias, SP3 5RJ, on lane opposite Black Horse ☎ (01722) 716392, *Fax (01722) 716820*, ≤, « Part 17C former dower house », – rest, . VISA
Meals (dinner only and Sunday lunch)/dinner 25.00 **t.** 8.25 – **9 rm** 75.00/135.00 **t.** – SB.

at Stapleford *NW : 7 m. by A 36 – Y – on B 3083 – ✉ Salisbury.*

Elm Tree Cottage without rest., SP3 4LH, ☎ (01722) 790507, –
restricted opening November-March – **3 rm** 30.00/46.00 **s.**

at Little Langford *NW : 8 m. by A 36 – Y – and Great Wishford rd – ✉ Salisbury.*

Little Langford Farmhouse without rest., SP3 4NR, ☎ (01722) 790205, *Fax (01722) 790086*, ≤, « Working farm », , park – .
closed 24 to 26 and 31 December-1 January – **3 rm** 30.00/45.00 **st.**

ATS 155 Wilton Rd ☎ (01722) 336789
ATS 28 St. Edmund's Church St. ☎ (01722) 322390/322451

SALTASH *Cornwall* 403 H 32 *The West Country G.* – *pop. 14 139.*

Env. : *Tamar River*★★.

Exc. : *St. Germans Church*★, *SW : 7 m. by A 38 and B 3249.*

18, 18 *St. Mellion* ☎ *(01579) 351351* – 18 *China Fleet C.C.* ☎ *(01752) 848668.*

London 246 – Exeter 38 – Plymouth 5 – Truro 49.

Travelodge, Callington Rd, Carkeel, PL12 6LF, NW : 1 ½ m. by A 388 on A 38 at Saltash Service Area ☎ (01752) 848408, Reservations (Freephone) 0800 850950 – . VISA JCB.
Meals (grill rest.) – **31 rm** 49.95 **t.**

ATS 99 St. Stephens Rd ☎ (01752) 848469

SALTFORD *Bath & North East Somerset* 403 404 M 29 – *see Bristol.*

SAMLESBURY *Lancs.* 402 M 22 – *see Preston.*

SAMPFORD PEVERELL *Devon* 403 J 31 *The West Country G.* – *pop. 1 091* – ✉ *Tiverton.*

Env. : *Uffculme (Coldharbour Mill*★★*), SE : 3 m. by A 373, A 38 and minor roads.*

Exc. : *Knightshayes Court*★, *W : 7 m. by A 373 and minor roads.*

London 184 – Barnstaple 34 – Exeter 20 – Taunton 19.

Parkway House, EX16 7BJ, ☎ (01884) 820255, *Fax (01884) 820780*, – – 150. VISA JCB.
Meals *(closed Saturday lunch)* (buffet lunch)/dinner a la carte 9.35/16.70 **st.** 3.95 – **10 rm** 35.00/45.00 **st.** – SB.

Old Cottage Inn, ✉ Uffculme, EX15 3ES, E : 1 ¾ m. by A 361 on A 38 ☎ (01884) 840328 – . VISA.
Meals (in bar) a la carte approx. 9.00 **st.** 3.00 – **10 rm** 37.95 **st.**

SAMPFORD PEVERELL SERVICE AREA *Devon* 403 J 31 – ✉ *Tiverton.*

London 184 – Barnstaple 34 – Exeter 20 – Taunton 19.

Travelodge, EX16 7HD, M 5 junction 27 ☎ (01884) 821087, Reservations (Freephone) 0800 850950 – rm, . VISA JCB.
Meals (grill rest.) – **40 rm** 44.95 **t.**

SANDBACH *Ches.* 402 403 404 M 24 – *pop. 15 839.*

18 *Malkins Bank* ☎ *(01270) 765931.*

London 177 – Liverpool 44 – Manchester 28 – Stoke-on-Trent 16.

Chimney House, Congleton Rd, CW11 0ST, E : 1 ½ m. on A 534 ☎ (01270) 764141, *Fax (01270) 768916*, , – – 100. VISA JCB.
Meals 12.00/18.00 **st.** and a la carte 6.95 – 8.95 – **48 rm** 73.00/85.00 **st.** – SB.

🏛 **Old Hall,** High St., CW11 1AL, ℰ (01270) 761221, *Fax (01270) 762551*, « 17C coaching inn », ☞ – 钟 rest, 📺 ☎ 🅿 – 🔏 30. 🐼 🖭 *VISA*
Meals *(closed Sunday dinner)* (dinner only) 17.95 **t.** and a la carte – **14 rm** ⌷ 50.00/70.00 **t.**

🏛 **Saxon Cross,** Holmes Chapel Rd, CW11 1SE, E : 1 ¼ m. by A 534 ℰ (01270) 763281, *Fax (01270) 768723* – 📺 ☎ 🅿 – 🔏 80. 🐼 🖭 ⓪ *VISA*. ⅔
Meals *(closed Saturday lunch and Sunday dinner)* 8.60/15.00 **st.** and dinner a la carte ⌁ 5.50 – **52 rm** ⌷ 55.00/65.00 **st.** – SB.

at Wheelock S : 1½ m. by A 534 – ⊠ Sandbach.

✕✕ **Grove House** with rm, Mill Lane, CW11 4RD, ℰ (01270) 762582, *Fax (01270) 759465* – 📺 ☎ 🅿. 🐼 🖭 *VISA*. ⅔
closed 27 to 30 December – **Meals** *(closed Monday, Tuesday and Saturday lunch and Sunday dinner)* 12.00/16.50 **t.** and a la carte ⌁ 5.75 – **9 rm** ⌷ 45.00/70.00 **t.**

SANDGATE Kent🔢 X 30 – *see Folkestone.*

SANDIACRE Derbs. 🔢 🔢 🔢 Q 25 – *see Nottingham (Notts.).*

SANDIWAY Ches. 🔢 🔢 🔢 M 24 – ⊠ *Northwich.*
London 191 – Liverpool 34 – Manchester 22 – Stoke-on-Trent 26.

🏛 **Nunsmere Hall** ⅔, Tarporley Rd, CW8 2ES, SW : 1 ½ m. by A 556 on A 49 ℰ (01606) 889100, *Fax (01606) 889055*, ≼, 斎, « Part Victorian house on wooded peninsula », ☞, park – 📲 钟 📺 ☎ 🅿 – 🔏 50. 🐼 🖭 ⓪ *VISA* *JCB*. ⅔
Meals *(bar lunch Saturday)* 19.50 **st.** (lunch) and dinner a la carte 19.50/42.75 **st.** ⌁ 8.00 – ⌷ 13.50 – **31 rm** 110.00/150.00 **st.**, 1 suite.

SANDPLACE Cornwall – *see Looe.*

SANDRINGHAM Norfolk🔢 🔢 V 25 *Great Britain G.* – *pop. 430* – ⊠ *King's Lynn.*
See : *Sandringham House★ AC.*
London 111 – King's Lynn 8 – Norwich 50.

🏛 **Park House** ⅔, PE35 6EH, ℰ (01485) 543000, *Fax (01485) 540663*, ≼, « Former Royal residence » *Restricted to physically disabled and their companions*, ⌁, ☞ – 📲 钟 📺 ☎ 🅖 🅿. 🐼 *VISA*. ⅔
Meals (buffet lunch)/dinner 14.50 **st.** ⌁ 5.60 – **16 rm** ⌷ (dinner included) 80.00/142.00 **st.**

SANDWICH Kent🔢 Y 30 *Great Britain G.* – *pop. 4 164.*
See : *Town★.*
🔱 *The Guildhall, Cattle Market, CT13 9AH* ℰ *(01304) 613565 (summer only).*
London 72 – Canterbury 13 – Dover 12 – Maidstone 41 – Margate 9.

🏛 **Bell,** The Quay, CT13 9EF, ℰ (01304) 613388, *Fax (01304) 615308* – 钟 rm, 📺 ☎ 🅿 – 🔏 120. 🐼 🖭 ⓪ *VISA*
closed 24 and 25 December – **Meals** 9.95/16.50 **t.** and a la carte ⌁ 5.50 – **33 rm** ⌷ 70.00/130.00 **st.** – SB.

SANDY Beds. 🔢 T 27 – *pop. 8 554.*
London 49 – Bedford 8 – Cambridge 24 – Peterborough 35.

🏛 **Holiday Inn Garden Court,** Girtford Bridge, London Rd, SG19 1DH, W : ¾ m. by B 1042 at junction of A 1 with A 603 ℰ (01767) 692220, *Fax (01767) 680452* – 钟 rm, 📺 ☎ 🅿 – 🔏 200. 🐼 🖭 ⓪ *VISA* *JCB*. ⅔
Meals *(closed lunch Saturday and Sunday)* 10.00 **st.** and a la carte – ⌷ 6.00 – **56 rm** 45.00 **st.**

🏠 **Highfield Farm** without rest., Great North Rd, SG19 2AQ, N : 2 m. by B 1042 on A 1 (southbound carriageway) ℰ (01767) 682332, *Fax (01767) 692503*, park – 钟 🅿
6 rm ⌷ 30.00/45.00 **st.**

Halten Sie beim Betreten des Hotels oder des Restaurants den Führer in der Hand.
Sie zeigen damit, daß Sie aufgrund dieser Empfehlung gekommen sind.

SANDYPARK Devon **403** I 31 – see Chagford.

SARISBURY Hants. **403** **404** Q 31 – pop. 5 805 – ✉ Southampton.
London 90 – Portsmouth 16 – Southampton 6.

⌂ **Dormy House**, 21 Barnes Lane, Sarisbury Green, SO31 7DA, S : 1 m. ℰ (01489) 572626,
Fax (01489) 573370, ☞ – 📺 ☎ 🅿. 📵 VISA JCB.
Meals (by arrangement) 10.95 **st.** – **12 rm** ☑ 37.60/46.00 **st.**

SARK **403** P 33 and **230** ⑩ – see Channel Islands.

SAUNTON Devon **403** H 30 – ✉ Braunton.
Env. : Braunton★ – St. Brannock's Church★, E : 2 ½ m. on B 3231 – Braunton Burrows★,
E : ½ m. on B 3231.
🏌, 🏌 Saunton ℰ (01271) 812436.
London 230 – Barnstaple 8 – Exeter 48.

🏨 **Preston House**, EX33 1LG, ℰ (01271) 890472, Fax (01271) 890555, ≤ Saunton Sands,
⚓s, ⅃, ☞ – 📺 ☎ 🅿. 📵 VISA JCB. ✍
closed mid January-mid February – Meals (bar lunch)/dinner 16.50 **st.** ⚬ 5.00 – **15 rm**
☑ 45.00/95.00 **st.** – SB.

*Le Guide change, changez de **guide Michelin** tous les ans.*

SAWBRIDGEWORTH Herts. **404** U 28 – pop. 9 432.
London 26 – Cambridge 32 – Chelmsford 17.

✗✗ **The Shoes**, 52 Bell St., CM21 9AN, ℰ (01279) 722554, Fax (01279) 832494 – 📵 AE VISA
closed lunch Monday and Saturday, Sunday, first 2 weeks August, 2 weeks after Christmas
and Bank Holiday Mondays – Meals 11.00/17.00 **t.** and a la carte ⚬ 6.95.

SAWLEY Lancs. **402** M 22 – pop. 237.
London 242 – Blackpool 39 – Leeds 44 – Liverpool 54.

✗ **Spread Eagle** with rm, BB7 4NH, ℰ (01200) 441202, Fax (01200) 441973 – ✂ rest, 📺 ☎
🅿. 📵 AE ① VISA. ✍
closed 25 December – Meals 11.25 **st.** (dinner) and a la carte 11.00/17.95 **st.** ⚬ 6.00 – **10 rm**
☑ 35.00/50.00 **st.** – SB.

SCALBY N. Yorks. **402** S 21 – see Scarborough.

SCARBOROUGH N. Yorks. **402** S 21 – pop. 38 809.
🏌 Scarborough North Cliff, North Cliff Av., Burniston Rd ℰ (01723) 360786, NW : 2 m. by
A 165 Y – 🏌 Scarborough South Cliff, Deepdale Av., off Filey Rd ℰ (01723) 360522, S : 1 m.
by A 165 Z.
🛈 Unit 3, Pavilion House, Valley Bridge Rd, YO11 1UY ℰ (01723) 373333.
London 253 – Kingston-upon-Hull 47 – Leeds 67 – Middlesbrough 52.

Plan on next page

🏨 **Crown**, 7-11 Esplanade, YO11 2AG, ℰ (01723) 373491, Fax (01723) 362271 – 🛗 ✂ 📺 ☎ –
🔬 160. 📵 AE ① VISA   Z i
Meals (bar lunch Monday to Saturday) 17.45 **t.** and a la carte ⚬ 6.50 – ☑ 9.25 – **77 rm**
55.00/85.00 **t.**, 1 suite – SB.

🏨 **Palm Court**, St. Nicholas Cliff, YO11 2ES, ℰ (01723) 368161, Fax (01723) 371547, ⚓s, 🖼 –
🛗 📺 ☎ ⟺ – 🔬 100. 📵 AE ① VISA. ✍   Z e
Meals 9.25/13.50 **t.** and dinner a la carte ⚬ 5.00 – **46 rm** ☑ 39.00/82.00 **t.**, 1 suite – SB.

🏨 **Bradley Court**, 7-9 Filey Rd, YO11 2SE, ℰ (01723) 360476, Fax (01723) 376661 – 🛗 📺 ☎
🅿 – 🔬 120. 📵 AE ① VISA. ✍   Z r
Meals 5.95/11.95 **st.** – **40 rm** ☑ (dinner included) 39.50/79.00 **st.** – SB.

🏨 **Old Mill**, Mill St., YO11 1SW, by Victoria Rd ℰ (01723) 372735, Fax (01723) 372735,
« Restored 18C windmill » – 📺 🅿. 📵 VISA   Z u
Meals (dinner only) 10.00 – **13 rm** ☑ 27.50/55.00 **st.**

✗✗ **Jade Garden**, 121 Falsgrave Rd, YO12 5EG, ℰ (01723) 369099, Fax (01723) 375193 – 📵
AE VISA   Z v
closed 25 and 26 December – Meals - Chinese - (dinner only) a la carte approx. 10.50 **t.**

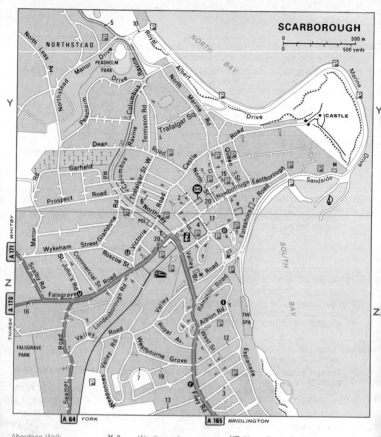

SCARBOROUGH

at Scalby *NW : 3 m. by A 171 – Z –* ⊠ *Scarborough.*

🏠 **Wrea Head** ◈, Barmoor Lane, YO13 0PB, N : 1 m. by A 171 on Barmoor Lane,
℘ (01723) 378211, *Fax* (01723) 371780, ≤, « Victorian country house », 🥀, park – 📺 ☎ 🅿
– 🔬 25. ⦿⦿ 🆎 ① 𝘝𝘐𝘚𝘈. 🦶
Meals 12.50/22.50 **t.** and dinner a la carte 🍴 6.00 – **20 rm** ⊇ 57.50/135.00 **t.**, 1 suite – SB.

at Hackness *NW : 7 m. by A 171 – Z –* ⊠ *Scarborough.*

🏛 **Hackness Grange** ◈, YO13 0JW, ℘ (01723) 882345, *Fax* (01723) 882391, « 18C
country house », ⛵, 🦢, 🥀, park, 🎾 – 📺 ☎ 🅿. ⦿⦿ 🆎 ① 𝘝𝘐𝘚𝘈 𝘑𝘊𝘉. 🦶
Meals 12.50/22.50 **t.** 🍴 6.95 – **27 rm** ⊇ 67.50/145.00 **t.**, 1 suite.

SCILLY (Isles of) *Cornwall* [403] [30] *The West Country G.* – *pop. 2 048.*

See : *Islands★ - The Archipelago (⇐★★★).*

Env. : *St. Agnes : Horsepoint★.*

Helicopter service from St. Mary's and Tresco to Penzance : ℘ (01736) 363871.

✈ *St. Mary's Airport : ℘ (01720) 422677, E : 1 ½ m. from Hugh Town.*

⛴ *from Hugh Town to Penzance (Isles of Scilly Steamship Co. Ltd) (summer only) (2 h 40 mn).*

[i] *Porthcressa Bank, St. Mary's, TR21 0JL ℘ 01720 (Scillonia) 422536.*

Bryher *The West Country G.* – *pop. 78* – ✉ *Scillonia.*

See : *Watch Hill (⇐★) – Hell Bay★.*

🏨 **Hell Bay** 🔇, TR23 0PR, ℘ (01720) 422947, *Fax (01720) 423004,* 🌳 – 🚭 rest, [TV] ☎. [MC] [VISA] [JCB]. 🐕
March-October – **Meals** (bar lunch)/dinner 21.00 **st.** 🍷 6.50, **13 suites** ☕ (dinner included) 73.00/146.00 **st.** – SB.

🏠 **Bank Cottage** 🔇, TR23 0PR, ℘ (01720) 422612, *Fax (01720) 422612,* ⇐, 🌳 – 🚭 rest, [TV]. 🐕
April-October – **5 rm** ☕ (dinner included) 36.00/82.00 **st.**

St. Martin's *The West Country G.* – *pop. 113.*

See : *St. Martin's Head (⇐★★).*

🏨 **St. Martin's on the Isle** 🔇, TR25 0QW, ℘ (01720) 422092, *Fax (01720) 422298,* ⇐ Tean Sound and islands, « Idyllic island setting », 🏊, 🌳, 🎾 – 🚭 rest, [TV] ☎. [MC] [AE] [D] [VISA]
March-October – ***Tean :*** **Meals** (bar lunch)/dinner 35.00 **st.** – **28 rm** ☕ (dinner included) 270.00 **st.**, 2 suites – SB.

St. Mary's *The West Country G.* – *pop. 1 607.*

See : *Gig racing★★ – Garrison Walk★ (⇐★★) – Peninnis Head★ – Hugh Town - Museum★*

⛳9 ℘ *(01720) 422692.*

🏨 **Star Castle** 🔇, TR21 0JA, ℘ (01720) 422317, *Fax (01720) 422343,* « Elizabethan fortress », 🏊, 🌳, 🎾 – 🚭 rest, [TV] ☎ [P]. [MC] [D] [VISA]
March-mid October – **Meals** (bar lunch)/dinner 23.00 **st.** 🍷 4.25 – **31 rm** ☕ (dinner included) 60.00/150.00 **st.**, 3 suites – SB.

🏨 **Tregarthen's,** Hugh Town, TR21 0PP, ℘ (01720) 422540, *Fax (01720) 422089,* ⇐ – 🚭 [TV] ☎. [MC] [AE] [D] [VISA]. 🐕
mid March-late October – **Meals** (bar lunch)/dinner 21.00 **t.** 🍷 6.10 – **33 rm** ☕ 55.00/144.00 **t.**

🏨 **Atlantic,** Hugh St., Hugh Town, TR21 0PL, ℘ (01720) 422417, *Fax (01720) 423009,* ⇐ St. Mary's Harbour – 🚭 rest, [TV] ☎. [MC] [VISA]
closed January and December – **Meals** (dinner only) 21.00 **t.** 🍷 6.70 – **24 rm** ☕ (dinner included) 73.00/159.00 **t.**

🏠 **Carnwethers** 🔇, Pelistry Bay, TR21 0NX, ℘ (01720) 422415, *Fax (01720) 422415,* [sauna], 🏊, 🌳 – 🚭 [TV]. 🐕
May-September – **Meals** 🍷 3.50 – **9 rm** ☕ (dinner included) 52.00/114.00 **st.**

🏠 **Carn Warvel** 🔇, Church Rd, Old Town, TR21 0NA, ℘ (01720) 422111, 🌳 – 🚭 rest, [TV]. 🐕
March-October – **Meals** (by arrangement) 12.00 **st.** 🍷 3.25 – **5 rm** ☕ (dinner included) 37.00/80.00 **st.**

🏠 **Crebinick House,** Church St., TR21 0JT, ℘ (01720) 422968 – 🚭. 🐕
April-October – **Meals** (by arrangement) 9.00 **st.** 🍷 4.80 – **6 rm** ☕ (dinner included) 84.00 **t.**

🏠 **Evergreen Cottage** without rest., Parade, High Town, TR21 0LD, ℘ (01720) 422711 – 🚭
closed 25 and 26 December – **5 rm** ☕ 25.50/51.00 **st.**

Tresco *The West Country G.* – *pop. 167* – ✉ *New Grimsby.*

See : *Island★ - Abbey Gardens★★ AC (Lighthouse Way ⇐★★).*

🏨 **The Island** 🔇, Old Grimsby, TR24 0PU, ℘ (01720) 422883, *Fax (01720) 423008,* ⇐ St. Martin's and islands, « Idyllic island setting, sub-tropical gardens », 🏊, park, 🎾 – [TV] ☎. [MC] [AE] [VISA] [JCB]. 🐕
March-October – **Meals** (bar lunch)/dinner 31.50 **st.** 🍷 10.75 – **38 rm** ☕ (dinner included) 110.00/304.00 **st.**, 2 suites.

🏨 **New Inn,** TR24 0QQ, ℘ (01720) 422844, *Fax (01720) 423200,* ⇐, 🏊, 🌳 – 🚭 rest, [TV] ☎. [MC] [VISA] [JCB]. 🐕
Meals (booking essential) (bar lunch)/dinner 16.50/21.00 **st.** – **14 rm** ☕ (dinner included) 79.00/158.00 **st.** – SB.

SCOLE Norfolk 404 X 26 – see Diss.

SCOTCH CORNER N. Yorks. 402 P 20 – ⊠ Richmond.

🖸 Granada Services, A 1, DL10 6PQ ℘ (01325) 377677.

London 235 – Carlisle 70 – Middlesbrough 25 – Newcastle upon Tyne 43.

🏨 **Quality Scotch Corner**, DL10 6NR, ℘ (01748) 850900, Fax (01748) 825417, ℔, ⓢ, ⊠
– 쉭 rm, 📺 ☎ ☻ – 🔬 280. ⓪ 🅰🅴 ⓪ 𝘝𝘐𝘚𝘈 𝘑𝘊𝘉
Meals 7.95/14.50 st. and dinner a la carte ⅜ 4.50 – 🖙 8.75 – **90 rm** 60.00/70.00 st. – SB.

🏨 **Travelodge**, Middleton Tyas Lane, D10 6PQ, ℘ (01325) 377719, Fax (01325) 377890,
Reservations (Freephone) 0800 850950 – 쉭 rm, 📺 & ☻. ⓪ 🅰🅴 ⓪ 𝘝𝘐𝘚𝘈 𝘑𝘊𝘉. ⊛
Meals (grill rest.) – **50 rm** 42.95 t.

🏨 **Travelodge**, Skeeby, DL10 5EQ, S : 1 m. on A 1 (northbound carriageway)
℘ (01748) 823768, Reservations (Freephone) 0800 850950 – 쉭 rm, 📺 & ☻. ⓪ 🅰🅴 ⓪ 𝘝𝘐𝘚𝘈
𝘑𝘊𝘉. ⊛
Meals (grill rest.) – **40 rm** 44.95 t.

SCUNTHORPE North Lincolnshire 402 S 23 – pop. 75 982.

℔ Ashby Decoy, Burringham Rd ℘ (01724) 842913 – ℔ Kingsway ℘ (01724) 840945 –
℔, ℔ Grange Park, Butterwick Rd, Messingham ℘ (01724) 762945.

✈ Humberside Airport : ℘ (01652) 688456, E : 15 m. by A 18.

London 167 – Leeds 54 – Lincoln 30 – Sheffield 45.

🏨 **Royal**, Doncaster Rd, DN15 7DE, ℘ (01724) 282233, Fax (01724) 281826 – 쉭 rm, 📺 ☎ ☻
– 🔬 200. ⓪ 🅰🅴 ⓪ 𝘝𝘐𝘚𝘈
Meals (closed Saturday lunch) 8.95/14.95 st. and a la carte ⅜ 5.25 – 🖙 7.95 – **33 rm** 59.50/
79.50 st. – SB.

🏨 **Wortley House**, Rowland Rd, DN16 1SU, ℘ (01724) 842223, Fax (01724) 280646 – 📺 ☎
☻ – 🔬 300. ⓪ 🅰🅴 ⓪ 𝘝𝘐𝘚𝘈 𝘑𝘊𝘉
Meals (bar lunch Monday to Saturday)/dinner 13.50 st. and a la carte ⅜ 5.50 – **38 rm**
🖙 65.00/70.00 st. – SB.

at Broughton E : 7 m. by A 18 – ⊠ Scunthorpe.

🏨 **Briggate Lodge Inn**, Ermine St., DN20 0AQ, S : 1 m. ℘ (01652) 650770,
Fax (01652) 650495, ℔, 🖈 – ⬥, 쉭 rm, 📺 ☎ & ☻ – 🔬 60. ⓪ 🅰🅴 ⓪ 𝘝𝘐𝘚𝘈 𝘑𝘊𝘉. ⊛
Meals 18.50 st. and a la carte ⅜ 7.50 – **84 rm** 🖙 76.00/84.00 st., 2 suites – SB.

ⓐ ATS Grange Lane North ℘ (01724) 868191

SEACROFT W. Yorks. 402 ⑩ – see Leeds.

SEAFORD E. Sussex 404 U 31 – pop. 19 622.

℔ Seaford Head, Southdown Rd ℘ (01323) 890139.

🖸 Station Approach, BN25 2AR ℘ (01323) 897426.

London 65 – Brighton 14 – Folkestone 64.

✕✕ **Quincy's**, 42 High St., BN25 1PL, ℘ (01323) 895490 – ⓪ 🅰🅴 𝘝𝘐𝘚𝘈 𝘑𝘊𝘉
closed Sunday dinner and Monday – **Meals** (dinner only and Sunday lunch)/dinner 23.00 t.
⅜ 4.25.

at Westdean E : 3 ¼ m by A 259.

⌂ **Old Parsonage** ⌾ without rest., BN25 4AL, ℘ (01323) 870432, « 13C King John
house », 🖈 – 쉭 ☻. ⊛
closed Christmas and New Year – **3 rm** 🖙 37.50/70.00.

SEAHOUSES Northd 401 402 P 17 Great Britain G..

Env. : Farne Islands★ (by boat from harbour).

℔ Beadnell Rd ℘ (01665) 720794.

🖸 Car Park, Seafield Rd, NE68 7SR ℘ (01665) 720884 (summer only).

London 328 – Edinburgh 80 – Newcastle upon Tyne 46.

🏨 **Olde Ship**, 9 Main St., NE68 7RD, ℘ (01665) 720200, Fax (01665) 721383, « Nautical
memorabilia » – 📺 ☎ ☻. ⓪ 𝘝𝘐𝘚𝘈 𝘑𝘊𝘉. ⊛
closed December and January – **Meals** (bar lunch)/dinner 14.00 st. ⅜ 5.25 – **12 rm**
🖙 36.50/73.00 st., 4 suites – SB.

🏠 **Beach House,** 12a St. Aidans, Seafront, NE68 7SR, ✆ (01665) 720337, Fax (01665) 720921, ≤, 🛜 – ✻ rest, 📺 ☎ ஃ 🅿. ⓦⓢ ᴀᴇ 𝘝𝘐𝘚𝘈 ᴊᴄʙ. ⅙
April-October – **Meals** (dinner only) 15.75 **t.** ≬ 4.95 – **14 rm** ⚏ (dinner included) 49.00/104.00 **t.** – SB.

SEALAND Flintshire 402 403 L 24 – see Chester (Ches.).

SEATOLLER Cumbria – see Keswick.

SEATON BURN Tyne and Wear 402 P 18 – see Newcastle upon Tyne.

SEATON CAREW Hartlepool 402 Q 20 – see Hartlepool.

SEAVIEW I.O.W. 403 404 Q 31 – see Wight (Isle of).

SEAVINGTON ST. MARY Somerset 403 L 31 The West Country G. – pop. 367 – ⊠ Ilminster.
Env.: Ilminster★ - Minster★★, W: 2 m.
London 142 – Taunton 14 – Yeovil 11.

🏨 **Pheasant,** Water St., TA19 0QH, ✆ (01460) 240502, Fax (01460) 242388, 🛜 – 📺 ☎ 🅿. ⓦⓢ ᴀᴇ 𝘝𝘐𝘚𝘈. ⅙
closed 24-25 December and 1 January – **Meals** (closed Sunday dinner) (dinner only and Sunday lunch)/dinner a la carte 22.70/31.45 **t.** ≬ 7.60 – **8 rm** ⚏ 70.00/120.00 **st.** – SB.

SEDGEFIELD Durham 401 402 P 20 – pop. 90 530.
London 270 – Carlisle 83 – Middlesbrough 15 – Newcastle upon Tyne 27 – Sunderland 23.

🏠 **Travelodge,** A 689 Roundabout, TS21 2JX, SE : ¾ m. on A 689 ✆ (01740) 623399, Fax (01740) 623540, Reservations (Freephone) 0800 850950 – ✻ rm, 📺 🅿. ⓦⓢ ᴀᴇ ⓞ 𝘝𝘐𝘚𝘈 ᴊᴄʙ. ⅙
Meals (grill rest.) – **40 rm** 44.95 **t.**

SEDGEMOOR SERVICE AREA Somerset.
🅱 Somerset Visitor Centre, M 5 South, BS26 2UF ✆ (01934) 750833.

🏠 **Welcome Lodge** without rest., BS24 0JL, M 5 (northbound carriageway) between junctions 22 and 21 ✆ (01934) 750831, Fax (01934) 750808, Reservations (Freephone) 0800 7314466 – ✻ 📺 ஃ 🅿. ⓦⓢ ᴀᴇ ⓞ 𝘝𝘐𝘚𝘈 ᴊᴄʙ. ⅙
40 rm 40.00 **t.**

SEDLESCOMBE E. Sussex 404 V 31 – pop. 1 631 (inc. Whatlington) – ⊠ Battle.
London 56 – Hastings 7 – Lewes 26 – Maidstone 27.

🏨 **Brickwall,** The Green, TN33 0QA, ✆ (01424) 870253, Fax (01424) 870785, ⅀, 🛜 – 📺 ☎ 🅿. ⓦⓢ ᴀᴇ ⓞ 𝘝𝘐𝘚𝘈 ᴊᴄʙ.
Meals 12.50/23.50 **t.** ≬ 5.30 – **23 rm** ⚏ 50.00/75.00 **t.** – SB.

SELSIDE Cumbria – see Kendal.

SETTLE N. Yorks. 402 N 21 – pop. 3 082.
🎯 Giggleswick ✆ (01729) 825288.
🅱 Town Hall, Cheapside, BD24 9EJ ✆ (01729) 825192.
London 238 – Bradford 34 – Kendal 30 – Leeds 41.

🏨 **Falcon Manor,** Skipton Rd, BD24 9BD, ✆ (01729) 823814, Fax (01729) 822087, 🛜 – ✻ rest, 📺 ☎ 🅿 – ⚬ 50. ⓦⓢ ᴀᴇ ⓞ 𝘝𝘐𝘚𝘈
Meals (bar lunch Monday to Saturday)/dinner 19.50 **st.** and a la carte ≬ 5.95 – **19 rm** ⚏ 55.00/104.00 **st.** – SB.

SEVENOAKS Kent 404 U 30 Great Britain G. – pop. 24 489.
Env.: Knole★★ AC, SE : ½ m. - Ightham Mote★ AC, E : 5 m. by A 25.
🎯 Woodlands Manor, Tinkerpot Lane ✆ (01959) 523805 – 🎯 Darenth Valley, Station Rd, Shoreham ✆ (01959) 522944.
🅱 Buckhurst Lane, TN13 1LQ ✆ (01732) 450305.
London 26 – Guildford 40 – Maidstone 17.

🏨 **Royal Oak,** Upper High St., TN13 1HY, ☎ (01732) 451109, Fax (01732) 740187, ✗ – 📺 ☎
🅿 – 🛦 35. 🐠 🖭 ⓪ 𝘝𝘐𝘚𝘈, ✗
Meals 12.95 t. (lunch) and a la carte 17.85/22.70 t. ⅄ 6.95 – ☲ 8.95 – **36 rm** 79.00/85.00 st.
– SB.

✗✗ **Sun Do,** 61 High St., TN13 1JF, ☎ (01732) 453299, Fax (01732) 461289 – 🔳. 🐠 🖭 ⓪ 𝘝𝘐𝘚𝘈
closed 25 and 26 December – **Meals** - Chinese - 6.50/17.50 t. and a la carte ⅄ 6.50.

at Ivy Hatch E : 4 ¾ m. by A 25 on Coach Rd – ⊠ Sevenoaks.

🏠 **The Plough,** High Cross Rd, TN15 0NL, ☎ (01732) 810268, Fax (01732) 810268, 🎇, 🛲 –
🔳 🅿. 🐠 𝘝𝘐𝘚𝘈
Meals 13.95 t. and a la carte.

SEVERN VIEW SERVICE AREA South Gloucestershire – ⊠ Bristol.
Severn Bridge (toll).

🏨 **Travelodge** without rest., BS12 3BH, M 4 junction 21 ☎ (01454) 633199,
Fax (01454) 632482, Reservations (Freephone) 0800 850950 – ✾ 📺 ☎ ㆔ 🅿. 🐠 🖭 ⓪ 𝘝𝘐𝘚𝘈
🄹🄲🄱, ✗
51 rm 46.95 t.

SHAFTESBURY Dorset 🟦🟦 N 30 The West Country G. – pop. 6 203.
See : Gold Hill★ (≼★) – Local History Museum★ AC.
Env. : Wardour Castle★ AC, NE : 5 m.
🄸 8 Bell St., SP7 8AE ☎ (01747) 853514.
London 115 – Bournemouth 31 – Bristol 47 – Dorchester 29 – Salisbury 20.

🏨 **Royal Chase,** Royal Chase Roundabout, SP7 8DB, SE : at junction of A 30 with A 350
☎ (01747) 853355, Fax (01747) 851969, 🔦, 🛲 – 📺 ☎ 🅿 – 🛦 130. 🐠 🖭 ⓪ 𝘝𝘐𝘚𝘈
Meals 19.00 t. and a la carte ⅄ 7.00 – ☲ 9.00 – **32 rm** 72.00/100.00 t. – SB.

🏠 **Paynes Place Barn** without rest., New Rd, SP7 8QL, NW : ½ m. off B 3081
☎ (01747) 855016, Fax (01747) 855016, ≼ Vale of Blackmore, 🛲 – ✾ 📺 🅿
closed Christmas – **2 rm** ☲ 30.00/46.00, 1 suite.

✗✗ **La Fleur de Lys,** 25 Salisbury St., SP7 8EL, ☎ (01747) 853717, 🎇 – 🐠 🖭 ⓪ 𝘝𝘐𝘚𝘈
closed Monday lunch, Sunday dinner and restricted opening in January – **Meals**
23.50 t. (dinner) and a la carte 23.00/30.50 t. ⅄ 5.50.

at Compton Abbas S : 4 m. on A 350 – ⊠ Shaftesbury.

🏠 **Old Forge** without rest., Chapel Hill, SP7 0NQ, ☎ (01747) 811881, Fax (01747) 811881,
« Blacksmiths forge museum », 🛲 – ✾ 🅿. ✗
3 rm ☲ 27.50/50.00 s.

at Motcombe NW : 2½ m. by B 3081 – ⊠ Shaftesbury.

🏨 **Coppleridge Inn** 📎, SP7 9HW, N : 1 m. on Mere rd ☎ (01747) 851980,
Fax (01747) 851858, 🛲, park, ✗ – 📺 ☎ 🅿 – 🛦 50. 🐠 𝘝𝘐𝘚𝘈
Meals 10.50 t. and a la carte ⅄ 4.75 – **10 rm** ☲ 42.50/72.50 t. – SB.

SHALDON Devon 🟦 J 32 – see Teignmouth.

SHANKLIN I.O.W. 🟦🟦 Q 32 – see Wight (Isle of).

SHAW Wilts. 🟦🟦 N 29 – see Melksham.

SHEDFIELD Hants. 🟦🟦 Q 31 – pop. 3 558 – ⊠ Southampton.
🏌, 🏌 Meon Valley Hotel, Sandy Lane, ☎ (01329) 833455, off A 334.
London 75 – Portsmouth 13 – Southampton 10.

🏨 **Marriot Meon Valley H. and Resort,** Sandy Lane, SO32 2HQ, off A 334
☎ (01329) 833455, Fax (01329) 834411, 🕩, ⊜, 🔦, 🏌, park, ✗, squash – ✾ 📺 ☎ 🅿 –
🛦 100. 🐠 🖭 ⓪ 𝘝𝘐𝘚𝘈, ✗
Meals 14.00/17.00 st. and dinner a la carte – **80 rm** ☲ 65.00/75.00 st., 3 suites – SB.

*Keine Aufnahme in den **Michelin-Führer** durch*
- falsche Information oder
- Bezahlung!

SHEEPWASH *Devon* 💷 *H 31 – see Hatherleigh.*

SHEFFIELD *S. Yorks.* 💷💷💷 *P 23 Great Britain G. – pop. 431 607.*

See : *Cutlers' Hall★* **CZ A** – *Cathedral Church of SS. Peter and Paul* **CZ B** : *Shrewsbury Chapel (Tomb★)*.

🏌 *Tinsley Park, High Hazel Park, Darnall* ℘ *(0114) 256 0237,* **BY** – 🏌 *Beauchief Municipal, Abbey Lane* ℘ *(0114) 236 7274/262 0040,* **AZ** – 🏌 *Birley Wood, Birley Lane* ℘ *(0114) 264 7262,* **BZ** – 🏌 *Concord Park, Shiregreen Lane* ℘ *(0114) 257 0274/257 0053,* **BY** – 🏌 *Hillsborough, Worrall Rd* ℘ *(0114) 234 3608,* **AY** – 🏌 *Abbeydale, Twentywell Lane, Dore* ℘ *(0114) 236 0763,* **AZ** – 🏌 *Lees Hall, Hemsworth Rd, Norton* ℘ *(0114) 255 4402,* **AZ**.

🛈 *Peace Gdns., S1 2HH* ℘ *(0114) 273 4671/2 – Railway Station, Sheaf St., S1 2BP* ℘ *(0114) 279 5901.*

London 174 – Leeds 36 – Liverpool 80 – Manchester 41 – Nottingham 44.

Plans on following pages

🏨 **Swallow,** Kenwood Rd, S7 1NQ, ℘ *(0114) 258 3811, Fax (0114) 250 0138,* Ⅼ₅, ⌂, 🔲, ⌇, 🛋, park – 🔄 ⇆ 🔟 ☎ 🅿 – 🔬 200. 🆗 🇦🇪 ⓞ *VISA*
AZ **r**
Meals 14.50/19.00 **st.** and a la carte – **115 rm** ⛌ 95.00/120.00 **st.** – SB.

🏨 **Holiday Inn Sheffield,** Victoria Station Rd, S4 7YE, ℘ *(0114) 276 8822, Fax (0114) 272 4519* – 🔄, ⇆ rm, 🔟 ☎ 🅿 – 🔬 400. 🆗 🇦🇪 ⓞ *VISA* 𝗝𝗖𝗕
DY **a**
Meals 13.00/16.50 **st.** and a la carte ⓐ 5.95 – ⛌ 9.95 – **100 rm** 85.00/120.00 **st.**

🏨 **Charnwood,** 10 Sharrow Lane, S11 8AA, ℘ *(0114) 258 9411, Fax (0114) 255 5107* – 🔟 ☎ 🅿 – 🔬 100. 🆗 🇦🇪 ⓞ *VISA*. ⌖
CZ **u**
closed 24 to 31 December – **Brasserie Leo :** Meals *(closed Sunday)* (dinner only) a la carte 12.00/18.00 **t.** ⓐ 6.75 – **Henfrey's :** Meals *(closed Sunday)* (dinner only) 25.00 **t.** ⓐ 8.25 – **22 rm** ⛌ 75.00/90.00 **t.**

🏨 **Beauchief,** 161 Abbeydale Road South, S7 2QW, SW : 3½ m. on A 621 ℘ *(0114) 262 0500, Fax (0114) 235 0197* – ⇆ rm, 🔟 ☎ 🅿 – 🔬 100. 🆗 🇦🇪 ⓞ *VISA*. ⌖
Meals 11.50/18.70 **t.** and a la carte ⓐ 7.25 – ⛌ 9.25 – **41 rm** 80.00/110.00 **t.** – SB.

🏨 **Harley,** 334 Glossop Rd, S10 2HW, ℘ *(0114) 275 2288, Fax (0114) 272 2383* – ⇆ rm, ▤ rest, 🔟 ☎ – 🔬 25. 🆗 🇦🇪 *VISA*. ⌖
CZ **e**
closed Bank Holidays – Meals *(closed Saturday lunch and Sunday)* (dancing Friday and Saturday evenings) 17.95 **t.** (dinner) and a la carte 21.45/28.45 **t.** ⓐ 8.50 – ⛌ 7.50 – **22 rm** 62.50/80.00 **t.**

🏨 **Forte Posthouse Sheffield,** Manchester Rd, Fulwood, S10 5DX, ℘ *(0114) 267 0067, Fax (0114) 268 2620,* ⬉, Ⅼ₅, 🔲 – 🔄, ⇆ rm, 🔟 ☎ 🅿 – 🔬 300. 🆗 🇦🇪 ⓞ *VISA*
AZ **a**
Meals a la carte 16.40/21.85 **st.** ⓐ 6.50 – ⛌ 8.95 – **133 rm** 69.00 **st.,** 2 suites – SB.

🏨 **Novotel,** Arundel Gate, S1 2PR, ℘ *(0114) 278 1781, Fax (0114) 278 7744,* 🔲 – 🔄, ⇆ rm, ▤ 🔟 ☎ 🅿 – 🔬 170. 🆗 🇦🇪 ⓞ *VISA* 𝗝𝗖𝗕
DZ **a**
Meals 14.95 **st.** (dinner) and a la carte 16.00/19.00 **st.** ⓐ 6.50 – ⛌ 8.50 – **144 rm** 72.50/110.00 **st.** – SB.

🏨 **Westbourne House** without rest., 25 Westbourne Rd, S10 2QQ, ℘ *(0114) 266 0109, Fax (0114) 266 7778,* 🛋 – 🔟 ☎ 🅿. 🆗 🇦🇪 *VISA* 𝗝𝗖𝗕
AZ **c**
closed 20 December-3 January – **9 rm** ⛌ 43.00/75.00 **st.**

🏨 **Travel Inn,** Attercliffe Common Rd, S9 2LU, ℘ *(0114) 242 2802, Fax (0114) 242 3703* – 🔄, ⇆ rm, 🔟 ⓓ 🅿. 🆗 🇦🇪 ⓞ *VISA*. ⌖
BY **a**
Meals (grill rest.) – **61 rm** 36.50 **t.**

🏨 **Travelodge,** 340 Prince of Wales Rd, S2 1FF, ℘ *(0114) 253 0935, Fax (0114) 264 2731,* Reservations (Freephone) 0800 850950 – ⇆ rm, 🔟 ⓓ 🅿 – 🔬 80. 🆗 🇦🇪 ⓞ *VISA* 𝗝𝗖𝗕.
BZ **a**
⌖
Meals (grill rest.) – **60 rm** 44.95 **t.**

🏨 **Coniston** without rest., 90 Beechwood Rd, Hillsborough, S6 4LQ, ℘ *(0114) 233 9680* – 🔟 🅿. ⌖
AY **a**
closed 1 week Christmas – **4 rm** ⛌ 17.00/34.00 **st.**

🍴🍴 **Rafters,** 220 Oakbrook Rd, Nether Green, S11 7ED, SW : 2½ m. by A 625 and Rustlings Rd, turning left at roundabout ℘ *(0114) 230 4819* – 🇦🇪
closed Sunday, Tuesday, 25-26 December and 1-2 January – Meals (dinner only) 18.95 **t.** ⓐ 6.95.

🍴 **Smith's of Sheffield,** 34 Sandygate Rd, S10 5RY, W : 2¼ m. by A 57, turning left at Crosspool Tavern ℘ *(0114) 266 6096* – ⇆ rm, 🆗 🇦🇪 *VISA*
closed dinner Sunday and Monday – Meals (booking essential Friday and Saturday) (dinner only and Sunday lunch)/dinner a la carte 17.50/24.00 **st.** ⓐ 6.95.

SHEFFIELD
BUILT UP AREA

Meadowhall
  Shopping Centre . . . . **BY**

Barrow Road . . . . **BY** 4

Bawtry Road . . . . **BY** 5
Bradfield Road . . . . **AY** 7
Brocco Bank . . . . **AZ** 8
Broughton Lane . . . . **BY** 10
Burngreave Road . . . . **AY** 12
Handsworth Road . . . . **BZ** 24
Holywell Road . . . . **BY** 29
Main Road . . . . **BZ** 32

Meadow Hall Road . . . . **BY** 33
Middlewood Road . . . . **AY** 34
Newhall Road . . . . **BY** 36
Westbourne Road . . . . **AZ** 47
Western Bank . . . . **AZ** 48
Whitham Road . . . . **AZ** 49
Woodbourn Road . . . . **BYZ** 50
Woodhouse Road . . . . **BZ** 51

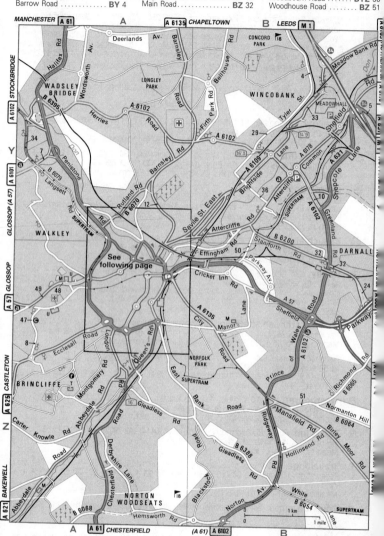

Gli alberghi o ristoranti ameni sono indicati nella guida
con un simbolo rosso.

Contribuite a mantenere
la guida aggiornata segnalandoci
gli alberghi ed i ristoranti dove avete soggiornato piacevolmente.

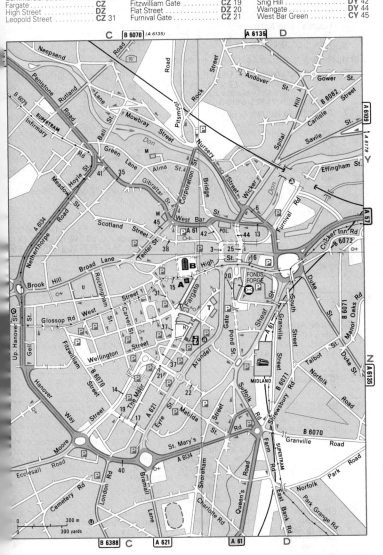

No confondete :

Confort degli alberghi :

Confort dei ristoranti :

Qualità della tavola :

547

at Grenoside N : 4½ m. on A 61 – AY – ⊠ Sheffield.

🏛 **Whitley Hall** ⌂, Elliott Lane, S35 8NR, E : 1 m. off Whitley Lane ℘ (0114) 245 4444, Fax (0114) 245 5414, « Part 16C Elizabethan manor house », ⌖, park – 📺 ☎ 🅿 – 🕴 70. 🕮 🖭 VISA. ⌖
closed Bank Holidays – Meals (closed Saturday lunch) 13.50/20.50 t. and a la carte 🛆 6.00 – 18 rm ⊇ 65.00/160.00 t.

⌂ **Holme Lane Farm** without rest., 38 Halifax Rd, S30 3PB, on A 61 ℘ (0114) 246 8858, Fax (0114) 246 8888, ⌖ – 🌤 📺 ☎ 🅿. 🕮 VISA. ⌖
7 rm ⊇ 26.00/45.00 s.

at Chapeltown N : 6 m. on A 6135 – AY – ⊠ Sheffield.

🏛 **Staindrop Lodge,** Lane End, S35 3UH, NW : ½ m. on High Green rd ℘ (0114) 284 6727, Fax (0114) 284 6783, ⌖ – 📺 ☎ 🅿 – 🕴 90. 🕮 🖭 ① VISA. ⌖
closed Bank Holidays – Meals (closed lunch Saturday and Monday, Sunday dinner and Bank Holidays) 13.25/21.50 t. and a la carte 🛆 4.75 – 13 rm ⊇ 65.00/83.00 t. – SB.

🕱🕱 **Greenhead House,** 84 Burncross Rd, S35 1SF, ℘ (0114) 246 9004 – 🌤 🅿. 🕮 🖭 VISA
closed lunch Wednesday to Saturday, Sunday to Tuesday, 2 weeks Easter, 2 weeks August and 1 week Christmas-New Year – Meals (booking essential) (dinner only) 28.50/30.50 t. 🛆 5.50.

at Ridgeway (Derbs.) SE : 6¾ m. by A 616 off B 6054 – BZ – ⊠ Sheffield.

🕱🕱🕱 **Old Vicarage,** Ridgeway Moor, S12 3XW, on Marsh Lane rd ℘ (0114) 247 5814, Fax (0114) 247 7079, ⌖ – 🌤 🅿. 🕮 🖭 ① VISA JCB. ⌖
closed Saturday lunch, Sunday dinner, Monday, 1 January, 26 and 31 December – Meals 28.00/38.00 t. 🛆 8.00.

at Meadow Head S : 5¼ m. on A 61 – AZ – ⊠ Sheffield.

🏛 **Sheffield Moat House,** Chesterfield Rd South, S8 8BW, ℘ (0114) 282 9988, Fax (0114) 237 8140, 🗲, ⌖, ☒ – 🕴 🌤, 🍴 rest, 📺 ☎ 🕭 🅿 – 🕴 500. 🕮 🖭 ① VISA. ⌖
Meals (bar lunch Saturday) 17.95 st. (dinner) and a la carte 18.45/24.75 st. 🛆 6.75 – ⊇ 9.50 – 89 rm 115.00/140.00 st., 5 suites – SB.

🅰 ATS Unit 9, Surbiton St. ℘ (0114) 244 9750/ 244 9759   ATS Herries Rd ℘ (0114) 234 3986/7

SHELLEY W. Yorks. 402 404 O 23 – pop. 4 424 (inc. Shepley) – ⊠ Huddersfield.
London 193 – Leeds 22 – Manchester 30 – Sheffield 20.

🏛 **Three Acres Inn,** Roydhouse, HD8 8LR, NE : 1 ½ m. on Flockton rd ℘ (01484) 602606, Fax (01484) 608411 – 🌤 rm, 📺 ☎ 🅿. 🕮 🖭 VISA. ⌖
closed 25 December – Meals (closed Saturday lunch) 14.95/20.00 t. and dinner a la carte 🛆 6.75 – 19 rm ⊇ 47.50/60.00 t. – SB.

SHENINGTON Oxon. – see Banbury.

SHEPTON MALLET Somerset 403 404 M 30 The West Country G. – pop. 7 581.
See : Town★ - SS. Peter and Paul's Church★.
Env. : – Downside Abbey★ (Abbey Church★) N : 5 ½ m. by A 37 and A 367.
Exc. : Longleat House★★★ AC, E : 15 m. by A 361 and B 3092 – Wells★★ - Cathedral★★★ Vicars' Close★, Bishop's Palace★ AC (≤★★★) W : 6 m. by A 371 – Wookey Hole★ (Caves★ AC Papermill★) W : 6 ½ m. by B 371 – Glastonbury★★ - Abbey★★ (Abbot's Kitchen★) AC St. John the Baptist★★, Somerset Rural Life Museum★ AC – Glastonbury Tor★ (≤★★★) SW 9 m. by B 3136 and A 361 - Nunney★, E : 8 ½ m. by A 361.
🏌 Mendip, Gurney Slade ℘ (01749) 840570.
London 127 – Bristol 20 – Southampton 63 – Taunton 31.

🏛 **Charlton House,** BA4 4PR, E : 1 m. on A 361 (Frome rd) ℘ (01749) 342008 ❀ Fax (01749) 346362, « Interior designed part Georgian country house », 🗲, ⌖ – 🌤 rest 📺 ☎ 🅿. 🕮 🖭 ① VISA JCB. ⌖
Mulberry : Meals 18.50/29.50 t. and a la carte 34.00/40.50 t. 🛆 11.00 – ⊇ 5.00 – 17 rm 85.00/285.00 t. – SB
Spec. Crab cake with tomato couscous, mango and onion salsa and langoustine oil. Rack of lamb with aubergine galette, pesto crushed potatoes and thyme sauce. Fig tart Tatin anglaise sauce and vanilla ice cream.

🏛 **Shrubbery,** Commercial Rd, BA4 5BU, ℘ (01749) 346671, Fax (01749) 346581, ⌖ – 📺 ☎ 🅿. 🕮 🖭 ① VISA
Meals (closed Sunday dinner to non-residents) 13.95/14.95 t. and a la carte 🛆 4.50 – 7 rm ⊇ 45.00/75.00 t.

XX **Bowlish House** with rm, Wells Rd, BA4 5JD, W : ½ m. on A 371 ℰ (01749) 342022, Fax (01749) 342022, 🐴 – 📺 🅿. ⁂ 🅰🅴 ᴠɪsᴀ. ⁂
closed 1 week in spring and 1 week in autumn – Meals (booking essential) (dinner only) 22.50 t. ⧍ 4.75 – 🖃 3.50 – **3 rm** 48.00 t.

X **Blostin's**, 29 Waterloo Rd, BA4 5HH, ℰ (01749) 343648, Fax (01749) 343648 – ⁂ ᴠɪsᴀ ᴊᴄв
closed Sunday, Monday, 2 weeks January and 1 week July – **Meals** (dinner only) 15.95 t. and a la carte ⧍ 5.95.

at Doulting E : 1½ m. on A 361 – ✉ Shepton Mallet.

XX **Brottens Lodge** ⌂ with rm, BA4 4RB, S : 1 m. turning right at Abbey Barn Inn, following sign for Evercreech ℰ (01749) 880352, Fax (01749) 880601, ≤, 🐴 – ᵁ⁺⁺ rest, 📺 🅿. ⁂ ᴠɪsᴀ. ⁂
Meals (closed Sunday and Monday) (dinner only) 20.25 st. ⧍ 4.25 – **3 rm** ⊇ 45.00/65.00 st.

at Evercreech SE : 4 m. by A 371 on B 3081 – ✉ Shepton Mallet.

🏠 **Pecking Mill Inn** with rm, BA4 6PG, W : 1 m. on A 371 ℰ (01749) 830336, Fax (01749) 831316 – 📺 ☎ 🅿. ⁂ 🅰🅴 ⓘ ᴠɪsᴀ ᴊᴄв. ⁂
closed 25 and 26 December – **Meals** (closed lunch Monday and Tuesday) a la carte 10.50/ 20.70 st. ⧍ 3.95 – **6 rm** ⊇ 33.00/48.00 st. – SB.

SHERBORNE Dorset 🄬🄬🄬 🄬🄬🄬 M 31 The West Country G. – pop. 7 606.

See : Town★ - Abbey★★ - Castle★ AC.
Env. : Sandford Orcas Manor House★ AC, NW : 4 m. by B 3148 – Purse Caundle Manor★ AC, NE : 5 m. by A 30.
Exc. : Cadbury Castle (≤★★) N : 8 m. by A 30.
🛇 Clatcombe ℰ (01935) 812475.
🔲 3 Tilton Court, Digby Rd, DT9 3NL ℰ (01935) 815341.
London 128 – Bournemouth 39 – Dorchester 19 – Salisbury 36 – Taunton 31.

🏨 **Eastbury**, Long St., DT9 3BY, ℰ (01935) 813131, Fax (01935) 817296, 🐴 – 📺 ☎ 🅿 – 🛤 60. ⁂ 🅰🅴 ᴠɪsᴀ. ⁂
Meals 12.95/16.95 t. and dinner a la carte ⧍ 5.50 – **15 rm** ⊇ 54.50/95.00 t. – SB.

🏨 **Antelope**, Greenhill, DT9 4EP, ℰ (01935) 812077, Fax (01935) 816473 – 📺 ☎ 🅿 – 🛤 80. ⁂ 🅰🅴 ⓘ ᴠɪsᴀ
Meals (dinner only) a la carte 14.20/20.10 t. ⧍ 4.95 – **19 rm** ⊇ 39.95/78.00 t. – SB.

XX **Pheasants** with rm, 24 Greenhill, DT9 4EW, ℰ (01935) 815252, Fax (01935) 815252 – 📺 🅿. ⁂ ᴠɪsᴀ. ⁂
closed 2 weeks January – **Meals** (closed Sunday dinner and Monday) 14.00/25.00 t. ⧍ 7.20 – **6 rm** ⊇ 40.00/55.00 t. – SB.

at Oborne NE : 2 m. by A 30 – ✉ Sherborne.

XX **Grange** ⌂ with rm, DT9 4LA, ℰ (01935) 813463, Fax (01935) 817464, ≤, 🐴, ⁂ – 📺 ☎ 🅿. ⁂ 🅰🅴 ᴠɪsᴀ ᴊᴄв. ⁂
closed 1 to 8 January and Bank Holiday Mondays – **Meals** - Italian - (closed Sunday dinner) (dinner only and Sunday lunch)/dinner a la carte 16.50/23.80 t. ⧍ 6.00 – **5 rm** ⊇ 48.00/ 70.00 t. – SB.

at Milborne Port NE : 3 m. on A 30 – ✉ Sherborne.

🏠 **Old Vicarage**, Sherborne Rd, DT9 5AT, ℰ (01963) 251117, Fax (01963) 251515, ≤, 🐴 – 📺 ☎ 🅿. ⁂ ᴠɪsᴀ. ⁂
closed January – **Meals** (closed dinner Sunday and Monday to non-residents) (dinner only and Sunday lunch) 12.50/19.50 st. and a la carte – **7 rm** ⊇ 29.50/84.00 st. – SB.

at Hermitage S : 7½ m. by A 352 – ✉ Sherborne.

⌂ **Almshouse Farm** ⌂ without rest., DT9 6HA, ℰ (01963) 210296, Fax (01963) 210296, ≤, « Former monastery, working farm », 🐴 – 📺 🅿. ⁂
closed January and December – **3 rm** ⊇ 28.00/46.00.

at Yetminster SW : 5½ m. by A 352 and Yetminster rd – ✉ Sherborne.

⌂ **Manor Farmhouse**, DT9 6LF, ℰ (01935) 872247, « 17C », 🐴 – ᵁ⁺⁺ 📺 🅿. ⁂ ᴠɪsᴀ. ⁂
closed 2 weeks in autumn – **Meals** (by arrangement) 15.00 t. – **3 rm** ⊇ 30.00/55.00 t.

at Leigh SW : 6¼ m. by A 352 – ✉ Sherborne.

⌂ **Huntsbridge Farm** ⌂ without rest., DT9 6JA, SE : ¼ m. on Batcombe rd ℰ (01935) 872150, Fax (01935) 872150, ≤, « Working farm », 🐴 – ᵁ⁺⁺ 📺 🅿. ⁂ ᴠɪsᴀ. ⁂
March-October – **3 rm** ⊇ 20.00/40.00 s.

SHERBOURNE Warks. – see Warwick.

SHERE Surrey 404 S 30 – see Guildford.

SHIFNAL Shrops. 402 403 404 M 25 – pop. 5 893 – ✉ Telford.
London 150 – Birmingham 28 – Shrewsbury 16.

🏨 **Park House,** Park St., TF11 9BA, ℘ (01952) 460128, Fax (01952) 461658, ☎, 🔍, 🐾 – 📳,
↻ rm, 📺 ☎ ও 🅿 – 🔏 180. 🅾 🖭 ⓪ 💳
Meals *(closed Saturday lunch)* 12.50/20.95 **st.** and dinner a la carte 🕯 5.25 – ☑ 8.50 – **52 rm**
90.00/118.00 **st.**, 2 suites – SB.

SHINFIELD Wokingham 404 R 29 – see Reading.

SHIPBOURNE Kent 404 U 30 – pop. 1 129.
London 35 – Maidstone 14 – Royal Tunbridge Wells 14.

🍽 **Chaser Inn** with rm, Stumble Hill, TN11 9PE, ℘ (01732) 810360, Fax (01732) 810941, 😷,
🐾 – 📺 ☎ ও 🅿. 🅾 🖭 💳
Meals *(closed Saturday lunch, Sunday dinner and Monday)* 15.95/18.95 **t.** and dinner
a la carte 🕯 8.20 – **15 rm** ☑ 45.00/65.00 **t.**

SHIPHAM Somerset 403 L 30 *The West Country G.* – pop. 1 094 – ✉ Winscombe.
Env. : Cheddar Gorge★★ (Gorge★★, Caves★, Jacobs's Ladder ✳★) – Axbridge★★ – King
John's Hunting Lodge★ – St. John the Baptist★, SW : 5 m. on A 38 – St. Andrew's Church★
S : 2 ½ m.
🏌, 🏌 Mendip Spring, Honeyhall Lane, Congresbury, Avon ℘ (01934) 853337/852322.
London 135 – Bristol 14 – Taunton 20.

🏨 **Daneswood House,** Cuck Hill, BS25 1RD, ℘ (01934) 843145, Fax (01934) 843824, ≤, 🐾
– ↻ rest, 📺 ☎ 🅿. 🅾 🖭 ⓪ 💳. ✸
closed 26 December-4 January – Meals 27.50 **st.** 🕯 4.50 – **9 rm** ☑ 59.50/89.50 **t.**, 3 suites –
SB.

Les prix	Pour toutes précisions sur les prix indiqués dans ce guide, reportez-vous aux pages de l'introduction.

SHIPLEY W. Yorks. 402 O 22 – pop. 28 165.
🏌 Northcliffe, High Bank Lane ℘ (01274) 584085.
London 216 – Bradford 4 – Leeds 12.

🏨 **Marriott Hollins Hall** ⊛, Hollins Hill, Baildon, BD17 7QW, NE : 2 ½ m. on A 603?
℘ (01274) 530053, Fax (01274) 530187, ≤, ☎, 🐾, park – 📳, ↻ rm, 📺 ☎ ও 🅿 – 🔏 200.
🅾 🖭 ⓪ 💳 🇯🇵 ✸
closed 5 January-5 February – **Meadows :** Meals *(bar lunch Saturday)* 18.95 **t.** *(dinner)*
and a la carte 21.40/27.65 **t.** 🕯 7.25 – ☑ 10.95 – **58 rm** 75.00/88.00, 1 suite.

✗ **Aagrah,** 27 Westgate, BD18 3QX, ℘ (01274) 530880 – 🅾 🖭 💳
closed 25 December – Meals - Indian - *(booking essential) (dinner only)* a la carte 10.80
16.30 **t.**

SHIPTON GORGE Dorset – see Bridport.

SHIPTON-UNDER-WYCHWOOD Oxon. 403 404 P 28 – pop. 1 154.
London 81 – Birmingham 50 – Gloucester 37 – Oxford 25.

🏨 **Lamb Inn,** High St., OX7 6DQ, ℘ (01993) 830465, Fax (01993) 832025 – ↻ 📺 ☎ 🅿. 🅾
🖭 💳 🇯🇵 ✸
Meals *(buffet lunch) (in bar Sunday and Monday dinner)/dinner* 21.00 **t.** and a la carte
🕯 5.95 – **5 rm** ☑ 58.00/85.00 **t.** – SB.

SHIRLEY W. Mids. 403 404 O 26 – see Solihull.

SHOTTISHAM Suffolk 404 X 27 – see Woodbridge.

SHREWLEY Warks. 403 404 P 27 – see Warwick.

SHREWSBURY *Shrops.* 402 403 L 25 *Great Britain G.* – *pop. 64 219.*

See : *Abbey★* **D.**

Exc. : *Ironbridge Gorge Museum★★* **AC** *(The Iron Bridge★★ - Coalport China Museum★★ - Blists Hill Open Air Museum★★ – Museum of the River and Visitor Centre★) SE : 12 m. by A 5 and B 4380.*

🇹🇸 *Condover* ℘ *(01743) 872976 –* 🇹🇸 *Meole Brace* ℘ *(01743) 364050.*

🇪 *The Music Hall, The Square, SY1 1LH* ℘ *(01743) 350761.*

London 164 – Birmingham 48 – Chester 43 – Derby 67 – Gloucester 93 – Manchester 68 – Stoke-on-Trent 39 – Swansea 124.

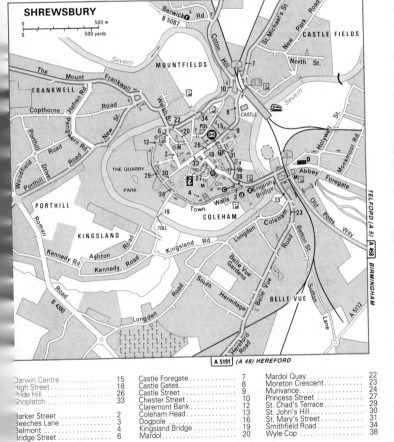

🏨 **Lion,** Wyle Cop, SY1 1UY, ℘ *(01743) 353107, Fax (01743) 352744* – 📶 ⤬ 📺 ☎ 🄿 – 🔺 200. 🅾🄾 🄰🄴 🄾 *VISA* JCB c
Meals 8.00 **st.** (lunch) and dinner a la carte 14.45/21.65 **st.** 🍷 6.75 – ⚏ 9.25 – **59 rm** 65.00/85.00 **st.** – SB.

🏨 **Prince Rupert,** Butcher Row, SY1 1UQ, ℘ *(01743) 499955, Fax (01743) 357306* – 📶,
▤ rest, 📺 ☎ 🄿 – 🔺 70. 🅾🄾 🄰🄴 🄾 *VISA* n
Meals 13.00/19.00 **st.** and a la carte 🍷 8.50 – **62 rm** ⚏ 70.00/80.00 **st.**, 3 suites – SB.

🏨 **Pinewood House** without rest., Shelton Park, The Mount, SY3 8BL, NW : 1 ½ m. on
A 458 ℘ *(01743) 364200,* 🌾 – 📺 🄿
closed 25 December and restricted opening in winter – **4 rm** ⚏ 38.00/54.00 **s.**

Lion and Pheasant, 49-50 Wyle Cop, SY1 1XJ, ✆ (01743) 236288, *Fax (01743) 244475* – ⇔ rest, TV ☎ P. MC AE ⓓ VISA JCB x
closed 24 to 30 December – **Meals** *(closed Sunday lunch)* 15.00 **st.** and a la carte 5.75 – **19 rm** ⊐ 45.00/60.00 **st.** – SB.

Fieldside without rest., 38 London Rd, SY2 6NX, E : 1 ¼ m. by Abbey Foregate on A 5064 (via Shirehall) ✆ (01743) 353143, *Fax (01743) 358645*, – ⇔ TV ☎ P. MC VISA.
closed 2 weeks November – **4 rm** ⊐ 28.00/44.00 **st.**

Sandford House without rest., St. Julians Friars, SY1 1XL, ✆ (01743) 343829, *Fax (01743) 343829*, – TV. MC VISA a
11 rm ⊐ 35.00/50.00 **st.**

Travelodge, Bayston Hill Service Area, SY3 0DA, S : 3 m. by A 5112 and A 49 at junction with A 5 ✆ (01743) 874256, Reservations (Freephone) 0800 850950 – ⇔ rm, TV ♿ P. MC AE ⓓ VISA JCB.
Meals (grill rest.) – **40 rm** 44.95 **t.**

Tudor House without rest., 2 Fish St., SY1 1UR, ✆ (01743) 351735, « 15C » – TV. e
closed 24 to 26 December – **3 rm** ⊐ 26.00/48.00 **st.**

Roseville without rest., 12 Berwick Rd, SY1 2LN, ✆ (01743) 236470 – ⇔ P. r
closed 19 December-31 January – **3 rm** ⊐ 23.00/46.00 **st.**

Jacky Chan, Barracks Passage, Wyle Cop, SY1 1XA, ✆ (01743) 242188 – MC VISA JCB c
closed lunch Monday to Thursday and Sunday – **Meals** - Chinese (Peking) - 5.70/13.00 **t.** and a la carte.

at Albrighton *N : 3 m. on A 528 – ✉ Shrewsbury.*

Albrighton Hall, Ellesmere Rd, SY4 3AG, ✆ (01939) 291000, *Fax (01939) 291123*, , , , park, squash – |♦|, ⇔ rm, TV ☎ ♿ P – 400. MC AE ⓓ VISA
Meals *(closed Saturday lunch)* 11.95/21.95 **t.** and a la carte 6.00 – ⊐ 8.50 – **70 rm** 85.00/95.00 **st.** – SB.

Albright Hussey , Ellesmere Rd, SY4 3AF, ✆ (01939) 290571, *Fax (01939) 291143*, <, « 16C moated manor house », – ⇔ TV ☎ ♿ P – 300. MC AE ⓓ VISA JCB.
Meals (bar lunch Monday to Saturday)/dinner 19.50 **t.** and a la carte 5.50 – **13 rm** ⊐ 65.00/120.00 **t.**, 1 suite – SB.

at Dorrington *S : 7 m. on A 49 – ✉ Shrewsbury.*

Country Friends with rm, SY5 7JD, ✆ (01743) 718707, *Fax (01743) 718707*, – ⇔ rest, P. MC VISA JCB.
closed 2 weeks mid July and 26 to 30 December – **Meals** *(closed Sunday and Monday)* 28.00 **t.** 9.20 – **3 rm** ⊐ (dinner included) 68.00/110.00 **t.**

at Hanwood *SW : 4 m. on A 488 – ✉ Shrewsbury.*

White House, SY5 8LP, ✆ (01743) 860414, *Fax (01743) 860414*, – ⇔ P.
Meals (by arrangement) 19.00 **st.** 4.75 – **6 rm** ⊐ 26.00/56.00 **st.** – SB.

ATS Lancaster Rd, Harlescott ✆ (01743) 443954/442231

SHURDINGTON *Glos.* 403 404 N 28 – *see Cheltenham.*

SIBSON *Leics.* – *see Nuneaton (Warks.).*

SIDFORD *Devon* 403 K 31 – *see Sidmouth.*

SIDMOUTH *Devon* 403 K 31 *The West Country G.* – *pop. 10 767.*

Env. : Bicton★ (Gardens★) AC, SW : 5 m.

Cotmaton Rd ✆ (01395) 513023.

Ham Lane, EX10 8XR ✆ (01395) 516441.

London 176 – Exeter 14 – Taunton 27 – Weymouth 45.

Riviera, The Esplanade, EX10 8AY, ✆ (01395) 515201, *Fax (01395) 577775*, < – |♦|, rest TV ☎ ♿ – 85. MC AE ⓓ VISA
Meals 13.50/23.00 **t.** and a la carte 5.25 – **27 rm** ⊐ (dinner included) 85.00/198.00 **t.** – SB.

Belmont, The Esplanade, EX10 8RX, ✆ (01395) 512555, *Fax (01395) 579101*, <, – |♦| ⇔ rest, TV ☎ P. MC AE ⓓ VISA.
Meals (dancing Saturday evening) 12.50/21.50 **st.** and a la carte 6.50 – **51 rm** ⊐ (dinner included) 65.00/130.00 **st.** – SB.

🏨 **Salcombe Hill House** ⊗, Beatlands Rd, EX10 8JQ, ℰ (01395) 514697, Fax (01395) 578310, 🔼, 🌫, ℅ – 🛗, ℅ rest, 📺 ☎ 🅿, ⓂⓈ VISA JCB
March-October – **Meals** (bar lunch Monday to Saturday)/dinner a la carte 15.50/19.20 t. – **28 rm** ⇆ (dinner included) 58.00/116.00 t. – SB.

🏨 **Fortfield** ⊗, Station Rd, EX10 8NU, ℰ (01395) 512403, Fax (01395) 512403, ☎, ▣, 🌫 – 🛗, ℅ rest, 📺 ☎ 🅿, ⓂⓈ ᴬᴱ ① VISA JCB
Meals 4.95/16.50 st. ⑧ 8.00 – ⇆ 5.50 – **55 rm** 38.00/76.00 st.

🏨 **Hunters Moon**, Sid Rd, EX10 9AA, ℰ (01395) 513380, Fax (01395) 514270, 🌫 – ℅ rest, 📺 ☎ 🅿, ⓂⓈ VISA JCB
March-November – **Meals** (booking essential to non-residents) (dinner only) 14.95 st. – **18 rm** ⇆ (dinner included) 43.00/86.00 st.

🏨 **Littlecourt**, Seafield Rd, EX10 8HF, ℰ (01395) 515279, 🔼, 🌫 – ℅ rm, 📺 🅿, ⓂⓈ ᴬᴱ VISA JCB, ℅
mid March-November and 5 days at Christmas – **Meals** (bar lunch)/dinner 15.00 st. ⑧ 3.95 – **20 rm** ⇆ (dinner included) 49.90/100.00 st. – SB.

🏨 **Abbeydale**, Manor Rd, EX10 8RP, ℰ (01395) 512060, Fax (01395) 515566, 🌫 – 🛗, ℅ rest, 📺 ☎ 🅿, ⓂⓈ VISA, ℅
restricted opening December and January – **Meals** (bar lunch Monday to Saturday and carving lunch Sunday)/dinner 13.00 st. and a la carte ⑧ 4.00 – **18 rm** ⇆ 49.00/116.00 st. – SB.

🏨 **Mount Pleasant**, Salcombe Rd, EX10 8JA, ℰ (01395) 514694, 🌫 – ℅ 📺 🅿, ℅
March-October – **Meals** (residents only) (dinner only) 15.50 st. ⑧ 4.95 – **16 rm** ⇆ (dinner included) 45.00/90.00 st. – SB.

🏨 **Woodlands**, Station Rd, Cotmaton Cross, EX10 8HG, ℰ (01395) 513120, Fax (01395) 513292, 🌫 – ℅ rest, 📺 🅿, ⓂⓈ VISA
Meals 5.95/12.50 st. ⑧ 5.00 – **28 rm** ⇆ 18.50/37.00 t.

at Sidford N : 2 m. – ✉ Sidmouth.

🏨 **Salty Monk**, Church St., EX10 9QP, on A 3052 ℰ (01395) 513174, « Part 16C », 🌫 – ℅ rest, 📺 ☎ 🅿, ⓂⓈ ᴬᴱ ① VISA, ℅
Meals (closed Monday) (light lunch)/dinner 11.50 t. and a la carte ⑧ 3.95 – **7 rm** ⇆ 18.50/45.00 t.

🔘 ATS Vicarage Rd ℰ (01395) 512433

SILCHESTER Hants. 403 404 Q 29 – pop. 1 428 – ✉ Reading (Berks.).
London 62 – Basingstoke 8 – Reading 14 – Winchester 26.

🏨 **Romans**, Little London Rd, RG7 2PN, ℰ (01189) 700421, Fax (01189) 700691, ℔, ☎, 🔼, 🌫, ℅ – 📺 ☎ 🅿 – ⓐ 80, ⓂⓈ ᴬᴱ ① VISA
closed 26 December-2 January – **Meals** (booking essential Sunday dinner) 18.00 st. and a la carte ⑧ 8.10 – **25 rm** ⇆ 89.00/135.00 st.

SIMONSBATH Somerset 403 I 30 The West Country G. – ✉ Minehead.
Env. : Exmoor National Park★★ – Exford (Church★) E : 5 ½ m. by B 3223 and B 3224.
London 200 – Exeter 40 – Minehead 19 – Taunton 38.

🏨 **Simonsbath House**, TA24 7SH, ℰ (01643) 831259, Fax (01643) 831557, ≤, « 17C country house », 🌫 – ℅ rest, 📺 ☎ 🅿, ⓂⓈ ᴬᴱ ① VISA JCB, ℅
closed December and January – **Meals** (dinner only) 22.50 t. ⑧ 4.95 – **7 rm** ⇆ 54.00/92.00 t. – SB.

SINDLESHAM Wokingham – see Reading.

SINGLETON Lancs. 402 L 22 – see Blackpool.

SINNINGTON N. Yorks. 402 R 21 – see Pickering.

SISSINGHURST Kent 404 V 30 – see Cranbrook.

Groß-London (GREATER LONDON) besteht aus der City und 32 Verwaltungsbezirken (Borough). Diese sind wiederum in kleinere Bezirke (Area) unterteilt, deren Mittelpunkt ehemalige Dörfer oder Stadtviertel sind, die oft ihren eigenen Charakter bewahrt haben.

SITTINGBOURNE Kent 404 W 29.

London 44 – Canterbury 18 – Maidstone 15 – Sheerness 9.

🏠 **Hempstead House**, London Rd, Bapchild, ME9 9PP, E : 2 m. on A 2 𝒫 (01795) 428020, Fax (01795) 428020, ⤳, 🐴 – ⇌ rm, 🆅 ☎ 🅿. 🕮 🆎 ⓪ 𝓥𝓘𝓢𝓐 𝒥𝒸𝒃
Meals (booking essential) (communal dining) 19.50 **st.** and a la carte ╽ 3.75 – **7 rm** �> 62.00/72.00 **st.** – SB.

🏠 **Beaumont** without rest., 74 London Rd, ME10 1NS, 𝒫 (01795) 472536, Fax (01795) 425921 – ⇌ 🆅 ☎ 🅿. 🕮 🆎 ⓪ 𝓥𝓘𝓢𝓐 𝒥𝒸𝒃
9 rm �> 28.00/54.00 **st.**

SIX MILE BOTTOM Cambs. – see Newmarket (Suffolk).

SKELTON N. Yorks. 402 Q 22 – see York.

SKELWITH BRIDGE Cumbria 402 K 20 – see Ambleside.

SKIPTON N. Yorks. 402 N 22 Great Britain G. – pop. 13 583.

See : Castle★ AC.

🖊 𝒫 (01756) 795657.

🛈 The Old Town Hall, 9 Sheep St., BD23 1JH 𝒫 (01756) 792809.

London 217 – Kendal 45 – Leeds 26 – Preston 36 – York 43.

🏛 **Hanover International H. and Club**, Keighley Rd, BD23 2TA, S : 1 ¼ m. on A 629 𝒫 (01756) 700100, Fax (01756) 700107, ⤳, ℺, ⓵, ⬜, squash – ⧘ ⇌ 🆅 ☎ 🅿 – ⚿ 400. 🕮 🆎 ⓪ 𝓥𝓘𝓢𝓐
Meals (bar lunch Saturday) 11.25/16.20 **st.** and dinner a la carte ╽ 8.75 – �> 9.50 – **76 rm** 78.00/110.00 **st.** – SB.

🏠 **Unicorn**, Devonshire Pl., Keighley Rd, BD23 2LP, 𝒫 (01756) 794146, Fax (01756) 793376 – 🆅 ☎. 🕮 🆎 𝓥𝓘𝓢𝓐. ⌖
Meals (residents only) (dinner only) a la carte 9.45/13.20 **st.** ╽ 4.00 – **9 rm** �> 44.00/ 51.00 **st.** – SB.

🏠 **Travelodge**, Gargrave Rd, BD23 1UD, W : 1 ¾ m. by Water St. at A 65/A 59 roundabout 𝒫 (01756) 798091, Reservations (Freephone) 0800 850950 – ⇌ rm, 🆅 ♿ 🅿. 🕮 🆎 ⓪ 𝓥𝓘𝓢𝓐 𝒥𝒸𝒃. ⌖
Meals (grill rest.) – **32 rm** 44.95 **t.**

🍴 **Aagrah**, Unit 4, Unicorn House, Devonshire Pl., Keighley Rd, BD23 2LP, 𝒫 (01756) 790807 – 🕮 🆎 𝓥𝓘𝓢𝓐
closed 25 December – Meals - Indian - (dinner only) a la carte 10.80/16.30 **t.**

at Rylstone N : 5 m. on B 6265 – ✉ Skipton.

🏠 **The Manor House** without rest., BD23 6LH, 𝒫 (01756) 730226, ⤳, 🐴, park – 🆅 🅿
3 rm �> 45.00/60.00 **t.**

at Hetton N : 5 ¾ m. by B 6265 and Hetton rd on Settle rd – ✉ Skipton.

🍴🍴🍴 **Angel Inn**, BD23 6LT, 𝒫 (01756) 730263, Fax (01756) 730363, « Characterful 18C inn » – ⇌, 🍽 rest. 🅿. 🕮 🆎 𝓥𝓘𝓢𝓐
closed Sunday – Meals (dinner only) 18.50/27.75 **t.** ╽ 5.55 - (see also *Bar Brasserie* below).

🍴 **Bar Brasserie** (at Angel Inn), BD23 6LT, 𝒫 (01756) 730263, Fax (01756) 730363 – ⇌ 🅿 🕮 🆎 𝓥𝓘𝓢𝓐
Meals (in bar) a la carte 14.20/23.95 **t.** ╽ 5.55.

at Elslack W : 4½ m. by A 59 off A 56 – ✉ Skipton.

🏠 **Tempest Arms**, BD23 3AY, 𝒫 (01282) 842450, Fax (01282) 843331 – 🆅 ☎ 🅿 – ⚿ 80. 🕮 🆎 𝓥𝓘𝓢𝓐. ⌖
Meals a la carte 10.40/20.95 **t.** ╽ – **10 rm** �> 49.00/57.50 **t.** – SB.

🅐 ATS Carleton Rd Garage, Carleton Rd 𝒫 (01756) 795741/2

SKIRMETT Bucks. – see Henley-on-Thames (Oxon.).

Wenn Sie ein ruhiges Hotel suchen,
benutzen Sie zuerst die Karte in der Einleitung
oder wählen Sie im Text ein Hotel mit dem Zeichen ॐ oder ॐ

SLAIDBURN *Lancs.* 402 M 22 – *pop. 302* – ⊠ *Clitheroe.*
London 249 – Burnley 21 – Lancaster 19 – Leeds 48 – Preston 27.

🏠 **Parrock Head** ⤜, BB7 3AH, NW : 1 m. ℰ (01200) 446614, *Fax (01200) 446313,*
⪚ *Bowland Fells*, 🌲 – ⤜ rest, 📺 ☎ 🅿. 🐄🐄 *VISA*. 🦟
closed 6 January-3 February – **Meals** (bar lunch Monday to Saturday)/dinner 21.50 **t.** ₰ 5.75
– **9 rm** ⊂ 50.00/80.00 **t.** – SB.

SLALEY *Northd.* 401 402 N 19 – *see Hexham.*

SLEAFORD *Lincs.* 402 404 S 25 – *pop. 10 388.*
🛆 *Willoughby Rd, South Rauceby* ℰ (01529) 488273.
🯁 *The Mill, Money's Yard, Carre St., NG34 7TW* ℰ (01529) 414294.
London 119 – Leicester 45 – Lincoln 17 – Nottingham 39.

🏨 **Lincolnshire Oak,** East Rd, NG34 7EH, NE : ¾ m. on B 1517 ℰ (01529) 413807,
Fax (01529) 413710, 🌲 – ⤜ rest, 📺 ☎ 🅿 – 🔏 140. 🐄🐄 🖭 *VISA*. 🦟
Meals (booking essential) 15.95 **st.** and a la carte – **17 rm** ⊂ 47.00/65.00 **st.** – SB.

🏠 **Travelodge,** NG34 8NP, NW : 1 m. on A 15 at junction with A 17 ℰ (01529) 414752,
Fax (01529) 414752, Reservations (Freephone) 0800 850950 – ⤜ rm, 📺 ⅃ 🅿. 🐄🐄 🖭 ⓞ
VISA *JCB*. 🦟
Meals (grill rest.) – **40 rm** 44.95 **t.**

🍴 **Tally Ho Inn** with rm, Aswarby, NG34 8SA, S : 4 ½ m. on A 15 ℰ (01529) 455205, ⪚, 🌲 –
📺 🅿. 🐄🐄 *VISA*
closed 25-26 December and 1 January – **Meals** (bar lunch Monday to Saturday) (in bar
Sunday dinner) a la carte 15.50/19.50 **t.** ₰ 3.75 – **6 rm** ⊂ 33.00/50.00 **t.**

⚙ ATS 40 Albion Terr., off Boston Rd ℰ (01529) 302908

SLINFOLD *W. Sussex – see Horsham.*

SLOUGH 404 S 29 – *pop. 110 708.*
London 29 – Oxford 39 – Reading 19.

🏰 **Copthorne,** Cippenham Lane, SL1 2YE, SW : 1 ¼ m. by A 4 on A 355 off M 4 junction 6
ℰ (01753) 516222, *Fax (01753) 516237,* ₭, ⌖, ⬛ – ▐, ⤜ rm, 🗏 📺 ☎ ⅃ 🅿 – 🔏 200. 🐄🐄
🖭 ⓞ *VISA* *JCB*. 🦟
Reflections : Meals *(closed Sunday)* (dinner only) 19.50 **t.** and a la carte ₰ 7.95 – **Veranda :**
Meals *(closed lunch Saturday, Sunday and Bank Holidays)* (dancing Saturday evening)
19.50 **st.** (dinner) and a la carte ₰ 7.95 – ⊂ 11.50 – **217 rm** 140.00/160.00 **t.**, 2 suites.

🏰 **Heathrow/Slough Marriott,** Ditton Rd, Langley, SL3 8PT, SE : 2 ½ m. on A 4
ℰ (01753) 544244, *Fax (01753) 540272,* ₭, ⌖, ⬛, ℀ – ▐, ⤜ rm, 🗏 📺 ☎ ⅃ 🅿 –
🔏 300. 🖭 ⓞ *VISA*. 🦟
Meals (bar lunch Saturday and Sunday) 16.00/19.95 **st.** and dinner a la carte ₰ 7.50 –
⊂ 11.75 – **379 rm** 110.00/119.00 **st.** – SB.

🏨 **Courtyard by Marriott,** Church St., Chalvey, SL1 2NH, SW : 1 ¼ m. by A 4 on A 355 off
M 4 junction 6 ℰ (01753) 551551, *Fax (01753) 553333,* ₭ – ▐, ⤜ rm, 🗏 📺 ☎ ⅃ 🅿 –
🔏 40. 🐄🐄 🖭 ⓞ *VISA*. 🦟
Meals *(closed lunch Saturday and Sunday)* a la carte 16.00/25.00 **st.** ₰ 6.50 – ⊂ 8.95 –
148 rm 89.00 **st.** – SB.

⚙ ATS 1A Furnival Av. ℰ (01753) 524214

SMITE *Worcestershire – see Droitwich.*

SOAR MILL COVE *Devon – see Salcombe.*

Particularly pleasant hotels and restaurants
are shown in the Guide by a **red symbol**.

Please send us the names
of anywhere you have enjoyed your stay.

Your **Michelin Guide** will be even better.

🏰 ... 仚

ⵣⵣⵣⵣⵣ ... ℀

SOLIHULL W. Mids. 403 404 O 26 – pop. 94 531.

🄱 Central Library, Homer Rd, B91 3RG ℘ (0121) 704 6130/704 6134.

London 109 – Birmingham 7 – Coventry 13 – Warwick 13.

Solihull Moat House, Homer Rd, B91 3QD, ℘ (0121) 623 9988, Fax (0121) 711 2696, Ⅰ₅, ⇆s, ⬜ – ☒, ⅙ rm, ☰ rest, ☒ ☎ & ☻ – 🄰 200. ⬤⑨ 🄰🄴 ⑩ VISA JCB
Meals (closed Saturday lunch) 14.50/18.75 st. and a la carte ⅟ 7.95 – ⌲ 10.50 – **115 rm** 140.00/200.00 st. – SB.

St. John's Swallow, 651 Warwick Rd, B91 1AT, ℘ (0121) 711 3000, Fax (0121) 705 6629, Ⅰ₅, ⇆s, ⬜, ⊰ – ☒, ⅙ rm, ☰ rest, ☒ ☎ ☻ – 🄰 700. ⬤⑨ 🄰🄴 ⑩ VISA
Meals (closed lunch Saturday) (dancing Saturday evening) 14.50/20.50 st. and a la carte ⅟ 8.00 – **176 rm** ⌲ 110.00/125.00 st., 1 suite – SB.

Jarvis International, The Square, B91 3RF, ℘ (0121) 711 2121, Fax (0121) 711 3374 – ☒, ⅙ rm, ☒ ☎ ☻ – 🄰 200. ⬤⑨ 🄰🄴 ⑩ VISA
Meals 14.90/18.50 st. and dinner a la carte – ⌲ 9.50 – **135 rm** 109.00/115.00 st., 10 suites – SB.

Shimla Pinks, 44 Station Rd, B91 3RX, ℘ (0121) 704 0344 – ☰. ⬤⑨ 🄰🄴 ⑩ VISA
closed lunch Saturday and Sunday, 25 December and 1 January – Meals - Indian - 6.95/19.95 t. and a la carte.

Rajnagar, 256 Lyndon Rd, Olton, B92 7QW, ℘ (0121) 742 8140, Fax (0121) 743 3147 – ☰. ⬤⑨ 🄰🄴 ⑩ VISA
closed 25 and 26 December – Meals - Indian - (dinner only) 17.95 t. and a la carte ⅟ 5.95.

at Shirley W : 2½ m. by B 4025 – ⊠ Solihull.

Regency, Stratford Rd, B90 4EB, SE : 2 m. on A 34 ℘ (0121) 745 6119, Fax (0121) 733 3801, Ⅰ₅, ⇆s, ⬜, ⊰ – ☒, ☰ rest, ☒ ☎ ☻ – 🄰 150. ⬤⑨ 🄰🄴 ⑩ VISA
Meals (closed Saturday lunch) 11.95/18.95 st. and a la carte ⅟ 8.95 – ⌲ 9.25 – **110 rm** 105.00/120.00 st., 2 suites – SB.

Travel Inn, Stratford Rd, B90 4PT, SE : 2 ½ m. on A 34 ℘ (0121) 744 2942, Fax (0121) 733 7075 – ⅙ rm, ☒ & ☻. ⬤⑨ 🄰🄴 ⑩ VISA. ⅋
Meals (grill rest.) – **51 rm** 36.50 t.

Chez Julien, 1036 Stratford Rd, Monkspath, B90 4EE, SE : 2 ½ m. on A 34 ℘ (0121) 744 7232, Fax (0121) 745 4775, 😊 – ☻. ⬤⑨ 🄰🄴 ⑩ VISA JCB
closed Saturday lunch and Sunday – Meals - French - 10.50/12.90 t. and a la carte ⅟ 4.95.

SOMERTON Somerset 403 L 30 The West Country G. – pop. 4 489.

See : Town★ - Market Place★ (cross★) – St. Michael's Church★.

Env. : Long Sutton★ (Church★★) SW : 2 ½ m. by B 3165 – Huish Episcopi (St. Mary's Church Tower★★) SW : 4 ½ m. by B 3153 – Lytes Cary★, SE : 3 ½ m. by B 3151.

Exc. : Muchelney★★ (Parish Church★★) SW : 6 ½ m. by B 3153 and A 372 – High Ham (≤★★, St. Andrew's Church★), NW : 9 m. by B 3153, A 372 and minor rd – Midelney Manor★ AC, SW : 9 m. by B 3153 and A 378.

London 138 – Bristol 32 – Taunton 17.

Lynch Country House without rest., 4 Behind Berry, TA11 7PD, ℘ (01458) 272316, Fax (01458) 272590, ≤, « Attractively converted Regency house », ⊰, park – ☒ ☎ ☻. ⬤⑨ 🄰🄴 VISA. ⅋
closed Christmas – **5 rm** ⌲ 45.00/75.00 t.

⓪ ATS Bancombe Rd Trading Est. ℘ (01458) 273467

SONNING-ON-THAMES Wokingham 404 R 29 – pop. 1 354.

London 48 – Reading 4.

French Horn with rm, Thames St., RG4 6TN, ℘ (01189) 692204, Fax (01189) 442210, ≤ River Thames and gardens – ☒ ☎ & ☻. ⬤⑨ 🄰🄴 ⑩ VISA. ⅋
closed 26 December and Good Friday – Meals (booking essential) 18.00/30.00 st. and a la carte ⅟ 6.75 – **15 rm** ⌲ 80.00/95.00 st., 5 suites.

GREEN TOURIST GUIDES

Picturesque scenery, buildings

Attractive routes

Touring programmes

Plans of towns and buildings.

SOUTHAMPTON 403 404 P 31 *Great Britain G. – pop. 210 138.*

See : *Old Southampton* AZ : *Bargate*★ B - *Tudor House Museum*★ M1.

ˌ₁₈ , ˌ₉ *Southampton Municipal, Golf Course Rd, Bassett* ℘ *(01703) 768407,* AY – ˌ₁₈ *Stoneham, Monks Wood Close, Bassett* ℘ *(01703) 768151,* AY – ˌ₁₈ *Chilworth Golf Centre, Main Rd, Chilworth* ℘ *(01703) 740544,* AY.

Itchen Bridge (toll) AZ.

✈ *Southampton/Eastleigh Airport :* ℘ *(01703) 620021, N : 4 m.* BY.

⚓ *to France (Cherbourg) (Stena Line) 1-2 daily (5 h) – to the Isle of Wight (East Cowes) (Red Funnel Ferries) frequent services daily (55 mn).*

⚓ *to Hythe (White Horse Ferries Ltd) frequent services daily (12 mn).*

🛈 *9 Civic Centre Rd, SO14 7LP* ℘ *(01703) 221106.*

London 87 – Bristol 79 – Plymouth 161.

Plans on following pages

🏨 **De Vere Grand Harbour,** West Quay Rd, SO15 1AG, ℘ (01703) 633033, *Fax (01703) 633066,* ˌⅰ, ≘, ⬚ – ⯊ ✦ ≡ 🅣🆅 ☎ & 🅿 – ⏚ 500. 🅞🅞 🅐🅔 ⓪ 𝘝𝘐𝘚𝘈. ⌖
Brewster's : Meals (dinner only and Sunday lunch) 21.50 **st.** and a la carte ⅃ 7.00 – (see also **Allerton's** below) – **169 rm** ⌥ 130.00/170.00 **st.**, 3 suites – SB.   AZ **a**

🏨 **Hilton National,** Bracken Pl., Chilworth, SO16 3RB, ℘ (01703) 702700, *Fax (01703) 767233,* ˌⅰ, ≘, ⬚ – ⯊, ✦ rm, ≡ rest, 🅣🆅 ☎ & 🅿 – ⏚ 200. 🅞🅞 🅐🅔 ⓪ 𝘝𝘐𝘚𝘈
🅙🅒🅑   AY **e**
Meals *(closed Saturday lunch)* 14.00/18.50 **t.** and a la carte ⅃ 6.50 – ⌥ 11.50 – **133 rm** 105.00 **st.**, 2 suites.

🏨 **Novotel,** 1 West Quay Rd, SO15 1RA, ℘ (01703) 330550, *Fax (01703) 222158,* ≼, ˌⅰ, ≘, ⬚ – ⯊, ✦ rm, ≡ 🅣🆅 ☎ & 🅿 – ⏚ 450. 🅞🅞 🅐🅔 ⓪ 𝘝𝘐𝘚𝘈   AZ **x**
Meals a la carte 12.50/21.20 **st.** ⅃ 4.50 – ⌥ **121 rm** 72.50 **st.** – SB.

🏨 **Southampton Park,** 12-13 Cumberland Pl., SO15 2WY, ℘ (01703) 343343, *Fax (01703) 332538,* ˌⅰ, ≘, ⬚ – ⯊, ✦ rm, ≡ rest, 🅣🆅 ☎ – ⏚ 175. 🅞🅞 🅐🅔 ⓪ 𝘝𝘐𝘚𝘈. ⌖
closed 24 to 26 December – **Number 12 Cumberland Place :** Meals (dinner only and Sunday lunch)/dinner 16.95 **st.** ⅃ 6.25 – ⌥ 7.50 – **72 rm** 60.00/80.00 **st.** – SB.   AZ **u**

🏨 **Dolphin,** 35 High St., SO14 2NH, ℘ (01703) 339955, *Fax (01703) 333650* – ⯊, ✦ rm, 🅣🆅 ☎ 🅿 – ⏚ 75. 🅞🅞 🅐🅔 𝘝𝘐𝘚𝘈   AZ **i**
Meals *(bar lunch Monday to Saturday)/dinner* 15.00 **t.** and a la carte ⅃ 5.50 – ⌥ 8.95 – **73 rm** 60.00/80.00 **t.** – SB.

🏨 **Forte Posthouse Southampton,** Herbert Walker Av., SO15 1HJ, ℘ (01703) 330777, *Fax (01703) 332510,* ≼, ˌⅰ, ≘, ⬚ – ⯊, ✦ rm, 🅣🆅 ☎ & 🅿 – ⏚ 200. 🅞🅞 🅐🅔 ⓪ 𝘝𝘐𝘚𝘈. ⌖
Meals *(closed Saturday lunch)* a la carte 17.00/21.00 **st.** ⅃ 8.00 – ⌥ 8.95 – **126 rm** 69.00 **st.**, 2 suites.   AZ **o**

🏨 **County H. Southampton,** 119 Highfield Lane, Portswood, SO17 1AQ, ℘ (01703) 359955, *Fax (01703) 583910,* ˌⅰ, ≘ – 🅣🆅 ☎ 🅿 – ⏚ 200. 🅞🅞 🅐🅔 ⓪ 𝘝𝘐𝘚𝘈. ⌖
Meals *(bar lunch)/dinner* 16.50 **st.** and a la carte ⅃ 6.00 – ⌥ 9.50 – **66 rm** 65.00/80.00 **st.** – SB.   BY **e**

🏨 **Travel Inn,** Romsey Rd, Nursling, SO16 0XJ, NW : 4 m. on A 3057 ℘ (01703) 732262 – ✦ rm, 🅣🆅 & 🅿. 🅞🅞 🅐🅔 ⓪ 𝘝𝘐𝘚𝘈. ⌖   AY **a**
Meals (grill rest.) – **32 rm** 36.50 **t.**

XXX **Allerton's** (at De Vere Grand Harbour H.), West Quay Rd, SO15 1AG, ℘ (01703) 633033, *Fax (01703) 633066* – ✦ ≡ 🅿. 🅞🅞 🅐🅔 ⓪ 𝘝𝘐𝘚𝘈   AZ **a**
closed Sunday – Meals (booking essential) 15.50 **st.** (lunch) and a la carte 25.75/38.40 **st.**

🕼 ATS West Quay Rd ℘ (01703) 333231   ATS 88-94 Portswood Rd ℘ (01703) 582727

Pour voyager en EUROPE utilisez :

les cartes Michelin grandes routes.

les cartes Michelin détaillées.

les guides Rouges Michelin (hôtels et restaurants) :
Benelux - Deutschland - España Portugal - Europe - France - Great Britain and Ireland - Italia - Suisse.

les guides Verts Michelin (paysages, monuments et routes touristiques) :
Allemagne - Autriche - Belgique Grand-Duché de Luxembourg - Canada - Espagne - France - Grande-Bretagne - Grèce - Hollande - Italie - Irlande - Londres - Portugal - Rome - Suisse
... et la collection sur la France.

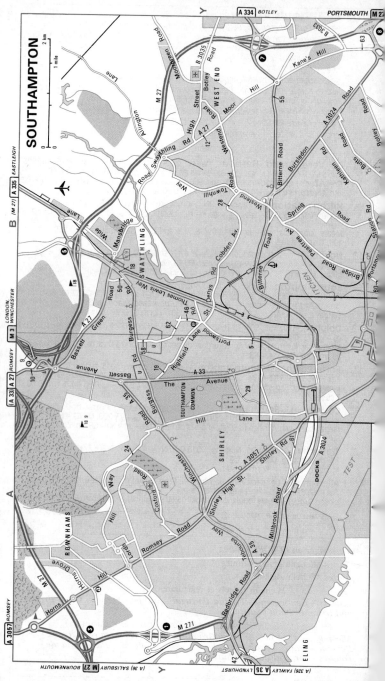

SOUTHAMPTON

0 1 mile
0 1 2 km

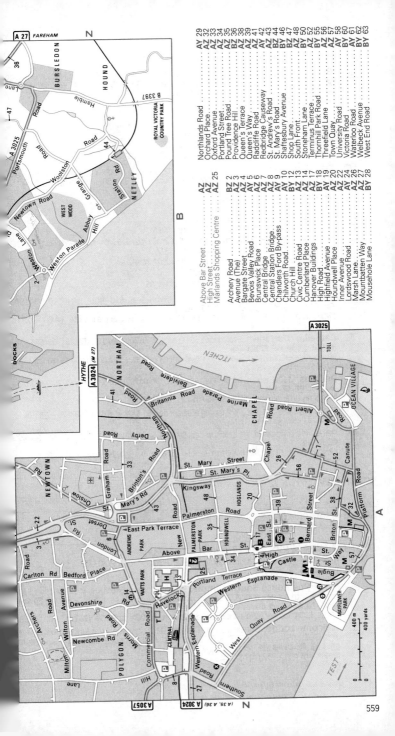

SOUTH BRENT Devon 403 I 32 *The West Country G. – pop. 2 087.*

Env. : *Dartmoor National Park★★.*

London 227 – Exeter 29 – Plymouth 16 – Torquay 16.

🏠 **Brookdale House** ⟫, North Huish, TQ10 9NR, SE : 4½ m. by B 3210 via Avonwick village
& (01548) 821661, Fax (01548) 821606, *☞* – ⁕ rm, 📺 ☎ 🅿. ⬛ 🆎 *VISA* ᴊᴄв, ⅍
Meals 12.50 **t.** (lunch) and dinner a la carte approx. 18.95 **t.** ⅃ 7.20 – **8 rm** ⌗ 50.00/
100.00 **t.** – SB.

SOUTH CAVE East Riding 402 S 22 – *pop. 2 669.*

⛳ *Cave Castle Hotel &* (01430) 421286/422245.

London 176 – Kingston-upon-Hull 12 – Leeds 40 – York 30.

🏠 **Travelodge,** Beacon Service Area, HU15 1RZ, SW : 2½ m. on A 63 (eastbound carriageway) *&* (01430) 424455, Reservations (Freephone) 0800 850950 – ⁕ rm, 📺 ૠ. 🅿. ⬛ 🆎
⓪ *VISA* ᴊᴄв, ⅍
Meals (grill rest.) – **40 rm** 35.95 **t.**

SOUTHEND-ON-SEA Southend 404 W 29 – *pop. 158 517.*

⛳ Belfairs, Eastwood Rd North, Leigh-on-Sea *&* (01702) 525345 – ⛳ Ballards Gore G & C.C.,
Gore Rd, Canewdon, Rochford *&* (01702) 258917.

✈ Southend-on-Sea Airport : *&* (01702) 340201, N : 2 m.

🛈 19 High St., SS2 1JE *&* (01702) 215120.

London 39 – Cambridge 69 – Croydon 46 – Dover 85.

🏠 **Balmoral,** 32-36 Valkyrie Rd, Westcliff-on-sea, SS0 8BU, *&* (01702) 342947
Fax (01702) 337828 – 📺 ☎ 🅿. ⬛ 🆎 *VISA* ⅍
Meals *(closed Sunday dinner)* (bar lunch)/dinner 12.95 **t.** and a la carte ⅃ 4.00 – **28 rm**
⌗ 39.00/68.00 **t.**, 1 suite.

🏠 **Camelia,** 178 Eastern Esplanade, SS1 3AA, *&* (01702) 587917, Fax (01702) 585704 –
▤ rest, 📺 ☎. ⬛ 🆎 *VISA* ᴊᴄв
Meals (dinner only and Sunday lunch)/dinner 12.95 **st.** and a la carte – **16 rm** ⌗ 46.00/
80.00 **st.** – SB.

⌂ **Pebbles,** 190 Eastern Esplanade, SS1 3AA, *&* (01702) 582329, Fax (01702) 582329 –
⁕ rest, 📺. ⬛ *VISA* ⅍
Meals (by arrangement) 12.50 **s.** – **5 rm** ⌗ 25.00/40.00 **s.**

⌂ **Moorings** without rest., 172 Eastern Esplanade, SS1 3AA, *&* (01702) 587575 – 📺. ⅍
3 rm ⌗ 26.50/40.00 **st.**

XX **Paris,** 719 London Rd, Westcliff-on-Sea, SS0 9ST, *&* (01702) 344077, Fax (01702) 344077 –
⬛ 🆎 *VISA*
closed Sunday dinner, Monday and Bank Holidays – **Meals** 14.95/24.95 **st.** ⅃ 6.00.

SOUTH KILVINGTON N. Yorks. – *see Thirsk.*

SOUTH LEIGH Oxon. 403 404 P 28 – *see Witney.*

SOUTH MIMMS SERVICE AREA Herts. 404 T 28 – ✉ Potters Bar.

🛈 Welcome Break, M 25 Motorway Services, EN6 3QQ *&* (01707) 643233.

London 21 – Luton 17.

🏠 **Forte Posthouse South Mimms,** Bignells Corner, EN6 3NH, M 25 junction 23 a
junction with A 1 (M) *&* (01707) 643311, Fax (01707) 646728, Ⅰઠ, ☎, ◨ – ⁕ rm, 📺 ☎ 🅿
– 🜲 170. ⬛ 🆎 ⓪ *VISA*
Meals 8.95 **t.** (dinner) and a la carte 15.35/21.95 **t.** ⅃ 7.25 – ⌗ 9.95 – **120 rm** 89.00 **t.** – SB.

🏠 **Welcome Lodge,** Bignells Corner, EN6 3QQ, M 25 junction 23 at junction with A 1 (M
& (01707) 665440, Fax (01707) 660189, Reservations (Freephone) 0800 7314466 – ⁕ rm
📺 ᕕ 🅿. ⬛ 🆎 ⓪ *VISA* ⅍
Meals (grill rest.) – **52 rm** 55.00 **t.**

For maximum information from town plans:
consult the conventional signs key.

SOUTH MOLTON Devon **403** I 30 – pop. 4 066.

🖪 1 East St., EX36 3BU ℰ (01769) 574122 (summer only).

London 210 – Exeter 35 – Taunton 39.

🏨 **Whitechapel Manor** ⤸, EX36 3EG, E : 4 m. by B 3227 and Whitechapel rd ℰ (01769) 573377, Fax (01769) 573797, ≤, « Elizabethan manor house built by Robert de Bassett, gardens », park – ⇄ rest, 📺 ☎ 🅿 – 🔏 30. 🐠 ⓞ *VISA* *JCB*. 🕸
Meals (booking essential) 34.00 **st.** (dinner) and lunch a la carte 19.50/28.95 **st.** 🖢 7.60 – **10 rm** ⊐ 70.00/150.00 **st.**, 1 suite – SB.

🏨 **Park House** ⤸, EX36 3ED, N : ½ m. on North Molton rd ℰ (01769) 572610, ≤, « Victorian country house, gardens », ⤬, park – ⇄ 📺 ☎ 🅿. 🐠 *VISA*. 🕸
closed February – **Meals** (light lunch) 18.50 **st.** (dinner) and lunch a la carte 10.00/18.50 **st.** 🖢 4.60 – **8 rm** ⊐ 51.00/92.00 **st.** – SB.

🏨 **Marsh Hall Country House** ⤸, EX36 3HQ, NE : 1 ½ m. on North Molton rd ℰ (01769) 572666, Fax (01769) 574230, ≤, ⤬ – ⇄ rest, 📺 ☎ 🅿. 🐠 *VISA* *JCB*. 🕸
Meals (dinner only) 19.50 **st.** 🖢 5.00 – **7 rm** ⊐ 45.00/95.00 **st.** – SB.

at East Buckland NW : 6 ¼ m. by B 3226 and Filleigh rd, turning right at Stags Head – ✉ Barnstaple.

✕✕ **Lower Pitt** ⤸ with rm, EX32 0TD, ℰ (01598) 760243, Fax (01598) 760243, ⤬ – ⇄ 🅿.
🐠 🖭 *VISA*. 🕸
closed Christmas and January – **Meals** (booking essential) (dinner only) a la carte 15.75/20.70 **t.** 🖢 6.00 – **3 rm** ⊐ (dinner included) 65.00/120.00 **t.** – SB.

SOUTH NORMANTON Derbs. **402** **403** **404** Q 24 – pop. 13 044 (inc. Pinxton).

London 130 – Derby 17 – Nottingham 15 – Sheffield 31.

🏨 **Swallow,** Carter Lane East, DE55 2EH, on A 38 ℰ (01773) 812000, Fax (01773) 580032, 🗚, ⟺, 🔲 – ⇄ rm, 📺 ☎ 🕭 🅿 – 🔏 200. 🐠 🖭 ⓞ *VISA*
Meals 11.95/21.00 **t.** 🖢 7.00 – **157 rm** ⊐ 95.00/120.00 **t.** – SB.

SOUTHPORT Mersey. **402** K 23 – pop. 90 959.

🖫 Southport Municipal, Park Road West ℰ (01704) 535286.

🖪 112 Lord St., PR8 1NY ℰ (01704) 533333.

London 221 – Liverpool 20 – Manchester 38 – Preston 19.

🏨 **Scarisbrick,** 239 Lord St., PR8 1NZ, ℰ (01704) 543000, Fax (01704) 533335 – 📢 📺 ☎ 🅿 – 🔏 180. 🐠 🖭 ⓞ *VISA*. 🕸
Meals (dancing Saturday evening) 8.70/12.00 **t.** and a la carte 🖢 5.95 – **77 rm** ⊐ 70.00/150.00 **st.** – SB.

🏨 **Stutelea,** Alexandra Rd, PR9 0NB, ℰ (01704) 544220, Fax (01704) 500232, 🗚, ⟺, 🔲, ⤬ – 📢 📺 ☎ 🅿. 🐠 🖭 ⓞ *VISA* *JCB*. 🕸
closed 25 December – **Meals** (bar lunch)/dinner 14.00 **st.** and a la carte 🖢 5.00 – **22 rm** ⊐ 50.00/120.00 **st.** – SB.

🏨 **Cambridge House,** 4 Cambridge Rd, PR9 9NG, NE : 1 m. on A 565 ℰ (01704) 538372, Fax (01704) 547183, ⤬ – ⇄ 📺 ☎ 🅿. 🐠 🖭 ⓞ *VISA*
Meals (dinner only and Sunday lunch)/dinner 14.50 **t.** and a la carte 🖢 5.75 – **18 rm** ⊐ 33.00/60.00 **t.** – SB.

🏠 **Ambassador,** 13 Bath St., PR9 0DP, ℰ (01704) 543998, Fax (01704) 536269 – ⇄ 📺 🅿.
🐠 🖭 *VISA*
closed Christmas and New Year – **Meals** 10.00 – **8 rm** ⊐ 30.00/50.00.

✕✕ **Warehouse Brasserie,** 30 West St., PR8 1QN, ℰ (01704) 544662, Fax (01704) 500074 – ▤. 🐠 🖭 *VISA*
closed Sunday and 25 December – **Meals** (light lunch)/dinner a la carte 13.95/26.45 **t.**

✕✕ **Ho'Lee Chow's,** Rotton Row, Victoria Park, PR8 2BZ, ℰ (01704) 551167, Fax (01704) 550519 – ▤ 🅿. 🐠 🖭 *VISA*
closed 25 and 26 December – **Meals** - Chinese - (dinner only) a la carte 12.00/32.50 **st.**

🅐 ATS 69 Shakespeare St. ℰ (01704) 534434

SOUTHSEA Portsmouth **403** **404** Q 31 – see Portsmouth and Southsea.

SOUTHWAITE SERVICE AREA Cumbria **401 402** L 19 – ✉ Carlisle.

▨ M 6 Service Area, CA4 0NS ℰ (016974) 73445/73446.

London 300 – Carlisle 14 – Lancaster 58 – Workington 48.

🏦 **Travelodge**, CA4 0NT, M 6 between junctions 41 and 42 ℰ (016974) 73131, Fax (016974) 73669, Reservations (Freephone) 0800 850950 – ❄ 📺 ☎ 🕭 🅿. 🐵 🖭 ① 💳 JCB. ❀
  Meals (grill rest.) – **39 rm** 46.95 t.

SOUTH WALSHAM Norfolk **404** Y 26 Great Britain G. – pop. 1 612 – ✉ Norwich.

Env. : The Broads★.

London 120 – Great Yarmouth 11 – Norwich 9.

🏨 **South Walsham Hall H. & Country Club** ⌖, The Street, NR13 6DQ, ℰ (01603) 270378, Fax (01603) 270519, ≼, ♨, ♒, ⌂, park, ❀ – 📺 ☎ 🅿 – 🔬 25. 🐵 🖭 ① 💳 JCB. ❀
  Meals 16.50 t. and a la carte ▯ 4.50 – **17 rm** ☲ 45.00/180.00 st. – SB.

SOUTHWATER W. Sussex **404** T 30 – see Horsham.

SOUTHWELL Notts. **402 404** R 24 Great Britain G. – pop. 6 498.

See : Minster★★ AC.

London 135 – Lincoln 24 – Nottingham 14 – Sheffield 34.

🏨 **Saracen's Head**, Market Pl., NG25 0HE, ℰ (01636) 812701, Fax (01636) 815408, 🎤 – ❄ rm, 📺 ☎ 🅿 – 🔬 120. 🐵 🖭 ① 💳
  Meals (bar lunch)/dinner 17.95 st. and a la carte ▯ 6.50 – ☲ 8.95 – **27 rm** 75.00/120.00 st.

🏠 **Old Forge** without rest., 2 Burgage Lane, NG25 0ER, ℰ (01636) 812809, Fax (01636) 816302, ☞ – ❄ 📺 ☎ 🅿. 🐵 🖭 💳
  6 rm ☲ 32.00/50.00.

SOUTHWOLD Suffolk **404** Z 27 – pop. 3 905.

🏌 The Common ℰ (01502) 723234.

▨ Town Hall, Market Pl., IP18 6EF ℰ (01502) 724729 (summer only).

London 108 – Great Yarmouth 24 – Ipswich 35 – Norwich 34.

🏨 **Swan**, Market Pl., IP18 6EG, ℰ (01502) 722186, Fax (01502) 724800, ☞ – ▐, ❄ rest, 📺 ☎ 🅿 – 🔬 40. 🐵 🖭 ① 💳. ❀
  Meals (bar lunch Monday to Friday November-Easter) 15.50/21.00 t. ▯ 5.35 – **43 rm** ☲ 53.00/123.00 t., 2 suites – SB.

🏨 **Crown**, 90 High St., IP18 6DP, ℰ (01502) 722275, Fax (01502) 727263 – 📺 ☎ 🅿 – 🔬 40. 🐵 🖭 ① 💳 JCB. ❀
  closed 1 week January – Meals 16.25/21.50 t. – ☲ 3.10 – **12 rm** 43.00/65.00 t.

at Reydon NW : 1 m. by A 1095 on B 1126 – ✉ Southwold.

🏠 **Cricketers** with rm, Wangford Rd, IP18 6PZ, ℰ (01502) 723603, Fax (01502) 722194, ☞ – ❄ rest, 📺 ☎ 🅿. 🐵 💳 JCB. ❀
  Meals (in bar) a la carte 11.55/13.35 t. ▯ 4.00 – **8 rm** ☲ 38.00/55.00 t. – SB.

SPALDING Lincs. **402 404** T 25 – pop. 18 731.

▨ Ayscoughfee Hall, Churchgate, PE11 2RA ℰ (01775) 725468/761161.

London 111 – Lincoln 40 – Leicester 56 – Norwich 65.

🏠 **Bedford Court** without rest., 10 London Rd, PE11 2TA, ℰ (01775) 722377, Fax (01775) 722377, ☞ – ❄ 📺 🅿. ❀
  4 rm ☲ 25.00/40.00.

🏠 **Queensgate** with rm, Westlode St., PE11 2AF, ℰ (01775) 711929, Fax (01775) 724205 ❄ rm, 📺 ☎ 🅿. 🐵 🖭 ① 💳 ❀
  closed 1 week Christmas – Meals (closed Bank Holiday Mondays) (in bar) 6.95/7.85 st. ▯ 3.9 – **11 rm** ☲ 35.00/45.00 st.

🅰 ATS 10 Gosberton Rd ℰ (01775) 680251

SPEEN *Bucks. –* ⊠ *Princes Risborough.*
London 41 – Aylesbury 15 – Oxford 33 – Reading 25.

XX **Old Plow** (Restaurant), Flowers Bottom, HP27 0PZ, W : ½ m. by Chapel Hill and Highwood Bottom 𝒫 (01494) 488300, *Fax* (01494) 488702, ☞ – **℗**, 🐙 🖭 *VISA*
closed Sunday dinner, Monday, 25 December, 1 January and 2 weeks August – **Meals** 19.95/25.00 t. ⑧ 10.95.

X **Bistro : Meals** (booking essential) a la carte 15.40/24.85 t. ⑧ 10.95.

SPORLE *Norfolk – see Swaffham.*

SPRATTON *Northants.* 404 R 27 *– see Northampton.*

STADDLEBRIDGE *N. Yorks. – see Northallerton.*

STAFFORD *Staffs.* 402 403 404 N 25 *– pop. 61 885.*
🇮🇸 *Brocton Hall, Brocton* 𝒫 (01785) 662627 *–* 🇫🇸 *Stafford Castle, Newport Rd* 𝒫 (01785) 223821.
🄑 *The Ancient High House, Greengate St., ST16 2HS* 𝒫 (01785) 240204.
London 142 – Birmingham 26 – Derby 32 – Shrewsbury 31 – Stoke-on-Trent 17.

🏨 **De Vere Tillington Hall,** Eccleshall Rd, ST16 1JJ, NW : 1 ½ m. on A 5013 𝒫 (01785) 253531, *Fax* (01785) 259223, 🛵, 🚄, 🔼, ☞, 🞥 – 🛗, 🚿 rm, 🗏 rest, 🖭 ☎ ᵫ **℗** – 🕸 200. 🐙 🖭 ⓪ *VISA*
Meals *(closed Saturday lunch)* (buffet lunch) 15.50 **st.** and a la carte ⑧ 6.75 – **90 rm** ⊇ 95.00/140.00 **st.** – SB.

🏨 **Garth,** Wolverhampton Rd, Moss Pit, ST17 9JR, S : 2 m. on A 449 𝒫 (01785) 256124, *Fax* (01785) 255152, ☞ – 🚿 rm, 🗏 rest, 🖭 ☎ **℗** – 🕸 120. 🐙 🖭 ⓪ *VISA*. 🞥
Meals (bar lunch Saturday) 16.50 **t.** and dinner a la carte ⑧ 5.65 – ⊇ 9.25 – **60 rm** 65.00/75.00 **st.**

🏨 **Vine,** Salter St., ST16 2JU, 𝒫 (01785) 244112, *Fax* (01785) 246612 – 🖭 ☎ **℗**. 🐙 🖭 *VISA*. 🞥
Meals (in bar) a la carte 8.50/14.00 **st.** ⑧ 7.00 – **27 rm** ⊇ 40.00/50.00 **st.**

🄐 ATS Kenworthy Rd, Astonfields Ind. Est.   🄐 ATS Sandon Rd 𝒫 (01785) 253200
𝒫 (01785) 223832

STAFFORD SERVICE AREA *Staffs. –* ⊠ *Stafford.*

🄐 **Travelodge** without rest., Stone, ST15 0EU, M6 between junctions 14 and 15 (northbound carriageway) 𝒫 (01785) 811188, *Fax* (01785) 810500, Reservations (Freephone) 0800 850950 – 🚿 🖭 ☎ ᵫ **℗**. 🐙 🖭 ⓪ *VISA* 🄓🄒🄑. 🞥
49 rm 46.95 **t.**

STAINES *Middx.* 404 S 29 *– pop. 51 167.*
London 26 – Reading 25.

🏨 **Thames Lodge,** Thames St., TW18 4SF, 𝒫 (01784) 464433, *Fax* (01784) 454858, ≤ – 🚿, 🗏 rest, 🖭 ☎ **℗** – 🕸 50. 🐙 🖭 ⓪ *VISA*
Meals a la carte 13.65/18.85 **st.** – ⊇ 9.75 – **47 rm** 110.00/125.00 **st.**

STAITHES *Redcar & Cleveland* 402 R 20 *–* ⊠ *Saltburn (Cleveland).*
London 269 – Middlesbrough 22 – Scarborough 31.

X **Endeavour,** 1 High St., TS13 5BH, 𝒫 (01947) 840825
closed Sunday except dinner July and August, mid January-early March and 25-26 December – **Meals** - Seafood - (lunch booking essential) a la carte 19.45/23.75 **t.**

When travelling for business or pleasure
in **England, Wales, Scotland** *and* **Ireland** *:*

– use the series of five maps
  (nos 401*,* 402*,* 403*,* 404 *and* 923*) at a scale of 1:400 000*

– they are the perfect complement to this Guide

STAMFORD Lincs. 402 404 S 26 *Great Britain G. – pop. 17 492.*

See : Town★★ - St. Martin's Church★ – Lord Burghley's Hospital★ – Browne's Hospital★ AC.
Env. : Burghley House★★ AC, SE : 1½ m. by B 1443.
🛈 Stamford Arts Centre, 27 St. Mary's St., PE9 2DL ℘ (01780) 755611.
London 92 – Leicester 31 – Lincoln 50 – Nottingham 45.

🏨 **The George of Stamford,** 71 St. Martin's, PE9 2LB, ℘ (01780) 755171,
Fax (01780) 757070, 🏤, « Part 16C coaching inn with walled monastic garden » – 📺 ☎ 🅿
– 🛦 50. 🐵 🖭 ⓪ 𝘃𝘐𝘚𝘈
Meals 16.50 st. (lunch) and a la carte 27.10/39.90 st. – **46 rm** ⊊ 78.00/160.00 st., 1 suite –
SB.

🏨 **Garden House,** 42 High St., St. Martin's, PE9 2LP, ℘ (01780) 763359, Fax (01780) 763339,
🏤, ➽ – 📺 ☎ 🅿 – 🛦 25. 🐵 🖭 𝘃𝘐𝘚𝘈
Meals (bar lunch Monday to Saturday)/dinner 15.00 st. and a la carte ░ 4.25 – **20 rm**
⊊ 55.00/85.00 st. – SB.

🏨 **Ram Jam Inn,** Great North Rd, Stretton, LE15 7QX, NW : 8 m. by B 1081 on A 1
(northbound carriageway) ℘ (01780) 410776, Fax (01780) 410361, ➽ – 📺 ☎ 🅿 – 🛦 25.
🐵 🖭 ⓪ 𝘃𝘐𝘚𝘈 ⚘
closed 25 December and 1 January – **Meals** 7.95 (lunch) and a la carte 14.75/19.70 ░ 9.00 –
⊊ 5.00 – **7 rm** 47.50/57.50 s.

🏨 **Lady Anne's,** 37-38 High St., St. Martin's Without, PE9 2LJ, ℘ (01780) 481184,
Fax (01780) 765422, ➽ – ⤢ rest, 📺 ☎ 🅿 – 🛦 100. 🐵 🖭 ⓪ 𝘃𝘐𝘚𝘈
closed 27 to 31 December – **Meals** (booking essential Saturday lunch) 10.95/17.50 t. ░ 6.75
– **29 rm** ⊊ 49.50/82.50 t. – SB.

XX **Raj of India,** 2 All Saints St., PE9 2PA, ℘ (01780) 753556, – 🗏. 🐵 🖭 ⓪ 𝘃𝘐𝘚𝘈
closed 25 December – **Meals** - Indian - a la carte 10.20/17.10 st. ░ 4.80.

at Tallington E : 5 m. by A 6121 on A 16 – ✉ Stamford.

⌂ **Old Mill** ⤢, Mill Lane, PE9 4RR, ℘ (01780) 740815, Fax (01780) 740280, « Converted 17C
mill », park – ⤢ 📺 🅿
Meals (by arrangement) – **5 rm** ⊊ 30.00/55.00 s.

at Ketton SW : 4 m. on A 6121 – ✉ Stamford.

⌂ **The Priory,** Church Rd, PE9 3RD, ℘ (01780) 720215, Fax (01780) 721881, « Part 16C
prebendal manor house », ➽ – ⤢ 📺 ☎ 🅿. 🐵 𝘃𝘐𝘚𝘈 ⚘
closed 23 to 30 December – **Meals** 19.50 t. – **3 rm** ⊊ 58.00/75.00 t. – SB.

at Duddington SW : 5½ m. on A 43 – ✉ Stamford.

🍴 **Royal Oak** with rm, High St., PE 9 3QE, on A 43 ℘ (01780) 444267, Fax (01780) 444369 –
📺 ☎ 🅿. 🐵 🖭 𝘃𝘐𝘚𝘈. ⚘
closed 25 and 26 December – **Meals** (in bar) a la carte 11.10/18.10 st. ░ 4.95 – ⊊ 4.25 –
6 rm 30.00/45.00 st.

at Empingham (Leics.) W : 5¾ m. on A 606 – ✉ Oakham.

🍴 **White Horse** with rm, 2 Main St., LE15 8PS, ℘ (01780) 460221, Fax (01780) 460521, ➽ –
⤢ rest, 📺 ☎ 🅿 – 🛦 60. 🐵 🖭 ⓪ 𝘃𝘐𝘚𝘈. ⚘
Meals (closed Sunday dinner) (bar lunch Monday to Saturday)/dinner 16.95 t. ░ 6.95 –
14 rm ⊊ 45.00/58.00 t. – SB.

at Normanton Park (Leics.) W : 6½ m. by A 606 on Edith Weston Rd – ✉ Oakham.

🏨 **Normanton Park** ⤢, South Shore, LE15 8RP, ℘ (01780) 720315, Fax (01780) 721086,
≼, « Converted Georgian stables on shores of Rutland Water », ➼, ➽ – ⤢ rm, 🗏 rest
📺 ☎ 🅿 – 🛦 30. 🐵 𝘃𝘐𝘚𝘈 𝖩𝖢𝖡
Meals a la carte 14.70/25.15 t. ░ 5.00 – **23 rm** ⊊ 58.50/85.00 t. – SB.

STANDISH Gtr. Manchester 402 404 M 23 – pop. 12 196 – ✉ Wigan.
London 210 – Liverpool 22 – Manchester 21 – Preston 15.

🏨 **Kilhey Court,** Chorley Rd, WN1 2XN, E : 1¾ m. by B 5239 on A 5106 ℘ (01257) 472100
Fax (01257) 422401, 🖪, 🏊, 🗏, ➽ – 🛊 ⤢, 🗏 rest, 📺 ☎ 🅿 – 🛦 180. 🐵 🖭 ⓪ 𝘃𝘐𝘚𝘈
Laureate : Meals (closed Saturday lunch) 13.75/24.00 and a la carte ░ 5.95
Kilhey's Brasserie : Meals (closed Sunday lunch) a la carte 17.40/21.90 ░ 5.95 – **62 rm**
⊊ 90.00/155.00 st. – SB.

🏨 **Wigan/Standish Moat House,** Almond Brook Rd, WN6 0SR, W : 1 m. on A 520
℘ (01257) 499988, Fax (01257) 427327, 🖪, 🏊, 🗏 – 🛊, ⤢ rm, 🗏 rest, 📺 ☎ & 🅿
🛦 150. 🐵 🖭 ⓪ 𝘃𝘐𝘚𝘈
Meals (closed Saturday lunch) (carving rest.) a la carte approx. 13.95 st. ░ 5.50 – ⊊ 9.95
124 rm 80.00/95.00 st. – SB.

🏛 **Wrightington**, Moss Lane, Wrightington (Lancs.), WN6 9PB, W : 1 ¾ m. by A 5209 ℰ (01257) 425803, Fax (01257) 425830, **₤₆**, **☎**, **◧**, squash – ✿ rm, **㆒** **☎** **℗** – **⚑** 180. **◑**
Æ **◉** **VISA**
Meals (bar meals) approx. 9.95 t. 🍷 5.75 – **Blazers :** Meals (closed Sunday) (dinner only) 17.50 t. 🍷 5.95 – **47 rm** ☲ 62.00/90.00 **t.** – SB.

🏛 **Ashfield House**, Ashfield Park Drive, WN6 0EQ, SE : ¾ m. by A 49 ℰ (01257) 473500, Fax (01257) 400311, ☞ – **㆒** **☎** **℗**. **Æ** **VISA** **JCB**
Meals 11.95/17.95 **t.** and a la carte 🍷 7.95 – **15 rm** ☲ 60.00/75.00 **t.**

ⓐ ATS 23 Market St. ℰ (01257) 423146/423732

STANNERSBURN Northd. **401 402** M 18 – ✉ Hexham.
London 363 – Carlisle 56 – Newcastle upon Tyne 46.

🍴 **Pheasant Inn** ⑳ with rm, Falstone, NE48 1DD, ℰ (01434) 240382, Fax (01434) 240382 – ✿ **㆒** **℗**. **◑** **VISA** **JCB**
closed 25 and 26 December – **Meals** (bar lunch Monday to Saturday)/dinner a la carte 13.45/18.70 **t.** 🍷 4.25 – **8 rm** ☲ 40.00/58.00 **t.** – SB.

STANSTEAD ABBOTTS Herts. **404** U 28 – pop. 1 909 – ✉ Ware.
☗ Briggens House Hotel, Briggens Park, Stanstead Rd ℰ (01279) 793742.
London 22 – Cambridge 37 – Luton 32 – Ipswich 66.

🏰 **County H. Stanstead Abbotts Briggens House**, Stanstead Rd, SG12 8LD, E : 2 m. by A 414 ℰ (01279) 829955, Fax (01279) 793685, ≼, **⃟**, **☗**, ☞, park, ✿ – **⃣** **㆒** **☎** **℗** – **⚑** 100. **◑** **Æ** **◉** **VISA** **JCB**. ✿
Bridgemans : Meals 18.50/23.50 **st.** 6and a la carte 🍷 8.50 – ☲ 9.50 – **53 rm** 99.00/125.00 **st.**, 1 suite – SB.

STANSTED AIRPORT Essex **404** U 28 – ✉ Stansted Mountfitchet.
London 37 – Cambridge 29 – Chelmsford 18 – Colchester 29.

🏛 **Hilton National**, Round Coppice Rd, CM24 8SE, ℰ (01279) 680800, Fax (01279) 680890, **₤₆**, **☎**, **◧** – **⃣**, ✿ rm, **▤** **㆒** **☎** **�** **℗** – **⚑** 250. **◑** **Æ** **◉** **VISA** **JCB**. ✿
Meals (bar lunch Saturday) 13.75/17.50 **t.** and a la carte 🍷 8.00 – ☲ 10.75 – **235 rm** 103.00/157.00 **st.**, 5 suites.

🏠 **Welcome Lodge** without rest., Birchanger Service Area, Old Dunmow Rd, CN23 5QZ, at junction 8 of M 11 ℰ (01279) 656477, Fax (01279) 656590, Reservations (Freephone) 0800 7314466 – ✿ **㆒** **ㄴ** **℗**. **◑** **Æ** **◉** **VISA**. ✿
60 rm 55.00 **t.**

at Broxted NE : 3 ¾ m. by Broxted rd – ✉ Great Dunmow.

🏛 **Whitehall**, Church End, CM6 2BZ, on B 1051 ℰ (01279) 850603, Fax (01279) 850385, ≼, « Part 12C and 15C manor house, walled garden », ✿ – **㆒** **☎** **℗** – **⚑** 100. **◑** **Æ** **◉** **VISA**. ✿
closed 26 to 31 December – **Meals** – (see below) – **25 rm** ☲ 85.00/115.00 **st.** – SB.

XXX **Whitehall** (at Whitehall H.), Church End, CM6 2BZ, on B 1051 ℰ (01279) 850603, Fax (01279) 850385 – **℗**. **◑** **Æ** **◉** **VISA**
closed Saturday lunch and 26 to 31 December – **Meals** 18.50/21.00 **st.** and dinner a la carte 🍷 7.50.

STANTON Suffolk **404** W 27 – pop. 2 490.
London 88 – Cambridge 38 – Ipswich 40 – King's Lynn 38 – Norwich 39.

X **Leaping Hare**, Wyken Vineyards, IP31 2DW, S : 1 ¼ m. by Wyken Rd ℰ (01359) 250287, Fax (01359) 252256, « Converted 17C barn », ☞ – **℗**. **◑**
closed Saturday lunch, Sunday dinner to Wednesday and 25 December-1 February – **Meals** (booking essential) a la carte 17.00/20.50 **t.**

STANTON FITZWARREN Wilts. – see Swindon.

STANTON ST. JOHN Oxon. **403 404** Q 28 – see Oxford.

STANTON WICK Bath & North East Somerset **403 404** M 29 – see Bristol.

STAPLEFORD Wilts. **403 404** O 30 – see Salisbury.

STAVERTON Devon 403 I 32 – pop. 682 – ⊠ Totnes.
London 220 – Exeter 20 – Torquay 33.

🏠 **Kingston House** ♨, TQ9 6AR, NW : 1 m. on Kingston rd ✆ (01803) 762235, Fax (01803) 762444, ≤, « Georgian mansion, antiques and marquetry staircase », 🐖, park – ⩳⁚≈ 🕿 🄿. 🐠 🅰🄴 🄾 VISA JCB. ⅋
closed Christmas and New Year – **Meals** (residents only) (lunch by arrangement)/dinner 26.50 **s.** and a la carte – **3 rm** ⊇ 65.00/115.00 **s.**

🍴 **Sea Trout Inn** with rm, TQ9 6PA, ✆ (01803) 762274, Fax (01803) 762506, 🦢 – 🄣 🕿 🄿. 🐠 🅰🄴 VISA
accommodation closed 24 to 26 December – **Meals** (closed Sunday dinner) (bar lunch Monday to Saturday)/dinner 18.50 **t.** and a la carte ₷ 4.25 – **10 rm** ⊇ 45.00/68.00 **t.** – SB.

STAVERTON Glos. – see Cheltenham.

STEDHAM W. Sussex 404 R 31 – see Midhurst.

STEEPLE ASTON Oxon. 403 404 Q 28 – pop. 874 – ⊠ Bicester.
London 69 – Coventry 38 – Oxford 10.

🏨 **Hopcrofts Holt,** OX6 3QQ, SW : 1 ¼ m. at junction of A 4260 with B 4030 ✆ (01869) 340259, Fax (01869) 340865, 🐖 – ⩳⁚≈ 🄣 🕿 🄿 – 🕍 140. 🐠 🅰🄴 🄾 VISA
Meals 11.00/23.00 **st.** and dinner a la carte ₷ 6.75 – **88 rm** ⊇ 75.00/145.00 **st.** – SB.

Es ist empfeblenswert, in der Hauptsaison und vor allem
in Urlaubsorten, Hotelzimmer im voraus zu bestellen.
Benachrichtigen Sie sofort das Hotel, wenn Sie ein bestelltes
Zimmer nicht belegen können.

Wenn Sie an ein Hotel im Ausland schreiben, fügen Sie Ibrem Brief
einen internationalen Antwortschein bei (im Postamt erhältlich).

STEVENAGE Herts. 404 T 28 Great Britain G. – pop. 76 064.
Env. : Knebworth House* AC, S : 2 ½ m.
🛇, 🛇 Aston Lane ✆ (01438) 880424 – 🛇, 🛇 Chesfield Downs Golf Centre, Jack's Hill, Graveley ✆ (01462) 482929.
London 36 – Bedford 25 – Cambridge 27.

🏨 **County H. Stevenage Cromwell,** High St., Old Town, SG1 3AZ, ✆ (01438) 779954, Fax (01438) 742169, 🐖 – ⩳⁚≈ rm, 🔳 rest, 🄣 🕿 🄿 – 🕍 220. 🐠 🅰🄴 🄾 VISA. ⅋
Meals (bar lunch Monday to Saturday)/dinner 17.25 **t.** and a la carte ₷ 8.00 – ⊇ 9.75 – **56 rm** 95.00/112.00 **st.**

🏨 **County H. Stevenage Hertfordpark,** Danestrete, SG1 1EJ, ✆ (01438) 779955, Fax (01438) 741880 – 🛗, ⩳⁚≈ rm, 🄣 🕿 – 🕍 250. 🐠 🅰🄴 🄾 VISA. ⅋
Meals (closed Saturday lunch) a la carte 11.25/15.00 **st.** ₷ 5.00 – ⊇ 8.75 – **98 rm** 63.00/79.00 **st.** – SB.

🏨 **Novotel Stevenage,** Knebworth Park, SG1 2AX, SW : 1 ½ m. by A 602 at junction with A 1 (M) ✆ (01438) 742299, Fax (01438) 723872, 🏊 – 🛗, ⩳⁚≈ rm, 🔳 rest, 🄣 🕿 ఈ 🄿 – 🕍 120. 🐠 🅰🄴 🄾 VISA
Meals 12.50/15.50 **st.** and a la carte ₷ 6.55 – ⊇ 8.95 – **100 rm** 75.00 **st.**

🏠 **Travel Inn,** Corey's Mill Lane, SG1 4AA, NW : 2 m. on A 602 ✆ (01438) 351318, Fax (01438) 721609 – 🛗, ⩳⁚≈ rm, 🔳 rest, 🄣 ఈ 🄿. 🐠 🅰🄴 🄾 VISA. ⅋
Meals (grill rest.) – **39 rm** 36.50 **t.**

🔘 ATS 4-8 Norton Rd ✆ (01438) 313262

STEYNING W. Sussex 404 T 31 – pop. 8 692 (inc. Upper Beeding).
London 52 – Brighton 12 – Worthing 10.

🏨 **The Old Tollgate,** The Street, Bramber, BN44 3WE, SW : 1 m. ✆ (01903) 879494, Fax (01903) 813399 – 🛗 🄣 🕿 ఈ 🄿. 🐠 🅰🄴 🄾 VISA. ⅋
Meals (carving rest.) 12.95/18.50 **t.** ₷ 5.50 – ⊇ 6.95 – **31 rm** 61.00/83.00 **t.** – SB.

🏠 **Springwells** without rest., 9 High St., BN44 3GG, ✆ (01903) 812446, Fax (01903) 879823, ⤨⤨, 🏊, 🐖 – 🄣 🕿 🄿. 🐠 🅰🄴 🄾 VISA. ⅋
closed 24 December-1 January – **11 rm** ⊇ 39.00/80.00 **st.**

STILTON *Cambs.* [404] T 26 – *pop. 2 219* – ⊠ *Peterborough.*
London 76 – Cambridge 30 – Northampton 43 – Peterborough 6.

🏠 **Bell Inn**, Great North Rd, PE7 3RA, ℘ (01733) 241066, *Fax (01733) 245173*, « Part 16C »,
🌳 – ⇌ rm, 🔟 ☎ 🅿 – 🔬 100. ◐◑ 🆎 ◍ 𝗩𝗜𝗦𝗔 𝗝𝗖𝗕
closed 25 December – **Meals** (bar lunch Saturday) 17.95 **t.** ◊ 6.00 – **19 rm** ⊑ 64.00/99.00 **t.**

STOCKBRIDGE *Hants.* [403] [404] P 30 – *pop. 570.*
London 75 – Salisbury 14 – Winchester 9.

⤴ **Carbery**, Salisbury Hill, SO20 6EZ, on A 30 ℘ (01264) 810771, *Fax (01264) 811022*, ⤳, 🌳 –
🔟 🅿. ⅏
closed 2 weeks Christmas – **Meals** (by arrangement) 12.50 **st.** ◊ 3.50 – **11 rm** ⊑ 25.00/
51.00 **t.**

STOCKPORT *Gtr. Manchester* [402] [403] [404] N 23 – *pop. 132 813.*
🏌 Heaton Moor, Mauldeth Rd ℘ (0161) 432 2134 - 🏌 Romiley, Goosehouse Green ℘ (0161)
430 2392 – 🏌 Ladythorn Rd, Bramhall ℘ (0161) 439 4057 – 🏌 Hazel Grove ℘ (0161) 483
3217 – 🏌 Offerton Rd, Offerton ℘ (0161) 427 2001.
🛈 *Graylaw House, Chestergate, SK1 1NH ℘ (0161) 474 3320/1.*
London 201 – Liverpool 42 – Manchester 6 – Sheffield 37 – Stoke-on-Trent 34.

🏠 Old Rectory, Churchgate, SK1 1YG, E : ¼ m. by Wellington St. ℘ (0161) 429 0060,
Fax (0161) 474 0076 – |≡|, ≡ rest, 🔟 ☎ 🕹 🅿
46 **rm**

🏠 **Jarvis Alma Lodge**, 149 Buxton Rd, SK2 6EL, S : 1 ¼ m. on A 6 ℘ (0161) 483 4431,
Fax (0161) 483 1983 – ⇌ rm, 🔟 ☎ 🅿 – 🔬 200. ◐◑ 🆎 ◍ 𝗩𝗜𝗦𝗔 𝗝𝗖𝗕
Meals (carving rest.) (bar lunch Saturday) 10.50 **st.** and a la carte ◊ 7.00 – ⊑ 8.00 – **52 rm**
79.00/110.50 **st.** – SB.

🏠 **Saxon Holme**, 230 Wellington Rd North, SK4 2QN, N : 1 m. on A 6 ℘ (0161) 432 2335,
Fax (0161) 431 8076 – |≡| ⇌ 🔟 ☎ 🕹 🅿. ◐◑ 🆎 ◍ 𝗩𝗜𝗦𝗔. ⅏
Meals (closed Sunday) (dinner only) 12.95 **t.** and a la carte ◊ 5.25 – **33 rm** ⊑ 45.00/65.00 **t.**

🏠 **Wycliffe**, 74 Edgeley Rd, Edgeley, SK3 9NQ, W : 1 m. on B 5465 ℘ (0161) 477 5395,
Fax (0161) 476 3219 – 🔟 ☎ 🅿 – 🔬 30. ◐◑ 🆎 ◍ 𝗩𝗜𝗦𝗔. ⅏
closed 26 December and 1 January – **Meals** - Italian - (closed Saturday lunch) 7.00/
15.00 **t.** and a la carte ◊ 4.75 – **28 rm** ⊑ 40.00/52.00 **st.**

🏠 **Travel Inn**, Buxton Rd, SK2 6NB, S : 1 m. on A 6 ℘ (0161) 480 2968, *Fax (0161) 477 8320* –
⇌ rm, ≡ rest, 🔟 🕹 🅿. ◐◑ 🆎 ◍ 𝗩𝗜𝗦𝗔. ⅏
Meals (grill rest.) – **40 rm** 36.50 **t.**

◎ ATS Hollingworth Rd, Bredbury ℘ (0161) 430 5221

STOCKTON-ON-TEES *Stockton-on-Tees* [402] P 20 – *pop. 83 576.*
🏌 Eaglescliffe, Yarm Rd ℘ (01642) 780098 – 🏌, 🏌 Knotty Hill Golf Centre, Sedgefield
℘ (01740) 620320 – 🏌 Norton, Junction Rd ℘ (01642) 676385.
✈ Teesside Airport : ℘ (01642) 219444, SW : 6 m. by A 1027, A 135 and A 67.
🛈 *Theatre Yard, off High St., TS18 1AT ℘ (01642) 615080.*
London 251 – Leeds 61 – Middlesbrough 4.

🏠 **Swallow**, 10 John Walker Sq., TS18 1AQ, ℘ (01642) 679721, *Fax (01642) 601714*, ✦₅, ≋,
⟨⟩ – |≡|, ⇌ rm, ≡ rest, 🔟 ☎ 🅿 – 🔬 300. ◐◑ 🆎 ◍ 𝗩𝗜𝗦𝗔
Portcullis : **Meals** (dinner only) 17.50 **t.** ◊ 7.25 – *Matchmaker Brasserie :* **Meals** (closed
Sunday) a la carte 13.95/22.45 **t.** ◊ 7.25 – **125 rm** ⊑ 95.00/125.00 **st.** – SB.

🏠 **Travel Inn**, Yarm Rd, TS18 3RT, SW : 1 ¾ m. on A 135 ℘ (01642) 633354,
Fax (01642) 633339 – ⇌ rm, 🔟 🕹 🅿. ◐◑ 🆎 ◍ 𝗩𝗜𝗦𝗔. ⅏
Meals (grill rest.) – **40 rm** 36.50 **t.**

at Eaglescliffe *S : 3½ m. on A 135* – ⊠ *Stockton-on-Tees.*

🏠 **Parkmore**, 636 Yarm Rd, TS16 0DH, ℘ (01642) 786815, *Fax (01642) 790485*, ✦₅, ≋, ⟨⟩
– ⇌ 🔟 ☎ 🅿 – 🔬 140. ◐◑ 🆎 ◍ 𝗩𝗜𝗦𝗔 𝗝𝗖𝗕
Meals 12.50/16.75 **st.** and dinner a la carte ◊ 5.20 – ⊑ 6.95 – **55 rm** 57.00/78.00 **st.** – SB.

◎ ATS 18 Brunswick St. ℘ (01642) 675733   ATS 112 Norton Rd ℘ (01642) 604477

STOKE BRUERNE Northants. 404 R 27 – pop. 347 – ⊠ Towcester.
London 69 – Coventry 33 – Northampton 9 – Oxford 33.

※ **Bruerne's Lock,** 5 The Canalside, NN12 7SB, ℘ (01604) 863654, Fax (01604) 863654, « Canalside setting » – ⊕⊗ AE VISA
closed Saturday lunch, Sunday dinner, Monday and 26 December-5 January –
Meals 16.50 t. (lunch) and dinner a la carte 21.75/28.25 t. ⅃ 6.75.

STOKE BY NAYLAND Suffolk 404 W 28.
London 70 – Bury St. Edmunds 24 – Cambridge 54 – Colchester 11 – Ipswich 14.

⌂ **Ryegate House** without rest., CO6 4RA, ℘ (01206) 263679, ≤, ⋒ – ⊁ TV ❶. ⅍
closed Christmas and 1 week spring and autumn – **3 rm** ⊇ 29.00/42.00 t.

※※ **Angel Inn** with rm, Polstead St., CO6 4SA, ℘ (01206) 263245, Fax (01206) 263373, « Part timbered 17C inn » – TV ☎ ❶. ⊕⊗ AE ① VISA. ⅍
closed 25-26 December and 1 January – **Meals** a la carte 12.25/20.85 t. ⅃ 4.50 – **6 rm** ⊇ 46.00/60.00 st.

STOKE CANON Devon 403 J 31 – see Exeter.

Halten Sie beim Betreten des Hotels oder des Restaurants
den Führer in der Hand.
Sie zeigen damit, daß Sie aufgrund dieser Empfehlung gekommen sind.

STOKE D'ABERNON Surrey 404 ⑫ – see Cobham.

STOKE FLEMING Devon 403 J 33 – see Dartmouth.

STOKE GABRIEL Devon 403 J 32 – see Totnes.

STOKE HOLY CROSS Norfolk 404 X 26 – see Norwich.

STOKE-ON-TRENT Staffs. 402 403 404 N 24 Great Britain G. – pop. 266 543.
See : Museum and Art Gallery★ Y M – Gladstone Pottery Museum★ AC V.
Env. : Wedgwood Visitor's Centre★ AC, S : 5 ½ m. by A 500 and A 34 V.
Exc. : Little Moreton Hall★★ AC, N : 8 ½ m. by A 500 on A 34 U.
⁊8 Greenway Hall, Stockton Brook ℘ (01782) 503158, U – ⁊8 Parkhall, Hulme Rd, Weston Coyney ℘ (01782) 599584, V.
🛈 Potteries Shopping Centre, Quadrant Rd, Hanley, ST1 9HR ℘ (01782) 284600.
London 162 – Birmingham 46 – Leicester 59 – Liverpool 58 – Manchester 41 – Sheffield 53.

Plans on following pages

🏨 **Stoke-on-Trent Moat House,** Etruria Hall, Festival Park, Etruria, ST1 5BQ ℘ (01782) 609988, Fax (01782) 284500, ⅃δ, ≘s, ◨ – ⁍, ⊁ rm, ▤ TV ☎ ❶ – 🔏 600. ⊕⊗ AE ① VISA JCB. ⅍
U n
Meals (bar lunch Saturday) 17.95 st. (dinner) and a la carte 14.70/23.40 st. ⅃ 7.50 – ⊇ 9.50 – **143 rm** 110.00/175.00 st. – SB.

🏨 Stakis Stoke-on-Trent, 66 Trinity St., Hanley, ST1 5NB, ℘ (01782) 202361 Fax (01782) 286464, ⅃δ, ≘s, ◨ – ⁍, ⊁ rm, TV ☎ & ❶ – 🔏 300
Y c
122 rm, 3 suites.

🏨 **North Stafford,** Station Rd, ST4 2AE, ℘ (01782) 744477, Fax (01782) 744580 – ⁍ TV ☎ ❶ – 🔏 450. ⊕⊗ AE ① VISA JCB
X a
Meals (closed Saturday lunch) 9.50/16.00 st. and a la carte – ⊇ 7.50 – **69 rm** 85.00/99.00 st. – SB.

at Burslem N : 3½ m. by A 500 and A 53 on A 50 – ⊠ Stoke-on-Trent.

🏨 **The George,** Swan Sq., ST6 2AE, ℘ (01782) 577544, Fax (01782) 837496 – ⁍ TV ☎ ❶ – 🔏 200. ⊕⊗ AE ① VISA. ⅍
U e
closed 25 and 26 December – **Meals** (bar lunch Saturday) 10.95/15.95 t. and a la carte ⅃ 5.50 – **39 rm** ⊇ 60.00/90.00 st. – SB.

STOKE-ON-TRENT
NEWCASTLE-UNDER-LYME
BUILT UP AREA

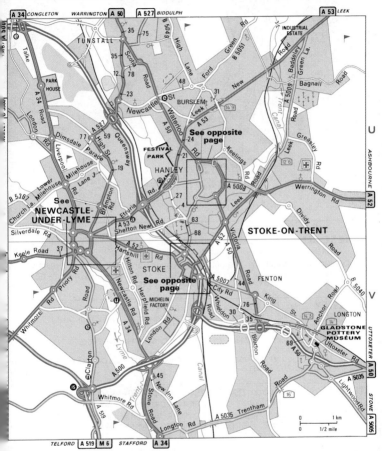

at **Basford** NW : 1 ¾ m. by A 500 off A 53 – ⊠ Stoke-on-Trent.

Haydon House, 9 Haydon St., ST4 6JD, ℰ (01782) 711311, Fax (01782) 717470 – 📺 ☎ 🅿
– 🔬 80. 🐿 🖭 ⓪ 𝐕𝐈𝐒𝐀 𝐉𝐂𝐁. U a
Clock : Meals *(closed Sunday dinner to non-residents)* 10.50/14.90 **st.** and a la carte –
⊇ 6.00 – **24 rm** 52.50/75.00 **st.**, 6 suites.

at **Talke** NW : 4 m. on A 500 at junction with A 34 – ⊠ Stoke-on-Trent.

Travelodge, Newcastle Rd, ST7 1UP, ℰ (01782) 777000, Fax (01782) 777000, Reservations (Freephone) 0800 850950 – ⊁ rm, 📺 ☎ &. 🅿. 🐿 🖭 ⓪ 𝐕𝐈𝐒𝐀 𝐉𝐂𝐁. 🛠 U e
Meals (grill rest.) – **62 rm** 44.95 **t.**

🔘 ATS 25 Smithpool Rd, Fenton ℰ (01782) 847081   ATS 87/89 Waterloo Rd, Burslem
ℰ (01782) 838493/836591

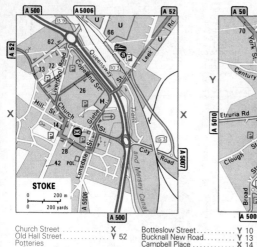

STOKE ST. GREGORY Somerset **403** L 30 – ⊠ Taunton.
London 147 – Bristol 39 – Taunton 8.

↑ **Slough Court** ⊗ without rest., Slough Lane, TA3 6JQ, ℰ (01823) 490311, Fax (01823) 490311, « 14C moated manor house, working farm », ⌅, ⌖, ⚙ – ⊡ ⦿. ⚙ restricted opening in winter – **3 rm** ⊇ 30.00/52.00 **st.**

STOKESLEY N. Yorks. **402** Q 20 Great Britain G. – pop. 4 008 – ⊠ Middlesbrough.
Env. : Great Ayton (Captain Cook Birthplace Museum★ AC), NE : 2 ½ m. on A 173.
London 239 – Leeds 59 – Middlesbrough 8 – York 52.

✗ **Chapter's** with rm, 27 High St., TS9 5AD, ℰ (01642) 711888, Fax (01642) 713387 – ↨⚟ rm ⊡ ☎. ⠀⠀ ⠀ 🆚
Meals (closed Sunday lunch, 25 December and 1 January) a la carte 13.90/26.95 **t.** ⸱ 5.50 – **13 rm** ⊇ 50.00/63.00 **t.**

STOKE-UPON-TERN Shrops. **402** **403** **404** M 25 – pop. 1 500 – ⊠ Market Drayton.
London 167 – Birmingham 49 – Chester 34 – Stoke-on-Trent 25 – Shrewbury 17.

↑ **Stoke Manor** ⊗ without rest., TF9 2DU, E : ½ m. on Wistanswick rd ℰ (01630) 685222 Fax (01630) 685666, « Vintage tractor collection », ⌖ – ↨⚟ ⊡ ⦿. ⚙ closed December – **3 rm** ⊇ 25.00/50.00 **st.**

STONE Staffs. **402** **403** **404** N 25 – pop. 12 305.
▫ Barlaston, Meaford Rd ℰ (01782) 372795.
London 150 – Birmingham 36 – Stoke-on-Trent 9.

🏨 **Stone House,** ST15 0BQ, S : 1 ¼ m. by A 520 on A 34 ℰ (01785) 815531 Fax (01785) 814764, ⌁, ⓢ, ⌖, ⌖, ⚙ – ↨⚟ ⊡ ☎ ⦿ – ⚿ 180. ⠀⠀ ⠀ 🆚 🆎
Meals (bar lunch Saturday and Bank Holidays) a la carte 14.95/23.40 **st.** ⸱ 6.95 – ⊇ 8.95 – **47 rm** 78.00 **st.**

STON EASTON Somerset – pop. 579 – ⊠ Bath (Bath & North East Somerset).
London 131 – Bath 12 – Bristol 11 – Wells 7.

🏰 **Ston Easton Park** ⊗, BA3 4DF, ℰ (01761) 241631, Fax (01761) 241377, ≤, « Palladian mansion », ⌖, park, ⚙ – ↨⚟ rest, ⊡ ☎ ⦿ – ⚿ 30. ⠀⠀ ⠀ 🆚 🆎 ⚙
Meals 15.00/39.50 **st.** and a la carte ⸱ 15.00 – ⊇ 12.50 – **19 rm** 170.00/400.00 **st.**, 2 suites – SB.

STONOR *Oxon.* [404] R 29 – *see Henley-on-Thames.*

STONY STRATFORD *Bucks.* [404] R 27 – *pop. 55 733 (inc. Wolverton).*
London 58 – Birmingham 68 – Northampton 14 – Oxford 32.

Plans : see Milton Keynes

🍴🍴 **Peking,** 117 High St., MK11 1AT, ☎ (01908) 563120, *Fax (01908) 560084* – ▤. [MC] [AE] [VISA] [JCB] on Milton Keynes town plan AV p
closed 25 and 26 December – **Meals** - Chinese (Peking, Szechuan) - 14.00/25.00 **t.** and a la carte.

at Cosgrove *(Northants.) N : 2½ m. by A 508 – ✉ Milton Keynes.*

🏠 **Old Bakery,** Main St., MK19 7JL, ☎ (01908) 262255, *Fax (01908) 263620* – [TV] ☎ [P]. [MC] [AE] [D] [VISA]. ⊘ on Milton Keynes town plan AU q
Meals (by arrangement Friday to Sunday) (residents only) (dinner only) a la carte 12.50 **t.** and a la carte – **8 rm** ☕ 55.00/65.00 **t.**

STORRINGTON *W. Sussex* [404] S 31 – *pop. 7 429.*
London 54 – Brighton 20 – Portsmouth 36.

🏠 **Little Thakeham** 🐦, Merrywood Lane, Thakeham, RH20 3HE, N : 1 ¾ m. by B 2139 ☎ (01903) 744416, *Fax (01903) 745022,* ≤, « Lutyens house with gardens in the style of Gertrude Jekyll » – [TV] ☎ [P]. [MC] [AE] [D] [VISA]. ⊘
closed 2 weeks Christmas and New Year – **Meals** *(closed Monday lunch and Sunday dinner to non-residents)* (lunch by arrangement)/dinner 30.00 **s.** 🍷 6.50 – **7 rm** ☕ 90.00/150.00 **s.**, 2 suites – SB.

🍴🍴🍴 ✿ **Manley's** (Löderer), Manley's Hill, RH20 4BT, E : ¼ m. on A 283 ☎ (01903) 742331, *Fax (01903) 740649* – [P]. [MC] [AE] [VISA] [JCB]
closed Sunday and Tuesday dinner, Monday and 2 weeks January – **Meals** 19.60/38.70 **t.** 🍷 8.00
Spec. Roast saddle of rabbit and breast of pigeon with a truffle dressing. Venison steak with celeriac, apple and wild cherries with a red wine sauce. Chocolate pavé with fruit purée and crème anglaise.

🍴🍴 ☺ **Old Forge,** 6 Church St., RH20 4LA, ☎ (01903) 743402, *Fax (01903) 742540* – [MC] [AE] [D] [VISA] [JCB]
closed Saturday lunch, Sunday dinner, Monday, Tuesday, 3 weeks in spring and 3 weeks in autumn – **Meals** 15.00/22.00 **st.** and a la carte 22.00/25.50 **st.** 🍷 5.00.

STOURBRIDGE *W. Mids.* [403] [404] N26 – *pop. 55 624.*
London 147 – Birmingham 14 – Wolverhampton 10 – Worcester 21.

Plan : see Birmingham p. 2

🏠 Talbot, High St., DY8 1DW, ☎ (01384) 394350, *Fax (01384) 371318* – [TV] ☎ [P] – 🪑 150 **25 rm.** AU a

at Hagley *S : 2½ m. by A 491 – ✉ Stourbridge.*

🏠 **Travel Inn,** Birmingham Rd, DY9 9JS, NE : 1 ½ m. on A 456 (eastbound) ☎ (01562) 883120, *Fax (01562) 884416* – ⊬ rm, [TV] ♿ [P]. [MC] [AE] [D] [VISA]. ⊘ AU r
Meals (grill rest.) – **40 rm** 36.50 **t.**

at Kinver *(Staffs.) W : 5 m. by A 458 –* AU – *✉ Stourbridge.*

🍴🍴 **Berkley's,** 5-6 High St., DY7 6HG, ☎ (01384) 873679 – [MC] [AE] [D] [VISA]
closed Sunday, 2 weeks February and 26 to 31 December – **Meals** (dinner only) a la carte 20.45/25.00 **t.** 🍷 4.75.

STOURPORT-ON-SEVERN *Worcestershire* [403] [404] N 26 – *pop. 18 283.*
London 137 – Birmingham 21 – Worcester 12.

🏠 **Stourport Manor,** 35 Hartlebury Rd, DY13 9LT, E : 1 ¼ m. on B 4193 ☎ (01299) 289955, *Fax (01299) 878520,* 🏋, ≘s, 🏊, 🏊, 🌳, 🎾, squash – ⊬ [TV] ☎ [P] – 🪑 350. [MC] [AE] [D] [VISA]
Meals (bar lunch Saturday) 11.95/14.95 **t.** and a la carte 🍷 5.25 – ☕ 8.25 – **65 rm** 70.00/120.00 **st.**, 3 suites – SB.

When looking for a quiet hotel
use the maps found in the introduction
or look for establishments with the sign 🐦 *or* 🐦

STOWMARKET Suffolk ₄₀₄ W/X 27 – pop. 13 229.
 🛈 Wilkes Way, IP14 1DE ℰ (01449) 676800.
 London 81 – Cambridge 42 – Ipswich 12 – Norwich 38.

🏛 **Gipping Heights,** Creeting Rd, IP14 5BT, E : 1 m. by Station Rd East (B 1113)
 ℰ (01449) 675264 – 📺 **(P)**. 🎟 VISA. ⌘
 Meals (closed 25 December) (bar lunch)/dinner 12.00 s. ⌘ 5.20 – **5 rm** ⌷ 33.00/46.00 s.

🏛 **Travelodge,** IP14 3PY, NW : 2 m. by A 1038 on A 14 (westbound) ℰ (01449) 615347,
 Reservations (Freephone) 0800 850950 – ⌘ rm, 📺 ఉ **(P)**. 🎟 ㏂ ① VISA JCB. ⌘
 Meals (grill rest.) – **40 rm** 35.95 t.

at Mendlesham Green NE : 6¼ m. by B 1115, A 1120 and Mendlesham rd – ⌷ Stowmarket.

⌂ **Cherry Tree Farm,** Mendlesham Green, IP14 5RQ, ℰ (01449) 766376, « Part Elizabethan
 house », 🌿 – ⌘ **(P)**. ⌘
 closed December-January – **Meals** (by arrangement) (communal dining) 16.00 st. – **3 rm**
 ⌷ 48.00 st.

STOW-ON-THE-WOLD Glos. ₄₀₃ ₄₀₄ O 28 Great Britain G. – pop. 1 999.
 Exc. : Chastleton House★★, NE : 6½ m. by A 436 and A 44.
 🛈 Hollis House, The Square, Gl54 1AF ℰ (01451) 831082.
 London 86 – Birmingham 44 – Gloucester 27 – Oxford 30.

🏛🏛 **Wyck Hill House** ⌂, GL54 1HY, S : 2¼ m. by A 429 on A 424 ℰ (01451) 831936,
 Fax (01451) 832243, ≤, « Part Victorian country house », 🌿, park – ⌽, ⌘ rest, 📺 ☎ **(P)** –
 ⌸ 50. 🎟 ㏂ ① VISA JCB
 Meals 14.95/32.50 t. ⌘ 10.00 – **29 rm** ⌷ 90.00/175.00 t., 1 suite – SB.

🏛 **Grapevine,** Sheep St., GL54 1AU, ℰ (01451) 830344, Fax (01451) 832278, « Mature grapevine in restaurant » – ⌘ rest, 📺 ☎ **(P)** – ⌸ 25. 🎟 ㏂ ① VISA JCB
 Meals 11.95/24.00 st. ⌘ 5.50 – **22 rm** ⌷ (dinner included) 96.00/192.00 st. – SB.

🏛 **Fosse Manor,** Fosse Way, GL54 1JX, S : 1¼ m. on A 429 ℰ (01451) 830354,
 Fax (01451) 832486, ☎, 🌿 – ⌘ rest, 📺 ☎ **(P)** – ⌸ 40. 🎟 ㏂ ① VISA JCB
 closed 20 to 29 December – **Meals** 14.95/21.95 t. and dinner a la carte ⌘ 5.95 – **20 rm**
 ⌷ 57.00/160.00 t. – SB.

🏛 **Unicorn,** Sheep St., GL54 1HQ, ℰ (01451) 830257, Fax (01451) 831090 – ⌘ 📺 ☎ **(P)**. 🎟
 ㏂ ① VISA JCB
 Meals 12.95/20.50 st. and dinner a la carte ⌘ 6.75 – ⌷ 8.75 – **20 rm** 85.00/110.00 st. – SB.

🏛 **Stow Lodge,** The Square, GL54 1AB, ℰ (01451) 830485, Fax (01451) 831671, 🌿 – ⌘ 📺
 ☎ **(P)**. 🎟 ㏂ ① VISA JCB. ⌘
 closed Christmas and January – **Meals** (bar lunch)/dinner 16.00 t. and a la carte ⌘ 7.50 –
 21 rm ⌷ 65.00/105.00 t. – SB.

⌂ **Bretton House,** Fosseway, GL54 1JU, S : ½ m. on A 429 ℰ (01451) 830388, ≤, 🌿 – ⌘
 📺 **(P)**
 closed 25 and 26 December – **Meals** (by arrangement) 12.50 st. – **3 rm** ⌷ 45.00 st.

⌂ **Wyck Hill Lodge** without rest., Wyck Hill, GL54 1HT, S : 2 m. by A 429 on A 424
 ℰ (01451) 830141, ≤, 🌿 – ⌘ 📺 **(P)**. ⌘
 March-November – **3 rm** ⌷ 46.00.

at Broadwell NE : 1¾ m. by A 429 – ⌷ Moreton-in-Marsh.

⌂ **College House,** Chapel St., GL56 0TW, ℰ (01451) 832351, « 17C », 🌿 – ⌘ 📺 **(P)**. ⌘
 closed 25 and 26 December – **Meals** (by arrangement) (communal dining) 17.50 st. – **3 rm**
 ⌷ 40.00/62.00 st.

at Lower Oddington E : 3 m. by A 436 – ⌷ Stow-on-the-Wold.

🍴 **Fox,** GL56 0UR, ℰ (01451) 870555, 🌿 – **(P)**. 🎟 VISA
 Meals a la carte approx. 14.40 t. ⌘ 4.25.

at Bledington SE : 4 m. by A 436 on B 4450 – ⌷ Kingham.

🏛 **Kings Head,** OX7 6XQ, ℰ (01608) 658365, Fax (01608) 658902, « Part 15C inn » – ⌘ rm
 📺 ☎ **(P)**. 🎟 ㏂ ① VISA JCB. ⌘
 closed 24 and 25 December – **Meals** 9.95 t. and dinner a la carte ⌘ 4.50 – **12 rm** ⌷ 45.00/
 75.00 st.

STRATFIELD TURGIS Hants. – pop. 94 – ⌷ Basingstoke.
 London 46 – Basingstoke 8 – Reading 11.

🏛 **Wellington Arms,** RG27 0AS, on A 33 ℰ (01256) 882214, Fax (01256) 882934, 🌿 –
 ⌘ rm, 📺 ☎ **(P)** – ⌸ 80. 🎟 ㏂ ① VISA
 Meals (closed Saturday lunch and Sunday dinner) 19.95 t. and a la carte – **33 rm** ⌷ 80.00/
 105.00 t., 2 suites.

STRATFORD-UPON-AVON *Warks.* **403 404** *P 27 Great Britain G.* – *pop. 22 231.*

See : *Town★ - Shakespeare's Birthplace★ AC,* AB.

Env. : *Mary Arden's House★ AC, NW : 4 m. by A 3400* A.

Exc. : *Ragley Hall★ AC, W : 9 m. by A 422* A.

  Tiddington Rd ℘ (01789) 297296, B – *Welcombe Hotel, Warwick Rd ℘ (01789) 299021,* B – *Stratford Oaks, Bearley Rd, Snitterfield ℘ (01789) 731982,* B.

  Bridgefoot, CV37 6GW ℘ (01789) 293127.

  London 96 – Birmingham 23 – Coventry 18 – Oxford 40.

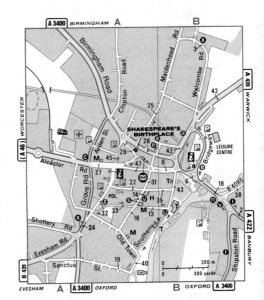

STRATFORD-UPON-AVON

For maximum information from town plans: consult the conventional signs key.

Welcombe H. & Golf Course, Warwick Rd, CV37 0NR, NE : 1 ½ m. on A 439 ℘ (01789) 295252, *Fax (01789) 414666,* ≤, « 19C Jacobean style mansion in park », ..., rest, ... – ... 80. ...
Meals 19.50/32.50 t. and dinner a la carte – **61 rm** ⊇ 115.00/275.00 t., 6 suites – SB.

Ettington Park ⊗, Alderminster, CV37 8BU, SE : 6 ¼ m. on A 3400 ℘ (01789) 450123, *Fax (01789) 450472,* ≤, « Victorian Gothic mansion », ..., park, ... – ..., rest, ... – ... 60. ...
Meals 15.00/30.50 t. and dinner a la carte ⅄ 8.95 – **43 rm** ⊇ 135.00/195.00 st., 5 suites – SB.

Stratford Moat House, Bridgefoot, CV37 6YR, ℘ (01789) 279988, *Fax (01789) 298589,* ..., ... rm, ... – ... 450. ...   B e
Meals (bar lunch Monday to Saturday)/dinner 14.50 st. and a la carte ⅄ 8.00 – ⊇ 9.50 – **245 rm** 108.00/136.00 t., 2 suites – SB.

Alveston Manor, Clopton Bridge, CV37 7HP, ℘ (01789) 204581, *Fax (01789) 414095,* « Part Elizabethan house », ... – ... rm, ... – ... 150. ...   B i
Manor : **Meals** a la carte 18.75/27.45 ⅄ 7.50 – ⊇ 9.75 – **105 rm** 95.00/120.00 st., 1 suite – SB.

Shakespeare, Chapel St., CV37 6ER, ℘ (01789) 294771, *Fax (01789) 415411,* « 17C timbered inn » – ... – ... 100. ...   A v
Meals a la carte approx. 18.50 st. – ⊇ 10.50 – **62 rm** 95.00/145.00 st., 1 suite – SB.

Arden Thistle, 44 Waterside, CV37 6BA, ℘ (01789) 294949, *Fax (01789) 415874,* ..., ... – ... 50. ...   B u
Bards : **Meals** 12.50/24.95 st. and a la carte ⅄ 6.70 – ⊇ 9.75 – **62 rm** 96.00/134.00 st. – SB.

Stratford Manor, Warwick Rd, CV37 0PY, NE : 3 m. on A 439 ℘ (01789) 731173, *Fax (01789) 731131,* ..., ..., park, ... – ..., rest, ... – ... 350. ... ...
Meals (bar lunch Saturday) 15.00/22.00 t. ⅄ 7.60 – ⊇ 8.50 – **103 rm** 85.00/104.00 t. – SB.

Stratford Victoria, Arden St., CV37 6QQ, ℘ (01789) 271000, *Fax (01789) 271001,* ▸ –
🛗, ❧← rm, ▤ rest, ▣ ☎ ₺ ◐ – ⅛ 140. ◑◎ ◭ ◑ ᴠɪ𝗌ᴀ
A c
Meals (carving lunch Sunday and carving dinner Saturday) a la carte 18.50/22.50 **st.** –
103 **rm** � 75.00/115.00 **st.**, 1 suite – SB.

Grosvenor, 12-14 Warwick Rd, CV37 6YT, ℘ (01789) 269213, *Fax (01789) 266087* – ▣ ☎
₺ ◐ – ⅛ 100. ◑◎ ◭ ◑ ᴠɪ𝗌ᴀ ᴊᴄʙ
B a
Meals 13.95 **st.** and a la carte ⅛ 6.25 – ⊂ 6.50 – **67 rm** 79.50/89.50 **st.** – SB.

Forte Posthouse Stratford-upon-Avon, Bridgefoot, CV37 7LT, ℘ (01789) 266761,
Fax (01789) 414547, ⊛ – ❧← rm, ▣ ☎ ◐ – ⅛ 150. ◑◎ ◭ ◑ ᴠɪ𝗌ᴀ ᴊᴄʙ
B v
Meals 8.95 **st.** (lunch) and a la carte 17.20/23.40 **st.** ⅛ 7.50 – ⊂ 9.95 – **60 rm** 79.00 **st.** – SB.

Dukes, Payton St., CV37 6UA, ℘ (01789) 269300, *Fax (01789) 414700,* ⊛ – ▣ ☎ ◐. ◑◎
◭ ᴠɪ𝗌ᴀ ᴊᴄʙ. ⅜
AB o
closed Christmas and New Year – **Meals** *(closed Sunday)* a la carte 15.45/24.95 **t.** ⅛ 5.50 –
22 **rm** ⊂ 52.50/115.00 **t.** – SB.

Stratford Court, Avenue Rd, CV37 6UX, ℘ (01789) 297799, *Fax (01789) 262449,*
« Edwardian house », ⊛ – ▣ ☎ ◐. ◑◎ ᴠɪ𝗌ᴀ
B x
closed 1 week Christmas – **Meals** (booking essential) (residents only) (dinner only) 16.50 **st.**
⅛ 6.50 – **13 rm** ⊂ 50.00/140.00 **st.** – SB.

Sequoia House without rest., 51-53 Shipston Rd, CV37 7LN, ℘ (01789) 268852,
Fax (01789) 414559, ⊛ – ❧← rm ◐ – ⅛ 40. ◑◎ ◭ ◑ ᴠɪ𝗌ᴀ ᴊᴄʙ. ⅜
B r
closed 21 to 27 December – **24 rm** ⊂ 45.00/72.00 **st.**

Caterham House without rest., 58-59 Rother St., CV37 6LT, ℘ (01789) 267309,
Fax (01789) 414836 – ▣ ◐. ◑◎ ᴠɪ𝗌ᴀ
A z
10 **rm** ⊂ 58.00/72.00 **st.**

Stratheden without rest., 5 Chapel St., CV37 6EP, ℘ (01789) 297119, *Fax (01789) 297119*
– ▣ ☎. ◑◎ ᴠɪ𝗌ᴀ. ⅜
A s
closed Christmas-New Year – **9 rm** ⊂ 37.00/62.00 **st.**

Twelfth Night without rest., Evesham Pl., CV37 6HT, ℘ (01789) 414595 – ❧← ▣ ◐. ◑◎
ᴠɪ𝗌ᴀ. ⅜
A x
6 **rm** ⊂ 58.00 **st.**

Payton without rest., 6 John St., CV37 6UB, ℘ (01789) 266442, *Fax (01789) 266442* – ❧←
▣. ◑◎ ◭ ᴠɪ𝗌ᴀ. ⅜
A e
closed 24 to 26 December – **5 rm** ⊂ 40.00/62.00 **s.**

Victoria Spa Lodge without rest., Bishopton Lane, CV37 9QY, NW : 2 m. by A 3400 on
Bishopton Lane turning left at roundabout with A 46 ℘ (01789) 267985,
Fax (01789) 204728, ⊛ – ❧← ▣ ◐. ◑◎ ᴠɪ𝗌ᴀ. ⅜
7 **rm** ⊂ 38.00/60.00 **t.**

Virginia Lodge without rest., 12 Evesham Pl., CV37 6HT, ℘ (01789) 292157, ⊛ – ❧← ▣
◐. ⅜
A x
closed 24 to 26 December – **8 rm** ⊂ 20.00/46.00 **st.**

Hussain's, 6a Chapel St., CV37 6EP, ℘ (01789) 267506, *Fax (01789) 415341* – ▤. ◑◎ ◭ ◑
ᴠɪ𝗌ᴀ
A s
closed 25 December – **Meals** - Indian - 5.95/30.95 **t.** and a la carte ⅛ 4.95.

The Boathouse, Swan's Nest Lane, CV37 7LS, ℘ (01789) 297733, *Fax (01789) 297733,* ⇐
« Riverside setting » – ◑◎ ᴠɪ𝗌ᴀ
B ▸
closed Monday lunch, Sunday, 25-26 December and 1 January – **Meals** a la carte 15.25
22.85 **t.** ⅛ 9.35.

at Charlecote E : 4¾ m. by B 4086 – B – ✉ Stratford-upon-Avon.

County H. Stratford Charlecote Pheasant, CV35 5EW, ℘ (01789) 279954
Fax (01789) 470222, 🏊, ⊛, ⅜ – ❧← rm, ▣ ☎ ₺ ◐ – ⅛ 120. ◑◎ ◭ ◑ ᴠɪ𝗌ᴀ. ⅜
Meals (bar lunch Saturday) 10.75/15.95 **st.** and a la carte ⅛ 7.95 – ⊂ 9.50 – **67 rm** 85.00
110.00 **st.** – SB.

at Wellesbourne E : 5¾ m. on B 4086 – B – ✉ Warwick.

Chadley House ⅖, Loxley Rd, CV35 9JL, SW : 1¼ m. by A 429 ℘ (01789) 840994
Fax (01789) 842977, « Part Georgian farmhouse », ⊛ – ▣ ◐ ᴠɪ𝗌ᴀ ◑. ⅜
closed 24 to 26 December – **Meals** (lunch by arrangement) (light dinner Sunday resident
only)/dinner a la carte 18.15/20.75 **t.** ⅛ 4.90 – **9 rm** ⊂ 45.00/80.00 **t.** – SB.

at Binton SW : 4½ m. by B 439 – A – ✉ Stratford-upon-Avon.

Graveside Barn ⅖ without rest., CV37 9TU, NW : ¾ m. by Binton H
℘ (01789) 750502, *Fax (01789) 298056,* ⇐, « Converted barn », ⊛, ⅜ – ❧← ▣ ◐. ◑◎ ᴠɪ𝗌ᴀ
⅜
3 **rm** ⊂ 40.00/60.00 **st.**

at Billesley *W : 4½ m. by A 422 – A – off A 46 – ✉ Stratford-upon-Avon.*

Billesley Manor ⛰, B49 6NF, ✆ (01789) 279955, *Fax (01789) 764145*, ←, « Part Elizabethan manor, topiary garden », 🏊, park, 🎾 – ⇔ rest, TV ☎ P – 🏛 90. MC AE ⓓ VISA. ✻
Meals *(closed Saturday lunch)* 30.00 **st.** (dinner) and a la carte 15.00/38.50 **st.** – ☕ 9.75 – **39 rm** 115.00/230.00 **st.**, 2 suites – SB.

at Wilmcote *NW : 3½ m. by A 3400 – A – ✉ Stratford-upon-Avon.*

Pear Tree Cottage ⛰ without rest., 7 Church Rd, CV37 9UX, ✆ (01789) 205889, *Fax (01789) 262862*, « Part Elizabethan », 🌳 – ⇔ TV P. ✻
closed Christmas-1 February – **5 rm** ☕ 30.00/46.00.

ATS Western Rd ✆ (01789) 205591

STRATTON *Glos.* 403 404 O 28 – *see Cirencester.*

STREATLEY *Newbury* 403 404 Q 29 *Great Britain G.* – *pop. 4 193 (inc. Goring)* – ✉ *Goring.*

Env. : *Basildon Park★ AC, SE : 2 ½ m. by A 329 – Mapledurham★ AC, E : 6 m. by A 329, B 471 and B 4526.*

Exc. : *Ridgeway Path★★.*

18 *Goring & Streatley, Rectory Rd ✆ (01491) 872688.*

London 56 – Oxford 16 – Reading 11.

Swan Diplomat, High St., RG8 9HR, ✆ (01491) 873737, *Fax (01491) 872554*, 🚣, « ← Thames-side setting », 🏋, 🧖, 🏊, 🌳 – TV ☎ ♿ P – 🏛 80. MC AE ⓓ VISA JCB
Meals (bar lunch)/dinner 30.00 **t.** and a la carte – ☕ 9.50 – **45 rm** 95.00/130.00 **t.**, 1 suite – SB.

Les prix — Pour toutes précisions sur les prix indiqués dans ce guide, reportez-vous aux pages de l'introduction.

STREET *Somerset* 403 L 30 *The West Country G.* – *pop. 10 539.*

See : *The Shoe Museum★.*

Env. : *Glastonbury★★ – Abbey★★ (Abbot's Kitchen★) AC, St. John the Baptist★★, Somerset Rural Life Museum★ AC, Glastonbury Tor★ (←★★★), NE : 2 m. by A 39.*

Exc. : *High Ham (←★★, St. Andrew's Church★), SW : 8 m. by A 39, A 361 and minor rd.*

London 138 – Bristol 28 – Taunton 20.

Bear Inn, 53 High St., BA16 0EF, ✆ (01458) 442021, *Fax (01458) 840007*, 🌳 – TV ☎ P – 🏛 100
16 rm, 1 suite.

STRETTON *Ches.* 402 403 404 M 23 – *see Warrington.*

STRETTON *Staffs.* 402 403 404 P 25 – *see Burton-upon-Trent.*

STROUD *Glos.* 403 404 N 28 – *pop. 38 835.*

18, 18, 18 *Minchinhampton ✆ (01453) 832642 (old course) (01453) 833866 (new course)* – 18 *Painswick ✆ (01452) 812180.*

ℹ *Subscription Rooms, George St., GL5 1AE ✆ (01453) 765768.*

London 113 – Bristol 30 – Gloucester 9.

Stonehouse Court, Stonehouse, GL10 3RA, W : 4 m. on A 419 ✆ (01453) 825155, *Fax (01453) 824611*, « Part 16C manor house », 🌳 – TV ☎ P – 🏛 150. MC AE ⓓ VISA JCB
Meals *(closed Saturday lunch)/dinner* 21.00 **t.** and a la carte 🍷 7.25 – **36 rm** ☕ 74.00/200.00 **t.**, 1 suite – SB.

Old Nelson - Premier Lodge, Stratford Lodge, Stratford Rd, GL5 4AF, N : ½ m. by A 46 ✆ (01453) 765821, *Fax (01453) 765964* – ⇔ rm, TV ☎ ♿ P. MC AE ⓓ VISA. ✻
Meals (grill rest.) a la carte 8.90/15.15 **st.** – ☕ 4.95 – **30 rm** 42.25 **st.**

at Brimscombe *SE : 2¼ m. on A 419 – ✉ Stroud.*

Burleigh Court ⛰, Burleigh Lane, GL5 2PF, S : ½ m. by Burleigh rd via The Roundabouts ✆ (01453) 883804, *Fax (01453) 886870*, ←, 🏊, 🌳 – ⇔ rest, TV ☎ P. MC ⓓ VISA JCB
Meals (light dinner Sunday) 16.95/21.50 **t.** 🍷 5.00 – **17 rm** ☕ 67.50/110.00 **t.** – SB.

at Amberley S : 3 m. by A 46 – ⊠ Stroud.

🏨 **Amberley Inn,** GL5 5AF, ℰ (01453) 872565, Fax (01453) 872738, 🐎 – 📺 ☎ 🅿. ⚠️ 🅰️🅴
VISA
Meals 12.95/18.95 **t.** and a la carte ⏐ 5.50 – **15 rm** ⊑ 35.50/80.00 **t.** – SB.

⚙ ATS Dudbridge Rd ℰ (01453) 758156/752191

STUCKTON Hants. – see Fordingbridge.

STUDLEY Warks. 403 404 O 27 – pop. 5 883 – ⊠ Redditch.
London 109 – Birmingham 15 – Coventry 33 – Gloucester 39.

XX **Pepper's,** 45 High St., B80 7HN, ℰ (01527) 853183 – ⊟. ⚠️ 🅰️🅴 VISA
closed Sunday and 25 December – **Meals** - Indian - (dinner only) a la carte 9.75/17.15 **t.**

STURMINSTER NEWTON Dorset 403 404 N 31 The West Country G. – pop. 2 155.
See : Mill★ AC.
London 123 – Bournemouth 30 – Bristol 49 – Salisbury 28 – Taunton 41.

🏠 **Stourcastle Lodge,** Gough's Close, DT10 1BU, (off the Market Place) ℰ (01258) 472320,
Fax (01258) 473381, 🐎 – ⇎ 📺 ☎ 🅿. ⚠️ VISA. ✑
Meals 16.00 **st.** – **5 rm** ⊑ 40.00/68.00 **st.**

XXX **Plumber Manor** ⌂ with rm, DT10 2AF, SW : 1 ¾ m. by A 357 on Hazelbury Bryan rd
ℰ (01258) 472507, Fax (01258) 473370, ≼, « 18C manor house », 🐎, park, ✑ – 📺 ☎ 🅿 –
🔏 25. ⚠️ 🅰️🅴 ⓪ VISA
closed February – **Meals** (dinner only and Sunday lunch)/dinner 21.50/27.50 **st.** ⏐ 5.00 –
16 rm ⊑ 70.00/130.00 **st.** – SB.

*Le Guide change, changez de **guide Michelin** tous les ans.*

SUDBURY Suffolk 404 W 27 Great Britain G. – pop. 19 512.
See : Gainsborough's House★ AC.
🅱 Town Hall, Market Hill, CO10 6TL ℰ (01787) 881320 (summer only).
London 59 – Cambridge 37 – Colchester 15 – Ipswich 21.

🏨 **Mill,** Walnut Tree Lane, CO10 6BD, ℰ (01787) 375544, Fax (01787) 373027, ≼, « Converted
19C mill » – ⊟ rest, 📺 ☎ 🅿 – 🔏 70. ⚠️ 🅰️🅴 VISA
Meals 13.25 **t.** (lunch) and dinner a la carte 18.65/23.70 **t.** ⏐ 5.25 – ⊑ 7.50 – **56 rm** 50.00/
78.00 **t.** – SB.

X **Red Onion Bistro,** 57 Ballingdon St., CO10 6DA, SW : ¾ m. on A 131 ℰ (01787) 376777,
Fax (01787) 883156, 🈸 – 🅿. ⚠️ VISA 🇯🇨🇧
closed Sunday and 25 December-1 January – **Meals** (booking essential) 7.50/9.75 **t.**
and a la carte ⏐ 3.50.

⚙ ATS Edgeworth Rd ℰ (01787) 374227

SULBY Isle of Man 402 G 21 – see Man (Isle of).

SUNDERLAND Tyne and Wear 401 402 P 19 – pop. 183 310.
🏌 Whitburn, Lizard Lane ℰ (0191) 529 2144.
🅱 50 Fawcett St., SR1 3RF ℰ (0191) 553 2000/1.
London 272 – Leeds 92 – Middlesbrough 29 – Newcastle upon Tyne 12.

Plan on next page

🏨 **Swallow Sunderland,** Queens Par., Seaburn, SR6 8DB, ℰ (0191) 529 2041,
Fax (0191) 529 4227, ≼, 🛁, 🛋, 🔲 – 🛗, ⇎ rm, ⊟ 📺 ☎ 🕭 🅿 – 🔏 300. ⚠️ 🅰️🅴 ⓪ VISA
Meals 15.95/24.00 **st.** and a la carte ⏐ 6.50 – **65 rm** ⊑ 90.00/130.00 **st.** – SB.   A

🏨 **Roker,** Roker Terrace, Roker, SR6 0PH, ℰ (0191) 567 1786, Fax (0191) 510 0289, ≼ – 📺 ☎
🅿 – 🔏 300. ⚠️ 🅰️🅴 ⓪ VISA. ✑
Meals (grill rest.) a la carte 9.55/17.35 **st.** – ⊑ 6.95 – **44 rm** 42.50 **t.**   A

🏠 **Travel Inn,** Wessington Way, SR5 3HR, NW : 3 ¾ m. by A 1231 ℰ (0191) 548 9384,
Fax (0191) 548 4148 – ⇎ rm, 📺 ఉ 🅿 – 🔏 25. ⚠️ 🅰️🅴 ⓪ VISA. ✑
Meals (grill rest.) – **41 rm** 36.50 **t.**

⚙ ATS Monkwearmouth Bridge ℰ (0191) 565 7694

SUNDERLAND

BUILT UP AREA

	1 km
0	
0	1/2 mile

A 1231 WASHINGTON
A 183 CHESTER-LE-STREET
A 690 (A 1 : M) DURHAM
A 1018 MIDDLESBROUGH

CENTRE

0	300 m
0	300 yards

A 183
A 1018
A 1231
A 183
A 690
A 1018

*Town plans: the names
of main shopping streets
are indicated in red
at the beginning
of the list of streets.*

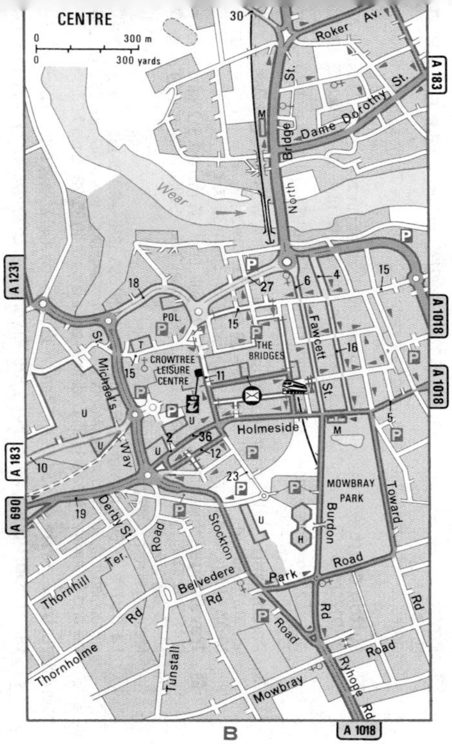

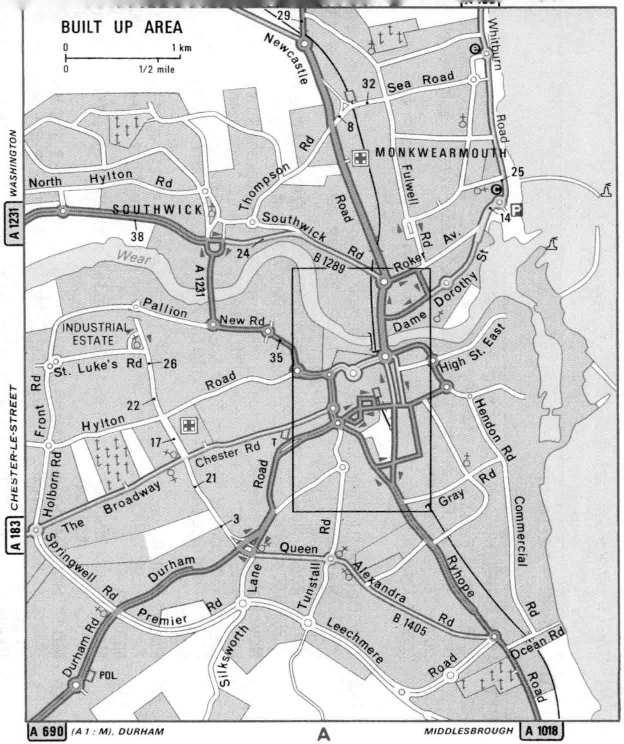

577

SUNNINGHILL *Windsor & Maidenhead* 404 S 29 – *see Ascot.*

SUTTON *W. Sussex – see Petworth.*

SUTTON COLDFIELD *W. Mids.* 403 404 O 26 – *pop. 106 001.*

🐾 Pype Hayes, Eachelhurst Rd, Walmley ℘ (0121) 351 1014, DT – 🐾 Boldmere, Monmouth Drive ℘ (0121) 354 3379, DT – 🐾 110 Thornhill Rd ℘ (0121) 353 2014, DT – 🐾, 🐾 The Belfry, Lichfield Rd, Wishaw ℘ (01675) 470301 DT.

London 124 – Birmingham 8 – Coventry 29 – Nottingham 47 – Stoke-on-Trent 40.

Plan : see Birmingham pp. 2 and 3

🏨 **The Belfry,** Lichfield Rd, Wishaw, B76 9PR, E : 6 ½ m. by A 453 on A 446 ℘ (01675) 470301, Fax (01675) 470178, ≤, 🛵, ≦s, 🔲, 🐾, 🐾, park, ⚓, squash – 🛗, 🌿 rm, 🍽 rest, 🔲 ☎ ♿ 🅿 – 🛐 450. 🕓 🕘 🆎 ⓪ 𝘝𝘐𝘚𝘈. ⚭ **Garden Room :** Meals (carving rest.) 15.50/21.50 **st.** ♦ 9.00 – **French Restaurant :** Meals 10.50/28.50 **st.** and a la carte ♦ 9.00 – **305 rm** ⊆ 99.00/195.00 **st.**, 15 suites – SB.

🏨 **New Hall** ⊁, Walmley Rd, B76 1QX, SE : 1 ½ m. by Coleshill St., Coleshill Rd and Reddicap Hill on B 4148 ℘ (0121) 378 2442, Fax (0121) 378 4637, ≤, « Part 13C moated manor house, gardens », 🐾, park, ⚓ – 🌿 rest, 🔲 ☎ 🅿 – 🛐 50. 🕓 🆎 ⓪ 𝘝𝘐𝘚𝘈 𝘑𝘊𝘉. ⚭ DT Meals (closed Saturday lunch) 19.50/35.50 **t.** ♦ 7.05 – ⊆ 12.50 – **55 rm** 120.00/174.00 **t.**, 5 suites – SB.

🏨 **Penns Hall,** Penns Lane, Walmley, B76 1LH, SE : 2 ¾ m. by A 5127 ℘ (0121) 351 3111, Fax (0121) 313 1297, 🛵, ≦s, 🔲, ⚓, ⚓, park, squash – 🛗, 🌿 rm, 🔲 ☎ ♿ 🅿 – 🛐 400. 🕓 🆎 ⓪ 𝘝𝘐𝘚𝘈 Meals (closed Saturday lunch) 11.95/16.95 **st.** and a la carte ♦ 7.00 – ⊆ 9.50 – **133 rm** 109.00/129.00 **st.**, 3 suites – SB.

🏨 **Moor Hall,** Moor Hall Drive, B75 6LN, NE : 2 m. by A 453 and Weeford Rd ℘ (0121) 308 3751, Fax (0121) 308 8974, 🛵, 🔲, ⚓ – 🛗, 🌿 rm, 🔲 ☎ 🅿 – 🛐 250. 🕓 🆎 ⓪ 𝘝𝘐𝘚𝘈. ⚭ Meals (carving lunch) 10.95/21.00 **st.** and dinner a la carte ♦ 6.50 – **74 rm** ⊆ 89.00/160.00 **st.** – SB.

🏨 **Royal,** High St., B72 1UD, ℘ (0121) 355 8222, Fax (0121) 355 1837 – 🔲 ☎ 🅿 – 🛐 50. 🕓 🆎 ⓪ 𝘝𝘐𝘚𝘈. ⚭ closed 25 December – Meals (grill rest.) a la carte 8.00/15.00 **t.** – **22 rm** ⊆ 51.45/68.40 **t.** – SB.

🏨 **Sutton Court,** 60-66 Lichfield Rd, B74 2NA, N : ½ m. at junction of A 5127 with A 453 ℘ (0121) 355 6071, Fax (0121) 355 0083 – 🌿 rm, 🔲 ☎ 🅿 – 🛐 90. 🕓 🆎 ⓪ 𝘝𝘐𝘚𝘈 𝘑𝘊𝘉 closed 26 to 30 December – Meals (bar lunch)/dinner 16.95 **t.** ♦ 4.95 – ⊆ 9.50 – **64 rm** 72.50/99.50 **st.** – SB.

🏨 **Parson and Clerk,** Chester Rd North, Streetly, B73 6SP, W : 3 ½ m. by A 453 on A 452 ℘ (0121) 353 1747, Fax (0121) 352 1340 – 🔲 ☎ 🅿. 🕓 🆎 ⓪ 𝘝𝘐𝘚𝘈. ⚭ CT Meals (grill rest.) a la carte 10.70/18.90 **t.** – ⊆ 6.00 – **36 rm** 39.00 **t.**

🏨 **Travelodge** without rest., Boldmere Rd, B73 5UP, SW : 1 ¼ m. by A 5127 and A 453 on B 4142 ℘ (0121) 355 0017, Reservations (Freephone) 0800 850950 – 🌿 rm, 🔲 ♿ 🅿. 🕓 🆎 ⓪ 𝘝𝘐𝘚𝘈 𝘑𝘊𝘉. ⚭ Meals (grill rest.) – **32 rm** 44.95 **t.**

🍴 **La Truffe,** 65 Birmingham Rd, B72 1QF, ℘ (0121) 355 5836 – 🕓 🆎 𝘝𝘐𝘚𝘈 DT closed Saturday lunch, Sunday, Monday, Easter Tuesday, last 2 weeks August, 25-26 December and 1 January – Meals 17.95 **t.** (dinner) and a la carte 10.85/28.20 **t.** ♦ 7.25.

at Curdworth SE : 6 ½ m. by A 5127, A 452 and A 38 – DT – on A 4097 – ✉ Sutton Coldfield.

🏠 **Old School House,** Kingsbury Rd, B76 9DR, on A 4097 ℘ (01675) 470177 – 🔲 🅿. 🕓 𝘝𝘐𝘚𝘈 𝘑𝘊𝘉 Meals (by arrangement) 15.50 **st.** ♦ 5.50 – **6 rm** ⊆ 39.50/48.00 **s.**

SUTTON COURTENAY *Oxon.* 403 404 Q 29 – ✉ Abingdon. *London 57 – Newbury 21 – Oxford 11 – Swindon 27.*

🍴 **The Fish** with rm, 4 Appleford Rd, OX14 4NQ, ℘ (01235) 848242, Fax (01235) 848014, ⚓ – 🔲 🅿 🆎 𝘝𝘐𝘚𝘈. ⚭ closed Sunday dinner January and February and 27 to 30 December – Meals 15.95/18.95 **st.** and a la carte ♦ 5.00 – ⊆ 7.50 – **2 rm** 35.00/45.00 **st.**

Les prix Pour toutes précisions sur les prix indiqués dans ce guide, reportez-vous aux pages de l'introduction.

SUTTON-ON-SEA *Lincs.* 402 404 U 24 – *pop. 9 719 (inc. Mablethorpe).*
London 151 – Boston 32 – Great Grimsby 30 – Lincoln 45.

⚲ **Athelstone Lodge,** 25 Trusthorpe Rd, LN12 2LR, ℘ (01507) 441521 – ⇷ rest, 📺 🅿 ⓪⑨
💳 *VISA*
March-October – **Meals** 8.00 **st.** – **6 rm** ☲ 19.00/38.00 **st.** – SB.

SUTTON SCOTNEY SERVICE AREA *Hants.* 403 404 P 30 – ✉ *Winchester.*
London 66 – Reading 32 – Salisbury 21 – Southampton 19.

🏠 **Travelodge,** SO21 3JY, on A 34 ℘ (01962) 761016 (northside), (01962) 760779 (south-side), Reservations (Freephone) 0800 850950 – ⇷ rm, 📺 ⅋ 🅿 ⓪⑨ 🇦🇪 ⓪ *VISA* *JCB*. ⚡
Meals (grill rest.) – **71 rm** 42.95 **t.**

SWAFFHAM *Norfolk* 404 W 26 *Great Britain G.* – *pop. 5 332.*
Exc. : *Oxburgh Hall*★★ *AC, SW : 7 ½ m.*
London 97 – Cambridge 46 – King's Lynn 16 – Norwich 27.

🏠 **Strattons,** Ash Close, PE37 7NH, off Market Sq. ℘ (01760) 723845, *Fax (01760) 720458,*
« Part Queen Anne house », 🌳 – ⇷ 📺 ☎ 🅿 ⓪⑨ *VISA.* ⚡
closed 25 and 26 December – **Meals** *(closed Sunday dinner)* (booking essential to non-residents) (light lunch residents only) 25.00 **st.** ⅋ 6.40 – **7 rm** ☲ 58.00/130.00 **st.**

🏠 **George,** Station St., PE37 7LJ, ℘ (01760) 721238, *Fax (01760) 725333* – ⇷ rest, 📺 ☎ 🅿 –
🅰 150. ⓪⑨ 🇦🇪 ⓪ *VISA*
Meals 15.95 **st.** and a la carte ⅋ 4.50 – **30 rm** ☲ 49.00/69.00 **st.**

at Sporle *NE : 3¼ m. by A 1065 and A 47* – ✉ *King's Lynn.*

⚲ **Corfield House,** PE32 2EA, on Necton rd ℘ (01760) 723636, 🌳 – ⇷ 📺 🅿. ⓪⑨ *VISA*
closed 18 December-28 March – **Meals** 12.50 **st.** – **4 rm** ☲ 29.00/43.00 **s.**

◉ ATS Unit 2a, Tower Meadow (off Station St.) ℘ (01760) 722543

In alta stagione, e soprattutto nelle stazioni turistiche,
è prudente prenotare con un certo anticipo.
Avvertite immediatamente l'albergatore se non potete più
occupare la camera prenotata.

Se scrivete ad un albergo all'estero, allegate alla vostra lettera
un tagliando-risposta internazionale
(disponibile presso gli uffici postali).

WANAGE *Dorset* 403 404 O 32 *The West Country G.* – *pop. 9 947.*
See : *Town*★.
Env. : *St. Aldhelm's Head*★★ *(⇽★★★), SW : 4 m. by B 3069 – Durlston Country Park (⇽★★),*
S : 1 m. – Studland (Old Harry Rocks★★*, Studland Beach (⇽★), St. Nicholas Church*★*),*
N : 3 m. – Worth Matravers (Anvil Point Lighthouse ⇽★★), S : 2 m. – Great Globe★*, S : 1 ¼ m.*
Exc. : *Corfe Castle*★ *(⇽★★) AC, NW : 6 m. by A 351 – Blue Pool*★*, NW : 9 m. by A 351 and*
minor roads – Lulworth Cove★*, W : 18 m. by A 351 and B 3070.*
🏌, 🏌 *Isle of Purbeck, Studland* ℘ (01929) 450361.
🚩 *The White House, Shore Rd, BH19 1LB* ℘ (01929) 422885.
London 130 – Bournemouth 22 – Dorchester 26 – Southampton 52.

🏨 **Purbeck House,** 91 High St., BH19 2LZ, ℘ (01929) 422872, *Fax (01929) 421194,*
« Former convent », 🌳 – 📺 ☎ 🅿 – 🅰 80. ⓪⑨ 🇦🇪 ⓪ *VISA*
Thomas Hardy : **Meals** (bar lunch Monday to Saturday)/dinner 18.50 **st.** and a la carte
⅋ 6.50 – **18 rm** ☲ 55.00/110.00 **st.** – SB.

✕ **Cauldron Bistro,** 5 High St., BH19 2LN, ℘ (01929) 422671 – ⓪⑨ 🇦🇪 ⓪ *VISA*
closed Tuesday lunch, Tuesday dinner in winter, Monday and January –
Meals a la carte 18.40/26.20 **t.** ⅋ 6.75.

✕ **The Galley,** 9 High St., BH19 2LN, ℘ (01929) 427299 – ⓪⑨ 🇦🇪 ⓪ *VISA* *JCB*
closed Monday and Tuesday in March, January and February and 3 weeks November –
Meals (dinner only) 18.50 **t.** ⅋ 4.25.

WAVESEY SERVICE AREA *Cambs.* 404 U 27 – *see Cambridge.*

WAY *Hants.* 403 404 P 31 – *see Brockenhurst.*

SWINDON 403 404 O 29 *The West Country G.* – *pop. 145 236.*

See : *Great Western Railway Museum*★ *AC* – *Railway Village Museum*★ *AC*Y **M**.

Env. : *Lydiard Park (St. Mary's*★*) W : 4 m.* U.

Exc. : *Ridgeway Path*★★*, S : 8 ½ m. by A 4361 – Whitehorse (*≤★*)E : 7 ½ m. by A 4312, A 420 and B 400 off B 4057.*

◯₁₈ , ◯₅ *Broome Manor, Pipers Way ℘ (01793) 532403 –* ◯₁₈ *Shrivenham Park, Penny Hooks ℘ (01793) 783853 –* ◯₁₈ *Wootton Bassett ℘ (01793) 849999 –* ◯₁₈ *Wrag Barn G & C.C., Shrivenham Rd, Highworth ℘ (01793) 861327.*

🄱 *37 Regent St., SN1 IJL ℘ (01793) 2530328.*

London 83 – Bournemouth 69 – Bristol 40 – Coventry 66 – Oxford 29 – Reading 40 – Southampton 65

SWINDON

SWINDON

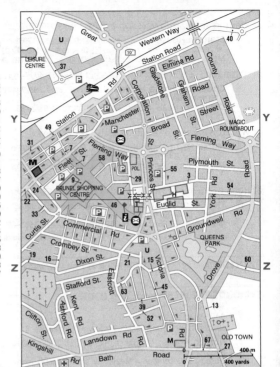

De Vere, Shaw Ridge Leisure Park, Whitehill Way, SN5 7DW, W : 2 ¾ m. by A 3102 and Tewkesbury Way (at Mannington junction) ℰ (01793) 878785, Fax (01793) 877822, **Ⅰ₆**, **≘s**, **◻**, – 🛗 ⅙⋇, ▤ rest, 📺 ☎ ⅍ Ⲣ – 🏝 400. **◍◍** **ⱯⒺ** **①** **𝘝𝘐𝘚𝘈**   U e
Meals (bar lunch Saturday) (carving lunch) 16.50/22.50 **st.** and dinner a la carte ⅋ 8.50 – **146 rm** ⇌ 115.00/125.00 **st.**, 8 suites – SB.

Swindon Marriott, Pipers Way, SN3 1SH, SE : 1 ½ m. by Marlborough Road off B 4006 ℰ (01793) 512121, Fax (01793) 513114, **Ⅰ₆**, **≘s**, **◻**, **⁒**, squash – 🛗, ⅙⋇ rm, ▤ 📺 ☎ ⅍ Ⲣ – 🏝 250. **◍◍** **ⱯⒺ** **①** **𝘝𝘐𝘚𝘈**   V s
Meals (closed Saturday lunch) 18.00/21.00 **st.** and a la carte – ⇌ 10.95 – **153 rm** 85.00/101.00 **st.** – SB.

Hilton National, Lydiard Fields, Great Western Way, SN5 8UZ, M 4 junction 16 ℰ (01793) 881777, Fax (01793) 881881, **Ⅰ₆**, **≘s**, **◻** – 🛗 ⅙⋇ rm, ▤ 📺 ☎ ⅍ Ⲣ – 🏝 350. **◍◍** **ⱯⒺ** **①** **𝘝𝘐𝘚𝘈**   V a
Meals (bar lunch Saturday) 12.75/18.50 **st.** and a la carte ⅋ 6.50 – ⇌ 11.50 – **150 rm** 136.00/160.00 **st.** – SB.

Forte Posthouse Swindon, Marlborough Rd, SN3 6AQ, ℰ (01793) 524601, Fax (01793) 512887, **Ⅰ₆**, **≘s**, **◻** – ⅙⋇ rm, 📺 ☎ Ⲣ – 🏝 70. **◍◍** **ⱯⒺ** **①** **𝘝𝘐𝘚𝘈** **𝗝𝗖𝗕**   V b
Meals 8.95 **st.** (lunch) and a la carte 16.45/25.90 **st.** ⅋ 7.50 – ⇌ 9.95 – **98 rm** 79.00/89.00 **st.** – SB.

Travel Inn, Lydiard Fields, Great Western Way, SN5 8UY, M 4 junction 16 ℰ (01793) 881490, Fax (01793) 886890 – ⅙⋇ rm, 📺 ⅍ Ⲣ. **◍◍** **ⱯⒺ** **①** **𝘝𝘐𝘚𝘈**   V e
Meals (grill rest.) – **63 rm** 36.50 **t.**

at Blunsdon N : 4½ m. on A 419 – ✉ Swindon.

Blunsdon House, SN2 4AD, ℰ (01793) 721701, Fax (01793) 721056, **Ⅰ₆**, **≘s**, **◻**, **Ⅰ₅**, ⋇, park, **⁒**, squash – 🛗 ⅙⋇ rm, 📺 ☎ ⅍ Ⲣ – 🏝 300. **◍◍** **ⱯⒺ** **①** **𝘝𝘐𝘚𝘈** **𝗝𝗖𝗕**. ⋇   U a
The Ridge : Meals (closed Saturday lunch) 14.50/20.00 **st.** and a la carte ⅋ 6.50 – **Carrie's : Meals** (carving rest.) 10.75/15.00 **st.** – ⇌ 10.00 – **86 rm** 85.00/130.00 **st.**, 1 suite – SB.

at Stanton Fitzwarren *NE : 5¼ m. by A 4312 and A 419 off A 361 –* ✉ *Swindon.*

🏨 **Stanton House** 🐦, The Avenue, SN6 7SD, ☎ (01793) 861777, *Fax (01793) 861857*, 🐦, 🌳, park, 🍴 – |‡|, 🚭 rm, ▤ rest, [TV] ☎ ♿ [P] – 🎓 110. [MC] [AE] [D] VISA JCB. 🐕 U c
Meals - Japanese - a la carte 15.00/40.00 **st.** 🍷 5.75 – **86 rm** 🛏 65.00/108.00 **st.**

at Chiseldon *S : 6¼ m. by A 4312, A 4259 and A 345 on B 4005 –* ✉ *Swindon.*

🏨 **Chiseldon House** 🐦, New Rd, SN4 0NE, ☎ (01793) 741010, *Fax (01793) 741059*, 🏊, 🌳 – [TV] ☎ [P]. [MC] [AE] [D] VISA. 🐕 V d
Orangery : Meals *(closed Saturday lunch)* 14.95/24.95 **t.** and dinner a la carte – **17 rm** 🛏 71.50/95.00 **t.** – SB.

at Wootton Bassett *W : 6¼ m. on A 3102 – V –* ✉ *Swindon.*

🏨 **Marsh Farm,** Coped Hall, SN4 8ER, N : 1 m. by A 3102 on Purton rd ☎ (01793) 848044, *Fax (01793) 851528*, 🌳 – 🚭 rest, [TV] ☎ [P] – 🎓 150. [MC] [AE] VISA. 🐕
Meals *(closed Saturday lunch)* 15.50/18.75 **st.** and a la carte 🍷 6.70 – **33 rm** 🛏 63.00/90.00 **st.**

at Hook *W : 6¼ m. by A 3102 – V, B 4534 and Hook rd –* ✉ *Swindon.*

🏨 **The School House,** Hook St., SN4 8EF, ☎ (01793) 851198, *Fax (01793) 851025*, 🌳 – 🚭 rest, [TV] ☎ [P]. [MC] [AE] VISA. 🐕
Meals 19.95/27.95 **st.** 🍷 8.95 – **12 rm** 🛏 79.00/89.00 **st.** – SB.

ATS Cheney Manor Ind. Est. ☎ (01793) 521171 ATS 86 Beatrice St. ☎ (01793) 534867/431620

SWINTON *Gtr.Manchester* [402] [403] [404] N 23 – *see Manchester.*

SYMONDS YAT WEST *Herefordshire* [403] [404] M 28 *Great Britain G.* – ✉ *Ross-on-Wye.*
See : *Town★ – Yat Rock (≤★).*
Env. : *S : Wye Valley★.*
London 126 – Gloucester 23 – Hereford 17 – Newport 31.

🏠 **Norton House,** Whitchurch, HR9 6DJ, ☎ (01600) 890046, *Fax (01600) 890045*, 🌳 – 🚭 [TV] [P]
closed 25 December – **Meals** (by arrangement) (communal dining) 14.95 **s.** – **3 rm** 🛏 30.00/44.00 **s.**

🏠 **Woodlea** 🐦, HR9 6BL, ☎ (01600) 890206, *Fax (01600) 890206*, 🌳 – 🚭 rest, ☎ [P]. [MC] VISA
Meals 15.50 **st.** 🍷 4.20 – **8 rm** 🛏 25.00/63.00 **st.** – SB.

TADCASTER *N. Yorks.* [402] Q 22 – *pop. 6 915.*
London 206 – Harrogate 16 – Leeds 14 – York 11.

🍴🍴 **Aagrah,** York Rd, Steeton, LS24 8EG, NE : 2½ m. on A 64 ☎ (01937) 530888 – [P]. [MC] [AE] VISA
closed 25 December – **Meals** - Indian - (dinner only) a la carte 10.80/16.30 **t.**

🍴 **Plough Inn,** Headwell Lane, Saxton, LS24 9PX, S : 5 m. by A 162 ☎ (01937) 557242 – 🚭 [P]. [MC] VISA. 🐕
closed Sunday dinner and Monday – **Meals** a la carte 15.40/20.95 **t.** 🍷 6.25.

ATS Station Road Ind. Est. ☎ (01937) 832626/833969

TADWORTH *Surrey* [404] T 30 – *pop. 37 245 (inc. Banstead).*
London 23 – Brighton 36 – Guildford 22 – Maidstone 41.

🍴🍴 **Gemini,** 28 Station Approach, KT20 5AH, ☎ (01737) 812179 – [MC] [AE] VISA
closed Saturday lunch, Sunday dinner, Monday and 1 week Christmas – Meals 14.50/24.50 **t.** 🍷 7.90.

TALKE *Staffs.* [402] [403] [404] N 24 – *see Stoke-on-Trent.*

TALLAND BAY *Cornwall* [403] G 32 – *see Looe.*

TALLINGTON *Lincs.* – *see Stamford.*

TAMWORTH Staffs. 402 403 404 O 26 – pop. 68 440.

  18 Eagle Drive, Amington ℘ (01827) 53850.

  🖪 Town Hall, Market St., B79 7LY ℘ (01827) 59134 (summer only).

  London 128 – Birmingham 12 – Coventry 29 – Leicester 31 – Stoke-on-Trent 37.

🏠 **Travel Inn,** Bitterscote, Bonehill Rd, B78 3HQ, on A 51 ℘ (01827) 54414, Fax (01827) 310420 – 🔆 rm, 📺 ぐ 🄿. 🕦🕄 🆎 ① 𝘝𝘐𝘚𝘈. ⋇
  Meals (grill rest.) – **40 rm** 36.50 **t.**

at Bodymoor Heath S : 6¾ m. by A 4091 – ⊠ Sutton Coldfield.

🏨 **Marston Farm,** B76 9JD, ℘ (01827) 872133, Fax (01827) 875043, ⤷, ⋇ – 🔆 rest, 📺 ☎ ぐ 🄿 – 🔬 50. 🕦🕄 🆎 ① 𝘝𝘐𝘚𝘈
  Meals (dinner only) 17.95 **st.** and a la carte – **37 rm** ⊏ 85.00/92.50 **st.** – SB.

  @ ATS Tame Valley Ind. Est., Watling St., Wilnecote ℘ (01827) 281983

TAMWORTH SERVICE AREA Staffs. – ⊠ Tamworth.

🏠 **Travelodge** without rest., Green Lane, B77 5PS, at junction 10 of M 42 ℘ (01827) 260120, Fax (01827) 260145, Reservations (Freephone) 0800 850950 – 🔆 📺 ☎ ぐ 🄿. 🕦🕄 🆎 ① 𝘝𝘐𝘚𝘈 𝙹𝙲𝙱. ⋇
  63 rm 46.95 **t.**

TANSLEY Derbs. – see Matlock.

> **Les prix**   Pour toutes précisions sur les prix indiqués dans ce guide, reportez-vous aux pages de l'introduction.

TAPLOW Windsor & Maidenhead 404 R 29.

  London 33 – Maidenhead 2 – Reading 12.

🏰 **Cliveden** ⤷, SL6 0JF, N : 2 m. by Berry Hill ℘ (01628) 668561, Fax (01628) 661837, « Mid-Victorian stately home, ≤ National Trust Gardens, parterre and River Thames », 𝗙𝟲, ≘s, ⊼, 🔲, ⤷, park, ⋇indoor/outdoor, squash – 📳, 🔆 rest, 📺 ☎ 🄿 – 🔬 40. 🕦🕄 🆎 ① 𝘝𝘐𝘚𝘈
  Terrace : Meals 28.00/39.00 **st.** and a la carte 35.50/62.50 **st.** ≬ 11.00 – (see also **Waldo's** below) – ⊏ 17.00 – **32 rm** 230.00/410.00 **t.,** 5 suites – SB.

💥💥💥 **Waldo's** (at Cliveden H.), SL6 0JF, N : 2 m. by Berry Hill ℘ (01628) 668561, Fax (01628) 661837 – 🔆 ☰ 🄿. 🕦🕄 🆎 ① 𝘝𝘐𝘚𝘈
  ⊛ closed Sunday and Monday – **Meals** (dinner only) 49.00/75.00 **st.** ≬ 11.00
  Spec. Ravioli of goat's cheese with soused vegetables in white bean broth. Pan fried John Dory with seared scallops, fennel purée and a red wine sauce. Hot mirabelle plum soufflé with liquorice ice cream.

TARPORLEY Ches. 402 403 404 M 24 – pop. 2 308.

  18 Portal G & C.C., Cobblers Cross Lane ℘ (01829) 733933 – 18 Portal Premier, Forest Rd ℘ (01829) 733884.

  London 186 – Chester 11 – Liverpool 36 – Shrewsbury 36.

🏠 **Swan,** 50 High St., CW6 0AG, ℘ (01829) 733838, Fax (01829) 732932 – 📺 ☎ 🄿 – 🔬 100. 🕦🕄 🆎 𝘝𝘐𝘚𝘈
  closed 25 December – **Bohars Brasserie :** Meals 13.95 **st.** and a la carte ≬ 7.00 – **20 rm** ⊏ 52.95/75.00 **t.**

TARRANT MONKTON Dorset 403 404 N 31 – see Blandford Forum.

TATTENHALL Ches. 402 403 404 L 24 – pop. 1 854.

  London 200 – Birmingham 71 – Chester 10 – Manchester 38 – Stoke-on-Trent 30.

🏠 **Higher Huxley Hall** ⤷, CH3 9BZ, N : 2 ¼ m. on Huxley rd ℘ (01829) 781484, Fax (01829) 781142, ≤, « Working farm », 🔲, �₣ – 🔆 📺 ☎ 🄿. 🕦🕄 🆎 𝘝𝘐𝘚𝘈 𝙹𝙲𝙱. ⋇
  booking essential – **Meals** (by arrangement) (communal dining) 20.00 **s.** ≬ 7.00 – **3 rm** ⊏ 40.00/80.00 **s.**

🏠 **Newton Hall** ⤷ without rest., CH3 9AY, N : 1 m. by Huxley rd on Gatesheath rd ℘ (01829) 770153, Fax (01829) 770655, « Working farm », 🌿 – 🔆 📺 🄿
  closed 24-25 December and 1 January – **3 rm** ⊏ 23.00/45.00 **s.**

TAUNTON Somerset **403** K 30 *The West Country G.* – pop. 55 855.

See : Town★ – St. Mary Magdalene★ – Somerset County Museum★ *AC* – St. James'★ – Hammett St.★ – The Crescent★ – Bath Alley★.

Env. : Trull (Church★), *S : 2½ m. by A 38*.

Exc. : Bishops Lydeard★ (Church★), *NW : 6 m.* – Wellington : Church★, Wellington Monument (≤★★), *SW : 7½ m. by A 38* – Combe Florey★, *NW : 8 m.* – Gaulden Manor★ *AC*, *NW : 10 m. by A 358 and B 3227*.

🏌 🏌 Taunton Vale, Creech Heathfield ℘ (01823) 412220 – 🏌 Vivary, Vivary Park ℘ (01823) 289274 – 🏌 Taunton and Pickeridge, Corfe ℘ (01823) 421240.

🛈 Paul St., TA1 3XZ ℘ (01823) 336344.

London 168 – Bournemouth 69 – Bristol 50 – Exeter 37 – Plymouth 78 – Southampton 93 – Weymouth 50.

🏨🏨 **The Castle,** Castle Green, TA1 1NF, ℘ (01823) 272671, *Fax (01823) 336066*, « Part 12C castle with Norman garden » – 🛏, ❀ rest, 📺 ☎ ⇐ 🅿 – 🕰 100. 🆗 🆎 ⓘ 💳. ✗
Meals 34.00/23.00 t. and lunch a la carte 🍴 10.00 – **36 rm** ⊑ 85.00/130.00 t. – SB.

🏨🏨 **Forte Posthouse Taunton,** Deane Gate Av., TA1 2UA, *E : 2½ m. by A 358 at junction with M 5* ℘ (01823) 332222, *Fax (01823) 332266*, 🏋, 🚶 – 🛏, ❀ rm, 🍽 rest, 📺 ☎ ὅ 🅿 – 🕰 300. 🆗 🆎 ⓘ 💳
Meals 14.95 st. (dinner) and a la carte 12.85/25.65 st. 🍴 7.25 – ⊑ 9.95 – **97 rm** 79.00 st. – SB.

🏠 **Orchard House** without rest., Fons George, Middleway, TA1 3JS, *off Wilton St.* ℘ (01823) 351783, *Fax (01823) 351785*, 🌿 – ❀ 📺 🅿. 🆗 💳. ✗
6 rm ⊑ 35.00/55.00 t.

🏠 **Travel Inn,** 81 Bridgwater Rd, TA1 2DU, *E : 1¾ m. by A 358* ℘ (01823) 321112, *Fax (01823) 322054* – ❀ rm, 📺 ὅ 🅿. 🆗 🆎 ⓘ 💳. ✗
Meals (grill rest.) – **40 rm** 36.50 t.

🏚 **Forde House** without rest., 9 Upper High St., TA1 3PX, ℘ (01823) 279042, *Fax (01823) 279042*, 🌿 – 📺 🅿.
closed Christmas and New Year – **5 rm** ⊑ 27.00/50.00 s.

at Henlade *E : 3½ m. on A 358* – ✉ Taunton.

🏨🏨 **Mount Somerset** ⟡, TA3 5NB, *S : ½ m. by Stoke Rd and Ash Cross rd* ℘ (01823) 442500, *Fax (01823) 442900*, ≤, « Regency country house », 🌿 – 🛏 📺 ☎ 🅿 – 🕰 60. 🆗 🆎 ⓘ 💳 🎴. ✗
Meals 16.95/24.50 t. 🍴 5.60 – **11 rm** ⊑ 65.00/140.00 – SB.

at Hatch Beauchamp *SE : 6 m. by A358* – ✉ Taunton.

🏨 **Farthings** ⟡, TA3 6SG, ℘ (01823) 480664, *Fax (01823) 481118*, « Georgian country house », 🌿 – ❀ 📺 ☎ 🅿. 🆗 🆎 💳
Meals *(closed Sunday)* 18.50 t. 🍴 4.65 – **8 rm** ⊑ 55.00/90.00 t. – SB.

🏚 **Frog Street Farm** ⟡, Beercrocombe, TA3 6AF, *SE : 1¼ m. by Beercrocombe Rd* ℘ (01823) 480430, *Fax (01823) 480430*, « 15C farmhouse, working farm », 🌿 – ❀ 🅿. ✗
April-October – **Meals** (by arrangement) 16.00 st. – **3 rm** ⊑ 30.00/54.00 st. – SB.

✗✗ **Nightingales,** Bath House Farm, West Hatch, TA3 5RH, *NW : 1½ m. by Village Rd on A 358* ℘ (01823) 480806, *Fax (01823) 480806*, 🌿 – 🅿. 🆗 💳
closed Monday to Thursday, 2 weeks February and 1 week October – **Meals** (dinner only and Sunday lunch)/dinner 22.50 🍴 4.50.

at Rumwell *SW : 2½ m. on A 38* – ✉ Taunton.

🏨 **Rumwell Manor,** TA4 1EL, ℘ (01823) 461902, *Fax (01823) 254861*, 🌿 – ❀ rest, 📺 ☎ 🅿 – 🕰 40. 🆗 🆎 💳. ✗
Meals 10.00/17.50 st. and dinner a la carte 🍴 5.00 – **19 rm** ⊑ 54.00/102.00 st. – SB.

at Bishop's Hull *W : 1¾ m. by A 38* – ✉ Taunton.

🏠 **Meryan House,** Bishop's Hull Rd, TA1 5EG, ℘ (01823) 337445, *Fax (01823) 322355*, 🌿 – ❀ 📺 ☎ 🅿. 🆗 💳 🎴
Meals *(closed Sunday)* (dinner only) 17.00 st. and a la carte 🍴 5.00 – **12 rm** ⊑ 45.00/65.00 st.

at West Bagborough *NW : 10½ m. by A 358* – ✉ Taunton.

🏚 **Bashfords Farmhouse** ⟡ without rest., TA4 3EF, ℘ (01823) 432015, *Fax (01823) 432520*, « 18C », 🌿 – ❀ 📺 🅿. ✗
3 rm ⊑ 22.00/39.00.

🏚 **Tilbury Farm** ⟡, Cothelstone, TA4 3DY, *E : ¾ m.* ℘ (01823) 432391, ≤, « 18C », 🌿 park – 📺 🅿. ✗
Meals (by arrangement) 15.00 – **3 rm** ⊑ 25.00/45.00 s.

🅐 ATS 138 Bridgwater Rd, Bathpool ℘ (01823) 412826

TAUNTON DEANE SERVICE AREA Somerset 403 K 31 – ⊠ Taunton.

▲ **RoadChef Lodge** without rest., TA3 7PF, ℰ (01823) 332228, Fax (01823) 338131, Reservations (Freephone) 0800 834719 – ≒ 🔟 🕭 🕭 🄿. 🚳 🖭 ⑨ 🚾. ⋘
closed 25 December and 1 January – **36 rm** 43.50 **st.**

TAVISTOCK Devon 403 H 32 The West Country G. – pop. 10 222.

Env. : Morwellham★ AC, SW : 4 ½ m.
Exc. : E : Dartmoor National Park★★ – Buckland Abbey★★ AC, S : 7 m. by A 386 – Lydford★★,
N : 8 ½ m. by A 386.
🟤 Down Rd ℰ (01822) 612049 – 🟤 Hurdwick, Tavistock Hamlets ℰ (01822) 612746.
🅱 Town Hall, Bedford Sq., PL19 0AE ℰ (01882) 612938 (restricted opening in winter).
London 239 – Exeter 38 – Plymouth 15.

↑ **Quither Mill** ≫, PL19 0PZ, NW : 5 ¾ m. by Chillaton rd on Quither rd ℰ (01822) 860160,
≤, « 18C corn mill », ☞, park – ≒ 🔟 🄿. 🚳 🚾. ⋘
Meals 17.50 ⅙ 4.50 – **3 rm** ⊆ 40.00/60.00, 1 suite.

↑ **April Cottage** without rest., Mount Tavy Rd, PL19 9JB, ℰ (01822) 613280 – ≒ 🔟 🄿
closed Christmas – **3 rm** ⊆ 28.00/36.00.

✗ **Neils,** 27 King St., PL19 0DT, ℰ (01822) 615550 – ≒, 🚳 🖭 🚾
closed Sunday and Monday – **Meals** (dinner only) 17.00 **t.** and a la carte ⅙ 8.50.

at Gulworthy W : 3 m. on A 390 – ⊠ Tavistock.

✗✗✗ **Horn of Plenty** ≫ with rm, PL19 8JD, ℰ (01822) 832528, Fax (01822) 832528, ≤ Tamar
Valley and Bodmin Moor, ☞ – ≒ 🔟 ☎ 🄿. 🚳 🖭 🚾. ⋘
❀ closed 25 and 26 December – **Meals** (closed Monday lunch) 17.50/29.50 **t.** ⅙ 7.00 – ⊆ 7.50
– **7 rm** 78.00/98.00 **t.** – SB.
Spec. Sesame scallops with roasted red pepper, seasonal salad and ginger dressing. Roast
lamb with wild mushrooms, garlic and rosemary polenta. Glazed lemon tart.

🔘 ATS 2 Parkwood Rd ℰ (01822) 612545

TEFFONT Wilts. – see Salisbury.

TEIGNMOUTH Devon 403 J 32 – pop. 13 528.

🅱 The Den, Sea Front, TQ14 8BE ℰ (01626) 779769.
London 216 – Exeter 16 – Torquay 8.

🏨 **Cliffden,** Dawlish Rd, TQ14 8TE, ℰ (01626) 770052, Fax (01626) 770594, ≤, Restricted to
the blind and their companions, 🔳, ☞ – 🖽 ≒ 🔟 ☎ 🄿. ⋘
closed January – **Meals** (residents only) (dinner only) a la carte 10.50 **t.** – **21 rm** ⊆ (dinner
included) 116.00/152.00 **t.** – SB.

▲ **Thomas Luny House** without rest., Teign St., TQ14 8EG, ℰ (01626) 772976, « Georgian
house built by Thomas Luny », ☞ – 🔟 🄿. ⋘
closed Christmas and January – **4 rm** ⊆ 35.00/70.00 **st.** – SB.

at Shaldon S : 1 m. on B 3199 – ⊠ Teignmouth.

🏨 **Ness House,** Marine Drive, TQ14 0HP, ℰ (01626) 873480, Fax (01626) 873486, ≤, ☞ – ≒
🔟 ☎ 🄿. 🚳 🖭 🚾 🥐. ⋘
closed 25 December – **Meals** (carving lunch Sunday) 17.50 **t.** and dinner a la carte ⅙ 6.50 –
12 rm ⊆ 39.00/85.00 **t.** – SB.

↑ **Glenside,** Ringmore Rd, TQ14 0EP, W : ½ m. on B 3195 ℰ (01626) 872448, ☞ – 🔟 🄿
Meals 13.00 **st.** ⅙ 4.00 – **9 rm** ⊆ 24.00/49.00 **st.** – SB.

TELFORD Wrekin 402 403 404 M 25 Great Britain G. – pop. 119 340.

Env. : Ironbridge Gorge Museum★★ AC (The Iron Bridge★★, Coalport China Museum★★,
Blists Hill Open Air Museum★★, Museum of the River and Visitor Centre★) S : 5 m. by B 4373.
Exc. : Weston Park★★ AC, E : 7 m. by A 5.
🟤, 🟤 Telford G & C.C. Moat House, Great Hay, Sutton Heights ℰ (01952) 429977 – 🟤 Wrekin,
Wellington ℰ (01952) 244032 – 🟤, 🟤, 🟤 The Shropshire, Muxton Grange, Muxton
ℰ (01952) 677866.
🅱 The Telford Centre, Management Suite, TF3 4BX ℰ (01952) 291370.
London 152 – Birmingham 33 – Shrewsbury 12 – Stoke-on-Trent 29.

🏨🏨 **Holiday Inn,** Telford International Centre, St. Quentin Gate, TF3 4EH, SE : ½ m.
ℰ (01952) 292500, Fax (01952) 291949, 🎿, ⌒, 🔳, ✗, squash – 🖽 ≒ rm, 🗐 rest, 🔟 ☎
🕭 🄿 – 🕿 250. 🚳 🖭 ⑨ 🚾 🥐
Meals (closed Saturday lunch) 10.50/15.95 **st.** and a la carte ⅙ 6.95 – ⊆ 9.95 – **100 rm**
104.00/115.00 **st.** – SB.

🏨 **County H. Telford Golf & Country Club,** Great Hay, Sutton Hill, TF7 4DT, S : 4 ½ m. by A 442 *₢* (01952) 429977, *Fax* (01952) 586602, ≤, *ฉ*, ☎, ◫, ╔, ╔, squash – ⅙ rm, ⊡ ☜ ◐ – ᦞ 240. ◐◉ ◪ ◑ ⅙
Meals (bar lunch Monday to Saturday)/dinner 15.95 **st.** and a la carte ╬ 6.00 – ☲ 9.95 – **85 rm** 99.00/115.00 **st.,** 1 suite – SB.

🏨 **Telford Moat House,** Forgegate, Telford Centre, TF3 4NA, *₢* (01952) 429988 *Fax* (01952) 292012, *₰*, ☎, ◫ – ▯, ⅙ rm, ▤ rest, ⊡ ☜ ◐ ◐ – ᦞ 400. ◐◉ ◪ ◑ Ⅵ⅟⅘
Meals a la carte 14.95/18.95 **st.** ╬ 6.00 – ☲ 9.50 – **143 rm** 95.00/105.00 **st.,** 4 suites – SB.

🏨 **Madeley Court** ⅗, Castlefields Way, Madeley, TF7 5DW, S : 4 ½ m. by A 442 and A 4169 on B 4373 *₢* (01952) 680068, *Fax* (01952) 684275, « Part 16C manor house », *₰* – ⊡ ☜ ◐ – ᦞ 200. ◐◉ ◪ ◑ ⅥⅩ⅘.
Meals a la carte 16.00/23.95 **st.** ╬ 7.95 – ☲ 9.50 – **47 rm** 95.00/150.00 **st.** – SB.

🏨 **Travelodge,** Shawbirch Crossroads, Shawbirch, TF1 3QA, NW : 5 ½ m. by A 442 at junction with B 5063 *₢* (01952) 251244, Reservations (Freephone) 0800 850950 – ⅙ rm ⊡ ☝ ◐. ◐◉ ◪ ◑ ⅥⅩ ⅉⅭⅫ. ⅘
Meals (grill rest.) – **40 rm** 44.95 **t.**

🏨 **White House,** Wellington Rd, Muxton, TF2 8NG, N : 4 ½ m. by A 442 off A 57? *₢* (01952) 604276, *Fax* (01952) 670336, *₰* – ⊡ ☜ ◐. ◐◉ ◪ ⅥⅩ
Meals *(closed Saturday lunch)* 8.50/12.50 **st.** and a la carte ╬ 4.95 – **30 rm** ☲ 55.00 66.00 **st.** – SB.

at Norton *S : 7 m. on A 442* – ⊠ *Shifnal.*

🏨 **Hundred House,** Bridgnorth Rd, TF11 9EE, *₢* (01952) 730353, *Fax* (01952) 730355 « Tastefully decorated inn, antiques », *₰* – ⊡ ☜ ◐. ◐◉ ◪ ⅥⅩ
Meals a la carte 14.85/36.85 **t.** ╬ 6.75 – **10 rm** ☲ 65.00/99.00 **t.** – SB.

at Wellington *W : 6 m. by M 54 on B 5061* – ⊠ *Telford.*

🏨 **Charlton Arms - Premier Lodge,** Church St., TF1 1DG, *₢* (01952) 25135? *Fax* (01952) 222077 – ⅙ rm, ⊡ ☜ ◐ – ᦞ 150. ◐◉ ◪ ◑ ⅥⅩ ⅘
Meals (grill rest.) 10.95 **st.** and a la carte ╬ 6.95 – ☲ 4.95 – **22 rm** 42.25 **t.** – SB.

ⓐ ATS Queen St., Madeley *₢* (01952) 582820   ATS Kensington Way, Oakengates
₢ (01952) 613810/612198

TEMPLE SOWERBY Cumbria ᨄᨄᨄ ᨄᨄᨄ M 20 – pop. 329 – ⊠ Penrith.
London 297 – Carlisle 31 – Kendal 38.

🏨 **Temple Sowerby House,** CA10 1RZ, *₢* (017683) 61578, *Fax* (017683) 61958, « Ear 18C farmhouse with Georgian additions », *₰* – ⅙ rest, ⊡ ☜ ◐. ◐◉ ◪ ⅥⅩ
Meals a la carte 21.20/26.85 **t.** ╬ 5.25 – **12 rm** ☲ 55.00/95.00 **t.** – SB.

TENBURY WELLS Worcestershire ᨄᨄᨄ ᨄᨄᨄ M 27 – pop. 2 219.
London 144 – Birmingham 36 – Hereford 20 – Shrewsbury 37 – Worcester 28.

🏨 **Cadmore Lodge** ⅗, St. Michaels, WR15 8TQ, SW : 2 ¾ m. by A 4112 *₢* (01584) 81004? *Fax* (01584) 810044, ≤, ╔, ⅌, park, ⅗ – ⅙ rm, ⊡ ☜ ◐ – ᦞ 100. ◐◉ ◪ ◑ ⅥⅩ ⅉⅭⅫ. ⅗
Meals 11.25/15.50 **t.** and a la carte – **14 rm** ☲ 30.00/140.00 **t.** – SB.

TENTERDEN Kent ᨄᨄᨄ W 30 – pop. 6 803.
🅱 *Town Hall, High St., TN30 6AN* *₢* (01580) 763572 *(summer only).*
London 57 – Folkestone 26 – Hastings 21 – Maidstone 19.

🏨 **Jarvis White Lion,** 57 High St., TN30 6BD, *₢* (01580) 765077, *Fax* (01580) 764157 ⅙ rm, ⊡ ☜ ◐ – ᦞ 50. ◐◉ ◪ ⅥⅩ
Meals 15.00 **t.** (dinner) and a la carte 11.15/19.20 **t.** ╬ 6.00 – **15 rm** ☲ 69.00/105.00 **t.** – S

🏨 **Little Silver Country,** Ashford Rd, St. Michaels, TN30 6SP, N : 2 m. on A 3 *₢* (01233) 850321, *Fax* (01233) 850647, *₰* – ⅙ rm, ⊡ ☜ ◐ – ᦞ 150. ◐◉ ◪ ⅥⅩ. ⅘
Meals (booking essential) (lunch residents only) 20.00 **t.** and a la carte ╬ 5.80 – **10 r** ☲ 60.00/110.00 **t.** – SB.

🏨 **Collina House,** 5 East Hill, TN30 6RL, *₢* (01580) 764852, *Fax* (01580) 762224 – ⅙ rm, ☜ ◐. ◐◉ ◪ ⅥⅩ. ⅘
closed 1 week Christmas – **Meals** (lunch by arrangement) 15.50 **st.** and a la carte – **14 r** ☲ 35.00/60.00 **st.** – SB.

🏠 **Brattle House,** Watermill Bridges, TN30 6UL, W : 1 m. by A 28 on Cranbrook ? *₢* (01580) 763565, ≤, *₰* – ⅙ ◐. ⅘
closed Christmas and New Year – **Meals** (by arrangement) (communal dining) 20.00 **s.** **3 rm** ☲ 35.00/60.00.

TETBURY *Glos.* [403] [404] N 29 *Great Britain G. – pop. 4 618.*
Env. : *Westonbirt Arboretum★* **AC**, *SW : 2 ½ m. by A 433.*
⛳9 *Westonbirt ✆ (01666) 880242.*
[i] *The Old Court House, 63 Long St., GL8 8AA ✆ (01666) 503552 (summer only).*
London 113 – Bristol 27 – Gloucester 19 – Swindon 24.

🏨 **The Close,** 8 Long St., GL8 8AQ, ✆ (01666) 502272, *Fax (01666) 504401,* « 16C town house with walled garden » – ⊁ rest, [TV] ☎ [P] – 🏛 30. [MO] [AE] [O] [VISA]. ⊁
Meals 18.50/29.50 **st.** and a la carte approx. 35.00 **st.** 🍷 8.50 – **15 rm** ☕ 100.00/180.00 **st.** – SB.

🏨 **Snooty Fox,** Market Pl., GL8 8DD, ✆ (01666) 502436, *Fax (01666) 503479* – ⊁ rest, [TV] ☎. [MO] [AE] [O] [VISA]. ⊁
Meals (bar lunch)/dinner 19.95 **t.** 🍷 5.95 – **12 rm** ☕ 65.00/120.00 **t.** – SB.

at Willesley *SW : 4 m. on A 433 – ✉ Tetbury.*

🏠 **Tavern House** without rest., GL8 8QU, ✆ (01666) 880444, *Fax (01666) 880254,* « Part 17C former inn and staging post », 🌳 – ⊁ [TV] ☎ [P]. [MO] [VISA]. ⊁
4 rm ☕ 45.00/66.00.

at Calcot *W : 3½ m. on A 4135 – ✉ Tetbury.*

🏨 **Calcot Manor** 🕊, GL8 8YJ, ✆ (01666) 890391, *Fax (01666) 890394,* 🏡, « Converted Cotswold farm buildings », 🏊, 🌳, 🎾 – ⊁ rest, [TV] ☎ [P] – 🏛 65. [MO] [AE] [O] [VISA]. ⊁
***Conservatory :* Meals** (buffet lunch) 12.50 **st.** and a la carte 19.25/34.00 **st.** 🍷 9.00 –
***Gumstool Inn :* Meals** a la carte 13.50/20.70 **st.** 🍷 9.00 – ☕ 6.50 – **25 rm** 95.00/150.00 **st.** – SB.

TEWKESBURY *Glos.* [403] [404] N 28 *Great Britain G. – pop. 9 488.*
See : *Town★ – Abbey★★ (Nave★★, vault★).*
Env. : *St. Mary's, Deerhurst★, SW : 4 m. by A 38 and B 4213.*
⛳18 *Tewkesbury Park Hotel, Lincoln Green Lane ✆ (01684) 295405.*
[i] *64 Barton St., GL20 5PX ✆ (01684) 295027.*
London 108 – Birmingham 39 – Gloucester 11.

🏨 **Tewkesbury Park H. & Country Club,** Lincoln Green Lane, GL20 7DN, S : 1 ¼ m. by A 38 ✆ (01684) 295405, *Fax (01684) 292386,* ≤, 🏋, 🏊, 🏊, ⛳18, park, 🎾, squash – ⊁ [TV] ☎ [P] – 🏛 150. [MO] [AE] [O] [VISA]. ⊁
Meals 19.50 **st.** (dinner) and a la carte 20.00/23.95 **st.** 🍷 7.50 – ☕ 9.50 – **78 rm** 82.00 **t.** – SB.

🏨 **Bell,** Church St., GL20 5SA, ✆ (01684) 293293, *Fax (01684) 295938* – ⊁ rest, [TV] ☎ [P] – 🏛 40. [MO] [AE] [VISA]
Meals (bar lunch)/dinner 18.95 **t.** and a la carte 🍷 5.95 – **24 rm** ☕ 63.50/82.00 **t.** – SB.

🏨 **Jessop House,** 65 Church St., GL20 5RZ, ✆ (01684) 292017, *Fax (01684) 273076* – [TV] ☎ [P]. [MO] [AE] [VISA]. ⊁
closed Christmas and New Year – **Meals** *(closed Sunday)* (bar lunch)/dinner 17.95 🍷 3.95 – **8 rm** ☕ 55.00/75.00 **st.** – SB.

🍴 **Bistrot André,** 78 Church St., GL20 5RX, ✆ (01684) 290357 – [MO] [VISA]
closed Sunday, Monday and first 3 weeks February – **Meals** - French - (dinner only) a la carte 15.35/23.75 **st.** 🍷 6.95.

at Puckrup *N : 2½ m. on A 38 – ✉ Tewkesbury.*

🏨 **Stakis Puckrup Hall,** GL20 6EL, ✆ (01684) 296200, *Fax (01684) 850788,* 🏋, 🏊, 🏊, ⛳18, 🌳, park – [lift], ⊁ rm, [TV] ☎ [P] – 🏛 200. [MO] [AE] [O] [VISA]
Meals 12.50/18.50 **st.** and a la carte 🍷 7.50 – ☕ 9.50 – **82 rm** 92.50/115.00 **st.**, 2 suites – SB.

at Kemerton *NE : 5¼ m. by A 46 – ✉ Tewkesbury.*

🏠 **Upper Court** 🕊, GL20 7HY, take right turn at stone cross in village ✆ (01386) 725351, *Fax (01386) 725472,* ≤, « Georgian manor house, antique furnishings, gardens », 🏊, 🎣, park, 🎾 – [TV] [P]. [MO] [VISA]
closed 1 week Christmas – **Meals** 27.00 **st.** 🍷 5.00 – **5 rm** ☕ 65.00/120.00 **st.**

at Corse Lawn *SW : 6 m. by A 38 and A 438 on B 4211 – ✉ Gloucester.*

🏨 **Corse Lawn House** 🕊, GL19 4LZ, ✆ (01452) 780771, *Fax (01452) 780840,* « Queen Anne house », 🏊, 🌳, 🎾 – [TV] ☎ [P] – 🏛 40. [MO] [AE] [O] [VISA]
***Bistro :* Meals** a la carte 14.85/23.85 **st.** 🍷 5.50 – (see also below) – **17 rm** ☕ 70.00/100.00 **st.**, 2 suites – SB.

🍴🍴🍴 **Corse Lawn House** (at Corse Lawn House), GL19 4LZ, ✆ (01452) 780771, *Fax (01452) 780840,* 🌳 – [P]. [MO] [AE] [O] [VISA]
Meals 16.95/24.50 **st.** and a la carte 🍷 5.50.

ATS Oldbury Rd ✆ (01684) 292461

THAME Oxon. **404** R 28 *The West Country G.* – *pop. 10 806.*

Exc.: Ridgeway Path★★.

🛈 Market House, North St., OX9 3HH 𝒫 (01844) 212834.

London 48 – Aylesbury 9 – Oxford 13.

🏦 **Spread Eagle,** 16 Cornmarket, OX9 2BW, 𝒫 (01844) 213661, Fax (01844) 261380 – 📺 🕿 🅿 – 🛦 250. 🐠 🖭 ① *VISA* 𝒥𝒞𝔹. 🛇

closed 28 to 30 December – **Meals** *(closed lunch Bank Holiday Mondays)* 18.95/22.95 **st.** and a la carte ⅃ 5.00 – 🖵 8.95 – **31 rm** 84.95/115.50 **st.**, 2 suites – SB.

🏛 **Travelodge,** OX9 3XA, NW : 1 m. by B 4445 on B 4011 at junction with A 418 𝒫 (01844) 218740, Fax (01844) 218740, Reservations (Freephone) 0800 850950 – ⇔ rm ▤ rest, 📺 & 🅿. 🐠 🖭 ① *VISA* 𝒥𝒞𝔹. 🛇
Meals *(grill rest.)* – **31 rm** 49.95 **t.**

✗ **The Old Trout,** 29-30 Lower High St., OX9 2AA, 𝒫 (01844) 212146, Fax (01844) 212614 « 15C thatched inn » – 🅿. 🐠 🖭 ① *VISA*
closed Sunday, 2 weeks August and 2 weeks December – **Meals** 10.95 **st.** *(lunch* and a la carte 17.50/24.25 **st.** ⅃ 5.75.

at Towersey *E : 2 m. by A 4129 –* ✉ *Thame.*

🏠 **Upper Green Farm** ⊱ without rest., Manor Rd, OX9 3QR, 𝒫 (01844) 212496 Fax (01844) 260399, « Part 15C and 16C thatched farmhouse, 18C barn », 🐾 – ⇔ 📺 & 🅿. 🛇
closed Christmas-New Year – **10 rm** 🖵 38.00/60.00 **st.**

Le Grand Londres (GREATER LONDON) est composé de la City et de 32 arrondissements administratifs (Borough) eux-mêmes divisés en quartiers ou en villages ayant conservé leur caractère propre (Area).

THANET WAY SERVICE AREA *Kent – see Whitstable.*

THATCHAM *Newbury* **403 404** Q 29 – *pop. 20 726 –* ✉ *Newbury.*

London 69 – Bristol 68 – Oxford 30 – Reading 15 – Southampton 40.

🏰 **Regency Park,** Bowling Green Rd, RG18 3RP, NW : 1 ¾ m. by A 4 and Northfield R 𝒫 (01635) 871555, Fax (01635) 871571, 🐾, 🛇 – 🛗 ⇔, ▤ rest, 📺 & 🅿 – 🛦 110. 🐠 🖪 *VISA*
Meals 16.95/24.50 **st.** and a la carte ⅃ 8.85 – 🖵 9.95 – **46 rm** 95.00/110.00 **st.** – SB.

🔘 ATS 29 High St. 𝒫 (01635) 865551

THAXTED *Essex* **404** V 28 – *pop. 1 899.*

London 44 – Cambridge 24 – Colchester 31 – Chelmsford 20.

🏛 **Four Seasons,** Walden Rd, CM6 2RE, NW : ½ m. on B 184 𝒫 (01371) 83012 Fax (01371) 830835 – ⇔ 📺 🕿 🅿. 🐠 🖭 *VISA* 𝒥𝒞𝔹. 🛇
Meals *(residents only Sunday dinner and Bank Holidays)* a la carte 16.75/24.25 **t.** ⅃ 5.20 🖵 8.50 – **9 rm** 50.00/65.00 **t.**

🏠 **Folly House,** Watling Lane, CM6 2QY, 𝒫 (01371) 830618, 🐾 – ⇔ 📺 🅿. 🛇
Meals *(by arrangement) (communal dining)* 15.00 **st.** – **3 rm** 🖵 35.00/50.00 **st.**

🏠 **Crossways** without rest., 32 Town St., CM6 2LA, 𝒫 (01371) 830348, 🐾 – ⇔ 📺
restricted opening in winter – **3 rm** 🖵 30.00/50.00 **st.**

THEBERTON *Suffolk – pop. 334.*

London 109 – Cambridge 75 – Ipswich 30 – Norwich 36.

🏛 **Theberton Grange Country House** ⊱, Theberton, IP16 4RR, SW : ½ m. off B 11 𝒫 (01728) 830625, Fax (01728) 830625, 🐾 – ⇔ 📺 🅿. 🐠 *VISA*. 🛇
closed Christmas – **Meals** *(closed Sunday) (residents only) (dinner only)* 20.00 **st.** ⅃ 5.50 **7 rm** 🖵 40.00/80.00 **st.**

THELBRIDGE *Devon* **403** I 31 – *pop. 261 –* ✉ *Crediton.*

London 220 – Barnstaple 21 – Exeter 20 – Taunton 34.

🏠 **Thelbridge Cross Inn** with rm, Thelbridge Cross, EX17 4SQ, on B 30 𝒫 (01884) 860316, Fax (01884) 860316, 🐾 – ⇔ 📺 🕿 🅿. 🐠 🖭 ① *VISA*. 🛇
Meals *(in bar)* a la carte 9.95/18.45 **t.** – **8 rm** 🖵 35.00/70.00 **t.** – SB.

THETFORD *Norfolk* [404] W 26 – *pop. 20 058.*
London 83 – Cambridge 32 – Ipswich 33 – King's Lynn 30 – Norwich 29.

🏨 **Bell,** King St., IP24 2AZ, ✆ (01842) 754455, *Fax (01842) 755552* – 🚭 [TV] ☎ [P] – 🏛 80. [MC] [AE] [D] [VISA] [JCB]
Meals (bar lunch Saturday) 11.95 **t.** (lunch) and dinner a la carte 16.00/23.00 **t.** 🍷 7.95 – ☕ 8.50 – **45 rm** 69.00/79.00 **st.**, 1 suite – SB.

Ⓜ ATS Canterbury Way ✆ (01842) 755529

THIRSK *N. Yorks.* [402] P 21 – *pop. 6 860.*
⛳ *Thornton-Le-Street* ✆ *(01845) 522170.*
[i] *14 Kirkgate, YO7 1PQ* ✆ *(01845) 522755 (summer only).*
London 227 – Leeds 37 – Middlesbrough 24 – York 24.

🏨 **Golden Fleece,** 42 Market Pl., YO7 1LL, ✆ (01845) 523108, *Fax (01845) 523996* – [TV] ☎ [P] – 🏛 80. [MC] [AE] [D] [VISA] [JCB]
Meals *(closed Saturday lunch)* 8.50/17.00 **t.** and a la carte 🍷 5.50 – **18 rm** ☕ 55.00/84.00 **t.**

🏠 **Sheppard's,** Front St., Sowerby, YO7 1JF, S : ½ m. ✆ (01845) 523655, *Fax (01845) 524720* – 🚭 rm, [TV] ☎ [P]. [MC] [VISA]. 🐕
closed first week January – ***Restaurant :*** **Meals** *(closed Sunday and Monday)* (dinner only) a la carte 20.75/27.25 **t.** 🍷 5.50 – ***Bistro :*** **Meals** a la carte 15.35/22.25 **t.** 🍷 5.50 – **8 rm** ☕ 65.00/90.00 **t.**

⌂ **Spital Hill** 🌿, York Rd, YO7 3AE, SE : 1 ¾ m. on A 19, entrance between 2 white posts ✆ (01845) 522273, *Fax (01845) 425970,* 🌳, park – 🚭 ☎ [P]. [MC] [AE] [VISA]. 🐕
Meals (by arrangement) (communal dining) 20.00 **st.** 🍷 2.75 – **3 rm** ☕ 39.00/66.00 **st.**

⌂ **St. James House** without rest., 36 The Green, YO7 1AQ, ✆ (01845) 524120 – 🚭 [TV]. 🐕
mid March-October – **4 rm** ☕ 25.00/42.00.

⌂ **Brook House** without rest., Ingramgate, YO7 1DD, at far end of drive ✆ (01845) 522240, *Fax (01845) 523133,* 🌳 – [TV] [P]. 🐕
closed 2 weeks Christmas-New Year – **3 rm** ☕ 24.00/32.00 **s.**

at South Kilvington *N : 1½ m. on A 61* – ✉ *Thirsk.*

⌂ **Thornborough House Farm,** YO7 2NP, N : ¼ m., entrance between roundabout and A 19 junction ✆ (01845) 522103, *Fax (01845) 522103,* 🌳 – 🚭 [TV] [P]. [MC] [VISA]. 🐕
Meals (by arrangement) (communal dining) 9.50 **st.** – **3 rm** ☕ 16.00/36.00 **st.**

at Asenby *SW : 5¼ m. by A 168* – ✉ *Thirsk.*

🍴 **Crab and Lobster,** Dishforth Rd, YO7 3QL, ✆ (01845) 577286, *Fax (01845) 577109,* 🍽, « Thatched inn, memorabilia », 🌳 – [P]. [MC] [AE] [VISA]
closed Sunday dinner and 25 December – **Meals** (booking essential) 14.95/21.50 **t.** and a la carte 17.50/24.00 **t.** 🍷 4.50.

Ⓜ ATS Long St. ✆ (01845) 522982/522923

THORALBY *N. Yorks.* [402] N/O 21 – *pop. 160* – ✉ *Leyburn.*
London 245 – Kendal 41 – Leeds 64 – York 57.

⌂ **Littleburn** 🌿, DL8 3BE, W : ½ m. by unmarked lane taking left fork after ¼ m. ✆ (01969) 663621, ≤, « 17C country house », 🌳 – 🚭 [P]. 🐕
Meals (by arrangement) (communal dining) 19.00 **st.** – **3 rm** ☕ 40.00/60.00 **st.**

⌂ **Low Green House** 🌿, DL8 3SZ, SE : ¼ m. on unmarked lane ✆ (01969) 663623, ≤, 🌳 – 🚭 [TV] [P]
closed mid January-mid February and Christmas – **Meals** (by arrangement) 14.00 **s.** – **3 rm** ☕ 27.50/45.00 **s.**

⌂ **High Green House,** DL8 3SU, ✆ (01969) 663420, *Fax (01969) 663420,* ≤, 🌳 – 🚭 [TV] ♿ [P]. [MC] [VISA]
April-October – **Meals** (by arrangement) 15.50 **st.** 🍷 3.00 – **3 rm** ☕ 34.00/48.00 – SB.

Don't confuse:

Comfort of hotels : 🏨🏨🏨🏨🏨 ... 🏠, ⌂
Comfort of restaurants : 🍴🍴🍴🍴🍴 ..... 🍴, 🍺
Quality of the cuisine : ✿✿✿, ✿✿, ✿, **Meals** 😋

THORNABY-ON-TEES *Stockton-on-Tees* [402] Q 20 – *pop. 12 108* – ✉ *Middlesbrough.*
London 250 – Leeds 62 – Middlesbrough 3 – York 49.

Forte Posthouse Teesside, Low Lane, Stainton Village, TS17 9LW, SE : 3 ½ m. by A 1045 on A 1044 ☎ (01642) 591213, *Fax (01642) 594989,* 🌳 – 🚭 rm, [TV] ☎ [P] – 🎤 120. [MC] [AE] [D] [VISA]
Meals *(closed Sunday lunch)* a la carte 14.20/25.90 **st.** 🍷 7.50 – ☕ 8.95 – **135 rm** 69.00 **st.** – SB.

THORNBURY *South Gloucestershire* [403] [404] M 29 – *pop. 12 108* – ✉ *Bristol.*
London 128 – Bristol 12 – Gloucester 23 – Swindon 43.

Thornbury Castle 🐴, Castle St., BS12 1HH, ☎ (01454) 281182, *Fax (01454) 416188,* « 16C castle, antiques, gardens and vineyard », park – 🚭 rest, [TV] ☎ [P]. [MC] [AE] [D] [VISA]. 🐕
closed 5 to 8 January – **Meals** 18.50/34.50 **t.** 🍷 8.80 – ☕ 8.95 – **17 rm** 75.00/225.00 **t.**, 2 suites.

THORNTHWAITE *Cumbria* [402] K 20 – *see Keswick.*

Se cercate un albergo tranquillo,
oltre a consultare le carte dell'introduzione,
rintracciate nell'elenco degli esercizi quelli con il simbolo 🐴 *o* 🐴.

THORNTON CLEVELEYS *Lancs.* [402] L 22 – *pop. 28 061.*
London 244 – Blackpool 6 – Lancaster 20 – Manchester 44.

🍴 **Didier's,** Victorian House, Trunnah Rd, Thornton, FY5 4HF, ☎ (01253) 860619, *Fax (01253) 865350,* ⛱, 🌳 – [P]. [MC] [AE] [VISA]
Meals (bookings not accepted) 8.50 **st.** and a la carte 13.40/18.00 **st.**

THORNTON HOUGH *Mersey.* [402] [403] K 24 – ✉ *Wirral.*
London 215 – Birkenhead 12 – Chester 17 – Liverpool 14.

Thornton Hall, L63 1JF, on B 5136 ☎ (0151) 336 3938, *Fax (0151) 336 7864,* 🌳 – [TV] ☎ [P] – 🎤 250. [MC] [AE] [VISA] [JCB]
closed 25 December – ***The Italian Room :*** **Meals** (bar lunch Saturday) 16.50/21.50 **st.** and dinner a la carte 🍷 7.75 – **62 rm** ☕ 75.00/85.00 **st.**, 1 suite – SB.

THORPE *Derbs.* [402] [403] [404] O 24 *Great Britain G.* – *pop. 201* – ✉ *Ashbourne.*
See : *Dovedale★★ (Ilam Rock★).*
London 151 – Derby 16 – Sheffield 33 – Stoke-on-Trent 26.

Peveril of the Peak 🐴, DE6 2AW, ☎ (01335) 350333, *Fax (01335) 350507,* ←, 🌳, 🎾 – 🚭 [TV] ☎ [P] – 🎤 50. [MC] [AE] [D] [VISA] [JCB]. 🐕
Meals 18.95 **st.** 🍷 8.25 – ☕ 9.75 – **46 rm** 80.00/90.00 **st.** – SB.

THORPE MARKET *Norfolk* [404] X 25 – *pop. 303* – ✉ *North Walsham.*
London 130 – Norwich 21.

Green Farm, North Walsham Rd, NR11 8TH, ☎ (01263) 833602, *Fax (01263) 833163* – 🚭 rest, [TV] ☎ [P]. [MC] [AE] [VISA]
Meals (bar lunch)/dinner 18.95 **st.** and a la carte 🍷 5.50 – **12 rm** ☕ 55.00/80.00 **st.** – SB.

Elderton Lodge 🐴, Gunton Park, NR11 8TZ, S : 1 m. on A 149 ☎ (01263) 833547 *Fax (01263) 834673,* 🌳 – 🚭 [TV] ☎ [P]. [MC] [D] [VISA]
Meals 18.50 **st.** (dinner) and a la carte 15.75/22.75 **st.** 🍷 5.00 – **8 rm** ☕ 55.00/90.00 **st.** – SB.

THRAPSTON SERVICE AREA *Northants.* [404] S 26 – ✉ *Kettering.*

Travelodge, NN14 4UR, at junction of A 14 with A 605 and A 45 ☎ (01832) 735199 *Fax (01832) 735199,* Reservations (Freephone) 0800 850950 – 🚭 rm, [TV] ♿ [P]. [MC] [AE] [D] [VISA] [JCB]. 🐕
Meals (grill rest.) – **40 rm** 44.95 **t.**

THREE BRIDGES *W. Sussex* – *see Crawley.*

THRELKELD *Cumbria* [402] K 20 – *see Keswick.*

THRUSSINGTON *Leics.* [402] [403] [404] Q 25 – *pop. 512* – ✉ *Leicester.*
London 101 – Leicester 10 – Nottingham 22 – Lincoln 50.

🏨 **Travelodge,** Green Acres Filling Station, LE7 8TF, on A 46 (southbound carriageway) ℘ (01664) 424525, *Fax (01664) 424525*, Reservations (Freephone) 0800 850950 – 🚭 rm, ▤ rest, [TV] ♿ [P]. [MC] [AE] [DC] [VISA] [JCB]. 🚫🐕
Meals (grill rest.) – **32 rm** 44.95 **t.**

THURLESTONE *Devon* [403] I 33 – *see Kingsbridge.*

THURROCK SERVICE AREA *Thurrock* [404] V 29 – ✉ *West Thurrock.*
⛳18 *Belhus Park, South Ockendon* ℘ *(01708) 854260.*
[B] *Granada Motorway Service Area (M 25), RM16 3BG* ℘ *(01708) 863733.*

🏨 **Travelodge,** RM16 3BG, ℘ (01708) 891111, *Fax (01708) 860971*, Reservations (Freephone) 0800 850950 – 🛗 🚭 [TV] ☎ ♿ [P]. [MC] [AE] [DC] [VISA] [JCB]. 🚫🐕
Meals (grill rest.) – **44 rm** 55.95 **t.**

ATS Units 13/14, Eastern Av., Waterglade Ind. Park, West Thurrock, Grays ℘ (01708) 862237

TICEHURST *E. Sussex* [404] V 30 – *pop. 3 118* – ✉ *Wadhurst.*
⛳18 *Dale Hill Hotel, Ticehurst* ℘ *(01580) 200112.*
London 49 – Brighton 44 – Folkestone 38 – Hastings 15 – Maidstone 24.

🏨 **Dale Hill H. and Golf Club,** TN5 7DQ, NE : ½ m. on A 268 ℘ (01580) 200112, *Fax (01580) 201249*, 🏋, ♨, 🏊, ⛳18, park – 🛗 [TV] ☎ [P] – 🪑 30. [MC] [AE] [VISA] [JCB]. 🚫🐕
Meals 15.95 **t.** (dinner) and a la carte 18.75/29.40 **t.** 🍷 5.75 – **25 rm** ☕ 58.00/116.00 **t.**, 1 suite – SB.

TICKTON *East Riding* – *see Beverley.*

TINTAGEL *Cornwall* [403] F 32 *The West Country G.* – *pop. 1 721.*
See : *Arthur's Castle (site★★★) AC – Church★ – Old Post Office★ AC.*
Exc. : *Camelford★, SE : 6 ½ m. by B 3263 and B 3266.*
London 264 – Exeter 63 – Plymouth 49 – Truro 41.

🏨 **Trebrea Lodge** 🐦, Trenale, PL34 0HR, SE : 1 m. by Boscastle Rd (B 3263) and Trenale Lane on Trewarmett rd ℘ (01840) 770410, *Fax (01840) 770092*, ≤, « Part 18C manor house, 14C origins », 🌳 – 🚭 [TV] ☎ [P]. [MC] [AE] [VISA]
restricted opening in winter – **Meals** (booking essential to non-residents) (dinner only) 21.00 **t.** 🍷 6.00 – **7 rm** ☕ 55.00/88.00 **t.** – SB.

🏨 **Wootons Country H.,** Fore St., PL34 0DD, ℘ (01840) 770170, *Fax (01840) 770978* – [TV] ☎ [P]. [MC] [AE] [DC] [VISA] [JCB]. 🚫🐕
Meals (bar lunch)/dinner 9.00 **st.** and a la carte 🍷 4.95 – **11 rm** ☕ 25.00/50.00 **st.**

🏠 **Polkerr,** Molesworth St., PL34 0BY, ℘ (01840) 770382, 🌳 – [TV] [P]. 🚫🐕
closed 25 and 26 December – **Meals** (by arrangement) 8.50 – **7 rm** ☕ 17.00/44.00 – SB.

🏠 **Old Borough House,** Bossiney Rd, PL34 0AY, NE : ½ m. on B 3263 ℘ (01840) 770475 – 🚭 rest, [P]. 🚫🐕
Meals (by arrangement) 12.00 **s.** – **6 rm** ☕ 42.00 **s.**

🏠 **Old Millfloor** 🐦, Trebarwith, PL34 0HA, S : 1 ¾ m. by B 3263 ℘ (01840) 770234, « Former flour mill », 🌳, park – 🚭 [TV] [P]. 🚫🐕
April-October – **Meals** (by arrangement) 15.00 – **3 rm** ☕ 20.00/40.00 **st.** – SB.

Für Ihre Reisen in ***Großbritannien***
- 5 Karten (Nr. [401], [402], [403], [404], [405]) im Maßstab 1 : 400 000
- Die auf den Karten **rot unterstrichenen** Orte sind im Führer erwähnt, benutzen Sie deshalb Karten und Führer zusammen.

TODDINGTON SERVICE AREA Beds. 404 S 28 – pop. 4 500 – ⊠ Luton.

🏠 **Travelodge** without rest., LU5 6HR, M 1 (southbound carriageway) ℰ (01525) 878424, Fax (01525) 878452, Reservations (Freephone) 0800 850950 – ⇛ 📺 ☎ ₺ 🅿. 🐵 ᴁ ① 🆅🆂🅰 JCB. ⨯
43 rm 49.95 t.

TODMORDEN W. Yorks. 402 N 22 – pop. 10 481.
London 218 – Burnley 10 – Leeds 35 – Manchester 22.

🏰 **Scaitcliffe Hall,** Burnley Rd, OL14 7DQ, NW : 1 m. on A 646 ℰ (01706) 818888, Fax (01706) 818825, « Part 17C country house », 🌳, park – 📺 ☎ 🅿 – 🔏 180. 🐵 ᴁ ①
🆅🆂🅰 JCB
Meals 19.65 st. (dinner) and lunch a la carte approx. 11.35 st. ₺ 7.35 – **11 rm** ⊇ 58.50/ 84.00 st., 1 suite.

TOFT Lincs. – see Bourne.

TOLLESHUNT KNIGHTS Essex – see Maldon.

---

*Pour voyager rapidement, utilisez les **cartes Michelin "Grandes Routes"** :*

970 Europe, 976 République Tchèque-République Slovaque, 980 Grèce,
984 Allemagne, 985 Scandinavie-Finlande, 986 Grande-Bretagne-Irlande,
987 Allemagne-Autriche-Benelux,
988 Italie, 989 France, 990 Espagne-Portugal, 991 Yougoslavie.

TONBRIDGE Kent 404 U 30 – pop. 34 260.
📗, 📗 Poult Wood, Higham Lane ℰ (01732) 364039.
🔼 Tonbridge Castle, Castle St., TN9 1BG ℰ (01732) 770929.
London 33 – Brighton 37 – Hastings 31 – Maidstone 14.

🏰 **Rose and Crown,** 125 High St., TN9 1DD, ℰ (01732) 357966, Fax (01732) 357194 – ⇛
📺 ☎ 🅿 – 🔏 100. 🐵 ᴁ ① 🆅🆂🅰 JCB
Meals (bar lunch Monday to Saturday)/dinner 15.95 t. and a la carte ₺ 5.75 – **48 rm**
⊇ 64.00/88.00 t. – SB.

🏠 **Langley,** 18-20 London Rd, TN10 3DA, N : on B 245 ℰ (01732) 353311
Fax (01732) 771471, 🌳 – ₺, ▦ rest, 📺 ☎ 🅿. 🐵 ᴁ ① 🆅🆂🅰. ⨯
Meals (closed Sunday dinner and Bank Holidays) 15.95 t. and a la carte ₺ 5.95 – **34 rm**
⊇ 59.50/82.50 t. – SB.

⌂ **Starvecrow Place** without rest., Starvecrow Hill, Shipbourne Rd, TN11 9NL, N : 2 m. on
A 227 ℰ (01732) 356863, ☒, 🌳 – ⇛ 📺 🅿. ⨯
closed Christmas and New Year – **3 rm** ⊇ 30.00/42.50 st.

🔘 ATS Unit 4, Sovereign Way ℰ (01732) 353800/352231

TORQUAY Torbay 403 J 32 The West Country G. – pop. 59 587.
See : Torbay★ – Kent's Cavern★ AC CX A.
Env. : Paignton Zoo★★ AC, SE : 3 m. by A 3022 – Cockington★, W : 1 m. AX.
📗 Petitor Rd, St. Marychurch ℰ (01803) 327471, B.
🔼 Vaughan Parade, TQ2 5JG ℰ (01803) 297428.
London 223 – Exeter 23 – Plymouth 32.

Plans on following pages

🏨 **Imperial,** Parkhill Rd, TQ1 2DG, ℰ (01803) 294301, Fax (01803) 298293, ≤ Torbay, 🛁, ≘s
☒, ☒, 🌳, ⨯, squash – ₺, ⇛ rm, ▦ rest, 📺 ☎ ₺ ⇦ 🅿 – 🔏 350. 🐵 ᴁ ①
🆅🆂🅰
CZ
Regatta : Meals (dinner only and Saturday and Sunday lunch)/dinner
27.50 st. and a la carte ₺ 10.00 – **Sundeck Brasserie :** Meals a la carte 17.25/28.25 st. –
⊇ 13.50 – **148 rm** 84.00/168.00 st., 17 suites – SB.

🏨 **Palace,** Babbacombe Rd, TQ1 3TG, ℰ (01803) 200200, Fax (01803) 299899, ≤, « Extensive
gardens », ≘s, ☒, ☒, 📗, park, ⨯indoor/outdoor, squash – ₺, ⇛ rm, 📺 ☎ ₺ ⇦ 🅿
🔏 350. 🐵 ᴁ ① 🆅🆂🅰. ⨯
CX
Meals 14.50/22.50 t. and a la carte ₺ 6.00 – **135 rm** ⊇ 65.00/150.00 st., 6 suites – SB.

Grand, Seafront, TQ2 6NT, ℰ (01803) 296677, Fax (01803) 213462, ≤, ₤₆, ≋ₛ, ☑, ☒, ※ –
▮⬤▮, ※ rest, ⓉⓋ ☎ ⟷ – 🛦 300. ⬤⬤ 🄰🄴 ⑩ 🆅🅸🆂🅰 🄹🄲🄱
Meals (bar lunch Monday to Saturday) 14.85/24.75 **st.** and a la carte ₤ 5.50 – **100 rm**
⟳ 70.35/157.50 **st.**, 11 suites – SB.
BZ z

Osborne, Hesketh Cres., Meadfoot, TQ1 2LL, ℰ (01803) 213311, Fax (01803) 296788, ≤,
« Regency town houses », ₤₆, ≋ₛ, ☑, ☒, ☞, ※ – ▮⬤▮, ※ rest, ⓉⓋ ☎ ℗ – 🛦 80. ⬤⬤ 🄰🄴
🆅🅸🆂🅰. ※
CX n
Langtry's : **Meals** (dinner only) 17.95 **st.** and a la carte ₤ 6.50 – **The Brasserie :** **Meals**
(bar lunch Monday to Thursday during January and February) a la carte 14.95/21.45 **t.**
₤ 6.50 – **29 rm** ⟳ (dinner included) 60.00/150.00 **t.** – SB.

Livermead House, Seafront, TQ2 6QJ, ℰ (01803) 294361, Fax (01803) 200758, ≤, ≋ₛ,
☑, squash – ▮⬤▮, ※ rest, ⓉⓋ ☎ ℗ – 🛦 350. ⬤⬤ 🄰🄴 ⑩ 🆅🅸🆂🅰
BZ e
Meals 9.75/19.75 **t.** and dinner a la carte ₤ 4.75 – **65 rm** ⟳ (dinner included) 60.00/
120.00 **st.** – SB.

Livermead Cliff, Seafront, TQ2 6RQ, ℰ (01803) 299666, Fax (01803) 294496, ≤, ☑, ☞ –
▮⬤▮ ⓉⓋ ☎ ℗ – 🛦 70. ⬤⬤ ⑩ 🆅🅸🆂🅰 🄹🄲🄱. ※
BX r
Meals 9.75/17.75 **st.** and a la carte ₤ 5.75 – **64 rm** ⟳ 45.00/105.00 **st.** – SB.

Albaston House, 27 St. Marychurch Rd, TQ1 3JF, ℰ (01803) 296758 – ⓉⓋ ☎ ℗. ⬤⬤ ⑩
🆅🅸🆂🅰 🄹🄲🄱
CY a
closed Christmas – **Meals** (dinner only) 12.00 **st.** ₤ 4.00 – **13 rm** ⟳ 32.00/72.00 **st.** – SB.

Fairmount House, Herbert Rd, Chelston, TQ2 6RW, ℰ (01803) 605446,
Fax (01803) 605446, ☞ – ※ rest, ⓉⓋ ℗. ⬤⬤ 🆅🅸🆂🅰
AX a
early March-early November – **Meals** (closed Sunday dinner Easter-September) (residents
only) (bar lunch)/dinner 12.50 **st.** ₤ 3.95 – **8 rm** ⟳ 32.00/64.00 **st.** – SB.

Cranborne, 58 Belgrave Rd, TQ2 5HY, ℰ (01803) 298046, Fax (01803) 298046 – ※ rest,
ⓉⓋ. ⬤⬤ 🆅🅸🆂🅰. ※
BY i
closed Christmas and New Year – **Meals** (by arrangement) 8.00 – **13 rm** ⟳ 23.00/50.00 **st.**

Belmont, 66 Belgrave Rd, TQ2 5HY, ℰ (01803) 295028, Fax (01803) 211668 – ※ rest, ⓉⓋ
℗. ⬤⬤ 🄰🄴 ⑩ 🆅🅸🆂🅰 🄹🄲🄱
BY i
Meals 8.00 **st.** ₤ 6.00 – **13 rm** ⟳ 18.00/44.00 **st.** – SB.

Glenorleigh, 26 Cleveland Rd, TQ2 5BE, ℰ (01803) 292135, Fax (01803) 292135, ☑, ☞ –
℗. ⬤⬤ 🆅🅸🆂🅰. ※
BY n
Easter-October – **Meals** (by arrangement) 10.00 **st.** ₤ 3.50 – **16 rm** ⟳ (dinner included)
25.00/76.00 **st.** – SB.

Cedar Court, 3 St. Matthews Rd, Chelston, TQ2 6JA, ℰ (01803) 607851 – ⓉⓋ ℗
closed 25 and 26 December – **Meals** (by arrangement) 7.00 **st.** – **9 rm** ⟳ 14.00/38.00 **st.** –
SB.
BY a

Remy's, 3 Croft Rd, TQ2 5UF, ℰ (01803) 292359 – ※. ⬤⬤ 🆅🅸🆂🅰 🄹🄲🄱
CY x
closed Sunday and Monday – **Meals** - French - (booking essential) (dinner only) 17.85 **t.**
₤ 5.50.

Mulberry House with rm, 1 Scarborough Rd, TQ2 5UJ, ℰ (01803) 213639 – ※ ⓉⓋ. ※
closed first 2 weeks January – **Meals** (closed Sunday dinner, Monday and Tuesday to
non-residents) (booking essential) 7.95 **st.** (lunch) and a la carte 12.50/16.50 **st.** ₤ 6.00 –
3 rm ⟳ 25.00/50.00 **st.**
CY x

Maidencombe N : 3½ m. by B 3199 – BX – ✉ Torquay.

Orestone Manor ⬥, Rockhouse Lane, TQ1 4SX, ℰ (01803) 328098, Fax (01803) 328336,
≤, ☑, ☞ – ※ rest, ⓉⓋ ☎ ℗. ⬤⬤ 🄰🄴 🆅🅸🆂🅰 🄹🄲🄱
closed first 2 weeks January – **Meals** (dinner only and Sunday lunch in low season)/
dinner 27.50 **t.** ₤ 6.00 – **18 rm** ⟳ (dinner included) 72.00/204.00 **t.** – SB.

Barn Hayes ⬥, Brim Hill, TQ1 4TR, ℰ (01803) 327980, Fax (01803) 327980, ≤, ☞ –
※ rest, ⓉⓋ ℗. ⬤⬤ 🆅🅸🆂🅰
booking essential November-March – **Meals** (bar lunch)/dinner 14.00 **st.** ₤ 3.50 – **12 rm**
⟳ 30.00/60.00 **st.** – SB.

Babbacombe NE : 1½ m. – ✉ Torquay.

Table, 135 Babbacombe Rd, TQ1 3SR, ℰ (01803) 324292, Fax (01803) 324292 – ⬤⬤ 🄰🄴 🆅🅸🆂🅰
closed lunch Sunday, Monday and May-August and 2 weeks early February, 2 weeks late
March and Christmas – **Meals** 26.50 **t.** ₤ 5.50.
CX a

🅐 ATS 20 Tor Church Rd ℰ (01803) 293985 | ATS 100 Teignmouth Rd ℰ (01803) 329495

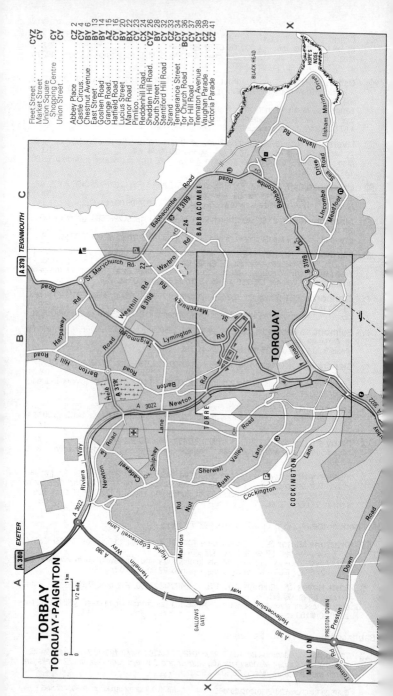

TORBAY

TORQUAY-PAIGNTON

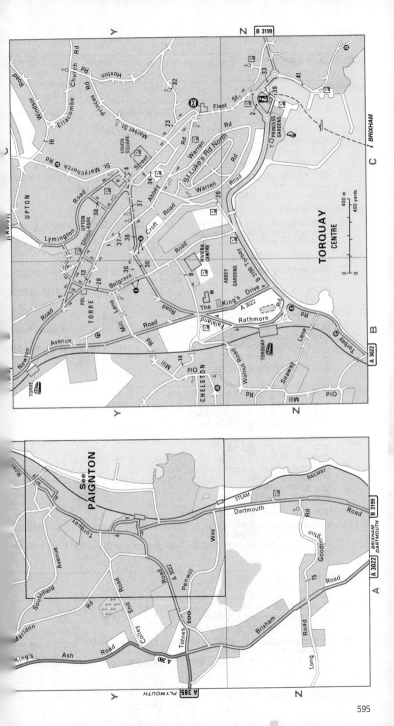

595

TORVER *Cumbria* 402 K 20 – *see Coniston*.

TOTLAND *I.O.W.* 403 404 P 31 – *see Wight (Isle of)*.

TOTNES *Devon* 403 I 32 *The West Country G.* – *pop. 6 929*.
See : *Town★ – St. Mary's★ – Butterwalk★ – Castle (≤★★★) AC*.
Env. : *Paignton Zoo★★ AC, E : 4½ m. by A 385 and A 3022 – British Photographic Museum*
Bowden House★ AC, S : 1 m. by A 381.
Exc. : *Dartmouth★★ (Castle ≤★★★) SE : 12 m. by A 381 and A 3122*.
🛇, 🛇 *Dartmouth G & C.C., Blackawton ℘ (01803) 712686*.
🔳 *The Plains, TQ9 5EJ ℘ (01803) 863168*.
London 224 – Exeter 24 – Plymouth 23 – Torquay 9.

⌂ **Old Forge at Totnes** without rest., Seymour Pl., TQ9 5AY, ℘ (01803) 862174
Fax (01803) 865385, « *14C working forge* », 🖘 – 🔆 🔟 ☎ 🅿. 🕮 *VISA*. ⅏
10 rm ☲ 40.00/70.00 **st.**

at Stoke Gabriel *SE : 4 m. by A 385 –* ⊠ *Totnes*.

🏨 **Gabriel Court** 🦢, Stoke Hill, TQ9 6SF, ℘ (01803) 782206, Fax (01803) 782333, 🛋, 🖘, ⅏
– 🔆 rest, 🔟 ☎ 🅿. 🕮 🆎 ① *VISA* JCB
Meals (dinner only and Sunday lunch)/dinner 24.00 **st.** ▯ 6.00 – **19 rm** ☲ 51.00/78.00 **st.**

at Ashprington *S : 3½ m. by A 381 –* ⊠ *Totnes*.

🏠 **Waterman's Arms**, Bow Bridge, TQ9 7EG, ℘ (01803) 732214, Fax (01803) 73221
« *Part 15C inn* », 🖘 – 🔆 rest, 🔟 ☎ 🅿. 🕮 🆎 *VISA*
Meals (bar lunch Monday to Saturday)/a la carte 10.15/19.85 ▯ 7.95 – **15 rm** ☲ 40.00
80.00 **t.**

at Dartington *NW : 2 m. by A 385 on A 384 –* ⊠ *Totnes*.

🍴 **Cott Inn** with rm, TQ9 6HE, S : ½ m. off A 385 ℘ (01803) 863777, Fax (01803) 86662
« *14C thatched inn* », 🖘 – 🔆 🔟 ☎ 🅿. 🕮 🆎 *VISA* JCB
closed 25 December – **Meals** (bar lunch)/dinner a la carte 15.50/20.50 **st.** ▯ 5.50 – **6 rm**
☲ 45.00/60.00 **st.** – SB.

🔧 ATS Babbage Rd ℘ (01803) 862086

TOWCESTER *Northants.* 403 404 R 27 – *pop. 7 006*.
🛇, 🛇 *West Park G. & C.C., Whittlebury, Towcester ℘ (01327) 858092 –* 🛇 *Farthingstone*
Hotel, Farthingstone ℘ (01327) 361291.
London 70 – Birmingham 50 – Northampton 9 – Oxford 36.

🏨 **Saracens Head**, 219 Watling St., NN12 7BX, ℘ (01327) 350414, Fax (01327) 359879 –
☎ 🅿 – 🔬 100. 🕮 🆎 ① *VISA*. ⅏
Meals 9.95/13.95 and a la carte ▯ 6.00 – **21 rm** ☲ 59.00/78.00 – SB.

🏠 **Travelodge**, East Towcester bypass, NN12 6TQ, SW : ½ m. by Brackley rd on A
℘ (01327) 359105, Fax (01327) 359105, Reservations (Freephone) 0800 850950 – 🔆 rm
🔟 ₰ 🅿. 🕮 🆎 ① *VISA* JCB. ⅏
Meals (grill rest.) – **33 rm** 44.95 **t.**

at Paulerspury *SE : 3¼ m. by A 5 –* ⊠ *Towcester*.

❌❌ **Vine House** with rm, 100 High St., NN12 7NA, ℘ (01327) 811267, Fax (01327) 811309,
– 🔆 rest, 🔟 ☎ 🅿. 🕮 *VISA*. ⅏
Meals *(closed Monday to Wednesday lunch and Sunday)* 16.95/23.95 **t.** ▯ 4.45 – **6 rm**
☲ 43.00/66.00.

TOWERSEY *Oxon.* 404 R 28 – *see Thame*.

TREGONY *Cornwall* 403 F 33 *The West Country G.* – *pop. 729 –* ⊠ *Truro*.
Env. : *Trewithen★★★ AC, N : 2½ m*.
London 291 – Newquay 18 – Plymouth 53 – Truro 10.

⌂ **Tregony House**, 15 Fore St., TR2 5RN, ℘ (01872) 530671, Fax (01872) 530671, 🖘 –
🅿. 🕮 *VISA*. ⅏
closed December and January – **Meals** (by arrangement) 11.25 **st.** – **5 rm** ☲ 30.00
67.50 **st.**

TREGREHAN *Cornwall* 403 F 32 – *see St. Austell*.

TRESCO Cornwall 403 ③ – see Scilly (Isles of).

TRING Herts. 404 S 28 – pop. 11 455.
London 38 – Aylesbury 7 – Luton 14.

🏨 **Pendley Manor,** Cow Lane, HP23 5QY, E : 1 ½ m. by B 4635 off B 4251 ℰ (01442) 891891, Fax (01442) 890687, ≤, ⅙, ☞, park, ℀ – ☖, ⅍ rest, ⓣⓥ ☎ ⅙ ⓟ – 🏛 220. ◍ ⌸ ⓪ 𝘝𝘐𝘚𝘈
Meals 21.00 **t.** and a la carte ⅙ 6.75 – **69 rm** ⊇ 90.00/120.00 **t.**, 2 suites.

🏨 **Rose and Crown,** High St., HP23 5AH, ℰ (01442) 824071, Fax (01442) 890735 – ⅍ rm, ⓣⓥ ☎ ⓟ – 🏛 80. ◍ ⌸ ⓪ 𝘝𝘐𝘚𝘈 𝘑𝘊𝘉
Meals (bar meals Saturday lunch and Sunday dinner) 12.95/21.95 **t.** and dinner a la carte ⅙ 6.70 – ⊇ 8.50 – **27 rm** 85.00/130.00 **t.** – SB.

🏨 **Travel Inn,** Tring Hill, HP23 4LD, W : 1 ½ m. on A 41 ℰ (01442) 824819, Fax (01442) 890787 – ⅍ rm, ⓣⓥ ⅙ ⓟ. ◍ ⌸ ⓪ 𝘝𝘐𝘚𝘈. ℀
Meals (grill rest.) – **30 rm** 36.50 **t.**

TROTTON W. Sussex – see Midhurst.

TROUTBECK Cumbria 402 L 20 – see Windermere.

TROWBRIDGE Wilts. 403 404 N 30 The West Country G. – pop. 29 334.
Env. : Westwood Manor★, NW : 3 m. by A 363 – Farleigh Hungerford Castle★ (St. Leonard's Chapel★) AC, W : 4 m.
Exc. : Longleat House★★★ AC, SW : 12 m. by A 363, A 350 and A 362 - Bratton Castle (≤★★) SE : 7 ½ m. by A 363 and B 3098 – Steeple Ashton★ (The Green★) E : 6 m. – Edington (St. Mary, St. Katherine and All Saints★) SE : 7 ½ m.
🖪 St. Stephen's Pl., BA14 8AH ℰ (01225) 777054.
London 115 – Bristol 27 – Southampton 55 – Swindon 32.

🏨 **Old Manor** ﹩, Trowle, BA14 9BL, NW : 1 m. on A 363 ℰ (01225) 777393, Fax (01225) 765443, « Queen Anne house of 15C origins », ☞ – ⅍ ⓣⓥ ☎ ⓟ. ◍ ⌸ ⓪ 𝘝𝘐𝘚𝘈 𝘑𝘊𝘉. ℀
closed 4 days Christmas – Meals (closed Sunday) (residents only) (dinner only) a la carte 12.80/20.95 **st.** ⅙ 3.95 – **14 rm** ⊇ 48.50/85.00 **st.**

🏠 **Hilbury Court,** Hilperton Rd, BA14 7JW, NE : ¼ m. on A 361 ℰ (01225) 752949, Fax (01225) 777990, ☞ – ⅍ rest, ⓣⓥ ☎ ⓟ. ◍ ⓪ 𝘝𝘐𝘚𝘈. ℀
Meals (lunch by arrangement)/dinner a la carte 14.35/16.70 **st.** – **13 rm** ⊇ 45.00/55.00 **st.** – SB.

↑ **Brookfield House** ﹩ without rest., Vaggs Hill, Wingfield, BA14 9NA, SW : 4 m. by A 366 on B 3109 ℰ (01373) 830615, Fax (01373) 830615, « Working farm », ☞, park – ⅍ ⓣⓥ ⓟ. ℀
closed 25 December – **3 rm** ⊇ 15.00/45.00 **st.**

↑ **Welam House** without rest., Bratton Rd, West Ashton, BA14 6AZ, SW : 2 m. by A 361 on West Ashton Rd ℰ (01225) 755908, ☞ – ⅍ ⓟ. ℀
April-October – **3 rm** ⊇ 32.00.

🅰 ATS Canal Rd, Ladydown Trading Est. ℰ (01225) 753469

TROWELL SERVICE AREA Notts. 404 Q 25 – ✉ Ilkeston.

🏠 **Travelodge** without rest., NG9 3PL, at junction 25/6 on M 1 (northbound carriageway) ℰ (0115) 932 0291, Fax (0115) 930 7261, Reservations (Freephone) 0800 850950 – ⅍ ⓣⓥ ☎ ⅙ ⓟ. ◍ ⌸ ⓪ 𝘝𝘐𝘚𝘈 𝘑𝘊𝘉. ℀
35 rm 46.95 **t.**

TRURO Cornwall 403 E 33 The West Country G. – pop. 18 966.
See : Royal Cornwall Museum★★ AC.
Env. : Trelissick garden★★ (≤★★) AC, S : 4 m. by A 39 – Feock (Church★) S : 5 m. by A 39 and B 3289.
Exc. : Trewithen★★★, NE : 7 ½ m. by A 39 and A 390.
🖪₈ Treliske ℰ (01872) 72640 – 🖪₈ Killiow Golf Park, Killiow, Kea ℰ (01872) 70246.
🖪 Municipal Buildings, Boscawen St., TR1 2NE ℰ (01872) 274555.
London 295 – Exeter 87 – Penzance 26 – Plymouth 52.

🏛 **Alverton Manor,** Tregolls Rd, TR1 1XQ, ✆ (01872) 276633, *Fax (01872) 222989*, « Mid 19C manor house, former Bishop's residence and convent », ☞ – ⬢, ⤩ rest, 🆃🆅 ☎ 🅿 🌲 200. 🏧 AE ⓞ VISA JCB
Meals 19.50 **st.** and dinner a la carte 19.50/25.00 **st.** ⌀ 5.20 – **30 rm** �☐ 63.00/123.00 **st.**
4 suites – SB.

🏛 **Royal,** Lemon St., TR1 2QB, ✆ (01872) 270345, Fax (01872) 242453 – ⤩ rm, 🆃🆅 ☎ 🅿 ⓞ
AE ⓞ VISA ⌕
closed 25 and 26 December – Meals (closed Sunday lunch) (grill rest.) 14.95 **t.** (dinner and a la carte 13.85/23.15 **t.** ⌀ 8.95 – **37 rm** ⊇ 52.00/90.00 **t.** – SB.

↑ **Laniley House** ⌕ without rest., Newquay Rd, nr. Trispen, TR4 9AU, NE : 3 ½ m. by A 39 and A 3076 on Frogmore rd ✆ (01872) 275201, ☞ – ⤩ 🆃🆅 🅿. ⌕
Easter-November – **3 rm** ⊇ 25.00/38.00.

↑ **Blue Haze** without rest., The Parade, Malpas Rd, TR1 1QE, ✆ (01872) 22355,
Fax (01872) 223553, ☞ – ⤩ 🆃🆅 🅿. ⌕
3 rm ⊇ 28.00/40.00 **s.**

↑ **Conifers** without rest., 36 Tregolls Rd, TR1 1LA, ✆ (01872) 279925 – ⤩ 🆃🆅 🅿. ⌕
4 rm ⊇ 21.00/37.00 **s.**

at Blackwater W : 7 m. by A 390 – ✉ Truro.

↑ **Rock Cottage,** TR4 8EU, ✆ (01872) 560252, Fax (01872) 560252 – ⤩ 🆃🆅 🅿. ⌕
closed Christmas and New Year – Meals (by arrangement) a la carte 10.15/13.10 **st.** – **3 rm**
⊇ 26.00/44.00 **st.**

🅐 ATS Tabernacle St. ✆ (01872) 74083   ATS Newham Rd ✆ (01872) 40353

Pour voyager rapidement, utilisez les **cartes Michelin "Grandes Routes"** :

970 Europe, **976** République Tchèque-République Slovaque, **980** Grèce,
984 Allemagne, **985** Scandinavie-Finlande, **986** Grande-Bretagne-Irlande,
987 Allemagne-Autriche-Benelux,
988 Italie, **989** France, **990** Espagne-Portugal, **991** Yougoslavie.

TRUSHAM *Devon* The West Country G. – pop. 152 – ✉ Newton Abbot.
Env. : Dartmoor National Park★★.
London 208 – Exeter 16 – Plymouth 36.

🍴 **Cridford Inn** with rm, TQ13 0NR, ✆ (01626) 853694, « 11C former hall house »
⤩ rest, 🆃🆅 🅿. 🏧 VISA
closed 25 December – Meals (booking essential) (lunch in bar) a la carte 9.80/21.50 **t.** ⌀ 7.
– **4 rm** ⊇ 45.00/65.00 – SB.

TUNBRIDGE WELLS *Kent* **404** U 30 – see Royal Tunbridge Wells.

TURNERS HILL *W. Sussex* **404** T 30 – pop. 1 534.
London 33 – Brighton 24 – Crawley 7.

🏛 **Alexander House** ⌕, East St., RH10 4QD, E : 1 m. on B 2110 ✆ (01342) 7149
Fax (01342) 717328, ≤, « Part 17C country house in extensive parkland », ☞, ⌘ –
⤩ rest, 🆃🆅 ☎ 🅿. 🏧 AE ⓞ VISA ⌕
Meals 22.00/29.50 **st.** and a la carte 42.00/55.00 **st.** ⌀ 7.50 – **9 rm** ⊇ 120.00/155.00 **s**
6 suites – SB.

TURVEY *Beds.* **404** S 27 – see Bedford.

TUTBURY *Staffs.* **402** **403** **404** O 25 Great Britain G. – pop. 5 646 (inc. Hatton) – ✉ Burton-upon Trent.
Env. : Sudbury Hall★★ AC, NW : 5 ½ m. by A 50.
London 132 – Birmingham 33 – Derby 11 – Stoke-on-Trent 27.

🏛 **Ye Olde Dog and Partridge,** High St., DE13 9LS, ✆ (01283) 8130
Fax (01283) 813178, « Part 15C timbered inn », ☞ – ⤩ rm, 🆃🆅 ☎ 🅿. 🏧 AE ⓞ VISA ⌕
closed 24-25 December and 1 January – Meals (carving rest.) 8.20 **t.** (dinner and a la carte ⌀ 5.95 – **17 rm** ⊇ 55.00/78.00 **t.**

↑ **Mill House** without rest., Cornmill Lane, DE13 9HA, SE : ¾ m. ✆ (01283) 8136
« Georgian house and watermill », ☞ – ⤩ 🆃🆅 🅿. ⌕
closed 25 and 26 December – **3 rm** ⊇ 35.00/55.00 **s.**

TWO BRIDGES *Devon* [403] I 32 *The West Country G.* – ✉ *Yelverton.*
Env. : *Dartmoor National Park★★.*
London 226 – Exeter 25 – Plymouth 17.

🏨 **Prince Hall** 🐦, PL20 6SA, E : 1 m. on B 3357 ☎ (01822) 890403, *Fax (01822) 890676*, ←, 🎣, 🌳 – ⊬ rest, [TV] ☎ [P]. [MC] [AE] [D] [VISA] [JCB]
closed 1 January-10 February and restricted opening in winter – **Meals** (booking essential to non-residents) (dinner only) 23.00 **st.** 🍷 4.95 – **9 rm** ⊐ (dinner included) 57.50/125.00 **st.** – SB.

TWO MILLS *Ches.* – *see Chester.*

TYNEMOUTH *Tyne and Wear* [401] [402] P 18 – *pop. 17 422.*
London 290 – Newcastle upon Tyne 8 – Sunderland 7.

🏨 **Grand,** Grand Par., NE30 4ER, ☎ (0191) 293 6666, *Fax (0191) 293 6665*, ←, « Victorian mansion » – 🛗 [TV] ☎ [P] – 🎤 75. [MC] [AE] [D] [VISA]. ✗
Meals *(closed dinner Sunday and 1 January)* 11.75/13.75 **t.** and a la carte 🍷 4.25 – **44 rm** ⊐ 65.00/85.00 **t.**

🏨 **Hope House,** 47 Percy Gdns., NE30 4HH, ☎ (0191) 257 1989, *Fax (0191) 257 1989*, ←, « Tastefully furnished Victorian house » – [TV] 🚗. [MC] [AE] [D] [VISA]. ✗
Meals (residents only) (communal dining) (dinner only) 17.50 **s.** 🍷 6.00 – **3 rm** ⊐ 39.50/65.00 **s.** – SB.

UCKFIELD *E. Sussex* [404] U 31 – *pop. 13 531.*
London 45 – Brighton 17 – Eastbourne 20 – Maidstone 34.

🏨 **Horsted Place** 🐦, Little Horsted, TN22 5TS, S : 2 ½ m. by B 2102 and A 22 on A 26 ☎ (01825) 750581, *Fax (01825) 750459*, ←, 🏛, « Victorian Gothic country house and gardens », [🏊], [18], park, 🎾 – 🛗, ⊬ rest, [TV] ☎ [P] – 🎤 100. [MC] [AE] [D] [VISA] [JCB]. ✗
Meals 17.95/30.00 **t.** and a la carte 🍷 9.75 – ⊐ 3.00 – **12 rm** 90.00/130.00 **t.**, 5 suites – SB.

🏨 **Hooke Hall,** 250 High St., TN22 1EN, ☎ (01825) 761578, *Fax (01825) 768025*, « Queen Anne town house » – [TV] ☎ [P]. [MC] [AE] [VISA]. ✗
closed 24 to 30 December – **Meals** – (see ***La Scaletta*** below) – ⊐ 7.75 – **9 rm** 45.00/120.00 **st.**

🍴🍴 **La Scaletta** (at Hooke Hall H.), 250 High St., TN22 1EN, ☎ (01825) 766844, *Fax (01825) 768025* – ⊬ [P]. [MC] [AE] [VISA]
closed Saturday lunch, Sunday, 2 weeks February, 24 to 30 December and Bank Holiday Mondays – **Meals** - Italian - 15.00 **t.** (lunch) and a la carte 19.00/30.50 **t.** 🍷 6.00.

UFFINGTON *Oxon.* [403] [404] P 29.
London 75 – Oxford 29 – Reading 32 – Swindon 17.

🏠 **Craven** 🐦, Fernham Rd, SN7 7RD, ☎ (01367) 820449, « 17C thatched house », 🌳 – ⊬ [P]. [MC] [AE] [VISA]. ✗
Meals (by arrangement) (communal dining) 14.50 🍷 3.25 – **7 rm** ⊐ 25.00/65.00.

ULLINGSWICK *Herefordshire* – *pop. 237* – ✉ *Hereford.*
London 134 – Hereford 12 – Shrewsbury 52 – Worcester 19.

🏨 **Steppes Country House** 🐦, HR1 3JG, ☎ (01432) 820424, *Fax (01432) 820042*, « Converted farmhouse of 14C origins », 🌳 – ⊬ [TV] ☎ [P]. [MC] [AE] [VISA] [JCB]
closed 2 weeks before Christmas and January – **Meals** (booking essential) (bar lunch)/dinner 25.00 **st.** 🍷 4.95 – **6 rm** ⊐ (dinner included) 84.00/138.00 – SB.

ULLSWATER *Cumbria* [402] L 20 – *pop. 1 199* – ✉ *Penrith.*
[i] *Main Car Park, Glenridding, CA11 0PA* ☎ *(017684) 82414 (summer only).*
London 296 – Carlisle 25 – Kendal 31 – Penrith 6.

Matterdale End *N : 2 ¾ m. on A 5091* – ✉ *Penrith.*

🏠 **Bank House Farm** 🐦 without rest., CA11 0LF, W : ¾ m. turning left after telephone box in village centre ☎ (017684) 82040, *Fax (017684) 82040*, ←, 🌳 – ⊬ [TV] [P]
restricted opening in winter – **4 rm** ⊐ 50.00 **s.**

Howtown *SW : 4 m. of Pooley Bridge* – ✉ *Penrith.*

🏨 **Howtown** 🐦, CA10 2ND, ☎ (017684) 86514, ←, 🌳 – [P]. ✗
mid March-October – **Meals** 7.00/13.25 **t.** 🍷 5.00 – **14 rm** ⊐ (dinner included) 42.00/84.00 **t.**

at Pooley Bridge on B 5320 – ✉ Penrith.

Sharrow Bay Country House ⛰, CA10 2LZ, S : 2 m. on Howtown r… ☎ (017684) 86301, Fax (017684) 86349, ≤ Ullswater and fells, « Lakeside setting, gardens » … – ⅔ ✈, ▤ rest, TV ☎ P. MC VISA JCB. ✂
closed December-mid February – **Meals** (booking essential) 33.75/44.75 **st.** 14.95 – **24 rm** (dinner included) 110.00/340.00 **st.**, 4 suites
Spec. Ravioli of lobster, scallops and truffles with saffron lemon pasta. Traditional roas… game. Vanilla parfait in a marzipan case with poached peaches.

at Watermillock on A 592 – ✉ Penrith.

Leeming House ⛰, CA11 0JJ, on A 592 ☎ (017684) 86622, Fax (017684) 86443, ≤ « Lakeside country house and gardens », park – ✈ TV ☎ & P – 35. MC AE D VISA JCB. ✂
Meals 31.50 **t.** (dinner) and lunch a la carte approx. 19.00 **t.** 8.50 – 11.95 – **40 rm** 80.00/145.00 **t.** – SB.

Rampsbeck Country House ⛰, CA11 0LP, ☎ (017684) 86442, Fax (017684) 8668… ≤ Ullswater and fells, « Lakeside setting », park – TV ☎ P. MC VISA. ✂
closed January-mid February – **Meals** – (see below) – **19 rm** 50.00/160.00 **t.**, 1 suite SB.

Old Church ⛰, CA11 0JN, ☎ (017684) 86204, Fax (017684) 86368, ≤ Ullswater and fell… « Lakeside setting », – ✈ rest, TV ☎ P. MC AE VISA. ✂
March-October – **Meals** *(closed Sunday)* (booking essential) (dinner only) a la carte 16.2… 22.40 **st.** 8.50 – **10 rm** 65.00/138.00 **st.** – SB.

Rampsbeck Country House (at Rampsbeck Country House H.), CA11 0L… ☎ (017684) 86442, Fax (017684) 86688, park – ✈ P. MC VISA
Meals (booking essential) (lunch by arrangement Monday to Saturday) 22.00/40.00 6.75.

Les prix — Pour toutes précisions sur les prix indiqués dans ce guide, reportez-vous aux pages de l'introduction.

ULVERSTON Cumbria 402 K 21 – pop. 11 866.

Bardsea Park ☎ (01229) 582824.
Coronation Hall, County Sq., LA12 7LZ ☎ (01229) 587120.
London 278 – Kendal 25 – Lancaster 36.

Trinity House, 1 Princes St., LA12 7NB, off A 590 ☎ (01229) 587639, Fax (01229) 58855… ✈ rest, TV ☎ P. MC AE D VISA JCB
Meals 11.95 **t.** (dinner) and a la carte 13.50/18.95 **t.** 5.95 – **6 rm** 45.00/65.00 **t.** – SB.

Church Walk House without rest., Church Walk, LA12 7EW, ☎ (01229) 582211 – ✈ **3 rm** 25.00/40.00 **st.**

Bay Horse ⛰ with rm, Canal Foot, LA12 9EL, E : 2 ¼ m. by A 5087, Morecambe Rd a… beyond Industrial area, on the coast ☎ (01229) 583972, Fax (01229) 5805… ≤ Morecambe bay – ✈ rest, TV ☎ P. MC VISA
Meals *(closed lunch Sunday and Monday)* (booking essential) 15.75 (lunch) and a la carte 21.70/25.85 **t.** – **7 rm** (dinner included) 80.00/150.00 **t.** – SB.

ATS The Gill ☎ (01229) 583442

UMBERLEIGH Devon 403 I 31.

London 218 – Barnstaple 7 – Exeter 31 – Taunton 49.

Rising Sun, EX37 9DU, on A 377 ☎ (01769) 560447, Fax (01769) 560764, – ✈ rm, ☎ P. MC VISA JCB
Meals 9.50/14.00 **st.** and dinner a la carte 4.50 – **9 rm** 40.00/77.00 **st.** – SB.

UNDERBARROW Cumbria 402 L 21 – see Kendal.

UP HOLLAND Lancs. 402 M 23 – see Wigan.

UPLYME Devon 403 L 31 – see Lyme Regis.

UPPER BENEFIELD Northants. – see Oundle.

UPPER QUINTON *Warks.* – ⊠ *Stratford-upon-Avon.*
London 95 – Cheltenham 24 – Oxford 43 – Stratford-upon-Avon 6.

⚘ **Winton House** without rest., The Green, CV37 8SX, ℘ (01789) 720500, « Victorian farmhouse », ☞ – ⑂ ℗
closed January, February and 25 December – **3 rm** ⊇ 35.00/48.00.

UPPER SLAUGHTER *Glos.* 403 404 O 28 – *see Bourton-on-the-Water.*

UPPINGHAM *Rutland* 404 R 26 – *pop. 3 140.*
London 101 – Leicester 19 – Northampton 28 – Nottingham 35.

⚘ **Rutland House** without rest., 61 High St. East, LE15 9PY, ℘ (01572) 822497, *Fax* (01572) 822497, ☞ – ⓉⓋ ℗. ⓐⓢ VISA
5 rm ⊇ 30.00/40.00 **t.**

✗✗ **Lake Isle** with rm, 16 High St. East, LE15 9PZ, ℘ (01572) 822951, *Fax* (01572) 822951 – ⓉⓋ ☎ ℗. ⓐⓢ ⒶⒺ ⓪ VISA
Meals *(closed Monday lunch)* 13.50/22.50 **t.** ¶ 6.00 – **10 rm** ⊇ 52.00/69.00 **st.**, 2 suites – SB.

at Morcott Service Area *E* : *4¼ m. by A 6003 on A 47* – ⊠ *Uppingham.*

🏨 **Travelodge,** Glaston Rd, LE15 8SA, ℘ (01572) 747719, *Fax* (01572) 747719, Reservations (Freephone) 0800 850950 – ⑂ rm, ⓉⓋ ⅙ ℗. ⓐⓢ VISA JCB. ✗
Meals *(grill rest.)* – **40 rm** 39.95 **t.**

UPTON ST. LEONARDS *Glos.* – *see Gloucester.*

UPTON SNODSBURY *Worcestershire* 403 404 N 27 – *see Worcester.*

UPTON-UPON-SEVERN *Worcestershire* 403 404 N 27 – *pop. 1 756.*
🄱 *4 High St., WR8 0HB* ℘ (01684) 594200 *(summer only).*
London 116 – Hereford 25 – Stratford-upon-Avon 29 – Worcester 11.

🏨 **Old Schoolhouse,** Severn Stoke, WR8 9JA, *N* : *3 ½ m. by A 4104 on A 38* ℘ (01905) 371368, *Fax* (01905) 371591, ⌧, ☞ – ⑂ ⓉⓋ ☎ ℗ – ⚬ 100. ⓐⓢ VISA
Meals *(closed Saturday lunch)* 12.50/17.50 **st.** and a la carte ¶ 7.95 – **13 rm** ⊇ 42.50/80.00 **t.** – SB.

🏨 **White Lion,** High St., WR8 0HJ, ℘ (01684) 592551, *Fax* (01684) 593333 – ⓉⓋ ☎ ℗. ⓐⓢ ⒶⒺ VISA
closed 25 and 26 December – **Meals** a la carte 17.00/21.30 **st.** ¶ 7.00 – **10 rm** ⊇ 49.95/69.95 **st.** – SB.

UTTOXETER *Staffs.* 402 403 404 O 25 *Great Britain G.* – *pop. 10 329.*
Env. : *Sudbury Hall* ★★ *AC, E* : *5 m. by A 518 and A 50.*
🄱 *Wood Lane* ℘ (01889) 565108.
London 145 – Birmingham 33 – Derby 19 – Stafford 13 – Stoke-on-Trent 16.

🏨 **White Hart,** Carter St., ST14 8EU, ℘ (01889) 562437, *Fax* (01889) 565099 – ⑂ rest, ⓉⓋ ☎ ℗ – ⚬ 50. ⓐⓢ ⒶⒺ ⓪ VISA. ✗
Meals 7.50 **t.** and a la carte ¶ 4.95 – ⊇ 6.00 – **21 rm** 44.00 **t.**

🏨 **Travelodge,** Ashbourne Rd, ST14 5AA, at junction of A 50 with B 5030 ℘ (01889) 562043, *Fax* (01889) 562043, Reservations (Freephone) 0800 850950 – ⑂ rm, ⓉⓋ ⅙ ℗. ⓐⓢ ⒶⒺ ⓪ VISA JCB. ✗
Meals *(grill rest.)* – **32 rm** 44.95 **t.**

at Doveridge *(Derbs.) NE* : *2½ m. by Derby rd on A 50* – ⊠ *Ashbourne.*

✗✗ **Beeches Farmhouse** ⚘ with rm, Waldley, DE6 5LR, *NE* : *2 m. by Marston Lane* ℘ (01889) 590288, *Fax* (01889) 590559, « Working farm », ☞ – ⓉⓋ ☎ ℗. ⓐⓢ ⒶⒺ ⓪ VISA. ✗
closed 5 days Christmas – **Meals** *(closed Sunday dinner)* 10.95 **t.** (lunch) and dinner a la carte 14.25/19.75 **t.** ¶ 4.75 – **10 rm** ⊇ 39.50/65.00 **t.**

◎ ATS Smithfield Rd ℘ (01889) 563848/565201

VAZON BAY *Guernsey (Channel Islands)* 403 P 33 and 230 ⑨ – *see Channel Islands.*

VENN OTTERY *Devon* [403] K 31 – ✉ *Ottery St. Mary.*
London 209 – Exeter 11 – Sidmouth 5.

Venn Ottery Barton ⛰, EX11 1RZ, ☎ (01404) 812733, *Fax (01404) 814713,* « Part 16C », 🌳 – ⊬ rest, [TV] ☎ [P]. [MC] [VISA] [JCB]
Meals (lunch booking essential) 12.95/15.00 **st.** and a la carte 🍷 5.00 – **16 rm** ☕ 36.00/76.00 **st.** – SB.

VENTNOR *I.O.W.* [403] [404] Q 32 – *see Wight (Isle of).*

VERYAN *Cornwall* [403] F 33 *The West Country G.* – *pop. 877* – ✉ *Truro.*
See : *Village★.*
London 291 – St. Austell 13 – Truro 13.

Nare ⛰, Carne Beach, TR2 5PF, SW : 1 ¼ m. ☎ (01872) 501279, *Fax (01872) 501856,* ≤ Carne Bay, ⛱, [Ls], ≘s, ⛱, ⛱, 🌳, 🎾 – [lift] [TV] ☎ [P]. [MC] [VISA]
closed 4 January-1 February – **Meals** 15.00/29.00 **t.** and a la carte 🍷 7.25 – **34 rm** ☕ 88.00/226.00 **t.**, 2 suites.

at Ruan High Lanes *W : 1¼ m. on A 3078* – ✉ *Truro.*

Hundred House, TR2 5JR, ☎ (01872) 501336, *Fax (01872) 501151,* 🌳 – ⊬ rest, [TV] ☎ [P]. [MC] [AE] [VISA]
March-October – **Meals** (dinner only) 22.50 **st.** – **10 rm** ☕ 60.00/120.00 **t.** – SB.

Crugsillick Manor ⛰, TR2 5LJ, SE : ¾ m. by A 3078 on Veryan rd ☎ (01872) 501214 *Fax (01872) 501228,* « Queen Anne manor house of Elizabethan origins », 🌳 – [P]. [MC] [VISA]
Meals (by arrangement) (communal dining) 20.00 **st.** 🍷 7.00 – **3 rm** ☕ 45.00/96.00 **st.**

VIRGINSTOW *Devon.*
London 227 – Bideford 25 – Exeter 41 – Launceston 11 – Plymouth 35.

Percy's at Coombeshead with rm, EX21 5EA, SW : 1 ¼ m. on Tower Hill rc ☎ (01409) 211236, *Fax (01409) 211275,* ≤, 🌳, park – ⊬ [TV] [P]. [MC] [AE] [O] [VISA]
Meals 19.50 **t.** 🍷 4.45 – **8 rm** ☕ 39.00/78.00 **t.** – SB.

WADDESDON *Bucks.* [404] R 28 – *pop. 1 864* – ✉ *Aylesbury.*
London 51 – Aylesbury 5 – Northampton 32 – Oxford 31.

Five Arrows, High St., HP18 0JE, ☎ (01296) 651727, *Fax (01296) 658596,* « Waddesdon Estate hotel », 🌳 – ⊬ [TV] ☎ [P]. [MC] [VISA]. ⊘
Meals a la carte 15.85/23.90 **t.** – **8 rm** ☕ 60.00/75.00 **t.**

WADDINGTON *Lancs.* [402] M 22 – *see Clitheroe.*

WADHURST *E. Sussex* [404] U 30 – *pop. 4 248.*
London 44 – Hastings 21 – Maidstone 24 – Royal Tunbridge Wells 6.

Newbarn ⛰ without rest., Wards Lane, TN5 6HP, E : 3 m. by B 2099 ☎ (01892) 782042 ≤ Bewl Water and countryside, 🌳 – ⊬ [P]. ⊘
closed 25 and 26 December – **3 rm** ☕ 22.00/50.00 **s.**

Kirkstone without rest., Mayfield Lane, TN5 6HX, ☎ (01892) 783204, 🌳 – [P]
3 rm ☕ 20.00/40.00 **st.**

WAKEFIELD *W. Yorks.* [402] P 22 *Great Britain G.* – *pop. 73 955.*
Env. : *Nostell Priory★ AC, SE : 4 ½ m. by A 638.*
⛳18 *City of Wakefield, Lupset Park, Horbury Rd ☎ (01924) 367442* – ⛳18 *28 Woodthorpe Lane Sandal ☎ (01924) 255104* – ⛳9 *Normanton, Snydale Rd ☎ (01924) 892943* – ⛳9 *Painthorpe House, Painthorpe Lane, Crigglestone ☎ (01924) 255083.*
[i] *Town Hall, Wood St., WF1 2HQ ☎ (01924) 305000.*
London 188 – Leeds 9 – Manchester 38 – Sheffield 23.

Cedar Court, Denby Dale Rd., Calder Grove, WF4 3QZ, SW : 3 m. on A 63 ☎ (01924) 276310, *Fax (01924) 280221,* [Ls] – [lift], ⊬ rm, ▤ [TV] ☎ [P] – 🎤 400. [MC] [AE] [O] [VISA]
Meals *(closed Saturday lunch)* 13.50/19.50 **t.** and a la carte – ☕ 8.95 – **146 rm** 90.00 **t**, 5 suites – SB.

Chasley, Queen St., WF1 1JU, ☎ (01924) 372111, *Fax (01924) 383648* – [lift], ⊬ rm, ▤ rest, [TV] ☎ [P] – 🎤 200. [MC] [AE] [O] [VISA]. ⊘
Meals 8.95/15.95 **st.** and dinner a la carte – **63 rm** ☕ 75.00/90.00 **st.** – SB.

🏨 **Forte Posthouse Wakefield,** Queen's Drive, Ossett, WF5 9BE, W : 2 ½ m. on A 638
𝒫 (01924) 276388, Fax (01924) 276437 – 📳, ⚥ rm, 🍽 rest, 📺 ☎ 🅟 – 🛦 150. 🐠 🅰🅴 🅾
🆅🅸🆂🅰 🅹🅲🅱. ⚖
Meals 9.95 **st.** (lunch) and a la carte 16.00/25.65 **st.** ⅙ 7.50 – ☱ 9.95 – **99 rm** 69.00/
79.00 **st.** – SB.

🏨 **Travel Inn,** Denby Dale Rd, Thornes Park, WF2 8DY, W : ½ m. on A 636 𝒫 (01924) 367901
– ⚥ rm, 📺 & 🅟. 🐠 🅰🅴 🅾 🆅🅸🆂🅰. ⚖
Meals (grill rest.) – **42 rm** 36.50 **t.**

at Newmillerdam S : 3 ½ m. on A 61 – ⊠ Wakefield.

🏨 **St. Pierre,** Barnsley Rd, WF2 6QG, 𝒫 (01924) 255596, Fax (01924) 252746 – 📳, ⚥ rm,
🍽 rest, 📺 ☎ & 🅟 – 🛦 100. 🐠 🅰🅴 🅾 🆅🅸🆂🅰 🅹🅲🅱. ⚖
Meals (bar lunch Saturday) 8.95/14.95 **t.** and dinner a la carte ⅙ 5.30 – ☱ 7.25 – **42 rm**
62.50 **st.,** 2 suites – SB.

🅾 ATS Bethel Pl., Thornes Lane 𝒫 (01924) 371638

WALBERSWICK Suffolk 🐧🐧🐧 Y 27 – pop. 1 648 – ⊠ Southwold.
London 97 – Great Yarmouth 28 – Ipswich 32 – Norwich 32.

🏨 **Anchor,** The Street, IP18 6UA, 𝒫 (01502) 722112, ☞ – ⚥ rest, 📺 🅟. 🐠 🆅🅸🆂🅰. ⚖
Meals a la carte 8.85/15.85 **t.** ⅙ 5.00 – **6 rm** ☱ 55.00 **t.**

WALBERTON W. Sussex – see Arundel.

Si vous cherchez un hôtel tranquille,
consultez d'abord les cartes de l'introduction
ou repérez dans le texte les établissements indiqués avec le signe 🕭 *ou* 🕭.

WALKINGTON East Riding 🐧🐧🐧 S 22 – see Beverley.

WALLASEY Mersey. 🐧🐧🐧 🐧🐧🐧 K 23 – pop. 15 642 – ⊠ Wirral.
London 222 – Birkenhead 3 – Liverpool 4.

🏨 **Grove House,** Grove Rd, L45 3HF, 𝒫 (0151) 639 3947, Fax (0151) 639 0028 – 📺 ☎ 🅟 –
🛦 100. 🐠 🅰🅴 🆅🅸🆂🅰. ⚖
Meals (closed Saturday lunch) 12.95/16.95 **t.** and a la carte – ☱ 5.95 – **14 rm** 49.50 **t.**

WALLINGFORD Oxon. 🐧🐧🐧 🐧🐧🐧 Q 29 The West Country G. – pop. 9 315.
Exc. : Ridgeway Path★★.
🅱 Town Hall, Market Place, OX10 0EG 𝒫 (01491) 7826972.
London 54 – Oxford 12 – Reading 16.

🏨 **George,** 84 High St., OX10 0BS, 𝒫 (01491) 836665, Fax (01491) 825359 – ⚥ rm, 📺 ☎ 🅟
– 🛦 120. 🐠 🅾 🆅🅸🆂🅰. ⚖
Meals (dinner only and Sunday lunch)/dinner 17.75 **t.** and a la carte ⅙ 5.75 – ☱ 9.75 –
39 rm 79.00/111.00 **t.** – SB.

at North Stoke S : 2 ¾ m. by A 4130 and A 4074 on B 4009 – ⊠ Wallingford.

🏨 **Springs** 🕭, Wallingford Rd, OX10 6BE, 𝒫 (01491) 836687, Fax (01491) 836877, ≤, ≘s, 🏊,
☞, park – 📺 ☎ 🅟 – 🛦 50. 🐠 🅰🅴 🅾 🆅🅸🆂🅰 🅹🅲🅱. ⚖
Meals 17.00/26.50 **st.** and a la carte ⅙ 9.50 – ☱ 9.50 – **28 rm** 76.00/135.00 **t.,** 2 suites – SB.

WALMERSLEY Gtr. Manchester – see Bury.

WALSALL W. Mids. 🐧🐧🐧 🐧🐧🐧 O 26 – pop. 174 739.
🅱 Calderfields, Aldridge Rd 𝒫 (01922) 640540 CT.
London 126 – Birmingham 9 – Coventry 29 – Shrewsbury 36.

Plan of enlarged area : see Birmingham pp. 2 and 3

🏨 **Quality Friendly,** 20 Wolverhampton Rd West, Bentley, WS2 0BS, W : 2 ½ m. on A 454
𝒫 (01922) 724444, Fax (01922) 723148, 🛋, ≘s, 🏊 – ⚥ rm, 📺 ☎ & 🅟 – 🛦 180. 🐠 🅰🅴
🅾 🆅🅸🆂🅰. ⚖
BT a
Meals (closed Saturday lunch) (carving rest.) 9.65/14.50 **st.** and a la carte ⅙ 5.25 – ☱ 8.75 –
153 rm 72.50/104.00 **st.** – SB.

Boundary, Birmingham Rd, WS5 3AB, SE : 1 ½ m. on A 34 $\mathscr{C}$ (01922) 33555, Fax (01922) 612034, $\%$ – $\boxed{!}$, $\leftthreetimes$ rm, $\blacksquare$ rest, $\boxed{tv}$ $\boxtimes$ $\mathbf{\Theta}$ – $\underline{\mathbf{\Delta}}$ 65. $\boxed{!!}$ $\boxed{AE}$ $\boxed{①}$ $\boxed{VISA}$ — CT e
Meals (bar lunch Monday to Saturday)/dinner 14.95 **st.** and a la carte $\frac{1}{6}$ 5.75 – $\rightleftarrows$ 9.95 – 94 rm 65.00/75.00 **st.** – SB.

Travel Inn, Bentley Rd North, WS2 0WB, W : 2 ¾ m. by A 454 and Bentley South rd $\mathscr{C}$ (01922) 724485, Fax (01922) 724098 – $\leftthreetimes$ rm, $\blacksquare$ rest, $\boxed{tv}$ $\mathbf{\&}$ $\mathbf{\Theta}$. $\boxed{!!}$ $\boxed{AE}$ $\boxed{①}$ $\boxed{VISA}$
Meals (grill rest.) – **40 rm** 36.50 **t.**
BT e

$\boxed{\text{ATS}}$ ATS Leamore Trading Est., Fryers Rd, Bloxwich $\mathscr{C}$ (01922) 478631

WALSGRAVE W. Mids. – see Coventry.

WALTHAM ABBEY Essex $\boxed{404}$ U 28 – pop. 15 629.
London 15 – Cambridge 44 – Ipswich 66 – Luton 30 – Southend-on-Sea 35.

Swallow, Old Shire Lane, EN9 3LX, SE : 1 ½ m. on A 121 $\mathscr{C}$ (01992) 717170, Fax (01992) 711841, I_6, $\cong$, $\boxed{\searrow}$ – $\leftthreetimes$ rm, $\blacksquare$ rest, $\boxed{tv}$ $\boxtimes$ $\mathbf{\&}$ $\mathbf{\Theta}$ – $\underline{\mathbf{\Delta}}$ 220. $\boxed{!!}$ $\boxed{AE}$ $\boxed{①}$ $\boxed{VISA}$. $\%$
Meals 14.50/18.50 **st.** and a la carte $\frac{1}{6}$ 7.50 – **163 rm** $\rightleftarrows$ 105.00/185.00 **st.** – SB.

$\boxed{\text{ATS}}$ ATS Unit 17, Lea Rd Ind. Park, Lea Rd $\mathscr{C}$ (01992) 788050

WALTON LE DALE Lancs. $\boxed{402}$ M 22 – see Preston.

WALTON-ON-THAMES Surrey $\boxed{404}$ S 29.
London 23 – Brighton 54 – Portsmouth 61 – Southampton 65.

Ashley Park, Ashley Park Rd, KT12 1JP, $\mathscr{C}$ (01932) 220196, Fax (01932) 248721 – $\boxed{tv}$ $\boxtimes$ $\mathbf{\Theta}$ – $\underline{\mathbf{\Delta}}$ 60. $\boxed{!!}$ $\boxed{AE}$ $\boxed{①}$ $\boxed{VISA}$
Meals (closed Sunday dinner)(bar lunch Monday to Saturday)/dinner a la carte 9.75/20.15 **t.** – $\rightleftarrows$ 6.00 – **29 rm** 64.00 **t.**

WANSFORD Peterborough $\boxed{404}$ S 26 – see Peterborough.

WANTAGE Oxon. $\boxed{403}$ $\boxed{404}$ P 29 – pop. 9 452.
London 71 – Oxford 16 – Reading 24 – Swindon 21.

Boar's Head, Church St., Ardington, OX12 8QA, E : 2 ½ m. by A 417 $\mathscr{C}$ (01235) 833254 – $\mathbf{\Theta}$. $\boxed{!!}$ $\boxed{①}$
closed Sunday dinner, Monday and 25 December – Meals a la carte 14.50/24.00 **t.** $\frac{1}{6}$ 4.50.

WARE Herts. $\boxed{404}$ T 28 – pop. 17 000.
$\boxed{18}$ Whitehill, Dane End $\mathscr{C}$ (01920) 438495.
London 24 – Cambridge 30 – Luton 22.

Marriott Hanbury Manor H. & Country Club, Thundridge, SG12 0SD, N : 1 ¾ m. b' A 1170 on A 10 $\mathscr{C}$ (01920) 487722, Fax (01920) 487692, $\leqslant$, $\widehat{\ominus}$, « Jacobean style mansior in extensive grounds, walled garden », I_6, $\cong$, $\boxed{\searrow}$, $\boxed{18}$, $\%$ – $\boxed{!}$, $\leftthreetimes$ rm, $\blacksquare$ rest, $\boxed{tv}$ $\boxtimes$ $\mathbf{\Theta}$ - $\underline{\mathbf{\Delta}}$ 100. $\boxed{!!}$ $\boxed{AE}$ $\boxed{①}$ $\boxed{VISA}$ $\boxed{JCB}$
Conservatory : Meals (closed lunch Saturday and Sunday and dinner Sunday to Thursday 25.00/31.50 **st.** and a la carte $\frac{1}{6}$ 15.00 – **Vardon :** Meals (closed dinner Sunday and Monday 19.50 **st.** (lunch) and a la carte 16.75/29.25 **st.** – (see also **Zodiac** below) – $\rightleftarrows$ 14.50 – **85 rm** 160.00/220.00 **st.**, 9 suites – SB.

Zodiac (at Marriott Hanbury Manor H. & Country Club), Thundridge, SG12 0SD, N : 1 ¾ m by A 1170 on A 10 $\mathscr{C}$ (01920) 487722, Fax (01920) 487692 – $\leftthreetimes$ $\mathbf{\Theta}$. $\boxed{!!}$ $\boxed{AE}$ $\boxed{①}$ $\boxed{VISA}$ $\boxed{JCB}$
Meals (dinner only and Sunday lunch)/dinner 31.50 **st.** and a la carte $\frac{1}{6}$ 15.00.

WAREHAM Dorset $\boxed{403}$ $\boxed{404}$ N 31 The West Country G. – pop. 2 454.
See : Town$\star$ – St. Martin's$\star\star$.
Env. : Blue Pool$\star$ AC, S : 3 ½ m. by A 351 – Bovington Tank Museum$\star$ AC, Woolbridg Manor$\star$, W : 5 m. by A 352.
Exc. : Moreton Church$\star\star$, W : 9 ½ m. by A 352 – Corfe Castle$\star$ ($\leqslant\star\star$) AC, SE : 6 m. by A 35 – Lulworth Cove$\star$, SW : 10 m. by A 352 and B 3070.
$\boxed{B}$ Trinity Church, South St., BH20 4LU $\mathscr{C}$ (01929) 552740.
London 123 – Bournemouth 13 – Weymouth 19.

🏨 **Priory** ⟋, Church Green, BH20 4ND, ℰ (01929) 551666, Fax (01929) 554519, ≤, ✿, « Part 16C priory, riverside gardens », ⟍ – ⬇, ✸ rest, 📺 ☎ 🅿. ⓦⓢ ⅀ ⓞ 𝘝𝘐𝘚𝘈 JCB. ✷
Meals 15.95/32.50 **t.** and a la carte 28.50/36.75 **t.** 🍷 7.00 – **17 rm** ⊇ 80.00/215.00 **t.**, 2 suites – SB.

🏨 **Springfield Country,** Grange Rd, BH20 5AL, S : 1 ¼ m. by South St. and West Lane ℰ (01929) 552177, Fax (01929) 551862, 𝟭₆, ⓢ, ⚊, ⬛, ✿, ✷, squash – ▮ ☎ 🅿 – 🔺 200. ⓦⓢ ⅀ ⓞ 𝘝𝘐𝘚𝘈
Meals (bar lunch)/dinner 18.50 **t.** and a la carte 🍷 6.00 – **48 rm** ⊇ 57.00/126.00 **t.** – SB.

🏠 **Kemps Country House,** East Stoke, BH20 6AL, W : 2 ¾ m. on A 352 ℰ (01929) 462563, Fax (01929) 405287, ✿ – ✸ rest, 📺 ☎ 🅿 – 🔺 70. ⓦⓢ ⅀ ⓞ 𝘝𝘐𝘚𝘈. ✷
Meals (closed Saturday lunch) 9.95/19.95 **t.** and a la carte 🍷 5.50 – **15 rm** ⊇ 61.00/86.00 **t.** – SB.

WAREN MILL Northd. – see Bamburgh.

WARMINSTER Wilts. 🄐🄑 N 30 The West Country G. – pop. 16 379.
Env. : Longleat House★★★ AC, SW : 3 m.
Exc. : Stonehenge★★★ AC, E : 18 m. by A 36 and A 303 – Bratton Castle (≤★★) NE : 6 m. by A 350 and B 3098.
🛈 Central Car Park, BA12 9BT ℰ (01985) 218548.
London 111 – Bristol 29 – Exeter 74 – Southampton 47.

🏨 **Bishopstrow House,** BA12 9HH, SE : 1 ½ m. on B 3414 ℰ (01985) 212312, Fax (01985) 216769, ≤, 𝟭₆, ⓢ, ⚊, ⬛, ⟍, ✿, park, ✷indoor/outdoor – ✸ rest, 📺 ☎ 🅿 – 🔺 60. ⓦⓢ ⅀ ⓞ 𝘝𝘐𝘚𝘈
Meals 16.50/29.50 **t.** and a la carte – ⊇ 5.50 – **27 rm** 80.00/175.00 **t.**, 3 suites – SB.

🏠 **Travelodge,** BA12 7RU, NW : 1 ¼ m. by B 3414 at junction of A 36 and A 350 ℰ (01985) 219539, Fax (01985) 214380, Reservations (Freephone) 0800 850950 – ✸ rm, 📺 ☎ 🅿. ⓦⓢ ⅀ ⓞ 𝘝𝘐𝘚𝘈 JCB. ✷
Meals (grill rest.) – **31 rm** 46.95 **t.**

at Heytesbury SE : 3 ¾ m. by B 3414 – ✉ Warminster.

🍴 **Angel Inn** with rm, High St., BA12 0ED, ℰ (01985) 840330, Fax (01985) 840931, « 17C » – 📺 ☎ 🅿. ⓦⓢ ⅀ 𝘝𝘐𝘚𝘈. ✷
Meals (bar lunch Monday to Saturday) a la carte 11.75/20.25 **t.** 🍷 5.95 – **3 rm** ⊇ 37.50/ 49.00 **t.**

at Crockerton S : 1 ¾ m. by A 350 – ✉ Warminster.

🏠 **Springfield House,** BA12 8AU, on Potters Hill rd ℰ (01985) 213696, ✿, ✷ – ✸ 🅿. ✷
closed 25 December – Meals (by arrangement) (communal dining) 16.00 **st.** – **3 rm** ⊇ 36.00/50.00 **st.**

at Horningsham SW : 5 m. by A 362 – ✉ Warminster.

🍴 Bath Arms with rm, BA12 7LY, ℰ (01985) 844308, Fax (01985) 844150, ✿ – 📺 🅿
7 rm.

WARREN STREET Kent 🄓 W 30 – see Lenham.

WARRINGTON Ches. 🄒🄐🄓 M 23 – pop. 82 812.
🛈₆ Hill Warren, Appleton ℰ (01925) 261620 – 🛈₆ Walton Hall, Warrington Rd, Higher Walton ℰ (01925) 266775 – 🛈₆ Birchwood, Kelvin Close ℰ (01925) 818819 – 🛈₆ Leigh, Kenyon Hall, Culcheth ℰ (01925) 763130 – 🛈₆ Alder Root, Alder Root Lane, Winwick ℰ (01925) 291919.
🛈 21 Rylands St., WA1 1EJ ℰ (01925) 442180.
London 195 – Chester 20 – Liverpool 18 – Manchester 21 – Preston 28.

🏨 Village H. & Leisure Club, Centre Park, WA1 1QA, ℰ (01925) 240000, Fax (01925) 445240, 𝟭₆, ⓢ, ⬛, ✷, squash – ▮ ✸, ⬛ rest, 📺 ☎ 🅿 – 🔺 250
87 rm.

🏨 **Holiday Inn Garden Court,** Woolston Grange Av., Woolston, WA1 4PX, E : 3 ¼ m. by A 57 on B 5210 at junction 21 of M 6 ℰ (01925) 838779, Fax (01925) 838859 – ▮, ✸ rm, ⬛ rest, 📺 ☎ 🅿. ⓦⓢ ⅀ ⓞ 𝘝𝘐𝘚𝘈
Meals (dinner only) 13.95 **st.** and a la carte – ⊇ 8.25 – **98 rm** 69.00 **st.** – SB.

🏠 **Travel Inn,** Woburn Rd, WA2 8RN, N : 2 ¼ m. on A 49 ℰ (01925) 414417, Fax (01925) 414544 – ✸ rm, ⬛ rest, 📺 ☎ 🅿. ⓦⓢ ⅀ ⓞ 𝘝𝘐𝘚𝘈. ✷
Meals (grill rest.) – **40 rm** 36.50 **t.**

at Stretton S : 3½ m. by A 49 on B 5356 – ⊠ Warrington.

🏛 **Park Royal International**, Stretton Rd, WA4 4NS, ℘ (01925) 730706,
Fax (01925) 730740, ℔, ≘s, 🔲 – 📳, ✳ rm, 🗐 rest, 🔟 ☎ 🅟 – 🔏 400. 🐠 🖭 ⓪ 🌆
The Harlequin : Meals a la carte 18.05/30.65 t. ⓰ 7.30 – 🖵 8.95 – **112 rm** 96.50/106.50 t.,
2 suites – SB.

🏠 Cat and Lion-Premier Lodge, Tarporley Rd, WA4 4NB, ℘ (01925) 730451,
Fax (01925) 730709 – ✳, 🗐 rest, 🔟 ☎ 🕭 🅟
29 rm.

🔘 ATS Grange Av., Latchford ℘ (01925) 632613

WARWICK Warks. 🔢🔢 P 27 Great Britain G. – pop. 22 476.

See : Town★ - Castle★★ AC Y – Leycester Hospital★ AC Y B – Collegiate Church of
St. Mary★ (Tomb★) Y A.

🏌 Warwick Racecourse ℘ (01926) 494316 Y.

🛈 The Court House, Jury St., CV34 4EW ℘ (01926) 492212.

London 96 – Birmingham 20 – Coventry 11 – Oxford 43.

Plan opposite

🏠 **Old Fourpenny Shop**, 27-29 Crompton St., CV34 6HJ, ℘ (01926) 491360
Fax (01926) 411892 – ✳ 🔟 ☎ 🅟. 🐠 🖭 ⓪ 🌆. ⌗ Y a
Meals (closed Sunday) (bar lunch)/dinner 12.95 t. and a la carte ⓰ 3.80 – **11 rm** 🖵 35.00/
65.00 t. – SB.

🏠 **Charter House**, 87 West St., CV34 6AH, ℘ (01926) 496965, Fax (01926) 411910, « 15C »
�──✳ 🔟 ☎ 🅟. 🐠 🌆 🗾. ⌗ Y c
Meals (by arrangement) 17.50 s. – **3 rm** 🖵 45.00/75.00 s.

🏠 **Park Cottage** without rest., 113 West St., CV34 6AH, ℘ (01926) 410319
Fax (01926) 410319 – ✳ 🔟 ☎ 🅟. 🐠 🌆. ⌗ Y e
closed Christmas – **4 rm** 🖵 50.00/60.00.

at Barford S : 3½ m. on A 429 – Z – ⊠ Warwick.

🏛 **Glebe**, Church St., CV35 8BS, on B 4462 ℘ (01926) 624218, Fax (01926) 624625, ℔, ≘s
🔲, �──📳, 🗐 rest, 🔟 ☎ 🅟 – 🔏 120. 🐠 🖭 ⓪ 🌆
Meals 16.50 t. (dinner) and a la carte 24.45/28.15 t. ⓰ 7.50 – **40 rm** 🖵 90.00/110.00 t.
1 suite – SB.

at Longbridge SW : 2 m. on A 429 – Z – ⊠ Warwick.

🏛 **Hilton National**, Stratford Rd, CV34 6RE, at junction of A 429 with M 4
℘ (01926) 499555, Fax (01926) 410020, ℔, ≘s, 🔲 – 📳, ✳ rm, 🗐 rest, 🔟 ☎ 🕭 🅟 ·
🔏 300. 🐠 🖭 ⓪ 🌆. ⌗
Meals (closed Saturday lunch) (carving lunch) 12.95/19.50 t. and dinner a la carte ⓰ 6.95 ·
🖵 11.50 – **181 rm** 120.00 t.

at Sherbourne SW : 2¾ m. by A 429 – Z – ⊠ Warwick.

🏠 **Old Rectory**, Vicarage Lane, CV35 8AB, at junction with A 46 ℘ (01926) 624562
Fax (01926) 624995, 🌮 – 🔟 ☎ 🅟. 🐠 ⓪ 🌆 🗾
Meals (dinner only) a la carte 14.00/19.50 st. ⓰ 2.90 – **14 rm** 🖵 35.00/70.00 st. – SB.

at Hatton NW : 3½ m. by A 425 on A 4177 – Z – ⊠ Warwick.

🏠 **Northleigh House** without rest., Five Ways Rd, CV35 7HZ, NW : 2 ½ m. by A 417
turning left at roundabout with A 4141 ℘ (01926) 484203, Fax (01926) 484006, 🌮 – ✳ 🅟
🅟. 🐠 🌆.
closed December and January – **7 rm** 🖵 33.00/58.00 st.

at Shrewley NW : 4¾ m. by A 425 and A 4177 – Z – on B 4439 – ⊠ Warwick.

🏠 **Shrewley House** without rest., Hockley Rd, CV35 7AT, on B 4439 ℘ (01926) 84254
Fax (01926) 842216, « Part 17C farmhouse », 🌮 – ✳ 🔟 ☎ 🅟. 🐠 🌆
4 rm 🖵 37.00/62.00 s.

at Honiley NW : 6¾ by A 425 on A 4177 – Z – ⊠ Warwick.

🏛 **Honiley Court**, CV8 1NP, on A 4177 ℘ (01926) 484234, Fax (01926) 484474 – 📳, ✳ rm
🔟 ☎ 🕭 🅟 – 🔏 150. 🐠 🖭 ⓪ 🌆 🗾
Meals (bar lunch Saturday) 16.00 t. (dinner) and a la carte 14.15/19.95 t. ⓰ 6.95 – 🖵 8.95
62 rm 75.00 st. – SB.

606

WARWICK
ROYAL
LEAMINGTON SPA

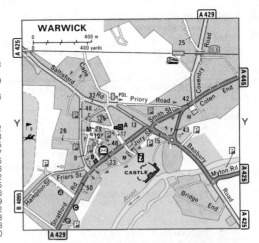

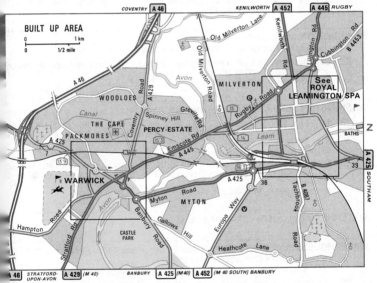

*Piante di città : i nomi delle principali vie commerciali sono scritti
in **rosso** all'inizio dell' indice toponomastico
delle piante di città.*

WARWICK SERVICE AREA Warks. **404** P 27.

🛈 *The Court House, Jury St., CV34 4EW* 𝒫 *(01926) 492212.*

🏨 **Welcome Lodge,** Banbury Rd, Ashorn, CV35 0AA, M 40 (northbound) between junctions
12 and 13 𝒫 (01926) 651681, *Fax (01926) 651634,* Reservations (Freephone) 0800 7314466
– ⇔ rm, 📺 & ℗. **◑❸ Æ ⓪ VISA**. ⬠
Meals (grill rest.) – **56 rm** 45.00 t.

🏨 **Welcome Lodge** without rest., Banbury Rd, Ashorn, CV35 0AA, M 40 (southbound)
between junctions 12 and 13 𝒫 (01926) 651699, *Fax (01926) 65160,* Reservations (Freephone) 0800 7314466 – ⇔ 📺 & ℗. **◑❸ Æ ⓪ VISA**. ⬠
40 rm 45.00 t.

WASDALE HEAD *Cumbria* 402 K 20 – ⊠ *Gosforth.*
London 324 – Kendal 72 – Workington 30.

⌂ **Wasdale Head Inn** ⌖, CA20 1EX, ℰ (019467) 26229, *Fax (019467) 26334,*
≤ Wasdale Head, ⇔ – ⁕ rest, ☎ ❷, ⓪ Ⅸ *VISA* *JCB*
Meals (bar lunch)/dinner 18.00 **st.** ⓵ 5.50 – **9 rm** ⊇ 39.00/78.00 **st.**, 5 suites.

WASHINGBOROUGH *Lincs.* 402 404 S 24 – *see Lincoln.*

WASHINGTON *Tyne and Wear* 401 402 P 19 – *pop. 56 848.*
⊓₈ Washington Moat House, Stone Cellar Rd , Usworth ℰ (0191) 417 2626.
London 278 – Durham 13 – Middlesbrough 32 – Newcastle upon Tyne 7.

⌂ **County H. George Washington,** Stone Cellar Rd, District 12, NE37 1PH,
ℰ (0191) 402 9988, *Fax (0191) 415 1166,* ℻, ⇔, ▢, ⊓₈, squash – ⁕ ⓣ ☎ ❷ – ₰ 200. ⓪
Ⅸ ⓪ *VISA*
Meals 16.50 **st.** and a la carte ⓵ 6.50 – ⊇ 9.75 – **102 rm** 95.00/120.00 **st.**, 1 suite – SB.

⌂ **Forte Posthouse Washington,** Emerson, District 5, NE37 1LB, at junction of A 1(M)
with A 195 ℰ (0191) 416 2264, *Fax (0191) 415 3371* – |≱|, ⁕ rm, ⓣ ☎ ❷ – ₰ 100. ⓪ Ⅸ
⓪ *VISA* *JCB*
Meals a la carte 13.85/25.65 **st.** ⓵ 7.25 – ⊇ 9.95 – **138 rm** 69.00 **st.** – SB.

⌂ **Campanile,** Emerson Rd, Emerson, District 5, NE37 1LE, at junction of A 1(M) with A 195
ℰ (0191) 416 5010, *Fax (0191) 416 5023* – ⁕ rm, ⓣ ☎ ❷ – ₰ 30. ⓪ Ⅸ ⓪ *VISA*
Meals 10.55 **t.** and a la carte ⓵ 4.75 – ⊇ 4.50 – **77 rm** 38.00 **t.**

WASHINGTON *W. Sussex* 404 S 31 – *pop. 1 035.*
London 47 – Brighton 14 – Portsmouth 32 – Worthing 6.

XX **Chardonnay,** Old London Rd, RH20 3BN, N : 1 ¼ m. off A 24 (northbound carriageway
ℰ (01903) 892271 – ⓪ Ⅸ *VISA*
closed Sunday and Monday – **Meals** 19.50/22.50 **t.** ⓵ 5.95.

WASHINGTON SERVICE AREA *Tyne and Wear* – ⊠ *Washington.*

⌂ **Travelodge** without rest., DH3 2SJ, on A 1(M) (southbound carriageway
ℰ (0191) 410 3436, *Fax (0191) 410 0057,* Reservations (Freephone) 0800 850950 – ⁕ ⓣ ☎
℥ ❷. ⓪ Ⅸ ⓪ *VISA* *JCB*. ⌀
36 rm 46.95 **t.**

⌂ **Travelodge,** DH3 2SJ, on A 1 (M) northbound carriageway ℰ (0191) 410 3436
Fax (0191) 410 9258, Reservations (Freephone) 0800 850950 – ⁕ rm, ⓣ ℥ ❷. ⓪ Ⅸ ⓪
VISA *JCB*. ⌀
Meals (grill rest.) – **31 rm** 46.95 **t.**

WATERHEAD *Cumbria* 402 L 20 – *see Ambleside.*

WATERHOUSES *Staffs.* 402 403 404 O 24 *Great Britain G.* – *pop. 1 182* – ⊠ *Stoke-on-Trent.*
Env. : *Dovedale★★ (Ilam Rock★) E : 6 m. by A 523.*
London 115 – Birmingham 63 – Derby 23 – Manchester 39 – Stoke-on-Trent 17.

XX **Old Beams** (Wallis) with rm, Leek Rd, ST10 3HW, ℰ (01538) 308254, *Fax (01538) 30815.*
⌀ ⇔ – ⁕ ⓣ ☎ ❷. ⓪ Ⅸ ⓪ *VISA*. ⌀
closed 2 weeks January and 1 week July – **Meals** *(closed lunch Saturday and Tuesda
Sunday dinner and Monday)* (booking essential) 21.00/39.50 **t.** ⓵ 8.50 – ⊇ 6.50 – **5 rm**
65.00/120.00 **t.**
Spec. Truffle scented risotto with a wild mushroom ravioli, tarragon beurre blanc. Braise
chicken breast with foie gras, olive potatoes and vermouth sauce. Strawberry parfait wit
pink champagne sorbet.

WATERINGBURY *Kent* 404 V 30 – *see Maidstone.*

WATERMILLOCK *Cumbria* 402 L 20 – *see Ullswater.*

WATER YEAT *Cumbria* – *see Coniston.*

WATFORD Herts. **404** S 29 – pop. 113 080.

🏌️₉ Bushey G & C.C., High St. ℰ (0181) 950 2283, BT – 🏌️ Bushey Hall, Bushey Hall Drive ℰ (01923) 222253, BT – 🏌️ Oxhey Park, Prestwick Rd, South Oxhey ℰ (01923) 248312, AT. London 21 – Aylesbury 23.

Plan : see Greater London (North-West)

🏨 **Hilton National**, Elton Way, WD2 8HA, Watford Bypass, E : 3 ½ m. on A 41 at junction with B 462 ℰ (01923) 235881, Fax (01923) 220836, **ᵣ₆**, **⤢**, **▨** – **⫸**, **⤢** rm, **▤** rest, **Ⅳ** **☎** **ℙ** – **🔏** 500. **◍❸** **Æ** **◍** **VISA**. **✾**
BT e
Patio rest. : Meals (closed Saturday lunch) 14.50/20.45 **t.** 🍴 6.50 – **Patio Brasserie :** Meals (closed Friday to Sunday) (dinner only) a la carte 18.70/30.25 **t.** 🍴 6.50 – ⇌ 11.25 – **194 rm** 116.00/126.00 **t.**, 1 suite – SB.

🏨 **Jarvis International**, Watford Bypass, WD2 8HQ, E : 4 m. on A 41 ℰ (0181) 950 6211, Fax (0181) 950 5804, **ᵣ₆**, **⤢**, **▨**, **✾** – **⤢**, **▤** rest, **Ⅳ** **☎** **&** **ℙ** – **🔏** 200. **◍❸** **Æ** **◍** **VISA**
BT a
Meals (carving rest.) (bar lunch Saturday) 12.50/18.50 **st.** 🍴 5.75 – ⇌ 9.25 – **217 rm** 119.00/150.00 **st.** – SB.

WATH-IN-NIDDERDALE N. Yorks. – see Pateley Bridge.

WEAVERHAM Ches. **402 403 404** M 24 – pop. 6 604.
London 191 – Chester 15 – Liverpool 28 – Manchester 28.

🏠 **Oaklands**, Millington Lane, Gorstage, CW8 2SU, SW : 2 m. by A 49 ℰ (01606) 853249, Fax (01606) 852419, **☞** – **Ⅳ** **☎** **ℙ**. **◍❸** **Æ** **VISA**. **✾**
Meals a la carte 17.40/22.85 **t.** – **11 rm** ⇌ 49.00/65.00 **st.**

🏠 **Tall Trees Lodge** without rest., Tarporley Rd, Lower Whitley, WA4 4EZ, N : 2 ¾ m. on A 49 at junction with A 533 ℰ (01928) 790824, Fax (01928) 791330 – **⤢** **Ⅳ** **☎** **&** **ℙ** – **🔏** 40. **◍❸** **Æ** **VISA**
20 rm 38.50 **st.**

WELLAND Worcestershire **403 404** N 27 – see Great Malvern.

WELLESBOURNE Warks. **403 404** P 27 – pop. 5 230 – see Stratford-upon-Avon.

WELLINGBOROUGH Northants. **404** R 27 – pop. 41 602.
🖪 Wellingborough Library, Pebble Lane, NN8 1AS ℰ (01933) 228101.
London 73 – Cambridge 43 – Leicester 34 – Northampton 10.

🏨 **Hind**, Sheep St., NN8 1BY, ℰ (01933) 222827, Fax (01933) 441921 – **⤢**, **▤** rest, **Ⅳ** **☎** **ℙ** – **🔏** 80. **◍❸** **◍** **VISA**. **✾**
Meals 8.50/13.50 **t.** and a la carte 🍴 5.25 – ⇌ 7.25 – **34 rm** 64.50/74.50 **t.** – SB.

🏠 **Travel Inn**, London Rd, NN8 2DP, SE : ¾ m. on A 5193 ℰ (01933) 278606, Fax (01933) 275947 – **⤢** rm, **Ⅳ** **&** **ℙ**. **◍❸** **Æ** **◍** **VISA**
Meals (grill rest.) – **40 rm** 36.50 **t.**

at Finedon NE : 3½ m. by A 510 – ✉ Wellingborough.

🏠 **Tudor Gate**, High St., NN9 5JN, ℰ (01933) 680408, Fax (01933) 680745 – **⤢** **Ⅳ** **☎** **ℙ** – **🔏** 45. **◍❸** **Æ** **◍** **VISA** **JCB**
Meals 18.00 **t.** (dinner) and a la carte 17.40/25.50 **t.** 🍴 4.95 – **27 rm** ⇌ 58.00/90.00 **t.** – SB.

WELLINGTON Wrekin **402 403 404** M 25 – see Telford.

WELLINGTON HEATH Herefordshire **403 404** M 27 – see Ledbury.

When visiting the West Country,
*use the **Michelin Green Guide** "**England: The West Country**".*
- *Detailed descriptions of places of interest*
- *Touring programmes by county*
- *Maps and street plans*
- *The history of the region*
- *Photographs and drawings of monuments,*
  beauty spots, houses...

WELLS Somerset 403 404 M 30 *The West Country G.* – *pop. 9 763.*

See : *City*★★ – *Cathedral*★★★ – *Vicars' Close*★ – *Bishop's Palace*★ (≼★★) *AC* – *St. Cuthbert's*★.

Env. : *Glastonbury*★★ – *Abbey*★★ (*Abbot's Kitchen*★) *AC*, *St. John the Baptist*★★, *Somerset Rural Life Museum*★ *AC*, *Glastonbury Tor*★ (≼★★★), SW : 5 ½ m. by A 39 – *Wookey Hole*★ (*Caves*★ *AC*, *Papermill*★), NW : 2 m.

Exc. : *Cheddar Gorge*★★ (*Gorge*★★, *Caves*★, *Jacob's Ladder* ⁂★) – *St. Andrew's Church*★, NW : 7 m. by A 371 – *Axbridge*★★ (*King John's Hunting Lodge*★, *St. John the Baptist Church*★), NW : 8 ½ m. by A 371.

🖼 *East Horrington Rd* ℘ *(01749) 672868.*

🛈 *Town Hall, Market Pl., BA5 2RB* ℘ *(01749) 672552.*

London 132 – Bristol 20 – Southampton 68 – Taunton 28.

🏥 **Swan**, 11 Sadler St., BA5 2RX, ℘ (01749) 678877, Fax (01749) 677647 – ⁖⁖ rest, 📺 ☎ 🅿 – 🔬 150. 🆗 🆎 ⓪ 𝕍𝕀𝕊𝔸
Meals 14.00/18.50 **t.** ⬧ 4.95 – **38 rm** ⊇ 72.50/89.50 **t.** – SB.

🏥 **The Market Place**, BA5 2RW, ℘ (01749) 672616, Fax (01749) 679670 – 📺 ☎ 🅿. 🆗 🆎 𝕍𝕀𝕊𝔸
Meals (booking essential) 19.50 **st.** (dinner) and a la carte 19.50/24.00 **st.** ⬧ 5.00 – **24 rm** ⊇ 72.50/89.50 **t.** – SB.

🏠 **Beryl** ⌂, BA5 3JP, E : 1 ¼ m. by B 3139 off Hawkers Lane ℘ (01749) 678738, Fax (01749) 670508, ≼, « Victorian Gothic country house, antique furnishings », ⌘, ⌿, park – 📺 ☎ 🅿 – 🔬 30. 🆗 𝕍𝕀𝕊𝔸
closed 25 December – **Meals** *(closed Sunday)* (booking essential) (residents only) (communal dining) (dinner only) 20.00 **st.** ⬧ 4.00 – **6 rm** ⊇ 50.00/85.00 **t.**

🏠 **Infield House** without rest., 36 Portway, BA5 2BN, ℘ (01749) 670989, Fax (01749) 679093, ⌿ – ⁖⁖ 📺 🅿. 🆗 𝕍𝕀𝕊𝔸. ⌘
3 rm ⊇ 34.50/49.00 **st.**

🏠 **White Hart**, Sadler St., BA5 2RR, ℘ (01749) 672056, Fax (01749) 672056 – ⁖⁖ rm, 📺 ☎ 🅿 – 🔬 60. 🆗 🆎 𝕍𝕀𝕊𝔸
Meals (grill rest.) 12.50/15.00 **t.** and a la carte ⬧ 5.25 – **12 rm** ⊇ 50.00/70.00 **t.** – SB.

🏠 **Littlewell Farm**, Coxley, BA5 1QP, SW : 1 ½ m. on A 39 ℘ (01749) 677914, ⌿ – ⁖⁖ 📺 🅿. ⌘
Meals (by arrangement) (communal dining) 17.50 – **5 rm** ⊇ 26.00/46.00 **st.** – SB.

at Wookey Hole *NW : 1 ¾ m. by A 371 –* ✉ *Wells.*

🏠 **Glencot House**, Glencot Lane, BA5 1BH, ℘ (01749) 677160, Fax (01749) 670210, ☎, ⌘, ⌿, park – ⁖⁖ 📺 ☎ 🅿 – 🔬 30. 🆗 🆎 𝕍𝕀𝕊𝔸
Meals *(closed Sunday and Monday to non-residents)* (dinner only) 24.50 **t.** ⬧ 5.40 – **12 rm** ⊇ 60.00/95.00 **t.** – SB.

at Priddy *NW : 6 ¼ m. by A 39 –* ✉ *Wells.*

🏠 **Highcroft** without rest., Wells Rd, BA5 3AU, SE : 1 ¼ m. ℘ (01749) 673446, ≼, ⌿, park – ⁖⁖ 🅿. ⌘
closed November-January – **4 rm** ⊇ 19.00/40.00 **st.**

WELLS-NEXT-THE-SEA Norfolk 404 W 25 *Great Britain G.* – *pop. 2 400.*

Env. : *Holkham Hall*★★ *AC*, W : 2 m. by A 149.

🛈 *Staithe St., NR23 1AN* ℘ *(01328) 710885 (summer only).*

London 117 – King's Lynn 31 – Norwich 36.

✕ **Moorings**, 6 Freeman St., NR23 1BA, ℘ (01328) 710949 – ⁖⁖
closed Sunday lunch, Tuesday, Wednesday, 2 weeks early June and 2 weeks early December – **Meals** - Seafood - (booking essential) 21.50 **t.** ⬧ 5.25.

WELWYN Herts. 404 T 28 – *pop. 10 512 (inc. Codicote).*

London 31 – Bedford 31 – Cambridge 31.

🏠 **Tewin Bury Farm**, AL6 0JB, SE : 3 ½ m. by A 1000 on B 1000 ℘ (01438) 717793, Fax (01438) 840440, ⌿, park – 📺 ☎ 🅿 – 🔬 70. 🆗 𝕍𝕀𝕊𝔸
closed Christmas-New Year – **Meals** 18.50 **t.** (dinner) and lunch a la carte 15.25/16.75 **t** ⬧ 5.50 – **21 rm** ⊇ 63.00/85.00 **t.** – SB.

Le Grand Londres (GREATER LONDON) est composé de la City et de 32 arrondissements administratifs (Borough) eux-mêmes divisés en quartiers ou en villages ayant conservé leur caractère propre (Area).

WEM *Shrops.* 402 403 L 25 – *pop. 4 882 –* ⊠ *Shrewsbury.*
  London 167 – Birmingham 50 – Chester 32 – Stoke-on-Trent 36 – Shrewsbury 8.

  🏠 **Soulton Hall,** SY4 5RS, E : 2 m. on B 5065 ℘ (01939) 232786, *Fax (01939) 234097,*
  « *16C manor house* », ⊰, ☞, park – ‡⊹ rm, 🆃🆅 ☎ 🅿. ⓌⓈ ① 𝗩𝗜𝗦𝗔 𝗝𝗖𝗕. ✷
  Meals (by arrangement) (dinner only) a la carte 19.00/35.00 t. ≬ 5.50 – **6 rm** ⊑ 33.50/
  66.00 t. – SB.

WENDLING *Norfolk* 404 W 25 – *see East Dereham.*

WENTBRIDGE *W. Yorks.* 402 404 Q 23 – ⊠ *Pontefract.*
  London 183 – Leeds 19 – Nottingham 55 – Sheffield 28.

  🏠🏠 **Wentbridge House,** Old Great North Rd, WF8 3JJ, ℘ (01977) 620444,
  Fax (01977) 620148, ☞, park – 🆃🆅 ☎ 🅿 – 🔬 120. ⓌⓈ 𝖠𝖤 ① 𝗩𝗜𝗦𝗔. ✷
  closed 25 December – **Meals** 14.50/21.00 t. and a la carte – **18 rm** ⊑ 69.00/99.00 t.

WEOBLEY *Herefordshire* 403 L 27 – *pop. 1 076 –* ⊠ *Hereford.*
  London 145 – Brecon 30 – Hereford 12 – Leominster 9.

  🏠 **Red Lion,** HR4 8SE, ℘ (01544) 318220, « *14C former inn* » – 🆃🆅 🅿. ⓌⓈ 𝗩𝗜𝗦𝗔. ✷
  closed 24 to 30 December – **Meals** (residents only) (dinner only) 19.50 s. ≬ 4.50 – **5 rm**
  ⊑ 42.50/62.50 – SB.

  ✕✕ **Ye Olde Salutation Inn** with rm, Market Pitch, HR4 8SJ, ℘ (01544) 318443,
  Fax (01544) 318216 – ‡⊹ 🆃🆅 🅿. ⓌⓈ 𝖠𝖤 ① 𝗩𝗜𝗦𝗔 𝗝𝗖𝗕. ✷
  closed 25 December – **Meals** (bar meals Sunday dinner and Monday) a la carte 19.60/
  26.15 t. ≬ 5.00 – **4 rm** ⊑ 40.00/65.00 t.

WEST BAGBOROUGH *Somerset* 403 K 30 – *see Taunton.*

WEST BEXINGTON *Dorset –* ⊠ *Dorchester.*
  London 150 – Bournemouth 43 – Bridport 6 – Weymouth 13.

  🏠🏠 **Manor,** Beach Rd, DT2 9DF, ℘ (01308) 897616, *Fax (01308) 897035,* ≼, ☞ – 🆃🆅 ☎ 🅿. ⓌⓈ
  𝖠𝖤 ① 𝗩𝗜𝗦𝗔. ✷
  Meals 17.45/22.45 t. – **13 rm** ⊑ 52.00/88.00 t. – SB.

WEST BRIDGFORD *Nottingham* 403 404 Q 25 – *see Nottingham.*

WEST BROMWICH *W. Mids.* 403 404 O 26 – *see Birmingham.*

WESTBURY *Wilts.* 403 404 N 30 – *pop. 9 939 (inc. Storridge).*
  🛈 *The Library, Edward St., BA13 3BD* ℘ (01373) 827158.
  London 110 – Bristol 32 – Salisbury 24 – Swindon 38 – Yeovil 40.

  🏠 **Cedar,** Warminster Rd, BA13 3PR, ℘ (01373) 822753, *Fax (01373) 858423,* ☞ – ‡⊹ rest,
  🆃🆅 ☎ 🅿. ⓌⓈ 𝖠𝖤 𝗩𝗜𝗦𝗔
  closed 27 and 28 December – **Meals** a la carte 11.25/19.95 t. ≬ 3.95 – **16 rm** ⊑ 45.00/
  60.00 t. – SB.

  🏠 **Westbury,** Market Pl., BA13 3DQ, ℘ (01373) 822500, *Fax (01373) 824144,* ☞ – 🆃🆅 ☎. ⓌⓈ
  𝖠𝖤 𝗩𝗜𝗦𝗔 𝗝𝗖𝗕. ✷
  closed 25 and 26 December – **Meals** (bar meals Sunday dinner) a la carte 11.00/21.00 t.
  ≬ 4.95 – **7 rm** ⊑ 43.50/69.50 s.

WEST CHILTINGTON *W. Sussex* 404 S 31 – *see Pulborough.*

WEST COKER *Somerset* 403 404 M 31 – *see Yeovil.*

WESTDEAN *E. Sussex – see Seaford.*

WEST DOWN Devon 403 H 30.

Env. : Exmoor National Park★★ – Ilfracombe : Hillsborough (≤★★) AC, Capstone Hill★ (≤★), St. Nicholas' Chapel★ (≤★★) AC, N : 3 m. by A 361 and minor rd.
London 221 – Exeter 52 – Taunton 59.

⌂ **Long House,** The Square, EX34 8NF, ℘ (01271) 863242, ☞ – TV. ℀
restricted opening in winter – **Meals** (by arrangement) 12.50 **st.** – **3 rm** ☐ 28.00/50.00 **st.** – SB.

WESTERHAM Kent 404 U 30 Great Britain G. – pop. 3 207.

Env. : Chartwell★ AC, S : 2 m. by B 2026.
London 24 – Brighton 45 – Maidstone 22.

🏨 **Kings Arms,** Market Sq., TN16 1AN, ℘ (01959) 562990, Fax (01959) 561240 – TV ☎ P. ◑◐
AE ◑ VISA JCB. ℀
Meals a la carte 18.85/33.75 **t.** ⬧ 8.50 – ☐ 8.75 – **17 rm** 75.00/95.00 **st.** – SB.

WEST HADDON Northants. 403 404 Q 26 – see Rugby.

WESTLETON Suffolk 404 Y 27 – pop. 1 317 – ⊠ Saxmundham.
London 97 – Cambridge 72 – Ipswich 28 – Norwich 31.

🏨 **Crown,** IP17 3AD, ℘ (01728) 648777, Fax (01728) 648239, ☞ – ⬧⬧ TV ☎ P. ◑◐ AE ◑ VISA JCB
Meals (bar lunch)/dinner 17.50 **t.** and a la carte ⬧ 5.95 – **19 rm** ☐ (dinner included) 57.50/107.50 **t.** – SB.

⌂ **Pond House** without rest., The Hill, IP17 3AN, ℘ (01728) 648773, ☞ – ⬧⬧ P. ℀
3 rm ☐ 24.00/42.00.

WEST LULWORTH Dorset 403 404 N 32 The West Country G. – pop. 838 – ⊠ Wareham.
See : Lulworth Cove★.
London 129 – Bournemouth 21 – Dorchester 17 – Weymouth 19.

🏨 **Cromwell House,** Main Rd, BH20 5RJ, ℘ (01929) 400253, Fax (01929) 400566, ≤, ⌁, ☞ – TV ☎ P. ◑◐ AE VISA
closed 22 December-4 January – **Meals** (dinner only) 14.00 **t.** and a la carte ⬧ 4.65 – **14 rm** ☐ 38.50/63.00 **t.**

🏨 **Gatton House** without rest., Main Rd, BH20 5RU, ℘ (01929) 400252, Fax (01929) 400252, ☞ – TV P. ◑◐ VISA
March-October – **8 rm** ☐ 37.50/58.00 **st.**

WESTON-SUPER-MARE North Somerset 403 K 29 The West Country G. – pop. 69 372.
See : Seafront (≤★★) BZ.
Exc. : Axbridge★★ (King John's Hunting Lodge★, St. John the Baptist Church★) SE : 9 m. by A 371 – BY – and A 38 – Cheddar Gorge★★ (Gorge★★, Caves★, Jacob's Ladder ☀★) – Clevedon★ (≤★★, Clevedon Court★), NE : 10 m. by A 370 and M 5 – St. Andrew's Church★, SE : 10 ½ m. by A 371.
🏌 Worlebury, Monks Hill ℘ (01934) 623214, BY – 🏌 Uphill Road North ℘ (01934) 626968 AZ.
🛈 Beach Lawns, BS23 1AT ℘ (01934) 888800/641741.
London 147 – Bristol 24 – Taunton 32.

Plan opposite

🏨 **Grand Atlantic,** Beach Rd, BS23 1BA, ℘ (01934) 626543, Fax (01934) 415048, ≤, ☞, ℀ – 🕴 ⬧⬧ TV ☎ P – ⚖ 200. ◑◐ AE ◑ VISA. ℀
BZ e
Meals (bar lunch Monday to Saturday)/dinner 16.95 **st.** and a la carte ⬧ 5.65 – ☐ 9.25 – **76 rm** 60.00/90.00 **st.** – SB.

🏨 **Old Colonial,** 30 Knightstone Rd, BS23 2AW, ℘ (01934) 620739, Fax (01934) 642725, ≤ – TV ☎ P. ◑◐ AE VISA. ℀
BZ a
closed 24 to 26 December – **Meals** (in bar) 12.95 **st.** and a la carte ⬧ 5.00 – **9 rm** ☐ 50.00/65.00 **st.** – SB.

🏨 **Commodore,** Beach Rd, Sand Bay, Kewstoke, BS22 9UZ, by Kewstoke rd (toll)
℘ (01934) 415778, Fax (01934) 636483 – TV ☎ P – ⚖ 120. ◑◐ VISA. ℀
AY e
closed Christmas-New Year – **Meals** (bar lunch Monday to Saturday)/dinner a la carte 12.65/19.00 **t.** – **18 rm** ☐ 50.00/65.00 **st.**

🏨 **Royal,** South Par., BS23 1JN, ℘ (01934) 623601, Fax (01934) 415135 – 🕴 TV ☎ P – ⚖ 250. ◑◐ AE ◑ VISA. ℀
BZ u
Meals (grill rest.) a la carte 9.00/22.50 **t.** – ☐ 6.95 – **37 rm** 40.95/73.90 **t.** – SB.

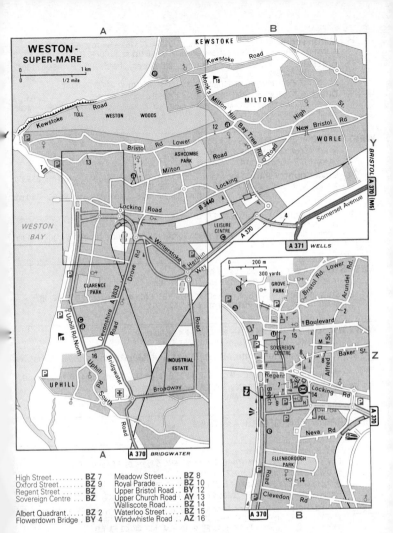

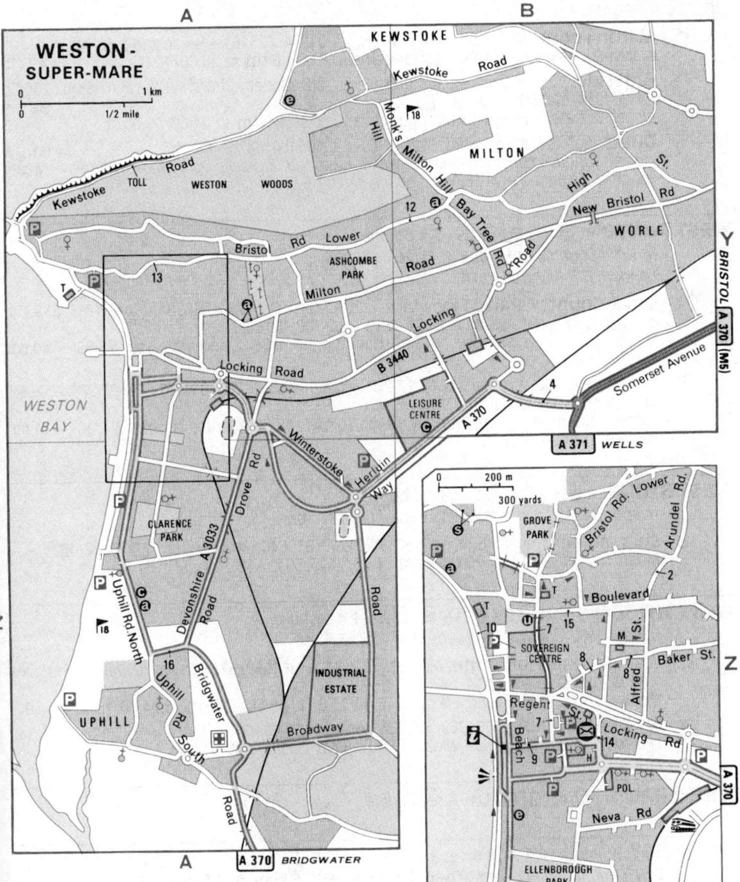
WESTON - SUPER-MARE
0 1 km
0 1/2 mile
KEWSTOKE
Kewstoke Road
Monk's Hill
MILTON
Milton Hill
High St.
New Bristol Rd
WORLE
Kewstoke Toll Road
WESTON WOODS
Bay Tree Rd
Road
Lower Bristol Rd
ASHCOMBE PARK
Milton Road
Locking
Locking Road
B 3440
Somerset Avenue
BRISTOL A 370 (M5)
WESTON BAY
LEISURE CENTRE
A 370
Winterstoke
Herluin Way
Drove Rd
CLARENCE PARK
A 3033
Devonshire Road
Uphill Rd. North
Road
INDUSTRIAL ESTATE
Bridgwater
Uphill Rd South
UPHILL
Broadway
Road
A 370 BRIDGWATER
A 371 WELLS
0 200 m
300 yards
GROVE PARK
Bristol Rd. Lower
Arundel Rd.
Boulevard
SOVEREIGN CENTRE
M St.
Baker St.
Alfred St.
Regent St.
Beach
Locking Rd
POL.
Neva Rd
ELLENBOROUGH PARK
Road
Clevedon Rd
A 370
A
B
Y
Z

Beachlands, 17 Uphill Rd North, BS23 4NG, ☎ (01934) 621401, *Fax (01934) 621966*, ≘, ⛱, – ⇔ rest, TV ☎ P – 🏃 25. MC AE VISA JCB. ✗ — AZ c
closed 23 December-3 January – **Meals** (bar lunch Monday to Saturday)/dinner 14.95 **t.** 6.75 – **17 rm** ☕ 37.50/85.00 **t.** – SB.

Queenswood, Victoria Park, BS23 2HZ, off Upper Church Rd ☎ (01934) 416141, *Fax (01934) 621759* – ⇔ rest, TV ☎. MC AE ⓓ VISA JCB — BZ s
Meals 12.50/14.50 **st.** 4.50 – **17 rm** ☕ 42.50/75.00 **st.** – SB.

Travel Inn, Hutton Moor Rd, BS22 8LY, E : 1 ½ m. by A 370 ☎ (01934) 622625, *Fax (01934) 627401*, – ⇔ rm, TV ♿ P. MC AE ⓓ VISA. ✗ — BY c
Meals (grill rest.) – **40 rm** 36.50 **t.**

Ormonde House without rest., 19 Uphill Rd North, BS23 4NG, ☎ (01934) 412315, ≘, ⛱, – TV P. MC VISA. ✗ — AZ a
6 rm ☕ 30.00/45.00 **st.**

Ashcombe Court, 17 Milton Rd, BS23 2SH, ☎ (01934) 625104, *Fax (01934) 625104* – ⇔ TV P. ✗ — AY a
Meals (by arrangement) 10.00 **st.** – **6 rm** ☕ 25.00/39.00 – SB.

⌂ **Milton Lodge**, 15 Milton Rd, BS23 2SH, ℘ (01934) 623161 – ↨ rest, 📺 🅿. ⌘
March-September – **Meals** (by arrangement) 8.00 – **6 rm** ⌷ 25.00/40.00.   AY a

⌂ **Braeside**, 2 Victoria Park, BS23 2HZ, off Upper Church Rd ℘ (01934) 626642,
Fax (01934) 626642 – ↨ rest, 📺   BZ s
closed October – **Meals** (by arrangement) 10.00 st. – **9 rm** ⌷ 24.00/48.00 st.

✗ **Duets**, 103 Upper Bristol Rd, BS22 8ND, ℘ (01934) 413428 – 🆎 🆅🆂🅰   BY a
closed Sunday dinner, Monday, 1 week June and 2 weeks October-November – **Meals**
(lunch by arrangement) 16.95 **t.** and a la carte ₰ 6.95.

WEST RUNTON *Norfolk* **404** X 25 – ✉ *Cromer*.
  ⛳ *Links Country Park Hotel* ℘ (01263) 838383.
  London 135 – King's Lynn 42 – Norwich 24.

🏨 **Links Country Park**, Sandy Lane, NR27 9QH, ℘ (01263) 838383, *Fax (01263) 838264*,
🌅, 🔲, ⛳, ☞, ✗ – ⑂, 🍽 rest, 📺 ☎ 🅿 – 🔬 200. 🆎 🆅🆂🅰
Meals (bar lunch Monday to Saturday)/dinner 19.75 **t.** and a la carte ₰ 5.65 – **40 rm**
⌷ 62.50/135.00 **t.** – SB.

🏠 **Dormy House**, Cromer Rd, NR27 9QA, on A 149 ℘ (01263) 837537, *Fax (01263) 837537*,
☞ – ⑂ 📺 ☎ 🅿. 🆎 🆎🅴 🆅🆂🅰. ⌘
Meals (dinner only and Sunday lunch)/dinner 15.50 **t.** and a la carte ₰ 4.20 – **14 rm**
⌷ 46.50/73.00 **t.** – SB.

WEST STOUR *Dorset – pop. 159 – ✉ Gillingham*.
  London 119 – Bournemouth 35 – Salisbury 28 – Yeovil 15.

🍴 **Ship Inn** with rm, SP8 5RP, on A 30 ℘ (01747) 838640, ☞ – ↨ rest, 📺 🅿. 🆎 🆅🆂🅰
Meals a la carte 9.40/17.70 **t.** – **7 rm** ⌷ 29.50/47.50 **t.** – SB.

WEST WITTON *N. Yorks.* **402** O 21 – *pop. 325* – ✉ *Leyburn*.
  London 241 – Kendal 39 – Leeds 60 – York 53.

🏠 **Wensleydale Heifer Inn**, Main St., DL8 4LS, ℘ (01969) 622322, *Fax (01969) 624183*, ☞
– 📺 ☎ 🅿. 🆎 🆅🆂🅰
Meals 23.50 **t.** (dinner) and a la carte 15.40/23.85 **t.** ₰ 5.50 – **15 rm** ⌷ 54.00/75.00 **t.** – SB.

⌂ **Ivy Dene**, DL8 4LP, ℘ (01969) 622785, ☞ – ↨ 📺 🅿. ⌘
closed 24 to 26 December – **Meals** 13.00 – **5 rm** ⌷ 39.00/48.00 – SB.

WETHERAL *Cumbria* **401** **402** L 19 – *see Carlisle*.

WETHERBY *W. Yorks.* **402** P 22 *Great Britain G.* – *pop. 8 154*.
  Env. : *Harewood House★★ (The Gallery★) AC, SW : 5 ½ m. by A 58 and A 659*.
  ⛳ *Linton Lane, Linton* ℘ (01937) 580089.
  🛈 *Council Offices, 24 Westgate, LS22 6NL* ℘ (01937) 582706.
  London 208 – Harrogate 8 – Leeds 13 – York 14.

🏨 **Wood Hall** ⌘, Trip Lane, Linton, LS22 4JA, SW : 3 m. by A 661 and Linton Rd
℘ (01937) 587271, *Fax (01937) 584353*, ≤, « Part Jacobean and Georgian country house in
park », 🗴, 🔲, ☞, ☞ – ⑂, 🍽 rest, 📺 ☎ 🅿 – 🔬 140. 🆎 🆎🅴 🆎 🆅🆂🅰
Meals *(closed Saturday lunch)* 15.95/29.95 **t.** ₰ 9.95 – ⌷ 9.95 – **41 rm** 99.00/130.00 **t.**,
1 suite – SB.

🏨 **Linton Springs** ⌘, Sicklinghall Rd, LS22 4AF, W : 1 ¾ m. by A 661 ℘ (01937) 585353,
Fax (01937) 587579, ☞, park, ✗ – 📺 ☎ 🅿 – 🔬 70. 🆎 🆎🅴 🆎 🆅🆂🅰. ⌘
closed 1 January – **Meals** *(closed Sunday dinner)* a la carte 16.70/22.45 ₰ 4.95 – **11 rm**
⌷ 65.00/85.00, 1 suite.

🏨 **Jarvis Wetherby**, Leeds Rd, LS22 5HE, W : ½ m. on A 58 ℘ (01937) 583881,
Fax (01937) 580062 – ↨ rm, 📺 ☎ 🅿 – 🔬 150. 🆎 🆎🅴 🆎 🆅🆂🅰
Meals (carving lunch) 11.00/14.95 **t.** and dinner a la carte ₰ 7.00 – ⌷ 10.95 – **72 rm** 79.00/
89.00 **st.** – SB.

WETHERSFIELD *Essex* **404** V 28 – *pop. 1 204* – ✉ *Braintree*.
  London 52 – Cambridge 31 – Chelmsford 19 – Colchester 22.

✗✗ **Dicken's**, The Green, CM7 4BS, ℘ (01371) 850723, « Part 17C house » – 🅿. 🆎 🆅🆂🅰
closed Sunday dinner, Monday and Tuesday – **Meals** 9.50 **t.** (lunch) and a la carte 18.65/
24.20 **t.**

WEYBRIDGE Surrey 404 S 29 – *pop. 52 802 (inc. Walton)*.
London 23 – Crawley 27 – Guildford 17 – Reading 33.

Oatlands Park, Oatlands Drive, KT13 9HB, NE : ¾ m. by A 317 on A 3050
ℰ (01932) 847242, *Fax (01932) 842252,* ₤₅, ≈, park, ℅ – ⁅▮⁆, ⁅✦⁆ rm, 🆅 ☎ 🅿 – 🔬 300. 🆎
🆎 ⓪ VISA
Meals (bar lunch Saturday) 19.50/21.50 **t.** and a la carte ₫ 5.95 – **123 rm** ☑ 100.00/
145.00 **t.,** 5 suites – SB.

Ship Thistle, Monument Green, High St., KT13 8BQ, off A 317 ℰ (01932) 848364,
Fax (01932) 857153 – ⁅✦⁆, ▤ rest, 🆅 ☎ 🅿 – 🔬 150. 🆎 🆎 ⓪ VISA. ℅
Meals *(closed 26 December-2 January)* (bar lunch Saturday) 13.95/18.25 **t.** and a la carte
₫ 7.95 – ☑ 11.00 – **39 rm** 110.00/125.00 **t.** – SB.

Casa Romana, 2 Temple Hall, Monument Hill, KT13 3RH, on A 317 ℰ (01932) 843470,
Fax (01932) 845221 – ▤ 🅿. 🆎 ⓪ VISA JCB
closed Saturday lunch and 25-26 December – **Meals** - Italian - 14.95/18.95 **t.** and a la carte
₫ 6.00.

WEYMOUTH Dorset 403 404 M 32 *The West Country G.* – *pop. 46 065.*
See : Town★ – Timewalk★ **AC** – Nothe Fort (≤★) **AC** – Boat Trip★ (Weymouth Bay and
Portland Harbour) **AC**.
Env. : Chesil Beach★★ – Portland★ - Portland Bill (✳★★) S : 2 ½ m. by A 354.
Exc. : Maiden Castle★★ (≤★) N : 6 ½ m. by A 354 – Abbotsbury★★ (Swannery★ **AC**,
Sub-Tropical Gardens★ **AC**, St. Catherine's Chapel★) NW : 9 m. by B 3157.
₆ Links Road ℰ (01305) 773981.
🅱 The King's Statue, The Esplanade, DT4 7AN ℰ (01305) 785747.
London 142 – Bournemouth 35 – Bristol 68 – Exeter 59 – Swindon 94.

Rex, 29 The Esplanade, DT4 8DN, ℰ (01305) 760400, *Fax (01305) 760500* – ⁅▮⁆ 🆅 ☎ ⟨⟩.
🆎 🆎 ⓪ VISA
closed 24 to 30 December – **Meals** (bar lunch)/dinner 11.50 **t.** and a la carte ₫ 3.95 – **30 rm**
☑ 55.00/90.00 **t.** – SB.

Bay Lodge, 27 Greenhill, DT4 7SW, ℰ (01305) 782419, *Fax (01305) 782828* – ⁅✦⁆ rest, 🆅
☎ 🅿. 🆎 🆎 ⓪ VISA JCB
closed November – **Meals** (dinner only) a la carte 11.85/21.85 **t.** ₫ 3.95 – **12 rm** ☑ 29.50/
70.00 **t.** – SB.

Chatsworth, 14 The Esplanade, DT4 8EB, ℰ (01305) 785012, *Fax (01305) 766342* – 🆅 ☎.
🆎 VISA. ℅
Meals 16.00 **st.** – **7 rm** ☑ 34.00/68.00 **st.,** 1 suite – SB.

Perry's, The Old Harbour, 4 Trinity Rd, DT4 8TJ, ℰ (01305) 785799 – 🆎 VISA
*closed lunch Monday and Saturday, Sunday dinner October-March, 1 January and
25-26 December* – **Meals** a la carte 11.45/23.00 **t.** ₫ 6.00.

Mallams at the Quay, The Old Harbour, 5 Trinity Rd, DT4 8TJ, ℰ (01305) 776757 – 🆎 🆎
VISA
closed Saturday lunch and Sunday except June-September and 25-26 December –
Meals 15.95/18.95 **t.** ₫ 6.00.

at Moonfleet NW : 4½ m. by B 3157 – ⊠ Weymouth.

Moonfleet Manor ⌂, DT3 4ED, ℰ (01305) 786948, *Fax (01305) 774395,* ≤, ≈, ℅,
squash – 🆅 ☎ 🅿 – 🔬 60. 🆎 🆎 ⓪ VISA JCB
Meals (dinner only) 15.50 **t.** and a la carte – **38 rm** ☑ 40.00/150.00 **t.**

WHALLEY Lancs. 402 M 22 – *pop. 5 364* – ⊠ Blackburn.
₆ Long Leese Barn, Clerkhill ℰ (01254) 822236.
London 233 – Blackpool 32 – Burnley 12 – Manchester 28 – Preston 15.

Foxfields Country, Whalley Rd, Billington, BB7 9HY, SW : 1 ¼ m. ℰ (01254) 822556,
Fax (01254) 824613, ₤₅, ≋, ⬚, ≈ – ⁅✦⁆, ▤ rest, 🆅 ☎ ♿ 🅿 – 🔬 150. 🆎 🆎 ⓪ VISA. ℅
***Expressions :* Meals** (bar lunch Saturday) (dancing Saturday evening) 11.50/
18.95 **t.** and a la carte ₫ 6.00 – **18 rm** ☑ 90.00/100.00 **t.,** 26 suites 115.00/120.00 **t.** – SB.

WHAPLODE Lincs. 402 404 T 25 – *pop. 1 929* – ⊠ Spalding.
London 106 – Lincoln 45 – Leicester 61 – Norwich 60.

Guy Wells ⌂, Eastgate, PE12 6TZ, E : ½ m. by A 151 ℰ (01406) 422239, « Queen Anne
house », ≈ – ⁅✦⁆ 🅿. ℅
closed 20 to 27 December – **Meals** (by arrangement) 10.00 **st.** – **3 rm** ☑ 25.00/42.00 **st.**

WHARRAM-LE-STREET N. Yorks. – *see Malton.*

ENGLAND

WHEATLEY *Oxon.* 403 404 Q 28 – *see Oxford.*

WHEELOCK *Ches. – see Sandbach.*

WHIMPLE *Devon* 403 J 31 – *see Exeter.*

WHITBY *N. Yorks.* 402 S 20 – *pop. 13 640.*
        ⋒ *Sandsend Rd, Low Straggleton* ℘ *(01947) 602768.*
        🛈 *Langborne Rd, YO21 1YN* ℘ *(01947) 602674.*
        London 257 – Middlesbrough 31 – Scarborough 21 – York 45.

🏨 **Larpool Hall Country House** ⤬, Larpool Lane, YO22 4ND, SE : 1 m. by A 171
        ℘ (01947) 602737, Fax (01947) 820204, ≤, ☞, park – 📺 ☎ 🅿 – 🔬 200. 🐵 🔤 *VISA*. ⤬
        Meals *(closed Sunday lunch)* 21.95 **t.** (dinner) and a la carte 16.00/28.15 **t.** ⌽ 4.55 – **20 rm**
        ⌸ 55.00/120.00 **t.** – SB.

at Dunsley *W : 3¼ m. by A 171* – ⊠ *Whitby.*

🏨 **Dunsley Hall** ⤬, YO21 3TL, ℘ (01947) 893437, Fax (01947) 893505, ≤, 🛵, ⭍, 🔲, ☞,
        ⤬ – ⭍⤬ 📺 ☎ 🅿. 🐵 🔤 *VISA*. ⤬
        Meals (light lunch Monday to Saturday) 12.95/22.95 **st.** and dinner a la carte ⌽ 7.45 – **18 rm**
        ⌸ 54.50/130.00 **st.** – SB.

WHITEPARISH *Wilts.* 403 404 P 30 – *see Salisbury.*

WHITEWELL *Lancs.* 402 M 22 – *pop. 5 617* – ⊠ *Clitheroe.*
        London 281 – Lancaster 31 – Leeds 55 – Manchester 41 – Preston 13.

🏨 **Inn at Whitewell,** Forest of Bowland, BB7 3AT, ℘ (01200) 448222, Fax (01200) 448298,
        ≤, « Memorabilia », 🎣, ☞ – 📺 ☎ 🅿. 🐵 🔤 ⓘ *VISA* 🔤
        Meals (bar lunch)/dinner a la carte 21.10/27.40 **st.** ⌽ 5.00 – **10 rm** ⌸ 58.00/89.00 **st.**,
        1 suite.

WHITLEY BAY *Tyne and Wear* 401 402 P 18 – *pop. 33 335.*
        🛈 *Park Rd, NE26 1EJ* ℘ *(0191) 200 8535.*
        London 295 – Newcastle upon Tyne 10 – Sunderland 10.

🏨 **Windsor,** South Par., NE26 2RF, ℘ (0191) 251 8888, Fax (0191) 297 0272 – ▯, 🍽 rest, 📺
        ☎ 🅿 – 🔬 100. 🐵 🔤 ⓘ *VISA*
        Meals (bar lunch)/dinner 12.75 **t.** and a la carte ⌽ 5.00 – **63 rm** ⌸ 59.00/70.00 **st.**
        ⓐ ATS John St., Cullercoats ℘ (0191) 253 3903

WHITNEY-ON-WYE *Herefordshire* 403 K 27 – *pop. 133* – ⊠ *Hereford.*
        London 150 – Birmingham 56 – Cardiff 73 – Hereford 17.

🏠 **Rhydspence Inn,** HR3 6EU, W : 1½ m. on A 438 ℘ (01497) 831262, Fax (01497) 831751,
        « Part 14C », ☞ – 📺 🅿. 🐵 🔤 *VISA*. ⤬
        closed 2 weeks January – **Meals** a la carte 20.25/30.25 **t.** ⌽ 4.95 – **7 rm** ⌸ 32.50/65.00 **t.** –
        SB.

WHITSTABLE *Kent* 404 X 29 – *pop. 28 907* – ⊠ *Whitstable.*
        London 68 – Dover 24 – Maidstone 37 – Margate 12.

✗ **Whitstable Oyster Fishery Co.,** Royal Native Oyster Stores, The Horsebridge, CT5
        1BU, ℘ (01227) 276856, Fax (01227) 770666, ≤, « Converted warehouse on beach » – 🐵
        🔤 ⓘ *VISA*
        closed Monday except 20 July, 5 September and 24 to 26 December – **Meals** - Seafood -
        a la carte 17.45/26.45 **t.** ⌽ 6.00.

at Wraik Hill *SW : 2 m. by A 290 and A 299 on Wraik Hill Rd* – ⊠ *Whitstable.*

🏠 **Barnfield at Windyridge** ⤬, CT5 3BY, ℘ (01227) 263506, Fax (01227) 771191, ≤, ☞
        – 📺 ☎ 🅿. 🐵 🔤 ⓘ *VISA*
        Meals (by arrangement) 15.00 **s.** ⌽ 5.00 – **8 rm** ⌸ 25.00/50.00 **s.**

at Thanet Way Service Area *SW : 3¼ m. by A 290 on A 299* – ⊠ *Faversham.*

🏠 **Travelodge,** ME13 9EL, (eastbound carriageway) ℘ (01227) 770980, Reservations (Free-
        phone) 0800 850950 – ⭍⤬ rm, 📺 🅿. 🐵 🔤 ⓘ *VISA* 🔤. ⤬
        Meals (grill rest.) – **40 rm** 44.95 **t.**

616

WHITTLE-LE-WOODS Lancs. 🎟️ M 23 – see Chorley.

WICKFORD Essex 🎟️ V 29 – see Basildon.

WICKHAM Hants. 🎟️ 🎟️ Q 31 – pop. 2 941.
London 74 – Portsmouth 12 – Southampton 11 – Winchester 16.

🏠 **Old House,** The Square, PO17 5JG, ℰ (01329) 833049, Fax (01329) 833672, « Queen Anne house », 🌳 – 📺 ☎ 🅿. 🐾 🝊 ⓪ 𝘝𝘐𝘚𝘈. ⚜
closed 1 week Easter, 2 weeks August, and 10 days Christmas – **Meals** - French - (closed lunch Monday and Saturday and Sunday) 27.00 **st.** 🝊 7.00 – 🖙 10.00 – **12 rm** 65.00/80.00 **st.** – SB.

WIDEGATES Cornwall 🎟️ G 32 – see Looe.

WIDNES Halton 🎟️ 🎟️ 🎟️ L 23 – pop. 57 162.
🏌️ Highfield Rd ℰ (0151) 424 2440.
London 205 – Liverpool 19 – Manchester 27 – Stoke-on-Trent 42.

🏠 **Everglades Park,** Derby Rd, WA8 3UJ, NE : 3 m. by A 568 on A 5080 ℰ (0151) 495 2040, Fax (0151) 424 6536 – 🐾 rm, 🍽 rest, 📺 ☎ 🅿 – 🔬 200. 🐾 🝊 ⓪ 𝘝𝘐𝘚𝘈 𝘑𝘊𝘉. ⚜
Meals (bar lunch)/dinner 14.95 **st.** and a la carte 🝊 5.85 – 🖙 8.50 – **68 rm** 60.00/72.00 **st.**

at Cronton NW : 2 m. by A 568 on A 5080 – ✉ Widnes.

🏠 **Hillcrest,** Cronton Lane, WA8 9AR, ℰ (0151) 424 1616, Fax (0151) 495 1348 – 🛗 📺 ☎ 🅿 – 🔬 120. 🐾 🝊 𝘝𝘐𝘚𝘈 𝘑𝘊𝘉
Meals (bar lunch Saturday) (carving lunch Sunday) 14.95 **st.** (dinner) and a la carte 12.25/ 26.45 **t.** 🝊 5.65 – **49 rm** 🖙 59.00/125.00 **t.** – SB.

🔧 ATS Tanhouse Lane ℰ (0151) 424 3011/2945

WIGAN Gtr. Manchester 🎟️ M 23 – pop. 85 819.
London 203 – Liverpool 18 – Manchester 24 – Preston 18.

🏠 **The Bellingham,** 149 Wigan Lane, WN1 2NB, N : 1 ¼ m. on A 49 ℰ (01942) 243893, Fax (01942) 821027 – 🛗 🐾 📺 ☎ 🅿 – 🔬 100. 🐾 🝊 ⓪ 𝘝𝘐𝘚𝘈. ⚜
Meals (bar lunch Sunday) 15.75 **st.** and a la carte – **32 rm** 🖙 58.00/68.00 **st.**

🏠 **Wigan Oak,** Riverway, WN1 3SS, access by Orchard St. ℰ (01942) 826888, Fax (01942) 825800 – 🛗, 🐾 rm, 📺 ☎ 🅿 – 🔬 200. 🐾 🝊 ⓪ 𝘝𝘐𝘚𝘈
Meals 15.95 **st.** and a la carte 🝊 7.95 – 🖙 7.50 – **88 rm** 65.00/75.00 **st.** – SB.

🏠 **Travel Inn,** Warrington Rd, Marus Bridge, WN3 6XB, S : 2 ¾ m. on A 49 ℰ (01942) 493469, Fax (01942) 498679 – 🐾 rm, 📺 🕭 🅿. 🐾 🝊 ⓪ 𝘝𝘐𝘚𝘈
Meals (grill rest.) – **41 rm** 36.50 **t.**

🏠 **Travel Inn,** Orrell Rd, Orrell, WN5 8HQ, W : 3 ½ m. on A 577 ℰ (01942) 211516, Fax (01942) 215002 – 🐾 📺 🕭 🅿 – 🔬 80. 🐾 🝊 ⓪ 𝘝𝘐𝘚𝘈. ⚜
Meals (grill rest.) – **40 rm** 36.50 **t.**

at Up Holland W : 4 ¾ m. on A 577 – ✉ Wigan.

🏠 Lancashire Manor, Prescott Rd, WN8 9PU, SW : 2 ¾ m. by A 577 and Stannanought Rd ℰ (01695) 720401, Fax (01695) 50953 – 🐾 rm, 🍽 rest, 📺 ☎ 🕭 🅿 – 🔬 200
55 rm.

XXX **Churchills,** Lafford Lane, WN8 0QZ, ℰ (01695) 624426, Fax (01695) 622433 – 🅿. 🐾 🝊 ⓪ 𝘝𝘐𝘚𝘈
closed 25-26 December and 1 January – **Meals** (dinner only and Wednesday and Sunday lunch) 21.95 **t.** and a la carte 🝊 8.90.

🔧 ATS 98 Warrington Rd, Newtown ℰ (01942) 242017/242442

WIGHT (Isle of) 🎟️ 🎟️ PQ 31 32 Great Britain G. – pop. 124 577.
See : Island★★.
Env. : Osborne House, East Cowes★★ AC – Carisbrooke Castle, Newport★★ AC (Keep ≤★) – Brading★ (Roman Villa★ AC, St. Mary's Church★, Nunwell House★ AC) – Shorwell : St. Peter's Church★ (wall paintings★).
🚢 from East Cowes to Southampton (Red Funnel Ferries) frequent services daily (55 mn) – from Yarmouth to Lymington (Wightlink Ltd) frequent services daily (30 mn) – from Fishbourne to Portsmouth (Wightlink Ltd) frequent services daily (35 mn).
🚢 from Ryde to Portsmouth (Hovertravel Ltd) frequent services daily (10 mn) – from Ryde to Portsmouth (Wightlink Ltd) frequent services daily (15 mn).

WIGHT (Isle of)

Alverstone – ⊠ Isle of Wight.

⌂ **Grange** ॐ, PO36 0EZ, ℘ (01983) 403729, Fax (01983) 403729, 氣 – ⥲ ℗. ※
closed December and January – **Meals** 13.50 **st.** – **7 rm** ⊇ 19.00/52.00 **st.**

Chale – pop. 717 – ⊠ Isle of Wight.
Newport 9.

🏛 **Clarendon H. and Wight Mouse Inn,** Newport Rd, PO38 2HA, ℘ (01983) 730431,
Fax (01983) 730431, ≤, 氣 – ⊺ⅴ ℗. ◍◍ 𝘝𝘐𝘚𝘈
Meals 10.00/13.50 **st.** and a la carte 🛦 4.75 – **12 rm** ⊇ 50.00/90.00 **st.**, 1 suite.

Cowes – pop. 16 335 – ⊠ Isle of Wight.
🟥 Osborne, Osborne House Estate, East Cowes ℘ (01983) 295421.
🔋 The Arcade, Fountain Quay, PO31 3AR ℘ (01983) 291914.
Newport 4.

🏛 New Holmwood, Queens Rd, Egypt Point, PO31 8BW, ℘ (01983) 292508,
Fax (01983) 295020, ≤, 🏡, ⤨ – ▤ rest, ⊺ⅴ ☎ ℗ – 🛦 150
24 rm, 2 suites.

Freshwater – pop. 7 317 (inc. Totland) – ⊠ Isle of Wight.
Newport 13.

🏠 **Yarlands Country House** ॐ, Victoria Rd, PO40 9PP, ℘ (01983) 752574, 氣 – ⥲ rest,
⊺ⅴ ℗. ◍◍ 𝘝𝘐𝘚𝘈 𝘑𝘊𝘉. ※
March-October – **Meals** (dinner only) 12.00 **t.** 🛦 4.95 – **6 rm** ⊇ 33.00/54.00 **t.**

⌂ **Rockstone Cottage,** Colwell Chine Rd, PO40 9NR, NW : ¾ m. by A 3055 off A 3054
℘ (01983) 753723, 氣 – ⥲ rest, ⊺ⅴ ℗
Meals (by arrangement) 11.00 **st.** – **5 rm** ⊇ 22.00/44.00 **st.**

Niton – ⊠ Isle of Wight.

🏠 **Windcliffe Manor** ॐ, Sandrock Rd, Undercliff, PO38 2NG, ℘ (01983) 730215,
Fax (01983) 730215, 🏡, 氣 – ⥲ rest, ⊺ⅴ ☎ ℗. ◍◍ 𝘈𝘌 ① 𝘝𝘐𝘚𝘈 𝘑𝘊𝘉
closed 2 weeks November – **Meals** (light lunch Monday to Saturday) 11.95/17.95 **t.**
and a la carte 🛦 5.85 – **14 rm** ⊇ (dinner included) 51.50/103.00 **t.** – SB.

⌂ **Pine Ridge,** The Undercliff, PO38 2LY, ℘ (01983) 730802, Fax (01983) 731001, 氣 –
⥲ rest, ⊺ⅴ ☎ ℗. ◍◍ 𝘝𝘐𝘚𝘈
Meals 17.95 **st.** 🛦 4.00 – **7 rm** ⊇ 38.50/75.00 **st.**

Ryde – ⊠ Isle of Wight.
🟥 Binstead Rd ℘ (01983) 614809.
🔋 81-83 Union St., PO33 2LW ℘ (01983) 562905.
Newport 7.

⌂ **Little Upton Farm** ॐ without rest., Gatehouse Rd, Ashey, PO33 4BS, SW : 2 m. by Wes
St. ℘ (01983) 563236, Fax (01983) 563236, ≤, « 17C farmhouse, working farm », 氣, park –
⊺ⅴ ℗
3 rm ⊇ 20.00/40.00.

St. Lawrence – ⊠ Isle of Wight.
Newport 16.

⌂ **Little Orchard** without rest., Undercliffe Drive, PO38 1YA, W : 1 m. on A 305
℘ (01983) 731106, 氣 – ⥲ ⊺ⅴ ℗. ※
3 rm ⊇ 25.00/37.00.

Seaview – pop. 2 181 – ⊠ Isle of Wight.

🏛 **Seaview,** High St., PO34 5EX, ℘ (01983) 612711, Fax (01983) 613729 – ⥲ rest, ⊺ⅴ ☎ ℗
◍◍ 𝘈𝘌 ① 𝘝𝘐𝘚𝘈 𝘑𝘊𝘉
Meals (bar dinner Sunday except Bank Holidays) a la carte 18.85/24.10 **t.** 🛦 4.40 – **14 rm**
⊇ 45.00/100.00 **t.**, 2 suites – SB.

Shanklin – pop. 17 305 (inc. Sandown) – ⊠ Isle of Wight.
🟥 Fairway Lake, Sandown ℘ (01983) 403217.
🔋 67 High St., PO37 6JJ ℘ (01983) 862942.
Newport 9.

Brunswick, Queens Rd, PO37 6AN, *ℰ* (01983) 863245, *Fax (01983) 868398,* ☎, ⊿, ◨,
⇌ – ⇺ rest, ◲ ☎ ℗. ◍◉ ▦
March-October and Christmas – **Meals** (bar lunch)/dinner 12.00 **st.** ⓘ 4.00 – **32 rm**
⌴ 39.00/92.00 – SB.

Bourne Hall Country ⌂, Luccombe Rd, PO37 6RR, *ℰ* (01983) 862820,
Fax (01983) 865138, ◨, ⇌, ⅏ – ◲ ☎ ℗. ◍◉ ⁂ ◐ ▦. ⅏
closed January and December except Christmas – **Meals** (bar lunch)/dinner
a la carte 16.85/22.40 **t.** ⓘ 6.95 – **30 rm** ⌴ (dinner included) 40.00/90.00 **t.** – SB.

Rylstone Manor ⌂, Rylstone Gdns., PO37 6RG, *ℰ* (01983) 862806, ⇌ – ⇺ ◲ ℗. ◍◉
▦.
April-October – **Meals** (residents only) (dinner only) 14.50 **st.** ⓘ 6.50 – **9 rm** ⌴ 32.00/
64.00 **st.**

Luccombe Chine Country House ⌂, Luccombe Chine, PO37 6RH, S : 2 ¼ m. by
A 3055 *ℰ* (01983) 862037, *Fax (01983) 862037,* ≼, ⇌ – ⇺ rest, ◲ ℗. ◍◉ ▦. ⅏
closed January and December – **Meals** (dinner only) 14.00 **t.** ⓘ 5.00 – **6 rm** ⌴ (dinner
included) 68.00/96.00 **t.** – SB.

Queensmead, 12 Queens Rd, PO37 6AN, *ℰ* (01983) 862342, ⊿, ⇌ – ⇺ rest, ◲ ℗. ◍◉
⁂ ▦ ⌨. ⅏
April-October – **Meals** (bar lunch)/dinner 9.50 **st.** and a la carte ⓘ 5.00 – **30 rm** ⌴ (dinner
included) 47.00/88.00 **st.** – SB.

Grange Bank, Grange Rd, PO37 6NN, *ℰ* (01983) 862337, *Fax (01983) 862337* – ⇺ ◲ ℗.
⅏
April-October – **Meals** (by arrangement) 6.00 **st.** – **9 rm** ⌴ 23.00/46.00 **st.** – SB.

Delphi Cliff, 7 St. Boniface Cliff Rd, PO37 6ET, *ℰ* (01983) 862179, *Fax (01983) 862179,* ≼,
⇌ – ⇺ rest, ◲ ℗
10 rm.

otland – pop. 7 317 (inc. Freshwater) – ⊠ Isle of Wight.
Newport 13.

Sentry Mead, Madeira Rd, PO39 0BJ, *ℰ* (01983) 753212, *Fax (01983) 753212,* ⇌ –
⇺ rest, ◲ ℗. ◍◉ ⁂ ▦
closed December – **Meals** (bar lunch)/dinner 12.50 **t.** – **14 rm** ⌴ 35.00/70.00 **t.**

Littledene Lodge, Granville Rd, PO39 0AX, *ℰ* (01983) 752411 – ⇺ rest, ℗. ◍◉ ▦
Meals (by arrangement) – **6 rm** ⌴ (dinner included) 30.00/60.00 **st.**

entnor – pop. 5 978 – ⊠ Isle of Wight.
⌗ Steephill Down Rd *ℰ* (01983) 853326.
◻ 34 High St., PO38 1RZ *ℰ* (01983) 853625 (summer only).
Newport 10.

Winterbourne ⌂, Bonchurch, PO38 1RQ, via Bonchurch Shute *ℰ* (01983) 852535,
Fax (01983) 853056, « Country house ≼ gardens and sea », ⊿ – ⇺ rest, ◲ ☎ ℗. ◍◉ ⁂
▦
April-October – **Meals** (bar lunch)/dinner 16.95 **st.** ⓘ 7.80 – **13 rm** ⌴ (dinner included)
53.00/124.00 **t.**, 1 suite.

Lake ⌂, Shore Rd, Bonchurch, PO38 1RF, *ℰ* (01983) 852613, *Fax (01983) 852613,* ⇌ –
⇺ rest, ◲ ℗
March-October – **Meals** (dinner only) 8.50 **st.** ⓘ 4.50 – **20 rm** ⌴ 25.00/50.00 **st.** – SB.

Highfield, 87 Leeson Rd, Upper Bonchurch, PO38 1PU, on A 3055 *ℰ* (01983) 852800, ≼,
⇌ – ⇺ rest, ◲ ☎ ℗. ◍◉ ▦. ⅏
March-October – **Meals** *(closed Monday)* 8.95/10.95 **t.** and dinner a la carte – **12 rm**
⌴ (dinner included) 39.00/84.00 **t.** – SB.

armouth – ⊠ Isle of Wight.
Newport 10.

George, Quay St., PO41 0PE, *ℰ* (01983) 760331, *Fax (01983) 760425,* ≼, 🌳, « 17C former
governors residence », ⇌ – ◲ ☎ – ⌂ 40. ◍◉ ⁂ ▦ ⌨
Brasserie : Meals a la carte 14.50/23.50 **t.** ⓘ 7.50 – (see also below) – **16 rm** ⌴ 80.00/
175.00 **t.**, 1 suite – SB.

George (at George H.), Quay St., PO41 0PE, *ℰ* (01983) 760331, *Fax (01983) 760425* – ▤.
◍◉ ⁂ ▦
closed Sunday dinner, Monday and 2 weeks from 16 February – **Meals** (booking essential)
(dinner only and Sunday lunch)/dinner 34.50 **t.** ⓘ 7.50.

WIGSTON Leics. 402 403 404 Q 26 – see Leicester.

WILLERBY East Riding 402 S 22 – see Kingston-upon-Hull.

WILLERSEY Glos. 403 404 O 27 – see Broadway (Worcestershire).

WILLERSEY HILL Glos. 403 404 O 27 – see Broadway (Worcestershire).

WILLESLEY Glos. 403 404 N 29 – see Tetbury.

WILLITON Somerset 403 K 30 The West Country G. – pop. 2 025 – ⊠ Taunton.
Env. : Exmoor National Park★★ – Cleeve Abbey★★ AC, W : 2 m. by A 39.
London 177 – Minehead 8 – Taunton 16.

🏠 **White House,** 11 Long St., TA4 4QW, ℘ (01984) 632306 – ⁕⊱ rest, 📺 ☎ 🄿
June-October – **Meals** (dinner only) 29.50 **t.** ⌀ 7.00 – **12 rm** ⌻ 41.00/90.00 **t.** – SB.

🏠 **Curdon Mill** ⌂, Lower Vellow, TA4 4LS, SE : 2 ½ m. by A 358 on Stogumber ro
℘ (01984) 656522, Fax (01984) 656197, ≤, « Converted water mill on working farm », 🗷
🝏, 🛋, park – ⁕⊱ 📺 🄿. 🆀 ⒶⒺ 💳 🄹🄲🄱. 🛇
Meals (closed Sunday dinner to non-residents) (booking essential to non-residents) (dinner
only and Tuesday and Sunday lunch) 22.50 **t.** ⌀ 4.05 – **6 rm** ⌻ 40.00/70.00 **t.**

WILMCOTE Warks. 403 404 O 27 – see Stratford-upon-Avon.

WILMINGTON Devon 403 K 31 – see Honiton.

WILMINGTON East Sussex 404 U 31 – see Eastbourne.

WILMSLOW Ches. 402 403 404 N 24 – pop. 28 604.
🛢 Great Warford, Mobberley ℘ (01565) 872148.
London 189 – Liverpool 38 – Manchester 12 – Stoke-on-Trent 27.

🏨 **Stanneylands,** Stanneylands Rd, SK9 4EY, N : 1 m. by A 34 ℘ (01625) 525225
Fax (01625) 537282, « Gardens » – ⁕⊱ rm, 📺 ☎ ও 🄿 – ⚄ 100. 🆀 ⒶⒺ ① 💳. 🛇
Meals – (see **The Restaurant** below) – ⌻ 10.50 – **32 rm** 89.00/120.00 **t.**

🏨 **Manchester Airport Moat House,** Oversley Ford, Altrincham Rd, SK9 4LR
NW : 2 ¾ m. on A 538 ℘ (01625) 889988, Fax (01625) 531876, ⌘, ≋ₛ, 🔲, squash – 🛗
⁕⊱ rm, 📺 ☎ 🄿 – ⚄ 300. 🆀 ⒶⒺ ① 💳
Meals (closed Saturday lunch) 14.50/17.50 **st.** and a la carte ⌀ 6.50 – ⌻ 9.25 – **126 rm**
99.00/135.00 **st.** – SB.

🏨 **Boddington Arms,** Racecourse Rd, SK9 5LR, W : 1 m. by A 538 ℘ (01625) 525849
Fax (01625) 548382 – 🛗 ⁕⊱, 🍴 rest, 📺 ☎ ও 🄿. 🆀 ⒶⒺ ① 💳. 🛇
Meals (grill rest.) 6.55 **st.** (lunch) and a la carte 10.00/14.50 **st.** ⌀ 5.25 – ⌻ 4.95 – **37 rm**
44.25 **st.** – SB.

XXX **The Restaurant** (at Stanneylands H.), Stanneylands Rd, SK9 4EY, N : 1 m. by A 3
℘ (01625) 525225, Fax (01625) 537282, « Gardens » – 🍴 rest, 🄿. 🆀 ⒶⒺ ① 💳
closed Sunday dinner to non-residents – **Meals** (buffet dinner Sunday) 14.50/32.00
and a la carte ⌀ 6.00.

X **Bank Square,** 4-6 Bank Sq., SK9 1AN, ℘ (01625) 539754 – 🍴. 🆀 ⒶⒺ 💳
closed Sunday dinner – **Meals** (booking essential) 14.50/18.50 **st.** and a la carte.

at Handforth N : 3 m. on A 34 – ⊠ Wilmslow.

🏨 **Pinewood Thistle,** 180 Wilmslow Rd, SK9 3LG, S : 1 m. on A 34 ℘ (01625) 52921
Fax (01625) 536812, ≋ – 🛗 ⁕⊱, 🍴 rest, 📺 ☎ 🄿 – ⚄ 200. 🆀 ⒶⒺ ① 💳
Meals 18.00 **st.** (dinner) and a la carte 19.95/25.95 **st.** ⌀ 5.80 – ⌻ 10.50 – **58 rm** 94.00
110.00 **st.** – SB.

🏨 **Belfry,** Stanley Rd, SK9 3LD, ℘ (0161) 437 0511, Fax (0161) 499 0597 – 🛗, ⁕⊱ rm, 📺 ☎
– ⚄ 180. 🆀 ⒶⒺ ① 💳. 🛇
closed 25-26 December and 1 January – **Meals** (dancing Friday and Saturda
evenings) 16.50/19.50 **t.** and a la carte ⌀ 8.00 – **78 rm** ⌻ 85.00/105.00 **t.**, 2 suites – SB.

WIMBORNE MINSTER *Dorset* 403 404 O 31 *The West Country G. – pop. 15 274.*

See : *Town★ – Minster★ – Priest's House Museum★ AC.*

Env. : *Kingston Lacy★★ AC, NW : 3 m. by B 3082.*

🛈 *29 High St., BH21 1HR* ℘ *(01202) 886116.*

London 112 – Bournemouth 10 – Dorchester 23 – Salisbury 27 – Southampton 30.

🏠 **Beechleas,** 17 Poole Rd, BH21 1QA, ℘ (01202) 841684, Fax (01202) 849344, « Georgian townhouse » – ఫ rest, 📺 ☎ 🅿. 🚗 🅰🅴 🆅🅸🆂🅰. 🛇
closed 3 weeks Christmas – Meals *(dinner only)* 19.75 **t.** ᵻ 5.95 – **9 rm** ⊐ 68.00/98.00 **t.** –

🍴🍴 **Les Bouviers,** Oakley Hill, Merley, BH21 1RJ, S : 1 ¼ m. on A 349 ℘ (01202) 889555, *Fax (01202) 889555* – 🅿. 🚗 🅰🅴 ⓸ 🆅🅸🆂🅰
Meals 12.75/23.95 **st.** and a la carte ᵻ 8.25.

THE CHANNEL TUNNEL Map Guide

260 *French edition*
  with tourist sights in England

261 *English edition*
  with tourist sights on the Continent

WINCHCOMBE *Glos.* 403 404 O 28 – *pop. 4 243.*

London 100 – Birmingham 43 – Gloucester 26 – Oxford 43.

🏠 **Isbourne Manor House** without rest., Castle St., GL54 5JA, ℘ (01242) 602281, « Part Georgian and Elizabethan manor house », 🌳 – ఫ 📺 🅿. 🛇
closed 1 week Christmas – **3 rm** ⊐ 45.00/65.00 **s.**

🏠 **Sudeley Hill Farm** 🦢 without rest., GL54 5JB, E : 1 m. by Castle St. ℘ (01242) 602344, *Fax (01242) 602344,* ⩽, « Part 15C house, working farm », 🌳, park – ఫ 📺 🅿. 🛇
closed Christmas – **3 rm** ⊐ 28.00/44.00 **st.**

🍴🍴 **Wesley House** with rm, High St., GL54 5LJ, ℘ (01242) 602366, « Part 15C » – ఫ 📺 ☎.
🚗 🅰🅴 🆅🅸🆂🅰. 🛇
closed 12 January-12 February – Meals *(closed Sunday dinner except at Bank Holidays)* 15.00/26.00 **t.** and lunch a la carte ᵻ 7.00 – **5 rm** ⊐ 48.00/80.00 **t.** – SB.

WINCHELSEA *E. Sussex* 404 W 31 *Great Britain G.*

See : *Town★ – St. Thomas Church (effigies★).*

London 64 – Brighton 46 – Folkestone 30.

🏠 **Strand House,** The Strand, TN36 4JT, E : ¼ m. on A 259 ℘ (01797) 226276, *Fax (01797) 224806,* « Part 14C and 15C », 🌳 – ఫ 📺 🅿. 🚗 🆅🅸🆂🅰 🅹🅲🅱
Meals *(by arrangement)* 12.50 **st.** ᵻ 3.50 – **10 rm** ⊐ 34.00/58.00 **st.**

WINCHESTER *Hants.* 403 404 P 30 *Great Britain G. – pop. 36 121.*

See : *City★★ - Cathedral★★★ AC* B *– Winchester College★ AC* B B *– Castle Great Hall★* B D *– God Begot House★* B A.

Env. : *St. Cross Hospital★★ AC* A.

🛈 *Guildhall, The Broadway, SO23 9LJ* ℘ *(01962) 840500.*

London 72 – Bristol 76 – Oxford 52 – Southampton 12.

Plan on next page

🏨 **Lainston House** 🦢, Sparsholt, SO21 2LT, NW : 3 ½ m. by B 3049 (old A 272)
℘ (01962) 863588, *Fax (01962) 776672,* ⩽, « 17C manor house », 🌳, park, 🎾 – 📺 ☎ 🅿 –
🦺 80. 🚗 🅰🅴 ⓸ 🆅🅸🆂🅰 🅹🅲🅱. 🛇
Meals 19.00 **t.** (lunch) and a la carte 39.70/46.80 **t.** ᵻ 20.00 – ⊐ 11.00 – **37 rm** 95.00/
245.00 **t.**, 1 suite – SB.

🏨 **Wessex,** Paternoster Row, SO23 9LQ, ℘ (01962) 861611, *Fax (01962) 841503,* ⩽ – 📶,
ఫ rm, 🍴 rest, 📺 ☎ 🅿 – 🦺 100. 🚗 🅰🅴 ⓸ 🆅🅸🆂🅰 🅹🅲🅱   B C
Wessex : Meals 15.00/21.00 **st.** and a la carte ᵻ 7.95 – **Explorer :** Meals *(lunch only and dinner Friday and Saturday)* a la carte 9.85/19.85 **st.** ᵻ 7.95 – ⊐ 10.85 – **93 rm** 79.00/
99.00 **t.**, 1 suite – SB.

WINCHESTER

Brooks Shopping Centre . . . . . **B** 8
High Street. . . . . **B**

Alresford Road . . . . **A** 2
Andover Road . . . . **B** 3
Bereweeke Road . . . . **A** 5
Bridge Street . . . . **B** 6
Broadway (The) . . . . **B** 7
Chilbolton Avenue . . . . **A** 9
City Road . . . . **B** 10
Clifton Terrace . . . . **B** 12
East Hill . . . . **B** 15
Eastgate Street . . . . **B** 16
Easton Lane . . . . **A** 18
Friarsgate . . . . **B** 19
Kingsgate Road . . . . **A** 22
Magdalen Hill . . . . **B** 23
Middle Brook Street . . . . **B** 24
Park Road . . . . **A** 26
St. George's Street . . . . **B** 32
St. Paul's Hill . . . . **B** 33
St. Peter's Street . . . . **B** 34
Southgate Street . . . . **B** 35
Stoney Lane . . . . **A** 36
Stockbridge Road . . . . **B** 37
Sussex Street . . . . **B** 38
Union Street . . . . **B** 39
Upper High Street . . . . **B** 40

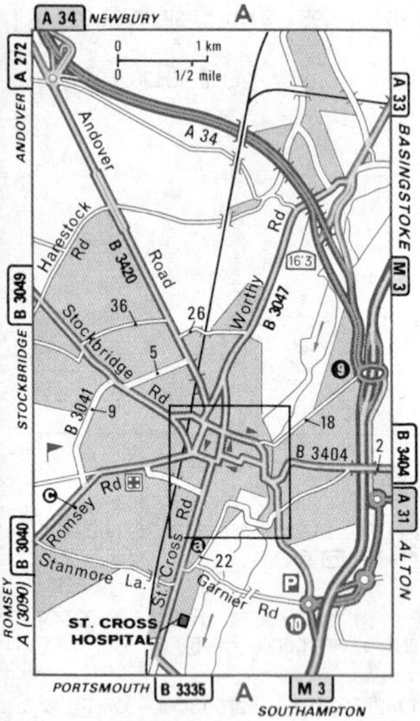

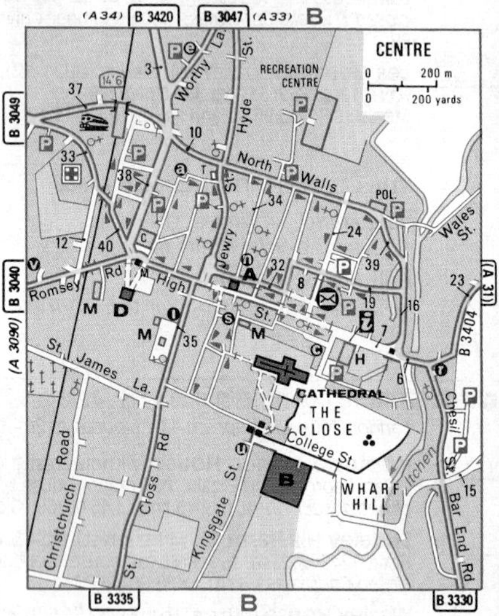

Hotel du Vin, 14 Southgate St., SO23 9EF, ✆ (01962) 841414, *Fax (01962) 842458*, « Georgian town house, wine themed interior », – TV ☎ P – 40. MC AE D VISA.
Meals – (see ***Bistro*** below) – 9.50 – **19 rm** 85.00/110.00 **t.** — B i

Royal, St. Peter St., SO23 8BS, ✆ (01962) 840840, *Fax (01962) 841582*, – rest, TV ☎ P – 100. MC AE D VISA JCB — B n
Meals 11.00/21.00 **st.** 8.50 – 10.50 – **75 rm** 75.00/105.00 **st.** – SB.

Winchester Moat House, Worthy Lane, SO23 7AB, ✆ (01962) 709988, *Fax (01962) 840862*, rm, TV ☎ P – 200. MC AE D VISA — B e
Meals 16.00 **st.** (dinner) and a la carte 13.50/20.00 **st.** 6.95 – 9.50 – **71 rm** 90.00/105.00 **st.** – SB.

Wykeham Arms, 75 Kingsgate St., SO23 9PE, ✆ (01962) 853834, *Fax (01962) 854411*, « Traditional 18C inn, memorabilia », rm, TV ☎ P. MC AE D VISA JCB
closed 25 December – **Meals** *(closed Sunday)* (booking essential) (in bar) a la carte 13.85/22.40 **t.** 5.85 – **13 rm** 69.50/89.50 **t.** — B u

East View without rest., 16 Clifton Hill, SO22 5BL, ✆ (01962) 862986, *Fax (01962) 862986*, – TV P. MC VISA. — B v
3 rm 38.00/48.00 **st.**

Portland House without rest., 63 Tower St., SO23 8TA, ✆ (01962) 865195, *Fax (01962) 865195* – TV. — B a
4 rm 38.00/48.00 **st.**

Dawn Cottage without rest., Romsey Rd, SO22 5PQ, ✆ (01962) 869956, – TV P. MC VISA JCB. — A c
3 rm 40.00/50.00 **s.**

Florum House, 47 St. Cross Rd, SO23 9PS, ✆ (01962) 840427, *Fax (01962) 862287*, – TV P. MC VISA — A a
closed 24 to 26 December – **Meals** (by arrangement) 13.50 **st.** – **9 rm** 42.00/58.00 **st.** – SB.

Nine The Square, 9 Great Minster St., The Square, SO23 9HA, ✆ (01962) 864004 *Fax (01962) 879586* – MC AE D VISA — B s
closed Sunday, 1 January and 25 to 28 December – **Meals** a la carte 23.50/29.65 **st.**

🍴 **Bistro** (at Hotel du Vin), 14 Southgate St., SO23 9EF, ☎ (01962) 841414, *Fax (01962) 842458*, 🌳 – [P]. [MC] [AE] [O] [VISA] B i
Meals a la carte 20.00/28.00 **t.** 🍾 9.50.

🍴 **Old Chesil Rectory,** Chesil St., SO23 8HU, ☎ (01962) 851555, *Fax (01962) 869704*, « 15C » – [MC] [O] [VISA] [JCB] B r
closed Sunday, Monday, 2 weeks August and 2 weeks Christmas – **Meals** 19.50/30.00 **t.** 🍾 6.75.

🛞 ATS 61 Bar End Rd ☎ (01962) 865021

WINDERMERE *Cumbria* [402] L 20 *Great Britain G.* – *pop. 6 847.*

Env. : *Lake Windermere*★★ – *Brockhole National Park Centre*★ *AC, NW : 2 m. by A 591.*

⛳18 *Cleabarrow* ☎ *(015394) 43123, E : 1 ½ m. by A 5074 – Z – on B 5284.*

[i] *Victoria St., LA23 1AD* ☎ *(015394) 46499 at Bowness, Glebe Rd, LA23 3HJ* ☎ *(015394) 42895 (summer only).*

London 274 – Blackpool 55 – Carlisle 46 – Kendal 10.

Plan on next page

🏨 **Langdale Chase** 🐦, LA23 1LW, NW : 3 m. on A 591 ☎ (015394) 32201, *Fax (015394) 32604*, ⩽ Lake Windermere and mountains, « Victorian country house in lakeside setting, carvings and artefacts », 🐟, 🌳, 🎾 – 🚭 rest, ▤ rest, [TV] ☎ [P] – 🏛 25. [MC] [AE] [O] [VISA] [JCB]
Meals 15.00/27.00 **st.** and a la carte 🍾 6.00 – **29 rm** 🛏 (dinner included) 55.00/195.00 **st.**, 1 suite – SB.

🏨 **Holbeck Ghyll** 🐦, Holbeck Lane, LA23 1LU, NW : 3 ¼ m. by A 591 ☎ (015394) 32375, *Fax (015394) 34743*, ⩽ Lake Windermere and mountains, « Former Victorian hunting lodge, gardens », 🏋, ♨, 🎾 – 🚭 rest, [TV] ☎ [P]. [MC] [AE] [O] [VISA] [JCB]
Meals (light lunch)/dinner 25.00 **t.** 🍾 7.75 – **13 rm** 🛏 (dinner included) 90.00/220.00 **t.**, 1 suite – SB.

🏨 **Miller Howe,** Rayrigg Rd, LA23 1EY, ☎ (015394) 42536, *Fax (015394) 45664*, ⩽ Lake Windermere and mountains, 🌳 – 🚭 rest, ▤ rest, [TV] ☎ [P]. [MC] [AE] [O] [VISA]. 🚫🐕 Y s
closed December-late February – **Meals** (booking essential) 15.00/32.00 **t.** 🍾 8.00 – **12 rm** 🛏 (dinner included) 95.00/250.00 **t.** – SB.

🏨 **Quarry Garth,** Troutbeck Bridge, LA23 1LF, NW : 2 m. on A 591 ☎ (015394) 88282, *Fax (015394) 46584*, 🌳 – 🚭 rest, [TV] ☎ [P]. [MC] [AE] [O] [VISA]
Meals 15.00 **st.** (dinner) and a la carte 12.50/17.50 **st.** 🍾 8.00 – **12 rm** 🛏 (dinner included) 65.00/150.00 **st.** – SB.

🏨 **Glenburn,** New Rd, LA23 2EE, ☎ (015394) 42649, *Fax (015394) 88998* – 🚭 [TV] ☎ [P]. [MC] [VISA] [JCB]. 🚫🐕 Y u
Meals (dinner only) 16.50 **st.** 🍾 5.50 – **16 rm** 🛏 35.00/65.00 **st.**

🏨 **Cedar Manor,** Ambleside Rd, LA23 1AX, ☎ (015394) 43192, *Fax (015394) 45970*, 🌳 – 🚭 rest, [TV] ☎ [P]. [MC] [VISA] Y i
Meals *(closed lunch Monday and Tuesday)* (light lunch)/dinner 18.50 **st.** 🍾 6.60 – **12 rm** 🛏 50.00/80.00 **st.** – SB.

🏨 **Woodlands,** New Rd, LA23 2EE, ☎ (015394) 43915, *Fax (015394) 48558* – 🚭 [TV] [P]. [MC] [VISA] [JCB]. 🚫🐕 Y u
restricted opening in winter – **Meals** (residents only) (dinner only) 14.50 **t.** 🍾 4.00 – **14 rm** 🛏 27.00/60.00 **t.** – SB.

⌂ **Archway,** 13 College Rd, LA23 1BU, ☎ (015394) 45613 – 🚭 [TV] ☎. [MC] [VISA] [JCB]. 🚫🐕
closed 1 week early December – **Meals** (by arrangement) 12.50 **st.** 🍾 6.20 – **4 rm** 🛏 54.00 **st.** Y e

⌂ **Braemount House,** Sunny Bank Rd, LA23 2EN, by Queens Drive ☎ (015394) 45967, *Fax (015394) 45967* – 🚭 [TV] [P]. [MC] [VISA]. 🚫🐕 Z u
closed Christmas and February – **Meals** 17.50 **st.** 🍾 5.25 – **5 rm** 🛏 40.00/70.00 **st.** – SB.

⌂ **Hawksmoor,** Lake Rd, LA23 2EQ, ☎ (015394) 42110, 🌳 – 🚭 [TV] [P]. [MC] [VISA] [JCB]. 🚫🐕
closed 5 January-12 February and 24 November-27 December – **Meals** (dinner only) 11.75 **st.** 🍾 3.95 – **10 rm** 🛏 27.00/62.00 **st.** – SB. Z s

⌂ **Beaumont** without rest., Holly Rd, LA23 2AF, ☎ (015394) 47075, *Fax (015394) 47075* – 🚭 [TV] [P]. [MC] [VISA]. 🚫🐕 Y n
10 rm 🛏 32.00/70.00 **st.**

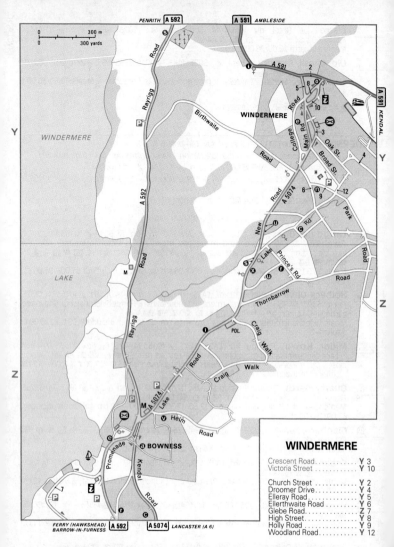

WINDERMERE

↑ **Fir Trees** without rest., Lake Rd, LA23 2EQ, ℘ (015394) 42272, Fax (015394) 42272 – ⅍✕
📺 🄿 🌂🅜🅢 🄰🄴 𝗩𝗜𝗦𝗔. ✂%   **Z** x
8 rm ⊇ 40.00/54.00 st.

↑ **Glencree** without rest., Lake Rd, LA23 2EQ, ℘ (015394) 45822, Fax (015394) 45822 – ⅍✕
📺 🄿. 🌂🅜🅢 𝗩𝗜𝗦𝗔. ✂%   **Z** s
Easter-late October and weekends January-March – **5 rm** ⊇ 39.00/75.00 **s.**

↑ **Kirkwood** without rest., Prince's Rd, LA23 2DD, ℘ (015394) 43907, Fax (015394) 43907 –
⅍✕ 📺. 🌂🅜🅢 𝗩𝗜𝗦𝗔 🄹🄲🄱. ✂%   **YZ** n
closed 1 week November and 2 weeks January – **7 rm** ⊇ 30.00/60.00 **st.**

↑ **Oldfield House** without rest., Oldfield Rd, LA23 2BY, ℘ (015394) 88445
Fax (015394) 43250 – ⅍✕ 📺 🌂🄿. 🌂🅜🅢 𝗩𝗜𝗦𝗔 🄹🄲🄱. ✂%   **Y** o
closed January – **8 rm** ⊇ 32.50/64.00 **st.**

✕✕ **Roger's**, 4 High St., LA23 1AF, ℘ (015394) 44954 – 🌂🅜🅢 🄰🄴 🄾 𝗩𝗜𝗦𝗔 🄹🄲🄱   **Y** o
closed Sunday – **Meals** (dinner only) 16.50 **t.** and a la carte 15.70/26.50 **t.** ♦ 5.50.

624

at Bowness-on-Windermere *S : 1 m. – ✉ Windermere.*

Old England, Church St., LA23 3DF, ☎ (015394) 42444, *Fax (015394) 43432,* ≤ Lake Windermere, ⛱, 🌳 – |‡|, ⇔ rm, TV ☎ P – 🚹 120. MC AE D VISA JCB. ⛔ Z e
Meals (bar lunch Monday to Saturday)/dinner 21.95 **t.** 7.50 – ☐ 8.95 – **76 rm** 70.00/150.00 **t.** – SB.

Linthwaite House ⛰, Crook Rd, LA23 3JA, S : ¾ m. by A 5074 on B 5284 ☎ (015394) 88600, *Fax (015394) 88601,* ≤ Lake Windermere and fells, « Extensive grounds and private lake », ⇔ – ⇔ TV ☎ P. MC AE VISA JCB. ⛔
Meals (light lunch Monday to Saturday)/dinner 32.00 **st.** 7.50 – **18 rm** ☐ 100.00/180.00 **st.** – SB.

Gilpin Lodge ⛰, Crook Rd, LA23 3NE, SE : 2 ½ m. by A 5074 on B 5284 ☎ (015394) 88818, *Fax (015394) 88058,* ≤, 🌳, park – TV ☎ P. MC AE D VISA JCB. ⛔
Meals (booking essential) 27.50 **st.** (dinner) and a la carte 11.50/18.50 **st.** 9.50 – **13 rm** ☐ 85.00/170.00 **st.** – SB.

Lindeth Fell ⛰, Lyth Valley Rd, LA23 3JP, S : 1 m. on A 5074 ☎ (015394) 43286, *Fax (015394) 47455,* ≤ Lake Windermere and mountains, « Country house atmosphere, gardens », ⇔, ⚔ – ⇔ rest, TV ☎ P. MC VISA. ⛔
closed 6 to 27 January – **Meals** (light lunch Monday to Saturday)/dinner 19.00 **st.** 4.25 – **14 rm** ☐ (dinner included) 60.00/140.00 **st.**

Burnside, Kendal Rd, LA23 3EP, ☎ (015394) 42211, *Fax (015394) 43824,* Fб, ≘s, ⛱, 🌳, squash – |‡| ⇔ TV ☎ ♿ P – 🚹 100. MC AE D VISA JCB Z c
Meals (bar lunch Monday to Saturday) (carving lunch Sunday and dinner Monday-Tuesday) 18.00 **t.** and a la carte 6.50 – **57 rm** ☐ (dinner included) 73.00/146.00 **t.** – SB.

Fayrer Garden House ⛰, Lyth Valley Rd, LA23 3JP, S : 1 m. on A 5074 ☎ (015394) 88195, *Fax (015394) 45986,* ≤, 🌳 – ⇔ rest, ▤ rest, TV ☎ P. MC AE VISA
Meals (bar lunch)/dinner 19.95 5.95 – **18 rm** ☐ (dinner included) 65.00/160.00 **t.** – SB.

Craig Manor, Lake Rd, LA23 2JF, ☎ (015394) 88877, *Fax (015394) 88878,* ≤ – ⇔ rest, TV ☎ P. MC AE VISA Z i
Meals (dinner only and Sunday lunch) (carving lunch Sunday) 17.50 **t.** and a la carte 6.50 – **16 rm** ☐ 57.00/108.00 **st.** – SB.

Burn How Garden House, Back Belsfield Rd, LA23 3HH, ☎ (015394) 46226, *Fax (015394) 47000,* 🌳 – ⇔ rest, TV ☎ P. MC AE D VISA JCB. ⛔ Z r
closed early January – **Meals** (bar lunch)/dinner 19.50 **st.** 7.50 – **26 rm** ☐ 59.00/88.00 **st.** – SB.

Wild Boar, Crook Rd, LA23 3NF, SE : 4 m. by A 5074 on B 5284 ☎ (015394) 45225, *Fax (015394) 42498,* 🌳 – ⇔ TV ☎ P – 🚹 35. MC AE D VISA JCB
Meals 19.95 **t.** (dinner) and a la carte 29.90/33.35 **t.** 5.75 – ☐ 9.50 – **36 rm** 49.00/110.00 **t.** – SB.

Crag Brow Cottage, Helm Rd, LA23 3BU, ☎ (015394) 44080, *Fax (015394) 46003,* 🌳 – ⇔ TV ☎ P. MC VISA JCB. ⛔ Z v
Meals 7.95/14.95 **st.** and dinner a la carte 5.95 – **11 rm** ☐ (dinner included) 60.00/110.00 **st.** – SB.

Lindeth Howe ⛰, Storrs Park, LA23 3JF, S : 1 ¼ m. by A 592 off B 5284 ☎ (015394) 45759, *Fax (015394) 46368,* ≤, ≘s, 🌳 – ⇔ rest, TV ☎ P. MC VISA JCB. ⛔
Meals (dinner only and Sunday lunch)/dinner 19.95 **t.** 5.50 – **15 rm** ☐ (dinner included) 48.50/108.00 **t.**

White Foss ⛰ without rest., Longtail Hill, LA23 3JD, S : ¾ m. by A 592 on B 5284 ☎ (015394) 46593, ≤, 🌳 – P. ⛔
March-October – **3 rm** ☐ 40.00/56.00 **st.**

Laurel Cottage without rest., St. Martins Sq., Kendal Rd, LA23 3EF, ☎ (015394) 45594, *Fax (015394) 45594* – TV P. ⛔ Z a
closed Christmas – **15 rm** ☐ 24.00/56.00 **st.**

at Troutbeck *N : 4 m. by A 592 – Y – ✉ Windermere.*

Broadoaks ⛰, Bridge Lane, LA23 1LA, S : 1 m. ☎ (015394) 45566, *Fax (015394) 88766,* 🌳 – ⇔ rest, TV ☎ P. MC VISA. ⛔
April-October – **Meals** (lunch by arrangement)/dinner 27.95 **st.** and a la carte 6.50 – **10 rm** ☐ 59.50/140.00 **st.** – SB.

Mortal Man ⛰, LA23 1PL, ☎ (015394) 33193, *Fax (015394) 31261,* ≤ Garburn Hill and Troutbeck Valley, 🌳 – ⇔ rest, TV ☎ P
21 February-21 November – **Meals** (bar lunch Monday to Saturday) 22.00 **st.** 5.95 – **12 rm** ☐ (dinner included) 58.00/116.00 **st.** – SB.

Queens Head with rm, LA23 1PW, E : ¼ m. on A 592 ☎ (015394) 32174, *Fax (015394) 31938,* ≤, « 17C inn » – ⇔ rm, TV P. MC VISA
closed 25 December – **Meals** (lunch in bar) a la carte 10.65/22.25 **t.** 6.00 – **8 rm** ☐ 40.00/60.00 **st.**

WINDLESHAM Surrey **404** S 29 – pop. 4 525.
London 37 – Basingstoke 26 – Reading 16 – Southampton 55.

🏠 **Brickmakers Arms,** Chertsey Rd, GU20 6HT, ℰ (01276) 472267, Fax (01276) 451014 – **℗ ⓂⓈ ⅍ ⓪ 𝚅𝙸𝚂𝙰**
closed 25 December and 1 January – Meals 9.95/17.95 **t.** and a la carte ₰ 6.75.

WINDSOR Windsor & Maidenhead **404** S 29 Great Britain G. – pop. 30 136 (inc. Eton).
See : Town★ – Castle★★★ : St. George's Chapel★★★ AC (stalls★★★), State Apartments★★ AC,
North Terrace (≼★★) Z – Eton College★★ AC (College Chapel★★, Wall paintings★) Z.
Env. : Windsor Park★ AC Y.
🅱 24 High St., SL4 1LH ℰ (01753) 852010.
London 28 – Reading 19 – Southampton 59.

Plan opposite

🏨 **Oakley Court** ♨, Windsor Rd, Water Oakley, SL4 5UR, W : 3 m. on A 308
ℰ (01753) 609988, Fax (01628) 37011, ≼, « Part Gothic mansion on banks of River
Thames », ₤ₔ, ≋s, ⧄, ₨, ♒, ⇝, park, ✗ – ⇔ rm, 𝚃𝚅 ☎ ₺ ℗ – 🔬 160. ⓂⓈ ⅍ ⓪ 𝚅𝙸𝚂𝙰.
✗
Le Boulestin : Meals 24.00/36.00 **st.** and a la carte – **Boaters Brasserie** : Meals (closed
Sunday lunch) a la carte 15.00/45.00 **st.** ₰ 4.95 – ⊯ 15.00 – **113 rm** 175.00/195.00 **st.**,
1 suite – SB.

🏨 **Castle,** High St., SL4 1LJ, ℰ (01753) 851011, Fax (01753) 830244 – ⏸ ⇔ 𝚃𝚅 ☎ ₺ ℗ – 🔬 400.
ⓂⓈ ⅍ ⓪ 𝚅𝙸𝚂𝙰   Z c
Castle restaurant : Meals (closed Wednesday lunch) a la carte 14.85/24.40 **st.** ₰ 9.00 –
Grand Cafe : Meals (closed dinner Sunday to Tuesday) a la carte 15.50/25.50 **st.** ₰ 9.00 –
⊯ 10.50 – **104 rm** 120.00/200.00 **st.**, 1 suite – SB.

🏨 **Aurora Garden,** 14 Bolton Av., SL4 3JF, ℰ (01753) 868686, Fax (01753) 831394, ⇝ – 𝚃𝚅
☎ ℗ – 🔬 90. ⓂⓈ ⅍ ⓪ 𝚅𝙸𝚂𝙰 𝙹𝙲𝙱   Z a
Meals 15.95 **t.** and dinner a la carte ₰ 5.95 – **19 rm** ⊯ 80.00/100.00 **t.** – SB.

WINEHAM W. Sussex **404** T 31 – see Henfield.

WINGFIELD Suffolk – see Diss.

WINKLEIGH Devon **403** I 31 – pop. 1 063.
London 218 – Barnstaple 25 – Exeter 23 – Plymouth 43 – Truro 76.

✗ **Pophams,** Castle St., EX19 8HQ, ℰ (01837) 83767 – ⓂⓈ 𝚅𝙸𝚂𝙰
⊚ closed February – Meals (closed Sunday to Tuesday) (booking essential) (lunch only)
(unlicensed) a la carte 16.85/24.65 **t.**

WINSCOMBE Somerset **403** L 30 The West Country G. – pop. 4 192.
Env. : Axbridge★★ (King John's Hunting Lodge★, St. John the Baptist Church★), S : 1 ¾ m.
by A 38 and A 371.
London 137 – Bristol 16 – Taunton 22.

🏨 **The Sidcot - Premier Lodge,** Bridgwater Rd, BS25 1NN, on A 38 ℰ (01934) 844145,
Fax (01934) 844192 – ⇔ rm, 𝚃𝚅 ☎ ₺ ℗. ⓂⓈ ⅍ ⓪ 𝚅𝙸𝚂𝙰. ✗
Meals (grill rest.) 6.55/12.95 **st.** and a la carte – ⊯ 4.95 – **31 rm** 42.25 **st.** – SB.

WINSFORD Somerset **403** J 30 The West Country G. – pop. 270 – ✉ Minehead.
See : Village★.
Env. : Exmoor National Park★★.
London 194 – Exeter 31 – Minehead 10 – Taunton 32.

🏨 **Royal Oak Inn,** Exmoor National Park, TA24 7JE, ℰ (01643) 851455, Fax (01643) 85100,
« Attractive part 12C thatched inn », ⇝ – 𝚃𝚅 ☎ ℗. ⓂⓈ ⅍ ⓪ 𝚅𝙸𝚂𝙰
Meals (dinner only and Sunday lunch)/dinner 18.50 **t.** – **14 rm** ⊯ 85.00/110.00 **t.** – SB.

✗✗ **Savery's at Karslake House** with rm, Halse Lane, Exmoor National Park, TA24 7J_,
⊚ ℰ (01643) 851242, Fax (01643) 851242, ⇝ – ⇔ 𝚃𝚅 ℗. ⓂⓈ 𝚅𝙸𝚂𝙰 𝙹𝙲𝙱
closed February – Meals (closed Sunday and Monday to non-residents) (booking essential)
(dinner only) 23.95 **st.** ₰ 7.50 – **7 rm** ⊯ 37.00/80.00 **st.** – SB.

WINDSOR

North is at the top
on all town plans.

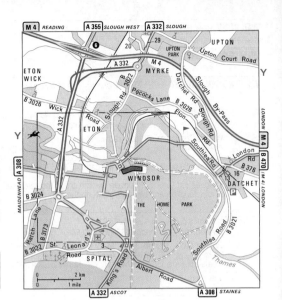

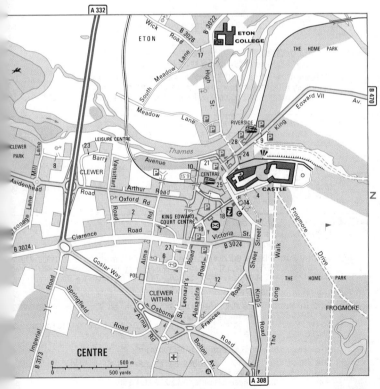

CENTRE

627

WINSLEY *Wilts.* 403 404 N 29 – *see Bradford-on-Avon.*

WINTERBOURNE *South Gloucestershire* 403 404 M 29 – *see Bristol.*

WINTERBOURNE STEEPLETON *Dorset* – *see Dorchester.*

WINTERINGHAM *North Lincolnshire* 402 S 22 – *pop. 4 714* – ⊠ *Scunthorpe.*
London 176 – Kingston-upon-Hull 16 – Sheffield 67.

XXXX **Winteringham Fields** (Schwab) with rm, Silver St., DN15 9PF, ℘ (01724) 733096,
❀ Fax (01724) 733898, « Part 16C manor house », ☞ – ✤ 📺 ☎ 📵. ⬥❾ 🆑 *VISA*. ℅
closed first week August and 2 weeks Christmas – **Meals** *(closed Sunday, Monday and Bank
Holidays)* 20.00/29.00 **st.** and a la carte 45.60/57.20 **st.** 🍴 6.75 – ☲ 8.50 – **6 rm** 65.00/
135.00 **st.**, 1 suite
Spec. Grilled turbot, mouclade of clam crust, mustard seed sauce. Gateau of rabbit with
smoked shallots and cep juice. Winteringham corn tart.

WISBECH *Cambs.* 404 U 25 – *pop. 24 981.*
London 103 – Cambridge 43 – Norwich 58.

🏠 **White Lion,** 5 South Brink, PE13 1JD, ℘ (01945) 463060, Fax (01945) 463069 – ✤ rest
📺 ☎ 📵 – 🔏 100. ⬥❾ 🆑 *VISA* *JCB*. ℅
Meals a la carte 15.05/26.70 **t.** 🍴 6.50 – **12 rm** ☲ 54.95/82.45 **t.**
⊚ ATS North End ℘ (01945) 583214

WITCOMBE *Glos.* – *see Gloucester.*

WITHERSLACK *Cumbria* 402 L 21 – *see Grange-over-Sands.*

WITHINGTON *Glos.* 403 404 O 28 – *pop. 486.*
London 91 – Gloucester 15 – Oxford 35 – Swindon 24.

🏠 **Halewell** ⤬, GL54 4BN, ℘ (01242) 890238, Fax (01242) 890332, ≼, « Part 15C
monastery », 🛆, ❧, ☞, park – ✤ rest, 📺 ᕕ 📵. ⬥❾ 🆑 *VISA*. ℅
Meals *(by arrangement)* (communal dining) 22.50 **st.** – **6 rm** ☲ 55.50/85.00 **st.**

WITHYPOOL *Somerset* 403 J 30 *The West Country G.* – *pop. 196* – ⊠ *Minehead.*
Env. : Exmoor National Park★★ – Tarr Steps★★, SE : 4 m. by B 3223 and minor roads
Exford (Church★) NE : 4 m. by B 3223 and B 3224.
London 204 – Exeter 34 – Taunton 36.

🏠 **Royal Oak Inn** with rm, TA24 7QP, ℘ (01643) 831506, Fax (01643) 831659, « Part 17C »
❧ – 📺 ☎ 📵. ⬥❾ 🆑 *VISA* *JCB*
Meals (bar lunch Monday to Saturday)/dinner 18.50 **t.** and a la carte – **8 rm** ☲ 33.00
88.00 **t.**

WITNEY *Oxon* 403 404 P 28 – *pop. 20 377.*
🛈 Town Hall, 51A Market Sq., OX8 6AG ℘ (01993) 775802.
London 69 – Gloucester 39 – Oxford 13.

🏛 **Witney Four Pillars,** Ducklington Lane, OX8 7TJ, S : 1½ m. on A 415 ℘ (01993) 77977
Fax (01993) 703467, 🏋, ⌔, ◻ – ✤ rm, 📺 ᕕ 📵 – 🔏 160. ⬥❾ 🆑 🅾 *VISA*. ℅
Meals 12.95/14.95 **st.** and a la carte – ☲ 6.95 – **74 rm** 74.00/86.00 **st.** – SB.

at Hailey *N : 1¼ m. on B 4022* – ⊠ *Witney.*

🏠 **Bird in Hand,** White Oak Green, OX8 5XP, N : 1 m. on B 4022 ℘ (01993) 86832
Fax (01993) 868702 – ✤ rm, 📺 ☎ ᕕ 📵. ⬥❾ *VISA*
closed 25 and 26 December – **Meals** a la carte 14.00/20.50 **t.** 🍴 6.00 – **16 rm** ☲ 55.0
75.00 **t.** – SB.

at Barnard Gate *E : 3¼ m. by B 4022 off A 40* – ⊠ *Eynsham.*

🏠 **The Boot Inn,** OX8 6XE, ℘ (01865) 881231, Fax (01865) 358910, « Collection
celebrities boots » – 📵. ⬥❾ *VISA*
closed 25 December – **Meals** a la carte 18.40/22.20 **t.** 🍴 4.50.

at South Leigh *SE : 3 m. by A 4022 – ✉ Witney.*

✗ **Mason Arms** with rm, OX8 6XN, ✆ (01993) 702485, « 15C thatched inn », – TV P. AE.
closed 25 and 26 December – **Meals** *(closed Sunday dinner and Monday)* a la carte 19.60/31.40 **t.** – **2 rm** 35.00/50.00.

ATS Orchard Way, off Corn St. ✆ (01993) 704273

WITTERSHAM *Kent* 404 W 30 – *pop. 1 431* – ✉ *Tenterden.*
London 59 – Brighton 54 – Folkestone 22 – Maidstone 28.

Wittersham Court, The Street, TN30 7EA, ✆ (01797) 270425, *Fax (01797) 270425*, – rm, P. MC VISA.
closed Christmas and New Year – **Meals** (by arrangement) (communal dining) 20.00 **s.** 6.00 – **3 rm** 45.00/60.00.

WIVELISCOMBE *Somerset* 403 K 30 *The West Country G. – pop. 1 753* – ✉ *Taunton.*
Env. : *Gaulden Manor★ AC, NE : 3 m. by B 3188.*
London 185 – Barnstaple 38 – Exeter 37 – Taunton 14.

Langley House, Langley Marsh, TA4 2UF, NW : ½ m. ✆ (01984) 623318, *Fax (01984) 624573*, – rest, TV ☎ P. MC AE VISA
Meals (booking essential) (dinner only) 25.00 **st.** 7.00 – **8 rm** 72.50/118.50 **st.** – SB.

Jews Farm House, Huish Champflower, TA4 2HL, NW : 2 ½ m. turning right opposite postbox in wall onto rd marked as unsuitable for heavy vehicles; 2nd on left ✆ (01984) 624218, « 13C », park – rm, P.
closed December and January – **Meals** (by arrangement) (communal dining) 20.00 **s.** – **3 rm** 42.00/60.00 **s.**

WIX *Essex* 404 X 28 – ✉ *Manningtree.*
London 70 – Colchester 10 – Harwich 7 – Ipswich 16.

Dairy House Farm without rest., Bradfield Rd, CO11 2SR, NW : 1 m. ✆ (01255) 870322, *Fax (01255) 870186*, park – TV P.
closed 1 week Christmas – **3 rm** 26.00/40.00.

WOBURN *Beds.* 404 S 28 *Great Britain G. – pop. 1 534* – ✉ *Milton Keynes.*
See : *Woburn Abbey★★.*
London 49 – Bedford 13 – Luton 13 – Northampton 24.

Bedford Arms Thistle, 1 George St., MK17 9PX, ✆ (01525) 290441, *Fax (01525) 290432* – rm, rest, TV ☎ P – 60. MC AE VISA.
Meals 17.95/21.00 **st.** and a la carte 7.25 – 11.00 – **51 rm** 95.00/135.00 **st.**, 2 suites – SB.

Bell Inn, 21 Bedford St., MK17 9QB, ✆ (01525) 290280, *Fax (01525) 290017* – rest, TV ☎ P. MC AE VISA.
Meals (bar meals Saturday lunch and Sunday dinner) a la carte 15.90/20.90 **st.** 4.95 – **23 rm** 59.00/69.00 **st.** – SB.

✗✗✗ **Paris House,** Woburn Park, MK17 9QP, SE : 2 ¼ m. on A 4012 ✆ (01525) 290692, *Fax (01525) 290471*, « Reconstructed timbered house in park », – P. MC AE VISA
closed Sunday dinner, Monday, 26 December and February – **Meals** 25.00/42.00 **t.** 6.00.

WOKINGHAM 404 R 29 – *pop. 38 063.*
18 Sand Martins, Finchampstead Rd ✆ (01734) 792711 – 9 Hurst, Sandford Lane ✆ (01734) 344355.
London 43 – Reading 7 – Southampton 52.

Stakis St. Anne's Manor, London Rd, RG40 1ST, E : 1 ½ m. on A 329 ✆ (01189) 772550, *Fax (01189) 772526*, park, – rm, rest, TV ☎ P – 200. MC AE VISA.
closed 26 to 30 December – **Meals** *(closed Saturday lunch)* (carving lunch) 14.95/22.50 **st.** and dinner a la carte 6.50 – 12.45 – **156 rm** 140.00/150.00 **st.**, 3 suites – SB.

Edward Court, Wellington Rd, RG40 2AN, ✆ (01189) 775886, *Fax (01189) 772018* – TV ☎ P – 40
25 rm.

✗ **Rose Street Wine Bar,** Rose St., RG40 1XU, ✆ (01189) 788025 – MC AE VISA
closed Bank Holiday lunch, Sunday, 25-26 December and 1 January – **Meals** a la carte 17.50/24.95 **t.** 6.95.

WOLVERHAMPTON W. Mids. 402 403 404 N 26 – pop. 257 943.

8 18 Queen Sq., WV1 1TQ ℰ (01902) 312051.

London 132 – Birmingham 15 – Liverpool 89 – Shrewsbury 30.

Plan of Enlarged Area : see Birmingham pp. 2 and 3

Mount ⌖, Mount Rd, Tettenhall Wood, WV6 8HL, W : 2 ½ m. by A 454 ℰ (01902) 752055, Fax (01902) 745263, ⇄ – ⌖ rm, 🆃🆅 ☎ 🅿 – 🔏 200. 🆖🅾 🆀🅴 ⓪ 𝐕𝐈𝐒𝐀 A a
Meals (bar lunch Saturday) 12.95/17.50 **st.** ⌗ 7.75 – ⇋ 8.50 – **55 rm** 79.00/95.00 **st.**, 1 suite – SB.

Goldthorn, 126 Penn Rd, WV3 0ER, ℰ (01902) 29216, Fax (01902) 710419, 𝐿ℰ, ⇋, 🔲 –
⌖ 🆃🆅 ☎ 🅿 – 🔏 120. 🆖🅾 🆀🅴 ⓪ 𝐕𝐈𝐒𝐀, ⌖ B c
Meals (closed Saturday lunch) 11.95/16.50 **st.** and a la carte ⌗ 5.50 – ⇋ 9.50 – **91 rm** 75.00/100.00 **st.** – SB.

Novotel, Union St., WV1 3JN, ℰ (01902) 871100, Fax (01902) 870054, 🔰 – 🛗, ⌖ rm
▤ rest, 🆃🆅 & 🅿 – 🔏 200. 🆖🅾 🆀🅴 ⓪ 𝐕𝐈𝐒𝐀 B a
Meals 9.95/15.50 **st.** and a la carte ⌗ 7.50 – ⇋ 8.50 – **132 rm** 61.00 **st.**

Park Hall, Park Drive, Ednam Rd, WV4 5AJ, off Goldthorn Hill ℰ (01902) 331121
Fax (01902) 344760, ⇄ – 🆃🆅 ☎ 🅿 – 🔏 400. 🆖🅾 🆀🅴 ⓪ 𝐕𝐈𝐒𝐀 A e
Meals (bar lunch Monday to Saturday)/dinner 13.95 **t.** and a la carte ⌗ 6.50 – ⇋ 8.50 –
56 rm 69.00/79.00 **t.**, 1 suite – SB.

WOLVERHAMPTON

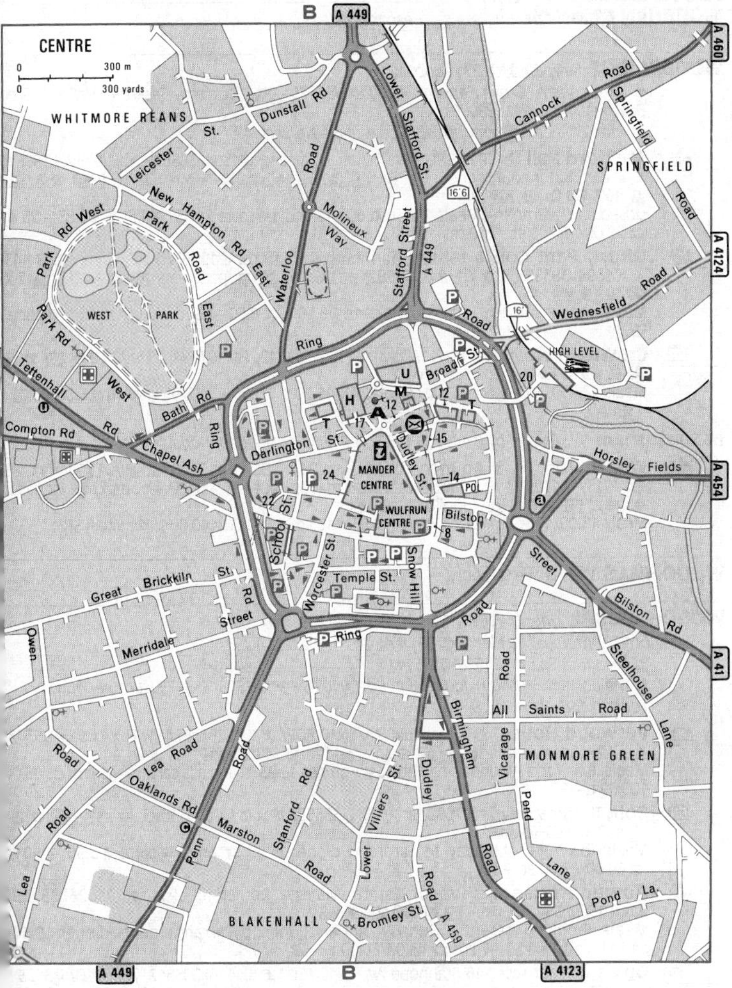

B
A 449
CENTRE
0 300 m
0 300 yards
WHITMORE REANS
Dunstall Rd
St.
Leicester
New Hampton Rd East
Park Rd West
Park
Road
WEST
PARK
Park Rd
Tettenhall
West
Bath Rd
Ring
Compton Rd
Rd
Chapel Ash
Waterloo
Road
Molineux Way
Lower
Stafford St.
Stafford Street
A 449
Ring
Road
Cannock Road
Springfield
SPRINGFIELD
Road
A 460
A 4124
Wednesfield Road
HIGH LEVEL
Broad St.
U
M
H
A
T
12
17
15
20
Darlington St.
MANDER CENTRE
Dudley St.
14
POL
WULFRUN CENTRE
Bilston
8
7
24
22
School St.
Worcester St.
Snow Hill
Temple St.
Horsley Fields
A 454
Street
Bilston Rd
A 41
Steelhouse Lane
Great Brickkiln St.
Rd Street
Merridale
Owen
Ring
Road
Road
All Saints Road
MONMORE GREEN
Vicarage
Birmingham
Dudley
Road
Lea Road
Road
Oaklands Rd
Road
Marston Road
Penn
Stanford Rd
Villiers St.
Lower
Road
Pond
Lane
Pond La.
Lea
Road
BLAKENHALL
Bromley St.
A 459
A 449
B
A 4123

Holiday Inn Garden Court, Dunstall Park, WV6 0PE, N : 1 ¾ m. by A 449 ✆ (01902) 713313, *Fax (01902) 714364* – |‡|, ⇹ rm, TV ☎ ♿ P – 🏛 50. MC AE ⓓ VISA. ✂
Meals a la carte 12.00/21.85 **st.** – ☕ 7.50 – **54 rm** 52.00 **st.** A c

Ely House, 53 Tettenhall Rd, WV3 9NB, ✆ (01902) 311311, *Fax (01902) 421098* – TV ☎ P. MC AE ⓓ VISA. ✂ B u
closed 24 to 26 December – **Meals** (lunch by arrangement) 12.95 **t.** and a la carte 🍷 5.95 – **18 rm** ☕ 45.00/68.00 **t.**

ATS 35-39 Wednesfield Rd ✆ (01902) 455055 ATS 2 Willenhall Rd ✆ (01902) 871417

Pour vos déplacements en ***Grande-Bretagne*** *et en* ***Irlande :***
- cinq cartes détaillées nos 401, 402, 403, 404, 405 à 1/400 000
- utilisez-les conjointement avec ce guide,
un souligné rouge signale toutes les localités dans ce guide.

WOOBURN COMMON Bucks. – see Beaconsfield.

WOODBRIDGE Suffolk **404** X 27 – pop. 10 950.

🇫 Cretingham, Grove Farm ℰ (01728) 685275 – 🇫 Seckford, Seckford Hall Rd, Great Bealings ℰ (01394) 388000.

London 81 – Great Yarmouth 45 – Ipswich 8 – Norwich 47.

🏨 **Seckford Hall** ⏴, IP13 6NU, SW : 1 ¼ m. by A 12 ℰ (01394) 385678, Fax (01394) 380610, ≤, « Part Tudor country house », ♨, 🔲, 🇫, ⚓, ☞, park – ⬥ rm, 🍽 rest, 📺 ☎ ♿ ❷ – 🔏 100. ◑ 🖭 ① 𝘝𝘐𝘚𝘈 𝘑𝘊𝘉
closed 25 December – **Meals** 12.50 **st.** (lunch) and a la carte 24.55/38.75 **st.** ⑅ 6.85 – **25 rm** ⊐ 79.00/150.00 **st.**, 7 suites – SB.

🏨 **Ufford Park Golf & Leisure,** Yarmouth Rd, Ufford, IP12 1QW, NE : 2 m. on B 1438 ℰ (01394) 383555, Fax (01394) 383582, ≤, ♨, ⚍, 🔲, 🇫, park – ⬥ 📺 ☎ ♿ ❷ – 🔏 200. ◑ 🖭 ① 𝘝𝘐𝘚𝘈. ⌘
Meals (carving rest.) 16.00 **t.** and a la carte ⑅ 6.50 – ⊐ 8.50 – **43 rm** 70.00/90.00 **t.**, 1 suite – SB.

🏨 **Crown,** Thoroughfare, IP12 1AD, ℰ (01394) 384242, Fax (01394) 387192 – ⬥ 📺 ☎ ❷ ◑ 🖭 ① 𝘝𝘐𝘚𝘈 𝘑𝘊𝘉
Meals 12.95 **t.** (dinner) and a la carte 10.45/16.20 **t.** ⑅ 5.65 – ⊐ 8.95 – **20 rm** 65.00/80.00 **t.** – SB.

at Shottisham SE : 5 ¾ m. by B 1438, A 1152 on B 1083 – ✉ Woodbridge.

🏨 **Wood Hall H. & Country Club** ⏴, IP12 3EG, on B 1083 ℰ (01394) 411283, Fax (01394) 410007, ≤, « Part Elizabethan manor house », ⚍, 🔲, ☞, park, ⌘, squash – ⬥ rest, 📺 ☎ ❷ – 🔏 150. ◑ 🖭 ① 𝘝𝘐𝘚𝘈
Meals 15.00/17.95 **t.** and a la carte ⑅ 4.95 – **13 rm** ⊐ 83.00/140.00 **t.**, 1 suite – SB.

WOODFALLS Wilts. – see Salisbury.

WOODHALL SPA Lincs. **402 404** T 24 Great Britain G. – pop. 3 337.

Env. : Tattershall Castle★ AC, SE : 4 m. by B 1192 and A 153.

🇫 Woodhall Spa ℰ (01526) 352511.

🎫 The Cottage Museum, Iddlesleigh Rd, LN10 6SH ℰ (01526) 353775 (summer only).

London 138 – Lincoln 18.

🏨 **Petwood House** ⏴, Stixwould Rd, LN10 6QF, ℰ (01526) 352411, Fax (01526) 353473, ≤, « Gardens », park – 📗 ⬥ 📺 ☎ ❷ – 🔏 120. ◑ 🖭 ① 𝘝𝘐𝘚𝘈
Meals (bar lunch Monday to Saturday)/dinner 16.95 **t.** and a la carte – **45 rm** ⊐ 65.00/105.00 **t.** – SB.

🏨 **Golf,** The Broadway, LN10 6SG, ℰ (01526) 353535, Fax (01526) 353096, ☞, ⌘ – 📺 ☎ ❷ 🔏 150. ◑ 🖭 ① 𝘝𝘐𝘚𝘈
Meals (bar lunch Monday to Saturday)/dinner 15.95 **st.** and a la carte ⑅ 5.95 – **50 rm** ⊐ 69.00/99.00 **st.** – SB.

🏠 **Dower House** ⏴, Manor Estate, via Spa Rd, LN10 6PY, ℰ (01526) 352588, Fax (01526) 354045, ☞ – 📺 ❷. ◑ 🖭 ① 𝘝𝘐𝘚𝘈
Meals (booking essential Sunday dinner) (lunch by arrangement)/dinner 16.50 and a la carte ⑅ 4.50 – **7 rm** ⊐ 43.00/66.00 **t.** – SB.

🏠 **Oglee** without rest., 16 Stanhope Av., LN10 6SP, ℰ (01526) 353512, Fax (01526) 353511 ☞ – 📺 ❷
5 rm ⊐ 20.00/40.00 **st.**

WOODSTOCK Oxon. **403 404** P 28 Great Britain G. – pop. 2 898.

See : Blenheim Palace★★★ (The Grounds★★★) AC.

🎫 Hensington Rd, OX20 1JQ ℰ (01993) 811038 (summer only).

London 65 – Gloucester 47 – Oxford 8.

🏨 **Bear,** Park St., OX20 1SZ, ℰ (01993) 811511, Fax (01993) 813380, « Part 16C inn » – ⬥ 📺 ☎ ❷ – 🔏 30. ◑ 🖭 ① 𝘝𝘐𝘚𝘈 𝘑𝘊𝘉
Meals 17.50/23.50 **t.** and dinner a la carte ⑅ 7.50 – ⊐ 10.50 – **41 rm** 100.00/150.00 **st.**, 3 suites – SB.

🏨 **Feathers,** Market St., OX20 1SX, ℰ (01993) 812291, Fax (01993) 813158, « Tastefully furnished 17C houses » – ⬥ rest, 🍽 rest, 📺 ☎ ◑ 🖭 ① 𝘝𝘐𝘚𝘈 𝘑𝘊𝘉
Meals 22.00 **t.** (lunch) and a la carte 22.70/33.90 **t.** ⑅ 5.90 – ⊐ 8.25 – **16 rm** 88.00/155.00 **t.**, 1 suite – SB.

WOOKEY HOLE Somerset **403** L 30 – see Wells.

WOOLACOMBE Devon **403** H 30 *The West Country G..*

    Env. : *Exmoor National Park*★★ – *Mortehoe*★★ *(St. Mary's Church★, Morte Point – vantage point★) N :* ½ *m – Ilfracombe : Hillsborough (*≤★★*) AC, Capstone Hill★ (*≤★*), St. Nicholas' Chapel (*≤★*) AC, NE :* 5 ½ *m. by B 3343 and A 361.*

    Exc. : *Braunton★ (St. Braunton's Church★, Braunton Burrows★), S :* 8 *m. by B 3343 and A 361.*

    🛈 *Red Barn Cafe Car Park, Barton Rd* ℘ *(01271) 870553 (summer only).*

    London 237 – Barnstaple 15 – Exeter 55.

🏨 **Woolacombe Bay**, South St., EX34 7BN, ℘ *(01271) 870388,* Fax *(01271) 870613,* ≤, **Ɫⅎ**, ⩥s, ⟂, ⧉, *☞,* ⋇, squash – ☖ ⏺ ☎ **ℙ** – 🔥 200. **⊙⊙ ㏂ ⓪ 𝙑𝙄𝙎𝘼 𝙅𝘾𝘽. ⅏**
    closed 4 January-14 February – Meals *(dancing Tuesday evening) (light lunch Monday to Saturday)/dinner* 20.00 **st.** and a la carte ▯ 6.00 – **65 rm** ⊇ *(dinner included)* 95.00/205.00 **st.** – SB.

🏠 **Little Beach**, The Esplanade, EX34 7DJ, ℘ *(01271) 870398,* Fax *(01271) 870051,* ≤ – ⅙⅞
    ⏺ ☎ **ℙ**. **⊙⊙ 𝙑𝙄𝙎𝘼**
    29 March-October – Meals *(residents only) (dinner only)* 24.95 **t.** ▯ 4.50 – **10 rm** ⊇ 44.00/110.00 **st.** – SB.

at Mortehoe *N :* ½ *m.* – ✉ *Woolacombe.*

🏨 **Watersmeet**, The Esplanade, EX34 7EB, ℘ *(01271) 870333,* Fax *(01271) 870890,*
    ≤ Morte Bay, ⧉, ⏺, *☞,* ⋇ – ⅙⅞ rest, ⏺ ☎ **ℙ**. **⊙⊙ ㏂ 𝙑𝙄𝙎𝘼. ⅏**
    closed December-mid February – Meals *(bar lunch Monday to Saturday)* 21.00 **t.**
    and a la carte ▯ 5.25 – **23 rm** ⊇ *(dinner included)* 95.00/198.00 **st.** – SB.

🏠 **Cleeve House**, EX34 7ED, ℘ *(01271) 870719,* Fax *(01271) 870719, ☞ –* ⅙⅞ rest, ⏺ **ℙ**.
    ⊙⊙ 𝙑𝙄𝙎𝘼 𝙅𝘾𝘽. ⅏
    April-October – Meals *(dinner only and light lunch in summer)/dinner* 15.75 **s.** ▯ 5.00 – **6 rm** ⊇ *(dinner included)* 26.00/82.00 **st.** – SB.

🏠 **Sunnycliffe**, Chapel Hill, EX34 7EB, ℘ *(01271) 870597,* Fax *(01271) 870597,* ≤ Morte Bay – ⅙⅞ ⏺ **ℙ**. ⅏
    March-October – Meals *(dinner only) (residents only)* 15.00 – **8 rm** ⊇ 64.00 **st.** – SB.

The Guide is updated annually so renew your Guide every year.

WOOLLEY EDGE SERVICE AREA *W. Yorks.* – ✉ *Wakefield.*

🏠 **Travelodge** without rest., WF4 4LQ, M 1 between junctions 38 and 39 ℘ *(01924) 830569,* Fax *(01924) 830609,* Reservations *(Freephone)* 0800 850950 – ⅙⅞ ⏺ ☎ ⅙ **ℙ**. **⊙⊙ ㏂ ⓪ 𝙑𝙄𝙎𝘼 𝙅𝘾𝘽. ⅏**
    32 rm 46.95 **t.**

WOOLSTASTON *Shrops.* **402 403** L 26 – *see Church Stretton.*

WOOLSTONE *Glos.* – *see Cheltenham.*

WOOLTON *Newbury* **402 403** L 23 – *see Liverpool.*

WOOLTON HILL *Newbury* – *see Newbury.*

WOOTTON BASSETT *Wilts.* **403 404** O 29 – *see Swindon.*

WOOTTON WAWEN *Warks.* **403 404** O 27 – *pop. 2 056*
    London 105 – Birmingham 18 – Stratford-upon-Avon 5 – Warwick 11 – Worcester 23.

🍴 **Bull's Head**, Stratford Rd, B95 6BD, ℘ *792511,* ㏂, *☞,* – **ℙ**. **⊙⊙ 𝙑𝙄𝙎𝘼**
    closed 25 and 26 December – Meals - *Seafood specialities* - a la carte 14.25/18.15 **st.** ▯ 4.75.

WORCESTER *Worcestershire* **403 404** N 27 *Great Britain G.* – *pop. 82 661.*
    See : *City★ – Cathedral★★ – Royal Worcester Porcelain Works★ (Dyson Perrins Museum★)* M.
    Exc. : *The Elgar Trail★ –* ⌷ₛ *Perdiswell Municipal, Bilford Rd* ℘ *(01905) 754668.*
    🛈 *The Guildhall, High St., WR1 1BA* ℘ *(01905) 726311.*
    London 124 – Birmingham 26 – Bristol 61 – Cardiff 74.

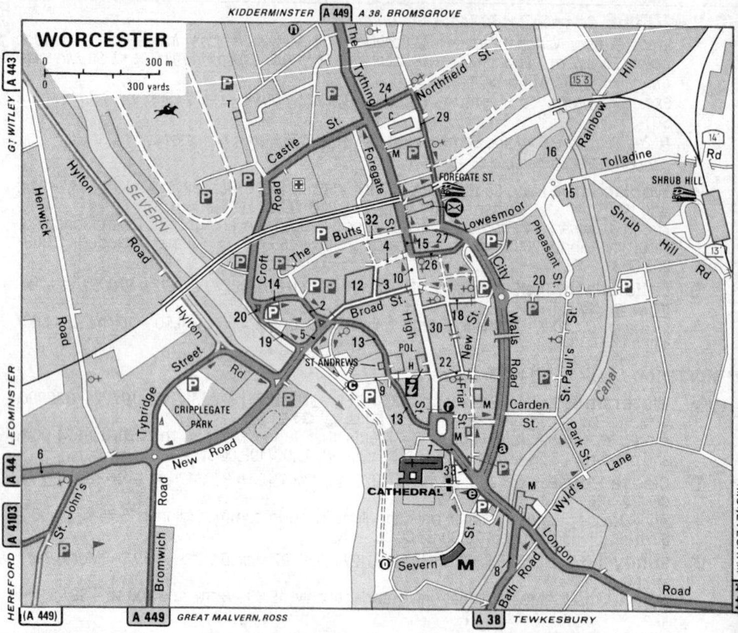

Broad Street		Angel Street	4	Mealcheapen Street	1
Cross (The)	10	Bridge Street	5	North Parade	1
Crowngate Centre	12	Bromyard Road	6	North Quay	2
Foregate (The)	15	College Street	7	St. Martin's Gate	2
High Street		Commandery Road	8	St. Mary's Street	2
Pump Street	22	Copenhagen Street	9	St. Nicholas Street	2
Shambles (The)	30	Deansway	13	Sansome Street	2
		Dolday	14	Sansome Walk	2
All Saints Road	2	Lowesmoor Place	16	Shaw Street	3
Angel Place	3	Lowesmoor Terrace	17	Sidbury	3

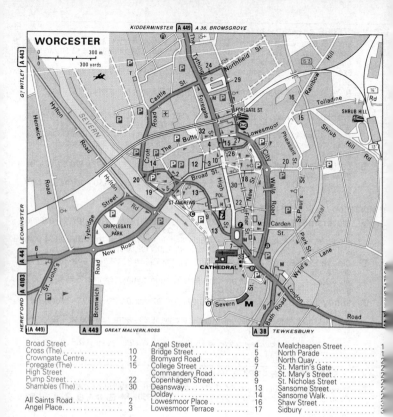

Fownes, City Walls Rd, WR1 2AP, ℘ (01905) 613151, *Fax (01905) 23742,* « Converte glove factory » – |‡|, ⇹ rest, TV ☎ ♿ P – 🏛 100. MC AE ① VISA
Meals (bar lunch Monday to Saturday)/dinner 15.95 **st.** and a la carte – ☕ 8.00 – **58 r** 85.00/95.00 **st.**, 3 suites – SB.

Giffard, High St., WR1 2QR, ℘ (01905) 726262, *Fax (01905) 723458* – |‡| ⇹, ▤ rest, TV P – 🏛 140. MC AE ① VISA
Meals 13.00 **t.** and a la carte 14.85/21.50 **t.** 🍷 7.95 – ☕ 7.95 – **96 rm** 59.00/69.00 s 2 suites – SB.

Diglis House, Severn St., WR1 2NF, ℘ (01905) 353518, *Fax (01905) 767772,* « Georgian house on banks of River Severn », 🏞 – TV ☎ P. MC AE ① VISA. ⛔
Meals 11.50/17.50 **st.** and a la carte – **25 rm** ☕ 60.00/120.00 **st.** – SB.

Number 40 without rest., 40 Britannia Sq., WR1 3DN, ℘ (01905) 61192 *Fax (01905) 27152,* « Regency townhouse » – TV. MC AE VISA. ⛔
3 rm ☕ 45.00/65.00 **st.**

Heathside, 172 Droitwich Rd, Fernhill Heath, WR3 7UA, NE : 3 m. by A 449 on A ℘ (01905) 458245, *Fax (01905) 458245,* 🏞 – ⇹ rest, TV P. MC ① VISA. ⛔
Meals (by arrangement) 11.50 **st.** 🍷 3.50 – **9 rm** ☕ 22.00/48.00 **t.**

Brown's, 24 Quay St., WR1 2JJ, ℘ (01905) 26263, « Converted riverside corn mill » – AE VISA JCB
closed Saturday lunch, Sunday dinner, Monday and 1 week Christmas – **Meals** 18.5 33.50 **st.** 🍷 5.50.

Il Pescatore, 34 Sidbury, WR1 2HZ, ℘ (01905) 21444 – MC VISA
closed Monday lunch, Sunday, 25 to 27 December and 2 weeks in summer – **Meals** - Itali a la carte 13.00/23.50 **t.** 🍷 5.25.

at Upton Snodsbury E : 6 m. by A 44 on A 422 – ⊠ Worcester.

⌂ **Upton House**, WR7 4NR, on B 4082 (beside church) ℰ (01905) 381226, Fax (01905) 381775, « Part 13C timbered house », ⊒, ≈ – ⇎ ᵀᵛ ₽. ⋘ closed Easter and Christmas – **Meals** (by arrangement) (communal dining) 25.00 st. – **3 rm** ⊇ 34.00/68.00 st.

@ ATS Little London, Barbourne ℰ (01905) 24009/28543

WORFIELD Shrops. – see Bridgnorth.

WORKSOP Notts. **402 403 404** C 24 – pop. 37 247.

ᴵ₈ Kilton Forest, Blyth Rd ℰ (01909) 472488 – ᴵ₈ Windmill Lane ℰ (01909) 472696.
🛈 Worksop Library, Memorial Av., S80 2BP ℰ (01909) 501148.
London 163 – Derby 47 – Lincoln 28 – Nottingham 30 – Sheffield 19.

🏨 **Clumber Park**, Clumber Park, S80 3PA, SE : 6 ½ m. by B 6040 and A 57 on A 614 ℰ (01623) 835333, Fax (01623) 835525 – ⇎ ᵀᵛ ☎ ⅙ ₽ – ▵ 220. ⁰⁹ ᴬᴱ ⓞ ᵛⁱˢᴬ ᴶᶜᴮ. ⋘
Meals 8.50/16.00 t. and a la carte ⅙ 6.95 – ⊇ 8.95 – **47 rm** 59.00 t., 1 suite – SB.

🏨 **Travelodge**, Dukeries Mill, St. Anne's Drive, S80 3QD, W : ½ m. by A 57 ℰ (01909) 501528, Reservations (Freephone) 0800 850950 – ⇎ rm, ᵀᵛ ⅙ ₽. ⁰⁹ ᴬᴱ ⓞ ᵛⁱˢᴬ ᴶᶜᴮ. ⋘
Meals (grill rest.) – **40 rm** 44.95 t.

@ ATS 44-46 Carlton Rd ℰ (01909) 501818

WORMINGTON Glos. **403 404** O 27 – see Broadway (Worcestershire).

WORSLEY Gtr. Manchester **402 403 404** MN 23 – see Manchester.

WORTHING W. Sussex **404** S 31 – pop. 95 732.

ᴵ₈ Hill Barn, Hill Barn Lane ℰ (01903) 237301, BY – ᴵ₈, ᴵ₈ Links Rd ℰ (01903) 260801 AY.
✈ Shoreham Airport : ℰ (01273) 452304, E : 4 m. by A 27 BY.
🛈 Chapel Rd, BN11 1HL ℰ (01903) 210022 – Marine Parade ℰ (01903) 210022 (summer only).
London 59 – Brighton 11 – Southampton 50.

Plan on next page

🏨🏨 **Beach**, Marine Par., BN11 3QJ, ℰ (01903) 234001, Fax (01903) 234567, ≼ – |⧢| ᵀᵛ ☎ ₽ – ▵ 180. ⁰⁹ ᴬᴱ ⓞ ᵛⁱˢᴬ. ⋘
Meals 18.50 st. (dinner) and a la carte 10.75/27.50 st. ⅙ 6.30 – **77 rm** ⊇ 53.25/89.50 st., 3 suites – SB.   **AZ e**

🏨 **Chatsworth**, Steyne, BN11 3DU, ℰ (01903) 236103, Fax (01903) 823726 – |⧢|, ⇎ rest, ᵀᵛ ☎ ₽ – ▵ 150. ⁰⁹ ᴬᴱ ⓞ ᵛⁱˢᴬ
Meals (carving lunch) 9.95/15.95 t. (dinner) and a la carte 4.95/15.95 t. ⅙ 5.50 – **105 rm** ⊇ 49.90/79.00 t. – SB.   **BZ x**

🏨 **Berkeley**, 86-95 Marine Par., BN11 3QD, ℰ (01903) 820000, Fax (01903) 821333, ≼ – |⧢| ᵀᵛ ☎ ⅙ ₽ – ▵ 150. ⁰⁹ ᴬᴱ ⓞ ᵛⁱˢᴬ. ⋘
Meals (bar lunch/dinner) 12.50 t. – **84 rm** ⊇ 59.00/92.00 t. – SB.   **BZ a**

🏨 **Windsor House**, 14-20 Windsor Rd, BN11 2LX, ℰ (01903) 239655, Fax (01903) 210763, ≈ – ▤ rest, ᵀᵛ ☎ ₽ – ▵ 120. ⁰⁹ ᴬᴱ ⓞ ᵛⁱˢᴬ ᴶᶜᴮ. ⋘
Meals 14.95 t. (dinner) and a la carte 12.50/23.00 t. ⅙ 4.95 – **30 rm** ⊇ 52.00/95.00 t. – SB.   **BY i**

🏨 **Kingsway**, 117-119 Marine Par., BN11 3QQ, ℰ (01903) 237542, Fax (01903) 204173 – |⧢| ᵀᵛ ☎ ₽ – ▵ 40. ⁰⁹ ᴬᴱ ⓞ ᵛⁱˢᴬ
Meals 8.95/15.95 t. and a la carte ⅙ 5.50 – **29 rm** ⊇ 49.50/90.00 t.   **AZ i**

⌂ **Beacons** without rest., 18 Shelley Rd, BN11 1TU, ℰ (01903) 230948, Fax (01903) 230948 – ⇎ ᵀᵛ ☎ ₽. ⁰⁹ ᴬᴱ ⓞ ᵛⁱˢᴬ ᴶᶜᴮ
8 rm ⊇ 29.00/52.00 s.   **BZ e**

⌂ **Bonchurch House**, 1 Winchester Rd, BN11 4DJ, ℰ (01903) 202492 – ⇎ rest, ᵀᵛ ₽. ⁰⁹ ᵛⁱˢᴬ ᴶᶜᴮ. ⋘
Meals 14.50 st. ⅙ 5.00 – **6 rm** ⊇ 20.00/42.00 st.   **AZ v**

⌂ **Upton Farm House** without rest., Upper Brighton Rd, Sompting Village, BN14 9JU, ℰ (01903) 233706, ≈ – ⇎ ᵀᵛ ₽
3 rm ⊇ 25.00/45.00 st.   **BY a**

WORTHING

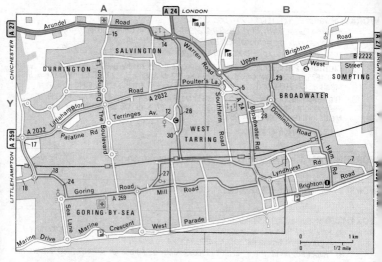

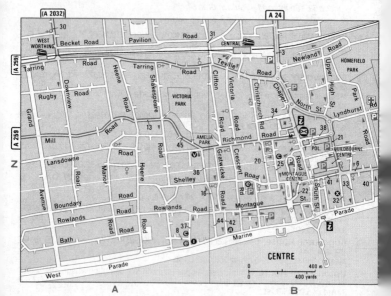

XX **Trenchers,** 118-120 Portland Rd, BN11 1QA, ℰ (01903) 820287 – ⓒ VISA   BZ **c**
closed Sunday dinner – **Meals** 15.50/21.50 **t.** and a la carte ⓘ 5.00.

XX **Parsonage,** 6-10 High St., Tarring, BN14 7NN, ℰ (01903) 820140, Fax (01903) 219386,
☂, « 15C cottages » – ⓒ AE ⓞ VISA   AY **c**
closed Saturday lunch, Sunday, 1 January, 25-26 December and Bank Holidays – **Meals**
19.50 **t.** and a la carte 24.65/31.60 **t.** ⓘ 7.00.

XX **Paragon,** 9-10 Brunswick Rd, BN11 3NG, ℰ (01903) 233367, Fax (01903) 233367 – ⓒ AE
ⓞ VISA   AZ **c**
closed Sunday, 24 June-8 July, 23 December-8 January and Bank Holidays – **Meals** 14.95/
18.95 **t.** and a la carte ⓘ 5.50.

ⓐ ATS Units 1/2, Hazelwood Trading Est., Dominion Way ℰ (01903) 237640/820971

WRAIK HILL Kent – see·Whitstable.

WRESSLE East Riding 402 R 22 Great Britain G. – ✉ Selby (N. Yorks.).
Env. : Selby (Abbey Church★), W : 5 m. by minor road and A 63.
London 208 – Kingston-upon-Hull 31 – Leeds 31 – York 19.

🏛 **Loftsome Bridge Coaching House,** YO8 7EN, S : ½ m. ℰ (01757) 630070,
Fax (01757) 630070, ☂ – ⑭ rm, ⓣ ☎ ⓟ, ⓒ VISA, ⅍
closed Bank Holidays – **Meals** (dinner only and Sunday lunch)/dinner 16.95 **st.** ⓘ 4.25 –
15 rm ⊡ 37.50/65.00 **st.**

WROTHAM HEATH Kent 404 U 30 – pop. 1 767 – ✉ Sevenoaks.
London 35 – Maidstone 10.

🏨 **Forte Posthouse Maidstone/Sevenoaks,** London Rd, TN15 7RS,
ℰ (01732) 883311, Fax (01732) 885850, ℹ6, ☎, 🔲, ☂ – ⑭ rm, ⓣ ☎ ⓺ ⓟ – ⓐ 60. ⓒ AE
ⓞ VISA JCB
Meals a la carte 17.85/25.65 **st.** ⓘ 8.45 – ⊡ 9.95 – **106 rm** 89.00/129.00 **st.** – SB.

🏨 **Travel Inn,** London Rd, TN15 7RX, ℰ (01732) 884214, Fax (01732) 780368 – ⑭ rm, ⓣ ⓺
ⓟ. ⓒ AE ⓞ VISA. ⅍
Meals (grill rest.) – **40 rm** 36.50 **t.**

WROXHAM Norfolk 404 Y 25 Great Britain G. – pop. 3 247 (inc. Hoveton).
Env. : The Broads★.
London 118 – Great Yarmouth 21 – Norwich 7.

🏠 **Garden Cottage,** 96 Norwich Rd, NR12 8RY, ℰ (01603) 784376, Fax (01603) 783192 –
⑭ ⓣ ⓟ. ⓒ AE VISA JCB
closed 25 to 26 December and 1 week January – **Meals** (by arrangement) 12.50 **st.** ⓘ 5.00 –
3 rm ⊡ 30.00/50.00 **st.** – SB.

WROXTON Oxon. 403 404 P 27 – see Banbury.

WYCH CROSS E. Sussex 404 U 30 – see Forest Row.

WYE Kent 404 W 30 – pop. 1 608 – ✉ Ashford.
London 60 – Canterbury 10 – Dover 28 – Hastings 34.

XX **Wife of Bath** with rm, 4 Upper Bridge St., TN25 5AW, ℰ (01233) 812540,
Fax (01233) 813630, ☂ – ⑭ rm, ⓣ ☎ ⓟ. ⓒ ⓞ VISA JCB. ⅍
closed 1 week after New Year – **Meals** (closed Sunday and Monday) 9.50/23.00 **t.** and
dinner a la carte ⓘ 10.50 – ⊡ 5.00 – **6 rm** 40.00/80.00 **t.**

WYMONDHAM Norfolk 404 X 26 – pop. 10 869.
London 102 – Cambridge 55 – King's Lynn 49 – Norwich 12.

🏨 **Wymondham Consort,** 28 Market St., NR18 0BB, ℰ (01953) 606721,
Fax (01953) 601361, ☎, ☂ – ⑭ rest, ⓣ ☎ ⓟ – ⓐ 35. ⓒ AE ⓞ VISA JCB
Meals 10.95/16.95 **t.** and a la carte ⓘ 5.95 – **20 rm** ⊡ 55.00/75.00 **t.** – SB.

WYNDS POINT Worcestershire 403 404 M 27 – see Great Malvern.

YARCOMBE Devon 403 K 31 – see Honiton.

YARM Stockton-on-Tees 402 P 20 – pop. 8 929.
London 242 – Middlesbrough 8.

🏨 **Crathorne Hall** ⌘, Crathorne, TS15 0AR, S : 3 ½ m. by A 67 ℘ (01642) 700398, Fax (01642) 700814, ≤, « Converted Edwardian mansion », ⌘, ☞, park – ⇔ rm, 🆅 ☎ ☯ – 🔬 140. ◑ 𝔸𝔼 �ⓞ 𝚅𝙸𝚂𝙰
Leven : Meals 14.95/24.95 **st.** and a la carte ⬧ 9.50 – **37 rm** ⥿ 108.00/190.00 **st.** – SB.

YARMOUTH I.O.W. 403 404 P 31 – see Wight (Isle of).

YATELEY Surrey 404 R 29 – pop. 15 663 – ⊠ Camberley.
London 37 – Reading 12 – Southampton 58.

🏨 **Casa Dei Cesari,** Handford Lane, Cricket Hill, GU17 7BA, ℘ (01252) 873275, Fax (01252) 870614, ☞ – 🆅 ☎ ☯. ◑ 𝔸𝔼 ⓞ 𝚅𝙸𝚂𝙰. ⅍
closed 26 December – **Meals** - Italian - 15.50 **t.** and a la carte ⬧ 5.25 – **34 rm** ⥿ 67.50/ 87.50 **t.**, 2 suites.

YATTENDON Newbury 403 404 Q 29 – pop. 288 – ⊠ Newbury.
London 61 – Oxford 23 – Reading 12.

XX **Royal Oak** with rm, The Square, RG18 0UG, ℘ (01635) 201325, Fax (01635) 201926, ☞ – ⇔ rest, 🆅 ☎ ☯. ◑ 𝔸𝔼 ⓞ 𝚅𝙸𝚂𝙰
Meals (booking essential) 35.00 **t.** and a la carte ⬧ 9.75 – ⥿ 9.50 – **5 rm** 75.00/105.00 **t.** – SB.

YEADON W. Yorks. 402 O 22 – see Leeds.

YEALMPTON Devon 403 I 32 – see Plymouth.

YELVERTON Devon 403 H 32 The West Country G. – pop. 3 609 (inc. Horrabridge).
See : Yelverton Paperweight Centre★.
Env. : Buckland Abbey★★ AC, SW : 2 m.
Exc. : E : Dartmoor National Park★★.
🅱 Golf Links Rd ℘ (01822) 853618.
London 234 – Exeter 33 – Plymouth 9.

🏨 **Moorland Links** ⌘, PL20 6DA, S : 2 m. on A 386 ℘ (01822) 852245, Fax (01822) 85500-, ≤, ☞, ⅍ – ⇔ 🆅 ☎ ☯ – 🔬 200. ◑ 𝔸𝔼 ⓞ 𝚅𝙸𝚂𝙰
Meals (closed 25 and 26 December) (bar lunch Saturday and Bank Holidays) 20.95 **t.** – **43 rm** ⥿ 70.00/100.00 **t.**, 1 suite – SB.

⌂ **Harrabeer Country House,** Harrowbeer Lane, PL20 6EA, ℘ (01822) 853302, Fax (01822) 853302, ☞ – ⇔ rm, 🆅 ☎ ☯. ◑ 𝚅𝙸𝚂𝙰
closed 24 December-2 January – **Meals** 11.50 **s.** ⬧ 4.50 – **7 rm** ⥿ 19.00/53.00 **s.** – SB.

YEOVIL Somerset 403 404 M 31 The West Country G. – pop. 38 805.
See : St. John the Baptist★.
Env. : Monacute House★★ AC, W : 4 m. on A 3088 – Fleet Air Arm Museum, Yeovilton★ AC, NW : 5 m. by A 37 – Tintinhull House Garden★ AC, NW : 5 ½ m. – Ham Hill (≤★★ AC) W : 5 ¼ m. by A 3088 – Stoke sub-Hamdon (parish church★) W : 5 ½ m. by A 3088.
Exc. : Muchelney★★ (Parish Church★★) NW : 14 m. by A 3088, A 303 and B 3165 – Lyte Cary★, N : 7 ½ m. by A 37, B 3151 and A 372 – Sandford Orcas Manor House★, NW : 8 m. b A 359 – Cadbury Castle (≤★★) NE : 10 ½ m. by A 359 – East Lambrook Manor★ AC, W : 12 m by A 3088 and A 303.
🅱, 🅱 Sherborne Rd ℘ (01935) 75949.
🅸 Petter's House, Petter's Way, BA20 1SH ℘ (01935) 471279 – at Podimore, Sou Somerset Visitor Centre, Forte Services (A 303), BA22 8JG ℘ (01935) 841302 (summer only
London 136 – Exeter 48 – Southampton 72 – Taunton 26.

🏨 **Yeovil Court,** West Coker Rd., BA20 2NE, SW : 2 m. on A 30 ℘ (01935) 86374, Fax (01935) 863990 – 🆅 ☎ ☯ – 🔬 60. ◑ 𝔸𝔼 ⓞ 𝚅𝙸𝚂𝙰 𝙹𝙲𝙱
Meals (closed Saturday lunch and Sunday dinner) a la carte 14.15/22.10 **st.** ⬧ 5.95 – **25 rm** ⥿ 59.00/69.00 **st.**, 1 suite – SB.

🏛 **Holywell House** ⌂, Holywell, East Coker, BA22 9NQ, SW : 2 ¾ m. by A 30 on Hardington rd ℘ (01935) 862612, Fax (01935) 863035, « Georgian manor house », ⚘, ✗ – 📺 📞. ✗ *closed 2 weeks Christmas and New Year* – **Meals** *(booking essential) (residents only) (communal dining) (dinner only) (unlicensed)* 17.00 **st.** – **2 rm** ⊃ 35.00/65.00 **s.**, 1 suite – SB.

at Podimore N : 9½ m. by A 37 off A 303 – ⊠ Yeovil.

🏛 **Travelodge,** BA22 8JG, W : ½ m. ℘ (01935) 840074, Reservations (Freephone) 0800 850950 – ⬧✗ rm, 📺 👤 📞. 🆗 Ⓐ🅴 ⓪ 𝗩𝗜𝗦𝗔 𝖩𝖢𝖡. ✗
Meals (grill rest.) – **31 rm** 44.95 **t.**

at Barwick S : 2 m. by A 30 off A 37 – ⊠ Yeovil.

✗✗ **Little Barwick House** ⌂ with rm, BA22 9TD, ℘ (01935) 423902, Fax (01935) 420908, « Georgian dower house », ⚘ – ⬧✗ rest, 📺 ☎ 📞. 🆗 Ⓐ🅴 𝗩𝗜𝗦𝗔 𝖩𝖢𝖡 *closed Christmas-New Year* – **Meals** *(closed Sunday to non-residents)* (booking essential) (dinner only) 25.90 **st.** ▲ 5.50 – **6 rm** ⊃ 54.50/89.00 **st.**

at West Coker SW : 3½ m. on A 30.

✗ **Skittles in the Square,** 1 Church St., BA22 9AH, ℘ (01935) 863986 – ⬧✗. 🆗 Ⓐ🅴 ⓪ 𝗩𝗜𝗦𝗔 𝖩𝖢𝖡
Meals 7.50 **t.** (lunch) and a la carte 13.50/23.50 **t.** ▲ 6.00.

at Montacute W : 5½ m. by A 3088 – ⊠ Martock.

🏛 **Kings Arms,** Bishopston, TA15 6UU, ℘ (01935) 822513, Fax (01935) 826549, ⚘ – ⬧✗ 📺 ☎ 📞. 🆗 Ⓐ🅴 𝗩𝗜𝗦𝗔. ✗
closed 25 December-5 January – **Meals** (buffet lunch Monday to Saturday and bar dinner Sunday) 21.00 **t.** (dinner) and a la carte 15.95/19.95 **t.** ▲ 5.90 – **13 rm** ⊃ 53.00/85.00 **t.** – SB.

✗✗ **Milk House** with rm, The Borough Sq., TA15 6XB, ℘ (01935) 823823, ⚘ – ⬧✗. ✗
closed January and Christmas – **Meals** *(closed Sunday to Tuesday)* (dinner only) 20.00 **st.** and a la carte ▲ 5.00 – ⊃ 5.00 – **2 rm** 40.00/50.00 **st.** – SB.

ⓐ ATS Lyde Rd, Penmill Trading Est. ℘ (01935) 475580

YETMINSTER Dorset 🄃🄀🄃 🄃🄀🄃 M 31 – see Sherborne.

YORK N. Yorks. 🄃🄀🄃 Q 22 Great Britain G. – pop. 124 609.

See : City★★★ – Minster★★★ (Stained Glass★★★ , Chapter House★★ , Choir Screen★★) CDY – National Railway Museum★★★ CY – The Walls★★ CDXYZ – Castle Museum★ AC DZ M2 – Jorvik Viking Centre★ AC DY M1 – Fairfax House★ AC DY A – The Shambles★ DY 54.

🄵 Lords Moor Lane, Strensall ℘ (01904) 491840, BY – 🄵 Heworth, Muncaster House, Muncastergate ℘ (01904) 424618 BY.

🄳 The De Grey Rooms, Exhibition Sq., YO1 2HB ℘ (01904) 621756 – York Railway Station, Outer Concourse, YO2 2AY ℘ (01904) 621756 – TIC Travel Office, 6 Rougier St., YO1 1JA ℘ (01904) 620557.

London 203 – Kingston-upon-Hull 38 – Leeds 26 – Middlesbrough 51 – Nottingham 88 – Sheffield 62.

Plan on next page

🏨 **Middlethorpe Hall,** Bishopthorpe Rd, YO2 1QB, S : 1 ¾ m. ℘ (01904) 641241, Fax (01904) 620176, ⩽, « William and Mary house, gardens », park – 📶, ⬧✗ rest, 📺 ☎ 📞 – 🄰 50. 🆗 Ⓐ🅴 𝗩𝗜𝗦𝗔. ✗
Meals (booking essential to non-residents) 12.50/26.95 **st.** and a la carte 34.95/45.00 **st.** ▲ 7.00 – **Grill** : **Meals** *(May-September)* (dinner only Friday and Saturday) 26.95 **st.** ▲ 7.00 – ⊃ 11.50 – **23 rm** 95.00/145.00 **st.**, 7 suites – SB.

🏨 **Swallow,** Tadcaster Rd, YO2 2QQ, ℘ (01904) 701000, Fax (01904) 702308, 🄵ỗ, 🕸, 🔲, ⚘ – 📶, ⬧✗ rm, 📺 ☎ 📞 – 🄰 170. 🆗 Ⓐ🅴 ⓪ 𝗩𝗜𝗦𝗔. ✗   AZ **a**
Meals 14.50/20.45 **st.** and a la carte ▲ 7.25 – **111 rm** ⊃ 99.00/140.00 **t.**, 1 suite – SB.

🏨 **York Viking Moat House,** North St., YO1 1JF, ℘ (01904) 459988, Fax (01904) 641793, ⩽, 🄵ỗ, 🕸 – 📶, ⬧✗ rm, ▤ rest, 📺 ☎ 📞 – 🄰 300. 🆗 Ⓐ🅴 ⓪ 𝗩𝗜𝗦𝗔 𝖩𝖢𝖡. ✗   CY **n**
Meals (bar lunch Monday to Saturday)/dinner 14.95 **t.** and a la carte ▲ 5.95 – ⊃ 9.50 – **199 rm** 120.00/145.00 **t.**, 1 suite – SB.

🏛 **The Grange,** Clifton, YO3 6AA, ℘ (01904) 644744, Fax (01904) 612453, « Regency town house » – 📺 ☎ 📞 – 🄰 45. 🆗 Ⓐ🅴 ⓪ 𝗩𝗜𝗦𝗔   CX **u**
The Ivy : **Meals** 11.50/24.00 **t.** and dinner a la carte ▲ 8.00 – **The Brasserie** : **Meals** a la carte 15.95/18.40 **t.** ▲ 7.00 – **29 rm** ⊃ 99.00/160.00 **st.**, 1 suite – SB.

🏛 **Ambassador,** 123-125 The Mount, YO2 2DA, ℘ (01904) 641316, Fax (01904) 640259, ⚘ – 📶, ⬧✗ rest, 📺 📞 – 🄰 50. 🆗 Ⓐ🅴 ⓪ 𝗩𝗜𝗦𝗔. ✗   AZ **c**
Meals (dinner only) 20.50 **t.** and a la carte ▲ 6.45 – **24 rm** ⊃ 98.00/128.00 **t.** – SB.

YORK

🏨 **York Pavilion,** 45 Main St., Fulford, YO1 4PJ, S : 1 m. on A 19 , *℘ (01904) 622099,
Fax (01904) 626939 – ⇔ rest, 📺 ☎ 🅿 – 🕍 30. 🐝 🆎 ⓪ 𝗩𝗜𝗦𝗔 𝗝𝗖𝗕. ⅜
Meals a la carte 16.90/26.95 **t.** – **34 rm** ⊇ 84.00/126.00 **t.** – SB.

🏨 **Forte Posthouse York,** Tadcaster Rd, YO2 2QF, *℘ (01904) 707921, Fax (01904) 702804,*
🐎 – 📲, ⇔ rm, 🔲 rest, 📺 ☎ 🅿 – 🕍 100. 🐝 🆎 ⓪ 𝗩𝗜𝗦𝗔 𝗝𝗖𝗕   AZ r
Meals a la carte 13.95/23.85 **t.** ⍭ 7.95 – ⊇ 8.95 – **142 rm** 69.00 **st.** – SB.

🏨 **Dean Court,** Duncombe Pl., YO1 2EF, *℘ (01904) 625082, Fax (01904) 620305* – 📲, ⇔ rm,
📺 ☎ 🅿 – 🕍 50. 🐝 🆎 ⓪ 𝗩𝗜𝗦𝗔 𝗝𝗖𝗕. ⅜   CY c
Meals 13.50/21.00 **st.** ⍭ 6.25 – **41 rm** ⊇ 75.00/115.00 **st.** – SB.

🏨 **Judges' Lodging,** 9 Lendal, YO1 2AQ, *℘ (01904) 638733, Fax (01904) 679947* – 📺 ☎ 🅿.
🐝 🆎 ⓪ 𝗩𝗜𝗦𝗔. ⅜   CY x
Meals a la carte 14.95/23.45 **st.** ⍭ 5.95 – **13 rm** ⊇ 75.00/130.00 **t.**

🏨 **Novotel,** Fishergate, YO1 4AD, *℘ (01904) 611660, Fax (01904) 610925,* 🔲 – 📲, ⇔ rm,
🔲 rest, 📺 ☎ 🕭 🅿 – 🕍 210. 🐝 🆎 ⓪ 𝗩𝗜𝗦𝗔   DZ o
Meals (bar lunch Monday to Saturday)/dinner 15.50 **st.** and a la carte ⍭ 5.35 – ⊇ 8.50 –
124 rm 80.00/95.00 **st.** – SB.

🏨 **Monkbar,** St. Maurice's Rd, YO3 7JA, *℘ (01904) 638086, Fax (01904) 629195* – 📲, ⇔ rest,
📺 ☎ 🅿 – 🕍 70. 🐝 🆎 ⓪ 𝗩𝗜𝗦𝗔 𝗝𝗖𝗕. ⅜   DX a
Meals (dinner only and Sunday lunch)/dinner 16.50 **st.** and a la carte ⍭ 6.95 – **47 rm**
⊇ 75.00/125.00.

🏠 **Arndale** without rest., 290 Tadcaster Rd, YO2 2ET, *℘ (01904) 702424,* 🐎 – 📺 🅿. 🐝. ⅜
closed Christmas and New Year – **10 rm** ⊇ 59.00/70.00 **st.**   AZ i

🏠 **23 St. Mary's** without rest., 23 St. Mary's, Bootham, YO3 7DD, *℘ (01904) 622738* – ⇔ 📺
☎. ⅜   CX a
closed 24 to 31 December – **9 rm** ⊇ 28.00/66.00 **t.**

🏠 **Holmwood House** without rest., 114 Holgate Rd, YO2 4BB, *℘ (01904) 626183,*
Fax (01904) 670899 – ⇔ 📺 ☎ 🅿. 🐝 🆎 𝗩𝗜𝗦𝗔. ⅜   AZ x
11 rm ⊇ 45.00/70.00 **t.**

🏠 **Curzon Lodge and Stable Cottages** without rest., 23 Tadcaster Rd, YO2 2QG,
℘ (01904) 703157 – 📺 🅿. 🐝 𝗩𝗜𝗦𝗔 𝗝𝗖𝗕. ⅜   AZ a
closed 24 to 26 December – **10 rm** ⊇ 42.00/65.00 **st.**

🏠 **Kilima,** 129 Holgate Rd, YO2 4DE, *℘ (01904) 625787, Fax (01904) 612083,* 🐎 – ⇔ rest,
📺 ☎ 🕭 🅿. 🐝 🆎 𝗩𝗜𝗦𝗔   AZ n
Meals (lunch by arrangement)/dinner 18.95 **t.** ⍭ 4.75 – **15 rm** ⊇ 50.00/90.00 **t.** – SB.

🏠 **Grasmead House** without rest., 1 Scarcroft Hill, YO2 1DF, *℘ (01904) 629996,*
Fax (01904) 629996 – ⇔ 📺. 🐝 🆎 𝗩𝗜𝗦𝗔 𝗝𝗖𝗕. ⅜   CZ a
5 rm ⊇ 45.00/60.00 **st.**

🏠 **Clifton Bridge,** Water End, YO3 6LL, *℘ (01904) 610510, Fax (01904) 640208* – 📺 ☎ 🅿.
🐝 🆎 ⓪ 𝗩𝗜𝗦𝗔   AY e
closed 24 to 26 December – **Meals** (dinner only) 10.00 **st.** and a la carte ⍭ 5.25 – **14 rm**
⊇ 42.00/68.00 **t.** – SB.

🏠 **Cottage,** 3 Clifton Green, YO3 6LH, *℘ (01904) 643711, Fax (01904) 611230* – ⇔ rest, 📺
☎ 🅿. 🐝 🆎 ⓪ 𝗩𝗜𝗦𝗔. ⅜   AY v
closed Christmas – **Meals** (dinner only) 11.50 and a la carte ⍭ 4.95 – **18 rm** ⊇ 45.00/75.00 **t.**
– SB.

🏠 **Black Bull,** Hull Rd, YO1 3LF, *℘ (01904) 411856, Fax (01904) 430667* – 📺 ☎ 🕭 🅿. 🐝 🆎
𝗩𝗜𝗦𝗔 𝗝𝗖𝗕. ⅜   BZ e
Meals (bar lunch Monday to Saturday)/dinner 10.50 **st.** and a la carte ⍭ 3.95 – ⊇ 5.00 –
40 rm 45.00/55.00 **st.**

⌂ **4 South Parade** without rest., 4 South Par., YO2 2BA, *℘ (01904) 628229,*
Fax (01904) 628229, « Georgian town house » – ⇔ 📺 ☎ 🅿. ⅜   CZ n
closed 1 week Christmas – **3 rm** ⊇ 73.00/93.00 **st.**

⌂ **18 St. Paul's Square,** 18 St. Paul's Sq., YO2 4BD, *℘ (01904) 629884,* 🐎 – ⇔.
⅜   AZ z
Meals (by arrangement) (communal dining) 18.50 **s.** – **3 rm** ⊇ 45.00/70.00 **s.**

⌂ **Ashbury** without rest., 103 The Mount, YO2 2AX, *℘ (01904) 647339, Fax (01904) 647339,*
🐎 – ⇔ 📺. ⅜   CZ e
closed 20 December-5 January – **6 rm** ⊇ 35.00/55.00 **st.**

⌂ **Crook Lodge,** 26 St. Mary's, Bootham, YO3 7DD, *℘ (01904) 655614* – ⇔ 📺 🅿.
⅜   CX z
closed Christmas and January – **Meals** 12.00 **st.** ⍭ 4.00 – **7 rm** ⊇ 25.00/50.00 **st.** – SB.

↑ **Hobbits** without rest., 9 St. Peter's Grove, Clifton, YO3 6AQ, ℰ (01904) 624538, Fax (01904) 651765 – ⇔ �📺 🅿. ◑◐ ⑩ *VISA*. ⅍
closed 1 week Christmas – **6 rm** ☟ 30.00/55.00 **st.**
· CX e

XX **Melton's**, 7 Scarcroft Rd, YO2 1ND, ℰ (01904) 634341, Fax (01904) 635115 – ⇔. ◑◐ *VISA*
closed Monday lunch, Sunday dinner, 1 week late August and 3 weeks Christmas-New Year
– **Meals** (booking essential) 15.00/19.50 **st.** and a la carte ₰ 6.00.
CZ c

at Kexby *E : 6¾ m. on A 1079 –* B *–* ⊠ *York.*

🏥 **Kexby Bridge**, Hull Rd, YO4 5LD, ℰ (01759) 388223, Fax (01759) 388822, ⤜, ⇌ – 📺 ☎ 🅿. ◑◐ *VISA*. ⅍
Meals (bar lunch)/dinner a la carte 10.00/20.85 **st.** ₰ 6.50 – **32 rm** ☟ 50.00/75.00 **st.** – SB.

at Escrick *S : 5¾ m. on A 19 –* B *–* ⊠ *York.*

🏥 **Parsonage Country House**, Main St., YO4 6LF, ℰ (01904) 728111 Fax (01904) 728151, ⇌ – ⇔ rest, 📺 ☎ 🅿 – 🔬 160. ◑◐ ⒶⒺ *VISA* *JCB*. ⅍
Meals 17.50 **t.** (dinner) and lunch a la carte 9.80/15.80 **t.** ₰ 4.50 – **13 rm** ☟ 70.00/145.00 **st**
SB.

at Bilbrough *SW : 5½ m. by A 1036 –* AZ *– off A 64 –* ⊠ *York.*

🏨 **Travel Inn**, Bilbrough Top, Colton, YO2 3PP, S : ½ m. on A 64 (westbound carriageway ℰ (01937) 835067, Fax (01937) 835934 – ⧈, ⇔ rm, 📺 ♿ 🅿 – 🔬 35. ◑◐ ⒶⒺ ⑩ *VISA*. ⅍
Meals (grill rest.) – **60 rm** 36.50 **t.**

🏨 **Travelodge**, Steeton, LS24 8EG, SW : ¾ m. on A 64 (eastbound carriageway ℰ (01937) 531823, Reservations (Freephone) 0800 850950 – ⇔ rm, 📺 ♿ 🅿. ◑◐ ⒶⒺ ⑩ *VISA* *JCB*. ⅍
Meals (grill rest.) – **40 rm** 44.95 **t.**

at Long Marston *W : 7 m. on B 1224 –* AZ *–* ⊠ *York.*

↑ **Gill House Farm** without rest., Tockwith Rd, YO5 8PJ, N : ½ m. ℰ (01904) 738379
« Working farm », ⇌ – ⇔ 📺 🅿. ◑◐ *VISA*
closed Christmas-Easter – **4 rm** ☟ 35.00/46.00 **st.**

at Skelton *NW : 3 m. on A 19 –* A *–* ⊠ *York.*

🏩 Fairfield Manor, Shipton Rd, YO3 6XW, ℰ (01904) 670222, Fax (01904) 670311, ⇌ – ⧈
⇔, 🍽 rest, 📺 ☎ 🅿 – 🔬 200
83 rm, 6 suites.

ⓘ ATS 2 James St. ℰ (01904) 412372/410375   ATS 110 Layerthorpe ℰ (01904) 628479/625884
ATS 36 Holgate Rd ℰ (01904) 654411

GREEN TOURIST GUIDES

Picturesque scenery, buildings
Attractive routes
Touring programmes
Plans of towns and buildings.

Scotland

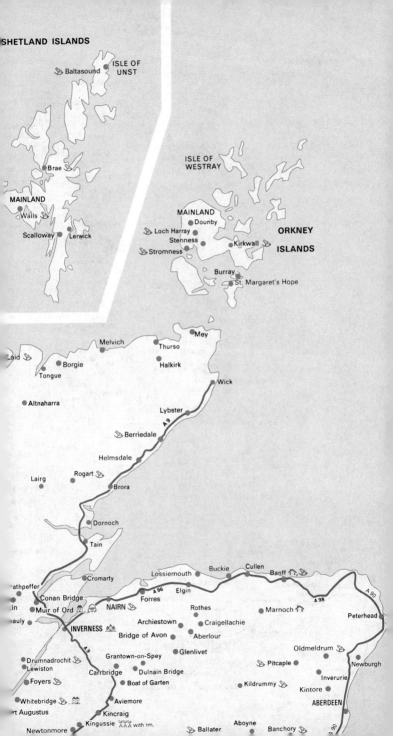

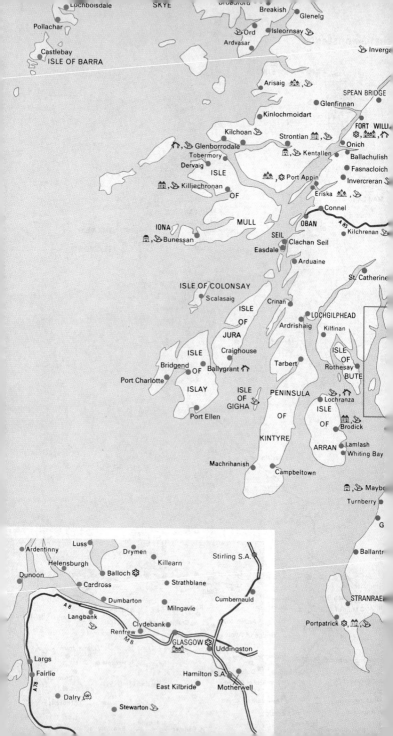

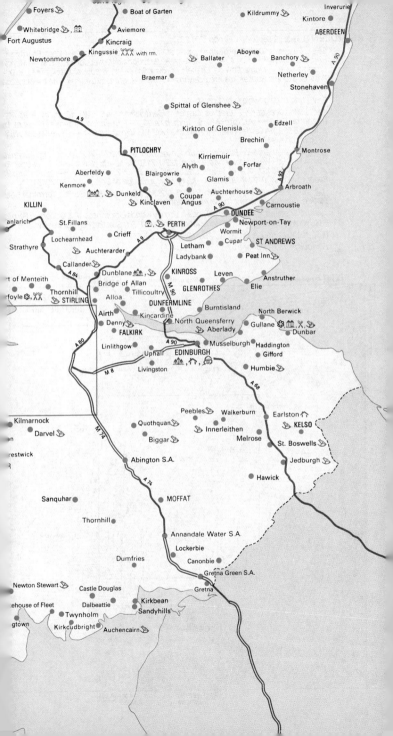

ABERDEEN 401 N 12 *Scotland G. – pop. 204 885.*

See : *City★★ – Old Aberdeen★★* X *– St. Machar's Cathedral★★ (West Front★★★, Heraldic Ceiling★★★)* X A *– Art Gallery★★ (Macdonald Collection★★)* Y M *– Mercat Cross★★* Y B *– King's College Chapel★ (Crown Spire★★★, medieval fittings★★★)* X D *– Provost Skene's House★ (painted ceilings★★)* Y E *– Maritime Museum★* Z M1 *– Marischal College★* Y U.

Env. : *Brig o' Balgownie★, by Don St.* X.

Exc. : *SW : Deeside★★ – Crathes Castle★★ (Gardens★★★)* AC*, SW : 16 m. by A 93* X *– Dunnottar Castle★★* AC *(site★★★)*, *S : 18 m. by A 90* X *– Pitmedden Garden★★*, *N : 14 m. by A 90 on B 999* X *– Castle Fraser★ (exterior★★)* AC*, W : 16 m. by A 944* X *– Fyvie Castle★, NW 26 ½ m. on A 947.*

🏌, 🏌 *Royal Aberdeen, Balgownie, Bridge of Don* ℘ *(01224) 702571,* X *–* 🏌 *Auchmill Bomyview Rd, West Heatheryfold* ℘ *(01224) 715214,* X *–* 🏌 *Balnagask, St. Fitticks Rd* ℘ *(01224) 876407,* X *–* 🏌 *King's Links, Golf Rd* ℘ *(01224) 632269,* X *–* 🏌 *Portlethen Badentoy Rd* ℘ *(01224) 782575,* X*–*🏌, 🏌 *Murcar, Bridge of Don* ℘ *(01224) 704345,* X.

✈ *Aberdeen Airport, Dyce :* ℘ *(01224) 722331, NW : 7 m. by A 96* X *–* **Terminal :** *Bus Station, Guild St. (adjacent to Railway Station).*

⛴ *to Shetland Islands (Lerwick) and via Orkney Islands (Stromness) (P & O Scottish Ferries) – to Norway (Bergen) via Shetland Islands (Lerwick) (P & O Scottish Ferries) weekly.*

🛈 *St. Nicholas House, Broad St., AB9 1DE* ℘ *(01224) 632727.*

Edinburgh 130 – Dundee 67.

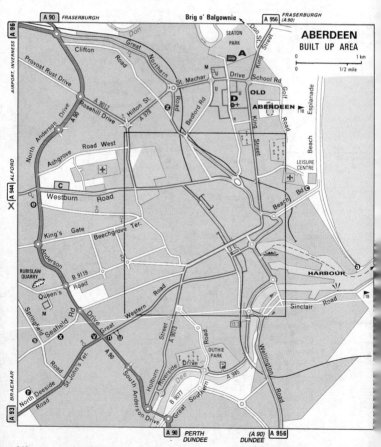

ABERDEEN

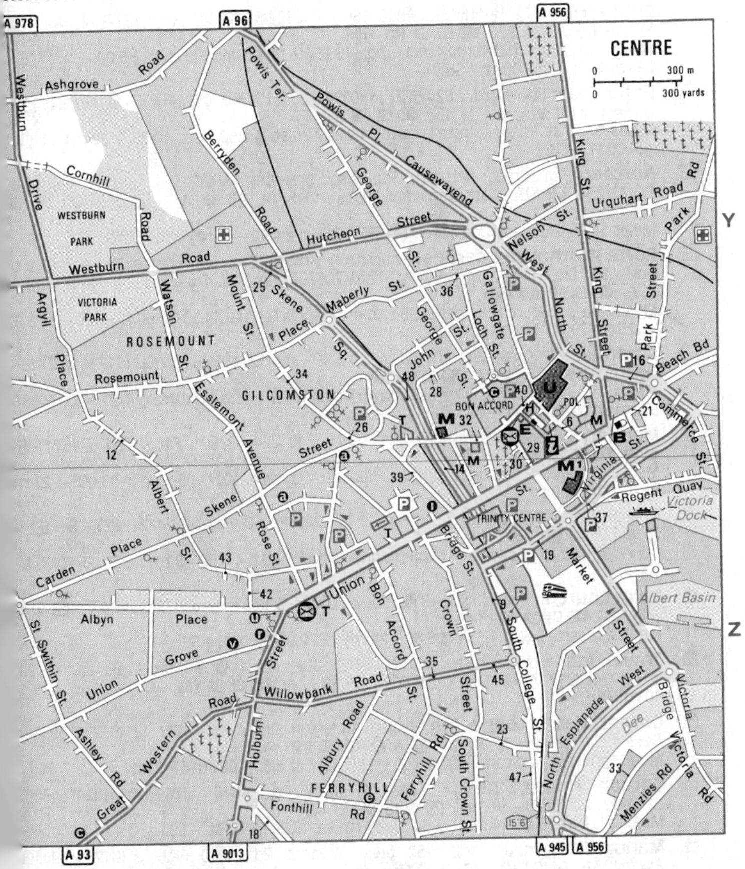

Marcliffe at Pitfodels, North Deeside Rd, AB15 9YA, ✆ (01224) 861000, *Fax (01224) 868860*, rest, – 400.
VISA
Invery Room **:** Meals (dinner only) a la carte 24.50/41.50 **st.** 8.50 – ***Conservatory*** **:** Meals a la carte 21.70/27.70 **st.** 8.50 – **42 rm** 135.00/290.00 **st.** – SB. X r

Skene House Holborn without rest., 6 Union Grove, AB10 6SY, ✆ (01224) 580000, *Fax (01224) 585193* – VISA JCB. Z v
35 suites 94.50/140.00 **st.**.

Ardoe House, South Deeside Rd, Blairs, AB12 5YP, SW: 5 m. on B 9077 ✆ (01224) 867355, *Fax (01224) 861283*, ←, « Part 19C baronial mansion », , park – – 120. VISA
Meals *(closed Saturday lunch)* a la carte 26.75/34.40 **t.** 7.00 – 12.50 – **69 rm** 125.00/145.00 **t.**, 2 suites – SB.

🏨 **Caledonian Thistle**, 10-14 Union Terr., AB10 1WE, ℰ (01224) 640233,
Fax (01224) 641627 – |≋|, ✸ rm, 🆚 ☎ 🅿 – 🔬 35. 🆚 ⒶⒺ ⓪ 𝘝𝘐𝘚𝘈 𝘑𝘊𝘉
Meals *(closed lunch Saturday and Sunday)* 13.95/21.00 **t.** and a la carte ⓙ 6.25 – ⚏ 11.75 –
78 rm 115.00/150.00 **t.**, 2 suites – SB.

🏨 **Stakis Aberdeen Tree Tops**, 161 Springfield Rd, AB15 7AQ, ℰ (01224) 313377,
Fax (01224) 312028, ℹ₆, ⚏, ☒, ☞, ℀ – |≋|, ✸ rm, 🆚 ☎ 🅿 – 🔬 900. 🆚 ⒶⒺ ⓪ 𝘝𝘐𝘚𝘈,
Meals 10.00/17.50 **t.** and dinner a la carte ⓙ 7.50 – ⚏ 9.50 – **111 rm** 105.00/115.00 **st.**,
1 suite – SB.

🏨 **Copthorne**, 122 Huntly St., AB10 1SU, ℰ (01224) 630404, *Fax (01224) 640573* – |≋|,
✸ rm, 🆚 ☎ 🅿 – 🔬 220. 🆚 ⒶⒺ ⓪ 𝘝𝘐𝘚𝘈 𝘑𝘊𝘉
Meals *(closed lunch Saturday and Sunday)* 8.95/16.95 **st.** and a la carte ⓙ 5.00 – ⚏ 11.25 –
89 rm 124.00/164.00 **st.** – SB.

🏨 **Patio**, Beach Boulevard, AB24 5EF, ℰ (01224) 633339, *Fax (01224) 638833*, ℹ₆, ⚏, ☒,
|≋|, ✸ rm, 🆚 ☎ & 🅿 – 🔬 150. 🆚 ⒶⒺ ⓪ 𝘝𝘐𝘚𝘈 𝘑𝘊𝘉
Meals 16.50 **st.** (dinner) and a la carte 14.95/27.20 **st.** ⓙ 6.50 – ⚏ 10.25 – **92 rm** 111.00/
184.00 **st.** – SB.

🏨 **Northern**, 1 Great Northern Rd, Kitty Brewster, AB24 3PS, ℰ (01224) 483342,
Fax (01224) 276103, « Art Deco building » – ✸ rm, 🆚 ☎ & – 🔬 350. 🆚 ⒶⒺ ⓪
𝘝𝘐𝘚𝘈
Meals 10.95 **t.** (dinner) and a la carte 8.85/18.50 **t.** ⓙ 4.40 – **30 rm** ⚏ 53.00/60.00 **t.** – SB.

🏨 **Forte Posthouse Aberdeen**, Aberdeen Exhibition and Conference Centre, Bridge of
Don, AB23 8BL, N : 3 m. on A 90 ℰ (01224) 706707, *Fax (01224) 823923* – |≋|, ✸ rm, 🆚 ☎
& 🅿. 🆚 ⒶⒺ ⓪ 𝘝𝘐𝘚𝘈 𝘑𝘊𝘉
Meals *(closed Saturday lunch)* 14.95 **t.** (dinner) and a la carte 14.50/28.50 **t.** ⓙ 7.50 – ⚏ 8.95
– **123 rm** 79.00/149.00 **st.** – SB.

🏨 **Amatola**, 448 Great Western Rd, AB10 6NP, ℰ (01224) 318724, *Fax (01224) 312716* –
✸ rm, 🆚 ☎ 🅿 – 🔬 400. 🆚 ⒶⒺ ⓪ 𝘝𝘐𝘚𝘈
Meals *(bar lunch Monday to Saturday)/dinner* 13.95 **t.** and a la carte ⓙ 7.50 – ⚏ 8.95 –
53 rm 84.00/104.00 **t.** – SB.

🏨 **Mariner**, 349 Great Western Rd, AB10 6NW, ℰ (01224) 588901, *Fax (01224) 571621* – 🆚
☎ 🅿. 🆚 ⒶⒺ ⓪ 𝘝𝘐𝘚𝘈 𝘑𝘊𝘉. ℀
Meals - Seafood - *(closed Saturday lunch)* a la carte 10.00/25.50 **t.** ⓙ 13.00 – **22 rm**
⚏ 65.00/95.00 **t.**

🏨 **Craiglynn**, 36 Fonthill Rd, AB11 6UJ, ℰ (01224) 584050, *Fax (01224) 212225* – ✸ 🆚
🅿. 🆚 ⒶⒺ ⓪ 𝘝𝘐𝘚𝘈 𝘑𝘊𝘉. ℀
closed 25 and 26 December – **Meals** *(dinner only)/*15.50 **t.** ⓙ 4.50 – **9 rm** ⚏ 30.00/70.00 **t.** –
SB.

🏨 **Palm Court**, 81 Seafield Rd, AB15 7YU, ℰ (01224) 310351, *Fax (01224) 312707* – 🆚 ☎
– 🔬 100. 🆚 ⒶⒺ ⓪ 𝘝𝘐𝘚𝘈. ℀
Meals a la carte 9.60/21.35 **t.** ⓙ 6.80 – **24 rm** ⚏ 70.00/90.00 **t.** – SB.

🏨 **Travel Inn** without rest., Murcar, AB23 8BP, N : 4 ½ m. on A 90 and B 99
ℰ (01224) 821217, *Fax (01224) 706869* – ✸ 🆚 & 🅿. 🆚 ⒶⒺ ⓪ 𝘝𝘐𝘚𝘈. ℀
40 rm 36.50 **t.**

🏨 **Cocket Hat - Lodge Inn**, North Anderson Drive, AB2 6DW, ℰ (01224) 695684,
Fax (01224) 692438 – |≋|, ✸ rm, 🆚 🅿. 🆚 ⒶⒺ ⓪ 𝘝𝘐𝘚𝘈. ℀
Meals *(grill rest.)* a la carte 7.20/15.60 **st.** ⓙ 3.95 – ⚏ 5.50 – **60 rm** 37.50 **st.**

🏠 **Corner House**, 385-387 Great Western Rd, AB10 6NY, ℰ (01224) 313063,
Fax (01224) 313063 – ✸ rest, 🆚 ☎ 🅿. 🆚 ⒶⒺ 𝘝𝘐𝘚𝘈
Meals a la carte 8.15/14.30 **st.** ⓙ 3.75 – **17 rm** ⚏ 48.00/58.00 **st.** – SB.

🏠 **Manorville** without rest., 252 Great Western Rd, AB10 6PJ, ℰ (01224) 594190,
Fax (01224) 594190, ☞ – 🆚 🅿. 🆚 𝘝𝘐𝘚𝘈. ℀
3 rm ⚏ 25.00/44.00.

🏠 **Fourways** without rest., 435 Great Western Rd, AB10 6NJ, ℰ (01224) 310218,
Fax (01224) 310218 – 🆚 🅿. 🆚 ⒶⒺ 𝘝𝘐𝘚𝘈. ℀
6 rm ⚏ 25.00/40.00 **s.**

✕✕ **Q Brasserie**, 9 Alford Pl., AB1 1YD, ℰ (01224) 595001, *Fax (01224) 582245* – 🆚 ⒶⒺ 𝘝𝘐𝘚𝘈
closed Saturday lunch and Sunday – **Meals** a la carte 24.00/31.00 **st.**

✕✕ **Rendezvous**, 210-212 George St., AB1 1BS, ℰ (01224) 633610, *Fax (01224) 649389* –
🆚 ⒶⒺ 𝘝𝘐𝘚𝘈
closed Sunday lunch – **Meals** - Chinese (Peking) and Thai - 8.90/17.00 **st.** and a la carte
ⓙ 6.00.

✕✕ **Courtyard on the Lane**, 1 Alford Lane, AB1 1YD, ℰ (01224) 21379,
Fax (01224) 212961 – 🆚 ⒶⒺ 𝘝𝘐𝘚𝘈. ℀
closed Sunday, Monday, 25 December and first week January – **Meals** a la carte 12.85/
20.15 **t.** ⓙ 6.95.

🍴🍴 **Nargile**, 77-79 Skene St., AB1 1QD, ☎ (01224) 636093, *Fax (01224) 636202* – [MC] [AE] [①] [VISA]
closed 25-26 December and 1 January – **Meals** - Turkish - (dinner only) 20.95 **t.** and a la carte 🍷 5.80. Y a

🍴 **Silver Darling**, Pocra Quay, North Pier, AB11 5DQ, ☎ (01224) 576229, *Fax (01224) 791275* – [MC] [AE] [①] [VISA] [JCB] X a
closed Saturday lunch, Sunday, 2 weeks Christmas-New Year – **Meals** - French Seafood - (booking essential) a la carte 27.90/63.50 **t.** 🍷 7.40.

at Altens *(Aberdeenshire) S : 3 m. on A 956 – X – ✉ Aberdeen.*

🏨 **Aberdeen Thistle**, Souter Head Rd, AB12 3LF, ☎ (01224) 877000, *Fax (01224) 896964*, 🏊 – 🛗, 🚭 rm, ▤ rest, [TV] ☎ ♿ 🅿 – 👥 400. [MC] [AE] [①] [VISA]
Meals 9.50/17.50 **st.** and a la carte 🍷 6.20 – ☕ 10.25 – **220 rm** 95.00/135.00, 1 suite – SB.

at Portlethen *(Aberdeenshire) S : 6 m. on A 90 – X – ✉ Aberdeen.*

🏨 **Travel Inn**, Mains of Balquuarn, AB12 4QS, ☎ (01224) 783856, *Fax (01224) 783836* – [MC] [AE] [①] [VISA]
Meals (grill rest.) – **40 rm** 36.50 **t.**

at Cults *(Aberdeenshire) SW : 4 m. on A 93 – X – ✉ Aberdeen.*

🍴 **Faraday's**, 2 Kirk Brae, AB1 9SQ, ☎ (01224) 869666, *Fax (01224) 869666* – 🅿. [MC] [AE] [VISA]
closed Sunday, Monday and 26 December-6 January – **Meals** (booking essential) 25.95 **t.** (dinner) and lunch a la carte 9.65/13.10 **t.** 🍷 6.60.

at Maryculter *(Aberdeenshire) SW : 8 m. on B 9077 – X – ✉ Aberdeen.*

🏨 **Maryculter House** 🐦, South Deeside Rd, AB12 5GB, ☎ (01224) 732124, *Fax (01224) 733510*, « Part 13C house on River Dee », 🌳 – 🚭 [TV] ☎ 🅿 – 👥 200. [MC] [AE] [①] [VISA]
Meals (bar lunch)/dinner 27.50 **t.** 🍷 6.00 – **23 rm** ☕ 105.00/120.00 **t.** – SB.

at Bankhead *(Aberdeenshire) NW : 3½ m. by A 96 – X – ✉ Aberdeen.*

🏨 **Craighaar**, Waterton Rd, AB21 9HS, ☎ (01224) 712275, *Fax (01224) 716362* – 🚭 rm, [TV] ☎ 🅿 – 👥 90. [MC] [AE] [①] [VISA]. 🐕
Meals *(closed Saturday lunch)* 18.95 **t.** (dinner) and a la carte 9.80/24.65 **t.** 🍷 6.80 – **49 rm** ☕ 69.50/105.00 **t.**, 6 suites – SB.

at Bucksburn *(Aberdeenshire) NW : 4 m. by A 96 – X – on A 947 – ✉ Aberdeen.*

🏨 **Holiday Inn Crown Plaza Aberdeen**, Malcolm Rd, AB21 9LN, ☎ (01224) 409988, *Fax (01224) 714020*, 🏋, ♨, 🏊 – 🛗, 🚭 rm, [TV] ☎ 🅿 – 👥 180. [MC] [AE] [①] [VISA]
Meals *(bar lunch Monday to Saturday)/dinner* 17.50 **st.** and a la carte 🍷 6.95 – ☕ 10.95 – **144 rm** 105.00/120.00 **st.** – SB.

at Dyce *(Aberdeenshire) NW : 5½ m. by A 96 – X – on A 947 – ✉ Aberdeen.*

🏨 **Aberdeen Marriott**, Overton Circle, AB21 7AZ, ☎ (01224) 770011, *Fax (01224) 722347*, 🏋, ♨, 🏊 – 🚭 rm, ▤ [TV] ☎ ♿ 🅿 – 👥 400. [MC] [AE] [①] [VISA] [JCB]. 🐕
Meals 15.95 **t.** and dinner a la carte 🍷 9.00 – ☕ 10.95 – **154 rm** 99.00 **t.**, 1 suite – SB.

🏨 **Travel Inn**, Burnside Drive, AB21 7HW, off Riverview Drive via Wellheads Rd ☎ (01224) 772787, *Fax (01224) 772968*, 🌳 – 🚭 rm, [TV] ♿ 🅿. [MC] [AE] [①] [VISA]. 🐕
Meals (grill rest.) – **40 rm** 36.50 **t.**

at Aberdeen Airport *(Aberdeenshire) NW : 6 m. by A 96 – X – ✉ Aberdeen.*

🏨 **Aberdeen Airport Thistle**, Argyll Rd, AB21 7DU, ☎ (01224) 725252, *Fax (01224) 723745*, 🏊 – 🚭 rm, [TV] ☎ ♿ 🅿 – 👥 550. [MC] [AE] [①] [VISA]
Meals 12.50/18.50 **st.** and a la carte 🍷 5.95 – ☕ 10.25 – **146 rm** 95.00/137.00 **st.**, 1 suite – SB.

🏨 **Speedbird Inn**, Argyll Rd, AB21 0AF, ☎ (01224) 772884, *Fax (01224) 772560* – 🚭 rm, [TV] ☎ ♿ 🅿 – 👥 35. [MC] [AE] [①] [VISA]
Meals *(closed lunch Saturday and Sunday)* (bar lunch)/dinner a la carte 11.70/14.95 **st.** – ☕ 3.95 – **99 rm** 42.50 **st.**

Ⓜ ATS Beach Boulevard ☎ (01224) 592727 ATS 214 Hardgate ☎ (01224) 589461

ABERDEEN AIRPORT *Aberdeenshire* [401] N 12 – *see Aberdeen.*

Bitte beachten Sie die Geschwindigkeitsbeschränkungen in Großbritannien
- 60 mph (= 96 km/h) außerhalb geschlossener Ortschaften
- 70 mph (= 112 km/h) auf Straßen mit getrennten Fahrbahnen und Autobahnen.

ABERFELDY Perthshire and Kinross **401** I 14 Scotland G. – pop. 4 083.

See : Town★.

Env. : St. Mary's Church (painted ceiling★) NE : 2 m. by A 827.

Exc. : Loch Tay★★, SW : 6 m. by A 827 – Ben Lawers★★, SW : 16 m. by A 827 – Blair Castle★★ AC, N : 20 ½ m. by A 827 and A 9.

🛗 Taybridge Rd ℰ (01887) 820535.

🖪 The Square, PH15 2DD ℰ (01887) 820276.

Edinburgh 76 – Glasgow 73 – Oban 77 – Perth 32.

🏨 **Farleyer House** ⟨⟩, PH15 2JE, W : 2 m. on B 846 ℰ (01887) 820332, Fax (01887) 829430, ⟨, ⟨, 🐎, park – ᢟ rest, 📺 ⟨ ⟨ ⟨, 🕮 AE ⟨ ⟨ VISA JCB, ⟨
Menzies : Meals (booking essential) (dinner only) 29.00 t. ⟨ 7.50 – **Bistro** : Meals 29.00 t. and a la carte ⟨ 7.50 – **11 rm** ⟨ 90.00/190.00 t. – SB.

🏨 **Guinach House** ⟨⟩, Urlar Rd, PH15 2ET, off Crieff Rd ℰ (01887) 820251, Fax (01887) 829607, ⟨, 🐎 – ᢟ rest, 📺 ⟨, 🕮 VISA, ⟨
closed 3 days Christmas – Meals (dinner only) 25.00 st. ⟨ 8.45 – **7 rm** ⟨ 42.50/85.00 st.

ABERFOYLE Stirling **401** G 15 Scotland G. – pop. 936 – ⊠ Stirling.

Env. : The Trossachs★★★ (Loch Katherine★★) N : 5 m. by A 821 – Hilltop Viewpoint★★★ (✳★★★) N : 2 ½ m. by A 821 – Inchmahone Priory (double effigy★) AC, E : 4 m. by A 81.

Exc. : Ben Lomond★★, W : 9 m. by B 829 – Loch Lomond★★, SW : 14 m. by A 81, A 811 and B 837.

🛗 Braeval ℰ (018772) 382493.

🖪 Main St., ℰ (01877) 382352 (summer only).

Edinburgh 56 – Glasgow 27.

XX **Braeval** (Nairn), FK8 3UY, E : 1 m. by A 821 on A 81 ℰ (01877) 382711, Fax (01877) 382400,
✿ « Converted mill », 🐎 – ⟨ ⟨ VISA
closed Sunday dinner, Wednesday lunch, Monday, Tuesday, 1 week February, June and October – Meals (booking essential) 19.50/31.50 t.
Spec. Risotto of seared scallops with asparagus and pesto oil. Roast rump of lamb with aubergine purée, couscous and a rosemary jus. Chilled chocolate cake with mascarpone sorbet.

ABERLADY East Lothian **401** L 15 – pop. 1 033.

Edinburgh 16 – Haddington 5 – North Berwick 7.5.

🏨 **Green Craigs** ⟨⟩, EH32 0PY, SW : ¾ m. on A 198 ℰ (01875) 870301, Fax (01875) 870440, ⟨, 🐎 – 📺 ⟨ ⟨ 🕮 AE ⟨ VISA JCB, ⟨
Meals 25.00 t. (dinner) and a la carte 12.75/29.25 t. ⟨ 6.00 – **6 rm** ⟨ 66.00/130.00 t. – SB.

🏨 **Kilspindie House,** Main St., EH32 0RE, ℰ (01875) 870682, Fax (01875) 870504 – 📺 ⟨ ⟨
🕮 VISA JCB
Meals a la carte 9.40/17.85 t. ⟨ 5.70 – **26 rm** ⟨ 47.00/68.00 t. – SB.

ABERLOUR Aberdeenshire **401** K 11 Scotland G. – pop. 1 780.

Env. : Dufftown (Glenfiddich Distillery★) SE : 6 m. by A 95 and A 941.

Edinburgh 192 – Aberdeen 60 – Elgin 15 – Inverness 55.

🏨 **Dowans,** AB38 9LS, SW : ¾ m. by A 95 ℰ (01340) 871488, Fax (01340) 871038, ⟨, 🐎 – ⟨
⟨ ⟨ 🕮 AE VISA
closed 20 December-15 March – Meals 19.95 st. (dinner) and a la carte 13.35/22.50 st. ⟨ 4.20 – **19 rm** ⟨ 39.00/90.00 st.

ABINGTON SERVICE AREA South Lanarkshire – ⊠ Biggar.

Edinburgh 43 – Dumfries 37 – Glasgow 38.

🏨 **Welcome Lodge,** ML12 6RG, at junction of A 74 with M 74 ℰ (01864) 502782, Fax (01864) 502759, Reservations (Freephone) 0800 7314466 – 📺 ⟨ ⟨, 🕮 AE ⟨ VISA, ⟨
Meals (grill rest.) – **56 rm** 45.00 t.

ABOYNE Aberdeenshire **401** L 12 Scotland G. – pop. 3 793 (inc. Cromar).

Exc. : Craigievar Castle★ AC, NE : 12 m. by B 9094, B 9119 and A 980.

🛗 Formanston Park ℰ (013398) 86328.

🖪 The Square ℰ (013398) 86060 (summer only).

Edinburgh 131 – Aberdeen 30 – Dundee 68.

Birse Lodge ⛰, Charleston Rd, AB34 5EL, ☏ (013398) 86253, *Fax (013398) 87796*, – TV ☎ P. MC VISA.
Meals a la carte 9.35/19.45 **t.** 5.50 – **12 rm** 39.00/70.00 **t.** – SB.

Hazlehurst Lodge, Ballater Rd, AB34 5HY, ☏ (013398) 86921, *Fax (013398) 86660*, « Contemporary art collection », – P. MC AE VISA
April-November – **Meals** 26.00 – **3 rm** 40.00/85.00 **st.** – SB.

Struan Hall without rest., Ballater Rd, AB34 5HY, ☏ (013398) 87241, *Fax (013398) 87241*, – TV P. MC VISA.
March-October – **3 rm** 24.00/48.00.

Arbor Lodge without rest., Ballater Rd, AB34 5HY, ☏ (013398) 86951, *Fax (013398) 86951*, – TV P. MC VISA
March-November – **3 rm** 24.00/48.00 **st.**

White Cottage, AB34 5BP, E : ½ m. on A 93 ☏ (013398) 86265, *Fax (013398) 86265* – P. MC VISA
closed Monday, 25 to 30 December, 1 week after Easter and 1 week October – **Meals** 26.70 **t.** dinner and a la carte 15.60/25.95 **t.** 5.90.

ACHILTIBUIE *Highland* 401 D 9.
Edinburgh 243 – Inverness 84 – Ullapool 25.

Summer Isles ⛰, IV26 2YG, ☏ (01854) 622282, *Fax (01854) 622251*, « Picturesque setting < Summer Isles », – rest, ☎ P. MC VISA
8 April-11 October – **Meals** (booking essential) (light seafood lunch) 35.00 **st.** (dinner) and lunch a la carte 11.50/38.00 **st.** – **11 rm** 57.00/106.00 **st.**, 1 suite
Spec. Ravioli verde stuffed with crabmeat. Breast of wood pigeon with celeriac purée and mushrooms. Selection of Scottish cheeses.

ACHMORE *Highland* 401 D 11 – ✉ *Stromeferry.*
Edinburgh 205 – Inverness 70 – Ullapool 75.

Soluis Mu Thuath ⛰ without rest., Braeintra, IV53 8UN, SE : 1 m. ☏ (01599) 577219, <, – TV ♿ P.
closed December and January – **4 rm** 25.00/40.00 **s.**

AIRTH *Falkirk* 401 I 15 – *pop. 1 519* – ✉ *Falkirk.*
Edinburgh 30 – Dunfermline 14 – Falkirk 7 – Stirling 8.

Radisson SAS Airth Castle ⛰, FK2 8JF, ☏ (01324) 831411, *Fax (01324) 831419*, <, « Part 13C and 17C castle and stables in extensive grounds », , park, – TV ☎ P – 380. MC AE VISA JCB.
Meals 12.95/21.50 **t.** and a la carte 7.10 – **129 rm** 105.00/160.00 **st.** – SB.

ALLOA *Clackmannanshire* 401 I 15 *Scotland G.* – *pop. 26 691.*
Exc. : *Culross★★ (Village★★★, Palace★★ AC, Study★ AC), SE : 7 m. by A 907, A 977 and B 9037 – Castle Campbell★ (site★★★, <★) AC, NE : 8 m. by A 908 and A 91 – Stirling★★, W : 8 m. by A 907.*
Edinburgh 33 – Dundee 48 – Glasgow 35.

Gean House ⛰, Gean Park, Tullibody Rd, FK10 2HS, NW : 1 m. on B 9096 ☏ (01259) 219275, *Fax (01259) 213827*, <, – rest, TV ☎ P – 50. MC AE VISA JCB.
Meals a la carte 13.50/21.50 **t.** – **7 rm** 80.00/140.00 **t.** – SB.

ATS Union St. ☏ (01259) 724253

ALLOWAY *South Ayrshire* 401 402 G 17 – *see Ayr.*

ALTENS *Aberdeenshire* – *see Aberdeen.*

ALTNAHARRA *Highland* 401 G 9 *Scotland G.* – ✉ *Lairg.*
Exc. : *Ben Loyal★★, N : 10 m. by A 836 – Ben Hope★ (<★★★) NW : 14 m.*
Edinburgh 239 – Inverness 83 – Thurso 61.

Altnaharra ⛰, IV27 4UE, ☏ (01549) 411222, *Fax (01549) 411222*, <, – rest, P. MC VISA.
March-mid October – **Meals** (bar lunch)/dinner a la carte 13.50/22.00 **t.** 4.00 – **15 rm** (dinner included) 63.50/127.00 **t.**

ALYTH Perthshire and Kinross 401 J 14 – pop. 4 650.

ᴮ Pitcrocknie ℘ (01828) 632268.

Edinburgh 63 – Aberdeen 69 – Dundee 16 – Perth 21.

🏛 **Lands of Loyal** ⌂, Loyal Rd, PH11 8JQ, N : ½ m. by B 952 ℘ (01828) 633151, Fax (01828) 633313, ≤, 🐎 – 🗹 ☎ 🅿. 🐵 🕮 💳
Meals 21.95 **t.** (dinner) and a la carte 12.00/23.95 **t.** 🍷 7.50 – **14 rm** ♀ 49.50/79.00 **t.** – SB.

🏠 **Drumnacree House,** St. Ninians Rd, PH11 8AP, ℘ (01828) 632194, Fax (01828) 632194, 🐎 – ⅙ 🗹 🅿. 🐵
April-November – Meals (booking essential) (dinner only) a la carte 17.00/23.50 **t.** 🍷 5.00 – **6 rm** ♀ 43.50/80.00 **t.** – SB.

ANNANDALE WATER SERVICE AREA Dumfries and Galloway – ✉ Lockerbie.

🏠 **Annandale Water Lodge,** Johnstonebridge, DG11 1HD, junction 16 A 74 (M) ℘ (0800) 470870, Fax (01576) 470644, ≤ – ⅙ rm, 🗹 ☎ ♿ 🅿. 🐵 🕮 ⓓ 💳
Meals (grill rest.) a la carte 8.90/11.40 **t.** – ♀ 4.25 – **42 rm** 39.95 **t.**

ANSTRUTHER Fife 401 L 15 Scotland G. – pop. 1 307.

See : Scottish Fisheries Museum★★ AC.

Env. : The East Neuk★★ – Crail★★ (Old Centre★★, Upper Crail★) NE : 4 m. by A 917.

Exc. : Kellie Castle★ AC, NW : 7 m. by B 9171, B 942 and A 917.

ᴮ Marsfield Shore Rd ℘ (01333) 310956.

🛈 Scottish Fisheries Museum ℘ (01333) 311073 (summer only).

Edinburgh 46 – Dundee 23 – Dunfermline 34.

↑ **Spindrift,** Pittenweem Rd, KY10 3DT, ℘ (01333) 310573, Fax (01333) 310573 – ⅙ 🗹 ☎ 🅿. 🐵 🕮 💳. 🌾
closed 25 December and restricted opening in January – Meals 13.50 **st.** 🍷 4.95 – **8 rm** ♀ 45.00/62.00 **st.** – SB.

✕ Cellar, 24 East Green, KY10 3AA, ℘ (01333) 310378, Fax (01333) 312544 – ⅙
Meals - Seafood rest.

There is no paid advertising in this Guide.

ARBROATH Angus 401 M 14 Scotland G. – pop. 24 002 (inc. St. Vigeans).

See : Town★ – Abbey★ AC.

Env. : St. Vigeans★, N : 1 ½ m. by A 92.

ᴮ Elliot ℘ (01241) 872069.

🛈 Market Pl., DD11 1HR ℘ (01241) 872609.

Edinburgh 72 – Aberdeen 51 – Dundee 16.

✕ **But 'n' Ben,** Auchmithie, DD11 5SQ, NE : 3 m. by A 92 ℘ (01241) 877223, « Converted fishermens cottages » – ⅙ 🐵 💳 🇯🇨🇧
closed Sunday dinner and Tuesday – Meals (light lunch) a la carte 8.65/15.20 **st.** 🍷 7.00.

ARCHIESTOWN Moray 401 K 11 – ✉ Aberlour (Aberdeenshire).

Edinburgh 194 – Aberdeen 62 – Inverness 49.

🏠 **Archiestown,** AB38 7QX, ℘ (01340) 810218, Fax (01340) 810239, ⌧, 🐎 – ☎ 🅿. 🐵 🕮 💳
11 February-September – Meals – (see **Bistro** below) – **9 rm** ♀ 35.00/85.00 **t.**

✕ **Bistro** (at Archiestown H.), AB38 7QX, ℘ (01340) 810218, Fax (01340) 810239 – 🅿. 🐵 🕮 💳
11 February-September – Meals a la carte 15.00/26.00 **t.** 🍷 5.00.

ARDENTINNY Argyll and Bute 401 F 15 Scotland G. – ✉ Dunoon.

Env. : The Clyde Estuary★.

Edinburgh 107 – Dunoon 13 – Glasgow 64 – Oban 71.

🏠 **Ardentinny** ⌂, PA23 8TR, ℘ (01369) 810209, Fax (01369) 810241, ≤ Loch Long, « Loch side setting », 🐎 – ⅙ 🗹 ☎ 🅿. 🐵 💳
Meals (bar lunch)/dinner 25.50 **t.** and a la carte 🍷 6.50 – **11 rm** ♀ 52.00/100.00 **t.** – SB.

ARDEONAIG Perthshire and Kinross 401 H 14 – see Killin (Stirling).

ARDRISHAIG *Argyll and Bute* 401 D 15 – *pop. 1 315* – ⊠ *Lochgilphead.*
Edinburgh 132 – Glasgow 86 – Oban 40.

⌂ **Allt-na-Craig,** Tarbert Rd, PA30 8EP, on A 83 ℘ (01546) 603245, ≼, ⩇ – **℗**
closed 2 weeks Christmas and New Year – **Meals** (by arrangement) 15.00 **s.** ⫶ 4.50 – **6 rm**
☑ (dinner included) 45.00/90.00 **s.** – SB.

ARDUAINE *Argyll and Bute* 401 D 15 *Scotland G.* – ⊠ *Oban.*
Exc. : *Loch Awe*★★ , *E : 12 m. by A 816 and B 840.*
Edinburgh 142 – Oban 20.

🏨 **Loch Melfort** ⬠, PA34 4XG, ℘ (01852) 200233, *Fax (01852) 200214*, ≼ Sound of Jura,
⩇, park – ⇆ rest, 🆅 ☎ **℗**. ⓪ 🅐🅔 *VISA*. ⅏
closed 5 January-28 February – **Meals** (bar lunch)/dinner 29.50 ⫶ 7.50 – **26 rm** ☑ 49.50/
130.00 – SB.

ARDVASAR *Highland* 401 C 12 – *see Skye (Isle of).*

ARDVOURLIE *Western Isles (Outer Hebrides)* 401 Z 10 – *see Lewis and Harris (Isle of).*

ARISAIG *Highland* 401 C 13 *Scotland G.*
See : *Village*★.
Env. : *Silver Sands of Morar*★ , *N : 5 ½ m. by A 830.*
🯅 *Traigh* ℘ (01687) 450337.
Edinburgh 172 – Inverness 102 – Oban 88.

🏨 **Arisaig House** ⬠, Beasdale, PH39 4NR, SE : 3 ¼ m. on A 830 ℘ (01687) 450622,
Fax (01687) 450626, ≼ Loch nan Uamh and Roshven, « Gardens », park – ⇆ rest, 🆅 ☎ **℗**.
⓪ *VISA*. ⅏
April-October – **Meals** (booking essential)/dinner 38.00 **t.** (dinner) and lunch a la carte
approx. 18.85 **t.** ⫶ 9.50 – **12 rm** ☑ 60.00/230.00 **t.**, 2 suites – SB.

🏠 **Arisaig,** PH39 4NH, ℘ (01687) 450210, *Fax (01687) 450310*, ≼ – ⇆ rest, 🆅 ☎ **℗**. ⓪ *VISA*
Meals (bar lunch)/dinner 21.50 **t.** and a la carte ⫶ 5.50 – **13 rm** ☑ 31.00/62.00 **t.** – SB.

✕ **Old Library Lodge** with rm, High St., PH39 4NH, ℘ (01687) 450651, *Fax (01687) 450219*,
≼ Loch nan Ceall and Inner Hebridean Isles – 🆅 ☎. ⓪ 🅐🅔 *VISA* 🅹🅲🅱. ⅏
April-October – **Meals** *(closed Tuesday lunch)* 22.50 **st.** (dinner) and lunch a la carte
approx. 11.25 **st.** – **6 rm** ☑ 45.00/68.00 **st.**

ARRAN (Isle of) *North Ayrshire* 401 402 DE 16 17 *Scotland G.* – *pop. 4 474.*
See : *Island*★★ - *Brodick Castle*★★ *AC.*
🚢 from Brodick to Ardrossan (Caledonian MacBrayne Ltd) 4-6 daily (55 mn) – from
Lochranza to Kintyre Peninsula (Claonaig) (Caledonian MacBrayne Ltd) frequent services
daily (30 mn) – from Brodick to Isle of Bute (Rothesay) via Largs (Mainland) (Caledonian
MacBrayne Ltd) 3 weekly (2 h 5 mn).

Brodick – *pop. 822.*
🯅 *Brodick* ℘ (01770) 302349 – 🯅 *Machrie Bay* ℘ (01770) 850232.
🄱 *The Pier KA27 8AU* ℘ (01770) 302140/302401.

🏨 Auchrannie Country House, KA27 8BZ, ℘ (01770) 302234, *Fax (01770) 302812*, 🆚, 🇸,
🔲, ⩇ – ⇆ rest, 🆅 ☎ ⅊ **℗**
26 rm, 2 suites.

🏨 **Kilmichael Country House** ⬠, Glen Cloy, KA27 8BY, W : 1 m. by Shore Rd, taking left
turn opposite Golf Club ℘ (01770) 302219, *Fax (01770) 302068*, ⩇, park – ⇆ 🆅 ☎ **℗**. ⓪
VISA
closed 1 week Christmas – **Meals** (booking essential) 28.50 **t.** (dinner) and a la carte
approx. 25.70 **t.** ⫶ 7.90 – **7 rm** ☑ 60.00/111.50 **t.**, 2 suites.

⌂ **Dunvegan House,** Shore Rd, KA27 8AJ, ℘ (01770) 302811, *Fax (01770) 302811*, ≼, ⩇ –
⇆ rm, 🆅 **℗**. ⅏
closed January and February – **Meals** 14.50 **st.** ⫶ 5.00 – **9 rm** ☑ 35.00/57.00 **st.**

⌂ **Glen Cloy Farmhouse** ⬠, KA27 8DA, W : 1 m. ℘ (01770) 302351, ⩇ – ⇆ rest, 🆅 **℗**.
⓪ *VISA*
March-14 November – **Meals** 14.00 – **5 rm** ☑ 21.00/50.00 – SB.

ARRAN (Isle of)

Lamlash – *pop. 900* – ✉ *Brodick.*

Lamlash ✆ (01770) 600296.

Glenisle, Shore Rd, KA27 8LS, ✆ (01770) 600559, *Fax (01770) 600966,* ≤, – TV ☎ P. MC VISA
closed January and November – **Meals** 14.50 **t.** (dinner) and a la carte 11.00/18.00 **t.** 4.60 – **13 rm** (dinner included) 46.00/92.00 **t.** – SB.

Lilybank, Shore Rd, KA27 8LS, ✆ (01770) 600230, *Fax (01770) 600230,* ≤, – TV P
March-October – **Meals** 15.00 **t.** – **6 rm** 22.50/60.00 **t.** – SB.

XX **Carraig Mhor,** Shore Rd, KA27 8LS, ✆ (01770) 600453, *Fax (01770) 600453* – . MC VISA
closed Sunday and 11 January-12 February – **Meals** (dinner only) 20.50 **t.** 7.50.

Lochranza.

Lochranza ✆ (01770) 830273.

Apple Lodge, KA27 8HJ, ✆ (01770) 830229, *Fax (01770) 830229,* – TV P.
minimum stay 2 nights May-October – **Meals** 15.50 **st.** – **3 rm** 45.00/58.00 **st.**, 1 suite – SB.

Butt Lodge, KA27 8JF, SE : ½ m. by Brodick Rd ✆ (01770) 830240, ≤, – rest, P. MC VISA.
March-October – **Meals** 14.00 **s.** – **5 rm** 29.00/56.00 **s.** – SB.

Whiting Bay – ✉.

Whiting Bay, Golf Course Rd ✆ (017707) 487.

Royal, Shore Rd, KA27 8PZ, ✆ (01770) 700286, *Fax (01770) 700286,* ≤, – rest, TV ☎ P
April-October – **Meals** 13.00 **st.** – **6 rm** 24.00/48.00 **s.**

Argentine House, Shore Rd, KA27 8PZ, ✆ (01770) 700662, *Fax (01770) 700693,* ≤, – rest, TV P. MC VISA JCB
closed 25 December-10 January – **Meals** (by arrangement) 21.00 **st.** – **6 rm** 21.00/40.00 **st.** – SB.

AUCHENCAIRN *Dumfries and Galloway* 401 402 I 19 – ✉ *Castle Douglas.*
Edinburgh 94 – Dumfries 21 – Stranraer 60.

Balcary Bay, DG7 1QZ, SE : 2 m. on Balcary rd ✆ (01556) 640217, *Fax (01556) 640272,* ≤, – TV ☎ P. MC AE VISA
March-mid November – **Meals** (bar lunch Monday to Saturday)/dinner 22.50 **st.** and a la carte 5.25 – **17 rm** 54.00/108.00 **st.** – SB.

AUCHTERARDER *Perthshire and Kinross* 401 I 15 *Scotland G.* – *pop. 3 910.*
Env. : Tullibardine Chapel★, NW : 2 m.
Ochil Rd ✆ (01764) 662804 – Dunning, Rollo Park ✆ (01764) 684747.
90 High St. PH3 1BJ ✆ (01764) 663450.
Edinburgh 55 – Glasgow 45 – Perth 14.

Gleneagles, PH3 1NF, SW : 2 m. by A 824 on A 823 ✆ (01764) 662231 *Fax (01764) 662134,* ≤, , « Championship golf courses and extensive leisure facilities », , , , , , , park, , squash – , rm, rest, TV ☎ & P – 360. MC AE D VISA JCB
Meals (light lunch)/dinner a la carte 20.00/35.00 **st.** 8.00 – ***Strathearn :*** **Meals** (dinner only and Sunday lunch)/dinner 41.00 **st.** and a la carte 12.00 – **216 rm** 135.00/295.00 **t.**, 18 suites.

Auchterarder House, PH3 1DZ, N : 1 ½ m. on B 8062 ✆ (01764) 663646 *Fax (01764) 662939,* ≤, « Scottish Jacobean house », , park – rest, TV ☎ P. MC AE D VISA JCB
Meals (booking essential) 27.50 **t.** (dinner) and a la carte 11.70/42.50 **t.** 6.50 – **13 rm** 110.00/250.00 **t.**, 2 suites – SB.

Duchally House, PH3 1PN, S : 4 m. by A 824 off A 823 ✆ (01764) 663071 *Fax (01764) 662464,* ≤, , park – TV ☎ P – 40. MC AE D VISA.
closed 1 week Christmas – **Meals** (bar lunch)/dinner a la carte 12.50/25.00 **st.** 5.75 – **11 rm** 52.50/80.00 **t.** – SB.

Cairn Lodge, Orchil Rd, PH3 1LX, ✆ (01764) 662634, *Fax (01764) 664866,* – rest TV ☎ P. MC AE VISA.
Meals a la carte 11.00/35.00 **t.** 6.50 – **7 rm** 60.00/120.00 **t.** – SB.

🏠 **Collearn House,** PH3 1DF, ℰ (01764) 663553, Fax (01764) 662376, ☞ – ﹡⇔ rm, 📺 ☎ 🅿 – 🔏 60. 🕦 🄰🄴 🄾 ⓥⓘⓢⓐ. ℅
closed 25-26 December and 1 to 4 January – **Meals** a la carte 11.00/25.50 **t.** ⓛ 5.25 – **8 rm** � 65.00/99.00 **t.** – SB.

AUCHTERHOUSE Angus 🄰🄾🄹 K 14 – pop. 794 – ✉ Dundee.
Edinburgh 69 – Dundee 7 – Perth 24.

🏯 **Old Mansion House** ♨ with rm, DD3 0QN, ℰ (01382) 320366, Fax (01382) 320400, ≤, « Part 15C and 17C country house », ⛱, ☞, park, ℀, squash – ﹡⇔ rest, 📺 ☎ 🅿. 🕦 🄰🄴 🄾 ⓥⓘⓢⓐ. ℅
closed 25 December-10 January – **Meals** 17.50/23.50 **t.** and a la carte ⓛ 5.50 – **6 rm** ⊭ 75.00/120.00 **t.** – SB.

AULDEARN Highland 🄰🄾🄹 I 11 – see Nairn.

AULTBEA Highland 🄰🄾🄹 D 10 Scotland G..
Env. : Wester Ross★★★ – Inverewe Gardens★★★ AC, S : 5 ½ m. by A 832.
Exc. : Loch Maree★★★, S : 10 m. by A 832.
Edinburgh 234 – Inverness 79 – Kyle of Lochalsh 80.

🏠 **Aultbea,** IV22 2HX, ℰ (01445) 731201, Fax (01445) 731214, ≤ Loch Ewe, ☞ – 📺 ☎ 🅿. 🕦 🄰🄴 ⓥⓘⓢⓐ 🄹🄲🄱
closed 25 December – **Meals** (bar lunch)/dinner 21.00 **t.** and a la carte ⓛ 4.25 – **11 rm** ⊭ 36.00/82.00 **t.** – SB.

🏡 **Cartmel,** Birchburn Rd, IV22 2HZ, ℰ (01445) 731375, ☞ – ﹡⇔ 🅿
4 rm.

AVIEMORE Highland 🄰🄾🄹 I 12 Scotland G. – pop. 2 214 – Winter sports.
See : Town★.
Exc. : The Cairngorms★★ (≤★★★) – ﹡★★★ from Cairn Gorm, SE : 11 m. by B 970 – Landmark Visitor Centre (The Highlander★) AC, N : 7 m. by A 9 – Highland Wildlife Park★ AC, SW : 7 m. by A 9.
🅱 Grampian Rd, PH22 1PP ℰ (01479) 810363.
Edinburgh 129 – Inverness 29 – Perth 85.

🏯 **Stakis Four Seasons,** PH22 1PF, ℰ (01479) 810681, Fax (01479) 810534, ≤ Cairngorms, Ⅰ₆, ☎, ⛌ – 🛗, ﹡⇔ rm, 📺 ☎ 🅿 – 🔏 110. 🕦 🄰🄴 🄾 ⓥⓘⓢⓐ
Meals (dancing Saturday evening) (bar lunch)/dinner 19.95 **st.** and a la carte ⓛ 6.50 – ⊭ 9.50 – **89 rm** 75.00/90.00 **st.** – SB.

🏠 **Corrour House** ♨, Inverdruie, PH22 1QH, SE : 1 m. on B 970 ℰ (01479) 810220, Fax (01479) 811500, ≤, ☜, ☞ – ﹡⇔ rest, 📺 ☎ 🅿. 🕦 🄾 ⓥⓘⓢⓐ
closed November-27 December – **Meals** (dinner only) 20.00 **t.** ⓛ 4.50 – **7 rm** ⊭ 35.00/70.00 **t.** – SB.

🏡 **Lynwilg House,** Lynwilg, PH22 1PZ, S : 2 m. by B 9152 on A 9 ℰ (01479) 811685, Fax (01479) 811685, ≤, ☜, ☞ – ﹡⇔ 📺 🅿. 🕦 🄾 ⓥⓘⓢⓐ. ℅
closed November-28 December – **Meals** (by arrangement) 20.00 **st.** – **4 rm** ⊭ 28.00/70.00 **st.**

AYR South Ayrshire 🄰🄾🄹 🄰🄾🄲 G 17 Scotland G. – pop. 47 872.
Env. : Alloway★ (Burns Cottage and Museum★ AC) S : 3 m. by B 7024 BZ
Exc. : Culzean Castle★ AC (setting★★★, Oval Staircase★★) SW : 13 m. by A 719 BZ
🏌 Belleisle, Bellisle Park, Doonfoot Rd ℰ (01292) 441258, BZ – 🏌 Dalmilling, Westwood Av. ℰ (01292) 263893, BZ – 🏌 Doon Valley, Hillside, Patna ℰ (01292) 531607, BZ
🅱 Burns House, Burns Statue Square, KA7 1UD ℰ (01292) 288688.
Edinburgh 81 – Glasgow 35.

Plan on next page

🏯 **Fairfield House,** 12 Fairfield Rd, KA7 2AR, ℰ (01292) 267461, Fax (01292) 261456, Ⅰ₆, ☎, ⛌, ☞ – ﹡⇔ 📺 ☎ 🅿 – 🔏 50. 🕦 🄰🄴 🄾 ⓥⓘⓢⓐ   AY a
Meals a la carte 16.25/30.25 **st.** ⓛ 6.50 – **33 rm** ⊭ 100.00/190.00 **t.** – SB.

🏠 **Kylestrome,** 11 Miller Rd, KA7 2AX, ℰ (01292) 262474, Fax (01292) 260863 – 📺 ☎ 🅿 – 🔏 25. 🕦 🄰🄴 🄾 ⓥⓘⓢⓐ. ℅   AY e
Meals 9.95/17.95 **t.** and a la carte ⓛ 5.50 – **12 rm** ⊭ 55.00/95.00 **st.** – SB.

🏡 **No. 26 The Crescent** without rest., 26 Bellevue Cres., KA7 2DR, ℰ (01292) 287329, Fax (01292) 286779 – ﹡⇔ 📺 🕦 ⓥⓘⓢⓐ. ℅   BZ c
closed late November-5 January – **4 rm** ⊭ 30.00/50.00 **t.**

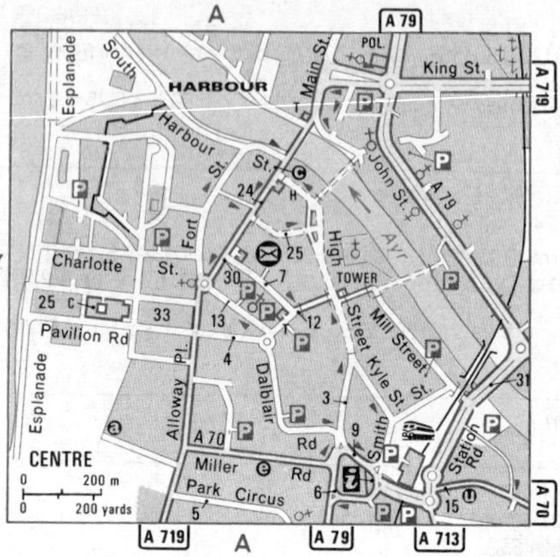

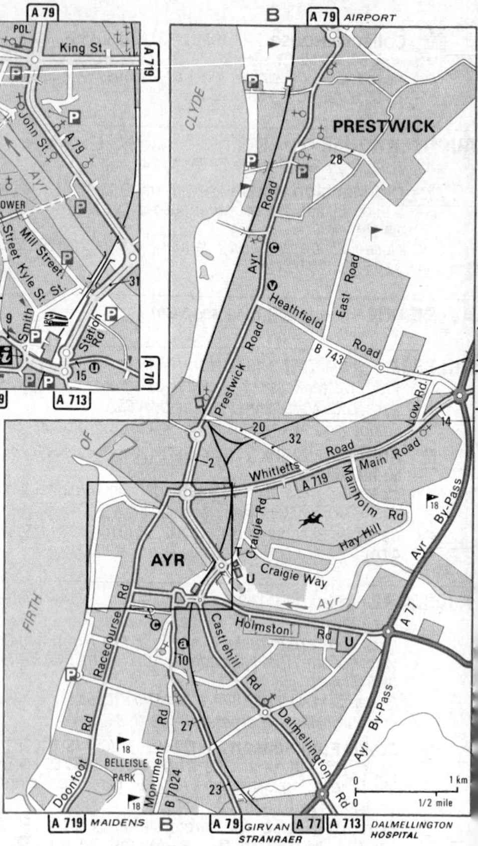

AYR AND PRESTWICK

⌂ **Glenmore** without rest., 35 Bellevue Cres., KA7 2DP, ☎ (01292) 269830, *Fax (01292) 269830* – [TV]. ⊁
5 rm ☕ 25.00/45.00 **st.** BZ c

⌂ **Coila** without rest., 10 Holmston Rd, KA7 3BB, ☎ (01292) 262642, *Fax (01292) 262642* – [TV] [P]. [MC] [AE] [VISA]
4 rm ☕ 25.00/45.00 **st.** AY u

⌂ **Langley Bank** without rest., 39 Carrick Rd, KA7 2RD, ☎ (01292) 264246, *Fax (01292) 282628* – [TV] ☎ [P]. [MC] [AE] [VISA]. ⊁
6 rm ☕ 45.00/50.00 **s.** BZ a

⌂ **Chaz-Ann** without rest., 17 Park Circus, KA7 2DJ, ☎ (01292) 611215, *Fax (01292) 285491* – ⊁ [TV]
closed 24 December-5 January – **3 rm** ☕ 28.00/40.00 **st.** AY s

🍴 **Fouters,** 2a Academy St., KA7 1HS, ☎ (01292) 261391, *Fax (01292) 619323* – [MC] [AE] [D] [VISA] AY c
closed Sunday, Monday, 25 to 27 December and 1 to 3 January – **Meals** 25.00 **t.** (dinner) and a la carte 16.25/25.40 **t.** 🍷 5.50.

at Alloway *S : 3 m. on B 7024* – **BZ** – ✉ *Ayr.*

🏠 **Northpark House,** 2 Alloway, KA7 4NL, ☎ (01292) 442336, *Fax (01292) 445572* – [TV] ☎ [P]. [MC] [AE] [D] [VISA] [JCB]. ⊁
Meals 17.50/21.50 **t.** and a la carte 🍷 6.25 – **5 rm** ☕ 67.50/125.00 **t.**

To visit a town or region: use the ***Michelin Green Guides.***

BALLACHULISH Highland **401** E 13 Scotland G..

Exc. : Glen Coe★★, E : 6 m. by A 82.

🖪 PA39 4JR ℰ (01855) 811296 (summer only).

Edinburgh 117 – Inverness 80 – Kyle of Lochalsh 90 – Oban 38.

🏨 **Ballachulish**, PA39 4JY, W : 2 ¼ m. by A 82 on A 828 ℰ (01855) 811606, Fax (01855) 821463, ≤, 🐾 – 📺 ☎ 🅿. 🕮 𝘝𝘐𝘚𝘈
Meals (bar lunch)/dinner 27.50 st. and a la carte ᾗ 6.95 – **52 rm** ⊊ (dinner included) 75.50/ 166.00, 2 suites – SB.

🏨 **Isles of Glencoe**, PA39 4HL, ℰ (01855) 811602, Fax (01855) 821463, ≤ Loch Leven and the Pap of Glencoe, « Lochside setting », ≊, 🔲, 🐾, park – 📺 ☎ & 🅿. 🕮 𝘝𝘐𝘚𝘈
Meals 11.00/21.50 st. and a la carte ᾗ 6.95 – **39 rm** ⊊ (dinner included) 75.50/151.00 st. – SB.

🏠 **Ballachulish House** ♨, PA39 4JX, W : 2 ½ m. by A 82 on A 828 ℰ (01855) 811266, Fax (01855) 811498, ≤, 🐾 – ⅍ 🅿. 🕮 𝘝𝘐𝘚𝘈 𝗝𝗖𝗕. ⅙
closed January and December – **Meals** 25.00 st. ᾗ 5.25 – **6 rm** ⊊ 50.00/80.00 st.

🏠 **Lyn Leven**, White St., PA39 4JP, ℰ (01855) 811392, Fax (01855) 811600, ≤, 🐾 – ⅍ rest, 📺 🅿. 🕮 𝘝𝘐𝘚𝘈
closed Christmas – **Meals** (by arrangement) 10.00 ᾗ 3.80 – **8 rm** ⊊ 25.00/48.00 st.

BALLANTRAE South Ayrshire **401 402** E 18 – pop. 672 – ⊠ Girvan.

Edinburgh 115 – Ayr 33 – Stranraer 18.

🏠 **Cosses Country House** ♨, KA26 0LR, E : 2 ¼ m. by A 77 (south) taking first turn left after bridge ℰ (01465) 831363, Fax (01465) 831598, « Part 16C former shooting lodge », 🐾, park – ⅍ 🅿. 🕮 𝘝𝘐𝘚𝘈
closed 15 December-15 January – **Meals** (by arrangement) (communal dining) 20.00 st. ᾗ 4.20 – **1 rm**, **2 suites** ⊊ 42.00/78.00 st..

🏠 **Balkissock Lodge** ♨, KA26 0LP, E : 4 m. by A 77 (south) taking first turn left after bridge ℰ (01465) 831537, Fax (01465) 831537, 🐾 – ⅍ 📺 🅿. 🕮 𝘝𝘐𝘚𝘈. ⅙
restricted opening in winter – **Meals** (by arrangement) 15.50 st. – **3 rm** ⊊ 32.50/45.00 st.

BALLATER Aberdeenshire **401** K 12 – pop. 1 362.

🏌 Victoria Rd ℰ (013397) 55567.

🖪 Station Sq. ℰ (013397) 55306 (summer only).

Edinburgh 111 – Aberdeen 41 – Inverness 70 – Perth 67.

🏨 **Stakis Craigendarroch**, Braemar Rd, AB35 5XA, on A 93 ℰ (013397) 55858, Fax (013397) 55447, ≤ Dee Valley and Grampians, 𝗙₅, ≊, 🔲, 🐾, ⅍, squash – ᛔ 📺 ☎ 🅿 – ⅍ 110. 🕮 🕮 ⑩ 𝘝𝘐𝘚𝘈. ⅙
closed 6 to 10 January – **Meals** 20.00 t. (dinner) and a la carte 13.35/22.85 t. ᾗ 7.00 – (see also **Oaks** below) – **38 rm** ⊊ 89.00/129.00 t., 6 suites – SB.

🏨 **Darroch Learg**, Braemar Rd, AB35 5UX, ℰ (013397) 55443, Fax (013397) 55252, ≤ Dee Valley and Grampians, 🐾 – ⅍ 📺 ☎ 🅿. 🕮 🕮 ⑩ 𝘝𝘐𝘚𝘈
closed 3 weeks January and Christmas – **Meals** - (see **Conservatory** below) – **18 rm** ⊊ (dinner included) 72.00/164.00 st.

🏨 **Balgonie Country House** ♨, Braemar Pl., AB35 5NQ, ℰ (013397) 55482, Fax (013397) 55482, ≤, 🐾 – ⅍ rest, 📺 ☎ 🅿. 🕮 🕮 𝘝𝘐𝘚𝘈. ⅙
closed 5 January-12 February – **Meals** (booking essential) 16.50/28.50 t. ᾗ 9.50 – **9 rm** ⊊ 61.50/105.00 t. – SB.

🏨 **Glen Lui** ♨, Invercauld Rd, AB35 5RP, ℰ (013397) 55402, Fax (013397) 55545, ≤, 🐾 – ⅍ 📺 🅿. 🕮 🕮 𝘝𝘐𝘚𝘈
Meals 10.50/21.00 st. and a la carte ᾗ 6.50 – **17 rm** ⊊ 29.00/78.00 st., 2 suites – SB.

🏠 **Auld Kirk**, Braemar Rd, AB35 5RQ, ℰ (013397) 55762, Fax (013397) 55707, « Former 19C church » – 📺 ☎ 🅿. 🕮 𝘝𝘐𝘚𝘈
Meals 15.95 t. (dinner) and a la carte 10.50/16.80 ᾗ 4.95 – **6 rm** ⊊ 35.00/54.00 st. – SB.

🏠 **Alexandra**, 12 Bridge Sq., AB35 5QJ, ℰ (013397) 55376, Fax (013397) 55466 – 📺 ☎. 🕮 🕮 ⑩ 𝘝𝘐𝘚𝘈
Meals (bar lunch)/dinner 17.50 t. and a la carte ᾗ 5.50 – **7 rm** ⊊ 30.00/60.00 t. – SB.

🏠 **Moorside House** without rest., 26 Braemar Rd, AB35 5RL, ℰ (013397) 55492, Fax (013397) 55492, 🐾 – ⅍ 📺 🅿. 🕮 𝘝𝘐𝘚𝘈. ⅙
April-October – **9 rm** ⊊ 25.00/40.00 st.

🏠 **Oaklands** without rest., 30 Braemar Rd, AB35 5RL, ℰ (013397) 55013, 🐾 – 📺 🅿
May-September – **3 rm** ⊊ 33.00/44.00 st.

XXX **Oaks** (at Stakis Craigendarroch H.), Braemar Rd, AB35 5XA, on A 93 ℰ (013397) 55858, Fax (013397) 55447 – ⅍ ▤ 🅿. 🕮 🕮 ⑩ 𝘝𝘐𝘚𝘈
Meals (dinner only and Sunday lunch)/dinner 25.00 t. and a la carte ᾗ 9.00.

🍴🍴 **Conservatory** (at Darroch Learg H.), Braemar Rd, AB35 5UX, ✆ (013397) 55443, *Fax (013397) 55252* – 🚭. [MC] [AE] [D] [VISA]
closed Christmas and 3 weeks January – **Meals** (light lunch Monday to Saturday) 27.50 **st.** (dinner) and lunch a la carte approx. 19.00 **st.** 🍷 9.00.

🍴🍴 **Green Inn** with rm, 9 Victoria Rd, AB35 5QQ, ✆ (013397) 55701, *Fax (013397) 55701* – 🚭 [TV]. [MC] [AE] [VISA]
closed 2 November and 24 to 26 December – **Meals** (dinner only and Sunday lunch in summer)/dinner 23.50 **t.** 🍷 7.50 – **3 rm** ☕ (dinner included) 59.50/99.00 **t.** – SB.

BALLOCH *West Dunbartonshire* [401] G 15 *Scotland G.* – ✉ *Alexandria.*
Env. : *N : Loch Lomond★★.*
[i] *Balloch Rd, JH3 8LQ ✆ (01389) 753533 (summer only).*
Edinburgh 72 – Glasgow 20 – Stirling 30.

🏨 **Cameron House** 🐦, Loch Lomond, G83 8QZ, NW : 1 ½ m. by A 811 on A 82 ✆ (01389) 755565, *Fax (01389) 759522*, ≤ Loch Lomond, « Lochside setting », 🏋, ♨, 🏊, ⛳9, 🎣, 🌳, park, 🎾, squash – 🛗, 🚭 rm, ▤ rest, [TV] ☎ [P] – 🎤 300. [MC] [AE] [D] [VISA]. 🐕
Brasserie : **Meals** (dinner only and Sunday lunch)/dinner 21.50 **t.** and a la carte 🍷 7.50 – (see also ***Georgian Room*** below) – **93 rm** ☕ 140.00/180.00 **st.**, 7 suites – SB.

⌂ **Sheildaig Farm** 🐦, Upper Stoneymollen Rd, G83 8QX, W : 1 m. by A 811 off A 82 ✆ (01389) 752459, *Fax (01389) 753695*, 🌳, park – 🚭 [TV] [P]. [MC] [VISA] [JCB]. 🐕
Meals (by arrangement) 15.00 **st.** 🍷 3.50 – **5 rm** ☕ 35.00/55.00 **st.** – SB.

🍴🍴🍴🍴 ✿ **Georgian Room** (at Cameron House H.), Loch Lomond, G83 8QZ, NW : 1 ½ m. by A 811 on A 82 ✆ (01389) 755565, *Fax (01389) 759522*, ≤ Loch Lomond, « Lochside setting », 🌳 – 🚭 ▤ [P]. [MC] [AE] [D] [VISA]
closed lunch Saturday and Sunday – **Meals** (booking essential) 18.50/37.50 **t.** and a la carte 41.75/53.95 **t.** 🍷 10.00
Spec. Sweet red pepper and lentil soufflé, vegetable boudin. Oven roasted lobster with scallop and caviar timbale, watercress sauce. Warm chocolate fondant, orange and tea ice cream.

[Prices] For notes on the prices quoted in this Guide, see the introduction.

BALLYGRANT *Argyll and Bute* [401] B 16 – *see Islay (Isle of).*

BALTASOUND *Shetland Islands* [401] R 1 – *see Shetland Islands (Island of Unst).*

BANAVIE *Highland* [401] E 13 – *see Fort William.*

BANCHORY *Aberdeenshire* [401] M 12 *Scotland G.* – *pop. 6 230.*
Env. : *Crathes Castle★★ (Gardens★★★) AC, E : 3 m. by A 93 – Cairn o'Mount Road★ (≤★★) S : by B 974.*
Exc. : *Dunnottar Castle★★ (site★★★) AC, SW : 15 ½ m. by A 93 and A 957 – Aberdeen★★ NE : 17 m. by A 93.*
⛳18 *Kinneskie ✆ (01330) 822365 –* ⛳9 *Torphins ✆ (013398) 82115.*
[i] *Bridge St. AB31 3SX ✆ (01330) 822000.*
Edinburgh 118 – Aberdeen 17 – Dundee 55 – Inverness 94.

🏨 **Raemoir House** 🐦, AB31 4ED, N : 2 ½ m. on A 980 ✆ (01330) 824884, *Fax (01330) 822171*, ≤, « 18C mansion with 16C Ha-House », 🌳, park, 🎾 – 🚭 rest, [TV] ☎ ♿ [P] – 🎤 50. [MC] [AE] [D] [VISA]. 🐕
closed 25 to 27 December – **Meals** (bar lunch Monday to Saturday)/dinner 26.50 **t** and a la carte 🍷 6.00 – **19 rm** ☕ 55.00/130.00 **t.** – SB.

🏨 **Banchory Lodge** 🐦, Dee St., AB31 5HS, ✆ (01330) 822625, *Fax (01330) 825019*, ≤ « Part 18C house on River Dee », 🎣, 🌳 – [TV] ☎ [P] – 🎤 30. [MC] [AE] [D] [VISA]
Meals 13.50/24.00 **st.** 🍷 4.00 – **22 rm** ☕ 80.00/130.00 **st.** – SB.

🏨 **Tor-na-Coille,** Inchmarlo Rd, AB31 4AB, ✆ (01330) 822242, *Fax (01330) 824012*, 🌳 – 🛗 [TV] ☎ [P] – 🎤 90. [MC] [AE] [D] [VISA]
closed 25 to 28 December – **Meals** (bar lunch)/dinner 24.50 **t.** and a la carte 🍷 10.00 – **22 rm** ☕ 71.50/104.50 **t.** – SB.

⌂ **Old West Manse,** 71 Station Rd, AB31 5UD, ✆ (01330) 822202, *Fax (01330) 822202*, ≤ – 🚭 [TV]. [MC] [VISA]. 🐕
Meals (by arrangement) 16.00 🍷 6.50 – **3 rm** ☕ 35.00/50.00.

BANFF Aberdeenshire **401** M 10 *Scotland G.* – *pop. 4 402.*
See : Town★ – *Duff House*★★ *(baroque exterior*★*) AC* – *Mercat Cross*★.
🏌 *Royal Tarlair, Buchan St., Macduff* ℰ *(01261) 832548/832897* – 🏌 *Duff House Royal, The Barnyards* ℰ *(01261) 812062.*
🛈 *Collie Lodge, AB45 1AU* ℰ *(01261) 812419 (summer only).*
Edinburgh 177 – Aberdeen 47 – Fraserburgh 26 – Inverness 74.

⌂ **Eden House** ⌖, AB45 3NT, S : 5 m. by A 98 and A 947 on Scatterty Dunlugas rd
ℰ *(01261) 821282, Fax (01261) 821283,* « *Part 18C former shooting lodge overlooking River Deveron Valley* », 🐾, 🌳, park, ℀ – ⥂ 🅿. ℀
closed Christmas and New Year – **Meals** *(by arrangement) (communal dining)* 20.00 **s.** –
5 rm ⊵ 34.00/72.00 **s.** – SB.

🔧 ATS Carmelite St. ℰ *(01261) 812234*

BANKHEAD Aberdeenshire **401** N 12 – *see Aberdeen.*

BARRA (Isle of) Western Isles **401** X 12/13 – *pop. 1 316* – ✉ *Castlebay.*
⛴ *from Castlebay to Oban and South Uist (Lochboisdale) (Caledonian MacBrayne Ltd)*
(summer only).

Castlebay.

🏠 **Castlebay,** HS9 5XD, ℰ *(01871) 810223, Fax (01871) 810455,* ≼, ⥄ – 📺 ☎ 🅿. 🆎 *VISA*
Meals 15.00 **st.** *(dinner) and a la carte* 11.85/25.90 **st.** ⅃ 5.50 – **12 rm** ⊵ 30.00/60.00 **st.** –
SB.

⌂ **Tigh na Mara** without rest., HS9 5XD, ℰ *(01871) 810304, Fax (01871) 810304* – ⥂ 📺 🅿.
℀
May-September – **5 rm** ⊵ 20.00/40.00 **s.**

BEATTOCK Dumfries and Galloway **401 402** J 18 – *see Moffat.*

BEAULY Highland **401** G 11 – *pop. 1 154.*
Edinburgh 169 – Inverness 13 – Wick 125.

🏨 **Lovat Arms,** High St., IV4 7BS, ℰ *(01463) 782313, Fax (01463) 782862* – ⥂ rest, 📺 ☎ 🅿
– 🔏 60. 🆎 *VISA*
Meals 21.00 **t.** *(dinner) and a la carte* 9.25/25.00 **t.** ⅃ 5.00 – **21 rm** ⊵ 35.00/100.00 **t.** – SB.

🏨 **Priory,** The Square, IV4 7BX, ℰ *(01463) 782309, Fax (01463) 782531* – ⧐ 📺 ☎. 🆎 🆎 ①
VISA. ℀
Meals *(dinner only)* 19.50 **t.** *and a la carte* ⅃ 4.40 – **23 rm** ⊵ 42.50/87.50 **t.** – SB.

⌂ **Chrialdon House,** Station Rd, IV4 7EH, ℰ *(01463) 782336,* 🌳 – ⥂ 📺 🅿. 🆎 *VISA*
closed 25 December – **Meals** 18.00 **st.** ⅃ 4.90 – **9 rm** ⊵ 40.00/60.00 **st.** – SB.

BENBECULA Western Isles **401** X/Y 11 – *see Uist (Isles of).*

BERRIEDALE Highland **401** J 9
Edinburgh 251 – Inverness 94 – Thurso 28 – Wick 14.

⌂ **The Factor's House** ⌖, Langwell, KW7 6HD, take private road to Langwell House - 2.9
m. ℰ *(01593) 751280, Fax (01593) 751251,* ≼, 🌳, park – ⥂ 🅿
Meals *(communal dining)* 17.00 **t.** – **3 rm** ⊵ 43.00/66.00 **t.**

BIGGAR South Lanarkshire **401** J 17 – *pop. 2 238.*
🏌 *The Park, Broughton Rd* ℰ *(01899) 220618/220319.*
🛈 *155 High St.* ℰ *(01899) 22106.*
Edinburgh 31 – Dumfries 49 – Glasgow 40.

🏠 **Lindsaylands** ⌖, Lindsaylands Rd, ML12 6NR, SW : ¾ m. via Park Place and The Wynd
ℰ *(01899) 220033, Fax (01899) 221009,* ≼, 🌳, park, ℀ – ⥂ rest, 🅿. ℀
March-November – **Meals** *(by arrangement) (unlicensed) (dinner only)* 13.00 **st.** – **3 rm**
⊵ 26.00/46.00 **st.**

BLAIRGOWRIE Perthshire and Kinross **401** J 14 *Scotland G.* – *pop. 5 208.*
EXC. : Scone Palace★★ *AC, S : 12 m. by A 93.*
🛈 *26 Wellmeadow, PH10 6AS* ℰ *(01250) 872960.*
Edinburgh 60 – Dundee 19 – Perth 16.

Kinloch House ⛰, PH10 6SG, W : 3 m. on A 923 ☎ (01250) 884237, *Fax (01250) 884333*, ≤, « Country house atmosphere », 🌳, park – ⇎ rest, TV ☎ P. MC AE ◑ VISA
closed 15 to 30 December – **Meals** 15.95/29.90 **st.** and lunch a la carte 🍷 6.45 – **21 rm** ☕ (dinner included) 89.00/185.00 **st.**

Altamount House ⛰, Coupar Angus Rd, PH10 6JN, on A 923 ☎ (01250) 873512, *Fax (01250) 876200*, 🌳 – ⇎ rest, TV ☎ P. MC AE VISA
closed 25 December – **Meals** (bar lunch)/dinner 17.50 **t.** and a la carte 🍷 7.00 – **7 rm** ☕ 45.00/80.00 **t.** – SB.

Laurels, PH10 6LH, SW : 1 ¼ m. on A 93 ☎ (01250) 874920, 🌳 – ⇎ TV P. MC AE ◑ VISA. ✂
closed December-first week January – **Meals** (by arrangement) 9.00 – **6 rm** ☕ 19.00/38.00.

BLAIRLOGIE *Stirling – see Stirling.*

BOAT OF GARTEN *Highland* 401 I 12.
Boat of Garten ☎ (01479) 831282.
Edinburgh 133 – Inverness 28 – Perth 89.

The Boat, PH24 3BH, ☎ (01479) 831258, *Fax (01479) 831414*, 🌳 – ⇎ rest, TV ☎ P – 🏛 30. MC AE ◑ VISA JCB
Meals (bar lunch)/dinner 19.50 **st.** 🍷 5.75 – **30 rm** ☕ 40.00/80.00 **st.** – SB.

Heathbank - The Victorian House, Spey Av., PH24 3BD, ☎ (01479) 831234, 🌳 – ⇎ P. ✂
April-October and 26 December-mid January – **Meals** 20.00 **s.** 🍷 5.00 – **7 rm** ☕ 35.00/80.00 **s.**

BONNYRIGG *Midlothian* 401 K 16 – *see Edinburgh.*

BORGIE *Highland* 401 H 8.
Edinburgh 262 – Inverness 93 – Thurso 31.

Borgie Lodge ⛰, KW14 7TH, ☎ (01641) 521332, *Fax (01641) 521332*, ≤, 🐟, 🌳 – ⇎ rest, P. MC VISA
restricted opening November-February – **Meals** (bar lunch)/dinner 23.50 **t.** 🍷 5.00 – **8 rm** ☕ 50.00/100.00 **t.** – SB.

BRAE *Shetland Islands* 401 P 2 – *see Shetland Islands (Mainland).*

BRAEMAR *Aberdeenshire* 401 J 12 *Scotland G.*
Env. : *Lin O'Dee*★, *W : 5 m.*
Cluniebank Rd ☎ (013397) 41618.
The Mews, Mar Rd ☎ (013397) 41600.
Edinburgh 85 – Aberdeen 58 – Dundee 51 – Perth 51.

Invercauld Arms Thistle, Invercauld rd, AB35 5YR, ☎ (013397) 41605 *Fax (013397) 41428* – |♦|, ⇎ rm, TV ☎ ♿ P – 🏛 60. MC AE ◑ VISA
Meals (bar lunch)/dinner 18.50 **st.** and a la carte – **68 rm** ☕ 79.00/120.00 **st.**

Braemar Lodge, Glenshee Rd, AB35 5YQ, ☎ (013397) 41627, *Fax (013397) 41627*, 🌳 – ⇎ TV P. MC VISA JCB
Meals (dinner only) a la carte 12.85/19.15 **st.** – **7 rm** ☕ 36.00/72.00 **st.**

BREAKISH *Highland* 401 C 12 – *see Skye (Isle of).*

BREASCLETE *Western Isles (Outer Hebrides)* 401 Z 9 – *see Lewis and Harris (Isle of).*

BRECHIN *Angus* 401 M 13 – pop. 8 315.
Exc. : *Aberlemno Stones*★, *SW : 1 m. by B 966 on B 9134 – Cairn O'Mount Road*★, *N : 1 m by B 9667 on A 94.*
Trinity ☎ (01356) 622383.
St. Ninians Pl. ☎ (01356) 623050 (summer only).
Edinburgh 83 – Aberdeen 42 – Dundee 28 – Perth 44.

⌂ **Doniford,** 26 Airlie St., DD9 6JX, ☎ (01356) 622361, 🏡 – ⊭ [TV] [P]
closed Christmas and New Year – **Meals** (by arrangement) 10.00 **s.** – **3 rm** ☐ 25.00/39.00 **s.**

⌂ **Blibberhill Farmhouse** 🏞, DD9 6TH, SW : 5 m. by A 935 and B 9134 off Melgund rd ☎ (01307) 830323, *Fax (01307) 830323*, « Working farm », 🏡, park – ⊭ [TV] [P]. ✗
closed 24 and 25 December – **Meals** (by arrangement) 10.50 **st.** – **3 rm** ☐ 24.00/50.00 **st.**

BRIDGEND *Argyll and Bute* [401] B 16 – *see Islay (Isle of).*

BRIDGE OF ALLAN *Stirling* [401] I 15.
Edinburgh 40 – Glasgow 32 – Perth 30.

🏠 **Old Manor,** 129 Henderson St., FK9 4RQ, ☎ (01786) 832169, *Fax (01786) 833990*, 🏡 – [TV] ☎ [P]. [MC] [AE] [VISA]
Meals 11.50 **t.** (lunch) and dinner a la carte 12.95/26.55 **t.** 🍷 4.95 – **7 rm** ☐ 30.00/80.00 **t.** – SB.

BRIDGE OF AVON *Aberdeenshire* [401] J 11 – ✉ *Ballindalloch (Moray).*
Edinburgh 157 – Inverness 50.

🏠 **Delnashaugh Inn,** AB37 9AS, on A 95 ☎ (01807) 500255, *Fax (01807) 500389*, ≤ – [TV] ☎ [P]. [MC] [VISA]. ✗
Easter-late October – **Meals** (bar lunch)/dinner 22.50 **t.** 🍷 6.50 – **9 rm** ☐ (dinner included) 65.00/130.00 **t.**

BROADFORD *Highland* [401] C 12 – *see Skye (Isle of).*

BRODICK *North Ayrshire* [401] [402] E 17 – *see Arran (Isle of).*

BRORA *Highland* [401] I 9 – *pop. 1 687.*
⛳18 *Golf Rd* ☎ *(01408) 621417.*
Edinburgh 234 – Inverness 78 – Wick 49.

🏨 **Royal Marine,** Golf Rd, KW9 6QS, ☎ (01408) 621252, *Fax (01408) 621181*, Lб, ≘s, 🏊, 🎣, 🏡 – ⊭ rest, [TV] ☎ ♿ [P] – 🎪 50. [MC] [AE] [O] [VISA]
Meals a la carte 14.00/24.00 **t.** 🍷 6.00 – **16 rm** ☐ 55.00/100.00 **t.** – SB.

🏨 **Links** 🏞, Golf Rd, KW9 6QS, ☎ (01408) 621225, *Fax (01408) 621383*, ≤, 🎣, 🏡 – [TV] ☎ [P]. [MC] [AE] [O] [VISA]
April-October – **Meals** (bar lunch)/dinner 20.00 **t.** and a la carte 🍷 6.00 – **20 rm** ☐ 55.00/100.00 **t.**, 2 suites – SB.

⌂ **Lynwood,** Golf Rd, KW9 6QS, ☎ (01408) 621226, *Fax (01408) 621226*, 🏡 – ⊭ [TV] [P]. [MC] [VISA]
restricted opening in winter – **Meals** (by arrangement) 12.00 **s.** – **4 rm** ☐ 26.00/44.00 **s.**

⌂ **Tigh Fada** without rest., Golf Rd, KW9 6QS, ☎ (01408) 621332, *Fax (01408) 621332*, ≤, 🏡 – ⊭ [P]. ✗
restricted opening in winter – **3 rm** ☐ 19.50/39.00 **s.**

BROUGHTY FERRY *Dundee City* [401] L 14 – *see Dundee.*

BUCKIE *Moray* [401] L 10 – *pop. 8 324.*
⛳18 *Buckpool, Barhill Rd* ☎ *(01542) 832236* – ⛳18 *Strathlene* ☎ *(01542) 31798.*
[i] *Cluny Sq.* ☎ *(01542) 834853 (summer only).*
Edinburgh 195 – Aberdeen 66 – Inverness 56.

🍴🍴 **Old Monastery,** Drybridge, AB56 5JB, SE : 3 ½ m. by A 942 on Deskford rd ☎ (01542) 832660, *Fax (01542) 832660*, ≤, « Former chapel overlooking Spey Bay » – [P]. [MC] [AE] [VISA]
closed Sunday, Monday, 25 December, 1-2 January, first 2 weeks November and last 3 weeks January – **Meals** a la carte 16.25/21.45 **t.** 🍷 5.75.

BUCKSBURN *Aberdeenshire* [401] N 12 – *see Aberdeen.*

BUNCHREW *Highland* – *see Inverness.*

BUNESSAN *Argyll and Bute* [401] B 15 – *see Mull (Isle of).*

BURNTISLAND *Fife* [401] K 15 *Scotland G. – pop. 5 951.*

Env. : *Aberdour★ – Aberdour Castle★* **AC**, *W : 3 m. by A 921.*

⛳ *Burntisland Golf House Club, Dodhead ☎ (01592) 873247 –* ⛳ *Kinghorn Municipal, McDuff Cres., Kingham ☎ (01592) 890345.*

ℹ *4 Kirkgate, KY3 9BB ☎ (01592) 872667.*

Edinburgh 20 – Dunfermline 10 – Kirkcaldy 6.

🏨 **Kingswood,** Kinghorn Rd, KY3 9LL, E : 1 m. ☎ (01592) 872329, *Fax (01592) 873123* – 🚭 [TV] ☎ [P] – 👥 100. [MC] [AE] VISA
Meals (bar lunch)/dinner a la carte 15.25/25.50 **st.** 🍷 4.00 – **9 rm** ☕ 48.00/70.00 **st.** – SB.

BURRAY *Orkney Islands* [401] L 7 – *see Orkney Islands.*

BUSBY *East Renfrewshire* [401] [402] H 16 – *see Glasgow.*

BUTE (Isle of) *Argyll and Bute* [401] [402] E 16 – *pop. 7 354.*

⛴ *from Rothesay to Wemyss Bay (Mainland) (Caledonian MacBrayne Ltd) frequent services daily (30 mn) – from Rhubodach to Colintraive (Mainland) (Caledonian MacBrayne Ltd) frequent services daily (5 mn) – from Rothesay to Isle of Arran (Brodick) via Largs (Mainland) (Caledonian MacBrayne Ltd) 3 weekly (2 h 5 mn).*

Rothesay.

⛳ *Canada Hill ☎ (01700) 502244.*

ℹ *15 Victoria St., Rothesay, PA20 0AJ ☎ (01700) 502151.*

🏨 **Ardmory House,** Ardmory Rd, Ardbeg, PA20 0PG, N : 1 ¾ m. by A 866 ☎ (01700) 502346, *Fax (01700) 505596,* <, 🌳 – 🚭 [TV] ☎ [P]. [MC] [AE] [D] VISA JCB
Meals (carving lunch Sunday) (bar lunch Monday to Saturday)/dinner 17.50 **t.** 🍷 4.85 – **5 rm** ☕ 40.00/60.00 **t.** – SB.

CAIRNBAAN *Argyll and Bute* [401] D 15 – *see Lochgilphead.*

CALLANDER *Stirling* [401] H 15 *Scotland G. – pop. 3 268.*

See : *Town★.*

Exc. : *The Trossachs★★★ (Loch Katrine★★) – Hilltop Viewpoint★★★ (✳★★★) W : 10 m. by A 821.*

⛳ *Aveland Rd ☎ (01877) 330090.*

ℹ *Rob Roy & Trossachs Visitor Centre, Ancaster Sq., FK17 8ED ☎ (01877) 330342.*

Edinburgh 52 – Glasgow 43 – Oban 71 – Perth 41.

🏨 **Roman Camp** 🔇, Main St., FK17 8BG, ☎ (01877) 330003, *Fax (01877) 331533,* <, « Part 17C hunting lodge in extensive gardens », 🎣, park – 🚭 rest, [TV] ☎ ♿ [P]. [MC] [AE] [D] VISA
Meals 19.00/34.00 **t.** and a la carte 🍷 8.50 – **11 rm** ☕ 85.00/140.00 **t.**, 3 suites – SB.

🏨 **Arran Lodge,** Leny Rd, FK17 8AJ, ☎ (01877) 330976, 🎣, 🌳 – 🚭 [TV] [P]. 🐕
mid March-mid November – **Meals** (residents only) (dinner only) (unlicensed) 27.50 **s.** – **4 rm** ☕ 63.00/75.00 **s.** – SB.

🏨 **Invertrossachs Country House** 🔇, Invertrossachs Rd, FK17 8HG, SW : 5 ½ m. by A 81 and Invertrossachs rd taking no through road after 1 ¾ m. ☎ (01877) 331126 *Fax (01877) 331229,* <, « Edwardian hunting lodge in extensive grounds », 🎣, 🌳 – 🚭 rest, [TV] ☎ [P]. [MC] [AE] VISA
closed mid December-6 January – **Meals** (by arrangement) (dinner only) (unlicensed 19.95 **st.** – **3 rm** ☕ 55.00/150.00 **st.** – SB.

🏨 **Lubnaig,** Leny Feus, FK17 8AS, ☎ (01877) 330376, *Fax (01877) 330376,* 🌳 – 🚭 rest, [TV] [P]. [MC] VISA JCB. 🐕
April-mid October – **Meals** (residents only) (dinner only) a la carte 16.25/19.75 **t.** 🍷 7.15 – **10 rm** ☕ 48.00/66.00 **t.** – SB.

🏠 **Priory** 🔇, Bracklinn Rd, FK17 8EH, ☎ (01877) 330001, *Fax (01877) 330001,* 🌳 – 🚭 [TV] [P]. 🐕
Easter-October – **Meals** (by arrangement) 14.50 **t.** 🍷 4.75 – **8 rm** ☕ 27.00/54.00 **t.** – SB.

🏠 **Brook Linn** 🔇, Leny Feus, FK17 8AU, ☎ (01877) 330103, *Fax (01877) 330103,* <, 🌳 – 🚭 [TV] [P]
mid March-mid November – **Meals** (by arrangement) 13.00 **st.** 🍷 4.00 – **7 rm** ☕ 21.00/52.00 **st.**

🏠 **East Mains House** without rest., Bridgend, FK17 8AG, 📞 (01877) 330535, *Fax (01877) 330535*, 🌳 – 🚭 [TV] [P]. [MC] [VISA] [JCB]. 🚫🐕
closed 25 December and 1 January – **4 rm** ☕ 30.00/46.00 **s.**

🏠 **Dunmore** without rest., Leny Rd, FK17 8AL, 📞 (01877) 330756 – 🚭 [TV] [P]
May-October – **4 rm** ☕ 27.00/44.00.

CAMPBELTOWN *Argyll and Bute* [401] D 17 – *see Kintyre (Peninsula).*

CANNICH *Highland* [401] F 11 – ✉ *Beauly.*
Edinburgh 184 – Inverness 28 – Kyle of Lochalsh 54.

🏨 **Mullardoch House** 🌿, IV4 7LX, W : 8 ½ m. 📞 (01456) 415460, *Fax (01456) 415460*, < Loch Sealbanach and Affric Hills, « Converted shooting lodge », 🎣, 🌳 – 🚭 rest, [TV] [P]. [MC] [AE] [VISA]
Meals (bar lunch)/dinner 24.00 **t.** 🍷 5.95 – **6 rm** ☕ 55.00/96.00 **t.**

CANONBIE *Dumfries and Galloway* [401] [402] L 18 – *pop. 1 144.*
Edinburgh 80 – Carlisle 15 – Dumfries 34.

🍴 **Riverside Inn** with rm, DG14 0UX, 📞 (013873) 71295 – 🚭 rest, [TV] [P]. [MC] [VISA]. 🚫🐕
closed 25 and 26 December, 1 January, 2 weeks February and 2 weeks November – **Meals** (booking essential) (bar meals Sunday and Monday) 18.50 **t.** 🍷 4.50 – **7 rm** ☕ 55.00/85.00 **st.** – SB.

CARDROSS *Argyll and Bute* [401] G 16 *Scotland G.*
Env. : *The Clyde Estuary★.*
Edinburgh 63 – Glasgow 17 – Helensburgh 5.

🏠 **Kirkton House** 🌿, Darleith Rd, G82 5EZ, 📞 (01389) 841951, *Fax (01389) 841868*, <, 🌳 – [TV] ☎ [P]. [MC] [AE] [VISA]
closed 5 December-25 January – **Meals** 18.25 **st.** 🍷 4.00 – **6 rm** ☕ 38.50/62.00 **st.** – SB.

CARNOUSTIE *Angus* [401] L 14 – *pop. 12 337.*
⛳18, ⛳18 Monifieth Golf Links, Medal Starter's Box, Princes St., Monifieth 📞 (01382) 532767 – ⛳18 Panmure, Barry 📞 (01241) 853120.
ℹ 1b High St., DD7 6AN 📞 (01241) 852258 (summer only).
Edinburgh 68 – Aberdeen 59 – Dundee 12.

🍴🍴 **11 Park Avenue,** 11 Park Av., DD7 7JA, 📞 (01241) 853336, *Fax (01241) 853336* – [MC] [AE] [VISA] [JCB]
closed lunch Saturday and October-March, Sunday, Monday and first week January – **Meals** a la carte 16.75/24.15 **t.** 🍷 9.30.

CARRBRIDGE *Highland* [401] I 12.
⛳9 Carrbridge 📞 (01479) 841623.
ℹ Main St. 📞 (01479) 841630 (summer only).
Edinburgh 135 – Aberdeen 92 – Inverness 23.

🏨 **Fairwinds,** PH23 3AA, 📞 (01479) 841240, *Fax (01479) 841240*, 🌳 – 🚭 rest, [TV] ☎ [P]. [MC] [VISA]. 🚫🐕
closed November-19 December – **Meals** (dinner only) 15.00 **st.** and a la carte 🍷 6.75 – **5 rm** ☕ 27.00/56.00 **st.**

🏠 **Feith Mho'r Country House** 🌿 without rest., Station Rd, PH23 3AP, W : 1 ¼ m. 📞 (01479) 841621, <, 🌳 – 🚭 rest, [TV] [P]
closed 1 to 27 December – **6 rm** ☕ 26.00/52.00.

CASTLEBAY *Western Isles* [401] X 12/13 – *see Barra (Isle of).*

CASTLE DOUGLAS *Dumfries and Galloway* [401] [402] I 19 *Scotland G.* – *pop. 4 187.*
Env. : *Threave Garden★★ **AC**, SW : 2 ½ m. by A 75 – Threave Castle★ **AC**, W : 1 m.*
⛳9 Abercromby Rd 📞 (01556) 502801.
ℹ Markethill Car Park 📞 (01556) 502611 (summer only).
Edinburgh 98 – Ayr 49 – Dumfries 18 – Stranraer 57.

↑ **Longacre Manor** ⌂, Ernespie Rd, DG7 1LE, NE : ¾ m. on A 745 ℘ (01556) 503576, Fax (01556) 503886, ≤, ✿ – ⅙✕ rest, 📺 ☎ 🅟, 🕪 VISA
Meals (by arrangement) (communal dining) 16.00 s. ⅙ 5.00 – **4 rm** ⌂ 35.00/75.00 st.

🅐 ATS Station Yard ℘ (01556) 503121/2

CLACHAN SEIL Argyll and Bute **401** D 15 – see Seil (Isle of).

CLEISH Perthshire and Kinross **401** J 15 – see Kinross.

CLYDEBANK West Dunbartonshire **401** G 16 – pop. 45 717.

🔓 Clydebank Municipal, Overtoun Rd, Dalmuir ℘ (0141) 952 8698 – 🔓 Clydebank & District, Hardgate ℘ (01389) 873289.
Edinburgh 52 – Glasgow 6.

🏨 **Beardmore**, Beardmore St., G81 4SA, off A 814 ℘ (0141) 951 6000, Fax (0141) 951 6018, ⅙₆, ≘ₛ, 🏊, 🗚 – 🛗, ⅙✕ rm, 🍴 📺 ☎ 🕭 🅟 – 🔬 170. 🕪 🅰🇪 ① VISA. ⅙✕
Symphony : **Meals** (dinner only Friday and Saturday) 27.50 t. ⅙ 8.00 – **Brasserie** : **Meals** (closed Saturday lunch) (buffet only) 13.50 t. ⅙ 8.00 – ⌂ 10.95 – **162 rm** 90.00/115.00 t., 6 suites.

🏨 **Patio**, 1 South Av., Clydebank Business Park, G81 2RW, ℘ (0141) 951 1133, Fax (0141) 952 3713 – 🛗, ⅙✕ rm, 🍴 rest, 📺 ☎ 🕭 🅟 – 🔬 150. 🕪 🅰🇪 ① VISA. ⅙✕
closed 25-26 December and 1 January – **Meals** (closed lunch Saturday and Sunday) 12.95/15.50 st. and a la carte ⅙ 5.50 – ⌂ 10.25 – **80 rm** 73.00/83.00 st. – SB.

COLONSAY (Isle of) Argyll and Bute **401** B 15 – pop. 106 (inc. Oronsay).

🔓 Isle of Colonsay ℘ (01951) 200316.
⚓ – from Scalasaig to Oban (Caledonian MacBrayne Ltd) 3 weekly (2 h 10 mn) – from Scalasaig to Kintyre Peninsula (Kennacraig) via Isle of Islay (Port Askaig) (Caledonian MacBrayne Ltd) weekly.

Scalasaig – ✉ Colonsay.

🏠 **Isle of Colonsay** ⌂, PA61 7YP, ℘ (01951) 200316, Fax (01951) 200353, ≤, ✿ – ⅙✕ rest, 📺 🅟, 🕪 🅰🇪 ① VISA JCB
March-4 November – **Meals** (booking essential) (bar lunch)/dinner 23.00 st. ⅙ 4.85 – **11 rm** ⌂ (dinner included) 75.00/150.00 st. – SB.

CONAN BRIDGE Highland **401** G 11.
Edinburgh 168 – Inverness 12.

🏠 **Kinkell House** ⌂, Easter Kinkell, IV7 8HY, E : 3 m. by B 9163 and A 835 on B 9169 ℘ (01349) 861270, Fax (01349) 865902, ≤, ✿ – ⅙✕ rest, 📺 🕭 🅟, 🕪 ⅙✕
Meals (booking essential) (residents only Saturday lunch and Sunday dinner) a la carte 10.65/22.25 t. ⅙ 5.00 – **7 rm** ⌂ 54.00/78.00 st. – SB.

CONNEL Argyll and Bute **401** D 14 – ✉ Oban.
Edinburgh 118 – Glasgow 88 – Inverness 113 – Oban 5.

↑ **Ards House**, PA37 1PT, on A 85 ℘ (01631) 710255, ≤, ✿ – ⅙✕ 🅟 🕪 VISA. ⅙✕
mid February-mid November – **Meals** 18.50 t. ⅙ 5.25 – **6 rm** ⌂ (dinner included) 54.00/92.00 t. – SB.

↑ **Ronebhal** without rest., PA37 1PJ, on A 85 ℘ (01631) 710310, Fax (01631) 710310, ≤, ✿ – 📺 🅟, 🕪 VISA. ⅙✕
mid March-mid October – **6 rm** ⌂ 24.00/65.00 s.

CONTIN Highland **401** G 11 – pop. 1 194 – ✉ Strathpeffer.
Edinburgh 175 – Inverness 19.

🏨 **Coul House** ⌂, IV14 9EY, ℘ (01997) 421487, Fax (01997) 421945, ≤, ✿ – ⅙✕ rest, 📺 ☎ 🅟, 🕪 🅰🇪 ① VISA
Meals (lunch by arrangement)/dinner 27.50 t. and a la carte ⅙ 6.50 – **19 rm** ⌂ 61.75/109.50 t., 1 suite – SB.

🏠 **Achilty**, IV14 9EG, NW : ¾ m. on A 835 ℘ (01997) 421355, Fax (01997) 421923 – ⅙✕ rest, 📺 ☎ 🅟, 🕪 VISA
Meals 8.95 st. (lunch) and a la carte 10.15/17.20 st. – **12 rm** ⌂ 45.00/65.00 st. – SB.

COUPAR ANGUS *Perthshire and Kinross* 401 K 14 – pop. 3 844 – ⊠ *Blairgowrie.*
Edinburgh 63 – Dundee 14 – Perth 13.

🏠 **Moorfield House,** Myreiggs Rd, PH13 9HS, NW : 2 ½ m. by A 923 ℘ (01828) 627303, *Fax* (01828) 627339, 絲 – ❄ rm, 📺 ☎ **❷** – 🔬 120. ⚠️ AE *VISA* ❄️
closed 22 to 26 December – **Meals** (booking essential) (bar lunch)/dinner 25.50 **t.** ❅ 6.80 –
12 rm ⊇ 42.50/80.00 **t.** – SB.

CRAIGELLACHIE *Moray* 401 K 11 *Scotland G.*
Env. : *Dufftown (Glenfiddich Distillery★), SE : 5 m. by A 941.*
Edinburgh 190 – Aberdeen 58 – Inverness 53.

🏠 **Craigellachie,** Victoria St., AB38 9SR, ℘ (01340) 881204, *Fax* (01340) 881253, ⅃, ☎ – 📺
☎ **❷** – 🔬 35. ⚠️ AE ⓪ *VISA*
Meals a la carte 18.45/40.00 **st.** – **29 rm** ⊇ 54.50/130.00 **st.** – SB.

CRAIGHOUSE *Argyll and Bute* 401 C 16 – *see Jura (Isle of).*

CRIANLARICH *Stirling* 401 G 14.
Edinburgh 82 – Glasgow 52 – Perth 53.

🏠 **Allt-Chaorain House** ⌂, FK20 8RU, NW : 1 m. on A 82 ℘ (01838) 300283, *Fax* (01838) 300238, ≤, 絲 – ❄ rm ☎ **❷**. ⚠️ AE *VISA*
April-October – **Meals** (residents only) (communal dining) (dinner only) 18.00 **t.** – **7 rm**
⊇ 48.00/78.00 **t.** – SB.

CRIEFF *Perthshire and Kinross* 401 I 14 *Scotland G.* – pop. 6 096.
See : *Town★.*
Env. : *Drummond Castle Gardens★ AC, S : 2 m. by A 822 – Comrie (Scottish Tartans Museum★) W : 6 m. by A 85.*
Exc. : *Scone Palace★★ AC, E : 16 m. by A 85 and A 93.*
🏌 , 🏌 *Perth Rd* ℘ (01764) 652909 – 🏌 *Muthill, Peat Rd* ℘ (01764) 681523.
🛈 *Town Hall, High St., PH7 3HU* ℘ (01764) 652578.
Edinburgh 60 – Glasgow 50 – Oban 76 – Perth 18.

🏠 **Murraypark,** Connaught Terr., PH7 3DJ, ℘ (01764) 653731, *Fax* (01764) 655311, 絲 –
❄ rest, 📺 ☎ **♿ ❷** – 🔬 25. ⚠️ AE ⓪ *VISA*
closed 25 December and 1-2 January – **Meals** (bar lunch)/dinner a la carte 11.70/22.00 **t.** –
19 rm ⊇ 50.00/80.00 **t.**, 1 suite – SB.

↑ **Gwydyr House** *without rest.*, Comrie Rd, PH7 4BP, on A 85 ℘ (01764) 653277, *Fax* (01764) 653277, ≤, 絲 – 📺 **❷**. ⚠️ *VISA*
closed 1 week Christmas – **8 rm** ⊇ 28.00/64.00.

CRINAN *Argyll and Bute* 401 D 15 *Scotland G.* – ⊠ *Lochgilphead.*
See : *Hamlet★.*
Exc. : *Kilmory Knap (Macmillan's Cross★) SW : 14 m.*
Edinburgh 137 – Glasgow 91 – Oban 36.

🏠 **Crinan,** PA31 8SR, ℘ (01546) 830261, *Fax* (01546) 830292, « Commanding setting, ≤ Loch
Crinan and Sound of Jura », 絲 – ▯, ❄ rest, 📺 ☎ **❷**. ⚠️ AE *VISA*
Meals (bar lunch)/dinner 32.50 **t.** ❅ 7.50 – (see also **Lock 16** below) – **22 rm** ⊇ (dinner
included) 105.00/240.00 **t.**

XX **Lock 16** (at Crinan H.), PA31 8SR, ℘ (01546) 830261, *Fax* (01546) 830292, « Commanding
setting, ≤ Loch Crinan and Sound of Jura » – ❄ **❷**. ⚠️ AE *VISA*
closed Sunday, Monday and October-May – **Meals** - Seafood - (booking essential) (dinner
only) 42.50 **t.** ❅ 8.75.

CROMARTY *Highland* 401 H 10 *Scotland G.* – pop. 865.
See : *Town★.*
Exc. : *Fortrose (Cathedral Church setting★), SW : 10 m. by A 832.*
🏌 *Fortrose & Rosemarkie, Ness Road East* ℘ (01381) 620529.
Edinburgh 182 – Inverness 26 – Wick 126.

🏠 **Royal,** Marine Terr., IV11 8YN, ℘ (01381) 600217, ≤ – 📺 **❷**. ⚠️ AE *VISA* JCB
Meals a la carte 9.25/19.25 **st.** ❅ 5.00 – **10 rm** ⊇ 32.00/55.00 **st.** – SB.

CROSSFORD *Fife* 401 J 15 – *see Dunfermline.*

CULLEN Moray **401** L 10 *Scotland G. – pop. 1 522.*

See : *Cullen Auld Kirk★ (Sacrament house★, panels★).*

Env. : *Deskford Church (Sacrament house★) S : 4 m. by A 98 and B 9018 – Portsoy★, E : 5 ½ m. by A 98.*

18 *The Links ℘ (01542) 840685.*

B *20 Seafield St., AB56 2FH ℘ (01542) 840757 (summer only).*

Edinburgh 189 – Aberdeen 59 – Banff 12 – Inverness 61.

Bayview, Seafield St., AB56 4SU, ℘ (01542) 841031, Fax (01542) 841731, ≤ – ✦✿ **TV** ☎. **WO AE VISA**

closed 25 December – **Meals** a la carte 9.60/25.95 **t.** ▯ 6.50 – **6 rm** ⊐ 45.00/95.00 **t.** – SB.

CULLODEN Highland **401** H 11 – *see Inverness.*

CULNAKNOCK Highland **401** B 11 – *see Skye (Isle of).*

CULTS Aberdeenshire **401** N 12 – *see Aberdeen.*

CUMBERNAULD North Lanarkshire **401** I 16 – *pop. 62 412.*

Edinburgh 40 – Glasgow 11 – Stirling 13.

Westerwood H. Golf and Country Club, St. Andrews Drive, G68 0EW, N : 2 m. by A 8011 ℘ (01236) 457171, Fax (01236) 738478, ▯6, ⬜, **18**, ✾ – ▯ ✦✿ rm, **TV** ☎ **P** – **24** 180. **WO AE ① VISA**. ✾

Meals *(closed Saturday lunch)* 9.95/16.50 **st.** and a la carte – **45 rm** ⊐ 82.50 **st.**, 4 suites – SB.

Travel Inn, 4 South Muirhead Rd, G67 1AX, off A 8011 ℘ (01236) 725339, Fax (01236) 736380 – ✦✿ rm, **TV** & **P**. **WO AE ① VISA**. ✾

Meals (grill rest.) – **37 rm** 36.50 **t.**

CUPAR Fife **401** K 15 – *pop. 8 174.*

B *The Granary, Coal Rd, PY15 5YQ ℘ (01334) 652874.*

Edinburgh 45 – Dundee 15 – Perth 23.

Ostler's Close, Bonnygate, KY15 4BU, ℘ (01334) 655574, Fax (01334) 654036 – **WO AE VISA JCB**. ✾

closed Sunday, Monday, 1 January, 25-26 December and first 2 weeks June – **Meals** (lunch by arrangement) a la carte 15.85/30.45 **t.** ▯ 5.95.

⑩ ATS St. Catherine St. ℘ (01334) 654003

DALBEATTIE Dumfries and Galloway **401 402** I 19 *Scotland G. – pop. 4 421.*

Env. : *Kippford★, S : 5 m. by A 710.*

18 *Dalbeattie ℘ (01556) 611421.*

B *Town Hall, DJ5 ℘ (01556) 610117 (summer only).*

Edinburgh 94 – Ayr 56 – Dumfries 14 – Stranraer 62.

Auchenskeoch Lodge ⊱, DG5 4PG, SE : 5 m. on B 793 ℘ (01387) 780277 Fax (01387) 780277, ✎, ✿, park – ✦✿ rest, **TV** & **P**. **WO VISA**

March-November – **Meals** (by arrangement) (communal dining) 17.00 **st.** ▯ 6.50 – **2 rm** ⊐ 37.00/60.00 **st.**, 1 suite.

Broomlands House ⊱, Haugh Rd, DG5 4AR, W : ½ m. by Auchencairn rd (A 711 ℘ (01556) 611463, Fax (01556) 611462, ✿ – ✦✿ **TV** **P**

closed November and December – **Meals** (by arrangement) 10.00 **st.** – **3 rm** ⊐ 32.00. 44.00 **st.**

Briardale House, 17 Haugh Rd, DG5 4AR, W : ½ m. by Auchencairn rd (A 711 ℘ (01556) 611468, ✿ – ✦✿ **TV** **P**

closed November and December – **Meals** (by arrangement) 12.00 **s.** – **3 rm** ⊐ 42.00 **s.**

DALCROSS Highland – *see Inverness.*

Si vous cherchez un hôtel tranquille,
consultez d'abord les cartes de l'introduction
ou repérez dans le texte les établissements indiqués avec le signe ⊱ ou ⊱

DALRY *North Ayrshire* 401 402 F 16.
Edinburgh 70 – Ayr 21 – Glasgow 25.

XX **Braidwoods** ⌂, Drumastle Mill Cottage, KA2 44LN, SW : 1½ m. by A 737 on Saltcoats rd
℘ (01294) 833544, Fax (01294) 833553 – ✳ 🅿 ⬤ 🆎 VISA
*closed Tuesday lunch, Sunday dinner, Monday, 25 December, first 3 weeks January and
2 weeks September-October* – **Meals** (booking essential) 16.00/25.00 **t.** ⟡ 6.25.

DARVEL *East Ayrshire* 401 402 H 17.
Edinburgh 60 – Ayr 22 – Glasgow 21.

🏠 **Scoretulloch House** ⌂, KA17 0LR, E : 1 m. on A 71 ℘ (01560) 323331,
Fax (01560) 323441, ≤, 🌿 – ✳ 📺 ☎ 🅿. ⬤ 🆎 VISA JCB
closed 25, 26 and 31 December and 1 January – **Meals** 26.00 **t.** (dinner)
and lunch a la carte 12.00/12.75 – **4 rm** ⊡ 59.00/150.00 **t.** – SB.

DENNY *Falkirk* 401 I 15 *Scotland G.* – pop. 11 061.
Exc. : Stirling★★, N : 8 m. by A 872.
Edinburgh 34 – Glasgow 25 – Stirling 7.

🏠 **Topps Farm** ⌂, Fintry Rd, FK6 5JF, W : 4 m. on B 818 ℘ (01324) 822471,
Fax (01324) 823099, ≤ – ✳ 📺 ☎ & 🅿. ⬤ VISA
closed 24 to 26 December – **Meals** (by arrangement) 16.00 **t.** ⟡ 5.50 – **8 rm** ⊡ 34.00/
44.00 **t.** – SB.

For the quickest route use the **Michelin Main Road Maps:**

970 Europe, 974 Poland, 976 Czech Republic-Slovak Republic, 980 Greece,
984 Germany, 985 Scandinavia-Finland, 986 Great Britain and Ireland,
987 Germany-Austria-Benelux, 988 Italy, 989 France,
990 Spain-Portugal.

DERVAIG *Argyll and Bute* 401 B 14 – *see Mull (Isle of).*

DORNIE *Highland* 401 D 12 *Scotland G.* – ✉ Kyle of Lochalsh.
See : Eilean Donan Castle★ AC (site★★).
Env. : Glen Shiel★, SE : 4 m. on A 87.
Edinburgh 212 – Inverness 74 – Kyle of Lochalsh 8.

🏠 **Conchra House** ⌂, Ardelve, IV40 8DZ, N : 1 ¾ m. by A 87 on Conchra rd
℘ (01599555) 555233, Fax (01599555) 555433, ≤ Loch Long, « Part Georgian country
house », 🌿 – ✳ 🅿 – 🔬 40. ⬤ 🆎 VISA. ✳
closed Christmas and New Year – **Meals** (by arrangement) a la carte 12.50/18.50 **t.** ⟡ 5.50 –
6 rm ⊡ 30.00/70.00 **t.** – SB.

DORNOCH *Highland* 401 H 10 *Scotland G.* – pop. 2 042.
See : Town★.
🟦, 🟦 Royal Dornoch, Golf Rd ℘ (01862) 810219.
🅱 The Square, IV25 3SD ℘ (01862) 810400.
Edinburgh 219 – Inverness 63 – Wick 65.

🏠 **Highfield** without rest., Evelix Rd, IV25 3HR, ℘ (01862) 810909, Fax (01862) 810909, ≤,
🌿 – ✳ 📺 🅿
3 rm ⊡ 38.00/50.00.

DOUNBY *Orkney Islands* 401 K 6 – *see Orkney Islands (Mainland).*

DRUMBEG *Highland* 401 E 9 – ✉ Lairg.
Edinburgh 262 – Inverness 105 – Ullapool 48.

🏠 **Drumbeg**, IV27 4NW, ℘ (01571) 833236, Fax (01571) 833333, ≤ – ✳ rest, 📺 🅿. ⬤ VISA
April-October – **Meals** (booking essential to non-residents) (bar lunch) 20.00 **t.** – **6 rm**
⊡ 38.00/66.00 **t.**

🏠 **Taigh Druimbeag** ⌂, IV27 4NW, ℘ (01571) 833209, 🌿 – ✳ 🅿. VISA. ✳
April-October – **Meals** (by arrangement) (communal dining) 15.00 – **3 rm** ⊡ 60.00.

DRUMNADROCHIT *Highland* **401** G 11 *Scotland G.* – pop. 852 – ⊠ *Milton*.
Env. : *Loch Ness*★★ – *Loch Ness Monster Exhibition*★ **AC** – *The Great Glen*★.
Edinburgh 172 – Inverness 16 – Kyle of Lochalsh 66.

🏠 **Polmaily House** ⟩, IV3 6XT, W : 2 m. on A 831 ℰ *(01456) 450343, Fax (01456) 450813,*
« Country house atmosphere », ⬛, 🐎, park, ⚒ – ⟨⟩ rest, 📺 ☎ 🅿. 💳 *VISA*
Meals (bar lunch)/dinner 25.00 t. and a la carte ⅋ 9.00 – **11 rm** ⊇ 59.00/138.00 t. – SB.

🏠 **Drumbuie Farm**, Drumbuie, IV3 6XP, E : ¾ m. by A 82 ℰ *(01456) 450634,*
Fax (01456) 450595, ⟨, « Working farm », park – ⟨⟩ 📺 🅿. ⚒
Meals (by arrangement) 12.00 – **3 rm** ⊇ 40.00 st. – SB.

DRYMEN *Stirling* **401** G 15 *Scotland G.* – pop. 1 565.
Env. : *Loch Lomond*★★, W : 3 m.
🅱 *Drymen Library, The Square, J63 0BL* ℰ *(01360) 660068 (summer only).*
Edinburgh 64 – Glasgow 18 – Stirling 22.

🏨 **Buchanan Arms**, Main St., G63 0BQ, ℰ *(01360) 660588, Fax (01360) 660943,* 🏋, ⓢ, ⬛,
🐎, squash – ⟨⟩ 📺 ☎ 🅿 – 🕭 150. 💳 *AE* ⓞ *VISA* *JCB*
Meals 10.50/19.95 t. and a la carte ⅋ 5.25 – **51 rm** ⊇ 78.00/116.00 t. – SB.

DULNAIN BRIDGE *Highland* **401** J 12 – ⊠ *Grantown-on-Spey*.
Edinburgh 140 – Inverness 31 – Perth 96.

🏠 **Muckrach Lodge** ⟩, PH26 3LY, ℰ *(01479) 851257, Fax (01479) 851325,* ⟨, 🐎, park –
⟨⟩ rest, 📺 ☎ 🅿. 💳 *VISA* *JCB*. ⚒
Meals (bar lunch Monday to Saturday)/dinner 24.50 st. ⅋ 6.50 – **11 rm** ⊇ 45.00/90.00 st.,
2 suites – SB.

🏠 **Auchendean Lodge**, PH26 3LU, S : 1 m. on A 95 ℰ *(01479) 851347, Fax (01479) 851347,*
⟨ Spey Valley and Cairngorms, 🐎 – ⟨⟩ rest, 📺 🅿. 💳 *AE* ⓞ *VISA* *JCB*
closed January-early February – Meals (dinner only) 25.00 st. ⅋ 4.00 – **8 rm** ⊇ 39.50/
73.00 st. – SB.

The Guide is updated annually so renew your Guide every year.

DUMBARTON *West Dunbartonshire* **401** G 16 *Scotland G.* – pop. 77 173.
See : *Dumbarton Castle (site*★*)* **AC**.
Env. : *Loch Lomond*★★, N : 5 ½ m. by A 82.
🅱 *Vale of Leven, Northfield Rd, Bonhill* ℰ *(01389) 752351.*
🅱 *Milton, by Dumbarton A 82 (northbound)* ℰ *(01389) 742306 (summer only).*
Edinburgh 64 – Glasgow 12 – Greenock 17.

🏠 **Travelodge**, Milton, G82 2TY, E : 3 m. by A 814 on A 82 ℰ *(01389) 65202, Reservations*
(Freephone) 0800 850950 – ⟨⟩ rm, 📺 🅿. 💳 *AE* ⓞ *VISA* *JCB*. ⚒
Meals (grill rest.) – **32 rm** 44.95 t.

DUMFRIES *Dumfries and Galloway* **401** **402** J 18 *Scotland G.* – pop. 21 164.
See : *Town*★ – *Midsteeple*★ **A** **A**.
Env. : *Lincluden College (Tomb*★*)* **AC**, N : 1 ½ m. by College St. **A**.
Exc. : *Drumlanrig Castle*★★ *(cabinets*★*)* **AC**, NW : 16 ½ m. by A 76 **A** – *Shambellie House,*
Museum of Costume (Costume Collection★*) S : 7 ¼ m. by A 710* **A** – *Sweetheart Abbey*★
AC, S : 8 m. by A 710 **A** – *Caerlaverock Castle*★ *(Renaissance façade*★★*)* **AC**, SE : 9 m. by A
725 **B** – *Glenkiln (Sculptures*★*) W : 9 m. by A 780* – **A** *– and A 75 – Ruthwell Cross*★, SE : 12 m
by A 780 – **B** – A 75 and B 724.

🅱 *Dumfries & Galloway, 2 Laurieston Av., Maxwelltown* ℰ *(01387) 253582 A –* 🅱 *Crichton*
Bankend Rd ℰ *(01387) 247894,* **B**.
🅱 *64 Whitesands, DG1 2RS* ℰ *(01387) 253862,* **A**.
Edinburgh 80 – Ayr 59 – Carlisle 34 – Glasgow 79 – Manchester 155 – Newcastle upon
Tyne 91.

Plan opposite

🏨 **Cairndale**, English St., DG1 2DF, ℰ *(01387) 254111, Fax (01387) 250555,* 🏋, ⓢ, ⬛ –
⟨⟩ rm, ▤ rest, 📺 ☎ 🅿 – 🕭 160. 💳 *AE* ⓞ *VISA*. ⚒
Meals 10.50/18.95 t. and a la carte ⅋ 6.50 – **76 rm** ⊇ 79.50/99.50 st. – SB. **B**

🏠 **Station**, 49 Lovers Walk, DG1 1LT, ℰ *(01387) 254316, Fax (01387) 250388 –* 📶 📺 ☎ 🅿
🕭 70. 💳 *AE* ⓞ *VISA* *JCB*
Meals (bar lunch)/dinner 16.95 st. and a la carte ⅋ 4.50 – **32 rm** ⊇ 75.00/90.00 st. – SB. **B**

DUMFRIES

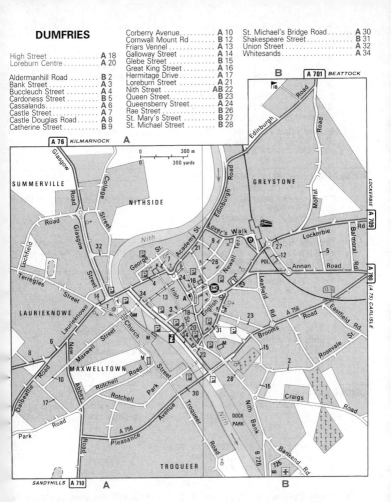

🏨 **Travelodge,** Annan Rd, DG1 3SE, E: 2 ¼ m. on A 75 ✆ (01387) 750658, Fax (01387) 750658, Reservations (Freephone) 0800 850950 – ⇌ rm, 📺 & 🅿. 🆖 🆎 ⓪ VISA JCB. ✗
Meals (grill rest.) – **40 rm** 39.95 **t.**

⌂ **Orchard House** without rest., 298 Annan Rd, DG1 3JE, E: 1 ½ m. on A 780 (Carlisle rd) ✆ (01387) 255099, 🐎 – ⇌ 📺 & 🅿
3 rm ☔ 25.00/40.00.

🔘 ATS Glasgow St. ✆ (01384) 266154   ATS 4 Downsway Ind. Est., Heathall
                                             ✆ (01387) 263837/8

DUNAIN PARK Highland – see Inverness.

SCOTLAND

DUNBAR East Lothian **401** M 15 Scotland G. – pop. 5 812.

See : Tolbooth★ – John Muir's Birthplace★.

Exc. : Tantallon Castle★★ (clifftop site★★★) AC, NW : 10 m. by A 1087, A 1 and A 198 – Fast Castle (site★★), SE : 13 m. by A 1087, A 1, A 1107 and minor rd – Preston Mill★, W : 6 m. by A 1087, A 1 and B 1407 – Tyninghame★, NW : 6 m. by A 1 and A 198 – Museum of Flight★, W : 7 m. by A 1087, A 1 and B 1377.

🏨 East Links ℘ (01386) 862317 – 🏨 Winterfield, St. Margarets, North Rd ℘ (01386) 862280.

🏢 143 High St., EH42 1ES ℘ (01368) 863353.

Edinburgh 28 – Newcastle upon Tyne 90.

⌂ **St. Laurence** without rest., North Rd, EH42 1AU, off Wood Gate (north end of High St.) ℘ (01368) 862527, ⇐ – 🅿. ⟨⟩
restricted opening November-Easter – **3 rm** ⊊ 23.00/40.00 st.

DUNBLANE Stirling **401** I 15 Scotland G. – pop. 8 007 (inc. Lecropt).

See : Town★ – Cathedral★ (west front★).

Env. : Doune★ (castle★ AC) W : 4 ½ m. by A 820 – Doune Motor Museum★ AC, W : 5 ½ m. by A 820 and A 84.

🏢 Stirling Rd ℘ (01786) 824428 (summer only).

Edinburgh 42 – Glasgow 33 – Perth 29.

🏰 **Cromlix House** ⟨⟩, Kinbuck, FK15 9JT, N : 3 ½ m. on B 8033 ℘ (01786) 822125, Fax (01786) 825450, ⇐, « Antique furnishings, 19C chapel », 🐟, 🎾, park, ⟨⟩ – ⇔ rest, 📺 ☎ 🅿 – 🔬 40. 🆗 🆎 ⓪ 🗺 ⟨⟩
closed 2 to 29 January – **Meals** (booking essential) (lunch by arrangement Monday to Friday mid October-April)/dinner 36.50 **t.** ⟨⟩ 9.00 – **6 rm** ⊊ 125.00/200.00 **t.**, **8 suites** 200.00/280.00 **t.** – SB.

Per spostarvi più rapidamente utilizzate le **carte Michelin "Grandi Strade"** :

n° **970** Europa, n° **976** Rep. Ceca/Slovacchia, n° **980** Grecia,
n° **984** Germania, n° **985** Scandinavia-Finlandia,
n° **986** Gran Bretagna-Irlanda, n° **987** Germania-Austria-Benelux,
n° **988** Italia, n° **989** Francia, n° **990** Spagna-Portogallo, n° **991** Jugoslavia.

DUNDEE **401** L 14 Scotland G. – pop. 165 873.

See : The Frigate Unicorn★ AC Y A – Discovery Point★ AC Y B – McManus Galleries★.

🏨, 🏨, 🏨 Caird Park, Mains Loan ℘ (01382) 453606 – 🏨 Camperdown, Camperdown Park ℘ (01382) 623398.

Tay Road Bridge (toll) Y .

✈ Dundee Airport : ℘ (01382) 643242, SW : 1 ½ m. Z .

🏢 4 City Sq., DD1 3BA ℘ (01382) 434664.

Edinburgh 63 – Aberdeen 67 – Glasgow 83.

Plan opposite

🏰 **Stakis Dundee**, Earl Grey Pl., DD1 4DE, ℘ (01382) 229271, Fax (01382) 200072, ⇐, 🚵 ⇔, 🏊 – |𝄐|, ⇔ rm, 🍴 rest, 📺 ☎ 🕭 🅿 – 🔬 400. 🆗 🆎 ⓪ 🗺 ⟨⟩ Y a
Meals (carving lunch) 9.95/18.00 **t.** and dinner a la carte – ⊊ 9.50 – **129 rm** 98.00/136.00 **st.** – SB.

🏨 **Swallow**, Kingsway West (Dundee Ring Rd), DD2 5JT, W : 4 ¾ m. at junction of A 85 with A 90 ℘ (01382) 641122, Fax (01382) 568340, 🚵, ⇔, 🏊, 🎾 – ⇔ rm, 🍴 rest, 📺 ☎ 🕭 🅿 – 🔬 80. 🆗 🆎 ⓪ 🗺
Meals 10.95/19.00 **st.** and a la carte ⟨⟩ 7.25 – **106 rm** ⊊ 90.00/115.00 **st.**, 1 suite – SB.

🏨 **Shaftesbury**, 1 Hyndford St., DD2 1HQ, ℘ (01382) 669216, Fax (01382) 641598 ⇔ rest, 📺 ☎. 🆗 🆎 🗺 Z e
Meals (lunch by arrangement) (Sunday dinner residents only) 8.90/15.50 **st.** and a la carte **12 rm** ⊊ 49.50/76.00 **st.** – SB.

🏨 **Travel Inn**, Discovery Quay, Riverside Drive, DD1 4XA, ℘ (01382) 203240 Fax (01382) 203237, ⇐ – ⇔ rm, 📺 ⟨⟩ 🅿. 🆗 🆎 ⓪ 🗺. ⟨⟩ Z c
Meals (grill rest.) – **40 rm** 36.50 **t.**

🏨 **Travel Inn**, Kingsway West, Invergowrie, DD2 5JU, NW : on A 90 ℘ (01382) 561115 Fax (01382) 568431 – ⇔ rm, 📺 ⟨⟩ 🅿. 🆗 🆎 ⓪ 🗺. ⟨⟩
Meals (grill rest.) – **40 rm** 36.50 **t.**

⌂ **Hillside** without rest., 43 Constitution St., DD3 6JH, ℘ (01382) 223443 Fax (01382) 223443 – ⇔ 📺 🅿. 🆗 🗺 Y n
4 rm ⊊ 21.00/48.00.

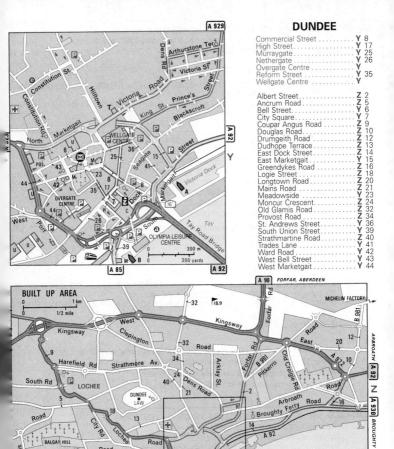

DUNDEE

at **Broughty Ferry** E : 4½ m. by A 930 – **Z** – (Dundee Rd) – ⊠ Dundee.

🏥 **Broughty Ferry,** 16 West Queen St., DD5 1AR, ℰ (01382) 480027, Fax (01382) 477660, ⅃ᵭ, ≦ₛ, ⬛ – ﹕ᷓ ⠧ 🕾 ℗, ⬟⬤ 🖭 𝘝𝘐𝘚𝘈. ⅏
     Meals (closed Sunday) a la carte 11.40/21.85 t. – **15 rm** ⊊ 59.00/74.00 t.

⌂ **Invermark House** without rest., 23 Monifieth Rd, DD5 2RN, ℰ (01382) 739430, ⏦ – ﹕ᷓ ⠧ ℗. ⅏
     4 rm ⊊ 30.00/40.00 s.

⌂ **Beach House,** 22 Esplanade, DD5 2EN, ℰ (01382) 776614, Fax (01382) 480241 – ﹕ᷓ rest, ⠧ 🕾, ⬤⬤ 𝘝𝘐𝘚𝘈. ⅏
     Meals 12.50 st. ⅃ 4.25 – **5 rm** ⊊ 38.00/48.00 st.

     ⓪ ATS 332 Clepington Rd ℰ (01382) 858327

Your recommendation is self-evident if you always walk into a hotel Guide in hand.

DUNDONNELL Highland **401** E 10 Scotland G. – ✉ Garve.

Env. : Wester Ross★★★ – Loch Broom★★, N : 4 ½ m. via Allt na h–Airbhe.

Exc. : Falls of Measach★★, SE : 10 m. by A 832 – Corrieshalloch Gorge★, SE : 11 ½ m. by A 832 and A 835.

Edinburgh 215 – Inverness 59.

🏨 **Dundonnell,** IV23 2QR, ✆ (01854) 633204, Fax (01854) 633366, ≤ Dundonnell Valley – ⅍⅍ 🆃🆅 ☎ 🅿 – 🔏 60. 🆀🆁 🆀🅴 🆅🅸🆂🅰
closed January – **Meals** (booking essential in winter) (bar lunch)/dinner 20.00 **t.** ⬧ 5.95 – 28 rm ⊆ 60.00/105.00 **t.** – SB.

DUNFERMLINE Fife **401** J 15 Scotland G. – pop. 29 436.

See : Town★ – Abbey★ (Abbey Church★★) AC.

Env. : Forth Bridges★★, S : 5 m. by A 823 and B 980.

Exc. : Culross★★ (Village★★★, Palace★★ AC, Study★ AC), W : 7 m. by A 994 and B 9037.

🏌 Canmore, Venturefair ✆ (01383) 724969 – 🏌 Pitreavie, Queensferry Rd ✆ (01383) 722591 – 🏌 Saline, Kinneddar Hill ✆ (01383) 852591.

🅱 13-15 Maygate, KY12 7NE ✆ (01383) 720999.

Edinburgh 16 – Dundee 48 – Motherwell 39.

🏨 **King Malcolm Thistle,** Queensferry Rd, KY11 5DS, S : 1 m. on A 823 ✆ (01383) 722611, Fax (01383) 730865 – ⅍⅍ rm, ▤ rest, 🆃🆅 ☎ 🅿 – 🔏 150. 🆀🆁 🆀🅴 🆀 🆅🅸🆂🅰 🅹🅲🅱. ⅍
Meals (closed lunch Saturday and Sunday) 9.50/16.50 **st.** and a la carte ⬧ 5.20 – ⊆ 9.75 – 48 rm 76.00/111.00 **st.** – SB.

at Crossford SW : 1 ¾ m. on A 994 – ✉ Dunfermline.

🏨 **Keavil House** ⌂, Main St., KY12 8QW, ✆ (01383) 736258, Fax (01383) 621600, 🄵🅂, ≋, 🄽, ☞ – ⅍⅍ 🆃🆅 ☎ & 🅿 – 🔏 300. 🆀🆁 🆀🅴 🆀 🆅🅸🆂🅰. ⅍
Meals (bar lunch)/dinner 21.50 **t.** and a la carte ⬧ 6.50 – ⊆ 8.75 – 33 rm 58.00/100.00 **t.** – SB.

🅖 ATS 14 Dickson St., Elgin St. Est. ✆ (0·1383) 722802

Le Grand Londres (GREATER LONDON) est composé de la City et de 32 arrondissements administratifs (Borough) eux-mêmes divisés en quartiers ou en villages ayant conservé leur caractère propre (Area).

DUNKELD Perthshire and Kinross **401** J 14 Scotland G. – pop. 4 069.

See : Village★ – Cathedral Street★.

🏌 Dunkeld & Birnam, Fungarth ✆ (01350) 727524.

🅱 The Cross, PH8 0AN ✆ (01350) 727688 (March-December).

Edinburgh 58 – Aberdeen 88 – Inverness 98 – Perth 14.

🏯 **Kinnaird** ⌂, Dalguise, PH8 0LB, NW : 6 ¾ m. by A 9 on B 898 ✆ (01796) 482440, Fax (01796) 482289, ≤ Tay valley and hills, « Sporting estate, antique furnishings », ≋, ☞, park, ⅍ – 🛗, ⅍⅍ rest, 🆃🆅 ☎ 🅿. 🆀🆁 🆀🅴 🆅🅸🆂🅰. ⅍
closed Monday to Wednesday January-March – **Meals** 28.00/42.00 **t.** ⬧ 8.00 – 8 rm ⊆ 230.00/300.00 **t.**, 1 suite.

🏨 **Stakis Dunkeld** ⌂, PH8 0HX, ✆ (01350) 727771, Fax (01350) 728924, ≤, « Taysid setting », 🄵🅂, ≋, 🄽, ≋, ☞, park, ⅍ – 🛗, ⅍⅍ rm, 🆃🆅 ☎ & 🅿 – 🔏 85. 🆀🆁 🆀🅴 🆀 🆅🅸🆂🅰 🅹🅲🅱 ⅍
Meals (bar lunch)/dinner 30.00 **st.** – ⊆ 9.75 – 83 rm 100.00/110.00 **st.**, 3 suites – SB.

🏠 **Bheinne Mhor,** Perth Rd, Birnam, PH8 0DH, SE : ¾ m. by A 923 ✆ (01350) 727779, ☞ – ⅍⅍ 🅿. 🆀🆁 🆅🅸🆂🅰. ⅍
closed mid December-mid January – **Meals** (by arrangement) 15.00 **s.** – 3 rm ⊆ 34.00/ 44.00 **st.** – SB.

DUNOON Argyll and Bute **401** F 16 Scotland G. – pop. 13 781 (inc. Kilmun).

Env. : The Clyde Estuary★.

🏌 Innellan, Knockamillie Rd ✆ (01369) 830242.

⚓ from Dunoon Pier to Gourock Railway Pier (Caledonian MacBrayne Ltd) frequent services daily (20 mn) – from Hunters Quay to McInroy's Point, Gourock (Western Ferrie (Clyde) Ltd) frequent services daily (20 mn).

🅱 7 Alexandra Par., PA23 8AB ✆ (01369) 703785 (closed weekends in winter).

Edinburgh 73 – Glasgow 27 – Oban 77.

Enmore, Marine Par., Kirn, PA23 8HH, N : 1 ¼ m. on A 815 ℰ (01369) 702230, Fax (01369) 702148, ≤ Firth of Clyde, ☞, squash – ☆ rest, 📺 ☎ 🅿. 🆖 ᴁ 𝘝𝘐𝘚𝘈 closed 20 to 29 December and 4 to 12 January – **Meals** 12.50/25.00 **st.** and a la carte ⓘ 6.50 – **10 rm** 39.00/150.00 **st.** – SB.

Anchorage, Shore Rd, Ardanadam, PA23 8QG, N : 3 m. on A 815 ℰ (01369) 705108, Fax (01369) 705108, ≤, ☞ – ☆ 📺 🕹 🅿. 🆖 𝘝𝘐𝘚𝘈. ❀ closed last week October, November and 25 December – **Meals** 15.00 **t.** (dinner) and a la carte 16.75/21.75 **t.** ⓘ 6.00 – **5 rm** ⇌ 55.00/75.00 **t.** – SB.

◎ ATS 247 Argyll St. ℰ (01369) 702853

DUNVEGAN Highland⁴⁰¹ A 11 – see Skye (Isle of).

DYCE Aberdeenshire⁴⁰¹ N 12 – see Aberdeen.

EARLSTON Borders⁴⁰¹ ⁴⁰² L 17 – pop. 1 968.
Edinburgh 34 – Hawick 22 – Newcastle upon Tyne 71.

Birkhill ❧, Earlston, TD4 6AR, N : 3 ¼ m. by A 68 and Birkenside rd on Lauder rd ℰ (01896) 849307, Fax (01896) 848206, ≤, ➾, ☞, park – ☆ 🅿 𝘝𝘐𝘚𝘈. ❀ closed Christmas and New Year – **Meals** (by arrangement) (communal dining) 20.00 **s.** – **3 rm** ⇌ 40.00/60.00 **st.** – SB.

EASDALE Argyll and Bute⁴⁰¹ D 15 – see Seil (Isle of).

EAST KILBRIDE South Lanarkshire⁴⁰¹ ⁴⁰² H 16 – pop. 73 378.
⌧ Torrance House, Strathaven Rd ℰ (01355) 248638.
Edinburgh 46 – Ayr 35 – Glasgow 10.

Stakis East Kilbride, Stewartfield Way, G74 5LA, NW : 2 ¼ m. on A 726 ℰ (01355) 236300, Fax (01355) 233552, Ⅰₛ, ⓢ, ▨ – ▮, ☆ rm, ▤ rest, 📺 ☎ 🕹 🅿 – ⓐ 400. 🆖 ᴁ ① 𝘝𝘐𝘚𝘈. ❀ **Meals** 16.50 **st.** and a la carte ⓘ 5.25 – ⇌ 10.50 – **97 rm** 95.00/110.00 **st.**, 2 suites.

Bruce Swallow, 34 Cornwall St., G74 1AF, ℰ (01355) 229771, Fax (01355) 242216 – ▮, ☆ rm, 📺 ☎ 🅿 – ⓐ 40. 🆖 ᴁ ① 𝘝𝘐𝘚𝘈 **Meals** (bar lunch Monday to Saturday)/dinner 16.65 **st.** and a la carte ⓘ 8.00 – **78 rm** ⇌ 80.00/99.00 **st.** – SB.

Crutherland House ❧, Strathaven Rd, G75 0QZ, SE : 2 m. on A 726 ℰ (01355) 237633, Fax (01355) 20855, ☞, park – 📺 ☎ 🅿 – ⓐ 40. 🆖 ᴁ ① 𝘝𝘐𝘚𝘈 **Meals** (booking essential) (dinner only)/a la carte 23.25/29.00 **t.** ⓘ 6.95 – **18 rm** ⇌ 85.00/110.00 **t.**, 1 suite.

Travel Inn, Brunel Way, The Murray, G75 0JY, ℰ (01355) 222809, Fax (01355) 230517 – ☆ rm, 📺 🕹 🅿. 🆖 ᴁ ① 𝘝𝘐𝘚𝘈. ❀ **Meals** (grill rest.) – **40 rm** 36.50 **t.**

Peel Park - Lodge Inn, Eaglesham Rd, G75 8LW, NW : 1 ½ m. on A 726 ℰ (01355) 222747, Fax (01355) 234346 – ☆ rm, 📺 🕹 🅿. 🆖 ᴁ ① 𝘝𝘐𝘚𝘈. ❀ **Meals** a la carte 8.30/13.90 **t.** ⓘ 3.95 – ⇌ 5.50 – **40 rm** 37.50 **t.** – SB.

EDINBURGH

401 K 16 *Scotland G. – pop. 418 914.*

Glasgow 46 – Newcastle upon Tyne 105.

TOURIST INFORMATION

🛈 *Edinburgh & Scotland Information Centre, 3 Princes St., EH2 2QP ℘ (0131) 557 1700.*
🛈 *Edinburgh Airport, Tourist Information Desk ℘ (0131) 333 2167.*

PRACTICAL INFORMATION

🛈, 🛈 *Braid Hills, Braid Hills Rd ℘ (0131) 447 6666, BX.*
🛈 *Craigmillar Park, 1 Observatory Rd ℘ (0131) 667 2837, BX.*
🛈 *Carrick Knowe, Glendevon Park ℘ (0131) 337 1096, AX.*
🛈 *Duddingston, Duddingston Road West ℘ (0131) 661 1005, BV.*
🛈 *Silverknowes, Parkway ℘ (0131) 336 3843, AV.*
🛈 *Liberton, 297 Gilmerton Rd ℘ (0131) 664 3009, BX.*
🛈, 🛈 *Dalmahoy Hotel C.C., Kirknewton ℘ (0131) 333 4105/1845, AX.*
🛈 *Portobello, Stanley St. ℘ (0131) 669 4361, BV.*
✈ *Edinburgh Airport : ℘ (0131) 333 1000, W : 6 m. by A 8 AV –* **Terminal :** *Waverley Bridge.*

SIGHTS

See : *City*★★★ *– Edinburgh International Festival*★★★ *(August) – National Gallery of Scotland*★★ *DY* **M4** *– Royal Botanic Garden*★★★ *AV – The Castle*★★ *AC DYZ : Site*★★★ *– Palace Block (Honours of Scotland*★★★ *) – St. Margaret's Chapel (※*★★★ *) – Great Hall (Hammerbeam Roof*★★ *) – ≼*★★ *from Argyle and Mill's Mount DZ – Abbey and Palace of Holyroodhouse*★★ *AC (Plasterwork Ceilings*★★★ *, ※*★★ *from Arthur's Seat) BV – Royal Mile*★★ *: St. Giles' Cathedral*★★ *(Crown Spire*★★★ *) EYZ – Gladstone's Land*★ *AC EYZ* **A** *– Canongate Tolbooth*★ *EY* **B** *– New Town*★★ *(Charlotte Square*★★★ *CY* **14** *– Royal Museum of Scotland*★★ *EZ* **M2** *– The Georgian House*★ *AC CY* **D** *– Scottish National Portrait Gallery*★ *EY* **M3** *– Dundas House*★ *EY* **E** *) – Scottish National Gallery of Modern Art*★ *AV* **M1** *– Victoria Street*★ *EZ* **84** *– Scott Monument*★ *(≼*★*) AC EY* **F** *– Craigmillar Castle*★ *AC BX – Calton Hill (※*★★★ *AC from Nelson's Monument) EY.*

Env. : *Edinburgh Zoo*★★ *AC AV – Hill End Ski Centre (※*★★*) AC, S : 5½ m. by A 702 BX – The Royal Observatory (West Tower ≼*★*) AC BX – Ingleston, Scottish Agricultural Museum*★*, W : 6½ m. by A 8 AV.*

Exc. : *Rosslyn Chapel*★★ *AC (Apprentice Pillar*★★★ *) S : 7½ m. by A 701 – BX – and B 7006 – Forth Bridges*★★*, NW : 9½ m. by A 90 AV – Hopetoun House*★★ *AC, NW : 11½ m. by A 90 – AV – and A 904 – Dalmeny*★ *– Dalmeny House*★ *AC, St. Cuthbert's Church*★ *(Norman South Doorway*★★ *) NW : 7 m. by A 90 AV – Crichton Castle (Italianate courtyard range*★ *) AC, SE : 10 m. by A 7 – X – and B 6372.*

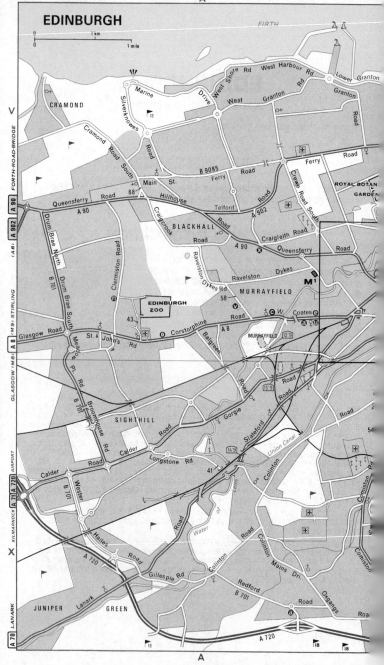

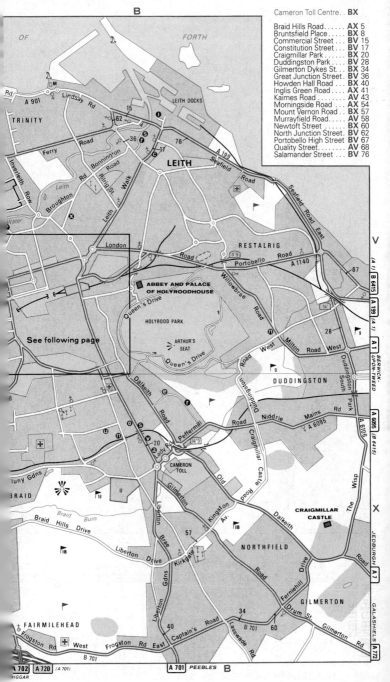

679

EDINBURGH
CENTRE

680

Castle Street .... DY
Frederick Street .... DY
George Street .... DY
Hanover Street .... DY
High Street .... EYZ 37
Lawnmarket .... EYZ 46
Princes Street .... DY
St. James Centre .... DY
Waverley Market .... EY

Bernard Terrace .... EZ 3
Bread Street .... DZ 6
Bristo Place .... EZ 7
Candlemaker Row .... EZ 9
Castlehill .... DZ 10
Chambers Street .... EZ 12
Chapel Street .... EZ 13
Charlotte Square .... CY 14
Deanhaugh Street .... CY 23
Douglas Gardens .... CY 25
Drummond Street .... EZ 27
Forrest Road .... EZ 31
Gardner's Crescent .... CZ 32
George IV Bridge .... EZ 33
Grassmarket .... DZ 35
Home Street .... DZ 38
Hope Street .... CY 39
Johnston Terrace .... DZ 42
King's Bridge .... DZ 44
King's Stables Road .... DZ 45
Leith Street .... EY 47
Leven Street .... DZ 48
Lothian Street .... EZ 51
Mound (The) .... DY 55
North Bridge .... EY 61
North St. Andrew Street .... EY 66
Raeburn Place .... CY 69
Randolph Crescent .... CY 71
St. Andrew Square .... EY 73
St. Mary's Street .... EY 75
Shandwick Place .... CYZ 77
Shandwick Place .... DY 78
South Charlotte Street .... DEY 78
South St. David Street .... DZ 79
Spittal Street .... DZ 83
Victoria Street .... EZ 84
Waterloo Place .... EY 87
Waverley Bridge .... EY 89

Balmoral, Princes St., EH2 2EQ, ℘ (0131) 556 2414, *Fax (0131) 557 3747,* Ⅰ₅, ⇔s, ◰ – ‖,
⇔ rm, ▤ Ⅳ & ⅙ ⇔ – ⅍ 350. ⑨ Ⓐ ① *VISA* ⒿⒸⒷ. ⅏　　　　　　　　　　EY n
Hadrian's : Meals a la carte 28.75/41.00 **st.** ⅛ 7.25 – (see also ***Number One*** below) –
⌑ 15.00 – **165 rm** 170.00/205.00 **st.,** 21 suites – SB.

Caledonian, Princes St., EH1 2AB, ℘ (0131) 459 9988, *Fax (0131) 225 6632* – ‖, ⇔ rm,
▤ Ⅳ ☎ & ⅙ ⅌ – ⅍ 300. ⑨ Ⓐ ① *VISA.*　　　　　　　　　　　　　　　CY n
Carriages : Meals *(closed Saturday lunch)* a la carte 19.40/27.85 **st.** ⅛ 6.95 – (see also
Pompadour below) – ⌑ 14.95 – **223 rm** 147.00/275.00 **t.,** 11 suites – SB.

Sheraton Grand, 1 Festival Sq., EH3 9SR, ℘ (0131) 229 9131, *Fax (0131) 229 6254,* Ⅰ₅,
⇔s, ◰ – ‖, ⇔ rm, ▤ Ⅳ ☎ & ⅙ ⅌ – ⅍ 500. ⑨ Ⓐ ① *VISA* ⒿⒸⒷ. ⅏　　CDZ v
Terrace : Meals 20.50 **t.** and a la carte – (see also ***Grill Room*** below) – ⌑ 14.00 – **244 rm**
180.00/220.00 **st.,** 17 suites.

George Inter-Continental, 19-21 George St., EH2 2PB, ℘ (0131) 225 1251,
Fax (0131) 226 5644 – ‖, ⇔ rm, Ⅳ ☎ ⅙ ⅌ – ⅍ 200. ⑨ Ⓐ ① *VISA.* ⅏　　　　DY z
Le Chambertin : Meals *(closed Saturday lunch and Sunday)* 23.50/26.00 **t.** – *Carvers*
(℘ (0131) 459 2305) : Meals 17.95 **t.** and a la carte ⅛ 7.50 – ⌑ 11.85 – **193 rm** 145.00/
200.00 **st.,** 2 suites – SB.

Marriott Dalmahoy H. & Country Club ⌕, Kirknewton, EH27 8EB, SW : 7 m. on A 71
℘ (0131) 333 1845, *Fax (0131) 333 1433,* ⇐, Ⅰ₅, ⇔s, ◰, Ⅰ₅, ♒, park, ⅏, squash – ‖ ⇔ Ⅳ
☎ & ⅙ ⅌ – ⅍ 400. ⑨ Ⓐ ① *VISA* ⒿⒸⒷ. ⅏
Pentland : Meals *(closed lunch Saturday and Sunday)* 15.00 **st.** (lunch) and a la carte 21.50/
27.00 **st.** ⅛ 7.45 – *Long Weekend :* Meals (grill rest.) a la carte 10.75/19.25 **st.** ⅛ 7.45 –
150 rm 130.00/140.00 **st.,** 1 suite – SB.

Carlton Highland, North Bridge St., EH1 1SD, ℘ (0131) 556 7277, *Fax (0131) 556 2691,*
Ⅰ₅, ⇔s, ◰, squash – ‖, ⇔ rm, ▤ rest, Ⅳ ☎ & ⅙ ⅌ – ⅍ 280. ⑨ Ⓐ ① *VISA*　　EY s
Quills : Meals *(closed Saturday lunch and Sunday)* 10.45/17.50 **t.** and a la carte ⅛ 5.95 –
Eureka : Meals (carving rest.) 10.45/17.50 **t.** and a la carte ⅛ 5.95 – **193 rm** ⌑ 119.00/
204.00 **t.,** 4 suites – SB.

Swallow Royal Scot, 111 Glasgow Rd, EH12 8NF, W : 4 ½ m. on A 8 ℘ (0131) 334 9191,
Fax (0131) 316 4507, Ⅰ₅, ⇔s, ◰ – ‖, ⇔ rm, ▤ Ⅳ ☎ & ⅙ ⅌ – ⅍ 300. ⑨ Ⓐ ① *VISA*
Meals 16.00/22.50 **st.** and a la carte ⅛ 7.50 – **255 rm** 110.00/145.00 **st.,** 4 suites – SB.

The Howard, 34 Great King St., EH3 6QH, ℘ (0131) 557 3500, *Fax (0131) 557 6515,*
« Georgian town houses » – ‖, ⇔ rest, ▤ rest, Ⅳ ☎ ⅌ – ⅍ 40. ⑨ Ⓐ ① *VISA.* ⅏　DY s
36 : Meals *(closed Saturday lunch)* a la carte 17.65/29.70 **st.** ⅛ 11.50 – **15 rm** ⌑ 110.00/
275.00 **st.**

Holiday Inn Crowne Plaza, 80 High St., EH1 1TH, ℘ (0131) 557 9797,
Fax (0131) 557 9789, Ⅰ₅, ⇔s, ◰ – ‖, ⇔ rm, Ⅳ ☎ & ⅙ ⅌ – ⅍ 200. ⑨ Ⓐ ① *VISA* ⒿⒸⒷ.
⅏　　　　　　　　　　　　　　　　　　　　　　　　　　　　　　　　　EY z
closed 25 to 28 December – Meals *(closed Saturday lunch and Sunday)* 16.50 **st.** (dinner)
and a la carte 11.50/29.50 **st.** ⅛ 8.00 – ⌑ 13.50 – **229 rm** 165.00/190.00 **st.,** 9 suites.

Hilton National, 69 Belford Rd, EH4 3DG, ℘ (0131) 332 2545, *Fax (0131) 332 3805* – ‖,
⇔ rm, Ⅳ ☎ & ⅙ ⅌ – ⅍ 130. ⑨ Ⓐ ① *VISA* ⒿⒸⒷ.　　　　　　　　　　CY i
Meals (bar lunch)/dinner 17.50 **t.** and a la carte ⅛ 6.30 – ⌑ 11.50 – **144 rm** 115.00/
250.00 **st.**

Channings, South Learmonth Gdns., EH4 1EZ, ℘ (0131) 315 2226, *Fax (0131) 332 9631,*
♒ – ‖ ⇔ Ⅳ ☎ – ⅍ 35. ⑨ Ⓐ ① *VISA* ⒿⒸⒷ. ⅏　　　　　　　　　　　CY e
closed 24 to 28 December – Meals *(closed lunch Saturday and Sunday)* 9.95/21.00 **st.**
and a la carte ⅛ 5.75 – **48 rm** ⌑ 105.00/220.00 **t.** – SB.

Malmaison, 1 Tower Pl., Leith, EH6 7DB, NE : 2 m. by A 900 ℘ (0131) 555 6868,
Fax (0131) 555 6999, « Contemporary interior » – ‖, ▤ rest, Ⅳ ☎ ⅌ – ⅍ 100. ⑨ Ⓐ ①
VISA　　　　　　　　　　　　　　　　　　　　　　　　　　　　　　　　BV i
Meals - Brasserie - 13.00 **st.** and a la carte ⅛ 6.00 – ⌑ 10.50 – **54 rm** 90.00/100.00 **st.,**
6 suites.

Prestonfield House ⌕, Priestfield Rd, EH16 5UT, ℘ (0131) 668 3346,
Fax (0131) 668 3976, ⇐, « Part 17C country house », Ⅰ₅, ♒ – ⇔ rm, Ⅳ ☎ ⅌. ⑨ Ⓐ ①
VISA ⒿⒸⒷ.　　　　　　　　　　　　　　　　　　　　　　　　　　　　BX r
Meals 17.00/28.00 **t.** and dinner a la carte ⅛ 7.00 – **31 rm** ⌑ 185.00/295.00 **t.** – SB.

King James Thistle, 107 Leith St., EH1 3SW, ℘ (0131) 556 0111, *Fax (0131) 557 5333* –
‖, ⇔ rm, Ⅳ ☎ ⅌ – ⅍ 250. ⑨ Ⓐ ① *VISA* ⒿⒸⒷ. ⅏　　　　　　　　　　EY u
Meals *(closed Sunday lunch)* 10.20/15.20 **st.** ⅛ 7.50 – *Saint Jacques :* Meals (dinner only)
21.50 **st.** and a la carte 21.50/29.00 **st.** – ⌑ 10.75 – **138 rm** 115.00/162.00 **st.,** 5 suites – SB.

Royal Terrace, 18 Royal Terr., EH7 5AQ, ℰ (0131) 557 3222, Fax (0131) 557 5334, ℐ₆, ⇆s,
☒, ☞ – ☝ ⓣⓥ ☎ – 🔬 80. ⓞⓞ ⒶⒺ ⓞ 𝘝𝘐𝘚𝘈. ⅌
EY i
Meals 17.90 **st.** and a la carte ≬ 7.50 – 🖙 10.50 – **93 rm** 120.00/180.00 **st.**, 1 suite – SB.

Stakis Edinburgh Grosvenor, Grosvenor St., EH12 5EF, ℰ (0131) 226 6001,
Fax (0131) 220 2387 – ☝ ⓣⓥ ☎ – 🔬 500. ⓞⓞ ⒶⒺ ⓞ 𝘝𝘐𝘚𝘈
CZ a
Meals (closed Sunday lunch) 11.00/20.00 **t.** and a la carte ≬ 8.00 – 🖙 9.50 – **186 rm** 108.00/
135.00 **t.**, 1 suite – SB.

Point, 34 Bread St., EH3 9AF, ℰ (0131) 221 9919, Fax (0131) 221 9929 – ☝ ⓣⓥ ☎. ⓞⓞ ⒶⒺ ⓞ
𝘝𝘐𝘚𝘈. ⅌
DZ a
closed 25 and 26 December – **Meals** (closed Sunday lunch) 7.90/10.80 **t.** ≬ 6.00 – 🖙 8.00 –
94 rm 80.00/145.00 **st.** – SB.

Edinburgh Capital Moat House, Clermiston Rd, EH12 6UG, ℰ (0131) 535 9988,
Fax (0131) 334 9712, ℐ₆, ⇆s, ☒ – ☝ ⅍ ⓣⓥ ☎ & ☻ – 🔬 300. ⓞⓞ ⒶⒺ ⓞ 𝘝𝘐𝘚𝘈. ⅌
AV n
Meals 16.50 **t.** ≬ 6.00 – 🖙 10.50 – **111 rm** 89.00/155.00 **t.** – SB.

Holiday Inn Garden Court, 107 Queensferry Rd, EH4 3HL, ℰ (0131) 332 2442,
Fax (0131) 332 3408, ≼, ℐ₆ – ☝ ⅍ rm, ☰ rest, ⓣⓥ ☎ & ☻ – 🔬 60. ⓞⓞ ⒶⒺ ⓞ 𝘝𝘐𝘚𝘈
ⒿⒸⒷ
AV x
Meals 10.95/14.95 **st.** and a la carte ≬ 5.05 – 🖙 9.45 – **118 rm** 89.50/140.00 **st.**, 1 suite –
SB.

Forte Posthouse Edinburgh, Corstorphine Rd, EH12 6UA, W : 3 m. on A 8
ℰ (0131) 334 0390, Fax (0131) 334 9237 – ☝ ⅍ rm, ☰ rest, ⓣⓥ ☎ ☻ – 🔬 120. ⓞⓞ ⒶⒺ ⓞ
𝘝𝘐𝘚𝘈 ⒿⒸⒷ. ⅌
AV c
Meals a la carte 14.00/21.00 **t.** – 🖙 9.95 – **204 rm** 79.00/99.00 **st.** – SB.

Jarvis Ellersly House, 4 Ellersly Rd, EH12 6HZ, ℰ (0131) 337 6888, Fax (0131) 313 2543
☞ – ☝ ⅍ rm, ⓣⓥ ☎ ☻ – 🔬 70. ⓞⓞ ⒶⒺ ⓞ 𝘝𝘐𝘚𝘈
AV v
Meals (Saturday lunch by arrangement) 10.95/14.95 **t.** and dinner a la carte ≬ 7.00 –
🖙 8.50 – **57 rm** 109.00/135.00 **t.** – SB.

Apex International, 31-35 Grassmarket, EH1 2HS, ℰ (0131) 300 3456
Fax (0131) 220 5345 – ☝, ⅍ rm, ☰ rest, ⓣⓥ ☎ ☻. ⓞⓞ ⒶⒺ ⓞ 𝘝𝘐𝘚𝘈. ⅌
DZ e
Meals (carving rest.) (bar lunch)/dinner 14.50 **st.** and a la carte ≬ 6.50 – 🖙 6.95 – **99 rm**
74.95 **st.** – SB.

Maitland without rest., 25a Shandwick Pl., EH2 4RG, ℰ (0131) 229 1467
Fax (0131) 229 7549 – ☝ ⅍ ⓣⓥ ☎. ⓞⓞ ⒶⒺ ⓞ 𝘝𝘐𝘚𝘈 ⒿⒸⒷ. ⅌
CY z
65 rm 🖙 69.50/130.00 **st.**

Lodge, 6 Hampton Terr., West Coates, EH12 5JD, ℰ (0131) 337 3682, Fax (0131) 313 170
– ⅍ ⓣⓥ ☎ ☻. ⓞⓞ 𝘝𝘐𝘚𝘈. ⅌
AV e
closed 20 to 26 December – **Meals** (closed Sunday) (booking essential) (residents only
(dinner only) 14.50 **st.** ≬ 5.25 – **10 rm** 🖙 40.00/80.00 **st.**

Kildonan Lodge, 27 Craigmillar Park, EH16 5PE, ℰ (0131) 667 2793, Fax (0131) 667 977
– ⅍ ⓣⓥ ☻. ⓞⓞ ⒶⒺ 𝘝𝘐𝘚𝘈 ⒿⒸⒷ. ⅌
BX v
Meals (closed Sunday) (dinner only) 12.95 **t.** and a la carte ≬ 4.25 – **12 rm** 🖙 35.00/90.00 **s**
– SB.

Travel Inn, 1 Morrison Link, EH3 8DN, ℰ (0131) 228 9819, Fax (0131) 228 9836 – ☝ ⅍
☰ rest, ⓣⓥ & ☻. ⓞⓞ ⒶⒺ ⓞ 𝘝𝘐𝘚𝘈. ⅌
CZ v
Meals (grill rest.) – **128 rm** 36.50 **t.**

Greenside, 9 Royal Terr., EH7 5AB, ℰ (0131) 557 0022, Fax (0131) 557 0022, ☞ – ⓣⓥ ☎
ⓞⓞ ⒶⒺ ⓞ 𝘝𝘐𝘚𝘈. ⅌
EY v
Meals (bar lunch)/dinner 11.50 **t.** ≬ 4.75 – **14 rm** 🖙 35.00/75.00 **t.**

Travel Inn, 228 Willowbrae Rd, EH8 7NG, ℰ (0131) 661 3396, Fax (0131) 652 2789
⅍ rm, ⓣⓥ & ☻. ⓞⓞ ⒶⒺ ⓞ 𝘝𝘐𝘚𝘈. ⅌
BV v
Meals (grill rest.) – **39 rm** 36.50 **t.**

Travelodge, 48 Dreghorn Link, City Bypass, EH13 9QR, ℰ (0131) 441 4296, Reservation
(Freephone) 0800 850950 – ⅍ rm, ⓣⓥ & ☻. ⓞⓞ ⒶⒺ ⓞ 𝘝𝘐𝘚𝘈 ⒿⒸⒷ. ⅌
AX v
Meals (grill rest.) – **40 rm** 49.95 **t.**

Thain Inn without rest., 123 Grove St., Fountainbridge, EH3 8AA, ℰ (0131) 229 923
Fax (0131) 229 9250 – ☝ ⅍ ⓣⓥ &. ⓞⓞ ⒶⒺ 𝘝𝘐𝘚𝘈. ⅌
CZ v
22 rm 54.95 **t.**

Drummond House without rest., 17 Drummond Pl., EH3 6PL, ℰ (0131) 557 918
Fax (0131) 557 9189, « Georgian town house » – ⅍ ⓣⓥ. ⓞⓞ 𝘝𝘐𝘚𝘈. ⅌
DY v
closed Christmas – **4 rm** 🖙 60.00/90.00 **st.**

17 Abercromby Place, 17 Abercromby Pl., EH3 6LB, ℰ (0131) 557 803
Fax (0131) 558 3453, « Georgian town house » – ⅍ ⓣⓥ ☎ ☻. ⓞⓞ 𝘝𝘐𝘚𝘈. ⅌
DY v
Meals (by arrangement) 25.00 – **6 rm** 🖙 45.00/90.00 **t.**

↑ **Sibbet House** without rest., 26 Northumberland St., EH3 6LS, ℰ (0131) 556 1078, *Fax (0131) 557 9445*, « Georgian town house » – ⬥ TV ☎ 🕼 VISA. ⅍   DY x
5 rm ⌣ 75.00/120.00 s., 1 suite.

↑ **27 Heriot Row** without rest., 27 Heriot Row, EH3 6EN, ℰ (0131) 225 9474, *Fax (0131) 220 1699*, « Georgian town house », ⌇ – ⬥ TV ☎ 🕼 VISA. ⅍   DY v
3 rm ⌣ 50.00/90.00.

↑ **Seven Danube Street** without rest., EH4 1NN, ℰ (0131) 332 2755, *Fax (0131) 343 3648*, « Georgian house », ⌇ – ⬥. 🕼 VISA JCB   CY r
April-24 December – **3 rm** ⌣ 45.00/90.00 st.

↑ **16 Lynedoch Place** without rest., EH3 7PY, ℰ (0131) 225 5507, *Fax (0131) 332 0224*, « Georgian house », ⌇ – TV. 🕼 VISA. ⅍   CY s
3 rm ⌣ 35.00/80.00 st.

↑ **22 Murrayfield Gardens**, EH12 6DF, ℰ (0131) 337 3569, *Fax (0131) 337 3803*, « Victorian house », ⌇ – ⬥ 🅿. 🕼 VISA JCB   AV c
Meals (by arrangement) 20.00 – **3 rm** ⌣ 40.00/80.00 s.

↑ **Number Two Saxe Coburg Place** without rest., 2 Saxe Coburg Pl., EH3 5BR, ℰ (0131) 315 4752, *Fax (0131) 332 4934*, ⌇ – TV ☎. 🕼 VISA. ⅍   BV v
closed November and 1 week Christmas – **3 rm** ⌣ 45.00/80.00 st.

↑ **Kew** without rest., 1 Kew Terr., Murrayfield, EH12 5JE, ℰ (0131) 313 0700, *Fax (0131) 313 0747* – ⬥ TV ☎ 🅿. 🕼 AE VISA. ⅍   AV a
6 rm ⌣ 40.00/80.00 st.

↑ **Stuart House** without rest., 12 East Claremont St., EH7 4JP, ℰ (0131) 557 9030, *Fax (0131) 557 0563* – ⬥ TV ☎. 🕼 AE VISA JCB. ⅍   BV x
closed 1 week Christmas – **7 rm** ⌣ 35.00/80.00 t.

↑ **Teviotdale** without rest., 53 Grange Loan, EH9 2ER, ℰ (0131) 667 4376, *Fax (0131) 667 4376* – ⬥ TV ☎. 🕼 AE VISA. ⅍   BX u
closed 23 to 28 December – **7 rm** ⌣ 45.00/74.00 st.

↑ **Ben-Craig House** without rest., 3 Craigmillar Park, EH16 5PG, ℰ (0131) 667 2593, *Fax (0131) 667 1109*, ⌇ – TV. ⅍   BX v
5 rm ⌣ 30.00/70.00 s.

↑ **International** without rest., 37 Mayfield Gdns., EH9 2BX, ℰ (0131) 667 2511, *Fax (0131) 667 1112* – TV. 🕼 VISA. ⅍   BX s
9 rm ⌣ 40.00/75.00 st.

↑ **Classic** without rest., 50 Mayfield Rd, EH9 2NH, ℰ (0131) 667 5847, *Fax (0131) 662 1016* – ⬥ TV. 🕼 AE ⓪ VISA JCB. ⅍   BX n
7 rm ⌣ 30.00/60.00 st.

↑ **Dorstan**, 7 Priestfield Rd, EH16 5HJ, ℰ (0131) 667 6721, *Fax (0131) 668 4644* – TV ☎ 🅿. 🕼 AE VISA. ⅍   BX e
Meals (by arrangement) 14.00 t. – **14 rm** ⌣ 37.00/76.00 t.

↑ **Parklands** without rest., 20 Mayfield Gdns., EH9 2BZ, ℰ (0131) 667 7184, *Fax (0131) 667 2011* TV. ⅍   BX o
6 rm ⌣ 38.00/56.00 st.

XXXX **Number One** (at Balmoral H.), 1 Princes St., EH2 2EQ, ℰ (0131) 556 6727, *Fax (0131) 557 3747* – ▤. 🕼 AE ⓪ VISA JCB   EY n
closed lunch Saturday and Sunday – **Meals** 16.95/21.50 st. and a la carte ₰ 7.25.

XXXX **Pompadour** (at Caledonian H.), Princes St., EH1 2AB, ℰ (0131) 459 9988, *Fax (0131) 225 6632* – 🅿. 🕼 AE ⓪ VISA   CY n
closed Sunday and Monday – **Meals** (dinner only) a la carte 35.95/49.90 ₰ 9.95.

XXX **Grill Room** (at Sheraton Grand H.), 1 Festival Sq., EH3 9SR, ℰ (0131) 229 9131, *Fax (0131) 229 6254* – ▤ 🅿. 🕼 AE ⓪ VISA JCB   CDZ v
closed Saturday lunch and Sunday – **Meals** 25.50/34.00 t. and a la carte ₰ 13.00.

XX **Haldanes**, 39A Albany St., EH1 3QY, ℰ (0131) 556 8407, 斎 – 🕼 VISA   EY e
closed Saturday and Sunday lunch – **Meals** 13.95 st. (lunch) and dinner a la carte approx. 30.00 st. ₰ 6.50.

XX **Kelly's**, 46 West Richmond St., EH8 9DZ, ℰ (0131) 668 3847 – ⬥. 🕼 VISA   EZ u
closed Sunday to Tuesday, 25-26 December and 1 January – **Meals** 25.00 t. (dinner) and lunch a la carte 12.50/17.50 t. ₰ 7.70.

XX **L'Auberge**, 56 St. Mary's St., EH1 1SX, ℰ (0131) 556 5888, *Fax (0131) 556 2588* – ▤. 🕼 AE ⓪ VISA JCB   EYZ c
closed Monday, 25 December and 1-2 January – **Meals** - French - 13.50/26.50 t. and a la carte ₰ 6.50.

XX **Martins,** 70 Rose St., North Lane, EH2 3DX, ℰ (0131) 225 3106 – ✦. 🕲 AE ⓞ VISA
JCB
DY n
closed Saturday lunch, Sunday, Monday, 1 week in spring, 1 week in autumn, and 24 December-19 January – **Meals** (booking essential) a la carte 19.10/36.50 **t.** ⓵ 5.90.

XX **(fitz)Henry,** 19 Shore Pl., Leith, EH6 6SW, ℰ (0131) 555 6625, *Fax (0131) 228 2998,* « Part 17C warehouse » – 🕲 AE VISA
BV s
closed Sunday, 25-26 December and 1-2 January – **Meals** 13.50/22.00 **t.** ⓵ 7.25.

XX **Raffaelli,** 10 Randolph Pl., EH3 7TA, ℰ (0131) 225 6060, *Fax (0131) 225 8830* – 🕲 AE ⓞ VISA
CY c
closed Saturday lunch, Sunday, 25-26 December, 1-2 January and Bank Holiday Monday – **Meals** - Italian - a la carte 16.60/32.40 **t.** ⓵ 5.90.

XX **Indian Cavalry Club,** 3 Atholl Pl., EH3 8HP, ℰ (0131) 228 3282, *Fax (0131) 225 1911* – 🕲 AE ⓞ VISA
CZ c
Meals - Indian - 6.95 **t.** (lunch) and a la carte 9.55/17.85 **t.**

XX **Vintners Room,** The Vaults, 87 Giles St., Leith, EH6 6BZ, ℰ (0131) 554 6767, *Fax (0131) 467 7130* – ✦. 🕲 AE VISA
BV r
closed Sunday and 2 weeks Christmas-New Year – **Meals** a la carte 13.00/28.25 **t.** ⓵ 5.00.

XX **Yumi,** 2 West Coates, EH12 5JQ, ℰ (0131) 337 2173, *Fax (0131) 337 2818* – ✦ ⓟ. 🕲 VISA
JCB
AV e
closed Sunday and 2 weeks Christmas-New Year – **Meals** - Japanese - (dinner only) 36.00 **t.** ⓵ 5.00.

XX **Denzler's 121,** 121 Constitution St., EH6 7AE, ℰ (0131) 554 3268, *Fax (0131) 467 7239* – 🕲 AE ⓞ VISA JCB
BV c
closed Saturday lunch, Sunday, Monday and 2 weeks late July – **Meals** 10.40/17.95 **st.** and a la carte ⓵ 5.50.

XX **Merchants,** 17 Merchant St., EH1 2QD, off Candlemaker Row, (under bridge) ℰ (0131) 225 4009, *Fax (0131) 557 9318* – 🕲 AE ⓞ VISA JCB
EZ x
closed Sunday and 26 December – **Meals** (booking essential) 10.50/17.50 **t.** and a la carte ⓵ 5.50.

X **Atrium,** 10 Cambridge St., EH1 2ED, ℰ (0131) 228 8882, *Fax (0131) 228 8808* – 🍴. 🕲 AE VISA
DZ c
closed Saturday lunch, Sunday and 1 week Christmas-New Year – **Meals** a la carte 18.50/27.00 **t.** ⓵ 8.50.

X **Blue,** 10 Cambridge St., EH1 2ED, ℰ (0131) 221 1222, *Fax (0131) 228 8808* – 🕲 AE VISA
DZ c
closed 25 and 26 December – **Meals** a la carte 11.50/15.50 **t.** ⓵ 6.00.

X **Café Saint-Honoré,** 34 North West Thistle Street Lane, EH2 1EA, ℰ (0131) 226 2211 – 🕲 AE ⓞ VISA JCB
DY c
closed Saturday lunch, Sunday except August, 3 days Christmas, 2 weeks Easter and 1 week October – **Meals** (booking essential) a la carte 15.20/26.40 **t.** ⓵ 4.75.

at Bonnyrigg *(Midlothian) SE : 8 m. by A 7 on A 6094* – EZ – ✉ Edinburgh.

🏰 **Dalhousie Castle,** EH19 3JB, SE : 1 ¼ m. on B 704 ℰ (01875) 820153, ≤, « Part 13C and 15C castle with Victorian additions », ☞ – ✦ 🆃🆅 🕲
ⓟ – ⚖ 120. 🕲 AE ⓞ VISA JCB. ⚶
closed 3 weeks January – **Meals** 25.00 **st.** (dinner) and lunch a la carte 13.45/18.05 **st.** ⓵ 7.75 – **28 rm** ⛋ 90.00/210.00 **st.** – SB.

at Edinburgh International Airport *W : 7½ m. by A 8* – AV – ✉ Edinburgh.

🏨 **Stakis Edinburgh Airport,** EH28 8LL, ℰ (0131) 519 4400, *Fax (0131) 519 4422* – |≝
✦ rm, 🍴 rest, 🆃🆅 ☎ & ⓟ – ⚖ 220. 🕲 AE ⓞ VISA. ⚶
Meals (grill rest.) 7.25/15.00 **t.** and a la carte ⓵ 5.00 – ⛋ 9.75 – **134 rm** 120.00/135.00 **st.** SB.

at Ingliston *W : 7¾ m. on A 8* – AV – ✉ Edinburgh.

🏨 **Norton House** ⤸, EH28 8LX, on A 8 ℰ (0131) 333 1275, *Fax (0131) 333 5305,* ≤, ☞
✦ rm, 🆃🆅 ☎ ⓟ – ⚖ 300. ⚶
Meals *(closed Saturday lunch)* 25.50 **t.** (dinner) and a la carte 23.25/35.40 **t.** ⓵ 7.50 – **46 rm** ⛋ 115.00/145.00 **t.,** 1 suite – SB.

🅐 ATS 167 Bonnington Rd, Leith ℰ (0131) 554 6617   ATS 6 Gylemuir Rd, Corstorphine
ℰ (0131) 334 6174

Great Britain and *Ireland* is now covered
by an *Atlas* at a scale of 1 inch to 4.75 miles.

Three easy to use versions: Paperback, Spiralbound and Hardback.

EDINBURGH INTERNATIONAL AIRPORT *Edinburgh City* **401** J 16 – *see Edinburgh.*

EDZELL *Angus* **401** M 13 *Scotland G.* – *pop. 830.*
Env. : *Castle★ AC (The Pleasance★★★) W : 2 m.*
Exc. : *Glen Esk★, NW : 7 m.*
Edinburgh 94 – Aberdeen 36 – Dundee 31.

🏠 **Glenesk,** High St., DD9 7TF, ℰ (01356) 648319, *Fax (01356) 647333,* **‰**, **≘s**, **⬛**, **☞** – **📺**
☎ 𝐏 – **⬚** 100. **◑❸ 𝔸𝔼 ⓞ 𝘝𝘐𝘚𝘈 𝘑𝘊𝘉**
Meals 12.50/16.00 **t.** and a la carte ⭑ 4.00 – **23 rm** ⌑ 50.00/82.00 **st.** – SB.

ELGIN *Moray* **401** K 11 *Scotland G.* – *pop. 11 855.*
See : *Town★ – Cathedral★ (Chapter house★★)AC.*
Exc. : *Glenfiddich Distillery★, SE : 10 m. by A 941.*
‰, **‰** *Moray, Stotfield Rd, Lossiemouth* ℰ *(01343) 812018 –* **‰** *Hardhillock, Birnie Rd*
ℰ *(01343) 542338 –* **‰** *Hopeman, Moray* ℰ *(01343) 830578.*
🛈 *17 High St., IV30 1EG* ℰ *(01343) 542666.*
Edinburgh 198 – Aberdeen 68 – Fraserburgh 61 – Inverness 39.

🏛 **Mansion House,** The Haugh, IV30 1AW, via Haugh Rd and Murdocks Wynd
ℰ (01343) 548811, *Fax (01343) 547916,* **‰**, **≘s**, **⬛**, **☞** – **➤❀** rest, **📺 ☎ 𝐏** – **⬚** 200. **◑❸ 𝔸𝔼**
ⓞ 𝘝𝘐𝘚𝘈 𝘑𝘊𝘉. **✵**
Meals 12.95/23.50 **st.** and a la carte ⭑ 8.00 – **22 rm** ⌑ 80.00/150.00 **st.** – SB.

🏠 **Mansefield House,** 2 Mayne Rd, IV30 1NY, ℰ (01343) 540883, *Fax (01343) 552491* – **❚❘**
➤❀ 📺 ☎ 𝐏. **◑❸ 𝔸𝔼 𝘝𝘐𝘚𝘈**. **✵**
Meals a la carte 20.70/25.75 **t.** ⭑ 6.20 – **21 rm** ⌑ 65.00/100.00 **t.**

🏠 **Travel Inn,** Linkwood Industrial Estate, East Rd, IV30 1XB, ℰ (01343) 550747,
Fax (01343) 540635 – **➤❀** rm, **📺 ⅙ 𝐏**. **◑❸ 𝔸𝔼 ⓞ 𝘝𝘐𝘚𝘈**
Meals (grill rest.) – **40 rm** 36.50 **t.**

⌂ **Lodge,** 20 Duff Av., IV30 1QS, ℰ (01343) 549981, **☞** – **➤❀ 📺 𝐏**. **◑❸ 𝘝𝘐𝘚𝘈**. **✵**
Meals (by arrangement) 14.00 **s.** – **8 rm** ⌑ 23.00/44.00 **s.**

◎ ATS Moycroft ℰ (01343) 546333

Per spostarvi più rapidamente utilizzate le **carte Michelin "Grandi Strade"** :
*n° * **970** Europa, *n° * **976** Rep. Ceca/Slovacchia, *n° * **980** Grecia,
*n° * **984** Germania, *n° * **985** Scandinavia-Finlandia,
*n° * **986** Gran Bretagna-Irlanda, *n° * **987** Germania-Austria-Benelux,
*n° * **988** Italia, *n° * **989** Francia, *n° * **990** Spagna-Portogallo, *n° * **991** Jugoslavia.

ELIE *Fife* **401** L 15 *Scotland G.* – *pop. 903.*
Env. : *The East Neuk★★.*
Exc. : *Kellie Castle★, NE : 9 m. by A 917, B 942, B 9171 and minor roads.*
Edinburgh 41 – Dundee 29 – Dunfermline 29.

💥💥 **Bouquet Garni,** 51 High St., KY9 1BZ, ℰ (01333) 330374, *Fax (01333) 330374* – **◑❸ 𝔸𝔼**
𝘝𝘐𝘚𝘈
closed Sunday, 25-26 December, 1-2 and last 2 weeks January – **Meals** a la carte 10.40/
29.90 **t.** ⭑ 6.50.

ERBUSAIG *Highland* **401** C 12 *Scotland G.* – **✉** *Kyle of Lochalsh.*
Env. : *Wester Ross★★★.*
Skye Bridge (toll).
Edinburgh 206 – Dundee 184 – Inverness 84 – Oban 127.

💥 **Old Schoolhouse** with rm, IV40 8BB, ℰ (01599) 534369, *Fax (01599) 534369,* **☞** –
➤❀ rest, **📺 𝐏**. **◑❸ 𝔸𝔼 𝘝𝘐𝘚𝘈 𝘑𝘊𝘉**
April-mid November – **Meals** (booking essential) (dinner only) a la carte 16.55/26.05 **t.**
⭑ 4.60 – **3 rm** ⌑ 30.00/52.00 **t.**

ERISKA (Isle of) *Argyll and Bute* **401** D 14 – **✉** *Oban.*

🏛 **Isle of Eriska** **❦**, Ledaig, PA37 1SD, ℰ (01631) 720371, *Fax (01631) 720531,* **≤** *Lismore*
and mountains, « *Country house atmosphere* », **‰**, **≘s**, **⬛**, **‰**, **❧**, **☞**, park, **✗** –
➤❀ rest, **📺 ⅙ 𝐏**. **◑❸ 𝔸𝔼 𝘝𝘐𝘚𝘈**. **✵**
closed January – **Meals** (booking essential) (bar lunch residents only)/dinner 37.50 **t.** ⭑ 6.10
– **17 rm** ⌑ 160.00/230.00 **t.**

FAIRLIE *North Ayrshire* 401 402 F 16.

Edinburgh 75 – Ayr 50 – Glasgow 36.

✗ **Fins,** Fencebay Fisheries, Fencefoot Farm, KA29 0ED, S : 1 ½ m. on A 78 ℘ (01475) 568989 – **P** ⁄⁄ 🄰🄴 ① *VISA* JCB

closed Sunday dinner, Monday, 25 December and 1 week January-February – **Meals** - Seafood - a la carte 14.85/24.85 **st.**

FALKIRK 401 I 16 – *pop. 42 353.*

🄸🄶 *Grangemouth, Polmonthill* ℘ (01324) 711500 – 🄻🄶 *Polmont, Manuel Rigg, Maddiston* ℘ (01324) 711277.

🄱 2-4 Glebe St., SK1 1HU ℘ (01324) 620244.

Edinburgh 26 – Dunfermline 18 – Glasgow 25 – Motherwell 27 – Perth 43.

🏛 **Grange Manor**, Glensburgh Rd, FK3 8XJ, NE : 2 m. by A 904 on A 905 ℘ (01324) 474836, Fax (01324) 665861 – 📺 ☎ **P** – 🔬 120. ⁄⁄ 🄰🄴 ① *VISA* ⁄⁄

Meals 11.95/19.65 **t.** and a la carte ⁑ 4.90 – **7 rm** 🖙 59.00/89.00 **t.** – SB.

🏛 **Stakis Falkirk**, Camelon Rd, Arnothill, FK1 5RY, W : ¼ m. on A 803 ℘ (01324) 628331, Fax (01324) 611593 – ⁙, ⁖ rm, 📺 ☎ **P** – 🔬 300. ⁄⁄ 🄰🄴 ① *VISA* ⁄⁄

Meals (bar lunch Saturday) 11.00/17.00 **st.** and a la carte – 🖙 8.95 – **55 rm** 79.00/89.00 **st.** – SB.

at Polmont *SE : 3 m. on A 803.*

🏨 **Inchyra Grange**, Grange Rd, FK2 0YB, Kirk entry via Boness Rd ℘ (01324) 711911, Fax (01324) 716134, ⁙₄, ⁖s, 🔲 – ⁙ ⁖ rm 📺 ☎ **P** – 🔬 200. ⁄⁄ 🄰🄴 ① *VISA*

Meals *(closed Saturday lunch)* 12.50/27.50 **st.** and a la carte ⁑ 9.00 – 🖙 9.50 – **109 rm** 69.00/160.00 **st.** – SB.

🄰 ATS Burnbank Rd ℘ (01324) 622958

FASNACLOICH *Argyll and Bute* – ⁖ Appin.

Edinburgh 133 – Fort William 34 – Oban 19.

⌂ **Lochside Cottage** ⁖, PA38 4BJ, ℘ (01631) 730216, Fax (01631) 730216, ≤ Loch Baile Mhic Chailen and mountains, « Lochside setting », ⁖ – ⁖ 📺 **P**

Meals (by arrangement) (communal dining) 17.00 **s.** – **3 rm** 🖙 20.00/50.00 **s.**

FIONNPHORT *Argyll and Bute* 401 A 15 – *Shipping Services : see Mull (Isle of).*

FLODIGARRY *Highland* – *see Skye (Isle of).*

FORFAR *Angus* 401 L 14 *Scotland G.* – *pop. 14 159.*

Env. : *Aberlemno Stones★, NE : 5 m. by B 9134.*

Exc. : *Brechin (Round Tower★), NE : 9 ½ m. by B 9134.*

🄸🄶 *Cunninghill, Arbroath Rd* ℘ (01307) 462120.

🄱 40 East High St., ℘ (01307) 467876 (summer only).

Edinburgh 53 – Aberdeen 55 – Dundee 12 – Perth 31.

🏛 **Chapelbank House**, 69 East High St., DD8 2EP, ℘ (01307) 463151, Fax (01307) 461922 – ⁖ 📺 ☎ **P**. ⁄⁄ 🄰🄴 *VISA* JCB. ⁄⁄

closed first 2 weeks January and first week October – **Meals** *(closed Sunday dinner and Monday)* 18.95 **t.** (dinner) and a la carte 10.95/24.65 **t.** ⁑ 5.50 – **4 rm** 🖙 55.00/80.00 **st.**

⌂ **Finavon Farmhouse**, Finavon, DD8 3PX, NE : 5 ½ m. by B 9128 off A 90 ℘ (01307) 850269, ⁖ – 📺 **P**

closed January and December – **Meals** (by arrangement) (communal dining) 9.00 – **3 rm** 🖙 24.00/40.00 – SB.

⌂ **Quarrybank Cottage**, Balgavies, DD8 2TF, E : 5 m. on B 9113 ℘ (01307) 830303, Fax (01307) 830414, ⁖ – ⁖ **P**. 🄰🄴

March-October – **Meals** (by arrangement) (communal dining) 12.50 **st.** – **3 rm** 🖙 27.00/45.00 **st.**

🄰 ATS Queenswell Rd ℘ (01307) 464501

FORRES *Moray* **401** J 11 *Scotland G. – pop. 5 559.*

See : *Town.*

Env. : *Sueno's Stone*★★, N : ½ m. by A 940 on A 96 – Brodie Castle★ *AC*, W : 3 m. by A 96.

Exc. : *The Road The Isles*★★, N : 1 m. by A 940 on A 96 – Elgin★ (Cathedral★, Chapter House★★ *AC*), E : 10 ¼ m. by A 96.

🏌 *Muiryshade* ℰ *(01309) 672949.*

🚩 *116 High St., IV6 0NP* ℰ *(01309) 672938 (summer only).*

Edinburgh 165 – Aberdeen 80 – Inverness 27.

🏨 **Knockomie** ⌘, Grantown Rd, IV36 0SG, S : 1 ½ m. on A 940 ℰ *(01309) 673146, Fax (01309) 673290, ㈜, park – ⇔ rest, TV ☎ ఈ ➋ – 🔏 50.* **◍◎ 🅰🅴 ⓪ 𝘝𝘐𝘚𝘈 🅹🅲🅱**
closed 25 and 26 December – **Meals** *15.00/26.00* **t.** *and a la carte* ⌗ *9.50 –* **15 rm** ⌷ *65.00/ 145.00* **t.**, *1 suite – SB.*

🏠 **Ramnee**, Victoria Rd, IV36 0BN, ℰ *(01309) 672410, Fax (01309) 673392, ㈜ – TV ☎ ➋ – 🔏 100.* **◍◎ 🅰🅴 ⓪ 𝘝𝘐𝘚𝘈 🅹🅲🅱**
closed 25 December and 1 to 3 January – **Meals** *12.50/22.50* **st.** *and dinner a la carte* ⌗ *5.00 –* **20 rm** ⌷ *55.00/99.00* **t.** *– SB.*

FORT AUGUSTUS *Highland* **401** F 12 *Scotland G. – pop. 902 (inc. Glenmoriston).*

Exc. : *Loch Ness*★★ – *The Great Glen*★.

🚩 *Car Park* ℰ *(01320) 366367 (summer only).*

Edinburgh 166 – Fort William 32 – Inverness 36 – Kyle of Lochalsh 57.

🏠 **Brae**, PH32 4DG, ℰ *(01320) 366289, Fax (01320) 366702, ㈜ – ⇔ TV ➋.* **◍◎ 🅰🅴 𝘝𝘐𝘚𝘈 🅹🅲🅱**
mid March-October – **Meals** *(dinner only) 24.00* **st.** ⌗ *7.00 –* **7 rm** ⌷ *(dinner included) 53.00/116.00* **st.**

🏠 **Sonas** *without rest.,* PH32 4DH, on A 82 ℰ *(01320) 366291, Fax (01320) 366291, ㈜ – ⇔ ➋.* ⌗
3 rm ⌷ *40.00.*

Le Guide change, changez de **guide Michelin** *tous les ans.*

FORT WILLIAM *Highland* **401** E 13 *Scotland G. – pop. 10 391.*

See : *Town*★.

Exc. : *The Road to the Isles*★★ (Neptune's Staircase (≤★★), Glenfinnan★ ≤★, Arisaig★, Silver Sands of Morar★, Mallaig★), NW : 46 m. by A 830 – Ardnamurchan Peninsula★★ - Ardnamurchan Point★ (≤★★), NW : 65 m. by A 830, A 861 and B 8007 – SE : Ben Nevis★★ (≤★★) - Glen Nevis★.

🏌 *North Rd* ℰ *(01397) 704464.*

🚩 *Cameron Centre, Cameron Sq., PH33 6AJ* ℰ *(01397) 703781.*

Edinburgh 133 – Glasgow 104 – Inverness 68 – Oban 50.

🏰 **Inverlochy Castle** ⌘, Torlundy, PH33 6SN, NE : 3 m. on A 82 ℰ *(01397) 702177, Fax (01397) 702953, ≤ loch and mountains, « Victorian castle in extensive park », ⚲, ㈜, ✿ – ⇔ rest, TV ☎ ➋.* **◍◎ 🅰🅴 ⓪ 𝘝𝘐𝘚𝘈**
closed January-13 February – **Meals** *(booking essential) 25.00/55.00* **st.** ⌗ *7.50 –* **16 rm** ⌷ *210.00/330.00* **t.**, *1 suite – SB*
Spec. Terrine of roasted lamb fillets with Provençale vegetables. Roast loin of venison with fig ravioli and port sauce. Vanilla crème fraîche mousse with strawberries.

🏠 **Travel Inn**, An Aird, PH33 6AN, NW : ½ m. by A 82 ℰ *(01397) 703707, Fax (01397) 703618 – |🛗|, ⇔ rm, ▤ rest, TV ఈ ➋.* **◍◎ 🅰🅴 ⓪ 𝘝𝘐𝘚𝘈**
Meals *(grill rest.) –* **40 rm** *36.50* **t.**

🏠 **Distillery House** *without rest.,* Nevis Bridge, North Rd, PH33 6LR, ℰ *(01397) 700103, Fax (01397) 702980 – TV ☎ ➋.* **◍◎ 𝘝𝘐𝘚𝘈**
7 rm ⌷ *38.00/64.00* **st.**

🏠 **The Grange** *without rest.,* Grange Rd, PH33 6JF, by Ashburn Lane ℰ *(01397) 705516, ≤, ㈜ – ⇔ TV ➋.* **𝘝𝘐𝘚𝘈**. ⌗
April-October – **3 rm** ⌷ *70.00.*

🏠 **Crolinnhe** *without rest.,* Grange Rd, PH33 6JF, by Ashburn Lane ℰ *(01397) 702709, ≤, ㈜ – ⇔ TV ➋.* ⌗
April-October – **4 rm** ⌷ *70.00* **s.**

🏠 **Ashburn House** *without rest.,* 8 Achintore Rd, PH33 6RQ, S : ½ m. on A 82 ℰ *(01397) 706000, Fax (01397) 706000, ㈜ – ⇔ TV ➋.* **◍◎ 𝘝𝘐𝘚𝘈**. ⌗
March-October – **7 rm** ⌷ *35.00/70.00.*

🏠 **Cabana House** *without rest.,* Union Rd, PH33 6RB, ℰ *(01397) 705991, Fax (01397) 705991, ㈜ – ⇔ TV ➋.* ⌗
closed February and November – **3 rm** ⌷ *35.00/52.00* **s.**

at Banavie N : 3 m. by A 82 and A 830 on B 8004 – ✉ Fort William.

🏨 **Moorings**, PH33 7LY, 𝓟 (01397) 772797, Fax (01397) 772441, ≤, 🌳 – 🍴 rest, 📺 ☎ 🄿. 🚫 🆎 ① 𝗩𝗜𝗦𝗔 𝗝𝗖𝗕
Jacobean : Meals (lunch by arrangement)/dinner 26.00 **t.** ≬ 7.95 – **21 rm** ⇆ 56.00/84.00 **t.** – SB.

↑ **Torbeag House** ⚘, Muirshearlich, PH33 7PB, NE : 2 m. on B 8004 𝓟 (01397) 772412, Fax (01397) 772412, ≤, 🌳 – 🍴 📺 🄿. 🚫 𝗩𝗜𝗦𝗔 𝗝𝗖𝗕
Meals (by arrangement) 21.00 **st.** – **3 rm** ⇆ 48.00/76.00 **st.** – SB.

FOYERS Highland 𝟦𝟢𝟣 G 12 Scotland G. – ✉ Loch Ness.
Env. : Loch Ness★★ – The Great Glen★.
Edinburgh 175 – Inverness 19 – Kyle of Lochalsh 63 – Oban 96.

🏠 **Craigdarroch** ⚘, IV1 2XU, N : ¼ m. on B 852 𝓟 (01456) 486400, Fax (01456) 486444, ≤, 🌳, park – 🍴 rest, 📺 ☎ ♿ 🄿. 🚫 🆎 𝗩𝗜𝗦𝗔
closed 3 January-13 February – Meals 14.50/24.50 **st.** and dinner a la carte ≬ 7.00 – **15 rm** ⇆ 60.00/120.00 **st.** – SB.

🏠 **Foyers Bay House**, Lower Foyers, IV1 2YB, W : 1 ¼ m. by B 852 on Lower Foyers rd 𝓟 (01456) 486624, Fax (01456) 486337, ≤, 🌳 – 📺 ☎ 🄿. 🚫 🆎 𝗩𝗜𝗦𝗔 ⚘
closed first 2 weeks January – Meals (dinner only) (unlicensed) 9.95 **t.** and a la carte – **3 rm** ⇆ 35.00/47.00 **t.** – SB.

Les prix	Pour toutes précisions sur les prix indiqués dans ce guide, reportez-vous aux pages de l'introduction.

GAIRLOCH Highland 𝟦𝟢𝟣 C 10 Scotland G. – pop. 2 194.
Env. : Wester Ross★★★ – Loch Maree★★★, E : 5 ½ m. by A 832.
Exc. : Inverewe Gardens★★★ AC, NE : 8 m. by A 832 – Victoria Falls★, SE : 8 m. by A 832.
🏌 Gairloch 𝓟 (01445) 712407.
🛈 Auchtercairn 𝓟 (01445) 712130.
Edinburgh 228 – Inverness 72 – Kyle of Lochalsh 68.

🏨 **Creag Mor**, Charleston, IV21 2AH, 𝓟 (01445) 712068, Fax (01445) 712044, ≤, 🌳 – 📺 ☎ 🄿 🚫 𝗩𝗜𝗦𝗔
March-mid November – Meals (bar lunch)/dinner 27.00 **t.** and a la carte ≬ 5.45 – **18 rm** ⇆ 44.00/88.00 **t.**, 1 suite – SB.

↑ **Little Lodge** ⚘, North Erradale, IV21 2DS, NW : 6 m. on B 8021 𝓟 (01445) 771237 ≤ Torridon Mountains and Skye, 🌳 – 🍴 🄿. ⚘
Easter-October – Meals (by arrangement) 18.00 **st.** – **3 rm** ⇆ (dinner included) 96.00 **st.**

↑ **Birchwood** without rest., IV21 2AH, 𝓟 (01445) 712011, ≤ – 🍴 🄿
April-October – **6 rm** ⇆ 35.00/50.00.

GALSON Western Isles (Outer Hebrides) 𝟦𝟢𝟣 A 8 – see Lewis and Harris (Isle of).

GATEHOUSE OF FLEET Dumfries and Galloway 𝟦𝟢𝟣 𝟦𝟢𝟤 H 19 – pop. 919.
🏌 Gatehouse of Fleet 𝓟 (01557) 814766.
🛈 Car Park, DG7 2AE 𝓟 (01557) 814212 (summer only).
Edinburgh 113 – Dumfries 33 – Stranraer 42.

🏩 **Cally Palace** ⚘, DG7 2DL, E : ½ m. on B 727 𝓟 (01557) 814341, Fax (01557) 814522, ≤ « Part 18C country mansion », 🚇, ⬛, 🏌, ⚘, 🌳, park, ※ – 🛗, 🍴 rest, 📺 ☎ 🄿 – 🔬 80 🚫 𝗩𝗜𝗦𝗔. ⚘
closed 3 January-8 March – Meals 11.00/23.50 **st.** and a la carte ≬ 6.00 – **50 rm** ⇆ 66.00/142.00 **t.**, 6 suites – SB.

GIFFNOCK East Renfrewshire 𝟦𝟢𝟣 ④ – see Glasgow.

GIFFORD East Lothian 𝟦𝟢𝟣 L 16 Scotland G. – pop. 688 – ✉ Haddington.
See : Village★.
Exc. : Northern foothills of the Lammermuir Hills★★, S : 10 ½ m. by B 6355 and B 6368.
🏌 Edinburgh Rd 𝓟 (01620) 810267.
Edinburgh 20 – Hawick 50.

🏠 **Tweeddale Arms,** High St., EH41 4QU, ✆ (01620) 810240, Fax (01620) 810488 – 📺 ☎.
MC AE VISA
Meals 12.75/19.75 **t.** ↥ 4.50 – **16 rm** � 47.50/85.00 **t.** – SB.

✗✗ **Bonars,** Main St., EH41 4QH, ✆ (01620) 810264, Fax (01620) 810264 – **MC VISA**
closed Sunday dinner and Monday mid September-late May and 2 weeks late January –
Meals 11.55/21.95 **t.** ↥ 8.40.

GIGHA (Isle of) Argyll and Bute **401** C 16.
  Edinburgh 168.

🏠 **Gigha** ⌂, PA41 7AA, ✆ (01583) 505254, Fax (01583) 505244, ≼ Sound of Gigha and
Kintyre Peninsula, 🐴 – ⅗ rest, 📺 ☎ ❷. **MC ◑ VISA**
early March-October – Meals (bar lunch)/dinner 21.00 **t.** ↥ 4.25 – **13 rm** ☲ 60.00/120.00 **t.**
– SB.

GIRVAN South Ayrshire **401 402** F 18 – pop. 7 719.
  🏌 Brunston Castle, Dailly ✆ (01465) 811471 – 🏌 Golf Course Rd ✆ (01465) 714272/714346.
  Edinburgh 100 – Ayr 20 – Glasgow 56 – Stranraer 31.

🏠 **Glendrissaig** ⌂, Newton Stewart Rd., KA26 0HJ, S : 1 ¾ m. by A 77 on A 714
✆ (01465) 714631, ≼, 🐴 – ⅗ ❷. ⅗
March-October – Meals (by arrangement) 14.00 **st.** – **3 rm** ☲ 30.00/52.00 **s.** – SB.

✗✗ **Wildings,** 56 Montgomerie St., KA26 9HE, ✆ (01465) 713481 – ⅗
closed Sunday dinner, Monday, Tuesday, last 2 weeks September, 2 weeks October and
3 weeks Christmas-New Year – Meals (booking essential) 11.95/20.50 **t.**

GLAMIS Angus **401** K 14 Scotland G. – pop. 648 – ✉ Forfar.
  See : Village★ - Castle★★ **AC** – Angus Folk Museum★ **AC**.
  Exc. : Meigle Museum★★ (early Christian Monuments★★) **AC**, SW : 7 m. by A 94.
  Edinburgh 60 – Dundee 11 – Perth 25.

✗✗✗ **Castleton House** with rm, DD8 1SJ, W : 3 ¾ m. on A 94 ✆ (01307) 840340,
Fax (01307) 840506, 🐴 – ⅗ rest, 📺 ☎ ❷. **MC AE VISA**. ⅗
Meals 12.95/19.50 **t.** and a la carte ↥ 7.25 – **6 rm** ☲ 70.00/100.00 **t.** – SB.

GLASGOW

401 402 H 16 *Scotland G. – pop. 662 853.*

Edinburgh 46 – Manchester 221.

TOURIST INFORMATION

🛈 *11 George Square, G2 1DY ℘ (0141) 204 4400.*
🛈 *Glasgow Airport, Tourist Information Desk, Paisley ℘ (0141) 848 4440.*

PRACTICAL INFORMATION

🏌 *Littlehill, Auchinairn Rd ℘ (0141) 772 1916.*
🏌 *Deaconsbank, Rouken Glen Park, Stewarton Rd, Eastwood ℘ (0141) 638 7044* **AX**.
🏌 *Linn Park, Simshill Rd ℘ (0141) 637 5871,* **BX**.
🏌 *Lethamhill, Cumbernauld Rd ℘ (0141) 770 6220,* **BV**.
🏌 *Alexandra Park, Dennistown ℘ (0141) 556 3991* **BV**.
🏌 *King's Park, 150a Croftpark Av., Croftfoot ℘ (0141) 630 1597,* **BX**.
🏌 *Knightswood, Lincoln Av. ℘ (0141) 959 6358* **AV**.
🏌 *Ruchill, Brassey St. ℘ (0141) 946 7676.*
Access to Oban by helicopter.
Erskine Bridge (toll) **AV**.
✈ *Glasgow Airport : ℘ (0141) 887 1111, W : 8 m. by M 8* **AV** – **Terminal** : *Coach service from Glasgow Central and Queen Street main line Railway Stations and from Anderston Cross and Buchanan Bus Stations.*
✈ *see also Prestwick.*

SIGHTS

See : *City*★★★ – *Cathedral*★★★ *(⇐★)* **DZ** – *The Burrell Collection*★★★ **AX M1** – *Hunterian Art Gallery*★★ *(Whistler Collection*★★★ – *Mackintosh Wing*★★★ *)* **AC CY M4** – *Museum of Transport*★★ *(Scottish Built Cars*★★★, *The Clyde Room of Ship Models*★★★ *)* **AV M3** – *Art Gallery and Museum Kelvingrove*★★ **CY** – *Pollok House*★ *(The Paintings*★★ *)* **AX D** – *Tolbooth Steeple*★ **DZ A** – *Hunterian Museum (Coin and Medal Collection*★ *)* **CY M1** – *City Chambers*★ **DZ C** – *Glasgow School of Art*★ **AC, CY B** – *Necropolis (⇐★ of Cathedral)* **DYZ**.
Env. : *Paisley Museum and Art Gallery (Paisley Shawl Section*★ *), W : 4 m. by M 8* **AV**.
Exc. : *The Trossachs*★★★, *N : 31 m. by A 879 –* **BV** *– A 81 and A 821 – Loch Lomond*★★, *NW : 19 m. by A 82* **AV**.

GLASGOW
BUILT UP AREA

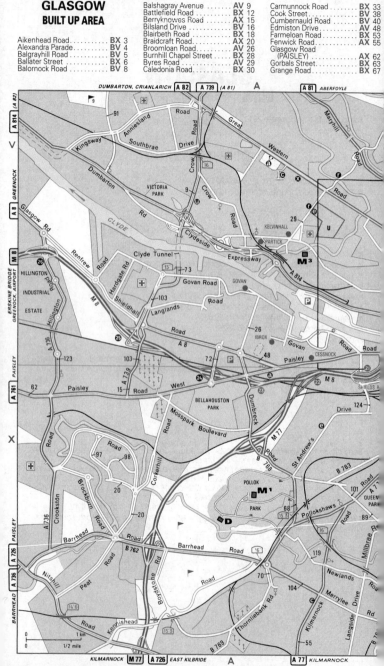

692

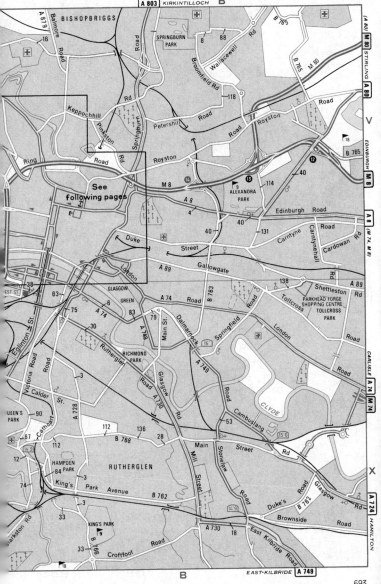

693

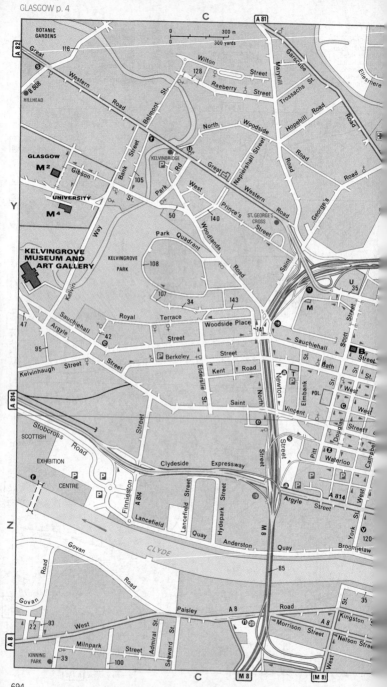

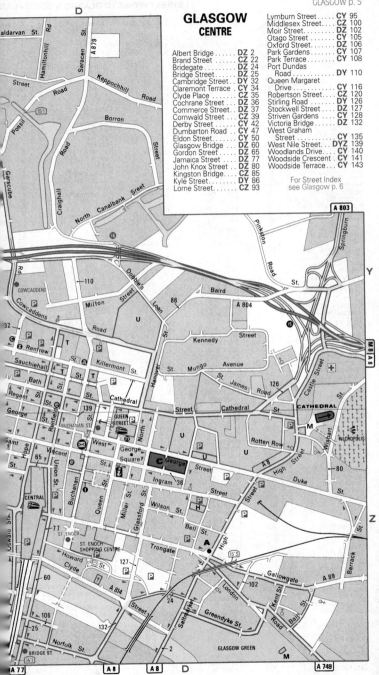

GLASGOW
CENTRE

For Street Index
see Glasgow p. 6

695

Glasgow Hilton, 1 William St., G3 8HT, ℰ (0141) 204 5555, Fax (0141) 204 5004, ≼, ₤₅, ⇌, ⬛ – ∣🛉∣, ⥼ rm, 🖭 ☎ ዼ 🅟 – 🔬 1000. 🐵 🆎 ⓞ 𝘝𝘐𝘚𝘈 𝘑𝘊𝘉. ⅏
CZ s
Minsky's : Meals a la carte 15.70/30.20 **st.** ₤ 8.50 – (see also *Camerons* below) – ⌑ 13.50 –
315 rm 171.00 **st.**, 4 suites.

One Devonshire Gardens, 1 Devonshire Gdns., G12 0UX, ℰ (0141) 339 2001,
Fax (0141) 337 1663, « Victorian town houses, opulent interior design » – ⥼ rest, 🖭 ☎ –
🔬 50. 🐵 🆎 ⓞ 𝘝𝘐𝘚𝘈. ⅏
AV a
Meals *(closed Saturday lunch)* 25.00/40.00 **t.** ₤ 10.00 – ⌑ 14.50 – **25 rm** 150.00/210.00 **t.**,
2 suites
Spec. Seared spiced scallops with lemon grass couscous. Roasted Bresse pigeon, confit of
cabbage and root vegetables, thyme jus. Iced vanilla parfait with roasted strawberries and
balsamic vinegar.

Glasgow Moat House, Congress Rd, G3 8QT, ℰ (0141) 306 9988, Fax (0141) 221 2022,
≼, ₤₅, ⇌, ⬛ – ∣🛉∣, ⥼ rm, 🖭 ☎ ዼ 🅟 – 🔬 800. 🐵 🆎 ⓞ 𝘝𝘐𝘚𝘈. ⅏
CZ r
Mariners : Meals *(closed Saturday lunch, Sunday and 26 December-13 January)*
16.50 (lunch) and dinner a la carte – *Pointhouse :* Meals 16.95/19.95 **st.** and a la carte
– ⌑ 10.95 – **267 rm** 132.00/162.00 **st.**, 16 suites.

Glasgow Marriott, 500 Argyle St., Anderston, G3 8RR, ℰ (0141) 226 5577,
Fax (0141) 221 7676, ₤₅, ⇌, squash – ∣🛉∣, ⥼ rm, 🖭 ☎ ዼ 🅟 – 🔬 720. 🐵 🆎 ⓞ 𝘝𝘐𝘚𝘈
𝘑𝘊𝘉. ⅏
CZ a
Terrace : Meals *(closed Saturday lunch)* 17.95 **t.** (dinner) and a la carte 16.95/26.15 **t.** ₤ 7.25
– ⌑ 10.95 – **296 rm** 94.00/104.00 **st.**, 4 suites.

Glasgow Thistle, 36 Cambridge St., G2 3HN, ℰ (0141) 332 3311, Fax (0141) 332 4050 –
∣🛉∣, ⥼ rm, ⬛ rest, 🖭 ☎ ዼ 🅟 – 🔬 1500. 🐵 🆎 ⓞ 𝘝𝘐𝘚𝘈 𝘑𝘊𝘉
DY z
Garden Cafe : Meals (carving rest.) 13.00/18.50 **st.** and a la carte – *Prince of Wales :*
Meals *(closed Saturday lunch and Sunday)* 19.00/27.50 **st.** and a la carte – ⌑ 13.00 –
299 rm 99.00/164.00 **st.**, 3 suites – SB.

Forte Posthouse Glasgow City, Bothwell St., G2 7EN, ℰ (0141) 248 2656,
Fax (0141) 221 8986, ≼ – ∣🛉∣, ⥼ rm, ⬛ 🖭 ☎ 🅟 – 🔬 800. 🐵 🆎 ⓞ 𝘝𝘐𝘚𝘈 𝘑𝘊𝘉
CZ z
The Carvery : Meals (dinner only) a la carte approx. 15.75 **t.** – *Jules Verne :* Meals *(closed
lunch Saturday and Sunday)* 13.20 **st.** ₤ 6.75 – ⌑ 10.95 – **246 rm** 79.00 **st.**, 1 suite.

Devonshire, 5 Devonshire Gdns., G12 0UX, ℰ (0141) 339 7878, Fax (0141) 339 3980 – 🖭
☎ – 🔬 50. 🐵 🆎 ⓞ 𝘝𝘐𝘚𝘈. ⅏
AV a
Meals a la carte 22.50/35.00 **st.** ₤ 8.00 – ⌑ 12.75 – **14 rm** 115.00/165.00 **st.** – SB.

Malmaison, 278 West George St., G2 4LL, ℰ (0141) 572 1000, Fax (0141) 572 1002,
« Contemporary interior » – ∣🛉∣ 🖭 🖭 ☎ 🅟 – 🔬. 🐵 🆎 ⓞ 𝘝𝘐𝘚𝘈. ⅏
CY c
Meals - Brasserie - a la carte 16.95/22.90 **t.** – ⌑ 10.50 – **69 rm** 90.00 **st.**, 4 suites.

Copthorne Glasgow, George Sq., G2 1DS, ℰ (0141) 332 6711, Fax (0141) 332 4264 – ∣🛉∣,
⥼ rm, 🖭 ☎ – 🔬 100. 🐵 🆎 ⓞ 𝘝𝘐𝘚𝘈 𝘑𝘊𝘉
DZ n
closed 25 and 26 December – Meals *(closed Saturday and Sunday lunch)* a la carte 24.40/
29.90 **t.** ₤ 7.00 – ⌑ 11.50 – **135 rm** 118.00/128.00 **st.**, 5 suites.

Stakis Glasgow Grosvenor, Grosvenor Terr., Great Western Rd, G12 0TA,
ℰ (0141) 339 8811, Fax (0141) 334 0710 – ∣🛉∣, ⥼ rm, 🖭 ☎ 🅟 – 🔬 450
CY s
94 rm, 2 suites.

Holiday Inn Garden Court Glasgow, Theatreland, 161 West Nile St., G1 2RL,
ℰ (0141) 353 2595, Fax (0141) 332 7447 – ⥼ rm, 🖭 ☎ – 🔬 80
DY a
80 rm.

County H. Glasgow Kelvin Park Lorne, 923 Sauchiehall St., G3 7TE,
ℰ (0141) 314 9955, Fax (0141) 337 1659 – ∣🛉∣, ⥼ rm, 🖭 ☎ 🅟 – 🔬 300. 🐵 🆎 ⓞ 𝘝𝘐𝘚𝘈. ⅏
Meals 9.95 **st.** (lunch) and a la carte approx. 17.85 **st.** ₤ 6.50 – ⌑ 8.50 – **97 rm** 85.00/
CY e
105.00 **st.**, 1 suite.

Swallow Glasgow, 517 Paisley Road West, G51 1RW, ℰ (0141) 427 3146,
Fax (0141) 427 4059, ₤₅, ⇌, ⬛ – ∣🛉∣, ⥼ rm, ⬛ rest, 🖭 ☎ 🅟 – 🔬 350. 🐵 🆎 ⓞ 𝘝𝘐𝘚𝘈
Meals *(closed Saturday lunch)* (carving lunch) 11.00/17.50 **st.** ₤ 7.50 – ⌑ 95.00/
AX a
135.00 **st.** – SB.

Stakis Glasgow City, Hill St., G3 6PR, ℰ (0141) 333 1515, Fax (0141) 333 1221 – ∣🛉∣,
⥼ rm, 🖭 ☎ ዼ – 🔬 35. 🐵 🆎 ⓞ 𝘝𝘐𝘚𝘈. ⅏
DY c
Meals (grill rest.) (bar lunch)/dinner 12.50 **st.** ₤ 7.00 – ⌑ 8.95 – **93 rm** 63.00/
73.00 **st.**

Tinto Firs Thistle, 470 Kilmarnock Rd, G43 2BB, ℰ (0141) 637 2353, Fax (0141) 633 1340
– ⥼ rm, 🖭 ☎ 🅟 – 🔬 200. 🐵 🆎 ⓞ 𝘝𝘐𝘚𝘈 𝘑𝘊𝘉
AX c
Meals (bar lunch Monday and Saturday) 12.95/19.95 **st.** and a la carte ₤ 5.95 – ⌑ 9.95 –
25 rm 82.00/102.00 **st.**, 2 suites – SB.

Charing Cross Tower, Elmbank Gdns., G2 4PP, pedestrianised area off Bath St.
ℰ (0141) 221 1000, Fax (0141) 248 1000, ≼ – ∣🛉∣, ⥼ rm, 🖭 ☎. 🐵 🆎 ⓞ 𝘝𝘐𝘚𝘈. ⅏
CY a
Meals (bar lunch)/dinner a la carte 10.40/19.20 **t.** ₤ 5.25 – ⌑ 6.95 – **281 rm** 44.50/49.50 **st.**

🏠 **Deauville's**, 62 St. Andrew's Drive, Pollok Shields, G41 5EZ, ℰ (0141) 427 1106, Fax (0141) 427 1106, 🚗 – ⅍ rest, 📺 ☎ 🅿. 🐵 🖭 ⓪ 𝓥𝓘𝓢𝓐
AX e
Meals (closed Sunday and Monday) 12.00/16.95 **t.** and dinner a la carte ᵻ 6.25 – **6 rm** ⚌ 40.00/80.00 **st.** – SB.

🏠 **Terrace House**, 14 Belhaven Terr., G12 0TG, (off Great Western Rd) ℰ (0141) 337 3377, Fax (0141) 337 3377 – ⅍ rest, 📺 ☎. 🐵 🖭 ⓪ 𝓥𝓘𝓢𝓐
AV x
Meals (booking essential Saturday and Sunday) (dinner only) a la carte 8.65/14.70 **t.** ᵻ 3.95 – **13 rm** ⚌ 62.00/78.00 **st.** – SB.

🏠 **Town House**, 4 Hughenden Terr., G12 9XR, ℰ (0141) 357 0862, Fax (0141) 339 9605 – ⅍ rest, 📺 ☎. 🐵 𝓥𝓘𝓢𝓐. ✂
AV i
booking essential December and January – **Meals** (dinner only) a la carte 15.50/20.45 **st.** ᵻ 5.45 – **10 rm** ⚌ 58.00/68.00 **st.**

🏠 **Manor Park**, 28 Balshagray Drive, G11 7DD, ℰ (0141) 339 2143, Fax (0141) 339 5842 – ⅍ rest, 📺 ☎. 🖭 𝓥𝓘𝓢𝓐 𝓙𝓒𝓑. ✂
AV u
Meals (lunch by arrangement) 7.95/16.75 **st.** and a la carte – **9 rm** ⚌ 45.00/65.00 **st.** – SB.

🏠 **Albion**, 405-407 North Woodside Rd, G20 6NN, ℰ (0141) 339 8620, Fax (0141) 334 8159 – ⅍ rest, 📺 ☎. 🐵 🖭 ⓪ 𝓥𝓘𝓢𝓐. ✂
CY u
Meals (residents only) (dinner only) 10.00 **st.** and a la carte ᵻ 4.00 – **16 rm** ⚌ 42.00/52.00 **st.** – SB.

🏠 **Kirklee** without rest., 11 Kensington Gate, G12 9LG, ℰ (0141) 334 5555, Fax (0141) 339 3828 – 📺 ☎. 🐵 🖭 ⓪ 𝓥𝓘𝓢𝓐. ✂
AV c
9 rm ⚌ 48.00/64.00 **t.**

🏠 **Travelodge**, 251 Paisley Rd, G5 8RA, ℰ (0141) 420 3882, Fax (0141) 420 3884, Reservations (Freephone) 0800 850950 – ⅍ rm, 📺 ☎ ⅕ 🅿. 🐵 🖭 ⓪ 𝓥𝓘𝓢𝓐 𝓙𝓒𝓑. ✂ CZ n
Meals (grill rest.) – **43 rm** 49.95 **t.**

🍴🍴🍴🍴 **Camerons** (at Glasgow Hilton H.), 1 William St., G3 8HT, ℰ (0141) 204 5511 Fax (0141) 204 5004 – 🔲 🅿. 🐵 🖭 ⓪ 𝓥𝓘𝓢𝓐 𝓙𝓒𝓑
CZ s
Meals (closed Saturday lunch, Sunday and Bank Holidays) 19.50 **st** (lunch) and a la carte 21.45/39.20 **st.** ᵻ 8.50.

🍴🍴🍴 **Buttery**, 652 Argyle St., G3 8UF, ℰ (0141) 221 8188, Fax (0141) 204 4639 – 🅿. 🐵 🖭 𝓥𝓘𝓢𝓐
CZ e
closed Saturday lunch, Sunday, 25-26 December and 1 January – **Meals** 15.85 **st** (lunch) and a la carte 23.05/29.80 **t.** ᵻ 9.25.

🍴🍴🍴 **Yes**, 22 West Nile St., G1 2PW, ℰ (0141) 221 8044, Fax (0141) 248 9159 – 🔲. 🐵 🖭 ⓪ 𝓥𝓘𝓢𝓐
DZ e
closed Sunday, 25-26 December, 1-2 January and Bank Holidays – **Meals** 15.95/24.50 and a la carte.

🍴🍴🍴 **Rogano**, 11 Exchange Pl., G1 3AN, ℰ (0141) 248 4055, Fax (0141) 248 2608, « Art Deco » – 🔲. 🐵 🖭 ⓪ 𝓥𝓘𝓢𝓐 𝓙𝓒𝓑
DZ e
closed 25 December and 1 January – **Meals** - Seafood - 16.50 **t.** (lunch) and a la carte 26.00/36.00 **t.** ᵻ 7.00.

🍴🍴 **Puppet Theatre**, 11 Ruthven Lane, off Byres Rd, G12 9BG, ℰ (0141) 339 8444 Fax (0141) 339 7666 – 🐵 🖭 𝓥𝓘𝓢𝓐
AV r
closed Saturday lunch, Monday, 25-26 December and 1-2 January – **Meals** 14.95/24.95 **t.** ᵻ 6.75.

🍴🍴 **Ho Wong**, 82 York St., G2 8LE, ℰ (0141) 221 3550, Fax (0141) 248 5330 – 🔲. 🐵 🖭 ⓪ 𝓥𝓘𝓢𝓐
CZ v
closed Sunday lunch and 3 days Chinese New Year – **Meals** - Chinese (Peking) - 8.50 (lunch) and a la carte approx. 19.00 **t.** ᵻ 5.95.

🍴🍴 **Amber Regent**, 50 West Regent St., G2 2QZ, ℰ (0141) 331 1655, Fax (0141) 353 3398 – 🔲. 🐵 🖭 ⓪ 𝓥𝓘𝓢𝓐 𝓙𝓒𝓑
DY e
closed Sunday, 1 January and 3 days Chinese New Year – **Meals** 8.45/24.00 **t.** and a la carte ᵻ 5.95.

🍴🍴 **Killermont Polo Club**, 2022 Maryhill Rd, G20 0AB, NW : 3 m. on A 81 ℰ (0141) 946 541: – 🅿. 🐵 🖭 ⓪ 𝓥𝓘𝓢𝓐
Meals 6.95 **t.** (lunch) and a la carte 14.20/20.00 **t.**

🍴 **Ubiquitous Chip**, 12 Ashton Lane, off Byres Rd, G12 8SJ, ℰ (0141) 334 5007 Fax (0141) 337 1302 – 🐵 🖭 ⓪ 𝓥𝓘𝓢𝓐
AV e
closed 25 and 31 December-2 January – **Meals** 23.60/31.60 **t.** ᵻ 5.50.

🍴 **La Parmigiana**, 447 Great Western Rd, Kelvinbridge, G12 8HH, ℰ (0141) 334 0686 Fax (0141) 332 3533 – 🔲. 🐵 🖭 ⓪ 𝓥𝓘𝓢𝓐 𝓙𝓒𝓑
CY e
closed Sunday and Bank Holidays – **Meals** - Italian - 7.50 **st.** (lunch) and a la carte 12.30/27.70 **st.** ᵻ 7.80.

at Stepps (North Lanarkshire) NE : 5½ m. by M 8 on A 80 – BV – ✉ Glasgow.

🏨 Garfield House, Cumbernauld Rd, G33 6HW, ℰ (0141) 779 2111, Fax (0141) 779 2111 – 📺 ☎ 🅿 – ⅍ 150
46 rm.

at Giffnock (East Renfrewshire) S : 5¼ m. by A 77 – **AX** – ⊠ Glasgow.

✗ **Turban Tandoori,** 2 Station Rd, G46 6JF, ℘ (0141) 638 0069 – ✇ ◱ *VISA*
closed 1 January – **Meals** - Indian - (dinner only) a la carte 10.40/16.15 **t.** ⅃ 6.95.

at Busby (East Renfrewshire) S : 7¼ m. by A 77 – **AX** – on A 726 – ⊠ Glasgow.

🏠 **Busby,** 1 Field Rd, Clarkston, G76 8RX, ℘ (0141) 644 2661, Fax (0141) 644 4417 – 📧,
⇚ rm, ⊡ ☎ ❷ – ⚒ 200. ✇ ◱ ◎ *VISA* ᴊᴄв. ✋
Meals 8.25/14.65 **t.** and a la carte – **32 rm** ⊇ 64.00/90.00 **t.** – SB.

at Glasgow Airport (Renfrewshire) W : 8 m. by M 8 – **AV** – ⊠ Paisley.

🏠 **Travel Inn,** Whitecart Rd, PA3 2TH, M 8 junction 28 ℘ (0141) 842 1563,
Fax (0141) 842 1570 – ⇚ rm, ⊡ ⅚ ❷ – ⚒ 30. ✇ ◱ ◎ *VISA*. ✋
Meals (grill rest.) (dinner only) – **81 rm** 36.50 **t.**

⓪ ATS 192 Finnieston St. ℘ (0141) 248 6761   ATS 1 Sawmillfield St., off Garscube Rd
ATS Rutherglen Ind. Est., Glasgow Rd, Rutherglen   ℘ (0141) 332 1945
℘ (0141) 647 9341

GLASGOW AIRPORT Renfrewshire 401 402 G 16 – see Glasgow.

GLENBORRODALE Highland 401 C 13 – ⊠ Acharacle.
Edinburgh 190 – Inverness 116 – Oban 106.

⩘ **Feorag House** ⌂, PH36 4JP, ℘ (01972) 500248, Fax (01972) 500285, ⩽ Loch Sunart,
« Lochside setting », ⌇, park – ⇚ ❷. ✇ *VISA*. ✋
Meals 20.00 **st.** – **3 rm** ⊇ (dinner included) 69.00/118.00 **st.** – SB.

When looking for a quiet hotel
use the maps found in the introduction
or look for establishments with the sign ⌂ or ⌂.

GLENCARSE Perthshire and Kinross 401 K 14 – see Perth.

GLENELG Highland 401 D 12.
Edinburgh 229 – Inverness 75 – Kyle of Lochalsh 25.

🏠 **Glenelg Inn,** IV40 8JR, ℘ (01599) 522273, Fax (01599) 522373, ⩽ Glenelg Bay, ⌇, ⟲ – ❷
Easter-mid November – **Meals** (bar lunch)/dinner 22.00 **st.** – **6 rm** ⊇ (dinner included)
69.00/158.00 **st.** – SB.

GLENFINNAN Highland 401 D 13 – ⊠ Fort William.
Edinburgh 150 – Inverness 85 – Oban 66.

🏠 **Prince's House,** PH37 4LT, W : ¾ m. on A 830 ℘ (01397) 722246, Fax (01397) 722307, ⩽
– ⇚ ⊡ ☎ ❷. ✇ ◱ *VISA*
closed Christmas and restricted opening November-March – **Meals** (bar lunch Monday to
Saturday)/dinner 25.00 **st.** and a la carte ⅃ 6.50 – **9 rm** ⊇ 45.00/99.00 **st.** – SB.

GLENLIVET Moray 401 J 11 – pop. 3 559 – ⊠ Ballindalloch.
Edinburgh 180 – Aberdeen 59 – Elgin 27 – Inverness 49.

🏠 **Minmore House** ⌂, AB37 9DB, S : ¾ m. on Glenlivet Distillery rd ℘ (01807) 590378,
Fax (01807) 590472, ⩽, ⟲, ✗ – ⇚ rest, ☎ ❷. ✇ *VISA*
May-September – **Meals** (booking essential to non-residents) (dinner only) 25.00 **st.** –
10 rm ⊇ (dinner included) 65.00/130.00 **st.**

GLENROTHES Fife 401 K 15 Scotland G. – pop. 38 650.
Env. : Falkland★ (Village★, Palace of Falkland★ AC, Gardens★ AC) N : 5 ½ m. by A 92 and
A 912.
🖫 Thornton, Station Rd ℘ (01592) 771111 – 🖫 Golf Course Rd ℘ (01592) 754561/758686 –
🖫 Balbirnie Park, Markinch ℘ (01592) 612095 – 🖫 Auchterderran, Woodend Rd, Cardenden
℘ (01592) 721579 – 🖫 Leslie, Balsillie Laws ℘ (01592) 620040.
🖪 Rothes Halls, Rothes Sq., Kingdom Centre, ℘ (01592) 610784/754954.
Edinburgh 33 – Dundee 25 – Stirling 36.

699

Balbirnie House ☜, Markinch, KY7 6NE, NE : 1 ¾ m. by A 911 and A 92 on B 9130 – *℘* (01592) 610066, *Fax (01592) 610529*, « Part 18C mansion », 斧, park – ⑮ rest, ⦿ ☎ ❷ – ⚑ 150. ⓪ ⅅ ⓪ 🆅🆂🅰. ⅏
Meals 28.50 **st.** (dinner) and lunch a la carte 12.25/20.25 **st.** ⬧ 6.25 – **28 rm** ⇌ 110.00/199.50 **st.**, 2 suites – SB.

Travel Inn, Beaufort Drive, Bankhead Roundabout, KY7 4UJ, E : 1 ¾ m. by A 911 at junction of A 92 and B 921 *℘* (01592) 773473, *Fax (01592) 773453* – ⑮ rm, ⦿ ⅍ ❷ – ⚑ 30. ⓪ ⅅ ⓪ 🆅🆂🅰. ⅏
Meals (grill rest.) – **40 rm** 36.50 **t.**

at Leslie *W : 3 m. by A 911.*

Rescobie, 6 Valley Drive, KY6 3BQ, *℘* (01592) 742143, *Fax (01592) 620231*, 斧 – ⦿ ☎ ❷. ⓪ ⅅ ⓪ 🆅🆂🅰. ⅏
closed 25 and 26 December – **Meals** 17.50 **t.** (dinner) and a la carte 16.75/24.45 **t.** ⬧ 5.75 – **10 rm** ⇌ 50.00/76.00 **t.** – SB.

GRANTOWN-ON-SPEY Highland 401 J 12 – pop. 2 391
▣ Abernethy, Nethy Bridge *℘* (01479) 821305.
▤ High St., PH26 3EH *℘* (01479) 872773 (summer only).
Edinburgh 143 – Inverness 34 – Perth 99.

Ravenscourt House, Seafield Av., PH26 3JG, *℘* (01479) 872286, *Fax (01479) 873260* – ⑮ rest, ⦿ ❷. ⓪ 🆅🆂🅰
restricted opening in winter – **Meals** *(closed Sunday and Monday lunch)* (Sunday dinner residents only) (light lunch)/dinner 12.00 **st.** and a la carte ⬧ 6.00 – **6 rm** ⇌ 35.00/80.00 **st** – SB.

Culdearn House, Woodlands Terr., PH26 3JU, *℘* (01479) 872106, *Fax (01479) 873641* 斧 – ⑮ ⦿ ❷. ⓪ ⅅ ⓪ 🆅🆂🅰 🅹🅲🅱. ⅏
March-October – **Meals** (residents only) (dinner only) ⬧ 5.90 – **9 rm** ⇌ (dinner included) 60.00/120.00 **st.** – SB.

Ardconnel, Woodlands Terr., PH26 3JU, *℘* (01479) 872104, *Fax (01479) 872104*, 斧 – ⑮ ⦿ 🅼🅾 🆅🆂🅰. ⅏
Easter-October – **Meals** 16.50 **st.** ⬧ 4.75 – **6 rm** ⇌ 30.00/65.00 **st.**

Ardlarig, Woodlands Terr., PH26 3JU, *℘* (01479) 873245, *Fax (01479) 873245*, 斧 – ⑮ ⦿
closed 22 December-2 January and restricted opening in winter – **Meals** (by arrangement) 18.50 **st.** ⬧ 5.25 – **7 rm** ⇌ 26.50/53.00 **st.**

GRETNA Dumfries and Galloway 401 402 K 19 – pop. 2 678.
▤ The Old Blacksmith's Shop *℘* (01461) 337834 (summer only).
Edinburgh 91 – Carlisle 10 – Dumfries 24.

Garden House, Sarkfoot Rd, DG16 5EP, SE : ½ m. on B 7076 *℘* (01461) 337621 *Fax (01461) 337692*, ⌕, ⬚ – ▤ rest, ⦿ ☎ ⅍ ❷ – ⚑ 150
21 rm.

Gretna Chase, DG16 5JB, SE : ¾ m. on B 7076 *℘* (01461) 337517, *Fax (01461) 337766* « Gardens » – ⦿ ☎ ❷. ⓪ ⅅ 🆅🆂🅰
Meals *(closed Sunday)* a la carte 16.95/24.40 **st.** ⬧ 4.50 – **9 rm** ⇌ 39.00/95.00 **st.** – SB.

GRETNA GREEN SERVICE AREA Dumfries and Galloway 401 402 K 18 – ✉ Gretna.
▤ Welcome Break Service Area, M 74, Gretna Green DG16 5HQ *℘* (01461) 338500.

Welcome Lodge, DG16 5HQ, on A 74 (M) (northbound carriageway) *℘* (01461) 337566 *Fax (01461) 337823*, Reservations (Freephone) 0800 7314466 – ⑮ rm, ⦿ ⅍ ❷. 🅼🅾 ⅅ ⓪ 🆅🆂🅰. ⅏
Meals (grill rest.) – **64 rm** 45.00 **t.**

GRIMSAY Western Isles (Outer Hebrides) 401 Y 11 – see Uist (Isles of).

Bitte beachten Sie die Geschwindigkeitsbeschränkungen in Großbritannien
- 60 mph (= 96 km/h) außerhalb geschlossener Ortschaften
- 70 mph (= 112 km/h) auf Straßen mit getrennten Fahrbahnen und Autobahnen.

GULLANE *East Lothian* **401** L 15 *Scotland G.* – *pop. 2 229.*

Env. : *Dirleton★ (Castle★) NE : 2 m. by A 198.*

🏌, 🏌, 🏌 *Gullane* ℘ *(01620) 843115.*

Edinburgh 19 – North Berwick 5.

🏨 **Greywalls** ⌂, Duncur Rd, Muirfield, EH31 2EG, ℘ *(01620) 842144, Fax (01620) 842241,* ≼ gardens and golf course, « Lutyens house, gardens by Gertrude Jekyll », ✗ – ☆ rest,

📺 ☎ 🅿 – 🛗 30. 📵 🆀 🆎 ⑩ 𝗩𝗜𝗦𝗔

April-October – **Meals** 15.00/35.00 **t.** ₰ 6.50 – **22 rm** � 95.00/190.00 **t.** – SB.

✗ **La Potinière** (Hilary Brown), Main St., EH31 2AA, ℘ *(01620) 843214, Fax (01620) 843214*

❀ ☆

closed lunch Friday and Saturday, dinner Sunday to Thursday, Wednesday, 25 December, 1 January, 1 week June and October – **Meals** (booking essential) 20.00/30.00 **t.** ₰ 6.50

Spec. Tomato and mint soup. Breast of maize fed chicken on a bed of spinach with asparagus and morels. Warm almond and polenta cake with rhubarb sorbet.

HADDINGTON *East Lothian* **401** L 16 *Scotland G.* – *pop. 7 342.*

See : *Town★* - *High Street★.*

Env. : *Lennoxlove★ AC, S : 1 m.*

EXC. : *Tantallon Castle★★ (clifftop site★★★) AC, NE : 12 m. by A 1 and A 198 – Northern foothills of the Lammermuir Hills★★, S : 14 m. by A 6137 and B 6368 – Stenton★, E : 7 m.*

🏌 *Amisfield Park* ℘ *(01620) 823627.*

Edinburgh 17 – Hawick 53 – Newcastle upon Tyne 101.

🏨 **Maitlandfield House**, 24 Sidegate, EH41 4BZ, ℘ *(01620) 826513, Fax (01620) 826713,* 🌸 – 📺 ☎ 🅿 – 🛗 200. 🆀 🆎 ⑩ 𝗩𝗜𝗦𝗔 𝗝𝗖𝗕

Meals 22.00 **st.** (dinner) and a la carte 12.40/20.00 **st.** – **22 rm** � 60.00/110.00 **st.** – SB.

✗✗ **Brown's** with rm, 1 West Rd, EH41 3RD, ℘ *(01620) 822254, Fax (01620) 822254* – 📺 ☎

🅿. 🆀 🆎 ⑩ 𝗩𝗜𝗦𝗔. ✗

Meals (booking essential) (dinner only and Sunday lunch)/dinner 27.50 **t.** ₰ 4.50 – **5 rm** � 60.00/84.00 **t.**

HALKIRK *Highland* **401** J 8 – *pop. 1 913.*

Edinburgh 285 – Thurso 8 – Wick 17.

↑ **Bannochmore Farm** ⌂, Harpsdale, KW12 6UN, S : 3 ¼ m. ℘ *(01847) 841216,* « Working farm », park – ☆ 🅿. ✗

Meals 10.00 **st.** – **3 rm** � 17.00/34.00.

HAMILTON SERVICE AREA *South Lanarkshire.*

🏌 *Larkhall, Burnhead Rd* ℘ *(01698) 881113* – 🏌 *Strathclyde Park, Mote Hill* ℘ *(01698) 266155.*

🅱 *Road Chef Services, M 74 northbound, ML3 6JW* ℘ *(01698) 285590.*

Edinburgh 38 – Glasgow 12.

🏨 **RoadChef Lodge** without rest., ML3 6JW, M 74 between junctions 6 and 5 (northbound carriageway) ℘ *(01698) 891904, Fax (01698) 891682,* Reservations (Freephone) 0800 834719 – ☆ 📺 ☎ ₺ 🅿 – 🛗 25. 🆀 🆎 ⑩ 𝗩𝗜𝗦𝗔. ✗

36 rm 43.50 **st.**

HARRIS (Isle of) *Western Isles (Outer Hebrides)* **401** Z 10 – *see Lewis and Harris (Isle of).*

HAWICK *Borders* **401** **402** L 17 *Scotland G.* – *pop. 16 127.*

EXC. : *Jedburgh Abbey★★ AC, SW : 12 ½ m. by A 698 – Waterloo Monument (※★★) NE : 12 m. by A 698, A 68 and B 6400 – Hermitage Castle★, S : 16 m. by B 6399.*

🏌 *Hawick, Vertish Hill* ℘ *(01450) 72293* – 🏌 *Minto, Denholm* ℘ *(01450) 870220.*

🅱 *Drumlanrig's Tower* ℘ *(01450) 372547 (summer only).*

Edinburgh 51 – Ayr 122 – Carlisle 44 – Dumfries 63 – Motherwell 76 – Newcastle upon Tyne 62.

🏨 **Kirklands,** West Stewart Pl., TD9 8BH, ℘ *(01450) 372263, Fax (01450) 370404,* 🌸 – 📺 ☎

🅿. 🆀 🆎 ⑩ 𝗩𝗜𝗦𝗔

closed 26 December and 1 January – **Meals** 17.50 **t.** (dinner) and a la carte 11.50/20.20 **t.** ₰ 4.75 – **9 rm** � 49.50/75.00 **t.**

◎ ATS Victoria Rd ℘ *(01450) 373369*

HEITON *Borders* – *see Kelso.*

HELENSBURGH *Argyll and Bute* **401** F 15 *Scotland G.* – *pop. 12 972.*

See : *Hill House* ★ *AC.*
Env. : *Loch Lomond* ★★ , *NE : 4 ½ m. by B 832.*
Exc. : *The Clyde Estuary* ★ .
🚢 to Gourock and via Kilcreggan (Caledonian MacBrayne Ltd and Clyde Marine Motoring Co. Ltd) (except Sunday).
🛈 *The Clock Tower, J84 7NY* ℰ *(01436) 672642 (summer only).*
Edinburgh 68 – Glasgow 22.

🏨 Commodore Toby, 112-117 West Clyde St., G84 8ES, ℰ (01436) 676924, Fax (01436) 676233, ≤ – 📶 ❄ 📺 ☎ 🅿 – 🔬 200
44 rm, 1 suite.

HELMSDALE *Highland* **401** J 9.

🛈 *Coupar Park* ℰ *(01431) 821640 (April-Sept).*
Edinburgh 227 – Inverness 71 – Thurso 45 – Wick 37.

🏠 **Navidale House** ❧, KW8 6JS, N : ½ m. on A 9 ℰ (01431) 821258, Fax (01431) 821531, ≤, 🚗 – ❄ 📺 🅿. 🐾 😊 *VISA*
restricted opening November-mid January – **Meals** (bar lunch Monday to Saturday)/dinner 21.00 ⓐ 5.50 – **9 rm** ⌖ (dinner included) 57.00/126.00 **st.** – SB.

HUMBIE *East Lothian* **401** L 16 *Scotland G.* – *pop. 376.*

Env. : *Crichton Castle (Italianate courtyard range* ★ *), W : 6 m. by B 6457, A 68 and minor roads.*
Edinburgh 19 – Hawick 44 – Newcastle upon Tyne 92.

🏨 **Johnstounburn House** ❧, EH36 5PL, S : 1 m. on B 6368 ℰ (01875) 833696, Fax (01875) 833626, ≤, « Part 17C country house in extensive gardens », 🔦, park – 📺 ☎ 🅿 – 🔬 30. 🐾 🖭 ① *VISA* *JCB*
Meals 18.00/29.00 **t.** ⓐ 5.85 – **20 rm** ⌖ 112.00/157.00 **t.** – SB.

INGLISTON *Edinburgh City* **401** K 16 – *see Edinburgh.*

INNERLEITHEN *Borders* **401 402** K 17 *Scotland G.*

Env. : *Traquair House* ★★ , *S : 1 m. on B 709 – Tweed Valley* ★★ .
Edinburgh 30 – Galashiels 12 – Peebles 6.

🏠 **The Ley** ❧, EH44 6NL, N : 2 ¼ m. on B 709 ℰ (01896) 830240, Fax (01896) 830240, 🚗 park – ❄ 🅿. 🛁
April-September – **Meals** (by arrangement) (residents only) (dinner only) 22.00 ⓐ 6.00 – **3 rm** ⌖ 48.00/78.00.

INVERCRERAN *Argyll and Bute* **401** E 14 – ✉ *Appin.*
Edinburgh 142 – Fort William 29 – Oban 19.

🏨 **Invercreran Country House** ❧, Glen Creran, PA38 4BJ, ℰ (01631) 730414 Fax (01631) 730532, ≤ Glen Creran and mountains, 🚗, park – ❄ rest, 📺 ☎ 🅿 🐾 *VISA*. 🛁
16 March-14 November – **Meals** 30.00 **t.** (dinner) and lunch a la carte 20.00/31.00 **t.** ⓐ 8.0(– **9 rm** ⌖ 70.00/170.00 **t.** – SB.

INVERGARRY *Highland* **401** F 12 *Scotland G.* – ✉ *Inverness.*

Env. : *The Great Glen* ★ .
Edinburgh 159 – Fort William 25 – Inverness 43 – Kyle of Lochalsh 50.

🏨 **Glengarry Castle** ❧, PH35 4HW, on A 82 ℰ (01809) 501254, Fax (01809) 501207, ≤, 🔦 🚗, park, 🛁 – ❄ rest, 📺 ☎ 🅿. 🐾 *VISA*
3 April-2 November – **Meals** (light lunch Monday to Saturday)/dinner 22.00 **st.** ⓐ 6.00 – **26 rm** ⌖ 50.00/120.00 **st.** – SB.

🏠 **Ardochy Lodge** ❧, Glengarry, PH35 4HR, W : 7 ½ m. by A 87 on Tomdoun r(ℰ (01809) 511232, Fax (01809) 511233, 🔦, 🚗, park – ❄ rest, 🅿. 🐾
Meals (residents only) (dinner only) ⓐ 4.00 – **8 rm** ⌖ (dinner included) 60.00/90.00 **t.** – SB.

🏠 **Invergarry,** PH35 4HJ, ℰ (01809) 501206, Fax (01809) 501236, 🔦 – ❄ rest, 📺 ☎ 🅿. 🐾 🖭 *VISA*
closed 5 days Christmas – **Meals** (bar lunch)/dinner 16.00 **st.** ⓐ 5.50 – **10 rm** ⌖ 41.0(70.00 **st.** – SB.

INVERNESS Highland **401** H 11 *Scotland G.* – pop. 62 186.

See : *Town★ – Museum and Art Gallery★* Y **M**.

Exc. : *Loch Ness★★*, SW : by A 82 Z – *Clava Cairns★*, E : 9 m. by Culcabock Rd, B 9006 and B 851 Z – *Cawdor Castle★* **AC**, NE : 14 m. by A 96 and B 9090 Y.

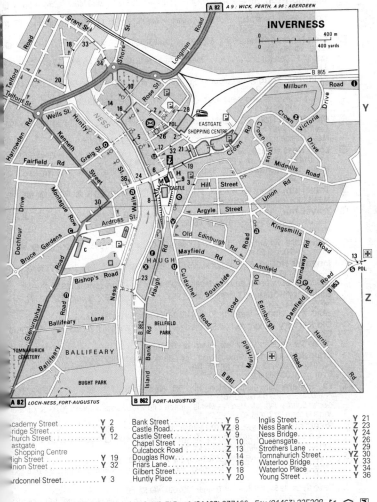

🛇 Culcabock Rd ℘ (01463) 239882 Z – 🛇 Torvean, Glenurquhart Rd ℘ (01463) 711434.

✈ Inverness Airport, Dalcross : ℘ (01463) 232471, NE : 8 m. by A 96 Y.

🛈 Castle Wynd, IV2 3BJ ℘ (01463) 234353 Y.

Edinburgh 156 – Aberdeen 107 – Dundee 134.

🏨🏨 **Kingsmills**, Culcabock Rd, IV2 3LP, ℘ (01463) 237166, Fax (01463) 225208, 🗗, ⊜s, 🔲, ♨ – 🛊 ⇆ 📺 ☎ & 🅿 – 🔬 60. 🆗 🐵 AE ① VISA JCB   Z S
Meals 13.00/22.00 **st.** and a la carte ↥ 6.50 – **76 rm** ⇌ 110.00/155.00 **st.**, 1 suite – SB.

🏨🏨 **Inverness Thistle**, Millburn Rd, IV2 3TR, E : 1 m. on B 865 ℘ (01463) 239666, Fax (01463) 711145 – 🛊, ⇆ rm, 📺 ☎ 🅿 – 🔬 230. 🆗 🐵 AE ① VISA JCB
Meals 9.75/17.95 **t.** and dinner a la carte 6.75 – ⇌ 9.75 – **117 rm** 88.00/130.00 **t.**, 1 suite – SB.

🏨 **Caledonian,** 33 Church St., IV1 1DX, ☎ (01463) 235181, *Fax (01463) 711206,* ♣, ⇔, ▨ –
|஖|, ⇔ rm, ▥ ☎ ৬ ₽ – 🖄 300. ◍ 🆎 ◑ 𝚅𝙸𝚂𝙰
Y u
Meals (bar lunch Monday to Saturday)/dinner 16.95 **t.** and a la carte – ☲ 8.50 – **103 rm**
105.00/134.00 **t.**, 3 suites – SB.

🏨 **Craigmonie,** 9 Annfield Rd, IV2 3HX, ☎ (01463) 231649, *Fax (01463) 233720,* ♣, ⇔, ▨ –
|஖| ⇔ ▥ ☎ ₽ – 🖄 140. ◍ 🆎 ◑ 𝚅𝙸𝚂𝙰. ⅏
Z e
closed 24 to 27 and 31 December-3 January – **Bistro : Meals** 9.50 **t.** (lunch)
and a la carte 10.95/20.00 **t.**, ⌀ 5.75 – **Chardonnay : Meals** (dinner only and Sunday lunch)/
dinner 24.00 **t.** ⌀ 6.50 – **32 rm** ☲ 75.50/104.00 **t.**, 3 suites – SB.

🏨 **Glenmoriston,** 20 Ness Bank, IV2 4SF, ☎ (01463) 223777, *Fax (01463) 712378* – ▥ ☎ ₽
– 🖄 30. ◍ ◑ 𝚅𝙸𝚂𝙰. ⅏
Z x
closed 25-26 December and 1-2 January – **Meals** – (see **La Riviera** below) – **15 rm**
☲ 68.00/130.00 **st.** – SB.

🏨 **Glen Mhor,** 9-12 Ness Bank, IV2 4SG, ☎ (01463) 234308, *Fax (01463) 713170* – ▥ ☎ ₽.
◍ 🆎 ◑ 𝚅𝙸𝚂𝙰. ⅏
Z r
closed 31 December-2 January – **Meals** a la carte 9.10/28.00 **t.** ⌀ 5.50 – **30 rm** ☲ 62.00/
110.00 **t.** – SB.

🏨 **Culduthel Lodge,** 14 Culduthel Rd, IV2 4AG, ☎ (01463) 240089, *Fax (01463) 240089* –
⇔ ▥ ☎ ₽. ◍ 𝚅𝙸𝚂𝙰
Z u
closed Christmas and New Year – **Meals** (by arrangement) 18.00 **st.** ⌀ 5.00 – **11 rm**
☲ 45.00/90.00 **st.**, 1 suite.

🏨 **Glendruidh House** 🏡, Old Edinburgh Rd South, IV1 2AA, SE : 2 m. ☎ (01463) 226499,
Fax (01463) 710745, ⪽ – ⇔ ▥ ☎ ₽. ◍ 🆎 ◑ 𝚅𝙸𝚂𝙰 𝙹𝙲𝙱. ⅏
Meals (residents only) 19.50/24.50 **st.** ⌀ 9.50 – **7 rm** ☲ 50.00/90.00 **t.** – SB.

🏨 **Loch Ness House,** Glenurquhart Rd, IV3 6JL, SW : 1 ½ m. on A 82 ☎ (01463) 231248,
Fax (01463) 239327, ⪽ – ▥ ☎ ₽ – 🖄 100. ◍ 🆎 ◑ 𝚅𝙸𝚂𝙰
Meals (bar lunch Monday to Saturday)/dinner 16.50 **t.** and a la carte – **22 rm** ☲ 52.50/
110.00 – SB.

🏨 **Travel Inn,** Milburn Rd, IV2 3QX, ☎ (01463) 712010 – ⇔ rm, ▥ ৬ ₽. ◍ 🆎 ◑ 𝚅𝙸𝚂𝙰. ⅏
Meals (grill rest.) – **39 rm** 36.50 **t.**
Y

🏨 **Travel Inn,** Beechwood Retail Park, IV2 3BW, E : 2 m. on A 9 ☎ (01463) 232729
Fax (01463) 231553 – ⇔ rm, ৬ ₽. ◍ 🆎 ◑ 𝚅𝙸𝚂𝙰
40 **rm** 36.50 **t.**

🏠 **Braemore** without rest., 1 Victoria Drive, IV2 3QB, ☎ (01463) 243318, ⪽ – ⇔ ₽. ⅏
3 rm 45.00/55.00 **st.**
Y z

🏠 **Moyness House,** 6 Bruce Gdns., IV3 5EN, ☎ (01463) 233836, *Fax (01463) 233836,* ⪽ –
⇔ rest, ▥ ₽. ◍ 𝚅𝙸𝚂𝙰
Z c
closed 24 December-3 January – **Meals** 18.00 **st.** ⌀ 4.50 – **7 rm** ☲ 34.00/68.00 **st.** – SB.

🏠 **Ballifeary House,** 10 Ballifeary Rd, IV3 5PJ, ☎ (01463) 235572, *Fax (01463) 717583,* ⪽ –
⇔ ▥ ₽. ◍ 𝚅𝙸𝚂𝙰. ⅏
Z r
Easter-mid October – **Meals** 18.50 **st.** ⌀ 4.50 – **5 rm** ☲ 55.00/70.00 **s.**

🏠 **Old Rectory** without rest., 9 Southside Rd, IV2 3BG, ⪽ – ⇔ ▥ ₽
◍ 𝚅𝙸𝚂𝙰. ⅏
Z a
closed Christmas and New Year – **4 rm** ☲ 26.00/44.00.

🏠 **Craigside Lodge** without rest., 4 Gordon Terr., IV2 3HD, ☎ (01463) 231576,
Fax (01463) 713409, ≤ – ⇔ ▥. ◍ 𝚅𝙸𝚂𝙰
Z v
6 rm ☲ 20.00/38.00 **t.**

XX **La Riviera** (at Glenmoriston H.), 20 Ness Bank, IV2 4SF, ☎ (01463) 223777
Fax (01463) 712378 – ◍ 🆎 𝚅𝙸𝚂𝙰
Z z
closed Sunday January-March – **Meals** - Italian - (lunch by arrangement) 20.95 **st.** (dinner
and a la carte 21.70/28.30 **st.** ⌀ 5.75.

X **Riverhouse,** 1 Greig St., IV5 3PT, ☎ (01463) 222033 – ⇔. ◍ 𝚅𝙸𝚂𝙰
Y c
closed Sunday lunch, Monday and January – **Meals** (booking essential) 22.50 **t.** (dinner
and lunch a la carte approx. 13.25 **t.** ⌀ 6.50.

X **Riva,** 4-6 Ness Walk, IV3 5NE, ☎ (01463) 237377 – ◍ ◑ 𝚅𝙸𝚂𝙰
Y z
closed Sunday lunch, 25-26 December and 1-2 January – **Meals** a la carte 9.85/16.35 **t.**
⌀ 4.95.

X **Cafe 1,** Castle St., IV2 3EA, ☎ (01463) 226200 – ◍ 🆎 𝚅𝙸𝚂𝙰
Y e
closed Sunday lunch, Sunday dinner October-May, 25-26 December and 1-2 January -
Meals 8.95 **t.** (lunch) and a la carte 14.50/26.85 **t.**

at Dalcross NE : 9 m. by A 96 – Y– , B 9039 and Ardersier rd – ✉ Inverness.

🏠 **Easter Dalziel Farm** 🏡, IV1 2JL, on B 9039 ☎ (01667) 462213, *Fax (01667) 462213*
« Working farm », ⪽ – ₽. ◍ 𝚅𝙸𝚂𝙰 𝙹𝙲𝙱
closed 20 December-6 January and booking essential in winter – **Meals** (by arrangement)
(communal dining) 12.00 – **3 rm** ☲ 26.00/38.00.

at Culloden *E : 3 m. by A 96 – Y – ✉ Inverness.*

Culloden House ⛳, IV1 2NZ, ☎ (01463) 790461, *Fax (01463) 792181*, ≤, « Georgian mansion », ⛰, 🎾, park, 🎾 – ⇔ 📺 ☎ 🅿. 🅜 🅐 🅞 VISA JCB. ✗
Meals 35.00 **st.** (dinner) and lunch a la carte 19.70/26.30 **st.** 🌢 10.65 – **22 rm** ☐ 135.00/230.00 **st.**, 6 suites – SB.

at Dunain Park *SW : 2½ m. on A 82 – Z – ✉ Inverness.*

Dunain Park ⛳, IV3 6JN, ☎ (01463) 230512, *Fax (01463) 224532*, ≤, « Country house, gardens », ⛰, 🏊, park – ⇔ rest, 📺 ☎ 🅿. 🅜 🅐 🅞 VISA JCB
Meals (lunch by arrangement)/dinner 27.50 **t.** 🌢 7.50 – **8 rm** ☐ 100.00/150.00 **t.**, 6 suites – SB.

at Bunchrew *W : 3 m. on A 862 – Y – ✉ Inverness.*

Bunchrew House, IV3 6TA, ☎ (01463) 234917, *Fax (01463) 710620*, ≤, « 17C Scottish mansion », 🌳, park – ⇔ rest, 📺 ☎ 🅿. 🅜 🅐 VISA JCB
closed first 2 weeks January – **Meals** a la carte 15.25/27.00 **t.** 🌢 7.00 – **11 rm** ☐ 70.00/150.00 **t.** – SB.

ATS Carsegate Rd North, The Carse ☎ (01463) 236167

INVERURIE *Aberdeenshire* 401 M 12 *Scotland G.* – *pop. 8 647.*

Exc. : *Castle Fraser★ (exterior★★) AC, SW : 6 m. by B 993 – Pitmedden Gardens★★, NE : 10 m. by B 9170 and A 920 – Haddo House★, N : 14 m. by B 9170 and B 9005 – Fyvie Castle★, N : 13 m. by B 9170 and A 947.*

18 Blackhall Rd ☎ (01467) 620207 – 18 Kintore ☎ (01467) 632631 – 18 Kemnay, Monymusk Rd ☎ (01467) 642225.

Town Hall, Market Pl., AB51 9SN ☎ (01467) 620600 (summer only).

Edinburgh 147 – Aberdeen 17 – Inverness 90.

Thainstone House H. & Country Club ⛳, AB51 5NT, S : 2 m. by B 993 on A 96 ☎ (01467) 621643, *Fax (01467) 625084*, 🏋, 🏊, park – 🛗, ⇔ rest, 📺 ☎ 🅿 – 🏛 300. 🅜 🅐 🅞 VISA
***Simpson's* :** **Meals** 15.50/29.95 **t.** and dinner a la carte 🌢 6.75 – ☐ 10.50 – **47 rm** ☐ 97.00/112.00 **t.**, 1 suite – SB.

Strathburn, Burghmuir Drive, AB51 4GY, NW : 1 ¼ m. by A 96 ☎ (01467) 624422, *Fax (01467) 625133*, 🌳 – ⇔, ▤ rest, 📺 ☎ ♿ 🅿 – 🏛 30. 🅜 🅐 VISA. ✗
closed 25-26 December and 1-2 January – **Meals** 21.75 **st.** (dinner) and a la carte 12.05/23.75 **st.** 🌢 5.75 – **25 rm** ☐ 65.00/85.00 **st.** – SB.

IRVINE *North Ayrshire* 401 402 F 17 *Scotland G.* – *pop. 23 275.*

Env. : *Kilmarnock (Dean Castle, arms and armour★, musical instruments★) AC, E : 5 ½ m. by A 71 and B 7038.*

18 Western Gailes, Gailes ☎ (01294) 311649 – 18 Irvine Ravenspark, Kidsneuk Lane ☎ (01294) 271293 – 18 Bogside ☎ (01294) 78139.

Edinburgh 75 – Ayr 14 – Glasgow 29.

Hospitality Inn, 46 Annick Rd, KA11 4LD, SE : 1 m. on B 7081 ☎ (01294) 274272, *Fax (01294) 277287*, « Exotic indoor garden with 🏊 », 9, – ⇔ rm, 📺 ☎ ♿ 🅿 – 🏛 300. 🅜 🅐 🅞 VISA JCB
Meals (carving lunch) 14.50 **st.** (dinner) and a la carte 12.00/26.00 **st.** 🌢 5.70 – ☐ 9.75 – **126 rm** 84.00/128.00 **st.** – SB.

ATS 9 Kyle Rd Ind. Est. ☎ (01294) 278727

Pour voyager rapidement, utilisez les ***cartes Michelin "Grandes Routes" :***

970 Europe, **976** République Tchèque-République Slovaque, **980** Grèce, **984** Allemagne, **985** Scandinavie-Finlande, **986** Grande-Bretagne-Irlande, **987** Allemagne-Autriche-Benelux, **988** Italie, **989** France, **990** Espagne-Portugal, **991** Yougoslavie.

ISLAY (Isle of) *Argyll and Bute* **401** B 16 – pop. 3 840.

🛏 *Machrie Hotel, Port Ellen* ℰ *(01496) 302310.*

✈ *Port Ellen Airport :* ℰ *(01496) 302022.*

🚢 *from Port Askaig to Isle of Jura (Feolin) (Western Ferries (Argyll) Ltd) frequent services daily (5 mn) – from Port Ellen or Port Askaig to Kintyre Peninsula (Kennacraig) (Caledonian MacBrayne Ltd) 1-3 daily – from Port Askaig to Oban via Isle of Colonsay (Scalasaig) (Caledonian MacBrayne Ltd) weekly (3 h 45 mn) – from Port Askaig to Isle of Colonsay (Scalasaig) and Kintyre Peninsula (Kennacraig) (Caledonian MacBrayne Ltd) weekly.*

🛈 *at Bowmore, The Square* ℰ *(01496) 810254.*

Ballygrant.

⌂ **Kilmeny Farmhouse** ⬦, PA45 7QW, SW : ½ m. on A 846 ℰ *(01496) 840668, Fax (01496) 840668,* ≤, « Working farm », �, park – 😄 **℗**
closed Christmas and New Year – **Meals** *(by arrangement) (communal dining) 23.00* **s.** –
3 rm ⊒ *38.00/60.00* **s.** – SB.

🍴 **Ballygrant Inn** with rm, PA45 7QR, ℰ *(01496) 840277, Fax (01496) 840277,* � – 😄 **℗**.
◯◯ **VISA**. ✂
Meals *10.00/17.50* **st.** *and lunch a la carte* ⏚ *4.00* – **3 rm** ⊒ *22.50/50.00* **st.** – SB.

Bridgend – ✉ *Bowmore.*

🏨 **Bridgend,** PA44 7PQ, ℰ *(01496) 810212, Fax (01496) 810960,* � – **TV** ☎ **℗**. **◯◯** **VISA** **JCB**
Meals *(bar lunch)/dinner 20.00* **t.** *and a la carte* **t.** ⏚ *5.50* – **10 rm** ⊒ *42.00/84.00* **t.** – SB.

Port Charlotte.

🏨 **Port Charlotte,** Main St., PA48 7TU, ℰ *(01496) 850360, Fax (01496) 850361,* ≤ – 😄 **TV**
☎ **℗**. **◯◯** **VISA** **JCB**. ✂
Meals *(light lunch) a la carte 16.45/33.45* **t.** ⏚ *7.50* – **10 rm** ⊒ *45.00/79.00* **t.**

Port Ellen.

⌂ **Glenmachrie Farmhouse,** PA42 7AW, NW : 4 ½ m. on A 846 ℰ *(01496) 302500, Fax (01496) 302560,* « Working farm », 🐎, �, park – 😄 **TV** **℗**. ✂
Meals *(by arrangement) 20.00* **st.** – **5 rm** ⊒ *38.00/56.00* **st.**

ISLEORNSAY *Highland* **401** C 12 – see Skye (Isle of).

JEDBURGH *Borders* **401** **402** M 17 *Scotland G.* – pop. 4 768.

See : Town★ - Abbey★★ **AC** – Mary Queen of Scots House Visitor Centre★ **AC** –
The Canongate Bridge★.

Env. : Waterloo Monument (❄★★) N : 4 m. by A 68 and B 6400.

🏌 *Jedburgh, Dunion Rd* ℰ *(01835) 863587.*

🛈 *Murray's Green, TD8 6BE* ℰ *(01835) 863435/863688.*

Edinburgh 48 – Carlisle 54 – Newcastle upon Tyne 57.

🏨 **Glenfriars,** The Friars, TD8 6BN, ℰ *(01835) 862000, Fax (01835) 862000,* � – **TV** **℗**. **◯◯**
AE **VISA**
closed Christmas and New Year – **Meals** *(booking essential) (dinner only) 17.50* **t.** ⏚ *4.65* –
6 rm ⊒ *35.00/80.00* **t.** – SB.

⌂ **Hundalee House** ⬦ without rest., TD8 6PA, S : 1 ½ m. by A 68 ℰ *(01835) 863011, Fax (01835) 863011,* ≤, 🐎, �, park – 😄 **TV** **℗**. ✂
April-October – **3 rm** ⊒ *35.00/40.00.*

⌂ **Spinney** without rest., Langlee, TD8 6PB, S : 2 m. on A 68 ℰ *(01835) 863525, Fax (01835) 864883,* � – 😄 **TV** **℗**. ✂
March-mid November – **3 rm** ⊒ *40.00/42.00* **st.**

JOHN O'GROATS *Highland* **401** K 8 – Shipping Services : see Orkney Islands.

JURA (Isle of) *Argyll and Bute* **401** C 15 – pop. 196.

🚢 *from Feolin to Isle of Islay (Port Askaig) (Western Ferries (Argyll) Ltd) frequent services daily (5 mn).*

Craighouse – ✉ *Jura.*

🏨 **Jura,** PA60 7XU, ℰ *(01496) 820243, Fax (01496) 820249,* ≤ Small Isles Bay, 🌻 – **℗**. **◯◯** **A**
◯ **VISA**
closed mid December-mid January – **Meals** *(bar lunch)/dinner 17.00* **st.** *and a la carte* -
17 rm ⊒ *30.00/95.00* **st.**

KELSO Borders **401 402** M 17 *Scotland G.* – pop. 6 167.

See : *Town*★ – *The Square*★★ – ≤★ *from Kelso Bridge.*
Env. : *Tweed Valley*★★ – *Floors Castle*★ *AC*, NW : 1 ½ m. by A 6089.
Exc. : *Mellerstain*★★ (Ceilings★★★, Library★★★) *AC*, NW : 6 m. by A 6089 – Waterloo Monument (※★★), SW : 7 m. by A 698 and B 6400 – *Jedburgh Abbey*★★ *AC*, SW : 8 ½ m. by A 698 – *Dryburgh Abbey*★★ (setting★★★), SW : 10 ½ m. by A 6089, B 6397 and B 6404 – *Scott's View*★★, W : 11 m. by A 6089, B 6397, B 6404 and B 6356 – *Smailholm Tower*★ (※★★), NW : 6 m. by A 6089 and B 6397 – Lady Kirk (Kirk o'Steil★), NE : 16 m. by A 698, A 697, A 6112 and B 6437.

☗ Berrymoss Racecourse Rd ℰ (01573) 23009.
🛈 Town House, The Square, PD5 7HC ℰ (01573) 223464 (summer only).
Edinburgh 44 – Hawick 21 – Newcastle upon Tyne 68.

🏰 **Ednam House,** Bridge St., TD5 7HT, ℰ (01573) 224168, Fax (01573) 226319, ≤, « 18C », 🐾 – 📺 ☎ ℗ – 🔏 200. 🆗 💳
closed 24 December-9 January – Meals 11.00/20.00 st. 🍴 6.00 – **32 rm** ⊇ 51.00/102.00 st. – SB.

at Heiton SW : 3 m. by A 698 – ⊠ Kelso.

🏰 **Sunlaws House** ⊗, TD5 8JZ, ℰ (01573) 450331, Fax (01573) 450611, ≤, « Victorian country house », ☖, 🐾, park, ※ – ⅔ rest, 📺 ☎ ℗. 🆗 🆎 ① 💳
closed 25 and 26 December – Meals 14.00/28.50 st. 🍴 9.50 – **22 rm** ⊇ 98.00/150.00 st. – SB.

🔧 ATS The Butts ℰ (01573) 224997/8

KENMORE Perthshire and Kinross **401** I 14 *Scotland G.* – pop. 596.

See : *Village*★ – Env. : *Loch Tay*★★ – Exc. : *Ben Lawers*★★, SW : 8 m. by A 827.
☗ Taymouth Castle, Aberfeldy ℰ (01887) 830228 – ☗s, ☗☗ Mains of Taymouth ℰ (01887) 830226.
Edinburgh 82 – Dundee 60 – Oban 71 – Perth 38.

🏨 **Kenmore,** PH15 2NU, ℰ (01887) 830205, Fax (01887) 830262, ☎s, 🔲, ☗☗, 🐾, 🐾, ※ – 🛗, ⅔ rest, 📺 ☎ ℗ – 🔏 35. 🆗 🆎 💳 JCB
Meals 15.50/27.50 t. and lunch a la carte 🍴 6.95 – **44 rm** ⊇ 35.00/70.00 t. – SB.

KENTALLEN Highland **401** E 14 – ⊠ Appin (Argyll and Bute).
Edinburgh 123 – Fort William 17 – Oban 33.

🏠 **Ardsheal House** ⊗, PA38 4BX, SW : ¾ m. by A 828 ℰ (01631) 740227, Fax (01631) 740342, ≤, « Country house atmosphere », 🐾, park – ⅔ rest, ☎ ℗. 🆗 💳
March-November – Meals (residents only) (dinner only) 23.00 🍴 9.00 – **6 rm** ⊇ (dinner included) 60.00/120.00 st.

KEOSE (CEOS) Western Isles (Outer Hebrides) **401** A 9 – see Lewis and Harris (Isle of).

KILCHOAN Highland **401** B 13 – ⊠ Acharacle.
Edinburgh 163 – Inverness 120 – Oban 84.

🏠 **Meall Mo Chridhe Country H.** ⊗, PH36 4LH, ℰ (01972) 510238, Fax (01972) 510238, ≤ Sound of Mull, « 18C former manse », 🐾, park – ⅔ ℗
April-October – Meals (by arrangement) (communal dining) 27.95 – **3 rm** ⊇ (dinner included) 69.00/138.00 s. – SB.

🏠 **Far View Cottage** ⊗, Mingary Pier Rd, PH36 4LH, ℰ (01972) 510357, ≤ Sound of Mull, 🐾 – ⅔ rest, 📺 ℗. 🐾
Easter-October – Meals 16.00 s. – **3 rm** ⊇ (dinner included) 70.00/90.00 – SB.

KILCHRENAN Argyll and Bute **401** E 14 *Scotland G.* – ⊠ Taynuilt.
Env. : *Loch Awe*★★, E : 1 ¼ m..
Edinburgh 117 – Glasgow 87 – Oban 18.

🏰 **Ardanaiseig** ⊗, PA35 1HE, NE : 4 m. ℰ (01866) 833333, Fax (01866) 833222, ≤ gardens and Loch Awe, « Country house in extensive informal gardens beside Loch Awe », 🐾, park, ※ – ⅔ rest, 📺 ☎ ℗. 🆗 🆎 ① 💳
closed 2 January-14 February – Meals (dinner only and Sunday lunch)/dinner 25.00 st. and a la carte 🍴 7.00 – **14 rm** ⊇ 95.00/168.00 st., 1 suite – SB.

🏨 **Taychreggan** ⊗, PA35 1HQ, SE : 1 ¼ m. ℰ (01866) 833211, Fax (01866) 833244, ≤ Loch Awe and mountains, « Lochside setting », 🐾, 🐾, park – ⅔ rest, ☎ ℗. 🆗 🆎 💳. 🐾
Meals 17.00/32.00 t. 🍴 4.50 – **20 rm** ⊇ (dinner included) 90.00/200.00 t. – SB.

KILDRUMMY Aberdeenshire **401** L 12 Scotland G. – ⊠ Alford.

See : Castle★ AC.

Exc. : Huntly Castle (Heraldic carvings★★★) N : 15 m. by A 97 – Craigievar Castle★, SE : 13 m. by A 97, A 944 and A 980.

Edinburgh 137 – Aberdeen 35.

🏨 **Kildrummy Castle** ⌕, AB33 8RA, S : 1 ¼ m. on A 97 ℰ (019755) 71288, Fax (019755) 71345, ≤ gardens and Kildrummy Castle, « 19C mansion in extensive park », ⌕ – ⌕ rest, 🆀 ☎ ❿. 🆀🆀 🆀🆀 🆀🆀 🆀🆀

closed 4 January-5 February – **Meals** 14.95/28.00 **st.** and a la carte ₆ 6.00 – **16 rm** ⌕ 80.00/ 150.00 **st.** – SB.

KILFINAN Argyll and Bute **401** E 16 – pop. 906 – ⊠ Tighnabruaich.

Edinburgh 124 – Glasgow 78 – Oban 78.

🏨 **Kilfinan** ⌕, PA21 2EP, ℰ (01700) 821201, Fax (01700) 821205, ⌕ – 🆀 ☎ ❿. 🆀🆀 🆀🆀 🆀🆀 ⌕

closed February – **Meals** – (see below) – **11 rm** ⌕ 48.00/96.00 **st.** – SB.

✕✕ **Kilfinan** (at Kilfinan H.), PA21 2EP, ℰ (01700) 821201, Fax (01700) 821205, ⌕ – ⌕ ❿. 🆀🆀 🆀🆀 🆀🆀

closed February – **Meals** (bar lunch)/dinner 28.00 **st.** ₆ 5.80.

KILLEARN Stirling **401** G 15 – ⊠ Glasgow.

Edinburgh 60 – Glasgow 19 – Perth 55 – Stirling 22.

✕ **Black Bull** with rm, 2 The Square, G63 9NG, ℰ (01360) 550215, Fax (01360) 550143, ⌕ – ⌕ 🆀 ☎ ❿. 🆀🆀 🆀🆀 🆀🆀 ⌕

Conservatory : Meals 22.00 **st.** (dinner) and lunch a la carte approx. 16.00 ₆ 5.95 –

Brasserie : Meals a la carte approx. 18.95 **t.** ₆ 5.95 – **11 rm** ⌕ 47.00/60.00 **t.** – SB.

KILLIECHRONAN Argyll and Bute **401** C 14 – see Mull (Isle of).

KILLIECRANKIE Perthshire and Kinross **401** I 13 – see Pitlochry.

KILLIN Stirling **401** H 14 Scotland G. – pop. 1 108.

Exc. : Loch Tay★★, Ben Lawers★★, NE : 8 m. by A 827 – Loch Earn★★, SE : 7 m. by A 827 and A 85.

🆀 Killin ℰ (01567) 820312.

🆀 Breadalbane Folklore Centre, Falls of Dochart, FK21 8XE ℰ (01567) 820254 (March December).

Edinburgh 72 – Dundee 65 – Perth 43 – Oban 54.

🏨 **Dall Lodge Country House,** Main St., FK21 8TN, ℰ (01567) 820217 Fax (01567) 820726, ⌕ – ⌕ rest, 🆀 ☎ ❿. 🆀🆀 🆀🆀 ⌕

March-October – **Meals** (dinner only) 22.50 **t.** ₆ 5.25 – **10 rm** ⌕ 45.00/91.00 **t.**

⌂ Breadalbane House, Main St., FK21 8UT, ℰ (01567) 820386, Fax (01567) 820386 – ⌕ 🆀 ❿

5 rm.

at Ardeonaig (Perthshire and Kinross) NE : 6 ¾ m. – ⊠ Killin (Stirling).

🏨 **Ardeonaig** ⌕, South Lochtayside, FK21 8SU, ℰ (01567) 820400, Fax (01567) 820282, ≤ ⌕, ⌕, park – ⌕ rest, ❿. 🆀🆀 🆀🆀

restricted opening November to March – **Meals** (closed lunch Tuesday to Thursday) 28.50 **t.** (dinner) and lunch a la carte 19.75 **t.** ₆ 6.75 – **13 rm** ⌕ (dinner included) 74.00/136.00 **t.** – SB.

KILMARNOCK East Ayrshire **401** **402** G 17 Scotland G.

See : Dean Castle (arms and armour★, musical instruments★).

🆀 62 Bank St., KA1 1ER ℰ (01563) 539090.

Edinburgh 64 – Ayr 13 – Glasgow 25.

🏨 **Travelodge,** Kilmarnock bypass, Bellfield Interchange, KA1 5LQ, at junction of A 71 with A 76 and A 77 ℰ (01563) 573810, Fax (01563) 573810, Reservations (Freephone) 0800 850950 – ⌕ rm, 🆀 ⌕ ❿. 🆀🆀 🆀🆀 🆀🆀 🆀🆀 🆀🆀 ⌕

Meals (grill rest.) – **40 rm** 35.95 **t.**

KILMORE Argyll and Bute **401** D 14 – see Oban.

KILNINVER Argyll and Bute **401** D 14 – see Oban.

KINCARDINE Fife 401 I 15 *Scotland G. – pop. 1 089.*

Env. : *Culross*★★ (*Village*★★★, *Palace*★★ AC, *Study*★ AC) E : 4 m. by B 9037.

🏌 Tulliallan ℘ (01259) 30396.

Edinburgh 30 – Dunfermline 9 – Glasgow 25 – Stirling 12.

✗ **Unicorn Inn,** 15 Excise St., FK10 4LN, ℘ (01259) 730704, *Fax* (01259) 731567 – ◍◍ ⅄ ◍

closed Sunday lunch, Monday, 1-3 January, 2 weeks July and 25-26 December – **Meals** (booking essential) a la carte 11.70/21.35 t. ⏧ 6.25.

KINCLAVEN Perthshire and Kinross 401 J 14 – *pop. 394 –* ⌧ *Stanley.*

Edinburgh 56 – Perth 12.

🏡 **Ballathie House** 🦢, PH1 4QN, ℘ (01250) 883268, *Fax* (01250) 883396, ≼, « Country house in extensive grounds on banks of River Tay », ➘, 🚜 – ⅛✗ rest, 🕎 ☎ & ℗. ◍◍ ⅄

◍ 𝓥𝓘𝓢𝓐 𝒥𝒞𝒷

Meals 26.50 t. (dinner) and lunch a la carte 11.25/14.75 t. ⏧ 6.50 – **26 rm** ⌸ 80.00/ 180.00 t., 1 suite – SB.

KINCRAIG Highland 401 I 12 *Scotland G. –* ⌧ *Kingussie.*

See : *Highland Wildlife Park*★ AC.

Exc. : *The Cairngorms*★★ (≼★★★) – ✳★★★ *from Cairn Gorm,* E : 14 m. by A 9 and B 970.

Edinburgh 119 – Inverness 37 – Perth 75.

🏠 **Ossian,** The Brae, PH21 1QD, ℘ (01540) 651242, *Fax* (01540) 651633, ≼, ➘, 🚜 – ⅛✗ rest,

🕎 ☎ ℗. ◍◍ 𝓥𝓘𝓢𝓐 𝒥𝒞𝒷

closed January and November – **Meals** (bar lunch)/dinner a la carte 15.00/22.00 t. ⏧ 5.75 –

9 rm ⌸ 30.00/60.00 st.

KINGUSSIE Highland 401 H 12 *Scotland G. – pop. 1 298.*

Env. : *Highland Wildlife Park*★ AC, NE : 4 m. by A 9.

Exc. : *Aviemore*★, NE : 11 m. by A 9 – *The Cairngorms*★★ (≼★★★) – ✳★★★ *from Cairn Gorm,* NE : 18 m. by B 970.

🏌 Gynack Rd ℘ (01540) 661374.

🛈 King St., PH21 1HP ℘ (01540) 661297 (summer only).

Edinburgh 117 – Inverness 41 – Perth 73.

🏡 **Scot House,** Newtonmore Rd, PH21 1HE, ℘ (01540) 661351, *Fax* (01540) 661111 –

⅛✗ rest, 🕎 ☎ ℗. ◍◍ 𝓥𝓘𝓢𝓐 𝒥𝒞𝒷

closed 25-26 December and 4 January-8 February – **Meals** (bar lunch)/dinner 18.50 t. and a la carte ⏧ 6.00 – **9 rm** ⌸ (dinner included) 57.50/102.00 t. – SB.

🏠 **Columba House,** Manse Rd, PH21 1JF, ℘ (01540) 661402, *Fax* (01540) 661652, 🚜 – 🕎

☎ ℗. ◍◍ ⅄ 𝓥𝓘𝓢𝓐 𝒥𝒞𝒷

Meals 18.00 t. (dinner) and lunch a la carte 7.70/14.85 ⏧ 4.30 – **7 rm** ⌸ 40.00/60.00 t. – SB.

⌂ **Avondale,** Newtonmore Rd, PH21 1HF, ℘ (01540) 661731, *Fax* (01540) 661731, 🚜 – ⅛✗

🕎 ℗

Meals (by arrangement) 9.00 st. – **6 rm** ⌸ 25.00/42.00.

⌂ **St. Helens** without rest., Ardbroilach Rd, PH21 1JX, ℘ (01540) 661430 – ⅛✗ ℗. ✀

3 rm ⌸ 40.00.

✗✗✗ **The Cross** 🦢 with rm, Tweed Mill Brae, Ardbroilach Rd, PH21 1TC, ℘ (01540) 661166, *Fax* (01540) 661080, « Converted tweed mill » – ⅛✗ ☎ ℗. ◍◍ 𝓥𝓘𝓢𝓐. ✀

closed 5 January-28 February and 1 to 26 December – **Meals** (closed Tuesday) (booking essential) (dinner only) 35.00 st. ⏧ 7.50 – **9 rm** ⌸ (dinner included) 105.00/190.00 st.

KINLOCHMOIDART Highland 401 C 13 – ⌧ *Lochailort.*

Edinburgh 153 – Inverness 110 – Oban 74.

✗ **Kinacarra,** PH38 4ND, ℘ (01967) 431238, ≼ – ⅛✗ ℗

Easter-October – **Meals** (closed Monday) (booking essential) (light lunch) a la carte 10.60/ 21.50 t.

Entrez à l'hôtel le Guide à la main, vous montrerez ainsi,
qu'il vous conduit là en confiance.

KINROSS *Perthshire and Kinross* **401** *J 15 – pop. 5 047.*

🏌, 🏌 *Green Hotel, 2 The Muirs* ℘ *(01577) 863407 –* 🏌 *Milnathort, South St.* ℘ *(01577) 864069 –* 🏌 *Bishopshire, Kinnesswood* ℘ *(01592) 780203.*

🎫 *Kinross Service Area (junction 6, M 90) KY13 7BA* ℘ *(01577) 863680.*

Edinburgh 28 – Dunfermline 13 – Perth 18 – Stirling 25.

🏨 **Green,** 2 The Muirs, KY13 7AS, ℘ *(01577) 863467, Fax (01577) 863180,* 🖙, 🔲, 🏌, 🏐, 🚗, ✖, squash – 📺 ☎ 🅿 – 🔏 140. 🐵 🖭 *VISA*
Meals (bar lunch)/dinner 22.50 **st.** and a la carte – **47 rm** � 73.00/150.00 **st.** – SB.

🏨 **Windlestrae,** KY13 7AS, ℘ *(01577) 863217, Fax (01577) 864733,* 🏋, 🖙, 🔲, 🚗 – 📺 ☎ 🕭 🅿 – 🔏 350. 🐵 🖭 🔘 *VISA*
Meals 12.95/23.50 **t.** and a la carte ⓘ 8.95 – **43 rm** ⊟ 80.00/118.00 **t.**, 2 suites – SB.

🏠 **Travelodge** without rest., Kincardine Rd, KY13 7NQ, W : 1 m. by A 922 on A 977 ℘ *(01577) 863123, Fax (01577) 864108,* Reservations (Freephone) 0800 850950 – ✷ 📺 ☎ 🕭 🅿 – 🔏 90. 🐵 *VISA JCB* ✖
35 rm 46.95 **t.**

✗ **Croftbank House,** Station Rd, KY13 7TG, ℘ *(01577) 863819* – ✷ 🅿 🐵 *VISA*
closed Monday, 1-2 January and 1 week February – Meals a la carte 15.70/23.65 **t.** ⓘ 7.50.

🍴 **Lomond Country Inn,** with rm, Kinnesswood, KY13 7HN, E : 4 ½ m. by A 922 on A 911 ℘ *(01592) 840253, Fax (01592) 840693,* ← – 📺 ☎ 🕭 🅿 🐵 🖭 🔘 *VISA.* ✖
Meals 12.50 **t.** and a la carte ⓘ 4.25 – **11 rm** ⊟ 40.00/60.00 **t.** – SB.

at Cleish SW : 4½ m. by B 996 off B 9097 – ⊠ Kinross.

🏨 **Nivingston House** 🏠, KY13 7LS, ℘ *(01577) 850216, Fax (01577) 850238,* ←, 🚗, park – 📺 ☎ 🅿 🐵 🖭 🔘 *VISA JCB*
closed 4 to 18 January – Meals 15.50/25.00 **t.** and a la carte ⓘ 7.40 – **17 rm** ⊟ 77.50/135.00 **t.** – SB.

Les prix	Pour toutes précisions sur les prix indiqués dans ce guide, reportez-vous aux pages de l'introduction.

KINTORE *Aberdeenshire* **401** *M 12.*

Edinburgh 136 – Aberdeen 14 – Inverness 91.

🏠 **Torryburn,** School Rd, AB51 0XP, ℘ *(01467) 632269, Fax (01467) 632271,* 🚗, ✖ – 📺 ☎ 🅿 – 🔏 90. 🐵 🖭 *VISA*
closed 1 January – Meals (bar lunch Monday to Friday) a la carte 12.50/19.10 **st.** – **9 rm** ⊟ 39.50/55.00 **st.** – SB.

KINTYRE (Peninsula) *Argyll and Bute* **401** *D 16 Scotland G.*

See : *Carradale*★ – *Saddell (Collection of grave slabs*★*).*

🏌, 🏌 *Machrihanish, Campbeltown* ℘ *(01586) 810213.*

✈ *Campbeltown Airport :* ℘ *(01586) 553797.*

⚓ from Claonaig to Isle of Arran (Lochranza) (Caledonian MacBrayne Ltd) frequent services daily (30 mn) – from Kennacraig to Isle of Islay (Port Ellen or Port Askaig) (Caledonian MacBrayne Ltd) 1-3 daily – from Kennacraig to Oban via Isle of Colonsay (Scalasaig) and Isle of Islay (Port Askaig) weekly – from Campbeltown to Ballycastle (Argyll and Antrim Steam Packet Co.) 2 daily (3 h).

Campbeltown.

🎫 *MacKinnon House, The Pier, PA28 6EF* ℘ *(01586) 552056.*
Edinburgh 176.

🏨 **Seafield,** Kilkerran Rd, PA28 6JL, ℘ *(01586) 554385, Fax (01586) 552741* – 📺 ☎ 🅿 🐵
Meals a la carte 15.00/24.35 **t.** ⓘ 5.95 – **9 rm** ⊟ 40.00/60.00 **t.** – SB.

🏠 **Balegreggan Country House** 🏠, Balegreggan Rd, PA28 6NN, NE : 1 m. by A 83 ℘ *(01586) 552062, Fax (01586) 552062,* ←, 🚗 – ✷ 📺 🅿 🐵 *VISA.* ✖
Meals 25.00 **s.** – **4 rm** ⊟ 50.00/80.00 **s.** – SB.

🏠 **Rosemount** without rest., Low Askomil, PA28 6EN, ℘ *(01586) 553552,* ←, 🚗 – 📺 🅿
5 rm ⊟ 22.00/40.00 **s.**

Machrihanish – *pop. 5 722* – ⊠ Campbeltown.

Edinburgh 182 – Oban 95.

🏠 **Ardell House** without rest., PA28 6PT, ℘ *(01586) 810235, Fax (01586) 810235,* ←, 🚗 – 🅿 🐵 *VISA*
March-October – **10 rm** ⊟ 28.00/60.00.

Tarbert.

🏌 Kilberry Rd, Tarbert 🖉 (01880) 820565.

🖪 Harbour St. 🖉 (01880) 820429 (summer only).

🏨 **Columba,** East Pier Rd, PA29 6UF, E : ¾ m. 🖉 (01880) 820808, Fax (01880) 820808, ≤, ≤ₛ
– ६♣ rest, 📺 **⚙**. **◑⊙** **VISA**
closed 25 and 26 December – **Meals** (bar lunch Monday to Saturday)/dinner 19.50 ₰ 5.50 –
9 rm ⊏ 33.95/77.90 **st.**, 1 suite – SB.

✗ **Anchorage,** Harbour St., PA29 6UD, 🖉 (01880) 820881, Fax (01880) 820881 – **◑⊙** **VISA** **JCB**
restricted opening in winter – **Meals** (dinner only) a la carte 20.40/23.40 **t.** ₰ 8.95.

🛈 ATS Burnside St., Campbeltown 🖉 (01586) 554404

KIRKBEAN Dumfries and Galloway **401** **402** J 19 – ⊠ Dumfries.
Edinburgh 89 – Carlisle 41 – Dumfries 12.

🏠 **Cavens Country House** ⤬, DG2 8AA, 🖉 (01387) 880234, Fax (01387) 880234, ☞ –
६♣ rest, 📺 **⚙**. **◑⊙** **VISA**. ⫶
Meals (by arrangement) 16.50 **st.** – **6 rm** ⊏ 35.00/57.00 **st.**

KIRKCOLM Dumfries and Galloway **401** **402** E 19 – see Stranraer.

KIRKCUDBRIGHT Dumfries and Galloway **401** **402** H 19 Scotland G. – pop. 4 188.
See : Town★.
Env. : Dundrennan Abbey★ AC, SE : 5 m. by A 711.
🏌 Stirling Cres. 🖉 (01557) 330314.
🖪 Harbour Sq., DG6 4HY 🖉 (01557) 330494 (summer only).
Edinburgh 108 – Dumfries 28 – Stranraer 50.

🏨 **Selkirk Arms,** Old High St., DG6 4JG, 🖉 (01557) 330402, Fax (01557) 331639, ☞ – ६♣ 📺
☎ **⚙**. **◑⊙** **AE** **①** **VISA** **JCB**. ⫶
Meals (bar lunch)/dinner 21.75 **st.** ₰ 4.25 – **16 rm** ⊏ 49.00/80.00 **st.** – SB.

🏠 **Gladstone House** without rest., 48 High St., DG6 4JX, 🖉 (01557) 331734,
Fax (01557) 331734, ☞ – ६♣ 📺. **◑⊙** **VISA**. ⫶
3 rm ⊏ 29.00/58.00 **s.**

🏠 **Baytree House,** 110 High St., DG6 4JQ, 🖉 (01557) 330824, ☞ – ६♣ 📺 **⚙**
Meals (by arrangement) (communal dining) 15.00 **s.** – **3 rm** ⊏ 50.00/56.00 **s.** – SB.

KIRKTON OF GLENISLA Angus **401** K 13.
Edinburgh 73 – Aberdeen 60 – Arbroath 32 – Pitlochry 28.

🏨 **Glenisla** ⤬, PH11 8PH, on B 951 🖉 (01575) 582223, Fax (01575) 582223 – ६♣ rm, **⚙**. **◑⊙**
VISA. ⫶
closed 21 to 28 December – **Meals** a la carte 11.15/21.55 **t.** ₰ 4.75 – **6 rm** ⊏ 45.00/75.00 **t.**
– SB.

KIRKWALL Orkney Islands **401** L 7 – see Orkney Islands (Mainland).

KIRRIEMUIR Angus **401** K 13 – pop. 6 347.
Edinburgh 65 – Aberdeen 50 – Dundee 16 – Perth 30.

🏠 **Purgavie Farm** ⤬, Lintrathen, DD8 5HZ, W : 6 ¾ m. on B 951 🖉 (01575) 560213,
Fax (01575) 560213, ≤ – ६♣ 📺 **⚙**
Meals (communal dining) 12.00 **s.** – **3 rm** ⊏ 25.00/40.00 **s.**

KYLESKU Highland **401** E 9 Scotland G.
Env. : Loch Assynt★★, S : 6 m. by A 894.
Edinburgh 256 – Inverness 100 – Ullapool 34.

🏨 **Kylesku** ⤬, IV27 4HW, 🖉 (01971) 502231, Fax (01971) 502313, ≤ Loch Glencoul and
mountains, ⤬, ☜ – ६♣ rest, 📺. **◑⊙** **VISA** **JCB**
March-October – **Meals** 19.50 **t.** and a la carte ₰ 3.50 – **8 rm** ⊏ 35.00/60.00 **t.** – SB.

🏨 **Newton Lodge** ⤬, IV27 4HW, S : 2 m. on A 894 🖉 (01971) 502070, ≤ Loch Glencoul and
mountains – ६♣ 📺 **⚙**. **◑⊙** **VISA**. ⫶
March-mid October – **Meals** (residents only) (dinner only) 13.00 **t.** ₰ 5.50 – **7 rm** ⊏ 58.00 **t.**

SCOTLAND

LADYBANK Fife **401** K 15 Scotland G. – pop. 1 373.
Env. : Falkland★ – Palace of Falkland★ – Gardens★ – Village★, S : ½ m. by A 914 on A 912.
Edinburgh 38 – Dundee 20 – Stirling 40.

⚑ **Redlands Country Lodge** ⌂ without rest., KY15 7SH, E : ¾ m. by Kingskettle rd taking first left after railway bridge on unmarked road ℰ (01337) 831091, Fax (01337) 831091, ⚞ – 📺 **℗**
4 rm.

LAID Highland **401** F 8 – ✉ Lairg.
⚐ Balnakeil, Durness ℰ (01971) 511364.
Edinburgh 242 – Thurso 59 – Ullapool 95.

⚑ **Port-na-Con House** ⌂, Loch Eribol, IV27 4UN, ℰ (01971) 511367, Fax (01971) 511367, ≼ Loch Eribol – ⚞⚞, **MO** **VISA**
March-October – **Meals** (dinner only) 12.00 st. and a la carte – **3 rm** ⚏ 24.00/36.00 st.

LAIRG Highland **401** G9 – pop. 857.
Edinburgh 218 – Inverness 61 – Wick 72.

⚑ **Park House**, IV27 4AU, ℰ (01549) 402208, Fax (01549) 402208, ≼, ⚞ – 📺 **℗**. **MO** **VISA**
closed Christmas and New Year – **3 rm** ⚏ (dinner included) 47.00/74.00 – SB.

LAMLASH North Ayrshire **401** E 17 – see Arran (Isle of).

LANGBANK Renfrewshire **401** G 16 Scotland G.
Env. : Greenock (≼★★), W : 6 m. by A 8.
Edinburgh 63 – Glasgow 17 – Greenock 7.

🏰 Gleddoch House ⌂, PA14 6YE, SE : 1 m. by B 789 ℰ (01475) 540711, Fax (01475) 540201, ≼ Clyde and countryside, ⚐s, ⚑, ⚞, park, squash – ⚞⚞ rm, 📺 ☎ **℗** – 🕭 80
39 rm.

LARGS North Ayrshire **401 402** F 16 Scotland G. – pop. 11 297.
See : Largs Old Kirk★ AC.
⚐ Irvine Rd ℰ (01475) 674681.
⚓ to Great Cumbrae Island (Cumbrae Slip) (Caledonian MacBrayne Ltd) frequent service daily (10 mn) – to Isle of Bute (Rothesay) and Isle of Arran (Brodick) (Caledonian MacBrayne Ltd) 3 weekly.
🛈 Promenade, KA30 8BG ℰ (01475) 673765.
Edinburgh 76 – Ayr 32 – Glasgow 30.

🏨 **Brisbane House**, 14 Greenock Rd, Esplanade, KA30 8NF, ℰ (01475) 687200 Fax (01475) 676295, ≼ – 📺 ☎ **℗** – 🕭 50. **MO** **AE** **①** **VISA**, ⚞
Meals (bar lunch)/dinner 19.75 t. and a la carte ⚇ 5.90 – **23 rm** ⚏ 65.00/140.00 – SB.

LERWICK Shetland Islands **401** Q 3 – see Shetland Islands (Mainland).

LETHAM Fife **401** K 15 – ✉ Cupar.
Edinburgh 42 – Dundee 14 – Perth 28.

🏨 **Fernie Castle** ⌂, KY15 7RU, NE : ½ m. on A 914 ℰ (01337) 810381, Fax (01337) 810422 « Part 14C », ⚞, park – ⚞⚞ rm, 📺 ☎ **℗** – 🕭 120. **MO** **AE** **VISA**
Meals (bar lunch Monday to Friday)/dinner 19.50 t. and a la carte ⚇ 6.95 – **15 rm** ⚏ 58.50/98.50 t. – SB.

LESLIE Fife **401** K 15 – see Glenrothes.

LEVEN Fife **401** K 15.
Edinburgh 33 – Dundee 33 – Stirling 42.

🏨 **Old Manor**, Leven Rd, Lundin Links, KY8 6AJ, E : 2 m. on A 915 ℰ (01333) 320368 Fax (01333) 320911, ≼, ⚞ – ⚞⚞ rest, 📺 ☎ **℗**. **MO** **AE** **VISA** **JCB**
Meals (grill dinner Sunday) 12.50/25.00 st. and a la carte ⚇ 5.50 – **23 rm** ⚏ 75.00/160.00 st., 1 suite – SB.

LEVERBURGH Western Isles (Outer Hebrides) **401** Y 10 – see Lewis and Harris (Isle of).

712

LEWIS and HARRIS (Isle of) *Western Isles (Outer Hebrides)* **401** A 9 *Scotland G.*

See : *Callanish Standing Stones*★★ – *Carloway Broch*★ – *St. Clement's Church, Rodel (tomb*★*).*

🚢 *from Stornoway to Ullapool (Mainland) (Caledonian MacBrayne Ltd) (2 h 45 mn) – from Kyles Scalpay to the Isle of Scalpay (Caledonian MacBrayne Ltd) (10 mn) – from Tarbert to Isle of Skye (Uig) (Caledonian MacBrayne Ltd) 1-3 daily (1 h 45 mn) – from Tarbert to Portavadie (Caledonian MacBrayne Ltd) (summer only) frequent services daily (20 mn) – from Leverburgh to North Uist (Otternish) (Caledonian MacBrayne Ltd) (1 h 20 mn).*

LEWIS.

Breasclete.

↑ **Eshcol** ⌂, 21 Breasclete, HS2 9ED, ℰ (01851) 621357, *Fax* (01851) 621357, ≤, 🌴 – 🖘 📺 ⓟ
March-October – **Meals** 18.00 **st.** – **3 rm** ⊇ 27.00/54.00 **st.**

Galson.

↑ **Galson Farm** ⌂, South Galson, HS2 0SH, ℰ (01851) 850492, *Fax* (01851) 850492, ≤, « Working farm », 🌴, park – 🖘 ⓟ, 🅜🅒 VISA
Meals (communal dining) (by arrangement) 16.00 **s.** ⓵ 3.75 – **3 rm** ⊇ 35.00/88.00 **s.**

Keose (Ceos).

↑ **Handa** ⌂, 18 Keose Glebe, HS2 9JX, ℰ (01851) 830334, ≤, 🎣, 🌴 – 🖘 ⓟ
3 rm.

Stornoway.

🛈 *Lady Lever Park* ℰ (01851) 702240.
🛈 *26 Cromwell St.*, HS1 2DD ℰ (01851) 703088.

🏨 **Cabarfeidh**, Manor Park, HS1 2EU, N : ½ m. on A 859 ℰ (01851) 702604, *Fax* (01851) 705572 – 🛗, 🍽 rest, 📺 ☎ ⓟ – 🖄 300. 🅜🅒 🅐🅔 ⓞ VISA
Meals (bar lunch)/dinner 19.75 **st.** and a la carte ⓵ 8.00 – **46 rm** ⊇ 69.00/92.00 **st.** – SB.

↑ **Ravenswood** without rest., 12 Matheson Rd, HS1 2LR, ℰ (01851) 702673, 🌴 – 🖘 📺 ⓟ. 🎴
closed 2 weeks October and Christmas-New Year – **3 rm** ⊇ 20.00/40.00.

HARRIS.

Ardvourlie.

🏨 **Ardvourlie Castle** ⌂, HS3 3AB, ℰ (01859) 502307, *Fax* (01859) 502348, ≤ Loch Seaforth and mountains, « Restored Victorian hunting lodge on shore of Loch Seaforth », 🌴, park – 🖘 rest, ⓟ. 🎴
April-October – **Meals** (residents only) (dinner only) 25.00 ⓵ 7.00 – **4 rm** ⊇ (dinner included) 85.00/150.00 **s.**

Leverburgh.

↑ **Carminish** ⌂, 1a Strond, HS5 3UD, S : 1 m. on Srandda rd ℰ (01859) 520400, ≤, 🌴 – 🖘 ⓟ
closed December and January – **Meals** (by arrangement) (communal dining) 13.50 **st.** – **3 rm** ⊇ 38.00/56.00 **st.**

Tarbert – *pop. 795* – ✉ *Harris.*

↑ **Leachin House** ⌂, HS3 3AH, NW : 1 ¼ m. on A 859 ℰ (01859) 502157, ≤ Loch Tarbert, 🌴 – 🖘 📺 VISA. 🎴
closed 15 December-15 January – **Meals** (communal dining) 23.00 **st.** – **3 rm** ⊇ 37.00/74.00 **st.**

↑ **Allan Cottage**, HS3 3DJ, ℰ (01859) 502146 – 🖘 📺
April-September – **Meals** (communal dining) 18.00 **s.** – **3 rm** ⊇ 30.00/60.00 **s.**

Particularly pleasant hotels and restaurants
are shown in the Guide by a red symbol.

Please send us the names
of anywhere you have enjoyed your stay.

Your **Michelin Guide** will be even better.

🏨🏨🏨 … ↑

ⅩⅩⅩⅩⅩ … Ⅹ

LEWISTON *Highland* **401** G 12 *Scotland G.*

Env. : *Loch Ness*★★ – *The Great Glen*★.
Edinburgh 173 – Inverness 17.

⌂ **Woodlands,** East Lewiston, IV3 6UL, ℰ (01456) 450356, ⇌ – ⅍ 🔟 🅿. 🕮 *VISA*. ⅍
closed 25 and 26 December – **Meals** 9.00 – **3 rm** ⊇ 18.00/36.00.

⌂ **Glen Rowan** without rest., West Lewiston, IV3 6UW, ℰ (01456) 450235
Fax (01456) 450817, ⇌ – ⅍ 🔟 🅿. 🕮 ᴀᴇ *VISA*. ⅍
closed 25-26 and 31 December and 1 January – **3 rm** ⊇ 42.00/45.00 st.

LINICLATE *Western Isles (Outer Hebrides)* **401** X/Y 11 – *see Uist (Isles of).*

LINLITHGOW *West Lothian* **401** J 16 *Scotland G.* – *pop. 13 689.*

See : *Town*★★ – *Palace*★★ *AC* : *Courtyard (fountain*★★*), Great Hall (Hooded Fireplace*★★*)*
Gateway★ – *Old Town*★ – *St. Michaels*★.
Env. : *Cairnpapple Hill*★ *AC, SW : 5 m. by A 706 – House of the Binns (plasterwork ceilings*★
AC, NE : 4 ½ m. by A 803 and A 904.
Exc. : *Hopetoun House*★★ *AC, E : 7 m. by A 706 and A 904 – Abercorn Parish Churcl*
(Hopetoun Loft★★*) NE : 7 m. by A 803 and A 904.*
🛅 Braehead ℰ (01506) 842585 – 🛅 West Lothian, Airngath Hill ℰ (01506) 826030.
🖪 Burgh Halls, The Cross, EH49 7EJ ℰ (01506) 844600.
Edinburgh 19 – Falkirk 9 – Glasgow 35.

XXX **Champany Inn,** Champany, EH49 7LU, NE : 2 m. on A 803 at junction with A 90₄
ℰ (01506) 834532, Fax (01506) 834302, « Converted horse mill », ⇌ – 🅿. 🕮 ᴀᴇ ① *VISA*
ᴊᴄʙ
closed Saturday lunch, Sunday, 25 December and 1 January – **Meals** (Beef Specialities
15.75 **t.** (lunch) and a la carte 31.50/48.90 **t.** ᵻ 12.50.

XX **Livingston's,** 52 High St., EH49 7AE, ℰ (01506) 846565, ⇌ – ⅍. 🕮 *VISA*
closed Sunday, Monday, 3 weeks January and 1 week October – **Meals** 10.00 **t**
(lunch) and a la carte 19.85/27.15 **t.** ᵻ 5.50.

LIVINGSTON *West Lothian* **401** J 16 – *pop. 22 357.*

🛅 Bathgate, Edinburgh Rd ℰ (01506) 652232 – 🛅 Deer Park C.C., Knightsridge ℰ (01506)
438843.
Edinburgh 16 – Falkirk 23 – Glasgow 32.

🏢 **Hilton National,** Almondview, Almondvale, EH54 6QB, ℰ (01506) 431222
Fax (01506) 434666, ᵻₛ, ≘ₛ, 🔲 – ⅍ 🔟 ☎ & 🅿 – 🔬 120. 🕮 ᴀᴇ ① *VISA* ᴊᴄʙ
Meals 12.50/17.50 **t.** and a la carte ᵻ 6.50 – ⊇ 10.25 – **120 rm** 129.00/145.00 **t.** – SB.

🏛 **Travel Inn,** Deer Park Av., Deer Park, Knightsridge, EH54 8AD, on A 899 at junction 3 o₁
M 8 ℰ (01506) 439202, Fax (01506) 438912 – ⅍ 🔟 ☎ & 🅿. 🕮 ᴀᴇ ① *VISA*. ⅍
Meals (grill rest.) – **52 rm** 36.50 **t.**

LOCHBOISDALE *Western Isles (Outer Hebrides)* **401** Y 12 – *see Uist (Isles of).*

LOCHCARRON *Highland* **401** D 11 *Scotland G.* – *pop. 870.*

Env. : *Wester Ross*★★★ – *Loch Earn*★★.
🖪 Main St. ℰ (01520) 722357 (summer only).
Edinburgh 221 – Inverness 65 – Kyle of Lochalsh 23.

⌂ **Rockvilla,** Main St., IV54 8YB, ℰ (01520) 722379, Fax (01520) 722379, ≼ Loch Carron –
⅍ rest, 🔟. 🕮 ᴀᴇ *VISA* ᴊᴄʙ. ⅍
closed 25 December and 1 January – **Meals** approx. 16.50 **t.** ᵻ 5.90 – **4 rm** ⊇ 37.00/54.00 **t**

LOCHEARNHEAD *Stirling* **401** H 14 *Scotland G.*

Env. : *Loch Earn*★★.
Edinburgh 65 – Glasgow 56 – Oban 57 – Perth 36.

🏛 **Mansewood Country House,** FK19 8NS, S : ½ m. on A 84 ℰ (01567) 830213, ⇌ –
⅍ rest, 🔟 🅿. 🕮 *VISA*. ⅍
Meals (residents only) (dinner only) 18.00 st. ᵻ 5.95 – **6 rm** ⊇ 29.00/44.00 st. – SB.

LOCHEPORT *Western Isles (Outer Hebrides)* **401** Y 11 – *see Uist (Isles of).*

LOCHGILPHEAD *Argyll and Bute* **401** D 15 *Scotland G. – pop. 2 421.*

Env. : *Loch Fyne*★★, *E : 3 ½ m. by A 83.*

🏌9 *Blarbuie Rd* ♟ *(01546) 602340.*

🛈 *Lochnell St., PA31 8JN* ♟ *(01546) 602344 (summer only).*

Edinburgh 130 – Glasgow 84 – Oban 38.

🏠 **Empire Travel Lodge** *without rest., Union St., PA31 8JS,* ♟ *(01546) 602381 –* 📺 ዿ **ₚ**.
◍❾ VISA. ⅍
closed 24 December-2 January **– 9 rm** ⌑ *23.00/46.00* **st.**

at Cairnbaan *NW : 2¼ m. by A 816 on B 841 –* ✉ *Lochgilphead.*

🏨 **Cairnbaan,** *PA31 8SQ,* ♟ *(01546) 603668, Fax (01546) 606045 –* ✑ 📺 ☎ **ₚ** – 🔏 *120.* **◍❾**
AE VISA. ⅍
closed first 2 weeks November and first 2 weeks February – **Meals** *(bar lunch)/dinner*
a la carte 13.95/24.15 **t.** ▯ *6.95 –* **11 rm** ⌑ *55.00/95.00* **st.**

LOCH HARRAY *Orkney Islands* **401** K 6 – *see Orkney Islands (Mainland).*

LOCHINVER *Highland* **401** E 9 *Scotland G. –* ✉ *Lairg.*

See : *Village*★.

Env. : *Loch Assynt*★★, *E : 6 m. by A 837.*

🛈 *Main St., ID27 4LF* ♟ *(01571) 844330 (summer only).*

Edinburgh 251 – Inverness 95 – Wick 105.

🏨🏨 **Inver Lodge,** *IV27 4LU,* ♟ *(01571) 844496, Fax (01571) 844395,* ≤ *Loch Inver Bay, Suilven*
and Canisp mountains, ⌸, ⌇, ☞, *park –* ✑ *rest,* 📺 ☎ **ₚ**. **◍❾ AE ① VISA JCB**
11 April-October – **Meals** *(bar lunch)/dinner 27.50* **st.** *and a la carte* ▯ *4.75 –* **20 rm**
⌑ *80.00/130.00* **st.** *– SB.*

🏠 **The Albannach** ⌇, *Baddidarroch, IV27 4LP, W : 1 m. by Baddidarroch rd*
♟ *(01571) 844407, Fax (01571) 844407,* ≤ *Loch Inver Bay and Suilven,* ☞ *–* ✑ **ₚ VISA**.
⅍
booking essential, closed January and February and restricted opening November and
December – **Meals** *(booking essential) (dinner only) 25.00* **t.** ▯ *8.00 –* **5 rm** ⌑ *(dinner*
included) 77.00/132.00 **t.**

⌂ **Davar** *without rest., Baddidarroch Rd, IV27 4LJ, W : ½ m. on Baddidarroch rd*
♟ *(01571) 844501,* ≤ *Loch Inver Bay and Suilven –* 📺 **ₚ**. ⅍
April-October – **3 rm** ⌑ *33.00/42.00.*

LOCHMADDY *Western Isles (Outer Hebrides)* **401** Y 11 – *see Uist (Isles of).*

LOCHRANZA *North Ayrshire* **401 402** E 16 – *see Arran (Isle of).*

LOCKERBIE *Dumfries and Galloway* **401 402** J 18 – *pop. 2 301.*

🏌18 *Corrie Rd* ♟ *(01576) 203363 –* 🏌18 *Lochmaben, Castlehill Gate* ♟ *(01387) 810552.*

Edinburgh 74 – Carlisle 27 – Dumfries 13 – Glasgow 73.

🏨🏨 **Dryfesdale,** *DG11 2SF, NW : 1 m. on B 7068* ♟ *(01576) 202427, Fax (01576) 204187,* ≤,
☞ *–* ✑ 📺 ☎ ዿ **ₚ**. **◍❾ AE VISA**
Meals *10.95/18.95* **st.** *and a la carte* ▯ *6.50 –* **15 rm** ⌑ *55.00/87.00* **st.** *– SB.*

LOSSIEMOUTH *Moray* **401** K 10.

🛈 *Station Park, Pitgaveny St.* ♟ *(01343) 814804 (May-September).*

Edinburgh 181 – Aberdeen 70 – Fraserburgh 66 – Inverness 44.

🏨🏨 **Stotfield,** *Stotfield Rd, IV31 6QS,* ♟ *(01343) 812011, Fax (01343) 814820,* ≤, ▯◦, ⌸ *–* ✑
📺 ☎ **ₚ** – 🔏 *150.* **◍❾ AE VISA**. ⅍
Meals *(bar lunch Monday to Saturday)/dinner a la carte 18.50/31.50* **st.** ▯ *5.00 –* **45 rm**
⌑ *41.00/62.00* **st.**

Prices	For notes on the prices quoted in this Guide, see the introduction.

LUSS Argyll and Bute **401** G 15 Scotland G. – pop. 402.

See : Village★.
Env. : E : Loch Lomond★★.
Edinburgh 89 – Glasgow 26 – Oban 65.

🏨 **Lodge on Loch Lomond**, G83 8PA, ℘ (01436) 860201, Fax (01436) 860203, ≤ Loch Lomond, « Lochside setting », ☎ – ⇔ rest, ⊤ ☎ ⅖ ℗, ⅏ Æ ▨▨
Meals a la carte 15.50/20.50 t. – ⌑ 7.50 – **28 rm** 79.00/110.00 t., 1 suite – SB.

🏠 **Inverbeg Inn**, Loch Lomond, G83 8PD, N : 3 ½ m. on A 82 ℘ (01436) 860678, Fax (01436) 860686, ≤ – ⊤ ☎ ℗, ⅏ Æ ▨▨
Meals 9.95/21.50 t. and a la carte ⅊ 6.95 – **12 rm** ⌑ 70.00/98.00 t. – SB.

LYBSTER Highland **401** K 9 Scotland G.

Env. : The Hill o'Many Stanes★, NE : 3 ½ m. by A 9 – Grey Cairns of Camster★, N : 6 m. by A 9 and minor rd.
Edinburgh 251 – Inverness 94 – Thurso 28 – Wick 14.

🏠 **Portland Arms**, KW3 6BS, on A 9 ℘ (01593) 721208, Fax (01593) 721446 – ⊤ ☎ ⇐ ℗ – 🔬 200, ⅏ Æ ① ▨▨
closed 1 and 2 January – Meals (bar lunch Monday to Saturday) a la carte 9.50/17.85 st. ⅊ 4.95 – **23 rm** ⌑ 45.00/68.50 st.

MACHRIHANISH Argyll and Bute **401** C 17 – see Kintyre (Peninsula).

MARNOCH Aberdeenshire **401** L 11 Scotland G. – pop. 1 706 – ✉ Huntly.

Exc. : Huntly Castle (elaborate Heraldic Carvings★★★) AC, SW : 10 ½ m. by B 9117, B 9118 and B 9022.
Edinburgh 170 – Aberdeen 40 – Fraserburgh 39 – Inverness 77.

🏠 **Old Manse of Marnoch** ⌂, AB54 5RS, on B 9117 ℘ (01466) 780873, Fax (01466) 780873, ⌖ – ⇔ rest, ⊤ ℗, ⅏ ▨▨
closed 2 weeks October and November, Christmas and New Year – Meals 27.00 t. ⅊ 8.00 – **5 rm** ⌑ 65.00/94.00 t. – SB.

MARYCULTER Aberdeenshire **401** N 12 – see Aberdeen.

MAYBOLE South Ayrshire **401** 402 F 17 Scotland G. – pop. 8 749.

Env. : Culzean Castle★ AC (setting★★★, Oval Staircase★★) W : 5 m. by B 7023 and A 719.

🏠 **Ladyburn** ⌂, KA19 7SG, S : 5 ½ m. by B 7023 off B 741 (Girvan rd) ℘ (01655) 740585, Fax (01655) 740580, ≤, ⌖, park – ⇔ ⊤ ☎ ℗, ⅏ Æ ▨▨, ⅍
closed 2 weeks November and restricted opening January-March – Meals (closed Sunday to Tuesday to non-residents) (booking essential) (lunch by arrangement) 15.50/27.50 t. ⅊ 6.50 – **5 rm** ⌑ 105.00/160.00 t. – SB.

MELROSE Borders **401** **402** L 17 Scotland G. – pop. 2 414.

See : Town★ - Abbey★★ (decorative sculpture★★★) AC.
Env. : Eildon Hills (⅍★★★) – Scott's View★★ – Abbotsford★★ AC, W : 4 ½ m. by A 6091 and B 6360 – Dryburgh Abbey★★ AC (setting★★★), SE : 4 m. by A 6091 – Tweed Valley★★.
Exc. : Bowhill★★ AC, SW : 11 ½ m. by A 6091, A 7 and A 708 – Thirlestane Castle (plasterwork ceilings★★) AC, NE : 21 m. by A 6091 and A 68 – ⌖ Melrose, Dingleton ℘ (01896) 822855.
🛈 Abbey House ℘ (01896) 822555 (summer only).
Edinburgh 38 – Hawick 19 – Newcastle upon Tyne 70.

🏨 **Burts**, Market Sq., TD6 9PN, ℘ (01896) 822285, Fax (01896) 822870, ⌖ – ⊤ ☎ ℗ – 🔬 30, ⅏ Æ ① ▨▨ ᴊᴄʙ
closed 26 December – Meals – (see below) – **20 rm** ⌑ 49.00/84.00 t. – SB.

🏨 **Bon Accord**, Market Sq., TD6 9PQ, ℘ (01896) 822645, Fax (01896) 823474 – ⊤ ☎, ⅏ ▨▨, ⅍
closed 25 December – Meals (bar lunch)/dinner a la carte 10.15/20.40 t. ⅊ 4.95 – **9 rm** ⌑ 42.00/70.00 t. – SB.

🏠 **Dunfermline House** without rest., Buccleuch St., TD6 9LB, ℘ (01896) 822148, Fax (01896) 822148 – ⇔ ⊤, ⅍
5 rm ⌑ 24.00/48.00 st.

XX **Burts** (at Burts H.), Market Sq., TD6 9PN, ℘ (01896) 822285, Fax (01896) 822870, ⌖ – ⇔ ℗, ⅏ Æ ① ▨▨ ᴊᴄʙ
closed 26 December – Meals 17.50/25.00 t. and dinner a la carte ⅊ 6.50.

MELVICH Highland **401** I 8 Scotland G. – ⊠ Thurso.
Env. : Strathy Point★ (⩽★★★, Ben Loyal★★), NW : 5 m. by A 836 and minor rd.
Edinburgh 267 – Inverness 110 – Thurso 18 – Wick 40.

⌂ **The Sheiling** without rest., KW14 7YJ, on A 836 𝒫 (01641) 531256, Fax (01641) 531256,
⩽, 🌹 – 🔆 ℗
March-October – **3 rm** ⊊ 30.00/48.00 **st.**

MEY Highland **401** K 8.
Edinburgh 302 – Inverness 144 – Thurso 13 – Wick 21.

🏠 **Castle Arms**, KW14 8XH, 𝒫 (01847) 851244, Fax (01847) 851244 – 🔟 ☎ ♿ ℗. 🆗 🆎 𝘝𝘐𝘚𝘈
🇯🇨🇧
Meals (bar lunch Monday to Saturday)/dinner 15.00 **st.** and a la carte ♦ 3.95 – **8 rm**
⊊ 39.00/58.00 **st.** – SB.

MILNGAVIE East Dunbarton **401** H 16 – pop. 12 592 – ⊠ Glasgow (Glasgow City).
Edinburgh 53 – Glasgow 7.

🏠🏠 **Black Bull Thistle**, 1-5 Main St., G62 6BH, 𝒫 (0141) 956 2291, Fax (0141) 956 1896 – 🔟
☎ ℗ – 🔬 100. 🆗 🆎 ⓞ 𝘝𝘐𝘚𝘈
Meals (bar lunch)/dinner 19.00 **t.** and a la carte ♦ 7.25 – ⊊ 10.50 – **27 rm** 78.00/100.00 **t.** –
SB.

*Piante di città : i nomi delle principali vie commerciali sono scritti
in rosso all'inizio dell' indice toponomastico
delle piante di città.*

MOFFAT Dumfries and Galloway **401 402** J 17 Scotland G. – pop. 2 647.
Exc. : Grey Mare's Tail★★, NE : 9 m. by A 708.
🏌 Coatshill 𝒫 (01683) 220020.
🄳 Churchgate, DG10 9EG 𝒫 (01683) 220620 (summer only).
Edinburgh 61 – Dumfries 22 – Carlisle 43 – Glasgow 60.

🏠🏠 **Moffat House**, High St., DG10 9HL, 𝒫 (01683) 220039, Fax (01683) 221288, 🌹 – 🔆 🔟
☎ ℗. 🆗 𝘝𝘐𝘚𝘈
Meals (bar lunch)/dinner 21.00 **t.** and a la carte ♦ 5.75 – **20 rm** ⊊ 57.00/87.50 **t.** – SB.

🏠 **Buccleuch Arms**, High St., DG10 9ET, 𝒫 (01683) 220003, Fax (01683) 221291, 🌹 –
🔆 rest, 🔟 ☎ ℗. 🆗 🆎 𝘝𝘐𝘚𝘈
Meals a la carte 13.00/19.25 **t.** ♦ 4.75 – **18 rm** ⊊ 39.00/65.00 **st.**

🏠 **Beechwood Country House** ⌖, Harthope Pl., DG10 9RS, N : ½ m. by A 701
𝒫 (01683) 220210, Fax (01683) 220889, ⩽, 🌹 – 🔆 rest, 🔟 ☎ ℗. 🆗 🆎 𝘝𝘐𝘚𝘈
closed 2 January-20 February – **Meals** (closed lunch Monday to Wednesday) (dinner
booking essential) 14.50/23.00 **t.** ♦ 5.95 – **7 rm** ⊊ (dinner included) 66.00/110.00 **t.** – SB.

⌂ **Fernhill** without rest., Grange Rd, DG10 9HT, N : ¼ m. by A 701 𝒫 (01683) 220077, 🌹 –
🔟. 🌺
April-September – **3 rm** ⊊ 20.00/40.00.

⌂ **Alba House** without rest., 20 Beechgrove, DG10 9RS, NW : ½ m. by A 701
𝒫 (01683) 220418, Fax (01683) 220418, 🌹 – 🔆 🔟. 🌺
restricted opening in winter – **3 rm** ⊊ 40.00 **st.**

⌂ **Hartfell House**, Hartfell Cres., DG10 9AL, NE : ½ m. by Well St. and Old Well Rd
𝒫 (01683) 220153, 🌹 – 🔆 rest, 🔟 ℗
restricted opening November-February – **Meals** (by arrangement) 12.00 **t.** ♦ 6.00 – **8 rm**
⊊ 25.00/45.00 **t.**

✗✗ **Well View** ⌖ with rm, Ballplay Rd, DG10 9JU, E : ¾ m. by Selkirk rd (A 708)
𝒫 (01683) 220184, Fax (01683) 220088, ⩽, 🌹 – 🔆 🔟 ℗. 🆗 🆎 𝘝𝘐𝘚𝘈. 🌺
Meals (closed Saturday lunch) (booking essential) 13.00/27.50 **st.** ♦ 8.00 – **5 rm** ⊊ 50.00/
82.00 **st.**, 1 suite – SB.

at Beattock SW : 2¼ m. by A 701 – ⊠ Moffat.

🏠🏠 **Auchen Castle** ⌖, DG10 9SH, N : 2 m. by A 74 𝒫 (01683) 300407, Fax (01683) 300667,
⩽, ♦, 🌹, park – 🔟 ☎ ℗ – 🔬 60. 🆗 🆎 ⓞ 𝘝𝘐𝘚𝘈 🇯🇨🇧
closed 22 December-12 January – **Meals** 9.65/19.50 **t.** ♦ 6.50 – **25 rm** ⊊ 48.50/86.00 **t.** –
SB.

⌂ **Broomlands Farm** without rest., DG10 9SH, S : ½ m. by A 74 𝒫 (01683) 300320,
Fax (01683) 300320, « Working farm », 🌹 – 🔆 🔟 ℗
April-October – **3 rm** ⊊ 20.00/40.00.

MONTROSE *Angus* [401] M 13 *Scotland G. – pop. 8 473.*

Exc. : *Edzell Castle★ (The Pleasance★★★)* **AC**, *NW : 17 m. by A 935 and B 966 – Cairn O'Mount Road★ (≤★★) N : 17 m. by B 966 and B 974 – Brechin (Round Tower★) W : 7 m. by A 935 – Aberlemno (Aberlemno Stones★, Pictish sculptured stones★) W : 13 m. by A 935 and B 9134.*

⛳18, ⛳18 *Traill Drive ✆ (01674) 672932.*

[i] *Bridge St., ✆ (01674) 672000 (summer only).*

Edinburgh 92 – Aberdeen 39 – Dundee 29.

⌂ **Oaklands** without rest., 10 Rossie Island Rd, DD10 9NN, on A 92 ✆ (01674) 672018, *Fax (01674) 672018* – [TV] [P]. MC VISA
7 rm ☕ 20.00/35.00 **s.**

MOTHERWELL *North Lanarkshire* [401] I 16.

[i] *Library, Hamilton Rd, ML1 3DZ ✆ (01698) 267676.*

Edinburgh 38 – Glasgow 12.

🏨 Holiday Inn Express without rest., Strathclyde Country Park, Hamilton Rd, ML1 3RB, NW : 4 ¼ m. by A 721 and B 7070 off A 725 ✆ (01698) 858585, *Fax (01698) 852375* – [lift] 🚭 [TV] ☎ ♿ [P] – 🎤 30
80 rm.

🏨 **Travel Inn** without rest., Glasgow Rd, Newhouse, ML1 5SY, NE : 4 ¼ m. by A 723 and A 73 on A 775 ✆ (01698) 860277, *Fax (01698) 861353* – 🚭 [TV] ♿ [P] – 🎤 100. MC AE [D] VISA. 🚫🐕
40 rm 36.50 **t.**

MUIR OF ORD *Highland* [401] G 11 – *pop. 2 033.*

⛳18 *Great North Rd ✆ (01463) 870825.*

Edinburgh 173 – Inverness 10 – Wick 121.

🏨 **Dower House** 🌿, Highfield, IV6 7XN, N : 1 m. on A 862 ✆ (01463) 870090, *Fax (01463) 870090*, « Part 17C », 🌳 – 🚭 [TV] ☎ [P]. MC VISA. 🚫🐕
Meals (lunch by arrangement)/dinner 25.00 **st.** 🍷 6.50 – **4 rm** ☕ 55.00/120.00 **st.**, 2 suites – SB.

MULL (Isle of) *Argyll and Bute* [401] BC 14/15 *Scotland G. – pop. 2 838.*

See : *Island★ - Calgary Bay★★ – Torosay Castle* **AC** *(Gardens★ ≤★).*

Env. : *Isle of Iona★ (Maclean's Cross★, St. Oran's Chapel★, St. Martin's High Cross★ Infirmary Museum★* **AC** *(Cross of St. John★)).*

⛳9 *Craignure, Scallastle ✆ (01680) 812487/812416.*

⛴ *from Craignure to Oban (Caledonian MacBrayne Ltd) (40 mn) – from Fishnish to Lochaline (Mainland) (Caledonian MacBrayne Ltd) frequent services daily (15 mn) – from Tobermory to Isle of Tiree (Scarinish) via Isle of Coll (Arinagour) (Caledonian MacBrayne Ltd 3 weekly (2 h 30 mn) – from Tobermory to Kilchoan (Caledonian MacBrayne Ltd 4-6 daily (summer only) (35 mn) – from Tobermory to Oban (Caledonian MacBrayne Ltd 3 weekly (1 h 30 mn).*

⛴ *from Fionnphort to Isle of Iona (Caledonian MacBrayne Ltd) frequent services dail (5 mn).*

[i] *Main St., Tobermory ✆ 01688 (Tobermory) 302182.*

Bunessan – ✉ *Fionnphort.*

🏨 **Ardfenaig House** 🌿, PA67 6DX, W : 3 m. by A 849 ✆ (01681) 700210 *Fax (01681) 700210*, ≤ Loch Scridain, 🌳, park – 🚭 [P]. MC VISA. 🚫🐕
April-October – **Meals** (booking essential to non-residents) (dinner only) 27.50 **st.** 🍷 6.75 – **5 rm** ☕ (dinner included) 89.00/178.00 **st.** – SB.

🏨 **Assapol House** 🌿, PA67 6DW, SE : 1 ½ m. by A 849 ✆ (01681) 700258 *Fax (01681) 700445*, ≤, « Lochside setting », 🎣 – 🚭 [TV] ☎ [P]. MC VISA JCB. 🚫🐕
April-October – **Meals** (residents only) (dinner only) 17.00 **st.** 🍷 4.50 – **5 rm** ☕ (dinner included) 49.00/112.00 **st.** – SB.

Dervaig – ✉ *Tobermory.*

🏨 **Druimard Country House** 🌿, PA75 6QW, on Salen rd ✆ (01688) 400345 *Fax (01688) 400345*, ≤, 🌳 – 🚭 rest, [TV] ☎ [P]. MC VISA
April-October – **Meals** *(closed Sunday to non-residents)* (dinner only) 22.50 **t.** 🍷 8.50 – **5 rm** ☕ (dinner included) 74.00/139.00 **t.**, 1 suite – SB.

⌂ **Balmacara,** PA75 6QN, E : ¼ m. on B 8073 ✆ (01688) 400363, *Fax (01688) 400363*, ≤, 🌳 – 🚭 rm, [TV] [P]. 🚫🐕
Meals (by arrangement) 13.50 **st.** – **3 rm** ☕ 30.00/54.00 **st.**

Killiechronan.

🏠 **Killiechronan House** ⌕, PA72 6JU, on B 8073 ℰ (01680) 300403, Fax (01680) 300463, ⇐, ⌇, ⓟ, park – 🐾 🕿 ⓟ, ⓦⓢ AE ⅥSA, ⌇
March-14 November – **Meals** (booking essential to non-residents) (dinner only and Sunday lunch)/dinner 25.00 **t.** ⓘ 7.70 – **6 rm** ⌷ (dinner included) 65.00/118.00 **t.** – SB.

Tobermory – pop. 2 708.

🛇 *Tobermory* ℰ (01688) 2020.

🏛 **Western Isles,** PA75 6PR, ℰ (01688) 302012, Fax (01688) 302297, ⇐ Tobermory harbour and Calve Island – 🐾 rest, 🆃🆅 🕿 ⓟ, ⓦⓢ AE ⅥSA
closed 18 to 28 December – **Meals** (bar lunch)/dinner 24.50 **t.** ⓘ 8.50 – **Spices :** Meals - Asian - *(closed Monday and Tuesday)* (dinner only) a la carte 14.75/20.00 **st.** – **24 rm** ⌷ 45.00/145.00 **st.**, 1 suite – SB.

🏠 **Tobermory,** 53 Main St., PA75 6NT, ℰ (01688) 302091, Fax (01688) 302254, ⇐ – 🐾 rest, 🆃🆅 ⓦⓢ ⌇
closed 14 to 28 December and restricted opening in winter – **Waters Edge :** Meals (booking essential to non-residents) (dinner only) 21.50 **t.** ⓘ 5.30 – **16 rm** ⌷ 34.00/90.00 **t.** – SB.

🏠 **Fairways Lodge** ⌕ without rest., Golf Course, PA75 6PS, NE : ½ m. by B 882 ℰ (01688) 302238, Fax (01688) 302238, ⇐ Calve Island and Sound of Mull, 🛇, ⓟ – 🐾 🆃🆅 ⓟ
closed Christmas and restricted opening in winter – **5 rm** ⌷ 34.00/68.00 **t.**

🏠 **Ulva House,** Strongarbh, PA75 6PR, ℰ (01688) 302044, ⇐ Tobermory harbour and Calve Island, ⓟ – 🐾 ⓟ
March-October – **Meals** 19.50 **t.** ⓘ 4.90 – **6 rm** ⌷ (dinner included) 63.00/106.00 **st.**

MUSSELBURGH East Lothian 401 K 16 – pop. 18 425.

🛇 *Monktonhall* ℰ (0131) 665 2005 – 🛇 *Royal Musselburgh, Prestongrange House, Preston-pans* ℰ (01875) 810276 – 🛇 *Musselburgh Old Course, Silver Ring Clubhouse, Millhill* ℰ (0131) 665 6981.
🛈 *Brunton Hall, EH21 6AF* ℰ (0131) 665 6597 (summer only).
Edinburgh 6 – Berwick 54 – Glasgow 53.

🏠 **Travel Inn,** Carberry Rd, Inveresk, EH21 8PT, ℰ (0131) 665 3005, Fax (0131) 653 2270 – 🐾 rm, 🆃🆅 ⅋ ⓟ, ⓦⓢ AE ⓞ ⅥSA
Meals (grill rest.) – **40 rm** 36.50 **t.**

🏠 **Travelodge,** Old Craighall, EH21 8RE, S : 1 ½ m. by B 6415 at junction with A 1 ℰ (0131) 653 6070, Fax (0131) 653 6106, Reservations (Freephone) 0800 850950 – 🐾 rm, 🆃🆅 🕿 ⅋ ⓟ, ⓦⓢ AE ⓞ ⅥSA JCB, ⌇
Meals (grill rest.) – **45 rm** 49.95 **t.**

NAIRN Highland 401 I 11 Scotland G. – pop. 3 367.

Env. : *Forres (Sueno's Stone★★) E :* 11 m. by A 96 and B 9011 – *Cawdor Castle★ AC, S :* 5 ½ m. by B 9090 – *Brodie Castle★ AC, E :* 6 m. by A 96.
Exc. : *Fort George★, W :* 8 m. by A 96, B 9092 and B 9006.
🛇, 🛇 *Seabank Rd* ℰ (01667) 452103 – 🛇 *Nairn Dunbar, Lochloy Rd* ℰ (01667) 452741.
🛈 *62 King St.* ℰ (01667) 452753 (summer only).
Edinburgh 172 – Aberdeen 91 – Inverness 16.

🏛 **Golf View,** 63 Seabank Rd, IV12 4HD, ℰ (01667) 452301, Fax (01667) 455267, ⇐, 🛵, ⌇s, 🛇, ⓟ, ⌇ – 🛗, 🐾 rest, 🆃🆅 🕿 ⓟ – 🛥 120. ⓦⓢ AE ⓞ ⅥSA
Meals 24.75 **t.** (dinner) and a la carte 9.95/20.90 **t.** ⓘ 7.50 – **46 rm** ⌷ 90.00/130.00 **t.**, 1 suite – SB.

🏛 **Newton** ⌕, IV12 4RX, ℰ (01667) 453144, Fax (01667) 454026, ⓟ – 🛗, 🐾 rest, 🆃🆅 🕿 ⓟ – 🛥 60. ⓦⓢ AE ⓞ ⅥSA
Meals (bar lunch Monday to Saturday)/dinner 23.50 **t.** – ⌷ 9.50 – **29 rm** 90.00/200.00 **st.** – SB.

🏠 **Claymore House,** 45 Seabank Rd, IV12 4EY, ℰ (01667) 453731, Fax (01667) 455290, ⓟ – 🐾 rest, 🆃🆅 🕿 ⓟ, ⓦⓢ AE ⓞ ⅥSA
Meals a la carte 9.90/19.35 **st.** ⓘ 4.50 – **15 rm** ⌷ 42.50/85.00 **st.**, 1 suite – SB.

🏠 **Clifton House** ⌕, Viewfield St., IV12 4HW, ℰ (01667) 453119, Fax (01667) 452836, ⇐, « Antiques », ⓟ – ⓟ, ⓦⓢ AE ⓞ ⅥSA
mid February-mid November – **Meals** (booking essential) a la carte 19.50/27.00 **t.** ⓘ 4.00 – **12 rm** ⌷ 60.00/105.00 **st.**

🏨 **Links,** 1 Seafield St., IV12 4HN, ☎ (01667) 453321, *Fax (01667) 456092*, ≤, 🌳 – ⚡ rest, [TV] ☎ [P]. [MC] [AE] [VISA]
Meals (dinner only) 16.50 **t.** and a la carte 🍷 6.50 – **10 rm** ☕ 37.50/75.00 **t.** – SB.

🏠 **Inveran Lodge** without rest., Seabank Rd, IV12 4HG, ☎ (01667) 455666, *Fax (01667) 455666*, 🌳 – ⚡ [TV] [P]. [MC] [AE] [VISA]. 🚫
3 rm ☕ 50.00/100.00 **t.**

at Auldearn *E : 2 m. on A 96 – ✉ Nairn.*

🏠 **Boath House,** IV12 5TE, ☎ (01667) 454896, *Fax (01667) 454896*, « Georgian mansion », 🚲, 🎣, 🌳 – ⚡ [TV] ☎ [P]. [MC] [AE] [DC] [VISA]. 🚫
Meals a la carte 13.95/29.50 **st.** 🍷 4.85 – **6 rm** ☕ 55.00/85.00 **st.** – SB.

NETHERLEY *Aberdeenshire* [401] N 12 *Scotland G. – ✉ Stonehaven.*

Env. : *Muchalls Castle (plasterwork ceilings★★) AC, SE : 5 m. by B 979 – Deeside★★, N : 2 m. by B 979 – Aberdeen★★, NE : 3 m. by B 979 and B 9077.*
Exc. : *Aberdeen★★, NE : 12 m. by – Dunnottar Castle★★ (site★★★) AC, S : 7 m. by B 979 – Crathes Castle★★ (Gardens★★★) AC, NW : 13 m. by B 979, B 9077 and A 93.*
Edinburgh 117 – Aberdeen 12 – Dundee 54.

🍴🍴 **Lairhillock,** AB39 3QS, NE : 1 ½ m. by B 979 on Portlethan rd ☎ (01569) 730001, *Fax (01569) 731175* – [P]. [MC] [AE] [DC] [VISA] [JCB]. 🚫
closed 25-26 December and 1-2 January – **Meals** (bar lunch Monday to Saturday)/dinner 27.95 **t.** and a la carte 🍷 6.10.

NEWBURGH *Aberdeenshire* [401] N 12 *Scotland G.*

Exc. : *Pitmedden Gardens★★ AC, W : 6 ½ m. by B 9000 – Haddo House★ AC, NW : 14 m. by B 900, A 92 and B 9005.*
⛳18 *McDonald, Ellon ☎ (01358) 720576* – ⛳9 *Newburgh-on-Ythan, Ellon ☎ (01358) 789058.*
Edinburgh 144 – Aberdeen 14 – Fraserburgh 33.

🏨 **Udny Arms,** Main St., AB41 6BL, ☎ (01358) 789444, *Fax (01358) 789012*, 🌳 – [TV] ☎ [P] – 🎤 45. [MC] [AE] [DC] [VISA]
Meals – (see below) – **24 rm** ☕ 59.00/79.00 **t.** – SB.

🍴🍴 **Udny Arms,** Main St., AB41 6BL, ☎ (01358) 789444, *Fax (01358) 789012* – [P]. [MC] [AE] [DC] [VISA]
Meals a la carte 12.55/30.75 **t.** 🍷 10.95.

Pour les grands voyages d'affaires ou de tourisme,
Guide Rouge ***MICHELIN : EUROPE.***

NEWPORT-ON-TAY *Fife* [401] L 14.

Edinburgh 55 – Dundee 4 – Perth 23 – St. Andrews 11.

🏠 Forgan House 🐦, DD6 8RB, SE : 2 ½ m. by B 995 and A 92 on Tayport rd ☎ (01382) 542760, *Fax (01382) 542760*, 🌳 – ⚡ [TV] [P]
4 rm.

NEW SCONE *Perthshire and Kinross* [401] J 14 – *see Perth.*

NEWTONMORE *Highland* [401] H 12 – *pop. 1 044.*

⛳18 *Newtonmore ☎ (01540) 673328.*
Edinburgh 113 – Inverness 43 – Perth 69.

🏠 **The Pines** 🐦, Station Rd, PH20 1AR, ☎ (01540) 673271, ≤, 🌳 – ⚡ [TV] [P]. 🚫
early April-October – **Meals** 10.00 **s.** – **6 rm** ☕ 24.50/49.00 **s.** – SB.

NEWTON STEWART *Dumfries and Galloway* [401] [402] G 19 *Scotland G. – pop. 2 543.*

Env. : *Galloway Forest Park★, Queen's Way★ (Newton Stewart to New Galloway) N : 19 m. by A 712.*
⛳18, *Kirroughtree Av., Minnigaff ☎ (01671) 402172.*
ℹ *Dashwood Sq., DG8 6DQ ☎ (01671) 402431 (summer only).*
Edinburgh 131 – Dumfries 51 – Glasgow 87 – Stranraer 24.

🏨 **Kirroughtree House** 🐦, DG8 6AN, NE : 1 ½ m. by A 75 on A 712 ☎ (01671) 40214, *Fax (01671) 402425*, ≤ woodland and Wigtown Bay, « 18C mansion in landscaped gardens », 🎾, 🌳 – ⚡ rest, [TV] ☎ [P]. [MC] [VISA]. 🚫
closed 3 January-13 February – **Meals** 27.50 **st.** (dinner) and lunch a la carte 17.00/21.00 **st.** – **15 rm** ☕ 70.00/140.00 **st.**, 2 suites – SB.

🏠 **Creebridge House** ॐ, Minnigaff, DG8 6NP, ℰ (01671) 402121, Fax (01671) 403258, 🎄 – ❄ rest, 🔟 ☎ 🅿. ⓿ 🗛 *VISA* JCB
Meals 22.00 **st.** (dinner) and a la carte 11.25/19.95 **st.** – **19 rm** ⌷ 50.00/84.00 **t.** – SB.

🏠 **Crown,** 101 Queen St., DG8 6JW, ℰ (01671) 402727, Fax (01671) 402727 – 🔟 ☎ 🅿. ⓿ *VISA*
Meals (bar lunch)/dinner 15.00 **st.** and a la carte ₰ 7.00 – **11 rm** ⌷ 30.00/50.00 **st.** – SB.

NORTH BERWICK *East Lothian* 𝟜𝟘𝟙 L 15 *Scotland G.* – pop. 5 871.

Env. : *North Berwick Law* (✱★★★) *S : 1 m. - Tantallon Castle★★ (clifftop site★★★) AC, E : 3 ½ m. by A 198 – Dirleton★ (Castle★ AC) SW : 2 ½ m. by A 198.*

Exc. : *Museum of Flight★, S : 6 m. by B 1347 – Preston Mill★, S : 8½m. by A 198 and B 1047 – Tyninghame★, S : 7 m. by A 198 – Coastal road from North Berwick to Portseton★, SW : 13 m. by A 198 and B 1348.*

🝖 *North Berwick, West Links, Beach Rd ℰ (01620) 892135 –* 🝖 *Glen, East Links ℰ (01620) 892221.*

🛈 *Quality St., EH39 4HJ ℰ (01620) 892197.*

Edinburgh 24 – Newcastle upon Tyne 102.

🏠🏠 **Marine,** 18 Cromwell Rd, EH39 4LZ, ℰ (01620) 892406, Fax (01620) 894480, ⩽ *golf course and Firth of Forth,* ⓕ, 🏊, 🎄, ✕ – 📵 ❄ 🔟 ☎ 🅿 – 🔬 250. ⓿ 🗛 ⓞ *VISA*
Meals (booking essential Sunday dinner) (bar lunch Monday to Saturday)/dinner 21.50 **t.** and a la carte ₰ 6.00 – ⌷ 10.25 – **78 rm** 70.00/90.00 **t.**, 5 suites – SB.

🏠 **Point Garry,** 20 West Bay Rd, EH39 4AW, ℰ (01620) 892380, Fax (01620) 892848, ⩽ – 🔟 ☎ 🅿. ⓿ *VISA*
May-mid October – **Meals** (bar lunch Monday to Thursday)/dinner 15.00 **t.** and a la carte 15 **rm** ⌷ 45.00/100.00 **t.**

🛖 **Glebe House** ॐ *without rest.,* Law Rd, EH39 4PL, ℰ (01620) 892608, « *Georgian manse* », 🎄 – ❄ 🅿. ✂
closed Christmas and New Year – **4 rm** ⌷ 30.00/55.00 **st.**

🛖 **Craigview** *without rest.,* 5 Beach Rd, EH39 4AB, ℰ (01620) 892257 – ❄ 🔟. ✂
3 rm ⌷ 25.00/40.00 **st.**

✕✕ **The Grange,** 35 High St., EH39 4NN, ℰ (01620) 895894 – 🅿. ⓿ 🗛 *VISA*. ✂
closed Tuesday lunch, Sunday dinner and Monday in winter and first 3 weeks January – **Meals** 7.00/15.00 **t.** and a la carte ₰ 6.95.

NORTH QUEENSFERRY *Fife* 𝟜𝟘𝟙 J 15 *Scotland G.* – ✉ *Inverkeithing.*

Env. : *Forth Bridges★★ (toll).*

Edinburgh 13 – Dunfermline 7 – Glasgow 42 – Kirkcaldy 16 – Perth 33.

🏠 **Queensferry Lodge,** St. Margarets Head, KY11 1HP, N : ½ m. on B 981 ℰ (01383) 410000, Fax (01383) 419708, ⩽ – 📵 ❄ 🔟 ☎ 🅿 – 🔬 130. ⓿ 🗛 ⓞ *VISA* JCB
Outside Inn : Meals (grill rest.) 6.95/9.95 **st.** and a la carte ₰ 3.95 – **Pentlands :** Meals (dinner only) a la carte approx. 23.40 **st.** ₰ 3.95 – ⌷ 9.50 – **32 rm** 80.00/109.00 **st.**

NORTH UIST *Western Isles (Outer Hebrides)* 𝟜𝟘𝟙 XY 10/11 – *see Uist (Isles of).*

OBAN *Argyll and Bute* 𝟜𝟘𝟙 D 14 *Scotland G.* – pop. 8 203.

Exc. : *Loch Awe★★, SE : 17 m. by A 85 – Bonawe Furnace★, E : 12 m. by A 85 – Cruachan Power Station★ AC, E : 16 m. by A 85 – Sea Life Centre★ AC, N : 14 m. by A 828.*

🝖 *Glencruitten, Glencruitten Rd ℰ (01631) 62868/64115.*

Access to Glasgow by helicopter.

🛥 *to Isle of Mull (Craignure) (Caledonian MacBrayne Ltd) (40 mn) – to South Uist (Loch-boisdale) via Isle of Barra (Castlebay) (Caledonian MacBrayne Ltd) (summer only) – to Isle of Tiree (Scarinish) via Isle of Mull (Tobermory) and Isle of Coll (Arinagour) (Caledonian Mac-Brayne Ltd) – to Isle of Islay (Port Askaig) and Kintyre Peninsula (Kennacraig) via Isle of Colonsay (Scalasaig) (Caledonian MacBrayne Ltd) (summer only) – to Isle of Lismore (Ach-nacroish) (Caledonian MacBrayne Ltd) 2-5 daily (except Sunday) (50 mn) – to Isle of Colonsay (Scalasaig) (Caledonian MacBrayne Ltd) 3 weekly (2 h 10 mn) – to Isle of Mull (Tobermory) (Caledonian MacBrayne Ltd) 3 weekly (1 h 30 mn).*

🛈 *Boswell House, Argyll Sq., PA34 4AN ℰ (01631) 563122.*

Edinburgh 123 – Dundee 116 – Glasgow 93 – Inverness 118.

🏠🏠 **Manor House,** Gallanach Rd, PA34 4LS, ℰ (01631) 562087, Fax (01631) 563053, ⩽, 🎄 – ❄ 🔟 ☎ 🅿. ⓿ 🗛 *VISA*
closed Sunday and Monday November-March – **Meals** (lunch by arrangement)/dinner 23.90 **t.** and a la carte ₰ 7.10 – **11 rm** ⌷ (dinner included) 110.00/160.00 **t.** – SB.

🏠 **Barriemore** without rest., Corran Esplanade, PA34 5AQ, ℘ (01631) 566356, Fax (01631) 566356, ≤ – 😾 📺 **P**. 🏧 ⚫ *VISA*
April-November – **13 rm** ☑ 25.00/56.00 **st.**

🏠 **Glenburnie** without rest., Corran Esplanade, PA34 5AQ, ℘ (01631) 562089, Fax (01631) 562089, ≤ – 😾 📺 **P**. 🏧 ⚫ *VISA*
April-October – **15 rm** ☑ 30.00/70.00 **st.**

🏠 **Kilchrenan House** without rest., Corran Esplanade, PA34 5AQ, ℘ (01631) 562663, Fax (01631) 562663, ≤ – 📺 ☎ **P**. 🏧 ⚫ *VISA*. ℀
Easter-October – **10 rm** ☑ 30.00/60.00 **t.**

at Kilmore S : 4 m. on A 816 – ✉ Oban.

🏠 **Invercairn** ℁ without rest., Musdale Rd, PA34 4XX, ℘ (01631) 770301, ≤, 🚗 – **P**
May-September – **3 rm** ☑ 36.00/48.00 **s.**

at Kilninver SW : 8 m. by A 816 on B 844 – ✉ Oban.

🏨 **Knipoch**, PA34 4QT, NE : 1 ½ m. on A 816 ℘ (01852) 316251, Fax (01852) 316249, ≤, 🚗 – 📺 ☎ **P**. 🏧 ⚫ 🅰🅴 ⚫ *VISA*. ℀
March-October – **Meals** (lunch by arrangement)/dinner 29.50 **st.** ⅙ 8.00 – **16 rm** ☑ 77.00/ 200.00 **st.**

OLDMELDRUM Aberdeenshire 401 N 11 Scotland G.
Exc. : Haddo House★, NE : 9 m. by B 9170 on B 9005.
Edinburgh 140 – Aberdeen 17 – Inverness 87.

🏨 **Meldrum House** ℁, AB51 0AE, N : 1 ½ m. on A 947 ℘ (01651) 872294, Fax (01651) 872464, ≤, « Part 13C baronial house », 🚗, park – 😾 rest, 📺 ☎ **P** – 🅰 50 🏧 *VISA*
closed 1 week January – **Meals** 25.50 **t.** (dinner) and lunch a la carte 25.50/29.50 **t.** ⅙ 7.00 - **9 rm** ☑ 80.00/115.00 **t.** – SB.

🏠 **Cromlet Hill**, South Rd, A51 0AB, ℘ (01651) 872315, Fax (01651) 872164 – 😾 📺 ☎ **P**
closed Christmas, 2 weeks in spring and 2 weeks in autumn – **Meals** (by arrangement) (communal dining) 17.50 – **2 rm** ☑ 35.00/65.00, 1 suite.

ONICH Highland 401 E 13 – ✉ Fort William.
Edinburgh 123 – Glasgow 93 – Inverness 79 – Oban 39.

🏨 **The Lodge on the Loch**, Creag Dhu, PH33 6RY, on A 82 ℘ (01855) 821237 Fax (01855) 821238, ≤ Loch Linnhe and mountains, 🚗 – 😾 rest, 📺 ☎ ♿ **P**. 🏧 *VISA*
closed January – **Meals** 11.00/29.50 **st.** and lunch a la carte ⅙ 6.95 – **18 rm** ☑ (dinne included) 79.50/174.00 **st.**, 1 suite – SB.

🏨 **Allt-Nan-Ros**, PH33 6RY, on A 82 ℘ (01855) 821210, Fax (01855) 821462, ≤ Loch Linnhe and mountains, 🚗 – 😾 rest, 📺 ☎ **P**. 🏧 🅰🅴 ⚫ *VISA*
closed mid November-December – **Meals** a la carte approx. 25.00 **t.** ⅙ 6.75 – **20 rm** ☑ 49.50/99.00 **t.** – SB.

🏨 **Onich**, PH33 6RY, on A 82 ℘ (01855) 821214, Fax (01855) 821484, ≤ Loch Linnhe an mountains, « Lochside setting », 🚗 – 😾 rest, 📺 ☎ **P**. 🏧 🅰🅴 ⚫ *VISA*
closed 1 week Christmas – **Meals** 22.00 **t.** (dinner) and lunch a la carte 12.85/22.00 **t.** ⅙ 5.2 – **25 rm** ☑ (dinner included) 71.00/132.00 **t.** – SB.

ORD Highland 401 C 12 – see Skye (Isle of).

ORKNEY ISLANDS Orkney Islands 401 KL 6/7 Scotland G. – pop. 19 612.
See : Old Man of Hoy★★★ – Islands★★ – Maes Howe★★ AC – Skara Brae★★ AC – Corrig. Farm Museum★ AC – Brough of Birsay★ AC – Birsay (≤★) – Ring of Brodgar★ – Unsta Cairn★.

≫ see Kirkwall.

⚓ service between Isle of Hoy (Longhope), Isle of Hoy (Lyness), Isle of Flotta and Houto (Orkney Ferries Ltd) – from Stromness to Scrabster (P & O Scottish Ferries) (1 h 45 mn) from Stromness to Shetland Islands (Lerwick) and Aberdeen (P & O Scottish Ferries) – fro Kirkwall to Westray, Stronsay via Eday and Sanday (Orkney Ferries Ltd) – from Tingwall t Wyre via Eglisay and Rousay (Orkney Ferries Ltd) – from Kirkwall to Shapinsay (Orkney Ferrie Ltd) (25 mn) – from Stromness to Isle of Hoy (Moness) (Orkney Ferries Ltd) – from Kirkwall t North Ronaldsay (Orkney Ferries Ltd) – from Houton to Isle of Hoy (Lyness) (Orkney Ferrie Ltd) – from Stromness to Graemsay via Isle of Hoy (Orkney Ferries Ltd).

⚓ from Burwick (South Ronaldsay) to John O'Groats (John O'Groats Ferries) 1-4 da. (45 mn).

Burray.

⌂ **Ankersted**, KW17 2SS, E : ½ m. on A 961 ℘ (01856) 731217, *Fax (01856) 731298*, ⩽, 🐎 – ⇔ rm, �📺 **℗**. 🆚. ⅍
Meals (by arrangement) 9.00 **st.** – **4 rm** ⌷ 16.00/32.00 **st.**

Dounby.

🏠 **Smithfield**, KW17 2HT, ℘ (01856) 771215, *Fax (01856) 771494* – ⇔ rest, 📺 **℗**. 🆆🆂 🇦🇪
🆚. ⅍
May-October – **Meals** a la carte 7.10/17.50 **st.** – **6 rm** ⌷ 25.00/50.00 **st.**

Kirkwall *Scotland G.* – pop. 5 952.

See : Kirkwall★★ – St. Magnus Cathedral★★ – Western Mainland★★, Eastern Mainland (Italian Chapel★) – Earl's Palace★ *AC* – Tankerness House Museum★ *AC* – Orkney Farm and Folk Museum★.

🏌 *Grainbank* ℘ (01856) 872457.

✈ *Kirkwall Airport* : ℘ (01856) 872421, S : 3 ½ m.

🅱 *6 Broad St., Kirkwall, KW15 1DH* ℘ (01856) 872856.

🏨 **Ayre**, Ayre Rd, KW15 1QX, ℘ (01856) 873001, *Fax (01856) 876289* – 📺 ☎ **℗** – 🛎 200. 🆆🆂
🇦🇪 🆚
Meals (bar lunch)/dinner a la carte 8.75/25.50 **st.** ⌀ 4.30 – **33 rm** ⌷ 54.00/88.00 **st.**

🏠 **Albert**, Mounthoolie Lane, KW15 1JZ, pedestrian area off Junction Rd ℘ (01856) 876000,
Fax (01856) 875397 – 📺 ☎. 🆆🆂 🇦🇪 🆚
Meals (bar lunch)/dinner 15.00 **t.** and a la carte ⌀ 4.00 – **19 rm** ⌷ 45.00/75.00 **t.**

🏠 **Foveran** ⑳, St. Ola, KW15 1SF, SW : 3 m. on A 964 ℘ (01856) 872389,
Fax (01856) 876430, « Overlooking Scapa Flow », 🐎, park – ⇔ rest, 📺 ☎ **℗**. 🆆🆂 🆚
closed January – **Meals** *(closed Sunday to non-residents)* (dinner only) a la carte 17.00/
25.00 **t.** ⌀ 4.50 – **8 rm** ⌷ 45.00/70.00 **t.**

🏠 **Queens**, Shore St., KW15 1LG, ℘ (01856) 872200, *Fax (01856) 873871* – ⇔ rest, 📺 ☎. 🆆🆂
🇦🇪 🆚. ⅍
Meals (in bar) a la carte 7.50/18.00 **t.** – **9 rm** ⌷ 30.00/42.00 **t.**

🏠 **St. Ola** without rest., Harbour St., KW15 1LE, ℘ (01856) 875090, *Fax (01856) 875090* – 📺 ☎
6 rm.

🏠 **West End**, Main St., KW15 1BU, ℘ (01856) 872368, *Fax (01856) 876181* – 📺 ☎ **℗**. 🆆🆂 🇦🇪
🆚. ⅍
closed 23 December-4 January – **Meals** *(closed Sunday lunch)* (in bar) a la carte 7.50/
15.80 **st.** ⌀ 4.50 – **16 rm** ⌷ 34.00/54.00 **st.**

⌂ **Royal Oak**, Holm Rd, KW15 1PY, S : 1 m. by A 960 on A 961 ℘ (01856) 877177,
Fax (01856) 877177 – ⇔ rest, 📺 **℗**. 🆆🆂 🆚 🏧. ⅍
Meals (by arrangement) 11.00 **st.** – **8 rm** ⌷ 26.00/50.00 **st.**

⌂ **Polrudden**, Peerie Sea Loan, KW15 1UH, W : ¾ m. by Pickaquoy Rd ℘ (01856) 874761,
Fax (01856) 874761 – ⇔ rest, 📺 **℗**. ⅍
closed Christmas and New Year – **Meals** (by arrangement) 12.00 **st.** – **7 rm** ⌷ 27.00/
42.00 **st.**

⌂ **Brekk-Ness** without rest., Muddisdale Rd, KW15 1RS, W : 1 m. by Pickaquoy Rd
℘ (01856) 874317, *Fax (01856) 874317* – 📺 **℗**
11 rm ⌷ 28.00/48.00 **t.**

🅰 ATS Junction Rd, Kirkwall ℘ (01856) 872361

Loch Harray.

🏠 **Merkister** ⑳, KW17 2LF, off A 986 ℘ (01856) 771366, *Fax (01856) 771515*, ⩽ Loch Harray,
🎣, 🐎 – ⇔ rest, 📺 ☎ **℗**. 🆆🆂 🇦🇪 🆚 🏧
restricted opening in winter – **Meals** (bar lunch Monday to Saturday)/dinner 15.00 **t.**
and a la carte ⌀ 5.00 – **14 rm** ⌷ 39.50/87.00 **t.** – SB.

St. Margaret's Hope.

✕✕ **Creel** with rm, Front Rd, KW17 2SL, ℘ (01856) 831311, ⩽ – ⇔ 📺 **℗**. 🆆🆂 🆚. ⅍
closed Monday to Friday October-March, 3 weeks October and January – **Meals** (dinner only) 24.00 **t.** ⌀ 4.50 – **3 rm** ⌷ 35.00/60.00 **t.**

Stenness.

🏨 **Standing Stones**, KW16 3JX, on A 965 ℘ (01856) 850449, *Fax (01856) 851262*, 🎣, 🐎 –
⇔ rm, 📺 ☎ **℗**. 🆆🆂 🇦🇪 🆚 🏧
closed 25-26 December and 1 to 4 January – **Meals** (booking essential) (bar lunch)/dinner
a la carte approx. 10.00 **t.** ⌀ 4.70 – **17 rm** ⌷ 39.00/74.00.

723

Stromness Scotland G.

See : Town★ - Pier Gallery (collection of abstract art★).

⌂ **Stenigar** without rest., Ness Rd, KW16 3DW, S : ½ m. by Main St. ✆ (01856) 850438, ≼, 🐎 – 📺 🅿
3 rm.

⌂ **Thira** ⊗, Innertown, KW16 3JP, NW : 1 ½ m. by Back Rd, turning right at mini round-about, taking first right onto unmarked road and then left at two junctions ✆ (01856) 851181, Fax (01856) 851182, ≼ Hoy Island and Sound, 🐎 – ⅏ 📺 🅿. ⅏
Meals (by arrangement) 8.00 st. – **4 rm** ⊇ 23.00/46.00 st.

PEAT INN Fife **401** L 15 Scotland G. – ⊠ Cupar.

Exc. : Kellie Castle★, SE : 7 ½ m. by B 940 and minor roads.
Edinburgh 45 – Dundee 21 – Perth 28.

XXX **The Peat Inn** ⊗ with rm, KY15 5LH, ✆ (01334) 840206, Fax (01334) 840530, 🐎 – ⅏ rest, 📺 🕭 🅿. 🕮 🆎 ⓞ 🆅🆂🅰 🇯🇨🇧
closed Sunday, Monday, 25 December and 1 January – **Meals** (booking essential) 18.50/28.00 st. and dinner a la carte ▮ 7.00 – **1 rm** 95.00 st., **7 suites** 135.00 st. – SB.

PEEBLES Borders **401** **402** K 17 Scotland G. – pop. 7 065.

Env. : Tweed Valley★★.
Exc. : Traquair House★★ AC, SE : 7 m. by B 7062 – Rosslyn Chapel★★ AC, N : 16 ½ m. by A 703, A 6094, B 7026 and B 7003.
🏌 Kirkland St. ✆ (01721) 720197.
🛈 High St., EH45 8AG ✆ (01721) 720138.
Edinburgh 24 – Hawick 31 – Glasgow 53.

🏨 **Peebles Hydro,** Innerleithen Rd, EH45 8LX, ✆ (01721) 720602, Fax (01721) 722999, ≼, ℩₅, ⅗, ◻, 🐎, park, ⅏, squash – ▮≡ 📺 🕭 🅿 – ▲ 450. 🕮 🆎 🆅🆂🅰. ⅏
Meals 15.00/22.00 st. – **135 rm** ⊇ (dinner included) 71.00/135.00 st., 2 suites – SB.

🏨 **Park,** Innerleithen Rd, EH45 8BA, ✆ (01721) 720451, Fax (01721) 723510, 🐎 – 📺 🕭 🅿 🕮 🆎 ⓞ 🆅🆂🅰
Meals (bar lunch)/dinner 19.20 t. and a la carte ▮ 7.75 – **24 rm** ⊇ (dinner included) 60.00.118.00 st. – SB.

🏨 **Cringletie House** ⊗, EH45 8PL, N : 3 m. on A 703 ✆ (01721) 730233
Fax (01721) 730244, ≼, « Victorian country house in extensive grounds », 🐎, ⅏ – ▮≡ ⅏ rest, 📺 🅿. 🕮 🆎 🆅🆂🅰
closed 2 January-early March – **Meals** 26.00 t. (dinner) and lunch a la carte – **13 rm** ⊇ 57.50/125.00 t. – SB.

PERTH Perthshire and Kinross **401** J 14 Scotland G. – pop. 123 495.

See : City★ – Black Watch Regimental Museum★ Y M1 – Georgian Terraces★ Y – Museum and Art Gallery★ Y M2.
Env. : Scone Palace★★ AC, N : 2 m. by A 93 Y – Branklyn Garden★ AC, SE : 1 m. by A 85 Z Kinnoull Hill (≼★) SE : 1½ m. by A 85 Z – Huntingtower Castle★ AC, NW : 3 m. by A 85 Y Elcho Castle★ AC, SE : 4 m. by A 912 – Z – and Rhynd rd.
Exc. : Abernethy (11C Round Tower★), SE : 8 m. by A 912 – Z – and A 913.
🏌 Craigie Hill, Cherrybank ✆ (01738) 624377 Z – 🏌 King James VI, Moncreiffe Island ✆ (01738) 625170/632460 Z – 🏌 Murrayshall, New Scone ✆ (01738) 551171 Y – 🏌 North Inch, c/o Perth & Kinross Council, 5 High St. ✆ (01738) 636481 Y.
🛈 45 High St., PH1 5TJ ✆ (01738) 638353 – Inveralmond, A 9 Western City bypass ✆ (01738) 638481.
Edinburgh 44 – Aberdeen 86 – Dundee 22 – Dunfermline 29 – Glasgow 64 – Inverness 112 Oban 94.

Plan opposite

🏨 **Kinfauns Castle** ⊗, PH2 7JZ, E : 3 m. on A 90 ✆ (01738) 620777, Fax (01738) 620778 « Renovated 17C castle », ⅏, 🐎, park – ⅏ 📺 🕭 🅿 – ▲ 60. 🕮 🆎 🆅🆂🅰
Meals 15.50/28.00 t. ▮ 7.00 – **14 rm** ⊇ 110.00/240.00 t., 2 suites.

🏨 **Hunting Tower** ⊗, Crieff Rd, PH1 3JT, W : 3 ½ m. by A 85 ✆ (01738) 583771 Fax (01738) 583777, 🐎 – 📺 🕭 🅿. 🕮 🆎 🆅🆂🅰. ⅏
Meals 12.50/19.95 t. ▮ 6.95 – **15 rm** ⊇ 75.00/125.00 t., **12 suites** 78.00/125.00 t.

🏨 **Parklands,** St. Leonard's Bank, PH2 8EB, ✆ (01738) 622451, Fax (01738) 622046, 🐎 ⅏ rest, 📺 🕭 🅿 – ▲ 25. 🕮 🆎 ⓞ 🆅🆂🅰 Z
closed 25 December-6 January – **Meals** 15.50/24.95 st. and a la carte ▮ 8.25 – **14 rm** ⊇ 79.00/135.00 st. – SB.

Stakis Perth, West Mill St., PH1 5QP, ✆ (01738) 628281, *Fax (01738) 643423* – ⟿ rm, TV ☎ P – 🧑‍🏫 150. MC AE O VISA JCB Y a
Meals 15.50 **st.** (dinner) and a la carte 12.05/21.40 **st.** 🍾 7.75 – ☕ 8.50 – **74 rm** 71.00/81.00 **st.**, 2 suites – SB.

Dupplin Castle ⛵, PH2 0PY, SW : 6 ¼ m. on A 9 ✆ (01738) 623224, *Fax (01738) 444140*, ≤, « Country house atmosphere, gardens », park – ⟿ rm, ☎ P. MC VISA JCB
Meals (booking essential) (residents only) (communal dining) (dinner only) 28.00 **st.** – **6 rm** ☕ 110.00 **t.**

Sunbank House, 50 Dundee Rd, PH2 7BA, ✆ (01738) 624882, *Fax (01738) 442515*, 🪑 – ⟿ TV ☎ ♿ P. MC VISA. ✗ Z a
Meals (dinner only) 19.50 **t.** and a la carte 🍾 6.75 – **9 rm** ☕ 30.00/70.00 **t.**

Park Lane without rest., 17 Marshall Pl., PH2 8AG, ✆ (01738) 637218, *Fax (01738) 643519* – ⟿ TV P. MC AE VISA JCB. ✗ Z e
closed 7 December-19 January – **6 rm** ☕ 23.00/46.00.

Aberdeen without rest., Pitcullen Cres., PH2 7HT, ✆ (01738) 633183 – TV P. ✗ Y u
3 rm ☕ 20.00/40.00.

Pitcullen without rest., 17 Pitcullen Cres., PH2 7HT, ✆ (01738) 626506, *Fax (01738) 628265* – ⟿ TV P. MC VISA. ✗ Y r
6 rm ☕ 25.00/50.00 **st.**

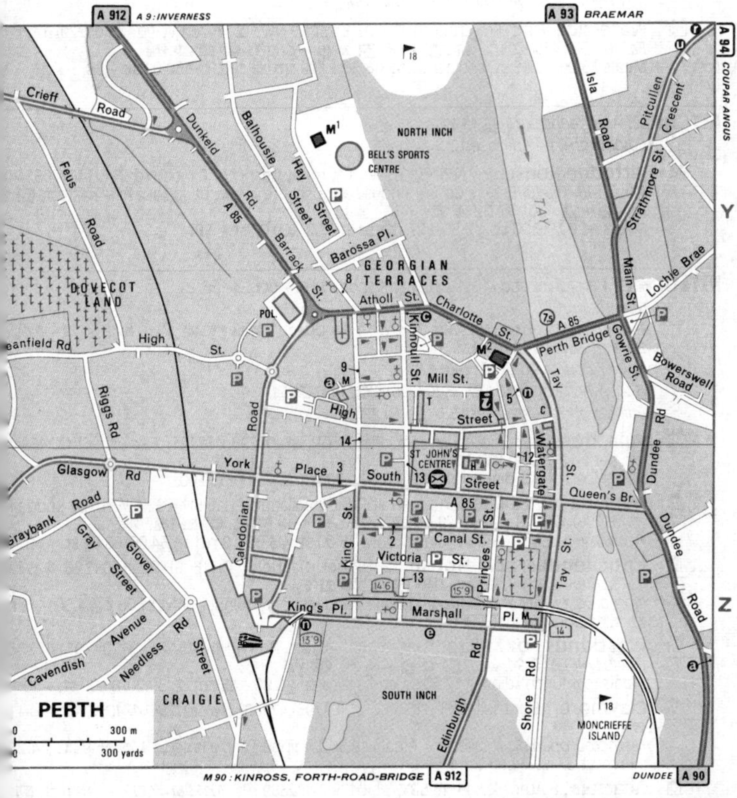

✗ **Let's Eat,** 77-79 Kinnoull St., PH1 5EZ, ℰ (01738) 643377, Fax (01738) 621464 – ⬤⬤ ⬛ 𝗩𝗜𝗦𝗔
closed Sunday, Monday, 25-26 December, 1-2 January and 2 weeks July – **Meals**
a la carte 13.55/22.95 **t.** ⬧ 6.50.
Y c

✗ **Number Thirty Three,** 33 George St., PH1 5LA, ℰ (01738) 633771 – ⬤⬤ 𝗩𝗜𝗦𝗔 𝗝𝗖𝗕
closed Sunday, Monday, 25-26 December, 1-2 and last 2 weeks January and first week
February – **Meals** - Seafood - a la carte 11.50/23.75 **t.** ⬧ 7.60.
Y n

at New Scone NE : 2½ m. on A 94 – Y – ✉ Perth.

🏨 **Murrayshall Country House** ⬥, PH2 7PH, E : 1 ¼ m. by Murraysall Ro
ℰ (01738) 551171, Fax (01738) 552595, ≤, ⬥, ⬥, ⬥, 🌹, park, ※ – �📺 ☎ 🅟 – 🔬 180. ⬤⬤
⬛ ⓘ 𝗩𝗜𝗦𝗔
Meals (bar lunch)/dinner 18.30 **st.** ⬧ 6.95 – **23 rm** ⬚ 85.00/130.00 **st.,** 3 suites – SB.

at Glencarse E : 6¼ m. on A 85 – Y – off A 90 – ✉ Perth.

🏨 **Newton House,** PH2 7LX, ℰ (01738) 860250, Fax (01738) 860717, 🌹 – ✼ rest, �📺 ☎
🅟. ⬤⬤ ⬛ ⓘ 𝗩𝗜𝗦𝗔 𝗝𝗖𝗕. ※
Meals a la carte 15.25/22.50 **st.** ⬧ 4.50 – **10 rm** ⬚ 65.00/95.00 **st.** – SB.

⬤ ATS Inveralmond Ind. Est., Ruthvenfield Rd ℰ (01738) 629481

PETERHEAD Aberdeenshire 𝟰𝟬𝟭 O 11 – pop. 20 789.
⬥, ⬥ Cruden Bay ℰ (01779) 812285 – ⬥, ⬥ Craigewan Links ℰ (01779) 472149.
🅑 54 Broad St., AB42 ℰ (01779) 471904 (summer only).
Edinburgh 165 – Aberdeen 35 – Fraserburgh 18.

🏨 **Waterside Inn,** Fraserburgh Rd, AB42 3BN, NW : 2 m. on A 90 ℰ (01779) 47112₁
Fax (01779) 470670, ⬥, ⬥, ☐, ✼ �📺 ☎ 🅟 – 🔬 100. ⬤⬤ ⬛ ⓘ 𝗩𝗜𝗦𝗔
Meals 15.00/18.95 **st.** and a la carte ⬧ 8.50 – **109 rm** ⬚ 110.00/130.00 **st.** – SB.

PITCAPLE Aberdeenshire 𝟰𝟬𝟭 M 12.
Edinburgh 51 – Aberdeen 21.

🏨 **Pittodrie House** ⬥, AB51 5HS, SW : 1 ¾ m. by Chapel of Garioch rd ℰ (01467) 68144₄
Fax (01467) 681648, ≤, « Country house atmosphere », 🌹, park, squash – ✼ rest, �📺 ☎
⬝ 🅟 – 🔬 120. ⬤⬤ ⬛ ⓘ 𝗩𝗜𝗦𝗔 𝗝𝗖𝗕
Meals 16.00/29.00 **st.** ⬧ 8.50 – **27 rm** ⬚ 126.00/169.00 **st.** – SB.

PITLOCHRY Perthshire and Kinross 𝟰𝟬𝟭 I 13 Scotland G. – pop. 3 126.
See : Town★.
Exc. : Blair Castle★★ AC, NW : 7 m. by A 9 – Queen's View★★, W : 7 m. by B 8019 – Falls ₒ
Bruar★, NW : 11 m. by A 9.
⬥ Golf Course Rd ℰ (01796) 472792.
🅑 22 Atholl Rd, PH16 5BX ℰ (01796) 472215/472751.
Edinburgh 71 – Inverness 85 – Perth 27.

🏨 **Pine Trees** ⬥, Strathview Terr., PH16 5QR, ℰ (01796) 472121, Fax (01796) 472460, ·
🌹, park – �📺 ☎ 🅟. ⬤⬤ ⬛ 𝗩𝗜𝗦𝗔. ※
Meals (bar lunch)/dinner 11.90 **t.** ⬧ 6.00 – **20 rm** ⬚ 75.00/160.00.

🏨 **Dunfallandy House** ⬥, Logierait Rd, Dunfallandy, PH16 5NA, S : 1 ¼ m. by Bridge R
ℰ (01796) 472648, Fax (01796) 472017, ≤, 🌹 – ✼ �📺 ☎ 🅟. ⬤⬤ ⬛ 𝗩𝗜𝗦𝗔. ※
February-October – **Meals** (dinner only) 16.00 **st.** ⬧ 3.95 – **8 rm** ⬚ 34.00/68.00 **st.** – SB.

🏨 **Knockendarroch House,** 2 Higher Oakfield, PH16 5HT, ℰ (01796) 47347
Fax (01796) 474068, ≤, 🌹 – ✼ �📺 ☎ 🅟. ⬤⬤ ⬛ 𝗩𝗜𝗦𝗔
closed December and January – **Meals** (residents only) (dinner only) 21.00 **t.** ⬧ 4.50 – **12 r**
⬚ (dinner included) 67.00/104.00 **t.** – SB.

🏨 **Westlands of Pitlochry,** 160 Atholl Rd, PH16 5AR, ℰ (01796) 4722₆
Fax (01796) 473994, 🌹 – �📺 ☎ 🅟 – 🔬 50. ⬤⬤ 𝗩𝗜𝗦𝗔
Meals (bar lunch)/dinner 17.50 **st.** and a la carte ⬧ 6.80 – **15 rm** ⬚ 39.00/84.00 **st.** – SB.

🏨 **Claymore,** 162 Atholl Rd, PH16 5AR, ℰ (01796) 472888, Fax (01796) 474037, 🌹 – ✼
☎ 🅟. ⬤⬤ 𝗩𝗜𝗦𝗔
restricted opening in winter – **Meals** 18.50 **t.** (dinner) and a la carte 9.20/16.95 **t.** ⬧ 4.2₅
11 rm ⬚ 37.00/74.00 **t.** – SB.

🏨 **Acarsaid,** 8 Atholl Rd, PH16 5BX, ℰ (01796) 472389, Fax (01796) 473952 – ✼ rest, �📺
🅟. ⬤⬤ 𝗩𝗜𝗦𝗔. ※
closed 6 January-6 March – **Meals** (light lunch)/dinner 17.00 **t.** ⬧ 5.50 – **18 rm** ⬚ (dinn
included) 55.00/110.00 **t.** – SB.

🏠 **Queens View** ⚜, Strathtummel, PH16 5NR, E : 3 ¼ m. on B 8019 ℰ (01796) 473291, Fax (01796) 473515, ≤ Loch Tummel and Hills, ⚞, – 🕿 🅿. ⬛ⓈVISA. ⚞
closed 24-25 December, 2 weeks January and February – **Meals** 23.50 **t.** (dinner) and lunch a la carte – **10 rm** ☲ (dinner included) 70.00/140.00 **t.** – SB.

🏠 **Balrobin**, Higher Oakfield, PH16 5HT, ℰ (01796) 472901, Fax (01796) 474200, ≤, ⚞ – ⚞ rest, 📺 🅿. ⬛ⓈVISA
April-October – **Meals** (residents only) (dinner only) 15.50 **t.** – **15 rm** ☲ 44.00/90.00 **t.** – SB.

🏠 **Birchwood**, 2 East Moulin Rd, PH16 5DW, ℰ (01796) 472477, Fax (01796) 473951, ⚞ – ⚞ rest, 📺 🕿 🅿. ⬛ⓈVISA – ⚞
closed January and February – **Meals** (dinner only) 21.00 **t.** 🟏 4.50 – **12 rm** ☲ 39.50/79.00 **t.** – SB.

🏠 **East Haugh House**, East Haugh, PH16 5JS, SE : 2 m. by A 924 ℰ (01796) 473121, Fax (01796) 472473, ⚞ – ⚞ rest, 📺 🕿 🅿 🅿. ⬛ⓈVISA. ⚞
closed 24 to 26 December and first 3 weeks February – **Meals** (bar lunch)/dinner 26.95 **t.** and a la carte 🟏 6.95 – **8 rm** ☲ 49.00/110.00 **t.** – SB.

↑ **Torrdarach**, Golf Course Rd, PH16 5AU, ℰ (01796) 472136, ⚞ – ⚞ rest, 📺 🅿. ⚞
Easter-October – **Meals** (by arrangement) 15.00 **st.** 🟏 5.95 – **7 rm** ☲ 25.00/52.00 **st.** – SB.

↑ **Dundarave**, Strathview Terr., PH16 5AT, ℰ (01796) 473109, ≤, ⚞ – ⚞ rest, 📺 🅿
29 April-November – **Meals** (by arrangement) 15.95 **s.** – **7 rm** ☲ 30.00/60.00 **st.** – SB.

at Killiecrankie NW : 4 m. by A 924 and B 8019 on B 8079 – ✉ Pitlochry.

🏠🏠 **Killiecrankie** ⚜, PH16 5LG, ℰ (01796) 473220, Fax (01796) 472451, ≤, ⚞ – ⚞ 📺 🕿 🅿. ⬛ⓈVISA
closed 3 January-7 March and 10 days December – **Meals** (bar lunch)/dinner 28.00 **t.** 🟏 8.25 – **9 rm** ☲ (dinner included) 79.00/158.00 **t.**, 1 suite – SB.

PLOCKTON Highland 🔢🔢🔢 D 11 Scotland G.
See : Village★.
Env. : Wester Ross★★★.
Edinburgh 210 – Inverness 88.

🏠 **Haven**, 3 Innes St., IV52 8TW, ℰ (01599) 544223, Fax (01599) 544467, ≤, ⚞ – ⚞ rest, 📺 🕿 🅿. ⬛ⓈVISA
closed 20 December-1 February – **Meals** (lunch by arrangement)/dinner 23.50 **t.** 🟏 4.75 – **13 rm** ☲ 35.00/74.00 **t.**, 2 suites – SB.

🍴 **Plockton** with rm, Harbour St., IV52 8TN, ℰ (01599) 544274, Fax (01599) 544475, ≤ Loch Carron and mountains, ⚞ – ⚞ rest, 📺 ⬛Ⓢ ⒶⒺ VISA ⒿⒸⒷ. ⚞
Meals (in bar) a la carte 10.40/20.85 **t.** 🟏 4.75 – **8 rm** ☲ 27.50/55.00 **t.**

POLLACHAR Western Isles (Outer Hebrides) – see Uist (Isles of).

POLMONT Falkirk 🔢🔢🔢 🔢🔢🔢 I 16 – see Falkirk.

POOLEWE Highland 🔢🔢🔢 D 10 Scotland G.
Env. : Wester Ross★★★ – Inverewe Gardens★★★, N : 1 m. on B 8057 – Loch Maree★★★.
Edinburgh 234 – Inverness 78 – Kyle of Lochalsh 74.

🏠 **Pool House**, IV22 2LE, ℰ (01445) 781272, Fax (01445) 781403, ≤ Loch Ewe – ⚞ rm, 📺 🕿 🅿. ⬛ⓈVISA. ⚞
restricted opening December and January – **Meals** (bar lunch)/dinner 19.50 **t.** and a la carte 🟏 5.05 – **13 rm** ☲ 42.00/88.00 **t.** – SB.

PORT APPIN Argyll and Bute 🔢🔢🔢 D 14 – ✉ Appin.
Edinburgh 136 – Ballachulish 20 – Oban 24.

🏠🏠🏠 **Airds** (Allen) ⚜, PA38 4DF, ℰ (01631) 730236, Fax (01631) 730535, ≤ Loch Linnhe and
⚜ mountains of Kingairloch, « Former ferry inn », ⚞ – ⚞ rest, 📺 🕿 🅿. ⬛ⓈVISA. ⚞
closed 7 to 28 January – **Meals** (booking essential) (light lunch)/dinner 35.00 **t.** – **12 rm** ☲ 81.00/206.00 **t.** – SB
Spec. Mousseline of rabbit and truffle, with a grain mustard sabayon. Fillet of monkfish with a lobster mousse, champagne and chervil sauce. Coconut and cardamom mousse, pineapple and mango purée.

PORT CHARLOTTE Argyll and Bute 🔢🔢🔢 A 16 – see Islay (Isle of).

PORT ELLEN Argyll and Bute 🔢🔢🔢 B 17 – see Islay (Isle of).

PORTLETHEN Aberdeenshire **401** N 12 – see Aberdeen.

PORT OF MENTEITH Stirling **401** H15 Scotland G.

Env. : Inchmahome Priory (double effigy★), W : 1 m. by A 81.

Edinburgh 53 – Glasgow 30 – Stirling 17.

🏠 **Lake** ⮞, FK8 3RA, 𝒫 (01877) 385258, Fax (01877) 385671, ≤, « Lakeside setting » –
🔆 rest, 📺 ☎ 𝐏. **◑◐** 𝔸𝔼 𝓥𝓘𝓢𝓐
April-October, Christmas and New Year – **Meals** (closed lunch Monday and Tuesday and
Sunday dinner) 12.75/23.90 **t.** and lunch a la carte 🍴 4.95 – **16 rm** ☲ (dinner included)
79.00/170.00 **t.** – SB.

PORTPATRICK Dumfries and Galloway **401 402** E 19 – pop. 842 – ✉ Stranraer.

🏌, 🏌 Golf Course Rd 𝒫 (01776) 810273.

Edinburgh 141 – Ayr 60 – Dumfries 80 – Stranraer 9.

🏠 **Knockinaam Lodge** ⮞, DG9 9AD, SE : 5 m. by A 77 off B 7042 𝒫 (01776) 810471
✿ Fax (01776) 810435, ≤, « Country house in picturesque coastal setting », 🐟, 🐦, park –
🔆 rest, 📺 ☎ 𝐏. **◑◐** 𝔸𝔼 **◑** 𝓥𝓘𝓢𝓐
Meals (booking essential) 27.00/38.00 **t.** 🍴 9.00 – **10 rm** ☲ (dinner included) 125.00/
250.00 **t.** – SB
Spec. Assiette of quail with grated truffle. Seared scallops with Parma ham, lemon oil and
balsamic dressing. Bitter chocolate tart with pineapple sorbet, coconut custard.

🏠 **Fernhill**, Heugh Rd, DG9 8TD, 𝒫 (01776) 810220, Fax (01776) 810596, ≤, 🐦 – 🔆 rest, 📺
☎ 🕹 𝐏. **◑◐** 𝔸𝔼 **◑** 𝓥𝓘𝓢𝓐 𝓙𝓒𝓑
closed 25 and 26 December – **Meals** 21.00 **t.** (dinner) and a la carte 15.65/27.70 **t.** 🍴 4.85 –
19 rm ☲ 57.00/100.00 **t.** – SB.

🏠 **Crown**, DG9 8SX, 𝒫 (01776) 810261, Fax (01776) 810551, ≤ – 🔆 rest, 📺 ☎. **◑◐** 𝔸𝔼 **◑**
𝓥𝓘𝓢𝓐
Meals 12.50 **st.** (dinner) and a la carte 10.00/32.95 **st.** – **12 rm** ☲ 48.00/96.00 **st.** – SB.

🏠 **Blinkbonnie** without rest., School Brae, DG9 8LG, 𝒫 (01776) 810282, ≤, 🐦 – 🔆 📺 𝐏.
🦅
closed December – **5 rm** ☲ 21.00/37.00 **st.**

PORTREE Highland **401** B 11 – see Skye (Isle of).

PRESTWICK South Ayrshire **401 402** G 17 – pop. 13 705.

✈ Prestwick International Airport : 𝒫 (01292) 479822 – BY – **Terminal** : Buchanan Bus
Station.

✈ see also Glasgow.

Edinburgh 78 – Ayr 2 – Glasgow 32.

Plan of Built up Area : see Ayr

🏠 **Carlton Toby**, 187 Ayr Rd, KA9 1TP, 𝒫 (01292) 476811, Fax (01292) 474845 – 🔆 rm, 📺
☎ 𝐏 – 🔺 25. **◑◐** 𝔸𝔼 𝓥𝓘𝓢𝓐 BY
Meals (carving rest.) 8.95 **t.** and a la carte 🍴 4.45 – **34 rm** ☲ 55.00/70.00 **t.** – SB.

🏠 **Travel Inn**, Kilmarnock Rd, Monkton, KA9 2RJ, NE : 3 m. by A 79 at junction of A 77 with
A 78 𝒫 (01292) 678262, Fax (01292) 678248 – 🔆 rm, 📺 & 𝐏 – 🔺 70. **◑◐** 𝔸𝔼 **◑** 𝓥𝓘𝓢𝓐. 🦅
Meals (grill rest.) – **40 rm** 36.50 **t.**

QUOTHQUAN South Lanarkshire **401** J 27 Scotland G. – ✉ Biggar.

Env. : Biggar★ (Gladstone Court Museum★ AC – Greenhill Covenanting Museum★ AC)
SE : 4 ½ m. by B 7016.

Edinburgh 32 – Dumfries 50 – Glasgow 36.

🏠 **Shieldhill** ⮞, ML12 6NA, NE : ¾ m. 𝒫 (01899) 220035, Fax (01899) 221092, ≤, « Victorian
country house, 12C origins », 🐦 – 🔆 rm, 📺 ☎ 𝐏 – 🔺 25. **◑◐** 𝓥𝓘𝓢𝓐. 🦅
Meals 17.50/30.00 **t.** 🍴 12.00 – **11 rm** ☲ 74.00/162.00 **t.**

THE CHANNEL TUNNEL Map Guide

260 French edition
with tourist sights in England

261 English edition
with tourist sights on the Continent

RENFREW Renfrewshire **401** G 16 Scotland G. – pop. 24 116.

Env. : Paisley Museum and Art Gallery (Paisley Shawl Section★) SW : 2 ¾ m. by A 741.

Edinburgh 53 – Glasgow 7.

Glynhill, 169 Paisley Rd, PA4 8XB, ℘ (0141) 886 5555, Fax (0141) 885 2838, ₤₅, ≘s, ⬜, ≪ rm, 🔟 ☎ ℗ – ⚞ 450. ⬢➒ AE ① VISA JCB. ⅍
Palm Court : Meals (carving rest.) 9.95/15.95 st. and a la carte ⅍ 7.00 – **Le Gourmet :** Meals (closed Sunday) (dancing Friday and Saturday evenings) 9.95/16.95 st. and a la carte ⅍ 7.00 – **125 rm** ⊆ 76.00/144.00 **t.** – SB.

RHICONICH Highland **401** F 8 Scotland G. – ✉ Lairg.

Exc. : Cape Wrath★★★ (≤★★) AC, N : 21 m. (including ferry crossing) by A 838 and minor rd.

Edinburgh 249 – Thurso 87 – Ullapool 57.

Rhiconich, IV27 4RN, ℘ (01971) 521224, Fax (01971) 521732, ≤ Loch Inchard, ≈ – ⚞ rest, 🔟 ☎ ℗. ⬢➒ VISA JCB
Meals (bar lunch)/dinner a la carte 10.30/19.85 st. ⅍ 4.50 – **11 rm** ⊆ 33.50/68.00 st.

ROGART Highland **401** H 9 – pop. 419.

Edinburgh 229 – Inverness 73 – Wick 63.

Sciberscross Lodge ⑧, Strath Brora, IV28 3YQ, N : 7 m. by Balnacoil rd ℘ (01408) 641246, Fax (01408) 641465, ≤ Brora valley and hills, ≈, ⚞ – ℗. ⬢➒ VISA. ⅍
Meals (booking essential) (communal dining) (dinner only) 45.00 – **4 rm** ⊆ 85.00 st.

ROTHES Moray **401** K 11 Scotland G. – pop. 1 520.

Exc. : Glenfiddich Distillery★, SE : 7 m. by A 941.

⛳ Dufftown ℘ (01340) 820325.

Edinburgh 192 – Aberdeen 62 – Fraserburgh 58 – Inverness 49.

Rothes Glen ⑧, AB38 7AQ, N : 3 m. on A 941 ℘ (01340) 831254, Fax (01340) 831566, ≤, « Country house atmosphere », ⚞, park – ⚞ rest, 🔟 ☎ ℗. ⬢➒ AE VISA. ⅍
Meals 15.95/30.00 **t.** and lunch a la carte ⅍ 7.50 – **14 rm** ⊆ 70.00/130.00 **t.**, 2 suites – SB.

ROTHESAY Argyll and Bute **401 402** E 16 – see Bute (Isle of).

ROYBRIDGE Highland **401** F 13 – see Spean Bridge.

ST. ANDREWS Fife **401** L 14 Scotland G. – pop. 11 136.

See : City★★ – Cathedral★ (⛪★★) AC B – West Port★ A.

Env. : Leuchars (parish church★), NW : 6 m. by A 91 and A 919.

Exc. : The East Neuk★★, SE : 9 m. by A 917 and B 9131 B – Crail★★ (Old Centre★★, Upper Crail★) SE : 9 m. by A 917 B – Kellie Castle★ AC, S : 9 m. by B 9131 and B 9171 B – Ceres★, SW : 9 m. by B 939 - E : Inland Fife★ A.

⛳ (x5), ⛳ Eden, Jubilee, New, Old, Strathtyrum and Balgove Courses ℘ (01334) 466666 – ⛳ Duke's, Craigtoun Park ℘ (01334) 479947.

🛈 70 Market St., KY16 9NU ℘ (01334) 472021.

Edinburgh 51 – Dundee 14 – Stirling 51.

Plan on next page

The Old Course H. Golf Resort and Spa, Old Station Rd, KY16 9SP, ℘ (01334) 474371, Fax (01334) 477668, ≤ golf courses and sea, ₤₅, ≘s, ⬜, ⛳ – ⧫, ≡ rest, 🔟 ☎ ♿ ℗ – ⚞ 195. ⬢➒ AE ① VISA JCB. ⅍
closed Christmas – **Conservatory :** Meals (May-October) 15.50/36.50 st. and a la carte ⅍ 9.50 – **Road Hole Grill :** Meals (closed lunch May-October) 15.50/36.50 st. and dinner a la carte – **108 rm** ⊆ 195.00/280.00 st., 17 suites – SB.

Rusacks, 16 Pilmour Links, KY16 9JQ, ℘ (01334) 474321, Fax (01334) 477896, ≤, ≘s – ⧫, ≪ rest, 🔟 ☎ ℗ – ⚞ 150. ⬢➒ AE ① VISA JCB   A a
Meals (light lunch Monday to Saturday)/dinner 28.95 **t.** and a la carte ⅍ 6.50 – ⊆ 10.50 – **48 rm** 100.00/150.00 **t.**, 2 suites – SB.

Rufflets Country House, Strathkinness Low Rd, KY16 9TX, W : 1 ½ m. on B 939 ℘ (01334) 472594, Fax (01334) 478703, ≤, « Country house, gardens » – ⚞ rm, 🔟 ☎ ℗ – ⚞ 30. ⬢➒ AE ① VISA JCB. ⅍
Meals (bar lunch Monday to Friday) 17.00/29.00 st. ⅍ 8.00 – **25 rm** ⊆ 80.00/150.00 st. – SB.

ST ANDREWS

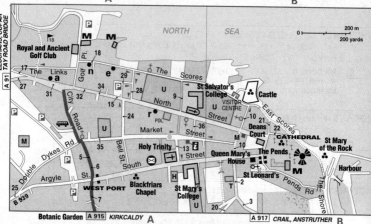

St. Andrews Golf, 40 The Scores, KY16 9AS, ℰ (01334) 472611, Fax (01334) 472188, ≤ –
|𝄐|, ↝ rest, 🆃🆅 ☎ 🅿 – 🔬 200. ◐◐ 🄰🄴 ① 𝘝𝘐𝘚𝘈
closed 24 to 28 December – **Meals** 15.00/27.50 **t.** and a la carte – **22 rm** ⊇ 78.00/165.00 **t**
– SB.

The Scores, 76 The Scores, KY16 9BB, ℰ (01334) 472451, Fax (01334) 473947, ≤, 🝖 – |𝄐|
↝ rest, 🆃🆅 ☎ 🅿 – 🔬 160. ◐◐ 🄰🄴 ① 𝘝𝘐𝘚𝘈 🄹🄲🄱. ⅏
Meals (bar lunch)/dinner 18.00 **t.** and a la carte – **29 rm** ⊇ 80.00/150.00 **t.**, 1 suite – SB.

Aslar House without rest., 120 North St., KY16 9AF, ℰ (01334) 473460
Fax (01334) 477540, 🝖 – ↝ 🆃🆅. ◐◐ 𝘝𝘐𝘚𝘈. ⅏
closed 2 weeks July and 1 week October – **5 rm** ⊇ 27.00/56.00.

at Strathkinness W : 3¾ m. on B 939 – A – ✉ St. Andrews.

Fossil House and Cottage without rest., 12-14 Main St., KY16 9RU, ℰ (01334) 850639
Fax (01334) 850639 – ↝ 🆃🆅 🅿. ◐◐ 𝘝𝘐𝘚𝘈. ⅏
4 rm ⊇ 25.00/44.00 **st.**

ST. BOSWELLS Borders 401 402 L 17 Scotland G. – pop. 2 092.

Env. : Dryburgh Abbey★★ AC (setting★★★), NW : 4 m. by B 6404 and B 6356 – Twee
Valley★★.

Exc. : Bowhill★★ AC, SW : 11 ½ m. by A 699 and A 708.

🆃🆂 St. Boswells ℰ (01835) 823858/823527.

Edinburgh 39 – Glasgow 79 – Hawick 17 – Newcastle upon Tyne 66.

Dryburgh Abbey ⟫, Dryburgh, TD6 0RQ, N : 3 ½ m. by B 6404 on B 635
ℰ (01835) 822261, Fax (01835) 823945, ≤, 🔲, 🝱, 🝖 – |𝄐|, ↝ rest, 🆃🆅 ☎ 🅿 – 🔬 120. ◐
🄰🄴 𝘝𝘐𝘚𝘈 🄹🄲🄱
Meals (dinner only) 22.50 **st.** ⅊ 5.50 – **23 rm** ⊇ 65.00/110.00 **st.**, 2 suites – SB.

ST. CATHERINES Argyll and Bute 401 E 15 Scotland G. – ✉ Cairndow.

Env. : Loch Fyne★★.

Exc. : Inveraray★★ : Castle★★ (interior★★★) AC, NW : 12 m. by A 815 and A 83
Auchindrain★, NW : 18 m. by A 815 and A 83.

Edinburgh 99 – Glasgow 53 – Oban 53.

⌂ **Arnish Cottage** ⊗ without rest., Poll Bay, PA25 8BA, SW : 2 m. on A 815 *ℰ* (01499) 302405, Fax (01499) 302405, ≤ Loch Fyne, « Lochside setting », 🌿 – ✲✲ ℗ *closed Christmas and New Year* – **3 rm** ⊐ 25.00/60.00 **st.**

⌂ **Thistle House** without rest., PA25 8AZ, on A 815 *ℰ* (01499) 302209, Fax (01499) 302531, ≤, 🌿 – 📺 ℗. ⁰⁹ *VISA* *April-October* – **4 rm** ⊐ 47.00.

ST. FILLANS *Perthshire and Kinross* **401** H 14 *Scotland G.*
Env. : *Loch Earn*★★.
Edinburgh 67 – Glasgow 57 – Oban 64 – Perth 30.

🏠 **Achray House,** PH6 2NF, *ℰ* (01764) 685231, Fax (01764) 685320, ≤ Loch Earn and mountains, 🌿 – ✲✲ rest, 📺 ☎ ℗. ⁰⁹ AE *VISA*. ⁄
Meals (bar lunch Monday to Saturday)/dinner 17.50 **t.** and a la carte ⅄ 4.85 – **9 rm** ⊐ 46.50/ 69.00 **t.**

ST. MARGARET'S HOPE *Orkney Islands* **401** K 6 – *see Orkney Islands.*

SANDYHILLS *Dumfries and Galloway* **401 402** I 19 – ⊠ *Dalbeattie.*
Edinburgh 99 – Ayr 62 – Dumfries 19 – Stranraer 68.

🏠 **Cairngill House** ⊗, DG5 4NZ, *ℰ* (01387) 780681, ≤, 🌿 – ✲✲ rest, 📺 ℗
Meals (bar lunch)/dinner 12.00 **t.** and a la carte ⅄ 5.00 – **6 rm** ⊐ 32.00/54.00 **t.**

SANQUHAR *Dumfries and Galloway* **401 402** I 17 *Scotland G.* – *pop. 2 680.*
Exc. : *Drumlanrig Castle*★★ *(cabinets★), SE : 8 m. by A 76.*
🏌 *Blackaddie Rd ℰ* (01659) 50577.
🏢 *Tolbooth, High St. ℰ* (01659) 50185 *(summer only).*
Edinburgh 58 – Dumfries 27 – Glasgow 24.

🏠 **Blackaddie House** ⊗, Blackaddie Rd, DG4 6JJ, N : ¼ m. by A 76 *ℰ* (01659) 50270, Fax (01659) 50270, « Riverside setting », ⌘, 🌿 – 📺 ℗. ⁰⁹ *VISA*. ⁄
closed 25 to 27 December – **Meals** (lunch by arrangement) a la carte 8.45/24.75 **t.** ⅄ 5.50 – **12 rm** ⊐ 36.00/62.00 **t.** – SB.

SCALASAIG *Argyll and Bute* **401** B 15 – *see Colonsay (Isle of).*

SCALLOWAY *Shetland Islands* **401** Q 3 – *see Shetland Islands (Mainland).*

SCOURIE *Highland* **401** E 8 *Scotland G.* – ⊠ *Lairg.*
Exc. : *Cape Wrath*★★★ *(≤★★) AC, N : 31 m. (including ferry crossing) by A 894 and A 838 – Loch Assynt*★★, *S : 17 m. by A 894.*
Edinburgh 263 – Inverness 107.

🏠 **Eddrachilles** ⊗, Badcall Bay, IV27 4TH, S : 2 ½ m. on A 894 *ℰ* (01971) 502080, Fax (01971) 502477, ≤ Badcall Bay and islands, ⌘, 🌿, park – 📺 ☎ ℗. ⁰⁹ *VISA*. ⁄
March-October – **Meals** (bar lunch)/dinner 11.60 **st.** and a la carte ⅄ 3.20 – **11 rm** ⊐ 50.00/ 80.00 **st.** – SB.

SEIL (Isle of) *Argyll and Bute* **401** D 15 – ⊠ *Oban.*

Clachan Seil – ⊠ *Oban.*

🏠 **Willowburn** ⊗, PA34 4TJ, *ℰ* (01852) 300276, Fax (01852) 300597, ≤, 🌿 – ✲✲ rest, 📺 ℗. ⁰⁹ *VISA*
closed early January-early April – **Meals** (bar lunch)/dinner 22.50 **st.** ⅄ 5.95 – **7 rm** ⊐ (dinner included) 55.00/110.00 **st.**

Easdale – ⊠ *Oban.*

🏠 **Inshaig Park** ⊗, PA34 4RF, *ℰ* (01852) 300256, Fax (01852) 300256, ≤ Inner Hebridean Islands, 🌿 – ✲✲ rest, 📺 ℗
Easter-mid October – **Meals** (bar lunch)/dinner 15.00 **t.** and a la carte – **6 rm** ⊐ 36.00/ 57.00 **t.**

SHETLAND ISLANDS Shetland Islands 401 PQ 3 Scotland G. – pop. 22 522.

See : Islands★ - Up Helly Aa★★ (last Tuesday in January) – Mousa Broch★★★ AC (Mousa Island) – Jarlshof★★ - Lerwick to Jarlshof★ (≤★) – Shetland Croft House Museum★ AC.

✈ Tingwall Airport : ℰ (01595) 840306, NW : 6 ½ m. of Lerwick by A 971.

⛴ from Lerwick (Mainland) to Aberdeen and via Orkney Islands (Stromness) (P & O Scottish Ferries) – from Lerwick (Mainland) to Skerries (Shetland Islands Council) booking essential 2 weekly (2 h 30 mn) – from Lerwick (Mainland) to Norway (Bergen) weekly (13 h 30 mn) – from Lerwick (Mainland) to Bressay (Shetland Islands Council) frequent services daily (5 mn) – from Laxo (Mainland) to Isle of Whalsay (Symbister) (Shetland Islands Council) frequent services daily (30 mn) – from Toft (Mainland) to Isle of Yell (Ulsta) (Shetland Islands Council) frequent services daily (20 mn) – from Isle of Yell (Gutcher) to Isle of Fetlar (Oddsta) and via Isle of Unst (Belmont) (Shetland Islands Council) – from Fair Isle to Sumburgh (Mainland) (Shetland Islands Council) weekly (2 h 40 mn).

MAINLAND.

Brae.

🏨 **Busta House** ⬥, ZE2 9QN, SW : 1 ½ m. ℰ (01806) 522506, Fax (01806) 522588, ≤, « Part 16C and 18C country house », ☞ – 🔟, ✵ rest, 🔟 ☎ 🅿, 🐶 AE ⓪ VISA
closed 22 December-3 January – Meals (bar lunch)/dinner 19.00 t. 🍷 5.00 – 20 rm ☑ 68.00/110.00 t. – SB.

Lerwick Scotland G. – pop. 7 590.

See : Clickhimin Broch★.

Env. : Gulber Wick (≤★), S : 2 m. by A 970.

🏌 Lerwick ℰ (01595) 840369.

🖪 The Market Cross, Lerwick, ZE1 0LU ℰ (01595) 693434.

🏨 **Kveldsro House,** Greenfield Pl., ZE1 0AQ, ℰ (01595) 692195, Fax (01595) 696595 – 🔟 ☎ 🅿, 🐶 AE ⓪ VISA ✵
closed 24 December-7 January – Meals (bar lunch)/dinner 23.50 t. and a la carte 🍷 6.50 – 17 rm ☑ 88.50/105.50 st. – SB.

🏨 **Shetland,** Holmsgarth Rd, ZE1 0PW, ℰ (01595) 695515, Fax (01595) 695828, ≤ – 🕴 ✵ 🔟 ☎ & 🅿 – 🔬 250. 🐶 AE ⓪ VISA ✵
Meals (bar lunch)/dinner 23.50 st. 🍷 4.50 – 63 rm ☑ 75.00/88.50 st., 1 suite – SB.

🏨 **Lerwick,** 15 South Rd, ZE1 0RB, ℰ (01595) 692166, Fax (01595) 694419, ≤, ☞ – 🔟 ☎ 🅿 – 🔬 60. 🐶 AE VISA 🍷
Meals 21.50 st. (dinner) and a la carte 12.85/18.40 st. 🍷 4.50 – 34 rm ☑ 69.50/79.50 st. 1 suite – SB.

🏠 **Glen Orchy House,** 20 Knab Rd, ZE1 0AX, ℰ (01595) 692031, Fax (01595) 692031 – ✵ rest, 🔟 & 🅿
Meals (residents only) (dinner only) 14.00 t. 🍷 4.25 – 14 rm ☑ 34.00/58.00 t.

🅰 ATS 3 Gremista Ind. Est., Lerwick ℰ (01595) 693857

Scalloway.

🏠 **Scalloway,** Main St., ZE1 0TR, ℰ (01595) 880444, Fax (01595) 880445, ≤ – ✵ 🔟 ☎ 🅿 🐶 AE ⓪
Meals (dinner only)/a la carte 10.60/18.80 st. 🍷 4.90 – 24 rm ☑ 50.00/70.00 st.

🏡 **Hildasay** without rest., Upper Scalloway, ZE1 0UP, NE : ½ m. by A 970 taking unmarked road on left after school ℰ (01595) 880822 – 🔟 & 🅿 ✵
4 rm ☑ 22.00/40.00.

Walls.

🏠 **Burrastow House** ⬥, ZE2 9PD, SW : 2 ½ m. ℰ (01595) 809307, Fax (01595) 809213 « Part 18C house overlooking Vaila Sound », ⬥, park – ✵ & 🅿 🐶 VISA ✵
restricted opening October-March – Meals (closed dinner Sunday and Monday) a la carte 15.25/24.70 t. 🍷 4.00 – 5 rm ☑ (dinner included) 80.00/160.00 t.

ISLAND OF UNST.

Baltasound.

🏡 **Buness House** ⬥, ZE2 9DS, E : ½ m. by A 968 ℰ (01957) 711315, Fax (01957) 711815 ≤ Balta Sound, ☞ – ✵ 🅿 ✵
Meals (communal dining) 21.00 st. 🍷 3.50 – 3 rm ☑ 30.00/50.00 st.

SHIELDAIG *Highland* [401] D 11 *Scotland G.* – ✉ *Strathcarron.*

Env. : *Wester Ross*★★★.

Edinburgh 226 – Inverness 70 – Kyle of Lochalsh 36.

🏨 **Tigh-An Eilean,** IV54 8XN, ☎ (01520) 755251, *Fax (01520) 755321,* ≤ Shieldaig Islands and Loch, « Attractively furnished inn » – [MC] VISA
April-late October – **Meals** (bar lunch)/dinner 22.50 **t.** 🍷 5.00 – **11 rm** ☕ (dinner included) 68.00/145.50 **t.** – SB.

SKYE (Isle of) *Highland* [401] B 11 /12 *Scotland G.* – *pop. 8 868.*

See : *Island*★★ – *The Cuillins*★★★ – *Skye Museum of Island Life*★ *AC.*

Env. : *N : Trotternish Peninsula*★★ – *W : Duirinish Peninsula*★ – *Portree*★.

Skye Bridge (toll).

⛴ – *from Mallaig to Armadale (Caledonian MacBrayne Ltd) 3-7 daily (30 mn) – from Uig to North Uist (Lochmaddy) or Isle of Harris (Tarbert) (Caledonian MacBrayne Ltd) 1-3 daily – from Sconser to Isle of Raasay (Caledonian MacBrayne Ltd) 9-10 daily (except Sunday) (15 mn).*

⛴ *from Mallaig to Isles of Eigg, Muck, Rhum and Canna (Caledonian MacBrayne Ltd) 3-7 daily – from Mallaig to Kyle of Lochalsh (Caledonian MacBrayne Ltd) (summer only) weekly (2 h).*

Ardvasar

🏨 **Ardvasar,** IV45 8RS, ☎ (01471) 844223, ≤, 🌳 – [TV] ☎ [P]. [MC] VISA. 🚫
closed Christmas-New Year and restricted opening January and February – **Meals** (bar lunch) a la carte 11.00/25.00 **t.** 🍷 8.00 – **9 rm** ☕ 45.00/80.00 **t.**

Breakish.

🍴 **Seagull,** IV42 8PY, ☎ (01471) 822001 – [P]. [MC] [AE] VISA
4 April-4 October – **Meals** (dinner only and Sunday lunch) a la carte 14.75/23.70 **st.**

Broadford.

🏠 **Corry Lodge** 🐚, Liveras, IV49 9AA, N : 1 m. by An Acarsaid rd ☎ (01471) 822235, *Fax (01471) 822318,* ≤, « Part 18C house », 🌳, park – 🚭 [TV] [P]. [MC] VISA. 🚫
April-October – **Meals** (by arrangement) (communal dining) 17.50 **st.** – **4 rm** ☕ 50.00/60.00 **st.**

🏠 **Ptarmigan** without rest., Harrapool, IV49 9AQ, E : ¾ m. on A 850 ☎ (01471) 822744, *Fax (01471) 822745,* ≤ Broadford Bay and islands, « Waterside setting », 🌳 – [TV] ☎ [P]. [MC] [AE] VISA
closed 2 weeks in winter – **3 rm** ☕ 35.00/54.00 **s.**

🏠 **Earsary** without rest., 7-8 Harrapool, IV49 9AQ, E : ¾ m. on A 850 ☎ (01471) 822697, *Fax (01471) 822781,* ≤, 🌳, park – 🚭 [TV] [P]
3 rm ☕ 25.00/44.00 **st.**

🏠 **Westside** without rest., Elgol Rd, IV49 9AB, on B 8083 ☎ (01471) 822320, 🌳 – [TV] [P]. 🚫
3 rm ☕ 19.00/42.00.

Culnaknock – ✉ *Portree*

🏨 **Glenview Inn,** IV51 9JH, ☎ (01470) 562248, *Fax (01470) 562211,* ≤ – 🚭 rest, [P]. [MC] VISA
April-October – **Meals** a la carte 13.45/23.00 **t.** 🍷 5.00 – **4 rm** ☕ 70.00 **t.**

Dunvegan.

🏨 **Harlosh House** 🐚, IV55 8ZG, SE : 6 m. by A 863 ☎ (01470) 521367, *Fax (01470) 521367,* ≤ Loch Bracadale and Islands – 🚭 [P]. [MC] VISA. 🚫
Easter-late October – **Meals** - Seafood - *(closed Wednesday)* (booking essential) (lunch by arrangement and dinner Wednesday residents only) 25.00 **t.** 🍷 8.50 – **6 rm** ☕ 67.50/95.00 **t.**

🏨 **Dunorin House** 🐚, Herebost, IV55 8GZ, SE : 2 ½ m. by A 863 on Roag rd ☎ (01470) 521488, *Fax (01470) 521488,* ≤, 🌳 – 🚭 [TV] [P]. [MC] VISA. 🚫
mid March-mid November – **Meals** (booking essential) (dinner only) a la carte 16.20/25.60 **st.** 🍷 4.00 – **10 rm** ☕ 42.00/78.00 **st.** – SB.

🍴 **Three Chimneys,** Colbost, IV55 8ZT, NW : 5 ¾ m. by A 863 on B 884 ☎ (01470) 511258, *Fax (01470) 511358* – 🚭 [P]. [MC] VISA
closed Sunday except Easter and late May Bank Holiday and November-March – **Meals** (booking essential) a la carte 9.70/36.70 **t.** 🍷 6.80.

Flodigarry – ⊠ Staffin.

🏛 **Flodigarry Country House** ⤸, IV51 9HZ, ℰ (01470) 552203, Fax (01470) 552301,
≤ Staffin Island and coastline, ㈜ – ⇆ **P**. **M0** **VISA**
Meals 16.50/28.00 **st.** ⓵ 8.50 – **18 rm** ⊇ 49.00/120.00 **t.**, 1 suite.

Isleornsay – ⊠ Sleat

🏛🏛 **Kinloch Lodge** ⤸, IV43 8QY, N : 3½ m. by A 851 ℰ (01471) 833333, Fax (01471) 833277
≤ Loch Na Dal, « 17C former shooting lodge », ⤸, ㈜, park – ⇆ ☎ **P**. **M0** **AE** **VISA**. ⅍
2 March-19 December – Meals (dinner only) 35.00 **t.** ⓵ 7.00 – **10 rm** ⊇ 50.00/190.00.

🏛 **Eilean Iarmain** ⤸, Sleat, IV43 8QR, ℰ (01471) 833332, Fax (01471) 833275, ≤,
« 19C inn », ㈜ – ⇆ ☎ **P**. **M0** **AE** **VISA**
Meals (lunch by arrangement) 16.50/29.50 **t.** ⓵ 6.50 – **12 rm** ⊇ 70.00/95.00 **t.** – SB.

Ord – ⊠ Sleat.

⌂ **Fiordhem** ⤸, IV44 8RN, ℰ (01471) 855226, ≤ Loch Eishort and The Cuillins, « Idyllic
setting on shores of Loch Eishort », ㈜ – ⇆ **P**. ⅍
Easter-October – Meals (communal dining) – **3 rm** ⊇ (dinner included) 37.00/80.00.

Portree – pop. 2 126.

🚺 Meall House, Portree, IV51 9BZ ℰ (01478) 612137.

🏛🏛 **Cuillin Hills** ⤸, IV51 9LU, NE : ¾ m. by A 855 ℰ (01478) 612003, Fax (01478) 613092, ≤,
㈜, park – ⇆ rest, **tv** ☎ **P** – 🔬 40. **M0** **AE** **VISA**
Meals (bar lunch Monday to Saturday) (buffet lunch Sunday)/dinner 24.00 **t.** ⓵ 5.25 – **25 rm**
⊇ 52.00/104.00 **t.** – SB.

🏛🏛 **Bosville**, Bosville Terr., IV51 9DG, ℰ (01478) 612846, Fax (01478) 613434, ≤ – ⇆ **tv** ☎ **P**
M0 **AE** **VISA**
Chandlery : Meals 11.00/21.00 **st.** and a la carte ⓵ 5.00 – **13 rm** ⊇ 60.00/90.00 **st.**
2 suites.

🏛 **Rosedale**, Beaumont Cres., IV51 9DF, ℰ (01478) 613131, Fax (01478) 612531, ≤ harbour
㈜ – ⇆ rest, **tv** ☎ **P**. **M0** **VISA** **JCB**. ⅍
May-15 October – Meals (dinner only) 20.00 **t.** ⓵ 6.15 – **23 rm** ⊇ 45.00/120.00 **t.** – SB.

⌂ **Almondbank** without rest., Viewfield Rd, IV51 9EU, SW : ¾ m. on A 85
ℰ (01478) 612696, Fax (01478) 613114, ≤ Portree Bay, ㈜ – **tv** ☎ **P**. **M0** **VISA**
4 rm ⊇ 30.00/65.00 **t.**

⌂ **Burnside** without rest., 5 Budmhor, IV51 9DJ, NE : ½ m. by A 855 ℰ (01478) 612669, ㈜
tv **P**
May-October – **3 rm** ⊇ 20.00/40.00 **st.**

⌂ **Kings Haven** without rest., 11 Bosville Terr., IV51 9DG, ℰ (01478) 612290, ㈜ – **tv**. **M0**
VISA. ⅍
closed Christmas, January and February – **6 rm** ⊇ 64.00 **t.**

Talisker – ⊠ Carbost.

⌂ **Talisker House** ⤸, IV47 8SF, ℰ (01478) 640245, Fax (01478) 640214, ≤, « Part 18C
country house », ⤸, ㈜, park – ⇆ ₺ **P**. **M0** **VISA**. ⅍
mid March-mid November – Meals (by arrangement) 20.00 **st.** – **3 rm** ⊇ 54.00/79.00 **t.**

Treaslane – ⊠ Skeabost Bridge.

⌂ **Auchendinny** ⤸, IV51 9NX, S : 1 m. on A 850 ℰ (01470) 532470, Fax (01470) 532470
≤ Loch Snizort Beag, ㈜ – ⇆ ₺ **P**. **M0** **VISA**. ⅍
Easter-mid October – Meals (by arrangement) 13.00 **s.** – **7 rm** ⊇ 30.00/54.00.

Uig.

🏠 **Ferry Inn** with rm, IV51 9XP, ℰ (01470) 542242 – **tv** **P**. **M0** **VISA**
closed 1 January – Meals (bar lunch) a la carte 10.50/14.50 **t.** ⓵ 4.75 – **6 rm** ⊇ 30.00/
54.00 **st.** – SB.

SOUTH UIST Western Isles (Outer Hebrides) **401** XY 11/12 – see Uist (Isles of).

Bitte beachten Sie die Geschwindigkeitsbeschränkungen in Großbritannien
- 60 mph (= 96 km/h) außerhalb geschlossener Ortschaften
- 70 mph (= 112 km/h) auf Straßen mit getrennten Fahrbahnen und Autobahnen.

SPEAN BRIDGE Highland **401** F 13.

Edinburgh 143 – Fort William 10 – Glasgow 94 – Inverness 58 – Oban 60.

🏠 **Corriegour Lodge,** Loch Lochy, PH34 4EB, N : 8 ¾ m. on A 82 ℘ (01397) 712685, *Fax (01397) 712696,* ≤, *☞* – *☆* rest, 🔟 **℗**, **⬤③** **AE** **VISA**, *☆*
29 January-mid November and weekends only February and March – **Meals** (dinner only) 21.50 **t.** ⓘ 5.50 – **9 rm** ⊐ (dinner included) 63.00/126.00 **t.** – SB.

🏠 **Coinachan,** Gairlochy Rd, PH34 4EG, NW : 1 ¼ m. by A 82 on B 8004 ℘ (01397) 712417, *Fax (01397) 712417,* ≤, *☞* – *☆* **℗**
closed 25 December and 2 weeks November – **Meals** 12.50 **st.** – **3 rm** ⊐ 30.00/45.00 **st.** – SB.

%% **Old Station,** Station Rd, PH34 4EP, ℘ (01397) 712535, « Former Victorian railway station » – *☆* **℗**, **⬤③** **VISA**
closed Monday in summer and restricted opening in winter – **Meals** (booking essential) (dinner only) 21.50 **t.** and a la carte ⓘ 6.25.

% **Old Pines** ⊜ with rm, PH34 4EG, NW : 1 ½ m. by A 82 on B 8004 ℘ (01397) 712324, *Fax (01397) 712433,* ≤, park – *☆* & **℗**, **⬤③** **AE** **VISA** **JCB**, *☆*
closed 2 weeks late November-early December – **Meals** *(closed Sunday to non-residents)* 13.50/25.00 **t.** – **8 rm** ⊐ (dinner included) 60.00/120.00 **st.** – SB.

at Roybridge E : 3 m. on A 86.

🏠🏠 **Glenspean Lodge** ⊜, PH31 4AW, E : 2 m. on A 86 ℘ (01397) 712223, *Fax (01397) 712660,* ≤, *☞* – *☆* rest, 🔟 **☎** **℗**, **⬤③** **VISA**, *☆*
Meals 12.50/22.50 **t.** and a la carte ⓘ 4.95 – **17 rm** ⊐ 50.00/140.00 **t.** – SB.

SPITTAL OF GLENSHEE Perthshire and Kinross **401** J 13 Scotland G. – ✉ Blairgowrie.

Env. : Glenshee (☀☀★★) *(chairlift AC).*
Edinburgh 69 – Aberdeen 74 – Dundee 35.

🏠 **Dalmunzie House** ⊜, PH10 7QG, ℘ (01250) 885224, *Fax (01250) 885225,* ≤, **⌞₃**, **⟋**, *☞*, park, ☀ – **⌐** **☎** **℗**, **⬤③** **VISA**
closed 1 to 28 December – **Meals** (bar lunch)/dinner 22.00 **t.** and a la carte ⓘ 5.50 – **17 rm** ⊐ 50.00/94.00 **t.** – SB.

STENNESS Orkney Islands **401** K 7 – see Orkney Islands.

STEPPS North Lanarkshire **401** H 16 – see Glasgow.

STEWARTON East Ayrshire **401** **402** G 16 Scotland G. – pop. 7 091.

Env. : Kilmarnock (Dean Castle, arms and armour★, musical instruments★ AC) S : 5 ½ m. by A 735 and B 7038.
Edinburgh 68 – Ayr 21 – Glasgow 22.

%%% **Chapeltoun House** ⊜ with rm, KA3 3ED, SW : 2 ½ m. by A 735 off B 769 ℘ (01560) 482696, *Fax (01560) 485100,* « Country house in extensive grounds », *⟋*, *☞* – *☆* rest, 🔟 **☎** **℗** – **⛴** 50. **⬤③** **AE** **VISA**, *☆*
Meals 24.80 **st.** (dinner) and lunch a la carte approx. 12.85 **st.** ⓘ 5.95 – **8 rm** ⊐ 85.00/145.00 **st.** – SB.

STIRLING **401** I 15 Scotland G. – pop. 30 515.

See : Town★★ – Castle★★ *AC* (Site★★★, external elevations★★★, Stirling Heads★★, Argyll and Sutherland Highlanders Regimental Museum★) B – Argyll's Lodging★ (Renaissance decoration★) B **A** – Church of the Holy Rude★ B **B**.
Env. : Wallace Monument (☀★★) NE : 2 ½ m. by A 9 – A – and B 998.
Exc. : Dunblane★ (Cathedral★★, West Front★★), N : 6 ½ m. by A 9 A.
🛈 41 Dumbarton Rd, FK8 2LQ ℘ (01786) 475019 – Royal Burgh Stirling Visitor Centre, The Esplanade ℘ (01786) 479901 – Motorway Service Area, M 9/M 80, junction 9 ℘ (01786) 814111 (summer only).
Edinburgh 37 – Dunfermline 23 – Falkirk 14 – Glasgow 28 – Greenock 52 – Motherwell 30 – Oban 87 – Perth 35.

Plan on next page

🏠🏠 **Stirling Highland,** Spittal St., FK8 1DU, ℘ (01786) 475444, *Fax (01786) 462929,* **⌞₆**, **≘s**, **⌐**, squash – **⌐** *☆* 🔟 **☎** & **℗** – **⛴** 150. **⬤③** **AE** **①** **VISA** **JCB**   B **e**
Scholars : **Meals** *(closed Saturday lunch)* 18.95 **t.** (dinner) and a la carte 10.30/29.95 **t.** ⓘ 5.75 – *Rizzios* : **Meals** - Italian - a la carte 9.20/20.35 **t.** ⓘ 5.75 – **74 rm** ⊐ 95.00/123.00 **t.**, 2 suites – SB.

STIRLING

Dumbarton Road . . . . . . B 10
Leisure Centre . . . . . . B
Murray Place . . . . . . B 15
Port Street . . . . . . B
Thistle Centre . . . . . . B
Upper Craigs . . . . . . B 29
Barnton Street . . . . . . B 2
Borestone Crescent . . . . . . A 3
Causewayhead Road. . . . . A, B 4
Corn Exchange Road . . . . . . B 5
Cornton Road. . . . . . A 7
Coxithill Road. . . . . . A 8
Drummond Place . . . . . . B 9
Goosecroft Road . . . . . . B 12
King Street . . . . . . B 13
Newhouse . . . . . . A 16
Park Place. . . . . . A 18
Queen Street . . . . . . B 20
Randolph Terrace . . . . . . A 22
St. John Street. . . . . . B 23
St. Mary's Wynd . . . . . . B 24
Seaforth Place . . . . . . B 25
Shirra's Brae Road . . . . . . A 26
Spittal Street . . . . . . B 27
Union Street. . . . . . B 28
Weaver Row . . . . . . A 31

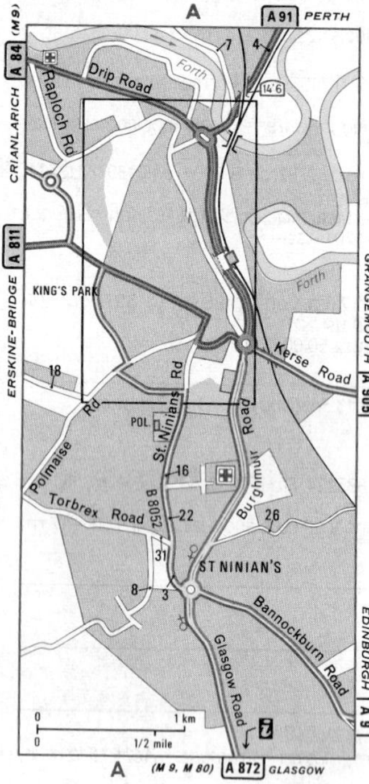

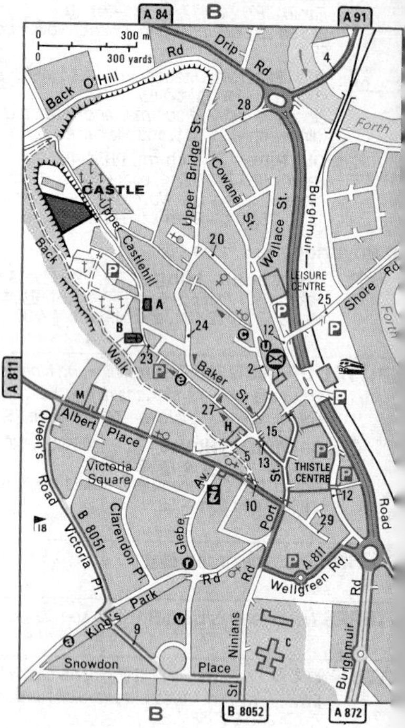

Park Lodge, 32 Park Terr., FK8 2JS, ✆ (01786) 474862, *Fax (01786) 449748,* « Georgia house, antiques », – TV ☎ P – 40. MC VISA. B
closed Christmas and New Year – **Meals** 9.50/14.75 **st.** and a la carte 4.75 – **10 rr** 50.00/160.00 **st.** – SB.

Travel Inn, Whins of Milton, Glasgow Rd, FK7 8EX, S : 3 m. by A 9 on A 87 ✆ (01786) 811256 – rm, TV P. MC AE VISA.
Meals (grill rest.) – **40 rm** 36.50 **t.**

Ashgrove House without rest., 2 Park Av., FK8 2LX, ✆ (01786) 47264 *Fax (01786) 474340* – TV B
closed 15 December-5 January – **3 rm** 27.50/55.00 **s.**

Number 10 without rest., Gladstone Pl., FK8 2NN, ✆ (01786) 472681, – TV. B
3 rm 30.00/40.00.

West Plean House without rest., FK7 8HA, S : 3 ½ m. on A 872 (Denny r ✆ (01786) 812208, *Fax (01786) 812208,* « Working farm », park – P.
closed December and January – **3 rm** 30.00/48.00 **st.**

Fairfield without rest., 14 Princes St., FK8 1HQ, ✆ (01786) 472685 – TV. B
March-October – **5 rm** 30.00/42.00.

East India Company, 7 Viewfield Pl., FK8 1NQ, ✆ (01786) 471330 – MC AE VI JCB B
closed 25 December and 1 January – **Meals** - Indian - (dinner only) 9.95 **t.** and a la car 6.50.

at Blairlogie NE : 4½ m. by A 9 on A 91 – A – ⊠ Stirling.

🏛 **Blairlogie House,** FK9 5QE, ℰ (01259) 761441, Fax (01259) 761441, ☞, park – 🖵 ☎ 🅿.
📶 VISA
closed 2 weeks Christmas – Meals (closed Sunday) (bar lunch)/dinner 18.50 st. ⒜ 4.15 –
7 rm ⊑ 52.50/72.00 st. – SB.

🔘 ATS 45 Drip Rd ℰ (01786) 450770

STIRLING SERVICE AREA Stirling 401 I 15 – ⊠ Stirling.

🏛 **Travelodge** without rest., Pirnhall roundabout, Snabhead, FK7 8EU, at junction 9 of M 9
with M 80 ℰ (01786) 813614, Fax (01786) 815900, Reservations (Freephone) 0800 850950 –
🔆 🖵 ☎ ⅛ 🅿. 📶 🆀 ⓪ VISA JCB. ⅙
37 rm 42.95 t.

STONEHAVEN Aberdeenshire 401 N 13 Scotland G.
Env. : Dunnottar Castle★★ (site★★★), SE : 1 m.
Exc. : Crathes Castle★★ (Gardens★★★), NW : 14 ½ m. by A 957 and A 93.
Edinburgh 114 – Aberdeen 16 – Dundee 51.

🍴 **The Tolbooth,** Old Pier Rd, AB39 1JU, ℰ (01569) 762287 – 📶 VISA
closed Monday and first 2 weeks January – Meals - Seafood - (dinner only and Sunday
lunch)/dinner a la carte 18.20/27.70 t. ⒜ 6.95.

🔘 ATS 64-72 Barclay St. ℰ (01569) 762077

STORNOWAY Western Isles (Outer Hebrides) 401 A 9 – see Lewis and Harris (Isle of).

STRANRAER Dumfries and Galloway 401 402 E 19 Scotland G. – pop. 11 348.
Exc. : Logan Botanic Garden★ AC, S : 11 m. by A 77, A 716 and B 7065.
🏌 Creachmore, Leswalt ℰ (01776) 870245.
⛴ to Northern Ireland (Belfast) (Stena Line) (3 h 15 mn) – to Northern Ireland (Belfast)
(Sea Containers Ferries Scotland Ltd) 4-5 daily (1 h 30 mn).
🛈 Burns House, Harbour St., DG9 7RA ℰ (01776) 702595.
Edinburgh 132 – Ayr 51 – Dumfries 75.

🏨 **North West Castle,** Port Rodie, DG9 8EH, ℰ (01776) 704413, Fax (01776) 702646, ⓢ,
⬛ – 🛗, 🔆 rest, 🖵 ☎ 🅿 – ⚒ 100. 📶 VISA. ⅙
Meals 21.00 st. (dinner) and a la carte 16.75/23.50 st. ⒜ 6.60 – **71 rm** ⊑ 45.00/100.00 st. –
SB.

🏠 **Kildrochet House** ⌂, DG9 9BB, S : 3 ¼ m. by A 77 on A 716 at junction with B 7077
(Newton Stewart rd) ℰ (01776) 820216, Fax (01776) 820216, « 18C former dower house »,
☞ – 🔆 🅿. 📶 VISA. ⅙
Meals (by arrangement) 15.00 s. – **3 rm** ⊑ 30.00/50.00.

🏠 **Windyridge Villa** without rest., 5 Royal Cresent, DG9 8HB, off Port Rodie (A77 Ayr rd)
ℰ (01776) 889900 – 🔆 🖵 ⇔
closed 25 December and 2 weeks November – **3 rm** ⊑ 20.00/40.00 st.

at Kirkcolm NW : 6 m. by A 718 – ⊠ Stranraer.

🏛 **Corsewall Lighthouse** ⌂, Corsewall Point, DG9 0QG, NW : 4 ¼ m. by B 738
ℰ (01776) 853220, Fax (01776) 854231, ≼, park – 🔆 🖵 ☎ 🅿. 📶 🆀 ⓪ VISA JCB. ⅙
Meals (dinner only) 25.00 t. ⒜ 7.95 – **6 rm** ⊑ (dinner included) 80.00/250.00 t. – SB.

🔘 ATS Commerce Rd Ind. Est. ℰ (01776) 702131

STRATHBLANE Stirling 401 H 16 – pop. 2 355 – ⊠ Glasgow.
Edinburgh 52 – Glasgow 11 – Stirling 26.

🏛 **Kirkhouse Inn,** Glasgow Rd, G63 9AA, ℰ (01360) 770621, Fax (01360) 770896 – 🖵 ☎ 🅿
– ⚒ 30. 📶 🆀 ⓪ VISA. ⅙
Meals 12.50/18.50 st. and dinner a la carte ⒜ 4.95 – **15 rm** ⊑ 48.00/65.00 st. – SB.

STRATHCONON Highland 401 F 11 Scotland G. – ⊠ Muir of Ord.
Exc. : Wester Ross★★★.
Edinburgh 184 – Inverness 28.

🏨 **East Lodge** ⌂, IV6 7QQ, W : 11 m. from Marybank off A 832 ℰ (01997) 477222,
Fax (01997) 477243, ≼, 🐟, ☞, park – 🔆 rest, 🖵 ☎ 🅿. 📶 VISA
Meals (bar lunch)/dinner 24.00 st. ⒜ 4.50 – **10 rm** ⊑ 55.00/110.00 st. – SB.

STRATHKINNESS Fife 🔢 L 14 – see St. Andrews.

STRATHPEFFER Highland 🔢 G 11 – pop. 966.
  🔢 Strathpeffer Spa ℘ (01997) 421219.
  🔢 The Square, IV14 9DW ℘ (01997) 421415 (April-November).
  Edinburgh 174 – Inverness 18.

⬆ **Craigvar** without rest., The Square, IV14 9DL, ℘ (01997) 421622, 🌼 – 📺 ☎ 🅿. 𝘝𝘐𝘚𝘈. ⚡
  closed Christmas and New Year – **3 rm** ⌑ 27.00/50.00.

STRATHYRE Stirling 🔢 H 15 Scotland G. – ✉ Callander.
  EXC.: The Trossachs★★★ (Loch Katherine★★) SW: 14 m. by A 84 and A 821 – Hilltop
  viewpoint★★★ (✳★★★) SW: 16 ½ m. by A 84 and A 821.
  Edinburgh 62 – Glasgow 53 – Perth 42.

⬆ **Ardoch Lodge** ॐ, FK18 8NF, W: ¼ m. ℘ (01877) 384666, Fax (01877) 384666, ≤, 🌼,
  park – ✳ rest. 🅿. 🆖 𝘝𝘐𝘚𝘈 𝘑𝘊𝘉
  restricted opening in winter – **Meals** (by arrangement) 19.50 **st.** – **3 rm** ⌑ 33.50/58.00 **st.**

✗ **Creagan House** with rm, FK18 8ND, on A 84 ℘ (01877) 384638, Fax (01877) 384319, ≤ –
  ✳ 🅿. 🆖 🆎 𝘝𝘐𝘚𝘈
  closed February and 1 week October – **Meals** (booking essential) (dinner only and Sunday
  lunch)/dinner 22.50 **t.** ⌑ 7.50 – **5 rm** ⌑ 45.00/70.00 **t.** – SB.

STROMNESS Orkney Islands 🔢 K 7 – see Orkney Islands.

STRONTIAN Highland 🔢 D 13.
  🔢 Village Square, PH36 ℘ (01967) 402131 (summer only).
  Edinburgh 139 – Fort William 23 – Oban 66.

🏨 **Kilcamb Lodge** ॐ, PH36 4HY, ℘ (01967) 402257, Fax (01967) 402041, ≤, « Lochside
  setting », ◣, 🌼 – ✳ 📺 🅿. 🆖 𝘝𝘐𝘚𝘈 𝘑𝘊𝘉. ⚡
  March-November and New Year – **Meals** (light lunch)/dinner 25.00 **t.** ⌑ 7.00 – **11 rm**
  ⌑ (dinner included) 69.50/170.00 **t.** – SB.

TAIN Highland 🔢 H 10 – pop. 4 540.
  🔢 Tain ℘ (01862) 892314.
  Edinburgh 191 – Inverness 35 – Wick 91.

🏨 **Morangie House,** Morangie Rd, IV19 1PY, ℘ (01862) 892281, Fax (01862) 892872, 🌼 –
  ✳ rm, 📺 ☎ 🅿. 🆖 🆎 ⓪ 𝘝𝘐𝘚𝘈
  Meals 10.50/18.70 **t.** and a la carte ⌑ 4.60 – **26 rm** ⌑ 50.00/80.00.

🏨 **Mansfield House,** Scotsburn Rd, IV19 1PR, ℘ (01862) 892052, Fax (01862) 892260, 🌼 –
  ✳ 📺 🅿 – 🔬 35. 🆖 🆎 𝘝𝘐𝘚𝘈
  Meals (bar lunch)/dinner a la carte 12.50/20.95 **st.** ⌑ 4.80 – **18 rm** ⌑ 55.00/100.00 **st.** – SB

⬆ **Aldie House** ॐ, IV19 1LZ, SE: 1 ½ m. by B 9174 off A 9 ℘ (01862) 893787,
  Fax (01862) 893787, ≤, 🌼, park – ✳ 📺 🅿. 🆖 𝘝𝘐𝘚𝘈
  Meals (by arrangement) 13.00 **st.** – **3 rm** ⌑ 26.00/44.00 **st.**

⬆ **Golf View House** without rest., 13 Knockbreck Rd, IV19 1BN, ℘ (01862) 892856
  Fax (01862) 892856, ≤, 🌼 – ✳ 📺 🅿. ⚡
  closed 16 December-15 January – **5 rm** ⌑ 20.00/40.00.

TALISKER Highland 🔢 A 12 – see Skye (Isle of).

TALLADALE Highland 🔢 D 10 Scotland G. – ✉ Achnasheen.
  ENV.: Wester Ross★★★ – Loch Maree★★★ – Victoria Falls★, N: 2 m. by A 832.
  Edinburgh 218 – Inverness 62 – Kyle of Lochalsh 58.

⬆ **Old Mill Highland Lodge** ॐ, IV22 2HL, ℘ (01445) 760271, 🌼 – ✳ 🅿
  closed 15 October-15 December – **Meals** (by arrangement) 25.00 **st.** ⌑ 7.50 – **6 rm**
  ⌑ (dinner included) 130.00 **st.** – SB.

TARBERT Argyll and Bute 🔢 D 16 – see Kintyre (Peninsula).

TARBERT Western Isles (Outer Hebrides) 🔢 Z 10 – see Lewis and Harris (Isle of).

THORNHILL *Dumfries and Galloway* **401 402** I 18 *Scotland G. – pop. 1 633.*
Env. : *Drumlanrig Castle*★★ *(cabinets*★*) AC, NW : 4 m. by A 76.*
Edinburgh 64 – Ayr 44 – Dumfries 15 – Glasgow 63.

🏨 **Trigony House**, Closeburn, DG3 5EZ, S : 1 ½ m. on A 76 ℰ (01848) 331211,
Fax (01848) 331303, 🐴 – ᐟᐟ rest, 🆃🆅 ☎ 🄿. 🆆🆂 *VISA* JCB. ℘
closed 25-26 December and 2-3 January – **Meals** (bar lunch Monday to Saturday)/dinner
18.95 t. ⅃ 5.50 – **8 rm** ⊊ 40.00/80.00 t. – SB.

THORNHILL *Stirling* **401** H 15 – *pop. 550 –* ✉ *Stirling.*
Edinburgh 46 – Glasgow 36.

⛫ **Corshill Cottage** ⌂, FK8 3QD, E : 1 m. on A 873 ℰ (01786) 850270, 🐴 – ᐟᐟ 🄿. ℘
April-October – **Meals** (by arrangement) 15.00 – **3 rm** ⊊ 28.00/50.00 s.

THURSO *Highland* **401** J 8 *Scotland G. – pop. 8 488.*
Exc. : *Strathy Point*★ *(*≤★★★*) W : 22 m. by A 836.*
🏌 *Newlands of Geise* ℰ (01847) 893807.
⛴ *from Scrabster to Stromness (Orkney Islands) (P & O Scottish Ferries) (1 h 45 mn).*
🖪 *Riverside, KW14 8BU* ℰ (01847) 892371 *(summer only).*
Edinburgh 289 – Inverness 133 – Wick 21.

🏛 **Forss House** ⌂, Bridge of Forss, KW14 7XY, W : 5 ½ m. on A 836 ℰ (01847) 861201,
Fax (01847) 861301, 🐟, 🐴, park – ᐟᐟ rest, 🆃🆅 ☎ & 🄿. 🆆🆂 *VISA*
closed 1 week Christmas – **Meals** (bar lunch)/dinner 19.50 t. ⅃ 5.20 – **10 rm** ⊊ 49.50/
100.00 t.

⛫ **Murray House** without rest., 1 Campbell St., KW14 7HD, ℰ (01847) 895759 – ᐟᐟ 🆃🆅 🄿.
℘
closed 1 week Christmas – **4 rm** ⊊ 16.00/40.00 s.

TILLICOULTRY *Clackmannanshire* **401** I 15 – *pop. 4 586.*
🏌 *Alva Rd* ℰ (01259) 50124.
Edinburgh 35 – Dundee 43 – Glasgow 38.

🏨 **Harviestoun Country Inn**, Dollar Rd, FK13 6PQ, on A 91 ℰ (01259) 752522,
Fax (01259) 752523 – ᐟᐟ 🆃🆅 ☎ 🄿 – 🕭 70. 🆆🆂 🆀🅴 *VISA*
closed 25 December and 1-2 January – **Meals** a la carte 12.15/24.70 st. ⅃ 6.95 – **10 rm**
⊊ 49.95/65.00 st.

TOBERMORY *Argyll and Bute* **401** B 14 – *see Mull (Isle of).*

TONGUE *Highland* **401** G 8 *Scotland G. – pop. 552 –* ✉ *Lairg.*
Exc. : *Cape Wrath*★★★ *(*≤★★*) W : 44 m. (including ferry crossing) by A 838 – Ben Loyal*★★,
S : 8 m. by A 836 – Ben Hope★ *(*≤★★★*) SW : 15 m. by A 838 – Strathy Point*★ *(*≤★★★*)*
E : 22 m. by A 836 – Torrisdale Bay★ *(*≤★★*) NE : 8 m. by A 836.*
Edinburgh 257 – Inverness 101 – Thurso 43.

🏨 **Ben Loyal**, Main St., IV27 4XE, ℰ (01847) 611216, *Fax* (01847) 611212, ≤ Ben Loyal and
Kyle of Tongue – ᐟᐟ rest, 🆃🆅 🄿. 🆆🆂 *VISA*
16 March-14 November – **Meals** (bar lunch)/dinner 24.00 t. ⅃ 6.95 – **12 rm** ⊊ 40.00/
76.00 t. – SB.

TORRIDON *Highland* **401** D 11 *Scotland G. –* ✉ *Achnasheen.*
Env. : *Wester Ross*★★★.
Edinburgh 234 – Inverness 62 – Kyle of Lochalsh 44.

🏰 **Loch Torridon** ⌂, IV22 2EY, S : 1 ½ m. on A 896 ℰ (01445) 791242, *Fax* (01445) 791296,
≤ Upper Loch Torridon and mountains, « 19C former shooting lodge », 🐟, 🐴, park – 🛗
ᐟᐟ 🆃🆅 ☎ 🄿 – 🕭 25. 🆆🆂 🆀🅴 🅾 *VISA*. ℘
Meals (bar lunch)/dinner 37.50 st. ⅃ 6.50 – **19 rm** ⊊ 80.00/235.00 st., 2 suites – SB.

TREASLANE *Highland – see Skye (Isle of).*

TROON *South Ayrshire* **401 402** G 17 – *pop. 15 116.*
🏌, 🏌, 🏌 *Troon Municipal, Harling Drive* ℰ (01292) 312464.
🖪 *Municipal Buildings, South Beach* ℰ (01292) 317696 *(summer only).*
Edinburgh 77 – Ayr 7 – Glasgow 31.

Marine Highland, 8 Crosbie Rd, KA10 6HE, ☏ (01292) 314444, Fax (01292) 316922, ≤, ₤₅, ⌨s, ⌧, squash – |₰|, ⇔ rm, ⊡ ☎ ℗ – ₳ 200. ⃝ ⒶⒺ ① ⒱ⒾⓈⒶ. ⅔
Rizzio's: Meals a la carte 12.30/22.45 t. ₰ 5.45 – **Fairways**: Meals (closed lunch Monday and Tuesday) 21.50 t. (dinner) and a la carte 13.45/35.45 ₰ 5.95 – **66 rm** ⊆ 90.00/144.00 t., 6 suites – SB.

Lochgreen House ⇖, Monktonhill Rd, Southwood, KA10 7EN, SE : 2 m. on B 749 ☏ (01292) 313343, Fax (01292) 318661, « Edwardian house, antiques », ⌨, park, ⅔ – ⊡ ☎ ₰ ℗ – ₳ 30. ⃝ ⒶⒺ ⒱ⒾⓈⒶ
Meals 18.95/29.95 st. and lunch a la carte ₰ 9.95 – **14 rm** ⊆ 99.00/150.00 st., 1 suite – SB.

Piersland House, 15 Craigend Rd, KA10 6HD, ☏ (01292) 314747, Fax (01292) 315613, ⌨ – ⊡ ☎ ℗ – ₳ 100. ⃝ ⒶⒺ ① ⒱ⒾⓈⒶ
Meals 11.95/19.95 st. and a la carte ₰ 5.95 – **17 rm** ⊆ 82.50/120.00 st., 11 suites – SB.

Highgrove House, Old Loans Rd, Loans, KA10 7HL, E : 2½ m. by A 759 on Dundonald rd ☏ (01292) 312511, Fax (01292) 318228, ≤, ⌨ – ⊡ ☎ ℗. ⃝ ⒶⒺ ⒱ⒾⓈⒶ. ⅔
Meals a la carte 15.40/27.40 t. ₰ 6.50 – **9 rm** ⊆ 70.00/90.00 st.

Glenside, 2 Darley Pl., KA10 6JQ, ☏ (01292) 313677, Fax (01292) 313677, ⌨ – ⇔ rest, ⊡ ℗
Meals (by arrangement) 12.00 st. ₰ 3.50 – **5 rm** ⊆ 28.00/51.00 st.

TURNBERRY South Ayrshire ⓋⓀⓁ ⓋⓀⓂ F 18 Scotland G. – ✉ Girvan.
  Env. : Culzean Castle★ AC (setting★★★, Oval Staircase★★) NE : 5 m. by A 719.
  Edinburgh 97 – Ayr 15 – Glasgow 51 – Stranraer 36.

Turnberry ⇖, KA26 9LT, on A 719 ☏ (01655) 331000, Fax (01655) 331706, « Part Edwardian, ≤ golf courses, bay, Ailsa Craig and Mull of Kintyre », ₤₅, ⌨s, ⌧, ⌨₈, ⌨, ⅔, squash – |₰| ⊡ ☎ ₰ ℗ – ₳ 150. ⃝ ⒶⒺ ① ⒱ⒾⓈⒶ ⒿⒸⒷ. ⅔
Turnberry: Meals (dinner only and Sunday lunch)/dinner 45.50 t. and a la carte ₰ 10.50 – **Bay at Turnberry**: Meals (closed dinner November-March) 22.00/33.00 t. ₰ 10.50 – **The Clubhouse**: Meals (lunch only) a la carte 13.00/21.00 t. ₰ 10.50 – **122 rm** ⊆ 215.00/330.00 t., 10 suites – SB.

TWYNHOLM Dumfries and Galloway ⓋⓀⓂ H 19 – pop. 1 068.
  Edinburgh 107 – Ayr 54 – Dumfries 27 – Stranraer 48.

Fresh Fields ⇖, Arden Rd, DG6 4PB, SW : ¾ m. by Burn Brae ☏ (01557) 860221, Fax (01557) 860221, ⌨ – ⇔ ℗.
March-October – Meals (by arrangement) ₰ 4.25 – **5 rm** ⊆ (dinner included) 41.00/82.00 st.

UDDINGSTON South Lanarkshire ⓋⓀⓁ ⓋⓀⓂ H 16 – pop. 5 367 – ✉ Glasgow.
  ⌨₈ Coatbridge, Townhead Rd ☏ (01236) 28975.
  Edinburgh 41 – Glasgow 10.

Redstones, 8-10 Glasgow Rd, G71 7AS, ☏ (01698) 813774, Fax (01698) 815319 – ⊡ ☎ ℗ ⃝ ⒶⒺ ① ⒱ⒾⓈⒶ. ⅔
closed 1 January – Meals (bar lunch and Sunday dinner)/dinner 15.50 t. and a la carte ₰ 5.25 – **18 rm** ⊆ 52.00/74.50 t.

Travel Inn, 601 Hamilton Rd, G71 7SA, N : 2 m. by B 7071 off A 74 ☏ (01698) 773 1133, Fax (01698) 771 8354, ⌨ – |₰|, ⇔ rm, ⊡ ₰ ℗. ⃝ ⒶⒺ ① ⒱ⒾⓈⒶ. ⅔
Meals (grill rest.) – **40 rm** 36.50 t.

UIG Highland ⓋⓀⓁ B 11 and 12 - see Skye (Isle of).

UIST (Isles of) Western Isles (Outer Hebrides) ⓋⓀⓁ XY 10 /11/12 – pop. 3 510.
  ✈ see Liniclate.
  ⌁ from Lochboisdale to Oban via Isle of Barra (Castlebay) and Malaig (Mainland) (Caledonian MacBrayne Ltd) (summer only) – from Lochmaddy to Isle of Skye (Uig) (Caledonian MacBrayne Ltd) 1-3 daily (1 h 50 mn) – from Otternish to Berneray (Caledonian MacBrayne Ltd) – from Otternish to Isle of Lewis and Harris (Leverburgh) (Caledonian MacBrayne Ltd) (1 h 20 mn).

NORTH UIST.

Grimsay.

Glendale ⇖, 7 Kallin, HS6 5HY, ☏ (01870) 602029, ≤ – ⇔ ℗. ⅔
closed Christmas and New Year – Meals (communal dining) 12.00 – **3 rm** ⊆ 21.00/36.00 st – SB.

Locheport.

🏠 **Langass Lodge** ⚘, HS6 5HA, NW : 4 ½ m. by B 894 off A 867 φ (01876) 580285, *Fax (01876) 580385*, ⚘, ⚘ – ☎ 🅿. ⓌⓈ 𝘝𝘐𝘚𝘈
closed February – **Meals** 10.00/18.00 t. and dinner a la carte – **6 rm** 🍽 31.00/56.00 t.

Lochmaddy.

🏠 **Lochmaddy**, HS6 5AA, φ (01876) 500331, *Fax (01876) 500210* – 📺 ☎ 🅿. ⓌⓈ 𝘼𝙀 𝘝𝘐𝘚𝘈
Meals (bar lunch)/dinner 15.00 t. and a la carte ⓘ 5.50 – **15 rm** 🍽 40.00/75.00 t.

BENBECULA.

Liniclate.

🛬 Benbecula Airport : φ (01870) 602051.

🏨 **Dark Island**, HS7 5PJ, φ (01870) 603030, *Fax (01870) 602347* – 📺 ☎ 🅿. ⓌⓈ 𝘝𝘐𝘚𝘈
closed 26 December and 1 January – **Meals** 9.75/17.75 st. and dinner a la carte ⓘ 4.00 –
42 rm 🍽 60.00/84.00 st. – SB.

SOUTH UIST.

Lochboisdale.

↑ **Brae Lea** ⚘, Lasgair, HS8 5TH, NW : 1 m. by A 865 φ (01878) 700497, *Fax (01878) 700497*,
⚘ – 🅿
Meals 12.00 st. – **6 rm** 🍽 25.00/50.00 st. – SB.

Pollachar.

🏠 **Polochar Inn**, HS8 5TT, φ (01878) 700215, *Fax (01878) 700768*, ⚘ Sound of Barra – ⬇
⚘ 📺 ☎ 🅿. ⓌⓈ 𝘝𝘐𝘚𝘈. ⚘
closed 31 December – **Meals** a la carte 9.75/29.45 st. – **10 rm** 🍽 40.00/65.00 st.

Die Preise   Einzelheiten über die in diesem Reiseführer angegebenen Preise
finden Sie in der Einleitung.

ULLAPOOL *Highland* 𝟜𝟘𝟙 E 10 *Scotland G.* – *pop. 1 231.*

See : *Town*★.
Env. : *Wester Ross*★★★ – *Loch Broom*★★.
Exc. : *Falls of Measach*★★, *S* : 11 m. by A 835 and A 832 - *Corrieshalloch Gorge*★, SE : 10 m.
by A 835 – Northwards to Lochinver★★, Morefield (⚘★★ *of Ullapool*), ⚘★ *Loch Broom*.
🚢 to Isle of Lewis (Stornoway) (Caledonian MacBrayne Ltd) (2 h 45 mn).
🛈 Argyle St., IV26 2UR φ (01854) 612135 (April-November).
Edinburgh 215 – Inverness 59.

🏨 **Altnaharrie Inn** (Gunn Eriksen) ⚘, IV26 2SS, SW : ½ m. by private ferry
φ (01854) 633230, « *Former drovers' inn on banks of Loch Broom*, ⚘ *Ullapool* », ⚘ – ⚘.
❀❀   ⓌⓈ 𝘝𝘐𝘚𝘈. ⚘
Easter-early November – **Meals** (booking essential) (residents only) (dinner only) 65.00/
75.00 st. ⓘ 7.50 – **8 rm** 🍽 (dinner included) 165.00/400.00 st.
Spec. Young monkfish with thin slices of crisp celeriac and two sauces. "Soup" of lobster
with summer truffles. Squab pigeon and foie gras with roasted kohlrabi and chanterelles.

🏠 **Ardvreck** ⚘ *without rest.*, Morefield Brae, IV26 2TH, NW : 2 m. by A 835
φ (01854) 612028, *Fax (01854) 613000*, ⚘ Loch Broom and mountains, ⚘ – ⚘ 📺 🅿. ⓌⓈ
𝘝𝘐𝘚𝘈. ⚘
March-November – **10 rm** 🍽 25.00/50.00 st.

↑ **The Sheiling** *without rest.*, Garve Rd, IV26 2SX, φ (01854) 612947, *Fax (01854) 612947*,
⚘ Loch Broom, ⚘, ⚘ – ⚘ 🅿. ⚘
closed Christmas and New Year – **7 rm** 🍽 35.00/50.00 st.

↑ **Dromnan** *without rest.*, Garve Rd, IV26 2SX, φ (01854) 612333, *Fax (01854) 612333*, ⚘,
⚘ – ⚘ 📺 🅿. ⓌⓈ 𝘝𝘐𝘚𝘈. ⚘
7 rm 🍽 30.00/50.00 st.

↑ **Point Cottage** *without rest.*, West Shore St., IV26 2UR, φ (01854) 612494, ⚘ Loch
Broom, ⚘ – ⚘ 📺 🅿
closed December and January – **3 rm** 🍽 45.00/50.00 s.

UNST (Island of) *Shetland Islands* 𝟜𝟘𝟙 R 1 – *see Shetland Islands.*

UPHALL *West Lothian* [401] J 16 – *pop. 14 600.*

⛳18 *Uphall, Houston Mains* ☎ *(01506) 856404.*

Edinburgh 13 – Glasgow 32.

Houstoun House, EH52 6JS, ☎ (01506) 853831, *Fax (01506) 854220,* « Gardens », park – ⊭ rm, 📺 ☎ 🅿 – 🏛 400. [MC] [VISA]. ✻

Meals 16.50/32.50 **st.** and dinner a la carte 🍷 7.00 – ☕ 10.00 – **73 rm** 115.00/180.00 **st.** – SB.

WALKERBURN *Borders* [401] [402] K 17 *Scotland G. – pop. 1 038 (inc. Traquair).*

Env. : *The Tweed Valley★★ – Traquair House★★, W : 4 m. by A 72 and B 709.*

Exc. : *Abbotsbury★★ AC, W : 10 ½ m. by A 72, A 6091 and B 6360.*

⛳9 *Innerleithen, Leithen Water, Leithen Rd* ☎ *(01896) 830951.*

Edinburgh 32 – Galashiels 10 – Peebles 8.

Tweed Valley 🐕, Galashiels Rd, EH43 6AA, ☎ (01896) 870636, *Fax (01896) 870639,* <, ≘s, 🎣, 🌳 – ⊭ rest, 📺 ☎ 🅿. [MC] [AE] [VISA]

Meals 12.00/19.00 **st.** and a la carte 🍷 7.50 – **16 rm** ☕ (dinner included) 54.00/108.00 **st.** – SB.

WALLS *Shetland Islands* [401] PQ 3 – *see Shetland Islands (Mainland).*

WHITEBRIDGE *Highland* [401] G 12 *Scotland G.*

Env. : *Loch Ness★★ – The Great Glen★.*

Edinburgh 171 – Inverness 23 – Kyle of Lochalsh 67 – Oban 92.

Knockie Lodge 🐕, IV1 2UP, SW : 3 ½ m. by B 862 ☎ (01456) 486276, *Fax (01456) 486389,* < Loch Nan Lann and mountains, « Converted hunting lodge », 🎣, park – ⊭ ☎ 🅿. [MC] [AE] [DC] [VISA]. ✻

May-October – **Meals** (booking essential to non-residents) (bar lunch)/dinner 33.00 **st** 🍷 7.50 – **10 rm** ☕ 60.00/160.00 **st.**

WHITING BAY *North Ayrshire* [401] [402] E 17 – *see Arran (Isle of).*

WICK *Highland* [401] K 8 *Scotland G. – pop. 9 713.*

Exc. : *Duncansby Head★ (Stacks of Duncansby★★) N : 14 m. by A 9 – Grey Cairns of Camster★ (Long Cairn★★) S : 17 m. by A 9 – The Hill O'Many Stanes★, S : 10 m. by A 9.*

⛳18 *Reiss* ☎ *(01955) 2726.*

✈ *Wick Airport :* ☎ *(01955) 602215, N : 1 m.*

ℹ *Whitechapel Rd, KW1 4EA* ☎ *(01955) 602596.*

Edinburgh 282 – Inverness 126.

Clachan without rest., South Rd, KW1 5NH, S : ¾ m. on A 9 ☎ (01955) 605384, 🌳 – ⊭ 📺. ✻

closed 2 weeks Christmas-New Year – **3 rm** ☕ 25.00/40.00 **s.**

Meadowbank House without rest., Thurso Rd, KW1 5LE, W : 1 m. on A 88 ☎ (01955) 603760 – ⊭ 📺 🅿

April-September – **3 rm** ☕ 20.00/40.00 **s.**

WIGTOWN *Dumfries and Galloway* [401] G 19 *Scotland G. – pop. 1 344 –* ✉ *Newton Stewart.*

Exc. : *Whithorn Museum (early Christian crosses★★) S : 10 m. by A 746.*

⛳9 *Wigtown & Bladnoch, Lightlands Terr.* ☎ *(01988) 403354.*

Edinburgh 137 – Ayr 61 – Dumfries 61 – Stranraer 26.

Corsemalzie House 🐕, DG8 9RL, SW : 6 ½ m. by A 714 on B 7005 ☎ (01988) 860254, *Fax (01988) 860213,* 🎣, 🌳, park – ⊭ rest, 📺 ☎ 🅿. [MC] [AE] [VISA]

closed mid January-early March and 25-26 December – **Meals** 10.75/19.95 **st.** and a la carte 🍷 4.50 – **15 rm** ☕ 49.00/94.00 **t.** – SB.

WORMIT *Fife* [401] L 14 – ✉ *Newport-on-Tay.*

⛳18 *Scotscraig, Golf Rd, Tayport* ☎ *(01382) 552515.*

Edinburgh 53 – Dundee 6 – St. Andrews 12.

Sandford 🐕, DD6 8RG, S : 2 m. at junction of A 914 with B 946 ☎ (01382) 541802, *Fax (01382) 542136,* <, 🌳 – ⊭ rest, 📺 ☎ 🅿 – 🏛 60. [MC] [AE] [DC] [VISA]

Meals 21.00 **t.** and a la carte 🍷 5.90 – **16 rm** ☕ 80.00/95.00 **t.** – SB.

Wales

Place with at least

- a hotel or restaurant   ● Ruthin
- a pleasant hotel or restaurant   🏨, ↷, ✗, 🕭
- a quiet, secluded hotel
- a restaurant with   ⌘, ⌘⌘, ⌘⌘⌘, 🕭   **Meals**
- See this town for establishments located in its vicinity   **NEATH**

Localité offrant au moins

- une ressource hôtelière   ● Ruthin
- un hôtel ou restaurant agréable   🏨, ↷, ✗, 🕭
- un hôtel très tranquille, isolé
- une bonne table à   ⌘, ⌘⌘, ⌘⌘⌘, 🕭   **Meals**
- Localité groupant dans le texte les ressources de ses environs   **NEATH**

La località possiede come minimo

- una risorsa alberghiera   ● Ruthin
- Albergo o ristorante ameno   🏨, ↷, ✗, 🕭
- un albergo molto tranquillo, isolato
- un'ottima tavola con   ⌘, ⌘⌘, ⌘⌘⌘, 🕭   **Meals**
- La località raggruppa nel suo testo le risorse dei dintorni   **NEATH**

Ort mit mindestens

- einem Hotel oder Restaurant   ● Ruthin
- ein angenehmes Hotel oder Restaurant   🏨, ↷, ✗, 🕭
- einem sehr ruhigen und abgelegenen Hotel
- einem Restaurant mit   ⌘, ⌘⌘, ⌘⌘⌘, 🕭   **Meals**
- Ort mit Angaben über Hotels und Restaurants in der Umgebung   **NEATH**

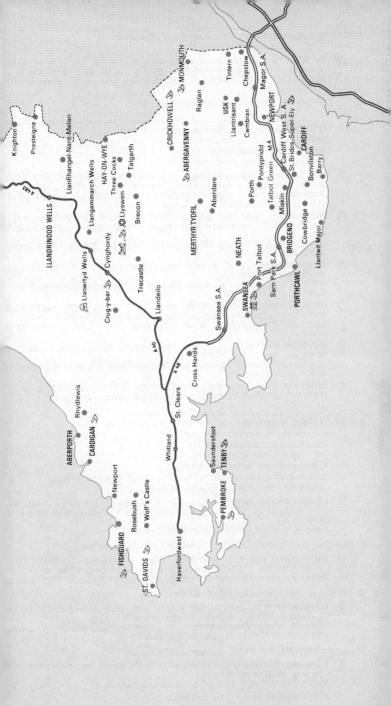

ABERDARE (Aberdâr) *Rhondda Cynon Taff* 403 J 28 – *pop. 29 040.*
London 178 – Cardiff 23 – Swansea 27.

🏨 **Ty Newydd Country,** Penderyn Rd, Hirwaun, CF44 9SX, NW : 5 m. on A 405⁵
℘ *(01685) 813433, Fax (01685) 813139,* 🖈 – 📺 ☎ ℗ – 🔬 300. 👁 🆎 ① *VISA* JCB. ⬤
Meals *(closed Sunday dinner)* 9.60/12.60 **st.** and a la carte ⓘ 4.10 – **26 rm** ⌂ 47.00.
67.00 **st.,** 1 suite – SB.

ⓐ ATS Canal Rd, Cwmbach ℘ *(01685) 873914/875491*

ABERDOVEY (Aberdyfi) *Gwynedd* 403 H 26 *Wales G.* – *pop. 869.*
Env. : *Snowdonia National Park***.
🏌 *Aberdovey* ℘ *(01654) 767210.*
London 230 – Dolgellau 25 – Shrewsbury 66.

🏨 **Plas Penhelig Country House** ⏩, LL35 0NA, E : 1 m. by A 493 ℘ *(01654) 767676*
Fax (01654) 767783, ≤, « Terraced gardens », park – 📺 ☎ ℗ – 🔬 35. 👁 ① *VISA* JCB
March-mid December – **Meals** *(bar lunch Monday to Saturday)/dinner* 19.50 **t.** ⓘ 8.50
11 rm ⌂ *(dinner included)* 63.00/126.00 – SB.

🏨 **Trefeddian,** Tywyn Rd, LL35 0SB, W : 1 m. on A 493 ℘ *(01654) 767213*
Fax (01654) 767777, ≤ golf course and sea, 🏐, 🖈, park, ❀ – 📇, ⇔ rest, 📺 ☎ ⇐ ℗. ⬤
VISA
closed 2 January-27 February – **Meals** 10.75/16.25 **t.** ⓘ 7.50 – **46 rm** ⌂ *(dinner included)*
49.00/122.00 **t.** – SB.

🏛 **Penhelig Arms,** LL35 0LT, ℘ *(01654) 767215, Fax (01654) 767690,* ≤, « Part 18C inn »
⇔ rm, 📺 ☎ ℗. 👁 *VISA* JCB
closed 25 and 26 December – **Meals** *(bar lunch Monday to Saturday)/dinner* 19.00 **t.**
10 rm ⌂ 39.50/79.00 **t.** – SB.

🏛 **Harbour,** LL35 0EB, ℘ *(01654) 767250, Fax (01654) 767792,* ≤ – ⇔ 📺 ☎. 👁 🆎 ① *VISA*
Meals *(booking essential) (residents only Sunday to Wednesday in winter) (meals in ba*
November-February) 15.50 **st.** *(dinner)* and a la carte ⓘ 8.30 – **8 rm** ⌂ 45.00/90.00 **st**
1 suite.

🏛 **Maybank,** 4 Penhelig Rd, LL35 0PT, E : 1 m. on A 493 ℘ *(01654) 767500,* ≤ – ⇔ 📺 ℗
👁 *VISA* JCB. ❀
14 February-7 November – **Meals** *(booking essential) (dinner only)* 19.95 **st.** ⓘ 7.00 – **6 rm**
⌂ 36.95/61.90 **st.** – SB.

⌂ **Brodawel,** LL35 0SA, W : 1 ¼ m. on A 493 ℘ *(01654) 767347,* ≤, 🖈 – ⇔ 📺 ℗. ❀
March-October – **Meals** *(by arrangement)* 14.00 ⓘ 3.50 – **6 rm** ⌂ 24.00/48.00 **t.**

ABERGAVENNY (Y-Fenni) *Monmouthshire* 403 L 28 *Wales G.* – *pop. 14 092.*
See : *Town* – *St. Mary's Church* *(Monuments**).*
Env. : *Brecon Beacons National Park**.*
Exc. : *Raglan Castle* *AC, SE : 9 m. by A 40.*
🏌 *Monmouthshire, Llanfoist* ℘ *(01873) 852606.*
🛈 *Swan Meadow, Monmouth Rd, NP7 5HH* ℘ *(01873) 857588 (summer only).*
London 163 – Gloucester 43 – Newport 19 – Swansea 49.

🏨 **Llansantffraed Court,** Llanvihangel Gobion, NP7 9BA, SE : 6 ½ m. by A 40 and B 459
off old Raglan rd ℘ *(01873) 840678, Fax (01873) 840674,* ≤, 🖈, park – 📇 ⇔ 📺 ☎ ℗. ⬤
🆎 ① *VISA* JCB
Meals 14.50/19.50 **t.** – **21 rm** ⌂ 68.00/95.00 **t.** – SB.

at Llanfihangel Crucorney *N : 6½ m. by A 40 on A 465 –* ⊠ *Abergavenny.*

⌂ **Penyclawdd Court** ⏩, NP7 7LB, S : 1 ¼ m. by Pantygelli rd ℘ *(01873) 89071*
Fax (01873) 890848, ≤, « Tudor manor house », 🖈 – ⇔ rm, 📺 ℗. 👁 *VISA*. ❀
Meals *(by arrangement) (communal dining)* 22.00 **st.** ⓘ 4.50 – **4 rm** ⌂ 45.00/74.00 **st.**

at Govilon *W : 5¼ m. by A 465 on B 4246 –* ⊠ *Abergavenny.*

🏛 **Llanwenarth House** ⏩, NP7 9SF, N : 1 m. on B 4246 ℘ *(01873) 83028*
Fax (01873) 832199, ≤, « 16C manor house », 🖈 – ⇔ rest, 📺 ℗
closed mid January-February – **Meals** *(by arrangement) (residents only) (communal dinin*
(dinner only) 22.50 **st.** ⓘ 6.85 – **4 rm** ⌂ 58.00/78.00 **s.** – SB.

at Llanwenarth *NW : 3 m. on A 40 –* ⊠ *Abergavenny.*

🏛 **Llanwenarth Arms,** Brecon Rd, NP8 1EP, ℘ *(01873) 810550, Fax (01873) 811880,* ≤,
– 📺 ☎ ℗. 👁 🆎 ① *VISA.* ❀
Meals a la carte 14.95/21.95 **st.** ⓘ 4.95 – **18 rm** ⌂ 59.00/69.00 **st.**

ⓐ ATS 11 Monmouth Rd ℘ *(01873) 854348/855829*

ABERPORTH *Ceredigion* **403** G 27 – *pop. 1 431* – ⊠ *Cardigan.*
London 249 – Carmarthen 29 – Fishguard 26.

🏛 **Penrallt**, SA43 2BS, SW : 1 m. by B 4333 *℘ (01239) 810227, Fax (01239) 811375,* ≼, *Ⅰ₅,*
⊆s, ⊒, 屛, ℀ – 🔟 ☎ 🅿. 🕮 🕮 *VISA*. ℀
closed 24 to 31 December – **Meals** *(bar lunch)/dinner 18.00* **st.** *and a la carte* ⅙ *6.75* – **16 rm**
⊒ *50.00/80.00* **st.** – SB.

at Tresaith *NE : 1¾ m.* – ⊠ *Cardigan.*

🏛 **Glandwr Manor** ⊸, SA43 2JH, *℘ (01239) 810197,* 屛 – ⅍ 🅿. ℀
Easter-October – **Meals** *(dinner only) 11.50* **t.** *and a la carte* ⅙ *3.80* – **7 rm** ⊒ *25.00/50.00* **t.**

ABERSOCH *Gwynedd* **402** **403** G 25 *Wales G.* – *pop. 805* – ⊠ *Pwllheli.*
Env. : *Lleyn Peninsula★★ – Plas-yn-Rhiw★ AC, W : 6 m. by minor roads.*
Exc. : *Bardsey Island★, SW : 15 m. by A 499 and B 4413 – Mynydd Mawr★, SW : 17 m. by*
A 499, B 4413 and minor roads.
🇫 *Golf Rd ℘ (01758) 712622.*
London 265 – Caernarfon 28 – Shrewsbury 101.

🏛 **Abersoch Harbour**, Lon Engan, LL53 7HR, *℘ (01758) 712406,* ≼ – 🔟 ☎ 🅿. 🕮 🕮 *VISA*. ℀
Meals *(closed Sunday lunch) a la carte approx. 13.40* **st.** ⅙ *4.95* – **14 rm** ⊒ *45.00/70.00* **st.**

🏛 **White House**, LL53 7AG, *℘ (01758) 713427, Fax (01758) 713512,* ≼, 屛 – ⅍ rm, 🔟 ☎
🅿 – 🔬 *100.* 🕮 *VISA*
closed 2 weeks February and 25 December – **Meals** *(dinner only) 19.50* **t.** *and a la carte*
⅙ *6.00* – **11 rm** ⊒ *33.50/80.00* **t.** – SB.

🏠 **Riverside**, LL53 7HW, *℘ (01758) 712419, Fax (01758) 712671,* 🖰, 屛 – 🔟 ☎ 🅿. 🕮 🕮 🕮
VISA
March-October – **Meals** *(bar lunch)/dinner 23.50* **st.** ⅙ *5.75* – **12 rm** ⊒ *52.00/88.00* **t.** – SB.

🏠 **Neigwl**, Lon Sarn Bach, LL53 7DY, *℘ (01758) 712363, Fax (01758) 712363,* ≼ *Cardigan Bay*
– 🔟 🅿. 🕮 🕮 *VISA*. ℀
Meals *(dinner only) 19.00* **st.** ⅙ *5.00* – **9 rm** ⊒ *46.00/77.00* **st.** – SB.

at Bwlchtocyn *S : 2 m.* – ⊠ *Pwllheli.*

🏛 **Porth Tocyn** ⊸, LL53 7BU, *℘ (01758) 713303, Fax (01758) 713538,* ≼ *Cardigan Bay and*
mountains, ⊒, 屛, ℀ – 🔟 ☎ 🅿. 🕮 *VISA*
Easter-mid November – **Meals** *(bar lunch Monday to Saturday)/dinner 27.75* **t.** ⅙ *5.75* –
⊒ *4.50* – **17 rm** *58.50/108.00* **t.** – SB.

🏠 **Crowrach Isaf** ⊸, LL53 7BY, *℘ (01758) 712860,* ≼, 屛, *park* – ⅍ 🔟 🅿. ℀
closed November and December – **Meals** *(by arrangement) 12.95* **st.** – **3 rm** ⊒ *22.00/*
44.00 **st.**

ABERYSTWYTH *Ceredigion* **403** H 26 *Wales G.* – *pop. 11 154.*
See : *Town★★ – The Seafront★ – National Library of Wales★ (Permanent Exhibition★).*
Env. : *Vale of Rheidol★ (Railway★★ AC) – St. Padarn's Church★, SE : 1 m. by A 44.*
Exc. : *Devil's Bridge (Pontarfynach)★, E : 12 m. by A 4120 – Strata Florida Abbey★ AC (West*
Door★), SE : 15 m. by B 4340 and minor rd.
🇫 *Bryn-y-Mor ℘ (01970) 615104.*
🅱 *Terrace Rd, SY23 2AG ℘ (01970) 612125.*
London 238 – Chester 98 – Fishguard 58 – Shrewsbury 74.

🏛🏛 **Belle Vue Royal**, Marine Terrace, SY23 2BA, *℘ (01970) 617558, Fax (01970) 612190,* ≼ –
⅍ rm, 🔟 ☎ ⟵ – 🔬 *40.* 🕮 🕮 🕮 *VISA*. ℀
closed 25 and 26 December – **Meals** *11.00/19.50* **st.** *and a la carte* ⅙ *5.50* – **37 rm** ⊒ *50.00/*
84.00 **st.** – SB.

🏠 **Four Seasons**, 50-54 Portland St., SY23 2DX, *℘ (01970) 612120, Fax (01970) 627458* –
⅍ *rest,* 🔟 ☎ 🅿. 🕮 *VISA*. ℀
closed 1 week Christmas – **Meals** *(bar lunch Monday to Saturday)/dinner 16.00* **t.** ⅙ *5.50* –
15 rm ⊒ *52.00/75.00* **t.** – SB.

🏠 **Sinclair**, 43 Portland St., SY23 2DX, *℘ (01970) 615158, Fax (01970) 615158* – ⅍ 🔟 🅿. ℀
closed 2 weeks Christmas-New Year – **Meals** *(by arrangement) 15.00* **st.** – **3 rm** ⊒ *30.00/*
45.00 **s.**

at Chancery (Rhydgaled) *S : 4 m. on A 487* – ⊠ *Aberystwyth.*

🏛 **Conrah Country House** ⊸, SY23 4DF, *℘ (01970) 617941, Fax (01970) 624546,* ≼,
« *Part 18C* », ⊆s, 🖰, 屛, *park* – ▮, ⅍ *rest,* 🔟 ☎ 🅿 – 🔬 *50.* 🕮 🕮 🕮 *VISA* 🕮. ℀
closed 23 to 31 December – **Meals** *16.00/26.00* **st.** ⅙ *6.50* – **20 rm** ⊒ *61.00/120.00* **st.** – SB.

🕘 ATS Glanyrafon Ind. Est., Llanbadarn *℘ (01970) 611166*

ARTHOG Gwynedd **402 403** I 25 – see Dolgellau.

BALA Gwynedd **402 403** J 25 Wales G. – pop. 1 922.
Env. : Snowdonia National Park★★★ – Bala Lake★.
Exc. : Bwlch y Groes★★, SE : 11 m. by A 494, B 4403 and minor rd.
🏌 Bala Lake Hotel ℰ (01678) 520344/520111.
🛈 Penllyn, Pensarn Rd, LL23 7SR ℰ (01678) 521021 (Friday to Sunday only in winter).
London 216 – Chester 46 – Dolgellau 18 – Shrewsbury 52.

⌂ **Fron Feuno Hall** ⦂, LL23 7YF, SW : 1 m. on A 494 ℰ (01678) 521115
Fax (01678) 521151, ≤ Bala Lake, ⬟, ✿, park, ✼ – ⬛, ✼ rest, ⓟ. ✼
April-October – **Meals** (by arrangement) (communal dining) 16.00 st. – **3 rm** ⊇ 34.00/
68.00 st.

⌂ **Melin Meloch,** LL23 7DP, E : 1 ¾ m. by A 494 on B 4401 ℰ (01678) 520101, « Part 13C
converted water mill », ✿ – ✼ ⓣⓥ ⓟ. ✼
April-November – **Meals** (by arrangement) (communal dining) 13.00 t. – **4 rm** ⊇ 25.00/
46.00 st. – SB.

⌂ **Llidiardau Mawr** ⦂ without rest., Llidiardau, LL23 7SG, NW : 4 ¼ m. by A 421?
ℰ (01678) 520555, ≤, « 17C stone-built mill house », ✿ – ⓟ. ✼
Easter-October – **3 rm** ⊇ 20.00/40.00.

at Fron-Goch NW : 2 ¾ m. on A 4212 – ✉ Bala.

⌂ **Cysgod Y Garn,** LL23 7NT, ℰ (01678) 520483, Fax (01678) 521457, park – ✼ ⓣⓥ ⓟ. ✼
Easter-October – **Meals** (by arrangement) 12.00 s. – **3 rm** ⊇ 22.00/50.00 s.

BANGOR Gwynedd **402 403** H 24 Wales G. – pop. 12 330.
Env. : Snowdonia National Park★★★ – Penrhyn Castle★★ AC, E : 3 m. by A 5122 – Menai
Bridge★, SW : 1 ½ m. by A 5122.
Exc. : Anglesey★★ – Plas Newydd★★ AC, SW : 7 ½ m. by A 5122 and A 4080 – Anglesey Se
Zoo★ AC, SW : 10 m. by A 5122, A 4080 and B 4419 – Llangefni (Oriel Ynys Mon★ AC), NW
7 m. by A 5122 and B 5420.
🏌 St. Deiniol, Penybryn ℰ (01248) 353098.
London 247 – Birkenhead 68 – Holyhead 23 – Shrewsbury 83.

🏨 **Menai Court,** Craig-y-Don Rd, LL57 2BG, ℰ (01248) 354200, Fax (01248) 354200, ≤, ✿
✼ rest, ⓣⓥ ☎ ⓟ. ⓪ ⓥⓘⓢⓐ ⓙⓒⓑ
Meals (closed lunch Saturday and Sunday) 12.95/21.95 t. and dinner a la carte ⓵ 6.50
13 rm ⊇ 50.50/83.00 t. – SB.

🏠 **Travelodge,** One Stop Services, Llandegai, LL57 4BG, SE : 2 ½ m. by A 5122, at junction c
A 5 with A 55 ℰ (01248) 370345, Fax (01248) 370345, Reservations (Freephone) 080
850950 – ✼ rm, ⓣⓥ ⓺ ⓟ. ⓪ ⓐⓔ ⓞ ⓥⓘⓢⓐ ⓙⓒⓑ
Meals (grill rest.) – **30 rm** 44.95 t.

⌂ **Country Bumpkin** without rest., Cefn-y-Coed, Llandegai, LL57 4BG, S : 3 m. on A 512
ℰ (01248) 370477, Fax (01248) 354166, ≤ – ⓣⓥ ⓟ. ⓪ ⓥⓘⓢⓐ
closed mid December-mid January – **3 rm** ⊇ 30.00/40.00 st.

BARMOUTH (Abermaw) Gwynedd **402 403** H 25 Wales G. – pop. 2 306.
See : Town★ – Bridge★ AC.
Env. : Snowdonia National Park★★★.
🛈 The Old Library, Station Rd, LL42 1LU ℰ (01341) 280787 (summer only).
London 231 – Chester 74 – Dolgellau 10 – Shrewsbury 67.

⌂ **Llwyndû Farmhouse** ⦂, LL42 1RR, NW : 2 ¼ m. on A 496 ℰ (01341) 28014
Fax (01341) 281236, « Part 17C farmhouse and 18C barn conversion », ✿ – ✼ ⓣⓥ ⓟ
restricted opening in winter – **Meals** (by arrangement) 15.95 t. ⓵ 6.00 – **7 rm** ⊇ 50.0
60.00 t. – SB.

BARRY (Barri) Vale of Glamorgan **403** K 29 – pop. 49 887.
🏌 Brynhill, Port Rd ℰ (01446) 735061 – 🏌 RAF St. Athan ℰ (01446) 751043.
🛈 The Triangle, Paget Rd, Barry Island, CF62 5TQ ℰ (01446) 747171 (summer only).
London 167 – Cardiff 10 – Swansea 39.

🏛 **Egerton Grey Country House,** CF62 3BZ, SW : 4 ½ m. by A 4226 and Porthkerry rd \
Cardiff Airport ℰ (01446) 711666, Fax (01446) 711690, ≤, « Country house atmosphere
✿, park, ✼ – ✼ rest, ⓣⓥ ☎ ⓟ – ⓐ 40. ⓪ ⓐⓔ ⓞ ⓥⓘⓢⓐ ⓙⓒⓑ
Meals 22.00 st. ⓵ 7.50 – **10 rm** ⊇ 60.00/120.00 st. – SB.

Mount Sorrel, Porthkerry Rd, CF62 7XY, ℰ (01446) 740069, Fax (01446) 746600, ▐⌀, ☎, ⬛ – ⬛ ☎ ⓟ – ⚿ 150. ⬛ AE ⓞ VISA
closed 24 to 26 December – Meals 12.50/17.50 **st.** ⬧ 5.50 – **43 rm** ⬜ 70.00/80.00 **st.** – SB.

Aberthaw House, 28 Porthkerry Rd, CF62 7AX, ℰ (01446) 737314, Fax (01446) 732376 – ⬛, ☎, ⬛ VISA
closed 24 December-4 January – Meals (residents only Sunday) (dinner only) 8.95 **t.** and a la carte ⬧ 4.50 – ⬜ 5.50 – **10 rm** 35.00/60.00 **t.**

Cwm Ciddy Toby, Airport Rd, CF62 3BA, NW : 1 ½ m. by B 4266 ℰ (01446) 700075, Fax (01446) 700075 – ⬿ rest, ⬛ ☎ ⓟ, ⬛ AE VISA. ⬿
Meals (grill rest.) a la carte approx. 10.95 ⬧ 3.95 – **14 rm** ⬜ 49.00/59.00 **t.** – SB.

XX **Six Bells Inn**, Penmark, CF62 3BP, NW : 4 ¼ m. by B 4266 on the Penmark rd
ℰ (01446) 710229, Fax (01446) 710671 – ▤ ⓟ – ⚿ 70. ⬛ AE VISA JCB
closed Sunday dinner – Meals a la carte 11.00/18.00 **st.** ⬧ 5.00.

BEAUMARIS Anglesey **402 403** H 24 *Wales G.* – *pop. 1 561*.

See : *Town★ – Castle★★ AC.*

Env. : *Anglesey★★ – Penmon Priory★, NE : 4 m. by B 5109 and minor roads.*

Exc. : *Plas Newydd★ AC, SW : 7 m. by A 545 and A 4080.*

London 253 – Birkenhead 74 – Holyhead 25.

Ye Olde Bull's Head Inn, Castle St., LL58 8AP, ℰ (01248) 810329, Fax (01248) 811294 – ⬿ ⬛ ☎ ⓟ, ⬛ AE VISA JCB, ⬿
closed 25-26 December and 1 January – Meals – (see below) – **15 rm** ⬜ 49.00/92.00 **t.** – SB.

Bishopsgate House, 54 Castle St., LL58 8BB, ℰ (01248) 810302, Fax (01248) 810166 – ⬿ ⬛ ☎ ⓟ, ⬛ AE VISA, ⬿
closed 3 weeks January – Meals (dinner only and Sunday lunch)/dinner 16.55 **t.** – **9 rm** ⬜ 40.00/70.00 **st.** – SB.

Plas Cichle ⬙ without rest., LL58 8PS, NW : 2 ¾ m. by B 5109 and Llanfaes Rd
ℰ (01248) 810488, Fax (01248) 810488, ≼, « Working farm », ⚞, park – ⬿ ⬛ ⓟ, ⬛ VISA. ⬿
February-November – **3 rm** ⬜ 30.00/50.00 **s.**

XX **Ye Olde Bull's Head Inn** (at Ye Olde Bull's Head Inn H.), Castle St., LL58 8AP,
ℰ (01248) 810329, Fax (01248) 811294 – ⓟ, ⬛ AE VISA JCB
closed 25-26 December and 1 January – Meals (bar lunch Monday to Saturday)/dinner 20.95 **t.** and a la carte ⬧ 6.95.

BEDDGELERT Gwynedd **402 403** H 24 *Wales G.* – *pop. 535*.

Env. : *Snowdonia National Park★★★ – Aberglaslyn Pass★, S : 1 ½ m. on A 498.*

London 249 – Caernarfon 13 – Chester 73.

Royal Goat, LL55 4YE, ℰ (01766) 890224, Fax (01766) 890422, ⬞ – ▐⬙ ⬿ ⬛ ☎ ⓟ, ⬛ AE ⓞ VISA
Meals 10.00/17.00 **st.** and a la carte ⬧ 6.50 – **29 rm** ⬜ 43.00/75.00 **st.**, 1 suite – SB.

Sygun Fawr Country House ⬙, LL55 4NE, NE : ¾ m. by A 498 ℰ (01766) 890258, ≼ mountains and valley, « Part 16C stone built house », ☎, ⚞, park – ⓟ, ⬛ VISA JCB
Meals (by arrangement) 15.00 **st.** ⬧ 4.45 – **8 rm** ⬜ 30.00/54.00 **t.** – SB.

BERRIEW (Aberriw) Powys **402 403** K 26 – *pop. 1 305* – ✉ *Welshpool*.

London 190 – Chester 49 – Shrewsbury 26.

Lion, SY21 8PQ, ℰ (01686) 640452, Fax (01686) 640604, « Part 17C inn » – ⬛ ☎ ⓟ, ⬛ AE VISA JCB, ⬿
closed 25 and 26 December – Meals (booking essential) (bar lunch Monday to Saturday)/dinner 18.95 **t.** and a la carte ⬧ 5.95 – **7 rm** ⬜ 50.00/90.00 **t.** – SB.

BETWS-Y-COED Conwy **402 403** I 24 *Wales G.* – *pop. 848*.

See : *Town★.*

Env. : *Snowdonia National Park★★★.*

Exc. : *Blaenau Ffestiniog★ (Llechwedd Slate Caverns★ AC), SW : 10 ½ m. by A 470 – The Glyders and Nant Ffrancon (Cwm Idwal★), W : 14 m. by A 5.*

▐⬙ *Clubhouse ℰ (01690) 710556.*

🅱 *Royal Oak Stables, LL24 0AH ℰ (01690) 710426.*

London 226 – Holyhead 44 – Shrewsbury 62.

🏨 **Waterloo**, LL24 0AR, on A 5 ℘ (01690) 710411, *Fax (01690) 710666*, *Lₒ*, ≘s, 🔲 – 📺 ☎ 🄿, 🕪 AE *VISA* JCB. ✵
closed 25 and 26 December – **Meals** (bar lunch Monday to Saturday)/dinner 16.95 **t.** and a la carte 🕴 5.55 – **39 rm** 🖙 51.00/91.00 **t.** – SB.

🏛 **Tan-y-Foel Country House** ⤧, LL26 0RE, E : 4 m. by A 5 and A 470 on Nebo rd ℘ (01690) 710507, *Fax (01690) 710681*, ≼ Vale of Conwy and Snowdonia, « Part 16C country house », 🛲, park – ⥲ 📺 🄿, 🕪 AE ① *VISA* JCB. ✵
closed Christmas and restricted opening December-February – **Meals** (booking essential) (dinner only) 25.00 **t.** 🕴 6.80 – **7 rm** 🖙 65.00/150.00 **t.** – SB.

🏛 **Park Hill**, Llanrwst Rd, LL24 0HD, NE : 1 m. by A 5 on A 470 ℘ (01690) 710540, *Fax (01690) 710540*, ≼ Vale of Conwy, ≘s, 🔲, 🛲 – ⥲ rest, 📺 🄿, 🕪 AE ① *VISA* JCB. ✵
Meals (residents only) (dinner only) 14.50 **t.** 🕴 4.30 – **11 rm** 🖙 19.50/62.00 **t.** – SB.

⤒ **Henllys**, Old Church Rd, LL24 0AL, ℘ (01690) 710534, « Former Victorian magistrates court », 🛲 – ⥲ 📺 🄿, 🕪 *VISA* JCB. ✵
closed November-24 December and 2 January-1 March – **Meals** (by arrangement) 15.95 **st.** – **10 rm** 🖙 30.00/60.00 **st.** – SB.

⤒ **Bryn Bella** without rest., Llanrwst Rd, LL24 0HD, ℘ (01690) 710627, ≼ Vale of Conwy – 📺 🄿. ✵
4 rm 🖙 18.00/45.00 **st.**

🍴 **White Horse Inn** with rm, Capel Garmon, LL26 0RW, NE : 2 ¼ m. by A 470 on Capel Garmon rd ℘ (01690) 710271, *Fax (01690) 710271*, « 16C » – ⥲ 📺 🄿, 🕪 *VISA*
Meals (closed Monday and Tuesday) (bar lunch Wednesday and Saturday) a la carte 14.45/ 18.25 **st.** – **6 rm** 🖙 30.00/48.00 **st.**

at Penmachno SW : 4¾ m. by A 5 on B 4406 – ✉ Betws-y-Coed.

⤒ **Penmachno Hall** ⤧, LL24 0PU, ℘ (01690) 760207, *Fax (01690) 760207*, ≼, 🛲 – ⥲ rm, 🄿, 🕪 *VISA*. ✵
Meals (by arrangement) (communal dining) 15.00 **st.** 🕴 3.25 – **4 rm** 🖙 30.00/50.00 **st.**

BLAENAU FFESTINIOG Gwynedd 402 403 I 25.
🄱 Isallt, High St., LL41 3HD ℘ (01766) 830360 (summer only).
London 237 – Bangor 32 – Caernarfon 32 – Dolgellau 23 – Chester 70.

🏛 **Queens**, 1 High St., LL41 3ES, ℘ (01766) 830055, *Fax (01766) 830046* – ⥲ rest, 📺 ☎ 🄿 – 🔬 100. 🕪 *VISA*. ✵
closed 25 December – **Meals** (bar lunch Monday to Saturday)/dinner a la carte 11.30/ 16.20 **st.** 🕴 4.30 – **12 rm** 🖙 40.00/80.00 **st.** – SB.

BONTDDU Gwynedd 402 403 I 25 – see Dolgellau.

BONVILSTON (Tresimwn) Vale of Glamorgan 403 J 29.
London 164 – Cardiff 9 – Swansea 25.

⤒ **Great Barn** ⤧ without rest., Lillypot, CF5 6TR, NW : 1 m. by A 48 off Tre-Dodridge rd ℘ (01446) 781010, ≼ – 📺 🄿
4 rm 🖙 25.00/44.00 **s.**

BRECON (Aberhonddu) Powys 403 J 28 Wales G. – pop. 7 523.
See : Town★ – Cathedral★ AC.
Env. : Brecon Beacons National Park★★.
Exc. : Dan-yr-Ogof Showcaves★ AC, SW : 20 m. by A 40 and A 4067 – Pen-y-Fan★★, SW : b... A 470.
🄽 Cradoc, Penoyre Park ℘ (01874) 623658 – 🄽 Newton Park, Llanfaes ℘ (01874) 622004.
🄱 Cattle Market Car Park, LD3 9DA ℘ (01874) 622485.
London 171 – Cardiff 40 – Carmarthen 31 – Gloucester 65.

🏨 **Peterstone Court**, Llanhamlach, LD3 7YB, SE : 3 ¼ m. on A 40 ℘ (01874) 665387 *Fax (01874) 665376*, ≼, « Georgian manor house », *Lₒ*, ≘s, 🔲, 🛲 – 📺 ☎ 🄿, 🕪 AE ① *VISA* JCB
Meals 6.95/21.95 **st.** and a la carte 🕴 5.95 – 🖙 7.95 – **12 rm** 75.00/135.00 **st.** – SB.
🍴 ATS The Watton ℘ (01874) 624496/624163

BRIDGEND (Pen-y-Bont) 403 J 29 – pop. 35 841.
London 177 – Cardiff 20 – Swansea 23.

🏨 **Heronston**, Ewenny Rd, CF35 5AW, S : 2 m. on B 4265 ℘ (01656) 66881... *Fax (01656) 767391*, ≘s, 🔲, 🔲 – 🛏 📺 ☎ 🄿 – 🔬 200. 🕪 AE ① *VISA* JCB
Meals 15.95 **t.** and a la carte 🕴 5.95 – **75 rm** 🖙 70.00/90.00 **st.**

at Pencoed NE : 4½ m. by A 473.

🏠 **Travel Inn,** Pantruthyn Farm, CF35 5HY, E : 1 m. by A 473 at junction 35 on M 4
ℰ (01656) 860133, Fax (01656) 864792 – ❄ rm, 📺 👌 🅿. 🅌 🆎 ① 𝗩𝗜𝗦𝗔. ❄
Meals (grill rest.) – **40 rm** 36.50 t.

🏠 **Travelodge,** CF3 5HU, E : 1 ¼ m. by Felindre rd ℰ (01656) 864404, Reservations (Free-phone) 0800 850950 – 📺 👌 🅿. 🅌 🆎 ① 𝗩𝗜𝗦𝗔 𝗝𝗖𝗕. ❄
Meals (grill rest.) – **40 rm** 35.95 t.

at Coychurch (Llangrallo) E : 2¼ m. by A 473 – ✉ Bridgend.

🏨 **Coed-y-Mwstwr** ﹩, CF35 6AF, N : 1 m. ℰ (01656) 860621, Fax (01656) 863122, ≼, ⅃,
🐎, park, ※ – ▐, ❄ rm, 📺 ☎ 🅿 – 🔬 150. 🅌 🆎 ① 𝗩𝗜𝗦𝗔. ❄
Meals 24.00 st. and a la carte 🔖 8.95 – **21 rm** ⌑ 85.00/130.00 st., 2 suites – SB.

at Southerndown SW : 5½ m. by A 4265 – ✉ Bridgend.

✗ **Frolics,** Beach Rd, CF32 0RP, ℰ (01656) 880127 – 🅌 𝗩𝗜𝗦𝗔
closed Sunday dinner, Monday, 25 to 30 December and 10 days in summer – **Meals** (dinner only and Sunday lunch)/dinner 16.50 t. and a la carte 🔖 7.00.

at Laleston W : 2 m. on A 473 – ✉ Bridgend.

✗✗ **Great House** with rm, High St., CF32 0HP, on A 473 ℰ (01656) 657644,
Fax (01656) 668892, ℔, ☎, ❄ rest, 📺 ☎ 🅿. 🅌 🆎 ① 𝗩𝗜𝗦𝗔 𝗝𝗖𝗕. ❄
closed 25-26 December and 1 January – **Meals** (closed Sunday dinner) 19.95 t. (dinner) and a la carte 10.00/25.00 t. 🔖 6.25 – **10 rm** ⌑ 75.00/95.00 st.

🅖 ATS 122 Coity Rd ℰ (01656) 658775/6

The Guide is updated annually so renew your Guide every year.

BWLCHTOCYN Gwynedd 🐴🐴🐴 🐴🐴🐴 G 25 – see Abersoch.

CADOXTON Neath Port Talbot 🐴🐴🐴 I 29 – see Neath.

CAERNARFON Gwynedd 🐴🐴🐴 🐴🐴🐴 H 24 Wales G. – pop. 9 695.
See : Town★★★ – Castle★★★ AC – Town Walls★.
Env. : Snowdonia National Park★★★.
🏌 Aberforeshore, Llanfaglan ℰ (01286) 673783/678359.
🅩 Oriel Pendeitsh, Castle St., LL55 2NA ℰ (01286) 672232.
London 249 – Birkenhead 76 – Chester 68 – Holyhead 30 – Shrewsbury 85.

🏨 **Seiont Manor** ﹩, Llanrug, LL55 2AQ, E : 3 m. on A 4086 ℰ (01286) 673366,
Fax (01286) 672840, ℔, ☎, ⅃, 🐎, park – ❄ 📺 ☎ 🅿 – 🔬 100. 🅌 🆎 ① 𝗩𝗜𝗦𝗔 𝗝𝗖𝗕
Meals 13.25/23.50 t. and a la carte 🔖 5.75 – **28 rm** ⌑ 83.00/210.00 t. – SB.

🏠 **Pengwern** ﹩, Saron, LL54 5UH, SW : 3 ½ m. by A 487 on Llanfaglan rd
ℰ (01286) 831500, Fax (01286) 831500, « Working farm », 🐎, park – ❄ 📺 🅿. ❄
closed December and January – **Meals** (by arrangement) 15.00 st. – **3 rm** ⌑ 40.00/50.00 st. – SB.

🏠 **Isfryn,** 11 Church St., LL55 1SW, ℰ (01286) 675628, Fax (01286) 675628 – ❄ rest, 📺. ❄
March-October – **Meals** (by arrangement) 17.50 s. – **6 rm** ⌑ 18.50/42.00 s.

at Seion NE : 5½ m. by A 406 and B 4366 on Seion rd – ✉ Caernarfon.

🏠 **Ty'n Rhos Country House** ﹩, Llanddeiniolen, LL55 3AE, SW : ¼ m. ℰ (01248) 670489,
Fax (01248) 670079, ≼, 🐎, park – ❄ 📺 ☎ 🅿. 🅌 🆎 ① 𝗩𝗜𝗦𝗔. ❄
closed 23 to 30 December – **Meals** (by arrangement) (residents only Sunday and Monday) (dinner only and Sunday lunch)/dinner 19.50 t. and a la carte 🔖 5.75 – **14 rm** ⌑ 45.00/90.00 t. – SB.

🅖 ATS Bangor Rd ℰ (01286) 673110

CAERSWS Powys 🐴🐴🐴 🐴🐴🐴 J 26.
London 194 – Aberystwyth 39 – Chester 63 – Shrewsbury 42.

🏨 **Maesmawr Hall** ﹩, SY17 5SF, E : 1 m. on A 489 ℰ (01686) 688255, Fax (01686) 688410,
« Part 16C hunting lodge », 🐎 – 📺 ☎ 🅿 – 🔬 120. 🅌 🆎 ① 𝗩𝗜𝗦𝗔
closed 26 to 30 December – **Meals** (bar lunch)/dinner 21.50 t. and a la carte 🔖 6.50 – **17 rm** ⌑ 51.00/78.00 t. – SB.

CARDIFF (Caerdydd) 403 K 29 *Wales G.* – pop. 272 129.

See : *City*★★★ – *National Museum and Gallery*★★★ *AC (Evolution of Wales*★★, *Picture galleries*★★ *(Galleries 12 and 13*★★*), Pottery and Porcelain*★*)* BY – *Castle*★★ *AC* BZ – *Civic Centre*★ BY – *Llandaff Cathedral*★ AV B – *Cardiff Bay*★ *(Welsh Industrial and Maritime Museum*★ *AC, Techniquest*★ *AC)* AX.

Env. : *Museum of Welsh Life*★★★ *AC, St. Fagan's, W : 5 m. by A 4161* AV – *Castell Coch*★★ *AC, NW : 5 m. by A 470* AV.

Exc. : *Caerphilly Castle*★★ *AC, N : 7 m. by A 469* AV – *Dyffryn Gardens*★ *AC, W : 8 m. by A 48* AX.

🏌 Dinas Powis, Old Highwalls ℰ (01222) 512727, AX.

✈ Cardiff (Wales) Airport : ℰ (01446) 711111, SW : 8 m. by A 48 AX – **Terminal** : Central Bus Station.

🚩 Central Station, CF1 1QY ℰ (01222) 227281.

London 155 – Birmingham 110 – Bristol 46 – Coventry 124.

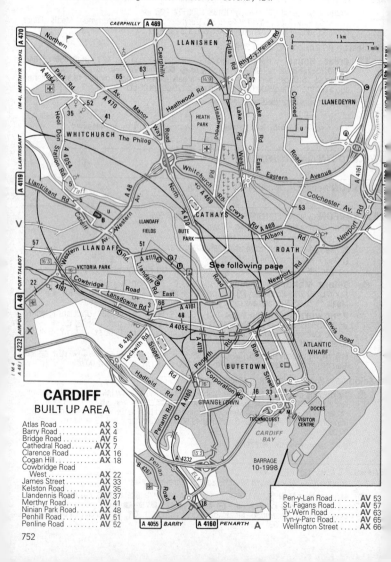

CARDIFF
BUILT UP AREA

Atlas Road	**AX** 3
Barry Road	**AX** 4
Bridge Road	**AV** 5
Cathedral Road	**AVX** 7
Clarence Road	**AX** 16
Cogan Hill	**AX** 18
Cowbridge Road West	**AX** 22
James Street	**AX** 33
Kelston Road	**AV** 35
Llandennis Road	**AV** 37
Merthyr Road	**AV** 41
Ninian Park Road	**AX** 48
Penhill Road	**AV** 51
Penline Road	**AV** 52
Pen-y-Lan Road	**AV** 53
St. Fagans Road	**AV** 57
Ty-Wern Road	**AV** 63
Tyn-y-Parc Road	**AV** 65
Wellington Street	**AX** 66

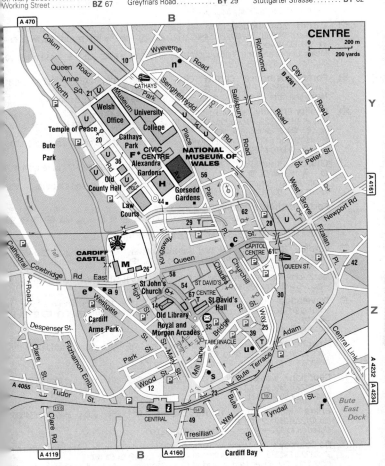

CENTRE

Copthorne, Copthorne Way, Culverhouse Cross, CF5 6XJ, W : 4 ¾ m. by A 4161 and A 48 at junction with A 4232 ℘ (01222) 599100, *Fax (01222) 599080*, **I₅**, **≘s**, **◻**, **⌖** – **|✿|**, **⇌** rm, ▤ rest, ⊡ ☎ & ❷ – 🕍 300. **◍◎ ◭ ⓪ ▨▨ ⌖**
  Raglan's : Meals (dinner only) 17.50 **t.** and a la carte – *Beauchamps* : Meals a la carte 12.95/16.85 **st.** – ⌷ 11.25 – **134 rm** 110.00/130.00 **st.**, 1 suite – SB.

Cardiff Marriott, Mill Lane, CF1 1EZ, ℘ (01222) 399944, *Fax (01222) 395578*, ≼, **I₅**, **≘s**, **◻** – **|✿|**, **⇌** rm, ▤ ⊡ ☎ & ❷ – 🕍 300. **◍◎ ◭ ⓪ ▨▨ JCB**
  BZ **s**
Meals 10.25/15.50 **t.** and dinner a la carte ▯ 7.95 – ⌷ 10.75 – **178 rm** 110.00/125.00 **st.**, 4 suites.

Park, Park Pl., CF1 3UD, ℘ (01222) 383471, *Fax (01222) 399309* – **|✿|**, **⇌** rm, ▤ rest, ⊡ ☎ ❷ – 🕍 300. **◍◎ ◭ ⓪ ▨▨**. ⌖
  BZ **c**
Meals 12.95/16.95 **st.** and a la carte ▯ 4.95 – ⌷ 10.00 – **132 rm** 90.00/115.00 **st.**, 4 suites – SB.

🏯 **Angel,** Castle St., CF1 2QZ, ☎ (01222) 232633, *Fax (01222) 396212*, ⅃₅, ☎ – |≢|, ⅙⇔ rm, 🔟
☎ 🅿 – ⚫ 300. 🔞 🝣 ⑩ 𝘝𝘐𝘚𝘈
BZ a
Meals (bar lunch Monday to Saturday)/dinner 16.95 **t.** ⅄ 5.95 – ☑ 9.25 – **102 rm** 84.00/
99.00 **st.**, 1 suite – SB.

🏯 **Jurys Cardiff,** Mary Ann St., CF1 2EQ, ☎ (01222) 341441, *Fax (01222) 223742* – |≢|
⅙⇔ rm, ■ rest, 🔟 ☎ ⅄ 🅿 – ⚫ 40. 🔞 🝣 ⑩ 𝘝𝘐𝘚𝘈. ❤
BZ u
Meals (bar lunch Monday to Saturday)/dinner 15.50 **t.** and a la carte ⅄ 5.50 – ☑ 10.50 –
140 rm 110.00/120.00 **st.**, 3 suites – SB.

🏯 **Cardiff Moat House,** Circle Way East, Llanedeyrn, CF3 7XF, NE : 3 m. by A 48
☎ (01222) 589988, *Fax (01222) 549092*, ⅃₅, ☎, 🔲 – |≢|, ⅙⇔ rm, ■ rest, 🔟 ☎ ⅄ 🅿 –
⚫ 300. 🔞 🝣 ⑩ 𝘝𝘐𝘚𝘈
AV n
Meals (dinner only and Sunday lunch)/dinner 16.95 **st.** ⅄ 6.00 – ☑ 9.50 – **130 rm** 85.00/
99.00 **st.**, 2 suites – SB.

🏯 **Forte Posthouse Cardiff City,** Castle St., CF1 2XB, ☎ (01222) 388681
Fax (01222) 371495 – |≢|, ⅙⇔ rm, 🔟 ☎ 🅿 – ⚫ 150. 🔞 🝣 ⑩ 𝘝𝘐𝘚𝘈 𝖩𝖢𝖡
BZ e
Meals (a la carte) 19.85/24.70 **st.** ⅄ 7.50 – ☑ 8.95 – **153 rm** 69.00 **st.**, 2 suites – SB.

🏯 **Quality Friendly,** Merthyr Rd, CF4 7LD, NW : 5 m. by A 470 on A 4054 at junction with
M 4 ☎ (01222) 529988, *Fax (01222) 529977*, ⅃₅, ☎, 🔲 – |≢|, ⅙⇔ rm, ■ rest, 🔟 ☎ ⅄ 🅿 –
⚫ 180. 🔞 🝣 ⑩ 𝘝𝘐𝘚𝘈 𝖩𝖢𝖡. ❤
Meals *(closed Saturday lunch)* (carving rest.) 9.95/14.50 **st.** and dinner a la carte ⅄ 4.50 –
☑ 8.75 – **95 rm** 74.50/110.00 **st.** – SB.

🏛 **Churchills,** Cardiff Rd, CF5 2AD, ☎ (01222) 562372, *Fax (01222) 568347* – ■ rest, 🔟 ☎ ⅄
🅿 – ⚫ 110. 🔞 🝣 ⑩ 𝘝𝘐𝘚𝘈
AV r
Meals *(closed Saturday lunch and Bank Holidays)* 9.50/16.50 **st.** and a la carte ⅄ 4.10 –
28 rm ☑ 70.00/115.00 **st.**, 7 suites – SB.

🏛 **Forte Posthouse Cardiff,** Pentwyn Rd, CF2 7XA, NE : 4 m. by A 48 ☎ (01222) 731212
Fax (01222) 549147, ⅃₅, ☎, 🔲 – |≢|, ⅙⇔ rm, ■ rest, 🔟 ☎ ⅄ 🅿 – ⚫ 120. 🔞 🝣 ⑩ 𝘝𝘐𝘚.
𝖩𝖢𝖡
Meals a la carte 14.85/25.65 **st.** ⅄ 7.85 – ☑ 8.95 – **142 rm** 69.00 **st.** – SB.

🏛 **Cardiff Bay,** Schooner Way, Atlantic Wharf, CF1 5RT, ☎ (01222) 465888
Fax (01222) 481491, « Converted warehouse », ⅃₅, ☎ – |≢|, ⅙⇔ rm, ■ rest, 🔟 ☎ 🅿 –
⚫ 350. 🔞 🝣 ⑩ 𝘝𝘐𝘚𝘈 𝖩𝖢𝖡. ❤
BZ s
Meals *(closed lunch Saturday and Bank Holidays)* 12.00/16.50 **t.** and dinner a la carte ⅄ 8.9*
– ☑ 8.75 – **157 rm** 105.00/140.00 **st.**, 6 suites – SB.

🏠 **Travelodge,** Circle Way East, Llanedeyrn, CF3 7ND, on Coed-y-Gores r
☎ (01222) 549564, Reservations (Freephone) 0800 850950 – ⅙⇔ rm, 🔟 ⅄ 🅿. 🔞 🝣 ⑩ 𝘝𝘚
𝖩𝖢𝖡. ❤
AV v
Meals (grill rest.) – **32 rm** 44.95 **t.**

⌂ **Townhouse** without rest., 70 Cathedral Rd, CF1 9LL, ☎ (01222) 239399
Fax (01222) 223214 – 🔟 ☎ 🅿. 🔞 𝘝𝘐𝘚𝘈
AV x
closed 24 to 31 December – **6 rm** ☑ 39.50/59.50 **t.**

⌂ **Georgian** without rest., 179 Cathedral Rd, CF1 9PL, ☎ (01222) 232594
Fax (01222) 232594 – 🔟. ❤
AV c
8 rm ☑ 27.50/40.00 **st.**

⌂ **Briars** without rest., 126-128 Cathedral Rd, CF1 9LQ, ☎ (01222) 340888
Fax (01222) 230122 – 🔟 ☎. ❤
AV e
closed 25 to 30 December – **10 rm** ☑ 18.00/38.00.

XXXX **De Courcey's,** Tyla Morris Av., Pentyrch, CF4 8QN, NW : 6 m. by A 4119 on Pentyrch r
☎ (01222) 892232, *Fax (01222) 891949* – 🅿 – ⚫ 100. 🔞 🝣 ⑩ 𝘝𝘐𝘚𝘈
closed Sunday dinner, Monday and 24 to 30 December – **Meals** (dinner only and Sunda
lunch)/dinner 21.95 **st.** and a la carte ⅄ 6.25.

X **Le Cassoulet,** 5 Romilly Cres., Canton, CF1 9NP, ☎ (01222) 221905, *Fax (01222) 221905*
🔞 🝣 ⑩ 𝘝𝘐𝘚𝘈 𝖩𝖢𝖡
AX s
closed Saturday lunch, Sunday, Monday, August and 1 week Christmas – **Meals** - Frenc
- 15.00/26.00 **t.** and a la carte ⅄ 7.50.

X **Quayle's,** 6-8 Romilly Cres., Canton, CF1 9NR, ☎ (01222) 341264 – 🔞 🝣 𝘝𝘐𝘚𝘈
AX n
closed Sunday dinner, Tuesday, 26 December and Bank Holidays – **Meals** - Bistro - 11.95
12.95 **t.** and a la carte ⅄ 5.95.

X **Armless Dragon,** 97 Wyeverne Rd, Cathays, CF2 4BG, ☎ (01222) 38235*
Fax (01222) 382357 – 🔞 🝣 ⑩ 𝘝𝘐𝘚𝘈
BY o
closed Saturday lunch, Sunday, Monday and 25 December-1 January – **Meals** 9.90
(lunch) and a la carte 15.70/21.70 **t.** ⅄ 3.95.

at Thornhill *N : 5¼ m. by A 470 on A 469 – AV – ✉ Cardiff.*

🏨 **New House Country,** Caerphilly Rd, CF4 5UA, on A 469 ☎ (01222) 520280, *Fax (01222) 520324,* ≤, 🌳, park – [TV] ☎ [P] – 👥 200. [MC] [AE] [VISA] [JCB]. 🚫🐕
Meals 15.50/19.50 **t.** and a la carte 🍷 5.95 – **33 rm** ☕ 78.50/165.00 **t.** – SB.

🏨 **Manor Parc,** Thornhill Rd, CF4 5UA, on A 469 ☎ (01222) 693723, *Fax (01222) 614624,* 🌳, 🎾 – [TV] ☎ [P] – 👥 120. [MC] [AE] [VISA]. 🚫🐕
closed 1 January and 24 to 26 December – **Meals** *(closed Sunday dinner)* a la carte 21.25/30.00 **t.** 🍷 7.00 – **12 rm** ☕ 58.50/110.00 **t.**

at Castleton (Cas-Bach) *(Newport) NE : 7 m. on A 48 – AV – ✉ Cardiff.*

🏨 **Travel Inn,** Newport Rd, CF3 8UQ, ☎ (01633) 680070, *Fax (01633) 681143* – 🚭 rm, [TV] ♿ [P]. [MC] [AE] [DC] [VISA]. 🚫🐕
Meals (grill rest.) – **47 rm** 36.50 **t.**

[ATS] ATS Hadfield Rd ☎ (01222) 228251/226336

CARDIFF WEST SERVICE AREA *Cardiff – ✉ Pontycwn (Rhondda Cynon Taff).*
[i] *Central Station, CF1 1QY ☎ (01222) 227281.*

🏨 **Travelodge** without rest., CF72 8SA, M 4 junction 33 ☎ (01222) 891141, *Fax (01222) 892497,* Reservations (Freephone) 0800 850950 – 🚭 [TV] ♿ [P] – 👥 30. [MC] [AE] [DC] [VISA] [JCB]. 🚫🐕
50 rm 44.95 **t.**

*Le Guide change, changez de **guide Michelin** tous les ans.*

CARDIGAN **(Aberteifi)** *Ceredigion* [403] G 27 *Wales G.* – *pop. 3 758.*
Env. : *Pembrokeshire Coast National Park★★.*
⛳18 *Gwbert-on-Sea ☎ (01239) 612035.*
[i] *Theatr Mwldan, Bath House Rd, SA43 2JY ☎ (01239) 613230.*
London 250 – Carmarthen 30 – Fishguard 19.

🏨 **Penbontbren Farm** 🌙, Glynarthen, SA44 6PE, NE : 9½ m. by A 487 ☎ (01239) 810248, *Fax (01239) 811129,* park – [TV] ☎ ♿ [P] – 👥 30. [MC] [AE] [DC] [VISA] [JCB]. 🚫🐕
closed 24 to 28 December – **Meals** (dinner only) a la carte 16.70/18.20 **t.** 🍷 4.50 – **10 rm** ☕ 43.00/74.00 **t.** – SB.

t Cilgerran *(Pembrokeshire) S : 3 m. by A 478 and Cilgerran rd – ✉ Cardigan.*

🏨 **Allt-y-Rheini Mansion** 🌙, SA43 2TJ, S : ½ m. on Crymmych rd ☎ (01239) 612286, ≤, 🌳 – [TV] [P]. [MC] [VISA]. 🚫🐕
Meals (bar lunch Monday to Saturday)/dinner a la carte 14.35/16.00 **t.** 🍷 3.90 – **5 rm** ☕ 32.00/56.00 **t.**

t St. Dogmaels *W : 1 m. by A 487 on B 4568 – ✉ Cardigan.*

⌂ **Berwyn** 🌙 without rest., Cardigan Rd, SA43 3HS, ☎ (01239) 613555, ≤, 🌳 – [TV] [P]. 🚫🐕
closed 1 week Christmas – **3 rm** ☕ 22.00/39.00 **st.**

t Gwbert on Sea *NW : 3 m. on B 4548 – ✉ Cardigan.*

🏨 **Gwbert,** SA43 1PP, on B 4548 ☎ (01239) 612638, *Fax (01239) 621474,* ≤ Cardigan Bay – [lift] [TV] ☎ [P]. [MC] [AE] [VISA] [JCB]. 🚫🐕
Meals (bar lunch Monday to Saturday)/dinner 14.95 **t.** and a la carte – **16 rm** ☕ 46.50/117.00 **t.** – SB.

[ATS] ATS 4 Bath House Rd ☎ (01239) 612917

ASTLETON **(Cas-Bach)** *Newport* [403] K 29 – *see Cardiff.*

EMAES *Anglesey* [402] [403] G 23 *Wales G.*
Env. : *Anglesey★★.*
London 272 – Bangor 25 – Caernarfon 32 – Holyhead 16.

⌂ **Hafod Country House,** LL67 0DS, S : ½ m. on Llanfechell rd ☎ (01407) 710500, ≤, 🌳 – 🚭 [TV] [P]. 🚫🐕
April-September – **Meals** (by arrangement) 15.00 **t.** – **3 rm** ☕ 39.00/45.00 **t.** – SB.

HANCERY **(Rhydgaled)** *Ceredigion* [403] H 26 – *see Aberystwyth.*

CHEPSTOW Monmouthshire 403 404 M 29 Wales G. – pop. 9 461.

See : Town★ – Castle★★ AC (Great Tower★★).

Env. : Wynd Cliff★, N : 2 ½ m. by A 466 – Caerwent★ (Roman Walls★), SW : 4 m. by A 48.

☍₁₈, ☍₁₈ St. Pierre, St. Pierre Park ℘ (01291) 625261.

🛈 Castle Car Park, Bridge St., NP6 5EY ℘ (01291) 623772 (summer only).

London 131 – Bristol 17 – Cardiff 28 – Gloucester 34.

🏯 **Marriott St. Pierre H. & Country Club,** St. Pierre Park, NP6 6YA, SW : 3 ½ m. on A 48 ℘ (01291) 625261, Fax (01291) 629975, ☖, ⇌ₛ, ☒, ☍₁₈, park, ※ – ⇔ �📺 ☎ 🅿 – 🔬 220. 🐴🐴 🅰🅴 ⓪ 🆅🅸🆂🅰 🅹🅲🅱 ※
Meals a la carte 20.00/22.00 ⅃ 7.00 – ⊆ 10.75 – **127 rm** 69.00/78.00 t., 16 suites – SB.

🏢 **George,** Moor St., NP6 5DB, ℘ (01291) 625363, Fax (01291) 627418 – ⇔ 📺 ☎ 🅿 – 🔬 30. 🐴🐴 🅰🅴 ⓪ 🆅🅸🆂🅰 🅹🅲🅱
Meals (bar lunch Monday to Saturday)/dinner 17.50 **st.** and a la carte – ⊆ 8.95 – **14 rm** 70.00/85.00 **st.** – SB.

🏠 **Beaufort,** Beaufort Sq., NP6 5EP, ℘ (01291) 622497, Fax (01291) 627389 – 📺 ☎ 🅿 – 🔬 35. 🐴🐴 🅰🅴 ⓪ 🆅🅸🆂🅰 ※
Meals 12.95 **st.** and a la carte ⅃ 4.35 – ⊆ 5.45 – **19 rm** 38.00/49.00 **st.**

🍴 **Castle View** with rm, 16 Bridge St., NP6 5EZ, ℘ (01291) 620349, Fax (01291) 627397, ⇌ – ⇔ rest, 📺 ☎. 🐴🐴 🅰🅴 ⓪ 🆅🅸🆂🅰
Meals (bar lunch Monday to Saturday) (Sunday dinner residents only)/dinner 14.95 **st** ⅃ 7.00 – ⊆ 5.95 – **13 rm** 39.95/59.95 **st.** – SB.

CILGERRAN Pembrokeshire 403 G 27 – see Cardigan (Cardiganshire).

COLWYN BAY (Bae Colwyn) Conwy 402 403 I 24 Wales G. – pop. 29 883.

See : Welsh Mountain Zoo★ AC (←★).

Env. : Bodnant Garden★★ AC, SW : 6 m. by A 55 and A 470.

☍₁₈ Abergele and Pensarn, Tan-y-Goppa Rd, Abergele ℘ (01745) 824034 – ☍₅ Old Colwyn Woodland Av. ℘ (01492) 515581.

🛈 40 Station Rd, LL29 8BU ℘ (01492) 530478 – The Promenade, Rhos-on-Sea, LL28 4E ℘ (01492) 548778 (summer only).

London 237 – Birkenhead 50 – Chester 42 – Holyhead 41.

🏢 **Norfolk House,** 39 Princes Drive, LL29 8PF, ℘ (01492) 531757, Fax (01492) 533781, ⇌ ※ 📺 ☎ 🅿 – 🔬 35. 🐴🐴 🅰🅴 ⓪ 🆅🅸🆂🅰 🅹🅲🅱
closed Christmas and New Year – **Meals** (dinner only) 15.75 **t.** and a la carte ⅃ 4.90 – **22 rm** ⊆ 45.00/60.00 **t.** – SB.

🏠 **Hopeside,** 63-67 Princes Drive, West End, LL29 8PW, ℘ (01492) 533244, Fax (01492) 532850 – ⇔ rm, 📺 ☎ 🅿 – 🔬 50. 🐴🐴 🅰🅴 ⓪ 🆅🅸🆂🅰
Meals 12.00/14.00 **t.** and a la carte ⅃ 4.75 – **18 rm** ⊆ 39.00/56.00 **t.** – SB.

※※ **Café Niçoise,** 124 Abergele Rd, LL29 7PS, ℘ (01492) 531555 – 🐴🐴 🅰🅴 🆅🅸🆂🅰 🅹🅲🅱
closed lunch Monday and Tuesday, Sunday, 25-26 December, 1 week January and 1 week June – **Meals** 13.95 **t.** and a la carte ⅃ 4.95.

at Rhos-on-Sea (Llandrillo-yn-Rhos) NW : 1 m. – ⊠ Colwyn Bay.

🏠 **Ashmount,** College Av., LL28 4NT, ℘ (01492) 544582, Fax (01492) 545479 – ⇔ rest, 📺 ☎ 🅿. 🐴🐴 🅰🅴 ⓪ 🆅🅸🆂🅰
Meals (bar lunch)/dinner 13.50 **st.** ⅃ 4.00 – **17 rm** ⊆ 33.50/59.00 **st.** – SB.

CONWY 402 403 I 24 Wales G. – pop. 3 627.

See : Town★★★ – Castle★★★ AC – Town Walls★★ – Plas Mawr★★.

Env. : Snowdonia National Park★★★ – Bodnant Garden★★ AC, S : 8 m. by A 55 and A 470 – Conwy Crossing (suspension bridge★).

☍₅ Morfa ℘ (01492) 593400 – ☍₅ Penmaenmawr, Conway Old Rd ℘ (01492) 623330.

🛈 Conwy Castle Visitor Centre, LL32 8LD ℘ (01492) 592248.

London 241 – Caernarfon 22 – Chester 46 – Holyhead 37.

🏢 **Berthlwyd Hall** ⌂, Llechwedd, LL32 8DQ, SW : 2 ¼ m. by B 5106 and Sychnant rd, off Hendre Rd ℘ (01492) 592409, Fax (01492) 572290, ←, ☒, ⇌ – ⇔ rm, 📺 ☎ 🅿. 🐴🐴 🅰🅴 ⓪ 🆅🅸 🅹🅲🅱
Meals 10.95/17.95 **st.** and a la carte ⅃ 6.50 – ⊆ 4.95 – **8 rm** 58.00/85.00 **st.** – SB.

at Roewen S : 3 m. by B 5106 – ⊠ Conwy.

🏠 **Tir-y-Coed Country House** ⌂, LL32 8TP, ℘ (01492) 650219, ←, ⇌ – ⇔ rest, 📺 🅿. 🅰🅴
March-October – **Meals** 12.25 **st.** ⅃ 3.75 – **7 rm** ⊆ 29.00/54.00 **st.** – SB.

at Tyn-y-Groes *(Gwynedd) S : 3¾ m. on B 5106 –* ⊠ *Conwy.*

Groes Inn, LL32 8TN, S : 1 ½ m. on B 5106 ℰ (01492) 650545, *Fax (01492) 650855*, ≼, « Part 17C », ℛ – ⅙ rm, 🖭 ☎ 🅿. ⓂⓈ AE ① *VISA*. ⅗
Meals 7.50 t. (dinner) and a la carte 12.45/20.45 t. ⓐ 8.00 – **14 rm** ⊡ 55.00/95.00 t. – SB.

at Tal-y-Bont *S : 5¾ m. on B 5106 –* ⊠ *Conwy.*

Lodge, LL32 8YX, ℰ (01492) 660766, *Fax (01492) 660534*, ℛ – ⅙ rest, 🖭 ☎ 🅿 – 🛦 30.
ⓂⓈ *JCB*
restricted opening in winter – **Meals** *closed Monday lunch* 6.25/14.95 t. and a la carte
ⓐ 5.10 – **10 rm** ⊡ 39.50/70.00 t. – SB.

CORWEN *Denbighshire* 402 403 J 25.
London 205 – Chester 34 – Dolgellau 30 – Llandudno 40 – Shrewsbury 40.

Powys House Estate, Bonwm, LL21 9EG, E : 1 ½ m. on A 5 ℰ (01490) 412367, ℛ, ⅗ –
🖭 🅿. ⅗
closed 24 to 27 December – **Meals** (by arrangement) 16.00 s. – **3 rm** ⊡ 25.00/40.00 s.

COWBRIDGE *Vale of Glamorgan* 403 J 29 – *pop. 3 682.*
London 167 – Cardiff 12 – Swansea 30.

Bear, 63 High St., CF71 7AF, ℰ (01446) 774814, *Fax (01446) 775425*, « 18C coaching inn, 12C origins » – 🖭 ☎ 🅿 – 🛦 100. ⓂⓈ AE *VISA*
Meals *(closed Sunday dinner)* (dinner only) a la carte 13.75/19.75 st. ⓐ 3.95 – **34 rm**
⊡ 47.50/75.00 st. – SB.

COYCHURCH (Llangrallo) *Bridgend* 403 J 29 – *see Bridgend.*

CRICCIETH *Gwynedd* 402 403 H 25 *Wales G. – pop. 1 720.*
Env. : *Lleyn Peninsula★★ – Ffestiniog Railway★★.*
🖪 *Ednyfed Hill* ℰ (01766) 522154.
London 249 – Caernarfon 17 – Shrewsbury 85.

Mynydd Ednyfed Country House ⌂, Caernarfon Rd, LL52 0PH, NW : ¾ m. on B 4411 ℰ (01766) 523269, ≼, 🖪, ℛ, ⅗ – 🖭 ☎ 🅿. ⓂⓈ AE *VISA*
closed 25 and 26 December – **Meals** (dinner only) a la carte 15.10/20.45 st. ⓐ 5.95 – **9 rm**
⊡ 36.00/62.00 st. – SB.

CRICKHOWELL *Powys* 403 K 28 *Wales G. – pop. 2 166.*
Env. : *Brecon Beacons National Park★★.*
Exc. : *Llanthony Priory★★, NE : 10 m. by minor roads.*
London 169 – Abergavenny 6 – Brecon 14 – Newport 25.

Gliffaes Country House ⌂, NP8 1RH, W : 3 ¾ m. by A 40 ℰ (01874) 730371, *Fax (01874) 730463*, ≼, « Country house and gardens on the banks of the River Usk », 🐟, park, ⅗ – ⅙ rest, 🖭 ☎ 🅿. ⓂⓈ AE ① *VISA*. ⅗
Meals (light lunch Monday to Saturday)/dinner 22.50 st. – **22 rm** ⊡ 49.00/114.00 st. – SB.

Bear, High St., NP8 1BW, ℰ (01873) 810408, *Fax (01873) 811696* – 🖭 ☎ 🅿 – 🛦 50. ⓂⓈ AE *VISA JCB*
Meals (lunch booking essential) (bar meal Sunday dinner) a la carte 16.20/23.90 t. ⓐ 4.25 –
27 rm ⊡ 42.00/100.00 t., 1 suite.

Nantyffin Cider Mill Inn, NP8 1SG, W : 1 ½ m. on A 40 ℰ (01873) 810775, *Fax (01873) 810775*, « Converted 16C cider mill » – ⓂⓈ AE *VISA*
closed Monday, 1 week January and 1 week November – **Meals** a la carte 13.65/24.00 t. ⓐ 7.85.

at Llangenny *E : 3 m. by A 40 via Glangrwyney –* ⊠ *Crickhowell.*

Gellirhydd Farm ⌂, NP8 1HF, N : 1 ½ m. taking unmarked road before bridge ℰ (01873) 810466, ≼, 🐟, ℛ, park – ⅙ 🅿. ⓂⓈ *VISA*. ⅗
closed Christmas and New Year – **Meals** (by arrangement) (communal dining) 12.50 s. –
3 rm ⊡ 20.00/40.00 s. – SB.

at Llangattock *SW : 1¼ m. by A 4077 and Llangynidr rd –* ⊠ *Crickhowell.*

Ty Croeso ⌂, The Dardy, NP8 1PU, ℰ (01873) 810573, *Fax (01873) 810573*, ≼, ℛ – 🖭 ☎ 🅿. ⓂⓈ AE *VISA JCB*
closed 24 to 26 December – **Meals** (dinner only and Sunday lunch)/dinner 15.95 t. and a la carte ⓐ 3.75 – **8 rm** ⊡ 30.00/70.00 t. – SB.

CROSSGATES *Powys* **403** J 27 – see Llandrindod Wells.

CROSS HANDS *Carmarthenshire* **403** H 28 – pop. 9 520.
London 208 – Fishguard 63 – Swansea 19.

🏠 **Travelodge,** SA14 6NW, on A 48 ℰ (01269) 845700, Reservations (Freephone) 0800
850950 – ✳️ rm, 📺 ♿ 🅿, 🕮 🆑 ⬛ 🚾 ᴊᴄʙ. ✳️
Meals (grill rest.) – **32 rm** 44.95 **t.**

CRUGYBAR *Carmarthenshire* **403** I 27 – ✉ Llanwrda.
London 213 – Carmarthen 26 – Swansea 36.

🏠 **Glanrannell Park** ⬎, SA19 8SA, SW : ½ m. by B 4302 ℰ (01558) 685230,
Fax (01558) 685784, ≤, ⬎, 🐎, park – ✳️ rest, 📺 🅿, 🕮 🚾 ᴊᴄʙ
April-October – Meals (bar lunch)/dinner 17.00 **t.** ⱥ 4.00 – **8 rm** ⱬ 41.00/72.00 **t.** – SB.

CWMBRAN *Torfaen* **403** K 29 – pop. 46 021.
London 149 – Bristol 35 – Cardiff 17 – Newport 5.

🏨 **Parkway,** Cwmbran Drive, NP44 3UW, S : 1 m. by A 4051 ℰ (01633) 871199,
Fax (01633) 869160, ⱥ, ⇌, ⬛, – ✳️ rm, 📺 🕿 ♿ 🅿 – ⱥ 500. 🕮 🆑 ⬛ 🚾. ✳️
restricted opening Christmas – Meals (light lunch Monday to Saturday)/dinner 15.00 **t.**
and a la carte – ⱬ 9.40 – **69 rm** 81.00/91.00 **t.**, 1 suite – SB.

🔧 ATS Station Rd ℰ (01633) 484964

CWM TAF *Merthyr Tydfil* – see Merthyr Tydfil.

CYNGHORDY *Carmarthenshire* **403** I 27 – ✉ Llandovery.
London 210 – Carmarthen 31 – Swansea 41.

⌂ **Llanerchindda Farm** ⬎, SA20 0NB, N : 2 ½ m. by Station rd and under viaduct
ℰ (01550) 750274, Fax (01550) 750300, ≤ Black Mountains, « Working farm », 🐎
✳️ rest, 📺 🅿
Meals (by arrangement) 10.00 ⱥ 3.00 – **9 rm** ⱬ 22.00/44.00 **st.**

DEGANWY *Conwy* **402 403** I 24 – see Llandudno.

DENBIGH (Dinbych) *Denbighshire* **402 403** J 24 – pop. 8 529.
🔝 Henllan Rd ℰ (01745) 814159.
London 217 – Chester 30 – Colwyn Bay 21 – Shrewsbury 53.

⌂ **Berllan Bach** ⬎, Fford Las, LL16 4LR, SE : 5 ¾ m. by Ruthin Rd and Llandyrnog rd o
Llangynhafel rd ℰ (01824) 790732, 🐎 – 📺 🅿
Meals 12.50 **s.** – **3 rm** ⱬ 32.50/45.00 **s.** – SB.

DOLGELLAU *Gwynedd* **402 403** I 25 *Wales G.* – pop. 2 396.
See : Town★.
Env. : Snowdonia National Park★★★ – Cadair Idris★★★ – Precipice Walk★, NE : 3 m. on minc
roads.
🔝 Pencefn Rd ℰ (01341) 422603.
🅱 Ty Meirion, Eldon Sq., LL40 1PU ℰ (01341) 422888.
London 221 – Birkenhead 72 – Chester 64 – Shrewsbury 57.

🏨 **Penmaenuchaf Hall** ⬎, Penmaenpool, LL40 1YB, W : 1 ¾ m. on A 49
ℰ (01341) 422129, Fax (01341) 422129, ≤, « Victorian mansion in extensive gardens »,
🐎, park – ✳️ rest, 📺 🕿 🅿 – ⱥ 50. 🕮 🆑 ⬛ 🚾 ᴊᴄʙ. ✳️
closed 5 to 12 January – Meals 14.95/25.00 **t.** and a la carte ⱥ 6.95 – **14 rm** ⱬ 65.00
150.00 **st.** – SB.

🏠 **Dolserau Hall** ⬎, LL40 2AG, NE : 2 ¾ m. by A 494 ℰ (01341) 422522, Fax (01341) 42240
≤, 🐎 – ⧄, ✳️ rest, 📺 🕿 🅿. 🕮 🚾
closed 9 November-13 February except Christmas and New Year – Meals (residents only
(dinner only) 19.50 **t.** ⱥ 7.50 – **15 rm** ⱬ (dinner included) 61.50/123.00 **t.** – SB.

🏠 **George III,** Penmaenpool, LL40 1YD, W : 2 m. by A 493 ℰ (01341) 422525,
Fax (01341) 423565, ≤ Mawddach estuary and mountains, ⇌ – ✳️ rest, 📺 🕿 🅿. 🕮 🚾
ᴊᴄʙ. ✳️
Meals (bar lunch Monday to Saturday)/dinner a la carte 16.40/25.85 **t.** ⱥ 6.20 – **11 rm**
ⱬ 50.00/88.00 **t.** – SB.

at Ganllwyd *N : 5½ m. on A 470 –* ⊠ *Dolgellau.*

🏛 **Dolmelynllyn Hall** ⚜, LL40 2HP, ℘ (01341) 440273, *Fax (01341) 440273*, ≤, ⚓, 🚗, park – ✠ 📺 ☎ 📵. ⓂⓈ ⒶⒺ ⓪ 𝒱𝐼𝒮𝒜. ✧
March-November – **Meals** (bar lunch)/dinner 23.50 **st.** and a la carte ⬧ 7.50 – **10 rm** ⊑ 47.50/110.00 **st.** – SB.

at Llanfachreth *NE : 3¾ m. –* ⊠ *Dolgellau.*

🏠 **Ty Isaf Farmhouse** ⚜, LL40 2EA, ℘ (01341) 423261, ≤, « 17C longhouse », 🚗 – ✠
📵. ✧
Meals (by arrangement) (communal dining) 13.50 **s.** – **3 rm** ⊑ 36.00/52.00 **s.**

at Arthog *SW : 7 m. on A 493 –* ⊠ *Dolgellau.*

🏠 **Cyfannedd Uchaf** ⚜, LL39 1LX, S : 4 ½ m. by A 493 Cregennan Lakes rd, taking right turn at T. junction at end of road (gated roads) ℘ (01341) 250526, ≤ Barmouth, Mawddach estuary and mountains, park – ✠ 📵. ✧
May-September – **Meals** (communal dining) 6.50 **st.** – **3 rm** ⊑ 37.00 **st.**

at Bontddu *W : 5 m. on A 496 (Barmouth Rd) –* ⊠ *Dolgellau.*

🏛🏛 **Bontddu Hall Country House,** LL40 2UF, ℘ (01341) 430661, *Fax (01341) 430284,*
≤ Mawddach estuary and mountains, « Victorian mansion in extensive gardens » –
✠ rest, 📺 ☎ 📵. ⓂⓈ ⒶⒺ ⓪ 𝒱𝐼𝒮𝒜 𝒿𝒸𝒷
April-October – ***Garden :*** **Meals** 23.50 **t.** (dinner) and a la carte 13.45/23.50 **t.** ⬧ 6.50 –
Brasserie : **Meals** 23.50 **t.** (dinner) and a la carte 13.45/23.50 **t.** ⬧ 6.50 – **17 rm**
⊑ 52.50/100.00 **st.,** 3 suites – SB.

🏛 **Borthwnog Hall,** LL40 2TT, E : 1 m. on A 496 ℘ (01341) 430271, *Fax (01341) 430682,*
≤ Mawddach estuary and mountains, « Part Regency house, art gallery », 🚗, park –
✠ rest, 📵. ⓂⓈ 𝒱𝐼𝒮𝒜. ✧
closed 23 to 27 December – **Meals** (booking essential) (dinner only) 17.50 **t.** and a la carte
⬧ 5.00 – **3 rm** ⊑ 46.00/112.00 **t.** – SB.

DRENEWYDD YN NOTAIS (Nottage) Bridgend – *see Porthcawl.*

DYFFRYN ARDUDWY *Gwynedd* **402 403** H 25 *Wales G. – pop. 1 452 (inc. Tal-y-Bont).*
Env. : *Snowdonia National Park★★★.*
London 237 – Dolgellau 16 – Caernarfon 44.

🏛 **Ystumgwern Hall Farm** ⚜ without rest., LL44 2DD, NW : 1 m. by A 496
℘ (01341) 247249, *Fax (01341) 247171*, « Working farm », 🚗, park – 📺 📵
6 suites ⊑ 20.00/44.00.

EWLOE *Flintshire* **402 403** K 24 – *pop. 3 263.*
🛈 *Autolodge Site, Gateway Services, A 55 Expressway westbound, Northophall, CH7 6HE*
℘ (01244) 541597 (summer only).
London 200 – Chester 8.5 – Shrewsbury 48.

🏛🏛🏛 **St David's Park,** St. David's Park, CH5 3YB, on B 5125 at junction with A 494
℘ (01244) 520800, *Fax (01244) 520930*, 𝖎𝖆, ⚌, 🏊, 🏋, 🚗, ✕ – ⧈, ✠ rm, 🍴 rest, 📺 ☎ 🕭
📵 – 🔬 270. ⓂⓈ ⒶⒺ ⓪ 𝒱𝐼𝒮𝒜 𝒿𝒸𝒷
Fountains : **Meals** 17.50 **st.** and a la carte ⬧ 11.95 – ⊑ 8.95 – **145 rm** 92.00/142.00 **st.** –
SB.

🝆 ATS Holywell Rd (Nr. Queensferry) ℘ (01244) 520380

LES GUIDES VERTS MICHELIN

Paysages, monuments
Routes touristiques
Géographie
Histoire, Art
Itinéraires de visite
Plans de villes et de monuments

FISHGUARD (Abergwaun) Pembrokeshire **403** F 28 Wales G. – pop. 2 679.

Env. : Pembrokeshire Coast National Park★★.

⚓ to Republic of Ireland (Rosslare) (Stena Line) 2 daily (3 h 30 mn).

🚩 4 Hamilton St., SA65 9HL ℰ (01348) 873484.

London 265 – Cardiff 114 – Gloucester 176 – Holyhead 169 – Shrewsbury 136 – Swansea 76.

🏠 **Plas Glyn-Y-Mel** ॐ without rest., Lower Town, SA65 9LY, ℰ (01348) 872296, Fax (01348) 874521, ≤, 🔲, 🌳, park – 📺 ℗
March-November – 5 rm ⇆ 45.00/72.00 t.

🏠 **Manor House,** 11 Main St., SA65 9HG, ℰ (01348) 873260, Fax (01348) 873260, 🌳 – 📺 ⓪ⓔ 𝑉𝐼𝑆𝐴
closed Christmas, 2 weeks in spring and 2 weeks in autumn – **Meals** (dinner only) 17.00 st ↑ 5.00 – 6 rm ⇆ 27.00/52.00 st. – SB.

XX **Three Main Street** with rm., 3 Main St., SA65 9HG, ℰ (01348) 874275 – 🍴 🍴
closed February (closed Tuesday in winter, Sunday and Monday) a la carte 12.95/22.50 t. ↑ 8.25 – 3 rm ⇆ 35.00/60.00 t.

at Pontfaen SE : 5½ m. by B 4313.

🏠 **Tregynon Country Farmhouse** ॐ, Cwm Gwaun, SA65 9TU, E : 6 ¼ m. ℰ (01239) 820531, Fax (01239) 820808, 🌳, park – 🍴 📺 ☎ ℗. ⓪ⓔ 𝑉𝐼𝑆𝐴 𝐽𝐶𝐵. 🍴
closed 2 weeks in winter – **Meals** (booking essential) (dinner only) 18.95 t. – 8 rm ⇆ 50.00/72.00 t. – SB.

at Letterston S : 5 m. by A 40.

⭡ **Heathfield Mansion** ॐ, SA62 5EG, NW : 1 ½ m. by B 4331 ℰ (01348) 840263 Fax (01348) 840263 – 🍴 📺 ℗
April-October – **Meals** (by arrangement) 10.00 – 3 rm ⇆ 25.00/40.00 – SB.

at Welsh Hook SW : 7½ m. by A 40 – ✉ Haverfordwest.

XX **Stone Hall** ॐ with rm, SA62 5NS, ℰ (01348) 840212, Fax (01348) 840815, « Part 14C manor house with 17C extension », 🌳 – 📺 ℗. ⓪ⓔ ⒶⒺ ⑪ 𝑉𝐼𝑆𝐴. 🍴
Meals (dinner only) 18.00 t. and a la carte ↑ 5.50 – 5 rm ⇆ 48.00/70.00 t. – SB.

ⓐ ATS Scleddau ℰ (01348) 873522

FRON-GOCH Gwynedd **402 403** J 25 – see Bala.

GANLLWYD Gwynedd **402 403** I 25 – see Dolgellau.

GOVILON Monmouthshire – see Abergavenny.

GUILSFIELD Powys **402 403** K 26 – see Welshpool.

GWBERT ON SEA Ceredigion **403** F 27 – see Cardigan.

HANMER Wrexham **402 403** L 25 – pop. 565 – ✉ Whitchurch (Shrops.).

London 237 – Chester 26 – Shrewsbury 27 – Stoke-on-Trent 28.

🏨 **Hanmer Arms,** SY13 3DE, ℰ (01948) 830532, Fax (01948) 830740, 🌳 – 🍴 rest, 📺 ☎ ℗
– 🔑 80. ⓪ⓔ ⒶⒺ ⑪ 𝑉𝐼𝑆𝐴. 🍴
Meals a la carte 9.20/21.70 t. ↑ 4.80 – 20 rm ⇆ 38.00/48.00 t., 6 suites.

HARLECH Gwynedd **402 403** H 25 Wales G. – pop. 1 233.

See : Castle★★ AC.

Env. : Snowdonia National Park★★★.

🛏 Royal St. David's ℰ (01766) 780203.

🚩 Gwyddfor House, High St., LL46 2YA ℰ (01766) 780658 (summer only).

London 241 – Chester 72 – Dolgellau 21.

⭡ **Gwrach Ynys,** LL47 6TS, N : 2 ¼ m. on A 496 ℰ (01766) 780742, Fax (01766) 781199, 🌳
🍴 📺 ℗. 🍴
March-October – **Meals** (by arrangement) 12.00 t. – 7 rm ⇆ 23.00/46.00 t. – SB.

XX **Castle Cottage** with rm, Pen Llech, LL46 2YL, off B 4573 ℰ (01766) 780479 Fax (01766) 780479 – 🍴 rest. ⓪ⓔ ⒶⒺ 𝑉𝐼𝑆𝐴
closed 3 weeks January – **Meals** (booking essential) (dinner only and Sunday lunch) dinner 21.00 t. ↑ 6.00 – 6 rm ⇆ 26.00/56.00 t. – SB.

HAVERFORDWEST (Hwlffordd) *Pembrokeshire* **403** F 28 *Wales G. – pop. 13 454.*

Env. : *Pembrokeshire Coast National Park★★.*
Exc. : *Skomer Island and Skokholm Island★, SW : 14 m. by B 4327 and minor roads.*
🏌 *Arnolds Down* ℰ *(01437) 763565.*
🛈 *2 Old Bridge, SA61 2EZ* ℰ *(01437) 763110.*
London 250 – Fishguard 15 – Swansea 57.

🏨 **Mariners,** Mariners Sq., SA61 2DU, ℰ *(01437) 763353, Fax (01437) 764258 –* 📺 ☎ 🅿 –
🛗 35. **MO** 🆎 ① *VISA* . 🛇
closed 24 to 28 December and 1 January – **Meals** (bar lunch)/dinner 14.00 **t.** and a la carte
🍴 5.50 – **29 rm** ⊑ 47.75/73.50 **t.** – SB.

🏠 **Wilton House,** 6 Quay St., SA61 1BG, ℰ *(01437) 760033, Fax (01437) 760297,* 🏊, 🐴 – 📺
☎ 🅿 **MO** 🆎 *VISA* . 🛇
Meals a la carte 8.20/15.45 **st.** 🍴 3.50 – **9 rm** ⊑ 35.00/52.50 **st.** – SB.

🔘 *ATS Back Lane, Prendergast* ℰ *(01437) 763756*

HAY-ON-WYE *Powys* **403** K 27 *Wales G. – pop. 1 407.*

See : *Town★.*
Env. : *Brecon Beacons National Park★★.*
Exc. : *Llanthony Priory★★, SE : 12 m. by minor roads.*
🏌 *Rhosgoch, Builth Wells* ℰ *(01497) 851251.*
🛈 *Oxford Rd Car Park, HR3 5DG* ℰ *(01497) 820144.*
London 154 – Brecon 16 – Hereford 21 – Newport 62.

🏨 **Swan,** Church St., HR3 5DQ, ℰ *(01497) 821188, Fax (01497) 821424,* 🖥, 🐴 – ❀ rest, 📺
☎ 🅿 – 🛗 160. **MO** 🆎 ① *VISA* 🇯🇨🇧
Meals 18.50 **st.** (dinner) and a la carte 🍴 7.00 – **18 rm** ⊑ 50.00/90.00 **st.** – SB.

🏠 **Old Black Lion,** Lion St., HR3 5AD, ℰ *(01497) 820841, « Part 13C and 17C inn » –*
❀ rest, 📺 ☎ 🅿. **MO** 🆎 *VISA*
Meals a la carte 17.35/22.90 **st.** 🍴 5.25 – **10 rm** ⊑ 25.00/52.50 **st.** – SB.

🏠 **York House,** Hardwick Rd, Cusop, HR3 5QX, E : ½ m. on B 4348 ℰ *(01497) 820705,* 🐴 –
❀ 📺 🅿. **MO** 🆎
Meals (dinner only by arrangement) (unlicensed) 13.50 **s.** – **4 rm** ⊑ 23.75/47.50 **s.** – SB.

at Llanigon *SW : 2½ m. by B 4350 –* ✉ *Hay-on-Wye.*

🏠 **Old Post Office** without rest., HR3 5QA, ℰ *(01497) 820008, « 17C house » –* ❀ 🅿
closed January – **3 rm** ⊑ 25.00/40.00.

HOLYHEAD (Caergybi) *Anglesey* **402** **403** G 24 *Wales G. – pop. 11 796.*

Env. : *South Stack Cliffs★, W : 3 m. by minor roads.*
⛴ *to Republic of Ireland (Dun Laoghaire) (Stena Line) 4-5 daily (1 h 40 mn) – to Republic
of Ireland (Dublin) (Irish Ferries) 2 daily (3 h 15 mn) – to Republic of Ireland (Dublin) (Stena
Line) daily (4 h).*
London 269 – Birkenhead 94 – Cardiff 215 – Chester 88 – Shrewsbury 105 – Swansea 190.

🏠 **Yr Hendre,** Porth-y-Felin Rd, LL65 1AH, NW : ¾ m. by Prince of Wales Rd off Waltham Av.
ℰ *(01407) 762929 –* ❀ 📺 🅿. 🛇
closed 25 and 26 December – **Meals** (by arrangement) 10.00 **st.** – **3 rm** ⊑ 25.00/40.00.

HOLYWELL (Treffynnon) *Flintshire* **402** **403** K 24 *Wales G. – pop. 7 531.*

See : *Town★.*
🏌 *Holywell, Brynford* ℰ *(01352) 710040/713937.*
London 217 – Chester 19 – Liverpool 34.

🏨 **Kinsale Hall** 🛇, Llanerchymor, CH8 9DX, N : 3 ½ m. by B 5121 off A 548
ℰ *(01745) 560001, Fax (01745) 561298,* ≼, 🏌, 🐴, *park –* 📶, ❀ rest, 🖥 rest, 📺 ☎ 🅿 –
🛗 350. **MO** 🆎 *VISA* 🇯🇨🇧. 🛇
Meals 18.00 **st.** and a la carte 🍴 8.10 – **28 rm** ⊑ 69.00 **st.**, 1 suite – SB.

🏠 **Travelodge,** Halkyn, CH8 8RF, SE : 3 ½ m. on A 55 (westbound carriageway)
ℰ *(01352) 780952, Reservations (Freephone) 0800 850950 –* ❀ rm, 📺 🛇 🅿. **MO** 🆎 ① *VISA*
🇯🇨🇧. 🛇
Meals (grill rest.) – **31 rm** 39.95 **t.**

HOWEY *Powys – see Llandrindod Wells.*

KNIGHTON (Trefyclawdd) *Powys* 403 K 26 *Wales G.* – pop. 2 972.

See : *Town*★.

Exc. : *Offa's Dyke*★, NW : 9 ½ m.

🏌 *Little Ffrydd Wood* ℰ (01547) 528646.

🛈 *The Offas Dyke Centre, West St., LD7 1EW* ℰ (01547) 528753.

London 162 – Birmingham 59 – Hereford 31 – Shrewsbury 35.

🏠 **Milebrook House,** Ludlow Rd, Milebrook, LD7 1LT, E : 2 m. on A 4113 ℰ (01547) 528632, Fax (01547) 520509, ⤴, 🚗 – 🖭 📺 **℗**, ⚫⓪ AE VISA JCB
Meals *(closed Monday lunch)* 10.95/17.50 **t.** 🍷 5.80 – **10 rm** ⌁ 48.50/78.50 **t.** – SB.

LAKE VYRNWY *Powys* 402 403 J 25 *Wales G.* – ✉ Llanwddyn.

See : *Lake*★.

🛈 *Unit 2, Vyrnwy Craft Workshops, SY10 0LY* ℰ (01691) 870346 *(summer only)*.

London 204 – Chester 52 – Llanfyllin 10 – Shrewsbury 40.

🏰 **Lake Vyrnwy** ⤴, SY10 0LY, ℰ (01691) 870692, Fax (01691) 870259, ≤ Lake Vyrnwy, « Victorian sporting estate », ⤴, 🚗, park, 🎾 – ⅙ rest, 🖭 ☎ **℗** – 🔒 80. ⚫⓪ AE ⓪ VISA
Meals *(lunch booking essential)* 15.95/25.50 **t.** – **34 rm** ⌁ 68.00/150.00 **t.**, 1 suite – SB.

LALESTON *Bridgend* 403 J 29 – see Bridgend.

LAMPHEY *Pembrokeshire* 403 F 28 – see Pembroke.

LANGSTONE *Newport* 403 L 29 – see Newport.

LETTERSTON *Pembrokeshire* 403 F 28 – see Fishguard.

LLANARMON DYFFRYN CEIRIOG *Wrexham* 402 403 K 25 – ✉ Llangollen (Denbighshire).

London 196 – Chester 33 – Shrewsbury 32.

🏠 **West Arms,** LL20 7LD, ℰ (01691) 600665, Fax (01691) 600622, ⤴, 🚗 – 🖭 ☎ **℗** – 🔒 30. ⚫⓪ AE ⓪ VISA JCB
Meals *(bar lunch Monday to Saturday)*/dinner 17.50 **st.** and a la carte 🍷 6.50 – **12 rm** ⌁ 40.00/70.00 **st.**, 1 suite – SB.

LLANBEDR *Gwynedd* 402 403 H 25 *Wales G.* – pop. 1 101.

Env. : *Snowdonia National Park*★★★.

London 262 – Holyhead 54 – Shrewsbury 100.

🏠 **Pensarn Hall** ⤴, LL45 2HS, N : ¾ m. on A 496 ℰ (01341) 241236, ≤, 🚗 – ⅙ rest, 🖭 **℗** ⚫⓪ VISA
March-October – **Meals** *(residents only) (dinner only)* 12.50 **s.** – **7 rm** ⌁ 28.50/48.50 **s.** – SB.

🍴 **Victoria Inn** with rm, LL45 2LD, ℰ (01341) 241213, Fax (01341) 241644, 🚗 – ⅙ rest, 🖭 **℗**. ⚫⓪ VISA JCB
Meals 8.50/14.50 **st.** and a la carte – **5 rm** ⌁ 28.00/50.00 **st.**

LLANBERIS *Gwynedd* 403 H 24 *Wales G.* – pop. 1 859.

See : *Town*★ – *Welsh Slate Museum*★ *AC* – *Power of Wales*★.

Env. : *Snowdonia National Park*★★★ *(Snowdon*★★★, *Snowdon Mountain Railway*★★ *AC* – panorama★★★).

🛈 *41a High St., LL55 4EH* ℰ (01286) 870765.

London 243 – Caernarfon 7 – Chester 65 – Shrewsbury 78.

🍴🍴 **Y Bistro,** 43-45 High St., LL55 4EU, ℰ (01286) 871278 – ⅙, ⚫⓪ VISA JCB
closed Sunday except at Bank Holidays and Monday in winter – **Meals** *(booking essential) (dinner only)* 23.50 **st.** 🍷 6.75.

LLANDEGLA *Denbighshire* 402 403 K 24 – ✉ Wrexham.

London 201 – Birkenhead 31 – Caernarfon 66 – Chester 22 – Llandudno 43 – Shrewsbury 40.

🏠 **Bodidris Hall** ⤴, LL11 3AL, NE : 1 ½ m. on A 5104 ℰ (01978) 790434, Fax (01978) 790335, « 15C manor of 12C origins », ⤴, 🚗, park – ⅙ rest, 🖭 ☎ **℗** – 🔒 50. ⚫⓪ AE ⓪ VISA JCB
Meals 16.00/30.00 **t.** 🍷 6.00 – **8 rm** ⌁ 80.00/140.00 **t.** – SB.

LLANDEGLEY *Powys – see Llandrindod Wells.*

LLANDEILO *Carmarthenshire* [403] I 28 *Wales G. – pop. 1 666.*

See : *Town★ – Dinefwr Park★ AC.*

Env. : *Brecon Beacons National Park★★ – Black Mountain★, SE : by minor roads – Carreg Cennen Castle★ AC, SE : 4 m. by A 483 and minor roads.*

⛳18 *Glynhir, Glynhir Rd, Llandybie, Ammanford ☎ (01269) 850472.*

London 218 – Brecon 34 – Carmarthen 15 – Swansea 25.

⌂ **Plough Inn,** Rhosmaen, SA19 6NP, N : 1 m. on A 40 ☎ (01558) 823431, *Fax (01558) 823969,* ≤, Lб, ≘s – [TV] ☎ ♿ [P] – 🏛 45. [MC] [AE] [VISA] [JCB]. ✂
closed 25 December – **Meals** (in bar Sunday dinner) a la carte 17.50/28.00 **t.** 🍷 5.50 – ☕ 5.00 – **12 rm** 47.50/67.50 **t.**

ATS Towy Terr., Ffairfach ☎ (01558) 822567

LLANDRILLO *Denbighshire* [402] [403] J 25 – *pop. 1 048 –* ✉ *Corwen.*

London 210 – Chester 40 – Dolgellau 26 – Shrewsbury 46.

⌂ **Tyddyn Llan Country House** 🌿, LL21 0ST, ☎ (01490) 440264, *Fax (01490) 440414,* « Part Georgian country house », 🎣, 🌳 – ⊁ rest, [TV] ☎ [P]. [MC] [AE] [DC] [VISA] [JCB]
closed 2 weeks January – **Meals** *(closed Monday lunch)* 15.50/25.00 **t.** 🍷 8.00 – **10 rm** ☕ 64.00/110.00 **t.** – SB.

Per spostarvi più rapidamente utilizzate le ***carte Michelin "Grandi Strade"*** *:*

n° [970] **Europa,** *n°* [976] **Rep. Ceca/Slovacchia,** *n°* [980] **Grecia,**
n° [984] **Germania,** *n°* [985] **Scandinavia-Finlandia,**
n° [986] **Gran Bretagna-Irlanda,** *n°* [987] **Germania-Austria-Benelux,**
n° [988] **Italia,** *n°* [989] **Francia,** *n°* [990] **Spagna-Portogallo,** *n°* [991] **Jugoslavia.**

LLANDRINDOD WELLS *Powys* [403] J 27 *Wales G. – pop. 4 362.*

Exc. : *Elan Valley★★ (Dol-y-Mynach and Claerwen Dam and Reservoir★★, Caban Coch Dam and Reservoir★, Garreg-ddu Viaduct★, Pen-y-Garreg Reservoir and Dam★, Craig Goch Dam and Reservoir★), NW : 12 m. by A 4081, A 470 and B 4518.*

⛳18 *Llandrindod Wells ☎ (01597) 822010/823873.*

[i] *Old Town Hall, Memorial Gardens, LD1 5DL ☎ (01597) 822600.*

London 204 – Brecon 29 – Carmarthen 60 – Shrewsbury 58.

⌂ **Metropole,** Temple St., LD1 5DY, ☎ (01597) 823700, *Fax (01597) 824828,* ≘s, 🏊, 🌳 – [lift] [TV] ☎ [P] – 🏛 250. [MC] [AE] [VISA]
Meals 9.95/17.95 **t.** 🍷 5.00 – **120 rm** ☕ 66.00/87.00 **t.**, 2 suites – SB.

⌂ **Montpelier,** Temple St., LD1 5HW, ☎ (01597) 822388, *Fax (01597) 825600* – [TV] ☎ [P]. [MC] [VISA]. ✂
Meals (bar lunch)/dinner 12.95 **st.** and a la carte – **11 rm** ☕ 35.00/70.00 **st.** – SB.

⌂ **Charis** without rest., Pentrosfa, LD1 5AL, S : ¾ m. by A 470 ☎ (01597) 824732 – ⊁ [TV] [P]
closed 24-31 December – **3 rm** ☕ 18.00/32.00.

at Crossgates *NE : 3½ m. at junction of A 483 with A 44 –* ✉ *Llandrindod Wells.*

⌂ **Guidfa House,** LD1 6RF, ☎ (01597) 851241, *Fax (01597) 851875,* 🌳 – ⊁ [TV] [P]. [MC] [VISA]. ✂
Meals (residents only) (dinner only) 16.00 **st.** 🍷 4.25 – **7 rm** ☕ 21.00/49.00 **st.** – SB.

at Llandegley *E : 7 m. by A 483 on A 44 –* ✉ *Llandrindod Wells.*

⌂ **Ffaldau Country House,** LD1 5UD, ☎ (01597) 851421, *Fax (01597) 851421,* « 16C origins », 🌳 – ⊁ [P]. [MC] [VISA]. ✂
Meals (booking essential) (residents only) (dinner only) 15.00/18.00 🍷 5.50 – **4 rm** ☕ 30.00/48.00.

at Howey *S : 1½ m. by A 483 –* ✉ *Llandrindod Wells.*

⌂ **Brynhir Farm** 🌿, Chapel Rd, LD1 5PB, NE : 1 m. ☎ (01597) 822425, *Fax (01597) 822425,* ≤, « Working farm », 🎣, 🌳, park – [P]
Meals (by arrangement) 9.00 **st.** 🍷 3.25 – **6 rm** ☕ 20.00/40.00 **s.** – SB.

⌂ **Holly Farm** 🌿, LD1 5PP, W : ½ m. ☎ (01597) 822402, « Working farm », 🌳 – ⊁ rest, [P]. ✂
April-November – **Meals** 9.00 **st.** – **3 rm** ☕ 20.00/38.00 **st.** – SB.

LLANDUDNO Conwy **402 403** | 24 Wales G. – pop. 14 576.

See : Town★ – Seafront★ (Pier★) B – The Great Orme★ (panorama★★, Tramway★, Ancient Copper Mines★ AC) AB.

Exc. : Bodnant Garden★★ AC, S : 7 m. by A 470 B.

Rhos-on-Sea, Penrhyn Bay ℘ (01492) 549641, A – Rhos 72 Bryniau Rd, West Shore ℘ (01492) 875325 A – Rhos Hospital Rd ℘ (01492) 876450 B.

1-2 Chapel St., LL30 2YU ℘ (01492) 876413.

London 243 – Birkenhead 55 – Chester 47 – Holyhead 43.

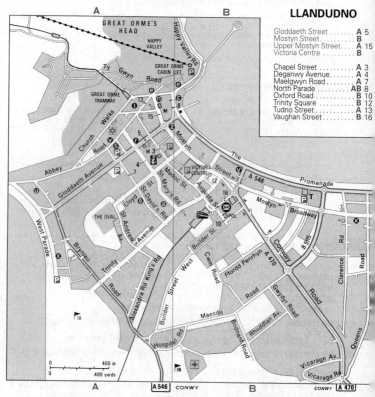

LLANDUDNO

Bodysgallen Hall ⟨⟩, LL30 1RS, SE : 2 m. on A 470 ℘ (01492) 584466, Fax (01492) 582519, ≤ gardens and mountains, « Part 17C and 18C hall with terraced gardens », Ⅰ⑥, ≘s, ⬛, park, ⅏ – ⅏ rest, ⅏ ☎ ℗ – 益 50. ⅏ 歴 ⅦSA ⅏
Meals (booking essential) 13.50/27.50 **st.** and dinner a la carte 27.50/36.00 **st.** ⟨ 11.75 –
⟐ 10.50 – **20 rm** 95.00/210.00 **st.**, 15 suites 155.00/210.00 **st.** – SB.

Imperial, The Promenade, LL30 1AP, ℘ (01492) 877466, Fax (01492) 878043, Ⅰ⑥, ≘s, ⬛,
⟐⟐⟐ ⅏ ☎ ℗ – 益 150. ⅏ 歴 ⅦSA
Meals 12.00/20.00 **st.** ⟨ 9.00 – **96 rm** ⟐ 65.00/105.00 **st.**, 4 suites – SB.

Empire, 73 Church Walks, LL30 2HE, ℘ (01492) 860555, Fax (01492) 860791, « Collection of Russell Flint prints », ≘s, ⬛, ⬛ – ⅏, ⅏ rest, ⅏ ☎ ℗ – 益 40. ⅏ 歴 ① ⅦSA ⅉCB ⅏
closed 20 to 30 December – **Watkins :** Meals (dinner only and Saturday and Sunday lunch)/dinner 22.50 **st.** ⟨ 7.50 – **43 rm** ⟐ 60.00/100.00 **st.**, 7 suites – SB.

Empire (No 72), 72 Church Walks, LL30 2HE, ℘ (01492) 860555, Fax (01492) 860791 « Victoriana » – ⅏ ⅏ ☎ ℗. ⅏ 歴 ① ⅦSA ⅉCB ⅏
closed 20 to 30 December – **8 rm** ⟐ 65.00/120.00 **st.** – SB.

St. Tudno, North Par., LL30 2LP, ℘ (01492) 874411, Fax (01492) 860407, ≤, ⬛ – ⅏, ⅏ ☎
⅏ 歴 ① ⅦSA ⅏
Meals – (see **Garden Room** below) – **19 rm** ⟐ 75.00/160.00 **st.**, 1 suite – SB.

🏛 **Dunoon,** Gloddaeth St., LL30 2DW, ℘ (01492) 860787, Fax (01492) 860031, ⇌ – 🛏 📺 ☎
🅿. 🆖 VISA. ✳   A   r
mid March-mid November – **Meals** 9.00/14.00 t. ▯ 5.00 – **55 rm** ⫤ 36.00/80.00 t. – SB.

🏛 **Bedford,** Promenade, Craig-y-Don, LL30 1BN, E : 1 m. on B 5115 ℘ (01492) 876647,
Fax (01492) 860185 – 🛏 📺 ☎ 🅿. 🆖 VISA
Gigolos : **Meals** - Italian - 12.00 **st.** and a la carte ▯ 5.00 – **27 rm** ⫤ 28.00/60.00 **st.**
– SB.

🏠 **Bryn Derwen,** 34 Abbey Rd, LL30 2EE, ℘ (01492) 876804, Fax (01492) 876804, ⬆s, ⇌ –
✳← 📺 🅿. 🆖 VISA. ✳   A   v
March-October – **Meals** (dinner only) 15.00 **t.** – **9 rm** ⫤ 38.50/73.00 t. – SB.

🏠 **Wilton,** 14 South Par., LL30 2LN, ℘ (01492) 876086, Fax (01492) 876086 – 📺 ☎   AB   z
March-November – **Meals** (dinner only) 10.00 **st.** and a la carte ▯ 4.50 – **14 rm** ⫤ 24.00/
48.00.

🏠 **Belle Vue,** 26 North Par., LL30 2LP, ℘ (01492) 879547, Fax (01492) 870001, ≼ – 🛗,
✳← rest, 📺 ☎ 🅿. 🆖 VISA. ✳   B   e
13 February-9 November – **Meals** (dinner only) 12.00 ▯ 4.25 – **15 rm** ⫤ 29.00/58.00 **st.**
– SB.

🏠 **Sunnymede,** West Par., West Shore, LL30 2BD, ℘ (01492) 877130, Fax (01492) 871824 –
📺 🅿. 🆖 VISA JCB   A   x
April-November – **Meals** (bar lunch)/dinner 14.00 **st.** ▯ 4.35 – **16 rm** ⫤ (dinner included)
36.00/74.00. – SB.

🏠 **Tan Lan,** 14 Great Orme's Rd, West Shore, LL30 2AR, ℘ (01492) 860221,
Fax (01492) 870219 – ✳← rest, 📺 🅿. 🆖 VISA   A   u
31 March-October – **Meals** 8.00/13.50 **t.** ▯ 4.75 – **16 rm** ⫤ 35.00/50.00 t. – SB.

↑ **Epperstone,** 15 Abbey Rd, LL30 2EE, ℘ (01492) 878746, Fax (01492) 871223 – ✳← 📺 ☎
🅿. 🆖 VISA   A   s
closed January-mid February – **Meals** (by arrangement) 15.00 **st.** ▯ 4.00 – **8 rm** ⫤ (dinner
included) 34.00/72.00 **st.** – SB.

↑ **Hollybank,** 9 St. David's Pl., LL30 2UG, ℘ (01492) 878521 – ✳← 📺 🅿. 🆖 VISA   A   a
April-October – **Meals** (by arrangement) 9.00 – **7 rm** ⫤ 26.00/42.00.

↑ **Craiglands,** 7 Carmen Sylva Rd, LL30 1LZ, E : 1 m. by B 5115 ℘ (01492) 875090 – ✳← rest,
📺
April-October – **6 rm** ⫤ (dinner included) 38.00 **st.** – SB.

↑ **Banham House,** 2 St. David's Rd, LL30 2UL, ℘ (01492) 875680, Fax (01492) 875680 – ✳←
📺 🅿. ✳   A   o
Meals 10.00 **st.** – **6 rm** ⫤ 31.00/52.00 **st.**

XX **Garden Room** (at St. Tudno H.), North Par., LL30 2LP, ℘ (01492) 874411,
Fax (01492) 860407 – ✳← 🍽. 🆖 AE ⓞ VISA JCB   A   c
Meals 16.50/25.00 **st.** ▯ 7.00.

XX **Martin's,** 11 Mostyn Av., LL30 1YS, ℘ (01492) 870070, Fax (01492) 876661, ⌂ – 🆖 AE
VISA. ✳   B   x
closed Sunday, Monday and 2 weeks January – **Meals** (booking essential) (dinner only)
16.95 **st.** and a la carte.

X **Richard's Bistro,** 7 Church Walks, LL30 2HD, ℘ (01492) 877924 – 🆖 AE VISA   A   n
Meals (dinner only) a la carte 16.15/23.85 **st.** ▯ 4.50.

X **Number 1's Bistro,** 1 Old Rd, LL30 2HA, ℘ (01492) 875424, Fax (01492) 875424 – 🆖 VISA
JCB   A   i
closed Monday lunch, Sunday, 25-26 December and 1 week January – **Meals** 15.75 **t.**
(dinner) and a la carte 14.70/20.95 **t.** ▯ 6.45.

t Deganwy S : 2 ¾ m. on A 546 – A – ✉ Llandudno.

X **Paysanne,** Station Rd, LL31 9EJ, ℘ (01492) 582079, Fax (01492) 583848 – 🆖 VISA
closed Sunday and Monday – **Meals** (booking essential) (dinner only) 15.00/17.50 **t.**
▯ 6.50.

LANERCHYMEDD Anglesey 402 403 G 24 Wales G.
Env. : Anglesey★★.
London 262 – Bangor 18 – Caernarfon 23 – Holyhead 15.

↑ **Llwydiarth Fawr** ⌂, LL71 8DF, N : 1 m. on B 5111 ℘ (01248) 470321, ≼, « Georgian
farmhouse », ⬎, ⇌, park – ✳← 📺 🅿. 🆖 VISA. ✳
closed Christmas – **Meals** (by arrangement) 12.50 **st.** – **4 rm** ⫤ 25.00/50.00 **st.**, 1 suite –
SB.

⌂ **Drws-Y-Coed** ⌖, LL71 8AD, E : 1 ½ m. by B 5111 on Benllech rd ℘ (01248) 470473, ≤, ⚘, park – ✹ TV 🅿. ⓦⓢ VISA. ✄
closed Christmas – **Meals** (by arrangement) 12.50 **s.** – **3 rm** ⊇ 25.00/45.00 **s.**

⌂ **Tre'r Ddôl** ⌖, LL71 7AR, SW : 3 ½ m. by B 5112 ℘ (01248) 470278, ≤, « 17C farmhouse », ⚘, park – ✹ TV 🅿. ✄
Meals (by arrangement) 12.00 **s.** – **4 rm** ⊇ 30.00/44.00.

LLANFACHRETH *Gwynedd* 402 403 I 25 – *see Dolgellau.*

LLANFIHANGEL *Powys* 402 403 J 25 – *see Llanfyllin.*

LLANFIHANGEL CRUCORNEY *Monmouthshire* 403 L 28 – *see Abergavenny.*

LLANFIHANGEL-NANT-MELAN *Powys.*
  London 180 – Brecon 20 – Carmarthen 40 – Shrewsbury 74.

🍴 **Red Lion**, LD8 2TN, on A 44 ℘ (01544) 350220, Fax (01544) 350220 – ✹ 🅿. ⓦⓢ VISA JCB
closed 25 December, Tuesday in winter, 1 week February and 1 week November –
Meals a la carte 11.40/16.40 **t.** ⓘ 4.00.

LLANFYLLIN *Powys* 402 403 K 25 *Wales G.* – *pop. 1 267.*
  Exc. : *Pistyll Rhaeadr★, NW : 8 m. by A 490, B 4391, B 4580 and minor roads.*
  London 188 – Chester 42 – Shrewsbury 24 – Welshpool 11.

✂ **Seeds**, 5 Penybryn Cottages, High St., SY22 5AP, ℘ (01691) 648604, « 16C cottages », ⚘
  – ✹ ⓦⓢ VISA
  closed Monday October-April and 2 weeks January – **Meals** (Sunday dinner booking
  essential) 17.95 **t.** (dinner) and lunch a la carte 12.30/22.70 **t.** ⓘ 5.75.

at Llanfihangel *SW : 5 m. by A 490 and B 4393 on B 4382* – ✉ *Llanfyllin.*

⌂ **Cyfie Farm** ⌖, SY22 5JE, S : 1 ½ m. by B 4382 ℘ (01691) 648451, Fax (01691) 648451
  ≤ Meifod valley, « Restored 17C longhouse, working farm », ⚘, park – ✹ rm, TV 🅿. ✄
  closed Christmas and January-March – **Meals** (by arrangement) (communal
  dining) 13.00 **st.** – **1 rm** ⊇ (dinner included) 22.50/45.00 **st.**, **3 suites** 51.00/53.00 **st.** – SB

LLANGAMMARCH WELLS *Powys* 403 J 27.
  London 200 – Brecon 17 – Builth Wells 8.

🏛 **Lake Country House** ⌖, LD4 4BS, E : ¾ m. ℘ (01591) 620202, Fax (01591) 620457, ≤
  « Country house in extensive grounds », ⌖, ⚘, ✂ – ✹ TV ☎ 🅿. ⓦⓢ ⒶⒺ ⓞ VISA JCB
  Meals 12.50/28.50 **st.** ⓘ 6.45 – **9 rm** ⊇ 75.00/140.00 **st.**, **10 suites** 155.00/190.00 **st.** – SB

LLANGATTOCK *Powys* 403 K 28 – *see Crickhowell.*

LLANGENNY *Powys* 403 K 28 – *see Crickhowell.*

LLANGOLLEN *Denbighshire* 402 403 K 25 *Wales G.* – *pop. 3 267.*
  See : *Town★ – Railway★ AC – Plas Newydd★ AC.*
  Env. : *Pontcysyllte Aqueduct★★, E : 4 m. by A 539 – Castell Dinas Bran★, N : by footpath
  Valle Crucis Abbey★ AC, N : 2 m. by A 542.*
  Exc. : *Chirk Castle★★ AC (wrought iron gates★), SE : 7 ½ m. by A 5 – Rug Chapel★ AC
  W : 11 m. by A 5 and A 494.*
  🏌 *Vale of Llangollen, Holyhead Rd* ℘ (01978) 860613.
  🎫 *Town Hall, Castle St., LL20 5PD* ℘ (01978) 860828.
  London 194 – Chester 23 – Holyhead 76 – Shrewsbury 30.

🏨 **Bryn Howel**, LL20 7UW, E : 2 ¾ m. on A 539 ℘ (01978) 860331, Fax (01978) 860119, ≤
  ≤s, ⌖, ⚘ – 🛗 TV ☎ 🅿 – 🔏 300. ⓦⓢ ⒶⒺ VISA JCB. ✄
  closed 24 to 26 December and 1-2 January – ***Cedar Tree :* Meals** a la carte 21.00/27.00
  ⓘ 7.90 – **35 rm** ⊇ 80.00/110.00 **t.**, 1 suite – SB.

🏨 **Royal**, Bridge St., LL20 8PG, ℘ (01978) 860202, Fax (01978) 861824, ≤, ⌖ – ✹ TV ☎ 🅿
  🔏 60. ⓦⓢ ⒶⒺ ⓞ VISA
  Meals (bar lunch Monday to Saturday)/dinner 13.95 **t.** ⓘ 6.75 – ⊇ 9.25 – **33 rm** 55.00/
  85.00 **t.** – SB.

🏠 **Gales Wine Bar,** 18 Bridge St., LL20 8PF, ✆ (01978) 860089, *Fax (01978) 861313* – ✝∞ rm, 📺 ☎ 🅿. 🆄🆁 AE VISA JCB. ⚘
closed 25 December-2 January – **Meals** *(closed Sunday)* (in bar) a la carte 7.65/15.45 **t.**
🍴 5.50 – **13 rm** ⌑ 40.00/50.00 **t.**, 2 suites.

🏠 **Hillcrest,** Hill St., LL20 8EU, ✆ (01978) 860208, *Fax (01978) 860208* – ✝∞ 📺 🅿. ⚘
Meals 9.00 **st.** – **7 rm** ⌑ 30.00/42.00 **st.**

🏠 **Oakmere** without rest., Regent St., LL20 8HS, on A 5 ✆ (01978) 861126, 🌳, ⚘ – ✝∞ 📺
🅿. ⚘
6 rm ⌑ 35.00/42.00 **st.**

LLANGYBI *Monmouthshire – see Usk.*

LLANIGON *Powys* 403 K 27 – *see Hay-on-Wye.*

LLANNEFYDD *Conwy* 402 403 J 24 – *pop. 567* – ✉ *Denbigh (Denbighshire).*
London 225 – Chester 37 – Shrewsbury 63.

🏠 **Hawk and Buckle Inn,** LL16 5ED, ✆ (01745) 540249, *Fax (01745) 540316*, ≤, « Part 18C
coaching inn » – ✝∞ 📺 ☎ 🅿. 🆄🆁 ① VISA JCB. ⚘
closed 25 December – **Meals** *(closed Sunday and Monday)* (bar lunch)/dinner
a la carte 9.85/19.85 **t.** 🍴 4.95 – **10 rm** ⌑ 38.00/50.00 **t.** – SB.

LLANRHIDIAN *Swansea – see Swansea.*

LLANRWST *Conwy* 402 403 I 24 *Wales G. – pop. 3 012.*
Env. : *Snowdonia National Park★★★.*
London 230 – Holyhead 50 – Shrewsbury 66.

🍴🍴 **Cae'r Berllan** ⚶ with rm, Betws Rd, LL26 0PP, S : 1 m. on A 470 ✆ (01492) 640027,
Fax (01492) 640027, « 16C manor house », 🌳 – ✝∞ 📺 🅿. 🆄🆁 VISA. ⚘
March-October – **Meals** *(closed Sunday to Thursday to non-residents)* (booking essential)
(dinner only) 15.00 **t.** and a la carte 15.00/22.00 **t.** 🍴 4.50 – **3 rm** ⌑ 80.00 **t.**

at Trefriw *NW : 2 m. on B 5106 –* ✉ *Llanrwst.*

🏠 **Hafod Country H.,** LL27 0RQ, ✆ (01492) 640029, *Fax (01492) 641351,* 🌳 – ✝∞ 📺 ☎ 🅿.
🆄🆁 AE VISA. ⚘
closed January – **Meals** *(closed Tuesday lunch)* (Tuesday dinner residents only) 8.50/
14.50 **t.** and dinner a la carte 🍴 4.50 – **7 rm** ⌑ 32.50/69.00 **t.** – SB.

🍴 **Chandler's Brasserie,** LL27 0JH, ✆ (01492) 640991 – ✝∞ 🅿. 🆄🆁 VISA
⚶ *closed Saturday lunch, dinner Sunday and Wednesday, Monday, Tuesday, New Year and
restricted opening in winter* – Meals (light lunch)/dinner a la carte 14.95/21.15 🍴 6.75.

LLANSANFFRAID GLAN CONWY *Conwy* 402 403 I 24 *Wales G. – pop. 2 194* – ✉ *Aberconwy.*
Env. : *Snowdonia National Park★★★ – Bodnant Garden★★ AC, S : 2 ½ m. by A 470.*
London 241 – Colwyn Bay 4 – Holyhead 42.

🏠 **Old Rectory** ⚶, Llanrwst Rd, LL28 5LF, on A 470 ✆ (01492) 580611, *Fax (01492) 584555,*
⚶ ≤ Conwy estuary, « Georgian country house with antique furnishings », 🌳 – ✝∞ 📺 ☎ 🅿.
🆄🆁 AE ① VISA JCB. ⚘
closed January and December – **Meals** (booking essential) (dinner only) 25.00 **st.** 🍴 7.90 –
6 rm ⌑ 79.00/139.00 – SB.

LLANTRISANT *Monmouthshire* 403 L 28 – *pop. 9 136 (inc. Pontyclun)* – ✉ *Usk.*
London 148 – Bristol 34 – Gloucester 43 – Newport 8.

🏠 **Greyhound Inn,** NP5 1LE, NE : ½ m. on Usk rd ✆ (01291) 672505, *Fax (01291) 673255,*
🌳 – 📺 ☎ 🅿. 🆄🆁 VISA JCB. ⚘
accommodation closed 24 and 25 December – **Meals** *(closed Sunday dinner)* a la carte 8.40/
17.40 **t.** 🍴 4.40 – **10 rm** ⌑ 42.00/65.00 **t.** – SB.

LLANTWIT MAJOR *Vale of Glamorgan* 403 J 29 – *pop. 12 909.*
London 175 – Cardiff 18 – Swansea 33.

🏠 **West House Country,** West St., CF61 1SP, ✆ (01446) 792406, *Fax (01446) 796147,* 🌳 –
📺 ☎ 🅿. 🆄🆁 AE VISA JCB
Meals *(closed Monday lunch)* 10.95/14.95 **t.** and a la carte 🍴 4.25 – **21 rm** ⌑ 48.00/68.00 **t.**
– SB.

LLANWENARTH *Monmouthshire – see Abergavenny.*

LLANWRTYD WELLS *Powys* 403 J 27 *Wales G. – pop. 649.*

Exc. : *Abergwesyn-Tregaron Mountain Road*★, *NW : 19 m. on minor roads.*

London 214 – Brecon 32 – Carmarthen 39.

Carlton House, LD5 4RA, ✆ (01591) 610248, *Fax (01591) 610242* – ⇔ rest, TV. MC VISA
closed 24 December-1 January – **Meals** (dinner only) 21.50 **t.** and a la carte 23.50/30.00 **t.** 5.00 – **6 rm** 30.00/70.00 **st.** – SB.

Lasswade Country House, Station Rd, LD5 4RW, ✆ (01591) 610515, *Fax (01591) 610611,* ≤, ⇔ – ⇔ TV ☎ P. MC VISA
Meals (dinner only) 14.95 **t.** and a la carte 4.95 – **8 rm** 27.50/55.00 **t.** – SB.

LLWYNGWRIL *Gwynedd* 402 403 H 25 *Wales G.* – ✉ *Dolgellau.*

Env. : *Snowdonia National Park*★★★.

London 226 – Aberystwyth 44 – Birkenhead 80 – Chester 72 – Shrewsbury 67.

Pentre Bach ⛰, LL37 2JU, ✆ (01341) 250294, *Fax (01341) 250885,* ≤, – ⇔ TV P. MC VISA.
closed 1 January, November, 24 to 26 and 31 December – **Meals** (by arrangement) 13.95 – **3 rm** 40.00/52.00.

LLYSWEN *Powys* 403 K 27 *Wales G.* – ✉ *Brecon.*

Env. : *Brecon Beacons National Park*★★.

London 188 – Brecon 8 – Cardiff 48 – Worcester 53.

Llangoed Hall ⛰, LD3 0YP, NW : 1 ¼ m. on A 470 ✆ (01874) 754525, *Fax (01874) 754545,* ≤, « Edwardian mansion by Sir Clough Williams-Ellis of 17C origins », park, – ⇔ rest, TV ☎ P – 50. MC AE VISA.
Meals (booking essential to non-residents) 17.00/32.50 **t.** and a la carte 27.50/38.50 **t** 11.00 – **20 rm** 100.00/215.00 **t.**, 3 suites – SB
Spec. Fillet of rabbit on confit potato with a sweet pimento oil. An assiette of Welsh lamb with a lemon grass sauce. Plate of summer fruit desserts.

Griffin Inn, LD3 0UR, on A 470 ✆ (01874) 754241, *Fax (01874) 754592,* « Part 15C », – ⇔ rest, ☎ P. MC AE VISA JCB
closed 25 and 26 December – **Meals** (Sunday dinner residents only) (bar lunch Monday to Saturday)/dinner 17.50/25.00 **t.** 7.95 – **7 rm** 40.00/80.00 **t.** – SB.

MACHYNLLETH *Powys* 402 403 I 26 *Wales G. – pop. 2 033.*

See : *Town*★ – *Celtica*★ *AC* – Env. : *Snowdonia National Park*★★★ – *Centre for Alternative Technology*★★ *AC, N : 3 m. by A 487.*

Ffordd Drenewydd ✆ (01654) 702000.

Canolfan Owain Glyndwr, SY20 8EE ✆ (01654) 702401.

London 220 – Shrewsbury 56 – Welshpool 37.

Ynyshir Hall ⛰, Eglwysfach, SY20 8TA, SW : 6 m. on A 487 ✆ (01654) 781209 *Fax (01654) 781366,* ≤, « Part Georgian country house, gardens », park – ⇔ TV ☎ P. MC AE VISA JCB.
closed 5 to 20 January – **Meals** (booking essential) 19.50/31.00 **st.** 7.50 – **6 rm** 85.00 150.00 **st.**, 2 suites – SB.

MAGOR SERVICE AREA *Newport* 403 L 29 – ✉ *Newport (Newport).*

First Services & Lodge, Junction 23a, M 4, NP6 3YL ✆ (01633) 881122.

First Motorway Services without rest., NP6 3YL, M 4 junction 23A ✆ (01633) 88188 *Fax (01633) 881896* – ⇔ TV ☎ ♿ P. MC AE VISA
5.00 – **43 rm** 42.95 **st.**

MERTHYR TYDFIL 403 J 28 *Wales G. – pop. 39 482* – Env. : *Brecon Beacons National Park*★★.

Exc. : *Ystradfellte*★, *NW : 13 m. by A 4102, A 465, A 4059 and minor roads.*

Morlais Castle, Pant, Dowlais ✆ (01685) 722822 – *Cilsanws Mountain, Cefn Coed ✆ (01685) 723308.*

14a Glebeland St., CF47 8AU ✆ (01685) 379884.

London 179 – Cardiff 25 – Gloucester 59 – Swansea 33.

Tregenna, Park Terr., CF47 8RF, ✆ (01685) 723627, *Fax (01685) 721951* – TV ☎ P. MC VISA JCB
Meals 9.65 **t.** and a la carte 5.00 – **24 rm** 45.00/60.00 **t.** – SB.

at Cwm Taf NW : 6 m. on A 470 – ⊠ Merthyr Tydfil.

▥ **Nant Ddu Lodge**, CF48 2HY, on A 470 𝒫 (01685) 379111, Fax (01685) 377088, ➱ – ▥
☎ ❶ – 🛦 25. 🆀🆁 🅰🅴 𝓥𝓘𝓢𝓐
closed 1 week Christmas and New Year – **Meals** a la carte 13.60/20.35 **t.** ⓝ 4.95 – **16 rm**
⊐ 45.00/60.00 **t.**

MISKIN Rhondda Cynon Taff – ⊠ Cardiff.
London 169 – Cardiff 22 – Swansea 31.

▥ **Miskin Manor**, CF72 8ND, E : 1 ¾ m. by A 4119 (Groesfaen rd) 𝒫 (01443) 224204,
Fax (01443) 237606, <, ↳ò, ☎ò, 🔲, ➱, park, squash – ↤↦ rm, ▥ ☎ ❶ – 🛦 200. 🆀🆁 🅰🅴 ⓞ
𝓥𝓘𝓢𝓐. ⅍
Meals (closed Saturday lunch) a la carte 19.85/33.40 **t.** ⓝ 5.35 – **31 rm** ⊐ 85.00/110.00 **t.**,
1 suite – SB.

MOLD (Yr Wyddgrug) Flintshire ▦▫▨ ▨▫▨ K 24 Wales G. – pop. 8 745.
See : St. Mary's Church★.
▥ Pantmywyn 𝒫 (01352) 740318/741513 – ▥, ▥ Old Padeswood, Station Rd 𝒫 (01244)
547401 – ▥ Padeswood & Buckley, The Caia, Station Lane, Padeswood 𝒫 (01244) 550537 –
▥ Caerwys 𝒫 (01352) 720692.
🄳 Library, Museum and Art Gallery, Earl Rd, CH7 1AP 𝒫 (01352) 759331 (summer only).
London 211 – Chester 12 – Liverpool 29 – Shrewsbury 45.

▥ **Soughton Hall** ⅍, CH7 6AB, N : 2 ½ m. by A 5119 𝒫 (01352) 840811,
Fax (01352) 840382, <, « Early 18C Italianate mansion », ➱, ⅍ – ↤↦ rest, ▥ ☎ ❶. 🆀🆁 🅰🅴
𝓥𝓘𝓢𝓐. ⅍
Meals 19.95 **t.** (dinner) and a la carte 16.00/25.00 **t.** ⓝ 9.00 – **13 rm** ⊐ 80.00/150.00 **t.**
– SB.

▥ **Tower** ⅍ without rest., Nercwys, CH7 4ED, S : 1 m. by B 5444 and Nercwys rd
𝒫 (01352) 700220, « 15C fortified house », ➱, park – ▥ ❶. 🆀🆁 🅰🅴 𝓥𝓘𝓢𝓐. ⅍
closed 15 December-6 January – **3 rm** ⊐ 40.00/60.00 **st.**

🄰 ATS Wrexham Rd 𝒫 (01352) 753682

MONMOUTH (Trefynwy) Monmouthshire ▨▫▨ L 28 Wales G. – pop. 7 246.
See : Town★.
Exc. : Raglan Castle★ AC, SW : 7 m. by A 40.
▥ The Rolls of Monmouth, The Hendre 𝒫 (01600) 715353 – ▥ Leasebrook Lane 𝒫 (01600)
712212.
🄳 Shire Hall, Agincourt Sq., NP5 3DY 𝒫 (01600) 713899 (summer only).
London 147 – Gloucester 26 – Newport 24 – Swansea 64.

▥ **Riverside**, Cinderhill St., NP5 3EY, 𝒫 (01600) 715577, Fax (01600) 712668 – ▥ ☎ ❶ –
🛦 150. 🆀🆁 𝓥𝓘𝓢𝓐
Meals (bar lunch)/dinner 13.95 **t.** – **17 rm** ⊐ 48.00/68.00 **t.** – SB.

at Whitebrook SE : 8½ m. by A 466 – ⊠ Monmouth.

✕✕ **Crown at Whitebrook** ⅍ with rm, NP5 4TX, 𝒫 (01600) 860254, Fax (01600) 860607,
➱ – ▥ ☎ ❶. 🆀🆁 🅰🅴 ⓞ 𝓥𝓘𝓢𝓐 𝓙𝓒𝓑
closed 2 weeks January and 2 weeks August – **Meals** (closed Monday lunch and Sunday
dinner to non-residents) 15.95/26.95 **t.** and lunch a la carte ⓝ 5.00 – **10 rm** ⊐ 50.00/
80.00 **t.** – SB.

🄰 ATS Wonastow Rd, Wonastow Ind. Est. 𝒫 (01600) 716832

MONTGOMERY (Trefaldwyn) Powys ▨▫▨ K 26 Wales G. – pop. 1 059.
See : Town★.
London 194 – Birmingham 71 – Chester 53 – Shrewsbury 30.

▥ **Dragon**, Town Square, SY15 6PA, 𝒫 (01686) 668359, Fax (01686) 668359, 🔲 – ↤↦ rm, ▥
☎ ❶. 🆀🆁 🅰🅴 𝓙𝓒𝓑
Meals 17.25 **t.** and a la carte ⓝ 4.50 – **15 rm** ⊐ 42.00/72.00 **t.** – SB.

⌂ **Little Brompton Farm** ⅍ without rest., SY15 6HY, SE : 2 m. on B 4385
𝒫 (01686) 668371, « Working farm », park – ↤↦ ▥ ❶. ⅍
3 rm ⊐ 20.00/40.00.

MOYLGROVE Pembrokeshire **403** F 27 – see Newport.

MUMBLES (The) Swansea **403** I 29 – see Swansea.

NANNERCH Flintshire **402** **403** K 24 – pop. 513 – ⊠ Mold.
London 218 – Chester 19 – Liverpool 36 – Shrewsbury 52.

🏠 **Old Mill,** Melin-y-Wern, Denbigh Rd, CH7 5RH, NW : ¾ m. on A 451 ℰ (01352) 741542, Fax (01352) 740254, « Converted 19C corn mill and stables », 斎 – ↝ 🆀 ☎ 🅿. 🕮 🆎 ⓪ **VISA** **JCB**
closed 23 December-1 January and restricted opening during winter – **Meals** (residents only) (dinner only) 17.50 **st.** ▯ 4.75 – **6 rm** � 41.00/60.00 **st.** – SB.

NEATH (Castell-Ned) Neath Port Talbot **403** I 29 Wales G. – pop. 45 965.
Env. : Aberdulais Falls★ AC, NE : 2 ½ m. by B 4434 and A 4109.
📷 Swansea Bay, Jersey Marine ℰ (01792) 812198.
London 188 – Cardiff 40 – Swansea 8.

🏛 **Castle,** The Parade, SA11 1RB, ℰ (01639) 641119, Fax (01639) 641624 – ↝ rm, 🆀 ☎ 🚗 🅿 – 🔏 120. 🕮 🆎 ⓪ **VISA**. ⛭
Meals a la carte 11.85/17.15 **t.** – � 4.95 – **28 rm** 49.50/59.50 **t.** – SB.

at Cadoxton NW : 1½ m. by A 474 – ⊠ Neath.

↑ **Cwmbach Cottages** 🈂 without rest., Cwmbach Rd, SA10 8AH, ℰ (01639) 639825, ≼, 斎 – ↝ 🆀 ☐ 🅿. **VISA**. ⛭
5 rm ⊄ 26.00/45.00 **st.**

NEFYN Gwynedd **402** **403** G 25 Wales G. – pop. 1 987.
Env. : Lleyn Peninsula★★ – Tre'r Ceiri★, NE : 5 ½ m. by B 4417 – Porth Dinllaen★, W : 1 ½ m. by B 4417.
📷, 📷 Nefyn & District, Morfa Nefyn ℰ (01758) 720218.
London 265 – Caernarfon 20.

🏠 **Caeau Capel** 🈂, Rhodfar Mor, LL53 6EB, ℰ (01758) 720240, 斎, ⛭ – 🆀 🅿. 🕮 **VISA**
Easter-October – **Meals** (bar lunch)/dinner 13.00 **t.** ▯ 5.10 – **18 rm** ⊄ 25.75/51.50 **t.** – SB.

NEWPORT Pembrokeshire **403** F 27 Wales G. – pop. 1 162.
Env. : Pembrokeshire Coast National Park★★.
📷 Newport ℰ (01239) 820244.
London 258 – Fishguard 7.

↑ **Llysmeddyg,** East St., SA42 0SY, on A 487 ℰ (01239) 820008, 斎 – ↝ 🅿. ⛭
closed Christmas – **Meals** (by arrangement) 13.50 **st.** – **4 rm** ⊄ 18.50/42.00 **st.**

↑ **Grove Park,** Pen-y-bont, SA42 0LT, on Moylegrove rd ℰ (01239) 820122 – ↝ 🆀
closed Christmas and New Year – **Meals** 13.50 **st.** ▯ 3.50 – **4 rm** ⊄ 19.00/43.00 **st.** – SB.

✗ **Cnapan** with rm, East St., SA42 0SY, on A 487 ℰ (01239) 820575, Fax (01239) 820878, 斎 – ↝ rest, 🅿. 🕮 ⛭
closed January, February and 25-26 December – **Meals** (closed Tuesday) (booking essential) (dinner only) a la carte 17.00/20.50 **t.** ▯ 5.50 – **5 rm** ⊄ 36.00/52.00 **t.**

at Moylgrove NE : 6 m. – ⊠ Cardigan (Cardiganshire).

🏠 **Old Vicarage Country** 🈂, SA43 3BN, S : ¼ m. on Glanrhyd rd ℰ (01239) 881231, Fax (01239) 881341, 斎 – ↝. ⛭
Easter-October – **Meals** (by arrangement) (dinner only) (unlicensed) 13.50 **s.** – **3 rm** ⊄ 30.00/48.00 **s.**

NEWPORT (Casnewydd-Ar-Wysg) **403** L 29 Wales G. – pop. 115 522.
See : Museum and Art Gallery★ – Transporter Bridge★ AC – Civic Centre (murals★).
Env. : Caerleon Roman Fortress★★ AC (Fortress Baths★ – Legionary Museum★ – Amphi-theatre★), NE : 2 ½ m. by B 4596 – Tredegar House★★ (Grounds★ – Stables★), SW : 2 ½ m. by A 48.
Exc. : Penhow Castle★, E : 8 m. by A 48.
📷 Tredegar Park, Bassaleg Rd ℰ (01633) 895219 – 📷 Caerleon, Broadway ℰ (01633) 42034 – 📷 Parc, Church Lane, Coedkernew ℰ (01633) 680933.
🚹 Museum and Art Gallery, John Frost Sq., NP9 1HZ ℰ (01633) 842962.
London 145 – Bristol 31 – Cardiff 12 – Gloucester 48.

Celtic Manor H. & Country Club, Coldra Woods, NP6 2YA, E : 3 m. on A 48
℘ (01633) 413000, Fax (01633) 412910, ⅃₅, ⇌, ▨, ⅂₈, park – ⁅, ⅙ rm, ▤ ▨ ☎ ℗ –
⅍ 500, ⓂⓈ ◭ ⓄⒹ ⅥⅠⒺⒶ, ⅌
Meals *(closed Saturday lunch and Sunday)* a la carte 16.00/23.00 t. – (see also *Hedley's*
below) – � 9.95 – **70 rm** 110.00 st.

Hilton National, The Coldra, NP6 2YG, E : 3 m. on a A 48 ℘ (01633) 412777,
Fax (01633) 413087, ⅃₅, ⇌, ▨ – ⅙ rm, ℡ ☎ ℗ – ⅍ 350, ⓂⓈ ◭ ⓄⒹ ⅥⅠⒺⒶ
Meals 12.50/14.75 st. and dinner a la carte ⅃ 6.50 – ⊊ 10.50 – **117 rm** 95.00 st.

NEWPORT

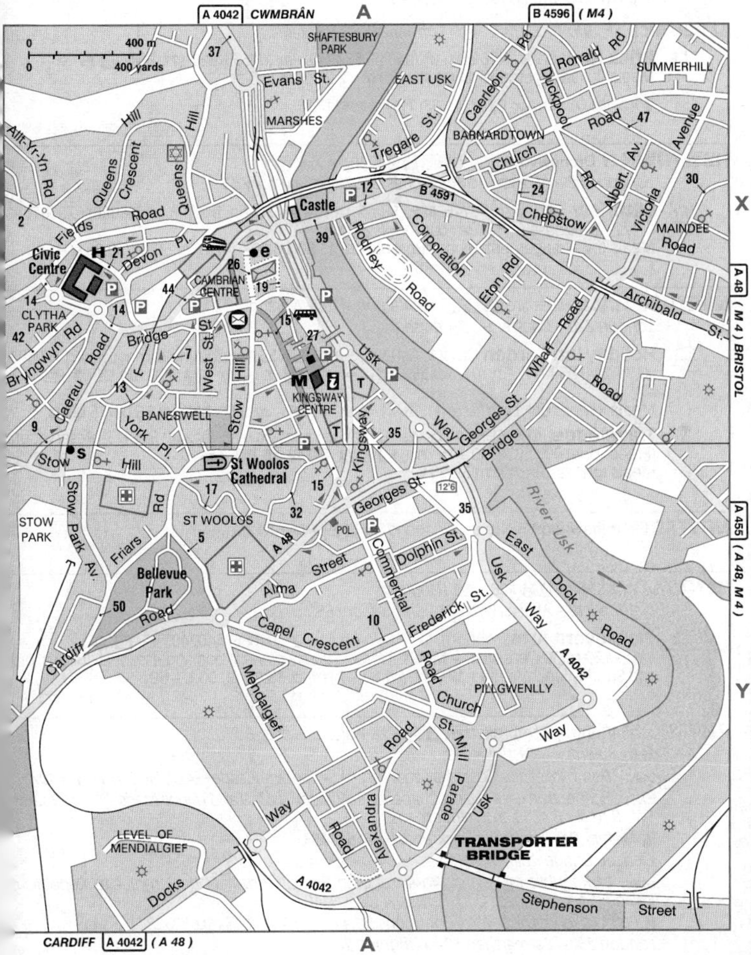

Kings, High St., NP9 1QU, ℰ (01633) 842020, Fax (01633) 244667 – 🛗 🔟 ☎ 🅿 – 🔬 200.
🕮 🗚 𝗩𝗜𝗦𝗔. 🛠
AX e
Meals *(closed Saturday)* (dinner only) a la carte 11.50/18.50 **st.** ⏐ 4.50 – ⌧ 8.00 – **47 rm**
49.00/75.00 **st.**

Newport Lodge, 147 Bryn Bevan, Brynglas Rd, NP9 5QN, N : ¾ m. by A 4042 off A 4051
ℰ (01633) 821818, Fax (01633) 856360 – 🔟 ☎ 🅿. 🕮 🗚 ① 𝗩𝗜𝗦𝗔 𝗝𝗖𝗕. 🛠
Meals *(closed Sunday dinner)* (bar lunch)/dinner a la carte 16.25/21.45 **st.** ⏐ 4.75 – **27 rm**
⌧ 67.00/87.00 **st.** – SB.

Kepe Lodge, 46a Caerau Rd, NP9 4HH, ℰ (01633) 262351, 🌫 – 🔟 🅿. 🛠
AY s
Meals (by arrangement) 10.00 **st.** – **8 rm** ⌧ 19.00/38.00 **st.** – SB.

Hedley's (at Celtic Manor H. & Country Club), Coldra Woods, NP6 2YA, E : 3 m. on A 48
ℰ (01633) 413000, Fax (01633) 412910 – 🅿. 🕮 🗚 ① 𝗩𝗜𝗦𝗔
Meals *(closed Saturday lunch and Sunday)* 16.00/23.00 **t.** and a la carte ⏐ 12.00.

at Langstone E : 4½ m. on A 48 – AX – ⌧ Newport.

Stakis Newport, Chepstow Rd, NP6 2LX, ℰ (01633) 413737, Fax (01633) 413713, 🎣,
🛌s, 🏊, 🌫 – ↪️ rm, 🍴 rest, 🔟 ☎ 🖧 🅿 – 🔬 90. 🕮 🗚 ① 𝗩𝗜𝗦𝗔
Meals (bar lunch Monday to Saturday)/dinner 17.25 **st.** and a la carte ⏐ 5.95 – ⌧ 9.95 –
138 rm 95.00/105.00 **st.**, 2 suites – SB.

at Redwick SE : 9½ m. by M 4 – AY – off B 4245 – ⌧ Magor.

Brick House 🦢, NP6 3DX, ℰ (01633) 880230, Fax (01633) 882441 – ↪️ 🔟 🅿. 🛠
Meals (by arrangement) 14.00 **st.** – **7 rm** ⌧ 25.00/42.00 **st.**

🅐 ATS 101 Corporation Rd ℰ (01633) 216115/216117

NEWTOWN (Y Drenewydd) *Powys* 402 403 K 26.
London 188 – Aberystwyth 43 – Chester 57 – Shrewsbury 35.

Cilthriew 🦢, Kerry, SY16 4PF, SE : 5 m. by A 489 on B 4368 ℰ (01686) 670667, ≼,
« 17C farmhouse », 🍃, 🌫, park – ↪️ 🖧 🅿
Meals (by arrangement) (communal dining) 13.50 ⏐ 4.00 – **7 rm** ⌧ 30.00/50.00 **s.** – SB.

NORTHOP HALL *Flintshire* 402 403 K 24 – *pop. 4 155 (Northop).*
London 220 – Chester 9 – Shrewsbury 52.

Holiday Inn Garden Court, Gateway Services, A 55 (westbound carriageway), CH7 6HB,
ℰ (01244) 550011, Fax (01244) 550763 – ↪️ rm, 🔟 ☎ 🖧 🅿 – 🔬 200. 🕮 🗚 ① 𝗩𝗜𝗦𝗔 𝗝𝗖𝗕
🛠
Meals (dinner only) a la carte 11.15/21.40 **st.** ⏐ 6.85 – ⌧ 8.50 – **55 rm** 55.00/75.00 **st.**

Travelodge, CH7 6HB, A 55 (eastbound carriageway) ℰ (01244) 816473, Reservations
(Freephone) 0800 850950 – ↪️ rm, 🔟 🖧 🅿. 🕮 🗚 ① 𝗩𝗜𝗦𝗔 𝗝𝗖𝗕. 🛠
Meals (grill rest.) – **40 rm** 39.95 **t.**

NOTTAGE (Drenewydd Yn Notais) *Bridgend* 403 I 29 – *see Porthcawl.*

PANT MAWR *Powys* 403 I 26 – ⌧ Llangurig.
London 219 – Aberystwyth 21 – Shrewsbury 55.

Glansevern Arms with rm, SY18 6SY, on A 44 ℰ (01686) 440240, ≼ – 🔟 🅿
closed 20 to 30 December – Meals *(closed Sunday dinner)* (booking essential) (dinner only
and Sunday lunch)/dinner 17.00 **t.** ⏐ 4.60 – **7 rm** ⌧ 35.00/60.00 **t.** – SB.

PEMBROKE (Penfro) *Pembrokeshire* 403 F 28 *Wales G.* – *pop. 6 773.*
See : *Town★★ – Castle★★ AC.*
Env. : *Pembrokeshire Coast National Park★★ – Carew★ (Castle★ AC), NE : 4 m. by A 4075.*
Exc. : *Bosherston (St. Govan's Chapel★), S : 7 m. by B 4319 and minor roads – Stack Rocks★*
SW : 9 m. by B 4319 and minor roads.
🏌 *Military Rd, Pembroke Dock ℰ (01646) 621453.*
Cleddau Bridge (toll).
🚢 *to Republic of Ireland (Rosslare) (Irish Ferries) 2 daily (3 h 45 mn) – to Republic of*
Ireland (Cork) (Swansea Cork Ferries) 4 weekly (10 h).
🅱 *Pembroke Visitor Centre, Commons Rd, SA71 4EA ℰ (01646) 622388.*
London 252 – Carmarthen 32 – Fishguard 26.

🏛 **Underdown Country House** ≫, Grove Hill, SA71 5PR, ℘ (01646) 622900, *Fax (01646) 621229,* « Antiques and gardens » – 📺 ☎ 🅿. ⓌⓈ ⑩ 𝘝𝘐𝘚𝘈. ✼
closed 23 December-3 January – **Meals** *(closed Sunday lunch)* (booking essential) 21.95 **st.**
– **6 rm** ⊆ 39.50/75.00 **t.** – SB.

🛏 **Coach House** with rm, 116 Main St., SA71 4HN, ℘ (01646) 684602, *Fax (01646) 687456,*
�── 📺 ☎ 🅿. ⓌⓈ 𝘈𝘌 𝘝𝘐𝘚𝘈
Meals a la carte 13.50/23.20 **t.** ⫶ 4.95 – **13 rm** ⊆ 45.00/75.00 **st.** – SB.

at Lamphey *E : 1 ¾ m. on A 4139* – ⊠ *Pembroke.*

🏛 **Court** ≫, SA71 5NT, ℘ (01646) 672273, *Fax (01646) 672480,* ₤₆, ⇌ₛ, ⊠, �──, park, ✼ –
⊱ rest, 📺 ☎ 🅿 – 🏛 80. ⓌⓈ 𝘈𝘌 ⑩ 𝘝𝘐𝘚𝘈 𝘑𝘊𝘉. ✼
Meals 9.95/18.75 **st.** and a la carte ⫶ 5.95 – **37 rm** ⊆ 67.00/130.00 **st.** – SB.

🏛 **Bethwaite's Lamphey Hall,** SA71 5NR, ℘ (01646) 672394, *Fax (01646) 672369,* �,
�── 📺 ☎ 🅿. ⓌⓈ 𝘈𝘌 𝘝𝘐𝘚𝘈 𝘑𝘊𝘉. ✼
Meals *(closed Sunday dinner)* (dinner only and Sunday lunch)/dinner 17.50 **t.** and a la carte
⫶ 4.50 – **10 rm** ⊆ 35.00/50.00 **t.** – SB.

at Pembroke Dock *NW : 2 m. on A 4139* – ⊠ *Pembroke.*

🏛 **Cleddau Bridge,** Essex Rd, SA72 6UT, NE : 1 m. by A 4139 on A 477 (at Toll Bridge)
℘ (01646) 685961, *Fax (01646) 685746,* ⊠ – 📺 ☎ 🅿 – 🏛 175. ⓌⓈ 𝘈𝘌 ⑩ 𝘝𝘐𝘚𝘈. ✼
Meals 10.50 **t.** and a la carte ⫶ 4.10 – **22 rm** ⊆ 55.00/64.50 **t.**, 2 suites – SB.

Ⓐ ATS Well Hill Garage, Well Hill ℘ (01646) 683217/683836

PEMBROKE DOCK Pembrokeshire 𝟦𝟢𝟥 F 28 – *see Pembroke.*

PENALLY (Penalun) Pembrokeshire 𝟦𝟢𝟥 F 29 – *see Tenby.*

PENCOED Bridgend 𝟦𝟢𝟥 J 29 – *see Bridgend.*

PENMACHNO Conwy 𝟦𝟢𝟤 𝟦𝟢𝟥 I 24 – *see Betws-y-Coed.*

PONTFAEN Pembrokeshire – *see Fishguard.*

PONTYPRIDD Rhondda Cynon Taff 𝟦𝟢𝟥 K 29 *Wales G.* – pop. 28 487.
Exc. : Caerphilly Castle★★ AC, SE : 7 m. by A 470 and A 468 – Llancaiach Fawr Manor★ AC,
NE : 6 ½ m. by A 4054, A 472, B 4255 and B 4254.
London 164 – Cardiff 9 – Swansea 40.

🏛 **Llechwen Hall,** Llanfabon, CF37 4HP, NE : 4 ¼ m. by A 4223 off A 4054
℘ (01443) 742050, *Fax (01443) 742189,* �── 📺 ☎ 🅿 – 🏛 80. ⓌⓈ 𝘈𝘌 ⑩ 𝘝𝘐𝘚𝘈
Meals 10.95 **t.** and a la carte ⫶ 4.95 – **12 rm** ⊆ 48.50/68.50 **st.** – SB.

Ⓐ ATS Nile St., off Broadway ℘ (01443) 403796

PORTH Rhondda Cynon Taff 𝟦𝟢𝟥 J 29 *Wales G.* – pop. 6 225 – ⊠ *Pontypridd.*
Env. : Trehafod (Rhondda Heritage Park★), E : 1 ½ m. by A 4058.
London 168 – Cardiff 13 – Swansea 45.

🏛 **Heritage Park,** Coed Cae Rd, Trehafod, CF37 2NP, on A 4058 ℘ (01443) 687057,
Fax (01443) 687060, ₤₆, ⇌ₛ, ⊠ – 🍽 rest, 📺 ☎ ⅙ 🅿 – 🏛 200. ⓌⓈ 𝘈𝘌 𝘝𝘐𝘚𝘈
Meals 5.95/13.50 **t.** and a la carte ⫶ 4.50 – **44 rm** ⊆ 49.00/70.00 **t.** – SB.

PORTHCAWL Bridgend 𝟦𝟢𝟥 I 29 *Wales G.* – pop. 15 922.
Env. : Glamorgan Heritage Coast★.
🇧 The Old Police Station, John St., CF36 3DT ℘ (01656) 786639 (summer only).
London 183 – Cardiff 28 – Swansea 18.

🏛 **Atlantic,** West Drive, CF36 3LT, ℘ (01656) 785011, *Fax (01656) 771877,* ≼ – ▐▌ 📺 ☎ 🅿.
ⓌⓈ 𝘈𝘌 ⑩ 𝘝𝘐𝘚𝘈 𝘑𝘊𝘉. ✼
Meals *(closed Sunday dinner in winter)* (bar lunch Monday to Saturday and dinner Sunday)/
dinner 12.95 **t.** and a la carte ⫶ 4.50 – **19 rm** ⊆ 54.00/82.00 **t.** – SB.

🏠 **Minerva,** 52 Esplanade Av., CF36 3YU, ℘ (01656) 782428 – 📺. ⓌⓈ 𝘝𝘐𝘚𝘈. ✼
closed 2 weeks Christmas-New Year – **Meals** (by arrangement) 9.50 **s.** ⫶ 3.00 – **9 rm**
⊆ 23.00/38.00 **s.**

at Nottage N : 1 m. by A 4229 – ⊠ Porthcawl.

🏠 **Rose and Crown,** Heol-y-Capel, CF36 3ST, N : 1 m. by A 4229 🖉 (01656) 784850,
Fax (01656) 772345 – ᕱ rest, 📺 ☎ 🅿. 🝓 🖭 ① 🖾. ✸
Meals (carving rest.) 11.00 **t.** – **8 rm** 🖙 41.95/47.90 **t.** – SB.

PORTHGAIN Pembrokeshire 🛄 E 28 – see St. Davids.

PORTMEIRION Gwynedd 🛄🛄 H 25 Wales G.
See : Village★★★ AC.
Env. : Snowdonia National Park★★★ – Lleyn Peninsula★★ – Ffestiniog Railway★★ AC.
London 245 – Caernarfon 23 – Colwyn Bay 40 – Dolgellau 24.

🏯 **Portmeirion** ♨, LL48 6ET, 🖉 (01766) 770228, Fax (01766) 771331, ≤ village and estuary,
« Private Italianate village, antiques », 🏊, 🌿, park, ✸ – ᕱ rest, 📺 ☎ 🅿 – 🔬 120. 🝓 🖭
① 🖾 🝓. ✸
Meals 13.50/26.50 🝓 9.00 – 🖙 9.00 – **28 rm** 80.00/135.00 **t.,** 9 suites – SB.

PORT TALBOT Neath Port Talbot 🛄 I 29 Wales G. – pop. 37 647.
Env. : Margam Park★ AC (Orangery★), SE : 4 m. by A 48.
London 193 – Cardiff 35 – Swansea 11.

🏠 **Travel Inn,** Baglan Rd, SA12 8ES, M 4 junction 41 🖉 (01639) 813017, Fax (01639) 823096 –
ᕱ rm, 📺 ⅃ 🅿. 🝓 🖭 ① 🖾. ✸
Meals (grill rest.) – **40 rm** 36.50 **t.**

🔘 ATS Afan Way 🖉 (01639) 883895/885747

PRESTATYN Denbighshire 🛄🛄 J 23 – pop. 15 020.
London 230 – Bangor 35 – Birkenhead 43 – Chester 35 – Holyhead 56.

🏠 **Traeth Ganol,** 41 Beach Rd West, LL19 7LL, 🖉 (01745) 853594, Fax (01745) 886687 – ᕱ
📺 ⅃ 🅿. 🝓 🖾 🝓. ✸
Meals (closed Monday and Tuesday to non-residents) (booking essential) (dinner only and
Sunday lunch)/dinner 12.50 **t.** and a la carte 🝓 7.00 – **9 rm** 🖙 35.00/60.00 **t.** – SB.

PRESTEIGNE Powys 🛄 K 27 Wales G. – pop. 1 815.
Env. : Old Radnor (St. Stephen's Church★), SW : 6 m. by B 4355, B 4362 and minor rd.
🚩 Shire Hall, LD8 2AD 🖉 (01544) 260650 (summer only).
London 159 – Llandrindod Wells 20 – Shrewsbury 39.

🏛 **Radnorshire Arms,** High St., LD8 2BE, 🖉 (01544) 267406, Fax (01544) 260418, 🌿 – ᕱ
📺 ☎ 🅿 – 🔬 30. 🝓 🖭 ① 🖾 🝓
Meals 11.95/17.95 **st.** 🝓 5.75 – 🖙 9.25 – **16 rm** 65.00/80.00 **st.** – SB.

PWLLHELI Gwynedd 🛄🛄 G 25 Wales G. – pop. 3 974.
Env. : Lleyn Peninsula★★.
🏌 Golf Rd 🖉 (01758) 701644.
🚩 Min-y-Don, Station Sq., LL53 5HG 🖉 (01758) 613000.
London 261 – Aberystwyth 73 – Caernarfon 21.

🍴🍴🍴 **Plas Bodegroes** ♨ with rm, LL53 5TH, NW : 1 ¾ m. on A 497 🖉 (01758) 612363,
Fax (01758) 701247, « Georgian country house », 🌿, park – ᕱ 📺 ☎ 🅿. 🝓 🖭 🖾 🝓
🝓
closed Monday and November-March – **Meals** (booking essential) (dinner only and Sunday
lunch)/dinner 33.00 **t.** 🝓 8.00 – **11 rm** 🖙 (dinner included) 70.00/200.00 **t.** – SB.

RAGLAN Monmouthshire 🛄 L 28 Wales G. – pop. 1 857 – ⊠ Abergavenny.
See : Castle★ AC.
London 154 – Gloucester 34 – Newport 18 – Swansea 58.

🍴 **Clytha Arms** with rm, NP7 9BW, W : 3 m. on Clytha rd (old Abergavenny Rd)
🖉 (01873) 840206, Fax (01873) 840206 – ᕱ rest, 📺 🅿. 🝓 🖾
Meals (closed Sunday dinner and Monday lunch except in summer) a la carte 12.00/27.00
🝓 6.50 – **3 rm** 🖙 55.00/75.00 **t.**

REDWICK Newport 🛄 L 29 – see Newport (Newport).

RHOSCOLYN Anglesey **402 403** G 24 *Wales G.* – *pop. 539* – ✉ *Holyhead*.
  Env. : *Anglesey***.
  Exc. : *Barclodiad y Gawres Burial Chamber★* , *SE : 10 m. by B 4545, A 5 and A 4080.*
  London 269 – Bangor 25 – Caernarfon 30 – Holyhead 5.5.

⚰ **Old Rectory** ⌂, LL65 2SQ, ☎ *(01407) 860214,* ≤, 龠 – ⭑⭑ ⊤⊻ ℗. ⓪⑨ *VISA*
    closed 21 December-3 January and restricted opening in autumn – **Meals**
    (by arrangement) (communal dining) 16.00 **st.** – **5 rm** ⊆ 32.00/56.00 **st.**

RHOS-ON-SEA (Llandrillo-Yn-Rhos) Conwy **402 403** I 24 – *see Colwyn Bay.*

RHYDLEWIS Ceredigion **403** G 27 *Wales G.* – ✉ *Llandysul.*
  Exc. : *Aberaeron★, NE : 11 ½ m. by B 4334 and A 487.*
  London 235 – Carmarthen 26 – Fishguard 38.

⚰ **Broniwan** ⌂, SA44 5PF, NE : ¼ m. by Pentregat rd, taking first turn right onto
    unmarked road ☎ *(01239) 851261, Fax (01239) 851261,* « Working farm », 龠, park – ⭑⭑
    ℗
    restricted opening January and February – **Meals** (by arrangement) 11.00 **st.** – **3 rm**
    ⊆ 20.00/40.00 **st.** – SB.

ROEWEN Conwy – *see Conwy.*

ROSEBUSH Pembrokeshire **403** F 28 – ✉ *Clynderwen (Carmarthenshire).*
  London 252 – Fishguard 9 – Haverfordwest 12.

🏠 **Tafarn Newydd,** SA66 7RA, W : 1 m. at junction of B 4313 and B 4329 ☎ *(01437) 532542,*
    « 17C former coaching inn » – ⭑⭑ ℗. ⓪⑨ *VISA*
    Meals 10.00 **t.** (lunch) and a la carte 16.00/22.70 **t.** ⅄ 6.25.

ROSSETT (Yr Orsedd) Wrexham **402 403** L 24 – *pop. 1 986.*
  London 203 – Chester 8 – Shrewsbury 39.

🏛 **Llyndir Hall** ⌂, Llyndir Lane, LL12 0AY, N : ¾ m. by B 5445 ☎ *(01244) 571648,*
    Fax (01244) 571258, « Part Strawberry Gothic country house », ₤₅, ⊠, 龠 – ⭑⭑ rm, ⊤⊻ ☎
    ₤ ℗ – 益 120. ⓪⑨ ℀℮ ① *VISA*. ℀
    Meals *(closed Saturday lunch)* 14.50/18.95 **t.** and a la carte ⅄ 6.25 – **37 rm** ⊆ 74.00/
    110.00 **t.**, 1 suite – SB.

🏛 **Rossett Hall,** Chester Rd, LL12 0DE, ☎ *(01244) 571000, Fax (01244) 571505,* 龠 – ⭑⭑ ⊤⊻
    ☎ ₤ ℗ – 益 120. ⓪⑨ ℀℮ ① *VISA* JᴄB. ℀
    Meals *(closed Saturday lunch)* a la carte 17.85/23.85 **st.** ⅄ 5.95 – ⊆ 8.50 – **29 rm** 70.00/
    90.00 **st.**, 1 suite – SB.

RUTHIN (Rhuthun) Denbighshire **402 403** K 24 *Wales G.* – *pop. 5 029.*
  Env. : *Llandyrnog (St. Dyfnog's Church★),* Llanrhaeder-yng-Nghinmeirch *(Jesse Window★★), N : 5 ½ m. by A 494 and B 5429.*
  Exc. : *Denbigh★ (Castle★), NW : 7 m. on A 525.*
  ⛳ *Ruthin-Pwllglas* ☎ *(01824) 702296.*
  🛈 *Ruthin Craft Centre, Park Rd, LL15 1BB* ☎ *(01824) 703992.*
  London 210 – Birkenhead 31 – Chester 23 – Shrewsbury 46.

⚰ **Eyarth Station** ⌂, Llanfair Dyffryn Clwyd, LL15 2EE, S : 1 ¾ m. by A 525
    ☎ *(01824) 703643, Fax (01824) 707464,* ≤, ⊠, 龠 – ⭑⭑ rm, ℗. ⓪⑨ *VISA*
    Meals 14.00 **s.** ⅄ 4.00 – **6 rm** ⊆ 30.00/44.00 **s.**

🏠 **Ye Olde Anchor Inn** with rm, Rhos St., LL15 1DX, ☎ *(01824) 702813, Fax (01824) 703050*
    – ⭑⭑ rest, ⊤⊻ ☎ ℗. ⓪⑨ *VISA* JᴄB
    Meals 12.95/18.95 **st.** and a la carte ⅄ 5.95 – **14 rm** ⊆ 37.50/65.00 **st.** – SB.

ST. ASAPH (Llanelwy) Denbighshire **402 403** J 24 *Wales G.* – *pop. 3 399.*
  See : *Cathedral★.*
  Env. : *Rhuddlan Castle★★ AC, N : 2 ½ m. by A 525 and A 547 – Bodelwyddan★★ AC, W : 2 ½ m. by A 55 – Denbigh★ (Castle★), S : 6 m. by A 525 and A 543.*
  London 225 – Chester 29 – Shrewsbury 59.

🏛 **Oriel House,** Upper Denbigh Rd, LL17 0LW, S : ¾ m. on A 525 ☎ *(01745) 582716,*
    Fax (01745) 585208, 龠 – ⊤⊻ ☎ ℗ – 益 250. ⓪⑨ ℀℮ ① *VISA*
    closed 26 December-1 January – **Meals** 11.00/15.95 **t.** and a la carte ⅄ 5.50 – **19 rm**
    ⊆ 41.00/68.00 **t.** – SB.

Plas Elwy, The Roe, LL17 0LT, N : ½ m. at junction of A 525 with A 55 ℰ (01745) 582263, Fax (01745) 583864 – 📺 ☎ 📵. 📶 🅰🅴 🆅🅸🆂🅰 🅹🅲🅱. ✶
closed 26 to 30 December – **Meals** *(closed Sunday dinner to non-residents)* (lunch by arrangement Monday to Saturday)/dinner a la carte 11.00/25.00 **t.** ⅄ 4.75 – **13 rm** ☵ 45.00/ 68.00 **t.**

ST. BRIDES-SUPER-ELY *Vale of Glamorgan.*
London 155 – Bristol 51 – Cardiff 9 – Newport 22.

Sant-Y-Nyll ⌂ without rest., CF5 6EZ, ℰ (01446) 760209, Fax (01446) 760897, ≼, 🖾, park – 📺 📵. 🅰🅴
6 rm ☵ 25.00/45.00 **st.**

ST. CLEARS (Sancler) *Carmarthenshire*▩ G 28 *Wales G.* – pop. 3 014.
Env. : *Laugharne*★ *(Castle*★, *The Boat House*★*)*, S : 4 m. on A 4066.
London 229 – Carmarthen 9 – Fishguard 37.

Forge Lodge, SA33 4NA, E : 1 m. on A 40 ℰ (01994) 230300, Fax (01994) 231577, 🅵🅰, 🈴, 🈲, 🖾, 🚗 – 📺 ☎ 📵. 📶 🆅🅸🆂🅰
closed 25 and 26 December – **Meals** (grill rest.) a la carte 7.75/17.45 **t.** ⅄ 4.00 – **18 rm** ☵ 39.50/55.00 **t.**

ST. DAVIDS (Tyddewi) *Pembrokeshire*▩ E 28 *Wales G.* – pop. 1 627 – ✉ *Haverfordwest.*
See : *Town*★★ – *Cathedral*★★ – *Bishop's Palace*★ *AC.*
Env. : *Pembrokeshire Coast National Park*★★.
⛳ *St. Davids City, Whitesands Bay* ℰ (01437) 721751.
🛈 *City Hall, SA62 6SD* ℰ (01437) 720392.
London 266 – Carmarthen 46 – Fishguard 16.

Warpool Court ⌂, SA62 6BN, W ℰ (01437) 720300, Fax (01437) 720676, ≼, 🖾, 🚗, ✶ – ✦ rest, 📺 ☎ 📵. 📶 🅰🅴 ⓪ 🆅🅸🆂🅰
closed January – **Meals** 19.95/33.50 **st.** ⅄ 5.00 – **25 rm** ☵ 84.00/158.00 **st.** – SB.

Old Cross, Cross Sq., SA62 6SP, ℰ (01437) 720387, Fax (01437) 720394, 🚗 – ✦ rm, 📺 ☎ 📵. 📶 🆅🅸🆂🅰
March-23 December – **Meals** (bar lunch)/dinner 15.00 **t.** and a la carte ⅄ 4.75 – **16 rm** ☵ 36.00/76.00 **t.** – SB.

St. Nons, Catherine St., SA62 6RJ, ℰ (01437) 720239, Fax (01437) 721839 – ✦ rest, 📺 ☎ 📵. 📶 🆅🅸🆂🅰
closed December – **Meals** (bar lunch)/dinner 19.50 **st.** ⅄ 5.50 – **21 rm** ☵ 61.00/98.00 **st.** – SB.

Ramsey House, Lower Moor, SA62 6RP, SW : ½ m. on Porthclais rd ℰ (01437) 720321 Fax (01437) 720025, 🚗 – ✦ 📺 📵. 📶 🆅🅸🆂🅰 🅹🅲🅱
Meals (by arrangement) 14.00 **st.** ⅄ 4.95 – **7 rm** ☵ (dinner included) 86.00 **st.** – SB.

Y-Gorlan, 77 Nun St., SA62 6NU, ℰ (01437) 720837, Fax (01437) 720837 – ✦ rm, 📺. 📶 🆅🅸🆂🅰. ✶
Meals (by arrangement) 19.50 – **5 rm** ☵ 20.00/39.00.

✗ **Morgan's Brasserie,** 20 Nun St., SA62 6NT, ℰ (01437) 720508 – 📶 🅰🅴 🆅🅸🆂🅰
closed Sunday and Monday – **Meals** (dinner only) a la carte 18.00/22.00 **t.** ⅄ 6.00.

at Porthgain NE : 7¾ m. by A 487 via Llanrian – ✉ *Haverfordwest.*

✗ **Harbour Lights,** SA62 5BW, ℰ (01348) 831549 – 📶 🆅🅸🆂🅰 🅹🅲🅱
closed 2 weeks Christmas – **Meals** (booking essential) (dinner only) 22.50 **t.** ⅄ 9.50.

ST.DOGMAELS *Ceredigion*▩ G 27 – *see Cardigan.*

In this guide

a symbol or a character, printed in red or **black**, in **bold** or light type, does not have the same meaning.
Pay particular attention to the explanatory pages.

SARN PARK SERVICE AREA Bridgend – ⊠ Bridgend.
🖪 M 4, Junction 36, CF32 9SY ℰ (01656) 654906.
London 174 – Cardiff 17 – Swansea 20.

🏨 **Welcome Lodge**, CF32 9RW, M 4 junction 36 ℰ (01656) 659218, Fax (01656) 768665,
Reservations (Freephone) 0800 7314466 – 📺 ⅋ 🅿. 🐵 🆎 ⓪ 𝘝𝘐𝘚𝘈. ⅍
40 rm 40.00 t.

SAUNDERSFOOT Pembrokeshire 🖪🖪🖪 F 28 Wales G. – pop. 3 221.
Env. : Pembrokeshire Coast National Park★★.
London 245 – Carmarthen 25 – Fishguard 34 – Tenby 3.

🏨 **St. Brides**, St. Brides Hill, SA69 9NH, ℰ (01834) 812304, Fax (01834) 813303, ≤, ⊒ –
↳⅍ rm, 🍽 rest, 📺 ☎ 🅿 – 🔬 150. 🐵 🆎 ⓪ 𝘝𝘐𝘚𝘈. ⅍
closed 1 and 2 January – Meals 19.50 st. (dinner) and a la carte 20.90/28.20 st. ╏ 6.50 –
41 rm ⊒ 60.00/108.00 st., 2 suites – SB.

⌂ **Vine Farm**, The Ridgeway, SA69 9LA, ℰ (01834) 813543, 🚗 – 📺 🅿
March-October – Meals (by arrangement) 11.00 – 5 rm ⊒ 22.00/48.00 st. – SB.

SEION Gwynedd 🖪🖪🖪 🖪🖪🖪 H 24 – see Caernarfon.

SOUTHERNDOWN Bridgend 🖪🖪🖪 J 29 – see Bridgend.

*Ask your bookshop for the catalogue of **Michelin Publications**.*

SWANSEA (Abertawe) 🖪🖪🖪 I 29 Wales G. – pop. 171 038.
See : Town★ – Maritime Quarter★ B – Maritime and Industrial Museum★ B M – Glynn Vivian
Art Gallery★ – Guildhall (British Empire Panels★).
Env. : Gower Peninsula★★ (Rhossili★★), W : by A 4067 A.
Exc. : The Wildfowl and Wetlands Trust★, Llanelli, NW : 6½m. by A 483 and A 484 A – Kidwelly
Castle★, NW : 19 m. by A 483 and A 484 A.
🏌 Morriston, 160 Clasemont Rd ℰ (01792) 771079, A – 🏌 Clyne, 120 Owls Lodge Lane,
Mayals ℰ (01792) 401989, A – 🏌 Langland Bay, (01792) 366023, A – 🏌 Fairwood Park,
Blackhills Lane, Upper Killay ℰ (01792) 203648, A – 🏌 Inco, Clydach ℰ (01792) 844216, A.
⛴ to Republic of Ireland (Cork) (Swansea Cork Ferries) (10 h).
🖪 P.O. Box 59, Singleton St., SA1 3QG ℰ (01792) 468321.
London 191 – Birmingham 136 – Bristol 82 – Cardiff 40 – Liverpool 187 –
Stoke-on-Trent 175.

Plan on following page

🏨 **Swansea Marriott**, Maritime Quarter, SA1 3SS, ℰ (01792) 642020, Fax (01792) 650345,
≤, ┢₆, 🛁, ◨ – ▐, ↳⅍ rm, 🍽 📺 ☎ ⅋ 🅿 – 🔬 250. 🐵 🆎 ⓪ 𝘝𝘐𝘚𝘈. ⅍   B e
Meals 12.50/18.50 st. and a la carte ╏ 7.25 – ⊒ 11.25 – **117 rm** 87.00 t.

🏨 **Forte Posthouse Swansea**, 39 The Kingsway, SA1 5LS, ℰ (01792) 651074,
Fax (01792) 456044, ┢₆, 🛁, ◨ – ▐, ↳⅍ rm, 📺 ☎ 🅿 – 🔬 250. 🐵 🆎 ⓪ 𝘝𝘐𝘚𝘈 𝗃𝖼𝖻. ⅍
Meals a la carte 14.55/26.65 t. ╏ 8.45 – ⊒ 9.95 – **97 rm** 79.00 t., 2 suites – SB.   B a

🏨 **Beaumont**, 72-73 Walter Rd, SA1 4QA, ℰ (01792) 643956, Fax (01792) 643044 – 📺 ☎ 🅿.
🐵 🆎 ⓪ 𝘝𝘐𝘚𝘈 𝗃𝖼𝖻   A n
Meals (closed Sunday dinner) 17.50/22.50 t. – **17 rm** ⊒ 52.50/65.00 t.

🏨 **Windsor Lodge**, Mount Pleasant, SA1 6EG, ℰ (01792) 642158, Fax (01792) 648996 – 📺
☎ 🅿. 🐵 🆎 ⓪ 𝘝𝘐𝘚𝘈 𝗃𝖼𝖻   B r
closed 25 and 26 December – Meals (lunch by arrangement) (bar meals Sunday) 12.50/
22.30 t. ╏ 5.25 – **18 rm** ⊒ 47.50/62.50 t. – SB.

⌂ **Alexander** without rest., 3 Sketty Rd, Uplands, SA2 0EU, ℰ (01792) 470045,
Fax (01792) 476012 – ↳⅍ 📺 ☎. 🐵 🆎 ⓪ 𝘝𝘐𝘚𝘈. ⅍   A c
closed 24 December-2 January – **6 rm** ⊒ 30.00/45.00 st.

✗ **Annie's**, 56 St. Helen's Rd, SA1 4BE, ℰ (01792) 655603 – 🐵 𝘝𝘐𝘚𝘈   A o
closed Sunday, Monday and 25-26 December – Meals (booking essential) (dinner only)
18.80 st. ╏ 4.45.

t Swansea Enterprise Park NE : 4 m. by A 4067 – A – off A 48 – ⊠ Swansea.

🏨 **Hilton National**, Phoenix Way, SA7 9EG, ℰ (01792) 310330, Fax (01792) 797535, ┢₆, 🛁,
◨ – ↳⅍ rm, 🍽 rest, 📺 ☎ ⅋ 🅿 – 🔬 180. 🐵 🆎 ⓪ 𝘝𝘐𝘚𝘈 𝗃𝖼𝖻. ⅍
Meals (bar lunch)/dinner 15.50 st. and a la carte ╏ 6.50 – ⊒ 10.25 – **120 rm** 85.00 st.

SWANSEA

College Street . . . . B 13
Kingsway (The) . . . . B
Oxford Street . . . . B
Parc Tawe
  Shopping Centre . . . . B
Princess Way . . . . B
Quadrant Centre . . . . B
St. David's Square . . . . B

Alexandra Road . . . . B 2
Belle Vue Way . . . . B 4
Carmarthen Road . . . . B 7
Castle Street . . . . B 8
Christina Street . . . . B 9
Clarence Terrace . . . . B 10
De la Beche Street . . . . B 15
Dillwyn Street . . . . B 17

East Bank Way . . . . C 18
Grove Place . . . . B 22
Nearth Road . . . . B 25
Nelson Street . . . . B 26
New Cut Bridge . . . . C 27
St. Mary's Square . . . . B 42
Tawe Bridge . . . . C 43
Union Street . . . . B 47
Wellington Street . . . . B 54
West Way . . . . B 55

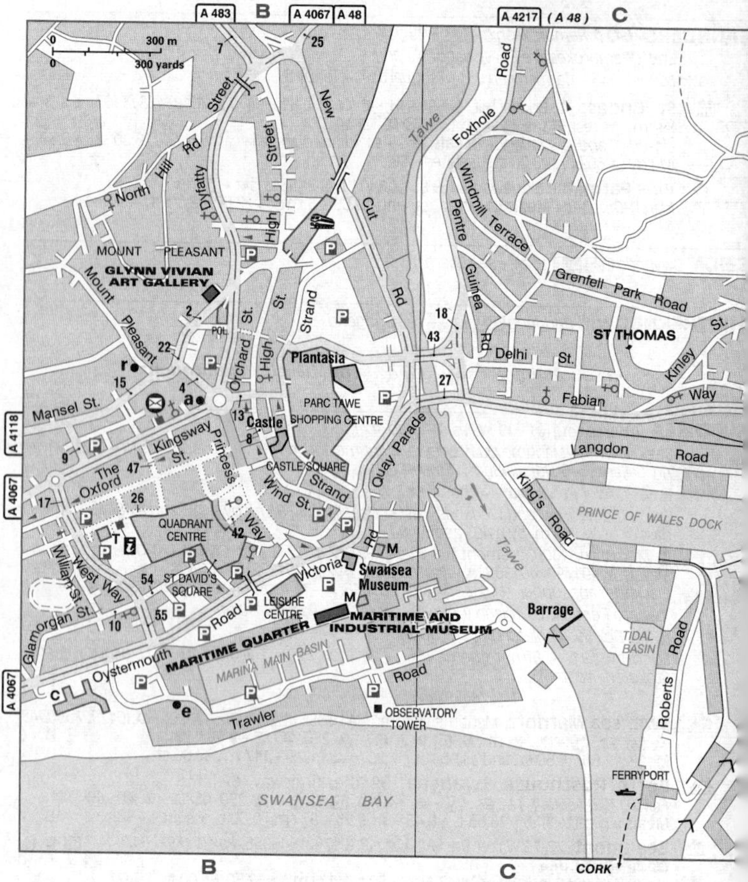

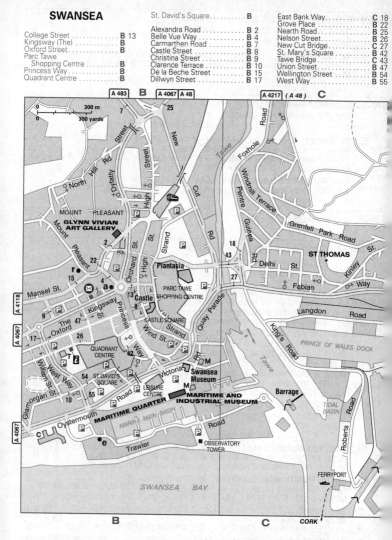

at The Mumbles *SW : 7 ¾ m. by A 4067 – A – ✉ Swansea.*

🏠 **Norton House,** 17 Norton Rd, SA3 5TQ, ☎ (01792) 404891, *Fax (01792) 403210* – TV ☎ Ⓟ – 🚶 25. MC AE ⓓ VISA. ✂
Meals (dinner only) 24.50 **t.** 🌢 4.50 – **15 rm** ☕ 57.50/85.00 **t.**

🏠 **Osborne,** Rotherslade Rd, Langland Bay, SA3 4QL, W : ¾ m. ☎ (01792) 366274 *Fax (01792) 363100,* ⇐ – |♦|, ✂ rm, TV ☎ Ⓟ – 🚶 50. MC AE ⓓ VISA JCB
March-late December – **Meals** 17.50/22.50 **t.** and a la carte – ☕ 11.50 – **32 rm** 85.00/130.00 **t.** – SB.

🏠 **Hillcrest House,** 1 Higher Lane, SA3 4NS, W : ¾ m. on Langland rd ☎ (01792) 363700 *Fax (01792) 363768* – ✂ rest, TV ☎ Ⓟ. MC AE VISA. ✂
closed 23 December-1 January and 2 weeks January-February – **Meals** *(closed Sunday)* (dinner only) 17.00 **st.** – **7 rm** ☕ 45.00/65.00 **t.** – SB.

✕✕ **L'Amuse,** 2 Woodville Rd, SA3 4AD, ☎ (01792) 366006 – MC VISA
closed Sunday, Monday, 1 week July and January – **Meals** - Bistro - 12.50/19.50 **t.** 🌢 4.00.

Clase Road .... **A** 12
Martin Street .... **A** 24
Pen-y-Graig Road .... **A** 30
Plasmarl By-Pass .... **A** 32
Ravenhill Road .... **A** 35
Station Road .... **A** 37
St. Helen's Road .... **A** 40
Terrace Road .... **A** 45
Uplands Crescent ...... **A** 49
Walter Road .... **A** 52
Woodfield Street .... **A** 60

*This Guide is not a
comprehensive list of
all hotels and
restaurants, nor even
of all good hotels and
restaurants in Great
Britain and Ireland.*

*Since our aim is to be
of service to
all motorists, we must
show establishments in
all categories and so
we have made
a selection
of some in each.*

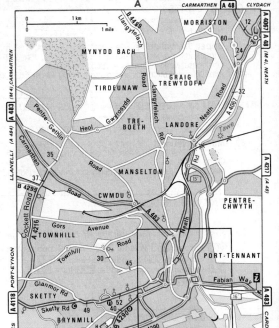

at Llanrhidian *W : 10½ m. by A 4118 –* **A** *– and B 4271 on B 4295 –* ⊠ *Reynoldston.*

🏛 **Fairyhill** ⌖, Reynoldston, SA3 1BS, W : 2 ½ m. by B 4295 (Llangennith rd)
℘ (01792) 390139, Fax (01792) 391358, ☞, park – 🆃🆅 ☎ 🅿 – 🔼 35. 🆗🅾 🅰🅴 𝘝𝘐𝘚𝘈 🅹🅲🅱
closed 26 to 31 December – **Meals** 14.50/29.50 **st.** ⓛ 8.50 – **8 rm** ⌖ 90.00/150.00 **st.** – SB.

🅐 ATS 139 Neath Rd, Hafod ℘ (01792) 456379

SWANSEA SERVICE AREA *Swansea* 🆘🅾🅱 🅸 28.
🅱 *P.O. Box 59, Singleton St., SA1 3QG* ℘ *(01792) 468321.*

🏛 **Travelodge** *without rest.,* Penllergaer, SA4 1GT, M 4 junction 47 ℘ (01792) 896222,
Fax (01792) 898806, Reservations (Freephone) 0800 850950 – ✥ 🆃🆅 & 🅿. 🆗🅾 🅰🅴 🅾 𝘝𝘐𝘚𝘈
🅹🅲🅱. ✥
50 rm 44.95 **t.**

TALBOT GREEN *Rhondda Cynon Taff – pop. 2 405.*
London 163 – Cardiff 9 – Swansea 34.

✕ **Woods Bistro,** 79 Talbot Rd, CF72 8AE, ℘ (01443) 222458, Fax (01443) 222458 – 🆗🅾 🅰🅴
𝘝𝘐𝘚𝘈 🅹🅲🅱
*closed Monday and Saturday lunch, Sunday, 25-26 December, 1 to 8 January and Bank
Holidays –* **Meals** 8.45 **t.** (lunch) and dinner a la carte 14.40/23.40 **t.** ⓛ 5.50.

*Le Grand Londres (GREATER LONDON) est composé de la City
et de 32 arrondissements administratifs (Borough)
eux-mêmes divisés en quartiers ou en villages
ayant conservé leur caractère propre (Area).*

TALGARTH Powys **403** K 28 *Wales G. – pop. 1 818.*
　　Env. : *Brecon Beacons National Park*★★.
　　London 182 – Brecon 10 – Hereford 29 – Swansea 53.

↑　**Upper Trewalkin** ⊗, Pengenffordd, LD3 0HA, S : 2 m. by A 479 (turn right onto unmarked road after 1 m.) ℰ (01874) 711349, Fax (01874) 711349, « Part Georgian farmhouse, working farm », ☞, park – ⇔ ℗. ℅
　　April-October – **Meals** (by arrangement) 12.00 – **3 rm** ⊇ 20.00/40.00 – SB.

TALSARNAU Gwynedd **402 403** H 25 *Wales G. – pop. 647 –* ⊠ *Harlech.*
　　Env. : *Snowdonia National Park*★★★.
　　London 236 – Caernafon 33 – Chester 67 – Dolgellau 25.

🏛　**Maes-y-Neuadd** ⊗, LL47 6YA, S : 1 ½ m. by A 496 off B 4573 ℰ (01766) 780200, Fax (01766) 780211, ≼, « Part 14C country house », ☞, park – ⇔ rest, 🖵 ☎ ℗ – ♨ 25. ➌ ⒶⒺ ⓪ 𝗩𝗜𝗦𝗔 𝗝𝗖𝗕
　　Meals 13.25/25.00 **st.** ▯ 5.50 – **15 rm** ⊇ (dinner included) 80.00/220.00 **st.**, 1 suite – SB.

TAL-Y-BONT Conwy **402 403** I 24 – *see Conwy.*

For the quickest route use the **Michelin Main Road Maps:**
　970 Europe, **974** Poland, **976** Czech Republic-Slovak Republic, **980** Greece, **984** Germany, **985** Scandinavia-Finland, **986** Great Britain and Ireland, **987** Germany-Austria-Benelux, **988** Italy, **989** France, **990** Spain-Portugal.

TAL-Y-LLYN Gwynedd **402 403** I 25 *Wales G. –* ⊠ *Tywyn.*
　　Env. : *Snowdonia National Park*★★★ *– Cadair Idris*★★★.
　　London 224 – Dolgellau 9 – Shrewsbury 60.

🏛　**Tynycornel**, LL36 9AJ, on B 4405 ℰ (01654) 782282, Fax (01654) 782679, ≼ Tal-y-Llyn Lake and mountains, ⇌, ☜, ☞ – ⇔ rest, 🖵 ☎ ℗, ➌ ⒶⒺ ⓪ 𝗩𝗜𝗦𝗔 𝗝𝗖𝗕
　　closed 2 to 8 January – **Meals** (lunch by arrangement Monday to Saturday)/dinner 20.00 **t.** ▯ 7.20 – **15 rm** ⊇ (dinner included) 65.00/130.00 **t.**, 2 suites – SB.

🏠　**Minfford**, LL36 9AJ, NE : 2 ¼ m. by B 4405 on A 487 ℰ (01654) 761665 Fax (01654) 761517, ≼, ☞ – ⇔ rest, ☎ ℗, ➌ 𝗩𝗜𝗦𝗔
　　March-October and weekends only in November – **Meals** (booking essential) (dinner only) 18.95 **st.** ▯ 6.50 – **6 rm** ⊇ (dinner included) 65.00/110.00 **st.** – SB.

↑　**Dolffanog Fawr**, LL36 9AJ, NE : 1 ¼ m. on B 4405 ℰ (01654) 761247, ≼ Tal-y-Llyn Lake and mountains, ☞ – ⇔ 🖵 ℗. ℅
　　Meals (communal dining) 14.50 **st.** – **4 rm** ⊇ 38.00/50.00 **st.** – SB.

TENBY (Dinbych-Y-Pysgod) Pembrokeshire **403** F 28 *Wales G. – pop. 5 619.*
　　See : *Town*★★ – *Harbour and seafront*★★.
　　Env. : *Pembrokeshire Coast National Park*★★ – *Caldey Island*★, S : by boat.
　　🏌 The Burrows ℰ (01834) 842787/842978.
　　🛈 The Croft, SA70 8AP ℰ (01834) 842402.
　　London 247 – Carmarthen 27 – Fishguard 36.

🏛　**Waterwynch House** ⊗, Narberth Rd, SA70 8TJ, N : 1 ¾ m. on A 478 ℰ (01834) 842464, Fax (01834) 845076, ≼, ☞, park – ⇔ rest, 🖵 ☎ ℗, ➌ 𝗩𝗜𝗦𝗔
　　11 March-October – **Meals** (dinner only and Sunday lunch)/dinner 15.00 **t.** – **13 rm** ⊇ (dinner included) 52.00/96.00 **t.**, 3 suites.

🏛　**Atlantic**, Esplanade, SA70 7DU, ℰ (01834) 842881, Fax (01834) 842881 (ext. 256), ▨, ☞ – ‖ 🖵 ☎ 👤 ℗, ➌ ⒶⒺ 𝗩𝗜𝗦𝗔, ℅
　　closed 21 December-17 January – **Meals** (bar lunch)/dinner 18.00 **t.** and a la carte ▯ 4.95 – **40 rm** ⊇ 58.00/110.00 **t.**

🏛　**Broadmead**, Heywood Lane, SA70 8DA, NW : ¾ m. ℰ (01834) 842641 Fax (01834) 845757, ☞ – 🖵 ☎ ℗, ➌ 𝗩𝗜𝗦𝗔 𝗝𝗖𝗕, ℅
　　closed January, February and November – **Meals** (bar lunch)/dinner 13.00 **st.** ▯ 4.75 – **20 rm** ⊇ 28.00/56.00 **st.** – SB.

🏨 **Fourcroft,** North Beach, SA70 8AP, ℰ (01834) 842886, Fax (01834) 842888, ≤, ☎, ⌁,
☞ – ⬛, ✳ rest, 📺 ☎ – 🔥 80. 🕮 VISA JCB
Meals (bar lunch)/dinner 15.00 **st.** and a la carte ⓘ 4.50 – **46 rm** ⊑ 37.00/84.00 **st.** – SB.

⌂ **Myrtle House,** St. Marys St., SA70 7HW, ℰ (01834) 842508, Fax (01834) 842508 – ✳ 📺
⌑. 🕮 VISA JCB. ⅙
March-September – Meals 10.00 **s.** – **8 rm** ⊑ 24.00/50.00 **s.**

at Penally (Penalun) *SW : 2 m. by A 4139* – ✉ *Tenby.*

🏨 **Penally Abbey** ⌑, SA70 7PY, ℰ (01834) 843033, Fax (01834) 844714, ≤, ☞ – ✳ rest,
📺 ☎ ⌑. 🕮 AE VISA JCB. ⅙
Meals (lunch by arrangement) 24.50 **st.** ⓘ 5.45 – **11 rm** ⊑ 74.00/120.00 **st.**, 1 suite – SB.

THORNHILL *Cardiff* 403 K 29 – *see Cardiff.*

THREE COCKS (Aberllynfi) *Powys* 403 K 27 *Wales G.* – ✉ *Brecon.*
Env. : *Brecon Beacons National Park★★.*
London 184 – Brecon 11 – Hereford 25 – Swansea 55.

✕✕ **Three Cocks** with rm, LD3 0SL, on A 438 ℰ (01497) 847215, Fax (01497) 847215,
« Part 15C inn », ☞ – ⌑. 🕮 VISA. ⅙
closed December-14 February – Meals *(closed Sunday lunch and Tuesday)* (lunch
by arrangement) 27.00 **st.** and a la carte ⓘ 6.95 – **7 rm** ⊑ 50.00/65.00 **st.** – SB.

TINTERN (Tyndyrn) *Monmouthshire* 403 404 L 28 *Wales G.* – pop. 749 – ✉ *Chepstow.*
See : *Abbey★★ AC.*
London 137 – Bristol 23 – Gloucester 40 – Newport 22.

🏨 **Beaufort,** NP6 6SF, on A 466 ℰ (01291) 689777, Fax (01291) 689727, ☞ – 📺 ☎ ⌑ –
🔥 50. 🕮 AE VISA
Meals (bar lunch Monday to Saturday)/dinner 14.95 **st.** ⓘ 5.25 – **24 rm** ⊑ 69.00/89.00 **st.** –
SB.

🏨 **Royal George,** NP6 6SF, on A 466 ℰ (01291) 689205, Fax (01291) 689448, ☞ – ✳ rm,
📺 ☎ ⌑. 🕮 AE ⓞ VISA JCB
Meals 11.95/20.00 **t.** ⓘ 4.00 – **19 rm** ⊑ 60.00/85.00 **t.** – SB.

✕✕ **Parva Farmhouse** with rm, NP6 6SQ, on A 466 ℰ (01291) 689411, Fax (01291) 689557 –
📺 ☎ ⌑. 🕮 AE VISA JCB
Meals (bar lunch)/dinner 17.50 **st.** ⓘ 5.80 – **9 rm** ⊑ 44.00/66.00 **st.** – SB.

TREARDDUR BAY *Anglesey* 402 403 G 24 *Wales G.* – ✉ *Holyhead.*
Env. : *Anglesey★★.*
Exc. : *Barclodiad y Gawres Burial Chamber★, SE : 10 m. by B 4545, A 5 and A 4080.*
London 269 – Bangor 25 – Caernarfon 29 – Holyhead 3.

🏨 **Trearddur Bay,** LL65 2UN, ℰ (01407) 860301, Fax (01407) 861181, ◳, ☞ – 📺 ☎ ⌑ –
🔥 120. 🕮 AE ⓞ VISA JCB
Meals (bar lunch)/dinner 18.50 **t.** ⓘ 9.95 – **45 rm** ⊑ 68.00/130.00 **t.** – SB.

TRECASTLE *Powys* 403 J 28.
London 192 – Aberystwyth 60 – Cardiff 47 – Carmarthen 37 – Gloucester 81.

🏚 **Castle Coach Inn** with rm, LD3 8UH, ℰ (01874) 636354, Fax (01874) 636457 – 📺 ☎ ⌑.
🕮 VISA JCB
Meals (bar lunch)/dinner 14.95 **t.** and a la carte ⓘ 4.45 – **9 rm** ⊑ 38.50/45.00 **t.**, 1 suite –
SB.

TREFRIW *Conwy* 402 403 I 24 – *see Llanrwst.*

TREMEIRCHION *Denbighshire* 402 403 J 24 – ✉ *St. Asaph.*
London 225 – Chester 29 – Shrewsbury 59.

⌂ **Bach-Y-Graig** without rest., LL17 0UH, SW : 2 m. by B 5429 and Heol Y Brenin off Dinbych
rd ℰ (01745) 730627, Fax (01745) 730627, « 16C brick built house, working farm », ☞,
park – ✳ 📺 ⌑. ⅙
closed Christmas and New Year – **3 rm** ⊑ 27.00/45.00 **s.**

TRESAITH *Ceredigion* – *see Aberporth.*

TYN-Y-GROES Gwynedd – see Conwy (Aberconwy and Colwyn).

USK (Brynbuga) Monmouthshire 403 L 28 Wales G. – pop. 2 187.
Exc. : Raglan Castle★ AC, NE : 7 m. by A 472, A 449 and A 40.
🏌, 🏌 Alice Springs, Bettws Newydd ℘ (01873) 880772.
London 144 – Bristol 30 – Gloucester 39 – Newport 10.

🏥 **Glen-yr-Afon House**, Pontypool Rd, NP5 1SY, ℘ (01291) 672302, Fax (01291) 672597,
🐾 – 🕴 ❄️ rm 📺 🕿 & 🅿 – 🔬 150. 🐾 🝙 ⓪ 🆅🆂🅰
Meals (residents only Sunday dinner) 18.25 **t.** and a la carte ⓵ 7.60 – **26 rm** �, 61.30/
120.00 **t.** – SB.

at Llangybi S : 2½ m. on Llangybi rd – ✉ Usk.

🏰 **Cwrt Bleddyn**, NP5 1PG, S : 1 m. ℘ (01633) 450521, Fax (01633) 450220, 🏊, ☎, 🔲, 🐾,
park, ❄️, squash – 🕴 ❄️ rm 📺 🕿 🅿 – 🔬 200. 🐾 🝙 🆅🆂🅰 ❄️
Nicholls : Meals 16.50/24.50 **t.** and a la carte ⓵ 6.75 – **32 rm** �. 90.00/130.00 **st.**, 4 suites –
SB.

WELSH HOOK Pembrokeshire – see Fishguard.

WELSHPOOL (Trallwng) Powys 402 403 K 26 Wales G. – pop. 5 725.
See : Town★.
Env. : Powis Castle★★★ AC, SW : 1 ½ m. by A 483.
🏌 Golfa Hill ℘ (01938) 83249.
🛈 Vicarage Gdn, Church St., SY21 7DD ℘ (01938) 552043.
London 182 – Birmingham 64 – Chester 45 – Shrewsbury 19.

🏥 **Royal Oak**, The Cross, SY21 7DG, ℘ (01938) 552217, Fax (01938) 556652 – 📺 🕿 🅿 –
🔬 150. 🐾 🝙 🆅🆂🅰 ⓪
Meals a la carte 10.70/14.40 **t.** – **24 rm** �. 55.00/80.00 **st.** – SB.

🏠 **Moat Farm** ❄️, SY21 8SE, S : 2 ¼ m. on A 483 ℘ (01938) 553179, « Working farm », 🐾,
park – ❄️ rest, 📺 🅿. ❄️
March-November – **Meals** (by arrangement) (communal dining) 11.00 **st.** – **3 rm** �. 25.00/
42.00 **st.**

at Guilsfield N : 3 m. by A 490 on B 4392 – ✉ Welshpool.

🏠 **Lower Trelydan** ❄️, SY21 9PH, S : ¾ m. by B 4392 on unmarked road
℘ (01938) 553105, Fax (01938) 553105, « 16C farmhouse, working farm », 🐾, park – ❄️
📺 🅿. ❄️
closed Christmas and New Year – **Meals** (by arrangement) (communal dining) 13.00 **t**
⓵ 3.50 – **3 rm** �. 27.00/44.00.

WHITEBROOK Monmouthshire – see Monmouth.

WHITLAND (Hendy-Gwyn) Carmarthenshire 403 G 28 – pop. 1 518.
London 235 – Carmarthen 15 – Haverfordwest 17.

🏠 **Cilpost Farm** ❄️, SA34 0RP, N : 1 ¼ m. by North Rd ℘ (01994) 240280, ≼, « Working
dairy farm », ☎, 🔲, 🐾 – 🅿. ❄️
April-September – **Meals** (by arrangement) 15.00 **st.** – **7 rm** �. 17.00/46.00 **st.**

🅖 ATS Emporium Garage, Market St. ℘ (01994) 240587

WOLF'S CASTLE (Cas-Blaidd) Pembrokeshire 403 F 28 Wales G. – pop. 616 – ✉ Haverfordwest
Env. : Pembrokeshire Coast National Park★★.
London 258 – Fishguard 7 – Haverfordwest 8.

🏥 **Wolfscastle Country H.**, SA62 5LZ, on A 40 ℘ (01437) 741225, Fax (01437) 741383, 🐾
squash – ❄️ rest, 📺 🕿 🅿 🐾 🝙 🆅🆂🅰 🝙
closed 24 to 26 December – **Meals** (lunch by arrangement)/dinner a la carte 14.30/23.35 **t**
⓵ 6.95 – **20 rm** �. 39.00/73.00 **t.** – SB.

WREXHAM (Wrecsam) 402 403 L 24 Wales G. – pop. 40 614.

See : St. Giles Church★.

Env. : Erddig★★ AC (Gardens★★), SW : 2 m – Gresford (All Saints Church★), N : 4 m. by A 5152 and B 5445.

🔒 Holt Rd ℰ (01978) 261033 – 🔒, 🔒 Chirk ℰ (01691) 774407.

🅱 Lambpit St., LL11 1WN ℰ (01978) 292015.

London 192 – Chester 12 – Shrewsbury 28.

🏨 **Llwyn Onn Hall** 🦢, Cefn Rd, LL13 0NY, 2 ½ m. by A 534 off Cefn Rd ℰ (01978) 261225, Fax (01978) 363233, ≤, 🍴, 🌳 – ✹ rm, 📺 ☎ 🅿 – 🔏 25. 🆎 ䷂ VISA JCB. ✸

Meals 16.00 st. and a la carte ⌕ 5.00 – **13 rm** ⌑ 59.00/80.00 st. – SB.

🏨 **Cross Lanes**, Marchwiel, LL13 0TF, SE : 3 ½ m. on A 525 ℰ (01978) 780555, Fax (01978) 780568, ☎s, 🔲, 🌳, park – 📺 ☎ 🅿 – 🔏 100. 🆎 ䷂ ⓪ VISA JCB. ✸

closed 25 and 26 December – **Meals** 12.50/19.50 t. and a la carte ⌕ 5.75 – ⌑ 7.95 – **15 rm** 64.00/99.00 st. – SB.

🏨 **Travel Inn**, Chester Rd, LL12 8PW, NE : 2 ½ m. by A 483 on B 5445 ℰ (01978) 853214 – |⧈|, ✹ rm, 📺 ⅙ 🅿. 🆎 ䷂ ⓪ VISA. ✸

Meals (grill rest.) – **38 rm** 36.50 t.

🏨 **Travelodge**, Croes-Foel roundabout, Rhostyllen, LL14 4EJ, SW : 2 ½ m. off A 483 (Wrexham bypass) ℰ (01978) 365705, Reservations (Freephone) 0800 850950 – ✹ rm, 📺 ⅙ 🅿. 🆎 ䷂ ⓪ VISA JCB. ✸

Meals (grill rest.) – **32 rm** 39.95 t.

🔧 ATS Dolydd Rd, Croesnewydd ℰ (01978) 352301/352928

The **video cassette**
CHÂTEAUX OF THE LOIRE, from Chambord to Chinon,
is a film to complement the **Michelin Green Guide Châteaux of the Loire**. It portrays the Châteaux and the elegant lifestyle of the Touraine.

Available in six versions:
0751 in French SECAM
0752 in French PAL
1752 in English PAL
1753 in English NTSC

2752 in German PAL
3752 in Italian PAL

Ireland

Northern Ireland

Place with at least
a hotel or restaurant ● Londonderry
a pleasant hotel or restaurant 🏨, ⌂, 🍴
a quiet, secluded hotel 🐴
a restaurant with ✿, ✿✿, ✿✿✿, ☺ **Meals**
See this town for establishments located in its vicinity **BELFAST**

La località possiede come minimo
una risorsa alberghiera ● Londonderry
Albergo o ristorante ameno 🏨, ⌂, 🍴
un albergo molto tranquillo, isolato 🐴
un'ottima tavola con ✿, ✿✿, ✿✿✿, ☺ **Meals**
La località raggruppa nel suo testo le risorse dei dintorni **BELFAST**

Localité offrant au moins
une ressource hôtelière ● Londonderry
un hôtel ou restaurant agréable 🏨, ⌂, 🍴
un hôtel très tranquille, isolé 🐴
une bonne table à ✿, ✿✿, ✿✿✿, ☺ **Meals**
Localité groupant dans le texte les ressources de ses environs **BELFAST**

Ort mit mindestens
einem Hotel oder Restaurant ● Londonderry
ein angenehmes Hotel oder Restaurant 🏨, ⌂, 🍴
einem sehr ruhigen und abgelegenen Hotel 🐴
einem Restaurant mit ✿, ✿✿, ✿✿✿, ☺ **Meals**
Ort mit Angaben über Hotels und Restaurants in der Umgebung **BELFAST**

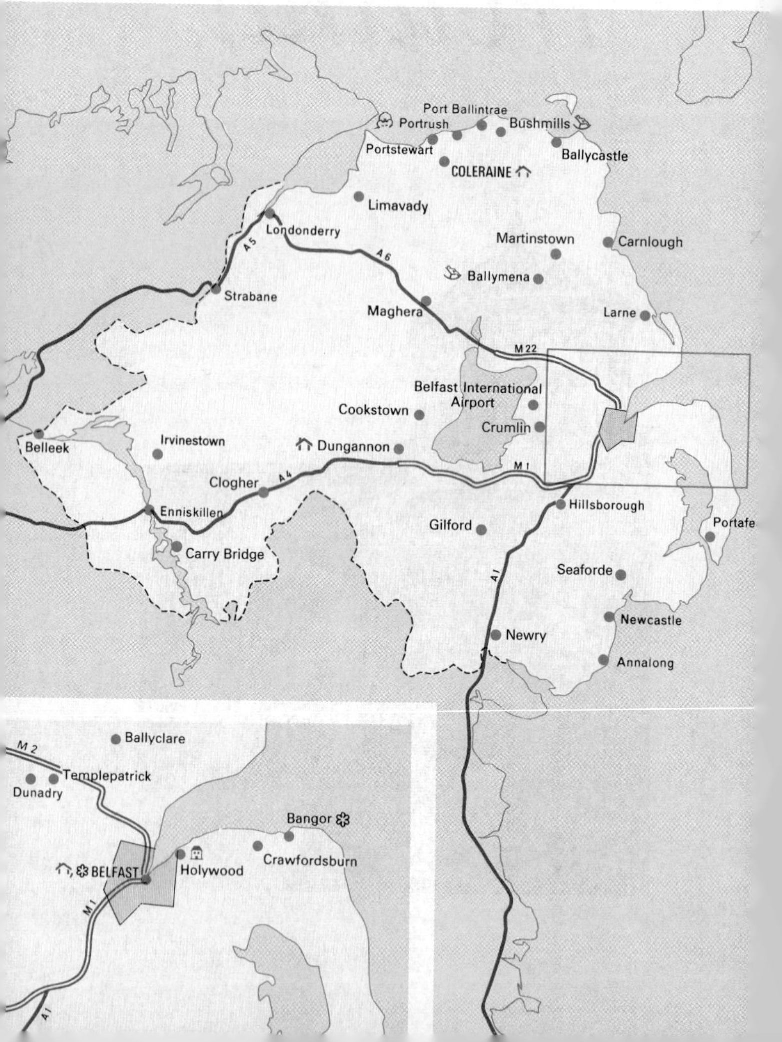

ANNALONG (Áth na Long) *Down* 923 O 5 *Ireland G.* – pop. 1 937.

EXC. : W : *Mourne Mountains*★★ :– *Bryansford, Tollymore Forest Park*★★ *AC, Annalong Marine Park and Cornmill*★ *AC – Silent Valley Reservoir*★ (≤★) – *Spelga Pass and Dam*★ – *Drumena Cashel and Souterrain*★ – *Kilbroney Forest Park (viewpoint*★ *)*.

Belfast 37 – Dundalk 36.

🏨 **Glassdrumman Lodge** ﹩, 85 Mill Rd, BT34 4RH, ℰ (013967) 68451, Fax (013967) 67041, ≤ Irish Sea and Mourne mountains, ☞, park – 💥 rest, 📺 ☎ 🅿. **꘏** **VISA**. ﹪

Meals (booking essential) (dinner only) 29.50 t. ⬧ 7.00 – **8 rm** ⬤ 85.00/125.00 t., 2 suites – SB.

BALLYCASTLE (Baile an Chaistil) *Antrim* 923 N 2.

🏌 *Cushendall Rd* ℰ (012657) 62536.

⛴ *to Campbeltown (Argyll and Antrim Steam Packet Co.) 2 daily (3 h).*

🛈 *Sheskburn House, 7 Mary St. BT54 6QH* ℰ (012657) 62024.

Belfast 55 – Ballymena 27 – Coleraine 22.

🏨 **Marine,** North St., BT64 6BN, ℰ (012657) 62222, Fax (012657) 69507, ≤ Fair Head and Rathlin Island, ⅓, ⬧, 🔳 – 🏢, 💥 rm, 📺 ☎ 🅿 – 🛆 150. **꘏** **AE** **①** **VISA**. ﹪

Meals (bar lunch Monday to Saturday)/dinner 14.00 **t.** and a la carte ⬧ 3.95 – **32 rm** ⬤ 50.00/70.00 **st.** – SB.

BALLYCLARE (Bealach Cláir) *Antrim* 923 N/O 3.

🏌 *25 Springvale Rd* ℰ (01960) 342352.

Belfast 10 – Ballymena 14 – Larne 10.

✗✗ **Ginger Tree,** 29 Ballyrobert Rd, BT39 9RY, S : 3 ¼ m. by A 57 on B 56 ℰ (01232) 848176 – 🅿. **꘏** **AE** **①** **VISA** **JCB**

closed Sunday, 11 to 13 July and 24 to 26 December – **Meals** - Japanese - 6.80/12.95 **t.** and a la carte ⬧ 3.95.

BALLYMENA (An Baile Meánach) *Antrim* 923 N 3 *Ireland G.* – pop. 28 717.

EXC. : *Antrim Glens*★★★ :– *Murlough Bay*★★★ *(Fair Head* ≤★★★ *) Glengariff Forest Park*★★ *AC (Waterfall*★★ *) Glengariff*★, *Glendun*★, *Rathlin Island*★ – *Antrim (Shane's Castle Railway*★ *AC, Round Tower*★ *) S : 9 ½ m. by A 26.*

🏌 *128 Raceview Rd* ℰ (01266) 861207/861487.

🛈 *Council Offices, 80 Galgorm Rd, BT42 1AB* ℰ (01266) 44111 – *Morrows Shop, 17 Bridge St., BT43 5EJ* ℰ (01266) 653663 *(summer only).*

Belfast 28 – Dundalk 78 – Larne 21 – Londonderry 51 – Omagh 53.

🏨 **Galgorm Manor** ﹩, BT42 1EA, W : 3 ¾ m. by A 42 on Cullybackey rd ℰ (01266) 881001, Fax (01266) 880080, ≤, « Part 19C country house on banks of River Main », 🏌, ⬧, ☞, park – 📺 ☎ 🅿 – 🛆 500. **꘏** **AE** **①** **VISA**. ﹪

Meals a la carte 22.00/26.50 **st.** ⬧ 11.00 – **20 rm** ⬤ 95.00/125.00 **st.**, 3 suites – SB.

🏨 **Country House** ﹩, 20 Doagh Rd, BT42 3LZ, SE : 6 m. by A 36 on B 59 ℰ (01266) 891663, Fax (01266) 891477, ⅓, ⬧, ☞ – 📺 ☎ & 🅿 – 🛆 300. **꘏** **AE** **①** **VISA**. ﹪

Meals *(closed Saturday lunch and Bank Holiday dinner)* 11.95/17.95 **st.** and dinner a la carte ⬧ 4.95 – **39 rm** ⬤ 75.00/130.00 **st.** – SB.

🏨 **Adair Arms,** Ballymoney Rd, BT43 5BS, ℰ (01266) 653674, Fax (01266) 40436 – 📺 ☎ 🅿 – 🛆 250. **꘏** **AE** **①** **VISA**. ﹪

closed 25 December – **Meals** (buffet lunch)/dinner 15.95 **t.** and a la carte ⬧ 4.50 – **40 rm** ⬤ 56.00/78.00 **st.** – SB.

Ⓜ ATS Antrim Rd ℰ (01266) 652888

BANGOR (Beannchar) *Down* 923 O/P 4.

🛈 *34 Quay St. BT20 5ED* ℰ (01247) 270069.

Belfast 14 – Newtownards 5.

🏨 **Marine Court,** 18-20 Quay St., BT20 5ED, ℰ (01247) 451100, Fax (01247) 451200, ⅓, 🔳 – 🏢, 💥 rm, 📺 ☎ & 🅿 – 🛆 350. **꘏** **AE** **①** **VISA**. ﹪

Meals 10.00/17.00 **st.** and a la carte – **51 rm** ⬤ 80.00/100.00 **st.** – SB.

🏨 **Clandeboye Lodge,** Estate Rd, Clandeboye, BT19 1UR, SW : 3 m. by A 2 and B 170 following signs for Blackwood Golf Centre ℰ (01247) 852500, Fax (01247) 852772, 🏌, ☞ – 🏢, 💥 rm, 📺 ☎ & 🅿 – 🛆 350. **꘏** **AE** **①** **VISA**

closed 24 to 26 December – **Meals** (bar lunch)/dinner 18.50 **t.** – **43 rm** ⬤ 46.00/85.00 **t.** – SB.

🏨 **Royal,** 26 Quay St., BT20 5ED, ℰ (01247) 271866, *Fax (01247) 467810*, ≤ – 📶, 🍴 rest, 📺 ☎
– 🔏 60. 🆎 🆎 ① 𝘝𝘐𝘚𝘈 ※
closed 25 December – Meals 17.50 **t.** (dinner) and a la carte 9.25/24.50 **t.** ▐ 4.00 – **50 rm**
⚏ 75.00/95.00 **t.** – SB.

↑ **Cairn Bay Lodge,** 278 Seacliffe Rd, BT20 5HS, E : 1 ¼ m. by Quay St. ℰ (01247) 467636,
Fax (01247) 457728, ≤, 🐴 – ↳ 📺 ☎ 🅿. 🆎 𝘝𝘐𝘚𝘈 ※
closed 1 week Christmas – Meals (by arrangement) (communal dining) 14.00 **st.** – **3 rm**
⚏ 37.50/70.00 **st.** – SB.

↑ **Shelleven,** 61 Princetown Rd, BT20 3TA, ℰ (01247) 271777, *Fax (01247) 271777* – ↳ 📺
☎ 🅿. 🆎 𝘝𝘐𝘚𝘈 ※
Meals (by arrangement) 12.50 – **12 rm** ⚏ 25.00/50.00 **s.** – SB.

XX **Shanks** (Millar), The Blackwood, Crawfordsburn Rd, Clandeboye, BT19 1GB, SW : 3 ¼ m.
₷ by A 2 and B 170 following signs for Blackwood Golf Centre ℰ (01247) 853313,
Fax (01247) 853785, 🏌 – 🅿. 🆎 🆎 𝘝𝘐𝘚𝘈
*closed Saturday lunch, Sunday, Monday, Easter Tuesday, 2 weeks mid July, 24 to
26 December and 1 January* – Meals 16.95/28.50 **t.** ▐ 6.75
Spec. Millefeuille of smoked chicken and foie gras, orzo, apple and cassis. Éminc é of
sweetbreads, potato galette, tarragon, broad beans and morels. Gratin of raspberries with
an apricot compote, almond ice cream.

ⓐ ATS 161 Clandeboye Rd ℰ (01247) 271736

GRÜNE REISEFÜHRER
Landschaften, Baudenkmäler
Sehenswürdigkeiten
Touristenstraßen
Tourenvorschläge
Stadtpläne und Übersichtskarten

BELFAST - (Béal Feirste)

Antrim 923 O 4 *Ireland G. – pop. 279 237.*

Dublin 103 – Londonderry 70.

TOURIST INFORMATION

🚹 *St. Anne's Court, 59 North St., BT1 1NB ℘ (01232) 246609.*
🚹 *Belfast International Airport, BT29 4AB ℘ (01849) 422888.*
🚹 *Belfast City Airport, Sydenham Bypass, BT3 9JH ℘ (01232) 457745.*

PRACTICAL INFORMATION

🛇 *Balmoral, 518 Lisburn Rd ℘ (01232) 381514, AZ.*
🛇 *Belvoir Park, Church Rd, Newtonbreda ℘ (01232) 491693 AZ.*
🛇 *Fortwilliam, Downview Av. ℘ (01232) 370770, AY.*
🛇 *The Knock Club, Summerfield, Dundonald ℘ (01232) 482249.*
🛇 *Shandon Park, 73 Shandon Park ℘ (01232) 793730.*
🛇 *Cliftonville, Westland Rd ℘ (01232) 744158/746595, AY.*
🛇 *Ormeau, 50 Park Rd ℘ (01232) 641069, AZ.*
   ✈ *Belfast International Airport, Aldergrove : ℘ (01849) 422888, W : 15½ m. by A 52 AY –*
Belfast City Airport : ℘ (01232) 457745 – **Terminal** : *Coach service (Ulsterbus Ltd.) from*
Great Victoria Street Station (40 mn).
   ⛴ *to Isle of Man (Douglas) (Isle of Man Steam Packet Co. Ltd) (summer only) (4 h 30 mn) –*
to Stranraer (Stena Line) (3 h 15 mn), (Sea Containers Ferries Scotland Ltd and Stena Line)
4-5 daily (1 h 30 mn) – to Liverpool (Norse Irish Ferries Ltd) weekly (11 h).

TOURIST INFORMATION

See : *City★ - Ulster Museum★★ (Spanish Armada Treasure★★ , Shrine of St. Patrick's Hand★)*
AZ M1 – *City Hall★* BZ – *Donegall Square★* BZ 20 – *Botanic Gardens (Palm House★)* AZ –
St Anne's Cathedral★ BY – *Crown Liquor Saloon★* BZ – *Sinclair Seaman's Church★* BY –
St Malachy's Church★ BZ.
Env. : *Belfast Zoological Gardens★★ AC, N : 5 m. by A 6 AY.*
Exc. : *Carrickfergus (Castle★★ AC, St. Nicholas' Church★) NE : 9 ½ m. by A 2 – Talnotry*
Cottage Bird Garden, Crumlin★ AC, W : 13½ m. by A 52.

Europa, Great Victoria St., BT2 7AP, ℰ (01232) 327000, *Fax (01232) 327800* – 🛗, ⇔ rm, 🍴 rest, 📺 ☎ ♿ 🅿 – 🔬 1000. 🆗 🆎 ① 💳. ⬚
BZ e
closed 24 and 25 December – **Gallery : Meals** *(closed Saturday lunch and Sunday)* 15.75/24.50 **t.** and a la carte ⬙ 6.00 – **Brasserie : Meals** a la carte 11.70/21.40 **t.** ⬙ 3.00 – 🖃 10.00 – **182 rm** 110.00/150.00 **st.**, 2 suites.

Stormont, Upper Newtownards Rd, BT4 3LP, E : 4½ m. by A 2 on A 20 ℰ (01232) 658621, *Fax (01232) 480240* – 🛗, ⇔ rm, 🍴 rest, 📺 ☎ ♿ 🅿 – 🔬 400. 🆗 🆎 ① 💳. ⬚
closed 25 December – **McMaster's : Meals** *(closed Saturday lunch and Sunday)* 15.50/21.00 **st.** and dinner a la carte ⬙ 7.50 – **La Scala : Meals** a la carte 12.35/20.90 **st.** ⬙ 6.50 – 🖃 11.00 – **109 rm** 97.00/180.00 **st.**

Holiday Inn Garden Court, 15 Brunswick St., BT2 7GE, ℰ (01232) 333555, *Fax (01232) 232999* – 🛗, ⇔ rm, 🍴 rest, 📺 ☎ ♿ 🅿 – 🔬 70. 🆗 🆎 ① 💳. ⬚
BZ a
Meals 7.95 **t.** (lunch) and a la carte 14.95/20.35 **t.** ⬙ 6.00 – 🖃 6.95 – **76 rm** 79.00/99.00 **t.** – SB.

Jurys Inn, Fisherwick Pl., Great Victoria St., BT2 7AP, ℰ (01232) 533500, *Fax (01232) 533511* – 🛗, ⇔ rm, 🍴 rest, 📺 ☎ ♿ – 🔬 35. 🆗 🆎 ① 💳. ⬚
BZ c
closed 24 to 26 December – **Meals** (grill rest.) (carving bar lunch)/dinner 15.00 **t.** and a la carte ⬙ 6.00 – 🖃 6.50 – **190 rm** 57.00 **st.**

Holiday Inn Express, 106A University St., BT7 1HP, ℰ (01232) 311909, *Fax (01232) 311910* – 🛗, ⇔ rm, 📺 ☎ ♿ 🅿 – 🔬 200. 🆗 🆎 ① 💳 💳. ⬚
AZ z
closed 25 and 26 December – **Meals** 5.95 **st.** (lunch) and a la carte 9.95/16.25 **st.** ⬙ 5.50 – 🖃 5.95 – **114 rm** 54.95 **st.**

Madison's, 59-63 Botanic Av., BT7 1JL, ℰ (01232) 330040, *Fax (01232) 328007* – 🛗, 🍴 rest, 📺 ☎ ♿. 🆗 💳. ⬚
AZ s
closed 25 December – **Meals** a la carte 14.80/22.30 **t.** – **35 rm** 🖃 59.00/69.00 **st.**

Dukes, 65 University St., BT7 1HL, ℰ (01232) 236666, *Fax (01232) 237177*, ⬙, ⬚ – 🛗, ⇔ rm, 🍴 rest, 📺 ☎ – 🔬 130. 🆗 🆎 ① 💳. ⬚
AZ a
Meals (bar lunch Saturday to Tuesday) 10.50/16.50 **st.** ⬙ 5.50 – **21 rm** 🖃 90.00/130.00 **st.** – SB.

Stranmillis Lodge, 14 Chlorine Gdns., BT9 5DJ, ℰ (01232) 682009, *Fax (01232) 683334* – 📺 ☎ 🅿. 🆗 🆎 ① 💳. ⬚
AZ x
Meals 12.50 **st.** ⬙ 3.95 – **6 rm** 🖃 45.00/56.00 **st.** – SB.

Ash Rowan, 12 Windsor Av., BT9 6EE, ℰ (01232) 661758, *Fax (01232) 663227*, ⬙ – 📺 ☎ 🅿. 🆗 💳. ⬚
AZ c
closed 23 December-4 January – **Meals** (by arrangement) 25.00 **st.** – **5 rm** 🖃 46.00/79.00 **t.**

Malone without rest., 79 Malone Rd, BT9 6SH, ℰ (01232) 669565 – 📺 🅿. ⬚
AZ n
8 rm 🖃 33.00/48.00 **t.**

Deanes, 38-40 Howard St., BT1 6PD, ℰ (01232) 560000, *Fax (01232) 560001* – 🍴. 🆗 🆎 💳
BZ n
closed Tuesday, Wednesday and Saturday lunch, Sunday, Monday, July Bank Holidays and Christmas – **Meals** 19.00/33.50 **t.**
Spec. Parfait of foie gras, roast squab pigeon and girolles. Clear soup of rabbit, spiced beans and coriander. Fillet of beef with braised oxtail and celeriac mash.

Downstairs at Deanes : Meals *(closed Sunday, 1 week July, Christmas and New Year)* (bookings not accepted) 14.25/21.40 **t.**

Roscoff (Rankin), 7 Lesley House, Shaftesbury Sq., BT2 7DB, ℰ (01232) 331532, *Fax (01232) 312093* – 🍴. 🆗 🆎 ① 💳
AZ r
closed Saturday lunch, Sunday, 1 January, 12-13 July and 25-26 December – **Meals** 16.50/28.95 **t.** ⬙ 12.00
Spec. Summer salad "Roscoff" with Parma ham and roast pepper mayonnaise. Roast turbot with tomatoes, olives and thyme. Crème brûlée Catalan with orange compote.

Mizuna, 99 Botanic Av., BT7 1JN, ℰ (01232) 230063, *Fax (01232) 244808* – 🆗 💳
closed Easter Monday, 12-13 July and 25-26 December – **Meals** (dinner only and lunch Friday and Sunday)/dinner 17.95 **t.** and a la carte ⬙ 5.95.
AZ e

Nick's Warehouse, 37-39 Hill St. (1st Floor), BT1 2LB, ℰ (01232) 439690, *Fax (01232) 230514* – 🍴. 🆗 🆎 ① 💳
BY a
closed Saturday lunch, Monday dinner, 12 July, 25-26 December and Easter Monday – **Meals** 18.95 **t.** (dinner) and lunch a la carte 15.05/22.50 **t.** ⬙ 5.70.

La Belle Epoque, 61-63 Dublin Rd, BT2 7HE, ℰ (01232) 323244, *Fax (01232) 323244* – 🆗 🆎 ① 💳
AZ o
closed Saturday lunch, Sunday, 1 week July and 25-26 December – **Meals** 15.00 **t.** (dinner) and a la carte 14.70/21.90 **t.** ⬙ 5.00.

Manor House, 43-47 Donegall Pass, BT7 1DQ, ℰ (01232) 238755, *Fax (01232) 238755* – 🍴. 🆗 💳
AZ u
closed 11 to 13 July and 25-26 December – **Meals** - Chinese (Canton) - 5.50/14.50 **t.** and a la carte.

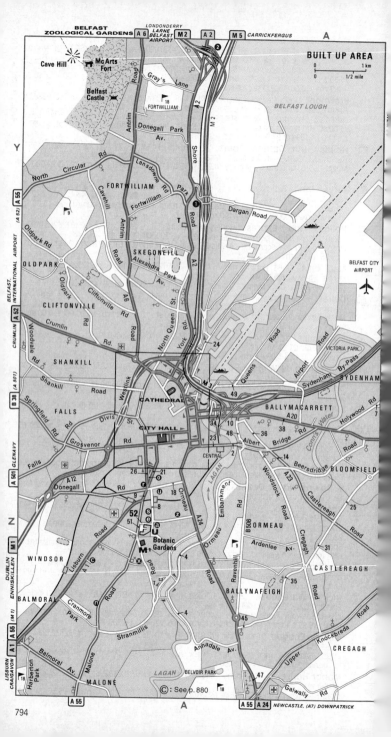

BELFAST

Castlecourt Shopping
Centre .... **BYZ**
Castle Place .... **BZ**
Donegal Place .... **BZ**
Royal Avenue .... **BYZ**

Albert Bridge .... **AZ** 2
Albert Square .... **BY** 3
Annadale Embankment ..... **AZ** 4
Ann Street .... **BZ** 5
Belmont Road .... **AZ** 7
Botanic Avenue .... **AZ** 8
Bradbury Place .... **AZ** 9
Bridge End .... **AZ** 10

Bridge Street .... **BZ** 12
Castlereagh Street .... **AZ** 14
Clifton Street .... **BY** 15
Corporation Square .... **BY** 16
Donegal Pass .... **AZ** 18
Donegall Quay .... **BYZ** 19
Donegall Square .... **BZ** 20
Dublin Road .... **AZ** 21
East Bridge Street .... **AZ** 23
Garmoyle Street .... **AY** 24
Grand Parade .... **AZ** 25
Great Victoria Street ...... **BZ** 26
High Street .... **BYZ** 28
Howard Street .... **BZ** 29
Ladas Drive .... **AZ** 31
Lagan Bridge .... **BY** 32

Middlepath St. .... **AZ** 34
Mount Merrion Avenue .... **AZ** 35
Mountpottinger Road ..... **AZ** 36
Newtownards Road .... **AZ** 38
Queen Elizabeth Bridge ... **BZ** 40
Queen's Bridge .... **BZ** 41
Queen's Square .... **BY** 42
Rosemary Street .... **BZ** 44
Rosetta Park .... **AZ** 45
Saintfield Road .... **AZ** 47
Short Strand .... **AZ** 48
Sydenham Road .... **AZ** 49
University Road .... **AZ** 51
University Square .... **AZ** 52
Waring Street .... **BY** 54
Wellington Place .... **BZ** 55

n Northern Ireland traffic and parking are controlled in the town centres. No vehicle may be left
nattended in a Control Zone.

The names of main shopping streets are indicated in **red**
at the beginning of the list of streets.

at Dundonald *E : 5½ m. on A 20–* AZ – ✉ *Belfast.*

⌂ **Cottage** without rest., 377 Comber Rd, BT16 0XB, SE : 1 ¾ m. on Comber Rd (A 22) ℰ (01247) 878189, 🐾 – ✻ ❋ 🅿. ❄
3 rm ☞ 22.00/40.00.

at Carryduff *S : 6 m. by A 24–* AZ – ✉ *Belfast.*

🏨 **Ivanhoe,** 556 Saintfield Rd, BT8 8EU, N : 1 m. on A 24 ℰ (01232) 812240, *Fax (01232) 815516* – ▮┃ ☎ ♿ 🅿 – 🔬 150. 🆇 ᴀᴇ 𝘝𝘐𝘚𝘈. ❄
closed 25 December – **Meals** 13.95/19.95 **t.** and a la carte ♟ 4.95 – **21 rm** ☞ 70.00/95.00 **st.**

at Dunmurry *SW : 5½ m. on A 1–* AZ – ✉ *Belfast.*

🏨 **Forte Posthouse Belfast,** 300 Kingsway, BT17 9ES, on A 1 ℰ (01232) 612101, *Fax (01232) 626546,* 🐾, park – ▮┃ ✻ rm, 🗏 rest, 🆃🆅 ☎ 🅿 – 🔬 400. 🆇 ᴀᴇ ◍ 𝘝𝘐𝘚𝘈. ❄
Meals (bar lunch Monday to Saturday) (carving lunch Sunday) a la carte 13.90/24.15 **st.** ♟ 6.25 – ☞ 9.95 – **82 rm** 79.00 **st.** – SB.

🏨 **Beechlawn House,** 4 Dunmurry Lane, BT17 9RR, ℰ (01232) 612974, *Fax (01232) 623601* – 🆃🆅 ☎ 🅿 – 🔬 300. 🆇 ᴀᴇ ◍ 𝘝𝘐𝘚𝘈. ❄
Meals 10.95/13.95 **t.** and a la carte ♟ 4.50 – **34 rm** ☞ 66.00/76.00 **t.** – SB.

🅐 ATS 4 Duncrue St. ℰ (01232) 749531   ATS 37 Boucher Rd ℰ (01232) 663623

BELFAST INTERNATIONAL AIRPORT (Aerphort Béal Feirste) *Antrim* 𝟿𝟸𝟹 N 4 – ✉ *Aldergrove.*
✈ Belfast International Airport, Aldergrove : ℰ (01849) 422888.
Belfast 15 – Ballymena 20 – Larne 23.

🏨 **Aldergrove,** Aldergrove, BT29 4ZY, ℰ (01849) 422033, *Fax (01849) 423500,* 🕭, 🚇s, 🐾 – ▮┃, ✻ rm, 🗏 🆃🆅 ☎ ♿ 🅿 – 🔬 230. 🆇 ᴀᴇ ◍ 𝘝𝘐𝘚𝘈. ❄
Meals 8.95/14.95 **t.** and dinner a la carte ♟ 4.50 – ☞ 7.50 – **108 rm** 75.00 **st.** – SB.

BELLEEK (Béal Leice) *Fermanagh* 𝟿𝟸𝟹 H 4 – *pop. 550.*
Belfast 117 – Londonderry 56.

🏨 **Carlton,** Main St., BT93 3FX, ℰ (013656) 58282, *Fax (013656) 59005* – ✻ rm, 🆃🆅 ☎ – 🔬 200. 🆇 𝘝𝘐𝘚𝘈. ❄
closed 25 December – **Meals** (bar lunch)/dinner a la carte 9.00/14.95 **st.** ♟ 5.00 – **19 rm** ☞ 45.00/70.00 **st.** – SB.

⌂ **Moohan's Fiddlestone** without rest., Main St., BT93 3FY, ℰ (013656) 58008 – 🆃🆅
5 rm.

BUSHMILLS (Muileann na Buaise) *Antrim* 𝟿𝟸𝟹 M 2 *Ireland G.* – *pop. 1 348* – ✉ *Bushmills.*
Exc.: *Causeway Coast*★★ : *Giant's Causeway*★★★ *(Hamilton's Seat* ≤★★*), Carrick-a-rede Rope Bridge*★★★, *Dunluce Castle*★★ *AC, Gortmore Viewpoint*★★ – *Magilligan Strand*★★ *Downhill*★ *(Mussenden Temple*★ *).*
🛇 *Bushfoot, Bushfoot Rd, Portballintrae* ℰ (012657) 31317.
Belfast 57 – Ballycastle 12 – Coleraine 10.

🏨 **Bushmills Inn,** 25 Main St., BT57 8QA, ℰ (012657) 32339, *Fax (012657) 32048* « Part 18C » – 🆃🆅 ☎ 🅿 – 🔬 60. 🆇 𝘝𝘐𝘚𝘈
Meals (carving lunch Sunday) 9.25/15.00 **t.** and a la carte ♟ 5.80 – **30 rm** ☞ 48.00/98.00 **t.** 1 suite – SB.

⌂ **Craig Park** 🐾 without rest., 24 Carnbore Rd, BT57 8YF, SE : 2 ½ m. by B 66 and Ballycastle rd (B 17), off How Rd ℰ (012657) 32496, *Fax (012657) 32479,* ≤, 🐾 – ✻ 🆃🆅 🅿 🆇 𝘝𝘐𝘚𝘈. ❄
closed 1 week Christmas and New Year – **3 rm** ☞ 30.00/50.00 **st.**

CARNLOUGH (Carnlach) *Antrim* 𝟿𝟸𝟹 O 3 – *pop. 1 493.*
Belfast 35 – Ballymena 16 – Larne 14.

🏨 **Londonderry Arms,** 20 Harbour Rd, BT44 0EU, ℰ (01574) 885255, *Fax (01574) 885263* ▮┃ 🆃🆅 ♿ 🅿 – 🔬 120. 🆇 ᴀᴇ ◍ 𝘝𝘐𝘚𝘈. ❄
closed 25 December – **Meals** 12.00/15.00 **t.** and dinner a la carte ♟ 5.25 – **35 rm** ☞ 45.00/75.00 **t.** – SB.

CARRY BRIDGE *Fermanagh* 𝟿𝟸𝟹 J 5 – ✉ *Lisbellaw.*
Belfast 80 – Dundalk 62 – Londonderry 60.

⌂ **Aghnacarra House,** BT94 5HX, ℰ (01365) 387077, 🐾, 🐾 – 🅿. ❄
April-October – **Meals** (by arrangement) 9.00 – **7 rm** ☞ 23.00/36.00 – SB.

CARRYDUFF (Ceathrî Aodha Dhuibh) *Antrim – see Belfast.*

CASTLEROCK (Carraig Ceasail) *Londonderry – see Coleraine.*

CLOGHER (Clochar) *Tyrone* 923 K 4.
Belfast 73 – Londonderry 55.

🏠 **Corick House** 🐾, 20 Corick Rd, BT76 0BZ, NE : 2 ½ m. by A 4 on unclassified rd
℘ (016625) 48216, Fax (016625) 49531, ≤, ⚲, 🐾, park – 📺 ☎ ₺ 🅿. 🐵 🗚 𝗩𝗜𝗦𝗔. ⚘
Meals *(closed Monday)* (dinner only and Sunday lunch)/dinner a la carte 18.00/45.00 **st.**
₺ 4.95 – **10 rm** ⊇ 40.00/70.00 **st.** – SB.

COLERAINE (Cîll Raithin) *Londonderry* 923 L 2 *Ireland G.* – pop. 20 721.
Exc. : *Antrim Glens*★★★ :– *Murlough Bay*★★★ (Fair Head ≤★★★), *Glenariff Forest Park*★★ AC
(Waterfall★★*)* – *Glenariff*★, *Glendun*★, *Rathlin Island*★ – *Causeway Coast*★★ : *Giant's Cause-
way*★★★ (Hamilton's Seat ≤★★) – *Carrick-a-rede Rope Bridge*★★★ – *Dunluce Castle*★★ AC –
Gortmore Viewpoint★★ – *Magilligan Strand*★★ – *Downhill*★ (Mussenden Temple★).
🏌18 , 🏌9 Castlerock, Circular Rd ℘ (01265) 848314 – 🏌9 Brown Trout, 209 Agivey Rd ℘ (01265)
868209.
🚉 Railway Rd, BT52 1PE ℘ (01265) 44723.
Belfast 53 – Ballymena 25 – Londonderry 31 – Omagh 65.

🏠 **Bushtown House,** 283 Drumcroone Rd, BT51 3QT, S : 2 ½ m. on A 29 ℘ (01265) 58367,
Fax (01265) 320909, 🖪, ☎s, 🏊, 🐾 – 📺 ☎ ₺ 🅿 – 🕍 300. 🐵 🗚 𝗩𝗜𝗦𝗔
closed 26 December – Meals 7.50/17.50 **t.** and a la carte ₺ 5.75 – **40 rm** ⊇ 48.00/85.00 **t.** –
SB.

🏠 **Brown Trout Golf and Country Inn,** 209 Agivey Rd, Aghadowey, BT51 4AD, SE : 9 m.
on A 54 ℘ (01265) 868209, Fax (01265) 868878, 🍽, 🖪, 🏌9, ⚲, park – ⁂⁂ rest, 📺 ☎ ₺ 🅿 –
🕍 40. 🐵 🗚 𝗩𝗜𝗦𝗔
Meals (bar lunch Monday to Saturday)/dinner a la carte 14.40/19.50 **t.** ₺ 5.50 – **16 rm**
⊇ 60.00/85.00 **t.** – SB.

🏠 **Greenhill House** 🐾, 24 Greenhill Rd, Aghadowey, BT51 4EU, S : 9 m. by A 29 on B 66
℘ (01265) 868241, Fax (01265) 868365, 🐾, park – ⁂⁂ rest, 📺 ☎ 🅿. 🐵 𝗩𝗜𝗦𝗔. ⚘
March-October – Meals (by arrangement) 16.00 – **6 rm** ⊇ 29.00/48.00 – SB.

at Castlerock NW : 6 m. by A 2 on B 119 – ✉ Castlerock.

🏠 **Maritima House** without rest., 43 Main St., BT51 4RA, ℘ (01265) 848388, ≤, 🐾 – 🅿. ⚘
restricted opening in winter – **3 rm** ⊇ 22.00/39.00.

🔧 ATS Loguestown Ind. Est., Bushmills Rd ℘ (01265) 42329

COOKSTOWN (An Chorr Chráochach) *Tyrone* 923 L 4.
🏌18 Killymoon, 200 Killymoon Rd ℘ (016487) 63762/62254.
🚉 48 Molesworth St. BT80 8TA ℘ (016487) 66727.
Belfast 45 – Ballymena 27 – Londonderry 49.

🏠 **Tullylagan Country House** 🐾, 40B Tullylagan Rd, Sandholes, BT80 8UP, S : 4 m. by
A 29 ℘ (016487) 65100, Fax (016487) 61715, ⚲, 🐾, park – ⁂⁂ rm, 📺 ☎ ₺ 🅿 – 🕍 180.
🐵 𝗩𝗜𝗦𝗔. ⚘
closed 24 to 26 December – Meals (bar lunch Saturday) 15.95/16.95 **t.** and a la carte ₺ 5.95
– **15 rm** ⊇ 45.00/90.00 **t.** – SB.

CRAWFORDSBURN (Sruth Chráfard) *Down* 923 O 4 *Ireland G.* – pop. 572.
Env. : *Heritage Centre, Bangor*★, E : 3 m. by B 20.
Exc. : – *Priory (Cross Slabs*★) – *Mount Stewart*★★★ AC, SE : 12 m. by A 2, A 21 and A 20 –
Scrabo Tower★ (≤ ★★★), SW : 8 m. – *Ballycopeland Windmill*★ AC, E : 13 m. by A 2, A 21 and
B 172 – *Strangford Lough*★ (Castle Espie Centre★ AC - Nendrum Monastery★) – *Grey
Abbey*★ AC, SE : 14 m. by A 2, A 21 and A 20.
Belfast 10 – Bangor 3.

🏠 **Old Inn,** 15 Main St., BT19 1JH, ℘ (01247) 853255, Fax (01247) 852775, 🐾 – 📺 ☎ 🅿 –
🕍 100. 🐵 🗚 ⓸ 𝗩𝗜𝗦𝗔. ⚘
Meals 20.00/25.00 **t.** and a la carte ₺ 5.50 – **33 rm** ⊇ 70.00/150.00 **t.** – SB.

*Halten Sie beim Betreten des Hotels oder des Restaurants
den Führer in der Hand.
Sie zeigen damit, daß Sie aufgrund dieser Empfehlung gekommen sind.*

CRUMLIN (Cromghlinn) Antrim **923** N 4 – pop. 2 697.
Belfast 14 – Ballymena 20.

↑ **Caldhame Lodge,** 102 Moira Rd, Nutts Corner, BT29 4HG, SE : 1 ¼ m. on A 26
  📞 (01849) 423099, Fax (01849) 422378, 🌿 – ⤶ 📺 ☎ ♿ 𝓕. %
  Meals (by arrangement) 15.00 **st.** – **6 rm** ⇌ 25.00/45.00 **st.** – SB.

↑ **Caldhame House,** 104 Moira Rd, Nutts Corner, BT29 4HG, SE : 1 ¼ m. on A 26
  📞 (01849) 422378 – ⤶ 📺 ☎ ɕƀ © 𝓕
  Meals (by arrangement) 20.00 – **3 rm** ⇌ 28.00/40.00 **st.** – SB.

DUNADRY (Dîn Eadradh) Antrim **923** N 3 Ireland G..
Env. : *Antrim (Round tower★, Shane's Castle Railway★ AC) NW : 4 m. by A 6.*
Exc. : *Crumlin : Talnotry Cottage Bird Garden★ AC, SW : 10 ½ m. by A 5, A 26 and A 52.*
Belfast 15 – Larne 18 – Londonderry 56.

🏨 **Dunadry,** 2 Islandreagh Drive, BT41 2HA, *📞 (01849) 432474, Fax (01849) 433389, ł
,* 🖼
  💨, 🎢, park – ⤶ rm, 📺 ☎ ☏ – ♕ 300. ɕƀ Æ © 𝓕. %
  closed 24 to 26 December – **Meals** (buffet lunch Saturday) 9.50/17.95 **st.** and dinner
  a la carte § 4.85 – ⇌ 6.00 – **66 rm** 92.50/115.00 **st.**, 1 suite – SB.

DUNDONALD (Dîn Dénaill) Antrim **923** O 4 – see Belfast.

DUNGANNON (Dîn Geanainn) Tyrone **923** L 4.
Belfast 42 – Ballymena 37 – Dundalk 47 – Londonderry 60.

🏨 **Inn on the Park,** Parkmount, Moy Rd, BT71 6BS, S : ¾ m. on A 29 *📞 (01868) 725151*
  Fax (01868) 724953, 🎢 – 📺 ☎ ☏ – ♕ 120. ƀ Æ © 𝓕
  closed 25 December – **Meals** (bar lunch Saturday) 10.95/18.95 **t.** and dinner a la carte
  § 5.95 – **13 rm** ⇌ 45.00/70.00 **t.** – SB.

🏨 **Cohannon Inn & Auto Lodge,** 212 Ballynakelly Rd, BT71 6HJ, E : 6 ¼ m. by A 29 and M
  on A 45 *📞 (01868) 724488, Fax (01868) 724488 – 📺 ♿ ☏ – ♕ 150. ƀ Æ © 𝓕. %*
  Meals (carving lunch)/dinner a la carte 7.45/18.45 **t.** § 3.50 – ⇌ 3.95 – **50 rm** 31.95/65.00 **t**
  – SB.

↑ **Grange Lodge** ♿, Grange Rd, BT71 7EJ, SE : 3 ½ m. by A 29 *📞 (01868) 784212*
  Fax (01868) 723891, 🎢 – ⤶ 📺 ☎ ☏
  closed 20 December-1 February – **Meals** (by arrangement) 20.00 **t.** § 6.00 – **5 rm** ⇌ 49.00
  69.00 **st.**

  ⓐ ATS 51 Oaks Rd *📞 (01868) 723772*

DUNMURRY (Dún Muirígh) Antrim **923** N 4 – see Belfast.

ENNISKILLEN (Inis Ceithleann) Fermanagh **923** J 4 Ireland G. – pop. 11 436.
Env. : *Castle Coole★★★ AC, SE : 1 m.*
Exc. : *NW : Lough Erne★★ ; Cliffs of Magho Viewpoint★★★ AC – Devenish Island★ AC*
Castle Archdale Country Park★ – White Island★ – Janus Figure★ – Tully Castle★ AC
Florence Court★★ AC, SW : 8 m. by A 4 and A 32 – Marble Arch Caves and Forest Natur
Reserve★★ AC, SW : 10 m. by A 4 and A 32.
ł
 Castlecoole 📞 (01365) 325250.
🖹 *Fermanagh Tourist Information Centre, Wellington Rd, BT74 7EF 📞 (01365) 323110.*
Belfast 87 – Londonderry 59.

🏨 **Killyhevlin,** Killyhevlin, BT74 6RW, SE : 1 ¾ m. on A 4 *📞 (01365) 32348*
  Fax (01365) 324726, ≤, 🎢 – 📺 ☎ ♿ ☏ – ♕ 500. ƀ Æ © 𝓕. %
  closed 25 December – **Meals** (bar lunch Saturday and Bank Holidays) 13.50/19.50 **s**
  and a la carte § 5.50 – **42 rm** ⇌ 60.00/90.00 **st.**, 1 suite – SB.

🏨 **Manor House Country** ♿, Killadeas, BT94 1NY, N : 7 ½ m. by A 32 on B 8
  *📞 (01365 6) 21561, Fax (01365 6) 21545, ≤, ł
, 🏊, 🖼, 🎢 – ⇕ 📺 ☎ ♿ ☏ – ♕ 300. ƀ*
  𝓕. %
  Meals 10.95/19.50 **st.** § 4.95 – **46 rm** ⇌ 55.00/80.00 **st.** – SB.

GILFORD (Áth Mhic Giolla) Down **923** M 4 – pop. 1 639.
Belfast 30 – Dundalk 32.

XX **Yellow Door,** Whinney Hill, BT63 6EP, *📞 (01762) 831543 – ⤶. ƀ Æ 𝓕*
  closed Sunday dinner, Monday, second week July and 25 December – **Meals** 14.95
  (lunch) and dinner a la carte approx. 23.95 § 6.00.

HILLSBOROUGH (Cromghlinn) *Down* 923 N 4 *Ireland G.*

See : *Town★ – Fort★*.

Exc. : – *The Argory★*, *W : 25 m. by A 1 and M 1*.

Belfast 13.

🏨 **White Gables,** 14 Dromore Rd, BT26 6HS, SW : ½ m. ✆ (01846) 682755, *Fax* (01846) 689532 – ✲ rm, ▤ rest, 🆃🆅 ☎ 🅿 – 🔬 120. 🕒 🆎 ⓞ 𝘝𝘐𝘚𝘈. ✜
closed 25 December – **Meals** *(closed Saturday lunch and Sunday)* 16.50/22.00 **t.** and a la carte ⓘ 6.25 – ☲ 9.50 – **31 rm** 76.50/100.00 **t.**

↑ **Fortwilliam** without rest., 210 Ballynahinch Rd, BT26 6BH, SE : 3 ½ m. on B 177 ✆ (01846) 682255, *Fax* (01846) 689608, « Working farm », 🞄, park – ✲ 🆃🆅 🅿. 𝘝𝘐𝘚𝘈. ✜
3 rm ☲ 30.00/50.00.

✗ **Hillside,** 21 Main St., BT26 6AE, ✆ (01846) 682765, *Fax* (01846) 689880 – 🕒 🆎 ⓞ 𝘝𝘐𝘚𝘈
closed Sunday – **Meals** *(dinner only)* a la carte 10.40/23.45 **t.** ⓘ 4.85.

HOLYWOOD (Ard Mhic Nasca) *Down* 923 O 4 *Ireland G.* – pop. 9 252.

Env. : *Cultra : Ulster Folk and Transport Museum★★ AC*, *NE : 1 m. by A 2.*

Belfast 5 – Bangor 6.

🏨 **Culloden,** 142 Bangor Rd, BT18 0EX, E : 1 ½ m. on A 2 ✆ (01232) 425223, *Fax* (01232) 426777, ≼, « Part Victorian Gothic manor », 🞄🞄, 🔲, 🞄, park, ✗, squash – 🛗, ✲ rm, 🆃🆅 ☎ 🅿 – 🔬 500. 🕒 🆎 ⓞ 𝘝𝘐𝘚𝘈. ✜
closed 24 and 25 December – **Mitre :** Meals *(closed Saturday lunch)* 22.50 **t.** (lunch) and a la carte 23.75/28.65 **t.** ⓘ 9.00 – **Cultra Inn :** Meals *(closed Good Friday and 25 December)* (grill rest.) a la carte 13.50/18.50 **t.** – ☲ 13.00 – **79 rm** 127.00/160.00 **t.**, 1 suite – SB.

🏨 **Rayanne House,** 60 Demesne Rd, BT18 9EX, by High St. and Downshire Rd ✆ (01232) 425859, *Fax* (01232) 423364, ≼, 🞄 – ✲ 🆃🆅 🅿. 🕒 🆎 𝘝𝘐𝘚𝘈. ✜
closed 1 week Christmas – **Meals** *(closed Sunday)* (booking essential) (dinner only) a la carte 21.50/28.95 **t.** ⓘ 5.95 – **6 rm** ☲ 75.00/95.00 **st.** – SB.

↑ **Beech Hill** ≶ without rest., 23 Ballymoney Rd, Craigantlet, BT23 4TG, SE : 4 ½ m. by A 2 on Craigantlet rd ✆ (01232) 425892, *Fax* (01232) 425892, 🞄, park – ✲ 🆃🆅 🅿. 🕒 𝘝𝘐𝘚𝘈. ✜
3 rm ☲ 35.00/60.00 **st.**

✗ **Sullivans,** Unit 5, Sullivan Pl., BT18 9JF, ✆ (01232) 421000, *Fax* (01232) 421000 – 🕒 🆎 𝘝𝘐𝘚𝘈
closed Sunday, 12 to 19 July and 25-26 December – **Meals** (restricted lunch) (unlicensed) 10.95/22.95 **t.** and a la carte.

IRVINESTOWN (Baile an Irbhinigh) *Fermanagh* 923 J 4 *Ireland G.* – pop. 1 906.

Exc. : *NW : Lough Erne★★ – Cliffs of Magho Viewpoint★★★ AC – Devenish Island★ AC – Castle Archdale Country Park★ – White Island★ – Janus Figure★ – Tully Castle★ AC.*

Belfast 78 – Dublin 132 – Donegal 27.

🏨 **Mahon's,** 2-10 Mill St., BT94 1GS, ✆ (013656) 21656, *Fax* (013656) 28344 – 🆃🆅 ☎ 🅿. 🕒 🆎 𝘝𝘐𝘚𝘈
closed 25 December – **Meals** 9.50/14.50 **t.** and a la carte ⓘ 4.75 – **18 rm** ☲ 35.00/60.00 – SB.

LARNE (Latharna) *Antrim* 923 O 3 *Ireland G.* – pop. 17 575.

Env. : *Glenoe Waterfall★, S : 5 m. by A 2 and B 99 – SE : Island Magee (Ballylumford Dolmen★).*

Exc. : *NW : Antrim Glens★★★ – Murlough Bay★★★ (Fair Head≼ ★★★), Glenariff Forest Park★★ AC (Waterfall★★), Glenariff★, Glendun★, Rathlin Island★.*

🏌 *Cairndhu, 192 Coast Rd, Ballygally* ✆ (01574) 583248.

⛴ *– to Cairnryan (P & O European Ferries Ltd) 4-6 daily (1 h).*

🅑 *Narrow Gauge Rd, BT40 1XB* ✆ (01574) 260088 – *Carnfunnock Country Park, Coast Road, BT40 2QZ* ✆ (01574) 270541.

Belfast 23 – Ballymena 20.

↑ **Derrin House** without rest., 2 Prince's Gdns., BT40 1RQ, off Glenarm Rd (A 2) ✆ (01574) 273269, *Fax* (01574) 273269 – 🆃🆅 🅿. 🕒 🆎 𝘝𝘐𝘚𝘈
closed 25 and 26 December – **7 rm** ☲ 21.00/36.00 **s.**

🅐 ATS Narrow Gauge Rd ✆ (01574) 274491

Les prix Pour toutes précisions sur les prix indiqués dans ce guide, reportez-vous aux pages de l'introduction.

LIMAVADY **(Léim an Mhadaidh)** *Londonderry* [923] L 2.
Belfast 62 – Ballymena 39 – Coleraine 13 – Londonderry 17 – Omagh 50.

🏨 **Radisson Roe Park H. & Golf Resort** 🌿, Roe Park, BT49 9LB, W : ½ m. on A 2 ☎ (015047) 22212, *Fax (015047) 22313*, Ꮀ, ≘s, [🏊], 🏌18, 🎣, park – [lift] [TV] ☎ ♿ [P] – 🧑‍🏫 440. [MC] [AE] [D] [VISA]. 🚫
Meals (bar lunch)/dinner a la carte 12.50/17.00 **t.** 🍷 4.95 – ***The Courtyard :*** Meals *(closed Sunday in winter)* (dinner only) 23.50 **t.** and a la carte 🍷 6.95 – **63 rm** ☕ 90.00/130.00 **t.** 1 suite – SB.

LONDONDERRY **(Doire)** *Londonderry* [923] K 2-3 *Ireland G. – pop. 72 334.*
See : *Town★ – City Walls and Gates★★ – Guildhall★ – St. Columb's Cathedral★ AC – Long Tower Church★ – Tower Museum★.*
Env. : *Grianan of Aileach★★ (≤ ★) (Republic of Ireland) NW : 5 m. by A 2 and N 13.*
Exc. : *SE : by A 6 – Sperrin Mountains★ : Ulster-American Folk Park★★ – Glenshane Pass★★ (✳★★) – Sawel Mountain Drive★ (≤★★) – Roe Valley Country Park★ – Ness Wood Country Park★ – Sperrin Heritage Centre★ AC – Beaghmore Stone Circles★ – Ulster History Park★ – Oak Lough Scenic Road★ – Eglinton★ – Gortin Glen Forest Park★ AC.*
🏌18, 🏌9 *City of Derry, 49 Victoria Rd ☎ (01504) 311610/46369.*
✈ *Eglinton Airport : ☎ (01504) 810784, E : 6 m. by A 2.*
[i] *8 Bishop St., BT48 6PW ☎ (01504) 267284.*
Belfast 70 – Dublin 146.

🏨 **Everglades,** Prehen Rd, BT47 2PA, S : 1 ½ m. on A 5 ☎ (01504) 346722 *Fax (01504) 349200* – [lift], ▤ rest, [TV] ☎ [P] – 🧑‍🏫 400. [MC] [AE] [D] [VISA]. 🚫
closed 25 December – ***The Satchmo :*** **Meals** (buffet lunch)/dinner 19.50 **st.** and a la carte 🍷 10.50 – **63 rm** ☕ 75.00/95.00 **st.**, 1 suite – SB.

🏨 **Waterfoot H. & Country Club,** 14 Clooney Rd, Caw Roundabout, BT47 1TB, NE : 3 ¾ m. at junction of A 39 with A 5 and A 2 ☎ (01504) 345500, *Fax (01504) 311006*, Ꮀ, ≘s, [🏊] – [TV] ☎ ♿ [P] – 🧑‍🏫 100. [MC] [AE] [D] [VISA]. 🚫
closed 25 and 26 December – **Meals** a la carte 13.35/20.15 **st.** 🍷 4.95 – ☕ 6.00 – **48 rm** 60.00/70.00 **st.** – SB.

🏨 **Trinity,** 22-24 Strand Rd, BT48 7AB, ☎ (01504) 271271, *Fax (01504) 271277* – [lift], ▤ rest [TV] ☎ ♿ [P] – 🧑‍🏫 55. [MC] [AE] [VISA]. 🚫
Meals (bar lunch)/dinner 14.95 **t.** and a la carte 🍷 5.95 – **37 rm** ☕ 75.00/90.00 **t.**, 3 suites SB.

🏨 **Beech Hill House** 🌿, 32 Ardmore Rd, BT47 3QP, SE : 3 ½ m. by A 6 ☎ (01504) 349279 *Fax (01504) 345366*, « 18C merchant's house », 🎣, 🌳, park, 🎾 – 🚭 rest, [TV] ☎ [P] 🧑‍🏫 100. [MC] [AE] [VISA] [JCB]. 🚫
closed 24 and 25 December – **Meals** 15.95/22.95 **t.** and a la carte 🍷 6.00 – **17 rm** ☕ 67.50/130.00 **t.** – SB.

🏨 **White Horse,** 68 Clooney Rd, BT47 3PA, NE : 6 ½ m. on A 2 (Coleraine rd) ☎ (01504) 860606, *Fax (01504) 860371* – [TV] ☎ [P] – 🧑‍🏫 500. [MC] [AE] [D] [VISA]. 🚫
Meals (grill rest.) a la carte 8.50/14.25 **st.** – ☕ 5.50 – **43 rm** 50.00/60.00 **st.** – SB.

MAGHERA **(Machaire Rátha)** *Londonderry* [923] L 3.
Belfast 40 – Ballymena 19 – Coleraine 21 – Londonderry 32.

🏨 **Ardtara Country House** 🌿, 8 Gorteade Rd, Upperlands, BT46 5SA, N : 3 ¼ m. by A 29 off B 75 ☎ (01648) 44490, *Fax (01648) 45080*, ≤, « 19C », 🌳, 🎾 – 🚭 rest, [TV] ☎ [P]. [MC] [AE] [VISA]. 🚫
closed 25 and 26 December – **Meals** *(closed Saturday lunch)* (booking essential) 12.95/25.00 **t.** and dinner a la carte 🍷 11.00 – **8 rm** ☕ 80.00/140.00 **st.** – SB.

MARTINSTOWN **(Baile Uí Mháirtán)** *Antrim* [923] N 3 – ✉ *Ballymena.*
Belfast 36 – Dundalk 86 – Larne 28 – Londonderry 58 – Omagh 61.

🏠 **Caireal Manor** without rest., 90 Glenravel Rd, Glen's of Antrim, BT43 6QQ ☎ (012667) 58465, *Fax (012667) 58465* – [TV] ♿ [P]. [MC] [AE] [D] [VISA]. 🚫
5 rm ☕ 25.00/50.00 **t.** – SB.

Particularly pleasant hotels and restaurants are shown in the Guide by a **red symbol**.
Please send us the names of anywhere you have enjoyed your stay.
Your **Michelin Guide** will be even better.

🏨🏨🏨🏨🏨 ... 🏠

🍴🍴🍴🍴🍴 ... 🍴

NEWCASTLE (An Caisleán Nua) *Down* 923 O 5 *Ireland G. – pop. 7 214.*
Env. : *Castlewellan Forest Park★★ AC, NW : 4 m. by A 50 – Dundrum Castle★ AC, NE : 4 m. by A 2.*
Exc. : *SW : Mourne Mountains★★ : Bryansford, Tollymore Forest Park★★ AC – Annalong Marine Park and Cornmill★ AC – Silent Valley Reservoir★ (≼★) – Spelga Pass and Dam★ – Drumena Cashel and Souterrain★ – Kilbroney Forest Park (viewpoint★) – Loughinisland Churches★, NE : 10 m. by A 2 and A 24.*
🖫 *The Newcastle Centre, 10-14 Central Promenade, BT30 6LZ ℰ (013967) 22222.*
Belfast 30 – Londonderry 101.

🏨 **Burrendale H. & Country Club,** 51 Castlewellan Rd, BT33 0JY, N : 1 m. on A 50 ℰ (013967) 22599, Fax (013967) 22328, 🏌, ≊, 🔲, ☞ – ⫯, 🍴 rest, 🔟 ☎ ⅙ 🄿 – 🔏 150. 🐠 🖭 ⑩ 𝑽𝑰𝑺𝑨. ⅍
Meals 19.00 t. (dinner) and a la carte 20.00/25.00 t. ⅙ 6.95 – **67 rm** ⫘ 55.00/100.00 t., 1 suite – SB.

🏠 **Briers** ⅍, 39 Middle Tollymore Rd, BT33 0JJ, N : 1 ½ m. by Bryansford Rd (B 180) and Tollymore Rd ℰ (013967) 24347, Fax (013967) 24347, ≼, ☞ – ⅏ rm, 🔟 ☎ ⅙ 🄿. 🐠 🖭 𝑽𝑰𝑺𝑨. ⅍
Meals a la carte 9.25/18.00 st. – **9 rm** ⫘ 35.00/50.00 st. – SB.

NEWRY (An tIúr) *Down* 923 M 5 – *pop. 22 975.*
Belfast 37 – Dundalk 16.

🏨 **Mourne Country,** 52 Belfast Rd, BT34 1TR, N : 1 ¼ m. ℰ (01693) 67922, Fax (01693) 60896 – 🔟 ☎ 🄿 – 🔏 400. 🐠 🖭 ⑩ 𝑽𝑰𝑺𝑨. ⅍
closed 25 December – Meals (bar lunch Monday to Saturday)/dinner a la carte 12.35/ 23.15 st. ⅙ 4.95 – **41 rm** ⫘ 49.50/65.00 t., 2 suites – SB.

PORTAFERRY (Port an Pheire) *Down* 923 P 4 *Ireland G. – pop. 2 324.*
See : *Aquarium★.*
Env. : *Castle Ward★★ AC, SW : 4 m. by boat and A 25.*
Exc. : *SE : Lecale Peninsula★★ – Struell Wells★, Quoile Pondage★, Ardglass★, Strangford★, Audley's Castle★.*
🖫 *Shore St., Nr Strangford Ferry Departure Point (summer only).*
Belfast 29 – Bangor 24.

🏨 **Portaferry,** 10 The Strand, BT22 1PE, ℰ (012477) 28231, Fax (012477) 28999, ≼, « Part 18C, loughside setting » – 🔟 ☎. 🐠 🖭 ⑩ 𝑽𝑰𝑺𝑨. ⅍
closed 24 and 25 December – Meals (bar lunch Monday to Saturday)/dinner 22.50 t. ⅙ 5.85 – **13 rm** ⫘ 55.00/90.00 t. – SB.

PORT BALLINTRAE (Port Bhaile an Trá) *Antrim* 923 M 2 *Ireland G. – pop. 756 –* ⊠ *Bushmills.*
Exc. : *Causeway Coast★★ : Giant's Causeway★★★ (Hamilton's Seat ≼★★) – Carrick-a-rede Rope Bridge★★★ – Dunluce Castle★★ AC – Gortmore Viewpoint★★ – Magilligan Strand★★ – Downhill★ (Mussenden Temple★).*
Belfast 68 – Coleraine 15.

🏠 **Bayview,** 2 Bayhead Rd, BT57 8RZ, ℰ (012657) 31453, Fax (012657) 32360, ≼, ≊, 🔲 – 🔟 ☎ 🄿 – 🔏 200. 🐠 𝑽𝑰𝑺𝑨
Meals a la carte 13.00/22.00 st. ⅙ 5.00 – **16 rm** ⫘ 45.00/75.00 st. – SB.

PORTRUSH (Port Rois) *Antrim* 923 L 2 *Ireland G. – pop. 5 703.*
Exc. : *Causeway Coast★★ : Giant's Causeway★★★ (Hamilton's Seat ≼★★) – Carrick-a-rede Rope Bridge★★★ – Dunluce Castle★★ AC – Gortmore Viewpoint★★ – Magilligan Strand★★ – Downhill★ (Mussenden Temple★).*
🖪₈, 🖪₈, 🖪 *Royal Portrush, Dunluce Rd ℰ (01265) 822311.*
🖫 *Dunluce Centre, Sandhill Dr., BT56 8BT ℰ (01265) 823333 (summer only).*
Belfast 58 – Coleraine 4 – Londonderry 35.

🏨 **Magherabuoy House,** 41 Magheraboy Rd, BT56 8NX, SW : 1 m. by A 29 ℰ (01265) 823507, Fax (01265) 824687, ≼, ≊, ☞ – ⅏ rest, 🔟 ☎ 🄿 – 🔏 400. 🐠 🖭 ⑩ 𝑽𝑰𝑺𝑨. ⅍
closed 25 December – Meals (bar lunch)/dinner a la carte 8.50/15.00 t. – **38 rm** ⫘ 60.00/ 100.00 t. – SB.

🏨 **O'Neill's Causeway Coast,** 36 Ballyreagh Rd, BT56 8LR, NW : 1 ¼ m. on A 2 (Portstewart rd) ℰ (01265) 822435, Fax (01265) 824495, ≼ – 🔟 ☎ 🄿 – 🔏 500. 🐠 🖭 𝑽𝑰𝑺𝑨. ⅍
Meals (bar lunch)/dinner 14.00 st. and a la carte ⅙ 5.95 – **21 rm** ⫘ 53.00/95.00 st. – SB.

PORTRUSH

XX Ramore, The Harbour, BT56 8BN, 𝒫 (01265) 824313, Fax (01265) 823194, ≤ – 🗐 🅿. 🆎
🅰 VISA
closed Sunday, Monday, 24 to 26 December and 1 January – Meals (booking essential)
(dinner only) a la carte 16.25/28.40 t. ≬ 5.50.

PORTSTEWART (Port Stíobhaird) Londonderry 📖 L 2 Ireland G. – pop. 6 459.
Exc. : Causeway Coast★★ : Giant's Causeway★★★ (Hamilton's Seat ≤★★) – Carrick-a-rede
Rope Bridge★★★ – Dunluce Castle★★ AC – Gortmore Viewpoint★★ – Magilligan Strand★★ –
Downhill★ (Mussenden Temple★).
🛈 Town Hall, The Crescent, BT55 7AB 𝒫 (01265) 832286 (summer only).
Belfast 67 – Coleraine 6.

🏢 Edgewater, 88 Strand Rd, BT55 7LZ, 𝒫 (01265) 833314, Fax (01265) 832224, ≤, ₤₅, �. –
📺 ☎ 🅿 – 🔬 150. 🆎 🅰 🅾 VISA. 🛠
Meals 9.50/16.00 t. and dinner a la carte ≬ 4.45 – 31 rm �]= 40.00/90.00 t. – SB.

SEAFORDE (Baile Forda) Down 📖 O 5 – pop. 186 – ✉ Downpatrick.
Belfast 25 – Dundalk 45 – Dungannon 53.

⌂ Drumgooland House ⊗ without rest., 29 Dunnanew Rd, BT30 8PJ, N : 2 m. by A 24
𝒫 (01396) 811956, Fax (01396) 811265, ≤, 🦢, 🌳, park – 📺 🅿. 🆎 VISA. 🛠
3 rm ☐ 24.50/39.00 st.

STRABANE (An Srath Bán) Tyrone 📖 J 3 Ireland G. – pop. 11 981.
Exc. : Sperrin Mountains★ : Ulster-American Folk Park★★ – Glenshane Pass★★ (⛰★★) –
Sawel Mountain Drive★ (≤★★) – Roe Valley Country Park★ – Ness Wood Country Park★ –
Sperrin Heritage Centre★ AC – E : Beaghmore Stone Circles★ – Ulster History Park★ –
Oak Lough Scenic Road★ – Eglinton★ – Gortin Glen Forest Park★ AC.
🆙 Ballycolman 𝒫 (01504) 382271/382007.
🛈 Abercorn Square, BT82 8DY 𝒫 (01504) 883735 (summer only) – Council Offices
47 Derry Rd, BT82 8DY 𝒫 (01504) 382204.
Belfast 87 – Donegal 34 – Dundalk 98 – Londonderry 14.

🏨 Fir Trees, Melmount Rd, BT82 9JT, S : 1 ¼ m. on A 5 𝒫 (01504) 382382
Fax (01504) 383116 – 📺 ☎ 🅿. 🆎 🅰 🅾 VISA. 🛠
closed 25 December – Meals (bar lunch Monday to Saturday)/dinner 12.95 st. and a la carte
≬ 3.50 – 26 rm ☐ 35.00/55.00 st. – SB.

TEMPLEPATRICK (Teampall Phádraig) Antrim 📖 N 3 – pop. 1 414 – ✉ Ballyclare.
Belfast 12 – Ballymena 16 – Dundalk 65 – Larne 16.

🏨 Templeton, 882 Antrim Rd, BT39 0AH, 𝒫 (01849) 432984, Fax (01849) 433406, 🌳 – 📺
☎ 🅿 – 🔬 300. 🆎 🅰 🅾 VISA
closed 25 and 26 December – **Templeton :** Meals (closed Saturday lunch and Bank Holidays) 10.50/17.95 t. and dinner a la carte ≬ 6.05 – **Upton Grill :** Meals (grill rest.) a la carte
6.65/17.40 t. ≬ 6.05 – 24 rm ☐ 85.00/125.00 st. – SB.

Republic of Ireland

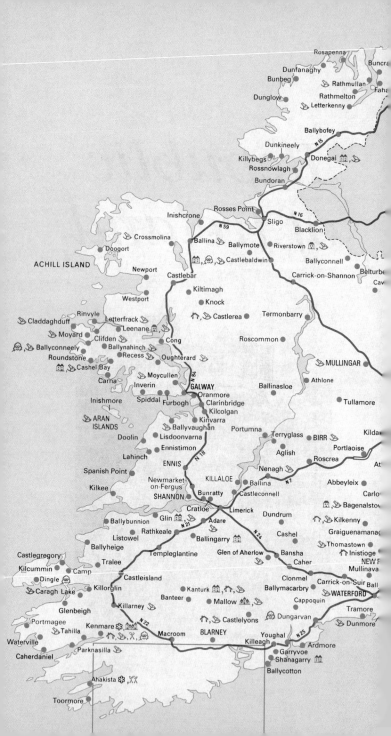

Place with at least

a hotel or restaurant • Adare
a pleasant hotel or restaurant 🏨, ↑, ✗
a quiet, secluded hotel ⊗
a restaurant with ✿, ✿✿, ✿✿✿, 🍴 **Meals**
*See this town for establishments
  located in its vicinity* **DUBLIN**

Localité offrant au moins

une ressource hôtelière • Adare
un hôtel ou restaurant agréable 🏨, ↑, ✗
un hôtel très tranquille, isolé ⊗
une bonne table à ✿, ✿✿, ✿✿✿, 🍴 **Meals**
*Localité groupant dans le texte
  les ressources de ses environs* **DUBLIN**

La località possiede come minimo

una risorsa alberghiera • Adare
Albergo o ristorante ameno 🏨, ↑, ✗
un albergo molto tranquillo, isolato ⊗
un'ottima tavola con ✿, ✿✿, ✿✿✿, 🍴 **Meals**
*La località raggruppa nel suo testo
  le risorse dei dintorni* **DUBLIN**

Ort mit mindestens

einem Hotel oder Restaurant • Adare
ein angenehmes Hotel oder Restaurant 🏨, ↑, ✗
einem sehr ruhigen und abgelegenen Hotel ⊗
einem Restaurant mit ✿, ✿✿, ✿✿✿, 🍴 **Meals**
*Ort mit Angaben über Hotels und Restaurants
  in der Umgebung* **DUBLIN**

● *Prices quoted in this section of the guide are in Irish pounds (punt)*

● *Dans cette partie du guide, les prix sont indiqués en monnaie irlandaise «Punt»*

● *In questa parte della guida, i prezzi sono indicati in livres irlandesi «Punt»*

● *In diesem Teil des Führers sind die Preise in irländischer Währung «Punt» angegeben*

ABBEYLEIX (Mainistir Laoise) *Laois* 923 J 9 – pop. 1 299.
Dublin 60 – Kilkenny 22 – Limerick 67.

🏛 **Hibernian**, Pembroke Terr., ℘ (0502) 31252, Fax (0502) 31888 – 📺 ☎. 🐵③ ① 🚾. ⅜
closed 25 and 26 December – **Meals** 7.00/10.00 st. and dinner a la carte – **10 rm** ⌷ 25.00/50.00 st. – SB.

↑ **Preston House**, Main St., ℘ (0502) 31432, Fax (0502) 31662, ✿ – ⅜, 📺 ☎ 🅿. 🐵③ 🚾
Meals – (see *Preston House Cafe* below) – ⌷ 5.00 – **4 rm** 30.00/50.00.

✗ **Preston House Cafe** (at Preston House H.), Main St., ℘ (0502) 31432, Fax (0502) 31662
✿ – 🅿. 🐵③ 🚾
closed Sunday dinner, Monday and 1 week Christmas – **Meals** a la carte 9.00/18.50 ₰ 2.60.

ACHILL ISLAND (Acaill) *Mayo* 923 B 5/6 *Ireland G.*
See : Island★.
🚹 Achill Sound ℘ (098) 45384 (1 July-31 August).

Doogort (Dumha Goirt) – ✉ Achill Island.
🏌 Keel ℘ (098) 43456.

↑ **Gray's** ⤫, ℘ (098) 43244, ✿ – ⅜ rest, 📺 🅿
closed 25 December – **Meals** (by arrangement) 17.00 t. – **15 rm** ⌷ 25.00/50.00 t.

ADARE (Áth Dara) *Limerick* 923 F 10 *Ireland G.* – pop. 1 042.
See : Town★ – Adare Friary★.
Exc. : Rathkeale (Castle Matrix★ AC) W : 7 ½ m. by N 21 – Newcastle West★, W : 16 m. by N 21 – Glin Castle★ AC, W : 29 m. by N 21, R 518 and N 69.
🚹 ℘ (061) 396255 (1 June-30 October).
Dublin 131 – Killarney 59 – Limerick 10.

🏨 **Adare Manor** ⤫, ℘ (061) 396566, Fax (061) 396124, ≼, « 19C Gothic mansion in extensive parkland », ₤ᵟ, ≘ₛ, 🛆, ⌷ₛ, ◪, ✿ – ⋕ 📺 ☎ 🅿 – 🕹 180. 🐵③ ① 🚾. ⅜
Meals 32.50 t. (dinner) and a la carte 19.50/45.00 t. ₰ 13.30 – ⌷ 12.10 – **64 rm** 240.00/335.00 st. – SB.

🏨 **Dunraven Arms**, Main St., ℘ (061) 396633, Fax (061) 396541, ₤ᵟ, 🛆, ✿ – ⋕ 📺 ☎ 🅿 –
🕹 400. 🐵③ 🅰🅴 ① 🚾. ⅜
Meals – (see *Maigue* below) – ⌷ 9.95 – **76 rm** 85.00/160.00 t. – SB.

🏨 **Woodlands House**, Knockanes, SE : 2 m. by N 21 on Croom rd ℘ (061) 396118,
Fax (061) 396073, ✿ – 📺 ☎ 🅿 – 🕹 350. 🐵③ 🅰🅴 ① 🚾
closed 24 and 25 December – **Meals** a la carte 8.00/16.15 st. ₰ 7.50 – **57 rm** ⌷ 50.00/120.00 st. – SB.

↑ **Foxhollow House** without rest., Knockanes, SE : 2 ¼ m. by N 21 on Croom rd
℘ (061) 396776, Fax (061) 396776, ✿ – ⅜ 📺 🅿. 🐵③ 🚾. ⅜
4 rm ⌷ 25.00/40.00 t.

↑ **Adare Lodge** without rest., Kildimo Rd, ℘ (061) 396629, Fax (061) 395060 – ⅜ 📺 🅿
🐵③ 🚾. ⅜
6 rm ⌷ 30.00/45.00 st.

↑ **Carrabawn Guesthouse** without rest., Killarney Rd, SW : ½ m. on N 21
℘ (061) 396067, Fax (061) 396925, ✿ – ⅜ 📺 ☎ 🅿. 🐵③ 🚾
closed 24 to 26 December – **8 rm** ⌷ 37.00/50.00 st.

↑ **Village House** without rest., Main St., ℘ (061) 396554, Fax (061) 396903 – ⅜ 🅿. 🐵
🚾. ⅜
restricted opening in winter – **6 rm** ⌷ 18.00/40.00.

⌂ **Sandfield House** without rest., Castleroberts, SE : 3 ¼ m. by N 21 on Croom rd ☎ (061) 396119, *Fax (061) 396119*, 🌳 – [P]. [MC] [VISA]. ✗
28 February-30 November – **4 rm** 24.00/44.00.

⌂ **Abbey Villa** without rest., Kildimo Rd, ☎ (061) 396113, *Fax (061) 396969* – [TV] [P]. [MC] [VISA]. ✗
closed 24 to 26 December – **6 rm** 25.00/40.00 **st.**

🍴🍴 **Maigue** (at Dunraven Arms H.), Main St., ☎ (061) 396633, *Fax (061) 396541*, 🌳 – [P]. [MC] [AE] [D] [VISA]
Meals (dinner only and Sunday lunch)/dinner 22.95 **t.**

🍴🍴 **The Wild Geese,** Main St., ☎ (061) 396451, *Fax (061) 396451* – [MC] [AE] [D] [VISA]
closed Sunday, Monday, 25 December and 4 to 27 January – **Meals** (light lunch May-September) a la carte 12.40/29.95 **t.** 🍷 8.00.

AGLISH (An Eaglais) *Tipperary* [923] H 8 – ✉ *Borrisokane.*
Dublin 114 – Galway 53 – Limerick 43.

⌂ **Ballycormac House** 🐦, ☎ (067) 21129, *Fax (067) 21200*, 🎣, 🌳, park – ✗ [P]. [MC] [VISA]. ✗
Meals (by arrangement) (communal dining) 24.00 **t.** 🍷 10.00 – **4 rm** 35.00/70.00 **t.**, 1 suite.

AHAKISTA (Áth an Chiste) *Cork* [923] D 13 – ✉ *Bantry.*
Dublin 217 – Cork 63 – Killarney 59.

🍴🍴 **Shiro** (Kei Pilz), ☎ (027) 67030, *Fax (027) 67206*, ≤ Dunmanus Bay, 🌳 – [P]. [MC] [AE] [D] [VISA]
✿ **Meals** - Japanese - (booking essential) (dinner only) 43.00 **st.**
Spec. Sashimi. Tempura. Sushi.

ARAN ISLANDS (Oileáin Árann) *Galway* [923] CD 8 *Ireland G.*
See : *Islands★ – Inishmore (Dun Aenghus★★★).*
Access by boat or aeroplane from Galway city or by boat from Kilkieran, Rossaneel or Fisherstreet (Clare) and by aeroplane from Inverin.
[i] ☎ *(099) 61263 (30 May-15 September).*

Inishmore – ✉ *Aran Islands.*

⌂ **Ard Einne** 🐦, Killeany, ☎ (099) 61126, *Fax (099) 61388*, ≤ Killeany Bay – [P]. [MC] [AE] [VISA]. ✗
March-6 November – **Meals** (by arrangement) 13.00 **t.** 🍷 12.00 – **12 rm** 25.00/36.00 **t.**

⌂ **Kilmurvy House** 🐦, Kilmurvy, ☎ (099) 61218, *Fax (099) 61397*, ≤, park – ☎. [MC] [VISA]
April-October – **Meals** (by arrangement) 13.50 **t.** 🍷 7.50 – **12 rm** 25.00/40.00 **t.**

ARDMORE (Aird Mhór) *Waterford* [923] I 12 *Ireland G. – pop. 436.*
See : *Town★ – Round Tower★ – Church★ (arcade★).*
Env. : *Whiting Bay★, W : 2 m. by the coast road.*
[i] *Ardmore Tourist Office* ☎ *(024) 94444 (mid May-mid September).*
Dublin 133 – Cork 57 – Waterford 45.

🏠 **Cliff House,** ☎ (024) 94106, *Fax (024) 94496*, ≤, 🌳 – ☎ [P]. [MC] [AE] [D] [VISA]. ✗
March-October – **Meals** 9.95/19.50 **t.** and a la carte 🍷 6.50 – **13 rm** 50.00/80.00 **t.** – SB.

ATHLONE (Baile Átha Luain) *Westmeath* [923] I 7 *Ireland G. – pop. 7 691.*
Exc. : *Clonmacnois★★★ (Grave Slabs★, Cross of the Scriptures★) S : 13 m. by N 6 and N 62 – N : Lough Ree (Ballykeeran Viewpoint★★, Glassan★) – Clonfinlough Stone★, S : 11 ½ m. by N 6 and N 62.*
⛳18 *Hodson Bay* ☎ *(0902) 92073/92235.*
[i] *Tourist Office, The Castle* ☎ *(0902) 94630/92856 (May-mid October).*
Dublin 75 – Galway 57 – Limerick 75 – Roscommon 20 – Tullamore 24.

🏨 **Hodson Bay,** NW : 4 ¾ m. by N 61 ☎ (0902) 92444, *Fax (0902) 92688*, ≤, 🏋, ♨, 🏊, ⛳18, 🎣, 🌳, 🍴 – [lift] [TV] ☎ ♿ [P] – 🎤 750. [MC] [AE] [D] [VISA]. ✗
L'Escale : **Meals** 12.00/22.00 **st.** and dinner a la carte 🍷 6.00 – **95 rm** 102.00/119.00 **st.**, 2 suites – SB.

⌂ **Riverview House,** Summerhill, Galway Rd, W : 3 m. by N 61, R 362, on N 6 ☎ (0902) 94532 – [TV] [P]
closed 14 December-1 February – **Meals** (by arrangement) 13.00 **st.** – **5 rm** 20.00/32.00 **st.** – SB.

🏠 **Shelmalier House,** Retreat Rd, Cartrontroy, E : ½ m. by Dublin rd (N 6) ☎ (0902) 72245, *Fax (0902) 73190,* 🌳 – [TV] 📞 [P]. [MC] VISA. 🐕
closed Christmas – **Meals** (by arrangement) 15.00 **st.** – **7 rm** ⊒ 23.50/34.00 **st.** – SB.

🏠 **The Mill,** Tuam Rd, NW : 3 ½ m. by Roscommon rd on R 362 ☎ (0902) 92927 – [TV] [P]. 🐕
closed 22 December-7 January – **Meals** (by arrangement) 15.00 – **6 rm** ⊒ 20.00/34.00 **st.** – SB.

🍴🍴 **Wineport,** NE : 4 ¼ m. by N 55 ☎ (0902) 85466, *Fax (0902) 85471,* « Loughside setting < Lough Ree » – ⚓ [P]. [MC] [AE] VISA
closed Good Friday, 25-26 December and 1 January – **Meals** (dinner only and Sunday lunch)/dinner a la carte 16.45/28.95 **t.** 🌡 5.95.

🍴 **Left Bank Bistro,** Bastion St., ☎ (0902) 94446, *Fax (0902) 94446,* ⛱ – [MC] VISA
closed Sunday, 1 week Christmas and Bank Holiday Mondays except August – **Meals** (light lunch)/dinner a la carte 12.85/20.85 **t.** 🌡 5.00.

ATHY (Baile Átha Á) *Kildare* [923] L 9 – *pop. 5 306.*

Dublin 40 – Kilkenny 29 – Wexford 59.

🏨 **Tonlegee House** 🔕, SW : 2 ¼ m. by N 78 ☎ (0507) 31473, *Fax (0507) 31473,* 🌳 – [TV] 📞 [P]. [MC] [AE] VISA
closed first 2 weeks November and 24 to 27 December – **Meals** – (see below) – **9 rm** ⊒ 45.00/65.00 **st.** – SB.

🍴🍴 **Tonlegee House** (at Tonlegee House H.),, SW : 2 ¼ m. by N 78 ☎ (0507) 31473, *Fax (0507) 31473,* 🌳 – [P]. [MC] [AE] VISA
closed Sunday and Monday to non-residents, first 2 weeks November and 24 to 27 December – **Meals** (dinner only) 20.00 **st.** 🌡 5.50.

AUGHRIM (Eachroim) *Wicklow* [923] N 9 – *pop. 745.*

[i] ☎ *(0905) 73939 (2 April-9 October).*
Dublin 46 – Waterford 77 – Wexford 60.

🏨 **Lawless's,** ☎ (0402) 36146, *Fax (0402) 36384,* 🎣 – [TV] 📞 [P]. [MC] [AE] [D] VISA. 🐕
closed 24 to 26 December – **Meals** (bar lunch Monday to Saturday)/dinner a la carte 9.50/22.75 **t.** 🌡 5.45 – **15 rm** ⊒ 59.50/81.00 **t.** – SB.

AVOCA (Abhóca) *Wicklow* [923] N 9 – *pop. 490.*

Dublin 47 – Waterford 72 – Wexford 55.

🏠 **Keppel's Farmhouse** 🔕, Ballanagh, S : 2 m. by unmarked road ☎ (0402) 35168, <, « Working farm », 🌳, park – 🚭. [MC] VISA. 🐕
April-14 October – **Meals** (by arrangement) 15.00 **st.** – **5 rm** ⊒ 28.00/40.00 **st.** – SB.

BAGENALSTOWN (Muine Bheag) *Carlow* [923] L 9 – *pop. 2 553.*

Dublin 63 – Carlow 10 – Kilkenny 13 – Wexford 37.

🏨 **Kilgraney Country House** 🔕, S : 4 m. by R 705 ☎ (0503) 75283, *Fax (0503) 75595,* < « Late Georgian house with collection of Far Eastern furnishings and artefacts », 🌳 – 🚭 rm, [P]. [MC] VISA. 🐕
March-November – **Meals** *(closed Sunday to Thursday, except June-August)* (booking essential) (residents only) (communal dining) (dinner only) 24.00 **st.** 🌡 7.50 – **5 rm** ⊒ 27.50/75.00 **st.** – SB.

BALLINA (Béal an Átha) *Mayo* [923] E 5 *Ireland G.* – *pop. 6 852.*

Env. : *Rosserk Abbey*★, *N : 4 m. by R 314.*
Exc. : *Moyne Abbey*★, *N : 7 m. by R 314 – Downpatrick Head*★, *N : 20 m. by R 314.*
⛳18 *Mossgrove, Shanaghy* ☎ *(096) 21050.*
[i] ☎ *(096) 70848 (3 May-30 September).*
Dublin 150 – Galway 73 – Roscommon 64 – Sligo 37.

🏨 **Mount Falcon Castle** 🔕, Foxford Rd, S : 4 m. on N 26 ☎ (096) 70811, *Fax (096) 71517* <, 🎣, park, 🎾 – 📞 [P]. [MC] [AE] [D] VISA
closed February, March and 1 week Christmas – **Meals** (by arrangement) (communal dining) (dinner only) 25.00 **t.** 🌡 6.00 – **10 rm** ⊒ 60.00/120.00 **t.**

🏠 **Brigown** without rest., Quay Rd, NE : 1 ¾ m. by N 59 on Enniscrone rd (R 297) ☎ (096) 22609, *Fax (096) 71247,* 🌳 – [TV] [P]
4 rm ⊒ 18.00/34.00.

BALLINA (Béal an Átha) Tipperary 🔡🔡🔡 G 9 – *pop. 598.*
Dublin 107 – Galway 62 – Limerick 16 – Tullamore 58.

🏛 **Waterman's Lodge**, 🖉 (061) 376333, Fax (061) 376333, 🌊 – ⅙⅙ rm, ☎ 🅿. 🐧🔵 VISA. 🛠
closed 20 December-10 March – **Meals** *(closed Sunday and Monday)* (booking essential to non-residents) (dinner only) 26.50 **s.** ⋀ 12.95 – **10 rm** 🖙 83.00/116.50 **st.** – SB.

BALLINADEE (Baile na Daibhche) Cork 🔡🔡🔡 G 12 – ✉ Bandon.
Dublin 174 – Cork 20.

⌂ **Glebe Country House** 🐪, 🖉 (021) 778294, Fax (021) 778456, « Georgian rectory »,
🌊 – ☎ 🅿. 🐧🔵 ① VISA
Meals (by arrangement) (communal dining) 16.50 **st.** – **4 rm** 🖙 30.00/55.00 **st.** – SB.

BALLINASLOE (Béal Átha na Sluaighe) Galway 🔡🔡🔡 H 8 *Ireland G.* – *pop. 5 634.*
Exc. : *Turoe Stone, Bullaun★, SW : 18 m. by R 348 and R 350.*
🏌 *Rossgloss* 🖉 (0905) 42126 – 🏌 *Mountbellew* 🖉 (0905) 79259.
🅱 *Main St.* 🖉 (0905) 42131 (1 July-31 August).
Dublin 91 – Galway 41 – Limerick 66 – Roscommon 36 – Tullamore 34.

🏨 **Haydens**, Dunlo St., 🖉 (0905) 42347, Fax (0905) 42895, 🌊 – ⎸🛗⎸, 🔳 rest, 📺 ☎ 🅿 –
🔬 250. 🐧🔵 AE ① VISA. 🛠
closed 24 to 27 December – **Meals** 11.00/14.00 **t.** and dinner a la carte ⋀ 5.25 – 🖙 6.00 –
48 rm 32.00/66.00 **t.** – SB.

Le Grand Londres (GREATER LONDON) est composé de la City
et de 32 arrondissements administratifs (Borough)
eux-mêmes divisés en quartiers ou en villages
ayant conservé leur caractère propre (Area).

BALLINCLASHET Cork 🔡🔡🔡 G 12 – *see Kinsale.*

BALLINGARRY (Baile an GharraÁ) Limerick 🔡🔡🔡 F 10 – *pop. 389.*
Dublin 141 – Killarney 56 – Limerick 18.

🏨 **Mustard Seed at Echo Lodge** 🐪, 🖉 (069) 68508, Fax (069) 68511, 🌊 – 📺 ☎ 🕭 🅿 –
🔬 25. 🐧🔵 AE VISA. 🛠
closed 24 to 26 December and mid January-March – **Meals** (communal dining Sunday and Monday residents only) (dinner only) 28.00 **t.** ⋀ 8.50 – **11 rm** 🖙 80.00/150.00 **st.**, 1 suite – SB.

BALLYBOFEY (Bealach Féich) Donegal 🔡🔡🔡 I 3 – *pop. 3 047 (inc. Stranorlar).*
🏌 *Ballybofey & Stranorlar* 🖉 (074) 31093.
Dublin 148 – Londonderry 30 – Sligo 58.

🏨 **Kee's**, Main St., Stranorlar, NE : ½ m. on N 15 🖉 (074) 31018, Fax (074) 31917, 🏋, 🛋, 🔳 –
📺 ☎ 🅿. 🐧🔵 AE ① VISA
Meals (bar lunch Monday to Saturday)/dinner 21.00 **t.** and a la carte ⋀ 6.60 – **36 rm**
🖙 38.50/85.00 **t.** – SB.

🏨 **Jackson's**, 🖉 (074) 31021, Fax (074) 31096, 🏋, 🛋, 🔳, 🌊 – ⎸🛗⎸, ⅙⅙ rm, 🔳 rest, 📺 ☎ 🕭
🅿. 🐧🔵 AE ① VISA
Meals (carvery lunch) 10.50/19.00 and a la carte ⋀ 6.00 – **88 rm** 🖙 52.00/89.00 **st.** – SB.

BALLYBUNNION (Baile an Bhuinneánaigh) Kerry 🔡🔡🔡 D 10 *Ireland G.* – *pop. 1 470.*
Exc. : *Carrigafoyle Castle★, NE : 13 m. by R 551 – Glin Castle★ AC, E : 19 m. by R 551 and N 69.*
🏌, 🏌 *Ballybunnion, Sandhill Rd* 🖉 (068) 27146.
Dublin 176 – Limerick 56 – Tralee 26.

🏛 **Marine Links**, Sandhill Rd, 🖉 (068) 27139, Fax (068) 27666, ⬱ – 📺 ☎ 🅿. 🐧🔵 AE ① VISA
13 March-October – **Meals** (bar lunch Monday to Saturday)/dinner 19.00 **t.** and a la carte
⋀ 6.50 – **11 rm** 🖙 50.00/75.00 – SB.

⌂ **Teach de Broc** without rest., Link Rd, S : 1 ½ m. by Golf Club rd 🖉 (068) 27581,
Fax (068) 27919, ⬱ – ⅙⅙ 📺 ☎ 🕭 🅿. 🐧🔵 VISA. 🛠
6 rm 🖙 30.00/50.00 **st.**

BALLYCONNEELY (Baile Conaola) *Galway* 923 B 7 – ✉ *Clifden.*
Dublin 189 – Galway 54.

Erriseask House ⛰, ✆ (095) 23553, *Fax (095) 23639*, ≤ Mannin Bay and Twelve Bens park – ☎ P. MC AE ⓓ VISA. ✻
Easter-October – **Meals** – (see below) – **12 rm** ⊡ 59.50/97.00 **st.** – SB.

Erriseask House (at Erriseask House H.), ✆ (095) 23553, *Fax (095) 23639* – ✻ P. MC AE ⓓ VISA
Easter-October – **Meals** *(closed lunch Monday to Thursday and Wednesday dinner to non-residents)* (booking essential) 15.00/19.00 **t.** and a la carte 24.00/31.50 **t.** ⅰ 7.50.

BALLYCONNELL (Béal Atha Conaill) *Cavan* 923 J 5 – *pop. 433.*
Dublin 89 – Drogheda 76 – Enniskillen 23.

Slieve Russell H. Golf and Country Club,, SE : 1 ¾ m. on R 200 ✆ (049) 26444 *Fax (049) 26474*, ≤, Fø, ≘s, ⊡, ⛳18, ⛱, park, ✂, squash – |$|, ≡ rest, TV ☎ & P – 🏛 800 MC AE ⓓ VISA. ✻
Conall Cearnach : **Meals** (dinner only and Sunday lunch)/dinner 25.00 **st.** and a la carte ⅰ 5.50 – ***Brackley :*** **Meals** *(closed Sunday lunch)* a la carte 12.70/19.60 **st.** ⅰ 5.25 – **151 rm** ⊡ 70.00/130.00 **st.** – SB.

BALLYCOTTON (Baile Choitán) *Cork* 923 H 12 – *pop. 477.*
Dublin 165 – Cork 27 – Waterford 66.

Bayview, ✆ (021) 646746, *Fax (021) 646075*, ≤ Ballycotton Bay, harbour and island, ⛱ – |$| TV ☎ P – 🏛 40. MC AE ⓓ VISA. ✻
10 April-28 October – **Meals** (bar lunch Monday to Saturday)/dinner 25.00 **st.** ⅰ 8.40 – **33 rm** ⊡ 70.00/116.00 **st.**, 2 suites – SB.

Spanish Point with rm, ✆ (021) 646177, *Fax (021) 646179*, ≤ Ballycotton Bay – TV ☎ P MC ⓓ VISA
closed 1 January-13 February and 1 week Christmas – **Meals** *(closed lunch Monday to Saturday October-April)* 11.00/20.00 **st.** and a la carte ⅰ 6.50 – **5 rm** ⊡ 25.00/40.00 **st.**

BALLYHACK (Baile Hac) *Wexford* 923 L 11 – *pop. 212* – ✉ *New Ross.*
Dublin 105 – Waterford 8.5.

Neptune, Ballyhack Harbour, ✆ (051) 389284, *Fax (051) 389284* – ✻. MC AE ⓓ VISA JCB
closed Sunday, Monday September-June and 20 December-14 February – **Meals** (dinner only) a la carte 17.90/25.50 **t.** ⅰ 7.50.

BALLYHEIGE (Baile Uí Thaidhg) *Kerry* 923 C 10 – *pop. 679.*
Dublin 186 – Limerick 73 – Tralee 11.

White Sands, ✆ (066) 33102, *Fax (066) 33357* – TV ☎ P. MC AE VISA. ✻
mid April-mid October – **Meals** (bar lunch Monday to Saturday)/dinner 16.00 **st.** and a la carte ⅰ 6.80 – **81 rm** ⊡ 39.00/70.00 **st.** – SB.

BALLYLICKEY (Béal Átha Leice) *Cork* 923 D 12 *Ireland G.* – ✉ *Bantry.*
Env. : *Bantry Bay★ – Bantry House★ AC, S : 3 m. by R 584.*
Exc. : *Glengarriff★ (Garinish Island★★, access by boat) NW : 8 m. by N 71 – Healy Pass★ (≤★★) W : 23 m. by N 71, R 572 and R 574 – Slieve Miskish Mountains (≤★★) W : 29 m. by N 71 and R 572 – Lauragh (Derreen Gardens★ AC) NW : 27 ½ m. by N 71, R 572 and R 574 – Allihies (copper mines★) W : 41 ½ m. by N 71, R 572 and R 575 – Garnish Island (≤★) W : 44 m. by N 71 and R 572.*
⛳9 *Bantry Park, Donemark* ✆ *(027) 50579.*
Dublin 216 – Cork 55 – Killarney 45.

Ballylickey Manor House ⛰, ✆ (027) 50071, *Fax (027) 50124*, ≤, « Extensive gardens », ⛱, 🎣, park – TV ☎ P. MC AE VISA. ✻
April-3 November – ***Le Rendez-vous :*** **Meals** (light lunch)/dinner 28.00 **t.** and a la carte ⅰ 9.00 – **5 rm** ⊡ 100.00/120.00 **t.**, **7 suites** 150.00/180.00 **t.** – SB.

Sea View House ⛰, ✆ (027) 50462, *Fax (027) 51555*, ≤, ⛱ – TV ☎ & P. MC AE ⓓ VISA. ✻
mid March-mid November – **Meals** (bar lunch Monday to Saturday)/dinner 23.50 **t.** ⅰ 4.50 – **16 rm** ⊡ 65.00/110.00 **st.** – SB.

Reendesert, ✆ (027) 50153, *Fax (027) 50597* – TV ☎ P – 🏛 100. MC AE ⓓ VISA
14 March-1 November – **Meals** (bar lunch Monday to Saturday)/dinner 9.50 **st.** and a la carte ⅰ 5.00 – **19 rm** ⊡ 32.50/61.00 **st.** – SB.

XX **Larchwood House** ♨ with rm, Pearsons Bridge, NE : 1 ¾ m. by R 584 ℰ (027) 66181, ≤, 🌧 – **🅿**. ⬛️ 🅰🅴 ⓞ 𝑽𝑰𝑺𝑨. ✀
restricted opening in winter – Meals *(closed Sunday)* (dinner only) 24.00 **t**. ⓘ 6.00 – **4 rm** ⌑ 25.00/50.00 **t**.

BALLYMACARBRY (Baile Mhac Cairbre) Waterford 923 I 11 Ireland G. – pop. 381 – ⊠ Clonmel.
Exc. : W : Nier Valley Scenic Route★★.
Dublin 118 – Cork 49 – Waterford 39.

↑ **Hanora's Cottage** ♨, Nire Valley, E : 4 m. by Nire Drive rd and Nire Valley Lakes rd ℰ (052) 36134, Fax (052) 36540, 🌧 – ⬛️ ☎ **🅿**. ⬛️ 𝑽𝑰𝑺𝑨. ✀
closed 20 to 27 December – Meals (by arrangement) 20.00 **st**. ⓘ 5.50 – **8 rm** ⌑ 40.00/70.00 **t**. – SB.

BALLYMOTE (Baile an Mhóta) Sligo 923 G 5 – pop. 994 – ⊠ Sligo.
Dublin 124 – Longford 48 – Sligo 15.

↑ **Mill House** without rest., Keenaghan, ℰ (071) 83449, 🌧, ✗ – ❖ ⬛️ **🅿**. ✀
closed 20 December-6 January – **5 rm** ⌑ 17.00/32.00 **st**.

BALLYNABOLA Wexford 923 L 10 – see New Ross.

The Guide is updated annually so renew your Guide every year.

BALLYNAHINCH (Baile na hInse) Galway 923 C 7 – ⊠ Recess.
Dublin 140 – Galway 41 – Westport 49.

🏨 **Ballynahinch Castle** ♨, ℰ (095) 31006, Fax (095) 31085, ≤ Owenmore River and woods, ♨, 🌧, park – ⬛️ ☎ **🅿**. ⬛️ 🅰🅴 ⓞ 𝑽𝑰𝑺𝑨. ✀
closed February and 20 to 26 December – Meals (bar lunch)/dinner 23.00 **t**. and a la carte ⓘ 7.50 – **28 rm** ⌑ 82.00/124.00 **t**.

BALLYVAUGHAN (Baile Uí Bheacháin) Clare 923 E 8 Ireland G. – pop. 257.
Env. : The Burren★★ (Cliffs of Moher★★★, Scenic Routes★★, Aillwee Cave★ AC (Waterfall★), Corcomroe Abbey★, Kilfenora Crosses★).
Dublin 149 – Ennis 34 – Galway 29.

🏨 **Gregans Castle** ♨, SW : 3 ¾ m. on N 67 ℰ (065) 77005, Fax (065) 77111, ≤ countryside and Galway Bay, ♋, 🌧, park – ☎ **🅿**. ⬛️ 𝑽𝑰𝑺𝑨. ✀
10 April-mid October – Meals (bar lunch)/dinner 30.00 **t**. and a la carte ⓘ 11.50 – **18 rm** ⌑ 90.00/180.00 **t**., 4 suites.

🏨 **Hyland's**, ℰ (065) 77037, Fax (065) 77131 – ❖ rm, ⬛️ ☎ **🅿**. ⬛️ 🅰🅴 ⓞ 𝑽𝑰𝑺𝑨. ✀
closed 1 week Christmas and January – Meals (bar lunch)/dinner 15.00 and a la carte ⓘ 5.75 – **30 rm** ⌑ 57.50/94.00 **st**. – SB.

🏠 **Rusheen Lodge** without rest., SW : ¾ m. on N 67 ℰ (065) 77092, Fax (065) 77152, 🌧 – ❖ ⬛️ ☎ **🅿**. ⬛️ 🅰🅴 𝑽𝑰𝑺𝑨. ✀
February-November – **8 rm** ⌑ 40.00/60.00 **st**.

↑ **Cappabhaile House** without rest., SW : 1 m. on N 67 ℰ (065) 77260, Fax (065) 77300, ≤, 🌧 – ⬛️ ☎ **🅿**. ⬛️ 𝑽𝑰𝑺𝑨. ✀
March-October – **8 rm** ⌑ 40.00/50.00 **st**.

BALTIMORE (Dîn na Séad) Cork 923 D 13 – pop. 232.
Dublin 214 – Cork 59 – Killarney 77.

🏨 **Baltimore Harbour**, ℰ (028) 20361, Fax (028) 20466, 🌧 – ⬛️ ☎ **🅿** – 🔬 130. ⬛️ 🅰🅴 ⓞ 𝑽𝑰𝑺𝑨. ✀
April-November – Meals (bar lunch)/dinner 18.00 **st**. and a la carte ⓘ 6.00 – **30 rm** ⌑ 60.00/90.00 **st**. – SB.

↑ **Rathmore House**, N : 1 ½ m. on R 595 (Skibbereen Rd) ℰ (028) 20362, Fax (028) 20362, ≤, 🌧 – ⬛️ 🅰🅴 ⓞ 𝑽𝑰𝑺𝑨. ✀
Meals (by arrangement) 14.00 **st**. ⓘ 5.50 – **6 rm** ⌑ 18.00/32.00 **st**. – SB.

🏠 **Casey's of Baltimore** with rm, ℰ (028) 20197, Fax (028) 20509, ≤ – ⬛️ ☎. ⬛️ 🅰🅴 ⓞ 𝑽𝑰𝑺𝑨. ✀
closed 23 to 27 December – Meals 15.80 **t**. (dinner) and a la carte 19.05/25.05 **t**. ⓘ 5.30 – **14 rm** ⌑ 55.00/75.00 **t**. – SB.

BANDON (Droichead na Bandan) *Cork* 923 F 12 – *pop. 1 697.*
Dublin 174 – Cork 19.

🏨 **Munster Arms,** Oliver Plunkett St., ℘ (023) 41562, *Fax (023) 41562* – 📺 ☎ – 🔏 200. 📧③
AE ⓪ VISA. ⌘
closed Good Friday and 25-26 December – **Meals** 10.00 **st.** (lunch) and dinner
a la carte 11.50/18.95 **st.** ‖ 6.50 – **34 rm** ⊆ 35.00/60.00 **st.** – SB.

⌂ **St. Anne's** without rest., Clonakilty Rd, ℘ (023) 44239, *Fax (023) 44239,* ☞ – ⭑⭒ ℗. 📧③
VISA. ⌘
5 rm ⊆ 22.50/36.00 **st.**

BANSHA (An Bháinseach) *Co. Tipperary* 923 H 10 – *pop. 288.*
Dublin 103 – Cork 55 – Limerick 30 – Waterford 48.

⌂ **Bansha House** ⌀, ℘ (062) 54194, *Fax (062) 54215,* ☞, park – ⭑⭒ ℗. 📧③ VISA. ⌘
closed 20 to 28 December – **Meals** 15.00 **t.** ‖ 5.00 – **8 rm** ⊆ 28.00/50.00 **t.** – SB.

BANTEER (Bántár) *Cork* 923 F 11 – *pop. 257.*
Dublin 158 – Cork 30 – Killarney 29 – Limerick 48.

🏠 **Clonmeen Lodge** ⌀, E : 2 m. on Mallow rd ℘ (029) 56238, *Fax (029) 56294,* ⌇, ☞
park – ℗. 📧③ AE ⓪ VISA
closed 21 to 31 December – **Meals** (residents only) (dinner only) 18.00 **st.** ‖ 5.50 – **6 rm**
⊆ 35.00/60.00.

BANTRY (Beanntraá) *Cork* 923 D 12 *Ireland G.* – *pop. 2 936.*
See : Bantry House★ AC (Bantry Bay★).
🄸 *Wolfe Tone Sq.* ℘ (027) 50229 (May-September).
Dublin 210 – Cork 56 – Killarney 53.

🏨 **Bantry House** ⌀, ℘ (027) 50047, *Fax (027) 50795,* ≤, ⌂, « Georgian country house
formal gardens, extensive parkland », ⌇, ⌘ – ⭑⭒ ☎ ℗. 📧③ AE VISA
March-October – **Meals** (closed dinner Saturday and Sunday) (light lunch)/dinner 20.25 **t.**
‖ 7.00 – **9 rm** ⊆ 70.00/140.00 **t.** – SB.

BAREFIELD (Gort Lomán) *Clare* 923 F 9 – *see Ennis.*

BARRELLS CROSS *Cork* – *see Kinsale.*

BELTURBET (Béal Tairbirt) *Cavan* 923 J 5 – *pop. 1 248.*
Dublin 89 – Drogheda 76 – Enniskillen 23.

🏠 **International Fishing Centre** ⌀,, N : 1 ½ m. ℘ (049) 22616, *Fax (049) 22616*
« Riverside setting », ⌇, ☞, ⌘ – ⬛ ℗. 📧③ VISA. ⌘
15 March-15 November – **Meals** (dinner only) 14.00 **st.** and a la carte ‖ 6.00 – **18 rm**
⊆ (dinner included) 38.00/76.00 **st.** – SB.

BETTYSTOWN (Baile an Bhiataigh) *Meath* 923 N 6.
Dublin 43 – Drogheda 6 – Dundalk 28.

✕✕ **Bacchus at the Coastguard,** Bayview, ℘ (041) 28251, *Fax (041) 28251,* ≤ Bettystown
Bay – ℗. 📧③ AE ⓪ VISA
closed Monday, 25 December, February and 1 week October – **Meals** (dinner only and
Sunday lunch) 14.00 **t.** and a la carte ‖ 5.50.

BIRR (Biorra) *Offaly* 923 I 8 *Ireland G.* – *pop. 3 355.*
See : Town★ – Birr Castle Demesne★★ AC (Telescope★).
Exc. : Roscrea★ (Damer House★ AC) S : 12 m. by N 62 – Slieve Bloom Mountains★, E : 13 m.
by R 440 – Clonfert Cathedral★ (West doorway★★), NW : 15 m. by R 439, R 356 and minor
roads.
🄸₈ *The Glenns* ℘ (0509) 20082.
🄸 ℘ (0509) 20110 (16 May-11 September).
Athlone 28 – Dublin 87 – Kilkenny 49 – Limerick 49.

🏨 **County Arms,** Railway Rd, S : ½ m. on N 62 ℘ (0509) 20791, *Fax (0509) 21234,* ☞
squash – ℗ ☎ ⅙ ℗ – 🔏 300. 📧③ AE ⓪ VISA JCB. ⌘
closed 24 to 26 December – **Meals** 12.00/19.00 **st.** and a la carte ‖ 8.00 – **24 rm** ⊆ 55.00/
110.00 **st.** – SB.

🏛 **Dooly's**, Emmet Sq., ℰ (0509) 20032, Fax (0509) 21332 – 📺 ☎ – 🔬 300. ⬦⬧ 🅰🅴 ⓪ 𝘝𝘐𝘚𝘈.
🛇
Meals (bar lunch Monday to Saturday)/dinner 16.50 **t**. and a la carte 🅸 6.50 – **18 rm**
⇌ 35.00/60.00 **t**. – SB.

🏛 **The Maltings**, Castle St., ℰ (0509) 21345, Fax (0509) 21345, 🛦, ⇌ – 📺 ☎ Ⓟ. ⬦⬧ 𝘝𝘐𝘚𝘈.
🛇
Meals 7.90/14.95 **st**. and dinner a la carte 🅸 4.95 – **10 rm** ⇌ 26.50/45.00 **st**. – SB.

🏠 **Emmet Guest House** without rest., Emmet Sq., ℰ (0509) 20395 – 📺
closed 24 December-21 January – **6 rm** ⇌ 20.00/40.00 **t**.

🏠 **Spinners House**, Castle St., ℰ (0509) 21673, Fax (0509) 21673 – ☎. ⬦⬧ 🅰🅴 ⓪ 𝘝𝘐𝘚𝘈. 🛇
closed February – Meals – (see **Spinners Bistro** below) – **8 rm** ⇌ 21.00/35.00 **st**. – SB.

🍴 **Spinners Bistro** (at Spinners House), Castle St., ℰ (0509) 21673, Fax (0509) 21673 – ⬦⬧
🅰🅴 ⓪ 𝘝𝘐𝘚𝘈
closed December and January – Meals (closed Sunday to Wednesday November-March)
(dinner only) a la carte 12.00/19.35 **t**.

at Kinnitty E : 8¼ m. on R 440 – ⊠ Birr.

🏰 **Kinnitty Castle** 🛇,, E : 1 m. on R 440 ℰ (0509) 37318, Fax (0509) 37284, « 12C
origins », 🛦, ⇌, 🏹, 🌧, park, 🦌 – ☎ Ⓟ – 🔬 250. ⬦⬧ 🅰🅴 𝘝𝘐𝘚𝘈
Meals (bar lunch Monday to Saturday)/dinner 25.00 **t**. and a la carte 🅸 10.00 – **37 rm**
⇌ 95.00/200.00 **t**. – SB.

BLACKLION (An Blaic) Cavan 📗 I 5 – pop. 153.
Dublin 121 – Drogheda 106 – Enniskillen 12.

🍴🍴 **Mac Nean House & Bistro** with rm, ℰ (072) 53022, Fax (072) 53404 – 🍴 rest, 📺 ☎.
𝘝𝘐𝘚𝘈
closed 24 to 26 December – Meals (closed Monday) (dinner only and Sunday lunch)/
dinner 15.95 **t**. and a la carte 🅸 6.50 – **6 rm** ⇌ 26.00/46.00 **t**. – SB.

Si vous cherchez un hôtel tranquille,
consultez d'abord les cartes de l'introduction
ou repérez dans le texte les établissements indiqués avec le signe 🛇 ou 🛇

BLARNEY (An Bhlarna) Cork 📗 G 12 Ireland G. – pop. 1 963 – ⊠ Cork.
See : Blarney Castle★★ AC – Blarney House★ AC.
Dublin 167 – Cork 6.

🏛 **Blarney Park**, ℰ (021) 385281, Fax (021) 381506, 🛦, ⇌, 🖾, 🌧, 🦌 – 📺 ☎ 🕭 Ⓟ –
🔬 300. ⬦⬧ 🅰🅴 ⓪ 𝘝𝘐𝘚𝘈. 🛇
Meals a la carte 10.00/20.00 – **76 rm** ⇌ 55.00/118.00 **st**. – SB.

🏠 **Killarney House** without rest., Station Rd, NE : 1 m. ℰ (021) 381841, 🌧 – 🍴 📺 Ⓟ. 🛇
5 rm ⇌ 24.00/36.00 **st**.

at Tower W : 2 m. on R 617 – ⊠ Cork.

🏠 **Ashlee Lodge**, ℰ (021) 385346, Fax (021) 22312, 🌧 – 🍴 Ⓟ. ⬦⬧ 🅰🅴 𝘝𝘐𝘚𝘈. 🛇
closed 22 December-5 January – Meals (by arrangement) 12.00 **st**. – **6 rm** ⇌ 26.00/
36.00 **st**.

BLESSINGTON (Baile Coimán) Wicklow 📗 M 8 – pop. 1 860.
Dublin 19 – Kilkenny 56 – Wexford 70.

🏛 **Tulfarris House** 🛇, S : 6 m. by N 81 ℰ (045) 867555, Fax (045) 867561, ≤, 🛦, ⇌, 🖾,
🕖, 🏹, 🌧, park, 🦌 – 🍴 📺 ☎ Ⓟ – 🔬 150. ⬦⬧ 🅰🅴 ⓪ 𝘝𝘐𝘚𝘈. 🛇
closed 21 to 27 December – Meals (bar lunch Monday to Saturday)/dinner 25.00 **st**. 🅸 6.50 –
20 rm ⇌ 90.00/156.00 **st**. – SB.

BRAY (Bré) Wicklow 📗 N 8 Ireland G. – pop. 25 252.
Env. : Powerscourt★★ (Waterfall★★★ AC) W : 4 m. - Killruddery House and Gardens★ AC,
S : 2 m. by R 761.
🛦 Woodbrook, Dublin Rd ℰ (01) 282 4799 – 🛦 Old Conna, Ferndale Rd ℰ (01) 282 6055.
Dublin 13 – Wicklow 20.

🍴🍴 **Tree of Idleness**, Seafront, ℰ (01) 286 3498, Fax (01) 282 8183 – ⬦⬧ 🅰🅴 𝘝𝘐𝘚𝘈
closed Monday, 2 weeks late August and 1 week Christmas – Meals - Greek-Cypriot -
(dinner only) 19.50 **t**. and a la carte 🅸 7.00.

REPUBLIC OF IRELAND

BUNBEG (An Bun Beag) *Donegal* 923 H 2 – *pop. 1 400 (inc. Derrybeg).*
Dublin 195 – Donegal 66 – Londonderry 55.

🏨 **Ostan Gweedore** ≶, ℰ *(075) 31177, Fax (075) 31726,* ≼, ℎ₅, ≘₅, 🔲, park – 🔲 ☎ ❷ –
🛁 50. ⬛ ⒶⒺ 𝗩𝗜𝗦𝗔. ✁
mid March-October – **Meals** (bar lunch)/dinner 22.50 ⅄ 8.00 – **33 rm** 🖙 55.00/85.00 **st.**,
3 suites – SB.

BUNCRANA (Bun Cranncha) *Donegal* 923 J 2 *Ireland G.* – *pop. 3 312.*
Exc. : – *Malin Head★★★ (≼★★★), NE : 31 ½ m. by R 238 and R 242 – Inishowen Peninsula★★*
– *Carndonagh High Cross★, NE : 18 ½ m. by R 238 – Gap of Mamore★, NW : 8 m. – Lag Sand*
Dunes★, NE : 24 ½ m. by R 238 and R 242.
Dublin 160 – Londonderry 15 – Sligo 99.

🏨 **Lake of Shadows,** Grianan Park, ℰ *(077) 61005, Fax (077) 62131* – 🔲 ☎ ❷. ⬛ ⒶⒺ 𝗩𝗜𝗦𝗔.
✁
closed 24 and 25 December – **Meals** (dinner only and Sunday lunch)/dinner 14.50 **st.**
and a la carte ⅄ 5.70 – **23 rm** 🖙 30.00/60.00 **st.** – SB.

BUNDORAN (Bun Dobhráin) *Donegal* 923 H 4 – *pop. 1 707.*
🄱 *Main St.* ℰ *(072) 41350 (June-September).*
Dublin 161 – Donegal 17 – Sligo 23.

🏨🏨 **Great Northern** ≶, N : ¼ m. ℰ *(072) 41204, Fax (072) 41114,* ≼, ℎ₅, ≘₅, 🔲, ℎ₈, ≈, ✗
– ▮ 🔲 ☎ ⅋ ❷. ⬛ 𝗩𝗜𝗦𝗔. ✁
Meals 10.00/22.00 **t.** and lunch a la carte – **118 rm** 🖙 60.00/180.00 **t.** – SB.

🏨 **Holyrood,** Main St., ℰ *(072) 41232, Fax (072) 41100* – ▮ 🔲 ☎ ⅋ ❷. ⬛ ⒶⒺ 𝗩𝗜𝗦𝗔. ✁
closed 1 week Christmas – **Meals** (bar lunch Monday to Saturday)/dinner 16.50
and a la carte ⅄ 7.50 – **100 rm** 🖙 55.00/80.00 **st.** – SB.

🏨 **Allingham Arms,** ℰ *(072) 41075, Fax (072) 41171* – ▮, ✦⇆ rm, 🔲 ☎ ⅋ ❷. ⬛ ⒶⒺ ❶
𝗩𝗜𝗦𝗔. ✁
closed Monday to Thursday 5 to 31 January and 22 to 27 December – **Meals** (bar lunch).
dinner 18.00 **st.** and a la carte ⅄ 5.00 – **118 rm** 🖙 37.50/75.00 **st.**

🏠 **Bay View** without rest., Main St., ℰ *(072) 41296, Fax (072) 41147,* ≼, ≘₅ – 🔲 ☎ ❷. ⬛
𝗩𝗜𝗦𝗔. ✁
19 rm 🖙 24.00/36.00 **st.**

⌂ **Leitrim House** without rest., Kinlough Rd, ℰ *(072) 41904, Fax (072) 41452,* ≈ – 🔲 ☎
❷. ⬛ 𝗩𝗜𝗦𝗔. ✁
March-October – **8 rm** 🖙 22.50/35.00 **st.**

✗✗ **Le Chateaubrianne,** Sligo Rd, W : 1 m. on N 5 ℰ *(072) 42160, Fax (072) 42160* – ❷. ⬛
ⒶⒺ 𝗩𝗜𝗦𝗔. ✁
closed Monday and January – **Meals** (dinner only and Sunday lunch)/dinner 21.00 **t.** ⅄ 7.50

BUNRATTY (Bun Raite) *Clare* 923 F 9 *Ireland G.*
See : *Castle and Folk Park★★ AC – Town★★.*
Dublin 129 – Ennis 15 – Limerick 8.

🏨 **Fitzpatrick Bunratty,** ℰ *(061) 361177, Fax (061) 471252,* ℎ₅, ≘₅, 🔲, ≈ – ✦⇆ rm, 🔲
☎ ❷ – 🛁 1200. ⬛ ⒶⒺ 𝗩𝗜𝗦𝗔. ✁
closed 24 to 26 December – **Meals** (closed Saturday lunch) 10.50/19.50 **t.** and a la carte
⅄ 6.50 – 🖙 9.00 – **115 rm** 88.00/125.00 **t.** – SB.

⌂ **Bunratty Lodge** without rest., N : 1 ½ m. ℰ *(061) 369402, Fax (061) 369363,* ≈ – ✦⇆
🔲 ❷. ⬛ 𝗩𝗜𝗦𝗔. ✁
mid March-October – **6 rm** 🖙 30.00/37.00 **st.**

⌂ **Shannon View** without rest., NW : 1 m. on N 18 (south-eastbound carriageway
completing U-turn at junction with R 471 ℰ *(061) 364056, Fax (061) 364056,* ≈ – ❷. ⬛
𝗩𝗜𝗦𝗔. ✁
17 March-November – **4 rm** 🖙 23.50/35.00 **s.**

✗✗ **MacCloskey's,** Bunratty House Mews, ℰ *(061) 364082, Fax (061) 364350,* « Cellars of
Georgian house » – ❷. ⬛ ⒶⒺ ❶ 𝗩𝗜𝗦𝗔
closed Sunday, Monday, 25-26 December and January – **Meals** (dinner only) 26.00 **t.** ⅄ 6.00

Bitte beachten Sie die Geschwindigkeitsbeschränkungen in Großbritannien
- 60 mph (= 96 km/h) außerhalb geschlossener Ortschaften
- 70 mph (= 112 km/h) auf Straßen mit getrennten Fahrbahnen und Autobahnen.

BUTLERSTOWN (Baile an Bhuitléaraigh) *Cork* 923 F 13 *Ireland G.* – ⊠ *Bandon.*
  Env. : *Courtmacsherry*, *N : 3 m.*
  Dublin 193 – Cork 32.

  ↑ **Atlantic Sunset** ☞ without rest., ℰ (023) 40115, ⩽ – ⅙⇆ ❷
    4 rm ⊆ 15.00/34.00 st.

  ✗ **Dunworley Cottage,** Dunworley, S : 2 m. ℰ (023) 40314, Fax (023) 40314 – ❷. ⓦ AE
    ① VISA
    closed Monday, Tuesday and November-mid March except Christmas – **Meals** (lunch
    by arrangement)/dinner 21.75 **st.**

BUTLERSTOWN (Baile an Bhuitléaraigh) *Waterford* – see Waterford.

CAHERDANIEL (Cathair Dónall) *Kerry* 923 B 12 – ⊠ *Killarney.*
  Dublin 238 – Killarney 48.

  ↑ **Derrynane Bay House,** W : ½ m. on N 70 ℰ (066) 75404, Fax (066) 75436, ⩽ – ⅙⇆ rm,
    ⊡ ☎ ❷ VISA. ✀
    closed February – **Meals** 13.50 **s.** ⟨ 6.00 – **6 rm** ⊆ 24.00/38.00 **s.** – SB.

CAHIR/CAHER (An Chathair) *Tipperary* 923 I 10 *Ireland G.* – pop. 2 236.
  See : *Caher Castle*★★ *AC* – *Town Square*★ – *St. Paul's Church*★.
  Env. : *Swiss Cottage*★ *AC*, *S : 1 m. by R 670.*
  Exc. : *Clonmel*★ *(County Museum*★, *St. Mary's Church*★, *Riverside*★, *Quay*★ *) E : 10 m. by
  N 24.
  ☖ Cahir Park, Kilcommon ℰ (052) 41474.
  ☐ Castle Street ℰ (052) 41453 (1 May-1 October).
  Dublin 114 – Limerick 39 – Cork 47 – Waterford 39.

  🏨 **Cahir House,** The Square, ℰ (052) 42727, Fax (052) 42727, ᾄ – ⊡ ☎ ❷ – 🔥 500. ⓦ AE
    ① VISA. ✀
    closed Good Friday and 25 December – **Meals** (bar lunch Monday to Saturday)/dinner
    18.00 **st.** and a la carte ⟨ 6.50 – **14 rm** ⊆ 60.00/80.00 **st.** – SB.

CAMP (An Com) *Kerry* 923 C 11 – ⊠ *Tralee.*
  Dublin 195 – Killarney 44 – Limerick 76 – Tralee 10.

  ↑ **Barnagh Bridge** without rest., Cappaclough, W : 2 m. on R 560 ℰ (066) 30145,
    Fax (066) 30299, ⩽, ᾄ – ⅙⇆ ⊡ ☎ ❷. ⓦ VISA. ✀
    April-October – **5 rm** ⊆ 36.00/52.00 **st.**

CAPPOQUIN (Ceapach Choinn) *Waterford* 923 I 11 *Ireland G.* – pop. 780.
  Env. : *Lismore*★ *(Lismore Castle Gardens*★ *AC, St. Carthage's Cathedral*★ *), W : 4 m. by N 72 –
  Mount Melleray Abbey*★, *N : 4 m. by R 669.*
  Exc. : *The Gap*★ *(⩽*★ *) NW : 9 m. by R 669.*
  Dublin 136 – Cork 31 – Waterford 40.

  ✗✗ **Richmond House** ☞ with rm, SE : ½ m. on N 72 ℰ (058) 54278, Fax (058) 54988,
    « Georgian house », ᾄ – ⊡ ☎ ❷. ⓦ ① VISA
    closed 23 December-1 March – **Meals** (closed Sunday and Monday to non-residents)
    (dinner only) 28.00 **t.** ⟨ 9.00 – **9 rm** ⊆ 50.00/100.00 **t.** – SB.

CARAGH LAKE (Loch Cárthaí) *Kerry* 923 C 11 *Ireland G.*
  See : *Lough Caragh*★.
  Exc. : *Iveragh Peninsula*★★★ *(Ring of Kerry*★★ *).*
  ☖ Dooks, Glenbeigh ℰ (066) 68205/68200.
  Dublin 212 – Killarney 22 – Tralee 25.

  🏨 **Caragh Lodge** ☞, ℰ (066) 69115, Fax (066) 69316, ⩽, « Lakeside setting », ➤s, 🎣, ᾄ,
    ✗ – 📖 ☎ ❷. ⓦ AE VISA. ✀
    May-October – **Meals** (residents only) (dinner only) 25.00 **t.** ⟨ 6.00 – **14 rm** ⊆ 60.00/
    120.00 **t.**, 1 suite.

  🏨 **Ard-Na-Sidhe** ☞, ℰ (066) 69105, Fax (066) 69282, ⩽, « Lakeside setting », 🎣, ᾄ, park
    – ⅙⇆ rest. ☎ ❷. ⓦ AE ① VISA. ✀
    May-September – **Meals** (dinner only) 23.50 **st.** – **20 rm** ⊆ 70.00/146.00 **st.**

↑ **Carrig House** ॐ, ℰ (066) 69100, Fax (066) 69166, « Lakeside setting », ⌕, ✍ – ⬇ ☎
℗. ⱽ⑨ ₥₥. ℀. *closed 24 to 26 December* – **Meals** (by arrangement) approx. 21.00 **t.** ₦ 6.50 – **6 rm**
⚏ 53.00/110.00 **t.** – SB.

CARLINGFORD (Cairlinn) *Louth* ⑨②③ N 5 *Ireland G.* – *pop. 647.*
See : *Town★*.
Exc. : *Windy Gap★, NW : 8 m. by R 173.*
Dublin 66 – Dundalk 13.

🏛 **McKevitt's Village,** Market Sq., ℰ (042) 73116, Fax (042) 73144, ✍ – ⬚ ☎. ⱽ⑨ ₥₥. ℀
Meals 9.50/17.50 **st.** and a la carte ₦ 5.50 – **13 rm** ⚏ 35.00/120.00 **st.** – SB.

✗✗ **Jordan's** with rm, Newry St., ℰ (042) 73223, Fax (042) 73827, ≼ – ⬚ ☎ ℗. ⱽ⑨ ₥₥ ₥₥. ℀
closed last 3 weeks January and 3 days Christmas – **Meals** (bar lunch)/dinner 19.50 **st.**
and a la carte ₦ 7.00 – **5 rm** ⚏ 45.00/85.00 **st.** – SB.

CARLOW (Ceatharlach) *Carlow* ⑨②③ L 9 – *pop. 11 721.*
Dublin 50 – Kilkenny 23 – Wexford 47.

🏨 **Dolmen,** Kilkenny Rd, SW : 1 ¾ m. on N 9 ℰ (0503) 42002, Fax (0503) 42375, ✍ – ▤ rest,
⬚ ☎ ₺ ℗ – ⚐ 800. ⱽ⑨ ₥₥ ⓞ ₥₥. ℀
Meals (carving lunch Monday to Saturday)/dinner 18.50 **t.** and a la carte ₦ 7.00 – **37 rm**
⚏ 45.00/120.00 **st.** – SB.

🏛 **Seven Oaks,** Athy Rd, ℰ (0503) 31308, Fax (0503) 32155, ✍ – ▤ ⬚ ☎ ℗ – ⚐ 300. ⱽ⑨
₥₥ ⓞ ₥₥. ℀
closed 25 December – **Meals** (carving lunch Saturday) 11.50/15.00 **st.** and a la carte – **32 rm**
⚏ 50.00/110.00 **st.** – SB.

🏛 **Barrowville Town House** without rest., Kilkenny Rd, ℰ (0503) 43324
Fax (0503) 41953, ✍ – ℀⣿ ⬚ ☎ ℗. ⱽ⑨ ₥₥ ₥₥. ℀
7 rm ⚏ 22.50/44.00 **st.**

↑ **Goleen** without rest., Milford, SW : 5 ¼ m. on N 9 ℰ (0503) 46132, Fax (0503) 46132, ✍ –
℀⣿ ⬚ ☎ ℗. ⱽ⑨ ₥₥ ₥₥. ℀
May-September – **6 rm** ⚏ 18.00/36.00 **st.**

✗ **Danette's Feast,** Urglin Glebe, E : 3 m. by R 726 (Hacketstown rd) turning left after
petrol station onto Burton Hall rd ℰ (0503) 40817, Fax (0503) 40817 – ℀⣿ ℗
closed Sunday dinner to Wednesday and 23 to 30 December – **Meals** (dinner only and
Sunday lunch)/dinner 24.00 **t.** ₦ 5.75.

CARNA *Galway* ⑨②③ C 8 *Dublin 186.*
Cork 169 – Galway 48 – Limerick 112.

🏛 **Carna Bay** ॐ, ℰ (095) 32255, Fax (095) 32530, ≼, ⌕, ✍ – ⬚ ☎ ℗. ⱽ⑨ ₥₥ ₥₥
Meals (bar lunch Monday to Saturday)/dinner 19.00 **t.** and a la carte ₦ 6.00 – **26 rm**
⚏ 50.00/70.00 **t.** – SB.

CARRICKCARNON *Louth* – *see Dundalk.*

CARRICKMACROSS (Carraig Mhachaire Rois) *Monaghan* ⑨②③ L 6 *Ireland G.* – *pop. 1 926.*
Env. : *Dún a' Rá Forest Park★, SW : 5 m. by R 179 – St. Mochta's House★, E : 7 m. by R 178.*
🟤 *Nuremore* ℰ (042) 61438.
Dublin 57 – Dundalk 14.

🏨 **Nuremore** ॐ, S : 1 m. on N 2 ℰ (042) 61438, Fax (042) 61853, ≼, ₤₼, ≋, ▨, 🟤, ⌕, ✍
park, squash – ▤ ▤ rest, ⬚ ☎ ₺ ℗ – ⚐ 600. ⱽ⑨ ₥₥ ⓞ ₥₥. ℀
Meals 13.50/24.50 **st.** and a la carte – **69 rm** ⚏ 80.00/150.00 **st.** – SB.

CARRICK-ON-SHANNON (Cora Droma Rúisc) *Leitrim* ⑨②③ H 6 *Ireland G.* – *pop. 1 868.*
See : *Town★*.
Exc. : *Lough Rynn Demesne★.*
Dublin 97 – Ballina 50 – Galway 74 – Roscommon 26 – Sligo 34.

↑ **Hollywell** ॐ without rest., Liberty Hill, ℰ (078) 21124, Fax (078) 21124, ≼, « Part 18
country house », ✍ – ℗. ⱽ⑨ ₥₥. ℀
closed 1 week Christmas – **4 rm** ⚏ 37.50/70.00 **t.**

CARRICK-ON-SUIR (Carraig na Siúire) Tipperary 𝟵𝟮𝟯 J 10 – *pop. 5 172.*

> ⌔ *Garravone* ⌀ *(051) 40047.*
> *Dublin 95 – Cork 68 – Limerick 62 – Waterford 16.*

🏨 **Carraig,** Main St., ⌀ *(051) 641455, Fax (051) 641604* – ▤ rest, 📺 ☎ 🅿. 🆎 🝁 ⓪ 𝚅𝙸𝚂𝙰. ⌘
closed Good Friday and 25 December – **Meals** 17.95 **st.** (dinner) and a la carte 14.95/
21.40 **st.** ⓘ 5.50 – **14 rm** � 35.00/60.00 **st.** – SB.

🏨 **Bell and Salmon Arms,** 95-97 Main St., ⌀ *(051) 645555, Fax (051) 641293* – 📺 ☎ 🅿.
🆎 ⓪ 𝚅𝙸𝚂𝙰. ⌘
closed 25 December – **Meals** (dinner only and Sunday lunch)/dinner 16.00 **st.** and a la carte
– **13 rm** ⊑ 33.00/55.00 **st.** – SB.

CARRIGALINE (Carraig Uí Leighin) Cork 𝟵𝟮𝟯 G 12 – *pop. 7 827.*

> *Dublin 163 – Cork 9.*

⌂ **Glenwood House** without rest., Ballinrea Rd, N : ¾ m. by R 611 (Cork rd)
⌀ *(021) 373878, Fax (021) 373878,* ☞ – 📺 ☎ ⅙ 🅿. 🆎 ⓪ 𝚅𝙸𝚂𝙰. ⌘
closed 25 to 31 December – **8 rm** ⊑ 32.00/54.00 **st.**

⌂ **Raffeen Lodge** without rest., Ringaskiddy Rd, Monkstown, NE : 2 ½ m. by R 611 and
N 28 off R 610 ⌀ *(021) 371632, Fax (021) 371632* – 📺 🅿. 🆎 𝚅𝙸𝚂𝙰
March-October – **6 rm** ⊑ 22.00/40.00 **st.**

CASHEL (Caiseal) Tipperary 𝟵𝟮𝟯 I 10 *Ireland G.* – *pop. 2 346.*

> See : *Town*★★★ – *Rock of Cashel*★★★ *AC* – *Cormac's Chapel*★★ – *Round Tower*★ –
> *Museum*★ – *Cashel Palace Gardens*★ – *Cathedrals*★ – *GPA Bolton Library*★ *AC* – *Hore*
> *Abbey*★ – *Dominican Friary*★.
> Env. : *Holy Cross Abbey*★★, *N : 9 m. by R 660* – *Athassel Abbey*★, *W : 5 m. by N 74.*
> 🅱 *Bolton Library* ⌀ *(062) 61333 (1 April-1 October).*
> *Dublin 101 – Cork 60 – Kilkenny 34 – Limerick 36 – Waterford 44.*

⌂ **Ros Guill House** without rest., NE : ¾ m. on R 691 ⌀ *(062) 61507, Fax (062) 61507,* ☞ –
⅙≒ 🅿. 🆎 𝚅𝙸𝚂𝙰. ⌘
May-20 October – **5 rm** ⊑ 26.00/38.00 **st.**

XXX **Chez Hans,** Rockside, ⌀ *(062) 61177,* « Converted synod hall » – 🅿. 🆎 𝚅𝙸𝚂𝙰
closed Sunday, Monday, 1 week Christmas and 3 weeks January – **Meals** (dinner only)
a la carte 25.20/28.50 **t.** ⓘ 8.00.

X **The Spearman,** 97 Main St., ⌀ *(062) 61143* – 🆎 🝁 ⓪ 𝚅𝙸𝚂𝙰
closed Sunday dinner and Monday October-June, November and 25 to 27 December –
Meals (restricted lunch Monday to Saturday) a la carte 11.95/20.50 **t.** ⓘ 4.95.

CASHEL BAY (Cuan an Chaisil) Galway 𝟵𝟮𝟯 C 7 *Ireland G.*

> See : *Town*★.
> *Dublin 173 – Galway 41.*

🏨 **Cashel House** ⌂, ⌀ *(095) 31001, Fax (095) 31077,* ≤, « Country house and gardens »,
≒, park, ⌘ – 📺 ☎ 🅿. 🆎 🝁 ⓪ 𝚅𝙸𝚂𝙰. ⌘
closed 10 January-10 February – **Meals** (booking essential to non-residents) (bar lunch)/
dinner a la carte approx. 31.40 **t.** ⓘ 7.95 – **32 rm** ⊑ 75.00/190.00 **t.** – SB.

🏨 **Zetland Country House** ⌂, ⌀ *(095) 31111, Fax (095) 31117,* ≤ Cashel Bay, « Gardens », ⌘ – 📺 ☎ 🅿. 🆎 ⓪ 𝚅𝙸𝚂𝙰
2 April-October – **Meals** – (see below) – **19 rm** ⊑ 80.50/157.00 **t.** – SB.

🏨 **Glynsk House** ⌂, SW : 5 ¾ m. on R 340 ⌀ *(095) 32279, Fax (095) 32342,* ≤ – 📺 ☎ 🅿.
🆎 🝁 𝚅𝙸𝚂𝙰
April-October – **Meals** 19.00 **t.** (dinner) and a la carte ⓘ 6.00 – **12 rm** ⊑ 38.00/55.00 **t.** – SB.

XX **Zetland Country House** (at Zetland Country House H.), ⌀ *(095) 31111,*
Fax (095) 31117, ≤ Cashel Bay, ☞ – ⅙≒ 🅿. 🆎 🝁 ⓪ 𝚅𝙸𝚂𝙰
2 April-October – **Meals** (booking essential) (dinner only) 29.50 **t.** ⓘ 8.00.

Particularly pleasant hotels and restaurants
are shown in the Guide by a **red symbol**.

🏨🏨🏨 ... ⌂

Please send us the names
of anywhere you have enjoyed your stay.
Your **Michelin Guide** will be even better.

XXXXX ... X

CASTLEBALDWIN (Béal Átha na gCarraigíní) *Sligo* 923 G 5 *Ireland G.* – ⊠ *Boyle (Roscommon)*.
Env. : *Carrowkeel Megalithic Cemetery (⩽★★), S : 3 m.*
Exc. : *Arigna Scenic Drive★★, N : 2 m. by N 4 – Lough Key Forest Park★★ AC, SE : 10 m. by N 4 – View★★, N : 9 m. by N 4 on R 280 – Mountain Drive★, N : 6 m. on N 4 – Boyle Abbey★ AC, SE : 8 m. by N 4.*
Dublin 118 – Longford 42 – Sligo 15.

Cromleagh Lodge ⌂, Ballindoon, SE : 3 ½ m. ℰ (071) 65155, Fax (071) 65455, ⩽ Lough Arrow and Carrowkeel Cairns, ⌕, ⌖, park – ⇌ 📺 ☎ 🅿, ⬤ 𝔸𝔼 ⓪ 𝘝𝘐𝘚𝘈
6 February-1 November – Meals (dinner only) a la carte 25.00/36.00 t. ⌕ 6.50 – **10 rm** ⊇ 99.50/139.00 t. – SB.

CASTLEBAR (Caisléan an Bharraigh) *Mayo* 923 E 6 – *pop. 6 585.*
Dublin 161 – Galway 49 – Sligo 47.

Breaffy House ⩨,, SE : 3 m. on N 60 ℰ (094) 22033, Fax (094) 22276, ⌔, ⌖, park – ⧊ 📺 ☎ ⅋ 🅿 – ⩘ 300. ⬤ 𝔸𝔼 ⓪ 𝘝𝘐𝘚𝘈. ⬤
closed 23 to 27 December – Meals 11.00/20.00 st. and dinner a la carte ⌕ 5.00 – **62 rm** ⊇ 57.50/93.00 t. – SB.

CASTLEBELLINGHAM (Baile an Ghearlánaigh) *Louth* 923 M 6 – *pop. 792 (inc. Kilsaran).*
Dublin 43 – Dundalk 8 – Drogheda 14.

Bellingham Castle ⌂, ℰ (042) 72176, Fax (042) 72766, ⌕, park – 📺 ☎ 🅿, ⬤ 𝔸𝔼 𝘝𝘐𝘚𝘈
closed 24 and 25 December – Meals 8.00/12.50 st. and dinner a la carte – **21 rm** ⊇ 35.00/70.00 st. – SB.

CASTLEBLAYNEY (Baile na Lorgan) *Monaghan* 923 L 5 – *pop. 1 884.*
⌖ Muckno Park ℰ (042) 40197.
Dublin 68 – Belfast 58 – Drogheda 39 – Dundalk 17 – Londonderry 80.

Glencarn, Monaghan Rd, ℰ (042) 46666, Fax (042) 46521, ⌔, ⬛ – ▤ rest, 📺 ☎ 🅿, ⬤ 𝔸𝔼 ⓪ 𝘝𝘐𝘚𝘈. ⬤
closed 24 and 25 December – Meals (carving lunch) 9.75/16.00 t. and a la carte ⌕ 5.8 – **27 rm** ⊇ 35.00/65.00 t. – SB.

CASTLECONNELL (Caisléan Uí Chonaill) *Limerick* 923 G 9 *Ireland G.* – *pop. 1 414* – ⊠ *Limerick*.
See : *Town★*.
Dublin 111 – Limerick 9.

Castle Oaks House ⌂, ℰ (061) 377666, Fax (061) 377717, ⩽, ⌔, ⩵, ⬛, ⌕, ⌖, park – ⬤ – 📺 ☎ 🅿 – ⩘ 200. ⬤ 𝔸𝔼 ⓪ 𝘝𝘐𝘚𝘈. ⬤
closed 24 to 26 December – Meals (bar lunch Monday to Saturday)/dinner 20.00 and a la carte ⌕ 5.25 – **20 rm** ⊇ 54.00/120.00 t. – SB.

CASTLEDERMOT (Díseart Diarmada) *Kildare* 923 L 9 *Ireland G.* – *pop. 733.*
Exc. : *Carlow Cathedral (Marble Monument★) NE : 7 m. by N 9.*
Dublin 44 – Kilkenny 30 – Wexford 54.

Kilkea Castle ⌂, Kilkea, NW : 3 m. by R 418 ℰ (0503) 45156, Fax (0503) 45187, ⩽, « Part 12C », ⌔, ⬛, ⌕⌖, ⌕, ⌖, park, ⬤ – ⧊ 📺 ☎ 🅿 – ⩘ 200. ⬤ 𝔸𝔼 ⓪ 𝘝𝘐𝘚𝘈 𝘑𝘊𝘉. ⬤
closed 1 week Christmas – Meals 16.50/28.50 t. ⌕ 6.50 – **29 rm** ⊇ 90.00/160.00 t., 7 suites – SB.

CASTLEGREGORY (Caisleán Ghriaire) *Kerry* 923 B 11 – *pop. 163.*
Dublin 203 – Killarney 36 – Limerick 85 – Tralee 16.

The Shores Country House, ℰ (066) 39196, Fax (066) 39196, ⩽, ⌖ – ⇌ 🅿. ⬤ 𝘝𝘐𝘚 ⬤
18 March-18 November – Meals (communal dining) 15.50 st. – **3 rm** ⊇ 22.00/40.00 st. – SB.

CASTLEISLAND (Oileán Ciarraá) *Kerry* 923 D 11 – *pop. 2 233.*
Dublin 170 – Cork 59 – Killarney 16 – Limerick 52 – Tralee 12.

River Island, Lower Main St., ℰ (066) 42555, Fax (066) 42544 – ⧊ 📺 ☎ – ⩘ 200. ⬤ ⓪ 𝘝𝘐𝘚𝘈. ⬤
Meals *(closed 25-26 December and Good Friday)* 9.50/16.50 t. and a la carte ⌕ 6.75 – **52 rm** ⊇ 55.00/140.00 t. – SB.

CASTLELYONS (Caisleán Ó Liatháin) *Cork* 𝟵𝟮𝟯 H 11 – *pop. 164.*
  Dublin 136 – Cork 19 – Killarney 65 – Limerick 40.

  ⌂ **Ballyvolane House** ⌛, ℘ (025) 36349, Fax (025) 36781, ≼, « 18C Italianate mansion,
    extensive parklands », ⌖ – **℗**. 🆖 ⒶⒺ ⓪ 𝚅𝙸𝚂𝙰. ⌖
    Meals (by arrangement) 23.00 **t.** ⌬ 6.00 – **6 rm** ⌸ 45.00/90.00 **t.**

CASTLEREA (An Caisleán Riabhach) *Roscommon* 𝟵𝟮𝟯 G 6 – *pop. 1 790.*
  Dublin 108 – Galway 62 – Limerick 105.

  ⌂ **Clonalis House** ⌛,, W : ½ m. on N 60 ℘ (0907) 20014, ≼, « Victorian Italianate mansion
    in extensive grounds », ⌖, ⌨, ⌖ – **℗**. 🆖 𝚅𝙸𝚂𝙰. ⌖
    April-September (booking essential) – **Meals** (by arrangement) (communal dining) 22.50
    ⌬ 8.15 – **4 rm** ⌸ 51.00/90.00.

CAVAN (An Cabhán) *Cavan* 𝟵𝟮𝟯 J 6 *Ireland G.* – *pop. 3 509.*
  Env. : Killykeen Forest Park★, W : 6 m. by R 198.
  🛈 Farnham St. ℘ (049) 31942 (June-September).
  Dublin 71 – Drogheda 69 – Enniskillen 40.

  🏨 **Kilmore**, Dublin Rd, E : 2 m. on N 3 ℘ (049) 32288, Fax (049) 32458 – 📺 ☎ ⌖ **℗** – ⚖ 550.
    🆖 ⒶⒺ ⓪ 𝚅𝙸𝚂𝙰. ⌖
    Meals 9.50/18.50 **st.** and dinner a la carte ⌬ 5.25 – **39 rm** ⌸ 45.00/72.00 **st.** – SB.

Le Guide change, changez de guide Michelin tous les ans.

CHEEKPOINT (Pointe na Ságe) *Waterford* 𝟵𝟮𝟯 K/L 11 – *see Waterford.*

CLADDAGHDUFF (An Cladach Dubh) *Galway* 𝟵𝟮𝟯 B 7 – ✉ *Clifden.*
  Dublin 189 – Ballina 85 – Galway 58.

  ⌂ **Acton's** ⌛, Leegaun, SE : 1 ¾ m. ℘ (095) 44339, Fax (095) 44309, ≼, ⌨ – ⌖ rm, 📺 ☎
    ℗. 🆖 ⒶⒺ ⓪ 𝚅𝙸𝚂𝙰. ⌖
    13 March-October – **Meals** (by arrangement) 21.00 **t.** – **6 rm** ⌸ 30.00/60.00 **t.** – SB.

CLARINBRIDGE (Droichead an Chláráin) *Galway* 𝟵𝟮𝟯 F 8.
  Dublin 145 – Galway 11.

  🏨 **Oyster Manor**, ℘ (091) 796777, Fax (091) 796770 – 📺 ☎ ⌖ **℗** – ⚖ 80. 🆖 ⒶⒺ ⓪ 𝚅𝙸𝚂𝙰. ⌖
    closed 25 December – **Meals** (bar lunch Monday to Saturday)/dinner 19.50 **st.** and a la carte
    ⌬ 5.95 – **14 rm** ⌸ 60.00/90.00 **st.** – SB.

CLIFDEN (An Clochán) *Galway* 𝟵𝟮𝟯 B 7 *Ireland G.* – *pop. 920.*
  Exc. : Connemara★★★, NE : by N 59 – Sky Road★★★, NE : by N 59 – Connemara National
  Park★, NE : 1 m by N 59.
  🛈 Market St. ℘ (095) 21163 (3 May-30 September).
  Dublin 181 – Ballina 77 – Galway 49.

  🏨 **Rock Glen Manor House** ⌛, S : 1 ¼ m. by R 341 ℘ (095) 21035, Fax (095) 21737, ⌨,
    ⌖ – ⌖ rest, 📺 ☎ ⌖. 🆖 ⒶⒺ ⓪ 𝚅𝙸𝚂𝙰. ⌖
    16 March-27 October – **Meals** (bar lunch)/dinner a la carte approx. 26.00 **t.** ⌬ 9.00 – **29 rm**
    ⌸ 70.00/110.00 **t.** – SB.

  🏨 **Ardagh** ⌛, Ballyconneely rd, S : 1 ¾ m. on R 341 ℘ (095) 21384, Fax (095) 21314,
    ≼ Ardbear Bay – 📺 ☎ ⌖. 🆖 ⒶⒺ ⓪ 𝚅𝙸𝚂𝙰. ⌖
    April-October – **Meals** (bar lunch)/dinner 28.50 **st.** ⌬ 7.50 – **21 rm** ⌸ 70.00/115.00 **st.** – SB.

  ⌂ **Mal Dua** without rest., Galway Rd, E : ½ m. on N 59 ℘ (095) 21171, Fax (095) 21739, ⌨ –
    ⌖ 📺 ☎ ⌖. 🆖 ⒶⒺ 𝚅𝙸𝚂𝙰. ⌖
    February-October – **14 rm** ⌸ 30.00/60.00 **st.**

  ⌂ **Sunnybank House** ⌛ without rest., Church Hill, ℘ (095) 21437, Fax (095) 21976, ⌖,
    ⌨, ⌨, ⌖ – 📺 ☎ ⌖. 🆖 𝚅𝙸𝚂𝙰. ⌖
    March-November – **9 rm** ⌸ 40.00/70.00.

  ✗ **Quay House** with rm, Beach Rd, ℘ (095) 21369, Fax (095) 21608, ≼ – 📺 ☎. 🆖 𝚅𝙸𝚂𝙰. ⌖
    closed Sunday and November-15 March – **Meals** (booking essential to non-residents)
    (dinner only and light lunch July and August)/dinner 22.00 **t.** ⌬ 6.50 – **10 rm** ⌸ 45.00/
    80.00 **t.** – SB.

  ✗ **O'Grady's**, Market St., ℘ (095) 21450, Fax (095) 21994 – 🆖 ⒶⒺ 𝚅𝙸𝚂𝙰
    April-November – **Meals** - Seafood - (light lunch)/dinner a la carte 18.85/27.85 **t.** ⌬ 6.00.

CLONAKILTY (Cloich na Coillte) *Cork* 923 F 13 *Ireland G. – pop. 2 724.*
See : *West Cork Regional Museum★ AC.*
Env. : *Timoleague★ (Franciscan Friary★) E : 5 m. by R 600.*
Dublin 193 – Cork 32.

⌂ **Árd na Gréine Farm House** ⌖, Ballinascarthy, NW : 5 ¾ m. by N 71 ℰ (023) 39104, Fax (023) 39397, « Working farm », ☞ – 📺 **P**. 🐾 *VISA*
Meals 16.00 **st.** ⌀ 5.00 – **6 rm** ⌷ 21.00/40.00 – SB.

CLONMEL (Cluain Meala) *Tipperary* 923 I 10 – *pop. 15 215.*
See : *Town★ – County Museum★, St. Mary's Church★, Riverside★ (quay★).*
🏌 *Lyreanearla, Mountain Rd ℰ (052) 21138.*
🛈 *Community Office, Town Centre ℰ (052) 22960.*
Dublin 108 – Cork 59 – Kilkenny 31 – Limerick 48 – Waterford 29.

🏨 **Minella** ⌖, Coleville Rd, ℰ (052) 22388, Fax (052) 24381, ⟋, ☞, park – 📺 ☎ **P** – ⛵ 550. 🐾 🏧 ⑩ *VISA*. ✂
closed 23 to 27 December – **Meals** 13.00/22.00 **st.** and a la carte ⌀ 6.50 – **67 rm** ⌷ 65.00/120.00 **st.**, 3 suites – SB.

🏨 **Clonmel Arms,** Sarsfield St., ℰ (052) 21233, Fax (052) 21526 – 🛗 📺 ☎ – ⛵ 450. 🐾 🏧 ⑩ *VISA*
Meals 10.00/14.00 **t.** and dinner a la carte ⌀ 5.50 – ⌷ 6.50 – **31 rm** 70.00/80.00 **t.** – SB.

Groß-London (GREATER LONDON) besteht aus der City und 32
Verwaltungsbezirken (Borough). Diese sind wiederum in kleinere
Bezirke (Area) unterteilt, deren Mittelpunkt ehemalige Dörfer
oder Stadtviertel sind, die oft ihren eigenen Charakter bewahrt haben.

COBH (An Cóbh) *Cork* 923 H 12 – *pop. 6 468.*
Dublin 173 – Cork 13 – Waterford 71.

⌂ **Tearmann** ⌖, Ballynoe, N : 1 ½ m. by R 624 ℰ (021) 813182, Fax (021) 814011, ☞ – **P** ✂
March-October – **Meals** (by arrangement) 12.00 **s.** – **3 rm** ⌷ 23.50/34.00 **s.** – SB.

CONG (Conga) *Mayo* 923 E 7 *Ireland G. – pop. 197.*
See : *Town★.*
Env. : *Lough Corrib★★.*
Exc. : *Ross Abbey★★ (Tower ⩽★) – Joyce Country★★ (Lough Nafooey★★) W : by R 345.*
Dublin 160 – Ballina 49 – Galway 28.

🏰 **Ashford Castle** ⌖, ℰ (092) 46003, Fax (092) 46260, ⩽, « Part 13C and 18C castle, i extensive formal gardens on shores of Lough Corrib », ₭, ⛵, ₰, ⟋, park, ✗ – 🛗 ⟻ rest, 📺 ☎ **P** – ⛵ 110. 🐾 🏧 ⑩ *VISA*. ✂
George V Room : **Meals** *(closed 24 December-2 January to non-residents)* 22.00 37.00 **t.** and dinner a la carte ⌀ 10.00 – *Connaught Room :* **Meals** (booking essentia (residents only) (dinner only May-September) a la carte 50.00/60.00 **t.** ⌀ 10.00 ⌷ 13.50 – **77 rm** 220.00/400.00 **st.**, 6 suites – SB.

CORK (Corcaigh) *Cork* 923 G 12 *Ireland G. – pop. 127 187.*
See : *City★★ – Shandon Bells★★ EY, St. Fin Barre's Cathedral★★ AC Z, Cork Publ Museum★★ X M – Grand Parade★ Z , South Mall★ Z , St. Patrick Street★ Z , Crawfor Art Gallery★ Y – Christ the King Church★ X D , Elizabethan Fort★ Z , Cork Lough★ X.*
Env. : *Dunkathel House★ AC, E : 5 ¾ m. by N 8 and N 25 X.*
Exc. : *Fota Island★★ (Fota House★★) E : 8 m. by N 8 and N 25 X – Cobh★ (St. Colmar Cathedral★, Lusitania Memorial★) SE : 15 m. by N 8, N 25 and R 624 X.*
🏌 *Douglas ℰ (021) 891086, X –* 🏌 *Mahon, Cloverhill, Blackrock ℰ (021) 362480 X* 🏌 *Monkstown, Parkgarriffe ℰ (021) 841376, X –* 🏌 *Harbour Point, Clash, Little Islar ℰ (021) 353094, X.*
✈ *Cork Airport : ℰ (021) 313131, S : 4 m. by L 42 X – Terminal : Bus Station, Parnell Pl.*
⛴ *to France (Le Havre) (Irish Ferries) (summer only) weekly (22 h), (Roscoff) (Brittar Ferries and Irish Ferries) weekly, (St. Malo) (Brittany Ferries) weekly (17 h 30 mn) – Pembroke (Swansea Cork Ferries) 4 weekly (10 h) – to Swansea (Swansea Cork Ferries) (10 l*
🛈 *Cork City, Grand Parade ℰ (021) 273251.*
Dublin 154.

CORK
BUILT UP AREA

Baker's Road . . . . X 4
Commons Road . . . . X 12
Curragh Road . . . . X 14
Dublin Street . . . . X 16
Gardiner's Hill . . . . X 20
Great William
O'Brien Street . . . . X 22
Horgan Quay . . . . X 23
Lower Mayfield Road . . . . X 31
Thomas Davis Street . . . . X 49
Victoria Cross Rd. . . . . X 50
Watercourse Road . . . . X 52
Western Road . . . . X 53
Wilton Road . . . . X 55

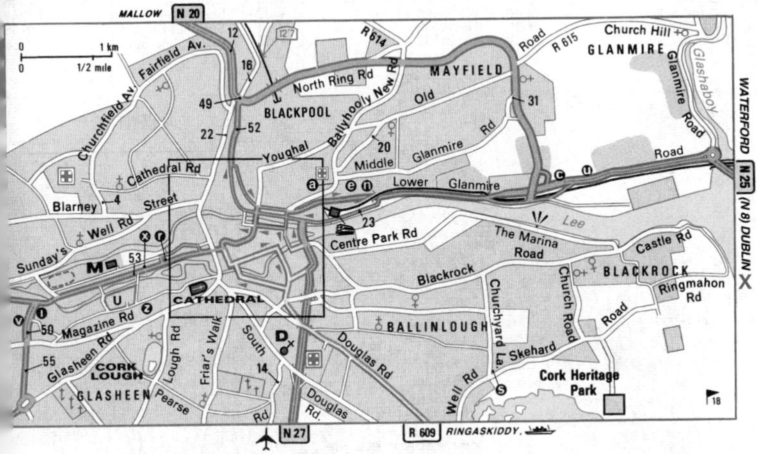

Rochestown Park, Rochestown Rd, Douglas, SE : 3 m. by R 609 ℘ (021) 892233, *Fax (021) 892178*, – 900. VISA.
Windsor **:** **Meals** 12.00/18.00 **t.** and a la carte 6.75 – **114 rm** 70.00/100.00 **t.**, 1 suite – SB.

Fitzpatrick Cork, Tivoli, E : 2½ m. on N 8 ℘ (021) 507533, *Fax (021) 507641*, park, squash – rm, rest, – 800. VISA JCB.
closed 25 December – **Meals** a la carte 20.00/35.00 6.95 – 8.50 – **106 rm** 85.00/121.00, 3 suites – SB. X c

Ambassador, Military Hill, ℘ (021) 551996, *Fax (021) 551997* – rm, – 80. VISA X a
closed 25 December – **Meals** 16.00 **st.** (dinner) and a la carte 9.00/26.00 **st.** 5.95 – **59 rm** 85.00/105.00 **st.**, 1 suite – SB.

Shandon Court, Shandon, ℘ (021) 551793, *Fax (021) 551665* – rest, – 150. VISA. Y e
closed 24 to 26 December – **Meals** (bar lunch Monday to Saturday)/dinner 24.50 **st.** and a la carte 7.00 – ***The Belfry*** **: Meals** 13.50 **st.** (lunch) and dinner a la carte 21.75/27.25 **st.** 7.00 – **6 rm** 70.00/95.00 **st.**, **18 suites** 110.00/140.00 **st.** – SB.

Jurys, Western Rd, by Washington St., ℘ (021) 276622, *Fax (021) 274477*, squash – rm, rest, – 500. VISA. Z v
closed 25 and 26 December – ***Glandore*** **: Meals** 13.00/19.00 **st.** and a la carte 8.15 – ***Fastnet*** **: Meals** *(closed Monday)* (dinner only) 27.00 and a la carte 8.15 – 10.05 – **184 rm** 125.00/145.00, 1 suite – SB.

Hayfield Manor, Perrott Av., College Rd, ℘ (021) 315600, *Fax (021) 316839*, – – 120. VISA. X z
Meals (bar lunch Saturday) 16.50/30.00 **st.** and dinner a la carte 6.95 – **51 rm** 100.00/150.00 **st.**, 2 suites – SB.

Morrisons Island, Morrisons Quay, ℘ (021) 275858, *Fax (021) 275833* – rest, VISA Z a
closed 4 days Christmas – ***Riverbank*** **: Meals** 13.85/18.95 **t.** and a la carte 7.00 – 9.00 – **12 rm** 65.00/150.00 **st.**, **28 suites** 75.00/165.00 **st.** – SB.

Arbutus Lodge, Middle Glanmire Rd, Montenotte, ℘ (021) 501237, *Fax (021) 502893*, – – 100. VISA. X e
closed 24 to 28 December – **Meals** – (see ***Arbutus Lodge*** below) – **16 rm** 52.00/125.00 **st.**, 4 suites – SB.

Imperial, South Mall, ℘ (021) 274040, *Fax (021) 275375* – – 500. VISA Z n
closed 1 week Christmas – **Meals** a la carte 10.25/13.25 **t.** 6.00 – 7.95 – **98 rm** 55.00/150.00 **t.** – SB.

CORK

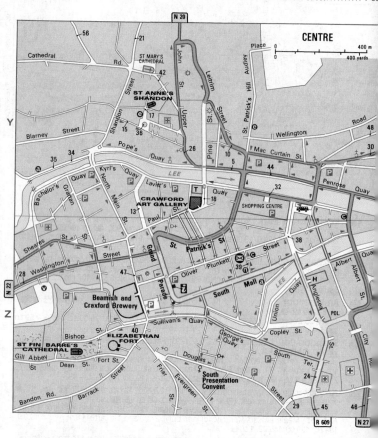

CENTRE

🏨 **Country Club**, Middle Glanmire Rd, Montenotte, ℰ (021) 502922, Fax (021) 502082, 🚗
📺 ☎ 🅿 – 🛗 300. 🔘 🔘 AE ① _VISA_. 🛠
X
closed 23 to 28 December – **Meals** (bar lunch Monday to Saturday)/dinner 13.50 s
and a la carte – **60 rm** 🖙 40.00/80.00 **st.** – SB.

🏨 **Jurys Cork Inn**, Anderson's Quay, ℰ (021) 276444, Fax (021) 276144 – 📳, 🖘 rm, 📺
🔘 🅿 – 🛗 40. 🔘 🔘 AE ① _VISA_. 🛠
Y
closed 24 to 27 December – **Meals** (carving lunch)/dinner 15.50 **st.** and a la carte 🍴 6.25
🖙 6.00 – **133 rm** 55.00 **st.**

🏨 **The Commons Inn**, Commons Rd, N : 1½ m. on N 20 ℰ (021) 210300, Fax (021) 2103
– 📺 ☎ 🔘 🅿 – 🛗 45. 🔘 🔘 AE ① _VISA_. 🛠
Meals _(closed Sunday dinner)_ (by arrangement Bank Holidays) (grill rest.) 4.50 s
(lunch) and a la carte 11.60/15.10 **st.** 🍴 5.50 – 🖙 4.50 – **40 rm** 37.50 **st.**

🏨 **Victoria Lodge** without rest., Victoria Cross, ℰ (021) 542233, Fax (021) 542572, 🚗 –
🖘 📺 ☎ 🅿. 🔘 🔘 AE _VISA_. 🛠
X
closed 24 to 28 December – **30 rm** 🖙 33.00/50.00 **st.**

⌂ **Ibis Cork,** Dunkette Roundabout, E : 4 ¾ m. by N 8 and N 25 on R 639 ℘ (021) 354354, Fax (021) 354202 – 📶, ✦✦ rm, 📺 ☎ ♿ ℗ – 🔏 90. ⬛ 𐄂 ⓞ 𐄂 𐄂. ✦
Meals (dinner only) 11.50 st. ↥ 5.50 – ☲ 5.25 – **100 rm** 49.50 st.

⌂ **Travelodge,** Blackash, S : 2 ¼ m. by R 600 ℘ (021) 310722, Reservations (Freephone) 0800 850950 (UK), 1800 709709 (Republic of Ireland) – ✦✦ rm, 📺 ♿ ℗. ⬛ 𐄂 ⓞ 𐄂 𐄂 𐄂. ✦
Meals (grill rest.) – **40 rm** 39.95 t.

⌂ **Garnish House** without rest., Western Rd, ℘ (021) 275111, Fax (021) 273872 – ✦✦ 📺 ☎ ℗. ⬛ 𐄂 ⓞ 𐄂. ✦   X   r
14 rm ☲ 20.00/60.00 st.

⌂ **Seven North Mall** without rest., 7 North Mall, ℘ (021) 397191, Fax (021) 300811 – 📺 ☎ ℗. ⬛ 𐄂. ✦   Y   a
closed 19 December-8 January – **5 rm** ☲ 45.00/70.00 st.

⌂ **Killarney House** without rest., Western Rd, ℘ (021) 270290, Fax (021) 271010 – ✦✦ 📺 ☎ ℗. ⬛ 𐄂 𐄂. ✦   X   x
closed 25 and 26 December – **19 rm** ☲ 50.00/55.00 st.

⌂ **Acorn House** without rest., 14 St. Patrick's Hill, ℘ (021) 502474 – 📺. ⬛ 𐄂 𐄂. ✦   Y   e
closed 20 December-12 January – **9 rm** ☲ 30.00/50.00 st.

XXX **Flemings** with rm, Silver Grange House, Tivoli, E : 2 ¾ m. on N 8 ℘ (021) 821621, Fax (021) 821800, 🌳 – 📺 ☎ ℗. ⬛ 𐄂 ⓞ 𐄂.   X   u
closed 23 to 26 December – **Meals** 14.00 t. (lunch) and a la carte 23.50/31.00 t. ↥ 7.00 –
4 rm ☲ 45.00/65.00 st.

XXX **Arbutus Lodge** (at Arbutus Lodge H.), Middle Glanmire Rd, Montenotte, ℘ (021) 501237, Fax (021) 502893, 🌳 – ▤ ℗. ⬛ 𐄂 ⓞ 𐄂   X   e
closed Sunday and 24 to 28 December – **Meals** 15.50/23.20 st. and a la carte ↥ 8.55.

XX **Lovetts** (Restaurant), Churchyard Lane, off Well Rd, Douglas, ℘ (021) 294909, Fax (021) 294024 – ℗. ⬛ 𐄂 ⓞ 𐄂   X   s
closed Saturday lunch, Sunday, Monday June-August, 1 week Christmas and Bank Holidays – **Meals** 14.50/24.00 t. and dinner a la carte ↥ 6.95.

XX **Wylam,** Victoria Cross, ℘ (021) 341063, Fax (021) 272146 – ▤ ℗. ⬛ 𐄂 ⓞ 𐄂 𐄂. ✦   X   i
closed 24 and 25 December – **Meals** - Chinese - (dinner only) 16.00 t. and a la carte ↥ 6.50.

X **Jacques,** 9 Phoenix St., ℘ (021) 277387, Fax (021) 270634 – ▤. ⬛ 𐄂 𐄂 𐄂   Z   c
closed Saturday lunch, Sunday, 1 week Christmas and Bank Holidays – **Meals** 10.90/19.90 t. and a la carte ↥ 6.90.

CRATLOE (An Chreatalach) Clare 923 F 9 – pop. 557 – ✉ Bunratty.
Dublin 127 – Ennis 17 – Limerick 7.

⌂ **Bunratty View** without rest., ℘ (061) 357352, Fax (061) 357491, ←, 🌳 – ✦✦ 📺 ☎ ℗. ⬛ 𐄂. ✦
6 rm ☲ 25.00/38.00.

CROOKEDWOOD (Tigh Munna) Westmeath 923 K 7 – see Mullingar.

CROSSMOLINA (Crois Mhaoilíona) Mayo 923 E 5 Ireland G. – pop. 1 103.
Env. : Errew Abbey★, SE : 6 m. by R 315.
Exc. : Broad Haven★, NW : 27 m. by N 59 and R 313.
Dublin 157 – Ballina 6.5.

⌂ **Enniscoe House** ⬥, Castlehill, S : 2 m. on R 315 ℘ (096) 31112, Fax (096) 31773, ←, « Georgian country house, antiques », 🔻, park – ✦✦ ℗. ⬛ 𐄂 𐄂. ✦
April-14 October – **Meals** (dinner only) 25.00 st. ↥ 8.00 – **6 rm** ☲ 60.00/112.00 st. – SB.

DELGANY (Deilgne) Wicklow 923 N 8 – pop. 6 682 (inc. Greystones) – ✉ Bray.
🏌 Delganny ℘ (01) 287 4536.
Dublin 19.

▲▲ **Glenview,** Glen of the Downs, NW : 2 m. by L 164 on N 11 ℘ (01) 287 3399, Fax (01) 287 7511, ←, ⅙, ☂, 🔳, 🌳, park – 📶 📺 ☎ ♿ ℗ – 🔏 250. ⬛ 𐄂 ⓞ 𐄂 𐄂. ✦
Woodlands : Meals 16.00 t. (lunch) and dinner a la carte 16.00/27.50 t. ↥ 7.00 – **40 rm** ☲ 90.00/175.00 t. – SB.

Les prix   Pour toutes précisions sur les prix indiqués dans ce guide, reportez-vous aux pages de l'introduction.

DINGLE (An Daingean) *Kerry* 923 B 11 *Ireland G.* – *pop. 1 536*.

See : *Town★* – *Pier★*, *St. Mary's Church★*.

Env. : *Gallarus Oratory★★★*, NW : *5 m. by R 559* – NE : *Connor Pass★★* – *Kilmalkedar★*, NW : *5 ½ m. by R 559*.

Exc. : *Mount Eagle (Beehive Huts★★) W : 9 m. by R 559* – *Slea Head★★*, W : *10 ½ m. by R 559* – *Stradbally Strand★★*, NE : *10 ½ m. via Connor Pass* – *Ballyferriter Heritage Centre★ AC*, NW : *8 m. by R 559* – *Mount Brandon★*, N : *12 ½ m. by R 559 via Kilmalkedar* – *Blasket Islands★*, W : *13 m. by R 559 and ferry from Dunquin*.

🛈 *Main St.* 𝒫 *(066) 51188 (April-October)*.

Dublin 216 – *Killarney 51* – *Limerick 95*.

🏨 **Dingle Skellig**, SE : ½ m. by T 68 𝒫 (066) 51144, *Fax (066) 51501*, ≤, 🛏, 🚗, ⬜, 🌳, ✖ – 🛗 📺 ☎ 🅿 – 🔬 250. 🆗 🆎 ⑩ *VISA*. ✘
closed 5 January-1 March – Meals (bar lunch Monday to Saturday)/dinner 25.00 **t.** and a la carte 🍴 8.00 – **109 rm** ⚌ 80.00/130.00 **st.**, 1 suite – SB.

🏨 **Milltown House** 🦢 without rest., W : ¾ m. by Slea Head Drive 𝒫 (066) 51372, *Fax (066) 51095*, ≤, 🌳 🅱 🅿. 🆗 *VISA*. ✘
10 rm ⚌ 30.00/60.00 **st.**

🏨 **Greenmount House** without rest., Gortonora, by John St. 𝒫 (066) 51414 *Fax (066) 51974*, ≤ – 📺 ☎ 🅿. 🆗 *VISA*. ✘
closed 20 to 26 December – **12 rm** ⚌ 35.00/70.00 **st.**

🏨 **Doyle's Townhouse**, 5 John St., 𝒫 (066) 51174, *Fax (066) 51816* – 📺 ☎. 🆗 ⑩ *VISA*. ✘
mid March-mid November – Meals – (see **Doyle's Seafood Bar** below) – 8 rm ⚌ 44.00/ 68.00

⌂ **Captains House** without rest., The Mall, 𝒫 (066) 51531, *Fax (066) 51079*, 🌳 – 📺 ☎. 🆗 🆎 ⑩ *VISA*. ✘
April-November – **7 rm** ⚌ 30.00/44.00 **st.**

⌂ **Cleevaun** without rest., Lady's Cross, Milltown, W : 1 ¼ m. on R 559 following signs for Slea Head Drive 𝒫 (066) 51108, *Fax (066) 51108*, ≤, 🌳 – 📺 ☎ 🅿. 🆗 *VISA*. ✘
March-November – **9 rm** ⚌ 42.00/48.00 **st.**

⌂ **Bambury's** without rest., Mail Rd, E : on T 68 𝒫 (066) 51244, *Fax (066) 51786*, ≤ – 📺 ☎ 🅿. 🆗 *VISA*
12 rm ⚌ 40.00/50.00 **st.**

⌂ **Alpine House** without rest., Mail Rd, E : on T 68 𝒫 (066) 51250, *Fax (066) 51966*, 🌳 – 📺 ☎ 🅿. 🆗 *VISA*. ✘
closed 15 to 25 December – **10 rm** ⚌ 35.00/45.00 **st.**

XX **Beginish**, Green St., 𝒫 (066) 51588, *Fax (066) 51591*, 🌳 – 🆗 🆎 ⑩ *VISA*
mid March-mid November – Meals - Seafood - (closed Monday) (light lunch)/dinner a la carte 18.30/26.30 **t.** 🍴 5.50.

X **Doyle's Seafood Bar**, 4 John St., 𝒫 (066) 51174, *Fax (066) 51816* – 🆗 ⑩ *VISA*
⊛ mid March-mid November – Meals (closed Sunday) (dinner only) 15.00 **t.** and a la carte 18.00/26.00 **t.**

DONEGAL (Dún na nGall) *Donegal* 923 H 4 *Ireland G.* – *pop. 2 296*.

See : *Donegal Castle★ AC*.

Exc. : *Cliffs of Bunglass★★★*, W : *30 m. by N 56 and R 263* – *Glencolumbkille Folk Village★ AC*, W : *33 m. by N 56 and R 263* – *Trabane Strand★★*, W : *36 m. by N 56 and R 263* – *Glenmalin Court Cairn★*, W : *37 m. by N 56 and R 263 at Malin Beg*.

✈ *Donegal Airport* 𝒫 *(075) 48232*.

🛈 *The Quay* 𝒫 *(073) 21148 (April-October)*.

Dublin 164 – *Londonderry 48* – *Sligo 40*.

🏨 **St. Ernan's House** 🦢, St. Ernan's Island, SW : 2 ¼ m. by N 15 𝒫 (073) 21065 *Fax (073) 22098*, « Wooded island setting ≤ Donegal Bay », park – ✄ rest, 📺 ☎ 🅿. 🆗 *VISA*. ✘
13 April-28 October – Meals (dinner only) 27.00 🍴 7.00 – **12 rm** ⚌ 168.00 **t.** – SB.

🏨 **Harvey's Point Country H.** 🦢, Lough Eske, NE : 4 ½ m. by T 27 (Killibegs rd) 𝒫 (073) 22208, *Fax (073) 22352*, ≤, « Loughside setting », 🐟, 🌳, park, ✖ – 📺 ☎ 🅿 🔬 50. 🆗 🆎 ⑩ *VISA*
April-October and restricted opening November-March – Meals – (see below) – **20 rm** ⚌ 66.00/121.00 **st.** – SB.

⌂ **Island View House** without rest., Ballyshannon rd, SW : ¾ m. on N 15 𝒫 (073) 22411 ≤, 🌳 – 🅿. ✘
4 rm ⚌ 25.00/34.00.

XX **Harvey's Point Country H.** (at Harvey's Point Country H.), Lough Eske, NE : 4 ½ m. by N 56 (Killibegs rd) *&* (073) 22208, *Fax (073) 22352*, ≤, « Loughside setting », *₷* – **P**. **M③** **AE** **①** **VISA**
April-October and restricted opening November-March – **Meals** 13.75/27.50 **st.** and a la carte ▯ 7.70.

DOOGORT (Dumha Goirt) *Mayo* **923** B 5/6 – *see Achill Island.*

DOOLIN (Dúlainn) *Clare* **923** D 8.
Dublin 171 – Galway 43 – Limerick 50.

🏠 **Aran View House** ⬧, NE : ½ m. *&* (065) 74061, *Fax (065) 74540*, ≤, « Working farm », *₷*, park – *⤫* **TV** **☎** **P**. **M③** **AE** **①** **VISA**
10 April-26 October – **Meals** (dinner only) 20.00 **t.** and a la carte ▯ 4.95 – **19 rm** ☲ 45.00/ 70.00 **t.** – SB.

↑ **Doonmacfelim House** without rest., *&* (065) 74503, *Fax (065) 74129*, *⤫* – **☎** **P**. **M③** **VISA**. *₷*
closed 24 to 29 December – **6 rm** ☲ 23.00/40.00 **st.**

DROGHEDA (Droichead Átha) *Louth* **923** M 6 *Ireland G.* – pop. 24 460.
Env. : *Monasterboice★★, N : 6 ½ m. by N 1 – Boyne Valley★★, on N 51 – Termonfeckin (Tower House★) NE : 5 m. by R 166.*
Exc. : *– Newgrange★★, W : 3 m. by N 51 on N 2 – Old Mellifont★.*
Dublin 29 – Dundalk 22.

🏨🏨 **Boyne Valley H. and Country Club**, SE : 1 ¼ m. on N 1 *&* (041) 37737, *Fax (041) 39188*, ▯₅, ≘₅, ⬚, *₷*, park, ※ – *⤫* rm, **TV** **☎** **P** – ▱ 350. **M③** **AE** **①** **VISA**. *₷*
Meals 10.95/21.00 **st.** and a la carte – **37 rm** ☲ 49.00/150.00 **st.** – SB.

🏨🏨 **Westcourt**, West St., *&* (041) 30965, *Fax (041) 30970* – *⤫* rm, **TV** **☎** ⬤ – ▱ 350. **M③** **AE** **①** **VISA**
closed 25 December – **Meals** (carving lunch) 10.95/11.95 and dinner a la carte ▯ 5.95 – **27 rm** ☲ 37.50/75.00 **st.** – SB.

↑ **Tullyesker House** without rest., Tullyesker, Monasterboice, N : 3 ½ m. by N 1 *&* (041) 30430, *Fax (041) 32624*, ≤, *₷* – *⤫* **TV** **P**. *₷*
March-October – **5 rm** ☲ 33.00/38.00 **st.**

↑ **Boynehaven House** without rest., Dublin Rd, SE : 2 ½ m. on N 1 *&* (041) 36700, *₷* – *⤫* **TV** **P**. **M③** **VISA**. *₷*
4 rm ☲ 44.00 **st.**

XX **Abbotts Bistro**, 32 Shop St., *&* (041) 30288, *Fax (041) 30288* – **M③** **AE** **VISA**
closed Saturday lunch, Sunday dinner, Monday, 1 week spring, 1 week September and 25 December – **Meals** 9.95/23.00 **t.** and dinner a la carte ▯ 6.50.

When in EUROPE never be without

Michelin Main Road Maps;

Michelin Regional Maps;

Michelin Red Guides :
 Benelux, Deutschland, España Portugal, Europe, France,
 Great Britain and Ireland, Italia, Switzerland
 (Hotels and restaurants listed with symbols; preliminary pages in English);

Michelin Green Guides :
 Austria, Belgium, Berlin, Scandanavia/Finland, Pyrenees Languedoc/Tarn
 Gorges, Tuscany, Vienna. Disneyland Paris, England : The West Country, France,
 Germany, Great Britain, Greece, Ireland, Italy, London, Netherlands,
 Portugal, Rome, Scotland, Spain, Switzerland, Vienna, Wales.
 Atlantic Coast, Auvergne/Rhône Valley, Brittany, Burgundy/Jura,
 Châteaux of the Loire, Dordogne, Northern France the Paris Region,
 French Riviera, Normandy, Paris, Provence
 (Sights and touring programmes described fully in English; town plans).

DUBLIN - (Baile Átha Cliath)

Dublin 🔲🔲🔲 *N 7 Ireland G. – pop. 859 976.*

Belfast 103 – Cork 154 – Londonderry 146.

TOURIST INFORMATION

🛈 *Baggot Street Bridge, D2 – Arrivals Hall, Dublin Airport – Tallaght, D24.*

PRACTICAL INFORMATION

🏌 *Elm Park G. & S.C., Nutley House, Donnybrook ₤ (01) 269 3438/269 3014,* GV.
🏌 *Milltown, Lower Churchtown Rd ₤ (01) 467 6090.*
🏌 *Royal Dublin, North Bull Island, Dollymount ₤ (01) 833 6346.*
🏌 *Forrest Little, Cloghran ₤ (01) 840 1183/840 1763.*
🏌 *Lucan, Celbridge Rd, Lucan ₤ (01) 628 0246.*
🏌 *Edmondstown, Rathfarnham ₤ (01) 493 2461.*
🏌 *Coldwinters, Newtown House, St. Margaret's ₤ (01) 864 0324.*
✈ *Dublin Airport : ₤ (01) 844 4900, N : 5 ½ m. by N 1* BS – **Terminal :** *Busaras (Central Bus Station) Store St.*
⛴ *to Holyhead (Irish Ferries) 2 daily (3 h 15 mn) – to Holyhead (Stena Line) daily (4 h) – to the Isle of Man (Douglas) (Isle of Man Steam Packet Co. Ltd) (4 h 30 mn).*

SIGHTS

See : *City*★★★ – *Trinity College*★★★ *(Library*★★★ *AC)* JY – *Chester Beatty Library*★★★ FV – *Phoenix Park*★★★ AS – *Dublin Castle*★★ HY – *Christ Church Cathedral*★★ HY – *St. Patrick's Cathedral*★★ HZ – *Marsh's Library*★★ HZ – *National Museum*★★ *(Treasury*★★*),* KZ – *National Gallery*★★ KZ – *Merrion Square*★★ KZ – *Rotunda Hospital Chapel*★★ JX – *Kilmainham Hospital*★★ AT – *Kilmainham Gaol Museum*★★ AT M6 – *National Botanic Gardens*★★ BS – *No 29*★ KZ D – *Liffey Bridge*★ JY – *Tailors' Hall*★ HY – *City Hall*★ HY – *St. Audoen's Gate*★ HY B – *St. Stephen's Green*★ JZ – *Grafton Street*★ JYZ – *Powerscourt Centre*★ JY – *Civic Museum*★ JY M1 – *Bank of Ireland*★ JY – *O'Connell Street*★ *(Anna Livia Fountain*★*)* JX – *St. Michan's Church*★ HY E – *Hush Lane Municipal Gallery of Modern Art*★ JX M4 – *Pro-Cathedral*★ JX – *Garden of Remembrance*★ JX – *Custom House*★ KX – *Bluecoat School*★ BS F – *Guinness Museum*★ BT M7 – *Marino Casino*★ CS – *Zoological Gardens*★ AS – *Newman House*★ AC JZ.

Exc. *Powerscourt*★★ *(Waterfall*★★★ *AC), S : 14 m. by N 11 and R 117* EV – *Russborough House*★★★ *, SW : 22 m. by N 81* BT – *Rathfarnham Castle*★ *, S : 3 m. by N 81 and R 115* BT.

The Merrion, Upper Merrion St., D2, ℰ (01) 603 0600, Fax (01) 603 0700, « Carefully restored Georgian town houses, collection of contemporary Irish art », ₤₅, ☐ – 📳, ✻ rm, ▤ 📺 ☎ ⇔ – 🏊 45. 🐾 🅰🄴 ⓞ 𝗩𝗜𝗦𝗔 ᴊᴄʙ. ✻
Mornington : Meals 16.00/23.00 **st.** and a la carte 21.45/35.50 **st.** ₤ 8.00 – ⛌ 13.00 – **135 rm** 190.00/255.00 **t.**, 10 suites – SB.
KZ e

Conrad International Dublin, Earlsfort Terr., D2, ℰ (01) 676 5555, Fax (01) 676 5424 – 📳, ✻ rm, ▤ 📺 ☎ 🄿 – 🏊 310. 🐾 🅰🄴 ⓞ 𝗩𝗜𝗦𝗔 ᴊᴄʙ. ✻
Alexandra : Meals (closed Saturday lunch and Sunday) 17.50/29.50 **t.** and a la carte ₤ 7.00 –
Plurabelle Brasserie : Meals 15.00/17.50 **t.** and a la carte ₤ 7.00 – ⛌ 12.00 – **182 rm** 185.00/210.00 **t.**, 9 suites.
JZ w

The Shelbourne, 27 St. Stephen's Green, D2, ℰ (01) 676 6471, Fax (01) 661 6006 – 📳, ✻ rm, 📺 ☎ ⇔ – 🏊 400. 🐾 🅰🄴 ⓞ 𝗩𝗜𝗦𝗔 ᴊᴄʙ. ✻
No. 27 The Green : Meals 17.50/26.50 **t.** and a la carte ₤ 8.50 – **The Side Door :** Meals a la carte 10.50/20.20 **t.** ₤ 7.50 – ⛌ 13.50 – **181 rm** 169.00/225.00 **t.**, 9 suites.
JZ s

Berkeley Court, Lansdowne Rd, Ballsbridge, D4, ℰ (01) 660 1711, Fax (01) 661 7238, ₤₅ – 📳, ✻ rm, ▤ rest, 📺 ☎ ₠ ⇔ 🄿 – 🏊 450. 🐾 🅰🄴 ⓞ 𝗩𝗜𝗦𝗔 ✻
FU c
Berkeley Room : Meals 17.75/27.50 **t.** and a la carte ₤ 6.75 – **Conservatory Grill :** Meals 12.00 **t.** (lunch) and a la carte 17.75/28.35 **t.** ₤ 6.75 – ⛌ 11.00 – **182 rm** 145.00/185.00 **t.**, 6 suites – SB.

The Westbury, Grafton St., D2, ℰ (01) 679 1122, Fax (01) 679 7078 – 📳, ✻ rm, ▤ rest, 📺 ☎ ⇔ – 🏊 150. 🐾 🅰🄴 ⓞ 𝗩𝗜𝗦𝗔. ✻
Meals 16.50/28.50 **t.** and a la carte ₤ 5.90 – ⛌ 9.95 – **195 rm** 185.00/205.00 **t.**, 8 suites.
JY b

The Burlington, Upper Leeson St., D4, ℰ (01) 660 5222, Fax (01) 660 3172 – 📳, ✻ rm, ▤ rest, 📺 ☎ ₠ 🄿 – 🏊 1000. 🐾 🅰🄴 ⓞ 𝗩𝗜𝗦𝗔 ᴊᴄʙ. ✻
EU e
Meals (carving lunch) 12.00/18.00 **t.** and dinner a la carte ₤ 7.45 – ⛌ 10.50 – **531 rm** 138.00/160.00 **t.**, 4 suites.

Jurys, Pembroke Rd, Ballsbridge, D4, ℰ (01) 660 5000, Fax (01) 660 5540, ☒ – 📳, ✻ rm, ▤ rest, 📺 ☎ ₠ 🄿 – 🏊 850. 🐾 🅰🄴 ⓞ 𝗩𝗜𝗦𝗔. ✻
FU p
Meals – **Raglans :** Meals 24.00 **t.** (dinner) and a la carte 21.50/30.70 **t.** ₤ 6.00 – ⛌ 9.25 – **290 rm** 140.00/180.00 **t.**, 4 suites – SB.

The Towers, Lansdowne Rd, D4, ℰ (01) 667 0033, Fax (01) 660 5540, ☎, ☒ – 📳, ✻ rm, ▤ 📺 ☎ ₠ 🄿. ✻
Meals – (see **Jurys H.** above) – ⛌ 9.25 – **100 rm** 180.00/210.00 **t.**, 4 suites – SB.

The Clarence, 6-8 Wellington Quay, D2, ℰ (01) 670 9000, Fax (01) 670 7800, « Contemporary interior design » – 📳 📺 ☎ 🄿 – 🏊 60. 🐾 🅰🄴 ⓞ 𝗩𝗜𝗦𝗔. ✻
HY
The Tea Room : Meals (closed lunch Saturday, Sunday and Bank Holidays 17.50 **st.** (lunch) and a la carte 20.00/35.00 **st.** ₤ 15.00 – ⛌ 13.00 – **45 rm** 175.00/190.00 **st.**, 4 suites.

Brooks, Drury St., D2, ℰ (01) 670 4000, Fax (01) 670 4455 – 📳, ✻ rm, ▤ 📺 ☎ ₠ 🄿 – 🏊 70. 🐾 🅰🄴 𝗩𝗜𝗦𝗔. ✻
JY
Francesca's : Meals (dinner only) 17.95 **t.** and a la carte ₤ 7.25 – **Brasserie 59 :** Meals a la carte 14.00/23.45 **t.** ₤ 5.95 – ⛌ 10.50 – **75 rm** 125.00/195.00 **t.**

DUBLIN
BUILT UP AREA

Herbert Park, Ballsbridge, D4, ℰ (01) 667 2200, *Fax (01) 667 2595*, ⅃₆ – ⅀, ⅍ rm, 🖵 📺 ☎ ℗ – ⚷ 100. 🆖 ﹠ ④ 𝘝𝘐𝘚𝘈. ﹩ FU **m**
The Park : Meals 11.50/23.50 **t.** and a la carte ⅃ 6.50 – ⚌ 10.50 – **149 rm** 135.00/175.00 **t.**, 4 suites – SB.

Red Cow, Naas Rd, D22, SW : 5 m. on N 7 ℰ (01) 459 3650, *Fax (01) 459 1588* – ⅀, ⅍ rm, 🖵 📺 ☎ ﹠ ℗ – ⚷ 700. 🆖 ﹠ ④ 𝘝𝘐𝘚𝘈. ﹩
closed 25 December – Meals 12.50/19.75 **t.** and dinner a la carte ⅃ 7.50 – **120 rm** ⚌ 75.00/150.00 **t.**, 3 suites – SB.

Doyle Green Isle, Naas Rd, D22, SW : 7 ¾ m. off N7 (eastbound carriageway) ℰ (01) 459 3406, *Fax (01) 459 2178* – ⅀, ⅍ rm, 📺 ☎ ﹠ ℗ – ⚷ 250. 🆖 ﹠ ④ 𝘝𝘐𝘚𝘈 𝗝𝗖𝗕. ﹩
Meals 13.95/18.95 **t.** and a la carte ⅃ 6.00 – ⚌ 7.50 – **90 rm** 89.00 **t.**

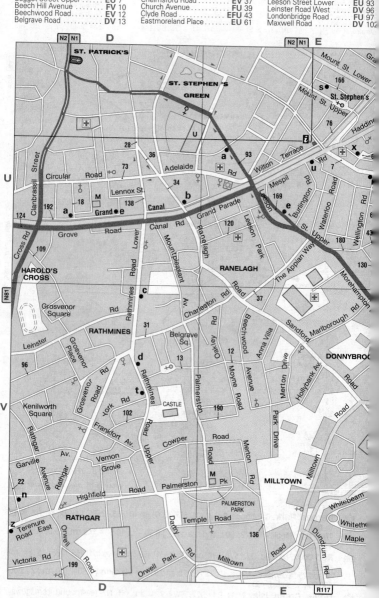

If you find you cannot take up a hotel booking you have made,
please let the hotel know immediately.

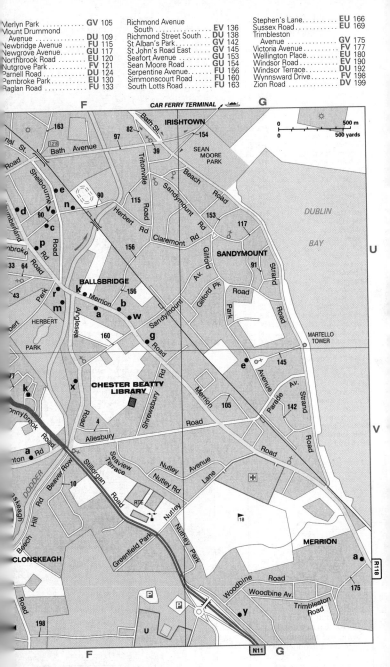

Prévenez immédiatement l'hôtelier si vous ne pouvez pas occuper la chambre que vous avez retenue.

DUBLIN
CENTRE

When looking
for a quiet hotel
use the maps found
in the introduction
or look
for establishments
with the sign 🛏 or 🛏.

832

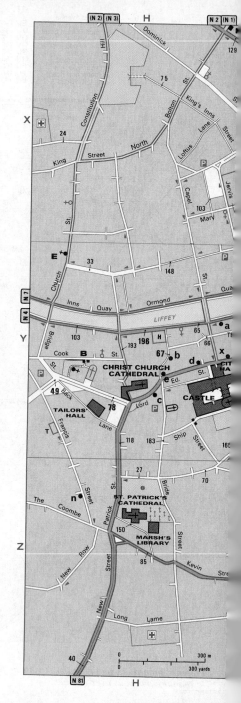

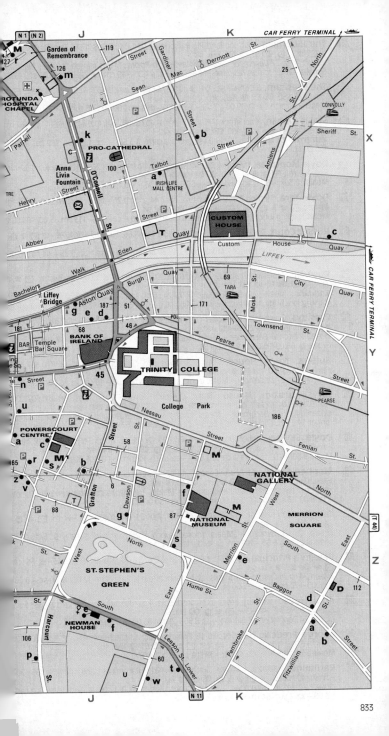

🏨🏨🏨 **The Hibernian,** Eastmoreland Pl., Ballsbridge, D4, ℘ (01) 668 7666, Fax (01) 660 2655 –
🛗 📺 ☎ 🅗 🅟 🙎 🆎 ⓞ 𝐕𝐈𝐒𝐀 𝐉𝐂𝐁. ℅
EU
closed 24 to 27 December – **Patrick Kavanagh Room :** Meals (closed Saturday lunch and
Sunday dinner to non-residents) 14.95/25.95 **t.** 🍷 7.00 – **40 rm** ⊥ 110.00/160.00 **st.** – SB.

🏨🏨🏨 **The Gresham,** O'Connell St., D1, ℘ (01) 874 6881, Fax (01) 878 7175 – 🛗, 🗏 rest, 📺 ☎
⇔ – 🙎 250. 🅼🅢 🆎 ⓞ 𝐕𝐈𝐒𝐀. ℅
JX
Meals à la carte 19.00/39.00 🍷 7.00 – ⊥ 15.00 – **198 rm** 200.00 **t.**, 6 suites – SB.

🏨🏨🏨 **Stakis Dublin,** Charlemont Pl., D2, ℘ (01) 402 9988, Fax (01) 402 9966 – 🛗, ⇜ rm
🗏 rest, 📺 ☎ ⇔ – 🙎 400. 🅼🅢 🆎 ⓞ 𝐕𝐈𝐒𝐀. ℅
DU
Waterfront : Meals 16.00/18.00 **st.** and à la carte 🍷 5.50 – ⊥ 11.00 – **189 rm** 135.00
155.00 **st.** – SB.

🏨🏨🏨 **Doyle Montrose,** Stillorgan Rd, D4, SE : 4 m. by N 11 ℘ (01) 269 3311, Fax (01) 269 116-
– 🛗, ⇜ rm, 📺 ☎ 🅟 – 🙎 70. 🅼🅢 🆎 ⓞ 𝐕𝐈𝐒𝐀 𝐉𝐂𝐁. ℅
GV
Meals 10.50/18.50 **t.** and à la carte 🍷 6.70 – ⊥ 6.50 – **179 rm** 85.00/130.00 **t.**

🏨🏨 **Doyle Tara,** Merrion Rd, D4, SE : 4 m. on T 44 ℘ (01) 269 4666, Fax (01) 269 1027 – 🛗
🗏 rest, 📺 ☎ 🅗 🅟 – 🙎 300. 🅼🅢 🆎 ⓞ 𝐕𝐈𝐒𝐀 𝐉𝐂𝐁. ℅
GV
Meals (carving lunch) 8.40/15.50 **t.** and à la carte 🍷 5.20 – ⊥ 6.75 – **113 rm** 85.00/105.00 **t**

🏨🏨 **Russell Court,** 21-25 Harcourt St., D2, ℘ (01) 478 4066, Fax (01) 478 1576 – 🛗 📺 ☎ 🅟
🙎 150. 🅼🅢 🆎 ⓞ 𝐕𝐈𝐒𝐀. ℅
JZ
closed 24 to 26 December – Meals 10.95/18.50 **st.** and à la carte – ⊥ 5.25 – **41 rm** 65.00
87.00 **t.**, 6 suites – SB.

🏨🏨 **Buswells,** Molesworth St., D2, ℘ (01) 614 6500, Fax (01) 676 2090 – 🛗, ⇜ rm, 📺 ☎ 🅗
🅟 – 🙎 80. 🅼🅢 🆎 ⓞ 𝐕𝐈𝐒𝐀. ℅
KZ
Trumans : Meals (closed Sunday) 12.95/24.50 **st.** and à la carte 🍷 6.00 – **Grill :** Meal
(carving lunch)/dinner à la carte 9.40/24.50 **st.** 🍷 6.00 – **67 rm** ⊥ 97.00/155.00 **st.**, 2 suites

🏨🏨 **Cassidys,** Cavendish Row, Upper O'Connell St., D1, ℘ (01) 878 0555, Fax (01) 878 0687 –
🛗, ⇜ rm, 📺 ☎ 🅗 🅟 𝐕𝐈𝐒𝐀. ℅
JX
closed 24 to 26 December – Meals (bar lunch)/dinner à la carte 14.95/17.95 **t.** 🍷 5.25 –
67 rm ⊥ 68.00/95.00 **t.**, 1 suite – SB.

🏨🏨 **Butlers Town House,** 44 Lansdowne Rd, Ballsbridge, D4, ℘ (01) 667 4022
Fax (01) 667 3960 – 🗏 📺 ☎ 🅗. 🅼🅢 🆎 ⓞ 𝐕𝐈𝐒𝐀. ℅
FU
closed 24 to 27 December – Meals (room service only) 🍷 7.50 – **19 rm** ⊥ 90.00/129.00 **st.**

🏨🏨 **Jurys Custom House Inn,** Custom House Quay, D1, ℘ (01) 607 5000
Fax (01) 829 0400, 🍴 – 🛗, ⇜ rm, 📺 ☎ ⇔ – 🙎 100. 🅼🅢 🆎 ⓞ 𝐕𝐈𝐒𝐀. ℅
KX
closed 24 to 26 December – Meals (closed lunch Saturday and Sunday) (buffet lunch)
dinner 14.50 **st.** and à la carte 🍷 5.25 – ⊥ 6.00 – **234 rm** 57.00 **st.**

🏨🏨 **Doyle Skylon,** Upper Drumcondra Rd, D9, N : 2 ½ m. on N 1 ℘ (01) 837 912
Fax (01) 837 2778 – 🛗, ⇜ rm, 🗏 rest, 📺 ☎ 🅟. 🅼🅢 🆎 ⓞ 𝐕𝐈𝐒𝐀. ℅
BS
Meals 9.50/14.00 **t.** and à la carte 🍷 5.20 – ⊥ 6.50 – **88 rm** 85.00/105.00 **t.**

🏨🏨 **Stephen's Hall,** Earlsfort Centre, 14-17 Lower Leeson St., D2, ℘ (01) 661 0585
Fax (01) 661 0606 – 🛗 ⇜ 📺 ☎ 🅟. 🅼🅢 🆎 ⓞ 𝐕𝐈𝐒𝐀. ℅
JZ
restricted service 24 December-2 January – Meals – (see **Morels at Stephen's Hall** below
– ⊥ 8.00 – **3 rm** 105.00/150.00 **st.**, 34 suites 150.00 **st.**

🏨🏨 **Temple Bar,** Fleet St., D2, ℘ (01) 677 3333, Fax (01) 677 3088 – 🛗, ⇜ rm, 📺 ☎ 🅟
🙎 30. 🅼🅢 🆎 ⓞ 𝐕𝐈𝐒𝐀. ℅
JY
closed 25 December – Meals (closed lunch Saturday and Sunday) 9.75/15.00
and à la carte 🍷 6.50 – **108 rm** ⊥ 95.00/125.00 **t.** – SB.

🏨🏨 **Bewley's Principal,** 19-20 Fleet St., D2, ℘ (01) 670 8122, Fax (01) 670 8103 – 🛗, ⇜ rm
📺 ☎ 🅼🅢 🆎 ⓞ 𝐕𝐈𝐒𝐀. ℅
JY
closed 24 to 26 December – Meals (closed Sunday dinner) à la carte 12.00/19.00 **st.** 🍷 6.00
⊥ 6.00 – **70 rm** 75.00/95.00 **st.** – SB.

🏨🏨 **Ariel House** without rest., 52 Lansdowne Rd, Ballsbridge, D4, ℘ (01) 668 5551
Fax (01) 668 5845, 🍴 – ⇜ 📺 ☎ 🅟. 🅼🅢 𝐕𝐈𝐒𝐀. ℅
FU
closed 24 December-12 January – ⊥ 8.60 – **28 rm** 68.00/169.00 **st.**

🏨🏨 **George Frederic Handel,** 16-18 Fishamble St., Christchurch, D2, ℘ (01) 670 9400
Fax (01) 670 9410 – 🛗, ⇜ rm, 🗏 rest, 📺 ☎ 🅗. 🅼🅢 🆎 ⓞ 𝐕𝐈𝐒𝐀. ℅
HY
Meals à la carte 10.00/25.00 **st.** – **39 rm** ⊥ 95.00/160.00 **st.**

🏨🏨 **Rathmines Plaza,** Lower Rathmines Rd, Rathmines, D6, ℘ (01) 496 696
Fax (01) 491 0603 – 🛗 📺 ☎ 🅗 🅟. 🅼🅢 🆎 ⓞ 𝐕𝐈𝐒𝐀. ℅
DV
closed 24 to 26 December – Meals (carving lunch) 6.00/11.00 **st.** and dinner à la cart
🍷 3.00 – ⊥ 7.50 – **54 rm** 70.00/90.00 **st.** – SB.

Grafton Plaza, Johnsons Pl., D2, ℘ (01) 475 0888, *Fax (01) 475 0908* – |🛗| 📺 ☎ &. 🆖 🆎 ⓪ 𝘝𝘐𝘚𝘈. ⚗
JZ v
closed 25 and 26 December – **Meals** *(closed Sunday lunch and Good Friday)* (bar lunch)/ dinner a la carte 11.00/21.50 **st.** ⓪ 7.00 – ☑ 7.50 – **75 rm** 95.00/115.00.

Jurys Christchurch Inn, Christchurch Pl., D8, ℘ (01) 454 0000, *Fax (01) 454 0012* – |🛗|, ⚲ rm, 🍽 rest, 📺 ☎ ⊕ ❷. 🆖 🆎 ⓪ 𝘝𝘐𝘚𝘈. ⚗
HY c
closed 24 to 26 December – **Meals** (carving lunch Monday to Saturday)/dinner 15.00 **t.** and a la carte ⓪ 6.00 – ☑ 6.50 – **182 rm** 75.00 **t.**

Mespil, 50-60 Mespil Rd, D4, ℘ (01) 667 1222, *Fax (01) 667 1244* – |🛗|, ⚲ rm, 🍽 rest, 📺 ☎ ❷ – ⚖ 50. 🆖 🆎 ⓪ 𝘝𝘐𝘚𝘈. ⚗
EU u
closed 24 to 26 December – **Meals** (carving lunch)/dinner 16.95 **st.** and a la carte ⓪ 5.90 – ☑ 8.00 – **153 rm** 75.00/95.00 **st.**

Drury Court, 28-30 Lower Stephens St., D2, ℘ (01) 475 1988, *Fax (01) 478 5730* – |🛗| 📺 ☎. 🆖 🆎 ⓪ 𝘝𝘐𝘚𝘈. ⚗
JYZ z
closed 25 December – **Meals** 15.00 **st.** (dinner) and a la carte 9.85/16.50 **st.** ⓪ 5.95 – **32 rm** ☑ 87.00/139.00 **st.** – SB.

Central, 1-5 Exchequer St., D2, ℘ (01) 679 7302, *Fax (01) 679 7303* – |🛗| 📺 ☎. – ⚖ 80. 🆖 🆎 ⓪ 𝘝𝘐𝘚𝘈. ⚗
JY u
Meals *(closed 25 December)* (bar lunch)/dinner 12.50 **t.** and a la carte ⓪ 4.75 – ☑ 7.50 – **68 rm** 95.00/135.00 **st.**, 2 suites – SB.

Adams Trinity, 28 Dame St., D2, ℘ (01) 670 7100, *Fax (01) 670 7101* – |🛗| 📺 ☎. 🆖 🆎 ⓪ 𝘝𝘐𝘚𝘈 𝗝𝗖𝗕
JY n
closed 25 and 26 December – **Meals** 10.95 **st.** and a la carte ⓪ 6.00 – **28 rm** ☑ 82.00/ 132.00 **st.** – SB.

Parliament, Lord Edward St., D2, ℘ (01) 670 8777, *Fax (01) 670 8787* – |🛗|, ⚲ rm, 🍽 rest, 📺 ☎. 🆖 🆎 𝘝𝘐𝘚𝘈. ⚗
HY d
Meals (bar lunch)/dinner 14.95 **st.** and a la carte ⓪ 5.25 – ☑ 6.75 – **63 rm** 100.00/140.00.

Bewley's, Newlands Cross, D22, SW : 7 m. by N 7 on R 113 ℘ (01) 464 0140, *Fax (01) 464 0900* – |🛗|, ⚲ rm, 📺 ☎ & ❷. 🆖 🆎 ⓪ 𝘝𝘐𝘚𝘈. ⚗
closed 25 and 26 December – **Meals** (carving lunch) a la carte 11.15/19.90 **st.** ⓪ 6.25 – ☑ 4.25 – **165 rm** 49.00 **st.**

Kylemore Park, Kylemore Rd, D12, SW : 4 ¾ m. by N 7 ℘ (01) 460 1055, *Fax (01) 460 1880,* 🗜, 🕿 – |🛗| 📺 ☎ ❷ – ⚖ 400. 🆖 🆎 ⓪ 𝘝𝘐𝘚𝘈. ⚗
closed 25 December – **Meals** (carving lunch)/dinner a la carte 12.00/22.00 **t.** ⓪ 4.50 – **72 rm** ☑ 55.00/79.00 **st.** – SB.

Longfield's, 10 Lower Fitzwilliam St., D2, ℘ (01) 676 1367, *Fax (01) 676 1542* – |🛗| 📺 ☎. 🆖 🆎 ⓪ 𝘝𝘐𝘚𝘈. ⚗
KZ d
closed 24 to 27 December – **Meals** – (see *Number 10* below) – **26 rm** ☑ 90.00/123.00 **st.** – SB.

Aberdeen Lodge, 53-55 Park Av., D4, ℘ (01) 283 8155, *Fax (01) 283 7877,* 🌸 – ⚲ 📺 ☎ ❷. 🆖 🆎 ⓪ 𝘝𝘐𝘚𝘈. ⚗
GV e
Meals (residents only) (dinner only) 22.00 **t.** ⓪ 8.50 – **16 rm** ☑ 60.00/125.00 **st.** – SB.

Uppercross House, 26-30 Upper Rathmines Rd, Rathmines, D6, ℘ (01) 4975486, *Fax (01) 4975361* – 📺 ☎ ❷. 🆖 🆎 𝘝𝘐𝘚𝘈
DV d
Meals *(closed lunch Monday to Friday)* (light meals) 9.95 **st.** (dinner) and a la carte 9.70/ 20.40 **t.** ⓪ 4.95 – **25 rm** ☑ 39.50/75.00 **st.**

Glenogra House without rest., 64 Merrion Rd, D4, ℘ (01) 668 3661, *Fax (01) 668 3698* – ⚲ 📺 ☎ ❷. 🆖 🆎 ⓪ 𝘝𝘐𝘚𝘈. ⚗
FU w
closed 20 to 31 December – **9 rm** ☑ 55.00/85.00.

The Leeson Inn without rest., 24 Lower Leeson St., D2, ℘ (01) 661 2002, *Fax (01) 662 1567* – |🛗| ☎. 🆖 🆎 ⓪ 𝘝𝘐𝘚𝘈. ⚗
EU a
closed 25 and 26 December – ☑ 5.00 – **16 rm** 55.00/75.00 **st.**

Number Eighty Eight without rest., 88 Pembroke Rd, Ballsbridge, D4, ℘ (01) 660 0277, *Fax (01) 660 0291* – |🛗| ⚲ rm, 📺 ☎ & ❷. 🆖 🆎 ⓪ 𝘝𝘐𝘚𝘈. ⚗
FU f
closed 22 to 30 December – **50 rm** ☑ 65.00/140.00 **st.**

Stauntons on the Green without rest., 83 St. Stephen's Green South, D2, ℘ (01) 478 2300, *Fax (01) 478 2263,* 🌸 – 📺 ☎ 🌫. 🆖 🆎 ⓪ 𝘝𝘐𝘚𝘈. ⚗
JZ f
closed 24 to 26 December – **39 rm** ☑ 61.00/96.00 **st.**

Ibis Dublin, Monastery Rd, Clondalkin, D22, SW : 5 ¼ m. off N 7 ℘ (01) 464 1480, *Fax (01) 464 1484* – |🛗|, ⚲ rm, 📺 ☎ & ❷ – ⚖ 40. 🆖 🆎 ⓪ 𝘝𝘐𝘚𝘈. ⚗
Meals (bar lunch)/dinner 11.50 **st.** and a la carte ⓪ 4.95 – ☑ 5.25 – **150 rm** 49.50 **st.**

Aston without rest., 7-9 Aston Quay, D2, ℘ (01) 677 9300, *Fax (01) 677 9007* – |🛗| 📺 ☎ &. 🆖 🆎 𝘝𝘐𝘚𝘈. ⚗
JY g
closed 25 December – **27 rm** ☑ 55.00/80.00 **st.**

DUBLIN

Harding, Copper Alley, Fishamble St., Christchurch, D2, ℰ (01) 679 6500,
Fax (01) 679 6504 – 🛗 📺 ☎ ⅐. 🐵 𝘝𝘐𝘚𝘈. ⅌
HY e
closed 24 to 26 December – **Meals** 10.50/16.00 **t.** and a la carte ↕ 7.00 – ☑ 5.50 – **53 rm**
45.00/60.00 **st.**

Travelodge, Auburn Av. roundabout, Castleknock, D15, NW : 5 ½ m. on N 3
ℰ (01) 820 2626, Fax (01) 820 2808, Reservations (Freephone) 0800 850950 (UK), 1800
709709 (Republic of Ireland) – ⅓× rm, 📺 ☎ ⅐. 🐵 𝘈𝘌 ① 𝘝𝘐𝘚𝘈 𝘑𝘤𝘣. ⅌
Meals (grill rest.) – **60 rm** 44.95 **t.**

Merrion Hall without rest., 54-56 Merrion Rd, Ballsbridge, D4, ℰ (01) 668 1426,
Fax (01) 668 4280, ⌂ – 📺 ☎ 🅿. 🐵 𝘝𝘐𝘚𝘈. ⅌
FU b
closed 24 December-3 January – **25 rm** ☑ 50.00/100.00 **st.**

Cedar Lodge Guesthouse without rest., 98 Merrion Rd, Ballsbridge, D4,
ℰ (01) 668 4410, Fax (01) 668 4533, ⌂ – ⅓× 📺 ☎ 🅿. 🐵 𝘈𝘌 𝘝𝘐𝘚𝘈. ⅌
FU g
15 rm ☑ 75.00/120.00 **st.**

Talbot without rest., 95-98 Talbot St., D1, ℰ (01) 874 9202, Fax (01) 874 9672 – 🛗 📺 ☎
🅿. 🐵 𝘈𝘌 𝘝𝘐𝘚𝘈.
JX a
closed 24 to 28 December – **48 rm** ☑ 36.00/65.00 **st.**

Lansdowne Lodge without rest., 6 Lansdowne Terr., Shelbourne Rd, D4
ℰ (01) 660 5755, Fax (01) 660 5662, ⌂ – 📺 ☎ 🅿. 🐵 𝘝𝘐𝘚𝘈
FU e
closed 24 to 28 December – **12 rm** ☑ 60.00/80.00 **st.**

Morehampton Lodge without rest., 113 Morehampton Rd, Donnybrook, D4
ℰ (01) 283 7499, Fax (01) 283 7595 – 📺 ☎ 🅿. 🐵 𝘝𝘐𝘚𝘈. ⅌
EV b
closed 25 December – **15 rm** ☑ 60.00/75.00 **st.**

Raglan Lodge without rest., 10 Raglan Rd, off Pembroke Rd, Ballsbridge, D4
ℰ (01) 660 6697, Fax (01) 660 6781, ⌂ – 📺 ☎ 🅿. 🐵 𝘈𝘌 ① 𝘝𝘐𝘚𝘈. ⅌
FU z
closed Christmas – **7 rm** ☑ 60.00/100.00 **st.**

Anglesea Town House without rest., 63 Anglesea Rd, Ballsbridge, D4
ℰ (01) 668 3877, Fax (01) 668 3461 – 📺 ☎ 🅿. 🐵 𝘈𝘌 ① 𝘝𝘐𝘚𝘈. ⅌
FV x
closed 15 December-8 January – **7 rm** ☑ 45.00/90.00 **t.**

Grafton House without rest., 26-27 South Great Georges St., D2, ℰ (01) 679 2041
Fax (01) 677 9715 – 📺 ☎. 🐵 𝘝𝘐𝘚𝘈. ⅌
JY a
closed 23 to 30 December – **15 rm** ☑ 45.00/80.00.

Astonvale House without rest., 55 Eglinton Rd, Donnybrook, D4, ℰ (01) 269 3199
Fax (01) 283 7991, ⌂ – 📺 ☎
FV a
7 rm.

Glenveagh Town House without rest., 31 Northumberland Rd, Ballsbridge, D4
ℰ (01) 668 4612, Fax (01) 668 4559 – 📺 ☎ 🅿. 🐵 𝘝𝘐𝘚𝘈. ⅌
FU b
closed 22 to 29 December – **10 rm** ☑ 60.00/80.00 **st.**

Roslyn House without rest., 63 Terenure Rd East, Rathgar, D6, ℰ (01) 492 5807
Fax (01) 492 9378 – 📺 ☎ 🅿. 🐵 𝘝𝘐𝘚𝘈. ⅌
DV a
7 rm ☑ 37.00/70.00 **st.**

Northumberland Lodge without rest., 68 Northumberland Rd, Ballsbridge, D4
ℰ (01) 660 5270, Fax (01) 668 8679, ⌂ – 📺 ☎ 🅿. 🐵 𝘝𝘐𝘚𝘈. ⅌
FU c
7 rm ☑ 55.00/120.00 **st.**

St. Aiden's without rest., 32 Brighton Rd, Rathgar, D6, ℰ (01) 4906178, Fax (01) 492023
– 📺 ☎ 🅿. 🐵 𝘝𝘐𝘚𝘈. ⅌
DV b
closed 22 to 31 December – **8 rm** ☑ 33.00/77.00 **st.**

The Glen without rest., 84 Lower Gardiner St., D1, ℰ (01) 855 1374 – 📺 ☎ 🅿. 🐵 𝘝𝘐𝘚𝘈. ⅌
KX b
15 rm ☑ 30.00/65.00 **st.**

XXXX **Patrick Guilbaud,** 21 Upper Merrion St., D2, ℰ (01) 676 4192, Fax (01) 661 0052 – ▤. 🐵
❀❀ 𝘈𝘌 ① 𝘝𝘐𝘚𝘈
KZ c
closed Sunday, Monday, 25 to 29 December and 1 week January – **Meals** a la carte 38.00/
55.00 **st.** ↕ 13.00
Spec. Poached Connemara lobster, green apple juice. Roast saddle of Wicklow lamb with
honey roast apricots. Hot rhubarb soufflé.

XXX **The Commons,** Newman House, 85-86 St. Stephen's Green, D2, ℰ (01) 478 0530
Fax (01) 478 0551, « Contemporary collection of James Joyce inspired Irish Art » – 🐵 𝘈
① 𝘝𝘐𝘚𝘈
JZ a
closed Saturday lunch, Sunday, 2 weeks Christmas and Bank Holidays – **Meals** 20.00/
35.00 **st.** and a la carte ↕ 8.50.

XXX **Le Coq Hardi,** 35 Pembroke Rd, D4, ℰ (01) 668 9070, Fax (01) 668 9887 – 🅿. 🐵 𝘈𝘌 ①
𝘝𝘐𝘚𝘈 𝘑𝘤𝘣
EU n
closed Saturday lunch, Sunday, 2 weeks August, 10 days Christmas and Bank Holidays –
Meals 19.00/34.00 **t.** and a la carte ↕ 8.10.

XXX ❀❀❀ ❀ **Thornton's** (Thornton), 1 Portobello Rd, D8, ℘ (01) 454 9067, Fax (01) 453 2947 – 🖻. 🕸
DU e
closed Sunday, Monday and 2 weeks January – **Meals** (booking essential) (dinner only and Friday lunch) 18.95 **t.** (lunch) and a la carte 34.95/41.30 **t.** ⋀ 8.50
Spec. Langoustine bisque with truffle sabayon. Suckling pig with trotter, Maxim potatoes and poitin jus. Nougat pyramid with glazed fruit and orange sauce.

XX ❀ **Chapter One,** The Dublin Writers Museum, 18-19 Parnell Sq., D1, ℘ (01) 873 2266, Fax (01) 873 2330 – 🖻. 🕸 🕸 ① 🅥🅸🅢🅰
JX r
closed Saturday lunch, Monday dinner, Sunday and 24 December-6 January – Meals 13.50 **t.** (lunch) and dinner a la carte 22.00/27.00 **t.** ⋀ 8.50.

XX ❀ **L'Ecrivain,** 109 Lower Baggot St., D2, ℘ (01) 661 1919, Fax (01) 661 0617, 🍴 – 🖻. 🕸 🅰🅴
① 🅥🅸🅢🅰
KZ b
closed Saturday lunch, Sunday, 25-26 December and Bank Holidays – Meals (booking essential) 15.50/25.00 **t.** and dinner a la carte approx. 31.50 **t.** ⋀ 7.00.

XX ❀❀❀ ❀ **Peacock Alley** (Gallagher), 47 South William St., ℘ (01) 677 0708, Fax (01) 671 8854 – 🕸
🅰🅴 ① 🅥🅸🅢🅰
JY s
closed 25 December and Bank Holidays – **Meals** (booking essential) 14.95 **t.** (lunch) and a la carte 22.40/40.40 **t.** ⋀ 8.00
Spec. Ravioli of lobster with lemon grass vinaigrette and lobster cream. Daube of beef with rosemary mashed potato and madeira cream. Warm chocolate fondant with pistachio ice cream.

XX ❀ **Ernie's,** Mulberry Gdns., off Morehampton Rd, Donnybrook, D4, ℘ (01) 269 3300, Fax (01) 269 3260, « Contemporary Irish Art collection » – 🖻. 🕸 🅰🅴 ① 🅥🅸🅢🅰
FV k
closed Saturday lunch, Sunday, Monday and 24 December-1 January – Meals 13.95/25.00 **t.** and a la carte 26.20/36.15 **t.** ⋀ 8.00.

XX **Les Frères Jacques,** 74 Dame St., D2, ℘ (01) 679 4555, Fax (01) 679 4725 – 🕸 🅰🅴 ①
🅥🅸🅢🅰
HY x
closed Saturday lunch, Sunday, 24 December-2 January and Bank Holidays – **Meals** - French - 13.50/20.00 **t.** and a la carte ⋀ 5.50.

XX **Morels at Stephen's Hall,** 14-17 Lower Leeson St., D2, ℘ (01) 662 2480, Fax (01) 662 8595 – 🖻. 🕸 🅰🅴 ① 🅥🅸🅢🅰
JZ t
closed Saturday lunch, Sunday, 5 days Christmas and Bank Holidays – **Meals** (booking essential) 12.50/23.00 **t.** and a la carte ⋀ 7.00.

XX **Locks,** 1 Windsor Terr., Portobello, D8, ℘ (01) 4543391, Fax (01) 4538352 – 🕸 🅰🅴 ① 🅥🅸🅢🅰
closed Saturday lunch, Sunday, last week July-first week August, 1 week Christmas and Bank Holidays – **Meals** 14.95/25.00 **t.** and a la carte ⋀ 6.00.
DU a

XX **Old Dublin,** 90-91 Francis St., D8, ℘ (01) 4542028, Fax (01) 4541406 – 🕸 🅰🅴 ① 🅥🅸🅢🅰
closed Saturday lunch, Sunday, 25 December and Bank Holidays – **Meals** - Russian-Scandinavian - 12.50/21.00 **t.** and dinner a la carte ⋀ 8.25.
HZ n

XX **La Stampa,** 35 Dawson St., D2, ℘ (01) 677 8611, Fax (01) 677 3336, « 19C former ballroom » – 🖻. 🕸 🅰🅴 ① 🅥🅸🅢🅰
JZ g
closed lunch Saturday and Sunday, Good Friday and 25-26 December – **Meals** 12.50 (lunch) and dinner a la carte 21.45/31.40 **t.** ⋀ 8.00.

XX **Popjoys,** 4 Rathfarnham Rd, Terenure, D6, S : 3 m. on N 81 ℘ (01) 492 9346, Fax (01) 492 9293 – 🕸 🅰🅴 ① 🅥🅸🅢🅰
BT a
closed Saturday lunch, Good Friday and 1 week Christmas – **Meals** 11.95/21.00 **t.** and a la carte ⋀ 6.75.

XX **L'Epee d'Or,** 112 Lower Baggot St., D2, ℘ (01) 662 5511, Fax (01) 676 7488 – 🕸 🅰🅴 ①
🅥🅸🅢🅰
KZ a
closed Saturday lunch, Sunday, 25 December and Bank Holidays – **Meals** 13.50/24.00 **t.** and a la carte ⋀ 5.75.

XX **Zen,** 89 Upper Rathmines Rd, D6, ℘ (01) 4979428 – 🖻. 🕸 🅰🅴 ① 🅥🅸🅢🅰
DV t
closed lunch Monday to Wednesday, Saturday and 25 to 28 December – **Meals** - Chinese (Szechuan) - 8.50 (lunch) and a la carte 12.50/21.00.

XX **Number 10** (at Longfield's H.), 10 Lower Fitzwilliam St., D2, ℘ (01) 676 1060, Fax (01) 676 1542 – 🕸 🅰🅴 ① 🅥🅸🅢🅰
KZ d
closed Saturday lunch, Sunday and Bank Holidays and 24 to 27 December – **Meals** 15.00/27.50 **st.** ⋀ 8.00.

XX **Coopers Cafe,** The Sweepstakes Centre, Ballsbridge, D4, ℘ (01) 660 1525, Fax (01) 660 1537 – 🖻. 🕸 🅰🅴 ① 🅥🅸🅢🅰
FU k
closed 25 and 26 December – **Meals** 9.95 **t.** and a la carte 18.80/25.35 **t.** ⋀ 6.00.

XX **Fitzers Café,** RDS, Merrion Rd, Ballsbridge, D4, ℘ (01) 667 1301, Fax (01) 667 1303 – 🅿.
🕸 🅰🅴 ① 🅥🅸🅢🅰
FU a
closed Sunday dinner and 4 days Christmas – **Meals** (booking essential) 11.25 **t.** (lunch) and a la carte 18.25/29.75 **t.** ⋀ 7.95.

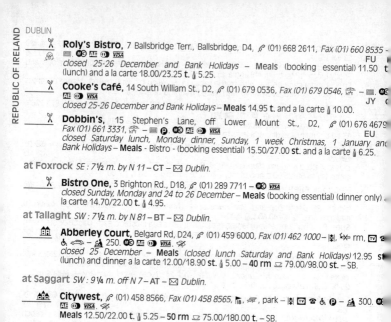

✗ **Roly's Bistro**, 7 Ballsbridge Terr., Ballsbridge, D4, ℰ (01) 668 2611, Fax (01) 660 8535 –
🖻, **M©** AE ⓪ VISA   FU
closed 25-26 December and Bank Holidays – Meals (booking essential) 11.50 t
(lunch) and a la carte 18.00/23.25 t. ⅟ 5.25.

✗ **Cooke's Café**, 14 South William St., D2, ℰ (01) 679 0536, Fax (01) 679 0546, 🍴 – 🖻. **M©**
AE ⓪ VISA   JY (
closed 25-26 December and Bank Holidays – Meals 14.95 t. and a la carte ⅟ 10.00.

✗ **Dobbin's**, 15 Stephen's Lane, off Lower Mount St., D2, ℰ (01) 676 4679
Fax (01) 661 3331, 🍴 – 🖻 ❾. **M©** AE ⓪ VISA   EU
closed Saturday lunch, Monday dinner, Sunday, 1 week Christmas, 1 January and
Bank Holidays – Meals - Bistro - (booking essential) 15.50/27.00 st. and a la carte ⅟ 6.25.

at Foxrock SE : 7½ m. by N 11 – CT – ✉ Dublin.

✗ **Bistro One**, 3 Brighton Rd., D18, ℰ (01) 289 7711 – **M©** VISA
closed Sunday, Monday and 24 to 26 December – Meals (booking essential) (dinner only) .
la carte 14.70/22.00 t. ⅟ 4.95.

at Tallaght SW : 7½ m. by N 81 – BT – ✉ Dublin.

🏨 **Abberley Court**, Belgard Rd, D24, ℰ (01) 459 6000, Fax (01) 462 1000 – 🛗, ⋇ rm, �📺 🕿
🕭 ⇌ – 🔏 250. **M©** AE ⓪ VISA
closed 25 December – Meals (closed lunch Saturday and Bank Holidays) 12.95 st
(lunch) and dinner a la carte 12.00/18.90 st. ⅟ 5.00 – 40 rm ⇌ 79.00/98.00 st. – SB.

at Saggart SW : 9¼ m. off N 7 – AT – ✉ Dublin.

🏨 **Citywest**, ℰ (01) 458 8566, Fax (01) 458 8565, 📃, 🐎, park – 🛗 📺 🕿 🕭 ❾ – 🔏 300. **M©**
AE ⓪ VISA, ⋇
Meals 12.50/22.00 t. ⅟ 5.25 – 50 rm ⇌ 75.00/180.00 t. – SB.

DUBLIN AIRPORT Dublin 923 N 7 – ✉ Dublin.

🏨 **Forte Posthouse Dublin Airport**, ℰ (01) 844 4211, Fax (01) 844 6002 – ⋇ rm
🖻 rest, 📺 🕿 🕭 ❾ – 🔏 130. **M©** AE ⓪ VISA, ⋇
closed 24 and 25 December – **Bistro** : Meals (closed Saturday lunch) 12.95
17.95 t. and dinner a la carte ⅟ 6.50 – **Sampan's** : Meals - Chinese - (closed Bank Holiday:
(dinner only) 15.50 t. and a la carte ⅟ 6.50 – ⇌ 9.95 – 249 rm 99.00 t. – SB.

DUNDALK (Dun Dealgan) Louth 923 M 5/6 – pop. 25 762.
Dublin 51 – Drogheda 22.

🏨 **Ballymascanlon**, N : 3 ½ m. by N 1 on R 173 ℰ (042) 71124, Fax (042) 71598, ⅃₆, ⇌
🖳, 📃, 🐎, ⋇ – 🛗 📺 🕿 🕭 ❾. **M©** AE ⓪ VISA
closed 24 to 26 December – Meals 13.00/23.00 t. and a la carte ⅟ 6.00 – 54 rm ⇌ 58.00
99.00 st. – SB.

🏨 **Fairways**, S : 3 m. on N 1 ℰ (042) 21500, Fax (042) 21511, ⇌, 🖳, 🐎, ⋇, squash – 📺 🕿
❾ – 🔏 400. **M©** AE ⓪ VISA
closed 24 and 25 December – Meals (carving lunch) 11.75/17.00 st. and dinner a la carte
⅟ 5.00 – 45 rm ⇌ 55.00/80.00 st. – SB.

at Carrickcarnon N : 8 m. on N 1 – ✉ Dundalk.

🏨 **Carrickdale**, ℰ (042) 71397, Fax (042) 71740, ⅃₆, ⇌, 🖳, 🐎 – 📺 🕿 ❾ – 🔏 40. **M©** AE
⓪ VISA, ⋇
closed 25 December – Meals (carving lunch) 8.95/10.95 st. and a la carte – 54 rm ⇌ 40.00
75.00 st. – SB.

DUNDRUM (Dîn Droma) Tipperary 923 H 10 – pop. 219 – ✉ Cashel.
Dublin 104 – Cork 66 – Limerick 33.

🏨 **Dundrum House** ⏦, SE : ¾ m. on R 505 ℰ (062) 71116, Fax (062) 71366, 📃, 🐎, par
⋇ – 🛗 📺 🕿 ❾ – 🔏 150. **M©** AE ⓪ VISA, ⋇
Meals (bar lunch Monday to Saturday)/dinner a la carte 16.00/26.50 t. ⅟ 8.00 – 60 rm
⇌ 55.00/98.00 – SB.

DUNFANAGHY (Dîn Fionnachaidh) Donegal 923 I 2 Ireland G. – pop. 290 – ⌧ Letterkenny.
Env. : Horn Head Scenic Route★, N : 2 ½ m.
Exc. : Doe Castle★, SE : 7 m. by N 56 – The Rosses★, SW : 25 m. by N 56 and R 259.
Dublin 172 – Donegal 54 – Londonderry 43.

🏦 **Arnold's**, Main St., ℘ (074) 36208, Fax (074) 36352, ≤, ☞, ℀ – 🆃🆅 ☎ 🅿. ᗌᑕ 🅰🅴 ① 💳.
⚅⚄
mid March-November – *Tramore rest.* : Meals (dinner only) 25.00 t. ⌗ 7.00 –
Garden bistro : Meals a la carte 10.75/20.50 t. ⌗ 7.00 – 30 rm ⌁ 41.00/82.00 t. – SB.

🏠 **Carrig Rua**, Main St., ℘ (074) 36133, Fax (074) 36277, ≤ – 🆃🆅 ☎ 🅿. ᗌᑕ 🅰🅴 💳
17 March-October and restricted opening in winter – *Sheephaven Room :* Meals (dinner
only) 22.00 t. ⌗ 8.00 – *Copper grill :* Meals a la carte 16.00/23.50 t. ⌗ 8.00 – 22 rm
⌁ 35.00/70.00 t. – SB.

DUNGARVAN (Dún Garbháin) Waterford 923 J 11 – pop. 7 175.
🅡🅱 Knocknagrannagh ℘ (058) 41605/43310 – 🅡🅰 Gold Coast, Ballinacourty ℘ (058) 42249.
Dublin 118 – Cork 44 – Waterford 30.

🏦 **Lawlors**, Meagher St., ℘ (058) 41122, Fax (058) 41000 – 📶, 🍽 rest, 🆃🆅 ☎ – 🚗 150. ᗌᑕ 🅰🅴
① 💳
closed 25 December – Meals 8.95/15.95 t. and dinner a la carte ⌗ 5.50 – 89 rm ⌁ 34.00/
90.00 t. – SB.

❌❌ **The Tannery**, 10 Quay St., via Parnell St. ℘ (058) 45420, Fax (058) 44025, « 19C former
⚄ tannery » – ᗌᑕ 🅰🅴
closed Sunday, Monday, late January-early February, 25-26 December and 1 January –
Meals a la carte 12.10/24.45 t. ⌗ 6.50.

There is no paid advertising in this Guide.

DUNGLOW (An Clochán Liath) Donegal 923 G 3 – pop. 1 042.
Dublin 173 – Londonderry 51 – Sligo 76.

🏦 **Ostan na Rosann**, Mill Rd, ℘ (075) 21088, Fax (075) 21365, ≤, 🛋, 🏊 – 🆃🆅 ☎ 🅿. ᗌᑕ 🅰🅴
💳 💳
closed 6 January-28 February – Meals (bar lunch)/dinner 14.95 st. ⌗ 6.50 – 48 rm ⌁ 40.00/
70.00 st. – SB.

DUNKINEELY (Dún Cionnaola) Donegal 923 G 4 – pop. 395.
Dublin 157 – Londonderry 56 – Sligo 50.

❌❌ **Castle Murray House** with rm, St. Johns Point, SW : 1 ¼ m. by N 56 and St. Johns Point
rd turning left at T junction ℘ (073) 37022, Fax (073) 37330, ≤ McSweeney Bay – 🆃🆅 ☎ 🅿.
ᗌᑕ 💳
closed 3 weeks January-February, Monday and Tuesday mid October-17 March and
24 to 26 December – Meals - French - (dinner only and Sunday lunch)/dinner a la carte
18.00/26.00 st. ⌗ 7.00 – 10 rm ⌁ 34.00/56.00 s. – SB.

DUN LAOGHAIRE (Dún Laoghaire) Dublin 923 N 8 Ireland G. – pop. 55 540.
Env. : – ≤★★ of Killiney Bay from coast road south of Sorrento Point.
🚢 to Holyhead (Stena Line) 4-5 daily (1 h 40 mn).
🅱 St. Michaels Wharf.
Dublin 9.

Plan on next page

🏨 **Royal Marine**, Marine Rd, ℘ (01) 280 1911, Fax (01) 280 1089, ≤, ☞ – 📶, 🍽 rest, 🆃🆅 ☎
🅿 – 🚗 500. ᗌᑕ 🅰🅴 ① 💳. ⚄
n
Meals (bar lunch Saturday) 12.10/18.40 t. and a la carte ⌗ 8.85 – ⌁ 10.35 – 103 rm 180.00 –
SB.

🏠 **Chestnut Lodge** without rest., 2 Vesey Pl., Monkstown, ℘ (01) 280 7860,
Fax (01) 280 1466, « Regency house, antiques », ☞ – 🆃🆅 ☎. ᗌᑕ 💳. ⚄
u
4 rm ⌁ 50.00/65.00 t.

❌❌ **Morels Bistro**, 1st floor (above Eagle House pub), 18 Glasthule Rd, ℘ (01) 230 0210,
⚄ Fax (01) 230 0466 – ᗌᑕ 🅰🅴 ① 💳 🍱
c
closed 25 and 26 December – Meals (dinner only and Sunday lunch)/dinner 12.95 t.
and a la carte 18.20/23.95 t. ⌗ 8.95.

DUN LAOGHAIRE

George Street
Mulgrave Street
Patrick Street

Cumberland Street 2

Dunleary Hill 4
Longford Place 5
Marine Road. 7
Monkstown Avenue .. 8
Monkstown
    Road 9
Mount Town Upper... 10
Pakenham Road...... 13

XX **Brasserie Na Mara,** 1 Harbour Rd, ℰ (01) 280 6767, Fax (01) 284 4649 – ⓜⓞ ⒜Ⓔ ① ⓥⓘⓢⓐ
closed Saturday lunch, Sunday, Good Friday, 25-26 December, 1 January and Bank Holidays
Meals 10.95/17.95 **t.** and a la carte ⓐ 6.75.

X **Cavistons,** 59 Glasthole Rd, ℰ (01) 280 9120, Fax (01) 284 4054 – ✗ ⓜⓞ ⓥⓘⓢⓐ ⒿⒸⒷ
closed Sunday, Monday and 1 week Christmas – **Meals** - Seafood - (booking essentia
(lunch only) a la carte 15.00/18.00 **t.** ⓐ 4.50.

DUNLAVIN (Dún Luáin) Wicklow ⑨②③ L 8 – pop. 693.
Dublin 31 – Kilkenny 44 – Wexford 61.

⌂⌂ **Rathsallagh House** ⌖, SW : 2 m. on Grangecon Rd ℰ (045) 403112, Fax (045) 40334
≤, « 18C converted stables, walled garden », ⓢ, ☒, ⓡ, park, ✗ – ⓣⓥ ☎ ⓟ – 🔺 50. ⓜⓞ
① ⓥⓘⓢⓐ ⒿⒸⒷ
closed 23 to 27 December – **Meals** (dinner only) 35.00 **t.** ⓐ 6.00 – **16 rm** ⌂ 65.00/190.00 ◆
1 suite – SB.

DUNMANWAY (Dún Mánmhaí) Cork ⑨②③ E 12 – pop. 1 427.
Dublin 191 – Cork 37 – Killarney 49.

⌂ **Dún Mhuire House,** Kilbarry Rd, W : ½ m. by R 586 taking first right at fork junctic
ℰ (023) 45162, Fax (023) 45162, ⌖ – ⓣⓥ ☎ ⓟ. ⓜⓞ ① ⓥⓘⓢⓐ. ✗
closed 25 to 27 December – **Meals** (closed Sunday to Tuesday) (booking essentia
(dinner only) a la carte 14.00/19.00 **t.** ⓐ 7.00 – **6 rm** ⌂ 30.00/50.00 **t.** – SB.

DUNMORE EAST (Dún MÉr) *Waterford* 923 L 11 *Ireland G.* – *pop. 1 430* – ⊠ *Waterford*.
　　See : *Village★*.
　　Dublin 108 – Waterford 12.

� **Lakefield House** ⚐, Dunmore East Rd, Rosduff, NW : 5 m. on R 684 ℘ (051) 382582,
　　Fax (051) 382582, ≤, ⚒, 🐎, park – 💥 rest, 🆃🆅 🅿. ⚙ 🅰🅴 𝘝𝘐𝘚𝘈
　　March-October – **Meals** (by arrangement) 15.00 – **6 rm** ⊇ 25.00/38.00 **s.** – SB.

✗ **The Ship,** Dock Rd, ℘ (051) 383141 – ⚙ 🅰🅴 𝘝𝘐𝘚𝘈
　　Meals - Seafood - *(closed Sunday and Monday November-March)* (dinner only and lunch
　　Monday to Saturday June-August) a la carte 10.50/19.50 **t.** ⋀ 6.75.

DUNSHAUGHLIN (Dún Seachlainn) *Meath* 923 M 7 – *pop. 2 139*.
　　Dublin 17 – Drogheda 19.

⚏ **Old Workhouse,** Ballinlough, S : 1 ½ m. on N 3 ℘ (01) 8259251, 🐎 – 💥 rm, 🆃🆅 🅿. ⚙
　　𝘝𝘐𝘚𝘈 ⚸
　　closed 15 December-1 January – **Meals** (by arrangement) (communal dining) 22.00 **st.** –
　　4 rm ⊇ 35.00/60.00 **st.**

⚏ **Gaulstown House** ⚐, NE : 1 ½ m. by Ratoath rd ℘ (01) 825 9147, « Working farm »,
　　🐎, park – 💥 🆃🆅 🅿. ⚙ 𝘝𝘐𝘚𝘈 ⚸
　　April-October – **Meals** (by arrangement) 14.00 **s.** – **4 rm** ⊇ 25.00/40.00 **s.**

DURRUS (Dúras) *Cork* 923 D 13 – *pop. 204*.
　　Dublin 210 – Cork 56 – Killarney 53.

✗✗ **Blairs Cove,** SW : 1 m. on L 56 ℘ (027) 61127, *Fax (027) 61127*, « Converted barn », 🐎 –
　　🅿. ⚙ 𝘝𝘐𝘚𝘈
　　closed Sunday, Monday except July and August and November-March – **Meals** (booking
　　essential) (dinner only) 29.00 **st.**

There is no paid advertising in this Guide.

ENNIS (Inis) *Clare* 923 F 9 *Ireland G.* – *pop. 15 333*.
　　See : *Ennis Friary★ AC*.
　　Env. : *Clare Abbey★, SE : 1 m. by R 469.*
　　Exc. : *Quin Franciscan Friary★, SE : 6 ½ m. by R 469 – Knappogue Castle★ AC, SE : 8 m. by
　　R 469 – Carrofin (Clare Heritage Centre★ AC), N : 8 ½ m. by N 85 and R 476 – Craggauno-
　　wen Centre★ AC, SE : 11 m. by R 469 – Kilmacduagh Churches and Round Tower★, NE :
　　11 m. by N 18 – Scattery Island★, SW : 27 m. by N 68 and boat from Kilrush – Bridge of Ross,
　　Kilkee★, SW : 35 ½ m. by N 68 and N 67.*
　　🏌 *Drumbiggle Rd* ℘ (065) 24074.
　　🇮 *Clare Rd* ℘ (065) 28366.
　　Dublin 142 – Galway 42 – Limerick 22 – Roscommon 92 – Tullamore 93.

🏨 **West Country,** Clare Rd, SE : ¾ m. on N 18 ℘ (065) 23000, *Fax (065) 23759*, *Fb*, ⚒s, 🔲 –
　　🔋, 🍽 rest, 🆃🆅 ☎ ⅊ 🅿 – 🔏 1000. ⚙ 🅰🅴 ⓘ 𝘝𝘐𝘚𝘈. ⚸
　　Meals 8.75/12.50 **st.** and a la carte ⋀ 6.00 – **153 rm** ⊇ 65.00/100.00 **st.** – SB.

🏨 **Old Ground,** ℘ (065) 28127, *Fax (065) 28112*, 🐎 – 🔋, 💥 rm, 🆃🆅 🅿 ⅊ 🅿 – 🔏 70. ⚙ 🅰🅴
　　ⓘ 𝘝𝘐𝘚𝘈. ⚸
　　closed 25 December – **Meals** 11.00/19.00 **t.** and dinner a la carte ⋀ 7.75 – **85 rm** ⊇ 76.00/
　　150.00 **t.** – SB.

🏨 **Auburn Lodge,** Galway Rd, N : 1 ½ m. on N 18 ℘ (065) 21247, *Fax (065) 21202*, 🐎 – 🆃🆅
　　☎ 🅿. ⚙ 🅰🅴 ⓘ 𝘝𝘐𝘚𝘈. ⚸
　　Meals (carving lunch Monday to Saturday)/dinner 16.00 **st.** and a la carte ⋀ 6.00 – **99 rm**
　　⊇ 48.00/99.00 **t.** – SB.

🏨 **Temple Gate,** The Square, ℘ (065) 23300, *Fax (065) 23322* – 🔋 🆃🆅 ☎ 🅿. ⚙ 🅰🅴 ⓘ 𝘝𝘐𝘚𝘈.
　　⚸
　　closed 25 December – **Meals** (carvery lunch Monday to Saturday)/dinner 18.50 **st.**
　　and a la carte ⋀ 6.50 – **34 rm** ⊇ 53.00/90.00 **st.** – SB.

⚏ **Cill Eoin House** without rest., Killadysert Cross, Clare Rd, SE : 1 ½ m. at junction of N 18
　　with R 473 ℘ (065) 41668, *Fax (065) 20224*, 🐎, ⚒ – 💥 🆃🆅 ☎ 🅿. ⚙ 🅰🅴 𝘝𝘐𝘚𝘈
　　closed 22 December-10 January – **14 rm** ⊇ 22.00/40.00 **st.**

at Barefield NE : 3½ m. on N 18 – ⊠ *Ennis*.

⚏ **Carraig Mhuire,** NE : 1 ¾ m. on N 18 ℘ (065) 27106, *Fax (065) 27375*, 🐎 – 🅿. ⚙ 🅰🅴 𝘝𝘐𝘚𝘈.
　　⚸
　　closed 20 December-4 January – **Meals** 12.00 **s.** – **5 rm** ⊇ 19.00/34.00 **st.** – SB.

ENNIS

at Inch SW : 4 m. on R 474 (Kilmaley rd) – ⊠ Ennis.

🏛 **Magowna House** ⊗, W : 1 m. by R 474 ℘ (065) 39009, Fax (065) 39258, ≤, ⌕, ✵ – ▣
☎ 🅿, 🆚 AE ⓪ *VISA*
closed 24 and 25 December – Meals 9.50/16.50 **st.** and dinner a la carte ⓸ 5.00 – **10 rm**
⌕ 37.00/56.00 **st.** – SB.

ENNISCORTHY (Inis CÉrthaidh) Wexford 🔢 M 10 – pop. 3 788.
🔢 Knockmarshal ℘ (054) 33191.
Dublin 76 – Kilkenny 46 – Waterford 34 – Wexford 15.

🏛 **Ballinkeele House** ⊗, Ballymurn, SE : 6 ½ m. by unmarked road on Curracloe r
℘ (053) 38105, Fax (053) 38468, ≤, « 19C country house », ✵, park – ⵜ rm, 🅿, 🆚 A
VISA JCB, ✼
March-13 November – Meals (booking essential) (residents only) (communal dining
(dinner only) 20.00 **st.** – **5 rm** ⌕ 55.00/90.00 **st.**

ENNISKERRY (Áth an Sceire) Wicklow 🔢 N 8 – pop. 1 275.
Dublin 16 – Wicklow 20.

🏛🏛 **Summerhill House,** Cookstown Rd, S : ½ m. ℘ (01) 286 7928, Fax (01) 286 7929 – ⒤ ⵜ
📺 ☎ 🅿 – 🔏 220. 🆚 *VISA*, ✼
Meals (bar lunch Monday to Saturday)/dinner 16.50 **st.** and a la carte ⓸ 5.95 – **57 rm**
⌕ 45.00/80.00 **st.** – SB.

*Le Grand Londres (GREATER LONDON) est composé de la City
et de 32 arrondissements administratifs (Borough)
eux-mêmes divisés en quartiers ou en villages
ayant conservé leur caractère propre (Area).*

ENNISTIMON (Inis Dáomáin) Clare 🔢 E 9 – pop. 920.
Dublin 158 – Galway 52 – Limerick 39.

⌂ **Grovemount House** without rest., Lahinch Rd, W : ½ m. on N 67 ℘ (065) 7143
Fax (065) 71823, ✵ – 📺 ☎ 🅿, 🆚 *VISA*, ✼
April-October – **8 rm** ⌕ 25.00/40.00 **st.**

FAHAN (Fathain) Donegal 🔢 J 2 Ireland G. – pop. 284 – ⊠ Inishowen.
Exc. : Inishowen Peninsula★★ : (Dun Ree Fort★ AC), N : 11 m. by R 238.
🔢 North West, Lisfannon ℘ (077) 61027.
Dublin 156 – Londonderry 11 – Sligo 95.

✕✕ **St. John's** with rm, ℘ (077) 60289, Fax (077) 60612, ≤, « Loughside setting », ✵
ⵜ rest, ▦ rest, 📺 ☎ 🅿, 🆚 ⓪ *VISA* JCB, ✼
closed Sunday dinner, Monday and 24 to 26 December – Meals (dinner only and Sunda
lunch) 22.00 **t.** and a la carte ⓸ 5.95 – **5 rm** ⌕ 35.00/110.00 **st.** – SB.

FERNS (Fearna) Wexford 🔢 M 10 Ireland G. – pop. 915 – ⊠ Enniscorthy.
Exc. : – Mount Leinster★, NW : 17 m.
Dublin 69 – Kilkenny 53 – Waterford 41 – Wexford 22.

⌂ **Clone House** ⊗, S : 2 m. by Boolavogue rd off Monageer rd ℘ (054) 6611
Fax (054) 66225, « Working farm », ⌕, ✵, park – ⵜ 📺 🅿, *VISA*, ✼
March-October – Meals (by arrangement) (communal dining) 13.00 **st.** – **4 rm** ⌕ 25.0
50.00.

FOXROCK (Carraig an tSionnaigh) Dublin 🔢 N 7 – see Dublin.

FURBOGH/FURBO (Na Forbacha) Galway 🔢 E 8.
Dublin 42 – Galway 7.

🏛🏛 **Connemara Coast,** ℘ (091) 592108, Fax (091) 592065, ≤, ⌖, ≋, ◲, ✵, ✕ – 📺 ☎
– 🔏 500. 🆚 AE ⓪ *VISA*, ✼
closed 24 and 25 December – Meals (bar lunch)/dinner a la carte 22.50/31.00 **st.** ⓸ 6.95
111 rm ⌕ 60.00/116.00 **st.**, 1 suite – SB.

GALWAY (Gaillimh) *Galway* 923 E 8 *Ireland G. – pop. 57 241.*

See : *City*★★ – *Lynch's Castle*★ BY – *St. Nicholas' Church*★ BY – *Roman Catholic Cathedral*★ AY – *Eyre Square : Bank of Ireland Building (Mace*★) BY D.

Env. : *NW : Lough Corrib*★★ .

Exc. : *W : by boat, Aran Islands (Inishmore – Dun Aenghus*★★★)BZ – *Thoor Ballylee*★★ , SE : 21 m. by N 6 and N 18 BY – Athenry*★ , E : 14 m. by N 6 and R 348 BY – Dunguaire Castle, Kinvarra*★ AC, S : 16 m. by N 6, N 18 and N 67 BY – Knockmoy Abbey*★ , NE : 19 m. by N 17 and N 63 BY – Coole Park (Autograph Tree*★), SE : 21 m. by N 6 and N 18 BY – St. Mary's Cathedral, Tuam*★ , NE : 21 m. by N 17 BY – Loughrea (St. Brendan's Cathedral*★), SE : 22 m. by N 6 BY.*

🟍 *Galway, Blackrock, Salthill* ℘ *(091) 522033.*

✈ *Carnmore Airport :* ℘ *(091) 752874, NE : 4 m.*

🚩 *Victoria Pl., Eyre Sq.* ℘ *(091) 63081.*

Dublin 135 – Limerick 64 – Sligo 90.

Plan on next page

🏨 **Glenlo Abbey,** Bushypark, NW : 3 ¼ m. on N 59 ℘ (091) 526666, *Fax (091) 527800,* ≤, « Restored part 18C house and church », 🏌, ⚲, park – ❘≢❘, 🍴 rest, 📺 ☎ ℗ – 🕍 90. ◔◑ AE ➊ VISA. 🟥
Meals (bar lunch Monday to Saturday)/dinner a la carte 24.50/28.00 t. ⓗ 11.00 – ⌂ 12.00 – **40 rm** 115.00/180.00 t., 5 suites – SB.

🏨 **Great Southern,** Eyre Sq., ℘ (091) 564041, *Fax (091) 566704,* ⇌, 🔲 – ❘≢❘, ≒ rm, 📺 ☎ – 🕍 450. ◔◑ AE ➊ VISA. 🟥
BY **a**
closed 25 and 26 December – Meals (carving lunch)/dinner 20.00 t. and a la carte ⓗ 7.50 – ⌂ 7.50 – **115 rm** 83.00/126.00 t., 1 suite – SB.

🏨 **Corrib Great Southern,** Merlin Park, E : 1 ¾ m. on N 6 ℘ (091) 755281, *Fax (091) 751390,* 🔲 – ❘≢❘, ≒ rm, 🍴 rest, 📺 ☎ ⅚ ℗ – 🕍 750. ◔◑ AE ➊ VISA. 🟥
closed 25 and 26 December – Meals (carving lunch Monday to Saturday)/dinner 18.00 t. and dinner a la carte ⓗ 6.00 – **175 rm** ⌂ 76.50/125.00 t., 4 suites.

🏨 **Ardilaun House,** Taylor's Hill, W : 1 ½ m. on R 336 ℘ (091) 521433, *Fax (091) 521546,* 🏌, ⇌, ⬚ – ❘≢❘, ≒ rm, 📺 ☎ ⅚ ℗ – 🕍 450. ◔◑ AE ➊ VISA
closed 22 to 28 December – Meals (bar lunch Saturday) 11.75/22.00 t. and dinner a la carte ⓗ 6.00 – **89 rm** ⌂ 65.00/110.00, 1 suite – SB.

🏦 **Jurys Galway Inn,** Quay St., ℘ (091) 566444, *Fax (091) 568415,* ⬚ – ❘≢❘, ≒ rm, 🍴 rest, 📺 ☎ ⅚ – 🕍 40. ◔◑ AE ➊ VISA. 🟥
BZ **c**
closed 24 to 26 December – Meals (carving lunch)/dinner 15.00 t. and a la carte ⓗ 6.00 – ⌂ 6.50 – **128 rm** 62.00 t.

🏦 **Park House,** Forster St., Eyre Sq., ℘ (091) 564924, *Fax (091) 569219* – ❘≢❘, 🍴 rest, 📺 ☎ ⅚ ℗ – 🕍 35. ◔◑ AE ➊ VISA JCB. 🟥
BY **c**
closed 24 to 26 December – Meals (carving lunch)/dinner 22.95 t. and a la carte – **57 rm** ⌂ 75.00/125.00 st. – SB.

🏦 **Brennan's Yard,** Lower Merchants Rd, ℘ (091) 568166, *Fax (091) 568262* – ❘≢❘ 📺 ☎. ◔◑ AE ➊ VISA. 🟥
BZ **e**
closed 25 and 26 December – Meals (booking essential) (bar lunch)/dinner 15.95 st. and a la carte ⓗ 4.50 – **24 rm** ⌂ 60.00/95.00 st. – SB.

🏦 **Galway Ryan,** Dublin Rd, E : 1 ¼ m. on N 6 ℘ (091) 753181, *Fax (091) 753187,* 🏌, ⇌, 🔲, ⬚, 🍴 – ❘≢❘, ≒ rm, 🍴 rest, 📺 ☎ ℗ – 🕍 30. ◔◑ AE ➊ VISA. 🟥
Meals (bar lunch)/dinner a la carte 15.00/35.00 st. ⓗ 6.00 – ⌂ 10.00 – **96 rm** 90.00/130.00 st. – SB.

🏛 **Spanish Arch,** Quay St., ℘ (091) 569600, *Fax (091) 569191,* « Part 18C Carmelite convent » – ❘≢❘ 📺 ☎. ◔◑ AE ➊ VISA. 🟥
BZ **u**
closed 25 and 26 December – Meals (closed Sunday dinner) a la carte 11.50/19.00 t. ⓗ 5.00 – ⌂ 7.00 – **20 rm** 80.00/90.00 st. – SB.

🏛 **Ibis,** Headford Rd, NE : 1 ¼ m. by N 84 (Castlebar rd) ℘ (091) 771166, *Fax (091) 771646* – ❘≢❘, ≒ rm, 📺 ☎ ⅚ ℗. ◔◑ AE ➊ VISA
Meals (dinner only) 11.50 st. ⓗ 4.95 – ⌂ 5.25 – **100 rm** 49.50 st.

🏠 **Adare House** without rest., 9 Father Griffin Pl., ℘ (091) 582638, *Fax (091) 583963* – ≒ 📺 ☎ ℗. ◔◑ VISA. 🟥
AZ **n**
closed 23 to 27 December – **12 rm** ⌂ 35.00/60.00 st.

🍴🍴 **Casey's Westwood,** Newcastle, NW : 1 ¾ m. on N 59 ℘ (091) 521442, *Fax (091) 521400* – ℗. ◔◑ AE ➊ VISA. 🟥
Meals 11.95 st. (lunch) and a la carte 19.50/23.95 st. ⓗ 6.50.

🍴🍴 **de Burgos,** 15-17 Augustine St., ℘ (091) 562188, *Fax (091) 520364,* « Cellars of 16C house » – ◔◑ AE VISA
BY **e**
closed Sunday and 25-26 December – Meals (dinner only) 22.50 t. and a la carte ⓗ 8.95.

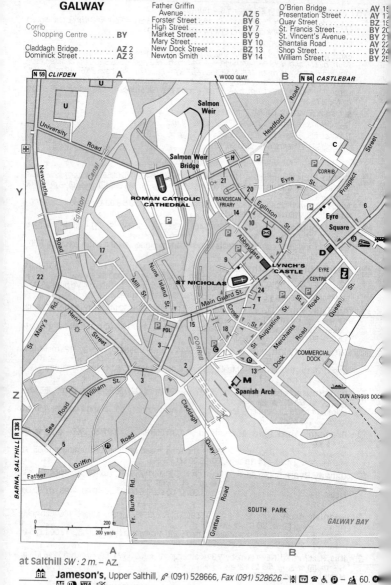

GALWAY

Corrib
Shopping Centre .... **BY**

Claddagh Bridge......... **AZ** 2
Dominick Street .... **AZ** 3

Father Griffin
Avenue............... **AZ** 5
Forster Street .... **BY** 6
High Street .... **BY** 7
Market Street .... **BY** 9
Mary Street .... **BY** 10
New Dock Street .... **BZ** 13
Newton Smith .... **BY** 14

O'Brien Bridge .... **AY** 1
Presentation Street ...... **AY** 1
Quay Street .... **BZ** 1
St. Francis Street........ **BY** 2
St. Vincent's Avenue...... **BY** 2
Shantalia Road .... **AY** 2
Shop Street .... **BY** 2
William Street......... **BY** 2

at Salthill SW : 2 m. – AZ.

Jameson's, Upper Salthill, ✆ (091) 528666, Fax (091) 528626 – 📶 📺 ☎ ✆ 🅿 – 🔬 60. ●
AE ⓪ VISA. ✦
closed 24 to 26 December – **Meals** (carving lunch)/dinner 18.95 **st.** and a la carte ⌁ 5.5
20 rm ⊇ 50.00/110.00 **st.** – SB.

Devondell without rest., 47 Devon Park, Lower Salthill, off Lower Salthill R
✆ (091) 528306 – ✦. ✦
March-October – **4 rm** ⊇ 20.00/40.00.

Benutzen Sie die Grünen Michelin-Reiseführer.
wenn Sie eine Stadt oder Region kennenlernen wollen.

844

GARRYVOE (Garraí Uí Bhuaigh) Cork **923** H 12 – ⊠ Castlemartyr.
Dublin 161 – Cork 23 – Waterford 62.

🏠 **Garryvoe**, ℘ (021) 646718, Fax (021) 646824, ≤, ⛲, ℀ – 🖵 ☎ 🅿 – 🔏 300. ⬤⑨ 🆎 ①
𝑉𝐼𝑆𝐴. ℁
closed 25 December – Meals 10.00/19.00 st. and dinner a la carte ⌄ 6.00 – **19 rm** ⊇ 35.00/
120.00 st. – SB.

GLENBEIGH (Gleann Beithe) Kerry **923** C 11 – pop. 251.
Dublin 197 – Killarney 21 – Tralee 24.

⌂ **Foxtrot** without rest., Mountain Stage, SW : 3 m. on N 70 ℘ (066) 68417, Fax (066) 68552,
≤ Coomasaharn lake and mountains – ℁⊱ 🅿. 𝑉𝐼𝑆𝐴. ℁
May-September – **4 rm** ⊇ 23.50/35.00.

GLENDALOUGH (Gleann dá Loch) Wicklow **923** M 8.
Dublin 28 – Kilkenny 68 – Wexford 63.

🏠 **Glendalough**, ℘ (0404) 45135, Fax (0404) 45142, ⛲ – 🛗 🖵 ☎ ও 🅿 – 🔏 200. ⬤⑨ 🆎 ①
𝑉𝐼𝑆𝐴. ℁
closed 5 January-6 February and 1 to 26 December – Meals 8.75/20.00 t. and a la carte
⌄ 5.00 – **42 rm** ⊇ 57.20/88.00 st. – SB.

GLENGARRIFF (An Gleann Garbh) Cork **923** D 12.
🅱 ℘ (027) 63084 (July-August).
Dublin 213 – Cork 60 – Killarney 37.

⌂ **Cois Coille** ॐ without rest., ℘ (027) 63202, ≤, ⛲ – ℁⊱ 🅿. ℁
April-October – **6 rm** ⊇ 22.50/35.00 st.

GLEN OF AHERLOW (Gleann Eatharlaí) Tipperary **923** H 10 Ireland G. – ⊠ Tipperary.
See : Glen of Aherlow★.
Exc. : Caher Castle★★ AC – Town Square★ – St. Paul's Church★ – Swiss Cottage★ AC, SE :
7 m. by N 24 and R 670 – Clonmel★ (County Museum★, St. Mary's Church★, Riverside★,
Quay★), NE : 16 m. by N 24 – Kilmallock★★ :- Abbey★, Collegiate Church★, Blossom's Gate★,
Town Walls★, King's Castle★ – W : 27½m. by R 664 and R 515.
Dublin 118 – Cahir 6 – Tipperary 9.

🏠 **Aherlow House** ॐ, ℘ (062) 56153, Fax (062) 56212, ≤ Galty Mountains, park – ℁⊱ rest,
🖵 ☎ 🅿 – 🔏 150. ⬤⑨ 🆎 ① 𝑉𝐼𝑆𝐴. ℁
restricted opening January-March – Meals 10.95/18.50 st. ⌄ 7.50 – ⊇ 7.50 – **30 rm** 45.00/
70.00 st. – SB.

GLIN (An Gleann) Limerick **923** E 10 – pop. 554.
Dublin 152 – Limerick 32 – Tralee 32.

🏠 **Glin Castle** ॐ, ℘ (068) 34112, Fax (068) 34364, ≤, « Georgian castle in extensive
parkland », ⛲ – ☎ 🅿. ⬤⑨ 🆎 𝑉𝐼𝑆𝐴. ℁
restricted opening December and January – Meals (booking essential) (lunch
by arrangement) 15.00/25.00 t. ⌄ 9.00 – **9 rm** ⊇ 85.00/250.00 t.

GOREY (Guaire) Wexford **923** N 9 Ireland G. – pop. 2 150.
Exc. : Ferns★, SW : 11 m. by N 11.
🖽 Courtown, Kiltennel ℘ (055) 25166/25432.
🅱 Town Centre ℘ (055) 21248 (July and August).
Dublin 58 – Waterford 55 – Wexford 38.

🏠 **Marlfield House** ॐ, Courtown Rd, SE : 1 m. on R 742 ℘ (055) 21124, Fax (055) 21572,
≤, « Regency mansion, extensive gardens and woodland », ⇔s, ℀ – ℁⊱ 🖵 ☎ 🅿. ⬤⑨ 🆎
① 𝑉𝐼𝑆𝐴. ℁
closed 20 December-25 January – Meals (light lunch Monday to Saturday)/dinner 35.50 st.
⌄ 9.00 – **18 rm** ⊇ 95.00/165.00 st., 1 suite.

Great Britain and Ireland is now covered
by an Atlas at a scale of 1 inch to 4.75 miles.

Three easy to use versions: Paperback, Spiralbound and Hardback.

GRAIGUENAMANAGH (Gráig na Manach) *Kilkenny* 923 L 10 – *pop. 1 374 (inc. Tinnahinch).*
Dublin 77 – Kilkenny 20 – Waterford 25 – Wexford 34.

X **Waterside** with rm, The Quay, ℰ (0503) 24246, Fax (0503) 24733, « 19C former grain store on banks of River Barrow » – ▯ ☎ ● ● ● ●
closed Sunday to Tuesday to non-residents March-May and October-November and December-mid March – **Meals** 13.95/22.95 **t.** ▯ 6.50 – **10 rm** ☲ 32.00/76.00 **t.** – SB.

GREYSTONES (Na Clocha Liatha) *Wicklow* 923 N 8 – *pop. 9 995.*
Dublin 22.

X **Hungry Monk,** Southview Church Rd, ℰ (01) 287 5759, Fax (01) 287 7183 – ● ● ●
closed Monday, Tuesday and 24 to 26 December – **Meals** (dinner only and Sunday lunch)/dinner a la carte 20.45/24.45 **t.** ▯ 6.95.

HOWTH (Binn Éadair) *Dublin* 923 N 7 *Ireland G.* – ✉ Dublin.
See : Town★ – The Summit★.
▯₈, ▯₈, ▯₉ Deer Park Hotel, Howth Castle ℰ (01) 832 2624.
Dublin 10.

🏨 **Marine,** Sutton Cross, D13, W : 1½ m. ℰ (01) 839 0000, Fax (01) 839 0442, ≼, ☎s, ▥, ☞
– ▯ ☎ ● – ▵ 175. ● ● ●
closed 25 to 27 December – **The Meridian :** Meals 13.00 **st.** (lunch) and dinner a la carte 15.00/22.25 **st.** ▯ 5.75 – **26 rm** ☲ 90.00/140.00 **st.** – SB.

🏨 **Howth Lodge,** W : ½ m. ℰ (01) 832 1010, Fax (01) 832 2268, ≼, ▯₆, ☎s, ▥ – ▤ ▯ ☎ ▵
● – ▵ 200. ● ● ●
closed 23 to 29 December – **Meals** (closed Sunday dinner) (bar lunch Monday to Saturday)/dinner 25.00 **st.** ▯ 5.50 – **46 rm** ☲ 50.00/120.00 **t.** – SB.

🏨 **Deer Park,** W : ¾ m. ℰ (01) 832 2624, Fax (01) 839 2405, ≼, ☎s, ▥, ▯₈, ▯₉, park – ▦ rest,
▯ ☎ ▵ ● – ▵ 100. ● ● ● ● jcb. ☞
closed 24 to 26 December – **Meals** 11.50/18.50 **t.** and dinner a la carte ▯ 5.00 – **77 rm**
☲ 65.00/96.00 **st.** – SB.

XX **King Sitric,** Harbour Rd, East Pier, ℰ (01) 832 5235, Fax (01) 839 2442 – ● ● ● ●
closed Sunday, 2 weeks January and Bank Holidays – **Meals** - Seafood - (light lunch Monday to Saturday May-September) (dinner only October-April)/dinner 26.00 **t.** and a la carte ▯ 6.25.

INCH (An Inis) *Clare* – see Ennis.

INISHANNON (Inis Eonáin) *Cork* 923 G 12 – *pop. 498.*
Dublin 169 – Cork 15.

🏨 **Innishannon House** ⑤, S : ¾ m. on R 605 ℰ (021) 775121, Fax (021) 775609, ≼,
« Riverside setting, gardens », ⚓, park – ▯ ▯ ☎ ● – ▵ 150. ● ● ● ● jcb
closed 15 January-15 March – **Meals** 12.00/25.00 **t.** and a la carte ▯ 7.50 – **13 rm** ☲ 85.00/250.00 **st.** – SB.

INISHCRONE (Inis Crabhann) *Sligo* 923 E 5 – *pop. 692.*
Dublin 160 – Ballina 8 – Galway 79 – Sligo 34.

⌂ **Ceol na Mara,** Main St., ℰ (096) 36351, Fax (096) 36642, ≼ – ▯ ☎ ● ● ● ● ☞
restricted opening in winter – **Meals** (by arrangement) 14.00 – **9 rm** ☲ 22.00/36.00 – SB.

INISHMORE (Inis Mór) *Galway* 923 CD 8 – see Aran Islands.

INISTIOGE (Inis Tíog) *Kilkenny* 923 K 10.
Dublin 82 – Kilkenny 16 – Waterford 19 – Wexford 33.

⌂ **Berryhill** ⑤, SE : ¾ m. by R 700 ℰ (056) 58434, Fax (056) 58434, ≼, « Working farm »,
⚓, ☞, park – ☞ rm, ● ● ● ● ● ☞
mid April-early November – **Meals** (by arrangement) (communal dining) 25.00 **s.** ▯ 7.00 –
3 rm ☲ 50.00/80.00 **s.**

⌂ **Rathsnagadan House** ♠, SE : 4 ½ m. by R 700 ℘ (051) 423641, ≤, ≋, park – ⤢ ❷.
MO AE VISA
closed December and January – **Meals** *(by arrangement)* 20.00 **st.** ⑂ 6.00 – **3 rm** ⇄ 18.00/
40.00 **st.**

XX **The Motte**, Plass Newid, NW : ¼ m. on R 700 ℘ (056) 58655 – ❷. **MO VISA**
closed Sunday, Monday and 1 week Christmas – **Meals** *(dinner only)* 21.00 **t.** ⑂ 8.50.

INVERIN (Indreabhán) *Galway* 923 D8.
Dublin 149 – Galway 17.

⌂ **Tigh Chualain** *without rest.*, Kilroe East, on R 336 ℘ (091) 553609 – ⤢ ⊡ ☎ ❷. ⅏
April-October – **9 rm** ⇄ 20.00/36.00.

KANTURK (Ceann Toirc) *Cork* 923 F 11 *Ireland G. –* pop. 1 666.

See : *Town★ · Castle★.*

🏌 *Fairy Hill* ℘ (029) 50534.

Dublin 161 – Cork 33 – Killarney 31 – Limerick 44.

🏛 **Assolas Country House** ♠, E : 3 ¼ m. by R 576 off R 580 ℘ (029) 50015,
Fax (029) 50795, ≤, « Part 17C and 18C country house, gardens, riverside setting », ♒,
park, ⅍ – ☎ ❷. **MO AE ① VISA**. ⅏
March-October – **Meals** *(booking essential) (dinner only)* 30.00 **st.** ⑂ 7.50 – **9 rm** ⇄ 79.00/
164.00 **st.**

⌂ **Glenlohane** ♠, ℘ (029) 50014, *Fax* (029) 51100, ≤, « Georgian country house,
extensive parkland, working farm », ≋ – ❷. **MO VISA**. ⅏
Meals *(by arrangement) (communal dining)* 25.00 **st.** – **4 rm** ⇄ 45.00/100.00 **st.**

🍴 **The Vintage**, O'Brien St., ℘ (029) 50549, *Fax* (029) 51209 – **MO VISA**
closed 25 December – **Meals** *a la carte* 7.50/18.00 **t.** ⑂ 5.95.

KENMARE (Neidín) *Kerry* 923 D 12 *Ireland G. –* pop. 1 420.

See : *Site★.*

Exc. : *Iveragh Peninsula★★★ (Ring of Kerry★★) – Healy Pass★★ (≤★★), SW : 19 m. by R 571
and R 574 – Mountain Road to Glengarriff (≤★★) S : by N 71 - Slieve Miskish Mountains
(≤★★), SW : 30 m. by R 571 - Gougane Barra Forest Park★★, SE : 10 m. – Lauragh (Derreen
Gardens★ AC), SW : 14 ½ m. by R 571 – Allihies (Copper Mines★), SW : 35 ½ m. by R 571 and
R 575 – Garnish Island (≤★), SW : 42½m. by R 571, R 575 and R 572.*

🏌 *Kenmare* ℘ (064) 41291.

🗓 *Heritage Centre, The Square* ℘ (064) 41233 *(April-October).*

Dublin 210 – Cork 58 – Killarney 20.

🏨 **Park** ♠, ℘ (064) 41200, *Fax* (064) 41402, ≤ Kenmare Bay and hills, « Antiques,
❀ paintings », Ɫ₅, 🏌, ♒, ≋, park, ⅍ – 🛗 ⊡ ☎ ὧ ❷ – ⚄ 35. **MO AE VISA**
15 April-1 November and 24 December-1 January – **Meals** *(dinner only)* 39.00 **t.**
and a la carte 39.00/47.70 **t.** ⑂ 9.50 – **47 rm** ⇄ 146.00/268.00 **st.**, 2 suites – SB
Spec. Foie gras on smoked aubergine compote, caramelised apple and thyme jus. Fillet of
turbot in a pine kernel crust with salsify and red wine butter sauce. Apple bavarois with
apple petals and Calvados sabayon.

🏨 **Sheen Falls Lodge** ♠, SE : 1 ¼ m. by N 71 ℘ (064) 41600, *Fax* (064) 41386, « Wooded
❀ setting on banks of Sheen River and Kenmare Bay, ≤ Sheen Falls », Ɫ₅, ≊, ▣, ♒, ≋,
park, ⅍ – 🛗 ⊡ ☎ ὧ ❷ – ⚄ 120. **MO AE ① VISA JCB.** ⅏
closed 4 January-7 February and 30 November-23 December – **La Cascade :** **Meals** *(dinner
only)* 37.50 **t.** ⑂ 11.50 – ⇄ 13.00 – **52 rm** 165.00/245.00 **t.**, 8 suites – SB
Spec. Fillet of sea perch with butternut pumpkin in a plum tomato essence. Noisettes of
lamb on smoked aubergine purée with caponata. Sugar glazed cardamom custard with
spiced seasonal fruit.

🏛 **Dromquinna Manor** ♠, Blackwater Bridge P.O., W : 3 m. on N 70 ℘ (064) 41657,
Fax (064) 41791, ≤, « Situated on the banks of Kenmare River », ♒, ≋, park, ⅍ – 🖃 ⊡ ☎
❷ – ⚄ 30. **MO AE ① VISA**
Meals *(bar lunch Monday to Saturday)/dinner* 19.00 **t.** *and a la carte* ⑂ 6.00 – **Boathouse
Bistro :** **Meals** *(May-September) a la carte approx.* 12.00 **t.** – **46 rm** ⇄ 42.00/130.00 **t.** – SB.

🏠 **Shelburne Lodge**, E : ½ m. on R 569 (Cork Rd) ℘ (064) 41013, *Fax* (064) 42135, « Styl-
ishly decorated 18C house », ≋, ⅍ – ⊡ ☎ ❷. **MO VISA**. ⅏
11 April-7 October – **Meals** *– (see Packie's below) –* **8 rm** ⇄ 45.00/80.00 **t.**

🏠 **Dunkerron** ♠, Sneem Rd, W : 2 ½ m. on N 70 ℘ (064) 41102, *Fax* (064) 41102,
« 12C fortified castle in grounds », ≋, park – ☎ ❷. **MO VISA**. ⅏
April-October – **Meals** *(booking essential) (dinner only)* 21.00 **t.** *and a la carte* ⑂ 8.00 – **10 rm**
⇄ 45.00/70.00 **t.**

KENMARE

🏠 **The Rosegarden,** W : ¾ m. by N 71 on Sneem rd ℰ (064) 42288, *Fax (064) 42305*, ⇔ – 📺 ☎ 🅿. 📇 AE ⑨ VISA
April-October – **Meals** (dinner only) 11.95 **t**. and a la carte ᵇ 6.00 – **8 rm** ⊆ 27.50/45.00 **t**.

⚄ **Sallyport House** without rest., S : ¼ m. on N 71 ℰ (064) 42066, *Fax (064) 42067*, ≤, « Antique furnishings », ⇔ – ⇔ 🅿. ⑨
Easter-October – **5 rm** ⊆ 60.00/80.00.

⚄ **Mylestone House** without rest., Killowen Rd, E : ¼ m. ℰ (064) 41753, ⇔ – 🅿. 📇 VISA ⚐
March-mid November – **5 rm** ⊆ 26.00/36.00 **st**.

⚄ **Rosewood House** without rest., E : ½ m. on R 569 (Cork Rd) ℰ (064) 41699, ⇔ – ⇔ 🅿. 📇 VISA
May-September – **4 rm** ⊆ 30.00/35.00.

⚄ **Ceann Mara** ⚙, E : 1 m. on R 569 (Cork Rd) ℰ (064) 41220, ≤ Kenmare Bay and hills, ⇔ – 🅿. ⚐
May-September – **Meals** (by arrangement) 14.00 **st**. – **4 rm** ⊆ 24.00/36.00.

⚄ **Ard Na Mara** without rest., Pier Rd, ℰ (064) 41399, *Fax (064) 41399*, ≤ Kenmare Bay and hills, ⇔ – 🅿. ⚐
closed 25 December – **4 rm** ⊆ 20.00/32.00 **st**.

XX **d'Arcys** with rm, Main St., ℰ (064) 41589, *Fax (064) 41589* – 📇 VISA
🍴 *closed Monday and Tuesday October-Easter* – **Meals** (dinner only) 17.50 **st**. and a la carte 15.90/26.00 **st**. ᵇ 6.00 – **5 rm** ⊆ 20.00/34.00 **st**. – SB.

X **Lime Tree,** Shelbourne St., ℰ (064) 41225, *Fax (064) 41402*, « Characterful former schoolhouse » – 🅿. 📇 VISA
late March-early November – **Meals** (dinner only) a la carte 22.00/26.00 **t**. ᵇ 7.00.

X **Packies,** Henry St., ℰ (064) 41508 – 📇 VISA
🍴 *closed Sunday and mid November-Easter* – **Meals** (dinner only) a la carte 18.40/26.70 **t**. ᵇ 5.50.

X **An Leath Phingin,** 35 Main St., ℰ (064) 41559 – ⇔. 📇 VISA
🍴 *closed 15 November-15 December* – **Meals** - Italian - (dinner only) a la carte 12.30/16.00 **t**. ᵇ 5.50.

📗 **Foleys** with rm, Henry St., ℰ (064) 41361, *Fax (064) 41799* – 📺. 📇 VISA. ⚐
Meals (bar lunch)/dinner 13.95 **st**. and a la carte – **10 rm** ⊆ 25.00/50.00 **st**.

KILCOLGAN (Cill Cholgáin) *Galway* 923 F 8 – ⊠ *Oranmore*.
Dublin 137 – Galway 11.

📗 **Moran's Oyster Cottage,** The Weir, NW : 1 ¼ m. by N 18 ℰ (091) 796113, *Fax (091) 796503*, 🌳, « Part 18C thatched cottage » – 📇 AE ⑨ VISA
Meals a la carte 15.40/31.20 **t**.

KILCUMMIN (Cill Chuimán) *Kerry* 923 B 11.
Dublin 203 – Killarney 34 – Limerick 85 – Tralee 21.

⚄ **Strand View House** without rest., Conor Pass Rd, ℰ (066) 38131, *Fax (066) 39434*, ≤ – 📺 🅿. AE ⚐
closed November-February – **4 rm** ⊆ 25.00/40.00.

KILDARE (Cill Dara) *Kildare* 923 L 8 – *pop. 4 278*.
Dublin 32 – Kilkenny 50 – Galway 112.

🏛 **Curragh Lodge,** Dublin Rd, ℰ (045) 522144, *Fax (045) 522098* – 📺 ☎. 📇 AE ⑨ VISA. ⚙
Meals 7.00/11.95 **t**. and a la carte ᵇ 4.50 – **21 rm** ⊆ 29.50/55.00 **st**. – SB.

KILKEE (Cill Chaoi) *Clare* 923 D 9 – *pop. 1 331*.
Dublin 177 – Galway 77 – Limerick 58.

🏠 **Halpin's,** Erin St., ℰ (065) 56032, *Fax (065) 56317* – ⇔ rest, 📺 ☎ 🅿. 📇 AE ⑨ VISA. ⚙
15 March-10 November – **Meals** (bar lunch Monday to Saturday)/dinner 21.00 **t**. and a la carte ᵇ 8.50 – **12 rm** ⊆ 40.00/80.00 **t**. – SB.

Bitte beachten Sie die Geschwindigkeitsbeschränkungen in Großbritannien
- 60 mph (= 96 km/h) außerhalb geschlossener Ortschaften
- 70 mph (= 112 km/h) auf Straßen mit getrennten Fahrbahnen und Autobahnen.

KILKENNY (Cill Chainnigh) *Kilkenny* 923 K 10 *Ireland G.* – *pop. 8 507.*

See : *Town*★★ – *St. Canice's Cathedral*★★ – *Kilkenny Castle and Grounds*★★ *AC* – *Cityscope*★ *AC* – *Black Abbey*★.

Exc. : *Dunmore Cave*★ *AC, N : 7 m. by N 77 and N 78* – *Kells Priory*★, *S : 9 m. by R 697.*

🛐₈ *Glendine* ℘ *(056) 65400* – 🛐₉ *Callan, Geraldine* ℘ *(056) 25136* – 🛐₉ *Castlecomer, Drumgoole* ℘ *(056) 41139.*

🇧 *Rose Inn St.* ℘ *(056) 51500.*

Dublin 71 – *Cork 86* – *Killarney 115* – *Limerick 69* – *Tullamore 52* – *Waterford 29.*

🏛 **Kilkenny,** College Rd, SW : ¾ m. at junction with N 76 ℘ *(056) 62000, Fax (056) 65984,* 🖿, ⇌s, 🗆, 🐾, 🛠 – 🔟 🖾 🅿 – 🔬 400. 🌑🟢 🆎 ⓪ 𝖵𝖨𝖲𝖠. 🛠
Meals 17.50 **st.** (dinner) and a la carte 17.75/23.00 **st.** ╏ 5.00 – **80 rm** ⚌ 55.00/95.00 – SB.

🏛 **Springhill Court,** Waterford Rd, S : 1 ¼ m. on N 10 ℘ *(056) 21122, Fax (056) 61600* – 🔟 ☎ 🅿 – 🔬 400. 🌑🟢 🆎 ⓪ 𝖵𝖨𝖲𝖠
Meals 10.95/15.95 **st.** and dinner a la carte ╏ 7.50 – **44 rm** ⚌ 50.00/90.00 **st.** – SB.

🏛 **Newpark,** Castlecomer Rd, N : 1 m. on N 77 ℘ *(056) 22122, Fax (056) 61111,* 🖿, ⇌s, 🗆, 🐾, park – ▤ rest, 🔟 ☎ 🕭 🅿 – 🔬 600. 🌑🟢 🆎 ⓪ 𝖵𝖨𝖲𝖠. 🛠
Meals 13.50/19.95 **t.** and a la carte – ╏ 7.50 – **84 rm** 40.00/80.00 **t.** – SB.

🏛 **Langton's House,** 69 John St., ℘ *(056) 65133, Fax (056) 63693* – ▤ 🔟 ☎ 🅿. 🌑🟢 🆎 ⓪ 𝖵𝖨𝖲𝖠
closed 25 December – **Meals** *(closed Good Friday)* 18.50 **st.** (dinner) and a la carte 11.50/ 20.00 **st.** ╏ 6.00 – **10 rm** ⚌ 65.00/180.00 **st.** – SB.

🏠 **Butler House** without rest., 15-16 Patrick St., ℘ *(056) 65707, Fax (056) 65626,* 🐾 – 🔟 ☎ 🅿 – 🔬 100. 🌑🟢 🆎 ⓪ 𝖵𝖨𝖲𝖠. 🛠
closed 24 to 29 December – **12 rm** ⚌ 49.00/109.00 **st.**, 1 suite.

🏠 **Berkeley House** without rest., 5 Patrick St., ℘ *(056) 64848, Fax (056) 64829* – 🔟 ☎ 🅿. 🌑🟢 𝖵𝖨𝖲𝖠. 🛠
closed 24 to 30 December – **10 rm** ⚌ 30.00/55.00 **st.**

↑ **Blanchville House** ⤴, Dunbell, Maddoxtown, SE : 7 ½ m. by N 10 turning right ½ m. after the Pike Inn ℘ *(056) 27197, Fax (056) 27636,* ≼, « Georgian country house », 🐾, park – ⇌ rest, 🅿. 🌑🟢 🆎 𝖵𝖨𝖲𝖠. 🛠
March-October – **Meals** *(by arrangement) (communal dining)* 22.00 **st.** – **6 rm** ⚌ 30.00/ 65.00 **st.** – SB.

↑ **Shillogher House** without rest., Callan Rd, SW : 1 m. on N 76 ℘ *(056) 63249, Fax (056) 64865,* 🐾 – ⇌ 🔟 ☎ 🅿. 🌑🟢 𝖵𝖨𝖲𝖠. 🛠
5 rm ⚌ 30.00/37.00 **st.**

🟅🟅 **Lacken House** with rm, Dublin Rd, E : ¾ m. on N 10 ℘ *(056) 61085, Fax (056) 62435,* 🐾 – ▤ rest, 🔟 ☎ 🅿. 🌑🟢 🆎 𝖵𝖨𝖲𝖠 𝖩𝖢𝖡. 🛠
closed 2 weeks Christmas – **Meals** *(closed Sunday and Monday) (dinner only)* 23.00 **st.** and a la carte ╏ 8.00 – **9 rm** ⚌ 36.00/60.00 **st.** – SB.

🟅🟅 **Ristorante Rinuccini,** 1 The Parade, ℘ *(056) 61575, Fax (056) 51288* – ▤. 🌑🟢 🆎 ⓪ 𝖵𝖨𝖲𝖠
closed 25 and 26 December – **Meals** - Italian - a la carte 7.35/24.90 **st.** ╏ 5.95.

KILL (An Chill) *Kildare* 923 M 8 – *pop. 1 711.*
Dublin 15 – *Carlow 36.*

🏛 **Ambassador,** on N 7 ℘ *(045) 877064, Fax (045) 877515* – 🔟 ☎ 🅿 – 🔬 280. 🌑🟢 🆎 ⓪ 𝖵𝖨𝖲𝖠. 🛠
Meals *(carving lunch Monday to Saturday)/dinner* 18.50 **st.** and a la carte ╏ 5.50 – **36 rm** ⚌ 54.00/85.00 **t.** – SB.

KILLALOE (Cill Dalua) *Clare* 923 G 9 *Ireland G.* – *pop. 972.*

See : *Town*★ – *St. Flannan's Cathedral*★.

Env. : *Graves of the Leinstermen*★, *N : 4 ½ m. by R 494.*

Exc. : *Nenagh*★ *(Heritage Centre*★★ *AC, Castle*★ *), NE : 12 m. by R 496 and N 7* – *Holy Island*★ *AC, N : 8 m. by R 463 and boat from Tuamgraney.*

🇧 *Lock House* ℘ *(061) 376866 (1 June-11 September).*

Dublin 109 – *Ennis 32* – *Limerick 13* – *Tullamore 58.*

🏛 **Kincora Hall,** N : ¾ m. on R 463 ℘ *(061) 376000, Fax (061) 376665,* 🐾 – ▤ rest, 🔟 ☎ 🕭 🅿. 🌑🟢 🆎 ⓪ 𝖵𝖨𝖲𝖠. 🛠
closed 23 to 27 December – **Meals** *(bar lunch Monday to Saturday)/dinner* 19.95 **t.** and a la carte ╏ 6.50 – **25 rm** ⚌ 63.00/115.00 **t.** – SB.

at Ogonnelloe *N : 6 ¼ m. on R 463.*

↑ **Lantern House** ⤴, ℘ *(061) 923034, Fax (061) 923139,* ≼, 🐾 – ⇌ rm, 🔟 ☎ 🅿. 🌑🟢 🆎 ⓪ 𝖵𝖨𝖲𝖠. 🛠
15 February-October – **Meals** *(by arrangement)* 17.50 **t.** ╏ 4.75 – **6 rm** ⚌ 26.00/40.00 **t.**

KILLARNEY **(Cill Airne)** *Kerry* [923] **D 11** *Ireland G. – pop. 8 809.*

See : *Town★★ – Knockreer Demesne★ – St. Mary's Cathedral★.*

Env. : *Killarney National Park★★★ – Muckross House★★* **AC**, *S : 3 ½ m. by N 71 – Torc Waterfall★★, S : 5 m. by N 71 – Gap of Dunloe★★, SW : 6 m. by R 582 – Muckross Abbey★, S : 3 ½ m. by N 71.*

Exc. : *Iveragh Peninsula★★★ (Ring of Kerry★★) – Ladies View★★, SW : 12 m. by N 71 – Moll's Gap★, SW : 15 ½ m. by N 71.*

⛳18, ⛳18 *Mahoney's Point ✆ (064) 31034.*

✈ *Kerry (Farranfore) Airport : ✆ (066) 64644, N : 9 ½ m. by N 22.*

[i] *Town Hall ✆ (064) 31633.*

Dublin 189 – Cork 54 – Limerick 69 – Waterford 112.

🏨🏨🏨🏨 **Europe** 🌙, Fossa, W : 3 ½ m. on R 562 ✆ (064) 31900, *Fax (064) 32118*, ≤ Lough Leane and mountains, 🏋, 🏊, ⛱, 🎣, 🌳, park, 🎾 – 🛗 ⚓ [TV] ☎ [P] – 👥 500. [MC] [AE] ⊙ VISA. 🚫
April-October – **Meals** (light lunch)/dinner 23.50 **st.** and a la carte – **202 rm** ☕ 88.00/146.00 **st.**, 3 suites.

🏨🏨🏨 **Killarney Park,** Kenmare Pl., ✆ (064) 35555, *Fax (064) 35266*, 🏋, 🏊, ⛱ – 🛗, ❄ rest, [TV] ☎ ♿ [P] – 👥 70. [MC] [AE] ⊙ VISA. 🚫
closed 24 to 26 December – ***Park :*** **Meals** (dinner only and Sunday lunch)/dinner 27.00 **st.** and a la carte 🍷 6.50 – **66 rm** ☕ 105.00/150.00 **st.**, 1 suite – SB.

🏨🏨🏨 **Aghadoe Heights** 🌙, NW : 3 ½ m. by N 22 ✆ (064) 31766, *Fax (064) 31345*, ≤ Lough Leane, Macgillycuddy's Reeks and countryside, 🏊, ⛱, 🌳, 🎾 – [TV] ☎ ♿ [P] – 👥 100. [MC] [AE] ⊙ VISA. 🚫
Meals – (see ***Fredrick's at the Heights*** below) – **57 rm** ☕ 130.00/215.00 **t.**, 3 suites – SB.

🏨🏨🏨 **Great Southern,** East Avenue Rd, ✆ (064) 31262, *Fax (064) 31642*, 🏋, 🏊, ⛱, 🌳, park, 🎾 – 🛗 [TV] ☎ ♿ [P] – 👥 900. [MC] [AE] ⊙ VISA
closed 3 January-14 February – ***Dining Room :*** **Meals** (dinner only) 20.00 **st.** and a la carte 🍷 7.00 – **178 rm** ☕ 73.00/120.00 **st.**, 3 suites – SB.

🏨🏨🏨 **Dunloe Castle** 🌙, Beaufort, W : 6 m. by R 562 ✆ (064) 44111, *Fax (064) 44583*, ≤ Gap of Dunloe, countryside and mountains, 🏊, ⛱, 🎣, 🌳, park, 🎾 – 🛗 [TV] ☎ [P] – 👥 250. [MC] [AE] ⊙ VISA. 🚫
16 April-14 October – **Meals** 23.00 **st.** (dinner) and a la carte 19.50/30.50 **st.** 🍷 10.00 – **102 rm** ☕ 88.00/110.00 **st.**, 1 suite – SB.

🏨🏨🏨 **Muckross Park,** S : 2 ¾ m. on N 71 ✆ (064) 31938, *Fax (064) 31965*, 🌳 – [TV] ☎ [P] – 👥 200. [MC] [AE] ⊙ VISA. 🚫
March-3 November – **Meals** (bar lunch)/dinner 23.00 and a la carte 🍷 6.50 – **25 rm** ☕ 80.00/120.00, **47 suites** 200.00/350.00 – SB.

🏨🏨🏨 **Randles Court,** Muckross Rd, ✆ (064) 35333, *Fax (064) 35206* – 🛗 [TV] ☎ [P]. [MC] [AE] ⊙ VISA. 🚫
closed 25 December and late January-mid February – **Meals** (bar lunch)/dinner 22.00 **st.** and a la carte 🍷 6.00 – **49 rm** ☕ 35.00/100.00 – SB.

🏨🏨 **The Killarney Heights,** Cork Rd, ✆ (064) 31158, *Fax (064) 35198* – 🛗 [TV] ☎ [P] – 👥 400. [MC] ⊙ VISA. 🚫
closed 25 to 27 December – **Meals** a la carte 12.50/22.00 **st.** 🍷 6.75 – **38 rm** ☕ 55.00/90.00 **st.** – SB.

🏨🏨 **Killeen House,** Aghadoe, W : 4 m. by R 562 ✆ (064) 31711, *Fax (064) 31811*, 🌳 – [TV] ☎ [P]. [MC] [AE] ⊙ VISA
March-October – **Meals** (dinner only) 25.00 **st.** 🍷 8.50 – **19 rm** ☕ 40.00/90.00 **t.**

🏨🏨 **Foley's Townhouse,** 23 High St., ✆ (064) 31217, *Fax (064) 34683* – ❄ rest, [TV] ☎ [P]. [MC] [AE] VISA. 🚫
accommodation closed November-Easter – **Meals** *(closed 23 to 26 December)* (bar lunch)/dinner 25.00 **st.** and a la carte 🍷 7.95 – **12 rm** ☕ 49.50/82.50 **st.**

🏨🏨 **Cahernane** 🌙, Muckross Rd, S : 1 m. on N 71 ✆ (064) 31895, *Fax (064) 34340*, ≤, 🌳, 🎾 – ☎ [P]. [MC] [AE] ⊙ VISA JCB. 🚫
April-4 November – **Meals** (bar lunch)/dinner a la carte 24.00/31.50 **st.** 🍷 6.50 – **48 rm** ☕ 90.00/130.00 **st.**

🏨🏨 **Ross,** Kenmare Pl., ✆ (064) 31855, *Fax (064) 31139*, 🏋, 🏊, ⛱ – 🛗, ❄ rest, [TV] ☎ [P]. [MC] [AE] ⊙ VISA. 🚫
March-October – **Meals** 11.00/17.50 **st.** and a la carte – **32 rm** ☕ 65.00/90.00 **st.** – SB.

🏨🏨 **Royal,** College St., ✆ (064) 31853, *Fax (064) 34001* – 🛗 [TV] ☎. [MC] [AE] ⊙ VISA
closed 1 week Christmas – **Meals** (bar lunch Monday to Saturday)/dinner 16.95 **st.** and a la carte 🍷 6.95 – **49 rm** ☕ 55.00/120.00 **st.** – SB.

🏨🏨 **Torc Great Southern,** Park Rd, ✆ (064) 31611, *Fax (064) 31824*, 🏊, ⛱, 🌳, 🎾 – [TV] ☎ ♿ [P]. [MC] [AE] ⊙ VISA. 🚫
Easter-mid October – **Meals** (bar lunch)/dinner 16.00 **t.** 🍷 6.00 – **94 rm** ☕ 65.00/96.00 **t.** – SB.

▣▣ **Castle Oaks House** without rest., Muckross Rd, S : 2 ½ m. on N 71, ℰ (064) 34154, Fax (064) 36980 – 🖵 ☎ ♿ 🅿. 🝠 ⓪ 𝑉𝐼𝑆𝐴. ⅀
closed 22 to 27 December – **16 rm** ⊑ 35.00/50.00 **st.**

▣ **Gleann Fia Country House** ⤴ without rest., Deerpark, N : 1 ½ m. by N 22 bypass ℰ (064) 35035, Fax (064) 35000, « Riverside setting, extensive woodlands », 🌳 – 🖳 🖵 ☎ 🅿. 🝠 𝐴𝐸 𝑉𝐼𝑆𝐴. ⅀
March-November – **14 rm** ⊑ 38.00/60.00 **st.**

▣ **Earls Court** without rest., Woodlawn Junction, Muckross Rd, S : ¾ m. by N 71 ℰ (064) 34009, Fax (064) 34366 – 🖳 🖵 ☎ 🅿. 🝠 𝑉𝐼𝑆𝐴. ⅀
11 March-4 November – **11 rm** ⊑ 50.00/80.00 **st.**

▣ **Fuchsia House** without rest., Muckross Rd, S : ¾ m. on N 71, ℰ (064) 33743, Fax (064) 36588, 🌳 – 🖳 🖵 ☎ 🅿. 🝠 𝑉𝐼𝑆𝐴. ⅀
March-November – **10 rm** ⊑ 56.00/76.00 **st.**

▣ **Old Weir Lodge** without rest., Muckross Rd, S : ¾ m. on N 71, ℰ (064) 35593, Fax (064) 35583 – 🖳 🖵 ☎ 🅿. 🝠 𝑉𝐼𝑆𝐴. ⅀
15 rm ⊑ 35.00/56.00 **st.**

▣ **Killarney Lodge** without rest., Countess Rd, ℰ (064) 36499, Fax (064) 31070 – ▤ rm, 🖵 ☎ ♿ 🅿. 🝠 𝐴𝐸 ⓪ 𝑉𝐼𝑆𝐴. ⅀
restricted opening in winter – **12 rm** ⊑ 60.00/70.00 **st.**

▣ **Kathleens Country House** without rest., Tralee Rd, N : 2 m. on N 22, ℰ (064) 32810, Fax (064) 32340, ≼, 🌳 – 🖳 🖵 ☎ 🅿. 🝠 𝐴𝐸 𝑉𝐼𝑆𝐴. ⅀
8 March-13 November – **17 rm** ⊑ 47.50/75.00 **st.**

▣ **Victoria House** without rest., Muckross Rd, S : 1 ¼ m. on N 71, ℰ (064) 35430, Fax (064) 35439 – 🖳 🖵 ☎ 🅿. 🝠 𝐴𝐸 𝑉𝐼𝑆𝐴. ⅀
closed December and January – **15 rm** ⊑ 32.00/48.00 **st.**

▣ **Beaufield House** without rest., Park Rd, E : 1 m. ℰ (064) 34440, Fax (064) 34663, 🌳 – 🖵 🅿. 🝠 𝐴𝐸 𝑉𝐼𝑆𝐴. ⅀
closed 16 to 28 December – **14 rm** ⊑ 29.00/44.00 **st.**

▣ **Lime Court**, Muckross Rd, S : ¾ m. on N 71, ℰ (064) 34547, Fax (064) 34121 – 🖵 ☎ 🅿. 🝠 𝑉𝐼𝑆𝐴. ⅀
closed 20 to 28 December – **Meals** (dinner only) 14.50 **st.** ₰ 6.00 – **12 rm** ⊑ 21.00/52.00 **st.** – SB.

⌂ **Naughton's Villa** without rest., Muckross Rd, ℰ (064) 36025 – 🖵 ☎ 🅿. 🝠 𝑉𝐼𝑆𝐴. ⅀
March-12 November – **5 rm** ⊑ 25.00/44.00 **st.**

⌂ **Lohans Lodge** without rest., N : 3 ½ m. on N 22, ℰ (064) 33871, Fax (064) 33871, 🌳 – 🖳 🖵 🅿. 𝑉𝐼𝑆𝐴. ⅀
closed December and January – **5 rm** ⊑ 30.00/35.00 **st.**

⌂ **Sika Lodge** without rest., Ballydowney, W : 1 m. on R 562, ℰ (064) 36304, Fax (064) 36746 – 🖵 ☎ 🅿. 🝠 𝑉𝐼𝑆𝐴. ⅀
closed 1 week Christmas – **6 rm** ⊑ 30.00/40.00 **st.**

⌂ **Avondale House** without rest., Tralee Rd, N : 3 m. on N 22, ℰ (064) 35579, ≼, 🌳 – 🖵 🅿. ⅀
closed December and January – **5 rm** ⊑ 25.00/35.00 **st.**

⌂ **Lake Lodge** without rest., Muckross Rd, S : ¾ m. on N 71, ℰ (064) 33333, Fax (064) 35109 – 🖵 ☎ 🅿. 🝠 𝑉𝐼𝑆𝐴. ⅀
March-October – **13 rm** ⊑ 25.00/40.00 **st.**

⌂ **McCarthy's Town House**, 19 High St., ℰ (064) 35655, Fax (064) 35745 – 🖵 ☎ 🅿. 🝠 𝐴𝐸 ⓪ 𝑉𝐼𝑆𝐴. ⅀
Meals 13.50 **st.** ₰ 5.20 – **8 rm** ⊑ 30.00/50.00 **st.**

XXX **Fredrick's at the Heights** (at Aghadoe Heights H.), NW : 3 ½ m. by N 22 ℰ (064) 31766, Fax (064) 31345, ≼ Lough Leane, Macgillycuddy's Reeks and countryside – ▤ 🅿. 🝠 𝐴𝐸 ⓪ 𝑉𝐼𝑆𝐴
Meals (booking essential) (buffet lunch Sunday) 21.50/33.50 **t.** and a la carte ₰ 8.00.

XX **Gaby's**, 27 High St., ℰ (064) 32519, Fax (064) 32747 – 🝠 𝐴𝐸 ⓪ 𝑉𝐼𝑆𝐴
closed Sunday, 10 days Christmas and 15 February-12 March – **Meals** - Seafood - (dinner only) a la carte 19.00/34.00 **st.** ₰ 8.00.

XX **Strawberry Tree**, 24 Plunkett St., ℰ (064) 32688, Fax (064) 32689 – 🝠 𝐴𝐸 ⓪ 𝑉𝐼𝑆𝐴
closed Sunday in winter, Monday, January and February – **Meals** (dinner only) a la carte 26.25/31.50 **st.** ₰ 7.50.

Bitte beachten Sie die Geschwindigkeitsbeschränkungen in Großbritannien

- 60 mph (= 96 km/h) außerhalb geschlossener Ortschaften
- 70 mph (= 112 km/h) auf Straßen mit getrennten Fahrbahnen und Autobahnen.

KILLEAGH (Cill Ia) Cork 923 H 12 – pop. 362.
Dublin 151 – Cork 23 – Waterford 53.

⌂ **Ballymakeigh House** 🦢, N : 1 m. ℘ (024) 95184, Fax (024) 95370, « Working farm », 🌿, park, ℀ – 🅿. ⓪❸ 𝖵𝖨𝖲𝖠
10 February-1 November – **Meals** (by arrangement) 20.00 st. ⓵ 8.00 – **5 rm** ⏥ 35.00/60.00 st. – SB.

KILLINEY (Cill Iníon Léinín) Dublin 923 N 8.
🏌 Killiney, Ballinclea Rd ℘ (01) 285 1983.
Dublin 8 – Bray 4.

🏰 **Fitzpatrick Castle**, ℘ (01) 284 0700, Fax (01) 285 0207, ⎰s, 🛋, 🔲, 🌿 – 🛗, ⤲ rm, ▤ rest, 📺 ☎ 🅿 – 🔬 500. ⓪❸ 𝔸𝔼 ⓞ 𝖵𝖨𝖲𝖠 𝖩𝖢𝖡. ℀
Meals 15.50 st. (lunch) and dinner a la carte 12.40/24.50 t. ⓵ 7.50 – ⏥ 9.00 – **106 rm** 85.00/130.00 t., 6 suites.

🏰 **Court**, Killiney Bay, ℘ (01) 285 1622, Fax (01) 285 2085, ≤, 🌿 – 🛗, ⤲ rm, 📺 ☎ 🅿 – 🔬 250. ⓪❸ 𝔸𝔼 ⓞ 𝖵𝖨𝖲𝖠. ℀
Meals 11.50/21.95 t. and a la carte – ⏥ 5.95 – **86 rm** 80.00/95.00 t. – SB.

KILLORGLIN (Cill Orglan) Kerry 923 C 11 – pop. 1 278.
Dublin 207 – Killarney 12 – Tralee 16.

🏨 **Grove Lodge** without rest., Killarney Rd, E : ½ m. on R 562 ℘ (066) 61157 Fax (066) 62330, « Riverside setting », 🎣, 🌿 – 🔟 📺 ☎ 🅿. ⓪❸ ⓞ 𝖵𝖨𝖲𝖠. ℀
closed December – **10 rm** ⏥ 30.00/56.00 st.

⌂ **Westfield House**, Glenbeigh Rd, W : ¾ m. by N 70 ℘ (066) 61909, Fax (066) 61996, ⎰s 🌿 – ⤲ rm, 📺 ☎ 🅿. ⓪❸ ⓞ 𝖵𝖨𝖲𝖠
Meals (by arrangement) 13.50 st. – **10 rm** ⏥ 25.00/40.00 st. – SB.

📁 **Bianconi** with rm, Annadale Rd, ℘ (066) 61146, Fax (066) 61950, 🎣 – 📺 ☎. ⓪❸ 𝔸𝔼 ⓞ 𝖵𝖨𝖲𝖠. ℀
closed February, March and 23 to 28 December – **Meals** (closed Sunday) (bar lunch)/dinner 18.50 t. and a la carte ⓵ 5.75 – **15 rm** ⏥ 35.00/54.00 t.

KILLYBEGS (Na Cealla Beaga) Donegal 923 G 4 Ireland G. – pop. 1 408.
Exc. : – Glengesh Pass★★★, SW : 15 m. by N 56 and R 263 – Gweebarra Estuary★, NE : 19 m by R 262 and R 252.
Dublin 181 – Donegal 17 – Londonderry 64 – Sligo 57.

🏨 **Bay View**, Main St., ℘ (073) 31950, Fax (073) 31856, ≤, ⎰s, 🛋, 🔲 – 🛗, ▤ rest, 📺 ☎ 🅿 ፈ – 🔬 200. ⓪❸ 𝖵𝖨𝖲𝖠. ℀
Meals (bar lunch Monday to Friday)/dinner 15.50 st. and a la carte ⓵ 5.50 – **42 rm** ⏥ 48.00/79.00 st. – SB.

KILMUCKRIDGE (Cill Mhucraise) Wexford 923 N 10.
Dublin 70 – Waterford 47 – Wexford 21.

💥💥 **The Rafters**, ℘ (053) 30391, Fax (053) 30181, « Converted 19C corn store » – ⓪❸ 𝔸𝔼 𝖵𝖨𝖲𝖠
closed Monday October-March, Good Friday and 25 December – **Meals** (dinner only and Sunday lunch)/dinner a la carte 16.95/25.45 st. ⓵ 6.50.

KILTIMAGH (Coillte Mach) Mayo 923 EF 6 – pop. 917.
Dublin 138 – Galway 52 – Westport 26.

🏨 **Cill Aodain**, ℘ (094) 81761, Fax (094) 81838 – 📺 ☎. ⓪❸ 𝖵𝖨𝖲𝖠. ℀
closed 25 December – **Meals** 9.00/16.50 st. and dinner a la carte ⓵ 4.75 – **15 rm** ⏥ 53.50/82.00 st. – SB.

KINNITTY (Cionn Eitigh) Offaly 923 I 8 – see Birr.

KINSALE (Cionn Eitigh) Cork 923 G 12 *Ireland G.* – pop. 2 007.

See : Town★★ – St. Multose Church★ – Kinsale Regional Museum★ *AC.*

Env. : Summercove★ (≤★) E : 1 ½ m. – Charles Fort★ *AC*, E : 1 ¾ m.

🛈 Pier Rd 🖉 (021) 772234 (March-November).

Dublin 178 – Cork 17.

🏨🏨🏨 Actons, Pier Rd, 🖉 (021) 772135, Fax (021) 772231, ≤, 🗗, 🚖, 🖾, 🐎 – 🛊 📺 ☎ 🅿 – 🔬 300. 🌐 🝙 ⓪ 🚾
Meals (bar lunch Monday to Saturday)/dinner 20.00 **st.** and a la carte 🛓 6.25 – **56 rm** ⚏ 90.00/135.00 **st.** – SB.

🏨🏨 Blue Haven, 3 Pearse St., 🖉 (021) 772209, Fax (021) 774268 – 📺 ☎. 🌐 🝙 ⓪ 🚾 🥢
⛛ closed 25 December and 8 to 25 January – **Meals** - Seafood - (bar lunch)/dinner 28.00 **st.** and a la carte 🛓 7.50 – **18 rm** ⚏ 70.00/140.00 **st.** – SB.

🏠 Old Bank House without rest., 11 Pearse St., 🖉 (021) 774075, Fax (021) 774296 – 📺 ☎. 🌐 🝙 🚾. 🥢
closed 23 to 26 December – **9 rm** ⚏ 65.00/130.00 **st.**

🏠 Moorings without rest., Scilly, 🖉 (021) 772376, Fax (021) 772675, ≤ Kinsale harbour – 📺 ☎ 🅿. 🌐 ⓪ 🚾. 🥢
closed 1 week Christmas – **6 rm** ⚏ 70.00/90.00 **st.**

🏠 Scilly House Inn without rest., Scilly, 🖉 (021) 772413, Fax (021) 774629, ≤, 🐎 – ☎ 🅿. 🌐 🝙 🚾. 🥢
10 April-October – **6 rm** ⚏ 70.00/100.00 **st.**, 1 suite.

🏠 Quayside House without rest., Pier Rd, 🖉 (021) 772188, Fax (021) 772664 – 📺 ☎. 🌐 🚾. 🥢
6 rm ⚏ 55.00 **st.**

🏠 Kilcaw Guesthouse without rest., E : 1 m. on R 600 🖉 (021) 774155, Fax (021) 774755, 🐎 – 🥢 📺 ☎ 🅿. 🌐 🝙 🚾
April-mid November – **7 rm** ⚏ 35.00/44.00 **st.**

🏠 Murphys Farm House without rest., NE : 1 ¼ m. by R 600 🖉 (021) 772229, Fax (021) 774176, 🐎 – 🅿. 🥢
March-November – **4 rm** ⚏ 19.00/38.00 **st.**

XX Chez Jean Marc, Lower O'Connell St., 🖉 (021) 774625, Fax (021) 774680 – 🌐 🝙 ⓪ 🚾 🥢
closed Monday except June-August, 15 February-15 March and 24 to 26 December – **Meals** (dinner only) a la carte 16.00/26.00 **t.**

XX Vintage, Main St., 🖉 (021) 772502, Fax (021) 774828 – 🗏. 🌐 🝙 ⓪ 🚾 🥢
closed Sunday and Monday in low season and January-1 March – **Meals** (dinner only) 27.50 **t.** and a la carte 🛓 9.00.

XX Annelie's, 18-19 Lower O'Connell St., 🖉 (021) 773074, Fax (021) 773075 – 🗏. 🌐 🝙 🚾
closed 24 to 27 December – **Meals** (dinner only) 15.00 **t.** and a la carte 🛓 6.95.

X Max's, Main St., 🖉 (021) 772443 – 🌐 🚾
March-October – **Meals** 12.00 **t.** and a la carte 🛓 7.50.

at Ballinclashet E : 5 m. by R 600 – ⊠ Kinsale.

XX Oystercatcher, 🖉 (021) 770822, Fax (021) 770822 – 🅿. 🌐 🚾
closed 25 December, November and January-Easter – **Meals** (closed Sunday and Monday in low season) (dinner only) 26.95 **t.** 🛓 6.95.

at Barrells Cross SW : 3 m. on R 600 – ⊠ Kinsale.

🏠 Rivermount House without rest., 🖉 (021) 778033, Fax (021) 778225, 🐎 – 🥢 📺 ☎ 🅿. 🌐 🚾. 🥢
February-4 November – **6 rm** ⚏ 30.00/40.00 **st.**

KINSALEY Dublin 923 N 7 – see Malahide.

KINVARRA (Cinn Mhara) Galway 923 F 8 – pop. 432.
Dublin 142 – Galway 17 – Limerick – 37.

🏨🏨 Merriman Inn, Main St., 🖉 (091) 638222, Fax (091) 637686 – 🛊, 🥢 rm, 📺 ☎ 🕭 🅿. 🌐 🝙 ⓪ 🚾. 🥢
closed January and February – **Meals** (bar lunch Monday to Saturday)/dinner 19.00 **t.** and a la carte 🛓 8.50 – **32 rm** ⚏ 55.00/70.00 **t.** – SB.

KNOCK (An Cnoc) Mayo 923 F 6 *Ireland G.* – pop. 575.
See : Basilica of our Lady, Queen of Ireland★.
✈ Knock (Connaught) Airport : 🖉 (094) 67222, NE : 9 m. by N 17.
🛈 Knock Airport 🖉 (094) 67247 (June-September).
Dublin 132 – Galway 46 – Westport 32.
Hotel see : **Cong** SW : 36 m. by N 17, R 331, R 334 and R 345.

LAHINCH (An Leacht) Clare 923 D 9 Ireland G. – pop. 580.
Env. : Cliffs of Moher★★★.

🏊, 🏊 Lahinch ℘ (065) 81003 – 🏌 Spanish Point, Miltown Malbay ℘ (065) 84198.

Dublin 162 – Galway 49 – Limerick 41.

🏛 **Aberdeen Arms**, ℘ (065) 81100, Fax (065) 81228, 🚗 – 🍽 rest, 📺 ☎ 🅿 – 🔬 200. 🐵
🖭 ⓪ 𝘷𝘪𝘴𝘢, ⅏
Meals (bar lunch Monday to Saturday)/dinner 16.00 st. and a la carte ᑲ 6.50 – 55 rm
⚏ 60.00/92.00 st. – SB.

🏛 **Atlantic**, Main St., ℘ (065) 81049, Fax (065) 81029 – ⅏ rm, 📺 ☎ 🅿. 🐵 𝘷𝘪𝘴𝘢, ⅏
Meals (bar lunch Monday to Saturday)/dinner 22.00 st. and a la carte ᑲ 5.50 – 14 rm
⚏ 45.00/120.00 st. – SB.

LARAGH (Láithreach) Wicklow 923 N 8 – pop. 267 – ✉ Wicklow.
Dublin 26 – Kilkenny 70 – Wexford 61.

🏠 **Laragh Trekking Centre** ⊗ without rest., Glendalough East, NW : 1 ½ m.
on Sallygap rd ℘ (0404) 45282, Fax (0404) 45204, ≼, 🌾, park – ⅏ 📺 ☎ 🅿. 🐵 𝘷𝘪𝘴𝘢, ⅏
closed Christmas – 6 rm ⚏ 34.00/48.00 st.

✗ **Mitchell's** with rm, The Old Schoolhouse, ℘ (0404) 45302, Fax (0404) 45302 – 🅿. 🐵 🖭 🖭
𝘷𝘪𝘴𝘢, ⅏
closed Sunday dinner, Monday and Tuesday November-17 March, Good Friday, 24 to 26
December and 3 weeks January – Meals 17.95 t. (dinner) and lunch a la carte 9.95/23.50 t.
ᑲ 4.50 – 5 rm ⚏ 37.00 st. – SB.

LEENANE (An Líonán) Galway 923 C 7 Ireland G. – ✉ Clifden.
See : Killary Harbour★.

Env. : Joyce Country★★ – Aasleagh Falls★, NE : 2 ½ m.

Exc. : Lough Nafooey★★, SE : 8 ½ m. by R 336 – Doo Lough Pass★, NW : 9 m. by N 59 and
R 335.

Dublin 173 – Ballina 56 – Galway 41.

🏛 **Delphi Lodge** ⊗, NW : 8 ¼ m. by N 59 on Louisburgh rd ℘ (095) 42211,
Fax (095) 42296, ≼, « Georgian sporting lodge, loughside setting », 🎣, park – ☎ 🅿 –
🔬 30. 🐵 🖭 𝘷𝘪𝘴𝘢, ⅏
closed mid December-mid January – Meals (residents only) (communal dining)
(dinner only) 27.00 t. ᑲ 7.00 – 12 rm ⚏ 50.00/120.00 st.

🏠 **Portfinn Lodge**, ℘ (095) 42265, Fax (095) 42315, ≼ – ☎ 🅿. 🐵 ⓪ 𝘷𝘪𝘴𝘢, ⅏
April-15 October – Meals (by arrangement) 16.00 t. – 8 rm ⚏ 40.00 t.

LEIXLIP (Léim an Bhradáin) Kildare 923 M 7 – pop. 13 451.
Dublin 14 – Drogheda 39 – Galway 125 – Kilkenny 73.

🏛 **Leixlip House**, Captain's Hill, ℘ (01) 624 2268, Fax (01) 624 4177, « Georgian house » –
📺 ☎ 🅿 – 🔬 100. 🐵 🖭 ⓪ 𝘷𝘪𝘴𝘢, ⅏
closed 25 December – Meals – (see The Bradaun below) – 15 rm ⚏ 90.00/140.00 st. – SB.

✗✗ **The Bradaun** (at Leixlip House H.), Captain's Hill, ℘ (01) 624 2268, Fax (01) 624 4177 – 🅿.
🐵 🖭 ⓪ 𝘷𝘪𝘴𝘢
closed 25 December – Meals 13.95/24.50 st. and dinner a la carte ᑲ 6.95.

LETTERFRACK (Leitir Fraic) Galway 923 C 7.
Dublin 189 – Ballina 69 – Galway 57.

🏛 **Rosleague Manor** ⊗, W : 1 ½ m. on N 59 ℘ (095) 41101, Fax (095) 41168, ≼ Ballynakill
harbour and Tully mountain, 🚗, 🌾, park, 🎾 – ⅏ rest, ☎ 🅿. 🐵 🖭 𝘷𝘪𝘴𝘢
Easter-October – Meals (bar lunch)/dinner 27.00 st. and a la carte ᑲ 8.50 – 20 rm ⚏ 80.00/
150.00 st. – SB.

---

*Für Ihre Reisen in **Großbritannien***

- 5 Karten (Nr. 401, 402, 403, 404, 405) im Maßstab 1 : 400 000
- Die auf den Karten rot unterstrichenen Orte sind im Führer erwähnt,
  benutzen Sie deshalb Karten und Führer zusammen.

LETTERKENNY (Leitir Ceanainn) *Donegal* 923 I 3 *Ireland G.* – pop. 7 606.

ExC. : *Glenveagh National Park★★ (Gardens★★), NW : 12 m. by R 250, R 251 and R 254 – Grianan of Aileach★★ (≤★) NE : 17 ½ m. by N 13 – Church Hill (Colmcille Heritage Centre★ AC, Glebe House and Gallery★ AC) NW : 10 m. by R 250.*

🍃 *Barnhill* 🖉 *(074) 21150* – 🍃 *Dunfanaghy* 🖉 *(074) 36335.*

Dublin 150 – Londonderry 21 – Sligo 72.

🏠 **Castlegrove House** ⌖, Ramelton Rd, NE : 4 ½ m. by N 13 off R 245 🖉 (074) 51118, *Fax (074) 51384, ≤, « Late 17C country house », ⌁, ☞, park – ✦ ☎ 🄿. ⏀ 🝙 ⓪ 𝘝𝘐𝘚𝘈. ✠ closed 24 to 28 December and 6 to 30 January –* **Meals** *(closed Sunday and Monday September-June) (dinner only) 18.50* **t.** *and a la carte* ⌁ *6.00 –* **15 rm** ⌑ *35.00/120.00* **t.** – SB.

🏠 **Gleneany House**, Port Rd, 🖉 (074) 26088, *Fax (074) 26090 –* ▤ *rest,* 📺 ☎ 🄿. ⏀ 🝙 𝘝𝘐𝘚𝘈. ✠
Meals *16.50* **t.** *(dinner) and a la carte 9.00/16.00* **t.** ⌁ *5.00 –* **22 rm** ⌑ *38.00/64.00* **t.** – SB.

LIMERICK (Luimneach) *Limerick* 923 G 9 *Ireland G.* – pop. 52 039.

See : *City★★ - St Mary's Cathedral★★* Y *– Limerick Museum★★* Z *– King John's Castle★ AC* Y *– John Square★* Z 20 *– St. John's Cathedral★* Z.

Env. : *Hunt Museum, Limerick University★ AC, E : 2 m. by N 7* Y *– Cratloe Wood (≤★) NW : 5 m. by N 18* Z.

Exc. : *Lough Gur Interpretive Centre★ AC, S : 11 m. by R 512 and R 514* Z *– Clare Glens★, E : 13 m. by N 7 and R 503* Y *– Monasterenenagh Abbey★, S : 13 m. by N 20* Z.

✈ *Shannon Airport :* 🖉 *(061) 471444, W : 16 m. by N 18* Z *–* **Terminal** *: Limerick Railway Station.*

🄑 *Arthur's Quay* 🖉 *(061) 317522* Y.

Dublin 120 – Cork 58.

Plan on next page

🏨 **Castletroy Park**, Dublin Rd, E : 2 ¼ m. by N 7 🖉 (061) 335566, *Fax (061) 331117,* Ⅰ₆, ⇌, 🔲, ☞ *–* 📶, ✦ rm, 📺 🝙 & 🄿 *–* 🔏 *450.* ⏀ 🝙 ⓪ 𝘝𝘐𝘚𝘈. ✠
closed 26 and 27 December – **McLaughlin's** *:* **Meals** *(closed Sunday dinner) (dinner only and Sunday lunch)/dinner 26.00* **st.** *and a la carte* ⌁ *7.95 –* **105 rm** ⌑ *135.00/180.00* **st.,** *2 suites – SB.*

🏨 **Limerick Inn**, Ennis Rd, NW : 4 m. on N 18 🖉 (061) 326666, *Fax (061) 326281,* Ⅰ₆, ⇌, 🔲, ☞, ✕ *–* 📶, ▤ *rest,* 📺 🝙 🄿 *–* 🔏 *600.* ⏀ 🝙 ⓪ 𝘝𝘐𝘚𝘈. ✠
closed 24 and 25 December – **Meals** *13.00/25.00* **t.** *and dinner a la carte* ⌁ *7.00 –* ⌑ *8.00 –* **149 rm** *98.00/116.00* **t.,** *4 suites – SB.*

🏨 **Jurys**, Ennis Rd, 🖉 (061) 327777, *Fax (061) 326400,* Ⅰ₆, ⇌, 🔲, ☞, ✕ *–* ✦ rm, ▤ *rest,* 📺 🝙 🄿 *–* 🔏 *200.* ⏀ 🝙 ⓪ 𝘝𝘐𝘚𝘈. ✠ Y Z
closed 24 to 29 December – **Copper Room** *:* **Meals** *(dinner only) 23.00* **t.** *and a la carte* ⌁ *6.00 –* ⌑ *7.00 –* **93 rm** *100.00/120.00* **t.,** *1 suite – SB.*

🏨 **Limerick Ryan**, Ennis Rd, NW : 1 ¼ m. on R 587 🖉 (061) 453922, *Fax (061) 326333,* ☞ *–* 📶, ✦ rm, ▤ *rest,* 📺 🝙 & 🄿 *–* 🔏 *120.* ⏀ 🝙 ⓪ 𝘝𝘐𝘚𝘈. ✠
Meals *12.50* **t.** *(lunch) and dinner a la carte 21.15/28.95* **t.** ⌁ *7.75 –* ⌑ *9.00 –* **179 rm** *90.00/120.00* **st.,** *2 suites – SB.*

🏨 **Greenhills**, Ennis Rd, NW : 2 ¼ m. on R 587 🖉 (061) 453033, *Fax (061) 453307,* Ⅰ₆, ⇌, 🔲, ✕ *–* ✦ rm, 📺 🝙 🄿 *–* 🔏 *600.* ⏀ 🝙 ⓪ 𝘝𝘐𝘚𝘈. ✠
closed 25 December – **Meals** *(carvery lunch) 9.95* **t.** *and dinner a la carte 15.00/25.00* **t.** ⌁ *5.50 –* ⌑ *8.80 –* **58 rm** *71.00/102.00* **st.** – SB.

🏨 **Jurys Inn Limerick**, Lower Mallow St., 🖉 (061) 207000, *Fax (061) 400966,* ≤ *–* 📶, ✦ rm, ▤ *rest,* 📺 🝙 & ⇌ *–* 🔏 *40.* ⏀ 🝙 ⓪ 𝘝𝘐𝘚𝘈. ✠ Z a
closed 24 to 27 December – **Meals** *(closed lunch Saturday and Sunday) (carving lunch)/ dinner 15.00* **st.** *and a la carte* ⌁ *6.50 –* ⌑ *6.00 –* **151 rm** *49.00* **st.**

🏨 **Kilmurry Lodge**, Castletroy, E : 3 ¼ m. by N 7 🖉 (061) 331133, *Fax (061) 330011 –* 📺 🝙 & 🄿 *–* 🔏 *300.* ⏀ 🝙 ⓪ 𝘝𝘐𝘚𝘈 𝘑𝘊𝘉. ✠
closed 25 December – **Meals** *9.75/16.00* **st.** *and dinner a la carte* ⌁ *7.00 –* **43 rm** ⌑ *45.00/ 64.00* **t.** – SB.

🏠 **Clifton House** *without rest.,* Ennis Rd, NW : 1 ¼ m. on R 587 🖉 (061) 451166, *Fax (061) 451224,* ☞ *–* 📺 🝙 🄿. ⏀ 𝘝𝘐𝘚𝘈. ✠
closed 20 December-7 January – **16 rm** ⌑ *28.00/40.00* **t.**

⌂ **Clonmacken House** *without rest.,* Clonmacken Rd, off Ennis Rd, NW : 2 m. by N 18 🖉 (061) 327007, *Fax (061) 327785,* ☞ *–* ✦ 📺 🝙 🄿. ⏀ ⓪ 𝘝𝘐𝘚𝘈. ✠
closed 22 December-4 January – **10 rm** ⌑ *28.00/50.00* **t.**

XX **Quenelle's**, Upper Henry St., 🖉 (061) 411111, *Fax (061) 400111 –* ⏀ 🝙 𝘝𝘐𝘚𝘈 Z r
closed Sunday, Monday, Good Friday, 25-26 December and 1 January – **Meals** *(dinner only) 24.50* **t.** ⌁ *7.50.*

LIMERICK

LISDOONVARNA (Lios Dúin Bhearna) *Clare* [923] E 8 *Ireland G.* – *pop. 890.*
Env. : *The Burren★★ (Cliffs of Moher★★★, Scenic Routes★★, Aillwee Cave★* AC *(Waterfall★), Corcomroe Abbey★, Kilfenora Crosses★).*
Dublin 167 – Galway 39 – Limerick 47.

Ballinalacken Castle ⛰, NW : 3 m. by N 67 (Doolin rd) on R 477 ☎ (065) 74025, *Fax (065) 74025*, ≤, park – ⊬ rest, [TV] ☎ [P]. [MC] [AE] [VISA]. ✻
6 April-4 October – **Meals** (bar lunch)/dinner a la carte 20.00/23.00 **t.** 🍷 6.00 – **13 rm** ☕ 60.00/70.00 **t.**

Sheedy's Spa View, Sulphir Hill, ☎ (065) 74026, *Fax (065) 74555*, 🌳, 🎾 – ☎ [P]. [MC] [AE] [D] [VISA] ✻
May-September – **Meals** – (see ***Orchid*** below) – **10 rm** ☕ 51.50/81.50 **t.**, 1 suite – SB.

Woodhaven without rest., Doolin Coast Rd, W : 1 m. by N 67 (Doolin rd) off R 477 ☎ (065) 74017, 🌳 – [P]. [MC] [VISA]. ✻
4 rm ☕ 23.50/34.00.

🍴🍴 **Orchid** (at Sheedy's Spa View H.), Sulphir Hill, ☎ (065) 74026, *Fax (065) 74555* – [P]. [MC] [AE] [D] [VISA]
May-September – **Meals** (dinner only) a la carte 17.50/32.00 **t.** 🍷 6.50.

LISTOWEL (Lios Tuathail) *Kerry* [923] D 10 – *pop. 3 393.*
Dublin 168 – Killarney 34 – Limerick 47 – Tralee 17.

Allo's, 41 Church St., ☎ (068) 22880 – [MC] [AE] [VISA]
closed Monday dinner, Sunday, Good Friday, 25 December and Bank Holiday Mondays – **Meals** (booking essential) a la carte 8.95/21.70 **t.** 🍷 7.50.

MACROOM (Maigh Chromtha) *Cork* [923] F 12 – *pop. 2 457.*
⛳18 *Lackaduve ☎ (026) 41072.*
Dublin 186 – Cork 25 – Killarney 30.

Castle, Main St., ☎ (026) 41074, *Fax (026) 41505*, 🏋, 🏊, squash – [TV] ☎ – 🎤 60. [MC] [AE] [D] [VISA]. ✻
closed 25 to 27 December – **Meals** 9.50/17.50 **t.** and a la carte 🍷 6.50 – **42 rm** ☕ 59.50/81.50 **st.** – SB.

MALAHIDE (Mullach Íde) *Dublin* [923] N 7 *Ireland G.* – *pop. 13 539.*
See : *Castle★.*
⛳18, ⛳9 *Beechwood, The Grange ☎ (01) 846 1611.*
Dublin 9 – Drogheda 24.

Grand, ☎ (01) 845 0000, *Fax (01) 845 0987*, 🏋, ♨, 🏊 – 🛗, ⊬ rm, [TV] ☎ [P] – 🎤 500. [MC] [AE] [D] [VISA]. ✻
closed 25 and 26 December – **Meals** 12.00/22.50 **t.** and a la carte 🍷 6.20 – **100 rm** ☕ 110.00/144.00 **t.** – SB.

🍴🍴 **Siam Thai,** Gas Yard Lane, off Strand St. ☎ (01) 845 4698, *Fax (01) 478 4798* – ▤. [MC] [AE] [D] [VISA]
closed Good Friday and 25-26 December – **Meals** - Thai - (dinner only) 18.50 **t.** and a la carte 🍷 6.95.

at Kinsaley *SW : 2½ m. on Dublin rd (L 87)* – ✉ *Malahide.*

Belcamp Hutchinson without rest., Carrs Lane, Balgriffin, D17, S : 1 m. by L 87 ☎ (01) 846 0843, *Fax (01) 848 5703*, « Georgian house », 🌳, park – [TV] ☎ [P]. [MC] [VISA]
closed 22 to 30 December – **8 rm** ☕ 38.00/76.00 **st.**

Liscara without rest., Malahide Rd, D17, S : ½ m. ☎ (01) 848 3751, *Fax (01) 848 3751*, 🌳 – ⊬ [P]
March-November – **6 rm** ☕ 28.00/40.00.

MALLOW (Mala) *Cork* [923] F 11 *Ireland G.* – *pop. 6 434.*
See : *Town★ – St. James' Church★.*
Exc. : *Doneraile Wildlife Park★* AC, *NE : 6 m. by N 20 and R 581 – Buttevant Friary★, N : 7 m. by N 20.*
⛳18 *Ballyellis ☎ (022) 21145.*
Dublin 149 – Cork 21 – Killarney 40 – Limerick 41.

Longueville House ⛰, W : 3 ½ m. by N 72 ☎ (022) 47156, *Fax (022) 47459*, ≤, « Part Georgian mansion in extensive grounds, working farm », 🎣, 🌳 – ⊬ [TV] ☎ [P]. [MC] [AE] [D] [VISA]. ✻
closed January-13 February – ***Presidents :*** **Meals** (booking essential) (bar lunch Monday to Saturday)/dinner 30.00 **t.** 🍷 7.00 – **20 rm** ☕ 59.00/164.00 **t.** – SB.

Springfort Hall ⊗, N : 4 ¾ m. by N 20 on R 581 ℰ (022) 21278, Fax (022) 21557, ⅏, park – ⛏ ☎ ℗ – ⅍ 300. ⬤⬤ ΑΕ ⓪ 𝗩𝗜𝗦𝗔. ⅏
closed 24 December-2 January – **Meals** (closed Sunday) 14.20/18.20 **st.** ⅊ 6.00 – **24 rm** ⊆ 41.00/75.00 **st.** – SB.

Central, Main St., ℰ (022) 21527, Fax (022) 21527 – ⛏ ☎ ℗ – ⅍ 350. ⬤⬤ ΑΕ ⓪ 𝗩𝗜𝗦𝗔
closed 24 and 25 December – **Meals** 9.95/16.95 **t.** and dinner a la carte ⅊ 5.00 – **20 rm** ⊆ 35.00/70.00 **st.** – SB.

MAYNOOTH (Maigh Nuad) Kildare **923** M 7 Ireland G. – pop. 8 528.
Env. : Castletown House★★ AC, SE : 4 m. by R 405.
Dublin 15.

Moyglare Manor ⊗, Moyglare, N : 2 m. ℰ (01) 628 6351, Fax (01) 628 5405, ≼, « Georgian country house, extensively furnished with antiques », ⅏, park – ⛏ ☎ ℗ – ⅍ 35. ⬤⬤ ΑΕ ⓪ 𝗩𝗜𝗦𝗔. ⅏
closed 3 days Christmas – **Meals** (closed Saturday lunch) 15.00/25.95 **t.** and a la carte ⅊ 8.95 – **16 rm** ⊆ 95.00/150.00 **t. 1 suite.**

Glenroyal, Straffan Rd, ℰ (01) 629 0909, Fax (01) 629 0919, ℩ₛ, ≋ₛ, ▨ – ▮, ▤ rest, ⛏ ☎ ℗ – ⅍ 450. ⬤⬤ ΑΕ ⓪ 𝗩𝗜𝗦𝗔
Meals (carving lunch) 15.00 **st.** and a la carte ⅊ 6.50 – **52 rm** ⊆ 55.00/85.00 **st.**, **18 suites** 75.00/100.00 **st.** – SB.

MIDLETON (Mainistir na Corann) Cork **923** H 12 – pop. 3 266.
▣ East Cork, Gortacrue ℰ (021) 631687.
🛈 Jameson Heritage Centre ℰ (021) 613702 (April-September).
Dublin 161 – Cork 12 – Waterford 61.

Midleton Park, Old Cork Rd, ℰ (021) 631767, Fax (021) 631605, ⅏ – ▤ rest, ⛏ ☎ ⅊ ℗ – ⅍ 400. ⬤⬤ ΑΕ ⓪ 𝗩𝗜𝗦𝗔. ⅏
closed 24 and 25 December – **Meals** 11.25/19.95 **st.** and dinner a la carte ⅊ 4.75 – **39 rm** ⊆ 60.00/80.00 **st.**, 1 suite – SB.

MONAGHAN (Muineachán) Monaghan **923** L 5 – pop. 5 628.
Dublin 83 – Belfast 43 – Drogheda 54 – Dundalk 22 – Londonderry 75.

Hillgrove, Old Armagh Rd, SE : ¾ m. by N 2 ℰ (047) 81288, Fax (047) 84951 – ▮, ▤ rest, ⛏ ☎ ⅊ ℗ – ⅍ 800. ⬤⬤ ΑΕ ⓪ 𝗩𝗜𝗦𝗔 𝗝𝗖𝗕.
Cavendish : **Meals** (dinner only) 18.50 **t.** and a la carte ⅊ 8.00 – **Bracken** : **Meals** 10.50/ 18.50 **t.** and a la carte ⅊ 6.00 – **44 rm** ⊆ 50.00/100.00 **t.** – SB.

Four Seasons, Coolshannagh, N : 1 m. on N 2 ℰ (047) 81888, Fax (047) 83131, ℩ₛ, ▨. ⅏ – ⛏ ☎ ℗. ⬤⬤ ΑΕ ⓪ 𝗩𝗜𝗦𝗔
closed 25 December – **Meals** (carving lunch) 11.50/18.50 **t.** and dinner a la carte ⅊ 5.50 – **44 rm** ⊆ 45.00/110.00 **t.** – SB.

MOYARD (Maigh Ard) Galway **923** B/C 7.
Dublin 190 – Galway 53 – Sligo 97.

Garraunbaun House ⊗,, W : 1 m. off N 59 ℰ (095) 41649, Fax (095) 41649, ≼, « 19C manor house », ⌇, ⅏, park – ℗. ⬤⬤ 𝗩𝗜𝗦𝗔. ⅏
Meals (by arrangement) 15.00 **t.** – **3 rm** ⊆ 20.00/60.00 **s.**

MOYCULLEN (Maigh Cuilinn) Galway **923** E 7 – pop. 601.
Dublin 139 – Galway 7.

Knockferry Lodge ⊗, Knockferry (on Lough Corrib), NE : 6 ½ m. by Knockferry rd ℰ (091) 550122, Fax (091) 550328, ≼, ⌇, ⅏ – ⅍ rest, ℗. ⬤⬤ ΑΕ ⓪ 𝗩𝗜𝗦𝗔. ⅏
Meals 16.00/17.50 **t.** ⅊ 5.00 – **10 rm** ⊆ 29.00/44.00 **t.** ⅏

Moycullen House ⊗, SW : 1 m. by Spiddle rd ℰ (091) 555566, Fax (091) 555566, ⅏ – ⅍⅏ ℗. ⬤⬤ ΑΕ 𝗩𝗜𝗦𝗔. ⅏
March-October – **Meals** (communal dining) (by arrangement) 20.00 **st.** – **5 rm** ⊆ 45.00/ 75.00 **st.**

XX **Drimcong House**, NW : 1 m. on N 59 ℰ (091) 555115, Fax (091) 555836, « 17C estate house », ⅏ – ℗. ⬤⬤ ΑΕ ⓪ 𝗩𝗜𝗦𝗔
closed Sunday, Monday and Christmas-March – **Meals** (booking essential) (dinner only) 18.50 **st.** and a la carte ⅊ 6.50.

MULLINAVAT (Muileann an Bhata) *Kilkenny* 923 K 10 – *pop. 275.*
Dublin 88 – Kilkenny 21 – Waterford 8.

🏠 **Rising Sun,** Main St., ℰ (051) 898173, Fax (051) 898435 – 📺 ☎ 🅿. ⬛⬛ 𝘝𝘐𝘚𝘈
closed 23 to 28 December – **Meals** (bar lunch) (residents only Sunday dinner) 14.00 **st.**
and a la carte 🍴 5.00 – **10 rm** ⊑ 28.00/48.00 **st.** – SB.

MULLINGAR (An Muileann gCearr) *Westmeath* 923 JK 7 *Ireland G.* – *pop. 8 040.*
Env. : *Belvedere House and Gardens*★ *AC, S :* 3 ½ m. by N 52.
Exc. : *Multyfarnhan Franciscan Friary*★, *N :* 8 m. by N 4 – *Tullynally Castle*★ *AC, N :* 13 m.
by N 4 and R 394 – *Fore Abbey*★, *NE :* 17 m. by R 394.
🛏 *Belvedere* ℰ (044) 48366/48629.
🪧 *Dublin Road* ℰ (044) 48650.
Dublin 49 – Drogheda 36.

🏨 **Greville Arms,** Pearse St., ℰ (044) 48563, Fax (044) 48052 – ▤ rest, 📺 ☎ 🅿 – 🔏 100.
⬛⬛ 𝘈𝘌 ⬤ 𝘝𝘐𝘚𝘈. ✻
closed 25 December – **Meals** 9.85 **st.** (lunch) and dinner a la carte approx. 22.25 **st.** 🍴 6.85 –
39 rm ⊑ 38.00/90.00 **st.,** 1 suite – SB.

🏠 **Marlinstown Court** without rest., Dublin Rd, E : 1 ½ m. on Dublin Rd (N 4)
ℰ (044) 40053, Fax (044) 41358, ☞ – 📺 🅿. ✻
closed 25 and 26 December – **5 rm** ⊑ 23.50/34.00.

🏠 **Hilltop Country House** without rest., Rathconnell, NE : 2 ½ m. by N 52 ℰ (044) 48958,
Fax (044) 48013, ☞ – ✾ 📺 🅿. ✻
restricted opening in winter – **5 rm** ⊑ 24.00/36.00 **st.**

at Crookedwood *N :* 6 ½ m. on R 394 – ✉ *Mullingar.*

🏨 **Crookedwood House** ⌖, *E :* 1 ½ m. on Delvin rd, turning right at The Wood pub
ℰ (044) 72165, Fax (044) 72166, ⩽, ☞, ✾ – ✾ 📺 ☎ 🅿. ⬛⬛ 𝘈𝘌 ⬤ 𝘝𝘐𝘚𝘈. ✻
closed 4 days Christmas and 2 weeks January – **Meals** – (see below) – **8 rm** ⊑ 50.00/
100.00 **st.**

✕✕ **Crookedwood House** (at Crookedwood House H.), *E :* 1 ½ m. on Delvin rd, turning
right at The Wood pub ℰ (044) 72165, Fax (044) 72166, « Cellars of 18C rectory », ☞ – 🅿.
⬛⬛ 𝘈𝘌 ⬤ 𝘝𝘐𝘚𝘈
closed Sunday dinner, Monday, 4 days Christmas and 2 weeks January – **Meals** (dinner only
and Sunday lunch)/dinner 14.95 **st.** and a la carte 🍴 6.50.

at Rathconrath *W :* 7 ¾ m. on R 392 – ✉ *Mullingar.*

🏠 **Meares Court** ⌖, *NW :* 3 ¾ m. on Moyvore rd ℰ (044) 55112, Fax (044) 55112, ⩽,
« Georgian mansion in parkland », ☞ – 🅿. ⬛⬛ 𝘝𝘐𝘚𝘈. ✻
closed 1 week Christmas – **Meals** (by arrangement) 18.00 **st.** 🍴 6.00 – **6 rm** ⊑ 32.00/50.00.

NAVAN (An Uaimh) *Meath* 923 L 7 – *pop. 3 447.*
Env. : *Bective Abbey*★, *S :* 4 m. by R 161.
Exc. : *Trim*★ *(castle*★★*) SW :* 8 m. by R 161.
Dublin 30 – Drogheda 16 – Dundalk 32.

🏠 **Killyon,** Dublin Rd, S : 1 m. on N 3 ℰ (047) 71224, Fax (047) 72766 – 📺 ☎ 🅿. ⬛⬛ 𝘝𝘐𝘚𝘈
Meals (by arrangement) 14.00 **s.** 🍴 6.00 – **10 rm** ⊑ 25.00/40.00 **s.** – SB.

✕ **Hudson's Bistro,** 30 Railway St., ℰ (046) 29231, Fax (046) 73382 – ⬛⬛ 𝘈𝘌 𝘝𝘐𝘚𝘈
*closed lunch Saturday and Sunday, Monday dinner, 24 to 26 December, 1 January and
Good Friday* – **Meals** (light lunch)/dinner a la carte 13.70/21.00 **t.** 🍴 5.50.

NENAGH (An tAonach) *Tipperary* 923 H 9 – *pop. 5 645.*
Dublin 96 – Galway 63 – Limerick 26.

🏨 **St. David's Country House** ⌖, Puckane, NW : 7 ½ m. by N 52 and R 493 turning left
after church in Puckane ℰ (067) 24145, Fax (067) 24388, ⩽, « Loughside setting », ⌖, ☞,
park – ✾ rm, ☎ 🅿. ⬛⬛ 𝘈𝘌 𝘝𝘐𝘚𝘈. ✻
closed mid January-mid March – **Meals** (booking essential) (dinner only) 30.00 **st.** 🍴 13.00 –
10 rm ⊑ 170.00 **st.**

La **carta stradale** Michelin è costantemente aggiornata.

NEWBRIDGE (An Droichead Nua) *Kildare* 923 L 8 *Ireland G.* – *pop. 12 970.*

See : *Town★.*

Env. : *Tully★★★ (Japanese Gardens★★★ AC, Irish National Stud★★ AC) SW : 6 m. by N 7 – Kildare★ (Cathedral★★) SW : 5 ½ m. by N 7.*

🛅 *Curragh ℰ (045) 441238/441714.*

🖪 *Main St. ℰ (045) 33835 (July-August).*

Dublin 28 – Kilkenny 57 – Tullamore 36.

🏛 **Keadeen**, Ballymany, SW : 1 m. ℰ (045) 431666, Fax (045) 434402, ⅙, ≘s, ☒, ☞ – ☜ ⊡
🕭 🄿 – 🛃 800. 🐵 🖭 ⓞ 🖾. 🛠
The Derby Room : Meals 15.00/25.00 **t.** and a la carte ⅄ 6.75 – **54 rm** ☲ 75.00/135.00 **t.**,
1 suite – SB.

NEWMARKET-ON-FERGUS (Cora Chaitlán) *Clare* 923 F 7 – *pop. 1 542.*

Dublin 136 – Ennis 8 – Limerick 15.

🏛 **Dromoland Castle** ⏚, NW : 1½ m. on N 18 ℰ (061) 368144, Fax (061) 363355, ≼, 🎇,
« Converted castle », ⅙, ≘s, 🛅, 🔾, ☞, park, 🛠 – 🕸 rest, ⊡ 🕭 🄿 – 🛃 450. 🐵 🖭 ⓞ
🖾. 🛠
Earl of Thormond : Meals 16.50/35.00 **t.** and a la carte ⅄ 9.00 – ☲ 12.50 – **67 rm**
220.00 **st.**, 6 suites – SB.

🏛 **Clare Inn**, NW : 2 m. on N 18 ℰ (065) 23000, Fax (065) 23759, ⅙, ≘s, ☒, 🛅, 🛠 – ⊡ 🕭
🄿 – 🛃 400. 🐵 🖭 ⓞ 🖾. 🛠
Meals (bar lunch Monday to Saturday) 8.00/18.75 **st.** ⅄ 6.00 – **161 rm** ☲ 65.00/100.00 **st.** –
SB.

🏚 **Carrygerry Country House** ⏚, SW : 8 m. by N 18 ℰ (061) 472339, Fax (061) 472123,
☞, park – 🕸 rm, ⊡ 🕭 🄿. 🐵 🖭 ⓞ 🖾
restricted opening in winter – **Meals** (closed Sunday) (dinner only) 24.00 **t.** – **12 rm**
☲ 48.50/85.00 **t.** – SB.

Les prix	Pour toutes précisions sur les prix indiqués dans ce guide, reportez-vous aux pages de l'introduction.

NEWPORT (Baile Uí Fhiacháin) *Mayo* 923 D 6 *Ireland G.* – *pop. 567.*

Env. : *Burrishoole Abbey★, NW : 2 m. by N 59 – Furnace Lough★, NW : 3 m. by N 59.*

Dublin 164 – Ballina 37 – Galway 60.

🏛 **Newport House** ⏚, ℰ (098) 41222, Fax (098) 41613, « Antique furnished country
house », 🔾, ☞, park – 🕸 rest, 🕭 🐵 🖭 ⓞ 🖾. 🛠
19 March-early October – **Meals** (dinner only) 30.00 **st.** ⅄ 8.00 – **18 rm** ☲ 73.00/146.00 **st.** –
SB.

NEW ROSS (Ros Mhic Thriúin) *Wexford* 923 L 10 *Ireland G.* – *pop. 5 012* – ✉ *Newbawn.*

See : *St. Mary's Church★.*

Exc. : *Kennedy Arboretum, Campile★ AC, S : 7 ½ m. by R 733 – Dunbrody Abbey★ , S : 8 m. by R 733 – Inistioge★, NW : 10 m. by N 25 and R 700 – Graiguenamanagh★ (Duiske Abbey★ , N : 11 m. by N 25 and R705.*

🛅 *Tinneranny ℰ (051) 421433.*

🖪 *Town Centre ℰ (051) 21857 (mid June-August).*

Dublin 88 – Kilkenny 27 – Waterford 15 – Wexford 23.

🏛 **Brandon House**, S : ¾ m. on N 25 ℰ (051) 421703, Fax (051) 421567, ☞, park – ▤ rest,
⊡ 🕭 🄿 – 🛃 200. 🐵 🖭 ⓞ 🖾. 🛠
closed Good Friday and 25 December – **Meals** (carving lunch) 10.95/18.00 **st.** and a la carte
⅄ 7.00 – **35 rm** ☲ 49.00/70.00 **st.** – SB.

🏚 **Riversdale House** without rest., Lower William St., ℰ (051) 422515, Fax (051) 422800,
☞ – 🕸 ⊡ 🄿.
March-October – **4 rm** ☲ 34.00 **st.**

at Ballynabola SE : 6 m. on N 25 – ✉ New Ross.

🏛 **Cedar Lodge**, Carrigbyrne, E : 3 m. on N 25 ℰ (051) 428386, Fax (051) 428222, ☞ – ⊡
🕭 🄿. 🐵 🖭 🖾. 🛠
closed December and January – **Meals** (bar lunch)/dinner 25.00 **st.** ⅄ 6.95 – **28 rm**
☲ 60.00/105.00 **st.** – SB.

OGONNELLOE (Tuath Ó gConaále) *Clare* 923 G 9 – *see Killaloe.*

OMEATH (Ó Méith) *Louth* 923 *N 5 – pop. 249.*
Dublin 63 – Dundalk 10.

🏨 **Omeath Park** 🦢, NW : ½ m. on B 79 ℘ (042) 75116, Fax (042) 75116, ≼, 🐎, park – ❄️ rm, 📺 ☎ 🅿. 🕦 *VISA*. 🍽️
Meals (bar lunch Monday to Saturday)/dinner a la carte 11.00/19.00 **st.** 🍷 5.95 – **13 rm** ⌕ 35.00/55.00 **st.** – SB.

🏠 **Granvue House,** ℘ (042) 75109, Fax (042) 75415, ≼ – 📺 ☎ 🅿. 🕦 *VISA*. 🍽️
closed 1 week Christmas – Meals (bar lunch Monday to Saturday)/dinner 15.00 **t.** – **8 rm** ⌕ 30.00/48.00 **t.** – SB.

ORANMORE (Órán Mór) *Galway* 923 *F 8 – pop. 1 410.*
🏌️ Athenry, Palmerstown ℘ (091) 994466/790795.
Dublin 131 – Galway 7.

🏠 **Mooring's,** Main St., ℘ (091) 790462, Fax (091) 790462 – 📺 ☎ 🅿 – 🕍 30. 🕦 🆎 *VISA*. 🍽️
Meals (dinner only) a la carte 14.85/23.40 **t.** 🍷 6.60 – **6 rm** ⌕ 25.00/45.00 **st.**

OUGHTERARD (Uachtar Ard) *Galway* 923 *E 7 Ireland G. – pop. 751.*
See : *Town★*.
Env. : *Lough Corrib★★ (Shore road – NW – ≼★★) – Aughnanure Castle★ AC, SE : 2 m. by N 59.*
🏌️ Gortreevagh ℘ (091) 552131.
🅱️ Main St. ℘ (091) 82808.
Dublin 149 – Galway 17.

🏨 **Connemara Gateway,** SE : ¾ m. on N 59 ℘ (091) 552328, Fax (091) 552332, ☎, 🏊,
🐎, 🍽️ – 🍴 rest, 📺 ☎ 🅿. 🕦 🆎 ⓪ *VISA*. 🍽️
restricted opening in winter – Meals (bar lunch)/dinner 24.50 **st.** and a la carte 🍷 6.75 –
61 rm ⌕ 85.00/116.00 **st.**, 1 suite – SB.

🏠 **Currarevagh House** 🦢, NW : 4 m. ℘ (091) 552312, Fax (091) 552731, ≼, « Country
house atmosphere », 🎣, 🐎, park, 🍽️ – ❄️ rest, 🅿. 🍽️
10 April-24 October – Meals (booking essential) (dinner only) 21.00 **t.** 🍷 4.90 – **15 rm**
⌕ 47.50/100.00 **t.** – SB.

🏠 **Ross Lake House** 🦢, Rosscahill, SE : 4 ½ m. by N 59 ℘ (091) 550109, Fax (091) 550184,
🐎, 🍽️ – 📺 ☎ 🅿. 🕦 🆎 ⓪ *VISA*
17 March-October – Meals (dinner only) 16.00 **t.** 🍷 6.50 – **13 rm** ⌕ 44.00/88.00 **st.** – SB.

🏠 **Boat Inn,** ℘ (091) 552196, Fax (091) 552694 – 📺 ☎. 🕦 🆎 *VISA*. 🍽️
Meals (bar lunch)/dinner a la carte 10.00/18.25 **st.** 🍷 6.25 – **11 rm** ⌕ 30.00/50.00 **st.** – SB.

PARKNASILLA (Páirc na Saileach) *Kerry* 923 *C 12 Ireland G.*
Env. : *Sneem★, NW : 2 ½ m. by N 70.*
Exc. : *Iveragh Peninsula★★★ (Ring of Kerry★★) – Staigue Fort★, W : 13 m. by N 70.*
Dublin 224 – Cork 72 – Killarney 34.

🏨 **Great Southern** 🦢, ℘ (064) 45122, Fax (064) 45323, ≼ Kenmare River, bay and
mountains, ☎, 🏊, 🏌️, 🐎, park, 🍽️ – 🛗 🔽 📺 ☎ 🚾 🅿 – 🕍 80. 🕦 🆎 ⓪ *VISA*. 🍽️
closed 4 January-13 February – Meals (bar lunch)/dinner 25.00 **st.** and a la carte 🍷 7.50 –
⌕ 8.25 – **83 rm** 96.00/152.00 **st.**, 1 suite – SB.

The **video cassette**
CHÂTEAUX OF THE LOIRE, from Chambord to Chinon,
is a film to complement the **Michelin** Green Guide **Châteaux of the Loire.** It
portrays the Châteaux and the elegant lifestyle of the Touraine.

Available in six versions:
0751 in French SECAM
0752 in French PAL
1752 in English PAL
1753 in English NTSC

2752 in German PAL
3752 in Italian PAL

PORTLAOISE (Port Laoise) *Laois* 923 K 8 *Ireland G.* – pop. *3 531*.
 Env. : *Rock of Dunamase★* (*<★*), E : *4 m. by N 80* – *Emo Court★ AC*, NE : *7 m. by N 7*.
 Exc. : *Stradbally★*, E : *6 ½ m. by N 80* – *Timahoe Round Tower★*, SE : *8 m. by R 426*.
 ☐₈ *The Heath* ℘ *(0502) 46533*.
 ☐ *James Fintan Lawlor Av.* ℘ *(0502) 21178* *(May-December)*.
 Dublin 54 – *Kilkenny 31* – *Limerick 67*.

🏨 **Killeshin,** Dublin Rd, E : 1 ¼ m. on N 7 ℘ *(0502) 21663*, Fax *(0502) 21976* – ⇔ rm, 🖵 ☎ 🅿 – 🔏 350. 🐟 🗚 ⓪ *VISA*. ⅍
 Meals (carving lunch Saturday) 9.90/18.50 **st.** and a la carte ⅄ 5.50 – **44 rm** ⊇ 40.50/70.00 **t.** – SB.

⌂ **Chez Nous,** Kilminchy, NE : 2 ¼ m. by N 7 ℘ *(0502) 21251*, ⌨ – ⇔ 🅿. ⅍
 closed 20 December-3 January – **Meals** (by arrangement) 12.50 – **5 rm** ⊇ 25.00/40.00.

⌂ **Aspen** without rest., Dunamase, E : 4 ½ m. by N 80 ℘ *(0502) 25405*, Fax *(0502) 25442*, ⌨ – ⇔ 🅿. ⅍
 April-October – **4 rm** ⊇ 24.50/37.00.

PORTMAGEE (An Caladh) *Kerry* 923 A 12.
 Dublin 227 – *Killarney 48* – *Tralee 51*.

🍴 **Moorings** with rm, ℘ *(066) 77108*, Fax *(066) 77220*, ⇐ – ☎ 🅿. 🐟 *VISA*. ⅍
 Easter-September – **Meals** *(closed Monday)* (bar lunch)/dinner 19.00 **t.** and a la carte ⅄ 5.60 – **6 rm** ⊇ 25.00/38.00 **st.** – SB.

PORTMARNOCK (Port Mearnóg) *Dublin* 923 N 7 – pop. *9 145*.
 Dublin 5 – *Drogheda 28*.

🏨 **Portmarnock H. and Golf Links,** ℘ *(01) 846 0611*, Fax *(01) 846 2442*, ⇐, ☐₈, ⌨ – 🕴 ⇔ rm, 🍴 rest, 🖵 ☎ & 🅿 – 🔏 250. 🐟 🗚 ⓪ *VISA*. ⅍
 The Links : **Meals** a la carte 12.70/23.95 **st.** ⅄ 7.00 – **The Osborne** : **Meals** (dinner only and Sunday lunch)/dinner 30.00 **st.** ⅄ 7.00 – **101 rm** ⊇ 125.00/195.00 **st.**, 2 suites – SB.

PORTUMNA (Port Omna) *Galway* 923 H 8 – pop. *984*.
 Dublin 114 – *Galway 42* – *Limerick 45*.

🏨 **Shannon Oaks H. and Country Club,** ℘ *(0509) 41777*, Fax *(0509) 41357*, ℟₆, ≦₅, 🔲, ⌨ – 🕴, ⇔ rm, 🖵 ☎ & 🅿 – 🔏 600. 🐟 🗚 ⓪ *VISA*
 Meals (dinner only and Sunday lunch)/dinner 20.95 **st.** and a la carte ⅄ 7.65 – **61 rm** ⊇ 82.00/102.00 **st.**, 2 suites – SB.

RATHCONRATH (Ráth Conarta) *Westmeath* 923 J 7 – *see Mullingar*.

RATHDRUM (Ráth Droma) *Wicklow* 923 N 9 – pop. *1 234*.
 Dublin 29 – *Kilkenny 76* – *Wexford 60*.

🏛 **Whaley Abbey** ⑊, Ballinaclash, S : 3 ½ m. by Wexford rd and Aughrim rd taking unmarked centre road just beyond Ballinaclash Bridge and following signs ℘ *(0404) 46529*, Fax *(0404) 46793*, ⌨, park, ⅍ – ☎ 🅿. 🐟 🗚 ⓪ *VISA* *JCB*. ⅍
 March-November – **Meals** (Sunday to Wednesday dinner by arrangement) (residents only) (communal dining) 25.00 **t.** – **7 rm** ⊇ 60.00/90.00 **t.**

RATHKEALE (Ráth Caola) *Limerick* 923 F 10 – pop. *1 546*.
 Dublin 138 – *Killarney 31* – *Limerick 18*.

🏨 **Rathkeale House,** ℘ *(069) 63333*, Fax *(069) 63300*, ⌨ – 🕴 🖵 ☎ 🅿 – 🔏 400. 🐟 🗚 ⓪ *VISA*
 Meals (bar lunch Monday to Saturday)/dinner a la carte 20.00/23.00 **st.** ⅄ 6.00 – **26 rm** ⊇ 45.00/70.00 **st.** – SB.

RATHMELTON (Ráth Mealtain) *Donegal* 923 J 2.
 Dublin 154 – *Donegal 37* – *Londonderry 27* – *Sligo 76*.

⌂ **Ardeen** ⑊ without rest., ℘ *(074) 51243*, ⌨, ⅍ – 🅿. 🐟 *VISA*. ⅍
 Easter-October – **4 rm** ⊇ 18.50/37.00 **st.**

RATHMULLAN (Ráth Maoláin) Donegal 923 J 2 Ireland G. – pop. 491 – ✉ Letterkenny.
EXC. : Knockalla Viewpoint★★, N : 8 m. by R 247 – Rathmelton★, SW : 7 m. by R 247.
🏌 Otway, Saltpans ℘ (074) 58319.
Dublin 165 – Londonderry 36 – Sligo 87.

🏠 **Rathmullan House** ⑤, N : ½ m. on R 247 ℘ (074) 58188, Fax (074) 58200, ≤,
« Part 19C country house, gardens », 🚗, 🔲, 🔾, park, 🎾 – 📺 ☎ 🅿. 🐠 🖭 ⑩ 𝘝𝘐𝘚𝘈. 🎇
closed 25 and 26 December and 3 January-14 March – Meals 10.00/25.00 t. ⅃ 8.00 – 24 rm
☲ 45.00/135.00 t. – SB.

🏠 **Fort Royal** ⑤, N : 1 m. by R 247 ℘ (074) 58100, Fax (074) 58103, ≤, 🌿, park, 🎾,
squash – ⇔ rest, 📺 ☎ 🅿. 🐠 🖭 ⑩ 𝘝𝘐𝘚𝘈
April-October – Meals (bar lunch Monday to Saturday)/dinner 21.00 t. ⅃ 8.00 – 15 rm
☲ 83.00/116.50 st. – SB.

RATHNEW (Ráth Naoi) Wicklow 923 N 8 – see Wicklow.

RECESS (Sraith Salach) Galway 923 C 7 Ireland G.
EXC. : Lough Nafooey★★, NE : by N 59 on R 345 – Lough Corrib★★, SE : by R 336 on N 59.
Dublin 173 – Ballina 72 – Galway 36.

🏠 **Lough Inagh Lodge** ⑤, NW : 4 ¾ m. by N 59 on R 344 ℘ (095) 34706, Fax (095) 34708,
≤ Lough Inagh and The Twelve Bens, 🔾, 🌿 – 📺 ☎ 🅿. 🐠 🖭 ⑩ 𝘝𝘐𝘚𝘈
April-October – Meals (bar lunch)/dinner 25.30 st. – 12 rm ☲ 75.00/158.80 st. – SB.

RINVYLE/RENVYLE (Rinn Mhaoile) Galway 923 C 7.
Dublin 193 – Ballina 73 – Galway 61.

🏠 **Renvyle House** ⑤, ℘ (095) 43511, Fax (095) 43515, ≤ Atlantic Ocean, 🔼, 🏌, 🔾, 🌿,
park, 🎾 – ⇔ rm, 📺 ☎ 🅿 – 🔬 120. 🐠 🖭 ⑩ 𝘝𝘐𝘚𝘈 𝐉𝐂𝐁.
closed January and February – Meals (light lunch Monday to Saturday)/dinner 23.00 t.
⅃ 7.00 – 64 rm ☲ 100.00/140.00 st., 1 suite – SB.

RIVERSTOWN (Baile idir Dhá Abhainn) Sligo 923 G 5 – pop. 266.
Dublin 123 – Sligo 13.

🏠 **Coopershill** ⑤, ℘ (071) 65108, Fax (071) 65466, ≤, « Georgian country house », 🔾,
🌿, park, 🎾 – ⇔ rm, ☎ 🅿. 🐠 🖭 ⑩ 𝘝𝘐𝘚𝘈 𝐉𝐂𝐁. 🎇
April-October – Meals (residents only) (dinner only) 25.00 st. ⅃ 5.50 – 8 rm ☲ 62.50/
105.00 st. – SB.

ROSAPENNA (Rosapenna) Donegal 923 I 2 Ireland G.
Env. : N : Rosguill Peninsula Atlantic Drive★.
🏌 Downings ℘ (074) 55301.
Dublin 216 – Donegal 52 – Londonderry 47.

🏠 **Rosapenna** ⑤, Downings, ℘ (074) 55301, Fax (074) 55128, ≤, 🏌, 🎾 – 📺 ☎ 🅿. 🐠 🖭
⑩ 𝘝𝘐𝘚𝘈
13 March-25 October – Meals (dinner only) a la carte 14.50/22.50 t. ⅃ 6.50 – 46 rm
☲ 60.00/100.00 t. – SB.

ROSCOMMON (Ros Comáin) Roscommon 923 H 7 Ireland G. – pop. 1 432.
See : Castle★.
EXC. : Castlestrange Stone★, SW : 7 m. by N 63 and R 362 – Famine Museum★, Strokestown
Park House★ AC, N : 12 m. by N 61 and R 368 – Castlerea : Clonalis House★ AC, NW : 19 m.
by N 60.
🏌 Moate Park ℘ (0903) 26382.
🛈 ℘ (0903) 26342 (20 June-4 September).
Dublin 94 – Galway 57 – Limerick 94.

🏠 **Abbey** ⑤, on N 63 (Galway rd) ℘ (0903) 26240, Fax (0903) 26021, 🌿 – 📺 ☎ 🅱 🅿 –
🔬 200. 🐠 🖭 ⑩ 𝘝𝘐𝘚𝘈. 🎇
closed 25 and 26 December – Meals 11.00/22.50 st. and dinner a la carte – 25 rm
☲ 60.00/120.00 st. – SB.

En saison, surtout dans les stations fréquentées,
il est prudent de retenir à l'avance.
Cependant, si vous ne pouvez pas occuper la chambre
que vous avez retenue, prévenez immédiatement l'hôtelier.

Si vous écrivez à un hôtel à l'étranger, joignez à votre lettre
un coupon-réponse international (disponible dans les bureaux de poste).

ROSCREA (Ros Cré) Tipperary 923 I 9 – pop. 4 170.
Dublin 76 – Kilkenny 37 – Limerick 95.

🏨 **Grant's**, Castle St., ℰ (0505) 23300, Fax (0505) 23209 – TV ☎ ℗ – 🔬 550. 🆚 🖽 ① VISA. ⋘
Meals 9.95/18.50 **t.** and a la carte – **25 rm** ⊇ 40.00/68.00 **st.** – SB.

🏨 **The Tower**, Church St., ℰ (0505) 21774, Fax (0505) 22425 – TV ☎ ℗. 🆚 🖽 ① VISA. ⋘
closed 25 and 26 December – **Meals** a la carte 11.00/17.50 **st.** ⌗ 5.50 – **10 rm** ⊇ 25.00/50.00 **st.** – SB.

⌂ **Monaincha House** ⧍ without rest., Monaincha, E : 1 ½ m. on N 7 ℰ (0505) 23181, « Georgian house, working farm », 🗮, park, ⋘ – ℗. ⋘
April-October – **3 rm** ⊇ 25.00/44.00.

ROSSCARBERY (Ros Ó gCairbre) Cork 923 E 13 – pop. 406.
Dublin 194 – Cork 39 – Killarney 75.

🏨 **Celtic Ross**, ℰ (023) 48722, Fax (023) 48723, ≤ Rosscarbery Bay, 🛦, 🖾, ⌷ – 🛗 TV ☎ 🕭 ℗ – 🔬 250. 🆚 🖽 ① VISA. ⋘
Meals (bar lunch Monday to Saturday)/dinner 18.00 **st.** and a la carte ⌗ 6.50 – **66 rm** ⊇ 70.00/120.00 **st.**, 1 suite – SB.

ROSSES POINT (An Ros) Sligo 923 G 5 – pop. 799.
Dublin 139 – Belfast 132 – Sligo 6.

🏨 **Yeats Country H.**, ℰ (071) 77211, Fax (071) 77203, ≤, 🛦, 🖾, ⌷, ⋇ – 🛗, ⋉ rm, TV ☎ ℗. 🆚 🖽 ① VISA. ⋘
Meals (bar lunch)/dinner 17.00 **t.** and a la carte ⌗ 5.00 – **99 rm** ⊇ 76.00/122.00 – SB.

ROSSLARE (Ros Láir) Wexford 923 M 11 – pop. 929.
🛦, 🛦 Rosslare Strand ℰ (053) 32113.
🖪 Rosslare Terminal ℰ (053) 33622.
Dublin 104 – Waterford 50 – Wexford 12.

🏨 **Kelly's Resort**, ℰ (053) 32114, Fax (053) 32222, ≤, 🛦, 🖾, ⌷, 🗮, ⋇indoor/outdoor, squash – 🛗, 🍽 rest, TV ☎ ⅙ ℗. 🆚 🖽 VISA. ⋘
March-November – **Kelly's :** Meals (dancing nightly) 14.00/23.00 **t.** and a la carte ⌗ 6.00 –
La Marine : Meals (light lunch) a la carte approx. 15.00 **t.** ⌗ 6.00 – **99 rm** ⊇ 68.00/130.00 **t.**
– SB.

ROSSLARE HARBOUR (Calafort Ros Láir) Wexford 923 N 11 Ireland G. – pop. 1 023.
Env. : Lady's Island★, SW : 6 m. by N 25 and R 736 – Tacumshane Windmill★, SW : 6 m. by N 25 and R 736.
⛴ to France (Cherbourg, Le Havre and Roscoff) (Irish Ferries) – to Fishguard (Stena Line) 2 daily (3 h 30 mn) – to Pembroke (Irish Ferries) 2 daily (3 h 45 mn).
🖪 Kilrane ℰ (053) 33232 (May-mid September).
Dublin 105 – Waterford 51 – Wexford 13.

🏨 **Great Southern**, ℰ (053) 33233, Fax (053) 33543, 🖾, ⋇ – 🛗 TV ☎ ℗ – 🔬 230. 🆚 🖽 ① VISA. ⋘
closed 4 January-6 March – **Meals** (bar lunch Monday to Saturday)/dinner a la carte 20.25/32.00 **t.** ⌗ 8.00 – ⊇ 7.00 – **100 rm** 62.00/84.00 **st.** – SB.

🏨 **Tuskar House**, St. Martins Rd, ℰ (053) 33363, Fax (053) 33363, ≤, 🗮 – ⋉ rest, 🍽 rest TV ☎ ℗. 🆚 🖽 ① VISA. ⋘
Meals 15.95 **st.** (dinner) and a la carte 7.90/21.95 **st.** ⌗ 5.00 – **30 rm** ⊇ 40.00/68.00 **t.** – SB

🏨 **Rosslare**, ℰ (053) 33110, Fax (053) 33386, ≤, « Nautical memorabilia », 🖾, 🛦, squash – TV ☎ ℗. 🆚 🖽 ① VISA. ⋘
closed 25 December – **Meals** 17.50 **st.** (dinner) and a la carte 8.80/23.00 **st.** ⌗ 3.95 – **25 rm** ⊇ 59.00/98.00 **st.** – SB.

⌂ **Devereux**, Wexford Rd, ℰ (053) 33216, Fax (053) 33301 – TV ☎ ℗. 🆚 🖽 VISA
closed 24 and 25 December – **Meals** (bar lunch)/dinner 17.50 **st.** and a la carte – **24 rm** ⊇ 44.00/66.00 **t.** – SB.

⌂ **Ferryport House** without rest., on N 25 ℰ (053) 33933, Fax (053) 33363 – TV ☎ ℗. 🆚 VISA
closed Christmas – **17 rm** ⊇ 35.00/56.00 **st.**

at Tagoat W : 2½ m. on N 25 – ⊠ Rosslare.

🏠 **Churchtown House** ⮳, N : ½ m. on Rosslare rd 𝒫 (053) 32555, Fax (053) 32555, 🚗 –
🔆 rm, 📺 ☎ 🅿, ⬥❾ 🆎 𝗩𝗜𝗦𝗔. ⬥
mid March-mid November – **Meals** (booking essential) (residents only) (dinner only)
18.00 st. ⅄ 7.50 – **12 rm** ⌕ 39.00/70.00 st. – SB.

ROSSNOWLAGH (Ros Neamhlach) Donegal 923 H 4 Scotland G.
See : Rossnowlagh Strand★★.
Dublin 153 – Donegal 14 – Sligo 31.

🏨 **Sand House** ⮳, 𝒫 (072) 51777, Fax (072) 52100, ≤ bay, beach and mountains, ⬥, ⬥ –
🔆 rm, ☎ 🅿, ⬥❾ 🆎 ⓪ 𝗩𝗜𝗦𝗔. ⬥
Easter-late October – **Meals** 12.50/23.50 t. and dinner a la carte ⅄ 7.50 – **45 rm** ⌕ 50.00/
200.00 t. – SB.

ROUNDSTONE (Cloch na Rón) Galway 923 C 7 – pop. 241.
Dublin 193 – Galway 47.

🏠 **Eldon's**, 𝒫 (095) 35933, Fax (095) 35722, ≤, 🚗 – 📱 📺 ☎. ⬥❾ 🆎 ⓪ 𝗩𝗜𝗦𝗔. ⬥
closed 5 January-10 March and 5 November-25 December – **Meals** (bar lunch)/dinner
a la carte 15.45/20.80 ⅄ 5.00 – **19 rm** ⌕ 40.00/80.00 t.

SAGGART (Teach Sagard) Dublin 923 M 8 – see Dublin.

SALTHILL (Bóthar na Trá) Galway 923 E 8 – see Galway.

SHANAGARRY (An Seangharrai) Cork 923 H 12 Ireland G. – pop. 230 – ⊠ Midleton.
Env. : Ballycotton★, SE : 2 ½ m. by R 629 – Cloyne Cathedral★, NW : 4 m. by R 629.
Exc. : Rostellan Wood★, W : 9 m. by R 629 and R 631 on R 630.
Dublin 163 – Cork 25 – Waterford 64.

🏨 **Ballymaloe House** ⮳, NW : 1 ¾ m. on L 35 𝒫 (021) 652531, Fax (021) 652021, ≤,
« Part 16C, part Georgian country house », ⬥, 🚗, park, ⬥ – ☎ 🅿, ⬥❾ 🆎 ⓪ 𝗩𝗜𝗦𝗔. ⬥
closed 24 to 26 December – **Meals** (buffet Sunday) 16.50/31.50 t. ⅄ 7.00 – **32 rm** ⌕ 80.00/
150.00 t. – SB.

SHANNON (Sionainn) Clare 923 F 9 – pop. 7 811.
🏌 Shannon Airport 𝒫 (061) 471020.
✈ Shannon Airport : 𝒫 (061) 471444. ⬥
🛈 Shannon Airport 𝒫 (061) 471644.
Dublin 136 – Ennis 16 – Limerick 15.

🏨 **Oak Wood Arms**, on N 19 𝒫 (061) 361500, Fax (061) 361414, ☎ – 🔆 rm, ▤ 📺 ☎ 🅿 –
🕺 400. ⬥❾ 🆎 ⓪ 𝗩𝗜𝗦𝗔. ⬥
closed 24 and 25 December – **Meals** (carving lunch Monday to Saturday) a la carte 15.00/
31.00 t. ⅄ 5.95 – **73 rm** ⌕ 70.00/96.00 st., 2 suites – SB.

at Shannon Airport SW : 2½ m. on N 19 – ⊠ Shannon.

🏨 **Great Southern**, 𝒫 (061) 471122, Fax (061) 471982 – 📱, 🔆 rm, ▤ rest, 📺 ☎ 🅿 –
🕺 200. ⬥❾ 🆎 ⓪ 𝗩𝗜𝗦𝗔. ⬥
closed 25 December – **Meals** (carving lunch)/dinner a la carte 14.20/25.95 st. ⅄ 6.50 –
⌕ 7.50 – **113 rm** 68.00/96.00 st., 2 suites – SB.

SHANNON AIRPORT Clare 923 F 9 – see Shannon.

When visiting the West Country,
*use the **Michelin Green Guide** "**England: The West Country**".*
- *Detailed descriptions of places of interest*
- *Touring programmes by county*
- *Maps and street plans*
- *The history of the region*
- *Photographs and drawings of monuments,*
  beauty spots, houses...

SKERRIES (Na Sceirí) *Dublin* [923] N 7 – *pop. 7 339.*

Skerries ☎ (01) 849 1204.

Community Office ☎ (01) 849 0888.

Dublin 19 – Drogheda 15.

Redbank Lodge without rest., 12 Convent Lane, ☎ (01) 849 0439, *Fax (01) 849 1598*, – [TV] ☎. [MC] [AE] [DC] [VISA].
5 rm 35.00/60.00 **t.** – SB.

Redbank, 7 Church St., ☎ (01) 849 1005, *Fax (01) 849 1598* – [MC] [AE] [DC] [VISA]
closed Sunday dinner, Monday and 24 to 26 December – **Meals** - Seafood - (dinner only and Sunday lunch)/dinner 23.00 and a la carte 5.75.

SKIBBEREEN (An Sciobairán) *Cork* [923] E 13 – *pop. 1 926.*

Dublin 205 – Cork 51 – Killarney 64.

Liss Ard Lake Lodge, SE : 2 ¾ m. by R 596 on Tragumna rd ☎ (028) 40000, *Fax (028) 40001*, <, « Minimalistic interior, themed feature gardens », park, – rm, [TV] ☎ [P] – 25. [MC] [AE] [DC] [VISA].
closed 16 January-15 February – **Meals** *(closed Tuesday to non-residents)* (booking essential) (dinner only) 33.00 **t.** 14.00 – **10 rm** 100.00/260.00 **t.** – SB.

SKULL/SCHULL (An Scoil) *Cork* [923] D 13 – *pop. 595.*

Dublin 226 – Cork 65 – Killarney 64.

Corthna Lodge Country House without rest., W : ¾ m. by R 592 ☎ (028) 28517, *Fax (028) 28517*, <, – ☎ [P].
April-October – **6 rm** 25.00/40.00 **st.**

Restaurant in Blue, W : 2 ½ m. on R 592 ☎ (028) 28305 – [P]. [MC] [AE] [DC] [VISA]
closed early December and January-March – **Meals** (booking essential) (dinner only) 24.50 **t.**

SLIEVEROE (Sliabh Rua) *Waterford* – *see Waterford.*

SLIGO (Sligeach) *Sligo* [923] G 5 *Ireland G.* – *pop. 17 786.*

See : *Town★★ – Abbey★.*

Env. : *SE : Lough Gill★★ – Carrowmore Megalithic Cemetery★ AC, SW : 3 m. – Knocknarea★ (<★★★) SW : 6 m. by R 292.*

Exc. : *Parke's Castle★★ AC, E : 9 m. by R 286 – Glencar Waterfall★, NE : 9 m. by N 16 – Creevelea Abbey, Dromahair★, SE : 11 ½ m. by N 4 and R 287 – Creevykeel Court Cairn★ N : 16 m. by N 15.*

Rosses Point ☎ (071) 77134/77186.

Sligo Airport, Strandhill : ☎ (071) 68280.

Temple St. ☎ (071) 61201.

Dublin 133 – Belfast 126 – Dundalk 106 – Londonderry 86.

Sligo Park, Pearse Rd, S : 1 m. on N 4 ☎ (071) 60291, *Fax (071) 69556*, , , , , – rm, rest, [TV] ☎ [P] – 150. [MC] [AE] [DC] [VISA].
Meals (bar lunch Saturday) (24 to 26 December residents only) 10.00/18.00 **st.** and dinner a la carte 4.75 – **110 rm** 61.00/99.00 **st.** – SB.

Tower, Quay St., ☎ (071) 44000, *Fax (071) 46888* – [TV] ☎ [P] – 150. [MC] [AE] [DC] [VISA].
closed 24 to 29 December – **Meals** (bar lunch Monday to Saturday)/dinner a la carte 9.50/19.95 **st.** 6.75 – **58 rm** 65.00/80.00 **st.** – SB.

Tree Tops without rest., Cleveragh Rd, S : ¼ m. by Dublin rd ☎ (071) 60160, *Fax (071) 62301*, – [TV] ☎ [P]. [MC] [AE] [VISA].
closed 16 December-7 January – **5 rm** 23.50/34.00 **st.**

Benwiskin Lodge without rest., Shannon Eighter, N : 2 m. by N 15 ☎ (071) 41088, [TV] [P]. [MC] [VISA].
5 rm 18.00/35.00.

Lisadorn without rest., Donegal Rd, N : 2 m. by N 15 ☎ (071) 43417, *Fax (071) 46418*, – [TV] ☎ [P]. [MC] [VISA]
Meals – **7 rm** 28.00/39.00 **t.**

SPANISH POINT **(Rinn na Spáinneach)** *Clare* [923] D 9 – ✉ *Milltown Malbay.*

Dublin 171 – Galway 65 – Limerick 52.

Armada, ☎ (065) 84110, *Fax (065) 84632* – 🛗 📺 ☎ 🅿 – 🎤 300. [MC] [VISA]. ✗
April-December – **Meals** (bar lunch Monday to Saturday)/dinner a la carte 9.00/21.00 **t.** 🍷 5.95 – **24 rm** ☕ 40.00/80.00 **st.** – SB.

SPIDDAL/SPIDDLE **(An Spidéal)** *Galway* [923] E 8.

Dublin 143 – Galway 11.

Bridge House, Main St., ☎ (091) 553118, *Fax (091) 553435,* 🌳 – 📺 ☎ 🅿. [MC] [AE] [VISA]. ✗
closed 22 December-1 March – **Meals** 10.95/12.95 **t.** and a la carte – **10 rm** ☕ 45.00/95.00 **t.** – SB.

Ardmor Country House without rest., W : ½ m. on R 336 ☎ (091) 553145, *Fax (091) 553596,* ≤, 🌳 – 🚭 📺 🅿. [MC] [VISA]. ✗
closed January and February – **7 rm** ☕ 20.00/40.00 **st.**

STRAFFAN **(Teach Srafáin)** *Kildare* [923] M 8 – *pop. 341.*

⛳ *Naas, Kerdiffstown* ☎ *(045) 874644.*

Dublin 15 – Mullingar 47.

Kildare H. & Country Club 🔇, ☎ (01) 627 3333, *Fax (01) 627 3312,* 🏨, « Part early 19C country house overlooking River Liffey, riverside gardens and arboretum », 🏋, ♨, 🏊, ⛳, 🎣, park, 🎾indoor/outdoor, squash – 🛗 📺 ☎ 🅿 – 🎤 130. [MC] [AE] [DC] [VISA] [JCB]. ✗
Byerley Turk* :** **Meals** (dinner only and Sunday lunch)/dinner 39.40 **t.** and a la carte 39.00/60.00 **t.** 🍷 8.00 – ***Legends (in K Club) **: Meals** a la carte 20.00/30.00 **t.** 🍷 8.00 – ☕ 15.00 – **38 rm** 280.00/320.00 **t.**, 7 suites – SB.

Barberstown Castle, N : ½ m. ☎ (01) 628 8157, *Fax (01) 627 7027,* « Part Elizabethan, part Victorian house with 13C castle keep », 🌳 – 🚭 rest, 📺 ☎ ♿ 🅿 – 🎤 30. [MC] [AE] [DC] [VISA]. ✗
closed 24 to 26 December – **Meals** (booking essential) (dinner only) 32.00 **t.** and a la carte 🍷 15.00 – **23 rm** ☕ 93.50/175.00 **st.**, 1 suite – SB.

Barberstown House without rest., N : ½ m. on R 403 ☎ (01) 627 4007, « Georgian house », 🌳 – 📺 🅿. [MC] [VISA]. ✗
April-October – **4 rm** ☕ 50.00 **s.**

SWORDS **(Sord)** *Dublin* [923] N 7 – *pop. 22 314.*

⛳ *Balcarrick, Corballis, Donabate* ☎ *(01) 843 6228.*

Dublin 8 – Drogheda 22.

Travelodge, Miltons Field, S : ½ m. on N 1 ☎ (01) 840 9233, *Fax (01) 840 9235,* Reservations (Freephone) 0800 850950 (UK), 1800 709709 (Republic of Ireland) – 🚭 rm, 📺 ♿ 🅿. [MC] [AE] [DC] [VISA] [JCB]. ✗
Meals (grill rest.) – **40 rm** 44.95 **t.**

Old Schoolhouse, Well Rd, off Main St. ☎ (01) 840 4160, *Fax (01) 840 5060* – ▤ 🅿. [MC] [AE] [DC] [VISA]
closed Saturday lunch, Sunday, Bank Holiday Monday, Easter, Christmas and New Year – **Meals** 13.95/23.95 **t.** and a la carte 🍷 6.95.

TAGOAT **(Teach Gót)** *Wexford* [923] M 11 – *see Rosslare Harbour.*

TAHILLA **(Tathuile)** *Kerry* [923] C 12 *Ireland G.*

Exc. : *Iveragh Peninsula★★★ (Ring of Kerry★★).*

Dublin 222 – Cork 70 – Killarney 32.

Tahilla Cove 🔇, ☎ (064) 45204, *Fax (064) 45104,* ≤ Tahilla Cove and mountains, « Waterside setting », 🎣, 🌳, park – ⚓ 📺 ☎ 🅿. [MC] [AE] [DC] [VISA]
Easter-September – **Meals** (bar lunch)/dinner 17.50 **st.** – **9 rm** ☕ 51.00/72.00 **st.** – SB.

TALLAGHT **(Tamhlacht)** *Dublin* [923] N 8 – *see Dublin.*

TEMPLEGLANTINE (Teampall an Ghleanntáin) Limerick 923 E 10 Ireland G.

Exc. : Newcastle West★, NE : 4 ½ m. by N 21.
🏌 Newcastle West, Ardagh ℰ (069) 76500.
Dublin 154 – Killarney 36 – Limerick 33.

🏛 **Devon Inn,,** on N 21 ℰ (069) 84122, Fax (069) 84255 – 📺 ☎ 🅿 – 🔬 500. 🐵 🖭 ⑩ 𝚅𝙸𝚂𝙰
closed 24 to 26 December – **Meals** 9.00/14.00 **st.** and dinner a la carte ⅃ 5.50 – **59 rm**
⊊ 35.00/75.00 **st.** – SB.

TERMONBARRY Longford 923 I 6.

Dublin 81 – Galway 85 – Roscommon 22 – Sligo 62.

⌂ **Shannonside House,** ℰ (043) 26052 – 📺 ☎ 🅿. 🐵 𝚅𝙸𝚂𝙰
Meals (by arrangement) 18.20 **st.** ⅃ 5.00 – **9 rm** ⊊ 18.00/35.00 **st.**

TERRYGLASS (Tír Dhá Ghlas) Tipperary 923 H 8 Scotland G. – ✉ Nenagh.

Exc. : Portumna★ (castle★), N : 9 m. by R 493 and N 65.
Dublin 114 – Galway 51 – Limerick 43.

⌂ **Riverrun House** 📎 without rest., ℰ (067) 22125, Fax (067) 22187, 🐄, 🎋 – ☎ 🅿. 🐵
🖭 𝚅𝙸𝚂𝙰
closed 25 December – **6 rm** ⊊ 30.00/45.00 **st.**

⌂ **Tír na Fiúise** 📎 without rest., SE : 1 ½ m. ℰ (067) 22041, Fax (067) 22041, « Working
farm », 🐄, park – ✂ 🅿. 🐵 𝚅𝙸𝚂𝙰 🎋
Easter-October – **4 rm** ⊊ 25.00/40.00 **s.**

THOMASTOWN (Baile Mhic Andáin) Kilkenny 923 K 10 Ireland G. – pop. 1 581 – ✉ Kilkenny.

See : Ladywell Water Garden★ AC.
Env. : Jerpoint Abbey★★, SW : 1 ½ m. by N9.
🏌 Mount Juliet ℰ (056) 24455.
Dublin 77 – Kilkenny 11 – Waterford 30 – Wexford 38.

🏨 **Mount Juliet** 📎, W : 2 ½ m. by N 9 on Stonyford rd ℰ (056) 24455, Fax (056) 24522
« 18C manor and sporting estate, ≼ River Nore and park », 🛌, 😫, 🏊, 🏌, 🐎, 🐄, 🎾 –
✂ rest, 📺 ☎ 🅿 – 🔬 40. 🐵 🖭 ⑩ 𝚅𝙸𝚂𝙰 🎋
Lady Helen McCalmont : Meals (dinner only) 33.00 **st.** and a la carte ⅃ 8.00 – ⊊ 12.50 –
30 rm 160.00/225.00 **st.**, 2 suites – SB.

🏛 **Hunters Yard at Mount Juliet,** W : 2 ½ m. by N 9 on Stonyford rd ℰ (056) 24455,
Fax (056) 24522, « Converted 18C stables », 🛌, 😫, 🏊, 🏌, 🐎, 🐄, park, 🎾 – 📺 ☎ 🅿 –
🔬 40. 🐵 🖭 ⑩ 𝚅𝙸𝚂𝙰 🎋
February-October – **The Loft :** Meals (June-September) (dinner only and Sunday lunch)
a la carte 15.00/25.00 **st.** ⅃ 8.00 – ⊊ 12.50 – **13 rm** 140.00 **st.**

⌂ **Abbey House,** Jerpoint Abbey, SW : 1 ¼ m. on N 9 ℰ (056) 24166, Fax (056) 24192, 🐄 –
☎ 🅿. 🐵 𝚅𝙸𝚂𝙰
closed 20 to 31 December – **Meals** (by arrangement) 16.00 **st.** – **7 rm** ⊊ 25.00/44.00 **t.** –
SB.

TOORMORE (An Tuar Mór) Cork 923 D 13 – ✉ Goleen.

Dublin 221 – Cork 68 – Killarney 65.

⌂ **Fortview House** 📎, Gurtyowen, NE : 1 ½ m. on Durrus rd (R 591) ℰ (028) 35324
✂ rest, 🅿. 🎋
March-October – **Meals** (by arrangement) 15.00 **st.** – **5 rm** ⊊ 20.00/50.00 **st.** – SB.

TOWER Cork 923 G 12 – see Blarney.

TRALEE (Trá Lí) Kerry 923 C 11 Ireland G. – pop. 19 056.

Env. : Blennerville Windmill★★ AC, SW : 2 m. by N 86 – Ardfert Cathedral★, NW : 5 ½ m. by
R 551.
Exc. : Banna Strand★★, NW : 8 m. by R 551 – Crag Cave★★ AC, W : 13 m. by N 21 – Rattoo
Round Tower★, N : 12 m. by R 556.
🚹 Ashe Memorial Hall, Denny St. ℰ (066) 21288.
Dublin 185 – Killarney 20 – Limerick 64.

🏨 **Ballyseede Castle** 📎,, SE : 3 ¼ m. by N 22 ℰ (066) 25799, Fax (066) 25287, « 15C castle
in extensive parklands », 🐄 – 📺 ☎ 🅿. 🐵 ⑩ 𝚅𝙸𝚂𝙰 🎋
Meals 20.00 **t.** (dinner) and a la carte 18.95/25.50 **t.** ⅃ 6.95 – ⊊ 7.50 – **14 rm** 80.00/
160.00 **t.**

🏠 **Grand,** Denny St., ℰ (066) 21499, Fax (066) 22877 – ▦ rest, 📺 ☎ – 🔥 250. 🆖 🆑 💳. ℀
closed 24 to 26 December – **Meals** 10.00/15.00 **st.** and a la carte ⓐ 6.00 – **44 rm** ⌷ 35.00/
72.00 **st.** – SB.

🏠 **Brook Manor Lodge** without rest., Fenit Rd, Spa, NW : 2 ¼ m. by R 551 on R 558
ℰ (066) 20509, Fax (066) 27552, 🌳 – ⇆ 📺 ☎ 🅿. 🆖 🆑 💳. ℀
April-October – **6 rm** ⌷ 38.00/64.00 **st.**

↑ **Barnakyle** without rest., Clogherbrien, NW : 1 ½ m. on R 551 ℰ (066) 25048,
Fax (066) 25048, 🌳 – ⇆ 📺 🅿. 🆖 💳. ℀
March-October – **4 rm** ⌷ 25.00/32.00 **st.**

↑ **Kilteely House** 🕭, Ballyard, S : 1 m. via Princes St. ℰ (066) 23376, Fax (066) 25766, 🌳 –
⇆ rest, ☎ 🅿. 🆖 🆑 💳. ℀
Meals (by arrangement) 17.00 **st.** ⓐ 5.00 – **11 rm** ⌷ 28.00/56.00 **st.**

↑ **Knockanish House** without rest., The Spa, NW : 3 m. by R 551 on R 558 ℰ (066) 36268,
🌳 – 🅿. ℀
April-October – **6 rm** ⌷ 22.00/36.00 **s.**

XX **Aisling Gheal,** Ivy House, Ivy Terr., ℰ (066) 29292, Fax (066) 23880 – 🆖 🆑 🅞 💳
closed Monday in winter – **Meals** (dinner only and Sunday lunch)/dinner 17.50 **t.**
and a la carte ⓐ 8.50.

TRAMORE (Trá Mhór) Waterford 923 K 11 – pop. 6 536.
Dublin 106 – Waterford 6.

↑ **Glenorney** without rest., Newtown, SW : 1 m. by R 675 ℰ (051) 381056,
Fax (051) 381103, ≤, 🌳 – ⇆ 📺 🅿. 🆖 💳. ℀
March-November – **5 rm** ⌷ 23.00/42.00 **st.**

TRIM (Baile Átha Troim) Meath 923 L 7 Ireland G. – pop. 1 740.
See : Trim Castle★★ – Town★.
Env. : Bective Abbey★, NE : 4 m. by R 161.
Dublin 27 – Drogheda 26 – Tullamore 43.

↑ **Crannmór** 🕭 without rest., Dunderry Rd, N : 1 ¼ m. ℰ (046) 31635, Fax (046) 31635, 🌳
– ⇆ 🔥 🅿. 🆖 💳. ℀
April-September – **4 rm** ⌷ 23.50/36.00.

TULLAMORE (Tulach Mhór) Offaly 923 J 8 – pop. 9 221.
Dublin 65 – Kilkenny 52 – Limerick 80.

↑ **Sea Dew House** without rest., Clonminch Rd, SE : ½ m. on N 80 ℰ (0506) 52054,
Fax (0506) 52054, 🌳 – ⇆ 📺 ☎ 🅿. 🆖 💳. ℀
closed 23 December-5 January – **10 rm** ⌷ 30.00/50.00 **st.**

↑ **Pine Lodge** 🕭, Screggan, SW : 4 ½ m. by N 52 on Mountbolus rd ℰ (0506) 51927,
Fax (0506) 51927, ☎s, 🔲, 🌳 – ⇆ rm, 🅿. ℀
closed 15 December-15 February – **Meals** (by arrangement) approx. 17.50 **st.** – **4 rm**
⌷ 27.00/44.00 **st.** – SB.

VIRGINIA (Achadh an Iúir) Cavan 923 K 6 – pop. 811.
Dublin 51 – Drogheda 39 – Enniskillen 60.

🏠 **Sharkey's,** Main St., ℰ (049) 47561, Fax (049) 47761, 🌳 – 📺 ☎ 🅿. 🆖 💳. ℀
Meals (carving lunch) 11.00/15.00 **st.** and dinner a la carte – **13 rm** ⌷ 30.00/75.00 **st.**

WATERFORD (Port Láirge) Waterford 923 K 11 Ireland G. – pop. 42 540.
See : Town★ – City Walls★ – City Hall Z H – Theatre Royal★ Z T.
Env. : Waterford Crystal★, SW : 1 ½ m. by N 25 Y.
Exc. : Tramore★, S : 9 m. by R 675 Y – Duncannon★, E : 12 m. by R 683, ferry from Passage
East and R 374 (south) Z – Dunmore East★, SE : 12 m. by R 684 Z – Tintern Abbey★, E : 13 m.
by R 683, ferry from Passage East, R 733 and R 734 (south) Z.
🖥 Newrath ℰ (051) 74182.
✈ Waterford Airport, Killowen : ℰ (051) 75589.
🅱 41 The Quay ℰ (051) 75788 Y.
Dublin 96 – Cork 73 – Limerick 77.

WATERFORD

When visiting the West Country,
*use the **Michelin Green Guide** "**England: The West Country**".*

- *Detailed descriptions of places of interest*
- *Touring programmes by county*
- *Maps and street plans*
- *The history of the region*
- *Photographs and drawings of monuments,*
  beauty spots, houses...

🏨🏨🏨🏨 **Waterford Castle** 🐚, The Island, Ballinakill, E : 2 ½ m. by R 683, Ballinakill Rd and private ferry ✆ (051) 878203, *Fax (051) 879316*, <, « Part 15C and 19C castle, river island setting », 🎾, ⛳18, 🎣, 🌳, park, 🍴 – ⇕, 🚭 rest, [TV] ☎ [P]. [MO] [AE] ◑ [VISA]. 🚫
Meals (light lunch October-May)/dinner 34.50 **t.** 🍾 12.50 – ☕ 11.00 – **14 rm** 160.00/220.00 **st.**, 5 suites – SB.

🏨🏨🏨🏨 **Granville,** Meagher Quay, ✆ (051) 855111, *Fax (051) 870307* – ⇕, ▤ rest, [TV] ☎ – 👥 200. [MO] [AE] ◑ [VISA] [JCB]. 🚫 Y a
closed 25 and 26 December – **Meals** 7.50/16.50 **st.** and a la carte 🍾 5.30 – ***Bells :*** **Meals** *(closed Sunday and Bank Holidays)* (dinner only) a la carte 17.25/21.25 **st.** 🍾 5.30 – **74 rm** ☕ 62.50/140.00 **st.** – SB.

🏨🏨🏨 **Jurys,** Ferrybank, ✆ (051) 832111, *Fax (051) 832863*, < City, 🏋, ≘s, 🏊, 🌳, park, 🎾 – ⇕ [TV] ☎ [P] – 👥 800. [MO] [AE] ◑ [VISA]. 🚫 Y c
closed 25 and 26 December – **Meals** 13.00/14.00 and a la carte 🍾 6.60 – ☕ 8.75 – **97 rm** 80.00/110.00 **t.**, 1 suite – SB.

🏨🏨🏨 **Dooley's,** The Quay, ✆ (051) 873531, *Fax (051) 870262* – ⇕, 🚭 rm, ▤ rest, [TV] ☎ – 👥 30. [MO] [AE] ◑ [VISA]. 🚫 Y s
closed 25 to 27 December – **Meals** (carvery lunch Monday to Saturday)/dinner 15.50 **st.** and a la carte 🍾 5.95 – **113 rm** ☕ 50.00/90.00 **t.** – SB.

🏨🏨🏨 **Bridge,** The Quay, ✆ (051) 877222, *Fax (051) 877229* – ⇕ [TV] ☎ [P] – 👥 250. [MO] [AE] ◑ [VISA]. 🚫 Y e
closed 25 December – **Meals** (carvery lunch Monday to Saturday)/dinner 17.95 **st.** and a la carte 🍾 4.95 – **110 rm** ☕ 40.00/94.00 **st.** – SB.

🏨 **Ivory Lodge Inn,** Tramore Rd, SW : 1 ¼ m. by N 25 on Tramore Rd ✆ (051) 358888, *Fax (051) 358899*, 🌳 – 🚭 rm, [TV] ☎ ♿ [P]. [MO] ◑ [VISA]. 🚫
Meals 9.95/12.95 **t.** and a la carte – ☕ 6.25 – **40 rm** 49.50/59.50 **t.** – SB.

🏨 **Travelodge,** Cork Rd, SW : 1 ¼ m. on N 25 ✆ (051) 358885, *Fax (051) 358890*, Reservations (Freephone) 0800 850950 (UK), 1800 709709 (Republic of Ireland) – 🚭 rm, ▤ rest, [TV] ☎ ♿ [P]. [MO] [AE] ◑ [VISA] [JCB]. 🚫
Meals (grill rest.) – **32 rm** 39.95 **t.**

🏠 **Foxmount Farm** 🐚, SE : 4 ½ m. by R 683, off Cheekpoint rd ✆ (051) 874308, *Fax (051) 854906*, <, « Working farm », 🌳, park, 🎾 – 🚭 rest, [P]. 🚫
11 March-October – **Meals** (by arrangement) 17.50 **st.** – **6 rm** ☕ 30.00/50.00 **st.** – SB.

🏠 **Brown's Town House** without rest., 29 South Par., ✆ (051) 870594, *Fax (051) 871923* – [TV] ☎. [MO] [VISA]. 🚫 Z i
closed 20 December-5 January – **4 rm** ☕ 30.00/44.00 **st.**

🍴🍴 **Dwyer's,** 8 Mary St., ✆ (051) 877478, *Fax (051) 871183* – [MO] [AE] ◑ [VISA]
closed Sunday, 1 week Christmas and Bank Holidays – **Meals** (dinner only) 15.00 **t.** and a la carte 🍾 6.00.

🍴 **Wine Vault,** High St., ✆ (051) 853444, *Fax (051) 853777*, « Converted bonded warehouse » – ▤. [MO] [AE] [VISA] Z n
closed Sunday and 25 December – **Meals** a la carte 19.95/26.95 **t.** 🍾 6.95.

🍴 **McCluskeys,** 18 High St., ✆ (051) 857766 – [MO] [VISA] Z n
closed Sunday, Monday, 1 week Christmas and Bank Holidays – **Meals** 14.95 **t.** (dinner) and a la carte 12.40/22.45 **t.** 🍾 6.25.

at Slieveroe *NE : 2 ¼ m. by N 25* – **Z** – ✉ *Waterford.*

🏠 **Diamond Hill,** ✆ (051) 832855, *Fax (051) 832254*, 🌳 – 🚭 rest, [TV] ☎ [P]. [MO] [AE] ◑ [VISA]
Meals (by arrangement) 12.00 **st.** – **10 rm** ☕ 25.00/50.00 **st.**

at Cheekpoint *E : 7 m. by R 683* – **Z** – ✉ *Waterford.*

🏨 **Three Rivers** 🐚 without rest., ✆ (051) 382520, *Fax (051) 382542*, < – 🚭 ☎ [P]. [MO] [AE] ◑ [VISA]. 🚫
closed 23 December-5 January – **14 rm** ☕ 25.00/56.00 **st.**

at Butlerstown *SW : 5 ¼ m. by N 25* – **Y** – ✉ *Waterford.*

🏨 **Coach House** 🐚, Butlerstown Castle, Cork Rd, ✆ (051) 384656, *Fax (051) 384751*, <, « Butlerstown Castle in grounds », ≘s, 🌳 – [TV] ☎ [P]. [MO] [AE] ◑ [VISA]. 🚫
closed 3 weeks Christmas and New Year – **Meals** *(closed Sunday and Monday)* (booking essential) (residents only) (dinner only) 16.00 **st.** 🍾 6.00 – **7 rm** ☕ 39.50/59.00 **st.**

WATERVILLE (An Coireán) Kerry 923 B 12 *Ireland G.* – pop. 466.

Exc. : *Iveragh Peninsula*★★★ *(Ring of Kerry*★★) – *Skellig Islands*★★, W : 8 m. by N 70 , R 567 *and ferry from Ballinskelligs* – *Derrynane National Historic Park*★★ *AC*, S : 9 m. by N70 – *Leacanabuaile Fort* (≤★★), N : 13 m. by N 70 – *Cahergall Fort*★, N : 12 m. by N 70.

🅱 *Ring of Kerry* ℰ (066) 74102.
Dublin 238 – Killarney 48.

🏛 **Butler Arms,** ℰ (066) 74144, Fax (066) 74520, ≤, 🐟, 🐀, ℅ – 📺 ☎ ℗, 🆖 🅰🅴 🆅🅸🆂🅰. ℅
mid April-mid October – **Meals** (bar lunch)/dinner 25.00 **t.** and a la carte ⅃ 6.00 – **30 rm**
☲ 55.00/150.00 **t.** – SB.

🏛 **Waterville House and Golf Links** without rest., ℰ (066) 74244, Fax (066) 74567, ≤, ⩘, 🏊, 🅱, 🐀, 🐀 – 📺 ☎ ℗. 🆖 🅰🅴 🆅🅸🆂🅰. ℅
15 April-October – **6 rm** ☲ 60.00/120.00, 4 suites.

⌂ **Golf Links View** without rest., Murreigh, N : 1 m. on N 70 ℰ (066) 74623,
Fax (066) 74623 – 📺 ℗. 🆖 🆅🅸🆂🅰. ℅
March-October – **4 rm** ☲ 23.50/34.00 **st.**

⌂ **Klondyke House** without rest., New Line Rd, N : ½ m. on N 70 ℰ (066) 74119,
Fax (066) 74666, ≤ – ℗. 🆖 🆅🅸🆂🅰. ℅
6 rm ☲ 21.00/32.00 **st.**

WESTPORT (Cathair na Mart) Mayo 923 D 6 *Ireland G.* – pop. 4 253.

See : *Town*★★ *(Centre*★) – *Westport House*★★ *AC.*
Exc. : SW : *Murrisk Peninsula*★★ – *Silver Strand*★★, SW : 21 m. by R 335 – *Ballintubber Abbey*★, SE : 13 m. by R 330 – *Croagh Patrick*★, W : 6 m. by R 335 – *Bunlahinch Clapper Bridge*★, W : 16 m. by R 335.

🅱 *Carowholly* ℰ (098) 28262/27070.
🅱 *The Mall* ℰ (098) 25711.
Dublin 163 – Galway 50 – Sligo 65.

🏛 **Westport Woods,** Louisburgh Rd, W : ½ m. ℰ (098) 25811, Fax (098) 26212, 🐀, ℅ –
📺 ☎ ℗ – 🕍 300. 🆖 🅰🅴 ⓪ 🆅🅸🆂🅰. ℅
Meals (bar lunch Monday to Saturday)/dinner 16.00 **t.** and a la carte ⅃ 4.95 – **111 rm**
☲ 63.00/150.00 **t.** – SB.

⌂ **Wilmaur** ⬙ without rest., Rosbeg, N : 2 m. by R 335 ℰ (098) 25784, Fax (098) 26224, ≤,
🐀 – ℗
Easter-September – **5 rm** ☲ 27.50/35.00 **st.**

WEXFORD (Loch Garman) Wexford 923 M 10 *Ireland G.* – pop. 9 533.

See : *Town*★ – *Main Street*★ – *Franciscan Friary*★.
Env. : *Irish Agricultural Museum, Johnstown Castle*★★ *AC*, SW : 4 ½ m. – *Irish National Heritage Park, Ferrycarrig*★ *AC*, NW : 2 ½ m. by N 11 – *Curracloe*★, NE : 5 m. by R 741 and R 743.
Exc. : *Tacumshane Windmill*★, S : 11 m. by N 25 – *Lady's Island*★, S : 11 m. by N 25 – *Kilmore Quay*★, W : 15 m. by N 25 and R 739 *(Saltee Islands*★ - access by boat) – *Enniscorth Castle*★ *(County Museum*★ *AC)* N : 15 m. by N 11.

🅱 *Mulgannon* ℰ (053) 42238.
🅱 *Crescent Quay* ℰ (053) 23111 (1 March-4 November).
Dublin 88 – Kilkenny 49 – Waterford 38.

🏛🏛 **Ferrycarrig,** Ferrycarrig Bridge, NW : 2 ¾ m. on N 11 ℰ (053) 20999, Fax (053) 20982, ≤, 🅵🕭, �·, 🅇, 🐀 – 🛗, ✳rm, 🍽 rest, 📺 ☎ ℗ – 🕍 400. 🆖 🅰🅴 ⓪ 🆅🅸🆂🅰. ℅
Tides : **Meals** (closed Sunday dinner) (dinner only and Sunday lunch) a la carte 17.45 25.15 **t.** ⅃ 4.75 – *Boathouse Bistro :* **Meals** 10.95/23.50 **t.** and a la carte ⅃ 4.75 – **86 rm**
☲ 46.00/150.00 **st.**, 4 suites – SB.

🏛 **Talbot,** Trinity St., ℰ (053) 22566, Fax (053) 23377, 🅵🕭, �·, 🅇 – 🛗, 🍽 rest, 📺 ☎ 🕭 ℗
🕍 400. 🆖 🅰🅴 ⓪ 🆅🅸🆂🅰. ℅
Meals (carving lunch)/dinner a la carte 12.70/18.00 **st.** ⅃ 7.00 – **99 rm** ☲ 62.50/110.00 **st.** – SB.

🏛 **Whitford House,** New Line Rd, W : 2 ¼ m. on R 733 ℰ (053) 43444, Fax (053) 46399, 🅇,
🐀, ℅ – 📺 ☎ ℗. 🆖 🆅🅸🆂🅰. ℅
closed 23 December-14 January – **Meals** (bar lunch)/dinner 13.95 **st.** and a la carte ⅃ 5.35 –
23 rm ☲ 27.00/70.00 **st.** – SB.

🏛 **White's,** George St., ℰ (053) 22311, Fax (053) 45000, 🅵🕭, �· – 🛗 📺 ☎ ℗ – 🕍 600. 🆖 🅰
⓪ 🆅🅸🆂🅰. ℅
closed 24 to 26 December – **Meals** (light lunch Monday to Saturday)/dinner 18.00 **st.**
and a la carte ⅃ 6.50 – **81 rm** ☲ 55.00/90.00 **t.**, 1 suite – SB.

Slaney Manor ⌂, Ferrycarrig, W : 3 m. on N 25 ℰ (053) 20051, Fax (053) 20510, ≼, 🐎, park – 🛏 ↔ 📺 ☎ 🅿. 🐧 VISA. ⌘
closed December and January – **Meals** (residents only) (bar lunch)/dinner 15.00 **st.** ₪ 5.00 – 28 **rm** ⟺ 35.00/80.00 **st.** – SB.

Farmers Kitchen, Drinagh, S : 2 ½ m. on Rosslare Rd ℰ (053) 43295, Fax (053) 45827, 🐎, squash – 📺 ☎ 🅿. 🐧 AE VISA. ⌘
closed Good Friday and 25 December – **Meals** (bar lunch Monday to Saturday)/dinner 15.00 **t.** and a la carte ₪ 5.00 – 11 **rm** ⟺ 30.00/54.00 **t.** – SB.

Rathaspeck Manor ⌂ without rest., Rathaspeck, SW : 4 m. by Rosslare Rd off Bridgetown rd ℰ (053) 42661, « Georgian country house », 🏌, 🐎, ⌘ – 📺 🅿. ⌘
2 May-6 November – 6 **rm** ⟺ 25.00/40.00 **st.**

Clonard House ⌂, Clonard Great, SW : 2 ½ m. by R 733 ℰ (053) 43141, Fax (053) 43141, ≼, « Georgian country house, working farm », 🐎, park – ↔ 📺 🅿. 🐧 VISA. ⌘
Easter-mid November – **Meals** (by arrangement) 14.00 **st.** – 9 **rm** ⟺ 25.00/40.00 **st.**

Ardruadh Manor ⌂ without rest., Spawell Rd, ℰ (053) 23194, Fax (053) 23194, 🐎 – 📺 🅿. 🐧 VISA. ⌘
closed 24 to 29 December – 5 **rm** ⟺ 25.00/50.00 **st.**

McMenamin's Townhouse without rest., 3 Auburn Terr., Redmond Rd, ℰ (053) 46442, Fax (053) 46442 – 📺 🅿. 🐧 VISA. ⌘
closed 20 to 28 December – 4 **rm** ⟺ 27.00/45.00 **st.**

CKLOW (Cill Mhantáin) *Wicklow* 923 N 9 *Ireland G.* – pop. 6 416.

Env. : *Mount Usher Gardens, Ashford★ AC, NW : 4 m. by R 750 and N 11 – Devil's Glen★, NW : 8 m. by R 750 and N 11.*

Exc. : *Glendalough★★★ :– Lower Lake★★★, Upper Lake★★, Cathedral★★, Round Tower★, St. Kevin's Church★, St. Kieran's Church★, St. Kevin's Cross★, St. Saviour's Priory★ – W : 14 m. by R 750, N 11, R 763, R 755 and R 756 – Wicklow Mountains★★ :– Avondale Forest Park★★ AC, Wicklow Gap★★, Sally Gap★★, Meeting of the Waters★, Glenmacnass Waterfall★, Glenmalur★ – Loughs Tay and Dan★.*

🏌 *Blainroe ℰ (0404) 68168.*

🛈 *Fitzwilliam St. ℰ (0404) 69117.*

Dublin 33 – Waterford 84 – Wexford 67.

Grand, Abbey St., ℰ (0404) 67337, Fax (0404) 69607 – 📺 ☎ 🅿 – 🔬 300. 🐧 VISA. ⌘
Meals 10.60 **t.** (lunch) and dinner a la carte 12.30/20.45 **t.** ₪ 6.00 – 32 **rm** ⟺ 50.00/82.00 **st.** – SB.

Old Rectory, NW : ¼ m. on R 750 ℰ (0404) 67048, Fax (0404) 69181, 🖐, 🚭, 🐎 – ↔ rest, 📺 ☎ 🅿. 🐧 AE VISA. ⌘
closed January-5 March – **Meals** (booking essential) (dinner only) 29.50 **st.** and a la carte 29.00/33.00 **st.** ₪ 8.00 – 7 **rm** ⟺ 75.00/100.00 **st.** – SB.

The Bakery, Church St., ℰ (0404) 66770 – 🐧 VISA
closed 25 December – **Meals** (dinner only and Sunday lunch)/dinner a la carte 13.50/28.00 **t.** ₪ 5.00.

Rathnew *NW : 2 m. on R 750* – ✉ *Wicklow.*

Tinakilly House ⌂, on R 750 ℰ (0404) 69274, Fax (0404) 67806, ≼, « Part Victorian country house », 🐎, ⌘ – ↔ rest, 🍴 rest, 📺 🏧 🅿 – 🔬 80. 🐧 AE ① VISA JCB. ⌘
The Brunel Room : **Meals** (booking essential) 18.50/30.00 **st.** and dinner a la carte 29.75/35.25 **st.** ₪ 8.00 – 38 **rm** ⟺ 108.00/136.00 **st.**, 2 suites – SB.

Hunter's, Newrath Bridge, N : ¾ m. by N 11 on R 761 ℰ (0404) 40106, Fax (0404) 40338, « Converted 18C inn, gardens » – ↔ 📺 ☎ 🅿. 🐧 AE ① VISA. ⌘
closed 24 to 26 December – **Meals** 15.00/22.50 **t.** ₪ 5.50 – 16 **rm** ⟺ 52.50/120.00 **t.**

In this guide

a symbol or a character, printed in red or black, in **bold** or light type, does not have the same meaning.
Pay particular attention to the explanatory pages.

WOODENBRIDGE *Wicklow* 923 N 9.

Dublin 46 – Waterford 68 – Wexford 41.

Woodenbridge, Vale of Avoca, ℘ (0402) 35146, Fax (0402) 35573, ☞ – ☑ ☎ ℗ - ⅍ 250. ⓾ Æ *VISA* . ℀

Meals 11.00/17.50 **st.** and dinner a la carte ⅃ 7.50 – **23 rm** ⵣ 50.00/80.00 **st.** – SB.

YOUGHAL (Eochaill) *Cork* 923 I 12 *Ireland G.* – pop. 5 630.

See : *Town★ – St. Mary's Collegiate Church★★ – Town Walls★★ – Clock Gate★ – The Red House★.*

Exc. : *Helvick Head★★ (≤★★), NE : 22 m. by N 25 and R 674 – Ringville (≤★★), NE : 20 m. by N 25 and R 674 – Dungarvan★ (King John's Castle★) NE : 19 m. by N 25 – Ardmore★ – Round Tower★ – Church★ (arcade★), N : 10 m. by N 25 and R 673 – Whiting Bay★, SE : 12 m. by N 25, R 673 and the coast road.*

ⁱ₈ *Knockaverry* ℘ (024) 92787.

🏛 *Heritage Centre* ℘ (024) 92390 (June-mid September).

Dublin 146 – Cork 30 – Waterford 47.

Aherne's, 163 North Main St., ℘ (024) 92424, Fax (024) 93633 – ☑ ☎ ຣ ℗. ⓾ Æ ⓪ *VISA* . ℀

closed 6 days Christmas – **Meals** – (see **Aherne's Seafood Bar** below) – **12 rm** ⵣ 80.00/120.00 **st.** – SB.

Devonshire Arms, Pearse Sq., ℘ (024) 92827, Fax (024) 92900 – ☑ ☎ ℗. ⓾ Æ ⓪ *VISA* ᴊᴄʙ . ℀

Meals 9.00/17.00 **t.** and a la carte – **10 rm** ⵣ 45.00/77.00 **st.** – SB.

XX **Aherne's Seafood Bar** (at Aherne's H.), 163 North Main St., ℘ (024) 92424, Fax (024) 93633 – ℗. ⓾ Æ ⓪ *VISA*

closed 6 days Christmas – **Meals** 16.00/28.00 **t.** and a la carte.

Major hotel groups
Central reservation telephone numbers

Principales chaînes hôtelières
Centraux téléphoniques de réservation

Principali catene alberghiere
Centrali telefoniche di prenotazione

Die wichtigsten Hotelketten
Zentrale für telefonische Reservierung

COUNTRY CLUB HOTEL GROUP (Country Club Resorts/Hotels)	01582 562256
DE VERE HOTELS PLC	01925 639499
FORTE HOTELS	0345 404040 or 0800 404040 (Freephone)
FRIENDLY HOTELS	0500 616263 (Freephone)
GRANADA LODGES	0800 555300 (Freephone)
HILTON HOTELS	0990 445866
HOLIDAY INN WORLDWIDE	0800 897121 (Freephone)
HYATT HOTELS	0345 581666
INTERCONTINENTAL HOTELS LTD	0181 847 2277 or calls from outside London 0345 581444
JARVIS HOTELS	0345 581811
MARRIOTT HOTELS	0800 221222 (Freephone)
MILLENNIUM COPTHORNE HOTELS	0645 455445
MOUNT CHARLOTTE/THISTLE HOTELS	0800 181716 (Freephone)
NOVOTEL	0181 283 4500
PREMIER LODGES & INNS	0800 118833 (Freephone)
QUEENS MOAT HOUSES PLC	0500 213214 (Freephone) or 01708 766677
RADISSON EDWARDIAN HOTELS	0800 374411 (Freephone)
RAMADA INTERNATIONAL	0800 181737 (Freephone)
REGAL HOTEL GROUP	0345 334400
SHERATON HOTELS	0800 353535 (Freephone)
STAKIS HOTELS	0990 383838
SWALLOW HOTELS LTD	0191 419 4666
TRAVEL INNS	01582 414341
TRAVELODGES	0800 850950 (Freephone)
VIRGIN HOTELS	0800 716919 (Freephone)

Distances

All distances in this edition are quoted in miles. The distance is given from each town to other nearby towns and to the capital of each region as grouped in the guide.
To avoid excessive repetition some distances have only been quoted once – you may therefore have to look under both town headings.
The distances in miles quoted are not necessarily the shortest but have been based on the roads which afford the best driving conditions and are therefore the most practical.

Distances en miles

Pour chaque région traitée, vous trouverez au texte de chacune des localités sa distance par rapport à la capitale et aux villes environnantes.
La distance d'une localité à une autre n'est pas toujours répétée aux deux villes intéressées : voyez au texte de l'une ou de l'autre.
Ces distances ne sont pas nécessairement comptées par la route la plus courte mais par la plus pratique, c'est-à-dire celle offrant les meilleures conditions de roulage.

Belfast											
261	Cork										137 Miles
106	154	Dublin									
53	208	54	Dundalk						Dublin - Sligo		
196	122	139	155	Galway							
288	54	181	235	134	Killarney						
228	57	121	175	65	70	Limerick					
72	296	143	102	174	299	230	Londonderry				
68	262	110	69	157	255	187	34	Omagh			
125	202	137	107	89	215	145	85	68	Sligo		
142	126	68	84	82	141	72	158	127	95	Tullamore	
206	71	100	154	135	112	77	241	208	177	82	Waterford

Distanze in miglia

Per ciascuna delle regioni trattate, troverete nel testo di ogni località la sua distanza dalla capitale e dalle città circostanti.
Le distanza da una località all'altra non è sempre ripetuta nelle due città interessate : vedere nel testo dell'una o dell'altra.
Le distanze non sono necessariamente calcolate seguendo il percorso più breve, ma vengono stabilite secondo l'itinerario più pratico, che offre cioè le migliori condizioni di viaggio.

Entfernungsangaben in meilen

Die Entfernungen der einzelnen Orte zur Landeshauptstadt und zu den nächstgrößeren Städten in der Umgebung sind im allgemeinen Ortstext angegeben.
Die Entfernung zweier Städte voneinander können Sie aus den Angaben im Ortstext der einen oder der anderen Stadt ersehen.
Die Entfernungsangaben gelten nicht immer für den kürzesten, sondern für den günstigsten Weg.

Distances between major towns
Distances entre principales villes
Distanze tra le principali città
Entfernungen zwischen den größeren Städten

431 Miles   Edinburgh – Southampton

Distance chart (in miles) between: Aberdeen, Ayr, Birmingham, Blackpool, Brighton, Bristol, Cambridge, Cardiff, Carlisle, Coventry, Dover, Dumfries, Dundee, Edinburgh, Glasgow, Inverness, Ipswich, Kingston-upon-Hull, Leeds, Leicester, Liverpool, London, Manchester, Middlesbrough, Newcastle, Norwich, Nottingham, Oban, Oxford, Plymouth, Portsmouth, Sheffield, Southampton, Stoke-on-Trent, Swansea, Wick.

To \ From	Aberdeen	Ayr	Birm.	Black.	Brigh.	Brist.	Camb.	Card.	Carl.	Cov.	Dover	Dumf.	Dund.	Edin.	Glas.	Inv.	Ips.	K-u-Hull	Leeds	Leic.	Liv.	Lond.	Manch.	Middl.	Newc.	Norw.	Nott.	Oban	Oxf.	Plym.	Ports.	Sheff.	South.	Stoke	Swan.
Ayr	186																																		
Birmingham	425	307																																	
Blackpool	317	199	133																																
Brighton	593	474	166	301																															
Bristol	505	387	87	214	159																														
Cambridge	467	369	99	226	121	152																													
Cardiff	529	411	111	238	192	44	186																												
Carlisle	442	96	203	95	379	290	252	314																											
Coventry	586	330	22	128	155	95	79	124	181																										
Dover	202	503	128	340	57	232	121	198	340	202																									
Dumfries	69	113	297	150	465	378	399	461	34	373	399																								
Dundee	124	82	356	249	524	437	378	440	128	252	518	134																							
Edinburgh	150	34	297	150	524	437	342	402	98	373	460	77	56																						
Glasgow	106	34	190	106	465	378	358	404	96	317	460	77	77	46																					
Inverness	209	155	300	234	540	467	467	576	192	429	586	148	192	155	171																				
Ipswich	361	145	90	207	55	207	61	129	270	79	91	324	399	326	385	525																			
K-u-Hull	324	226	55	123	195	167	102	124	234	77	287	171	248	221	289	385	132																		
Leeds	422	326	129	57	247	118	105	177	90	99	256	167	399	218	289	416	107	61																	
Leicester	351	232	59	167	125	79	44	98	207	25	127	201	223	222	225	354	103	102	75																
Liverpool	542	423	102	70	294	161	110	207	145	93	287	205	473	238	289	473	201	132	79	129															
London	346	228	118	234	55	118	57	154	324	99	75	345	399	365	416	576	77	205	205	99	220														
Manchester	274	199	90	55	270	171	167	223	90	248	311	179	309	250	264	381	201	124	44	89	36	207													
Middlesbrough	230	165	129	121	324	207	167	429	55	277	381	148	104	148	264	309	210	73	55	78	115	260	42												
Newcastle	490	392	165	143	323	294	207	525	145	309	473	192	155	192	277	309	226	134	85	177	93	292	230	42											
Norwich	394	296	128	196	67	234	90	305	199	179	216	326	289	289	289	429	43	136	162	98	177	115	259	162	122										
Nottingham	179	181	53	143	207	196	91	171	181	45	224	124	104	201	248	429	118	73	73	25	98	129	73	136	190	107									
Oban	494	82	324	294	586	470	452	541	194	557	586	167	124	130	92	118	493	315	309	345	315	493	344	270	226	475	379								
Oxford	624	206	78	276	57	75	82	105	273	57	146	426	366	426	369	529	136	172	174	58	172	55	232	261	344	149	91	459							
Plymouth	577	206	151	355	95	140	213	140	285	140	305	289	435	289	435	508	179	302	302	228	353	228	389	418	418	339	262	589	197						
Portsmouth	360	151	86	48	48	86	140	86	158	35	57	235	449	235	452	611	164	256	256	78	242	70	315	315	395	155	99	542	67	138					
Sheffield	559	262	97	121	267	97	132	176	97	67	249	168	235	255	255	395	169	35	39	67	88	169	39	99	128	169	55	345	151	345	183				
Southampton	380	89	132	267	46	42	152	75	140	46	191	253	434	253	431	593	134	243	237	88	224	58	297	326	326	175	134	523	64	143	22	202			
Stoke-on-Trent	522	121	47	128	215	79	159	140	128	58	267	191	312	191	312	556	189	91	64	46	58	164	46	155	183	199	55	345	151	247	199	52	152		
Swansea	212	79	89	221	41	300	257	267	300	159	332	275	454	271	415	556	171	192	192	171	192	171	329	358	303	303	191	487	172	191	172	235	152	187	
Wick	712	315	565	457	733	646	608	669	364	587	777	342	234	265	501	108	563	486	370	414	631	535	225	486	631	501	634	225	764	717	717	501	699	520	662

424	452	595	718	298	*Amsterdam*
1025	1052	1195	1319	898	*Barcelona*
617	644	787	911	490	*Basel*
778	806	949	1073	652	*Berlin*
676	704	847	970	550	*Bern*
534	516	570	832	612	*Bordeaux*
1063	1091	1234	1357	937	*Bratislava*
1449	1477	1620	1743	1323	*Brindisi*
322	350	493	617	196	*Bruxelles-Brussel*
138	120	315	439	81	*Cherbourg*
640	668	811	934	513	*Clermont-Ferrand*
447	474	617	741	320	*Düsseldorf*
575	602	745	869	448	*Frankfurt am Main*
663	690	833	957	536	*Genève*
674	702	845	968	547	*Hamburg*
869	896	1039	356	742	*København*
267	294	437	561	140	*Lille*
1270	1251	1306	1567	1348	*Lisboa*
456	484	627	750	330	*Luxembourg*
663	691	834	957	537	*Lyon*
965	947	1001	1263	1043	*Madrid*
1291	1273	1327	1589	1369	*Málaga*
856	884	1027	1150	730	*Marseille*
831	858	1001	1125	704	*Milano*
796	824	967	1090	669	*München*
333	314	369	630	276	*Nantes*
1311	1338	1482	1605	1184	*Palermo*
376	404	547	671	250	*Paris*
1150	1132	1186	1448	1228	*Porto*
878	905	1048	1172	751	*Praha*
1183	1210	1354	1477	1056	*Roma*
684	666	720	982	762	*San Sebastián*
582	609	752	876	455	*Strasbourg*
811	668	722	1105	684	*Toulouse*
1240	1009	1063	1534	1113	*Valencia*
1124	1151	1294	1418	997	*Warszawa*
1013	1041	1184	1307	886	*Wien*
1135	1163	1306	1429	1009	*Zagreb*

Birmingham · Cardiff · Dublin · Glasgow · London

For distances refer to the colour key in the table
Les distances sont indiquées dans la couleur du point de passage
Le distanze sono indicate con il colore del punto di passaggio
Die Entfernungen sind angegeben in der Farbe des betroffenen Passagepunktes

● **FOLKESTONE**
  (CHANNEL TUNNEL)
● SOUTHAMPTON
● **TYNEMOUTH**

Glasgow - Barcelona | 1319 Miles

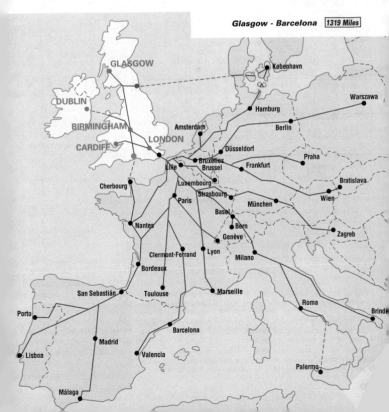

Major roads and principal shipping routes

Motorway	—⧫—
Road number	A 4.T 35. N 2
Mileage	20

Principales routes et liaisons maritimes

Autoroute	—⧫—
Nº de route	A 4.T 35. N 2
Distance en miles	20

Principali strade e itinerari marittimi

Autostrada	—⧫—
Numero di strada	A 4.T 35. N 2
Distanza in miglia	20

Hauptverkehrsstrassen und Schiffverbindungen

Autobahn	—⧫—
Straßennummer	A 4.T 35. N 2
Entfernung in Meilen	20

Illustrations Cécile Imbert/MICHELIN : pages 4 à 48 – Narratif Systèmes/Geneclo :
pages 50 à 55, 60, 62 - Rodolphe Corbel pages 116, 336, 383, 436, 676, 690, 785, 792.

Manufacture française des pneumatiques Michelin
Société en commandite par actions au capital de 2 000 000 000 de francs
Place des Carmes-Déchaux – 63 Clermont-Ferrand (France)
R.C.S. Clermont-Fd B 855 200 507

Michelin et Cie, Propriétaires-Éditeurs 1998
Dépôt légal Janvier 98 – ISBN 2.06.006579-8

Printed in E.C. – 12-97

Photocomposition : APS, Tours – Impression : MAURY Imprimeur S.A., Malesherbes
Reliure : A.G.M., Forges-les-Eaux

International dialling codes

Note : When making an international call to the UK do not dial the first "0" of the city codes.

Indicatifs téléphoniques internationaux

Important : Pour les communications d'un pays étranger vers le Royaume-Uni, le zéro (0) initial de l'indicatif interurbain n'est pas à chiffrer.

from \ to	A	B	CH	CZ	D	DK	E	FIN	F	GB	GR
A Austria		0032	0041	00420	0049	0045	0034	00358	0033	0044	0030
B Belgium	0043		0041	00420	0049	0045	0034	00358	0033	0044	0030
CH Switzerland	0043	0032		00420	0049	0045	0034	00358	0033	0044	0030
CZ Czech Republic	0043	0032	0041		0049	0045	0034	00358	0033	0044	0030
D Germany	0043	0032	0041	00420		0045	0034	00358	0033	0044	0030
DK Denmark	0043	0032	0041	00420	0049		0034	00358	0033	0044	0030
E Spain	0043	0032	0041	00420	0049	0045		00358	0033	0044	0030
FIN Finland	0043	0032	0041	00420	0049	0045	0034		0033	0044	0030
F France	0043	0032	0041	00420	0049	0045	99034	00358		0044	0030
GB United Kingdom	0043	0032	0041	00420	0049	0045	0034	00358	0033	044	0030
GR Greece	0043	0032	0041	00420	0049	0045	0034	00358	0033	0044	
H Hungary	0043	0032	0041	00420	0049	0045	0034	00358	0033	0044	0030
I Italy	0043	0032	0041	00420	0049	0045	0034	00358	0033	0044	0030
IRL Ireland	0043	0032	0041	00420	0049	0045	0034	00358	0033	0044	0030
J Japan	00143	00132	00141	00142	0149	00145	00134	001358	00133	00130	0030
L Luxembourg	0043	0032	0041	00420	0049	0045	0034	00358	0033	0044	0030
N Norway	0043	0032	0041	00420	0049	0045	0034	00358	0033	0044	0030
NL Netherlands	0043	0032	0041	00420	0049	0045	0034	00358	0033	0044	0030
PL Poland	0043	0032	0041	00420	0049	0045	0034	00358	0033	0044	0030
P Portugal	0043	0032	0041	00420	0049	0045	0034	00358	0033	0044	0030
RUS Russia	81043	81032	81041	6420	81049	81045	*	009358	81033	81044	*
S Sweden	0043	0032	0041	00420	0049	0045	00934	00358	0033	0044	0030
USA	1143	01132	01141	011420	01149	01145	01134	01358	01133	01144	01130

* *Direct dialing not possible* *   * *Pas de sélection automatique*

Indicativi telefonici internazionali

Importante : per comunicare con il Regno Unito da un paese straniero non bisogna comporre lo zero (0) iniziale dell'indicativo interurbano.

International Telefon-Vorwahlnummern

Wichtig : Bei Auslandsgesprächen von und nach Vereinigtes Königreich darf die voranstehende Null (0) der Ortsnetzkennzahl nicht gewählt werden.

(H)	(I)	(IRL)	(J)	(L)	(N)	(NL)	(PL)	(P)	(RUS)	(S)	(USA)	
0036	0039	00353	0081	00352	0047	0031	0048	00351	007	0046	001	**Austria A**
0036	0039	00353	0081	00352	0047	0031	0048	00351	007	0046	001	**Belgium B**
0036	0039	00353	0081	00352	0047	0031	0048	00351	007	0046	001	**Switzerland CH**
0036	0039	00353	0081	00352	0047	0031	0048	00351	007	0046	001	**Czech CZ Republic**
0036	0039	00353	0081	00352	0047	0031	0048	00351	007	0046	001	**Germany D**
0036	0039	00353	0081	00352	0047	0031	0048	00351	007	0046	001	**Denmark DK**
0036	0039	00353	0781	00352	0047	0031	0048	00351	077	0046	071	**Spain E**
0036	0039	00353	0081	00352	0047	0031	0048	00351	9907	0046	001	**Finland FIN**
0036	0039	00353	0081	00352	0047	0031	0048	00351	007	0046	001	**France F**
0036	0039	00353	0081	00352	0047	0031	0048	00351	007	0046	001	**United GB Kingdom**
0036	0039	00353	0081	00352	0047	0031	0048	00351	007	0046	001	**Greece GR**
	0039	00353	0081	00352	0047	0031	0048	00351	007	0046	001	**Hungary H**
0036		00353	0081	00352	0047	0031	0048	00351	*	0046	001	**Italy I**
0036	0039		0081	00352	0047	0031	0048	00351	007	0046	001	**Ireland IRL**
00136	00139	001353		01352	00147	00131	00148	01351	*	01146	0011	**Japan J**
0036	0039	00353	0081		0047	0031	0048	00351	007	0046	001	**Luxembourg L**
0036	0039	00353	0081	00352		0031	0048	00351	007	0046	001	**Norway N**
0036	0039	00353	0081	00352	0047		0048	00351	007	0046	001	**Netherlands NL**
0036	0039	00353	0081	00352	0047	0031		00351	007	0046	001	**Poland PL**
0036	0039	00353	0081	00352	0047	0031	0048		007	0046	001	**Portugal P**
636	*	*	*	*	*	81031	648	*		*	*	**Russia RUS**
0036	0039	00353	00981	00352	0047	0031	0048	00935	097		0091	**Sweden S**
01136	01139	011353	01181	011352	01147	01131	01148	*	011351	01146		**USA**

* Selezione automatica impossibile ** Automatische Vorwahl nicht möglich*

Notes
Appunti
Notizen

Notes
Appunti
Notizen